Peter Mühle

DICTIONARY OF IMAGING

German-English · English-German

2005

OSCAR BRANDSTETTER VERLAG · WIESBADEN

Peter Mühle

WÖRTERBUCH DER BILDTECHNIK

Deutsch-Englisch · Englisch-Deutsch

2005

OSCAR BRANDSTETTER VERLAG · WIESBADEN

Die Deutsche Bibliothek - CIP-Einheitsaufnahme

Ein Titeldatensatz für diese Publikation ist bei
Der Deutschen Bibliothek erhältlich

In diesem Wörterbuch werden, wie in allgemeinen Nachschlagewerken üblich, etwa bestehende Patente, Gebrauchsmuster oder Warenzeichen nicht erwähnt. Wenn ein solcher Hinweis fehlt, heißt das also nicht, dass eine Ware oder ein Warenname frei ist.

In this dictionary, as in reference works in general, no mention is made of patents, trademark rights, or other proprietary rights which may attach to certain words or entries. The absence of such mention, however, in no way implies that the words or entries in question are exempt from such rights.

Dieses Werk ist urheberrechtlich geschützt. Die dadurch begründeten Rechte, insbesondere die der Übersetzung, des Nachdruckes, der Funksendung, der Wiedergabe auf fotomechanischem oder ähnlichem Wege und der Speicherung in Datenverarbeitungsanlagen bleiben, auch bei nur auszugsweiser Verwertung, vorbehalten.

All rights reserved. No part of this book may be translated, reproduced, stored in information retrieval systems, or transmitted, in any form or by any means - electronic, mechanical, photocopying, recording, or otherwise - without the prior written permission of the publishers.

1. Auflage 2005

Copyright © 2005 by
OSCAR BRANDSTETTER VERLAG GMBH & CO. KG, WIESBADEN

Datentechnische Verarbeitung: Acolada GmbH, Nürnberg
Druck: Druckwerkstätte H. Kunze GmbH und Partner KG, Mainz-Hechtsheim
Buchbinderische Verarbeitung: Leipziger Großbuchbinderei Treuleben & Bischof GmbH

ISBN 3-87097-207-6

Printed in Germany

WIEDER FÜR MARIANNE

Preface

This book with its more than 35,000 entries in either language section presents the most comprehensive bilingual collection of imaging terms published so far.

Among the wealth of material used in the compilation of this dictionary Joseph P. Hornak's Encyclopedia of Imaging Science and Technology proved to be a particularly useful source.

Spelling is based on Merriam-Webster's Collegiate Dictionary and the German Duden, in cases of doubt I adopted the spelling that prevails in scientific usage.

I wish to thank Dirk Schmidt for his generous assistance in preparing the machine-readable text.

Any suggestions for enhancing a possible further edition of this book will be appreciated and should be directed to Oscar Brandstetter Verlag, D-65007 Wiesbaden, Postfach 1708.

Lübeck
January 2005   Peter Mühle

Vorwort

Mit mehr als 35.000 Eintragungen je Sprachrichtung bietet dieses Buch die bislang umfangreichste Sammlung von Fachbegriffen der Bildtechnik in englischer und deutscher Sprache.

In der Fülle des verwendeten Materials hat sich Joseph P. Hornaks Encyclopedia of Imaging Science and Technology als besonders ergiebige Quelle erwiesen.

Orthografisch folgt das Wörterbuch dem Duden und Merriam-Webster's Collegiate Dictionary; in Zweifelsfällen wurde die fachsprachlich dominierende Schreibweise gewählt.

Mein Dank gilt Herrn Dirk Schmidt für die uneigennützige Hilfe bei der maschinellen Typoskriptbearbeitung.

An Mitteilungen zur Verbesserung und Ergänzung der vorliegenden Ausgabe bin ich selbstverständlich interessiert und bitte, diese an den Oscar Brandstetter Verlag, D-65007 Wiesbaden, Postfach 1708, zu richten.

Lübeck
Januar 2005   Peter Mühle

Abkürzungen/Abbreviations

bes./esp.	besonders/especially
f	Femininum/feminine noun
fpl	Femininum pluralis/feminine plural
m	Maskulinum/masculine noun
mpl	Maskulinum pluralis/masculine plural
n	Neutrum/neuter noun
npl	Neutrum pluralis/neuter plural
pl	Plural/plural
s.	siehe/see
s.a.	siehe auch/see also
z.B./e.g.	zum Beispiel/for example

Zeichen/Signs

/	digitize/to = to digitize
( )	lens set (line) = lens set *or* lens line
[ ]	special[-purpose] film = special film *or* special-purpose film
( )	Diese Klammern enthalten Erklärungen
	These brackets contain explanations

WÖRTERBUCH DER BILDTECHNIK

TEIL I

DEUTSCH-ENGLISCH

Abbildungsaufgabe

A

abaxial abaxial, off-axis, extra-axial
Abbe-Kondensor *m* Abbe condenser *(optical microscope)*
Abbe-Prisma *n* Abbe prism
Abbe-Refraktometer *n* Abbe refractometer
Abbe-Zahl *f* Abbe [V-]number, Abbe constant, V value (number), constringence, reciprocal relative dispersion *(optics)*
Abbild *n s.* Abbildung 2.
abbildbar portrayable
Abbildbarkeit *f* portrayability
abbilden to image; to depict, to portray, to picture; to delineate; to map
~/**aufeinander** to map onto
~/**ineinander** to [re]image onto itself
~/**optisch** to image optically
Abbildung *f* 1. imaging, image formation; depiction, delineation; mapping *(s.a. under Darstellung)*; 2. [pictorial] image, picture; depiction, delineation; figure, [pictorial] illustration; map *(s.a. under Bild)*
~/**affine** 1. affine mapping *(computational geometry)*; 2. affine map (image)
~/**afokale** afocal imaging
~/**anamorphotische** anamorph[ot]ic image formation
~/**aplanatische** aplanatic imaging
~/**außeraxiale** off-axis image
~/**beugungsbegrenzte** diffraction-limited image
~/**bilineare** bilinear mapping
~/**biquadratische** biquadratic mapping
~/**dreidimensionale** three-dimensional imaging
~/**flächige** planar imaging
~/**fotografische** photographic image
~/**ganzseitige** full-page illustration
~/**Gaußsche** 1. Gaussian image formation; 2. Gaussian image
~/**geometrische** geometric mapping *(video modeling)*
~/**grafische** graphic[al] image; graph, plot
~/**harmonische** harmonic imaging (function) *(ray optics)*
~/**hochauflösende** high-resolution imaging, HRI
~/**holografische** holographic imaging
~/**ideale [geometrisch-optische]** ideal image *(optics)*
~/**inkohärente** incoherent imaging
~/**inverse** inverse (backward) mapping *(geometric transformation)*
~/**ionenoptische** ion-optical imaging
~/**kinematografische** cinematographic imaging
~/**kohärente** coherent [light] imaging
~/**kollineare** *s.* ~/Gaußsche
~/**konfokale** confocal imaging
~/**lineare** 1. linear imaging; 2. *s.* ~/affine 1. and 2.
~/**mehrdimensionale** multidimensional imaging
~/**mikroskopische** microscopic (microscope) imaging, microscopic image formation
~/**multispektrale** multispectral imaging
~/**nachbarschaftserhaltende** topographic (topology-preserving) map, feature (geometric) map *(pattern recognition)*
~/**nichtaffine (nichtlineare)** nonlinear imaging
~/**nichtperspektivische** nonperspective imaging
~/**optische** 1. optical imaging; 2. optical image, [visible-]light image
~/**panchromatische** panchromatic imaging
~/**partiell kohärente** partially coherent imaging
~/**perfekte** *s.* ~/beugungsbegrenzte
~/**perspektivische** perspective mapping; perspective projection
~/**polynomiale** polynomial mapping
~/**projektive** projection imaging; projective mapping
~/**pseudoperspektivische** pseudo-perspective mapping
~/**punktförmige** point (spot) image, spot diagram *(optics)*
~/**radiometrische** radiometric imaging
~/**räumliche** spatial map
~/**retinotope** retinotopic (topographic) mapping
~/**scharfe** sharp image (picture), crisp (blur-free) image
~/**stigmatische** stigmatic imaging
~/**teleskopische** telescopic imaging
~/**tomografische** tomographic imaging (mapping)
~/**topografische** 1. topographic mapping; 2. topograph[al] map; 3. *s.* ~/retinotope
~/**topologieerhaltende** *s.* ~/nachbarschaftserhaltende
~/**unverzerrte** 1. distortion-free imaging; isotropic mapping; 2. undistorted (distortion-free) image, undistorted picture
~/**vektorielle** vector image
~/**verwandte** *s.* ~/affine
~/**verzerrte** 1. anamorph[ot]ic image formation; anisotropic mapping; 2. anamorphic [image], distorted image (picture)
~/**verzerrungsfreie** *s.* ~/unverzerrte
Abbildungsalgebra *f* imaging algebra
Abbildungsalgorithmus *m* imaging (mapping) algorithm
Abbildungsapparat *m* imaging apparatus
Abbildungsaufgabe *f* imaging task

Abbildungsaufwärtsvektor

Abbildungsaufwärtsvektor *m* view-up vector *(world coordinate space)*
Abbildungsbedingungen *fpl* imaging conditions
Abbildungsbeschreibung *f* view representation *(computer graphics)*
Abbildungsebene *f* image-forming [conjugate] plane, imaging plane *(optics)*; view[ing] plane *(computer graphics)*; camera target *(video modeling)*
Abbildungseigenschaft *f* imaging (image-forming) property *(e.g. of a lens)*
Abbildungsfehler *m* 1. imaging aberration, [image] aberration, optical defect (aberration); imaging defect; 2. *s.* Bildfehler
~/**außeraxialer** off-axis aberration, transverse (lateral) aberration
~/**axialer** on-axis aberration, longitudinal aberration
~/**geometrischer** geometrical aberration
~/**monochromatischer** monochromatic aberration
~/**optischer** optical defect (aberration)
~/**Seidelscher** [von] Seidel aberration, primary aberration (image defect), third-order aberration *(optics)*
abbildungsfehlerfrei aberrationless
Abbildungsfehlerrest *m* residual aberration
Abbildungsfenster *n* view window *(computer graphics)*
Abbildungsfläche *f* imaging surface
Abbildungsfunktion *f* mapping function
Abbildungsgenauigkeit *f* imaging precision
Abbildungsgeometrie *f* imaging (mapping) geometry
Abbildungsgeschwindigkeit *f* imaging speed
Abbildungsgesetz *n* imaging law
Abbildungsgleichung *f* imaging (image) equation
~/**Newtonsche** Newtonian lens equation
Abbildungsgröße *f* mapping value *(photogrammetry)*
Abbildungsgüte *f s.* Abbildungsqualität 1. and 2.
Abbildungsindex *m* view index *(computer graphics)*
Abbildungskette *f* imaging chain, image [processing] chain
~/**digitale** digital imaging chain
Abbildungskörper *m* view volume *(computer graphics)*
Abbildungsleistung *f* imaging (image) performance; imaging efficiency
Abbildungslichtweg *m* image-forming [light] path
Abbildungslinse *f* imaging lens
Abbildungsmaßstab *m* scale of reproduction, reproduction ratio; [image] scale; [optical] magnification

Abbildungsmedium *n* imaging (image-display) medium
Abbildungsmethode *f* imaging method
Abbildungsmode *f* imaging mode *(e.g. in electron microscopy)*
Abbildungsmodus *m* imaging mode
Abbildungsobjekt *n* imaged object
Abbildungsoptik *f* imaging optic[s]
Abbildungsorientierungsmatrix *f* view orientation matrix *(computer graphics)*
Abbildungsprinzip *n* mapping principle; imaging principle
Abbildungsprojektionsmatrix *f* view mapping matrix *(computer graphics)*
Abbildungsprozess *m* imaging process
Abbildungsqualität *f* 1. imaging quality; 2. image quality
Abbildungsraum *m* imaging space; mapping space
Abbildungsreferenzkoordinatensystem *n* view reference coordinate system *(computer graphics)*
Abbildungsreferenzpunkt *m* view reference point *(computer graphics)*
Abbildungsrichtung *f* imaging direction
Abbildungsschärfe *f* image (picture) sharpness, acutance
Abbildungssituation *f* imaging situation
Abbildungsspeicher *m s.* Bildwiederholspeicher
Abbildungsstrahl *m* imaging ray, image-forming ray [of light], image-carrying ray; image[-forming] beam; imaging electron beam *(electron microscopy)*
Abbildungsstrahlengang *m* image-forming ray path
Abbildungssystem *n* imaging (image-forming) system, image formation system
~/**beugungsbegrenztes** diffraction-limited imaging system
~/**digitales** digital imaging system
~/**einlinsiges** single-lens imaging system
~/**elektrooptisches** electro-optical imaging system
~/**kohärentes** coherent imaging system
~/**optisches** optical imaging system
Abbildungsszenario *n* imaging scenario
Abbildungstabelle *f* view table *(computer graphics)*
Abbildungstechnik *f* 1. imaging [technology]; 2. imaging (image formation) technique
Abbildungstheorie *f* imaging theory
Abbildungstiefe *f* depth of focus (field); imaging depth *(e.g. in sonography)*
Abbildungstreue *f* image (visual) fidelity
Abbildungsumgebung *f* viewing environment *(computer graphics)*
Abbildungsverfahren *n* imaging process (procedure), imaging technique; image-forming process; imaging modality

Abbildungsverhalten *n* imaging behavior *(e.g. of a lens)*
Abbildungsverhältnis *n* scale ratio
Abbildungsvermögen *n* imaging [cap]ability
Abbildungsvorgang *m* imaging process
Abbildungsvorrichtung *f* imaging device (tool)
Abblätterbuch *n* flip-book
Abblende *f* fade[-out], fading out (down) *(cinema)*
~ **nach Schwarz** fade[-out] to black
abblenden to stop down, to diaphragm; to fade down; to iris out *(a motion-picture camera)*
Abblendtaste *f* [all-mode] depth-of-field preview button
Abblendung *f* 1. stopping down, diaphragming; 2. fading out (down), fade[-out] *(cinema)*
abblocken to block [out] *(e.g. rays of light)*
ABCD-Matrix *f* ray-transfer matrix
Abdeckband *n* masking tape
abdecken to mask [out], to block [out], to knock out *(e.g. image elements)*; to opaque
Abdeckfahne *f* flag, gobo; headscreen
Abdeckfarbe *f* masking ink; opaquing paint
Abdeckfilm *m*, **Abdeckfolie** *f* masking film (sheet), tissue overlay
Abdecklack *m* masking lacquer
Abdeckmaske *f* [printing] mask
Abdeckschablone *f* dodging (shading) tool
Abdeckstift *m* masking (opaquing) pen
Abdruck *m* 1. replica; reprint; print; copy; 2. impression; indentation
abdruckbar printable
Abdruckbarkeit *f* printability
Abdruckfilm *m* replica film
abdunkeln to darken, to obscure
Abdunkelung *f* darkening
Abendmahlsformat *n* Last Supper format *(visual telephony)*
Abenteuerspiel *n* adventure game *(interactive video)*
Aberration *f* aberration; image (imaging) aberration
~/**asymmetrische** asymmetrical aberration
~/**axiale chromatische** axial (longitudinal) chromatic aberration, chromatic variation of focus, longitudinal color
~/**chromatische** chromatic [lens] aberration, chromatic error (defect), color aberration (distortion)
~/**geometrische** geometrical aberration
~/**monochromatische** monochromatic aberration
~/**optische** optical aberration (defect)
~/**sphärische** spherical aberration, SA
aberrationsfrei aberration-free, unaberrated
Aberrationsfunktion *f* aberration function

Aberrationskoeffizient *m* aberration coefficient
Aberrationskorrektion *f*, **Aberrationskorrektur** *f* aberration[al] correction
aberrationskorrigiert aberration-corrected
Aberrationstheorie *f* aberration theory
Abfahrzeichen *n* changeover cue [mark], cue dot (mark), reel change mark *(cinema)*
abfallend bled off *(layout)*
Abfallzeit *f* fall time *(of a pulse)*
Abfangradar *n* interception radar
abfilmen to film off
Abformung *f s.* Duplikatdruckform
abfragen to query *(e.g. an image database)*
Abfragesprache *f* query language *(database system)*
abgleichen to match *(e.g. colors)*
Abgleichung *f* matching
abhalten *s.* abwedeln
Abhängigkeitslänge *f* constraint length *(block coding)*
Abhörlautsprecher *m* box
A-Bild *n* A-scan [image] *(sonography)*
A-Bild-Sonografie *f* A-mode (amplitude-mode) ultrasound scanning, A-mode (A-scan) process
abkaschen to mask [off], to mask out
Abkaschen *n*, **Abkaschung** *f* masking [off]
AB-Kopieren *n* AB printing *(film or video)*
Ablageblatt *n*, **Ablagehülle** *f* storage sheet *(e.g. for transparencies)*
Ablation *f* ablation
~ **mit Lasern** laser ablation
Ablaufkante *f* drain edge *(computational geometry)*
Ablaufplan *m* storyboard *(film production)*
Ablegen *n* setoff, offset *(printing defect)*
Ableitung *f* 1. derivation; 2. derivative
Ableitungsfilter *n s.* Ableitungsoperator
Ableitungsoperator *m* derivative operator
Ablenkebene *f* deflection plane
Ablenkeinheit *f* deflection (deflecting) yoke, magnetic-deflection coil pair *(cathode-ray tube)*
Ablenkeinrichtung *f*/**akustooptische** acousto-optic deflector, AOD
Ablenkelektrode *f* deflecting electrode *(cathode-ray tube)*
Ablenkempfindlichkeit *f* deflection sensitivity
ablenken to deflect; to deviate
Ablenkfehler *m* deflection aberration
Ablenkfrequenz *f*/**horizontale** horizontal [sweep] frequency, horizontal scan rate, horizontal (line) scanning frequency, line frequency (rate)
~/**vertikale** vertical (field) scanning frequency, vertical [sweep] frequency, vertical scan rate *(s.a.* Bildwiederholfrequenz*)*
Ablenkgenerator *m* sweep generator
Ablenkjoch *n s.* Ablenkeinheit

Ablenkkondensator *m* deflecting capacitor
Ablenkmagnet *m s.* Ablenkspule
Ablenkplatte *f* deflection (deflecting) plate
Ablenkprisma *n* deflection prism
Ablenkschaltung *f* deflection circuit[ry]
Ablenkspannung *f* deflection voltage
Ablenkspiegel *m* deflection mirror; reflex mirror
Ablenkspule *f* deflecting (scan) coil, deflection (deflector) coil, magnetic-deflection coil pair
Ablenkstrom *m* deflection (deflecting) current
Ablenksystem *n* deflection system
Ablenkung *f* deflection; deviation
~/**elektrostatische** electrostatic deflection
~/**magnetische** magnetic deflection
Ablenkvermögen *n* deflection power
Ablenkwinkel *m* deflection angle, angle of deflection
ablesbar readable
Ablesbarkeit *f* readability
Ablesefernrohr *n* reading telescope
ablichten to photostat *(s.a.* fotokopieren, fotografieren*)*
Ablichtung *f* 1. photomechanical transfer, PMT *(diffusion transfer process)*; 2. photostat[ic] copy, [photo]stat
abliegen to sett off, to offset *(printing defect)*
Abmagnetisierungsdrossel *f* demagnetizer
abmischen to mix *(e.g. sound tracks)*
Abmischen *n*, **Abmischung** *f* mixdown
Abmusterung *f* color matching (adjustment)
Abnahmekopie *f* reference print *(cinema)*
Abofernsehen *n*, **Abonnement[s]fernsehen** *n* subscription television (TV) *(s.a.* Bezahlfernsehen*)*
abpausen to trace
abquetschen to squeegee
Abquetscher *m* squeegee
Abquetschrolle *f* squeegee roll[er]
Abquetschung *f* squeegeeing
abrakeln to doctor off, to scrape [off] *(e.g. printing ink)*
abrastern to raster scan, to scan [off]; to sample
Abreibeschrift *f* transfer (instant) lettering
Abreißblatt *n* tear sheet
Abreißpunkt *m* break point *(ophthalmic optics)*
Abrieb *m* abrasion
abriebbeständig, abriebfest abrasion-resistant, rub-proof
Abriebfestigkeit *f* abrasion resistance *(e.g. of photographic material)*
Abriebschutz *m* abrasion protection
Abriebschutzschicht *f* antiabrasion coating
Abrollmenü *n* pull-down menu *(display)*
Abrufdatei *f* demand file
abrufen to retrieve *(e.g. image data)*
Absatz *m* paragraph *(text layout)*
Absatzeinzug *m* paragraph indent

abscannen to scan [off]
Abschaltautomatik *f* sleep timer *(e.g. of a television set)*
abschatten to shade
Abschattung *f* shading, shadowing
Abschattungseffekt *m* shading effect
Abschließung *f* closure *(binary image processing)*
Abschneidefehler *m* truncation error *(digital filtering)*
Abschneidefrequenz *f* cutoff frequency *(e.g. in image filtering)*
Abschneiden *n* clipping *(computer graphics)*; truncation *(digital filtering)*
abschneiden to cut (trim) off; to clip; to truncate
AB-Schnitt *m* AB editing (cutting), A&B roll editing, checkerboard (A&B) cutting *(video)*
Abschnittlänge *f* cutoff *(web printing)*
Abschnüren *n* lacing *(a film screen)*
abschwächen to attenuate; to reduce
Abschwächer *m* attenuator; reducer
~/**Farmerscher** Farmer's (proportional) reducer
~/**kontrasterhaltender** subtractive (cutting) reducer
~/**kontrastmindernder** flattening (superproportional) reducer
~/**kontraststeigernder** sub-proportional reducer
~/**optischer** optical attenuator
Abschwächung *f* attenuation; reduction
Abschwächungseffekt *m* attenuation effect
Abschwächungskoeffizient *m* attenuation (extinction) coefficient
Absolutblendung *f* blinding glare
Absorbanz *f* absorbance, absorbancy
Absorber *m* absorber
absorbieren to absorb
Absorption *f* absorption
~/**absolute** absolute absorption
~/**elektromagnetische** electromagnetic absorption
~/**fotochemische** photochemical absorption
~/**fotoelektrische** photoelectric absorption
~/**optische** optical (light) absorption
~/**selektive** selective absorption
~/**spektrale** spectral absorption
~/**teilweise** partial absorption
~/**wahre** true absorption
Absorptionsbande *f* absorption band
Absorptionsbereich *m* absorption region
Absorptionsbild *n* absorption image
Absorptionsdichteverteilung *f* absorption density distribution
Absorptionsdruckfarbe *f* pressure-set ink
Absorptionseffizienz *f* absorption efficiency
Absorptionsenergie *f* absorption energy
Absorptionsfaktor *m* absorption factor

Absorptionsfilter *n* absorption filter
Absorptionsfotometrie *f* absorption photometry
Absorptionsgrad *m* absorptance
~/spektraler spectral absorptance
Absorptionshologramm *n* absorption hologram
Absorptionsindex *m* absorption index
Absorptionskante *f* absorption edge
Absorptionskoeffizient *m* absorption coefficient *(of a medium)*
~/fotoelektrischer photoelectric absorption coefficient
~/linearer linear absorption coefficient
~/molarer molar absorption coefficient
~/relativer relative absorption coefficient
Absorptionskonstante *f* absorption constant
Absorptionskontrast *m* absorption contrast *(X-ray microscopy)*
Absorptionskurve *f* absorption curve *(e.g. of a filter)*
Absorptionslinie *f* absorption line
Absorptionslinienspektrum *n* absorption line spectrum
Absorptionsmaximum *n* absorption maximum (peak)
Absorptionsspektralfotometrie *f* absorption photometry
Absorptionsspektroskopie *f* absorption spectroscopy
Absorptionsspektrum *n* absorption (absorptance) spectrum, spectral window of absorption
Absorptionsverlust *m* absorption loss
Absorptionsvermögen *n* absorptivity; absorptance
absorptiv absorptive
Abspann *m* 1. trailer; 2. end title; [end] credits, closing credits
abspeichern to store, to save *(e.g. image data)*
Abspeicherung *f* storage
abspielbar playable
Abspielbarkeit *f* playability
Abspielelektronik *f* playback electronics
abspielen 1. to play [out]; 2. to replay, to play back
Abspieler *m s.* Abspielgerät
Abspielformat *n* playback[-only] format
Abspielgerät *n* playback[-only] machine, playback device, player [device]
Abspielgeschwindigkeit *f* playback [frame] rate, display [frame] rate, playback speed *(of film or video sequences)*
Abspielkopf *m* play[back] head, replay (reproducing) head
Abspielmaschine *f s.* Abspielgerät
Abspielmodus *m* play[back] mode *(camcorder)*
Abspielqualität *f* playback quality
Abspielung *f* playback; replay *(e.g. of a videotape)*

~/laserabgetastete laser-scanned playback
Abspielvorgang *m* playback [process]
Abspielzeit *f* playback (playing) time, program duration *(e.g. of a videodisk)*
abspulen to unreel, to unwind
Abstand *m*/**algebraischer** algebraic distance
~/Euklidischer Euclidean distance *(pattern recognition)*
~/gewichteter Euklidischer weighted Euclidean distance
Abstandsbild *n* [Euclidean] distance map
Abstandsgesetz *n* [/**quadratisches**] *s.* Abstandsquadratgesetz
Abstandsmaß *n* distance measure (metric)
~/Euklidisches Euclidean metric (norm)
Abstandsmessradar *n* distance radar
Abstandsquadratgesetz *n* inverse-square law [of distance], law of inverse squares *(radiant intensity)*
Abstandstransformation *f* distance transform[ation] *(binary image processing)*
Abstandsverhältnis *n* spacing ratio
Abstandsverlust *m* spacing loss *(tape recording)*
Abstandswarnradar *n* anticollision (collision avoidance) radar
Abstandswert *m* distance value
abstimmbar tunable
Abstimmbarkeit *f* tunability
Abstimmbereich *f* tuning range
abstimmen to tune *(e.g. a laser)*
Abstimmspule *f* alignment coil *(cathode-ray tube)*
Abstimmung *f* tuning
abstrahlen to radiate; to emit; to beam
Abstrahlung *f* 1. radiation; emission; 2. *s.* ~/spezifische spektrale
~/spezifische spektrale [radiant] exitance, emissivity, emittance
Abstrahlwinkel *m* angle of radiation, radiation angle
Abstraktion *f* abstraction
Abstraktionshierarchie *f* abstraction hierarchy *(logical structure)*
Abstraktionsniveau *n* abstraction level (layer) *(e.g. of a multimedia system)*
abstreifen to squeegee
Abstreifer *m* squeegee
Abstreifrakel *f* doctor [blade], scraper *(gravure printing)*
Abszissenachse *f* x-axis, horizontal axis *(coordinate system)*
Abtastabstand *m* sampling distance, sample spacing
Abtastalgorithmus *m* sampling algorithm
Abtastauflösung *f* scanning resolution; sampling (sample) resolution *(s.a.* Abtastfrequenz*)*
Abtastbandbreite *f* sampling bandwidth
abtastbar scannable
Abtastbereich *m* scanning area

Abtastbewegung

Abtastbewegung *f* scanning movement, scan[ning] motion
Abtastblende *f* scanning aperture (diaphragm)
Abtastdichte *f* sampling density; scanning density
Abtasteffekt *m* scanning effect *(radar)*
Abtasteffizienz *f* sampling efficiency
Abtasteinheit *f* scanning unit
Abtastelektrode *f* scan electrode
Abtastelektronenmikroskop *n* scanning [electron] microscope, SEM
abtasten to scan [off]; to sample, to probe
Abtaster *m* scanner *(s.a.* Scanner*)*; sampler
~/**mechanischer** mechanical scanner
~/**optomechanischer** optical-mechanical scanner
Abtastfehler *m* scanning error (artifact), sampling error (artifact), discretization error
Abtastfilter *n* sampled data filter
Abtastfläche *f* scan[ning] area
Abtastfolge *f* scan[ning] order, scanning sequence; sample[d] sequence
Abtastformat *n* sampling format; scanning format
Abtastfrequenz *f* scan[ning] rate, scanning frequency; sampling (sample) rate, sampling frequency
~/**horizontale** horizontal scanning frequency, horizontal [sweep] frequency, horizontal scan rate, line frequency (rate)
~/**vertikale** vertical scanning frequency, vertical [sweep] frequency, vertical scan rate; field frequency (repetition rate) *(interlaced video)*; frame rate *(noninterlaced video)*
Abtastfunktion *f* sampling function
Abtastgebiet *n* scan[ning] area
Abtastgenauigkeit *f* sampling (sample) precision
Abtastgeometrie *f* sampling geometry; scan[ning] geometry
Abtastgerät *n* scanning device (machine), scanner; image scanner
Abtastgeräusch *n s.* Abtastrauschen
Abtastgeschwindigkeit *f* scan[ning] speed, scan velocity
Abtastgitter *n* sampling lattice (grid)
Abtast-Halte-Glied *n* sample-and-hold unit
Abtast-Halte-Schaltung *f*,
Abtast-Halte-Stufe *f* sample-and-hold circuit
Abtastimpuls *m* sampling pulse; scanning impulse
Abtastintervall *n* scanning (digitizing) interval; scan phase; sampling (sample) interval, sampling period
Abtastkopf *m* scan[ning] head
Abtastlaser *m* scanning laser
Abtastlichtpunkt *m* scanning light spot
Abtastlichtquelle *f* scanning light source scanning lamp

Abtastlücke *f s.* Austastlücke
Abtastmatrix *f* sampling (generating) matrix; scan matrix
Abtastmechanismus *m* scanning mechanism
Abtastmethode *f* scanning method
Abtastmodus *m* scan[ning] mode
Abtastmuster *n* scan[ning] pattern; sampling (sample) pattern; raster scan[-type] pattern
Abtastnorm *f* scanning standard
Abtastobjektiv *n*, **Abtastoptik** *f* scanning optics; laser disk objective
Abtastort *m* scan position; sampling site
Abtastparameter *m* scan[ning] parameter
Abtastpassband *n* sampling passband
Abtastperiode[ndauer] *f s.* Abtastintervall
Abtastposition *f* scan position
Abtastpräzision *f* sampling (sample) precision
Abtastprinzip *n* scanning principle
Abtastprisma *n* scanning prism
Abtastpunkt *m* scanning spot, scanned point; sample (sampling) point
Abtastpunkte *mpl* **pro Zoll** samples per inch, spi
Abtastraster *m(n)* scan[ning] raster, scanned raster; sampling raster
~/**äquidistanter** equidistant scanning raster
~/**rechteckförmiger** rectangular raster (lattice)
Abtastrate *f* scan[ning] rate, scanning frequency; sampling (sample) rate, sampling frequency
Abtastratenkonversion *f*,
Abtastratenumsetzung *f* scan-rate (frame-rate) conversion, sampling-rate conversion, field-rate (temporal-rate) conversion
Abtastratenverhältnis *n* sampling structure
Abtastratenwandler *m* sampling rate converter
Abtastrauschen *n* scanning noise
Abtastreihe *f* sampling series
Abtastreihenfolge *f* grid scan order
Abtastrichtung *f* scan[ning] direction, direction of scan
Abtaströhre *f* scanning tube
Abtastschaltung *f* scanning circuit[ry]
Abtastschema *n* scan[ning] scheme
Abtastschrittweite *f* sampling step size
Abtastsignal *n* scan[ning] signal; sampled[-data] signal, discrete[-time] signal
Abtastsonde *f* scanning probe
Abtastspalt *m* scanning slit
Abtastspektrum *n* sampling spectrum
Abtastspiegel *m* scan[ning] mirror
Abtaststandard *m* scanning standard
Abtaststeuerung *f* 1. sampling control; scanning control; 2. scanning control circuit

Abtaststrahl m scanning [electron] beam, raster beam
Abtaststrahlapertur f scanning beam slit
Abtaststruktur f scanning structure; sampling structure
Abtastsystem n scanning system
Abtasttakt m sample [rate] clock, sampling clock
Abtasttechnik f scan[ning] technique
Abtasttheorem n sampling theorem *(signal theory)*
Abtasttheorie f sampling theory
Abtastthermograf m scanning thermograph
Abtasttiefe f sampling depth; scanning depth *(sonography)*
Abtastung f 1. sampling, probing *(signal processing)*; 2. scan[ning] *(of structures or spectra)*
~/**aliasfreie** alias-free sampling
~/**asymmetrische** asymmetric[al] sampling
~/**bildpunktsequentielle (bildpunktweise)** point-by-point scanning
~/**digitale** digital sampling
~/**diskrete** discrete sampling
~/**dynamische** dynamic scanning
~/**eindimensionale** unidimensional sampling
~/**elektronische** electronic scanning
~/**feine** fine scanning
~/**fotoelektrische** photoelectric scanning
~/**getaktete** clocked sampling
~/**grobe** coarse scanning
~/**hexagonale** hexagonal sampling
~/**holografische** holographic scanning
~/**ideale** ideal sampling
~ **im Zeilensprungverfahren (Zwischenzeilenverfahren)** interlaced [video] scanning, interlaced scan[ning] system, interlacing
~/**mechanische** mechanical scanning *(sonography)*
~/**mehrdimensionale** multidimensional sampling
~/**optische** optical scanning
~/**orthogonale** orthogonal sampling (scanning)
~/**pixelsynchrone** pixel-synchronous scan[ing]
~/**progressive** progressive [video] scanning, sequential (noninterlaced) scanning, progressive scan [mode]
~/**punktweise** point scan[ning]
~/**räumliche** spatial sampling
~/**rechteckförmige** rectangular sampling
~/**rotierende** rotational scanning *(sonography)*
~/**spektrale** spectral sampling
~/**stochastische** stochastic sampling
~/**zeilenweise** line[-by-line] scanning
~/**zeitliche** temporal sampling
~/**zeitlich-räumliche** spatiotemporal sampling
~/**zweidimensionale** two-dimensional scanning
Abtastungenauigkeit f sampling inaccuracy (imperfection)
Abtastverfahren n scanning method; sampling method
Abtastverhalten n scanning behavior
Abtastverhältnis n sampling ratio
Abtastvolumen n 1. sampling volume; 2. scan volume *(tomography)*
Abtastvorgang m scan[ning] process, scan[ning] operation; sampling process
Abtastvorlage f scanning copy
Abtastvorrichtung f scanning device; sampling device
Abtastweg m scanning path
Abtastwert m sample [value]
~/**spektraler** spectral sample
Abtastwinkel m scan[ning] angle; sampling angle
Abtastzeile f scan[ning] line, raster line; gate line *(liquid-crystal display)*
Abtastzeilenfrequenz f scanning line frequency (rate)
Abtastzeit f scan[ning] time; sampling time (window)
Abtastzeitpunkt m sampling instant (moment)
Abtastzyklus m scan[ning] cycle
Abtastzylinder m scanning cylinder
Abtönung f shade, nuance
abtragen to plot
Abtragung f s. 1. Erosion; 2. Ablation
abwärtskompatibel downward (backward) compatible
Abwärtskompatibilität f downward (backward) compatibility
Abwärtskonverter m downconverter
abwärtskonvertieren to down-convert *(a digital signal)*
Abwärtskonvertierung f downconversion
Abwärtsskalierung f downscaling
Abwärtsstrecke f downlink, down path *(signal transmission)*
abwärtstasten to down-sample
Abwärtstaster m downsampler
Abwärtstastung f downsampling *(image filtering)*
Abwedelmaske f dodging (shading) tool
abwedeln to dodge [out], to hold back
Abweichung f 1. deviation; 2. s. Aberration
~/**mittlere quadratische** mean-square deviation, mean-square[d] error, MSE, root-mean-square error, rms error *(assessment parameter)*
Abweichungsquadrat n/**mittleres** s. Abweichung/mittlere quadratische
Abweisungsrate f **berechtigter Personen** false rejection rate, FRR *(authentication)*
Abwickelmagazin n supply (feed) magazine
Abwickelspule f feed (source) reel, source (supply) spool
Abziehbild n decal

Abziehbilderpapier *n* [decal] transfer paper
Abziehen *n* stripping [off]; peeling [off]
Abziehfilm *m* stripping film, peel-apart film
Abziehlack *m* masking (stripping) lacquer, stripping varnish *(reprography)*
Abzug *m* 1. [positive] print, photo[graphic] print, paper [positive] print, duplicate print; 2. extractor *(darkroom appliance)*
~/**großformatiger** large-format print
~/**randloser** borderless print
~/**verblasster (verblichener)** faded print
Abzugsformat *n* print format (size)
Abzugsvergrößerung *f* print enlargement
Abzweigverstärker *m* active amplifier *(cable television)*
Academy-Format *n* academy (sound) aperture, Academy ratio *(film format)*
Acetat *n* acetate
Acetatfilm *m* acetate[-base] film, [cellulose] triacetate [safety] film, safety [base] film
Acetatfilter *n* acetate-base filter
Acetatfolie *f* acetate [film]
Acetatrollfilm *m* acetate roll film
Acetatschlauch *m* acetate sleeve [protector]
Acetatunterlage *f* acetate base, [tri]acetate film base
Aceton *n* acetone, dimethylketone *(solvent)*
Acetylcellulose *f* acetyl[ated] cellulose, [cellulose] acetate
Achromasie *f s.* Achromatopsie
Achromasiebedingung *f* condition of achromatism
Achromat *m* achromat [objective], achromatic lens (objective), achromatic system
achromatisch 1. achromatic, uncolored, neutral; 2. achromatic, color-corrected *(lens)*
achromatisieren to achromatize, to color-correct
Achromatisierung *f* achromatization
Achromatismus *m s.* Achromatopsie
Achromatopsie *f* achromatism, achromatopsia
Achse *f* axis
~/**optische** 1. optical axis *(lens optics)*; 2. optic axis *(uniaxial birefringent crystal)*; 3. *s.* Augenachse[/optische]
~/**parallaktische** parallactic axis
~/**visuelle** visual axis
Achsenabstand *m* interaxial distance
achsenentfernt, achsenfern off-axis, abaxial, extra-axial
achsennah near-axis, paraxial
achsenparallel axis-parallel, axially parallel, parallel to the axis; orthogonal
Achsenparallelstrahl *m* ray parallel to the axis
Achsensprungregel *f* 180-degree rule *(cinematography)*
Achsenstrahl *m* axial ray

Achsensymmetrie *f* axisymmetry, axial symmetry
achsensymmetrisch axisymmetric[al], axially symmetrical
Achsenverschwenkung *f* tilt *(e.g. of a view camera)*
achsfern *s.* achsenentfernt, achsenfern
Achsparallelbündel *n* on-axis bundle
Acht-auf-Vierzehn-Modulation *f* eight-to-fourteen modulation, EFM *(channel encoding)*
Acht-Bit-Bild *n* eight-bit image; eight-bit gray-scale image
Acht-Bit-Farbbild *n* color eight-bit image
Acht-Bit-Farbtiefe *f* eight-bit color depth
Acht-Bit-Quantisierung *f* eight-bit quantization
Acht-Bit-Wort *n* eight-bit [PCM] codeword
Acht-Charakteristik *f* figure eight [shaped pattern] *(of microphone directivity)*
Achterbaum *m* octree *(data structure)*
Achterbaumcodierung *f* octree encoding [procedure]
Achterbaumdarstellung *f* octree representation
Achterbaumquantisierung *f* octree quantization
Achternachbarschaft *f*, **Achterumgebung** *f* octagonal (eight-connection) neighborhood, eight-adjacency, 8-neighborhood *(of pixels)*
Acht-Millimeter-Farbfilm *m* eight-mm color movie film
Acht-Millimeter-Film *m* eight millimeter (mm) film, regular eight mm *(home-movie format)*
Acmade-Codierung *f* Acmade code (number), ink number *(on motion-picture dailies)*
Acmade-Numeriermaschine *f* Acmade [machine], ink number printer
Acrylglas *n* acrylic glass
Actionfotografie *f* action photography
A-D-..., A/D-... *s.* Analog-Digital...
Adaptabilität *f* adaptability
Adaptation *f* adaptation, adaption; visual (eye) adaptation
~/**chromatische** chromatic (color) adaptation *(of the eye)*
~/**neuronale** neural adaptation
Adaptations[daten]feld *n* adaptation field
Adaptationsfeldsteuerung *f* adaptation field control
Adaptationsleuchtdichte *f* adaptation luminance
Adaptationsparameter *m* adaptation parameter
Adaptationsvermögen *n* adaptability
Adaptationszeit *f* adaptive time
Adaptationszustand *m* adaptation state, state of adaptation
Adapter *m* [coupling] adapter, adaptor
~ **für Verbindungskabel** connector adapter
Adapterkabel *n* adapter cord (cable)

Akkommodationszustand

Adapterkassette f adapter cassette
Adapterring m adapter ring
Adaptertubus m adapter tube
adaptieren to adapt
Adaption f s. Adaptation
adaptiv adaptive
Adaptivität f adaptivity
Adaptometer n adaptometer
Add/Drop-Filter n/**optisches** optical add/drop filter
~/**Drop-Multiplexer** m/**optischer** optical add/drop multiplexer
Additionsbild n sum image *(radiography)*
Additionsfarbe f additive color
Additivität f additivity
Aderhaut f choroid [coat] *(of the eye)*
Adhäsion f adhesion
Adhäsionskraft f adhesion (adhesive) force
adjazent adjacent
Adjazenz f adjacency *(s.a. under Nachbarschaft)*
Adjazenzgraph m adjacency (neighborhood) graph
Adjazenzmatrix f adjacency matrix *(graph theory)*
Adressbus m address bus *(computer)*
Adresse f address
~/**absolute** absolute address
~/**relative** relative address
Adressencode m address code
Adressencodierung f/**relative** relative address coding, RAC *(image compression)*
Adressfeld n address field
adressierbar addressable
~/**wahlfrei** randomly addressable
Adressierbarkeit f addressability
Adressiersignal n [vertical interval control] address signal *(video disk)*
Adressierung f addressing *(e.g. of pixels in a liquid-crystal display)*
~/**absolute** direct adressing
~/**aktive** active[-matrix] addressing
~/**direkte** direct addressing
~/**passive** passive[-matrix] addressing
Adressraum m address[ing] space
Adressspur f time-code channel
Adsorber m adsorbent, adsorber
adsorbieren to adsorb
Adsorption f adsorption
adsorptiv adsorptive
Aerofotografie f aerophotography, aerial (air) photography
Aerofotogrammetrie f aerophotogrammetry, aerial photogrammetry
Aerogeologie f photogeology
Aerograf m airbrush
Aerografie f airbrushing
Aerokartograf m aerocartographer
Aerotriangulation f aerotriangulation
AF... s.a. Autofokus...
AF-Kupplung f AF coupling
afokal afocal; focusless

AF-Starttaste f AF start button
Agentenkamera f spy camera, spycam
Agenturaufnahme f, **Agenturbild** n, **Agenturfoto** n stock picture (photograph)
Agenturfotograf m stock photographer
Agglomeration f agglomeration *(s.a. Cluster)*
Aggregationszustand m state of aggregation
AgX s. Silberhalogenid
Ähnlichkeitsbedingung f similarity constraint *(image modeling)*
Ähnlichkeitserkennung f similarity recognition
Ähnlichkeitsfunktion f similarity function
Ähnlichkeitsgrad m degree of similarity
Ähnlichkeitsmaß n similarity measure
Ähnlichkeitsmatrix f similarity matrix
Ähnlichkeitsmessung f similarity measurement
Ähnlichkeitsmetrik f similarity metrics
Ähnlichkeitsmodell n similarity model
Ähnlichkeitssatz m similarity theorem
Ähnlichkeitssuche f similarity search
Ähnlichkeitsterm m similarity term
Ähnlichkeitstransformation f similarity transform[ation]; isotropic mapping *(computer graphics)*
Ähnlichkeitsverteilung f similarity distribution
Airbrush-Technik f airbrushing
Airport-Rundsichtradar n airport surveillance radar, ASR
Airy-Beugungsscheibchen n s. Airy-Scheibchen
Airy-Funktion f Airy function
Airy-Scheibchen n, **Airy-Scheibe** f Airy disk, diffraction disk *(refractive optics)*
Akaziengummi n gum arabic (acacia), acacin[e]
Akima-Interpolation f Akima interpolation *(computer graphics)*
Akkolade f brace, curly bracket *(punctuation mark)*
Akkommodation f [visual] accommodation, ocular accommodation
Akkommodationsbereich m accommodation [range]
Akkommodationsbreite f accommodation width
Akkommodationsfähigkeit f accommodative ability
Akkommodationsgebiet n s. Akkommodationsbereich
Akkommodationskraft f power of accommodation
Akkommodationsnahpunkt m near point (limit)
Akkommodationsreflex m accommodation reflex (response)
Akkommodationszeit f accommodation time
Akkommodationszustand m accommodation state (condition)

akkommodativ accommodative
akkommodieren to accommodate, to refocus
Akku *m s.* Akkumulator
Akkuanzeige *f* battery remaining indicator
Akkugürtel *m* battery belt
Akkukapazität *f* battery power
Akkumulator *m* accumulator, secondary cell; battery *(s.a.* Batterie*)*
Akkupack *m* battery pack
Akkuscheinwerfer *m* sun gun
akquirieren to acquire
Akquisition *f* acquisition *(e.g. of image data)*
Akquisitionsdauer *f*, **Akquisitionszeit** *f* [image] acquisition time
Akt *m* motion-picture roll, spool
aktinisch actinic
Aktinität *f* actinism, actinity
Aktinometer *n* actinometer
Aktionsaufnahme *f* action shot
Aktionsfilm *m* actioner
Aktionspotential *n* action potential, nerve impulse, spike *(neuroinformatics)*
aktiv/optisch optically active
Aktivator *m* activator
Aktivatorbad *n* activator bath (solution)
Aktivierungsenergie *f* activation energy *(photodetector)*
Aktivierungszustand *m* activation level *(neural network)*
Aktivität *f*/**optische** optical activity
Aktivlautsprecher *m* active [loud]speaker
Aktivmatrixbildschirm *m* active-matrix display, TFT (thin-film transistor) display
Aktivmatrix-Dünnfilmtransistor *m* active-matrix thin-film transistor
Aktivmatrix-Flüssigkristallanzeige *f* active-matrix LCD (liquid-crystal display), AMLCD
Aktivspeicher *m* active storage
Aktor *m s.* Aktuator
Aktualisierungsmodus *m* deferral mode *(graphics workstation)*
Aktuator *m* actuator
Akustikkoppler *m* acoustic coupler *(telecommunications)*
Akustooptik *f* acoustooptics
akustooptisch acousto-optic[al]
Akustothermometrie *f* acoustothermometry
Akut *m* acute accent *(diacritic)*
Akzentbuchstabe *m* accented character
Akzentuierung *f* accentuation
Akzeptanzwinkel *m* [light] acceptance angle, angle of acceptance *(e.g. of an objective)*
Akzidenzdruck *m* short-run work, job printing
Akzidenzfarbdruck *m* short-run color printing
Akzidenzmaschine *f* jobbing [printing] press; short-run lithographic press
Akzidenzsatz *m* job composition

Albada-Sucher *m* [van] Albada [view]finder, bright-frame [view]finder, suspended-frame finder
Albedo *f* albedo, reflective power, reflectivity; diffuse reflectance *(of a Lambertian surface)*
Albert-Effekt *m* Albert effect *(photographic reversal image production)*
Albertotypie *f* 1. Albertypy *(an early photomechanical process)* 2. albertype *(print)*
Album *n* album
Albuminabzug *m* albumen [positive] print
Albuminpapier *n* albumen[ized] paper
Albuminpapierabzug *m s.* Albuminabzug
Albuminplatte *f* albumen [glass] plate
Albuminverfahren *n* albumen [negative] process
Albumseite *f* album page
Alexandritlaser *m* alexandrite laser
Algebra *f*/**Boolesche** Boolean algebra (logic)
~/**geometrische** geometric algebra
Algorithmenanimation *f* algorithm animation
algorithmieren to algorithmize
algorithmisch algorithmic
Algorithmus *m* algorithm
~/**adaptiver** adaptive algorithm
~/**asymmetrischer** asymmetrical algorithm
~/**bikubischer** bicubic algorithm
~/**diskreter** discrete algorithm
~/**Euklidischer** Euclidean algorithm
~/**evolutionärer** evolutionary algorithm
~/**genetischer** genetic algorithm *(stochastic search method)*
~/**gieriger** greedy algorithm *(computer graphics)*
~/**globaler** global algorithm
~/**hierarchischer** hierarchical algorithm
~/**iterativer** iterative algorithm
~/**konservativer** conservative algorithm
~/**lernender** learning algorithm
~/**morphologischer** morphological algorithm
~/**rechenintensiver** computationally intensive algorithm
~/**robuster** robust algorithm
~/**schneller** fast algorithm *(e.g. for geometric transforms)*
Algorithmusanimation *f* algorithm animation
Alias[effekt] *m s.* Aliasing
Aliasfehler *m* aliasing error (defect)
aliasfrei alias-free
Aliasing *n* aliasing [effect], alias *(sampling artifact; s.a.* Treppeneffekt*)*; wraparound artifact *(magnetic resonance imaging)*
~/**zeitliches** temporal alias[ing]
Aliasing-Effekt *m s.* Aliasing
Aliasing-Frequenz *f* aliased (aliasing) frequency
Aliaskomponente *f* alias[ing] component

Aliasspektrum *n* aliasing spectrum
Aliasstörung *f*, **Aliasstruktur** *f* aliasing [artifact]
Aliasunterdrückung *f* suppression of aliasing
Alkali *n* alkali
Alkalibatterie *f* alkaline battery
Alkalicarbonat *n* alkali carbonate
Alkalihalogenid *n* alkali halide
Alkalihalogenidlösung *f* alkali halide solution
Alkalimetall *n* alkali metal
Alkali-Mignonzelle *f* AA-type alkaline battery
Alkalinitrat *n* alkali nitrate
alkalisch alkaline
Alkalität *f* alkalinity
Alkoholfeuchtung *f* alcohol damping system *(printing)*
Alles-oder-nichts-Transformation *f* hit-or-miss transformation *(binary image processing)*
Allgemeinbeleuchtung *f* general lighting
Allgemeinempfindlichkeit *f* overall sensitivity *(e.g. of a photographic emulsion)*
Allgemeinkontrast *m* overall (general) contrast, total contrast
Allgemeinlicht *n* overall (ambient) light
Allgemeinschärfe *f* overall sharpness
Allonge *f* clear (protective) leader; trailer
Allpassfilter *n* allpass filter
Allwetterkamera *f* weatherized (winterized) camera
Allzweckfilter *n* general-purpose filter
Allzweckkollimator *m* general-purpose collimator *(radiography)*
Allzweckobjektiv *n* general-purpose lens
Alphabet *n* alphabet *(e.g. of pixel values in image compression)*
~/binäres binary alphabet
Alpha-Blending *n* alpha mix[ing], alpha blending
alphageometrisch alphageometric[al]
Alphakanal *m* alpha (matte) channel *(video, computer graphics)*
Alphakanalsteuerung *f* alpha channeling
alphamerisch *s.* alphanumerisch
Alphanumerik *f* alphanumerics
alphanumerisch alphanumeric[al], alphameric
Alphastrahlen *mpl*, **Alphastrahlung** *f* alpha radiation
Alphateilchen *n* alpha [particle], alpha ray
Alpha-Wert *m* alpha value
Altazimut *m(n)* altazimuth *(astronomical optics)*
Altchemietank *m* old chemistry tank
Alters[weit]sichtig presbyopic
~[weit]sichtigkeit *f* presbyopia, limited accommodation, old eye *(vision defect)*
Alterungsbeständigkeit *f* age resistance *(e.g. of photo paper)*
Altfilmmaterial *n* scrap (reject) films

Alukoffer *m* aluminum case
aluminieren to aluminize
Aluminierung *f* aluminizing
Aluminiumchlorid *n* aluminum chloride
Aluminiumfilter *n* aluminum filter
Aluminiumspiegel *m* aluminum (aluminized) mirror, aluminum-coated surface mirror
Aluminiumtreppe *f* aluminum [metal] step tablet *(brightness normalization)*
Alychne *f* alychne *(colorimetry)*
Amacrinzelle *f* amacrine (association) cell *(retinal neuron)*
amagnetisch nonmagnetic
Amateur *m*/**ambitionierter (engagierter)** devoted (high-end) amateur, serious amateur
Amateur-Astrofotografie *f* amateur astrophotography
Amateurbereich *m* amateur field
Amateurcamcorder *m* consumer [video] camcorder
Amateur-Digitalkamera *f* consumer-grade digital camera
Amateurfarbfilm *m* amateur color film
Amateurfarbfoto *n* amateur color picture
Amateur-Farbfotografie *f* amateur color photography
Amateur-Farbvideokamera *f* color home video camera
Amateurfilm *m* 1. amateur film; 2. amateur (home) movie
Amateurfilmen *n* amateur moviemaking
Amateurfilmer *m* amateur filmmaker
Amateurfilmproduktion *f* amateur filmmaking (production)
Amateurfoto *n* amateur photograph
Amateurfotofilm *m* amateur still film
Amateurfotograf *m* amateur photographer
Amateurfotografie *f* amateur (consumer) photography
amateurfotografisch amateur photographic
Amateurkamera *f* amateur (nonprofessional) camera, consumer camera
Amateurkameraobjektiv *n* amateur camera lens
Amateurkinematografie *f* amateur cinematography
Amateurschmalfilm *m* amateur home motion picture, [amateur] home movie
Amateurschmalfilmen *n* amateur home moviemaking
Amateur-Schnappschusskamera *f* amateur snapshot camera
Amateurstudio *n* amateur studio
Amateurteleskop *n* amateur telescope
Amateurvideo *n* amateur video
Amateurvideoband *n* consumer (home) videotape
Amateur-Videokamera *f* consumer[-level] video camera

Amateur-Videorecorder *m* home (consumer-grade) video recorder, domestic (consumer) videocassette recorder, home (domestic) VCR
Amaurose *f* amaurosis, loss of sight
amblyop amblyopic
Amblyopie *f* amblyopia, dimness of sight, low vision, lazy eye
Ambrotypie *f* 1. ambrotype process; 2. ambrotype, positive on glass, collodion positive *(chiefly British)*
Ametropie *f* ametropia, disorder of vision
Amici-Prisma *n* Amici (direct-vision) prism, roof prism
Amidol *n s.* Diamidophenolhydrochlorid
Aminophenol *n* aminophenol *(developing chemical)*
Ammoniak *n* ammonia
Ammoniakdampf *m* ammonia fume (vapor)
Ammoniakemulsion *f* ammoniacal emulsion *(film manufacture)*
Ammoniumbichromat *n* ammonium bichromate (dichromate)
Ammoniumbromid *n* ammonium bromide
Ammoniumchlorid *n* ammonium chloride
Ammoniumeisencitrat *n*, **Ammoniumferricitrat** *n* ferric ammonium citrate *(image toner)*
Ammoniumiodid *n* ammonium iodide
Ammoniumoxalat *n* ammonium oxalate *(developing chemical)*
Ammoniumpersulfat-Abschwächer *m* ammonium persulfate reducer
Ammoniumthiosulfat *n* ammonium thiosulfate *(fixing agent)*
A-Mode-Verfahren *n s.* A-Bild-Sonografie
Ampere *n* ampere, amp *(basic unit of electric current intensity)*
Amplitude *f* amplitude
~/**diskrete** discrete amplitude
~/**komplexe** complex amplitude *(wave optics)*
~/**konjugierte** conjugate amplitude *(holography)*
~/**kontinuierliche** continuous amplitude
~/**nichtsymmetrische** nonsymmetrical amplitude
~/**phasencodierte** phase-encoded amplitude
~/**reflektierte** reflected amplitude
~/**zeitabhängige** time-dependent amplitude
Amplitudenabtastung *f* amplitude sampling
Amplitudenanalyse *f* amplitude analysis *(ground penetrating radar)*
Amplitudenauflösung *f* amplitude resolution
Amplitudenbegrenzer *m* amplitude limiter
Amplitudenbereich *m* 1. amplitude domain; 2. amplitude range
Amplitudenbild *n* amplitude presentation
~/**quadratisches** square root intensity image
Amplitudendämpfung *f* amplitude damping (reduction), amplitude attenuation
Amplitudendarstellung *f* amplitude presentation
Amplitudendichte *f* amplitude density
Amplitudendichteverteilung *f* amplitude density distribution
~/**Gaußsche** Gaussian (normal) distribution
Amplitudendifferenz *f* amplitude difference
Amplituden-Doppler *m* Doppler power imaging, amplitude (power) Doppler *(sonography)*
Amplitudenfehler *m* amplitude error
Amplitudenfilterung *f* amplitude filtering
Amplitudenfluktuation *f* amplitude fluctuation (variation)
Amplitudenfrequenzgang *m* amplitude[-frequency] response, amplitude-frequency characteristic, magnitude response
Amplitudenfunktion *f* frequency function
Amplitudengang *m s.* Amplitudenfrequenzgang
Amplitudengeschwindigkeit *f* amplitude velocity
Amplitudengitter *n* amplitude diffraction grating
Amplitudengradient *m* amplitude gradient
Amplitudenhistogramm *n* amplitude histogram
Amplitudenhöhe *f* amplitude level
Amplitudenhologramm *n* amplitude hologram
Amplituden-Hüllkurve *f* amplitude envelope
Amplitudenirrelevanz *f* amplitude irrelevancy
Amplitudenkontrast *m* amplitude contrast *(electron microscopy)*
Amplitudenkontrastmikroskop *n* amplitude-contrast microscope
Amplitudenlinearität *f* amplitude linearity
Amplitudenmodulation *f* amplitude modulation, AM
Amplitudenmodus *m* A-mode *(sonography)*
Amplitudenobjekt *n* amplitude object; amplitude specimen *(bright-field microscopy)*
Amplituden-Phasendiagramm *n* amplitude-phase diagram *(electron diffraction)*
Amplitudenprojektion *f* amplitude projection
Amplitudenquantisierung *f* amplitude quantization, banding
Amplitudenrauschen *n* amplitude noise
Amplitudenreflexionskoeffizient *m* amplitude reflection coefficient

Amplitudenschrift *f* variable-area sound track, amplitude trace *(motion-picture sound)*
Amplitudenschwankung *f* amplitude fluctuation (variation)
Amplitudensieb *n* amplitude (sync) separator
Amplitudenskala *f* amplitude scale
Amplitudenskalierung *f* amplitude scaling
Amplitudenspektrum *n* amplitude (power) spectrum *(Fourier analysis)*
Amplitudenstabilität *f* amplitude stability
Amplitudenstruktur *f* amplitude structure
Amplitudenstufe *f* amplitude step
Amplitudentastung *f s.* Amplitudenumtastung
Amplitudenteilung *f* division of amplitude
Amplitudentiefe *f s.* Amplitudenauflösung
Amplitudentransmission *f* amplitude transmittance *(holography)*
Amplitudentransmissionskoeffizient *m* amplitude transmission coefficient
Amplitudenumtastung *f* amplitude shift keying, ASK
Amplitudenvektor *m* amplitude vector
Amplitudenverhältnis *n* amplitude ratio
Amplitudenverlauf *m* amplitude response
Amplitudenverteilung *f*/**komplexe** complex amplitude distribution
Amplitudenverzerrung *f* amplitude distortion (bias)
Amplitudenvorverzerrung *f* amplitude predistortion
Amplitudenwert *m* amplitude value
Amplitudenzonenplatte *f* amplitude zone plate *(X-ray microscopy)*
AM-Rasterung *f s.* Rasterung/amplitudenmodulierte
Anaglyphenbild *n* anaglyph, stereoanaglyph image; red-green image
Anaglyphenbrille *f* anaglyph glasses; red-green goggles
Anaglyphendruck *m* anaglyphic print
Anaglyphenverfahren *n* anaglyph[ic] method, anaglyph system *(of stereoscopic viewing)*
analog analog, analogue *(chiefly British)*
Analoganzeige *f* analog display
Analogaufzeichnung *f* 1. analog recording; 2. analog record[ing]
Analogband *n* analog tape
Analogbereich *m* analog domain
Analogbild *n* analog (continuous) image
Analogbildschirm *m* analog [CRT] monitor; analog display
Analogdaten *pl* analog data
Analog-Digital-Schnittstelle *f* analog-digital interface ADI
Analog-Digital-Signalwandler *m*, **Analog-Digital-Umsetzer** *m* analog-[to-]digital [signal] converter, A-to-D converter, ADC
Analog-Digital-Umsetzung *f*, **Analog-Digital-Wandlung** *f* analog-[to-]digital conversion [process], AD conversion, digitization
Analogeingabe[einheit] *f* analog input *(process computing system)*
Analogeingang *m* analog input
Analogempfänger *m* analog receiver
Analogfernsehen *n* analog television
Analogfilter *n* analog filter, continuous-time filter
Analogfilterung *f* analog filtering
Analogfotografie *f* analog photography *(s.a.* Silberfotografie*)*
Analogkamera *f* analog camera
Analogmischer *m* analog [video] switcher
Analogmonitor *m* analog [CRT] monitor
Analogproof *m* analog proof *(printing)*
Analogrechner *m* analog computer
Analogrecorder *m* analog recorder
Analogsignal *n* analog (continuous-time) signal, analytic signal
Analogsignalverarbeitung *f* analog signal processing
Analogtechnik *f* analog technology
Analogton *m* analog sound
Analog-Tonbandaufzeichnung *f* analog magnetic tape recording
Analogtonspur *f* analog sound track
Analogübertragung *f* analog transmission
Analogvideo *n* analog video
Analogwert *m* analog value
Analysator *m* analyzer
Analyse *f* analysis
~/**dreidimensionale** three-dimensional analysis
~/**harmonische** harmonic (Fourier) analysis, Fourier transform[ation]
~/**lokale** local analysis
~/**mikroskopische** microscopic[al] analysis
~/**spektrale** spectral (spectrum) analysis
~/**visuelle** visual analysis
Analysefenster *n* analysis window
Analysefilter *n* analysis filter
Analysefilterbank *f* analysis [filter] bank
Analysenspektrometer *n* analytical spectrometer
Analyse-Synthese-Codierung *f*/**objektbasierte** object-based analysis-synthesis coding, OBASC
~/**wissensbasierte** knowledge-based analysis-synthesis coding, KBASC
anamorph *s.* anamorphotisch
Anamorphose *f* anamorphosis
Anamorphot *m* anamorphote [lens], anamorphic [squeeze] lens, anamorphic optics (system), distorting (squeeze) lens
anamorphotisch anamorphic, anamorphotic
Anastigmat *m(n)* anastigmat, anastigmatic lens
~/**symmetrischer** symmetrical anastigmat
anastigmatisch anastigmat[ic], stigmatic
anätzen to pre-etch
anaxial anaxial

Änderungsdetektion

Änderungsdetektion f, **Änderungserkennung** f change detection
Änderungsliste f change list *(e.g. in film editing)*
Andruck m 1. proof; press proof, trial (strike off) proof; 2. s. ~/echter
~/echter composite (final) proof, imposition (stripping) proof
andrucken to proof
Andruckergebnis n proofing result
Andruckersatz m prepress proof, dry (off-press) proof
Andruckkufe f skid
Andruckmaschine f proof[ing] press
Andruckpapier n proof paper
Andruckplatte f pressure plate; camera pressure plate, pressure pad
Andruckrolle f pinch (pressure) roller, pad roller, intermittent shoe
Andruckschiene f guide rail
Andruckskala f proofing scale, progressive proof, progressives, progs
Andruckwalze f/**beheizte** heated pressure roller *(electrophotography)*
Anfangsallonge f leader
Anfangsaufnahme f establishing shot *(motion-picture photography)*
Anfangsband n leader
Anfangsbildpunkt m seed pixel
Anfangsbuchstabe m initial [capital letter]
Anfangskennsatz m header [record] *(of a data frame)*
Anfangsklappe f head (front) slate *(filming)*
Anfangskontrast m initial contrast
Anfangsöffnung f maximum aperture
Anfangsphase f initial phase *(e.g. of a light wave)*
Anfangspunkt m starting (initial) point *(e.g. in chain coding)*
Anfangstitel m opening credits (title); main and credit title *(cinema)*
Anfasser m handle *(computer graphics)*
Anfeuchtungslösung f pre-moistening solution
Anfragebild n query image *(image retrieval)*
Anfragesprache f query language *(database system)*
Anfügeschnitt m 1. assemble editing *(videography)*; 2. assemble edit
Anführungszeichen n quotation (quote) mark *(punctuation mark)*
~/halbes single quotation mark
Angel f fishpole, microphone (boom) pole
Anger-Kamera f Anger[-type] camera, [single-crystal] gamma camera, scintillation camera
angeschnitten bled off *(layout)*
Angiografie f angiography, angiographic (vascular) imaging
~/biplane biplane angiography
~/computertomografische computed tomography angiography
~/interventionelle interventional angiography
Angiografiekassette f angiography cassette
Angiografiekatheter m angiographic catheter
angiografisch angiographic
Angiogramm n angiogram
Angiokardiografie f angiocardiography, cardioangiography
angiokardiografisch angiocardiographic
Angiokardiogramm n cardioangiogram
Angioskop n angioscope
Angioskopie f angioscopy
~/virtuelle virtual angioscopy
Angleich m match
Angström n angstrom *(a metric unit of length)*
angular, angulär angular
Angulierung f angulation *(radiology)*
Anhaltspunkt m witness point
Anilindruck m 1. aniline printing (process); 2. s. Flexodruck
Anilinfarbe f, **Anilinfarbstoff** m aniline dye
Anilingummidruck m s. Flexodruck
Anilinrot n s. Magenta
Aniloxfarbwerk n, **Aniloxwalze** f anilox inking system, anilox roll *(flexography)*
Animation f 1. [traditional] animation; 2. s. ~/computerbasierte
~/computerbasierte computer[-enhanced] animation, computer-assisted animation
~/computererzeugte computer-generated animation
~/digitale digital animation
~/dreidimensionale three-dimensional animation; stop-motion animation (photography)
~/dynamische dynamics
~/einbildweise frame-by-frame animation
~/elektronische electronic animation
~/lippensynchrone lip-sync animation
~/verhaltensbedingte behavioral animation
~/zielgerichtete goal-directed animation
~/zweidimensionale two-dimensional animation, 2-D animation
Animationsbild n animation image, [animation] frame
Animationsdatei f animation file
Animationsdesigner m animation designer *(s.a. Animator)*
Animationseffekt m animation effect
Animationsfigur f animatronic, animated figure, animation character
Animationsfilm m animated (trick) film, animation, effects film, special-effects movie
Animationsfotografie f animation photography
Animationskamera f animation camera, process motion-picture camera

Animationskinematografie f animation cinematography
Animationsmodell n animation model
Animationsprogramm n animation program
Animationspuppe f [animation] puppet
Animationssequenz f animation (animated) sequence
Animationssoftware f animation software
Animationsspezialist m animator
Animationsstudio n animation studio
Animationssystem n animation system
Animationstechnik f animation technique
Animationsverfahren n animation technique
Animator m animator
animierbar animatable
animieren to animate
Anion n anion
Anionenleerstelle f anion vacancy
Aniseikonie f aniseikonia *(defect of binocular vision)*
aniseikonisch aniseikonic
Anisometropie f anisometropia *(disorder of vision)*
anisometropisch anisometropic
anisotrop anisotropic, nonisotropic, directionally dependent, directional
Anisotropie f [directional] anisotropy, anisotropism
~/**dielektrische** dielectric anisotropy
~/**lineare** linear anisotropy
~/**magnetische** magnetic anisotropy
~/**planare** planar anisotropy
Ankerpunkt m anchor point *(computer graphics)*
anklickbar clickable *(interface)*
anklicken to click
Anlagekante f edge guide, guided edge
Anlagemaß n flange focal distance *(of a lens)*
Anlaufzeit f 1. warm-up time *(e.g. of a copier)*; 2. *s.* Hochlaufzeit
Anlegeapparat m *s.* Anleger
Anlegearbeit f *s.* Anlegen[/synchrones]
anlegen to conform *(film or video editing)*
Anlegen n [/**synchrones**] conforming, syncing-up *(film editing)*
~ **von Ton zu Bild** sync-sound *(film editing)*
Anleger m feeding unit, feeder *(printing press)*
Anmerkungszeichen n reference mark; dagger
Annäherungszünder m proximity fuze *(radar)*
Annihilation f annihilation [radiation] *(particle physics)*
Annotation f annotation
Anode f anode, ultor
Anodengitter n anode grid
Anodenmaterial n anode material, target [material] *(X-ray tube)*
Anodenneigungswinkel m anode angle
Anodenplatte f anode panel (disk)

Anodenspannung f anode (target) voltage
Anodenverlustleistung f anode dissipation power
Anodenzylinder m anode cylinder
Anomaloskop n anomaloscope
Anop[s]ie f ano[o]psia
Anordnung f array, arrangement, order *(s.a.* Array*)*
~/**flächenhafte (flächige)** area array *(e.g. of photodiodes)*
anpassen to adapt; to accommodate; to fit; to match
Anpassring m adapter ring
Anpassung f adaptation, adaption; accommodation; fit; match
anregbar excitable
anregen to stimulate; to excite, to pump *(e.g. atoms or molecules)*
Anregung f stimulation; excitation
~/**codierte** coded excitation *(sonography)*
~/**optische** optical stimulation
~/**selektive** selective excitation
Anregungsenergie f excitation energy
Anregungsfrequenz f excitation frequency
Anregungsimpuls m excitation [im]pulse
Anregungsintegral n excitation integral
Anregungssignal n excitation signal
Anregungsstrahlung f exciting radiation
Anregungstemperatur f excitation temperature
Anregungsvolumen n excitation volume
Anreicherung f/**fokale** hot spot *(scintigraphy)*
Ansatz m approach
anschallen to insonify
Anschallfrequenz f insonifying frequency
Anschaulichkeit f descriptiveness; iconicity
Anschlagdrucker m impact [dot-matrix] printer
anschließen to interface
Anschluss m 1. terminal; port; 2. *s.* Schnittstelle
~/**serieller** serial port [connection] *(data transmission)*
anschlussfähig interfaceable
Anschlussfehler m bridging error
Anschlussgewinde n mounting head *(objective)*
Anschlusskabel n connecting cord
Anschlussring m mounting ring
Anschlusssockel m socket mount
Anschlusstechnik f interconnection technology
Anschnitt m bleed *(typography)*
Anschriftenlesegerät n address reader (reading machine)
Ansetzkamera f eyepiece (microscope) camera *(photomicrography)*
Ansicht f view
~/**orthogonale** orthogonal view
~/**perspektivische** perspective view
Ansichtsebene f view[ing] plane *(computer graphics)*

Ansichtsfenster *n* viewport
Ansichtskopie *f* viewing print
Ansichtsmodus *m* viewing mode
ANSI-Lumen *n* ANSI (American National Standards Institute) lumen *(a unit of luminous flux)*
Ansprechempfindlichkeit *f* responsivity, sensitivity, sensitiveness *(photodetector)*
Ansprechzeit *f* response (reaction) time *(e.g. of a photodetector)*
Ansteckmikro[fon] *n* 1. lapel [microphone]; 2. lavalier[-style] microphone, lavaliere (chest) microphone, lav
ansteuerbar addressable *(e.g. pixels)*
Ansteuerbarkeit *f* addressability
Ansteuerelektronik *f* driving (control) electronics, drive[r] electronics
Ansteuerimpuls *m* drive pulse
Ansteuersignal *n* driving signal
Ansteuerung f/passive passive addressing
Anstiegszeit *f* rise time *(of a pulse)*
anstrahlen to spotlight
Antenne *f* antenna, aerial *(chiefly British)*
~/**adaptive** adaptive antenna *(radar)*
~/**empfangende** receiving antenna (aerial)
~/**gerichtete** directional antenna (aerial)
~/**phasengesteuerte** phased-array antenna
~/**reale** real antenna *(radar)*
~/**reziproke** reciprocal antenna *(radar)*
~/**synthetische** synthetic antenna *(radar)*
~/**terrestrische** terrestrial antenna
Antennenapertur *f* antenna aperture *(radar)*
Antennenausrichtung *f* antenna orientation
Antennenbewegung *f* antenna motion *(radar)*
Antennencharakteristik *f*, **Antennendiagramm** *n* antenna [radiation] pattern
Antenneneingang *m* antenna (aerial) input
Antennenfeld *n* antenna array *(radar)*
Antennenfernsehen/digitales *s.* Digitalfernsehen/terrestrisches
Antennenfläche *f s.* Antennenapertur
Antennenfrequenz *f* antenna frequency
Antennengeometrie *f* antenna geometry
Antennengewinn *m* antenna (aerial) gain
Antennenkabel *n* antenna lead (cable)
Antennenkeule *f* antenna beam (lobe) *(radar)*
Antennenrauschen *n* antenna noise
Antennenrichtcharakteristik *f* antenna directivity diagram *(radar)*
Antennenschwenkung *f* antenna sweep
Antennensignal *n* antenna signal
Antennenspannung *f* antenna voltage
Antennenspule *f* antenna (aerial) coil; pickup coil *(e.g. of a SQUID sensor)*
Antennenstrahlbreite *f* antenna beam width
Antennenstrahlungskeule *f s.* Antennenkeule
Anthropometrie *f* anthropometry
anthropometrisch anthropometric
Antialiasing *n* antialiasing, dejagging *(digital filtering operation)*
Antialiasing-Filter *n* antialias[ing] filter
Antialiasing-Technik *f s.* Antialiasing
Antibeschlagschicht *f* antifog coating
Anticurl-Schicht *f s.* Antiroll[rück]schicht
Antielektron *n* antielectron, positron
Antihalofarbstoff *m* antihalation pigment (dye)
Antihaloschicht *f* antihalation layer (coating), remjet (anti-halo) backing, gel coat
Antikdruckpapier *n* antique paper
Antimontrisulfid *n* antimony trisulfide *(photoresistor)*
Antinewtonglas *n* anti-Newton-ring glass, anti-Newton mount
Antioxidans *n* antioxidant
Antiqua *f* [/**klassizistische**], **Antiqua[druck]schrift** *f* roman type, old-style roman type[face]
Antiquellmittel *n s.* Härtemittel
Antireflex[ions]beschichtung *f* 1. antireflection (antireflective) coating, antireflex coating; 2. *s.* Antireflexionsschicht
Antireflexbelag *m s.* Antireflexionsschicht
Antireflexionsschicht *f* antireflection layer (film), antireflection (antireflective) coating, ARC
Antireflex-Mehrfachvergütung *f* antireflection multiple coating, multilayer antireflection coating
Antireflexschicht *f*, **Antireflexvergütung** *f s.* Antireflexionsschicht
Antiroll[rück]schicht *f* anticurl layer (backing), noncurl backing (coat) *(photographic film)*
Antirotaugenstift *m* red eye pen (remover)
Antischleiereffekt *m* antifogging effect
Antischleiermittel *n* antifoggant [compound], fog inhibitor (inhibiting agent) *(s.a. Entwicklungshemmer)*
Antisensibilisierung *f* reduction sensitization
Antistatikmittel *n* antistatic agent
Antistatikschicht *f* antistatic layer (coating); antistatic backing
Antistatiktuch *n* anti-static cloth
antistatisch antistatic[al]
Antiverwacklungssystem *n* image stabilization system
Antivignettierungsfilter *n* antivignetting filter
Antivirenprogramm *n* antivirus program *(software)*
Antwortfunktion f/lineare linear response function
Antwortsignal *n* response signal
Antwortzeit *f* response (reaction) time

anvisieren to sight; to aim [at], to point *(e.g. a camera)*
Anweisung *f* instruction, command, statement *(computer program)*
Anwender... *s.* Anwendungs...
Anwendungsfenster *n* application window
Anwendungsprogramm *n* [application] program, user program
Anwendungsprogrammierschnittstelle *f* application programming (programmer's) interface, API
Anwendungsschicht *f* application layer (level) *(data transmission)*
Anwendungsschnittstelle *f* application program interface, API
Anwendungssoftware *f* application software
Anwendungssymbol *n* [application] icon *(graphical user interface)*
anwinkeln to angle
anzeigbar displayable
Anzeige *f* display, readout *(s.a.* Display*)*
~/**digitale** digital display
~/**elektronische** electronic display
~/**grafische** graphics display
~/**optische** optical display
~/**passive** passive display
Anzeigebereich *m* display area
Anzeigedauer *f* display duration
Anzeigeelektronik *f* display electronics
Anzeigeelement *n* indicator element
Anzeigefehler *m* readout error
Anzeigefeld *n* display field, display [panel]
Anzeigefläche *f* display area (surface)
Anzeigegerät *n* display [device], readout
Anzeigemodus *m* display mode
anzeigen to display
Anzeigepulver *n* [magnetic flaw] detection powder
Anzeigeschnittstelle *f*/**digitale** digital visual interface *(graphics display card)*
Anzeigesystem *n* display (soft copy) system
Anzeigetafel *f* billboard
Anzeigetechnik *f* display technology
Anzeigevorrichtung *f* display device
Aortografie *f* aortography
aortografisch aortographic
Apertometer *n* apertometer
Apertur *f* 1. aperture *(optics)*; 2. [antenna] aperture *(radar)*
~/**effektive** effective aperture
~/**gaußförmige** Gaussian aperture
~/**numerische** numerical aperture, NA
~/**nutzbare** useful (clear) aperture, free (optimum) aperture
~/**reale** real aperture *(radar)*
~/**rechteckförmige** rectangular (square) aperture
~/**relative** *s.* Blendenzahl
~/**synthetische** synthetic aperture *(radar, X-ray telescope)*
Aperturabbildung *f* aperture imaging
Aperturblende *f* aperture diaphragm, aperture stop (vignette), mask; aperture plate *(cine camera)*
~/**einstellbare (verstellbare)** adjustable aperture diaphragm
Aperturblendenöffnung *f* aperture diaphragm opening [size]
Aperturform *f* aperture shape
Apertur-Jitter *m* aperture jitter *(sample-and-hold unit)*
Aperturkorrektur *f* aperture correction
Aperturproblem *n* aperture problem *(motion estimation)*
Aperturradar *n*/**synthetisches** synthetic-aperture radar, SAR
Apertursonde *f* aperture probe
Apertursynthese *f* aperture synthesis *(radio astronomy)*
Aperturwinkel *m* aperture angle, angular aperture
Apex *m* apex, vertex, tip
Aplanasiebedingung *f* condition of aplanatism *(optics)*
Aplanat *m(n)* aplanat [lens], aplanatic lens
~/**beugungsbegrenzter** diffraction-limited aplanat [lens]
aplanatisch aplanatic
Aplanatismus *m* aplanatism
APM-Maschine *f s.* Plattenmessmaschine/automatische
Apochromat *m* apochromat [objective], apochromatic lens (objective)
apochromatisch apochromatic
Apodisation *f* apodization *(optics, signal processing)*
~/**duale** dual apodization
~/**ortsvariante** space-variant apodization, spatially variant apodization
a-posteriori-Wahrscheinlichkeit *f* a posteriori probability *(Bayesian statistics)*
Apostilb *n* apostilb *(a unit of luminance)*
Apostroph *m* apostrophe *(punctuation mark)*
Apparaterauschen *n* device noise
Apparition *f* apparition; [optical] phenomenon
Approximation *f* approximation
~/**binomiale** binomial approximation
~/**diskrete** discrete approximation
~/**finite** finite approximation
~/**Gaußsche** Gaussian approximation
~/**lineare** linear approximation
~/**polygonale** polygonal approximation
~/**schrittweise (sukzessive)** stepwise (successive) approximation
Approximationsfehler *m* approximation error
Approximationsfilter *n* approximation filter
Approximationsgerade *f* approximating line
approximativ approximative
approximieren to approximate

a-priori-Wahrscheinlichkeit f prior [probability] *(image restoration)*
a-priori-Wissen n a priori knowledge (information), prior knowledge *(image understanding)*
Äqualisation f s. Äqualisierung
äqualisieren to equal[ize]
Äqualisierung f equalization *(image-processing operation)*
Aquarellpapier n aquarelle paper
Aquarienfotografie f aquarium photography
Aquatinta[ätzung] f 1. aquatint [process] *(etching technique)*; 2. aquatint, aquatinta engraving
Aquatondruck m aquatone process *(printing)*
Äquatorialmontierung f equatorial mount[ing] *(telescope)*
äquibikonvex equibiconvex *(lens)*
Äquidensite f isodensity line *(line of equal photographic effect)*
Äquidensitenfilm m equidensity film
Äquidensitenherstellung f density slicing *(image enhancement)*
Äquidensitometrie f equidensitometry
äquidistant equidistant, equally distant *(e.g. sample values)*
Äquidistanzkarte f equidistance map
äquikonkav equiconcave *(lens element)*
äquikonvex equiconvex *(lens element)*
äquiluminant equiluminant, equiluminous, isoluminant
Äquivalent n equivalent
~/fotochemisches photochemical equivalent
~/fotometrisches photometric equivalent
Äquivalentbrennweite f equivalent focal length, EFL; power *(of an optical system)*
Äquivalentdosis f equivalent dose *(radiography)*
Äquivalentlinse f equivalent lens
Äquivalentzeit f effective exposure time *(of a shutter)*
Äquivalenzbreite f equivalent width, EW
Äquivalisierung f s. Äqualisierung
Arbeitsabstand m [**/freier**] working distance *(microscopy)*
Arbeitsbereich m region (area) of interest *(e.g. in image analysis)*
Arbeitsblende f working (taking) aperture
Arbeitskanal m working channel *(endoscope)*
Arbeitskopie f [positive] work print, film work print, cutting copy *(cinema)*
~/angelegte conformed work print
~/geschnittene edited work print
Arbeitslicht n working light
Arbeitslösung f working[-strength] solution, processing solution; tank solution *(photographic processing)*
Arbeitsplatz m**/grafischer** graphics [computer] workstation, image (imaging computer) workstation

Arbeitsplatzcomputer m, **Arbeitsplatzrechner** m workstation
Arbeitsplatzdrucker m desktop (tabletop) printer
Arbeitsprojektor m overhead projector
Arbeitsspeicher m active (core) memory, base memory; random-access memory, RAM
Arbeitsstation/grafische graphical workstation
Arbeitswellenlänge f working wavelength *(confocal microscopy)*
Archäologiefotografie f archaeological photography
Architektur f**/datenparallele** data-parallel architecture
Architekturaufnahme f architectural photograph
Architekturfotograf m architectural photographer
Architekturfotografie f architectural photography
Architekturfotogrammetrie f architectural photogrammetry
Archiv n archive
~/elektronisches electronic archive
~/multimediales multiple media archive
archivalisch archival
Archivar m archivist
Archivaufnahme f stock (library) shot *(cinema)*
Archivbild n archival image
Archivdatei f archive file
Archivfähigkeit f archival quality
archivfest archive-proof, storage-proof
Archivfestigkeit f archival stability (quality)
Archivfoto n stock picture (shot)
Archivfotografie f archival (archive) photography
Archivierbarkeit f archival quality
archivieren to archive, to file
Archivierfähigkeit f archival quality
Archivierung f archiving, filing, archival storage (keeping)
Archivierungseigenschaft f archival property
Archivierungssystem n filing system
archivisch archival
Archivmaterial n stock (archival) footage *(cinema)*
Archivpapier n archival paper
Archivschrank m filing cabinet
Archiv-Server m archive server
archivsicher archive-proof, storage-proof
Areografie f areography
Argon[ionen]laser m argon[-ion] laser
Aristopapier n gelatin chloride printing-out paper
Aristotypie f aristotype
Arithmetikeinheit f arithmetic [logic] unit, ALU *(processor)*
Armierung f armoring
ARPA-Anlage f, **ARPA-Gerät** n automatic radar plotting aid, ARPA

Array *n* / **dreidimensionales** three-dimensional array
Arrayprozessor *m* array processor
Arretierstift *m* register (registration) pin, pilot pin
Artefakt *n* artifact, artefact
~/**kreisförmiges** 1. ring[-shaped] artifact, ringing [artifact], circular artifact *(image coding)*; 2. *s.* Gibbs-Artefakt
Artefaktbeseitigung *f* artifact elimination, removal of artifacts
artefaktfrei artifact-free
Artefaktreduktion *f* artifact suppression
Arteriografie *f* arteriography, arterial imaging
arteriografisch arteriographic
Arteriogramm *n* arteriogram
Arthrogramm *n* arthrogram
Arthroskop *n* arthroscope
Arthroskopie *f* arthroscopy
arthroskopisch arthroscopic
Aryldiazoniumsalz *n* aryl diazonium salt
ASA-Empfindlichkeit *f* ASA [film] speed
ASA-Skala *f* ASA scale
ASA-Wert *m* ASA rating
A-Scan *m* A[-mode] scan *(sonography)*
ASCII-Code *m* ASCII code *(text interchange format; from American Standard Code for Information Interchange)*
ASCII-Datenbank *f* ASCII database
ASCII-Zeichen *n* ASCII character
ASCII-Zeichensatz *m* ASCII [standard] character set
Ascorbinsäure *f* ascorbic acid *(developer constituent)*
Aspektanzeiger *m* aspect source flag, ASF *(computer graphics)*
Aspektgraph *m* aspect graph
Aspektverhältnis *n* aspect ratio *(s.a. Bildseitenverhältnis)*
Aspektwinkel *m* aspect angle
Asphaltkopierverfahren *n* bitumen process
Asphaltlack *m* asphalt varnish
Asphäre *f* aspheric [optical] surface
Asphären-Objektiv *n* aspherical [photographic] lens
asphärisch aspheric[al], nonspherical
Asphärisierung *f* aspherizing
Assemble-Schnitt *m* 1. assemble editing *(videography)*; 2. assemble edit
assoziativ associative *(e.g. an image-processing operator)*
Assoziativität *f* associativity
Assoziativschraffur *f* associative hatching *(computer graphics)*
Assoziativspeicher *m* associative memory (storage), content-addressable memory, CAM
~/**bidirektionaler** bidirectional associative memory, BAM
Asteriskus *m* asterisk *(reference mark)*
asthenop asthenopic

Asthenopie *f* asthenopia
Astigmat *m* astigmat, astigmatic lens
astigmatisch astigmatic[al]
Astigmatismus *m* astigmatism, astigmatic aberration (error)
~/**anisotroper** anisotropic astigmatism
~/**axialer** axial astigmatism
~/**dynamischer** dynamic astigmatism
~/**regelmäßiger** regular astigmatism
~/**unregelmäßiger** irregular astigmatism
Astrobeobachtung *f* astronomical observation (viewing)
Astrofoto *n* astrophotograph, astronomical photograph
Astrofotograf *m* astrophotographer
Astrofotografie *f* 1. astrophotography, astronomical (celestial) photography; 2. *s.* Astrofoto
astrofotografisch astrophotographic
Astrograf *m* astrograph
Astrografenobjektiv *n* astrograph lens
Astrokamera *f* astronomical camera
Astrometrie *f* astrometry
Astrometrie-Astrograf *m* astrometric astrograph
astrometrisch astrometric
Astronomie *f* / **optische** optical astronomy
Astroobjektiv *n* astronomical objective
Astrooptik *f* astronomical optics
Astroplatte *f* astronomical plate
Astrospektrograf *m* astronomical spectrograph
Astrospektroskopie *f* astronomical spectroscopy, astrospectroscopy
Astrostereogramm *n* astrostereogram
Asymmetrie *f* asymmetry; dissymmetry
Asymmetriefehler *m* meridional coma *(s.a. Koma)*
asymmetrisch asymmetric[al], nonsymmetric
asynchron asynchronous, nonsynchronous, out of sync
Asynchronität *f* asynchrony, asynchronism
Asynchronmotor *m* wild motor *(cinema)*
ATA-Radaranlage *f* automated tracking aid, ATA *(navigational system)*
Atelier *n* studio *(s.a. under Studio)*
Atelierarbeiter *m* grip
Atelieraufnahme *f* studio shot
Atelierbeleuchtung *f* studio lighting
Atelierkamera *f* studio [view] camera
Atelierlichtquelle *f* studio light source
Atelierszene *f* studio scene
Atemartefakt *n* respiratory motion artifact *(medical imaging)*
Atemeffekt *m s.* Atmen
Atemkompensation *f* respiratory compensation (phase reordering), respiratory-ordered phase encoding, ROPE *(magnetic resonance imaging)*
Atmen *n* breathing *(motion-picture projection)*
ATM-Netz *n* ATM (asynchronous transfer mode) network *(data transmission)*

Atmo f s. Atmosphäre 2.
Atmosphäre f 1. atmosphere *(e.g. as depth cue in images)*; 2. presence, ambience, aura; room tone
Atmosphärentrübung f atmospheric (sky) fog
Atom n atom
Atomabsorptionsspektrofotometrie f atomic absorption spectrophotometry
Atomabsorptionsspektroskopie f atomic absorption spectroscopy, AAS
Atombindung f atomic bond
Atomemissionsspektrometrie f atomic emission spectrometry
Atomemissionsspektroskopie f atomic emission spectroscopy, AES
Atomfluoreszenzspektroskopie f atomic fluorescence spectroscopy, AFS
Atomkern m atomic nucleus
Atomkraftmikroskopie f s. Rasterkraftmikroskopie
Atommasse f atomic mass (weight)
Atommodell n/**Bohrsches** Bohr atom model
Atomoptik f atom optics
Atomradius m atomic radius
Atomspektroskopie f atomic spectroscopy
Attribut n attribute *(s.a. under* Merkmal, Deskriptor*)*
Attributelement n attribute element *(metafile element)*
Attributmenge f set of attributes
Ätzalkalien npl caustic alkalies
Ätzbad n etching bath
Ätzchemikalie f etching chemical
ätzen to etch
Ätzen n/**chemisches** chemical etching
~/**elektrochemisches** electrochemical etching
~/**fotochemisches** photochemical etching
~/**nasschemisches** wet-chemical etching
Ätzflüssigkeit f etching liquid
Ätzgrübchen n etch pit
Ätzgrund m etching ground
Ätzkali n caustic potash, potassium hydroxide *(developer constituent)*
Ätzmaschine f etching machine
Ätzmaske f etching mask
Ätzmittel n etchant
Ätznatron n caustic [soda], sodium hydroxide *(developer constituent)*
Ätztechnik f 1. etching technology ; 2. etching technique
Ätztiefe f etch depth
Ätzung f etching *(printing)*
Ätzverfahren n etch[ing] process
Audio... s.a. Ton...
Audioaufzeichnung f 1. sound recording; 2. sound record
Audiobearbeitung f sound editing
Audiobuchse f audio jack
Audiocodierer m audio encoder
Audiocodierung f audio encoding
Audiodaten pl audio (sound) data

Audioeffektgerät n audio effects device
Audioeingang m audio input
Audioformat n audio format
Audiofrequenz f audio frequency
Audiogramm n audiogram
Audio-Hilfsträger m audio subcarrier
Audiokanal m audio (sound) channel
Audiokarte f sound board (card) *(computer)*
Audiokassette f audio cassette
Audiokassettengerät n,
Audiokassettenrecorder m [audio] cassette recorder, audio cassette player *(magnetic tape recorder)*
Audiokompression f audio compression
Audiolängsspur f linear audio track
Audiomischer m, **Audiomischpult** n audio mixer, mic[rophone] mixer, audio (sound) mixing console
Audiopost[produktion] f s. Nachvertonung
Audioprozessor m audio processing unit, APU *(television)*
Audiorecorder m sound recorder, record[ing] machine
Audiosignal n audio (aural) signal, acoustic (sound) signal
Audiospur f sound track, audio [data] track
Audiosystem n audio system
Audio-Video-Ausgang m audio-video output, AV out[put]
Audio-Video-Kreuzschiene f,
Audio-Video-Kreuzschienenverteiler m audio-video crosspoint
Audio-Video-Mischer m audio-video mixer
Audio-Video-Signal n composite signal
Audio-Video-Synchronisation f audio-video synchronization
Audio-Video-Technik f audio-video technique
Audiovision f audiovision
audiovisuell audiovisual
Audio-Zeitcode m audio time code
auditiv auditory, audile
Aufbau m/**mikrofotografischer** photomicrographic setup
~/**optischer** optical design
Aufbaueffekt m dose buildup *(X-ray dosimetry)*
Aufbelichtungskamera f [film] identification camera, photographic marker *(radiography)*
Aufblende f fade-in *(cinema)*
~ **aus Schwarz** fade-in from black
aufblenden to fade in (up); to iris in *(a motion-picture camera)*
Aufblendung f s. Aufblende
Aufblick m/**schräger** oblique view
aufblitzen to flash
Aufdruck m stamp, imprint, impress; overprint
aufdrucken to stamp, to imprint, to impress; to overprint
Aufdruckkontrolle f, **Aufdruckprüfung** f label inspection

Auffangebene f interception plane *(optics)*
Aufforderung f prompt *(computer)*
Auffrischspeicher m refresh memory (buffer), frame buffer [memory], image buffer
auffüllbar refillable *(e.g. ink)*
Aufgabemedium n output medium
Aufhängeklammer f hanger chip
Aufhärtung f beam hardening *(X-ray absorption)*
Aufhellblitz m fill[-in] flash
Aufhellblitzen n fill-flash photography
Aufhellen n fill-in
aufhellen to lighten, to brighten [up] *(e.g. a picture)*
Aufheller m 1. reflecting screen; 2. s. ~/optischer
~/optischer [optical] brightener, whitener, whitening agent
Aufhellfolie f retroreflective foil
Aufhellicht n fill[-in] light
Aufhellschirm m reflecting screen
Aufhellung f brightening; lightening; fill-in lighting
Aufklärung f reconnaissance, recon; intelligence
~/elektronische electronic intelligence, elint
~/fotografische photoreconnaissance
Aufklärungsbild n reconnaissance image
Aufklärungsflugzeug n reconnaissance aircraft
Aufklärungsfoto n reconnaissance photo[graph]
Aufklärungsfotografie f reconnaissance photography; surreptitious photography
Aufklärungskamera f reconnaissance camera
Aufklärungssatellit m [photo]reconnaissance satellite, imaging satellite
aufkleben to mount *(e.g. photographs)*
Aufladezeit f recycle time *(e.g. of a flashgun)*
Aufladung f/**elektrostatische** 1. electrostatic charging; 2. s. Ladung/elektrostatische
Aufladungsgerät n corona charging apparatus *(electrophotography)*
Auflage f 1. support, rest *(e.g. for stabilizing a camera)*; 2. [press]run *(as a number of copies)*
Auflagemaß n flange focal distance; back focus (focal distance)
Auflagendruck m 1. production printing (run); 2. production print
Auflagendrucker m pressman, printer
Auflagenpapier n house (floor) sheet, printing stock
Auflegemaske f, **Aufleger** m overlay
Auflicht n incident light; reflected light
~/seitliches bias light
Auflichtbeleuchtung f incident-light illumination, reflected-light illumination
Auflichtbeobachtung f,
Auflichtbetrachtung f observation by reflected light
Auflichtbild n reflected-light image
Auflichtdensitometer n reflection densitometer
Auflicht-Dunkelfeldbeleuchtung f dark-field reflected-light illumination
Auflicht-Fluoreszenzmikroskopie f reflected-light fluorescence microscopy
Auflicht-Hellfeldbeleuchtung f bright-field reflected-light illumination
Auflichtmikroskop n reflected-light microscope, reflecting (reflection light) microscope
Auflichtmikroskopie f reflected[-light] microscopy, incident-light microscopy, epi-illumination microscopy
Auflichtprojektion f s. Aufprojektion
Auflichtprojektor m episcopic (opaque) projector, episcope
Auflichtvorlage f reflective copy (material), reflection (reflex) copy
Auflichtwand f s. Auflichtbildwand
auflösbar resolvable
Auflösbarkeit f resolvability
auflösen 1. to resolve *(optics)*; 2. to solve *(mathematics)*; 3. to dissolve, to pass into solution *(chemicals)*
Auflösung f 1. resolution *(s.a. Bildauflösung)*; 2. dissolution *(e.g. of chemicals)*
~/atomare atomic resolution
~/axiale axial resolution, axial point spread function
~/azimutale azimuthal resolution *(radar)*
~/beugungsbegrenzte diffraction-limited resolution
~/bildschirmbedingte display (screen) resolution
~/darstellbare displayable resolution
~/diagonale diagonal resolution
~/digitale digital resolution
~/dynamische 1. dynamic (moving) resolution; 2. s. Farbauflösung
~/elektromechanische electromechanical resolution
~/feine fine resolution
~/geometrische geometric[al] resolution
~/grobe coarse resolution
~/horizontale horizontal resolution
~/interpolierte interpolated resolution
~/isotrope isotropic resolution
~/laterale lateral resolution
~/lineare linear resolution
~/neuronale neural resolution
~/optische optical resolution
~/örtliche spatial (positional) resolution
~/ortsabhängige space-variant resolution
~/physikalische physical resolution
~/radiale radial resolution *(radar)*
~/radiometrische radiometric resolution
~/räumliche spatial (positional) resolution

Auflösung

~/**reale** 1. actual resolution *(display)*; 2. s. ~/optische
~/**senkrechte** vertical resolution
~/**spektrale** spectral resolution
~/**statische** static resolution
~/**thermische** thermal resolution
~/**ultrahohe** superhigh resolution
~/**vertikale** vertical resolution
~/**visuelle** visual (eye) resolution
~/**waagerechte** horizontal resolution
~/**zeitliche** temporal (time) resolution
Auflösungsbandbreite f resolution bandwidth
auflösungsbegrenzt resolution-limited
Auflösungserhöhung f resolution enhancement
Auflösungsfähigkeit f s. Auflösungsvermögen
Auflösungsfehler m resolution error (artifact)
Auflösungsfeinheit f definition
Auflösungsgenauigkeit f accuracy of resolution
Auflösungsgrad m degree of resolution
Auflösungsgrenze f resolution limit, limit of resolution
Auflösungskeil m resolution wedge
Auflösungsmaß n resolution measure (metric); unit of resolution
Auflösungsmessung f resolution measurement (testing)
Auflösungspyramide f resolution pyramid
Auflösungssteigerung f resolution enhancement
Auflösungsstufe f resolution level
Auflösungsunabhängigkeit f resolution independence *(e.g. of graphics software)*
Auflösungsverlust m resolution loss (degradation), loss of (in) resolution
Auflösungsverminderung f resolution reduction
Auflösungsvermögen n resolving power (frequency), resolving [cap]ability, resolution [capability]; definition *(e.g. of a video screen)*
~/**axiales** axial resolving power, depth of field, zone of focus *(objective)*
~/**instrumentelles** instrumental resolving power
~/**örtliches** spatial resolving power
~/**radiales** radial resolving power *(radar)*
~/**räumliches** spatial resolving power
~/**spektrales** spectral resolving power
~/**zeitliches** time resolving limit
Auflösungszelle f [azimuth] resolution cell *(radar)*
Aufmerksamkeit f/**visuelle** visual attention
Aufmerksamkeitszuwendung f attentional blink *(eye movement)*
aufmodulieren to modulate [up]on
Aufnahme f 1. recording *(e.g. on magnetic tape; s.a. Aufzeichnung)*; 2. record[ing]; acquisition; 3. exposure; shot *(photography)*; take *(cinema, video)*; 4. exposure, shot *(s.a. under Foto)*; take; 5. acquisition, exposure *(esp. in radiography)*

~ **aus der Hand** handheld shooting
~/**einzelbildweise** frame-by-frame recording (shooting)
~/**elektronenmikroskopische** electron micrograph, electron microscope (microscopy) image
~/**fotografische** 1. photographic recording; 2. photographic record, photorecord
~/**holografische** holographic recording
~/**kurz[zeit]belichtete** short-exposure photograph; short X-ray exposure
~/**lang[zeit]belichtete** long-exposure photograph
~/**makrofotografische** photomacrograph
~/**mikrofotografische** photomicrograph, microphotograph
~ **mit nichtsynchronisierter Kamera** wild take
~/**multisensorale** multisensoral data acquisition
~/**multitemporale** multitemporal data acquisition
~/**radiografische** radiograph[ic image], radio image, radiogram, skiagram
~/**rasterelektronenmikroskopische** scanning electron microscope photograph, SEM photograph
Aufnahmeabstand m s. Aufnahmedistanz
Aufnahmeachse f optical axis; camera[-to subject] axis
Aufnahmeanordnung f/**holografische** holographic recording setup
Aufnahmeapparatur f recording equipment
Aufnahmeband n record[ing] tape; master tape
Aufnahmebedingungen fpl picture-taking conditions
Aufnahmebelichtung f recording exposure
aufnahmebereit ready to record; ready for exposure
Aufnahmebericht m camera report (sheet); camera exposure chart, dope sheet *(cinema)*
Aufnahmebildformat n,
Aufnahmebildgröße f recording image size
Aufnahmebildröhre f s. Aufnahmeröhre
Aufnahmeblende f shooting aperture
Aufnahmebrennweite f exposure focal length
Aufnahmecharakteristik f microphone polar pattern
Aufnahmedauer f recording time
Aufnahmedistanz f taking (working) distance
Aufnahmeelektronik f record[ing] electronics
Aufnahmeempfindlichkeit f recording sensitivity

Aufnahmeentfernung f taking (working) distance
Aufnahmefilm m record[ing] film; camera (picture-taking) film
Aufnahmefilmmaterial n [film] stock; motion-picture [film] stock
Aufnahmefilter n camera filter
Aufnahme-Folgezeit f exposure interval
Aufnahmefolie f exposure screen *(radiography)*
Aufnahmeformat n 1. picture format; 2. recording (acquisition) format; 3. s. Filmformat
Aufnahmefotografie f record photography
Aufnahmefrequenz f capture (recording) rate, acquisition [frame] rate, framing rate, camera frame-per-second rate
Aufnahmefunktion f record function
Aufnahmegegenstand m object, subject
Aufnahmegeometrie f exposure geometry
Aufnahmegerät n recording (acquisition) device, record machine, recorder
Aufnahmegeschwindigkeit f record[ing] speed; acquisition speed; framing (shooting) speed *(cinema)*
Aufnahmeintervall n exposure interval
Aufnahmekamera f recording (production) camera, taking camera; cine[matographic] camera, [motion-]picture camera, movie camera; imaging camera *(radiography)*; live television camera
~ **mit Revolverkopf** turret-front camera
Aufnahmekopf m record[ing] head, magnetic recording head, sensing head; video recording head
~/**digitaler** digital record head
Aufnahmekopfbreite f record-head width
Aufnahmelampe f exposure lamp
Aufnahmeleistung f record performance
Aufnahmeleiter m production supervisor, line producer, location manager *(film crew)*
~/**Erster** [first] assistant director, AD
Aufnahmelicht n exposing light
Aufnahmemaßstab m taking scale
Aufnahmematerial n recorded material, recording (capture) material; photographic (negative) material
Aufnahmemedium n recording (capture) medium; shooting medium
Aufnahmemodus m recording (capture) mode, [ready-to-]record mode
Aufnahmeobjekt n object, subject
Aufnahmeobjektiv n, **Aufnahmeoptik** f [picture-]taking lens
Aufnahmeort m [shooting] location *(s.a. Drehort)*
Aufnahmeplattform f shooting platform; [remote] sensing platform
Aufnahmeposition f shooting position
Aufnahmequalität f recording quality

Aufnahmerecorder m editing recorder, record (edit) VTR, record machine; master recorder
Aufnahmereihe f s. Aufnahmesequenz
Aufnahmerichtung f acquisition direction; direction of shooting
Aufnahmeröhre f [camera] pickup tube, camera picture tube, camera [video] tube; television camera tube
Aufnahmeschicht f recording layer
Aufnahmesequenz f, **Aufnahmeserie** f burst images
Aufnahmesituation f photographic (picture-making) situation, shooting (picture-taking) situation
Aufnahmestab m motion-picture production crew
Aufnahmestandort m, **Aufnahmestandpunkt** m camera [exposure] station
Aufnahmestart m record start; record in point *(taping)*
Aufnahmestopp m record stop *(taping)*
Aufnahmestudio n recording studio; soundstage *(motion-picture production)*; capture stage *(esp. in computer-enhanced imaging)*
Aufnahmesystem n recording system; pickup system
Aufnahmeszene f input scene
Aufnahmetaste f record button, recording key
Aufnahmeteam n shooting crew
Aufnahmetechnik f 1. recording technology; 2. s. ~/fotografische
~/**fotografische** shooting (picture-taking) technique; photographic technique
Aufnahmetechniker m recordist
Aufnahmetisch m background table
Aufnahmeverfahren n recording technique, method of recording
~/**digitales** digital recording technique
Aufnahmevermögen n recording capability
Aufnahmevorgang m recording process; capturing process
Aufnahmewellenlänge f recording wavelength *(holography)*
Aufnahmewinkel m 1. [recording] angle of view; 2. [light] acceptance angle, angle of acceptance *(e.g. of an objective)*; 3. s. Kamera[blick]winkel
Aufnahmezeit f recording time
aufnehmbar recordable
aufnehmen to record; to acquire; to shoot; to capture; to take
~/**auf Band** to tape[-record]
~/**in eine Datei** to capture
~/**nachträglich** to postrecord; to rerecord; to retake
Aufnehmer m 1. receptor *(s.a. Sensor)*; 2. pickup [device]
~/**optischer** optical pickup
Aufprojektion f front projection [process], reflex projection

aufrastern

aufrastern to dither, to pixelate
Aufrasterung f dithering, dither technique, halftoning *(electronic imaging; s.a.* Streurasterung*)*
Aufrichteprisma n image-erecting prism
Aufschärfung f sharpening, deblurring *(digital image processing)*
Aufschmelzen n fusing *(of the toner to paper)*
Aufsetzkamera f eyepiece (microscope) camera *(photomicrography)*
Aufsicht f direct viewing
Aufsichtdensitometer n reflection densitometer
Aufsichtdensitometrie f reflection densitometry
Aufsicht-Farbkopie f reflection color print
Aufsichtkopie f s. Aufsichtsbild
Aufsichtsbild n reflection (reflective) print, reflection copy
Aufsichtsmaterial n reflection display material, directly viewed material
Aufsichtsmontage f 1. pasteup [process]; 2. pasteup, hard mechanical
Aufsichtsucher m brilliant (waist-level) finder
Aufsichtsvorlage f reflective copy (material), reflection (reflex) copy
Aufspießanfrage f stabbing problem *(computational geometry)*
Aufspuleinrichtung f winder
aufstauben to dust on
Aufsteckblitz m, **Aufsteckblitzgerät** n hotshoe flash, on-camera flash (gun), on-camera [portable electronic] flash unit
Aufsteckfilter n slip-on filter
Aufsteckfuß m, **Aufsteckschuh** m hot shoe
Aufstrich m s. Haarstrich
Auftragsfotografie f commissioned photography
Auftragstasche f 1. order envelope, [film] processing envelope *(photofinishing service)*; 2. s. ~/konventionelle
~/konventionelle job ticket, docket *(printing business)*
Auftreffpunkt m point of incidence
Auftreffwinkel m angle of arrival; incidence (incident) angle, angle of incidence, AOI
Auftrittswahrscheinlichkeit f probability of occurence *(statistical encoding)*
aufwärtskompatibel upward compatible
Aufwärtskompatibilität f upward compatibility
aufwärtskonvertieren to up-convert *(a lower conversion video)*
Aufwärtskonvertierung f up-conversion
Aufwärtsskalierung f upscaling
Aufwärtsstrecke f uplink *(signal transmission)*
aufwärtstasten to upsample
Aufwärtstaster m upsampler
Aufwärtstastung f upsampling, zero padding *(image filtering)*

Aufwärtsverbindung f uplink, up path *(signal transmission)*
Aufweitung f expansion, spreading *(e.g. of a laser beam)*
Aufweitungsfaktor m, **Aufweitungsverhältnis** n expansion ratio
Aufwickeldorn m [spiral] reel *(developing tank)*
Aufwickelkern m take-up core, [winding] core, bobbin
Aufwickelmagazin n lower (take-up) magazine, spool box
Aufwickelrolle f, **Aufwickelspule** f take-up reel (spool), pickup reel
Aufwickeltrommel f s. Aufwickelrolle
Aufzählungspunkt m, **Aufzählungszeichen** n bullet [point] *(typography)*
aufzeichenbar recordable
aufzeichnen to record; to prerecord, to prescore *(e.g. a television show)*
~/auf Band to tape[-record]
~/auf Videoband to videotape
Aufzeichnung f 1. recording *(s.a. under* Aufnahme*)*; 2. record[ing]
~/audiovisuelle audiovisual recording
~/bandlose tapeless recording
~/digitale digital recording
~/digitale optische digital optical recording, DOR
~/elektronische electronic recording
~/magnetische magnetic recording
~/magnetooptische magneto-optical recording
Aufzeichnungsdichte f recording density
Aufzeichnungsformat n recording (acquisition) format
Aufzeichnungsgerät n recording (acquisition) device, record machine, recorder
Aufzeichnungsgeschwindigkeit f record speed; [relative] tape-to-head speed, head-to-tape speed
Aufzeichnungskopf m s. Aufnahmekopf
Aufzeichnungsmaterial n recorded material, recording (capture) material
Aufzeichnungsmedium n recording medium
Aufzeichnungsmodus m recording (capture) mode, [ready-to-]record mode
Aufzeichnungsnorm f recording standard
Aufzeichnungspause f record[ing] pause *(video)*
Aufzeichnungsqualität f recording quality
Aufzeichnungssignal n record signal
Aufzeichnungsspur f recorded (recording) track
Aufzeichnungsstörung f recording artifact
Aufzeichnungsträger/magnetisierbarer magnetic recording medium
Aufzeichnungsverfahren n recording technique
Aufzeichnungsverstärker m recording amplifier

Aufzeichnungs-Wiedergabe-Kopf *m* magnetic recording/reproducing head
Aufziehblock *m* mounting board
Aufziehen *n* **von Fotos** mounting of photographs
Aufziehfolie *f* laminating film
Aufziehkarton *m* mount[ing] board
aufzoomen to zoom in
Aufzugshebel *m* winding (film-advance) lever
Aufzugsknopf *m* winding (film-advance) knob
Augapfel *m* eyeball
Auge *n* 1. eye; 2. bowl *(character part)*; 3. *s.* Punze
~/**bewaffnetes** aided eye
~/**bewegtes** tracking eye
~/**dunkeladaptiertes** dark-adapted eye
~/**fernakkommodiertes** unaccommodate eye
~/**helladaptiertes** light-adapted eye
~/**menschliches** human eye
~/**raumfest ruhendes** fixed eye
~/**schematisches** schematic eye
~/**unbewaffnetes** unaided (naked) eye
Augenabstand *m* eye (interocular) distance
Augenachse *f* optic axis
Augenbasis *f* eye base
Augenbewegung *f* eye movement (motion)
~/**konjugierte** conjugate eye movement
~/**ruckartige (sakkadierte)** saccadic [eye] movement, saccadic motion, saccade
Augenbewegungsgeschwindigkeit *f* eye motion (movement) speed
Augenbulbus *m* eyeball
Augendiagramm *n* eye pattern
Augendrehpunkt *m* center of rotation of the eye
Augenempfindlichkeit *f* eye sensitivity, sensitivity of the [human] eye
Augenempfindlichkeitskurve *f* sensitivity curve of the eye
Augenermüdung *f* eyestrain, fatigue
Augenfarbe *f* eye color
Augenfolgebewegung *f* tracking movement of the eye
Augenhaut *f*/**harte** sclera, sclerotic [coat], white of the eye
Augenheilkunde *f* ophthalmology
Augenhintergrund *m* [eye] fundus, ocular fundus, back (fundus) of the eye
Augenhöhe *f* eye level
Augenhöhle *f* eye socket, eyehole, orbit
Augenhornhaut *f* [eye] cornea
Augeninnere *n* internal ocular surfaces
Augeniris *f* iris *(of the eye)*
Augenkammer *f*/**hintere** posterior chamber *(of the eye)*
~/**vordere** anterior chamber *(of the eye)*
Augenkapsel *f s.* Augenhöhle
Augenkorrektionslinse *f,*
Augenkorrekturlinse *f* eyepiece correction lens

Augenkurve *f* spectral sensitivity function
Augenlicht *n* 1. [eye]sight *(s.a.* Sehen*)*; 2. eyelight; 3. *s.* Augenlichtlampe
Augenlichtlampe *f* eyelight, obie
Augenlid *n* eyelid
Augenlinie *f s.* Blicklinie
Augenlinse *f* 1. [crystalline] lens *(of the eye)*; 2. eye lens *(of an eyepiece)*
Augenmaß *n* visual estimate
Augenmittelpunkt *m*/**optischer** optical center of the eye
augenmotorisch oculomotor
Augenmuschel *f* eye cup (guard), eye shield
Augenmuskel *m* eye muscle
Augenmuskelfunktion *f* oculomotor function
Augennetzhaut *f* retina [of the eye]
Augenoptik *f* ophthalmic (eye's) optics; ocular optics; optometry
Augenoptiker *m* optometrist, oculist
augenoptisch optometric[al]
Augenort *m* eye location
Augenposition *f* eye position
Augenpunkt *m* eye point
Augenpupille *f* pupil [of the eye]
Augenrückwand *f s.* Augenhintergrund
Augen-Scan *m* iris scan
Augenschädigung *f* eye injury
Augenspiegel *m* ophthalmoscope
Augenstellung *f* eye position
Augensteuerung *f* eye [motion] tracking
Augenstörung *f* eye[-related] disorder
Augenszintigrafie *f* eye scintigraphy
Augenzittern *n* ocular tremor, nystagmus [movement]
Äugigkeit *f* eyedness, dominance *(of one eye over the other)*
Augpunkt *m s.* Augenpunkt
Aurafotografie *f s.* Kirlian-Fotografie
aural, aurikulär aural, auricular
Ausbildungsmikroskop *n* teaching (student) microscope
Ausbleichen *n* bleaching away (out); fading
ausbleichen to bleach away (out); to fade
ausblenden to block [out] *(optics)*; to fade out *(film, video)*
~/**weich** to fade out
Ausblendung *f* fade-out
Ausblendzeichen *n* changeover cue [mark], cue dot (mark), reel change mark *(cinema)*
Ausbreitung *f*/**quasioptische** line-of-sight propagation *(of signals)*
Ausbreitungsanomalie *f* anomalous propagation *(e.g. of a radar beam)*
Ausbreitungsgeschwindigkeit *f* propagative speed (velocity)
Ausbreitungskonstante *f* propagation constant
Ausbreitungsmedium *n* propagation medium

Ausbreitungsrichtung

Ausbreitungsrichtung f propagative (propagation) direction, direction of propagation *(e.g. of waves)*
Ausbreitungsverzögerung f propagation delay
Ausdehnung f s. Dilatation
Ausdruck m 1. term, expression *(mathematics)*; 2. printout; [paper] hard copy; hard-copy image
~/**Boolescher** Boolean expression *(e.g. in information retrieval)*
~/**eingliedriger** monomial
~/**farbiger** color output
~/**logischer** logical expression
~/**mehrgliedriger** polynomial
ausdrucken to print out
Ausdruckvorrichtung f printout device
Ausdünnen n, **Ausdünnung** f decimation *(e.g. of a polygonal mesh)*
Ausdünnungsalgorithmus m decimation algorithmus
ausentwickeln to develop out
Ausentwicklung f full (finality) development, developing-out process
ausfällen to precipitate out
Ausfallstelle f drop-out
Ausfallswinkel m angle of reflection, reflection (emergent) angle
ausfiltern to filter out
ausfixieren to fix out
Ausfleckarbeit f spotting
ausflecken to spot; to opaque
Ausflecken n spotting
Ausfleckfarbe f spotting color (compound); opaquing paint
Ausfleckretusche f spotting
Ausfüllung f/**leere** empty (hollow) interior style *(computer graphics)*
Ausgabe f 1. output *(e.g. of image data)*; 2. edition *(e.g. of printed matter)*
Ausgabeauflösung f output resolution
Ausgabebild n output image; output frame *(video)*
Ausgabedateiformat n s. Ausgabeformat
Ausgabeelement n s. Ausgabeprimitiv
Ausgabeformat n output format
Ausgabegerät n output device
~/**grafisches** graphical output device
~/**rasterorientiertes** raster (pixel-based) output device
Ausgabehistogramm n output histogram
Ausgabematerial n output material
Ausgabemedium n output medium
Ausgabeprimitiv n output primitive [element] *(image description)*
Ausgabepuffer[speicher] m output buffer
Ausgabeschicht f output layer *(artificial neural network)*
Ausgabevektor m output vector
Ausgangsbild n 1. source image (picture) *(image processing)*; 2. output image
Ausgangsebene f output plane *(ray optics)*
Ausgangsfrequenz f output frequency

Ausgangshauptebene f rear principal (nodal) plane *(of a thick lens)*
Ausgangshelligkeit f output brightness *(electronic imaging)*
Ausgangsimpuls m output pulse
Ausgangsleuchtschirm m output [fluorescent] screen, output phosphor screen, [image intensifier] output phosphor *(radiography)*
Ausgangsmedium n transmitted medium
Ausgangs-Multiplexfilter n output multiplex filter, OMUX
Ausgangsmuster n output pattern *(pattern classification)*
Ausgangspixel n output pixel
Ausgangspolarisation f output polarization axis
Ausgangspuffer m output buffer
Ausgangspunkt m starting point; seed point *(region-growing method)*
Ausgangsschicht f output layer *(artificial neural network)*
Ausgangsschirm m s. Ausgangsleuchtschirm
Ausgangsschnittstelle f output interface *(e.g. for video)*
Ausgangssignal n output signal
Ausgangssymbol n output symbol *(coding)*
Ausgangsszene f output scene
Ausgangstakt m output clock
Ausgangsvektor m output vector
Ausgangsverstärker m output amplifier
Ausgangsverstärkerrauschen n output amplifier noise
Ausgangsvideobild n output video image
ausgeschlossen justified [full-out] *(lines of text)*
Ausgleichsbit n stuffing bit
Ausgleichsentwickler m compensating developer; soft[-working] developer
Ausgleichsfilter n balancing filter *(radiography)*
Ausgleichsimpuls m equalization (equalizer) pulse *(television signal)*
Ausgleichsschleife f Latham loop *(film passage)*
Ausgleichsspur f balance stripe *(opposite from the magnetic track of motion-picture film)*
aushärten to cure, to set *(e.g. optical adhesives by ultraviolet light)*
Ausklappbild n foldout [picture], gatefold, pullout
Auskopieremulsion f print-out emulsion
auskopieren to print out
Auskopierpapier n print[ing]-out paper, POP, direct-writing paper
Auskopierprozess n printing-out process, developing-out process
Auskoppelfenster n output window *(laser)*
Auskoppelmodulation f cavity dumping
auskoppeln to couple out *(e.g. light out of optical fibers)*

Auskoppelspiegel *m* output coupler [mirror], [laser] output mirror
Auslagerungsdatei *f,*
Auslagerungsspeicher *m* swap file, virtual memory (storage)
Auslagetrommel *f* sheet transfer cylinder *(offset lithographic press)*
Auslassungspunkte *mpl* ellipsis, suspension points *(punctuation mark)*
Auslassungszeichen *n* apostrophe *(punctuation mark)*
Auslaufbereich *m* lead-out area, program end signal area *(video disk)*
Ausleger *m* boom [arm], jib arm *(e.g. of a camera crane)*
Auslesebandbreite *f* readout bandwidth
Auslese-CCD *f* readout CCD
Ausleseelektrode *f* readout electrode
Ausleseelektronik *f* readout electronics (circuitry)
Auslesefrequenz *f* readout rate
Auslesegeschwindigkeit *f* readout speed; readout rate
Auslesegradient *m* readout (frequency-encoding) gradient *(magnetic resonance imaging)*
Ausleseimpuls *m* readout pulse
Auslesemodus *m* readout mode
Auslesemultiplexer *m* readout multiplexer
auslesen to read out (off) *(e.g. image data or signals)*
Auslesen *n* readout
Auslesephase *f* readout phase (period)
Ausleserauschen *n* read[out] noise
Ausleseregister *n* readout [shift] register
Ausleserichtung *f* readout direction
Auslesestrahl *m* readout beam
Ausleseverstärker *m* readout amplifier
Auslesevorgang *m* readout process, read
Auslesevorrichtung *f* readout device
Auslesewert *m* readout value
Auslesezeile *f* readout line
Auslesezeit *f* readout time
Auslesezyklus *m* read cycle
Auslesung *f* readout *(e.g. of image data)*
ausleuchten to illuminate
Ausleuchtung *f* illumination *(s.a. under Beleuchtung)*
~/**frontale** front (flat) lighting
~/**gleichmäßige** uniform (homogenous) illumination, even illumination
~/**kreuzpolarisierte** crossed polarized illumination
~/**schattenfreie** shadowless illumination
~/**ungerichtete** nondirectional (scattered) illumination
~/**ungleichmäßige** nonuniform illumination
Ausleuchtzone *f* 1. illumination patch; 2. footprint *(of a broadcasting satellite)*
Auslöschung *f* extinction
Auslöschungsverhältnis *n* extinction ratio
Auslöseimpuls *m* trigger pulse
Auslösekabel *n* cable release

Auslöseknopf *m* shutter [release] button, release button
Auslösekontakt *m* release contact
auslösen to trigger, to release, to trip, to snap *(e.g. a shutter)*
Auslösepriorität *f* shutter priority [mode], release priority
Auslöser *m* shutter [button], shutter release [button]; trigger
~/**elektromagnetischer** electromagnetic release
~/**elektronischer** electronic trigger
Auslöserverriegelung *f,* **Auslösesperre** *f* double-exposure lock (prevention device)
Auslösesystem *n* triggering system *(electronic flash)*
Auslösetaste *f* release button
Auslöseverzögerung *f* shutter lag, delayed action *(camera)*
Auslösevorrichtung *f* triggering device
Auslösezählrohr *n* Geiger-Müller [counting] tube *(dosimetry)*
Auslösung *f* shutter release
Ausmischung *f* matching *(of colors)*
Ausreißer *m* outlier, rogue *(statistics)*
Ausreißererkennung *f* outlier detection
ausrichten to align; to orient[ate]; to register
Ausrichtlaser *m* alignment laser
Ausrichtung *f* alignment, orientation; registration *(e.g. of images)*
~/**optische** optical alignment
~/**räumliche** spatial orientation
Ausrichtungsschicht *f* alignment layer *(of a liquid-crystal display)*
Ausrufungszeichen *n* exclamation point (mark)
Ausrundungsfläche *f* fillet surface *(image processing)*
Ausrüstung *f* 1. equipment ; 2. finish *(e.g. of paper)*
Aussagenkalkül *n(m)* propositional (sentential) calculus
Aussagenlogik *f* propositional logic
Ausschaltung *f/***automatische** automatic power-down mode *(e.g. of a camera)*
ausschießen to impose
Ausschießen *n* [plate] imposition *(prepress area)*
Ausschießschema *n* imposition scheme
ausschließen to justify *(typesetting)*
Ausschließen *n* justification *(typesetting)*
Ausschließkeil *m* justification wedge; [wedged] spaceband, justifying spacer
Ausschließvorgang *m* justification [process]
ausschneiden to cut out
Ausschneiden *n* **und Einfügen** *n* cut-and-paste *(computer operation)*
Ausschnittbild *n* cutout [image]
Ausschnitte *mpl* trims *(film editing)*
Ausschnittsbestimmung *f* framing
Ausschnittsucher *m* viewmeter

Ausschnittvergrößern

Ausschnittvergrößern *n* cropping
Ausschnittvergrößerung *f* selective enlargement
Ausschnittwahl *f* framing
aussehen to look
Aussehen *n* look, appearance
Außenantenne *f* outdoor antenna (aerial)
Außenaufnahme *f* 1. location shoot[ing], exterior; 2. outdoor exposure; outdoor photograph
~ **bei Nacht** night exterior
Außenaufnahmekamera *f* field television camera
Außenaufnahmeort *m* exterior (outdoor) location
Außenbeleuchtung *f* outdoor lighting
Außendekoration *f* outdoor setting
aussenden to transmit [out], to send out; to emit
Außendreh *m*, **Außendreharbeit** *f* exterior shooting, [on-]location filming (shooting); field recording *(video)*
Außendrehort *m* exterior (outdoor) location
Außeneinheit *f* outdoor unit *(filming)*
Außeneinsatz *m* field use *(video recording)*
Außenhüllenelektron *n* [outer-]shell electron
Außenkante *f* outer edge
Außenkoma *f* negative coma *(optics)*
Außenmotiv *n s.* Außendrehort
Außenproduktion *f* field (location) production *(filming)*
~/**elektronische** electronic field production, EFP
Außenszene *f* outdoor scene
Außentrommelbelichter *m* external drum recorder
Außenübertragung *f* field (outside) broadcast
außeraxial off-axis, extra-axial, abaxial
Aussetz[fehl]er *m* drop-out
Ausstattungsmerkmal *n* feature *(e.g. of a camera)*
Ausstellungsbild *n*, **Ausstellungsfoto** *n* exhibition print
Aussteuerungsanzeige *f* recording level indication
Aussteuerungsinstrument *n* hi-peaker *(studio camera)*
Ausstiegspunkt *m* out point *(tape editing)*
ausstrahlen 1. to radiate [out]; 2. to broadcast, to air
Ausstrahlung *f* 1. radiation; 2. broadcast[ing]
~/**digital terrestrische** digital terrestrial broadcasting
~/**gleichzeitige (parallele)** simultaneous broadcast, simulcast
~/**spezifische [spektrale]** radiant exitance (emittance) *(radiometry)*
~/**terrestrische** terrestrial broadcast[ing], over-the-air broadcast

Ausstrahlungsrichtung *f* direction of radiation
Ausstrahl[ungs]winkel *m* radiation angle
Austastblende *f* blanking aperture
austasten to blank [out], to turn off *(video signal)*
Austastimpuls *m* blanking pulse
Austastlücke *f* blanking interval
~/**horizontale** horizontal blanking interval, HBI
~/**vertikale** vertical blanking interval, VBI, field blanking interval, FBI
Austastpegel *m s.* Austastwert
Austastsignal *n* blank[ing] signal, blank timing control signal
Austastung *f* blanking
~/**horizontale** horizontal blanking
~/**vertikale** vertical blanking
Austastwert *m* blanking level, [black] pedestal *(video signal)*
Austastzeichen *n s.* Austastsignal
Austastzeit *f* blanking period (time) *(s.a.* Austastlücke*)*
Austauschformat *n* interchange format *(data processing)*
Austragungsfläche *f* sweep surface *(surface modeling)*
Austrittsapertur *f* exit aperture
Austrittsdosis *f* exit dose *(radiology)*
Austrittsecho *n* [ultrasound] echo trailing edge *(sonography)*
Austrittsfenster *n* exit window *(X-ray tube)*
Austrittslinse *f* output lens
Austrittsluke *f* exit window
Austrittspupille *f* exit pupil, Ramsden circle; eye point *(Köhler illumination of microscope)*
~ **des Objektivs** objective back focal plane *(Köhler Ilumination)*
Austrittspupillendurchmesser *m* exit pupil diameter
Austrittspupillenebene *f* exit pupil plane
Austrittsstrahl *m* emergent (emerging) ray, exiting ray; emergent beam; output beam
Austrittswelle *f* exit wave
Austrittswinkel *m* exit (emergence) angle; output angle
Auswähler *m* choice device
Auswahlschlüssel *m* selective key *(image analysis)*
Auswahlwerkzeug *n* selection tool *(digital imaging)*
auswaschen to wash away (up) *(e.g. an offset plate)*
auswässern to wash out
Auswässern *n*, **Auswässerung** *f* water wash (rinse), washing
Ausweis-Fälschungssicherheit *f* ID card security
Ausweisfotografie *f* identification photography
ausweiten to expand *(e.g. a laser beam)*
auswertbar interpretable

Auswertbarkeit f interpretability *(e.g. of imagery)*
Auswertekamera f, **Auswertekammer** f plotting (restitution) camera *(photogrammetry)*
auswerten to evaluate; to plot; to interpret
Auswerter m [plotter] operator
Auswerterechner m evaluating computer
Auswertung f evaluation; interpretation
~/fotogrammetrische photogrammetrical restitution
~/halbautomatische semiautomatic interpretation
auszeichnen to mark up *(copy preparation)*
Auszeichnungsbefehl m tag *(data structure)*
Auszeichnungsschrift f display face (type) *(typography)*
Auszeichnungssprache f markup language
Ausziehstativ n telescopic tripod
auszoomen to zoom out
Auszug m extension *(camera)*
Auszugsfarbe f separation color
Auszugsfilter n separation filter
Auszugsnegativ n separation negative *(color processing)*
Auszugspositiv n separation positive (master) *(dye transfer process of color printing)*
Auszugsverlängerung f extension tube
Authentie f s. Authentizität
Authentifikation f authentication
authentifizieren to authenticate
Authentifizierung f, **Authentikation** f authentication
authentisieren to authenticate
Authentisierung f s. Authentifikation
Authentizität f authenticity
Authentizitätsprüfung f s. Authentifikation
Autoadapter m car adapter (charger)
Autoassoziation f autoassociation *(pattern recognition)*
autoassoziativ autoassociative *(neural network)*
Autobatterie-Anschlusskabel n s. Autoadapter
Autochromie f autochrome process (system) *(early color photography)*
Autochromplatte f autochrome [plate] *(positive color transparency)*
Autochromplattentechnik f s. Autochromie
Autofluoreszenz f autofluorescence, primary fluorescence
Autofluoroskop n multicrystal camera
Autofokus m autofocus [system], autofocus[ing] device, automatic focus, autofocus mechanism (facility) *(s.a. under* AF-...*)*
~/aktiver active autofocus [system]
~/kontinuierlicher continuous autofocus
~/mehrstrahliger multibeam autofocus
~/passiver passive autofocus [device]
Autofokusbetrieb m autofocus operation

Autofokus-Diaprojektor m autofocus slide projector, automatic-focus projector
Autofokuseinrichtung f s. Autofokus
Autofokusfunktion f autofocus capability
Autofokusgenauigkeit f autofocus accuracy
Autofokusgeschwindigkeit f autofocus speed
Autofokushilfslicht n autofocus illumination
Autofokuskamera f autofocus camera
Autofokus-Kompaktkamera f autofocus compact camera
Autofokusmodul n autofocus (AF) module
Autofokusmotor m focus motor
Autofokusobjektiv n autofocus (AF) lens
Autofokussensor m autofocus sensor
Autofokussierung f autofocusing, automatic focusing
Autofokussperre f autofocus lock
Autofokusspiegel m autofocus mirror
Autofokussystem n autofocus[ing] system *(s.a. under* Autofokus*)*
Autofokusvergrößerer m autofocus enlarger
Autofokus-Zoomobjektiv n autofocus zoom lens
autograf s. autografisch
Autograf m autograph, autographic recorder
Autografie f autography
autografisch autographic[al]
Autoirisobjektiv n auto iris lens
autokatalytisch autocatalytic *(development process)*
Autokino n drive-in theater
Autokollimation f autocollimation
Autokollimationsfernrohr n autocollimation telescope, autocollimator
Autokollimationsmikroskop n autocollimating microscope
Autokollimationsprisma n autocollimation prism
Autokollimationsspektrograf m autocollimating spectrograph
Autokollimator m 1. [reflex] autocollimator; 2. s. Autokollimationsfernrohr
autokollimieren to autocollimate
Autokorrelation f autocorrelation
Autokorrelationsbild n autocorrelation image
Autokorrelationsfunktion f autocorrelation function, ACF
Autokorrelationshistogramm n autocorrelation histogram
Autokorrelationskoeffizient m autocorrelation coefficient
Autokorrelationsmatrix f autocorrelation matrix
Autokorrelationstheorem n autocorrelation theorem
Autokorrelator m autocorrelator

Autokovarianzmatrix f autocovariance matrix
Autoladekabel n car adapter (charger)
Autolithografie f s. Autografie
Autolumineszenz f autoluminescence
Automat m/**endlicher (finiter)** finite[-state] automaton, finite-state machine
~/**gewichteter endlicher** weighted finite automaton
Automatenfoto n photobooth picture
Automatikblende f s. Blendenautomatik 1.
Automatikblitz m auto[matic] flash
Automatikfunktion f automatic function *(e.g. of a camera)*
Automatikmodus m auto mode *(video camera)*
Automatverschluss m self-cocking shutter
Autoradiografie f autoradiography
autoradiografisch autoradiographic
Autoradiogramm n autoradiograph [image], autoradiogram, radioautograph
Autorensystem n, **Autorenwerkzeug** n authoring tool *(multimedia design)*
Autorisierung f authorization
Autostereogramm n autostereogram, magic-eye stereogram; single-image random dot stereogram, SIRDS
Autostereoskopie f autostereoscopy
autostereoskopisch autostereoscopic
Autotransformator m autotransformer
Autotypie f 1. autotypy; 2. autotype *(copy)*
Autotypieraster m(n) [halftone] screen
autotypisch autotypic
Autoxidation f autoxidation, self-oxidation
AV s. Audio-Video
Avatar m avatar, natural resident *(virtual environment)*; cyborg, cybernetic organism, cybercitizen *(esp. as movie character)*
Avogadro-Konstante f Avogadro's constant, Avogadro['s] number *(number of atoms or molecules per mole)*
A-Wicklung f A wind (type) *(motion-picture film)*
axial axial, axal
Axialität f axiality
Axialsymmetrie f axial symmetry, axisymmetry
axialsymmetrisch axisymmetric[al], axially symmetrical
Axonometrie f axonometric projection
~/**dimetrische** dimetric projection
~/**trimetrische** trimetric projection
axonometrisch axonometric
Azimut n(m) azimuth
azimutal azimuthal
Azimutalprojektion f azimuthal [equidistant] projection
Azimutauflösung f azimuth resolution *(radar)*
Azimutdarstellung f azimuth display *(radar)*
Azimutdurchlauf m azimuth sweep
Azimuteffekt m azimuthal effect
Azimuteinstellung f azimuth adjustment
Azimutfehler m azimuth error
Azimutprojektion f [/**mittabstandstreue**] azimuthal [equidistant] projection
Azimutverlust m azimuth loss
Azimutversatz m slanted azimuth
Azimutwinkel m azimuth[al] angle
Azofarbstoff m azo dye (pigment)
Azomethinfarbstoff m azomethine dye *(image dye)*

B

Babyspot[scheinwerfer] *m* baby spot (light) *(studio lamp)*
Badbewegung *f* agitation [of the bath]
Bäderverschleppung *f* carryover *(of processing solutions)*
Badtemperatur *f* bath temperature
Bahn *f* 1. [paper] web, continuous [paper] roll *(printing)*; 2. *s.* Bahnkurve
Bahnelektron *n* orbital (orbiting) electron
Bahnkurve *f* trajectory
Bahnspannung *f* web tension
Bajonett *n* bayonet
Bajonettanschluss *m* bayonet mount (coupling), K-mount
Bajonetthalterung *f* bayonet holder
Bajonettverschluss *m s.* Bajonettanschluss
Bake *f* beacon
Bakterizid *n* bactericide, antibacterial [agent] *(developer additive)*
Balgen *m* [corrugated] bellows, camera bellows
Balgenauszug *m* 1. bellows [extension], extendable bellows; 2. lens-to-film distance (spacing), bellows extension (draw)
~/**doppelter** double-extension bellows
~/**dreifacher** triple-extension bellows
Balgen[einstell]gerät *n* [extension] bellows; bellows attachment (unit)
Balgenkamera *f* bellows (folding) camera
Balgenkompendium *n* compendium hood, matte box
Balgennaheinstellgerät *n* closeup bellows (tube)
Balgenzwischenstück *n* bellows connection
Balkencode *m* bar code
Balkendetektor *m* bar detector
Balkendiagramm *n* bar graph (chart) *(s.a.* Histogramm*)*
Balkenraster *m(n)* bar pattern
Ballard-Verfahren *n* Ballard process *(of copper-coating gravure cylinders)*
Ballempfang *m* relay reception *(broadcasting)*
Ballettfotografie *f* dance photography
Band *n* 1. tape; 2. band, range *(e.g. of frequencies)*
~/**bespieltes** used tape
~/**codiertes** time-coded tape
~/**freies (freilaufendes)** open reel tape
~/**Internationales** international tape (sound track), music and effect track, M&E [mix] *(cinema)*
~/**nachzubearbeitendes** edit tape
~/**oberes** high (upper) band *(e.g. as frequency range in satellite reception)*
~/**sendefertiges** broadcast (television) videotape, broadcast[-quality] tape, professional tape
~/**unbespieltes** blank [magnetic] tape *(s.a.* Frischband*)*
~/**unperforiertes** unperforated (nonperforated) tape
~/**unteres** low[er] band *(frequency range)*
Bandabrieb *m* tape abrasion
Bandabspielgeschwindigkeit *f* tape playback speed
Bandabspielsystem *n* tape playback system
Bandabstand *m s.* Bandlücke
Bandabtastung *f* 1. tape scanning; 2. *s.* Bandpassabtastung
Bandandruck *m* tape pressure
Bandanfang *m* beginning of a tape
Bandantrieb *m* tape drive
Bandantriebsachse *f*, **Bandantriebswelle** *f* capstan
Bandarchiv *n* tape archive (library)
Bandaufnahme *f* 1. tape recording, taping; 2. tape [recording]
Bandaufnahmegerät *n* tape recorder
Bandaufnahmezeit *f* tape record time
Bandausnutzung *f* tape utilization
bandbegrenzt band-limited
Bandbegrenzung *f* band limitation (limiting)
Bandbegrenzungsfilter *n* band-limiting filter
Bandbeschichtung *f* tape coating
Bandbreite *f* 1. bandwidth, frequency range capability; 2. tape width
~/**elektrische** electrical (power) bandwidth *(photodetector)*
~/**optische** optical (voltage) bandwidth *(photodetector)*
~/**ortsfrequente** spatial-frequency bandwidth *(e.g. of the eye)*
~/**rauschäquivalente** noise-equivalent bandwidth
~/**spektrale** spectral bandwidth
~/**wirksame** effective bandwidth
Bandbreitenausnutzung *f* 1. bandwidth use; 2. spectral efficiency
Bandbreitenbedarf *m* bandwidth requirement
bandbreitenbegrenzt bandwidth-limited, bandwidth-constrained
Bandbreitenbegrenzung *f*, **Bandbreitenbeschränkung** *f* bandwidth limitation (limiting)
Bandbreiteneffizienz *f* spectral efficiency
Bandbreitenexpansion *f* bandwidth expansion
Bandbreitenfilter *n s.* Bandpassfilter
Bandbreitenfluktuation *f* bandwidth fluctuation
Bandbreitenkompression *f* bandwidth compression
Bandbreitenreduktion *f* bandwidth reduction

Bandbreitenschwankung *f* bandwidth fluctuation
Bandbreitensegment *n* bandwidth segment
Bandbreitenverbrauch *m* bandwidth consumption
Bandbreitenverfügbarkeit *f* bandwidth availability
Bändchenmikrofon *n* ribbon microphone
Banddehnung *f* tape stretch
Banddicke *f* tape thickness
Banddrucker *m* band (belt) printer
Banddurchlauf *m* tape pass
Bandeinlegen *n* tape installation process
Bandende *n* end of tape
Bandendeabschaltung *f* end search
Bandenspektrum *n* band spectrum
Bändermodell *n*, **Bänderschema** *n* band model (theory) *(of solid-state physics)*
Bandfehler *m* tape defect
Bandfilter *n s.* Bandpassfilter
Bandformat *n* tape [recording] format
Bandführung *f* tape guide
Bandführungsrolle *f*, **Bandführungstrommel** *f* head drum
Bandgerät *n* tape-based device
Bandgeschwindigkeit *f* tape speed (velocity)
~/**effektive** effective tape speed
Bandkante *f* tape edge
Bandkassette *f* tape cassette (cartridge)
Bandklebestelle *f* tape splice
Bandkopf *m* tape head
Bandkopie *f* copy tape
Bandkuchen *m* pancake
Bandlängenzählwerk *n* tape [machine] counter
Bandlauf *m* tape travel (run)
Bandlaufgeschwindigkeit *f* tape speed
Bandlaufrichtung *f* direction of tape travel (motion)
Bandlaufwerk *n* tape drive; streamer
~/**schnelles** streamer
Bandleiterlaser *m* slab laser
bandlos tapeless *(video server)*
Bandlöschgerät *n* bulk eraser
Bandlöschung *f* tape erasure
Bandlücke *f* band (forbidden) gap *(photodetector)*
Bandmaschine *f* tape machine (recorder), tape player; [tape] deck
Bandmaterial *n* tape stock, tape[d] material
Bandoberfläche *f* tape surface
Bandpass *m* band-pass
Bandpassabtastung *f* band-pass sampling
Bandpasscharakteristik *f s.* Bandpassverhalten
Bandpassfilter *n* band-pass [frequency] filter
Bandpassfilterung *f* band-pass filtering [operation]
Bandpassfunktion *f* band-pass function
Bandpassignal *n* band-pass signal
Bandpassverhalten *n* band-pass response (characteristic)
Bandrauschen *n* tape noise
Bandrecorder *m* tape recorder
Bandreibung *f* tape path friction
Bandrestanzeige *f* remaining tape counter
Bandriss *m* tape breakage
Bandrücklauf *m* [tape] rewind
Bandschleife *f* continuous (endless) loop, infinite loop
Bandschlupf *m* tape slippage
Bandschnitt *m* tape editing
Bandspeicher *m* tape store
Bandspeicherung *f* tape-based storage
Bandsperre *f*, **Bandsperrfilter** *n* band-stop (band-reject) filter, band elimination filter
Bandsperrfilterung *f* band-stop (bend-reject) filtering
Bandspieler *m* tape player, tape machine (recorder)
Bandspule *f* tape reel
Bandspur *f* tape track
Bandstellensuche *f*/**automatische** automatic program search, APS, automatic picture finder, APF
Bandsuchlaufeinrichtung *f* [/**automatische**] auto locator
Bandteller *m* tape reel
Bandträger *m* tape support
Bandtransport *m* tape transport
Bandtransportantrieb *m* capstan
Bandtransportgeschwindigkeit *f* tape speed
Bandtransportmechanismus *m* tape transport mechanism
Bandtransportsystem *n* tape transport system, transport
Bandüberlappungseffekt *m* aliasing [effect]
Bandumschlingung *f* tape wrap
Bandverbrauch *m* tape consumption
Bandvorlauf *m* black[ed] tape, preblacked (striped) tape
Bandwechsel *m* tape change
Bandweg *m* tape path
Bandwickel *m* pancake
Bandzählwerk *n* tape [machine] counter,
Bandzug *m* tape tension; skew
Bandzugfehler *m* skew error
Bandzugkraft *f*, **Bandzugspannung** *f s.* Bandzug
Bank *f*/**optische** 1. optical (lens) bench, lens board; 2. optical printer *(cinema)*
Banknotenpapier *n* banknote paper
Bankpostpapier *n* bond (business) paper, communication (correspondence) paper
Banküberwachungskamera *f* bank surveillance camera
Bannerdruck *m* banner printing
Bannerwerbung *f* banner ad[vertising] *(Internet)*
Barcode *m* bar code
Barcodelesen *n* bar-code reading

Barcodeleser *m*, **Barcodescanner** *m* bar-code reader (scanner), wand
Baritkronglas *n* barium crown [glass]
Baritleichtkron *n* light barium crown [glass]
Baritschwerkron *n* dense barium crown [glass]
Bariumbetaborat *n* beta-barium borate, BBO
Bariumsulfat *n* barium sulfate, baryta *(pigment, X-ray contrast agent)*
Barlow-Linse *f* Barlow lens *(telescope)*
Bartlett-Fenster *n*, **Bartlett-Filter** *n* Bartlett window *(signal processing)*
Baryt *m* 1. barite, baryte[s], heavy spar; 2. *s*. Bariumsulfat
barytbeschichtet baryta-coated, clay-coated
Barytbeschichtung *f* baryta coating
Baryt[foto]papier *n* baryta[-coated] paper
Barytschicht *f* baryta layer (coating)
Barytweiß *n* baryta white, blanc fixe *(pigment)*
Baryzentrum *n* barycenter, center of mass
Base *f* base
BAS-Fernsehsignal *n* composite [encoded video] signal, composite video [signal], composite TV signal
Basis *f*/**stereoskopische** stereo base
Basisband *n* baseband *(frequency)*
Basisbandbreite *f* base bandwidth
Basisbandfilter *n* baseband filter
Basisbandmodulation *f* baseband modulation
Basisbandsignal *n* baseband [video] signal
Basisbandübertragung *f* baseband transmission
Basisbild *n* 1. basis image (picture), basis matrix *(digital image processing)*; 2. *s*. Schlüsselbild
Basiscode *m* base code *(image compression)*
Basiseinheit *f* [/**internationale**] base unit [in the International System of Units]
Basisfunktion *f* basis function *(digital image processing)*
Basisfunktionsnetz *n*/**radiales** radial basis functions [neural] net[work], RBFNN
Basisnetz *n* backbone
Basisstation *f s*. Kamerakontrolleinheit
Basisvektor *m* base (basis) vector, unit vector
Basis-Wavelet *n* wavelet basis, mother wavelet
Bassanhebung *f* bass boosting
BAS-Signal *n s*. BAS-Fernsehsignal
bathochrom bathochromic
Bathochromie *f* bathochromism
Bathymetrie *f* bathymetry, water depth measurement
Batterie *f* battery, primary cell *(s.a.* Akkumulator*)*
~/**wiederaufladbare** rechargeable battery
Batteriebetrieb *m* battery mode

batteriebetrieben battery-powered
Batteriefach *m* battery compartment
Batteriefachdeckel *m* battery cover
batteriegespeist battery-powered
Batteriegürtel *m* battery belt
Batteriehandgriff *m* power grip [kit]
Batteriekontrolle *f s*. Batterieprüfung
Batterieladegerät *n* battery charger
Batteriemagazin *n* battery holder
Batterieprüfung *f* battery check (power confirmation)
Batterietester *m* [battery] charge tester
Batteriewarnanzeige *f* low-battery warning
Bauchhöhlenspiegel *m* laparoscope
Bauch[höhlen]spiegelung *f* laparoscopy
Baud *n* baud, bit per second *(unit of data rate)*
Baudrate *f* baud rate
Baudratengenerator *m* baud rate generator
Bauelement *n*/**elektromechanisches** actuator
~/**ladungsgekoppeltes** charge-coupled device (detector), CCD
~/**ladungsinjizierendes** charge-injection device, CID
~/**optisch abbildendes**, ~/**optisches** optical element
~/**optoelektronisches** optoelectronic component
Bauernfeind-Prisma *n* Bauernfeind prism
Baulänge *f* construction (physical) length *(of an objective)*
Baum *m* tree, dendrogram *(data structure)*
~/**ausgeglichener** balanced tree
~/**binärer** binary tree
~/**geordneter** ordered tree
~/**hierarchischer** hierarchical tree
~/**logischer** logical tree
~/**quaternärer** quad (quartic) tree
Baumcode *m* tree-base code
Baumcodierung *f* tree [en]coding
Baumdarstellung *f* tree representation, dendrogram *(pattern recognition)*
Baumklassifikator *m* hierarchical classifier
Baumknoten *m* tree node
Baumstruktur *f* tree structure *(e.g. of image data)*; tree-and-branch design (architecture) *(e.g. of a cable television system)*
~/**hierarchische** hierarchical tree structure
Baumsuche *f* tree search [technique] *(vector quantization)*
Bauteilidentifikation *f* workpiece recognition, components detection, industrial parts verification
Bauten *mpl* props *(e.g. in motion-picture production)*
Bayer-Mosaik *n* Bayer pattern *(charge-coupled device)*
Bayes-Klassifikation *f* Bayesian classification *(pattern recognition)*
Bayes-Klassifikator *m* Bayes[ian] classifier

Bayes-Netz *n* Bayesian network (framework) *(information theory)*
Bayes-Regel *f* Bayes [decision] rule, Bayes optimal discriminant function
Bayes-Schätzung *f* Bayesian estimation
Bayes-Statistik *f* Bayesian statistics
Bayes-Theorem *n* Bayes' theorem *(probability theory)*
B-Bild *n* 1. B picture (frame), bidirectional[ly predictive] coded picture, bidirectional frame *(video encoding)*; 2. [ultrasound] B-scan [image], B-mode [ultrasound] image
B-Bild-Sonografie *f*, **B-Bildverfahren** *n* [ultrasound] B-mode imaging, B-mode ultrasound [scanning], B-scan [pulse echo mode of] imaging
bearbeiten to edit *(e.g. motion pictures, sound)*
Bearbeitungsmodus *m* edit mode
bebildern to illustrate, to pictorialize, to picture; to image *(a printing plate)*
Bebilderung *f* [pictorial] illustration, pictorialization; imaging *(esp. of printing plates)*
~/**digitale** digital imaging
~/**direkte** direct imaging
~/**elektronische** electronic imaging
~ **in der Druckmaschine** computer-to-press
Beck-Effekt *m* Beck effect *(optics)*
Becquerel-Effekt *m* Becquerel effect *(exposure phenomenon)*
Bedienbarkeit *f* operability, practicability *(e.g. of a camera)*
Bedienelement *n*/**nutzerfreundliches** user-friendly control
Bediener *m* operator
Bedienerführung/menügesteuerte menu-driven [operator] prompting
Bedienerschnittstelle *f* operator interface
Bedienfehler *m* operator error
Bedienfeld *n* control (front) panel, operator console
Bedienkomfort *m* ease of operation
Bedienoberfläche *f* user[-computer] interface, operating interface, user agent *(s.a. under Benutzerschnittstelle)*
Bedienungselement *n* [user] control
Bedienungsfehler *m* manipulative error
Bedienungskomfort *m s.* Bedienkomfort
Bedingung *f*/**Hornsche** Horn constraint equation *(motion detection)*
bedruckbar printable
Bedruckbarkeit *f* printability
bedrucken to print [on]
~/**beidseitig** to back up
Bedruckmaterial *n*, **Bedruckstoff** *m* print support material, [printing] substrate, matter (material) to be printed
bedruckt/beidseitig printed both sides
Beeinflussungslänge *f* constraint length *(video signal processing)*

Befehl *m* command, instruction, statement *(computer program)*
Befehlsfolge *f* sequence of instructions
Befehlsmenü *n* command menu
Befehlssatz *m s.* Befehlsvorrat
Befehlssprache *f* command language
Befehlsvorrat *m* command (instruction) set, set of instructions
Begießanlage *f* coating apparatus *(film manufacture)*
Begleitton *m* accompanying sound
Begrenzer *m* [de]limiter
Begrenzungsfläche *f* boundary surface *(three-dimensional visualization)*
Begrenzungsflächendarstellung *f* boundary representation, B-rep
Begrüßungsbildschirm *m s.* Eröffnungsbildschirm
Beguss *m* [film] coating
beidäugig binocular
Beidäugigkeit *f* binocularity
Beifilm *m* fill-up [film], supplementary film
Beilage *f* insert, interleaves *(additional printed item within a publication)*
B-Einstellung *f* B-setting
Beispiel[s]bild *n* example image
Beistelldecoder *m* set-top [box], STB, video set-top unit, set-top converter (box decoder), integrated receiver-decoder, IRD
Beistellgerät *n* set-top appliance
Belederung *f* leather facing *(of a camera)*
Belegleser *m* document reader
Belehrung *f* teach-in *(e.g. of a neural network)*
beleuchten to light, to illuminate
Beleuchter *m* [set] lighting technician, lighting electrician; best boy [electric]
Beleuchterbrücke *f s.* Beleuchtungsbrücke
Beleuchtung *f* lighting, illumination *(s.a. under Ausleuchtung)*
~/**aktive** active illumination
~/**diffuse** diffuse[d] illumination, diffuse[d] lighting
~/**direkte** direct lighting (illumination)
~/**faseroptische** fiber[-optic] lighting
~/**fluoreszierende** fluorescent lighting (illumination)
~/**gedämpfte** subdued lighting
~/**gegenseitige** mutual illumination
~/**gerichtete** directional lighting
~/**globale** global illumination
~/**harte** hard (harsh) lighting
~/**indirekte** indirect (bounce) lighting, indirect illumination
~/**inkohärente** incoherent illumination
~/**interaktive** interactive lighting
~/**koaxiale** coaxial illumination
~/**kohärente** coherent illumination
~/**Köhlersche** Köhler illumination [technique]
~/**kollimierte** collimated lighting
~/**kontrastarme** flat lighting (illumination)
~/**kontrastreiche** high-contrast lighting

~/**künstliche** artificial lighting (illumination), man-made illumination
~/**monochromatische** monochromatic illumination
~/**orthoskopische** orthoscopic illumination
~/**partiell kohärente** partially coherent lighting
~/**schattenlose** shadowless lighting
~/**schiefe (schräge)** oblique illumination
~/**seitliche** side lighting
~/**spiegelnde** specular lighting
~/**stroboskopische** stroboscopic illumination
~/**strukturierte** structured illumination
~/**teilkohärente** partially coherent illumination
~/**ungleichmäßige** nonuniform (uneven) lighting, uneven illumination
~/**weiche** soft lighting
Beleuchtungberechnung f [/**computergrafische**] light field rendering
Beleuchtungsachse f lighting axis
Beleuchtungsalgorithmus m/**globaler** global illumination algorithm
Beleuchtungsänderung f illumination change (variation)
Beleuchtungsanlage f lighting installation; lighting equipment; lighting kit
Beleuchtungsanordnung f lighting arrangement (setup)
Beleuchtungsapertur f illuminating (condenser) aperture
Beleuchtungsart f kind of lighting; lighting style
Beleuchtungsassistent m best boy [electric], assistant chief lighting technician
Beleuchtungsaufbau m lighting setup (arrangement)
Beleuchtungsbedingungen fpl lighting conditions
Beleuchtungsbrücke f [lighting] bridge, grid
Beleuchtungsbündel n illumination bundle
Beleuchtungseffekt m illumination (lighting) effect
Beleuchtungseinheit f lighting unit, illumination (illuminating) unit
Beleuchtungseinrichtung f illuminating apparatus *(e.g. of a microscope)*; lighting rig (setup)
Beleuchtungsfarbe f lighting (illumination) color
Beleuchtungsfilter n lighting filter
Beleuchtungsgeometrie f illumination geometry, geometry of illumination
Beleuchtungsgerät n illuminating device (apparatus), illuminant
Beleuchtungsgerüst n track lighting system
Beleuchtungsimpuls m illuminating pulse
Beleuchtungsingenieur m illuminating engineer
Beleuchtungsintensität f lighting level; illumination intensity
Beleuchtungskasten m illumination (light) box
Beleuchtungskegel m illumination cone, cone of illumination
Beleuchtungskompensation f illumination compensation
Beleuchtungskonstanz f constancy of illumination
Beleuchtungskontrast m lighting contrast
Beleuchtungskörper m luminaire, lighting instrument, light[ing] fixture, light
Beleuchtungskorrektur f illumination correction
Beleuchtungslicht n illuminating light
Beleuchtungslichtkegel m illuminating light cone
Beleuchtungslichtleiter m s. Chefbeleuchter
Beleuchtungslichtweg m illuminating light path
Beleuchtungslinse f condenser [lens]
Beleuchtungsmesser m s. Beleuchtungsstärkemesser
Beleuchtungsmilieu n lighting environment
Beleuchtungsmodell n illumination (lighting) model *(computer graphics)*
~/**geometrisches** geometric illumination model
~/**globales** global illumination model
~/**lokales** local illumination model
~/**Phongsches** Phong's illumination model
~/**spektrales** spectral illumination model
Beleuchtungsmodellierung f illumination (lighting) modelling
Beleuchtungsmodul n lighting module
Beleuchtungsniveau n lighting (illumination) level
Beleuchtungsoptik f illumination system optics, light source optics
Beleuchtungsplan m lighting plan
Beleuchtungspraxis f lighting practice
Beleuchtungsquelle f lighting source, illumination (illuminating) source, source of illumination
Beleuchtungsrichtung f illumination (lighting) direction
Beleuchtungssituation f lighting situation
Beleuchtungsspektrum n illumination spectrum
Beleuchtungsspiegel m illuminating mirror
Beleuchtungsstärke f illuminance, illumination, light level, intensity *(photometry)*
Beleuchtungsstärkemesser m, **Beleuchtungsstärkemessgerät** n illuminance meter, [il]luminometer, lux[o]meter; incident-light [exposure] meter, inciden[-light] meter

Beleuchtungsstärkeverhältnis *n* illuminance ratio
Beleuchtungsstärkeverteilung *f* illumination distribution
Beleuchtungsstil *m* lighting style
Beleuchtungsstrahlengang *m* illuminating ray path
Beleuchtungssystem *n* lighting (illumination) system
Beleuchtungtechnik *f* 1. illuminating (lighting) engineering; 2. lighting (illumination) technique
Beleuchtungstechniker *m* [set] lighting technician, lighting electrician
Beleuchtungsverfahren *n*/**Köhlersches** Köhler illumination [technique]
Beleuchtungsverhältnis *n* lighting ratio
Beleuchtungswinkel *m* lighting (illumination) angle, angle of illumination
Beleuchtungszubehör *n* lighting accessories
belichten to expose [to light]
~/**partiell (teilweise)** to dodge [out], to hold back
Belichter *m* 1. imagesetter; [film] recorder; 2. *s.* Belichtungsgerät
Belichterpixel *n* [laser] dot, laser point
Belichtung *f* light exposure, illumination, quantity of illuminance *(photometry)*; [light] exposure, exposure to light *(photography)*
~/**automatische** automatic exposure
~/**bildmäßige** image light exposure, imagewise (image-forming) exposure
~/**fotografische** photographic exposure
~/**holografische** holographic exposure
~/**intermittierende** intermittent exposure
~/**kontinuierliche** time exposure
~/**kurzzeitige** short[-duration] exposure
~/**optimale** optimum exposure
~/**richtige** correct (proper) exposure
~/**sensitometrische** sensitometric exposure
~/**spektrale** spectral exposure
Belichtungsänderung *f* exposure change
Belichtungsanpassung *f* exposure adjustment
Belichtungsausgleich *m* exposure compensation
Belichtungsautomat *m* light-integrating timer *(typography)*
Belichtungsautomatik *f* auto[matic] exposure [system], autoexposure feature, AE [system]
~ **mit Blendenvorwahl** aperture priority [mode], focus priority
~ **mit Zeitvorwahl** shutter priority [mode], release priority
Belichtungsblitz *m* [optical] flash
Belichtungscomputer *m* exposure computer
Belichtungsdaten *pl* exposure data
Belichtungsdauer *f* exposure duration
Belichtungseffekt *m* exposure effect (phenomenon)
Belichtungseinheit *f* exposure unit, unit of exposure
Belichtungseinstellung *f* exposure [time] setting, exposure timing
~/**automatische** *s.* Belichtungsautomatik
Belichtungsempfehlung *f* exposure recommendation
Belichtungsempfindlichkeit *f* exposure sensitivity, exposure [film] speed
Belichtungsfächer *m* exposure series (wedge)
Belichtungsfaktor *m* exposure factor
Belichtungsfehler *m* exposure error
Belichtungsfenster *n* exposure gate
Belichtungsfilter *n* exposure filter
Belichtungsfunktion *f* exposure mode
Belichtungsgenauigkeit *f* exposure accuracy
Belichtungsgerät *n* exposing (exposure) device, exposure tool *(lithography)*
Belichtungsgeschwindigkeit *f* exposure speed
Belichtungsgröße *f s.* Belichtungswert
Belichtungsindex *m* exposure index, EI
Belichtungsinnenmessung *f* through-the-lens metering, TTL metering
Belichtungsintensität *f* exposure (exposing light) intensity
Belichtungsintervall *n* exposure interval
Belichtungskeim *m* exposure nucleus
Belichtungskompensation *f* exposure compensation
Belichtungskontrolle *f* exposure check
Belichtungskorrektur *f* exposure correction; exposure compensation
Belichtungskorrekturfaktor *m* exposure correction factor
Belichtungskorrekturtaste *f* exposure compensation button
Belichtungskorrekturwert *m* exposure compensation value
Belichtungsmenge *f* exposure
Belichtungsmessart *f* exposure mode
Belichtungsmesser *m* exposure (light) meter
~/**eingebauter** built-in exposure (camera) meter, in-camera [exposure] meter
~/**elektronischer** electronic exposure meter
~/**externer** external exposure meter
~/**fotoelektrischer (lichtelektrischer)** photoelectric exposure meter
Belichtungsmessergenauigkeit *f* exposure meter accuracy
Belichtungsmesserkupplung *f* exposure meter coupling
Belichtungsmessfeld *n* exposure metering field
Belichtungsmessgerät *n s.* Belichtungsmesser
Belichtungsmesssystem *n* exposure metering (measurement) system

Belichtungsmessung f exposure measurement, light (exposure) metering
~ **durch das Objektiv** s. Belichtungsinnenmessung
~/**integrale** integrating metering
~/**mittenbetonte** center-weighted metering
~/**punktuelle** spot metering
Belichtungsmodus m exposure mode
Belichtungsmuster n exposure pattern
Belichtungsoptik f exposing optics
Belichtungsparameter m exposure parameter
Belichtungspräzision f exposure accuracy
Belichtungsprobe f exposure test
Belichtungsprogrammautomatik f programmed auto[matic] exposure, program exposure system
Belichtungspunkt m dot *(halftone printing)*
Belichtungsregelung f exposure control
Belichtungsreihe f exposure series (wedge)
Belichtungsreihenautomatik f, **Belichtungsreihenfunktion** f bracketing function, auto-bracketing [function] *(camera)*
Belichtungsrichtzahl f exposure index number, EI number (film speed rating) *(motion-picture film)*
Belichtungsschaltuhr f s. Belichtungsuhr
Belichtungsschleier m exposure-induced fog, optical fog
Belichtungsserie f exposure series (wedge)
Belichtungsskale f exposure-value scale
Belichtungsspalt m exposure slit
Belichtungsspielraum m [log-]exposure range; exposure latitude
Belichtungsstärke f exposure level
Belichtungssteuergerät n exposure controller (control unit)
Belichtungssteuerung f exposure control; integration control *(CCD technology)*
~/**automatische** automatic exposure control
Belichtungssteuerungssystem n exposure control system
Belichtungsstrahlung f exposing radiation
Belichtungsstufe f exposure level (step)
Belichtungssystem n exposure system
Belichtungstabelle f exposure table (chart)
Belichtungstechnik f exposure technique
Belichtungstest m [light] exposure test
Belichtungstrommel f exposure drum; photoconductive rotating drum *(laser printer)*
Belichtungsuhr f exposure timer; [darkroom] timer
Belichtungsumfang m [exposure] latitude; [log-]exposure range
Belichtungsverlängerungsfaktor m exposure increase factor
Belichtungsverteilung f exposure distribution
Belichtungsvorgang m exposure process
Belichtungswahl f exposure mode selection
Belichtungswellenlänge f exposure wavelength
Belichtungswert m [/**relativer**] exposure value, EV
Belichtungszeit f exposure time; integration time *(CCD technology)*
~/**effektive** effective exposure time
~/**eingestellte** set exposure time
~/**ultrakurze** ultrashort framing exposure
Belichtungszeitbestimmung f exposure time determination
Belichtungszeitenbereich m exposure range
Belichtungszeiteneinstellring m, **Belichtungszeitenwähler** m exposure setting ring
Belichtungszeitpunkt m instant (moment) of exposure
Belichtungszeitraum m exposure period
Belichtungszeitschaltuhr f s. Belichtungsuhr
Belichtungszeitverlängerung f exposure increase
Bell-Howell-Perforation f BH (Bell and Howell) barrel-shaped perforation, negative perf[oration] *(motion-picture film)*
Benham-Farben fpl subjective (Fechner's) colors
Benham-Scheibe f Benham['s] disk *(for generating chromatic sensations)*
Benton-Hologramm n Benton (rainbow) hologram
Benutzereinstellung f user setting
benutzerfreundlich user-friendly
Benutzerfreundlichkeit f user convenience
Benutzerführung f user prompting
Benutzergruppe f/**geschlossene** closed user group
Benutzerkomfort m user convenience
Benutzermenü n user menu
Benutzeroberfläche f s. Benutzerschnittstelle
Benutzerschnittstelle f user[-computer] interface, operating interface, user agent
~/**grafische** graphical (graphics-based) user interface, GUI, graphics controller interface, graphic[al] interface, graphical front-end
Benutzungsoberfläche f, **Benutzungsschnittstelle** f s. Benutzerschnittstelle
Benzol n benzene *(solvent)*
Benzolderivat n benzene derivative *(developing chemical)*
Benztriazol n benzotriazole *(antifoggant)*
beobachtbar observable, viewable
Beobachtbarkeit f observability
beobachten to observe, to watch, to monitor

Beobachter *m*/**durchschnittlicher (normalsichtiger)** normal [human] observer, average (standard) observer
Beobachtermetamerie *f* observer metamerism *(colorimetry)*
Beobachtung *f*/**einäugige** monocular observation
~/**orthoskopische** orthoscopic viewing (observation)
~/**visuelle** visual observation
Beobachtungs... *s.a.* Betrachtungs...
Beobachtungsapertur *f* viewing aperture
Beobachtungsbereich *m* viewing range
Beobachtungsebene *f* observation plane, plane of observation
Beobachtungsentfernung *f* view[ing] distance
Beobachtungsfernrohr *n* observatory (observation) telescope, viewing telescope
Beobachtungsgerät *n* observational tool
Beobachtungsmikroskop *n* observation microscope
Beobachtungsokular *n* framing eyepiece
Beobachtungsort *m*, **Beobachtungspunkt** *m* observation (observing) point, observation site
Beobachtungsrichtung *f* view[ing] direction, direction of view[ing], look direction
Beobachtungssatellit *m* observation[al] satellite
Beobachtungsschirm *m* viewing screen
Beobachtungsstation *f*/**astronomische** astronomical observatory
Beobachtungswinkel *m* observation angle; view[ing] angle, angle of view (field)
Berandung *f* boundary
berechnen to calculate, to compute, to figure *(e.g. optical elements)*
Bereich *m* 1. domain, realm; 2. region *(s.a.* Region*)*; blob; 3. range, extent
~/**aktiver** active region *(semiconductor)*
~/**bildfreier** nonimage [surface] area *(printing)*
~/**interessierender (signifikanter)** region of interest, ROI
Bereichfrage *f s.* Bereichsabfrage
Bereichsabfrage *f* [exact] range query *(computer graphics)*
Bereichsanalyse *f* region analysis
Bereichsanfrage *f s.* Bereichsabfrage
Bereichsauffüllung *f* region filling [method]
Bereichsbeschreibung *f* region description
Bereichscharakterisierung *f* region characterization
Bereichscodierung *f* region encoding
Bereichsdeskriptor *m* region descriptor
Bereichsdetektion *f* region detection (finding), binary segmentation
Bereichseckpunkt *m* region corner point
Bereichsextraktion *f* region extraction
Bereichsisolierung *f* region isolation
Bereichsklassifikator *m* region classifier
Bereichskontur *f* region contour (boundary), region border
Bereichskorrekturalgorithmus *m* region correction algorithm *(binary image processing)*
Bereichsmerkmal *n* region [shape] feature
Bereichsmodell *n* region model
Bereichsprimitiv *n* region primitive
Bereichspunkt *m* region point
Bereichsunterteilungsalgorithmus *m* region splitting algorithm
Bereichsverschmelzung *f* region merging
Bereichswachstum[sverfahren] *n* region-growing [method], region-growing procedure, magic wand approach *(segmentation technique)*
Bereichszuordnung *f* block matching *(image coding)*
Bereitschaftslampenkontakt *m* readylight contact
Bereitschaftsmodus *m*, **Bereitschaftsschaltung** *f* standby mode *(e.g. of a video camera)*
Bereitschaftsstellung *f* standby position
Bereitschaftstasche *f* ever-ready [camera] case
Bereitschaftszeichen *n* prompt [character] *(computer)*
Berichterstattung *f* [news] coverage
~/**elektronische** electronic news gathering, ENG
~ **via Satellit[/elektronische]** satellite news gathering, SNG
Bernoulli-Verteilung *f s.* Binomialverteilung
Bernsteinbildschirm *m* amber screen
Bernstein-Polynom *n* Bernstein polynomial *(computer graphics)*
Bertrand-Linse *f* Bertrand lens *(phase-contrast microscopy)*
Berufsfilmformat *n* professional [film] format
Berufsfotograf *m* professional photographer
Berufsfotografie *f* professional photography
Beruhigungsschleife *f* Latham loop *(film passage)*
Berührungsbildschirm *m* touch[-sensitive] screen, tactile (pressure-sensitive) screen; touch screen monitor
beschallen to insonify *(sonography)*
Beschattung *f* shadowing
Beschauer *m s.* Betrachter
beschichten to coat
Beschichtung *f* coating
~/**dielektrische** dielectric coating
~/**mehrlagige** multilayer coating
~/**schmalbandige** narrow-band coating
Beschleuniger *m* 1. [development] accelerator; 2. *s.* Beschleunigerkarte
Beschleunigeranode *f* accelerating anode *(cathode-ray tube)*

Beschleunigerkarte f [graphics] accelerator card, video accelerator *(s.a. Grafikkarte, Videokarte)*
Beschleunigungselektrode f accelerating electrode
Beschleunigungsgitter n accelerating grid *(cathode-ray tube)*
Beschleunigungskarte f s. Beschleunigerkarte
Beschleunigungspotential n acceleration potential
Beschleunigungsspannung f acceleration (accelerating) voltage, tube [kilo]voltage *(cathode-ray tube)*
beschneiden to crop, to trim, to clip *(e.g. a photograph)*
Beschneidung f, **Beschnitt** m trimming, cropping, clipping; scissoring *(computer graphics)*
Beschnittkante f trimming edge
Beschnittmarke f, **Beschnittzeichen** n trim (crop) mark, cut (tic) mark, corner mark
beschreibbar recordable
Beschreibbarkeit f acceptance of writing *(photographic paper)*
Beschreibung f/**codierte** coded description
~/**parametrische** parametric description
~/**syntaktische** syntactic description *(e.g. in object classification)*
Beschreibungssprache f markup language
Beschriftung f lettering
Beschriftungslaser m marking laser
Besetzungsinversion f population inversion *(laser)*
bespielbar recordable
~/**mehrfach** rewritable
Bespurungsband n sound stripe *(motion-picture film)*
Bessel-Filter n Bessel filter
Bessel-Funktion f Bessel function *(frequency modulation)*
~ **erster Ordnung** first-order Bessel function, Bessel function of order one, Bessel function of the first kind
~ **nullter Ordnung** order n Bessel function
bestrahlen to irradiate
Bestrahlung f irradiation; radiant exposure *(radiometry)*
Bestrahlungsstärke f [incident] irradiance *(radiometry)*
~/**relative** relative irradiance
Beta n s. Betawert
Betafluorografie f beta fluorography
Betalumineszenz f betaluminescence
Betaprobenwechsler m liquid scintillation counter *(nuclear medicine)*
Betaradiografie f beta radiography
Betastrahlung f beta radiation (ray)
Betateilchen n beta particle (ray)
Betatron n betatron *(electron accelerator)*
Betawert m beta, relativistic velocity
Betazerfall m beta decay
Betitelung f titling
betrachten to view

Betrachter m viewer, spectator, observer
~/**hörgeschädigter** hearing-impaired viewer
~/**idealer** ideal (Bayesian) observer *(mathematical model)*
~/**synthetischer** synthetic observer *(computer graphics)*
Betrachterabstand m s. Betrachtungsabstand
Betrachterperspektive f viewer-centered perspective
Betrachterposition f, **Betrachterstandpunkt** m viewer position
Betrachtung f viewing
~/**beidäugige** binocular viewing
~/**stereoskopische** stereoscopic (three-dimensional) viewing
Betrachtungsabstand m view[ing] distance; screen-to-audience distance
Betrachtungsachse f viewing axis
Betrachtungsapparat m s. Betrachtungsgerät
Betrachtungsbedingungen pl viewing conditions
Betrachtungsdistanz f, **Betrachtungsentfernung** f view[ing] distance; screen-to-audience distance
Betrachtungsentfernung f view[ing] distance
Betrachtungsfeld n viewing area
Betrachtungsfernrohr n viewing telescope, observatory (observation) telescope
Betrachtungsfilter n viewing (panchromatic vision) filter, PV filter
Betrachtungsgeometrie f viewing geometry, geometry of viewing
Betrachtungsgerät n viewing device (apparatus), viewer
Betrachtungshilfe f viewing aid
Betrachtungskasten m film viewing box; X-ray viewing box
Betrachtungskegel m viewing (vision) cone
Betrachtungskreis m circle of vision
Betrachtungslicht n viewing illuminant
Betrachtungsmedium n viewing medium
Betrachtungsmikroskop n observation microscope
Betrachtungsmodus m viewing mode
Betrachtungsparallaxe f viewing (observation) parallax
Betrachtungsparameter m viewing parameter
Betrachtungsposition f viewing (observation) position, viewing point
Betrachtungsrichtung f view[ing] direction, direction of view[ing], look direction
Betrachtungsschirm m viewing screen; [image intensifier] output phosphor, output [fluorescent] screen, output phosphor screen *(radiography)*
Betrachtungssituation f viewing situation

Betrachtungstechnik 40

Betrachtungstechnik *f* 1. viewing technique; 2. viewing equipment
Betrachtungstransformation *f* rendering (viewing) pipeline
Betrachtungsumgebung *f* viewing environment
Betrachtungsvorgang *m* viewing process
Betrachtungswinkel *m* view[ing] angle, angle of view (field); observation angle
Betrachtungszeit[dauer] *f* viewing time
Betrieb *m*/**fotovoltaischer** photovoltaic (no bias) mode *(photodetector)*
Betriebsart *f* mode [of operation]
Betriebsarten-Einstellrad *n* command dial
Betriebsartenschalter *m* mode selector
Betriebsartenwahl *m* function selection
Betriebsmessband *n* alignment tape *(video)*
Betriebsmode *f* mode [of operation] *(e.g. of a laser)*
Betriebsstatus *m* operational state
Betriebssystem *n* operating system, OS
beugen to bend, to diffract
Beugung *f* diffraction, bending
~/**akustooptische** acousto-optic diffraction
~ **am Doppelspalt** diffraction by a double slit
~/**Braggsche** Bragg diffraction
~/**Fraunhofersche** Fraunhofer diffraction
~/**Fresnelsche** Fresnel (near-field) diffraction
~/**konische** conical diffraction
~/**skalare** scalar diffraction
Beugungsamplitude *f* diffraction amplitude
Beugungsauflösung *f* diffraction resolution
beugungsbegrenzt diffraction-limited, aperture-limited *(lens)*
Beugungsbegrenzung *f* diffraction limitation
Beugungsberechnung *f* diffraction calculation
Beugungsbild *n* diffraction image; diffraction pattern (figure)
~/**Airysches** Airy pattern
~/**Fraunhofersches** Fraunhofer diffraction pattern
~/**Fresnelsches** Fresnel diffraction pattern
Beugungsdiagramm *n* diffraction diagram
Beugungsebene *f* diffraction plane
Beugungseffekt *m* diffraction effect
Beugungseffektivität *f* diffraction efficiency
Beugungserscheinung *f* diffraction phenomenon
Beugungsfächer *m* diffraction fan
Beugungsfehler *m* diffraction artifact
Beugungsfigur *f s.* Beugungsbild
Beugungsfleck *m* diffraction spot
Beugungsformel *f*/**Kirchhoffsche** Kirchhoff['s] formula
Beugungsgeometrie *f* diffraction geometry
Beugungsgitter *n* diffraction grating (grid)
Beugungsgrenze *f* diffraction limit

Beugungsintegral *n* diffractive integral
Beugungsintensität *f* diffraction intensity
Beugungsinterferenz *f* diffraction interference
Beugungskante *f* diffracting edge
Beugungskontrast *m* diffraction (orientation) contrast *(electron microscopy)*
Beugungskontrastbild *n* diffraction-contrast image
Beugungslaufzeittechnik *f* time-of-flight diffraction method
Beugungsmagnet *m* bending magnet
Beugungsmaximum *n* diffraction maximum
~/**zentrales** *s.* Airy-Scheibchen
Beugungsmikroskop *n* diffraction microscope
Beugungsmodus *m* diffraction mode
Beugungsmuster *n* diffraction pattern (figure)
Beugungsoptik *f* 1. diffractive optics; 2. diffraction optic[s] *(optical system)*
beugungsoptisch diffractive-optical, diffraction-optical
Beugungsordnung *f* diffraction order, order of diffraction
~/**erste** first order of diffraction
~/**minus erste** minus first order of diffraction
~/**nullte** zeroth order of diffraction
~/**plus erste** plus first order of diffraction
Beugungsring *m* 1. diffraction ring; 2. *s.* Newton-Ringe
Beugungssaum *m* diffraction fringe
Beugungsscheibchen *n*, **Beugungsscheibe** *f* diffraction disk, Airy disk *(refractive optics)*
Beugungsspektrum *n* diffraction spectrum
Beugungsstrahl *m* diffracted beam
Beugungsstreifen *m* diffraction fringe
Beugungstheorie *f* diffraction theory
Beugungsunschärfe *f* diffraction blur
Beugungsvektor *m* diffraction vector
Beugungswinkel *m* diffraction angle, angle of diffraction
Beugungswirkung *f* diffraction effect
Beugungswirkungsgrad *m* diffraction efficiency
bewegen to move *(e.g. geometric elements)*
Bewegtbild *n* moving picture (image), motion image (picture)
Bewegtbildcodierer *m* moving-image encoder, video encoder
Bewegtbildcodierung *f* motion-picture coding, moving-image coding, video coding
Bewegtbilddarstellung *f* motion-picture display, video display
Bewegtbildfolge *f* moving[-image] sequence; motion video sequence

Bewegtbildkommunikation *f* moving-image communication; moving-picture telecommunication
Bewegtbildkompression *f* motion image compression, moving-image compression
Bewegtbildsequenz *f* moving[-image] sequence; motion video sequence
Bewegtbildspeicherung *f*/**digitale** moving-image digital storage
Bewegtbildübermittlung *f*, **Bewegtbildübertragung** *f* moving-image transmission; videophone transmission
Bewegtbildverarbeitung *f* dynamic image processing
Bewegtbildvideo *n* [full-]motion video, FMV, movie video
Bewegtzielanzeige *f* moving-target indication *(radar)*
Bewegtzielanzeiger *m* moving-target indicator, MIT *(radar)*
Bewegtzieldetektion *f* moving-target detection
Bewegtzieldetektor *m* moving-target detector
Bewegtzielerkennung *f* detection of moving-targets
Bewegung *f* motion, movement
~/**abgetastete** *s.* ~/scheinbare
~/**affine** affine motion
~/**bilineare** bilinear motion
~/**Brownsche** Brownian motion *(of small particles)*
~/**gebrochene Brownsche** fractional Brownian motion
~/**isotrope** isotropic motion
~/**rotatorische** rotational (rotary) motion, rotation
~/**scheinbare** [stroboscopic] apparent motion, stroboscopic motion; phi motion (phenomenon)
~/**translatorische** translational motion
~/**zielgerichtete** goal-directed motion *(computer animation)*
~/**zusammenhängende** coherent motion
bewegungsadaptiv motion-adaptive
Bewegungsanalyse *f* motion (kinematic) analysis
~/**fotografische** photographic motion analysis
~/**globale** global motion analysis
~/**objektorientierte** object-based motion analysis
~/**stroboskopische** stroboscopic motion analysis
Bewegungsanalysetechnik *f* motion analysis technique
Bewegungsanpassung *f* movement adaptation
Bewegungsartefakt *n* motion artifact
Bewegungsauflösung *f* motion resolution
Bewegungsaufnahme *f* motion record
Bewegungsbeschreibung *f*/**interpolative** control grid interpolation, CGI, quadrangle-based motion compensation, QBMC
Bewegungscodierung *f* motion coding
Bewegungsdarstellung *f* motion representation (portrayal) *(s.a.* Bewegungswiedergabe*)*
~/**bereichsbasierte** region-based motion representation; object-based motion representation
~/**blockbasierte** block-based motion representation
~/**globale** global motion representation
~/**zeitdiskrete** time-sampled motion portrayal
Bewegungsdetektion *f* motion detection
Bewegungsdetektionsfilter *n* motion-detection filter
Bewegungsdetektor *m* motion (movement) detector
Bewegungserfassung *f* motion capturing (capture), performance capture *(special-effects cinematography)*
Bewegungserkennung *f* motion detection
Bewegungsfeld *n* motion (velocity) field
Bewegungsfeldsegmentierung *f*/**prädiktive** predictive motion field segmentation
Bewegungsfotografie *f* cinephotography
Bewegungsgeschwindigkeit *f* speed of motion
Bewegungsgradient *m* motion gradient
Bewegungsillusion *f s.* Bewegungstäuschung
Bewegungsinformation *f* motion information
Bewegungsinterpolation *f* motion interpolation
Bewegungskompensation *f* motion compensation
~/**blockbasierte** block-based motion compensation
~/**globale** global motion compensation
~/**pixelbasierte** pixel-based motion compensation
~/**translatorische** translational motion compensation
Bewegungskompensationsfilter *n* motion compensation filter
Bewegungskomponente *f* motion component
Bewegungskonstanz *f* motion (velocity) constancy *(perceptual phenomenon)*
Bewegungsmelder *m* motion (movement) detector
Bewegungsmodell *n* motion model *(motion detection)*
~/**parametrisches** parametric motion model
Bewegungsmodus *m* M mode, M scan *(ultrasound imaging)*
Bewegungsnacheffekt *m* movement (motion) aftereffect *(vision)*
Bewegungsparallaxe *f* motion parallax

Bewegungsparameter *m* motion parameter
Bewegungsperspektive *f* motion perspective
Bewegungspfad *m* motion path
Bewegungsprädiktion *f* motion prediction
Bewegungsrichtung *f* motion direction, direction of motion (movement)
Bewegungsruckeln *n* [motion] judder, jutter, jerkiness [of motion] *(video)*
Bewegungsschätzalgorithmus *m* motion estimation algorithm
Bewegungsschätzer *m* motion estimator
Bewegungsschätzgenauigkeit *f* motion estimation accuracy
Bewegungsschätzung *f* motion estimation
~/**Bayessche** Bayesian motion estimation
~/**bereichsbasierte** region-based motion estimation
~/**blockbasierte** block[-based] motion estimation
~/**globale** global motion estimation
~/**iterative** iterative motion estimation
~/**merkmalsbasierte** feature-based motion estimation
~/**objektorientierte** object-oriented motion estimation
~/**pixelbasierte** pixel-based motion estimation
~/**pixelrekursive** pel-recursive motion estimation
Bewegungsschätzwert *m* motion estimate, estimated motion parameter
Bewegungssegmentierung *f* motion (optical flow) segmentation
~ *f* motion segmentation
Bewegungssehen *n* perception of visual motion
Bewegungssensor *m* motion sensor *(s.a.* Bewegungsmelder*)*
Bewegungssignal *n* motion signal
Bewegungssimulation *f* motion simulation
Bewegungsstudie *f* motion study
Bewegungstäuschung *f* cinematic illusion, illusion of movement (motion), illusory movement
~/**stroboskopische** stroboscopic effect
Bewegungstrajektorie *f* motion trajectory
bewegungsunscharf motion-blurred
Bewegungsunschärfe *f* motion blur (smear), movement blur, movement (kinetic) unsharpness, motion[al] unsharpness
Bewegungsvektor *m* motion vector
Bewegungsvektorcodierer *m* motion vector coder
Bewegungsvektorcodierung *f* motion vector coding
Bewegungsvektorfeld *n* motion vector field, MVF *(optical flow)*
Bewegungsvektorhistogramm *n* motion vector histogram, MV histogram
Bewegungsvektorschätzung *f* motion vector estimation

Bewegungsverfolgung *f* motion tracking
~/**modellfreie** model-free motion tracking
Bewegungswahrnehmung *f* motion perception, perception of motion
~/**visuelle** visual motion perception
Bewegungswiedergabe *f* motion rendition (reproduction), motion rendering
Beweisfoto *n* evidence photograph
Beweismittelfotografie *f* [civil] evidence photography
Bezahlfernsehen *n* pay-TV, pay television *(s.a.* Abonnementsfernsehen*)*
Bezahlfernsehsender *m* pay channel
Bezahlung *f* **pro Programmbeitrag** pay-per-view, PPV
~ **pro Programmkanal** pay-per-channel, PPC
~ **pro Programmpaket** pay-per-package, PPP
Bezeichner *m* identifier; label
Bézier-Approximation *f* Bézier approximation
Bézier-Fläche *f* Bézier surface
~/**bikubische** Bézier bicubic patch
Bézier-Flächensegment *n* Bézier patch
Bézier-Funktion *f s.* Bézier-Kurve
Bézier-Hyperfläche *f* Bézier hyperpatch
Bézier-Kurve *f* Bézier curve (spline)
Bézier-Kurvensegment *n* Bézier segment
Bézier-Polynom *n s.* Bézier-Kurve
Bézier-Segment *n* Bézier segment
Bézier-Vektor *m* Bézier geometry vector
Bezold-Abney-Effekt *m* Abney effect *(color metrics)*
Bezold-Brücke-Effekt *m* Bezold-Brücke phenomenon *(color perception)*
Bezugs... *s.a.* Referenz...
Bezugsband *n* calibration (alignment) tape; reference tape (video)
Bezugsbild *n* reference image (picture); reference frame, frame of reference, R-frame; key frame *(computer graphics)*
Bezugsebene *f* reference plane
Bezugsfarbe *f* 1. reference color; 2. *s.* Primärvalenz
Bezugsfläche *f* reference area
Bezugsfrequenz *f* reference frequency
Bezugskante *f* reference edge
Bezugskoordinatensystem *n* reference coordinate system
Bezugskugel *f* reference sphere *(wave optics)*
Bezugslichtart *f* reference illuminant
Bezugsobjekt *n* reference object
Bezugspegel *m* alignment level
Bezugsphase *f* reference phase
Bezugspixel *n* reference pixel
Bezugspunkt *m* reference point
Bezugsrahmen *m* frame of reference
Bezugsrichtung *f* reference orientation (direction)
Bezugssehweite *f* normal viewing distance
Bezugssignal *n* reference signal
Bezugsspur *f* reference track

Bezugsstrahl *m* reference ray (beam); holographic reference beam
Bezugssystem *n* reference system
~/**Frenetsches** Frenet frame *(geometric modeling)*
Bezugsweiß *n* reference white [color]
Bezugswellenfront *f* reference wave front *(e.g. of an interferometer)*
Bias *m* bias
bichrom bichrome, bicolor[ed], two-color[ed]; dichromatic, dichroi[ti]c
Bichromat *n s.* Dichromat
bidirektional bidirectional; two-way, duplex
Biegekontur *f* equi-inclination contour, bent contour *(electron microscopy)*
Bifokalbrille *f* bifocal [spectacles]
Bifokalglas *n*, **Bifokallinse** *f* bifocal [eyeglass] lens; split-field lens
bikonkav biconcave, concavo-concave, double-concave *(lens)*
Bikonkavität *f* biconcavity
Bikonkavlinse *f* biconcave (double-concave) lens
bikonvex biconvex, convexo-convex, double-convex *(lens)*
Bikonvexität *f* biconvexity
Bikonvexlinse *f* biconvex (double-convex) lens
bikubisch bicubic
Bild *n* 1. [visual] image, picture; icon *(s.a. under Abbildung)*; 2. frame [of picture] *(film strip, imaging screen)*
~/**aberrationsfreies** aberration-free image
~/**abfallendes** *s.* ~/angeschnittenes
~/**abgetastetes** scanned image
~/**achs[en]fernes** off-axis image
~/**achs[en]nahes** paraxial image
~/**aktuelles** current frame *(motion estimation)*
~/**akustisches** acoustic (sonic) image
~/**analoges** analog (continuous) image
~/**anamorph[otisch]es** anamorphic [image], squeezed (distorted) image; anamorphic [frame] *(cinema)*
~/**angeschnittenes** crossover, gutter jump (bleed), bridge *(layout, typography)*
~/**animiertes** animated image
~/**aperiodisches** aperiodic image
~/**auflösungsbegrenztes** limited-resolution image
~/**aufrechtes** upright (erect) image
~/**ausentwickeltes** well-developed image
~/**auswertbares** interpretable image
~/**beständiges** permanent image (picture)
~/**bewegtes** motion (moving) picture
~/**bidirektional [prädiktiv] codiertes** bidirectional[ly predictive] coded picture, B picture, bidirectional frame, B frame *(video encoding)*
~/**binäres** binary image (picture), bilevel (two-level) image, bistable image
~/**binarisiertes** binarized image
~/**bipolares** bipolar image
~/**bitebenencodiertes** bit-plane coded image
~/**bitonales** bitonal (bilevel) image
~/**bleibendes** permanent image (picture)
~/**blockcodiertes** block-[en]coded image
~/**codiertes** [en]coded image
~/**computeranimiertes** computer-animated image
~/**computererzeugtes (computergeneriertes)** computer-generated (computer-produced) image, synthetic (computer-synthesized) picture, computer-graphic[s] image, CG image; computer[ized] image
~/**computersimuliertes** computer-simulated image
~/**dauerhaftes** permanent image (picture)
~/**detailliertes** detailed image (picture)
~/**diagnostisches** diagnostic image
~/**dichtegewichtetes** proton-density-weighted image *(magnetic resonance imaging)*
~/**digitales** digital image (picture); [image] scene, picture scene *(s.a.* Bitmap-Bild*)*
~/**digitalisiertes** digitized image; image matrix
~/**diskretes** discrete image *(s.a.* ~/digitales*)*
~/**dreidimensionales** three-dimensional image, 3-D [image]
~/**durchscheinendes** diaphanous image
~/**durchscheinendes fotografisches** diapositive; [positive] transparency
~/**dynamisches** dynamic image
~/**ebenes** planar image
~/**eidetisches** eidetic image
~/**eindimensionales** one-dimensional image
~/**einfarbiges** monochrome [image], monochromatic (monotone) image *(s.a.* Schwarzweißbild*)*
~/**einseitig umgekehrtes** *s.* ~/seitenverkehrtes
~/**elektrisches** electric image
~/**elektromagnetisches** electromagnetic image
~/**elektronisches** electronic image
~/**elektrostatisches** electrostatic image
~/**endgültiges** final image (picture)
~/**endoskopisches** endoscopic image
~/**entzifferbares** decipherable image
~/**farbcodiertes** color-coded image
~/**farbfotografisches** color photographic image
~/**farbgetreues** *s.* ~/farbrichtiges
~/**farbiges** colored image
~/**farbrichtiges** color-corrected image
~/**feinkörniges** fine-grain[ed] image
~/**filmisches** [motion-]picture image, movie picture
~/**flächiges** planar image (picture)
~/**flaues** flat (low-contrast) image

Bild 44

~/**flimmerfreies** flickerless (flicker-free) image
~/**flüchtiges** soft copy
~/**fotoähnliches** near-photographic quality image
~/**fotografisches** photographic image
~/**fotogrammetrisches** photogrammetric image
~/**fotorealistisches** photorealistic image
~/**fouriertransformiertes** Fourier-transform image
~/**fraktales** fractal image (pattern); fractal figure (construct)
~/**Gaußsches** Gaussian image
~/**gedrucktes** printed image
~/**gefälschtes** faked picture
~/**gefiltertes** filtered image
~/**geometrisches** geometric image
~/**gepixeltes** pixelated image
~/**gerastertes** 1. halftone [screened image], [halftone] dot image, screened image *(reprography)*; 2. *s.* Bitmap-Bild
~/**gescanntes** scanned image
~/**gespeichertes** stored image
~/**gespiegeltes** mirror[ed] image, reflex
~/**gestochen scharfes** high-acutance image, pin-sharp image, razor-sharp picture
~/**gleichmäßig ausgeleuchtetes** evenly lit picture
~/**grafisches** graphic[al] image; graph, plot
~/**grobkörniges** high-granularity image
~/**hochaufgelöstes** highly resolved image, high-resolution image
~/**hochauflösendes** high-resolution image
~/**höhenrichtiges** uninverted top-to-bottom image
~/**höhenverkehrtes** top-to-bottom reversed image
~/**holografisches** holograph[ic image], hologram
~/**homophotisches** homophotic image
~/**hyperspektrales** hyperspectral image
~/**ideales** ideal image *(optics)*
~/**ikonisches** iconic image (picture)
~/**infrarotes** infrared image (picture)
~/**intermediär gewichtetes** intermediate-weighted image *(magnetic resonance imaging)*
~/**intracodiertes** intracoded (independent) frame, intraframe [coded] picture, I-frame, I-picture *(video coding)*
~/**intrinsisches** intrinsic image
~/**kantenverstärktes** edge-enhanced image
~/**kinematografisches** cinematographic image
~/**kombiniertes** combined image *(s.a. Kombinationsbild)*
~/**komprimiertes** compressed image
~/**konfokalmikroskopisches** confocal microscope image
~/**konjugiertes** conjugate image

~/**konoskopisches** conoscopic image
~/**kontinuierliches** continuous image
~/**kontrastarmes** flat (low-contrast) image
~/**kontrastreiches** contrasty (high-contrast) image
~/**konturcodiertes** contour-coded image
~/**kopfstehendes** inverted (upside down) image
~/**körniges** grainy (granular) image
~/**kornloses** grainfree image
~/**laplacegefiltertes** Laplacian[-filtered] image
~/**latentes** latent [photographic] image, invisible image
~/**lebensgroßes** life-sized image
~/**lichtschwaches** dim (faint) image; low-key picture
~/**linksäugiges** left-eye image
~/**logisches** logical image
~/**lotrechtes** upright (erect) image
~/**makroskopisches** macroscopic image
~/**maßstabgerechtes (maßstabsgleiches)** same-size image
~/**mehrdimensionales** multidimensional image, scene *(e.g. in medical imaging)*
~/**mehrkanaliges** *s.* ~/multispektrales
~/**mikroskopisches** microscopic (microscope) image, microscope picture, micrograph
~/**monochromes** monochrome [image], monochromatic (monotone) image *(s.a. Schwarzweißbild)*
~/**multispektrales** multispectral (multichannel) image, multiband image; multispectral photograph
~/**multivariates** multivariate image
~/**natürliches** natural image (picture), non-computer-generated image, real-world (real-life) image, surface (solid) image
~/**nichtikonisches** noniconic image
~/**nichtpermanentes** soft copy
~/**nichtstatisches** nonstationary image
~/**niedrigaufgelöstes** low-resolution image; FPO (for position only) image *(prepress)*
~/**nuklearmedizinisches** nuclear-medicine image
~/**optisches** optical image, [visible-]light image
~/**orthoskopisches** orthoscopic image
~/**ortsdiskretes** discrete-space image
~/**ortskontinuierliches** continuous-space image
~/**ortszeitliches** spatiotemporal image
~/**parallel polarisiertes** parallel-polarized image *(radar)*
~/**parametrisches** parametric image
~/**paraxiales** paraxial image
~/**periodisches** periodic image
~/**perspektivisches** perspective image (picture)
~/**physikalisches** physical image

~/**pixelorientiertes** bit-mapped image, bit-map
~/**polarisiertes** polarized image
~/**prädiktiv codiertes**, ~/**prädiziertes** predicted frame (image), P frame, predictive[-coded] picture, P picture
~/**primäres** primary (first) image *(optics)*
~/**projiziertes** projected image
~/**protonengewichtetes** proton-density-weighted image *(magnetic resonance imaging)*
~/**pseudoskopisches** pseudoscopic image *(holography)*
~/**quantisiertes** quantized image
~/**radiologisches** radiological image
~/**randabfallendes** *s.* ~/angeschnittenes
~/**rastersondenmikroskopisches** scanning probe microscopy image
~/**räumliches** spatial (three-dimensional) image,
~/**raumzeitliches** spatio-temporal image
~/**rauscharmes** low-noise image
~/**rauschfreies** noiseless (noise-free) image
~/**reales** *s.* 1. ~/natürliches; 2. ~/reelles
~/**realistisches** realistic image
~/**rechtsäugiges** right-eye image
~/**redundantes** redundant image
~/**reelles** real image *(optics)*
~/**reflektiertes** reflected (reflection) image, reflection
~/**rekonstruiertes** reconstructed image
~/**retinales** retinal image
~/**röntgenologisches** roentgenological image
~/**rückprojiziertes** back-projected image
~/**scharfes** sharp image (picture), crisp (blur-free) image
~/**scheinbares** virtual image
~/**segmentiertes** segmented image
~/**seitenkorrektes (seitenrichtiges)** laterally correct[ed] image, right-reading image, correct-reading image
~/**seitenverkehrtes** laterally reversed image, reverted (wrong-reading) image
~/**sekundäres** secondary image
~/**selbstähnliches** self-similar image
~/**sichtbares** visible image (picture)
~/**silberfotografisches** silver photographic image
~/**skalares** scalar image
~/**sonografisches** ultrasound (ultrasonic) image, sonogram
~/**spektrales** spectral (spectrum) image
~/**spektroskopisches** spectroscopic image
~/**spiegelverkehrtes** reversed image
~/**statisches** static (stationary) image
~/**stehendes** still image (picture)
~/**stereoskopisches** stereo[scopic] image, stereo[scopic] picture, stereograph, stereogram
~/**stigmatisches** stigmatic image
~/**symbolisches** symbolic picture (image)
~/**synthetisches** *s.* ~/computererzeugtes

~/**technisches** technical image
~/**tiefpassgefiltertes** low-pass filtered image
~/**topografisches** topographic image, topographical map
~/**transformiertes** transformed image
~/**unbewegtes** still image (picture), nonmoving image
~/**unkomprimiertes** noncompressed image, uncompressed picture
~/**unscharfes** blurred (unsharp) image, fuzzy image; indistinct (out-of-focus) image
~/**unsichtbares** invisible (nonvisible) image
~/**unverarbeitetes** as-acquired image
~/**unverrauschtes** noise-free image, clean image
~/**unverzeichnetes** orthoscopic image (picture)
~/**unverzerrtes** undistorted (distortion-free) image, undistorted picture
~/**vektorielles** vector image
~/**verblasstes** faded image
~/**verborgenes** *s.* ~/latentes
~/**verdecktes** occluded image
~/**vergilbtes** yellowed image
~/**vergrößertes** enlarged (magnified) image
~/**verkleinertes** diminished (minified) image, reduced image
~/**verrauschtes** noisy (noised) image, [noise-]corrupted image
~/**verschmiertes** smeared image
~/**verschneites** snowy picture
~/**verschwommenes** blurry (blurred) image
~/**verwackeltes** blurry (blurred) image
~/**verwaschenes** washed-out picture
~/**verwischtes** blurry (blurred) image
~/**verzeichnetes** aberrated image
~/**verzerrtes** distorted (squeezed) image, anamorphic [image] anamorphic [image]
~/**verzerrungsfreies** *s.* ~/unverzerrtes
~/**vielfarbiges** multicolored image
~/**virtuelles** virtual image
~/**visuelles** visual image
~/**vollständig umgekehrtes** *s.* ~/kopfstehendes
~/**volumetrisches** volume[tric] image, image volume
~/**vorangehendes** preceding (previous) frame, before image *(video coding)*
~/**vorverdünntes** pre-thinned image
~/**wahres** real (true) image
~/**wahrgenommenes** perceived image
~/**wärmefixierbares** heat-fixable image *(electrophotography)*
~/**xerografisches** xerographic image
~/**zeitsequentielles** time-sequential image
~/**zeitveränderliches** time-varying image
~/**zusammengesetztes** composite image

Bild

~/**zweidimensionales** two-dimensional image
Bild... s.a. Abbildung[s]..., Foto...
Bildabdeckung f image coverage; frame coverage
Bildabfrage f image query; image querying
Bildabgleich m image matching
Bildabgrenzung f image boundary
Bildablenkgenerator m vertical time-base generator
Bildablenkspule f frame coil
Bildablenkung f image deflection; frame (field) deflection
Bildabmessung f image dimension
Bildabschattung f image shading
Bildabschnitt m image section (portion)
Bildabstand m 1. image spacing; 2. s. Bildentfernung 1.
Bildabtaster m, **Bildabtastgerät** n [image] scanner
Bildabtastmuster n image sampling pattern
Bildabtastung f image scan, [image] scanning; image sampling (s.a. Abtastung)
~/**elektronische** electronic image scanning
Bildabtastzeit f frame scanning time
Bildabzug m photo[graphic] print, paper [positive] print, [positive] print
Bildachse f image axis
Bildaddition f image-frame addition
Bildadresse f image address
Bildagentur f [stock] picture agency; stock house (agency)
Bildähnlichkeit f image similarity
Bildakquisition f image (picture) acquisition, image gathering (capture), imaging (s.a. Bildaufnahme)
Bildakquisitionszeit f [image] acquisition time; scan time (magnetic resonance imaging)
Bildalgebra f image algebra
Bildamplitude f image amplitude
~/**vertikale** vertical image amplitude
Bildamplitudenbereich m image amplitude range
Bildamplitudenhistogramm n image amplitude histogram
Bildanalysator m image analyzer
Bildanalyse f image (picture) analysis (s.a. Bilderkennung)
~/**beispielsbasierte** example-based image analysis
~/**computergestützte (digitale)** computer-assisted image analysis
~/**fraktale** fractal image analysis
~/**medizinische** medical image analysis
~/**mehrdimensionale** multidimensional image analysis
~/**modellbasierte (modellgesteuerte)** model-based image analysis
~/**morphologische** morphological image analysis

~/**morphometrische** morphometric image analysis
~/**objektbezogene** object-related image analysis
~/**quantitative** quantitative image analysis
~/**spektrale** spectral image analysis
~/**statistische** statistical image analysis
~/**volumetrische** volumetric image analysis
~/**wissensbasierte** knowledge-based image analysis
~/**wissenschaftliche** scientific image analysis
~/**wissensgestützte** s. ~/wissensbasierte
Bildanalysealgorithmus m image analysis algorithm
Bildanalysearbeitsplatz m image analysis workstation
Bildanalysecomputer m image analysis computer
Bildanalysefunktion f image analysis function
Bildanalyseprogramm n image analysis program
Bildanalysesystem n image-analysis system
Bildanalyseverfahren n analytical imaging technique
Bildanalysewerkzeug n image-analysis tool
Bildanalytiker m image analyst
bildanalytisch image-analytical
Bildänderungsprinzip n image variation principle
Bildanimation f image animation
Bildanmutung f s. Bildeindruck
Bildannotation f image annotation
Bildanordnung f image arrangement (array)
Bildanwahl f crosspoint (video editing)
Bildanzeige f 1. image display; 2. image display device
Bildarbeitsplatz m image (imaging computer) workstation, graphics [computer] workstation
~/**radiologischer** radiological imaging workstation
Bildarchiv n image (pictorial) archive
Bildarchivierung f image (picture) archiving, archival image storage
Bildarchivierungs- und kommunikationssystem n picture archiving and communication[s] system, PACS (medical imaging)
Bildarchivierungssystem n photo archiving system
Bildareal n image area
Bildarithmetik f image arithmetics
bildarithmetisch image arithmetic
Bildart f image (picture) type, kind of image
Bildartefakt n image artifact (s.a. Bildfehler)
Bildattribut n image attribute

Bildaufbau *m* 1. image construction; picture composition; image structure; 2. image completion *(e.g. in instant photography)*; display build-up *(video)*
bildaufbauend image-forming
Bildaufbereiter *m* image editor *(software)*
Bildaufbereitung *f* image editing; print finishing
Bildauffrischfrequenz *f s.* Bildwiederholfrequenz
Bildaufklärung *f* photoreconnaissance
Bildauflösung *f* image resolution (definition), picture resolution (definition); frame resolution *(s.a. under* Auflösung*)*
Bildaufmachung *f* picture preparation
Bildaufnahme *f* 1. picture-taking [process], picture making, image taking (capture) *(s.a.* Bilderfassung*)*; image (picture) recording, imaging; 2. picture record; photographic record, photorecord
~/**digitale** digital imaging
~/**dreidimensionale** 3-D [image] acquisition *(magnetic resonance imaging)*
~/**elektronische** electronic imaging
Bildaufnahmechip *m* imaging chip
Bildaufnahmefrequenz *f* image-acquisition rate, framing (frame) rate, picture-capture rate
Bildaufnahmegerät *n* image recording (capture) device, image acquisition device, imaging (image-capturing) device
Bildaufnahmekamera *f s.* Aufnahmekamera
Bildaufnahmekarte *f* frame grabber card, [video] frame grabber, digitizing board *(high-speed memory device)*
Bildaufnahmematerial *n* image-capture material, image-recording material
Bildaufnahmemedium *n* image-recording medium, image capture medium
Bildaufnahmeradar *n* imaging radar
Bildaufnahmeröhre *f* camera picture tube, [camera] pickup tube, camera [video] tube; television camera tube
Bildaufnahmesensor *m* image (picture) sensor, imaging sensor (detector), imager *(s.a. under* Bildsensor*)*
Bildaufnahmesituation *f* picture-making situation
Bildaufnahmesystem *n* image recording (capture) system
Bildaufnahmetechnik *f* 1. picture-taking technique; 2. image acquisition hardware
Bildaufnahmezeit *f* [image] acquisition time; scan time *(magnetic resonance imaging)*
Bildaufnehmer *m* 1. image receptor; 2. *s.* Bildaufnahmesensor
Bildaufrasterung *f* dithering, dither technique, halftoning *(electronic imaging; s.a.* Streurasterung*)*
Bildaufrichtung *f* erection of image

Bildaufruf *m* image retrieval
Bildaufteilung *f* partition
Bildaufzeichnung *f* 1. image (picture) recording; 2. picture record; photographic record, photorecord
~/**elektronische** electronic video recording
~/**holografische** holographic image recording
~/**magnetische** magnetic image (picture) recording
~/**optische** optical image recording
Bildaufzeichnungsgerät *n* image recorder, image-capturing device; photorecorder
Bildaufzeichnungssystem *n* image-recording system
Bildausfall *m* [image] dropout, picture breakup
Bildausgabe *f* image output
~/**permanente** hard-copy output
Bildausgabe-Array *n*/**LWL-gekoppeltes** fiber-linked array image formatter, FLAIR
Bildausgabeeinheit *f*, **Bildausgabegerät** *n* image output unit (device)
Bildauslesung *f* image readout [process]
Bildausleuchtung *f* image illumination (illuminance)
Bildausrichtung *f* image alignment; image orientation
Bildausschnitt *m* image sector, frame; window *(digital image processing)*
~/**interessierender** region of interest, ROI, area of interest, AOI
Bildausschnittvergrößerung *f* selective enlargement
Bildausschnittwahl *f* framing
Bildaussetzer *m* [image] dropout, picture breakup
Bildaustastlücke *f* field (vertical) blanking interval *(video)*
Bild-Austast-Synchron[isier]-Signal *n s.* BAS-Signal
Bildaustastung *f* field (frame) blanking, video blanking
Bildaustauschformat *n* interchange format
Bildauswertegerät *n* [image] restitution machine
Bildauswerter *m* image analyst; photographic interpreter, photointerpreter
Bildauswertung *f* image interpretation; image restitution; photointerpretation; image exploitation *(s.a. under* Bildinterpretation*)*
Bildauswertungsalgorithmus *m* image exploitation algorithm
Bildauthentifikation *f*, **Bildauthentifizierung** *f* image authentication
Bildband *n* 1. picture tape; filmstrip; 2. picture book, book of reproductions
Bildbandbreite *f* image bandwidth
Bildbandgerät *n* video tape machine (unit)
Bildbank *f* image bank

Bildbaum

Bildbaum *m*/**quartärer** quadtree
Bildbearbeiter *m* image (picture) editor
Bildbearbeitung *f* image (picture) editing, imaging *(s.a.* Bildverarbeitung*)*
~/**digitale** digital imaging
~/**elektronische** electronic imaging
Bildbearbeitungscomputer *m* image processing computer (PC)
Bildbearbeitungsdatei *f* electronic image file
Bildbearbeitungsmethode *f* imaging method
Bildbearbeitungsprogramm *n* image manipulation [software] program, picture-editing program; image-processing program
Bildbearbeitungssoftware *f* image-editing software, [computer] imaging software, image-manipulating software; photo-processing (photo-editing) software; image management software
Bildbearbeitungssystem *n* imaging (image-processing) system
Bildbeeinträchtigung *f* image (picture) impairment
Bildbegrenzung *f* image limitation; image boundary
Bildbehandlung *f* image handling
Bildbeispiel *n* pictorial example, example image
Bildbeleuchtung *f* image illumination
Bildbeleuchtungsstärke *f* image illuminance
Bildbelichtung *f* image exposure
Bildbeobachtung *f* image observation
Bildberechnung *f* image arithmetic (computation); rendering *(computer-graphic simulation process)*
Bildbereich *m* 1. image area (region); image domain; 2. *s.* Darstellungsbereich
~/**aktiver** active picture portion *(television screen)*
~/**interessierender** region of interest, ROI
Bildbericht *m* photoreport, pictorial record
Bildberichterstatter *m s.* Fotoreporter
Bildbeschleunigung *f* upspeed
Bildbeschneidung *f*, **Bildbeschnitt** *m* image clipping, picture cropping (trimming)
Bildbeschreibung *f* image description
~/**abstrakte** *s.* ~/symbolische
~/**hierarchische** hierarchic[al] image description
~/**ikonische (konkrete)** iconic image description
~/**rationale** relational image description
~/**strukturelle** structural image description
~/**symbolische** symbolic image description
Bildbeschreibungssprache *f* image description language
Bildbeschriftung *f* caption, legend, cutline
Bildbestand *m* image assets

Bildbeständigkeit *f* image permanence (longevity); print permanence
Bildbestandteil *m* image component
Bildbetrachter *m* 1. picture viewer; 2. mute head *(cinematography)*
Bildbetrachtung *f* image (picture) viewing
Bildbeurteilung *f* image judgment
Bildbewegung *f* image move[ment], image motion
Bildbewegungsausgleich *m* image motion compensation, IMC
Bildbewegungsgenauigkeit *f* image movement accuracy
Bildbewegungsunschärfe *f* image motion blur
Bildbewertung *f* image evaluation
Bildbibliothek *f* image library *(s.a.* Bilddatenbank*)*
Bildbinarisierung *f* image binarization
Bildblock *m* image (picture) block
Bildbreite *f* image (picture) width, image length; frame width
Bildbrennpunkt *m* second (rear) focal point
Bildbrennweite *f* back focal length
Bildbrillanz *f* image (picture) brilliance
Bildbühne *f* [film] gate; camera gate
Bild-CD *f* picture CD
Bildcharakterisierung *f* image characterization
Bildchip *m* imaging chip
Bildcode *m* image [processing] code
Bildcodieralgorithmus *m* image coding algorithm
~/**pixelbasierter (pixelweiser)** pixel-by-pixel image coding algorithm
Bildcodierer *m* image coder
Bildcodierung *f* 1. image (picture) coding; image encoding (remapping) *(s.a. under* Codierung*)*; 2. *s.* Bildkompression
~/**fraktale** fractal image coding
~/**modellbasierte** model-based image coding, analysis-synthesis [image] coding
~/**objektbasierte** object-based image coding
~/**prädiktive** predictive image coding
~/**wahrnehmungsbasierte** perception-based image coding
~/**waveletbasierte** wavelet-based image coding
Bildcodierungsschema *n* image coding scheme
Bildcodierungsstandard *m* image coding standard
Bildcodierungssystem *n* image coding system
Bildcodierungsverfahren *n* image coding technique
Bilddarbietung *f* image (picture) presentation
Bilddarstellung *f* image (pictorial) representation; image (picture) presentation; image display (portrayal); depiction

Bilddatei f [graphics] image file, picture file
Bilddateielement n metafile element
Bilddateiformat n image [file] format, imaging (graphic) file format
Bilddateifunktion f image file function
Bilddateigenerator m metafile generator
Bilddateiinterpreter m metafile interpreter
Bilddateiverzeichnis n image file directory
Bilddaten pl image data, picture (pictorial) data, imagery *(s.a. under Daten)*
~/**binäre** binary image data
~/**hyperspektrale** hyperspectral [image] data
~/**medienneutrale** device-independent image data
~/**mehrdimensionale (multidimensionale)** multidimensional image data
~/**multimodale** multimodal image data
~/**multiparametrische** multiparametric image data
~/**multispektrale** multispectral image data
~/**multitemporale** multitemporal image data
Bilddatenanalyse f image data analysis
Bilddatenbank f image database [system], picture database, pictorial (image retrieval) database
Bilddatenbankentwickler m image database developer
Bilddatenbankprogramm n image database [management] routine
Bilddatenbankschnittstelle f image database interface
Bilddatenbanksystem n image database system, pictorial information system
Bilddatenbankverwaltung f image database management
Bilddatenblock m block of image data
Bilddatenbus m image [data] bus
Bilddatendarstellung f image data representation
Bilddatendatei f s. Bilddatei
Bilddatenerfasssung f image-data acquisition
Bilddatenfilterung f imaging data mining
Bilddatenformat n image-data format
Bilddatenkompression f image [data] compression *(s.a. under Bildkompression, Kompression)*
Bilddatenmatrix f s. Bildmatrix
Bilddatenrekonstruktion f s. Bildrekonstruktion
Bilddatensatz m image data set, set of image data
Bilddatenschnittstelle f image data interface, IDI
Bilddatenspeicher m image data store
Bilddatenspeicherung f picture-data storage
Bilddatenstrom m video image data stream, video [bit] stream, stream of video data
Bilddatenstruktur f image data structure

Bilddatentransfer m, **Bilddatenübertragung** f image data transfer (transmission)
Bilddatenverarbeitung f image data processing
Bilddatenverwaltung f image asset management
Bilddatenvorverarbeitung f image data preprocessing
Bilddauer f frame period (duration), frame time
Bilddecodierung f image decoding
Bilddefekt m s. Bildfehler
Bilddefinition f [image] definition, fineness of detail
Bilddeformation f image deformation
Bilddegradation f image (picture) degradation
Bilddehnung f image stretching
Bilddekomposition f image decomposition (dissection)
Bilddekompression f, **Bilddekomprimierung** f image decompression
Bilddemodulation f image demodulation
Bilddeskriptor m image descriptor
Bilddetail n image detail, picture (pictorial) detail
~/**feinstrukturiertes** fine image detail
Bilddeutung f image interpretation
Bilddiagnose f medical-image diagnosis
Bilddiagnostik f imaging [medical] diagnostics
bilddiagnostisch medical-image diagnostic
Bilddiagonale f image diagonal
Bilddichte f image density
Bilddienst m picture service
Bilddienstleistung f/**digitale** digital image service
Bilddifferenz f image difference
Bilddifferenzierung f image differentiation (differencing)
Bilddigitalisierer m image digitizer; digitizing board, [video] frame grabber, frame grabber card *(high-speed memory device)*
Bilddigitalisierung f image digitization (digitizing)
Bilddimensionalität f image dimensionality
Bilddiskretisierung f s. Bildabtastung
Bilddissektorröhre f image dissector tube
Bilddokument n image document
Bilddokumentation f image (pictured) documentation
Bilddokumentationssystem n hard copy camera
Bilddokumentdatei f s. Bilddatei
Bilddrehung f image (picture) rotation; frame rotation
Bilddurchlauf m frame roll
Bildebene f image (picture) plane; focal plane; film plane; layer *(special-effects cinematography)*

Bildebene

~/**Gaußsche** Gaussian (paraxial) image plane, Gauss plane, [Gaussian] cardinal plane
~/**geometrische** geometric image plane
~/**paraxiale** paraxial image plane
~/**sagittale** sagittal image plane
~/**tangentiale** tangential image plane
Bildebenenmarkierung *f* film plane indicator
Bildebnung *f s.* Bildfeldebnung
Bildecke *f* picture corner
Bildeditor *m* image editor *(program)*
Bildeffekt *m* picture (pictorial) effect, special [picture] effect; screen [change] effect *(video)*
~/**digitaler** digital [picture] effect
Bildeffektgerät *n*/**digitales** digital video effects device, video effects machine
Bildeigenschaft *f* image property (attribute)
Bildeinblendung *f* insert
Bildeindruck *m* image impression (appearance), impact
Bildeingabe *f* image input
Bildeingabegerät *n* image-input device
Bildeinordnung *f* image classification
Bildeinstellen *n* framing
Bildeinstellung *f* 1. framing; 2. [single] shot *(cinema, video)*
Bildeinzelheit *f* image (picture) detail
Bildeinzugskarte *f s.* Bilderfassungskarte
Bildelement *n* 1. image element, picture (pictorial) element; object *(esp. in vector files)*; 2. picture element, [image] pixel, pel *(s.a. under Pixel)*
Bildelementmatrix *f* pixel array
Bildelementtakt *m* pixel (dot) clock
bildelementweise pixelwise, pixel-by-pixel
Bildelementwiederholfrequenz *f* refresh rate
Bildempfang *m* image receiving
Bildempfänger *m* image receiver; image receptor
Bildempfängerchip *m* CCD imaging chip, CCD [camera] chip
Bildempfängerunschärfe *f* intrinsic (photographic) unsharpness *(radiography)*
Bildempfangsgerät *n* picture receiver; video receiver
Bildempfangsschicht *f* [image-]receiving layer, receptor layer *(instant photography)*
Bildende *n* last frame of action, LFOA *(on a film reel)*; end (last frame) of picture, EOP, LFOP
Bildendgerät *n* display terminal
Bildendstufe *f* video output stage
Bildenergie *f* image energy (power)
Bildentfernung *f* 1. image distance (conjugate); camera (bellows) extension; lens-to-film distance; 2. throw *(projection)*
Bildentstehung *f* image formation
~/**kohärente** coherent image formation
~/**optische** optical image formation
~/**paraxiale** paraxial image formation
~/**physikalische** physical image formation
Bildentstehungsmodell *n* image formation model
Bildentstehungsprozess *m* image formation process, image-forming process
Bildentstehungszeit *f* image reconstruction time *(computed tomography)*
Bildentwicklung *f* image development
Bildentzerrung *f* image distortion correction, image rectification
Bilder *npl* **pro Sekunde** frames per second, fps *(cinematography)*
Bilderbuch *n s.* Bildband 2.
Bilderdienst *m* picture processing service
Bilderdruck *m* image printing
Bilderdruckpapier *n* art [printing] paper
Bilderdrucktechnik *f* image printing technology
Bilderfassung *f* image capture (gathering), image (picture) acquisition, imaging; frame capture (grab) *(video)*
Bilderfassungsgerät *n* image-gathering (capture) device, imaging (image-capturing) device, image acquisition device
Bilderfassungsgeschwindigkeit *f* image acquisition speed
Bilderfassungshardware *f* image acquisition hardware
Bilderfassungskarte *f* frame grabber (capture) card, [video] frame grabber, video digitizer, digitizing board *(high-speed memory device)*
Bilderfassungsprozess *m* image gathering process
Bilderfassungsrate *f s.* Bildaufnahmefrequenz
Bilderfassungssystem *n* image capturing (capture) system
Bilderfluss *m s.* Bildfluss
Bilderfolge *f s.* Bildfolge
Bildergebnis *n* final image, final (finished) picture
Bildergruppe *f* group of pictures, GOP *(esp. as MPEG data structure)*
Bilderkennung *f* image recognition; image detection *(s.a. Bildanalyse)*
~/**automatische** automated image detection
~/**maschinelle** computer (machine) vision
Bilderkennungsmodul *m* vision module
Bilderkennungssoftware *f* image analysis software
Bilderkennungssystem *n* image detection scheme
Bilderneuerungsfrequenz *f s.* Bildwiederholfrequenz
Bilderrate *f s.* Bildfrequenz
Bilderschrift *f* picture script, hieroglyphic[s]

Bilderstapel *m* image stack
Bilderstellung *f s.* Bilderzeugung
Bildertrommel *f* wheel of life, zoetrope *(early cinematography)*
Bilderwascher *m* print washer
Bilderzange *f* print tongs
bilderzeugend image-forming, imaging
Bilderzeuger *m* imager
Bilderzeugnis *n* image product
Bilderzeugung *f* image generation (formation), image production, image-making, picture-making; imaging
~/**algorithmische** algorithmic image generation
~/**fotorealistische** rendering *(computer-graphic simulation process)*
Bilderzeugungsprozess *m* image-forming process, imaging process (procedure)
Bilderzeugungstechnik *f* imaging technique
Bilderzeugungsverfahren *n s.* Bilderzeugungsprozess
Bildfaltung *f* image convolution
Bildfarbe *f* image (picture) color
Bildfarbstoff *m* image[-forming] dye
~/**subtraktiver** subtractive image dye
Bildfarbstofffreisetzung *f* image dye release
Bildfehler *m* image (picture) defect, image error (imperfection), image fault; image artifact; [image] aberration
~ **fünfter Ordnung** fifth-order aberration
~ **höherer Ordnung** higher-order aberration
~/**magnetischer** magnetic aberration *(electron optics)*
~/**Seidelscher** Seidel [monochromatic] aberration
bildfehlerbehaftet aberrated
bildfehlerfrei aberration-free, unaberrated
Bildfehlerkoeffizient *m* aberration coefficient
Bildfehlerkorrektur *f* aberration correction
Bildfehlermaß *n* image error measure
Bildfehlertheorie *f* aberration theory
Bildfehlertoleranz *f* aberration tolerance
Bildeinheit *f* image definition
Bildfeld *n* image (picture) field; frame; film (motion-picture) frame
Bildfeldausleuchtung *f* image illuminance
Bildfeldauswahl *f* framing
Bildfeldblende *f* field stop (diaphragm)
Bildfeldebner *m* field flattener [element]
Bildfeldebnung *f* field flattening
Bildfeldgröße *f* field coverage *(of a lens);* frame size
Bildfeldkorrektur *f* field correction
Bildfeldverzerrung *f* field distortion
Bildfeldwinkel *m* [image] field angle; angular field
Bildfeldwölbung *f* curvature of field, field curvature [aberration], Petzval curvature
~/**meridionale** meridional curvature of field
~/**sagittale** sagittal curvature of field
Bildfeldzerlegung *f* [image] field dissection
Bildfenster *n* [image] window; film (exposure) gate, [image] gate *(camera)*; picture aperture (gate) *(projector)*
Bildfenstermaske *f* film-gate mask
Bildfensterverschluss *m* focal-plane shutter
Bildfernsprechen *n* video[tele]phony, video (visual) telephony
Bildfernsprecher *m* videophone, VP, picturephone, video (visual) telephone, screen phone
Bildfernübermittlung *f,*
Bildfernübertragung *f* facsimile (picture) transmission
Bildfilm *m* 1. picture (pictorial) film; image-containing film *(cinema)*; 2. print film
Bildfilter *n* image filter
Bildfilterung *f* image filtering *(s.a. under* Filterung*)*
Bildfilterungsverfahren *n* image filtering technique
Bildfixierung *f* image fusing *(xerography)*
Bildfläche *f* 1. image (picture) area; frame area; 2. *s.* Bildschirmfläche
~/**aktive** active picture area
Bildfleck *m* image patch
Bildflimmern *n* [image] flicker[ing]; frame [rate] flicker *(cinema, video)*
Bildflug *m* [aerial] survey flight
Bildflugzeug *n* photographic (camera-carrying) aircraft
Bildfluss *m* 1. image stream; 2. *s.* Fluss/optischer
Bildfolge *f* image sequence, succession of images, series (sequence) of pictures *(s.a. under* Bildsequenz*)*; sequence (series) of photographs; frame sequence, sequence of frames *(cinema, video)*
~/**dreidimensionale (räumliche)** spatial image sequence
~/**zeitliche** temporal image sequence
Bildfolgefrequenz *f* frame frequency (rate)
Bildfolgenanalyse *f* image-sequence analysis
Bildfolgenfilter *n* image-sequence filter
Bildfolgenfilterung *f* image-sequences filtering
Bildfolgenstabilisierung *f* image-sequence stabilization
Bildfolgeregler *m* intervalometer
Bildfolgezeit *f* exposure interval
Bildform *f* image shape
Bildformat *n* image (picture) format; [image] aspect ratio, aspect, [picture] width-to-height ratio
~/**anamorphotisches** anamorphic picture format
Bildformatdiagonale *f* format diagonal
Bildformatierung *f* image formatting
Bildformatkonversion *f* image format conversion

bildfrei

bildfrei nonimage *(e.g. area of a gravure plate)*
Bildfrequenz *f* image (picture) frequency, image [frame] rate; frame[-per-second] rate, framing speed (rate) *(s.a. Bildwiederholfrequenz)*
Bildfrequenzunterschied *m* frame-rate difference
Bildführung *f* 1. image guidance *(e.g. of surgical operations)*; 2. camera operation
Bildfunk *m* radiophotography
~/**digitaler** digital video broadcast [system], DVB
~/**digitaler terrestrischer** digital terrestrial video broadcast system, DVB-T
Bildfunktion *f*/**diskrete** discrete image function
Bildfusion *f* image fusion
bildgebend image-forming, imaging
Bildgeber *m* imager, imaging device
Bildgebung *f* imaging
~/**akustische** acoustic imaging
~/**biochemische** biochemical imaging, tomochemistry
~/**biomagnetische** biomagnetic imaging
~/**biomedizinische** biomedical imaging
~/**biophotonische** biophotonic imaging
~/**diagnostische** diagnostic imaging *(s.a. ~/medizinische)*
~/**dreidimensionale** three-dimensional imaging
~/**echoplanare** echo-planar imaging, EPI *(magnetic resonance imaging)*
~/**elektromagnetische** electromagnetic imaging
~/**elektrooptische** electro-optic imaging
~/**filmlose** filmless imaging
~/**funktionelle** functional imaging
~/**hochauflösende** high-resolution imaging
~/**kardiologische** cardiac (cardiological) imaging
~/**medizinische** medical imaging [technology]; clinical (diagnostic medical) imaging, [medical] diagnostic imaging
~/**molekulare** molecular imaging
~/**morphologische** morphological imaging
~/**nichtinvasive** noninvasive imaging
~/**nuklearmedizinische** nuclear medicine imaging
~/**optische** optical imaging
~/**planare** planar imaging *(e.g. in nuclear medicine)*
~/**schnelle** fast imaging
~/**seismische** seismic imaging
~/**spektroskopische** spectroscopic imaging
~/**szintigrafische** scintigraphic imaging
~/**tomografische** tomographic imaging, tomography
~/**ultraschnelle** ultrafast imaging
~/**zerebrale** neuroimaging, brain imaging

Bildgebungsausrüstung *f* imaging equipment
Bildgebungslinse *f* imaging lens
Bildgebungsmaterial *n* imaging material
Bildgebungsmethode *f* imaging method
Bildgebungsprozess *m* imaging process
Bildgebungssystem *n* imaging system
Bildgebungstechnik *f* imaging (image formation) technique
Bildgebungsverfahren *n* image-forming process, imaging process (procedure)
~/**diagnostisches** diagnostic imaging modality
~/**medizinisches** medical imaging modality
Bildgebungszweck *m* imaging purpose
Bildgedächtnis *n* picture memory
Bildgegenstand *m* image object, pictorial subject
Bildgehalt *m s.* Bildinhalt
bildgenau frame-accurate *(e.g. synchronization)*
Bildgenauigkeit *f* image fidelity (accuracy); frame accuracy *(e.g. in film-to-video transfer)*
Bildgenerator *m* image generator; field (pattern) generator
Bildgenerierung *f* image generation (formation) *(s.a. Bilderzeugung)*
Bildgeometrie *f* image geometry
Bildgerät *n* imaging (video) device
Bildgeschwindigkeit *f* image velocity
Bildgestaltung *f* image creation; pictorial composition
Bildgestaltungsrechner *m s.* Bildrechner
Bildgewinnung *f* image gathering (capture), image (picture) acquisition, imaging
Bildgewinnungsprozess *m* image gathering process
Bildglättung *f* image smoothing (blurring)
Bildglättungsfilter *n* image-smoothing filter *(s.a. Glättungsfilter)*
Bildgleichheit *f* picture sameness
Bildgradient *m* image gradient
Bildgraph *m* image graph
Bildgrauwert *m* image gray-level [value]
Bildgröße *f* image (picture) size
Bildgrößenschwankung *f* variation of image size
Bildgrößenverhältnis *n* ratio of image sizes
Bildgruppe *f* group of frames, GOF, group of pictures, GOP *(video encoding)*
Bildgüte *f* image (picture) quality, image performance *(s.a. Bildqualität)*
Bildgüteanforderung *f* image quality requirement
Bildgütemaß *n* image quality metric (measure)
Bildgütemerkmal *n* image quality characteristic (criterion)
Bildgüteprüfkörper *m* [image] quality control phantom, image quality indicator

Bildgütetest *m*, **Bildgüteuntersuchung** *f* image quality assessment
Bildgüteverlust *m* image quality loss, loss of image quality
Bildgütezahl *f* image quality value
bildhaft pictorial; iconic
Bildhaftigkeit *f* pictorialness; iconicity
Bildhälfte *f* image half
Bildhaltbarkeit *f* image permanence (longevity); print permanence
Bildhauptpunkt *m* rear principal point
Bildhelligkeit *f* image (picture) brightness, image luminance
Bildhelligkeits-Austast-Synchronsignal *n*/**kombiniertes** composite TV signal, composite video [signal]
Bildhelligkeitssignal *n* luminance (luma) signal, black-[and-]white [video] signal, monochrome (gray-scale) video signal, Y [signal]
Bildherstellung *f* image production, image-making
Bildhierarchie *f* picture hierarchy
Bildhintergrund *m* image background
Bildhistogramm *n* image histogram
Bildhöhe *f* image (picture) height; frame height
Bildhöhenaberration *f* image height aberration
~/**meridionale** meridional image height aberration
~/**sagittale** sagittal image height aberration
~/**tangentiale** tangential image height aberration
~ **windschiefer Strahlen** image height aberration of skew rays
Bildidentifizierung *f* image identification *(image analysis)*
Bild-im-Bild-... *s.* Bild-in-Bild-...
Bildimpuls *m* frame pulse *(video)*
Bild-in-Bild-Funktion *f*, **Bild-in-Bild-Modus** *m* picture-in-picture mode, PIP
Bild-in-Bild-Prozessor *m* picture insertion processor
Bild-in-Bild-Technik *f* picture-in-picture mode, PIP
Bildindexierung *f* image indexing
Bildinformatik *f* image informatics
Bildinformation *f* image information, picture (pictorial) information
Bildinformationsverarbeitung *f* pictorial information processing
Bildinformationsverlust *m* loss of image information
Bildinhalt *m* image content, picture (pictorial) content
~/**aktiver** active picture information; active video [signal], active region
Bildinhaltsanalyse *f* image content analysis
Bildinhaltsmerkmal *n* image content feature
Bildinnere *n s.* Bildmitte

Bildinstabilität *f* jitter
Bildintegration *f* image integration
Bildintensität *f* image intensity
Bildintensitätshistogramm *n* image intensity histogram
Bildinterpolation *f* image (frame) interpolation
Bildinterpretation *f* image interpretation; photointerpretation *(s.a. under* Bildauswertung*)*
~/**visuelle** visual image interpretation
Bildinterpretationssprache *f s.* Bildanalysesprache
Bildintervall *n* frame interval
Bildinversion *f* image inversion (reversal), image negation
Bildjournalismus *f* photojournalism
Bildjournalist *m* photojournalist
Bildjustierung *f* image registration (registering)
Bildkabel *n s.* Bildleitkabel
Bildkader *m* [film] frame, motion-picture frame
Bildkalibrierung *f* image calibration
Bildkammer *f* photogrammetric camera
Bildkanal *m* video channel
Bildkante *f* image (picture) edge, image border (boundary) *(s.a. under* Kante*)*
Bildkantenversteilerung *f* edge crispening
Bildkarte *f* 1. photomap, photographic map *(photogrammetry)*; 2. *s.* Bilddigitalisierer
Bildkennung *f* identification caption
Bildkennzeichnung *f* image label[l]ing
Bildkippen *n* [/**vertikales**] *n* frame roll
Bildkippfrequenz *f* vertical [sweep] frequency, field frequency (repetition rate) *(s.a.* Bildwiederholfrequenz*)*
Bildklasse *f* class of images, image class
Bildklassifikation *f*, **Bildklassifizierung** *f* image classification
Bildkoinzidenz *f* image coincidence
Bildkolorierung *f* image coloration
Bildkombination *f* 1. image combination; image merging; 2. composite [image], composite picture
Bildkommunikation *f*/**digitale** digital image communication
Bildkommunikationssystem *n* image (visual) communication system
Bildkomplexität *f* picture complexity
Bildkomponente *f* image component
Bildkomposition *f* image composition; pictorial composition; photo composition
Bildkompression *f* 1. image [data] compression *(esp. lossless compression)*; 2. *s.* Bildcodierung
~/**differentielle** differential image compression
~/**digitale** digital image compression
~/**fraktale** fractal image compression
~/**kontextbasierte** context-based image compression

Bildkompression

~/**progressive** progressive image compression
~/**statistische** statistical image compression
~/**verlustbehaftete** lossy image compression
Bildkompressionsalgorithmus m image compression algorithm
Bildkompressionsstandard m image compression standard
Bildkompressionsverfahren n image compression method (technique)
Bildkomprimierbarkeit f image compressibility
Bildkomprimierung f s. Bildkompression
Bildkonferenz f videoconference, video meeting (session)
Bildkonstruktion f image construction (optics)
Bildkontrast m image (pictorial) contrast (s.a. under Kontrast)
~/**lokaler** local image contrast
Bildkontrastmessung f image contrast measurement
Bildkontrastvergleich m image contrast comparison
Bildkontrastverstärkung f image contrast amplification
Bildkontrolle f image control
Bildkontrollempfänger m [picture] monitor
Bildkontur f image contour
Bildkoordinate f image coordinate
Bildkoordinatenmessung f image coordinate measurement
Bildkoordinatensystem n image coordinate system, image reference frame; screen space (computer graphics)
Bildkopie f 1. image copy, copy image; 2. mute (silent) print, picture only print (cinema)
Bildkorn n image (picture) grain
Bildkörnigkeit f image graininess
Bildkörnung f image granularity
Bildkorrektur f image correction
~/**dynamische** dynamic picture control
Bildkorrelation f/**digitale** digital image correlation
Bildkorrelationsfilterung f image correlation filtering
Bildkorrelationsspektroskopie f image correlation spectroscopy, ICS
Bildkorrelationstechnik f image correlation technique
Bildkreis m image circle, circle of coverage
Bildkreisdurchmesser m image circle diameter
Bildkrümmung f image curvature (optics)
Bildkurve f image curve
Bildlage f image position
Bildlageänderung f image position shift
Bildlageregelung f centering control (display)
Bildlauffeld n scroll box
Bildlaufleiste f scroll bar (display)

Bildlaufpfeil m scroll arrow
Bildlegende f caption, legend
Bildleistung f image (picture) performance (e.g. of a cathode-ray tube)
Bildleitbündel n s. Bildleitkabel
Bildleitkabel n imaging [fiber] bundle
Bildleitung f image guide; video circuit
Bildleuchtdichte f image luminance
bildlich pictorial
Bildlinearität f image linearity
Bildlinie f image line
Bildlöschung f image erasure
Bildmanipulation f image (picture) manipulation
~/**computergestützte** computer-controlled image manipulation
Bildmanipulationsprogramm n image manipulation [software] program
Bildmanipulator m image manipulator
Bildmarke f 1. document mark, blip (microfilming); 2. s. Logo
Bildmarkierung f image label[l]ing
Bildmaske f framing mask; image mask (digital image processing)
Bildmaskierung f image masking
Bildmaß n image dimension
bildmäßig pictorial; imagewise
Bildmäßigkeit f pictorialness
Bildmaßstab m image scale; photo scale; scale of reproduction
Bildmaßstabsfehler m distortion error
Bildmaterial n image (picture) material, pictorial material, imagery; image footage (cinema); illustrative material (matter) (typography)
~/**computerbearbeitetes** computer-enhanced imagery
~/**computergeneriertes** s. ~/rechnererzeugtes
~/**ideales** ideal imagery
~/**künstliches** s. ~/rechnererzeugtes
~/**medizinisches** medical imagery
~/**reales** real imagery
~/**rechnererzeugtes** computer-generated imagery, [synthetic] CG imagery, CGI
~/**vorgedrehtes** stock footage (cinema)
Bildmatrix f image [data] matrix, picture matrix; digitized image; display matrix
Bildmedium n image (imaging) medium, picture medium
Bildmenge f image set
Bildmerkmal n image feature (characteristic) (s.a. under Merkmal)
Bildmerkmalsanalyse f image feature analysis
Bildmerkmalspunkt m image feature point
Bildmessfilm m photogrammetric film
Bildmessgerät n photogrammetric apparatus
Bildmessung f image measurement (mensuration); photographic mensuration, photomensuration
Bildmesswesen n photometrology; photogrammetry, phototopography

Bildmetamorphose f/**merkmalsbasierte** feature-based image metamorphosis
Bildmischeinrichtung f video mixer
Bildmischen n image mixing (merging)
Bildmischer m 1. video mixer *(person)*; 2. s. Bildmischpult
Bildmischpult n video switcher, video (vision) mixer; [studio] production switcher
~/**analoges** analog switcher (vision mixer)
~/**digitales** digital switcher (vision mixer)
Bildmitte f image (picture) center
Bildmitteilung f picture message
Bildmittelpunkt m image center
Bildmittelung f image (frame) averaging *(inhomogeneous point operation)*
Bildmodell n image model *(e.g. in video modeling)*
~/**stochastisches** stochastic image model
Bildmodellierung f image modeling
Bildmodifikation f image modification
Bildmodulation f image modulation *(s.a. under Modulation)*
Bildmodus m image mode
Bildmonitor m image [display] monitor, picture monitor
Bildmontage f image assembly, stripping [operation] *(photomechanical reproduction)*; image overlay
Bildmosaik n image mosaic *(s.a. under Mosaik)*
Bildmotiv n pictorial subject
Bildmuster n 1. image (pictorial) pattern; 2. image specimen
Bildmustererkennung f image (pictorial) pattern recognition
Bildmustergenerator m test pattern generator
Bildmusterkontrast m image pattern contrast
Bildnachbearbeitung f, **Bildnachverarbeitung** f image postprocessing
Bildnachweis m picture credit
Bildnachziehen n comet tail *(motion artifact)*
Bildnavigation f/**volumetrische** volumetric image navigation
Bildnavigationssystem n image navigation system
Bildnegativ n image (picture) negative, pictorial negative
Bildnegativfilm m pictorial negative film, negative pictorial film
Bildneigung f image inclination
Bildner m image maker
Bildnerei f image-making, pictorial works
bildnerisch imaging
Bildnumerierung f frame count
Bildnummer f picture number; frame number
Bildnummernfenster n viewing (red safety) window *(e.g. of a roll-film camera)*
Bildoberfläche f image (picture) surface

Bildobjekt n image object, pictorial object (subject) *(s.a. under Objekt...)*
Bildobjektsegmentierung f s. Bildsegmentierung
Bildoperation f imaging (image) operation
Bildoperator m image operator *(s.a. under Operator)*
Bildoptimierung f image optimization
Bildorientierung f image orientation
Bildort m image location *(optics)*
~/**paraxialer** paraxial image location
Bildorthikon n image-orthicon [tube], IO
Bildpaar n image pair, pair of images
Bildparallelität f image parallelism
Bildparameter m image parameter; image format parameter
Bildpartie f image (picture) area
Bildpasser m register *(printing)*
Bildpegel m picture level, video [signal] level
Bildperspektive f pictorial perspective
Bildperzeption f s. Bildwahrnehmung
Bildpixel n image (imaging) pixel, pel *(s.a. under Pixel, Bildpunkt)*
Bildplan m aerial mosaic *(photogrammetry)*
Bildplankarte f aerial mosaic map
Bildplatte f 1. image[-bearing] plate; 2. optical (laser) disk; videodisc, videodisk *(s.a. under DVD)*
~/**analoge** optical (laser) disk
~/**digitale** digital videodisc *(comprehensive term, s.a. under DVD)*
~/**einschichtige** single-layer disk
~/**löschbare** erasable laser optical disk
~/**magnetische** magneto-optic[al] disk
~/**optisch reflektierende** optical reflective videodisk
~/**optische** optical disk
~/**rillenlose** grooveless video disk
Bildplattengerät n s. Bildplattenspieler
Bildplattenlaufwerk n optical disk drive
Bildplattenspeicher m optical disk memory
~/**digitaler** digital optical disk, DOD
Bildplattenspeicherung f optical disk storage
Bildplattenspieler m videodisc player
Bildposition f image position
Bildpositionierung f image positioning
Bildpositiv n positive image (picture)
Bildpostkarte f picture [post]card
Bildpräparation f picture preparation
Bildpräsentation f image presentation
Bildprimitiv n image primitive
Bildproduktion f image production *(s.a. Bilderzeugung)*
Bildprofil n image [projection] profile, image signature *(binary image analysis)*
Bildprojektion f image projection
Bildprojektionssystem n image projecting system
Bildprojektor m picture projector, image projection device

Bildprozedur f display subroutine
Bildprozessor m image processor
~ **mit zellularer Logikstruktur** cellular logic image processor, CLIP
~/**parallel arbeitender** parallel image processor
~/**programmierbarer** programmable image processor
Bildpuffer[speicher] m frame buffer [memory], image buffer, refresh memory (buffer)
Bildpunkt m image (picture) point; image dot *(reprography);* picture element, [image] pixel, pel *(s.a. under* Pixel*)*
~/**Gaußscher** Gaussian image point, Gauss (cardinal) point
~/**unabhängig identisch verteilter** independent identically distributed picture element
~/**zugehöriger** conjugate image point
Bildpunktadresse f pixel address
Bildpunktdarstellung f pixel representation
Bildpunktdistanz f pixel [separation] distance, pixel pitch, pel spacing
Bildpunkte mpl **pro Zoll** pixel per inch, ppi *(measure of resolution)*
Bildpunktfarbe f pixel color
Bildpunkthelligkeit f pixel brightness (luminosity), pixel intensity [value]
Bildpunktoperation f image point operation *(s.a.* Punktoperation*)*
Bildpunktposition f pixel position (location)
Bildpunktraster m(n) raster, bit-map *(array of binary data)*
Bildpunktverschiebung f pixel shifting
bildpunktweise pixelwise, pixel-by-pixel
Bildpyramide f image pyramid
Bildquadrant m image quadrant
Bildqualität f image (picture) quality, image performance *(s.a.* Bildgüte*)*
~/**fotorealistische** near-photographic image quality
Bildqualitätsbeurteilung f image (picture) quality evaluation, judg[e]ment of image quality, image quality assessment
Bildqualitätseinbuße f picture quality constraint
Bildqualitätskennzeichnung f image quality characterization
Bildqualitätsmaß n image quality measure (metric)
Bildqualitätssicherung f image quality assurance
Bildqualitätsverbesserung f image quality improvement, picture quality improvement (enhancement)
Bildquantisierung f image quantization
Bildquelle f image (picture) source, source of imagery
Bildradar n imaging (mapping) radar
Bildrahmen m picture frame
Bildrahmenmarke f fiducial (reference) mark *(photogrammetry)*
Bildrand m image border (boundary), image (picture) edge; image periphery
Bildraster m(n) image raster, picture grid
Bildrasterung f image halftoning
Bildrate f s. Bildfrequenz
Bildraum m image (picture) space
Bildraumalgorithmus m image space algorithm
Bildraumbrechzahl f image space refractive index
Bildraumdarstellung f image space representation
Bildraum-Hauptebene f image space principal plane
Bildraumkoordinatensystem n image space coordinate system
Bildraumverfahren n image space method *(computer graphics)*
Bildrauschabstand m image signal-to-noise ratio, sensitivity
Bildrauschen n image [optical] noise, pictorial noise; [frame] noise; snow, snowstorm [effect] *(interference)*
Bildrauschquelle f image noise source
Bildrauschunterdrückung f noise suppression
Bildrecherche f image [search and] retrieval *(s.a.* Bildsuche*)*
Bildrecherchesystem n image retrieval system
Bildrecherchetechnik f image search and retrieval technology
Bildrechner m image acquisition computer; imaging (image processing) computer
Bildredakteur m picture editor, photo[graphic] editor
Bildredundanz f image redundancy
Bildregelung f framing control
Bildregie f 1. vision (master) control *(television);* 2. s. Bildregieraum
Bildregieraum m vision control room
Bildregion f image region (area)
Bildregisseur m/**Zweiter** director of photography, DOP
Bildregistration f image registration (registering)
Bildregistrationstechnik f image registration technique
Bildregistrierung f s. Bildregistration
Bildreihe f 1. image row; 2. picture series, series of images (pictures)
Bildreihenaufnahme f framing
Bildrekonstruktion f image reconstruction (deconvolution) *(s.a. under* Rekonstruktion*)*
Bildrekonstruktionsalgorithmus m image reconstruction algorithm
Bildrekonstruktionsfilter n image reconstruction filter
Bildrekonstruktionstechnik f image reconstruction technique

Bildrekonstruktionszeit f image reconstruction time
Bildrektifikation f image rectification, image distortion correction
Bildreporter m press (newspaper) photographer, daily news photographer
Bildrepräsentation f s. Bilddarstellung
Bildreproduktion f image reproduction
~/**fotomechanische** photomechanical reproduction
Bildrestauration f image restoration (recovery)
~/**lineare** linear image restoration, image deconvolution
Bildrestaurationsalgorithmus m image-restoration algorithm
Bildrestaurierung f s. Bildrestauration
Bildresultat n final image, final (finished) picture
Bildretrieval n image retrieval
Bildrichtung f image direction; image (picture) orientation
Bildrohdaten pl raw image data
Bildröhre f picture (image) tube, kinescope; display tube
~/**elektromagnetische** electromagnetic image tube
Bildröhren-Ablenkschaltung f picture tube deflection circuitry
Bildröhrendiagonale f picture tube diagonal
Bildröhrenfront f [CRT-]faceplate
Bildröhrengamma n monitor gamma, [CRT] gamma
Bildröhrengerät n CRT television [set]
Bildröhrenhals m CRT neck
Bildröhrenkennlinie f [characteristic] display curve, characteristic curve of a CRT [monitor], tube characteristic
Bildröhrenmaske f s. Bildschirmmaske
Bildröhrenmonitor m cathode-ray tube monitor, CRT screen (display)
Bildröhrenoberfläche f tube face
Bildröhrenrecycling n picture tube recycling
Bildröhrensteuereinheit f cathode-ray tube controller, CRTC
Bildrollen n scrolling, screen rolling
Bildrotation f image (picture) rotation; frame rotation
Bildruckeln n jerkiness, choppiness (display)
Bildrücklauf m frame flyback, vertical retrace [time]
Bildrückteil n rear standard (of a technical camera)
Bildruhe f picture steadiness, steadiness [of the image]
Bildsammlung f image collection
Bildsandwich n [image] overlay
Bildscanner m [image] scanner
Bildschale f image surface (optics)
~/**meridionale** meridional image surface
~/**sagittale** sagittal image surface
~/**tangentiale** tangential image surface
Bildschaltmatrix f video switching matrix
Bildschärfe f image (picture) sharpness, acutance; image focus
Bildschärfe- und Belichtungsspeicher m aperture-exposure lock, AE lock
Bildschärferegulierung f [image] sharpness adjustment, picture sharpness control
Bildschärfung f image sharpening, [image] crispening
Bildschicht f image (picture) layer; image slice (magnetic resonance imaging)
Bildschirm m image (imaging) screen, [viewing] screen, display [screen] (s.a. under Display, Sichtschirm, Monitor)
~/**aktiver** active-matrix display, TFT (thin film transistor) display
~/**analoger** analog [CRT] monitor; analog display
~/**berührungsempfindlicher (berührungssensitiver)** touch[-sensitive] screen, tactile (pressure-sensitive) screen; touch-screen monitor
~/**digitaler** digital [image] display; digitally controlled CRT monitor
~/**dreidimensionaler** s. Display/stereoskopisches
~/**externer** desktop (stand-alone) monitor
~/**flacher** flat[-screen] display, flat-panel display, FPD; flat-panel monitor
~/**flexibler** flexible display
~/**gekachelter** tiled display
~/**geteilter** split screen, continuous presence (visual telephony)
~/**grafikfähiger** graphic display
~/**großflächiger** large screen [display], large[-format] display
~/**hochauflösender** high-resolution display (screen), high-definition screen
~/**kurznachleuchtender** short-persistent screen
~/**langnachleuchtender** long-persistent screen
~/**niedrigauflösender** low-resolution display
~/**passiver** passively addressed display
~/**reflexionsarmer** low-reflective screen
~/**selbstleuchtender** self-luminous display
~/**strahlungsarmer** low-radiation screen
Bildschirmabstand m screen distance; viewer-to-screen distance
Bildschirmadapter m s. Bildschirmkarte
Bildschirmansteuerung f display addressing
Bildschirmanzeige f 1. on-screen display, OSD; 2. soft [copy] display
Bildschirmanzeigegerät n display [device], readout
Bildschirmarbeit f screen work
Bildschirmarbeitsplatz m display (terminal) workstation
Bildschirmauflösung f display (screen) resolution

Bildschirmaufnahme

Bildschirmaufnahme f screen shot, off-screen photograph
Bildschirmaufteilung f screen splitting
Bildschirmausdruck m printout; [paper] hard copy; hard copy image
Bildschirmausgabe f soft [copy] display
Bildschirmausleuchtung f screen illumination
Bildschirmbild n screen (display) image; monitor image; cathode-ray tube image
Bildschirmbreite f screen width
Bildschirmbrille f head-mounted (helmet-mounted) display, HMD
Bildschirmdarstellung f 1. display representation, screen presentation; 2. [computer-]screen image
Bildschirmdesign n screen design
Bildschirmdiagonale f screen diagonal; screen diagonal size, diagonal screen size
~/sichtbare viewable (visible) screen diagonal
Bildschirmebene f screen plane
Bildschirmecke f screen corner
Bildschirmeditor m screen editor
Bildschirmeinstellung f display setting
Bildschirmfarbe f screen (display) color, monitor color
Bildschirmfenster n display window, [screen] window
Bildschirmfläche f display area; screen space; viewing surface *(display screen)*
Bildschirmflimmern n screen (display) flicker, screen flare
Bildschirmfluoreszenz f screen fluorescence
Bildschirmformat n screen format
Bildschirmfoto n off-screen photograph, screen shot
Bildschirmfotografie f 1. television/computer-screen photography 2. s. Bildschirmfoto
Bildschirmgerät n [image-]display device; visual display unit (terminal), VDU, VDT *(s.a. Monitor, Display)*
Bildschirmgestaltung f screen management
Bildschirmgrafik f [on-]screen graphics
Bildschirmgröße f screen (display) size, monitor size
Bildschirmhelligkeit f screen (display) brightness
Bildschirmhelm m virtual reality helmet; head-mounted (helmet-mounted) display, HMD
Bildschirmhintergrund m screen background
Bildschirmhöhe f screen height
Bildschirminhalt m screen content
Bildschirminstallation f grouping of screens
Bildschirmkalibrierung f monitor calibration (alignment), color calibration
Bildschirmkarte f display board (adapter), graphics [display] card, graphics board (adapter), graphics engine (controller) *(s.a. Videokarte)*
Bildschirmkoordinate f screen coordinate
Bildschirmkoordinatensystem n screen (display) coordinate system, viewing coordinate system
Bildschirmkrümmung f screen curvature
Bildschirmleuchtdichte f screen (display) luminance
Bildschirmleuchtstoff m 1. fluorescent screen material; 2. s. Bildschirmphosphor
Bildschirmmaske f screen mask, CRT (cathode-ray tube) mask, display map, bezel
Bildschirmmedium n display medium
Bildschirmmenü n display (on-screen) menu, on-screen display, OSD
Bildschirm-Miniaturisierung f screen miniaturization
Bildschirmmitte f screen center
Bildschirmneigung f screen tilt
Bildschirmoberfläche f display surface
Bildschirmobjekt n [on-]screen object
Bildschirmphosphor m screen (monitor) phosphor, display (cathode-ray-tube) phosphor
Bildschirmpixel n screen pixel, display (monitor) pixel
Bildschirmprojektor m beamer
Bildschirmprozess m display process
Bildschirmprozessor m display processor
Bildschirmrahmen m s. Bildschirmmaske
Bildschirmrand m screen border
Bildschirmraster m(n) raster
Bildschirmrauschen n [image-]display noise
Bildschirmschoner m screen saver
Bildschirmschrift f screen font
Bildschirmseite f [display] screen page
Bildschirmsichtgerät n display [device], readout
Bildschirmsignal n display signal
Bildschirmspeicher m display[-processor] memory; screen store (memory); frame buffer
Bildschirmspiegelung f screen glare
Bildschirmspiel n video game
Bildschirm-Splitting n s. Bildschirmaufteilung
Bildschirmstation f display terminal
Bildschirmsteuereinheit f [video] display controller
Bildschirmsteuerung f display control
Bildschirmstrahlung f screen radiation
Bildschirmtechnik f display technology
Bildschirmtechniker m monitor engineer
Bildschirmteiler m screen splitter
Bildschirmteilung f screen split
Bildschirmtelefon n s. Bildtelefon
Bildschirmterminal n display terminal, terminal screen
Bildschirmtext[dienst] m [interactive] videotex; viewdata

Bildschirmtreiber *m* [video] display driver, screen driver, display drive electronics
Bildschirmwinkel *m* screen angle *(radar)*
Bildschirmzeile *f* screen line
Bildschirmzeitung *f s.* Videotext
Bildschirmzyklus *m* refresh (display) cycle
Bildschleier *m* image fog
Bildschnitt *m* picture editing [process] *(cinema, video)*
Bildschnittstelle *f* picture edit (cut)
Bildschnittweite *f* back focus (focal distance)
Bildschritt *m*, **Bildschritthöhe** *f* frame gauge
Bildschrittschaltung *f* Geneva movement, intermittent [movement]
Bildschutz *m* image protection
Bildschwankung[en] *f[pl]* [picture] jitter *(cinema, video)*
Bildschwarz *n* picture black, shade
Bildschwärzung *f* image density
Bildsegment *n* image (pictorial) segment
Bildsegmentierung *f* image (picture) segmentation *(s.a. under* Segmentierung*)*
~/**adaptive** adaptive image segmentation
~/**linienbasierte** line-based image segmentation
~/**morphologische** morphological image segmentation
~/**regionenorientierte** region-oriented image segmentation
~/**schwellenwertbasierte** threshold-based image segmentation
~/**überwachte** supervised image segmentation
Bildsegmentierungsalgorithmus *m* image segmentation algorithm
Bildseite *f* image side *(e.g. of a paper print)*
Bildseitenlänge *f* image side length
Bildseitenverhältnis *n* [image] aspect ratio, aspect, [picture] width-to-height ratio
Bildseitenverhältniswandlung *f* aspect ratio accommodation
bildseitig image-side
Bildsektor *m* image section (portion)
Bildsemantik *f* image semantics
Bildsender *m* video transmitter *(television)*
Bildsensor *m* image (picture) sensor, imaging sensor (detector), imager
~/**elektronischer** electronic image (imaging) sensor
~/**flugzeuggetragener** airborne imager
Bildsequenz *f* image sequence, sequence (series) of pictures, sequence (succession) of images *(s.a. under* Bildfolge*)*
Bildsequenzcodierer *m* frame sequence coder
Bildsequenzcodierung *f* image sequence coding, [image] sequence compression
Bildsequenzkamera *f* framing camera
Bildsequenzverarbeitung *f* image sequence processing

Bildserie *f* picture series, series of images (pictures)
Bildserienkamera *f* multiexposure camera
Bildsicherung *f* image backup
Bildsignal *n* 1. image (picture) signal; video signal *(s.a. under* Videosignal, Signal*)*; 2. *s.* ~/vollständiges; 3. *s.* FBAS-Signal
~/**diskretes** discrete image signal
~/**vollständiges** complete picture signal *(s.a.* BAS-Signal*)*
Bildsignalmodell *n* image signal model
Bildsignalverstärker *m* image-signal amplifier
Bildsignalverstärkung *f* gain *(camcorder)*
Bildsignatur *f* image signature, image [projection] profile *(binary image analysis)*
Bildsilber *n* image[-forming] silver
Bildsimulation *f* image simulation
Bildskalierung *f* image scaling *(s.a.* Skalierung*)*
Bildskelettierung *f* image skeletonization *(computer graphics)*
Bildskizze *f* [aerial] mosaic *(remote sensing)*
Bildsondenröhre *f* [image] dissector tube
Bildspeicher *m* image (picture) memory, image (picture) store; iconic store; frame [store] memory, frame (still) store *(video)*
~/**digitaler** digital picture memory
~/**logischer** bit map
~/**physikalischer** *s.* Bildwiederholspeicher
Bildspeicheradressierung *f* image store addressing
Bildspeichereinheit *f* frame (image) storage unit
Bildspeicherfunktion *f* image storage function
Bildspeicherkarte *f* [/**digitale**] frame grabber (capture) card, digital picture card, DPC
Bildspeicherplatte *f* optical (laser) disk; videodisc, videodisk *(s.a. under* DVD*)*
Bildspeicherraum *m* image storage space
Bildspeicherröhre *f* [storage] camera tube
Bildspeichersoftware *f* picture filing software
Bildspeichersystem *n* image stor[ag]e system, visual storage system
Bildspeichertechnik *f* 1. image storage technology; 2. frame storage technique
Bildspeichertiefe *f* frame memory depth
Bildspeicherung *f* image storage
~/**elektronische** electronic image storage
~/**magnetische** magnetic image storage
Bildspeichervorrichtung *f* image storage device
Bildspektrometer *n* imaging spectrometer
Bildspektrometrie *f* imaging spectrometry
Bildspektroskopie *f* spectrographic imaging
Bildspektrum *n* image spectrum
Bildspiegel *m* image (picture) area *(typography)*

Bildsprache

Bildsprache *f* image language
Bildsprung *m* jump cut *(cinematography)*
Bildspur *f* image (picture) track
Bildstabilisation *f* image stabilization
Bildstabilisator *m* image (picture) stabilizer
~/**digitaler (elektronischer)** digital (electronic) image stabilizer, DIS, EIS
~/**optischer** optical image stabilizer
Bildstabilisierung *f* image (optical) stabilization
Bildstabilisierungssystem *n* image stabilization system
Bildstabilität *f* image stability
Bildstand *m* picture steadiness, steadiness [of the image]
Bildstandsausgleich *m* image[-motion] compensation, IMC
Bildstandsfehler/seitlicher [film] weave, gate weave
~/**vertikaler** projection jump
Bildstapel *m* image stack
Bildstärke *f* image strength
Bildstart *m* start (sync) mark
Bildstatistik *f* 1. image statistics *(image data processing)*; 2. pictorial statistics *(graphic design, visualization)*
bildstatistisch image statistical
Bildstelle *f* image location (patch); image area *(e.g. of an offset plate)*
~/**druckende** printing image area
~/**fehlende** missing dots *(printing imperfection)*
~/**nichtdruckende** nonimage [surface] area *(printing)*
Bildsteuereinheit *f* graphics [display] controller *(computer)*
Bildsteuerung *f* picture (framing) control
Bildstillstand *m* picture rest [period]
Bildstörung *f* image disturbance (perturbation), [image] interference
Bildstrahl *m* image ray
Bildstreifen *m* image strip
Bildstreifenbreite *f* flight-line spacing *(aerophotogrammetry)*
Bildstrich *m* frame line
Bildstruktur *f* image (picture) structure
Bildsubtraktion *f* image subtraction
Bildsuchalgorithmus *m* image retrieval algorithm
Bildsuche *f* image search[ing]; image [search and] retrieval
~/**inhaltsbasierte** content-based image retrieval
Bildsuchlauf *m* tape review
Bildsuchmaschine *f* image search engine
Bildsuchvorgang *m* image search process
Bildsymbol *n* [pictorial] icon, graphical icon
bildsynchron frame-synchronous
Bildsynchronisation *f* frame (image) synchronization
Bildsynchronisierimpuls *m*,
Bildsynchronsignal *n* frame synchronization (synchronizing) pulse, control track pulse

Bildsynthese *f* image synthesis *(s.a. Rendering)*
Bildsynthetisierer *m* image synthesizer
Bildsystem *n*/**technisches** technical image system
Bildszene *f* [image] scene, picture scene
Bildszenerie *f* image scenery
Bildtechnik *f* 1. imaging [technology], image technology; 2. image technique; 3. studio editing environment
~/**elektronische** electronic imaging technology
bildtechnisch technical imaging
Bildteil *m(n)* image part (area)
Bildteiler *m* image splitter
Bildteilung *f* image partition
Bildteilungstrick *m* split screen effect *(cinema)*
Bildtelefon *n* videophone, VP, picturephone, video (visual) telephone, screen phone
Bildtelefonanalage *f* visual telephony installation
Bildtelefondienst *m* videophone (video telephone) service
Bildtelefongerät *n* videophony terminal
Bildtelefonie *f* video[tele]phony, video (visual) telephony
~/**paketvermittelte** packet-switched videophony
Bildtelefonsignal *n* visual telephony signal
Bildtelefonverbindung *f* visual telephony link
Bildtelefonzelle *f* visual telephony kiosk
Bildtelegrafie *f* phototelegraphy, picture telegraphy, facsimile
~/**drahtlose** radiophotography
Bildtelegramm *n* phototelegram, facsimile [telegram]
Bild-Text-Dokument *n* compound document *(including both text and images)*
Bildtextur *f* image texture
Bildtexturanalyse *f* image texture analysis
Bildtexturdeskriptor *m* image texture descriptor
Bildtexturklassifikation *f* image texture classification
Bildtexturmerkmal *n* image textural feature
Bildtiefe *f* image depth
Bildton *m* image tone *(photographic printing paper)*
~/**dunkler** low key
~/**farbiger** image color
~/**heller** high key
Bild-Ton-Abstand *m s.* Bild-Ton-Versatz
Bild-Ton-Kamera *f* sound camera
Bild-Ton-Trägerabstand *m* visual/aural separation *(television signal)*
Bildtonung *f* toning
Bild-Ton-Versatz *m* picture-to-sound offset, [sound] advance, pull-up
Bildtopografie *f* image topography

Bildtopologie f [digital] image topology
Bildträger m 1. image (picture) carrier, image[-bearing] support; 2. s. Bildträgerfrequenz
Bildträgerfrequenz f vision carrier [frequency], picture carrier frequency
Bildträger-Tonträger-Abstand m s. Bild-Ton-Trägerabstand
Bildtransfer m image (picture) transfer
Bildtransferstruktur f frame-transfer structure *(charge-coupled device)*
Bildtransformation f image transform[ation]
~/**analoge** analog image transformation
~/**digitale** digital image transformation
~/**geometrische** geometric [image] transformation
~/**radiometrische** radiometric [image] transformation
Bildtranslation f image translation
Bildtransport m/**ruckweiser** intermittent [film] movement *(cinema)*
Bildtrennung f image separation
Bildtriangulation f photogrammetric triangulation, air (aerial) triangulation
Bildtrick m s. Bildeffekt
Bildtyp m frame type *(image coding)*
Bildüberblendung f [lap] dissolve, cross fade
Bildüberdeckung f overlap *(photogrammetry)*
Bildübergang m image transition
Bildüberlagerung f [image] superimposition
Bildüberlappung f image overlap
Bildübermittlung f s. Bildübertragung
Bildübersicht f thumbnails
Bildübersprechen n image cross talk, image lag, ghosting
Bildübertragung f image (picture) transmission; image (picture) transfer
~/**automatische** automatic picture transmission, APT
~/**progressive** progressive image transmission
~/**schmalbandige** narrow-band picture transmission
Bildübertragungskette f image-transmission chain
Bildübertragungsrate f s. Bildwiederholfrequenz
Bildübertragungssystem n image transfer system
Bildübertragungstechnik f image transmission technique; image transfer technique
Bildübertragungsverfahren n image transfer process (technique)
Bildumcodierung f image transcoding
Bildumfang/nutzbarer useful density *(radiography)*
Bildumgebung f image environment

Bildumkehr[ung] f 1. image reversal (inversion), image negation; 2. s. Solarisation
Bildumrandung f submount
Bildumsortierung f image rearrangement
Bildumwandlung f image conversion
Bildungsfernsehen n educational television, ETV
Bildunruhe f unsteadiness; float *(motion-picture projection)*
Bildunschärfe f image unsharpness (fuzziness), image blur[ring], blur
Bildunterbrechung f picture disruption
Bildunterscheidung f image discrimination
Bildunterschied m image difference
Bildunterschrift f caption, legend, cutline
Bilduntreue f image infidelity
Bildvariabilität f image variability
Bildvariable f image (spatial) variable
Bildvektor m image vector
Bildvektorquantisierung f image vector quantization
Bildveränderung f image alteration (transformation)
Bildverarbeiter m 1. image-processing engineer; 2. image processor, imager *(machine)*
~/**fraktaler** fractal imager
Bildverarbeitung f image (picture) processing, imaging *(s.a. Bildbearbeitung)*
~/**analoge** analog image processing
~/**bewegugsadaptive** motion-adaptive image processing
~/**digitale** digital image processing, DIP
~/**dreidimensionale** three-dimensional image processing
~/**elektronische** electronic image processing, electronic imaging
~/**ikonische** iconic [image] processing; low-level [image] processing
~/**industrielle** industrial image processing; [industrial] machine vision
~/**interaktive** interactive image processing
~/**lineare** linear image processing
~/**logarithmische** logarithmic image processing
~/**medizinische** medical imaging (imaging processing)
~/**modellbasierte** model-based image processing
~/**morphologische** morphological image processing
~/**multidimensionale** multidimensional image processing
~/**multispektrale** multispectral image processing
~/**nichtlineare** nonlinear image processing
~/**optische** optical image processing
~/**ortsvariante** space-variant image processing
~/**parallele** parallel image processing
~/**parametrische** parametric image processing

Bildverarbeitung

~/**pixelbasierte** pixel-based image processing
~/**raumzeitliche** spatiotemporal image processing
~/**rechnergestützte** computer-assisted image processing
~/**schnelle** fast image processing
~/**sequentielle (serielle)** sequential image processing
~/**transformationsbasierte** transform-based image processing
~/**wissensbasierte** knowledge-based image processing
~/**wissenschaftliche** scientific image processing
~/**zeitveränderliche** time-varying image processing
~/**zweidimensionale** two-dimensional image processing
Bildverarbeitungsalgorithmus m image processing algorithm
Bildverarbeitungsanlage f image processing workstation
Bildverarbeitungsanwendung f image processing application, vision application
Bildverarbeitungsarchitektur f image processing architecture
Bildverarbeitungsaufgabe f image processing task
Bildverarbeitungsbefehl m image processing instruction, imaging command
Bildverarbeitungsbibliothek f image processing library
Bildverarbeitungscomputer m imaging (image processing) computer
Bildverarbeitungseinheit f picture processing unit, PPU
Bildverarbeitungsfachkraft f image processing engineer
Bildverarbeitungsfilter n image processing filter
Bildverarbeitungsfunktion f image processing function
Bildverarbeitungsgerät n image processing device
Bildverarbeitungshardware f image processing hardware
Bildverarbeitungsingenieur m image processing engineer
Bildverarbeitungskette f image [processing] chain, imaging chain
Bildverarbeitungslabor[atorium] n image processing laboratory
Bildverarbeitungsleistung f image processing performance
Bildverarbeitungsmessgerät n imaging instrument
Bildverarbeitungsmodul n image processing module
Bildverarbeitungsoperation f image processing operation
Bildverarbeitungsoperator m image (picture) processing operator *(s.a. under Operator, Filter)*
Bildverarbeitungsparameter m image processing parameter
Bildverarbeitungsprogramm n image processing program
Bildverarbeitungsprogrammierung f image processing programming
Bildverarbeitungsprozessor m image processor
Bildverarbeitungsrechner m imaging (image processing) computer
Bildverarbeitungsroutine f image processing routine
Bildverarbeitungsschritt m image processing step
Bildverarbeitungssoftware f image processing software, [computer] imaging software
Bildverarbeitungssoftwarepaket n image processing software package
Bildverarbeitungsstation f/**digitale** digital imaging workstation
Bildverarbeitungssystem n image processing system, imaging system
~/**digitales** digital image processing system
Bildverarbeitungstechnik f 1. image processing technology; 2. image processing technique
Bildverarbeitungsverfahren n image processing technique (procedure)
Bildverarbeitungswerkzeug n image processing tool
Bildverarbeitungszeit f image processing time
Bildverbesserung f image (picture) improvement; image enhancement
Bildverbreiterung f image widening
Bildverdeutlichung f image enhancement
Bildverdopp[e]lung f image doubling
Bildveredelung f s. Bildverdeutlichung
Bildvereinfachung f image simplification
Bildverfälschung f image corruption
Bildverfremdung f [electronic] image distortion
Bildvergleich m image (picture) comparison, [image] matching
Bildvergrößerung f image magnification (enlargement)
Bildverkleinerung f image reduction (minification)
Bildverknüpfung f image coupling
Bildverlust m frame loss
Bildvermessung f image measurement (mensuration)
Bildversand m **per Mobilfunk** multimedia messaging service, MMS
Bildversatz m image displacement
Bildverschärfung f image sharpening, [image] crispening
Bildverschiebung f image shift; image translation

Bildverschlechterung f image (picture) degradation, image deterioration
Bildverschmelzung f image fusion
Bildverschmierung f image smear[ing]; image blurring
Bildversetzung f/**axiale** axial image dislocation
Bildverständlichkeit f image intelligibility
Bildverstärker m image intensifier (amplifier); image-amplification device; image enhancer
~/**fluoroskopischer** fluoroscopic image intensifier
~/**fotoelektrischer** s. Bildverstärker
Bildverstärkerausgangsschirm m [image intensifier] output phosphor, output [fluorescent] screen, output phosphor screen *(radiography)*
Bildverstärkereingangsschirm m input fluorescent (phosphor) screen, [image intensifier] input phosphor *(radiography)*
Bildverstärkerfernsehen n image-intensifier television
Bildverstärker-Fernsehkette f television fluoroscopy system
Bildverstärkerfluoroskopie f image intensification fluoroscopy
Bildverstärkerröhre f image intensifier tube
Bildverstärkung f image intensification (amplification)
Bildverstehen n image understanding
Bildverteilung f image irradiance *(radiometry)*
Bildvervielfachung f image multiplication
Bildverwaltung f image management
Bildverwaltungs- und kommunikationssystem n image management and communication system, IMACS
Bildverwaltungsprogramm n image management program
Bildverwaltungssystem n image management system
Bildverzeichnung f, **Bildverzerrung** f image distortion; image warping, rubber sheeting *(computer graphics)*
Bildverzögerung f 1. image lag, frame delay *(video)*; 2. s. Bildübersprechen
Bildvibration f image vibration
Bildviertel n image quadrant
Bildvisualisierung f image visualization
Bildvordergrund m image foreground
Bildvorführung f image presentation
Bildvorlage f copy image, source (input) image; original
Bildvorschau f preview
Bildvorverarbeitung f image preprocessing
Bildwackeln n [projection] jitter
Bildwahrnehmung f image perception
Bildwand f [projection] screen, [projection] wall
~/**akustisch [hoch]transparente** perforated screen
~/**diffuse** matt screen, surface diffuser
~/**durchscheinende** translucent screen
~/**ebene** plane screen
~/**geprägte** lenticular screen
~/**hinterleuchtete** rear-lit screen
~/**metallisierte** metalized (aluminized) screen; silver (specular) screen
~/**reflektierende** reflecting screen
Bildwandabdeckung f screen mask *(film projection)*
Bildwandausleuchtung f screen luminance
Bildwandern n crawl *(interference)*
Bildwanderung f image motion *(e.g. in remote sensing)*
Bildwanderungsausgleich m image-motion compensation
Bildwandler m image converter, imaging transducer
~/**fotoelektrischer** photoelectric image converter
~/**ladungsgekoppelter** charge-coupled device (detector), CCD
Bildwandlerchip m CCD imaging chip, CCD [camera] chip
Bildwandlerkamera f image-converter camera
Bildwandlerröhre f image-converter tube
Bildwandleuchtdichte f screen luminance
Bildwandlung f image conversion
Bildwechsel m image (picture) change
Bildwechselfrequenz f s. Bildwiederholfrequenz
Bildwechselprinzip n image change principle *(dynamic-graphic simulation)*
Bildwechselrate f, **Bildwechselzahl** f s. Bildwiederholfrequenz
bildweise imagewise
Bildweiß n picture white
Bildweite f image distance (conjugate); camera (bellows) extension
Bildwelle f image wave *(holography)*
Bildwerfer m [optical] projector
~/**elektronischer** beamer
Bildwerferraum m projection booth (box) *(cinema)*
Bildwert m image value
Bildwiederauffindung f image retrieval
Bildwiedergabe f image reproduction; image rendition (rendering), image output; image display
Bildwiedergabeeinheit f s. Bildwiedergabegerät
Bildwiedergabegerät n image display device (unit)
Bildwiedergabemaßstab m image scale of reproduction
Bildwiedergabemedium n image display medium
Bildwiedergabequalität f image fidelity
Bildwiedergaberöhre f picture tube, kinescope; display tube
Bildwiedergabesystem n image reproduction system; image display (portrayal) system

Bildwiedergewinnung f image regeneration, image (picture) recovery
Bildwiederholfrequenz f picture repetition rate, repetition frequency, frame refresh rate, screen (video) refresh rate *(s.a.* Bildfrequenz, Vertikalfrequenz*)*
Bildwiederholgeschwindigkeit f, **Bildwiederholrate** f s. Bildwiederholfrequenz
Bildwiederholspeicher m frame buffer [memory], image buffer, refresh buffer (memory)
Bildwiederholung f image replication
Bildwinkel m [**/nutzbarer**] angle (field) of coverage *(of a lens)*; field angle, angle of view (field); image angle
Bildwirksamkeit f s. Fotogenität
Bildwirkung f pictorial effect
Bildwissenschaft f imaging (image) science
Bildwissenschaftler m imaging scientist
Bildwölbung f 1. image warping, rubber sheeting *(computer graphics)*; 2. s. Bildfeldwölbung
Bildzähler m film (exposure) counter; frame counter
Bildzählung f frame count
Bildzählwerk n s. Bildzähler
Bildzange f print tongs
Bildzeichen n graphical symbol, pictorial character *(s.a.* Piktogramm, Icon*)*
bildzeichnend image-forming, imaging
Bildzeile f 1. picture (image) line *(television)*; 2. s. Bildunterschrift
Bildzelle f picture cell
Bildzentrum n image (picture) center
Bildzerlegung f image dissection (decomposition)
Bildzittern n image jitter, [frame] jitter
Bild-zu-Bild-Codierung f frame-to-frame coding, interframe [en]coding, interpicture coding
Bild-zu-Bild-Transformation f image-to-image transformation
Bild-zu-Bild-Variation f image-to-image variation
Bild-zu-Bild-Verarbeitung f s. Bildverarbeitung/ikonische
Bildzuordnung f image matching; image correlation
~/**merkmalsbasierte** feature-based image matching
~/**objektbasierte** object-based image matching
Bildzusammenhang f pictorial continuity
Bildzusammensetzung f image composition
Bildzustand m image state
Bildzyklus m image cycle
Bi-Linse f [/**symmetrische**] bispheric lens
Billigkamera f inexpensive (low-priced) camera, low-cost camera
Bimetallplatte f bimetal plate *(printing)*
bimodal bimodal
Bimodalität f bimodality
binär binary, bilevel
Binäranzeige f binary display
Binärbaum m binary [search] tree
Binärbild n binary image (picture), bilevel (two-level) image, bistable image
Binärbildanalyse f binary image analysis
Binärbilddarstellung f binary image representation
Binärbildkompression f binary image compression (coding)
Binärbildpunkt m bi-level pixel
Binärbildskelettierung f binary image skeletonization
Binärbildverarbeitung f binary [digital] image processing
Binärcode m binary code, PCM (pulse code modulation) code
~/**komplementärer** complementary binary code
~/**natürlicher** natural (straight) binary code
Binärcodierung f binary [en]coding
Binärdarstellung f binary representation
Binärdatei f binary file
Binärdatencodierung f binary data coding
Binärelement n s. Binärzahl
Binärgrafik f binary (bilevel) graphics
Binärgruppenzeichen n binary group flag
binarisieren to binarize
Binarisierung f, **Binärisierung** f binarization
~/**globale** global binarization
Binarisierungsschwelle f binarizing threshold
Binärkanal m binary channel
Binärmaske f binary mask
Binärmaskenbild n binary mask image
Binärmatrix f binary (Boolean) matrix
Binärmuster n binary (bit) pattern
Binärobjekt n binary object
Binärobjekterkennung f binary [image] object detection
Binärrepräsentation f binary representation
Binärschwelle f binary threshold
Binärsegmentierung f binary segmentation
Binärsignal n binary signal
Binärsystem n binary [numbering] system, base 2
Binärverarbeitung f binary [image] processing
Binärwert m binary value
Binärwort n [binary] word, multi-digit binary number
Binärzahl f, **Binärzeichen** n, **Binärziffer** f binary digit (number), binary unit, bit
Bindemittel n binding agent, binding medium (compound), binder
Bindestrich m hyphen *(punctuation mark)*
Bindung f/**heteropolare** heteropolar (ionic) bond, electrovalent bond
~/**kovalente** covalent bond[ing] *(e.g. of silver halides)*
Bindungsenergie f [nuclear] binding energy

Binnenkontrast *m* surface contrast
Binokel *n s.* Binokular
binokular binocular, two-eyed
Binokular *n* binocular *(optical instrument)*
Binokularansatz *m*, **Binokularaufsatz** *m* binocular body *(microscope, telescope)*
Binokularmikroskop *n* [stereoscopic] binocular microscope
Binokularsehen *n* binocular (two-eyed) vision, binocular viewing
Binokularteleskop *n* binocular telescope
Binokulartubus *m* binocular tube
Binomialfilter *n* binomial filter
Binomialverteilung *f* binomial (Bernoulli) distribution
Bioinformatik *f* bioinformatics
Biolumineszenz *f* bioluminescence
Biometrie *f*, **Biometrik** *f* biometry, biometrics
biometrisch biometric[al]
Biomikroskop *n* biomicroscope
Bionik *f* bionics
Biopsie *f*/**optische** optical biopsy, elastic scattering spectroscopy, ESS
Biorthogonalitätsbedingung *f* biorthogonality constraint (requirement) *(reconstruction filtering)*
Bipack *n(m)* bipack [film]
bipolar bipolar
Bipolarsignal *n* bipolar signal
Bipolarzelle *f* [retinal] bipolar cell
Biprisma *n* [/**Fresnelsches**] *n* [Fresnel] biprism
Bireflexion *f* bireflection
Bispektrum *n* bispectrum
bistabil bistable
Bistabilität *f*/**optische** [optical] bistability
Bit *n* bit, binary digit (number), binary unit
~/**höchstwertiges** most significant bit, MSB *(sequential coding)*
~/**niederwertigstes** least significant bit, LSB *(sequential coding)*
Bitabbildung *f* bit-mapping
Bitauflösung *f* bit resolution
Bitbild *n s.* Bitmap-Bild
Bitblocktransfer *m*, **Bitblocktransport** *m* bit block transfer, bit blit
Bitbreite *f* bit width
Bitbündelübertragung *f* burst transmission
Bitdichte *f* bit density
Bitebene *f* bit plane
~/**niederwertige** least significant bit plane
Bitebenencodierung *f* bit-plane coding
Bitebenenskalierung *f* bit-plane scaling
Bitebenenzerlegung *f* bit-plane decomposition
Bitfehler *m* bit error
Bitfehlerhäufigkeit *f*, **Bitfehlerquote** *f*, **Bitfehlerrate** *f* bit error rate, BER *(probability of error per bit)*
Bitfehlerverhältnis *n* bit error ratio, BER
Bitfehlerwahrscheinlichkeit *f* bit error probability

Bitfehlerzahl *f* **pro Sekunde** *s.* Bitfehlerhäufigkeit
Bitfolge *f* string of bits, bit string
Bitfolgefrequenz *f* bit clock rate
Bitfrequenz *f s.* Bitrate
Bitgrafik *f s.* Bitmap-Grafik
Bitmap *f* 1. bit-map, raster *(array of binary data)*; 2. *s.* Bitmap-Bild
Bitmap-Animation *f* bit-map animation
Bitmap-Bild *n* bit-map [representation], raster (bit-mapped) image, pixel map (image), pixmap
Bitmap-Datei *f* bit-map file
Bitmap-Daten *pl* bit-map data
Bitmap-Format *n* bit-map format
Bitmap-Grafik *f* bit-mapped graphics; pixel (raster) graphics
Bitmap-Grafikprogramm *n* bit-mapped [graphics] program
Bitmap-Schrift *f* bit-mapped font
Bitmap-Textur *f* bit-map texture
Bitmap-Zeichensatz *m* bit-mapped font
Bitmaske *f* bit mask
Bitmaskierung *f* bit masking
Bitmatrix *f* bit matrix (array)
Bitmuster *n* bit (binary) pattern; bit-map *(s.a. under* Bitmap*)*
Bitmustergrafik *f* bit-mapped graphics
Bitpaar *n* pair of bits
bitparallel bit parallel
Bitperiode *f* bit period
Bitposition *f* bit position (location)
Bitrate *f* bit [transfer] rate, coding rate
~/**konstante** fixed bit rate, FBR, constant bit rate, CBR
~/**mittlere** average bit rate
~/**variable** variable bit rate, VBR
Bitratencodierung *f*/**variable** variable bit rate [en]coding, VBR
Bitratenkompression *f*, **Bitratenkomprimierung** *f* bit rate compression
Bitratenminimierung *f* bit rate minimization
Bitratenprofil *n* bit rate profile
Bitratenreduktion *f*, **Bitratenreduzierung** *f* bit rate reduction *(s.a. under* Kompression*)*
Bitratensteuerung *f* bit rate control
Bitratenübertragung *f*/**variable** VBR (variable bit rate) transmission
Bitratenvariabilität *f* bit rate variability
Bitratenvariation *f* bit rate variation
Bits *npl* **pro Sekunde** bits per second, bps *(designating the speed of data transmission)*
bitseriell bit-serial
Bitspiegelung *f* bit reverse shuffling
Bitstopfen *n* bit stuffing
Bitstrom *m* [transport] bitstream
~/**kontinuierlicher** continuous bit stream
~/**serieller** serial bitstream
Bitstromsyntax *f* bitstream syntax
Bittakt *m*, **Bittaktfrequenz** *f* bit clock rate

Bittiefe *f* bit (pixel) depth *(s.a.* Farbtiefe*)*
Bitumkehr *f* bit reversal
Bitumordnung *f* bit interleaving
Bitverschachtelung *f* bit interleaving
Bitzuordnung *f* bit allocation *(image compression)*
~/**rückwärtsadaptive** backward-adaptive bit allocation
~/**vorwärtsadaptive** forward-adaptive bit allocation
Bitzuweisung *f* bit assignment
Bjerrum-Schirm *m* Bjerrum screen *(ophthalmic instrument)*
BK-Netz *n s.* Breitbandkabelnetz
Black Burst *m* black burst, house sync (reference), house (reference) black *(composite video signal)*
Blähmittel *n* blowing agent
Blankfilm *m* blank (clear) film
Blankodruck *m* single-sheet proof *(color printing)*
Blankseite *f* non-emulsion side, back of the film
Bläschenbild *n* vesicular (bubble) image *(vesicular process)*
Bläschenkopierverfahren *n* vesicular process
Blasenbild *n s.* Bläschenbild
Blasengrafik *f* bubble chart
Blasenkammer *f* bubble chamber
Blasenkammerfoto *n* bubble chamber photograph
Blasenkammerfotografie *f* bubble chamber photography
Blasenkammerholografie *f* bubble chamber holography
Blasenkammeroptik *f* bubble chamber optics
Blasenspiegel *m* cystoscope
Blasepinsel *m* blower brush
Blatt *n* leaf *(as a sheet of paper)*
~/**fliegendes** flyleaf, free endpaper *(of a book)*
Blattdrucker *m* page printer
blättern to scroll
Blättertrick *m* page flip, page-turn [effect] *(digital video)*
Blattfilm *m* sheet film; cut (flat) film
Blattknoten *m* leaf node *(e.g. of a binary tree)*
Blattrückseite *f* verso [page] *(layout)*
Blattvorderseite *f* recto [page]; right-hand page *(layout)*
Blattzuführung *f* sheet feed
Blau *n* blue *(primary color)*
~/**genormtes** cyan
Blauauszug *m* blue [light] record *(color photography)*
blaublind blue-blind, tritanopic
Blaublindheit *f* blue[-yellow color] blindness, tritanopia
Blaudruck *m* blueprint

blauempfindlich blue-sensitive, monochromatic, color-blind *(photographic emulsion)*
Blauempfindlichkeit *f* blue[-light] sensitivity, blue speed
Blaufilter *n* blue [light] filter; cool-down filter
Blau-Gelb-Blindheit *f s.* Blaublindheit
Blau-Gelb-Störung *f*/**angeborene** *s.* Blauschwäche
Blaugrün *n* blue-green, cyan *(subtractive primary color)*
Blaugrünfilter *n* cyan (blue-green) filter
Blaugrünkuppler *m* cyan[-forming] coupler, cyan dye-forming coupler
Blaugrünschicht *f*/**rotempfindliche** red-sensitive layer
Blaukanal *m* blue channel, blue component (record)
Blaulicht *n* blue light
Blaupause *f* 1. blueprint; 2. blueline [proof], brownline *(prepress photographic proof)*
blaupausen to blueprint
Blauphosphor *m* blue phosphor
Blauraum *m* blue box
Blauschirm *m s.* Blauwand
Blauschwäche *f* tritanomaly, decreased blue sensitivity *(color-vision deficiency)*
Blausignal *n* blue signal *(video)*
Blaustanze *f s.* Bluescreen-Verfahren
Blaustich *m* blue (bluish) cast, blue bias
Blaustrahl *m* blue beam *(cathode-ray tube)*
Blauteilbild *n* blue [light] record *(color photography)*
Blautoner *m* blue toner
Blautonung *f* blue toning
Blauwand *f* blue screen; blue box *(television)*
Blaze-Gitter *n* blazed grating, blaze grid, echelette [grating]
Blaze-Wellenlänge *f* blaze wavelength
Blaze-Winkel *m* blaze angle
Bleiabschirmung *f* lead shielding
Bleichbad *n* bleach[ing] bath, bleach[ing] solution *(reversal processing)*
Bleichbad-Auffrischlösung *f* bleach regenerator
Bleichbad-Nachfüllösung *f* bleach replenisher
Bleichbad-Starter *m* bleach starter
Bleichbeschleuniger *m* bleaching accelerator
bleichen to bleach
Bleicher *m s.* Bleichmittel
Bleichfixage *f*, **Bleichfixierbad** *n* bleach-fix[ing] bath, blix
Bleichfixierlösung *f* bleach-fix solution
Bleichlösung *f* bleach[ing] solution
Bleichmittel *n* bleaching agent, bleach [chemical], bleacher
Bleichprozess *m* bleach-out process
Bleifolie *f s.* Bleiverstärkerfolie
Bleiglas *n* lead glass
Bleigleichwert *m* lead equivalent

Bleikristallglas *n* lead crystal glass
Bleisatz *m* lead composition
Bleistiftkeule *f* pencil beam *(radar)*
Bleistiftretusche *f* pencil retouching
Bleitype *f* lead type
Bleiverstärkerfolie *f* lead [intensifying] foil, lead screen *(radiography)*
Blendart *f* transition type *(video, cinema)*
Blenddauer *f* transition rate *(editing)*
Blende *f* 1. [lens] diaphragm; aperture; shutter *(cinema)*; 2. fade *(cinema, video)*; 3. *s.* Blendenzahl
~/**bündelbegrenzende** beam-limiting aperture
~/**effektive** effective aperture (f-number), entrance pupil
~/**elektromagnetische** electromagnetic shutter
~/**elektronische** fader; fade control
~/**feldbegrenzende** field stop (diaphragm)
~/**förderliche** useful (optimum) aperture, clear (free) aperture
~/**gewählte** working (taking) aperture
~/**kleinste** minimum aperture
~/**kreisförmige** circular aperture (stop)
~/**kritische** critical aperture (stop), *(s.a.* ~/förderliche*)*
~/**maximale** full (maximum) aperture, largest aperture
~/**natürliche** natural diaphragm
~/**optische** optical aperture
~/**rechteckige** rectangular (square) aperture
~/**ringförmige** annular (ring) aperture
~/**variable** adjustable aperture
blenden to glare
Blendenautomatik *f* 1. automatic iris mechanism, automatic diaphragm system; auto iris [control] *(camera feature)*; 2. [auto] shutter priority *(exposure mode)*
Blendenbereich *m* aperture range
Blendenbild *n* aperture (stop) image
Blendendifferenz *f* focal shift
Blendendurchmesser *m* aperture diameter
~/**maximaler** maximum aperture
Blendenebene *f* aperture plane
Blendeneffekt *m* 1. aperture effect; 2. wipe [transition]
Blendeneinstellring *m* aperture (iris) ring, diaphragm control (setting) ring
Blendeneinstellung *f* [lens-]aperture setting, diaphragm setting, aperture adjustmen; f-number setting
Blendeneinstellvorrichtung *f* diaphragm setting device
Blendenfleck *m* stop spot
Blendenfunktion *f* aperture [transmission] function, pupil function *(ray optics)*
Blendengitter *n* aperture grating *(color picture tube)*
Blendenhalbwinkel *m* aperture half-angle
Blendenkörper *m* iris mount
Blendenlamelle *f* iris blade

Blendenloch *n s.* Blendenöffnung
Blendenmaske *f* aperture mask
Blendenöffnung *f* diaphragm opening; [diaphragm] aperture opening
~/**effektive** effective aperture (f-number), entrance pupil
~/**maximale** maximum diaphragm opening
Blendenpriorität *f* aperture priority
Blendenproblem *n* aperture problem *(motion estimation)*
Blendenrechner *m* exposure calculator
Blendenreihe *f s.* Blendenskale
Blendenring *m* 1. aperture annulus; 2. *s.* Blendeneinstellring
Blendenschalter *m* fade button *(camcorder)*
Blendenschieber *m* shutter *(spotlight)*
Blendenschließhebel *m* iris [closing] lever
Blendenskale *f* [lens] diaphragm scale, aperture [value] scale
Blendensteuerring *m s.* Blendeneinstellring
Blendensteuerung *f* aperture control
Blendenstufe *f* [aperture] stop, f-stop
Blendentrick *m* wipe [transition]
Blendenverschluss *m* diaphragm (aperture) shutter
Blendenvorwahl *f* depth-of-field preview, preset diaphragm
Blendenwahl *f* aperture choice
Blendenwert *m s.* Blendenzahl
Blendenzahl *f* [diaphragm] f-number, F number, stop [number], relative aperture, aperture number, focal (aperture) ratio
~/**belichtungskorrekte** exposure stop, e-stop
~/**effektive** effective f-number, effective relative aperture, T-stop, t-stop
~[en]**reihe** *f s.* Blendenskale
Blenden-Zeit-Stufe *f* exposure value, EV
blendfrei nonglare *(e.g. glass)*
Blendschutz[schirm] *m* [anti-]glare screen, glare guard (filter) *(computer)*
Blendung *f* glare
~/**indirekte** reflected glare
~/**physiologische** disability glare
~/**psychologische** discomfort glare
Blendungsgrad *m* degree of glare
Blendungszahl *f* flare factor, glare index (number)
Blendwinkel *m* glare angle
Blendwirkung *f* glare effect
Blick *m* look; gaze; view, sight; glance
~/**linksäugiger** left-eye view
~/**rechtsäugiger** right-eye view
Blickachse *f* gaze axis, axis of gaze *(s.a.* Blicklinie, Sehachse*)*
Blickbewegung *f* coarse saccade
Blickdauer *f* gaze duration
blicken to look; to view; to gaze *(s.a.* fixieren*)*
Blickfeld *n* field [of view], view field *(s.a.* Gesichtsfeld*)*

Blickfeld 68

~/**binokulares** binocular field [of view]
~/**monokulares** monocular field [of view]
Blickfolgebewegung f pursuit eye movement
Blicklinie f line of sight (vision), view (visual) line, sight (eye) line
Blicklinienmessung f line-of-sight registration
Blicklinienvektor m line-of-sight vector
Blickpunkt m viewpoint, point of view, vantage point, stationpoint
blickpunktabhängig view-dependent *(e.g. object shapes)*
Blickrichtung f view[ing] direction, direction of view[ing], look direction; direction of gaze
Blicksprung m s. Blickzielbewegung
Blicksteuerung f eye [motion] tracking
Blickstrahl m viewing ray
Blickwinkel m view[ing] angle, angle of view (field), observation (look) angle
Blickzielbewegung f saccade, saccadic [eye] movement, saccadic motion
Blickzieluntersuchung f s. Blicklinienmessung
Blimp m blimp *(soundproof camera housing)*
Blinddruck m s. Blindprägung
Blindgeschwindigkeit f blind speed *(of radar targets)*
Blindheit f blindness
Blindmaterial n reglet *(typography)*
blindprägen to blind emboss
Blindprägung f relief embossing
Blindzeile f empty line *(typography)*
Blinken n flashing
Blinkkomparator m blink comparator *(astronomical optics)*
Blisterpackung f blister pack
Blitz m 1. flash [of light]; 2. lightning
Blitz... s.a. Blitzlicht...
Blitz/ausklappbarer flip-up flash, pop-up flash
~/**eingebauter** built-in [electronic] flash, integrated flash
~/**indirekter** bounce flash, bounced electronic flash
~/**stroboskopischer** stroboscopic flash, strobe light (flash)
Blitzabschaltung f flash on/off facility
Blitzadapter m flash adapter (adaptor)
Blitzanschluss m flash fixture; flash sync socket
Blitzanschlusskabel n flash (sync) cord, flash connector (sync cord), sync[hronization] lead
Blitzaufnahme f flash shot (picture), flash[light] photograph
Blitzausleuchtung f flash illumination (lighting)
Blitzauslöser m flash trigger
Blitzauslösung f flash triggering
Blitzausrüstung f flash equipment

Blitzautomatik f [built-in] automatic flash exposure control
Blitzbatterie f flashlight battery
Blitzbeleuchtung f flash illumination (lighting)
Blitzbelichtung f flash exposure
Blitzbelichtungsmesser m [electronic] flash meter, flashlight exposure meter
Blitzbelichtungsmessung f flash exposure measurement
Blitzbelichtungsreihe f flash [exposure] bracketing
Blitzbelichtungssteuerung f s. Blitzsteuerung
Blitzbereitschaftsanzeige f 1. [flash] readylight indication; 2. s. Blitzbereitschaftslampe
Blitzbereitschaftslampe f [flash] readylight, flash-ready indicator light
Blitzbetrieb m flash operation
Blitzbetriebsart f flash [sync] mode
Blitzbirne f flash bulb
Blitzdauer f flash duration (time)
Blitzeinsatz m flash use
Blitzeinstelllicht n modeling flash
blitzen to flash
Blitzentladung f flash discharge
Blitzer mpl pinholes *(printing defect)*
Blitzfigur f static mark *(on an radiographic image)*
Blitzfotografie f flash photography; electronic flash photography
Blitzfrequenz f flashing frequency (rate)
Blitzgerät n flash unit, flashgun, speedflash, speedlight
~/**eingebautes** built-in flash [unit], built-in speedlight
~/**externes** separable (off-camera) flash unit, external flash
~/**integriertes (internes)** s. ~/eingebautes
Blitzgerätehersteller m flash manufacturer
Blitzintensität f flash intensity
Blitzkabel n flash (sync) cord, flash connector (sync cord), sync[hronization] lead
Blitzkondensator m flash capacitor
Blitzkontakt m flash contact, sync terminal
Blitzkontrollanzeige f s. Blitzbereitschaftsanzeige
Blitzkopf m [electronic-]flash head
Blitzkurve f flash curve
Blitzlämpchen n s. Blitzlampe
Blitzlampe f flashbulb; photoflash [lamp]; flashlamp; photo[graphic] flashlamp
Blitzlampen-Farbstofflaser m flashlamp-pumped dye laser
Blitzlampenlaser m flashlamp-pumped laser
Blitzlampensystem n [photographic] flash lamp array
Blitzleistung f flashlamp performance; flash output [level], flash effectiveness
Blitzleitzahl f [flash] guide number, GN, flash factor

Blitzleuchtdauer f s. Blitzleuchtzeit
Blitzleuchte f flash[bulb] fixture; flash[gun]
Blitzleuchtzeit f flash time (duration)
Blitzlicht n flashlight
~/indirektes bounce light
Blitzlichtaufnahme f flash shot (picture), flashlight
Blitzlichtfoto n s. Blitzlichtaufnahme
Blitzlichtfotografie f flash photography
Blitzlichtgerät n photoflash unit
Blitzlichtintensität f flash luminous intensity
Blitzlichtkamera f flash camera
Blitzlichtlampe f s. Blitzlampe
Blitzlichtleistung f flash output [level]
Blitzlichtpulver n flash[light] powder
Blitzlichtquelle f flash light (illumination) source, [photo]flash source; electronic-flash light source
Blitzlichtreichweite f flash range
Blitzlicht-Steckverbindung f flash connector
Blitzlichtsteuerung f flash control
Blitzmodus m flash [sync] mode
Blitzneiger m bounce flash adapter
Blitzortung f lightning location
Blitzortungssystem n lightning position system; lightning locator (strike mapper)
Blitzpulver n flash[light] powder
Blitzreflektor m flash reflector (head); electronic-flash reflector, bounce card
Blitzreichweite f flash range
Blitzröhre f flashtube
Blitzschiene f flash bracket
~/abgewinkelte folding flash bracket
~/gerade straight flash bracket
Blitzschirm m flash umbrella
Blitzschuh m hot shoe [contact], flash shoe
Blitzsensor m flash sensor
Blitzsteuerung f flash[-exposure] control
~/autofokusgekoppelte semiautomatic flash-exposure control
~/kabellose off-camera flash control
Blitzsynchronisation f flash synchronization
Blitzsynchronisationsmodus m flash [sync] mode
Blitzteiler m flash divider
Blitzüberwachung f lightning sensing
Blitzverlängerungskabel n flash extension lead, flash synchronization cable
Blitzwarnsystem n lightning warning system
Blitzwinkel m angle of flash coverage
Blitzwürfel m flash-cube
Blitzzeit f s. Blitzleuchtzeit
Blitzzubehör n flash accessories
Blitzzündung f flash ignition
Blix n s. Bleichfixierbad
Blob m blob, binary large object *(group of pixels; item of binary data)*
blobähnlich blob-like
Block m block *(e.g. of data, signals or pixels)*

Blockanfangskennsatz m block header
Blockanpassung f block matching *(motion estimation)*
Blockartefakt n block[ing] artifact *(image coding)*
Blockbegrenzer m block delimiter
Blockbegrenzung f block boundary
Blockbildung f/digitale s. Mosaikeffekt
Blockbitmuster n block bit pattern
Blockbuchstabe m block letter
Blockcode m block[-type] code
Blockcodebit n block code bit
Blockcodierer m block coder
Blockcodierung f block[-based] coding, area character coding *(class of image compression techniques)*
~/fraktale fractal block coding
~/gefilterte filtered block compression
Blockdiagramm n [graphical] block diagram; equipment block diagram
Blockebene f block layer
Blockecke f block corner, node
Blockentropie f block entropy
Blockfehler m burst error
Blockfehlerkorrektur f block error correction
Blockfehlerrate f block error rate, BLER
Blockgrafik f block graphic
Blockgröße f block size
Blockgruppe f group of blocks, GOB
Blockierung f blocking
Blockkante f block edge
Blockkosinustransformation f block cosine transform
Blocklängenfehler m block length error, BLE
Blocklücke f [inter]block gap
Blockmatching[-Verfahren] n block matching [technique] *(motion estimation)*
Blockmitte f block center
Blockmittelwert m block mean value
Blockprüfung f block check
Blockprüfzeichen n block check character, BCC
Blockprüfzeichenfolge f frame check sequence
Blockquantisierer m block quantizer
Blockquantisierung f block quantization
~/adaptive adaptive block quantization
Blocksatz m [full] justification, justified type *(typography)*
Blockschaltbild n [graphical] block diagram; equipment block diagram
Blockserife f square (slab) serif *(s.a. Serife/ungekehlte)*
Blocksicherung f/zyklische cyclic redundancy check, CRC
Blocksortierung f block sort
Blockstruktur f blocking
Blocktransformation f block transform[ation]
Blocktransformationscodierung f block transform coding

Blocküberlappung *f* block overlapping *(transform coding)*
Blockübertragung *f* block transfer
Blockumsetzer *m* [/**rauscharmer**] low-noise block converter, LNB *(satellite television)*
Blockung *f* blocking
Blockvarianz *f* block variance
Blockvergleich *m* block matching [technique] *(motion estimation)*
~/**hierarchischer** hierarchical block matching
~/**szenenadaptiver** scene-adaptive block matching
Blockvergleichsalgorithmus *m* block-matching algorithm, BMA
Blockwelt *f* blocks world *(computer vision)*
Blockzerlegung *f* block decomposition
Blooming-Effekt *m* blooming effect, [image] blooming
Bluescreen-Aufnahme *f* blue-screen shot
Bluescreen-Verfahren *n* blue-screen process (photography); blue screen[ing]; blue-box process *(videography)*
Blühen *n s.* Blooming-Effekt
Blutflussdarstellung *f* blood flow image
Blutlaugensalz *n*/**rotes** red prussiate of potash, potassium ferrycyanide *(bleaching agent)*
B-Mode-Bild *n* [ultrasound] B mode image, B scan image
B-Mode-Scanner *m* B mode scanner *(sonography)*
B-Mode-Verfahren *n* B scan modality (process), B mode imaging
BMP-Format *n s.* Bitmap-Format
BNC-Stecker *m* BNC pin (connector) *(from Bayonet Neil-Concelman)*
Bobby *m* bobbin, [winding] core, take-up core
Bodenauflösung *f* ground resolution
Bodenclutter *m* ground clutter *(interfering radar echoes)*
Bodenclutterkarte *f* ground clutter map
Bodendämpfung *f* ground attenuation
Bodendurchdringungsradar *n* ground-penetrating (surface-penetrating) radar, subsurface radar, georadar
Bodenecho *n s.* Bodenclutter
Bodenkarte *f* soil map
Bodenkontrollpunkt *m* ground [control] point *(remote sensing)*
Bodenkörper *m* bottom sediment *(e.g. of a developer solution)*
Bodennutzungskarte *f* land use map
Bodenradar *n* ground[-based] radar
Bodenspinne *f* spider, triangle, tripod (floor) spreader
Bodenstation *f* [/**empfangende**] ground[-based] receiving station, ground (earth) station
Bodenstativ *n* hi-hat, top hat
Bodenstreifen *m* [ground] swath *(radar)*
Bodenwellenradar *n* ground-wave radar

Bogen *m* 1. arc; 2. arch *(component)*; 3. sheet *(of paper)*
~/**gedruckter** printed sheet
Bogenanlage *f,* **Bogenanleger** *m* feeding unit, feeder; register unit *(printing press)*
Bogenauslage *f* delivery stack *(printing press)*
Bogendruck *m* sheet-fed printing
Bogendruckmaschine *f* sheet-fed [printing] machine, sheet-fed press
Bogenentladungslampe *f* arc-discharge lamp
Bogenlampe *f* arc [lamp]
Bogenlänge *f* arc length
Bogenlicht *n* arc light
Bogenmaschine *f* cut sheet machine *(s.a.* Bogendruckmaschine*)*
Bogenminute *f* minute of arc
Bogenmontage *f* imposition
Bogenoffset[druck]maschine *f* sheet-fed [rotary] offset press (machine), rotary sheet-fed offset press
Bogenrotationsmaschine *f* sheet-fed rotary [press]
Bogensekunde *f* arc-second, sec[ond of arc]
Bogenstapel *m* pile of sheets
Bogentiefdruck *m* sheet-fed gravure
Bogentiefdruckmaschine *f* sheet-fed gravure press
Bogenzähler *m* sheet counter
Bogenzuführung *f* sheet feeding
Boid *m(n)* boid *(computer animation)*
Bolograf *n* bolograph
Bolometer *n* bolometer [detector], bolometer element
Bolometerschicht *f* bolometer film
Bolometerwiderstand *m* bolometer resistance
bolometrisch bolometric
Boltzmann-Faktor *m* Boltzmann factor
Boltzmann-Konstante *f* Boltzmann['s] constant
Boltzmann-Maschine *f* Boltzmann machine *(single-layer neural network)*
Boltzmann-Statistik *f* [Maxwell-]Boltzmann statistics
Borax *n* borax, sodium tetraborate *(developer improver)*
Bordradar *n* onboard radar
Borkron *m* borosilicate crown [glass], BK
Borsäure *f* boric acid *(development additive)*
Borsilikatglas *n* borosilicate glass
Borsilikat-Kronglas *n* borosilicate crown [glass], BK
Bouguer-Fotometer *n* Bouguer photometer
Bouncen *n s.* Blitzen/indirektes
Bouncer *m,* **Bounce-Reflektor** *m* bounce flash adapter
Box[kamera] *f* box camera
Bragg-Reflektor *m* Bragg reflector
Bragg-Reflexion *f* Bragg reflection

Bragg-Streuung *f* Bragg scattering
Bragg-Winkel *m* Bragg angle
brechen to refract
Brechkraft *f* **[/optische]** refractive (refracting) power, dioptric (diopter) power, diopter number *(optics)*
brechkraftändernd refractive, refractile
Brechung *f* **[/optische]** [optical] refraction
Brechungsfehler *m* refractive (refraction) error
Brechungsgesetz *n* law of refraction
~**/Snell[ius]sches** [Snell's] refraction law, Snell's law [of refraction]
Brechungsindex *m s.* Brechzahl
Brechungsinvariante *f* refraction invariant
Brechungsverhältnis *n* relative refractive index, refractive index ratio
Brechungswinkel *m* angle of refraction, refraction (refracting) angle
Brechwert *m s.* Brechzahl
Brechwerteinstellung *f* **[/des Auges]** accommodation
Brechzahl *f* index of refraction, refractive index
~**/absolute** absolute refractive index
~**/relative** relative refractive index
~**/wellenlängenabhängige** wavelength-dependent refractive index
Brechzahlanpassung *f* index (phase) matching *(nonlinear optics)*
Brechzahlbestimmung *f* refractive index determination
Brechzahldifferenz *f* [refractive] index difference
Brechzahlgradient *m* refractive index gradient, index-of-refraction gradient
Brechzahlmesser *m* refractometer
Brechzahlmessung *f* refractometry
Brechzahlprofil *n s.* Brechzahlverteilung
Brechzahlverteilung *f* refractive index distribution
Breitbahnpapier *n* grain short paper, short grain paper, wide web paper
Breitband *n* broadband, wideband
Breitbandanschluss *m* broadband connection
Breitbandbeschichtung *f* broadband coating
Breitbandcodierung *f* broadband coding
Breitbanddatennetz *n* broadband network
Breitbanddienst *m* broadband service
Breitbandempfang *m* broadband reception
Breitbandfilter *n* broadband filter
breitbandig broadband, wideband, wide-bandwidth, high-bandwidth
Breitbandinterferenzfilter *n* broadband interference filter
Breitband-Internet *n* broadband Internet
Breitband-ISDN *n* Broadband ISDN (Integrated Services Digital Network), B-ISDN
Breitbandkabel *n* broadband (wideband) cable
Breitbandkabelnetz *n* broadband network; cable television system
Breitbandkabel-Verstärkerstelle *f***/benutzerseitige** bridger amplifier
Breitbandkanal *m* broadband channel
Breitbandkommunikation *f* broadband communication
Breitbandkommunikationsnetz *n* broadband network
Breitbandmedium *n* broadband medium
Breitband-Multimedia-Informationsabrufdienst *m* broadband multimedia information retrieval service
Breitbandnetz *n* broadband network
Breitbandnutzer *m* broadband user
Breitbandportal *n* broadband portal
Breitbandrauschen *n* broadband (wideband) noise; white noise
Breitbandsignal *n* broadband [electrical] signal, wide-bandwidth signal
Breitbandtechnik *f* broadband technology
Breitbandübertragung *f* broadband transmission
Breitbandverbindung *f* broadband (wide-bandwidth) connection, high-bit-rate connection
Breitbandverstärker *m* broadband (wideband) amplifier
Breitbandverteilernetz *n* cable television system
Breitbandzugang *m* broadband access
Breitbild *n* wide picture
Breitbilddarstellung *f* wide-screen presentation
Breitbildempfänger *m s.* Breitbildfernseher
Breitbildfernsehen *n* wide-screen television
Breitbildfernseher *m*,
Breitbildfernsehgerät *n* wide-screen receiver
Breitbildformat *n* wide-picture format; wide-screen format
Breitbildkino *n* wide-screen cinema
Breitbild-Kinofilm *m* wide-screen [motion] picture, wide-screen movie
Breitbildschirm *m* wide screen
Breitbildverfahren *n* [motion picture] wide-screen process
Breitentabelle *f s.* Dicktentabelle
Breitenvergrößerung *f* transverse magnification
Breitfilmverfahren *n s.* Breitbildverfahren
Breitformatfernseher *m* wide-screen receiver
Breitstrahler *m* broad-beam lamp
Breitwand *f* wide screen; wide canvas *(film presentation)*
Breitwandbild *n* wide-screen image (picture)
Breitwand-Bildseitenverhältnis *n* wide-screen ratio
Breitwandfilm *m* wide-format film; wide-screen [motion] picture,

wide-screen movie; wide-screen feature [film]
~/**anamorphotischer** anamorphosed movie
Breitwandfilmverfahren *n s.* Breitwandverfahren
Breitwandformat *n* wide-screen movie format, wide-screen [film] format, anamorphic [film] format
breitwandig wide-screen
Breitwandkamera *f* wide-screen camera
Breitwandkinematografie *f* wide-screen movie photography
Breitwandkino *n* wide-screen cinema
Breitwand-Kinofilm *m s.* Breitwandfilm
Breitwandprojektion *f* wide-screen [movie] projection
Breitwandsystem *n* wide-screen system
Breitwandverfahren *n* [motion picture] wide-screen process, motion-picture wide-screen system
Breitwandvorführung *f* wide-screen presentation (show)
Bremsmittel *n* restrainer, development inhibitor *(s.a. Antischleiermittel)*
Bremsspektrum *n* [/**kontinuierliches**] bremsstrahlung [X-ray] spectrum, X-ray continuum
Bremsstrahlung *f* bremsstrahlung [radiation], braking (decelerated) radiation
Bremszeit *f* post-roll [time] *(video recorder)*
Brenndauer *f* lighting hours *(lamp)*
Brennebene *f* focal (focus) plane, plane of focus; image (picture) plane
~/**bildseitige** rear (back) focal plane
~/**Gaußsche** Gaussian focal plane
~/**hintere** *s.* ~/bildseitige
~/**objektseitige** front focal plane
~/**paraxiale** paraxial focal plane
Brennfläche *f* caustic (focal) surface, caustic [curve]; catacaustic; diacaustic surface *(ray optics)*
Brennfleck *m* focal spot *(e.g. of a X-ray tube)*
~/**optisch wirksamer** effective focal spot
~/**thermischer** thermal focal area
~/**wahrer** actual focal spot
Brennfleckbahn *f* focal track
Brennfleckbewegung *f* focal spot movement (motion)
Brennglas *n* burning glass
Brennlinie *f* [cata]caustic (focal) line; diacaustic line *(formed by refraction)*
Brennpunkt *m* [principal] focus, focal (focus) point
~/**bildseitiger** second (rear) focal point
~/**dingseitiger (objektseitiger)** first focal point
~/**virtueller** virtual focus, center of dispersion
brennpunktlos focusless; afocal
Brennpunktschnittweite *f*/**bildseitige** back focus (focal distance)

Brennpunktstrahl *m* focal ray
Brennpunktverschiebung *f* focus shift
Brennstrahl *m* focal ray
Brennweite *f* focal length (distance), focusing distance, focus
~/**bildseitige** back (rear) focal length
~/**effektive** effective (equivalent) focal length, power
~/**hintere** *s.* ~/bildseitige
~/**nutzbare** useful focal length
~/**objektseitige** front focal length (distance)
~/**rückwärtige** *s.* ~/bildseitige
~/**tatsächliche** effective (equivalent) focal length, EFL
~/**vordere** front focal length
Brennweitenaberration *f*, **Brennweitenabweichung** *f* defocus
Brennweitenbereich *m* focus range, focal[-length] range
Brennweitendifferenz *f*/**chromatische** chromatic difference (variation) of magnification, transverse chromatic aberration, TCA, lateral color (chromatic aberration)
Brennweiteneinstellring *m* focus[ing] ring, zoom ring
Brennweiteneinstellung *f* focus (focal length) setting
Brennweitenfahrt *f* zoom shot (effect) *(filming)*
Brennweitenmesser *m* focometer, focimeter
Brennweitenmessung *f* focometry
Brennweitenring *m* focus[ing] ring, zoom ring
Brennweitenskale *f* focusing (zoom) scale
Brennweitenspanne *f s.* Brennweitenbereich
Brennweitenspektrum *n s.* 1. Brennweitenbereich; 2. Brennweitenspanne
Brennweitenverhältnis *n* focal[-length] ratio
Brenzcatechin *n* [pyro]catechol, pyrocatechin[ic acid], pyro *(developing chemical)*
B-Rep-Liste *f* boundary representation list *(computational geometry)*
Bresenham-Algorithmus *m* Bresenham's algorithm *(computer graphics)*
Brewster-Bedingung *f* Brewster's law
Brewster-Fenster *n* Brewster [angle] window *(laser)*
Brewster-Prisma *n* Brewster's angle dispersing prism
Brewster-Winkel *m* Brewster angle [of incidence], polarization (polarizing) angle *(optics)*
Bridgekamera *f* bridge camera, hybrid
Briefkopf *m* letterhead
Briefpapier *n* letter paper; stationery
Briefqualität *f* letter quality, LQ *(printed image)*

brillant brilliant
Brillantsucher *m* brilliant (waist-level) finder
Brillanz *f* brilliance, brilliancy *(e.g. of an image)*
Brille *f* [pair of] glasses, eyeglasses, spec[tacle]s
~/verordnete prescription glasses
Brillenglas *n* spectacle (eyeglass) lens
Brillenoptik *f* ophthalmic (spectacle lens) optics
Brillenträger *m* spectacle wearer
Brillouin-Streuung *f* Brillouin scattering *(quantum optics)*
Bristolkarton *m* bristol [board]
Brodatz-Textur *f* Brodatz texture *(texture segmentation)*
Bromablaufeffekt *m* bromide-streak effect *(e.g. of tank-processed sheet film)*
Bromakzeptor *m* bromine acceptor
Bromammonium *n* ammonium bromide
Bromgelatinepapier *n* gelatin bromide paper
Bromid *n* bromide
Bromidabzug *m* bromide [print]
Bromidemulsion *f* bromide emulsion
Bromidfahne *f* bromide streak (drag)
Bromidpapier *n* [silver-]bromide paper
Bromidstreifen *m s.* Bromidfahne
Bromion *n* bromide ion
Bromöldruck *m* 1. bromoil process (printing); 2. bromoil print
Bromöldruckfotografie *f* bromoil process photography
Bromsilber *n* silver bromide
Bromsilberdruck *m* 1. bromide printing; 2. [silver] bromide print
Bromsilberemulsion *f* silver bromide emulsion
Bromsilbergelatine *f* gelatinobromide, silver bromide gelatin
Bromsilber-Gelatine-Emulsion *f* gelatin-silver bromide emulsion, silver bromide gelatin emulsion
Bromsilber-Gelatine-Papier *n s.* Bromsilber[vergrößerungs]papier
Bromsilber-Gelatine-Platte *f* silver bromide gelatin plate
Bromsilber-Gelatine-Trockenplatte *f* gelatin silver bromide glass dry plate
Bromsilber-Kollodium-Platte *f* silver bromide collodion plate
Bromsilberkristall *m* silver bromide crystal
Bromsilbervergrößerungspapier *n* [silver-]bromide paper, bromide [printing] paper
Bronchoskop *n* bronchoscope
Bronchoskopie *f* bronchoscopy
bronchoskopisch bronchoscopic
Bronzieren *n* bronzing
Brotschrift *f* bread-and-butter type, body face *(typography, printing)*
Browser *m* browser *(client software program)*

Bruch *m s.* Falz
Brüchigkeit *f* brittleness *(e.g. of a photographic emulsion)*
Bruchschrift *f s.* Fraktur[schrift]
Brücke-Bezoldsches Phänomen *n* Bezold-Brücke phenomenon *(color perception)*
Brückenstecker *m* [/kleiner] jumper *(circuit board)*
Brummspannung *f* ripple
Brummstörung *f* hum trouble
Brustbild *n* bust shot, half-length portrait
Bruststativ *n* chestpod
B-Signal *n s.* Bildsignal
BSP-Baum *m* binary space partitioning *(data structure)*
B-Spline *n s.* B-Spline-Kurve
B-Spline-Fläche *f* B-spline [surface] patch *(computer graphics)*
~/bikubische bicubic B-spline surface patch
~/dreieckige triangular B-spline surface patch
B-Spline-Interpolation *f*/**kubische** cubic B-spline interpolation
B-Spline-Kurve *f* B-spline [curve], basis spline
~/kubische cubic B-spline
~/rationale *s.* NURBS-Kurve
B-Spline-Transformation *f* B-spline transform
BTX *s.* Bildschirmtext
Buchdecke *f*, **Buchdeckel** *m* book cover
Buchdruck *m* 1. letterpress [printing], typography, relief (block) printing; 2. book printing
Buchdruckmaschine *f* letterpress [printing] machine, letterpress press
Buchdruckplatte *f* letterpress [printing] plate
Buchdruck-Rotationsmaschine *f* letterpress rotary
Bucheinband *m* book cover
Bücher[schreib]papier *n* book paper
Buchfertigung *f*, **Buchherstellung** *f* bookmaking
Buchkassette *f* book-type cassette *(radiophotography)*
Buchseite *f* book page
Buchstabe *m* [alphabet] letter, character
Buchstabenabstand *m* letter spacing
Buchstabenbild *n* letter image, letterform
Buchstabenbreite *f* 1. set size *(of a type)*; 2. [advance] width *(typography)*
Buchstabenform *f* matrix, die
Buchstabengießmaschine *f* [type]caster, typecasting machine
Buchstabenlinie *f* stroke *(typography)*
Buchstabensetz- und -gießmaschine *f* typecasting compositor
Bucky-Raster *m(n)* Bucky diaphragm *(flat-film X-ray imaging)*
Bühnenbeleuchtung *f* 1. theatrical lighting; 2. stage lights

Bühnenfoto *n* performance photograph, onstage picture
Bühnenfotografie *f* theatrical photography
Bühnenlautsprecher *m* screen speaker, stage [loud]speaker *(cinema)*
Bühnenlichtfilter *n* theatrical-lighting filter
Bühnenprojektion *f* stage projection
Bühnenscheinwerfer *m* stage light; theatrical spotlight
Bühnentechniker *m* theater technician
Bump-Mapping *n* bump [texture] mapping *(computer graphics)*
Bund *m* binding *(of a book or magazine)*
Bündel *n* 1. [ray] bundle, bundle of rays; 2. bundle *(e.g. as a set of attributes in computer graphics)*
~/**achsparalleles** on-axis bundle
~/**divergentes** diverging bundle
~/**einfallendes** incident bundle
~/**homozentrisches** homocentric beam
~/**inkohärentes** incoherent (noncoherent) bundle
~/**kohärentes** coherent (aligned) bundle *(fiber optics)*
~/**kollimiertes** collimated bundle [of rays]
~/**konvergentes** converging bundle [of rays]
~/**paralleles** parallel bundle [of rays]; collimated beam
~/**schiefes (schräges)** oblique bundle
Bündelausgleichung *f*/**fotogrammetrische** *s.* Bündelblockausgleich
Bündelaustastung *f* burst blanking
Bündelblock *m* bundle block
Bündelblockausgleich *m*, **Bündelblockausgleichung** *f* bundle [block] adjustment
Bündelfehler *m* burst error
Bündelfokussierung *f* beam focusing
Bündelindex *m* bundle index *(computer graphics)*
Bündelkollimation *f*, **Bündelkollimierung** *f* beam collimation
Bündelöffnung *f* beam aperture
Bündelöffnungswinkel *m* beam aperture angle
Bündeloptik *f* beam optics
Bündeltabelle *f* bundle table
Bündeltabelleneintrag *m* bundle table entry
Bundsteg *m* gutter, inside margin[s] *(layout)*
Bunsen-Fotometer *n* Bunsen photometer, grease-spot [photo]meter
Bunsen-Gesetz *n* Bunsen Roscoe law, [Bunsen-Roscoe] reciprocity law
bunt chromatic *(color)*; varicolored, brightly colored
Buntaufbau *m* chromatic composition *(reprographic technology)*
Buntfarbe *f* chromatic (dye) color, pigmented color
Buntfarbenaddition *f* undercolor addition, UCA *(reprography)*

Buntfotografie *f* color photography *(s.a. Farbfotografie)*
Buntglas *n* stained glass
Buntheit *f* chromaticity; chromaticness, chromatic content; [Munsell] chroma
Buntheitssignal *n s.* Chrominanzsignal
Buntlabor *n s.* Farblabor
Buntpapier *n* tinted (colored) paper
Buntsehen *n* color (chromatic) vision
Buntton *m* [color] hue, dye hue, [color] tone, tint
Bunttonbild *n* hue image
Bunttonstufe *f* hue step
Bunttonwinkel *m* hue angle
Burgers-Vektor *m* Burgers vector *(electron microscopy)*
Bürodokumente-Architektur *f* office document architecture, ODA
Bürodokumente-Austauschformat *n* office document interchange format, ODIF
Bürodruck *m* office printing
Bürodrucker *m* office printer
Bürodruckmaschine *f* duplicating machine (device), duplicator, manifolder
Bürofarbdrucker *m* office color-printing device
Bürografik *f* office graphics
Bürokommunikation *f* office communication
Bürokopie *f* office copy
Bürokopierer *m*, **Bürokopiergerät** *n* office [photo]copier, office copy[ing] machine
Bürokopiertechnik *f*, **Bürokopierverfahren** *n* office [convenience] copying
Bürovervielfältigung *f* office copying
Burst *m* [color synchronizing] burst, [color] burst signal, color burst
~/**alternierender** alternating burst
Burstamplitude *f* [color] burst amplitude
Burstfehler *m* burst error
Burstgenerator *m* burst generator
Burst-Kennimpuls *m* burst flag (gate), burst key
Burstphase *f* burst phase
Burstrauschen *n* burst noise
Burstsignal *n* burst signal
Burststörung *f* burst-type interference
Burstsynchronisation *f* burst synchronization
Bus *m* [data] bus, main bus *(signal transmission path in a computer system)*
~/**bidirektionaler** bidirectional bus
~/**lokaler** local (system) bus
~/**unidirektionaler** unidirectional bus
~/**universeller serieller** universal serial bus, USB *(for connecting peripheral devices)*
Busadresse *f* bus address
Busanschluss *m* [data] bus connector
Busbandbreite *f* bus bandwidth
Busbreite *f* bus width
Büschelfehler *m s.* Burstfehler
Buselektrode *f* bus electrode
Busfehler *m* bus error

Buslaufzeit *f* transmission path delay, response propagative time
Busnetz *n* bus network
Busschnittstelle *f* bus interface
Busstandard *m* bus standard
Bussystem *n* bus system
Busverwaltung *f* bus arbitration
Butterworth-Filter *n* Butterworth [low-pass] filter, BLPF
Butterworth-Hochpass *m* Butterworth high-pass filter, BHPF
Butterworth-Tiefpass *m* Butterworth low-pass filter, BLPF
Butzen *m* hot spot, hickey, bulls (fish) eye *(printing defect)*
Buzz-Track-Tonspur *f* buzz track *(optical sound test film)*
B-Verstärker *m* bridger amplifier *(cable television)*
B-Wicklung *f* B wind (type) *(of a motion-picture film)*
Byte *n* [data] byte, octet *(group of eight bits)*
Bytefolge *f* byte order
Byteumfang *m* byte size

C

C C [programming] language, C *(compiler language)*
Cache *m s.* 1. Kasch; 2. Cachespeicher
Cachespeicher *m* cache [memory], data cache
CAD-Bildschirm *m* computer-aided design display
Cadmiumsulfid-Belichtungsmesser *m* cadmium sulfide meter, CdS exposure meter
Cadmiumsulfid-Widerstand *m* cadmium sulfide photoelectric cell, cadmium sulfide [photo]cell, CdS [cell]
Cadrage *f* framing *(cinema)*
Caesiumdampflampe *f* cesium vapor lamp
Caesiumiodid *n* cesium iodide
Caesiumoxidzelle *f* cesium oxide cell *(photoemissive detector)*
Calcit *m* calcite, calcareous spar
Calcit-Interferenzmikroskop *n* calcite interference microscope
Calciumfluorid *n* calcium fluoride *(optical material)*
Calciumiodid *n* calcium iodide
Calciumwolframat *n* calcium tungstate
Calciumwolframat-Verstärkerfolie *f* calcium tungstate intensifying screen
Callier-Effekt *m* Callier effect *(selective scattering of light)*
Callier-Quotient *m* Callier coefficient, Q factor
Camcorder *m* camcorder, camera-recorder
~/**digitaler** digital camcorder
Camcorderbatterie *f* camcorder battery
Camcorderkabel *n* camcorder cable
Camcorderkassette *f* camcorder cassette
Camcorderobjektiv *n* camcorder lens
Camera *f* **lucida** camera lucida *(early drawing aid)*
~ **obscura** camera [obscura], pinhole camera
Candela *f* candela, standard candle, [new] candle, sd *(SI unit of luminous intensity)*
~ **pro Quadratmeter** candela per square meter, nit *(SI unit of luminance)*
Canny-Filter *n*, **Canny-Operator** *m* Canny edge detector, Canny [edge] operator, Canny filter *(computer vision)*
C-Anschluss *m* C-mount *(objective)*
Capriblaueffekt *m* Capri-blue effect
Carbocyanin *n* carbocyanine *(dye)*
Carbon... *s.* Karbon...
Carbrodruck *m* 1. carbro process; 2. carbro print
Carcinotron *n* carcinotron, backward-wave oscillator (tube)
Cassegrain-Antenne *f* Cassegrain antenna
Cassegrain-Coudé-Teleskop *n* Cassegrain-Coudé telescope
Cassegrain-Fokus *m*/**modifizierter** modified Cassegrain focus
Cassegrain-Spektrograf *m* Cassegrain spectrograph
Cassegrain-Spiegel *m* Cassegrain mirror
Cassegrain-Spiegelteleskop *n* Cassegrain reflecting telescope, Cassegrainian telescope
Cassegrain-System *n* Cassegrain [lens] system
CCD *f* CCD, charge-coupled device *(s.a. Bauelement/ladungsgekoppeltes)*
CCD-Abtaster *m s.* CCD-Filmabtaster
CCD-Astrokamera *f* astronomical CCD camera
CCD-Bauelementanordnung *f* CCD array
CCD-Bildsensor *m*, **CCD-Bildwandler** *m* CCD imager (image sensor), CCD imaging device, CCD image array, image-sensing CCD
CCD-Chip *m* CCD [camera] chip, CCD imaging chip
CCD-Detektor *m s.* CCD-Sensor
CCD-Element *n* charge-coupled device (detector), CCD
CCD-Farbkamera *f* color CCD camera
CCD-Farbscanner *m* CCD color scanner
CCD-Farbsensor *m* color CCD
CCD-Fernsehkamera *f* CCD television (TV) camera
CCD-Filmabtaster *m* CCD (charge-coupled device) telecine
CCD-Flächenchip *m*, **CCD-Flächensensor** *m* CCD wafer (receptor plate); area charge-coupled device, area array CCD [imager], two-dimensional CCD array
CCD-Kamera *f* CCD[-type] camera, [CCD-]chip camera, charge-coupled [device] camera
~/**gekühlte** cooled CCD camera
~/**hochempfindliche** high sensitivity CCD camera
~/**rauscharme** low-noise CCD camera
~/**verstärkende** intensified charge-coupled device camera, ICCD camera
CCD-Matrix *f* CCD array
CCD-Matrixkamera *f* [matrix] array camera, area array camera
CCD-Pixel *n* CCD pixel
CCD-Sensor *m* CCD sensor, CCD [photo]detector
~/**frontbestrahlter** front[-side]-illuminated CCD
~/**handelsüblicher (kommerzieller)** commercial-grade CCD
~ **mit Bildauswahl** frame transfer [CCD] imager, frame-transfer device
~/**rückseitenbestrahlter** backlit CCD, back[side]-illuminated CCD, back-thinned CCD

~/wissenschaftlicher scientific-grade CCD, scientific charge-coupled device
CCD-Spalte f CCD column
CCD-Technik f, **CCD-Technologie** f CCD technology
CCD-Videokamera f CCD video camera
CCD-Wandler m s. CCD-Sensor
CCD-Zeile f linear CCD [detector array], linear array CCD [imager]; single-line CCD
CCD-Zeilenkamera f linear array [CCD] camera
CCD-Zeilensensor m linear CCD image sensor *(s.a.* CCD-Zeile*)*
CC-Filter n s. Farbkorrekturfilter
CCIR-Norm f CCIR standard *(digital component video)*
CD f compact disc, CD
CD/beschreibbare recordable compact disc, compact disc recordable, CD-R
CD/interaktive compact disc interactive, CD-I
CD/löschbare compact disc erasable, CD-E
CD/wiederbeschreibbare compact disc rewritable, CD-RW
CD-Brenner m CD (compact disc) burner, CD writer
CD-Platte f compact disc, CD
CD-ROM f CD-ROM, compact disc read-only memory
CD-ROM-Laufwerk n CD-ROM drive
CD-Schreiber m s. CD-Brenner
CD-Spielfilm m CD movie
CdS-Widerstand m cadmium sulfide [photo]cell, CdS
CD-Video n CD (compact disc) video, CDV, video compact disc, video CD, VCD
Cedille f cedilla *(diacritic)*
Cellofolie f cel[l], animation (overlay) cel, acetate cel (sheet)
Celluloid n celluloid *(thermoplastic)*
Celluloidrollfilm m celluloid [roll] film
Cellulose f cellulose *(polysaccharide)*
Celluloseacetat n [cellulose] acetate, acetyl[ated] cellulose
Celluloseacetatfilm m [cellulose] acetate film
Cellulosediacetat n cellulose diacetate
Celluloseester m cellulose ester
Cellulosenitrat n cellulose nitrate, nitrocellulose *(film base)*
Cellulosenitratfilm m [cellulose] nitrate film, nitrate-based film
Cellulosepropionat n cellulose propionate
Cellulosetriacetat n cellulose triacetate, triacetate cellulose *(film material)*
Ceriumoxid n cerium oxide *(polishing material)*
C-Fassung f C mount *(standard screw-type lens mount)*
CGA-Grafikkarte f color graphics adapter, CGA
C-Gewinde n s. C-Fassung

Chalkogenidglas n chalcogenide glass *(optical material)*
Charakter m/**computergenerierter** computer graphics character, computer-generated actor; cyborg, avatar *(cinema)*
Chefbeleuchter m chief lighting technician, [chief set] electrician, gaffer *(cinema)*; lighting supervisor (director) *(esp. in computer graphics)*
Chefkameramann m director of photography, DP *(esp. USA)*; lighting cameraman *(chiefly British)*
Chemie f/**fotografische** photographic chemistry
Chemiefilm m s. Silberhalogenidfilm
Chemiegraf m photoengraver
Chemiegrafie f 1. photoengraving [process]; 2. photoengraving, photoengraved plate; 3. photoengraving *(print)*
Chemiekalienmixer m chemical automixer *(film processing)*
Chemieverschleppung f carryover *(of processing solutions)*
chemilumineszent chemiluminescent
Chemilumineszenz f chemiluminescence
Chemisorption f chemisorption
Chemolumineszenz f s. Chemilumineszenz
Chiasma n optic chiasm[a]
Child-Langmuir-Strom m Child-Langmuir current *(cathode-ray tube)*
Chip m chip ; microprocessor
Chipkamera f chip (solid-state) camera *(s.a.* CCD-Kamera*)*
Chipkarte f smart card
Chipoberfläche f chip surface
Chipsatz m chip set
Chi-Quadrat-Verteilung f chi-square distribution *(probability density function)*
Chirp m chirp, frequency sweep *(laser)*
Chirurgie f/**bildgeführte (bildgestützte)** image-guided surgery, IGS
~/computergestützte computer-assisted surgery, CAS
Chlor n chlorine
Chlorbromemulsion f chlorobromide emulsion
Chlorbrompapier n chlorobromide paper
Chlorbromsilber n silver chlorobromide, silver bromochloride
Chlorbromsilberpapier n chlorobromide paper
Chloridpapier n s. Chlorsilberpapier
Chloriodidemulsion f chloroiodide (iodochloride) emulsion
Chlorion n chlorine ion
Chlorsilber n silver chloride
Chlorsilbergelatine f gelatinochloride, silver chloride gelatin
Chlorsilber-Gelatine-Emulsionspapier n gelatin-silver chloride paper; gelatin chloride printing-out paper

Chlorsilberkollodium *n* silver chloride collodion
Chlorsilberpapier *n* [silver] chloride paper
Cholangiografie *f* cholangiography
Cholangioskop *n*, **Choledochoskop** *n* choledochoscope
Choroplethe *f s.* Karte/choroplethische
Christiansen-Filter *n* Christiansen [effect] filter; dispersion filter
Chromakanal *m* chrominance channel
Chromakey-Gerät *n*, **Chromakey-Mischer** *m* chroma keyer
Chromakey-Technik *f*, **Chromakey-Verfahren** *n* chroma key[ing], keying; electronic matting
Chromalaun *n* chrome alum, chromic potassium sulfate *(gelatin hardener)*
Chromalaunfixierer *m* chrome alum fixer
Chromasignal *n s.* Chrominanzsignal
Chromat *n* chromate, chromium salt
Chromatik *f* chromatics *(colorimetry)*
chromatisch chromatic, nonachromatic *(lens)*
Chromatizität *f* chromaticity; chromaticness, chromatic content, colorfulness
Chromatizitätswert *m* chromaticity coordinate
Chromatopsie *f* chromatopsia, colored vision
Chromatoskop *n s.* Chromoskop
Chromatverfahren *n* chromate process
Chromdioxid *n* chromium dioxide
Chromdioxidbandmaterial *n* chromium dioxide magnetic material
Chromgelatine *f* dichromate[d] gelatin, DCG, bichromated gelatin
Chrominanz *f* 1. chrominance, chroma, C; 2. *s.* Chrominanzsignal
Chrominanzamplitude *f* chrominance amplitude
Chrominanzauflösung *f* chrominance (chroma) resolution
Chrominanzbandbreite *f* chrominance bandwidth
Chrominanzbild *n* chrominance frame
Chrominanzblock *m* chrominance block *(image sequence coding)*
Chrominanzinformation *f* chrominance information
Chrominanzkanal *m* chrominance channel
Chrominanzkoeffizient *m* chrominance coefficient
Chrominanzkomponente *f* chrominance component
Chrominanzparameter *m* chrominance parameter
Chrominanzsignal *n* chrominance (chroma) signal, color information signal, C [signal] *(video)*
Chrominanz-Störabstand *m* chrominance signal-to-[random-]noise ratio, chroma noise, color[ed] noise

Chrominanz-Übersprechen *n* cross-color [artifact], color crossover
Chrominanzverzerrung *f* chrominance distortion
chromogen chromogenic
Chromogenentwicklung *f* chromogenic (color-coupling) development
Chromolithografie *f* 1. chromolithography; 2. chromolithograph *(print)*
chromolithografisch chromolithographic
chromolytisch chromolytic
Chromophor *n(m)* chromophore
Chromoskop *n* chromoscope
Chromosomenbildanalyse *f* chromosome analysis
Chromsalz *n* chromium salt, chromate
Chromsäure *f* chromic acid *(developer constituent)*
Chronofotografie *f* chronophotography
chronofotografisch chronophotographic
Chronokinematografie *f* chronocinematography
CID-Bildaufnehmer *m* CID imager
CID-Sensor *m* charge-injection device, CID
CIE-Farbdiagramm *n*, **CIE-Farbendreieck** *n* CIE [standard] chromaticity diagram
CIE-Farbraum *m* CIE color space
CI-Einschubschacht *m* CI (common-interface) slot
CIE-Kegel *m* [der sichtbaren Farben] *s.* CIE-Farbraum
CIELAB-Farbmodell *n*, **CIELAB-Farbraum** *m* CIELAB [color] space, CIELAB system
CIELUV-Farbmodell *n* CIELUV color space, CIELUV system
CIE-Normfarbtafel *f* CIE [standard] chromaticity diagram
CIE-Normlichtart *f* CIE [standard] illuminant, CIE source
CIE-Normvalenzsystem *n* CIE [standard primary reference] system *(colorimetry)*
Cinch-Stecker *m* Cinch (RCA) plug, RCA [phono] connector
Cinch-Verbindung *f* Cinch connection *(video)*
Cine... *s.a.* Kine...
Cinemascope[verfahren] *n* Cinemascope, C-scope, Scope, 1:2.35 anamorphic system
CI-Wert *m* CI (contrast index) value
Clayden-Effekt *m*, **Clayden-Entwicklungseffekt** *m* Clayden effect, black lightning
Clip *m* clip *(of filmed or videotaped material)*
Cliparts *pl* clip art
Clipping *n* clipping *(computer graphics)*
Clipping-Algorithmus *m* clipping algorithm
Clipping-Anzeiger *m* clipping indicator
Clipping-Modus *m* clipping mode
Clipping-Operation *f* clipping operation
Clipping-Rechteck *n* clip rectangle

Codierung

Clique f clique *(e.g. as neighborhood structure of pixels)*
Close-up n s. Nahaufnahme
Closing n, **Closing-Operation** f closing *(binary image processing)*
Cluster m/**unscharfer** fuzzy cluster
Clusteralgorithmus m clustering algorithm
~/**hierarchischer** hierarchical clustering algorithm
Clusteranalyse f 1. cluster analysis; 2. s. Klassifikation/unüberwachte
~/**histogrammbasierte** histogram-based cluster analysis
Clusteranalysealgorithmus m clustering algorithm
Clusteranalyseverfahren n cluster analysis method
Clustergeometrie f cluster geometry
Clustern n, **Clusterung** f clustering, clumping
Clusterzentrum n cluster center
Clutter m [radar] clutter, clutter interference
Clutterspektrum n clutter spectrum
Clutterunterdrückung f clutter suppression
CMOS-Bildsensor m, **CMOS-Sensor** m CMOS imager, complementary metal oxide semiconductor [image] sensor, active pixel sensor, APS
CMOS-Technologie f CMOS technology
CMY-Farbmodell n, **CMY-Farbraum** m CMY (cyan-magenta-yellow) color space, subtractive color system
CMYK-Farbmodell n, **CMYK-Farbraum** m CMYK model (color space) *(from cyan, magenta, yellow, black)*
Cobaltglas n cobalt (woods) glass
Code m code
~/**bewegungsadaptiver** motion-adaptive code
~/**binärer** binary code; PCM (pulse code modulation) code
~/**digitaler** digital code
~/**fehlerkorrigierender** error-correcting code, error correction (protection) code, ECC
~/**fraktaler** fractal code
~/**grafischer** graphical code
~/**größenvariabler** s. ~/längenvariabler
~/**kanonischer** canonical code
~/**kompakter** compact (optimum) code, minimum redundancy code
~/**längenvariabler** variable-length code, variable-size code
~ **mit fester Symbollänge** fixed-length code, run-length-limited code
~/**präfixfreier** prefix code, instantaneously decodable code
~/**redundanter** redundant code
~/**sequentieller** sequential code
~/**sofort decodierbarer** instantaneously decodable code, prefix code
~/**zyklischer** cyclic code

Codealphabet n code alphabet
Codebit n code bit
Codeblock m code block
Codebuch n codebook, [coding] dictionary
Codec m(n) 1. codec, [en]coder-decoder *(hardware device)*; 2. compression-decompression algorithm
Codec-Filter n codec filter
Codeelement n code element
Codeerweiterung f code extension
Codefolge f coding (code) sequence
Codehandschuh m s. Datenhandschuh
Codeklasse f class of codes
Codekompatibilität f code compatibility
Codelänge f code length
Codenummer f code number
Coder m s. Codierer
Coderate f code rate
Codesatz m code set
Codesignal n code signal
Codespreizung f interleaving
Codesteuerzeichen n code extension character
Codesymbol n code symbol
Codetabelle f code table
Codeumsetzer m decoder
Codevektor m code vector
Codewert m code value
Codewort n code word *(sequence of binary bits)*
~/**binäres** binary code word
~/**längenvariables** variable-length code word
Codewortlänge f code word length
~/**mittlere** average code word length, bit rate
Codieralgorithmus m coding algorithm
Codierartefakt m coding artifact
codierbar codable
Codierbarkeit f codability
Codiereffizienz f coding (code) efficiency
Codiereinheit f coding unit
~ /**kleinste** minimum coded unit, MCU
codieren to [en]code; to encode *(esp. by the transmitting unit)*
Codierer m [en]coder; [data] compressor
~/**arithmetischer** arithmetic coder
~/**szenenadaptiver** scene-adaptive coder
Codiererschleife f encoder loop
Codierfehler m [en]coding error
Codierfolge f [en]coding order
Codiergewinn m coding gain, compression factor
Codierhierarchie f coding hierarchy
Codierschema n [en]coding scheme
Codierstandard m coding standard
Codiertechnik f coding technique
Codierung f [en]coding *(s.a. under Kompression)*
~/**adaptiv-arithmetische** adaptive arithmetic coding
~/**adaptive** adaptive [en]coding
~/**algebraische** algebraic coding
~/**arithmetische** arithmetic coding

Codierung

~/**asymmetrische** asymmetrical coding
~/**bewegungskompensierende** motion-compensated coding
~/**binäre** binary [en]coding
~/**binäre arithmetische** binary arithmetic coding
~/**blockweise** block[-based] coding, area character coding *(class of image compression techniques)*
~/**differentielle** 1. differential (relative) coding, differencing, predictive (previous-pixel) coding; 2. *s.* Differenzpulscodemodulation
~/**digitale** digital [en]coding
~/**dynamische** dynamic coding
~/**fraktale** fractal [en]coding
~/**generische** generic coding
~/**geschaltete** switchable coding
~/**hierarchische** hierarchical[-mode] coding *(s.a. ~/mehrstufige)* layered (embedded) coding
~/**hybride** hybrid [transform/waveform] coding
~/**inhaltsbasierte arithmetische** content-based arithmetic encoding, CAE
~/**interpolative** interpolative coding
~/**kontextbasierte binäre arithmetische** context-based binary arithmetic coding
~/**lineare** linear encoding (mapping)
~/**mehrdimensionale** multidimensional coding
~/**mehrstufige** multiple [en]coding, layered (embedded) coding
~ **mit [sehr] kleiner Bitrate** [very] low-bit-rate coding
~ **mit variabler Wortlänge** variable-length [statistical] coding, VLC, entropy [en]coding
~/**modellbasierte** model-based coding
~/**nahezu verlustlose** near-lossless coding
~/**nichtlineare** nonlinear encoding
~/**n-wertige** n-ary encoding
~/**objektbasierte** object-based coding
~/**objektorientierte** object-oriented coding
~/**prädiktive** *s.* ~/differentielle 1.
~/**progressive** progressive [en]coding, pyramidal [en]coding, sequential [en]coding
~/**räumliche** spatial [en]coding
~/**relative** *s.* ~/differentielle 1.
~/**schaltbare** switchable coding
~/**segmentierte** segmented coding
~/**semantische** semantic[al] coding
~/**semiadaptive** semiadaptive [en]coding
~/**skalierbare** scalable coding
~/**speicherlose** memoryless coding
~/**statistische** 1. statistical [en]coding; entropy [en]coding; 2. *s.* ~ mit variabler Wortlänge
~/**syntaxbasierte arithmetische** syntax-based arithmetic coding, SAC
~/**verlustbehaftete** lossy [en]coding
~/**verlustfreie (verlustlose)** lossless [symbol] coding, lossless (exact) encoding; lossless compression
~/**verzögerungsarme** low-delay coding
~/**voll adaptive** *s.* ~/dynamische
~/**wahrnehmungsbasierte** perceptual (perceptive) coding, perception-based [image] coding
~/**waveletbasierte** wavelet-based coding
~/**wissensbasierte** knowledge-based coding
~/**zonale** zonal coding (sampling)
~/**zweiwertige** binary encoding
Codierungsalgorithmus *m* [en]coding algorithm
Codierungsansatz *m* coding approach
Codierungsart *f* coding type
Codierungsartefakt *n* coding artifact
Codierungs-Decodierungspaar *n* encoder/decoder, codec
Codierungseffizienz *f* coding (code) efficiency
Codierungseinheit *f* coding unit *(e.g. of a video sequence)*
Codierungsentscheidung *f* coding-mode decision
Codierungsfehler *m* coding error
Codierungsfunktion *f* encoding function
Codierungsleistung *f* coding performance
Codierungsmethode *f* [en]coding method
Codierungsmodus *m* coding mode
Codierungsparameter *m* [en]coding parameter
Codierungsredundanz *f* coding redundancy
Codierungsregel *f* [en]coding rule
Codierungsreihenfolge *f* [en]coding order
Codierungsschaltung *f* encoding circuitry
Codierungsschema *n* [en]coding scheme, compression scheme
Codierungsschicht *f* coding layer *(e.g. of a neural network)*
Codierungsschleife *f* [en]coding loop
Codierungsschritt *m* coding step
Codierungssequenz *f* [en]coding sequence
Codierungssoftware *f* encoding software
Codierungsstil *m* coding style
Codierungsstrategie *f* coding strategy
Codierungssyntax *f* coding syntax
Codierungssystem *n* coding system
Codierungstabelle *f* [en]coding table, dictionary
Codierungstechnik *f* coding technique
Codierungstheorem *n* coding theorem
~/**rauschbehaftetes** noisy [channel] coding theorem, Shannon's second theorem
~/**rauschfreies** noiseless [source] coding theorem, Shannon's first theorem
Codierungstheorie *f* coding (structural information) theory
Codierverfahren *n* [en]coding process; coding technique
Codierverzögerung *f* [en]coding delay

Codiervorgang *m* encoding procedure, [en]coding process
Codierwerkzeug *n* coding tool
Collage *f* collage, papier collé
collagieren to collage
Collotypeverfahren *n* collotype [process], photogelatin process
Color... *s.a.* Farb...
Coloraufsichtsbild *n* color print
Colorfilm *m* color [photographic] film, photographic color film
Colorfilter *n* color filter
Colormaterial *n* [photographic] color material
Color-Negativmaterial *n* negative color material
Colorpapier *n* color [print] paper, color photographic paper
Colorpositiv *n* color positive, positive color image
Colorpositivverarbeitung *f* color print processing, color printing
Colorsofortbild *n* instant color image; instant color print
Colorumkehrmaterial *n* color reversal material
Colorverarbeitung *f* color processing
COM-Film *m* computer output microfilm, COM
Compiler *m* compiler *(data processing)*
Compton-Effekt *m s.* Compton-Streuung
Compton-Elektron *n* Compton electron
Compton-Linie *f* Compton line
Compton-Streuung *f* Compton scattering (effect) *(X-ray attenuation)*
Computer *m* computer, processor *(binary logic device)*
~/**analoger** analog computer
~/**digitaler** digital computer
~/**[kohärenter] optischer** optical computer
~/**tragbarer** portable computer; laptop [computer]; notebook [computer]
Computeralgorithmus *m* computer algorithm
Computerangiografie *f* CT (computed tomography) angiography, CTA, digital subtraction angiography, DAS
computerangiografisch CT angiographic
Computeranimateur *m s.* Computeranimator
Computeranimation *f* computer[-enhanced] animation, computer-assisted animation; computer-generated animation
Computeranimationssoftware *f* computer animation software
Computeranimationssystem *n* computer animation system
Computeranimationtechnik *f* computer animation technique
Computeranimator *m* computer animator, digital (computer graphics) animator, CG animator

Computeranschluss *m* [personal] computer link system
Computeranschlusszubehör *n* computer connection accessories
Computerarbeitsplatz *m*/**grafischer** graphics workstation
Computerauflösung *f* computer [monitor] resolution
Computerausdruck *m* printout; [paper] hard copy; hard copy image
Computerausgabe *f* computer[ized] output
Computerausgabe-Mikrofilm *m* computer output microfilm
Computerausgabe-Mikrofilmrecorder *m* computer output microfilm recorder, COM recorder
Computer-Betriebssystem *n* computer's operating system
Computerbild *n* computer[ized] image, computer-generated (computer-produced) image, synthetic (computer-synthesized) picture; computer-graphic[s] image, CG image
~/**bittiefenbegrenztes** limited-bit-depth CG image
Computerbildanalyse *f* computer [image] analysis
Computerbildbearbeitung *f* computer image (picture) processing, computer imaging
Computerbildbearbeitungssystem *n* computer imaging (image-processing) system
Computerbilddatei *f* computer image file
Computerbilderzeugung *f* computer image generation, CIG
Computerbildgenerator *m* computer image (graphics) generator
Computerbildröhre *f* computer-monitor CRT (cathode-ray tube)
Computerbildschirm *m* computer [image] display, computer [display] screen
Computerbildseite *f* computer image page
Computerbildsynthese *f* computer image synthesis, computer synthesis of images
Computerbildverarbeitung *f* computer image (picture) processing, computer imaging
Computerbildverarbeitungssystem *n* computer imaging (image processing) system
Computerbildwelt *f s.* Realität/virtuelle
Computerblitz *m* computer flash
Computerchip *m* computer chip *(s.a. Mikrochip)*
Computerdarstellung *f* computer representation *(e.g. of an object system)*
Computerdateiformat *n* computer file format
Computerdiskette *f* floppy disk, FD, diskette
Computerdruck *m* computer printing
Computerdrucker *m* computer printer *(s.a. under Drucker)*

Computereingabegerät *n* computer input device
Computerfarbbildschirm *m* multicolor display, color display [terminal]
Computerfestplatte *f* computer (hard) disk
Computerfigur *f* computer-generated actor, computer graphics character
Computerfilm *m* computer-animated film, computer-generated film (movie), [full] CG feature
Computerfoto *n* photo-quality CG image
computergeneriert computer-generated, CG, computer-produced, computer-synthesized
Computergeometrie *f* computational geometry
computergeometrisch computational geometric
Computergrafik *f* 1. computer graphics [technology], computational graphics, CG *(s.a. under* Grafik*)*; 2. computer[-generated] graphic, computer graphics image (construct)
~/**dreidimensionale** three-dimensional graphics, 3-D [computer] graphics
~/**fotorealistische** photo-quality CG image
~/**interaktive** interactive computer graphics
~/**zweidimensionale** two-dimensional graphics, 2-D [computer] graphics
Computergrafikalgorithmus *m* [computer] graphics algorithm
Computergrafikarbeitsplatz *m* computer graphics workstation
Computergrafikbild *n s.* Computergrafik 2.
Computergrafiker *m* computer graphics worker (professional), [computer] graphicist, [computer] graphics practitioner
Computergrafikhardware *f* computer graphics hardware
Computergrafik-Metadatei *f* computer graphics metafile, CGM
Computergrafikprogramm *n* computer graphics program
Computergrafikschnittstelle *f* computer graphics interface, CGI
Computergrafikspiel *n s.* Computerspiel
Computergrafiksystem *n* computer graphics system
computergrafisch computer-graphic
Computerholografie *f* computer-generated holography
Computerhologramm *n* computer-generated hologram, CGH
Computerisierung *f* computerization
Computerkunst *f* computer art
Computerlaufwerk *n* computer drive
Computerlayout *n* computer layout
Computerleistung *f* computer [processing] power
computerlesbar computer-readable, machine-readable *(e.g. image data)*
Computerlink *m(n) s.* Computeranschluss

Computer-Malprogramm *n* [computer] paint program
Computermaus *f* [computer] mouse, puck *(handheld input device)*
Computermodell *n* computer model *(as a system of mathematical equations)*
Computermodellierer *m* computer modeler
Computermodellierung *f* computer modeling
Computermodem *n(m)* computer modem (modulator/demodulator)
Computermonitor *m* computer [display] monitor; desktop computer monitor
Computernetz *n* computer network, network of computers
~/**lokales** local area network, LAN
~/**unternehmensinternes** intranet *(nonpublic computer network)*
Computerplatine *f* [computer] motherboard, logic board, main computer circuit board
Computerprogramm *n* computer [software] program
Computerprogrammfehler *m* bug
Computerradiografie *f* computed radiography, CR
Computerradiologie *f* computed radiology
Computerretusche *f* computer enhancement
Computersatz *m* computer[ized] typesetting, electronic (programmed) composition, electronic front end
Computersatzsystem *n* computerized [photo]typesetting system
Computerschirmbild *n* computer screen image
Computerschnittstelle *f* computer interface
Computersehen *n* computer vision; [industrial] machine vision
Computersimulation *f* computer[-generated] simulation
Computerspeicher *m* computer memory [device], computer storage
Computerspeicherchip *m* computer memory chip
Computerspeicherung *f* computer storage
Computerspiel *n* computer game
Computerspielfigur *f* game character
Computerspielgrafik *f* game graphics
Computersprache *f* 1. computer (machine) language; 2. computer parlance (lingo), computerese
Computersteckkarte *f* plug-in computer board
Computersteuerung *f* computer control
Computertastatur *f* computer keyboard
Computertechnologie *f* computer technology
Computertomograf *m* comput[eriz]ed tomography scanner, C[A]T scanner, CT machine

Computertomografie f comput[eriz]ed tomography, CT, computer-assisted tomography, comput[eriz]ed axial tomography, CAT; CAT [scan] recording, CAT scanning, CT scan
~/**industrielle** industrial comput[eriz]ed tomography
~/**ultraschnelle** ultrafast CT
Computertomografiegerät n s. Computertomograf
computertomografisch comput[eriz]ed tomographic
Computertomogramm n computed tomogram, C[A]T scan, CT image
Computertrick m computer-generated [special] effect, computer (digital) special effect
Computertrickfilm m s. Computerfilm
Computertypografie f computer typography
Computerverarbeitung f computer processing *(e.g. of image data)*
Computervideo n computer video
Computervisualisierung f computer visualization
Computervolumenhologramm n computer-generated volume hologram, CGVH
Cooke-Objektiv n Cooke lens (objective)
Cook-Torrance-Schattierungsmodell n Cook and Torrance [reflection] model, Cook-Torrance shading model *(computer graphics)*
Coolidge-Röhre f Coolidge tube *(X-ray tube)*
Copyright n copyright
Cordband n sprocketed magnetic tape
Cornea f [eye] cornea
Cornu-Doppelprisma n Cornu double prism
Coronardraht m s. Koronadraht
Cortex m/**visueller** visual (striate) cortex *(of the brain)*
Cosinus... s. Kosinus...
Coudé-Fokus m coudé focus *(telescope)*
Coudé-System n coudé [optical] system, coudé arrangement
Coulomb-Streuung f Coulomb scattering *(of charged particles)*
covalieren to lubricate *(processed print film)*
CPS-Emitron n s. Orthikon
Cross-Color-Effekt m cross-color [artifact], color crossover
Crossfilter n s. Gitterfilter
Cross-Luminanz-Effekt m cross-luminance [artifact], cross-luma artifact
CRT-Fotosetzanlage f cathode-ray-tube phototypesetter
CSG-Baum m CSG (constructive solid geometry) tree *(computer graphics)*
CT s. Computertomografie
CT-Aufnahme f, **CT-Bild** n CT image, CT slice [image], CAT scan

CTL-Impuls m control track pulse (signal) *(videotape)*
CTL-Schnitt m control track editing
CT-Scanner m s. Computertomograf
Cursor m cursor, [screen] pointer
~/**mausgesteuerter** mouse-controlled cursor
Cursorpfeil m [cursor] arrow
Cut-in m s. Einschnittszene
cutten to edit, to cut
Cutter m [film] editor, cinema (motion-picture) editor, cutter
Cutterassistent m assistant [film] editor, assistant picture editor
Cutterbericht m script *(s.a. Drehbericht)*
cuttern s. cutten
CW-Doppler m continuous-wave Doppler [ultrasound]
CW-Laser m cw laser, continuous-wave laser
CW-Radar n cw radar, continuous-wave radar
Cyan n cyan, blue-green *(subtractive primary color)*; process blue *(printing)*
cyanblau cyan, blue-green, green-blue
Cyanentwickler m cyan [dye] developer
Cyanfarbstoff m cyan dye
Cyanin n, **Cyaninfarbstoff** m cyanine [dye]
Cyankuppler m cyan[-forming] coupler, cyan dye-forming coupler
Cyanoferrat n ferricyanide *(bleaching agent)*
Cyanometer n cyanometer
Cyanometrie f cyanometry
Cyanotypie f 1. cyanotype (ferro-prussiate) process, blueprint (Prussian-blue) process; 2. cyanotype, blueprint
Cyantoner m cyan toner
Cyberianer m cyber[ian] citizen, cyborg *(virtual reality)*
Cyberkrankheit f cybersickness
Cyberspace m cyberspace, virtual space (reality system); Internet, net

D

Dachansatz *m* beak terminal *(letterface)*
Dachantenne *f* roof antenna (aerial)
Dachkant[en]prisma *n* roof (Amici) prism
Daguerreotypie *f* 1. daguerreotype [photographic] process, daguerreotypy; 2. daguerreotype [image], daguerreotype picture
Daguerreotypiekamera *f* daguerreotype camera
Daguerreotypieplatte *f* daguerreotype plate
daguerreotypieren to daguerreotype
Daguerreotypist *m* daguerreotypist
Dakryozystografie *f* dacryocystography
Daktylogramm *n* dactylogram, dactylograph, fingerprint
Daktyloskop *m* dactyloscopist
Daktyloskopie *f* dactyloscopy
daktyloskopisch dactyloscopic
Daltonismus *m* 1. Daltonism, red-green blindness; 2. *s.* Farbenblindheit
Dammarlack *m* dam[m]ar varnish
Dämmerlicht *n* dim light
Dämmerung *f* twilight
Dämmerungsleistung *f* twilight efficiency *(telescope)*
Dämmerungssehen *n* 1. dim-light vision, mesopic vision; 2. *s.* Dunkelsehen
Dämmerungszahl *f* twilight factor *(binocular)*
Dampfblasenstrahl *m* bubble jet *(ink jet printer)*
Dampfblasenverfahren *n* bubble-jet process *(ink-jet printing)*
Dämpfung *f* attenuation; damping
Dämpfungsartefakt *n* attenuation artifact
Dämpfungskoeffizient *m* attenuation (extinction) coefficient
Dämpfungskonstante *f* attenuation (damping) constant
Dämpfungskorrektur *f* attenuation correction *(emission tomography)*
Dämpfungskraft *f* damping force
Dämpfungsmaß *n* attenuation constant
Dämpfungsmatrix *f* damping matrix
Danebenschauen *n*/**gezieltes** averted vision *(viewing technique in astronomy)*
Darmspiegel *m* enteroscope
Darmspiegelung *f* enteroscopy
darstellbar representable; displayable
darstellen to represent; to display
~/**bildlich** to pictorialize, to picturize, to depict, to render *(s.a.* abbilden*)*
~/**computergrafisch** to render
~/**grafisch** to graph
~/**optisch** to visualize

Darsteller *m*/**digitaler (virtueller)** computer-generated actor, computer graphics character; cyborg, avatar *(cinema)*
Darstellung *f* representation, portrayal *(s.a. under* Abbildung*)*; display
~/**audiovisuelle** audiovisual presentation
~/**axonometrische** axonometric representation
~/**bereichsbasierte** region-based representation
~/**bildbasierte** image-based representation
~/**bilddokumentarische** pictorial documentary representation
~/**bildliche** pictorial representation, pictorialization, depiction, rendition, view
~/**blockbasierte** block-based representation *(motion estimation)*
~/**codierte** coded representation
~/**digitale** digital representation
~/**dreidimensionale** three-dimensional representation
~/**explizite** explicit representation
~/**fotografische** photographic depiction
~/**fotorealistische** near-photographic representation; photorealistic rendering (rendition) *(computer graphics)*
~/**fraktale** fractal-based representation
~/**geometrische** geometric representation
~/**grafische** graphic[al] representation (depiction), graphic[al] presentation; graph, plot
~/**hierarchische** hierarchical representation
~/**implizite** implicit representation
~/**kartografische** cartographic representation
~/**mehrdimensionale** multidimensional representation
~/**merkmalsgestützte** feature-based representation
~/**numerische** numerical representation *(e.g. of an image)*
~/**objektbasierte** object-based (object-centered) representation
~/**optische** visualization
~/**parametrische (parametrisierte)** parametric representation
~/**perspektivische** perspective representation; perspective plot
~/**pixelorientierte** pixel[-based] representation
~/**raumbildliche (räumliche)** spatial representation
~/**relationale** *s.* ~/symbolische
~/**röntgenografische** roentgenographic visualization
~/**schematische** schematic[al] representation; schematic illustration; schematic [diagram]; schematic drawing
~/**spiegelbildliche** mirror imaging
~/**statische** static (stationary) representation

~/**symbolische** symbolic representation
~/**syntaktische** grammar
~/**vektorielle (vektororientierte)** vectorial representation
~/**vierdimensionale** four-dimensional representation
~/**visuelle** visual [re]presentation
~/**von Rohrsche** aberration curve *(of a lens)*
~/**voxelbasierte** voxel-based representation
~/**zweidimensionale** two-dimensional representation
Darstellungsattribut *n* display attribute; primitive attribute
Darstellungsbereich *m* display space
Darstellungsebene view plane
Darstellungselement *n* display element
~/**grafisches** graphical primitive element, graphic (output) primitive
~/**verallgemeinertes** generalized drawing primitive, GDP *(computer graphics)*
~/**zusammengesetztes** compound primitive
Darstellungsfeld *n* viewport
~/**effektives** effective viewport
Darstellungsfenster *n* presentation (view) window *(display)*
Darstellungsfläche *f* display (presentation) surface
Darstellungskörper *m* view volume *(computer graphics)*
Darstellungsmedium *n* display (presentation) medium
Darstellungsmodus *m* display mode
Darstellungsquader *m* bounding rectangle (box) *(computer graphics)*
Darstellungsqualität *f* representation quality
Darstellungsraum *m* representation space *(e.g. of audiovisual objects)*
Darstellungsreihenfolge *f* imaging order
Darstellungsschicht *f* presentation layer
Darstellungsstruktur *f* representational structure
Darstellungstabelle *f* view table *(computer graphics)*
Darstellungstechnik *f* representation technique
Darstellungsvermögen *n* display ability *(e.g. of a monitor)*
Darstellungsziel *n* representational goal
Datagramm *n* datagram *(packet switching)*
DAT-Band *n* Digital Audio Tape, DAT *(audio tape recording format)*
Datei *f* [data] file
~/**binäre** binary file
~/**digitale** digital file
~/**gepackte (komprimierte)** compressed file
~/**permanente** permanent file
~/**sequentielle** sequential file
~/**vektorisierte** vectorized file

Dateiaustauschformat *n* file interchange format
Dateibetrachter *m* viewer
Dateielement *n* file element
Dateiformat *n* [data] file format
~/**herstellerspezifisches (proprietäres)** proprietary file format
Dateigröße *f* file size
Dateikoordinaten *f*p*l* file coordinates
Dateiname *m* file name
Dateinamenerweiterung *f* file format (name) extension
Dateiserver *m* file server
Dateisicherheit *f* file security
Dateispeicherung *f* file storage
Dateistruktur *f* file structure
Dateityp *m* type of file, file type
Dateiübertragungsprotokoll *n* File Transfer Protocol, FTP *(client software)*
Dateiverwaltung *f* file management
Dateiverzeichnis *n* directory
Dateivorspann *m* file header *(e.g. of a digital image)*
Dateizugriff *m* file access
Daten *pl* data
~/**analoge** analog data
~/**anwenderbestimmte (benutzerdefinierte)** user-defined data
~/**codierte** encoded (compressed) data
~/**digitale** digital (discrete) data
~/**fehlerhafte** erroneous data
~/**formatierte** formatted data
~/**geocodierte** geocoded data
~/**gestreute** scattered data
~/**grafische** graphical (graphics) data
~/**ikonische** iconic data
~/**kanalcodierte** channel-coded data
~/**komprimierte** compressed (encoded) data
~/**logarithmische** logarithmic data
~/**paketierte** packet[ized] data
~/**periodische** periodic data
~/**räumliche** spatial data
~/**redundante** redundant data
~/**serielle** serial data
~/**spektrale** spectral data
~/**strukturierte** structured (regular) data
~/**unstrukturierte** unstructured (irregular) data
~/**verteilte** scattered data
Datenabgleich *m* data matching
Datenanalyse *f* data analysis
Datenanzeige *f* [/**optische**] 1. data display; 2. [data] display, data screen
Datenanzug *m* data suit *(virtual reality)*
Datenaufteilung *f* data partitioning
Datenaufzeichnung *f* data recording
Datenauslesung *f* [data] readout
Datenaustausch *m* data exchange
Datenautobahn *f* communication highway
Datenbank *f* database, data bank
~/**hybride** hybrid database
~/**multimediale** multimedia database

Datenbank

~/**objektorientierte** object-oriented database
~/**relationale** relational database
Datenbankabfrage f query
Datenbank-Anfragesprache f database query language
Datenbankbild n database image
Datenbank-Diensterbringer m database server
Datenbankebene f s. Speicherungsebene
Datenbankformat n database format
Datenbankserver m search engine
Datenbankspeichersystem n database storage system
Datenbanksprache f database language
Datenbanksuche f database search[ing]
Datenbanksystem n database system, flat-file database
Datenbankverwaltung f database management
Datenbankverwaltungssystem n database management system
Datenbasis f database (s.a. Datenbank)
Datenbildschirm m alphanumeric screen (display)
Datenbit n data bit
Datenbitstrom m data bit stream
Datenblock m data block, block of data, chunk
Datenbrille f head-mounted (helmet-mounted) display, HMD
Datenbündel n, **Datenburst** m data burst
Datenbus m data bus (s.a. under Bus)
Datenbustechnik f data bus technology
Datenbyte n data byte
Datencodierung f data [en]coding
Datendarstellung f data [re]presentation
Datendichte f data density
Datendienst m data service
~/**interaktiver** interactive data service
Datendisplay n [data] display, data screen
Datendruck m/**variabler** variable data printing, VDP
Datendurchsatz m data throughput
Dateneinbelichtung f data imprinting
Dateneingabe f data entry (input)
Dateneingabefehler m data entry error
Dateneinheit f data unit
~/**logische** logical data unit, LDU
Datenelement n data element
Datenendstation f data [display] terminal; terminal device
Datenentschlüssler m decoder
Datenerfassung f data acquisition (capture), data recording
Datenerfassungsgerät n data capture (acquisition) device
Datenerfassungssystem n data acquisition system, DAS
Datenextraktion f data extraction
Datenfehler m data error
Datenfeld n 1. data display; 2. [data] field (e.g. of a database)

Datenfernübertragung f remote data transmission
Datenfluss m data flow (stream)
Datenflussplan m data flow diagram
Datenfolge f string of data
Datenformat n data format
~/**plattformunabhängiges** portable document format, PDF
Datenfusion f data fusion
Datengruppe f data group
Datenhandschuh m data (sensor) glove, glove input device, cyber glove (navigational tool)
Datenhelm m virtual reality helmet; head-mounted (helmet-mounted) display, HMD
Datenkanal m data channel
Datenkapazität f s. Datenspeicherkapazität
Datenkommunikation f data communication
Datenkompatibilität f data compatibility
Datenkompression f data compression (s.a. under Kompression)
Datenkompressionsalgorithmus m data compression algorithm
Datenkompressionsverfahren n data compression technique
Datenkomprimierung f s. Datenkompression
Datenkorrektur f data correction
Datenmatrix f data matrix
Datenmenge f amount (set) of data; data set (s.a. Datenvolumen)
Datenmodell n data[base] model (s.a. under Modell)
Datenmodellierung f data modeling
Datenmonitor m data monitor (e.g. on camcorders)
Datenmultiplexer m data multiplexer
Datennetz n data network (grid)
~/**lokales** local area network, LAN (data communication)
~/**paketvermitteltes** packet-switched network
~/**schnelles** high-speed [data] network
Datenobjekt n data object (resource); datum
Datenpaket n data package, [data] packet; datagram (packet switching)
Datenpaketvermittlung f packet switching
Datenpfad m data path
Datenprojektion f data projection
Datenprojektor m data projection system
Datenpunkt m data point
Datenquelle f data source
Datenrahmen m [data] frame
Datenrate f data [transfer] rate, data [transfer] speed
Datenraum m data space
Datenrecorder m data recorder
Datenreduktion f data [rate] reduction, subsampling
Datenreduktionsfaktor m data reduction factor; compression factor (ratio)

Datenreduktionsrate f,
Datenreduktionsstufe f data compression level
Datenreduktionsverfahren n data reduction process
Datenredundanz f data redundancy
Datenreduzierung f s. Datenreduktion
Datenrückgewinnung f data recovery
Datenrückwand f data[-recording] back (35-mm camera)
Datenrundfunk m data broadcast
Datensatz m data set; [data] record
~/**dreidimensionaler** three-dimensional data set
Datensatzattribut n data set attribute
Datenschnittstelle f data [transport] interface (s.a. under Schnittstelle)
Datensenke f data sink
Datensicherheit f data security
Datensicherung f backup
Datensicherungskopie f backup [copy]
Datensichtgerät n desktop [data] display monitor; data [display] terminal; terminal [device]
Datensichthelm m s. Datenhelm
Datensignal n data signal
Datenspeicher m data storage [device], data memory (s.a. under Speicher)
~/**digitaler** digital data storage
Datenspeicherformat n data storage format
Datenspeicherkapazität f data-storage capacity
Datenspeicherkarte f [data] storage card, memory [storage] card
Datenspeichermedium n data storage medium
Datenspeichertechnik f data storage technology
Datenspeicherung f data storage
~/**holografische** holographic data storage
~/**optische** optical data storage
Datenspektrum n data spectrum
Datenspreizung f/**räumliche** interleaving
Datenspur f data track
Datenstation f data station; [data] terminal
Datenstrom m data stream (flow)
~/**multimedialer** streaming [multi]media
~/**paralleler** parallel data stream
~/**serieller** serial data stream
Datenstromformat n data stream format
Datenstrom-Nutzlast f data stream payload, useful data rate
Datenstruktur f data structure
~/**baumartige** tree-like data structure
~/**geometrische** geometric data structure
~/**hierarchische** hierarchical data structure
~/**pyramidenförmige** pyramid data structure
~/**räumliche** spatial data structure
Datensynchronisation f data synchronization
Datentiefe f bit (pixel) depth (s.a. Farbtiefe)

Datenträger m data carrier (medium), volume
Datenträgersatz m volume set
Datentransfer m s. Datenübertragung
Datentyp m data type
Datenübermittlung f data communication (s.a. Datenübertragung)
Datenübertragung f data transmission (transfer) (s.a. under Übertragung)
~/**automatische** automatic data transmission, ADT
~/**digitale** digital data transmission
~/**paketweise** packetized data transfer
~/**parallele** parallel data transfer
~/**serielle** serial data transfer
Datenübertragungsblock m [transmission] frame
~/**fehlerhafter** improper frame
Datenübertragungseinrichtung f data transmision equipment
Datenübertragungsgeschwindigkeit f,
Datenübertragungskapazität f s. Datenübertragungsrate
Datenübertragungsprotokoll n data transmission protocol
Datenübertragungsrate f data [transfer] rate, data [transfer] speed
Datenübertragungssystem n data transmission system
Datenumfang m data size
Datenvektor m data vector
Datenverarbeiter m data processor
Datenverarbeitung f data processing, DP
~/**geometrische** computational geometry
~/**grafische** computer graphics [technology], computational graphics, CG
~/**optische** optical data processing
Datenverarbeitungstechnik f 1. data processing technology; 2. data processing technique
Datenverarbeitungswerkzeug n data processing tool
Datenverdichtung f data compression
Datenverkettung f data chaining
Datenverlust m data loss
Datenvermittlung f data switching
Datenverschachtelung f data interleaving
Datenverschlüsselung f data encryption
Datenverstümmelung f data truncation
Datenverwaltung f data management
Datenvisualisierung f data (numerical) visualization
Datenvolumen n data volume (s.a. Datenmenge)
Datenvorverarbeitung f data preprocessing
Datenwandler m data converter (transducer)
Datenwiedergewinnung f,
Datenwiederherstellung f data recovery
Datenwort n 1. [data] word; 2. s. Byte
Datenwortbreite f wordlength
Datenzeile f data line

Datenzugriffszeit

Datenzugriffszeit *f* data access time
Datenzwischenspeicher *m* data cache (buffer)
Datumsanzeige *f* data display
Datumsdruck *m* date stamp
Daubechies-Wavelet *n* Daubechies wavelet
Daubresse-Prisma *n* Daubresse prism *(optics)*
Dauerbeleuchtung *f* sustained (long-term) illumination
Dauerbelichtung *f* time exposure
Dauerlicht *n* continuous[-burning] light
Dauerlichtlampe *f* continuous-burning lamp
Dauerlichtquelle *f* continuous[-burning] light source, continuous-duration [light] source
Dauermagnet *m* permanent magnet
Dauermagnetfeld *n* permanent-magnetic field
Dauerstrichlaser *m* continuous-wave laser, cw laser
Dauerstrichleistung *f* cw (continuous-wave) power
Dauerstrichradar *n* continuous-wave radar, cw radar
~/frequenzmoduliertes frequency-modulated continuous-wave radar, FMCW radar
Daumenkino *n* flip-book
Daumenrad *n* thumbwheel
Davis-Gibson-Doppelflüssigkeitsfilter *n* Davis-Gibson [liquid] filter
Dawes-Grenze *f* Dawes limit *(of the resolving power of telescopes)*
dB *s.* Dezibel
Deakzentuierung *f s.* Deemphasis
Debot-Effekt *m* Debot effect *(latent-image formation)*
Debye-Scherrer-Kamera *f* Debye-Scherer X-ray camera
Debye-Scherrer-Röntgenfilm *m* Deby-Scherer X-ray film
de-Casteljau-Algorithmus *m* de Casteljau algorithm *(computer graphics)*
Deckblatt *n* cover sheet; fax cover page
Deckelektrode *f* top electrode *(photoconductor)*
Deckenkamera *f* overhead (ceiling-mounted) camera
Deckenmonitor *m* ceiling-mounted monitor
Deckenschienensystem *n* ceiling rail system, roof track system; track lighting system *(studio equipment)*
Deckfarbe *f* opaquing paint
Deckglas *n*, **Deckgläschen** *n* cover glass, [glass] coverslip *(microscopy)*
Deckglasdicke *f* cover glass thickness, coverslip thickness
Deckmaske *f* slide mount aperture (window)
Deckung *f* density, extinction

Decoder *m* decoder; digital-[to-]analog converter, DAC
Decoderausgang *m* decoder output
Decodergerät *n s.* Decoder
decodierbar decodable, decryptable
Decodierbarkeit *f* decodability
decodieren to decode
Decodierer *m s.* Decoder
Decodiermatrix *f* decoder matrix
Decodierung *f* decoding
~/digitale digital decoding
~/fraktale fractal decoding
~/iterative iterative decoding
Decodierungsalgorithmus *m* decoding algorithm
Decodierungsgeschwindigkeit *f* decoding speed
Decodierungsschicht *f* decoding layer *(of a neural network)*
Decodierungsschleife *f* decoding loop
Decodierungsschritt *m* decoding step
Decodierungssystem *n* decoding system
Decodiervorgang *m* decoding process
Deemphasis *f* deemphasis, post-emphasis, postequalization *(frequency modulation)*
Deep-Sky-Fotografie *f* deep-sky photography
Defektanalyse *f* flaw analysis
Defektelektron *n* defect electron, [photogenerated] hole *(photodetector)*
Defekterkennung *f* damage detection
Defektoskop *n* defectoscope
Defektoskopie *f* defectoscopy, flaw detection
Definitionsbereich *m* domain [of definition], DOD
Definitionshelligkeit *f* [/**Strehlsche**] Strehl [intensity] ratio, Strehl definition *(image quality criterion)*
Deflektometrie *f* deflectometry
Deflektor *m* deflector
defokussieren to defocus
Defokussierung *f* defocusing
Deformation *f* deformation, warping *(e.g. of shapes in computer graphics)*
Defuzzifikation *f s.* Defuzzifizierung
defuzzifizieren to defuzzify
Defuzzifizierung *f* defuzzification
Dehnrichtung *f* against (across) the grain, cross grain *(of paper)*
Dehnungslinienbild *n* fringe pattern
Dejustage *f* misalignment
dejustieren to misalign
Dekamired-Wert *m* decaMIRED value *(designating a light source)*
Dekomposition *f s.* Wavelet-Analyse
Dekompression *f* decompression *(e.g. of image data)*
Dekompressionsalgorithmus *m* decompression algorithm (program), decoder
Dekompressor *m* decompressor
dekomprimieren to decompress, to uncompress, to expand

Dekomprimierung f s. Dekompression
Dekonvolution f deconvolution, inverse filtering (image reconstruction)
Dekoration f decoration; set[ting]
~/**virtuelle** virtual set
Dekorationsleuchte f set-lighting fixture
Dekorationslicht n set light
Dekorationsteil n set piece
Dekorationswechsel m set turnover
Dekorrelation f decorrelation
Dekorrelationsfilter n decorrelation filter
Dekorrelationstransformation f decorrelation transform
dekorrelieren to decorrelate (e.g. image data)
dekrementieren to decrement (data)
Delaunay-Dreieck n Delaunay triangle
Delaunay-Netz n Delaunay mesh
Delaunay-Triangulation f, **Delaunay-Triangulierung** f Delaunay triangulation
Delone-... s. Delaunay-...
Delta n/**Kroneckersches** s. Deltafunktion/diskrete
Deltabaum m delta tree (data structure)
Deltabaumdarstellung f delta tree representation
Deltabild n delta frame
Deltafunktion f [/**Diracsche**] delta (impulse) function, Dirac [delta] function (signal processing)
~/**diskrete** discrete delta (impulse) function, Kronecker delta, unit sample sequence
Deltafunktional n s. Deltafunktion[/Diracsche]
Deltakompression f delta compression
Deltamodulation f delta modulation, DM (image compression)
Deltamodulator m delta modulator
Deltapunkt m s. Objektpunkt
Deltaregel f delta rule (learning rule for feedforward networks)
~/**generalisierte** generalized delta rule [for learning by backpropagation]
Deltaröhre f delta tube
Deltavektor m delta vector
Demodulation f demodulation
~/**inkohärente** incoherent demodulation
~/**kohärente** coherent demodulation
Demodulator m demodulator
demodulieren to demodulate; to detect
Dempster-Shafer-Theorie f Dempster-Shafer theory, evidence theory
Demultiplexen n s. Demultiplexierung
Demultiplexer m demultiplexer
demultiplexieren to demultiplex
Demultiplexierung f demultiplexing
DEMUX s. Demultiplexer
Densität f density
Densitometer n densitometer
~/**fotoelektrisches** photoelectric (electronic) densitometer
~/**optisches** visual densitometer

Densitometerfehler m densitometer error
Densitometerfilter n densitometer filter
Densitometrie f densitometry
~/**digitale** digital densitometry
densitometrisch densitometric
Densograf m recording densitometer
Dentalfilm n dental film
Dentalfotograf m dental photographer
Dentalfotografie f dental photography
Dentalmikroskop n dental microscope
Dentalradiografie f dental radiography
Dentalröntgeneinrichtung f dental X-ray machine (unit)
dephasieren to dephase
Dephasierung f dephasing
Dephasierungseffekt m dephasing effect
Depolarisation f depolarization
Depolarisator m depolarizer
depolarisieren to depolarize
Depressionswinkel m depression angle
dequantisieren to dequantize
Dequantisierer m dequantizer
Dequantisierung f dequantization
Deriche-Filter n, **Deriche-Kantenfilter** n Deriche filter
Desensibilisator m desensitizer
desensibilisieren to desensitize
Desensibilisierung f desensitization
Desensibilisierungseffekt m desensitization effect
Deskriptor m descriptor, feature (s.a. under Merkmal, Attribut)
~/**audiovisueller** audiovisual descriptor
~/**geometrischer** geometric[al] descriptor
~/**globaler** global descriptor
~/**qualitativer** qualitative descriptor
~/**quantitativer** quantitative descriptor
~/**regionaler** regional descriptor
~/**relationaler** relational descriptor
~/**semantischer** semantic descriptor
~/**statistischer** statistical descriptor
~/**topologischer** topological descriptor
Desktoppublishing n desktop publishing, DTP
Desktop-Video n desktop video, DTV
Desktop-Videokonferenzsystem n desktop videoconference system, DVC
Desorption f desorption
Detail n detail
~/**feinstrukturiertes** fine detail
~/**lichtschwaches** faint detail
Detailauflösung f detail resolution, resolution of detail
Detailaufnahme f detail shot; extreme close-up, XCU; big close-up, BCU
Detailbild n detail image
Detaileinstellung f detail shot (cinema)
Detailerkennbarkeit f detail detectability, visibility of detail[s], acuity to detail
Detailinformation f detail information
Detailkontrast m [image-]detail contrast, local contrast
Detaillierung f detailing

Detaillierungsebene f level of detail, LOD (computer graphics)
Detailrestaurierung f detail enhancement
Detailschärfe f [image] definition, fineness of detail
Detailtreue f accuracy in detail[s], fidelity, exactness
Detailverlust m detail loss, loss (degradation) of detail[s]
Detailwahrnehmung f perception of detail
Detailwiedergabe f detail rendering, rendition of detail
Detailzeichnung f detail drawing
detektierbar detectable
Detektierbarkeit f detectability
Detektierbarkeitsfaktor m detectability factor
detektieren to detect; to sense
Detektion f detection
~/**computergestützte** computer-aided detection
~/**optische** optical detection
Detektionsalgorithmus m detection algorithm
Detektionsbandbreite f detection bandwidth
Detektionseffizienz f detection efficiency, efficiency of detection
Detektionsempfindlichkeit f detection sensitivity
Detektionsfilter n detection filter
Detektionsgüte f detection quality
Detektionsleistung f detection performance
Detektionsmaske f detection mask
▸**Detektionsschwelle** f detection threshold
Detektionswahrscheinlichkeit f detection probability, probability (likelihood) of detection
Detektionszyklus m detection cycle
Detektivität f detectivity, detection capability
Detektivkamera f detective (clandestine) camera, secret camera
Detektor m detector [element], detecting element (s.a. under Sensor)
~/**bildgebender** imaging detector
~/**digitaler** digital detector
~/**diskreter** discrete detector
~/**flächenauflösender (flächiger)** area (planar) detector, [two-dimensional] array detector, flat-panel array (detector)
~/**fotovoltaischer** photovoltaic detector
~/**hochauflösender** high-resolution detector
~/**ladungsgekoppelter** charge-coupled detector
~/**lichtelektrischer** photoelectric (electro-optic) detector
~/**optischer** optical (light) detector, photodetector; photon detector
~/**pyroelektrischer** pyroelectric detector
~/**stationärer** stationary detector
~/**thermischer** thermal [radiation] detector
~/**vorgespannter** biased detector
~/**zeilenauflösender** line[ar] array detector; linear array transducer
Detektoranordnung f, **Detektorarray** n detector array
Detektorartefakt n detector artifact
Detektorauflösung f detector resolution
Detektorbandbreite f detector bandwidth
Detektordunkelstrom m detector dark current
Detektorebene f detector plane
Detektorelektronik f detector electronics
Detektorelement n [/**diskretes**] detector element, del
Detektorempfindlichkeit f detector sensitivity; [detector] responsivity
Detektorfenster n detector window
Detektorfläche f detector area
Detektorgeometrie f detector geometry
Detektorkranz m ring of detectors (tomograph)
Detektorleistung f detector performance
Detektormaterial n detector material
Detektormatrix f detector array
Detektoroberfläche f detector surface
Detektorparameter m detector parameter
Detektorpixel n detector pixel
Detektorrauschen n detector [intrinsic] noise
Detektorrauschstrom m detector noise current
Detektorring m ring detector (computed tomography)
Detektorsegment n detector segment
Detektorsignal n detector signal
Detektorspannung f detector voltage
Detektorstrom m detector current
Detektorsystem n detector system
Detektorwiderstand m detector resistance
Deutanstörung f s. Deuteranopie
Deuteranomalie f deuteranomaly, decreased green sensitivity (color-vision deficiency)
deuteranop deuteranopic, green-blind
Deuteranopie f deuteranopia, [red-]green blindness (color-vision deficiency)
Dezentrierung f decentration
Dezentrierungsfehler m decentration aberration
Dezibel n decibel, dB
Dezimalziffer f decimal digit
Dezimation f decimation; subsampling; downconversion (video signal processing)
~/**horizontale** horizontal decimation
~/**räumliche** spatial decimation
Dezimationsfilter n decimation filter, decimator
Dezimationsfilterung f decimation filtering
Dezimationstiefpass m, **Dezimator** m s. Dezimationsfilter
Dezimeterwellenbereich m decimeter (ultra-high frequency) wave range
dezimieren to decimate

Dia *n* [photographic] slide, projection (transparent) slide, film (lantern) slide *(s.a.* Diapositiv*)*
~/gerahmtes slide [transparency]
~/glasgerahmtes (plangeglastes) glass[-mounted] slide
Diaabtaster *m s.* Diascanner
Diaabzug *m* transprint
Diaarchiv *n* slide archive
Diaarchivhülle *f* slide sheet (storage sheet)
Diaarchivkassette *f* slide archive cassette
Dia-Aufbewahrung *f* slide storage
Diabetrachter *m* transparency (slide) viewer, [transparency] illuminator; tabletop slide viewer
Diabild *n* slide image (picture)
Diaduplikat *n* duplicate slide (transparency)
Diaduplikatfilm *m* slide-duplication film, [slide-]duplicating [color] film
Diaduplikation *f* slide duplication
Diaduplikator *m* slide duplicator, slide-duplicating device
Diafenster *n* slide gate
Diafilm *m* slide (reversal) film, transparency film
Diaformat *n* transparency (slide) format
Diagnoseverfahren *n*/**bildgebendes** diagnostic imaging procedure
Diagnostik *f*/**bildgebende** imaging [medical] diagnostics
Diagnostik-Röntgenröhre *f* diagnostic X-ray tube
diagonal diagonal
Diagonale *f* diagonal
Diagonalisierung *f* diagonalization
Diagonalmatrix *f* diagonal[ized] matrix
Diagramm *n* diagram, diagrammatic representation
Diaherstellung *f* slide making (production)
Diahülle *f* slide [storage] page; slide holder
Diakasten *m* slide [storage] box
Diakaustik *f* diacaustic *(optics)*
diakaustisch diacaustic
Diakopie *f* slide duplicate, duplicate transparency, dupe
Diakopieradapter *m* slide copying adaptor
Diakopierer *m*, **Diakopiergerät** *n* slide copier, slide-copying device; transparency printer
Diakopierung *f* slide duplicating
Diakopiervorsatz *m* slide copying adaptor
Dialog *m* dialogue, dialog
~/asynchroner wild lines
Dialogband *n* dialogue line (track)
Dialogbearbeitung *f* dialogue editing
Dialogfeld *n* dialogue box
Dialogfenster *n* dialogue window
Dialogmonitor *m* interactive display [device]
Dialogpassage *f* line of dialogue
Dialogrechner *m* transputer, transaction computer
Dialogspur *f* dialogue track *(cinema)*

Dialogstück *n s.* Dialogpassage
Dialytprisma *n* dialyte prism
Diamagazin *n* slide tray (magazine)
diamagnetisch diamagnetic
Diamantstichel *m* diamond[-tipped] stylus
Diamidophenolhydrochlorid *n* 2,4-diaminophenol dihydrochloride *(developing agent)*
diaphan diaphanous, sheer
Diaphanbild *n*, **Diaphanie** *f* diaphanous image
Diaphanität *f* diaphaneity, diaphanousness
Diaphragma *n s.* Blende 1.
Diaplatte *f* [projection] slide plate; lantern plate
Diapositiv *n* diapositive; [positive] transparency *(s.a.* under Dia*)*
Diapositivfilm *m s.* Diafilm
Diapositivplatte *f s.* Diaplatte
Diapositivprojektor *m* still[-picture] projector, lantern *(s.a.* Diaprojektor*)*
Diapositivretusche *f* transparency retouching
Diapräsentation *f* slide presentation
Diapräsentationshülle *f* slide holder
Diaprojektion *f* transparency projection; slide projection
Diaprojektionsabstand *m* slide projection distance
Diaprojektionsanlage *f* slide projection system
Diaprojektionsbild *n* projected image
Diaprojektions-Zoomobjektiv *n* slide projector zoom lens
Diaprojektor *m* slide [transparency] projector
Diarähmchen *n s.* Diarahmen
Diarahmen *m* slide mount (frame)
~/geglaster glass mount
~/glasloser glassless [slide] mount
Diarahmung *f* slide mounting
Diascanner *m* slide scanner (digitizer), transparency scanner; slide[-to-video] converter; slide scanning equipment
Diaschau *f* slide show (presentation)
Diaschneidegerät *n* slide cutter
Diaserie *f* slide series (set)
Diaskop *n* 1. diascope, overhead projector; 2. *s.* Diaprojektor
Diasortierpult *n* light box
Diastreifen *m* filmstrip, slide film, strip film
Diastreifenprojektor *m* filmstrip (strip film) projector
Diatonbildschau *f* [synchronized] sound-slide program
Diaüberblendschau *f* multiple projector slide show, multiple slide projector presentation, multimedia slide show
Diaüberspielung *f* slide-to-video conversion
Diavorführer *m* slide-show lecturer
Diavorführung *f* slide presentation (show)
Diawechsel *m* slide change
Diawechselzeit *f* recovery time

Diawechsler

Diawechsler *m* slide-changing mechanism
Diazin *n* diazine *(developing chemical)*
Diazobeschichtung *f s.*
 Diazo-Kopierschicht
Diazoemulsion *f* diazo emulsion
Diazofilm *m* diazo [duplicating] film
Diazokopie *f* diazo copy
Diazo-Kopierschicht *f* diazo coating *(printing plate)*
Diazomikrofilm *m* diazo microfilm
Diazoniumsalz *n* diazonium salt
Diazoniumsalz-Druckplatte *f* diazo plate
Diazopapier *n* diazo[-treated] paper
Diazotechnik *f s.* 1. Diazoverfahren; 2. Diazotypie 1.
Diazotypie *f* 1. diazo[type] process, diazotyping [process]; 2. diazotype, diazo copy
Diazoverbindung *f* diazo[nium] compound
Diazoverfahren *n* diazo [copying] process, diazonium (dyeline) process
Dibit *n* dibit
Dichroidfilter *n* dichroi[ti]c filter; interference filter
Dichroismus *m* dichroism
dichroitisch dichroic
Dichromasie *f* dichromatism, dichromatic vision, partial color blindness
Dichromat *m* 1. dichromat *(optical system)*; 2. dichromat, partially color-blind person
~ *n* dichromate, bichromate *(chromium salt)*
Dichromatgelatine *f* dichromate[d] gelatin, DCG, bichromated gelatin
dichromatisch dichromatic *(optics)*
Dichromatkolloid *n* dichromated (bichromated) colloid
Dichromatopsie *f s.* Dichromasie
Dichromatverfahren *n* dichromated-colloid process, dichromate (bichromate) process
Dichroskop *n* dichroscope
Dichte *f* 1. [mass] density; 2. [optical] density; photographic density, blackening *(s.a. under* Schwärzung, Grauwert*)*
~ **der Strahlungsleistung/spektrale** *s.* Strahlungsfluss/spektraler
~/**fotografische** photographic density, D
~/**Gaußsche** Gaussian density
~/**maximale** maximum density, D-max *(densitometry)*
~/**minimale** minimum density, D-min *(densitometry)*
~/**mittlere optische** average optical density, AOD
~/**optische** optical density, absorbance, absorbancy
~/**spektrale** [power] spectral density, power spectrum
Dichteänderung *f* density change
Dichtebereich *m s.* Dichteumfang
Dichtefilter *n s.* Graufilter

Dichtefunktion *f* [probability] density function, PDF
Dichtegradient *m* density gradient
Dichtekorrektur *f* density correction
Dichtekurve *f* [/**fotografische**] density (characteristic) curve, [photographic] response curve, [characteristic] D-log H curve
Dichtemesser *m*, **Dichtemessgerät** *n* densitometer
Dichtemessung *f* density measurement; densitometry
Dichtemittel *n* mode, modal value *(statistics)*
Dichteschwankung *f* density variation (fluctuation)
Dichteskala *f* density scale
Dichteumfang *m* density range *(s.a.* Tonwertbereich*)*
Dichteunterschied *m* density difference
Dichteverteilung *f* density distribution
Dichtewert *m* density value
Dickdarmspiegel *m* colonoscope
Dickdarmspiegelung *f* colonoscopy
Dicke *f*/**optische** optical thickness
Dickfilm-Siebdruck *m* thick-film screen printing
Dickkernfaser *f* fat fiber *(fiber optics)*
Dickte *f* 1. set size *(of a type)*; 2. [advance] width *(typography)*
dicktengleich monospaced
Dicktentabelle *f* width table *(typography)*
Didot-Punkt *m* Didot point, [typographical] point
Didot-System *n* typographical point system
Didymfilter *n* didymium [glass] filter
Dielektrikum *n* dielectric [material]
dielektrisch dielectric
Dielektrizitätskonstante *f* [complex] dielectric constant, permittivity
Dienst *m*/**audiovisueller** audiovisual service
~/**multimedialer** multimedia service
Diensteanbieter *m*, **Diensterbringer** *m* server; service provider *(data communication)*
Differentialentzerrungsgerät *n* orthoprojector
Differentialinterferenzkontrastmikroskopie *f* differential interference contrast microscopy, DIC microscopy, Nomarski interference microscopy
Differentialinterferometer *n* differential interferometer
Differenzbild *n* difference image (picture), differential image; subtraction image
Differenzbildung *f* differencing *(data processing)*
Differenzblock *m* difference block *(video compression)*
Differenzcodierung *f* 1. differential (relative) coding, differencing, predictive

(previous-pixel) coding; 2. s. Differenzpulscodemodulation
~/**informationserhaltende** information-preserving differential coding
Differenzdeskriptor m difference descriptor
Differenzfilter n difference filter, differencing mask
Differenzfrequenz f difference frequency (e.g. of two lasers)
Differenzhistogramm n difference histogram
Differenzoperation f difference operation, subtraction (minus) operation (pixel processing)
Differenzoperator m/**linearer** linear difference operator
~/**symmetrischer** symmetric difference operator
Differenzpulscodemodulation f differential pulse code modulation, differential PCM, DPCM (data compression technique)
Differenzsignal n difference (differential) signal
Diffraktion f diffraction, bending
Diffraktionstomografie f diffraction tomography
Diffraktometer n diffractometer
Diffraktometrie f diffractometry
diffraktometrisch diffractometric
diffundieren to diffuse
diffus diffuse
Diffusion f 1. diffusion (as of liquids or gases); 2. [light] diffusion, optical diffusion, scatter[ing] [of light]
~/**anisotrope** anisotropic diffusion (e.g. in pattern analysis)
~/**eckenerhaltende** corner-preserving diffusion
~/**inhomogene** inhomogeneous diffusion (image modeling)
~/**isotrope** isotropic diffusion
~/**nichtlineare** nonlinear diffusion
Diffusionsalgorithmus m diffusion algorithm
Diffusionsbildgebung f diffusion imaging (magnetic resonance imaging)
diffusionsfähig diffusible, diffusable
Diffusionsfähigkeit f diffusibility
Diffusionsfilter n [frosted] diffusion filter, diffusing (fog) filter; soft-focus attachment (filter)
Diffusionsfilterung f diffusion filtering
Diffusionsfolie f diffusion sheet, scattering foil, scrim
Diffusionsfotostrom m diffusion current (photodetector)
Diffusionsgeschwindigkeit f diffusion velocity (rate)
Diffusionsgrad m degree of diffusion
Diffusionsgradient m diffusion gradient
Diffusionskoeffizient m diffusion coefficient

Diffusionskreis m circle of least confusion
Diffusionskugel f diffusing sphere (incident-light meter)
Diffusionslichthof m diffuse halo
Diffusionsmaterial n diffusing material (lighting accessory)
Diffusionsmodell n diffusion model (image modeling)
Diffusionsstrom m diffusion current (photodetector)
Diffusionstensor m diffusion tensor
Diffusionswinkel m diffusion angle
Diffusor m diffuser, diffusor; diffusion disk (s.a. Diffusionsfilter)
~/**sphärischer** hemispherical diffuser
Diffusorkalotte f s. Diffusionskugel
Diffusorscheibe f diffuser disk (photometer)
Digigrafie f s. Digitalfotografie
Digit n digit
digital digital
Digital-Analog-Konverter m, **Digital-Analog-Wandler** m digital-[to-]analog [signal] converter, DAC
Digital-Analog-Wandlung f digital-[to-]analog conversion, D/A conversion, DAC
Digitalanzeige f digital display
Digitalaufzeichnung f 1. digital recording; 2. digital record[ing]
Digitalausgang m digital output
Digitalausstrahlung f digital broadcast[ing]
Digitalband n digital [video]tape
Digitalbereich m digital domain (realm)
Digitalbild n digital image (picture); [image] scene, picture scene (s.a. Bitmap-Bild)
Digitalbildauflösung f digital image resolution
Digitalbildaufnahme f digital image acquisition
Digitalbildbearbeiter m digital imager
Digitalbildbearbeitung f digital imaging
Digitalbildbearbeitungstechnik f digital image processing technique
Digitalbildcodierung f digital image coding
Digitalbilddatei f digital image file
Digitalbilddaten pl digital image data
Digitalbilddatensatz m digital-image data set
Digitalbildmanipulation f digital [image] manipulation
Digitalbildmanipulator m digital picture manipulator
Digitalbildschirm m digital [image] display; digitally controlled CRT monitor
Digitalbildsensor m digital imaging sensor
Digitalbildspeicher m digital framestore [device] (cinema)
Digitalbildspeicherung f digital image storage
Digitalbildtechnik f digital imaging [technology], electronic digital imaging,

Digitalbildverarbeitung

digital image processing technology; digital image technique
Digitalbildverarbeitung f digital image processing, DIP
Digitalbildverarbeitungseinheit f digital image processing unit
Digitalcamcorder m digital camcorder
Digitaldaten pl digital data
Digitaldatensatz m digitized data set
Digitaldatenspeicherung f digital data storage, DDS
Digitaldecoder m digital decoder
Digitaldruck m 1. digital printing; 2. digital print
Digitaldrucker m digital printer
Digitaldruckplatte f digital [printing] plate
Digitaleffekt m digital [picture] effect
Digitaleingang m digital input
Digitalelektronik f digital electronics
Digitalelement n digit
Digitalempfänger m digital receiver
Digitalfarbbild n color digital [electronic] image
Digitalfarbdruck m digital color printing
Digitalfarbdrucker m digital color printer
Digital-Farbkamera f digital color camera, color digital camera
Digitalfernsehempfänger m s. Digitalfernsehgerät
Digitalfernsehen n digital television [broadcasting], DTV, digital video broadcasting, DVB
~/**hochauflösendes** high-definition digital television
~/**terrestrisches** digital terrestrial television, terrestrial digital video broadcasting, DVB-T
Digitalfernsehgerät n digital TV set, digital television [broadcast] receiver, DVB (digital video broadcasting) receiver
Digitalfernsehsender m digital television broadcast station; digital TV transmitter
Digitalfernsehstandard m digital television standard
Digitalfernsehsystem n digital TV system
Digitalfernsehtechnik f digital television technology
Digitalfilm m digital film (picture)
Digitalfilmtechnik f digital film technology
Digitalfilter n digital filter, discrete-time filter
Digitalfilterung f digital filtering
Digitalformat n digital format
Digitalfoto n digital photograph[ic image], digital still image (picture)
Digitalfotoapparat m digital still camera, DSC
Digitalfotograf m digital photographer
Digitalfotografie f digital photography, digital still imaging
Digitalfotokamera f digital still camera
Digitalgradient m digital gradient
Digitalisiereinheit f s. Digitalisierer

digitalisieren to digitize, to digitalize; to capture (esp. video data)
Digitalisierer m, **Digitalisiergerät** n digitizer, digitizing device
Digitalisierstift m digitizing pen, pressure-sensitive pen, [electronic] stylus (graphics tablet)
Digitalisiertablett n digitizing (graphics) tablet, [electronic] tablet
Digitalisiertisch m 1. digitizing table; 2. s. Digitalisiertablett
Digitalisierung f digitization, analog-[to-]digital conversion [process]
~/**fotometrische** photometric digitization
Digitalisierungskarte f digitizing board, frame grabber board, [video] frame grabber
Digitalisierungsrauschen n digitization noise
Digitalkamera f digital[-imaging] camera, digicam, DC
~/**semiprofessionelle** prosumer digital camera
~/**wissenschaftliche** scientific-grade digital camera
Digitalkamerarückteil n digital[-image] back, electronic-imaging back
Digitalkamera-Speicherkarte f camera card, memory stick
Digitalkameratechnik f digital camera technology
Digitalkino n digital (electronic) cinema, D-cinema, E-cinema
Digitalkompaktkamera f digital compact camera
Digitalkopierer m digital copier
Digitalmikroskop n [/**optisches**] digital [light] microscope
Digitalmikroskopie f digital microscopy, digital microscope technology
Digitalnetz n/**breitbandiges diensteintegrierendes** Broadband ISDN (Integrated Services Digital Network), B-ISDN
~/**diensteintegrierendes (diensteintegriertes)** Integrated Services Digital Network, ISDN
Digitalprint n digital print
Digitalprojektion f digital projection
Digitalprojektor m digital projector; beamer
Digitalproof m digital proof (printing)
~/**immaterieller** digital soft proof
~/**materieller** digital hard proof
Digitalprozessor m digital signal processor, DSP
Digitalprüfdruck m s. Digitalproof
Digitalradar n digital radar
Digitalrechner m digital computer
Digitalrückteil n s. Digitalkamerarückteil
Digitalscankonverter m digital scan converter
Digitalscanner m digital scanner

Digitalschaltkreis *m* digital [switching] circuit
Digitalschnitt *m* digital editing (cut)
Digitalschnittstelle *f* digital [component] interface
Digitalsensor *m* digital sensor
Digital-Shearografie *f* digital shearography
Digitalsignal *n* digital [electric] signal
Digitalspeicher *m* digital memory
Digitalspeicherung *f* digital storage
Digitaltechnik *f* digital technology
Digitalton *m* digital sound (audio)
Digitaltuner *m* digital terrestrial broadcast tuner *(television)*
Digitalübertragung *f* digital transmission
Digitalvergrößerer *m* digital enlarger
Digitalvideo *n* digital video, DV, numerical video
Digitalvideokamera *f* digital video camera, DV camera, DVC
Digitalvideokassette *f* digital [video] cassette, DV (digital video) cartridge
Digitalvideorecorder *m* digital video recorder
Digitalvideotechnik *f* digital video technology
Digitalzahl *f* digit
Digitalzoom *n(m)* digital zoom [feature] *(video camera)*
Dilatation *f* dilation, Minkowski [set] addition *(binary image processing)*
Dilatationsfilter *n s.* Dilatationsoperator
Dilatationsgradient *m* dilation gradient
Dilatationsoperation *f* dilation operation
Dilatationsoperator *m* [binary] dilation filter, dilate filter
dilatieren to dilate
Dimension *f*/**fraktale (fraktionäre)** fractal dimension, Hausdorff-Besicovitch dimension *(computer graphics)*
~/**topologische** topological dimension
Dimensionalität *f* dimensionality
Dimensionierung *f* dimensioning
dimensionslos dimensionless
Dimensionsreduzierung *f* dimensionality reduction
Dimensionsstabilität *f* dimensional stability
Dimethylketon *n* dimethylketone, acetone *(solvent)*
Dimetrie *f* dimetric projection
dimetrisch dimetric
dimmbar dimmable
dimmen to dim
Dimmer *m* [lamp] dimmer
Dimmung *f* dimming
DIN-Filmempfindlichkeit *f* DIN film speed, DIN rating (speed value)
Dingebene *f* object (subject) plane; sample (specimen) plane
Dingpunkt *m* object (subject) point
~/**außeraxialer** off-axis object point
Dingraum *m* object (subject) space
dingseitig object-side

Dingwahrnehmung *f* perception of shape
Dingweite *f* object (subject) distance, object conjugate, working distance
Diode *f* diode
~/**lichtemittierende** light-emitting diode, LED, luminescent diode
~/**lichtempfindliche** light-sensitive diode, photodiode
~/**organische lichtemittierende** organic light-emitting diode, OLED
Diodenlaser *m* diode laser *(s.a. Halbleiterlaser)*
~/**blauer** blue diode laser
Diodenmatrix *f* diode matrix, two-dimensional photodiode array
Diodenmodulator *m* diode modulator
Diodenreihe *f*, **Diodenzeile** *f* series of diodes, linear photodiode array
Diopter *n* peep sight, [optical] sight, sighting hole
Dioptrie *f* diopter, dioptre
Dioptrienanpassung *f*, **Dioptrienausgleich** *m* dioptric compensation *(eyepiece; s.a. Dioptrieneinstellung)*
Dioptrieneinstellknopf *m* diopter adjustment knob
Dioptrieneinstellung *f* dioptric (diopter) adjustment
Dioptrienkorrektur[linse] *f* diopter correction [lens], dioptric correction
Dioptrienmesser *m* dioptometer
Dioptrienzahl *f* diopter number
Dioptrik *f* dioptrics
dioptrisch dioptric, [photo]refractive
Dioptrometer *n* dioptometer
Diorama *n* diorama; cyclorama
Diplexer *m* diplexer *(television)*
Diplopie *f* diplopia, double vision
Diplopiepunkt *m* break point *(ophthalmic optics)*
Dipol *m* dipole
~/**akustischer** acoustic dipole
~/**elektrischer** electric dipole
~/**magnetischer** magnetic dipole
Dipolantenne *f* dipole antenna, dipole [aerial]
Dipolmoment *n* dipole moment
~/**elektrisches** electric dipole moment
~/**induziertes** induced dipole moment
~/**kernmagnetisches** nuclear magnetic dipole moment
~/**magnetisches** magnetic [dipole] moment
Dipolstrahlung *f*/**elektrische** electric dipole radiation
Dirac-Delta *n* Dirac delta
Dirac-Filter *n* Dirac (impulse) filter, nearest-neighbor filter
Dirac-Funktion *f* Dirac [delta] function, delta (impulse) function *(signal processing)*
Dirac-Impuls *m* Dirac pulse; unit [im]pulse function *(signal processing)*
~/**diskreter** *s.* Einheitspuls

Dirac-Stoß *m s.* Dirac-Impuls
Direktabtastung *f* direct scanning
Direktadressierröhre *f* direct-view storage tube, DVST
Direktaufzeichnung *f* direct recording
Direktausdruck *m* direct print
Direktbebilderung *f* [in der Druckmaschine] direct imaging, DI
Direktbelichtung *f* direct exposure
Direktbetrachtung *f* direct viewing (visual observation)
Direktblendung *f* direct glare
Direktdruck *m* direct printing
Direktempfangssatellit *m* direct broadcast satellite, DBS
Direktfotografie *f* direct photography
Direktkopie *f* direct[-positive] copy
Direktkopierung *f* direct copying
Direktlicht *n* direct light
Direktpositiv *n* direct positive [image]
Direktpositivemulsion *f* [direct-]positive emulsion, positive-working emulsion
Direktpositivfilm *m* direct positive film, instant-print film
Direktpositivpapier *n* direct positive paper
Direktpositiv-Silberhalogenidemulsion *f* direct-positive [silver halide] emulsion
Direktpositivverfahren *n* direct positive process
Direktprojektion *f* direct [front] projection
Direktradiografie *f* direct radiography
Direktrix *f* directrix [curve]
Direktsendebetrieb *m* on-air broadcast use
Direktsichtdisplay *n*,
Direktsichtspeicherröhre *f* direct-view display, direct-view [storage] tube, direct-view CRT (cathode-ray tube)
Direkttoner *m* direct toner
Direkttonpositiv *n* direct sound positive
Direkttonung *f* direct toning
Direktübertragung *f* direct transfer; direct transmission; live broadcast
Direktumkehr *f* direct reversal
Direktumkehremulsion *f* direct-reversal emulsion
Direktumkehrfarbfilm *m* direct reversal color film
Direktumkehrfilm *m* direct-reversal film
Direktverarbeitung *f* straightforward processing
Direktzugriff *m* random (direct) access; nonlinear access
Direktzugriffsdatei *f* random[-access] file, direct-access file
Direktzugriffsmöglichkeit *f* random-access capability
Direktzugriffsspeicher *m* random-access memory, RAM, direct-access storage [device]
DIR-Farbkuppler *m s.* DIR-Kuppler
Dirichlet-Parkettierung *f* Dirichlet tiling (tessellation), Voronoi tiling (tessellation), *(computational geometry)*

DIR-Kuppler *m* developer-inhibitor-releasing coupler, DIR coupler
Disambiguierung *f* disambiguation *(character recognition)*
disjunkt disjunct, disjoint *(e.g. image regions)*
Diskette *f* floppy [disk], FD, diskette
Diskettenadapter *m* floppy disk adapter
Diskettenlaufwerk *n* [floppy] disk drive
Diskkamera *f* disc camera
Diskokugel *f* mirrored ball
Diskrepanz *f/perzeptuelle* perceptual discrepancy *(robotics)*
diskret discrete, noncontinuous, distinct
Diskretheit *f* discreteness
diskretisieren to discretize
Diskretisierung *f* discretization; sampling
~**/räumliche** spatial discretization
~**/zeitliche** time [direction] discretization
Diskretisierungsfehler *m* discretization error; sampling error (artifact), scanning error (artifact)
Diskretisierungsrauschen *n* discretization noise
Diskriminanzanalyse *f* discriminant (discriminatory) analysis
Diskriminanzfunktion *f* discriminant (decision) function
Diskriminanzmethode *f* discriminant (Otsu's) method *(of thresholding)*
Diskriminanzfähigkeit *f* discriminability, discriminatory ability, discriminatory (discriminative) power
Disparität *f* disparity
~**/angulare** angular disparity
~**/binokulare** binocular disparity
~**/retinale** retinal disparity (rivalry)
~**/vertikale** vertical disparity *(three-dimensional imaging)*
Disparitätsanalyse *f* disparity analysis
Disparitätsbereich *m* disparity range
Disparitätsschätzung *f* disparity estimation
Disparitätsvektor *m* disparity vector
Disparitätsverhältnis *n* disparity ratio
dispergierbar dispersible
dispergieren to disperse
Dispergierung *f* dispersion, dispersing
Dispergierungsmittel *n* dispersing agent, dispersant
dispers disperse
Dispersion *f* dispersion *(e.g. of optical materials)*
~**/anomale** anomalous dispersion
~**/atmosphärische** atmospheric
~**/chromatische** [chromatic] dispersion, color [light] dispersion
~**/kolloide** colloidal dispersion
~**/lineare** linear dispersion
~**/normale** normal dispersion
~**/optische** optical dispersion
~**/räumliche** spatial dispersion

Dispersionsfilter *n* dispersion filter; Christiansen [effect] filter
Dispersionsformel *f* dispersion formula (equation), Cauchy (Hartmann) formula
Dispersionskoeffizient *m* dispersion coefficient
Dispersionsprisma *n* dispersing prism
Dispersionsspektroskopie *f* dispersion spectroscopy
Dispersionsvermögen *n* dispersive power
Dispersionswinkel *m* dispersion angle
Dispersität *f* dispersity
dispersiv dispersive
Display *n* display, readout *(s.a.* under Anzeige, *Bildschirm, Monitor)*
~/**aktives** active-matrix display, TFT (thin-film transistor) display
~/**autokalibrierendes** autocalibrating display
~/**autostereoskopisches** autostereo[scopic] display
~/**berührungsempfindliches (berührungssensitives)** touch[-sensitive] screen; tactile (pressure-sensitive) screen; touch screen monitor
~/**flexibles** flexible display
~/**grafikfähiges (grafisches)** graphical (computer-graphic) display, graphics display [screen], graphics screen
~/**großflächiges** large[-format] display, large-screen [display]
~/**haptisches** *s.*
~/berührungsempfindliches
~/**hochauflösendes** high-resolution display
~/**niedrigauflösendes** low-resolution display
~/**organisches** organic display
~/**passives** passively addressed display
~/**stereoskopisches** stereoscopic display
~/**verformbares** flexible display
Displayfläche *f* display area
Displayforschung *f* display research
Displayholografie *f* display[-type] holography
Displaykennlinie *f* display function (characteristic curve)
Displayliste *f* display file
Displayprozessor *m* display processor
Displaysystem *n* display system
Displaytechnik *f*, **Displaytechnologie** *f* display technology
Dispo[sition] *f* call sheet *(filming)*
Dissektorröhre *f* dissector tube
Dissoziation *f* dissociation
Distanz *f*/**Euklidische** Euclidean distance
~/**hyperfokale** hyperfocal distance *(optics)*
~/**optische** optical distance
Distanzmaß *n* distance measure (metric)
Distanzraster *m(n)* glass [halftone] screen, ruled screen
Distanzring *m* distance ring

Distanztransformation *f* distance transform[ation] *(binary image processing)*
Distorsion *f* distortion *(an oblique aberration; s.a.* under Verzeichnung*)*
Distribution *f* distribution *(e.g. of television signals)*
distributiv distributive *(e.g. an image-processing operator)*
Distributivität *f* distributivity
Dithering *n*, **Dithering-Technik** *f* dithering, dither technique, halftoning *(electronic imaging; s.a.* Streurasterung*)*
Dithermatrix *f* dither[ing] matrix, dither[ing] pattern
divergent divergent
Divergenz *f* divergence, divergency *(e.g. of radiation)*
Divergenzoperator *m* divergence operator *(nonlinear filtering)*
Divergenzwinkel *m* divergence angle
divergieren to diverge *(e.g. lines)*
Divis *n* hyphen *(punctuation mark)*
DLP-System *n* DLP projector system *(digital cinema)*
DMD-Projektor *m*, **DMD-Videoprojektor** *m* DMD (digital micromirror device) video projector
Dobson-Teleskop *n* Dobsonian telescope
DoG-Filter *n* difference of Gaussians [filter]
Dokument *n*/**multimediales** multimedia (mixed media) document
~/**zusammengesetztes** compound document
Dokumentablichtungssystem *n* document-imaging system
Dokumentaraufnahme *f* documentary photograph
Dokumentarfilm *m* documentary [film]
Dokumentarfilmer *m* documentary filmmaker (camera person)
Dokumentarfilmproduktion *f* documentary film production
Dokumentarfilmteam *n* documentary crew
Dokumentarfotograf *m* documentary photographer
Dokumentarfotografie *f* documentary photography
dokumentarfotografisch documentary photographic
Dokumentarteam *n* documentary crew
Dokumentationsaufnahme *f* documentary photograph
Dokumentenanalyse *f* document [image] analysis
Dokumentenauszeichnungssprache *f* markup language *(data processing)*
Dokumentenbild *n* document image
Dokumentenbildverarbeitung *f* [/**elektronische**] electronic document image processing, EDIP
Dokumenteneinzug *m*/**automatischer** automatic document feeder, ADF

Dokumentenerfassung f document capture
Dokumentenerkennung f document recognition
Dokumentenfilm m microfilm; microfiche film
Dokumentenkamera f document[-copying] camera
Dokumentenkopierer m document copier, document-copying machine
Dokumentenlesegerät n, **Dokumentenleser** m document reader (viewer)
Dokumentenpapier n document (archive) paper
Dokumentenscanner m document scanner
Dokumentenübertragung f document transfer (interchange)
Dokumentenvervielfältigung f document reproduction; document copying
Dokumentenzuführung f 1. document feed; 2. document feeder *(device)*
dokumentieren to document
Dokumentseite f document page
Dokumentvorlage f 1. template; 2. style sheet
Dolly m [camera] dolly, truck; crab dolly *(mobile shooting platform)*
Dollyfahrer m dolly pusher
Domäne f domain *(data processing)*
Dominanz f dominance *(of one eye over the other)*, eyedness
Donnereffekt m thunder effect *(optical sound interference)*
Doppel-Acht-Film m standard double-8-mm film, double-run 8-mm
Doppelanastigmat m(n) double anastigmat [lens], double-anastigmatic objective
Doppelanodenröhre f double anode [X-ray] tube
doppelbelichten to double-burn *(esp. in reprography)*
Doppelbelichtung f double exposure, DX
Doppelbelichtungsholografie f double-exposure holography, holographic interferometry
Doppelbelichtungshologramm n double-exposure hologram
Doppelbelichtungsinterferometrie f s. Doppelbelichtungsholografie
Doppelbelichtungsmaske f double-exposure mask
Doppelbelichtungssperre f double-exposure lock (prevention device)
Doppelbelichtungstechnik f double-exposure method *(holographic interferometry)*
Doppelbeschichtung f double coating *(e.g. of videotape)*
Doppelbild n double image (picture)
Doppelbildmessung f stereophotogrammetry
Doppelbildmikroskopie f double-image microscopy
Doppelbildprisma n double-image prism, [Fresnel] biprism
Doppelbildschirm m double screen *(television)*
Doppelbildteiler m double image splitter
Doppelbit n dibit
Doppelblitz m double flash
Doppelbogenkontrolle f caliper *(sheet-fed press)*
doppelbrechen to doubly refract
doppelbrechend birefractive, birefracting, birefringent, doubly refracting
Doppelbrechung f double refraction, birefringence, birefraction
Doppelbrechzahl f double refractive index
Doppelbuchstabe m ligature, tied letters *(typography)*
Doppelbus m dual bus *(data transmission)*
Doppeleinlauf m double-jet precipitation, double-jet method (scheme) *(emulsion preparation)*
Doppeleinlaufemulsion f double-jet emulsion
Doppelfernrohr n [pair of] binoculars; field glass[es]
Doppelflüssigkeitsfilter n Davis Gibson filter
Doppelfokus[röntgen]röhre f double-focus tube (valve)
Doppelgängerfilter n dual-image filter
Doppelgitterprisma n double grating prism
Doppelhandfernrohr n field glass[es]
Doppel-Heterostruktur f double heterostructure *(e.g. of a light-emitting diode)*
Doppelimpulslaser m double-pulse laser
Doppelkamera f twin-lens camera, stereo[scopic] camera
Doppelklick m double-click
doppelklicken to double-click
Doppelkondensor m dual condenser
Doppelkontrast m double contrast *(fluoroscopy)*
Doppelkontur f ghosting
Doppelkreuz n double dagger *(character)*
Doppelkristallmonochromator m double-crystal monochromator
Doppellaufwerk n twin drive
Doppelmikroskop n split-field microscope
Doppelmodulation f dual (double) modulation
Doppelobjektiv n doublet [lens], lens doublet
Doppelokular n double eyepiece
Doppelphasenhologramm n double-phase hologram
Doppelpol[arisations]filter n fader
Doppelprisma n double (dual) prism
~/elektrooptisches electro-optic double prism
Doppelprojektion f double projection
Doppelprojektor m double projector

Doppelpufferung f double (ping-pong) buffering (image data processing)
Doppelreflexion f double reflection [effect]
Doppelschichtfilm m duplitized (double-coated) film, double-emulsion film
Doppelschichtfilter n double-layer filter
Doppelschicht-Röntgenfilm m duplitized (double-coated) X-ray film
Doppelseite f [full] spread, two-page spread (e.g. in a magazine)
doppelseitig double[-sided], two-sided
Doppelselbstauslöser m two-shot self-timer
Doppelspalt m double slit (optics)
Doppelspaltinterferenz f two-slit interference
Doppelspalt-Interferenzbild n two-slit interference pattern
Doppelspaltversuch m double-slit experiment
Doppelspur f dual track (film sound recording)
Doppelstrahlablenkung f double beam deflection
Doppelteleskop n binocular telescope
Doppeltonbild n bitonal (bi-level) image
Doppeltonfarbe f bitone ink (typography)
Doppeltonprobe f cross modulation test
Doppeltsehen n double vision, diplopia
Doppeltürschleuse f double-door system (light lock) (darkroom entrance)
Doppelwendel f double-coiled filament, coiled-coiled filament
Doppelzackenschrift f bilateral area track
Doppler-Auflösung f Doppler resolution
Doppler-Bild n Doppler (velocity) image
Doppler-Bildgebung f Doppler imaging
Doppler-Breite f Doppler width
Doppler-Dilemma n Doppler dilemma
Doppler-Echokardiografie f Doppler echocardiography
Doppler-Effekt m Doppler effect
~/**longitudinaler** longitudinal Doppler effect
~/**transversaler** transverse Doppler effect
Doppler-Frequenz f Doppler[-shift] frequency
Doppler-Frequenzverschiebung f Doppler [frequency] shift
Doppler-Lidar m(n) Doppler lidar
Doppler-Linienbreite f Doppler width
Doppler-Monitor m Doppler information display
Doppler-Prinzip n Doppler principle
Doppler-Radar n Doppler radar
Doppler-Raum m Doppler space (domain)
Doppler-Reflektor m Doppler reflector
Doppler-Signal n Doppler [ultrasonic] signal
Doppler-Sonograf m Doppler device
Doppler-Sonografie f 1. Doppler ultrasound imaging technology; 2. Doppler ultrasound imaging (technique)

~/**farbcodierte** ultrasound color Doppler system
Doppler-Spektroskopie f Doppler spectroscopy
Doppler-Spektrum n Doppler[-shifted] spectrum, Doppler power spectrum
Doppler-Tomografie f Doppler tomography
Doppler-Ultraschall m Doppler[-shifted] ultrasound
Doppler-Verbreiterung f Doppler broadening (widening)
Doppler-Verfahren n Doppler technique (sonography)
Doppler-Verschiebung f Doppler [frequency] shift
Doppler-Verschiebungsfrequenz f Doppler shift frequency
Doppler-Winkel m Doppler angle
Dosenentwicklung f small tank processing
Dosimeter n dosimeter, dosemeter, dosage meter
Dosimetrie f dosimetry
dosimetrisch dosimetric
Dosis f/**absorbierte** [absorbed] dose (X-ray dosimetry)
~/**effektive** effective dose
Dosiszuwachsfaktor m build-up factor
Dotand m dopant
dotieren to dope (semiconductor material)
Dotiermittel n, **Dotierstoff** m dopant
Dotierung f doping
Dove-Prisma n Dove prism
Download m download
Downloadzeit f download time
Drahtantenne f wire antenna
Drahtauslöser m [camera] cable release, antinous release
Drahtgaze f scrim (lighting accessory)
Drahtgittermodell n wire frame [model], wire frame object, net model
drahtlos wireless
Drahtmodell n s. Drahtgittermodell
Drahtstaffage f rig wires (movie set)
Drahtsteg m wire target [phantom] (radiography)
Draufsicht f top view
Dreh m shoot[ing] (filming; s.a. Videodreh)
Drehachse f axis of rotation (revolution), rotat[al] axis
Drehanode f rotating anode (X-ray tube)
Drehanodenröhre f s. Drehanoden-Röntgenröhre
Drehanoden-Röntgengenerator m rotating-anode X-ray generator
Drehanodenröntgenröhre f rotating-anode X-ray tube
Dreharbeit f production shooting
~ **vor Ort** location shoot[ing]
Drehbericht m camera report (sheet), camera exposure chart, dope sheet, shooting notes (cinema)
Drehbewegung f rotational (rotary) motion, rotation
Drehblende f rotary diaphragm

Drehbuch

Drehbuch n 1. [motion-picture] screenplay, scenario; 2. s. Filmskript
Drehbuchauszug m breakdown
Drehbuchautor m screenwriter, filmwright
Drehbuch-Vorstufe f treatment
drehen to shoot, to crank *(cinema)*
Drehen n **auf Schnitt** in-camera editing; cutting in the camera, triple-take
~ **ohne O-Ton** mit out sound, MOS *(cinema)*
Drehende f wrap *(filming)*
Drehfilter n rotary (rotating) filter
Drehfolge f shooting order
Drehinvarianz f rotation invariance *(pattern recognition)*
Drehkeilpaar n counterrotating wedges (prisms), Risley prisms
Drehkopf m swivel head *(e.g. of a tripod)*
Drehmaterial n [/originales] original (raw) footage; source material (tape) *(video)*
Drehmoment n angular momentum
Drehort m film location, [shooting] location; [motion-picture] set, setting; taping location *(video)*
Drehpause f shooting break
Drehplan m shooting schedule; shooting script (plan)
Drehplanung f scheduling
Drehprisma n rotating prism
Drehprotokoll n script *(s.a. Drehplan, Drehbericht)*
Drehpunkt m pivot point, fulcrum
Drehrichtung f direction of rotation
Drehschieberpumpe f rotary vane pump *(electron microscopy)*
Drehschluss m wrap *(filming)*
Drehsinn m sense of rotation
Drehsituation f shooting situation
Drehspiegel m rotating (spinning) mirror, pivoting mirror
Drehspiegelkamera f rotating-mirror camera
Drehspiegelsystem n rotating-mirror system
Drehstab m film crew, [motion-picture] production crew
Drehtag m shoot[ing] day, day of shooting
Drehtagebuch n continuity report *(s.a. Drehbericht, Drehprotokoll)*
Drehteam n film crew
Drehtürschleuse f rotating-door entrance *(e.g. for a darkroom)*
Drehung f rotation *(geometric transformation)*
~/**optische** optical rotation
Drehungsinvarianz f rotation[al] invariance *(pattern recognition)*
Drehverhältnis n shooting ratio
Drehvermögen n/**optisches** optical activity
Drehwinkel m rotation[al] angle, angle of rotation
Drehzeiger m phasor *(signal processing)*
Drehzeit f shooting time

Dreibadprozess m three-bath tray processing *(of photographic paper)*
Dreibein[stativ] n tripod, three-legged stand *(s.a. under Stativ)*
Dreibereichs-Farbmessgerät n tristimulus colorimeter
Dreibereichs-Farbtemperaturmesser m three-detector color-temperature meter, three-cell[-type] color temperature meter
Dreibereichsverfahren n tristimulus method *(colorimetry)*
Drei-Bildpunkte-Nachbarschaft f three-pixel neighborhood *(image processing)*
Dreichipkamera f three-chip [video] camera, three-chip DV camcorder, three-CCD [imaging-array color] camera, three-sensor [professional] camera
dreidimensional three-dimensional, tridimensional, three-D, 3-D
Dreidimensionalität f tridimensionality, three-dimensionality
Dreieck n triangle
~/**gleichschenkliges** isosceles triangle
~/**gleichseitiges** equilateral triangle
~/**Maxwellsches** Maxwell triangle *(chromaticity diagram)*
~/**rechtwinkliges** right triangle
~/**spitzwinkliges** acute triangle
~/**stumpfwinkliges** obtuse triangle
~/**ungleichseitiges** scalene triangle
dreieckig f triangular
Dreiecksfenster n Bartlett window *(signal processing)*
Dreiecksgitter n, **Dreiecksnetz** n triangular (triangle) mesh, triangle lattice, triangular [irregular] network
Dreiecksraster m(n) triangular dot pattern *(reprography)*
Dreierregel f rule of thirds
Dreifachauszug m triple extension *(view camera)*
Dreifach-Selbstauslöser m triple self-timer *(digital camera)*
Dreifachvergütung f triple coating
Dreifachzoom[objektiv] n triple zoom
Dreifarb... s. Dreifarben...
Dreifarbenauszug m three-color [separation] record
Dreifarbenbild n three-color image, tricolor image
Dreifarbendruck m 1. three-color printing [process], trichromatic printing; 2. trichromatic print
Dreifarbenfilm m/**subtraktiver** three-color subtractive reversal film
Dreifarbenfotografie f 1. [additive] trichromatic color photography, three-color photography, three-color photographic process; 2. trichromatic color photograph
Dreifarbenkinematografie f three-color cinematography
Dreifarbenkolorimeter n three-color meter

dreifarbenkolorimetrisch trichromatic colorimetric
Dreifarbenprojektion f three-color projection [method]
Dreifarbenröhre f tricolor CRT (cathode-ray tube), three-[single-]color CRT
Dreifarbensehen n trichromatic [color] vision, trichromacy, trichromatism
Dreifarbensystem n tricolor (trichromatic) system
Dreifarbentheorie f **des Lichts** three-color theory [of light], trichromacy (trichromatic) theory [of color vision], Young-Helmholtz theory [of color vision]
dreifarbig three-color; tricolor[ed]; trichromatic
Dreiflügel[zangen]blende f three-bladed shutter *(film projector)*
Dreifuß-Kleinstativ n small tripod, minipod
Dreikammer-Farbdruckpatrone f, **Dreikammer-Farbtintenpatrone** f tricolor ink-jet print cartridge
Dreikanalton m three-channel sound
Dreikantprisma n triangular [glass] prism
Drei-Kelvin-Strahlung f s. Hintergrundstrahlung/kosmische
Dreikomponententheorie f **des Farbensehens** trichromatic theory of color vision
Dreilinser m [optical lens] triplet; triplet objective; [photographic] triplet lens
Dreimesserautomat m s. Dreischneider
Dreiniveaulaser m three-level laser
Dreipassmethode f three-light method *(scanning)*
Dreipassscanner m triple sensor scanner
Drei-Phasen-CCD-Bildsensor m three-phase CCD image sensor
Dreipunkt-Abbildung f s. Abbildung/affine
Dreipunktperspektive f three-point perspective; oblique perspective
Dreiröhren[farb]kamera f three-tube [television color] camera
Dreischichtenfarbfilm m three-layer (triple-layer) color film; integral-tripack color film
~/**chromogener** three-color subtractive reversal film
Dreischichtenfilm m three [emulsion] layer film, triple-layer film
Dreischichten-Negativfilm m three-layer negative film
Dreischneider m three-knife trimmer
Dreisensorenkamera f s. Dreichipkamera
Dreistrahl-Lochmaskenbildröhre f, **Dreistrahlröhre** f three-gun cathode ray tube
Dreistreifenverfahren n three-strip process *(of early color motion-picture production)*
Dreistrichbogen m octavo
Dreiviertel-Frontallichtführung f three-quarter lighting
Dreiviertelporträt n, **Dreiviertelprofil** n three-quarter [face] view *(s.a. Brustbild)*

Dreiviertelzollband n three-quarter-inch [wide] tape, 19-mm tape *(video)*
Dreiviertelzoll-Kassette f three-quarter-inch cassette
Dreiwegekopf m three-way head *(tripod)*
Dreiweg-Fluideffekt-Videokopf m three-way video fluid effect head
Dreizylinder-Offsetpresse f three-cylinder offset press
Drittfarbe f tertiary color
Drive-in-Kino n drive-in theater
Drop-in-Ladeautomatik f drop-in loading system
Druck m 1. pressure; 2. printing; presswork; 3. print
~/**anastatischer** anastatic printing [procedure]
~/**bedarfsweiser** print on demand
~/**beidseitiger** double-face printing
~/**bidirektionaler** bidirectional printing
~/**digitaler** digital printing
~/**doppelseitiger** double-face printing
~/**dreidimensionaler** three-dimensional printing
~/**elektrofotografischer** electrophotographic printing
~/**elektrostatischer** electrostatic printing [process]
~/**leichter** kiss impression *(printing)*
~/**lithografischer** lithographic printing
~/**magnetografischer** magnetographic printing
~/**mehrfarbiger** multicolor (polychrome) printing
~/**xerografischer** xerographic printing, xerography *(electrophotography)*
Druckarbeit f print[ing] job, job
Druckauflage f [press]run
Druckauftrag m 1. printing order, production (work) order; print[ing] job, job; 2. job ticket, docket
Druckausgabe f printer output
druckbar printable
Druckbefehl m print command
Druckbeilage f insert, interleaves *(additional printed item within a publication)*
Druckbetrieb m printing office (plant), printing company (firm)
Druckbild n printed image
~/**wolkiges** mottled (mealy) image *(printing defect)*
Druckbildanzeige f preview
Druckbildelement n printing image area
druckbildfrei nonimage *(e.g. area of a gravure plate)*
Druckbildinspektion f, **Druckbildkontrolle** f printed image control
Druckbildspeicher m printed image store
Druckbildübertragung/digitale digital-to-plate process
~/**direkte** direct imaging, DI
Druckbildvorschau f preview
Druckblende f pressure diaphragm

Druckbogen *m* press sheet; printed sheet
Druckbogenmontage *f* imposition
Druckbreite *f* printing width
Druckbuchstabe *m* 1. printed letter; [hand-]printed character; 2. letter, printing type, [piece of] type, type piece
Druckdatei *f* print[er] file
Druckdichte *f* impression density
Druckdurchgang *m s.* Druckgang
Druckdüse *f* printing nozzle
Druckeinheit *f* printing unit
Druckempfänger *m* pressure microphone
drucken to print, to letter
~/**kursiv** to italicize
~/**nass-auf-trocken** to dry-trap
~/**nass-in-nass** to wet-trap
Drucken *n* printing
~/**anschlagfreies** nonimpact printing
~/**bedarfsweises** printing on demand, POD
~/**beidseitiges** double[-way] printing, duplex printing
~/**digitales** digital printing
~ **nach Bedarf** printing on demand, POD
~/**personalisiertes** customized printing
~/**randloses** borderless printing
Drucker *m* 1. [hard-copy] printer, printout device, [peripheral] printing device; 2. printer, pressman
~/**anschlagender** impact [dot-matrix] printer
~/**anschlagfreier (aufschlagfreier)** nonimpact (pressureless) printer
~/**bidirektionaler** bidirectional printer
~/**dielektrischer** dielectric printer
~/**dreidimensionaler** 3-D printer
~/**elektrofotografischer** electrophotographic printer
~/**elektrostatischer** electrostatic printer
~/**fotoelektrischer** *s.* ~/elektrofotografischer
~/**fotorealistischer** near-photographic printer
~/**grafikfähiger** graphics printer
~/**mechanischer** impact [dot-matrix] printer
~/**nichtmechanischer** *s.* ~/anschlagfreier
~/**vernetzter** networked printer
~/**xerografischer** xerographic printer
Druckeranschluss *m* printer port (interface)
Druckerauflösung *f* printer resolution
Druckerausgabe *f* printer (hard-copy) output
Druckerbeschreibungsdatei *f* printer description file
Druckerei *f* printing office (shop), printery
~/**firmeneigene (hauseigene)** inplant
Druckeremulation *f* printer emulation
Druckerfarbband *n s.* Farbband
Druckergebnis *n* printing result
Druckerkabel *n* printer cable
Druckerkalibrierung *f* printer calibration
Druckerlaubnis *f* imprimatur

Druckerleistungstest *m* printer performance test
Druckerpapier *n* printer paper
Druckerpatrone *f* print[er] cartridge
Druckerpresse *f* [printing] press
Druckerpuffer *m* print[er] buffer
Druckerschlange *f* printer queue
Druckerschnittstelle *f* printer interface (port)
Druckerschrift *f* printer font
Druckerschwärze *f* printer's ink, printing black
Druckersoftware *f* printer software
Druckerspeicher *m* printer buffer
Drucker[steuer]sprache *f* printer [control] language, printer command language
Druckertechnik *f* printer technology
Druckertreiber *m* printer driver
Druckerwarteschlange *f* printer queue
Druckerzeugnis *n* [final] printed product; printed material
druckfähig printable
Druckfähigkeit *f* printability
Druckfahne *f* galley [proof]
Druckfarbe *f* 1. printing [ink] color; 2. [printing] ink
~/**dick[flüssig]e** viscous ink; [thick] greasy ink
~/**dünn[flüssig]e** fluid [solvent] ink, low-viscosity ink
~/**hochviskose** *s.* ~/dick[flüssig]e
~/**kurze** short ink
~/**lasierende** transparent ink
~/**magnetische** magnetic ink
~/**niederviskose** *s.* ~/dünn[flüssig]e
~/**pigmentierte** pigmented ink
~/**scheuerfeste** rub-proof ink
~/**schnelltrocknende** fast-drying ink
~/**thermoplastische** thermoplastic ink
~/**thixotrope** thixotropic [printing] ink
~/**unter Hitzeeinwirkung verdunstende** heat-drying printing ink
~/**zähflüssige** *s.* ~/dick[flüssig]e
Druckfarbe-Feuchtmittel-Balance *f* ink-water balance
Druckfarbenaufnahmevermögen *n* ink receptivity
Druckfarbenentfernung *f* deinking
Druckfarbenpigment *n* printing ink pigment
Druckfehler *m* printer (typographical) error, typo; erratum, corrigendum *(s.a.* Druckschwierigkeit*)*
druckfertig ready for [the] press
Druckfilm *m* graphic arts film
Druckfolie *f* photopolymer plate (image carrier) *(gravure printing)*
Druckform *f* printing (press) form, typeform, form[e]
~/**äußere** outer form
~/**elastische** flexible plate
~/**innere** inner form
~/**löschbare** erasable [printing] form
Druckformat *n* style; print[ing] format

Druckverfahren

Druckformatvorlage f style sheet
Druckformfeuchtung f aqueous coating, moistening, wetting
Druckformherstellung f platemaking, printing-plate fabrication; photomechanics
~/**filmlose** computer-to-plate (metal), C2P
Druckformoberfläche f typeface
Druckformträger m chase; bed *(letterpress printing)*
Druckformzylinder m plate[-bearing] cylinder *(printing press)*
Druckfreigabe f imprimatur
Druckgang m printing step; pressrun
Druckgeschwindigkeit f printing speed (rate)
Druckgewerbe n graphic arts
Druckgrafik f print graphics
druckgrafisch print graphic
Druckgüte f print[ing] quality
Druckhilfsmittel n printing additive
Druckindustrie f printing (graphic arts) industry, print [industry]
Druckjob m print[ing] job, job
Druckkassette f print cartridge
Druckkennlinie f print characteristic
Druckklischee n s. Duplikatdruckform
Druckkontrast m [/**relativer**] print contrast
Druckkontrolleiste f, **Druckkontrollstreifen** m color control bar, [standard offset] color bar, color guide
Druckkopf m printhead, printer head
~/**piezoelektrischer** piezoelectric printer head
Druckkopfsteuerung f printhead control
Druckkopie f dye transfer (imbibition) print *(color photography)*
Druckkunst f art of printing; graphic arts
Drucklack m varnish, lacquer
Drucklegung f printing
Druckmanager m print manager *(software program)*
Druckmaschine f printing machine (press)
Druckmedium n printing medium
Druckmikrofon n pressure microphone
Drucknadel f printing needle
Drucköl n printing oil
Druckpapier n/**ungestrichenes** uncoated printing paper
Druckpaste f printing paste, paste ink
Druckplatte f [printing] plate *(s.a. under Platte)*
~/**diazobeschichtete** diazo plate
~/**digital zu bebildernde** digital plate
~/**elektrostatische** electrostatic plate
~/**flexible** flexible plate; wraparound [press] plate
~/**fotomechanische** photomechanical printing plate
~/**fotopolymere** photopolymer [printing] plate; photopolymer gravure plate
~/**geätzte** etched printing plate
~/**vorbeschichtete** precoated [printing] plate

~/**vorsensibilisierte** presensitized plate
Druckplattenätzung f plate etching
Druckplattenbelichtung f plate exposure
Druckplattenfertigung f, **Druckplattenherstellung** f printing-plate fabrication, platemaking; photomechanics *(s.a. under Druckformherstellung)*
Druckplattenherstellung/filmlose filmless platemaking
Druckpresse f [printing] press
Druckprinzip n printing principle
Druckprodukt n [final] printed product; printed material
Druckprozess m 1. printing process; 2. s. Druckverfahren 2.
Druckpufferspeicher m print[er] buffer
Druckpunkt m printing (printer) dot, [ink] dot
~/**digitaler** digital dot
Druckpunktzuwachs m dot (press) gain, dot growth (spread)
Druckqualität f print[ing] quality
Druckrad n daisy (type) wheel
Druckraster m(n) line screen
Druckrichtung f print direction
Drucksaal m pressroom
Drucksache f printed matter (piece), print
Druckschrift f [printed] type
Druckschwierigkeit f printing defect
Druckseite f printed page, page of type
Druckserver m print server
Druckservice m print service
Druckspalte f column
Druckspeicher m print storage
Druckstelle f pressure mark *(e.g. on film or paper)*
Druckstock m printing block; [printing] plate
Druckstreifen m printing nip
Drucksystem n printing system
Drucktechnik f 1. printing (graphic) technology; 2. printing technique
Drucktechniker m pressman
drucktechnisch typographic[al], print-technical
Drucktinte f printing ink
Drucktuch n [cylinder] blanket
Drucktuchzylinder m blanket[-covered] cylinder, offset (rubber blanket image transfer) cylinder
Drucktype f printing type, [piece of] type, letter
Druckverfahren n 1. printing process (technique), printing method; 2. dye transfer [printing] process *(photographic color printing method)*
~/**direktes** direct printing process
~/**fotografisches** photographic printing process
~/**fotomechanisches** photomechanical printing process
~/**indirektes** indirect printing process

Druckverfahren

~/**mechanisches** impact (plate, pressure) printing process
~/**nichtmechanisches** nonimpact (plateless, pressureless) printing process
~/**rasterloses** screenless printing process
Druckvoranzeige f print preview
Druckvoranzeigeprogramm n previewer
Druckvorbereitung f prepress work
Druckvorgang m printing operation
Druckvorlage f artwork, art; [printer's] copy
Druckvorstufe f prepress [area]; prepress printing process, preparation
~/**digitale** computer-to-plate system
~/**elektronische** electronic prepress
Druckvorstufenbetrieb m prepress plant
Druckvorstufenproof m prepress proof, dry (off-press) proof
Druckvorstufensystem n prepress system
Druckwalze f 1. platen [roller], platen drum *(e.g. of a thermal-transfer printer)*; 2. s. Druckzylinder
Druckwarteschlange f printer queue
Druckweite f pitch
Druckweiterverarbeitung f post-printing operations, post press operations, finish[ing]
Druckwerk n 1. [printing] unit, printing station; 2. s. Druckerzeugnis
Druckwesen n printing
Druckzeichen n [printed] character, type character
Druckzeichensatz m printed font
Druckzeile f printing line, line of print
Druckzeit f printing time
Druckzone f printing area; printing nip
Druckzylinder m impression cylinder, impression roll[er] *(printing press)*
~/**nahtloser** seamless impression roll
DTP s. Desktoppublishing
dual dual *(s.a. binär)*
Dualcode m s. Binärcode
Dualität f duality
Dualobjektiv n s. Doppelobjektiv
Dualsystem n binary [number] system
Dualzahl f, **Dualziffer** f binary digit (number), binary unit, bit
Dublett n doublet [lens], lens doublet
~/**achromatisches** achromatic doublet [lens]
~/**sphärisches** spherical doublet [lens]
Dublettlinse f s. Dublett
Dublieren n doubling *(printing defect)*
Dubray-Howell-Lochung f Dubray-Howell perforation, DH perf
Duettschnitt m synchro[nous] edit *(video)*
Dukalampe f s. Dunkelkammerlampe
Dukaleuchte f s. Dunkelkammerleuchte
Duktor m ductor, duct[or] roller *(printing press)*
dunkel dark, lightless
Dunkeladaptation f dark (rod) adaptation
Dunkeladaptationszustand m resting state of accommodation, dark focus

dunkeladaptiert dark-adapted, scotopic
Dunkelanpassung f s. Dunkeladaptation
Dunkelblitz m infrared flash
Dunkelentladung f dark discharge *(photoreceptor)*
Dunkelentsättigung f chroma black (dark)
dunkelfarbig dark-colored
Dunkelfeld n dark field
Dunkelfeldbeleuchtung f dark-field (darkground) illumination
Dunkelfeldbeobachtung f, **Dunkelfeldbetrachtung** f dark-field observation
Dunkelfeldbild n dark-field image *(electron microscopy)*
Dunkelfeldblende f dark-field stop
Dunkelfeldkondensor m dark-field condenser
Dunkelfeld-Mikrofotografie f 1. dark-field photomicrography; 2. dark-field photomicrograph
Dunkelfeldmikroskop n dark-field (dark-ground) microscope
Dunkelfeldmikroskopie f dark-field microscopy, ultramicroscopy
Dunkelfeldobjekt n dark-field object
Dunkelfeldprojektion f dark-field projection
Dunkelfotografie f s. Infrarotfotografie
Dunkelheit f darkness, lightlessness
Dunkel-Hell-Übergang m dark-to-light [image] transition
Dunkelkammer f [photographic] darkroom; chemical darkroom *(s.a. under Dunkelraum)*; dark chamber
Dunkelkammerarbeit f darkroom work (photography)
Dunkelkammerausrüstung f darkroom equipment (outfit)
Dunkelkammerbeleuchtung f darkroom (safelight) illumination; [darkroom] safelighting
Dunkelkammereingang m entrance (entry) to the darkroom
Dunkelkammerfilter n safelight filter
Dunkelkammergerät n darkroom appliance
Dunkelkammergerätschaften pl darkroom facilities
Dunkelkammerlampe f darkroom (safelight) lamp
Dunkelkammerleuchte f [darkroom] safelight, safelamp
Dunkelkammerlicht n [darkroom] safelight
Dunkelkammerpraxis f darkroom practice
Dunkelkammerschutzfilter n safelight filter
Dunkelkammertätigkeit f s. Dunkelkammerarbeit
Dunkelkammerverarbeitung f darkroom [photo] processing
Dunkelkammerzubehör n darkroom accessories
Dunkelladung f dark charge

Dunkelladungsrauschen *n s.* Dunkelstromrauschen
Dunkelleitfähigkeit *f* dark conductivity
Dunkelpause *f s.* Dunkelperiode
Dunkelperiode *f*, **Dunkelphase** *f* dark period (interval)
Dunkelprojektion *f s.* Dunkelraumprojektion
Dunkelraum *m* darkened room; [photographic] darkroom; chemical darkroom *(s.a.* Dunkelkammer*)*
Dunkelraumausleuchtung *f*, **Dunkelraumbeleuchtung** *f* darkroom illumination, safe[light] illumination
Dunkelraumbelüftung *f* darkroom ventilation
Dunkelraumkamera *f* darkroom [process] camera
Dunkelrauschen *n s.* Dunkelstromrauschen
Dunkelsack *m* changing (black) bag
Dunkelsehen *n* scotopic (dark-adapted) vision, night (rod) vision
dunkelsteuern *s.* dunkeltasten
Dunkelstrom *m* dark current *(photodetector)*
Dunkelstromdichte *f* dark current density
Dunkelstromrauschen *n* dark[-current] noise, dark-current shot noise
Dunkelstufe *f* value *(colorimetry; s.a.* Helligkeit*)*
Dunkeltasten *n* [retrace] blanking
dunkeltasten to blank [out], to turn off *(video signal)*
Dunkelwert *m s.* Grauwert
Dünndarmspiegel *m* enteroscope
Dünnfilm... *s.* Dünnschicht...
Dünnschicht *f*/**polymere** polymer thin-film layer
Dünnschichtelektronenlumineszenzdisplay *n* thin-film electroluminescence display
Dünnschichtfilm *m* thin-layer photographic film
Dünnschichtfilter *n* thin-film optical filter
Dünnschichtkondensator *m* thin-film capacitor
Dünnschichtpolarisator *m* thin-film polarizer
Dünnschicht-Strahl[en]teiler *m* pellicle beam splitter
Dünnschichttechnik *f* thin-film technology
Dünnschichttransistor *m* thin-film transistor, TFT
~/**organischer** organic thin film transistor
Dünnschnitt *m* thin section *(microscopy)*
~/**elektronenmikroskopischer** thin electron microscope section
Dünnspiegelteleskop *n* thin mirror telescope
Dünnungsverfahren *n* thinning method *(electron microscopy)*
Dunst *m*/**atmosphärischer** aerial (atmospheric) haze
Dunstfilter *n* haze filter
duobinär duobinary

Duodenoskop *n* duodenoscope
Duodenoskopie *f* duodenoscopy
Duodezimalziffer *f* duodecimal digit
Duotonabbildung *f* duotone [halftone image], duotone illustration, two-color halftone image
Duoton-Verfahren *n s.* Duplexdruck 1.
Dup *n s.* Duplikatfilm
Duplet *n* doublet *(esp. as a handheld magnifier)*
Duplexbetrieb *m* duplex operation (mode) *(e.g. in ultrasound imaging)*
Duplexdruck *m* 1. duotone [process]; 2. *s.* Duotonabbildung; 3. *s.* Druck/beidseitiger
~/**unechter** fake (false) duotone, dummy duotone, duplex (flat tint) halftone
Duplexer *m s.* Duplexgerät 1. *and* 2.
Duplexgerät *n* 1. duplexer [switch], transmit-receive device; 2. duplex scanner *(ultrasound imaging)*
Duplexpapier *n* duplex (double-faced) paper, two-tone paper
Duplikat *n* 1. duplicate [copy], dupe; 2. *s.* Duplikatfilm; 3. *s.* Duplikatdruckform
Duplikatbuchdruckplatte *f s.* Duplikatdruckform
Duplikatdruckform *f*, **Duplikatdruckplatte** *f* duplicate [relief] plate; stereotype [plate]
Duplikatfilm *m* duplicate film; motion-picture duplicate, dupe
Duplikatnegativ *n* duplicate negative, dupe [negative]
~/**kombiniertes** composite dup[licat]e negative
Duplikatpositiv *n*, **Duplikat-Positivkopie** *f* master positive, lavender print *(cinema)*
duplizierbar duplica[ta]able
duplizieren to duplicate, to dupe
Duplizierfarbfilm *m* duplicating color film
Duplizierfilm *m* 1. duplicating film; 2. *s.* Duplikatfilm
Dupliziergerät *n* duplicator
Dupliziermaterial *n* duplicating stock
Duplizierprozess *m* duplication process, duping
Duplizierstempel *m* rubber stamp tool, cloning tool *(digital imaging)*
Duplizierung *f* duplication
Dup-Negativ *n s.* Duplikatnegativ
Düppel *m*, **Düppelecho** *n* chaff, window *(radar)*
Durchbelichtungseffekt *m* crossover effect *(radiography)*
Durchblende *f* [lap] dissolve, cross fade
Durchdringungsfähigkeit *f*, **Durchdringungsvermögen** *n* penetration power (capacity) *(e.g. of X rays)*
Durchdruck *m* 1. porous printing; 2. [silk]screen printing, retigraphy
Durchgriff *m* inverse amplification factor *(electron tube)*
Durchhang *m* toe, foot *(of a characteristic curve)*

Durchlassband *n* passband
Durchlassbereich *m* transmission band, passband range (width) *(of a filter)*
Durchlassfrequenz *f* passband frequency
durchlässig transmissive
Durchlässigkeit *f* transmittance, transmissivity
~/spektrale spectral transmittance
Durchlässigkeitsgrad *m* degree of transmittance, transmittance factor
Durchlasskurve *f* transmission curve
Durchlassstrahlung *f* transmitted radiation
Durchlassvorspannung *f* forward bias[-voltage] *(light-emitting diode)*
Durchlaufalgorithmus *m* plane-sweep algorithm *(computer graphics)*
Durchlaufentwicklungsmaschine *f* continuous-strip processor, continuous-strand processor, continuous machine
Durchlaufkamera *f* rotary camera *(reprography)*
Durchlauf-Kontaktkopiermaschine *f s.* Durchlaufkopiermaschine
Durchlaufkopieren *n* continuous printing
Durchlaufkopiermaschine *f* continuous[-contact] printer, continuous processor
Durchlauftrockenmaschine *f*, **Durchlauftrockner** *m* continuous dryer
Durchlaufverarbeitung *f* continuous processing *(of film or paper)*
durchleuchten to transilluminate; to fluoroscope
Durchleuchter *m* fluoroscopist
Durchleuchtung *f* transillumination; fluoroscopy, transmission radiography
Durchleuchtungsbild *n* fluoroscopic image, fluoroscopy frame; radiograph[ic image], radiogram
Durchleuchtungsgerät *n* transilluminator; fluoroscope
Durchleuchtungsschirm *m* fluoroscopic (fluoroscope) screen, radiographic screen
Durchleuchtungszeit *f* fluoroscopic time
Durchlicht *n* transmitted [visible] light
Durchlichtanzeige *f* transmissive display
Durchlichtaufsatz *m* overhead transparency adapter *(scanner)*
Durchlichtbeleuchtung *f* transmitted (transmittent) illumination, diascopic illumination
Durchlichtbetrachtung *f* transmitted-light observation
Durchlichtbild *n* transmission (transmitted-light) image, transparency [image]
Durchlichtbildschirm *m*, **Durchlichtbildwand** *f* translucent screen
Durchlichteinheit *f s.* Durchlichtaufsatz
Durchlichtfluoreszenz *f* transmitted light fluorescence

Durchlichtholografie *f* transmitted-light holography
Durchlichtmakrofotografie *f* transmitted-light photomacrography
Durchlicht-Mikrofilmlesegerät *n* rear-projection microfilm reader
Durchlichtmikrofotografie *f* transmitted-light photomicrography
Durchlichtmikroskop *n* transmission microscope
Durchlichtmikroskopie *f* transmission (transmitted-light) microscopy
Durchlichtobjektiv *n* transmitted-light objective *(optical microscopy)*
Durchlicht-Rasterelektronenmikroskop *n* scanning transmission electron micoscope STEM
Durchlicht-Rasterelektronenmikroskopie *f* scanning transmission electron microscopy, STEM
Durchlichtverfahren *n* transmitted-light technique
Durchlichtwand *f* rear-projection screen
Durchprojektion *f* rear[-screen] projection, back[ground] projection, process projection
Durchsatz *m* throughput
Durchschallungstomografie *f* ultrasound transmission tomography, transmissive ultrasonic computerized tomography, acoustooptical (ultrasound-modulated optical) tomography
Durchscheinbild *n* transmission image
Durchscheinen *n* show[ing]-through *(esp. as a printing defect; s.a.* Durchschlagen*)*
durchscheinend translucent, lucid; diaphanous, sheer
Durchschlag *m* carbon copy
Durchschlagen *n* strike-through, bleed-through *(esp. as a printing defect; s.a.* Durchscheinen*)*
Durchschlagpapier *n* manifold paper
Durchschleifbetrieb *m* electronics-to-electronics [mode]
Durchschleiffilter *n* loop through [filter], bridging-type filter
Durchschnittshelligkeit *f* average brightness [level]
Durchschuss *m* line gap, [external] leading *(typography)*
Durchsichtdensitometer *n* transmission densitometer
durchsichtig transparent, pellucid
Durchsichtigkeit *f* transparency
Durchsichtsbetrachtung *f* eye-level viewing *(reflex camera)*
Durchsichtsbild *n* transparency [image]
Durchsichts-Grauskala *f* transmission gray-scale, transmission [step] tablet
Durchsichtsucher *m* 1. direct-vision viewfinder, eye-level viewfinder; 2. *s.* ~/optischer
~/optischer direct-vision optical viewfinder

Durchsichtvorlage f transparent copy
Durchsprudelung f turbulation, gas[eous]-burst agitation *(photoprocessing)*
durchstimmbar tunable
Durchstimmbarkeit f tunability
durchstimmen to tune *(e.g. a laser)*
Durchstoßpunkt m intersection point
durchstrahlen to radiograph *(esp. with invisible rays)*
Durchstrahlung f transmission
Durchstrahlungsaufnahme f, **Durchstrahlungsbild** n radiograph[ic image], radiogram
Durchstrahlungselektronenmikroskop n transmission [electron] microscope, TEM
Durchstrahlungselektronenmikroskopie f transmission electron microscopy, TEM
Durchstrahlungsoptik f transmission optics
Durchstrahlungsprotokoll n radiographic test report
Durchstrahlungsprüfung f/**industrielle** industrial radiography
Durchstrahlungs-Rasterelektronenmikroskop n scanning transmission electron microscope, STEM
durchsuchen to browse
durchzeichnen to trace
Durchzeichnung f 1. tracing; 2. [image] definition
DVB-Datenrundfunk m data broadcasting service, DBS
DVB-Empfänger m DVB receiver, multimedia terminal
DVB-Empfängerkarte f, **DVB-Karte** f DVB [receiving] card
DVD f 1. digital versatile disk, DVD; 2. s. Bildplatte/digitale
~/beschreibbare recordable DVD, DVD-R
DVD-Abtastung f DVD scanning
DVD-Anlage f DVD unit
DVD-Audio n DVD audio
DVD-Film m DVD movie
DVD-Player m DVD player
DVD-Recorder m DVD recorder
DVD-Scheibe f digital versatile (video) disk, DVD [disk]
DVD-Spieler m DVD player
DVD-Technik f DVD technology
DVD-Tonträger m DVD audio disk
DVD-Video n DVD video
DVD-Videorecorder m DVD recorder
DVD-Videospieler m DVD player
DVE-Gerät n digital video effects device, video effects machine
DV-Format n DV format, digital video format
DVI-Anschluss m, **DVI-Eingang** m DVI (Digital Visual Interface) connection port
DX-Code m DX code
DX-Codierung f DX coding [system]
dyadisch dyadic *(s.a. under binär)*

Dynamik f 1. dynamics; 2. s. Dynamikbereich
Dynamikbereich m dynamic [signal] range; dynamic range, [maximum-to-minimum] luminance range; latitude *(silver-halide photography)*
Dynamikkompression f dynamic range compression
Dynamikreduktion f dynamic range suppression
Dynamikumfang m s. Dynamikbereich
Dynode f dynode *(photomultiplier)*

E

eben plane, planar, flat
Ebene f/**konjugierte** conjugate plane *(optics)*
~/**lichtlose** alychne *(Kolorimetrie)*
~/**tomografische** tomographic plane
~/**verborgene** s. Schicht/verdeckte
Ebenheit f planarity, flatness *(shape feature)*
Ebenunterscheidbarkeit f just noticeable difference, JND, difference threshold; minimum perceptible color difference, MPCD
Eberhard-Effekt m Eberhard effect *(esp. due to developer exhaustion)*
~/**vertikaler** interimage effect
ebnen to flatten
Ebnungslinse f field flattener
EB-Schnitt m s. Schnitt/elektronischer
Echelettegitter n echelette [grating], blazed grating, blaze grid
Echellegitter n echelle [grating]
Echellespektrograf m echelle spectrograph
Echo n echo, return *(sonography, magnetic resonance imaging, radar)*
~/**asymmetrisches** asymmetric echo
~/**elektromagnetisches** electromagnetic echo *(radar)*
~/**rücklaufendes** returned echo
~/**schwaches** weak (low-level) echo
~/**stimuliertes** stimulated echo
~/**zweidimensionales** two-dimensional echo
Echoamplitude f echo [signal] amplitude
Echoanzeige f blip *(radar)*
echoarm hypoechoic
Echoaufhellung f echo brightening *(radar)*
Echoausblendung f echo cancellation
Echobild n echo image (pattern)
echobildend echogenic
Echobildung f echo formation
Echoenzephalografie f echoencephalography
echoenzephalografisch echoencephalographic
Echofeld n echo field
echofrei anechoic
Echograf m echograph
Echografie f echography *(s.a. Sonografie)*
echografisch echographic
Echogramm n echogram, [ultra]sonogram
Echo-Impuls-... s. Impuls-Echo-...
Echointensität f echo intensity
Echokardiografie f echocardiography
echokardiografisch echocardiographic
Echokardiogramm n echocardiogram, echocardiographic (echocardiac) image
Echokardiologie f echocardiology
Echolot n echo sounder
Echolotung f echo (sonic) sounding
Echomuster n s. Echostruktur
Echoplanarsequenz f echo planar imaging sequence, EPI sequence
Echoplanarverfahren n echo planar imaging
Echoquerschnitt m radar cross section, RCS
echoschwach hypoechoic
Echosignal n echo signal *(sonography)*; backscattered signal, returned signal, return *(radar)*
Echosignalverarbeitung f echo signal processing
Echoskop n echoscope
Echostruktur f echo pattern *(sonography)*
Echounterdrücker m echo suppressor
Echounterdrückung f echo suppression
Echovergrößerung f [/**künstliche**], **Echoverstärkung** f echo stretching (enhancement) *(sonography, radar)*
Echozeit f echo time, TE
~/**effektive** effective echo time
Echozug m echo train
Echtbildsucher m real-image viewfinder
~/**optischer** real-image optical [view]finder
~/**umgekehrter Galiläischer** reversed Galilean finder
Echtbildzoomsucher m real-image zoom [view]finder
Echtfarbe f true (real) color
Echtfarbenbild n true-color image (picture), 24-bit color image; true-color (full-color) photograph
Echtfarbenholografie f true-color holography
Echtheitsbestätigung f authentication *(e.g. by digital watermarking)*
Echtzeit f real time
Echtzeitanimation f real-time animation
Echtzeitaufnahme f real-time recording (capture)
Echtzeitauslesung f real-time readout
Echtzeitauslösung f real-time shutter release
Echtzeitbetrachtung f instantaneous (real-time) viewing
Echtzeit-Betriebssystem n real-time operating system
Echtzeit-Bewegungssegmentierung f real-time motion segmentation
Echtzeit-Bewegungsverfolgung f real-time motion tracking
Echtzeitbild n real-time image (picture)
Echtzeit-Bildcodierung f real-time image coding (compression)
Echtzeit-Bilddarstellung f real-time imaging (image formation), real-time rendition (display)
Echtzeitbildgeber m real-time imager

Echtzeit-Bildverarbeitungssystem *n* real-time image processing system
Echtzeitcodierung *f* real-time encoding
Echtzeitcomputer *m* real-time computer
Echtzeitdarstellung *f*/**computergrafische** real-time rendering
Echtzeitdigitalisierung *f* real-time digitization
Echtzeit-Disparitätsschätzer *m* real-time disparity estimator
Echtzeitfähigkeit *f* real-time [processing] capability
Echtzeitfernsehen *n* real-time video
Echtzeitfotogrammetrie *f* real-time photogrammetry
Echtzeitgeschwindigkeit *f* real-time speed
Echtzeit-Grauwertbild *n* real-time gray-scale image
Echtzeitholografie *f* real-time holography
Echtzeitkamera *f* real time camera
Echtzeitkonferenz *f* real-time conferencing
Echtzeitmedium *n* real-time medium
Echtzeitmikroskopie *f* real-time microscopy
Echtzeitmodus *m* real-time mode
echtzeitnah near-real-time
Echtzeitradiografie *f* real-time radiography
Echtzeitscanner *m* real-time scanner *(sonography)*
Echtzeitsensor *m* real-time sensor
Echtzeitsimulation *f* real-time simulation
Echtzeit-Spektralanalysator *m* real-time [spectrum] analyzer
Echtzeitsystem *n* real-time system
Echtzeittechnik *f* real-time method *(holographic interferometry)*
echtzeittomografisch real-time tomographic
Echtzeittomogramm *n* real-time tomographic image
Echtzeit-Transformationscodierung *f* real-time transform coding
Echtzeitübertragung *f* real-time transmission
Echtzeit-Ultraschallgerät *n* real-time ultrasonic scanner
Echtzeitverarbeitung *f* real-time processing
Echtzeitvideo *n* real-time video, live video
Echtzeit-Videosignalprozessor *m* real-time video signal processor
Echtzeitvisualisierung *f* real-time visualization
Echtzeitwiedergabe *f* real-time playback *(video)*
Echtzeitzählwerk *n* linear time counter *(video)*
Echtzeitzugriff *m* real-time access
Ecke *f* corner
Eckendetektor *m* corner detector
Eckenerkennung *f* corner detection
Eckfrequenz *f* corner frequency *(active filter)*
Eckpixel *n* corner pixel

Eckpunkt *m* corner point, vertex
Edeldruck *m* fine[-art] print
Edelgashalogenid *n* noble-gas halide
editierbar editable, live
editieren to edit, to redact
Editiergerät *n* editing device
Editierung *f* editing
Editiervorgang *m* editing process
Editor *m* editor *(software tool)*
EDTA *s.* Ethylendiamintetraessigsäure
E-E-Betrieb *m s.* Durchschleifbetrieb
EEG *s.* Elektroenzephalogramm
Effekt *m* effect *(s.a.* Trick*)*
~/**äußerer fotoelektrischer (lichtelektrischer)** external photoelectric effect
~/**bolometrischer** bolometric effect
~/**elektrooptischer** electro-optic effect
~/**filmischer** motion-picture optical effect
~/**fotoelektrischer** photoelectric effect, photoeffect
~/**fotoelektromagnetischer** photoelectromagnetic effect
~/**fotografischer** photographic effect
~/**fotomagnetoelektrischer** *s.* ~/fotoelektromagnetischer
~/**innerer fotoelektrischer** internal photoelectric effect
~/**lichtelektrischer** *s.* ~/fotoelektrischer
~/**magnetoresistiver** magnetoresistivity effect
~/**optischer** optical [effect], special visual effect, montage
~/**optoakustischer** optoacoustic effect
~/**piezoelektrischer** piezoelectric effect
~/**pyroelektrischer** pyroelectric effect
~/**stereokinetischer** stereokinetic effect
~/**stroboskopischer** stroboscopic effect
~/**umgekehrter piezoelektrischer** inverse piezoelectricity (piezoelectric effect)
~/**visueller** visual effect
Effektaufnahme *f* [special-]effects shot, trick (VFX) shot, process shot; special-effect photography
Effektbeleuchtung *f* effect lighting
Effektblende *f* wipe [transition]
Effektfarbe *f* spot color *(printing)*
Effektfilm *m* effects film, special-effects movie, trick (animated) film, animation
Effektfilter *m* effect (creative) filter; special-effects filter, optical effect filter
Effektfolie *f* texturizing film material, textured laminating material
Effektgenerator *m* special-effects generator, [postproduction] effects generator
Effektgerät *n* special-effects device (gear), effects machine
~/**digitales** digital video effects device, video effects machine
Effektgeräusch *n* sound effect
Effektgestaltung *f* visual effects production
Effektivbrennweite *f* effective (equivalent) focal length, power *(of a thin lens)*

Effektivzeit f effective exposure time *(of a shutter)*
Effektkanal m effects channel
Effektlicht n effects light
Effektprojektor m effects projector
Effektscheinwerfer m s. Effektstrahler
Effektschrift f fancy script font
Effektspur f effects track
Effektstudio n [special] effects studio, effects facility (house); digital effects studio
Effektverfahren n special-effect procedure
Effizienz f/**spektrale** spectral efficiency
EGA-Grafikkarte f enhanced-graphics adapter, EGA
Eichband n calibration tape
eichen to calibrate
Eichfehler m calibration error
Eichfilm m calibration film
Eichkonstante f calibration constant
Eichkurve f calibration curve (function)
Eichung f calibration
Eidophorprojektor m s. Eidophorgerät
Eigenachse f eigen axis
Eigenbild n eigenimage, eigenpicture, score image
Eigendrehimpuls m spin; nuclear spin
Eigenemission f eigenemission
Eigenfilterung f self-filtering *(of X rays)*
Eigenfotoleitung f intrinsic conductivity *(photodiode)*
Eigenfunktion f eigenfunction *(e.g. of an imaging system)*
Eigengrau n intrinsic gray
Eigenrauschen n inherent (inner) noise
Eigenrauschleistungsdichte f noise-equivalent power, NEP
Eigenschaftsbild n/**vektorielles** s. Mehrkanalbild
Eigenschatten m self-shadow, contained shadow
Eigenstrahlung f natural (characteristic) radiation *(X rays)*
Eigenvektor m eigenvector, characteristic vector *(of an operator)*
Eigenvektormatrix f eigenvector matrix
Eigenvektortransformation f eigenvector (Hotelling) transform, principal components analysis (transform), main axis transformation; Karhunen-Loève-transform[ation] (expansion) *(feature identification)*
Eigenwert m eigenvalue, characteristic value (root) *(scalar)*
Eigenwertanalyse f eigenvalue analysis
Eigenwertmatrix f eigenvalue matrix
Eikonal n eikonal; eikonal equation *(ray optics)*
Eimerkettenschaltung f bucket brigade device, BBD
einäugig monocular, monoculous
Einbad-Fixierentwickler m monobath developer-fixer, monobath [developer]
Einbein[stativ] n monopod, unipod

~[**stativ**]/**verstellbares** adjustable monopod
Einbildmessung f single-photograph measurement *(photogrammetry)*
Einbildstereogramm n single-image stereogram
einbildweise frame-by-frame *(animation)*
Ein-Bit-Quantisierung f one-bit quantization
Einblatt-Farbfilm m single-sheet color film
Einblattfilm m single-sheet film
einblenden[/weich] to fade in
Einblendung f 1. fade-in; 2. insert [sequence], insert material
Einbrenneffekt m s. Einbrennen
Einbrennen n burn[-in] *(esp. of still frames on display screens)*
Ein-Chip-Videokamera f single-chip camera, single-CCD camera
eindigitalisieren to load *(e.g. data into a memory)*
eindimensional one-dimensional, unidimensional
Eindimensionalität f one-dimensionality, unidimensionality
Eindringtiefe f penetration depth, depth of penetration *(e.g. of ultrasound)*
Einergang m single-frame exposure, frame-by-frame exposure
Einfachdrucker m simple printer
Einfachkamera f simple camera
Einfachklicken n single-clicking *(computer mouse)*
Einfach-MIT[-Filter] n single canceller *(radar signal processor)*
Einfachstkamera f least-expensive camera
einfachvergütet single-coated
Einfädelmechanismus m threading mechanism
Einfall m incidence *(ray, beam)*
~/**nichtsenkrechter** nonnormal incidence
~/**rechtwinkliger** normal incidence
~/**schräger** oblique (glancing) incidence
~/**senkrechter** normal incidence
~/**streifender** grazing incidence
Einfallsebene f plane of incidence
Einfallslot n [incidence] normal
Einfallsrichtung f direction of incidence
Einfallsstrahl m incident ray (beam), entrance (entering) beam, incoming beam
Einfallsstrahlung f incident radiation
Einfallsweg m incident path
Einfallswinkel m incidence (incident) angle, angle of incidence, AOI
Einfaltung f, **Einfaltungsartefakt** n wraparound artifact (error), [image] wrap *(binary image processing)*
Einfaltungsunterdrückung f phase oversampling *(magnetic resonance imaging)*
einfärben to color[ize], to tint *(e.g. a photographic positive)*; to ink *(a printing plate)*

Einfärben *n* colorization, coloring, tinting *(esp. of motion-picture films)*; colorization *(of video productions by electronic means)*; inking *(printing plates)*
Einfarbenmaschine *f* single-color press *(printing)*
Einfarbensehen *n* 1. monochromatic vision, monochromatism, monochromacy, complete color blindness; 2. *s.* Grauwertsehen
einfarbig single-color[ed], monochrome, monotint; monochrom[at]ic
Einfarbigkeit *f* monochromaticity
Einfärbung *f* inking *(printing)*
Einfrequenz-Halbleiterlaser *m* single-frequency semiconductor laser
Einfrequenzlaser *m* single-mode laser
Einfrieren *n* **[der Bewegung]** freezing [the movement]
Einfügemarke *f* insertion point; [screen] cursor; pointer
Einfügemodus *m* insert mode
einfügen to insert; to paste *(computer graphics)*
Einfügeschnitt *m* 1. insert editing; 2. insert edit
Einfügetaste *f* insert key
Einfügungszeichen *n* [/**keilförmiges**] caret [mark] *(in printed matter)*
Einführungstotale *f* establishing shot *(cinema)*
Eingabe *f* input; entry
Eingabeaufforderung *f* prompt
Eingabebild *n* input image
Eingabedatenmatrix *f* input data matrix
Eingabefeld *n* input field
Eingabeformat *n* input format
Eingabefunktion *f* input function
Eingabegerät *n* [user-]input device, intake device
~/**digitales** digital input device, DID
~/**grafisches** graphical input device
Eingabehistogramm *n* input histogram
Eingabemaske *f* input mask
Eingabemuster *n s.* Eingangsmuster
Eingabeprogramm *n* reader
Eingabescanner *m* input scanner
Eingabeschicht *f* input layer *(artificial neural network)*
Eingabetablett *n* graphics (digitizing) tablet, [electronic] tablet
Eingabetaste *f* enter (return) key
Eingabetisch *m* feed tray *(automatic processor)*
Eingabevektor *m* input vector
Eingabevektorraum *m* input vector space
Eingabewarteschlange *f* input (event) queue
Eingangsbandbreite *f* input bandwidth
Eingangsbild *n* input image
Eingangsbildauflösung *f* input image resolution
Eingangsbilddaten *pl* input image data

Eingangsbildgröße *f* input image size
Eingangsbildsignal *n* input image signal
Eingangsdatenkontrolle *f*/**drucktechnische** preflight procedure[s]
Eingangsdatensatz *m* input data set
Eingangsfeldgröße *f* entrance field size
Eingangsfrequenz *f* input frequency
Eingangshauptebene *f* frontal principal (nodal) plane *(of a thick lens)*
Eingangshelligkeit *f* input brightness *(electronic imaging)*
Eingangsimpuls *m* input pulse
Eingangsleuchtschirm *m* input fluorescent (phosphor) screen, input screen, [image intensifier] input phosphor *(radiography)*
Eingangsmedium *n* incident medium
Eingangs-Multiplexfilter *n* input multiplex filter, IMUX
Eingangsmuster *n* input pattern *(pattern classification)*
Eingangsnennleistung *f* nominal [anode] input power *(X-ray tube)*
Eingangsrauschen *n* input noise
Eingangsreiz *m* input stimulus
Eingangsschicht *f* input layer *(artificial neural network)*
Eingangsschirm *m s.* Eingangsleuchtschirm
Eingangsschnittstelle *f* input interface *(e.g. for video)*
Eingangssignal *n* input [signal], incoming signal
Eingangstakt *m* input clock
Eingangstaktfrequenz *f* incoming clock rate
Eingangsvektor *m* input vector
Eingangsverstärker *m* input amplifier
Eingangs-Videobild *n* input video picture
Eingangsvideosignal *n* input video signal
eingeben to input, to enter; to feed; to key [in], to keyboard
Eingießöffnung *f*/**lichtdichte** light-trapped opening *(of a developing tank)*
Eingriffsmöglichkeit *f* [/**manuelle**] [manual] override *(camera control)*
Einhand-Camcorder *m* handycam
Einheit *f*/**arithmetisch-logische** arithmetic [logic] unit, ALU *(processor)*
~/**fotometrische** photometric[al] unit
~/**lichttechnische** light unit
Einheitsimpuls *m* unit impulse *(s.a.* Impulsfolge*)*
Einheitsimpulsfunktion *f* unit [im]pulse function
Einheitskreis *m* unit[-radius] circle
Einheitskugel *f* unit sphere
Einheitsmatrix *f* unit[ary] matrix
Einheitsokular *n s.* Huygens-Okular
Einheitspuls *m s.* Einheitsimpuls
Einheitsraumwinkel *m* unit solid angle, steradian
Einheitsschritt *m* unit step *(causal signal)*
Einheitsvektor *m* unit vector, base (basis) vector)

Einheitswürfel

Einheitswürfel *m* unit cube *(colorimetry, computer graphics)*
Einheitszelle *f* unit cell *(of a reciprocal lattice)*
Einhüllende *f* envelope
einkleben to tip [in] *(an insert in a book)*
Einknopf-Abstimmungssystem *n* one-button tuning
Einkomponentensystem *n* monocomponent (single-component) system
Einkomponententoner *m* monocomponent (single-component) developer *(xerography)*; single-component magnetic toner *(ion-deposition printing)*
einkopieren to print in
Einkopieren *n* printing in
Einkopierraster *m(n)* mechanical tint *(prepress)*
einkoppeln to couple in[to] *(e.g. light into optical fibers)*
Einkreisen *n* [en]circling *(takes in motion-picture production)*
Einkristall *m* monocrystal, single crystal
Einkristall-Fotodetektor *m* single-crystal photodetector
Einkristall-Gammakamera *f* [single-crystal] gamma camera, Anger[-type] camera, scintillation camera
Einkristallhalbleiter *m* single-crystal semiconductor
einkristallin monocrystal[line]
Einkristallmonochromator *m* single-crystal monochromator
einladen to load into *(e.g. image data into a computer)*
Einlaufbereich *m* lead-in area *(video disk)*
Einlegefläche *f* platen, exposure glass *(copier, scanner)*
einlegen to load *(e.g. a film cartridge into a camera)*; to thread to lace *(e.g. a length of film)*
Einlegevorgang *m* loading procedure
Einlernen *n*, **Einlernvorgang** *m* teach-in *(neuroinformatics)*
einlesen to read in[to] *(e.g. image data)*
einleuchten to pre-light *(a film set)*
Einleuchten *n*, **Einleuchtung** *f* [pre-]lighting
Einlichtkopie *f* one-light [print] *(motion-picture print)*
einlinsig single-lens
Einloch-Kollimator *m* pinhole collimator *(gamma-ray camera)*
Einmalentwickler *m* one-use (one-shot) developer
Einmodenfaser *f* monomode [optical] fiber, single-mode fiber
Einmodenlaser *m* single-mode laser, single-frequency laser
Einmodenlaserstrahl *m* single-mode laser beam
Einpass-Scanner *m* single-pass scanner

Einplanbarkeit *f* schedulability *(multimedia data processing)*
Einpunktperspektive *f* one-point perspective, parallel (telecentric) perspective
Einraumkamera *f* gallery camera
Einrichtebogen *m* register sheet *(printing)*
Einrichtemitte *f* optical center *(layout)*
Einrichten *n* makeready, setup *(printing)*
einrücken to indent *(lines of text)*
Einrückung *f* indent, indent[at]ion
einscannen to scan in
Einschaltungszeichen *n* caret [mark] *(in printed matter)*
Einschichtfilm *m* 1. [photographic] single-emulsion film; 2. single-coated [X-ray] film, single-sided film; 3. *s.* Dünnschichtfilm
Einschicht-Perzeptron *n* single-layer perceptron *(artificial neural network)*
Einschicht-Spiral-Computertomograf *m* single-slice [CT] scanner
Einschichtvergütung *f* single-layer [low-reflection] coating
einschneiden 1. to cut into, to incise; 2. to intercut *(e.g. a contrasting shot into a film scene)*
Einschnittszene *f* insert [sequence], insert material; cut-in [shot] *(film editing)*
Einschraubfassung *f* screw-type [lens] mount, thread[ed] mount, screw thread
Einschraubfilter *n* screw-type filter, screw-in filter
Einschub *m* plug-in *(s.a. Einsteckmodul)*
Einseitenbandmodulation *f* single side band modulation
Einseitenbandübertragung *f* single-sideband transmission
einspeichern to store in *(e.g. data)*
einspiegeln to reflect into
Einspiegelungsverfahren *n*/**Schüfftansches** Schufftan process *(cinema)*
einspielen to dub [in] *(esp. sound effects to a film or video production)*; to intercut
Einspielung *f* contribution; intercut
Einspur-Tonaufzeichnung *f* single-track record[ing], one-track [sound] record[ing]
Einspur-Tonwiedergabegerät *n* single-track sound reproducer
einstanzen to key [in]
Einstanzen/weiches soft keying
einsteckbar pluggable
Einsteck-Chipkarte *f* plug-in card (board)
einstecken to nest, to inset *(folded signatures)*
Einsteckkarte *f s.* Einsteck-Chipkarte
Einsteckmodul *n* plug-in [module]
Einsteigerkamera *f* entry-level camera
Einstein-Koeffizient *m* Einstein's coefficient *(e.g. of spontaneous emission)*
Einstellbereich *m* setting range

Einstellebene *f* focal plane
Einstellentfernung *f* focusing distance
~/kürzeste closest (minimum) focusing distance, near focusing limit, minimum focus
Einsteller *m* fader *(sound control)*
Einstellfassung *f* focusing mount *(motion-picture camera lens)*
Einstellfehler *m* setting (adjustment) error
Einstellfernrohr *n* framing eyepiece
Einstellgenauigkeit *f* framing accuracy
Einstellhilfe *f*, **Einstellhilfsmittel** *n* focusing aid
Einstellicht *n* modeling light; focusing light
Einstellupe *f* focusing magnifier
Einstellmattscheibe *f* ground glass; focusing screen
Einstellmöglichkeit *f*/**manuelle** [manual] override *(camera control)*
Einstellrad *n* command dial
Einstellring *m* setting ring
Einstellscheibe *f* [ground-glass] viewing screen, [ground-glass] focusing screen, ground-glass [view]finder, [finder] screen
Einstellschnecke *f* helicoid extension tube
Einstellstufung *f* focusing scale
Einstelltuch *n* focusing (dark) cloth
Einstellung *f* 1. setting *(e.g. of a camera)*; 2. [single] shot; take, scene *(cinema, video)*
~/amerikanische thigh shot
~/halbtotale long (full) shot
Einstellungsfolge *f* shooting order
Einstellungsliste *f* shot sheet (list) *(filming)*; editing log *(videotaping)*
Einstellungsnummer *f* take number
Einstellungswiederholungen *fpl* coverage *(filmmaking)*
Einstiegskamera *f* entry-level camera
Einstiegspunkt *m* in point *(tape editing)*
Einstrahlhologramm *n* in-line hologram, Gabor hologram
Einstrahlspektrofotometer *n* single-beam spectrophotometer
Einstrahlung *f* irradiation, irradiance, flux density
Einstreifen-Ton-Bild-Aufzeichnung *f*, **Einstreifenverfahren** *n* single-system recording (shooting)
Einstreifenverfahren *n* single system [cinematography]
Eins-zu-eins-Kopieren *n* one-to-one printing
Einteilungsbogen *m* layout grid
Eintouren[druck]maschine *f* single revolution press
Eintrittsblende *f* entrance aperture (stop)
Eintrittsecho *n* [ultrasound] echo leading edge *(sonography)*
Eintrittsfenster *n* [glass] faceplate *(camera tube)*
Eintrittsluke *f* entrance window *(optics)*
Eintrittspupille *f* entrance pupil, effective aperture
Eintrittsspalt *m* entrance slit

Eintrittsspektrum *n* entrance spectrum *(radiography)*
Eintrittsstrahl *m* entrance (entering) beam, incident ray (beam), incoming (input) beam
Einwahlprogramm *n* dialer [program] *(Internet)*
Einwärtsdrehung *f* inward rotation *(e.g. of the eyes)*
Einwegkamera *f* single (one-time) use camera, disposable (throw-away) camera, film-with-camera
Einwickelpapier *n* wrapping paper
Einzelaufnahme *f* single (individual) shot
Einzel-Autofokus *m* single-point auto focus
Einzelbild *n* 1. single (individual) image; 2. [single] frame *(film, video)*; 3. *s.* Einzelaufnahme
Einzelbildanalyse *f* single-image analysis
Einzelbildanzeige *f* single-image display
Einzelbildaufnahme *f* single-frame exposure; frame record; still picture recording *(video)*
Einzelbildbelichtung *f* single-frame exposure, frame-by-frame exposure
Einzelbildfortschaltung *f s.* Einzelbildschaltung 1. *and* 2.
einzelbildgenau frame-accurate *(e.g. synchronization)*
Einzelbildkamera *f* single-frame camera
Einzelbildmotor *m* animation motor
Einzelbildpuffer *m* frame buffer
Einzelbildrate *f* frame rate
Einzelbildschaltung *f* 1. single-frame exposure (shooting); jogging *(video editing)*; 2. jogwheel, jog dial
Einzelbildspeicher *m* frame [store] memory, frame (still) store *(video)*
Einzelbildspeicherung *f* single-image storage; frame grabbing
Einzelbildstereogramm *n* single-image stereogram
Einzelbildtechnik *f* frame-by-frame technique; stop-motion (stop-action) cinematography, stop-motion photography technique
Einzelbildtransport *m* single-frame advance
einzelbildweise imagewise; frame-by-frame
Einzelbitbild *n s.* Pixelbild
Einzelbitfehler *m* single-bit error
Einzelblatteinzug *m* [cut-]sheet feeder, CSF
~/automatischer automatic [cut] sheet feeder, ASF
Einzelblattfilm *m* sheet film, cut (flat) film
Einzelbuchstaben-Setz- und -gießmaschine *f* [monotype] composition caster
Einzelbuchstabensetzmaschine *f* monotype (single-type) composing machine

Einzeleinlauf *m* single-jet scheme *(emulsion preparation)*
Einzeleinlaufemulsion *f* single-jet emulsion
Einzelfehler *m s.* Bitfehler
Einzelfeld-Autofokus *m* single-area AF mode
Einzelimpuls *m* single pulse
Einzelletter *f* piece of type
Einzellinse *f* single lens, [lens] element
~/**dünne** thin lens
Einzelphasentrick *m* stop-motion animation (photography), stop-action animation, stop motion (action)
Einzelphotonen-Emissionstomograf *m* [clinical] SPECT system
Einzelphotonen-Emissionstomografie *f* single-photon emission-computed tomography, SPECT [imaging] *(s.a. under SPECT)*
Einzelpixeloperation *f* single-pixel operation
Einzelplatzdrucker *m* desktop (tabletop) printer
Einzelrechner *m* standalone computer (workstation)
Einzelschichttomogramm *n* individual image slice
Einzelsensor *m* individual detector
Einzelsequenz *f* take *(cinema)*
Einzelspaltbeugung *f* single-slit diffraction
Einzelszene *f* individual scene; take *(cinema)*
Einzelträger *m* single-channel carrier *(signal transmission)*
einziehen to indent *(lines of text)*
Ein-Zoll-Band *n* one-inch tape, 1 in.videotape
einzoomen to zoom in
Einzug *m* indent[at]ion, indent *(layout)*
~/**hängender** hanging indent
~/**negativer** outdent
Einzugsscanner *m* feed (sheet-fed) scanner
Einzugwerk *n* unwind brake [system] *(of web-fed presses)*
Eisenblaudruck *m* [/**negativer**] 1. cyanotype (ferro-prussiate) process, blueprint (Prussian-blue) process; 2. cyanotype, blueprint
Eisenchlorid *n* ferric chloride *(etchant)*
Eisenoxalatentwickler *m* ferrous oxalate developer
Eisenoxid *n* iron oxide; ferric oxide
Eisenoxidammoniak *n* ferric ammonium citrate *(image toner)*
Eisensalzverfahren *n* iron [salt] process, ferric process *(early photography)*
Eisessig *m* glacial acetic acid *(stop bath)*
Eiweißpapier *n* albumen[ized] paper
E-Kamera *f* electronic[-imaging] camera
EKG-Steuerung *f*, **EKG-Triggerung** *f* electrocardiographic (ECG) gating, cardiac gating *(magnetic resonance imaging)*

Elastografie *f* elastography, sonoelasticity imaging, elasticity imaging [method]
~/**dynamische** dynamic elastography
~/**statische** static elastography
Elastogramm *n* elastogram
EL-Bildschirm *m*, **ELD**, **EL-Display** *n s.* Elektrolumineszenzanzeige
Elektret *n(m)* electret
Elektret-Kondensatormikrofon *n*, **Elektretmikrofon** *n* electret [condenser] microphone
Elektrizität *f*/**statische** static electricity
Elektrode *f* electrode
~/**ionenselektive** ion-selective electrode, ISE
Elektroenzephalograf *m* [electro]encephalograph
Elektroenzephalografie *f* electroencephalography
elektroenzephalografisch electroencephalographic
Elektroenzephalogramm *n* electroencephalogram, EEG
Elektrofotografie *f* 1. electrophotography, electrophotographic imaging; 2. *s.* Xerography
~/**indirekte** xerography
elektrofotografisch electrophotographic
Elektrografie *f* Electrofax [process] *(electrophotography)*
Elektroholografie *f* electroholography
Elektrokardiografie *f* electrocardiography, electrocardiographic imaging
elektrokardiografisch electrocardiographic
Elektrokardiogramm *n* electrocardiogram, ECG
elektrolumineszent electroluminescent
Elektrolumineszenz *f* electroluminescence
Elektrolumineszenzbildschirm *m*, **Elektrolumineszenzdisplay** *n* electroluminescent display, ELD
Elektrolumineszenzlampe *f* electroluminescent lamp
elektrolumineszierend electroluminescent
Elektrolyse *f* electrolysis
elektrolytisch electrolytic
Elektromagnet *m* electromagnet
elektromagnetisch electromagnetic, EM
Elektromyograf *m* electromyograph
Elektromyografie *f* electromyography, electrodiagnosis
elektromyografisch electromyographic[al]
Elektromyogramm *n* electromyogram, EMG
Elektron *n* electron, negatron
~/**angeregtes** excited electron
~/**freies** free electron
~/**positives** positron, antielectron
~/**strahlendes** luminous electron
~/**tunnelndes** tunneling electron
Elektronenakzeptor *m* electron acceptor
Elektronenanregung *f* electron excitation
Elektronenbelichtungsanlage *f* electron exposure system *(microlithography)*

Elektronenbeschleunigung f electron acceleration
Elektronenbild n electron image
Elektronenbildröhre f electron image (imaging) tube
Elektronenbildsimulation f electron image simulation
Elektronenblitz m 1. electronic flash, speedflash, speedlight; 2. s. Elektronenblitzgerät
Elektronenblitzdauer f electronic-flash duration
Elektronenblitzfotografie f electronic flash photography
Elektronenblitzgerät n electronic flash unit (system)
Elektronenblitzlampe f electronic flash lamp (tube)
Elektronenblitzlicht n s. Elektronenblitz 1.
Elektronendetektor m electron detector
Elektronendichte f electron density
Elektronendonator m electron donator
Elektroneneinfang m electron trapping (capture) *(photographic theory)*
Elektroneneinfangstelle f [electron] trapping site, electron trap
Elektronenemissionsmikroskop n/**ballistisches** ballistic electron emission microscope
Elektronenemitter m electron emitter
Elektronenenergie f electron energy
Elektronenfehlstelle f empty electron position, [electron] hole, vacancy
Elektronenfotografie f electronic photography
elektronenfotografisch electronic-photographic
Elektronenholografie f electron holography
Elektronenhülle f [atomic] electron shell
Elektronenkanone f electron [beam] gun *(cathode-ray tube)*
Elektronenkollektor m electron collector
Elektronenladung f electron[ic] charge
Elektronenleerstelle f s. Elektronenfehlstelle
Elektronenlinse f electron lens
Elektronenmetallografie f electron metallography
Elektronenmikrofotografie f 1. electron photomicrography; 2. electron photomicrograph
Elektronenmikrografie f 1. electron micrography; 2. electron micrograph
Elektronenmikrogramm n electron micrograph, electron microscope (microscopy) image
Elektronenmikroskop n electron microscope, EM
~/**analytisches** analytical electron microscope, AEM
~/**elektrostatisches** electrostatic electron microscope

~/**magnetisches** magnetic electron microscope
Elektronenmikroskopaufnahme f electron micrograph, electron microscope (microscopy) image
Elektronenmikroskopie f electron microscopy
~/**hochauflösende** high-resolution electron microscopy, HREM
Elektronenmikroskopie-Labor[atorium] n electron microscopy laboratory
Elektronenmikroskopiker m electron microscopist
elektronenmikroskopisch electron-microscopic[al]
Elektronenoptik f electron optics
elektronenoptisch electron-optical
Elektronenpaarbildung f electron-hole pair generation (creation), electron pair production *(electrophotography)*
Elektronenpaarbindung f electron-pair linkage (bond)
Elektronenquelle f electron source
Elektronenröhre f electron tube, [electron] valve
Elektronensonde f electron probe
Elektronenspeicherring m electron storage ring
Elektronenspektrometer n electron spectrometer
Elektronenspektroskopie f electron spectroscopy
Elektronenspender m electron donor
Elektronenspiegel m electron mirror
Elektronenspin m electron spin
Elektronenspinresonanz f electron spin resonance, ESR, electron [para]magnetic resonance, EPR, EMR
Elektronenstrahl m electron[ic] beam
Elektronenstrahlablenkung f electron beam deflection
Elektronenstrahlabtaster m electron beam scanner
Elektronenstrahlabtastung f electron beam scan[ning]
Elektronenstrahlaufzeichnung f electron beam recording, EBR
Elektronenstrahlbelichtung f electron beam exposure
Elektronenstrahlbild n electron beam image
Elektronenstrahlbildröhre f s. Elektronenstrahlröhre
Elektronenstrahl-Computertomograf m electron beam CT scanner, EBCT scanner
Elektronenstrahl-Computertomografie f electron beam [computed] tomography, electron beam CT, EBT *(s.a. Elektronentomografie)*
Elektronenstrahlenergie f electron beam energy
Elektronenstrahlerzeuger m, **Elektronenstrahl-Erzeugungssystem** n electron [beam] gun *(cathode-ray tube)*

Elektronenstrahl-Filmabtastung f electron beam film scanning
Elektronenstrahlgravur f electron beam gravure (engraving), EBG
Elektronenstrahlkanone f electron [beam] gun *(cathode-ray tube)*
Elektronenstrahl-Leuchtfleckbildabtaster m flying-spot scanner
Elektronenstrahllithografie f electron beam [micro]lithography, cathodolithography
Elektronenstrahlmodulation f electron beam modulation
Elektronenstrahloszilloskop n cathode-ray oscilloscope, oscilloscope [cathode-ray tube]
Elektronenstrahlquelle f electron beam source
Elektronenstrahl-Richtungssuche f cathode-ray detection finding, CRDF
Elektronenstrahlröhre f electron beam tube, cathode-ray tube, CRT
Elektronenstrahlrücklauf m retrace
Elektronenstrahlschreiben n electron beam [direct] writing
Elektronenstrahlsonde f electron[-beam] probe
Elektronenstrahlstrom m [electron] beam current, electron gun beam current
Elektronenstrahltomografie f s. Elektronentomografie
Elektronenstrahlvergütung f electron beam coating *(of lenses)*
Elektronenstrahlwandlerröhre f image-converter tube
Elektronenstrom m 1. electron stream (flow); 2. electron current
Elektronenteleskop n electron telescope
Elektronentomografie f electron[-beam] tomography, electron-beam computed tomography
elektronentomografisch electron tomographic
Elektronentransfer m electron transfer
Elektronentunneln n, **Elektronentunnelung** f electron tunnelling
Elektronenübergang m electron[ic] transition *(in an atom)*
Elektronenübertragung f electron transfer
Elektronenvervielfacher m photomultiplier [tube], multiplier phototube
Elektronenvolt n electron volt, eV *(unit of energy)*
Elektronenwelle f electron wave
Elektronenwolke f electron cloud
Elektronik f electronics
Elektronikbild n electronic image
Elektronikplatine f printed [circuit] board, circuit board
Elektronikrauschen n electronics noise, electronic circuit noise
Elektronikschrott m waste electronics, discarded (used) electronics
Elektronikverschluss m electronic (electronically controlled) shutter
elektronisch electronic
Elektron-Loch-Paar n electron-hole pair
Elektron-Loch-Paarbildung f electron-hole pair creation (production)
Elektron-Positron-Paarvernichtung f electron-positron annihilation
Elektronvolt n s. Elektronenvolt
Elektronystagmograf m electronystagmograph
Elektrookulogramm n electrooculogram, EOG
Elektrooptik f electro-optics, EO
elektrooptisch electro-optic[al], photoelectric
Elektrophorese f electrophoresis
Elektroradiografie f s. 1. Ionografie; 2. Xeroradiografie
elektroradiografisch electroradiographic; ionographic
Elektroretinogramm n electroradiogram
elektrostatisch electrostatic
Elektrothermografie f electrothermography
Element n/**beschreibendes** descriptor element *(metafile element)*
~/**faseroptisches** fiber-optic element
~/**geometrisches** geometric element
~/**holografisch-optisches** holographic optical element, HOE
~/**lichtbrechendes optisches** diffractive optical element, DOE
~/**optisches** optical element
~/**piezoelektrisches** piezoelectric element; piezo[electric] transducer
Elementarbild n elementary image
Elementarbitstrom m, **Elementardatenstrom** m elementary [bit] stream
~/**paketierter** packetized elementary stream, PES
Elementareinheit f neuron *(neuroinformatics)*
Elementarfarbe f s. Grundfarbe
Elementargerüst n/**linienhaftes** skeleton
Elementarmuster n [/**geometrisches**], **Elementarobjekt** n [geometric] primitive
Elementarprozess m/**fotografischer** photographic process
Elementarquader m volume [picture] element, volume pixel, voxel
Elementarquadrat n halftone cell *(digital printing)*
Elementarreflektor m scatterer *(radar)*
Elementarteilchen n elementary particle
Elementarwelle f elementary wave; wavelet
~/**Huygenssche** Huygens' wavelet
Elementarzelle f 1. elementary cell *(e.g. in image processing)*; 2. unit cell *(of a reciprocal lattice)*
Elevation f, **Elevationswinkel** m elevation [angle], angle of elevation

Elimination f verdeckter Flächen hidden-surface elimination (removal), visible-surface identification
~ verdeckter Kanten (Linien) hidden-line removal
Eliminationsschlüssel m elimination key *(image analysis)*
Ellipsenschere f ellipse (oval) scissors
Ellipsenspiegelscheinwerfer m ellipsoidal reflector floodlight, ERF; ellipsoidal reflector spotlight, ERS
Ellipsenwerkzeug n ellipse (oval) tool
Ellipsoid n ellipsoid
Ellipsoidspiegel m ellipsoidal mirror
Ellipsometer n ellipsometer
~/spektroskopisches spectroscopic ellipsometer
Ellipsometrie f ellipsometry
ellipsometrisch ellipsometric
Elliptizität f ellipticity
Eltern-Kind-Beziehung f parent-child relationship *(graphics programming)*
E-Mail f E-mail, electronic mail
Emanation f emanation
emanieren to emanate
Emission f emission *(e.g. of radiation)*
~/induzierte s. **~/stimulierte**
~/lichtelektrische photoelectric (photoelectron) emission, photoemission
~/spektrale spectral emission
~/spontane spontaneous emission
~/stimulierte stimulated (responsive) emission *(laser)*
~/thermionische thermionic emission
~/thermische thermal emission
Emissionsbild n emission image
Emissionsbildgebung f emission imaging
Emissionscomputertomograf m [clinical] SPECT system
Emissionscomputertomografie f single-photon emission-computed tomography, SPECT imaging *(s.a. under SPECT)*
Emissionselektronenmikroskop n emission [electron] microscope, electron emission microscope, EEM
Emissionsenergie f emission energy
Emissionsfilter n emission filter *(fluorescence microscope)*
Emissionsfläche f emitting surface
Emissionsgrad m [/spektraler] emissivity, emittance
Emissionsionenmikroskop n emission ion microscope, EIM
Emissionskennlinie f, **Emissionskurve** f emission characteristic *(e.g. of a light source)*
Emissionslicht n emission light
Emissionslinienspektrum n emission line spectrum
Emissionsmikroskop n s. Emissionselektronenmikroskop
Emissionsrasterelektronenmikroskop n emission scanning electron microscope

Emissionsrichtung f emission direction
Emissionsspektralfotometrie f emitted radiation spectral photometry
Emissionsspektrografie f emission spectrography
Emissionsspektroskopie f emission spectroscopy
Emissionsspektrum n emission spectrum
Emissionsstrom m 1. emission current; 2. s. Elektronenstrahlstrom
Emissionstheorie f des Lichts emission (corpuscular) theory of light
Emissionstomografie f 1. [radionuclide] emission tomography; 2. s. Emissionscomputertomografie
emissionstomografisch emission tomographic
Emissionsvermögen n [/spezifisches] emissivity, emittance
Emissionswellenlänge f emission wavelength
Emissivität f [/spezifische] s. Emissionsvermögen
Emitter m emitter
emittieren to emit
~/kohärentes Licht to lase
emittierend emissive
emmetrop emmetropic
Emmetropie f emmetropia, normal (corrected) vision
Empfang m reception
~/digital terrestrischer digital terrestrial reception
~/terrestrischer terrestrial reception
empfangbar receivable
Empfangbarkeit f receivability
empfangen to receive *(e.g. signals)*
Empfänger m receiver, receptor *(s.a. under Detektor, Sensor)*
~/fotoelektrischer (lichtelektrischer) photoelectric detector
~/optischer optical receiver
~/terrestrischer terrestrial receiver
Empfängerbandbreite f receiver bandwidth
Empfängerbildröhre f viewing tube
Empfängerempfindlichkeit f receiver sensitivity
Empfängerrauschen n receiver [circuit] noise
Empfängerspule f receiver coil *(magnetic resonance imaging)*
Empfangsantenne f receiving antenna (aerial)
Empfangsbild n received image
Empfangsdecoder m/**digitaler** integrated receiver-decoder, IRD, set-top converter (box decoder), set-top [box], STB, video set-top unit
Empfangsfrequenz f receiving frequency
Empfangsgerät n receiving set, receiver
Empfangskanal m receiving channel
Empfangskonverter m 1. receiving converter; 2. s. Blockumsetzer

Empfangsschicht

Empfangsschicht f receiving layer (s.a. Bildempfangsschicht)
Empfangsseite f receiver side, receiving end
empfangsseitig at the receiving end
Empfangssignal n received signal
Empfangsstation f receiving station
Empfangsstörung f/**nichtsynchrone** fruit, false replies unsynchronous in time (radar)
Empfangsverstärker m receiver (receiving) amplifier
empfindlich sensitive (e.g. to light)
Empfindlichkeit f sensitivity, sensitiveness; speed (of photographic material)
~/**fotografische** photographic sensitivity (speed)
~/**maximale** peak sensitivity
~/**radiografische** radiographic sensitivity
~/**relative** relative sensitivity (speed)
~/**relative spektrale** relative spectral sensitivity
~/**spektrale** spectral sensitivity (responsivity), spectral response, color sensitivity
~/**visuelle** visual sensitivity
Empfindlichkeitsangabe f **nach ISO** ISO [film] speed
Empfindlichkeitsbereich m sensitivity range
Empfindlichkeitseinstellung f film speed setting
Empfindlichkeitsgewinn m s. Empfindlichkeitssteigerung
Empfindlichkeitsgrenze f sensitivity limit
Empfindlichkeitskurve f sensitivity curve (function)
~/**spektrale** spectral sensitivity curve (function)
Empfindlichkeitsmaximum n sensitivity peak
Empfindlichkeitsmesser m sensitometer
Empfindlichkeitsmessung f sensitometry
Empfindlichkeitspunkt m sensitivity speck (sensitometry)
Empfindlichkeitsreduktion f speed reduction
Empfindlichkeitsspektrum n sensitivity spectrum
Empfindlichkeitsspielraum m sensitivity range
Empfindlichkeitssteigerung f sensitivity (speed) increase, increase in sensitivity
Empfindlichkeitsvektor m sensitivity vector
Empfindlichkeitsverlust m sensitivity (speed) loss
Empfindlichkeitsverteilung f/**spektrale** s. Empfindlichkeitskurve/spektrale
Empfindlichkeitswert m film-speed number (value), speed value
Empfindlichkeitszentrum n sensitivity center

Empfindung f [/**sinnliche**] sensation, sense impression
Empfindungsphänomen n sensible phenomenon
Emulation f emulation
Emulator m emulator
Emulgierung f emulsification
emulieren to emulate, to imitate
Emulsion f emulsion
~/**blauempfindliche** blue-sensitive emulsion
~/**fotografische** photographic emulsion, photoemulsion
~/**grünempfindliche** green-sensitive emulsion
~/**hochempfindliche** high-speed emulsion
~/**holografische** holographic emulsion
~/**infrarotempfindliche** infrared-sensitive emulsion
~/**kontrastarme** low-contrast emulsion
~/**kontrastreiche** high-contrast emulsion
~/**lichtempfindliche** light-sensitive emulsion
~/**monochromatische** monochromatic emulsion
~/**monodisperse** monodisperse[d] emulsion
~/**niederempfindliche** slow-speed emulsion
~/**orthochromatische** orthochromatic emulsion
~/**panchromatische** panchromatic [silver halide] emulsion
~/**polydisperse** polydisperse emulsion
~/**röntgenstrahlenempfindliche** X-ray-sensitive emulsion
~/**rotempfindliche** red-sensitive emulsion
~/**sensibilisierte** sensitized emulsion
~/**spektralsensibilierte** spectral sensitized emulsion
~/**unsensibilisierte** unsensitized emulsion
Emulsionsbeguss m emulsion coating
Emulsionsbereitung s. Emulsionsherstellung
Emulsionsbestandteil m emulsion ingredient (component)
Emulsionscharge f emulsion batch
Emulsionsdeckschicht f supercoat, top [emulsion] layer, overcoat, topcoat (photographic material)
Emulsionsdicke f emulsion thickness
Emulsionsempfindlichkeit f emulsion speed (sensitivity)
Emulsionsfällung f emulsion precipitation
Emulsionshaftung f emulsion adhesion
Emulsionshärtungsmittel n hardener for emulsion incorporation
Emulsionshersteller m emulsion maker
Emulsionsherstellung f [photographic] emulsion manufacture, emulsion making (preparation), emulsification
Emulsionskontrast m emulsion contrast
Emulsionskorn n emulsion grain
Emulsionskorngröße f emulsion grain size

Emulsionskristall m [photo]emulsion [micro]crystal, [photographic] grain
Emulsions-Laserspeicher m emulsion laser storage
Emulsionsnudel f noodle
Emulsionsnummer f emulsion number
Emulsionsoberfläche f emulsion surface
Emulsionsreaktor m emulsion reactor
Emulsionsschicht f emulsion layer; emulsion coat[ing]
Emulsionsschichtdicke f emulsion layer thickness
Emulsionsschleier m emulsion fog
Emulsionsseite f emulsion (front) side *(of film material)*; print (emulsion) side *(of photographic paper)*
Emulsionsstabilisator m emulsion stabilizer
Emulsionstechnik f [photographic] emulsion technology
Emulsionswäsche f emulsion washing
Emulsionszusatz[stoff] m emulsion additive
encodieren to encode
Endabmischung f 1. final mixing (mixdown) *(sound)*; 2. final mix
Endallonge f s. Endband
Endanwender m end user
Endband n tail leader; [run-out] trailer *(sound film print)*
Endbild n final image (picture), finished picture
~[leucht]schirm m final image fluorescent screen
Endeffektor m end effector *(computer animation)*
Endetitel m end title; [end] credits, closing credits
Ende-zu-Ende-Protokoll n end-to-end protocol *(data transmission)*
Ende-zu-Ende-Verzögerung f end-to-end delay
Endfensterröhre f end window tube *(X rays)*
Endfertigung f postproduction [work], [postproduction] editing
Endfertigungsphase f postproduction phase
Endfilm m output film *(reprography)*
Endformat n final format (size) *(e.g. of an enlargement)*; finished size, trim[med] size *(e.g. of a printed product)*
Endgerät n terminal [device]; data [display] terminal
Endgerätehersteller m terminal equipment manufacturer
Endikon n s. Vidikon
Endknoten m terminal (final) node, endpoint node *(e.g. in graph theory)*; peripheral node
Endkopie f final print
Endlosaufnahme f continuous (endless) recording

Endlosband n, **Endlosbandschleife** f s. Endlosschleife
Endlospapier n continuous-form paper
Endlosprojektion f continuous repetitive projection
Endlosprojektor m continuous [loop] projector
Endlosschleife f continuous (endless) loop, infinite loop
Endlosvordruck m continuous form
Endmarke f trailer *(data transmission)*
Endmischband n print[ing] master, complete sound track
Endmischung f s. Endabmischung
Endoskop n endoscope; optical endoscopic instrument
~/biegsames s. ~/faseroptisches
~/faseroptisches (flexibles) fiber-optic endoscope, fiberscope [device], flexible imagescope
~/starres rigid endoscope
Endoskopanwender m endoscopist
Endoskopaufnahme f endoscope (endoscopic) image; endoscope photograph
Endoskopie f endoscopy
~/chirurgische surgical endoscopy
~/industrielle industrial endoscopy
~/medizinische medical (clinical) endoscopy
~/stereoskopische stereoscopic endoscopy
~/technische industrial endoscopy
~/virtuelle virtual endoscopy
Endoskopieeinheit f endoscopy suite
Endoskopiekamera f endoscopic camera
Endoskopieobjektiv n endoscope lens
Endoskopierer m endoscopist
endoskopisch endoscopic
Endoskopsonde f endoscope probe
Endoskopspitze f endoscope tip (head)
Endosonografie f endoscopic [ultra]sonography
Endpunkt m endpoint, vertex *(e.g. of a line segment)*
Endschnitt m final cut *(cinema)*
Endspiegel m mirrored end *(laser tube)*
Endstrich m terminal *(character part)*
Endstrichlose f grotesque *(nonserif typeface)*
Endteilnehmer m subscriber
Endtitel m end title; [end] credits, closing credits
Endvergrößerung f final [image] magnification
Endverstärker m final (terminal) amplifier
Endwässerung f final wash[ing]; final rinse
Energie f/**elektromagnetische** electromagnetic energy
~/magnetische magnetic energy
Energieauflösung f energy resolution *(PET detector)*
Energiebändermodell n s. Bändermodell
Energiebilanz f energy balance

Energiedichte

Energiedichte f energy density
~/**spektrale, Energiedichtespektrum** n power-spectral density, energy-density spectrum
Energiedosis f absorbed dose
Energiedosisleistung f aborbed dose rate
Energiefenster n pulse height analyzer window *(gamma camera)*
Energiefluss m energy flux (flow)
Energieflussdichte f energy flux density
Energieniveau n energy level
Energiequant n energy quantum
Energiesparschaltung f power saving mode (device); energy save mode
Energiespektrum n energy (power) spectrum, [power] spectral density
Energiestromdichte f energy flux density
Energieverteilung f energy (power) distribution
~/**relative spektrale** relative spectral energy (power) distribution
~/**spektrale** spectral energy distribution
Energieverteilungskurve f frequency distribution
Energieverwischung f energy dispersal *(channel coding step)*
En-face-Aufnahme f [full] front view
Engelecho n angel echo *(radar)*
Engelshaar n angel hair, skivings *(defect of cinematographic film material)*
Engwinkeltomografie f narrow-angle tomography
Entdeckungswahrscheinlichkeit f detection probability, probability of [target] detection *(radar)*
Entelektrisator m static neutralizer *(e.g. on a printing press)*
Enteroskop n enteroscope
Enteroskopie f enteroscopy
enteroskopisch enteroscopic
entfalten to deconvolve
Entfaltung f deconvolution, inverse filtering *(image reconstruction)*
Entfärben n de-inking *(of waste paper)*
entfärben to decolorize; to de-ink
Entfernungsauflösung f range resolution *(radar)*
Entfernungsbereich m distance range *(of a lens)*
Entfernungseindruck m sense of distance
Entfernungseinstellbereich m s. Entfernungsbereich
Entfernungseinstellring m focus control ring
Entfernungseinstellung f distance setting
Entfernungsfehler m distance error
Entfernungsgesetz n/**fotometrisches (quadratisches)** law of inverse squares, inverse square law [of distance], fundamental law of photometry
Entfernungskrümmung f range curvature *(radar)*
Entfernungsmesser m rangefinder, distance gauge

~/**[objektiv]gekoppelter** coupled rangefinder
Entfernungsmesserkamera f rangefinder camera
Entfernungsmesssystem n distance measuring system, ranging system
Entfernungsmessung f 1. distance measurement; ranging; 2. telemetry
Entfernungsring m focus control ring
Entfernungsschätzung f distance estimation
Entfernungssensor m range [imaging] sensor
Entfernungsskale f distance scale
Entfernungsverhältnis n distance ratio, ratio of distances
Entfernungswahrnehmung f distance perception
entionisieren to deionize
Entkalkungsmittel n sequestering agent (compound), sequesterant *(development additive)*
Entladekurve f discharge curve
Entladestrom m discharge current
Entladungsbild n discharge image (pattern)
Entladungsenergie f discharge energy
Entladungslampe f [electric-]discharge lamp
Entladungszyklus m discharge cycle
entmagnetisieren to degauss, to demagnetize
Entmagnetisierer m degausser
Entmagnetisierung f degaussing, demagnetization
Entmagnetisierungsspule f, **Entmagnetisierungswicklung** f degaussing coil *(cathode-ray tube)*
entoptisch entoptic *(visual sensation)*
entrastern to descreen
Entrasterung f descreening
Entrauschung f denoising [procedure], noise removal (cleaning), noise cancel[l]ing
Entropie f entropy *(average information content of a source symbol)*
Entropiecodierer m entropy [en]coder
Entropiecodierung f entropy coding, variable-length [statistical] coding, VLC, entropy-based compression
~/**adaptive** universal coding
~ **nach Huffman** Huffman [en]coding
Entropiedecod[ier]er m entropy decoder
Entropiefunktion f/**binäre** binary entropy function *(image compression)*
entsättigen to desaturate *(e.g. colors)*
Entsättigung f desaturation, muddying *(of color)*
Entschäumer m defoamer, antifrothing (antifoaming) agent *(emulsion preparation)*
Entscheidungsbaum m decision (classification) tree *(data structure)*
Entscheidungsbereich m decision region

Entscheidungsebene f decision level (surface)
Entscheidungsfehler m decision error
Entscheidungsfindung f decision making
Entscheidungsfläche f decision surface *(image segmentation)*
Entscheidungsfunktion f decision (discriminant) function *(object recognition)*
Entscheidungsklasse f decision class
Entscheidungsklassifikator m decision classifier
Entscheidungsprozessor m decision processor
Entscheidungsraum m decision space
Entscheidungsregel f decision rule
Entscheidungsrückkopplung f decision feedback
Entscheidungsschwelle f decision threshold (boundary)
Entscheidungssymbol n decision box *(as a symbol in flowcharts)*
entscheidungstheoretisch decision-theoretic
Entscheidungstheorie f [/statistische] [statistical] decision theory
Entscheidungsvariable f decision variable
entschlüsselbar decryptable, decodable
Entschlüsseler m decoder; descrambler
entschlüsseln to decrypt, to decode; to descramble
Entschlüsselung f decryption, decoding; descrambling
Entsilberung f desilverization
Entspannungsmittel n surfactant, wetting (surface-active) agent, spreading agent
entspiegeln to antiglare
Entspiegelung f antireflection (antireflective) coating, antireflex coating
~/**breitbandige mehrlagige** broadband multilayer [antireflection] coating
~/**optische** optical coating
Entspiegelungsfolie f glare filter
Entspiegelungsschicht f antireflection layer (film), antireflection (antireflective) coating, ARC
Entwerfen n/**computergestütztes (computerunterstütztes)** computer-aided design, CAD
entwickelbar developable
Entwickelbarkeit f developability
entwickeln to develop *(s.a. verarbeiten)*
Entwickler m [chemical] developer; [photographic] developer, dev
~/**elektrofotografischer** electrophotographic developer
~/**fotografischer** photographic developer
~/**gerbender** tanning (hardening) developer
~/**handelsüblicher** commercial developer
~/**hart arbeitender** high-energy developer, high-contrast developer
~/**hochauflösender** high-definition developer
~/**höchstempfindlicher** super-speed developer
~/**physikalischer** physical developer
~/**schnell arbeitender** rapid[-working] developer, rapid-access developer, fast-acting developing agent; rapid film developer; rapid print developer
~/**verbrauchter** exhausted developer
~/**weich arbeitender** soft[-working] developer, low-energy (low-contrast) developer; compensating developer
Entwickleraktivität f developer activity
Entwickleralkali n developer alkali
Entwickleransatz m developer bath
Entwicklerbestandteil m developer component (constituent)
Entwicklerchemikalie f developing chemical
Entwicklereinheit f developer unit *(copier)*
Entwicklerelektron n developer electron
Entwicklererschöpfung f developer exhaustion
Entwicklerfahne f developer streak
Entwicklerfarbstoff m developer dye, dye developer
Entwicklerflüssigkeit f s. Entwicklerlösung
Entwicklerkonzentrat n developer concentrate
Entwicklerkonzentration f developer concentration
Entwicklerkristall m developer crystal
Entwicklerlöslichkeit f developer solubility
Entwicklerlösung f developer (developing) solution
Entwicklermaschine f 1. creation engine *(computer graphics)*; 2. s. Entwicklungsmaschine
Entwicklermolekül n developer (developing agent) molecule
Entwickler-Nachfüllösung f developer replenisher
Entwickleroxidationsprodukt n developer oxidation product
Entwicklerpaste f jellied processing agent
Entwicklerpinzette f print tongs
Entwicklerpulver n developer powder
Entwicklerreaktion f developer reaction
Entwicklerrezeptur f 1. developer formula; 2. developer formulation
Entwicklerschale f developer (developing) tray, developing dish
~/**beheizbare** dishwarmer
Entwicklersubstanz f developing agent (chemical), developer compound
Entwicklertank m developer (developing) tank
Entwicklertemperatur f developer temperature
Entwicklertrommel f, **Entwicklerwalze** f developer (developing) roller, development roll *(electrophotography)*
Entwicklerzange f print tongs
Entwicklerzusammensetzung f developer composition

Entwicklerzusatz *m* development additive, developer improver
Entwicklung *f* development
~/**chemische** chemical development
~/**chromogene** chromogenic [color] development, color-coupling (color-forming) development
~/**chromolytische** chromolytic development
~/**elektrofotografische** electrophotographic development
~/**elektrolytische** electrolytic development
~/**forcierte** forced development (processing), forcing, push[ed] development, pushing, push [film] processing, overdevelopment
~/**fotografische** photographic development
~/**gerbende** tanning development
~/**gesteigerte** *s.* ~/forcierte
~/**halbphysikalische** solution-physical development
~/**manuelle** manual (hand) processing
~/**maschinelle** [continuous] machine processing
~/**physikalische** physical (postfixation) development
~/**superadditive** superadditive development
~/**thermische** thermal development *(e.g. in vesicular processes)*
Entwicklungsanstalt *f* photofinisher
Entwicklungsautomat *m* automatic processor, automatic [film-]processing machine, automatic developing plant
Entwicklungsbad *n* developing (developer) bath, soup
Entwicklungsbeschleuniger *m* [development] accelerator
Entwicklungsbeschleunigung *f* development acceleration
Entwicklungsdauer *f* development (developing) time
Entwicklungsdose *f* [amateur] developing tank, film (daylight) developing tank
Entwicklungseffekt *m* development (processing) effect
entwicklungsfähig developable
Entwicklungsfähigkeit *f* developability
Entwicklungsflüssigkeit *f* developer (developing) solution
Entwicklungsgeschwindigkeit *f* development (developing) rate, rate of development *(of silver halide grains)*
Entwicklungshemmer *m* development inhibitor, restrainer *(s.a.* Antischleiermittel*)*
Entwicklungsinnenkeim *m* intragranular nucleus *(photographic process)*
Entwicklungskeim *m* development nucleus
~/**oberflächlicher** surface development center

Entwicklungskontrast *m* development contrast
Entwicklungslabor *n* photofinishing lab[oratory], [professional] processing lab
Entwicklungsmaschine *f* [photo] processing machine, machine processor
Entwicklungspapier *f* developing[out] paper, development paper
Entwicklungsprozess *m* development (developing) process
Entwicklungsreaktion *f* development reaction
Entwicklungsschleier *m* development (oxidative) fog, milkiness
Entwicklungsschritt *m* development step
Entwicklungsspielraum *m* development latitude
Entwicklungstank *m* developing (developer) tank
Entwicklungstechnik *f* developing technique
Entwicklungstemperatur *f* development temperature
Entwicklungstrommel *f* print drum
Entwicklungsumgebung *f*/**grafische** graphical development environment
Entwicklungsverfahren *n* developing procedure (technique)
Entwicklungsverzögerer *m* [silver] development inhibitor, developer restrainer
Entwicklungsvorgang *m* development process (action)
Entwicklungszeit *f* development (developing) time
Entwicklungszentrum *n* development center
Entwurf *m*/**rechnerunterstützter** computer-aided design, CAD
Entwürfeler *m* descrambler, descrambling device *(signal processing)*
entwürfeln to descramble
Entwürfelung *f* descrambling
Entwurfsmodus *m* draft mode *(dot-matrix printer)*
Entwurfsmuster *n* design pattern
Entwurfsqualität *f* draft quality *(dot-matrix printer)*
entzerren to equalize; to rectify; to unsqueeze, to uncompress *(an anamorphic image)*
Entzerrer *m* equalizer
Entzerrerfilter *n* filter-type equalizer
Entzerrung *f* distortion correction; dewarping; equalization
~/**absolute** georeferencing *(photogrammetry)*
~/**anamorphotische** unsqueezing
~/**direkte** direct method of rectification
~/**fotogrametrische** photogrammetric rectification
~/**geometrische** geometric distortion correction

~/**indirekte** indirct method of rectification
~/**kartografische** cartographic rectification
~/**relative** image registration
Entzerrungsfotogrammetrie f rectification photogrammetry
Entzerrungsgerät n phototransformer, [image] rectifier
Entzerrungsvorsatz m [/**optischer**] anamorphic projector (projection) lens, anamorphic expansion lens, de-squeeze lens
entzifferbar decipherable
entziffern to decipher
Enumerationsverfahren n/**räumliches** spatial occupancy enumeration *(computer graphics)*
Enveloppe f envelope
Environment-Mapping n environment mapping *(computer graphics)*
Enzephalografie f encephalography
enzephalografisch encephalographic
Enzephalogramm n encephalogram, encephalograph
Epidiaskop n 1. epidiascope; 2. *s.* Epiprojektor
Epifluoreszenz f epifluorescence
Epifluoreszenzmikroskop n epifluorescence microscope
epipolar epipolar
Epipolarebene f epipolar plane
Epipolargeometrie f epipolar geometry, geometry of stereo[psis]
Epipolarlinie f epipolar line *(motion estimation)*
Epiprojektion f episcopic projection
Epiprojektor m, **Episkop** n episcopic (opaque) projector, episcope
Epivorlage f reflective copy (material), reflection (reflex) copy
Epoxidkitt m epoxy cement *(lens manufacture)*
EPS-Bilddatei f, **EPS-Datei** f EPS (Encapsulated PostScript) file
Erblindung f loss of sight, amaurosis
Erdbeobachtung f *s.* Fernerkundung
Erdbeobachtungssatellit m earth observation satellite
Erdbildmesskammer f terrestrial camera
Erdbildmessung f terrestrial photogrammetry
Erdefunkstelle f ground[-based] receiving station, ground (earth) station
Erderkundungssatellit m earth observation satellite
Erdfernrohr n terrestrial (erecting) telescope, ground-based telescope
Ereignisfotografie f action photography
Ereignismodus m event mode *(of a logical input device)*
erfassen to acquire
Erfassung f acquisition; capture *(e.g. of image data)*
~/**visuelle** visual capture
Erfassungsradar n acquisition radar

Erfle-Okular n Erfle eyepiece
Erfragefunktion f inquiry function
Erg n erg *(a basic unit of energy)*
Ergänzung f/**amodale** amodal (visual) completion *(perception)*
Ergänzungsfarbe f complementary color (hue); opponent (opposite) color
Ergänzungswinkel m complementary angle
Ergebnisbild n result (final) image
ergodisch ergodic
Ergodizität f ergodicity *(of stochastic processes)*
Erhitzungsmikroskop n heating (high-temperature) microscope
erkennbar recognizable; detectable
Erkennbarkeit f recognizability; detectability
erkennen n to recognitize; to detect; to identify
Erkennen n recognition
~/**primäres** *s.* Einlernen
~/**sekundäres** *s.* Speicherlesen
~/**visuelles** visual recognition
Erkennung f recognition; identification; detection
~/**optische** optical recognition
Erkennungsalgorithmus m recognition (detection) algorithm
Erkennungsaufgabe f recognition task
Erkennungsbild n identification picture
Erkennungsfehler m recognition error
Erkennungsfoto n identification photo[graph], mug [shot]
Erkennungsfotografie f identification photography
Erkennungsgenauigkeit f recognition accuracy
Erkennungsgeschwindigkeit f recognition speed
Erkennungsleistung f recognition performance
Erkennungsrate f recognition rate
Erkennungssicherheit f probability of detection
erkennungstheoretisch detection theoretic
Erkennungsverfahren n recognition technique
Erkennungsvermögen n recognition capability
Erkennungsvorgang m recognition process
Erlang-Rauschen n Erlang (gamma) noise
Eröffnungsbildschirm m startup screen, banner screen (page)
Eröffnungseinstellung f establishing shot *(filming)*
Erosion f erosion [operation] *(binary image processing)*
~/**morphologische** morphological erosion, Minkowski [set] subtraction
Erosionsgradient m erosion gradient
Erosionsoperation f erosion operation
Erosionsoperator m erosion operator

Erratum

Erratum n erratum, corrigendum
Erregung f/**neuronale** neural excitation
Ersatzbild n surrogate image *(e.g. of a museum object)*
Ersatzkamera f back-up camera; spare camera
Erscheinung f/**optische** 1. optical phenomenon; apparition; 2. *s.* Erscheinungsbild
~/**visuelle, Erscheinungsbild** n [visual] appearance, [visual] look
Erschöpfung f exhaustion *(e.g. of developers)*
Erstaufführung f first (premium) run
Erstaufführungskino n, **Erstaufführungstheater** n first-run theater (house)
Erstbelichtung f first (initial) exposure
Erstentwickler m first developer *(reversal processing)*
Erstentwicklung f first development
Ersterfassung f enrolment *(authentication)*
Erstinstallation f/**automatische** auto[matic] start-up tuning *(e.g. of a video recorder)*
Erstkopie f first [trial] print, check (grading) print, [first] answer print, trial composite print, approval print *(cinema)*
Erstzeileneinzug m/**negativer** hanging indent *(layout)*
Erwartungsoperator m expectation (averaging) operator *(image quantization)*
Erwartungswert m expectation (expected) value; mean [value]
Erweiterbarkeit f extensibility *(e.g. of data transport formats)*
Erweiterungsbus m expansion bus, system input/output bus
Erweiterungskarte f expansion board (card); plug-in card (board)
Erweiterungsspeicher m extended (expanded) memory
Erweiterungssteckplatz m [expansion] slot
Essigsäure f acetic acid
Etalon n etalon, resonator, [resonant] cavity *(interferometry, laser)*
Ethernet n Ethernet *(local area network standard)*
Ethernet-Adapter m Ethernet adapter (connector)
Ethernet-Kabelanschluss m Ethernet cable port
Ethernet-Schnittstelle f, **Ethernet-Verbindung** f Ethernet connection (link)
Ethylendiamintetraessigsäure f ethylenediaminetetraacetic acid, EDTA *(bleach-fix bath additive)*
Ethylenglycol n [ethylene] glycol
Etikettendruck m label printing
Etikettenpapier n/**metallbedampftes** metallic paper
Et-Zeichen n ampersand

Euler-Gleichung f Euler['s] equation (formula) *(mathematical morphology)*
Euler-Operation f Euler operation *(computer graphics)*
Euler-Operator m Euler operator
Euler-Zahl f Euler number *(binary image processing)*
Euro-AV-Buchse f SCART connector (socket)
Euro-AV-Stecker m Euroconnector, SCART (Peritel) connector *(video)*
EUV *s.* Ultraviolett/extremes
Evaporograf m evaporograph *(sensor)*
Evaporografie f evaporography
Evidenztheorie f [**von Dempster und Shafer**] evidence theory, Dempster-Shafer theory
Ewald-Kugel f Ewald['s] sphere *(electron diffraction)*
Excimerlaser m excimer laser
EXKLUSIV-ODER n/**logisches**, **EXKLUSIV-ODER-Verknüpfung** f Boolean EX-OR
Expansion f expansion
Expansionspunkt m focus of expansion, FoE *(optical flow)*
Expansionsverhältnis n expansion ratio
Experimentalfotografie f experimental photography
Expertensystem n expert (knowledge-based) system *(data processing)*
~/**regelbasiertes** rule-based expert system
Expertenwissen n expert knowledge, human expertise
Explosionsdarstellung f, **Explosionszeichnung** f exploded diagram; exploded-view [photograph]
Exponentialfunktion f exponential [function]
~/**komplexe** phasor *(signal processing)*
exponieren to expose *(e.g. to radiant energy)*
Exposimeter n exposure (light) meter
Exposition f [radiant] exposure *(s.a. under Belichtung)*
Expositionszeit f exposure time *(radiology)*
Express-Fixierbad n fast-acting fixing agent, rapid[-acting] fixer
Extenderkarte f *s.* Erweiterungskarte
Extinktion f extinction
~/**atmosphärische** atmospheric extinction
Extinktionsbelichtungsmesser m extinction [exposure] meter
Extinktionskoeffizient m extinction (attenuation) coefficient
Extinktionsverhältnis n extinction ratio
extrafett ultra bold *(type)*
extrafokal out-of-focus
extrahart extra hard *(paper grade)*
Extrapolation f extrapolation
extrapolieren to extrapolate
extraweich extra soft *(paper grade)*

Extremwertoperator *m* extremum filter
(gray-scale image processing)
Extrusionsfläche *f* extruded surface
(surface modeling)
exzentrisch eccentric
Exzentrizität *f* eccentricity *(shape feature)*
Exzess *m* kurtosis *(histogram analysis)*

F

Fabry-Perot-Interferometer *n* Fabry-Perot interferometer
Fabry-Perot-Resonator *m* [Fabry-Perot] cavity, two-mirror planar resonator
Fabry-Perot-System *n* Fabry-Perot device
Facette *f* facet, facette *(s.a.* Polygonfläche*)*
Facettenmodell *n* facet model
Facettenspiegel *m* faceted mirror
facettieren to facet *(e.g. a lens)*
Facettierung *f* faceting *(e.g. in computer graphics)*
Fächerblende *f* fan fader
Fächerform *f* fan-like geometry *(e.g. of an ultrasound image)*
Fächerkeule *f* fan beam *(radar)*
Fächerstrahl *m* fan[-shaped] beam, fanned beam
Fächerstrahldetektor *m* fan beam detector *(tomography)*
Fächerstrahlkollimation *f* fan beam collimation
Fächerstrahlprojektion *f* fan beam projection
Fächerwinkel *m* fan angle
Fachfarblabor[atorium] *n* professional color laboratory
Fachfotograf *m* professional photographer; commercial photographer
Fachfotografie *f* commercial photography
Fachkamera *f* view (technical) camera
Fachkameraobjektiv *n* view camera lens
Fachkamera-Rückteil *n* view camera back
Fachlabor *n* photofinishing lab[oratory], commercial darkroom
Fachobjektiv *n* view camera lens
Fadenkreuz *n* crosshair, cross wire
Fadenkreuz-Cursor *m* crosshair cursor
Fadenkreuzokular *n* filar (crosshair) eyepiece
Fadenzähler *m* linen tester, loupe *(typography)*
Fahndungsbild *n* s. Fahndungsfoto
Fahndungsdatei *f* mug shot database
Fahndungsfoto *n* identification photo[graph], mug [shot]
Fahndungsfotografie *f* mug photography
Fahne *f*, **Fahnenabzug** *m* galley [proof]
Fahnenziehen *n* streaking, tailing *(television)*
Fahraufnahme *f* tracking (follow) shot, dolly (truck) shot, travel[ing] shot
Fahreffekt *m*, **Fahreffektaufnahme** *f* zoom shot (effect) *(filming)*
Fahrerassistenzsystem *n* driver assistance system
Fahrsimulator *m* driving simulator
Fahrspinne *f*, **Fahrstativ** *n* [camera] dolly, truck
Fahrt *f*/**optische** *s.* Fahreffekt
Fahrzeugnavigationssystem *n* vehicle (car) navigation system
Faksimile *n* facsimile
Faksimilecodierung *f* facsimile coding
Faksimiledarstellung *f* facsimile representation
Faksimiledruck *m* facsimile printing
Faksimilekompression *f* facsimile compression
Faksimileübertragung *f* facsimile transmission
faksimilieren to facsimile
Faktorenanalyse *f* factor (oblique) analysis
fällen to precipitate
Fallstudie *f* case study
Fällung *f* precipitation *(emulsion making)*
Fallverschluss *m* drop shutter
Falschakzeptanzrate *f* false acception rate, FAR *(authentication)*
Falschalarmrate *f* false alarm rate *(radar)*
fälschen to fake, to forge, to counterfeit
Falscherfassungsrate *f* false enrolment rate, FER *(authentication)*
Falschfarbe *f* false color *(s.a. under Pseudofarbe)*
Falschfarbenbild *n* false-color image (picture)
Falschfarbenfilm *m* [IR] false-color film, color infrared film, IR color film, false IR film
Falschfarbenfotografie *f* false-color photography
Falschfarben-Wärmebild *n* false-color thermograph
Falschlicht *n* false light *(s.a. Streulicht)*
Falschrückweisungsrate *f* false rejection rate, FRR *(authentication)*
Fälschungserkennung *f* forgery (tampering) detection
fälschungssicher tamperproof *(e.g. a photo identification system)*
Fälschungssicherheit *f* tamper resistance
Faltbalgen *m* corrugated bellows
falten to fold; to convolve *(e.g. signals)*
Faltenbalg *m* corrugated bellows
Faltkamera *f* folding bellows camera
Faltlichtschacht *m* folding viewing hood, folding [viewfinder] light shield *(twin-lens reflex camera)*
Faltprospekt *m* folder, broadside
Faltreflektor *m* folding mirror
Faltschachteldruck *m* folding carton printing
Faltung *f* convolution [filtering], folding *(signal processing mathematical operation)*
~/**aperiodische** *s.* ~/lineare
~/**binäre** binary convolution
~/**digitale** digital convolution
~/**diskrete** discrete convolution

~/**diskrete zweidimensionale** two-dimensional discrete convolution
~/**eindimensionale** one-dimensional convolution
~/**grafische** graphical convolution
~/**kaskadierte** cascaded convolution
~/**kontinuierliche** continuous convolution
~/**kubische** cubic convolution *(resampling technique)*
~/**lineare** linear convolution
~/**mehrdimensionale** multidimensional convolution
~/**nichtlineare** nonlinear convolution
~/**normalisierte** normalized convolution
~/**periodische** 1. periodic convolution; 2. *s.* ~/zyklische
~/**räumliche** spatial convolution
~/**rekursive** recursive convolution
~/**zeitdiskrete** discrete-time convolution
~/**zeitkontinuierliche** continuous-time convolution
~/**zirkulare** *s.* ~/zyklische
~/**zweidimensionale** two-dimensional convolution
~/**zyklische** cyclic (circular) convolution, wraparound convolution
Faltungsalgorithmus *m* convolution algorithm
Faltungscode *m* convolutional code
Faltungscodierer *m* convolutional [en]coder
Faltungscodierung *f* convolution[al] coding
Faltungsdecodierer *m* convolutional decoder
Faltungsergebnis *n* convolution result
Faltungsfilter *n s.* Faltungskern
Faltungsfläche *f* convolution surface
Faltungsfrequenz *f* aliased frequency
Faltungsfunktion *f* convolving (convolution) function
Faltungsgleichung *f* convolution [integral] equation
Faltungsintegral *n* convolution integral
Faltungsinterpolation/kubische cubic convolution interpolation *(image restoration)*
Faltungsinterpolationsfunktion *f* **höherer Ordnung** high-order convolutional interpolation function
Faltungskern *m* [convolution] kernel, convolution mask (filter), filter[ing] mask
~/**nichtrekursiver** nonrecursive convolution filter
~/**punktsymmetrischer** point-symmetric convolution kernel
Faltungsmaske *f s.* Faltungskern
Faltungsmatrix *f* convolution matrix
Faltungsoperation *f* convolution (blurring) operation
Faltungsoperator *m* convolution[al] operator
Faltungsprodukt *n* convolution product
Faltungsprozess *m s.* Faltungsoperation

Faltungsroutine *f* convolution routine
Faltungssatz *m* convolution theorem
Faltungssumme *f* convolution sum
Faltungssummierung *f* convolution summation
Faltungstechnik *f* convolution technique
Faltungstheorem *n* convolution theorem *(signal analysis)*
Falz *m* fold
Falzapparat *m* folder, folding system
Falzbogen *m* [folded] signature
falzen to fold *(e.g. printed sheets)*
Falzfolge *f* folding succession
Falzmarke *f* fold mark
Falzmaschine *f s.* Falzapparat
Falzreihenfolge *f* folding succession
Falzvorrichtung *f s.* Falzapparat
Familienalbum *n* family album
Fangbereich *m* catchment area *(visual navigation)*
Fangspiegel *m* secondary mirror *(e.g. of a catadioptric system)*; subreflector *(telescope)*
Fangstoff *m* getter
Faraday-Effekt *m* Faraday effect
Faraday-Käfig *m* Faraday cage
Faraday-Rotation *f* Faraday (magnetic) rotation, Kundt effect
Faraday-Rotator *m* Faraday rotator
Faraday-Verschluss *m* Faraday (magneto-optical) shutter
Farb... *s.a.* Farben...
Farbabbildungsfehler *m s.* Farbfehler
Farbabbildungstabelle *f s.* Farbindextabelle
Farbabgleich *m* 1. [color] matching *(electronic imaging)*; 2. *s.* Farbabmusterung
Farbabmusterung *f* color matching (adjustment)
Farbabschalter *m*, **Farbabschaltung** *f* color killer *(video)*
Farbabsorption *f* color absorption
Farbabstand *m* color distance (difference)
Farbabstandsmaß *n* color difference measure (unit)
Farbabstimmung *f* color matching (adjustment); color tuning
farbabstoßend ink-repellent
Farbabstufung *f* color gradation
Farbabtastung *f* chromatic (color) sampling; color scanning
Farbabweichung *f* color deviation *(s.a.* Farbfehler*)*
farbabweisend ink-repellent
Farbabzug *m* color [photo]print, photographic color print
Farbadaptation *f* color (chromatic) adaptation
Farbähnlichkeitsmaß *n* color similarity measure
Farbanalysator *m* [darkroom] color analyzer
Farbanalyse *f* color analysis

Farbandruck 128

Farbandruck *m* color proof
Farbangleichung *f* color matching (adjustment)
Farbannahme *f* ink reception *(printing)*
Farbannahmefähigkeit *f*,
Farbannahmevermögen *n* ink receptivity
farbannehmend ink-receptive
Farbanpassung *f s.* Farbangleichung
Farbanteil *m* color component; color portion *(e.g. of the video signal)*
Farbäquidensite *f* chromatic equidensity line
Farbart *f* 1. chrominance, chroma, C; 2. chromaticity
Farbartdiagramm *n* chromaticity diagram (chart)
Farbartinformation *f* chrominance (color) information
Farbartsignal *n* chrominance (chroma) signal, color information signal, C [signal] *(video)*
Farbarttafel *f* chromaticity chart (diagram)
Farbartunterscheidung *f* chromaticity discrimination
Farbatlas *m* color atlas
Farbätzung *f* color etching
Farbaufbau *m* color coupling
Farbauflösung *f* color (chromatic) resolution
Farbauflösungsvermögen *n* chromatic resolving power
Farbaufnahme *f* color shot, color photo[graph]
Farbaufnahmefilm *m* color [photographic] film, photographic color film *(s.a.* Farbfilm*)*
Farbaufnehmer *m* color picker *(imaging software)*
Farbaufspaltung *f* 1. color splitting (scission) *(perceptual phenomenon)*; 2. dispersion *(of polychromatic light)*
Farbauftrag[s]walze *f* ink (form) roller *(printing press)*
Farbausbleichverfahren *n* dye bleach process, dye destruction process *(color photography)*
Farbausdruck *m* color output
Farbausgleich *m* color compensation
Farbausgleichsfilter *m* color-compensating filter, CC filter, color balance filter
Farbauswahlfeld *n* color dialogue box
Farbauswahlmodus *m* color selection mode
Farbauszug *m* 1. color separation *(process)*; 2. color separation (record) *(monochrome image)*; 3. *s.* Farbdifferenzwert
Farbauszugkopieren *n* separation printing
Farbauszugsfilm *m* [color] separation film, panchromatic separation film
Farbauszugsfilter *n* color separation filter
Farbauszugsfotografie *f* color separation photography

Farbauszugsnegativ *n* [color] separation negative
Farbauszugspositiv *n* separation positive (master) *(dye transfer process of color printing)*
Farbauszugsverfahren *n* color-separation process
Farbbalance *f* color balance; ink balance *(printing)*
Farbbalancespeicher *m* color balance memory
Farbbalanceverschiebung *f* color balance shift
Farbbalken *m* color bar
Farbbalkenamplitude *f* color bar amplitude
Farbbalkenbild *n s.* Farbbalkentestbild
Farbbalkengenerator *m* color bar generator
Farbbalkenmuster *n s.* Farbbalkentestbild
Farbbalkensignal *n* color-bar waveform (test signal)
Farbbalkentestbild *n* color-bar test pattern, [color] bars
Farbband *n* 1. color band; 2. color[ed] ribbon; inked (dye donor) ribbon *(dye transfer printer)*
Farbbandfarbe *f* ribbon ink
Farbbandkassette *f* [inked] ribbon cartridge
Farbbbalkenprüfsignal *n s.* Farbbalkensignal
Farbbelichtungssystem *n* color exposure system
Farbbenennung *f* color naming
Farbbereich *m* 1. color region; 2. color range (gamut), gamut [of colors] *(e.g. of a printer)*
Farbbeschreibung *f* color description (specification)
farbbeständig color-consistent
Farbbeständigkeit *f* color consistency
Farbbestimmung *f s.* Farblichtbestimmung
Farbbetrachtung *f* color viewing
Farbbeurteilung *f* color judgement
Farbbezeichnungssystem *n* color-naming system, CNS
Farbbild *n* color image (picture), colored picture (image); color [photo]print
~/**indiziertes** indexed-color image, color-mapped image
Farbbildanalyse *f* color image analysis
Farbbildaufnahme *f* color image acquisition
Farb-Bild-Austast-Synchron[isier]-Signal *n* composite [video] signal, composite color [video] signal, composite TV signal
Farbbildbearbeitung *f* color imaging
Farbbildcodierung *f* color image coding
Farbbilddaten *pl* color image data
Farbbilddrucker *m* pictorial color printer
Farbbild-Elektronenstrahlröhre *f s.* Farbbildröhre
farbbildend chromogenic

Farbbildentstehung f color image formation
Farb-Bilderfassungskarte f color image digitizer
Farbbildfilterung f color image filtering
Farbbildgebung f color imaging
Farbbildglättung f color image smoothing
Farbbildkompression f, **Farbbildkomprimierung** f color image compression
Farbbildkontrollempfänger m color monitor [display]
Farbbildkopie f pictorial color copy
Farbbildmaterial n color imagery
Farbbildner m color (dye) former, color-forming agent, dye-forming agent
Farbbildpunkt m color[ed] pixel
Farbbildquantisierung f color image quantization
Farbbildrestauration f color image restoration
Farbbildröhre f color [picture] tube, color kinescope; color CRT (cathode-ray tube)
Farbbildschirm m color [picture] screen, color kinescope screen; multicolor display, color display [terminal]
Farbbildschirmgerät n color monitor [display]
Farbbildsegmentierung f color image segmentation
Farbbildsensor m color image sensor
Farbbildsignal n chrominance video signal, color picture signal
Farbbildteil m color insert *(as in books)*
Farbbildtransformation f color image transformation
Farbbildtreue f color image fidelity
Farbbildübertragung f color facsimile transmission
Farbbildung f color formation
Farbbildungsreaktion f dye formation reaction
Farbbildverarbeitung f color image processing
Farbbildverstehen n color image understanding
Farbbildwiedergabe f color image reproduction
Farbbildwiedergabegerät n color image reproduction device
Farbbit n color bit
Farbbleichbad n dye bleach solution
Farbbleichen n, **Farbbleichung** f, **Farbbleichverfahren** n dye bleaching, dye bleach (destruction) process, color bleaching process *(color print processing)*
Farbbrennweitenfehler m chromatic variation of focus, longitudinal (axial) chromatic aberration, longitudinal color
Farbbrillanz f color brilliance
Farbbrille f s. Farbfilterbrille
Farbbündelung f, **Farbburst** m s. Farbträgerburst

Farb-CCD-Kamera f color CCD camera
Farbcharakter m tone [of a color]
Farbcode m color code
farbcodieren to color-code
Farbcodierer m color [en]coder
Farbcodiersystem n color [television] encoding system, color-coding system (scheme), color-coding table
Farbcodierung f color [en]coding, chromatic coding; color keying *(video)*
Farbdarstellung f color representation
Farbdeckung f 1. registration *(color picture tube)*; 2. [ink] coverage *(printing)*
Farbdeckungsfehler m misregistration
Farbdecod[ier]er m chroma demodulator, color (chrominance) demodulator, color decoder
Farbdecodierung f color decoding
Farbdefinition f color definition *(bit-mapped image)*
Farbdemodulator m s. Farbdecod[ier]er
Farbdensitometer n color densitometer
Farbdensitometrie f color densitometry
Farbdeskriptor m color descriptor
Farbdetail n color (chrominance) detail
Farbdia n color [projection] slide
Farbdiafilm m color slide (transparency) film, chrome film
Farbdiafilmverarbeitung f color transparency processing
Farbdiagramm n chromaticity diagram (chart)
Farbdiamaterial n color transparency material
Farbdiapositiv n 1. [photographic] color transparency; 2. s. Farbdia
Farbdiaprojektor m color slide projector
Farbdichte f [color] density
~/**analytische** analytical density
~/**integrale** integral color density
~/**spektrale** spectral color density; excitation purity *(television)*
Farbdichtemessung f color density measurement
Farbdichteregelung f [ink] density control *(printing)*
Farbdifferenz f color difference (distance)
~/**empfindungsgemäße** perceptual color difference
Farbdifferenzierung f color differentiation
Farbdifferenzkanal m color difference channel
Farbdifferenzmessung f color difference measurement
Farbdifferenzsignal n color difference signal (component) *(video)*
~ **B-Y** blue-minus-luma signal, B-Y signal *(video)*
~ **R-Y** red-minus-luma signal, R-Y signal *(video)*
Farbdifferenzwert m chrominance, chroma, C
Farbdiffusion f s. Farbstoffdiffusion
Farbdisplay n color display

Farbdistanz

Farbdistanz f s. Farbabstand
Farb-Dithering n color dithering
Farb-Dokumentenkopierer m color document copier
Farb-Doppler m s. Farb-Doppler-Sonografie
Farb-Doppler-Echokardiografie f color Doppler echocardiography
Farb-Doppler-Sonografie f color Doppler [ultra]sonography, color Doppler ultrasound, color Doppler [method]
Farbdosiereinrichtung f/**nebenwirkungsfreie** split fountain *(printing press)*
Farbdosierkasten m [ink] fountain *(printing press)*
Farbdreieck n color triangle, triangle of color; chromaticity diagram (chart)
Farbdruck m 1. color printing; 2. color print, printed color reproduction
~/**kleinauflagiger** short-run color printing
Farbdrucker m color printer, color printing device
Farbdrucksystem n color printing system
Farb-Druckvorstufenbereich m color prepress
Farbdüse f ink nozzle
Farbdüsenplotter m ink jet plotter
Farbe f 1. color; hue; 2. paint; 3. s. Druckfarbe
~/**achromatische** achromatic (neutral) color
~/**bedingt gleiche** metameric color
~/**bezogene** related color
~/**blasse** pale color
~/**brillante** brilliant (bright) color
~/**bunte** chromatic (dye) color, pigmented color
~/**diffuse** diffuse color
~/**dunkle** dark color
~/**durchscheinende** transparent color
~/**emittierte** emissive color
~/**entsättigte** desaturated color
~/**flaue** flat (faint) color
~/**fluoreszente** fluorescent color
~/**freie** intrinsic hue
~/**gebundene** relative hue
~/**geräteunabhängige** device-independent color
~/**gesättigte** saturated (strong) color, vibrant (vivid) color, bright (brilliant) color
~/**getrübte** tint
~/**gleichaussehende** matched color
~/**graue** s. ~/unbunte
~/**gültige** valid color
~/**helle** light color
~/**hochgesättigte** highly saturated color, high-saturation color
~/**illegale** illegal color *(video)*
~/**indizierte** indexed (indirect) color *(digital image processing)*
~/**irreale** imaginary primary
~/**isomere** isomeric color
~/**kalte** cool color

~/**komplementäre** complementary (opposite) color
~/**kräftige** strong (vibrant) color
~/**lasierende** transparent color
~/**metamere** metameric color, metamer
~/**mischbare** miscible color
~/**monochromatische** monochromatic (monochrome) color, single-wavelength color
~/**naturgetreue (natürliche)** natural (normal) color
~/**nichtdruckbare** unprintable color
~/**nichtspektrale** nonspectral color (hue), purple color
~/**objektive** objective color
~/**originalgetreue** true color
~/**psychophys[iolog]ische** psychophysical color
~/**reale** real color
~/**reine** pure color *(s.a. ~/gesättigte)*
~/**reproduzierbare** reproducible color
~/**satte** s. ~/gesättigte
~/**sichtbare** visible color
~/**spektrale** spectral (spectrum) color
~/**spiegelnde** specular color
~/**subtraktive** subtractive color, reflecting (secondary) light source
~/**typografische** typographic color
~/**übersättigte** oversaturated color
~/**unbedingt gleiche** isomeric color
~/**unbezogene** unrelated color
~/**unbunte** achromatic (neutral) color
~/**ungesättigte** unsaturated (weak) color
~/**ungültige** invalid color
~/**verblasste** faded color
~/**vergraute** gray-shaded color
~/**wahrgenommene** perceived color (hue), recognized color
~/**warme** warm color
Farbebene f color plane
farbecht colorfast
Farbechtheit f colorfastness
Farbeffekt m color effect
Farbeffektfilter n color effect filter
Farbeigenschaft f chromatic (color) property
Farbeindruck m color impression (appearance)
Farbeingabe f, **Farbeintastung** f chroma keying *(video)*
Farbeinzelheit f color (chrominance) detail
Farbelektrolumineszenz f color electroluminescence
Färbemittel n colorant, coloring agent (material) *(s.a. Farbstoff)*
Farbempfang m color reception
Farbempfinden n s. Farbempfindung
farbempfindlich color-sensitive
Farbempfindlichkeit f color sensitivity, spectral sensitivity (responsivitiy), spectral response
Farbempfindung f chromatic (color) sensation, sensation of color
Farbemulsion f color emulsion

färben to color; to dye, to tint; to stain *(e.g. a biological specimen)*
Farben ... *s.a.* **Farb** ...
~ *fpl*/**subjektive** subjective (Fechner's) colors
farbenblind color-blind
Farbenblinder *m* color-blind person (individual), monochromat
~/**partiell** partially color-blind person, dichromat
Farbenblindheit *f* [/**angeborene**] color blindness, Daltonism
~/**partielle** partial color blindness, dichromatism
~/**totale** complete color blindness; achromatopsia, achromatism; monochromatic vision, monochromatism, monochromacy
Farbenentsättigung *f* desaturation, muddying *(of color)*
Farbenfehlsichtigkeit *f* defective color vision, deficient (anomalous) color vision, color-vision defect (deficiency)
Farbenfotografie *f s.* Farbfotografie
Farbenkarte *f* color chart
Farbenkegel *m* color cone
Farbenkreis *m s.* Farbkreis
Farbenkugel *f* color sphere
Farbenlehre *f* chromatics, color science, science of colors
Farbenmannigfaltigkeit *f* colorfulness
Farbenschwäche *f* color weakness, anomalous trichromacy (trichromatism) *(color-vision deficiency)*; color asthenopia
Farbensehen *n* color (chromatic) vision
~/**dichromatisches** dichromatic vision, dichromatism, partial color blindness
~/**extrafoveales (indirektes)** extrafoveal color vision
~/**normales** normal color vision
~/**trichromatisches** trichromatic [color] vision, trichromacy of vision, trichromatism
Farbensinn *m* color sense
Farbentheorie *f* theory of colors
Farbentwickler *m* color[-forming] developer, color-coupling developer
Farbentwicklerbad *n* color developer bath, color-developing solution
Farbentwickler-Starter *m* color developer starter
Farbentwicklersubstanz *f* color developing agent
Farbentwicklerzusatz *m* color developer additive
Farbentwicklung *f* color development (processing)
~/**chromogene** chromogenic [color] development, color-coupling development
Farbenwürfel *m* color cube, RGB [color] cube

Farbenzerlegung *f* 1. color separation; 2. *s.* Farbenzerstreuung
Farbenzerstreuung *f* color [light] dispersion
Farberfassung *f* color acquisition
Farberkennung *f* color identification
Farberscheinung *f* color appearance
Farberzeugung *f s.* Farbmischung
farbfähig color-capable
Farbfähigkeit *f* color capability
Farbfax *n* color fax (facsimile)
Farbfehler *m* chromatic [lens] aberration, chromatic error (defect), color aberration (distortion); color defect (error); color artifact, hue error, off-color *(video)*
~/**lateraler** *s.* Farbquerfehler
farbfehlerfrei chromatic aberration-free
Farbfehlerfreiheit *f* freedom from chromatic aberration, achromatism
Farbfehlerkorrektion *f*,
Farbfehlerkorrektur *f* chromatic [aberration] correction
farbfehlerkorrigiert chromatically corrected *(lens)*
farbfehlsichtig color deficient
Farbfehlsichtigkeit *f s.* Farbenfehlsichtigkeit
Farbfernsehbild *n* color television image (picture)
Farbfernsehbildröhre *f* color television [picture] tube, color television CRT (cathode-ray tube)
Farbfernsehbildschirm *m* color TV (picture) screen
Farbfernsehempfang *m* color television reception
Farbfernsehempfänger *m* color [television] receiver
Farbfernsehen *n* color television (TV)
Farbfernsehgerät *n* color television display device; color [television] receiver, color television (TV) set
Farbfernsehkamera *f* color television (TV) camera
Farbfernsehmonitor *m* color television monitor
Farbfernsehnorm *f* color television (video) standard, color video format
Farbfernsehröhre *f s.* Farbfernsehbildröhre
Farbfernsehrundfunk *m* color broadcast TV
Farbfernsehsendung *f* color [TV] broadcast, color program, colorcast
Farbfernsehsignal *n* color television (TV) signal
Farbfernsehstandard *m s.* Farbfernsehnorm
Farbfernsehsystem *n* color television [broadcast] system, color TV system
Farbfernsehtechnik *f* color television technology
Farbfernsehübertragung *f* color television transmission, color broadcasting

Farbfernsehwiedergabegerät *n* color television display device
Farbfilm *m* 1. color [photographic] film, photographic color film; 2. color movie (motion picture)
~/**additiver** additive color film
~/**subtraktiver** subtractive color film
Farbfilmaufbau *m* color-film structure
Farbfilmbleicher *m* color film bleach
Farbfilmempfindlichkeit *f* color film speed
Farbfilmemulsion *f* color film emulsion
Farbfilmentwicklung *f* color [film] processing
Farbfilmhersteller *m* color film manufacturer
Farbfilmmaterial *n* color film stock
Farbfilmrecorder *m* color film recorder
Farbfilmtechnik *f* color film technology
Farbfilmverarbeitung *f* color [film] processing
Farbfilter *n* color[ed] filter, light (ray) filter, color screen
~/**optisches** optical color filter
Farbfilterbrille *f* red-green goggles; anaglyph glasses
Farbfiltermosaik *n* color filter mosaic *(liquid crystal display)*
Farbfiltermuster *n* color pattern *(CCD technology)*
Farbfilterrad *n* color filter wheel
Farbfilterscheibe *f* color filter disk
Farbfilterung *f* color filtering (filtration)
~/**selektive** selective color filtering
Farb-Flachbettscanner *m* color flatbed scanner
Farbfläche *f* colored area; solid tint *(typography)*
Farbflächengenerator *m* matte
Farbflecktafel *f* pseudoisochromatic test target
Farbflimmern *n* color flicker
Farbfolie *f* colored foil
Farbfoto *n* colorphoto, color photograph[ic image], photographic color image
Farbfotoapparat *m* color camera
Farbfotograf *m* color photographer
Farbfotografie *f* 1. color photography; 2. *s.* Farbfoto
~/**additive** additive color photography
~/**Lippmannsche** Lippmann process *(color photography)*
~/**subtraktive** subtractive color photography
farbfotografisch color photographic
farbfotokopieren to color photocopy
Farbfotokopierer *m*, **Farbfotokopiergerät** *n* color photocopier
Farbfotopapier *n* [photographic] color paper, color photographic paper
Farbfotoverfahren *n* color [photography] process
Farbfrequenz *f s.* Farbton
farbfreundlich, farbführend ink-receptive
Farbgangkorrektur *f s.* Farbkorrektur

farbgebend chromogenic
Farbgebung *f* 1. coloring; 2. *s.* Farbart
Farbgebungstechnik *f* coloring technique
Farbgedächtnis *n* color memory
Farbgehalt *m* color content *(e.g. of a query image)*
farbgenau color-correct, color-grade
Farbgenauigkeit *f* 1. color accuracy (precision), hue accuracy *(s.a.* Farbtreue*)*; 2. *s.* Farbwiedergabegenauigkeit
Farbgeometrie *f* color geometry
Farbgerät *n* color device
Farbgesichtsfeld *n* color visual field [of the eyes]
Farbgestalter *m* color designer
Farbgestaltung *f* color design
Farbgitter *n* color (chromatic) grating; color mesh
Farbglas *n* stained (coloring) glass
Farbglasfilter *n* color[ed] glass filter
farbgleich isochromatic, like-colored; homochromatic
Farbgleichgewicht *n* color balance
Farbgleichheit *f* color match
Farbgleichung *f* color equation
Farbgradient *m* color gradient
Farbgrafik *f* color graphics
Farbgrafikadapter *m s.* Farbgrafikkarte
Farbgrafik-Bibliothek *f* color graphics library
Farbgrafikfeld *n* color graphics array, CGA
Farbgrafikkarte *f* color graphics adapter, CGA
Farbgrundeinstellungsdatei *f* color setting file *(file format extension)*
Farbharmonie *f* color harmony
Farbhelligkeit *f* color lightness; luminance, photometric brightness
Farbhilfsträger *m* color (chrominance) subcarrier *(video signal)*
Farbhilfsträgerfrequenz *f* color subcarrier frequency
Farbhistogramm *n* color histogram
Farbholografie *f* color holography
Farbhologramm *n* color hologram
farbig colored, chromatic *(s.a.* bunt*)*
Farbigkeit *f* colorfulness, chromaticness; chromaticity
Farbillustration *f* color illustration
Farbindex *m* color index
Farbindextabelle *f* color lookup table, CLUT, color map
Farbinformation *f* color (chromatic) information; chrominance [information] *(video)*
Farbinformationsverarbeitung *f* color information processing
Farbinfrarotbild *n* color infrared image
Farbinfrarotfilm *m* color infrared film, IR color film, [IR] false-color film, false IR film
Farbintensität *f* color intensity *(s.a.* Farbsättigung*)*
farbintensiv color-intensive

Farbinterpolation *f* color interpolation
Farbinvarianz *f s.* Farbkonstanz
Farbkalibrierung *f* [color] calibration
Farbkamera *f* color camera
Farbkanal *m* color (chroma) channel, chrominance channel, color track; chromatic channel *(opponent-colors theory)*
Farbkante *f* color edge
Farbkantendetektion *f* color edge detection
Farbkantendetektor *m* color edge detector
Farbkantenerkennung *f* color edge detection
Farbkantenextraktion *f* color edge extraction
Farbkarte *f* 1. color [test] chart, color rendition (control) chart, color plate (map); chromaticity chart (diagram); 2. *s.* Farbindextabelle
Farbkasten *m* [ink] fountain *(printing press)*
Farbkastenwalze *f* duct[or] roller, ductor
Farbkegel *m* color cone
Farbkeil *m* color wedge
Farbkennzeichnung *f* color labeling; color notation; color specification
Farbkinefilm *m* color motion-picture film
Farbkinefilmverarbeitung *f* color motion-picture processing
Farbkinematografie *f* color cinematography, color-motion picture photography
Farbklassifikation *f* color classification
Farbklassifikator *m* color classifier
Farbklassifizierung *f* color classification
Farbkohärenzvektor *m* color coherence vector, CCV
Farbkombination *f* color combination
Farbkompensation *f* color compensation
Farbkompensationsfilter *n* color-compensating filter, CC filter
Farbkomplement *n* color complement
Farbkomponente *f* color (chromatic) component
Farbkomponentensignal *n* color component signal
Farbkomposite *f* color composite *(analog image processing)*
Farbkomposition *f* color composition
Farbkonstanz *f* [chromatic] color constancy
Farbkontinuität *f* color continuity
Farbkontrast *m* color (chromatic) contrast
~/**fotometrischer** photometric color contrast
~/**simultaner** simultaneous [color] contrast
Farbkontrastfilter *n* color contrast filter *(optical microscopy)*
Farbkontrastregelung *f*/**automatische** automatic chrominance control, ACC *(video)*
Farbkontrasttäuschung *f* color contrast illusion

Farbkontrolle *f* color inspection
~/**automatische** *s.* Farbkontrastregelung/automatische
Farbkontrolltafel *f s.* Farbkarte
Farbkonversion *f* color conversion
Farbkonverter *m* color converter *(video processor)*
Farbkonzentration *f* dye concentration
Farbkoordinatensystem *n* color [space] coordinate system
Farbkopf *m* color head *(enlarger)*
Farbkopie *f* color print; color copy
Farbkopieren *n* color copying; color printing
Farbkopierer *m* color copier
Farbkopierfilm *m* color print film
Farbkopierfilter *n* color printing filter, CP filter
Farbkopiermaterial *n* color print[ing] material
Farbkopierpapier *n* color printing paper
Farbkopierung *f* color printing
Farbkopierverfahren *n* color printing process
Farbkorn *n* color grain
Farbkörper *m* 1. color solid (spindle); 2. [color] pigment
~/**kugelförmiger** color sphere *(colorimetry)*
farbkorrekt color-correct, color-grade
Farbkorrektion *f* 1. chromatic [aberration] correction; 2. *s.* Farbkorrektur
Farbkorrektur *f* color correction; [film] color timing, [color] timing, [color] grading
~/**globale** global color correction
~/**selektive** selective color correction
Farbkorrekturfilter *n* color correction filter, color corrector; color conversion filter; color-compensating filter, CC filter
Farbkorrekturfilterung *f* color compensating (correction) filtration
Farbkorrekturgerät *n* color corrector
Farbkorrekturkurve *f* color [correction] curve, timing curve
Farbkorrekturmaschine *f* color correcting machine
Farbkorrekturschicht *f* color-correction layer
Farbkorrekturtabelle *f* color correction table
farbkorrigieren to color-correct, to achromatize
farbkorrigiert color-corrected, achromatic *(lens)*
Farbkreis *m* color circle (cycle), color disk (wheel), hue circle (wheel), circular color palette
Farbkreisel *m* **[/Maxwellscher]** Maxwell disk *(additive color mixture)*
Farbkuppler *m* color[ed] coupler, color former (forming coupler), dye[-forming] coupler, [photographic] coupler

Farbkuppler

~/**diffusionsfester** nondiffusing (immobile) coupler
~/**eingebetteter (eingelagerter)** incorporated [color] coupler
~/**geschützter** protected coupler
~/**ölgeschützter** oil-protected coupler, fat-tail coupler
Farbkupplung f dye coupling
Farbkurve f s. Farbkorrekturkurve
Farblabor n color processing lab[oratory], [professional] color laboratory; custom color lab, color darkroom
Farblängsfehler m longitudinal (axial) chromatic aberration, chromatic variation of focus, longitudinal color
Farblängsfehlerkorrektur f longitudinal (axial) chromatic aberration correction
Farblaserdrucker m color laser printer
Farblaserkopierer m color laser copier
Farblehre f s. Farbenlehre
farblich coloristic
Farblicht n color[ed] light
farblichtbestimmen to color time
Farblichtbestimmer m [film] color timer, [laboratory] timer, color (negative) grader, colorist
Farblichtbestimmung f [film] color timing, [color] timing, [color] grading
Farblichtquelle f color[ed] light source
Farblithografie f lithographic color print
farblos colorless
Farblosigkeit f colorlessness
Farblosprägung f relief embossing
Farb-Luftaufnahme f, **Farb-Luftbild** n aerial color photograph
Farbmanagement n color management
Farbmanagementmodul n color management module, CMM
Farbmanagementsystem n color management system, CMS
Farbmanipulation f color manipulation
Farbmaske f color[ed] mask
Farbmaskierung f color masking
Farbmaß n color measure
Farbmaßstabsfehler m chromatic difference of magnification
Farbmaßzahl f/**trichromatische** tristimulus value *(colorimetry)*
Farbmaterial n color material
Farbmatrix f color matrix
Farbmatrizierung f color matrixing
Farbmerkmal n color feature (attribute)
Farbmessgerät n colorimeter, color meter
Farbmesskeil m color wedge
Farbmesslabor[atorium] n color measurement laboratory
Farbmessstreifen m color control bar, [standard offset] color bar, color guide
Farbmesstafel f s. Farbkarte 1.
Farbmessung f 1. color (colorimetric) measurement; color matching [experiment]; 2. s. Farbmetrik
~ **nach dem Gleichheitsverfahren** color matching [experiment]

Farbmessverfahren n color measurement method
Farbmetrik f colorimetry, color metrics, colorimetrics
~/**höhere** advanced colorimetry
~/**niedere** basic colorimetry
farbmetrisch colorimetric
Farbmikrofilm m color microfilm
Farbmikrofotografie f color photomicrography
Farbmikroskopie f color microscopy
Farbmischkopf m color head *(enlarger)*
Farbmischkurve f color-mixture curve *(television camera)*
Farbmischprojektor m additive color viewer *(analog image processing)*
Farbmischung f 1. color mixing (blending); 2. color mixture (blend)
~/**additive** additive color mixing (mixture), additive synthesis (composition); additive color matching *(colorimetry)*
~/**autotypische** halftone color synthesis
~/**multiplikative** s. ~/subtraktive
~/**optische** s. ~/additive
~/**substantielle** s. ~/subtraktive
~/**subtraktive** subtractive color mixing (mixture), subtractive synthesis; subtractive color matching *(colorimetry)*
Farbmischungsgesetz n color mixing law
Farbmodell n 1. color model (system); 2. s. Farbraum
~/**additives** additive [color] system, red-green-blue primary color system, RGB model
~/**subtraktives** subtractive [color] system, CMY (cyan-magenta-yellow) color space, CMY model
Farbmodulation f color modulation
Farbmodulationsfrequenz f color modulation frequency
Farbmodulator m color modulator
Farbmodus m color mode *(imaging software)*
Farbmoiré[muster] n color moiré pattern
Farbmoment n color moment
Farbmonitor m color monitor [display], color monitor display screen
Farbmuster n color pattern; color sample
Farbmusterbuch n, **Farbmustersammlung** f color atlas
Farbmusterfächer m s. Farbfächer
Farbnebeln n misting, flying ink *(printing defect)*
farbnegativ color-negative
Farbnegativ n color negative [image]
Farbnegativentwicklung f color-negative process
Farbnegativfilm m color-negative [slide] film, negative color film
Farbnegativ-Kinefilm m color-negative motion-picture film
Farbnegativmaterial n color-negative material; color-negative stock *(cinema)*

Farbnegativtechnik f,
Farbnegativverarbeitung f color-negative processing, negative color processing
Farbnomenklatur f color-naming system
Farbnormalsichtigkeit f normal color vision
Farbnormierung f color normalization
Farbnuance f color shade, hue
Farbordnungssystem n color order (specification) system
~/**Munsellsches** Munsell [color-order] system, Munsell system of color notation, Munsell system of perceptual color measurement
Farbort m spectral (spectrum) locus, color locus, locus of spectral colors *(colorimetrics)*
Farbortsfehler m longitudinal (axial) chromatic aberration, chromatic variation of focus, longitudinal color
Farbpalette f 1. [color] palette; paint palette; 2. color gamut (range), gamut [of colors] *(e.g. of a printer)*; color box *(graphics program)*; 3. s. Farbtabelle
Farbpapier n color [print] paper, color photographic paper
Farbpapierbild n color print
Farbpasser m butt register (fit), kiss register *(color printing)*
Farbpatrone f color cartridge
Farbperspektive f color perspective
Farbphysik f color physics, physics of color
Farbpigment n color pigment (solid); paint pigment
Farbpixel n color[ed] pixel
Farbplotter m color plotter
~/**elektrostatischer** color electrostatic plotter
Farbpositiv n color positive, positive color image
Farbpositivfilm m color positive film, positive color film; color print [still] film
Farbpositivpapier n color-positive material, color print material
Farbpositivtechnik f color-positive processing
Farbprobe f color sample
Farbprofil n color profile
Farbprojektionsgerät n, **Farbprojektor** m color projector (projection device)
Farbproof m color proof; full-color prepress proof
~/**digitaler** direct digital color proof, DDCP
~/**immaterieller** soft [digital] proof
~/**materieller** hard proof
Farbproofherstellung f color proofing
Farbproofsystem n color proofing system *(photochemical reproduction)*
Farbprüfdruck m test color reproduction *(s.a. Farbproof)*
Farbprüfleuchte f color evaluation lamp
Farbpunkt m color point, color[ed] dot
Farbqualität f color quality

Farbquantisierung f color quantization
Farbquerfehler m transverse chromatic aberration, lateral color (chromatic aberration), lateral chromatic error, chromatic aberration (difference, variation) of magnification
Farbradarbild n color radar image
Farbradierer m color replacer *(imaging software tool)*
Farbradiografie f color radiography
Farbrand m color boundary; [color] fringe *(convergence error)*
Farbraster m(n) color raster; color (dyed) screen
Farbrasterverfahren n screen color process
Farbraum m color space [space] *(s.a. Farbmodell)*
~/**diskreter** discrete color space
~/**dreidimensionaler** three-dimensional color space
~/**empfindungsgemäßer** perceptual color space
~/**geräteabhängiger** [display-]device-dependent color space
~/**geräteunabhängiger** [display-]device-independent color space
~/**Kartes[ian]ischer** Cartesian color space
~/**linearer** linear [color] space
~/**logarithmischer** logarithmic color space
~/**nichtlinearer** nonlinear color space
~/**perzeptueller** s. ~/empfindungsgemäßer
~/**RGB-verwandter** RGB-related color space
~/**uniformer** uniform color space
~/**zylindrischer** cylindrical color space
Farbraumanpassung f gamut mapping
Farbraumkonverter m color space converter, CSC
Farbraumtransformation f color space conversion (transformation)
Farbraumumfang m color gamut (range), gamut [of colors] *(e.g. of a printer)*
Farbraumumwandlung f s. Farbraumkonvertierung
Farbrauschen n color[ed] noise, chroma noise, chrominance signal-to[-random]-noise ratio
Farbreduktion f color reduction
Farbreflexion f color reflection
Farbregelung f color control
~/**automatische** automatic color control, ACC *(video)*
Farbregler m hue (tint) control, chroma control *(television)*
Farbreihenfolge f color (laydown) sequence, rotation *(printing)*
Farbreinheit f 1. color (chromatic) purity; 2. s. Farbsättigung
Farbreinheitseinstellung f color-purity adjustment *(television)*
Farbreiz m color[ed] stimulus, chromatic stimulus

~/**metamerer** metameric [color] stimulus, metamer
Farbreizfunktion f color stimulus function
Farbreproduktion f color reproduction (s.a. Farbwiedergabe)
Farbrestauration f color restoration
Farbrestfehler m residual chromatic aberration; secondary spectrum (optics)
Farbretusche f color retouching
Farbrezeptor m color receptor
farbrichtig color-correct, color-grade
Farbrichtigkeit f color accuracy (precision), hue accuracy (s.a. Farbtreue)
Farbringbildung f color ringing
Farb-Röhrenmonitor m color CRT monitor
Farbrolle f [flood] fill tool (computer graphics)
Farbrotation f color cycling (graphics program)
Farbrupfen n [surface] picking (printing defect)
farbsatt color-saturated, vivid, high in chroma
Farbsättigung f [color] saturation, [excitation] purity, chroma, intensity (colorimetry)
Farbsättigungsregler m chroma gain
Farbsatz m proofing scale, progressive proof, progressives, progs
Farbsatzprüfgerät n color proof
Farbsatzprüfung f color proofing
Farbsaum m [color] fringe (convergence error)
Farbsaumbildung f color fringing (edging)
Farbscankopf m color scan head
Farbscannen n color scanning
Farbscanner m [drum] color scanner
Farbschablonentechnik f s. Farbstanze
Farbschattierung f color shading
Farbschicht f 1. color layer; 2. paint layer; ink film (printing)
Farbschleier m dichroic fog
Farbschlieren fpl cross-color effect
Farb-Schmalfilm m amateur color motion picture film
Farb-Schnellkopierer m high-speed color copier
Farbschnittweitenfehler m s. Farblängsfehler
Farbschwankung f color fluctuation, color (chromatic) variation, variation of color
Farbschwelle f color threshold
Farbsechseck n hexcone HSV color model, color hexagon
Farbsegmentierung f color segmentation
Farbsehen n s. Farbensehen
Farbsehschwäche f color asthenopia
Farbsehstörung f s. Farbsinnstörung
Farbsehsystem n color vision system (of the eye)
Farbsehtest m color vision test
Farbselektion f color selection
Farbsendung f color [TV] broadcast, color program, colorcast

Farbsensibilisator m color (dye) sensitizer
farbsensibilisieren to color-sensitize
farbsensibilisiert color-sensitized, dye-sensitized
Farbsensibilisierung f coor sensitization
Farbsensitometrie f color sensitometry
Farbsensor m color sensor
Farbseparation f, **Farbseparierung** f color separation
Farbsichtgerät n s. Farbmonitor
Farbsignal n color signal; chrominance (chroma) signal, color information signal, C [signal] (video)
Farbsignalbandbreite f color bandwidth
Farbsignalverarbeitung f color signal processing
Farbsignalverstärkung f chroma gain
Farbsilberbleichen n, **Farbsilberbleichverfahren** n [silver-]dye-bleach process, silver dye bleach, dye bleach (destruction)
Farbsinn m color sense
Farbsinneseindruck m color impression
Farbsinnstörung f defective color vision, deficient (anomalous) color vision, color vision defect (deficiency)
~/**angeborene** congenital color vision defect
~/**erworbene** acquired color vision defect
Farbskala f 1. color (hue) scale; 2. s. Farbsatz
~/**kollimierte** collimated color scale
Farbsofortbild n instant color print
Farbsofortbildfilm m instant color film, color instant-picture film
~/**subtraktiver** subtractive instant color film
Farbsofortbildfotografie f instant color photography
Farbspeicher m color store
Farbspektrometer n color spectrometer
Farbspektrum n [color] spectrum
Farbspezifikation f color specification (description), specification of color
farbspezifisch color-specific
farbstabil colorfast
Farbstabilität f color stability (consistency)
Farbstanze f, **Farbstanztrick** m chroma (color) key, chroma keying, electronic matting
Farbsteuersystem n color management system, CMS
Farbsteuerung f color control
Farbstich m color cast (bias), cast
Farbstimmung f color (chromatic) adaptation (of the eye)
Farbstoff m dye[stuff]; colorant
~/**fotochromer** photochromic dye
~/**lichtabsorbierender** [light-]absorbing dye
~/**organischer** organic dye
~/**pigmentierter** pigmented dye
~/**sublimierbarer** sublimable dye
~/**subtraktiver** subtractive dye

Farbstoffabbau *m* dye destruction
farbstoffabbauend chromolytic
Farbstoffabbauverfahren *n* dye destruction process *(color photography)*
Farbstoffabsaugverfahren *n* s. Farbstoffübertragungsverfahren
farbstoffaufbauend chromogenic
Farbstoffaufbaufilm *m* chromogenic film, substantive-coupler film
Farbstoffausbleichung *f* 1. dye fading; 2. *s.* Farbstoffbleichung
Farbstoffbad *n* dye bath
Farbstoffbild *n* dye image
Farbstoffbildung *f* dye formation (generation)
Farbstoffbleichung *f* dye bleach[ing], dye bleach process
Farbstoffdesensibilisierung *f* dye desensitization
Farbstoffdichte *f* dye density
Farbstoffdiffusion *f* dye diffusion
Farbstoffdiffusionsverfahren *n* dye diffusion method (transfer process) *(color photography)*
Farbstoffentwickler *m* dye[-forming] developer
Farbstofffreisetzung *f* dye release
Farbstoffkontrast *m* dye contrast
Farbstoffkügelchen *n* dye globule
Farbstoffkuppler *m* s. Farbkuppler
Farbstofflaser *m* dye laser
~/**abstimmbarer** tunable dye laser
~/**blitzlampengepumpter** flashlamp-pumped dye laser
~/**gepulster** pulsed dye laser
Farbstofflösung *f* dye solution
Farbstoffmaske *f* dye mask
Farbstoffmaskierung *f* dye masking
Farbstoffmolekül *n* dye molecule
Farbstoffprisma *n* Kundt prism
Farbstoffschicht *f* dye layer
Farbstoffstabilität *f* dye stability
Farbstoffteilbild *n* color record, dye image
Farbstoffübertragung *f* dye transfer
Farbstoffübertragungsverfahren *n* dye transfer [printing] process, dye imbibition process
Farbstoffwolke *f* dye cloud
Farbstrahldruck *m* [ink-]jet printing
Farbstreuung *f* s. Farbzerlegung
Farbstufe *f* color step
Farbsublimationsdruck *m* [thermal] dye sublimation printing, dye diffusion thermal transfer printing
Farbsublimationsdrucker *m* [thermal] dye sublimation printer, thermal [sublimation] dye transfer printer, dye diffusion printer
Farbsucher *m* color viewfinder
Farbsynchronimpuls *m*, **Farbsynchron[isier]signal** *n* [color synchronizing] burst, [color] burst signal, color (chroma) burst
Farbsynthese *f* color synthesis

Farbsystem *n s.* 1. Farbordnungssystem; 2. Farbmodell
Farbtabelle *f* color table; color lookup table, CLUT, color map
Farbtafel *f* 1. color [test] chart, color rendition (control) chart, color plate (map); chromaticity chart (diagram); 2. *s.* Farbtabelle
Farbtafelteil *m* color insert *(as in books)*
Farbtechnik *f* color technology
Farbtechniker *m* color timer
Farbteil *m* color insert *(as in books)*
Farbteiler *m* color splitter
Farbtemperatur *f* color temperature
~/**ähnlichste (korrelierte)** approximate (correlated) color temperature, equivalent color temperature
Farbtemperaturmesser *m*, **Farbtemperaturmeßgerät** *n* color-temperature meter (measuring device)
Farbtemperaturmessung *f* color temperature measurement
Farbtemperaturmeßwert *m* color temperature value (metering reading)
Farbtemperaturskala *f* color temperature scale
Farbtemperaturverschiebung *f* color [temperature] shift
Farbtest *m* color test (check)
Farbtestbild *n* [/elektronisches] color test pattern; color television test card
Farbtesttafel *f* color test chart; pseudoisochromatic [test] plate
Farbtextur *f* color texture
Farbtheorie *f* color theory, theory of color
Farbthermogramm *n* color thermogram (thermograph)
Farb-Thermoprinter *m*, **Farbthermosublimationsdrucker** *m* s. Farbsublimationsdrucker
Farbtiefe *f* color depth (intensity) *(s.a. Bittiefe)*
Farbtinte *f* color[ed] ink, dye-based ink
Farbtintendrucker *m* s. Farbtintenstrahldrucker
Farbtintenpatrone *f* color ink cartridge
Farbtintenstrahldrucker *m* color ink-jet printer
Farbtoleranz *f* color tolerance
Farbton *m* [color] hue, dye hue, [color] tone, [color] shade, tint
Farbtonabstufung *f* scale of hues, hue scale
Farbtonbild *n* hue image
Farbtondifferenz *f* hue difference
Farbtoner *m* color[ed] toner
Farbtonerbild *n* color[ed] toner image
Farbtonkonstanz *f* hue constancy
Farbtonkreis *m* hue circle
farbtonrichtig orthochromatic, isochromatic
Farbton-Sättigungs-Helligkeits-Farbsystem *n* hue-saturation-intensity

Farbtonunterschied

color system, HSI system (space), HSV (hue-saturation-value) space
Farbtonunterschied *m* hue difference
Farbtonwinkel *m* hue angle
Farbträger *m* chrominance carrier
Farbträgerburst *m* color (chroma) burst, [color] burst signal, [color synchronizing] burst *(s.a. under Burst)*
Farbträgerfrequenz *f* chrominance carrier frequency, [color] subcarrier frequency
Farbträgerperiode *f* color subcarrier period
Farbtransformation *f* color transform[ation]
Farbtransformationsmatrix *f* color transformation matrix
Farbtrennung *f* color separation
Farbtreue *f* color[imetric] fidelity *(s.a. Farbgenauigkeit)*; chrominance fidelity *(video)*
Farbtrio *n s.* Farbtripel
Farbtripel *n* RGB triple[t], [color] triad, three-colored phosphor dot *(color picture tube)*
Farbtripel-Leuchtschicht *f* phosphor screen *(cathode-ray tube)*
Farbtüchtigkeit *f* color capability
Farbübereinstimmung *f* color conformance (conformity)
Farbübergang *m* color gradation
Farbüberlagerung *f s.* Farbübersprechen
Farbüberlappung *f* trapping *(multicolor printing)*
Farbübersprechen *n*, **Farbüberstrahlung** *f* cross-color [artifact], color crossover
Farbübertragung *f* 1. color transmission *(video)*; 2. ink transfer *(printing)*
Farbumfang *m* color gamut (range), gamut [of colors] *(e.g. of a printer)*
Farbumkehrentwicklung *f* reversal color development
Farbumkehrfilm *m* color reversal (transparency) film, reversal (transparency-type) color film, color slide film
~/**chromogener** substantive color film
Farbumkehr-Fotopapier *n s.* Farbumkehrpapier
Farbumkehr-Kinefilm *m* color reversal motion picture film
Farbumkehrpapier *n* reversal color paper, color reversal printing paper
Farbumkehrprozess *m*, **Farbumkehrtechnik** *f* color reversal process, reversal color process
Farbumstimmung *f* chromatic (color) adaptation *(of the eye)*
Farbumwandlung *f* color reversal
Farbunausgeglichenheit *f* color imbalance (nonuniformity)
farbunempfindlich color-insensitive
Färbung *f* coloration, coloring, tinge *(s.a. Farbton)*
farbungleich heterochromatic
Farbuniformität *f* color uniformity

Farbunreinheit *f* color impurity
Farb-Unterabtastung *f* color subsampling
Farbunterdrückung *f* color [spill] suppression
Farbunterscheidung *f* color (chromatic) discrimination
Farbunterscheidungsvermögen *n* chromatic selectivity
Farbunterschied *m* color difference (distance)
Farbunterschiedsschwelle *f* **nach MacAdam** MacAdam ellipse *(colorimetry)*
Farbunterschiedssignal *n s.* Farbdifferenzsignal
Farburteil *n* color judg[e]ment
Farbvalenz *f* tristimulus value
~/**gleichabständige** equidistant tristimulus value
~/**spektrale** spectral color stimulus
Farbvalenzberechnung *f* tristimulus value calculation
Farbvalenzmetrik *f* basic colorimetry
Farbvariation *f* color (chromatic) variation, color fluctuation, variation of color
Farbvektor *m* color vector
Farbvektorraum *m* color vector space
Farbveränderung *f* color change
Farbverarbeitung *f* color processing
Farbverfahren *n* color process
~ **mit additiver Farbmischung** additive color process
~/**subtraktives** subtractive [color] process
Farbverfälschung *f* color deviation
Farbvergleich *m* color comparison
Farbvergleichssignal *n s.* Farbsynchronimpuls
Farbvergrößerer *m* color enlarger
Farbvergrößern *n* color enlarging
Farbvergrößerung *f* color enlarging
Farbvergrößerungsdifferenz *f s.* Farbquerfehler
Farbvergrößerungsfehler *m* 1. color magnification error *(optics)*; 2. *s.* Farbquerfehler
Farbvergrößerungsgerät *n* color enlarger
Farbvergrößerungspapier *n* color enlarging paper
Farbvergrößerungssystem *n* color enlarging system
Farbverhältnis *n* chromaticity
Farbverkoppelungszeichen *n* color [lock] flag *(PAL time code)*
Farbverschiebung *f* color shift
Farbverteilung *f* color distribution
Farbverunreinigung *f* color contamination
Farbverwaltungssystem *n s.* Farbmanagementsystem
Farbverzerrung *f* color distortion
Farbverzögerung *f* chroma delay *(video recorder)*
Farbvideo *n* color video
Farbvideoanalysator *m* color video analyzer

Farbvideodrucker m video color printer
Farbvideokamera f color video camera
Farbvideokassettenabspielgerät n color videocassette player
Farbvideokassettenrecorder m color VCR (video cassette recorder)
Farbvideokompression f color video compression
Farbvideomonitor m color video monitor (screen)
Farbvideoprojektion f color video projection
Farbvideoprojektor m color video projector
Farbvideorecorder m color video recorder
Farbvideosequenz f color video sequence
Farbvideosignal n color video signal, RGB [video] signal
~/**kombiniertes** composite color [video] signal, composite [video] signal, composite TV signal
Farbvideoübertragung f color video transmission
Farbvielfalt f colorfulness
Farbvorlage f color copy *(reprography)*
Farbwachspapier n colored wax paper
Farbwahl f color choice (selection)
Farbwahrnehmung f color (chromatic) perception, perception of color[s]
Farbwalze f ink[ing] roller *(s.a. Farbkastenwalze)*
Farbwandlung f color change
Farbwanne f ink pan *(printing press)*
Farb-Wasser-Balance f, **Farb-Wasser-Gleichgewicht** n ink-water balance *(printing)*
Farbwechsel m color change
Farbwerk n inking system (mechanism), ink flooding mechanism *(printing press)*
Farbwert m 1. color value; tonal value; 2. tristimulus value *(colorimetry)*
Farbwertrekonstruktion f chroma mapping
Farbwertsignal n RGB signal
Farbwiedergabe f color reproduction, color rendition (rendering)
~/**äquivalente** equivalent color reproduction
~/**exakte** exact (colorimetric) color reproduction
~/**farbbildbezogene** color imagerelated color reproduction *(printing)*
~/**korrekte** s. ~/exakte
Farbwiedergabebereich m color reproduction range; reproducible color gamut
Farbwiedergabefehler m artifact of color reproduction
Farbwiedergabegenauigkeit f color rendition accuracy, accuracy of color rendering, fidelity of color reproduction
Farbwiedergabeindex m color rendering index, CRI, color quality index
Farbwiedergabequalität f color reproduction quality
Farbwiedergabetechnik f color reproduction technology
Farbwiedergabevermögen n color reproducibility, color reproduction ability, color rendering property
Farbwirkung f color effect
Farbwissenschaft f color science
Farbwissenschaftler m color scientist
Farbwürfel m color cube, RGB [color] cube
Farbxerografie f color xerography (electrophotography)
farbxerografisch color electrophotographic
Farbzerlegung f, **Farbzerstreuung** f [chromatic] dispersion, color [light] dispersion
Farbzuordnung f color assignment
~/**direkte** direct color
Farbzuordnungstabelle f s. Farbtabelle
Farbzusammensetzung f color (chromatic) composition *(e.g. of light)*
Farbzusammenstellung f color combination
Farbzwischenpositiv n color master positive [print]
Fase f bevel
Faser f/**optische** optical fiber; [single] fiber-optic strand
~/**selbstfokussierende [optische]** self-focusing fiber
~/**ummantelte** cladded fiber
Faserbündel n fiber[-optic] bundle
~/**kohärentes** coherent[-fiber] bundle
Faserendoskop n fiber-optic endoscope, fiberscope [device], flexible imagescope
Faserinterferometer m fiber interferometer
Faserkabel n fiber cable
Faserkern m fiber core
Faserkoppler m fiber coupler
Faserkopplung f fiber-optic coupling
Faserlaser m fiber laser
Faseroptik f 1. fiber optics; 2. fiber optic *(component)*
Faseroptikinstrument n fiberscope
Faseroptikkollimator m fiber optic collimator
Faseroptikplatte f fiber-optic plate
faseroptisch fiber-optic[al]
Faserplatte f s. Faseroptikplatte
Faserrichtung f grain [direction] *(s.a. Laufrichtung)*
Faserspektrograf m fiber spectrograph
Fassungsanschluss m screw-type [lens] mount, threaded mount, screw thread
FAT s. Filmabtaster
Fata Morgana f mirage, fata morgana *(optical illusion)*
Fax n fax, facsimile copy, [tele]facsimile, telecopy, phototelegraphy
Faxbild n s. Faxgrafik
Faxcodierung f facsimile [en]coding, fax coding; facsimile compression

Faxdaten *pl* facsimile data
Faxempfang *m* fax reception
faxen to fax
Faxgerät *n* facsimile transceiver (machine), fax machine, fax [terminal]
Faxgrafik *f* facsimile chart, fax chart (map)
Faxkarte *f* fax board (card)
Faxmitteilung *f* facsimile message
Faxmodem *n* [PC] fax modem
Faxpollen *n* polling *(fax transmission)*
Fax-Scan-Kopier-Laserdrucker *m* multifunction printer, all-in-one device
Fax-Software *f* fax (facsimile) software
Faxübertragung *f* facsimile (fax) transmission; fax telephony
Faxübertragungsformat *n* facsimile transmission format
FAZ *s.* Filmaufzeichnung 1.
FBAS-Signal *n* composite color [video] signal, composite [video] signal, composite TV signal
f-Blende *f* [f-]stop, [diaphragm] f-number, aperture stop (setting)
Fechner-Benhamsche Farben *fpl* Fechner's (subjective) colors
Federkonstante *f* spring constant
Federwerk *n* spring mechanism
Feedback *n* feedback
Fehlabsorption *f* unwanted (subsidiary) absorption *(color photography)*
Fehlabtastung *f* mistracking
Fehlausrichtung *f* misalignment; misregistration
Fehlbelichtung *f* misexposure, erroneous (erratic) exposure
Fehlecho *n* spurious echo *(radar, sonography)*
Fehleinstellung *f* misadjustment *(e.g. of a camera lens)*
Fehler *m* 1. error; failure; fault; defect; flaw; imperfection; bug; 2. *s.* ~/optischer
~/**chromatischer** chromatic [lens] aberration, chromatic error (defect), color aberration (distortion)
~/**geometrischer** geometrical aberration
~/**mittlerer absoluter** mean absolute difference, MAD *(distortion measure)*
~/**mittlerer quadratischer** mean square[d] error, MSE, mean-square deviation, root-mean-square error, rms error *(assessment parameter)*
~/**optischer** optical artifact (aberration), optical error
~/**sphärischer** spherical error, power *(of a lens)*
~/**systematischer** systematic (constant) error
~/**unkorrigierbarer** uncorrectable error
Fehlerbild *n* error image *(image compression)*
Fehlerburst *m* error burst
Fehlerdiffusion *f* error diffusion [rendering]; [dot] diffusion dithering *(halftoning technique)*

Fehlererkennung *f* error detection (recognition); fault detection; flaw detection
Fehlererkennungscode *m* error-detecting code, EDC
Fehlerfortpflanzung *f* error propagation
Fehlerfortpflanzungsgesetz *n* [/**Gaußsches**] error propagation theorem (law)
Fehlerfunktion *f* [/**Gaußsche**] [Gaussian] error function, defect (merit) function
Fehlerfunktionskurve *f* error function curve
Fehlergradient *m* error gradient
Fehlergrenze *f* error limit
Fehlerkennung *f* 1. misrecognition; 2. error indicator *(data processing)*
Fehlerkorrektur *f* 1. error correction; 2. aberration[al] correction *(optics)*
Fehlerkorrekturalgorithmus *m* error-correcting algorithm
Fehlerkorrekturcode *m* error correction (protection) code, error-correcting code, ECC
~/**äußerer** outer error correction code, outer ECC
~/**binärer** binary error-correcting code
~/**innerer** inner error correction code, inner ECC
Fehlerkorrekturcodierung *f* error correction coding, ECC
Fehlerkorrekturmodus *m* error correction mode, ECM *(facsimile transmission)*
Fehlermaß *n* error measure (metric)
Fehlermatrix *f* error matrix
Fehlerquadrat *n*/**minimales** least-squares error
~/**mittleres** *s.* Fehler/mittlerer quadratischer
Fehlerquadratminimierung *f* least-mean-square approximation
Fehlerrate *f* error rate
Fehlerratenanzeige *f* error rate display *(digital videotape recorder)*
Fehlerrückführung *f* [error] backpropagation, BP *(learning algorithm)*
Fehlerrückführungsnetz *n* backpropagation network
Fehlerrückmeldung *f*, **Fehlerrückverfolgung** *f*, **Fehlerrückvermittlung** *f s.* Fehlerrückführung
Fehlerschutz *m* error protection; error correction *(video encoding)*
~/**äußerer** outer error correction
~/**innerer** inner error correction
~/**ungleicher** unequal error protection
Fehlerschutzcode *m s.* Fehlerkorrekturcode
Fehlersegmentierung *f* error segmentation
Fehlersequenz *f* error sequence
Fehlersignal *n* error signal
Fehlertheorie *f*/**Seidelsche** aberration theory *(optics)*

Fehlertoleranz f error resilience (robustness)
Fehlerverdeckung f error concealment
Fehlervorwärtskorrektur f forward error correction, FEC
Fehlerwahrscheinlichkeit f probability of error
Fehlfarbenfotografie f near-infrared photography
Fehlfokussierung f misfocus
Fehlidentifikation f misidentification
Fehlinterpretation f misinterpretation
Fehlklassifikation f misclassification
fehlklassifizieren to misclassify
Fehlklassifizierung f misclassification
Fehlpassung f, **Fehlregistration** f misregister (prepress); misregistration; misfit
fehlsichtig ametropic
Fehlsichtigkeit f ametropia, disorder of vision
feinabstimmen to fine-tune
Feinabstimmung f/**automatische** automatic fine-tuning, AFT
Feinauflösung f fine resolution
Feinbereichsbeugung f selected-area diffraction, SAD (electron microscopy)
Feindruckpapier n fine paper
Feinfilter n fine filter
Feinfokussierung f 1. fine focusing; 2. fine-focusing mechanism (device)
Feinheit f fineness
Feinkitt m lens cement
Feinkorn n fine grain
Feinkornemulsion f fine-grain emulsion
Feinkornentwickler m fine-grain developer, high-definition developer
Feinkornentwicklung f fine-grain development
Feinkornfarbfilm m fine-grain color film
Feinkornfilm m fine-grained film, fine-grain [photographic] film
feinkörnig fine-grain[ed] (film)
Feinkörnigkeit f fineness of grain
Feinkornkopie f fine-grain copy (print) (motion-picture film)
Feinkorn-Positivfilm m fine-grain print film
Feinliniensiebdruck m fine-line screen printing
Feinoptik f precision optics
Feinpapier n fine (graphic) paper, cultural paper; wood-free paper, free sheet
Feinraster m(n) fine screen
Feinschnitt m fine (final) cut (cinema)
Feinsprüher m airbrush (imaging tool)
Feinstellschraube f s. Feintrieb
Feinstkornentwickler m superfine-grain developer, ultrafine-grain developer
Feinstrahl m fine beam (esp. of electrons)
Feinstrich m fine line
Feinstruktur f fine structure
Feinststrich m very fine line, hairline

Feintrieb m fine-focus control, fine-focus (adjustment) knob; microscope fine-adjustment knob
Feld n 1. field (e.g. as a data element); array (e.g. of pixels); 2. [film] frame, motion-picture frame; 3. cell (table, screen menu); 4. s. Datenfeld 2.
~/**elektromagnetisches** electromagnetic field
~/**elektrostatisches** electrostatic field
~/**programmierbares logisches** programmable logical array (device), PLA, PLD
~/**rezeptives** receptive field (of the retina)
~/**skalares** scalar field
~/**stationäres** s. ~/homogenes
Feldamplitude f field amplitude
Feldblende f field stop (diaphragm); film gate
Feldeffekt-Flüssigkristallanzeige f twisted nematic liquid crystal display, TN-LCD
Feldeffekttransistor m field effect transistor, FET (light detector)
~/**ionensensitiver** ion-sensitive field effect transistor
Feldelektronenmikroskop n field emission microscope
Feldemission f field emission (of electrons)
Feldemissionsanzeige f, **Feldemissionsdisplay** n field emission display [panel], FED
Feldemissions[elektronen]mikroskop n field emission microscope
Feldemissionsstrom m field emission current
Feldemitter m field emitter
Feldgradient m field gradient (electromagnetic imaging)
Feldgröße f field size (optics); field coverage (radiography)
Feldheterogenität f field heterogeneity
Feldhomogenität f field homogeneity
Feldinhomogenität f [magnetic] field inhomogeneity
Feldionenmikroskop n field ion microscope
Feldionenmikroskopie f field ion microscopy
Feldkonverter m/**optischer** optical field converter
Feldkrümmung f curvature of field, field curvature [aberration], Petzval [field] curvature
Feldlinse f field lens
Feldnetz n wall screen (cathode-ray tube)
Feldplatte f field plate (photodiode)
Feldrechner m array processor
Feldspektrograf m field spectrograph
Feldspule f field coil
Feldstärke f [/**magnetische**] magnetic field strength
Feldstativ n field tripod
Feldstecher m field glass[es]
Feldvektor m [electric-]field vector

Feldwinkel

Feldwinkel *m* field angle, angle of field (view)
~/**halber** semifield (half-field) angle *(lens)*
Fell-Windschutz *m* furry windscreen *(microphone)*
FEM *s.* Finite-Elemente-Methode
Femtosekundenlaser *m* femtosecond laser
Fenster *n* window *(e.g. in digital image processing)*
~/**aktives** active window *(graphical user interface)*
~/**atmosphärisches** atmospheric [spectral] window
~/**Gaußsches** Gaussian window
~/**optisches** optical window
~/**raumzeitliches** spatiotemporal window
~/**zeitliches** temporal window
Fensterfalz *m* gatefold
Fenster-Fourier-Transformation *f* window[ed] Fourier transform
Fensterfunktion *f* window[ing] function *(signal processing)*
Fensterglas *n* window glass
Fensterkoeffizient *m* window coefficient
Fensterlicht *n* window light
Fenstertechnik *f*, **Fensterung** *f* window-level transformation, window technique, windowing
Fensterverwaltung *f* window management
Fermi-Energie *f*, **Fermi-Niveau** *n* Fermi [energy] level *(semiconductor)*
Fernabfrage *f* relay broadcasting *(facsimile)*
Fernaufnahme *f* long (full-length) shot, distant (distance) shot
Fernauslösekabel *n* [remote] release cable
Fernauslöser *m* remote release, remote[-control] trigger
~/**kabelloser** wireless remote release
~/**pneumatischer** pneumatic bulb release
Fernauslöserkabel *n* remote cord
Fernauslösung *f* remote triggering
Fernbedienung *f* 1. remote control (operation); 2. remote control unit (device), remote control[ler], remote, handset, clicker
~/**sprachgesteuerte** speaker-driven handset
Fernbedienungskabel *n* remote control cable
Fernbild *n* telephoto
Fernbildlinse *f s.* Fernobjektiv
Fernchirurgie *f* telesurgery, remote surgery
Ferndrucker *m* teleprinter
Ferndunst *m* atmospheric haze
Fernerkennung *f* remote sensing [technology]
Fernerkundung *f* remote sensing [technology]
~/**multispektrale** multispectral remote sensing
~/**passive** passive remote sensing
Fernerkundungsbild *n* remote sensing image, remotely sensed image

Fernerkundungsdaten *pl* remote sensing data, remotely sensed data
Fernerkundungskamera *f* remote sensing camera
Fernerkundungs-Multispektralfotografie *f* remote-sensing multispectral photography
Fernerkundungssatellit *m* remote sensing satellite; earth-imaging satellite
Fernerkundungssystem *n* remote sensing system
Fernfeld *n* far-field *(ultrasound transducer, laser)*
Fernfotografie *f* long-distance aerial photography; long-distance [infrared] photography
Fernglas *n* binocular; field glass[es]
Fernkopie *f* fax, [tele]facsimile, telecopy, phototelegraphy
fernkopieren to fax
Fernkopierer *m* facsimile transceiver (machine), fax machine, fax [terminal]
Fernkopierer-Flachbettgerät *n* facsimile flatbed equipment
fernladen to download
Fernmeldesatellit *m* communication [technology] satellite, communications satellite
~/**ziviler** domestic communication satellite, DOMSAT
Fernmessung *f* 1. far-distance measurement; 2. telemetry
Fernnetz *n* wide area network, WAN
Fernobjektiv *n* telephoto[graphic] lens, tele-lens, telephoto, teleobjective, long tom
Fernproof *m* remote proof *(digital printing)*
Fernpunkt *m* far point *(visual acuity)*
Fernrohr *n* telescope *(s.a.* Teleskop*)*
~/**astronomisches** astronomical (Keplerian) telescope, astrotelescope
~/**binokulares** [pair of] binoculars
~/**Galileisches** Galilean (Dutch) telescope
~/**geodätisches** geodetic[al] telescope, geodesic telescope
~/**Holländisches** Dutch (Galilean) telescope
~/**Keplersches** Keplerian (astronomical) telescope
~/**pankratisches** pancratic telescope
~/**technisches** industrial telescope
~/**terrestrisches** terrestrial (erecting) telescope, ground-based telescope
~/**umgekehrtes Galileisches** reversed Galilean telescope
Fernrohrlupe *f* telescopic magnifier
Fernrohrobjektiv *n* telescope objective
~/**Gaußsches** Gauss lens
Fernrohrokular *n* telescopic (telescope) eyepiece
Fernrohrspiegel *m* telescope mirror
Fernrohrsucher *m* direct-vision optical viewfinder

Fernsehen

Fernrohrtubus *m* 1. telescope tube; 2. *s.* Teleskoptubus
Fernrohrvergrößerung *f* telescopic magnification
Fernsatz *m* teletypesetting, remote control composing
Fernschreibband *n* ticker tape
Fernschreiber *m*, **Fernschreibgerät** *n* teletypewriter, ticker; teleprinter
Fernschreibnetz *n* telex system (network)
Fernseh-... *s.a.* TV-...
Fernsehabtaster *m* television scanner
Fernsehabtastung *f* television scanning
Fernsehanstalt *f* television operation (broadcaster), telecaster
Fernsehantenne *f* television (TV set) antenna, TV aerial
Fernsehapparat *m s.* Fernsehgerät
Fernseharchiv *n* television archive[s]
Fernseharchivierung *f* television archiving
Fernsehauflösung *f* television resolution
Fernsehaufnahme *f* television recording
Fernsehaufnahmeröhre *f* television camera tube, TV pickup tube
~/**speichernde** [television] storage tube
Fernsehaufnahmestudio *n* television studio
Fernsehaufnahmewagen *m* television [camera] truck
Fernsehaufzeichnung *f* 1. television recording; 2. television record
Fernsehausrüstung *f* television equipment
Fernsehausstrahlung *f* television transmission; television broadcast[ing]
~/**digitale** digital video broadcasting, DVB
~/**terrestrische** terrestrial television broadcasting
Fernsehband *n* television band
Fernsehbegleitton *m* television (TV) sound
Fernsehbeitrag *m* television program (broadcast), telecast
Fernsehberichterstattung *f* television gathering; electronic news gathering, ENG
Fernsehbetrieb *m* television operation
Fernsehbild *n* television (TV set) image, [broadcast] television picture, TV [screen] image; television frame, frame [picture]
~/**überlagertes** ghost image (effect)
Fernsehbildauflösung *f* television image resolution
Fernsehbildaufnahmeröhre *f s.* Fernsehaufnahmeröhre
Fernsehbildaufzeichnung *f* television picture recording *(s.a.* Fernsehaufzeichnung*)*
Fernsehbildfolge *f* TV image sequence
Fernsehbildformat *n* TV screen format
Fernsehbildkanal *m* video channel
Fernsehbildkontrast *m* television image contrast
Fernsehbildmustergenerator *m* television test pattern generator

Fernsehbildprojektion *f* TV picture projection
Fernsehbildprojektor *m* telecine projector
Fernsehbildqualität *f* television image quality, TV picture quality
Fernsehbildröhre *f* television image (picture) tube
Fernsehbildschärfe *f* TV sharpness, definition
Fernsehbildschirm *m* telescreen, television (TV) screen, television display
Fernsehbildschirmformat *n* TV screen format
Fernseh-Bildseitenverhältnis *n* television aspect ratio
Fernsehbildsender *m* video transmitter *(television)*
Fernsehbildsequenz *f*, **Fernsehbildserie** *f* TV image sequence
Fernsehbildsignal *n* television-picture signal
Fernseh-Bildspeicherröhre *f* television camera tube
Fernsehbildverarbeitung *f* television image processing
Fernsehbildverbesserung *f* TV-picture enhancement
Fernsehbildwiedergabe *f* television picture reproduction
Fernsehbildzeile *f* television (TV) line, television scan[ning] line
Fernsehbreitbildstandard *m* wide-screen television standard
Fernsehcutter *m* television editor
Fernsehdekoration *f* television set
Fernsehdienst *m* television service
Fernsehdirektsendung *f* television live broadcast, live telecast (TV broadcast)
Fernsehdokumentation *f* television documentary
Fernseheinzelbild *n* [television] frame, frame picture
Fernsehempfang *m* television reception
Fernsehempfänger *m s.* Fernsehgerät
fernsehen to teleview, to watch television (TV)
Fernsehen *n* 1. television, TV, video; 2. [television] viewing
~/**analoges** analog television
~/**betriebliches** business television, BTV, business video
~/**digitales** digital television (video); digital television broadcasting, DTVB, digital video broadcasting, DVB
~/**digitales terrestrisches** digital terrestrial television, terrestrial digital video broadcasting, DVB-T
~/**dreidimensionales** *s.* ~/räumliches
~/**elektronisches** electronic television
~/**erdgebundenes** terrestrial television
~/**flimmerfreies** 100 Hz TV
~/**frei empfangbares** free television (TV)

Fernsehen 144

~/**hochauflösendes (hochzeiliges)** high-definition television, HDTV, advanced television, ATV
~/**immersives** immersive television
~/**industrielles** industrial (technical) television
~/**interaktives** interactive television (video), ITV
~/**lokales** local television
~/**mechanisches** mechanical television
~ **mit begrenzter Auflösung** limited definition television, LDTV
~ **mit verbesserter Auflösung** enhanced (extended) definition television, EDTV, improved definition television, IDTV
~ **mit Zuschauerbeteiligung** s. ~/interaktives
~/**niedrigauflösendes (niedrigzeiliges)** low-definition television, LDTV
~/**normalauflösendes** normal-definition TV, standard-definition television, SDTV
~/**öffentliches** public [service] television
~/**räumliches (stereoskopisches)** stereoscopic (three-dimensional) television, 3-D television
~/**terrestrisches digitales** s. ~/digitales terrestrisches
~/**verbessertes** enhanced television, ETV; improved-definition television
Fernseher m s. Fernsehgerät
Fernseh-Fernbedienung f television remote control, TV remote controller
Fernsehfilm m television film (motion picture), telefilm, television (TV) movie
Fernsehformat n television format
Fernsehfrequenz f TV (television frame) rate, video frequency, video [frame] rate
Fernseh-Füllsender m television transposer
Fernsehfunk m s. Fernsehrundfunk
Fernsehgerät n [broadcast] television receiver, television [receiving] set, TV [set], telly *(chiefly British)*
~/**analoges** analog television set
~/**internetfähiges** Internet-enabled television set
~/**kabelfähiges** cable-ready television receiver
~/**kabelloses** wireless TV [set]
~/**tragbares** portable TV, portable television [set]
Fernsehgerätehersteller m television set manufacturer
Fernsehgerätlautsprecher m television set speaker
Fernsehgesellschaft f television company
Fernseh-Großbildprojektor m large-screen television projector
Fernseh-Großsender m television transmission center
Fernseh-Halbbild n television (TV) field
Fernsehhaushalt m television household
Fernseh-Heimempfänger m, **Fernseh-Heimgerät** n home television (TV) receiver, home (entertainment) television set, home TV (screen), consumer television set
Fernsehindustrie f television (TV) industry, videoland
Fernseh-IOT-Röhre f image-orthicon [tube], IO
Fernsehjournalismus m television journalism
Fernsehjournalist m television journalist
Fernsehkabel n television cable
Fernsehkabelnetz n television cable network, cable TV network (distribution system)
Fernsehkamera f television (TV) camera, telecamera
Fernsehkamerabild n television camera picture
Fernsehkameramann m TV camera operator
Fernsehkameraröhre f television camera tube, TV pickup tube
Fernsehkanal m television (TV) channel; broadcast TV channel
Fernsehkarte f TV tuner card
Fernseh-Kasch m TV mask
Fernsehkette f television [supply] chain
Fernsehkonsument m TV user
Fernsehkopie f television print (copy)
Fernsehleitung f video circuit
Fernseh-Livesendung f television live broadcast, live telecast (TV broadcast)
Fernsehluminanzsignal n luminance signal, black-[and-]white signal, Y [signal] *(video)*
Fernseh-Mehrkanalton m multichannel television sound, MTS
Fernsehmikroskop n television microscope
Fernsehmikroskopie f television microscopy
Fernsehmonitor m television (TV) monitor
Fernsehnachrichten fpl television (TV) news
Fernsehnachrichtensendung f television newscast
Fernsehnachrichtenstudio f TV newsroom
Fernsehnetz n television network, video [broadcasting] network
Fernsehnorm f broadcast television standard, television [broadcast] standard
Fernsehnormwandler m television system converter, scan-format converter
Fernsehpixel n television (TV) pixel, television (video) pel
Fernsehportal n television (TV) portal
Fernsehproduktion f television production
Fernsehproduktionsfirma f television production company
Fernsehproduktionstechnik f television production equipment
Fernsehprogramm n 1. television [broadcast] program; 2. s. Fernsehprogrammplan; 3. s. Fernsehprogrammkanal

Fernsehprogrammkanal *m* television (TV) channel; broadcast TV channel
Fernsehprogrammmaterial *n* television programming
Fernsehprogrammplan *m* television programming schedule, lineup
Fernsehprojektion *f* television projection
Fernsehprojektor *m* television projector
Fernsehraster *m(n)* television (TV) raster
Fernsehrauschen *n* television noise
Fernseh-Richtantenne *f* directional television antenna (aerial)
Fernsehröhre *f* television [vacuum] tube, television cathode-ray tube; picture (image) tube, kinescope
Fernsehrundfunk *m* television (video) broadcasting, broadcast television [system], broadcast TV
~/**digitaler** digital video broadcasting, DVB
Fernsehrundfunkband *n* television broadcast band
Fernsehrundfunkdecoder *m* video broadcasting decoder
Fernsehrundfunksendung *f* television broadcast transmission
Fernsehsatellit *m* television satellite
Fernsehschirm *m* telescreen, television (TV) screen, television display
Fernsehschirmbild *n* screen shot, off-screen photograph
Fernsehschirmbildaufzeichnung *f* telerecording
Fernsehsendeanlage *f* television broadcasting system
Fernseh-Sendeantenne *f* television transmitting antenna
Fernsehsender *m* television broadcast[ing] station, TV station; television broadcaster (transmitter), telecaster
~/**lokaler** local TV (television broadcasting) station
Fernsehsendernetz *n* broadcast television network
Fernsehsendertechnik *f* television production equipment
Fernseh-Sendesignal *n* TV broadcast signal, broadcast television (TV) signal, broadcast video signal
Fernsehsendung *f* television program (broadcast), telecast; [television] show
Fernsehsequenz *f* television sequence
Fernsehserie *f* television series
Fernsehsignal *n* television (TV) signal
~/**analoges** analog television (TV) signal
~/**digitales** digital television (TV) signal
~/**komponentencodiertes** component-coded television signal
~/**zusammengesetztes** composite TV signal, composite [encoded video] signal, composite video
Fernsehspielfilm *m* s. Fernsehfilm
Fernsehspot *m* TV (television) commercial
Fernsehstandard *m* s. Fernsehnorm

Fernsehstation *f* television broadcast[ing] station, [broadcast] TV station
Fernsehstudio *n* television studio
~/**virtuelles** virtual studio
Fernsehstudiokamera *f* television studio camera
Fernsehstudiotechnik *f* studio video equipment
Fernsehsystem *n* television (TV) system
~/**analoges** analog television system
Fernsehszene *f* television scene
Fernsehtechnik *f* 1. television technology (engineering); TV broadcast technology; 2. television technique
Fernsehtechniker *m* television engineer
fernsehtechnisch television technical
Fernseh-Teilbild *n* TV field
Fernsehteilnehmer *m* television license-holder *(s.a. Fernsehzuschauer)*
Fernsehtestbild *n* television test pattern (chart)
Fernsehtext *m* broadcast videotex, teletext
Fernsehton *m* television (TV) sound
Fernsehtonsender *m* television sound transmitter
Fernsehtonübertragung *f* television sound transmission
Fernsehtuner *m* television (TV) tuner
Fernsehtunerkarte *f* TV tuner card
Fernsehturm *m* television tower
Fernsehübertragung *f* television transmission, telecast
Fernsehübertragungskanal *m* television transmission channel
Fernsehübertragungsnorm *f* television broadcast transmission standard *(s.a. Fernsehnorm)*
Fernsehübertragungstechnik *f* television transmission technology
Fernsehumsetzer *m* television transposer
Fernsehverbindung *f* television link
Fernsehversorgungskette *f* television supply chain
Fernseh-Videokanal *m* TV video channel
Fernseh-Werbefilm *m* TV (television) commercial
Fernsehwerbung *f* television ad[vertising]
Fernseh-Wettervorhersage *f* television weather forecast
Fernsehwiedergabe *f* television display (reproduction)
fernsehwirksam telegenic
Fernsehzeile *f* television (TV) line; television scan[ning] line
Fernsehzeilenraster *m(n)* television (TV) raster
Fernsehzuschauer *m* television viewer, [tele]viewer, televisor
Fernsetzmaschine *f* teletypesetter
~/**telegrafische** remote-control composing equipment
Fernsichtigkeit *f* s. Weitsichtigkeit
fernsteuerbar remotely controllable
Fernsteuerung *f* remote control

Fernsteuerungsbuchse f remote terminal
Fernsteuerungszubehör n remote control accessories
Fernübertragung f long-line transmission
Fernüberwachung f remote [video] surveillance
Fernzugriff m remote access
Ferritkern m ferrite core
ferromagnetisch ferromagnetic
Ferromagnetismus m ferromagnetism
Ferrotypie f 1. ferrotype [process], tintype process; 2. ferrotype, tintype, melanotype *(positive photograph)*
Ferrotypist m ferrotyper
Fertigbild n final image (picture), finished picture
Fertigung f/**rechnerintegrierte** computer-integrated manufacturing, CIM
~/**rechnerunterstützte** computer-aided manufacturing, CAM
Fertigungskontrolle f product assembly analysis
Fertigungsmesstechnik f production measuring technology
Fertigungssteuerung f production control
Festanode f stationary anode *(X-ray tube)*
Festanschluss m permanent connection
Festbild n still image (picture) nonmoving image *(s.a. Stehbild..., Standbild...)*
Festbildcodierung f still image coding
Festbildkommunikation f still image communication
Festbildkompressionsstandard m still-image compression standard
Festbild-Sende-Empfangs-Gerät n still-picture transceiver
Festbildübertragung f still-picture (still-image) transmission
Festblende f fixed diaphragm
Festbrennweite f fixed focal length (distance)
Festbrennweitenobjektiv n fixed-focal-length lens, fixed-focus lens
festbrennweitig fixed-focus
Festkommabild n fixed-point representation
Festkörperbauelement n solid-state component
Festkörper-Bildsensor m,
Festkörper-Bildwandler m solid-state imager (image sensor), *(s.a. Halbleiterkamera)*
Festkörperdetektor m solid-state detector, SSD
Festkörper-Fotoempfänger m solid-state photodetector
Festkörpergeometrie f/**konstruktive** constructive solid geometry, CSG
Festkörperlaser m solid-state laser
Festkörpermodellierung f/**analytische** analytic solid modeling, ASM
Festkörperphysik f solid-state physics
Festkörpersensor m solid-state sensor
Festmusterrauschen n pattern noise

Festobjektiv n fixed-focus lens, fixed-focal-length lens; prime lens
Festplatte f [fixed] hard disk, fixed disk
~/**herausnehmbare** removeable hard disk [storage device]
Festplattencamcorder m hard disk camcorder
Festplattenlaufwerk n hard disk drive, [computer] hard drive, Winchester drive
Festplattenrecorder m hard disk [video] recorder; hard-drive-based consumer VCR
Festplattenschnittstelle f hard drive interface
Festplattenspeicher m hard disk storage device
Festplatten-Videorecorder m s. Festplattenrecorder
Festpunktarithmetik f fixed-point arithmetic
Festspeicher m 1. solid-state memory [device]; 2. s. Festwertspeicher
Festtinte f solid (dry) ink
Festtintendrucker m solid-ink printer
Festwertspeicher m read-only [electronic] memory, ROM
~/**elektrisch lösch- und programmierbarer** electric erasable and programmable read-only memory, EEPROM
~/**lösch- und programmierbarer** erasable and programmable read-only memory, EPROM
~/**programmierbarer** programmable read-only memory, PROM
Festzielunterdrückung f fixed-target suppression *(radar)*
Fetografie f fetography, fetal imaging, fetal [ultra]sonography
Fetoskop n fetoscope
Fetoskopie f fetoscopy
fett bold[faced] *(typestyle)*
Fettblende f Bunsen screen *(photometer)*
Fettdruck m bold[face]
Fettfleckfotometer n grease-spot [photo]meter, Bunsen photometer
fettfreundlich grease-receptive, lipophilic; ink-receptive
fettgedruckt s. fett
Fettsättigung f fat saturation (suppression) *(magnetic resonance imaging)*
Fettschwanzkuppler m fat-tail coupler, oil-protected coupler
Fettstift m grease pencil, greasy crayon
Fettsuppression f s. Fettsättigung
Feuchtauftragswalze f s. Feuchtwalze
feuchten to dampen *(a printing plate)*
Feuchtentwicklung f liquid development
feuchtfeindlich water-repellent, hydrophobic
feuchtfreundlich water-receptive, hydrophilic
Feuchthaltemittel n humectant

**feuchtigkeitsabstoßend,
feuchtigkeitsabweisend** s.
feuchtfeindlich
feuchtigkeitsführend s. feuchtfreundlich
Feuchtmittel n fountain solution,
 dampener (dampening) solution
Feuchtmittelfilm m aqueous coating
Feuchtung f moistening, wetting, aqueous
 coating
Feuchtwalze f water (dampening) roller,
 wetting roller
Feuchtwerk n moistening (wetting)
 system, dampening system [rollers],
 dampening mechanism *(printing press)*
Feuerschutzklappe f douser, dowser, fire
 shutter *(projector, spotlight)*
FHS s. HSB-Farbmodell
Fiberoptik f s. Faseroptik
Fiche n(m) microfiche, filmcard
Figur f figure, figural shape
~/**ambivalente** ambiguous figure (design)
 (optical illusion)
~/**geschlossene** closed figure *(computer
 graphics)*
~/**Lichtenbergsche** Lichtenberg figure
 (image) *(charge pattern)*
Figur-Grund-Differenzierung f,
Figur-Grund-Gliederung f figure-ground
 organization
Figur-Grund-Verhältnis n relationship of
 figure to ground
Figursatz m runaround *(layout)*
Figurwahrnehmung f perception of shape
Film m 1. [photographic] film; 2.
 [cinematographic] film, motion-picture
 film, movie, pic; 3. s. Filmindustrie
~/**abendfüllender** feature-length film
 (motion picture); full-length picture
 (feature)
~/**belichteter** [light-]exposed film
~/**chromogener** chromogenic film,
 substantive-coupler film
~/**computeranimierter**
 computer-animated film,
 computer-generated film (movie), [full]
 CG feature
~/**doppelseitig perforierter**
 double-perforated film, twin-sprocket
 stock
~/**dreidimensionaler** stereographic
 motion picture
~/**einseitig perforierter** single-perforated
 film, single-perforation film,
 single-sprocket stock
~/**feinkörniger** fine-grained film, fine-grain
 [photographic] film
~/**feinstkörniger** finest-grain film
~/**folienloser** non-screen [X-ray] film,
 direct-exposure film, envelope-wrapped
 film
~/**fotografischer** photographic film; still
 [camera] film
~/**fototechnischer** process film,
 repro[graphic] film *(s.a.
 ~/lithografischer)*
~/**gammavariabler** s.
 ~/gradationsvariabler
~/**gealterter** aged film
~/**gradationsfester** fixed-grain film
~/**gradationsvariabler** variable-gain film
~/**grafischer** s. ~/lithografischer *(s.a.
 ~/fototechnischer)*
~/**grobkörniger** coarse-grain[ed
 photographic] film
~/**handelsüblicher** consumer film
~/**hoch[licht]empfindlicher** fast
 (high-speed) film
~/**hochauflösender** high-resolution film
~/**höchstempfindlicher** highest-speed
 film, ultraspeed film
~/**holografischer** holographic film
~/**infrarotempfindlicher** infrared-sensitive
 film, infrared [photographic] film
~/**integrierter** embedded movie
 (multimedia)
~/**kinematografischer** cine[matographic]
 film, motion-picture film, movie film
~/**kontrastreicher** high-contrast
 [photographic] film
~/**lithografischer** litho[graphic] film,
 lith[-type] film, graphic arts film *(s.a.
 ~/fototechnischer)*
~/**mittelempfindlicher** medium-speed film
~/**niedrigempfindlicher** [s]low-speed film
~/**orthochromatischer** ortho[chromatic]
 film, correct-color film
~/**panchromatischer** panchromatic
 [photographic] film, pan (all-color) film
~/**perforierter** perforated (sprocketed) film
~/**radiografischer** radiographic film,
 [photo]fluorographic film, X-ray[-type]
 film
~/**radiologischer** radiologic film
~/**randperforierter** edge-perforated film
~/**röntgenbelichteter** X-ray-exposed film
~/**seitengroßer** composite film
 (reprography)
~/**selbstentwickelnder** self-developing
 film
~/**silberfreier (silberloser)** nonsilver film
~/**spektroskopischer** spectroscopic film
~/**stereoskopischer** stereographic motion
 picture
~/**strahlungsempfindlicher**
 radiation-sensitive film
~/**technischer** process (reprographic) film
~/**teilbelichteter** partially exposed film
~/**ultrahochempfindlicher** ultra high
 speed film
~/**unbelichteter** unexposed film
~/**unentwickelter** undeveloped film
~/**unperforierter** nonperforated film
~/**untertitelter** subtitled film
~/**verarbeiteter** processed film
~/**vorgerasterter** prescreened film

Film 148

~/zweiseitig perforierter double-perforated film, twin-sprocket stock
Filmablaufumkehrung f reverse action
Filmabstreifer m, **Filmabstreifzange** film squeegee
Filmabtaster m film scanner (pickup), film-to-video [transfer] system *(s.a. Filmgeber)*
~/digitaler digital film scanner, film digitizer
~/optomechanischer cathode-ray tube [film] recorder, CRT-based [film] recorder, CRT [film] recorder
Filmabtastung f film scanning; film digitization; telecine (film-to-video) transfer
Filmakt m motion-picture roll, spool
Filmamateur m amateur filmmaker
Filmandruckplatte f film pressure plate
Filmanfang m [film] leader
Filmanimation f motion-picture animation, film (movie) animation
Filmantrieb m film drive
Filmarchitekt m set designer
Filmarchitektur f film architecture
Filmarchiv n film archive (library); cinematheque
Filmarchivar m film archivist
Filmarchivierung f film archiving
Filmart f film type, type (kind) of film
Film-Astrofotografie f film astrophotography
Filmatelier n movie (motion-picture) studio
Filmaufbau m film structure
Filmauffangspule f take-up spool
Filmaufhängeklammer f film clip
Filmauflösung f film resolution
Filmaufnahme f 1. motion-picture recording; 2. film record; movie shot, motion-picture [film] shot
Filmaufnahmearbeit f production shooting
Filmaufnahmekamera f s. Filmkamera
Filmaufnahmeleuchte f film luminaire
Filmaufnahmematerial n motion-picture [film] stock; [film] stock
Filmaufnahmetechnik f film recording technique
Filmaufnahmetrick m [in-]camera effect, optical effect *(cinema)*
Filmaufnahmeverfahren n film capture process
Filmaufwickelspule f take-up reel (spool)
Filmaufzeichnung f 1. film recording, telerecording; 2. film record
Filmaufzeichnungsanlage f film recorder
Filmaufzeichnungsverfahren n film captue process
Filmausleuchtung f film illumination
Filmausrüstung f cine (motion-picture) equipment
Filmausschnitt m film clip, [movie] clip
Filmauswahl f film choice (selection)

Filmauswertung f film analysis *(aerial photography)*
Filmauswurf m film ejection
Filmautor m screenwriter, filmwright
Filmband n film strip
Filmbearbeitung f 1. film (motion-picture) editing; postproduction; 2. film handling
Filmbearbeitungsbetrieb m motion picture [processing] laboratory, cinema laboratory, film lab[oratory]
Filmbegleitton m film (motion-picture) sound
Filmbehälter m film container
Filmbehandlung f film treatment; film handling
Filmbeleuchtung f film (movie) lighting
Filmbelichter m film recorder
Filmbelichtung f 1. film exposure; motion-picture film exposure; 2. s. Filmaufzeichnung 1.
Filmbelichtungssystem n film exposure system
Filmbelichtungszeit f film exposure time
Filmbeschädigung f film damage
Filmbetrachter m 1. film viewer; 2. s. Filmbetrachtungsgerät
Filmbetrachtung f film viewing, screening
Filmbetrachtungsgerät n film viewer (viewing box), [film] viewbox
Filmbewegung f film motion (movement)
Filmbewertungsraum m movie review room
Filmbibliothek f film library (archive)
Filmbild n [film] frame, motion-picture frame; [positive] film image; [motion-]picture image, movie picture
~/angehaltenes (stehendes) still [frame], freeze (stop) frame, held (hold) frame
Filmbildebene f film image plane
Filmbildformat n frame size
Filmbildfrequenz f film [frame] rate, framing (frame) rate
Filmbildnumerierung f film frame numeration
Filmbildseitenverhältnis n film aspect ratio
Filmbildsequenz f frame (film image) sequence
Filmblatt n film sheet
Filmbranche f s. Filmindustrie
Filmbreite f film [format] width *(s.a. Filmformat)*
Filmbüchse f s. Filmdose
Filmbühne f skid plate *(film scanner)*
Filmcharakteristik f film characteristic
Filmclip m [film] clip, movie clip
Filmcode m film code
Filmcodierung f film coding
Filmcrew f film crew, motion-picture production crew
Filmcutter m film (motion-picture) editor, [cinema] editor, cutter
Film-Datenformat n movie file format
Filmdekoration f [motion-picture] set, movie set, setting

Filmdicke *f* film gauge
Filmdigitalisierung *f* film digitization
Filmdokumentation *f* film documentation
Filmdose *f* film can[ister], can, reel case, magazine
Filmdosimeter *n* film dosimeter (badge), photographic badge, badge meter
Filmdosimetrie *f* film dosimetry
Filmdreh *m* movie shoot[ing]
Filmdruck *m* film printing
Filmdrucker *m* film (photo) printer
Filmdurchlauf *m* film passage
Filmebene *f* film plane
Filmeditor *m s.* Filmcutter
Filmeinfädelung *f* 1. film threading; 2. *s.* Filmeinlegen
Filmeinlegen *n*, **Filmeinspulen** *n* film loading [procedure]; camera loading
Filmeinstellung *f s.* Einstellung 2.
Filmeinzug *m* film feed
Filmemachen *n* filmmaking; moviemaking
Filmemacher *m* filmmaker; moviemaker; feature cinematographer
Filmempfindlichkeit *f* film speed (sensitivity), sensitivity (speed) of film *(s.a. under* Empfindlichkeit*)*
Filmempfindlichkeitsbereich *m* film speed range
Filmempfindlichkeitseinstellung *f* film speed setting
Filmempfindlichkeitsnorm *f* film speed standard
Filmempfindlichkeitstabelle *f* film speed table
Filmemulsion *f* film emulsion
Filmemulsionsschicht *f* film emulsion layer
filmen to film, to cinematograph, to lens
Filmende *n* film end
Filmentwickler *m* film developer; negative developer
Filmentwicklung *f* film development (processing)
Filmentwicklungsdose *f* film (daylight) developing tank, [amateur] developing tank
Filmentwicklungsmaschine *f* cine [film] processor, film processing machine
~ **nach dem Hängerprinzip** dip and dunk processor
Filmentwicklungstank *m* developing tank
Filmer *m* 1. filmer; 2. *s.* Filmemacher
Filmfachmann *m* cineast, cinephile
Filmfarbe *f* film color
Filmfarbstoff *m* film dye
Filmfeld *n* [film] frame, motion-picture frame
Filmfenster *n* [film] gate
Filmfensterpositionierung *f* gate positioning
Film-Filter-Kombination *f* film-and-filter combination
Filmfixierbad *n* film fixing bath, film fixer
Filmfixierung *f* film fixing
Filmfläche *f* film surface

Filmfolie *f* cold laminating film
Film-Folien-Kombination *f* [X-ray] film-screen combination, screen-film combination, double-screen film cassette *(radiography)*
Film-Folien-Mammografie *f* screen-film mammography
Film-Folien-Radiografie *f* screen-film radiography
Film-Folien-System *n* film-screen system, [intensifying] screen-film system
Filmformat *n* film format (size); film width, [film] gauge
Filmfortschalteinrichtung *f s.* Filmschaltwerk
Filmfotograf *m* cine (motion-picture) photographer
Filmfotografie *f* movie (motion-picture) photography
Filmgalgen *m* [trim] bin
Filmgeber *m* telecine scanner (machine), telecine [equipment], [motion-picture film] scanner *(s.a.* Filmabtaster*)*
Filmgelände *n* [studio] backlot, lot
Filmgerät *n* film handling device
Filmgerätehersteller *m* manufacturer of motion picture equipment
Filmgeschichte *f* cinema history
Filmgeschwindigkeit *f* film [running] speed, film velocity
Filmgießanlage *f* film casting line
Filmgießmaschine *f* film coating machine
Filmgruppe *f s.* Filmteam
Filmhalter *m* film holder
Filmhandhabung *f* film handling
Filmherauszieher *m* cassette film retriever, film leader retriever, film extractor
Filmhersteller *m* [photographic] film manufacturer, film maker
Filmherstellung *f* film manufacture, film production (making)
Filmhintergrund *m* cyclorama, backing, backdrop
Filmidentifizierung *f* film identification
Filmindustrie *f* film (motion-picture) industry, cinema (movie) industry, filmdom, screen[land], moviedom, movies
filmisch filmic, cinematic
Filmkader *m* [film] frame, motion-picture frame
Filmkamera *f* motion-picture [film] camera, cine[matographic] camera, motion (picture) camera
~/**geräuschgedämpfte** blimped camera
~/**professionelle** professional motion-picture camera
Filmkameramann *m* motion-picture cameraman, cinematographer
Filmkameraobjektiv *n* movie camera objective, motion-picture [camera] lens, cine camera lens
Filmkammer *f* film chamber
Filmkammerverriegelung *f* film door lock

Filmkanal

Filmkanal *m* 1. film path *(imaging camera)*; 2. movie channel *(television)*
Filmkante *f* film edge
Filmkasch *m* mask, matte
Filmkassette *f* film cassette
Filmkennlinie *f* film characteristic curve *(s.a.* Gradationskurve*)*
Filmkern *m* [film] core; bobbin
Filmkitt *m* film (cine) cement
Filmklammer *f* film clip
Filmklebeapparat *m* film splicer
Filmklebeband *n* splicing tape
~**/perforiertes** film patch
Filmklebefolie *f s.* Filmklebeband
Filmklebepresse *f* film splicer
Filmkleber *m* film (cine) cement
Filmklebestelle *f* [film] splice
Filmkolorierung *f* colorization, coloring, tinting
Filmkonservierung *f* film preservation
Filmkontrast *m* film contrast
Filmkontrollgerät *n* film inspection apparatus
Filmkopf *m* film head
Filmkopie *f* film copy; motion-picture copy (print); movie copy; film (motion-picture release) print
~**/anamorphotische** anamorphic [release] print
~**/entzerrte** unsqueezed [release] print
~**/fremdsprachige** foreign language release
~**/kombinierte** married (composite) print *(cinema)*
~**/vorführbereite (vorführfertige)** motion-picture release print, projection print, [exhibition] release print, release
Filmkopiermaschine *f* [cine] film printer, motion-picture printer
Filmkopierolle *f* print reel
Filmkopierung *f* motion-picture printing
Filmkopierverfahren *n* motion-picture duplicating process; motion-picture printing technique
Filmkopierwerk *n* motion-picture [processing] laboratory, cinema laboratory, film lab[oratory]
Filmkorn *n* film grain
Filmkörnigkeit *f* film graininess
Filmkornrauschen *n* film[-grain] noise, photographic grain noise
Filmkörnung *f* film granularity
Filmkratzer *m* film scratch
Filmkrümmung *f* film curvature
Filmkulisse *f* [motion-picture] set, setting
Filmkunde *f* motion-picture science
Filmkunst *f* film (motion-picture) art, art of cinematography
Filmkunsttheater *n* art[-house] theater
Filmkurve *f***/charakteristische** characteristic (density) curve, [photographic] response curve, [characteristic] D-log H curve

Filmlabor *n s.* 1. Filmkopierwerk; 2. Entwicklungslabor
Filmladegerät *n* [bulk] film-loader
Filmladen *n* film loading [procedure]; camera loading
Filmlader *m s.* Filmladegerät
Filmlager *n* film store
Filmlagerraum *m* film storeroom
Filmlagerung *f* film storage
Filmlänge *f* film length; [film] footage
Filmlängenmesser *m* footage counter
Filmlasche *f* [film] leader, [film] tongue
Filmlaufgeschwindigkeit *f* film [running] speed, film velocity
Filmlaufrichtung *f* direction of film travel
Filmlaufwerk *n* film-moving mechanism, camera movement
Filmlaufzeit *f* screen (running) time
Filmleinwand *f* film (motion-picture) screen, silver screen *(s.a.* Kinoleinwand*)*
Filmlesekopf *m* film reader
Filmlicht *n* 1. film lighting; 2. motion-picture lighting source
Filmlichtbestimmer *m* [film] color timer, [laboratory] timer, color (negative) grader, colorist
filmlos filmless
Filmmagazin *n* film magazine; spool box
Film-Mammogramm *n* film mammogram
Filmmaschine *f* motion-picture machine
Filmmaske *f* mask, matte
Filmmaterial *n* 1. film material; [film] stock; 2. [image] footage *(cinema)*
~**/stumm gedrehtes** wild footage, MOS footage
~**/unbelichtetes** unexposed film stock
Filmmeter *mpl* [film] footage
Filmmontage *f* on-line editing *(cinema)*
Filmmusik *f* [musical] score, sound track
Filmmuster *npl* [film] dailies, rushes *(chiefly British)*
Filmnachbearbeitung *f* [film] postproduction
Filmnegativ *n* film negative; motion-picture negative
Filmoberfläche *f* film surface
Filmobjektiv *n* cinematograph lens
Filmografie *f* filmography
Filmologie *f* motion-picture science
Filmoperateur *m s.* Filmvorführer
Filmothek *f* cinematheque; film archive (library)
Filmpack *m* film pack[et]
Filmpackung *f* film package
Filmpalast *m* movie palace, picture palace (show)
Filmpatrone *f* film cartridge
Filmperforation *f* film perforation
Filmpflege *f* film care
Filmplakat *n* movie poster
Filmplakette *f* film badge (dosimeter), photographic badge, badge meter
Filmplatte *f* film (photographic) plate, photoplate

Filmpraxis f film practice
Filmprobe f film sample
Filmprodukt n film product
Filmproduktion f film (motion-picture) production
~/**elektronische** electronic cinema
Filmproduktionsfirma f production company *(cinema)*
Filmproduktionstechnik f motion-picture production technique
Filmproduzent m film producer
Filmprojektion f film (motion-picture) projection
Filmprojektionsanlage f cine projection equipment
Filmprojektor m film (motion-picture) projector, cine [film] projector, cinematograph, [picture] projector
Filmprozessor m film processor (processing machine)
Filmrahmen m film holder
Filmrand m film border (edge)
Filmrauschen n film[-grain] noise, photographic grain noise
Filmrecorder m film recorder
Filmregie f film directing (direction)
Filmregisseur m film (motion-picture) director
Filmreibung f film friction
Filmreibungskoeffizient m film coefficient of friction
Filmreiniger m film cleaner
Filmrequisit n prop
Filmrestaurator m film preservationist
Filmrestaurierung f motion picture restoration, film (old movie) restoration
Filmriss m film fracture
Filmrolle f film reel; motion-picture roll, spool
Filmröntgen n radiophotography, radiographic (X-ray) photography, [photo]fluorography, fluororadiography, X[-ray] radiography, [fluoro]roentgenography
Filmröntgenbild n X-ray [photograph]
Filmrückholer m s. Filmherauszieher
Filmrückseite f back of the film, base (non-emulsion) side
Filmrückspulkurbel f film rewind crank
Filmrückspulung f, **Filmrücktransport** m, **Filmrückwicklung** f film rewind
Filmrückwand f s. Kamerarückwand
Filmsalat m jamming; camera jam
Filmsammlung f film collection
Filmsatz m s. Fotosatz
Filmscanner m s. Filmabtaster
Filmschachtel f [square] film box, photographic film box
Filmschaden m film damage
Filmschaffender m feature cinematographer; filmmaker, moviemaker
Filmschaltrolle f intermittent sprocket

Filmschaltwerk n intermittent [movement], Geneva movement
Filmschärfe f film sharpness
Filmschicht f film layer; film coating
Filmschichtträger m [film] support, [photographic] film base
Filmschleife f [film] loop
Filmschneidemaschine f film (motion-picture) editing machine
Filmschneideraum m film cutting (editing) room, [motion-picture] editing room, cutting room, editing suite
Filmschneidetisch m editing (cutting) table, edit bench
Filmschnitt m [film] cutting; film (motion-picture) editing; postproduction
~/**computergestützter** computer-controlled editing
~/**konventioneller (traditioneller)** traditional film editing
Filmschnittliste f film cut list *(s.a. Schnittliste)*
Filmschnittplatz m/**digitaler** digital edit bay
Filmschnitzel npl trims *(film editing)*
Filmschramme f film scratch
Filmschrank m film cabinet
Filmschrumpfung f film shrinkage
Filmschutzbeutel m lead-lined film pouch, X-ray film shield
Filmschwärzung f film blackening (darkening); film density
Filmschwärzungskurve f film characteristic curve *(s.a. Gradationskurve)*
Filmsendekopie f TV-motion-picture film
Filmsequenz f film (motion-picture) sequence *(s.a. Filmszene)*
Filmset m(n) [motion-picture] set, movie set, setting *(s.a. Drehort)*
Filmskript n [motion-picture] script, camera (shooting) script *(s.a. Drehbuch)*
Filmsorte f s. Filmtyp
Filmspeicher m photo-optical memory
Filmspeicherung f film storage; motion-picture storage
Filmspender m film dispenser
Filmspirale f [spiral] reel *(developing tank)*
Filmspule f film spool (reel)
Filmstab m film (motion-picture) crew, [motion-picture] production crew
Filmstandarte f rear standard *(view camera)*
Filmstandbild n film (movie) still, action still, still [frame]; production (publicity) still
Filmstartband n head leader, leader [strip]; countdown [head] leader *(motion-picture release print)*
Filmsteg m frame line
Filmstill n, **Filmstillstand** m filmstill
Filmstreifen m filmstrip, strip of film
Filmstreifenprojektor m filmstrip projector
Filmstruktur f film structure
Filmstück n piece of film

Filmstudio

Filmstudio n movie (motion-picture) studio
Filmszene f film (movie) scene, [motion-picture] scene, shot (s.a. Einstellung, Take)
~/**eingeschnittene** insert
Filmszenenbildner m set designer
Filmteam m film (motion-picture) crew, [motion-picture] production crew
Filmtechnik f 1. motion-picture technology, film technology; 2. film technique; 3. film (motion-picture) equipment
Filmtechniker m motion-picture engineer
Filmtechnologie f film technology
Filmteller m flange, cheek
Filmtheater n movie theater (house), [motion-picture] theater, cinema
Filmton m film (motion-picture) sound
~/**separat aufgenommener** separately recorded sound, wild (nonsynched) sound, wild track
Filmtonaufnahme f, **Filmtonaufzeichnung** f motion-picture sound recording; 2. motion-picture sound record
Filmtonspur f film[-based] sound track, [motion-picture] sound track
Filmtontechniker m [production] sound recordist, soundperson
Filmträger m [photographic] film base, [film] support, base
Filmträgermaterial n film base material
Filmtrailer m [movie] trailer, preview [trailer], prevue
Filmtransfer m film[-to-video] transfer; telecine transfer
Filmtransfergerät n s. Filmgeber
Filmtransport m film advance (transport)
~/**automatischer** 1. automatic film winding (transport); 2. autowinder, automated film transport system
~/**manueller** manual film transport
~/**motorischer (motorisierter)** motorized film advance
~/**ruckweiser** intermittent film movement
Filmtransportart f film advance mode
Filmtransporteinrichtung f film advance (transport) mechanism, film movement [mechanism]
Filmtransportgeschwindigkeit f film advance speed
Filmtransporthebel m winding (film-advance) lever
Filmtransportmechanismus m s. Filmtransporteinrichtung
Filmtransportsystem n film-transport system
Filmtransportwähler m film advance mode dial
Filmtrick m motion-picture [special] effect, cinematic (movie) special effect
~/**optischer** motion-picture optical effect (s.a. Spezialeffekt/optischer)
Filmtricktisch m [motion-picture] animation stand

Filmtrickverfahren n motion-picture animation [technique], motion-picture animation method
Filmtrockenschrank m film-drying cabinet
Filmtrocknung f film drying
Filmtrommel f film drum
Filmtyp m film type, type of film
Filmtypenfenster n film confirmation window (SLR camera)
Filmunterlage f [photographic] film base, [film] support, base
Filmuntertitel m motion-picture subtitle, caption
Filmverarbeitung f film processing
Filmverarbeitungsautomat m automatic film processor, automatic film-processing machine
Filmverarbeitungschemie f film processing chemistry
Filmverbrauch m film consumption
Filmverleih m movie distribution; theater (theatrical) distribution
Filmvertonung f film dubbing, motion-picture sound dubbing
Filmvorderseite f s. Emulsionsseite
Filmvorführer m theater (motion-picture) projectionist, motion-picture machine operator, cinematographer
Filmvorführgerät n film (motion-picture) projector, cine [film] projector, cinematograph, [picture] projector
Filmvorführraum m screening room
Filmvorführung f motion-picture screening, [film] screening, film presentation, motion-picture show[ing], cinema
Filmvorrat m 1. film load (e.g. of a camera); 2. film stock
Filmvorratsraum m reel case, magazine
Filmvorschub m film advance
Filmwahl f film choice (selection)
Filmwechsel m film change[over]
Filmwechsler m serial (spot-film) camera, rapid film changer, rapid-sequence camera (X-ray diagnostics)
Filmweg m film path (travel) (in a camera or projector)
Filmweitertransport m film advance (transport)
Filmwesen n cinema
Filmwiedergabe f film playback
Filmwindung f film coil
Filmwirtschaft f s. Filmindustrie
Filmwissenschaft f motion-picture science
Filmzählwerk n footage (film) counter, footage indicator
Film-Zahnrolle f sprocket
Film-zu-Band-Konversion f film[-to-tape] transfer (s.a. Filmtransfer)
Filmzug m film tension
Filmzunge f [film] tongue, [film] leader
Filmzuschauer m film viewer
Filter n(m) 1. filter (optics, photography); 2. filter, mask, kernel, template, window

(electronics, digital image processing; s.a Operator*)*
~/**abstimmbares akustooptisches** acousto-optic tunable filter
~/**adaptives** adaptive filter
~/**additives** additive filter
~/**afokales** afocal filter
~/**aktives** active filter
~/**akustooptisches** acousto-optic filter
~/**analoges** analog filter; continuous-time filter
~/**angepasstes** matched filter
~/**anisotropes** anisotropic filter
~/**asymmetrisches** asymmetric filter
~/**bewegungsadaptives** motion-adaptive filter
~/**bilineares** bilinear filter
~/**binomiales** binomial filter, Gaussian filter (kernel)
~/**biorthogonales** biorthogonal filter
~/**Boolesches** Boolean filter
~/**chromatisches** chromatic filter
~/**detailerhaltendes** detail-preserving filter
~/**dichroitisches** dichroi[ti]c [color] filter; interference filter
~/**dielektrisches** dielectric filter
~/**digitales** digital filter; discrete-time filter
~/**diskretes** discrete filter
~/**doppelbrechendes** birefringent filter
~/**eindimensionales** one-dimensional filter
~/**eindrehbares** screw-in filter, screw-type filter
~/**einpoliges** single-pole filter
~/**einstellbares** *s.* ~/steuerbares
~/**elektrisches** electrical filter
~/**elektronisches** electronic filter
~/**elektrooptisches** electro-optical filter
~/**elliptisches** elliptical filter
~/**fotografisches** photographic filter
~/**frequenzselektives** frequency-selective filter
~/**gekittetes** cemented filter
~/**geometrisches** geometric filter
~/**gerichtetes** directional (oriented) filter
~/**gewichtetes** weighted filter
~/**holografisches** holographic filter
~/**homomorphes** homomorphic filter
~/**hyperbolisches** hyperbolic filter
~/**ideales** ideal filter
~/**inverses** inverse filter
~/**isotropes** isotropic filter
~/**kantenerhaltendes** edge-preserving filter
~/**kantenverstärkendes** edge-enhancing filter, edge enhancer
~/**kausales** causal filter
~/**lineares** linear filter
~/**mathematisches** mathematical filter
~/**mehrdimensionales** multidimensional filter
~/**morphologisches** morphological filter (operator)
~/**neuronales** neural filter *(s.a.* Assoziativspeicher*)*
~/**nichtkausales** noncausal filter
~/**nichtlineares** nonlinear filter
~/**nichtorthonormales** nonorthonormal filter
~/**nichtrekursives** nonrecursive filter, finite-impulse-response filter, FIR filter
~/**nichtseparierbares** nonseparable filter
~/**nullphasiges** zero-phase-shift filter
~/**optimales** optimum (optimal) filter, optimal morphological operator *(image restoration)*
~/**optisches** optical (light) filter
~/**orthogonales** orthogonal filter
~/**orthonormales** orthonormal filter
~/**ortsinvariantes** space-invariant filter
~/**paradigmenbasiertes** paradigm-based filter
~/**passives** passive filter
~/**periodisches** periodic filter
~/**programmierbares** programmable filter
~/**pseudoinverses** pseudoinverse filter
~/**raumzeitliches** spatiotemporal (three-dimensional) filter
~/**rekursives** recursive [digital] filter, infinite-impulse-response filter
~/**richtungsempfindliches** direction-sensitive filter, orientation-selective filter
~/**rotationssymmetrisches** *s.* ~/isotropes
~/**schmalbandiges** narrow-band[pass] filter, spike filter
~/**separierbares** separable filter (mask)
~/**signalangepasstes** matched filter
~/**stabiles** stable filter
~/**steuerbares** steerable (tunable) filter
~/**subtraktives** subtractive filter
~/**symmetrisches** symmetric (symmetrical digital) filter
~/**systolisches** systolic filter
~/**ungerichtetes** nondirectional filter
~/**verkittetes** cemented filter
~/**zeitdiskretes** discrete-time filter, digital filter
~/**zeitinvariantes** time-invariant filter
~/**zeitkontinuierliches** continuous-time filter, analog filter
~/**zeitveränderliches** time-varying filter
~/**zusammengesetztes** composite filter
~/**zweidimensionales** two-dimensional filter, 2-D filter
Filterabsorption *f* filter absorption
Filteradapter *m* 1. filter adapter; 2. *s.* Filterhalter
Filteradapterring *m* filter adapter ring
Filteralgorithmus *m* filtering algorithm
Filteranordnung *f* filter arrangement
Filterantwort *f* filter response
Filterarchitektur *f* filter architecture
Filterausdehnung *f* filter width
Filterausgang *m* filter output
Filterausgangssignal *n* filter output [signal]
Filterbandbreite *f* filter bandwidth

Filterbank 154

Filterbank *f* filter bank, bank of filters
~/**biorthogonale** biorthogonal filter bank
~/**kaskadierte** cascaded filter bank
Filterbankanalyse *f* filter bank analysis
Filterbankkanal *m* filter bank channel
Filterbankkaskade *f* cascaded filter bank
Filterbild *n* filtered image
Filtercharakteristik *f* filter characteristic
Filterdesign *n* filter design
Filterdurchmesser *m* filter diameter
Filterebene *f* filter plane
Filtereffekt *m* filter[ing] effect, filtering action
Filtereinschub *m* filter slot
Filtereinstellung *f* filter setting
Filterempfehlung *f* filter recommendation
Filterentwurf *m* filter design
Filterergebnis *n* filter[ing] result
Filteretui *n* filter pocket
Filterfaktor *m* filter factor
Filterfarbe *f* filter color
Filterfarbstoff *m* filter dye
Filterfassung *f* filter mount
Filterfehler *m* filter error
Filterfenster *n* filter window; operator window
Filterfolie *f* 1. filter foil; 2. *s.* Gelatinefilter
Filterform *f* filter shape
Filterfrequenz *f* filter frequency
Filterfunktion *f* filter function
Filtergeometrie *f* filter geometry
Filtergewinde *n* [lens] filter thread
Filtergitter *n* filter grating
Filterglas *n* filter glass
Filtergröße *f* filter size
Filterhalter *m*, **Filterhalterung** *f* filter holder; filter clamp
Filterimpulsantwort *f* filter impulse response
Filterkern *m* filter (operator) kernel *(gray-scale image processing)*
Filterklasse *f* class of filters
Filterklemme *f* filter clamp
Filterkoeffizient *m* filter (mask) coefficient
Filterkombination *f* filter combination
Filterkonzept *n* filter concept
Filterkurve *f* filter function
Filterlänge *f* filter length
Filterleistung *f* filter performance, filtering power
Filtermaske *f* filter[ing] mask, convolution mask (kernel)
Filtermaterial *n* filter material
Filtermatrix *f* filter matrix
filtern to filter
Filternetzwerk *n*/**digitales** digital filter network
Filteroperation *f* filtering operation
Filteroperator *m* filter operator
Filterordnungsgrad *m* filter order
Filterpaar *n* filter pair
Filterpaket *n* filter pack
Filterparameter *m* filter parameter
Filterpolynom *n* filter polynomial
Filterprofil *n* filter profile
Filterprozess *m s.* 1. Filtervorgang; 2. Filterverfahren
Filterrad *n* filter wheel
Filterradius *m* filter radius
Filterraster *m(n)* filter raster
Filterreihe *f* filter line
Filterrevolver *m* filter turret (revolver)
Filterrichtblock *m* lens filter ring straightening block
Filterring-Richtzange *f* lens ring straightening pliers
Filtersatz *m* filter set, set of filters
Filterschaltung *f* filter circuit
Filterscheibe *f* filter disk
Filterschicht *f* filter layer; filter coating
Filterschublade *f* filter drawer (slider)
Filterskale *f* filter scale
Filtersoftware *f* filter software
Filtersortiment *n* 1. assortment of filters; 2. *s.* Filtersatz
Filterstruktur *f* filter structure
~/**rekursive** recursive filter structure
Filtersystem *n* filter system
Filtertechnik *f* filtering technique
Filtertheorie *f* filter[ing] theory
Filtertransmission *f* filter transmission
Filter-Transmissionsgrad *m* filter transmittance
Filtertyp *m* filter type
Filterübertragungsfunktion *f* filter transfer function
Filterung *f* filtration, filtering; filtering [procedure], mask processing *(of digital images)*
~/**adaptive** adaptive filtering
~/**adaptive raumzeitliche** adaptive spatiotemporal filtering
~/**additive** additive filtering
~/**analoge** analog filtering
~/**angepasste** matched filtering, signal-adaptive filtering
~/**bewegungskompensierte** motion-compensated filtering
~/**bilaterale** bilateral filtering
~/**bilineare** bilinear filtering
~/**binäre** binary filtering
~/**digitale** digital filtering
~/**diskret lineare** discrete linear filtering
~/**elektronische** electronic filtering
~/**faktorielle** factorial filtering
~/**homomorphe** homomorphic filtering
~/**inverse** inverse filtering, deconvolution *(image reconstruction)*
~/**kantenadaptive** edge-adaptive filtering
~/**kohärente** coherent filtering
~/**lineare** linear filtering
~/**mehrdimensionale** multidimensional filtering
~/**merkmalsbasierte** feature-based filtering
~/**morphologische** morphological filtering
~/**nichtlineare** nonlinear filtering
~/**optimale** optimal filtering

~/**optische** optical filtering (filtration)
~/**periodische** periodic filtering
~/**räumliche** spatial filtering
~/**raumzeitliche** spatiotemporal filtering
~/**rekursive** recursive filtering
~/**richtungsempfindliche** direction-sensitive filtering
~/**selektive** selective filtering (filtration)
~/**signalangepasste** *s.* ~/angepasste
~/**spektrale** spectral filtering
~/**subtraktive** subtractive filtering
~/**topologische** topological filtering
~/**zeitliche** temporal filtering
Filterungsartefakt *n* filter[ing] artifact
Filterverfahren *n* filtering technique (process), filtering method
Filterverhalten *n* filter behavior
Filtervorgang *m* filter operation
Filterwahl *f* filter choice (selection)
Filterwechsel *m* filter change[over]
Filterwerkzeug *n* filtering tool
Filterwert *m* filter value
Filterwirkung *f* filter[ing] effect, filtering action
Filterwürfel *m* filter cube
Filterzeit *f* filtering time
Filzseite *f* felt side *(paper)*
Finesse *f* finesse
Fingerabdruck *m* fingerprint, dactylogram, dactylograph; finger[print] mark *(e.g. on film material)*
Fingerabdruckanalyse *f* fingerprint analysis (recognition)
Fingerabdruckbild *n* fingerprint image
Fingerabdruckdaten *pl* fingerprint data
Fingerabdruckerkennung *f* fingerprint recognition (analysis)
Fingerabdruckkamera *f* fingerprint camera
Fingerabdrucklesegerät *n*,
  Fingerabdruckscanner *m* fingerprint reader
Fingerabdruckschablone *f* fingerprint template
Fingerabdrucksensor *m* fingerprint sensor
Fingerabdruckvergleich *m* fingerprint matching
Finish *n* finish *(e.g. of paper)*
Finisher *m s.* Fotodienstleister
Finite-Elemente-Methode *f* finite element method (analysis)
Firewire-Buchse *f*, **Firewire-Schnittstelle** *f* firewire interface *(for connecting peripheral devices)*
FIR-Filter *n* FIR (finite-impulse-response) filter
Firmenaufdruck *m*, **Firmenkopf** *m* letterhead
Firmenlogo *n* company logo (seal)
Firmen-TV *n* business television, BTV, business video
Fischauge *n s.* Fischaugenobjektiv
~/**Maxwellsches** Maxwell fish-eye
Fischaugenobjektiv *n* fish-eye lens; true fish-eye

Fischer-Entwicklung *f s.* Chromogenentwicklung
Fisheye[objektiv] *n s.* Fischaugenobjektiv
Fistulografie *f* fistulography
FIT-CCD-Bildwandler *m*, **FIT-Chip** *m* frame-interline-transfer device
Fixage *f* fixation, fixing *(photographic processing)*
Fixation *f* 1. [eye] fixation; 2. *s.* Fixage
Fixationsentfernung *f* fixation distance *(vision)*
Fixationsobjekt *n* object of fixation
Fixationspunkt *m* fixation point, point of fixation *(vision)*
~/**binokularer** binocular fixation point
Fixationsstelle *f* location of fixation
Fixationszeit *f* 1. fixation [dwell] time *(vision)*; 2. *s.* Fixierzeit
Fixativ *n* fixative *(protective coating)*
Fixfokuseinstellung *f* fixed (pan) focus arrangement, focus lock
Fixfokus-Farbkamera *f* fixed-focus[ed] color camera
Fixfokuskamera *f* fixed-focus[ed] camera, focus-free camera
Fixfokus-Kleinbildkamera *f* fixed-lens 35-mm camera
Fixfokusobjektiv *n* fixed-focus lens, fixed-focal-length lens, prime lens
Fixfokus-Schnappschusskamera *f* fixed-focus snapshot camera
Fixierbad *n* fixing (fixer) bath, hypo
Fixierbadentsilberung *f* recovering silver from used fixer solution
Fixierbadkontrolle *f* fixing bath test
fixierbar fixable
Fixierbeschleuniger *m* fixing accelerator
Fixierdauer *f* fixing time
fixieren 1. to fixate *(a visual object; s.a.* blicken*)*; 2. to fix *(e.g. photographic material)*
Fixierentwickler *m* fixing developer
Fixierentwicklung *f* fixing development
Fixierer *m* [chemical] fixer, fixing agent
Fixiergeschwindigkeit *f* fixing rate (speed), rate of fixation (fixing)
Fixierleistung *f* fixing performance
Fixierlösung *f* fixing solution
Fixiermittel *n* 1. fixing agent, [chemical] fixer; 2. *s.* Fixativ
Fixiernatron *n s.* Natriumthiosulfat
Fixierprozess *m* fixing process
Fixierpunkt *m* fixation point, point of fixation *(vision)*
Fixiersalz *n* fixing salt
Fixierschale *f* fixing (fixer) tray
Fixierung *f* fixation
Fixiervorgang *m* fixing process
Fixierwalze *f* fuser roller *(xerography)*
Fixierzeit *f* 1. fixing time; 2. *s.* Fixationszeit
Fixobjektiv *n s.* Fixfokusobjektiv
Fixpunktsatz *m*/**Banachscher** contraction mapping theorem *(fractal image compression)*

Fizeau-Interferometer *n* Fizeau interferometer
Fizeau-Linien *fpl*/**kreisförmige** *s.* Newton-Ringe
Flachbettabtaster *m* *s.* Flachbettscanner
Flachbett-Dokumentenscanner *m* flatbed document scanner
Flachbettgerät *n* flatbed device
Flachbettplotter *m* flatbed plotter; desktop plotter
Flachbettprojektor *m* platter [system] *(cinema)*
Flachbettscanner *m* flatbed (print) scanner, flatbed digitizer
Flachbettschneidetisch *m* flatbed [editing] table, flatbed editing machine, flatbed [viewer]
Flachbildröhre *f* flat square tube, FST
Flachbildschirm *m* flat[-screen] display, flat-panel display, FPD; flat-panel monitor
Flachdisplay *n* *s.* Flachbildschirm
Flachdruck *m* 1. planography, planographic printing; 2. *s.* ~/indirekter
~/**indirekter** offset printing [process], [offset] lithography, litho-offset
Flachdruckpapier *n* offset paper
Flachdruckplatte *f* planographic plate
Flachdruckverfahren *n* planographic [printing] process, offset lithographic process
Fläche *f* area *(shape feature)*; [sur]face *(s.a. under* Oberfläche*)*
~/**asphärische** aspheric [optical] surface
~/**bestrahlungsempfindliche** radiant sensitive area *(photodiode)*
~/**bikubische** bicubic surface
~/**brechende** refracting surface
~/**deformierbare** deformable surface *(computer graphics)*
~/**druckende** printing area
~/**ebene** plane [surface]
~/**effektive** effective area *(e.g. of a reflecting telescope)*
~/**extrudierte** extruded surface *(geometric modeling)*
~/**gekrümmte** curved surface
~/**geschlossene** closed surface
~/**ideal matte (weiße)** perfect (ideal isotropic) diffuser *(colorimetry)*
~/**Lambertsche** Lambertian surface (source), ideal diffuse surface *(photometry)*
~/**nichtdruckende** nonprinting area
~/**optisch wirksame,** ~/**optische** optical surface
~/**sphärische** spherical surface
~/**spiegelnde** specular surface
~/**verdeckte** hidden surface
~ **zweiter Ordnung**/**algebraische** quadric [surface] *(Euclidean geometry)*
Flächenabtastung *f* area sampling
~/**ungewichtete** unweighted area sampling
Flächenanpassung *f* surface fitting

Flächenapproximation *f* surface approximation
Flächenausleuchtung *f* area illumination
Flächenbildsensor *m* area [image] sensor, array sensor (imager), sensor (mosaic detector) array,
Flächenbildwandler *m* large-surface-area imager, large-area continuous photoconductor
Flächenchip *m* area-array CCD (charge-coupled device)
Flächenchipkamera *f* *s.* Flächenkamera
Flächendarstellung *f* surface representation
Flächendatenkompression *f*/**adaptive** adaptive surface data compression
Flächendeckung *f,* **Flächendeckungsgrad** *m* screen density (percentage), dot area *(of halftones)*
Flächendetektor *m* area (planar) detector, [two-dimensional] array detector, flat-panel array (detector)
Flächendiagramm *n* surface plot; plane (area) chart
Flächenebnung *f* surface flattening
Flächenelement *n* planar element; area (surface) element
Flächenextraktion *f* surface extraction
Flächenfluter *m* *s.* Fluter
Flächenfragment *n* surface fragment
Flächenfüllen *n* *s.* Flächenwachstum
Flächenfüllfaktor *m* fill[ing] factor
Flächenfunktion *f* area function
Flächengewicht *n* grams per square meter, gram[m]age, GSM *(paper specification)*
Flächenglättung *f* surface smoothing
flächenhaft planar, plane, flat
Flächenhelligkeit *f* luminance
Flächenintegral *n* planar integral
Flächenkamera *f* [area] array camera, matrix array camera
Flächenkrümmung *f* surface curvature
Flächenleuchte *f* broad [light]
Flächenlicht *n* area (broad) light
Flächenlichtquelle *f* area [light] source
Flächenmerkmal *n* area feature *(e.g. on a map)*
Flächenmesser *m* planimeter
Flächenmessung *f* planimetry
Flächenmodell *n* surface model
Flächenmodellierung *f* surface modelling
~/**interaktive** interactive surface modeling
Flächenmodifikation *f* surface modification
Flächennormale *f* surface normal, normal to the surface
Flächenobjekt *n* planar (plane) object
Flächenpolarisator *m* sheet polarizer, polarizing sheet (foil)
Flächenpolygon *n* planar polygon
Flächenprojektion *f* planar (surface) projection
Flächenrekonstruktion *f* surface reconstruction

Flugsimulator

Flächenscanner *m* [optical] surface scanner, area scanner
Flächenscheinwerfer *m* floodlight
Flächenschwerpunkt *m* [geometric] centroid of the area
Flächensensor *m s.* Flächenbildsensor
Flächenstrahler *m* surface emitter *(type of light-emitting diode)*
Flächenstück *n* surface patch; face
Flächenträgheitsmoment *n* areal moment of inertia
Flächentriangulation *f* surface triangulation
Flächenüberlappung *f* surface overlap
Flächenvereinfachungsalgorithmus *m* surface simplification algorithm *(computer graphics)*
Flächenwachstum *n* region-growing [method], region-growing procedure, magic wand approach *(segmentation technique)*
Flächenziel *n* area target *(radar)*
Flachform-Druckmaschine *f* flatbed [printing] press
Flachform-Offsetdruckmaschine *f* flatbed offset press
Flachglas *n* plate (sheet) glass
flächig planar, plane, flat
Flächigkeit *f* planarity
Flachkristall *m s.* Tafelkristall
Flachkristallmonochromator *m* flat crystal monochromator
Flachoffsetpresse *f* flatbed offset press; flatbed proof press
Flachpresse *f* flatbed print dryer
Flachspiegel *m* flat (plane) mirror
Flackern *n*, **Flackerstörung** *f* 1. flutter *(television image)*; 2. *s.* Flimmern
Flankensteilheit *f* slope steepness
Flatterrand *m* ragged setting *(typography, layout)*
Flattersatz *m* unjustified matter
~ **links** ragged left
~ **rechts** ragged right
~/**linksbündiger** align (flush) left
~/**rechtsbündiger** align (flush) right
flau flat, faint *(picture)*
Flauheit *f* flatness
FLC-Bildschirm *m* ferroelectric liquid crystal display, FLC display
Fleck *m*/**blinder** [retinal] blind spot, optic disk
~/**gelber** yellow spot, macula [lutea] *(in the human retina)*
~/**heller** hot spot *(esp. as an interference)*
~/**Poissonscher** bright point of Poisson *(Fresnel diffraction)*
Fleckgröße *f* spot size
Fleckigkeit *f*/**farbige** *s.* Farbrauschen
Fleckradius *m* beam waist *(Gaussian optics)*
Fleckretuschierstift *m* [photographic] spotting pen
Fleischfarbe *f* flesh (skin) tone

Flexodruck *m* flexography [process], flexographic (aniline) printing, flexo *(letterpress process)*
Flexodruckmaschine *f* flexographic [printing] press, flexopress
Flexodruckplatte *f* flexographic plate
Flexografie *f* flexography
flexografisch flexographic
Fliegenaugenlinse *f* fly's eye lens
Fließfertigungssystem *n* in-line system *(e.g. in printed-matter production)*
Fließkomma... *s.* Gleitkomma...
Fließmuster *n* flow pattern
Fließtext *m* flowed (continuous) text
Flimmerblende *f* flicker blade, chopper *(motion-picture projector)*
Flimmereffekt *m* flicker[ing] effect; moiré [effect]
Flimmerfarben *fpl* subjective (Fechner's) colors
Flimmerfotometer *n* flicker photometer
Flimmerfotometrie *f* flicker photometry
flimmerfrei flickerless, flicker-free
Flimmerfreiheit *f* absence of flicker
Flimmerfrequenz *f* flicker frequency (rate) *(s.a.* Flimmerverschmelzungsfrequenz*)*
~/**kritische, Flimmergrenze** *f* critical flicker frequency, CFF, [observer's] flicker threshold *(s.a.* Flimmerverschmelzungsfrequenz*)*
Flimmerkorrektur *f* flicker correction
Flimmern *n* flicker[ing]; flare
Flimmerstörung *f* flicker[ing] artifact
Flimmerverschmelzung *f* flicker fusion
Flimmerverschmelzungsfrequenz *f* [critical] fusion frequency *(s.a.* Flimmerfrequenz/kritische*)*
Flimmerwahrnehmung *f* flicker perception, perception of flicker
Flintglas *n* flint glass
Flintglaslinse *f* flint lens
Flipalbum *n* flip photo album
Flipflop *n(m)* flip-flop
Flipwinkel *m* flip (tip) angle *(magnetic resonance imaging)*
Floppydisk *f* floppy [disk], FD, diskette
Floyd-Steinberg-Dithering *n s.* Fehlersummen-Dithering
Fluchtfernrohr *n s.* Fluchtungsprüfernrohr
Fluchtgerade *f*, **Fluchtlinie** *f* vanishing line
Fluchtpunkt *m* vanishing point
Fluchtungsprüfernrohr *n* alignment telescope
Flugbahn *f* flight track
Flügelblende *f* blade (multibladed) shutter, sector aperture, sector-wheel shutter, rotary (disk) shutter, chopper
Flughafenüberwachungsradar *n* airport surveillance radar, ASR
Flugroutenüberwachungsradar *n* air route surveillance radar, ARSR
Flugscheinlesegerät *n* airline ticket reader
Flugsimulation *f* flight simulation
Flugsimulator *m* flight (aircraft) simulator

Flugstreckenüberwachungsradar *n* air route surveillance radar, ARSR
Flugstreifen *m* flight strip (line), line of flight
Flugweg *m* **über Grund** ground track, flight line *(remote sensing)*
Flugwegkarte *f* flight map
Flugzeitmessung *f*/**optische** *s.* Lichtradar
Flugzeugaufnahme *f* aircraft image
Flugzeug-Doppler-Radar *n* airborne Doppler radar
Flugzeugradar *n* airborne radar
Flugzeugscanner *m* airborne scanner
Flugzeug-Seitensichtradar *n* side-looking airborne radar, SLAR
Fluidkopf *m* fluid[-dampened tripod] head, hydraulic head
Fluoresceinisothiocyanat *n* fluorescein isothiocyanate *(fluorescent dye)*
fluoreszent *s.* fluoreszierend
Fluoreszenz *f* fluorescence
~ **bei Kaltkatode** cold cathode fluorescent light, CCFL
~/**laserinduzierte** laser-induced fluorescence, LIF
~/**parametrische** parametric downconversion
~/**sekundäre** secondary fluorescence
Fluoreszenzanregung *f* fluorescence excitation
Fluoreszenzanzeige *f* fluorescent display
Fluoreszenzaufnahme *f s.* Fluoreszenzbild
Fluoreszenzausbeute *f* fluorescent yield
Fluoreszenzbild *n* fluorescence (fluorescent) image
Fluoreszenzbildgebung *f* fluorescence imaging
Fluoreszenzdruckfarbe *f* fluorescent ink
Fluoreszenzeffekt *m* fluorescence effect
Fluoreszenzfarbstoff *m* 1. fluorescent dye, fluorescing stain, fluorochrome; 2. fluorophore
Fluoreszenzfärbung *f* fluorescence staining
Fluoreszenzfolie *f* fluorescing screen *(X-ray film)*; salt [intensifying] screen
Fluoreszenzfotografie *f* fluorescence (black-light) photography
Fluoreszenzintensität *f* fluorescence intensity
Fluoreszenz-Konfokalmikroskopie *f* fluorescence confocal microscopy
Fluoreszenzkontrastverfahren *n* fluorescence contrasting technique
Fluoreszenzkorrelationsspektroskopie *f* fluorescence correlation spectroscopy
Fluoreszenzlampe *f* fluorescent lamp (light source)
Fluoreszenzlicht *f* fluorescent light
Fluoreszenzmikrofotografie *f* fluorescence [photo]micrography
Fluoreszenzmikroskop *n* fluorescence (ultraviolet) microscope; ultraviolet microscope

~/**aufrechtes** upright fluorescence microscope
~/**inverses** inverted fluorescence microscope
Fluoreszenzmikroskopie *f* fluorescence [light] microscopy
Fluoreszenzröhre *f* fluorescent tube, [tubular] fluorescent lamp
Fluoreszenzscanner *m* fluorescence scanner
Fluoreszenzschicht *f* fluorescent layer *(e.g. of a picture tube)*
Fluoreszenzschirm *m* fluorescent screen
Fluoreszenzspektrometrie *f* fluorescence spectrometry
Fluoreszenzspektroskopie *f* fluorescence (fluorescence) spectroscopy
~/**laserinduzierte** laser-induced fluorescent spectroscopy, LIF
~/**zeitaufgelöste** time-resolved fluorescence spectroscopy
Fluoreszenzspektrum *n* fluorescence (fluorescent) spectrum
Fluoreszenzstoff *m* fluorescent substance (material), fluorescing substance *(s.a. Fluoreszenzträger)*
Fluoreszenzstrahlung *f* fluorescent (fluorescence) radiation
Fluoreszenzträger *m* fluorophore
Fluoreszenzvideomikroskopie *f* fluorescence videomicroscopy
fluoreszieren to fluoresce
fluoreszierend fluorescent
Fluoridglas *n* fluoride glass
Fluorit *m* fluorite, calcium fluoride, fluorspar *(optical crystal)*
Fluoritglas *n* fluorite (calcium fluoride) glass
Fluoritlinse *f*, **Fluoritobjektiv** *n* fluorite [objective], fluoride lens, semiapochromatic objective
Fluorometer *n* fluorometer
Fluorometrie *f* fluorometry
Fluorophor *m* fluorophore
Fluorosensor *m* fluorosensor
Fluoroskopie *f* fluoroscopy, transmission radiography
~/**digitale** digital fluorographic imaging, DFI
~/**interventionelle** interventional fluoroscopy
fluoroskopisch fluoroscopic
Flurkarte *f* terrain map; cadastral map
~/**digitale** digital terrain map
Fluss *m*/**magnetischer** magnetic flux
~/**optischer** optical flow *(computer vision)*
Flussartefakt *n* flow artifact *(magnetic resonance imaging)*
Flussäure *f* hydrofluoric acid
Flussdiagramm *n* flowchart, flow sheet, [information] flow diagram
Flussdichte *f* flux density, irradiance, irradiation
~/**magnetische** magnetic flux density

~/spektrale spectral flux density
Flussfeld n/optisches optical flow field
Flüssigemulsion f liquid emulsion
Flüssigentwickler m liquid developer
Flüssigkeit f/ferroelektrische ferroelectric liquid
Flüssigkeitsdeckel m floating lid
Flüssigkeitsfilter n liquid filter
Flüssigkeits-Kopierfenster n liquid gate
Flüssigkeitslaser m liquid laser
Flüssigkristall m liquid crystal
~/ferroelektrischer ferroelectric liquid crystal, FLC
~/gedrillter nematischer twisted nematic liquid crystal
~/nematischer nematic liquid crystal
~/smektischer smectic liquid crystal
Flüssigkristallanzeige f liquid-crystal [digital] display, LCD, liquid crystal readout
~/hintergrundbeleuchtete backlit LCD
~/plasmaadressierte liquid-plasma display, LPD
Flüssigkristallbildschirm m 1. liquid-crystal display projector, LCD [computer display] screen; 2. s. Flüssigkristallanzeige
Flüssigkristalldiode f liquid-crystal diode, LCD
Flüssigkristalldisplay n liquid-crystal [digital] display, LCD, liquid crystal readout
Flüssigkristallfilter n liquid-crystal filter
flüssigkristallin liquid crystalline
Flüssigkristallinität f liquid crystallinity
Flüssigkristall-Lichtventil n liquid-crystal light valve, LCLV
Flüssigkristallmatrix f liquid crystal matrix
Flüssigkristalloptik f liquid-crystal optics
Flüssigkristall-Projektionsgerät n, Flüssigkristallprojektor m LCD (liquid-crystal) projector
Flüssigkristallschiene f liquid-crystal shutter, LCS
Flüssigkristallschirm m s. Flüssigkristallanzeige
Flüssigkristallzelle f liquid crystal cell
Flüssiglaser m liquid laser
Flüssigtintenstrahldruck m liquid ink-jet print
Flüssigtintenstrahldrucker m liquid ink-jet printer
Flüssigtoner m liquid toner
Flusskompensation f flow compensation, gradient-moment nulling *(magnetic resonance imaging)*
Flussquant n [/magnetisches] flux quantum, quantum of flux, fluxon
Flussrauschen n flux noise
Flussspat m s. Fluorit
Flusswechsel m flux transition *(magnetism)*
Fluter m flood[light], reflector floodlight; broad [light]

Flutlicht n floodlight *(s.a.* Fluter*)*
Flying-Spot-Abtaster m flying-spot scanner (telecine) *(s.a.* Filmabtaster, Filmgeber*)*
FMCW-Radar n FMCW (frequency-modulated continuous-wave) radar
FM-Radar n FM (frequency-modulated) radar
FM-Rasterung f s. Rasterung/frequenzmodulierte
fokal focal
Fokalbereich m focus[ing] range, focal[-length] range; focal zone (region)
Fokaldistanz f focus distance
Fokalebene f s. Fokusebene
Fokalreduktor m focal reducer *(astronomical optics)*
Fokogramm n focogram
Fokometer n focometer, focimeter
Fokometrie f focometry
Fokus m [principal] focus, focal (focus) point
Fokusachse f focal axis
Fokusbereich m focus[ing] range, focal[-length] range; focal zone (region)
Fokus-Bildebenen-Abstand m focus-film distance, FFD *(radiography)*
Fokusdifferenz f focus difference
Fokusebene f focal plane, Fourier [transform] plane
Fokuseinstellung f focus setting (adjustment)
~/falsche misfocus
fokusfern not in focus, out of focus
Fokus-Film-Abstand m focus-film distance, FFD *(radiography)*
Fokusfläche f focal plane
Fokuskorrektion f focus correction
Fokuslage f focal position
Fokusnachführung f focus tracking
Fokus-Objekt-Abstand m focus-object distance, FOD
Fokuspunkt m s. Fokus
Fokusring m focus[ing] ring; zoom ring
Fokussensor m focus sensor
Fokusserie f through-focus series
Fokussieranode f focusing anode
Fokussierart f focus mode
Fokussierautomatik f s. Autofokus
fokussierbar focusable
Fokussierbarkeit f focusing capability, focusability
Fokussierbereich m focusing range
Fokussierbetriebsart f focus mode
Fokussierbewegung f focusing movement
Fokussierebene f focal plane
Fokussiereinrichtung f focusing mechanism
Fokussierelektrode f focus[ing] electrode
fokussieren to focus, to focalize
Fokussierer m focuser
Fokussierfähigkeit f focusing capability, focusability

Fokussierfehler *m* focus[ing] error
Fokussiergenauigkeit *f* focusing accuracy, accuracy of focus
Fokussierhilfe *f* focusing aid
Fokussierlinse *f* focus[ing] lens
Fokussiermechanik *f* focusing mechanism
Fokussiermotor *m* focus motor
Fokussieroptik *f* focusing optics
Fokussierring *m* focus[ing] ring; zoom ring
Fokussierschalter *m* focus mode selector
Fokussierschnecke *f*,
Fokussierschneckengang *m* helical [focusing] mount *(lens mount)*
Fokussierspannung *f* focus[ing] voltage *(cathode-ray tube)*
Fokussierspiegel *m* focusing mirror
Fokussierspule *f* focus[ing] coil, focus solenoid
Fokussiersystem *n* focusing system
Fokussierung *f* focusing
~/**automatische** autofocusing
~/**dynamische** dynamic focusing
~/**elektronische** electronic focusing *(sonography)*
~/**elektrooptische** electro-optical focusing
~/**elektrostatische** electrostatic focusing
~/**magnetische** magnetic focusing
~/**manuelle** manual focusing
~/**mechanische** mechanical focusing *(sonography)*
~/**parallaxenfreie** no-parallax focusing
~/**paraxiale** paraxial focusing
~/**selektive** selective focusing
~/**ungenaue** imprecise focusing
~/**visuelle** visual focusing
Fokussierungsgitter *n* focusing grid
Fokussierungsgrad *m* degree of focusing *(sonography)*
Fokussierungslinse *f* focus[ing] lens
Fokussierungsspule *f s.* Fokussierspule
Fokussierungswirkung *f* focal power *(of a symmetrical optical system)*
Fokussierzahl *f s.* Blendenzahl
Fokussteuerung *f* focus[ing] control
Fokustiefe *f* depth of focus (field)
Fokusverlagerung *f* defocusing
Folge *f* sequence, sequency *(s.a. unter Sequenz)*
Folgeabtastung *f* progressive [video] scanning, sequential (noninterlaced) scanning, progressive scan mode
Folgebewegung *f* smooth pursuit eye movement, pursuit movement
Folgebild *n* successive (consecutive) image, subsequent (past) picture
Folgebildanschluss *m* bridging
Folgefrequenz *f* [pulse] repetition rate *(of a laser)*
Folie *f* 1. foil, film; 2. cel[l], animation (overlay) cel, acetate cel (sheet); 3. [intensifying] screen *(X-ray film)*
~/**feinzeichnende** high-resolution screen
~/**hochempfindliche (hochverstärkende)** high-speed screen *(radiography)*

~/**lichtempfindliche** photosensitive foil
~/**piezoelektrische** piezoelectric foil
Foliendruck *m* [flexible] film printing, foil printing
Folienfilm *m* screen-type X-ray film, X-ray screen-type film
Folienfilter *n* gelatin filter, gel
Folienfilterhalter *m* gelatin filter holder
Folienkaschiermaschine *f* laminating press
Folienkaschierung *f* 1. film laminating; 2. film laminate
Folienklebepresse *f* tape splicer
Folienpolarisator *m* sheet polarizer, polarizing sheet (foil)
Folienschreiber *m* print marking pen; film marking pen
Folienspeicher *m s.* Floppydisk
Folienspiegel *m* foil mirror
Folienstrahlteiler *m* pellicle beam splitter
Folienunschärfe *f* screen blur *(radiography)*
forcieren to force-process *(underexposed film)*
Form *f* shape, form *(s.a. Druckform)*
~/**geschlossene** closed shape *(object description)*
Formähnlichkeit *f* shape similarity
Formaldehyd *m* formaldehyde
Formalin *n* formalin
Formanalyse *f* shape (morphological) analysis
Format *n* format *(s.a. Dateiformat)*; size *(e.g. of a printed product)*
~/**beschnittenes** finished size, trim[med] size *(e.g. of a printed product)*
Formatänderung *f* format change
Formatauswahl *f* format selection
Formatblende *f*/**verstellbare** adjustable (sliding) masking blade
Formatdiagonale *f* format diagonal; diagonal through the film
Formatersteller *m* format originator
formatieren 1. to format *(e.g. a printout)*; 2. to format, to initialize *(e.g. a data carrier)*
Formatierung *f* formatting
Formatkonversion *f*, **Formatkonvertierung** *f* format conversion
~/**verlustlose** lossless format conversion
Formatrahmen *m* film aperture
Formatsteuerzeichen *n* format effector; layout character
Formatumschaltung *f* format change, reframing
Formatvorlage *f* style sheet *(text processing)*
Formbeschreibung *f* shape description
Formbestimmung *f* **aus Grauwertverteilungen** shape-from-shading [technique], structure from shading
Formblatt *n* style sheet
Formcodierung *f* shape coding

~/**bitmapbasierte** bit-map-based shape coding
~/**polygonbasierte** polygon-based shape coding
Formdarstellung *f* shape representation
Formel *f*/**Beersche** Beer's law *(of radiation absorption)*
~/**Eulersche** Euler's formula (equation) *(mathematical morphology)*
Formeln *fpl*/**Fresnelsche** Fresnel's equations *(optics)*
Formen *n* [image] morphing, polymorphic tweening *(animation technique)*
Formenkonstanz *f* shape constancy
formerhaltend shape-preserving
Formerkennung *f* shape (form) recognition
Formfaktor *m* shape (form) factor, configuration factor
Formgebung *f* shaping
Formiergas *n* forming gas *(astrophotography)*
Forminvarianz *f* shape invariance
Formklassifikation *f*, **Formklassifizierung** *f* shape classification
Formkonstanz *f* shape constancy
Formmerkmal *n* shape feature (characteristic), form feature
~/**globales** global shape feature
~/**lokales** local shape feature
Formparameter *m* shape parameter
Formproof *m* [hard-copy] position proof, blackprint, blue[line]
Formrekonstruktion *f* shape reconstruction
Formsatz *m* runaround *(layout)*
Formsegmentierung *f* shape segmentation
Formulardruck *m* forms printing
Formularlesegerät *n* form reader (reading system)
Formveränderung *f s.* Formwandlung
Formwahrnehmung *f* shape perception
Formwandlung *f* shape shifting *(s.a. Morphing)*
Formzylinder *m* plate[-bearing] cylinder *(printing press)*
Forschungsfotografie *f* research photography
Forschungsmikroskop *n* research[-grade] microscope
Forschungsobservatorium *n* research observatory
Forschungsradaranlage *f* research radar system
Fortdruck *m* 1. production printing; 2. production print
Fortdruckmaschine *f* production[-type] press; rotary production-type press
Fortschaltmechanismus *m s.* Filmschaltwerk
Foto *n* photo[graph], pic, shot *(s.a. under Fotografie, Aufnahme, Bild)*
~/**arrangiertes** staged photo[graph]
~/**ausentwickeltes** developed-out photograph

~/**digitalisiertes** digitized photo[graph], digitized photographic image
~/**gerastertes** screened (rasterized) photograph
~/**gestelltes** staged photo[graph]
~/**kurzzeitbelichtetes** short-exposure photograph
~/**manipuliertes** manipulated photograph
~/**mehrfachbelichtetes** multiexposure photograph
~/**ungerastertes** unscreened photograph
~/**ungestelltes** unposed photograph, candid [photograph]
~/**unscharfes** fuzzy photo
~/**untertiteltes** captioned photo[graph]
~/**verblichenes** (**vergilbtes**) faded photograph
~/**verwackeltes** fuzzy photo
Fotoabsorption *f s.* Photonenabsorption
Fotoabteilung *f* photographic (photography) department
~/**betriebliche** company (industrial) photographic department
Fotoabwasser *n* photographic effluent
Fotoabzug *m* photo[graphic] print, silver halide print, paper [positive] print, [positive] print
Fotoagentur *f* photo [stock] agency, photographic agency
fotoähnlich near-photographic, photographlike *(image)*
fotoakustisch photoacoustic
Fotoalbum *n* photograph album
Fotoamateur *m* amateur photographer
fotoanalytisch photoanalytical
Fotoapparat *m* photographic (camera) apparatus; photographic [film] camera, still [picture] camera, [conventional] silver halide still camera
~/**digitaler** digital still camera, DSC
Fotoapparatereparatur *f* camera repair
Fotoarbeit *f* photographic work
Fotoarchiv *n* photographic archive
Fotoarchivar *m* photographic archivist
fotoarchivisch photographic archival
Fotoatelier *n* photography (photographic) studio
fotoätzen to photoetch
Fotoaufklärung *f* photo reconnaissance
Fotoaufnahme *f* photo shot
Fotoaufnahmeleuchte *f* photo luminaire
Fotoauftragstasche *f* [film] processing envelope, order envelope
Fotoausarbeitung *f* photofinishing
Fotoauslöser *m* photo button
Fotoausrüstung *f* photographic equipment, still photography equipment
Fotoausstellung *f* photographic exhibition
Fotoauswertung *f* photointerpretation; photo evaluation
Fotoautomat *m* photomaton booth
Fotobearbeitung *f* photo editing
Fotobearbeitungssoftware *f* photo-retouching software

Fotobericht *m* photo-narrative, picture story
Fotobibliothek *f* photo[graphic] library
Fotobild *n* photographic image (picture)
Fotoblitzgerät *n* photoflash device
Fotobuch *n* photographic book
Foto-CD *f* photo CD (compact disk), PCD
Fotochemie *f* photochemistry *(s.a. Chemie/fotografische)*
Fotochemikalie *f* photographic [processing] chemical, film-processing chemical
Fotochemiker *m* photochemist
fotochemisch photochemical
fotochrom photochromic
Fotochromie *f* photochromism
Fotochromoskop *n* photochromoscope
Fotocollage *f* photocollage, photographic collage
Fotodegradation *f* photodegradation
Fotodesign *n* photo design
Fotodetektor *m* photodetector, photon (photoconductive) detector, light (optical) detector
~/fasergekoppelter fiber-coupled photodetector
Fotodetektorrauschen *n* photodetector noise
Fotodienst *m* photographic service
Fotodienstleister *m* photofinisher
Fotodienstleistung *f* photofinishing (photographic) service
Fotodiode *f* photodiode, light-sensitive diode
~/flächige planar [photo]diode, diode area array
~/ladungsgekoppelte charge-coupled photodiode
~/selbstabtastende self-scanned photodiode
Fotodiodenarray *n* photodiode array, photodetector imaging array
Fotodiodendetektor *m* photodiode detector
Fotodokument *n* photographic document
Fotodokumentation *f* photographic (camera) documentation
Fotodruck *m* 1. photomechanical printing; 2. *s.* ~/direkter
~/direkter direct printing
Fotodrucker *m* photo[graphic] printer
Fotodrucktechnik *f* photographic printing technology
Fotoecke *f* photo [mounting] corner
Fotoeffekt *m* photoeffect, photoelectric effect
~/äußerer external photoeffect (photoelectric effect), extrinsic photoconduction
~/innerer internal photoeffect (photoelectric effect), intrinsic photoconduction
fotoelastisch photoelastic
Fotoelastizität *f* photoelasticity

fotoelektrisch photoelectric
Fotoelektrizität *f* photoelectricity
Fotoelektron *n* photoelectron
Fotoelektronenrauschen *n* photoelectron noise
Fotoelektronenstrom *m* photoelectron current
Fotoelektronenvervielfacher *m* photomultiplier [tube], PMT, multiplier phototube
fotoelektronisch photoelectronic
Fotoelektrophorese *f* photoelectrophoresis, PEP
Fotoelement *n* photovoltaic (barrier-layer) cell
Fotoemission *f* photoemission, photoelectric (photoelectron) emission
Fotoemissionsdetektor *m* photoemissive detector (sensor)
Fotoemissionseffekt *m* external photoeffect (photoelectric effect), extrinsic photoconduction
Fotoemissionsmikroskop *n* photoemission microscope
Fotoemitter *m* photoemitter
fotoemittierend photoemissive
Fotoempfänger *m* photoelectric receiver, photoreceiver
fotoempfindlich photosensitive, light-sensitive, sensitive to light
Fotoempfindlichkeit *f* photosensitivity, light sensitivity, sensitivity to light
~/spektrale spectral sensitivity *(s.a. Empfindlichkeit/spektrale)*
Fotoemulsion *f* photographic emulsion, photoemulsion
Fotoenthusiast *m* photographic enthusiast
Fotoentladung *f* photodischarge
Fotoerzählung *f* photo-narrative, picture story
Fotoerzeugnis *n* photoproduct, photographic product
Fotoessay *m(n)* photo[graphic] essay
Fotofachgeschäft *n* photographic (camera) store, photo supply store
Fotofachhändler *m* photographic (photography) dealer, photo retailer, cameraman
Fotofachlabor[atorium] *n* photofinishing lab[oratory], commercial darkroom
Fotofachmann *m* photographic expert
Fotofachsprache *f* photographic parlance
Fotofälschung *f* photo fakery, photographic fraud
Foto-Fibel *f* photoguide
Fotofilm *m* photographic film; still [camera] film
Fotofinish *n* photo finish
Fotofinisher *m* photofinisher, photographic finisher, photofinishing operation (firm)
Fotofinishing *n* photofinishing, commercial developing and printing
Fotofirma *f s.* Fotofinisher
Fotoformat *n* photo[graph] format

Fotogalerie f photographic (photography) gallery, photo gallery
fotogalvanisch photogalvanic
Fotogalvanografie f photogalvanography
Fotogelatine f photographic gelatin
fotogen photogenic
Fotogeologie f photogeology
fotogeologisch photogeologic[al]
Fotogerät n photographic device
Fotogerätehersteller m photographic manufacturer
Fotogerätetechnik f photoinstrumentation, photographic instrumentation
Fotogerätetechniker m photoinstrumentation engineer; photo equipment technician
Fotogeschichte f photographic history, history of photography
Fotogewehr n photographic gun
Fotogewerbe n photographic craft
Fotogoniometer n photogoniometer, scatterometer
Fotograf m [still] photographer, photo[graph]ist, photo, camerist, lensman
~/**kriminaltechnischer** forensic photographer
~/**semiprofessioneller** semi-professional photographer
~/**studiounabhängiger** location photographer
~/**technischer** technical photographer
Fotografenweste f photo vest
Fotografie f 1. photography; 2. [still] photograph, photographic (still-photography) image, photogram *(s.a. Foto)*
~/**abbildende** pictorial photography
~/**allgemeine** general photography
~/**anamorphotische** anamorph[ot]ic photography
~/**angewandte** applied photography
~/**ballistische** ballistic photography
~/**beweissichernde** [civil] evidence photography
~/**bildgebende (bildmäßige, bildnerische)** pictorial photography
~/**chemische** chemical photography
~/**chromogene** chromogenic photography
~/**digitale** digital photography
~/**dokumentierende** documentary photography
~/**dreidimensionale** three-dimensional photography, stereoscopic photography, stereophotography
~/**elektronische** electronic [still] photography
~/**endoskopische** endoscopic photography
~/**entzerrte** orthophoto[graph]
~/**experimentelle** experimental photography
~/**filmlose** filmless photography
~/**forensische** forensic photography
~/**freistehende** cutout photograph *(typography)*
~/**geologische** geological photography
~/**gestaltende** creative photography
~/**gewerbliche** commercial photography
~/**herkömmliche** conventional (ordinary) photography
~/**historische** historical photography
~ **in natürlichen Farben** Lippmann process *(color photography)*
~/**journalistische** journalistic photography
~/**kameralose** cameraless photography
~/**klinische** clinical photography
~/**kommerzielle** commercial photography
~/**konventionelle** conventional (ordinary) photography
~/**kreative** creative photography
~/**kriminaltechnische** forensic photography
~/**künstlerische** artistic photography
~/**medizinische** medical photography
~/**mobile** location photography
~/**multispektrale** multispectral photography
~/**professionelle** professional photography
~/**silberfreie** nonsilver [chemical] photography, paraphotography
~/**spektroskopische** spectroscopic photography
~/**synchroballistische** synchroballistic photography
~/**technische** technical photography
~/**wissenschaftliche** scientific photography
Fotografiedruck m s. Fotodruck
Fotografiefilm m photographic film; still [camera] film
Fotografiegeschichte f photographic history, history of photography
fotografierbar photographable
fotografieren to photo[graph], to shoot
Fotografik f 1. light graphics (drawing), photogenics; 2. photogram, photogenic drawing, cameraless photograph, photogrammatic image, Schadograph
fotografisch photographic, photo
Fotogramm n 1. photogrammetric image; 2. s. Fotografik 2.
Fotogrammeter m photogrammetrist
Fotogrammetrie f photogrammetry, phototopography
~/**analytische** analytical photogrammetry
~/**digitale** digital photogrammetry
~/**forensische** forensic photogrammetry
~/**forstliche** forest photogrammetry
~/**terrestrische** terrestrial photogrammetry
fotogrammetrisch photogrammetric[al]
Fotogravüre f 1. photogravure [process], photographic engraving, heliogravure; 2. photogravure, heliogravure *(print)*
Fotohalbleiter m phototransistor

Fotohändler

Fotohändler *m* photographic (photography) dealer, photo retailer, cameraman
Fotohandy *n* camera-cell phone, multimedia [cell] phone
Fotohistoriker *m* photohistorian, photographic historian
fotohistorisch photographic historical
Fotoillustration *f* photographic illustration
Fotoindex *m* index print, thumbnail images, thumbnails
Fotoindustrie *f* photographic [manufacturing] industry, photo[graphy] industry
Fotoingenieur *m* photographic engineer
Fotoinklinometer *n* photoclinometer
Fotointerview *n* photointerview
Fotoionisation *f* photoionization
Fotojournal *n* photographic journal
Fotojournalismus *m* photojournalism
Fotojournalist *m* photojournalist
fotojournalistisch photojournalistic
Fotokamera *f* photographic [film] camera, still [picture] camera, [conventional] silver halide still camera
~/**digitale** digital still camera, DSC
Fotokameraformat *n* still-camera format
Fotokameraobjektiv *n* camera objective (lens) *(s.a. under Objektiv)*
Fotokarton *m* mount[ing] board
Fotokatode *f* photocathode
Fotokeramik *f* photoceramics
Fotokleber *m*, **Fotoklebstoff** *m* photographic adhesive
Fotoklub *m* photographic (camera) club, photo[graphy] club
Fotokoffer *m* rigid camera case
Fotokompressionsalgorithmus *m* photographic image compression algorithm, PICA
Fotokopie *f* 1. photo[graphic] copy, photoduplicate, copy photograph; 2. photocopy, photoreproduction
Fotokopierautomat *m s.* Fotokopierer
fotokopieren to photoduplicate; to rephotograph; to photocopy
Fotokopieren *n* photographic copying; photocopying
~/**archivalisches** archival photocopying
Fotokopierer *m* photocopier; photocopy[ing] machine
Fotokopiererindustrie *f* photocopy machine industry
Fotokopiergerät *n s.* Fotokopierer
Fotokopierlack *m s.* Fotolack
Fotokopiermaschine *f* photocopy[ing] machine
Fotokopierpapier *n* photocopy[ing] paper
Fotokunst *f* photographic art
Fotokünstler *m* photographic artist
Fotolabor *n* [/**professionelles**] photographic lab[oratory], photo[processing] laboratory, photolab

Fotolaborant *m* darkroom technician; [professional] photofinisher
Fotolaborleuchte *f* safelight
Fotolack *m* photoresist, [photosensitive] resist; photopolymer resist
~/**negativer** negative[-working] photoresist
~/**positiver** positive[-working] photoresist
Fotolampe *f* photo[graphic] lamp; photoflood [lamp], photoflood bulb, floodlamp
Fotoleim *m* photo paper glue *(s.a. Fotokleber)*
Fotoleinen *n* photo linen
fotoleitend photoconductive
Fotoleiter *m* photoconductor; photoconductive element; photoconducting material
~/**anorganischer** inorganic photoconductor
~/**elektrofotografischer** electrophotographic photoconductor, [electrophotographic] photoreceptor
~/**elektrostatischer** electrostatic photoconductor
~/**organischer** organic photoconductor, OPC
~[**ober**]**fläche** *f* photoconductor surface
Fotoleiterschicht *f* photoconductor (photoconducting) layer
Fotoleitertrommel *f*, **Fotoleiterwalze** *f* photoconductor drum
fotoleitfähig photoconductive
Fotoleitfähigkeit *f* photoconductivity
Fotoleitung *f* photoconduction
Fotoleitungsbetrieb *m* photoconductive (reverse biased) mode *(photodiode)*
Fotoleitungseffekt *m* photoconductivity (photoconductive) effect
Fotoleitungssensor *m* photoconductor detector *(s.a. Fotowiderstand)*
Fotoleuchte *f* 1. photoflood lamp; 2. *s.* Fotolampe
Fotoliteratur *f* photographic literature
Fotolithograf *m* photolithographer
Fotolithografie *f* 1. photolithography, optical lithography *(printing process)*; 2. photo[litho] *(print)*
Fotolithografiemaske *f* photolithographic mask
fotolithografisch photolithographic
Fotolumineszenz *f* photoluminescence
fotolumineszierend photoluminescent
Fotolyse *f* photolysis, photodissociation
fotolytisch photolytic
Fotomagazin *n* photographic magazine
Fotomappe *f* [photography] portfolio
Fotomaske *f* photographic mask, [photo]mask
Fotomaterial *n* photo[graphic] material, photograph material
Fotomechanik *f* photomechanics
fotomechanisch photomechanical
Fotomechatronik *f* photo-mechatronics

Fotomedienlaborant m [professional] photofinisher
Fotomesse f photographic trade show, photographic [trade] fair
Fotometer n photometer, light meter
~/**fotoelektrisches** photoelectric (electro-optical) photometer
~/**heterochromes** heterochromatic photometer
~/**kolorimetrisches** colorimetric photometer
~/**lichtelektrisches** photoelectric photometer
~/**physikalisches** physical photometer
~/**thermoelektrisches** thermoelectric photometer
~/**visuelles** visual (comparison) photometer
~/**Webersches** Weber photometer
Fotometerbank f photometer bench
Fotometerfeld n photometric field
Fotometerkopf m photometer head
Fotometerlampe f photometer (photometric) lamp
Fotometerwürfel m photometric (Lummer-Brodhun) cube
Fotometrie f photometry, measurement of brightness
~/**fotografische** photographic photometry
~/**heterochrome** heterochromatic photometry
~/**objektive** s. ~/physikalische
~/**physikalische** physical photometry
~/**subjektive** s. ~/visuelle
~/**visuelle** visual photometry
fotometrisch photometric[al]
Fotomikrografie f photomicrography, microphotography, photomicroscopy *(s.a.* Mikrofotografie*)*
Fotomikroskop n photomicroscope, photographic microscope
Fotomodus m photo mode (function) *(video camera, copier)*
Fotomontage f 1. photomontage; 2. [photo]montage, composite photograph; composite print, pasteup
Fotomosaik n s. Mosaik 2.
Fotomotiv n photographic subject
Fotomultiplier m s. Fotoelektronenvervielfacher
Fotomuseum n photography (photographic) museum
Fotonegativ n photographic negative
Fotoobjekt n photographic subject
Fotoobjektiv n photographic objective (lens), photolens *(s.a. under* Objektiv*)*
Fotookular n projection eyepiece
Fotooptik f photo-optics, photographic optics
fotooptisch photo-optic[al]
Fotooxidation f photooxidation
fotooxidativ photooxidative
Fotopädagoge m photography (photographic) teacher

Fotopapier n photo paper, photographic [printing] paper, print[ing] paper; enlarging paper *(s.a. under* Papier*)*
Fotopapierrolle f roll of photographic paper
Fotophorese f photophoresis
Fotophysik f photophysics, light physics
fotophysikalisch photophysical
Fotopigment n photopigment, photosensitive pigment
fotopisch photopic, light-adapted
Fotoplastik f photosculpture
Fotoplatte f photoplate, photographic (film) plate
Fotoplethysmograf m photoplethysmograph
Fotoplethysmografie f photoplethysmography
fotoplethysmografisch photoplethysmographic
Fotoplotter m laser plotter
Fotopolymer n photopolymer, photosensitive polymer
Fotopolymerdruckplatte f photopolymer [printing] plate; photopolymer gravure plate
Fotopolymerfilm m photopolymer (photographic polymer) film
~/**holografischer** photopolymer holographic film
Fotopolymergravur f photopolymer gravure
Fotopolymerisation f photopolymerization, photochemical polymerization
fotopolymerisierbar photopolymerizable
fotopolymerisieren to photopolymerize
Fotopolymerklischee n, **Fotopolymerplatte** f s. Fotopolymerdruckplatte
Fotopolymerschicht f photopolymer coating, photoconductive polymeric layer
Fotopolymertechnik f photopolymer technology
Fotoporträt n photographic portrait
Fotopositiv n [photographic] transparency
Fotopostkarte f photographic postcard
Fotopraxis f photographic practice
Fotoprinter m photo[graphic] printer
Fotoproduktion f photofabrication
Fotoprojekt n photographic project
Fotoprozess m photographic procedure
Fotoqualität f photo quality, [true] photographic quality *(image rendition)*
Fotorahmen m photo frame
Fotoreaktion f photoreaction, photochemical reaction
Fotorealismus m photographic realism, photorealism
fotorealistisch photoreal[istic], photo-quality
Fotoredakteur m photo[graphic] editor, picture editor

fotorefraktiv [photo]refractive, dioptric
Fotoreihe f s. Fotosequenz, Fotoserie
Fotoreportage f photographic reportage, photoreportage
Fotoreporter m press (newspaper) photographer, daily news photographer
Fotoreproduktion f photographic reproduction
Fotoresist m photoresist, photosensitive resist; photopolymer resist
fotoresistiv photoresistive
Fotorestaurierung f photograph restoration, restoration of photographs
Fotoretusche f photographic retouching
Fotorezeption f photoreception
Fotorezeptor m photoreceptor, [light] receptor; photoreceptor cell, eye receptor
Foto-Ringalbum n ring[ed] binder
Fotorohpapier n photographic base paper
Fotorucksack m photo backpack
Fotosachverständiger m photographic expert
Fotosammler m photograph collector
Fotosammlung f photograph[y] collection, photographic collection
Fotosatz m photocomposition, phototypesetting, phototypography, filmsetting
~/tastaturgesteuerter keyboard-operated photocomposition
Fotosatzdrucker m phototypesetter
Fotosatzfilm m phototypesetting film
Fotosatzgerät n photocomposer, phototypesetter
Fotosatzmaschine f phototypesetting machine, phototypesetter
Fotosatzpapier n phototypesetting paper
Fotoscanner m photoscanner, photograph[ic] scanner
Fotoschablone f photomask
Fotoschale f processing dish (tray)
Fotoscheinwerfer m photoflood [lamp]
Fotoschicht f photographic layer
Fotoschule f photo[graphic] school
Foto-Sekundärelektronenvervielfacher m s. Fotoelektronenvervielfacher
fotosensibel photosensitive, light-sensitive, sensitive to light
Fotosensibilisator m photosensitizer
fotosensibilisieren to photosensitize
Fotosensibilisierung f photosensitization, light sensitization
fotosensitiv s. fotosensibel
Fotosensor m photosensor, light (optical) sensor
Fotosequenz f, **Fotoserie** f photographic series, sequence (series) of photographs
Fotoservice m photographic (photofinishing) service
Fotosession f photo shoot, photographic session (sitting)
Fotosetz... s.a. Fotosatz...

Fotosetzer m photocomposer; phototypesetter
Foto-Sichthülle f print sheet, photo pocket
Fotositzung f s. Fotosession
Fotoskulptur f photosculpture
Fotospannung f photovoltage
Fotostabilität f photostability, light stability (resistance), lightfastness
Fotostativ n camera stand
Fotostil m photographic style
Fotostrom m photocurrent, photoelectric current
Fotostudio n photography (photographic) studio
Foto-Stundenservice m one-hour [processing] lab, one-hour photolab
Fotosystem n photographic system
Fototapete f [photo]mural
Fototasche f 1. camera (photo) bag; soft camera case; 2. s. Fotoauftragstasche
Fototechnik f 1. photographic technology, phototechnology; photographic engineering; 2. photographic technique
Fototechniker m photographic technician, photomechanical worker; photo equipment technician
fototechnisch photo-technical, technical photographic
Fototechnologie f photographic technology, phototechnology
Fototeleskop n photographic telescope
Fotothek f photo[graphic] library
Fototheodolit m phototheodolite
fotothermisch photothermal
Fotothermografie f photothermography
fotothermografisch photothermographic
Fotothermometrie f photothermometry
Fototopografie f s. Fotogrammetrie
Fototransistor m phototransistor
Fototrick m photographic special effect
Fototrommel f s. Fotoleitertrommel
fototrop phototropic
Fototropie f phototropism, phototropy
Fotoüberwachung f photographic monitoring
Fotoverarbeitung f photographic processing, photoprocessing; photofinishing
~/digitale digital photofinishing
Fotoverarbeitungsindustrie f photofinishing industry
Fotoverarbeitungstechnik f photofinishing technology
Fotovergleich m photographic comparison
Fotoverlag m photographic publisher
Fotovernetzung f s. Fotopolymerisation
Fotoverschluss m photographic shutter
Fotovervielfacher m photomultiplier [tube], PMT, multiplier phototube
Foto-Volta-Effekt m photovoltaic effect
Fotovoltaik f photovoltaic[s]
fotovoltaisch photovoltaic
Fotovorlage f photographic (camera-ready) copy *(reprography)*

Fotowand f photomural
Fotowettbewerb m photo contest, print competition
Fotowiderstand m, **Fotowiderstandszelle** f photoresistor; photoconductive cell *(photoelectric sensor)*
Fotozeichnen n photogenic drawing
Fotozeitschrift f photographic journal (magazine), photography periodical
Fotozelle f photocell, photoelectric (pec) cell, photosensitive cell, electric eye
Fotozinkografie f photozincography
Fotozubehör n photographic accessories
Fourier-Analyse f Fourier (harmonic) analysis, Fourier transform[ation]
Fourier-Beschreibung f Fourier description
Fourier-Bild n Fourier image
Fourier-Bildanalyse f Fourier image analysis
Fourier-Bildgewinnung f Fourier [transform] imaging
Fourier-Darstellung f Fourier series representation
Fourier-Deskriptor m Fourier descriptor *(e.g. of a digital boundary)*
Fourier-Ebene f Fourier [transform] plane, focal plane
Fourier-Filter n Fourier filter
Fourier-Filterung f Fourier [domain] filtering
Fourier-Holografie f Fourier-transform holography
Fourier-Hologramm n Fourier-transform hologram
Fourier-Integral n Fourier integral
Fourier-Koeffizient m Fourier [transform] coefficient
~/**komplexer** complex Fourier coefficient
Fourier-Komponente f Fourier component
Fourier-Konstante f s. Fourier-Koeffizient
Fourier-Merkmal n Fourier descriptor
Fourier-Modell n Fourier model
Fourier-Optik f Fourier optics
fourieroptisch Fourier-optics, Fourier optical
Fourier-Raum m Fourier space (domain)
Fourier-Reihe f Fourier series (sequence)
Fourier-Reihenentwicklung f Fourier-series expansion
Fourier-Rekonstruktion f Fourier reconstruction
Fourier-Rücktransformation f inverse Fourier transform, Fourier inversion
~/**diskrete** inverse discrete Fourier transform, IDFT
Fourier-Scheibentheorem n s. Projektionstheorem
Fourier-Schnelltransformation f fast Fourier transform, FFT
Fourier-Spektrometer n Fourier-transform spectrometer
Fourier-Spektroskopie f Fourier-transform spectroscopy
Fourier-Spektrum n Fourier [power] spectrum, spatial-frequency spectrum
Fourier-Synthese f Fourier synthesis
Fourier-Theorie f Fourier theory
Fourier-Transformation f Fourier transform[ation], Fourier (harmonic) analysis
~/**allgemeine** s. ~/kontinuierliche
~/**analoge** analog Fourier transform
~/**diskrete** discrete (symmetric) Fourier transform, DFT
~/**diskrete schnelle** discrete fast Fourier transform, DFFT
~/**dreidimensionale** three-dimensional Fourier transform, 3-DFT
~/**eindimensionale** one-dimensional Fourier transform
~/**gefensterte** windowed Fourier transform, short-time Fourier transform, STFT
~/**inverse** inverse Fourier transform, IFT
~/**inverse diskrete** inverse discrete Fourier transform, IDFT
~/**kontinuierliche** continuous Fourier transform, CFT
~/**lokale** local Fourier transform
~/**mehrdimensional (multidimensional) diskrete** multidimensional discrete Fourier transform
~/**optische** optical Fourier transform
~/**ortsdiskrete** discrete-space Fourier transform, DSFT
~/**ortskontinuierliche** continuous-space Fourier transform
~/**räumliche** spatial Fourier transform
~/**schnelle** fast Fourier transform, FFT
~/**umgekehrte** s. ~/inverse
~/**zeitkontinuierliche** continuous-time Fourier transform
~/**zweidimensionale** two-dimensional Fourier transform, 2-DFT
~/**zweidimensionale diskrete** discrete spatial Fourier transform, DSFT
Fourier-Transformationshologramm n Fourier transform hologram
Fourier-Transformations-Infrarotspektroskopie f Fourier transform infrared spectroscopy
Fourier-Transformations-Objektiv n Fourier transform lens
Fourier-Transformationspaar n Fourier transform pair
fouriertransformieren to Fourier transform
Fourier-Transformierte f Fourier transform
~/**zeitdiskrete** discrete-time Fourier transform, DTFT
Fourier-Vorwärtstransformation f forward Fourier transform
Fourier-Zerlegung f Fourier decomposition *(wave optics)*
Fovea [centralis] f foveal center, [retinal] fovea
foveal foveal
Foveola f center of the fovea

Fragezeichen *n* question mark, interrogation point
Fragment *n* fragment
fragmentieren to fragment[ize]
fraktal fractal
Fraktal *n* fractal
~/deterministisches deterministic fractal
~/homogenes homogeneous (uniform) fractal
~/selbstähnliches self-similar fractal
Fraktalanalyse *f* fractal analysis
Fraktalbild *n* fractal image (pattern); fractal figure (construct)
Fraktalbildcodierung *f* fractal image coding
Fraktalbildkompression *f* fractal image compression
Fraktalgeometrie *f* fractal geometry
fraktalgeometrisch fractal geometric
Fraktalkompression *f* fractal[-based] compression
Fraktalprogramm *n* fractal program
Fraktaltheorie *f* fractal theory
Fraktur[schrift] *f* Fraktur, Fractur *(style of black letter)*
Frame *m(n)* frame *(esp. as an area of a computer image page)*
Framegrabber *m*, **Framegrabberkarte** *f* frame grabber (capture) card, [video] frame grabber, video digitizer, digitizing board *(high-speed memory device)*
Frame-Transfer-Bildaufnehmer *m* frame-transfer [CCD] imager, frame-transfer device
Fraunhofer-Beugung *f* Fraunhofer (far-field) diffraction
Fraunhofer-Beugungsbild *n* Fraunhofer (far-field) diffraction pattern
Fraunhofer-Holografie *f* Fraunhofer holography
Fraunhofer-Hologramm *n* Fraunhofer hologram
Fraunhofer-Linien *fpl* Fraunhofer (spectral) lines
Freeman-Code *m* Freeman [chain] code
Freeman-Kette *f* Freeman chain
Free-to-Air-Empfänger *m* free-to-air receiver
Freie-Elektronen-Laser *m* free-electron laser, FEL
Frei-Fernsehen *n* free television (TV)
Freiformfläche *f* free-form surface, arbitrarily shaped surface, arbitrary surface shape
Freiformflächendarstellung *f* free-form surface representation
Freiformobjekt *n* arbitrarily shaped object, freeform object
Freiformverformung *f* free-form deformation, FFD *(soft-object animation)*
Freiform-Wavelettransformation *f* arbitrary-shape wavelet transform
Freihandaufnahme *f* 1. handheld shot; 2. *s.* Freihandfilmen

Freihandeinsatz *m* handheld work
Freihandfilmen *n* handheld filming (shooting), off-the-cuff shooting
Freihandfotografie *f* handheld photography
Freihandschere *f* freehand scissors, lasso tool *(graphics program)*
Freihandzeichnen *n* freehand drawing *(computer graphics)*
Freiheitsgrad *m* degree of freedom, DOF *(statistics)*
Freilichtaufnahme *f* outdoor picture
Freilichtfotograf *m* outdoor photographer
Freilichtfotografie *f* outdoor photography
Freiraumübertragung *f* free-space propagation
Freistrahllaser *m* free-space laser
Freizeitfotograf *m* amateur photographer
Fremdatom *n* foreign atom
Fremdecho *n* [radar] clutter, clutter interference
Fremdgeräusch *n* extraneous [environmental] noise *(motion-picture production)*
Fremdleuchter *m* non-self-luminous source (surface)
Fremdlicht *n* extraneous light
Fremdspannung *f* noise
Fremdspannungsabstand *m* signal-to-noise ratio, SNR
Fremdstrahler *m* secondary (reflecting) light source, subtractive color
Fremdstrahlung *f* extraneous radiation
Frenkel-Defekt *m*, **Frenkel-Fehlstelle** *f* Frenkel defect (disorder)
Frenkel-Gleichgewicht *n* Frenkel equilibrium
Frequenz *f* frequency
~/abstimmbare tunable frequency *(laser)*
~/diskrete discrete frequency
~/dominante dominant wavelength *(colorimetry)*
~/harmonische harmonic frequency
~/kritische critical frequency
~/optische optical frequency
~/räumliche spatial frequency
~/zeitliche temporal frequency
Frequenzabtastung *f* frequency sampling
Frequenzachse *f* frequency axis
Frequenzanalysator *m* frequency analyzer
Frequenzanalyse *f* frequency[-domain] analysis *(e.g. of digital images)*
Frequenzänderung *f* frequency change
Frequenzanteil *m* frequency component *(e.g. of a Fourier transform)*
Frequenzauflösung *f* frequency resolution
Frequenzband *n* frequency band, band [of frequencies]
Frequenzbandbreite *f* frequency bandwidth
Frequenzbereich *m* 1. frequency range (span); frequency band; 2. frequency domain (plane); 3. *s.* Ortsfrequenzraum

Frequenzbereichsauflösung f frequency-domain resolution
Frequenzbereichsbild n frequency-domain image
Frequenzbereichsdarstellung f frequency-domain representation; frequency-space representation
Frequenzbereichsfilter n frequency-domain filter
Frequenzbereichsfilterung f frequency-domain filtering
Frequenzbereichsfunktion f frequency-domain function
Frequenzbereichssignal n frequency-domain signal
Frequenzbereichswert m frequency-domain value
Frequenzcodiergradient m s. Frequenzgradient
Frequenzcodierung f frequency encoding *(e.g. in magnetic resonance imaging)*
Frequenzcodierungsrichtung f frequency-encoding direction
Frequenzdifferenz f frequency difference
Frequenzebene f frequency plane (domain)
Frequenzfilter n frequency [weighting] filter
Frequenzfilterung f/**räumliche** spatial frequency filtering
Frequenzfunktion f frequency function
Frequenzgang m frequency response
Frequenzgehalt m frequency content
Frequenzgemisch n frequency spectrum
Frequenzgradient m frequency-encoding gradient, readout gradient *(magnetic resonance imaging)*
Frequenzhub m frequency sweep
Frequenzinterferenz f frequency interference
Frequenzintervall n frequency interval
Frequenzinversion f frequency inversion
Frequenzkoeffizient m frequency coefficient
Frequenzkomponente f frequency component *(e.g. of a Fourier transform)*
Frequenzkonversion f frequency conversion; rate conversion
Frequenzkurve f frequency response curve (function)
Frequenzmaskierung f frequency masking (dependence) *(video compression)*
Frequenzmischer m frequency mixer
Frequenzmodulation f frequency modulation, FM
~/**lineare** linear frequency modulation
~/**orthogonale** orthogonal frequency division modulation, OFDM
~/**sequentielle** sequential frequency modulation
frequenzmoduliert frequency-modulated
Frequenzmultiplexen n, **Frequenzmultiplextechnik** f, **Frequenzmultiplexverfahren** n frequency[-division] multiplexing, FDM

~/**orthogonales** orthogonal frequency division multiplex, OFDM
Frequenzraster m(n) frequency raster
Frequenzraum m frequency space, wave number domain
Frequenzraumdarstellung f frequency-space representation
Frequenzrauschen n frequency[-dependent] noise
Frequenzregelung f/**automatische** automatic frequency control, AFC
Frequenzschwankung f frequency change; frequency jitter
Frequenzsignal n frequency signal
Frequenzspektrum n frequency spectrum
~/**diskretes** discrete frequency spectrum
~/**kontinuierliches** continuous frequency spectrum
Frequenzsprungmodulation f s. Frequenzumtastung
Frequenzstabilität f frequency stability
Frequenzsteuerung f s. Frequenzregelung
Frequenzsynthese f frequency synthesis
Frequenzteiler m frequency divider; field divider *(television)*
Frequenztransformation f frequency transform[ation]
~/**selektive** subband coding (compression), SBC
Frequenzüberlappung f frequency overlap
Frequenzumfang m frequency range
Frequenzumtastung f frequency shift keying, FSK
Frequenzverdoppler m frequency doubler
Frequenzverdopplung f frequency doubling
Frequenzverdreifacher m frequency tripler
Frequenzverkämmung f frequency interleaving (interlace)
Frequenzverlauf m frequency response
Frequenzverschachtelung f s. Frequenzverkämmung
Frequenzverschiebung f frequency shift
Frequenzverteilung f frequency distribution
Frequenzverzerrung f frequency aliasing (distortion)
Frequenzwahl f frequency selection, choice of frequency
Frequenzzerlegung f frequency separation
Fresnel-Beugung f Fresnel (near-field) diffraction
~ **am Spalt** Fresnel diffraction from a slit
Fresnel-Effekt m Fresnel effect
Fresnel-Holografie f Fresnel holography
Fresnel-Hologramm n Fresnel hologram
Fresnel-Linse f Fresnel lens
Fresnel-Platte f [Fresnel] zone plate *(diffractive focusing element)*
Fresnel-Reflexion f Fresnel (mirror) reflection, specular (direct) reflection
Fresnel-Rhomboid n Fresnel rhomb
Fresnel-Scheibe f Fresnel screen
Fresnel-Spiegellinse f Fresnel mirror

Fresnel-Verlust

Fresnel-Verlust m Fresnel [reflection] loss
Fresnel-Zahl f Fresnel number *(wave optics)*
Friktionsantrieb m friction drive
Friktionskopf m friction head *(tripod)*
Friktionskupplung f friction clutch
Friktionstrieb m friction drive
Frischband n virgin stock (tape) *(s.a. Band/unbespieltes)*
Frontalaufnahme f [full] front view
Frontalbeleuchtung f front (flat) lighting
Frontalität f frontality
Frontallicht n front light
Frontalporträt n portrait *en face*
Frontansicht f frontal view
Frontglas n faceplate
Frontglied n front component, front element (optics) *(objective)*
Frontgruppe f front group *(lens)*
Frontlinse f front (foremost) lens
Frontlinsenschutzfilter n front lens protective filter
Frontplatte f faceplate, [monitor] front face
Frontprojektion f front projection [process], reflex projection
Frontprojektionseinrichtung f front projection setup
Frontprojektionswand f front-projection screen
Frontprojektor m front projector
Frontscheibe f faceplate, [monitor] front face
Frontstandarte f front [camera] standard, [front] lens standard *(view camera)*
Frosch m s. Froschstativ
Froschperspektive f worm's-eye view, mouse-eye's view
Froschstativ n hi-hat, top hat
Frühdruck m incunabulum, incunable
Frühwarnradar n early warning radar
FT-CCD-Bildwandler m s. Frame-Transfer-Bildaufnehmer
F-Theta-Korrektion f f theta correction *(e.g. in laser printers)*
F-Theta-Linse f, **F-Theta-Objektiv** n f theta lens *(of a scan system)*
FT-Sensor m s. Frame-Transfer-Bildaufnehmer
Führerscheinfoto n driver's license photo
Führungsbewegung f smooth-pursuit eye movement, pursuit movement
Führungsdraht m guide wire *(angiography)*
Führungsgriff m, **Führungshebel** m balance arm *(tripod)*
Führungskante f guided edge, edge guide
Führungslicht n key (primary) light, main (principal) light
Führungslichtquelle f key (dominant) light source, main (primary) light source, key
Führungs-Pit n(m) tracking pit *(videodisc)*
Führungsrille f pre-groove
Führungsrolle f guide roller; idle[r] roller
Führungssäule f [enlarger] column

Führungsschiene f guide rail; monorail *(view camera)*
Führungsstift m guide pin
Fulkrum m fulcrum, pivot point
Füllbit n stuffing bit
Fülldarstellungselement n fill primitive
Füllfaktor m [/**optischer**] fill[ing] factor
Füllfarbe f fill color
Füllfläche f, **Füllgebiet** n [solid-]fill area, solid [area] *(printing, computer graphics)*
Füllgebietsbündeltabelle f fill area bundle table
Füllgebietsfarbindex m fill area color index
Füllgebietsmenge f fill area set
Fülllicht n 1. fill [light]; 2. fill-light feature *(electroni flash unit)*
Füllmuster n key fill *(video)*
Füllsender m repeater, gap filler, intermediate broadcasting facility
Füllsignal n fill
Füllwerkzeug n [flood] fill tool
Fundamentaldifferenz f fundamental difference
Fundoskopie f funduscopy, fundoscopy
fundoskopisch funduscopic, fundoscopic
Fundusfotografie f [retinal] fundus photography
Funduskamera f fundus (ophthalmic) camera, retinal camera
Fünfseit[en]prisma n pentagonal (five-sided) prism, pentaprism
Fünfunddreißig-Millimeter-Film m thirty-five millimeter film, 35 mm film
Fungizid n fungicide, fungicidal agent *(developer additive)*
Funkauslöser m radio slave
Funkbild n radiophoto[graph], photoradiogram
Funkbildübertragung f radiophoto, photoradio
Funkelrauschen n flicker noise
Funkenbeleuchtung f spark illumination
Funkenblitzgerät n spark flash [unit]
Funkenlichtquelle f spark light (illumination) source
Funkfernauslöser m radio slave
Funkkamera f radio camera
Funkmaus f radio mouse *(handheld input device)*
Funkmikrofon n radio (wireless) microphone
Funkortung f radio location (position finding)
Funkstille f radio silence
Funktelefon n radiotelephone *(s.a. Mobiltelefon)*
Funktion f function
~/**amplitudenmodulierte** amplitude-modulated function
~/**analytische** analytic[al] function
~/**bandbreitenbegrenzte** band-limited function
~/**Boolesche** Boolean function
~/**harmonische** harmonic function

~/**komplexwertige** complex [valued] function
~/**monotone** monotonic function
~/**nichtperiodische** nonperiodic function
~/**periodische** periodic function
~/**trigonometrische** trigonometric (circular) function
~/**zweidimensionale** two-dimensional function
Funktionalbild *n* functional diagram
Funktionsaufruf *m* function call
Funktionsbaum *m*/**bandbreitenbegrenzter** band-limited functions tree
Funktionsspeicher *m* function[al] memory
Funktionssymbol *n* function symbol
Funktionsszintigrafie *f* functional scintigraphy
Funktionstaste *f* function key
Funktionsuntersuchung *f* functional imaging
Funkübertragung *f* radio transmission
Fusion *f* fusion
~/**binokulare** binocular fusion
~/**sensorische** sensory fusion
Fusionsfrequenz *f s.* Flimmerverschmelzungsfrequenz
Fusionspunkt *m* recovery point *(human vision)*
Fußempfindlichkeit *f s.* Durchhang
Fußnote *f* footnote
Fußnummer *f* [latent] edge number, footage number, negative (key) number *(motion-picture film)*
Fußrille *f* groove *(of a piece of type)*
Fußschalter *m* footswitch
Fußsteg *m* foot (tail) margin *(printed page)*
Fußstrich *m s.* Serife
Fußtitel *m* [motion-picture] subtitle, caption
Fußzeile *f* footer *(data structure)*
Fuzzifikation *f s.* Fuzzifizierung
fuzzifizieren to fuzzify
Fuzzifizierung *f* fuzzification
Fuzzy-Clusteranalyse *f* fuzzy cluster analysis
Fuzzy-Filter *n* fuzzy filter
Fuzzy-Logik *f* fuzzy logic
Fuzzy-Menge *f* fuzzy set
Fuzzy-Operator *m* fuzzy operator
Fuzzy-Regel *f* fuzzy rule
Fuzzy-System *n* fuzzy system
Fuzzy-Technik *f* fuzzy technique
Fuzzy-Theorie *f* fuzzy set theory
f-Zahl *f*, **F-Zahl** *f s.* f-Blende

G

GaAs-Laser m GaAs laser, gallium arsenide [semiconductor] laser
Gabor-Analyse f Gabor analysis
Gabor-Filter n Gabor [energy] filter
Gabor-Filterbank f Gabor filter bank
Gabor-Funktion f Gabor function *(texture visualization)*
Gabor-Hologramm n Gabor (in-line) hologram
Gabor-Textur f Gabor texture
Gabor-Transformation f Gabor [wavelet] transform
Gabor-Wavelet n Gabor wavelet
Gabriel-Graph m Gabriel graph, GG *(pattern recognition)*
Gadolinium n gadolinium *(heavy metal)*
Gadolinium-DTPA n gadolinium diethylenetriamine pentaacetic acid, Gd-DTPA *(contrast agent)*
Galaktografie f galactography
Galgen m boom [arm], jib arm *(studio lighting)*
Galilei-Fernrohr n Galilean (Dutch) telescope
Galilei-Sucher m reversed Galilean finder
Galilei-Teleskop n s. Galilei-Fernrohr
Gallengangspiegel m choledochoscope
Galliumarsenid-Feldeffekttransistor m gallium arsenide field effect transistor, GaAs FET
Galliumarsenid-Fotodiode f GaAs (gallium arsenide) photodiode
Galliumnitridlaser m gallium nitride laser
Galliumphosphid n gallium phosphide
Gallussäure f gallic acid
Galvano n electrotype
Galvanoformung f electrotyping
Galvanografie f galvanography
Galvanometer n/**registrierendes (schreibendes)** recording galvanometer
Gamma n s. 1. Gammawert; 2. Bildröhrengamma
Gammaaufnahme f gamma camera image (picture)
Gammabedingung f s. Goldberg-Bedingung
Gammadetektor m gamma ray detector
Gammadichtemesser m gamma densitometer
Gammadurchstrahlung f gamma [ray] radiography, gamma-ray imaging
Gammafehler m gamma error
Gammagrenzwert m gamma infinity
Gammakamera f [single-crystal] gamma camera, scintillation camera, Anger[-type] camera
Gammakameraaufnahme f gamma camera image (picture)
Gammakennlinie f s. Gammakurve
Gammakorrektor m gamma corrector
Gammakorrektur f gamma correction *(video signal processing)*
Gammakorrekturfaktor m gamma correction factor
Gammakorrekturtabelle f gamma correction table
Gammakurve f gamma characteristic (function) *(e.g. of a cathode-ray tube)*
Gammaquant n gamma quantum, gamma [ray] photon
Gammaradiografie f gamma [ray] radiography, gamma ray imaging
Gammarauschen n gamma (Erlang) noise
Gammaschaltung f s. Gammakorrektur
Gammaspektrometer n gamma ray spectrometer
Gammaspektroskopie f gamma spectroscopy
Gammaspektrum n gamma ray spectrum
Gammastrahl m gamma ray
Gammastrahlenbild n gamma ray image; gamma radiograph (ray photograph)
Gammastrahlenbündel n gamma ray beam
Gammastrahlenspektroskopie f gamma spectroscopy
Gammastrahlenteleskop n gamma imaging Cerenkov telescope
Gammastrahlentomografie f gamma ray tomography
Gammastrahlung f gamma [ray] radiation
Gammaverteilung f gamma distribution *(of random variables)*
Gammaverzerrung f gamma distortion
Gammavoreinstellung f,
Gammavorentzerrung f pre-knee
Gammawert m gamma [value], gamma factor *(e.g. as the straight-line slope of a D-log H curve)*
Gammawertanpassung f gamma adjustment (correction), gamma conversion
Gammawertberechnung f gamma calculation
Gamma-Zeit-Kurve f time-gamma curve, gamma-time curve
Ganglienzelle f ganglion cell, gangliocyte
Ganglienzelle/retinale retinal ganglion cell
Ganglienzellschicht f ganglion cell layer *(of the retina)*
Ganglion n [nerve] ganglion; nucleus
Ganglionzelle f s. Ganglienzelle
Gangunterschied m [/**optischer**] optical path difference, OPD
Gantry f [scanning] gantry *(tomography)*
Gantt-Diagramm n Gantt chart *(graphical tool)*

Ganzbild n [/optisches] complete (entire) image, full-sized image, full[-frame] image (s.a. Vollbild)
Ganzfoto n full photograph
Ganzgroßaufnahme f extreme close-up, XCU; tight close-up, choker close-up [shot]; big close-up, BCU
Ganzkörper-Abbildungssystem n whole-body imaging system
Ganzkörperantenne f body coil (magnetic resonance imaging)
Ganzkörperplethysmograf m total-body plethysmograph
Ganzkörperscan m whole-body scan
Ganzkörperscanner m whole-body scanner
Ganzkörperzähler m whole-body (human-body) counter
Ganzmetallgehäuse n all-metal housing
Ganzmetallkamera f all-metal camera
Ganzporträt n full-length portrait; full-length photograph
Ganzseitenanzeige f full-page display
Ganzseitenbildschirm m full-page display
Ganzseitenfilm m composite film (reprography)
Ganzseitenmontage f mechanical, pasteup, [art]board
Ganzseitenumbruch m full-page pagination, FPP
ganzseitig full-sheet
Gas n/**ionisiertes** ionized gas
Gasentladung f gas discharge
Gasentladungsbildschirm m gas discharge display
Gasentladungslampe f gas discharge lamp, vapor
Gasentladungslaser m gas laser
Gasentladungsröhre f gas discharge tube
Gaslaser m gas laser
Gasplasmabildschirm m gas plasma display
Gastransportlaser m gas transport laser
Gastroskop n gastroscope
Gastroskopie f gastroscopy
gastroskopisch gastroscopic
Gate-Elektrode f gate [electrode]
Gatterschaltung f gate circuit
Gauß n gauss, G (former unit of magnetic induction)
Gauß-Bündel n Gaussian beam (wave optics)
Gauß-Daten pl/**multivariate** multivariate Gaussian data
Gauß-Doppelobjektiv n double-Gauss lens
Gauß-Faltung f Gaussian convolution
Gauß-Fehler m spherochromatism, chromatic variation of spherical aberration
Gauß-Fehlerverteilung f Gaussian error distribution
Gauß-Fenster n Gaussian window
Gauß-Filter n Gaussian filter (kernel)

Gauß-Filterfunktion f Gaussian filter function
gaußförmig Gaussian
Gauß-Funktion f, **Gauß-Glocke** f Gaussian[-shape] function
Gauß-Hochpass m Gaussian highpass filter, GHPF
Gauß-Impuls m Gaussian (bell-shaped) pulse
Gauß-Maske f s. Gauß-Filter
Gauß-Objektiv n Gauss lens
Gauß-Pyramide f Gaussian pyramid
Gauß-Rauschen n Gaussian[-type] noise, normal noise
Gauß-Seidel-Verfahren n Gauss-Seidel method (of solving linear equations)
Gauß-Signal n s. Gauß-Impuls
Gauß-Strahl m Gaussian [ray]
Gauß-Tiefpass m Gaussian lowpass filter, GLPF
Gauß-Typ-Objektiv n Gauss-type lens
gaußverteilt Gaussian[-distributed]
Gauß-Verteilung f Gaussian distribution, normal [frequency] distribution
Gazefilter n gauze [filter] (lighting accessory)
Gebiet n/**achsnahes (paraxiales)** paraxial region (domain) (optics)
Gebietsmarkierung f region (domain) labeling, connected-component labeling (identification); blob coloring
Gebietsnachbarschaftsgraph m region adjacency graph, RAG
Gebietszerlegung f region segmentation, region-based (region-oriented) segmentation, area subdivision (computer graphics)
Gebrauchslösung f working[-strength] solution, processing solution
Gebrauchtkamera f used camera
Gedächtnis n/**neuronales** neural memory
~/**visuelles** visual memory
Gedankenskizze f scribble, scamp, [rough] sketch (layout)
Gedankenstrich m dash (punctuation mark)
gedeckt s. lichtundurchlässig
Gegenbild n s. Negativ 1.
Gegendruckzylinder m impression cylinder, impression rol[er] (printing press)
Gegenfarbe f opponent (opposite) color; complementary color (hue)
Gegenfarbensignal n s. Chrominanzsignal
Gegenfarbentheorie f opponent[-colors] theory, opponent process theory, [Hering's] opponent theory of color vision
Gegengewicht n counterbalance (e.g. on camera stands)
Gegenimpuls m blackset (electronic camera)
Gegenion n counterion
Gegenkasch m s. Gegenmaske

Gegenlicht *n* backlight[ing], contre-jour lighting
Gegenlichtaufnahme *f* backlighted [camera] shot, contre-jour [photograph]
Gegenlichtbeleuchtung *f* backlighting
Gegenlichtblende *f* lens hood (shade), sunshade
Gegenlichteffekt *m* against-the-light effect
Gegenlichtfotografie *f* backlight (contre-jour) photography
Gegenlichtkompensation *f*, **Gegenlichtkorrektur** *f* backlight compensation
Gegenlichtquelle *f* backlighting light source, backlight
Gegenlichttaste *f* backlight button, manual backlight control button *(camcorder)*
Gegenlichttubus *m s.* Gegenlichtblende
Gegenmaske *f* [background] countermatte, male (inverted) matte *(cinema)*
Gegenrichtung *f* reverse direction
Gegenstandsaufnahme *f* pack shot
Gegenstandsbild *n* object image; specimen image *(microscopy)*
Gegenstandsebene *f* subject (object) plane; sample (specimen) plane
Gegenstandsentfernung *f s.* Gegenstandsweite
Gegenstandspunkt *m* object (subject) point
Gegenstandsraum *n* object (subject) space *(optics)*
gegenstandsseitig object-side
Gegenstandsstrahl *m* object beam
Gegenstandswahrnehmung *f* perception of shape
Gegenstandsweite *f* object (subject) distance, object conjugate, working distance
Gegenstandswelle *f* object (original) wave, object (subject) beam *(holography)*
Gegenstrahlung *f* atmospheric radiation
Gegentakttonspur *f* push-pull track
Gegenuhrzeigersinn *m* counterclockwise sense
Gehäusebezug *m* leather facing *(e.g. of a camera)*
Gehäuseblitz *m* built-in flash [unit], integrated flash, built-in speedlight
Gehäusedeckel *m* body cap
Geheimkamera *f* clandestine (secret) camera, detective camera; candid camera
Geiger-Müller-Zähler *m* Geiger[-Müller] counter *(dosimetry)*
Geiger-Müller-Zählrohr *n* Geiger-Müller [counting] tube
Geigerzähler *m s.* Geiger-Müller-Zähler
Geisterartefakt *m* ghost[ing] artifact *(magnetic resonance imaging)*
Geisterbild *n* ghost image (effect)
Geisterbildentstehung *f* ghosting, image cross talk
Geisterbildunterdrückung *f* ghost cancellation
Geisterecho *n* ghost (second-trip) echo *(radar)*
Geistereffekt *m* ghosting, ghost halftone *(e.g. as printing defect)*
Gekrümmtheit *f* crookedness
Gel *n* gel
Geländeerkennungssystem *n* terrain recognition system
Geländefolgeradar *n* terrain-following radar
Geländekoordinatensystem *n* ground coordinate system
Geländemessradar *n* ground-mapping radar, GMR
Geländemodell *n*/**digitales** digital (digitized) terrain model
Geländepunkt *m* terrain point
Gelatine *f* gelatin[e]
~/wässrige aqueous gelatin
gelatinebeschichtet gelatin-coated
Gelatinebeschichtung *f* gelatin coating
Gelatine-Bindemittel *n* gelatin binder
Gelatineeffekt *m* gelatin effect, Ross effect *(photography)*
Gelatineemulsion *f* gelatin[-based] emulsion
Gelatineemulsionspapier *n* gelatin paper
Gelatineemulsionsschicht *f* gelatin emulsion layer
Gelatinefarbstoff *m* gelatin dye
Gelatinefilter *n* gelatin[-base] filter, dyed gelatin filter, [colored] gel, Wratten filter
Gelatinefolie *f* gelatin film
Gelatinehärtung *f* gelatin hardening
Gelatinehärtungsmittel *n* gelatin-hardening agent (compound)
Gelatinelösung *f* gelatin solution
Gelatinematrix *f* gelatin matrix
Gelatineplatte *f* gelatin [dry] plate
Gelatinequellung *f* gelatin swelling
Gelatinerelief *n* gelatin relief [image] *(dye transfer process of color printing)*
Gelatine-Rückguss *m* anticurl layer (backing), noncurl backing (coat) *(photographic film)*
Gelatineschicht *f* gelatin layer
Gelatineschutzschicht *f s.* Gelatineüberzug
Gelatinesilberabzug *m* silver gelatin print, gelatin-silver print
Gelatinetrocken[bild]platte *f* gelatin[-silver] dry plate
Gelatineüberzug *m* gelatin coating *(s.a. Überguss)*
Gelatineverfahren *n* gelatin process
Gelatine-Zwischenschicht *f* gelatin interlayer
Gelb *n* yellow *(subtractive primary color)*
Gelbentwickler *m* yellow [dye] developer
Gelbfarbstoff *m* yellow dye *(color photography)*
Gelbfilter *n* yellow filter, minus-blue filter
Gelbfilterschicht *f* yellow filter layer

Gelbkuppler *m* yellow [dye-forming] coupler, yellow-colored coupler
Gelbschicht *f*/**blauempfindliche** blue-sensitive yellow [dye] layer
Gelbstich *m* yellow cast (bias)
Gelegenheitsfotograf *m* point-and-shoot photographer, unsophisticated camera user
Gelenkspiegel *m* arthroscope
Gelenkspiegelung *f* arthroscopy
Gemeine *f s.* Kleinbuchstabe
Gemeinschaftsantenne[nanlage] *f* community antenna TV system, CATV
Gemeinschaftsantennenfernsehen *n* community antenna television (TV), CATV; master antenna television, MATV
Genauigkeit *f*/**fotometrische** photometric accuracy
Genauigkeitsstufe *f* level of detail, LOD *(computer graphics)*
Generation *f* generation
Generations-Rekombinations-Rauschen *n* trapping noise, g-r noise *(photodetector)*
Generationsverlust *m* generation[al] loss
generieren to render *(computer graphics)*
Genlock-Karte *f* genlock [board] *(for combining video with computer graphics)*
Geocodierung *f* geocoding
Geodäsie *f* geodesy
Geodät *m* geodesist
geodätisch geodetic[al], geodesic
Geoinformationssystem *n* geographic information system, GIS
Geometer *m* geodesist
Geometrie *f* geometry
~/**algorithmische** computational geometry
~/**analytische** analytic (coordinate) geometry
~/**darstellende** descriptive geometry
~/**diskrete** discrete geometry
~/**dreidimensionale** three-dimensional geometry
~/**ebene** planimetry
~/**Euklidische** Euclidean (parabolic) geometry
~/**fraktale** fractal geometry
~/**hyperbolische** hyperbolic geometry
~/**optische** optical geometry
~/**projektive** projective geometry
~/**Riemannsche** Riemannian geometry
~/**stochastische** stochastic geometry
Geometrieelement *n* geometry entity
Geometriefehler *m* geometric error
Geometriekompression *f* geometry compression
Geometriemodellierung *f* geometric (shape) modeling
Geometrieprozessor *m* geometry processor
geometrisch geometric[al]
Geometry/**nichteuklidische** non-Euclidean geometry
Georadar *n s.* Oberflächendurchdringungsradar
Georeferenzierung *f* georeferencing *(photogrammetry)*
Geradeausholografie *f* in-line holography
Geradeaushologramm *n* in-line hologram
Geraden *fpl*/**Juddsche** Judd correction *(colorimetry)*
Geradenapproximation *f* straight-line approximation
Geradenerkennung *f* straight-line recognition
Geradenstück *n* straight-line segment *(graphics primitive)*
geradestoßen *s.* glattstoßen
Geradführung *f* straight-line mechanism
Geradheit *f* straightness *(shape feature)*
geradlinig rectilinear; straight
Geradlinigkeit *f* linearity; straightness [of lines]
Geradmagazin *n* straight cartridge *(slide projector)*
Geradsichtprisma *n* [**nach Amici**] direct-vision prism, Amici (roof) prism
Geradsichtspektroskop *n* direct-vision [pocket] spectroscope
Gerät *n* device, appliance, contrivance
~/**audiovisuelles** audiovisual device
~/**bildgebendes** imaging device
~/**fotoelektrisches** photoelectric device
~/**grafisches** graphics device
~/**optisches** optical device
~/**peripheres** peripheral device (add-on), [external] peripheral
~/**virtuelles** virtual device
geräteabhängig device-dependent *(software)*
Geräteabhängigkeit *f* device (hardware) dependency
Geräteabschaltung *f* close-down
Gerätebereich *m* device space
Gerätedarstellungsfeld *n* device (workstation) viewport
Gerätefenster *n* workstation window
Gerätekoordinate *f* device coordinate
Gerätekoordinatensystem *n* [imaging] device coordinate system
Geräteschnittstelle *f*/**analoge** component analog interface
~/**grafische** graphical device interface, GDI, computer graphics interface, CGI
Gerätetransformation *f* workstation transformation
Gerätetreiber *m* device driver *(software)*
geräteunabhängig device-independent *(software)*
Geräusch *n* sound; noise *(s.a.* Rauschen*)*
Geräuscharchiv *n* [sound-]effects library
Geräuscheffekt *m* sound effect, Foley [sound] effect
Geräuschemacher *m* Foley artist (operator)
Geräuschetechniker *m* Foley editor
Geräuschkulisse *f* background noise
Geräuschpegel *m* noise level

Geräuschspannung f psophometric voltage
Geräuschstudio n Foley stage
Geräuschtonspur f effects track
Geräuschuntermalung f background noise
Gerbentwickler m tanning (hardening) developer
Gerbentwicklung f tanning development
Gerbwirkung f tanning action *(of developer)*
Gerichtetheit f directionality *(e.g. of textures)*
Gerichtsfoto n forensic photo[graph]
Gerichtsfotograf m forensic photographer
Gerichtsfotografie f forensic photography
gerichtsfotografisch forensic photographic
Germanium-Fotoleiter m germanium photoconductor
Gesamtaufhellung f overall light
Gesamtauflösung f overall resolution
Gesamtaufnahme f establishing shot *(cinema)*
Gesamtausleuchtung f, **Gesamtbeleuchtung** f total illumination
Gesamtbelichtung f, **Gesamtbelichtungszeit** f total (overall) exposure
Gesamtbild n total (overall) image, overall picture
Gesamtbrennweite f total (effective) focal length; combined (composite) focal length *(e.g. of camera lens and supplementary lens)*
Gesamtentwicklungszeit f total development time
Gesamtfehler m [/**optischer**] overall (total) aberration
Gesamthelligkeit f overall (total) brightness *(e.g. of a display)*
Gesamtklirrfaktor m total harmonic distortion
Gesamtkontrast m total (overall) contrast, general contrast
Gesamtleuchtkraft f, **Gesamtleuchtstärke** f total luminosity
Gesamtlöschung f bulk erasure
Gesamtrauschen n total (overall) noise; total (background) image noise
Gesamtreflexion f total reflection
Gesamtreflexionsgrad m total reflection factor, total reflectance
Gesamtschärfe f overall sharpness
Gesamtspin m total spin
Gesamttonspur f print[ing] master, complete sound track
Gesamtunschärfe f total image unsharpness
Gesamtverarbeitungszeit f overall processing time
Gesamtvergrößerung f total (overall) magnification *(e.g. of a microscope)*
Gesamtverstärkung f gain *(sonography)*

Gesamtzeilendauer f total line time *(television signal)*
Geschäftsdrucksache f business form
Geschäftsdrucksachenherstellung f business printing
Geschäftsgrafik f business graphics
Geschwindigkeit f velocity, speed
~/**linearkonstante** constant linear velocity, CLV
~/**relativistische** relativistic velocity, beta
Geschwindigkeitscodierung f velocity encoding *(phase-contrast angiography)*
Geschwindigkeitsfehler m velocity error
Geschwindigkeitsfehlerausgleicher m, **Geschwindigkeitsfehlerkorrektor** m velocity [error] compensator
Geschwindigkeitsfeld n velocity (motion) field
Geschwindigkeitskonstanz f velocity (motion) constancy
Geschwindigkeitsvektor m velocity (flow) vector, displacement vector
Gesetz n/**Abneysches** Abney law *(optics, photometry)*
~/**Beersches** Beer's law *(of radiation absorption)*
~/**Blochsches** Bloch's law *(light perception)*
~/**Bouguer-Lambertsches**, ~/**Bouguersches** Bouguer-Lambert law, Bouguer's law *(optics)*
~/**Brewstersches** Brewster's law
~/**Bunsen-Roscoesches** Bunsen Roscoe law, Bunsen-Roscoe reciprocity law
~/**Fechnersches** Fechner's law, Weber-Fechner law, Weber's law *(psychophysics)*
~/**Grothus-Drapersches** Grot[t]hus-Draper law, first law of photochemistry
~/**Kirchhoffsches** Kirchhoff's law
~/**Lambert-Beersches** Beer-Lambert [absorption] law, Beer's (Lambert's) law *(radiation attenuation)*
~/**Lambertsches** s. 1. ~/Bouguer-Lambertsches; 2. Kosinusgesetz[/Lambertsches]
~/**Riccos** Ricco's law *(visual perception)*
~/**Scheimpflugsches** Scheimpflug rule (law)
~/**Stefan-Boltzmannsches** Stefan-Boltzmann law (equation)
~/**Weber-Fechnersches** s. ~/Fechnersches
~/**Wiensches** Wien's radiation (displacement) law *(blackbody radiation)*
Gesetze npl/**Grassmannsche** Grassman's laws [of additive color mixture]
Gesichts[ausdrucks]animation f face (facial) animation, facial expressions (feature) animation
Gesichtsbild n face (facial) image
Gesichtsempfindung f visual sensation
Gesichtserkennung f face detection; face (facial) recognition

Gesichtserkennungsmerkmal *n* facial recognition feature
Gesichtserkennungssystem *n* face detection and recognition system
Gesichtsfeld *n* 1. visual field, field of vision, FOV *(s.a. Blickfeld)*; 2. lens coverage
~/**binokulares** binocular visual field, binocular field of vision
~/**momentanes** instantaneous field of view (vision), IFOV
~/**monokulares** monocular visual field, monocular field of vision
~/**scheinbares** apparent field [of view]
Gesichtsfeldblende *f* field stop (diaphragm)
Gesichtsfelddefekt *m* scotoma *(disorder of vision)*
Gesichtsfeldgröße *f* visual field size
Gesichtslinie *f s.* 1. Blicklinie; 2. Blickachse
Gesichtsmerkmal *n* facial feature
Gesichtsfeldmesser *m* campimeter, perimeter *(an eye test apparatus)*
Gesichtsfeldmessung *f* perimetry, campimetry
Gesichtsmodellierung *f* facial model[l]ing
Gesichtssinn *m* sense of sight, visual sense, [sense of] vision
Gesichtswahrnehmung *f* 1. visual perception; 2. face perception
Gesichtswinkel *m* visual angle
gesperrt justified loose *(line of text)*
Gestalt *f* shape; figure; hanging-togetherness, gestalt
~ **aus Schattierung** shape-from-shading [technique], structure from shading
~ **aus Textur** shape-from-texture [technique]
Gestaltfaktor *m* Gestalt factor *(human vision)*
Gestaltgesetz *n* gestalt law
Gestaltinformation *f* gestalt information
Gestaltmerkmal *n* shape feature
Gestaltmodellierung *f* shape modeling
Gestaltpsychologie *f* gestalt psychology
Gestalttheorie *f* gestaltism, gestalt theory *(of human perception)*
Gestaltungsraster *m(n)* grid *(typography)*
Gestaltungsvorlage *f* layout
Gestaltwahrnehmung *f* perception of shape, shape perception
Gestaltwandel (Gestaltwechsel) *m* [/**computeranimierter**] [image] morphing, polymorphic tweening *(animation technique)*
Gestenerkennung *f* [hand] gesture recognition
Getriebe[neige]kopf *m* geared head
Geviert *n* 1. quadrangle; quad[rat]; 2. [em] quad *(type-metal space)*
Geviertstrich *m* [em] dash, em rule *(typography)*
Gewässertiefenkarte *f* bathymetric map
Gewebecharakterisierung *f* tissue characterization

Gitter

Gewebediskriminierung *f* tissue discrimination
Gewebefarbband *n* fabric (textile) ribbon
Gewebeklassifikation *f* tissue classification
Gewebekontrast *m* tissue contrast
Gewebewichtungsfaktor *m* tissue[-specific] weighting factor *(X-ray dosimetry)*
Gewehrzielfernrohr *n* [gun]sight, rifle (gun) scope *(s.a. Zielfernrohr)*
Gewerbe *n*/**grafisches** graphic-design profession
Gewichtsfunktion *f* weighting function
Gewichtsmatrix *f* weight[ing] matrix
Gewichtsvektor *m* weight vector
Gewindeanschluss *m* thread[ed] mount, screw thread, screw-type lens mount
Gewinn *m*/**optischer** optical gain
Gewitterecho *n* thunderstorm echo *(radar)*
Gibbs-Artefakt *n*, **Gibbs-Phänomen** *n* Gibbs artifact (phenomenon), Gibbs effect, truncation (ringing) artifact
Gibbs-Verteilung *f*, **Gibbs-Zufallsfeld** *n* Gibbs distribution *(image segmentation)*
gieren to yaw
Gierwinkel *m* yaw angle *(e.g. of a camera)*
Gießkopf *m* coating head *(photosensitive materials manufacturing)*
Gießmaschine *f* 1. coating machine *(film manufacture)*; 2. [type]caster, typecasting machine
GIF *s.* GIF-Grafikformat
GIF-Animation *f* animated GIF
GIF-Datei *f* GIF file
~/**animierte** animated GIF
GIF-Grafikformat *n* graphics interchange format, GIF *(standard computer file format)*
Gigabyte *n* gigabyte, Gb
Gigahertz *n* gigahertz, GHz *(unit of frequency)*
Gitter *n* lattice, grating; grid; mesh
~/**abbildendes** imaging grating
~/**diffraktives** diffraction grating (grid)
~/**diskretes** discrete grid
~/**ebenes** plane grating
~/**geblaztes** blazed grating, blaze grid, echelette [grating] *(optics)*
~/**gleichmäßiges** regular grid (mesh), uniform grid, structured points
~/**hexagonales** hexagonal grid (lattice)
~/**holografisches** hologram grating, holographic lattice
~/**kartes[ian]isches** Cartesian grid
~/**kubisches** cubic lattice
~/**optisches** optical grating
~/**quadratisches** square grid (lattice)
~/**rechtwinkliges** rectilinear grid *(data structure)*
~/**reziprokes** reciprocal lattice
~/**szintillierendes** scintillation grid *(optical illusion)*
~/**unstrukturiertes** unstructured grid
~/**versetztes** staggered grid *(visualization)*

Gitter

~/**vollkommenes** perfect grating
Gitterabstand *m* grid (grating) spacing, lattice spacing
Gitteranordnung *f* grating array; lattice arrangement *(e.g. of atoms)*
Gitteraufstellung *f* mounting *(diffraction grating spectrography)*
Gitterausbeute *f* grating efficiency
Gitterbaufehler *m*, **Gitterbaufehlstelle** *f* lattice defect
Gitterbeugungsbild *n* diffraction grating pattern
Gitterbild *n* lattice image
Gitterbindung *f* lattice coupling (binding) *(of electrons)*
Gitterblock *m* grid block
Gitterdarstellung *f* mesh representation *(e.g. of surfaces)*
Gitterdatei *f* grid file *(as a data structure in image retrieval)*
Gitterebene *f* lattice plane
Gitterelektrode *f* grid electrode *(cathode-ray tube)*
Gitterfehler *m* lattice imperfection; grating imperfection
Gitterfilter *n* star [burst] filter, cross star (screen) filter
Gitterfrequenz *f* grating frequency
Gittergeometrie *f* grating geometry
Gittergleichung *f* grating equation
Gittergrafik *f* wire frame
Gitterion *n* lattice ion
Gitterknoten *m* grid node
Gitterkonstante *f* lattice constant
Gitterlinie *f* grid (grating) line, lattice line
Gitterlinienschnittpunkt *m* grid-line intersection
Gittermaske *f* grid mask
Gittermattscheibe *f* reticulated screen
Gittermodell *n* wire frame [model], wire frame object, net model *(computer graphics)*
Gittermuster *n* grid (grating) pattern
Gitternetz *n* grid [of] lines, grid, graticule; mesh *(s.a. Raster)*
Gitternetzdarstellung *f* mesh[-based] representation *(computer graphics)*
Gitteröffnung *f* grating aperture
Gitteroptimierung *f* mesh optimization
Gitterordnung *f* grating order
Gitterprisma *n* grating prism *(astronomical spectroscopy)*
Gitterprofil *n* grating profile
Gitterpunkt *m* grid (mesh) point, lattice point
~/**reziproker** reciprocal lattice point (node) *(electron diffraction pattern)*
Gitterquadrat *n* grid square
Gitterschnittpunkt *m* s. Gitterpunkt
Gitterschwingung *f* lattice vibration
~/**quantisierte** s. Phonon
Gitterspannung *f* grid voltage *(cathode-ray tube)*
Gitterspektrograf *m* [diffraction] grating spectrograph
Gitterspektrum *n* lattice spectrum
Gitterstelle *f* lattice site (position)
Gitterstruktur *f* lattice structure
Gittertestbild *n*, **Gittertesttafel** *f* convergence pattern
gittertheoretisch lattice-theoretic
Gittertheorie *f* lattice (grating) theory
Gittertopologie *f* grid topology
Gittervektor *m* grating (grid) vector
Gittervereinfachungsalgorithmus *m* mesh simplification algorithm *(image analysis)*
Gittervorsatz *m* egg crate [grid] *(lighting accessory)*
Gitterzelle *f* grid cell
Glamourfotografie *f* glamour photography
Glanz *m* gloss, sheen, shininess, luster, lustre
~/**binokularer (stereoskopischer)** binocular luster
Glanzdruckfarbe *f* gloss ink
glänzend glossy, shiny, lustrous
Glanzfarbe *f* gloss[y] ink *(printing)*
Glanzfolie *f* laminating film
Glanzfolienkaschierung *f* 1. film laminating; 2. film laminate
Glanzlicht *n* specular highlight, dropout highlight *(s.a. Spitzlicht, Hochlicht)*
Glanzpunkt *m* specular point
Glanzseite *f* non-emulsion side, back of the film
Glanzwinkel *m* glancing angle; Bragg angle
Glanzzahl *f*/**visuelle** luster number *(graphic arts)*
Glas *n* glass
~/**blendfreies** nonglare glass
~/**extremes** exotic optical glass
~/**fototropes** phototropic glass
~/**hochbrechendes** high-index glass
~/**niedrigbrechendes** low-index glass
~/**optisches** optical glass
~/**organisches** organic glass *(s.a. Kunststoff/optischer)*
~/**starkbrechendes** high-index glass
~/**unvergütetes** uncoated glass
~/**UV-absorbierendes** ultraviolet-absorbing glass
Glasart *f* kind of glass
Glasaufnahme *f* [painted] glass shot *(motion-picture effect)*
Glasblock *m* glass block
Glasdia *n* glass[-mounted] slide
Glasdiagramm *n* optical glass chart, diagram of optical glasses, glass map (veil)
Glasdiarahmen *m* glass mount
Glasfaser *f* glass (optical) fiber
Glasfaserendoskop *n* fiber-optic endoscope, fiberscope [device], flexible imagescope
Glasfaserkabel *n* fiber-optic cable, optical[-fiber] cable, light guide cable

Glasfasernetz *n* optical [fiber] network
Glasfaseroptik *f* fiber optics
Glasfilter *n* solid glass filter, glass[-mounted] filter
Glasgravurraster *m(n)* glass [halftone] screen, ruled screen
Glaskatalog *m* glass catalog
Glaskeramik *f* devitrified glass, glass ceramic
Glaskörper *m* vitreous [humor], vitreous body *(of the eye)*
Glaskörperkanal *m* hyaloid canal *(of the eye)*
Glaslaminat *n* glass laminate
Glaslinse *f* glass lens
Glas-Luft-Fläche *f* air-glass interface
Glasnegativ *n* glass[-plate] negative, [glass-]plate negative, negative plate
Glasplatte *f* glass plate
Glasprisma *n* [optical] glass prism
Glasrahmen *m* glass mount
Glasraster *m(n) s.* Glasgravurraster
Glasrezeptur *f* glass formulation
Glasrohling *m* glass blank
Glasschmelze *f* glass melt
Glassorte *f* glass type, type of glass
Glasspiegel *m* glass mirror
~/**silberbeschichteter (versilberter)** silver-on-glass mirror
Glastyp *m* glass type
Glasvorsatzaufnahme *f s.* Glasaufnahme
Glaszusammensetzung *f* glass formulation
glätten *n* to smooth *(e.g. a binary image)*
Glattheit *f* smoothness *(e.g. of a curve)*
Glattheitsbedingung *f* smoothness constraint *(image modeling)*
Glattheitsmaß *n* smoothness measure
Glattheitsterm *m* smoothness term
glattstoßen to jog *(printed sheets)*
Glättung *f* smoothing, fairing
~/**adaptive** adaptive smoothing
~/**kantenerhaltende** edge-preserving smoothing
~/**morphologische** morphological smoothing
~/**nichtlineare** nonlinear smoothing
~/**selektive** selective smoothing
Glättungsalgorithmus *m* smoothing algorithm
Glättungsfilter *n* smoothing filter (mask), smoother *(s.a. Tiefpassfilter)*
Glättungsfunktion *f* smooth[ing] function, smoothing filter function
Glättungskern *m* smoothing kernel
~ *m*/**Gaußscher** Gaussian smoothing kernel
Glättungsmaske *f s.* Glättungskern
Glättungsmatrix *f* smoothing matrix
Glättungsoperation *f* smoothing operation (procedure)
Glättungsoperator *m*/**Gaußscher** Gaussian smoothing operator
Glättungsparameter *m* smoothing parameter

Glättungswirkung *f* smoothing effect
gleichabständig equidistant, equally distant *(e.g. sample values)*
Gleichanteil *m* bias
Gleichenergieweiß *n* equal-energy white *(color television)*
gleichfarbig like-colored, isochromatic; homochromatic
Gleichfrequenznetz *n s.* Gleichwellennetz
gleichgestaltig isomorph[ic], isomorphous
Gleichgestaltigkeit *f* isomorphism
Gleichheitsfotometer *n* equality-of-brightness photometer
Gleichheitsverfahren *n* calibrated atlas method *(color measurement)*
gleichhell isoluminant, equiluminant, equiluminous
Gleichlauf *m* synchronism
Gleichlaufschwankung *f* wow and flutter *(distortion in reproduced sound)*
~/**langsame** wow
~/**schnelle** flutter
Gleichlaufsignal *n*, **Gleichlaufzeichen** *n* sync[chronizing] signal, synchronization signal, sync[hronization] pulse
Gleichphasigkeit *f* phase coherence
Gleichrichter *m* rectifier
Gleichstrom *m* direct current, DC, dc
Gleichung *f*/**Helmholtz-Lagrangesche** Helmholtz-Lagrange relationship *(refractive optics)*
Gleichungen *fpl*/**Fresnelsche** Fresnel['s] equations *(wave optics)*
Gleichverteilung *f* uniform distribution
Gleichwellennetz *n* single-frequency network, SFN
Gleitbahn *f* slideway *(cine camera)*
Gleitkommaarithmetik *f* floating-point arithmetic
Gleitkommabild *n* floating-point representation
Gleitkommafilter *n* floating-point filter
Gleitkommaoperation *f* floating-point [mathematical] operation
Gleitkommarechnung *f* floating-point calculation (computation)
Gleitmittel *n* lubricant
Gleitpunkt... *s.* Gleitkomma...
Gliederung *f*/**linienhafte** structural analysis
Glimmlampe *f* glow lamp
g-Linie *f* g-line
Glint *m* [specular] glint, specular flash *(radar)*
Globalstrahlung *f* global (total) radiation
Glockenkurve *f* bell-shaped curve (function), bell (normal distribution) curve, Gaussian (normal) curve *(s.a. Gauß-Verteilung)*
Gloriole *f s.* Haarlicht
Glühbirne *f s.* Glühlampe
Glühemission *f* thermionic emission
Glühfaden *m* thermal (heated) filament
Glühfadenlampe *f* filament lamp
Glühkatode *f* thermionic cathode

Glühkatodenröhre *f* thermionic (hot-cathode) tube
Glühlampe *f* incandescent [electric] lamp, filament lamp, [incandescent] lightbulb; tungsten lamp
~/**mattierte** frosted [white] bulb
Glühlampenlicht *n* incandescent light ; tungsten light
Glühlicht *n* incandescent light; tungsten light
Glühlichtquelle *f* incandescent (hot light) source
Glühwendel *f* coiled filament
Glühwendelbild *n* filament image
Glycerin *n*, **Glycerol** *n* glycerin[e], glycerol *(used e.g. as humectant)*
Glycin *n* glycin *(developing agent)*
Glyphe *f* glyph *(visualization)*
Glyphenhöhe *f* font (type) size, size of type, body size
Golay-Detektor *m s.* Golay-Zelle
Golay-Zelle *f* Golay cell *(thermal radiation detector)*
Goldberg-Bedingung *f* Goldberg condition
Goldberg-Keil *m* Goldberg wedge
Goldsalz *n* gold salt
Gold-Schwefel-Reifung *f* sulfur-plus-gold sensitization, gold and sulfur sensitization
Goldsensibilisator *m* gold sensitizer
Goldsensibilisierung *f* gold sensitization
Goldtoner *m* gold toner
Goldtonung *f* gold toning
Golomb-Code *m* Golomb code *(image compression)*
Goniofotometer *n* goniophotometer
goniofotometrisch goniophotometric
Goniometer *n* goniometer
goniometrisch goniometric[al]
Gotisch *f* gothic *(typeface)*
Gouraud-Schattierung *f* Gouraud (intensity interpolation) shading, color interpolation shading, smooth (linear) shading *(computer graphics)*
GPI-Schnittstelle *f* general-purpose interface, GPI
GPS *n*/**erweitertes (genaueres)** differential global positioning system, DGPS
Gradation *f* [photographic] gradation, local contrast ; gamma [value]
~/**flache** flat gradation
~/**weiche** smooth gradation
Gradationsentzerrung *f* gamma correction *(video signal processing)*
Gradationsfunktion *f* grading function
Gradationskurve *f* characteristic (density) curve, [photographic] response curve, [characteristic] D-log H curve
Gradationskurvenbereich *m*/**geradliniger** straight line [of the characteristic curve], straight line portion (region), mid-scale region
Gradationspapier *n* graded paper
Gradationsstufe *f* gradation level
Gradationswandelpapier *n* variable-contrast paper, VC paper
Gradationsziffer *f* grade number *(of photographic paper)*
Gradient *m* gradient
~/**biphasischer** biphasic gradient
~/**bipolarer** bipolar gradient
~/**digitaler** digital gradient
~/**lokaler** local gradient
~/**mittlerer** average gradient (slope), G bar *(densitometry)*
~/**morphologischer** morphological gradient
~/**optischer** optical gradient
~/**räumlicher** spatial gradient
~/**thermischer** thermal gradient (profile)
~/**ungerichteter** nondirectional gradient
~ **zweiter Ordnung** second-order gradient
Gradientenabstieg *m* gradient descent *(neuroinformatics)*
Gradientenabstiegsmethode *f*, **Gradientenabstiegsverfahren** *n* gradient descent method (procedure)
Gradientenamplitude *f* gradient amplitude
Gradientenanalyse *f* gradient analysis
Gradientenbetrag *m* gradient value (magnitude)
Gradientenbetragsbild *n*, **Gradientenbild** *n* 1. gradient image; 2. gradient echo image
Gradientendetektor *m* gradient detector
Gradientenecho *n* gradient[-recalled] echo, gradient-refocused echo
~/**multiplanares** multiplanar gradient echo
Gradientenechobild *n* gradient echo image
Gradientenechosequenz *f* gradient echo [pulse] sequence
~/**schnelle** rapid gradient echo pulse sequence
Gradientenfaser *f* graded-index [optical] fiber
Gradientenfeld *n* [/**magnetisches**] gradient [magnetic] field *(magnetic resonance imaging)*
Gradientenfilter *n* gradient filter
Gradientenindexglas *n* gradient index glass
Gradientenindex-Mikrolinse *f* gradient index micro lens
Gradientenoperator *m* gradient operator
~/**diskreter** discrete gradient operator
~/**lokaler** local gradient operator
Gradientenoptik *f* graded-index optics, GRIN optics
Gradientenorientierung *f s.* Gradientenrichtung
Gradientenpuls *m* gradient pulse
Gradientenquantisierung *f* gradient quantization
Gradientenraum *m* gradient space
Gradientenrefokussierung *f* gradient refocusing
Gradientenrichtung *f* gradient direction (orientation)

Gradientenschattierung f [gray-level] gradient shading
Gradientenschätzung f gradient estimation
Gradientenspule f gradient coil *(magnetic resonance imaging)*
Gradientensystem n gradient system
Gradiententäuschung f gradient illusion *(optical illusion)*
Gradientenvektor m gradient vector
~/**normalisierter** normalized gradient vector
~/**räumlicher** spatial gradient vector
Gradientenverstärker m gradient amplifier *(magnetic resonance imaging)*
Gradiometer n gradiometer
Grafik f 1. graphics *(s.a. under* Computergrafik*)*; 2. graphic; chart *(s.a.* Darstellung/grafische*)*
~/**animierte** animation
~/**anklickbare** clickable (image) map *(World Wide Web)*
~/**bildbasierte** image-based graphics
~/**digitale** digital graphics
~/**interaktive** interactive graphics
~/**objektorientierte** s. ~/vektororientierte
~/**repro[duktions]fähige** camera-ready art[work]
~/**vektororientierte** vector[-based] graphics, object-oriented graphics
Grafikadapter m s. Grafikkarte
Grafikalgorithmus m graphics algorithm
Grafikanschluss m/**beschleunigter** s. Grafikschnittstelle/beschleunigte
Grafikanwendung f graphics application
Grafikanwendungsprogramm n graphics application program
Grafikanzeige f s. Grafikbildschirm
Grafikarbeitsplatz[rechner] m graphics [computer] workstation, image (imaging computer) workstation
Grafikarchitektur f graphics architecture
Grafikauflösung f graphical resolution
Grafikausgabe f graphical output
Grafikaustauschformat n graphics interchange format, GIF *(standard computer file format)*
Grafikbefehl m graphics command (instruction)
Grafikbereich m/**erweiterter** extended graphics array, XGA *(display mode)*
Grafikbeschleuniger m graphics accelerator [card], video accelerator *(s.a.* Grafikkarte, Videokarte*)*
Grafikbeschleunigung f graphics acceleration
Grafikbetriebssystem n graphical operating system, graphic-based computer operating system
Grafikbibliothek f graphics library, GL
Grafikbildschirm m graphics screen, graphics display [screen], graphical (computer-graphic) display; cathode-ray graphic display

Grafikchip m graphics [controller] chip, graphics processor
Grafikcompiler m graphical compiler
Grafikcomputer m graphics computer
Grafik-Controller m graphics [display] controller
Grafikdarstellung f graphic[al] representation (depiction), graphic[al] presentation
Grafikdatei f graphics file
Grafikdateiformat n graphics [file] format
Grafikdaten pl graphics (graphical) data
Grafikdatenbank f graphics library, GL
Grafikdesign n graphic design
Grafikdesigner m graphic designer
Grafikdia[positiv] n graphic slide
Grafikdisplay n s. Grafikbildschirm
Grafikdrucker m graphics printer; image printer
Grafikeditor m graphical (graphics) editor
Grafikelement n graphic element
Grafikerkennung f graphics (graphic-object) recognition
Grafikfähigkeit f graphical (graphics) capability *(e.g. of a personal computer)*
Grafikformat n graphics [file] format
~/**digitales** digital graphics format
Grafikfunktion f graphics function
Grafikgestaltung f graphic design
Grafikhardware f graphics[-display] hardware
Grafikkarte f graphics [display] card, graphics board (adapter), graphics engine (controller), display board *(s.a.* Videokarte*)*
Grafikkartenspeicher m graphics card memory, video [storage] memory, video buffer
Grafikleistung f graphics[-card] performance, graphical performance (power) *(of a computer)*
Grafikmodellierung f graphics modeling
Grafikmodus m graphics mode
Grafikmonitor m s. Grafikbildschirm
Grafikobjekt n graphic[al] object
Grafikpaket n graphics package
Grafikprimitiv n graphic[s] primitive
Grafikprogramm n [computer] graphics program, graphics-oriented program
~/**pixelorientiertes** bit-mapped [graphics] program
Grafikprogrammierer m graphics program[m]er
Grafikprogrammierung f graphical programming
Grafikprozessor m graphics processor, graphics [controller] chip
Grafikrechner m graphics computer
Grafikscanner m [professional] graphic scanner, graphics (graphic arts) scanner; graphic arts drum scanner
Grafikschnittstelle f graphic[al] interface, graphics controller interface, graphical

Grafikschnittstelle (graphics-based) user interface, GUI, graphical front-end

~/**beschleunigte** accelerated graphic[s] port, AGP *(bus system)*

Grafiksoftware f graphics[-based] software

Grafikspeicher m graphics card memory, video [storage] memory, video buffer

Grafiksprache f graphics language

Grafikstandard m graphics standard

Grafikstift m digitizing pen, pressure-sensitive pen, [electronic] stylus *(graphics tablet)*

Grafiksymbol n [graphical] icon

Grafiksystem n graphic[s] system, graphic[s] processing system

~ **des Programmierers/hierarchisch-interaktives** programmer's hierarchical interactive graphics system, PHIGS

~/**interaktives** interactive graphics system

Grafiktablett n graphics (digitizing) tablet, [electronic] tablet *(input device)*

Grafiktransformation f graphics transformation

Grafiktreiber m s. Grafikkartentreiber

Grafikverarbeitung f graphics processing

Grafikwerkzeug n graphical (graphic production) tool

grafisch graphic[al]

Grammatik f grammar *(set of rules of syntax e.g. in pattern recognition)*

~/**generative** generative grammar

~/**kontextfreie** context-free grammar

~/**stochastische** stochastic grammar

Grammatom n gram atom, gram-atomic weight (mass)

Grammolekül n gram-molecule, gram-molecular weight (mass)

Granularrauschen n granular (grain) noise

Granulationsmuster n speckle pattern *(e.g. in ultrasound images)*

Granulometrie f/**algebraische** algebraic granulometry

~/**Euklidische** Euclidean granulometry

Graph m graph *(set of vertices and edges)*

~/**azyklischer** acyclic graph

~/**dualer** dual graph

~/**finiter** finite graph

~/**gerichteter** directed graph, digraph

~/**gerichteter azyklischer** directed acyclic graph, DAG

~/**gewichteter** weighted graph

~/**planarer** planar graph

~/**regulärer** regular graph

~/**relationaler** relational graph

~/**topologischer** topological graph

~/**ungerichteter** undirected (nonoriented) graph

Graph-Algorithmus n graph algorithm

Graphbild n s. Graphendarstellung

Graphem n grapheme *(as a kind of graphical primitive)*

Graphendarstellung f graph representation

graphentheoretisch graph-theoretic

Graphentheorie f graph theory

Graphsuche f graph search[ing]; graph search technique

~/**multihierarchische** multihierarchical graph search

Graphtransformation f graph transformation

Grauabgleich m 1. [neutral] gray balance; 2. s. Weißabgleich

Grauabstufung f gray shade, shade of gray

Graubalance f [neutral] gray balance

Graubalkendiagramm n gray-scale chart

Graubild n s. Grauwertbild

Graubildstatistik f s. Grauwertstatistik

Graubildverarbeitung f gray-scale [image] processing, gray-level processing

Graufeld n neutral density card

Graufilter n gray filter, neutral[-density] filter, ND filter

Grauglas n neutral glass

Graukarte f gray (neutral test) card, gray board, artificial midtone

Graukeil m gray-scale wedge, gray (neutral-density) step wedge, stepped [optical] wedge, [photographic] density wedge, step (tone) wedge, [silver] step tablet

Graukeilfotometer n wedge photometer

Graumaske f s. Silbermaske

Grauraster m(n) gray screen

Grauschleier m gray fog

Grauschwelle f gray-level threshold

Grauskala f gray[-stepped] scale, gray-level scale *(s.a. Graukeil)*

Graustabilisierung f gray stabilization *(four-color process printing)*

Graustufe f gray level; gray[-level] step, gray-scale step

Graustufenanalyse f gray-scale image analysis

Graustufenbild n gray-scale image (picture), gray-level picture; continuous-tone image (picture), tonal (continuous) image

Graustufenersatz m gray component replacement, GCR, achromatic color removal

Graustufengerät n gray-scale device

Graustufenkeil m s. Graukeil

Graustufenwert m s. Grauwert

Grauton m 1. gray [mid]tone, gray shade, tone (shade) of gray; 2. s. Grauwert

Grautonbild n graymap

Grautonwert m neutral tone *(s.a. Grauwert)*

Grautreppe f s. Grauskala

Grauwert m gray-scale [intensity] value, gray [tone] value, density; gray level [value], intensity [value] *(of a pixel)*

~/**konstanter** constant gray value

~/**mittlerer** average gray value (level), mid-scale gray, gray midtone

Grauwertabhängigkeitsmatrix f [gray-level] co-occurence matrix, two-point probability density function, 2P-PDF *(image analysis)*
Grauwertagglomeration f gray-value agglomeration
Grauwertamplitude f gray level amplitude
Grauwertänderung f gray-level change; gray-level variation
Grauwertäqualisation f, **Grauwertäqualisierung** f gray-scale equalization
Grauwertauflösung f gray-level resolution, gray-scale resolution
Grauwertauswertung f gray-value evaluation
Grauwertbereich m 1. gray[-level] range, gray-scale range; 2. gray-level region
Grauwertbild n gray-scale [digital] image, gray-value[d] image, intensity (gray-level) image, gray-level picture; gray pattern
Grauwertbildfilter n gray-level image filter
Grauwertbildkompression f gray-level image compression
Grauwertbildverarbeitung f gray-scale [image] processing, gray-level [image] processing
Grauwertcode m gray-scale code
Grauwertcodierung f gray-scale [en]coding
Grauwertdarstellung f gray rendition
Grauwertdifferenz f gray-level difference
Grauwertdilatation f gray-scale dilation
Grauwertdiskontinuität f gray-level discontinuity
Grauwertdynamik f gray-level dynamics
Grauwerterosion f gray-scale erosion
Grauwertgehalt m gray-level content
Grauwertgradient m gray-value (gray-level) gradient
Grauwertgradientenschattierung f [gray level] gradient shading
Grauwerthistogramm n gray-scale histogram, gray-level histogram
Grauwertintensität f gray-scale intensity
Grauwertinterpolation f gray-level interpolation
Grauwertintervall n gray-level interval, gray-scale spread
Grauwertkante f gray-scale edge, gray-value edge
Grauwertkantendetektion f gray-scale edge detection
Grauwertkennlinie f s. Gradationskurve
Grauwertkomponente f gray-scale component
Grauwertkonturierung f gray-scale contouring
Grauwertmatrix f gray-value matrix
Grauwert-Medianfilter n gray-level median filter
Grauwertmodifikation f gray-level modification, point operation *(pixel processing)*
Grauwertmorphologie f gray-scale morphology, gray-level mathematical morphology
Grauwertpixel n gray-level pixel, gray-scale pixel
Grauwertprofil n gray-level profile, gray-scale profile
Grauwertquantisierung f gray-level quantization, gray-scale quantization
Grauwertreproduktion f gray scale reproduction, tone reproduction
Grauwertrundung f gray-level rounding
Grauwertschattierung f gray-scale shading
Grauwertschwelle f gray-level threshold
Grauwertsehen n monochrome (black-white) vision, black-white vision
Grauwertskalierung f gray-level scaling
Grauwertskelettierung f gray-scale skeletonization
Grauwertstatistik f gray-level statistics
Grauwertstufe f gray level
Grauwerttiefe f gray-scale depth
Grauwerttransformation f gray-value (gray-level) transformation, gray-scale transform[ation], intensity (mapping) transformation
Grauwertübergang m, **Grauwertübergangsgebiet** n gray-level transition, gray-scale transition
Grauwertübergangsmatrix f [gray-level] co-occurence matrix, two-point probability density function *(image analysis)*
Grauwertüberlauf m overflow *(in digitized images)*
Grauwertunterlauf m underflow *(in digitized images)*
Grauwertunterschied m gray-value difference, gray-scale difference, gray-level difference
Grauwertvarianz f gray-level variance
Grauwertvariation f gray-scale variation
Grauwertveränderung f gray-value change
Grauwertverarbeitung f s. Grauwertbildverarbeitung
Grauwertverteilung f gray-level distribution, gray-scale distribution
Grauwertwiedergabe f gray-scale rendition (reproduction)
Grauwertzuordnung f gray-level assignment; gray-level allocation
Graveur m engraver
gravieren to engrave
~/**lichtelektrisch** to [photo]engrave
Graviermaschine f engraving machine, [electromechanical] engraver
Gravierstichel m engraving stylus
Gravur f engraving
~/**elektromechanische** electromechanical engraving, EME
~/**elektronische** electronic engraving
Gravurkopf m engraving head
Gray n gray, Gy *(unit of radiation dose)*

Gray-Code 184

Gray-Code *m* Gray code *(television)*
Greedy-Algorithmus *m* greedy algorithm
Gregory-System *n*, **Gregory-Teleskop** *n* Gregorian[-type] telescope
Greifer *m* 1. [pull-down] claw *(motion-picture projector)*; 2. gripper *(e.g. on sheet-fed presses)*; 3. *s.* Greifergetriebe
Greifergetriebe *n* claw-type mechanism, pull-down mechanism
Greiferkante *f* gripper edge, feeding (leading) edge *(sheet-fed printing)*
Greiferrand *m* gripper margin
Greiferwerk *n s.* Greifergetriebe
Grenzabtastfrequenz *f* Nyquist frequency (rate)
Grenzauflösung *f* limiting resolution
Grenzfläche *f* interface
Grenzflächenkontrast *m* interface (displacement fringe) contrast *(electron microscopy)*
Grenzflächenmikrofon *n* pressure-zone microphone, boundary layer microphone, BLM
Grenzfrequenz *f* cutoff (limiting) frequency *(e.g. in image filtering)*
~/**obere** high-frequency cutoff
~/**untere** low-frequency cutoff
Grenzstrahlen *mpl* grenz rays *(soft X-rays)*
Grenzwellenlänge *f* cutoff wavelength *(e.g. of a quantum detector)*
Grenzwellenzahl *f* Nyquist frequency *(sampling theorem)*
Grenzwinkel *m* critical angle
Griff *m s.* Griffpunkt
Griffmulde *f* finger grip *(e.g. of a focus ring)*
Griffpunkt *m* handle *(computer graphics)*
Grisma *n s.* Gitterprisma
Grobauflösung *f* coarse resolution
Grobfokussierung *f* 1. coarse focusing; 2. coarse focusing mechanism
Grobkontrast *m s.* Kontrastfaktor
grobkörnig coarse-grained *(film)*
Grobraster *m(n)* coarse screen *(printing)*
Grobschnitt *m* rough (first) cut *(film editing)*
Grobtrieb *m* coarse focus control, coarse adjustment knob
Groedel-Technik *f* air gap [technique] *(for minimizing scattered radiation in medical imaging)*
Großaufnahme *f* 1. [head and shoulder] close-up; head close-up [shot]; 2. *s.* Halbgroßaufnahme; 3. *s.* Nahaufnahme
Großbilddia *n s.* Großdia[positiv]
Großbildfernsehen *n* large-screen television
Großbildfotografie *f* large-format photography
Großbildkamera *f s.* Großformatkamera
Großbildleinwand *f* giant screen
Großbildmonitor *m* large-screen monitor

Großbildprojektion *f* large-screen projection
Großbild-Projektionsfernsehen *n* large-screen projection television
Großbildprojektor *m* large-screen projection unit
Großbildschirm *m* large screen [display], large[-format] display
Großbildsucher *m* big [view]finder
Großbild-Videoprojektior *m* videobeam
Großbildwand *f* giant screen
Großbuchstabe *m* capital uppercase) letter, cap, majuscule
Großdia[positiv] *n* large-format transparency; superslide, jumbo slide; display transparency
Großdruckausgabe *f* large-print book
Größe *f* 1. size; magnitude; dimension; 2. quantity *(e.g. in mathematics)*; 3. *s.* Größenklasse
~/**dimensionslose** dimensionless quantity
~/**konjugierte** conjugate *(optics)*
~/**lichttechnische** photometric quantity
~/**strahlungsphysikalische** radiometric quantity
größeninvariant size-invariant
Größenklasse *f* magnitude *(measure of star brightness)*
Größenkonstanz *f* size constancy
Größentäuschung *f* [/**optische**] size illusion
Größenverhältnis *n* ratio of sizes
Großfeldaufnahme *f* wide-field photograph (picture) *(astrophotography)*
Großfeldfotografie *f* wide-field astronomical photography
Großfeldkamera *f* wide-field camera; all-sky camera *(astrophotography)*
Großfeldobjektiv *n* wide-field lens
Großfeldokular *n* wide-field [of view] eyepiece
Großfeld-Schmidt-Teleskop *n* wide-field Schmidt telescope
Großfeldteleskop *n* wide-field telescope
Großfilm *m* feature-length film (motion picture), full-length picture (feature)
Großflächenflimmern *n* large-area flicker
Großformat *n* large format; giant format
Großformatdrucker *m* large-format (wide-format) printer
Großformat-Fachkamera *f* long-bellows camera
Großformat-Farbkopierer *m* large-format color copier
Großformatfotografie *f* large-format photography
großformatig large-format; large-size[d]
Großformatkamera *f* large-format camera; view (technical) camera
Großformatmikrofotografie *f* large-format photomicrography
Großformatnegativ *n* large-format negative
Großformatobjektiv *n* large-format lens

Großformat-Sucherkamera f large-format rangefinder camera
Großformat-Vergrößerungsapparat m large-format enlarger
Großhirnrinde f cerebral cortex
Großkopie f large print
Großlabor[atorium] n large-volume photofinishing lab, commercial (large-scala) lab, large-scale [commercial] processing laboratory, high-volume lab
Großlaborverarbeitung f [automated] photofinishing
Großleinwand f giant screen
Großleinwandkino n giant screen theater
großmaßstäbig, großmaßstäblich large-scale
Großobservatorium n large observatory
Großporträt n large-format portrait
Großprojektion f large-scale projection
Großrechenanlage f, **Großrechner** m mainframe [computer], central computer
Großserien-Kompaktkamera f compact mass-market camera
Großstativ n giant tripod
Großteleskop n large[-scale] telescope
Großvergrößerung f big (large photographic) enlargement
Grotesk f grotesque *(nonserif typeface)*
Grün n green *(primary color)*
~/**bläuliches** bluish green
Grünauszug m green [light] record *(color photography)*
grünblind green-blind, deuteranopic
Grünblinder m deuteranope
Grünblindheit f [red-]green blindness, deuteranopia *(color-vision deficiency)*
Grundbelichtungszeit f base exposure time
Grundbrett n baseboard *(e.g. of an enlarger)*
Grundeinstellung f default option
Grundelement n primitive [element]
~/**grafisches** graphic[s] primitive
Grundfarbe f primary color, [monochromatic] primary, basis (basic) color *(colorimetry)*
~/**additive (spektrale)** additive primary [color]
~/**subtraktive** subtractive primary [color]; process color *(esp. in the graphic arts)*
Grundfarbenfilter n primary-color filter
Grundfarbwert m primary color stimulus
Grundfeld n main field *(magnetic resonance imaging)*
Grundfilter n basic filter
Grundform f [/**geometrische**] basic shape; [geometric] primitive
Grundfrequenz f fundamental (basic) frequency
Grundgesetz n/**fotometrisches** fundamental law of photometry, law of inverse squares, inverse square law

~/**psychophysisches** s. Gesetz/Weber-Fechnersches
Grundgrauwert m bias
Grundhelligkeit f overall (ambient) light
Grundierungslack m s. Primer
Grundkarte f base map *(cartography)*
Grundkontrast m basic contrast
Grundkörper m [/**elementarer**] solid primitive
Grundlicht n ambient (overall) light
Grundlinie f baseline *(e.g. in typography)*
Grundmagnetfeld n s. Grundfeld
Grundmode f Gaussian (fundamental) mode *(laser)*
Grundobjektiv n prime (main) lens; prime camera lens
Grundplatte f base plate *(tripod)*
Grundrauschen n [back]ground noise
Grundrauschpegel m basic noise level, noise floor
Grundschleier m basic (gross) fog
Grundschrift f text type; body face, bread-and-butter type *(typography)*
Grundschriftgröße f current body size
Grundschwärze f, **Grundschwärzung** f base density
Grundstrich m stem *(letterface)*
Grundweiß n base white
Grundzahl f base number
Grundzeilenabstand m line spacing
grünempfindlich green-sensitive, orthochromatic *(photographic emulsion)*
Grünempfindlichkeit f green[-light] sensitivity
Grünfilter n green [light] filter
Grünkanal m green channel
Grünschwäche f deuteranomaly, decreased green sensitivity *(color-vision deficiency)*
Grünstich m green cast (bias)
Grünstrahl m green beam *(cathode-ray tube)*
Grünteilbild n green [light] record *(color photography)*
Gruppe f/**chromophore** s. Chromophor
Gruppenantenne f/**phasengesteuerte** phased-array antenna *(radar)*
Gruppenaufnahme f group shot
Gruppenbild n group picture; group portrait
Gruppencode m group code *(algebraic coding)*
Gruppencodierung f group coding
Gruppenfoto n s. 1. Gruppenaufnahme; 2. Gruppenbild
Gruppengeschwindigkeit f group velocity *(of a wave)*
Gruppenlaufzeit f group delay *(signal processing)*
Gruppenoperator m group operator
Gruppenporträt n group portrait
Gruppenverzögerung f s. Gruppenlaufzeit
Gruppierungsknoten m group node
Grußkartendruck m greeting card printing

Grußkartenpapier *n* greeting card paper
G-Strich *m s.* Gradient/mittlerer
Guckkasten *m* peep show
Guckkastenapparat *m* peep-show machine
Guckloch *n* peephole
Gummiabstreifer *m* rubber squeegee
Gummiarabikum *n* gum arabic (acacia), acacin[e]
Gummiarmierung *f* rubber armoring
Gummi-Augenmuschel *f* rubber eyecup
Gummi-Bichromat-Verfahren *n* gum bichromate [printing] process, photo-aquatint process
Gummidruck *m* gum[-bichromate] print
Gummidruckplatte *f* rubber [printing] plate; rubber stereo
Gummidrucktuch *n* rubber blanket *(offset press)*
Gummidrucktuchzylinder *m* rubber blanket image transfer cylinder, blanket[-covered] cylinder, offset cylinder
Gummidruckverfahren *n* gum print process
Gummifuß *m* rubber-tipped leg *(tripod)*
~ **mit einstellbarem Dorn** rubber foot with [a] retractable spike
Gummihandschuhe *mpl* rubber gloves
Gummiklischee *n* rubber stereotype, rubber duplicate [plate], molded rubber plate
Gummilinse *f* zoom [lens], varifocal (vario) lens
Gumminoppenlaufrolle *f* soft touch tyre
Gummisonnenblende *f* rubber [lens] hood
Gummistereo *n s.* Gummiklischee
Gummituch *n s.* Gummidrucktuch
Gummizylinder *m s.* Gummidrucktuchzylinder
Gurney-Mott-Theorie *f* Gurney-Mott theory *(of latent image formation)*
Gussletter *f* foundry type
Gusszeile *f* slug
Gütemodulation *f s.* Güteschalter
Güteschalter *m* Q-switch *(laser)*
~/**akustooptischer** acousto-optic Q-switch
Gyroskop *n* gyroscope, gyro
gyroskopisch gyroscopic

H

Haarlicht *n* hair light
Haarlinie *f* hairline, very fine line
Haarnadelkatode *f* hairpin filament *(electron microscope)*
Haarstrich *m s.* Haarlinie
Haar-Transformation *f* Haar [wavelet] transform *(image coding)*
Haar-Wavelet *n* Haar wavelet *(signal processing)*
Hadamard-Matrix *f* Hadamard matrix
Hadamard-Transformation *f*/**diskrete** discrete Hadamard transform, DHT
Hadernpapier *n* rag paper
Haftschicht *f* subbing (substrate) layer, adhesive layer, substratum *(film structure)*
Haftvermittler *m* adhesion promoter
Haidinger-Büschel *n* Haidinger brushes *(entoptic phenomenon)*
Halbapochromat *m* semiapochromatic objective
halbapochromatisch semiapochromatic
Halbbild *n* 1. half-frame [image]; double-35-mm *(cinema)*; 2. field [image], field-picture, image (picture) field *(video)*; 3. *s.* ~/stereoskopisches
~/**geradzahliges** even field
~/**oberes** top field
~/**stereoskopisches** stereophotograph
~/**ungeradzahliges** odd field
~/**unteres** bottom field
Halbbildabtastung *f* field scan
Halbbildauflösung *f* field resolution
Halbbildaustastperiode *f* field-blanking period
Halbbildaustastung *f* field blanking
Halbbilddauer *f* field period (time), field duration
Halbbilddominanz *f* field dominance
Halbbildfrequenz *f* field refresh rate, [picture] field rate, field frequency (repetition rate) *(interlaced video)*
Halbbildimpuls *m* field pulse
Halbbildinterpolation *f* field interpolation
Halbbildkennung *f* field identification
Halbbildmodus *m* interlaced mode
Halbbildpaar *n* [/**stereoskopisches**] stereo[scopic] image pair, stereo[photographic] pair, stereograph, stereogram
Halbbildprädiktion *f* field[-based] prediction
Halbbildrate *f s.* Halbbildfrequenz
Halbbildspeicher *m* field store (memory)
Halbbildspeicherung *f* field storage
Halbbildsynchronisation *f* field synchronization
Halbbildverarbeitung *f* field processing
Halbbildverfahren *n*,
Halbbildverkämmung *f* interlace[d] [video] scanning, interlaced scan[ning] system, interlacing
Halbbildwechselfrequenz *f s.* Halbbildfrequenz
Halbbildwiederholung *f* field repetition
Halbbyte *n* half byte, nibble
Halbdunkel *n* semidarkness, partial darkness
halbdurchsichtig semitransparent
Halbebene *f* halving plane *(Euclidean geometry)*
Halbebenenfilter *n*/**asymmetrisches** nonsymmetric half-plane filter *(image modeling)*
halbfett demibold[faced], medium-faced *(typestyle)*
Halbformatkamera *f* half-frame camera
Halbgeviert *n* en quad (space), en rule (leader) *(typography)*
Halbgeviertstrich *m* [en] dash *(typography)*
Halbgroßaufnahme *f* medium close-up [shot]
Halbleiter *m* semiconductor; semiconductor device
~/**amorpher** amorphous semiconductor
~/**direkter** direct-gap semiconductor
~/**dotierter** extrinsic semiconductor
~/**intrinsischer** intrinsic semiconductor
~/**optoelektronischer** opto[electronic] semiconductor
~/**undotierter** intrinsic semiconductor
Halbleiterbauelement *n*,
Halbleiterbaustein *m* semiconductor device
Halbleiterbildschirm *m* semiconductor display
Halbleiterbildsensor *m* solid-state image (imaging) sensor, SSIS, solid-state imaging chip (device)
Halbleiterbildwandler *m s.* 1. Halbleiterbildsensor; 2. CCD-Filmabtaster
Halbleiterchip *m* semiconductor [integrated] chip
Halbleiterdetektor *m* semiconductor[-based] detector, solid-state detector, SSD
Halbleiterdiode *f* semiconductor diode
Halbleiterdisplay *n* semiconductor display, CCD
Halbleiterelektronik *f* semiconductor (solid-state) electronics
Halbleiterelektronikindustrie *f* semiconductor electronics industry
Halbleiterelement *n* semiconductor device (element)
~/**ladungsgekoppeltes** charge-coupled device (detector), CCD
Halbleiter-Flächendetektor *m s.* Flächendetektor
Halbleiterfolie *f* semiconducting film

Halbleiterfotodetektor *m*
semiconductor[-based] photodetector, semiconductor photoemissive (photoelectric) detector

Halbleiterfotodiode *f* semiconductor photodiode [detector], photoconductive diode

Halbleiterfotoeffekt *m* internal photoeffect (photoelectric effect), intrinsic photoconduction

Halbleiterfotoelement *n* semiconductor [photo]cell; photovoltaic (barrier-layer) cell

Halbleiterfotowiderstand *m* s. Fotowiderstand

Halbleiterfotozelle *f* s. Halbleiterfotoelement

Halbleiterherstellung *f* semiconductor device fabrication

Halbleiterkamera *f* chip (solid-state) camera; CCD[-type] camera, CCD-chip camera, charge-coupled [device] camera

Halbleiterkristall *m* semiconductor crystal

Halbleiterlaser *m* semiconductor [injection] laser, semiconductor laser diode, semiconductor diode laser, semiconducting (injection) laser

~/**[frequenz]abstimmbarer** tunable semiconductor laser

Halbleiterlaserdiode *f* s. Halbleiterlaser

Halbleiter-Leuchtdiode *f* semiconductor LED (light-emitting diode)

Halbleiter-Lichtempfänger *m* solid-state photodetector

Halbleitermaterial *n* semiconductor material, semiconducting (semiconductive) material

Halbleitermatrix *f* semiconductor matrix

Halbleiteroptik *f* semiconductor optics

halbleiteroptisch semiconductor optical

Halbleiter-Optoelektronik *f* semiconductor optoelectronics

Halbleiterpulslaser *m* pulsed semiconductor laser

Halbleiterschaltkreis *m*/**integrierter** complementary metal-oxide semiconductor, CMOS

Halbleiterscheibe *f* [semiconductor] wafer

Halbleitersensor *m* solid-state sensor

Halbleiterspeicher *m* semiconductor memory

Halbleiter-Speicherkarte *f* semiconductor memory card

Halbleiter-Strahlungsdetektor *m* semiconductor radiation detector

Halbleitertechnik *f*, **Halbleitertechnologie** *f* semiconductor (solid-state) technology

Halbleiterwiderstand *m* semiconductor resistor

Halblinsen *fpl*/**Billetsche** Billet's split lens

halblogarithmisch semilogarithmic

halbmatt semimatt[e], semigloss *(e.g. photographic paper)*

Halbmetall *n* semimetal

Halbnahaufnahme *f* medium[-distance] shot, MS

Halbnahe *f*, **Halbnaheinstellung** *f* medium closeup, semi-closeup

halbopak translucent, lucid

Halbpixelgenauigkeit *f* half-p[ix]el accuracy, half-pixel precision *(video coding)*

Halbpixelinterpolation *f* half-pixel interpolation

Halbporträt *n*, **Halbporträtaufnahme** *f* half-length portrait, bust shot

Halbprofil-Aufnahme *f* semisilhouette profile portrait

Halbquader *m* hemicube *(computer graphics)*

Halbraum *m* half-space *(Euclidean geometry)*

~/**algebraischer** algebraic half-space

Halbschatten *m* half shade, partial shadow; penumbral shadow, penumbra

Halbschattenpolarisator *m* half-shade polarizer

Halbserife *f* half-serif terminal *(letterface)*

Halbspiegel *m* s. Spiegel/halbdurchlässiger

Halbton *m* [/**echter**] continuous tone, contone

~/**unechter** halftone

Halbtonapproximation *f* halftoning, dithering, dither technique *(electronic imaging; s.a.* Streurasterung*)*

Halbtonbild *n* 1. continuous-tone image (picture), tonal (continuous) image; gray-scale image (picture); 2. s. Mitteltonbild

~/**fotografisches** continuous-tone photographic image

Halbtonbildanalyse *f* gray-scale image analysis

Halbtonbildcodierung *f* continuous-tone-image coding

Halbtonbildkompression *f* continuous-tone image compression

Halbtondarstellung *f* continuous-tone representation

Halbtondia *n* continuous-tone slide

Halbton-Diafilm *m* continuous-tone slide film

Halbton-Digitalproof/materieller hard digital continuous-tone proof

Halbtondruck *m* continuous-tone printing

Halbtondrucker *m* continuous-tone printer

Halbtoneffekt *m* continuous-tone effect

Halbtonentwickler *m* continuous-tone type developer

Halbtonentwicklung *f* continuous-tone development

Halbton-Farbkopie *f* continuous-tone color print

Halbtonfestbild *n* continuous-tone still image

Halbtonfestbildkompression *f* continuous-tone still image compression

Halbtonfilm *m* continuous-tone [photographic] film; continuous-tone copy film
Halbtonfotografie *f* 1. continuous-tone photography; 2. continuous-tone photo[graphic image]
Halbtonkopierer *m* continuous-tone printer
Halbtonnegativ *n* continuous-tone negative
Halbtonoriginal *n* continuous-tone original
Halbtonpositiv *n* continuous-tone positive, positive continuous-tone image
Halbtonraster *m(n)* [halftone] screen
Halbtonrasterung *f* halftone screening; [digital] halftoning *(rendering digital images at two levels)*
Halbtonreproduktion *f* continuous-tone reproduction
Halbton-Schwarzweißvorlage *f* continuous-tone black-and-white copy *(printing)*
Halbtonverfahren *n* 1. halftone process *(photography)*; 2. continuous-tone process *(printing)*; 3. *s.* Halbtonrasterung
Halbtonvorlage *f* [continuous-]tone copy, contone
Halbtonwiedergabe *f* continuous-tone reproduction
Halbtonxerografie *f* continuous-tone xerography
Halbtotale *f* long (full) shot
halbtransparent semitransparent
Halbwelle *f* half-wave
Halbwellenantenne *f* half-wave antenna
Halbwellenlänge *f* one-half wavelength
Halbwellenlängenplättchen *n*, **Halbwellenplatte** *f* half-wave plate (retarder)
Halbwellenspannung *f* half-wave voltage
Halbwertsbreite *f* [/spektrale/] full-width-at-half-maximum, FWHM *(e.g. of a line-spread function)*
Halbwertsschicht *f* half-value layer, HVL *(radiography)*
Halbwertsschichtdicke *f s.* Halbwertsdicke
Halbwertszeit *f* half-life [period]
Halbwinkel *m* semiangle
Halbwinkelbreite *f* half-angular width
Halbwürfel *m* hemicube *(computer graphics)*
Halbwürfelprisma *n* hemicube prism
Halbzeile *f* half-line *(video)*
Halbzeilen-Offset *m*, **Halbzeilenversatz** *m* half-line offset
Halbzollband *n* half-inch [magnetic] tape *(video)*
Halbzollkassette *f* one-half-inch cassette
Hall *m* reverberation
Hall-Effekt *m* Hall effect *(magnetic field imaging)*
Hallgenerator *m* reverberator, echo unit
Hall-Konstante *f* Hall coefficient
Hall-Sensor *m* Hall generator (probe)

Hall-Spannung *f* Hall voltage
Hallzeit *f* reverberation time
Halo *m* halo
Halogen *n* halogen
Halogenakzeptor *m* halogen acceptor
Halogenglühlampe *f* [incandescent] halogen lamp; tungsten-halogen lamp; quartz-halogen lamp
Halogenid *n* halide, halogenide; halide salt
Halogenlampe *f s.* Halogenglühlampe
Halogenlicht *n* halogen [bulb] light
Halogen-Metalldampflampe *f* metal halide lamp; metal halide gas-discharge arc lamp, HMI lamp
Halogenrezeptor *m* halogen receptor *(e.g. gelatin)*
Halogensalz *n* halide salt
Halogensilber *n* silver halide, AgX
Halogensilberkorn *n* silver-halide grain
Halogensilbersalz *n s.* Halogensilber
Halogensilberverfahren *n* silver halide process
haltbar permanent
Haltbarkeit *f* permanence, permanency, keeping quality *(e.g. of photographic material)*
Halteglied *n* hold [element] *(signal processing)*
~ **nullter Ordnung** sample and hold
Haltekondensator *m* hold[ing] capacitor
Halter *m s.* Optikhalter
Hamming-Abstand *m s.* Hamming-Distanz
Hamming-Code *m* Hamming code
Hamming-Codierung *f* Hamming encoding
Hamming-Distanz *f* Hamming (signal) distance *(digital image processing)*
Hamming-Fenster *n* Hamming window
Hamming-Funktion *f* Hamming function
Hamming-Netz *n* Hamming net
Handauflage *f* wrist support (rest) *(in front of the computer keyboard)*
Handaufnahme *f* 1. handheld shooting; 2. handheld shot
Hand-Auge-Kalibrierung *f* hand-eye calibration *(robotics)*
Handauslösung *f* manual exposure
Handbelichtungsmesser *m* hand[held] light] meter, handheld [photoelectric] exposure meter, handheld reflected-light exposure meter
Handdruckverfahren *n* manual printing process
Handeinstellung *f* manual setting
Handentwicklung *f* hand (manual) processing
Handfernrohr *n* hand[held] telescope
Handgelenkschlaufe *f* [wrist] strap
Handhabungsfehler *m* manipulative error
Handhabungskomfort *m* ease of operation
Handkamera *f* hand[held] camera; handycam
Handkameraaufnahme *f* handheld photograph

Handklappe f clapboard, clapper [board], clapstick[s], sync stick; [clapping] slate, number board *(cinema)*
handkolorieren to hand-color, to hand-tint
Handkolorierstift m hand-coloring pen
Handkolorierung f hand-coloring, hand-tinting
Handkolorist m hand colorist
Handlampe f s. Handleuchte
Handlichkeit f handiness
Handlupe f hand lens
Handmikrofon n handheld microphone
Handretusche f hand (manual) retouching
Handsatz m hand composition *(typesetting)*
Handsatzletter f handset type
Handsatzschrift f handset type
Handsatztype f handset type
Handscanner m 1. handheld [mini]scanner; freehand scanner, handheld transducer *(sonography)*; 2. s. Handgeometrie-Scanner
Handschlaufe f [wrist] strap
Handschriftanalyse f handwriting analysis
Handschrifterkennung f handwriting (handwritten character) recognition, intelligent character recognition, ICR
Handschriftzeichen n handwritten (handprinted) character
Handschuh m/**sensorischer** sensor (data) glove, cyber glove, glove input device *(navigational tool)*
Handskizze f [rough] sketch, scribble, scamp
Handspektroskop n hand spectroscope
Handspiegel m hand glass
Handverarbeitung f manual (hand) processing
Handvergrößerungssystem n manual enlarging system
Handvideokamera f [/mobile] handheld video camera, camcorder, camera-recorder
Handy n cell[ular] [tele]phone, mobile phone
Handydisplay n cell-phone display
Hängebrücke f suspension bridge *(e.g. as a lighting setup)*
Hänger[entwicklungs]maschine f dip and dunk processor
Hängeregistratur f suspension file
Hanning-Fenster n Hanning (von Hann) window *(digital image processing)*
Haploskop n haploscope
haploskopisch haploscopic
Hardcopygerät n hard copy device
Hardware f hardware; hardware device
Harmonische f harmonic *(sine wave)*
Harnröhrenspiegel m urethroscope
Harnwegsröntgendarstellung f urography
hart hard *(paper grade)*; high-contrast, contrasty *(image)*
Härtebad n hardening bath
Härtefixierbad n hardening fixing bath

Härtefixierer m hardening fixer
Härtegrad m gradation
Härtemittel n, **Härter** m hardening agent, hardener
Härtestoppbad n stop and hardening bath
Hartgelatine f hardened gelatin
Hartley-Transformation f Hartley transform
Hartmann-Shack-Sensor m Hartmann-Shack [wave-front] sensor
Hartschnitt m straight (editorial) cut, abrupt cut (transition) *(film, video)*
Härtungsmittel n s. Härtemittel
Häufigkeitsverteilung f frequency distribution
Häufung f cluster
Hauptachse f major (principal) axis *(e.g. of an ellipse)*
Hauptachsen[aus]richtung f major axis orientation
Hauptachsentransformation f s. Hauptkomponentenanalyse
Hauptbeleuchtung f main lighting
Hauptbelichtung f main exposure
Hauptbild n main image
Hauptblitz m master (main) flash
Hauptbrechzahl f principal refractive index, principal index of refraction
Hauptdreh m principal photography, main-unit shoot *(motion-picture production)*
Hauptdruckverfahren n principal printing process
Hauptebene f principal (cardinal) plane, Gaussian plane *(optics)*
~/**bildseitige** rear principal (nodal) plane
~/**Gaußsche** s. Hauptebene
~/**objektseitige** frontal principal (nodal) plane
Hauptfarbe f principal color; primary color
Hauptfarbton m principal hue *(Munsell system of color notation)*
Hauptfilm m feature (main) film, feature-length film, feature [motion picture], [full-length] feature movie *(s.a. Spielfilm)*
Hauptgerät n master unit *(flash equipment)*
Hauptkamera f main camera *(filming)*
Hauptkeule f [central] main lobe, central lobe *(radar, ultrasound)*
Hauptkomponentenachse f principal component axis
Hauptkomponentenanalyse f principal components analysis (transform), principal axis transformation, eigenvector (Hotelling) transform, Karhunen-Loève-transform[ation] (expansion) *(feature identification)*
Hauptkomponentenbild n principal-component image
Hauptkopf m main header *(image data structure)*

Hauptleitungsträger *m* [data] bus, main bus *(signal transmission path in a computer system)*
Hauptlicht *n* key (primary) light, main (principal) light
Hauptlichtquelle *f* main (primary) light source, key (dominant) light source, key
Hauptmagnetfeld *n* main field *(magnetic resonance imaging)*
Hauptmaximum *n* principal maximum *(e.g. of a point-spread function)*
Hauptmotiv *n* main subject, principal (dominant) subject *(e.g. of a photograph)*
Hauptobjekt *n* main (principal) object *(e.g. of an image)*
Hauptobjektiv *n* prime (main) lens; prime camera lens
Hauptphasenanimation *f* key frame animation, key framing
Hauptphasenzeichner *m* key (senior) animator
Hauptplatine *f* [computer] motherboard, logic board, main computer circuit board
Hauptprozessor *m* [master] processor, mainframe; central processing unit, CPU *(computer module)*
Hauptpunkt *m* principal point *(e.g. of an optical lens)*
~/bildseitiger rear principal point
~/dingseitiger (objektseitiger) front principal point
Hauptpunktabstand *m* nodal space, nodal point separation
Hauptpunktstrahl *m* principal (chief) ray, pupil ray
Hauptrechner *m* main computer, host [computer]
Hauptschalter *m* power switch
Hauptsendezeit *f* prime time *(television)*
Hauptspeicher *m* main (central) memory; active (core) memory; random-access memory, RAM
Hauptspiegel *m* main (primary) mirror *(e.g. of a catadioptric system)*
~/sphärischer spherical primary [mirror]
Hauptstrahl *m* principal (chief) ray *(optics)*; main beam *(e.g. in radiography)*
Haupttaktgeber *m* master clock [signal] generator, main clock
Hauptteleskop *n* main telescope *(astrophotography)*
Haupttitel *m* main and credit title *(cinema)*
Haupttrabant *m* broad pulse
Hauptträgheitsachse *f* principal axis of inertia
Hausanschluss *m* drop cable *(cable television)*
Hausantenne *f* home antenna, roof antenna (aerial)
Hausdorff-Besikowitsch-Dimension *f* Hausdorff-Besicovitch dimension, fractal dimension *(computer graphics)*
Hausdruckerei *f* inplant

Haushaltsglühbirne *f*,
Haushaltsglühlampe *f* household light[bulb], house-lighting bulb, household tungsten lamp, domestic tungsten bulb
Hausschrift *f* house style *(typography)*
Hausüberwachung *f* home surveillance
Hautton[wert] *m* skin (flesh) tone
Hauttonwiedergabe *f* rendition of flesh tones
Haze-Filter *n* haze filter
HDTV-Format *n* HDTV format *(derived from high-definition television)*
Headline *f s.* 1. Schlagzeile; 2. Titelzeile; 3. Überschrift
Heat-set-Rollenoffsetpresse *f* heat-set web [press]
Hebb-Regel *f* Hebb's rule *(unsupervised learning)*
Hebelschneidemaschine *f* guillotine cutter (trimmer)
Heel-Effekt *m* heel effect *(radiography)*
Hefner-Kerze *f* Hefner candle *(photometry)*
Heimbildtechnik *f* consumer imaging
Heimcomputer *m* home [personal] computer, home PC
Heimelektronik *f* consumer electronics
Heimelektronikindustrie *f* consumer electronics industry
Heimempfang *m* home reception
Heimempfänger *m* home receiver
Heimfernsehen *n* home (domestic) television, consumer television
Heimfernseher *m*, **Heimfernsehgerät** *n* home television (TV) receiver, home (entertainment) television set, consumer television set
Heimfilmer *m* amateur filmmaker
Heimgerät *n* consumer device, home appliance
Heimkassettenrecorder *m* consumer VCR (video cassette recorder)
Heimkino *n* home cinema (movie), video home theater
Heimkinoanlage *f* home cinema installation (system)
Heimkinobildwand *f* home cinema screen
Heimkinoempfänger *m* home cinema receiver
Heimkinofilm *m* home movie [film]
Heimkinoformat *n* home-movie format
Heimkinoprojektor *m* home theater projector
Heimlabor *n* home (personal) darkroom
Heim-PC *m s.* Heimcomputer
Heimprojektion *f* home screening
Heimprojektionsanlage *f*, **Heimprojektor** *m* domestic projection equipment, home-use projector
Heimrecorder *m s.* Heimvideorecorder
Heimstudio *n* [in-]home studio
Heimverarbeitung *f* home (user) processing *(of photo material)*
Heimvideo *n* home (consumer) video

Heimvideogerät *n* consumer-grade (consumer-brand) video player
Heimvideoindustrie *f* consumer video industry
Heimvideokamera *f* home video camera
Heimvideorecorder *m* home (consumer-grade) video recorder, domestic (consumer) videocassette recorder, home (domestic) VCR
Heim-Videospiel *n* home game
Heimvideotechnik *f* consumer video recording technology
Heisenberg-Unschärfe *f* Heisenberg's uncertainty relation (principle)
Heißfolienprägedruck *m*, **Heißfolienprägung** *f* hot foil printing, [hot] foil stamping
Heißklebefolie *f* heat-activated laminating material
Heißklebepresse *f* hot (heat) splicer
Heißklebestelle *f* hot splice, film weld
Heißleiter *m* thermistor *(a semiconductor)*
Heißlicht *n* hot light
heißprägen to [hot] foil stamp, to foil emboss, to block print
Heißprägepresse *f* blocking press
Heißtrockenpresse *f* heated print dryer
Heizrolle *f*, **Heizwalze** *f* [heated] fuser roll, hot roll *(electrophotography)*
Hektograf *m* hectograph; spirit duplicator
Hektografie *f* spirit duplication (duplicating), fluid (direct) process
hektografieren to hectograph
Helicalscan *m* helical (spiral) scan
Heliochromie *f* heliochromy
Heliograf *m* [photo]heliograph
Heliografie *f* 1. heliography, heliographic process; 2. heliograph, photoengraving
heliografisch heliographic
Heliogravüre *f* 1. photogravure [process], heliogravure; 2. photogravure, heliogravure *(print)*
Heliogravurtechnik *f s.* Heliogravüre 1.
Heliostat *m* heliostat, coelostat *(solar observation)*
Helium-Neon-Laser *m* helium-neon laser
hell bright; light; luminous
Helladaptation *f* light adaptation
helladaptiert light-adapted, photopic
Hell-Dunkel-Übergang *m* light-to-dark [image] transition
Hellempfindlichkeit *f* luminosity
~/**fotopische** photopic [spectral] sensitivity
~/**relative** relative luminosity
~/**spektrale** spectral luminosity
Hellempfindlichkeitsgrad *m* luminous efficiency
~/**relativer** relative luminous efficiency
~/**spektraler** spectral luminous efficiency
Hellempfindlichkeitskurve *f* luminosity function (curve)
~/**spektrale** spectral luminosity function (curve), [spectral] luminous efficiency function
Hellempfindungsgrad *m s.* Hellempfindlichkeitsgrad
Hellentwickler *m* daylight developer
hellfarbig light-colored
Hellfeld-Auflichtmikroskopie *f* bright-field reflected-light microscopy
Hellfeldbeleuchtung *f* bright-field illumination (lighting)
Hellfeldbeobachtung *f* bright-field observation
Hellfeldbild *n* bright-field image
Hellfeldkondensor *m* bright-field condenser
Hellfeldmikroskop *n* bright-field microscope
Hellfeldmikroskopie *f* bright-field microscopy, BF microscopy
Hellicht *n* bright light
Helligkeit *f* brightness *(of a light source; s.a.* Leuchtdichte*)*; lightness *(of reflecting objects)*; value *(Munsell color-order system)*; intensity *(HSI color model)*
~/**empfindungsgemäße** perceived (subjective) brightness; perceived lightness
~/**gesehene** visual brightness
~/**mittlere** average brightness
~/**relative** relative brightness, luminosity
~/**spektrale** spectral brightness
~/**subjektive** *s.* ~/empfindungsgemäße
~/**wahrgenommene** perceived brightness
Helligkeitsabfall *m* brightness decrease
Helligkeitsabtastung *f* brightness scan, B scan
Helligkeitsadaptation *f* brightness adaptation; lightness adaptation *(s.a.* Helladaptation*)*
Helligkeitsänderung *f* brightness change; brightness variation
Helligkeitsauflösung *f* brightness (intensity) resolution
Helligkeitsbereich *m* brightness range
Helligkeitsdifferenz *f* brightness difference
Helligkeitseindruck *m*/**psychophysiologischer (subjektiver)** subjective percept of brightness
Helligkeitseinstellung *f* brightness setting *(e.g. of a monitor)*
Helligkeitsempfinden *n s.* Helligkeitsempfindung
Helligkeitsempfindlichkeit *f* brightness (luminous) sensitivity
Helligkeitsempfindung *f* [perceptual] brightness sensation, sensation of brightness
Helligkeitsflimmern *n* luminance flicker
Helligkeitsfunktion *f* brightness function
Helligkeitsgehalt *m* brightness content *(of an image)*
Helligkeitsgradient *m* brightness gradient

Helligkeitshistogramm *n* brightness histogram
Helligkeitsinformation *f* brightness information; luminance information *(video)*
Helligkeitskante *f* luminance edge
Helligkeitskonstanz *f* brightness constancy; lightness constancy
Helligkeitskontrast *m* luminance contrast
Helligkeitskorrekturfilter *n s.* Neutraldichtefilter
Helligkeitsmessung *f* measurement of brightness, photometry
Helligkeitsmodulation *f* brightness modulation
Helligkeitsmuster *n* brightness pattern
Helligkeitsniveau *n* brightness level
Helligkeitspixel *n* luminance pixel
Helligkeitsprofil *n* brightness profile
Helligkeitsregelung *f*/**automatische** automatic brightness control, ABC
Helligkeitsregler/stufenloser [lamp] dimmer
Helligkeitsschwankung *f* brightness variation (fluctuation); flutter *(television image)*
Helligkeitssehen *n* photopic (light-adapted) vision, daylight (bright-light) vision, cone[-mediated] vision
Helligkeitssignal *n* brightness signal; luminance (luma) signal, black-[and-]white signal, Y [signal] *(video)*
Helligkeitsskala *f* brightness scale; lightness scale
Helligkeits-Stanztrick *m* luminance (luma) keying
Helligkeitssteuerung *f* brightness control
Helligkeitsstufe *f* brightness level
Helligkeitsübersprecheffekt *m* cross-luminance [artifact], cross-luma artifact
Helligkeitsumfang *m* brightness range
Helligkeitsunterschied *m* brightness difference
Helligkeitsverfahren *n* tristimulus method *(colorimetry)*
Helligkeitsverlauf *m* brightness distribution curve
Helligkeitsverlust *m* brightness loss
Helligkeitsverstärkung *f* brightness gain
Helligkeitsverteilung *f* brightness distribution
Helligkeitswahrnehmung *f* brightness (luminance) perception; lightness perception
~/**subjektive** subjective perception of brightness
Helligkeitswert *m* luminous value *(colorimetry)*; brightness (intensity) value
Hellraumentwicklungsmaschine *f s.* Hellraummaschine
Hellraumfilm *m* daylight[-balanced] film, daylight-type film

Hellsektor *m* open portion [of the shutter], shutter opening
Helltastung *f* highlighting *(display)*
Helmdisplay *n s.* Datenhelm
Helmholtz[-Lagrange]-Invariante *f* Helmholtz invariant, Lagrange (optical) invariant
Helmholtz-Gleichung *f* Helmholtz equation *(wave optics)*
Hemeralopie *f* hemeralopia, day blindness
Hemmkörper *m* retarder
Hemmung *f s.* Inhibition
Henry *n* henry, H *(unit of inductance)*
heranfahren to dolly in, to truck (push) in *(the camera in filming)*
heranzoomen to zoom in
heraufladen to upload *(e.g. image data to Web sites)*
herausfiltern to filter out
Herausschnitt *m* trims *(film editing)*
Hermann-Gitter *n* Hermann grid illusion
Hermite-Interpolation *f* Hermitian interpolation *(geometric modeling)*
Herschel-Effekt *m* Herschel effect
Herschel-Teleskop *n* Herschelian telescope, off-axis reflector
Hertz *n* hertz, Hz *(unit of frequency)*
herunterladbar downloadable *(software)*
herunterladen to download
Herunterladen *n* download *(data from Web sites)*
Hervorheben *n* highlighting *(e.g. in photography)*; enhancing *(image processing)*
Hervorhebung *f* accent *(e.g. in layout)*
Hervorhebungszeichen *n* bullet [point] *(typography)*
Herzmuskelszintigramm *n* myocardial scintigram
Hesse-Matrix *f* Hessian matrix *(network optimization)*
heterochromatisch heterochromatic
Heterophorie *f* heterophoria
Heterostruktur-Fotodiode *f* heterostructure photodiode, heterojunction diode [array], heterojunction device
Heterostrukturlaser *m* heterostructure laser
Heteroübergang *m* heterojunction *(semiconductor)*
Heuristik *f* heuristic[s]
heuristisch heuristic
Hexacyanoferrat *n* ferricyanide *(bleaching agent)*
Hexadezimalsystem *n* hexadecimal [numbering] system, base 16
Hexadezimalzahl *f*, **Hexadezimalziffer** *f* hexadecimal
Hexaeder *n* hexahedron, cube *(geometric primitive)*
Hexagon *n* hexagon
hexagonal hexagonal

Hexagonalgitter

Hexagonalgitter *n*, **Hexagonalraster** *m* hexagonal lattice (grid)
HF-... *s.* Hochfrequenz...
Hidden-Markow-Modell *n* hidden Markov model, HMM *(pattern recognition)*
~/**semikontinuierliches** semi-continuous (tied-mixture) hidden Markov model
Hierarchieebene *f*, **Hierarchiestufe** *f* level of hierarchy
Highfidelity *f* high fidelity
High-Key-Bild *n* high-key picture, high-key photo[graph]
High-Key-Effekt *m* high-key effect
Hilbert-Filter *n* Hilbert filter *(signal processing)*
Hilbert-Kurve *f* Hilbert curve
Hilbert-Operator *m s.* Hilbert-Filter
Hilbert-Raum *m* Hilbert space
Hilbert-Transformation *f* Hilbert transform
Hilfsantenne *f* auxiliary antenna *(radar)*
Hilfsdaten *pl* ancillary (auxiliary) data
Hilfsdatenpaket *n* ancillary data packet
Hilfsentwickler *m* auxiliary developer, auxiliary developing agent
Hilfskoordinate *f* dummy coordinate
Hilfs-Massenspeicher *m* auxiliary bulk storage
Hilfsoszillator *m* auxiliary oscillator, klystron *(radar)*
Hilfstonspur *f* cue track
Hilfsträger *m* auxiliary information carrier, subcarrier
Hilfsträgeramplitude *f* subcarrier amplitude
Hilfsträgerfrequenz *f* subcarrier frequency
Hilfsträgermodulation *f* subcarrier modulation
Hilfsträgerphase *f* subcarrier phase
Hilfsträgersignal *n* subcarrier signal
Hilfszeitcode *m* ancillary time code
Himmel *m*/**bedeckter** overcast sky
Himmelsblau *n* sky blue
Himmelsfärbung *f* sky coloring
Himmelsfoto *n* celestial (astronomical) photograph
Himmelsfotografie *f* 1. astrophotography, celestial (astronomical) photography; 2. *s.* Himmelsfoto
Himmelskartierung *f* sky mapping, positional astronomy
Himmelsleuchten *n* sky glow
Himmelslicht *n* skylight, airlight
Himmelsstrahlung *f* sky [ir]radiance, celestial (skylight) radiation
H-Impuls *m* horizontal sync[hronization] pulse
Hin- und Herfahren *n* **des Videobandes** shuttling *(video editing)*
Hinderniserkennung *f* obstacle recognition
Hindernisvermeidung *f* obstacle avoidance
Hinkanal *m* forward channel
Hinterbandkontrolle *f* confidence
Hinterdeckel *m* back cover *(of a book)*

Hinterglied *n* rear element (member), rear group (component) *(of a lens)*
~/**zerstreuendes** negative rear element
Hintergliedfokussierung *f* rear focusing
Hintergrund *m* 1. background, BG; back plane; 2. [photographic] background, backdrop, backing *(studio accessory)*
~/**gemalter** matte painting
Hintergrundabzug *m* background subtraction
Hintergrundausleuchtung *f* 1. background illumination; 2. *s.* Hintergrundbeleuchtung
Hintergrundbeleuchtung *f* background lighting, backlight
Hintergrundbereich *m* background region
Hintergrundbild *n* background image; [background] plate, background element *(cinema)*
Hintergrunddetail *n* background detail
Hintergrundfarbe *f* background color; backing color *(traveling-matte process)*
Hintergrundfarbpuffer *m s.* Hintergrundpuffer
Hintergrundgeräusch[e] *n[pl]* background noise; background sound[s], ambient sound
Hintergrundhelligkeit *f* background luminosity
Hintergrundkarton *m* background paper, paper backdrop *(studio accessory)*
Hintergrundleuchtdichte *f* background luminance
Hintergrundlicht *n* background light; surround *(esp. in microscopy)*
Hintergrundmaske *f*, **Hintergrundmaskenfilm** *m* [background] countermatte, male (inverted) matte *(cinema)*
Hintergrundmaterial *n* backing
Hintergrundobjekt *n* background object (subject)
Hintergrundpixel *n* background pixel
Hintergrundprädiktion *f* background prediction
Hintergrundprimitiv *n* background primitive
Hintergrundprojektion *f* 1. background projection; 2. projected background
Hintergrundprojektor *m* background projector
Hintergrundpuffer *m* back buffer
Hintergrundpunkt *m* background point *(image segmentation)*
Hintergrundrauschen *n* background [radiation] noise, ambient noise, background density
Hintergrundrolle *f* seamless [roll], roll of background paper *(studio accessory)*
Hintergrundsignal *n* background signal
Hintergrundspeicher *m* cache [memory], data cache
Hintergrundstrahlung *f* 1. background radiation; 2. *s.* ~/kosmische

~/**kosmische** [cosmic] background radiation
Hintergrundsubtraktion *f* background subtraction
Hintergrundszene *f* background scene
Hintergrundvorhang *m* [photographic] background, backdrop *(studio accessory)*
Hintergrundzeichnung *f* background drawing *(animation)*
Hinterhauptlappen *m* occipital lobe (cortex), primary visual cortex *(of the brain)*
hinterleuchten to backlight
Hinterleuchten *n*, **Hinterleuchtung** *f* backlighting
Hinterlicht *n* back light, contre-jour lighting
Hinterlinse *f*/**axial verschiebbare** floating element
Hinterlinsenverschluss *m* rear shutter
Hinweiszeichen *n* reference mark, pointer
Hippus *m* hippus, tremor of the iris
Hirnperfusionsuntersuchung *f* brain perfusion study *(single-photon emission-computed tomography)*
Histogramm *n* histogram, staircase curve *(s.a.* Säulendiagramm*)*
~/**bimodales** bimodal histogram
~/**diskretes** discrete histogram
~/**globales** global histogram
~/**kumulatives** cumulative histogram
~/**lineares** linear histogram
~/**lokales** local histogram
~/**mehrdimensionales** multidimensional histogram
~/**multimodales** multimodal histogram
~/**normiertes** normalized histogram
~/**unimodales** unimodal histogram
~/**zweidimensionales** two-dimensional histogram
Histogrammanalyse *f* histogram analysis
Histogrammangleich *m* histogram matching
Histogrammanipulation *f* histogram manipulation (processing)
Histogrammäqualisation *f s.* Histogrammausgleich
Histogrammausgleich *m* histogram equalization (flattening), histogram smoothing *(nonlinear point operation)*
Histogrammberg *m* histogram peak
Histogrammbildung *f* histogramming
Histogrammdarstellung *f* histogram plot
Histogrammdehnung *f* histogram expansion (stretching)
Histogrammdifferenz *f* histogram difference
Histogrammegalisierung *f*, **Histogrammeinebnung** *f s.* Histogrammausgleich
Histogrammeinstellung *f* histogram adjustment
Histogrammfenster *n* histogram window
Histogrammfunktion *f* histogram function

Histogrammhyperbolisation *f*, **Histogrammhyperbolisierung** *f* histogram hyperbolization
Histogrammkompression *f* histogram compression (contraction)
Histogrammkurve *f* histogram function
Histogrammodifikation *f* histogram modification
Histogrammparametrisierung *f* histogram parametrization
Histogrammpyramide *f* histogram pyramid
Histogrammrückprojektion *f* histogram backprojection
Histogrammschätzung *f* histogram estimation
Histogrammschnitt *m* histogram intersection
Histogrammsegmentierung *f* histogram segmentation
Histogrammspezifikation *f* histogram specification
Histogrammspreizung *f* histogram stretching (expansion)
Histogrammstatistik *f* histogram statistics
Histogrammtal *n* histogram valley
Histogrammtransformation *f* histogram transform[ation]
Histogrammurne *f* [histogram] bin
Histogrammverarbeitung *f* histogram[-based] processing
Histogrammvergleich *m* histogram comparison; histogram matching (specification)
Histogrammverschärfung *f* histogram sharpening [operation]
Histogrammwert *m* histogram value
Histogrammzerlegung *f* histogram intersection
Historadiografie *f* historadiography
Hit-Miss-Operator *m* hit-or-miss operator *(morphological image processing)*
Hit-Miss-Transformation *f* hit-or-miss transform[ation]
HLS-Farbmodell *n*, **HLS-Farbsystem** *n* HLS (hue-lightness-saturation) color space, HLS coordinate system
HMI-Brenner *m*, **HMI-Lampe** *f* HMI lamp (light) *(from Hydrargyrum Medium Arc-Length Iodide)*
Hobby... *s.a.* Amateur...
Hobbylabor *n* home darkroom
Hobbylaborant *m* [home] darkroom enthusiast
Hobbyvideofilmer *m* videographer, videomaker
hochauflösend high-resolution
Hochauflösung *f* high resolution
Hochaufnahme *f s.* Hochformataufnahme
hochbrechend high-index *(e.g. optical glass)*
hochdimensional high-dimensionality
Hochdruck *m* 1. letterpress [printing], relief (block) printing; 2. high pressure

Hochdruck

~/**direkter** s. Hochdruck 1.
~/**indirekter** indirect letterpress [printing], letterset, letterpress (dry) offset
Hochdruckätzung f s. Chemigrafie 1.
Hochdruck-Entladungslampe f high-pressure [gas-]discharge lamp
Hochdruck-Halogenmetalldampflampe f s. HMI-Brenner
Hochdrucklampe f high-pressure lamp, arc lamp
Hochdruckmaschine f letterpress [printing] press
Hochdruck-Natriumdampflampe f high-pressure sodium lamp
Hochdruckpapier n letterpress paper
Hochdruckplatte f letterpress (relief printing) plate
~/**fotopolymere** photopolymer [printing] plate *(letterpress)*
Hochdruckplattennachformung f s. 1. Duplikatdruckform; 2. Galvano
Hochdruck-Quecksilberdampflampe f high-pressure mercury vapor lamp, HP
Hochdruckrotationsmaschine f web-fed letterpress machine
Hochdruckverfahren n relief [printing] process
hochempfindlich fast *(photographic material)*
Hochenergielaser m high-power laser
Hochenergiestrahlung f high-energy radiation
Hochformat n vertical orientation (format), portrait mode (fashion), portrait [orientation]
Hochformataufnahme f vertical-format picture
hochformatig portrait
Hochformatmonitor m portrait-mode monitor
hochfrequent high-frequency
Hochfrequenz f 1. high frequency, HF; 2. radio[-wave] frequency, RF
Hochfrequenzantenne f s. Hochfrequenzspule
Hochfrequenzbereich m radio-frequency range
Hochfrequenzfeld n radio-frequency magnetic field *(magnetic resonance imaging)*
Hochfrequenz-Filmkamera f high-speed motion picture camera
Hochfrequenzfotografie f high-speed [still] photography
Hochfrequenzimpuls m radio frequency [energy] pulse, RF pulse *(magnetic resonance imaging)*
~/**harter** hard (non-frequency-selective) RF pulse
~/**weicher** soft (frequency-selective) RF pulse
Hochfrequenzkamera f high-speed [framing] camera

Hochfrequenzkanal m high-frequency channel
Hochfrequenzkinematografie f high-speed cinematography
Hochfrequenzlautsprecher m high-frequency loudspeaker
Hochfrequenzradar n HF (high-frequency) radar
Hochfrequenzsignal n radio-frequency signal
Hochfrequenzspule f RF (radio-frequency) coil, radio-frequency antenna *(magnetic resonance imaging)*
Hochfrequenz-Ultraschall m high-frequency ultrasound
Hochgeschwindigkeitsaufnahme f high-speed recording
Hochgeschwindigkeitsbild n high-speed [still] picture, high-speed photograph
Hochgeschwindigkeits-Bildwandlerkamera f high-speed digital camera, digital high-speed camera
Hochgeschwindigkeits-Blitzfotografie f flash high-speed photography
Hochgeschwindigkeitsbus m high-speed bus
Hochgeschwindigkeitsdruck m high-speed printing
Hochgeschwindigkeitsfilmkamera f high-speed motion-picture camera
Hochgeschwindigkeitsfotografie f high-speed [still] photography, high-speed photographic imaging
hochgeschwindigkeitsfotografisch high-speed photographic
Hochgeschwindigkeitskamera f high-speed [framing] camera; high-speed still camera
Hochgeschwindigkeitskinematografie f high-speed cinematography, high-speed motion-picture photography
Hochgeschwindigkeitsnetz n high-speed network *(data transmission)*
Hochgeschwindigkeitsradiografie f high-speed radiography
Hochgeschwindigkeitsscanner m high-speed scanner
Hochgeschwindigkeitsschnittstelle f high-speed interface
Hochgeschwindigkeitsspeicher m high-speed memory device
Hochgeschwindigkeitsverbindung f s. Breitbandverbindung
Hochgeschwindigkeitsverschluss m high-speed shutter
Hochgeschwindigkeits-Videokamera f high-speed video camera
Hochglanz m high gloss
Hochglanzabzug m glossy [print]
Hochglanzbild n very glossy image
hochglänzend glossy *(e.g. photographic paper)*
Hochglanz-Farbfoto n color glossy photo
Hochglanzfoto n glossy [print]

Hochglanzkopie *f* glossy [print]
Hochglanzoberfläche *f* high-gloss surface
Hochglanzpapier *n* glossy[-surface] paper, highly polished paper, cast-coated paper
Hochglanzpresse *f* glazer
Hochkontrastauflösung *f* high-contrast resolution, HCR
Hochkontrastbeleuchtung *f* high-contrast lighting
Hochkontrastentwickler *m* high-contrast developer
Hochkontrastfilm *m* high-contrast film
hochladen to upload *(e.g. image data)*
Hochlauf *m*, **Hochlaufzeit** *f* preroll [time] *(tape editing)*
Hochleistungs[röntgen]röhre *f* high-rating X-ray tube, high-power [X-ray] tube
Hochleistungsdrucker *m* high-efficiency printer
Hochleistungsgrafik *f* high-performance graphics *(computer graphics)*
Hochleistungsinstrument *n* high-performance instrument
Hochleistungskamera *f* high-performance camera
Hochleistungs-Kernspintomograf *m* high-performance MRI scanner
Hochleistungslaser *m* high-power laser
Hochleistungsmikroskop *n* high-power microscope
Hochleistungsobjektiv *n*, **Hochleistungsoptik** *f* high-performance lens, superior lens
Hochlicht *n* highlight *(s.a. Glanzlicht, Spitzlicht)*
Hochlichtaufnahme *f* highlight exposure
Hochpass *m s.* Hochpassfilter
Hochpassbild *n* high-pass image
Hochpassfilter *n* high-pass filter; high-pass (high-frequency) kernel *(s.a. Schärfefilter)*
~/ideales ideal high-pass filter, IHPF
~/zonales zonal high-pass filter
Hochpassfilterung *f* high-pass filtering, enhancement
Hochpass-Zerlegungsfilter *n* highpass decomposition filter
Hochspannungselektronenmikroskopie *f* high-voltage electron microscopy
Hochspannungsfotografie *f s.* Kirlian-Fotografie
Höchstauflösung *f* ultrafine resolution
Höchstdichte *f* maximum density, D-max *(densitometry)*
Höchstschwärzung *f s.* Höchstdichte
Hochstspannungselektronenmikroskop *n* [extra-]high-voltage electron microscope
Hochtank *m* deep (sheet film) tank
Hochtemperaturverarbeitung *f* high-temperature processing
Hochverstellung *f* rise [movement] *(view camera)*
Hochvoltlampe *f* high-voltage lamp
hochweiß superwhite

Hochzeilenfernsehen *n* high-definition television, HDTV, advanced television, ATV
Hochzeilenkamera *f* high-line-rate camera
Hochzeitsfoto *n* wedding photograph
Hochzeitsfotograf *m* wedding photographer
Hochzeitsfotografie *f* wedding photography
Hof *m* halo, fringe *(e.g. of a halftone dot)*
Höhenabsenkung *f* deemphasis
Höhenanhebung *f* preemphasis
Höhenbild *n* high-altitude image (aerial photograph)
Höhenlinie *f* iso-elevation contour line, level contour line
Höhenliniendarstellung *f* 1. height contour curve; 2. *s.* Höhenlinienkarte
Höhenlinienkarte *f* contour map
Höhenmessradar *n* height-finding radar
Höhenmodell *n*/**digitales** digital elevation model, DEM *(photogrammetry)*
Höhennetz *n* 1. height field *(esp. as terrain representation)*; 2. sky map
Höhenobservatorium *n* mountaintop (high-altitude) observatory
höhenrichtig correct top to bottom *(image)*
Höhenstrahlung *f* [/**kosmische**] cosmic radiation (rays)
Höhensuchradar *n* height-finding radar
Höhenversatz *m* relief displacement
Höhenverstellung *f* height control (adjustment) *(e.g. of an enlarger)*
Höhenwinkel *m* elevation [angle], angle of elevation
Hohlkatodenlampe *f* hollow cathode source *(atomic absorption spectroscopy)*
Hohlkehle *f* sweep (cove), coving
Hohlraumresonator *m* resonant cavity
Hohlraumstrahler *m* cavity (blackbody) radiator, Planckian radiator
Hohlraumstrahlung *f* cavity (Planckian) radiation, blackbody [thermal] radiation
Hohlspiegel *m* concave (convergent) mirror, collecting mirror
Höllenstein *m* lunar caustic
Holograf *m* holographer
Holografie *f* holography
~/akustische acoustical holography
~/elektronische *s.* Speckle-Interferometrie/elektronische
~/helioseismische helioseismic holography
~/nichtlineare nonlinear holography
~/optische optical holography
holografieren to holograph
Holografiespeicher *m* holographic memory
holografisch holographic
Hologramm *n* hologram, holograph[ic image]
~/akustisches acoustical hologram
~/außeraxiales off-axis hologram
~/binäres binary hologram

Hologramm 198

~/**computererzeugtes** computer-generated hologram, CGH
~/**dreidimensionales** three-dimensional hologram
~/**durchlässiges** transmission hologram
~/**elektronisches** electronic hologram
~/**konjugiertes** conjugate (real) holographic image
~/**optisches** optical hologram
~/**stereografisches** stereographic hologram
~/**synthetisches** synthetic hologram
~/**zweidimensionales** two-dimensional hologram
Hologrammaufnahme f holographic recording
Hologrammbild n holograph[ic image], hologram
Hologrammebene f holographic plane, plane of [a] hologram
Hologramminterferometrie f holographic interferometry, double-exposure holography
Hologrammkamera f holographic camera
Hologrammplatte f holographic plate, holoplate
Hologrammrekonstruktion f, **Hologrammwiedergabe** f holographic (hologram) reconstruction
homochromatisch homochromatic
Homodiode f homojunction diode [array], homojunction device
Homogenität f 1. homogeneity *(e.g. of an image region)*; 2. s. Verschiebungsinvarianz
Homogenitätsgrad m degree of homogeneity
Homogenitätskriterium n homogeneity criterion
Homoübergang m homojunction *(semiconductor)*
Hopfield-Netz[werk] n Hopfield net[work], symmetric recurrent network *(image coding, pattern recognition)*
hörbar audible
Horizont m horizon
Horizontalablenkung f horizontal sweep (deflection), line sweep
Horizontalauflösung f horizontal resolution
Horizontalaustastung f horizontal (line) blanking; horizontal blanking period
Horizontalbeleuchtung f s. Hintergrundlicht
Horizontalentfernung f ground range *(radar)*
Horizontalfrequenz f horizontal [sweep] frequency, horizontal (line) scanning frequency, horizontal scan rate, line frequency (rate)
Horizontalimpuls m horizontal sync[hronization] pulse
Horizontalkamera f horizontal [process] camera, gallery camera

Horizontalrücklauf m horizontal retrace [time], line flyback
Horizontalschwenk m pan [move], pan[orama] shot
Horizontalsynchronimpuls m horizontal sync[hronization] pulse, horizontal synchronizing signal, HSYNC
Horizontalsynchronisation f horizontal sync[hronization]
Horizontalvergrößerungsgerät n horizontal enlarger
Horizontalwinkel m azimuth
Horizontalzelle f horizontal cell *(of the retina)*
Horizontebene f horizon plane
Horizontlinie f horizon line
Hörkopf m pickup head *(magnetic sound reproduction)*
Hornhaut f [eye] cornea
Hornhautkrümmung f corneal curvature
Hornhautmikroskop n corneal microscope
Hornstrahler m horn[-type] radiator *(radar)*
Horopter m horopter *(imaging geometry)*
~/**empirischer** empirical horopter
~/**geometrischer** geometric[al] horopter
Hörschall m audible sound
Hörschwelle f threshold of hearing (audibility), audible level
Hör-Sprech-Garnitur f headset
Hostbus m host bus
Hostcomputer m, **Hostrechner** m host [computer], main computer
Hough-Raum m Hough domain (space), Hough transform plane, accumulator array
Hough-Transformation f Hough transform[ation], Hough technique *(image segmentation)*
~ **für Geraden** linear Hough transform
~ **für Kreise** circular Hough transform
~/**probabilistische** probabilistic Hough transform
~/**randomisierte** randomized Hough transform
~/**unscharfe** fuzzy Hough transform
Hough-Transformierte f Hough transform
Hounsfield-Einheit f Hounsfield (H) unit, HU, CT number *(measure of amplitude resolution in computed tomography)*
Hounsfield-Skale f Hounsfield scale *(for absorption coefficients)*
HSB-Farbmodell n HSB color model *(from hue, saturation, brightness)*
HSI-Merkmalsraum m, **HSI-Raum** m HSI space (system), hue-saturation-intensity color system, HSV (hue-saturation-value) space
HSL-Farbmodell n s. HLS-Farbmodell
Hub m hub
Hubble-Teleskop n, **Hubble-Weltraumteleskop** n Hubble Space Telescope, HAST, Hubble telescope

Hubschraubersimulator *m* helicopter simulator
Hueckel-Operator *m* Hueckel operator *(edge detection)*
Hufeisenmontierung *f* horseshoe[-shaped] mounting *(telescope)*
Huffman-Algorithmus *m* Huffman [coding] algorithm *(image compression)*
Huffman-Baum *m* Huffman tree
Huffman-Code *m* Huffman [shift] code
~/**erweiterter** extended Huffman code
~/**kanonischer** canonical Huffman code
~/**modifizierter** modified Huffman code, MHC *(facsimile transmission)*
Huffman-Codierer *m* Huffman coder
Huffman-Codierung *f* Huffman [en]coding, Shannon-Fano-Huffman coding, variable-length coding, VLC
~/**adaptive** adaptive Huffman [en]coding
~/**dynamische** dynamic Huffman [en]coding
~/**statische** static Huffman [en]coding
Huffman-Tabelle *f* Huffman [code] table, Huffman coding table
Hülle *f*/**konvexe** convex hull *(computer graphics)*
Hüllenelektron *n* orbital (orbiting) electron
Hüllenstreifen *m* negative sleeve
Hüllfläche *f* envelope
Hüllkörper *m* bounding volume *(computer graphics)*
Hüllkugel *f* bounding sphere
Hüllkurve *f* envelope
Hüllkurvendemodulation *f* envelope demodulation
Hundert-Hertz-Fernsehen *n* 100 Hz TV
Hurenkind *n* widow [line] *(printing)*
Huygens-Helmholtz-Invariante *f s.* Helmholtz[-Lagrange]-Invariante
Huygens-Okular *n* Huygenian [microscope] eyepiece, negative eyepiece
Hyalotypie *f* hyalotype *(albumen-on-glass positive transparency)*
Hybrid[bild]codierer *m* hybrid [image] coder
Hybridcodierung *f* hybrid [transform/waveform] coding
Hybridfilter *n* hybrid filter
Hybridgerät *n* hybrid device (set)
Hybridmodellierung *f* hybrid modeling
Hybridobjektiv *n* hybrid [glass-polymer] lens
Hybridrecorder *m* hybrid recorder
Hydraulikkopf *m s.* Hydrokopf
Hydrazin *n* hydrazine *(developer additive)*
Hydrochinon *n* hydroquinone *(developing chemical)*
Hydrochinonentwickler *m* hydroquinone developer
Hydrokopf *m* hydraulic head, fluid[-dampened tripod] head
hydrophil hydrophilic, water-receptive
Hydrophilie *f* hydrophilicity
hydrophob hydrophobic, water-repellent
Hydrophobie *f* hydrophobicity
Hydroxydiaminobenzenhydrochlorid *n* diaminophenol dihydrochloride *(developing agent)*
Hydroxylaminsulfat *n* hydroxylammonium sulfate *(color developer additive)*
hyperbelförmig, hyperbolisch hyperbolic[al]
Hyperboloid *n* hyperboloid *(primitive object)*
Hyperbolspiegel *m* hyperbolic mirror
Hyperebene *f*, **Hyperfläche** *f* hyperplane, hypersurface, decision (separating) surface *(pattern classification)*; hyperpatch *(computer graphics)*
Hyperfokaldistanz *f* hyperfocal distance
Hyperfokaleinstellung *f* hyperfocal position
Hyperkugel *f* hypersphere
Hyperlink *m(n)* hyperlink *(for connecting hypertext or hypermedia)*
Hypermediasystem *n* hypermedia [system] *(database format)*
Hypermetropie *f* hyper[metr]opia, farsightedness, longsightedness, long sight
hypermetropisch hyper[metr]opic, farseeing, farsighted, longsighted
hyperop *s.* hypermetropisch
Hyperopie *f s.* Hypermetropie
hyperpanchromatisch hyperpanchromatic *(emulsion)*
Hyperpolarisation *f* hyperpolarization
hyperpolarisieren to hyperpolarize
hypersensibilisieren to hypersensitize
Hypersensibilisierung *f* hypersensitization
hyperspektral hyperspectral
Hyperspektralaufnahme *f* 1. hyperspectral imaging; 2. hyperspectral image
Hyperspektraldaten *pl* hyperspectral data
Hyperspektralsensor *m* hyperspectral sensor
Hyperstereoskopie *f* hyperstereoscopy
Hypertext *m* hypertext *(database format)*
Hypertextmaschine *f*/**abstrakte** hypertext abstract machine, HAM *(hypermedia system)*
Hypervoxel *n* hypervoxel *(computer graphics)*
Hypochromasie *f* hypochromia *(optics)*
Hypostereoskopie *f* hypostereoscopy
Hyposulfit *n* hypo[sulfite], sodium thiosulfate *(fixing agent)*
Hypothetisieren *n* **und Testen** *n* hypothetize-and-test *(image recognition)*
Hysterese *f* hysteresis
Hysterese-Binarisierung *f* hysteresis thresholding
Hystereseschleife *f* hysteresis loop
Hysterosalpingografie *f* hysterosalpingography

I-Bild *n s.* Intrabild
Icon *n* [graphical] icon, pictorial icon; computer (on-screen) icon; placeholder
~/animiertes motion (animated) icon, micon
Idealbild *n* ideal image *(optics)*
Ideenskizze *f* scribble
idempotent idempotent
Idempotentfilter *n* idempotent operator *(morphological image processing)*
Idempotenz *f* idempotence
identifizierbar identifiable; recognizable
Identifizierbarkeit *f* identifiability; recognizability
identifizieren to identify
Identifizierung *f* identification
Identitätsmatrix *f* identity matrix
Ideogramm *n* ideogram
IIR-Filter *n* IIR (infinite impulse response) filter
Ikone *f* icon *(s.a.* Icon*)*
Ikonenindexieren *n* iconic indexing *(pattern recognition)*
Ikonik *f* low-level [computer] vision
ikonisch iconic
Ikonizität *f* iconicity
Ikonografie *f* iconography
Ikonoskop *n* iconoscope, ike *(a camera tube)*
Illuminanz *f* illuminance, light level
Illumination *f* illumination *(s.a.* Ausleuchtung, Beleuchtung*)*
Illuminator *m* illuminator
illuminieren to illuminate
Illusion *f s.* Täuschung
Illustration *f* [pictorial] illustration
~/farbige color illustration
Illustrationsfotografie *f* illustration photography
Illustrationsprogramm *n* drawing program
Illustrator *m* illustrator
illustrieren to illustrate, to picture, to pictorialize
IL-Sensor *m s.* Interline-Transfer-Bildaufnehmer
imbibieren to imbibe
Imbibitionskopie *f* imbibition print
Imbibitions-Kopierfilm *m* film blank
Immersionsflüssigkeit *f* index-matching fluid
Immersionsgitter *n* immersion grating
Immersionslinse *f* immersion lens
Immersionsmedium *n* immersion medium
Immersionsmikroskop *n* immersion [electron] microscope
Immersionsobjektiv *n* immersed [microscope] objective, immersion objective (lens)
Immersionsöl *n* immersion oil *(microscopy)*
Immunfluoreszenzmikroskopie *f* immunofluorescence microscopy
Impedanz *f* impedance
~/akustische acoustic impedance *(sonography)*
Impedanzkardiografie *f* impedance cardiography
impedanzkardiografisch impedance-cardiographic
Impedanzplethysmograf *m* electric-impedance plethysmograph
Impedanzplethysmografie *f* [electric-]impedance plethysmography
Impedanzspektroskopie/elektrochemische electrochemical impedance spectroscopy
Impedanzsprung *m* impedance mismatch
Impedanztomografie *f* [electric-]impedance tomography
Impedanzwandler *m* impedance converter
imperzeptibel imperceptible
Implantationsmaske *f* implant mask
implodieren to implode
Implosion *f* implosion
Importieren to acquire *(e.g. image data)*
Impressum *n* masthead
Imprimatur *n(f)* imprimatur
Impuls *m* [im]pulse *(s.a. under* Puls*)*
~/elektrischer electrical impulse
~/elektromagnetischer electromagnetic pulse, EMP
~/elektronischer electronic [im]pulse
~/magnetischer magnetic impulse
impulsähnlich impulselike
Impulsanstiegszeit *f* rise time
Impulsantwort *f* impulse response
~/begrenzte (endliche) finite impulse response, FIR
~/Gaußsche Gaussian-shaped impulse response
~/infinite (unbegrenzte) infinite impulse response, IIR
~/lokale local impulse response
~/positionsunabhängige *s.* ~/verschiebungsinvariante
~/unbegrenzte *s.* ~/infinite
Impulsantwortfilter *n*/**endliches** finite impulse response filter, FIR, cosine filter
~/unendliches infinite impulse response filter, IIR
Impulsantwortfunktion *f* impulse response function
Impulsausbreitung *f* pulse propagation
Impulsdauer *f* pulse duration
Impuls-Doppler-Radar *n* pulse Doppler radar
Impuls-Echo-Bild *n* pulse echo [ultrasonic] image

Impuls-Echo-Bildwandler *m* pulse echo ultrasonic scanner, pulse-echo imaging transducer
Impuls-Echo-Methode *f s.* Impuls-Echo-Verfahren
Impuls-Echo-Prinzip *n* pulse echo principle
Impuls-Echo-Signal *n* pulse echo signal
Impuls-Echo-Verfahren *n* pulse echo mode (imaging)
Impuls-Echo-Verhalten *n* pulse echo behavior
Impulsfilter *n* impulse (Dirac) filter, nearest-neighbor filter
Impulsflanke *f* pulse edge
Impulsfolge *f* pulse sequence (train), train (series) of pulses
Impulsfolgefrequenz *f* pulse repetition frequency (rate), pulse recurrence frequency, PRF *(ultrasound, radar)*
Impulsformungsfilter *n* pulse shaping filter
Impulsfrequenz *f* pulse frequency (rate)
Impulsfunktion *f* impulse (delta) function, Dirac [delta] function *(signal processing)*
~/**diskrete** discrete impulse (delta) function, unit sample sequence, Kronecker delta [function]
~/**Gaußsche** Gaussian impulse function
~/**kontinuierliche** continuous impulse function
~/**rechteckförmige** rectangular impulse function
Impulsgeber *m*, **Impulsgenerator** *m* [synchronizing] pulse generator, impulse (clock) generator, pulser
Impulshöhenanalysator *m* pulse height analyzer *(gamma camera)*
Impulshöhenanalyse *f* pulse height analysis
Impulshöhenangleichung *f* pulse height equalization
Impulshöhendiskriminator *m s.* Impulshöhenanalysator
Impulshöhendiskriminierung *f* pulse height discrimination
Impulshöhenverteilung *f* pulse height distribution
Impulsintegration/inkohärente postdetection integration
~/**kohärente** predetection integration
Impulsinterferenz *f* intersymbol interference, ISI
Impulsinvarianz *f* impulse invariance
Impulslaser *m* pulsed laser
Impulslichtquelle *f* pulsed light source
Impulsmagnetron *n* pulsed magnetron
Impulsmodulation *f* pulse modulation
Impulsmodulator *m* pulse modulator
Impulsradar[verfahren] *m* pulse[d] radar
Impulsrauschen *n* impulse (impulsive) noise, speckle (speckling) noise, salt-and-pepper noise *(s.a.* Punktrauschen*)*
~/**bipolares** bipolar impulse noise, shot (spike) noise *(s.a.* Quantenrauschen*)*
~/**unipolares** unipolar impulse noise
Impulsschallverfahren *n s.* Impuls-Echo-Verfahren
Impulssequenz *f s.* Impulsfolge
Impulsspitzenverschiebung *f* peak shift
Impulsstörung *f s.* Impulsrauschen
Impulsthermografie *f* fast transient thermography (thermal imaging) *(nondestructive evaluation)*
Impulsunterdrückung *f* pulse suppression
Impulswiederholungsfrequenz *f s.* Impulsfolgefrequenz
Impulszählung *f* pulse counting
Index *m* 1. index; indication; 2. subscript; 3. quantitative invisibility *(computer graphics)*
Indexbild *n* index print, thumbnail [images]
Indexellipsoid *n* index ellipsoid, optical indicatrix *(crystal optics)*
indexieren to index *(e.g. image data)*
Indexprint *m s.* Indexbild
Indexprofil *n*/**parabelförmiges** parabolic index profile
Indexsignal *n* index signal *(video)*
Index-Suchlauf *m* index search
Indexverfahren *n* edge-intersection algorithm
Indikator[farbstoff] *m* indicator dye
Indikatormessstreifen *m* indicator strip
Indikatorpapier *n* indicator [test] paper
Indikatrix *f* 1. indicatrix; 2. *s.* ~/optische
~/**optische** *f* optical indicatrix, index ellipsoid *(crystal optics)*
Indiumantimonid *n* indium antimonide *(photon detector)*
Indiumgalliumarsenid *n* indium gallium arsenide *(photon detector)*
Indiumzinnoxid *n* indium tin oxide, ITO *(electrode material)*
Individualfunktion *f* custom setting
Individualverarbeitung *f* custom finishing
Induktion *f* induction
~/**magnetische** magnetic induction (flux density)
Induktionsperiode *f* induction period
Induktionsspule *f* induction coil
Induktionszerfall *m*/**freier** free induction decay, FID *(nuclear magnetic resonance)*
induktiv inductive
Induktivität *f* inductance
Industrieaufnahme *f* infrared image
Industrieendoskop *n* borescope [lens], probe lens, industrial endoscope
Industriefernsehen *n* industrial television (TV)
Industriefilm *m* industrial film
Industriefotograf *m* industrial photographer
Industriefotografie *f* [on-location] industrial photography
industriefotografisch industrial photographic
Industriefotogrammetrie *f* industrial photogrammetry

Industriekamera f industrial camera
Industriemikroskopie f industrial microscopy
Industrieroboter m industrial robot
Industrie-Röntgenfilm m industrial X-ray film
induzieren to induce
ineinanderkopieren to [re]image onto itself
Inferenzmaschine f inference machine (engine) *(artificial intelligence*
Inflow-Angiografie f inflow (time-of-flight) angiography
Infografik f information graphics *(s.a. under* Visualisierung*)*
Informatik f information (computer) science, informatics
~/**medizinische** medical image informatics, MII
Information f information
~/**bildhafte (bildliche)** pictorial (picture) information, image information
~/**binär codierte** binary coded information, BCI
~/**dienstebezogene** service information
~/**grafische** graphical information
~/**ikonische** iconic information
~/**optische** optical information
~/**programmspezifische** program-specific information, PSI
~/**redundante** redundant information
~/**spektrale** spectral information
~/**visuelle** visual information
Informationsanzeige f information display
Informationsdichte f information density
Informationseffizienz f information efficiency
Informationserhaltung f information preservation
Informationsgehalt m information content *(e.g. of an image)*
~/**mittlerer** average information content; entropy *(of a source symbol)*
Informationsgeschwindigkeit f information rate
Informationsgrafik f information graphics
Informationskanal m information channel
Informationsmaß n information measure
Informations-Pit n information pit
Informationsspeichersystem n information storage system
Informationsspeicherung f information storage
Informationsspeichervermögen n information storage capacity
Informationssystem n/**geografisches** geographic information system, GIS
~/**radiologisches** radiological information system, RIS
Informationstechnik f information technology, IT
informationstheoretisch information-theoretic[al], communication-theoretic
Informationstheorie f information theory, communication [engineering] theory
Informationsträger m information carrier
Informationsübertragung f information transfer (transmission)
Informationsübertragungssystem n information transmission system
Informationsverarbeitung f information processing
~/**visuelle** visual information processing
Informationsverlust m information loss, loss of information
Informationsvisualisierung f information visualization
Informationswiedergewinnung f information retrieval
infrarot infrared, ultrared
Infrarot n infrared, IR
~/**abbildendes** imaging infrared, IIR
~/**extremes** extreme infrared
~/**fernes** far infrared [region], far IR, FIR
~/**fotografisches** s. Infrarot/nahes
~/**kurzwelliges** short-wave[length] infrared, SWIR
~/**langwelliges** long-wave[length] infrared [region], LWIR
~/**mittleres** mid[-wavelength] infrared, medium[-wave] infrared, mid-IR region, MIR
~/**nahes** near-infrared [region], NIR, far red
~/**thermales (thermisches)** thermal infrared, THIR
Infrarotabsorber m infrared absorber *(thermal printing)*
Infrarotabsorptionsspektroskopie f infrared absorption spectroscopy
Infrarotabtastung f infrared scanning
Infrarot-Astronomie f infrared astronomy
Infrarotaufnahme f infrared photograph
Infrarotauslöser m infrared slave (trigger)
Infrarot-Autofokus m infrared autofocus
Infrarotbande f infrared (IR) band
Infrarot-Bandpassfilter n IR band-pass filter
Infrarotbeleuchtung f infrared illumination
Infrarotbelichtung f infrared exposure
Infrarot-Beobachtungssatellit m infrared observation satellite
Infrarotbereich m infrared (IR) range, infrared region (regime)
Infrarotbild n infrared image (picture); thermal image
Infrarotbildaufnahme f infrared (IR) imaging
Infrarotbilddaten pl IR image data
Infrarotbildsensor m infrared (IR) thermographic system, IR imager
Infrarotbildverarbeitung f infrared image processing
Infrarotbildwandler m infrared image converter
Infrarotblitz m infrared flash
Infrarotblitzfotografie f infrared flash photography

Infrarot-CCD *f* focal plane array imager, FPA imager (detector)
Infrarotdetektor *m* infrared [photo]detector, infrared diode (photon) detector, IR detection device; infrared image detector
Infrarotdiode *f* infrared diode
infrarotdurchlässig infrared transmitting
Infrarotemission *f* infrared emission
Infrarotemitterdiode *f* infrared-emitting diode
infrarotempfindlich infrared-sensitive, sensitive to infrared light
Infrarotempfindlichkeit *f* infrared sensitivity
Infrarotemulsion *f* infrared emulsion
Infrarotendoskopie *f* infrared endoscopy
Infrarotenergie *f* infrared energy
Infrarotfarbfilm *m* IR color film, color infrared film, [IR] false-color film, false IR film
Infrarot-Farbfoto *n* infrared (IR) color photograph, false color photograph, camouflage detection photograph
Infrarot-Farbfotografie *f* color infrared photography
Infrarot-Farbluftbild *n* infrared color [aerial] photograph
Infrarot-Fernauslöser *m* infrared slave (trigger)
Infrarot-Fernbedienung *f* infrared remote control [unit], infrared handset
Infrarotfernsteuerung *f s.* Infrarot-Fernbedienung
Infrarotfilm *m* infrared [photographic] film, infrared-sensitive film
Infrarotfilter *n* infrared[-transmitting] filter
Infrarotfluoreszenz *f* infrared fluorescence
Infrarotfluoreszenzfotografie *f* infrared fluorescence photography
Infrarotfoto *n* infrared (IR) photograph
Infrarotfotografie *f* infrared photography
Infrarot-Fotomaterial *n* infrared [photographic] material
Infrarotgerät *n* infrared device
Infrarotkamera *f* infrared [imaging] camera
Infrarotkanal *m* infrared channel
Infrarotkinefilm *m* infrared motion-picture film
Infrarotkinematografie *f* infrared cinematography
Infrarotlampe *f* infrared [emitting] lamp
Infrarotlaser *m* infrared laser
~/abstimmbarer tunable infrared laser
Infrarotlicht *n* infrared light
Infrarotlichtstrahl *m* infrared beam
Infrarotluftaufnahme *f* aerial infrared image (photograph)
Infrarot-Luftbildfotografie *f* infrared aerial photography
Infrarotlumineszenz *f* infrared luminescence
Infrarotmarke *f*, **Infrarotmarkierung** *f* infrared mark (focusing index)
Infrarotmikroskop *n* infrared microscope
Infrarotmikroskopie *f* infrared microscopy
Infrarotobjektiv *n* infrared optics
Infrarotoptik *f* infrared optics
infrarotoptisch infrared-optical
Infrarotplatte *f* infrared [photosensitive] plate
Infrarotpolarisationsfilter *n* infrared polarizing filter
Infrarotpyrometer *n* infrared pyrometer
Infrarotquant *n* infrared photon
Infrarotquelle *f* infrared [radiation] source
Infrarotreflektografie *f* infrared (IR) reflectography, near-IR-photography
infrarotreflektografisch infrared reflectographic
Infrarot-Satellitenbild *n* infrared satellite image, satellite infrared image
Infrarotscanner *m* infrared scanner
Infrarotschnittstelle *f* infrared interface
Infrarotsender *m* infrared transmitter; infrared emitter
Infrarotsensor *m* infrared sensor (receptor)
Infrarotsichtgerät *n* infrared scope; infrared visual display unit
Infrarotsignatur *f* infrared signature
Infrarotspektroskopie *f* infrared spectroscopy
Infrarotspektrum *n* infrared spectrum
Infrarotsperrfilter *n* infrared-blocking (infrared-reflecting) filter, IR absorbing filter, hot filter
Infrarotspiegel *m* infrared (IR) mirror, hot (heat-reflecting) mirror
Infrarotstrahl *m* infrared beam
~[en]teiler *m* infrared beam splitter
Infrarotstrahlung *f* infrared (IR) radiation
Infrarotstrahlungssensor *m* infrared photodetector
Infrarotsystem *n*/**abwärts gerichtetes** downward looking infrared [system], DLIR
Infrarottechnik *f* infrared technology
Infrarotteleskop *n* infrared telescope
Infrarotthermografie *f* infrared (IR) thermography
infrarotthermografisch IR thermographic
Infrarot-Transmissionsfilter *n s.* Infrarotfilter
infrarottransparent infrared transmitting
Infrarottrockner *m* infrared drier
Infrarotübertragung *f* infrared transmission
Infrarot-Videokamera *f* infrared video camera
Infrarot-Wärmebildverfahren *n* infrared thermal imaging technique
Infrarot-Wärmesensor *m* thermal infrared sensor
Infrarotwellenlänge *f* infrared wavelength
Infraschall[bereich] *m* infrasonic frequency range
Ingenieurarbeit *f*/**rechnerunterstützte** computer-aided engineering, CAE

Ingenieurzeichnung f engineer's drawing
Inhalteanbieter m content provider (server) *(electronic media)*
Inhaltseinsetzung f content insertion *(video-on demand)*
Inhibition f inhibition
~/**laterale** lateral inhibition *(vision)*
~/**zeitliche** temporal inhibition *(vision)*
Inhibitor m inhibitor, retardant
Initial n, **Initialbuchstabe** m s. Initiale
Initiale f initial [capital letter]; ornamental capital
~/**herausgestellte** raised cap[ital]
~/**hineingestellte** drop cap[ital]
initialisieren to initialize *(e.g. a video board)*; to initialize, to format *(e.g. a floppy disk)*
Initialisierungsdatei f initialization file
Initialpunkt m 1. initial (starting) point *(e.g. in chain coding)*; 2. s. Keimpunkt
Injektionslaser m injection (semiconducting) laser, semiconductor [injection] laser, semiconductor laser diode
In-Kamera-Effekt m [in-]camera effect, optical effect *(cinema)*
Ink-Jet-Drucker m ink-jet printer
Ink-Jet-Druckmaschine f ink-jet printer
Inklusionsinformation f inclusion updating information *(computational geometry)*
inkohärent incoherent
Inkohärenz f incoherence
inkompatibel incompatible
Inkompatibilität f incompatibility
Inkreis m inscribed circle
Inkrement n increment
inkrementell incremental
inkrementieren to increment
Inkubationszeit f s. Induktionsperiode
Inkunabel f incunabulum, incunable
In-line-Farbbildröhre f s. In-line-Röhre
In-line-Hologramm n in-line hologram
In-line-Röhre f [precision-]in-line tube, PIL tube
Innen[licht]messung f through-the-lens metering, TTL metering
Innenaufnahme f 1. interior recording; 2. indoor photograph (picture); interior shot
~ **bei Nacht** night interior
Innenausleuchtung f indoor illumination
Innenbeleuchtung f indoor illumination
Innenbildumkehrverfahren n internal-image [emulsion] reversal process
Innendekoration f s. Innendrehort
Innendreh m, **Innendreharbeit** f interior shooting *(filming)*
Innendrehort m interior location; interior set, indoor setting; cover set
Innenfokussierung f internal focusing
Innenkeim m intragranular nucleus *(photographic process)*
Innenkoma f positive coma

Innenraumantenne f indoor antenna (aerial)
Innenraumaufnahme f indoor photograph (picture); interior shot
Innenraumlicht n indoor light
Innenraum-Porträtaufnahme f indoor portrait shot
Innenszene f indoor (interior) scene
innenverspiegelt internal mirrored *(surface)*
Insert n insert [material], insert sequence
Insertschnitt m 1. insert editing *(videography)*; 2. insert [edit]
In-situ-Mikroskopie f in situ microscopy
installieren to install
Instantfotografie f instant[-picture] photography, instantaneous photography
instantiieren to instantiate
Instantiierung f, **Instanzierung** f instantiation *(computer graphics)*
instanziieren s. instantiieren
instationär nonstationary *(e.g. an image signal)*
Instationarität f nonstationarity *(e.g. of images)*
Instrument n/**faseroptisches** fiber-optic instrument
~/**optisches** optical instrument, optic
Instrumentenkonvergenz f s. Apparatekonvergenz
Intaglioplatte f intaglio image carrier
Integral n/**Fresnelsches** Fresnel sine integral *(diffractive optics)*
Integralbelichtungsmesser m integrating meter
Integralbelichtungsmessung f s. Integralmessung
Integralfilm m integral (single-sheet) film
Integralmessung f integrating metering
~/**mittenbetonte** center-weighted metering
Integrationsbedingung f integrability constraint
Integrationszeit f integration time (period) *(e.g. of an analog-to-digital converter)*
Integrierbarkeit f integrability
Intelligenz f/**künstliche** artificial intelligence, AI, machine intelligence *(computer science)*
Intensität f intensity; amount *(of achromatic light)*
Intensitätsabfall m/**anodenseitiger** heel effect *(radiography)*
Intensitätsauflösung f intensity resolution
Intensitätsbereich m intensity range
Intensitätsbild n intensity image; intensity plot (map)
Intensitätsebene f intensity plane *(gray-scale image)*
Intensitätsfunktion f intensity function
Intensitätsgradient m intensity gradient
Intensitätshistogramm n intensity histogram

Intensitätsintervall *n* intensity interval
Intensitätskante *f* intensity edge
Intensitätsmodulation *f* intensity modulation
Intensitätsmuster *n* intensity pattern
Intensitätsprofil *n* intensity profile, profile of intensity
Intensitätsrauschen *n* intensity noise *(of a light source)*
~/**relatives** relative intensity noise, RIN
Intensitätsschrift *f* variable-density [sound] track, push-pull system *(cinema)*
Intensitätsschwelle *f* intensity (gray-scale) threshold
Intensitätsskala *f* intensity scale
Intensitätsskalierung *f* intensity scaling
Intensitätstransformation *f* intensity transformation
Intensitätsübergang *m* intensity transition
Intensitätsumkehreffekt *m* latent image destruction effect
Intensitätsverfahren *n* variable-density system *(optical sound recording)*
Intensitätsverteilung *f* intensity distribution
~/**Gaußsche** Gaussian intensity distribution
Intensitätsverzerrung *f* intensity distortion
Intensitätswert *m* intensity (brightness) value
interagieren to interact
Interaktion *f*/**multimodale** multimodal interaction
Interaktionsbaustein *m* widget *(computer graphics)*
Interaktionsgerät *n* interactive input device
Interaktionskanal *m* interaction channel
interaktiv interactive
Interaktivität *f* interactivity
Interbild *n s.* P-Bild
intercodieren to intercode
Intercodierung *f s.* Interframe-Codierung
Intercomeinrichtung *f* intercom [system], intercommunication system
Intercomlautsprecher *m* intercom speaker, squawk box
Intercomsignal *n* intercom signal
Interface *n* interface; interface device, black box *(s.a.* Schnittstelle 1.*)*
Interferenz *f* interference
~/**destruktive** destructive interference
~/**elektromagnetische** electromagnetic interference
~/**kohärente** coherent interference
~/**konstruktive** constructive interference
~/**optische** optical (light) interference
Interferenzbild *n* interference figure (pattern) *(s.a.* Moiré*)*
Interferenzeffekt *m,* **Interferenzerscheinung** *f* interference effect (phenomenon)
Interferenzfarbe *f* interference color
Interferenzfeld *n* interference field

Interferenzfilter *n* interference filter; dichroi[ti]c filter
~/**dielektrisches** dielectric interference filter
Interferenzflimmern *n s.* Farbübersprechen
Interferenzfotografie *f* interference photography
Interferenzgitter *n* interference grating
Interferenzgleichung *f* interference equation
Interferenzholografie *f* interference holography
Interferenzkontrast *m* interference contrast
Interferenzlinie *f* interference fringe
Interferenzmikroskop *n* interference microscope, interferometric light microscope
~/**doppelbrechendes** birefringent interference microscope
Interferenzmikroskopie *f* interference microscopy
Interferenzmuster *n* interference pattern (figure) *(s.a.* Moiré*)*
Interferenzschicht *f* interference coating
Interferenzspektrum *n* interference spectrum
Interferenzstreifen *m* interference fringe
Interferenzstreifenmuster *n s.* Interferenzmuster
Interferenz-Wärmeschutzfilter *n* hot mirror
interferieren to interfere
Interferograf *m* interferograph
Interferografie *f* interferography
interferografisch interferographic
Interferogramm *n* interferogram
~/**holografisches** holographic interferogram
~/**shearografisches** shearographic interferogram
Interferometer *n* [optical] interferometer
~/**Mach-Zehndersches** Mach-Zehnder interferometer
~/**Voglsches** Vogl interferometer
Interferometrie *f* interferometry
~/**holografische** holographic interferometry, double-exposure holography
~/**shearografische** shearographic interferometry
interferometrisch interferometric
Interferrikum *n* air gap *(between field-magnet poles)*
Interframe-Codierung *f* interframe [en]coding, interpicture coding, frame-to-frame coding
~/**prädiktive** interframe predictive (differential) coding
Interieuraufnahme *f* indoor photograph (picture); interior shot
Interimage-Effekt *m* interimage effect
Interline-Transfer-Bildaufnehmer *m* interline transfer imager (CCD array)

Intermediatefilm *m* intermediate [film]
Intermittenzeffekt *m* intermittency effect
Intermodulation *f* intermodulation
Intermodulationsprodukt *n* intermodulation product
Intermodulationsstörung *f* intermodulation noise
Intermodulationsverzerrung *f* intermodulation distortion
Internegativ *n* intermediate (dupe) negative, interneg[ative]; dupe neg; color reversal intermediate, color internegative *(duplicate negative)*
Internegativfilm *m* internegative film *(s.a. Internegativ)*
Internet *n* 1. internet[work]; 2. Internet, net, cyberspace
Internetanschluss *m* Internet port (connection)
Internetanwendung *f* Internet application
Internetbereich *m* Internet domain
Internetbild *n* Internet image
Internetbildschirm *m* Internet screen
Internet-Datendienst *m* datacast[ing]
Internetdienst *m* Internet service
Internetdienstanbieter *m*, **Internet-Dienstleister** *m* Internet [service] provider, ISP
internetfähig Internet-enabled, Internet-ready
Internet-Fernsehen *n* Web TV; Web broadcasting
Internetgestalter *m* Web page designer
Internetgestaltung *f* Web design
Internetinhalt *m* Internet content
Internetkamera *f* webcam, Webcam
Internet-Multimedia *n* Internet multimedia
Internetportal *n* portal, walled garden
Internetprotokoll *n* Internet protocol, IP
Internetseite *f* Web page
Internet-Sicherheitsschleuse *f* firewall *(computer software)*
internettauglich Internet-enabled, Internet-ready
Internet-Trickfilm *m* animated GIF
Internetverbindung *f* Internet connection
Internetvideo *n* Internet (webcast) video
Internet-Videoanimation *f* [streaming] Internet animation, animacast
Internet-Videokonferenzbetrieb *m* Internet videoconferencing
Internetzugang *m* 1. Internet access; 2. Internet access link
Internetzugriff *m* Internet access
Interoperabilität *f* interoperability *(e.g. of an image database)*
Interpolation *f* interpolation *(image-processing operation)*
~/**bewegungsadaptive** motion-dependent interpolation, motion-adaptive interpolation *(narrow-band picture transmission)*
~/**bewegungskompensierte** motion-compensated interpolation
~/**bikubische** bicubic interpolation
~/**bilineare** bilinear interpolation
~/**digitale** digital interpolation
~/**elektronenoptische** electron-optical interpolation
~ **erster Ordnung** first-order interpolation
~/**formbasierte** shape-based interpolation
~/**geometrische** geometric interpolation
~/**hierarchische** hierarchical interpolation
~/**isoparametrische** isoparametric interpolation
~/**konsistente** consistent interpolation
~/**kubische** cubic interpolation
~/**lineare** linear interpolation, lerping
~/**logische** logical (logic-based) interpolation
~/**objektbasierte** object-based interpolation
~/**optimierte** optimized interpolation
~/**polynomiale (polynomische)** polynomial interpolation
~/**räumliche** spatial interpolation
~/**sphärische lineare** spherical linear interpolation, SLERP *(computer animation)*
~/**szenenbasierte** scene-based interpolation
~/**transfinite** transfinite interpolation
~/**trilineare** trilinear interpolation
~/**visuelle** visual interpolation
~/**zeitliche** temporal interpolation
Interpolationsalgorithmus *m* interpolation algorithm
Interpolationsansatz *m* interpolation approach
Interpolationsartefakt *n* interpolation artifact
Interpolationscodierung *f* interpolative coding
Interpolationsfaltungsmaske *f* interpolation mask
Interpolationsfehler *m* interpolation error
Interpolationsfilter *n* interpolation filter (operator), interpolating filter, interpolator
~ **nullter Ordnung** zero-order interpolation [reconstruction] filter
Interpolationsfunktion *f* interpolation (interpolating) function
Interpolationsgenauigkeit *f* interpolation accuracy
Interpolationsgitter *n* interpolation lattice
Interpolationskern *m* interpolation kernel
Interpolationskoeffizient *m* interpolation coefficient
Interpolationskurve *f* interpolating (interpolation) curve *(s.a. Interpolationsfunktion)*
Interpolationsmaske *f* interpolation mask
Interpolationsmatrix *f* interpolation matrix
Interpolationspassband *n* interpolation passband
Interpolationspolynom *n* interpolation polynomial

interpolativ interpolative
Interpolator *m* interpolator
~/linearer linear interpolator
interpolieren to interpolate
Interpositiv *n* interpositive [film], intermediate positive; master positive; interpositive print; color master positive [print]
Interpretationsfaktor *m* interpretation element
Interpretationsschlüssel *m* interpretation key *(image analysis)*
interpretierbar interpretable
Interpretierbarkeit *f* interpretability
interpretieren to interpret
Interpretoskop *n* interpretoscope *(photogrammetry)*
Interpunktionszeichen *n* punctuation mark
Interreflexion *f* interreflection
Intervall *n* interval; time (temporal) interval
~/optisches *s.* Tubuslänge/optische
~/räumliches spatial interval
Intervallbaum *m* interval tree *(geometrical data structure)*
Intervallometer *n* intervalometer
Intestinoskop *n* enteroscope
Intrabild *n* I-frame, I-picture, intraframe [coded] picture, intracoded (independent) frame *(video coding)*
intracodieren to intracode
Intracodierung *f s.* Intraframe-Codierung
Intraframe-Codierung *f* intraframe [en]coding, within-frame coding
Intraklassenvarianz *f* within-class variability
Intranet *n* intranet *(nonpublic computer network)*
Intraokularlinse *f* intraocular lens *(ophthalmology)*
invariant invariant
Invariante *f* invariant
~/Abbesche Abbe invariant *(optics)*
~/Helmholtz-Lagrangesche, ~/optische Lagrange (optical) invariant, Helmholtz invariant
~/projektive projective invariant
Invarianz *f* invariance
~/affine affine invariance
Inversfilterung *f* inverse filtering, deconvolution *(image reconstruction)*
Inversion *f* inversion
Inversionsfigur *f* ambiguous figure (design) *(optical illusion)*
Inversionsimpuls *m* inversion pulse *(magnetic resonance imaging)*
Inversionsrückkehr *f* inversion recovery *(magnetic resonance imaging)*
Inversschaltung *f s.* Negativ-Positiv-Umschaltung
Invertentfernungsmesser *m* inverted-image rangefinder
invertierbar invertible
invertieren to invert
invisibel invisible, nonvisible, viewless

In-vivo-Abbildung *f* in vivo imaging
inzident incident
Inzidienz *f* incidence
Iod *n* iodin[e]
Iodat *n* iodate
Iodid *n* iodide
Iodopsin *n* iodopsin, visual violet *(retinal pigment)*
Iodsilber *n* silver iodide
Iodsilberpapier *n* silver iodide paper
Ion *n* ion
Ionenaustausch *m* ion exchange
Ionenbeschussdrucker *m* ion-deposition printer
Ionenbindung *f* ionic bond[ing], electrovalent (heteropolar) bond
Ionendrucker *m* ion-deposition printer
Ionenemission *f* ion emission
Ionengitter *n* ionic lattice
Ionenkammer *f* ion chamber
Ionenkonzentration *f* ion[ic] concentration
Ionenkristall *m* ionic (polar) crystal
Ionenleitfähigkeit *f* ionic conductivity, ion conductance
Ionenmikroskop *n* ion microscope
Ionenmikroskopie *f* ion microscopy
Ionenoptik *f* ion optics
ionenoptisch ion-optical
Ionenpaar *n* ion pair
Ionenprodukt *n* ion[ic] product
Ionenreihe *f*/**Hofmeistersche** Hofmeister (lyotropic) series
Ionenstrahl *m* ion beam
Ionenstrahllithografie *f* ion beam lithography
Ionisation *f* ionization
Ionisationskammer *f* ionization chamber
ionisieren to ionize
Ionisierung *f* ionization
Ionografie *f* ionography, ion-flow electrophotography, ion-deposition printing
ionografisch ionographic; electroradiographic
IP-Adresse *f* dot address *(Internet)*
Iridiumsensibilisierung *f* iridium sensitization
Iris *f* iris *(of the eye)*
Irisblende *f* iris [diaphragm]
Iris-Erkennungsgerät *n* iris scanner
Irispigmentierung *f* iris pigmentation
Iris-Scan *m* iris scan
Iris-Scanner *m* iris scanner
Iriszittern *n* tremor of the iris, hippus
Irradianz *f s.* Bestrahlungsstärke
irrelevant irrelevant
Irrelevanz *f* irrelevance, irrelevancy
Isarithme *f* isarithm *(s.a.* Isolinie*)*
Isarithmenkarte *f* isarithmic map
Ishihara-Tafel *f* Ishihara plate *(color perception test equipment)*
isochrom *s.* isochromatisch
Isochromate *f* isochromat, isochromatic line

isochromatisch isochromatic, like-colored; homochromatic
isochron isochronous *(e.g. data transmission)*
Isodensitometrie *f* isodensitometry
ISO-Einstellung *f* film-speed dial
ISO-Empfindlichkeit *f* ISO [film] speed
Isofläche *f* isosurface, isovalue surface, contour surface *(computer graphics)*
Isoflächenalgorithmus *m* isosurface algorithm
Isoflächenbildung *f* isosurfacing *(image preprocessing operation)*
Isoflächenextraktion *f* isosurface extraction
Isoflächen-Extraktionsalgorithmus *m* isosurface extraction algorithm
ISO-Grad *m* ISO rating (index), ISO [film speed] number
Isohelie *f* isohelie
Isohypse *f s.* Höhenlinie
Isokline *f* isoclinic line
Isolator *m*/**optischer** optical isolator
Isolierschicht-Feldeffekttransistor *m* metal-oxide semiconductor field-effect transistor, MOSFET
Isolinie *f* isoline, isarithm, isogram, isovalue line; contour line
Isolinienkarte *f* isarithmic map
Isomerisierung *f* isomerization
Isometrie *f* isometry
isometrisch isometric
isomorph isomorph[ic], isomorphous
Isomorphie *f* isomorphism
Isomorphismus *m* isomorphism
Isopache *f* isopach
Isophote *f* isophote, isolux
Isoplanasie *f* isoplanatism, isoplanacity
isoplanatisch isoplanatic *(s.a. ortsinvariant)*
Isoplethenkarte *f* isopleth map
Isotop *n* isotope
Isotopenrenografie *f* renography
Isotopenzerfall *m* isotope decay
isotrop isotropic, directionally independent
Isotropie *f* isotropy
ISO-Wert *m*, **ISO-Zahl** *f s.* ISO-Grad
IT-Band *n* international tape (sound track), music and effect track, M&E [mix] *(cinema)*
Iteration *f* iteration
Iterationsalgorithmus *m* iterative (iteration) algorithm
Iterationsschleife *f* iteration loop
iterativ iterative
iterieren to iterate
IT-Fassung *f*, **IT-Mischung** *f s.* IT-Band

J

Jamin-Interferometer *n* Jamin interferometer
Jaulen *n* [wow and] flutter *(distortion in reproduced sound)*
Jitter *m* jitter *(of signals)*
~/**korrelierter** correlated jitter, pattern (systematic) jitter
~/**unkorrelierter** uncorrelated jitter, noise (nonsystematic) jitter
Jod... *s.* Iod...
Jog-Shuttle-Regler *m* jog/shuttle *(controller)*
Johnson-Rauschen *n* Johnson (system) noise, random thermal noise
Josephson-Kontakt *m*, **Josephson-Tunnelelement** *n* Josephson [tunnel] junction *(SQUID sensor)*
Joule *n* joule, J *(unit of energy)*
Joystick *m* joystick
JPEG-Algorithmus *m* JPEG [compression] algorithm *(digital imaging)*
JPEG-Datei *f* JPEG file
JPEG-Dateiformat *n*, **JPEG-Format** *n* JPEG [file interchange] format
JPEG-Kompression *f* JPEG [image] compression
JPEG-Standard *m* JPEG [image compression] standard *(for still image compression)*
JPEG-Verfahren *n* JPEG [compression] technique
Judäa-Asphalt *m* bitumen of Judea
Jupiterlampe *f* sun arc
justieren to adjust; to align
Justiergreifer *m* pilot (register) pin
Justierlaser *m* alignment laser
Justiermarke *f* adjustment mark
Justiermikroskop *n* alignment microscope
Justierspule *f* alignment coil *(cathode-ray tube)*
Juxtaposition *f* juxtaposition

K

Kabel *n*/**serielles** serial cable
Kabelanlage *f* cable [television] plant, CATV plant
Kabelanschluss *m* cable junction
Kabelauslöser *m* remote cord
Kabelbandbreite *f*/**nutzbare** usable cable bandwidth
Kabelbetreiber *m* s. Kabelnetzbetreiber
Kabel-Bezahlfernsehen *n* pay-cable
Kabelempfang *m* cable reception
Kabelempfänger *m* cable receiver
kabelfähig cable-ready *(e.g. a television receiver)*
Kabelfernauslöser *m* remote cord
Kabelfernbedienung *f* cable remote control
Kabelfernsehanbieter *m* cable television provider
Kabelfernsehdienst *m* cable television service
Kabelfernsehempfangsstation *f* cable television relay service station, CARS
Kabelfernsehen *n* cable [authority] television, cable TV, community antenna television, CATV; closed-circuit television, CCTV
~/digitales cable digital video broadcasting, C-DVB, DVB-C
Kabelfernsehkanal *m* cable TV channel
Kabelfernsehkopfstation *f* [cable] headend, CATV headend
Kabelfernsehnetz *n* cable TV network (distribution system), television cable network
Kabelfernsehsignal *n* cable television signal
Kabelfernsehsystem *n* CATV (cable television) system, closed-circuit television system
Kabelfernsehteilnehmer *m* CATV subscriber, cable customer (subscriber)
Kabelfernsehübertragung *f* cable television transmission
Kabelfernseh-Verteilsystem *n* cable TV distribution system, CATV
Kabelhaushalt *m* s. Kabelfernsehhaushalt
Kabelhelfer *m*, **Kabelhilfe** *f* dolly grip
Kabelkanal *m* cable channel (conduct)
Kabelkopfstation *f* [cable] headend, CATV headend
kabellos wireless *(e.g. video transmission)*
Kabelmodem *n(m)* cable modem (modulator/demodulator)
Kabelmodulator *m* cable modulator
Kabelnetz *n* cable network
Kabelnetzbetreiber *m* cable [system] operator, CATV operator *(television)*
Kabelrückkanal *m* cable return path

Kabelsender *m* cable broadcaster
Kabelsignal *n* cable [transmission] signal
kabeltauglich *s.* kabelfähig
Kabelübertragung *f* cable transmission
Kabelverbinder *m* cable connector
Kabelverstärker *m* CATV amplifier
Kabelverteiler *m* curb
Kabelzieher *m* dolly grip
Kabinenfenster *n*, **Kabinenfensteröffnung** *f* booth porthole; projection port
Kabinettprojektion *f* cabinet axonometry
Kachelung *f* s. Parkettierung
Kader *m* [film] frame, motion-picture frame
kadrieren to frame
Kadrierung *f* framing
Kaiser-Fenster *n* Kaiser window *(signal processing)*
Kalander *m* calender [roller]
kalandern, kalandrieren to calender *(e.g. paper)*
Kaleidoskop *n* kaleidoscope
kaleidoskopisch kaleidoscopic
Kalialaun *n* potassium alum, aluminum potassium sulfate *(gelatin hardener)*
kalibrieren to calibrate
Kalibrierung *f* calibration
~/radiometrische radiometric calibration
Kalibrierungslampe *f* calibration lamp *(e.g. in spectroscopy)*
Kaliumaluminiumsulfat *n* s. Kalialaun
Kaliumbichromat *n* s. Kaliumdichromat
Kaliumbromid *n* potassium bromide *(development restrainer)*
Kaliumcarbonat *n* potassium carbonate *(developer constituent)*
Kaliumcyanid *n* potassium cyanide *(fixing agent)*
Kaliumdichromat *n* potassium dichromate (bichromate) *(bleaching agent)*
Kaliumdisulfit *n* potassium metabisulfite *(fixer additive)*
Kaliumferricyanid *n* potassium ferricyanide (ferrocyanide), red prussiate of potash *(bleaching agent)*
Kaliumhydroxid *n* potassium hydroxide, caustic potash *(developer constituent)*
Kaliumiodid *n* potassium iodide *(restrainer)*
Kaliummetabisulfit *n* potassium metabisulfite *(fixer additive)*
Kaliumnitrat *n* potassium nitrate
Kaliumoxalat *n* potassium oxalate
Kaliumpermanganat-Abschwächer *m* potassium permanganate reducer
Kaliumrhodanid *n*, **Kaliumthiocyanat** *n* potassium rhodanide (thiocyanate) *(development additive)*
Kalkschutzmittel *n* sequestering agent (compound), sequesterant *(development additive)*
Kalkspat *m* calcite, calcareous spar
Kalkspatpolarisator *m* calcite polarizer
Kalman-Filter *n* Kalman filter *(image analysis)*

Kalman-Filterung f Kalman filtering
Kaloreszenz f calorescence
Kalotte f invercone *(photometry)*
Kalotypie f 1. calotype [process], talbotype *(photographic-negative process)*; 2. calotype, talbotype *(print)*
Kalotypist m calotypist
Kaltkaschierfolie f cold laminating foil
Kaltkatodenfluoreszenz f cold cathode fluorescent light, CFL
Kaltkatodenfluoreszenzanzeige f cold-cathode fluorescent display (device)
Kaltkatoden-Fluoreszenzlicht n cold cathode fluorescent light, CCFL
Kaltkatodenlampe f cold-cathode lamp
Kaltlicht n cold light
Kaltlichtbeleuchtung f cold light illumination
Kaltlichtlampe f cold-light lamp
Kaltlichtleuchte f cold-light illuminator
Kaltlichtquelle f cold-light source
Kaltlichtröhre f cold cathode fluorescent tube, CCFT
Kaltlichtspiegel m diathermic (cold) mirror; cold mirror (light) reflector
Kaltprägung f cold embossing *(stereotypy)*
Kaltsatz m cold[-type] composition *(typography)*
Kaltspiegellampe f cold mirror lamp, metal-oxide-vaporized mirror lamp
Kaltstart m cold boot (start), hard boot *(of a computer)*
Kaltstrahler m nonthermal radiator
Kalttonpapier n cold-tone paper
Kalvar-Verfahren n Kalvar process *(s.a.* Vesikularverfahren*)*
Kalzit m *s.* Kalkspat, Calcit
Kamelhaarpinsel m camel's hair brush
Kamera f camera [apparatus]
~/**affine** affine camera *(computer vision)*
~/**aktive** active camera
~/**analoge** analog camera
~/**astronomische** astronomical camera
~ **auf optischer Bank** monorail [view] camera
~/**aufgeschulterte** shoulder camera
~/**automatische** automatic (automated) camera
~/**bewegliche** mobile camera; hand-holdable camera
~/**computergesteuerte** computer-controlled camera; motion control camera, MOCO camera
~/**Daguerresche** daguerreotype camera
~/**deckenmontierte** overhead (ceiling-mounted) camera
~/**digitale** digital[-imaging] camera, digicam, DC
~/**dreiäugige** trinocular camera
~/**einäugige** single-lens camera
~/**elektronische (elektrooptische)** electronic[-imaging] camera
~/**endoskopische** endoscopic camera
~/**fernbedienbare** telerobotic (far-end) camera, remote-control camera
~/**fotografische** photographic camera; film-based camera
~/**fotogrammetrische** photogrammetric camera
~/**geräuschlose** noiseless camera
~/**halbautomatische** semiautomatic camera
~/**handelsübliche** off-the-shelf camera
~/**hochauflösende** high-resolution camera
~/**holografische** holographic camera
~/**industrielle** industrial camera
~/**intelligente** smart camera *(with integrated processing system)*
~/**interferometrische** interferometric camera
~/**kanonische** canonical camera
~/**kinematografische** cine[matographic] camera, motion-picture [film] camera, motion (picture) camera
~/**koronografische** coronographic camera
~/**makrofotografische** photomacrographic camera
~/**mechanische** manual camera
~/**mikrofotografische** photomicrographic camera
~/**mikrokinematografische** cinemicrographic (microcinematographic) camera
~/**mikroprozessorgesteuerte** microprocessor-controlled camera
~ **mit diskontinuierlichem Filmtransport** intermittent[-action] motion-picture camera
~/**mobile** mobile camera; hand-holdable camera
~/**multisensorische** multisensorial camera
~/**niedrigauflösende** low-resolution camera
~/**nuklearmedizinische** nuclear medical camera
~/**omnidirektionale** omnidirectional camera
~/**peltiergekühlte** Peltier-cooled camera
~/**professionelle** professional[-level] camera
~/**rauscharme** low-noise [CCD] camera
~/**robotergeführte** telerobotic (far-end) camera, robot (remote-control) camera
~/**selbstgeblimpte** self-blimped camera
~/**semiprofessionelle** semipro[fessional] camera, prosumer camera
~/**starre** fixed-lens camera
~/**statische** *s.* ~/unbewegte
~/**stumme** silent [camera]
~/**synchroballistische** synchroballistic camera, ballistic-synchro camera, image-synchro camera
~/**technische** technical (view) camera
~/**unbewegte** unmoving (locked-off) camera, static camera
~/**verdeckte (versteckte)** candid (covert) camera

Kamera

~/**virtuelle** virtual (synthetic) camera, CG (computer graphics) camera
~/**vollautomatische** fully automatic camera
~/**vollelektronische** all-electronic camera
~/**voreingestellte** prefocused camera
~/**zweiäugige** binocular camera
Kameraabstand *m* camera (subject) distance
Kameraabstützung *f* camera support [device]
Kameraabtastung *f* camera scanning
Kameraabteilung *f* camera crew *(cinema)*
Kameraachse *f* camera[-to-subject] axis; camera angle
Kameraadapter *m* camera adapter
Kameraanordnung *f* camera setup
Kameraarbeit *f* camera work
Kameraassistent *m* [/**Erster**] 1. [first] camera assistant, assistant cameraman (cameraperson), AC, camera operator; 2. *s.* Schärfezieher
~/**Zweiter** second assistant cameraman, 2nd AC, camera operator assistant, clapper[/loader]
Kameraaufbau *m* camera rig *(filmmaking)*
Kameraauflage *f* camera support
Kameraaufnahme *f* camera record; camera photograph (shot); scene
Kameraausgangsspannung *f* camera output voltage
Kameraausleger *m* camera boom
Kameraausrichtung *f* camera orientation
Kameraausrüstung *f* camera equipment (gear)
Kameraauszug *m* camera (bellows) extension, image distance (conjugate)
Kamerabatterie *f* [on-]camera battery
Kamerabau *m* camera manufacture
Kamerabauart *f* camera design
Kamerabauer *m* camera maker (manufacturer)
Kamerabaum *m s.* Kamerakran
Kamera-Bedienelement *n* camera control [feature]
Kamerabelichtung *f* camera[-type] exposure
Kamerabelichtungseinstellung *f* camera exposure setting
Kamerabelichtungsmesser *m* camera exposure meter, built-in light meter
Kamerabericht *m* camera report (sheet), camera exposure chart, dope sheet *(cinema)*
Kamerabeutel *m* camera bag (pouch)
Kamerabewegung *f* camera move[ment], camera motion; film camera move
Kamerabild *n* camera[-made] image, camera picture
Kamerabildebene *f* camera focal plane
Kamerabildfensterverschluss *m* camera focal plane shutter
Kamerablende *f* 1. camera [lens] diaphragm; 2. camera aperture

Kamerablendenöffnung *f* camera diaphragm opening
Kamerablickfeld *n* camera field of view, field of view of the camera
Kamerablickpunkt *m* camera viewpoint (interest), camera look-at
Kamerablickwinkel *m* camera angle; camera[-to-subject] axis
Kamerablitz *m* integrated flash, built-in [electronic] flash
Kamerabrennpunkt *m* camera focus (focal point)
Kamerabrennweite *f* camera focal length
Kameradesign *n* camera design
Kameradesigner *m* camera designer
Kameraebene *f* camera plane
Kameraeffekt *m* [in-]camera effect, optical effect *(cinema)*
Kameraeinstellung *f* 1. [camera] setup, camera setting; camera adjustment; 2. camera take, setup *(filming)*
Kameraelektronik *f* camera electronics
Kameraempfindlichkeit *f* camera sensitivity
Kameraende *n* front end *(motion-picture production)*
Kameraerschütterung *f* camera shake
Kamerafahrt *f* camera travel; [camera] tracking, trucking
Kamerafehler *m* camera defect
Kamerafenster *n* camera aperture (window), [camera] gate
Kamerafernauslösung *f* remote camera control
Kamerafernbediensystem *n* remote camera control
Kamerafertigung *f* camera manufacture
Kamerafilm *m* camera (picture-taking) film
Kamera-Filmabtaster *m* cathode-ray tube scanner, CRT-based [film] recorder
Kamerafilmebene *f* camera film plane
Kamerafilmempfindlichkeit *f* camera film speed
Kamerafilmformat *n* camera-film format
Kamerafilmrolle *f* cam[era roll] *(cinema)*
Kamerafilter *n* camera filter; still-camera filter
Kameraformat *n* camera format
Kamerafront *f* camera front
Kameraführung *f* camera operation
Kamerafunktion *f* 1. camera function; 2. camera feature
Kameragebrauchsanweisung *f* camera instruction manual
Kameragehäuse *n* camera housing (body)
~/**wasserdichtes** waterproof camera housing
Kamerageräusch *n* [mechanical] noise of the camera
Kamerageschichte *f* camera history
Kamerageschwindigkeit *f* camera [running] speed
Kamera-Gesichtsfeld *n s.* Kamerablickfeld
Kameragewicht *n* camera weight

Kameragriff *m* camera (pistol) grip
Kameragröße *f* camera size
Kameragrundeinstellung *f* camera's default setting
Kameragurt *m* camera [neck] strap
Kamerahandhabung *f* camera handling (manipulation)
Kamerahandy *n* camera-cell phone, multimedia [cell] phone
Kamerahersteller *m* camera manufacturer (maker)
Kamerahöhe *f* camera (lens) height
Kamerahülle *f* [/schalldichte] blimp
Kameraimitation *f* dummy camera
Kamerainnere *n* camera interior
kameraintern in-camera
Kamerajustierung *f* camera adjustment
Kamerakabel *n* camera cable
Kamerakalibrierung *f* camera calibration *(computer vision)*
~/**geometrische** geometric camera calibration
~/**parakatadioptrische** paracatadioptric camera calibration
Kamerakarte *f* camera card, memory stick
Kameraklinik *f* camera clinic
Kamerakonstante *f* camera constant
Kamerakonstrukteur *m* camera designer
Kamerakonstruktion *f* camera design
Kamerakontrolleinheit *f*, **Kamerakontrollgerät** *n* camera control unit, CCU
Kamerakoordinatensystem *n* camera (eye) coordinate system, camera space (reference frame)
Kamerakopf *m* camera head
Kamerakordel *f* camera sling
Kamerakörper *m* camera body
Kamerakran *m* camera boom, crane
Kamerakranführer *m* crane operator
Kamerakreisfahrt *f* rotation *(camera move in motion-picture photography)*
Kameralänge *f* [/**optische**] optical camera length
Kameralaufgeräusch *n* [mechanical] camera noise, camera-operating noise
Kameralicht *n* tally light
Kameralinse *f* camera lens *(s.a. Kameraobjektiv)*
kameralos cameraless
Kameramagazin *n* camera magazine
Kameramann *m* 1. [motion-picture] cameraman, cameraperson, lensman, camera operator, cinematographer; 2. *s.* ~/leitender; 3. *s.* ~/Erster
~/**Erster** operative (first) cameraman, principal cameraperson
~/**leitender (lichtbestimmender, verantwortlicher)** director of photography, DP *(esp. USA)*; lighting cameraman *(chiefly British)*
Kameramattscheibe *f* camera ground glass
Kameramechanismus *m* camera mechanism

Kameramesssystem *n* camera metering system
Kameramikro *n*, **Kameramikrofon** *n* [/**eingebautes**] on-camera microphone
Kameramikroskop *n* photomicroscope, photographic microscope
Kameramodell *n* camera model
~/**affines** affine camera model *(computer vision)*
Kameramodellierung *f* camera modeling
Kameramodul *n* camera module
Kameramodus *m* camera mode
Kameramonitor *m* camera monitor
Kameramotor *m* camera motor
Kameranegativ *n* camera negative
Kameranegativfilm *m* camera negative film
Kameraneigung *f* camera tilt
Kameraoberseite *f* camera top
Kamera-Objekt-Entfernung *f* camera-to-object (subject) distance
Kameraobjektiv *n* camera objective (lens) *(s.a. under Objektiv)*
Kameraobjektivbrennweite *f* camera lens focal length
Kameraobjektivhalter *m* camera lens mount
Kameraoptik *f* camera optics
Kameraorientierung *f* camera orientation
Kameraoriginal *n* [original] camera film, camera original [film] *(s.a. Originalnegativ)*
Kameraparameter *m* camera parameter
Kameraperspektive *f* camera point of view
Kamerapflege *f* camera care; camera maintenance
Kameraplattform *f*/**fahrbare** crab dolly
Kameraposition *f* camera position (location)
Kameraproduzent *m* camera manufacturer
Kameraprotokoll *m s.* Kamerabericht
Kamerarauschen *n* camera noise
Kamerarecorder *m* camera-recorder, camcorder
Kamerareparateur *m* camera-repair technician
Kamerareparatur *f* camera repair
Kamerarichten *n* [camera] pointing, aiming
Kamerarichtung *f* camera direction
Kameraeriemen *m* camera [neck] strap
Kameraroboter *m* robot (remote-control) camera, telerobotic (far-end) camera
Kameraröhre *f* camera [video] tube, camera picture tube, [camera] pickup tube; television camera tube
Kamerarolle *f* camera roll *(filming)*
Kamerarotation *f* camera rotation
Kamerarotlicht *n* tally light
Kamerarucksack *m* camera backpack
Kamerarückseite *f* camera back
Kamerarückteil *m(n)* 1. camera back; 2. rear (back) standard, film standard *(view camera)*
Kamerarückwand *f* camera back

Kamerarückwand

~/auswechselbare interchangeable back
Kamerascanner m camera scanner
Kameraschnittstelle f camera interface
Kameraschraube f camera retaining screw
Kameraschulterstativ n shoulder pod
Kameraschwenk m camera pan, pan [move]; pan shot; camera tilt, tilt [move]
Kameraschwenker m operative (first) cameraman, principal cameraperson *(motion-picture production)*
Kamera-Selbstkalibrierung f camera self-calibration
Kamerasensor m camera sensor
Kameraserie f line of cameras
Kamerasichtfeld n camera [field of] view
Kamerasignal n camera signal *(television)*
Kameraspeicher m camera memory
Kamerastabilisator m, **Kamerastabilisierer** m camera stabilization device
Kamerastabilisierung f camera stabilization
Kamerastabilisierungssystem n camera stabilizing (stabilization) system, camera support system
Kamerastabilität f camera stability
Kamerastandarte f camera standard
Kamerastandort m, **Kamerastandpunkt** m camera location (station)
Kamerastativ n camera stand; camera tripod
Kamerastellung f camera position (location)
Kamerasteuereinheit f camera control unit, CCU
Kamerasteuerung f camera control
Kamerastütze f camera support [device]
Kamerasucher m camera viewfinder
Kamerasystem n camera system
Kameratasche f camera case (bag)
Kamerateam n camera team; camera crew *(cinema)*
Kameratechnik f 1. camera technology; 2. camera technique
Kameratechniker m camera technician
Kameratechnologie f camera technology
Kameratrag[e]riemen m camera [neck] strap
Kameratranslation f camera translation
Kameratrick m [in-]camera effect, optical effect *(cinema)*
Kameratubus m camera barrel
Kameratyp m camera type, type of camera
Kameraverleih m camera rental house
Kameraverschluss m camera shutter
Kameravibration f camera vibration
Kamerawagen m [/höhenverstellbarer] [camera] dolly, truck; crab dolly *(mobile shooting platform)*
~/selbstfahrender camera car
Kamerawagenfahrer m dolly pusher
Kamerawinkel m camera angle *(s.a.* Kameraposition*)*; camera[-to-subject] axis
Kamerazoom n camera zoom [lens]

Kamerazubehör n camera accessories
Kammerkonstante f calibrated focal length *(photogrammetry)*
Kammerwasser n aqueous humor *(of the eye)*
Kammfilter/digitales digital comb filter, DCF
Kammfilterung f comb filtering
Kammfunktion f comb (shah) function, impulse train *(signal processing)*
Kanadabalsam m, **Kanadaterpentin** n Canada balsam *(lens cement)*
Kanal m channel; bandwidth channel, band *(communication theory)*
~/bandbegrenzter bandlimited channel
~/diskreter discrete channel
Kanalaufteilung f channel allocation
Kanalausgang m channel output
Kanalbandbreite f channel [band]width
Kanalbündelung f channel bundling
Kanalcode m channel code
Kanalcodierer m channel encoder
Kanalcodierung f channel [en]coding
Kanaldecod[ier]er m channel decoder
Kanaleffizienz f channel efficiency
Kanalelektronenvervielfacherplatte f microchannel plate, multichannel [multiplier] plate, MCP
Kanalfehler m channel [transmission] error
Kanalfilter n channel filter
Kanalhierarchie f channel hierarchy
Kanalkapazität f channel capacity
Kanalkonstanz f channel constancy
Kanalmultiplexer m channel multiplexer
Kanalplatte f channel plate *(s.a.* Mikrokanal-Elektronenvervielfacherplatte*)*
Kanalrauschen n [communication] channel noise
Kanalspeicher m channel buffer
Kanalstruktur f channel structure
Kanaltrennung f channel separation
Kanalübertragung f channel transmission
Kanalvervielfachung f channel multiplexing
Kanalwähler m tuner [dial] *(television set)*
Kanalwechsel m channel change
Kanalweiche f [channel] combiner, channel combining unit
Kanalzuordnung f channel allocation
Kanisza-Täuschung f visual (amodal) completion
Kante f edge *(s.a. under* Rand*)*
~/begrenzende boundary (realized) edge
~/beugende diffracting edge
~/brechende refracting edge
~/echte true (real) edge
~/falsche false edge
~/Gaußsche Gaussian edge
~/gekrümmte curved edge
~/geradlinige straight edge
~/reale real (true) edge
~/scharfe sharp (strong) edge
~/schließende trailing edge

~/**stufige** jagged edge (boundary)
~/**unscharfe** blurred edge, weak (soft) edge
~/**verdeckte** occluded edge, hidden line
~/**verrauschte** noisy edge
Kantenabstand *m* [edge] margin
kantenadaptiv edge-adaptive
Kantenanhebung *f*, **Kantenanschärfung** *f* edge enhancement; edge sharpening (crispening)
Kantenanstieg *m* edge slope
Kantenanzeiger *m* edge flag *(computer graphics)*
Kantenapproximation *f* edge approximation
Kantenausrichtung *f* edge orientation
Kantenbegradigung *f s.* Kantenglättung
Kantenbetonung *f* edge enhancement
Kantenbild *n* edge image (map) *(image segmentation)*
~/**binäres** binary edge image (map)
Kantenbildanalyse *f* edge gradient analysis
Kantenblockcodierung *f* edge block coding
Kantenbreite *f* edge width
Kantendarstellung *f* edge representation
Kantendetail *n* edge detail
Kantendetektion *f* edge detection (recognition)
~/**adaptive** adaptive edge detection
~/**binäre** binary edge detection
~/**gradientenbasierte** gradient[-based] edge detection
~/**morphologische** morphological edge detection
~/**pseudolaplacesche** pseudo-Laplacian edge detection
~/**subpixelgenaue** subpixel-precision edge detection
~/**waveletbasierte** wavelet-based edge detection
Kantendetektionsalgorithmus *m s.* Kantendetektor
Kantendetektionsfilter *n* edge-detection filter (operator)
Kantendetektor *m* edge detector, edge (border) detection algorithm
~/**richtungsempfindlicher** directionally sensitive edge detector
Kanteneffekt *m* edge (adjacency) effect
Kantenelement *n* edge element, edgel
Kantenendpunkt *m* edge endpoint
Kantenerhaltung *f* edge preservation
Kantenerkennbarkeit *f* edge detectability; edge recognizability
Kantenerkennung *f* edge detection; edge recognition
Kantenextraktion *f* edge extraction *(image segmentation)*
~/**parallele** parallel edge extraction
~/**sequentielle** sequential edge extraction, line following
Kantenfärbung *f* edge coloring
Kantenfilter *n* edge filter (operator)
Kantenfiltermaske *f* edge filter mask

Kantenfinder *m s.* Kantendetektor
Kantenfindung *f* edge finding
Kantenfindungstechnik *f* edge-finding technique
Kantenflackern *n* edge flicker
Kantenflimmern *n* interlace flicker
Kantenglättung *f* edge smoothing; antialiasing, dejagging *(computer graphics)*
Kantengradient *m* edge (boundary) gradient
Kantengüte *f* edge quality
Kantenhervorhebung *f* edge enhancement
Kantenhistogramm *n* edge histogram
Kantenidentifikation *f*, **Kantenidentifizierung** *f* edge identification
Kantenintensität *f* edge intensity
Kantenkohärenz *f* edge coherence
Kantenkontrast *m* edge contrast
Kantenkorrektur *f* aperture correction
Kantenkrümmung *f* edge curvature
Kantenlänge *f* edge length
Kantenlicht *n* edge light
Kantenliste *f* edge list *(polymesh)*
Kantenlokalisation *f*, **Kantenlokalisierung** *f* edge localization
Kantenlokalisierungsverhalten *n* edge locating behavior
Kantenmerkmal *n* edge feature
Kantenmittelpunkt *m* edge center
Kantenmodell/stochastisches stochastic edge model
Kantenmodellierung *f* edge modeling
Kantennormale *f* edge normal
Kantenoperator *m* edge [detection] operator
~/**rotationssymmetrischer (isotroper)** rotationally symmetric edge operator (filter)
Kantenorientierung *f* edge orientation
Kantenort *m* edge location
Kantenpixel *n* edge pixel, edgel
Kantenposition *f* edge position
Kantenprofil *n* edge profile
Kantenpunkt *m* edge point *(s.a.* Kantenelement*)*
Kantenpunktverknüpfung *f* edge-point linking
Kantenqualität *f* edge quality
Kantenrauschen *n* edge noise; mosquito noise
Kantenregion *f* edge region
Kantenrichtung *f* edge direction
Kantenschablone *f* edge template
Kantenschärfe *f* edge contrast (sharpness), edge acuteness (acuity), edge definition, acutance
Kantensegment *n* edge segment
Kantensegmentierung *f* edge segmentation
Kantensignal *n* edge signal
Kantensprungverhältnis *n* absorption edge jump ratio

Kantenstärke

Kantenstärke f edge strength (width)
Kantensteilheit f edge kurtosis
Kantenstruktur f edge structure
Kantentabelle f edge table
Kantentyp m edge type
Kantenübergang m edge transition
Kantenverdünnung f edge thinning
Kantenverfolgung f edge following (tracing)
Kantenverfolgungsalgorithmus m edge-following algorithm
Kantenverknüpfung f edge linking
Kantenverschmierung f edge corruption
Kantenverstärkung f edge enhancement (sharpening)
Kantenverstärkungsalgorithmus m edge enhancement algorithm
Kantenversteilerung f edge crispening
Kantenverzerrung f edge distortion
Kantenwelligkeit f wavy edge
Kantenwinkel m edge angle
Kapazität f capacitance *(of a conductor)*
Kapitälchen n small cap[ital] *(typography)*
Kapitale f, **Kapitalschrift** f all capital letters
Karbonatpuffer m carbonate buffer *(developer additive)*
Karbondruck m s. Kohledruck 1. *and* 2.
Kardinalpunkt m cardinal point *(optics)*
Kardioangiografie f cardiac angiography
Kardiogramm n cardiogram
Kardioidmikrofon n cardioid microphone
Karhunen-Loève-Transformation f Karhunen-Loève transform[ation] (expansion); principal components analysis (transform), principal axis transformation, eigenvector (Hotelling) transform *(feature identification)*
Karolus-Zelle f s. Kerr-Zelle
Karte f map
~/**choroplethische** choropleth map
~/**digitale** digital map
~/**elektronische** electronic map *(radar)*
~/**geodätische** geodetic map
~/**geografische** geographic map
~/**geologische** geologic[al] map
~/**hydrologische** hydrological map
~/**maßstäbliche** scaled map
~/**morphometrische** morphometric map
~/**nichtmaßstäbliche** unscaled map
~/**planimetrische** planimetric map
~/**qualitative** qualitative map
~/**quantitative** quantitative map
~/**selbstorganisierende** self-organizing [feature] map; topology-preserving map, Kohonen map (network) *(pattern recognition)*
~/**thematische** thematic map
~/**topografische** topographic map
~/**topologische** topological map
~/**winkeltreue** conformal (orthomorphic) map
Kartenadapter m card adapter
Kartenaufnahme f mapping
Kartenbild n map image

Kartenblatt n map sheet
Kartendigitalisierung f map digitization
Kartenebene f map plane
Karteninterpretation f interpretation of maps
Kartenlesegerät n, **Kartenleser** m card reader
Kartenmaßstab m map scale
Kartenmesskunde f cartometry
Kartennetzentwurf m map coordinates
Kartenprojektion f map projection
Kartenskizze f sketch map
Kartensteckplatz m card slot
Kartentisch m map table
Kartenzeichen n map symbol
kartieren to map, to chart
Kartiertisch m tracing table *(photogrammetry)*
Kartierung f mapping; mapmaking
~/**digitale** digital mapping
~/**fotogrammetrische** photogrammetric mapping
Kartierungsgenauigkeit f mapping accuracy
Kartograf m cartographer, mapmaker, mapper, projectionist
Kartografie f cartography, mapping science
kartografieren to map
kartografisch cartographic[al]
Kartometrie f cartometry
Karton m board [paper], paperboard, cardboard
kartonstark double-weight, DW *(printing paper)*
Kartusche f cartridge
Karyogramm n karyogram
Karzinotron n s. Carcinotron
Kasch m, **Kaschblende** f mask, matte
kaschieren 1. to mask [off], to mask out *(s.a. maskieren)*; 2. to laminate
Kaschierfolie f laminating film
Kaschierung f 1. lamination; 2. laminate
~/**einseitige** single-surface lamination
Kaskadenguss m hopper coating *(manufacture of photographic materials*
Kaskadenmethode f cascade processing *(washing system)*
Kaskadenverstärker m cascade[d] amplifier
kaskadierbar cascadable
kaskadieren to cascade
Kaskadierung f cascading
Kassenscanner m point-of-sale scanner; supermarket scanner terminal
Kassette f 1. cassette; cartridge; 2. s. Vergrößerungsrahmen
~/**radiografische** radiographic cassette
Kassettenadapter m adapter cassette
Kassettenauswurf m eject
Kassettenband n cassette (cartridge) tape
Kassettenbandgerät n cassette tape player
Kassettenbandmaschine f cartridge-based tape machine

Kassettenfach n cassette compartment
Kassettenfilm m cassette[-type] film
Kassettenformat n cassette format (size); cassette recording format
Kassettenladestation f cassette loading section
Kassettenmaschine f cassette machine
Kassettenmaul n cassette mouth
Kassettenöffner m cassette opener
Kassettenrahmen m cassette frame
Kassettenrecorder m cassette recorder
Kassettenschlitz m cassette entry slot, loading slot
Kassettenspeicher m cassette memory
Kassetten-Videobandgerät n videocassette recorder, VCR
Kassettenwechsler m cassette changer
kastenfrisch duct fresh *(printing ink)*
Kastenkamera f Giroux camera
Katadioptrik f catadioptrics
katadioptrisch catadioptric[al]
Katakaustik f [cata]caustic *(optics)*
Katalogdruck m catalog printing
Katalogfotograf m catalog photographer
Katalogfotografie f catalog photography
Katalogspeicher m s. Speicher/assoziativer
Katalysator m catalyst
katalysieren to catalyze
Katarakt[a] f cataract *(opacity of the eye's lens)*
Katasteraufnahme f cadastral survey
Katasterkarte f cadastral map
Katheter m/**angiografischer** angiographic catheter
Katheterangiografie f catheter angiography
Kathetometer n cathetometer
Katode f cathode, ka
~/imprägnierte impregnated (dispenser) cathode
Katodenelektron n cathode electron
Katodenfläche f cathode surface (area)
katodenlumineszent cathodoluminescent
Katodenlumineszenz f cathode luminescence, cathodoluminescence
Katodenspannung f cathode voltage
Katodenstrahl m cathode ray, CR
Katodenstrahlbelichter m cathode-ray tube scanner
Katodenstrahlbildröhre f cathode-ray picture tube
Katodenstrahlmaschine f cathode-ray-tube phototypesetter
Katodenstrahlmonitor m CRT (cathode-ray-tube) monitor, CRT-based display monitor
Katodenstrahloszillograf m cathode-ray oscillograph
Katodenstrahloszilloskop n cathode-ray oscilloscope, oscilloscope [cathode-ray tube]
Katodenstrahlröhre f cathode-ray tube, CRT, electron beam tube

Katodenstrahlrohrmaschine f s. Katodenstrahlmaschine
Katodenzylinder m cathode cylinder
katodolumineszent cathodoluminescent
Katodolumineszenz f cathodoluminescence, CL
Katoptrik f catoptrics
katoptrisch catoptric[al]
Katzenaugenblende f cat's-eye diaphragm
Kaufkassette f, **Kaufvideo** n commercial videotape *(esp. of a movie)*
Kaustik f caustic [curve], caustic (focal) surface; catacaustic; diacaustic surface *(ray optics)*
Kavalierperspektive f, **Kavalierprojektion** f cavalier projection (axonometry)
Kavitation f cavitation *(sonography)*
Keck-Teleskop n Keck telescope
Kegel m 1. cone; 2. point size *(of a piece of type)*
Kegelabtastverfahren n conical scan technique *(radar)*
Kegelfläche f conical surface
Kegelprojektion f conic projection *(cartography)*
Kegelschnitt m conic section
Kegelstrahl m cone beam
Kegelstrahlgeometrie f cone-beam [imaging] geometry
Kegelstrahltomografie f cone-beam tomography (CT)
Kegelwinkel m cone angle
Kehlkopfspiegel m laryngoscope
Kehlkopfspiegelung f laryngoscopy
Kehrbild n 1. inverted (upside down) image; 2. s. Negativ 1.
Kehrbildentfernungsmesser m inverted-image rangefinder
Keil m wedge; [wedged] spaceband, justifying spacer *(typesetting)*
~/Abatischer Abat's wedge
~/optischer optical wedge *(sensitometry)*
Keilplatte f wedge[d] [optical] plate
Keilspektrograf m wedge spectrograph
Keilspektrogramm n wedge spectrogram
Keimbildner m nucleating agent
Keimbildung f nucleation *(photographic theory)*
Keim-Korn-Modell n nucleation-and-growth model
Keimpunkt m seed point *(region-growing method)*
Kell-Faktor m Kell factor *(television resolution)*
Kellner-Okular n Kellner eyepiece
Kelvin n kelvin, K *(base unit of temperature)*
Kelvin-Skala f Kelvin [temperature] scale, absolute temperature scale
Kennungsbild n caption
Kennzeichnungsband n identification leader; identification trailer
Keramikfilter n [piezo]ceramic filter
Keratoskop n keratoscope

keratoskopisch keratoscopic
Kerbmarkierung f edge (film) notch *(e.g. of sheet film)*
Kerma n Kerma *(short for kinetic energy released in media; X-ray dosimetry)*
Kern m 1. kernel; core; 2. nucleus
Kernemulsion f nuclear emulsion
Kernfotografie f nuclear photography
Kernfotoplatte f s. Kernspurenplatte
Kernfusion f nuclear fusion
Kernladungszahl f atomic number
Kernmagnetismus m nuclear magnetism
Kernresonanzsignal n nuclear [magnetic] resonance signal, NMR signal
Kernschatten m umbra
Kernspin m nuclear spin
Kernspinaufnahme f, **Kernspinbild** n 1. MRI acquisition; 2. MR slice; MR image
Kernspinmammogramm n MRI mammogram
Kernspinresonanz f [/**magnetische**] f nuclear magnetic resonance, NMR *(s.a. under Magnetresonanz)*
Kernspinresonanzabbildung f nuclear magnetic resonance imaging, NMR imaging *(s.a. Kernspintomografie)*
Kernspinresonanzspektroskopie f s. Kernspinspektroskopie
Kernspinresonanztomografie f s. Kernspintomografie
Kernspinspektroskopie f magnetic resonance spectroscopy, MRS
Kernspintomograf m MRI scanner
Kernspintomografie f [nuclear] magnetic resonance imaging, MR (NMR) imaging, MRI
~/**funktionelle** functional MRI (magnetic resonance imaging), fMRI
~/**interventionelle** interventional MRI (magnetic resonance imaging)
kernspintomografisch magnetic resonance tomographic
Kernspintomogramm n s. Kernspinaufnahme 2.
Kernspuraufnahme f nuclear track photography
Kernspuraufzeichnung f nuclear-track recording
Kernspuremulsion f nuclear emulsion
Kernspurenplatte f nuclear [emulsion] plate
Kernspurfotografie f nuclear-track photography
Kernstrahlung f nuclear radiation
Kernsystem n/**grafisches** graphical kernel system, GKS
Kernverschmelzung f s. Kernfusion
Kerr-Effekt m Kerr [electro-optical] effect, quadratic electro-optic[al] effect
Kerr-Zelle f Kerr cell *(high-speed photography)*
Kerr-Zellenverschluss m Kerr cell shutter, electro-optical shutter
Kerze f/**Neue** s. Candela

Kette f/**bilderzeugende** image (imaging) chain
Kettencluster m chain cluster
Kettencode m chain code
Kettencodedarstellung f chain-code representation
Kettencodierung f chain coding
Kettendecodierung f chain decoding
Kettendrucker m band (belt) printer
Keulenbreite f elevation
Keulenmikrofon n shotgun (rifle) microphone, interference tube microphone
Keulensteuerung f beam control *(radar)*
Keulenverlust m beam shape loss *(radar)*
Keycode-Codierung f Key code [number] *(of film material)*
Keycode-Lesegerät n Key code reader
Keyframe-Animation f key frame animation, key framing
Kicker[scheinwerfer] m kicker *(a light source)*
Kieselgel n silica gel *(drying agent)*
Kieselglas n fused silica [glass], vitreous silica *(s.a.* Quarzglas*)*
Kilobit n kilobit, kb, Kb
Kilobyte n kilobyte, kB, KB
Kilohertz n kilohertz, kHz
K-Impuls m burst flag (gate), burst key *(video signal)*
Kindersicherung f child lock, parental control
Kindknoten m child node *(graph theory)*
Kineangiografie f cineangiography
Kineangiogramm n cineangiogram
Kineangiokardiografie f cineangiocardiography
Kinefilm m cine[matographic] film, motion[-picture] film, movie film; 35-mm cine film, standard 35-mm film
Kinefilmformat n cine film size, motion-picture [film] format, motion-picture film gauge
Kinefilmherstellung f motion-picture film manufacture
Kinefilmmaterial n motion-picture [film] stock, [film] stock
Kinefotogrammetrie f motion-picture photogrammetry
Kinekoronarografie f cinecoronary arteriography, cardiac cine MRI
Kinemathek f cinematheque; film archive (library)
Kinematik f kinematics *(study of motion)*
~/**inverse** inverse kinematics, goal-directed motion *(computer animation)*
~/**visuelle** visual kinematics
kinematisch 1. cinematic; 2. kinematic[al]
Kinematograf m cinematograph
Kinematografie f cinema[tography], kinematography, motion[-picture] photography

~/anamorphotische anamorphic cinematography
~/elektronische electronic cinematography
kinematografisch cinematographic[al], cine
Kinenegativfilm *m* motion picture negative film, negative movie (motion picture) film
Kineobjektiv *n*, **Kineoptik** *f* cinematograph lens
Kineösophagografie *f* cineoesophagography
Kineradiografie *f* cineradiography, cineroentgenography
kineradiografisch cineradiographic
Kineradiogramm *n* cineradiogram
Kineskop *n* kinescope, picture tube *(s.a. Bildröhre)*
Kineszintigrafie *f* cinescintigraphy
Kinetechnik *f* cinema technology
Kinetograf *m* kinetograph *(an early cinematographic camera)*
Kinetophon *n* kinetophone *(combining a kinetoscope and a phonograph)*
Kinetoskop *n* kinetoscope *(peep-show machine)*
Kino *n* movie theater (house), [motion-picture] theater, theatre, cinema
~/digitales digital (electronic) cinema, D-cinema, E-cinema
~/stereoskopisches stereoscopic cinema
Kinoapparat *m* cinematograph
Kinoausstatter *m* theater installer
Kinobesucher *m* filmgoer, picture-goer
Kinobetreiber *m* theater owner
Kinobild *n* [motion-picture] frame, movie frame; [motion-]picture image, cinema image, movie picture
Kinobildseitenverhältnis *n* theatrical (movie) aspect ratio
Kino-Digitalton *m* theater (cinema) digital sound
Kinofilm *m* [theatrical] motion picture, theatrical film (movie), cine[matographic] film, movie [film], picture, celluloid
Kinofilmbelichter *m* cine film recorder
Kinofilmbild *n* motion-picture image (frame)
Kinofilmformat *n* motion-picture format (film gauge), theatrical format
Kinofilmindustrie *f* film (motion-picture) industry, cinema (movie) industry, filmdom, screen[land], moviedom, movies
Kinofilmkamera *f* [professional] motion-picture camera, movie (feature film) camera *(s.a. Filmkamera)*
Kinofilmmaterial *n* movie footage
Kinofilmproduktion *f* theatrical film (motion-picture) production, cinema[tic] production, theatrical moviemaking
Kinofilmprojektion *f* movie projection
Kinofilmprojektor *m* movie (theatrical motion-picture) projector
Kinofilmreiniger *m* motion-picture film cleaner
Kinofilmton *m* theatrical movie's sound
Kinofilmverarbeitung *f* motion-picture [film] processing
Kinofilmverleih *m* theater distribution
Kinofotograf *m* cine photographer
Kinofotografie *f* movie (motion-picture) photography
Kinogänger *m s.* Kinobesucher
Kinokamera *f s.* Kinofilmkamera
Kinokameramann *m* motion-picture cameraman, cinematographer
Kinokameratechnik *f* motion-picture camera technique
Kinokette *f* theater (exhibition) chain
Kinoklang *m* theater sound
Kinokopie *f* theatrical [projection] print, [exhibition] release print, [theatrical] release [print]
Kinolautsprecher *m* theater speaker
Kinoleinwand *f* [movie] theater screen, movie (cinema) screen *(s.a. Filmleinwand)*
Kinomaschine *f* theater projector, cinematograph
Kinonegativfilm *m* motion-picture negative film
Kinoobjektiv *n* motion-picture projection objective, cine lens
Kinoprogramm *n* movie program
Kinoprojektion *f* cinema (theatrical) projection, motion-picture projection
~/digitale digital cinema projection
Kinoprojektionsobjektiv *n s.* Kinoobjektiv
Kinoprojektor *m* theater projector, theatrical (theater-type) projector, cine (motion-picture) projector
Kinopublikum *n* movie audience
Kinospielfilm *m* theatrical film (feature)
Kinostativ *n* cinema tripod
Kinotechnik *f* 1. cinema (motion-picture) technology; 2. motion-picture equipment (technics), filmmaking apparatus
Kinotechniker *m* motion-picture engineer
kinotechnisch film technical
Kinoton *m* theater sound
~/digitaler cinema digital sound, CDS
Kinotonanlage *f*, **Kinotonsystem** *n* theater sound system
Kinotrailer *m* movie trailer *(s.a. Filmtrailer)*
Kinoverleih *m* movie distribution; theater (theatrical) distribution
Kinovorführung *f* theatrical (movie theater) showing, theatrical presentation (exhibition), cinema performance, pictures
Kinowagen *m* cinemobile, cinema van *(chiefly British)*
Kinozentrum *n* multiplex [cinema], multiplex theater, cineplex
Kinozuschauer *m* cinema spectator
kippbar tiltable
Kippbild *n s.* Kippfigur

Kippentwicklung f tray rocking
Kippfigur f ambiguous figure (design) *(optical illusion)*
Kippfrequenz f toggle frequency
Kippgenerator m swept frequency generator
Kippglied n/**bistabiles** flip-flop
Kippmethode f tray rocking
Kippschaltung f/**bistabile [elektronische]** flip-flop
Kippspiegel m tilting mirror
Kippstativ n inclinable stand
Kippung f tilt *(e.g. of a view camera)*
Kippwinkel m tilting angle, angle of tilt, tilt [angle]
Kirlian-Fotografie f Kirlian [electro]photography, plasma (corona-discharge) photography
Kirlian-Fotogramm n Kirlian photograph
Kirlian-Generator m Kirlian generator
KI-Roboter m intelligent robot
Kirsch-Operator m Kirsch [edge] operator *(edge enhancement)*
Kissenentzerrung f correction of pincushion distortion
Kissenfehler m s. Kissenverzeichnung
Kissenverzeichnung f, **Kissenverzerrung** f pincushion (negative) distortion *(optics)*
Kitt m/**optischer** lens cement
kitten to cement
Kittfläche f cemented (cementing) surface *(e.g. of an objective)*
Kittkörper m pitch button *objective manufacture)*
Klammer f/**eckige** square bracket *(punctuation mark)*
~/**geschweifte** brace, curly bracket *(punctuation mark)*
~/**spitze** angle bracket
Klammerteil n(m) film clip
Klangdatei f sound (audio) file
Klappblende f s. Jalousieblende
Klappdiarahmen m folding clip mount
Klappe f clapboard, clapper [board], clapstick[s], sync stick; [clapping] slate, number board
~/**elektronische** electronic clapper
Klappenbeschriftung f slate
Klappennachlauf m [frame] handles, padding *(cinematography)*
Klappenreihenfolge f shooting order
Klappenvorlauf m s. Klappennachlauf
Klappkamera f folding (bellows) camera; folding roll-film camera
Klapplupe f folding magnifier
Klappspiegel m swinging (reflex) mirror, instant-return[-type reflex] mirror *(single-lens reflex camera)*
Klappstativ n collapsible stand
Klapp-Winkelschiene f folding flash bracket
Klärbad n clearing bath *(reversal processing)*
Klarglas n clear glass

~[**glüh**]**birne** f, **Klarglaslampe** f clear lamp (lightbulb), bare tungsten filament bulb
Klärmittel n clearing agent, clarifier
Klarschrifterkennung f, **Klarschriftlesen** n [optical] character recognition, OCR
Klarschriftleser m character reader
Klarsichtfilm m clear-base film
Klarsichthülle f, **Klarsichttasche** f acetate sleeve [protector]
Klartext m plaintext
Klärzeit f clearing time, time to clear *(photoprocessing)*
Klasse f class
~/**abstrakte** abstract class
~/**homogene** homogenous class
~/**konkrete** concrete class
~/**linear separierbare** linearly separable class
~/**nichtseparierbare** nonseparable class
~/**semantische** semantic class
Klasseneinteilung f binning
Klassengrenze f class boundary
Klassenhierarchie f class hierarchy
Klassenmitte f class center
Klassenmittelwert m class mean
Klassenrepräsentant m template, prototype *(pattern recognition)*
Klassenstruktur f class structure
Klassentrennbarkeit f class separability
Klassentrennung f class separation
Klassenunterbaum m class subtree
Klassenzimmer n/**virtuelles** virtual classroom
Klassenzugehörigkeit f class membership
Klassifikation f classification [procedure], class assignment, categorization
~/**automatische** automatic (automated) classification, machine classification
~/**digitale multispektrale** digital multispectral classification
~/**evidenztheoretische** evidential classification
~/**hierarchisch aufsteigende** hierarchical ascendant classification
~/**hierarchische** hierarchical classification
~/**kontextabhängige** contextual (context-based) classification
~/**kontextunabhängige** context-independent classification
~/**merkmalbasierte** feature-based classification
~/**multispektrale** multispectral classification
~/**nichtparametrische** nonparametric classification
~/**numerische** numerical classification
~/**objektbasierte** object-based classification
~/**parametrische** parametric classification
~/**pixelbasierte (pixelweise)** pixelwise (pixel-by-pixel) classification
~/**statistische** statistical classification
~/**strukturelle** structural classification

~/**texturbasierte** texture-based classification
~/**topologische** topological classification
~/**überwachte** supervised classification
~/**untrainierte** s. ~/unüberwachte
~/**unüberwachte [automatische]** unsupervised [automatic] classification, cluster analysis, clustering
Klassifikationaufgabe f classification task
Klassifikationsalgorithmus m classification algorithm, classifier (s.a. under Klassifikator)
Klassifikationserfolg m classification success
Klassifikationsfehler m [mis]classification error
Klassifikationsgenauigkeit f classification accuracy
Klassifikationsleistung f classification performance (power)
Klassifikationsphase f classification phase (image preprocessing)
Klassifikationsraum m classification space
Klassifikationsschema n classification scheme (system)
Klassifikationstechnik f classification technique
Klassifikationsvermögen n classification capability
Klassifikator m classifier, classification algorithm
~/**bayesoptimaler** Bayes[ian] classifier (pattern recognition)
~/**Euklidischer** Euclidean classifier
~/**geometrischer** geometric classifier
~/**hierarchischer** hierarchical classifier
~/**lernender** learning classifier
~/**linearer** linear classifier
~/**neuronaler** neural classifier
~/**nichtparametrischer** nonparametric classifier
~/**nichtparametrischer entscheidungstheoretischer** nonparametric decision theoretic classifier
~/**parametrischer** parametric classifier
~/**polynomialer** polynomial classifier
~/**probabilistischer** probabilistic classifier
~/**statistischer** statistical classifier
~/**unscharfer** fuzzy classifier
klassifizierbar classifiable (e.g. a pattern)
klassifizieren to classify, to class
Klassifizierung f classification (s.a. Klassifikation)
Klassifizierungsgeschwindigkeit f classification speed
Klassifizierungsverfahren n classification method
Klatschkopie f [positive] work print, film work print, cutting copy (cinema)
Klebeband n splicing (adhesive) tape
Klebebild n collage, papier collé
Klebefolie f cold laminating film
Klebekitt m cement

Klebelade f [film] splicer
Klebelayout n s. Klebespiegel
Klebelehre f s. Klebelade
Klebemontage f 1. pasteup [process]; 2. pasteup, hard mechanical
kleben to splice, to join (e.g. pieces of film)
Kleben n **der Druckbogen [im Stapel]** blocking [of printed sheets]
Klebepresse f mounting press (for photographic prints); [film] splicer
Klebespiegel m pasteup, hard mechanical
Klebestelle f splice
~/**keilförmig überlappte** bevelled overlapped splice
~/**überlappte** overlap splice
Klebestreifen m splicing (adhesive) tape
Klebeumbruch m s. Klebespiegel
Kleinbildaufnahmefilm m s. Kleinbildfilm
Kleinbilddia n s. Kleinbilddiapositiv
Kleinbilddiapositiv n 35-mm slide
Kleinbilddiaprojektor m miniature slide projector
Kleinbild-Diarahmen m 35-mm mount
Kleinbild-Farbdia n 35-mm color slide
Kleinbildfilm m small-format film; 35-mm [miniature] film
Kleinbildfotograf m 35-mm photographer
Kleinbildfotografie f miniature-format photography, miniature camera work; 35-mm [still] photography
Kleinbildkamera f small (miniature) format camera; thirty-five-millimeter [still] camera, [35-mm] miniature camera; candid camera
~/**vollautomatische** fully automatic 35-mm camera
Kleinbildnegativ n small-format negative; miniature (35-mm) negative
Kleinbildobjektiv n miniature camera lens; 35-mm [still] camera lens, 35-mm photography lens
Kleinbildpatrone f thirty-five-mm magazine (cassette), 35-mm standard cartridge
Kleinbildprojektor m miniature slide projector
Kleinbild-SLR-Kamera f, **Kleinbildspiegelreflexkamera** f thirty-five millimeter single-lens reflex camera
Kleinbildsucherkamera f thirty-five-millimeter viewfinder camera; 35-mm rangefinder camera
Kleinbild-Systemkamera f thirty-five millimeter systems camera
Kleinbildvergrößerer m, **Kleinbildvergrößerungsgerät** n small enlarger
Kleinbuchstabe m small (lowercase) letter, minuscule, miniscule
Kleinfeldinstrument n narrow-field instrument
kleinformatig small-size[d]
Kleingedruckte n fine print
Kleinkamera f 1. small (miniature) camera; 2. s. Kleinbildkamera

Kleinkino n small theater (movie house)
Kleinlabor n custom-finishing lab[oratory], custom lab
kleinmaßstäbig, kleinmaßstäblich small-scale
Kleinoffsetmaschine f [small] offset duplicating machine, duplicator
Kleinseriendruck m short-run work, job printing
Kleinspiegel m micromirror
Kleinstativ n small tripod, baby tripod (legs), minipod
~ **mit flexiblen Beinen** bendy leg tripod
Kleinstbild n microimage
Kleinstbildfilm m microfilm
Kleinstbildkamera f subminiature camera; ultraminiature camera
Kleinste-Quadrate-Ausgleichung f, **Kleinste-Quadrate-Bildzuordnung** f least-squares-matching
Kleinstkamera f s. Kleinstbildkamera
Kleinstprojektor m ultraminiature projector
Kleinstudio n small studio
Kleinwinkelstreuung f small-angle scattering
Kleinwinkeltomografie f narrow-angle tomography
Kleinzubehör n gadget
Klemmbrett n clipboard
Klemmleuchte f clamp-on light (socket)
Klemmschaltung f clamping [circuit], DC-restoration circuit *(television)*
Klemmstativ n clamp tripod, clamp-mount device
Klemmung f clamping, DC (direct current) restoration
klicken to click
Klinke f s. Klinkenstecker
Klinkenbuchse f jack
Klinkenstecker m jack plug
Klinometer n clinometer; inclinometer
Klipp... s. Clipping-...
Klirrfaktor m harmonic distortion [factor]
Klischee n duplicate [relief] plate, stereotype [plate]
Klischeeherstellung f/**fotomechanische** photoengraving [process]
Klonwerkzeug n cloning (rubber stamp) tool *(digital imaging)*
Klötzchenwelt f blocks world *(computer vision)*
Klystron n klystron *(electron tube)*
Knettrick m clay [figure] animation *(a stop-motion animation technique)*
Knickstelle f kink mark *(e.g. in film or paper)*
Kniefunktion f knee correction
Kniehöcker m [/**seitlicher**] lateral geniculate nucleus
Knieschaltung f/**automatische** auto knee *(electronic camera)*
Knipsfoto n candid [photograph], unposed photograph
Knipskamera f point-and-shoot camera, snapshot camera
Knoten m node *(graph theory, computer graphics)*
Knotenpunkt m nodal (node) point
~/**bildseitiger** rear nodal point
~/**hinterer** rear nodal point
~/**objektseitiger** front nodal point
Knotenpunktebene f nodal plane
Knotenpunktversatz m nodal point shift
Knotenvektor m nodal vector *(motion estimation, B-spline technique)*
Koax[ial]kabel n coax[ial] cable
koaxial coaxial
Kochanek-Bartels-Spline n Kochanek-Bartels spline, TCB (tension-continuity-bias) spline *(geometric modeling)*
Koch-Kurve f [von Koch] snowflake curve *(fractal geometry)*
Kochsalz n [common] salt, table salt, sodium chloride
Kode m s. Code
Koeffizientenmatrix f coefficients matrix, matrix of [the] coefficients
Koeffizientenquantisierung f coefficient quantization *(image coding)*
Koerzitivfeldstärke f, **Koerzitivkraft** f coercive force, coercivity
Kofferprojektor m portable projector
Kognition f cognition
Kognitionswissenschaft f cognitive science
kognitiv cognitive
kohärent coherent
Kohärenz f coherence, coherency
~/**optische** optical coherence
~/**partielle** partial coherence
~/**räumliche** spatial coherence
~/**zeitliche** temporal coherence
Kohärenzbandbreite f coherence bandwidth
Kohärenzfunktion f coherence function
Kohärenzgrad m degree of coherence, coherence degree
Kohärenzlänge f coherence (coherent) length *(e.g. of a light source)*
Kohärenzmaß n coherency measure
Kohärenzmatrix f coherence matrix *(partial polarization)*
Kohärenzoszillator m coherent [local] oscillator, COHO *(radar)*
Kohärenzradar n coherence [laser] radar
Kohärenztomografie f [/**optische**] optical coherence tomography, OCT
~/**spektraloptische** spectral optical coherence tomography
~/**transversale [optische]** transversal (en-face) optical coherence tomography
Kohärenztomogramm n OCT image
Kohärenzzeit f coherence time
Kohäsion f cohesion
Kohäsionskraft f cohesive force

Kohleaufdampfschicht f carbon film (electron microscopy)
Kohlebogenlampe f carbon-arc lamp
Kohlebogenlicht n carbon-arc light
Kohledruck m 1. carbon process; 2. carbon print
Kohlefaden[glüh]lampe f carbon filament incandescent lamp
Kohlekopierverfahren n carbon process
Kohlelichtbogen m carbon arc
Kohlendioxidlaser m carbon-dioxide [gas] laser
Kohlepapier n carbon paper
Kohleschicht f s. Kohleaufdampfschicht
Kohonen-Karte f, **Kohonen-Netz** n Kohonen map (network), self-organizing [feature] map, topology-preserving map (pattern recognition)
Kohonen-Schicht f output layer (artificial neural network)
koinzident coincident
Koinzidenzentfernungsmesser m coincidence[-type] rangefinder, superimposed-image rangefinder
Koinzidenz-Gammakamera f coincidence camera
Koinzidenzlinie f line of response, LOR (positron emission tomography)
Kolbenblitz m, **Kolbenblitzlampe** f flashbulb, [photo] flashlamp
Kollagen n collagen (scleroprotein)
kollationieren s. zusammentragen
Kollektivlinse f s. Feldlinse
Kollektor m collector; collector lens
Kollimation f collimation
~/**binokulare** binocular collimation
~/**elektronische** electronic collimation
Kollimationsfehler m collimation error
Kollimationsoptik f collimating optics
Kollimator m collimator (optical system)
~/**divergierender** diverging (fan-beam) collimator
~/**hochauflösender** high-resolution collimator
~/**konvergierender** converging (cone-beam) collimator
Kollimatorauflösung f collimator [spatial] resolution
Kollimatorkonstante f collimator constant
Kollimatorlinse f collimator (collimating) lens
Kollimatormarke f collimating mark
Kollimatorobjektiv n collimator objective
Kollimatorschlitz m collimator (collimating) slit
Kollimatorspiegel m collimator (collimating) mirror
Kollimatorwinkel m collimator angle
Kollimatorzylinder m collimating cylinder
kollimieren to collimate
Kollimiermodul n collimating module
kollinear collinear, colinear
Kollinearität f collinearity
Kollisionsanalyse f collision analysis

Kollisionserkennungstechnik f collision detection technique
Kollodium n collodion, collodium
Kollodiumabzug m collodion print
Kollodiumemulsion f collodion emulsion
Kollodiumfotografie f collodion photography
Kollodiumplatte f collodion [glass] plate
~/**nasse** wet-collodion plate, collodion wet plate
~/**trockene** dry-collodion plate, collodion dry plate
Kollodiumtanninplatte f tannin-coated collodion plate
Kollodiumverfahren n collodion [photographic] process
~/**nasses** wet-collodion process
~/**trockenes** dry-collodion process
Kollodiumwolle f collodion cotton, pyroxylin
Kolloid n colloid
kolorieren to color[ize], to tint
Kolorierstift m hand-coloring pen
Kolorierung f colorization, coloring, tinting
Kolorimeter n colorimeter, color meter
~/**fotoelektrisches (lichtelektrisches)** photoelectric colorimeter
Kolorimetrie f colorimetry, colorimetrics
kolorimetrisch colorimetric
Kolorist m colorist
Koloskop n colonoscope
Koloskopie f colonoscopy
Kolposkopie f colposcopy
kolposkopisch colposcopic
Kolumne f column (of printed matter)
Kolumnentitel m/**lebender** page header (printing)
Koma f coma [blur], comatic aberration (optics)
~/**anisotrope** anisotropic coma
~/**elliptische** elliptical coma
~/**meridionale** meridional coma
~/**sagittale** sagittal (off-axis) coma
~/**seitliche** lateral coma
~/**tangentiale** tangential coma
Komafehler m s. Koma
Komafigur f coma patch (pattern), comatic circle
komafrei coma-free
Komafreiheit f lack (absence) of coma
Komakorrektion f coma correction
Komarestfehler m residual coma[tic aberration]
Kombinationsaufnahme f composite photograph, [photo]montage; composite (process) shot, combined shot (cinema)
Kombinationsaufnahmeverfahren n compositing; keying; matting, matte photography (cinema)
Kombinationsbild n composite [image], composite picture (s.a. Überlagerungsbild)
Kombinationseffekt m composite (composition) effect

Kombinationsfilter *n* combination filter
Kombinationstrickverfahren *n s.*
Kombinationsaufnahmeverfahren
Kometeneffekt *m*, **Kometenschweif** *m*
comet tail *(motion artifact)*
Kommunikation *f*/**audiovisuelle**
audioivsual communication
~/**optische** optical communication
~/**visuelle** visual communication;
low-bit-rate telecommunication
Kommunikationskanal *m*
communication[s] channel
Kommunikationsmittel *n*
communication[s] medium;
communication tool
Kommunikationsnetz *n* communications network
~/**dienstintegrierendes digitales**
integrated services digital network, ISDN
Kommunikationssatellit *m*
communication [technology] satellite, communications satellite
Kommunikationsschnittstelle *f*
communication[s] interface
Kommunikationssignal *n* communication signal
Kommunikationstechnik *f*
communications technology
~/**optische** optical communications technology
Kommunikationstheorie *f s.*
Informationstheorie
kommutativ commutative *(e.g. an image-processing operator)*
Kommutativität *f* commutativity
Kompakt-Flash-Karte *f* compact flash card
Kompaktheit *f* compactness
Kompaktkamera *f* compact [camera], direct-vision camera
Kompakt-Magnetbandkassette *f* compact cassette, CC
Kompaktplatte *f* compact disc, CD
Komparator *m* [optical] comparator
Komparator-und-Vertauschungsmodul *n* compare-and-swap module
Kompassgradient *m* compass gradient *(image-processing operator)*
kompatibel compatible
Kompatibilität *f* compatibility; compliance, compliancy
Kompendium *n* compendium hood, matte box
Kompensationsfarbe *f* complementary color
Kompensationsfilter *n* 1. compensation (compensating) filter; 2. *s.* Korrekturfilter 1.
Kompensationsokular *n* compensating eyepiece *(microscope)*
Kompensatorplatte *f* 1. compensating (clear) glass, clear filter; 2. *s.* Korrektionsplatte[/Schmidtsche]
komplanar complanate
Komplanarität *f* complanarity

Komplement *n* complement
komplementär complementary
Komplementärbild *n* complementary image
Komplementärfarbe *f* complementary color (hue); opponent (opposite) color
Komplementärfarbfilter *n* complementary [color] filter, filter of complementary color
Komplementärfarbstoff *m* complementary dye
Komplementärfilter *n* complementary filter
Komplementärfilterung *f* complementary filtration
Komplementärkontrast *m* complementary contrast
Komplettbild *n* complete image *(s.a.* Vollbild*)*
Komplexbildner *m*, **Komplexierungsmittel** *n* complexing agent *(developer additive)*
Komplexbildung *f* complexation
Komplex-Ion *n* complex ion
Komplexsalz *n* complex salt
Komponenten *fpl*/**digital-serielle** digital serial components, DSC
Komponentenaufzeichnung *f* component signal recording *(video)*
~/**digitale** component digital recording
Komponentenbild *n* component image
Komponentencodierung *f*
[separate-]component coding *(digital television)*
Komponentenfernsehen *n* component television (video)
Komponenteninhaltsschicht *f*
within-component layer *(hypermedia system)*
Komponentensignal *n* [/**analoges**]
component [video] signal, YUV
~/**digitales** digital component video signal, component digital signal
Komponentenvektor *m* component vector
Komponentenvideo *n* component video
~/**analoges** component analog video, CAV
~/**digitales** digital component video, component digital video
Kompositsignal *n* composite [encoded video] signal, composite TV signal; composite color [video] signal, color (RGB) video signal
Kompression *f* compression, compaction *(e.g. of image data; s.a. under* Codierung*)*
~/**adaptive** adaptive compression
~/**arithmetische** arithmetic compression
~/**asymmetrische** asymmetrical compression
~/**auflösungsunabhängige**
resolution-independent compression
~/**fraktale** fractal[-based] compression
~/**lokal adaptive** locally adaptive compression
~/**progressive** progressive compression
~/**reversible** reversible compression

~/**semiadaptive** semi-adaptive compression
~/**sequentielle** sequential [data] compression
~/**skalierbare** scalable compression
~/**symmetrische** symmetrical compression
~/**verlustarme** near[-to]-lossless compression, transparent compression
~/**verlustbehaftete** lossy (irreversible) compression
~/**verlustfreie (verlustlose)** lossless (reversible) compression, nonlossy (error-free) compression
~/**waveletbasierte** wavelet[-transform]-based compression, wavelet compression
~/**wörterbuchbasierte** dictionary-based compression
Kompressionsalgorithmus m compression algorithm (program), encoder
Kompressionsart f compression type
Kompressionsartefakt n compression artifact
Kompressionsbereich m compression range
Kompressionseffizienz f compression efficiency
Kompressionsfaktor m compression factor, coding gain
Kompressionsfehler m compression error
Kompressionsformat n compression format
Kompressionsgewinn m compression gain
Kompressionsgrad m degree of compression
Kompressionsleistung f compression performance
Kompressionsparameter m compression parameter
Kompressionsrate f s. Kompressionsstufe
Kompressionssoftware f compression program
Kompressionsstandard m compression standard
~/**digitaler** digital compression standard, DCS
Kompressionsstufe f compression rate (level)
Kompressionssystem n compression system (scheme)
Kompressionstechnik f 1. compression technology; 2. compression technique
Kompressionstransformation f s. Karhunen-Loève-Transformation
Kompressionsverfahren n compression method (technique); compression procedure
~/**transformationsbasiertes** transform-based compression method
Kompressionsverhältnis n compression ratio
Kompressionsverlust m compression loss

Kompressionsverstärker m compression amplifier *(ultrasound scanner)*
Kompressionsverzerrung f compression distortion
Kompressionsvorgang m compression process
Kompressionszyklus m compression cycle
Kompressor m compressor
komprimierbar compressible
Komprimierbarkeit f compressibility
komprimieren to compress
Komprimierung f s. Kompression
Kondensation f condensation
Kondensator m capacitor, condenser
Kondensatormikrofon n capacitor (condenser) microphone
Kondensor m s. Kondensorlinse
~/**achromatischer** achromatic condenser
~/**aplanatischer** aplanatic condenser
~/**zweistufiger** two-lens Abbe [condenser]
Kondensorapertur f, **Kondensorblende** f condenser aperture [diaphragm], condenser diaphragm
Kondensor-Frontlinse f condenser front lens
Kondensorlinse f condenser [lens]
Kondensorlinsengruppe f condensor lens array
Kondensorträger m substage *(microscope)*
Kondensorvergrößerer m condenser[-type] enlarger
konditionieren to condition, to cure, to season, to mature *(e.g. printing paper)*
Konditionierungsbad n conditioner
Konferenzfernsehen n conference television (TV), video teleconferencing
Konfiguration f configuration
konfokal confocal
Konfokalmikroskop n confocal [optical] microscope, confocal scanning light microscope, CSLM
Konfokalmikroskopie f confocal microscopy
konfokalmikroskopisch confocal microscopic
Konfokaltomograf m confocal tomograph
kongruent congruent
Kongruenz f congruence, congruency
Konimeter n konimeter, coniometer
Konjugationsabstand m total conjugate distance, object-[to-]image distance, track length *(optics)*
Konjugationsverhältnis n conjugate ratio
konjugieren to conjugate
Konkatenation f concatenation, chaining *(e.g. of codes)*
konkav concave, dished, curved inward
Konkavgitter n concave [reflection] grating
~/**holografisches** concave holographic grating
Konkavität f concavity
konkavkonvex concavo-convex
Konkavkonvexlinse f concavo-convex lens, positive meniscus [lens]

Konkavlinse

Konkavlinse f concave (negative) lens, diverging (dispersive) lens
Konkavspiegel m concave (convergent) mirror, collecting mirror
Konnektionismus m connectionism
Konnektivität f connectivity *(e.g. of a network)*
Konoskop n conoscope
konoskopisch conoscopic
Konservierungsmittel n preservative *(developer additive)*
Konsole f console *(e.g. of an electron microscope)*
Konstante f/**Plancksche** Planck['s] constant *(quantum theory)*
Konstantenergie-Stimulus m equal-energy stimulus
Konstanz f constancy
Konstanzprüfung f constancy testing *(film processing)*
Konstruieren n/**computergestütztes, Konstruktion** f/**rechnerunterstützte** computer-aided design, CAD
Konsumelektronik f consumer electronics
Kontakt m/**optischer** optical contact
Kontaktabzug m 1. contact print (copy); 2. s. Indexbild
Kontaktbelichtung f [direct-]contact exposure
Kontaktbelichtungsgerät n contact printer
Kontaktbildschirm m touch[-sensitive] screen; touch screen monitor
Kontaktbildsensor m contact image sensor, CIS
Kontaktbogen m contact sheet
Kontaktdruck m contact printing
Kontakterscheinung f s. Geistereffekt
Kontaktfilm m/**UV-empfindlicher** ultraviolet-sensitive contact film
Kontaktkopie f contact print (copy)
kontaktkopieren to contact-print
Kontaktkopieren n contact printing, contacting
Kontaktkopierer m contact printer
Kontaktkopiergerät n contact printing device
Kontaktkopiermaschine f motion-picture contact printer
Kontaktkopierpapier n contact printing paper (material), contact speed paper
Kontaktkopierrahmen m [contact] printing frame, contact print frame
Kontaktkopierung f s. Kontaktkopieren
Kontaktkopierverfahren n contact [photographic] printing process
Kontaktlinie f matte line
Kontaktlinse f contact lens
Kontaktmikrofon n contact microphone
Kontaktmikroradiografie f [contact] microradiography; contact X-ray microscopy, X-ray micrography
Kontaktmikroskopie f contact microscopy
Kontaktpapier n contact [printing] paper, chloride paper
Kontaktprofilometer n contact profilometer
Kontaktraster m(n) contact screen, [halftone] screen
Kontaktverfahren n contact process
Konterfei n s. under Abbildung 2.
Kontern n reverse printing
Kontext m context
Kontextanalyse f contextual analysis *(optical character recognition)*
Kontextinformation f contextual information
Kontextmenü n context (object) menu
Kontextmerkmal n topological feature
Kontingenzmatrix f contingency matrix *(classification)*
Kontingenztafel f contingency table *(classification)*
Kontinuität f/**geometrische** geometric continuity
~/**parametrische** parametric continuity
Kontinuitätsbedingung f continuity constraint
Kontinuitätsgleichung f 1. continuity equation; 2. brightness change constraint equation, BCCE *(motion analysis)*
Kontrast m contrast, brightness range, gamma
~/**bildgebender** image-forming contrast
~/**binokularer** binocular contrast
~/**fotografischer** photographic contrast
~/**fotometrischer** objective contrast
~/**inhomogener** inhomogenous contrast
~/**lokaler** local contrast
~/**mittlerer** average contrast
~/**objektiver** objective contrast
~/**optischer** optical contrast
~/**physikalischer** physical contrast
~/**physiologischer** s. ~/subjektiver
~/**radiografischer** radiographic contrast
~/**räumlicher** spatial contrast
~/**regionaler** regional contrast
~/**relativer** relative contrast
~/**subjektiver** subjective contrast
~/**tonaler** tonal contrast
~/**visueller** visual contrast
Kontrastabfall m loss of contrast
Kontrastabnahme f, **Kontrastabschwächung** f contrast degradation, decrease in contrast
Kontraständerung f contrast change
Kontrastangiografie f contrast angiography
Kontrastangleich m, **Kontrastangleichung** f 1. contrast match[ing]; 2. s. Kontrastanpassung
Kontrastanhebung f contrast crispening *(s.a.* Kontrasterhöhung*)*
Kontrastanpassung f contrast adaptation (adjustment)
Kontrastanreicherung f s. Kontrastanhebung
kontrastarm low-contrast, flat
Kontrastarmut f lack of contrast, flatness

Kontrastauflösung f contrast resolution
Kontrastausgleich m contrast compensation; dodging
Kontrastbearbeitung f contrast editing
Kontrastbeeinflussung f contrast manipulation
Kontrastbereich m contrast range
Kontrastbild n contrast image
Kontrast-Booster m contrast booster
Kontrastdarstellung f 1. contrast display; 2. s. Kontrastmitteldarstellung
Kontrastdehnung f contrast stretch[ing], contrast expansion; full-scale histogram stretch
Kontrast-Detail-Diagramm n contrast-detail phantom *(image-quality assessment)*
Kontrasteinstellung f 1. contrast adjustment (setting); 2. contrast control
Kontrastempfindlichkeit f contrast sensitivity *(e.g. of the eye)*
Kontrastempfindung f subjective contrast
Kontrastentwickler m [high-]contrast developer
Kontrasterhöhung f contrast enhancement (increase), increase in contrast
Kontrasterkennung f contrast detection
Kontrastfaktor m s. Gradation
Kontrastfarbe f 1. contrasting color; 2. complementary color
Kontrastfilter n contrast filter
Kontrastfotometer n contrast photometer
Kontrastgradient m contrast gradient
kontrastieren to contrast
Kontrastindex m contrast index, CI; gamma index
Kontrastindexmeter n contrast-index meter
Kontrastindex-Zeit-Kurve f time-contrast index curve
Kontrastkonstanz f contrast constancy
Kontrastkorrektur f contrast correction
kontrastlos flat, lacking in contrast *(photograph or negative)*
Kontrastlosigkeit f flatness, lack of contrast
Kontrastmanipulation f contrast manipulation
Kontrastmaske f contrast mask
Kontrastmaskierung f contrast masking, luminance masking (dependence) *(video compression)*
Kontrastmechanismus m contrast mechanism
Kontrastmerkmal m contrast feature
Kontrastmessung f contrast measurement
Kontrastminderung f contrast reduction
Kontrastmittel n contrast agent (material), contrast [medium]; contrast-medium fluid; X-ray contrast agent (medium)
~/**diamagnetisches** diamagnetic contrast agent
~/**paramagnetisches** paramagnetic contrast agent

Kontrastmitteldarstellung f contrast[-uptake] imaging
Kontrastmodifikation f contrast modification
Kontrastmodulation f contrast modulation
Kontrastniveau n contrast level
Kontrastnormierung f contrast normalization
Kontrastoptimierung f contrast optimization
Kontrastreduzierung f contrast reduction
Kontrastregelung f contrast control
kontrastreich high-contrast, contrasty, hard
Kontrastsättigung f contrast saturation
Kontrastschärfe f definition
kontrastschwach low-contrast, flat, faint
Kontrastschwelle f contrast [detection] threshold
Kontrastskalierung f contrast scaling
Kontrastsonografie f contrast sonography
Kontrastspreizung f s. Kontrastdehnung
kontraststark high-contrast, contrasty, hard
Kontraststeigerung f contrast increase (enhancement), increase in contrast *(s.a. Kontrastverbesserung)*
Kontraststeuerung f contrast control
Kontraststufe f contrast level; contrast step (grade)
Kontrasttransferfunktion f s. Kontrastübertragungsfunktion
Kontrasttreue f contrast fidelity
Kontrastübertragbarkeit f contrast transferability
Kontrastübertragung f contrast transfer
Kontrastübertragungsfunktion f contrast (modulation) transfer function, CTF, MTF; modulation transfer [function] curve; contrast sensitivity function, CSF
Kontrastumfang m contrast range, luminance ratio
Kontrastumkehr f contrast reversal
Kontrastunterdrückung f suppression of contrast
Kontrastunterschied m contrast difference
kontrastvariabel variable-contrast *(photographic paper)*
Kontrastveränderung f contrast change; contrast variation
Kontrastverbesserung f contrast improvement *(s.a. Kontraststeigerung)*
Kontrastverhältnis n [optical] contrast ratio, CR
Kontrastverlust m loss of contrast
Kontrastverminderung f contrast reduction, reduction in contrast
Kontrastverringerung f s. Kontrastverminderung
Kontrastverschärfung f s. Kontrastverstärkung
Kontrastverstärker m contrast amplifier

Kontrastverstärkung f contrast enhancement (amplification), contrast intensification
Kontrastversteilerung f s. Kontrastverstärkung
Kontrastverteilung f contrast distribution
Kontrastverzerrung f contrast distortion
Kontrastwahl f/**automatische** automatic contrast selection *(video)*
Kontrastwahrnehmung f contrast perception
Kontrastwandelpapier n variable-contrast paper
Kontrastwert m contrast value
Kontrastwiedergabe f contrast rendering (rendition), contrast reproduction
Kontrastwirkung f contrast effect
Kontrastzerlegung f contrast decomposition
Kontrollanzeige f display, readout *(s.a. under* Display, Anzeige, Bildschirm*)*
Kontrollbild n control image *(printing)*
Kontrollbildschirm m monitor [screen]
Kontrollbit n check bit
Kontrollpolygon n control polygon *(computer graphics)*
Kontrollpunkt m control point *(e.g. in shape modeling)*; check point
Kontrollraum m control room
Kontrollspur f control (address) track *(magnetic image recording)*
Kontrollstreifen m control (test) strip
Kontur f contour, outline *(s.a. under* Umriss*)*
~/**aktive** active contour, [active] snake; spline fit, magic lasso *(computer graphics)*
~/**binäre** binary contour
~/**geodätische aktive** geodesic active contour
~/**geschlossene** closed (contiguous) contour, connected contour
~/**komplexe** complex-shaped contour
~/**planare** planar contour
~/**verformbare** deformable contour
Konturanalyse f contour analysis
Konturanpassung f contour fitting
Konturapproximation f contour approximation
Konturbereich m contour region
Konturbeschreibung f contour description
Konturbild n contour[-line] image
Konturcode m contour code
Konturcodierungsalgorithmus m contour coding algorithm
Konturdarstellung f 1. contour representation; 2. contour plot
Konturdiskontinuität f contour discontinuity
Konturenfilm m contour film
Konturensatz m runaround *(typography)*
konturenscharf sharp, crisp *(image)*
Konturenschärfe f [edge] sharpness, acutance *(esp. of photographic images)*; [image] definition
Konturextraktion f contour extraction
Konturfolgeverfahren n s. Konturverfolgung
Konturgenerator m contour generator
Konturglättung f contour smoothing
Konturgrafik f contour plot
konturieren to contour
Konturierung f contouring *(scalar visualization technique)*
Konturinformation f contour information
Konturkante f boundary
Konturklassifikator m contour classifier
Konturkorrektur f detailing, crispening *(electronic imaging)*
Konturkorrelation f contour correlation
Konturkrümmung f contour curvature
Konturkurve f contour (level) curve
Konturlänge f contour length
Konturlinie f contour line; boundary line; outline [edge]
~/**umschreibende** boundary contour
Konturliniensegment n contour line segment
Konturmerkmal n contour feature
Konturmodell n/**aktives** active (deformable) contour model
Konturnormale f contour normal
Konturpixel n contour pixel
Konturpolygon n circumscribing polygon
Konturpunkt m contour (boundary) point
Konturpunktauffindung f contour point detection
Konturrauschen n contour noise
Konturschärfe f s. Konturenschärfe
Kontursegment n contour segment
Kontursegmentierung f contour segmentation (decomposition)
Konturstück n s. Kontursegment
Konturverfolgung f contour[-based] tracking, contour tracing
Konturwahrnehmung f contour perception
Konturzeichnung f contour drawing
Konus m bevel, neck *(movable type)*
konvergent convergent, converging
Konvergenz f convergence, vergence, convergency
Konvergenzfehler m misconvergence, convergence error, beam convergence misalignment
Konvergenzgebiet n region of convergence, ROC *(signal theory)*
Konvergenzkorrektur f/**automatische** auto[matic] convergence
Konvergenzpunkt m point of convergence
Konvergenzwinkel m convergence angle, angle of convergence
konvergieren to converge *(e.g. lines)*
Konversionsfilter n [color] conversion filter; light-balancing filter
Konversionsgewinn m conversion gain, CG *(photodetector)*

Konversionsmatrix f conversion matrix
Konverter m 1. converter, convertor; 2. afocal converter, converter lens; 3. [television system] converter
konvertieren to convert
Konvertierung f conversion
konvex convex, curved outward
Konvexe-Hülle-Eigenschaft f convex hull property *(of geometrical objects)*
Konvexität f convexity
konvexkonkav convexo-concave
Konvexlinse f convex (converging) lens, collection (collector) lens, convergent (positive) lens
Konvexscanner m, **Konvexschallkopf** m curved-array scanner *(sonography)*
Konvexspiegel m convex mirror
Konvolutionscode m s. Faltungscode
konzentrisch concentric
Konzentrizität f concentricity
Koordinate f coordinate
~/**baryzentrische** barycentric coordinate
~/**homogene** homogeneous coordinate
~/**normierte** normalized device coordinate, NDC
~/**rechtwinklige** rectangular (rectilinear) coordinate
~/**virtuelle** virtual device coordinate, VDC
Koordinatenachsen fpl axes of coordinates, coordinate axes
Koordinatendarstellung f coordinate representation
Koordinatendatei f coordinate file
Koordinatenebene f coordinate plane
Koordinatengitter n coordinate grid
Koordinatengrafik f s. Liniengrafik
Koordinatenliste f lookup table [memory], LUT, index map
Koordinatenmessgerät n coordinate measuring machine, CMM
Koordinatenmeswsmikroskop n coordinate measuring microscope
Koordinatenmesstisch m coordinate table
Koordinatenpaar n coordinate pair
Koordinatenraum m coordinate space
Koordinatensystem n coordinate system
~/**betrachterzentriertes** viewer-centered coordinate system
~/**kartes[ian]isches** Cartesian coordinate system
~/**linkshändiges** left-handed coordinate system
~/**objektzentriertes** object-centered coordinate system
~/**polares** polar coordinate system
~/**rechtshändiges** right-handed coordinate system
~/**rechtwinkliges** rectangular coordinate system
~/**stereotaktisches** stereotactical coordinate system
~/**weltfestes** world (global) coordinate system, world reference frame, world (global) space, scene coordinate system
~/**zylindrisches** cylindrical coordinate system
Koordinatentransformation f transformation of coordinates; coordinate transform[ation] *(computer graphics)*
Koordinatenursprung m coordinate origin
Koordinatograf m coordinatograph *(photogrammetry)*
Koordinator m s. Koordinatograf
Kopf m head *(s.a. Magnetkopf)*; header [record] *(of a data frame)*
Kopfabrieb m head wear
Kopfazimut n(m) head azimuth
Kopfbogen m [sheet of] letterhead
Kopfdaten pl header data
Kopfdatenbereich m header [record] *(of a data frame)*
Kopfhörer m headphone[s], earphone
Kopfhörergeschirr n,
Kopfhörersprechgarnitur f headset
Kopflicht n s. Augenlicht
Kopfmonitor m head-mounted (helmet-mounted) display, HMD; virtual reality helmet
Kopfneigung f head tilt
Kopfrad n s. Kopftrommel
Kopfrauschen n head noise
Kopfscheibe f s. Kopftrommel
Kopfspalt m [magnetic] head gap
Kopfsprechgarnitur f headset
Kopfspule f head coil *(magnetic resonance imaging)*
Kopfspur f head track
Kopfsteg m head [margin], top edge *(layout)*
Kopftrommel f head drum (wheel) *(video recorder)*
Kopftrommel-Regeleinheit f head servo *(videotape machine)*
Kopftrommelrotation f head rotation
Kopftrommelumschlingungswinkel m wrap angle
Kopfumschaltung f head switch
Kopfzeile f page header *(printing, videotex)*
Kopfzusetzer m head clog
Kopie f copy; print *(film)*
~/**doppelseitige** two-sided copy
~/**elektrofotografische** photocopy, photoreproduction
~/**farbkorrigierte** timed (corrected) print
~/**fotografische** photo[graphic] copy, photoduplicate, copy photograph
~/**fotomechanische** photomechanical copy
~/**frische** green film *(cinema)*
~/**kombinierte** married (composite) print, combined print *(cinema)*
~/**kontrastverstärkte** contrast-amplified copy *(e.g. of a radiograph)*
~/**stoffliche** hard copy
~/**stumme** mute (silent) print, picture only print *(cinema)*
Kopieablage f copy (exit) tray *(copier)*

Kopiebeschädigung f print damage (cinema)
Kopieformat n print format (size)
Kopieranstalt f motion picture [processing] laboratory, cinema laboratory, film lab[oratory]
Kopierapparat m s. Kopierer
Kopierarbeit f copy[ing] work
Kopierautomat m automated [machine] printer
kopierbar printable
Kopierbelichtung f print[ing] exposure
Kopierbelichtungsmesser m enlarging [exposure] meter
Kopierbelichtungszeit f printing exposure time
Kopierdichte f printing density
Kopierdurchlauf m printing pass
Kopierebene f printing plane
Kopiereffekt m 1. printing effect; print through (magnetic tape technology); 2. optical printing effect (cinematography)
kopieren to copy; to print (film material); to dub (a videotape)
Kopieren n/**additives** additive printing
~/**digitales** digital copying
~/**elektrostatisches** electrostatic copying
~/**kombiniertes** composite printing (motion-picture film)
~ **mit anamorphotischer Entzerrung** unsqueezing, deanamorphotic printing
~/**optisches** optical (projection) printing
~/**subtraktives** subtractive printing, white-light printing [method]
Kopierer m 1. copier, copy machine; printer; 2. printed (circled) take, kept take, A neg (film editing)
~/**additiver** additive printer
~/**elektrostatischer** electrostatic copier
~/**xerografischer** xerographic copier, Xerox
Kopiererpapier n copy paper
kopierfähig printable
Kopierfähigkeit f printability
Kopierfehler m printing error
Kopierfenster n printer (printing) aperture
Kopierfilm m print film; motion-picture [theatrical] print film
Kopierfilmmaterial n print stock (material)
Kopierfilter n printing filter
Kopierfolie f copier (transparency) film
Kopierfunktion f copy function (e.g. of a fax machine)
Kopiergenauigkeit f reproduction accuracy
Kopiergerät n copier, copy machine; printer
kopiergeschützt copy-protected, CP
Kopiergeschwindigkeit f printing speed
Kopierkamera f copy[ing] camera
Kopierkarte f printer (printing) card, grading (timing) card, timing list (motion-picture printing)
Kopierkontrast m printing contrast
Kopierkopf m printer head

Kopierlampe f printing lamp
Kopierlicht n printing (printer) light
Kopierlichtwert m printing light value, printer point (light)
Kopiermaschine f copying (printing) machine, copy (copier) machine, machine printer
~/**optische** optical printer
Kopiermaschinenlampenhaus n printer lamphouse
Kopiermaske f printing mask
Kopiermaterial n copy[ing] material, printing material; motion-picture print film, print stock (cinema)
Kopiermedium n copying medium
Kopierobjektiv n copy[ing] lens
Kopierpapier n copy[ing] paper; [photographic] printing paper, print paper
Kopierpinsel m s. Klonwerkzeug
Kopierprozess m print[ing] process
Kopierrahmen m printing (masking) frame, [printing] easel, [adjustable] masking easel, multi-mask enlarging easel, enlarging paper holder
Kopier-Rohfilm m print stock (material)
Kopierschnittverfahren n time-code editing (video)
Kopierschutz m copy protection, copy prevention
Kopierschutzbit n copy prohibition bit
Kopierschutzstecker m dongle
Kopierschutzvorrichtung f copy protection mechanism
Kopierservice m photocopy[ing] shop
Kopierspalt m printing slit
Kopierstartmarke f printer startmark
Kopiertechnik f 1. printing technology; 2. printing technique; copying technique
Kopiertisch m printing stage
Kopiertrick m optical printing effect
Kopiertrickverfahren n motion-picture optical printing technique, optical compositing
Kopiertrommel f 1. printing drum; 2. s. Kopierzahntrommel
Kopieruhr f enlarger timer
Kopierung f printing
~/**optische** optical printing
Kopierverfahren n copying process; printing process (procedure)
~/**additives** additive printing
Kopierverlust m generation[al] loss
Kopiervorgang m printing process (procedure)
Kopiervorlage f art[work]
Kopierwerk n motion picture [processing] laboratory, cinema laboratory, film lab[oratory]
Kopierwerkserzeugnis n laboratory product
Kopierwerksrolle f lab roll
Kopierwerktest m lab[oratory] test
Kopierzahntrommel f sprocketed printing drum

Kopierzeit f print[ing] time *(photography)*
koplanar coplanar
Koppelbit n merging bit
Koppelfeld n patch panel
Koppelfeldprozess m neighborhood process (operation)
Kopplungselement n/**faseroptisches** fiber[-optic] coupler, optical fiber coupler
~/**optisches** optical coupling element
Koprozessor m coprocessor
Korn n 1. grain; 2. *s.* Körnigkeit
~/**fotografisches** photographic grain
~/**grobes** coarse grain
~/**mikrokristallines** microcrystalline grain
Kornea f [eye] cornea
Korngröße f grain size
Korngrößenverteilung f grain size distribution, GSD
körnig grainy, granular *(e.g. film material)*
Körnigkeit f graininess *(subjective term)*
kornlos grainless, grainfree
Kornoberfläche f grain surface
Kornraster m(n) grained (mezzograph) screen *(reprography)*
Kornrauschen n grain (granular) noise; granular quantization noise
Kornreifung f grain ripening
Kornstruktur f grain (granular) structure
Körnung f granularity *(objective correlate of graininess)*
Körnungswert m granularity level
Kornvergrößerung f grain growth
Kornvolumen n grain volume
Kornzusammenballung f grain cluster
Korona-Aufladung f corona charging *(electrophotography)*
Koronadraht m corona wire
Koronafotografie f *s.* Kirlian-Fotografie
Koronarangiografie f coronary angiography
Koronarangioskopie f coronary angioscopy
Koronararteriografie f coronary arteriography
Koronarentladung f corona[ry] discharge
Koronograf m [/**nach Lyot**] coronagraph, coronograph, disk telescope
Korotron n corotron *(electrophotography)*
Körper/**elastischer** soft body *(e.g. in computer graphics)*
~/**fotometrischer** light distribution solid, solid of luminous intensity distribution
~/**fraktaler** fractal solid
~/**konvexer** convex body
~/**platonischer** Platonic body (solid), regular polyhedron
~/**Schwarzer** blackbody [radiator], Planckian (cavity) radiator
~/**starrer** rigid solid (body) *(e.g. in computer graphics)*
Körperanimation f body animation; human body animation
Körperdiagramm n stereogram
Körperdosis f [whole-]body dose

Körperfarbe f subject (body) color, object (surface) color
Körpergeometrie f/**konstruktive** constructive solid geometry, CSG
Körpermodell n solid model
Körpermodellierung f solid modeling
Körperphantom n anthropomorphic phantom *(X-ray dosimetry)*
Körperquerschnittsbild n body cross-sectional image
Körperscheibe f body slice
Körperspule f [whole-]body coil *(magnetic resonance imaging)*
korpuskular corpuscular
Korpuskularoptik f particle optics
Korpuskularstrahlung f corpuscular radiation
Korpuskulartheorie f [**des Lichts**] corpuscular theory [of light], particle (emission) theory of light
Korrektion/**optische** optical correction
Korrektionsfilter n *s.* Korrekturfilter
Korrektionsgrad m degree (level) of correction
Korrektionslinse f corrective (correction) lens
Korrektionsoptik f correction optics
Korrektionsplatte f [/**Schmidtsche**] Schmidt (aspheric lens) correcting plate, corrector plate *(s.a.* Kompensatorplatte*)*
Korrektionszustand m state of correction
Korrektorfilter n printing filter
Korrektur f correction
~/**asphärische** aspheric[al] correction
~/**geometrische** geometric[al] correction
~/**optische** optical correction
~/**radiometrische** radiometric correction
Korrekturalgorithmus m correction algorithm
Korrekturaufnahme f *s.* Nachaufnahme
Korrekturbild n correction image
Korrekturfahne f galley [proof]
Korrekturfeld n stigmator *(electron microscope)*
Korrekturfilter n 1. correction filter, correcting (corrective) filter; 2. *s.* Kompensationsfilter 1.
Korrekturfilterung f corrective filtering (filtration)
Korrekturfunktion f correction function
Korrekturkopie f reference print *(cinema)*
Korrekturlinse f corrective (correction) lens
Korrekturmatrix f correction matrix; correction map *(emission tomography)*
Korrekturstern m update
Korrekturstufe f correction level *(e.g. of an objective)*
Korrekturverfahren n/**fotomechanisches** masking method
Korrekturzeichen n [proof] correction mark, proofreader mark
Korrelation f correlation
~/**diskrete** discrete correlation
~/**nichtlineare** nonlinear correlation

Korrelation 232

~/**räumliche** spatial correlation
~/**zeitliche** temporal correlation
Korrelationsfilter n matched filter
Korrelationsfilterung f correlation filtering (template matching)
Korrelationsfunktion f correlation function
Korrelationskoeffizient m correlation coefficient
Korrelationsmaß n correlation measure
Korrelationsmatrix f correlation matrix
Korrelationsspektroskopie f correlation spectroscopy
Korrelationstheorem n correlation theorem
Korrelationszeit f correlation time
Korrelogramm n correlogram
Korrespondenzanalyse f correspondence analysis
Korrespondenzmatrix f correspondence matrix
Korrespondenzproblem n correspondence problem (stereopsis); matching problem (computer vision)
Korrespondenzqualität f letter quality, LQ (printed image)
korrigierbar correctable
korrigieren to correct (e.g. lens aberrations)
Kosinusfunktion f cosine (signal processing)
Kosinusgesetz n [/**Lambertsches**] [Lambert's] cosine law [of illumination], Lambert's law (geometric optics)
Kosinusgitter n cosinusoidal (cosine wave) grating
Kosinus-hoch-vier-Gesetz n cosine[-to-the-]fourth law (optics)
Kosinusschwingung f s. Kosinusfunktion
Kosinustransformation f cosine transform (image coding)
~/**adaptive diskrete** adaptive DCT [coding]
~/**blockbasierte diskrete** block-based DCT
~/**diskrete** discrete cosine transform[ation], DCT
~/**inverse diskrete** inverse discrete cosine transform, IDCT
~/**kontinuierliche** continuous cosine transform
~/**zweidimensionale diskrete** two-dimensional DCT
Kosinustransformierte f cosine transform
Kosinuswelle f cosine wave
Koslowsky-Effekt m s. Goldeffekt
Kostenfunktion f cost function
Kostinsky-Effekt m Kostinsky effect (photography)
Kovarianzfunktion f covariance function
Kovarianzmatrix f covariance matrix
Kraftmikroskop n atomic force microscope, AFM
~/**elektrostatisches** Coulomb force microscope, CFM

Kraftmikroskopie f/**atomare** atomic force microscopy
Kraftrückkopplung f force feedback
Kran m crane
Kranaufnahme f crane shot
Kratzer m scratch (s.a. Schramme)
Kratzfestigkeit f scratch resistance (e.g. of light filters)
K-Raum m k-space (imaging mathematics)
Krawattenmikrofon n lavalier[-style] microphone, lavaliere (chest) microphone, lav
Kreativfilter n creative (effect) filter
Kreditkartenlesegerät n credit card reader
Kreis m circle (geometric primitive)
~/**Ramsdenscher** Ramsden circle (optics)
Kreisalgorithmus m **von Bresenham** Bresenham's algorithm (computer graphics)
Kreisbewegung f circular motion
Kreisblende f 1. circular aperture (stop); 2. iris wipe (motion-picture effect)
Kreisbogen-Bezugsprofil n arc reference profile (sprocket)
Kreisdiagramm n pie (circular) chart, circle graph (diagram)
Kreiselkompass m gyroscope
Kreiselkopf m gyro head (tripod)
Kreiselstabilisator m gyrostabilizer, gyroscope stabilizer, gyrostat
kreisförmig circular, round
Kreisförmigkeit f circularity, roundness (shape feature)
Kreisfrequenz f circular frequency
Kreispupille f circular pupil
Kreisring m torus
kreisrund s. kreisförmig
Kreissymmetrie f circular symmetry
kreissymmetrisch circularly symmetric[al] (e.g. a beam pattern)
Kreuzfaltung f French fold (of printed sheets)
Kreuzfalz m right-angle fold
Kreuzfeldröhre f crossed-field tube (radar)
Kreuzkorrelation f cross-correlation
Kreuzkorrelationsbild n cross-correlation[al] image
Kreuzkorrelationsfunktion cross-correlation function, CCF
Kreuzkovarianz f cross covariance
Kreuzluminanz f cross luminance (luma)
Kreuzmodulation f cross-mod[ulation], Xm
Kreuzpeilung f triangulation [procedure]
Kreuzpolarisation f cross polarization
Kreuzpolarisator m crossed polarizer
Kreuzraster m(n) crossline halftone; crossline screen
Kreuzschiene f [video] switcher
Kreuzschienenverteiler m crossbar [distributor], crossbar switch
Kreuzschnitt m cross cutting
Kreuztisch m mechanical stage (microscope)
Kriecheffekt m worming (temporal alias)

Kriechschrift f, **Kriechtitel** m crawling title
Kriegsfotograf m war photographer
Kriegsfotografie f combat photography
Kristall m crystal
~/**anisotroper** anisotropic crystal
~/**doppelbrechender** birefringent (doubly refracting) crystal
~/**elektrooptischer** electro-optic crystal
~/**fehlgeordneter** imperfect (faulted) crystal
~/**idealer** perfect crystal
~/**isotroper** isotropic crystal
~/**kubischer** cubic crystal
~/**lichtbrechender** photorefractive crystal
~/**optisch einachsiger** uniaxial crystal
~/**optisch zweiachsiger** biaxial crystal
~/**optischer** optical crystal
~/**piezoelektrischer** piezoelectric[al] crystal
~/**polarer** polar (ionic) crystal
~**[bau]fehler** m crystal defect (imperfection)
Kristallgitter n crystal[line] lattice, crystal space lattice
Kristallgitterfehler m crystal lattice defect
Kristallgitterkonstante f crystal lattice constant
Kristallgitterstruktur f crystal lattice structure
Kristallinse f crystalline lens (eye)
Kristallkeim m seed crystal, crystal nucleus
Kristallmikrofon n crystal microphone
Kristalloberfläche f crystal surface
Kristallografie f crystallography
kristallografisch crystallographic
Kristallogramm n crystallogram
Kristalloptik f crystal optics
Kristallperlwand f [glass-]beaded screen, pearl screen
Kristallspektrograf m crystal spectrograph
Kristallspektrometer n crystal spectrometer
Kristallstruktur f crystal[line] structure
Kristallwachstum n crystal growth
Kron-Effekt m Kron effect (photography)
Kronflint m crown flint glass
Kronglas n crown glass
krummlinig curvilinear
Krümmung f 1. curvature; 2. curl (of film or photographic paper)
~/**Gaußsche** Gauss[ian] curvature, Gaussian curve
~/**mittlere** mean curvature
~/**ortszeitliche** spatio-temporal curvature
Krümmungsdetektion f curve detection
Krümmungsenergie f curvature energy
Krümmungsgrad m degree of curvature
Krümmungskreis m circle of curvature
Krümmungsmaß n curvature measure
Krümmungsmessung f curvature measurement
Krümmungsmittelpunkt m center of curvature
Krümmungsoperator m curvature operator
Krümmungspunkt m curvature point
Krümmungsradius m radius of curvature
Krümmungsschätzung f curvature estimation
Krümmungstensor m curvature-augmented tensor
~/**Riemannscher** Riemann's [curvature] tensor
Krümmungsvektor m curvature vector
Krümmungszentrum n center of curvature
Kryoelektronenmikroskopie f cryo electron microscopy
Kryoelektronentomografie f cryoelectron tomography
Kryomikroskop n freeze-drying microscope
Kryomikroskopie f freeze-drying microscopy, FDM
kryomikroskopisch cryomicroscopic
Kryospektroskopie f cryospectroscopy
Kryptografie f cryptography
kryptografisch cryptographic
Kryptogramm n cryptogram, cryptograph
Kryptonlaser m krypton laser
Ku-Band n Ku band (satellite transmission)
kubisch cubic[al]
kubisch-flächenzentriert face-centered cubic (crystal structure)
Kubus m cube (geometric primitive)
Kugel f/**Ulbrichtsche** integrating sphere (photometry)
~/**umhüllende (umschließende)** bounding sphere (computer graphics)
Kugelabweichung f spherical aberration, SA (optics)
Kugelcharakteristik f omnidirectional microphone pattern
Kugelende n ball terminal (letterface)
Kugelfläche f spherical surface
kugelförmig spherical
Kugelförmigkeit f sphericity
Kugelfotometer n [nach Ulbricht] integrating sphere (photometry)
Kugelgelenk n, **Kugelgelenkkopf** m s. Kugelkopf
Kugelgeometrie f spherical geometry
Kugelgestaltsfehler m spherical aberration, SA
Kugelhülle f bounding sphere
Kugelkino n cinedome
Kugelkopf m ball and socket [tripod] head, ball joint head; gimbal head
Kugelkopfdrucker m [golf] ball printer
Kugellinse f spherical lens
Kugelmikrofon n omni[directional] microphone
Kugelneiger m s. Kugelkopf
Kugelschreibertinte f ball-point ink
Kugelspiegel m spherical mirror; spherical reflector
Kugelsymmetrie f spherical symmetry
Kugelwelle f spherical wave

Kugelwellenfront f spherical wave front
Kulisse/computergenerierte (virtuelle) virtual set
Kundenfoto n consumer image
Kundenverwaltung f subscriber management
Kunstdruck m 1. graphic arts printing; 2. art print
Kunstdruckfilm m graphic arts film
Kunstdruckpapier n fine-art paper
Kunstfotograf m [fine-]art photographer
Kunstfotografie f 1. [fine-]art photography; 2. art photograph
Kunstlicht n artificial light
Kunstlichtbedingungen pl tungsten conditions
Kunstlichtbeleuchtung f artificial lighting (illumination), man-made illumination
Kunstlichtdiafilm m tungsten-balanced reversal film
Kunstlichtfarbfilm m tungsten color film
Kunstlichtfilm m artificial-light[-balanced] film, tungsten[-balanced] film
Kunstlichtfotografie f artificial-light photography, photography by artificial light
Kunstlichtquelle f artificial light source
Kunstsiebdruck m serigraphy, creative silk-screen printmaking
Kunststoff m/**optischer** optical plastic (polymer), plastic optical material
Kunststofffilter m plastic filter
Kunststofflinse f plastic lens
Kunststoffobjektiv n plastic lens
Kunststoffpapier n plastic-laminated paper
Kunststoffrähmchen n, **Kunststoffrahmen** m plastic mount
Kunststoffstereo n stereoplastic (plastic duplicate) plate
Kupferchlorid n copper (cupric) chloride *(bleaching agent)*
Kupferdampflaser m copper vapor laser, CVL
Kupferdruck m s. Kupfertiefdruck
Kupferdruckplatte f copper printing plate
Kupferplatte f/**gestochene** [manual] copperplate intaglio engraving
Kupferrottoner m copper red toner
Kupferrottonung f copper red toning
Kupfertiefdruck m copperplate gravure
Kupfertoner m s. Kupferrottoner
Kupferverstärker m copper intensifier
Kuppler m coupler [compound]
~/**eingebetteter (eingelagerter)** incorporated coupler
~/**farbloser** colorless coupler
~/**fotografischer** photographic coupler
~/**vierwertiger** four-equivalent coupler
~/**zweiwertiger** two-equivalent coupler
Kupplermolekül n coupler molecule
Kurbelmittelsäule f geared center column, elevator *(tripod)*
Kurbelstativ n windup

Kurs m **über Grund** course over ground, COG
kursiv cursive, slanting; italic[ized] *(typestyle)*
Kursiv[e] f, **Kursivschrift** f italic [type]
Kursivschrifterkennung f cursive script (word) recognition; cursive handwriting recognition
Kursmikroskop n student (teaching) microscope, course microscope
Kurve f curve, curved line *(e.g. in geometric modeling)*
~/**approximierende** nonuniform rational B-spline, NURBS *(computer graphics)*
~/**charakteristische** characteristic (density) curve, [photographic] response curve, [characteristic] D-log H curve
~/**einhüllende** envelope
~/**fraktale** fractal curve
~/**glatte** smooth curve
~/**kontinuierliche** continuous curve
~/**kubische** cubic [polynomial] curve
~/**offene** open curve
~/**Plancksche** Planck['s] function, spectral radiance contrast
~/**polynomiale (polynomische)** polynomial curve
~/**sensitometrische** sensitometric curve *(s.a. ~/charakteristische)*
~/**stückweise polynomielle** spline
~/**verformbare** deformable curve
Kurvenanpassungstechnik f curve-fitting technique
Kurvenapproximation f curve approximation
Kurvenbeschreibung f curve description
Kurvenbild n curve representation
Kurvendetektion f curve detection
Kurvendiagramm n curve chart (diagram)
Kurvenfamilie f s. Kurvenschar
Kurvenfuß m toe, foot *(of a characteristic curve)*
Kurvengestaltbeschreibung f curve shape description
Kurvenglättung f curve smoothing
Kurveninterpolation f/**parametrische** parametric curve interpolation
Kurvenmerkmal n curve feature
Kurvenprimitiv n curve [segment] primitive
Kurvenpunkt m curve point *(s.a. Ankerpunkt)*
Kurvenschar f set (family) of curves
Kurvensegment n, **Kurvenstück** n curve segment
Kurventeil m/**geradliniger** straight-line portion *(of a characteristic curve)*
kurzbrennweitig short focal-length *(lens)*
Kurzdrehbuch n [/**illustriertes**] storyboard
Kurzfarbwerk n anilox inking system *(flexography)*
Kurzfilm m short [film]
Kurzpassfilter n short pass [filter], short-wave pass filter
Kurzpulsdetektor m short-pulse detector

Kurzpulslaser *m* short-pulse laser, ultrafast laser
Kurzschlussfluss *m* short-circuit flux *(magnetic tape)*
Kurzschrittperforation *f* short pitch
kurzsichtig nearsighted, shortsighted, myopic
Kurzsichtigkeit *f* nearsightedness, short sight, myopia
Kurzstreckenübertragung *f* short-haul transmission
Kurzvideo *n* video clip
Kurzwellenband *n* short-wave band, SWB
kurzwellig short-wave[length]
Kurzzeitbelichtung *f* short[-duration] exposure
Kurzzeitblitz *m* short-duration flash
Kurzzeitfehler *m* high-intensity reciprocity failure, HIRF
Kurzzeitfotografie *f* high-speed [still] photography, high-speed photographic imaging
Kurzzeit-Fourier-Transformation *f* short-time Fourier transform, STFT, windowed Fourier transform
Kurzzeitgedächtnis *n*/**visuelles** short-term visual memory
Kurzzeit-Lichtquelle *f s.* Kurzlichtquelle
Kurzzeitspeicher *m* short-term (short-time) memory, short-term store, primary memory
Kurzzeitsynchronisation *f* high-speed sync[hronization]
Kuwahara-Filter *n* Kuwahara filter *(binary image processing)*
Kybernetik *f* cybernetics
kybernetisch cybernetic[al]
Kymograf *m* kymograph
Kymografie *f* kymography
kymografisch kymographic
Kymogramm *n* kymogram
K-Zapfen *m* S cone, short-wavelength-sensitive cone *(of the retina)*

L

L*a*b*-Farbmodus m, **LAB-Farbraum** m
L*a*b* color coordinates
Laborant m lab[oratory] assistant
Laborausrüstung f, **Laborausstattung** f
laboratory equipment
Laborbericht m lab[oratory] report
Laborbildanalyse f laboratory image analysis
Laboreinrichtung f laboratory equipment
Laborflasche f laboratory bottle
Laborfotografie f laboratory[-based] photography
Laborgerät n laboratory apparatus
Laborlicht n [darkroom] safelight
Labormikroskop n laboratory microscope
Labor-Röntgenmikroskop n laboratory X-ray microscope
Laborsprache f laboratory parlance
Labortechniker m lab[oratory] technician, processing technician
Laborvergrößerer m laboratory enlarger
Laborzange f print tongs
Labyrintheingang m, **Labyrinthschleuse** f labyrinth entrance, light trap labyrinth, maze [light trap] *(darkroom)*
Lack m/**fotoempfindlicher** photosensitive resist, [photo]resist
Lackierung f varnishing *(e.g. of printed sheets)*
Lackmus m(n) litmus *(indicator dye)*
ladbar downloadable *(software)*
Ladegerät für Autoanschluss car charger (adapter)
~ n [/**externes**] [battery] charger, recharge unit
laden 1. to load *(e.g. data into a memory)*; 2. to charge *(e.g. batteries)*
Ladestrom m charging current
Ladung f/**elektrostatische** [electro]static charge
~/freie free charge
~/lichtinduzierte photogenerated (optically induced) charge, photon-generated charge
Ladungsakkumulation f charge accumulation
Ladungsbild n [/**elektrisches**] charge[-density] pattern, charge[d] image
~/elektrostatisches electrostatic charge pattern
~/latentes latent charge[d] image
Ladungsbürste f conductive brush
Ladungsdichte f charge density
Ladungsdiffusion f charge diffusion
Ladungseinfang m charge trapping
Ladungsempfänger m charge receiver
Ladungsinjektionswandler m charge-injection device, CID
Ladungsintegration f charge integration
Ladungskopplung f charge coupling
Ladungsmuster n s. Ladungsbild
Ladungspaar n charge pair
Ladungspaket n charge packet *(charge-coupled device)*
Ladungsschieberegister n shift (transfer) register *(charge-coupled device)*
Ladungsspeicher m charge-coupled storage
Ladungsspeicherkapazität f charge storage capacity
Ladungsspeicherstelle f charge storage location
Ladungsspeicherung f charge storage
Ladungsspektrograf m charge spectrograph
Ladungsspektrometer n charge spectrometer
Ladungsstabilisierung f charge stabilization
Ladungsteilchen n charged particle
Ladungsteilchendetektion f charged-particle detection
Ladungsteilchendetektor m charged-particle detector
Ladungsteilchenoptik f charged-particle optics
Ladungsträger m [electric-]charge carrier
~/fotogenerierter photogenerated (light-produced) charge carrier
~/freier free carrier
Ladungsträgerdichte f charge carrier density
Ladungsträgereinfang m charge[-carrier] trapping
Ladungsträgerinjektion f charge carrier injection
Ladungsträgerpaar n charge pair
Ladungsträgerrekombination f charge carrier recombination
Ladungsträgerschicht f charge-carrier layer
Ladungstransfer m charge transfer
Ladungstransferelement n charge-coupled device (detector), CCD
Ladungstransferrauschen n transmission[-induced] noise
Ladungstransport m charge transport
Ladungstransportschicht f charge-transport layer, CTL
Ladungsübertragung f, **Ladungsverschiebung** f charge transfer
Ladungsverschiebungsschaltung f bulk-channel CCD MOS capacitor, bulk-channel device
Ladungsverstärker m charge amplifier
Ladungsverteilung f charge distribution
Ladungswolke f charge cloud
Lagebestimmung f position fixing (finding)
Lagedaten pl position data
Lageerkennung f position sensing

Lagefehler *m* positional error; geometrical aberration
Lagekonstanz *f* position constancy *(perceptual phenomenon)*
Lagerungstisch *m s.* Patientenlagerungstisch
Lagesensor *m* position sensor (sensing device)
Lagesymmetrie *f* positional symmetry
Lagrange-Interpolation *f* Lagrange interpolation *(computer graphics)*
Lagrange-Polynom *n* Lagrange polynomial
Lainer-Effekt *m* Lainer effect
Lambdahalbedipol *m* half-wave dipole [antenna]
Lambdahalbeplatte *f*,
Lambda-Halbe-Verzögerungsplatte *f* half-wave plate (retarder)
Lambda-Viertelplättchen *n*,
Lambda-Viertelplatte *f*,
Lambda-Viertel-Verzögerungsplatte *f* quarter-wave[length] plate *(phase retarder)*
Lambert *n* lambert, l, equivalent phot *(a unit of luminance)*
Lambert-Beer-Gesetz *n* Beer-Lambert [absorption] law, Beer's (Lambert's) law *(radiation attenuation)*
Lambert-Reflektor *m s.* Lambert-Strahler
Lambert-Reflexionsmodell *n* Lambertian [surface] reflectance model, Lambertian model
Lambert-Strahler *m* Lambertian emitter (diffuser), Lambertian [light] source, [ideal] Lambertian reflector
Lamellenkollimator *m* laminated collimator
Lamellenschlitzverschluss *m* focal-plane shutter; slot (slit) shutter
Lamellenverschluss *m* leaf shutter
Laminargitter *n* laminar grating
Laminarströmung *f* laminar flow
laminieren to laminate
Laminierpresse *f* laminating press
Laminierung *f* lamination [process]
Lampe *f* lamp
~/**elektrische** electric lamp
~/**gepulste** pulsed lamp
Lampenalter *n* lamp age
Lampenfilter *n* lamp filter
Lampengehäuse *n s.* Lampenhaus
Lampenglühdraht *m s.* Lampenwendel
Lampenhaus *n* [projector] lamphouse, lamp housing
~/**additives** additive lamphouse
Lampenklappe *f* flap *(s.a. Lampentor)*
Lampenkondensor *m* lamp condenser
Lampenkopf *m* lamp head
Lampenlebensdauer *f* lamp life
Lampenleistung *f* lamp wattage
Lampenlicht *n* lamplight
Lampentor *n* barn door
Lampenwendel *f* lamp filament

Ländercode *m* country (area) code *(digital video production)*
Landkarte *f* [geographic] map
Landmarke *f* landmark
Landolt-Ring *m* Landolt ring, Landolt C *(visual test target)*
Landschaftsaufnahme *f* landscape shot
Landschaftsbild *n* landscape picture
Landschaftsfoto *n* landscape photograph
Landschaftsfotograf *m* landscape photographer
Landschaftsfotografie *f* [outdoor] landscape photography, scenic photography
Landschaftslinse *f* landscape lens
Landschafts-Rückprofilm *m* landscape film *(cinema)*
langbrennweitig long focal-length, long-focus, narrow-angle *(lens)*
Längencodierung *f*/**variable** variable-length [statistical] coding, VLC, entropy [en]coding
Längenwinkel *m* azimuth[al] angle
Längestrich *m* macron *(diacritic)*
Langfilm *m* full-length film, full-length picture (feature)
Langlebigkeit *f* longevity, long-term stability, [long-term] permanence *(e.g. of photographic material)*
Langpassfilter *n* long-pass [filter], long-wave[length] pass filter
Längsaberration *f* longitudinal (on-axis) aberration
~/**chromatische** longitudinal (axial) chromatic aberration, chromatic variation of focus, longitudinal color
~/**sphärische** longitudinal spherical aberration
Längsabweichung *f s.* Längsaberration
Längsdrehung *f* longitudinal twist *(tape defect)*
Längsmagnetisierung *f* longitudinal magnetization
Längsparitätsprüfung *f* longitudinal redundancy check, LRC
Langspielmodus *m* long play mode, LP mode *(video)*
Längsrelaxationszeit *f* longitudinal (spin-lattice) relaxation time, T one [time constant], T1 *(magnetic resonance imaging)*
Längsspuraufzeichnung *f*,
Längsspurverfahren *n* longitudinal [video] recording, LVR
Längsspur-Zeitcode *m* longitudinal time code
Längstonspur *f* linear audio track
Längsüberdeckung *f* forward overlap *(aerophotogrammetry)*
Längswelligkeit *f* longitudinal ripple *(tape defect)*
Längswinkligkeit *f* longitudinal angularity *(tape defect)*
Langwellenband *n* long wave band, LWB

langwellig long-wave[length]
Langzeitarchivierung f long-term archival use; extended-term keeping (storage)
Langzeitaufnahme f time exposure
Langzeitbelichtung f [long-]time exposure, long-term exposure [to light], long exposure
Langzeitfehler m low-intensity reciprocity failure, LIRF
Langzeitgedächtnis n/**visuelles** long-term visual memory
Langzeithaltbarkeit f, **Langzeit-Lagereigenschaft** f s. Langlebigkeit
Langzeitspeicher m long-term memory
Langzeitsynchronisation f slow sync[hronization] *(flash sync mode)*
Langzeit-Videorecorder m time-lapse [video] recorder
Lanthanhexaborid-Kristallelektrode f lanthanum hexaboride electron gun *(electron microscope)*
laparoendoskopisch laparoendoscopic
Laparoskop n laparoscope
Laparoskopie f laparoscopy
laparoskopisch laparoscopic
Laplace-Ableitung f Laplacian
Laplace-Filter n Laplacian filter (mask), Laplacian [operator]
~ **mit gleichzeitiger Tiefpasswirkung** s. Laplace-Gauß-Operator
Laplace-Filterung f Laplacian filtering
Laplace-Gauß-Operator m Laplacian-of-Gaussian [operator], LoG filter (operator), Mexican hat filter (kernel), sombrero filter, Marr-Hildreth operator *(edge detection)*
Laplace-Gradient m Laplacian gradient
Laplace-Operator m s. Laplace-Filter
Laplace-Pyramide f Laplacian (band pass) pyramid *(e.g. in motion analysis)*
Laplace-Transformation f Laplace transform *(signal processing)*
~/**einseitige** unilateral (one-sided) Laplace transform
~/**inverse** inverse Laplace transform
Laplace-Transformierte f Laplace transform
Laplace-Verteilung f Laplacian (Laplace) distribution *(of a random variable)*
Laptop m(n) laptop [computer] *(s.a. Notebook)*
Laptop-Bildschirm m laptop display (computer screen)
Laptopcomputer m s. Laptop
Larmor-Beziehung f s. Larmor-Gleichung
Larmor-Frequenz f Larmor [precessional] frequency, precession[al] frequency, resonant frequency *(magnetic resonance imaging)*
Larmor-Gleichung f Larmor equation (relationship), Larmor's formula
Larmor-Präzession f Larmor precession
Laryngoskop n laryngoscope

Laryngoskopie f laryngoscopy
laryngoskopisch laryngoscopic
Laser m laser *(short for light amplification by stimulated emission of radiation)*
~/**abstimmbarer** tunable laser
~/**axial durchströmter** axial-flow laser
~/**blauer** blue [light] laser, blue light-emitting solid-state laser
~/**blitzlampengepulster** flashlamp-pulsed laser
~/**chemischer** chemical laser
~/**diodengepumpter** diode-pumped laser
~/**gepulster** pulsed laser
~/**gewinngeführter** gain-guided laser
~/**gütegeschalteter** Q-switched laser
~/**indexgeführter** index-guided laser
~/**kontinuierlicher** continuous[-wave] laser, CW laser
~/**längsgeströmter** axial-flow laser
~/**optisch gepumpter** optically pumped laser
~/**quergeströmter** cross-flow laser
~/**roter** red [light] laser
~/**wissenschaftlicher** scientific laser
Laserabbildung f laser imaging
Laserabsorptionsspektrometer n laser absorption spectrometer
Laserabtaster m laser scanner
Laserabtastmikroskop n laser scanning microscope, LSM
Laserabtastmikroskopie f/**konfokale** confocal laser scanning microscopy, CLSM, laser scanning confocal microscopy, LSCM
Laserabtastung f laser scanning; laser beam recording *(video-to-film transfer)*
Laseranlage f laser unit
Laseranordnung f laser assembly
Laserätzen n laser etching
Laserbeleuchtung f laser illumination
Laserbelichter m laser exposure unit, laser imager; [laser] imagesetter
Laserbelichtung f laser [beam] exposure
Laserbeschriften n laser scribing (marking)
Laserbeschrifter m laser marker
Laserbeschriftung f laser marking
Laserblitz m laser spike
Laserbündel n laser [light] beam, laser jet *(s.a. under Laserstrahl)*
Laserdiode f laser diode
~/**indexgeführte** index-guided device
~/**verstärkungsgeführte** gain-guided laser diode
Laserdiodenbelichtung f laser diode exposure
Laserdiodenkollimator m laser diode collimator
Laserdiodensteuergerät n laser diode controller (driver)
Laserdiodenstrahl m laser diode beam
Laserdiodentreiber m s. Laserdiodensteuergerät
Laserdisk f laser (optical) disk; videodisc *(s.a. under DVD)*

Laserdisplay n laser display
Laser-Doppler-Anemometrie f laser Doppler anemometry, LDA
Laserdruck m laser printing
Laserdrucker m laser[jet] printer
Laserdruckerpatrone f laser printer cartridge
Laserdruckpapier n laser bond [paper], laser[jet] paper
Lasereffekt m laser effect
laserelektrofotografisch laser-electrophotographic
Laseremission f laser emission
Laserenergie f laser energy
Laser-Entfernungsmesser m laser rangefinder (ranger)
Laserfarbstoff m laser dye
Laserfernerkundung f laser[-based] remote sensing
Laserfilmabtaster m, **Laserfilmbelichter** m, **Laserfilmrecorder** m laser film scanner (printer), laser[-based] film recorder, laser recorder
Laserfleck m laser spot, laser dot (point)
Laserfokus m laser focus
Laserfotografie f s. Holografie
Laserfrequenz f laser frequency
Laser-Ganzkuppelprojektionssystem n laser all-dome projection system
Lasergas n laser gas
Lasergerät n laser device
Lasergravur f laser gravure (engraving)
Laserhalter m laser mount
Laserimpuls m laser pulse
Laserinterferometer n laser interferometer
Laserinterferometrie f laser interferometry
Laserkamera f laser imager
Laserkinematografie f s. Interferenzkinematografie
Laserkollimator m laser collimator
Laserkonfokalmikroskop n laser scanning confocal microscope, LSCM
Laserkopf m laser head
Laserkopfophthalmoskop n laser head ophthalmoscope
Laserkopierer m laser copier
Laser-Kraft-Mikroskop n laser force microscope, LFM
Laserkristall m laser crystal
Laserleistung f laser power (performance)
Laserlicht n laser light
~/**gepulstes** pulsed laser light
Laserlichtenergie f laser [light] energy
Laserlichtquelle f laser [light] source
Laserlichtstärke f laser intensity
Laserlichtstrahl m s. Laserstrahl
Laserlinie f laser line
Lasermarkierer m laser marker
Lasermaterial n laser material
Lasermedium n lasing medium
Lasermessmikroskop n laser measuring microscope
Lasermikrometer n laser micrometer
Lasermikroskop n laser microscope

Lasermikroskopie f laser [capture] microscopy, LM, LCM
Lasermode f laser mode
Lasermodulator m laser modulator
lasern to lase
Laserobjektiv n laser objective
Laserophthalmoskop n scanning laser ophthalmoscope
Laseroptik f laser [beam] optics
laseroptisch laser-optical
Laserpapier n s. Laserdruckpapier
Laserphoton n laser photon
Laserphysik f laser physics
Laserplatte f laser (optical) disk; [laser] videodisk
Laserplattenspieler m laserdisk player
Laserplotter m [/**elektrostatischer**] m laser plotter
Laserpointer m laser pointer
Laserprinter m laser printer
Laserprojektion f laser projection
Laserpuls m laser pulse
Laserpulsdauer f laser pulse duration (width)
Laserpumpe f laser pump
Laserpunkt m laser point (dot); laser spot
Laserradar n laser radar, lidar *(short for light detection and ranging)*, ladar *(short for laser detection and ranging)*
Laser-Raman-Spektroskopie f laser Raman spectroscopy
Laserraster m(n) laser grid
Laserrastermikroskop n laser scan microscope
Laserrauschen n laser noise
Laserresonator m laser resonator, [optical] resonator, laser (optical) cavity
Laserrohr n laser tube
Laser-Sättigungsspektroskopie f laser saturation spectroscopy
Laserscanner m/**abbildender** imaging laser scanner
Laserschutzbrille f laser protective eyewear (spectacles)
Laserschutzglas n laser protective glass
Lasersensor m laser sensor
Lasershow f laser show
Lasersignal n laser signal
Lasersintern n laser sintering
Lasersonde f laser probe
Laserspektroskopie f laser spectroscopy
laserspektroskopisch laser spectroscopic
Laserspiegel m laser mirror
Laserstab m laser rod
Laserstift m laser pointer
Laserstrahl m laser [light] beam, laser jet
~/**aufgeweiteter** expanded laser beam, laser sheet
Laserstrahlabtastung f laser beam scanning
Laserstrahlaufweiter m laser beam expander
Laserstrahlaufweitung f laser beam expansion

Laserstrahlquelle

Laserstrahlquelle *f* laser [beam] source
Laserstrahlrauschen *n* laser beam noise
Laserstrahlstabilisierung *f* laser beam stabilization
Laserstrahlung *f* laser radiation
Laserstroboskop *n* laser stroboscope
Laserstroboskopie *f* laser stroboscopy
Lasersystem *n* laser system
Lasertechnik *f* laser technology
Laserteleskop *n* laser telescope
Laser-Tischdrucker *m* desktop laser printer
Lasertriangulation *f* laser triangulation
Lasertriangulationssensor *m* laser triangulation sensor
Laserwellenlänge *f* laser wavelength
Laserwirkung *f* laser (lasing) action
Laserwirkungsgrad *m* laser efficiency
Laserziel[verfolgungs]gerät *n* laser tracker
lasierend *s.* durchscheinend
Lassoband *n* gaffer tape, grip (cloth) tape, duct tape
Lassowerkzeug *n* lasso tool, freehand scissors *(graphics program)*
Lastwiderstand *m* load resistance
Lasurfarbe *f* transparent color; transparent paint
Latensifikation *f* latensification, latent image intensification; flashing
latensifizieren to latensify
Latentbild *n* latent [photographic] image, invisible image
~/**elektrostatisches** electrostatic latent image
Latentbildentstehung *f* latent-image formation
Latentbildkeim *m* latent-image nucleus (center), development nucleus
Latentbildsilber *n* latent-image silver
Latentbildstabilität *f* latent-image stability, latent-image keeping [performance]
Latentbildtheorie *f* latent-image theory
Latentbildzentrum *n* latent-image center
Latenzzeit *f* latency [time]
Lateralauflösung *f* lateral resolution
Lateralvergrößerung *f* lateral magnification
Laterna magica *f* magic lantern
Latham-Schlaufe *f* Latham loop *(film passage)*
Laue-Diagramm *n* Laue pattern (photograph), Lauegram
Laue-Verfahren *n* Laue method *(structural analysis of crystals)*
Laufbild *n* motion picture (image), moving image (picture)
~/**synthetisiertes** synthesized motion video
Laufbildaufnahme *f* motion-picture recording
Laufbildfotografie *f* motion-picture photography, moving-image photography
Laufbildgeber *m* telecine [machine]
Laufbildgeschwindigkeit *f* frame rate

Laufbildkamera *f* motion-picture camera, cine[matographic] camera, motion (picture) camera
Laufbildprojektion *f* motion-picture projection
Laufbildprojektor *m* film (motion-picture) projector; cinematograph
Laufbildübertragung *f* moving-picture transmission
Laufbildvideo *n* [full-]motion video, FMV, movie video
~/**erfasstes** captured motion video
Laufbildwerfer *m s.* Laufbildprojektor
Laufboden *m* [flat]bed *(view camera)*
~/**herabklappbarer** drop bed
Laufbodenkamera *f* flatbed camera, sliding box camera; press[-type] camera
Laufgeschwindigkeit *f* running speed
~/**konstante** constant linear velocity, CLV
Lauflängencode *m* run-length code *(image data compression)*
Lauflängencodierer *m* run-lengh [en]coder
Lauflängencodierung *f* run-length [en]coding, chord encoding
Lauflängenmodus *m* run mode
Lauflinie *f* sweepline *(data structure)*
Laufrichtung *f* grain (machine) direction *(of paper)*
Laufrolle *f* idle[r] roller; guide roller
Laufschienensystem *n* ceiling rail system, roof track system; track lighting system *(studio equipment)*
Laufschramme *f* dig; cinch mark
Laufschrift *f* crawling title, moving caption
Laufstreifen *m s.* Laufschramme
Laufweite *f* letter spacing *(typography)*
Laufweitenänderung *f* tracking
Laufwerk *n* drive; tape drive (transport); tape deck; disk drive
~/**externes** external drive
Laufzeit *f* running time *(e.g. of a movie)*; time of flight *(e.g. of pulses)*
Laufzeitfehler *m* run time error
Laufzeitschicht *f* run-time layer *(hypermedia system)*
Laufzeittomografie *f* time-of-flight tomography
Lautheit *f* loudness
Lautsprecher *m* loudspeaker, [sound] speaker
Lautstärke *f* [sound] volume, sound level; loudness
Lautstärkebegrenzung *f* limiter
Lautstärkebereich *m* volume range
Lautstärkeregler *m* fader (level) control
Lavaliermikrofon *n* lavalier[-style] microphone, lavalier (chest) microphone, lav
Lavendel *n*, **Lavendelkopie** *f* lavender print, master positive *(cinema)*
Lawinenfotodiode *f* avalanche photodiode, APD
Layout *n* layout
Layout-Arbeitsstation *f* layout workstation

Layoutausdruck *m* [display] thumbnail
Layouter *m* layout man; page designer
Layoutfolie *f* layout sheet
Layoutgestaltung *f* layout work
Layoutprogramm *n s.* Layoutsoftware
Layout-Schnitt *m* offline (nonlinear) editing *(video)*
Layoutsoftware *f* page layout software (programs)
LC-Bildschirm *m* LCD screen
LCD-Chip *m* LD chip
LCD-Farbmonitor *m* LCD color monitor
LC-Display *n* liquid crystal [digital] display, LCD, liquid crystal readout
LCD-Monitor *m*/**schwenkbarer** fold-out LCD screen; flip-out color LCD viewfinder *(camcorder)*
LCD-Pixel *n* LCD pixel
LCD-Projektor *m* LCD projector, beamer
LCOS-Bildschirm *m*, **LCOS-Display** *n* LCOS (liquid crystal on silicon) display
Lebenderkennung *f* live check, liveness test *(authentication)*
lebensgroß life-size[d]
Lebensgröße *f* life size
Lebensmittelfotografie *f* food photography
Lebensrad *n* wheel of life, zoetrope *(early cinematography)*
Leckstrom *m* leakage (reverse) current *(e.g. of a semiconductor)*
LED *s.* Leuchtdiode
LED-Anzeige *f* LED display
Lederhaut *f* sclera, sclerotic [coat], white of the eye
LED-Linienlicht *n* LED line
Leerband *n* blank [magnetic] tape *(s.a.* Frischband*)*
Leerlaufrolle *f* idle[r] roller
Leerlaufspannung *f* open-circuit voltage *(photodiode)*
Leerraum *m* blank space, air *(e.g. between printed characters)*
Leerseite *f* blank [page]
Leervergrößerung *f* empty magnification *(microscopy)*
Leerzeichen *n* blank [space]
Leerzeile *f* empty line *(typography)*; blank line
Legende *f* caption, legend
Legetrick *m* cutout animation
Lehrfilm *m* educational film (motion picture), teaching (training) film, visual aid
Lehrsatz *m*/**Pythagoreischer** Pythagoras' theorem (theory)
Leica-Gewinde *n* Leica (universal) thread *(enlarger)*
Leichtflintglas *n* light flint glass
Leichtstativ *n* lightweight tripod
Leihkassette *f*, **Leihvideo** *n* rental video
Leinenprägung *f* linen finish *(on text paper)*
Leinwand *f* screen, canvas *(film presentation)*
~/geteilte split screen *(cinema)*
Leinwandbild *n* screen image (picture)
Leinwandbildseitenverhältnis *n* screen[-image] aspect ratio
Leinwandfläche *f* screen area; screen surface
Leinwandflimmern *n* screen flicker *(cinema)*
Leinwandformat *n* screen format
Leinwandhelligkeit *f* screen brightness (luminance)
Leinwandprojektion *f* screen projection
Leistung *f*/**optische** optical performance
~/rauschäquivalente noise-equivalent power, NEP
Leistungsbandbreite *f* power (electrical) bandwidth *(photodetector)*
Leistungsdichte *f* power density
~/spektrale, **Leistungsdichtespektrum** *n* [power] spectral density, power (energy) spectrum
Leistungsreflexion *f* power reflection
Leistungsspektrum *n s.* Leistungsdichtespektrum
Leistungstransmission *f* power transmission
Leistungsverstärker *m* power amplifier
leiten to pipe *(e.g. light)*
Leiterplatte *f* [/**gedruckte**] printed [circuit] board, circuit board
Leiterplattendruck *m* circuit board printing
Leiterplattendrucker *m* circuit printer
Leiterplattenfotolithografie *f* circuit-board photolithography
Leiterplattenherstellung *f* printed-circuit manufacture, circuits manufacturing
Leiterplatteninspektion *f* circuit board inspection
Leiterplattentechnik *f* printed-circuit technology, integrated-circuit technology
Leitfähigkeit *f* conductivity
Leitfernrohr *n* guidescope *(astrophotography)*
Leith-Upatniek-Hologramm *n* off-axis hologram
Leitstrahl *m* guiding beam
Leitung *f*/**symmetrische** balanced line
Leitungsband *n* conduction band
Leitungsbandelektron *n* conduction-band electron
Leitungselektron *n* conduction electron
Leitungsspeisung *f* constrained feed *(radar antenna)*
Leitungsvermittlung *f* circuit switching
Leitzahl *f* [flash] guide number, GN, flash factor
Lempel-Ziv-Codierung *f* Lempel-Ziv coding
Lempel-Ziv-Welch-Codierung *f* Lempel-Ziv-Welch coding, LZW [data] compression
Lenkradar *n* guidance radar
lentikulär lenticular

Leporellofalz *m* concertina fold *(of printed matter)*
Lernalgorithmus *m* learning algorithm *(pattern recognition)*
Lerndatensatz *m* learning (training) set, training class (population) *(neuroinformatics)*
Lernen *n* learning, training *(decision-theoretic method in objec recognition; s.a.under* Training*)*
~/kompetitives (konkurrierendes) competitive learning
~/überwachtes supervised learning (training) *(pattern recognition)*
~/unüberwachtes unsupervised learning (training)
lernfähig learnable, trainable
Lernfähigkeit *f* learnability
Lernmenge *f s.* Lerndatensatz
Lernmuster *n* training pattern
Lernregel *f* training rule
~/Hebbsche Hebb's rule *(unsupervised learning)*
Lernstichprobe *f s.* Lerndatensatz
Lerping *n s.* Interpolation/lineare
lesbar readable; legible
Lesbarkeit *f* readability, readableness; legibility
Leseabstand *m* reading distance
Lesebrille *f* reading glasses
Lesegerät *n* reading device, reader
Lesegeschwindigkeit *f* reading speed
Leseglas *n* reading glass; hand lens (magnifier)
Lesegradient *m* readout (frequency-encoding) gradient *(magnetic resonance imaging)*
Lesekopf *m* read[ing] head
~/kapazitiver capacitance pick-up
~/optischer optical read head, optical stylus
Lese-Kopiergerät *n* reader-printer
Leselampe *f* reading lamp
Leser *m*/**fotoelektrischer** photoelectric reader
leserichtig right reading *(printed matter)*
leserlich legible *(s.a.* lesbar*)*
Leserlichkeit *f* legibility
Lesespeicher *m s.* Nurlesespeicher
Lesestift *m* read pen, pin reader
Lesestrahl *m* reading beam
Lesetakt *m* read clock *(time compression)*
Letter *f* 1. letter, [piece of] type, type piece, printing type; 2. type body
~/bewegliche movable letter, movable type [character]
Letterbox-Bild *n* letterboxed picture
Letterbox-Format *n* letterbox [picture] format, letterbox
Letterbox-Verfahren *n* letterboxing
Letterbox-Wiedergabe *f* letterboxing
Letterngießmaschine *f* typecasting machine, [type]caster

Lettersetdruck *m* letterset, dry offset, indirect letterpress [printing], waterless lithography
Leuchtanzeige *f* illuminated display
Leuchtband *n* luminous row
Leuchtbild *n* luminous image
Leuchtdauer *f* flash duration (time)
Leuchtdichte *f* luminance, photometric brightness *(s.a. under* Luminanz*)*
~/äquivalente equivalent luminance
~/maximale maximum (peak) luminance, peak brightness
~/minimale minimum luminance
~/relative relative luminance
~/remittierte reflected luminance
Leuchtdichteabstufung *f* gradation
Leuchtdichtebereich *m* [maximum-to-minimum] luminance range, dynamic range
Leuchtdichtefaktor *m* luminance factor
Leuchtdichtegegensatz *m*, **Leuchtdichtekontrast** *m* luminance contrast
Leuchtdichtemesser *m*, **Leuchtdichtemessgerät** *n* luminance (reflected-light) meter; reflected-light [photographic] exposure meter
Leuchtdichtemessung *f* luminance measurement
Leuchtdichtenormal *n* luminance standard; regulated brightness source
Leuchtdichtesignal *n* luminance (luma) signal, black-[and-]white signal, Y [signal] *(video)*
Leuchtdichtespektrum *n* luminance spectrum
Leuchtdichteumfang *m* luminance ratio, contrast range
Leuchtdichteunterschied *m*/**relativer** objective contrast
Leuchtdichteunterschiedsempfindlichkeit *f* luminance difference sensitivity
Leuchtdichteverteilung *f* luminance distribution
Leuchtdichtewert *m* luminance value
Leuchtdiode *f* light-emitting diode, LED, luminescent diode *(semiconductor device)*
~/organische organic light-emitting diode, OLED
~/weiße white LED
Leuchtdiodenanzeige *f* light-emitting diode display, LED display
Leuchte *f* luminaire, lighting instrument, light[ing] fixture, lamp
Leuchtelektron *n* luminous electron
leuchten to emit light
leuchtend luminous, lucid
Leuchtenstativ *n* light[ing] stand, light support
Leuchtfarbe *f* luminous paint; fluorescent paint
Leuchtfeld *n* luminous field

Leuchtfeldblende *f* illuminated field diaphragm *(optical microscope)*
Leuchtfläche *f* area of illumination, illuminated area
Leuchtfleck *m* luminous (light) spot *(cathode-ray tube)*
Leuchtfleckabtaster *m* flying-spot scanner
Leuchtkasten *m* illumination (light) box, illuminated view box
Leuchtkörper *m* illuminant
Leuchtkraft *f* luminosity, luminous power
Leuchtphosphor *m s.* Leuchtstoff
Leuchtplatte *f* light panel
Leuchtpult *n* light (viewing) box
Leuchtpunkt *m* phosphor (fluorescent) dot
Leuchtpunkttripel *n* three-colored phosphor dot, RGB triple[t], triad *(color picture tube)*
Leuchtquelle *f* luminous source
Leuchtrahmensucher *m* bright-frame [view]finder, brightline viewfinder, suspended-frame finder, [van] Albada [view]finder
Leuchtrichtung *f* illumination (lighting) direction
Leuchtröhre *f* fluorescent tube, tubular fluorescent lamp
Leuchtschicht *f* fluorescent layer *(e.g. of a picture tube)*
Leuchtschirm *m* illumination screen; luminescent screen; fluorescent screen; phosphor[escent] screen, phosphorous (phosphor-coated) screen
Leuchtschirmbild *n* fluoroscopic (fluorescent screen) image
Leuchtstärke *f* luminosity, luminous power
Leuchtstoff *m* luminescent material, luminophor, [light-producing] phosphor *(s.a.* Phosphor*)*
Leuchtstoffalterung *f* phosphor aging (wear), phosphor degradation
Leuchtstoffbild *n* phosphor image
Leuchtstofflampe *f* fluorescent lamp (light source)
Leuchtstofflampenlicht *n* fluorescent [lamp] light
Leuchtstoffpunkt *m* phosphor (fluorecent) dot
Leuchtstoffröhre *f s.* Leuchtröhre
Leuchtstoffschicht *f* phosphor layer (coating)
Leuchttisch *m* light (luminous) table
Leuchtwinkel *m* angle of flash coverage
Leuco[cyan]farbstoff *m* leuco dye
Libelle *f*, **Libellennivellier** *n* level bubble
Licht *n* light
~/**achromatisches** achromatic light
~/**aktinisches** actinic (photographically active) light
~/**ambientes** ambient (overall) light
~/**amplitudenmoduliertes** amplitude-modulated light
~/**auftreffendes** impinging light
~/**ausgestrahltes** emitted light
~/**bildformendes** imaging (image-forming) light
~/**blendendes** glaring light
~/**chromatisches** chromatic light
~/**diffus reflektiertes** diffused (stray) light
~/**diffuses** diffuse (soft) light
~/**direktes** direct (undeviated) light
~/**dispergiertes** dispersed light
~/**einfallendes** incident (incoming) light
~/**einfarbiges** monochromatic light
~/**elliptisch polarisiertes** elliptically polarized light
~/**farbiges** color[ed] light
~/**faseroptisches** fiber-optic light
~/**fluoreszierendes** fluorescent light
~/**fokussiertes** focused light
~/**gebeugtes** diffracted (deviated) light
~/**gedämpftes** subdued (dimmed) light
~/**gepulstes** pulsed light
~/**gerichtetes** directed (directional) light
~/**gestreutes** scattered (diffused) light
~/**gleichfarbiges** homochromatic (isochromatic) light
~/**gleißendes** glaring light
~/**hartes** hard (harsh) light, specular light
~/**helles** bright light
~/**indirektes** indirect light; bounce[d] light
~/**infrarotnahes** near-infrared light
~/**inkohärentes** incoherent light
~/**kaltes** cold light
~/**katoptrisches** catoptric light
~/**kohärentes** coherent light
~/**kollimiertes** collimated light
~/**kopolarisiertes** copolarized light
~/**kreuzpolarisiertes** cross-polarized light
~/**künstliches** artificial light
~/**kurzwelliges** short-wavelength light
~/**langwelliges** long-wavelength light
~/**linear polarisiertes** linearly polarized light, plane-polarized light
~/**linkselliptisch polarisiertes** left-elliptically polarized light
~/**linkszirkular polarisiertes** left-circularly polarized light
~/**mehrfarbiges** polychromatic light
~/**moduliertes** modulated light
~/**monochromatisches** monochromatic light
~/**natürliches** natural light
~/**nichtabbildendes** non-image-forming light
~/**nichtpolarisiertes** nonpolarized (unpolarized) light
~ **nullter Ordnung** zero[th]-order light
~/**paralleles** parallel light
~/**partiell kohärentes** partially coherent light
~/**planpolarisiertes** plane-polarized light
~/**polarisiertes** polarized light
~/**polychromatisches** polychromatic (multicolored) light
~/**primärfarbiges** primary-colored light
~/**quasimonochromatisches** quasi-monochromatic light

Licht

~/**rechtselliptisch polarisiertes** right-elliptically polarized light
~/**rechtszirkular polarisiertes** right-circularly polarized light
~/**reflektiertes** reflected light
~/**regulär reflektiertes** specularly reflected light
~/**rückgestreutes** backscattered light
~/**schattenfreies** shadowless light
~/**schattenreiches** shadowy light
~/**schräg auffallendes** oblique (slanted) light, raking (obliquely-incident) light
~/**schwaches** low[-level] light, weak (faint) light
~/**sichtbares** visible (visual) light
~/**spektrales** spectral light
~/**spiegelnd reflektiertes** specularly reflected light
~/**stroboskopisches** stroboscopic light
~/**strukturiertes** structured light
~/**teilkohärentes** partially coherent light
~/**teilpolarisiertes** partially polarized light
~/**transmittiertes** transmitted light
~/**trichromatisches** trichromatic light
~/**ultraviolettes** ultraviolet (black) light
~/**unbuntes** s. ~/weißes
~/**ungebeugtes** undeviated light
~/**ungerichtetes** nondirectional light
~/**ungestreutes** unscattered light
~/**unmoduliertes** unmodulated light
~/**unpolarisiertes** unpolarized (nonpolarized) light
~/**unsichtbares** invisible light
~/**unzerlegtes** undispersed light
~/**verfügbares** available (exisiting) light
~/**verschiedenfarbiges** heterochromatic light
~/**vorhandenes** s. ~/verfügbares
~/**warmes** warm light
~/**weiches** soft (diffuse) light
~/**weißes** white (incandescent) light
~/**zerstreutes** scattered (diffused) light
~/**zirkular polarisiertes** circularly polarized light, circular-polarized light
Lichtabfall m light dissipation, [light] falloff, falloff of light
Lichtabgabe f light output
Lichtabklingzeit f light decay time (PET scintillator)
Lichtablenker m [light] deflector
Lichtablenkung f light [ray] deflection
~/**akustooptische** acousto-optic deflection
Lichtabschirmung f light shield[ing]
Lichtabschwächung f light attenuation
Lichtabsorber m light absorber
Lichtabsorption f light (optical) absorption
Lichtabstrahlung f light (optical) emission
Lichtabstufung f light gradation
Lichtachse f light axis
Lichtäquivalent n [/**fotometrisches**] light equivalent
Lichtarbeit f s. Lichtmenge
lichtarm faint, dim

Lichtarrangement n light[ing] arrangement
Lichtart f 1. type of light; 2. illuminant
Lichtaufbau m lighting setup (arrangement)
Lichtausbeute f light efficiency (yield), luminous efficiency; light output [ratio]
Lichtausbreitung f light spread (propagation)
Lichtausbreitungsrichtung f direction of propagation of light
Lichtausgleichsfilter n light-balancing filter, [color] conversion filter
Lichtausnutzung f light utilization
Lichtausrüstung f lighting equipment
Lichtaussendung f, **Lichtausstrahlung** f light (optical) emission
Lichtausstrahlung/spezifische luminous exitance, luminous power per area (photometry)
Lichtaustritt m light exit
Lichtaustrittsöffnung f light exit port
Lichtband n printing (timing) tape (motion-picture printing)
Lichtbank f light bank
Lichtbau m s. Lichtaufbau
lichtbeständig lightfast, light-stable, stable to light, photostable
Lichtbeständigkeit f lightfastness, light stability (resistance), photostability
Lichtbestimmer m [film] color timer, [laboratory] timer, color (negative) grader, colorist
Lichtbestimmung f [color] timing, film color timing, grading
Lichtbestimmungsgerät n color analyzer
Lichtbeugung f [light] diffraction, light rays bending
Lichtbild n [visible-]light image, optical image; photographic image; photo[graph]
Lichtbildabzug m photocopy, photoduplicate
Lichtbildaufklärung f photoreconnaissance
Lichtbildner m photographer
Lichtbildnerei f photoimaging
Lichtbildsammlung f photographic library
Lichtbildwand f projection screen
Lichtbildwerfer m [optical] projector
Lichtbildwesen n photoimaging
Lichtblende f 1. barn door; 2. gobo, flag
Lichtblitz m light flash, flash of light
Lichtblitzstroboskop n flash-type stroboscope
Lichtbogen m [light] arc
Lichtbogen-Filmprojektor m arc-lamp motion-picture projector
Lichtbogenlampe f arc (high-pressure) lamp, arc
lichtbrechend [photo]refractive, dioptric
Lichtbrechung f light refraction, refringence
Lichtbrechungsindex m index of refraction, refractive index

Lichtbrechungsvermögen *n* refractivity
Lichtbündel *n* [light] bundle; light beam
Lichtcharakter *m* key, tonality *(e.g. of a photograph)*
Lichtdegradation *f* light degradation
Lichtdesign *n* lighting design
Lichtdetektion *f* photodetection
Lichtdetektor *m* light (optical) detector, photodetector; photon detector
lichtdicht lightproof, lighttight
Lichtdichtheit *f* lightproofness
Lichtdiffusion *f* [light] diffusion, optical diffusion, scatter[ing] [of light]
Lichtdiffusor *m* light diffuser
Lichtdimmer *m* [lamp] dimmer
Lichtdruck *m* 1. light pressure; 2. photogelatin [printing]; collotype [printing]; aquatone [printing]; 3. collotype *(print)*
Lichtdruckfarbe *f* photogelatin ink
Lichtdurchgang *m* passage of light; light transmission
Lichtdurchlass[grad] *m* light transmittance
lichtdurchlässig transparent, pellucid; translucent
Lichtdurchlässigkeit *f* transparency; translucency
lichtecht lightfast, light-stable, stable to light, photostable
Lichtechtheit *f* lightfastness, light stability (resistance)
Lichteffekt *m* light effect
Lichteinfall *m* light entry
Lichteinfallöffnung *f s.* Eintrittspupille
Lichteinfallsrichtung *f* direction of incident light
Lichteinkopplung *f* optical coupling, coupling of light *(esp. to a photodetector)*
~/**faseroptische** fiber-optic coupling
~/**linsenoptische** optical lens coupling
Lichteinlass *m* light entry
Lichteinstrahlung *f* light irradiation (irradiance)
Lichteinwirkung *f* action of light
lichtelektrisch photoelectric, electro-optic[al]
Lichtemission *f* light (optical) emission
Lichtemissionsdiode *f s.* Lichtemitterdiode
Lichtemitter *m* light emitter
Lichtemitterdiode *f* light-emitting diode, LED, luminescent diode
~/**organische** organic light-emitting diode, OLED
Lichtempfänger *m* light receiver
lichtempfindlich light-sensitive; photosensitive; fast *(emulsion or film)*
Lichtempfindlichkeit *f* light sensitivity, sensitivity to light, photosensitivity; [optical] speed *(of an emulsion or film)*
Lichtempfindlichkeitsmesser *m* sensitometer
Lichtempfindlichkeitsmessung *f* sensitometry

Lichtempfindung *f* light sensing, sensation of light
Lichtenergie *f* light (optical) energy
Lichtenergiekalkül *n* radiosity
Lichter *pl* light areas; highlights
Lichterabschwächer *m* superproportional reducer
Lichterpunkt *m* highlight dot *(halftone printing)*
Lichterregung *f* light excitation
lichterzeugend light-producing, luminiferous; photogenic *(esp. applied to biological sources)*
Lichterzeugung *f* light production (generation)
Lichtexposition *f* light exposure, exposure to light
Lichtfalle *f* light trap; beam dump
Lichtfang *m* light absorption *(esp. in printed paper between halftone dots)*
Lichtfarbe *f* light[-source] color, color of light
Lichtfeld *n* light field
Lichtfilter *n* light (optical) filter
Lichtfilterung *f* light filtration
Lichtfläche *f* sheet (plane) of light, light plane
Lichtfleck *m* light patch; light spot, spot [of light]
Lichtfluss *m* 1. light flow; 2. *s.* Lichtstrom
Lichtfortpflanzung *f* light propagation (spread)
Lichtfrequenz *f* frequency of light
Lichtführung *f* lighting
Lichtgeschwindigkeit *f* speed (velocity) of light, light velocity
Lichtgestaltung *f* lighting design
Lichtgrafik *f* 1. light graphics (drawing), photogenics; 2. photogram, photogenic drawing, cameraless photograph, photogrammatic image, Schadograph
Lichtgravüre *f s.* Heliogravüre
Lichtgriffel *m* light pen
Lichthof *m* [/**fotografischer**] halation, halo
Lichthofbildung *f* halation
Lichthofschutz *m* [anti]halation protection, antihalo protection
Lichthofschutz-Farbstoff *m* antihalation dye
Lichthofschutzschicht *f* antihalation layer (coating); remjet (antihalo) backing, gel coat
Lichtimpuls *m* light [im]pulse, optical pulse, pulse of light
Lichtintensität *f* luminous (light) intensity, optical intensity
Lichtinterferenz *f* light (optical) interference
Lichtkante *f* rim of light
Lichtkarte *f* grading (timing) card, printer (printing) card, timing list *(motion-picture printing)*
Lichtkasten *m* light (illumination) box, illuminated view box

Lichtkegel *m* light cone, cone of light
Lichtklappe *f* flap; barn door
Lichtkontrast *m* highlight contrast
Lichtkranz *m* rim lighting effect
Lichtlehre *f* photology; optics
Lichtleistung *f* light (luminous) power, light (luminous) flux *(photometry)*; luminous (light) efficiency *(e.g. of an electronic flash unit)*
Lichtleiter *m* light guide (conduit)
~/**faseroptischer** fiber-optic light guide
Lichtleiterbündel *n* fiber[-optic] bundle
Lichtleitfaser *f* optical fiber
Lichtleitkabel *n* light guide cable, fiber-optic cable, optical[-fiber] cable
Lichtleitwert *m s.* Fluss/optischer
Lichtlithografie *f s.* Fotolithografie 1. *and* 2.
lichtlos lightless, dark
Lichtlosigkeit *f* lightlessness, darkness
Lichtmalerei *f s.* Lichtgrafik 1. *and* 2.
Lichtmarke *f* cursor
Lichtmaß *n* light measure
Lichtmenge *f* quantity (amount) of light, luminous energy *(photometry)*
Lichtmessgerät *n* light meter, photometer
Lichtmesstechnik *f* photometry
Lichtmessung *f* 1. light measurement (metering), photometry; 2. incident-light metering (reading)
Lichtmikroskop *n* [optical] light microscope, optical (conventional) microscope
Lichtmikroskopaufnahme *f*, **Lichtmikroskopbild** *n* light (optical) microscope image, optical micrograph
Lichtmikroskopie *f* [visible-]light microscopy, optical microscopy
lichtmikroskopisch optical microscopic
Lichtmischschacht *m* [light-]mixing box *(enlarger)*
Lichtmodulation *f* light modulation
~/**elektrooptische** electro-optic light modulation, EOLM
Lichtmodulator *m* light (optical) modulator; light valve
Lichtniveau *n* light level
Lichtoptik *f* light optics
lichtoptisch photooptical, light-optical
Lichtorgel *f* lighting console
Lichtpartie *f* highlights
Lichtpause *f* blueprint
Lichtpausfarbe *f* heliographic ink
Lichtpauslampe *f* blueprinting (photoprinting) lamp
Lichtpegel *m* light level
Lichtpendelgrafik *f* physiogram
Lichtpolarisator *m* light polarizer
Lichtpolarisierung *f* light polarization
Lichtpuls *m* light [im]pulse, optical pulse, pulse of light
Lichtpunkt *m* 1. light spot, spot [of light]; 2. hickey, bull's (fish) eye *(printing defect)*
~**[film]abtaster** *m* flying-spot scanner (telecine) *(s.a. Filmabtaster, Filmgeber)*

Lichtpunktprojektion *f* spot projection *(triangulation)*
Lichtqualität *f* light quality
Lichtquant *n* light quantum (particle), [visible-]light photon
Lichtquantenhypothese *f* [**/Einsteinsche**], **Lichtquantentheorie** *f* quantum theory of light
Lichtquelle *f* light (luminous) source
~/**ausgedehnte** extended light source
~/**diffuse** diffuse light source, diffused-light source
~/**gerichtete** directional light source
~/**kohärente** coherent light source
~/**kollimierte** collimated light source
~ **mit kontinuierlichem Spektrum** continuous-spectrum light source
~/**primäre** 1. primary (illuminating) light source, main light source; 2. *s.* ~/szenenbestimmende
~/**punktförmige** point light source, point source [of] light
~/**sekundäre** secondary light source
~/**szenenbestimmende** key [light source], dominant light source;
~/**theoretische** theoretical light source
~/**thermische** thermal light source, thermal source of light
~/**virtuelle** virtual light source
Lichtquellenabstand *m* light source distance
Lichtquellenbild *n* [light] source image
Lichtquellenfarbe *f* light source color
Lichtradar *n* lidar, *(short for light detection and ranging)*, laser radar, ladar *(short for laser detection and ranging)*
Lichtrand *m s.* Lichtsaum
Lichtrastermikroskop *n* laser scan microscope
Lichtreaktion *f* photochemical reaction
Lichtreduktionsfilter *n*, **Lichtreduzierfilter** *n s.* Neutraldichtefilter
Lichtreflektor *m* light reflector
Lichtreflex *m* flare
Lichtreflexion *f* light reflection
Lichtregie *f* lighting design
Lichtregler *m* fader
Lichtregulierung *f* light regulation
Lichtreiz *m* light (photic) stimulus
Lichtremission *f* diffuse (Lambertian) reflection
Lichtrezeptor *m* [light] receptor, photoreceptor
Lichtrichtung *f* direction of light, light direction
Lichtröhre *f* light tube *(optics)*
Lichtsammelfähigkeit *f* light-gathering ability
Lichtsammlung *f* light collection (gathering)
Lichtsatz *m* photocomposition; phototypesetting, phototypography, filmsetting

Lichtsatzmaschine f phototypesetting machine, phototypesetter
Lichtsatzsystem n photocomposition system
Lichtsaum m rim of light
Lichtschacht m fixed-mirror reflex housing, viewing hood *(of a twin-lens reflex camera)*
Lichtschachtsucher m brilliant (waist-level) finder
Lichtschleier m light fog
Lichtschleuse f 1. light trap; 2. *s.* Lichtventil 3. *s.* Lichtmodulator
Lichtschnittmikroskop n light-section microscope
Lichtschnittverfahren n light-section method, light-stripe method
Lichtschranke f light gate (valve)
Lichtschutz m light protection
Lichtschutzlack m light protecting varnish
Lichtschutzpapier n light-protecting paper
lichtschwach low-light-level, low-luminosity, low-luminance, faint, dim
Lichtschwächung f light attenuation
Lichtschwund m light dissipation, [light] falloff, falloff of light
Lichtsensor m light (optical) sensor, photosensor
Lichtsetzmaschine f *s.* Lichtsatzmaschine
Lichtsetzung f lighting *(cinema)*
Lichtsignal n light signal
Lichtsinn m *s.* Gesichtssinn
Lichtsinnesorgan n light receptor
Lichtsinneszelle f light sensing cell; light receptor
Lichtsituation f light situation
Lichtsonde f light probe *(confocal microscopy)*
Lichtspalt m light slit
Lichtspektrum n light spectrum
Lichtspielhaus n, **Lichtspieltheater** n [motion-picture] theater, movie theater (house), cinema
Lichtspielwesen n cinematography
lichtstabil light-stable, stable to light, lightfast, photostable
Lichtständer m light[ing] stand, light support
lichtstark fast *(camera lens)*; high-luminosity *(e.g. a projector)*
Lichtstärke f 1. luminous (light) intensity *(photometry)*; 2. light gathering power, speed *(of an objective)*; 3. *s.* ~/relative
~ in Candela candlepower, cp
~/relative, **Lichtstärkenverhältnis** n relative aperture, aperture ratio, [diaphragm] f-number, F-number *(of an objective)*
Lichtstärkeverteilung f intensity distribution
Lichtstärkeverteilungsdiagramm n/**polares** polar graph (diagram)
Lichtstellanlage f, **Lichtstellpult** n lighting console (board)

Lichtsteuerband n printing (timing) tape *(motion-picture printing)*
Lichtsteuerblende f fader
Lichtsteuereinrichtung f light-controlling device, lighting control board
Lichtsteuergerät n dimmer [switch]
Lichtsteuersystem n light control system
Lichtsteuerung f light control
Lichtstift m light pen
Lichtstil m lighting style
Lichtstimmung f mood of light (illumination) *(s.a.* Lichtcharakter*)*
Lichtstörung f light disturbance
Lichtstrahl m light ray (beam), ray of light
~/einfallender incident (incoming) light ray
Lichtstrahlablenker m [light] deflector
Lichtstrahlenbündel n bundle of light rays, light beam
Lichtstrahler m *s.* Lichtquelle
Lichtstrahlung f optical radiation
Lichtstreuung f light scatter[ing], scatter[ing] of light *(s.a. under* Streuung*)*
~/elastische Rayleigh scattering
Lichtstrom m luminous flux (power), light flux *(photometry)*
Lichtstromdichte f luminous-flux density, light flux density, intensity of light
Lichtsumme f light sum
Lichttechnik f illuminating (lighting) engineering
Lichttechniker m [set] lighting technician, lighting electrician
lichttechnisch photometric
Lichtteilchen n light particle (quantum), photon [quantum]
Lichttelefon n photophone
Lichtteleskop n optical (visible-light) telescope, visual telescope
Lichttheorie f theory of light
Lichttisch m light table
Lichtton m optical (photographic) sound
~/kombinierter composite optical [sound], comopt
Lichttonabtastgerät n optical [sound] head, optical-sound-reading equipment
Lichttonaufnahme f, **Lichttonaufzeichnung** f 1. optical (photographic) sound recording; 2. optical (photographic) sound record
Lichttonaufzeichnungsgerät n photographic sound recorder
Lichttongerät n optical sound head
Lichttonkamera f sound camera
Lichttonkopie f optical sound print
Lichttonnegativ n, **Lichttonnegativfilm** m optical sound negative
Lichttonqualität f optical sound quality
Lichtton-Sprossenschrift f variable-density [sound] track, push pull system *(cinema)*
Lichttonspur f optical (photographic) sound track, optical [audio] track

Lichtton-Testfilm *m* photographic sound test film
Lichttonverfahren *n* sound-on-film system
Lichtton-Vorverstärker *m* pre-amplifier for optical sound
Lichttonwiedergabe *f* optical sound reproduction
Lichttonwiedergabegerät *n* optical sound reproducer
Lichttor *n* barn door
Lichttransmission *f* light transmission
Lichttransmissionsgrad *m* light (luminous) transmittance
Lichtübertragung *f* illumination transfer, light transmission
lichtunbeständig photolabile
Lichtunbeständigkeit *f* photolability
Lichtundichtheit *f* light leakage
lichtundurchlässig opaque; lightproof
Lichtundurchlässigkeit *f* opacity; lightproofness
lichtunempfindlich light-insensitive
Lichtunterbrechung *f* light interruption
Lichtunterschiedsempfindlichkeit *f* luminance difference sensitivity
Lichtvektor *m* light vector
Lichtventil *n* light valve
Lichtventilprojektor *m* light valve[-based] projector
Lichtverhältnisse *pl* light[ing] conditions
Lichtverlust *m* light loss (leakage), loss of light
Lichtverlustfaktor *m* light loss factor
Lichtverschmutzung *f*, **Lichtverseuchung** *f* light pollution *(astrophotography)*
Lichtverstärker *m* light amplifier (intensifier), light amplification unit
Lichtverstärkung *f* light amplification (intensification)
~ **durch angeregte (stimulierte) Strahlungsemission** light amplification by stimulated emission of radiation, laser
Lichtverteilung *f* light distribution
Lichtverteilungskörper *m* light distribution solid, solid of luminous intensity distribution
Lichtverteilungskurve *f* light distribution curve
Lichtwahrnehmung *f* light perception
Lichtwandler *m* photoconverter
Lichtwandlung *f* light conversion, photoconversion
Lichtwanne *f* broad [light]
Lichtwechsel *m* light change
Lichtwechselfrequenz *f* light alternating frequency
Lichtweg *m* light path[way], optical path[way]; light[-travel] distance, optical distance (path length)
Lichtwegunterschied *m* optical path difference
Lichtwelle *f* light (optical) wave
~ /**stehende** stationary (standing) light wave

Lichtwellenausbreitung *f* light wave propagation
Lichtwellenlänge *f* light wavelength
Lichtwellenleiter *m* optical waveguide; [fiber-optic] light guide; optical fiber
Lichtwert *m* light value
Lichtwirkung *f* light action
Lichtzeichnung *f s.* 1. Fotografik 1. *and* 2.; 2. Fotografie 1. *and* 2.
Lichtzeiger *m* light [beam] pointer
Lichtzelt *n* lighting tent
Lichtzerlegung *f* light decomposition
Lichtzerstreuung *f* light scatter[ing] *(s.a. under* Streuung*)*
Lichtzusammensetzung *f* light composition
Lidar *s.* Lichtradar
Ligatur *f* ligature, tied letters *(typography)*
Likelihoodfunktion *f* likelihood function *(probability theory)*
Linac *m s.* Linearbeschleuniger
Lineament *n* lineation
Linearantiqua *f*/**serifenlose** grotesque; black letter, Gothic *(nonserif typeface)*
Linearbeschleuniger *m* linear accelerator, linac *(gamma ray production)*
Linearfaktor *m s.* Linearmaßstab
Lineargeschwindigkeit *f*/**konstante** constant linear velocity, CLV
linearisieren to linearize
Linearisierung *f* linearization
Linearität *f* linearity
Linearmaßstab *m* magnification factor
Linearmotor *m* linear motor
Linearperspektive *f* linear (central) perspective, convergence of parallels, pinhole perspective
Linearpolarisation *f* linear polarization
Linearpolarisationsfilter *n*, **Linearpolarisator** *m* linear[ly] polarizing filter, linear polarizer
Linearprojektion *f*/**klassenspezifische** class-specific linear projection
Lineation *f s.* Lineament
Linie *f* 1. line; 2. stroke *(typography)*
~ /**diakaustische** diacaustic line *(formed by refraction)*
~ /**dünne** thin line
~ /**gekrümmte** curved line
~ /**gerade** straight line
~ /**geschlossene** circuit
~ /**isochromatische** isochromatic line *(photoelastic stress analysis)*
~ /**isomagnetische** isomagnetic
~ /**katakaustische (kaustische)** [cata]caustic line
~ /**verdeckte** hidden line *(computer graphics)*
Linien *fpl*/**Fraunhofersche** Fraunhofer (spectral) lines
~ /**konvergierende** converging lines
~ **pro Zoll** lines per inch, lpi *(measure of fineness of halftone screen)*

~/**stürzende** converging verticals, architectural perspective
Linienabschnitt *m* line segment
Linienabstand *m* line spacing
Linienanpassung *f* line fitting
Linienapproximation *f* line approximation
Linienauflösung *f* line[-space] resolution
Linienausbreitungsfunktion *f s.* Linienbildfunktion
Linienbild *n* 1. line[-drawing] image; line illustration; 2. *s.* Spaltbild/optisches
Linienbildfunktion *f* **[eindimensionale]** *f* line-spread [response] function, LSF
~/**normierte** normalized line-spread function
Linienbreite *f* line width
Linienbreitenfaktor *m* linewidth scale factor
Liniencodierung *f* line coding
Liniendarstellung *f* line representation
Liniendetektion *f* line detection *(image segmentation)*
Liniendetektor *m* line detector
Liniendiagramm *n* line chart (diagram)
Linienelement *n* line element
Linienende *n*, **Linienendpunkt** *m* line end[ing], line termination
Linienfilter *n* narrow-band[pass] filter, spike filter
Liniengeber *m* stroke device *(logical input device)*
Liniengitter *n* line grating
~/**holografisches** holographic line grating
~/**optisches** optical line grating
Liniengrafik *f* line graphics (art), coordinate graphics
Linienintegral *n* line integral
Linienkontrast *m* line contrast
Linienkreuzung *f* line crossover
Linienmuster *n* line pattern
Liniennachbarschaftsgraph *m* line adjacency graph
Linienobjekt *n* line object
Linienpaar *n* line pair *(measure of resolution)*
Linienquelle *f* line source *(emission tomography)*
Linienraster *m(n)* 1. line raster (screen) *(printing)*; 2. line-scanning pattern *(television)*
Linienrasterung *f* line rastering
Linienrasterverfahren *n* line-screen process *(color photography)*
Linienrauschen *n* line noise
Linienrichtung *f* line orientation
Linienscan *m* line scan
Linienscanner *m* line scanner
Liniensegment *n* line segment
Liniensegmentierung *f* line segmentation
Liniensensor *m s.* Zeilensensor
Linienspektrum *n* line (discrete) spectrum, discontinuous spectrum
Linienstärke *f* line (stroke) width, line thickness

Linienstrahler *m* line radiator
Linien-Streufunktion *f s.* Linienverbreiterungsfunktion
Linienstruktur *f* line structure
Linienstück *n s.* Liniensegment
Linientyp *m* line type (style)
Linienverbreiterungsfunktion *f s.* Linienbildfunktion
Linienverfolgung *f* line following, sequential edge extraction
Linienverwaschungsfunktion *f s.* Linienverbreiterungsfunktion
Linienzug *m* polyline, chain, arc *(computer graphics)*
Linienzugfarbindex *m* polyline color index
linksäugig left-eyed
linksbündig left-aligned, left-adjusted, flush (ranged) left; ragged right
linksdrehend levorota[to]ry, levo, turning counterclockwise
Linksklick *m* left click
Linksklicken *n* left clicking
Linotype-Setzmaschine *f* Linotype *(a keyboard-operated typesetting machine)*
Linse *f* lens
~/**achromatische** achromatic (color-corrected) lens, achromat
~/**aplanatische** aplanatic lens, aplanat
~/**apochromatische** apochromatic lens, apochromat
~/**asphärische** aspheric[al] [single-element] lens, nonspherical lens
~/**bikonkave** biconcave lens
~/**bikonvexe** biconvex (double-convex) lens
~/**bitorische** bitoric lens
~/**dicke** thick lens; compound (complex) lens
~/**dünne** thin lens
~/**einfache** simple lens
~/**elektromagnetische** [electro]magnetic lens
~/**elektrostatische** electrostatic lens *(ion optics)*
~/**farbkorrigierte** *s.* ~/achromatische
~/**Fresnelsche** Fresnel lens
~/**gekrümmte** curved lens
~/**ideale** ideal (perfect) lens
~/**konische** conical lens
~/**konkave** concave (diverging) lens
~/**magnetische** magnetic lens
~/**negative** negative (diverging) lens, concave (dispersive) lens
~/**nichtideale** nonideal lens
~/**nichtzentrierte** decentered lens
~/**optische** optical lens
~/**perfekte** *s.* ~/ideale
~/**positive** positive (converging) lens
~/**sphärische** spherical lens
~/**symmetrische** symmetrical lens
~/**torische (toroidale)** toric (toroidal) lens
~/**vergütete** coated lens
~/**verkittete** cemented lens
~/**zentrierte** centered lens

Linse

~/**zylindrisch-plankonkave** cylindrical plano-concave lens
~/**zylindrisch-plankonvexe** cylindrical plano-convex lens
Linsenachse f lens axis, axis of a lens
Linsenanordnung f lens arrangement
Linsenaufspaltung f element splitting
Linsendicke f lens thickness
Linsendurchsichtssucher m direct-vision [optical] viewfinder, direct viewfinder
Linsenebene f lens plane
Linsenelement n [lens] element, single lens
~/**asphärisches** aspheric[al] lens element
Linsenfehler m lens error, lens [image] defect, [lens] aberration; lens imperfection
Linsenfernrohr n refracting telescope, refractor
Linsenfertigung f lens fabrication (manufacture)
Linsenfläche f 1. lens area; 2. lens surface
Linsenform f lens shape
Linsenformel f/**Gaußsche** s. Linsengleichung/Gaußsche
linsenförmig lenticular
linsenfrei lensless
Linsenglas n lens glass
Linsengleichung f/**Gaußsche** Gaussian lens equation (formula), lens [conjugate] equation
~/**Newtonsche** Newtonian lens equation
Linsengrenzfläche f lens interface
Linsengruppe f lens group
~/**bewegliche** floating element *(of a picture-taking lens)*
Linsenhalter m lens holder
Linsenhauptpunkt m principal point [of an optical lens]
Linsenkombination f lens combination (system), lens assembly
Linsenkorrektur f lens correction
Linsenkrümmung f lens curvature
Linsenmachergleichung f lensmakers' formula *(focal length determination)*
Linsenmaterial n lens (optical) material
Linsenmittelpunkt m lens center
Linsenmuskel m ciliary (iris) muscle *(of the eye)*
Linsennomogramm n lens nomogram
Linsenoberfläche f lens surface
Linsenoberflächenbehandlung f lens coating
Linsenoptik f refractive optics
linsenoptisch refractive optical
Linsenpaar n lens pair
Linsenpapier n s. Linsenputztuch
Linsenputztuch n lens tissue (paper), lens cleaning cloth (tissue), optics cleaning tissue (wipe)
Linsenrasterbildschirm m lenticular screen (sheet display)
Linsenrasterfarbfotografie f lenticular color photography
Linsenrasterfilm m lenticular (lenticulated) film, lenticular [color] motion-picture film
Linsenrasterschmalfilm m lenticular additive color amateur motion picture film
Linsenrasterverfahren n lenticular [color] process, lenticular method
Linsenreinigungsflüssigkeit f lens cleaning fluid
Linsenreinigungsstift m lens pen
Linsenrohling m [lens] blank
Linsensaugnapf m lens suction cup
Linsenscheinwerfer m focusing spotlight
Linsenscheitel m lens vertex (pole)
Linsenschleifer m lens grinder
Linsenschnitt m lens drawing
linsenslos lensless
Linsenstreuung f lens flare
Linsenstrom m lens current *(electron microscope)*
Linsensystem n lens system (combination), lens assembly
~/**anamorphotisches** anamorphic system (optics), anamorphote [lens]
~/**fokales** focal lens system
Linsentragkörper m lens block holder, [grinding] block
Linsenvergütung f lens coating
Linsenwerkstoff m lens (optical) material
Linsenzeichnung f lens drawing
lipophil lipophilic; grease-receptive; ink-receptive
Lippenstift-Objektivpinsel m lipstick lens brush
lippensynchron lip-sync
Lippensynchronisation f lip sync[hronization]
lippensynchronisieren to lip-sync[h]
Lippensynchronität f lip sync [relationship]
Lippmann-Bragg-Hologramm n transmission hologram
Lippmann-Emulsion f Lippmann emulsion *(color photography)*
Liste f list
~/**lineare** string
~/**verknüpfte** linked list
Lithentwickler m lith[ographic film] developer
Lithentwicklung f lith development
Lithfilm m lith[-type] film, litho[graphic] film, graphic arts film
Lithfilmfotografie f lith-film photography
Lithiumbatterie f lithium battery (cell)
Lithium-Ionen-Akku[mulator] m li[thium]-ion battery
Litho n lithograph, lithographic image
Lithofarbe f lithograph[ic] ink
Lithograf m lithographer
Lithografenstein m lithograph[ic] stone
Lithografie f 1. lithography, lithographic printing; 2. s. Offsetdruck 1.; 3. lithograph, lithographic image
~/**holografische** holographic lithography

~/**interferometrische** interferometric lithography
~/**lichtoptische** s. ~/optische
~/**optische** optical lithography, photolithography
~/**rasterlose** screenless lithography
Lithografiepapier n lithographic paper
lithografieren to lithograph
Lithografiestein m lithograph[ic] stone
lithografisch lithographic
live live (a broadcast)
Live-Aufzeichnung f live recording
Live-Dreh m live[-action] shoot, live-action photography (production)
Live-Fernsehen n live television, real-time on-site video
Live-Fotografie f photo reporting
Live-Mitschnitt m direct recording
Live-Produktion f live show production
Live-Sendung f live broadcast
Live-Ton m original [production] sound, production (direct) sound
Live-Übertragung f live broadcast
Loader m s. Materialassistent
Loch n hole; [photogenerated] hole defect electron (photodetector)
Lochband n perforated [paper] tape
Lochblende f 1. pinhole [aperture]; pinhole diaphragm; 2. doughnut, dount (esp. of a spotlight)
Lochblendenkamera f s. Lochkamera
Lochfilter n notch filter
Lochkamera f pinhole camera, camera obscura
Lochkamerabild n pinhole camera image
Lochkameramodell n pinhole camera model (video modeling)
Lochmaske f hole mask; circular-hole shadow mask (television)
Lochmaskenabstand m dot pitch
Lochmaskenbildröhre f,
Lochmasken[farbbild]röhre f three-gun shadow-mask color picture tube
Lochstreifen m perforated tape
Lochstreifenleser m punched-tape reader
LoG-Filter n LoG filter (operator), Laplacian-of-Gaussian [operator], Marr-Hildreth operator, sombrero filter, Mexican hat filter (kernel) (edge detection)
Logik f/**Boolesche** Boolean logic (algebra)
~/**kontinuierlichwertige (unscharfe)** fuzzy logic
Logikbaustein m/**programmierbarer** [field] programmable gate array, [F]PGA
Logikspeicher m logic memory
Logo n(m) logo[type] (s.a. Signet)
Logotype f logotype, logo (character)
Lokalantenne f local (surface) coil (magnetic resonance imaging)
Lokalfernsehen n local television (TV)
Lokalisierer m locator device (logical input device)
Lokalisierung f localization

Luftbildaufklärung

Lokalisierungsgüte f localization accuracy (e.g. in edge detection)
Lokalität f locality (e.g. of image structures)
Lokaloszillator m local oscillator (television)
Lokalsender m local broadcast station
Lokalzeichenkonstanz f position constancy
Longitudinalmagnetisierung f longitudinal magnetization
Longitudinalrelaxation f s. Längsrelaxation
Longitudinalwelle f longitudinal wave
Lookup-Tabelle f 1. lookup table [memory], LUT, index map; video lookup table; 2. s. Farbtabelle
Lorentz-Kraft f Lorentz [electromagnetic] force
löschbar erasable, reversible
Löschbarkeit f erasability
Löschbelichtung f erase exposure (electrophotography)
Löschdrossel f quenching coil
löschen to erase, to delete (e.g. unwanted data)
Löschfunktion f erase function
Löschkopf m erase (erasing) head
~/**fliegender (rotierender)** flying erase head
Löschkopfbreite f erase-head width
Löschlaser m eraser laser
Löschschutz m erasure protection
Löschstrom m erasing current
Löschtaste f delete (cancel) key
Löschung f 1. erasure; 2. s. Extinktion
Lösemittelfarbe f solvent ink
Löslichkeit f solubility
Lösung f/**gesättigte** saturated solution
~/**kolloidale** colloidal solution
~/**übersättige** supersaturated solution
Lösungsmittel n solvent
Low-Key-Bild n low-key picture, low-key photo[graph]
Low-Key-Effekt m low-key effect
LTI-System n/**[zeit]diskretes** linear time-invariant discrete-time system (digital filtering)
Lückenfüllsender m s. Füllsender
Luftabstand m airspace, air gap (between lens elements)
Luftaufklärung f aerial reconnaissance [survey], aerial survey
Luftaufklärungsfoto n aerial reconnaissance picture, overhead reconnaissance image
Luftaufklärungskamera f aerial reconnaissance camera; overhead surveillance camera
Luftaufnahme f s. Luftbild 2.
Luftbild n 1. aerial (virtual) image (optics); 2. aerial [surveillance] photo[graph], air[borne] photograph, aerophoto, aerial [shot], airborne (overhead) image
Luftbildarchäologie f aerial archaeology
Luftbildaufklärung f photoreconnaissance

Luftbildaufnahme f 1. aerial imaging; 2. s. Luftbild 2.
~ f **aus großer Höhe** high-altitude image (aerial photograph)
Luftbildauswertung f airphoto interpretation, aerial photo (image) interpretation
Luftbild-Farbaufnahme f color aerial photograph
Luftbildfarbfilm m aerial color film
Luftbild-Farbfotografie f color aerial photography
Luftbildfilm m aerial[-survey] film, aero[graphic] film
Luftbildfilmempfindlichkeit f aerial film speed
Luftbildfotografie f aerial (air) photography, aerophotography
Luftbildfotogrammetrie f aerial mapping photography
Luftbildgeologie f photogeology
Luftbildinterpretation f s. Luftbildauswertung
Luftbildkamera f, **Luftbildkammer** f aerial [technical] camera, airborne camera
Luftbildkarte f aerial map, photomap
Luftbildkartierung f aerial mapping
Luftbildlabor[atorium] n aerial photography laboratory
Luftbildmaterial n aerial imagery
Luftbildmessung f aerial photogrammetry, aerophotogrammetry
Luftbildobjektiv n aerial camera lens
Luftbildort m aerial image location *(optics)*
Luftbildsegmentierung f aerial image segmentation
Luftbildsequenz f aerial image sequence
Luftbildtriangulation f aerotriangulation
Luftdruck-Fernauslöser m pneumatic bulb release
Lufterkundung f aerial reconnaissance
Luftfeuchte f atmospheric humidity (moisture), humidity of [the] air, air moisture (humidity)
~/**relative** relative humidity [of the air], RH
Luftfeuchtigkeit f s. Luftfeuchte
Luftkerma n air Kerma, Kerma in air *(X-ray dosimetry)*
Luftlicht n atmospheric haze
Luftlinse f air lens *(objective)*
Luft-Nachtaufnahme f nighttime aerial photograph
Luftperspektive f aerial (atmospheric) perspective
Luftpinsel m 1. airbrush; 2. blower brush
Luftplattenspektroskop n s. Fabry-Perot-Interferometer
Luftpostpapier n air mail stationery, onion skin *(lightweight type of paper)*
Luftraum m airspace, air gap *(between lens elements)*
Luftraumüberwachung f overhead surveillance

Luftraumüberwachungsradar n air-surveillance radar
Luftruhe f steadiness of the air *(astrophotography)*
Luftschnittstelle f common air interface, CAI
Luftspalt m air gap *(e.g. between field-magnet poles)*
Luftstreuung f Rayleigh scattering
Lufttrocknung f air (atmospheric) drying *(e.g. of photographic paper)*
Luftüberwachung f aerial (air) surveillance
Luftüberwachungsfotografie f s. Luftbild 2.
Luftunruhe f 1. unsteadiness of the air, atmospheric scintillation *(astrophotography)*; 2. seeing *(astrophotography)*
Luftvermessung f photographic aerial survey
Lumen n lumen, lm *(SI unit of luminous power)*
~ **pro Quadratfuß** foot-candle, fc, lumen per square foot *(unit of illuminance)*
Lumensekunde f lumen second, Talbot *(unit of luminous energy)*
Lumenstunde f lumen hour
Luminanz f luminance, photometric brightness *(s.a. under Leuchtdichte)*
~/**gammakorrigierte** gamma-corrected luminance, luma *(video)*
Luminanzamplitude f luminance amplitude
Luminanzauflösung f luminance resolution
Luminanzband n luminance band
Luminanzbandbreite f luminance bandwidth
Luminanzbild n luminance image
Luminanzblock m luminance block *(image sequence coding)*
Luminanz-Chrominanz-Trennung f luma/chroma separation [technique], Y/C separation
Luminanzfilter n luminance filter
Luminanzhistogramm n luminance histogram
Luminanzinformation f luminance information
Luminanzkanal m luminance channel
Luminanzkomponente f luminance component
Luminanzmaskierung f luminance masking (dependence), contrast masking *(video compression)*
Luminanzmaß n luminance measure
Luminanzpegel m luminance level, video brightness level
Luminanzprofil n luminance profile
Luminanzrauschen n luminance noise
Luminanzsignal n luminance (luma) signal, black-[and-]white signal, Y [signal] *(video)*
Luminanztiefpassfilter n luminance low-pass filter

Luminanz-Übersprechen n cross-luminance [artifact], cross-luma artifact
Luminanzverhältnis n luminance ratio
Luminanzverstärker m video [processing] amplifier
Lumineszenz f luminescence
~/**lichtangeregte** photostimulated luminescence
~/**verzögerte** delayed luminescence
Lumineszenzdiode f luminescent diode, light-emitting diode, LED
~/**kantenemittierende** edge-emitting LED
Lumineszenzfarbstoff m luminescent dye
Lumineszenzlicht n luminescence light
Lumineszenzmikroskopie f luminescence microscopy
Lumineszenzmodulationsspektroskopie f luminescence modulation spectroscopy
Lumineszenzradiografie f/**digitale** digital luminescence radiography
Lumineszenzschirm m luminescence screen
Lumineszenzspektroskopie f luminescence spectroscopy
Lumineszenzspur f streak
Lumineszenzstrahler m luminescent (selective) radiator
Lumineszenzstrahlung f luminescence
lumineszieren to luminesce
lumineszierend luminescing; luminescent
Luminokopie f s. Luminografie
Luminophor m luminophor, lumophor, luminescent material
luminös, luminos luminous, lucid
Lummer-Brodhun-Würfel m Lummer-Brodhun cube (photometer), photometric cube
Lupe f loupe; magnifying glass, magnifier
~/**elektronische** s. Zoom/digitales
~/**Haidingersche** dichroscope
Lupenaufnahme f photomacrograph, macro photograph
Lupenbrille f binocular magnifier
Lupenfotografie f photomacrography, macrophotography
Lupenvergrößerung f loupe magnification
LUT s. Look-up-Tabelle
Lux n lux, lx, lumen per square meter *(SI unit of illuminance)*
Luxmeter n lux[o]meter, illuminance (incident-light) meter, illuminometer
Luxsekunde f lux second, lumen-second per square meter, meter-candle-second *(unit of exposure)*
Lymphangiografie f lymph[angi]ography
lymphangiografisch lymph[angi]ographic
Lymphangiogramm n lymph[angi]ogram
Lyot-Filter n birefringent filter
L-Zapfen m L cone, long-wavelength-sensitive cone *(retina)*
LZW-Codierung f s. Lempel-Ziv-Welch-Codierung

M

MacAdam-Ellipse f MacAdam ellipse *(colorimetry)*
Mach-Band n Mach band
Mach-Band-Effekt m, **Mach-Täuschung** f Mach [band] effect, Mach banding *(visual perception)*
Magazin n 1. [film] magazine; spool box; 2. magazine *(e.g. as a television program)* 3. magazine *(printed material)*
Magazinaufwicklung f magazine take-up
Magazindruck m magazine printing; publication gravure printing
Magazinkamera f magazine camera
Magenspiegel m gastroscope
Magenspiegelung f gastroscopy
Magenta n magenta *(subtractive primary color)*; process red *(in printing)*
Magentaentwickler m magenta [dye] developer
magentafarben, magentafarbig magenta
Magentafarbstoff m magenta dye
Magentafilter n magenta filter
Magentafilterschicht f magenta filter layer
Magentakuppler m magenta [dye-forming] coupler, magenta-colored coupler
Magentaraster m(n) magenta screen
magentarot magenta
mager light *(typeface)*
Magnesium n magnesium
Magnesiumblitz m, **Magnesiumblitzlicht** n magnesium flash (light)
Magnesium-Blitzpulver n magnesium flash powder
Magnesiumfluorid n magnesium fluoride *(optical material)*
Magnesiumoxid n magnesium oxide
Magnet m/**resistiver** resistive magnet
~/**supraleitender (supraleitfähiger)** superconducting magnet
Magnetaufzeichnung f 1. magnetic recording; 2. magnetic record[ing]
Magnetaufzeichnungsgerät n magnetic recorder
Magnetaufzeichnungssystem n magnetic recording system
Magnetband n mag[netic] tape
~/**perforiertes** sprocketed magnetic tape
Magnetbandaufzeichnung f magnetic tape recording
Magnetbandgerät n magnetic tape storage device; streamer
Magnetbandkassette f magnetic tape cassette (cartridge)
Magnetbandlaufwerk n [/**schnelles**] streamer
Magnetbandmedium n magnetic tape medium
Magnetbandrolle f pancake
Magnetbandspeicherkapazität f magnetic tape storage capacity
Magnetbandtechnik f magnetic tape technology
Magnetband-Tonaufnahmegerät n magnetic-tape sound recorder
Magnetband-Videorecorder m magnetic tape video recorder
Magnetbespurung f magnetic striping
Magnetbildaufzeichnung f magnetic image (picture) recording
Magnetbildaufzeichnungsgerät n video[tape] recorder, VTR
Magnetblasenspeicher m magnetic bubble memory
Magnetbürste f magnetic brush [roll]
Magnetenzephalografie f magnetoencephalography, MEG
Magnetenzephalogramm n magnetoelectroencephalogram, MEG
Magnetfeld n magnetic field
~/**äußeres** external magnetic field
~/**statisches** static magnetic field
~/**zeitveränderliches** time-varying magnetic field
Magnetfeldgradient m magnetic[-field] gradient
Magnetfeldinhomogenität f [magnetic] field inhomogeneity
Magnetfeldlinie f magnetic field line
Magnetfeldsensor m magnetic[-field] sensor
Magnetfeldstärke f magnetic-field strength
Magnetfeldvektor m magnetic-field vector
Magnetfilm m mag[netic] film, magnetic cord
~ **mit Tonaufzeichnung** separated magnetic [sound], SEPMAG
~/**perforierter** sprocketed magnetic film, magnetic sprocketed film
~/**voll beschichteter** full-coated magnetic film
Magnetfilmaufzeichnungsgerät n magnetic film recorder
Magnetfilmband n [magnetic] cord
Magnetfilmlaufwerk n magnetic film transport
Magnetfilmmaterial n magnetic film stock
Magnetfilmspeicher m magnetic-film memory
Magnetfilmstreifen m magnetic film stripe
Magnetfluss m magnetic flux
Magnetflussdichte f magnetic flux density
magnetisch magnetic, mag
magnetisierbar magnetizable
Magnetisierbarkeit f magnetizability
magnetisieren to magnetize
Magnetisierung f magnetization
~/**makroskopische** macroscopic magnetization
~/**remanente** residual (rest) magnetism, remanence
~/**transversale** transverse magnetization

Magnetisierungskurve f magnetization curve
Magnetisierungsrichtung f magnetization direction, direction of magnetization
Magnetisierungstransfer m magnetization transfer
Magnetisierungstransferkontrast n magnetization transfer contrast, MTC
Magnetisierungsvektor m magnetization vector
Magnetkopf m magnetic head (s.a. Aufnahmekopf)
Magnetkopfkern m magnetic head core
Magnetkopfspalt m magnetic head gap
Magnet-Kraft-Mikroskop n magnetic force microscope, MFM
Magnetlinse f magnetic lens
Magnetoenzephalografie f s. Magnetenzephalografie
Magnetografie f magnetography, magnetic imaging
magnetografisch magnetographic
Magnetokardiografie f magnetocardiography
Magnetokardiogramm n magnetocardiogram
Magnetometer n magnetometer
Magnetometrie f magnetometry
Magnetooptik f magneto-optics, magneto-optical technology
magnetooptisch magneto-optic[al]
Magnetorotation f magneto-optic rotation
Magnetostriktion f magnetostriction
magnetostriktiv magnetostrictive
Magnetplatte f magnetic [storage] disk
Magnetplattenlaufwerk n magnetic disk drive
Magnetplattenspeicher m magnetic disk memory
Magnetpulverprüfung f magnetic particle examination (inspection)
Magnetpulver-Rissprüfung f magnetic crack detection
Magnetrandspur f magnetic strip[e], magnetic sound stripe
Magnetresonanz f magnetic resonance, MR
Magnetresonanzangiografie f magnetic resonance angiography, MR angiography, MRA
~/**kontrastverstärkte** contrast-enhanced MRA, Gd-MRA
Magnetresonanzangiogramm n MR angiogram, MRA image
Magnetresonanzanlage f MRI (magnetic resonance imaging) system, MRI machine, MR imager (scanner)
Magnetresonanzaufnahme f, **Magnetresonanzbild** n magnetic resonance image, MR image
Magnetresonanzbild/dichtegewichtetes (protonengewichtetes) density-weighted MR image
Magnetresonanzbildgebung f magnetic resonance imaging, MR imaging, MRI
Magnetresonanzendoskopie f magnetic resonance endoscopy
Magnetresonanzgerät n s. Magnetresonanzanlage
Magnetresonanzmessung f magnetic resonance measurement
Magnetresonanzmikroskopie f magnetic resonance microscopy, MR microscopy
Magnetresonanzphänomen n magnetic resonance phenomenon
Magnetresonanzsignal n MR (magnetic resonance) signal
Magnetresonanzspektrometer n MR (magnetic resonance) spectrometer
Magnetresonanzspektroskopie f magnetic resonance spectroscopy, MRS
magnetresonanzspektroskopisch magnetic resonance spectroscopic, MR spectroscopic
Magnetresonanztomograf m MRI scanner
Magnetresonanztomografie f magnetic resonance imaging, MR imaging, MRI
~/**funktionelle** functional MRI (magnetic resonance imaging), fMRI
~/**struturelle** structural MRI (magnetic resonance imaging)
magnetresonanztomografisch magnetic resonance tomographic
Magnetresonanztomogramm n MR slice; MR image
Magnetron n magnetron (oscillator tube)
Magnetschicht f magnetic coating, magnetic layer (film) (e.g. on videotape)
Magnetspeicher m magnetic storage [medium], magnetic storage device, magnetic memory
Magnetspeicherung f magnetic storage
Magnetspule f magnetic [field] coil
Magnetspulenlöschgerät n bulk eraser
Magnetspur f mag[netic] track
Magnetstreifen m magnetic stripe
Magnetton m mag[netic] sound, magnetically recorded sound
~/**kombinierter** composite magnetic [sound], commag
Magnettonabtastgerät n magnetic sound head
Magnettonaufnahme f magnetic audio recording, magnetic [sound] recording
Magnettonband n audio magnetic tape, magnetic sound (audio) tape
Magnettonfilm m magnetic [sound] film
Magnettonkamera f magnetic film recorder
Magnettonkopf m magnetic sound head
Magnetton-Lichtton-Kopie f magoptical print
Magnettonspur f magnetic sound (audio) track, mag track (stock)
Magnettonstreifen m magnetic sound stripe, magnetic strip[e], mag stripe

Magnettonwiedergabe *f* magnetic sound reproduction
Magnettonwiedergabegerät *n* magnetic reproducer, penthouse
Magnitude *f* magnitude *(measure of star brightness)*
Mahalanobis-Abstand *m*, **Mahalanobis-Distanz** *f* Mahalanobis distance [measure] *(pattern classification)*
Mahalanobis-Klassifikator *m* Mahalanobis classifier
mailen to e-mail
Majuskel *f* majuscule, capital (uppercase) letter, cap
Majuskelschrift *f* all capital letters
Makro *m* macro [facility] *(computer technology)*
Makroaufnahme *f* photomacrograph, macrophotograph, macro image
Makroautomatik *f s.* Makroeinstellung/automatische
Makroblock *m* macroblock *(video compression)*
Makroblockadresse *f* macroblock address
Makroeinstellung *f*/**automatische** auto[matic] macro function, automatic macro setting
Makrofokussierung *f* macro-focusing
Makrofotografie *f* photomacrography, macrophotography
makrofotografisch photomacrographic
Makrokinematografie *f* macrocinematography, cinemacrography
makrokinematografisch macrocinematographic
Makrolinse *f s.* Nahlinse
Makromerkmal *n* macrofeature *(e.g. in image classification)*
Makromodus *m* macro mode
Makromolekül *n* macromolecule
Makroobjektiv *n* photomacrographic lens (objective), macro[photographic] lens, close-focusing lens
~/langbrennweitiges long focus length macro lens
Makropixel *n* [pixel] tile *(computational geometry)*
Makropsie *f* macropsia, macropsy
makroskopisch macroscopic[al], megascopic
Makrostativ *n* photomacrographic stand
Makro-Stereofotografie *f* stereo photomacrography
Makro-Teleobjektiv *n* telemacro lens
Makrotisch *m* macrostage *(microscopy)*
Makrotypografie *f* layout
Makrovorsatz *m*, **Makrovorsatzlinse** *f* closeup lens
Makrozoom[objektiv] *n* macro-zoom lens
Maksutow-Cassegrain-Teleskop *n* Maksutov-Cassegrain telescope
Maksutow-System *n* Maksutov (Bouwers) system *(mirror lens)*
Maksutow-Teleskop *n* Maksutov telescope
Makula *f* **lutea** macula [lutea], yellow spot *(in the human retina)*
Makuladegeneration *f* [/**altersbedingte**] macular degeneration
Makulapigment *n* macular pigment
Makulapigmentierung *f* macular pigmentation
Makulatur *f* makeready [paper], waste *(printing)*
Malmodus *m* paint mode
Malprogramm *n* [computer] paint program; paint software, paint package (system)
Malteserkreuz *n* Maltese (Geneva) cross
Malteserkreuzgetriebe *f*, **Malteserkreuzschaltung** *f* Maltese cross mechanism
Malteserscheibe *f* Geneva wheel
Malwerkzeug *f* paint tool *(image-processing program)*
Mammografie *f* mammography, breast imaging, radiography of the breast
~/computergestützte computer-aided mammography
~/digitale digital mammography
~/optische optical mammography
Mammografiefilm *m* mammographic (mammography) film
Mammografiegerät *n* mammography device (viewer); mammography equipment (unit)
mammografisch mammographic
Mammogramm *n* mammogram, mammographic image
Manchester-Code *m* Manchester code
Mandelbrot-Menge *f* Mandelbrot set *(fractal geometry)*
Mangin-Spiegel *m* Mangin [mirror] *(catadioptric system)*
manipulierbar manipulable *(e.g. images)*
Manipulierbarkeit *f* manipulability
Marching-Cubes-Algorithmus *m* marching cubes [contouring] algorithm *(visualization)*
Marionettenfilm *m* puppet animation
Markenlinie *f* fiducial line *(photogrammetry)*
Markenrahmen *m* fiducial frame *(photogrammetry)*
Markersubstanz *f* marking compound
Markierlaser *m* marking laser
Markierung *f* mark[ing], cue *(e.g. on film material)*; tag
Markierungssprache *f* markup language *(data processing)*
Markov-... *s.* Markow-...
Markow-Analyse *f* Markovian analysis
Markow-Codierung *f*/**dynamische** dynamic Markov coding
Markow-Kette *f* Markov chain
Markow-Modell *n* Markov model

Markow-Prozess m Markov process
~/zweidimensionaler two-dimensional Markov process
Markow-Zufallsfeld n Markov random field, MRF
Marr-Hildreth-Operator m Marr-Hildreth operator, Laplacian-of-Gaussian [operator], LoG filter (operator), Mexican hat filter *(edge detection)*
Marsgeografie f areography
Maschinenbefehl m computer command (instruction)
Maschinencode m machine[-specific] code, object code, machine language, low-level programming language
Maschinenentwickler m machine processor, [photo] processing machine
Maschinenentwicklung f [continuous] machine processing
maschinenlesbar machine-readable, computer-readable *(e.g. image data)*
Maschinenrichtung f machine (grain) direction *(of paper)*
Maschinensatz m machine composition *(printing)*
~/lochstreifengesteuerter tape-operated typesetting
~/tastaturgesteuerter keyboard-operated typesetting
Maschinenschrift f typescript
maschinenschriftlich machine-written
Maschinensehen n [industrial] machine vision
Maschinen-Sichtsystem n [automatic] machine vision system
Maschinenverarbeitung f [continuous] machine processing, [fully] mechanized processing *(e.g. of photographic material)*
maschinenverarbeitungsfähig machine-processable
Maske f 1. mask *(e.g. in photomechanical reproduction)*; matte, key *(cinematography)*; 2. s. Maskenoperator; 3. s. Alphakanal
~/unscharfe unsharp mask [filter], blur[ring] filter
Maskenaufbau m matte generation *(e.g. in computer animation)*
Maskenaufnahme f matte shot
Maskenbelichtung f mask exposure
Maskenbild n mask image; matte image *(cinematography)*
Maskeneinschub m matte box
Maskenfertigung f mask fabrication
Maskenfilm m mask film
Maskenhalter m mask holder
Maskenherstellung f mask fabrication
Maskenkanal m matte (alpha) channel *(computer graphics, video)*
Maskenkoeffizient m mask (filter) coefficient
Maskenkuppler m **[/gefärbter]** [colored] masking coupler

Maskenloch n mask aperture *(color cathode-ray tube)*
Maskenoperator m mask, kernel, local operator *(gray-scale image processing)*
Maskensatz m mask set
Maskenverfahren n 1. masking method *(photomechanical reproduction)*; matte extraction technique, matting [process] *(cinematography)*; 2. s. Wandermaskenverfahren
maskierbar maskable
maskieren to mask [out], to block [out], to knock out *(e.g. image elements)*
Maskierfolie f masking sheet (film)
Maskierung f masking
~/fotografische photographic masking
~/raumzeitliche spatiotemporal masking
~/unscharfe unsharp (soft-edge) masking, unsharp mask operation
Maskierungseffekt m masking effect
Maskierungsfarbstoff m masking dye *(color film)*
Maskierungstechnik f masking technique
maßanalytisch volumetric
Masse f**/flächenbezogene** gram[m]age, grams per square meter, GSM *(paper specification)*
Massefilter n absorption filter
Massenabsorptionskoeffizient m s. Massenschwächungskoeffizient
Massenkontrast m structure factor contrast *(electron microscopy)*
Massenkopie f [mass] release print; theatrical [projection] print *(motion-picture film)*
Massenkopierer m high-volume copier
Massenkopierung f mass (quantity) printing, volume printing; quantity (high-speed) release printing *(motion-picture film)*
Massenprojektionskopie f s. Massenkopie
Massenschwächungskoeffizient m mass attenuation coefficient, mass [energy] absorption coefficient, mass energy transfer coefficient
Massenspeicher m mass storage [device], high-capacity storage, bulk memory (storage), mass data storage medium
~/holografischer holographic mass storage
Massenspektrograf m mass spectrograph
~/Astonscher Aston's mass spectrograph
Massenspektrometer n**/doppeltfokussierendes** double focusing mass spectrometer
Massenspektrometrie f mass spectrometry (spectroscopy)
Massenszene f crowd scene *(filming)*
Masseschwerpunkt m center of mass, barycenter
maßhaltig dimensionally stable *(e.g. film material)*
Maßhaltigkeit f dimensional stability

Massiv[glas]filter n [solid] glass filter, glass-mounted filter
Massivspiegel m monolithic mirror
maßkonstant s. maßhaltig
Maßprüfung f dimensional checking
Maßstab m [spatial] scale
maßstäblich [true] to scale
Maßstabsänderung f scale change, change of scale
Maßstabsfaktor m scaling factor
Maßstabsfehler m scale error
maßstabsgerecht, maßstabsgleich [true] to scale
Maßstabsleiste f, **Maßstabs-Messstrecke** f scale bar
Maßstabstreue f trueness to scale
Masterband n master [tape], first-generation tape; work tape
~/**spiegelbildliches** mirror master tape
Mastereinstellung f master shot *(filming)*
Masterhologramm n master hologram
Mastermischband n s. Masterband
Material n/**fotografisches** photo[graphic] material, photograph material
~/**fotoresistives** photoresist, photosensitive resist
~/**lichtempfindliches** light-sensitive material, photosensitive material
Materialassistent m second assistant cameraman, 2nd AC, camera operator assistant, clapper[/loader]
Materialmikroskopie f materials microscopy
Materialprüfung f/**zerstörungsfreie** nondestructive material[s] testing, nondestructive testing (evaluation) of materials
Matrix f matrix
~/**aktive** active matrix *(liquid-crystal display)*
~/**Boolesche** Boolean (binary) matrix
~/**diagonale** diagonal matrix
~/**dreidimensionale** three-dimensional matrix
~/**hermitische** Hermitian matrix
~/**Hessesche** Hessian matrix
~/**homogene** homogeneous matrix
~/**Kartesi[ani]sche** Cartesian matrix
~/**orthogonale** orthogonal matrix
~/**orthonormale** orthonormal matrix
~/**passive** passive matrix *(liquid-crystal display)*
~/**quadratische** square matrix
~/**symmetrische** symmetrical matrix
Matrixaddition f matrix addition, addition of matrices
Matrixalgebra f matrix algebra
Matrixanordnung f matrix array
Matrixanzeige f matrix[-controlled] display
Matrixberechnung f matrix computation
Matrix-CCD f CCD array
Matrixdarstellung f matrix representation
Matrixdiagonalisierung f matrix diagonalization
Matrixdisplay n matrix[-controlled] display
~/**organisches** organic matrix display
Matrixdrucker m [dot-]matrix printer, dot-matrix line printer
Matrixelement n matrix element
Matrixfilm m matrix film *(color photography)*
Matrix-Flachbildschirm m flat-panel active-matrix display
Matrixform f matrix form *(e.g. of a transformed image)*
Matrixgleichung f matrix equation
Matrixgröße f matrix size
Matrixinversion f matrix inversion
Matrixkamera f [matrix] array camera, area array camera
Matrixkoeffizient m matrix coefficient
Matrixkonversion f matrix conversion
Matrixmessung f matrix metering
Matrixmultiplikation f matrix multiplication
Matrix-Nadeldrucker m dot-matrix wire printer
Matrixoperation f matrix operation (manipulation)
Matrixoptik f matrix optics
Matrixprodukt n matrix product
Matrixschreibweise f matrix notation
Matrixsensor m matrix sensor (detector)
Matrixtransformation f matrix transformation
Matrixtransponierung f matrix transposition
Matrixzeichen n matrix character
Matrize f matrix, mat, die *(type casting)*
Matrizenfilm m s. Matrixfilm
Matrizenrahmen m matrix (typecase) frame *(typesetter)*
matrizieren to matrix
Matrizierung f matrixing [operation]
matt faint *(e.g. a photographic negative)*; matt[e] *(e.g. a printing paper)*; dull
Mattebild n matte painting
Mattemaler m matte artist
Mattglanzfotopapier n matt-surface paper
Mattglanzkopie f matt-surface print
Mattglas n frosted glass, opal[ized] glass
Mattglasfilter n frosted glass filter
Mattglasglühbirne f, **Mattglaslampe** f opalized lamp [bulb]
mattgrau matt[e] gray
Mattiermittel n matting agent
mattiert matte-finished
Mattlack m matt varnish
Mattscheibe f [ground-glass] viewing screen, [ground-glass] focusing screen, [finder] screen
Mattscheibenbild n ground-glass image, [focusing] screen image
Mattscheibenebene f ground-glass plane
Mattscheibenkamera f screen focusing camera
Mattscheibensucher m ground-glass [view]finder, screen viewfinder

mattschwarz matt-black, matte black
Mattseite f emulsion (front) side (of film material)
Mattspray n dull[ing] spray, matt spray
mattweiß matt-white, white matt
Maus f [computer] mouse, puck (handheld input device)
~/**kabellose** wireless (cordless) mouse
~/**mechanische** mechanical mouse
~/**optische (optomechanische)** optical mouse
Mausklick m mouse click
Maussteuerung f mouse control
Maustaste f mouse button
~/**linke** primary mouse button
Mausunterlage f mouse pad (mat)
Mauszeiger m mouse pointer (cursor)
Maximaldichte f maximum density, D-max (densitometry)
Maximalkontrast m maximum [image] contrast
Maximalöffnung f maximum (widest) aperture
Maximalschwärzung f s. Maximaldichte
Maximum n/**lokales** peak
Maximumfilter n max[imum] filter
Maximum-Intensitäts-Profil n s. Maximumsprojektion
Maximum-Likelihood-Klassifikation f maximum likelihood classification, ML classification
Maximumsfilterung f maximum filtering
Maximumsprojektion f maximum intensity projection, MIP (visualization)
Maxwell-Gleichungen fpl Maxwell's equations (electromagnetic radiation)
MAZ s. Magnetbildaufzeichnung
MAZ-Band n video magnetic tape, [magnetic] videotape
MAZ-Bearbeitung f video postproduction
MAZ-Maschine f videotape machine
MAZ-Schnitt m videotape editing
M-Bildverfahren n M scan ultrasonography, [ultrasound] M mode imaging, M mode ultrasound (method)
McCollough-Effekt m McCollough effect, contingent color aftereffect
ME-Band n metal-evaporated tape, ME tape
Median m s. Medianwert
Medianfilter n median[-type] filter (image operator)
~/**achteckiges** octagonal median filter
~/**adaptives** adaptive median filter
~/**binäres** binary median filter, majority filter
~/**gewichtetes** weighted median [filter], WM
~/**hybrides** hybrid (edge-preserving) median filter
~/**zentral gewichtetes** center-weighted median filter
Medianfiltermaske f median filter mask
Medianfilterung f median filtering

Medianoperation f median operation
Medianoperator m s. Medianfilter
Medianpixel n median pixel
Medianschnittverfahren n median cut algorithm (color quantization)
Medianwert m median [value], middle value (statistics)
Medienarchiv n media archive
Mediendatei f media file
Mediendatendurchsatz m media data throughput
Mediendatenobjekt n media object (s.a. Multimediaobjekt)
Mediendatenstrom m media stream
Mediendienst m media service
Medienintegration f media integration
Medienobjekt n media object (s.a. Multimediaobjekt)
Medientechnik f media technology
Medientechnologie f media technology
Medienumsetzung f, **Medienwechsel** m media translation; medium interchange
Medienwirtschaft f [/angewandte] media management
Medienzugriffskontrolle f medium access control, MAC
Medium n medium; communications medium
~/**aktives** active medium (laser)
~/**anisotropes** anisotropic medium
~/**audiovisuelles** audiovisual medium
~/**brechendes** refractive medium
~/**dielektrisches** dielectric (nonconducting) medium
~/**dispersives** dispersive medium
~/**elektronisches** electronic medium
~/**hochbrechendes** high-index medium
~/**homogenes** homogeneous medium
~/**inhomogenes** inhomogeneous (graded-index) medium
~/**isotropes** isotropic medium
~/**kontinuierliches** continuous medium
~/**laseraktives** laser [active] material
~/**niedrigbrechendes** low-index medium
~/**optisch aktives** optically active medium
~/**optisch isotropes** optically isotropic medium
~/**optisches** optical medium
~/**rauschfreies** noise-free medium
~/**schmalbandiges** narrow-bandwidth medium
~/**zerstreuendes** scattering medium
Medizinbildgebung f medical imaging; clinical (diagnostic medical) imaging, [medical] diagnostic imaging
Medizinbildtechnik f medical imaging technology
Medizinfotograf m medical photographer
Medizinfotografie f medical photography
Meeresbodenkartierung f ocean mapping
Meeresfotografie f marine photography
Megabit n megabit, Mb
Megabyte n megabyte, MB

Megahertz *n* megahertz, MHz *(unit of frequency)*
Megapixel *n* megapixel
Megapixelkamera *f* megapixel camera
Mehraderkabel *n* multicore
Mehrbandfilter *n* multiband filter
Mehrbenutzer-Betriebssystem *n* multi-user computer system
Mehrbildfeldmittelung *f* multi-frame averaging
Mehrbildschirm *m* multi-image screen
Mehrbildtechnik *f*, **Mehrbildverfahren** *n* multi-image processing *(photogrammetry)*
mehrdimensional multidimensional
Mehrdimensionalität *f* multidimensionality
Mehrfachablenkung *f* multideflection *(e.g. of an ink jet)*
Mehrfachauflösung *f* multiresolution
Mehrfachauflösungsanalyse *f* multiresolution analysis
Mehrfachauflösungsfilter *n* multiresolution filter
Mehrfachauflösungspyramide *f* multiresolution pyramid
Mehrfachaufnahme *f* multiple image
Mehrfachbelichtung *f* multiple exposure
~/unbeabsichtigte (versehentliche) multiple accidental exposure
Mehrfachbelichtungskassette *f*, **Mehrfachbelichtungsrahmen** *m* test strip printer
Mehrfachbelichtungsverfahren *n* multiple exposure procedure
Mehrfachbeugung *f* multiple diffraction
Mehrfachbild *n* 1. multiple image; 2. split-screen [shot]
Mehrfachblitz *m* multiflash, multiple flash *(s.a. Multiblitz...)*
Mehrfachbündel *n* multiple beam *(optics)*
Mehrfachcodierung *f* multiple [en]coding
Mehrfachecho *n* multiple echo *(radar)*
Mehrfachexposition *f* multiple exposure
Mehrfachkopie *f* multiple copy
Mehrfachprisma *n* many-sided prism
Mehrfachprojektion *f* multiple projection
Mehrfachreflexion *f* multiple reflection
Mehrfachschichtpolarisator *m* multilayer polarizer
Mehrfachspeisung *f* multifeed *(satellite reception)*
Mehrfachsucher *m* universal [view]finder
Mehrfachumschalter *m* multiplexer, multiplexor, mux
mehrfachvergütet multicoated, multilayer [optically] coated
Mehrfachvergütung *f* multicoating, multiple (multilayer) coating
Mehrfarbdrucker *m* multicolor printer
Mehrfarbenband *n* multicolor[ed] ribbon
Mehrfarbenbild *n* multicolor (polychrome) image
Mehrfarben-Bogendruckmaschine *f* multicolor sheet-fed press

Mehrfarbendruck *m* multicolor (polychrome) printing
Mehrfarbendruckmaschine *f* multicolor press
Mehrfarbenfotometrie *f* multicolor photometry
Mehrfarben-Rasterbild *n* multicolor halftone image
Mehrfarben-Rotationsdruckmaschine *f* polychrome rotary
Mehrfarbentiefdruck *m* multicolor gravure printing
Mehrfarbentiefdruckrotationsmaschine *f* multicolor web press
mehrfarbig multicolor[ed], polychromatic
Mehrfarbigkeit *f* polychromy
Mehrfeld[belichtungs]messung *f* multi-pattern metering, multi-field measurement, area-weighted measurement
Mehrfeld-Autofokus *m* multi-zone autofocus
Mehrfrequenzbildschirm *m* multisync monitor, multisync [display]
Mehrfrequenznetz *n* multi-frequency network, MFN
Mehrgradationenpapier *n* multigraded paper
Mehrkameraproduktion *f* multicamera television production, multiple camera operation
Mehrkanalanordnung *f* multichannel array *(CCD technology)*
Mehrkanalbild *n* multichannel (multispectral) image, multiband image
Mehrkanalcodierung *f* multichannel coding
Mehrkanalempfänger *m* multichannel receiver
Mehrkanalfilterung *f* multichannel filtering
mehrkanalig multichannel
Mehrkanal-Punktoperation *f* multichannel point operation
Mehrkanalsignal *n* multichannel signal
Mehrkanalspektrometer *n* multichannel (simultaneous) spectrometer
Mehrkanalstereofonie *f* multichannel stereophony
Mehrkanal-Surroundton *m* multichannel surround sound
Mehrkanalton *m* multichannel sound; multichannel television sound, MTS
Mehrkanal-UV-Spektrofotometrie *f* multichannel UV spectrophotometry
Mehrkanalverstärker *m* multichannel amplifier
Mehrkomponenten-Punktoperation *f s.* Mehrkanal-Punktoperation
Mehrlinser *m* multielement (complex) lens, composite lens (objective), component lens
Mehrnormenempfänger *m* multistandard equipment

Mehrparteien-Videokonferenz f multiparty videoconference, multipoint videoconferencing
Mehrschichtaufnahme f 1. multislice acquisition, multislice (multiple slice) imaging *(magnetic resonance imaging)*; 2. multiple slice image
Mehrschichtcomputertomograf m multislice [X-ray CT] scanner
Mehrschichtenfarbfilm m multilayer color film
Mehrschichtenfilm m multilayer (multiple-layer) film
Mehrschichtenspiegel m multilayer[ed] mirror
mehrschichtenvergütet multilayer [optically] coated, multicoated
mehrschichtig multilayer[ed]; multiplanar
Mehrschichtplatte f/**metallische** multimetal plate *(offset printing)*
Mehrschicht-Spiral-Computertomograf m multislice [CT] scanner
Mehrschicht-Tonerbild n multilayer toner image
Mehrschichtvergütung f multilayer [antireflection] coating, multiple coating, multicoating
Mehrschrittbildverarbeitung f multistep image processing
Mehrschwellenverfahren n multilevel thresholding *(point operation)*
Mehrseitendruck m multiple-page printing
Mehrspiegelteleskop n multimirror telescope
Mehrspuraufzeichnung f multi[ple-]track recording
Mehrspurband n multitrack tape, multiple track tape
Mehrspurbandmaschine f multitrack machine
mehrspurig multitrack
Mehrspur-Recorder m multitrack [tape] recorder
Mehrspur-Tonaufzeichnung f multiple-track sound record
Mehrspur-Tontechnik f multitrack audio
Mehrstrahl-Farbbildröhre f s. Farbbildröhre
Mehrstrahlinterferenz f multiple-beam interference
Mehrstrahlscanner m raster [image] scanner
Mehrträgermodulation f, **Mehrträgerverfahren** n s. Multiträgerverfahren
Mehrwegeausbreitung f multipath propagation
Mehrwegeecho n multipath echo *(radar)*
Mehrzeilen-Computertomograf m multirow detector CT machine
Meisterfotograf m master photographer
Melanin n melanin *(pigment)*
Melanotypie f s. Ambrotypie

Meldeleitung f control (record) line, record circuit *(television broadcasting)*
Membranmodell n membrane model
Menge f set *(e.g. of pixels)*; class *(e.g. mathematical elements)*
~/**abgeschlossene** closed [point] set
~/**äquivalente** equivalent weight *(e.g. of photographic chemicals)*
~/**dyadische** dyadic set *(wavelet transform)*
~/**fraktale** fractal set
~/**unscharfe** fuzzy set
Mengenoperation f/**Boolesche** Boolean set operation *(computer graphics)*
Mengenoperator m set operator
Mengensatz m s. Brotschrift
mengentheoretisch set-theoretic
Mengentheorie f set theory *(mathematical morphology)*
Meniskus m meniscus, meniscus[-type] lens
~/**aplanatischer** aplanatic meniscus
~/**Hoeghscher** Hoegh meniscus [lens]
~/**konzentrischer** concentric meniscus
~/**negativer** negative meniscus lens, divergent (diverging) meniscus lens, convexo-concave lens
~/**positiver (sammelnder)** positive meniscus [lens], concavo-convex lens
Meniskuslinse f s. Meniskus
Menschenauge n human eye
Menschenfotografie f people (anthropological) photography
Mensch-Maschine-Kommunikation f human-computer interaction, HCI
Mensch-Maschine-Schnittstelle f human (man-machine) interface, human-computer interface *(s.a. under Schnittstelle)*
Menschmodell n biped *(computer animation)*
Mensel f s. Messtisch
Mensur f graduate[d cylinder]; measuring beaker
Menü n menu
Menüauswahl f menu selection
Menübalken m menu bar
Menübaum m menu tree
Menübefehl m menu instruction
Menübox f, **Menüfenster** n menu box
Menüführung f menu control
Menüfunktion f menu function
Menüleiste f menu bar
Menüsteuerung f menu control
Menütaste f menu key
Mercator-Karte f Mercator projection map
Mercatorprojektion f, **Mercator-Zylinderprojektion** f Mercator projection *(cartography)*
Meridionalebene f meridional plane *(optics)*
Meridionalkoma f meridional coma
Meridionalschnitt m s. Meridionalebene

Meridionalstrahl

Meridionalstrahl *m* meridional (tangential) ray
Merkmal *n* feature; characteristic; attribute; criterion *(s.a. under* Attribut, Deskriptor*)*
~/**abgeleitetes** derived feature
~/**biometrisches** biometrical feature
~/**diskretes** discrete feature
~/**formbeschreibendes** shape (form) feature, shape characteristic
~/**fotometrisches** photometrical feature
~/**geometrisches** geometric[al] feature
~/**globales** global feature
~/**interessierendes** feature of interest
~/**invariantes** invariant feature
~/**lokales** local feature
~/**morphometrisches** morphometric feature *(s.a.* ~/formbeschreibendes*)*
~/**numerisches** numerical feature
~/**objektbezogenes** object-related feature
~/**objektförmiges** object-shaped feature
~/**parametrisches** parametric feature
~/**segmentiertes** segmented feature
~/**strukturelles** structural feature
~/**topografisches** topographic feature
~/**topologisches** topological feature
~/**variantes** variant feature
~/**visuelles** visual feature
Merkmalsähnlichkeit *f* feature similarity
Merkmalsanalyse *f* feature analysis
~/**klassifikatorunabhängige** classifier-independent feature analysis, CIFA
Merkmalsauflösung *f* feature resolution
Merkmalsausrichtung *f* feature orientation
Merkmalsauswahl *f* feature (attribute) selection, description
Merkmalsbeobachtung *f* feature observation
Merkmalsbild *n* feature [domain] image
Merkmalscluster *m* feature cluster
Merkmalscode *m* feature code
Merkmalsdeskriptor *m* feature descriptor
Merkmalsdetail *n* feature detail
Merkmalsdetektor *m* feature detector
Merkmalseigenschaft *f* feature property
Merkmalserkennung *f* feature recognition (identification), [image] feature detection
Merkmalsextraktion *f* [image] feature extraction
~/**modellgestützte** model-based feature extraction
Merkmalsextraktor *m* feature extractor
Merkmalsfläche *f* feature area
Merkmalsform *f* feature shape
Merkmalsglättung *f* feature smoothing
Merkmalsgrenze *f* feature boundary
Merkmalsgröße *f* feature size
Merkmalsgruppierung *f* feature grouping
Merkmalshistogramm *n* feature histogram
Merkmalsidentifikation *f s.* Merkmalserkennung
Merkmalsintervall *n* feature interval
Merkmalskante *f* feature edge

Merkmalskarte *f* feature map
~/**selbstorganisierende** self-organizing [feature] map, topology-preserving map, Kohonen map (network) *(pattern recognition)*
Merkmalsklasse *f* feature class
Merkmalsklassifikation *f* feature classification
Merkmalskorrespondenz *f* feature correspondence
Merkmalslokalisierung *f* feature localization
Merkmalsmessung *f* feature measurement
Merkmalsmodellierung *f* feature modeling
Merkmalsparameter *m* feature parameter
Merkmalspixel *n* feature pixel
Merkmalspolygon *n* feature polygon
Merkmalsprimitiv *n* feature primitive
Merkmalspunkt *m* feature point
Merkmalsraum *m* feature (parameter) space
Merkmalsraumanalyse *f* feature space analysis
Merkmalsreduktion *f*, **Merkmalsreduzierung** *f* feature reduction
Merkmalssatz *m* feature set
Merkmalsselektion *f* feature (attribute) selection
Merkmalsüberlappung *f* feature overlap
Merkmalssuche *f* feature search
Merkmalsvektor *m* feature vector
Merkmalsverfolgung *f* feature tracking
Merkmalsverstärkung *f* feature enhancement
Merkmalsvolumen *n* feature volume
Merkmalswert *m* feature value
Merkmalszuordnung *f* feature matching
Merkspur *f* cue track
Merocyanin *n*, **Merocyaninfarbstoff** *m* merocyanine [dye]
mesopisch mesopic
Mesosphäre *f* mesosphere, chemosphere *(a level of the atmosphere)*
Mesostruktur *f* mesostructure
Messastrograf *m s.* Messkamera/astrografische
Messaufnahme *f s.* Messbild
Messband *n* alignment tape *(video)*
Messbereich *m* metering range
Messbild *n* [/**fotografisches**] mapping photograph, program
~/**terrestrisches** terrestrial photogram, ground photograph
Messbildaufnahme *f* Messbild
Messbildkamera *f* mapping (photogrammetric) camera
Messblende *f* measuring diaphragm, measurement aperture
Messblitz *m* monitor pre-flash
Messcharakteristik *f* metering feature
Messcharakteristikwähler *m* metering system selector *(SLR camera)*

Messerschneidenmethode f [nach Foucault] knife-edge technique, Foucault knife[-edge] test *(optics)*
Messfeld n metering field
Messfeld-Betriebsartenwähler m AF area mode selector
Messfeldwahl f focus area selection
Messfeldwähler m, **Messfeldwippe** f focus area selector
Messfernrohr n measuring telescope
Messfühler m [meter] sensor, sensing device *(s.a. Sensor, Detektor)*
Messgefäß n s. Messglas
Messgeometrie f measurement geometry
Messglas n graduate [cylinder]; measuring beaker
Messinglinie f brass rule *(letterpress composing)*
Messingtype f brass type
Messinstrument n/**optisches** optical measuring instrument
Messkamera f metric (measuring) camera
~/**astrografische** astrometric astrograph
Messkammer f [/**fotogrammetrische**] mapping (photogrammetric) camera
~/**terrestrische** terrestrial [photogrammetric] camera
Messkeil m measuring (compensating) wedge; split-image wedge (rangefinder), split-prism rangefinder *(focusing aid)*
Messkopf m measuring head; [sensing] probe
Messkreuz n measurement gratic[u]le *(as in optical instruments)*
Messlupe f 1. measuring magnifier; 2. s. Messkeil
Messmarke f measuring mark
Messmikroskop n measuring microscope
Messobjektiv n photogrammetric objective
Messokular n measuring eyepiece *(s.a. Okularmikrometer)*
Messprojektor m measuring projector
Messring m bearer *(press cylinder)*
Messstereoskop n measuring stereoscope
Messstrahl m measuring beam; line of response, LOR *(radiography)*
Messstreifenbreite f swath width *(remote sensing)*
Messtechnik f metrology
~/**fotoelektronische** photoelectronic metrology
~/**fotografische** photographic metrology
Messtisch m tracing table
Messtischblatt n plane-table sheet
Messtor n gate *(sonography)*
Messucher m [coupled] rangefinder
Messucherbild n rangefinder image
Messucherfehler m rangefinder error
Messucherkamera f rangefinder camera
Messung f/**berührungslose** noncontact measurement
~/**fotometrische** photometric measurement

~/**mittenbetonte** center-weighted metering *(automatic exposure)*
~/**optische** optical measurement
Messvolumen n sample volume *(sonography)*
Messwertdrucker m logger
Messwinkel m set square
Messsystem n metering system
Messzelle f 1. meter[ing] cell; 2. s. Lichtsensor
Messzylinder m s. Messglas
Metabisulfit n s. Natriumdisulfit
Metadatei f metafile
Metadaten pl metadata
Metallaustauschverfahren n silver recovery by metallic replacement
Metallband n metal particle tape
Metalldampf[entladungs]lampe f metal vapor lamp
Metalldetektor m metal detector
Metalldruckfarbe f metallic ink
Metall-Halbleiter-Diode f metal-semiconductor diode
Metallhalogen[id]lampe f metal halide lamp; metal halide gas-discharge arc lamp, HMI lamp
Metallkamera f metal camera
Metallograf m metallograph
Metallografie f metallography
metallografisch metallographic
Metalloxid-Feldeffekttransistor m metal-oxide-semiconductor field-effect transistor, MOSFET
Metalloxidhalbleiter m metal-oxide-semiconductor, MOS
Metallpartikelband n s. Metallband
Metallrahmen m metal frame
Metallspiegel m metallic mirror; speculum mirror *(esp. of early telescopes)*
Metallstativ n metal tripod
Metalltonband n metal particle tape
metamer metameric
Metamerie f metamerism, metamery
Metamerie-Index m metamerism index, index of metamerism
Metamorphose f/**computeranimierte** s. Morphing
Metasuchmaschine f meta-search engine, multisearch engine
Meterware f bulk film (lengths)
Meterwellenbereich m, **Meterwellenfrequenz** f metric wavelength range, very high frequency, VHF [range]
Methode f **der kleinsten Quadrate** method of least squares, least-squares method (approximation)
~ **der totalen kleinsten Quadrate** method of total least squares
Methylaminophenolsulfat n [para-]methylaminophenol sulfate, metol, elon *(developing agent)*
Metol n s. Methylaminophenolsulfat

Metol-Hydrochinon-Entwickler *m* metol-hydroquinone developer, MQ [developer]
Metrik *f*/**Euklidische** Euclidean metric (norm)
Metrologie *f*/**optische** optical metrology
Mettage *f* lockup, makeup *(printing)*
Metteur *m* lockup
Mexikanerhut-Operator *m* Mexican hat filter (kernel), sombrero filter, Laplacian-of-Gaussian [operator], LoG filter (operator), Marr-Hildreth operator *(edge detection)*
Mezzotinto *n* 1. mezzotint [technique] *(relief printing process)*; 2. mezzotint *(engraving)*
MH-Lampe *f s.* Metallhalogenidlampe
MHP *s.* System für interaktive Anwendungen
MHP-Endgerät *n*, **MHP-Gerät** *n* MHP device
MHP-Standard *m* MHP (Multimedia Home Platform) standard *(interactive television)*
Michelson-Interferometer *n* Michelson interferometer
Mie-Streuung *f* Mie scattering *(of light)*
Mikroamperemeter *n* microammeter
Mikroanalyse *f* microanalysis
mikroanalytisch microanalytical
Mikro-Angel *f s.* Mikrofonangel
Mikroaufnahme *f* microform; microimage
Mikrobild *n* microimage
Mikroblitz *m* microflash
Mikrobolometer *n* microbolometer *(photon absorber)*
Mikrochip *m* microchip, integrated circuit [chip], IC
Mikrocomputer *m* microcomputer
Mikro-Computertomograf *m s.* Mikrotomograf
Mikrodensitometer *n* microdensitometer
Mikrodensitometrie *f* microdensitometrie
mikrodensitometrisch microdensitometric
Mikrodisplay *n* microdisplay
Mikrodokumentation *f s.* Mikroreproduktion
Mikroelektronik *f* microelectronics
mikroelektronisch microelectronic
Mikrofacette *f* microfacet
Mikrofarbfilm *m* color microfilm
Mikrofiche *n(m)* microfiche, filmcard
Mikrofiche-Kamera *f* microfiche camera
Mikrofilm *m* microfilm; microfiche film
Mikrofilmaufnahme *f*, **Mikrofilmaufzeichnung** *f* 1. microfilm recording; 2. microfilm record
Mikrofilmbild *n* microfilm image
Mikrofilm-Dokumentationsfotografie *f* microfilm documentation
Mikrofilmduplikat *n* microfilm duplicate
Mikrofilmgerät *n s.* Mikrofilmlesegerät
Mikrofilmkamera *f* microfilm (microreduction) camera
Mikrofilmkarte *f* [microfilm] aperture card

Mikrofilmkopie *f* microfilm copy
Mikrofilmlesegerät *n* [projection] microfilm reader, microform reader, microreader
Mikrofilm-Lochkarte *f s.* Mikrofilmkarte
Mikrofilmspeicher *m* microfilm storage
Mikrofilmstreifen *m* microfilm strip
Mikrofilmtasche *f* microfilm jacket
Mikrofilmtechnik *f* microfilm technology (technics), micrographic film technology
Mikrofilm-Vergrößerungsgerät *n* microfilm enlarger
Mikrofilter *n* microfilter
mikrofokal microfocal
Mikrofokusradiografie *f* microfocus radiography
Mikrofokus-Röntgenröhre *f* microfocus X-ray tube
Mikrofon *n* microphone, mike
~/**drahtloses** wireless (radio) microphone
~/**dynamisches** [electro]dynamic microphone
~/**eingebautes** built-in microphone
~/**externes** external microphone
~/**kabelloses** radio microphone
~/**separates** external microphone
~/**separates** external microphone
~/**ungerichtetes** omnidirectional microphone
~/**zweiseitig gerichtetes** bidirectional microphone
Mikrofonangel *f* microphone (boom) pole, fishpole
Mikrofonausleger *m* boom [arm]
Mikrofonbuchse *f* mic[rophone] jack
Mikrofoncharakteristik *f* microphone polar pattern
Mikrofoneingang *m* mic[rophone] input *(video camera)*
Mikrofongalgen *m* microphone boom [apparatus], [mike] boom
Mikrofonhülle *f* gobo *(s.a.* Windschutzhülle*)*
Mikrofonkabel *n* microphone cable (cord), mike cable
Mikrofonkopfhörer *m* headset
Mikrofonmischer *m* microphone mixer
Mikrofonmultiplexer *m* microphone multiplexer
Mikrofonständer *m* microphone stand
Mikrofoto *n* photomicrograph
Mikrofotodiode *f* microphotodiode
Mikrofotograf *m* [photo]micrographer
Mikrofotografie *f* 1. photomicrography, microphotography, photomicroscopy; 2. photomicrograph; microimage
~/**digitale** digital photomicrography
mikrofotografieren to photomicrograph
mikrofotografisch photomicrographic[al]
Mikrofotogrammetrie *f* microphotogrammetry
Mikrofotometer *n* microphotometer
Mikrofotometrie *f* microphotometry
Mikro-Galgen *m s.* Mikrofongalgen

Mikro-Gradientenspiegel *m* graded reflectance micromirror
Mikrografie *f* micrographics
Mikrografiekamera *f* microfilm (microreduction) camera
mikrografisch micrographic
Mikrokamera *f s.* Mikroskopkamera
Mikrokanal-Bildverstärker *m* microchannel image intensifier
Mikrokanal-Elektronenvervielfacherplatte *f*, **Mikrokanalplatte** *f* microchannel plate, multichannel [multiplier] plate, MCP
Mikrokanalvervielfacher *m* multichannel multiplier
Mikrokapsel *f* microcapsule
Mikrokarte *f* microcard, microopaque
Mikrokassette *f* microcassette
Mikrokinematografie *f* cine[photo]micrography, microcinematography
mikrokinematografisch microcinematographic
Mikrokopie *f* microopy, microform, microreproduction
mikrokopieren to microcopy
Mikrokopierer *m* microcopier
Mikrokristall *m* microcrystal
Mikrolaser *m* microlaser
Mikrolinse *f* microlens, lenslet
Mikrolithografie *f* microlithography
mikrolithografisch microlithographic
Mikromerkmal *n* microfeature
Mikrometer *n* 1. [optical] micrometer; 2. micrometer, micron
Mikrometerauflösung *f* micrometer resolution
Mikrometerokular *n* micrometer ocular
Mikromotor *m* micromotor
Mikron *n s.* Mikrometer
Mikroobjektiv *n* microscope objective
Mikrooptik *f* micro-optics, miniaturized optics
mikrooptisch micro-optic[al]
Mikrooptoelektronik *f* microoptoelectronics
Mikropixel *n* micropixel
Mikroplanfilm *m* microfiche, filmcard
Mikropolarisator *m* micropolarizer
Mikropolygon *n* micropolygon
Mikroport *n* radio (wireless) microphone
Mikroprisma *n* microprism
Mikroprismenentfernungsmesser *m* microprism focus finder
Mikroprismenfeld *n* microprism area (array)
Mikroprismenraster *m(n)* microprism grid
Mikroprojektion *f* microprojection
Mikroprojektionsgerät *n*, **Mikroprojektor** *m* microprojector
Mikroprozessor *m* microprocessor, microprocessing unit *(e.g. of an autofocus system)*
Mikroprozessorsteuerung *f* microprocessor control

Mikropsie *f* micropsia, micropsy
Mikroradiografie *f* X-ray micrography, contact X-ray microscopy, [contact] microradiography
mikroradiografisch microradiographic
Mikroraster *m(n)* micro raster
Mikroreproduktion *f* 1. microreproduction, microform; 2. microreproduction, microform, microcopy
Mikroreziprokgrad *n s.* Mired
Mikroschaltkreis *m* microcircuit, microelectronic circuit
Mikroschaltkreisherstellung *f* microcircuit production
Mikrosensitometrie *f* microsensitometry
Mikrosensor *m* microsensor
~/**optischer** optical microsensor
Mikroskop *n* microscope
~/**einfaches** simple microscope
~/**fokussierendes** focusing microscope
~/**inverses** inverted microscope
~/**kohärentes** coherent microscope
~/**konfokales** confocal [optical] microscope, confocal scanning light microscope, CSLM
~/**metallografisches** metallographic microscope
~/**optisches** optical (conventional) microscope, [optical] light microscope
~/**zusammengesetztes** compound [light] microscope, two-lens microscope
Mikroskopadapter *m* microscope adapter, microadapter
Mikroskopauflösung *f* microscope resolution
Mikroskopaufnahme *f s.* Mikroskopbild
Mikroskopbeleuchtung *f* microscope illumination
Mikroskopbild *n* microscope (microscopic) image, microscope picture, micrograph
Mikroskopbildanalyse *f* microscope image analysis
Mikroskopbildverarbeitung *f* microscope image processing
Mikroskopeinstellung *f* microscope setting
Mikroskopfilter *n* microscopic filter
Mikroskopfotometer *n* microscope photometer
Mikroskopfotometrie *f* microscope photometry
Mikroskopie *f* microscopy
~/**akustische** acoustic microscopy
~/**analytische** analytical microscopy
~/**aperturbegrenzte optische** aperture-limited optical microscopy, AOM
~/**chemische** chemical microscopy
~/**computergestützte** computer-assisted microscopy
~/**dreidimensionale** three-dimensional microscopy
~/**elektrochemische** electrochemical microscopy

Mikroskopie 266

~/**elektronentomografische** electron tomographic microscopy
~/**holografische** holographic microscopy
~/**konfokale** confocal microscopy
~/**konventionelle** conventional microscopy
~/**lichtoptische** optical microscopy, [visible-]light microscopy
~/**nahfeldoptische** scanning near-field optical microscopy, SNOM, near-field [scanning optical] microscopy
~/**stereoskopische** stereoscopic microscopy, stereomicroscopy
~/**stroboskopische** stroboscopic microscopy
~/**virtuelle** virtual microscopy
~/**zeitaufgelöste** time-resolved microscopy
mikroskopieren to microscope
Mikroskopierer *m s.* Mikroskopist
Mikroskopierlampe *f,* **Mikroskopierleuchte** *f* microscope lamp, [microscope] illuminator
Mikroskopiermethode *f* mode of microscopy
Mikroskopiker *m* microscopist
mikroskopisch microscopic[al]
Mikroskopist *m* microscopist
Mikroskopkamera *f* eyepiece (microscope) camera *(photomicrography)*
Mikroskopkondensor *m* microscope condenser
Mikroskoplichtquelle *f* microscope light (illumination) source, microscope lamp (illuminator)
Mikroskopmikrometer *n* microscope [stage] micrometer, stage micrometer
Mikroskopmonitor *m* microscope monitor
Mikroskopobjektiv *n* microscope objective
Mikroskopobjektivhalter *m* microscope objective mount
Mikroskopokular *n* microscope eyepiece (ocular)
Mikroskopoptik *f* microscope optics
Mikroskopsäule *f* electron column *(scanning electron microscope)*
Mikroskopstativ *n,* **Mikroskopstativfuß** *m* microscope stand, base (foot) of the microscope
Mikroskoptheorie *f*/**Abbesche** Abbe's theory of the microscope
Mikroskoptubus *m* microscope tube; microscope objective barrel
Mikroskoptubuslänge *f* microscope body tube length
Mikrospektrofluoreszenz *f* microspectrofluorescence
Mikrospektrofotometer *n* microspectrophotometer
Mikrospektrofotometrie *f* microspectrophotometry
Mikrospektrometer *n* microspectrometer
Mikrospektroskopie *f* microspectroscopy
Mikrospiegel *m* micromirror

Mikrospiegelprojektor *m* micromirror projector
Mikrostereoskopie *f* microstereoscopy
Mikrostruktur *f* microstructure, micromorphology
Mikroteleskop *n* microtelescope
Mikrotexturmaske *f* microtexture mask
Mikrotom *n* microtome *(microscopy)*
Mikrotomograf *m* micro-CT scanner *(e.g. in cardiac image processing)*
Mikrotomografie *f* microtomography, micro computer tomography
mikroverfilmen to microfilm
Mikroverfilmung *f* microfilming, microcopying
Mikroverkleinerungskamera *f* microreduction (microfilm) camera *(photorepeater)*
Mikrowelle *f* microwave
Mikrowellenband *n* microwave band
Mikrowellenbild *n* microwave image
Mikrowellen-Bildgebung *f* microwave imaging
Mikrowellenempfänger *m* microwave receiver
Mikrowellenenergie *f* microwave energy
Mikrowellen-Fernerkundung *f* microwave remote sensing
Mikrowellenfrequenz *f* microwave frequency
Mikrowellenholografie *f* microwave holography
Mikrowellenkanal *m* microwave channel
Mikrowellenoptik *f* microwave optics
Mikrowellenphotonik *f* microwave photonics
Mikrowellenpuls *m* microwave pulse
Mikrowellenradar *n* microwave [ranging] radar
Mikrowellenröhre *f* microwave tube
Mikrowellensensor *m* microwave sensor (imager)
Mikrowellensignal *n* microwave signal
Mikrowellenstrahlung *f* microwave radiation
Mikrowellensystem *n*/**passives** passive microwave system
Mikrowellenthermografie *f* microwave thermography
Mikrowellen-Überwachungsradar *n* microwave surveillance radar
Mikrozonenplatte *f* micro zone plate *(X-ray microscopy)*
Mikrozonenplattenobjektiv *n* micro zone plate objective
Milchglas *n* milk glass *(s.a.* Mattglas*)*
Militärfotografie *f* military photography
Millimeterpapier *n* graph paper
Milliradian *n* milliradian *(resolution measure; image interpretation)*
Milzszintigrafie *f* splenic scintigraphy
Mindestauflösung *f* minimum resolution
Mindestbelichtungszeit *f* minimum exposure time

Mindestbetrachtungsabstand *m* minimum viewing distance
Mindestdichte *f s.* Minimaldichte
Miniaturabzug *m* miniature print
Miniaturansicht *f* thumbnail [screen display]
Miniaturbild *n* thumbnail [image]
Miniaturdekoration *f* movie miniature, miniature [set], scale model *(special-effects cinematography)*
Miniaturfoto *n* thumbnail [image]
Miniaturisierung *f* miniaturization
Miniaturkamera *f* miniature camera
Miniaturkulisse *f s.* Miniaturdekoration
Miniaturwandler *m* miniature transducer *(sonography)*
Mini-Blitzausleuchtung *f* mini flash illumination
Minicamcorder *m* minicamcorder
Minicomputer *m* minicomputer
Minifernseher *m* small TV receiver
Minikassette *f* small cassette
Minilab[or] *n* [photo development] minilab
Minilabzubehör *n* minilab photofinishing equipment
Minimalbelichtung *f* minimum exposure
Minimaldichte *f* minimum (minimal) density, D-min *(densitometry)*; base plus fog, fog level *(black-and-white film)*
Minimaldistanzklassifikation *f* minimum-distance classification
Minimaldistanzklassifikator *m* minimum-distance classifier
Minimalschwärzung *f s.* Minimaldichte
Minimalwertbaum *m* tag tree
Minimum *n* **separabile** minimum distinct border *(vision)*
Minimumfilter *n* min[imum] filter
Minimumfilterung *f* minimum filtering
Ministativ *n s.* Kleinstativ
Minkowski-Abstand *m* Minkowski distance
Minkowski-Addition *f* Minkowski [set] addition, dilation *(binary image processing)*
Minkowski-Distanz *f* Minkowski distance
Minkowski-Operator *m* Minkowski operator
Minkowski-Subtraktion *f* Minkowski [set] subtraction, morphological erosion, erosion [operation] *(binary image processing)*
Minkowski-Summe *f* Minkowski sum
Minoritätsträger *m* minority carrier *(photodetector)*
Minusfarbe *f* minus color
Minuskel *f* minuscule, miniscule, small (lowercase) letter
Mip-Mapping *n* mip mapping *(computer graphics, texture processing)*
Mired *n* MIRED, microreciprocal degree *(designating a light source)*
Mired-Wert *m* MIRED value
Mischbarkeit *f* miscibility *(e.g. of colors)*

Mischbeleuchtung *f* mixed illumination
Mischbild *n* mixed image; composite image
Mischbildentfernungsmesser *m* coincidence rangefinder
Mischbildszene *f* composite scene *(blue-screen effect)*
Mischer *m s.* Bildmischer 1. *and* 2.
Mischfarbe *f* mixed (composite) color
Mischhalbleiter *m s.* Mischungshalbleiter
Mischkristall *m* mixed crystal
Mischlicht *n* mixed (composite) light, blended light
Mischlichtbeleuchtung *f* mixed-light[ing] situation
Mischlichtquelle *f* mixed-light source
Mischpult *n* editing (mixing) console, mixing board
Mischschacht *m* [light-]mixing box *(enlarger)*
Mischsignatur *f* mixed signature *(image analysis)*
Mischung *f* mixing *(e.g. of sound sources)*
Mischungshalbleiter *m* compound (mixed) semiconductor
Mischverteilung *f* mixture density *(probability theory)*
Mitkopplungsnetz *n* feedforward network
Mitschwenk *m* pan [move]; sweeping pan; pan shot, follow tracking shot
Mittagslicht *n* midday (noon) daylight
~/mittleres average noon daylight, mean noon sunlight
Mittel *n*/**arithmetisches** [arithmetic] mean, arithmetic average
~/geometrisches geometric average (mean)
~/quadratisches root-mean-square, rms
Mittelachse *f* 1. center axis; 2. *s.* Mittelachsensatz
Mittelachsensatz *m* align center *(typography)*
Mittelachsentransformation *f* medial axis transform[ation], MAT, symmetric axis transform[ation], SAT
Mittelblende *f* central (center) stop *(of a lens)*
Mittelformat *n* medium format
Mittelformatdia[positiv] *n* medium-format slide
Mittelformatfotografie *f* medium-format photography
Mittelformatkamera *f* medium-format camera, medium-size hand camera
Mittelformatobjektiv *n* medium-format lens
Mittelformatprojektor *m* medium-format projector
Mittelformat-Rollfilmkamera medium-format roll-film camera
Mittelformat-Spiegelreflexkamera *f* medium-format SLR (single-lens reflex) camera, medium-format reflex camera

Mittelformat-Sucherkamera *f* medium-format rangefinder camera
mittelgrau middle (median) gray, mid-gray, medium gray
Mittelgrund *m* middle distance (ground)
Mittelguss *m* middle layer *(film manufacture)*
Mittellänge *f* half-line *(typography)*
Mittellautsprecher *m* center (central) speaker *(cinema)*
Mittellinie *f* 1. midline, median line; 2. x-line *(typography)*
mitteln to average
Mittelpunkt *m*/**optischer** optical center
Mittelpunktstrahl *m* principal (chief) ray *(optics)*
Mittelpunktsvalenz *f* basic stimulus
Mittelsäule *f* center column (pillar), central column, centerpost *(stand, tripod)*
Mittelstrebe *f* cross brace *(e.g. of a tripod)*
Mittelton *m* middle (medium) tone, midtone
Mitteltonbereich *m* midtone area (region)
Mitteltonbild *n* midtone image, middle-key image
Mitteltonkontrast *m* middle-tone contrast
Mittelung *f s.* Mittelwertbildung
Mittelwert *m* middle value; mean [value], average *(s.a. under Mittel)*
Mittelwertbild *n* average[d] image
Mittelwertbildung *f* averaging; averaging operation
Mittelwertfilter *n* [spatial] averaging filter, mean filter; box (uniform) filter
~/**arithmetisches** arithmetic mean filter
~/**geometrisches** geometric mean filter
~/**harmonisches** harmonic mean filter
~/**kontraharmonisches** contraharmonic mean filter
Mittelwertfilterung *f* mean value filtering
Mittelwertoperation *f* averaging operation
Mittelwertoperator *m* mean value operator
Mittenabschattung *f* central obscuration (obstruction) *(e.g. of an optical pupil)*
Mittenabstand *m* center-to-center distance (spacing), pitch *(e.g. of pixels)*
Mittendicke *f* center (central) thickness *(e.g. of a lens)*
Mittenfrequenz *f* center frequency
Mittenpunkt *m* midpoint, central (center) pixel, center pel *(binary image)*
Mittenpunktrekonstruktion *f* midpoint reconstruction
Mittenschärfe *f* central definition
Mittenspur *f* center track
Mittenwellenlänge *f* center wavelength *(laser)*
Mittigkeit *f* medialness
Mitziehen *n* **[der Kamera]** panning, tracking, trucking *(camera movement)*
Mitzieher *m s.* Mitschwenk
M-Mode-Verfahren *n s.* M-Bildverfahren
Mobildrucker *m* mobile printer

Mobil[funk]telefon *n* mobile phone, cell[ular] [tele]phone
Mobilcomputer *m* portable computer
Mobilfestplatte *f* removable [hard] disk
Mobilfunk *m* mobile radio
Möbius-Band *n* Möbius strip
Modalwert *m* modal value, mode *(statistics)*
Mode *f(m)* mode *(laser)*
~/**longitudinale** longitudinal mode
~/**transversale** transverse mode
Modeaufnahme *f* fashion photograph (picture)
Modefotografie *f* fashion photography
Modell *n* model *(e.g. in image analysis)*
~/**affines** affine model
~/**asymmetrisches** asymmetrical model
~/**autoregressives** autoregressive model
~/**Boolesches** Boolean model
~/**deformierbares** deformable model
~/**deterministisches** deterministic model
~/**dreidimensionales** three-dimensional model, 3-D model
~/**elastostatisches** elastostatic model
~/**formbasiertes** shape-based model
~/**fraktales** fractal model
~/**generisches** generic model
~/**geometrisch deformiertes** geometrically deformed model
~/**geometrisches** geometric model, graphic[al] model
~/**ikonisches** iconic model
~/**kinematisches** kinematic model
~/**kolorimetrisches** colorimetric model
~/**konnektionistisches** connectionist (parallel distributed processing) model, connectionist network, neural net[work], neuromorphic system
~/**kontextbasiertes** context-based model
~/**maßstab[s]gerechtes** scale model *(e.g. in film production)*
~/**merkmalsgestütztes** feature-based model *(object recognition)*
~/**neuronales** neuron model
~/**nichtparametrisches** nonparametric model
~/**numerisches** numerical model
~/**objektorientiertes** object-centered model
~/**parametrisches** parametric model
~/**polygonales** polygonal model
~/**räumliches** spatial model
~/**semantisches** semantic model
~/**spektrales** spectral model
~/**spezifisches** specific model
~/**statistisches** statistical model
~/**stereolithografisches** stereolithographic model
~/**stochastisches** stochastic model
~/**strukturelles** structural model
~/**symbolisches** symbolic model
~/**virtuelles** virtual model
~/**wissensbasiertes** knowledge-based model

~/**zufälliges** random model
Modellakquisition f model acquisition
Modellanimation f three-dimensional animation
Modellaufnahme f model (miniature) shot
Modellbau m model building
Modellbeleuchtung f model illumination *(video modeling)*
Modellbild n model image
Modellbildung f model generation (building)
Modellerstellung f model generation
Modellgeometrie f model geometry
Modellhierarchie f model hierarchy
modellieren to model
Modellieren n modeling
Modellierer m modeling program
Modellierlicht n modeling light
Modelliermethode f s. Modellierungsverfahren
Modellierung f modeling
~/**asymmetrische** asymmetrical modeling
~/**bildbasierte** image-based modeling, map-based modeling
~/**bildbasierte semantische** map-based semantic modeling
~/**dreidimensionale** three-dimensional modeling, 3-D modeling
~ **finiter Elemente** finite-element modeling
~/**geometrische** geometric (shape) modeling; computer-aided geometric design
~/**grafische** graphical modeling
~/**hierarchische** hierarchical modeling
~/**hybride** hybrid modeling
~/**implizite** implicit modeling
~/**kontextabhängige** context-dependent modeling
~/**mathematische** mathematical modeling *(e.g. in image restoration)*
~/**plenoptische** plenoptic modeling
~/**probabilistische** probabilistic modeling
~/**rechnergestützte** computer-aided modeling
~/**relationale** relational modeling
~/**robuste** robust modeling
~/**semantische** semantic[al] modeling
~/**statistische** statistical modeling
~/**stochastische** stochastic modeling
~/**symmetrische** symmetrical (reflective) modeling
Modellierungsfehler m modeling error
Modellierungsprogramm n modeling program
Modellierungstechnik f modeling technique
Modellierungsverfahren n modeling technique
Modellierungswerkzeug n modeling tool
Modellkoordinatensystem n model coordinate system
Modellmerkmal n model feature
Modellmethode f model method

Modellobjekt n model object *(video modeling)*
Modellparameter m model parameter
Modellprojektion f model projection
Modellraum m model space
Modellrepräsentation f model representation
Modellstruktur f model structure
Modellszene f model scene *(video modeling)*
Modelltextur f model texture *(video modeling)*
Modelltrick m model effect *(cinematography)*
Modellvereinfachung f model simplification
Modem n(m) modem, modulator/demodulator *(signal converter)*
~/**kabelloses** wireless modem
Modemkarte f modem board
Modemleitung f modem line
Modenblende f mode diaphragm *(laser)*
Modenrauschen n modal noise
Modenstruktur f mode structure
Modensynchronisation f mode locking *(laser)*
Modenverteilungsrauschen n mode competition noise
Moderator m anchorman *(as on a news program)*
Modul n(m) module
~/**optisches** optical module
modular modular
Modularität f modularity
Modulation f modulation
~/**akustooptische** acousto-optical modulation, AOM
~/**analoge** analog modulation
~/**digitale** digital modulation, keying
~/**elektrooptische** electro-optical modulation, EOM
~/**hierarchische** hierarchical modulation
~/**trelliscodierte** trellis-coded modulation, TCM
Modulationsanalyse f modulation analysis
Modulationsart f modulation scheme
Modulationsfrequenz f modulation frequency
Modulationsgeschwindigkeit f modulation rate
Modulationsgrad m modulation factor
Modulationsgrenze f modulation limit
Modulationsindex m modulation index
Modulationskennlinie f modulation characteristic
Modulationskontrast m modulation contrast
Modulationsmatrix f modulation matrix
Modulationsmodellierung f modulation modeling
Modulationsrauschen n modulation noise
Modulationsschema n modulation scheme
Modulationssignal n modulation signal

Modulationsspannung *f* modulation voltage
Modulationsstrom *m* modulation current
Modulationstechnik *f* modulation technique
Modulationsthermografie *f* steady-state [IR] thermography *(nondestructive evaluation)*
Modulationstiefe *f* modulation depth
Modulationstransferfunktion *f s.* Modulationsübertragungsfunktion
Modulationsübertragungsfaktor *m* modulation transfer factor
Modulationsübertragungsfunktion *f* modulation (contrast) transfer function, MTF, CTF; modulation transfer [function] curve; contrast sensitivity function, CSF
~/**beugungsbegrenzte** diffraction-limited modulation transfer function
~/**diffuse** diffuse modulation transfer function
Modulationsübertragungswert *m s.* Modulationsübertragungsfaktor
Modulationsverfahren *n* modulation scheme
Modulator *m* modulator
~/**akustooptischer** acousto-optic modulator, Bragg cell *(laser technology)*
~/**elektrooptischer** electro-optic modulator
~/**optischer** optical modulator
modulieren to modulate
Modulo-2-Addition *f s.* EXKLUSIV-ODER/logisches
Modulschacht *m* [expansion] slot
Moiré *n* [image] moiré, moire, moiré [fringe] pattern, moiré interference pattern
Moiré-Effekt *m*, **Moiré-Erscheinung** *f* moiré [pattern] effect
Moirégitter *n* moiré grating
Moiré-Interferometrie *f* moiré interferometry
Moirémuster *n s.* Moiré
Moiréstörung *f* moiré fringing
Moiréstreifen *mpl* moiré fringes
Moirétechnik *f* moiré technique (method) *(e.g. in materials testing)*
Mol *n* 1. mole, mol *(SI base unit of amount of pure substance)*; 2. gram molecular weight, gram-molecule
Molarität *f* molarity, molar concentration
Molekül *n* molecule
Molekularbewegung *f* molecular motion
Molekularmedizin *f* molecular medicine
Moleküldesign *n* molecular modeling, computer-aided molecular design, CAMD
Molekülgaslaser *m* molecular [gas] laser
Molekülmasse *f* molecular mass
Molekülspektroskopie *f* molecular spectroscopy
Moment *n* moment *(of a function)*
~/**magnetisches** magnetic moment
~/**zentrales** central moment

Momentanbild *n* current picture *(predictive coding)*
Momentaufnahme *f* instantaneous record; instantaneous photograph
Momentinvariante *f* moment invariant
Momentverschluss *m* instantaneous shutter
Mondsondenkamera *f* lunar probe camera
Mondtäuschung *f* moon illusion *(perceptual phenomenon)*
Monitor *m* [display] monitor; monitor screen
~/**externer** desktop (stand-alone) monitor
~/**hochauflösender** high-resolution monitor
~/**höchstauflösender** highest-resolution monitor
~/**lichtstarker** high-brightness monitor
Monitorarbeitsplatz *m* display (terminal) workstation
Monitorauflösung *f* monitor resolution
Monitorbild *n* monitor image; screen (display) image; cathode-ray tube picture
Monitorbildröhre *f* monitor display
Monitoreinstellung *f* 1. monitor setting; 2. *s.* Monitorkalibrierung
Monitorfenster *n* display window, [screen] window
Monitorfilm *m* radiation-monitoring film
Monitor-Fotodiode *f* monitor photodiode
Monitorkalibrierung *f* monitor calibration (alignment), color calibration
Monitorleistung *f* monitor performance
Monitorpixel *n* monitor (display) pixel, screen pixel
Monitorrauschen *n* monitor noise
Monitorweiß *n* monitor white
monochrom 1. monochrome, monotint, single-color[ed]; 2. *s.* monochromatisch 1.
Monochromabzug *m* monochrome print; black-and-white print
Monochromasie *f* monochromatism, monochromacy, monochromatic vision, complete color blindness
Monochromat *m* monochromat *(completely color-blind individual)*
monochromatisch 1. monochrom[at]ic; 2. *s.* monochrom 1.
Monochromatisierung *f* monochromatization
Monochromator *m* monochromator
~/**fokussierender** focusing monochromator
Monochrombild *n* monochrome [image], monochromatic (monotone) image; one-bit image *(s.a.* Schwarzweißbild*)*
Monochrombildröhre *f* monochrome picture tube, monochrome CRT (cathode-ray tube), bilevel (black-and-white) CRT
Monochrombildschirm *m* monochrome (black-and-white) screen; monochrome [graphics] display, bilevel display

Monochrombildverarbeitung f monochrome image processing
Monochromemulsion f monochrome emulsion
Monochromentwickler m monochrome developer
Monochromfilm m monochrome film
Monochromfilmmaterial n monochrome stock
Monochromgerät n monochrome device
Monochromie f monochromaticity
Monochromkamera f monochrome camera, black-and-white camera
Monochromlaser m monochromatic laser
monodispers monodisperse *(e.g. a photographic emulsion)*
Monoeinlauf m [/**konventioneller**] single-jet method *(emulsion preparation)*
monofon monophonic, monaural *(sound)*
Monokomparator m monocomparator *(remote sensing)*
monokular monocular, monoculous
Monom n monomial
Monometallplatte f monometal plate *(offset printing)*
Monomethyl-p-aminophenolsulfat n s. Methylaminophenolsulfat
Monomodefaser f monomode [optical] fiber, single-mode fiber
Monomodelaser m single-mode laser, single-frequency laser
Monomode-Stufenindexfaser f monomode step-index fiber
Mononom n s. Monom
Monopack n monopack, [integral] tripack, tripack color [negative] film
Monopuls-Sekundärradar n monopulse secondary surveillance radar, MSSR
Monoskop n monoscope
monoskopisch monoscopic
Monostativ n monopod, unipod
Monoton m monophonic (monaural) sound
Monotonfilm m monophonic movie
Monotonspur f mono (monaural) sound track
Montage f 1. stripping, [image] assembly, pasteup *(prepress operation)*; 2. [hard] mechanical, pasteup, [art]board; 3. s. Fotomontage; 4. s. Filmschnitt
~/**elektronische** electronic (soft) mechanical
Montagebogen m mounting board
Montagefolie f layout sheet
Montageschnitt m 1. assemble editing *(videography)*; 2. assemble edit
Montagetisch m lineup table *(prepress area)*
Montageunterlage f mounting board
Monte-Carlo-Methode f Monte Carlo method, Monte Carlo [computer] technique *(simulation)*
Monte-Carlo-Modell n Monte Carlo model

montieren to strip, to assemble *(prepress operation)*
Montierung f mount[ing] *(telescope)*
~/**altazimutale** altazimuth mounting
~/**äquatoriale** equatorial mounting
~/**deutsche** German [equatorial] mounting, Fraunhofer equatorial mounting
MOPA-Laser m MOPA (master oscillator power amplifier) laser
Morgenlicht n morning light
Morphing n [image] morphing, polymorphic tweening *(animation technique)*
Morphingeffekt m morphing animation effect
Morphingoperation f s. Morphing
Morphologie f morphology
~/**binäre** binary morphology
~/**mathematische** mathematical morphology
morphologisch morphological
Morphometrie f morphometry
morphometrisch morphometric
Mosaik n 1. mosaic, tessellation; 2. photomosaic *(set of aerial photographs)*
~/**dynamisches** dynamic mosaic
~/**kontrolliertes** controlled photomosaic
~/**statisches** static mosaic
Mosaikbild n mosaic [image]
Mosaikbildung f mosaic construction, mosaicking *(aerial mapping)*
~/**geometrische** geometric mosaicking
~/**radiometrische** radiometric mosaicking
Mosaikdrucker m [dot-]matrix printer
Mosaikeffekt m mosaicking *(digital pictorial effect)*
Mosaikfilter n mosaic filter
Mosaikfilterung f mosaic filtering
mosaikieren to mosaic
MOS-Diode f metal semiconductor diode
MOSFET s. Metalloxid-Feldeffekttransistor
MOS-Kondensator m MOS (metal oxide semiconductor) capacitor
~/**ladungsgekoppelter** charge-coupled MOS (metal-oxide semiconductor) capacitor
Mößbauer-Effekt m Mössbauer effect
Motion-Control-Kamera f motion control camera, MOCO camera
Motiv n 1. subject [matter]; motif; 2. s. Drehort
~/**fotografisches** photographic subject
~/**statisches** static subject
Motivbereich m subject area
Motivbewegung f subject motion
~ f subject motion
Motivdetail n subject detail
Motivdistanz f subject distance
Motivebene f subject plane
Motiventfernung f subject distance
Motivhelligkeit f subject (scene) brightness; subject luminance
Motivkontrast m object (subject) contrast

Motivlicht *n* light fro subject
Motivobjekt *n s.* Motiv
Motivstelle *f* subject area
Motivwahl *f* choice of subject
Motorantrieb *m* motor drive *(e.g. as battery-powered film transport)*
Motorzoomblitz *m* motorized-driven zoom flash head
Motorzoomobjektiv *n* motorized (power) zoom
Mottling *n s.* Wolkigkeit
Mouches volantes *pl s.* Mückensehen
MP-Band *n* metal particle tape
MPEG-Kompression *f* MPEG compression, MPEG [video] encoding, MPEG *(from Moving Pictures Experts Group)*
MPEG-Standard *m* MPEG standard *(for compressing image sequences)*
MR-... *s.* Magnetresonanz...
MRT-Bild *n* MR image; MR slice
Mückensehen *n* floaters
Multi-Access-Modul *n* multi-access module, MAM
Multiautomatik *f s.* Mehrfachautomatik
Multiblitzauslöser *m* flash sequencer
Multiblitzbuchse *f* multiple flash terminal
Multiblitzfotografie *f* multiflash photography
Multichipkamera *f* multichip camera
Multidetektor-Computertomografie *f* multidetector computed tomography
Multidetektorensystem *n* multidetector system
multifokal multifocal
Multiformatkamera *f* multiformat[ting] camera, video imager, hard copy unit *(esp. in medical imaging)*
Multifraktal *n* multifractal
Multifrequenzholografie *f* multifrequency holography
Multifrequenzmonitor *m* multisync monitor, multisync [display]
Multifunktionsdrucker *m*, **Multifunktionsgerät** *n* multifunction printer, all-in-one device
Multifunktionskarte *f* multifunction board
Multifunktionsmonitor *m* multifunction display, MFD
Multifunktionsradar *n* multifunction radar, MFR
Multikanalmagnetografie *f* multichannel magnetography
Multikristallkamera *f* multicrystal camera
Multimedia *n* multimedia, multiple media
~/**digitales** digital multimedia
~/**interaktives** interactive multimedia
~/**mobiles** mobile multimedia
~/**vernetztes** networked multimedia
Multimediaangebot *n* multimedia offering
Multimediaanwendung *f*, **Multimediaapplikation** *f* multimedia application
Multimediaarchiv *n* multiple media archive
Multimediabereich *m* multimedia field

Multimedia-Betriebssystem *n* multimedia operating system
Multimediacodierung *f* multimedia coding
Multimediacomputer *m* multimedia personal computer, multimedia (mixed-media) PC
Multimediadatei *f* multimedia [format] file, media file; multimedia database
Multimediadaten *pl* multimedia data
Multimediadatenbank *f* multimedia database
Multimediadesign *n* multimedia design
Multimediadesigner *m* multimedia designer (application developer)
Multimediadienst *m* multimedia service
Multimediadisplay *n* multimedia display
Multimediadokument *n* multimedia (mixed media) document
Multimediadrucker *m* multimedia printer
Multimedia-Endgerät *n* multimedia terminal
Multimediafernseher *m* multimedia television [set]
Multimediaformat *n* multimedia file format
Multimediagerät *n* multimedia device; multimedia receiver
Multimedia-Handy *n* multimedia [cell] phone, camera cell phone
Multimedia-Informationsabrufdienst *m* multimedia information retrieval service
Multimediainhalt *m* multimedia content
Multimediainstallation *f* media installation
Multimediakarte *f* multimedia card, MMC
Multimediakommunikation *f* multimedia communications
multimedial multimedia[-related], mixed-media
Multimediamaschine *f* multimedia machine
Multimediamaterial *n* multimedia material
Multimediamodus *m* multimedia mode
Multimedianetz *n* multimedia communications network
Multimediaobjekt *n* [multi]media object, mixed-mode object
Multimedia-PC *m s.* Multimediacomputer
Multimediapräsentation *f* multimedia[-based] presentation
Multimediaprodukt *n* multimedia product
Multimediaproduktion *f* multimedia production
Multimediaprogramm *n* multimedia program
Multimediaprojektor *m* beamer
Multimediaprozessor *m* media processor
Multimediaschau *f* multimedia slide show
Multimediaschnittstelle *f* multimedia interface
Multimediasektor *m* multimedia field
Multimedia-Server *m* multimedia server
Multimediasignalverarbeitung *f* multimedia signal processing
Multimediasoftware *f* multimedia software

Multimediastandard *m* multimedia standard
Multimediastudio *n* multimedia studio
Multimediasystem *n* multimedia [presentation] system
Multimediatechnik *f* multimedia technology; multimedia engineering
Multimedia-Terminal *n* multimedia terminal, DVB receiver
Multimediaübertragung *f*/**hoch[bit]ratige** high-rate multimedia transmission
Multimedia-Videoprozessor *m* multimedia video processor, MVP
multimodal multimodal
Multimodalität *f* multimodality
Multimodefaser *m* multimode [optical] fiber
Multimodelaser *m* multimode laser
Multimode-Stufenindexfaser *f* multimode step-index fiber
Multinormgerät *n* multistandard equipment
Multiphotonenspektroskopie *f* multiphoton spectroscopy
multiplanar multiplanar
Multiplex *n s.* 1. Multiplexkino; 2. Multiplexer; 3. Multiplexsignal
multiplex multiplex, multiple
Multiplexbetrieb *m* multiplex operation (mode)
Multiplexbildung *f* multiplexing
Multiplexeinrichtung *f* multiplexing equipment
multiplexen to multiplex, to combine multiple signals
Multiplexen *n*/**statistisches** statistical multiplexing, asynchronous time division multiplexing, ATDM
Multiplexer *m* multiplexer, multiplexor, mux
~/**optischer** optical multiplexer
~/**plesiochroner** plesiochronous multiplexer
Multiplexhierarchie *f* multiplexer hierarchy, hierarchy of multiplexing
Multiplexhologramm *n* multiplex hologram
Multiplexierung *f* multiplexing
Multiplexkino *n* multiplex [cinema], multiplex theater, cineplex
Multiplexsignal *n* multiplexed signal
Multiplexübertragung *f* multiplex transmission
Multiplexverfahren *n* multiplex[ing] technique, multiplexing method
Multiplier *m s.* Elektronenvervielfacher
Multiplikator *m*/**Lagrangescher** Lagrange multiplier, Lagrangean factor *(image restoration)*
Multipolarisationsradar *n* polarization diversity radar
Multiprogrammblitz *m* multi-program flash

Multiprojektor-Großbildsystem *n* multiprojector large-image system
Multiresolutions-Analysis *f* multiresolution analysis
Multiscan-Monitor *m* multisync monitor, multisync [display]
Multischalter *m* multiple switch, multiswitch *(satellite reception)*
Multisensoralverfahren *n* multisensoral method *(image merging)*
Multisensorverarbeitung *f* multisensor processing
multiskalar multiscalar
Multiskalenfilter *n* multiscale (multiorientation) filter, MOMS filter *(pattern recognition)*
multispektral multispectral
Multispektralanalyse *f* multispectral analysis
Multispektralaufnahme *f* multispectral data acquisition
Multispektralbild *n* multispectral (multichannel) image, multiband image; multispectral photograph
Multispektral-Fernerkundungsbild *n* remotely sensed multispectral image
Multispektralfotografie *f* 1. multispectral photography, MSP, multispectral imaging; 2. multispectral photograph
Multispektralkamera *f* multispectral (multiband) camera
Multispektralklassifizierung *f* multispectral classification
Multispektralscanner *m* multispectral scanner, multispectral scanning system
Multispektralsensor *m* multispectral sensor
Multitemporalverfahren *n* multitemporal method *(image merging)*
Multiträgermodulation *f* multicarrier modulation
Multiträgersignal *n* multicarrier signal
Multiträgerverfahren *n* multicarrier (multiple carrier) system
Multivisionsschau *f* multi-image slide-tape program
Munsell-Farbbaum *m* Munsell color tree
Munsell-Farbsystem *n*, **Munsell-System** *n* [**der Farbordnung**] Munsell [color-order] system, Munsell system of color notation, Munsell system of perceptual color measurement
Münzfotografie *f* coin photography
Münzkopierer *m* coin-operated copier
Museumsfotograf *m* museum photographer
Musikband *n* music track
Musikclip *m s.* Musikvideo
Musikspur *f* music track
Musikuntermalung *f* underscore *(s.a. Filmmusik)*
Musikvideo *n* music (pop) video
Muster *npl* [film] dailies, rushes *(cinema)*

Muster

~ *n* 1. pattern; template; 2. sample, specimen
~/**abstraktes** abstract pattern
~/**fraktales** fractal pattern
~/**gerichtetes** oriented pattern
~/**invariantes** invariant pattern
~/**isotropes** isotropic pattern
~/**konkretes** concrete pattern
~/**periodisches** periodic pattern
~/**räumliches** spatial pattern
~/**selbstähnliches** self-similar pattern
~/**skelettiertes** skeletonized pattern
~/**tieffrequentes** low-frequency pattern
~/**unterscheidbares** discernible pattern
~/**zelluläres** cellular pattern
Musterabgleich *m* pattern matching
Musterabtastung *f* pattern scanning
Musteranalyse *f* pattern analysis
~/**statistische** statistical pattern analysis
Musteranordnung *f* pattern arrangement
Musterassoziator *m* pattern associator
Musterbeschreibungssprache *f* pattern description language
Musterbibliothek *f* pattern library
Musterbild *n* sample image
Musterbildung *f* patterning
Musterblattkarte *f* standard form map *(photogrammetry)*
Musterdarstellung *f* pattern representation
Musterentdeckung *f s.* Mustererkennung
Musterergänzung *f* pattern completion
Mustererkennung *f* pattern recognition (identification)
~/**adaptive** adaptive pattern recognition
~/**automatische** automatic pattern recognition
~/**invariante** invariant pattern recognition
~/**kartografische** cartographic[al] pattern recognition
~/**konzeptionelle** conceptual pattern recognition
~/**modellbasierte** model-based pattern recognition
~/**numerische** numerical pattern recognition
~/**optische** optical pattern recognition
~/**statistische** statistical pattern recognition
~/**strukturelle** structural pattern recognition
~/**syntaktische** syntactic pattern recognition
~/**videobasierte** video-based pattern recognition
~/**wissensbasierte** knowledge-based pattern recognition
Mustererkennungsalgorithmus *m* pattern recognition algorithm
Mustererkennungsaufgabe *f* pattern recognition task
Mustererkennungsprogramm *n* pattern recognition software
Mustererkennungsroboter *m* pattern recognition robot

Mustererkennungssoftware *f* pattern recognition software
Mustererkennungssystem *n* pattern recognition system
Mustererkennungstechnik *f* 1. pattern recognition engineering; 2. pattern recognition technique
Mustererkennungsverfahren *n* pattern recognition technique (procedure)
Mustererzeugung *f* pattern generation
Musterfeld *n* texture map, texture (textural) image *(computer graphics)*
Mustergröße *f* pattern size
Musterklasse *f* pattern class
Musterklassenseparator *m* pattern class separator
Musterklassifikation *f* pattern classification
Musterklassifikator *m* pattern classifier *(s.a. under* Klassifikator*)*
Musterklassifizierung *f s.* Musterklassifikation
Musterkopie *f* one-light [print] *(motion-picture print)*
Mustermaske *f* template, prototype
Mustermorphologie *f* pattern morphology
Musterprimitiv *n* pattern primitive, morph
Musterprojektor *m* pattern projector
Musterpunkt *m* pattern point
Musterraum *m* pattern space
Musterreferenzpunkt *m* pattern [reference] point
Musterrekonstruktion *f* pattern reconstruction
Mustersegmentierung *f* pattern segmentation
Musterspektrum *n* pattern spectrum
Musterstruktur *f* pattern structure
Mustertabelle *f* pattern table
Musterteil *n* template *(object detection)*
Musterunterscheidbarkeit *f* pattern discriminability
Musterunterscheidung *f*/**visuelle** visual pattern discrimination
Mustervektor *m* pattern vector
Mustervergleich *m* pattern matching; template (matrix) matching, matched filtering *(pattern recognition)*
Musterverknüpfer *m* pattern associator
Musterverteilung *f* pattern distribution
Mustervervollständigung *f* pattern completion
Mustervorführung *f* dailies [screening]
Mustervorlage *f* template
Musterwiederauffindung *f* pattern retrieval
Musterzuordnung *f* pattern matching
Mutterplatine *f* [computer] motherboard, logic board, main computer circuit board
Mutter-Wavelet *n* mother wavelet, wavelet basis
Myelografie *f* myelography
Myokardperfusionsmessung *f* myocardial perfusion study *(single-photon emission-computed tomography)*

Myokardszintigrafie *f* myocardial perfusion imaging; myocardial infarct imaging
Myokardszintigramm *n* myocardial scintigram
myop myopic, nearsighted, shortsighted
Myopie *f* myopia, nearsightedness, short sight
M-Zapfen *m* M cone, middle-wavelength-sensitive cone *(retina)*

N

Nabla-Operator *m* gradient operator
nachabtasten to resample
Nachabtastung *f* resampling
Nachaufnahme *f* rerecording [session]; pickup [shot], retake *(s.a. Nachdreh)*
nachaufnehmen 1. to postrecord; to rerecord; to retake; 2. to rephotograph, to retake
Nachbar *m* neighbor
Nachbarbildpunkt *m s.* Nachbarpixel
Nachbarblock *m* adjacent block
Nachbareffekt *m* adjacency (edge) effect
Nachbarkanal *m* adjacent channel
Nachbarpixel *n* neighbor[ing] pixel, adjacent pixel (pel)
Nachbarpolygon *n* adjacent polygon
Nachbarschaft *f* neighborhood *(e.g. of pixels)*; adjacency *(topology)*
~/**einfache** single neighborhood
~/**konstante** constant neighborhood
~/**lokale** local neighborhood
~/**mehrfache** multiple neighborhood
~/**räumliche** spatial neighborhood
Nachbarschaftsalgorithmus *m* adjacency algorithm
Nachbarschaftsanalyse *f* neighborhood analysis
Nachbarschaftsfilter *n*/**adaptives** adaptive neighborhood filter
Nachbarschaftsfrage *f* nearest-neighbor query *(computer graphics)*
Nachbarschaftsgraph *m* neighborhood (adjacency) graph
~/**relativer** relative neighborhood graph, RNG
Nachbarschaftsoperation *f* neighborhood operation (process)
~/**globale** global neighborhood operation
~/**lokale** local neighborhood operation
Nachbarschaftsoperator *m* neighborhood operator
Nachbarschaftsrelation *f* neighborhood relation
Nachbarschaftsstruktur *f* neighborhood structure
nachbearbeiten to reprocess *(e.g. photographic materials)*; to postprocess, to reedit *(e.g. a film or video production)*
Nachbearbeitung *f* [video] editing, postproduction [work]; postprocessing [work]
Nachbearbeitungsalgorithmus *m* postprocessing algorithm
Nachbearbeitungseffekt *m* postproduction effect
Nachbearbeitungseinrichtung *f* [video] postproduction facility, editor
Nachbearbeitungsgerät *n* postproduction device
Nachbearbeitungskarte *f* [video] capture board
Nachbearbeitungsplatz *m* edit suite
Nachbearbeitungstrick *m* postproduction effect
Nachbehandlung *f* aftertreatment, posttreatment *(e.g. of negatives)*
nachbelichten to reexpose, to burn (print) in; to flash *(esp. cinematographic film)*
Nachbelichten *n*, **Nachbelichtung** *f* reexposure, postexposure; burning in; [post]flashing
Nachbild *n* [/**positives**] afterimage, persistent (residual) image
Nachbildung *f* emulation
Nachbildwirkung *f* persistence of vision [effect], vision persistence; afterimage effect
nachcodieren to re[en]code
Nachcodierung *f* reencoding
Nachdigestion *f s.* Nachreifung
Nachdreh *m* reshoot[ing], additional photography *(s.a. Nachaufnahme)*
nachdrehen to reshoot, to retake, to rephotograph
Nachdruck *m* reprint
~/**korrigierter (verbesserter)** makegood
nachdrucken to reprint
Nacheffekt *m* aftereffect *(vision)*
nachentwickeln to redevelop
Nachentwicklung *f* redevelopment
Nachentzerrung *f* de-emphasis, post-emphasis, postequalization *(frequency modulation)*
Nachfilter *n* postfilter
nachfiltern to postfilter
Nachfilterung *f* postfiltering
nachfixieren to refix
nachfokussieren to refocus
Nachfolgerbild *n* successive (consecutive) image, subsequent (past) picture
Nachführen *n*/**automatisches** autoguiding *(astrophotography)*
Nachführkamera *f* [/**automatische**] autoguider
Nachführkorrektur *f* guiding correction
Nachführung *f* guiding *(astrophotography)*; tracking *(radar)*
Nachfülllösung *f* replenisher
Nachhall *m* reverberation
Nachhallgerät *n* reverberator, echo unit
Nachhallzeit *f* reverberation time
nachjustieren to readjust
nachkopieren to reprint
Nachlauf *m* postroll
Nachlaufstreifen *m* tail[-cueing] leader *(motion-picture release print)*
Nachlaufzeit *f* post-roll [time]
Nachleuchtdauer *f* persistence [time], glow time; phosphor persistence *(e.g. of a television screen)*

Nachleuchten *n* afterglow, persistent luminescence, persistence, long-lived phosphorescence
Nachleuchtschleppe *f* target trail *(radar)*
Nachleuchtzeit *f s.* Nachleuchtdauer
nachmischen to remix
Nachmischung *f*/**additive (optische)** additive matching
Nachreifung *f* afterripening, digestion, chemical (second) ripening, chemical sensitization
Nachrichtennetz *n*/**Dienste integrierendes digitales** integrated services digital network, ISDN
Nachrichtensatellit *m* communication [technology] satellite, communications satellite
Nachrichtensendung *f* newscast, news broadcast
Nachrichtensignal *n* message (true) signal, useful (usable) signal, intelligence-bearing signal
Nachrichtentechnik *f* communication engineering
Nachrichtenvideo *n* news video
Nachschautabelle *f s.* Lookup-Tabelle
nachschneiden to recut *(a film)*; to reedit *(a videotape)*
Nachspann *m* 1. trailer; 2. end title; [end] credits, closing credits
Nachspannband *n* trailer tape
Nächster-Nachbar-Abstand *m* nearest-neighbor distance
Nächster-Nachbar-Filter *n* nearest-neighbor filter, Dirac (impulse) filter
Nächster-Nachbar-Interpolation *f* nearest-neighbor [gray-level] interpolation, zero-order interpolation, pixel replication *(image restoration)*
Nächster-Nachbar-Klassifikation *f* nearest-neighbor [pattern] classification
Nächster-Nachbar-Klassifikator *m* nearest-neighbor classifier
Nächster-Nachbar-Multikanalfilter *n* nearest-neighbor multichannel filter
Nächster-Nachbar-Problem *n* proximity (nearest-neighbor) problem
Nächster-Nachbar-Regel *f* nearest-neighbor [decision] rule, NNR
Nächster-Nachbar-Suche *f* nearest-neighbor search[ing]
Nachsynchronisation *f* postsynchronization, post-sync, resynchronization; automatic dialog[ue] replacement, ADR [editing], additional dialog[ue] recording, [dialogue] looping *(s.a.* Nachvertonung*)*
nachsynchronisieren to postsynch[ronize]; to resynchronize
Nacht *f*/**amerikanische** day-for-night [effect] *(film lighting)*
Nachtaufnahme *f* night shot (exposure); night photograph

Nachtaufnahmemodus *m* low-light mode *(camcorder)*
nachtblind nyctalopic
Nachtblinder *m* nyctalope
Nachtblindheit *f* night blindness, nyctalopia
Nachtfotografie *f* night photography
Nachtlicht *n* night light
Nachtporträtmodus *m* night portrait modus
Nachtrabant *m* postequalizing pulse *(composite video signal)*
Nachtsehen *n* night (dark-adapted) vision, scotopic (rod) vision
Nachtsichtaufnahme *f* night shot (exposure)
Nachtsichtbrille *f* night vision goggles
Nachtsichtfähigkeit *f s.* Nachtsehvermögen
Nachtsichtgerät *n* nightscope, night vision device (system)
Nachtsichtigkeit *f* scotopia
Nachtsichttechnik *f* night vision equipment
Nachtszene *f*, **Nachtszenerie** *f* night sequence *(cinema)*
Nachverarbeitung *f s.* Nachbearbeitung
nachvergrößern to reenlarge
Nachvergrößerung *f* reenlargement
nachvertonen to [post-]dub, to dub in, to postrecord; to rerecord
Nachvertonung *f* sound postproduction, [post-]dubbing, audio dubbing, post-]scoring, looping, rerecording *(s.a.* Nachsynchronisation*)*
~/**lippensynchrone** lip sync[hronization]
nachweisbar detectable
Nachweisbarkeit *f* detectability
Nachweisgrenze *f* detection limit
Nachweisvermögen *n* detectivity *(e.g. of photodetectors)*
Nachwickel[zahn]rolle *f*, **Nachwickler** *m* lower feed sprocket, holdback sprocket
Nachwirkungsbild *n* retained image *(television)*
nachzentrieren to recenter
Nachzieheffekt *m* 1. streak (lag) effect *(picture tube);* 2. *s.* Nachziehleuchtfahne
Nachziehen *n* **der Blende** pulling [the] aperture
Nachziehleuchtfahne *f* blooming effect, [image] blooming
Nadeldrucker *m* needle printer; [dot-]matrix printer
Nadelmatrixdrucker *m* [dot-]matrix printer
Nadelstrahl *m* pencil beam
Nadeltonverfahren *n* sound-on-disk recording *(cinema)*
Nadiraufnahme *f* nadir image *(aerophotogrammetry)*
Nahabstandspunkt *m* near point *(e.g. of a photographic lens)*

Nahaufnahme 278

Nahaufnahme *f* close-up [image], close-up photograph; close-up [shot], close shot *(cinema)*
~/extreme extreme close-up, ECU, XCU
Nahaufnahmegerät *n*,
Nahaufnahmekamera *f* close-up camera
Nahaufnahmezubehör *n* close-up accessories (equipment)
Nahbereich *m* close-up range *(of a lens)*
Nahbereichsfotografie *f s.* Nahfotografie
Nahbereichsfotogrammetrie *f* close-range (short-range) photogrammetry
Nahbereichsradar *n* short-range radar
Nahbildmessung *f s.* Nahbereichsfotogrammetrie
Nahe *f s.* Nahaufnahme
Nahechodämpfung *f* sensitivity time control, STC *(radar)*
Naheinstellgrenze *f* near focusing limit, closest (minimum) focusing distance, minimum focus
Naheinstellung *f* close focusing, close-up adjustment
~ auf Unendlich fixed (pan) focus arrangement, focus lock
Nahentfernung *f* near (close) distance
Näherung *f*/**paraxiale** paraxial approximation *(ray optics)*
Näherungsansatz *m* approximation approach
Näherungskurve *f* approximating curve (spline)
näherungsweise approximative
Nahfeld *n* near field *(Gaussian optics)*
Nahfeldabtastung *f* near-field scanning
Nahfeldbeugung *f* near-field diffraction, Fresnel diffraction
Nahfeldfokussierung *f* near-field focusing
Nahfeldholografie *f* [/**akustische**] near-field acoustic holography
Nahfeldhologramm *n* near-field hologram
Nahfeldmikroskop *n*/**optisches** scanning near-field optical microscope
Nahfeldmikroskopie *f*/**optische** scanning near-field optical microscopy, SNOM, near-field [scanning optical] microscopy
Nahfeldoptik *f* near-field optics
Nahfeld-Rastermikroskop *n*/**optisches** near-field optical scanning microscope, NFOSM
Nahfokus *m* close (near) focus
Nahfokussiergrenze *f s.* Naheinstellgrenze
Nahfokussierungsfähigkeit *f* close focusing ability
Nahfotograf *m* close-up photographer
Nahfotografie *f* near photography; close-up photography
Nahgerät *n s.* Nahaufnahmegerät
Nahgrenze *f s.* Naheinstellgrenze
Nahlinse *f s.* Nahvorsatz
Nahmessung *f* near-distance measurement
Nahporträt *n* close-up portrait
Nahpunkt *m* near point (limit) *(optics)*

Nahpunktabstand *m* near-point distance, distance of distinct vision
Nahsehen *n* near vision
Nah-Unendlich-Einstellung *f* close-up focusing at infinity
Nahunendlichpunkt *m* hyperfocal distance
Nahvorsatz *m*, **Nahvorsatzlinse** *f* close-up (close-range) attachment, close-up lens (filter), supplementary close-up lens, plus; portrait attachment lens
Nahzubehör *n s.* Nahaufnahmezubehör
Nanobildgebung *f* nano-scale imaging, nanoimaging
Nanodetektor *m* nanodetector
Nanoelektronik *f* nanoelectrics
Nanomechanik *f* nanomechanics
Nanometer *n(m)* nanometer, nm, millimicron
Nanooptik *f* nano-scale optics
Nanophotonik *f* nanophotonics
Nanosekunde *f* nanosecond, ns
nanoskopisch nanoscopic
Nanostruktur *f* nanostructure
Nanostrukturierungstechnologie *f* nano-structuring technology
Nanotechnik *f*, **Nanotechnologie** *f*, **Nanoverfahrenstechnik** *f* nanotechnology
Näpfchen *n s.* Rasternäpfchen
Naphtholkuppler *m* naphthol coupler
Nasenklammer *f* brace, curly bracket *(punctuation mark)*
Nassabtastung *f* wet-gate scanning
Nassätzen *n* wet dot-etching *(photomechanics)*; wet etching *(semiconductor processing)*
Nassbearbeitung *f* wet processing
Nassbereich *m* wet side *(darkroom)*
Nassbildplattenverfahren *n* [Archer's collodion] wet plate process
Nassentwicklung *f* wet development
Nassfensterkopierung *f s.* Nasskopierung
Nassfilm *m* wet film
Nassklebestelle *f* cement splice
Nasskollodiumkamera *f* wet-collodion camera
Nasskollodium-Stereokamera *f* wet-collodion stereograph camera
Nasskollodiumverfahren *n* wet-collodion process (photography)
Nasskopiereinrichtung *f* wet-gate printer
Nasskopierfenster *n* wet (liquid) gate
Nasskopiermaschine *f* wet-gate printer
Nasskopierung *f*, **Nasskopierverfahren** *n* wet-gate printing, liquid-gate [optical] printing, immersion printing
Nassplattenverfahren *n* wet-plate process
Nassreißfestigkeit *f* wet strength *(e.g. of photographic paper)*
Nassteil *m* wet side (equipment) *(darkroom)*
Nasstoner *m* liquid toner
Nasstonung *f* liquid toning

Nassverarbeitung *f* wet [film] processing, wet chemical processing
Nasszeit *f* wet time
Natrium *n*/**unterschwefligsaures** *s.* Natriumthiosulfat
Natriumacetat *n* sodium acetate
Natriumbisulfit *n s.* Natriumdisulfit
Natriumborat *n* sodium borate
Natriumcarbonat *n* sodium carbonate, soda *(developer improver)*
Natriumchlorid *n* sodium chloride, [common] salt
Natriumcitrat *n* sodium citrate
Natriumdampflampe *f* sodium [vapor] lamp, sodium arc lamp
Natriumdisulfit *n* sodium bisulfite *(fixer additive)*
Natriumdithionit *n* sodium dithionite
Natriumhochdrucklampe *f* high-pressure sodium lamp
Natriumhydroxid *n* sodium hydroxide, caustic [soda] *(developer constituent)*
Natriumhyposulfit *n s.* Natriumthiosulfat
Natriumiodidkristall *m* sodium iodide crystal, sodium iodide [scintillation] detector *(gamma camera)*
Natriumlicht *n*/**monochromatisches** monochromatic sodium light *(darkroom illumination)*
Natriummetabisulfit *n* sodium metabisulfite
Natriummetaborat *n* sodium metaborate *(developer additive)*
Natriummetaphosphat *n* sodium metaphosphate *(developer additive)*
Natriumniederdrucklampe *f* low-pressure sodium lamp
Natriumsulfat *n* sodium sulfate
Natriumsulfit *n* sodium sulfite *(developer additive)*
Natriumthiosulfat *n*, **Natron** *n*/**unterschwefligsaures** sodium thiosulfate, hypo[sulfite] *(fixing agent ,solvent)*
Naturfarbenbild *n* natural color image
Naturfarbenkamera *f* color camera
Naturfotograf *m* nature photographer
Naturfotografie *f* nature photography
Naturlicht *f* natural light
Naturpapier *n* fiber[-base] paper, uncoated (natural) paper; fiber-base[d] photographic paper
Navigation *f* navigation, wayfinding
~/**bildgestützte** image-based navigation
Navigationshilfe *f* navigational aid *(e.g. radar)*
Navigationsradar *n* navigation radar
Navigationssystem *n*/**chirurgisches** surgical navigational system
Navigationswerkzeug *n* navigational tool
navigieren 1. to navigate; 2. to scroll *(computer)*
NC-Schicht *f* noncurl[ing] coat[ing], noncurl backing *(of a film base)*
NCS-Modell *n* natural color system, NCS *(color order system)*
ND-Filter *n s.* Neutraldichtefilter
Nd-Glaslaser *m*, **Nd-Laser** *m* Nd (neodymium) glass laser, Nd laser
Nebel *m*/**atmosphärischer** atmospheric fog
Nebeleffektfilter *n* fog (diffusing) filter, [frosted] diffusion filter
Nebelfilter *n* 1. nebular filter *(astrophotography)*; 2. *s.* Nebeleffektfilter
Nebelkammer *f* cloud chamber
Nebelleinwand *f* fog screen
Nebelmaschine *f* fog machine
Nebelpunkt *m* blur spot (point) *(human vision)*
Nebenabsorption *f* subsidiary (unwanted) absorption
Nebenbild *n* phantom (ghost) image
Nebendichte *f s.* Nebenfarbdichte
Nebeneinanderstellung *f* juxtaposition
Nebengeräusch *n* ambient noise
Nebenkeule *f* side lobe *(ultrasound imaging, radar)*
~/**sekundäre** grating lobe
Nebenkeulenaustastung *f* side lobe cancellation (blanking)
Nebenkeulenecho *n* side [lobe] echo
Nebenkeulenpegel *m* side lobe level
Nebenkeulenunterdrückung *f* **auf dem Empfangsweg** receiving-path side lobe suppression
Nebenlicht *n* spill (unwanted) light
Nebenmaximum *n* secondary maximum *(diffractive optics)*
Nebensprechen *n* cross talk
Nebenzipfel *m s.* Nebenkeule
Negativ *n* 1. [photographic] negative, negative photograph; 2. *s.* Negativfilm 1. *and* 2.
~/**abgeschwächtes** low-density range negative, mask *(reprography)*
~/**dünnes** thin (light) negative
~/**fotografisches** photographic negative
~/**geschnittenes** edited camera negative
~/**kombiniertes** conformed (combined) negative *(cinema)*
Negativ-Ablageblatt *n* negative [storage] sheet
Negativabziehen *n* negative cut[ting] *(cinema)*
Negativbericht *m* camera exposure chart, camera report (sheet), dope sheet *(cinema)*
Negativbild *n* negative image *(s.a. under* Negativ*)*
Negativbühne *f* negative stage (carrier), film holder *(enlarger)*
Negativcutter *m* negative cutter
Negativdichte *f* negative (fog) density
Negativemulsion *f* negative[-working] emulsion
Negativentwickler *m* negative developer

Negativentwicklung

Negativentwicklung f negative development
Negativ-Farbfotografie f negative color photography
Negativfehler m negative defect
Negativfilm m 1. negative[-acting] film, film negative, nonreversal film: 2. picture negative *(cinema)*
Negativfixierer m negative fixer
Negativformat n negative size
Negativ-Fußnummer f [latent] edge number, negative (key) number, footage number *(motion-picture film)*
Negativhalter m negative holder (carrier) *(e.g. of an enlarger)*
Negativhülle f s. Negativtasche
Negativkontrast m negative contrast
Negativkontrastierung f negative staining *(electron microscopy)*
Negativkopie f printing (copy) negative
Negativkopiermaterial n negative printing material
Negativlack m negative[working] photoresist
Negativ-Lichtbestimmung f negative timing (grading) *(motion-picture printing)*
Negativlinse f negative (concave) lens, diverging (dispersive) lens
Negativmaterial n negative [photographic] material, negative-type material, negative stock; negative footage (film material)
Negativmodulation f negative [sense of] modulation *(television)*
Negativmontage f negative cut[ting] *(cinema)*
Negativ-Negativ-Verfahren n negative-to-negative process *(color photography)*
Negativokular n negative eyepiece, Huygenian [microscope] eyepiece
Negativordner m negative file binder
Negativpapier n negative[-working] paper
Negativperforation f negative perf[oration], BH (Bell and Howell) barrel-shaped perforation *(motion-picture film)*
Negativplatte f negative plate, [glass-]plate negative, glass[-plate] negative
Negativ-Positiv-Material n negative-positive material
Negativ-Positiv-Umschaltung f luminance reversal *(digital video processing)*
Negativ-Positiv-Verfahren n negative-positive [photographic] process, negative-positive color process
Negativprozess m negative-working process *(photography)*
Negativretusche f negative retouching
Negativ-Rohfilmmaterial n negative raw stock
Negativscanner m negative scanner
Negativschnitt m negative cut[ting] *(cinema)*
Negativschnittliste f [film] negative cut list

280

Negativschramme f negative scratch
Negativschwärzung f negative density
Negativstreifentasche f negative sleeve
Negativtasche f negative filing page, negative [storage] sheet, negative pocket
Negativtechnik f negative technique
Negativträger m negative carrier
Negativverarbeitung f negative processing
Negativverfahren n negative-working process *(photography)*
Negaton n s. Negatron
Negatron n negatron, electron *(s.a. under Elektron)*
Neger m 1. cue (idiot) card; 2. gobo, flag
neigbar tiltable
Neigekopf m tilt top; pan[-and]-tilt head *(camera stand)*
~/**motorgetriebener** power pan and tilt
neigen to tilt
Neigung f inclination, bias
Neigungswinkel m inclination angle
nematisch nematic *(liquid crystal)*
Neocognitron n neocognitron *(pattern recognition)*
Neodym[ium]laser m neodymium-type laser
Neodym-YAG-Laser m neodymium in yttrium-aluminum garnet laser, Nd:YAG laser
Neonlampe f neon [glow] lamp
Neonlicht n neon [light]
Nephrografie f nephrography
Nephrogramm n nephrogram
Nervenknoten m [nerve] ganglion; nucleus
Nervenzelle f nerve (neural) cell, neuron[e] *(s.a. Neuron)*
Nettobitrate f net bit rate
Nettomagnetisierung f net magnetization *(magnetic resonance imaging)*
Netz n 1. net[work] *(communication)*; 2. s. Gitternetz
~/**autoassoziatives neuronales** autoassociative neural network, AANN *(pattern recognition)*
~/**einschichtiges neuronales** single-layer neural network
~/**hausinternes** s. ~/lokales
~/**hierarchisches neuronales** hierarchical neural network
~/**kabelloses** wireless network
~/**kabelloses lokales** wireless local area network, wireless LAN, WLAN
~/**künstliches neuronales** artificial neural network, ANN
~/**leitungsvermitteltes** circuit-switched network *(video transmission)*
~/**lokales** local area network, LAN *(of personal computers)*
~/**mehrschichtiges künstliches neuronales** multilayer artificial neural network
~/**morphologisch organisiertes** s. ~/räumlich organisiertes

Neuron

~/**multimediales** multimedia communications network
~/**neuronales** neural net[work], neuromorphic system, connectionist (parallel distributed processing) model, connectionist network
~/**polygonales** polygonal net[work], polygon[al] mesh, polymesh
~/**räumlich organisiertes** topological mesh
~/**schmalbandiges** low-bandwidth network
~/**selbstorganisierendes neuronales** self-organizing neural network
~/**semantisches** semantic network *(graph data structure)*
~/**topologisch organisiertes** topological mesh
~/**vorwärtsgekoppeltes** feedforward network
~/**zellulares neuronales** cellular neural network, CNN
Netzadapter *m* [AC/DC] mains adapter
Netzätzung *f* 1. autotypy; 2. autotype *(copy)*
Netzbandbreite *f* network bandwidth
Netzbetreiber *m* network operator
Netzbrumm *m*, **Netzbrummen** *n* [power-]line hum
Netzdiagramm *n* trellis diagram
Netzentwurf *m* map coordinates
Netzfrequenz *f* power line frequency
Netzgerät *n* [AC/DC] mains adapter
Netzgitterraster *m(n)* reticle, [measurement] graticule
Netzhaut *f* retina *(of the eye)*
~/**periphere** peripheral retina
~/**zentrale** s. Fleck/gelber
Netzhautabbildung *f* retinal imaging
Netzhautareal *n* retinal area
Netzhautarterie *f* [/**zentrale**] central retinal artery
Netzhautbeleuchtungsstärke *f* retinal illuminance
Netzhautbereich *m* retinal area
Netzhautbild *n* retinal image
Netzhautbildgröße *f* retinal image size
Netzhautbildqualität *f* retinal image quality
Netzhautdensitometrie *f* retinal densitometry
Netzhautebene *f* retinal plane
Netzhautexzentrizität *f* retinal eccentricity
Netzhaut-Ganglienzelle *f* retinal ganglion [cell]
Netzhautgrube *f* [retinal] fovea, fovea centralis
~/**innere** center of the fovea
Netzhautkamera *f* fundus (ophthalmic) camera, retinal camera
Netzhautnervenzelle *f*, **Netzhautneuron** *n* retinal neuron
Netzhautoberfläche *f* retina[l] surface
Netzhautort *m* retinal locus (location)
Netzhautperipherie *f* retinal periphery

Netzhautpigment *n* retinal pigment
Netzhautpigmentepithel *n* retinal pigment epithelium
Netzhautprojektion *f* retinal projection
Netzhautrand *m* retinal periphery
Netzhautrezeptor *m* retinal photoreceptor, retinal [sensory] receptor, retinal sensor
Netzhautrivalität *f* retinal rivalry (disparity)
Netzhautscanner *m* retinal scanner; retinal pattern detector
Netzhautstäbchen *n* retinal (optic) rod, rhabdom[e]
Netzhautstelle *f* retinal locus (location), retinal position
Netzhautzäpfchen *n*, **Netzhautzapfen** *m* [retinal] cone, visual cone, cone [photo]receptor
Netzknoten *m* network node
Netzladeadapter *m* s. Netzstromadapter
Netzmittel *n* surfactant, wetting (surface-active) agent, spreading agent
Netzmodell *n* net model, wire frame [model] *(computer graphics)*
Netzschnittstelle *f* network interface; telecommunication interface
Netzstromadapter *m* [AC/DC] mains adapter
Netztasche *f* mesh pocket *(e.g. in a camera case)*
Netzteil *n* s. Netzgerät
Netzübertragung *f* network transmission
Netzwerk *n* network *(s.a. under Netz)*
Netzwerkanbindung *f* network access
Netzwerkarchitektur *f* network architecture
~/**neuronale** neural-net architecture
Netzwerkbetreiber *m* network operator
Netzwerkdrucker *m* network (remote) printer
Netzwerkeinbindung *f* s. Netzwerkanbindung
netzwerkfähig networkable
Netzwerkfähigkeit *f* networkability
Netzwerkrechner *m* network computer
Netzwerkschnittstelle *f* s. Netzschnittstelle
Netzwerktopologie *f* network topology, topology of networks
Neuabtastung *f* resampling
Neuaufzeichnung *f* rerecording
Neubebilderung *f* reimaging *(e.g. of a printing drum)*
Neubespielung *f* rerecording
Neukomprimierung *f* s. Rekompression
Neunspurband *n* nine-track tape
Neuroangiografie *f* neuroangiography
Neurochirurgie *f*/**bildgeführte** image-guided neurosurgery
Neurocomputer *m* neural computer
Neuroinformatik *f* neuroinformatics
Neuron *n* neuron, neurone, nerve (neural) cell
~/**bewegungserkennendes** motion-detecting neuron

~/**binokulares** binocular cell *(visual system)*
~/**formales** s. ~/künstliches
~/**künstliches** artificial neuron
~/**retinales** retinal ganglion cell
Neuronennetz *n* s. Netz/neuronales
Neurophysiologie *f* neurophysiology
neurophysiologisch neurophysiologic[al]
Neusatz *m* resetting *(typed matter)*
Neusynchronisation *f*, **Neusynchronisierung** *f* resynchronization *(s.a. Nachsynchronisation)*
Neutraldichte *f* neutral density
Neutraldichtefilter *n* neutral[-density] filter, [neutral-]gray filter, ND filter
Neutraldichte-Verlauffilter *n* neutral density graduated filter
Neutralfilter *n* s. Neutraldichtefilter
Neutralfilterung *f* neutral-density filtration
Neutralglas *n* neutral glass
neutralgrau neutral gray
Neutralgraufilter *n* s. Neutraldichtefilter
Neutralgraukeil *m* neutral-gray wedge *(sensitometry)*
Neutralisation *f* neutralization
Neutralisator *m* neutralizer
neutralschwarz neutral black
Neutralteilerschicht *f* neutral beam splitting coating
Neutralton *m* neutral tone
neutralweiß neutral white
Neutrino *n* neutrino
Neutrinospektroskopie *f* neutrino spectroscopy
Neutrinoteleskop *n* neutrino telescope
Neutron *n* neutron, nucleon
Neutronenabsorption *f* neutron absorption
Neutronenaktivierungsautoradiografie *f* neutron activation autoradiography, NAAR
Neutronenbeugung *f* neutron diffraction
Neutronenradiografie *f* neutron radiography
neutronenradiografisch neutron radiographic
Neutronenradiogramm *n* neutron radiograph (radiographic image)
Neutronenstrahl *m* neutron beam
Neutronenszintillator *m* neutron scintillator
Neutronentomografie *f* neutron tomography
neutronentomografisch neutron tomographic
Neutronentomogramm *n* neutron tomogram
Newton-Ringe *mpl* Newton's rings *(interference pattern)*
Newton-Sucher *m* Newton finder
Newton-Teleskop *n* Newtonian telescope (reflector)
NHS-Verfahren *n* s. Nichthalogensilberverfahren

Nibble *n* nibble
nichtaktinisch nonactinic *(radiation)*
nichtbelichtet nonexposed, unexposed
Nichtbildpartie *f*, **Nichtbildstelle** *f* nonimage [surface] area *(printing)*
nichtdruckbar nonprintable
nichtdruckend nonprinting
Nichtechtzeit *f* nonreal time
nichterkennbar unrecognizable
Nichthalogensilberverfahren *n* nonsilver process
Nicht-Kontakt-Rasterkraftmikroskopie *f* non-contrast atomic force microscopy, NC-AFM
Nichtkopierer *m* noncircled take, B neg *(film editing)*
nichtleuchtend nonluminous
nichtlinear nonlinear
Nichtlinearität *f* non-linearity
nichtlöschbar nonerasable
nichtmetrisch nonmetric
nichtparametrisch nonparametric
Nichtsehen *n* ano[o]psia
nichtselbstleuchtend non-self-luminous
Nichtselbstleuchter *m* non-self-luminous source (surface)
nichtspiegelnd nonspecular
Nichtstationarität *f* nonstationarity
Nichttemperaturstrahler *m* luminescent (selective) radiator
nichttransparent opaque
Nichtvertiefung *f* land *(compact disk)*
Nickel-Cadmium-Batterie *f* nickel-cadmium battery, NiCad (nicad) battery
Nickel-Metallhydrid-Akku[mulator] *m* nickel metal hydride battery
Nickelodeon *n* nickelodeon, juke-box *(early cinematography)*
Nickradar *n* nodding-beam radar
Nicol[-Prisma] *n* Nicol [prism]
niederbitratig low-bit-rate
Niederdruck[gas]entladungslampe *f* low-pressure [gas] discharge lamp
Niederdrucklampe *f* low-pressure lamp
niederempfindlich slow[-speed] *(film material)*
niederfrequent low-frequency
Niederkontrastauflösung *f* low-contrast resolution, LCR
Niederleistungsdetektor *m* low-power detector
Niederleistungs[röntgen]röhre *f* low-power [X-ray] tube
Niederschlagsradar *n* precipitation radar
Niedervoltlampe *f* low-voltage lamp
Niedervoltscheinwerfer *m* beam projector
niedrigbrechend low-index *(optical glass)*
niedrigempfindlich slow[-speed] *(film material)*
Nierenbeckenaufnahme *f* pyelography
Nierenbeckendurchleuchtung *f* pyelofluoroscopy

Nierencharakteristik f hypercardioid polar pattern *(of a microphone)*
Nierenmikrofon n cardioid microphone
Nierenröntgendarstellung f 1. nephrography; 2. nephrogram
Ni-MH-Akku m s. Nickel-Metallhydrid-Akku[mulator]
Nipkow-Scheibe f, **Nipkow-Spirallochscheibe** f Nipkow disk *(e.g. as a mechanical television scanner)*
Nit n nit, candela per square meter *(SI unit of luminance)*
Nitratcellulose f nitrocellulose, cellulose nitrate *(film base)*
Nitratfilm m s. Nitrofilm
Nitrocellulose f s. Nitratcellulose
Nitrofilm m [cellulose] nitrate film, nitrate-based film
Niveaulinie f s. Höhenlinie
Nivellierfernrohr n leveling telescope
Nivellierinstrument n leveling instrument
Nivellierlibelle f spirit level (bubble)
NMR s. Resonanz/kernmagnetische
NMR-Fourier-Zeugmatografie f zeugmatography
NMR-Spektroskopie f NMR (nuclear magnetic resonance) spectroscopy
NMR-Tomografie f [nuclear] magnetic resonance imaging, MR imaging, MRI
Nodalpunkt m, **Nodus** m nodal (node) point, Gauss point *(optics)*
Nomarski-Mikroskop n Nomarski [interference] microscope
Nomarski-Mikroskopie f Nomarski [interference] microscopy, differential interference contrast microscopy, DIC microscopy
Nominalempfindlichkeit f s. Nennempfindlichkeit
Nomogramm n nomogram, nomograph
Nonius m vernier
Nonius-Sehschärfe f vernier acuity, [visual] hyperacuity
Nonpareille f nonpareil *(size of type)*
NOR n/**exklusives** exclusive NOR *(computer logic circuit)*
Norm f/**Euklidische** Euclidean norm (metric) *(of a vector)*
normal normal *(paper grade)*
Normal... s.a. under Standard...
Normalbelichtung f normal exposure
Normalbeobachter m normal [human] observer, standard (average) observer
~ **1964**/**farbmetrischer** CIE 1964 supplementary standard colorimetric observer, 10° observer
~/**farbmetrischer** standard colorimetric observer, color normal observer
~/**fotometrischer** standard photometric observer, standard [human] observer
Normalbrennweite f normal (standard) focal length
Normaldispersion f normal dispersion
Normale f normal *(a unit vector)*
Normalempfindlichkeit f average sensitivity *(e.g. of photographic material)*
Normalentwickler m standard (ordinary) developer, general-purpose developer
Normalentwicklung f normal development
Normalenvektor m normal vector *(computer graphics)*
Normalfarbfilm m normal color film
Normalfarbfoto n normal color photograph
Normalfarbsichtiger m normal trichromat
Normalfarbsichtigkeit f normal color vision
Normalfilm m 1. normal (conventional) film, plain photographic film; 2. s. ~/kinematografischer
~/**kinematografischer** 35-mm cine film, standard 35-mm film
Normalfilmformat n academy format
Normalfilmverarbeitung f normal film processing
Normalfotografie f ordinary (standard) photography, normal photography; general[-purpose] photography
normalisieren to normalize
Normalisierung f normalization
Normalkontrast m normal contrast
Normallicht n normal (ordinary) light
Normallösung f normal solution
Normalobjektiv n standard objective; normal[-type] lens, normal design lens; ordinary (normal) camera lens, standard [photographic] lens
Normalpapier n plain (standard) paper, normal (ordinary) paper
Normalpapierkopierer m plain-paper copier
Normalperspektive f normal perspective
Normalprojektion f orthographic (orthogonal) projection, [orthographic] parallel projection
normalsichtig emmetropic
Normalsichtiger m emmetrope
Normalsichtigkeit f emmetropia, normal (corrected) vision
Normalsynchronisation f normal sync[hronization]
Normalton m standard tone
Normalvektor m s. Normalenvektor
Normalvergrößerung f normal magnification *(microscopy)*
Normalverteilung f [/**Gaußsche**] normal [frequency] distribution, Gaussian distribution
Normalwinkelkamera f, **Normalwinkelkammer** f normal-angle camera *(photogrammetry)*
Normalzoom[objektiv] n standard zoom; mid-range zoom
Normenwandler m standards converter; standards conversion equipment
Normenwandlung f standards conversion
Normfarbbalken m standard color bar

Normfarbbalkenfolge *f*,
Normfarbbalkenvorlage *f* color bar waveform (test signal); color bar test pattern
Normfarbe *f* standard color
Normfarbraum *m* standard color space
Normfarbtafel *f* standard chromaticity diagram
Normfarbwert *m* chromaticity value; CIE tristimulus value *(colorimetry)*
Normfarbwertanteil *m* chromaticity
Normfarbwerttafel *f s.* Normfarbtafel
normieren to normalize
Normierung *f* normalization
Normierungsfaktor *m* normalization factor, normalizing constant
Normierungsmatrix *f* normalization matrix
Normierungstransformation *f* normalization transformation
Normlichtart *f* standard[ized] illuminant, standard source of illumination, standard [light] source
Normsehweite *f* normal viewing distance
Normspektralfarbe *f* primary color, [monochromatic] primary, basis (basic) color *(colorimetry)*
Normspektralwertfunktion *f*,
Normspektralwertkurve *f* standardized color-matching function; CIE color-matching function
Normstartband *n* countdown [cueing] leader, [head] leader
Normvalenz *f s.* Normfarbwert
Normweiß *n*, **Normweißwert** *m* reference white [color]
Normzelle *f s.* Voxel
Notebook *n* notebook [computer] *(portable microcomputer)*
Notenanhang *m* back (end) matter *(layout)*
NRZI-Code *m* NRZI (non-return-zero-inverse) code
NRZ-Signal *n* NRZ (non-return-to-zero) signal
NTSC-Fernsehen *n* NTSC video *(derived from National Television Standards Committee)*
NTSC-Norm *f* NTSC standard
NTSC-Verfahren *n* NTSC process *(color television)*
Nuance *f* nuance, shade
Nudel *f* noodle, emulsion shred
Nuklearmedizin *f* nuclear medicine, nuc med
nuklearmedizinisch nuclear medical, nuclear-medicine
Nukleon *n* nucleon, proton; hydrogen nucleus
Nuklid *n*/**strahlendes** radionuclide, unstable nuclide
Nulldensitometer *n* null densitometer
Nulldurchgang *m* zero crossing
Nulldurchgangsoperator *m* zero-phase filter, phase-preserving filter
Nullebene *f* zero plane

Nullenunterdrückung *f* zero suppression
Nullfrequenz *f* zero (null) frequency
Nullkopie *f* first [trial] print, check (grading) print, [first] answer print, trial composite print, approval print *(cinema)*
Nullmatrix *f* null matrix
Nullode *f* nullode, electrodeless tube
Nullparallaxe *f* zero parallax
Nullpunktabfall *m* low-frequency drop, LFD *(modulation transfer function)*
Nullpunktsteilheit *f* zero crossover *(photodiode)*
Nullsetzen *n* setting to zero, zeroing *(e.g. a gradient)*
Nullstelle *f* zero, zeroth place *(transfer function)*
Nullvektor *m* zero vector
NURBS-Kurve *f* nonuniform rational B-spline, NURBS *(computer graphics)*
Nurlesespeicher *m* read-only [electronic] memory, ROM
~/**elektrisch löschbarer** electrically erasable programmable read-only memory, EEPROM
~/**löschbarer programmierbarer** erasable programmable read-only memory, EPROM, reprogrammable read-only memory, RPROM
~/**programmierbarer** programmable read-only memory, PROM
nuten *s.* rillen
Nutzbitrate *f* net bit rate
Nutzdaten *pl* useful data
Nutzdatenrate *f* data stream payload, useful data rate
Nutzen *m s.* Drucknutzen
Nutzerermittlung *f* user tracking
Nutzer-Netz-Schnittstelle *f* user [network] interface, consumer interface
Nutzinformation *f* useful information
Nutzlichtstrom *m* effective luminous flux
Nutzsignal *n* useful (usable) signal, message (true) signal, intelligence-bearing signal
Nyktalopie *f* nyctalopia, night blindness
Nyquist-Abtastung *f* Nyquist sampling
Nyquist-Bandbegrenzung *f* Nyquist band limit
Nyquist-Bandbreite *f* Nyquist bandwidth
Nyquist-Bedingung *f* Nyquist condition
Nyquist-Bereich *m* Nyquist [sample] spacing
Nyquist-Filter *n* Nyquist filter
Nyquist-Flanke *f* Nyquist slope
Nyquist-Frequenz *f* Nyquist frequency (rate)
Nyquist-Grenze *f* Nyquist [frequency] limit
Nyquist-Intervall *n* Nyquist interval
Nyquist-Kriterium *n* Nyquist['s] criterion, Nyquist sampling criterion
Nyquist-Punkt *m* Nyquist sample
Nyquist-Rate *f* Nyquist rate (frequency)
Nyquist-Rauschen *n s.* Johnson-Rauschen

Nyquist-Theorem *n* Nyquist [sampling] theorem, Nyquist rule
Nyquist-Wellenzahl *f* Nyquist frequency
nystagmisch nystagmic
Nystagmus *m* nystagmus [movement], ocular tremor
~/**optokinetischer** optokinetic nystagmus
~/**physiologischer** physiological nystagmus

O

Oberbeleuchter *m* chief lighting technician, [chief set] electrician, gaffer *(cinema)*; lighting supervisor (director) *(esp. in computer graphics)*
Oberfläche *f* surface *(s.a. under Fläche)*; surface area
~/**blendarme** antiglare surface
~/**brechende** refracting surface
~/**deformierbare** deformable surface
~/**ebene** planar surface
~/**facettierte** faceted surface
~/**gekrümmte** curved surface
~/**glänzende** glossy (shiny) surface
~/**hochglänzende** high-gloss surface
~/**Lambertsche** Lambertian surface (source), ideal diffuse surface *(photometry)*
~/**matte** dull surface
~/**nichtplanare** nonplanar surface
~/**optische** optical surface
~/**planare** planar surface
~/**spiegelnd reflektierende, Oberfläche/spiegelnde** specular surface
~/**streuende** scattering surface
~/**vollkommen matte** perfect (ideal isotropic) diffuser *(colorimetry)*
Oberflächenanalyse *f* surface analysis
Oberflächenbeschreibung *f* surface description
Oberflächendarstellung *f* [/**computergrafische**] 1. surface rendering; 2. surface rendition
~/**szenenbasierte** scene-based surface rendering
~/**voxelbasierte** voxel-based surface rendering
Oberflächendetektion *f* surface detection
Oberflächendurchdringungsradar *n* ground-penetration radar, GPR, surface-penetration radar, SPR, subsurface radar, georadar
Oberflächenebenheit *f* surface flatness
Oberflächeneinzelheit *f* surface detail
Oberflächenelektronenmikroskop *n* surface electron microscope
Oberflächenelement *n* surface element
Oberflächenentwickler *m* surface developer
Oberflächenentwicklung *f* surface development
Oberflächenfarbe *f* surface (object) color, subject (body) color
Oberflächenfehler *m* surface defect
Oberflächenform *f* surface shape
Oberflächengeometrie *f* surface geometry
Oberflächengitter *n* surface mesh
Oberflächenglanz *m* [surface] sheen, surface shininess, [surface] luster
Oberflächenglattheit *f* surface smoothness
Oberflächengradient *m* surface gradient
Oberflächenhelligkeit *f* surface brightness
Oberflächenkeim *m* surface development center
Oberflächenkrümmung *f* surface curvature
Oberflächenladung *f* surface charge *(electrophotography)*
Oberflächenladungsdichte *f* surface charge density
Oberflächenmodell *n* surface model
~/**deformierbares** deformable surface model
~/**digitales** digital surface model
Oberflächenmodellierung *f* surface modeling
Oberflächennormale *f* surface normal
Oberflächennormalenschätzung *f* surface normal estimation
Oberflächennormalenvektor *m* surface normal vector
Oberflächenorientierung *f* surface orientation
Oberflächenprimitiv *n* surface primitive
Oberflächenprofil *n* surface contour (profile) *(s.a. Tiefenbild)*
Oberflächenprüfung *f* surface inspection
Oberflächenpunkt *m* surface point *(computer graphics)*
Oberflächenrauh[ig]keit *f* surface roughness
Oberflächenreflexion *f* surface reflection
Oberflächenrekonstruktion *f* surface reconstruction
Oberflächenrelief *n* surface relief
Oberflächenrepräsentation *f s.* Oberflächendarstellung
Oberflächenschattierung *f* surface shading
Oberflächensegment *n* surface segment
Oberflächensegmentierung *f* surface segmentation
Oberflächenspiegel *m* front-surface[d] mirror, first-surface[d] mirror
Oberflächenspule *f* surface (local) coil *(magnetic resonance imaging)*
Oberflächenstreuung *f* surface scattering
Oberflächenstruktur *f* surface structure
Oberflächentextur *f* surface texture
Oberflächentopografie *f* surface topography
oberflächenverspiegelt surface-silvered *(mirror)*
Oberflächenverspiegelung *f* front-surface coating
Oberflächenwelle *f* surface wave
~/**akustische** surface acoustic wave, acoustic surface wave
Oberflächenwellenausbreitung *f* surface-wave propagation
Oberflächenwellenfilter *n* surface acoustic wave filter

Oberflächenwellenradar n surface wave radar, SWR
Oberguss m topcoat, top [emulsion] layer, supercoat, overcoat *(photographic material)*
Oberkante f top edge
Oberklasse f super class
Oberlänge f 1. ascender *(letterform)*; 2. ascender height
Oberlicht n 1. top light[ing]; 2. scoop *(floodlight)*
Oberseite f top side
Obersicht f direct viewing
~/**extreme** bird's-eye view
Obertischröhre f overtable [X-ray] tube
Oberwelle f/**harmonische** harmonic oscillation
Objekt n object *(e.g. in image analysis)*; sample, specimen *(microscopy)*
~/**abgeschattetes** shadowed object
~/**beliebiges** arbitrary object
~/**beugendes** diffracting object
~/**binäres** binary object
~/**digitales** digital object
~/**diskretes** discrete object
~/**farbcodiertes** color-coded object
~/**flächenhaftes** planar (plane) object
~/**flexibles** flexible object
~/**fraktales** fractal [object]
~/**geometrisches** geometric[al] object
~/**grafisches** graphical object; glyph *(visualization)*
~/**hierarchisches** hierarchic[al] object
~/**interessierendes** object of interest
~/**lichtschwaches** low-luminance subject
~/**mehrdimensionales** multidimensional object
~/**mikroskopisches** microscopic[al] object, microscope specimen
~/**räumliches** volumetric (solid) object
~/**relationales** relational object
~/**rotationssymmetrisches** rotationally symmetric object
~/**schattiertes** shadowed object
~/**selbstähnliches** self-similar object
~/**selbstleuchtendes** self-luminous object
~/**skaliertes** scaled object
~/**starres** rigid object
~/**statisches** static object
~/**strukturloses** primitive
~/**unscharfes** fuzzy object
~/**verformbares** deformable (soft) object
~/**virtuelles** virtual object
~/**visuelles** visual object
~/**visuelles** visual object
~/**voxelbasiertes** voxel-based object
~/**zusammengesetztes** aggregate object
~/**zweidimensionales** two-dimensional object
Objektabstand m object (subject) distance, object conjugate
Objektabtaster m object scanner
Objektabtastung f object scanning
Objektauflösung f object resolution

Objektausleuchtung f object illumination; specimen illumination
Objektausrichtung f object orientation
Objektbeleuchtung f subject lighting
Objektbereich m object region
Objektbeschreibung f object description
Objektbewegung f object motion (movement), subject motion (movement)
Objektbild n object image; specimen image *(microscopy)*
Objekt-Bild-Abstand m object-[to-]image distance, total conjugate distance, track length
Objektbrennpunkt m first focal point
Objekt-Clipping n object clipping *(computer graphics)*
Objektcodierung f object coding
Objektdarstellung f object representation
Objektdarstellungstechnik f object representation technique
Objektdetail n object (subject) detail; specimen detail *(microscopy)*
~/**kleines** fine detail
Objektdetektion f s. Objekterkennung
Objektdistanz f s. 1. Objektweite; 2. Objektentfernung
Objektdynamik f s. Objektumfang
Objektebene f object (subject) plane; sample (specimen) plane *(microscopy)*
Objektentfernung f object distance
Objekterkennbarkeit f object detectability
Objekterkennung f [visual] object recognition, object detection
~/**bildbasierte** image-based object recognition
~/**modellbasierte** model-based object recognition
~/**strukturbasierte** structure-based object recognition
Objektextraktion f object extraction
Objektfarbe f object (subject) color, body (surface) color
Objektfarbwert m subject color value
Objektfeinheit f s. Ortsfrequenz
Objektfeld n object field
Objektfeldblende f object field stop
Objektfeldwinkel m object field angle
Objekt-Film-Abstand m object-[to-]film distance
Objektfläche f object area
Objektform f object shape
Objektformanalyse f object shape analysis
Objektfotografie f object photography
Objektfrequenz f object frequency
Objektgeometrie f object geometry
Objektgeschwindigkeit f object speed
Objektgrafik f s. Vektorgrafik 1.
Objektgrenze f object boundary
Objektgröße f object (subject) size
Objekthauptpunkt m front principal point
Objekthelligkeit f object brightness
Objekthierarchie f object hierarchy
Objekthöhe f object height
Objektidentifikation f object identification

Objektidentifikator *m* object identifier; media object identifier, MOID
Objektisolierung *f* object isolation
Objektiv *n* [compound] lens ; objective *(esp. of a microscope or telescope)*
~/**achromatisches** achromatic objective (lens), achromatic system, achromat [objective]
~/**afokales** afocal lens
~/**anamorphotisches** anamorphic [squeeze] lens, distorting (squeeze) lens, anamorphote [lens], anamorphic optics (system)
~/**anastigmatisches** anastigmatic lens, anastigmat
~/**apochromatisches** apochromatic lens (objective), apochromat [objective]
~/**asphärisches** aspherical [photographic] lens
~/**asymmetrisches** unsymmetrical (asymmetrical) lens
~/**auswechselbares** interchangeable lens, detachable lens
~/**beugungsbegrenztes** diffraction-limited lens
~/**bilderzeugendes** imaging (picture-taking) lens
~/**dreilinsiges** [optical lens] triplet; triplet objective; [photographic] triplet lens
~/**farb[fehler]korrigiertes** chromatically corrected objective, color-corrected lens, achromatic lens
~/**festbrennweitiges** fixed-focus lens, fixed-focal-length lens, prime lens
~/**fotografisches** photographic objective (lens)
~/**fotolithografisches** photolithographic lens
~/**hochauflösendes** high-resolution lens
~/**hochkorrigiertes** highly corrected lens (objective)
~/**hochlichtstarkes** high-speed lens
~/**ideal korrigiertes** fully corrected lens
~/**infrarotkorrigiertes** infrared optics
~/**innenfokussiertes** internal focusing objective
~/**katadioptrisches** catadioptric lens, catadioptric [imaging] system, mirror (reflecting) lens
~/**kinematografisches** cinematograph lens
~/**korrigiertes** corrected lens
~/**kurzbrennweitiges** short-focus lens, short-focal-length lens
~/**langbrennweitiges** long-focus lens, long-focal-length lens
~/**längerbrennweitiges** longer focal-length lens
~/**lichtschwaches** low-power lens (objective), slow lens; low-numerical-aperture objective
~/**lichtstarkes** fast (powerful) lens, high-aperture lens, high-power objective, high-numerical-aperture objective
~/**mehrgliedriges** multiple-component lens
~/**mehrlinsiges** multielement (complex) lens, composite lens (objective), compound lens
~/**mehrschichtenvergütetes** multicoated lens
~/**mikrofotografisches** photomicrographic objective (lens)
~ **mit unendlicher Brennweite** infinity-corrected objective *(microscope)*
~/**normalbrennweitiges** normal-focus lens, normal-focal-length lens
~/**pankratisches** pancratic [lens] system, varifocal (vario) lens, variable-focal-length lens, zoom [lens]
~/**plankorrigiertes** plan-corrected objective
~/**quasisymmetrisches** quasi-symmetrical lens
~/**scharfzeichnendes** sharp-focus lens, high-definition lens
~/**schmalwinkliges** narrow-angle lens *(s.a. Teleobjektiv)*
~/**spannungsfreies** strain-free objective (lens)
~/**sphärisch korrigiertes** spherically corrected objective, spherical (flat) lens
~/**symmetrisches** symmetrical lens (objective)
~/**telezentrisches** telecentric lens
~/**ultralichtstarkes** ultrafast (ultrarapid) lens
~/**unkorrigiertes** uncorrected lens
~/**unsymmetrisches** unsymmetrical (asymmetrical) lens
~/**variofokales** variable-focal-length lens, varifocal (vario) lens, zoom [lens]
~/**verzeichnungsfreies** orthoscopic (distortion-free) lens, aberration-free lens, perfect lens
~/**viellinsiges** *s.* ~/mehrlinsiges
~/**viergliedriges** four-element lens
~/**wechselbares** *s.* ~/auswechselbares
~/**zweiteiliges** doublet lens system, two-part compound lens
Objektivabdeckung *f* front lens cap; lens cover
Objektivachse *f* lens axis, axis of a lens
Objektivadapter *m* lens adapter; body mount adapter
Objektivanschluss *m* lens mount
Objektivanschlussgewinde *n* objective [screw] thread
Objektivapertur *f* [lens] aperture, lens opening
~ **numerische** numerical objective aperture
Objektivaufbau *m* objective (lens) design
Objektivauflösung *f*, **Objektivauflösungsvermögen** *n* lens resolution
Objektivausführung *f* objective (lens) design

Objektivauszug *m* lens extension
Objektivbau *m* 1. lens manufacture; 2. lens configuration
Objektivbeutel *m* soft lens pouch
Objektivblende *f* lens diaphragm; lens (objective) aperture
Objektivblendenring *m* aperture (iris) ring, diaphragm control (setting) ring
Objektivbrennweite *f* lens [focal] length, lens focus, focal length [of the objective]
Objektivdeckel *m* lens cap
Objektivdeckelhalter *m* cap keeper
Objektivdurchmesser *m* lens diameter
Objektivebene *f* lens plane
Objektiveinstellung *f* lens setting
Objektiveintrittspupille *f* lens entrance pupil
Objektivelement *n* lens element
Objektiventriegelung[staste] *f* lens release button
Objektivfassung *f* lens mount
Objektivfehler *m* lens artifact
Objektiv-Film-Abstand *m* lens-to-film spacing (distance)
Objektivfilter *n* lens filter; camera lens filter
Objektivfilterung *f* lens filtration
Objektivfrontlinse *f* objective front lens
Objektivglied *n* lens element
Objektivhalter *m* lens mount
Objektivhalterung *f* bayonet
Objektivhersteller *m* lens producer
Objektivherstellung *f* lens manufacture
Objektivkappe *f* [front] lens cap
Objektivköcher *m* lens case
Objektivkompatibilität *f* lens compatibility
Objektivkompendium *n* compendium hood, matte box
Objektivkonstrukteur *m* lens designer
Objektivkonstruktion *f* lens design
Objektivlänge *f* lens length
Objektivleistung *f* lens performance
Objektivlichtstärke *f* lens speed, light gathering power [of a lens]
Objektivlichtweg *m* lens path
Objektivlinse *f* objective lens
Objektivmikroprozessor *m* lens microprocessor
Objektivöffnung *f* lens opening, [lens] aperture
Objektivparameter *m* lens parameter
Objektivpinsel *m* lens brush
~ **mit Blasebalg (Gummiball)** blower brush
Objektivplatine *f* lens stage *(enlarger)*
Objektivprisma *n* objective prism
Objektivprüfung *f* lens testing
Objektivqualität *f* lens quality
Objektivreihe *f* lens set (line)
Objektivreinigungspapier *n* lens cleaning tisse
Objektivreinigungstuch *n* lens cleaning cloth
Objektivrevolver *m* [lens] turret; revolving nosepiece *(microscopy)*

Objektivring *m* lens ring
Objektivrückdeckel *m* rear lens cap
Objektivsatz *m* lens set, set of lenses
Objektivschnittweite *f* vertex [focal] length [of a lens]
Objektivschutz *m* lens guard
Objektivschutzdeckel *m*,
Objektivschutzkappe *f* lens cap
Objektivstandarte *f* [front] lens standard, front [camera] standard *(view camera)*
Objektivstutzen *m s.* Objektivtubus
Objektivsystem *n* lens system
Objektivträger *m* lens stage; lens board
Objektivtubus *m* lens barrel (housing); objective barrel
Objektivtyp[us] *m* lens type
Objektivvergrößerung *f* objective magnification
Objektivvergütung *f* lens coating
Objektivverschluss *m* [inter]lens shutter, between[-the]-lens shutter; diaphragm (aperture) shutter
Objektivverschlusskamera *f* lens-shutter camera
Objektivverschwenkung *f* lens plane swing
Objektivverzeichnung *f* lens distortion; camera lens distortion
Objektivvorsatz *m* lens attachment (extender)
Objektivwahl *f* lens selection (choice)
Objektivwechsel *m* change of the objective
Objektivwechseleinrichtung *f* objective changer
Objektivwechselsystem *n* lens-changing system
Objektivwerkzeug *n* lens tool
Objektivwinkel *m* lens angle
Objektiv-Zonenplatte *f* objective zone plate *(scanning microscope)*
Objektivzubehör *n* lens accessories
Objektivzusatz *m s.* Objektivvorsatz
Objektkante *f* object edge
Objektklasse *f* object class (category), class of objects
Objektklassifikation *f* object classification
~/**iterative** iterative object classification
Objektkonstanz *f* object constancy
Objektkontrast *m* object (subject) contrast; specimen contrast *(microscopy)*
Objektkontur *f* object contour
Objektkonturverfolgung *f* object contour tracking
Objektkoordinatensystem *n* object (local) coordinate system, modeling coordinate system, local (object) space
Objektkreisdurchmesser *m* object circle diameter *(of a lens)*
Objektlage *f* object position
Objektleuchtdichte *f* object (subject) luminance

Objektlokalisation *f*, **Objektlokalisierung** *f* object loca[liza]tion
Objektluminanz *f* object luminance
Objektmenge/potentiell sichtbare potentially visible set, PVS *(computer graphics)*
Objektmerkmal *n* object feature (characteristic)
Objektmessung *f* reflected-light metering, reflected-light meter reading
Objektmikrometer *n* stage (object) micrometer
Objektmodell *n* object model *(computer vision; s.a. under Modell)*
~/**geometrisches** geometric[al] object model
Objektmodellierung *f* object modeling
Objektmodellierungssystem *n* object modeling system
Objektmodulation *f* object modulation
Objektmuster *n* object pattern
Objektoberfläche *f* object (subject) surface
Objektorientierung *f* object orientation
Objektort *m* object (subject) location *(optics)*
Objektpixel *n* object pixel
Objektpixelgruppe *f* blob
Objektposition *f* object position
Objektpunkt *m* object point; specimen point *(microscopy)*
~/**außeraxialer** off-axis object point
Objektrand *m* object boundary
Objektranderkennung *f* object boundary detection
Objektraum *m* object (subject) space; specimen space *(s.a. Objektkoordinatensystem)*
Objektraumalgorithmus *m* object-space algorithm
Objektraumfilterung *f* object-space filtering
Objektreflexion *f* object reflectance
Objektrekonstruktion *f* object reconstruction
Objektschärfe *f* specimen sharpness *(microscopy)*
Objektschicht *f* slice
Objektschwerpunkt *m* centroid
Objektsegmentierung *f* object segmentation
Objektseite *f* object side *(e.g. of a lens)*
objektseitig object-side
Objektsignatur *f* object signature *(image analysis)*
Objektstrahl *m* object beam *(holography)*
Objektstruktur *f* object structure
Objektsystem *n* object system
Objektszene *f* object scene
Objektteil *n(m)* subject part
Objekttisch *m* [specimen] stage, sample (microscope) stage
Objektträger *m* microscope (specimen) slide, subject slide
Objekttrennung *f* object segregation

Objektumfang *m* luminance ratio, contrast range
Objektumgebung *f* bounding volume *(computer graphics)*
Objektriss *m* object outline
Objektunterscheidung *f* object discrimination
Objektverdeckung *f* object occlusion
Objektvereinfachungsalgorithmus *m* object simplification algorithm
Objektverfolgung *f* [object] tracking *(computer vision)*; [target] tracking *(image sequence coding)*
Objektvergrößerung *f* object magnification
Objektverschiebung *f* object displacement
Objektverteilung *f* object radiance *(radiometry)*
Objektvisualisierung *f* object visualization
Objektwahrnehmung *f* object perception
Objektweite *f* object (subject) distance, object conjugate
Objektweitenverhältnis *n* ratio of object distances
Objektwelle *f* object (original) wave, object (subject) beam *(holography)*
Objektzugehörigkeit *f* objectness *(of pixel or voxel in image analysis)*
Objektzuordnung *f* object location
Observatorium *n* observatory
ODER *n* [/**logisches**] OR *(logical operator)*
ODER-Gatter *n* OR gate
Oesophagoskop *n* esophagoscope
Off *n* off-camera
Off-axis-Hologramm *n* off-axis hologram
Offenblenden-Innenmessung *f* TTL full-aperture exposure metering [system]
Offenblendenmessung *f* full-aperture exposure metering [system] *(SLR camera)*
Offenblitz *m*, **Offenblitzmethode** *f* open-flash [procedure]
Offline-Schnitt *m* offline (nonlinear) editing *(video)*
Offline-Schnittsystem *n* [digital] offline media composer
Öffnen *n* [/**morphologisches**] *n* opening; opening operation *(morphological image processing)*
Öffnung *f*/**maximale** maximum (full) aperture, largest aperture
~/**relative** s. Öffnungsverhältnis
~/**wirksame** effective [lens] aperture, entrance pupil
Öffnungsblende *f* aperture stop (diaphragm), aperture vignette, mask
Öffnungsfehler *m* spherical aberration, SA
~ **der Pupille** pupil aberration
Öffnungsverhältnis *n* aperture (focal) ratio, relative aperture, [diaphragm] f-number, F number, aperture number, stop [number] *(of an objective)*
~/**effektives** effective f-number

Öffnungswinkel *m* aperture angle, angular aperture *(optics)*; opening angle, angle of opening *(e.g. of a shutter)*
Öffnungszahl *f s.* Öffnungsverhältnis
Offset-Abtastung *f*/**vertikal-zeitliche** *s.* Zeilensprungabtastung
Offsetdruck *m* 1. offset printing process, offset lithography, litho-offset; 2. offset print
~/**wasserloser** waterless lithography, dry (letterpress) offset, letterset, indirect letterpress [printing]
Offsetdrucker *m* offset printer
Offsetdruckerei *f* offset print shop
Offsetdruckfarbe *f* offset ink
Offsetdruckmaschine *f* offset [printing] machine, offset [lithographic] press
Offsetdruckpapier *n* offset paper
Offsetdruckplatte *f* offset [printing] plate, lithographic [printing] plate
~/**gerasterte** screened offset plate
Offsetdruckplattenherstellung *f* offset plate making
Offsetdruckverfahren *n* offset [printing] process
Offseterzeugnis *n* offset product
Offsetherstellung *f* offset production
Offsetlithografie *f s.* Offsetdruck
Offsetmaschine *f s.* Offsetdruckmaschine
Offsetpapier *n* offset paper
Offset-Prinzip *n* offset principle
Offsetraster *m(n)* litho[graphic] screen
Offsetrollendruckmaschine *f*, **Offsetrotations[druck]maschine** *f* web offset press, rotary web-fed offset machine, offset rotary
Offsetvervielfältiger *m* offset duplicating machine, duplicator
Ohm *n* ohm *(basic unit of electric resistance)*
Ohrspiegel *m* otoscope
Ohrspiegelung *f* otoscopy
Okklusion *f* occlusion, interposition; overlap
Okklusionsbereich *m* occluded region
Oktagonbaum *m*, **Oktalbaum** *m* octree *(data structure)*
Oktalsystem *n* octal numbering system, base 8
Oktalziffer *f* octal digit
Oktant *m* octant
Oktav *n* octavo *(printing sheet)*
Oktavbandanalyse *f*, **Oktavbandzerlegung** *f* octave[-band] analysis
Oktavbogen *m s.* Oktav
Oktett *n* 1. octet; 2. *s.* Byte
Oktettregel *f*, **Oktetttheorie** *f* octet theory
okular ocular
Okular *n* ocular, eyepiece, eyeglass
~/**Huygenssches** Huygenian [microscope] eyepiece, negative eyepiece
~/**kurzbrennweitiges** short-focus eyepiece
~/**monozentrisches** monocentric eyepiece
~/**orthoskopisches** orthoscopic eyepiece
~/**symmetrisches** symmetrical (Plössl) eyepiece
~/**terrestrisches** terrestrial eyepiece
~/**zusammengesetztes** compound eyepiece
Okularadapter *m* eyepiece adapter
Okularauszug *m* eyepiece draw tube, eyetube
Okularblende *f* eyepiece diaphragm *(microscope)*
Okularbrennweite *f* focal length of the eyepiece
Okularfilter *n* eyepiece (ocular) filter
Okularkamera *f* eyepiece (microscope) camera *(photomicrography)*
Okularlinse *f* eyepiece (ocular) lens
Okularmikrometer *n* eyepiece micrometer, eyepiece (ocular) measuring graticule
Okularobjektiv *n* eyepiece optics
Okularprojektion *f* eyepiece projection
Okularrevolver *m* nosepiece turret, rotating nosepiece *(microscope)*
Okularskale *f* eyepiece scale (graticule)
Okulartubus *m* eyetube, eyepiece housing *(microscope)*
Okularvergrößerung *f* eyepiece magnification
okulomotorisch oculomotor
ölabweisend *s.* oleophob
Öldruck *m* oil printing process
oleophil oleophilic, oil-receptive, grease-receptive; ink-receptive
oleophob oleophobic, oil-repellent, grease-repellent; ink-repellent
Ölimmersionsmikroskopie *f* oil immersion microscopy
Ölimmersionsobjektiv *n*, **Ölimmersionsoptik** *f* oil-immersion objective (optics)
Ölkuppler *m* oil-protected coupler, fat-tail coupler
Online-Formular *n* electronic form, e-form
Online-Schnitt *m* on-line editing, linear [video] editing
Online-Speicher *m* on-line memory
Online-Speicherung *f* on-line storage
opak opaque; lightproof
Opaleszenz *f* opalescence
opaleszieren to opalesce
Opalglas *n* opal glass; milk glass
Opalglaslampe *f* opal [filament] lamp
opalisieren *s.* opaleszieren
Opallampe *f s.* Opalglaslampe
Opazität *f* opacity, opaqueness
Opening *n*, **Opening-Operation** *f s.* Öffnen
Operateur *m* [camera] operator
Operation *f* operation
~/**Boolesche** Boolean [logic] operation, spatial set operation *(modeling technique)*
~/**einstellige** point operation, gray-level modification *(pixel processing)*
~/**geometrische** geometrical operation

Operation

~/**globale** global operation
~/**ikonische** iconic operation
~/**lineare** linear (kernel) operation
~/**logische** logical operation
~/**lokale** local operation
~/**mengentheoretische** set-theoretic operation
~/**morphologische** morphological operation
~/**pixelweise** pixel-by-pixel operation
~/**topologische** topological operation
Operationsmikroskop *n* operating microscope
Operationsverstärker *m* operational amplifier, op-amp *(signal processing)*
Operativspeicher *m* operating memory
Operator *m* operator *(s.a. Filter)*
~/**arithmetischer** arithmetic operator
~/**aufbereitender** *s.* ~/extrahierender
~/**bildpunktbezogener** pixel-related operator
~/**Boolescher** Boolean (logical) operator
~/**dualer** dual operator
~/**dyadischer** dyadic operator
~/**geometrischer** geometric operator
~/**globaler** global operator
~/**kontextabhängiger** context-dependent operator
~/**linearer** linear operator
~/**logischer** *s.* ~/Boolescher
~/**lokaler** local operator, mask, kernel *(gray-scale image processing)*
~/**monotoner** monotonic operator
~/**morphologischer** morphological operator (filter)
~/**nichtlinearer** nonlinear operator
~/**optimaler** optimal operator
~/**pseudoinverser** pseudoinverse operator
~/**skalarer** scalar operator
~/**translationsinvarianter** translation-invariant (shift-invariant) operator
Operatorfenster *n* operator window; filter window
Operatorkern *m* operator (filter) kernel *(gray-scale image processing)*
Opernglas *n* opera glass[es]
ophthalmisch ophthalmic
Ophthalmologie *f* ophthalmology
Ophthalmometer *n* ophthalmometer, keratometer *(eye testing apparatus)*
Ophthalmoskop *n* ophthalmoscope
Ophthalmoskopie *f* ophthalmoscopy
ophthalmoskopisch ophthalmoscopic
Opsin *n* opsin *(protein)*
Optik *f* 1. optics *(science of light)*; 2. optic[s], optical system (components)
~/**abbildende** imaging optic[s]
~/**adaptive** adaptive optics
~/**aktive** active optics *(telescope control)*
~/**anamorphotische** anamorphic optics (system), anamorphic [squeeze] lens, distorting (squeeze) lens, anamorphote [lens]

~/**angewandte** applied optics
~/**astronomische** astronomical optics
~/**astrophysikalische** astrophysical optics
~/**binäre** binary optics
~ **des Paraxialgebietes** *s.* ~/Gaußsche
~/**diffraktive** diffractive optics
~/**elektromagnetische** electromagnetic optics
~ **erster Ordnung** *s.* ~/Gaußsche
~/**fliegende** moving (flying) optics
~/**fotografische** photographic optics, photooptics
~/**Gaußsche** Gaussian [beam] optics, paraxial [geometric] optics, first-order [geometric] optics
~/**geometrische** geometric[al] optics, ray optics
~/**holografische** holographic optics
~/**integrierte** integrated optics
~/**klassische** classical optics
~/**kohärente** coherent optics
~/**lineare** linear optics
~/**nichtlineare** nonlinear optics
~/**paraxiale** *s.* ~/Gaußsche
~/**physikalische** physical optics, [scalar] wave optics
~/**physiologische** physiological optics
~/**refraktive** refractive optics
~/**selbstkorrigierende** adaptive optics
~/**spektroskopische** spectroscopic optics
~/**statistische** statistical optics
~/**technische** technical optics
Optiker *m* optician
Optikhalter *m* optical mount
~/**kardanischer** gimbal [optical] mount
~/**kinematischer** kinematic [optical] mount
Optikhersteller *m* lens producer
Optikkomponente *f* optical component
Optikkonstrukteur *m* lens designer
Optikkonstruktion *f* optical design
Optiklabor *n* optics laboratory
Optikmodellierer *m* lens designer
Optikmodul *n* optical module
Optikrechnen *n* optical calculation[s]
Optikrechnung *f* optical computation (calculation)
Optikteil *n* optical component
Optikus *m* *s.* Sehnerv
Optikvergütung *f* optical coating
Optimalfarbe *f* [**Schrödingersche**] optimum color; optimal color [stimulus] *(colorimetry)*
Optimalfilter *n* optimum (optimal) filter, optimal morphological operator *(image restoration)*
~/**Wienersches** Wiener[-matrix] filter, least (minimum means) square error filter *(image restoration)*
Optimalfilterung *f* optimal (optimum) filtering
optimieren to optimize
Optimierung *f* optimization
Optimierungsalgorithmus *m* optimization algorithm

optisch optic *(relating to eye or vision);* optical *(relating to optics or vision)*
Optische-Bank-Kamera *f* monorail [view] camera
Optoelektronik *f* optoelectronics, optronics
optoelektronisch optoelectronic
Optohalbleiter *m* opto[electronic] semiconductor
optokinetisch optokinetic
Optokoppler *m* optocoupler, optoisolator
optomechanisch optical-mechanical, optomechanical
Optometer *n* optometer
Optometrie *f* optometry
optometrisch optometric[al]
Optosensor *m* optical (light) sensor, photosensor
Optotechnik *f* optical technology
Optotypen *pl* optotypes *(e.g. of a Snellen test chart)*
Optronik *f* optronics, optoelectronics
Orangefarbstich *m* orange cast (bias)
Orangefilter *n* orange filter
Orbita *f* orbit, eye socket, eyehole
Orbital *n(m)* orbital
Orbitalfernsehen *n s.* Satellitenfernsehen
Ordinatenachse *f* y-axis, vertical axis *(coordinate system)*
Organdarstellung *f*/**bildliche** organ imaging
Orientierbarkeit *f* orientability
orientieren to orient
Orientierung *f* orientation
~/lokale local orientation
Orientierungsdetektion *f* orientation (direction) detection
Orientierungskontrast *m* orientation (diffraction) contrast *(electron microscopy)*
Orientierungsvektor *m* orientation vector
Orientierungsverfolger *m* head tracker *(virtual reality)*
Original *n* original; master
Originalabzug *m* original print; vintage [photographic] print
Originalaufnahme *f* 1. photographic original, original photograph; original shot; 2. *s.* Originalaufzeichnung
Originalaufzeichnung *f* original recording
~ *f*/**ungeschnittene** master original
Originalband *n* source tape *(s.a.* Masterband*)*
Originalbild *n* original image
Originalbilddaten *pl* original image data
Original-Bildnegativ *n* color reversal intermediate (internegative), CRI
Originaldrehort *m* original (actual) location, real location
Originaleinzug *m*/**automatischer** automatic document feeder, ADF
Originalfarbe *f* original color
Originalfarbfoto *n* original color photograph

Originalfilm *m* original [film]; master film *(printing)*
Originalfilmbild *n* original motion-picture image
Originalfilmmaterial *n* original [film] footage
Originalfoto *n* original photograph, photographic original
Originalgeräusch *n* presence, ambience, aura, room tone
Original-Hochdruckplatte *f* [/**fotomechanische**] original photoengraving *(letterpress)*
Original-Kamerafilmmaterial *n* camera-original footage
Originalkopie *f* original copy
Originalnegativ *n* original negative [film], negative original; original camera negative, OCN, camera [original] negative
~/geschnittenes edited camera negative
~/ungeschnittenes uncut original negative
Originalpunkt *m s.* Objektpunkt
Originalschauplatz *m s.* Originaldrehort
Originalsendung *f* live broadcast
Originalsignal *n* original signal
Originalszene *f* original scene; live action *(filming)*
Originalton *m* original [production] sound, production (direct) sound
Originaltonaufnahme *f* production sound recording, onset [sound] recording, [on-]location recording
Originaltonfilmaufnahme *f* original sync-sound production recording
Originalumkehrfilm *m* reversal [original] film, reversal camera film
Originalvergrößerung *f* vintage [photographic] print
Originalvorlage *f* original copy
ortbar locatable
orten to locate, to position
Orthikon *n* orthicon *(a camera tube)*
Orthobild *n* ortho image *(photogrammetry);* orthoscopic image
Orthochromasie *f* orthochromatism
orthochromatisch orthochromatic, isochromatic; ortho[chromatic], [blue-and-]green-sensitive *(photographic material)*
Orthodiagrafie *f* orthodiagram *(radiography)*
Orthofilm *m* ortho[chromatic] film, correct-color film
Orthofoto *n* orthophotograph
Orthofotoelement *n* orthophoto element
Orthofotografie *f* orthophotography
Orthofotokarte *f* orthophoto map
Orthofotomosaik *n* orthophoto mosaic
orthogonal orthogonal; perpendicular
Orthogonalfilter *n* orthogonal filter
Orthogonalität *f* orthogonality
Orthogonalitätsbedingung *f* orthogonality condition

Orthogonalitätsprinzip *n* orthogonality principle
Orthogonalprojektion *f* orthographic (orthogonal) projection, [orthographic] parallel projection
Orthonormalität *f* orthonormality
orthopanchromatisch orthopanchromatic
Orthophenylendiamin *n* orthophenylenediamine *(developer substance)*
Orthoprojektorsystem *n* orthoprojector system *(photogrammetry)*
Orthorektifizierung *f* orthorectification, orthocorrection
Orthoröntgenografie *f s.* Orthodiagrafie
Orthoskop *n* orthoscope *(optics)*
Orthoskopie *f* orthoscopy
orthoskopisch orthoscopic
Ortsauflösung *f* spatial (positional) resolution
Ortsbereich *m* spatial (space) domain
Ortsbereichsbild *n* spatial-domain image
Ortsbereichsdarstellung *f* spatial[-domain] representation *(e.g. of image signals)*
Ortsbereichsfaltung *f* spatial-domain convolution
Ortsbereichsfilter *n* spatial-domain filter (operator), space-domain filter
Ortsbereichsfrequenz *f* spatial-domain frequency
Ortsbereichsnachbarschaft *f* spatial-domain neighborhood
Ortscodierung *f* spatial coding
ortsdiskret discrete-space, spatially discrete *(e.g. signals)*
Ortsdiskretisierung *f* spatial discretization
Ortsfrequenz *f* spatial frequency
ortsfrequenzabhängig spatial-frequency-dependent
Ortsfrequenzabhängigkeit *f* spatial-frequency dependence
Ortsfrequenzachse *f* spatial-frequency axis
Ortsfrequenzanalyse *f* spatial-frequency analysis
Ortsfrequenzauflösung *f s.* Ortsauflösung
Ortsfrequenzbereich *m* spatial-frequency domain; spatial-frequency range
Ortsfrequenzbild *n* spatial-frequency pattern
Ortsfrequenzdarstellung *f* spatial-frequency [domain] representation
Ortsfrequenzfilter *n* spatial[-frequency] filter
Ortsfrequenzfilterung *f* spatial[-frequency] filtering, spatial filtration
Ortsfrequenzgang *m* spatial-frequency response, SFR, normalized optical transfer function
Ortsfrequenzgehalt *m* spatial-frequency content
Ortsfrequenzkanal *m* spatial-frequency channel
Ortsfrequenzkoordinate *f* spatial-frequency coordinate
Ortsfrequenzquantisierung *f* space-frequency quantization
Ortsfrequenzraum *m* [spatial-]frequency domain, transform domain *(image processing)*
Ortsfrequenzrichtung *f* spatial frequency direction
Ortsfrequenzspektrum *n* spatial frequency spectrum, Fourier [power] spectrum
Ortsfrequenzvektor *m* spatial frequency vector
Ortsfrequenzverteilung *f* spatial frequency distribution, spectrum
Ortsfunktion *f* space (position) function, spatial response function
ortsinvariant space-invariant, spatially invariant, position-invariant; isoplanatic *(e.g. an operator)*
Ortsinvarianz *f* position invariance; isoplanatism, isoplanacity
Ortskonstanz *f* position constancy *(perceptual phenomenon)*
ortskontinuierlich continuous-space, spatially continuous
Ortskoordinate *f* spatial (position) coordinate
Ortsraum *m* spatial space (domain)
Ortssignal *n* position signal
Ortssignalbereich *m s.* Ortsbereich
Orts-Skalierbarkeit *f* spatial scalability
Ortsvariable *f* spatial (image) variable
ortsvariant space-variant, spatially varying *(signal)*
Ortsvektor *m* position vector
Orts-Zeit-Bild *n* spatiotemporal image
ortszeitlich spatiotemporal, space-time
Ortung *f* location
Ortungsgenauigkeit *f* location accuracy
Ostwald-Reifung *f* Ostwald ripening, physical (first) ripening *(silver-halide photography)*
Ostwald-System *n* Ostwald [color] system *(colorimetry)*
Oszillator *m* oscillator
~/**parametrischer** [optical] parametric oscillator, OTO
~/**spannungsgesteuerter** voltage-controlled oscillator
~/**zeitdiskreter** discrete-time oscillator, DTO
Oszillatorfrequenz *f* oscillator frequency
Oszillatorrauschen *n* oscillator noise
Oszillatorröhre *f* oscillator tube (valve)
oszillieren to oscillate
Oszillograf *m* oscillograph
Oszillografenröhre *f* oscillograph valve
Oszillografenschirm *m* oscillograph (oscilloscope) screen
Oszillografie *f* oscillography
oszillografisch oscillographic
Oszillogramm *n* oscillogram
Oszilloskop *n* oscilloscope [CRT]

Oszilloskopfotografie f oscilloscope photography
oszilloskopisch oscilloscopic
Oszilloskopkamera f oscilloscope camera
O-Ton m s. Originalton
Otoskop n otoscope
Otoskopie f otoscopy
otoskopisch otoscopic
Overheadfolie f overhead transparency
Overheadprojektion f 1. overhead projection; 2. overhead projected image
Overheadprojektor m overhead [projector]
Overlay-Karte f [video] overlay board
Oxidation f oxidation
Oxidationsmittel n oxidant, oxidizing agent
Oxidationsprodukt n oxidation product
Oxidationsschutzmittel n antioxidant
Oxidkatode f oxide cathode
Ozalidpapier n s. Lichtpauspapier
Ozalidverfahren n Ozalid process, brownline (blackline) process

P

Paarbildung f, **Paarerzeugungsprozess** m pair production process *(particle physics)*
Paarhäufigkeitsmatrix f [gray-level] co-occurence matrix, two-point probability density function, 2P-PDF *(image analysis)*
Paarvernichtungsprozess m annihilation process *(particle physics)*
Packfilm m pack film, film pack
Pagina f page number, folio [number]
paginieren to page, to paginate
Paginierung f pagination, paging
Painter's-Algorithmus m painter's algorithm *(computer graphics)*
Paket n packet *(e.g. of digital data)*
Paketdatenvermittlung f packet switching
Paketidentifikation f packet identification, PID
paketieren to packetize *(e.g. image data)*
Paketierung f packetization
Paketierungsverzögerung f packetization delay
Paketkopfdaten pl header data
Paketlänge f packet length
Paketverlust m packet loss
Paketvermittlung f packet switching
Paketvideoübertragung f packet video transmission
PAL-Auftrennstufe f, **PAL-Decoder** m PAL decoder *(derived from phase alternate line)*
Palette f [color] palette
PAL-Fernsehen n PAL (phase alternating line) television, PAL video
~/**erweitertes** s. PALplus-Fernsehen
Palladiotypie f palladium [printing] process, palladiotype
Palladium n palladium
Palladiumabzug m palladium print
PAL-Norm f PAL standard
PALplus-Fernsehen n PALplus television [system], enhanced 625-line phase alternative line television
PALplus-Format n, **PALplus-Norm** f PALplus standard
PAL-System n PAL (phase alternating line) system *(television)*
Panavision n Panavision *(motion-picture wide-screen process)*
panchromatisch panchromatic, pan *(emulsion)*
Panglas n neutral glass
Panikknopf m panic button *(prism reflex camera)*
Panmyelografie f panmyelography
Panorama n panorama
Panoramaaufnahme f panorama shot, panoramic photograph
Panoramabild n panoramic image (picture)
~/**autostereoskopisches** autostereoscopic panoramic image
Panoramadia[positiv] n panoramic slide
Panoramaeinstellung f 1. extreme long shot; 2. s. Panoramamodus
Panoramafilm m panoramic film
Panoramafilmleinwand f wraparound movie screen
Panoramafoto n panoramic photograph
Panoramafotografie f 1. panoramic photography; 2. panoramic photograph
Panoramakamera f panoramic camera
~/**echte** true panoramic camera
Panoramakopf m pan[oramic] head, swivel head
Panoramaradar n surveillance radar
Panoramaschwenk m rotation *(camera move)*
Panoramaverzerrung f panoramic distortion
Pantoffelspule f saddle coil *(picture tube)*
Pantograf m pantograph *(drawing copying device)*
pantografisch pantographic
Pantone-Matching-System n Pantone matching system, PMS *(an approved ink mixing and color matching system)*
Panum-Areal n, **Panum-Raum** m [Panum's] fusional area *(vision)*
Papier n paper
~/**digitales** s. ~/elektronisches
~/**doppelt logarithmisches** doubly logarithmic paper
~/**einseitig satiniertes** machine-glazed paper
~/**elektronisches** electronic paper
~/**elektrosensitives** burn-off paper
~/**fotografisches** photographic [printing] paper, photo paper, print[ing] paper; enlarging paper
~/**gelatinebeschichtetes (gelatiniertes)** gelatin-coated paper
~/**geprägtes** text paper
~/**gestrichenes** sized paper; coated paper
~/**gradationsfestes** graded paper
~/**gradationsvariables** variable-contrast paper, VC paper
~/**grafisches** graphic[al] paper
~/**gussgestrichenes** cast-coated paper, glossy[-surface] paper, highly polished paper
~/**halbmattes** semimatt paper
~/**hart[zeichnend]es** hard (high-contrast) paper
~/**hochglänzendes** glossy paper
~/**hochsatiniertes** supercalendered paper, SC paper
~/**holzfreies** wood-free paper, free sheet
~/**holzhaltiges** groundwood paper
~/**kunstharzbeschichtetes** resin-coated [photographic] paper, RC paper

Papierverarbeitung

~/kunststoffbeschichtetes plastic-laminated paper
~/leichtes lightweight paper
~/lichtempfindliches photosensitive (sensitized) paper
~/maschinengestrichenes s. ~/gestrichenes
~/maschinenglattes uncoated (offset) paper
~/mattes (mattgestrichenes) matt[e] paper
~/polyesterbeschichtetes polyester-coated paper, PE paper
~/polyethylenkaschiertes polyethylene-coated paper
~/satiniertes machine-glazed paper
~/säure- und holzfreies acid- and lignin-free paper
~/säurefreies acid-free paper, alkaline (neutral pH) paper
~/seidenmattes semimatt paper
~/selbstdurchschreibendes carbonless paper
~/sensibilisiertes sensitized paper
~/thermoaktives s. ~/wärmeempfindliches
~/ungestrichenes uncoated (offset) paper
~/wärmeempfindliches heat-sensitive paper, thermal (heat-copying) paper
~/wasserfestes waterproof paper
~/weiches soft paper
Papierablage f copy (exit) tray (copier)
Papierabstreifer m print squeegee
Papierabzug m paper [positive] print, paper reproduction, photo[graphic] print, [positive] print (s.a. Papierbild)
Papierart f paper type
Papierausdruck m [paper] hard copy, hard copy print, paper copy
Papierausgabe f hard copy output
Papierausgabefach n output tray (printer)
Papierausrüstung f [paper] finish
Papierausschuss m spoilage (printing)
Papierbahn f [paper] web, [continuous] paper roll (printing)
Papierbelichtung f paper exposure
Papierbelichtungsfehler m paper exposure error
Papierbild n paper [copy] image; hard copy (s.a. Papierabzug)
~/fotografisches photographic paper print
Papierbildabzug m s. Papierabzug
Papierdegradation f paper grade
Papierdicke f paper thickness (s.a. Papierstärke)
Papierdurchlauf m paper path
Papierdurchsatz m paper throughput
Papiereinzug m paper feed
Papierempfindlichkeit f paper sensitivity (speed)
Papieremulsion f [photographic] paper emulsion
Papierentwickler m [photographic] paper developer, [paper] print developer

Papierentwicklung f paper development, print processing
Papierentwicklungsmaschine f paper processor
Papierfarbe f paper color
Papierfaser f paper fiber
Papierfixierer m paper fixer
Papierflächengewicht n, **Papierflächenmasse** f grammage, basis weight [of paper], sub[stance] weight
Papierformat n paper size
Papierfoto n paper photograph (s.a. Papierabzug)
Papierführung f paper train (printer)
Papiergradation f paper [contrast] grade, contrast grade, degree of contrast
Papierhalter m paper holder (e.g. of a view camera)
Papierhärtegrad m paper [contrast] grade
Papierhintergrund m paper backdrop, background paper (studio accessory)
Papierkassette f paper tray (cassette)
Papierkontrast m paper contrast
Papierkopie f 1. paper copy, hard copy print, [paper] hard copy; 2. s. Papierabzug
Papierkorb m [/elektronischer] trash can, dumpster (computer)
Papierlaufrichtung f grain (machine) direction (of paper)
Papierleimung f sizing
Papiermontage f 1. pasteup [process]; 2. pasteup, hard mechanical
Papiernegativ n paper negative
Papieroberfläche f paper surface
Papierpositiv n paper [positive] print, photo[graphic] print, [positive] print
Papierrand m margin
~ **innen** inside margin[s], gutter
Papiersafe m dark box
Papierscanner m paper scanner
Papier-Schichtträger m paper base (support) (printing material)
Papierschutzband n backing paper (roll film)
Papiersorte f paper type, type (kind) of paper
papierstark single-weight (printing paper)
Papierstärke f paper weight (thickness); [paper] base thickness, caliper
Papierstau m paper jam[ming]
Papierton m, **Papiertönung** f [paper] stock tint
Papierträger m paper base (support) (printing material)
Papiertransport m paper feed; paper advance
Papiertrockner m print dryer
Papiertrommel f print drum
Papiertyp m paper type
Papierunterlage f paper base (support) (printing material)
Papierverarbeitung f paper (print) processing, paper development

Papierverzug

Papierverzug *m* curl; fanout
Papiervorratskassette *f* paper tray (cassette)
Papiervorschub *m* paper feed; paper advance
Papierweg *m* paper path
Papierweiß *n* paper white
Papierzange *f* print tongs
Papierzuführung *f* paper feed; paper input
Papille *f s.* Fleck/blinder
Pappe *f* paperboard, cardboard, board [paper]
Papprähmchen *n*, **Papprahmen** *m* cardboard mount
Paraaminophenol-Entwickler *m* para-aminophenol developer, paraminophenol
Parabol[empfangs]antenne *f* parabolic antenna, [receiving] dish *(s.a. Satellitenschüssel)*
parabolisch parabolic
parabolisieren to parabolize *(e.g. a telescope mirror)*
Paraboloid *n* paraboloid
Parabolreflektor *m* parabolic reflector
Parabolspiegel *m* paraboloid[al] mirror, parabolic mirror (reflector)
Parabolspiegelantenne *f s.* Parabol[empfangs]antenne
Parabolspiegelscheinwerfer *m* beam projector
parallaktisch parallactic
Parallaxe *f* parallax; viewpoint difference
~/**binokulare** binocular parallax
~/**horizontale** horizontal parallax
~/**negative** negative parallax
~/**optische** optical parallax
~/**positive** positive parallax
~/**stereoskopische** *s.* ~/binokulare
~/**vertikale** vertical parallax (disparity)
Parallaxenausgleich *m* 1. parallax [error] correction; 2. parallax-compensating device, parallax correction system; rack-over [viewfinder]
Parallaxenfehler *m* parallax (parallactic) error
Parallaxenfehlerkorrektur *f* parallax error correction
parallaxenfrei parallax-free, no-parallax
Parallaxenkorrektur *f* parallax [error] correction
Parallaxenstereogramm *n* parallax stereogram
Parallaxenunterschied *m* parallax difference
Parallaxenverschiebung *f* parallax shift (displacement)
Parallaxenverzerrung *f s.* Trapezverzerrung
Parallaxenwinkel *m* parallax (parallactic) angle
parallel zur Faserrichtung (Laufrichtung) with the grain, along (parallel to) the grain direction *(printing paper)*
Parallelabtastung *f* parallel scan[ning]

Parallel-Anschlussbuchse *f* parallel port, LPT port
Parallelbetrieb *m* simulcast *(television)*
Parallelbruchfalz *m* parallel fold
Parallelbündel *n* parallel bundle [of rays]; collimated beam
Parallelbus *m* parallel bus
Paralleldrucker *m* parallel (line) printer
Parallelepiped *n* parallelepiped
Parallelepipedklassifikation *f* parallelepiped classification, PE classification *(pattern recognition)*
Parallelfahrt *f* track *(camera motion)*
Parallelflach *n s.* Parallelepiped[on]
parallelisieren to parallelize; to deserialize *(e.g. samples)*
Parallelisierung *f* parallelization
Parallelität *f* parallelism
Parallellicht *n* collimated light
Parallellichtbündel *n* collimated beam
Parallellochkollimator *m* parallel-hole[s] collimator *(gamma camera)*
Parallelogramm *n* parallelogram
Parallelperspektive *f* parallel (one-point) perspective, telecentric perspective
Parallelplatte *f s.* Planparallelplatte
Parallelprojektion *f* [/**orthogonale**] [orthographic] parallel projection, orthographic (orthogonal) projection
~/**schiefwinklige (schräge)** oblique parallel projection
Parallelprozessor *m* parallel processor
Parallelrechner *m* parallel (simultaneous) computer
Parallel-Scan *m* parallel scan[ning]
Parallelschnittstelle *f* parallel interface (port)
Parallel-Seriell-Umsetzer *m* serializer
Parallelstrahl *m* parallel ray (beam)
Parallelstrahlenbündel *n* parallel bundle of rays
Parallelstrahlgerät *n* linear scanner *(tomography)*
Parallelstrahlprojektion *f*, **Parallelstrahlverfahren** *n* parallel-beam projection *(tomography)*
Parallelübertragung *f* parallel transmission
Parallelumsetzer *m* flash converter *(video processor)*
Parallelverarbeitung *f* parallel processing
Parallelverschiebung *f*, **Parallelversetzung** *f* parallel shift (displacement)
Parallelwandler *m* flash converter
Paramagnet *m* paramagnet
paramagnetisch paramagnetic
Paramagnetismus *m* paramagnetism
Parameter *m* parameter
~/**geschätzter** estimated parameter
~/**morphometrischer** morphometric parameter
Parametercodierung *f* parameter [en]coding
Parameterdarstellung *f* parametric representation

Parameterkurve *f* parametric [polynomial] curve
Parametermatrix *f* parameter matrix
Parameteroptimierung *f* parameter optimization
Parameterraum *m* parameter (parametric) space
Parameterschätzung *f* parameter estimation
Parametervektor *m* parameter vector
parametrierbar parametrizable
parametrieren to paramet[e]rize
Parametrierung *f s.* Parametrisierung
parametrisch parametric, parametr[ic]al
parametrisierbar parametrizable
parametrisieren to paramet[e]rize
Parametrisierung *f* paramet[e]rization
~/**äquidistante** equidistant paramet[e]rization
~/**chordale** chordal paramet[e]rization
~/**gleichmäßige** *s.* ~/äquidistante
~/**zentripetale** centripetal paramet[e]rization
paraperspektivisch paraperspective
Paraphenylendiamin *n* paraphenylenediamin *(developing agent)*
paraxial paraxial, near-axis
Paraxialgebiet *n* paraxial domain (region) *(optics)*
Paraxialstrahl *m* paraxial (near-axis) ray
parfokal parfocal
Parietallappen *m* parietal lobe *(of cerebral cortex)*
Parität *f* parity
~/**gerade** even parity
~/**ungerade** odd parity
Paritätsbit *n* parity [check] bit, parity *(coding redundancy)*
Paritätsprüfung *f* parity check
Parkettierung *f* tiling; tessellation; parquetry *(computational geometry)*
Parkettstein *m* [pixel] tile *(computational geometry)*
PAR-Lampe *f*, **PAR-Scheinwerfer** *m* PAR (parabolic aluminized reflector) light
Parseval-Theorem *n* Parseval's theorem *(signal processing)*
Partialbelichtungsmesser *m* spot meter
Partial-Lichttonspur *f* [optical] snake track *(sound track recording)*
Partialvolumeneffekt *m* partial volume effect, PVE *(image segmentation)*
Partikel... *s.a. under* Teilchen...
Partikelstrahlung *f s.* Teilchenstrahlung
Partikelverfolgung *f* particle tracing *(visualization)*
Partition *f* partition
PASCAL *n* Pascal [language] *(a high-level programming language)*
Passband *n* passband
Passbild *n* passport photo, passport[-size] photograph
Passbildautomat *m* photomaton booth
Passbildpapier *n* passport paper

Passelement *n s.* Passpunkt
Passepartout *n* passe-partout; ready-made frame; window mount, window [over]mat
Passer *m* register *(printing)*
passergenau in [perfect] register
Passergenauigkeit *f* register accuracy
Passerkontrolle *f* register control
Passerkreuz *n s.* Passkreuz
Passerungenauigkeit *f* misregistration
Passfotoporträt *n* passport portrait
passgenau, passgerecht in register
Passivierung *f* passivation [layer] *(photodiode)*
Passivmatrixbildschirm *m* passive matrix display
Passivmatrix-Flüssigkristallanzeige *f* passive-matrix LCD (liquid-crystal display)
Passkreuz *n* crossmark, register (position) mark
Passmarke *f s.* Passpunkt
Passpunkt *m* [photo] control point, premarked (panel) point *(photogrammetry)*; ground control point, GCP *(remote sensing)*
Passpunktnetz *n* control network
Passstift *m* registration (register) pin
Passsystem *n* register system
Passung *f* registration, alignment *(e.g. of images)*
Pastellfarbe *f* pastel [color], pale color
pastellfarben, pastellig pastel[-colored]
Pastellton *m* pastel hue (shade)
Pastenentwicklung *f* viscous processing
Patientenbildrecherche *f* patient-image retrieval
Patientenlagerungstisch *m*, **Patientenliege** *f* patient table (couch), [translation] couch, pallet *(computed tomography scanner)*
Patrize *f* male die, force card *(e.g. in embossing or debossing)*
pausen to trace
Pausenfunktion *f* pause feature *(camcorder)*
Pauspapier *n* blueprint paper; tracing paper
Pay-TV-Empfänger *m* pay-TV receiver
P-Bild *n* P-frame, predicted frame (image), predictive [coded] picture
P-Bus-Schnittstelle *f* P-bus interface
PC *m* PC, personal computer
PC-Anschlusskabel *n* personal computer connecting cord
PC-Bildverarbeitungssystem *n* computer imaging (image-processing) system
PC-Buchse *f* PC (pin cylinder) connector, PC terminal *(on a camera)*
PC-Grafikkarte *f s.* Grafikkarte
PCI-Bus *m* PCI (peripheral component interconnect) bus
PC-Karte *f* PC card *(standard interface)*
PC-Kartenadapter *m* PC card adapter

PC-Kartenschlitz *m* PC card slot
PC-Maus *f* [computer] mouse, puck *(handheld input device)*
PC-Nutzer *m* PC (personal computer) user
PC-Objektiv *n* PC (perspective-control) lens, shift lens
PC-Video-Karte *f* genlock [board] *(for combining video with computer graphics)*
PC-Video-Konverter *m* genlock device
Peltier-Element *n*, **Peltier-Kühler** *m* Peltier (thermoelectric) cooler
Pelzen *n* piling *(printing defect)*
PEM-Effekt *m* photoelectromagnetic effect
Pendelfotogramm *n s.* Lichtpendelgrafik
Pentadachkantenprisma *n* roof pentaprism, inverting pentagonal prism
Pentagonprisma *n*, **Pentaprisma** *n* pentaprism, pentagonal prism
Pentaprismensucher *m* pentaprism viewfinder [system]
Penumbra *f* penumbra, penumbral shadow; partial shadow, half shadow
PE-Papier *n* PE (polyester-coated) paper
Perche *f s.* Mikrofonangel
Perfektormaschine *f* [rotary] perfecting machine, perfecting [cylinder] press, perfector [press], duplex (blanket-to-blanket) press
Perfoband *n* sprocketed magnetic tape
Perforation *f* perforation, perf
~/**doppelseitige** double perforation
~/**einseitige** single perforation
Perforationsart *f* perforation type
Perforationsbereich *m* sprocket-hole area
Perforationsgeräusch *n* sprocket noise
Perforationsloch *n* sprocket (perforation) hole
Perforationslochabstand *m* [perforation] pitch
Perforationsschaden *m* perforation damage
Perforationsschritt *m* [perforation] pitch
Perforator *m* perforator
perforieren to perforate
Perforiermaschine *f* perforating machine
Perfo-Tonband *n* sprocketed magnetic tape
Perfusionsbild *n* perfusion image
Perfusionsbildgebung *f* perfusion imaging
Perfusionsszintigrafie *f* perfusion scintigraphy
Perfusionsszintigramm *n* perfusion scintigram
Pergamin[papier] *n* glassine
Peri-Anschluss *m s.* Scart-Anschluss
Perimeter *n* perimeter, campimeter *(an eye testing apparatus)*
Perimetrie *f* perimetry, campimetry
perimetrisch perimetric[al]
Periode *f*/**fundamentale** fundamental period *(signal processing)*
Periodendauer *f* **der Vertikalablenkung (des Halbbildwechsels)** field period (time), field duration

Periodizität *f* periodicity *(e.g. of a Fourier transform)*
Peripherie *f* 1. periphery; 2. peripheral equipment *(computer)*
Peripheriegerät *n* peripheral device (add-on), [external] peripheral
Periskop *n* 1. periscope; 2. periscopic lens
periskopisch periscopic
Perlen *n* mottle, sinkage; chalking, crocking *(printing defect)*
Perl[lein]wand *f* pearl screen, [glass-]beaded screen
Permanentspeicher *m* nonvolatile (involatile) memory
Permanentweiß *n* baryta white, blanc fixe *(pigment)*
Permeabilität *f* permeability *(magnetism)*
Peroxid *n* peroxide
Persistenz *f* persistence; persistent luminescence, long-lived phosphorescence, afterglow
Personalcomputer *m* personal computer, PC *(s.a. under PC-...)*
~/**fernsehtauglicher** TV-enabled PC
~ **im Buchformat** notebook [computer]
Personenaufnahme *f*/**erkennungsdienstliche** mug shot
Personenfotografie *f* people (anthropological) photography
Perspektive *f* perspective
~/**entozentrische** entocentric perspective
~/**flache** weak perspective, scaled orthography *(e.g. as a projection model)*
~/**fotografische** photographic perspective
~/**geometrische** geometric[al] perspective
~/**hyperzentrische** hypercentric perspective
~/**kanonische** canonical perspective
~/**lineare** linear (central) perspective, pinhole perspective, convergence of parallels
~/**räumliche** spatial perspective
~/**telezentrische** telecentric (parallel) perspective, one-point perspective
Perspektivekorrektur *f* perspective correction (control); perspective compensation
Perspektivekorrekturobjektiv *n* perspective-control lens, PC lens, shift lens
perspektivisch perspective
Perspektivität *f* perspectivity
Perspektivitätszentrum *n* perspective center, center of perspective
perzeptibel perceptible, perceivable
perzeptiv perceptive, discerning
Perzeptor *m s.* Perzeptron
Perzeptron *n* perceptron *(artificial neural network)*
~/**dreischichtiges** three-layer perceptron
~/**einschichtiges** single-layer perceptron
~/**mehrschichtiges** multilayer[ed] perceptron, MLP

Perzeptron-Lernregel f generalized delta rule [for learning by backpropagation]
perzipieren to perceive
PET s. Positronenemissionstomografie
PET-Gerät n, **PET-Scanner** m PET (positron-emission tomography) scanner, positron[-emission] tomograph
Petzval-Bedingung f Petzval contribution
Petzval-Krümmung f Petzval [field] curvature
Petzval-Objektiv n Petzval objective; Petzval [portrait] lens
Petzval-Schale f Petzval surface
Petzval-Summe f Petzval sum
Petzval-Wölbung f s. Petzval-Krümmung
Pfad m path *(computer graphics)*
~/**optischer** optical path
Pfaditerator m path iterator *(computer graphics)*
Pfeilhöhe f sag[itta] *(optics)*
Pfeiltaste f arrow key
Pflanzenfotografie f botanical photography
Pflanzenleim m vegetable glue (adhesive), paste
Pfortaderangiografie f portography
Phänakistiskop n phenakistoscope, phenakistiscope *(an early optical toy)*
Phänomen n/**elektrooptisches** electro-optic phenomenon *(e.g. Kerr effect)*
~/**Gibbssches** Gibbs phenomenon (effect), Gibbs artifact, truncation (ringing) artifact
Phantom n phantom
Phantombild n phantom (ghost) image
Phantomfoto n 1. 2. photofit
Pharmakoangiografie f pharmacoangiography
Phase f phase *(of a wave or a signal)*
~/**analytische** analytic phase *(e.g. of a compression algorithm)*
~/**cholesterinische** cholesteric phase *(liquid crystal)*
~/**differentielle** differential phase
~/**nematische** nematic phase *(liquid crystal)*
~/**smektische** smectic phase *(liquid crystal)*
Phasenanalyse f phase analysis
Phasenänderung f phase change
Phasenanpassung f index (phase) matching *(nonlinear optics)*
Phasenbeziehung f phase relationship
Phasenbild n phase image (map); sequential picture
Phasencodiergradient m phase-encoding [field] gradient
Phasencodierschritt m phase-encoding step
Phasencodierung f phase encoding
Phasencodierungsrichtung f phase-encoding direction
Phasendetektion f/**differentielle** differential phase detection
Phasendetektor m phase detector

Phasendifferenz f phase difference
Phasendifferenzcodierung f differential phase-shift keying, DPSK
Phasendrehung f angular phase shift
Phasenfaktor m phase factor
Phasenfehler m phase error
Phasenfilter n phase filter
Phasenfilterung f phase filtering
Phasenfluktuation f phase fluctuation
Phasenfotografie f stroboscopic (repetitive flash) photography
Phasenfrequenzgang m phase[-frequency] response
Phasenfrontsensor m wave-front sensor
Phasengang m s. Phasenfrequenzgang
Phasengeschwindigkeit f phase velocity *(of a wave)*
Phasengitter n phase grating
phasengleich cophasal, in-phase
Phasengradient m phase[-encoding] gradient *(magnetic resonance imaging)*
Phasenhologramm n phase hologram
Phasenhub m [maximum] phase deviation, phase swing
Phaseninformation f phase information
Phaseninterferenz f phase interference
phasenkohärent phase-coherent
Phasenkohärenz f phase coherence
Phasenkompensation f phase compensation
Phasenkongruenz f phase congruency
Phasenkonjugation f phase conjugation
Phasenkonstante f phase coefficient
Phasenkontrast m phase contrast
Phasenkontrastangiografie f phase-contrast [magnetic resonance] angiography, PC[MR]A
Phasenkontrastbeleuchtung f phase-contrast illumination
Phasenkontrastbild n phase-contrast image
Phasenkontrast-Fluoreszenzmikroskop n phase-contrast fluorescence microscope
Phasenkontrastmikroskop n phase[-contrast] microscope
Phasenkontrastmikroskopie f phase-contrast microscopy, PC microscopy
Phasenkontrastobjektiv n phase[-contrast] objective
Phasenkontrastoptik f phase-contrast optics
Phasenkontrast-Röntgenmikroskop n phase contrast X-ray microscope
Phasenkontrastverfahren n phase contrast method (imaging)
Phasenkorrektor m phase corrector
Phasenkorrelationsfunktion f phase correlation function, PCF
Phasenkurve f trajectory
Phasenlage f phase position
~/**zeilenweise wechselnde** phase alternating line, PAL

Phasenlaufzeit f phase delay *(signal processing)*
Phasenlinearität f phase linearity
Phasenmaske f phase mask
Phasenmodulation f phase modulation, PM
Phasenmodulator m phase modulator
Phasenobjekt n phase object
Phasen-Oversampling n s. Einfaltungsunterdrückung
Phasenplättchen n, **Phasenplatte** f phase plate (retarder) *(phase-contrast microscopy)*
Phasenproblem n phase problem *(diffraction optics)*
Phasenraum m s. Zustandsraum
Phasenrauschen n phase noise
Phasenregelkreis m phase-lock[ed] loop, PLL
Phasenregelung f/**automatische** automatic phase control, APC
phasenrichtig in-phase
Phasenrichtung f phase direction
Phasenschieber m phase shifter (modifier)
Phasenschiebe-Shearografie f [/**bildgebende**] phase-shifting shearography
Phasenspektrum n phase spectrum (angle)
Phasensprung m phase jump
Phasensteuerung f phase control
Phasenstruktur f phase structure
Phasensynchronisation f mode locking *(laser)*
Phasenteleskop n phase telescope
Phasenthermografie f lock-in thermography
Phasentrennung f phase separation
Phasenübergang m phase transition
Phasenübertragungsfunktion f phase transfer function, PTF
Phasenumkehr f/**zeilenweise** line-by-line phase reversal
Phasenumtastung f phase-shift keying, PSK
~/**differentielle vierwertige** differential quadrature phase shift keying, DQPSK
~/**vierwertige** quadrature phase-shift keying, QPSK
~/**zweiwertige** binary phase-shift keying, BPSK
Phasenveränderung f/**elektrooptische** electro-optic phase change, EOPC
Phasenvergleich m phase comparison
Phasenverschiebung f phase shift
phasenverschoben out of phase
Phasenverteilung f phase distribution
Phasenwechsel m phase change
~/**optischer** optical phase change, OPC *(DVD technology)*
Phasenwechseldrucker m phase change printer
Phasenwechselspeicher m phase change RAM (random-access memory)
Phasenwinkel m phase angle (spectrum)

Phasenzeichnung f cel[l] drawing, [animation] cel[l], acetate
Phenakistiskop n s. Phänakistiscope
Phenidon n s. Phenylpyrazolidon
Phenol n phenol
Phenolkuppler m phenol coupler
Phenylendiamin n phenylenediamine *(developer substance)*
Phenylpyrazolidon n phenylpyrazolid[in]one *(developer substance)*
Phi-Bewegung f, **Phi-Phänomen** n phi motion (phenomenon); [stroboscopic] apparent motion, stroboscopic motion
Phlebografie f phlebography *(s.a. Venografie)*
phlebografisch phlebographic
Phlebogramm n phlebogram
Phon n phon
Phong-Schattierung f Phong shading (interpolation), normal-vector interpolation [shading] *(computer graphics)*
Phonokardiografie f phonocardiography
phonokardiografisch phonocardiographic
Phonokardiogramm n phonocardiogram
Phonon n phonon *(quantum of vibrational energy)*
Phorometer n phorometer
Phosphen n [visual] phosphene *(luminous impression)*
Phosphor m 1. phosphor[e], phosphorescent substance; 2. [light-producing] phosphor, luminescent material, luminophor *(s.a. under Leuchtstoff)*; 3. phosphorus *(nonmetallic element)*
Phosphoreszenz f phosphorescence
Phosphoreszenzschirm m phosphor[escent] screen, phosphorous (phosphor-coated) screen
Phosphoreszenzstrahler m phosphorescent radiator
phosphoreszieren to phosphoresce
Phosphorleuchtpunkt m phosphor (fluorescent) dot
Phosphorleuchtstreifen m phosphor stripe
Phosphorpunkt m s. Phosphorleuchtpunkt
Phosphorschicht f phosphor coating, [storage] phosphor screen *(cathode-ray tube)*
Phot n phot, ph lumen per square centimeter *(unit of illuminance)*
Photon n photon [quantum]; [visible-]light photon, light quantum (particle)
Photonenabsorber m photon absorber
Photonenabsorption f photon absorption
Photonenanregung f photon excitation
Photonendetektion f photon detection
Photonendetektor m photon (quantum) detector
Photonendichte f photon[-flux] density; photon current density
Photoneneffekt m photon effect

Photonenemission *f* photon emission
Photonenenergie *f* photon energy
Photonenfluss *m* photon flux
Photonenhypothese *f s.*
  Lichtquantenhypothese
Photonenkorrelationsspektroskopie *f*
  photon correlation spectroscopy
Photonenquelle *f* photon source
Photonenrastertunnelmikroskop *n* photon
  scanning tunneling microscope, PSTM
Photonenrauschen *n* photon [image]
  noise, photon-induced noise; photon
  shot noise *(s.a.* Quantenrauschen*)*
Photonenspektrum *n* photon spectrum
Photonenstrahl *m* photon beam
Photonenstrahlung *f* photon radiation
Photonenstrom *m* photon flux (stream);
  photon[-produced] current,
  photon-generated current
Photonenzähler *m* photon counter,
  photon-counting detector
Photonenzählung *f* photon counting
Photonik *f* photonics
Photoniknetz *n* photonic network
photonisch photonic
Photophon *n* photophone
Phrasencodierung *f* dictionary-based
  compression
Phthalocyanin *n* phthalocyanine *(pigment)*
pH-Wert *m* pH [value], hydrogen-ion
  concentration
Physik *f* **des Lichts** light physics,
  photophysics
~/fotografische photographic physics
Physiologie *f* **des Sehens** visual physiology
Pica *f* pica *(unit of type size)*
Piepser *m* [sync-]pop, 2 pop *(film editing)*
Piezoantrieb *m* piezoelectric actuator
Piezoeffekt *m***/reziproker (umgekehrter)**
  inverse piezoelectric effect
piezoelektrisch piezoelectric
Piezoelektrizität *f* piezoelectricity
Piezoelement *n* piezoelectric element *(s.a.*
  Piezowandler*)*
Piezokristall *m* piezoelectric crystal
Piezo-Tintenstrahldrucker *m* piezoelectric
  ink-jet printer
Piezowandler *m* piezo[electric] transducer
Pigment *n* pigment
Pigmentbild *n* pigment image
pigmentbildend chromogenic
Pigmentdruck *m* 1. pigment process; 2.
  pigment print
Pigmentepithel *n* pigment[ed] epithelium
  (of the eye)
Pigmentgelatine *f* pigmented gelatin
pigmentiert pigmented
Pigmentierung *f* pigmentation
Pigmentpapier *n* carbon tissue
Pigmentschicht *f* pigment layer
Pikometer *m* picometer
Pikosekundenlaser *m* picosecond laser
piktografisch pictographic

Piktogramm *n* pictograph, pictogram;
  [graphical] icon
Piktoralismus *m* pictoralism, pictorial
  photography
Pilot *m***/ständiger** continual pilot, CP *(video
  signal)*
~/verstreuter scattered pilot, SP
Pilot-Bezugsband *n* test tape
Pilotfrequenzaufzeichnung *f* pilot frequeny
  recording
Pilotlicht *n s.* Einstelllicht
Pilotsendung *f* pilot program
Pilotsignal *n* pilot
Pilotton *m* pilot tone
Pilzbefall *m* fungal (fungi) attack
pin-Fotodiode *f* p-i-n photodiode
Pinholekollimator *m* pinhole collimator
Pinsel *m* brush [tool] *(electronic imaging)*
Pinselretusche *f* brush retouching
Pinselstrich *m* brush stroke
Pinzette *f* tweezers *(e.g. as hand tool in
  composing)*
Pipette *f* pipette
Pistolengriff *m* pistol grip *(e.g. of a camera)*
Pixel *n* pixel, pel, picture element *(s.a.
  under* Bildpunkt, Punkt*)*
~/adressierbares addressable pixel
~/aktives active pixel
~/ansteuerbares addressable pixel
~/logarithmisches logarithmic pixel
~/nichtquadratisches *s.* ~/rechteckiges
~/quadratisches square pixel
~/räumliches volume pixel, volume
  [picture] element, voxel
~/rechteckiges rectangular (nonsquare)
  pixel
Pixelabmessung *f s.* Pixelgröße
Pixelabstand *m* pixel [separation] distance,
  pixel separation (interval), pixel (dot)
  pitch, pixel (pel) spacing
Pixeladresse *f* pixel address
Pixeladressierung *f* pixel addressing
Pixelamplitude *f* pixel (pel) amplitude
Pixelanordnung *f* pixel array, array of pixels
  (dots)
Pixelauflösung *f* pixel resolution
Pixelausfall *m* pixel dropout
Pixelbearbeitung *f* pixel editing
Pixelbereich *m* pixel domain
Pixelbereichsdarstellung *f* pixel-domain
  representation
pixelbezogen pixel-related
Pixelbild *n* pixel image (map), pixmap,
  bit-map[ped image]; raster image
~/geräteabhängiges device-dependent
  bit-map
~/geräteunabhängiges
  device-independent bit-map
Pixelbinning *n* binning *(CCD imaging
  technology)*
Pixelblock *m* pixel block, block of pixels
  (pels)
Pixelbreite *f* pixel (pel) width
Pixelcache[speicher] *m* pixel cache

Pixelchip *m s.* CCD-Chip
Pixelcluster *m* pixel cluster
Pixelclusterung *f* pixel clustering
Pixelcodierung *f* pixel encoding
Pixeldarstellung *f* pixel[-based] representation
Pixeldatei *f s.* Pixelgrafikdatei
Pixeldaten *pl* pixel data
Pixeldefekt *m* pixel error (anomaly)
Pixeldichte *f* pixel density
Pixeldichtewert *m s.* Pixelgrauwert
Pixelebene *f* pixel plane (level)
Pixelelektrode *f* pixel electrode *(liquid crystal display)*
Pixelfarbe *f* pixel color
Pixelfarbwert *m* pixel color value
Pixelfehler *m* pixel error (anomaly)
Pixelfeld *n* pixel array (arrangement), array of dots
~/**beschnittenes** clipped p[ix]el array
Pixelfläche *f* 1. pixel area; 2. *s.* Bitmap 1.
~/**aktive** active pixel area
Pixelfrequenz *f* pixel frequency
pixelgenau pixel-precise
Pixelgenauigkeit *f* [integer-]pixel accuracy, integer-pel accuracy, full-pixel precision *(video coding)*
Pixelgitter *n* pixel grid
Pixelgrafik *f* 1. pixel (bit-mapped) graphics, raster graphics; 2. *s.* Pixelbild
Pixelgrafikdatei *f* bit-map file
Pixelgrafikprogramm *n* [computer] paint program, paint software
Pixelgrauwert *m* pixel gray value (level), gray pixel value, pixel intensity [value]
Pixelgröße *f* pixel size (dimension)
Pixelgruppe *f* pixel group, group of pixels
pixelig pixil[l]ated, blocky
Pixeligkeit *f* pixilation, blockiness
Pixelinhalt *m s.* Pixelwert
Pixelinterpolation *f* pixel interpolation
Pixeljitter *m* pixel jitter
Pixelkette *f* pixel chain
Pixelklasse *f* class of pixels
Pixelklassifikation *f*/**topografische** topographic pixel classification
Pixelkontrast *m* pixel contrast
Pixelkoordinate *f* pixel coordinate
Pixelladung *f* pixel charge
Pixelluminanz *f* pixel luminance [value]
Pixelmatrix *f* pixel matrix, matrix of pixels
Pixelmitte *f*, **Pixelmittelpunkt** *m* pixel center
Pixelmittelung *f* pixel averaging
Pixelmuster *n* pixel pattern
Pixelnachbarschaft *f* pixel neighborhood
Pixelnumerierung *f* pixel count
Pixeloptimierung *f* pixel optimization
Pixelpaar *n* pixel pair
Pixelposition *f* pixel position (location), pixel site
Pixelrand *m* pixel boundary (edge)
Pixelraster *m(n)* raster, bit-map *(array of binary data)*

Pixelraum *m* pixel space
Pixelrauschen *n* pixel noise
Pixelrepräsentation *f s.* Pixeldarstellung
Pixelschwankung *f* pixel variation
Pixelseitenverhältnis *n* pixel aspect ratio, PAR
Pixelsensor *m* pixel sensor (detector)
~/**aktiver** active pixel sensor, APS; CMOS (complementary metal oxide semiconductor) image sensor, CMOS imager
~/**passiver** passive pixel sensor, PPS
Pixelsignatur *f* pixel signature
Pixelspalte *f* pixel column
Pixelspannung *f* pixel voltage *(liquid-crystal display)*
Pixelstruktur *f* pixel structure
pixelsynchron pixel-synchronous
Pixeltabelle *f* pixel table
Pixeltakt *m* pixel (dot) clock
Pixeltaktrate *f* pixel clock rate
Pixeltiefe *f* pixel (bit) depth *(s.a. Farbtiefe)*
Pixeltopologie *f* pixel topology
Pixelunabhängigkeit *f* pixel independence
Pixel-Unterabtastung *f* pixel subsampling
Pixelvektor *m* pixel vector
Pixelverarbeitung *f* pixel (point) processing
Pixelverbindung *f* pixel connection; pixel linking
Pixelverdopp[e]lung *f* pixel duplication (replication)
Pixelvergleich *m* pixel comparison
Pixelverlust *m* pixel loss
Pixelverschiebung *f* pixel shift (offset)
Pixelverstärker *m* pixel amplifier *(CMOS sensor)*
Pixelverteilung *f* pixel distribution
pixelweise pixelwise, pixel-by-pixel
Pixelwert *m* pixel value; color value *(bit-mapped image)*
Pixelzahl *f* pixel count, number of pixels (dots)
Pixelzeile *f* line of pixels
Plakatfarbe *f* poster color (paint)
plan plane, planar, flat
Planachromat *m* plan achromat [objective], flat-field achromat
Planapochromat *m* planapochromat, plan apochromatic objective
planar planar, plane, flat
Planar-Bildschirm *m s.* Flachbildschirm
Planarität *f s.* Planheit
Plandiffusor *m* flat (cosine-corrected) diffuser *(incident-light meter)*
Planetarium *n* planetarium
Planfilm *m* sheet film, cut (flat) film
Planfilmhalter *m* 1. sheet-film holder; 2. [sheet-]film hanger *(tank processing)*
Planfilmkamera *f* sheet-film camera
Planfilmkassette *f* sheet-film holder *(of a technical camera)*
Planfläche *f* plane (flat) surface; optically flat surface
Plangitter *n* plane [reflection] grating

Plangitterspektrograf *m* plane grating spectrograph
Planglas *n* flat glass *(optics)*
Planheit *f* planarity
Planigrafie *f* planigraphy *(roentgenographic technique)*
Planigramm *n* planigram, planigraph
Planimeter *n* planimeter
Planimetrie *f* planimetry
planimetrisch planimetric
Planität *f s.* Planheit
plankonkav plano-concave
Plankonkavlinse *f* plano-concave lens
plankonvex plano-convex
Plankonvexlinse *f* plano-convex lens
Plankorrektur *f* flat-field correction, plan correction
Planlage *f* flatness
plano plane, flat *(esp. said of a press sheet)*
Planobjektiv *n* plan objective, flat-field lens
Planobogen *m* flat
Planoptik *f* folded optics
planparallel plane-parallel
Planparallelität *f* plane parallelism
Planparallelplatte *f* plane parallel plate, planar plate, [optical] flat
Planplatte *f s.* Planparallelplatte
Planpolarisation *f* planar polarization
Planpolarisator *m* plane polarizer
planpolarisiert plane-polarized, linearly polarized
Planspiegel *m* plane (planar) mirror, flat mirror
Planungsskizze *f* scribble
Plasma *n* plasma
Plasmaanzeige *f* plasma display [panel], PDP
Plasmabildschirm *m*, **Plasmadisplay** *n* plasma display (screen), plasma [display] panel, gas[-discharge] display
Plasma-Flachbildschirm *m s.* Plasmabildschirm
Plasma-Großbildschirm *m* large plasma display
Plasmaquelle *f* plasma source
Plasmaschirm *m s.* Plasmabildschirm
Plasmaspektroskopie/laserinduzierte laser-induced plasma spectroscopy, LIPS
Plasmatrockenätzen *n* plasma dry etching
Plasmon *n* plasmon
Plastiklinse *f* plastic lens
Platinabzug *m*, **Platindruck** *m* platinum print, platinotype
Platindruckverfahren *n* platinotype [process], platinum process (printing)
Platine *f* 1. printed [circuit] board, circuit board; 2. film pressure plate
Platinenfoto *n* circuit image
Platinotypie *f s.* Platindruckverfahren
Platinpapier *n* platinum [printing] paper, platinotype paper
Platte *f* 1. plate *(s.a. under* Druckplatte*)*; 2. disk, disc
~/**asphärische** aspherical plate
~/**doppelbrechende planparallele** phase (wave) plate, phase retarder
~/**eloxierte** anodized plate *(offset printing)*
~/**fotografische** photographic (film) plate, photoplate
~/**fotolithografische** photolithographic plate
~/**holografische** holographic plate, holoplate
~/**keilförmige** wedge[d] [optical] plate
~/**magnetooptische** magneto-optic[al] disk, magnetic-optical disk, MOD
~/**optische** optical disk
~/**panchromatische** panchromatic plate
~/**planparallele** plane parallel plate *(optics)*
~/**spektroskopische** spectroscopic plate
~/**vorbeschichtete** presensitized plate *(offset printing)*
~/**xeroradiografische** xeroradiographic plate
Plattenbelichtung *f* plate exposure
Plattenherstellung *f s.* Druckplattenherstellung
Plattenkamera *f* plate camera
Plattenlaufwerk *n* disk drive, hard [disk] drive; magnetic disk drive
Plattenmessmaschine *f*/**automatische** automatic plate measuring machine, APM *(astrophotography)*
Plattenspeicher *m* disk memory
~ *m*/**optischer** optical disk storage
Plattenspeicherung *f* disk[-based] storage
Plattenteller *m* turntable
Plattentiefdruck *m* plate gravure printing
Plattenwechsel *f*/**[voll]automatischer** automatic plate changing (loading) *(printing press)*
Plattenzylinder *m* plate[-bearing] cylinder *(printing press)*
Platzhalter *m*, **Platzhalter-Pixelbild** *n* placeholder, computer (on-screen) icon
Plausibilitätsprüfung *f* parity check
PLED-Display *n* PLED (polymer light-emitting diode) display, polymer[-based OLED-]display
Pleochroismus *m* pleochroism
plesiochron plesiochronous
Plethysmograf *m* plethysmograph
Plethysmografie plethysmography
plethysmografisch plethysmographic
Plethysmogramm *n* plethysmogram
Plössl-Okular *n* Plössl (symmetrical) eyepiece
Plot *m(n)* plot *(graphic representation)*
plotten to plot, to graph
Plotter *m* [drafting] plotter, plotting instrument; plotting machine
~/**digitaler** digital plotter
~/**elektrostatischer** electrostatic plotter
~/**fotogrammetrischer** photogrammetric plotter
Plotterdisplay *n* plotter display *(navigational data screen)*

Plotterstift *m* plotting pencil
Plug-In *n* plug-in [module], add-in
Plumbikon *n* plumbicon [tube], lead oxide vidicon (camera tube)
pn-Fotodiode *f* p-n [junction] photodiode
pn-Grenzschicht *f* p-n boundary
pn-Übergang *m* p-n junction, Schottky barrier *(photodiode)*
Pockels-Effekt *m* Pockels effect, linear electro-optic effect
Pockels-Zelle *f* Pockels cell *(electro-optical device)*
Pocketkamera *f* pocket[-size] camera
Poggendorff-Täuschung *f* Poggendorff illusion *(geometrical illusion)*
Poisson-Prozess *m* Poisson process
Poisson-Rauschen *n* Poisson [counting] noise, Poisson-distributed white noise
poissonverteilt Poisson-distributed
Poisson-Verteilung *f* Poisson [probability density] distribution, Poisson frequency distribution, Poisson statistics
Poisson-Voronoi-Mosaik *n* [Poisson-]Voronoi tessellation
Pol *m* pole *(transfer function)*
Polachse *f s.* Polarachse
Polafilter *n s.* Polarisationsfilter
Polarabstandsprojektion *f* distance-versus-angle signature
Polarachse *f* polar axis
Polarimeter *n*/**abbildendes** *n* imaging polarimeter
Polarimetrie *f* polarimetry
polarimetrisch polarimetric *(radar system)*
Polarisation *f* polarization
~/**elektrische** electric polarization
~/**elliptische** elliptic[al] polarization
~/**horizontale** horizontal [linear] polarization *(radar)*
~/**lineare** linear polarization
~/**linksdrehende (linkszirkulare)** left-hand[ed] polarization
~/**optische** optical polarization
~/**orthogonale** orthogonal polarization
~/**rechtsdrehende (rechtszirkulare)** right-hand[ed] polarization
~/**teilweise** partial polarization
~/**vertikale** vertical [linear] polarization *(radar)*
~/**zirkulare** circular polarization
Polarisationsachse *f* polarization (polarizing) axis, axis of polarization
Polarisationsanalysator *m* polarization analyzer
Polarisationsbeschichtung *f* polarization coating
Polarisationsbrille *f* polarized glasses, polarizing (polarization) goggles
Polarisationsdrehung *f* polarization rotation
Polarisationsdrehwinkel *m s.* Polarisationswinkel
Polarisationsebene *f* polarization plane, plane of polarization

Polarisationseffekt *m* polarization (polarizing) effect
Polarisationseigenschaft *f* polarization characteristic
Polarisationseinrichtung *f* polarization device
Polarisationsellipse *f* polarization ellipse
Polarisationselliptizität *f* polarization ellipticity
Polarisationsfarbfilter *n* colored polarizing filter
Polarisationsfilter *n* polarizing filter, pola screen, polarizer
Polarisationsfilterbrille *f s.* Polarisationsbrille
Polarisationsfilterfolie *f*, **Polarisationsfolie** *f* polarizing sheet (foil), sheet polarizer
Polarisationsfotografie *f* polarized-light photography
Polarisationsgerät *n* polarization device
Polarisationsgrad *m* degree of polarization, polarization degree
Polarisationsholografie *f* polarization holography
Polarisationshologramm *n* polarization hologram
Polarisationsinterferometrie *f* polarization interferometry
Polarisationskontrolle *f* polarization control
Polarisationslinse *f* polarizing lens
Polarisationsmessung *f* polarization measurement
Polarisationsmikrofotografie *f* polarization photomicrography
Polarisationsmikroskop *n* polarizing (polarized-light) microscope
Polarisationsmikroskopie *f* polarizing (polarized-light) microscopy
Polarisationsmodendispersion *f* polarization mode dispersion
Polarisationsmuster *n* polarization pattern
Polarisationsoptik *f* 1. polarizing (polarization) optics; 2. polarizing [optical] system
Polarisationsplatte *f* polarizing plate, sheet polarizer
Polarisationsprisma *n* polarizing prism, prism polarizer
Polarisationsrauschen *n* polarization noise
Polarisationsreinheit *f* polarization purity
Polarisationsrichtung *f* polarization direction (orientation)
Polarisations-Röntgenspektrometer *n* polarized excitation X-ray spectrometer
Polarisationsrotator *m* polarization rotator
Polarisationsvektor *m* polarization vector
Polarisationsverhältnis *n* polarization ratio
Polarisationsvermögen *n* polarization capability
Polarisationswinkel *m* polarization (polarizing) angle, Brewster['s] angle
Polarisationszustand *m* polarization state, state of polarization

Polarisator *m* polarizer
~/**dichroitischer** dichroic polarizer
polarisierbar polarizable
Polarisierbarkeit *f* polarizability
polarisieren to polarize
Polariskop *n* polariscope
Polarität *f* polarity
Polarkoordinaten *fpl* polar coordinates
Polarkoordinatenachse *f* polar coordinate axis
Polarkoordinatendarstellung *f* plan position indication, PPI *(radar)*; plan position indicator mode, PPI mode
Polarkoordinatensystem *n* polar coordinates system
Polaroid... *s.* Sofortbild...
Polarplanimeter *n* polar planimeter
Polarwinkel *m* polar angle
Polfilter *n s.* Polarisationsfilter
Polfilterbrille *f s.* Polarisationsbrille
Polfolie *f s.* Polarisationsfilterfolie
Poliermittel *n* polishing material
Polierpech *n* polishing pitch *(lens manufacture)*
Polierrot *n* jewelers' rouge *(lens manufacture)*
Polizeiaufnahme *f*, **Polizeifoto** *n* police photograph
Polizeifotograf *m* police photographer
Polybézierkurve *f* polybézier curve *(computer graphics)*
polychrom polychromatic, multicolor[ed]
Polychromasie *f* polychromaticity
polychromatisch *s.* polychrom
Polychromie *f* polychromy
polydispers polydisperse *(e.g. a photographic emulsion)*
Polyeder *n* polyhedron
~/**konvexes** convex polyhedron
~/**regelmäßiges** regular polyhedron, Platonic body (solid) *(geometric primitive)*
~/**umschließendes** bounding polyhedron
Polyederapproximation *f* faceting *(computer graphics)*
Polyederdarstellung *f* polyhedron representation
Polyederfläche *f* polyhedral face
Polyederobjekt *n* polyhedral object
Polyedersatz *m*/**Eulerscher** Euler['s] equation (formula) *(mathematical morphology)*
Polyester *m* polyester [resin]
Polyesterdruckfolie *f* polyester plate
Polyesterfilm *m* polyester[-based] film
Polyesterfilmträger *m* polyester film base
Polyethylen *n* polyethylene
Polyethylenazin *n* polyethylene azine *(development additive)*
Polyethylenterephthalat *n* polyethylene terephthalate, PET *(film base)*
Polygon *n* polygon
~/**beliebiges** arbitrary polygon
~/**ebenes** patch *(radiosity technique)*
~/**einfaches** simple polygon
~/**einfassendes** surrounding (circumscribing) polygon
~/**eingeschriebenes** inscribed polygon, inpolygon
~/**geschlossenes** closed polygon
~/**konkaves** concave polygon
~/**konvexes** convex polygon
~/**monotones** monotone polygon
~/**offenes** open polygon
~/**optisches** optical polygon
~/**orthogonales** orthogonal (rectilinear) polygon
~/**reguläres** regular polygon
~/**umschreibendes** *s.* ~/einfassendes
~/**unregelmäßiges** irregular polygon
Polygonabtaster *m* polygon scanner
polygonal polygonal
polygonalisieren to polygonalize
Polygonalisierung *f* polygonalization
Polygonalprisma *n s.* Polygonprisma
Polygonapproximation *f* polygonal approximation
Polygonbildung *f* polygonalization
Polygondarstellung *f* 1. polygon rendering; 2. polygonal (polymesh) representation
Polygondurchdringung *f* polygon intersection
Polygonebene *f s.* Polygonfläche
Polygonecke *f*, **Polygoneckpunkt** *m* polygon vertex
Polygonfläche *f* polygonal [sur]face
Polygonfüllalgorithmus *m* polygon filling algorithm
Polygonkante *f* polygon boundary
Polygonkontur *f* polygonal contour
Polygonmenge *f* polygon set
Polygonmodell *n* polygonal model
Polygonmodellierung *f* polygonal modeling, polygon[-based] modeling
Polygonnetz *n* polygon[al] mesh, polymesh, polygonal net[work]
Polygonoptimierung *f* polygon optimization
Polygonprisma *n* polygon[al] prism
Polygonreduktion *f* polygon reduction [technique], polygon thinning
Polygonschnittpunkt *m* polygon section point
Polygonspiegel *m* polygon[al] mirror
Polygontabelle *f* polygon table
Polygontriangulation *f* polygon triangulation
Polygonumrandung *f* polygonal contour
Polygonzerlegung *f* polygon decomposition, polygonal (rendering) subdivision, tessellation
Polygonzug *m* 1. polygonal curve; 2. [survey] traverse *(photogrammetry)*
Polygrafie *f* graphic arts
Polymarke *f* polymarker
Polymer *n* polymer

Polymer 308

~/**fotoleitfähiges** photoconductive polymer
~/**fotovernetzbares** photo-crosslinkable polymer
~/**lichtempfindliches** photosensitive polymer
~/**synthetisches** synthetic polymer
Polymerdisplay n polymer[-based OLED-]display, PLED (polymer light-emitting diode) display
Polymerfolie f polymer film
Polymerisation f polymerization
polymerisierbar polymerizable
polymerisieren to polymerize
Polymethinfarbstoff m polymethine dye *(sensitizer)*
Polymethiniminfarbstoff m s. Polymethin-Farbstoff
Polymethylmethacrylat n polymethyl methacrylate, acrylic *(optical plastic)*
polymorph polymorphic
Polynom n polynomial
~ **dritter Ordnung** s. ~/kubisches
~ **erster Ordnung** first-order polynomial, straight-line polynomial
~ **höherer Ordnung** higher-order polynomial, higher-degree polynomial
~/**kubisches** cubic polynomial, third-order polynomial
~/**trigonometrisches** trigonometric[al] polynomial
~ **vierter Ordnung** fourth-degree polynomial, quartic polynomial
~ **zweiter Ordnung** second-order polynomial, quadratic (second-degree) polynomial
Polynomfilter n polynomial filter *(image processing)*
polynomial polynomial
Polynominterpolation f polynomial interpolation
polynomisch polynomial
Polynomklassifikation f polynomial classification
Polynomklassifikator m polynomial classifier
Polynomkoeffizient m polynomial coefficient
Polynomverteilung f polynomial (multinomial) distribution
Polyphasenfilter n polyphase filter
Polypropylen n polypropylene
Polysilicium n polysilicon, polycrystalline silicon, poly-Si
Polyvinylchlorid n polyvinyl chloride, PVC *(e.g. as film base)*
Polyvinylzimtsäurepolymer n polyvinylcinnamate polymer
Pop[p]el m s. Butzen
Popularitätsmethode f popularity algorithm *(color quantization)*
Pop-up-Fenster n pop-up window *(on a computer screen)*

Porro-Prisma n **erster Art** Porro prism of the first type
~ **zweiter Art** Porro prism of the second type
Portal n s. Internetportal
Portografie f portography
Porträt n portrait
Porträtatelier n [photographic] portrait studio
Porträtaufnahme f portrait shot
Porträtbeleuchtung f portrait lighting
Porträteinstellung f portrait setting
Porträtfilm m portrait film
Porträtfotograf m portrait photographer
Porträtfotografie f portrait photography, portraiture
Porträtfunktion f portrait mode
porträtieren to portray
Porträtist m portrayer
Porträtmotiv n portrait subject
Porträtobjektiv n portrait lens
Porträtstudio n [photographic] portrait studio
Porträt-Teleobjektiv n portrait lens
Porträtzoom n portrait zoom
Positionierlaser m pilot laser
Positioniertisch m positioning table (stage)
Positionierung f positioning, placement
Positionierungsfehler m positioning error
Positionierungsgenauigkeit f placement accuracy
Positionierungskugel f trackball
Positionierungssystem n positioning system
Positionierungswerkzeug n positioning tool
Positionsdisplay n position display *(navigational data screen)*
Positionsgeber m position sensor (sensing device)
Positionsgenauigkeit f positional accuracy *(object recognition)*
Positionsmarke f 1. position mark *(s.a. Passkreuz)*; 2. cursor, [screen] pointer, arrow
Positionsrahmen m frame *(desktop publishing)*
Positionsregelung f positional control
Positionsvektor m position vector
Positiv n positive [photograph], positive [photographic] image, positive picture
~/**transparentes** [positive] transparency, diapositive
Positivabzug m s. Papierpositiv
Positivemulsion f [direct-]positive emulsion, positive-working emulsion
Positiventwickler m [photographic] paper developer, print developer
Positiventwicklung f positive development
Positiv-Farbfilm m positive color film, color positive film; color print [still] film
Positivfilm m positive film, reversal[-type] film, reversal transparency (working) film, knockout film

Positiv-Fotolack *m* positive[-acting] photoresist
Positivkopie *f* positive copy; positive [film] print; positive work print *(cinema)*
Positivlack *m* positive[-working] photoresist
Positivlinse *f* positive (convergent) lens, convex (converging) lens, collection (collector) lens
Positivmaterial *n* positive [photographic] material, positive stock; positive footage *(film material)*
Positivmodulation *f* positive modulation *(television)*
Positivpapier *n* positive paper
Positivperforation *f* positive perforation
Positiv-Perforationslochabstand *m*, **Positiv-Perforationsschritt** *m* long pitch *(film stock)*
Positivplatte *f* positive plate *(color photography)*
Positiv-Positiv-Verfahren *n* positive-positive procedure *(of color print processing)*
Positivprozess *m s.* Positivverfahren
Positivretusche *f* positive retouching
Positiv-Rohfilm *m* positive raw stock
Positivschicht *f* positive layer *(instant film)*
Positivtechnik *f s.* Positivverfahren
Positivverfahren *n* positive[-working] process, positive technique *(photography)*
Positron *n* positron, antielectron
Positronenemissionstomograf *m* positron[-emission] tomograph, PET (positron-emission tomography) scanner
Positronenemissionstomografie *f* positron-emission tomography, PET [scanning]
Positronenemissionstomogramm *n* positron-emission image, PET image
Positronenkamera *f* positron camera; PET camera
Positronenstrahler *m* positron radiator (emitter)
Positronentomograf *m s.* Positronenemissionstomograf
Positronenzerfall *m* positron decay
Post *f*/**elektronische** electronic mail, E-mail
Poster *n(m)* poster
Postereffekt *m s.* Tontrennung
Postkartenformat *n* postcard size
Postkartenfoto *n* postcard picture
Postkartenfotografie *f* postcard photography
Postproduktion *f* postproduction [work], postprocessing [work]; [postproduction] editing
Postproduktionsfirma *f* post house (department)
Postsortieranlage *f* postal mail sorter
Postsortierung *f* mail sorting
Potential *n*/**elektrostatisches** electrostatic potential

Potentialdifferenz *f* potential difference; electromotive force
Potentialmulde *f*, **Potentialsenke** *f*, **Potentialtopf** *m* potential well *(photodetector)*
Potentiometer *n* potentiometer, pot
Powerspektrum *n s.* Leistungsdichtespektrum
Poynting-Vektor *m* Poynting vector *(of energy flow)*
p-Phenylendiamin *n* p-phenylenediamine, PPD *(developing agent)*
PPI-Sichtgerät *n* PPI (plan-position indicator) display *(radar)*
Präcodierung *f s.* precoding
Prädikat *n* predicate *(logic)*
Prädikatenkalkül *n* predicate (functional) calculus
Prädikatenlogik *f* predicate logic
prädiktabel predictable
Prädiktabilität *f* predictability
Prädiktion *f* prediction
~/**adaptive** adaptive prediction
~/**bewegungskompensierte** motion-compensated prediction, MCP
~/**bidirektionale** bidirectional prediction
~/**deterministische** deterministic prediction
~/**disparitätskompensierte** disparity-compensated prediction
~/**dreidimensionale** three-dimensional prediction
~/**halbbildbasierte** field-based prediction
~/**hierarchische** hierarchic[al] prediction
~/**kantensensitive** edge-sensitive prediction
~/**lineare** linear prediction
~/**lokale** local prediction
~/**nichtlineare** nonlinear prediction
~/**ortszeitliche** spatiotemporal prediction
~/**rückwärtsgesteuerte adaptive** backward adaptive prediction
~/**unidirektionale** unidirectional prediction
~/**vorwärtsgesteuerte adaptive** forward adaptive prediction
~/**zeitliche** temporal prediction
Prädiktionsbild *n* prediction image; predictive (predicted) frame, prediction frame, P-frame *(video)*
Prädiktionsblock *m* prediction block
Prädiktionscodierer *m* predictive [en]coder
Prädiktionscodierung *f* 1. predictive (previous-pixel) coding, differential (relative) coding, differencing; 2. *s.* Pulscodemodulation/differentielle
~/**bewegungskompensierte** motion-compensated predictive coding
~/**lineare** linear predictive coding, LPC
Prädiktionsdifferenz *f* prediction difference
Prädiktionsfehler *m* prediction error; difference signal *(differential coding)*

Prädiktionsfehler 310

~/bewegungskompensierter motion-compensated prediction error
Prädiktionsfehlerbild *n* prediction error image
Prädiktionsfehlerblock *m* prediction error block
Prädiktionsfehlerfilter *n* analysis filter
~/inverses synthesis filter
Prädiktionsfehlersignal *n* prediction error signal
Prädiktionsfehlerspektrum *n* prediction error spectrum
Prädiktionsgenauigkeit *f* prediction accuracy
Prädiktionsgewinn *m* prediction gain
Prädiktionskoeffizient *m* predicition coefficient
Prädiktionsverfahren *n* prediction process
Prädiktionswert *m* prediction value
prädiktiv predictive
Prädiktor *m* predictor
~/adaptiver adaptive predictor
~/bewegungskompensierter motion-compensated predictor
~/linearer linear predictor
~/optimaler optimal predictor
Präfixcode *m* prefix (instantaneously decodable) code
~/binärer binary prefix code, tree-structured code
Prägebild *n* blind image
Prägedruck *m* blind stamping, blinding
Prägefoliendruck *m* hot foil printing, [hot] foil stamping
Prägehologramm *n* embossed hologram
prägen to emboss, to cameo; to deboss, to tool
Prägepresse *f* embossing press
Prägestock *m* male die, force card *(e.g. in embossing or debossing)*
Prägung *f*/**farblose** relief embossing
Prallelektrode *f* dynode *(photomultiplier)*
Präparatebene *f* sample (specimen) plane *(microscopy)*
Präparatefotografie *f* specimen photography
Präparateradiografie *f* specimen radiography
Präparation *f* [specimen] preparation
Präpariermikroskop *n* dissecting microscope
Präsentation *f* presentation
~/audiovisuelle audiovisual presentation
Präsentationsgrafik *f* presentation graphics
Präsentationsmappe *f* print presenter; portfolio
Präsentationsprojektor *m* [video] beamer
Präsentationssoftware *f* presentation software *(multimedia)*
Präsentationssystem *n* presentation system
Präsentationstechnik *f* presentation technology

prävisualisieren to previsualize *(filming)*
Prävisualisierung *f* previsualization, previz
Praxinoskop *n* praxinoscope *(an early optical toy)*
präzedieren to precess *(protons)*
Präzession *f*/**gyromagnetische** gyromagnetic precession
Präzessionsachse *f* axis of precession
Präzessionsbewegung *f* precessional motion
Präzessionsfrequenz *f* [spin] precession frequency, Larmor [precessional] frequency, resonant frequency *(magnetic resonance imaging)*
Präzessionskegel *m* precession cone
Präzessionsmatrix *f* precession matrix
Präzessionswinkel *m* precession angle
Präzisionsanflugradar *n* precision-approach radar, PAR
Präzisionsdruck *m* precision printing
Präzisionsgerät *n*/**optisches** precision optical device
Präzisionskamera *f* precision (high-quality) camera
Präzisionsmikrofotografie *f* precision photomicrography
Präzisionsobjektiv *n* high-quality [photographic] lens
Präzisionsoptik *f* precision (high-quality) optics; precision optical equipment
präzisionsoptisch precision optical
Präzisionsspiegel *m* precision[-ground] mirror
Precursor *m*/**farbstoffabspaltender** dye releaser *(color photography)*
Preemphasis *f* preemphasis; predistortion *(frequency modulation)*
Premierenkino *n* first-run theater (house)
Presbyopie *f* presbyopia, limited accommodation, old eye *(vision defect)*
Pressefoto *n* press photo, news photo[graph]
Pressefotograf *m* press (newspaper) photographer, daily news photographer
Pressefotografie *f* press (news) photography
Presseur *m* impression roll[er], impression cylinder *(printing press)*
Pressling *m* pressing *(optical manufacture)*
Pressung *f* squeeze *(e.g. of impression cylinders in printing)*
Prewitt-Filter *n*, **Prewitt-Operator** *m* Prewitt filter (mask), Prewitt kernel, Prewitt [edge gradient] operator, Prewitt edge detection mask
Primäranregung *f* primary excitation *(X-ray fluorescence)*
Primärelektronenstrahl *m* primary electron beam *(electron microscope)*
Primärfarbe *f* primary color, [monochromatic] primary, basis (basic) color *(colorimetry)*
~/additive additive primary [color]

~/**imaginäre** imaginary primary; hypothetical primary
~/**psychologische** psychological primary [color], unitary color
~/**subtraktive** subtractive primary [color]
Primärfarbenbild *n* primary color image
Primärfarbenfilter *n* primary color filter
primärfarbig pimary-colored
Primärfarbreiz *m* primary color stimulus
Primärfarbwert *m s.* Primärvalenz
Primärfokus *m* prime focus
Primärobjektiv *n* prime lens
Primärprozess *m*/**fotochemischer** primary photochemical process
~/**fotografischer** first stage of latent-image formation
Primärradar *n* primary [surveillance] radar
Primärreaktion *f*/**fotochemische** primary photochemical process
Primärreflexion *f* primary reflection
Primärspiegel *m* primary (main) mirror *(e.g. of a catadioptric system)*
Primärstrahl *m* primary beam *(e.g. of a laser)*
Primärstrahler *m* primary radiator, self-luminous object
Primärstrahlfilter *n* primary beam filter
Primärstrahlung *f* primary radiation *(e.g. from a X-ray source)*
Primärton *m* original *(filming)*
Primärvalenz *f* primary color, [monochromatic] primary, basis (basic) color *(colorimetry)*
~/**spektrale** spectral primary
~/**virtuelle** virtual primary
Primer *m* primer, prime coat
Primitiv *n* primitive [element]
~/**geometrisches** geometric primitive
~/**grafisches** graphic primitive
~/**semantisches** semantic primitive
Primitivkörper *m* solid (volumetric) primitive, primitive solid
Printer *m* printer, printout device
~/**digitaler** digital printer
~/**optischer** optical printer
Printmedium *n* print medium
Prinzip *n*/**Babinets** Babinet principle *(diffractive optics)*
~/**Fermatsches** Fermat's principle [of least time] *(ray optics)*
~/**Huygenssches** Huygens' principle *(wave theory)*
Priorisierung *f* priorization
Prioritätenlistenalgorithmus *m* painter's algorithm
Prioritätensuchbaum *m* priority search tree *(data structure)*
Prioritätswarteschlange *f* priority queue *(data processing)*
Prisma *n* prism
~/**achromatisches** achromatic prism
~/**Bauernfeindsches** Bauernfeind prism
~/**brechendes** refracting (refractive) prism

~/**doppelbrechendes (doppelreflektierendes)** constant-deviation prism
~/**dünnes** thin prism
~/**Foucaultsches** Foucault prism
~/**Nicolsches** Nicol [prism]
~/**rechtwinkliges** right-angle[d] prism, right-triangle prism
~/**rhombisches** rhombic prism
~/**totalreflektierendes** totally reflecting prism
~/**zusammengesetztes** composite prism *(s.a. Prismenkombination)*
prismatisch prismatic[al], prismal
Prismenblock *m* prism block
Prismenbrille *f* prism eyeglasses
Prismenfeldstecher *m*, **Prismenfernglas** *n* prism binocular[s]
Prismenfernrohr *n* prism telescope
Prismenfilter *n* prismatic filter
Prismenfläche *f* prism face; prismatic plane
Prismenhalter *m* prism table
Prismeninterferometer *n* prism interferometer
Prismenklemme *f* prism [table] clamp
Prismenkombination *f* prism combination, composite prism; train of prisms
Prismenkreuz *n* crossed-prism (double-prism) square
Prismenpaar *n* pair of prisms
~/**anamorphotisches** anamorphic prism pair
Prismenpolarisator *m* prism polarizer, polarizing prism
Prismensatz *m* set of prisms
Prismenspektrograf *m* prism spectrograph
Prismenspektrometer *n* prism spectrometer
Prismenspektroskop *n* prism spectroscope
Prismenspektrum *n* prism[atic] spectrum
Prismenstrahl[en]teiler *m* prismatic beam splitter
Prismensucher *m* [penta]prism finder
Prismensystem *n* prism system; composite prism
Prismentisch *m* prism table
Prismenwinkel *m* prism [interface] angle
Probe *f* 1. sample; specimen; 2. test
Probeabzug *m* 1. test [photographic] print; [contact] proof; 2. *s.* Probeandruck
Probeandruck *m* prepress proof; proof [print]
Probeaufnahme *f* test shot *(filming; s.a. Probebild)*
Probeausdruck *m* hard proof
Probebelichtung *f* test exposure
Probeblitz *m* [test] preflash
Probeglas *n* test glass *(lens manufacture)*
Probelayout *n* dummy, mock-up
Probenkammer *f* sample chamber *(electron microscope)*
Probestreifen *m* test strip
Probevorführung *f* test screening *(cinema)*

Produktaufnahme *f*, **Produktfoto** *n* pack shot
Produktfotografie *f* product photography
Produktion *f*/**dokumentarische** documentary [production] *(cinema, video)*
Produktionsassistent *m* assistant production manager, APM
Produktionsfirma *f* production company *(cinema)*
Produktionsgelände *n* [studio] backlot, lot
Produktionskamera *f* broadcast[-quality] camera
Produktionsleiter *m* production's director, [unit] production manager, [U]PM *(filming)*
Produktionsmischer *m* [studio] production switcher
Produktionsnachbearbeitung *f* postproduction [work], [postproduction] editing
Produktionsort *m* location; set
Produktionsstudio *n* production studio
Produktionsteam *n* production team (crew)
Profiausrüstung *f* professional[-grade] equipment
Proficamcorder *m* professional [digital] camcorder
Profikamera *f* professional[-level] camera
Profil *n*/**räumlich skalierbares** spatially scalable profile
Profilansicht *f* profile view
Profilaufnahme *f* profile photograph; profile portrait; profile shot
Profilmessgerät *n* profilometer
Profil-Nahaufnahme *f* profile close-up shot
Profilometer *n* profilometer
Profilometrie *f* profilometry
Profilprojektor *m* profile (contour) projector
Profilscheinwerfer *m* ellipsoidal [reflector] spotlight, ERF, ellipsoidal (profile) spot
Profiobjektiv *n* professional quality lens
Programm *n* program
~/**Twain-kompatibles** Twain-compliant program *(for scanners)*
Programmablaufplan *m s.* Flussdiagramm
Programmabsturz *m* software failure
Programmanbieter *m* content provider (server)
Programmausstrahlung *f* distribution *(e.g. of television signals)*
Programmaustausch *m*/**internationaler** international program distribution, international exchange of programs
Programmautomatik *f* programmed auto[matic] exposure, program exposure system
~/**variable** variable (flexible) program mode
Programmbearbeitung *f* program (broadcast) editing
Programmbefehl *m* program instruction

Programmbeitrag *m* 1. program; 2. *s.* Programmzuspielung
Programmbereich *m* program area *(video disk)*
Programmdatei *f* program file
Programmdatenstrom *m* program [transport] stream *(digital video)*
Programmfehler *m* program error, bug
Programmfenster *n* program window *(as a portion of the computer screen)*
Programmführer *m*/**elektronischer** electronic program[ming] guide, EPG
~/**interaktiver** interactive program[ming] guide, IPG
programmierbar programmable
~/**frei** user programmable
Programmierschnittstelle *f* programming (programmer's) interface
Programmiersprache *f* [computer] programming language
~/**höhere** high-level programming language; high-level compiler language
Programmierung *f*/**dynamische** dynamic programming
~/**lineare** linear programming *(optimization method)*
~/**objektorientierte** object-oriented programming
Programminformation[en] *f[pl]* programming information
Programminstallation *f*/**automatische** automatic channel installation, ACI
Programmkanal *m* program channel
Programmmaterial *n* program material; programming *(e.g. of a television broadcaster)*
Programmmonitor *m* program monitor
Programmpaket *n* bouquet
Programmproduktion *f* program production (origination) *(broadcast television)*
Programmsignal *n* program signal
Programmspeicher *m* program memory
Programmstrom *m* program [transport] stream *(digital video)*
Programmsymbol *n* computer (on-screen) icon; placeholder
Programmtaktreferenz *f* program clock reference, PCR *(television)*
Programmton *m* program sound
Programmverschiebung *f* program shift *(automatic exposure)*
Programmverschluss *m*/**elektronischer** programmed electronic shutter
Programmwählscheibe *f* program mode selector *(compact camera)*
Programmzeitschrift *f*/**elektronische** electronic program[ming] guide, EPG
Programmzuspielung *f* contribution
Projektion *f* projection; screening *(cinema)*
~/**affine** affine projection
~/**äquidistante** [azimuthal] equidistant projection
~/**axonometrische** axonometric projection

~/**diaskopische** diascopic projection (s.a. Diaprojektion)
~/**digitale** digital cinema projection
~/**dimetrische** dimetric projection
~/**elektronische** electronic projection
~/**episkopische** episcopic projection
~/**fächerförmige** fan-beam projection (tomography)
~/**geometrische** geometric projection
~/**gnomonische** gnomonic projection (cartography)
~/**hyperbolische** hyperbolic projection
~/**isometrische** isometric projection
~/**lineare** linear projection
~/**monometrische** monometric projection
~/**optische** optical projection
~/**orthogonale (parallele)** orthographic (orthogonal) projection, [orthographic] parallel projection
~/**perspektivische** perspective (polar) projection
~/**planimetrische** planimetric projection
~/**radiografische** radiographic projection
~/**schief[winklig]e** oblique projection
~/**sphärische** spherical projection
~/**stereografische** stereographic projection
~/**stereoskopische** stereoscopic projection
~/**täuschende** illusionistic projection
~/**topografische** topographical projection
~/**trimetrische** trimetric projection
~/**winkeltreue** conformal projection
~/**zentralperspektivische** centered perspective projection
Projektionsabstand m projection distance, projector-to-screen distance
Projektionsachse f projection axis
Projektionsanlage f projection facility (equipment)
Projektionsapparat m [optical] projector
Projektionsapparatur f projector equiment
Projektionsart f projection type
Projektionsbelichtung f projection printing
Projektionsbild n projection (projected) image, projection view
Projektionsbildebene f projection image plane
Projektionsbildentstehung f projection image formation
Projektionsbildschirm m projection display [device]
Projektionsblende f s. Projektionsmaske
Projektionsdaten pl projection data
Projektionsdatensatz m projection [data] set, projection image set, set of projection data
Projektionsdia[positiv] n projection transparency; projection slide
Projektionsdisplay n projection display
Projektionsdistanz f s. Projektionsentfernung
Projektionsdurchlauf m screening (of a motion picture)

Projektionsebene f projection (projective) plane; view[ing] plane (computer graphics)
Projektionseinheit f projection assembly (unit) (e.g. of an enlarger)
Projektionsempfänger m projection TV set
Projektionsentfernung f projection distance; projector-to-screen distance, image distance, throw
Projektionsfenster n projection port; booth porthole
Projektionsfernsehen n projection television (TV)
Projektionsfernseher m,
Projektionsfernsehgerät n projection TV set
Projektionsfernsehsystem n projection television system
Projektionsfilm m projection[-type] film
Projektionsfläche f projection area; projection surface
Projektionsformat n projection format
Projektionsfrequenz f projection [frame] rate, projected frame-per-second rate
Projektionsgeometrie f projection geometry
Projektionsgerät n projection device (s.a. Projektor)
Projektionsgeschwindigkeit f projection speed (rate)
Projektionsgleichung f projection equation
Projektionskabine f projection booth
Projektionskegel m projection cone
Projektionskondensor m projection condenser
Projektionskopie f projection print
Projektionskopieren n,
Projektionskopierung f projection printing
Projektionslampe f projection (projector) lamp, projector bulb
Projektionsleinwand f projection screen
Projektionslesegerät n projection reader
Projektionslicht n projector light
Projektionslichtkegel m projection cone
Projektionslichtquelle f projection source, projector light source
Projektionslichtstärke f projector luminosity
Projektionslichtstrahl m projecting light ray
Projektionslichtstrom m projection beam
Projektionslichtweg m projection path
Projektionslinie f projection line
Projektionslinse f projection lens
Projektionslithografie f projection lithography
Projektionsmaske f gobo, flag; pattern mask (s.a. Schattenwerfer)
Projektionsmaterial n projection material
Projektionsmatrix f projection matrix (computer vision)
Projektionsmikroskop n projection (projecting) microscope

Projektionsmodell

Projektionsmodell *n* projection model
Projektionsobjektiv *n* projection (projector) lens, projection optics
Projektionsoptik *f* 1. projection optics; 2. *s.* Projektionsobjektiv
projektionsoptisch projection optical
Projektionsprofil *n* projection profile
Projektionspunkt *m* projection point
Projektionsradiografie *f* [X-ray] projection radiography, X-ray projection imaging
~/digitale computed (scanned projection) radiography
Projektionsradiogramm *n* projection radiograph, X-ray projection image
Projektionsraum *m* 1. projection (projective) space *(object classification)*; 2. projection (screening) room
Projektionsrekonstruktion *f* projection reconstruction, projective imaging *(magnetic resonance imaging)*
Projektionsrichtung *f* projection direction, direction of projection
Projektionsrohdaten *pl* projection raw data
Projektionsröhre *f* projection [cathode-ray] tube, projection CRT
Projektionsröntgentechnik *f s.* Projektionsradiografie
Projektionsschirm *m* projection screen
Projektionsspiegel *m* projection mirror
Projektionsstrahl *m* projection ray (beam)
Projektionssystem *n* projection [optical] system
Projektionstechnik *f* 1. projection technology (technics); 2. projection technique
Projektionstheorem *n* projection theorem *(tomographic image formation)*
Projektionstisch *m* projector table
Projektionstrick *m* process shot *(cinema)*
Projektionsvergrößerung *f* projection enlargement
Projektionsverhältnis *n* throw ratio
Projektionswand *f* projection screen
Projektionswärme *f* heat of projection
Projektionswinkel *m* projection angle; screen angle
Projektionszentrum *n* projection center, center of projection
projektiv projective
Projektiv *n* projector lens *(microscope)*
Projektor *m* [optical] projector
~/digitaler digital projector; beamer
~ fester Auflösung fixed-resolution projector
~/gebläsegekühlter fan-cooled projector
~ mit kontinuierlichem Filmlauf continuous-motion projector
~ variabler Auflösung variable-resolution projector
Projektorbildfenster *n* projector gate (aperture), projection aperture
Projektorblende *f* projector shutter
Projektorfenster *n s.* Projektorbildfenster
Projektorformat *n* projector format

Projektorkoffer *m* projector case
Projektorkopf *m* projector (picture) head
Projektorlampe *f* projector (projection) lamp, projector bulb
Projektorlaufwerk *n* projector intermittent
Projektorlicht *n* projector light
Projektormagazin *n* projector magazine
Projektorobjektiv *n* projector (projection) lens, projection optics
Projektorraum *m* 1. projection room; projection booth (box); *(cinema)*; 2. *s.* Vorführraum 1.
Projektorstativ *n* projector stand
Projektortisch *m* projector table
~/fahrbarer projection cart
Projektorwechsel *m* projector change, changeover *(film screening)*
projizierbar projectable
Projizierbarkeit *f* projectability
projizieren to project, to image
Projizierung *f s.* Projektion
Promotionsfoto *n* publicity photo (still) *(cinema)*
Proof *m* proof; press proof, trial (strike off) proof
~/digitaler digital proof
~/farbverbindlicher color proof
~/fotografischer [prepress] photographic proof
Proofanfertigung *f* proofing
~/digitale digital proofing
Proofdruck *m* proof print
Proofdrucker *m* proof printer, proofer
Proofherstellung *f* proofing
Proofsystem *n* proofing system
Proportionalabschwächer *m* proportional reducer
Proportionalschrift *f* proportional [type]font, proportional spacing *(typography)*
Proportionalzählrohr *n* proportional counter *(detector)*
Proportionsempfinden *n* sense of scale
Prospekt *m* matte painting *(cinema)*
Prospektbeilage *f* newspaper advertising insert
Protanomalie *f* protanomaly, decreased red sensitivity *(color-vision deficiency)*
Protanop *m* protanope
Protanopie *f*, **Protanstörung** *f* protanopia, red[-green] blindness, red and bluish green confusion *(color-vision deficiency)*
Proteinkristallografie *f* protein crystallography
Protokoll *n* protocol *(data exchange)*
~/netzunabhängiges network-independent protocol *(digital video broadcasting)*
Protokolldateneinheit *f* protocol data unit, PDU
Proton *n* proton, nucleon; hydrogen nucleus
Protonendichte *f* proton density

Protonendonator m proton don[at]or, proton emitter
Protonen-Magnetresonanzspektroskopie f proton magnetic resonance spectroscopy
Protonenmikroskop n proton microscope
Protonenspektroskopie f proton spectroscopy
Protonenspender m s. Protonendonator
Prototyp m prototype, template (e.g. in pattern recognition)
Prototypenbau m/**digitaler** rapid prototyping
Prototypenklassifikation f, **Prototypenklassifizierung** f prototype classification
prototypisch prototypical
Proxy m proxy (server)
Prozess m/**fotografischer** photographic process; photographic procedure
Prozessfarbe f 1. process [ink] color; 2. process ink (printing)
Prozessfarbenmodell n CMYK model (color space) (from cyan, magenta, yellow, black)
Prozessor m processor
~/**parallel arbeitender** parallel (array) processor
Prozessorfeld n processor array
Prozessorgeschwindigkeit f processor speed
Prozessormodul n control module
Prozessüberwachung f process monitoring
Prüfandruck m prepress proof; proof [print]
Prüfbit n check bit
Prüfdruck m proof print
~/**digitaler** digital proof
Prüffernrohr n testing telescope
Prüffilm m test film
Prüflicht n inspection light
Prüfling m s. Prüfobjekt
Prüfmuster n test pattern
Prüfobjekt n [test] specimen
Prüfobjektiv n test lens
Prüfpapier n test paper
Prüfsumme f check sum
Prüfung f/**berührungslose** noncontact inspection
~/**eindringfreie** nonintrusive testing
~/**radioskopische** radioscopic testing
~/**zerstörungsfreie** nondestructive testing (evaluation)
Prüfzeile f test line (television)
Prüfzeilensignal n insertion test signal
pseudodreidimensional pseudo-three-dimensional
Pseudo-Echtzeitanimation f pseudo real-time animation
Pseudoeffekt m s. Raumeindruck/pseudoskopischer
Pseudofarbbild n pseudocolor image
Pseudofarbbildschirm m pseudocolor display
Pseudofarbbildverarbeitung f pseudocolor image processing
Pseudofarbcodierung f pseudocolor coding
Pseudofarbdarstellung f 1. pseudo-coloring; 2. pseudocolor[ed] map, pseudocolor rendition
Pseudofarbe f pseudocolor (s.a. under Falschfarbe)
Pseudofarbfolge f pseudocolor sequence
Pseudohalogenid n pseudohalide
pseudoisochromatisch pseudoisochromatic
Pseudokante f pseudo-edge
Pseudokolorierung f pseudo-coloring
Pseudo-Laplace-Operator m pseudo-Laplacian [operator]
Pseudomedianfilter n pseudomedian filter
Pseudooptik f pseudooptics
Pseudo-Reisen n surrogate traveling (multimedia application)
Pseudorelief n pseudorelief
Pseudoschnitt m match frame edit, tracking edit (video)
Pseudoskop n pseudoscope
Pseudoskopie f pseudoscopy
pseudoskopisch pseudoscopic
Pseudosolarisation f Sabattier effect (exposure effect)
Pseudostereoskopie f pseudosteroscopy
pseudostereoskopisch pseudostereoscopic
Pseudotriangulation f pseudotriangulation
Pseudozufallscode m pseudorandom code
Pseudozufallsfolge f/**binäre** pseudorandom binary sequence, PRBS
Pseudozufallsfolgengenerator m pseudorandom sequence (number) generator
Pseudozufallsrauschen n pseudorandom noise
Psophometer n psophometer, noise meter
psophometrisch psophometric
Psychoakustik f psychoacoustics
psychoakustisch psychoacoustic[al]
Psychometrie f psychometry, psychometrics
psychometrisch psychometric
psychooptisch psychovisual
Psychophysik f psychophysics
psychophysikalisch psychophysical
Psychophysiker m psychophysicist
psychophysiologisch psychophysiologic[al], physiopsychologic[al]
psychovisuell psychovisual
Publizieren n **am Schreibtisch** desktop publishing, DTP
~/**elektronisches** electronic publishing
Puffer m 1. buffer (e.g. as a fixer constituent); 2. s. Pufferspeicher
Pufferlösung f buffer solution

Pufferspeicher 316

Pufferspeicher m buffer memory, buffer storage (store), [frame] buffer
~/**schneller** cache [memory], data cache
Pufferspeicherplatz m buffer space
Puffersubstanz f buffer substance
Pufferung f/**doppelte** double (ping-pong) buffering *(image data processing)*
Pulfrich-Effekt m Pulfrich effect *(stereoscopic imaging)*
Pulfrich-Fotometer n Pulfrich (step) photometer
Puls ... *s.a.* Impuls ...
~ m/**optischer** optical pulse
Pulsabstand m pulse repetition interval, PRI *(radar)*
Pulsamplitude f pulse amplitude (height)
Pulsamplitudenmodulation f pulse-amplitude modulation, PAM
Pulsauskopplung f cavity dumping *(laser)*
Pulsbetrieb m pulsed [laser] action, pulse mode
Pulsbreite f pulse width
~/**kritische** critical pulse width
Pulsbreitenmessung f pulse width measurement
Pulsbreitenmodulation f pulse width modulation, PWM, pulse duration modulation, PDM, pulse length modulation, PLM
~/**binäre** binary pulse width modulation, PWM
Pulscharakteristik f pulse characteristic
Pulscodemodulation f pulse code modulation, PCM
~/**adaptive differentielle** adaptive differential pulse code modulation, ADPCM
~/**differentielle** differential pulse code modulation, differential PCM, DPCM
~/**logarithmische** logarithmic pulse code modulation, log-PCM
Pulsdauer m pulse duration
Pulsdauermodulation f s. Pulsbreitenmodulation
Pulsdispersion f pulse dispersion
Puls-Echo-... s. Impuls-Echo-...
pulsen to pulse
Pulsenergie f pulse energy
Pulsfolge f pulse sequence, sequence of pulses
Pulsfolgefrequenz f s. Pulswiederholfrequenz
Pulslänge f pulse length
Pulslaser m pulsed laser
Pulsleistung f pulse power
Pulsmodulation f pulse modulation
Pulsmodulator m pulse modulator
Pulsphasenmodulation f pulse-position modulation, PPM
Pulsradar n pulse[d] radar
Pulsreflexionsverfahren n pulse-echo imaging
Pulsschallverfahren n pulsed (pulse-wave) Doppler [ultrasound]

Pulssequenz f pulse sequence, sequence of pulses
Pulsspitzenleistung f peak pulse power, pulse peak power
Pulsverbreiterung f pulse broadening *(s.a. Pulsverlängerung)*; pulse spreading
Pulsverlängerung f pulse lengthening
Pulsweitenmodulation f s. Pulsbreitenmodulation
Pulswelle f pulse wave
Pulswiederholfrequenz f, **Pulswiederholrate** f pulse repetition frequency (rate), pulse recurrence frequency, PRF *(ultrasound, radar)*
Pulswinkel m flip (tip) angle *(magnetic resonance imaging)*
Pulverbild n powder image *(electrophotography)*
Pulverdiffraktometer n powder diffractometer
Pumpe f s. Pumpstativ
pumpen 1. to pump *(e.g. a fluid)*; 2. to pump, to energize *(e.g. a laser)*
Pumpen n/**optisches** optical pumping *(spectroscopy)*
Pumplaser m pumped laser
Pumplicht n pumping light
Pumplichtquelle f pumping light source
Pumppuls m pumping pulse
Pumpspiegel m pump mirror *(laser)*
Pumpstativ n pedestal
Punkt m 1. point *(geometric element)*; 2. period, full stop (point) *(punctuation mark)*; 3. dot *(e.g. in printing)*; 4. s. Bildpunkt; 5. s. Pixel; 6. s. ~/typografischer
~/**fokaler** focal point
~/**gemeinsamer (homologer)** homologous point *(e.g. in three-dimensional imaging)*
~/**isoelektrischer** isoelectric point, IEP
~/**konjugierter** conjugate point *(optics)*
~/**typografischer** [typographical] point, Didot point, p
Punktabstand m interdot distance; dot pitch *(display)*
Punktabtaster m spot-scanning apparatus
Punktabtastung f point scan[ning]
punktadressierbar all points addressable, APA
Punktantwort[funktion] f s. Punktbildfunktion
Punktätzlösung f dot-etching solution
Punktauflösung f point (structural) resolution
Punktausbreitung f spot spread
Punktbelichtungsmesser m spot meter
Punktbestimmung f point determination
Punktbild n point (spot) image, spot diagram *(optics)*
Punktbildentstehung f point image formation

Punktbildfunktion f point-spread function, PSF, blur[ring] function; spatial response, SR
~/**beugungsbegrenzte** diffraction-limited point-spread function
~/**beugungsbegrenzte** diffraction-limited point-spread function
~/**kohärente** coherent point-spread function
~/**optische** optical point-spread function, OPSF
Punktbildverwaschungsfunktion f s. Punktbildfunktion
Punktdatensatz m point data set
Punktdiagramm n scatter diagram, scattergram, scattergraph, scatterplot, feature space image (s.a. Punktwolke)
Punktdichte f point density; dot density (e.g. of a printer)
Punktdiffraktionsinterferometer n point diffraction interferometer, PDI
Punkt-Digital-Zoom n pinpoint digital zoom
Punkte mpl **pro Zoll** dots per [square] inch, dpi, DPI; pixels per inch, ppi, PPI (resolution measurement)
Punkterkennbarkeit f point visibility (measure of resolution)
Punkterkennung f point detection
Punktfrage f exact match query (computer graphics)
Punktgitter n grid of points
Punktgröße f point size (typography)
Punkthelligkeit f point brilliance
Punkt-im-Polygon-Test m point-in-polygon location (computational geometry)
Punktkontaktmikroskop n point contact microscope
Punktkoordinate f point coordinate
Punktlicht n point light; spotlight
Punktlichtabtaster m flying-spot scanner (telecine) (s.a. Filmabtaster, Filmgeber)
Punktlichtabtastung f flying-spot scanning
Punktlichtbeleuchtung f point source illumination; spotlighting
Punktlichtlampe f spot lamp
Punktlichtquelle f point light source, point source of light
Punktlichtscheinwerfer m spot[light]
Punktlokalisation f, **Punktlokalisierung** f point location
Punktlosigkeit f astigmatism, astigmatic aberration (error)
Punktmatrix f dot matrix, cell (electronic imaging)
Punktmatrixbild n dot-matrix image
Punktmatrixbildschirm m dot matrix display
Punktmatrixdrucker m [dot-]matrix printer, dot-matrix line printer
Punktmatrix-Druckkopf m dot-matrix printhead
Punktmenge f point set
Punktmessung f spot metering

Punktmuster n point (dot) pattern
Punktnachbarschaft f pixel neighborhood
Punktobjekt n point [source] object (optics)
Punktoperation f point operation, gray-level modification (pixel processing)
~/**allgemeine** general point operation
~/**dyadische** dyadic point operation
~/**homogene** homogeneous point operation
~/**inhomogene** inhomogeneous point operation
~/**lineare** linear point operation
~/**logarithmische** logarithmic point operation, point logarithmic operation
~/**nichtlineare** nonlinear point operation
~/**skalare** scalar point operation
Punktoperator m point operator
~/**homogener** homogeneous point operator
Punktquelle f point source
Punktquellenspektroskopie f point source spectroscopy
Punktraster m(n) dot matrix, cell (electronic imaging)
Punktrasterverfahren n dot-scanning method
Punktrauschen n spot (peak) noise (s.a. Rauschen/impulsförmiges)
Punktscheinwerfer m spot[light]
Punktsehschärfe f point acuity
Punktsignatur f point signature
Punktstörung f point defect
Punktstrahl m point beam (of electrons)
Punktstreuer m point scatterer
Punktstreufunktion f s. Punktantwort[funktion]
Punktsystem n/**typografisches** typographical point system
Punkttransformation f point transform[ation]
Punktüberhang m dot (press) gain, dot growth (spread)
Punktverschmierungsfunktion f s. Punktbildfunktion
Punktverteilung f point distribution
Punktverwaschungsfunktion f s. Punktbildfunktion
punktweise pointwise (image-processing operation)
Punktwolke f 1. point cloud, cloud of points; 2. s. Punktdiagramm
Punktzeiger m pointer
Punkt-zu-Multipunkt-Verteilsystem n point-to-multipoint distribution system
Punkt-zu-Punkt-Verteilsystem n point-to-point distribution system
Punktzuwachs m s. Punktüberhang
Punze f counter (character part)
Pupille f pupil
~/**kreisförmige (ringförmige)** circular pupil
Pupillenabbildungsmaßstab m pupillary ratio (magnification)
Pupillenaberration f pupil aberration

Pupillenabstand *m*, **Pupillendistanz** *f*
interpupillary distance
Pupillendurchmesser *m* pupil diameter
Pupillenebene *f* pupil plane
Pupillenfilterung *f s.* Ortsfrequenzfilterung
Pupillenfläche *f* pupil area
Pupillenform *f* pupil shape
Pupillenfunktion *f* pupil function, aperture [transmission] function *(ray optics)*
Pupillengröße *f* pupil size
Pupillenlichtstärke *f* retinal illuminance
Pupillenmaßstab *m* pupillary ratio (magnification)
Pupillenöffnung *f s.* Pupillengröße
Pupillenposition *f* pupil position (location)
Pupillenradius *m* pupil radius
Pupillenstrahl *m* pupil ray *(optics)*
~/**paraxialer** paraxial pupil ray, PPR
Pupillometrie *f* pupillometrics
Puppenfilm *m s.* Puppentrickfilm
Puppenfilmanimation *f* puppet animation
Puppentrickfilm *m* puppet animation
Purkinje-Phänomen *n* Purkinje effect (phenomenon), Purkinje shift *(human vision)*
Purpur *n* magenta *(subtractive primary color)*
Purpurfarbe *f* purple color, nonspectral color (hue)
Purpur-Farbkuppler *m s.* Purpurkuppler
Purpurfilter *n* purple (magenta) filter
Purpurgerade *f s.* Purpurlinie
Purpurkuppler *m* magenta [dye-forming] coupler, magenta-colored coupler
Purpurlinie *f* purple boundary *(colorimetry)*
Pushentwicklung *f* push[ed] development, push [film] processing, pushing, forced development (processing), forcing, overdevelopment
PW-Doppler-Verfahren *n s.* Pulsschallverfahren
Pyelofluoroskopie *f* pyelofluoroscopy
Pyelografie *f* pyelography
Pyramide *f* pyramid
Pyramidencodierung *f* pyramid coding
Pyramideninterpolation *f* pyramid interpolation
Pyramidenzerlegung *f* pyramid decomposition
Pyrazolonkuppler *m* pyrazolone coupler *(color photography)*
Pyrogallol *n* pyro[gallol], pyrogallic acid
Pyrogallolentwickler *m* pyro[gallol] developer
Pyrometrie *f*/**fotografische** photographic pyrometry

Q

QAM *s.* Quadraturmodulation
Q-Switch-Betrieb *m* Q-switching *(laser)*
Quaderhülle *f* bounding box *(computer graphics)*
Quaderklassifikation *f*, **Quadermethode** *f* parallelepiped classification, PE classification *(pattern recognition)*
Quadrangel *n* quadrangle, quad
Quadrant *m* quadrant
Quadrat *n* square, quadrate
Quadratmetergewicht *n s.* Masse/flächenbezogene
Quadratraster *m(n)* square grid
Quadraturamplitudenmodulation *f* quadrature amplitude modulation, QAM
~/**gleichförmige** uniform QAM
~/**ungleichförmige** nonuniform QAM
Quadraturdemodulation *f* quadrature demodulation
Quadraturdetektion *f* quadrature detection *(magnetic resonance imaging)*
Quadraturdetektor *m* quadrature detector
Quadraturfilter *n* quadrature filter
~/**konjugiertes** conjugate quadrature filter bank, CQF *(image coding)*
Quadraturfilterpaar *n* quadrature filter pair
Quadraturmodulation *f* 1. quadrature modulation; 2. *s.* Quadraturamplitudenmodulation
Quadraturmodulator *m* quadrature modulator
Quadraturphasenumtastung *f* quadrature phase shift keying, QPSK *(digital television)*
Quadraturspiegelfilter *n* quadrature mirror filter, QMF; conjugate quadrature filter, power-complementary filter
Quadraturspiegelfilterbank *f* quadrature mirror filter bank
Quadraturspule *f* quadrature coil *(magnetic resonance imaging)*
Quadraturtechnik *f* quadrature technique
Quadrik *f* quadric [surface] *(Euclidean geometry)*
Quadrofonie *f* quadrophony
Qualitätsdruck *m* 1. high-quality printing; 2. quality print
Qualitätsfarbdruck *m* high-quality color printing
Quant *n* [/elektromagnetisches] quantum
~/**rauschäquivalentes** noise-equivalent quantum
Quantelung *f s.* Quantisierung
Quantenausbeute *f* quantum yield, photon catch *(e.g. of an image sensor)*
Quantendetektor *m* quantum (photon) detector
Quanteneffizienz *f* quantum [detection] efficiency, detector quantum efficiency, DQE, photon [counting] efficiency
~/**absolute** absolute quantum efficiency
~/**differentielle** differential quantum efficiency
~/**relative** relative quantum efficiency
Quantenelektrodynamik *f* quantum electrodynamics, QED
Quantenenergie *f* quantum energy
Quantenfluss *m* quantum (photon) flux
Quanteninterferometer *n*/**supraleitendes** superconducting quantum interference device, SQUID [sensor]
Quantenmechanik *f* quantum mechanics
quantenmechanisch quantum-mechanical
Quantenoptik *f* quantum optics
Quantenrauschen *n* quantum noise (mottle) *(s.a.* Photonenrauschen, Schrotrauschen*)*
Quantensensor *m* quantum sensor
Quantensprung *m* quantum jump
Quantentheorie *f* quantum theory (electrodynamics), quantum physics
Quantentopf *m* quantum well
Quantenwirkungsgrad *m* quantum [detection] efficiency, QDE, detective quantum efficiency, DQE
quantisieren to quantize
Quantisierer *m* quantizer
~/**linearer** linear (uniform) quantizer
~/**nichtlinearer** nonlinear quantizer
~/**optimaler** optimum [scalar] quantizer
~/**prädiktiver** predictive quantizer
Quantisierung *f* quantization, quantizing *(digitizing the amplitude values of signals)*
~/**abgeleitete** derived quantization
~/**adaptive** adaptive quantization
~/**äquidistante** equidistant quantization
~/**baumstrukturierte** tree-structured quantization
~/**dynamische** dynamic quantization
~/**entropiecodierte** entropy-coded quantization
~/**explizite** explicit quantization
~/**frequenzgewichtete** frequency-weighted quantization
~/**gleichmäßige** uniform quantization
~/**globale** global quantization
~/**grobe** coarse (low-resolution) quantization
~/**implizite** implicit quantization
~/**lineare** linear (uniform) quantization
~/**logarithmische** logarithmic quantization, companding technique [of quantization]
~/**nichtlineare** nonlinear quantization
~/**optimale** optimum quantization
~/**örtliche** spatial quantization
~/**rückwärtsadaptive** backward adaptive quantization
~/**skalare** scalar quantization
~/**spektrale** spectral quantization

Quantisierung

~/**trelliscodierte** trellis-coded quantization
~/**ungleichförmige (ungleichmäßige)** nonuniform quantization
~/**uniforme** uniform quantization
~/**vorwärtsadaptive** forward adaptive quantization
~/**wahrnehmungsoptimierte** perceptual[ly] optimized quantization
~/**zeitliche** temporal quantization
Quantisierungsalgorithmus *m* quantization algorithm
Quantisierungsbereich *m* quantizing range
Quantisierungseffekt *m* quantization effect
Quantisierungsfehler *m* quantization (quantizing) error, quantization uncertainty (artifact) *(s.a.* Quantisierungsrauschen*)*
~/**mittlerer quadratischer** mean-square[d] quantization error, msqe
Quantisierungsfehlermaß *n* quantization error measure
Quantisierungsfehlerverzerrung *f* quantization error distortion
Quantisierungsfunktion *f* quantization function
Quantisierungsgenauigkeit *f* quantization accuracy
Quantisierungsindex *m* quantization index
Quantisierungsintervall *n* quantization interval
Quantisierungskennlinie *f* quantization curve
Quantisierungsmatrix *f* quantization matrix
Quantisierungsoperator *m* quantization operator
Quantisierungsparameter *m* quantization parameter
Quantisierungsrauschen *n* quantization (quantizing) noise, quantization distortion, digitization noise *(s.a.* Quantisierungsfehler*)*
Quantisierungsschema *n* quantization scheme
Quantisierungsschritt *m* quantization step
Quantisierungsstufe *f* quantization (quantizing) level, reconstruction level
Quantisierungsstufenhöhe *f* quantization step size
Quantisierungstabelle *f* quantization table, q-table
Quantisierungsverfahren *n* quantization techniqe
Quantisierungsverzerrung *f* quantization (quantizing) distortion
Quart[o] *n* quarto *(sheet folded twice)*
Quarz *m* quartz; fused quartz, [fused] silica
~/**synthetischer** synthetic fused silica
Quarzfilter *n* quartz filter
Quarzgenerator *m* piezoelectric generator (oscillator), crystal oscillator
Quarzglas *n* fused quartz, quartz glass *(s.a.* Kieselglas*)*

Quarzhalogen[glüh]lampe *f* quartz-halogen [filament] lamp, tungsten-halogen (tungsten-halide) lamp
Quarzkristall *m* quartz crystal, crystal quartz *(optical material)*
Quarzlampe *f* 1. quartz [filament] lamp; 2. *s.* Quarzhalogen[glüh]lampe
Quarzlinse *f* quartz lens
Quarzmotor *m* crystal[-controlled] motor
Quarz-Synchrontechnik *f* crystal sync *(filming)*
Quarz-Ultraviolett *n s.* Vakuum-Ultraviolett
quasiabbildend quasi-imaging
Quasi-Cassegrain-System *n* quasi-Cassegrain system
quasioptisch quasi-optical
Quaternio *m*, **Quaternion** *f(n)* quaternion *(e.g. as a vector of four elements)*
Quecksilberbogenlampe *f s.* Quecksilberdampflampe
Quecksilberdampf *m* mercury vapor (fume)
Quecksilberdampflampe *f* mercury [vapor] lamp; mercury arc lamp; high-intensity discharge lamp, HMI
Quecksilberhochdruck[entladungs]lampe *f* mercury high-pressure arc-discharge lamp, mercury burner
Quecksilber-Höchstdrucklampe *f* extra-high-pressure mercury [vapor] lamp
Quecksilbersalz *n* mercury salt
Quecksilberverstärker *m* mercury (mercuric chloride) intensifier
Quellbild *n* source image
Quelldatei *f* source file
Quellencode *m* source code
Quellencodierer *m* source [en]coder
Quellencodierung *f* source [en]coding
Quellencodierungstheorem *n* source-coding theorem
Quellendecodierer *m* source decoder
Quellendecodierung *f* source decoding
Quellenentropie *f* source entropy, marginal (first-order) entropy *(information theory)*
Quellenlaser *m* source laser
Quellenmodell *n* source model *(video coding)*
Quellenmodellierung *f* source modeling
Quellensignal *n* source signal
Quellpunkt *m* source point
Quellreliefverfahren *n* imbibition process *(photography)*
Quellung *f* swell[ing] *(e.g. of gelatin)*
Quenching *n* quenching *(photoconduction)*
quer zur Faserrichtung (Laufrichtung) across (against) the grain, cross direction *(printing paper)*
Queraberration *f* transverse (off-axis) aberration, lateral aberration
~/**chromatische** transverse chromatic aberration, lateral color (chromatic aberration), lateral chromatic error,

chromatic aberration (difference, variation) of magnification
~/**sphärische** transverse spherical aberration
Querabweichung *f s.* Queraberration
Querauflösung *f* transverse resolution; cross-range resolution *(radar)*
Queraufnahme *f s.* Querformataufnahme
Querdiffusion *f* transverse diffusion
Querdisparation *f*, **Querdisparität** *f* retinal rivalry (disparity)
Querformat *n* horizontal orientation (format), landscape mode, landscape [orientation]
Querformatanzeige *f* landscape display
querformatig landscape
Querkräuselung *f* transverse curl *(tape defect)*
Quermagnetisierung *f* transverse magnetization
Querparitätsprüfung *f* vertical redundancy check, VRC
Querrelaxation[szeit] *f*, **Querrelaxationszeitkonstante** *f* transverse (spin-spin) relaxation time, T-two [time constant], T2 *(magnetic resonance imaging)*
Querschnittsbild *n* cross-section[al] image
Querspuraufzeichnung *f*, **Querspurverfahren** *n* transverse tape recording
Querstreben *fpl* cross braced legs *(tripod)*
Quetschroller *m* squeegee roll[er]
Quincunx-Abtastung *f* quincunx sampling
Quincunx-Raster *m* quincunx (diamond) lattice *(signal sampling)*

R

Rad *n* rad *(unit of radiant energy; short for radiation absorbed dose)*
Radar *n* radar *(short for radio detection and ranging)*
~/**abbildendes** imaging (mapping) radar
~/**aktives** active radar
~/**bistatisches** bistatic radar [system]
~/**dreidimensionales** three-dimensional radar
~/**elektrooptisches** electro-optic radar
~/**flugzeuggetragenes** airborne radar
~/**frequenzmoduliertes** frequency-modulated radar, FM radar
~/**halbaktives** semiactive radar
~/**hochauflösendes** high-resolution radar, HRR
~/**kurzwelliges** short-wavelength radar
~/**langwelliges** long-wavelength radar
~ **mit inverser synthetischer Apertur** inverse synthetic-aperture radar, ISAR
~ **mit realer Antennenapertur (Apertur)** real-aperture radar, real-beam radar
~ **mit synthetischer Apertur** synthetic-aperture radar, SAR
~/**mobiles** mobile radar
~/**monostatisches** monostatic radar
~/**monotonfrequenzmoduliertes** chirp radar
~/**multistatisches** multistatic radar
~/**optisches** *s.* Lichtradar
~/**passives** passive radar
~/**phasengetastetes** phase-coded radar
~/**polarimetrisches** polarimetric radar
~/**quasimonostatisches** quasimonostatic radar
~/**satellitengetragenes** satellite-borne radar; spaceborne radar
~/**weitsichtiges** over-the-horizon radar, OTHR
Radarabbildung *f* radar imaging
Radarabstand *m* radar range
Radaranlage *f* radar unit (facility)
Radarantenne *f* radar[-dish] antenna, radar scanner
Radarantwortbake *f* radar beacon, racon
Radarastronomie *f* radar astronomy
Radaraufklärung *f* radar reconnaissance
Radaraufzeichnung *f* radar imagery
Radarausleuchtung *f* radar illumination
Radar-Ausleuchtzone *f* radar footprint
Radarbake *f s.* Radarantwortbake
Radarbandbreite *f* radar bandwidth
Radarbeobachter *m* radar observer
Radarbeobachtung *f* radar observation
Radarbetrieb *m* radar operation
Radarbild *n* radar [display] image, radar [screen] picture
Radarbildauswertegerät *n*/**automatisches** automatic radar plotting aid, ARPA
Radarbilddaten *pl* radar data
Radarbildröhre *f* radar [cathode-ray] tube, radar CRT
Radarbildverarbeitung *f* radar image processing
Radarcharakteristik *f* radar pattern
Radardaten *pl* radar data
Radardatenprozessor *m* radar data processor, RDP
Radarecho *n* radar echo (return)
Radarelektronik *f* radar electronics
Radarempfänger *m* radar receiver
~/**bistatischer** bistatic radar receiver
Radarenergie *f* radar energy
Radarfernerkundung *f* radar remote sensing
Radarfrequenz *f* radar [energy] frequency
Radar-Frühwarnsystem *n* early warning radar system
Radargerät *n* radar set; radar device
Radargleichung *f* radar [range] equation
Radargrammetrie *f* radargrammetry
Radarhöhenmesser *m* radar altimeter
Radarhorizont *m* radar horizon
Radarhydrografie *f* radar hydrography
Radarimpuls *m* radar [im]pulse, pulse of radar energy
Radarinformation *f* radar information
Radarinterferometer *n* radar interferometer
Radarinterferometrie *f* radar interferometry
Radarkarte *f* radar map
Radarkette *f* radar chain
Radarkeule *f* radar beam
Radarkopf *m* radar scanner
Radarkuppel *f* radar dome, radome [protective covering]
Radarmeteorologe *m* radar meteorologist
Radarmeteorologie *f* radar meteorology
radarmeteorologisch radar meteorological
Radarmodulator *m* radar modulator
Radarmodus *m* radar mode
Radarnavigation *f* radar navigation
Radarnetz *n* radar network
Radarortung *f* radar location (detection)
Radarpeilung *f* radar bearing
Radarpuls *m* radar [im]pulse, pulse of radar energy
Radarquerschnitt *m* radar cross section, RCS
Radarreflektivität *f* radar reflectivity
Radarreflektor *m* radar reflector
Radarreichweite *f* radar range
Radarrohdaten *pl* radar raw data
Radarröhre *f s.* Radarbildröhre
Radarrückstreufaktor *m* radar backscatter coefficient, radar reflectivity factor
Radarrückstreuung *f* radar backscatter (reflection)
Radarsatellit *m* radar satellite
Radarschatten *m* radar shadow

Radarschirm *m* radar screen (display), radarscope, scope
Radarschirmbild *n* s. Radarbild
Radarschirmfotografie *f* radarscope photography
Radarsender *m* radar transmitter
Radarsensor *m*/**bildgebender** *m* imaging radar sensor
Radarsichtgerät *n* radar[-display] indicator
Radarsignal *n* radar signal
Radarsignatur *f* radar signature
Radarsimulator *m* radar simulator
Radarstation *f* radar station
Radarstörung *f* radar jamming
Radarstrahl *m* radar beam
Radarstreuung *f* radar scatter
Radarsystem *n* radar system
Radartechnik *f* radar technology (engineering)
Radartechniker *m* radar operator
Radarteleskop *n* radar telescope
Radartriangulation *f* radar triangulation
Radarüberwachung *f* radar surveillance
Radarverfolgung *f* radar tracking
Radarvermessung *f* radar surveying
Radarwarnempfänger *m* radar warning receiver
Radarwelle *f* radar wave
~/**hochfrequente** high-frequency radar wave, short-wavelength radar wave
Radarwellenfront *f* radar wave front
Radarwellenlänge *f* radar wavelength
Radarzeichengerät *n*/**automatisches** automatic radar plotting aid, ARPA
Radarzelle *f* radar cell
Radarziel *n* radar target
Radial-Basis-Funktions-Netzwerk *n* radial basis functions neural network, RBF [neural] network
Radialgeschwindigkeit *f* radial velocity (speed), range rate *(radar)*
Radialsignal *n* radial signal *(video disk)*
Radiant *m* radian *(unit of plane angle)*
radiant radiant
Radierer *m* etcher
Radiergummi *m*/**elektronischer** electronic eraser
Radiernadel *f* etching needle
Radierung *f* 1. etching *(printmaking process)*; 2. etching *(original print)*
Radikal *n* radical
~/**freies** free radical
radioaktiv radioactive
Radioaktivität *f* radioactivity, activity
Radioaktivitätsverteilung *f* distribution of radioactivity
Radioastronom *m* radio astronomer
Radioastronomie *f* radio astronomy
radioastronomisch radio astronomical
Radiofenster *n* radio window
Radiofoto *n* radiophoto[graph]
Radiofotografie *f* [photo]fluorography
Radiofotogramm *n* radiophotogram

Radiofrequenz *f* radio[-wave] frequency, RF *(s.a. Hochfrequenz)*
Radiofrequenzidentifizierung *f* radio frequency identification, RFID
Radiofrequenzspektroskopie *f* radio frequency spectroscopy
Radiofrequenzstrahlung *f* RF (radio frequency) radiation
Radiograf *m* radiographer
Radiografie *f* 1. radiography, radiation imaging; 2. radiograph[ic image], radiogram; X-ray photograph; gamma ray photograph
~/**diagnostische** diagnostic radiography
~/**digitale** digital radiography, digital fluoroscopic imaging
~/**direkte** direct radiography
~/**dynamische [industrielle]** travel-ray radiography, in-motion radiography
~/**indirekte** indirect radiography
~/**industrielle** industrial radiography
~/**medizinische** medical radiography
~/**stereoskopische** stereoscopic radiography, stereoradiography
radiografieren to radiograph
radiografisch radiographic
Radiogramm *n* radiograph[ic image], radio image, radiogram, skiagram; X-ray [photograph] *(s.a. Röntgenbild)*; gamma ray photograph
Radiointerferometer *n* radio interferometer
Radiointerferometrie *f* radio interferometry
Radioisotopenkamera *f* radioisotope camera
Radiologe *m* radiologist
Radiologie *f* radiology
~/**computergestützte** computer-assisted (computer-aided) radiology, CAR
~/**diagnostische** diagnostic radiology
~/**filmlose** filmless radiology
radiologisch radiologic[al]
Radiolumineszenz *f* radioluminescence
Radiometer *n* radiometer
~/**goniometrisches** goniometric radiometer
Radiometrie *f* radiometry
Radiometrieverzerrung *f* radiometric distortion
radiometrisch radiometric
Radionuklid *n* radionuclide, unstable nuclide
Radioobservatorium *n* radio astronomy observatory
Radioisotop *n* radioisotope, radioactive isotope
Radiopharmakon *n* radiopharmaceutical, radioactive tracer, [radio]tracer
Radiosity *f* radiosity
Radiosity-Matrix *f* radiosity matrix
Radiosity-Verfahren *n* radiosity [technique], radiosity image generation *(computer graphics)*

Radioskopie f radioscopy
radioskopisch radioscopic[al]
Radiostrahlung f s. Radiofrequenzstrahlung
Radioteleskop n [radio] telescope
Radiowelle f radio wave
Radiowellenbereich m radio [wavelength] regime, radio wave portion *(of the electromagnetic spectrum)*
Radiusvektor m radius vector
Radmaus f wheel mouse *(input device)*
Radom m radome [protective covering], radar dome
Radon-Raum m Radon space *(object classification)*
Radon-Transformation f Radon transform[ation] *(tomographic image formation)*
rahmen to mount *(e.g. a transparency)*
Rahmen m 1. frame *(e.g. of a data structure);* 2. s. Diarahmen
~/**glasloser** glassless mount
Rahmenkopf m frame header *(data structure)*
Rahmenmarke f fiducial (reference) mark *(photogrammetry)*
Rahmenstruktur f frame structure
Rahmensucher m wire-frame viewfinder, frame [view]finder, sports viewfinder
Rahmungsmaschine f mounting machine
RAID-Konfiguration f RAID array
Rakel f, **Rakelmesser** n doctor [blade], scraper *(gravure printing)*
Rakelschlag m doctor blade [oscillation] stroke
Rakeltiefdruck m gravure [printing]; rotogravure
Rakelwalze f doctor roll
RAM f(n) random-access memory, RAM, direct-access storage [device]
Raman-Laser m Raman laser
Raman-Spektrometer n Raman spectrometer
Raman-Spektroskopie f Raman spectroscopy
Raman-Streuung f [electronic] Raman scattering
~/**aktive** active Raman scattering
~/**induzierte** stimulated Raman scattering
~/**inverse** inverse Raman scattering
~/**spontane** spontaneous Raman scattering
Rampenfilter n ramp filter
Rampenfunktion f ramp function
Rampenkante f ramp edge
Ramsden-Okular n Ramsden [microscope] eyepiece, positive eyepiece
Rand m border; boundary; margin; edge *(s.a. under Kante)*
~/**unterer** foot (tail) margin *(printed page)*
randabfallend bled off *(layout)*
Randabschattung f [peripheral] vignetting; vignetting effect
Randartefakt n s. Schichtdickenartefakt

Randaufhellung f rim lighting
Randauflösung f marginal resolution
Randausleuchtung f peripheral illumination
Randbedingung f boundary condition *(computational geometry)*
Randbeschnitt m cropping
Randbildschärfe f s. Randschärfe
Randdarstellung f boundary representation, b-rep *(computer graphics)*
Randdicke f edge thickness *(e.g. of a lens)*
Randeffekt m adjacency (border) effect, boundary effect
Rändelrad n thumbwheel
Randfeld n surrounding area *(e.g. of a display)*; fringing field *(charge-coupled device)*
Randhelligkeit f peripheral brightness
Randhelligkeitsabfall m hot spot *(television interference)*
Randkante f boundary edge
Randkennzeichnung f [film] edgeprint
Randkerbe f notch
Randkontrast m 1. edge contrast; 2. Mach banding (band effect)
Randkurve f boundary curve
Randlinie f boundary line, borderline
Randlöcher npl s. Randperforation
Randmerkmal n boundary feature
Randnumerierung f edge numbering
Randnummer f edge (key) number, footage number *(motion-picture film)*
Randobjekt n boundary object
Randperforation f edge perforation
Randpixel n border (boundary) pixel, peripheral pixel
Randpunkt m boundary (contour) point
Randschärfe f peripheral (edge) definition; boundary (contour) sharpness
Randschatten m edge shadow
Randschicht f s. Sperrschicht
Randschleier m marginal fog (veil)
Randsegment n boundary segment
Randsignatur f edge numbers
Randspur f edge track (stripe)
Randstrahl m peripheral (marginal) ray, rim (edge) ray
~/**paraxialer** paraxial marginal ray, PMR
Randunschärfe f edge softness
Randverletzung f edge damage
Randverzeichnung f edge distortion
Randvignettierung f cutoff
Randvoxel n border voxel
Randzahl f s. Randnummer
Rang[folge]operation f s. Rangordnungsfilterung
Rangoperator m s. Rangordnungsfilter
Rangordnungsähnlichkeit f rank-order similarity
Rangordnungsfilter n rank[-order] filter, rank[ing] operator
Rangordnungsfilterung f rank[-order] filtering, ranking operation

Rangordnungsoperator *m s.* Rangordnungsfilter
Rangordnungsverfahren *n s.* Rangordnungsfilterung
Rapidentwickler *m s.* Schnellentwickler
Rapidspiegel *m s.* Schwingspiegel
Rasen *m* 1. guard band *(videotape)*; 2. *s.* Bildstrich
Rastblende *f* click stop
Raste *f* click stop *(e.g. of an aperture ring)*
Raster *m(n)* 1. [scanning] raster *(display screen)*; 2. screen, grid
~/**amplitudenmodulierter (autotypischer)** amplitude-modulated raster
~/**bewegter** Bucky diaphragm *(flat-film X-ray imaging)*
~/**feiner** fine screen
~/**grober** coarse screen
~/**herkömmlicher** *s.* ~/amplitudenmodulierter
~/**hexagonaler** hexagonal lattice (grid)
~/**quadratischer** square [dot] screen *(halftone process)*
~/**rechteckiger** rectangular raster (lattice)
~/**typografischer** typographic grid
Rasterabstand *m* 1. raster distance (spacing); 2. screen distance, grid element spacing *(halftone process)*
Rasterabtastung *f* raster scan[ning]
Rasteralgorithmus *m* rasterization (screening) algorithm
Rasterätzung *f* 1. autotypy; 2. autotype *(copy)*
Rasterauflösung *f* 1. scanning resolution; 2. halftone resolution
Rasterbefehl *m* raster command
Rasterbild *n* 1. halftone [screened image], [halftone] dot image, screened image *(reprography)*; 2. *s.* Pixelbild
Rasterbilddatei *f* raster image file
Rasterbilddateiformat *n* raster image file format, RIFF
Rasterbilddaten *pl* raster[ized] image data
Rasterbildformat *n* raster image format
Rasterbildprozessor *m* raster image processor, RIP
Rasterbildpunkt *m* 1. graphic-arts halftone dot; 2. halftone pixel, [digital] halftone dot
Rasterbildrechner *m s.* Rasterbildprozessor
Rasterbildschirm *m* raster [display] screen, raster[-scanned] display, bit-map (raster graphics) display; raster-based monitor
Rasterbildspeicher *m* frame buffer [memory], image buffer, refresh memory (buffer)
Rasterbildverarbeitung *f* raster image processing
Rasterdarstellung *f* raster[-based] representation
Rasterdatei *f s.* Rasterbilddatei
Rasterdaten *pl* raster data
Raster-Digitalproof/materieller hard digital halftone proof, screened digital hard proof
Rasterdisplay *n s.* Rasterbildschirm
Rasterdrehung *f* raster rotation
Rasterdruck *m* halftone (screen) printing
Rasterdrucker *m* raster-based printingdevice, halftone (binary) printer, raster line printer, raster hardcopy device; [dot-]matrix printer; scanning printer
Rasterdrucksystem *n* raster printing system
Rasterdruckverfahren *n* halftone printing process
Rastereffekt *m* raster effect
Rasterelektronenmikroskop *n* scanning [electron] microscope, SEM
Rasterelektronenmikroskopie *f* scanning electron[ic] microscopy, SEM
Rasterelektronenstrahllithografie *f* scanning electron beam lithography
Raster-Farbauftragswalze *f* anilox roll *(flexography)*
Raster-Farbauszug *m* halftone color separation
Rasterfarbbildschirm *m* color raster display
Rasterfeinheit *f s.* Rasterfrequenz
Rasterfeld *n* 1. grid field *(typography)*; 2. *s.* Bitmap; 3. *s.* Target
Rasterfilm *m* halftone (line) film *(reprography)*
Rasterfläche *f* scan area
~/**verlaufende** vignette halftone, degrade
Rasterfolie *f* halftone screen
Rasterformat *n* raster format
Raster-Fotoemissionsmikroskop *n* scanning photoemission microscope, SPEM
Rasterfotografie *f* halftone photography; [glass] screen photography
Rasterfrequenz *f* 1. raster frequency; screen frequency (ruling); 2. *s.* Teilbildfrequenz
Rastergenerator *m* scan generator *(electron microscope)*
Rastergeometrie *f* raster geometry
Rastergeometriefehler *m* raster geometric error
Rastergerät *n* raster (pixel-based) output device
Rastergitter *n* raster grid *(computer graphics)*; halftone screen (grid) *(printing)*
Rastergrafik *f* 1. halftone graphics; 2. raster graphics, pixel (bit-mapped) graphics; 3. *s.* Pixelbild
Rastergrafiksystem *n* raster graphics system (package)
Rastergravur *f* halftone gravure
Rasterionenmikroskop *n* scanning ion microscope

Rasterionenmikroskopie f scanning ion microscopy, SIM
Rasterisierung f s. Rasterung 1.
Rasterkapazitätsmikroskop n scanning capacitance microscope, SCM
Rasterkarte f grid map
Rasterkassette f gridded cassette *(radiography)*
Rasterkeule f grating lobe *(radar)*
Rasterkonversion f, **Rasterkonvertierung** f scan conversion
Rasterkoordinate f raster coordinate
Rasterkraftmikroskop n scanning force microscope; atomic force microscope, AFM
Rasterkraftmikroskopie f/**dynamische** dynamic scanning force microscopy
Rasterlinie f raster line, scan[ning] line
Raster-Lumineszenzmikroskop n scanning luminescence microscope
Rastermakrofotografie f scanning photomacrography
Rastermaß n pitch
Rastermatrix f scanning matrix
Rastermikroskop n scanning microscope
~/**elektrochemisches** scanning electrochemical microscope, SECM
Rastermikroskopie f scanning microscopy
~/**akustische** scanning acoustic microscopy, SAM
~/**elektrochemische** scanning electrochemical microscopy, SECM
Rastermikrowellenmikroskop n scanning microwave microscope, SMWM
Rastermodulation f raster modulation
Rastermuster n scan pattern; raster pattern; screen pattern
Rastern n rasterizing; screening
rastern to raster[ize]; to screen, to halftone
Rasternäpfchen n [intaglio] cell, well *(gravure printing)*
Rasternegativ n halftone negative
Rasternetz n raster grid
Rasteroperation f raster operation
Rasterperiode f s. Rasterkonstante
Rasterplatte f screen (halftone) plate
Rasterplotter m electrostatic plotter
Rasterpositiv n halftone positive
Rasterprinzip n halftone principle
Rasterprozessor m s. Rasterbildprozessor
Rasterpunkt m halftone dot, dot [element]; raster point *(electrophotography)*
~/**elliptischer** elliptical (chain) dot
~/**konventioneller (quadratischer)** conventional (square) dot
~/**scharfer** hard dot
~/**unscharfer** soft dot
Rasterpunktabstand m interdot distance; raster unit
Rasterpunktgröße f [halftone] dot size, spot size
Rasterpunkthof m halo effect, halation
Rasterpunktmuster n halftone dot pattern
Rasterpunktschärfe f dot definition

Rasterpunktunschärfe f s. Rasterpunkthof
Rasterpunktverbreiterung f dot (press) gain, dot growth (spread); mechanical (physical) dot gain; optical dot gain
Rasterröntgenmikroskop n scanning X-ray microscope
Rasterscanformat n raster-scan format
Rasterscanner m raster [input] scanner
Rastersichtgerät n raster CRT (cathode-ray tube) output device
Rastersignal n raster signal
Rastersondenmikroskop n scanning probe microscope
Rastersondenmikroskopie f scanning (scanned) probe microscopy
Raster-SQUID-Mikroskop n scanning SQUID microscope
Rastersteg m land *(of a gravure cylinder)*
Rasterstrahl m raster beam, scanning [electron] beam
Rastersuche f raster[-order] search
Rastersystem n raster system; grid system *(typography)*
Rastertiefdruck m halftone gravure, photogravure printing
Rastertisch m s. Rasteraufnahmetisch
Rasterton m screen tint (tone)
Rastertonwert m screen density (percentage), dot area *(of halftones)*
Rastertonwertzunahme f s. Rasterpunktverbreiterung
Rastertransmissionselektronenmikroskop n scanning transmission electron microscope, STEM
Rastertransmissionselektronenmikroskopie f scanning transmission electron microscopy, STEM
Rastertransmissionsionenmikroskop n scanning transmission ion microscope, STIM
Rastertransmissionsröntgenmikroskop n scanning transmission X-ray microscope, STXM
Rastertunnelmikroskop n scanning tunneling microscope, STM
Rastertunnelmikroskopie f scanning tunneling microscopy, STM
~/**spannungsabhängige** voltage-dependent scanning tunneling microscopy, VDSTM
Rasterung f 1. rasterization; halftoning; 2. scanning *(of structures or spectra)*
~/**amplitudenmodulierte (autotypische)** halftone screening
~/**bildparallele** image-parallel rasterization
~/**fotoelektronische** electronic dot generation, EDG
~/**frequenzmodulierte** stochastic (frequency-modulated) screening, [dot] diffusion dithering, error diffusion *(halftoning technique)*
~/**nichtperiodische (stochastische)** s. ~/frequenzmodulierte

Rasterverfahren *n* 1. screen process *(early color photography)*; 2. halftone [screening] process, halftoning method *(printing)*
Rastervideosignal *n* raster video signal
Rastervorlage *f* halftone copy
Rasterwalze *f* gravure [printing] cylinder
Raster-Wärme-Mikroskop *n* near-field thermal microscope, NFTM
Rasterweite *f* screen ruling (frequency); raster frequency
Rasterwinkel *m* screen angle
Rasterzahl *f s.* Rasterweite
Rasterzeile *f* raster line, scan[ning] line
Rasterzeilenabstand *m* raster line spacing
Rasterzelle *f* halftone cell
Rastpunkt *m*, **Rastsperre** *f*, **Rastung** *f* click-stop *(e.g. of an aperture ring)*
RATAN-System *m* RATAN system *(short for radar and television aids to navigation)*
Ratiobild *n* ratio image *(remote sensing)*
Ratioverfahren *n* ratioing *(image merging)*
Raubkopie *f* pirate (illegal) copy, unauthorized copy
raubkopieren to pirate, to bootleg
Raubkopierer *m* [software] pirate
Raubkopierung *f* unauthorized duplication; software theft
Raum *m*/**abgedunkelter** darkened room
~/**achs[en]naher** paraxial region (domain)
~/**dreidimensionaler** three-dimensional space
~/**eindimensionaler** one-dimensional space
~/**Euklidischer** Euclidean space
~/**fadenförmiger** *s.* ~/achs[en]naher
~/**faktorieller** factorial space
~/**freier** blank space, air *(e.g. between printed characters)*
~/**Gaußscher** *s.* ~/achs[en]naher
~/**halbdunkler** semidarkened room
~/**kartes[ian]ischer** Cartesian space
~/**kontinuierlicher** continuous space
~/**mehrdimensionaler** multidimensional space, high-dimensionality space
~/**metrischer** metric space
~/**realer** real space
~/**reziproker** reciprocal space
~/**topologischer** topological space
~/**unbedruckter** white space *(e.g. between printed characters)*
~/**verdunkelter** darkened room
~/**virtueller** virtual space; cyberspace
Raumauflösung *f* spatial (positional) resolution
Raumausleuchtung *f* room illumination
Raumbeleuchtung *f* room lighting
Raumbild *n* stereograph, stereogram, stereoscopic image, stereo[scopic] picture
Raumbild-Entfernungsmesser *m* stereo[scopic] rangefinder

Raumbilder *npl*//**betretbare** *s.* Realität/virtuelle
Raumbildkamera *f* stereo[scopic] camera, twin-lens camera
raumbildlich stereographic
Raumbildmessung *f* stereo[photo]grammetry
Raumbildprojektion *f* stereo[scopic] projection
Raumbildtechnik *f* 1. three-dimensional imaging technique; 2. *s.* Raumbildwesen
Raumbildwahrnehmung *f s.* Raumwahrnehmung
Raumbildwesen *n* stereoscopy
Raumbildwiedergabe *f* stereo display
Raumfahrtfotografie *f* space photography
Raumfahrzeugradar *n* spaceborne radar; satellite-borne radar
Raumfilm *m* stereographic motion picture
Raumfilter *n* spatial [frequency] filter, spatial filter mask
~/**fünfachsiges** five-axis spatial filter
Raumfrequenz *f* spatial frequency
Raumgefühl *n* feeling of spaciousness
Raumgruppensymmetrie *f* space group symmetry *(of a crystal)*
Raumhelligkeit *f* volume brightness (luminance)
Rauminvarianz *f* space invariance
Raumklang *m* surround sound
Raumklangeffekt *m* stereophonic (binaural) effect
Raumkoordinate *f* spatial coordinate
Raumkurve *f* space curve
Raumladung *f* space charge
Raumladungszone *f* depletion region (layer), depletion zone, charge-depleted region *(photodiode)*
Raumlautsprecher *m* theater loudspeaker; surround speaker
räumlich spatial; three-dimensional, tridimensional
Räumlichkeit *f* spatiality; solidity
Raumlicht *n* 1. room light; 2. *s.* Hintergrundlicht
Raumlichtfilm *m* daylight[-balanced] film, daylight-type film
Raummultiplex *n* space [division] multiplex *(signal transmission)*
Raumprimitiv *n s.* Primitivkörper
Raumpunkt *m* space point
Raumrichtung *f* direction in space
Raumsehen *n* spatial (three-dimensional) vision, stereo[scopic] vision, stereopsis
Raumsinn *m* sense of perspective
Raumsondenaufnahme *f* space probe picture
Raumteilung *f* space subdivision *(computer graphics)*
Raumteleskop *n* space (extraterrestrial) telescope
Raumtiefe *f* spatial depth
Raumton *m* 1. room sound (tone) *(s.a. Raumklang...)*; 2. *s.* Stereoton

Raumunterteilungsbaum *m*/**binärer** binary space-partitioning tree *(computational geometry)*
Raumwahrnehmung *f* space (depth) perception, perception of space (depth), stereopsis
Raumwinkel *m* [three-dimensional] solid angle, cone angle
Raumwinkeleinheit *f*,
Raumwinkelelement *n* unit solid angle
raumzeitlich spatiotemporal, space-time
Rauschabstand *m* signal-to-noise ratio, SNR
rauschadaptiv noise-adaptive
rauschähnlich noise-like *(signal)*
Rauschakkumulation *f* noise accumulation
Rauschamplitude *f* noise amplitude
Rauschanteil *m* noise part (component)
Rauschäquivalentleistung *f* noise equivalent power, NEP
rauscharm low-noise
Rauscharmut *f* noiselessness
Rauschausbreitung *f* noise propagation
Rauschbandbreite *f* noise bandwidth
Rauschbefreiung *f* noise removal (cleaning), noise cancel[l]ing, denoising [procedure]
Rauschbegrenzer *m*/**selbsttätiger** automatic noise limiter, ANL
rauschbegrenzt noise-limited
rauschbehaftet noisy, noised
Rauschbeitrag *m* noise contribution (contributor)
Rauschbeseitigung *f s.* Rauschbefreiung
Rauschbewertungsfilter *n* noise filter
Rauschdämpfung *f* noise attenuation
Rauschdichte *f* noise density
Rauscheffekt *m* noise effect
Rauscheinbruch *m* noise bump, burst
Rauschelektron *n* noise electron
rauschempfindlich noise-sensitive
Rauschempfindlichkeit *f* noise sensitivity, sensitivity to noise
rauschen to noise
Rauschen *n* [interference] noise
~/**additives** additive [electronic] noise
~/**additives weißes Gaußsches (gaußverteiltes)** additive [white] Gaussian noise, AWGN
~/**akustisches** acoustical noise
~/**analoges** analog noise
~/**anatomisches** anatomic noise *(in a radiographic image)*
~/**binäres** binary noise
~/**digitales** digital noise
~/**diskretes** discrete noise
~/**eingefrorenes** fixed-pattern noise, FPN
~/**elektrisches** electrical noise
~/**elektromagnetisches** electromagnetic noise
~/**elektronisches** electronic noise
~/**farbiges** color[ed] noise, chroma noise, chrominance signal-to[-random] noise ratio

~/**Gaußsches (gaußverteiltes)** Gaussian[-type] noise, normal noise
~/**harmonisches** harmonic noise
~/**hochfrequentes** high-frequency noise
~/**impulsförmiges** impulse (impulsive) noise; salt-and-pepper noise, noise spikes
~/**kohärentes** coherent noise
~/**korreliertes** correlated noise
~/**kosmisches** cosmic noise
~/**künstliches** man-made noise
~/**lokales** local noise
~/**mechanisches** mechanical noise
~/**multiplikatives** multiplicative noise
~/**niederfrequentes** low-frequency noise
~/**normalverteiltes** normal noise, Gaussian[-type] noise *(s.a.* ~/additives weißes Gaußsches*)*
~/**optisches** optical noise
~/**ortszeitliches** spatiotemporal noise
~/**periodisches** periodic noise
~/**poissonverteiltes weißes** Poisson-distributed white noise, Poisson [counting] noise
~/**räumliches** spatial noise, spatially dependent noise
~/**rosa** pink noise *(a test noise signal)*
~/**schwaches** low[-level] noise
~/**schwarzes** black noise
~/**sichtbares** visible noise
~/**signalabhängiges** signal-dependent noise
~/**sinusförmiges** sinusoidal noise
~/**statistisches** statistical noise
~/**strukturiertes** structured noise
~/**subtraktives** subtractive noise
~/**thermisches** thermal [conductance] noise, temperature noise *(thermal sensor)*; random [thermal] noise, Johnson (system) noise
~/**tieffrequentes** low-frequency noise
~/**uniformes** uniform noise
~/**unkorreliertes** uncorrelated noise
~/**weißes** white noise
~/**weißes Gaußsches** white Gaussian noise
Rauschfaktor *m* noise factor
Rauschfehler *m* noise error
Rauschfilter *n* noise filter
Rauschfilterung *f* noise filtering
rauschfrei noise-free, noiseless
Rauschfreiheit *f* noise immunity
Rauschfrequenz *f* noise frequency
Rauschgehalt *m* noise content
Rauschgenerator *m* noise generator *(radar)*
Rauschglättung *f* noise smoothing (equalization)
Rauschglättungsfilter *n* noise smoothing filter
Rauschgrauwert *m* noise gray-level value
Rauschgrenze *f* noise limit
Rauschimpuls *m* noise impulse
Rauschkoeffizient *m* noise coefficient

Rauschleistung f noise power (performance)
~/**äquivalente** noise equivalent power, NEP
Rauschleistungsdichte f noise power [spectral] density
Rauschleistungsspektrum n noise-power spectrum, NPS, Wiener [noise-power] spectrum
Rauschmaß n noise figure, NF
Rauschmatrix f noise matrix
Rauschmerkmal n noise feature
Rauschmessung f noise measurement
Rauschminderer m noise reducer
Rauschminderung f s. Rauschreduktion
Rauschmodell n noise model
Rauschmuster n noise [interference] pattern
Rauschniveau n noise level
Rauschparameter m noise parameter
Rauschpegel m noise level
Rauschpixel n [random-]noise pixel
Rauschpunkt m noise point
Rauschquelle f noise source
Rauschreduktion f noise reduction, denoising
~/**bewegungskompensierte** motion-compensated noise reduction
~/**digitale** digital noise reduction, DNR
~/**örtliche** spatial noise reduction
~/**zeitliche** temporal noise reduction
Rauschreduktionsalgorithmus m noise-reduction algorithm
Rauschreduktionsfilter n noise-reduction filter
Rauschreduktionsfilterung f noise-reduction filtering
Rauschreduktionssystem n [audio] noise-reduction system
Rauschreduktionswert m s. Rauschreduktionsfaktor
Rauschreduzierung f s. Rauschreduktion
Rauschschwelle f noise threshold *(of a receiver)*
Rauschsignal n noise signal (impulse)
Rauschsignatur f noise signature
Rausch-Skalierbarkeit f SNR scalability
Rauschspannung f noise voltage
Rauschspektrum n noise spectrum
Rauschspitze f noise peak (spike)
Rauschstörquelle f s. Rauschquelle
Rauschstörung f noise disturbance; noise artifact
Rauschstrom m noise current
Rauschstromquelle f noise current source
Rauschtemperatur f noise temperature
Rauschübertragung f noise transmission (transfer)
Rauschumgebung f noise environment
rauschunempfindlich noise-resistant; noise-tolerant, robust to noise
Rauschunempfindlichkeit f noise insensitivity (immunity), insensitivity to noise

Rauschunterdrückung f noise suppression
~/**adaptive** adaptive noise suppression
~/**automatische** automatic noise limiter, ANL
~/**digitale** digital noise reduction, DNR
~/**dynamische** dynamic noise suppression, DNS
Rauschvarianz f noise variance
Rauschverhalten n noise performance
Rauschverminderung f s. Rauschreduktion
Rauschverstärkung f noise amplification (gain)
Rauschvorgang m noise process
Rauschwert m noise value
Rauschzahl f noise figure, NF
Rayleigh-Bereich m Rayleigh range *(Gaussian optics)*
Rayleigh-Gleichung Rayleigh equation *(color vision)*
Rayleigh-Kriterium n Rayleigh criterion (condition) *(optics, radar)*
Rayleigh-Länge f Rayleigh length *(laser)*
Rayleigh-Rauschen n Rayleigh noise
Rayleigh-Streuung f Rayleigh (coherent) scattering
~/**gefilterte** filtered Rayleigh scattering
~/**klassische** classical Rayleigh scattering
Rayleigh-Verteilung f Rayleigh distribution
RBF-Netz n radial basis function [neural] net[work], RBFNN
RCA-Stecker m RCA (Cinch) plug, RCA [phono] connector
RCA-Verbindung f RCA (Cinch) connection *(video)*
RC-Papier n RC (resin-coated) paper
Readaptation f readaptation
reakquirieren to reacquire
Reaktion f/**fotochemische** photochemical reaction, photoreaction
Reaktionszeit f reaction (response) time *(e.g. of a photodetector)*
Realaufnahme f 1. live-action shot (photograph); 2. s. Realdreh
Realbildsucher m s. Echtbildsucher
Realdarsteller m live actor, live-action character
Realdekoration f real setting; real (physical) location *(film production)*
Realdreh m live filming, live[-action] shoot, live-action photography (production)
Realfilm m live-action film (movie), live-action feature
Realfilmmaterial n live-action footage (material)
Realgeräusch n ambience, presence, aura, room tone
Realität f/**erweiterte** augmented (enhanced) reality, AR
~/**virtuelle** virtual reality, VR
Realkamera f real[-world] camera, physical camera
Realszene f real scene; live-action scene *(cinema)*

Realweltbildfolge *f*, **Realweltszene** *f* real-world video sequence, real-world scene
Realzeit *f s.* Echtzeit
Rechenaufwand *m* computational effort (burden), computational cost (load)
rechenaufwendig, rechenintensiv computationally intensive (expensive), compute[r]-intensive
Rechenleistung *f* computing power
Rechenvorschrift *f* algorithm
Rechenzeit *f* computation (computing) time, calculation time
Recherche *f* retrieval
Rechnerbildschirm *m* computer [image] display, computer [display] screen
Rechnerendknoten *m* terminal
Rechnernetz *n*/**lokales** local area network, LAN
Rechnerschnittstelle *f* computer interface
Rechnersehen *n* computer vision
Rechteck *n*/**umgebendes (umschließendes, umschreibendes)** bounding rectangle (box), delimiting rectangle *(shape analysis)*
Rechteckapertur *f s.* Rechteckblende
Rechteckblende *f* rectangular (square) aperture
Rechteckfilter *n* box (uniform) filter
Rechteckfunktion *f* rectangle (box) function, rectangular impulse function, rect[angular] function, *(digital signal processing)*
Rechteckgitter *n* rectangular (square) lattice, rectangular grid; gratic[u]le, retic[u]le *(optics)*
rechteckig rectangular; orthogonal; perpendicular
Rechteckimpuls *m* rectangular pulse *(s.a.* Rechteckfunktion*)*
Rechteckraster *m(n)* rectangular raster (lattice)
Rechtecksignal *n* rectangular signal, square [wave] signal
Rechteckwelle *f* square (rectangular) wave
Rechteckwellenamplitude *f* square-wave amplitude
Rechteckwellenfunktion *f* square-wave function
Rechte-Hand-Regel *f* [light] right-hand rule *(optics)*
rechtsäugig right-eyed
rechtsbündig right-aligned, right-adjusted, flush right; ragged left
Rechtschreibprüfprogramm *n* spell check[er]
rechtsdrehend dextrorota[to]ry, dextro[gyrate], turning clockwise
rechtsichtig emmetropic
Rechtsklick *m* right click
rechtsklicken to right-click
Rechtsklicken *n* right clicking
Rechtwinkelprisma *n* right-angle[d] prism, right-triangle prism
Rechtwinkelspiegel *m* right-angle mirror
rechtwinklig right-angled, rectangular; orthogonal
Rechtwinkligkeit *f* rectangularity; orthogonality; perpendicularity
Recorder *m* 1. recorder, recording device, record machine; 2. *s.* Belichter
Recorderrauschen *n* recorder noise
Recyclingpapier *n* recycled paper
Redaktionsfotograf *m* staff photographer
redigitalisieren to redigitze
Redoxeigenschaft *f* reduction-oxidation property
Redoxpotential *n* redox potential
Redoxprozess *m*, **Redoxreaktion** *f*, **Redoxvorgang** *m* redox reaction
Reduktion *f* reduction
~/**chemische** chemical reduction
Reduktionsfaktor *m s.* Kompressionsfaktor
Reduktionskamera *f* reduction camera
Reduktionsmittel *n* reducing agent, reductant, reducer
Reduktionsvorgang *m* reduction process
redundant redundant
Redundanz *f* redundancy
~/**örtliche** spatial (geometric) redundancy, intraframe redundancy (correlation)
~/**psychooptische (psychovisuelle)** psychovisual redundancy
~/**räumliche** *s.* ~/örtliche
~/**spektrale** spectral redundancy
~/**statistische** statistical redundancy
~/**zeitliche** temporal redundancy, interframe redundancy (correlation), frame-to-frame correlation (redundancy)
Redundanzbeseitigung *f* redundancy removal
redundanzfrei redundancy-free
Redundanzprüfung *f*/**zyklische** cyclic redundancy check, CRC
Redundanzreduktion *f*, **Redundanzreduzierung** *f* redundancy reduction
Reed-Solomon-Blockcode *m*, **Reed-Solomon-Code** *m* Reed-Solomon [block] code *(digital television)*
Reed-Solomon-Codierung *f* Reed-Solomon [en]coding
reemittieren to reemit
Referenz... *s.a.* Bezugs...
Referenzauge *n* dominant eye
Referenzbild *n* reference image (picture); reference frame, frame of reference, R frame; key frame *(computer graphics)*
Referenzbündel *n* reference beam
Referenz-Farbmodell *n* reference color model
Referenzleerband *n* reference tape
Referenzmatrix *f* reference matrix
Referenzmodell *n* reference model
Referenzmonitor *m* reference monitor
Referenzmuster *n* reference pattern
Referenzoszillator *m* reference oscillator *(television)*

Referenzpixel *n* reference pixel *(differential image compression)*
Referenzplatte *f* reference flat *(optics)*
Referenzpunkt *m* reference point
Referenzradar *n* reference radar
Referenzsignal *n* reference signal
Referenzstrahl *m* reference beam (wave) *(holography)*
Referenzstreifen *m* master strip
Referenzvektor *m* reference vector
Referenzwelle *f* reference wave (beam) *(holography)*
Reflektanz *f s.* Reflexionsgrad
reflektieren to reflect
reflektierend reflecting, reflective
Reflektivität *f* reflectivity, reflecting power
Reflektivitätsgleichung *f* image irradiance equation
Reflektografie *f* reflectography
Reflektometer *n* reflectometer
Reflektor *m* 1. reflector; 2. *s.* Spiegelteleskop
~/**diffuser** diffuse reflector
~/**Lambertscher** [ideal] Lambertian reflector *(s.a.* Strahler/Lambertscher*)*
~/**spiegelnder** mirror (specular) reflector
Reflektorlampe *f* reflector lamp
Reflektorwand *f* reflector board, reflecting screen
Reflex *m* reflex
~/**optokinetischer** optokinetic reflex
reflexarm *s.* reflexionsarm
Reflexautokollimator *m* [reflex] autocollimator
Reflexbelichtung *f* reflex (reflected) exposure
Reflexbild *n* reflection, reflected (reflection) image
Reflexblendung *f* reflected glare
Reflexfolie *f* retroreflective foil
Reflexfotografie *f* single-lens-reflex photography
reflexfrei nonreflecting, nonreflective
Reflexfreiheit *f* non-reflection
Reflexion *f* reflection, reflexion
~ **am Bildschirm** screen glare
~ **am optisch dichteren Medium** external reflection
~ **am optisch dünneren Medium** internal reflection
~/**ambiente** ambient reflection
~/**anisotrope** anisotropic reflection
~/**dielektrische** dielectric reflection
~/**diffuse** diffuse (Lambertian) reflection
~/**Fresnelsche** Fresnel reflection
~/**gemischte** mixed reflection
~/**gerichtete** direct reflection, [directional] specular reflection
~/**gestreute** diffuse (Lambertian) reflection
~/**hyperbolische** hyperbolic reflection *(radar)*
~/**Lambertsche** Lambertian (diffuse) reflection
~/**nichtspiegelnde** off-specular reflection
~/**polarisierte** polarized reflection
~/**regelmäßige** *s.* ~/gerichtete
~/**selektive** selective reflection
~/**spiegelnde** specular (mirror) reflection, glare [reflection]
~/**totale** total reflection
~/**ungerichtete** indirect reflection
reflexionsarm low-reflection, low-reflective
Reflexionsbedingung *f*/**Braggsche** Bragg [reflection] condition
Reflexionsbeugungsgitter *n s.* Reflexionsgitter
Reflexionsbild *n s.* Reflexbild
Reflexionsdensitometer *n* reflection densitometer
Reflexionsdensitometrie *f* reflection densitometry
Reflexionsdichte *f* reflection density
Reflexionsebene *f* plane of reflection
Reflexionselektronenmikroskop *n* reflection[-type] electron microscope
Reflexionselektronenmikroskopie *f* reflection [electron] microscopy
Reflexionsfähigkeit *f s.* Reflexionsvermögen 1.
Reflexionsfaktor *m s.* Reflexionsgrad
Reflexionsfilter *n* reflection filter
Reflexionsfläche *f* reflective (reflecting) surface
Reflexionsfleck *m* flare spot
Reflexionsformel *f*/**Fresnelsche** Fresnel reflection formula
reflexionsfrei nonreflecting, nonreflective
Reflexionsgesetz *n* reflection law, law of reflection
Reflexionsgitter *n* reflection [diffraction] grating, reflecting grating
~/**planes** plane reflection grating
Reflexionsgrad *m* reflectance [factor], reflectivity, reflection coefficient (factor)
~/**spektraler** spectral reflectance
reflexionsholografisch reflection holographic
Reflexionshologramm *n* reflection[-type] hologram
Reflexionskoeffizient *m* reflection coefficient
Reflexionskurve *f* reflection curve
Reflexionslicht *n s.* Reflexlicht
Reflexionslichthof *m* [reflection] halation
Reflexionsmatrix *f* reflection matrix
reflexionsmindernd reflection-diminishing
Reflexionsmodell *n* [surface] reflectance model, reflection model *(computer graphics, image analysis)*
Reflexionspolarisator *m* reflection polarizer
Reflexionsprisma *n* reflecting (reflector) prism, reflex prism
Reflexionsröntgengerät *n* backscatter X-ray unit
Reflexionsschicht *f* reflective [substratum] layer *(e.g. of an intensifying screen)*

Reflexionsseismik f reflection seismology
reflexionsspektrofotometrisch reflection spectrophotometric
Reflexionsspektrometer n reflectance spectrometer
Reflexionsspektroskopie f reflectance spectroscopy
Reflexionsspektrum n reflection spectrum
Reflexionsstrahl m reflected ray; reflection beam
Reflexionsstufengitter n reflection echelon
Reflexionsvektor m reflection vector
Reflexionsverlust m reflection (reflective) loss
Reflexionsvermögen n 1. reflecting power, reflective ability, reflectivity; 2. s. Reflexionsgrad
~/**ambientes** s. ~/unidirektionales
~/**bidirektionales** bidirectional [spectral] reflectivity
~/**unidirektionales** unidirectional reflectivity
Reflexionswand f s. Reflexwand
Reflexionswinkel m angle of reflection, reflection angle
Reflexlicht n reflected light; bounce light
reflexmindernd reflection-diminishing
Reflexminderung f reflectance glare reduction
Reflexradiografie f reflex radiography, X-ray emissiography
Reflexschirm m flash umbrella
Reflexsignal n echo signal *(ultrasound imaging)*
Reflexspiegel m reflex mirror
Reflexsucher m reflex [view]finder
Reflextafel f s. Reflexwand
Reflexwand f reflector board, reflecting screen
Refraktion f 1. [optical] refraction; 2. s. Fernpunktrefraktion
~/**atmosphärische** atmospheric refraction
~/**axiale** s. Fernpunktrefraktion
~/**konische** conic refraction
Refraktionsanomalie f ametropia *(disorder of vision)*
Refraktionswinkel m angle of refraction, refraction (refracting) angle
Refraktionszustand m refractive condition (state) *(of the eye)*
refraktiv refractive, refractile
Refraktometer n refractometer
Refraktometrie f refractometry
refraktometrisch refractometric
Refraktor m refractor, refracting telescope
~/**apochromatischer** apochromatic refractor
Regel f/**Parsevalsche** Parseval's theorem *(signal processing)*
~/**Scheimpflugsche** Scheimpflug rule
Regelfläche f lofted surface *(geometric modeling)*
Regelschaltkreis m regulation circuitry
Regenbogeneffekt m chromatic dispersion

Regenbogenhaut f iris *(of the eye)*
Regenbogenhologramm n rainbow (Benton) hologram
Regenclutter m, **Regenecho** n rain clutter (echo) *(radar)*
Regenenttrübung f/**maximale** anticlutter rain maximum *(radar)*
~/**minimale** anticlutter rain minimum
Regenerator m, **Regeneratorlösung** f replenisher [solution]
Regeneratortank m replenishment tank
regenerieren to regenerate; to replenish *(processing solutions)*
Regenerierung f regeneration; replenishment
Regenerierungsrate f replenishment rate
Regenschutzhaube f camera rain guard
Regie f direction; directing
Regieassistent m 1. personal assistant *(film crew)*; 2. [first] assistant director, AD *(film crew)*
Regiebuch n s. 1. Drehbuch; 2. Filmskript
Regiegerät n cueing device
Regieraum m control room
Regiesignal n cue
Region f region; blob *(s.a. Bereich)*
~/**interessierende** region of interest, ROI
Regionalstudio n local TV station
Regionenbild n label image
Regionendarstellung f region-based representation
Regionenidentifikation f region identification
Regionenklassifikation f region classification
Regionennachbarschaft f region adjacency
Regionennachbarschaftsgraph m region adjacency graph
Regionensegmentierung f region segmentation
Regionenwachstum n region-growing [method], region-growing procedure, magic wand approach *(segmentation technique)*
Regisseur m director *(cinema)*
Regisseur-Fassung f director's (first) cut
Register n register
Registerfehler m register (registration) error
Registergenauigkeit f registration accuracy
Registerstift m register (registration) pin, pilot pin
Registrat n record *(color photography)*
registrieren to register
Registrierpapier n [/**fotografisches**] recording paper
Registrierung f registration
~/**objektbasierte** object-based registration
~/**szenenbasierte** scene-based registration
Reglette f reglet *(typography)*
Regressionsanalyse f regression analysis
Regularisierung f regularization

Regulierung f/präventive preventive policing *(video transmission)*
Rehalogenierung f rehalogenation
Rehalogenierungsmittel n rehalogenizing agent
Reibungselektrizität f triboelectricity, static electricity
Reibungskupplung f friction clutch
Reichweite f range; propagative distance; coverage *(e.g. of radar)*
Reifekeim m sensitizing (ripening) center *(latent image)*
Reifkeim m s. Reifekeim
Reifmittel n ripening agent, ripener *(emulsion preparation)*
Reifung f ripening, cooking *(emulsion preparation)*
~/chemische chemical ripening (sensitization), second ripening, digestion, afterripening
~/physikalische physical (first) ripening, Ostwald ripening
Reihe f/trigonometrische Fourier series (sequence)
Reihenabtastung f row scanning
Reihenbelichtung f sequential exposure
Reihenbild n sequential image, serial image (picture), sequence photograph
Reihenbildschaltung f continuous shooting mode, multiple capture mode *(camera feature)*
Reihenentwicklung f series expansion
Reihenfotografie f chronophotography
Reihenmatrix f row matrix
Reihenmesskamera f, **Reihenmesskammer** f aerial frame camera
Reihenvektor m row vector
reihenweise rowwise *(e.g. image filtering)*
Reineisenband n metal particle tape
Reinheit f/kolorimetrische colorimetric purity
~/spektrale spectral purity
Reinigungsbürste f cleaning brush *(copying machine)*
Reinigungskassette f cleaning cassette, head cleaner tape *(video)*
Reinitialisierung f reinitialization
Reinraum m clean room
Reintransmissionsgrad m [/spektraler] [spectral] internal transmittance
Reinzeichnung f finished drawing
Reisefoto n travel photograph
Reisefotograf m travel[ing] photographer
Reisefotografie f travel photography
Reisekamera f flatbed camera, sliding box camera
Reisestativ n travel tripod
Reißfestigkeit f tear resistance *(e.g. of photographic papers)*
Reißschwenk m swish (whip) pan, flash pan *(filming)*
Reiz m stimulus
~/optischer visual stimulus
~/sensorischer sensory stimulus
~/visueller visual stimulus
Reizantwort f [stimulus] response
Reizdauer f stimulus duration
Reizintensität f stimulus intensity
Reizsteigerung f stimulus increase
Reizverarbeitung f stimulus processing
Reklamefoto n advertising photograph
Reklassifikation f reclassification
reklassifizieren to reclassify
Reklassifizierung f reclassification
Rekombination f recombination
Rekombinationsstrahlung f recombination radiation, p-n junction electroluminescence *(light-emitting diode)*
rekombinieren to recombine
Rekompression f recompression
rekomprimieren to recompress *(e.g. image data)*
Rekondensation f recondensation *(e.g. of printing ink)*
rekonstruieren to reconstruct
Rekonstruktion f reconstruction *(e.g. of image data)*
~/algebraische algebraic reconstruction
~/dreidimensionale three-dimensional reconstruction
~/holografische holographic reconstruction
~/iterative iterative reconstruction
~/merkmalsbasierte feature-based reconstruction
~/morphologische morphological reconstruction
~/multiplanare multiplanar reconstruction, MPR *(tomography)*
~/phasenerhaltende phase-preserving reconstruction
~/tomografische tomographic reconstruction
~/verzerrungsfreie distortion-free reconstruction
~/voxelbasierte voxel-based reconstruction
Rekonstruktionsalgorithmus m reconstruction (reconstructive) algorithm
Rekonstruktionsbild n reconstructed image
Rekonstruktionsergebnis n reconstruction result
Rekonstruktionsfarbe f reconstruction color *(laser)*
Rekonstruktionsfehler m reconstruction error
Rekonstruktionsfilter n reconstruction filter (operator)
Rekonstruktionsfilterbank f reconstruction filter bank
Rekonstruktionsgenauigkeit f reconstruction accuracy (fidelity)
Rekonstruktionsgleichung f s. Fenster-Fourier-Transformation/inverse
Rekonstruktionsleistung f reconstruction performance

Rekonstruktionsmatrix f reconstruction matrix (grid)
Rekonstruktionstechnik f/**arithmetische** arithmetic reconstruction technique, ART
Rekonstruktionswelle f reconstructed wave
Rekonstruktionszeit f reconstruction time
Rekristallisation f recrystallization
rektifizieren to rectify
Rektifizierung f rectification
~/**zylindrische** cylindrical rectification
Rekto n recto [page]; right-hand page (layout)
Rekursion f recursion
Rekursionstiefe f recursion depth
Rekursivfilter n recursive filter
Relais n relay
Relaisoptik f relay lens
Relaissender m relay transmitter (s.a. Füllsender)
relational relational
Relationenobjekt n relational object
Relativgeschwindigkeit f [relative] tape-to-head speed, head-to-tape speed
Relaxation f relaxation (image-processing operation)
~/**diskrete** discrete relaxation
~/**iterative** iterative relaxation
~/**kontinuierliche** continuous relaxation
~/**lineare** linear relaxation
~/**stochastische** stochastic relaxation
~/**transversale** transverse relaxation (magnetic resonance imaging)
Relaxationsalgorithmus m relaxation algorithm
Relaxationsmatrix f relaxation matrix
Relaxationstechnik f/**probabilistische** probabilistic relaxation technique
Relaxationsverfahren n relaxation method
Relaxationszeit f relaxation time
~/**longitudinale** longitudinal (spin-lattice) relaxation time, T-one [time constant], T1 (magnetic resonance imaging)
~/**transversale** transverse relaxation time, spin-spin relaxation time, T2 [time constant] (magnetic resonance imaging)
relaxieren to relax
relevant relevant, nonredundant
Reliefbild n relief image
Reliefdruck m relief (block) printing, letterpress [printing]
Reliefdruckplatte f letterpress (relief printing) plate
Reliefkarte f relief map
Relpunkt m reciprocal-lattice point (crystallography)
Relstab m relrod, reciprocal-lattice rod
Remanenz f remanence, residual (rest) magnetism
REM-Aufnahme f SEM (scanning electron microscope) photograph
Rembrandt-Beleuchtung f Rembrandt lighting

Remission f 1. reflectance [factor], reflectivity, reflection coefficient (factor); 2. s. Reflexion/diffuse
Remissionsfaktor m, **Remissionsgrad** m reflection factor (in case of diffuse reflection)
Remissionskurve f [diffuse] reflectance curve
remittieren to remit
Rendering n rendering (computer-graphic simulation process)
~/**bildbasiertes** image-based rendering
~/**geometriebasiertes** geometry-based rendering
~ **in Echtzeit** real-time rendering
~/**nichtfotorealistisches** nonphotorealistic rendering, NPR
~/**stochastisches** stochastic [halftone] rendering
Rendering-Algorithmus m rendering algorithm
Rendering-Gleichung f rendering equation
Rendering-Software f rendering software, 3-D rendering package
Rendering-Technik f rendering technique
Rendern n s. Rendering
rendern to render (computer graphics)
Renografie f renography
renografisch renographic
Renogramm n renogram
Reparametrisierung f reparametrization
Repetitionszeit f repetition time, time of repetition (magnetic resonance imaging)
rephasieren to rephase
Rephasierung f rephasing
Rephasierungsgradient m rephasing gradient
Reportagefotografie f reportage photography, photoreporting
Reportagekamera f news (reportage) camera; field recorder
Reposition[ierung] f reposition, repo (e.g. of image elements)
Repräsentation f representation (s.a. Darstellung)
Reprint m reprint
Reprisenkino n archival theater
Repro f(n) repro [proof], reproduction (press) proof (s.a. under Reproduktion)
Reproanstalt f [trade] camera service, prep service, service bureau, trade shop, output house
Reproarbeit f process work, copy[ing] work
Reproaufnahme f copy photograph
Reproaufnahmematerial n process material
Reproauszugsfilter n color separation filter
Reproduktion f 1. reproduction (s.a. under Repro...); 2. reproduction (copy)
~/**fotomechanische** photomechanical reproduction
Reproduktions... s.a. Repro...
Reproduktionsgerät n reproducer

Reproduktionsmaßstab *m* scale of reproduction
Reproduktionsobjektiv *n* copy (process) lens, reproduction objective
Reproduktionsqualität *f* reproduction quality, quality of reproduction
Reproduktionstechnik *f s.* Reprotechnik
Reproduktionsverfahren *n* reproduction process
Reproduktionsverhältnis *n* reproduction ratio
Reproduktionsvorlage *f* copy
reproduzierbar reproducible *(s.a.* reprofähig*)*
Reproduzierbarkeit *f* reproducibility
reproduzieren to reproduce
reprofähig camera-ready, reproducible *(artwork)*
Reprofilm *m* process film, repro[graphic] film *(s.a.* Lithfilm*)*
Reprofotografie *f* reproduction-related photography, process (graphic arts) photography, copy[ing] photography, photomechanical reproduction
Reprogestell *n* copy stand
Reprograf *m* reprographer
Reprografie *f* reprography
Reprografik *f* reprographics
reprografisch reprographic
Repro-Halbtonfilm *m* continuous-tone process film
Reprohersteller *m* reproductionist
Reprokamera *f* process [copy] camera, copy[ing] camera, graphic arts camera, reproduction (reprographic) camera
~/**kleinformatige** stat camera
reproreif *s.* reprofähig
Reproseite *f* repro page
Reproständer *m s.* Reprostativ
Reprostativ *n* copy stand
Reprostativbeleuchtung *f* copy-stand lighting
Reprotechnik *f* reprographic (reproduction) technology
Reprovorlage *f* camera-ready copy, reproduction copy, finished art
requantisieren to requantize
Requantisierung *f* requantization, requantizing, inverse quantization
Requisiten *pl* props, properties
Requisiteur *m* property man, propman *(cinema)*
Reseau-Gitter *n* reseau [marks]
Reseau-Kamera *f* reseau camera
Reseau-Platte *f* reseau plate *(photogrammetry)*
Reserveaufnahme *f* cover shot *(filming)*
Reservefilm *m* spare film
Reservekamera *f* spare camera
Resist *m* resist; photoresist, photosensitive resist
resistiv resistive
Resistmaske *f* resist mask
Resistron *n s.* Vidikon

Resistschicht *f* resist layer
reskalieren to rescale *(e.g. data)*
Resonanz *f* resonance
~/**elektronenmagnetische** *s.* Elektronenspinresonanz
~/**kernmagnetische** *s.* ~/nuklearmagnetische
~/**magnetische** magnetic resonance, MR
~/**nuklearmagnetische** nuclear magnetic resonance, NMR
~/**optische** optical resonance
Resonanzabsorption *f* resonance absorption
Resonanzamplitude *f* resonance amplitude
Resonanzartefakt *n* comet tail *(sonography)*
Resonanzbedingung *f* resonance condition *(magnetic resonance imaging)*
Resonanzbild *n* resonance image
Resonanzbildgebung *f* spin mapping
Resonanzfilter *n* resonance filter *(neighborhood operator)*
Resonanzfluoreszenz *f* resonant fluorescence
Resonanzfrequenz *f* resonance (resonant) frequency *(e.g. of a piezoelectric crystal)*
Resonanzkurve *f* resonance curve
Resonanzsignal *n* resonance signal
Resonanzspektroskopie *f*/**kernmagnetische** nuclear magnetic resonance spectroscopy
Resonanzstreuung *f* resonance scattering
Resonator *m* resonator, [resonant] cavity, etalon *(interferometry, laser)*
~/**gütegeschalteter** Q-switched laser cavity
~/**instabiler** unstable resonator
~/**konfokaler** confocal resonator
~/**optischer** optical resonator
~/**stabiler** stable resonator
Resonatorspiegel *m* resonator mirror
resonieren to resonate
Rest *m* 1. residue; 2. outtake *(film editing)*
Restaberration *f* residual aberration
Restastigmatismus *m* residual astigmatism
Restaurationsalgorithmus *m* restoration algorithm
Restaurationsfilter *n* [image] restoration filter, restoration operator, deconvolution filter
restaurieren to restore *(e.g. image data)*
Restbandanzeige *f* remaining tape counter
Restbild *n s.* Restladungsbild
Restbildfehler *m* residual aberration
Restfarbfehler *m* residual chromatic aberration
Restfehlerverdeckung *f* concealment *(electronic imaging)*
Restkoma *f* residual coma[tic aberration] *(optics)*
Restladung *f* residual electrostatic charge
Restladungsbild *n* residual electrostatic image *(electrophotography)*

Restleuchtdichte *f* residual luminance
Restlicht *n* residual light
Restlichtkamera *f* low-light-level camera
Restlichtverstärker *m* residual light amplifier
Restmagnetisierung *f* residual (rest) magnetism, remanence
Restöffnungsfehler *m* residual uncorrected spherical aberration
Restreflexion *f* residual reflection
Restsehvermögen *n* residual visual capability, blindsight
Restseitenband *n* vestigial (partially suppressed) sideband, VSB
Restseitenband-Demodulator *m* vestigial-sideband demodulator
Restseitenbandfilter *n* vestigial sideband filter
Restseitenbandmodulation *f* vestigial sideband modulation, VSB
Restseitenbandmodulator *m*/**digitaler** digital residual sideband modulator
Restseitenbandverfahren *n* vestigial sideband method
Resttoner *m* remaining toner
Restverzeichnung *f*, **Restverzerrung** *f* residual aberration
Resultatbild *n* result (final) image
Resynchronisation *f* resynchronization
resynchronisieren to resynchronize
Retarderfolie *f* retardation sheet *(of a liquid-crystal display)*
Retikel *n* retic[u]le, gratic[u]le *(optics)*
Retina *f* retina *(s.a. under Netzhaut)*
Retinabild *n* retinal image
Retinakamera *f* fundus (ophthalmic) camera, retinal camera
retinal retinal
Retinal *n* retinal[dehyde], retinene, vitamin A aldehyde
Retinascanner *m* retinal scanner; retinal pattern detector
Retinextheorie *f* retinex theory *(of color vision)*
Retinoskop *n* retinoscope
Retinoskopie *f* retinoscopy, sciascopy
retinoskopisch retinoscopic
retinotop retinotopic
Retransformation *f* retransformation
retransformieren to retransform
Retrieval *n* retrieval
Retrofokuskonstruktion *f* retrofocus construction (design)
Retrofokusobjektiv *n* retrofocus lens, reverse telephoto lens
Retrofokus-Weitwinkelobjektiv *n* retrofocus wide-angle lens, reverse-telephoto wide-angle lens
Retroobjektiv *n* reversed lens
retroreflektierend retroreflective
Retroreflektor *m* retroreflector, corner [cube] reflector, corner cube [prism]
Retusche *f* retouch, retouching [work]
~/elektronische electronic retouching
Retuschefarbe *f* retouching [dye] color
Retuschefarbstoff *m* retouching dye (colorant)
Retuschelack *m* retouching lacquer
Retuscheur *m* retoucher, retouching specialist
Retuschierbleistift *m* retouching pen
retuschieren to retouch
Retuschierfarbe *f s.* Retuschefarbe
Retuschiermaschine *f* retouching machine
Retuschiermesser *n* retouching (etching) knife
Retuschierpinsel *m* retouching brush
Retuschierpult *n* retouching desk
Retuschiersoftware *f* retouching software
Retuschierspray *n* retouching spray
Retuschierstift *m* retouching pen
Reversalintermediatefilm *m s.* Umkehrintermediatefilm
Reversibilitätsprinzip *n* reversibility principle *(geometrical optics)*
Reversionsprisma *n* reversing (derotation) prism, inversion (inverting) prism
Revolverblende *f* revolving diaphragm
Revolverkopf *m* [lens] turret
Revolverokular *n* turret eyepiece
Rezeptor *m* 1. receptor, receiver *(s.a. under Empfänger)*; 2. *s.* Rezeptor/lichtempfindlicher 1.
~/lichtempfindlicher 1. photoreceptor, [light] receptor; 2. *s.* Rezeptorzelle
Rezeptorpigment *n* receptor pigment
Rezeptorschicht *f* receptor layer
Rezeptorsignal *n* receptor signal
Rezeptorzelle *f* photoreceptor cell, visual (eye) receptor
Reziprozität *f* reciprocity
Reziprozitätseffekt *m* reciprocity effect
Reziprozitätsfehler *m* reciprocity [law] failure, reciprocity effect, Schwarzschild behavior
Reziprozitätsgesetz *n* **[nach Bunsen und Roscoe]**, **Reziprozitätsregel** *f* [Bunsen-Roscoe] reciprocity law, Bunsen Roscoe law
Reziprozitätskorrektur *f* reciprocity correction
Reziprozitätsprinzip *n* principle of reprocity
Reziprozitätsverhalten *n* reciprocity behavior
RGB-Bild *n* RGB (red-green-blue) image, trispectral (three-channel) image
RGB-Bildsignal *n* RGB [picture] signal
RGB-Farbmodell *n* RGB model, red-green-blue primary color system, additive [color] system
RGB-Farbraum *m* RGB color space
~/erweiterter extended RGB color space
RGB-Filter *n* three-color filter
RGB-Kamera *f* three-tube television color camera
RGB-Laser *m* RGB laser
RGB-Pixel *n* RGB pixel

RGB-Schema *n s.* RGB-System
RGB-Signal *n* RGB signal
RGB-System *n* RGB system
RGB-Videosignal *n s.* RGB-Signal
RGB-Würfel *m* RGB [color] cube, color cube
Rhabdom *n* rhabdom[e], rod [photo]receptor, optic[al] rod, [retinal] rod
Rheinberg-Beleuchtung *f* Rheinberg illumination *(microscopy)*
Rheostat *m* rheostat
RHI-Sichtgerät *n* RHI (range-height indicator) display *(radar)*
Rhodamin *n* rhodamine *(fluorescent dye)*
Rhodopsin *n* rhodopsin, rod [photo]pigment, retinal purple, visual purple [pigment]
Rhythmogramm *n s.* Lichtpendelgrafik
Rice-Codierung *f* Rice coding *(image compression)*
Richtantenne *f* directional antenna (aerial)
Richtcharakteristik *f* directivity (pickup) pattern, [microphone] polar pattern
Richtfunkübertragungsanlage *f* field pickup unit, FPU
Richtigkeit *f*/**fotometrische** photometric accuracy
Richtmikrofon *n* directional mic[rophone]; interference tube microphone, shotgun (rifle) microphone
richtungsabhängig directionally dependent, directional, anisotropic, nonisotropic
Richtungsabhängigkeit *f* [directional] anisotropy, anisotropism
Richtungscode *m* direction code
Richtungscodierung *f* directional coding
Richtungsdetektion *f* direction (orientation) detection
richtungsempfindlich directionally sensitive
Richtungsempfindlichkeit *f* directional sensitivity
Richtungsfilter *n* directional (orientation) filter
Richtungsfilterung *f* directional filtering
Richtungsinformation *f* orientation information
Richtungslicht *n* directional (directed) light
Richtungsquantisierung *f* space quantization
Richtungssensor *m* orientation sensor (sensing device)
richtungsunabhängig directionally independent, isotropic
Richtungsvektor *m* direction (polar) vector
Richtungswinkel *m* orientation angle; azimuth
Richtwirkung *f s.* Richtcharakteristik
Riemengleitschutz *m* shoulder (nonslip) pad
Riemenhalterung *f* camera strap eyelet
Ries *n* ream *(quantity of paper)*

Riesenbildwand *f*, **Riesenleinwand** *f* gigantic movie screen, giant screen
Riesenradioteleskop *n* giant telescope
Riffelwand *f* lenticulated screen
rillen to score, to crease *(printed matter)*
Ringalbum *n* ring[ed] binder
Ringartefakt *m* 1. ring[-shaped] artifact, ringing (circular) artifact, ringing *(image coding)*; 2. *s.* Verstümmelungsartefakt
Ringblende *f* ring (annular) aperture
Ringblitzgerät *n* ring-flash [unit]
Ringblitzleuchte *f* ringlight, circular flash tube
Ringdemodulator *m* ring demodulator *(video modulation)*
Ringdetektor *m* ring detector *(computed tomography)*
Ringe *mpl*/**Newtonsche** Newton's rings *(interference pattern)*
Ringelektrode *f* annular (ring-shaped) electrode
Ringleuchte *f*, **Ringlicht** *n* ringlight
Ringmagnet *m* annular magnet
Ringmodulator *m* ring modulator *(video modulation)*
Ringordner *m* ring[ed] binder
Ringspule *f* toroidal [resistance] coil, toroid *(picture tube)*
Rinnenfehler *m* sagittal (off-axis) coma
Rivalität *f*/**binokulare** binocular rivalry (suppression)
RLE-Kompression *f s.* Lauflängencodierung
RMS-Körnung *f*, **RMS-Wert** *m* RMS (root-mean-square) granularity *(densitometry)*
Roberts-Kantendetektor *m*, **Roberts-Operator** *m* Roberts [edge] operator, Roberts cross[-gradient] operator
Robinson-Operator *m* Robinson's operator
Roboter *m*/**ferngesteuerter** remotely controlled robot, waldo
~/optisch navigierter optically navigated robot
Roboterkamera *f* robot (remote-control) camera, telerobotic (far-end) camera
Roboternavigation *f* robot navigation
Robotersehen *n* robot[ic] vision
Robotertechnik *f* robotics
Roboterteleskop *n* robot telescope
Robotik *f* robotics
robust robust *(e.g. an image processing algorithm)*
Robustheit *f* robustness
Rohabzug *m* loose (first) proof, random (scatter) proof, show-color proof
Rohbild *n* input (initial) image; as-acquired image
Rohbilddaten *pl* raw image data
Rohdaten *pl* raw (original) data; unencoded data
Rohdatenbild *n s.* Rohbild
Rohdatenrate *f* raw data rate

Rohdrehbuch *n* treatment *(as an outline of a screenplay)*
Rohfilm *m* raw film; [motion-picture film] raw stock, film stock
Rohfilmherstellung *f* film manufacture (production)
Rohfilmmaterial *n* raw [film] stock
Rohlinse *f* [lens] blank
Röhre *f*/**Braunsche** Braun tube *(cathode-ray tube)*
Röhrenbildschirm *m* cathode-ray [viewing] screen, CRT[-based] display, CRT screen
Röhrenbildwandler *m* tube imager
Röhrenblitzgerät *n* electronic flash unit (system)
Röhrenentwicklung *f* pipe (tube) processing
Röhrenfernseher *f*, **Röhrenfernsehgerät** *n* CRT television [set]
Röhrenfotozelle *f* phototube
Röhrenhals *m* tube neck; CRT neck
Röhrenkamera *f* [image] tube camera, tube-based camera, [video] tube-type camera
Röhrenkolben *m* [cathode-ray] tube envelope, [glass] envelope
Röhrenmonitor *m* CRT (cathode-ray-tube) monitor, CRT-based display monitor
Röhrenprojektor *m* cathode-ray tube projector, CRT[-based] projector *(video)*
Röhrenraster *m(n)* [CRT] raster
Röhrensehen *n* tubular (tunnel) vision *(visual aberration)*
Röhrensensor *m* tube imager
Röhrenspannung *f* tube drive voltage, tube [kilo]voltage, acceleration (anode-cathode) voltage *(cathode-ray tube)*
Röhrenstrom *m* [X-ray] tube current
Röhrenvideokamera *f* tube-type video camera
Rohrichtmikrofon *n* interference tube microphone, shotgun (rifle) microphone
Rohschnitt *m* rough (first) cut *(film editing)*
Rohschnittabnahme *f s.* Schnittabnahme
Rohsegmentierung *f* raw segmentation
Rohvideo *n* raw video
Rohzeichnung *f* scribble
Rollbalken *m* scroll bar *(user interface component)*
Rollendruck *m* web (roll-fed) printing
Rollendruckmaschine *f* web (roll-fed) press, reel-fed press
Rollenkern *m s.* Spulenkern
Rollenoffsetdruck *m* web offset [printing]
Rollenoffsetdruckmaschine *f* web offset press, rotary web-fed offset machine, offset rotary
Rollenpaket *n*/**unteres** diabolos *(cine film processor)*
Rollenpapier *n* roll paper; continuous [paper] roll, [paper] web *(printing)*
Rollenpapierbreite *f* web width
Rollenquetscher *m* squeegee rollers

Rollenrotationsmaschine *f* roll-fed rotary [press], web-fed [rotary] press, roll-fed web press
Rollenrotationstiefdruck *m* web-fed rotogravure
Rollenrotations-Tiefdruckmaschine *f* rotogravure rotary (machine), photogravure rotary machine
Rollenscanner *m s.* Trommelscanner
Rollenschneidemaschine *f*, **Rollenschneider** *m* rotary trimmer
Rollentiefdruck *m* web-fed gravure printing
Rollentransportmaschine *f* roller-transport machine
Rollfilm *m* roll film
Rollfilmformat *n* roll-film size (format)
Rollfilmhalter *m* roll-film holder
Rollfilmkamera *f* roll[-film] camera
Rollfilmkassette *f* roll film cassette
Rollfilmmagazin *n* roll-film magazine (holder)
Rollfilmmaterial *n* roll film material
Rollfilmnegativ *n* roll-film negative
Rollfilmtank *m* roll-film tank
Rollfilmtransport *m* roll film transport
Rollkugel[einheit] *f* trackball *(pointing device)*
Rollo *n* [fabric] blind *(focal-plane shutter)*
Rollschutzschicht *f* anticurl layer *(of film material)*
Rollstativ *n* [camera] dolly, truck
Rolltitel *m* rolling title; crawling title, moving caption
Rollwagen *m* wagon; dolly *(e.g. in filming; s.a.* Dolly*)*
ROM *n* ROM, read-only [electronic] memory
Roman *f s.* Antiqua
röntgen to X-ray, to radiograph
Röntgen *n* 1. X-ray imaging; 2. roentgen *(unit of X-radiation or gamma radiation)*
~/**dreidimensionales** *s.* Röntgentomografie
~/**konventionelles** conventional X-ray imaging, conventional radiography
~/**planares** plane tomography
Röntgenabbildung *f* 1. X-ray imaging; 2. *s.* Röntgenbild
Röntgenabsorber *m* X-ray absorber
Röntgenabsorption *f* X-ray [quantum] absorption
Röntgenabsorptionsbild *n* X-ray absorption profile
Röntgenabsorptionstomografie *f* X-ray absorption tomography
Röntgenabteilung *f* X-ray department, radiography (radiology) department *(of a hospital)*
Röntgenanalyse *f* X-ray analysis
Röntgenangiografie *f* X-ray angiography
röntgenangiografisch X-ray angiographic
Röntgenangiogramm *n* [projection] X-ray angiogram

Röntgenanlage f X-ray unit (suite), Roentgen unit, X-ray gear
~/**digitale** digital X-ray suite
Röntgenapparat m, **Röntgenapparatur** f X-ray apparatus (machine)
Röntgenarteriogramm n X-ray arteriogram, luminogram
Röntgenastronom m X-ray astronomer
Röntgenastronomie f X-ray astronomy
Röntgenaufnahme f 1. radiographic (X-ray) exposure; 2. s. Röntgenbild
Röntgenaufnahmetechnik f/**zahnärztliche** dental radiology
Röntgenbelichtung f X-ray exposure, radiographic exposure
Röntgenbelichtungszeit f X-ray exposure time
Röntgenbereich m X-ray region (regime)
Röntgenbestrahlung f X-ray exposure
Röntgenbetrieb m s. Röntgenabteilung
Röntgenbeugung f X-ray diffraction
Röntgenbeugungsanalyse f X-ray diffraction analysis
Röntgenbeugungsaufnahme f, **Röntgenbeugungsbild** n X-ray diffraction pattern
Röntgenbeugungskamera f X-ray diffraction camera
Röntgenbeugungsspektrum n X-ray diffraction spectrum
Röntgenbild n X-ray image (map), [still] X-ray picture, X-radiograph, roentgenogram; X-ray [photograph]
~/**konventionelles** conventional X-ray image
~/**planares** X-ray planar image
Röntgenbildaufnahme f s. Röntgenaufnahme 1.
Röntgenbildaufnehmer m X-ray image pickup apparatus (s.a. Röntgensensor)
Röntgenbilddarstellung f roentgenographic visualization; X-ray imaging
Röntgenbildgebung f X-ray imaging
Röntgenbildtechnik f X-ray imaging [technology]
Röntgenbildverstärker m [X-ray] image intensifier, XRII; fluoroscopic image intensifier
Röntgen-Bildverstärkerröhre f X-ray image intensifier tube
Röntgenbildwandler m X-ray imaging detector
Röntgenblitz m X-ray flash
Röntgenbremsspektrum n bremsstrahlung [X-ray] spectrum
Röntgenbremsstrahlung f bremsstrahlung, braking (decelerated) radiation
Röntgencomputertograf m X-ray CT scanner
Röntgencomputertomografie f X-ray compute[rize]d tomography, X-ray CT, computerized X-ray tomography
röntgencomputertomografisch X-ray computed tomographic
Röntgendarstellung f X-ray depiction (s.a. Röntgenbild)
Röntgendetektion f X-ray detection
Röntgendetektor m X-ray [photon] detector, X-ray detection material (medium)
Röntgendiagnostik f X-ray diagnostic[s]
röntgendiagnostisch X-ray diagnostic
Röntgendiffraktometer n X-ray diffractometer, Roentgen diffraction apparatus
Röntgendosimetrie f X-ray dosimetry
Röntgendosis f X-ray dose, dose of X radiation
röntgendurchlässig transparent to X rays
Röntgendurchleuchtung f X-ray fluoroscopy, roentgenoscopy, transmission radiography
Röntgendurchleuchtungsanlage f [X-ray] fluoroscope
Röntgendurchleuchtungsbild n, **Röntgendurchstrahlungsbild** n X-ray fluorescent (fluoroscopy) image
Röntgendurchstrahlungsprüfung f roentgen examination
Röntgeneinheit f s. Röntgen 2.
Röntgeneinrichtung f X-ray equipment
~/**zahnärztliche** dental radiographic equipment
Röntgenemission f X-ray emission
röntgenempfindlich X-ray sensitive, sensitive to X rays
Röntgenemulsion f X-ray emulsion
Röntgenenergie f X-ray [photon] energy
Röntgenfächerstrahl m fan X-ray beam
Röntgenfächerstrahlwinkel m X-ray fan beam angle
Röntgenfarbbild n color-enhanced roentgenogram
Röntgenfilm m X-ray [type] film, [photo]fluorographic film, radiographic film
~/**doppelseitig begossener (beschichteter)** duplitized (double-coated) X-ray film, double-emulsion [X-ray] film
~/**einseitig beschichteter** single-coated X-ray film
~/**industrieller** industrial X-ray film
~/**medizinischer** medical (diagnostic) X-ray film
Röntgenfilmbild n film radiograph
Röntgenfilmdigitalisierer m X-ray film digitizer
Röntgenfilmdigitalisierung f X-ray film digitization
Röntgenfilmdigitalisierungsgerät n X-ray film digitizer
Röntgenfilmentwickler m, **Röntgenfilm-Entwicklungsmaschine** f X-ray film developer
Röntgenfilmkassette f X-ray cassette

Röntgenfilmträger *m* X-ray film base
Röntgenfluoreszenz *f* X-ray fluorescence, XRF
Röntgenfluoreszenzbild *n* X-ray fluorescent image
Röntgenfluoreszenzbildgebung *f* X-ray fluorescence (fluorescent) imaging
röntgenfluoreszenzholografisch X-ray fluorescent holographic
Röntgenfluoreszenzhologramm *n* X-ray fluorescent hologram
Röntgenfluoreszenz-Mikrosonde *f* X-ray fluorescence microprobe
Röntgenfluoreszenzspektrum *n* X-ray fluorescence (fluorescent) spectrum
Röntgenfluoreszenzstrahlung *f* X-ray fluorescence radiation; characteristic X-rays
Röntgenfluoroskopie *f* X-ray fluoroscopy
Röntgenfolienfilm *m* X-ray screen-type film, screen-type X-ray film
Röntgenfoto *n* X-ray [photograph]
Röntgenfotoemissionsspektroskopie *f* X-ray photoemission spectroscopy, XPS
Röntgenfotografie *f* 1. radiophotography, photoradiography, fluororadiography, radiographic (X-ray) photography, [fluoro]roentgenography, [photo]fluorography, X[-ray] radiography; 2. X-ray [photograph]
röntgenfotografisch roentgenographic, X-ray photographic, fluorographic
Röntgengenerator *m* X-ray generator
Röntgengerät *n* X-radiograph device *(s.a.* Röntgenanlage*)*
Röntgengerätehersteller *m* radiographic equipment manufacturer
Röntgenholografie *f* X-ray holography
Röntgenimpuls *m* X-ray pulse
Röntgeninspektion *f* X-ray inspection
Röntgenintensität *f* X-ray intensity
Röntgeninterferenz *f* X-ray interference
Röntgeninterferenzbild *n* X-ray interference pattern
Röntgeninterferometer *n* X-ray interferometer
Röntgeninterferometrie *f* X-ray interferometry
röntgeninterferometrisch X-ray interferometric
Röntgenkamera *f* X-ray camera
Röntgenkassette *f* X-ray cassette, radiographic cassette
Röntgenkinefilm *m* X-ray motion-picture film
Röntgenkinematografie *f* cineradiography, cinefluorography, X-ray cinematography, X-ray motion-picture photography
röntgenkinematografisch cinefluorographic
Röntgenkinokamera *f* X-ray cine camera
Röntgenkontaktmikroskopie *f* contact microscopy
Röntgenkontrastangiografie *f* X-ray contrast angiography, radioangiography
Röntgenkontrastbild *n* contrast radiogram
Röntgenkontrastdarstellung von Gebärmutter und Eileitern hysterosalpingography
Röntgenkontrastmittel *n* X-ray contrast agent (medium)
Röntgenkopie *f* facsimile (copy) radiograph, X-ray print
Röntgenkoronarangiogramm *m* X-ray coronary angiogram
Röntgenkristallografie *f* X-ray crystallography
Röntgenkunde *f* roentgenology
Röntgenlaser *m* X-ray laser
Röntgenleuchtschirm *m* [image intensifier] input phosphor, input fluorescent (phosphor) screen *(radiography)*
Röntgenleuchtstoff *m* X-ray phosphor
Röntgenlinienspektrum *n* characteristic X-ray lines
Röntgenlinse *f* X-ray lens
Röntgenlithografie *f* X-ray lithography
röntgenlithografisch X-ray lithographic
Röntgenmammografie *f* X-ray mammography
Röntgenmammografiegerät *n* mammographic X-ray unit
Röntgenmammogramm *n* X-ray mammogram
Röntgenmikroanalyse *f* X-ray microanalysis
Röntgenmikroaufnahme *f* X-ray micrograph, microradiograph, microradiogram
Röntgenmikrobeugung *f* X-ray microdiffraction
Röntgenmikrolithografie *f* X-ray microlithography
Röntgenmikroskop *n* X-ray microscope
Röntgenmikroskopie *f* X-ray microscopy
Röntgen-Mikrosonde *f* X-ray microprobe
Röntgenmikrotomograf *m* X-ray microtomograph
Röntgenmikrotomografie *f* X-ray microtomography
Röntgenmonochromator *m* X-ray monochromator
Röntgenniveau *n* quantum state
Röntgenobservatorium *n* X-ray observatory
Röntgenografie *f* [fluoro]roentgenography, radiographic (X-ray) photography, [photo]fluorography, X[-ray] radiography, radiophotography, fluororadiography
röntgenografisch roentgenographic, X-ray photographic, X-radiographic
Röntgenogramm *n* s. Röntgenbild
Röntgenologe *m* roentgenologist
Röntgenologie *f* roentgenology
röntgenologisch roentgenologic[al]
Röntgenoptik *f* X-ray optics
röntgenoptisch X-ray optical

Röntgenoskopie f roentgenoscopy, X-ray fluoroscopy, transmission radiography
Röntgenphoton n X-ray photon
Röntgenphysik f X-ray physics
Röntgenpixeldetektor m digital X-ray detector
Röntgenplanfilm m [medical] X-ray sheet film
Röntgenplatte f X-ray plate
Röntgenpraxis f X-ray practice
Röntgenprojektion f X-ray projection (profile)
Röntgenprüfung f roentgen examination
Röntgenpuls m X-ray pulse
Röntgenpulverkamera f X-ray powder camera
Röntgenquant n X-ray quantum
Röntgenquelle f X-ray [beam] source, X-radiation source
röntgenradiologisch X-radiological
Röntgenraum m X-ray room
Röntgenreihenuntersuchung f mass radiography
Röntgenröhre f X-ray tube, Roentgen-ray tube
~/**gittergesteuerte** grid X-ray tube
Röntgenröhrenkabel n X-ray tube cable
Röntgenröhrenspannung f X-ray tube [kilo]voltage
Röntgenröhrenstrom m X-ray tube current
Röntgenrollfilm m fluorographic roll film
Röntgenscanner m X-ray scanner
Röntgenschatten m X-ray shadow, radiographic shadow
Röntgenschirm m fluoroscopic (fluoroscope) screen, radiographic screen
Röntgenschleier m X-ray fog
Röntgenschutzkleidung f X-ray protective clothing
Röntgenschwächungskoeffizient m X-ray attenuation coefficient
Röntgensensor m X-ray sensor (detector), X-ray image (imaging) sensor, X-ray image detector
Röntgenspektrallinie f X-ray spectral line
Röntgenspektrofotometer n X-ray spectrophotometer
Röntgenspektrometer n X-ray spectrometer
~/**energiedispersives** energy-dispersive X-ray spectrometer
~/**kombiniertes** combined X-ray spectrometer
~/**offenes** open X-ray spectrometer
~/**wellenlängendispersives** wavelength-dispersive X-ray spectrometer
Röntgenspektrometrie f X-ray spectrometry
Röntgenspektroskopie f X-ray spectroscopy
röntgenspektroskopisch X-ray spectroscopic

Röntgenspektrum n X-ray [energy] spectrum
~/**kontinuierliches** X-ray continuum, bremsstrahlung [X-ray] spectrum
~/**monoenergetisches** monoenergetic (monochromatic) X-ray spectrum
~/**polyenergetisches** polyenergetic (polychromatic) X-ray spectrum
Röntgenspiegel m X-ray mirror
Röntgenstation f X-ray department, radiography (radiology) department (of a hospital)
Röntgenstrahl m X ray [beam], Roentgen ray
Röntgenstrahlabsorption f X-ray absorption
Röntgenstrahlbildwandler m X-ray imaging detector
Röntgenstrahlenbereich m X-ray band, X-ray region (of the electromagnetic spectrum)
Röntgenstrahlenbündel n X-ray beam
Röntgenstrahlendosis f X-ray dose, dose of X radiation
röntgenstrahlenempfindlich X-ray sensitive, sensitive to X-rays
Röntgenstrahlenerzeuger m X-ray generator
Röntgenstrahlenerzeugung f X-ray production
Röntgenstrahlenexposition f X-ray exposure
Röntgenstrahlenfilterung f X-ray filtration
Röntgenstrahlenfotografie f s. Röntgenfotografie
Röntgenstrahlenschwächung f X-ray [beam] attenuation
Röntgenstrahlfächer m fan X-ray beam
Röntgenstrahlgitter n X-ray grating
Röntgenstrahlröhre f s. Röntgenröhre
Röntgenstrahlschattenmikroskop n shadow microscope
Röntgenstrahlung f X-[ir]radiation, X-ray radiation, X-rays
~/**charakteristische** characteristic X-rays
~/**harte (hochenergetische)** hard (high-energy) X rays
~/**niederenergetische** lower-energy X-rays
~/**primäre** primary X-rays
~/**ultraharte** very hard X-rays, ultrahard X-rays
~/**weiche** soft (low-energy) X rays
Röntgenstrahlungsenergie f X-ray [photon] energy
Röntgenstreustrahlenraster m(n) radiographic (anti-scatter) grid
Röntgenstreuung f X-ray scattering
Röntgensystem n X-ray system; radiographic system
Röntgenszintillationsschirm m scintillating screen
Röntgenszintillator m X-ray scintillator
Röntgentechnik f X-ray technology

Röntgentechniker *m* radiological technologist, X-ray technician
Röntgenteleskop *n* X-ray telescope
~/abbildendes Wolter telescope
Röntgentisch *m* X-ray table
Röntgentomograf *m* X-ray tomograph, X-ray CT device
Röntgentomografie *f* X-ray tomography, X-ray CT
röntgentomografisch X-ray tomographic
Röntgentransmissionsmikroskop *n* X-ray transmission microscope, XTM
röntgenundurchlässig opaque to X rays
Röntgenuntersuchung *f* X-ray examination, X-radiographic examination
Röntgen-Verstärkerfolie *f* X-ray intensifying screen
Röntgen-Videosichtgerät *n* security X-ray machine
Röntgenwandler *m* X-ray imaging detector
Röntgenwelle *f* X-ray wave
Röntgenwellenlänge *f* X-ray wavelength
Root-Signal *n* fixed-point sequence
Rosafilter *n* pink filter
Rosarot *n s.* Magenta
Rosettenmuster *n* rosette pattern *(of halftone dots)*
Ross-Effekt *m* Ross effect, gelatin effect *(photography)*
Rot *n* red *(primary color)*
~/genormtes magenta
Rotation *f* 1. rotation *(geometric transformation)*; 2. *s.* Drehbewegung; 3. *s.* Rotationsdruckmaschine
Rotationsachse *f* axis of rotation (revolution), rotation[al] axis
Rotationsandruckmaschine *f* rotary-type proofing press
Rotationsdruck *m* rotary printing
Rotationsdruckmaschine *f* rotary-type [printing] press, rotary (cylinder) press
Rotationsdruckverfahren *n* rotary printing process
Rotationsebene *f* plane of rotation
Rotationsentwicklung *f* rotary processing
Rotationsentwicklunganlage *f*, **Rotationsentwicklungsmaschine** *f* rotary processor
Rotationsfläche *f* surface of revolution, SOR
Rotationshochdruck *m* rotary letterpress printing
rotationsinvariant rotation-invariant
Rotationsinvarianz *f* rotation[al] invariance *(pattern recognition)*
Rotationskamera *f* circuit-type panoramic camera
Rotationskörper *m* solid of revolution
Rotationslamellenverschluss *m* rotary lamellar shutter
Rotationsmaschine *f s.* Rotationspresse
Rotationsmatrix *f* rotation matrix
Rotationspresse *f* rotary (cylinder) press, rotary-type [printing] press
Rotationsscanner *m* rotary scanner, revolving optical system, ROS
Rotationssymmetrie *f* rotational symmetry
rotationssymmetrisch rotationally symmetric[al]
Rotationstampondruck *m* pad [transfer] printing
Rotationstiefdruck *m* rotogravure [printing], rotogravure [printing] process
Rotationstiefdruckmaschine *f* rotary intaglio press
Rotationstrick *m* rotate effect *(digital video effect)*
Rotationsvarianz *f* rotational variance
Rotationsverschluss *m* revolving shutter
Rotaugen... *s.* Rote-Augen-...
Rotauszug *m* red [light] record *(color photography)*
rotblind red-blind, protan[opic]
Rotblinder *m* protanope
Rotblindheit *f* red[-green] blindness, red and bluish green confusion, protanopia *(color-vision deficiency)*
Rote-Augen-Effekt *m* red-eye effect *(flash photography)*
Rote-Augen-Korrektur *f*, **Rote-Augen-Reduktion** *f* red-eye reduction
Röteltonung *f* gold toning
rotempfindlich red-sensitive, panchromatic *(photographic emulsion)*
Rotempfindlichkeit *f* red[-light] sensitivity, red speed *(e.g. of film material)*
Rotfilter *n* red filter
Rotfilterschicht *f* red filter layer
Rötgenbildentstehung *f* X-ray image formation
Rot-Grün-Blau-... *s.* RGB-...
Rotgrünblindheit *f* red-green blindness, Daltonism
Rotgrünbrille *f* red-green goggles; anaglyph glasses
Rotkanal *m* red channel
Rotlampe *f* red lamp
Rotlicht *n* red light
Rotlichtempfindlichkeit *f* red light sensitivity
Rotmarderhaarpinsel *m* red sable brush *(retouching tool)*
Rotorkamera *f s.* Rotationskamera
Rotoskop *n* rotoscope *(special-effects cinematography)*
Rotschwäche *f* protanomaly, decreased red sensitivity *(color-vision deficiency)*
Rotsignal *n* red signal *(video)*
Rotstich *m* red cast (bias)
Rotstrahl *m* red beam *(cathode-ray tube)*
Rotteilbild *n* red [light] record *(color photography)*
rotunempfindlich red-insensitive
Routinemikroskop *n* routine microscope
Routinemikroskopie *f* routine microscopy
Rowland-Gitter *n* concave grating

Rubinlaser m ruby [chromium aluminum] laser, chromium aluminum oxide laser
Rückansicht f rear view
Rückcodierung f decoding *(s.a.* Decodierung*)*
ruckelfrei jerk-free
ruckelig jerky, choppy, stuttery *(e.g. motion pictures)*
Rückenmarkröntgendarstellung f myelography
Rückfahrkamera f rear-view camera
Rückfaltungsverzerrung f aliasing [effect], alias *(sampling artifact)*
Rückflächenspiegel m back-surface (back-coated) mirror, back-silvered mirror
Rückflussdämpfung f/**optische** optical return loss, ORL *(photodetector)*
Rückfolie f s. Rückverstärkungsfolie
Rückgrat n spine *(e.g. in geometric modeling)*
Rückguss m backing layer *(s.a.* Gelatine-Rückguss*)*
Rückhänger m backdrop
Rückkanal m backchannel, reverse channel, return (backward) channel
Rückkaschierung f balancing coating *(of a film base)*
Rückkehrspiegel m s. Rückschwingspiegel
Rückkopplung f feedback
~ f/**akustische** acoustic feedback, howl round
~/**optische** optical feedback
~/**verteilte** distributed feedback, DFB
Rückkopplungsnetz[werk] n feedback (recurrent) network
Rückkopplungsrauschen n feedback noise
Rücklauf m retrace, flyback *(electron beam)*; rewind *(e.g. of tape)*
~/**langsamer** slow rewind
~/**schneller** fast rewind
Rücklaufaustastung f retrace (flyback) blanking
Rücklaufzeile f retrace line
Rücklaufzeit f retrace time, flyback period
Rückprojektion f rear[-screen] projection, back[ground] projection, process projection; back-projection imaging, summation *(radiography)*
~/**gefilterte** filtered back projection [reconstruction method] *(emission tomography)*
Rückprojektionsalgorithmus m back-projection algorithm
Rückprojektionsanlage f rear-projection unit
Rückprojektionsbild n back-projected image
Rückprojektionsgerät n s. Rückprojektor
Rückprojektionskamera f rear-projection camera
Rückprojektionsleinwand f rear-projection screen
Rückprojektionsobjektiv n rear-screen lens

Rückprojektionsschirm m rear-projection display (viewing screen)
Rückprojektionstechnik f back-projection technique
Rückprojektionstisch m rear-projection table
Rückprojektionsverfahren n rear-screen (rear-projection) process, blue-screening
Rückprojektionsvideowand f rear-projection [video] wall
Rückprojektor m rear (back) projector; process projector *(special-effects cinematography)*
rückprojizieren to back-project, to rear-project; to reproject
rückquantisieren to requantize
Rückquantisierer m inverse quantizer *(video compression)*
Rückquantisierung f requantization, requantizing, inverse quantization
Rückquantisierungsfilter n requantization filter
Rückreflexion f back reflection, narcissus
Rückschlusswahrscheinlichkeit f a posteriori probability *(Bayesian statistics)*
Rückschrägstrich m backslash
Rückschwingspiegel m instant-return mirror, swinging (reflex) mirror *(single-lens reflex camera)*
Rückseitenentfernung f backface culling (removal) *(computer graphics)*
Rücksetzer m backing flat
Rücksichtprisma n s. Reflexionsprisma
Rückspeicher m back buffer *(graphics computer)*
Rückspulautomatik f automatic rewind
Rückspulgeschwindigkeit f rewind speed
Rückspulknopf m rewind knob
Rückspulkurbel f [film] rewind crank
Rückspulung f rewind
~ **teilbelichteter Filme, Rückspulung/vorzeitige** mid-roll rewind
Rückspulvorrichtung f rewind[ing device], rewind mechanism
Rückstandarte f rear (back) standard, film standard *(view camera)*
Rückstrahl m return beam
Rückstrahlquerschnitt m radar cross section, RCS
Rückstrahlung f 1. reradiation; 2. s. Reflexion
Rückstrahlungsgrad m, **Rückstrahlungsvermögen** n reflectivity, reflective power, albedo *(s.a.* Reflexionsgrad*)*
Rückstreuelektron n backscattered electron
Rückstreuelektronenbild n backscattered electron image *(electron microscopy)*
rückstreuen to backscatter, to scatter back
Rückstreufläche f radar cross section, RCS
Rückstreukoeffizient m backscattering coefficient

Rückstreuquerschnitt *m s.*
Rückstreufläche
Rückstreuung *f* backscatter[ing]
Rückteil *m(n) s.* Rückstandarte
Rücktransformation *f* inverse transform[ation], reverse transform[ation]
Rücktransformationskern *m* inverse transform kernel
Rücktransformationsmatrix *f* inverse transformation matrix
rücktransformieren to retransform
Rücktransformierte *f* inverse transform
Rückübertragung *f* retransmission *(e.g. of image data)*
rückvergrößern to reenlarge
Rückvergrößerung *f* reenlargement *(e.g. of microfilm images)*
Rückverstärkungsfolie *f* back intensifying screen *(X-ray cassette)*
Rückwandentriegelung *f* camera back lock release lever
Rückwandlung *f* reconversion
Rückwärtsabbildung *f* backward (inverse) mapping *(geometric transformation)*
Rückwärtsabspielen *n*,
Rückwärtsabspielung *f* reverse playback, backward playout
Rückwärtsdifferenzenoperator *m* backward difference operator
rückwärtsgeneigt backslanting *(typeface)*
rückwärtskompatibel backward (downward) compatible
Rückwärtskompatibilität *f* backward compatibility
Rückwärtslauf *m* reverse action (run) *(filming)*
Rückwärtsprädiktion *f* backward predicition *(image sequence coding)*
Rückwärtsstreuung *f* backscatter[ing]
Rückwärtsverkettung *f* backward chaining
Rückwärtswiedergabe *f* reverse playback
Rückwickel... *s.* Rückspul...
Rufnummernverzeichnis *n* [electronic] phone directory *(fax machine)*
Ruhegeräuschspannungsabstand *m* dynamic [signal] range
rund round, circular
Rundfunk *m* broadcast[ing]
Rundfunkempfangsstelle *f s.*
Kabel[fernseh]kopfstation
Rundfunksatellit *m* direct broadcast satellite, DBS
Rundfunkschnittstelle *f* broadcast interface
Rundfunk-Videorecorder *m* broadcast digital videotape recorder
Rundheit *f* roundness, circularity *(shape feature)*
Rundhorizont *m* cyclorama, cyc
Rundkehle *f* sweep stage, coving
Rundmagazin *n* rotary magazine, circular slide tray
Rundmagazin-Diaprojektor *m*,
Rundmagazinprojektor *m* circular-tray projector
Rundpanoramakamera *f* circuit-type panoramic camera
Rundsatz *m* runaround *(layout)*
Rundsichtanzeige *f* plan position indicator [display], PPI display *(radarscope)*
Rundsichtradar *n* surveillance radar
Rundsuchradar *n* azimuth-scanning radar
Rundumbeleuchtung *f* wraparound lighting
Rundumprojektion *f* 360-degree projection
Rundumschwenk *m* rotation *(camera move)*
Rundumsicht *f* panoramic view
Rundumton *m* surround sound
Rundung *f* rounding
Runzelkorn *n* reticulation
Rupfen *n* [surface] picking *(printing defect)*
Ruß *m* soot, carbon black, lampblack *(pigment)*
Rüsten *n* makeready, setup *(printing)*
Rüstzeit *f* makeready time
rütteln to jog *(printed sheets)*

S

Saallautsprecher *m* auditorium loudspeaker
Saatpunkt *m* seed point *(region-growing method)*
Sabattier-Effekt *m* Sabattier effect *(exposure effect)*
Sachaufnahme *f* pack shot
Sachfotografie *f* object photography; still life photography; product photography
Sachtrick *m* practical effect *(cinema)*
Safety-Film *m s.* Sicherheitsfilm
Sägezahneffekt *m* stair-stepping [artifact], staircasing, jaggedness, jaggies *(spatial alias)*
Sägezahngenerator *m* sawtooth generator
Sägezahnimpuls *m* serration pulse *(television signal)*
Sägezahnkurve *f* sawtooth (triangular) waveform
sagittal sagittal
Sagittalbrennpunkt *m* sagittal focus
Sagittalebene *f* sagittal (radial) plane
Sagittalschnitt *m* sagittal [principal] section
Sagnac-Interferometer *n* Sagnac interferometer
Sakkade *f* saccade, saccadic [eye] movement, saccadic motion
sakkadiert saccadic *(eye movement)*
Salonfotografie *f* salon photography
Salpetersäure *f* nitric acid
Salz *n*/**Schlippesches** Schlippe's salt
Salzbildner *m* halogen
Salzfolie *f s.* Salzverstärkerfolie
Salzkopierverfahren *n* salted-paper process
Salzpapier *n* salted paper
Salzpapierabzug *m*, **Salzpapierkopie** *f* salt (salted-paper) print
Salzverstärkerfolie *f* salt [intensifying] screen; fluorescing screen *(X-ray film)*
Sammelelektrode *f* collection electrode *(photodetector)*
Sammellinse *f* collection (collector) lens, convex (converging) lens, convergent (positive) lens
sammeln to nest, to inset *(folded signatures)*
Sammelschiene *f* bus bar
Sammelspiegel *m* convergent (concave) mirror, collecting mirror
Sammlerkamera *f* collectible [camera]
Samplingtheorem *n* sampling theorem *(signal theory)*
sanddicht sand proof
SAR-Bilddaten *pl* synthetic aperture radar image data
Satellit *m* satellite, bird
~ *m*/**direktstrahlender** direct broadcast satellite, DBS
~/**geostationärer (geosynchroner)** geostationary (geosynchronous) satellite
Satellit-Druckeinheit *f* drum press
Satellitenantenne *f* satellite antenna
Satellitenaufklärung *f* satellite reconnaissance
Satellitenausstrahlung *f* satellite broadcasting
Satelliten-Berichterstattung *f*/**digitale** digital satellite news gathering, DSNG
Satellitenbetreiber *m* satellite operator
Satellitenbild *n* satellite image (picture), [satellite] scene, space image
Satellitenbildanalyse *f* satellite image analysis
Satellitenbildaufnahme *f* space imaging
Satellitenbildauswertung *f* satellite photo interpretation
Satellitenbilddaten *pl* satellite [image] data
Satellitenbilddatenbank *f* satellite image database
Satellitenbildgeber *m* satellite imager
Satellitenbildklassifizierung *f* satellite image classification
Satellitenbildmaterial *n* satellite imagery
Satellitenbildtechnik *f* satellite imaging technology
Satellitenblitz *m s.* Servoblitz
Satelliten-Direktausstrahlung *f* direct broadcast by satellite, DBS
Satellitendirektempfang *m* direct-to-home, DTH
Satelliten-Direktübertragung *f* direct satellite broadcast, direct broadcast satellite transmission
Satellitenempfang *m* satellite reception
Satellitenempfänger *m* satellite receiver
~/**digitaler** digital satellite receiver
Satellitenempfangsgebiet *n* footprint, serving (service) area *(television transmission)*
Satellitenempfangsgerät *n* satellite receiver
Satellitenfarbfoto *n* satellite color photograph
Satellitenfernerkundung *f* satellite [remote] sensing
Satellitenfernsehen *n* satellite television, live satellite TV
~/**digitales** digital satellite television, DST, satellite digital video broadcasting, S-DVB
Satellitenfernsehübertragung *f* satellite video transmission, satellite television broadcasting
Satellitenfoto *n* satellite photo[graph]
Satellitenfotografie *f* satellite[-based] photography
satellitengestützt spaceborne
Satellitenhaushalt *m* satellite-equipped household

Satelliten-Individualempfang *m s.*
Satellitendirektempfang
Satellitenkamera *f* satellite-tracking camera
Satellitenkameraobjektiv *n* satellite lens
Satellitenkanal *m* satellite channel
Satellitenmodulator *m* satellite modulator
Satellitennavigationssystem *n*/**weltweites** global positioning system, GPS
Satellitenradar *n* satellite-borne radar; spaceborne radar
Satellitenradarbild *n* satellite radar image
Satelliten-Rundfunkdienst *m* broadcast satellite service, BSS
Satellitenscanner *m* satellite scanner
Satellitenschüssel *f* [satellite] dish, satellite dish receiver, earth station
Satellitensender *m* satellite broadcaster
Satellitensignal *n* satellite [transmission] signal, satellite-transmitted signal
Satellitentechnik *f* satellite technology; satellite broadcasting technology
Satellitenübertragung *f* satellite transmission; satellite broadcasting
Satellitenübertragungsanlage *f* satellite transmission equipment
Satellitenüberwachungssystem *n* satellite surveillance system
Satellitenverbindung *f* satellite link
Satellit-Prinzip *n* common-impression-cylinder principle *(printing)*
Satikon *n* saticon [tube]
Satinage *f* satin (dull) finish *(on paper)*
satiniert calendered *(paper)*
Sattelfläche *f* saddle surface *(computer graphics)*
Sattelspule *f* saddle coil *(picture tube; magnetic resonance imaging)*
Sättigung *f* 1. saturation *(e.g. of a chemical compound)*; 2. [color] saturation, [excitation] purity, chroma, intensity *(colorimetry)*
Sättigungsabsorptionsspektroskopie *f* saturated absorption spectroscopy
Sättigungsbereich *m* saturation range (region) *(e.g. of a density curve)*
Sättigungsgrad *m* degree of saturation, vividness [of color]
Sättigungskonstanz *f* saturation constancy
Sättigungsladung *f* full well capacity *(image sensor)*
Sättigungspuls *m* saturation pulse
Sättigungsspektroskopie *f* saturation spectroscopy
Sättigungssperrstrom *m* dark current *(photodetector)*
Sättigungswert *m* saturation value
Saturation *f s.* Sättigung
Satz *m* 1. composition, typesetting
~/**ausgeschlossener** justified type, [full] justification *(typography)*
~/**Bayesscher** Bayes' theorem *(probability theory)*
~/**digitaler** digital typesetting; desktop publishing, DTP
~/**Malusscher** Malus' theorem (law) *(geometrical optics)*
~/**Riccoscher** Ricco's law *(visual perception)*
~/**zentrierter** align center *(typography)*
Satzanweisung *f* specs
Satzbelichter *m* phototypesetter
Satzbild *n* type area
Satzcomputer *m s.* Satzrechner
Satzgestalter *m* typesetter
Satzherstellung *f* typesetting
~/**maschinelle** mechanical typesetting
Satzmaschine *f* typesetting (composing) machine, typesetter
Satzobjektiv *n* convertible lens (objective)
Satzrechner *m* composition workstation
Satzspiegel *m* type area (page)
Satzsystem *n* typesetting unit
Satztechnik *f* 1. typesetting technology; 2. typesetting technique
Satzvorlage *f* copy
Satzzeichen *n* punctuation mark
Saugkassette *f*, **Saugmattscheibe** *f* vacuum back (board), vacuum easel *(process camera)*
Säule *f* column *(e.g. of an enlarger)*
Säulendiagramm *n* bar graph (chart) *(s.a.* Histogramm*)*
Säulenstativ *n* single-column stand, single-post stand
Saumeffekt *m* fringe effect
Säuregrad *m* [degree of] acidity
Scan *m* scan
~/**linearer** linear scan
Scanauflösung *f* scanning resolution
scanbar scannable
Scanbreite *f* scanning width
Scandaten *pl* scanning data
Scandruckfaxkopierer *m* multifunction printer, all-in-one device
Scanebene *f* scan[ning] plane *(tomography, sonography)*
Scan-Effizienz *f* sampling efficiency
Scanfläche *f* scan area; scanning array
Scanfrequenz *f* scan[ning] rate, scanning frequency
Scangeschwindigkeit *f* scan[ning] speed, scan velocity
Scangröße *f* scan size
Scankonverter *m* scan converter *(sonography)*
~/**analoger** analog scan converter
Scankonvertierung *f* scan conversion
Scankopf *m* scan header *(image data structure)*
Scanline-Algorithmus *m* scan-line (sweep-line) algorithm
Scanlinie *f* scan[ning] line, raster line
Scanmodus *m* scan[ning] mode
scannen to scan

Scanner *m* scanner, scanning device (machine); image scanner
~/**aktiver** flying-spot scanner
~/**akustooptischer** acousto-optic scanner
~/**diagnostischer** diagnostic (clinical) scanner
~/**elektronischer** electronic scanner
~/**elektrooptischer** electro-optical scanner
~/**faseroptischer** fiber-optic scanner
~/**hyperspektraler** imaging spectrometer
~/**mechanischer** mechanical scanner (scanning device)
~/**nuklearmedizinischer** nuclear-medicine scanning instrument
~/**optischer** optical scanner
~/**optoelektronischer** optoelectronic (pushbroom) scanner
~/**optomechanischer** optomechanical scanner
~/**piezoelektrischer** piezoelectric scanner
~/**rektilinearer** rectilinear scanner
Scannerauflösung *f* scanner resolution
Scannerbild *n* scanner image
Scannerbildschirm *m* scanner monitor
Scannerkamera *f* camera scanner
Scannerkoordinatensystem *n* scanner coordinate system
Scannerlampe *f* scanner illuminant
Scannermodul *n* scanner module
Scannerschnittstelle *f* scanner interface
Scannerspiegel *m* scanner mirror
Scannerzeile *f* scan[ning] line, raster line
Scanningelektronenmikroskop *n* scanning [electron] microscope, SEM
Scanning-Objektiv *n* scanning optics
Scansignal *n* scan[ning] signal, sampled[-data] signal; discrete[-time] signal
Scanstrahl *m* scanning [electron] beam, raster beam
Scanvorgang *m* scan[ning] process, scan[ning] operation
Scanvorlage *f* scanning copy
Scanzeit *f* scan[ning] time; sampling time
SCART-Anschluss *m* SCART (Peritel) connection *(video)*
SCART-Buchse *f* SCART socket
SCART-Kabel *n* SCART cable
SCART-Stecker *m* SCART connector
Schabemesser *n* retouching (etching) knife
Schaberetusche *f* abrasive (physical) reduction, physical etching
Schablone *f* 1. template; 2. mask, matte *(cinema; s.a. Maske)*
Schablonenabgleich *m*, **Schablonenanpassung** *f* template (matrix) matching, matched filtering *(pattern recognition)*
Schablonendruck *m* stencil printing
Schablonenkanal *m* alpha (matte) channel *(video, computer graphics)*
Schablonenmuster *n* template pattern *(pattern recognition)*

Schablonentrickverfahren *n* matte photography, matting *(s.a. Wandermaskenverfahren, Bluescreen-Verfahren, Stanzverfahren)*
Schablonenvergleich *m s.* Schablonenabgleich
Schabmanier *f s.* Mezzotinto 1.
Schabretusche *f s.* Schaberetusche
Schachbrettbearbeitung *f s.* Schachbrettschnitt
Schachbrettdistanz *f* chessboard distance *(binary image geometry)*
Schachbrettschnitt *m* checkerboard (A&B) cutting, A/B editing (cutting), A&B roll editing
Schadografie *f* Schadograph *(s.a. Fotografik, Fotogramm)*
Schalenentwicklung *f* tray (dish) development
Schalenverarbeitung *f* tray (dish) processing
Schalenwässerung *f* tray washing
Schall *m* sound *(s.a. under Ultraschall, Ton)*
Schallaufzeichnung *f* 1. sound (audio) recording; 2. sound record
Schallausbreitung *f* sound propagation
Schallausbreitungsrichtung *f* sound propagative direction, direction of sound
Schallbeugung *f* sound diffraction
Schallbild *n* acoustic (sonic) image
Schallbildgebung *f* acoustical imaging
Schalldämpfung *f* sound attenuation
Schalldetektion *f* sound detection
schalldicht soundproof *(e.g. a projection booth)*
Schalldruck *m* sound pressure, [sound] intensity
Schalldruckmessgerät *n* sound level meter
Schalldruckpegel *m* sound pressure level, SPL
schalldurchlässig sonolucent
Schalleitfähigkeit *f* sound conductivity
schallen to insonify
Schallenergie *f* sound (acoustical) energy
Schallfeld *n* acoustic (sound) field
Schallfeldgeometrie *f* transducer field pattern
Schallfenster *n* acoustic window *(sonography)*
Schallfrequenzbereich *m* sound frequency range
Schallgeschwindigkeit *f* speed of sound, sound velocity, sonic speed
Schallimpuls *m* acoustic pulse, sound [im]pulse; sound burst
Schallkopf *m* ultrasound scan head, ultrasound (ultrasonic) scanner
~/**mechanischer** mechanical transducer
~ **mit [elektronisch] variierbarem Schallfeld** phased-array transducer *(sonography)*
Schallkopfführung *f/freie* freehand scanning *(sonography)*

Schallkopfgeometrie

Schallkopfgeometrie *f* transducer geometry
Schallplatte *f* phonograph record[ing], record
Schallquant *n* phonon
Schallquelle *f* sound source
Schallreflexion *f* acoustic reflection
Schallschatten *m* sound shadow
schallschluckend sound-absorbent
Schallschutzgehäuse *n*,
Schallschutzhaube *f* sound absorbing box; blimp; barney
Schallsonde *f s.* Schallkopf
Schallstrahl *m* sound (acoustic) beam
Schallübertragung *f* sound transmission
Schallwandler *m* ultrasound (ultrasonic) transducer
Schallwelle *f* sound (acoustic) wave
Schallwellenfeld *n* acoustic (sound) field
Schallwellenfotografie *f* soundwave photography, sonophotography
Schallwellenwiderstand *m* acoustic impedance *(sonography)*
Schallwiedergabe *f s.* Tonwiedergabe
Schaltelement *n* switching element
Schalter *m*/**elektrooptischer** electro-optical switch
~/**optischer** optical (light-operated) switch
Schaltfläche *f* [push] button, action (command) button *(computer)*
Schaltgeschwindigkeit *f* switching rate
Schaltkreis *m* switching circuit
~/**analoger** analog circuit
~/**bistabiler** flip-flop
~/**digitaler** digital circuit
~/**gedruckter** printed circuit [board]
~/**integrierter** integrated circuit [chip], IC, microchip
Schaltkreisrauschen *n* circuit noise
Schaltröhre *f* switch[ing] tube
Schaltrolle *f* [/**gezähnte**] intermittent sprocket *(motion-picture projector)*
Schalttransistor *m* switching transistor
Schaltuhr *f* timer; darkroom timer
Schaltung *f*/**anwendungsspezifisch integrierte** application-specific integrated circuit, ASIC
~/**gedruckte** printed circuit [board]
~/**höchstintegrierte** very large-scale integrated circuit, VLSI circuit
~/**integrierte** integrated circuit, IC, microchip
~/**logische** logic circuit
~/**optoelektronische integrierte** opto-electronic integrated circuit, OEIC
Schaltwippe *f* rocker switch
scharf sharp, crisp, blur-free *(image)*
Schärfe *f* sharpness, acutance, crispness *(of images)*; acuity *(esp. of vision)*
Schärfebereich *m* depth of field (focus), zone of focus; axial resolving power *(objective)*
Schärfeeebene *f* focal plane

Schärfefilter *n* sharpening [spatial] filter, deblurring (crisp) filter, enhancement (enhancing) filter, high-pass filter
Schärfegrad *m* acutance value
Schärfeindikator *m* focus indication
Scharfeinstellgerät *n* focusing magnifier, focus finder
Scharfeinstellring *m* focus[ing] ring; zoom ring
Scharfeinstellung *f* sharpness adjustment; focus control, focusing
~/**automatische** 1. automatic focusing, autofocusing; 2. automatic focus, autofocus [system], autofocus[ing] device, autofocus mechanism (facility) *(s.a.* Autofokus..., AF-...)
~/**manuelle** 1. manual focusing; 2. manual focus, MF
Schärfekontrolle *f* sharpness control
Schärfeleistung *f* sharpness performance
Schärfenassistent *m s.* Schärfezieher
Schärfenbereich *m* focusing range
Schärfenebene *f* focal plane
Schärfennachführung *f* focus tracking (pull), follow focus *(cinematography)*
Schärfenregulierung *f s.* Scharfeinstellung
Schärfenspeicher *m* focus lock
Schärfenspeicherung *f* focus lock *(SLR camera)*
Schärfensteuerung *f* sharpness (focusing) control
Schärfentiefe *f* depth of field (focus), zone of focus; axial resolving power *(objective)*
Schärfentiefebereich *m* depth-of-field zone
Schärfentiefenanzeige *f* depth-of-field indicator
Schärfentiefenkontrolle *f* depth-of-field indicator
Schärfentiefenparameter *m* depth-of-field parameter
Schärfentiefenring *m* depth-of-field scale
Schärfentiefenskale *f* depth-of-field scale
Schärfentiefentabelle *f* depth-of-field table
Schärfenzone *f s.* Schärfentiefebereich
Schärfeprädiktion *f s.* Schärfevorausberechnung
Schärfepriorität *f* aperture priority [mode], focus priority
Schärferaum *m s.* Schärfentiefebereich
Schärfering *m* focus[ing] ring; zoom ring
Schärfeverlust *m* sharpness loss (degradation), loss of (in) sharpness
Schärfeverteilung *f* acuity distribution *(vision)*; sharpness distribution *(in a picture)*
Schärfewert *m* sharpness value
Schärfeziehen *n* follow focus *(cinema)*
Schärfezieher *m* focus puller, follow-focus assistant *(film crew)*
Scharfpunkt *m* point of sharpest focus
scharfstellen to focus, to focalize
Scharfsteller *m* focusing magnifier (glass); focus mechanism *(enlarger)*

Scharfstellhilfe f focusing aid
Scharfstellung f s. Scharfeinstellung
Schärfung f sharpening, deblurring *(digital image processing)*
Schärfungskoeffizient m sharpening coefficient
Scharfzeichnung f definition
Scharfzeichnungsfilter n s. Schärfefilter
Schatten m shadow; shade
~/**echter** cast shadow
~/**harter** hard[-edged] shadow, sharp[-edged] shadow, harsh (hard light) shadow
~/**weicher** soft (fuzzy) shadow
Schattenaufnahmetechnik f shadowgraph technique *(schlieren photography)*
Schattenberechnung f shadow computation, shading calculation
Schattenbild n shadow image (picture); shadowgraph; silhouette [image]
Schattenbildung f shadow formation (generation) *(computer graphics)*
Schattendetail n shadow detail
Schattendichte f shadow density
Schattendurchzeichnung f shadow definition
Schatteneffekt m shadow[ing] effect
schattenfrei shadowless
Schattenkante f shadow edge
Schattenkontrast m shadow contrast
Schattenlinie f shadow line
schattenlos shadowless
Schattenmaske f shadow (aperture) mask, grille *(color screen)*
Schattenmaskenröhre f shadow mask [color picture] tube, shadow mask CRT (cathode-ray tube)
Schattenmuster n shadow pattern
Schattenpartie f shadow area, shadows *(densitometry)*
Schattenprobe f/**Foucaultsche** Foucault knife[-edge] test, knife-edge technique *(optics)*
Schattenprojektion f shadow projection; proximity printing *(semiconductor manufacturing)*
Schattenriss m shadow silhouette
Schattenschwärzung f shadow density
Schattenseite f shadow (shaded) side
Schattenspieler m shadow puppeteer
Schattenverfahren n shadowgraph technique *(schlieren photography)*
Schattenwerfer m cookie, cookaloris, kukaloris, cuke *(cinema)*
Schattenwirkung f shadow[ing] effect
Schattenwurf m shadow[s] cast
Schattenwurfeffekt m shading effect
Schattenwurfhologramm n shadowgram
Schattenzeichnung f shadow definition
Schattenzone f 1. shadow area; 2. s. Schallschatten
schattieren to shade

Schattierung f shading; shading [operation]; shade; compositing *(computer graphics)*
~/**interpolative (interpolierte)** interpolate[d] shading, interpolative shading *(s.a. Gouraud-Schattierung)*
~/**konstante** constant shading, faceted (flat) shading
Schattierungsalgorithmus m shading (shade) algorithm
Schattierungsanalyse f shading analysis
Schattierungsberechnung f s. Schattenberechnung
Schattierungsfunktion f shading function
Schattierungskorrektur f shading correction
Schattierungsmodell n shading model
~/**analytisches** analytic[al] shading model
Schattierungsmuster n shading pattern
Schattierungsverfahren n shading technique
Schätzalgorithmus m estimation algorithm
Schätzbild n estimated image
schätzen to estimate, to assess
Schätzgenauigkeit f estimation accuracy
Schätzparameter m assessment parameter
schätztheoretisch estimation-theoretic
Schätztheorie f estimation theory, theory of estimation
Schätzung f estimation
~/**direkte** direct estimation
~/**erwartungstreue** unbiased estimation
~/**indirekte** indirect estimation
~/**rekursive** recursive estimation
~/**robuste** robust estimation
Schätzwert m estimate, guess
Schaubild n diagram, diagrammatic representation (layout)
Schaukasten m viewbox *(s.a. Betrachtungskasten)*
Schauplatzsuche f location scouting *(filming)*
Scheckscanner m [bank] check reader, check amount reading machine
Scheibe f 1. disk, disc; 2. slice *(image sequence coding)*
~/**Benhamsche** Benham['s] disk *(for generating chromatic sensations)*
~/**Maxwellsche** Maxwell disk *(additive color mixing)*
Scheibenlaufwerk n disk drive
Scheibenverschluss m disk shutter
Scheidenspiegelung f colposcopy
Scheimpflug-Bedingung f Scheimpflug condition (rule)
Scheiner-Grade npl Scheiner speed
Scheinwerfer m spot[light]
Scheinwerferlicht n spotlight
Scheinwerfermodus m spotlight mode *(synthetic aperture radar)*
Scheinwerfertor n barn door
Scheinwerfertubus m snoot *(e.g. of studio lights)*

Scheinwiderstand *m* **[/elektrischer]** impedance
Scheitel *m* vertex, apex, pole
Scheitelbrennweite *f* vertex [focal] length *(of a lens)*
Scheitellappen *m* parietal lobe *(of cerebral cortex)*
Scheitelpunkt *m* vertex, apex, pole
Scheitelwert *m* vertex value
Scheitelwinkel *m* vertex (apex) angle
Schemazeichnung *f* schematic drawing
Scherachse *f* axis of shear
Scherenfernrohr *n* telestereoscope, stereotelescope
Scherenschnittfilm *m* silhouette animation; cutout animation
Scher-Interferometer *n* shearing interferometer
Scherung *f* shear[ing] *(geometric transformation)*
Scherungsachse *f* axis of shear
Schicht *f* layer; slice *(tomography)*
~/**aktive** active layer *(semiconductor injection laser)*
~/**bildgebende** imaging (image-forming) layer
~/**blauempfindliche** blue-sensitive layer, yellow dye-forming layer
~/**eigenleitende** *s.* ~/intrinsische
~/**farbempfindliche** color-sensitive layer
~/**farbstoffbildende** dye-forming layer
~/**fotografische** photographic layer
~/**fotoleitende (fotoleitfähige)** photoconduction (photoconductive) layer
~/**grünempfindliche** green-sensitive layer, magenta dye forming layer
~/**holografische** holographic layer
~/**intrinsische** intrinsic region *(p-i-n photodiode)*
~/**lichtempfindliche** photosensitive layer
~/**physikalische** physical layer
~/**reflektierende** reflective layer
~/**reflex[ions]mindernde** antireflection coating (film), anti-reflex coating
~/**rotempfindliche** red-sensitive layer, cyan dye forming layer
~/**strahlungsempfindliche** radiosensitive layer
~/**thermoplastische** thermoplastic layer
~/**tomografische** tomographic slice *(s.a. Tomogramm)*
~/**verdeckte (versteckte)** hidden (intermediate) layer *(artificial neural network)*
Schichtabstand *m* slice spacing, interslice distance *(tomography)*
Schichtaufbau *m s.* Schichtfolge
Schichtaufnahme *f* slice, scan
Schichtbild *n* tomographic slice (image), slice [image], image slice, tomogram
Schichtdicke *f* 1. layer thickness; coating thickness; 2. slice thickness *(tomography)*

Schichtentwicklung *f* layer exposure
Schichtfolge *f* layer order (arrangement); emulsion sequence
Schichtintervall *n* slice interval
Schichtoberflächenentwickler *m* surface developer
Schichtseite *f* emulsion side (surface), image-bearing side *(of photo material)*
Schichtselektion *f* slice selection
Schichtsilber *n* coated silver
Schichttiefe *f* slice thickness *(tomography)*
Schichtträger *m* [film] support, [photographic] film base
~/**blaugefärbter** blue base
~/**ungefärbter** clear base
Schichtung *f* stratification *(e.g. of spectral data)*
Schichtwahl *f* slice selection
Schichtwahlgradient *m* slice selection gradient *(magnetic resonance imaging)*
schichtweise slice-by-slice *(e.g. tomographic scanning)*
Schichtzwischenraum *m* interslice gap
Schiebeblende *f* [transitional] wipe *(motion-picture optical effect)*; push *(digital video effect)*
Schiebeprisma *n* sliding prism
Schieberegister *n* [CCD] shift register, transfer register
Schieberegler *m* slide lever, slider; fader [control] *(esp. of sound equipment)*
Schiebeschalter *m* slide switch
Schiebetrick *m* 1. cutout animation; 2. *s.* Schiebeblende
Schiebezoom[objektiv] *n* continuous-zoom optical system
Schiefe *f*, **Schiefheit** *f* obliquity *(e.g. of a light ray)*; skewness *(e.g. of an image signal)*
Schiefspiegler *m* Brachyt telescope
schielen to squint
Schielen *n* squint, strabismus
Schiene *f*/**optische** optical rail
Schienendolly *m s.* Schienenwagen
Schießbaumwolle *f* 1. guncotton; 2. *s.* Cellulosenitrat
Schiffsradar *n* shipborne radar
Schirmbild *n* screen image
Schirmbildaufnahme *f* 1. screen shot; hard copy; 2. photofluorogram, photofluorographic image
Schirmbildbetrachtung *f* soft viewing
Schirmbildfilm *m* screen-type film *(X-ray film)*
Schirmbildfotografie *f* [photo]fluorography
schirmbildfotografisch [photo]fluorographic
Schirmbildkamera *f* photofluorographic camera
Schirmdiagonale *f* screen diagonal; screen diagonal size
Schirmfarbstoff *m* antihalation dye
Schirmgitter *n* screen grid

Schirmplatte f signal plate, target *(camera tube)*
Schirmreflektor m [lighting] umbrella
Schläfenlappen m temporal lobe *(of the brain)*
schläfenwärts temporal
Schlagschatten m cast shadow
Schlagzeile f headline; banner
Schleier m fog, veil *(of photographic negatives)*; nonimage silver
~/dichroitischer (zweifarbiger) dichroic fog
Schleieranstieg m fog increase
Schleierbildung f fog formation, [film] fogging
Schleierdichte f fog (negative) density
schleierfrei fog-free, fogless
Schleiergrenze f fog limit
Schleierkeim m fog center
Schleiermessung f fog measurement
Schleiermittel n fogging agent
Schleierschwärzung f fog density
Schleierwert m fog level *(s.a. Minimaldichte)*
Schleierwirkung f fogging effect
Schleife f loop *(e.g. of film material)*
Schleifenfilter n loop [low-pass] filter *(video encoder)*
Schleifenmagazin n [film] bin
Schleifenprojektor m continuous [loop] projector
Schleifenschrank m s. Schleifenmagazin
Schleifen-Tiefpassfilter n s. Schleifenfilter
Schleifenverziehen n buckle
Schleifmittel n abrasive
Schleppkurve f tractrix
Schleusengang m two-way trap *(e.g. as a darkroom entrance)*
Schliere f schliere; stria[tion]; streak
Schlierenaufnahmeanordnung f schlieren setup
Schlierenbild n schlieren image (pattern), schlieren photo[graph]
Schliereneffekt m schlieren effect
Schlierenfarbfoto n color schlieren photograph
Schlierenfotografie f schlieren photography
schlierenfrei striation-free
Schliereninterferometer n schlieren interferometer
Schlierenoptik f schlieren optics
schlierenoptisch schlieren-optical
Schlierenverfahren n [/**Toeplersches**] [Toepler] schlieren technique (method)
Schließen n [morphological] closing *(binary image processing)*
schließen 1. to close; 2. to quoin *(typesetting)*
Schließfeld n close box
Schließkeil m quoin *(typesetting)*
Schlitzantenne f slot antenna *(radar)*
Schlitzblende f slit aperture
Schlitzmaske f s. Streifenmaske

Schlitzverschluss m slot (slit) shutter; focal-plane shutter
~/vertikal ablaufender vertical-travel focal-plane shutter
Schlupf m slippage
Schlussbad n stabilizing (stabilization) bath
Schlussband n tail leader; [run-out] trailer
Schlüsselbild n key (reference) frame, key image *(e.g. in image coding)*
Schlüsselpunkt m key point *(e.g. in object recognition)*
Schlüsselverwirrung f garbling *(radar)*
Schlussklappe f tail [slate], end slate
Schlussschicht f final layer
Schlusstitel m end title; [end] credits, closing credits
Schlusswässerung f final wash[ing]
~/fließende final rinse
schmal 1. narrow; 2. condensed, narrow, justified tight *(typeface)*
Schmalbahnpapier n grain long paper, long grain paper, narrow web paper
Schmalband n s. Schmalspurband
Schmalbandfernsehen n narrowband television
Schmalbandfilter n narrow-band[pass] filter, spike filter
Schmalbandfilterung f narrow-band filtering
schmalbandig narrowband, narrow-bandwidth, low-bandwidth
Schmalbandkanal m narrowband channel
Schmalbandlaser m narrow-bandwidth laser, narrow-line laser
Schmalbandrauschen n narrowband noise
Schmalbandsignal n narrowband signal
Schmalfilm m substandard film; narrow-gauge cine film
Schmalfilmkamera f 16-mm camera; home movie camera
schmallaufend s. schmal 2.
Schmalspurband n [sound] stripe, sound (audio) track *(cinema)*
Schmalstrahlgeometrie f narrow-beam geometry
Schmalwinkelobjektiv n narrow-angle lens *(s.a. Teleobjektiv)*
Schmelzklebstoff m [/**thermoplastischer**] hot-melt *(adhesive)*
Schmetterlingsalgorithmus m butterfly algorithm *(discrete fast Fourier transform)*
Schmetterlingsantenne f batwing (turnstile) antenna *(television)*
Schmidt-Cassegrain-Teleskop n Schmidt-Cassegrain telescope
Schmidt-Kamera f Schmidt [telescope] camera *(astrophotography)*
Schmidt-Optik f Schmidt [projection] system, Schmidt objective
Schmidt-Platte f Schmidt (aspheric lens) correcting plate, corrector plate *(s.a. Kompensatorplatte)*
Schmidt-Spiegel m s. Schmidt-Optik

Schmidt-Teleskop *n* Schmidt[-type] telescope, Schmidt
Schmiereffekt *m* smear effect
Schmierskizze *f* scribble
Schmuckfarbe *f* spot color *(printing)*
Schnappschuss *m* snapshot [photograph], snap; candid shot, candid [photograph]
Schnappschusseinstellung *f* snapshot mode
Schnappschussfotograf *m* snapshot photographer, snapshooter
Schnappschussfotografie *f* [still] snapshot photography; candid shooting
Schnappschussjäger *m* snapshooter
Schnappschusskamera *f* snapshot (point-and-shoot) camera; candid camera
Schneckenführung *f*, **Schneckengang** *m*, **Schneckengangfassung** helical [focusing] mount *(lens mount)*
Schnee *m*, **Schneegestöber** *n* snow, snowstorm [effect] *(as spots on a television screen)*
Schneideimpuls *m* edit (frame) pulse
Schneidemaschine *f* 1. editing machine; 2. cutting machine; 3. [print] trimmer
schneiden to cut *(e.g. motion-picture film during editing)*; to edit *(esp. video material)*
~/**sich** to intersect *(e.g. lines)*
Schneiden[prüf]verfahren *n* [**/Foucaultsches**] knife-edge technique, Foucault knife[-edge] test *(optics)*
Schneideplatz *m* s. Schnittplatz
Schneidepult *n* edit[ing] deck
Schneideraum *m* editing room (suite); motion-picture editing room, [film] cutting room, film [editing] room
Schneidetisch *m* editing (cutting) table, edit[ing] bench
Schnellaufzugshebel *m* rapid-advance lever
Schnelldruck *m* quick printing; high-speed printing
Schnelldrucker *m* high-speed printer
Schnelldruckplatte *f* high-speed [printing] plate *(photomechanical reproduction)*
Schnellentwickler *m* rapid[-working] developer, rapid-access developer, fast-acting developing agent; rapid film developer; rapid print developer
Schnellentwicklung *f* rapid processing
Schnellfixierbad *n* rapid fixing bath
Schnellfixierer *m* fast-acting fixing agent, rapid[-acting] fixer
Schnellfotografie *f* quick photography
Schnellkopierer *m* high-speed copier
Schnellkopiermaschine *f* speed printer
Schnellkopierung *f* rapid copying
Schnellkupplung *f* quick-release adapter (device) *(e.g. on a tripod)*
Schnellkupplungsplatte *f* quick-release platform *(tripod)*
Schnellpresse *f* high-speed press *(printing)*
Schnellrücklauf *m* fast reverse (rewind)
Schnellrücklaufspiegel *m* instant-return-type reflex mirror *(SRL camera)*
Schnellrückstellung *f* two-button reset
Schnellschusskamera *f* snapshot (point-and-shoot) camera; candid camera
Schnellserienaufnahmetechnik *f* serial radiography, seriography
Schnellspannkameraplatte *f* quick-release platform *(tripod)*
Schnellstartlaufwerk *n* quick mechanism
Schnellsuchlauf *m* fast forward [movement] *(videocassette recorder)*
Schnelltrieb *m* coarse focus control, coarse adjustment knob *(microscope)*
Schnellverarbeitung *f* rapid (high-speed) processing *(e.g. of film material)*
Schnellverarbeitungspapier *n* rapid-processing paper
Schnellvorlauf *m* fast forward [movement]
Schnellwechselbajonett *n* quick-change bayonet
Schnellwechselplatte *f* s. Schnellspann[kamera]platte
Schnellzugriffsspeicher *m* rapid-access memory
Schnitt *m* 1. section *(e.g. in microscopy)*; 2. cutting; editing *(s.a. Filmschnitt, Videoschnitt)*; 3. cut; edit
~/**aneinanderfügender** 1. assemble editing; 2. assemble edit
~ **beim Drehen** in-camera editing; cutting in the camera, triple shot
~/**bildgenauer** frame-accurate editing; field-accurate editing
~/**Bild-Ton-versetzter** split (delay) edit
~/**computergesteuerter** computer-based editing; auto assembly [edit]
~/**digitaler** digital editing (cut)
~/**dünner** thin section
~/**einfügender** 1. insert editing; 2. insert edit
~/**elektronischer** electronic editing
~/**goldener** golden section (ratio), gold[en] mean, extreme and mean ratio
~/**harter** straight (editorial) cut, abrupt cut (transition)
~/**linearer** linear [video] editing, on-line editing
~/**manuell gesteuerter** manual editing
~/**nichtlinearer** nonlinear (offline) editing *(video)*
~/**springender** jump cut
~/**zeitcodierter** time code editing
Schnittabfall *m* outtakes, outs *(film editing)*
Schnittabteilung *f* editorial [department]
Schnittanfang *m* begin edit point *(video)*
Schnittansicht *f* sectional view; cutaway diagram (view)
Schnittarbeit *f* editorial work
Schnittart *f* type of editing

Schnittassistent *m* assistant [film] editor, AE, first assistant editor
Schnittausführung *f* editorial work
Schnittband *n* edit tape
Schnittbearbeitung *f* editorial refinement (manipulation), editing
Schnittbearbeitungsraum *m* editing room (suite)
Schnittbestimmung *f* edit decision
Schnittbild *n* 1. section[al] image, tomographic image, tomogram, slice [image], image slice; 2. cutaway diagram (view); 3. edit frame
Schnittbilddarstellung *f* tomographic imaging, tomography
Schnittbildebene *f* tomographic plane
Schnittbildentfernungsmesser *m*, **Schnittbildindikator** *m* split-prism rangefinder, split-image rangefinder (wedge) *(focusing aid)*
Schnittbildserie *f* serial section images
Schnittbildzentrum *n* medical-imaging department
Schnittcomputer *m* computer-controlled editing machine; computer editing suite; editing special-effects computer
Schnittebene *f* section (cut) plane; slice plane *(tomography)*
Schnittechnik *f* 1. editing technology; 2. editing technique; 3. editing equipment
Schnitteffekt *m* editing (cut) effect
Schnitteinrichtung *f* editing equipment, editor
Schnittende *n* end edit point
Schnitterkennung *f* cut detection
schnittfähig editable
Schnittfassung des Regisseurs *f* director's (first) cut
Schnittfestlegung *f* edit decision
Schnittgenauigkeit *f* editing accuracy
Schnittgerät *n* editing device
Schnittkontrolle *f* edit control
Schnittkopie *f* cutting copy, film work print, [positive] work print; edited work print
Schnittlänge *f s.* Schnittweite
Schnittlinie *f* line of intersection
Schnittliste *f* 1. log (cue) sheet, cut (assemble) list *(cinema)*; 2. *s.* ~/elektronische
~/**elektronische** edit [decision] list, EDL, edit[ing] script *(video)*
Schnittlücke *f* edit gap
Schnittmeister *m* [film] editor, cinema (motion-picture) editor, cutter
Schnittmethode *f* editing method (mode), type of editing
Schnittmonitor *m* edit monitor
Schnittnegativ *n* edited camera negative
Schnittplan *m* edit[ing] script; editorial script; edit decision list, EDL
Schnittplatz *m* editing [work]station, edit bay *(s.a. Schneideraum)*
~/**nichtlinearer** nonlinear editing workstation

Schnittprogramm *n* editing program
Schnittprogrammsoftware *f* editing software
Schnittprozess *m* edit[ing] process, editing operation
Schnittpult *n* edit[ing] deck
Schnittpunkt *m* 1. point of intersection; 2. edit[ing] point, cutting (trim) point, knot
Schnittrecorder *m* editing recorder, edit (record) VTR, record machine
Schnittrhythmus *m* cutting rhythm
Schnittsoftwarepaket *n* editing software package
Schnittstelle *f* 1. [data] interface; interface (interfacing) device, black box; 2. *s.* Schnittpunkt 2.
~/**analoge** analog interface
~/**bidirektionale** bidirectional [parallel] interface, two-way interface
~/**digitale** digital interface
~/**einheitlich definierte** common interface, CI
~/**grafische** graphic[al] interface, graphics controller interface, graphical (graphics-based) user interface, GUI, graphical front-end
~/**haptische** haptic (tactile) interface *(human-computer interaction)*
~/**interaktive** interactive interface
~/**normierte** standard interface
~/**parallele** parallel interface (port)
~/**seriell-digitale** serial digital interface, SDI
~/**serielle** serial [data] interface, serial [data] port
~/**unidirektionale** unidirectional (one-way) interface
~/**virtuelle** virtual interface
Schnittstellengeschwindigkeit *f* interface speed
Schnittstellenintegration *f* interface integration
Schnittstellenkabel *n* interface cable
Schnittstellenkarte *f* interface card
Schnittstellen-Steuerwort *n* interface control word
Schnittstellentechnologie *f* [user] interface technology
Schnittstellenvervielfacher *m* interface multiplier
Schnittsteuergerät *n* [tape] edit controller, editing station, editing (control) module; digital tape editor
Schnittsteuersoftware *f* edit controller software
Schnittsteuersystem *n s.* Schnittsystem
Schnittsteuerung *f* edit control
Schnittstudio *n* post[production] house
Schnittsynchronisierung *f* level (editorial) sync, dead sync *(motion-picture production)*
Schnittsystem *n* edit[ing] system, edit control system

~/computergestütztes computer-based edit system, computerized editing system
~/lineares linear editing system
~/nichtlineares [digitales] nonlinear (digital) editing system, [digital] nonlinear editor, [D]NLE
Schnittunterlage f cutting mat
Schnittverfahren n editing technique
Schnittvorgang m edit[ing] process, editing operation
Schnittweite f vertex [focal] length *(of a lens)*
~/bildseitige back focus (focal distance)
Schnittweitendifferenz f/**chromatische** chromatic variation of focus, longitudinal (axial) chromatic aberration
Schnittwerkzeug n/**elektronisches** electronic editing tool
Schnittwinkel m angle of intersection
Schnittzuspieler m s. Zuspieler
Schnorchelkamera f rostrum (snorkel) camera
Schnürsenkel m s. Schmalspurband
Schockwelle f shock wave
Schön- und Widerdruckmaschine f [rotary] perfecting machine, perfecting [cylinder] press, perfector [press], duplex (blanket-to-blanket) press
Schön[druck]seite f felt side *(paper)*
Schottky-Defekt m Schottky defect *(crystal imperfection)*
Schottky-Diode f Schottky [barrier photo]diode, metal semiconductor photodiode
Schottky-Effekt m Schottky effect
Schraffe f hatch *(typography, computer graphics)*
schraffieren to hatch, to hachure
Schraffur f hatching, hachure
~/assoziative associative hatching
Schraffurart f hatch style
schräg 1. oblique, inclined; 2. s. schräglaufend
Schrägauflichtbeleuchtung f oblique lighting (illumination)
Schrägaufnahme f s. Schrägluftbild
Schrägbetrachtung f oblique viewing
Schrägbildaufnahme f 1. oblique imaging; 2. s. Schrägluftbild
Schrägentfernung f slant range *(radar imaging)*
schräglaufend diagonal; slanting; cursive, italic[ized] *(typestyle)*
Schräglicht n oblique (slanted) light, raking (obliquely-incident) light
Schräglichtbeleuchtung f oblique lighting (illumination)
Schräglinie f diagonal
Schrägluftbild n oblique [aerial] photograph; high-oblique photograph *(aerophotogrammetry)*
Schrägprojektion f oblique projection
Schrägschrift f slanted typeface

Schrägspiegel m tilted mirror
Schrägspur f diagonal (slanting) track
Schrägspuraufzeichnung f helical-scan [magnetic] recording, transverse tape recording, azimuth (slant-track) recording, helical scanning
Schrägspuraufzeichnungsverfahren n helical scanning system
Schrägspurmaschine f helical-scan machine (recorder), helical videotape machine, helical [tape] machine
Schrägspurverfahren n helical scanning system
Schrägstrahl m oblique ray
Schrägstrich m diagonal, slash [mark], solidus, virgule; oblique stroke
Schramme f surface scratch, crush; abrasion [mark]
Schrammenfestigkeit f scratch resistance *(e.g. of light filters)*
Schrammschutzschicht f antiabrasion (anti-abrasive) layer, supercoat[ing]
Schraubenversetzung f screw dislocation *(electron microscopy)*
Schraubfassungsanschluss m thread[ed] mount, screw thread, screw-type [lens] mount
Schraubfilter n threaded filter
Schraubgewindeanschluss m s. Schraubfassungsanschluss
Schreibfolie f original film
schreibgeschützt write-protected
Schreibgeschwindigkeit f write (writing) speed, writing rate; [relative] tape-to-head speed, head-to-tape speed
Schreibkopf m write head
Schreib-Lese-Kopf m read-write head, record-playback head *(computer)*
Schreib-Lese-Speicher m read-write memory; random-access memory, RAM, direct-access storage [device]
~ mit wahlfreiem Zugriff/dynamischer dynamic random-access memory, DRAM
Schreib-Lese-Zyklus m read-write cycle
Schreibmarke f [screen] cursor; insertion point; pointer
Schreibmaschine f typewriter
Schreibmaschinenpapier n typing paper
Schreibpapier n writing paper *(s.a. Bankpostpapier)*
Schreibrichtung f text path
Schreibschrift f written script; script [typeface] *(style of printed letters)*
Schreibschutzschalter m write-protect tab *(e.g. on a video cassette)*
Schreibstrahl m writing beam
Schreibtakt m write clock *(time compression)*
Schreibtischdrucker m desktop printer
Schreibvorgang m writing operation
Schreib-Zyklus-Zeit f write cycle time *(random-access memory)*
Schrift f 1. writing; 2. type; 3. script; typeface, typestyle, font style

~/**breit[laufend]e** s. ~/gesperrte
~/**digitale** digital typeface
~/**digitalisierte** digitized font
~/**eingebaute** intrinsic (built-in) font *(computer)*
~/**gebrochene** Fraktur, Fractur *(style of black letter)*
~/**gedruckte** [printed] type
~/**geneigte** slanted typeface
~/**gesperrte** extended (expanded) type
~/**schattierte** shaded type
~/**schmale** condensed type
~/**serifenbehaftete** serif type[face], serif font
~/**serifenlose** sans [serif], sans serif font (type), nonserif typeface, block letters
~/**unterschnittene** condensed type
Schriftabbild *n*, **Schriftabbildung** *f* document image
Schriftalphabet *n* typeface alphabet
Schriftart *f* [type] font, set of type *(s.a.* Schriftgattung*)*
Schriftartfamilie *f* s. Schriftfamilie
Schriftartmetrik *f* font metrics
Schriftausrichtung *f* alignment *(typography)*
Schriftauszeichnung *f* weight *(type measurement)*
Schriftbild *n* 1. face *(of a letter)*; 2. typeface
Schriftdatensatz *m* font file
Schriftdesign *n* type design
Schrifteinblender *m* downstream keyer *(video)*
Schriftenbibliothek *f* font library, library of type fonts
Schrifterkennung *f* s. Schriftzeichenerkennung
Schriftfamilie *f* type family; font family
Schriftfont *m* s. 1. Schriftart; 2. Schriftgattung
Schriftgattung *f* [type]face, typestyle
Schriftgenerator *m* character generator, CG; font generator *(software)*
Schriftgießer *m* typefounder; typecaster
Schriftgießerei *f* [type]foundry
Schriftgrad *m* font (type) size, size of type; point size; body size
Schriftgrafiker *m* print (typeface) designer, typographer
Schriftgröße *f* s. Schriftgrad
Schriftgrundlinie *f* baseline
Schriftguss *m* typefounding; typecasting
Schriftgutverfilmung *f* filming of documents
Schrifthöhe *f* 1. type height; 2. font size
Schriftlinie *f* baseline
Schriftsatz *m* letterpress composition
Schriftschneider *m* type cutter
Schriftschnitt *m* typeface [design], typestyle, font style, face; weight *(esp. regarding boldness of a font)*
~/**aufrechter** s. Schriftschnitt/normaler
~/**fetter** bold typeface
~/**fett-kursiver** bold italic typeface
~/**kursiver** italic typeface
~/**normaler** plain typeface
Schriftsetzer *m* typesetter, compositor, composer
~/**gestaltender** s. Schriftgrafiker
Schriftsippe *f* s. Schriftfamilie
Schriftstil *m* s. Schriftschnitt
Schrifttyp *m* s. Schriftfamilie
Schriftunterschneidung *f* [character] kerning *(typography)*
Schriftzeichen *n* [graphic] character; letter; glyph
Schriftzeichenbild *n* character image (icon)
Schriftzeichenblock *m* character block
Schriftzeichenerkennung *f* character recognition
~/**magnetische** magnetic ink character recognition, MICR
~/**optische** optical character recognition, OCR
Schriftzumischer *m*, **Schriftzusetzer** *m* downstream keyer *(video)*
Schrittfunktion *f* step function *(signal processing)*
Schrittkamera *f* step-and-repeat camera, planetary camera
Schrittkopiermaschine *f* step printer
~/**optische** step optical printer, optical step printer
Schrittkopierung *f* step[-by-step] printing, intermittent printing *(motion-picture duplicating process)*
Schrittmotor *m* stepping (stepper) motor
Schrittschaltung *f* 1. intermittent motion; 2. s. Schrittschaltwerk
Schrittschaltwerk *n* Geneva movement, intermittent [movement]
Schrödinger-Gleichung *f* Schrödinger's [wave] equation
Schrotrauschen *n* shot (spike) noise, bipolar impulse noise, speckle noise *(s.a.* Quantenrauschen*)*
Schrumpfung *f* shrinkage
Schüfftan-Verfahren *n* Schufftan process *(trick cinematography)*
Schülermikroskop *n* student-grade microscope
Schulfernsehen *n* educational television, ETV
Schulfotograf *m* school photographer
Schulfotografie *f* school photography
Schulter *f* shoulder [part], shoulder region (zone) *(characteristic curve)*
Schulterauflage *f* [/**gepolsterte**] shoulder pod *(camera support device)*
Schulterkamera *f* shoulder camera
Schulterriemen *m* shoulder strap *(e.g. of a camera case)*
Schulterstativ *n* shoulder pod
Schulterstütze *f* shoulder rest; gun pod (stock support), rifle grip
Schulungsfilm *m* educational film (motion picture), teaching (training) film, visual aid

Schulungsvideo *n* training video
Schumann-Emulsion *f* Schumann emulsion
Schummerung *f s.* 1. Schattierung; 2. Schummerungsrelief
Schusterjunge *m* orphan [line] *(printing)*
schütteln to jog *(printed sheets)*
Schutzband *n* guard band
Schutzbit *n* protection bit
Schutzbrille *f* safety goggles, protective eyewear
Schutzfilm *m s.* Allonge
Schutzfilter *n* protective filter; safelight filter
Schutzkolloid *n* protective colloid
Schutzlicht *n* safelight
Schutzschicht *f* protective layer (coat), overcoat layer
~/antistatische antistatic layer (coating); antistatic backing
Schutzüberzug *m* protective overcoat; cladding *(videodisc)*
Schutzwulstring *m* track guard
Schwabbelburst *m* alternating burst *(television signal)*
Schwachlicht *n* low[-level] light, weak (faint) light
schwachsichtig amblyopic
Schwachsichtigkeit *f* amblyopia, dimness of sight, lazy eye, low vision *(s.a.* Sehschwäche*)*
Schwächung *f* attenuation
Schwächungsbild *n* attenuation map (image), attenuation profile
Schwächungsfilter *n* balancing filter *(radiography)*
Schwächungskoeffizient *m* attenuation (extinction) coefficient
~/linearer linear attenuation coefficient
Schwächungskontrast *m* attenuation contrast *(radiography)*
Schwächungsprofil *n s.* Schwächungsbild
Schwächungswert *m* attenuation value
Schwadbreite *f* swath width *(remote sensing)*
Schwarmelement *n* boid *(computer animation)*
Schwarzabgleich *m* black balance
~/automatischer automatic black control, ABC
Schwarzabhebung *f* pedestal, [black level] setup *(electronic imaging)*
Schwarzauszug *m* black separation *(reprography)*
Schwarzband *n* black[ed] tape, preblacked (striped) tape
Schwarzbezugswert *m* reference (house) black, black burst, house sync (reference) *(composite video signal)*
Schwarzdehnung *f* black stretch *(electronic camera)*
Schwärze *f* blackness
schwärzen to blacken

Schwarzentzerrer *m* black stretch *(CCD telecine)*
Schwarzfilm *m* black [emulsion] leader
Schwarzfilter *n* black filter
Schwarzgehalt *m* black content *(colorimetry)*
Schwarzkörperstrahler *m* blackbody [radiator], Planckian (cavity) radiator
Schwarzkörperstrahlung *f* blackbody [thermal] radiation, Planckian (cavity) radiation
Schwarzlichtfilter *n* black filter
Schwarzlichtlampe *f* black-light lamp
Schwarzlücke *f* blanking interval *(television image)*
Schwarzpatrone *f* black cartridge
Schwarzpegel *m* black (setup) level *(video signal)*
Schwarzpunkt *m* black point
Schwarzschild-Effekt *m* Schwarzschild effect *(exposure effect)*
Schwarzschild-Kamera *f* Schwarzschild camera
Schwarzschild-Objektiv *n* Schwarzschild objective
Schwarzschild-Verhalten *n* Schwarzschild behavior, reciprocity [law] failure, reciprocity effect
Schwarzschulter *f* black porch
~/hintere back porch
~/vordere front porch
Schwärzung *f* 1. blackening; 2. [optical] density
~/maximale maximum density, D-max
Schwärzungsbereich *m* density range
Schwärzungsdichte *f* photographic density
Schwärzungseffekt *m* blackening effect
Schwärzungskurve *f* characteristic (density) curve, [photographic] response curve, [characteristic] D-log H curve
Schwärzungsmesser *m* densitometer
Schwärzungsumfang *m* density range; negative contrast
schwarzweiß black-and-white, BW; monochrome
Schwarzweißabzug *m* black-and-white print, monochrome print
Schwarzweißarbeit *f* black-and-white work
Schwarzweißaufnahme *f,*
Schwarzweißbild *n* black-and-white image (picture), intensity picture *(s.a.* Schwarzweißabzug, Binärbild*)*
Schwarzweißbildcodierung *f* monochrome image encoding
Schwarzweißbildgeber *m* monochrome imager
Schwarzweißbildröhre *f* black-and-white CRT (cathode-ray tube), monochrome picture tube, monochrome (bilevel) CRT
Schwarzweißbildschirm *m* monochrome (black-and-white) screen; monochrome [graphics] display, bilevel display

Schwarzweißdia[positiv] *n* black-and-white slide (projection transparency), monochrome transparency
Schwarzweißdruck *m* monochrome printing
Schwarzweißdrucker *m* monochrome printer
Schwarzweißemulsion *f* black-and-white emulsion
Schwarzweißentwickler *m* black-and-white developer
Schwarzweißentwicklung *f* black-and-white development
Schwarzweiß-Fernsehempfänger *m s.* Schwarzweißfernsehgerät
Schwarzweißfernsehen *n* monochrome (black-and-white) television
Schwarzweißfernsehgerät *n* monochrome receiver (television set), black-and-white television receiver (set)
Schwarzweißfernsehkamera *f* monochrome TV camera
Schwarzweißfilm *m* black-and-white film
~/chromogener chromogenic black-and-white film
~/panchromatischer panchromatic black-and-white film, black-and-white pan[chromatic] film
Schwarzweißfilmbild *n* black-and-white film image
Schwarzweißfilmentwickler *m* black-and-white film developer
Schwarzweißfilmentwicklung *f s.* Schwarzweißfilmverarbeitung
Schwarzweißfilmkamera *f* black-and-white film camera
Schwarzweißfilmverarbeitung *f* black-and-white film processing
Schwarzweißfoto *n* black-and-white photographic image
Schwarzweißfotografie *f* black-and-white photography, monochromatic (monochrome) photography
Schwarzweißfotopapier *n s.* Schwarzweißpapier
Schwarzweiß-Halbtonpapier *n* black-and-white continuous-tone paper
Schwarzweißillustration *f* black-and-white illustration
Schwarzweiß-Infrarotfilm *m* black-and-white infrared (IR) film, infrared black-and-white film
Schwarzweißkamera *f* black-and-white camera, monochrome camera
Schwarzweiß-Kinefilm *m* black-and-white motion-picture film
Schwarzweißkontrast *m* black-and-white contrast
Schwarzweißkopie *f* black-and-white print (copy)
Schwarzweißkopieren *n* black-and-white printing

Schwarzweißkopierer *m* black-and-white copier
Schwarzweißlaserdrucker *m* monochrome (black-and-white) laser printer
Schwarzweißmaterial *n* black-and-white [photographic] material, noncolor material
Schwarzweißmikrofotografie *f* black-and-white photomicrography
Schwarzweißmodus *m* black-and-white mode *(CCD camera)*
Schwarzweißmonitor *m* black-and-white monitor, monochrome monitor
Schwarzweißnegativ *n* black-and-white negative
Schwarzweiß-Negativmaterial *n* black-and-white negative material (film)
Schwarzweißpapier *n* black-and-white [photographic] paper, black-and-white photographic printing paper
~/kontrastvariables variable-contrast [black-and-white] paper
Schwarzweißpixel *n* black-and-white pixel
Schwarzweißpositiv *n* black-and-white positive
Schwarzweißpositivfilm *m* black-and-white positive (print) film
Schwarzweißprozess *m* monochrome photographic process; black-and-white film processing
Schwarzweiß-Scanner *m* black-and-white scanner, monochrome [electronic] image scanner
Schwarzweißsehen *n* black-white vision, monochrome vision *(s.a.* Einfarbensehen 1.*)*
Schwarzweißsendung *f* monochrome broadcast, black-and-white transmission *(television)*
Schwarzweißsignal *n* black-[and-]white [video] signal, monochrome (gray-scale) video signal, luminance (luma) signal, Y [signal]
Schwarzweiß-Sofortfilm *m* black-and-white instant film
Schwarzweißsucher *m* monochrome viewfinder
Schwarzweißtechnik *f s.* Schwarzweißverarbeitung
Schwarzweißübergang *m* black-to-white transition
Schwarzweißübertragung *f* black-and-white transmission *(television)*
Schwarzweiß-Umkehrentwickler *m* reversal-type black-and-white developer
Schwarzweiß-Umkehrfilm *m* black-and-white reversal film, reversal black-and-white film
Schwarzweiß-Umkehrverarbeitung *f* black-and-white reversal processing
Schwarzweiß-Umkehrverfahren *n* black-and-white reversal process

Schwarzweißverarbeitung f
black-and-white processing
Schwarzweißvergrößerer m
black-and-white enlarger
Schwarzweißvergrößern n
black-and-white enlarging
Schwarzweißvergrößerungsgerät n
black-and-white enlarger
Schwarzweißvergrößerungspapier n
black-and-white enlarging paper
Schwarzweißvideo n monochrome video
Schwarzweißvideosignal n s.
Schwarzweißsignal
Schwarzweißvorlage f black-and-white copy *(printing)*
Schwarzweiß-Wärmebild n
black-and-white thermal image
Schwarzwert m black (setup) level *(video signal)*
Schwarzwertklemmung f black-level clamp[ing] *(video waveform)*
Schwebestativ n Steadicam *(trade name for a camera stabilizing system)*
Schwebung f beat *(wave optics)*
Schwebungslänge f beat length
Schwefelsäure f sulfuric acid
Schwefelsensibilisierung f sulfur sensitization
Schwefeltoner m sulfur toner
Schwefeltonung f sulfur toning
Schweißnahtabbildung f weld image
Schwelle f threshold *(s.a. Schwellenwert, Reizschwelle)*
Schwellenellipse f nach MacAdam
MacAdam ellipse *(colorimetry)*
Schwellenfestlegung f threshold setting
Schwellenintervall n threshold range
Schwellenmodulation f threshold modulation
Schwellenoperation f s.
Schwellenwertoperation
Schwellenstrom m threshold current *(laser diode)*
Schwellenwert m threshold [value]; threshold exposure *(characteristic curve)*
~/**adaptiver** adaptive threshold
Schwellenwertbildung f thresholding [procedure], thresholding process *(image-processing operation)*
~/**adaptive** adaptive (dynamic) thresholding
~/**binäre** binary thresholding
~/**globale** global thresholding
~/**harte** hard thresholding
~/**hierarchische** hierarchical thresholding
~/**lokale** local thresholding
~/**multispektrale** multispectral thresholding
~/**variable** variable thresholding
~/**weiche** soft thresholding
Schwellenwertcodierung f threshold coding
Schwellenwert-Dithering n threshold dithering *(computer graphics)*

Schwellenwertfestlegung f s.
Schwellenwertbildung
Schwellenwertfunktion f threshold[ing] function
Schwellenwertoperation f threshold[ing] operation
Schwellenwertsegmentierung f threshold segmentation
Schwellenwertverfahren n threshold procedure; thresholding [technique]
Schwellenwertzerlegung f threshold decomposition
Schwellwert... s. Schwellenwert...
Schwenk m pan [move]; sweeping pan; pan shot; tilt [move] *(filming)*
~/**schneller** swish (whip) pan, flash pan *(filming)*
schwenken to pan *(camera)*
Schwenker m operative (first) cameraman principal cameraperson *(motion-picture production)*
Schwenkkopf m pan[oramic] head, swivel head
Schwerflint m, **Schwerflintglas** n dense flint glass
Schwerpunkt m center of mass, barycenter
Schwerspat m heavy spar, barite, baryte[s]
Schwerstflint m extra dense flint [glass]
Schwinger m s. Ultraschallsender
Schwingquarz m quartz[-crystal-based] oscillator, crystal oscillator
Schwingspiegel m swinging (reflex) mirror *(reflex camera)*; vibrating mirror; oscillating mirror
Schwingung f/**harmonische** harmonic oscillation
Schwingungsamplitude f oscillation (oscillatory) amplitude
Schwingungsanalyse f vibration analysis
Schwingungsbild n vibrogram
Schwingungsebene f vibrational (oscillation) plane, plane of vibration
Schwingungsenergie f vibrational energy *(e.g. of an electron)*
Schwingungsknoten m vibration node
Schwingungsmuster n vibrogram
Schwingungsrichtung f vibrational direction
Schwingungsschreiber m oscillograph
Schwingungszahl f s. Frequenz
Schwingungszug m oscillation train
SC-Optik f s. Schmidt-Cassegrain-Optik
Scribble n scribble; [rough] sketch
SCSI-Festplatte f SCSI hard disk
SCSI-Gerät n SCSI device
SCSI-Schnittstelle f small computer systems interface, SCSI *(hard disk controller standard)*
SECAM-Identifikationssignale npl SECAM field identification bottles
SECAM-Verfahren n SECAM process *(color television; derived from Sequential Couleur A Mémoire)*

Sechseck *n* hexagon
sechseckig hexagonal
Sechsfarbendruck *m* six-color (six-ink) printing
Sechsflächner *m* [/**regelmäßiger**] hexahedron *(geometric primitive)*
Sechsspurmagnetton *m* six-track [magnetic] sound, six-channel sound
Sedezimalziffer *f* sexadecimal digit
Seeclutter *m*, **Seegangecho** *n* sea clutter *(radar)*
Seegangsenttrübung *f*/**maximale** anticlutter sea maximum
~/**minimale** anticlutter sea minimum
Seeing *n* seeing *(astrophotography; s.a. Luftunruhe)*
Seekarte *f* marine chart
~/**elektronische** electronic chart display and information system, ECDIS
Segment *n* 1. segment; 2. *s.* Bildprimitiv
segmental segmental
Segmentation *f s.* Segmentierung
segmentierbar segmentable *(e.g. a histogram)*
segmentieren to segment, to partition
Segmentierung *f* segmentation, partitioning *(image-processing operation)*
~/**adaptive** adaptive segmentation
~/**agglomerative** bottom-up segmentation
~/**autonome** autonomous segmentation
~/**bereichsbasierte (bereichsorientierte)** region-based (region-oriented) segmentation
~/**bewegungsbasierte** motion-based segmentation
~/**divisive** top-down segmentation
~/**histogrammgestützte** histogram-based segmentation
~/**kantenbasierte (kantenorientierte)** edge-based segmentation
~/**kontextabhängige** contextual segmentation
~/**kontexunabhängige** noncontextual segmentation
~/**merkmalsbasierte** feature-based segmentation
~/**modellbasierte** model-based segmentation
~/**oberflächenbasierte** surface-based segmentation
~/**pixelbasierte (punktorientierte)** pixel-based segmentation
~/**regionenbasierte (regionenorientierte)** region segmentation, region-based (region-oriented) segmentation
~/**szenenbasierte** scene-based segmentation
~/**texturbasierte** texture-based segmentation
~/**topologische** topological segmentation
~/**unscharfe** fuzzy segmentation
~/**vollständige** complete (knowledge-guided) segmentation
~/**volumetrische** volumetric segmentation
~/**wissensbasierte** knowledge-based segmentation
Segmentierungsalgorithmus *m* segmentation algorithm
Segmentierungsansatz *m* segmentation approach
Segmentierungsergebnis *n* segmentation result
Segmentierungsfehler *m* segmentation error
Segmentierungsgenauigkeit *f* segmentation accuracy
Segmentierungsleistung *f* segmentation performance
Segmentierungslinie *f* segmentation line
Segmentierungsmaske *f* segmentation mask
Segmentierungsmerkmal *n* segmentation feature
Segmentierungsmodell *n* segmentation model
Segmentierungsobjekt *n* segmentation object
Segmentierungsprozess *m* segmentation process
Segmentierungstechnik *f* segmentation technique
Segmentkontur *f* segment boundary
Segmentverschluss *m* leaf shutter
segmentweise segmental
Sehabstand *m* viewing distance
Sehachse *f* visual (view) axis, central visual ray *(s.a. Sichtlinie, Blickachse)*
Sehapparat *m* visual system (mechanism)
~/**menschlicher** human visual system
Sehaufgabe *f* visual detection task
Sehbahn *f* visual pathway
Sehbeeinträchtigung *f* visual discomfort
sehbehindert visually (sight) impaired
Sehbehinderung *f* visual impairment
Sehding *n* visual object
Seheindruck *m* visual impression (sensation)
Sehen *n* vision, viewing, [eye]sight, seeing
~/**aktives** active vision
~/**beidäugiges** binocular (two-eyed) vision, binocular viewing
~/**chromatisches** chromatic (color) vision
~/**deutliches** clear vision
~/**dichoptisches** dichoptic vision
~/**dreiäugiges** trinocular vision
~/**dreidimensionales** *s.* ~/**räumliches**
~/**dunkeladaptiertes** *s.* ~/**skotopisches**
~/**einäugiges** monocular vision (viewing)
~/**fotopisches** photopic vision, cone[-mediated] vision, daylight (daytime) vision, bright-light (light-adapted) vision
~/**foveales** foveal vision (viewing)
~/**maschinelles** [industrial] machine vision; computer vision
~/**menschliches** human vision

Sehen 360

~/**mesopisches** mesopic vision, dim-light vision
~/**modellbasiertes** model-based vision
~/**monokulares** monocular vision (viewing)
~/**peripheres** peripheral vision
~/**räumliches** spatial (three-dimensional) vision, stereo[scopic] vision, stereopsis
~/**scharfes** acute (high-acuity) vision
~/**skotopisches** scotopic (dark-adapted) vision, night (rod) vision
~/**stereoskopisches** s. ~/räumliches
~/**technisches dreidimensionales** three-dimensional computer vision
~/**unscharfes** nonsharp (unsharp) vision
~/**unverzügliches** preattentive vision
Sehentfernung f viewing distance
Seherfahrung f visual experience
Sehfähigkeit f visual [cap]ability
Sehfarbstoff m visual pigment
Sehfehler m vision (visual) defect, defect of vision; visual error
Sehfeld n visual field, field of vision, FOV
Sehfeldblende f field stop (diaphragm)
Sehfelddurchmesser m view-field diameter *(objective)*
Sehforschung f vision research (science)
Sehfunktion f visual function
Sehgrube f [retinal] fovea, fovea centralis
Sehhilfe f visual (optical) aid
Sehhügel m thalamus
Sehkraft f power of vision, [eye]sight
Sehkraftbestimmung f optometry
Sehkreis m circle of vision
Sehleistung f 1. visual performance; 2. s. Sehvermögen
Sehloch n pupil
Sehmechanismus m visual mechanism
Sehnerv m optic nerve; optic nerve bundle
Sehnervenfaser f optic nerve fiber
Sehnervenkreuzung f optic chiasm[a]
Sehnervensystem n visual nervous system
Sehobjekt n visual object
Sehorgan n organ of sight, visual organ
Sehpigment n visual pigment
Sehprobe f vision (visual) test
Sehprobentafel f eye chart; Snellen eye (test) chart, Snellen chart
Sehprozess m visual (vision) process
Sehpurpur m visual purple [pigment], retinal purple, rhodopsin, rod [photo]pigment
Sehraum m visual space
Sehreiz m visual stimulus
Sehrezeptor m visual (eye) receptor, photoreceptor cell
Sehrichtung f view[ing] direction, direction of view[ing], look direction
Sehrichtungsgemeinschaft f s. Korrespondenz
Sehrinde f visual (striate) cortex *(of the brain)*
Sehrindenmodul n cortical module
Sehrohr n periscope

Sehschärfe f [visual] acuity, acuity of the eye; keen eyesight
~/**anguläre** angular acuity
~/**stereoskopische** stereo acuity
Sehschärfebestimmung f visual acuity measurement
Sehschärfetest m acuity test
sehschwach asthenopic
Sehschwäche f asthenopia *(s.a. Schwachsichtigkeit)*
Sehschwelle f visibility (visual) threshold, threshold of vision
Sehsinn m visual sense, sense of sight, [sense of] vision
Sehstäbchen n optic[al] rod, rod [photo]receptor, [retinal] rod, rhabdom[e]
Sehstörung f disorder of vision, visual aberration
Sehstrahl m visual ray; viewing ray
Sehstrahlung f lateral geniculate nucleus
Sehsystem n visual (eye) system
~/**maschinelles** artificial vision system
~/**menschliches** human visual (eye) system, HVS
~/**technisches** artificial vision system
Sehtafel f/**Snellensche** Snellen eye (test) chart, Snellen chart
Sehtest m vision (visual) test
Sehverhalten n visual behavior
Sehvermögen n visual [cap]ability
Sehvorgang m visual (vision) process
Sehwahrnehmung f [human] visual perception
Sehweite f visual range *(s.a. Sichtweite)*
~/**deutliche** s. ~/konventionelle
~/**konventionelle** normal viewing distance
Sehweitenmesser m optometer
Sehwinkel m [apparent] visual angle, angle of vision
Sehzapfen m visual cone, [retinal] cone, cone [photo]receptor
Sehzeichen n optotype; visual test target
Sehzelle f visual cell
Sehzentrum n visual center *(of the brain)*
Seidel-Aberration f [von] Seidel aberration, primary aberration (image defect), third-order aberration *(optics)*
seidenmatt pearl *(e.g. a printing paper)*
Seidenraster m(n) silk screen
Seilschlinge f articulatory loop
Seismograf m seismograph
Seismografie f seismography
seismografisch seismographic
Seismogramm n seismogram
Seitblickendoskop n side-viewing endoscope
Seite f 1. side; 2. page
~/**emulsionsabgewandte** non-emulsion side, back of the film
~/**gerade** verso [page], left-hand page, even-numbered page *(layout)*
~/**ungerade** recto [page], right-hand page
Seitenansicht f side view
Seitenauflösung f lateral resolution

Seitenband n sideband
~/**oberes** upper sideband
~/**unteres** lower sideband
Seitenbandholografie f off-line holography
Seitenbeschreibungsbefehl m page description command
Seitenbeschreibungssprache f page description language, PDL
Seitenblättern n page flip, page-turn [effect] *(digital video)*
Seitendrucker m page printer
Seitenfensterröhre f side window [X-ray] tube
Seitenformat n page format
Seitengestaltung f page layout
Seitenkeule f side lobe *(radar, sonography)*
Seitenlayoutprogramm n page layout program
Seitenlicht n side light
~/**flaches** low side light
~/**gegenlichtiges** crosslight
Seitenmontage f s. Seitenumbruch
Seitennumerierung f pagination, paging
Seitenproof m page proof
Seitenradar n side-looking radar
seitenrichtig laterally correct, right reading
Seitenrichtung f side orientation
Seitensichtradar n side-looking radar
Seitensicht-Sonarverfahren n side-scan[ned] sonar
Seitenspeicher m page [area] memory
Seitentabelle f, **Seitentafel** f page table *(graphics file)*
Seitenumbruch m [page] makeup, page assembly, composition
Seitenumkehr[ung] f lateral reversal
Seitenvergrößerung f lateral (transverse) magnification
Seitenverhältnis n aspect [ratio], height-to-width ratio (proportion)
Seitenverhältnistransformierung f aspect ratio accommodation
seitenverkehrt laterally reversed, inverted laterally, wrong (reverse) reading, flopped
Seitenverkehrtheit f lateral reversal
Seitenvorschub m form feed *(printer)*
Seitenwechsel m page break *(printing)*
Seitenzahl f 1. page number, folio [number]; 2. page count, extent
Seitenzipfel m side lobe *(ultrasonography, radar)*
Sektorabtastung f sector scanning *(radar)*
Sektorbild n sector image *(sonography)*
Sektorenblende f sector aperture; disk (sector-wheel) shutter, blade (multi-bladed) shutter, rotary (rotating) shutter, chopper
~/**verstellbare** variable [camera] shutter, adjustable disk shutter
Sektorenscheibe f 1. sector disk *(e.g. in a sensitometer)*; 2. s. Sektorenblende
Sektorscanner m sector scanner *(sonography)*

Sektorverschluss m s. Sektorenblende
Sekundäranregung f secondary excitation *(X-ray fluorescence)*
Sekundärelektron n secondary electron
Sekundärelektronenabbildung f secondary electron imaging
Sekundärelektronenbild n secondary-electron image
Sekundärelektronenvervielfacher m photomultiplier [tube], multiplier phototube
Sekundäremission f secondary emission
Sekundärfarbe f secondary (nonprimary) color, overprint color
Sekundärfokus m virtual focus; Cassegrain focus *(telescope)*
Sekundärionen-Massenspektrometer n secondary ion mass spectrometer
Sekundärionen-Massenspektrometrie f secondary ion mass spectrometry
Sekundärlichtquelle f secondary light source
Sekundärmerkmal n secondary feature
Sekundärradar n secondary [surveillance] radar
Sekundärradarabfragegerät n interrogator
Sekundärreaktion f secondary reaction
Sekundärreflexion f secondary reflection
Sekundärspeicher m secondary storage *(s.a. Massenspeicher)*
Sekundärspiegel m secondary mirror *(e.g. of a catadioptric system)*
Sekundärstrahler m secondary radiator
Sekundärstrahlung f secondary radiation
Sekundärtarget n secondary target *(X-ray fluorescence)*
Sel n s. Sensorelement
selbstabbildend self-imaging
selbstähnlich self-similar *(fractal object)*
Selbstähnlichkeit f self-similarity
Selbstausarbeiter m s. Selbstverarbeiter
Selbstauslöser m self-timer [shutter release]
~/**selbstrückstellender** delayed-action self timer
Selbstauslöserablaufzeit f timing sequence *(self-timer)*
Selbstauslöserlampe f s. Selbstauslöseranzeige
Selbstauslöser-LED f self-timer indicator LED
Selbstauslöser-Vorlaufzeit f timer duration
Selbstdurchschreibpapier n carbonless paper
selbstemittierend self-emitting
Selbstfaltung f self-convolution
Selbstfokussierung f self-focusing
Selbstkalibrierung f self-calibration
Selbstklebeband n self-sticking tape, self-adhesive strip
Selbstleuchten n self-illumination
selbstleuchten to self-illuminate
selbstleuchtend self-luminous, self-illuminating

Selbstleuchter *m* self-luminous object, primary radiator
Selbststrahler *m* s. Selbstleuchter
selbsttaktend self-clocking *(e.g. video data)*
Selbsttransformation *f* self-transformation *(image coding)*
selbstverarbeitbar user-processable, user-processible *(photographic material)*
Selbstverarbeiter *m* [home] darkroom enthusiast
Selbstverarbeitung *f* home (user) processing
Selektionsfilter *n* color separation filter
Selektivität *f* selectivity
Selektivmessung *f* spot metering
Selektorblende *f* selector aperture *(electron microscope)*
Selen *n*/**amorphes** amorphous selenium, a-Se *(photoconductor)*
Selenfotoelement *n* s. Selenzelle
Selenpulver *n* selenium powder
Selentoner *m* selenium toner; selenium toning solution
Selentonung *f* selenium toning
Selenzelle *f* selenium [photo]cell, selenium photovoltaic cell
Seltenerdglas *n* rare-earth glass
Selwyn-Körnigkeit *f*, **Selwyn-Körnung** *f* Selwyn granularity
Semichinon *n* semiquinone *(chromogenic chemistry)*
Semigrafik *f* semigraphics
Semiprofikamera *f* semiprofessional camera
semitransparent semitransparent
Sendeanlage *f* broadcast (transmitting) facility, broadcast plant
Sendeanstalt *f* 1. broadcasting company; 2. broadcast operation, broadcaster
Sendeantenne *f* transmission antenna, transmitting antenna (aerial), radiating antenna (aerial)
Sendeband *n* broadcast (television) videotape, broadcast[-quality] tape, professional tape
Sendebandbreite *f* broadcast bandwidth
Sendebeitrag *m* [broadcast] program *(s.a. Sendung)*
Sendeeinrichtung *f* [professional] broadcast operation, broadcast-type facility
Sende-Empfangs-Duplexer *m*, **Sende-Empfangs-Umschalter** *m* transmit-receive device, duplexer [switch]
Sende-Empfangs-Verzögerung *f* transmit-to-receive delay
Sende-Empfangs-Weiche *f* s. Sende-Empfangs-Umschalter
sendefähig broadcast-quality, broadcast-level
Sendeformat *n* broadcast-quality format
Sendefrequenz *f* transmission frequency
Sendeimpuls *m* transmitted pulse
Sendekanal *m* broadcast[ing] channel, transmission channel
Sendekopie *f* television print (copy)
Sendeleistung *f* transmitting power
Sendelicht *n* broadcast illumination level
Sendemagnetband *n* s. Sendeband
senden to broadcast; to transmit, to send
~/**erneut** to rebroadcast
~/**gleichzeitig** 1. to simulcast; 2. to multiplex
~/**live** to broadcast live
~/**parallel** s. ~/gleichzeitig
Sendenorm *f* broadcast[ing] standard
Sendepuls *m* transmitted pulse
Sender *m* broadcaster; [broadcasting] transmitter, sender
~/**terrestrischer** terrestrial transmitter (broadcaster)
Senderegie *f* master control room, MCR
Senderkennung *f* station identification (ID)
Sendernetz *n* broadcast[ing] network
Senderöhre *f* transmitting (transmitter) tube
Senderseite *f* s. Sendeseite
Sendersuchlauf *m*/**automatischer** auto[matic] search tuning, auto channel programming
Sendeseite *f* transmitter side (end)
sendeseitig at the transmitting end
Sendesignal *n* broadcast signal
Sendestation *f* broadcast station
Sendestudio *n* broadcast studio
Sendesystem *n* broadcast system
Sendetag *m* broadcast day
Sendetechnik *f* 1. broadcast[ing] technology; broadcast (transmitting) engineering; 2. [professional] broadcast equipment; broadcast[-grade studio] equipment
Sendetechniker *m* broadcast engineer
Sendeton *m* program sound
Sendeturm *m* transmitting tower
Sendeverstärker *m* transmitting amplifier
Sendezentrale *f* [television] transmission center
Sendung *f* 1. transmission; broadcast; 2. broadcast [program], program, show
• **auf ~** on air
Senke *f* drain, sink
Senkel *m* [sound] stripe; sound (audio) track *(cinema)*
Senkrecht[bild]aufnahme *f*, **Senkrechtluftbild** *n* vertical [aerial] photograph
Sensibilisation *f* s. Sensibilisierung
Sensibilisator *m* sensitizer, sensitizing [re]agent, sensitizing compound
~/**optischer** optical sensitizer
~/**spektraler** spectral sensitizer
Sensibilisatorfarbstoff *m* [spectral] sensitizing dye
sensibilisierbar sensitizable
sensibilisieren to sensitize

Sensibilisierfarbstoff *m* [spectral] sensitizing dye
Sensibilisierung *f* sensitization
~/**chemische** chemical sensitization (ripening), second ripening, digestion, afterripening
~/**optische** *s.* ~/**spektrale**
~/**spektrale** spectral (optical) sensitization
Sensibilisierungsfarbe *f,*
Sensibilisierungsfarbstoff *m* [spectral] sensitizing dye
Sensibilisierungsvermögen *n* sensitizing power
Sensitometer *n* sensitometer
~/**monochromatisches** monochromatic sensitometer
Sensitometerstreifen *m* sensitometric strip
Sensitometrie *f* sensitometry
~/**elektronische** electronic sensitometry
sensitometrisch sensitometric
Sensor *m* [meter] sensor, sensing device *(s.a. under Detektor)*
~/**aktiv sendender** active sensor
~/**amplitudenmodulierter** amplitude-modulated sensor *(fiber optics)*
~/**bildaufnehmender (bildgebender)** image (picture) sensor, imaging sensor (detector), imager
~/**digitaler** digital sensor
~/**elektrischer** electric sensor
~/**elektronischer** electronic sensor
~/**elektrooptischer** electro-optical sensor, EO sensor
~/**faseroptischer** fiber-optic sensor
~/**faseroptischer** fiber-optic[al] sensor, fiber sensor
~/**flächiger** sensor array
~/**fotoelektrischer** photoelectric sensor
~/**heterogener** heterogeneous sensor
~/**hyperspektraler** hyperspectral sensor
~/**kapazitiver** capacitive sensor
~/**lichtempfindlicher** light-sensitive sensor
~/**multispektraler** multispectral sensor
~/**optischer** optical (light) sensor, photosensor
~/**optoelektronischer** optoelectronic sensor
~/**passiver** passive sensor
~/**piezoelektrischer** piezoelectric sensor
~/**thermischer** thermal [radiation] sensor
~/**thermoelektrischer** thermoelectric sensor
~/**ultraspektraler** ultraspektral sensor
~/**visueller** visual sensor
Sensorarchitektur *f* sensor architecture
Sensor-Array *n* sensor array
Sensorauflösung *f* detector resolution
Sensorbildschirm *m* touch[-sensitive] screen, tactile (pressure-sensitive) screen; touch screen monitor
Sensorblitzgerät *n* sensor auto flash
Sensorchip *m* sensor chip

Sensordaten *pl* sensor data
Sensorebene *f* sensor plane
Sensoreigenrauschen *n* sensor noise
Sensorelektronik *f* sensitive electronics
Sensorelement *n* sensor (sensing) element
Sensorfläche *f* sensor area; sensor array
Sensorgenauigkeit *f* sensor accuracy
sensoriell *s.* sensorisch
Sensorik *f* sensor technology (engineering)
sensorisch sensory, sensorial
Sensorkopf *m* sensor head
Sensormaterial *n* sensor (sensing) material
Sensormodell *n* sensor model
Sensorpixel *n* sensor pixel
Sensorposition *f* sensor position
Sensorrauschen *n* sensor noise; CCD noise
Sensorschaltung *f* sensor circuitry
Sensorschicht *f* detection layer *(charge-coupled device)*
Sensorspektrum *n* sensor spectrum
Sensorstrom *m* sensor current
Sensortablett *n* sensor array
Sensortastenfeld *n* touch pad
Sensortechnik *f* sensor technology (engineering)
Sensorverstärker *m* sensor amplifier
Sensorzeile *f* line (linear array) sensor, linear image sensor, linear detector array
Separationsnegativ *n* [color] separation negative
separierbar separable *(e.g. a transformation)*
Separierbarkeit *f* separability
separieren to separate
sepia sepia
Sepiaabzug *m* sepia [print], sepia image
sepiabraun sepia
Sepiaeffekt *m* sepia effect
Sepiafilter *n* sepia tone filter
Sepiapapier *n* sepia [receiving] paper
Sepiaton *m* sepia tone
Sepiatoner *m* sepia toner
Sepiatonung *f* sepia (sulfide) toning
Sequentialisierung *f* sequencing
Sequenz *f* sequence, sequency
~/**bitonische** bitonic sequence
Sequenzanalyse *f* sequence analysis
Sequenzspektrometer *n* sequential spectrometer
serialisieren to serialize *(e.g. samples)*
Serie *f* series
Seriellabtastung *f,* **Serienabtastung** *f* serial scanning
Serienaufnahme *f* sequential picture (image), burst image
Serienauslösung *f* burst capture
Serienbildfunktion *f,* **Serienbildmodus** *m,* **Serienbildschaltung** *f* continuous-shooting mode, multiple-capture mode *(camera feature)*
Serienbus *m*/**universeller** universal serial bus, USB
Seriendrucker *m* serial [impact] printer; character printer

Serienfotografie

Serienfotografie f sequence (serial) photograph
Serienkamera f 1. sequence[d] camera; 2. series camera
Serienobjektiv n series-produced lens
Serif n s. Serife
Serife f serif *(typography)*
~/ungekehlte abrupt serif *(s.a. Blockserife)*
Serifenform f serif shape
serifenlos nonserif[ed], sans [serif]
Serifenschrift f serif type[face], serif font
seriflos s. serifenlos
Serigrafie f serigraphy, creative silk-screen printmaking
serigrafisch serigraphic
Seriografie f seriography, serial radiography
Server m 1. server [software]; 2. server [machine] *(computer)*
Servo-Hochlaufzeit f servo lockup time *(magnetic tape technology)*
Servomotor m servomotor, relay
Servoregelung f servo[mechanism]
Set m(n) [motion-picture] set, movie set, setting *(s.a. Drehort)*
Set-Top-Box f set-top [box], STB, video set-top unit, set-top converter (box decoder), integrated receiver-decoder, IRD
~ mit Aufzeichnungsfunktion hard disk [video] recorder, hard-drive-based consumer VCR
setzen to compose, to typeset
~/kursiv to italicize
Setzer m typesetter, compositor, composer
Setzerei f composing room; typesetting department
Setzkasten m typecase
Setzlinie f brass rule *(typesetting device)*
Setzmaschine f typesetting (composing) machine, typesetter
~/tastaturgesteuerte keyboard[-operated] typesetting machine
Setzschiff n galley
Setzsystem n typesetting system
Shannon-Theorem n Shannon sampling theorem
Shearografie f shearography, speckle pattern shearing interferometry
~/digitale digital shearography
~/elektronische electronic shearography
~/stroboskopische stroboscopic shearography
shearografisch shearographic
Shiftobjektiv n shift lens, PC (perspective-control) lens
Shutterbrille f shutter glasses *(stereoscopy)*
Sicherheitsbeleuchtung f safelight illumination
Sicherheitsfilm m safety [base] film, [safety] acetate film, [cellulose] triacetate [safety] film
Sicherheitskasch m safety margin

Sicherheitskopie f 1. protection master *(motion-picture printing)*; 2. backup [copy]
Sicherheitstonband n protective track *(motion-picture production)*
Sicherheitsunterlage f safety base *(film support)*
Sicherungsdatei f backup file
Sicherungskopie f backup [copy]
sicherungskopieren to back up
Sicht f sight; view; visibility
~/perspektivische perspective view
sichtbar visible, visual; viewable
Sichtbarkeit f visibility, visibleness
Sichtbarkeitsalgorithmus m visible-surface algorithm *(computer graphics)*
~ m visible-surface algorithm
Sichtbarkeitsentscheid m visible-line determination; visible-surface determination *(computer graphics)*
Sichtbarkeitsverfahren n visibility operation *(computer graphics)*
Sichtbarkeits-Vorberechnung f visibility processing *(computer graphics)*
Sichtbarmachen n, **Sichtbarmachung** f visualization; visibility computation *(computer graphics)*
Sichtbereich m visibility range
Sichtfeld n field [of view], view field
~/endoskopisches endoscopic field
Sichtfläche f view surface; display surface
Sichtgerät n visual display unit (terminal), VDU, VDT; [image-]display device *(s.a. Monitor)*
Sichthülle f acetate sleeve [protector]
Sichtkontrolle f visual inspection
Sichtlinie f line of sight (vision), view (visual) line, sight (eye) line
Sichtprüfung f visual inspection
Sichtscanner m visual scanner
Sichtschirm m viewing screen, visual display *(s.a. Bildschirm, Monitor)*
Sichtsystem n**/industrielles** industrial machine vision, IMV
Sichtvektor m viewing vector
Sichtverbindung f s. Sichtlinie
Sichtvolumen n view[ing] volume *(computer graphics)*
Sichtweite f visual range; visibility
Sichtwinkel m view[ing] angle, angle of view (field), observation angle
Siderografie f s. Stichtiefdruck
Siebdruck m serigraphic printing, [silk]screen printing, retigraphy
~/künstlerischer serigraphy, creative silk-screen printmaking
Siebdruckfarbe f screen printing ink
Siebdruckgewebe n screen texture
Siebdruckpresse f screen press
Siebdruckrakel f squeegee
Siebdruckschablone f stencil
Siebenfarbendruck m seven-ink printing
Siebenlinser m seven-element lens

Siebenspur-Magnetton *m* seven-track magnetic sound
Siebschablone *f* stencil
Siebseite *f* wire side *(papermaking)*
Siebtest *m* screening study *(e.g. in radiography)*
Siebverfahren *n* screen color process
SI-Einheit *f* SI (International System) unit *(from Systéme International d' Unités, system of internatinal units of measurement)*
Siemensstern *m* Siemens star resolution chart
Sievert *n* sievert, Sv *(unit of X-ray exposure)*
SIF-Format *n* standard (source) input format, source intermediate [video] format, SIF
Sigma-Filter *n* sigma filter
Sigmaspiegel *m*, **Sigmoidoskop** *n* sigmoidoscope
Signal *n* signal
~/**abgetastetes** sampled signal
~/**akustisches** acoustic (sound) signal, audio (aural) signal
~/**amplitudenmoduliertes** amplitude-modulated signal
~/**analoges** analog (continuous-time) signal, analytic signal
~/**analytisches** *s.* ~/analoges
~/**artefaktfreies** artifact-free signal, true signal
~/**band[breiten]begrenztes** band[width]-limited signal
~/**bildgebendes** imaging signal
~/**binäres** binary signal
~/**codiertes** [en]coded signal
~/**decodiertes** decoded signal
~/**detektierbares** detectable signal
~/**determiniertes (deterministisches)** deterministic signal
~/**digitales** digital [electric] signal
~/**digitalisiertes** digitized signal
~/**diskretes** discrete (discontinuous) signal *(s.a.* ~/zeitdiskretes*)*
~/**dreidimensionales** three-dimensional signal
~/**eindimensionales** one-dimensional signal
~/**einkanaliges** single-channel signal
~/**elektrisches** electrical signal
~/**elektrochemisches** electrochemical signal
~/**elektromagnetisches** electromagnetic signal
~/**elektronisches** electronic[s] signal
~/**elektrooptisches** electro-optic signal
~/**farbcodiertes** color-coded signal
~/**fotoelektrisches** photoelectric signal
~/**frequenzmoduliertes** frequency-modulated signal
~/**gammakorrigiertes** gamma-corrected signal
~/**Gaußsches** Gaussian signal
~/**gefiltertes** filtered signal
~/**gerades** even signal
~/**hochaufgelöstes** high-definition signal
~/**hochfrequentes** high-frequency signal
~/**instationäres** *s.* ~/nichtstationäres
~/**isochrones** isochronous signal
~/**kausales** causal signal
~/**kohärentes** coherent signal
~/**komprimiertes** compressed signal
~/**kontinuierliches** continuous signal
~/**lichtelektrisches** photoelectric signal
~/**linear codiertes** linearly encoded signal
~/**linear frequenzmoduliertes** linear frequency-modulated signal, chirp signal *(radar)*
~/**mehrdimensionales** multidimensional signal
~/**moduliertes** modulated signal
~/**monofones** monophonic signal
~/**neuronales** neural signal
~/**nichtperiodisches** nonperiodic signal
~/**nichtstationäres** nonstationary signal
~/**niederfrequentes** low-frequency signal
~/**optisches** optical signal
~/**örtliches** spatial signal
~/**örtlich-zeitliches** spatiotemporal signal
~/**ortsdiskretes** discrete-space signal
~/**ortskontinuierliches** continuous-space signal
~/**ortsvariantes** spatially varying signal
~/**periodisches** periodic (repetitive) signal
~/**quantisiertes** quantized signal
~/**rekonstruiertes** reconstructed signal
~/**separierbares** separable signal
~/**sinusförmiges** sinusoidal (sine-wave) signal
~/**stationäres** stationary signal
~/**stochastisches** stochastic signal
~/**ternäres** ternary signal
~/**tieffrequentes** low-frequency signal
~/**ungerades** odd signal
~/**unharmonisches** nonharmonic signal
~/**unkomprimiertes** uncompressed signal
~/**unterabgetastetes** subsampled signal
~/**unverstärktes** unamplified signal
~/**verfälschtes** corrupted signal
~/**verrauschtes** noisy signal
~/**verwürfeltes [digitales]** scrambled signal
~/**visuelles** visual signal
~/**wertdiskretes** discrete-value signal
~/**wertkontinuierliches** continuous-value signal
~/**zeitdiskretes** discrete[-time] signal; sampled[-data] signal, scan signal
~/**zeitkontinuierliches** continuous-time signal, analog (analytic) signal
~/**zeitlich-räumliches** spatiotemporal signal
~/**zeitveränderliches** time-varying signal
~/**zusammengesetztes** composite signal
~/**zweidimensionales** two-dimensional signal

Signalabschwächung f signal attenuation (step-down)
Signalabtastung f signal sampling
Signalamplitude f signal amplitude
Signalanalyse f signal analysis
Signalanteil m signal portion
Signalauflösung f signal resolution
Signalausbreitung f signal propagation
Signalausfall m [signal] dropout
Signalauslesung f signal readout
Signalauswertung f signal diagnosis *(radar)*
Signalbandbreite f signal bandwidth
Signalbearbeitung f s. Signalverarbeitung
Signalbereich m signal range; signal region
Signalcode m signal code
Signalcodierer m signal encoder
Signalcodierung f signal [en]coding
Signaldämpfung f signal attenuation (step-down)
Signaldarstellung f signal representation
Signaldecodierung f signal decoding
Signaldegeneration f jitter
Signaldekorrelation f signal decorrelation
Signaldetektion f signal detection
Signaldetektor m signal detector
Signaldichte f signal density
Signaleinbruch m s. Signalausfall
Signaleingang m signal input
Signalelektrode f/**transparente [leitende]** transparent electrode *(camera tube)*
Signalelement n signal element
Signalenergie f signal energy
Signalentropie f source entropy, marginal (first-order) entropy *(information theory)*
Signalerfassung f signal acquisition
Signalerzeugung f signal generation
Signalfilterung f signal filtering
Signalflanke f signal edge
Signalfluss m signal flux
Signalfolge f signal sequence
Signalfrequenz f signal frequency
Signalfrequenzgang m signal frequency response
Signalgenerator m signal generator
Signalgewinnung f signal acquisition
Signalgleichförmigkeit f signal uniformity
Signalgradientenamplitude f signal gradient amplitude
Signalhelligkeit f signal brightness
Signalinhalt m signal content
Signalintensität f signal intensity
Signalinterpolation f signal interpolation
signalisieren to signal
Signalkomponente f signal component
Signalkompression f signal compression
Signalkontrast m signal contrast
Signalkontrolle f signal control
Signalkonvertierung f signal conversion
Signalkorrektur f signal correction
Signalladung f signal charge
Signalleistung f signal performance (power)

Signalmittelwert m signal average
Signalmodell n signal model
Signalmodellierung f signal modeling
Signalmodulation f signal modulation
Signalparameter m signal parameter
Signalpegel m signal level
Signalperiode f [signal] period
Signalplatte f signal plate, target *(camera tube)*
Signalprädiktion f signal prediction
Signalprozessor m/**digitaler** digital signal processor, DSP
Signalqualität f signal quality
Signalquantisierung f signal quantization
Signalquelle f signal source
Signalraum m signal space
Signal-Rausch-Abstand m s. Signal-Rausch-Verhältnis
Signalrauschen n signal-induced noise
Signal-Rausch-Verhältnis n signal-to-noise ratio, SNR; image signal-to-noise ratio, sensitivity
~/**gewichtetes** weighted SNR
Signalrechner m signal processor
Signalreflexion f signal reflection
Signalregeneration f signal regeneration
Signalrekonstruktion f signal reconstruction (recovery)
Signalrückgewinnung f signal recovery
signalschwach low-signal
Signalschwankung f jitter
Signalsequenz f signal sequence
Signalskalierung f signal scaling
Signalspannung f signal voltage
Signalspeicher m signal memory
Signalspeicherung f signal storage
Signalspektrum n signal spectrum
Signalsprung m signal step
Signalstärke f signal strength (intensity)
Signal-Störecho-Verhältnis n signal-to-clutter ratio *(radar)*
Signal-Stör-Verhältnis n s. Signal-Rausch-Verhältnis
Signalstrom m signal current
~/**lichtmodulierter** light-modulated signal current
Signalsynthese f signal synthesis
Signaltheorie f signal [processing] theory
Signaltransformation f signal transform (conversion)
Signaltreue f signal fidelity
Signalübertragung f signal transmission
Signalumformer m signal converter
Signalumsetzung f sampling
Signalunterdrückung f signal suppression
Signalvarianz f signal variance
Signalvariation f signal variation
Signalvektor m signal vector
Signalverarbeitung f signal processing
~/**adaptive** adaptive signal processing
~/**akustooptische** acousto-optic signal processing
~/**bewegungsadaptive** motion-adaptive signal processing

~/**biomedizinische** biomedical signal processing
~/**digitale** digital signal processing, DSP
~/**mehrdimensionale** multidimensional signal processing
~/**modellbasierte** model-based signal processing
~/**optische** optical signal processing
~/**statistische** statistical signal processing
~/**volldigitale** all-signal signal processing
~/**zeitdiskrete (zeitliche)** discrete-time signal processing
Signalverarbeitungskette f signal-processing chain
Signalverarbeitungstechnik f 1. signal processing technology; 2. signal processing technique
Signalverfälschung f signal aliasing; signal corruption
Signalverlust m signal loss, loss of signal
~/**artefaktbedingter** artifactual signal loss
Signalverschlechterung f signal degradation
Signalverschlüsselung f signal encryption
Signalverstärker m signal amplifier; repeater *(local area network)*
Signalverstärkung f signal amplification; [signal] gain
Signalverteilung f signal distribution
Signalverwürfelung f signal scrambling; signal shuffling
Signalverzerrung f signal distortion
Signalvorverarbeitung f signal preprocessing
Signalvorverzerrung f preemphasis *(frequency modulation)*
Signalwandler m [signal] transducer
Signalwandlung f signal conversion; signal transduction
Signalweg m signal path
Signalwelle f object (original) wave, object (subject) beam *(holography)*
Signalwellenlänge f signal wavelength
Signalwert m signal value (response)
Signalwiedergabe f signal reproduction
Signalzerlegung f signal decomposition
Signatur f 1. signature; 2. nick *(of a type body)*; 3. s. Kartenzeichen
~/**biometrische** biometric[al] signature
~/**digitale (elektronische)** digital signature
~/**fraktale** fractal signature
~/**optische** optical signature
~/**parametrische** parametric signature
~/**spektrale** spectral signature
Signet n signet; caption *(s.a. Logo)*
Sikkativ n siccative, drier
Silbenzeichen n logotype
Silber n silver
~/**bildaufbauendes** image[-forming] silver
~/**elementares** elemental (elementary) silver
~/**fotolytisches** photolytic silver
~/**kolloid[al]es** colloidal silver
~/**metallisches** metallic silver

~/**reduziertes** reduced silver
Silberaggregat n silver aggregate (cluster)
Silberatom n silver atom
Silberbild n [photographic] silver image, silver-based image, silver halide image; silver print
Silberbildentstehung f silver image formation
Silberbildung f silver formation
Silberbleichbad n silver bleach
Silberbleichung f silver bleaching [stage]
Silberbromid n silver bromide
Silberbromidemulsion f silver bromide emulsion
Silberbromidkristall m silver bromide crystal
Silberbromidpapier n bromide paper
Silberchlorid n silver chloride
Silberchloridbromidpapier n chlorobromide paper
Silberchloridemulsion f silver chloride emulsion, AgCl emulsion
Silberchloridpapier n [silver] chloride paper
Silbercluster m silver[-atom] cluster
Silberdichte f silver density
Silberemulsion f silver emulsion
Silberentwicklung f silver development
Silberfaden m silver [metal] filament, filamentary silver particle
Silberfarbbleichverfahren n [silver-]dye-bleach process, silver dye bleach, dye bleach (destruction)
Silberfilm m s. Silberhalogenidfilm
Silberfilmschicht f silver film layer
Silberfotografie f 1. silver halide photography; 2. silver [halide-based] photograph
silberfotografisch silver[-halide] photographic
silberfrei non-silver
Silbergehalt m silver content
Silbergelatine f silver gelatin, gelatin silver
Silbergelatineabzug m silver gelatin print, gelatin silver print
Silberglanz m silver glance, argentite; silver sulfide
Silberhalogenid n silver halide, AgX
Silberhalogenidausfällung f silver halide precipitation
Silberhalogeniddruckplatte f silver-halide-based [digital] printing plate
Silberhalogenidemulsion f silver-halide [photographic] emulsion, AgX emulsion
Silberhalogenidentwickler m silver halide developer
Silberhalogenid-Farbfotografie f 1. silver halide color photography; 2. silver halide color photograph
Silberhalogenidfilm m silver halide photographic film, silver halide[-based] film, silver-based film, AgX film
Silberhalogenidfotografie f s. Silberfotografie

Silberhalogenidgitter *n* silver halide lattice
Silberhalogenidkorn *n* silver-halide grain
Silberhalogenidkristall *m* silver halide crystal
Silberhalogenidlösungsmittel *n* silver halide solvent
Silberhalogenidmikrofilm *m* silver halide microfilm
Silberhalogenidmikrokristall *m* silver halide microcrystal
Silberhalogenidsalz *n* silver-halide salt
Silberhalogenid-Sofortbildfilm *m* silver halide instant film
Silberhalogenidverfahren *n* silver halide process
Silberiodchloridemulsion *f* silver iodochloride emulsion
Silberiodid *n* silver iodide
Silberiodidemulsion *f* silver iodide emulsion
Silberion *n* silver ion
Silberionenkonzentration *f* silver ion concentration, pAg
Silberkeim *m* silver nucleus
Silberkeimtheorie *f* nucleation-and-growth model
Silberkomplex *m* silver complex
Silberkorn *n* silver grain
Silberkristall *m* silver crystal
Silberleinwand *f s.* Silberwand
Silberlösungsmittel *n* silver solvent
Silberlösungsvermittler *m* silver-solubilizing agent
Silbernegativ *n* silver negative [image]
Silberniederschlag *m* silver deposit
Silbernitrat *n* silver nitrate
Silbernitratlösung *f* silver nitrate solution
Silbernitratpapier *n* silver nitrate paper
Silberoxid *n* silver oxide
Silberplatte *f* silver plate
Silberrhodanid *n s.* Silberthiocyanat
Silberrückgewinnung *f* silver recovery (reclamation)
~/elektrolytische electrolytic silver recovery
Silbersalz *n* silver salt *(s.a.* Silberhalogenid*)*
Silbersalzdiffusion *f* silver-salt diffusion
Silbersalzdiffusionsverfahren *n* silver [salt] diffusion transfer process, diffusion transfer copying system, diffusion transfer photographic process
Silbersalzkristall *m* silver salt crystal
Silberschicht *f* silver layer
Silberschwärzung *f* silver density
Silberselenid *n* silver selenide
Silberspiegel *m* silver mirror
Silberstruktur *f*/**fadenförmige** *s.* Silberfaden
Silbersulfid *n* silver sulfide
Silberthiocyanat *n* silver thiocyanate, silver rhodanate (rhodanide)
Silberthiosulfat *n* argentothiosulfate
Silberverbindung *f* silver compound

Silberverstärker *m* silver intensifier
Silberwand *f* silver (specular) screen
Silhouette *f* silhouette [image]; shadow image (picture)
Silhouettentrickfilm *m* silhouette animation
Silicagel *n* silica gel
Silicatglas *n* silicate glass
Silicium *n*/**amorphes** amorphous silicon
~/einkristallines (monokristallines) monocrystalline silicon, mono-Si
~/polykristallines polycrystalline silicon, polysilicon, poly-Si
Silicium-Bildsensor *m* silicon imaging sensor
Siliciumchip *m* silicon chip
Siliciumdiode *f* silicon diode
Siliciumfotodiode *f* silicon photodiode, SPD
Siliciumgleichrichter *m* silicon-controlled rectifier, SCR
Siliciumhalbleiter *m* silicon semiconductor
Siliciumkristall *m* silicon crystal
Siliciumscheibe *f* silicon wafer
Siliciumsensor *m* silicon detector
Siliciumwafer *m* silicon wafer
Siliciumzelle *f* silicon [photoconductive] cell, silicon photoelectric cell
Silikonkautschuk *m* silicon rubber
Simulation *f* simulation
~/computergestützte computer-assisted simulation
~/dynamische dynamic simulation
~/grafisch-dynamische dynamic graphic simulation
~/grafisch-dynamische dynamic-graphic simulation
~/numerische numerical simulation
~/visuelle visual simulation
Simulationsalgorithmus *m* simulation algorithm
Simulationsbildschirm *m* simulation display
Simulationsergebnis *n* simulation result
Simulationsmodell *n* simulation model
Simulationsprogramm *n* simulation program
Simulationstechnologie *f* simulation technology
Simulator *m* simulator
~[en]krankheit *f* simulator sickness *(subjective discomfort)*
simulieren to simulate; to mimic
Simultanauslösung *f* simultaneous shutter release
Simultanbelichtung *f* simultaneous exposure
Simultankalibrierung *f s.* Selbstkalibrierung
Simultankontrast *m* simultaneous contrast, lateral adaptation *(vision)*
Simultanschichtkassette *f* multisection cassette *(X-ray technology)*

Simultansehen *n* binocular (two-eyed) vision, binocular viewing
Simultanspektrometer *n* simultaneous (multichannel) spectrometer
sinc-Funktion *f* sinc function *(digital signal processing)*
Singulettzustand *m* singlet state
Sinneseindruck *m*, **Sinnesempfindung** *f* sense impression, sensation
Sinnesleistung *f* sensory performance
Sinnesorgan *n* sense organ, sensory system, receptor
Sinnesphysiologie *f* sensory physiology
Sinnespsychologie *f* sensory psychology
Sinnesreiz *m* sensory stimulus
Sinneswahrnehmung *f* sense (sensory) perception, perceptual sensation
Sinogramm *n* sinogram *(projection data set in emission tomography)*
Sinusbedingung *f* [/**Abbesche**] [Abbe] sine condition *(optics)*
sinusförmig sinusoidal
Sinusfunktion *f* sine (sinusoidal) function, sinusoid
Sinusgitter *n* sinusoidal [diffraction] grating, sine-wave grating
Sinuskurve *f* sine curve (wave) sinusoid
Sinusphasenfilter *n* sine-phase filter
Sinusschwingung *f* sinusoidal oscillation (vibration)
Sinustransformation *f* sinusoidal transform, sine transform[ation] *(image coding)*
~/**diskrete** discrete sine transform[ation], discrete sinusoidal transform[ation]
Sinuswelle *f* sine (sinusoidal) wave
Sinuswellenamplitude *f* sine-wave amplitude
Skala *f* 1. scale; interval scale; nominal scale; ratio scale; 2. *s.* Grauskala; 3. *s.* Skale
skalar scalar
Skalar *m* scalar *(mathematics)*
Skalarfeld *n* scalar field
Skalarprodukt *n* scalar (dot) product
Skalarquantisierer *m* scalar quantizer
Skale *f* scale, rule *(graduation)*
Skalen[an]druck *m* progressive proof, progressives, progs, proofing scale
Skalenraum *m* scale space
Skalenraumfilterung *f* scale-space filtering
skalierbar scalable
Skalierbarkeit *f* scalability
~/**inhaltsbasierte** content-based scalability
~/**objektbasierte** object-based scalability
~/**objektbasierte zeitliche** object-based temporal scalability, OTS
~/**räumliche** spatial scalability
~/**zeitliche** temporal scalability
skalieren to scale; to resize
Skalierung *f* scaling, zooming *(geometric transformation)*
~/**isotrope** isotropic scaling
~/**lineare** linear scaling
~/**multiplikative** multiplicative scaling
~/**psychophysikalische** psychophysical scaling *(image quality metrics)*
~/**räumliche** spatial scaling
Skalierungsfaktor *m* scaling factor
Skalierungsfilter *n s.* Skalierungsoperator
Skalierungsfunktion *f* scaling function
Skalierungskoeffizient *m* scaling (approximation) coefficient
Skalierungskonstante *f* scaling constant
Skalierungsmatrix *f* scaling matrix
Skalierungsoperator *m* scaling operator
Skalierungstransformation *f* scaling transformation
Skalierungsvektor *m* scaling vector
Skelett *n*/**morphologisches** morphological skeleton
skelettieren to skeletonize
Skelettierung *f* skeletonization, thinning *(binary image processing)*
~/**binäre** binary [image] skeletonization
~/**flexible** flexible skeletonization
~/**lineare** linear skeletonization
Skelettierungsalgorithmus *m* skeletonization algorithm
Skelettierungsoperator *m* skeletonization operator
Skelettierungsverfahren *n* skeletonization technique
Skelettlinie *f* skeleton line
Skelettmodell *n* wire frame [model], net model *(computer graphics)*
Skelettschwarz *n* skeleton black *(reprography)*
Skelettszintigrafie *f* bone scintigraphy
Skeletttransformation *f* skeleton transform[ation]
Skiaskop *n s.* Retinoskop
Skizze *f* [rough] sketch, scribble, scamp
skizzieren to sketch
Sklera *f* sclera, sclerotic [coat], white of the eye
Skorotron *n* scorotron *(electrophotography)*
Skotom *n* scotoma *(disorder of vision)*
skotopisch scotopic
Skriptgirl *n* script girl (supervisor); continuity girl *(filming)*
Skylightfilter *n* skylight filter
Slanttransformation *f* slant transform
Slave-Auslöser *m* slave cell *(flash accessory)*
Slave-Blitzgerät *n* slave [flash] unit
Slave-Maschine *f s.* Zuspielrecorder
Slevogt-Kamera *f*, **Slevogt-System** *n* flat-field camera *(astronomical imaging)*
SLR-Kamera *f s.* Spiegelreflexkamera/einäugige
SMPTE[/EBU]-Code *m* SMPTE time code *(from Society of Motion Picture and Television Engineers)*
Snellius-Brechungsgesetz *n* Snell's law [of refraction], Snell['s] refraction law

SNR-Codierung f/**skalierbare** scalable SNR encoding
S-NRZ-Code m scrambling non return zero code, S-NRZ code
Sobel-Filter n s. Sobel-Operator
Sobel-Filterung f Sobel operation
Sobel-Kantendetektor m, **Sobel-Maske** f s. Sobel-Operator
Sobel-Operator m Sobel [gradient] operator, Sobel [gradient] edge detector, Sobel kernel, Sobel filter (edge detection) mask
Sobel-Transformation f Sobel transform
Soda f(n) soda, sodium carbonate *developer improver)*
Soffitte[nlampe] f tubular lamp
Sofortbild n instant [film] picture, instant image (photograph)
Sofortbildabzug m instant photographic print
Sofortbild-Dia[positiv] n instant transparency (slide)
~[positiv]film m instant slide film
Sofortbildendoskopie f instant endoscopy
Sofortbild-Farbdiafilm m instant color transparency film
Sofortbild-Farbdiapositiv n instant color slide
Sofortbild-Farbfilm m instant color film
Sofortbild-Farbfotografie f instant color photography
Sofortbildfilm m instant[-picture] film, instant-imaging film
Sofortbildfotografie f instant[-picture] photography, instantaneous photography
Sofortbildholografie f real-time holography
Sofortbildkamera f instant[-picture] camera
Sofortbild-Kompaktkamera f compact instant camera
Sofortbild-Makrofotografie f instant photomacrography
Sofortbildmaterial n instant-picture material
Sofortbild-Papierfilm m instant-print color film, instant color print film
Sofortbildsystem n instant-image system
Sofortbildverfahren n instant-picture process, instant-print process
Sofortdiafilm m instant slide film
Sofortdiapositiv n autoprocess transparency
Sofortfoto n s. Sofortbild
Softcopy f soft copy
soften to soften
Softfokusobjektiv n, **Softlinse** f soft-focus lens
Softproof m soft [digital] proof *(printing)*
Software f software
~/bildverarbeitende image-processing software, [computer] imaging software

~/frei herunterladbare (verfügbare) freeware
~/grafische graphics[-based] software
~/raubkopierte pirated (bootleg) software
Softwarepaket n software package
Softwareprogramm n software program
Softwareprogrammierer m software programmer
Softwaretreiber m software driver
Solarisation f, **Solarisationseffekt** m solarization [effect], black sun effect
Solarisationsfilter n solarizing filter
solarisieren to solarize
Solarmikroskop n solar microscope
Solarstrahlung f solar radiation
Solarzelle f solar (silicon photovoltaic) cell
Solenoid n solenoid [coil] *(magnetic resonance imaging)*
Soller-Blende f, **Soller-Spalt** m s. Kollimator
Sombrerofilter n sombrero filter, Mexican hat filter (kernel), Laplacian-of-Gaussian [operator], LoG filter (operator), Marr-Hildreth operator *(edge detection)*
Sonarautofokus m sonar autofocus
Sonarbild n sonar image; underwater sonar image
Sonarecho n sonar backscatter
Sonargerät n sonar (sound navigation and ranging) device
Sonarimpuls m sonar pulse
Sonarsensor m sonar sensor
Sonartechnik f sonar technology
Sonde f probe
Sondenbewegungsartefakt n probe motion artifact *(sonography)*
Sondenmikroskopie f probe microscopy
Sondenspitze f [scanning] probe tip *(electron microscope)*
Sonderdruckverfahren n specialty printing process
Sonderfarbe f nonprocess color ink *(printing)*
Sonderfilter n s. Spezialfilter
Sonderglas n specialized glass
Sonderobjektiv n specialty lens, special[-purpose] lens
Sonderpapier n special[ty] paper, specially treated paper; specialized photographic paper
Sonderzeichen n dingbat; flag
Sonnenbeobachtung f [daytime] solar observation, sun viewing
Sonnenblende f sunshade, lens hood (shade)
Sonneneinstrahlung f solar irradiance
Sonnenfilter n solar filter
Sonnenfotografie f solar photography
Sonnenlicht n sunlight
~/sichtbares visible sunlight
Sonnenspektrum n solar spectrum
Sonnenstrahlung f solar radiation
Sonnenteleskop n solar telescope
Sonnenwinkel m solar (sun) angle

Sonograf *m* sonograph
Sonografie *f* [ultra]sonography, ultrasonic (sonographic) imaging, ultrasound [imaging technique], echography *(s.a.* Ultraschalluntersuchung*)*
~/**eindimensionale** A-mode (amplitude-mode) ultrasound scanning, A-mode (A-scan) process
~/**zweidimensionale** [ultrasound] B-mode imaging, B-mode ultrasound [scanning], B-scan [pulse echo mode of] imaging
Sonografiegerät *n* ultrasonic sensing device; ultrasonic imager (image recorder); ultrasound unit (machine)
sonografisch [ultra]sonographic
Sonogramm *n* sonogram, ultrasound (ultrasonic) image
Sonoholografie *f* sonoholography, ultrasound holography
Sonohologramm *n* sonohologram, ultrasound hologram
sonolumineszent sonoluminescent
Sonolumineszenz *f* sonoluminescence
Sonolumineszenzomografie *f* sonoluminescent tomography, SLT
Sonometer *n* sonometer
Sonotomografie *f s.* Ultraschalltomografie
Sortieralgorithmus *m* sort algorithm
Sortierproblem *n* sorting problem
Soundkarte *f* sound board (card), audio card (board) *(computer)*
Soundtrack *m* 1. film[-based] sound track, [motion-picture] sound track; 2. *s.* Filmmusik
Spalierdiagramm *n* trellis diagram
Spalt *m* slit
Spaltbild *n* [/**optisches**] slit image
Spaltblende *f* slit aperture
Spaltbreite *f* slit (gap) width
~/**endliche** finite slit width
Spalte *f* column
Spaltenbreite *f* column width, width of column *(typography)*
Spaltenmatrix *f* column matrix
Spaltenumbruch *m* column break
Spaltenvektor *m* column vector
spaltenweise columnwise *(e.g. image filtering)*
Spaltenzwischenraum *m* alley
Spaltfunktion *f* sinc function *(digital signal processing)*
Spaltkamera *f* slit camera *(high-speed photography)*
Spaltkollimator *m* slit collimator
Spaltlampe *f* slit lamp
Spaltlänge *f* gap length
Spaltmaske *f* sinc filter
Spaltöffnung *f* slit opening
Spaltspektrograf *m* slit spectrograph
Spalttiefe *f* gap depth
Spalttiefpass *m*, **Spalttiefpassfilter** *n* box (uniform) filter
Spaltverlust *m* gap loss

Spannungsanalyse *f* [/**fotoelastische**] [photoelastic] stress analysis
Spannungsbandbreite *f* voltage (optical) bandwidth *(photodetector)*
Spannungsdoppelbrechung *f* stress (mechanical) birefringence
Spannungsfigur *f* strain pattern
Spannungsimpuls *m* voltage pulse
Spannungskonstanthalter *m* voltage stabilizer
Spannungskontrast *m* 1. voltage contrast *(electron microscopy)*; 2. strain contrast *(electron microscopy)*
Spannungsmuster *n* stress pattern
Spannungsoptik *f* photoelastics, photoelasticity
spannungsoptisch photoelasticity
Spannungssignal *n* voltage signal
Spannungsspitze *f* voltage spike
Spannungsstabilisator *m* voltage stabilizer (regulator)
Spannungsteiler *m* voltage divider; potentiometer, pot
Spannverschluss *m* preset shutter
Spannvorrichtung *f* cocking device *(e.g. of a mechanical shutter)*
Spartenkabelkanal *m* specialized interest cable channel
Spartenkanal *m* special-interest channel *(television)*
Spartransformator *m* autotransformer
Spatialfilter *n s.* Raumfilter
Spatienkeil *m* justification wedge; [wedged] spaceband, justifying spacer
spatiieren *s.* spationieren
spationieren 1. to justify *(typesetting)*; 2. *s.* sperren
Spationierung *f* justification
Speckle-Dekorrelation *f* speckle decorrelation
Speckle-Effekt *m* speckle phenomenon
Speckle-Filter *n* speckle filter
Speckle-Filterung *f* speckle filtering
Speckle-Fotografie *f* speckle photography
Speckle-Holografie *f* speckle holography
Speckle-Interferogramm *n* speckle interferogram
Speckle-Interferometer *n* speckle interferometer
Speckle-Interferometrie *f*/**elektronische** electronic speckle pattern interferometry, ESPI
speckleinterferometrisch speckle-interferometric
Speckle-Messtechnik *f* speckle metrology
Speckle-Muster *n* speckle pattern *(e.g. in ultrasound images)*
Speckle-Rauschen *n* speckle noise
Speckle-Störung *f* speckle interference [artifact], acoustic speckle *(radar, sonography)*
SPECT *f* SPECT [imaging], single-photon emission-computed tomography *(s.a.* Einzelphotonen-Emissionstomografie*)*

SPECT-Bild

SPECT-Bild *n* SPECT image
SPECT-Gerät *n* [clinical] SPECT system
SPECT-Untersuchung *f* SPECT study (acquisition), SPECT procedure
Speicher *m* memory [device], storage [device], store; storage facility
~/**assoziativer** associative memory (storage), content-adressable memory, CAM
~/**autoassoziativer** auto-associative memory
~/**bidirektionaler assoziativer** bidirectional associative memory, BAM
~/**dauerhafter** resident storage
~/**digitaler** digital memory
~/**externer** external [computer] memory, auxiliary storage
~/**flüchtiger** volatile memory (storage)
~/**fotografischer** photographic storage
~/**gemeinsam genutzter** shared memory
~/**heteroassoziativer** hetero-associative memory
~/**ikonischer** iconic memory
~/**inhaltadressierter** content-addressable memory, CAM, associative memory (storage)
~/**interner** internal memory
~/**löschbarer** erasable memory
~/**magnetooptischer** magneto-optical storage, MO memory
~/**mikrografischer** micrographic storage
~/**nichtflüchtiger** nonvolatile (involatile) memory
~/**optischer** optical memory
~/**prozessübergreifender** shared memory
~/**schneller** fast memory
~/**sequientieller** sequential storage
~/**temporärer (transienter)** transient storage
~/**virtueller** virtual memory (storage), swap file
Speicherabfrage *f s.* Speicherlesen
Speicherabtaster *m s.* Speicherröhrenabtaster
Speicheradresse *f* memory address
Speicheradressierung *f* memory addressing
Speicherbandbreite *f* memory (storage) bandwidth
speicherbar storable
Speicherbaustein *m* [computer] memory chip
Speicherbedarf *m* storage requirement[s], storage demand
Speicherbelegung *f* memory occupation
Speicherbild *n* hologram, holograph[ic image]
Speicherbildröhre *f* [/**bistabile**] direct-view storage tube, DVST
Speicherbildschirm *m* storage phosphor [screen], storage monitor (tube display), long-persistence phosphor display screen
Speicherbit *n* memory (storage) bit

Speicherblock *m* memory block, block of memory
Speicherbus *m* memory bus
Speicherchip *m* [computer] memory chip
Speicherdatei *f* memory file
Speicherdichte *f* [data] storage density
Speicherdiskette *f* storage disk
Speichererweiterung *f* memory expansion
Speicherfähigkeit *f* storage capability
Speicherformat *n* storage format
speicherfrei memoriless
Speichergerät *n* storage device
Speichergitter *n* storage mesh
Speicherinhalt *m* memory content
Speicherkapazität *f* storage (memory) capacity; storage power
Speicherkarte *f* [data] storage card, memory [storage] card
Speicherkartencamcorder *m* disk-based camcorder
Speicherkarteneinschub *m s.* Speicherkartenschlitz
Speicherkartenlaufwerk *n* disk drive
Speicherkartenschlitz *m* [memory] card slot, memory stick slot
Speicherkondensator *m* storage capacitor
Speicherleistung *f* memory performance
Speicherlesen *n* reading from memory, memory readout process
Speicherleuchtstoff *m* storage (photostimulable) phosphor
Speichermatrix *f* memory (core) matrix
Speichermedium *n* storage (memory) medium
~/**digitales** digital storage medium
~/**hochauflösendes** high-resolution storage medium
~/**optisches** optical [storage] medium
Speichermodul *n* memory module
speichern to store, to save *(e.g. image data)*
Speicherorganisation *f* memory organization; storage architecture
Speicheroszilloskop *n* storage oscilloscope
Speicherphosphor *m s.* Speicherleuchtstoff
Speicherplatine *f s.* Speicherplatte
Speicherplatte *f* 1. storage disk; 2. storage target (plate) *(camera tube)*
~/**optische** optical disk
~/**wiederbeschreibbare optische** rewritable optical disk, ROD
Speicherplatz *m* 1. storage (memory) space; 2. *s.* Speicherstelle
Speicherplatzbedarf *m* storage requirement[s], storage demand
Speicherraum *m s.* Speicherplatz 1.
Speicherregister *n* storage register *(CCD array)*
Speicherröhre *f* [television] storage tube
Speicherröhrenabtaster *m* cathode-ray tube scanner, CRT-based [film] recorder

Speicher-Rollenwechsler *m* flying splice mechanism *(web-fed press)*
Speicherschicht *f* 1. [storage] phosphor screen, phosphor coating *(cathode-ray tube)*; 2. *s.* Speicherungsschicht
Speicherschnittstelle *f* memory interface
Speicherschreiben *n* 1. writing to memory; 2. teach-in *(neuroinformatics)*
Speicherstelle *f* storage site; memory (storage) location
Speichersteuerung *f* memory control
Speichersystem *n* memory system
Speichertabelle *f* lookup table [memory], LUT, index map; video lookup table
Speichertaste *f* storage key
Speichertechnik *f* storage (memory) technology
Speichertiefe *f* storage depth
Speicherung *f* [memory] storage
~/**analoge** analog storage
~/**digitale** digital storage
~/**elektronische** electronic storage
~/**elektrostatische** electrostatic storage
~/**gestreute** hashing *(data processing)*
~/**hierarchische** hierarchical storage
~/**magnetische** magnetic storage
~/**optische** optical storage
Speicherungsebene *f*, **Speicherungsschicht** *f* storage layer *(hypermedia system)*
Speicherverwaltung *f* memory management
Speichervolumen *n* storage capacity
Speicherzelle *f* memory (storage) cell
Speicherzugriff *m* memory access
~/**direkter** direct memory access, DMA
Speiseeinheit *f* feed unit, feedhorn *(satellite antenna)*
Speiseröhrenspiegel *m* esophagoscope
Speisesystem *n s.* Speiseeinheit
spektral spectral
Spektralanalysator *m* spectrum analyzer
Spektralanalyse *f* spectrum (spectral) analysis
Spektralantwort *f* spectral response
Spektralapparat *m* spectral apparatus
Spektralband *n*, **Spektralbande** *f* spectral band
Spektralbereich *m* spectral region; spectral range
~/**infraroter** infrared portion of the spectrum
~/**sichtbarer** visible spectral region, visible portion of the spectrum
Spektralbild *n* spectral (spectrum) image
Spektraldarstellung *f* spectral representation
Spektraldichte *f* spectral density
Spektraldichtekurve *f* spectral density curve
Spektralempfindlichkeit *f* spectral sensitivity (responsivity), spectral response, color sensitivity
Spektralfarbe *f* spectral (spectrum) color

Spektralfarbenfotografie *f* spectral color photography
Spektralfarbenzug *m* spectral (spectrum) locus, color locus, locus of spectral colors
Spektralfehler *m* spectral error
Spektralfilter *n* spectral filter
Spektralfilterung *f* spectral filtering
Spektralfotometer *n* spectrophotometer
~/**registrierendes** recording spectrophotometer
Spektralfotometrie *f* spectrophotometry
~/**fotografische** photographic spectrophotometry
spektralfotometrisch spectrophotometric[al]
Spektralfunktion *f* spectral [response] function, frequency function
Spektralgebiet *n* spectral region
Spektralhauptfarbe *f* primary [color], basis (basic) color
Spektralkanal *m* spectral channel
Spektralkoeffizient *m* spectral coefficient
Spektralkomponente *f* spectral component
Spektrallampe *f* spectral (spectroscopic) lamp
Spektrallicht *n* spectral light
Spektrallinie *f* spectral line
~/**astigmatische** astigmatic spectral line
~/**umgekehrte** inverted spectral line
Spektrallinienanalyse *f* spectral line analysis
Spektrallinienverteilung *f* spectral line distribution
Spektralmessung *f* spectral measurement
Spektralplatte *f* spectral plate
Spektralradiometer *n* spectroradiometer
Spektralradiometrie *f* spectroradiometry
spektralradiometrisch spectroradiometric
Spektralreflexion *f* spectral reflection
Spektralschätzung *f* estimation of spectrum
Spektralsensibilisator *m* spectral sensitizer
Spektraltransformation *f* spectral transform
Spektralverfahren *n* RGB color matching method *(color measurement)*
Spektralverhalten *n* spectral response
Spektralverschiebung *f* spectral (spectrum) shift
Spektralverteilung *f* spectral [power] distribution, spectral energy distribution
Spektralverteilungskurve *f* spectral energy distribution curve (chart), spectral curve
Spektralwertfunktion *f*, **Spektralwertkurve** *f* color-matching function, color-mixture curve (function)
Spektralzerlegung *f* spectral separation
Spektralzusammensetzung *f* spectral composition (content) *(e.g. of light)*
Spektrofluorometer *n* spectrofluorometer, spectrofluorimeter

Spektrofluorometrie f spectrofluorometry
spektrofluorometrisch spectrofluorometric
Spektrofotografie f spectrophotography
Spektrofotometrie f s. Spektralfotometrie
Spektrograf m spectrograph
~/**abbildender** imaging spectrograph
~/**faserabbildender** fiber spectrograph
Spektrografie f spectrography
spektrografisch spectrographic
Spektrogramm n spectrogram
Spektroheliograf m spectroheliograph
Spektroheliografie f spectroheliography
Spektroheliogramm n spectroheliogram
Spektrohelioskop n 1. spectrohelioscope; 2. s. Spektroheliograf
Spektrometer n spectrometer
~/**abbildendes** imaging spectrometer
~/**faseroptisches** fiber-optic spectrometer
Spektrometrie f spectrometry
spektrometrisch spectrometric
Spektromikroskopie f spectromicroscopy
Spektroradiometrie f spectroradiometry
Spektrosensitogramm n spectrosensitogram
Spektroskop n spectroscope, spectroscopic (dispersing) instrument
Spektroskopie f spectroscopy
~/**dynamische** dynamic spectroscopy
~/**elektronische** electronic spectroscopy
~/**nichtlineare** nonlinear spectroscopy
~/**optische** optical spectroscopy
~/**ultraschnelle** ultrafast spectroscopy
~/**zeitaufgelöste** time-resolved spectroscopy, TRS
Spektroskopiker m spectroscopist
spektroskopisch spectroscopic
Spektrum n spectrum
~/**asymmetrisches** asymmetric[al] spectrum
~/**charakteristisches** 1. characteristic spectrum; 2. characteristic X-ray lines
~/**diskontinuierliches** discontinuous (noncontinuous) spectrum
~/**diskretes** discrete (line) spectrum, discontinuous spectrum
~/**elektromagnetisches** electromagnetic [wave] spectrum, EM spectrum
~/**energiegleiches** equal-energy spectrum
~ **erster Ordnung** first-order spectrum
~/**frequenzkontinuierliches** continuous-frequency spectrum
~/**gaußförmiges** Gaussian spectrum
~/**infrarotnahes** near-infrared spectrum
~/**kontinuierliches** continuous spectrum
~ **nullter Ordnung** zero[th]-order spectrum
~/**optisches** optical spectrum
~/**periodisches** periodic spectrum
~/**raumzeitliches** spatiotemporal (three-dimensional) spectrum
~/**sekundäres** secondary spectrum; residual chromatic aberration
~/**sichtbares** visible [light] spectrum, visual (white light) spectrum
~/**solares** solar spectrum
~/**tertiäres** tertiary spectrum
~/**unsichtbares** invisible spectrum
Spektrumanalysator m spectrum analyzer
Spekulum n speculum
Sperrbereich m stop (rejection) band (of a filter)
sperren to letter space (layout)
Sperrfilter n 1. barrier filter (ultraviolet fluorescence photography); 2. band-stop (band-reject) filter
Sperrfrequenz f stop frequency
Sperrgreifer m pilot (register) pin
Sperr-Justier-Greifer m pin-registering mechanism
Sperrschicht f [internal] barrier layer, boundary layer (e.g. of a semiconductor photocell)
Sperrschicht-Fotoeffekt m photovoltaic effect
Sperrschicht-Fotoelement n, **Sperrschicht[foto]zelle** f photovoltaic (barrier-layer) cell, semiconductor cell
Sperrspannung f bias voltage, reverse bias (voltage) (photodiode)
Sperrstrom m bias current (s.a. Sättigungssperrstrom)
Sperrvorspannung f s. Sperrspannung
Spezialbrille f special spectacles (e.g. in stereoscopy)
Spezialeffekt m special effect, FX (cinema)
~/**digitaler** digital (computer) special effect, computer-generated [special] effect
~/**mechanischer** physical effect
~/**optischer** optical [effect], special visual effect, montage
Spezialeffektgenerator m special-effects generator, [postproduction] effects generator
Spezialentwickler m special[-formula] developer, special-purpose developer
Spezialfilm m special[-purpose] film
Spezialfilter n special[ty] filter, special-purpose filter
Spezialfotografie f special-purpose photography, specialty photography
Spezialglas n specialized glass
Spezialkamera f special[-purpose] camera, specialized camera
Speziallabor n specially equipped lab
Spezialmonitor m special-purpose monitor
Spezialobjektiv n specialty lens, special[-purpose] lens
Spezialoptik f special optics
Spezialpapier n special[ty] paper, specially treated paper; specialized photographic paper
Spezialvergrößerer m specialty-model enlarger
sphärisch spherical
Sphärometer n spherometer

Spiegel *m* 1. mirror, looking glass; 2. pastedown, end sheet *(outer leaf of an endpaper)*
~/**asphärischer** aspheric[al] mirror
~/**astronomischer** astronomical mirror
~/**Cassegrainscher** Cassegrain mirror [system]
~/**dichroitischer** dichroi[ti]c mirror, cold mirror
~/**dielektrischer** dielectric mirror
~/**ebener** flat mirror, plane (planar) mirror
~/**elliptischer** elliptical mirror
~/**farbzerlegender** *s.* ~/dichroitischer
~/**gekrümmter** curved mirror
~/**halbdurchlässiger** half-reflecting mirror, semitransparent (semireflecting) mirror, semisilvered (half-silvered) mirror
~/**hyperbolischer** hyperbolic mirror
~/**komafreier** coma-free mirror
~/**mehrschichtvergüteter** multilayer-coated mirror
~/**oberflächenversilberter** surface-silvered mirror; front-surface[d] mirror, first-surface[d] mirror
~/**optischer** optical mirror
~/**perfekter** perfect mirror
~/**phasenkonjugierender** phase-conjugating mirror
~/**sphärischer** spherical mirror
~/**strahl[en]teilender** beam-splitting mirror
~/**teildurchlässiger** partially transmitting (silvered) mirror, partially reflecting (reflective) mirror
~/**virtueller** virtual mirror
Spiegelanordnung *f* mirror arrangement
Spiegelapertur *f* mirror aperture
Spiegelausrichtung *f* mirror alignment
Spiegelbild *n* mirror[ed] image, reflex
spiegelbildlich mirror-image symmetrical, reverse
Spiegelbildlichkeit *f* mirror-image relationship, mirror-likeness
Spiegelbildstrahl *m* mirror-image ray
Spiegelblende *f* mirror shutter *(motion-picture camera)*
Spiegeldurchmesser *m* mirror diameter
Spiegelebene *f* mirror plane
Spiegelfacette *f* mirror facet
Spiegelfernrohr *n s.* Spiegelteleskop
Spiegelfläche *f* mirror [sur]face; mirror facet
Spiegelfleck *m* light spot
Spiegelgalvanometer *n* mirror galvanometer
Spiegelgesetz *n* reflection law, law of reflection
Spiegelgestalt *f* mirror figure
Spiegelglas *n* mirror glass (plate)
Spiegelhalter *m* mirror mount
Spiegelkamera *f* 1. mirror camera, reflector-type camera; 2. *s.* Spiegelreflexkamera
Spiegelkante *f* mirror edge

Spiegelkasten *m* mirror box
Spiegelkrümmung *f* mirror curvature
Spiegelkugel *f* mirrored ball
Spiegellinse *f* mirror lens, lens-mirror system
Spiegellinsenobjektiv *n s.* Spiegelobjektiv
Spiegelmetall *n* speculum metal
Spiegelmikroskop *n* mirror (reflecting) microscope
spiegeln to mirror
Spiegeln *n s.* Kontern
spiegelnd specular
Spiegelobjektiv *n* mirror (reflecting) lens, catadioptric lens, catadioptric [imaging] system
Spiegeloptik *f* mirror optics
Spiegelprisma *n* mirrored prism *(s.a.* Reflexionsprisma*)*
Spiegelprojektion *f* reflective projection
Spiegelprojektor *m* [/**digitaler**] digital mirror projector
Spiegelradabtastung *f* mirror drum scanning
Spiegelrahmensucher *m s.* Leuchtrahmensucher
Spiegelreflektor *m* mirror (specular) reflector
Spiegelreflexion *f* specular (mirror) reflection, glare [reflection] *(s.a.* Fresnel-Reflexion*)*
Spiegelreflexkamera *f* 1. [prism] reflex camera; 2. *s.* ~/einäugige
~/**einäugige** single-lens reflex [camera], SLR [camera]
~/**großformatige** large-format SLR
~/**zweiäugige** twin-lens-reflex [camera], TLR
Spiegelreflexsucher *m* reflecting [view]finder, reflex [view]finder, SLR viewfinder
Spiegelrichtung *f* mirror direction
Spiegelschlag *m* mirror slap (bounce), mirror flop (reflex action)
Spiegelstereoskop *n* mirror stereoscope
Spiegelsucher *m* triangulation rangefinder
Spiegelsymmetrie *f* specular (mirror) symmetry
Spiegelsystem *n* mirror system
Spiegeltele *n s.* 1. Spiegelteleobjektiv; 2. Spiegelteleskop
Spiegelteleskop *n* reflecting telescope, reflector
Spiegelteleskopoptik *f* reflecting telescope optics
Spiegeltrick *m* mirror (glass) shot *(cinema)*
Spiegeltrickverfahren *n* Schufftan process
Spiegelumlaufblende *f* [rotating] mirror shutter
Spiegelung *f* specular (mirror) reflection, glare [reflection]
Spiegelungseffekt *m* mirror effect
Spiegelungsrichtung *f* specular direction

spiegelverkehrt

spiegelverkehrt reverse (wrong) reading, laterally reversed, inverted laterally, flopped
Spiegelvorauslösung f mirror lock[up feature] *(single-lens reflex camera)*
Spiegelvorsatz m candid angle [lens] attachment
spielbar screenable *(film print)*
Spieldauer f playback (playing) time, program duration *(e.g. of a videodisc)*
Spieledesigner m game designer
Spieleentwickler m game developer
Spielekonsole f [video] game console, play station
Spieleprogrammierung f game programming
Spielfilm m [motion] picture, movie [film], photoplay, fiction film *(s.a. Hauptfilm)*
Spielfilmatelier n movie (motion-picture) studio
Spielfilmindustrie f feature film industry
Spielfilmkameramann m motion-picture cameraman, cinematographer
Spielfilmkopie f movie copy
Spielfilmnachbearbeitung f feature film editing
Spielfilmproduktion f feature [film] production
Spielfilmprojektion f theatrical projection
Spielfilmset m [motion-picture] set
Spielkonsole f s. Spielekonsole
Spielstätte f s. Drehort
Spielzeit f s. Spieldauer
Spin m spin; nuclear spin
Spindichte f spin density
Spindichtebild n spin density-weighted image
Spinecho n spin echo
Spinechobild n spin echo [MR] image
Spinechoerfassung f spin echo acquisition
Spinechosequenz f spin echo [imaging] sequence, spin echo [imaging] pulse sequence
~/**schnelle** fast spin echo pulse sequence
Spinechoverfahren n spin echo procedure (imaging) *(magnetic resonance imaging)*
Spin-Gitter-Relaxationszeit f spin-lattice relaxation time, longitudinal relaxation time, T-one [time constant], T1
Spinne f spider, triangle, tripod (floor) spreader
Spinpräzessionsgeschwindigkeit f spin precession speed
Spinsignal n spin signal
Spin-Spin-Relaxationszeit f spin-spin relaxation time, transverse relaxation [time], T-two [time constant], T2 *(magnetic resonance imaging)*
Spinsystem n spin system
Spinthariskop n spinthariscope
Spinzustand m spin state
Spionageflugzeug n spy plane
Spionagefotografie f espionage photography

Spionagekamera f spy camera, spycam
Spionagesoftware f spyware *(Internet)*
Spiral-Computerangiografie f spiral CT angiography
Spiral-Computertomografie f, **Spiral-CT** f spiral computed (volumetric computerized) tomography, helical computed tomography, spiral CT [scanning]
Spiral-CT-Datensatz m, **Spiraldatensatz** m helical scan data
Spiraleinsatz m [spiral] reel *(developing tank)*
Spiralkabel n coiled cord
Spiralscan m spiral (helical) scan
Spiralscanner m helical [CT] scanner, spiral scanner
Spiralsynchronkabel n coiled sync[hronized] cord
Spiralwendellampe f coil filament lamp
Spirit-Umdruck m spirit duplicating (duplication), fluid (direct) process
Spirit-Umdruckapparat m, **Spirit-Umdrucker** m spirit duplicator
Spitzenamplitude f peak amplitude
Spitzenbitrate f peak bit rate, PBR
Spitzendetektion f peak detection
Spitzenleuchtdichte f peak brightness, maximum (peak) luminance
Spitzenobjektiv n high-quality [photographic] lens
Spitzen-Signal-Rausch-Verhältnis n peak signal-to-noise ratio, PSNR
Spitzenspannungsmesser m peak meter
Spitzenwertanzeiger m peak meter
Spitzenwertbegrenzer m [peak] limiter
Spitzenwertbegrenzung f peak limiting
Spitzlicht n catchlight [effect] *(s.a. Glanzlicht, Hochlicht)*
Spline n(m) s. Spline-Kurve
Spline-Animation f spline-driven animation *(geometric modeling)*
Spline-Anpassung f spline fitting
Spline-Fläche f spline surface
Spline-Funktion f s. Spline-Kurve
Spline-Interpolation f spline interpolation
Spline-Kurve f spline [curve], spline function
~/**algebraische** algebraic spline, A-spline
~/**kubische** cubic spline [function]
Spline-Oberfläche f spline surface
Split-and-Merge-Algorithmus m split-and-merge algorithm (approach), quad-tree method *(image segmentation)*
Splitlinse f s. Teilnahlinse
Splitten n slitting *(film)*
Spontanentwicklung f spontaneous development
Sportfotograf m sports photographer (shooter)
Sportfotografie f sports photography
Sportsucher m sports viewfinder, frame [view]finder, wire frame viewfinder
Spot m 1. spot; 2. s. Spotlampe

Spotbeleuchtung f spotlighting
Spotbelichtungsmesser m spot meter
Spotbelichtungsmessung f spot metering
Spotdiagramm n spot diagram, point (spot) image *(optics)*
Spotfotometer n spot meter; telephotometer
Spotlampe f, **Spotlight** n spot [light], spot lamp
Spotmessung f spot metering
Spotmeter n s. Spotfotometer
Sprachband n dialogue line (track)
Sprachsteuerung f voice activation (actuation), voice input control *(e.g. of a television set)*
Sprachstreifen m dialogue line (track)
Sprachverständlichkeit f speech intelligibility
Sprachvisualisierung f speech visualization
Sprechanlage f intercom [system], intercommunication system
Sprechblase f balloon
Sprecher m/**digitaler** avatar, cybercitizen, natural resident *(software program)*
Sprechgarnitur f headset
Springblende f [/**automatische**] instant-return iris
Springspreizenkamera f folding roll-film camera
Spritzretusche f airbrushing
spritzwassergeschützt water-resistant
Sprossenschrift f variable-density [sound] track, push-pull system *(cinema)*
Sprühdose f spray can *(imaging software tool)*
Sprühkleber m spray adhesive, mounting spray
Sprühpistole f airbrush *(imaging tool)*
Sprungschnitt m jump cut *(screen change effect)*
Sprungsuchlauf m skip
Sprungtemperatur f transition (critical) temperature *(superconductor)*
Spule f spool
spulen to spool; to wind
Spulendose f reel container
Spuleneinsatz m s. Spiraleinsatz
Spulenkern m [winding] core, take-up core, bobbin
Spulenstrom m coil current *(electron lens)*
Spulentonbandgerät n reel-to-reel tape recorder
Spulenvideobandgerät n reel-to-reel [video] machine
Spülwasser n wash[ing] water
Spur f track
Spurabstand m track pitch (spacing)
Spurbreite f track width
Spurdichte f track density
Spureinstellung f tracking
Spurformat n track format
Spurkörper m sweep *(computer graphics)*
Spurlage f track position (configuration)

Spurlagenanordnung f track layout
Spurlagenfehler m tracking error, mistracking
Spurlagenregelung f tracking [adjustment]
~/**automatische** automatic track following, ATF, auto tracking
~/**dynamische** dynamic track following, DTF
Spurlagenregler m tracking mechanism
Spurnachführung f, **Spurregelung** f s. Spurlagenregelung
Spursteuerung f tracking control
Spurwinkel m track angle, skew
SQUID n SQUID [sensor], SQUID magnetometer, superconducting quantum interference device; SQUID chip
SQUID-Elektronik f SQUID electronics
SQUID-Vielkanalsystem n multichannel SQUID system
Stabanode f rod anode *(radiography)*
Stabantenne f rod antenna (aerial)
Stabblitz[licht]gerät n grip-type flash
Stäbchen n [retinal] rod, optic[al] rod, rod [photo]receptor, rhabdom[e]
Stäbchenmonochromasie f rod monochromacy (monochromatism)
Stäbchenpigment n rod [photo]pigment, rhodopsin
Stäbchenplan m lined script *(film production)*
Stäbchensehen n rod (scotopic) vision, night (dark-adapted) vision
Stäbchensystem n rod system
Stabilisator m stabilizer, stabilizing agent *(development improver)*
Stabilisatorbad n, **Stabilisierungsbad** n stabilizing (stabilization) bath
Stabilisier[ungs]verstärker m processing amplifier, proc amp *(video equipment)*
Stadtbereichsnetz n metropolitan arc network, MAN
Staffelbild n s. Histogramm
Stahlfilm m steel film
Stahlrakel f s. Rakel
Stamm m stem *(letterface)*
Stammlösung f stock solution
Standardbildformat n standard picture format
Standard... s.a. Normal...
Standardabtastung f standard sampling
Standardabweichung f standard deviation
Standardauflösung f standard resolution
Standardbeleuchtung f standard lighting
Standardbelichtungsmesser m standard light meter
Standard-Bildbearbeitungssoftware f off-the-shelf image-handling software
Standardbrennweite f standard focal length
Standarddateiformat n standard file format
Standard-Fernsehgerät n standard TV receiver

Standardformat

Standardformat *n* 1. standard format; 2. academy (sound) aperture, Academy ratio *(film format)*
Standardkamera *f* standard camera
Standardkassette *f* standard[-size] cassette *(digital video)*
Standardlichtquelle *f* s. Normlichtart
Standardobjektiv *n* standard objective; normal[-type] lens, normal design lens; ordinary (normal) camera lens, standard [photographic] lens
Standardokular *n* standard equipment eyepiece
Standardpapier *n* standard (plain) paper, normal (ordinary) paper
Standardreflektor *m* standard reflector
Standardröntgenröhre *f* general-purpose X-ray tube
Standardschnittstelle *f* standard interface
Standardsoftware *f* standard software
Standardvideosignal *n* standard video signal
Standardzeichensatz *m* **zum Informationsaustausch/Amerikanischer** American Standard Code for Information Interchange, ASCII
Standardzoom[objektiv] *n* standard zoom; mid-range zoom
Standarte *f* standard *(view camera)*
Standaufnahme *f* lockdown shot
Standbild *n* still image (picture), static (nonmoving) image *(s.a. under* Stehbild*)*; still [frame], freeze (stop) frame, held (hold) frame *(s.a.* Standfoto*)*
~/digitales digital still picture, DSP
~/elektronisches electronic standing picture, ESP
~/synthetisiertes synthesized still image
Standbildarchivierung *f* still image archiving
Standbildausgabe *f*/**digitale** digital still output
Standbilddatenbank *f* still picture database
Standbildfotografie *f*/**digitale** digital still video photography
Standbildkamera *f* [electronic] still camera, still video camera
Standbildmodus *m* still-picture mode *(video coding)*; freeze frame mode *(camcorder)*; playback pause mode *(video)*
Standbildprojektor *m* still[-picture] projector, lantern
Standbildspeicher *m* frame store [memory], still store; freeze buffer
Standbildübertragung *f* still-picture (still-image) transmission
Standbild-Video *n* still video
Standbogen *m* layout grid
Stand-by *n*, **Stand-by-Betrieb** *m* standby (pause) mode *(e.g. of a video camera)*
Standfoto *n* static (still) photograph; film (movie) still, action still, still [frame]; production (publicity) still

Standfotograf *m* still photographer, location photographer *(cinema)*
Standfotografie *f* production still photography
Standkopierung *f* freeze frame
Standlupe *f* standing magnifier; focusing magnifier
Standprojektion *f* still [picture] projection
Standsäule *f* column *(enlarger)*
Standverlängerung *f* freeze frame
Stanze *f* key
~/lineare linear key
Stanzen *n* keying
Stanzfarbe *f* [chroma] key color
Stanzfläche *f*, **Stanzhintergrund** *m* key fill
Stanzsignal *n* keying signal, key source (signal)
Stanzsignal-Umkehrung *f* key invert
Stanztrick *m* matte [effect]; blue-screen effect
Stanzverfahren *n* keying [technique]; electronic matting
Stanzwand *f*/**blaue** blue screen
Stapelaufnahme *f* s. Stapeldigitalisierung
Stapelauslage *f* delivery stack *(printing press)*
Stapeldatei *f* batch file *(data processing)*
Stapeldigitalisierung *f* batch digitizing (capture) *(of video material)*
Stapelfehler *m* stacking fault *(crystallography)*
Stapeltisch *m* collating table
Stapelverarbeitung *f* batch processing (mode), background process
Star *m*/**Grauer** cataract *(opacity of the eye's lens)*
Stärke starch, amylum *(polysaccharide)*
Stärkekorn *n*, **Stärkekörnchen** *n* starch grain (granule)
Starklichtquelle *f* high-powered light source
Starrkörpertransformation *f* rigid-body transformation *(geometric modeling)*
Startband *n* head (start) leader, leader [strip]; count-down [head] leader *(motion-picture release print)*
Startcode *m* start code *(video bit stream)*
Startknoten *m* start node *(graph theory)*
Startkreuz *n*, **Startmarkierung** *f* start (sync) mark
Startmenü *n* start menu
Startpunkt *m* starting (initial) point *(e.g. in chain coding)*; seed point *(region-growing method)*
Startseite *f* home page *(World Wide Web)*
Startstreifen *m* s. Startband
Startzeichen *n* s. Startkreuz
stationär stationary
Stationarität *f* stationarity
Stationaritätsbedingung *f* stationarity condition
Statistik *f* **erster Ordnung**, **~/univariate** first-order statistics
~ zweiter Ordnung second-order statistics

Stativ *n* stand; tripod; arm, limb *(of a compound microscope)*
~/**fahrbares** [camera] dolly, truck
~/**pneumatisches** pedestal
Stativablage *f* tripod tray
Stativanschluss *m* tripod mount (coupler), tripod connection
Stativaufnahme *f* tripod shot
Stativaufsatz *m* tripod head
Stativbein *n* stand (tripod) leg
Stativbeinarretierung *f*, **Stativbein-Schnellarretierung** *f* clip leg lock
Stativblitz *m* stand-mounted flash
Stativbuchse *f* tripod socket
Stativgewinde *n* tripod socket
Stativhalterung *f* tripod holder
Stativkamera *f* tripod[-mounted] camera
Stativklemme *f* tripod clamp
Stativkopf *m* tripod head
~/**flüssigkeitsgedämpfter** fluid[-dampened tripod] head, hydraulic head
Stativkopfplatte *f* tripod platform
Stativkupplung *f* tripod mount
Stativsäule *f* tripod column
Stativschraube *f* tripod screw
Stativschwenkarm *m* tripod head control arm
Stativspinne *f* crow's foot, triangle
Stativtasche *f* tripod case
Stativtraggurt *m* tripod strap
Stativuntersatz *m*/**fahrbarer**, **Stativwagen** *m* [camera] dolly, truck
Statusfilter *n* status filter *(densitometry)*
Statusvektor *m* state vector
Staubfleck *m* dust spot (speck)
Steadicam-Kameramann *m* steadicam operator
Steckblende *f* Waterhouse stop
Stecker *m*/**faseroptischer** fiber-optic connector
~/**mehrpoliger** multipin connector
Steckfeld *n* patch panel
Steckkabel *n* patch cable
Steckkarte *f* plug-in board (card); expansion board card
Steckplatz *m*, **Steckschacht** *m* [expansion] slot
Steckverteiler *m s.* Steckfeld
Stefan-Boltzmann-Konstante *f* Stefan-Boltzmann constant
Steg *m* land *(esp. as space between pits on an optical disk)*
Steganografie *f* steganography
steganografisch steganographic
Stehbild *n* still image (picture), static (nonmoving) image *(s.a. under Standbild)*
Stehbildfotograf *m* still photographer
Stehbildfotografie *f*/**elektronische** electronic still photography, still electronic photography
Stehbildkamera *f* still [picture] camera, still frame camera, [photographic] camera
~/**elektronische** electronic still [video] camera, still video camera
Stehbildprojektion *f* still projection
Stehbildprojektor *m*, **Stehbildwerfer** *m* still [picture] projector, lantern
Stehwelle *f* standing (stationary) wave
Steifigkeitsmatrix *f* stiffness matrix
Steiger *m* riser *(e.g. of a lamp stand)*
steil roman, upright *(typestyle)*
Steilheit *f* steepness, slope *(e.g. of a characteristic curve)*
Steilschrift *f* roman
Steindruck *m* lithography, lithographic printing
Steindrucker *m* lithographer
Steindruckform *f* lithographic plate
Steindruckpresse *f* lithographic press
Steiner-Baum *m* Steiner tree, minimum Steiner spanning tree *(computer graphics)*
Steinpresse *f s.* Steindruckpresse
Stellarfotografie *f* stellar photography *(s.a.* Sternbildfotografie, Sternfeldfotografie*)*
Stellmotor *m* servomotor, relay
Stellring *m* setting (adjusting) ring *(e.g. on optical devices)*
Stellwand *f* screen
Stempelfertigung *f* rubber stamp making
Stempelschneider *m* rubber stamp maker
Steradiant *m* steradian, unit solid angle
Stereo *n s.* Stereotypplatte
Stereoansicht *f* stereo view
Stereoauflösung *f* stereo resolution
Stereoauswertegerät *n s.* Stereoplotter
Stereoautograf *m* stereoautograph, analog stereoplotter
Stereobasis *f* stereo base
Stereobetrachtung *f s.* Stereobildbetrachtung
Stereobild *n* stereo[scopic] image, stereo[scopic] picture, stereograph, stereogram
Stereobildanalyse *f* stereo image analysis
Stereobildanzeige *f* stereoimage display
Stereobildarchiv *n* stereo picture (card) archive
Stereobildbetrachter *m* stereo[scopic] viewer, stereo[scopic] viewing device, 3-D [picture] viewer, stereoscope, stereopticon
Stereobildbetrachtung *f* stereo[scopic] viewing
Stereobildcodierer *m* stereo image (video) coder
Stereobildfolge *f* stereo[scopic] image sequence, stereo sequence
Stereobildgebung *f* stereo[scopic] imaging
Stereobildmaterial *n* stereoscopic imagery
Stereobildmessung *f* stereophotogrammetry

Stereobildpaar *n* stereo[scopic] image pair, pair of stereo pictures, stereo[photographic] pair, stereogram
Stereobildschirm *m* stereo display; stereoscopic computer screen
stereoblind stereo-blind
Stereoblindheit *f* stereoblindness
Stereobrille *f* stereobinocular, stereo glasses, 3-D glasses
Stereo-Computergrafik *f* stereo computer graphics
Stereo-Computertomografie *f* stereo computer tomography
Stereodaguerreotypie *f* stereo[scopic] daguerreotype
Stereodecoder *m* stereo decoder
Stereo-Diabetrachter *m* stereo slide viewer
Stereo-Diapositiv *n* stereo slide
Stereodisparität *f* stereo[scopic] disparity
Stereoeffekt *m* stereo[scopic] effect
Stereo-Farbdia[positiv] *n* color stereographic slide
Stereofernsehen *n* stereoscopic (three-dimensional) television, 3-D television
Stereofernsehsendung *f* stereo television show
Stereofilm *m* stereoscopic film (motion picture), three-dimensional [motion] picture, stereomovie
Stereofluoroskop *n* stereofluoroscope
stereofluoroskopisch stereofluoroscopic
stereofon stereophonic
Stereofonie *f* stereophony
stereofonisch stereophonic
Stereofoto *n* [still] stereo[scopic] photograph, [photographic] stereogram, stereograph
Stereofotografie *f* 1. stereophotography, stereoscopic (three-dimensional) photography; 2. *s.* Stereofoto
stereofotografisch stereophotographic
Stereofotogrammetrie *f* stereophotogrammetry
stereofotogrammetrisch stereophotogrammetric
stereografisch stereographic[al]
Stereogramm *n* 1. stereogram; 2. *s.* Stereobildpaar
~/**holografisches** holographic stereogram
Stereokalibrierung *f* stereo calibration
Stereokamera *f* stereo[scopic] camera, stereo-pair (twin-lens) camera
~/**hochauflösende** high-resolution stereo camera, HRSC
Stereokanal *m* stereo channel
Stereokinematografie *f* stereoscopic (three-dimensional) cinematography
Stereokomparator *m* stereocomparator
Stereokorrespondenz *f* stereo correspondence

Stereolithografie *f* stereolithography, three-dimensional printing; rapid prototyping
stereolithografisch stereolithographic
Stereologie *f* stereology
stereologisch stereolical
Stereo-Luftbild *n* aerial stereo pair
Stereo-Luftbildaufnahme *f* stereoscopic aerial photograph
Sterolupe *f* stereo[scopic] magnifier
Stereometrie *f* stereometry
stereometrisch stereometric
Stereomikrofon *n* stereo[phonic] microphone
Stereomikrofotografie *f* stereomicrography
Stereomikrometer *n* stereomicrometer
Stereomikroskop *n* stereomicroscope, stereoscopic microscope
Stereomikroskopie *f* stereomicroscopy, stereoscopic microscopy
stereomikroskopisch stereomicroscopic
Stereomodell *n* stereo[scopic] model
Stereomodus *m* stereo mode
Stereonachvertonung *f* stereo audio dubbing
Stereo-Nahfotografie *f* close-up stereophotography
Stereoplanigraf *m* stereoplanigraph
Stereoplotter *m* stereoplotter, stereoscopic plotting instrument
Stereoprojektion *f* stereoprojection, stereoscopic projection
Stereoprojektionsfläche *f* stereo projection surface
Stereopsis *f s.* Stereosehen
Stereoradiografie *f* stereoradiography, stereoscopic radiography
Stereorekonstruktion *f* stereo reconstruction
Stereosatellitenbild *n* stereo satellite image
Stereosehen *n* stereo[scopic] vision, stereopsis, spatial (three-dimensional) vision
~/**binokulares** binocular stereopsis (stereo vision), binocular depth perception
~/**fotometrisches** shape-from-shading [technique], shape from shading
~/**trinokulares** trinocular stereo vision
Stereosensor *m* stereo sensor
Stereosignal *n* stereo signal
Stereoskop *n* stereoscope, stereo[scopic] viewer, stereo[scopic] viewing device, 3-D [picture] viewer, stereopticon
Stereoskopbild *n s.* Stereobild
Stereoskopie *f* stereoscopy
stereoskopisch stereoscopic[al]
stereotaktisch stereotaxic, stereotactic[al]
Stereotaxie *f* stereotaxis, stereotaxy
Stereoteleskop *n* stereoscopic telescope
Stereoton *m* stereo[phonic] sound, stereo audio
Stereotonkanal *m* stereo audio channel

Stereotonspur f stereo sound track
Stereotypie f stereotypy
stereotypieren to stereotype
Stereotypplatte f stereotype [plate], duplicate [relief] plate
Stereoübersprechen n stereo cross talk
Stereovisualisierung f stereo visualization
Stereovorsatz m stereo attachment
Stereowahrnehmung f stereo perception
Sternabbildung f, **Sternaufnahme** f star image
Sternbildfotografie f 1. astrophotography, celestial (astronomical) photography; 2. astronomical photograph
Sternblende f central stop
Sterneffektfilter n star[burst] filter, cross star (screen) filter
Sternenlicht n starlight
Sternfeldfotografie f star field photography
Sternhelligkeit f star brightness
Sterninterferometer n very large telescope interferometer, VLTI
Sternpolygon n star-shaped polygon
Sternspektrografie f stellar spectrography
Sternspektroskop n stellar spectroscope
Sternspektroskopie f stellar spectroscopy
Sternverteiler m hub
Sternwarte f astronomical observatory
Sterry-Effekt m Sterry effect *(contrast reduction)*
Sterry-Verfahren n Sterry process *(contrast reduction)*
Stetigkeit f 1. steadiness; continuity; 2. s. Glattheit
Stetigkeitsbedingung f stationarity assumption, assumption of stationarity
Steuerbus m control bus
Steuercode m control code
Steuerelektrode f modulation (control) electrode
Steuerelektronik f control electronics
Steuerelement n tool *(computer software)*
Steuergerät n controller
Steuergitter n control grid *(cathode-ray tube)*
Steuerimpuls m control pulse
Steuerimpulsgeber m trigger circuit *(radar)*
Steuerknüppel f joystick
Steuerkugel f trackball
Steuermodul n control module
Steuerprogramm n control program
Steuerpunkt m control point (vertex) *(computer graphics)*
Steuerrechner m control computer
Steuerschnittstelle f control interface
Steuersignal n control signal
Steuerspannung f control[-circuit] voltage; control grid voltage *(cathode-ray tube)*
Steuerspur f control (address) track *(magnetic image recording)*
Steuerspursignal n control track signal (pulse) *(videotape)*

Steuertaste f control key; navigation key *(computer)*
Steuerung f / **servomotorische** servo[mechanism]
Steuerungsbit n control bit
Steuerungselektronik f control electronics
Steuerungsfolie f s. Schaltfolie
Steuerungshebel m s. Steuerknüppel
Steuerungsschicht f session layer *(data transmission)*
Steuerungsverfahren n **für Satelliteneinrichtungen/digitales** digital satellite equipment control, DiSEqC *(data transmission)*
Steuerzeichen n control character *(e.g. in an alphanumeric code)*
Stickstoffagitation f nitrogen burst agitation *(photoprocessing)*
Stickstofflaser m nitrogen laser
Stiftkante f spike edge
Stiftplotter m pen plotter
stigmatisch stigmatic
Stigmator m stigmator *(electron microscope)*
Stilb n stilb *(a unit of luminance)*
Stiles-Crawford-Effekt m Stiles-Crawford effect *(vision)*
Stilllebenaufnahme f still-life photograph
Stilllebenfotograf m still-life photographer
Stilllebenfotografie f still-life photography
Stillstandsprojektion f still [picture] projection
Stillvideokamera f still-video camera, electronic still[-video] camera
Stimmung f 1. mood, key *(of a photograph)*; 2. s. Lichtstimmung
Stirnfensterröhre f end window tube *(X rays)*
stirnparallel fronto-parallel
STIR-Pulssequenz f STIR (short tau inversion recovery) pulse sequence *(magnetic resonance imaging)*
Stöbern n browsing *(multimedia)*
stochastisch stochastic, random
Stoffdruck m textile printing
Stoffdrucker m textile printer
Stoffmengenkonzentration f molar concentration, molarity
Stopfbit n stuffing bit
Stopfbyte n stuffing byte
Stoppbad n stop bath, shortstop
Stoppbadschale f stop bath tray
Stoppbadtank m stop bath tank
Stoppcode m stop code
Stopptrick m stop-motion animation (photography), stop-action animation, stop motion (action)
Stopptrickfigur f stop-motion puppet
Stoppzeit f stop time
Stoppzylinder[druck]maschine f stop-cylinder press (printing machine)
Störabstand m signal-to-noise ratio, SNR
Störamplitude f noise amplitude

Störbefreiung

Störbefreiung f noise removal (cleaning), noise cancel[l]ing, de-noising [procedure]
Störbegrenzer m/**dynamischer** dynamic noise limiter, DNL
Storchschnabel m pantograph *(drawing copying device)*
Störecho n [radar] clutter, clutter interference
Störechogleichung f clutter equation
Störechokarte f clutter map
stören to disturb; to interfere [with]; to jam *(e.g. radar)*
Störer m jammer *(radar)*
~/**breitbandiger** barrage jammer
~/**schmalbandiger** spot jammer
~/**wobbelnder** swept jammer
~/**zielbegleitender** escort jammer, ESJ
Störfeld n disturbing field, interference (interfering) field *(magnetic interference imaging)*
Störgeräusch n noise
Störgeräuschregler m noise gate
Störimpuls m interference pulse; glitch *(digital-analog converter)*
Störleistung f noise power (performance)
Störlicht n stray light
Störlichtblende f shield
Störmuster n interference pattern (figure), objectionable pattern *(s.a. Moiré)*
Störpegel m interference level
Störpixel n pixel drop-out
Stör-Rausch-Abstand m interference-to-noise ratio, INR
Störsender m jammer *(radar)*
Störsignal n interfering (interference) signal; noise; jamming signal *(radar)*
Störsignalpegel m noise level
Störsignalunterdrückung f noise suppression
Störstelle f [lattice] impurity
Störstellenfotoleitung f extrinsic photoconduction
Störübertragungsfunktion f disturbance transfer function
Störung f/**elektromagnetische** electromagnetic interference
~/**nichtsynchrone** s. Empfangsstörung/nichtsynchrone
Störungsmuster n s. Störmuster
Störunterdrückung f interference suppression; noise suppression
~/**digitale** digital noise reduction, DNR
Storyboard n storyboard *(film production)*
Störzeile[n] f[pl] line-dropout
Stoßantwort f s. Impulsantwort
Stoßionisation f impact ionization
stoßweise bursty *(e.g. a bit stream)*
Strabismus m strabismus, squint
Strahl m 1. ray; beam [of rays], ray bundle; 2. jet *(of gases or liquids)*
~/**abgelenkter** deflected ray
~/**achs[en]ferner** abaxial (off-axis) ray, nonparaxial ray

~/**achs[en]paralleler** ray parallel to the axis
~/**achsennaher** paraxial (near-axis) ray
~/**aufgeweiteter** expanded beam
~/**auftreffender** impinging beam
~/**ausgezeichneter** principal (chief) ray
~/**außerordentlicher** extraordinary ray (beam)
~/**austretender** emergent ray
~/**beliebiger** arbitrary ray
~/**beugungsbegrenzter** diffraction-limited beam
~/**direkter** direct ray
~/**einfallender** incident ray (beam)
~/**endlicher** finite ray *(optics)*
~/**Gaußscher** Gaussian ray (beam)
~/**gebeugter** diffracted beam
~/**gebrochener** refracted ray
~/**kollimierter** collimated beam
~/**kontinuierlicher** continuous jet *(ink jet printer)*
~/**meridionaler** meridional (tangential) ray
~/**optischer** optical ray; optical beam
~/**ordentlicher** ordinary (stationary) ray, ordinary beam
~/**paraxialer** paraxial (near-axis) ray
~/**pulsierender** drop-on-demand jet *(ink jet printer)*
~/**randnaher (randseitiger)** peripheral (marginal) ray, rim (edge) ray
~/**reflektierter** reflected ray; reflection beam
~/**sagittaler** sagittal ray
~/**schräger** oblique ray
~/**spiegelreflektierter** specularly reflected beam
~/**transmittierter** transmitted ray
~/**windschiefer** skew (oblique) ray
Strahl... s.a. Strahlen...
Strahlaberration f ray aberration
Strahlablenker m ray deflector; beam deflector
Strahlablenkung f ray deflection; beam deflection; beam deviation
~/**magnetische** magnetic ray deflection
Strahlablenkwinkel m ray deflection angle
Strahlabschwächer m beam attenuator
Strahlabschwächung f beam attenuation
Strahlabtaster m/**holografischer** holographic beam sampler
Strahlachse f beam axis
Strahlaufteilung f s. Strahlenteilung
Strahlaufweitsystem n beam expanding system; expanding lens
Strahlaufweitung f 1. beam expansion, beam spread[ing]; 2. beam expander
Strahlausbreitung f ray propagation
Strahlbegrenzung f beam limiting
Strahlbegrenzungsblende f beam[-defining] aperture
Strahlbeugung f beam bending
Strahlbrechung f refraction
Strahlbreite f beam width
Strahldaten pl ray data

Strahldichte f radiance, radiancy *(radiometry)*
~ **des schwarzen Körpers/spektrale spezifische** blackbody emissive power
~/**spektrale** spectral radiance
Strahldichtefaktor (Strahldichtewert) m/**spektraler** spectral radiance factor
Strahldicke f beam thickness
Strahldivergenz f beam divergence (spread)
Strahldurchmesser m beam diameter *(laser)*
Strahldurchrechnung f ray tracing (casting)
Strahldurchstoß[ungs]punkt m ray intersection
Strahldurchzeichnung f [graphical] ray trace
strahlen to radiate; to beam *(e.g. light rays through an aperture)*
Strahlen... *s.a.* Strahl...
Strahlenaufhärtung f beam hardening *(X-ray absorption)*
Strahlenbelastung f radiation burden
Strahlenbeugung f beam bending
Strahlenbild n radiograph[ic image], radiation-produced image, radiogram; X-ray photograph; gamma ray photograph
Strahlenblende f beam[-defining] aperture
Strahlenbrechung f refraction
Strahlenbündel n ray bundle, beam [of rays] *(s.a. under Bündel)*
~/**kegelförmiges** cone beam
Strahlenbüschel n *s.* Strahlenbündel
strahlend radiant
Strahlendiagnostik f diagnostic radiology; diagnostic radiography
Strahlendiagnostiker m diagnostic radiologist
strahlendiagnostisch radiodiagnostic
Strahlendosis f radiation dose, dose of radiation *(s.a. under Dosis)*
strahlendurchlässig radiolucent, radioparent
Strahlendurchlässigkeit f radiolucency
Strahlenenergie f beam energy
Strahlenexposition f radiation exposure *(e.g. to patients)*
Strahlenfächer m fan[-shaped] beam, fanned beam
Strahlengang m ray path (trajectory); beam path
~/**optischer** optical path (train)
~/**telezentrischer** telecentric path of rays
~/**verketteter** relayed beam
Strahlenkegel m cone of rays
Strahlenkonstruktion f/**Listingsche** *s.* Bildkonstruktion
Strahlenkörper m ciliary body *(of the eye)*
Strahlenkunde f radiology
Strahlenoptik f [/**geometrische**] f ray optics, geometric[al] optics
strahlenoptisch ray-optics, geometric[al]-optics

Strahlenquelle f *s.* Strahlungsquelle
Strahlenraum m/**objektseitiger** object (subject) space; specimen space *(optical system)*
Strahlenrelief n *s.* Strahlenabsorptionsbild
Strahlenrisiko n radiation hazard
Strahlenrückverfolgung f ray tracing
Strahlenschaden m radiation damage
Strahlenschutz m radioprotection, radiation protection
Strahlenschutzkabine f radiation protection cabinet
Strahlenschutzplakette f film dosimeter (badge), photographic badge, badge meter
Strahlenschwächung f radiation attenuation
Strahlensicherheit f radiation safety; X-radiation safety
Strahlenteiler m beam (light) splitter, beam divider
~/**akustooptischer** acousto-optical beam splitter
~/**dichroitischer** dichroic beam splitter
~/**optischer** optical beam splitter
~/**stereoskopischer** stereoscopic beam splitter
Strahlenteilerkamera f beam-splitting camera, beam-splitter camera, one-shot camera *(instrument)*
Strahlenteiler-Vorsatz m image splitter *(stereo camera)*
Strahlenteilerwürfel m [optical] cube beam splitter
Strahlenteilung f beam division (partition), beam splitting
Strahlenteilungskamera f *s.* Strahlenteilerkamera
Strahlenteilungsoptik f beam-splitting optics
Strahlenteilungsprisma n beam-splitting (beam-division) prism, prism beam splitter
Strahlenteilungsverhältnis n beam-splitting ratio
Strahlentheorie f **des Lichts** ray theory of light
Strahlenumlenkung f beam bending
strahlenundurchlässig radiopaque, radio-opaque
Strahlenundurchlässigkeit f radiopacity
Strahler m radiator; emitter
~/**Grauer** gray body
~/**idealer** ideal (perfect) radiator
~/**isotroper** isotropic radiator
~/**kontinuierlicher** continuous radiator
~/**Lambertscher** Lambertian emitter (diffuser), Lambertian [light] source, [ideal] Lambertian reflector
~/**Planckscher** *s.* Strahler/Schwarzer
~/**Schwarzer** blackbody [radiator], Planckian (cavity) radiator
~/**selektiver** selective (luminescent) radiator

Strahlfokus *m* beam focus
Strahlfokussierung *f* beam focusing
Strahlformer *m* beam shaper
Strahlformung *f* beam shaping (forming)
Strahlführung *f* beam-guiding system
Strahlgeometrie *f* beam geometry
Strahlgeschwindigkeit *f* beam [scanning] speed, beam velocity
Strahlgleichung *f* ray equation
Strahlintegration *f* ray merging
Strahlintensität *f* s. Strahlstärke
Strahlkanone *f* electron [beam] gun *(cathode-ray tube)*
Strahlkonvergenz *f* beam convergence
Strahllage *f* beam position
Strahllagestabilität *f* beam position stability
Strahllänge *f* beam path length
Strahlleistung *f* beam power *(laser)*
Strahlmatrix *f* ray-transfer matrix
Strahlmatrixröhre *f* beam matrix tube
Strahlmischer *m* beam combiner
Strahlmodulation *f* beam modulation
Strahlprober *m* beam sampler
Strahlprobung *f* beam sampling
Strahlprofil *n* beam profile
Strahlprofilierung *f* beam profiling
Strahlprojektion *f* ray projection
Strahlpropagationsfaktor *m* beam propagation factor *(laser)*
Strahlquelle *f* beam source
Strahlquerschnitt *m*, **Strahlquerschnittsfläche** *f* beam [cross-sectional] area *(laser)*
Strahlradius *m* beam radius
Strahlrichtung *f* beam (ray) direction
Strahlrücklauf *m*, **Strahlrücksprung** *m* electron beam retrace, flyback
Strahlsegment *n* ray segment
Strahlspannung *f* beam voltage
Strahlstabilität *f* beam stability *(laser)*
Strahlstärke *f* radiant (beam) intensity *(radiometry)*
~/**spektrale** spectral radiant intensity
Strahlsteuerung *f* beam steering
Strahlstrom *m* [electron-]beam current, electron gun beam current
Strahlsymmetrie *f* beam symmetry
Strahltaille *f* [/**Gaußsche**] beam waist *(Gaussian optics)*
Strahlteiler *m* s. Strahlenteiler
Strahlumlenkblock *m* beam deflection cube
Strahlumlenkung *f* 1. beam steering; 2. beam steerer
Strahlung *f* radiation
~/**aktinische** actinic radiation
~/**bilderzeugende** image-forming radiation
~/**charakteristische** characteristic radiation (X rays)
~/**direkte** direct radiation
~/**durchdringende** penetrating-type radiation
~/**einfallende** incident radiation
~/**elektromagnetische** electromagnetic (EM) radiation, EMR
~/**elliptisch polarisierte** elliptical polarized radiation
~/**emittierte** emitted radiation
~/**gepulste** pulsed radiation
~/**harte** hard radiation
~/**infrarote** infrared (IR) radiation
~/**infrarotnahe** near-infrared radiation
~/**inkohärente** incoherent radiation
~/**ionisierende** ionizing (ionization) radiation
~/**kohärente** coherent radiation
~/**kollimierte** collimated radiation
~/**kontinuierliche** continuous-wave irradiation
~/**kosmische** cosmic radiation
~/**kurzwellige** short-wavelength radiation
~/**langwellige** long-wavelength radiation
~/**leuchtende (luminöse)** luminous radiation
~/**monochromatische** monochromatic radiation
~/**monoenergetische** monoenergetic (monochromatic) radiation
~/**nichtionisierende** nonionizing radiation
~/**nichtthermische** nonthermal radiation
~/**optische** optical radiation
~/**polychromatische** polychromatic radiation
~/**radioaktive** radioactive radiation
~/**rückgestreute** backscattered radiation
~/**schmalbandige** narrow-band radiation
~/**sichtbare** visible (visual) radiation
~/**spektrale** spectral radiation
~/**teilpolarisierte** partially polarized radiation
~/**transmittierte** transmitted radiation
~/**unpolarisierte** unpolarized (randomly polarized) radiation
~/**unsichtbare** invisible radiation
~/**unzusammenhängende** s. ~/inkohärente
~/**weiche** soft radiation
~/**willkürlich polarisierte** randomly polarized radiation
~/**zusammenhängende** s. ~/kohärente
Strahlungsabbildung *f* radiograph[ic image], radiogram
Strahlungsabschwächung *f* radiation attenuation
Strahlungsabsorption *f* radiation absorption
Strahlungsäquivalent *n* [/**fotometrisches**] photometric radiation equivalent, luminous efficacy, light yield
~/**mechanisches** mechanical radiation equivalent
strahlungsarm low-radiation *(e.g. a monitor)*
Strahlungsart *f* radiation type
Strahlungsausbeute *f* radiant (radiating) efficiency, radiation yield

Strahlungsdämpfung f radiation damping
Strahlungsdetektion f radiation detection
Strahlungsdetektor m radiation detector
Strahlungsdiagramm n radiative (radiation) pattern *(e.g. of an antenna)*
Strahlungsdichte f radiance, radiancy *(radiometry)*
Strahlungsdruck m radiation pressure
Strahlungsdurchgang m radiation transmission
Strahlungsempfänger m radiation receiver (detector)
~/**bildgebender** imaging photodetector
strahlungsempfindlich radiosensitive, radiation-sensitive
Strahlungsempfindlichkeit f radiosensitivity, radiation sensitivity
Strahlungsenergie f radiant (radiation) energy, radiative (radiating) energy
Strahlungsfeld n radiation (radiative) field, radiance field
Strahlungsfilter n/**optisches** optical radiation filter, spectral (color) filter
Strahlungsfluss m radiant (radiation) flux, radiant (radiation) power *(photometry)*
~/**auffallender spektraler** spectral incident radiant (luminous) flux
~/**reflektierter spektraler** spectral reflected radiant (luminous) flux
~/**spektraler** spectral radiant (luminous) flux
Strahlungsflussdichte f 1. radiant flux density, radiant exitance; 2. *s.* Bestrahlungsstärke
Strahlungsformel f/**Plancksche** *s.* Strahlungsgesetz/Plancksches
Strahlungsfunktion f relative spectral energy distribution
Strahlungsgesetz n/**Kirchhoffsches** Kirchhoff's law
~/**Plancksches** Planck's [radiation] law, Planck's formula
Strahlungsgröße f radiometric quantity
Strahlungsintensität f radiant intensity
Strahlungskeule f 1. radiation lobe; beam; 2. *s.* Radarkeule
Strahlungsleistung f radiant (radiation) power, radiant flux *(radiometry)*
~/**emittierte** emissive power
~/**rauschäquivalente** noise equivalent power, NEP
~/**relative spektrale** relative spectral power
Strahlungsmenge f radiation quantity *(s.a.* Strahlungsenergie*)*
Strahlungsmessung f radiometry
Strahlungsnachweis m radiation detection
Strahlungsphysik f radiation physics
Strahlungsquant n quantum of radiation; [light] quantum, photon
Strahlungsquelle f radiation (radiant) source, source of radiation
Strahlungsrichtung f direction of radiation

Strahlungsschwächung f radiation attenuation
Strahlungssensor m radiation sensor
Strahlungsspeisung f space feed *(radar antenna)*
Strahlungsspektrum n radiation (radiative) spectrum
Strahlungsstärke f radiant intensity
Strahlungstemperatur f radiating temperature
Strahlungsverlust m radiation (radiative) loss
Strahlungsverteilung f/**spektrale** spectral [power] distribution, spectral energy distribution
Strahlungswärme f radiant heat
Strahlungswellenlänge f radiation wavelength
Strahlvereiniger m,
Strahlvereinigungsoptik f combiner
Strahlverfolgung f ray tracing
~/**geometrische** geometrical ray tracing
~/**rekursive** recursive ray tracing
~/**vereinfachte** ray casting
Strahlverfolgungsalgorithmus m ray tracing algorithm
Strahlverfolgungsmodell n ray-tracing model
Strahlverlauf m ray path (trajectory); beam path
Strahlversatz m beam displacement
Strahlvervielfacher m beam multiplexer
Strahlvervielfachung f beam multiplexing
Strahlweg m beam path
Strahlweiche f beam deflector
Strahlweite f/**Gaußsche** beam waist *(Gaussian optics)*
Strahlwinkel m ray angle; beam angle
Straßenfotograf m street photographer
Straßenfotografie f street photography
Straßenkarte f road map; traffic map
Stratigrafie f stratigraphy
stratigrafisch stratigraphic
Streakaufnahme f, **Streakbild** n streak image
Streakfotografie f streak photography
Streakkamera f streak (velocity-recording) camera
Streakkameraufzeichnung f streak camera record
Streakröhre f/**fotoelektrische** *s.* Streakkamera
Streichmasse f, **Streichpaste** f size *(e.g. in papermaking)*
Streifen m/**Machscher** Mach band *(optics)*
~ mpl/**Brewstersche** Brewster's fringes *(interference pattern)*
Streifenartefakt n banding, contouring
Streifenbeseitigung f destriping
Streifenfilter n stripe[d] filter
Streifenkamera f strip camera
Streifenkontrast m fringe contrast *(holography, electron microscopy)*
Streifenlaser m ridge laser

Streifenmaske

Streifenmaske f aperture [grille] mask, stripe (slotted-shadow) mask, striped aperture *(picture tube)*
Streifenmaskenröhre f aperture grille CRT; [precision-]in-line tube, PIL tube
Streifenmodus m stripmap mode *(synthetic aperture radar)*
Streifenmuster n stripe[d] pattern; fringe pattern
Streifenrastermonitor m stripe raster monitor
Streifenstabilität f fringe stability *(holography)*
Streifentasche f negative sleeve
Streifentest m strip test *(exposure measurement)*
streifig streaky *(e.g. an underdeveloped print)*
Streuabsorption f Compton effect (scattering) *(X-ray attenuation)*
Streuabsorptionskontrast m structure factor contrast *(electron microscopy)*
Streuamplitude f scattered amplitude
Streubild n 1. light scattering image; 2. *s.* Streuungsdiagramm
Streuechos npl noise *(sonography)*
Streuelektron n stray (scatter) electron
streuen to scatter, to stray *(e.g. reflected light)*
Streuer m scatterer
Streufeld n stray [magnetic] field
Streufilter n diffusing filter
Streufolie f scattering foil, diffusion sheet, scrim
Streukalotte f diffusing sphere *(incident-light meter)*
Streukegel m scattering cone
Streukoeffizient m scattering coefficient; volumetric scattering cross section
Streukörper m scatterer
~/**punktförmiger** point scatterer
Streukreis m blur circle, circle of confusion
Streulicht n stray light; scattered (diffused) light; flare [light]
Streulichtanteil m scatter[ing] fraction
Streulichtblende f glare stop [diaphragm]; lens hood (shade), sunshade
Streulichtfaktor m flare factor, glare index (number)
Streulichtkompensation f flare correction *(electronic camera)*
Streulichtmessung f stray light measurement
Streulichtquelle f stray light source
Streulichtstrahl m stray ray
Streulinse f diverging (dispersive) lens, negative (concave) lens
Streumatrix f scatter[ing] matrix
Streuprozess m scattering process
Streurasterung f stochastic (frequency-modulated) screening, [dot] diffusion dithering, error diffusion [rendering] *(halftoning technique)*

Streurichtung f scattering direction, direction of scatter
Streuscheibe f diffuser disk; diffuser (bounce) card
Streuschirm m diffusing screen; lighting umbrella
Streustrahlenanteil m scatter[ing] fraction *(radiography)*
Streustrahlenraster m(n) radiographic (antiscatter) grid
Streustrahlung f stray (scattered) radiation; flare
~/**sekundäre** secondary radiation
Streuung f 1. scatter[ing], diffusion, dispersion *(of radiation)*; 2. dispersion *(statistics)*
~/**atmosphärische** atmospheric scattering
~/**diffuse** diffuse scattering
~/**elastische** elastic scattering
~/**inelastische** inelastic scattering
~/**inkohärente** incoherent (Compton) scattering, Compton effect *(X-ray attenuation)*
~/**klassische** classical scattering
~/**kohärente (lineare)** coherent (Rayleigh) scattering
~/**optische** optical scatter[ing]
~/**unelastische** inelastic scattering
Streuungsdiagramm n scatter diagram, scattergram, scattergraph, scatterplot, feature space image
streuungsfrei scatter-free
Streuungsmatrix f scatter matrix
Streuverlust m scattering loss
Streuvermögen n scattering strength (power)
~/**optisches** optical scattering power
Streuwinkel m scattering angle; angle of spread
Streuzentrum n scattering center
Strich m stroke; line
Strichabbildung f *s.* Strichbild
Strichätzung f line etching
Strichbild n line[-drawing] image; line illustration
Strichcode m bar code
Strichcode-Lesepistole f bar code pistol
Strichcodeleser m bar-code reader (scanner), wand
Strichcodierung f bar code labeling, bar coding
Strichdia n line slide
Strichdicke f *s.* Strichstärke
Strichfilm m line (halftone) film *(reprography)*
Strichgitter n gratic[u]le, retic[u]le
Strichgrafik f line graphics (art), coordinate graphics
Strichkante f line edge
Strichkopie f line copy; line-copy print
Strichmännchen n stick figure *(animation)*
Strichnegativ n line negative
Strichplatte f reticle, [measurement] graticule

Strichraster *m(n)* bar pattern *(television)*
Strichrasterverfahren *n* line-scanning method
Strichschärfe *f* line sharpness
Strichstärke *f* line (stroke) width, line thickness *(line metrics)*
Strichvorlage *f* line copy (original), line art (work)
Strichzeichnung *f* line drawing
Stripping-Film *m* stripping film, peel-apart film *(graphic-arts material)*
Strobo[blitz]fotografie *f* stroboscopic (repetitive flash) photography
Stroboblitz *m* stroboscopic flash, strobe light (flash), strobe
Stroboblitzgerät *n* stroboscopic flash unit
Stroboskop *n* stroboscope, strobe
~/**elektronisches** electronic stroboscope
~/**mechanisches** mechanical stroboscope
Stroboskopaufnahme *f* stroboscopic photograph
Stroboskopbeleuchtung *f* stroboscopic illumination
Stroboskopbild *n s.* Stroboskopaufnahme
Stroboskopblitz *m s.* Stroboblitz
Stroboskopeffekt *m* stroboscopic effect
Stroboskopfotografie *f s.* Strobofotografie
Stroboskopie *f* stroboscopy
stroboskopisch stroboscopic, strobe
Stroboskoplicht *n* strobe light *(s.a.* Stroboblitz*)*
Strom *f*/**faradischer** faradic current
~/**fotoelektrischer** photoelectric current, photocurrent
Stromband *n* stream ribbon *(visualization)*
Stromdichte *f* electron current density
Stromkreis *m*/**geschlossener** closed (integrating) circuit *(photodiode)*
Stromsparschaltung *f* power saving mode
Stromtor *n s.* Thyratron
Strömung *f*/**laminare** laminar flow
Strömungsanalyse *f* fluids motion analysis
Strömungsartefakt *n* flow artifact *(magnetic resonance imaging)*
Strömungsbild *n* flow pattern
Strömungsfeld *n*/**optisches** optical flow field
Strömungsfeldanalyse *f* flow field analysis
Strömungsfläche *f* stream surface
Strömungssimulation *f*/**numerische** computational fluid dynamics
Strömungsvisualisierung *f* flow imaging (mapping), [fluid] flow visualization
Stroop-Effekt *m* Stroop effect *(perceptual interference)*
Struktogramm *n* [program] structure chart
Struktur *f* structure *(s.a.* Muster*)*
Strukturanalyse *f* structural analysis
Strukturdiagramm *n s.* Struktogramm
Strukturebene *f* structure level
Strukturelement *n* structuring element *(morphological image processing)*
Strukturerkennung *f* structure recognition

Strukturfolie *f* texturizing film material, textured laminating material
Strukturierung *f* structuring *(data processing)*
Strukturmerkmal *n* structural feature
Strukturspeicher *m*/**zentraler** centralized structure store, CSS
Strukturtensor *m* structure tensor
Studio *n* studio *(s.a. under* Atelier*)*
~/**digitales** digital studio
~/**virtuelles** virtual studio
~**[frei]gelände** *n* [studio] backlot, lot
Studioanimation *f* studio animation
Studioarbeit *f* studio work
Studioarchiv *n* studio archive
Studioareal *n* [studio] backlot, lot
Studioaufbauten *pl* studio structures
Studioaufnahme *f* 1. studio shot; 2. *s.* Studioaufzeichnung 1. *and* 2.
Studioaufzeichnung *f* 1. studio recording; 2. studio record
Studioausleuchtung *f* studio illumination
Studioausrüster *m* studio supplier
Studioausrüstung *f* studio equipment
Studiobandmaschine *f* studio machine (deck)
Studiobeleuchtung *f* studio lighting
Studiobetrieb *m* studio business (operation)
Studiobild *n* studio picture *(television)*
Studioblitz *m* studio [electronic] flash
~**[licht]gerät** *n* studio[-type electronic] flash unit
Studioblitzanlage *f* studio flash system
Studiodecke *f* studio ceiling
Studiodekoration *f* studio setting
Studioeinrichtung *f* studio facility
Studio-Fachkamera *f* studio view camera
Studiofernsehen *n* studio television
Studiofilmmaterial *n* studio footage
Studioformat *n* studio format *(e.g. of tape stock)*
Studiofotograf *m* studio photographer
Studiofotografie *f* studio photography
Studiogerät *n* studio[-grade] device
Studiokabel *n* studio cable
Studiokamera *f* studio camera; broadcast[-quality] camera
Studiokamerastativ *n* studio-type camera stand, pedestal
Studiolampe *f* studio lamp
Studiolaufwerk *n* studio deck (machine)
Studioleuchte *f* studio-type lighting unit, studio light
Studiolicht *n* studio light
Studiomikrofon *n* studio microphone
Studiomonitor *m* studio monitor
Studionorm *f s.* Studiostandard
Studioporträt *n* studio portrait
Studioporträtfotograf *m* studio portrait photographer, studio portraitist
Studioporträtfotografie *f* studio portraiture
Studioproduktion *f* studio production

Studiopumpe

Studiopumpe f, **Studiopumpstativ** n pedestal
Studioqualität f [/**technische**] studio (broadcast) quality
Studioraumbeleuchtung f studio lighting
Studiorecorder m studio recorder
Studio-Referenzsignal n house (reference) black, house sync (reference), black burst *(composite video signal)*
Studioscheinwerfer m studio light
Studioschirm m [lighting] umbrella
Studioschnitt m studio editing
Studiosendung f studio broadcast
Studiostandard m studio [production] standard, broadcast industry standard
~/**digitaler** digital studio [production] standard
Studiostativ n studio stand, pedestal
Studioszene f studio scene
Studiotechnik f 1. studio engineering; 2. studio equipment
Studiotechniker m studio technician
Studioton m studio sound
Studiotonaufzeichnung f studio sound recording
Studio-Videokamera f studio video camera
Studio-Videotechnik f studio video equipment
Studio-Zeitcode m SMPTE time code *(from Society of Motion Picture and Television Engineers)*
Studiozubehör n studio accessories
Stufenbelichtung f step-tablet exposure
Stufeneffekt m, **Stufenfehler** m stair-stepping [artifact], staircasing, jaggedness, jaggies *(spatial alias)*
Stufenfilter n step filter *(e.g. in sensitometry)*
Stufenfotometer n step (Pulfrich) photometer
Stufengitter n echelon [grating]
Stufengraukeil m stepped [optical] wedge, gray (neutral-density) step wedge, step (tone) wedge, gray-scale wedge, [photographic] density wedge, [silver] step tablet
Stufenindexfaser f step-index fiber
Stufenkante f step edge
Stufenkeil m s. Stufengraukeil
Stufenlinse f [/**Fresnelsche**] Fresnel lens
Stufenlinsenscheinwerfer m, **Stufenlinser** m Fresnel[-lens spotlight]
stufig jagged
Stufigkeit f jaggedness *(s.a. Treppeneffekt)*
Stummfilm m silent [motion] picture, silent film, mute
Stummfilmzeit f silent era, silent film days
Stummkamera f silent [camera]
Stummschaltungsfunktion f, **Stummtaste** f mute
Stumpfkleben n butt (tape) splicing
Stumpfklebepresse f butt (guillotine) splicer
Stumpfklebestelle f butt (tape) splice

Stundenachse f s. Polarachse
Stützbild n anchor picture *(motion estimation)*
Stützkerbe f s. Raste
Stützpunkt m, **Stützstelle** f grid point
Stutzung f truncation *(e.g. of a distribution)*
Subbasskanal m subwoofer
Subbaum m subtree *(data structure)*
Subdivision f subdivision
~/**bilineare** bilinear (quad) subdivision
Subgraph m subgraph
Subkeim m ripening center *(latent image)*
Sublimationsdrucker m sublimation printer
sublimierbar sublimable *(dye)*
subliminal subliminal *(stimulus)*
Submenü n submenu
submikroskopisch submicroscopic
Submillimeter-Array n, **Submillimeter-Interferometer** n submillimeter array, SMA *(telescope)*
Subpixel n subpixel
Subpixelauflösung f subpixel (better-than-pixel) resolution
Subpixelgenauigkeit f subpixel accuracy (precision), fractional-pel accuracy
Subpixelinterpolation f subpixel interpolation
Subpixelschätzung f subpixel estimation
Subproportionalabschwächer m subproportional reducer
Subraum m subspace
Substrat n substrate, substratum *(e.g. of a photoresist)*
Substratschicht f substrate (subbing) layer, adhesive layer *(film structure)*
Subträger m subcarrier
Subträgerfrequenz f subcarrier frequency
Subtraktionsangiografie f/**digitale** digital subtraction angiography, DSA, CT angiography, CTA
Subtraktionsangiogramm n subtraction angiogram
Subtraktionsbild n subtraction image; difference image *(picture)*
Subtraktionsradiografie f/**digitale** digital subtraction radiography
Subtraktivabschwächer m subtractive (cutting) reducer
Suchalgorithmus m search[ing] algorithm
Suchanfrage f query
Suchaufgabe f search task
Suchaufwand m search effort
Suchbaum m/**binärer** binary [search] tree
Suchbaumalgorithmus m search tree algorithm
Suchbegriff m search term
Suchbereich m search area (region); search range
Suchbewegung f search movement *(of the eyes)*
Suchbild n search image; query image *(image retrieval)*
Suchdatei f search file

Suche f search, seek[ing]
~/**Boolesche** Boolean search (retrieval)
~/**globale** global search *(image coding)*
~/**gradientenbasierte** gradient-based search
~/**heuristische** heuristic search
~/**hierarchische** hierarchical search
~/**iterative** iterative search
~/**logarithmische** logarithmic search
Sucher m [view]finder, camera finder
~/**elektronischer** video (electronic) viewfinder
~/**optischer** optical viewfinder
Sucherachse f viewfinder axis
Sucheranzeige f viewfinder information
Sucherbild n [view]finder image, rangefinder image
Sucherbildrahmen m viewfinder frame
サウchereinstellung f viewfinder focusing
Sucherfehler m viewfinder (rangefinder) error, framing error
Sucherfeld n, **Sucherfeldgröße** f s. Suchergesichtsfeld
Sucherfenster n viewfinder window
Sucherfokussierung f viewfinder focusing
Suchergebnis n search result
Suchergesichtsfeld n viewfinder frame coverage
Sucherkamera f rangefinder[-type] camera, viewfinder camera
Sucherleistung f viewfinder performance
Sucherleuchtrahmen m illuminated lens viewfinder frame
Sucherlichtweg m viewfinder light path
Sucherlinse f finder lens
Sucherlupe f focusing magnifier (glass)
Suchermonitor m video assist [monitor], video tap, electronic viewfinder *(of a movie camera)*
Sucherobjektiv n viewing (viewfinder) lens, focusing lens *(medium-format camera)*
Sucherokular n [view]finder eyepiece
Sucheroptik f viewfinder optics (optical system); rangefinder optics
Sucherparallaxe f viewpoint difference
Sucherprisma n [view]finder prism
Sucherrahmen m viewfinder frame
Sucherscheibe f [ground-glass] viewing screen, ground-glass [view]finder, [ground-glass] focusing screen, [finder] screen
Sucherspiegel m viewfinder mirror
Suchersystem n finder system, viewing (viewfinder) system; rangefinder system
Suchervergrößerung f [view]finder magnification
Sucherzubehör n [view]finder accessories
Suchfenster n search (query) window
Suchfilter n/**optimales** matched filter
Suchfunktion f search function
Suchgenauigkeit f search precision
Suchgraph m search graph
Suchkapazität f search capacity

Suchkriterium n search criterion
Suchlauf m search [run], cueing
~/**sichtbarer** visible search
Suchlaufdrehknopf m jog (shuttle) dial *(video recorder)*
Suchlaufrad n jogwheel
Suchlaufzeit f cue time
Suchmaschine f search engine
Suchmuster n search pattern
Suchpunkt m search point
Suchquadrat n search square
Suchradar n search radar
Suchraum m search space
Suchscheinwerfer m searchlight
Suchschritt m search step
Suchstrategie f search[ing] strategy *(e.g. in pattern recognition)*
Suchverfahren n search procedure (technique)
Suchwerkzeug n search tool
Suchzeit f search (seek) time
Sukzessivkontrast m successive contrast
~/**farbiger** chromatic aftereffect *(vision)*
Sulfidtonung f sulfide (sepia) toning
Sulfitentwickler m sulfite developer
Sulfonamidkuppler m sulfonamide coupler
Summationsbild n sum image *(radiography)*
Summensignal n composite signal
Superachromat m superachromat
~ m superachromat, superachromatic lens
superachromatisch superachromatic
Super-Acht-Film m super-eight [mm] film *(home movie format)*
Super-Acht-Kamera f super-eight camera
Superadditivität f superadditivity *(photographic process)*
Superauflösung f superresolution
superglänzend superglossy
Supergroßfeldokular n superwide-field eyepiece *(optical microscopy)*
Superikonoskop n image iconoscope
Superimposition f super[im]position, superimposure, registration
Superkardioid-Mikrofon n hypercardioid microphone
Supernierencharakteristik f hypercardioid polar (directivity) pattern *(microphone)*
Superorthikon n image orthicon [tube], IO
superpanchromatisch superpanchromatic
superparamagnetisch superparamagnetic
superponieren to super[impose], to overlay
Superposition f superposition
Superpositionsprinzip n principle of superposition, superposition principle *(wave optics)*
Superproportionalabschwächer m superproportional (flattening) reducer
Supersensibilisator m supersensitizer
Supersensibilisierung f supersensitization
Supertele[objektiv] n super telephoto [lens], long-focal-length telephoto lens

Super-VHS *n* Super Video Home System, S-VHS *(enhanced version of VHS)*
Superweitwinkelobjektiv *n* super (extreme) wide-angle lens
Supplementwinkel *m* supplementary angle
Supraleiter *m* superconductor
Supraleitungsmagnet *m* superconducting magnet
Surround-Ton *m* surround sound *(a stereophonic sound system)*
Suspension *f* suspension
~/**kolloidale** colloidal suspension
Suszeptibilität *f*/**magnetische** magnetic susceptibility
Suszeptibilitätsartefakt *n* [magnetic] susceptibility artifact *(magnetic resonance imaging)*
SVGA-Monitor *m* SVGA (super visual graphics array) monitor, SVGA display
S-Video *n* S-video, Y/C video, separate video *(signal format)*
Sweep-Modell *n* sweep *(computer graphics)*
Sweep-Operation *f* sweeping
Symbol *n* symbol, token
Symbolalphabet *n* symbol alphabet
Symbolcode *m* symbol code
Symbolcodierer *m* symbol [en]coder
Symboldecodierer *m* symbol decoder
Symbolfehler *m* symbol error
symbolisch symbolic
Symbolleiste *f* icon (button) bar; tool bar *(display)*
Symbolsprache *f*/**grafische** graphics language
Symmetrie *f* symmetry
~/**axiale** axial symmetry
Symmetrieachse *f* symmetric (symmetry) axis, axis of symmetry, medial axis
Symmetrieachsentransformation *f* symmetric axis transform[ation], SAT, medial axis transform, MAT
Symmetriebedingung *f* symmetry assumption *(e.g. of quantization)*
Symmetriedetektion *f* symmetry detection *(e.g. in pattern recognition)*
Symmetrieebene *f* plane of symmetry
Symmetriewahrnehmung *f* symmetry perception
symmetrisch symmetric[al]
Synästhesie *f* synesthesia
synästhetisch synesthetic
Synchrokabel *n* flash synchronization cable
synchron synchronous, in sync
Synchronatelier *n* recording studio
Synchronaufzeichnung *f* synchronous recording
Synchronbearbeiter *m* automatic dialog[ue] replacement editor, ADR editor (mixer)
Synchronbearbeitung *f* automatic dialog[ue] replacement, ADR [editing], additional dialog[ue] recording, [dialogue] looping *(s.a.* Nachvertonung*)*
Synchronblitz *m* synchronized flash
Synchronfehler *m* sync error
Synchrongenerator *m* sync[hronous] generator, synchronization (sync-pulse) generator, genlock
Synchronimpuls *m* 1. sync beep, sound pulse *(filming)*; 2. *s.* Synchronisiersignal
Synchronisation *f* synchronization; sound synchronization, sync *(motion-picture production)*
~ **auf den zweiten Verschlussvorhang** second-curtain synchronization, tailflash (rear-curtain) synchronization
~/**bildgenaue** frame-accurate synchronization
~/**horizontale** horizontal sync[hronization]
Synchronisationsblock *m* sync block
Synchronisationsbyte *n* sync[hronization] byte
Synchronisationsgenerator *m* sync generator
Synchronisationsimpuls *m*, **Synchronisationssignal** *n s.* Synchronisiersignal
Synchronisationssteuerzeichen *n* initial alignment control, IAC
Synchronisationsverzögerung *f* synchronization delay
Synchronisationszeit *f* sync[hronization] speed
Synchronisator *m* synchronizer
synchronisieren to synchronize
Synchronisierer *m* synchronizer
Synchronisierimpuls *m s.* 1. Synchronimpuls 1.; 2. Synchronisiersignal
Synchronisiersignal *n* sync[hronizing] signal, synchronization signal, sync[hronization] pulse
~/**gemischtes** composite sync[hronization] pulse
~/**horizontales** horizontal synchronizing signal, horizontal sync[hronization] pulse, HSYNC, line drive, LD
~/**vertikales** vertical synchronizing signal, vertical sync[hronization] pulse
~/**voreilendes** advanced sync pulse
Synchronisierung *f s.* Synchronisaion
Synchronisierzeichen *n s.* Synchronisiersignal
Synchronismus *m*, **Synchronität** *f* synchronism, synchroneity, sync[h]
Synchronkabel *n* sync (flash) cord, flash connector (sync cord), sync[hronization] lead
Synchronklappe *f* 1. sync stick, clapstick[s], clapboard, clapper [board]; 2. *s.* Szenenklappe
Synchronkontakt *m* sync contact
Synchronkopie *f* dubbing print
Synchron-Leitband *n* lip-sync band

Synchronmarke *f* synchronization mark; level sync *(cinema)*
Synchronmotor *m* synchronous motor
Synchronpegel *m* sync level *(video signal)*
Synchronpuls *m s.* Synchronisiersignal
Synchronpunkt *m* synchronization point, sync [reference] point *(film editing)*
Synchronschnitt *m* conforming, syncing-up
Synchronsignal *n s.* Synchronisiersignal
Synchronspur *f* sync track
Synchronstartband *n* sync leader
Synchronstudio *n* recording studio
Synchronton *m* sync[hronous] sound, synchronized sound
Synchrontonaufnahme *f*, **Synchrontonaufzeichnung** *f* sync sound recording
Synchronumroller *m* synchronizer, synchrometer *(film editing device)*
Synchronverbund *m* [/elektronischer] crystal sync *(filming)*
Synchronzeichen *n* synchronization mark *(s.a.* Synchronpunkt*)*
Synchronzeichengeber *m* audio slate
Synchronzeit *f s.* Synchronisationszeit
Synchrotron *n* synchrotron [radiation facility]
Synchrotron-Röntgenstrahlung *f* synchrotron X rays
Synchrotron-Speicherring *m* synchrotron [radiation] storage ring
Synchrotronstrahlung *f* synchrotron radiation (emission)
Synchrotronstrahlungsquelle *f* synchrotron radiation source
Synergiespule *f* phased-array antenna *(magnetic resonance tomography)*
Synthese *f*/**harmonische** Fourier synthesis
Synthesefilter *n* synthesis filter
~/**kreuzmoduliertes** cross modulated synthesis filter
Synthesefilterbank *f* synthesis filter bank
Synthetische-Apertur-Fokussierungstechnik *f* synthetic aperture focusing technique
System *n*/**abbildendes** imaging (image-forming) system, image formation system
~/**abbildendes optisches** imaging (image-forming) optical system
~/**abbildungsfehlerfreies** unaberrated system
~/**achsensymmetrisches** axially symmetrical system
~/**afokales** afocal system (lens), zero-power system
~/**aplanatisches** aplanatic [lens] system
~/**apochromatisches** apochromatic system
~/**asphärisches** aspheric [lens] system
~/**bandbreitenbegrenztes** bandwidth-limited system
~/**beugendes** diffracting system

~/**beugungsbegrenztes [optisches]** diffraction-limited optical system
~/**bilderzeugendes (bildgebendes)** *s.* ~/abbildendes
~/**bildverarbeitendes** image-processing system
~/**binäres** binary [numbering] system, base 2
~/**bistabiles** bistable (two-state) system
~/**dioptrisches** dioptric system
~/**fokales** focal (nonzero-power) system
~ **für interaktive Anwendungen** multimedia home platform, MHP
~/**ideales optisches** ideal optical system
~/**katadioptrisches** catadioptric [imaging] system, catadioptric (mirror) lens, reflecting lens
~/**katoptrisches** catoptric system
~/**kohärentes** coherent (one-wavelength) optical system
~/**konfokales optisches** confocal optical system
~/**konnektionistisches** connectionist (parallel distributed processing) model, connectionist network, neural net[work], neuromorphic system
~/**lageabhängiges** position-dependent system
~/**lageunabhängiges** position-independent system
~/**linear zeitinvariantes diskretes** linear time-invariant discrete-time system *(digital filtering)*
~/**mehrlinsiges** multi-element system
~/**menschliches visuelles** human visual system, HVS
~/**öffnungsfehlerbegrenztes [optisches]** spherical aberration limited system
~/**okulomotorisches** oculomotor system
~/**optisches** optical system (train)
~/**pankratisches** pancratic [lens] system, varifocal (vario) lens, variable-focal-length lens, zoom [lens]
~/**rotationssymmetrisches** rotationally symmetrical system
~/**sammelndes** collecting optics
~/**visuelles** visual (eye) system
~/**wissensbasiertes** knowledge-based system, expert system *(data processing)*
~/**zeitdiskretes** discrete-time system
~/**zentriertes optisches** centered lens system
Systembeschreibungssprache *f* systems description language
Systembus *m* system bus *(computer)*
Systemdatei *f* system file *(computer)*
Systemfehler *m* system error (fault)
Systemkamera *f* system[s] camera, modular camera
Systemplatine *f* [computer] motherboard, logic board, main computer circuit board
Systemrauschen *n* system[atic] noise, ghosts
Systemspeicher *m* system memory

Systemtakt m, **Systemzeit** f system [time] clock, STC
Systemzubehör n system accessories
S-Zapfen m S cone, short-wavelength-sensitive cone *(of the retina)*
Szene f [object] scene; digital image (picture)
~/**audiovisuelle** audiovisual scene
~/**dreidimensionale** three-dimensional scene
~/**dynamische** dynamic scene
~/**natürliche** natural scene
~/**polygonale** polygonal scene
~/**räumliche** three-dimensional scene
~/**visuelle** visual scene
Szenegraph m scene graph
Szenenabschnitt m take *(cinema, video)*
Szenenanalyse f scene analysis
~/**wissensbasierte** knowledge-based scene analysis
Szenenaufnahme f take; shot *(cinema)*
Szenenausleuchtung f scene illumination
Szenenbereich m scene domain
Szenenbeschreibung f scene description
Szenenbeschreibungssprache f scene description language
Szenenbild n scenic image
Szenendauer f scene duration
Szeneneditor m scene editor *(computer graphics)*
Szenenelement n scene element
Szenenentfernung f scene distance
Szenenerkennung f scene recognition
Szenenfarbe f scene color
Szenenfolge f sequence of scenes
Szenenfoto n film (movie) still, action still, still [frame]; production (publicity) still
Szenengeometrie f scene geometry
Szenenhelligkeit f scene brightness (luminance)
Szenenheterogenität f scene heterogeneity
Szenenhintergrund m scene background
Szeneninformation f scene information
Szeneninhalt m scene content
Szenenintensitätsgradient m scene intensity gradient *(three-dimensional visualization)*
Szeneninterpolation f scene interpolation
Szenenklappe f [clapping] slate, number board *(filming)*
Szenenkontrast m scene contrast
Szenenkoordinatensystem n scene coordinate system, world (global) coordinate system, world reference frame, world (global) space
Szenenmerkmal n scene characteristic
Szenenmodell n scene model
Szenenmodellierung f scene modeling
Szenennummer f scene (sequence) number *(cinema)*
Szenenobjekt n scene object
Szenenparameter m scene parameter

Szenenpunkt m scene point
Szenenraum m scene space *(visualization)*
Szenenrekonstruktion f/**geometrische** geometric scene reconstruction
Szenensegmentierung f scene segmentation
Szenenstruktur f scene structure
Szenentafel f slate, number board
Szenentiefe f scene depth
Szenentransformation f scene transformation
Szenenübergang m [shot] transition, segue
Szenenwechsel m scene[ry] change
Szenenwechselerkenner m shot change detector *(film scanner)*
Szenerie f scenery
Szintigrafie f scintigraphy
~/**planare** planar scintigraphy
~/**tomografische** [radionuclide] emission tomography
szintigrafisch scintigraphic
Szintigramm n scintillation camera image
Szintillation f scintillation
Szintillationsdetektor m scintillation detector, scintillator-based X-ray detector
Szintillationskamera f scintillation camera, [single-crystal] gamma camera, Anger[-type] camera
Szintillationskristall m scintillation (scintillating) crystal
Szintillationslicht n scintillation light
Szintillationsmesskopf m, **Szintillationsmesssonde** f scintillation probe (head)
Szintillationsscanner m s. Szintillationsdetektor
Szintillationsschicht f scintillation (scintillating) layer
Szintillationsschirm m scintillation (scintillator) screen, gamma-ray camera detector screen
Szintillationssignal n scintillation signal
Szintillationszähler m scintillation counter, scaling device, scaler
Szintillationszeit f scintillation time
Szintillator m scintillator
Szintillatorfolie f scintillating screen
szintillieren to scintillate

T

T1 *s.* Spin-Gitter-Relaxationszeit
T2 *s.* Transversalrelaxationszeit
Tabellenblatt *n* spreadsheet
Tabellensatz *m* tabular setting
Tabellenspeicher *m* lookup table [memory], LUT; video lookup table
Tableau *n/***selbstorganisierendes** *s.* Karte/selbstorganisierende
Tabletop-Fotografie *f* tabletop photography
Tablett *n* [/**grafisches**] graphics (digitizing) table[t], [electronic] tablet
Tablettstift *m* stylus *(graphics tablet)*
Tabloid[format] *n* tabloid *(newspaper format)*
Tabukanal *m* taboo channel *(television)*
Tachistoskop *n* tachistoscope
tachistoskopisch tachistoscopic
Tachometer *m(n)* tachometer
Tachymeter *n* tachymeter
Tachymetrie *f* tachymetry
Tachyskop *n* Tachyscope *(early animated-picture machine)*
Tafel *f* plate *(e.g. as illustration)*
~/**pseudoisochromatische** pseudoisochromatic plate
Tafelbild *n* matte painting
Tafelglas *n* plate (sheet) glass
Tafelkristall *m* tabular crystal, tabular photoemulsion microcrystal, tabular [silver-halide] grain, T-grain
Tag-Außenaufnahme *f* outdoor daylight picture
Tagblindheit *f* day blindness, hemeralopia
Tagesdisposition *f* call sheet *(filming)*
Tageslicht *n/***fotografisches** photographic daylight
~/**künstliches mittleres** average artificial daylight
~/**mittleres** average daylight
Tageslichtatelier *n* daylight studio
Tageslichtbearbeitungssystem *n* daylight film-handling system *(radiography)*
Tageslichtbedingungen *fpl* daylight conditions
Tageslichtbeleuchtung *f* daylight[-type] illumination
Tageslichtbildschirm *m* daylight screen
Tageslichtblendung *f* daylight glare
Tageslichtdose *f s.* Tageslicht-Entwicklungsdose
Tageslichteinlegepackung *f* daylight-loading package
Tageslichtemulsion *f* daylight emulsion
Tageslicht-Entwicklungsdose *f* daylight [development] tank, daylight developing (processing) tank
Tageslichtfarbfilm *m* daylight[-balanced] color film, outdoor color film
Tageslicht-Farbtemperatur *f* daylight color temperature
Tageslichtfilm *m* daylight[-balanced] film, daylight-type film
Tageslichtfilter *n* daylight-balanced filter; daylight conversion light filter, daylight color temperature conversion filter; daylight correction gel
Tageslichtfoto *n* daylight photograph
Tageslichtfotografie *f* daylight photography
Tageslichtkassette *f* daylight-load roll cassette, daylight-loading magazine (cartridge)
Tageslichtlampe *f* 1. daylight lamp; 2. *s.* Tageslichtleuchte
Tageslichtleuchte *f* daylight-balanced lighting fixture, daylight illuminant
Tageslichtmagazin *n* daylight magazine
Tageslichtpapier *n* daylight paper
Tageslichtprojektor *m* overhead projector
Tageslicht-Rollfilmspule *f* daylight-loading film roll
Tageslichtspule *f* daylight loader
Tageslichtsystem *n* daylight [film-handling] system *(photofluorography)*
~/**dezentrales (modulares)** modular (integrated) daylight film-handling system
~/**zentrales** composite daylight [film-handling] system
Tageslichtverarbeitung *f* daylight processing
Tagesmuster *npl* [film] dailies, rushes *(cinema)*
Tagessehen *n* daylight (daytime) vision, bright-light (light-adapted) vision, photopic vision, cone[-mediated] vision
Tagessichtigkeit *f* photopia
Taillendurchmesser *m* [beam] waist diameter *(optics)*
Taillenradius *m* [beam] waist radius
Take *m(n)* take; [single] shot *(cinema, video)*
Takt *m* clock [cycle]
Taktabweichung *f* clock skew (phase deviation) *(digital video)*
takten to clock
Taktfrequenz *f* clock[ing] frequency, clock speed (rate)
Taktfrequenzgenerator *m s.* Taktgeber
Taktgeber *m* clock [pulse] generator, [synchronizing] pulse generator, impulse generator
Taktgeberfrequenz *f s.* Taktfrequenz
Taktgenauigkeit *f* clock accuracy
Taktgenerator *m s.* Taktgeber
Taktjitter *m* clock jitter
Taktperiode *f* clock cycle
Taktquelle *f* clock, source of clocking
Taktrate *f s.* Taktfrequenz

Taktrückgewinnung f clock (timing) recovery, reclocking
Taktsignal n clock[ing] signal, timing signal
Taktsteuerung f clock control
Taktung f clocking
Taktzyklus m clock cycle
Talbot-Effekt m Talbot effect *(optics)*
Talbotypie f s. Kalotypie 1. *and* 2.
Tampondruck m, **Tampondruckverfahren** n pad [transfer] printing
Tangensbedingung f/**Airysche** Airy's tangent condition *(optics)*
Tangensfehler m slope error
Tangente f tangent
Tangentenfehler m slope error
Tangentenfläche f tangent surface
Tangentenvektor m tangent vector, [tangent] handle *(computer graphics)*
tangential tangent; tangential
Tangentialebene f tangent[ial] plane; meridional plane *(optics)*
Tangentialsignal n tangential signal *(videodisc)*
Tankentwicklung f tank processing
Tankverarbeitung f tank processing
Tanninplatte f tannin[-coated collodion] plate
Tanzfotografie f 1. dance photography; 2. dance photograph
Tapedeck n tape deck
Tapetenillusion f wallpaper illusion *(stereopsis)*
Target n target, signal plate *(camera tube)*
Targetmaterial n target [material], anode material
Taschendiabetrachter m pocket slide viewer
Taschenfernglas n pocket binocular
Taschenfernseher m pocket television, handheld TV
Taschenkamera f pocket[-size] camera
~/**digitale** pocket digicam
Taschenlupe f pocket magnifier
Taschenstereoskop n pocket stereoscope
Taschenvideorecorder m pocket-size[d] video recorder
Taskleiste f task bar
Tastatur f keyboard *(input device)*
Tastatursperre f [keyboard] lockup, lockout
Tastenfeld n keypad, key panel
Tastung f 1. keying, digital modulation; 2. s. Umtastung
Tastverhältnis n duty cycle *(signal processing)*
Tatortaufnahme f, **Tatortfoto** n crime scene photograph
Tatortfotograf m crime scene photographer
Tatortfotografie f crime scene photography
Tatortvideo n crime scene video
Tauchbeschichtung f dip coating
Tauchspulenmikrofon n moving-coil microphone

Täuschung f/**Machsche** Mach [band] effect, Mach banding *(visual perception)*
~/**optische** optical (visual) illusion, trick
~/**perspektivische** perspective illusion
Taylor-Reihe f Taylor['s] series *(predicate calculus)*
T-Belag m s. Transparenzschicht
T-Blende f T-stop, t-stop, effective f-number, effective relative aperture
TCB-Spline n s. Kochanek-Bartels-Spline
Technik f/**digitale** digital technology
Technoskop n borescope [lens], probe lens, industrial endoscope
Teil n/**optisches** optical component
Teilabsorption f partial absorption
Teilband n/**örtliches** spatial subband
Teilbandanalyse f subband analysis
Teilband-Analysefilter n subband analysis filter
Teilbandbild n subband image (picture)
Teilband-Bildcodierung f subband image coding
Teilbandcodierer m sub-band coder
Teilbandcodierung f subband coding (compression), SBC
Teilbandcodierungsfilterbank f subband coding filter bank
Teilbandfilter n subband filter
Teilbandfilterung f subband filtering
Teilbandkoeffizient m subband coefficient
Teilbandsignal n subband signal
Teilbandsynthese f subband synthesis
Teilbandzerlegung f subband decomposition
Teilbaum m subtree *(data structure)*
teilbelichtet partially exposed
Teilbelichtung f partial (split) exposure
Teilbereich m subregion *(e.g. of an image)*
~[**sab**]**frage** f partial range query *(computer graphics)*
Teilbild n 1. partial image (picture); component image *(e.g. in color photography)*; subimage *(e.g. in image analysis)*; 3. s. Halbbild
~/**stereoskopisches** stereophotograph
Teilbildfläche f subimage area
Teilbildformat n subimage format
Teilbildfrequenz f s. Vertikalfrequenz
Teilbildgröße f subimage size
Teilbildtransformation f subimage transform
Teilbildverarbeitung f subimage processing
Teilbildzerlegung f subimage decomposition
Teilchen... s.a. *under* Partikel...
Teilchenbeschleuniger m particle accelerator
Teilchenmechanik f particle mechanics
Teilchenphysik f particle (high-energy) physics
Teilchenstrahlung f particle (corpuscular) radiation
Teilchenstreuung f particulate scattering

Teilchentheorie f **des Lichts** corpuscular (particle, emission) theory of light
Teildispersion f/**relative** relative partial dispersion *(optics)*
teildurchsichtig partially transparent
Teileerkennung f components detection, workpiece recognition, industrial parts verification
Teilerplatte f plate beam splitter
Teilerprisma n s. Strahlenteilungsprisma
Teilerspiegel m beam-splitting mirror
Teilertabelle f quantization table, q-table
Teilerwürfel m cube beam splitter
Teile-und-herrsche-Ansatz m divide-and-conquer strategy *(computer graphics)*
Teilfarbe f component color
Teilfarbenbild n color record *(color photography)*
Teilkettencode m substring code
teilkohärent partially coherent
Teilkohärenz f partial coherence
Teilkreis m divided circle, graduated circle (dial), circular scale
Teilkreisspektrometer n divided-circle spectrometer
Teillichtstrom m partial luminous flux
Teilmatrix f submatrix
Teilmenge f subset *(e.g. of features)*
Teilmuster n subpattern
Teilnahlinse f split-field filter
Teilnehmeranschlussleitung f subscriber line (drop cable)
~/**digitale** digital subscriber line, DSL
Teilnehmerleitung f/**asymmetrisch digitale** asymmetrical digital subscriber line, ADSL
Teilnehmerverwaltung f subscriber management
Teilobjekt n subobject
Teilpolarisation f partial polarization
Teilpunkt m subpixel
Teilpunktfrage f partial match query *(computer graphics)*
Teilreflexion f partial reflection
Teilsegmentierung f partial segmentation
Teilspektrum n subspectrum
Teilspiegel m partial mirror
Teilspur f half-track
Teilstrahl m partial beam
Teilszene f subscene
Teilungswürfel m cube beam splitter
teilverspiegelt partially mirrored
Teilverspiegelung f partial silvering
Teilwelle f subwave, partial wave
Teilwinkeltomografie f limited-angle tomography
T-Einstellung f T setting *(camera)*
Teleaufnahme f telephotograph
Telefax[gerät] n fax [terminal], fax machine, facsimile transceiver (machine)
Telefaxpapier n s. Thermopapier
Telefoto n telephoto

Telefotografie f 1. telephotography; 2. s. Telefoto
telefotografisch telephotographic
Telefotoobjektiv n s. Teleobjektiv
telegen telegenic
Telekommunikationsindustrie f telecommunications industry
Telekommunikationsnetz n telecommunications network
Telekommunikationsnorm f/**Europäische** European Telecommunication Standard, ETS
Telekonverter m teleconverter [lens]
Telemakroobjektiv n telemacro lens
Telemammografie f telemammography
Telemedizin f telemedicine
Telemeter n s. Mischbildentfernungsmesser
Telemetrieradar n telemetric radar
telemetrisch telemetric
Telemikroskop n telemicroscope
Telemikroskopie f telemicroscopy
telemikroskopisch telemicroscopic[al]
Telenegativ n 1. negative rear element; 2. s. Televorsatzlinse
Teleobjektiv n [/**echtes**] true telephoto[graphic] lens, tele[-lens], telephoto [lens], teleobjective, long lens (tom)
~/**langbrennweitiges** long focal-length telephoto lens, super telephoto [lens]
~/**mittellangbrennweitiges** medium telephoto lens
~/**umgekehrtes** reverse telephoto lens, retrofocus lens
Teleoptik f s. Teleobjektiv
Telepositiv n positive front element
Telepräsenz f telepresence *(virtual reality)*
Teleprompter m teleprompter, autocue
Teleradiologie f teleradiology
teleradiologisch teleradiologic[al]
Telerobotik f telerobotics
Tele-Röntgendiagnose f teleroentgen diagnosis
Teleskop n telescope *(s.a. Fernrohr)*
~/**abbildendes** imaging telescope
~/**achromatisches** achromatic telescope
~/**astrofotografisches** astrophotographic telescope
~/**astronomisches** astronomical (inverting) telescope
~/**automatisches fotometrisches** automatic photometric telescope, APT
~/**erdgebundenes** terrestrial (erecting) telescope, ground-based telescope
~/**extraterrestrisches** extraterrestrial (space) telescope
~ **mit Uhrwerksnachführung** clock-driven telescope
~/**optisches** optical telescope
~/**röntgeninterferometrisches** X-ray interferometric telescope
Teleskopadapter m telescopic adapter
Teleskopauflösung f telescope resolution

Teleskopbein *n* telescoping leg
Teleskopbild *n* telescope image, telescopic picture (image)
Teleskopdurchmesser *m* telescope diameter
Teleskopelektronik *f* telescope electronics
teleskopisch telescopic
Teleskopmontierung *f* telescope mount[ing]
Teleskopnachführung *f* [telescope] guiding
Teleskopobjektiv *n* telescope objective
Teleskopöffnung *f* telescope aperture
Teleskopokular *n* telescopic (telescope) eyepiece
Teleskopoptik *f* telescope optics
Teleskopspiegel *m* telescope mirror
Teleskopstativ *n* telescope stand
Teleskopsucher *m* telescopic rangefinder
~/**Keplerscher** Kepler telescope finder
Teleskoptubus *m* 1. telescoping tube, drawtube; 2. *s.* Fernrohrtubus
Teleskopvorsatz *m* telescope attachment
Telespektroradiometrie *f* telespectroradiometry
Telespiel *n* telegame
Telespielkonsole *f* [video] game console, play station
Telestereoskop *n* telestereoscope
Teletext *m s.* Videotext 1.
Televerhältnis *n* telephoto ratio (power)
Television *f* television, TV, video *(s.a. under* Fernsehen*)*
televisuell televisionary, televisual
Televorsatz *m*, **Televorsatzlinse** *f* telephoto attachment, telescopic (afocal) attachment
Telex *n* 1. telex; 2. telex system
telexen to [send by] telex
Telexgerät *n* teletypewriter; teleprinter
Telezentrik *f s.* Telezentrie
telezentrisch telecentric *(optics)*
Telezoom[objektiv] *n* long telephoto zoom
Temperatur *f*/**kritische** critical (transition) temperature *(superconductor)*
Temperaturdifferenz *f*/**minimale auflösbare** minimum resolvable temperature difference, MRTD *(thermal imaging)*
~/**rauschäquivalente** noise-equivalent temperature difference, NETD *(thermal imaging)*
Temperatureffekt *m* temperature exposure effect
Temperaturfeld *n* temperature field
Temperaturkoeffizient *m* temperature coefficient
Temperaturrauschen *n* temperature noise, thermal [conductance] noise *(of a thermal sensor)*
Temperaturregler *m* [/**automatischer**] thermostat
Temperaturskale *f* **nach Kelvin** Kelvin scale
Temperaturstrahler *m* thermal (temperature) radiator

Temperaturstrahlung *f* thermal (heat) radiation
temporal 1. temporal *(relating to time)*; 2. temporal *(relating to the temples of the skull)*
Tensor *m* tensor *(a generalized vector or matrix)*
~/**quadrifokaler** quadrifocal tensor
~/**Riemannscher** Riemann's [curvature] tensor
~/**symmetrischer** symmetrical tensor
~/**trifokaler** trifocal tensor
Tensorellipsoid *n* tensor ellipsoid *(type of glyph)*
Tensorfeld *n* tensor field
Tensorprodukt *n* tensor product
Terabyte *n* terabyte, Tb, TB *(a unit of information storage capacity)*
Terahertz-Bereich *m* terahertz portion [of the spectrum]
Terahertz-Bild *n* terahertz image, THz image, T-ray image
Terahertz-Bildgebungsverfahren *n* T-ray imaging modality
Terahertz-Lücke *f* terahertz gap
Terahertz-Mikroskop *n* terahertz wave microscope
Terahertz-Spektroskopie *f* terahertz [time-domain] spectroscopy
Terahertz-Strahlung *f* terahertz radiation, THz wave radiation
Terahertz-Welle *f* terahertz wave, T ray
Terminal *n* terminal [device]; data [display] terminal
Terrestrik *f* over-the-air broadcasting
terrestrisch terrestrial
Tertiärfarbe *f* tertiary color
Tesla *n* tesla, T *(unit of magnetic flux density)*
Tessellation *f s.* Parkettierung
Testaufnahme *f* test shot *(filming; s.a.* Probebild*)*
Testausdruck *m* hard proof
Testbelichtung *f* test exposure
Testbild *n* test (target) image, test chart (target), proof; test pattern [image], pattern
Testbildgenerator *m* test pattern generator
Testbildvorlage *f* test target
Testblitz *m* [test] preflash
Testfarbe *f* test color
Testfarbstreifen *m* color test strip
Testfilm *m* test film
Testfilmstreifen *m* film test strip
Testlicht *n* test light *(color matching)*
Testmuster *n* test pattern *(s.a.* Testbild*)*
Testnegativ *n* test negative
Testobjekt *n* test object
Testpapier *n* test paper
Testplatte *f* resolution [test] target, resolution chart
Testreihe *f* test series
Testsignal *n* test signal
Teststreifen *m* test strip

Testtafel f test chart
Testvorlage f test target
Tetrachlorkohlenstoff m carbon tetrachloride, tetrachloromethane
tetrachromatisch tetrachromatic, quadrichromatic, four-color
Tetraeder n tetrahedron
Texel n texel, texture element
Text m text
~/**elektronischer** electronic text, e-text
~/**formatierter** formatted text
~/**gedruckter** machine-printed text
~/**handgeschriebener (handschriftlicher)** handwritten text
~/**nichtlinearer** hypertext
~/**unformatierter** plain text
~/**unterschnittener** kerned text
~/**unverschlüsselter** plaintext
~/**verschlüsselter** scrambled text, cyphertext
Textabschnitt m string of text, field
Textanzeige f text display
Textauflösung f text resolution
Textausrichtung f text alignment
Textbaustein m boiler plate
Textbild n text image
Textblock m text block
Textblockbreite f width of a text block, measure
Textdatei f text file
Textdaten pl textual data
Textdatenbank f text database
Textdokument n [all-]text document
Textdrehbuch n dialog[ue] continuity
Textdrucker m text (line) printer
Texteile f text line
Texteinblendung f insert [title] *(cinema)*
Textelement n text element *(e.g. on the screen)*
Texterfassung f text entry
Texterkennung f text recognition
Textfarbenindex m text color index
Textfenster n text window (field) *(on a screen)*
Textgeber m [/**elektronischer**] m teleprompter, electronic cue card
Textgrafik f textual graphics
Textildruck m textile (fabric) printing
Textildruckpresse f textile press
Textilfarbband n textile (fabric) ribbon
Textilklebeband n gaffer tape, grip (cloth) tape
Textinformation f textual information
Textkompression f text compression
Textkontrast m text contrast
Textkörper m body
Textlesbarkeit f text legibility
textlich textual
Textmodus m text mode
Texton n s. Texturelement
Textschrift f body face, bread-and-butter type *(typography)*
Textseite f page of text, text page
Textspur f text track *(video)*

Textsuchmaschine f text search engine
Textübertragungssystem n/**interaktives** interactive text transmission system, ITTS
textuell textual
Textur f texture
~/**blockbasierte** block-based texture
~/**deterministische** deterministic texture
~/**globale** global texture
~/**periodische** periodic texture
~/**prozedurale** procedural texture
~/**statistische** statistic texture
~/**synthetische** synthetic texture
Texturabbildung f texture (pattern) mapping *(rendering technique)*
Texturabweichung f texture deviation *(coding artifact)*
Texturähnlichkeit f texture similarity
Texturalgorithmus m texture algorithm
Texturanalyse f textural (texture) analysis
~/**fourierbasierte** Fourier-based texture analysis
~/**fraktale** fractal texture analysis
~/**statistische** statistical (statistics-based) textural analysis
~/**transformationsbasierte** transform-based textural analysis
Texturanimation f texture animation
Texturauflösung f texture resolution
Texturbaum m texture tree *(data structure)*
Texturbeschreibung f texture (textural) description
Texturbestimmung f texture characterization
Texturbild n texture (textural) image, texture map *(computer graphics)*
Texturcodierer m texture coder
Texturcodierung f/**waveletbasierte** wavelet-based texture coding
Texturdarstellung f textural representation
Texturdecodierung f texture decoding
Texturdeskriptor m texture descriptor
Texturelement n texture element, texel, texton
texturell textural
Texturerzeugung f texture generation
~/**computergrafische** bump [texture] mapping
Texturextraktion f texture extraction
Texturfiltermaske f texture operator, texture-sensitive filter
Texturfilterungsalgorithmus m texture filtering algorithm
Texturgehalt m texture content
Texturgradient m textural (texture) gradient
Texturhomogenität f texture homogeneity
Texturidentifikation f texture identification
texturieren to texture
Texturinformation f texture information
Texturklassifikation f texture classification
Texturkontrast m texture contrast
Texturkoordinate f texture coordinate
Textur-Mapping n s. Texturabbildung

Texturmaskierung *f* texture (spatial) masking, activity masking, detail dependence *(video compression)*
Texturmaß *n* textural measure
Texturmerkmal *n* textural (texture) feature
~/**pixelbasiertes** pixel-based textural feature
Texturmerkmalsvektor *m* textural feature vector
Texturmodell *n* textural (texture) model
Texturmodellierung *f* texture modeling
Texturmuster *n* textural (texture) pattern
Texturmustererkennung *f* texture pattern recognition
Texturoperator *m* texture operator
Texturparameter *m* texture parameter
Texturprimitiv *n* texture primitive
Texturpufferspeicher *m* texture buffer
Texturpunkt *m* s. Texel
Texturschatten *m* texture shadow
Textursegmentierung *f* texture [image] segmentation, textural segmentation
~/**viererbaumbasierte** quad-tree-based textural segmentation
Textursynthese *f* texture synthesis
Texturunterscheidung *f* texture discrimination
Texturvektor *m* textural vector
Texturverarbeitung *f* texture processing
Texturwahrnehmung *f* texture perception
Textvektorisierungsalgorithmus *m* text vectorization algorithm
Textverarbeitung *f* word (text) processing
Textverarbeitungsprogramm *n* word processing program
Textzeichen *n* text character
Textzeile *f* text line, line [of text], string [of text]
TFT *s.* Dünnfilmtransistor
TFT-Bildschirm *m*, **TFT-Monitor** *m* TFT (thin-film transistor) display, active-matrix display
Thalamus *m* thalamus
Thalliumiodid *n* thallous iodide
Thaumatrop *n* thaumatrope *(an optical toy)*
Theaterfotografie *f* theatrical photography
Theaterglas *n* opera glass[es]
Theaterkopie *f* theatrical [projection] print, [exhibition] release print, [theatrical] release [print]
Themakarte *f* thematic map
Themenkanal *m* special-interest channel *(television)*
Theorem *n*/**Babinetsches** Babinet's principle *(diffractive optics)*
Theorie *f* **des Farbensehen/trichromatische** trichromatic theory [of color vision], tri-receptor theory of color vision, Young[-Helmholtz] theory [of color vision]
~/**dynamische** dynamical [diffraction] theory *(electron diffraction)*

~/**kinematische** kinematical [diffraction] theory
~ **linearer Systeme** linear-systems theory
~ **unscharfer Mengen** fuzzy set theory
~ **von Mott und Gurney** Gurney-Mott theory *(latent-image formation)*
Thermalbild *n* s. Thermobild
Thermalscanner *m* infrared scanner
Thermalstrahlung *f* thermal (heat) radiation
Thermistor *m* thermistor, thermal sensitive resistor *(thermal sensor)*
Thermobild *n* thermal (heat) image, thermogram, thermograph[ic image]
Thermochromie *f* thermochromism
Thermodiffusionsdruck *m* s. Thermosublimation
Thermodruck *m* thermal printing *(s.a. under* Thermografie*)*
Thermodrucker *m* [direct] thermal printer, thermographic printer
Thermodruckkopf *m* thermal [print] head
Thermodruckverfahren *n* thermographic (thermal printing) process
Thermoelement *n* thermocouple
Thermofarbband *n* thermal transfer ribbon
Thermofarbdrucker *m* color thermal printer, thermal-transfer color printer, thermal dye printer *(s.a.* Thermosublimationsdrucker*)*
Thermofaxgerät *n* thermal fax machine
Thermograf *m* thermographer
Thermografie *f* 1. thermography *(comprehensive term)*; 2. thermography, raised printing; 3. thermal printing
~/**indirekte** 1. heat-transfer printing, thermal [dye-]transfer printing; 2. *s.* Thermosublimationsdruck
Thermografiebild *n* s. Thermogramm
Thermografiekamera *f* thermal [image] camera, infrared (thermographic recording) camera, heat-sensing camera
thermografisch thermographic
Thermogramm *n* thermogram, thermograph[ic image], heat (thermal) image
Thermokamera *f* s. Thermografiekamera
Thermokaschieren *n* thermolamination, hot foil transfer
Thermokopie *f* thermal print
Thermokopierer *m* thermal printer
Thermokopiertechnik *f* thermal printing technology
Thermokopieverfahren *n* thermographic process
Thermolumineszenz *f* thermoluminescence
Thermolumineszenzdosimeter *n* thermoluminescent dosemeter, TLD
Thermolyse *f* thermolysis
thermolytisch thermolytic
Thermometrie *f*/**fotografische** photographic thermometry

Thermopapier *n* thermal (heat-copying) paper, heat-sensitive paper
Thermoplastfilm *m* thermoplastic film
Thermoreaktionsdrucker *m* s. Thermodrucker
Thermostat *m* thermostat
Thermosublimation *f*, **Thermosublimationsdruck** *m* [thermal] dye-sublimation printing, dye diffusion thermal transfer printing
Thermosublimationsdrucker *m* [thermal] dye-sublimation printer, thermal sublimation dye transfer printer, dye-diffusion printer
Thermotintenstrahldrucker *m* bubble jet printer
Thermotransferdruck *m* 1. heat-transfer printing, thermal [dye-]transfer printing; 2. s. Thermosublimation
Thermotransferdrucker *m* 1. thermal-transfer printer; 2. s. Thermosublimationsdrucker; 3. Thermowachsdrucker
Thermowachsdrucker *m* thermal wax printer (machine), wax-melt printer
Theta-Mikroskopie *f*/**konfokale** confocal theta microscopy
Thiessen-Diagramm *n* s. Voronoi-Diagramm
Thiosulfatlösung *f* thiosulfate solution *(fixing agent)*
Thixotropie *f* thixotropy
Thomson-Filter *n* Bessel filter *(television technology)*
Thomson-Streuung *f* Thomson scattering *(of X rays)*
Thoraxaufnahme *f* chest radiograph (X-ray)
Thoraxradiografie *f* chest radiography
Thyratron *n* thyratron *(a hot-cathode electron tube)*
Thyristor *m* thyristor *(semiconductor device)*
Ticker *m* ticker, teletypewriter
Tiefätz[druck]platte *f* deep-etch plate
Tiefbasslautsprecher *m* subwoofer
tiefbrechend low-index *(optical glass)*
Tiefdruck *m* 1. intaglio (recess) printing; gravure [printing]; rotogravure; 2. gravure print; 3. low pressure
~/**autotypischer** s. ~/flächenvariabler
~/**flächentiefenvariabler** Dultgen halftone intaglio process
~/**flächenvariabler** direct-transfer gravure, inverse halftone gravure, Henderson process
~/**konventioneller** conventional gravure, [roto]gravure
~/**tiefenvariabler** s. ~/konventioneller
Tiefdruckätzung *f* gravure etching
Tiefdruckbild *n* gravure image
Tiefdruckbogenmaschine *f* sheet-fed gravure press
Tiefdruckfarbe *f* gravure ink

Tiefdruckform *f* intaglio image carrier
Tiefdruckgravur *f* halftone gravure
Tiefdruckmaschine *f* gravure machine
Tiefdrucknäpfchen *n* gravure cell
Tiefdruckpapier *n* rotogravure paper
Tiefdruckplatte *f* gravure plate; intaglio [printing] plate, intaglio-engraved plate
Tiefdruckpresse *f* gravure [printing] press
Tiefdruckproof *m* gravure proof
Tiefdruckraster *m(n)* gravure [crosshatch] screen
Tiefdruckrotationsmaschine *f* rotary intaglio press
Tiefdruckverfahren *n* gravure printing process; intaglio [printing] process; rotogravure process
Tiefdruckvorstufe *f* gravure prepress
Tiefdruckzylinder *m* gravure [printing] cylinder
Tiefdruckzylinderätzung *f* gravure cylinder etching
Tiefe *f* [/**räumliche**] [stereoscopic] depth, stereodepth; spatial depth
~/**wahrgenommene** perceived depth
Tiefen *pl* shadows *(densitometry)*
Tiefenabschätzung *f* depth judg[e]ment (estimation)
Tiefenabtastung *f* depth scanning *(sonography)*
Tiefenauflösung *f* depth resolution, resolution in depth; axial resolution, axial point spread function
Tiefenausdehnung *f* extent (extension) in depth
Tiefenausgleich *m* time gain compensation *(sonography)*
Tiefenbereich *m* depth range
Tiefenbild *n* depth image (map), height map, range image, XYZ map *(computer vision)*
Tiefenbildanalyse *f* range image analysis
Tiefendosiskurve *f* dose (energy) deposition versus depth *(X-ray dosimetry)*
Tiefeneffekt *m* depth effect
~/**kinetischer** structure from motion
~/**stereoskopischer** stereo[scopic] depth effect
Tiefeneindruck *m* depth impression (sensation), impression (sense) of depth
Tiefenentwicklung *f* internal development
Tiefenhinweis *m* [pictorial] depth cue, depth clue
Tiefenholografie *f* volume holography
Tiefenhologramm *n* volume [transmission] hologram, thick hologram
Tiefeninformation *f* depth information (cue)
Tiefenkarte *f* s. Tiefenbild
Tiefenmultiplex *m* deep layer recording
Tiefenpuffer *m* depth buffer, z-buffer *(computer graphics)*
Tiefenpufferalgorithmus *m* depth buffer algorithm, z-buffering algorithm

Tiefenpufferverfahren *n* depth-buffering, z-buffering
Tiefenrekonstruktion *f* depth reconstruction
Tiefenring *m* depth-of-field scale
Tiefenschärfe *f s.* Schärfentiefe
Tiefenschattierung *f* depth shading
Tiefenschicht *f* depth layer
Tiefensehen *n* spatial (three-dimensional) vision, stereo[scopic] vision; stereopsis
~/**querdisparates** *s.* Stereosehen
Tiefensehvermögen *n* stereopsis, depth perception, perception of depth
Tiefenskalierung *f* depth scaling
Tiefenspeicherverfahren *n s.* Tiefenpufferverfahren
Tiefensuchbaum *m* depth-first search tree
Tiefensuche *f* depth-first search
Tiefentladen *n* deep discharging *(battery)*
Tiefenunterscheidung *f* depth discrimination
Tiefenunterscheidungsvermögen *n* depth discrimination ability
tiefenverkehrt pseudoscopic
Tiefenwahrnehmung *f* depth (space) perception, perception of depth, stereopsis
~/**binokulare** binocular depth perception, binocular stereopsis (stereo vision)
~/**stereoskopische** steroscopic depth perception
Tiefenwiedergabe *f* depth reproduction
Tiefenwirkung *f* depth effect, effect of depth
tieffrequent low-frequency
Tiefkühlkamera *f* cold camera *(astrophotography)*
Tiefpass *m s.* Tiefpassfilter
Tiefpassbild *n* low-pass image
Tiefpassfilter *n* low-pass [frequency] filter, high filter; suppressing filter *(s.a. Glättungsfilter)*
~/**Gaußsches** Gaussian low-pass filter
~/**gerichtetes** directional low-pass filter
~/**ideales** ideal low-pass filter, ILPF
~/**lineares** linear low-pass filter
~/**richtungsempfindliches** direction-sensitive low-pass filter
~/**rotationssymmetrisches** rotationally symmetric low-pass filter
~/**zonales** zonal low-pass filter
tiefpassfiltern to low-pass-filter
Tiefpassfilterung *f* low-pass filtering (smoothing)
~/**lineare** low-pass linear filtering
~/**örtliche** spatial low-pass filtering
~/**zeitliche** temporal low-pass filtering
Tiefpass-Rekonstruktionsfilter *n* lowpass reconstruction filter
Tiefpass-Vorfilter *n* low-pass pre-filter
Tiefpass-Vorfilterung *f* low-pass pre-filtering
tiefschwarz deep (dense) black, superblack
Tiefseefotografie *f* deep-sea photography
Tiefseekamera *f* deep-water camera
Tieftonlautsprecher *m* bass (low-frequency) loudspeaker, woofer
Tiegeldruckmaschine *f*, **Tiegel[druck]presse** *f* platen press
Tierfotograf *m* wildlife photographer
Tierfotografie *f* wildlife photography
Tierleim *m* animal glue
TIF-Format *n* tagged image file format, TIFF
Tilde *f* tilde *(diacritic)*; swung dash
Tilgung *f* quenching *(photoconduction)*
Timecode *m s.* Zeitcode
Timing *n* timing
Tinte *f* ink
~/**elektronische** electronic ink
~/**pigmentierte** pigmented ink
Tintendruck *m* ink-jet printing
~/**thermischer** bubble-jet printing
Tintendrucker *m* ink-jet printer
Tintendruckerpapier *n* ink-jet paper
Tintendruckpatrone *f s.* Tintenpatrone
Tintendüse *f* ink nozzle
Tintenkartusche *f*, **Tintenpatrone** *f* ink (print) cartridge
Tintenstrahlausdruck *m* ink-jet print
Tintenstrahldruck *m* ink-]jet printing
Tintenstrahldrucker *m* ink-jet printer
~ **nach dem Bubble-Jet-Verfahren** thermal bubble ink-jet printer
~/**piezoelektrischer** piezoelectric ink-jet printer
Tintenstrahldrucktechnik *f* ink-jet printing technology, IJP technology
Tintenstrahl-Farbdrucker *m* color ink-jet printer
Tintenstrahlkopf *m* ink-jet head
Tintenstrahlpapier *n* ink-jet paper
Tintenstrahlplotter *m* ink-jet plotter
Tintentank *m* ink tank (reservoir)
Tintometer *n s.* Kolorimeter
Tisch *m*/**optischer** optics (antivibration) table, [vibration-isolated] optical table, vibration-free table
Tischdrucker *m* desktop (tabletop) printer
Tischgerät *n* desktop device
Tisch-Klemmstativ *n* clamp table tripod
Tischmikrofon *n* tabletop (desk) microphone
Tischplotter *m* desktop plotter; flatbed plotter
Tischprozessor *m* tabletop processor
Tischrechner *m* desktop computer
Tischscanner *m* desktop [black-and-white] scanner; desktop color scanner
Tischstativ *n* table[top] tripod
Tischverschiebung *f* table feed *(spiral computed tomography)*
Tischzeichner *m s.* Tischplotter
Titelabspann *m* end title; [end] credits, closing credits
Titelbild *n* cover image
Titelei *f* front matter *(of a book)*
Titeleinkopierung *f* title insertion

Titelerzeugung *f* titling
Titelfoto *n* cover photo[graph], photographic cover
Titelgenerator *m*, **Titelgerät** *n* [title] character generator, caption generator, title writer (machine), titler
Titelherstellung *f* titling
Titelillustration *f* cover illustration
Titelliste *f* play list *(e.g. of a camcorder)*
Titelprägung *f* title embossing
Titelrolle *f* screen credit
Titelseite *f* title page
Titelsetzgerät *n* [photo]headliner *(typesetting)*
Titelspeicher *m* imposer *(camcorder)*
Titelvorlage *f* title card *(cinema)*
Titelvorspann *m* opening credits (title); main and credit title *(cinema)*
Titelzeile *f* headline
T-Kristall *m* tabular crystal, tabular [silver halide] grain, T-grain
T-Kristall-Emulsion *f* tabular grain emulsion
Tochterblitz *m* remote [electronic] flash unit
Tochter-Wavelet *n* daughter wavelet *(signal processing)*
Toluol[druck]farbe *f* solvent [printing] ink
Tomofotografie *f* tomophoto[fluoro]graphy
Tomograf *m* tomograph, tomographic machine
Tomografie *f* tomography, tomographic imaging
~/**akustische** acoustic tomography
~/**chirurgische** surgical tomography
~/**dreidimensionale** three-dimensional tomography
~/**elektronenmikroskopische** electron microscope tomography
~/**fluoreszenzvermittelte** fluorescence-mediated tomography
~/**fotoakustische** photoacoustic tomography
~/**geophysikalische** geophysical tomography
~/**hochauflösende** high-resolution tomography
~/**industrielle** industrial tomography
~/**interferometrische** interferometric tomography
~/**lineare** linear tomography
~/**medizinische** medical tomography
~/**nichtionisierende optische** nonionizing optical tomography
~/**nichtlineare** nonlinear tomography
~/**niedrigauflösende elektromagnetische** low-resolution electromagnetic tomography, LORETA
~/**optische** optical tomography, optical tomographic imaging
~/**seismische** seismic tomography
~/**stereoskopische** stereoscopic tomography
~/**szintigrafische** 1. [radionuclide] emission tomography; 2. *s.* Emissionscomputertomografie
~/**teleseismische** teleseismic tomography
Tomografiegerät *n* tomographic machine, tomograph
tomografisch tomographic
Tomogramm *n* tomogram, tomographic image, slice [image], image slice, section image
Tomosynthese *f* tomosynthesis
~/**digitale** digital tomosynthesis
~/**transversale** transverse tomosynthesis
Ton *m* sound
~/**asynchroner** wild sound (track), nonsynched (separately recorded) sound
~/**bildsynchroner** sync sound; locked audio
~/**dumpfer** muffled sound
~/**lippensynchroner** lip-sync[hronized] sound
Tonabmischung *f* sound mix
Tonabspielung *f* sound playback
Tonabstufung *f* tone gradation (scale)
Tonabtaster *m* sound scanner
Tonabtastung *f* sound scanning *(cinema)*
Tonangel *f* microphone (boom) pole, fishpole
Tonanlage *f* audio (sound) equipment
Tonanlegearbeit *f*, **Tonanlegen** *n* sound conforming, sync-sound *(film editing)*
Tonassistent *m* sound man, boom operator
Tonatelier *n* sound studio (stage), dubbing stage; sound effects house
Tonaufnahme *f* 1. sound (audio) recording; sound take *(filming)*; 2. sound record, sound (audio) pickup; sound take
~/**analoge** analog sound recording
~/**digitale** digital sound recording
Tonaufnahmegerät *n* sound recorder, recording machine
Tonaufnahmemöglichkeit *f* audio recording ability
Tonaufnahmetechnik *f* 1. sound recording technique; 2. sound recording equipment
Tonaufnahmeverfahren *n* sound-recording process, audio recording method
Tonaufzeichnung *f s.* Tonaufnahme
Tonaufzeichnungsspur *f s.* Tonspur
Tonausrüstung *f* sound equipment
Tonaussetzer *m* dropout
Tonbad *n* toning bath
Tonband *n* audiotape, sound tape
~/**Internationales** international tape (sound track), music and effect track, M&E [mix] *(cinema)*
Tonbandgerät *n* [audio] tape recorder, ATR
Tonbandmaschine *f* audio tape machine
Tonbearbeitung *f* sound processing; sound[-effects] editing; [audio] sweetening *(cinema)*

Tonbericht

Tonbericht *m* [production] sound log, sound report
Tonbildschau *f* tape-and-slide presentation
Toncodierung *f* audio coding
Toncutter *m* sound editor, [sound] mixer
Toneffekt *m* Foley (sound) effect
Toneffektschnitt *m* sound effects editing
tonen to tone
Tonendfertigung *f*, **Tonendmischung** *f* final mixing (mixdown) *(sound)*
Toner *m* toner [additive]
~/**chemischer** chemical toner
~/**magnetografischer** magnet[ograph]ic toner
~/**xerografischer** xerographic toner
Tonerauftrag *m* toner deposition
Tonerbild *n* toner [particle] image, toner-based image, toned image
Tonerdispersion *f* toner dispersion
Tonerentwicklung *f* toner development
Tonerfarbe *f* toner color
Tonerfarbteilchen *n* toner particle
Tonerhaftung *f* toner adhesion (sticking)
Tonerkartusche *f*, **Tonerkassette** *f* toner cartridge
Tonerkonzentration *f* toner concentration
Tonerladung *f* toner charge
Tonerlösung *f* toning (toner) solution
Tonerpartikel *n(f)* toner particle
Tonerpatrone *f* toner cartridge
Tonerpolymer *n* toner polymer
Tonerpulver *n* toner powder
Tonerschicht *f* toner layer
Tonerschichtdicke *f* toner layer thickness
Tonerstaub *m* toner powder
Tonerteilchen *n* toner particle
Tonerträger *m* toner support
Tonertransportwalze *f* toner drum
Tonerübertragung *f* toner transfer
Tonerwalze *f* toner drum
Tonfarbe *f* tint
Tonfeld *n* sound field
Tonfilm *m* 1. sound film (movie), sound [motion] picture, talking picture, talkie; 2. *s.* Tonnegativfilm
Tonfilmkopie *f* sound film print
Tonfilmprojektor *m* sound projector
Tonfilmwiedergabe *f* motion-picture sound reproduction
Tonfixierbad *n* fixing and toning bath
Tonfläche *f* fond *(printing)*
Tonfrequenz *f* audio frequency, audible frequency range
Tonfrequenzsignal *n* audio-frequency signal
Tongalgen *m* boom [arm] *(s.a. Tonangel)*
Tongestaltung *f* sound design
Tonhöhe *f* pitch
Tonigkeit *f* tonality, key *(of a photograph)*
Tonimpuls *m* sound pulse, sync beep *(filming)*
Toninformation *f* sound information
Toningenieur *m* sound engineer (recordist)
Tonkamera *f* sound camera

Tonkanal *m* sound (audio) channel; stem *(as part of a final mix)*
Tonklappe *f* sync stick, clapstick[s], clapboard, clapper [board]
Tonkopf *m* sound (audio) head
Tonlampe *f* exciter lamp *(optical sound reproduction)*
Tonlaufwerk *n* penthouse
Tonleitung *f* audio circuit, program line *(television)*
Tonmannschaft *f* sound crew *(filming)*
Tonmarkierung *f* cue tone *(video editing)*
Tonmaterial *n* audio material
Tonmeister *m* [supervising] sound editor, [sound] mixer
Tonmischanlage *f* audio mix equipment; production sound mixer
Tonmischpult *n* audio (sound) mixing console, audio mixer, mic[rophone] mixer
Tonmischung *f* sound mix[ing]
Tonmodulation *f* sound (audio) modulation
Tonnachbearbeitung *f s.* Nachvertonung
Tonnegativ *n* sound negative *(cinema)*
Tonnegativfilm *m* [negative] sound film
Tonnenverzeichnung *f*, **Tonnenverzerrung** *f* barrel (positive) distortion *(image defect)*
Ton-Original *n* [sound] stripe, sound (audio) track *(cinema)*
Tonpositiv *n* sound positive *(cinema)*
Tonprobe *f* sound test
Tonqualität *f* sound quality
Tonregler *m* fader [control] *(sound control)*
Tonreproduktion *f* tone (gray-scale) reproduction
Tonrolle *f* sound roll *(motion-picture production)*
Tonschneider *m* sound editor, [sound] mixer
Tonschnitt *m* sound editing; sound-effects editing
Tonsender *m* sound transmitter *(television)*
Tonsignal *n* audio (sound) signal, aural (acoustic) signal
Tonsignalverarbeitung *f* audio signal processing, ASP
Tonspalt *m* slit
Tonspur *f* sound track, audio [data] track
~/**monaurale** monaural (mono) sound track
Tonspurentwickler *m* sound track developer
Tonspurkopiergerät *n* sound track printer
Tonspurnegativ *n* sound track negative
Tonstartmarke *f* head sync
Tonstudio *n* sound studio (stage), dubbing stage; sound effects house
Tonsynchronisation *f* sound synchronization
Tontechnik *f* 1. sound (audio) technology; 2. sound (audio) engineering
Tontechniker *m* audio (sound) technician, soundman; sound engineer (recordist);

recording engineer; production sound mixer
Tonträger *m* audio (sound) carrier
~ *m* audio carrier
Tontrennung *f* tonal separation, posterization, banding
Tonübertragung *f* sound transmission
Tonung *f* 1. toning; 2. tint
~/**chemische** chemical toning
~/**direkte** direct toning
~/**indirekte** indirect toning
Tonungsbad *n* toning bath
Tonungslösung *f* toning solution
Tonungsmittel *n* image toner
Tonungstechnik *f* toning technique
Tonungsverfahren *n* toning method; toning procedure
Tonverstärker *m* audio amplifier
Tonverstärkung *f* sound amplification
Tonvormischung *f* sound premix[ing] *(s.a.* Vormischung*)*
Tonwert *m* 1. tone value, [tonal] value *(of an image)*; 2. s. Rastertonwert
Tonwertabstufung *f* tonal (tone) gradation; tonal differentiation
Tonwertbereich *m* tonal (tone) range, range of tones; key type *(of an image)*
Tonwertbeurteilung *f* tonal assessment
Tonwertkorrektur *f* tone correction, tonal modification (adjustment)
Tonwertreichtum *m* tonal quality
tonwertrichtig ortho[chromatic], [blue-and-]green-sensitive *(photographic material)*
Tonwertrichtigkeit *f* orthochromatism
Tonwertschwankung *f* tonal variation
Tonwertskala *f* tone (tonal) scale
Tonwertsteuerung *f* tonal control
Tonwerttrennung *f* tone (tonal) separation, separation of tones
Tonwertübergang *m* tone gradation
Tonwertumfang *m* s. Tonwertbereich
Tonwertumkehr *f* tone reversal, reversal of tones
Tonwertunterschied *m* tone (tonal) difference
Tonwertverteilung *f* tonal variation
Tonwertverzerrung *f* tone distortion
Tonwertwiedergabe *f* tone [scale] reproduction, tone (tonal) rendition
Tonwertzunahme *f*, **Tonwertzuwachs** *m* dot (press) gain, dot growth (spread); optical dot gain
Tonwiedergabe *f* sound (audio) reproduction
Tonwiedergabegerät *n* sound reproducer
Tonwiedergabesystem *n* sound [reproduction] system, audio system
Top-Hat-Filter *n* top hat filter, rolling-ball filter
Top-Hat-Transformation *f* top-hat transform (technique), rolling-ball technique *(morphological image processing)*

Töplitz-Matrix *f* Toeplitz matrix
Topograf *m* topographer
Topografie *f* topography
topografisch topographic[al]
Topogramm *n* topogram; scout view *(tomography)*
Topologie *f* topology
~/**digitale** digital topology
~/**finite** finite topology
~/**logische** logical topology
~/**physikalische** physical topology
~/**unregelmäßige** irregular topology
Topologieerhaltung *f* topology preservation
Topologiemerkmal *n* topological feature
Topologievergleich *m* topology matching
Topologievisualisierung *f* topology visualization
topologisch topological
Topometrie *f* topometry
topometrisch topometric
TOP-System *n* s. Videotext-Inhaltsübersicht
Tor *n* 1. gate; 2. flap *(e.g. of a floodlight)*
Torblende *f* barn door
Torelektrode *f* gate [electrode]
Toroid *n* s. Toroidspule
Toroidspule *f* toroidal [resistance] coil, toroid *(picture tube)*
Torse *f* s. Tangentenfläche
Tortendiagramm *n* pie chart
Torus *m* torus; toroid
Totalaufnahme *f*, **Totale** *f* long (full-length) shot, distant (distance) shot
Totalreflexion *f* total reflection
~/**abgeschwächte** attenuated total reflectance (reflection), ATR
~/**äußere** total external reflection
~/**gedämpfte** s. ~/abgeschwächte
~/**innere** total internal reflection, TIR
Totalreflexionsmonochromator *m* total reflection monochromator
Totalreflexions-Röntgenspektrometer *n* total reflection X-ray spectrometer
Totalreflexionswinkel *m* critical angle
Totzeit *f* dead time *(signal processing)*
Totzeitkorrektor *m* dead time correction
Totzonenquantisierer *m* dead zone quantizer
Totzonenquantisierung *f* dead zone quantization
Trabant *m* equalization (equalizer) pulse *(television signal)*
Tracer *m* tracer, label *(e.g. in nuclear medicine)*
Tracking *n* s. Schärfenachführung
Trackingfehler *m* tracking error, mistracking
Tragegurt *m* neck strap, [shoulder] strap
Träger *m* carrier; support
~/**amplitudenmodulierter** amplitude-modulated carrier
~/**frequenzmodulierter** frequency-modulated carrier

Trägeramplitude f carrier amplitude
Trägerelektrode f base-plate electrode
Trägerfolie f supporting foil
Trägerfrequenz f carrier [frequency]
Trägerfrequenzholografie f off-axis holography
Trägerfrequenzsystem n carrier-frequency system
Trageriemen m neck strap, [shoulder] strap
Trägermaterial n carrier material, support [material], base material *(e.g. in film manufacture)*
Trägermedium n carrying medium (agent)
Trägermodulation f carrier modulation
Trägerpolygon n billboard, impostor *(image-based rendering)*
Träger-Rauschabstand m, **Träger-Rausch-Verhältnis** n carrier-to-noise ratio, CNR
Trägerschicht f screen base *(intensifiying screen)*
Trägerschwingung f carrier wave
Trägersignal n carrier [signal]
Träger-Störsignal-Verhältnis n carrier-to-interference ratio, C/I
Trägerunterdrückung f carrier suppression
Trägervektor m s. Knotenvektor
Trägerwelle f carrier wave
Trageschlaufe f [wrist] strap
Trägheit f **des Auges** persistence of vision [effect]
Trägheitsmatrix f inertia matrix
Trägheitstensor m inertia tensor, tensor of inertia
Tragkörper m [grinding] block *(lens manufacture)*
Tragsäule f column *(enlarger)*
Tragstativ n [**/abgefedertes**] n Steadicam *(trade name for a camera stabilizing system)*
Trailer m [movie] trailer, preview trailer
Training n training, learning *(neuroinformatics, pattern recognition; s.a. unter Lernen)*
~/korrektives corrective training
Trainingsalgorithmus m training algorithm
Trainingsbild n training picture; training pattern
Trainingsdatensatz m training (learning) set, training class (population)
Trainingsgebiet n training area (field)
Trainingsobjekt n training object
Trainingsphase f training phase (period) *(image preprocessing)*
Trainingsvektor m training vector *(quantization)*
Trajektorie f trajectory
Traktrix f tractrix *(mathematics)*
Tränensackröntgendarstellung f dacryocystography
Transcoder m transcoder
transcodieren to transcode
Transcodierung f transcoding

~/kompressionsbasierte compression-based transcoding
Transferdruck m pad [transfer] printing
Transferfunktion f s. Übertragungsfunktion
Transferkanal m**/abgedeckter** buried channel *(charge-coupled device)*
Transferrauschen n transmission[-induced] noise
Transferthermografie f heat-transfer printing, thermal [dye-]transfer printing
Transferverfahren n transfer process *(electrophotography, thermography)*
transflektiv transflective *(display)*
Transfokator m s. Zoomobjektiv
Transformation f transform[ation], Xform *(e.g. as image processing operation)*
~/affine affine transformation
~/algebraische algebraic transformation
~/bilineare bilinear transformation
~/biorthogonale biorthogonal transform[ation]
~/diskrete discrete transformation
~/dreidimensionale three-dimensional transform[ation]
~/fraktale fractal transform[ation]
~/geometrische geometric[al] transform[ation], rubber sheet transformation
~/globale global transformation
~/hermitische Hermitian transform
~/inverse inverse transform[ation], reverse transform[ation]
~/iterative iterative transformation
~/lineare linear transformation
~/nichtlineare nonlinear transformation
~/orthogonale orthogonal transformation
~/orthonormale orthonormal transform
~/örtliche spatial transformation
~/polynomische polynomial transform
~/projektive projective transformation, collineation, homography
~/pseudoperspektivische pseudo-perspective transformation
~/sinusförmige sinusoidal transform[ation]
~/starre rigid transformation
~/suboptimale suboptimum transform
~/translationsinvariante translation-invariant transform
~/unitäre unitary transform[ation]
~/waveletbasierte wavelet-based transformation
~/zahlentheoretische number-theoretic transform, NTT
Transformationsalgorithmus m transform[ation] algorithm
Transformationsanalyse f transform analysis
Transformationsbild n transformed image
Transformationsblock m transformation block
Transformationscode f transform code
transformationscodieren to transform code

Transformationscodierer *m* transform coder
Transformationscodierung *f* transform [en]coding
~/**adaptive** adaptive transform coding
~/**blockweise** block-based transform coding
~/**hybride** hybrid transform coding
~/**nichtadaptive** nonadaptive transform coding
~/**zweidimensionale** two-dimensional transform coding
Transformationscodierungsfehler *m* transform coding error
Transformationsebene *f* transform plane
Transformationsfunktion *f* transformation function
Transformationsgleichung *f* transformation[al] equation
Transformationsinvarianz *f* transformational invariance
Transformationskern *m* transform[ation] kernel
Transformationskoeffizient *m* transform[ation] coefficient
Transformationsmatrix *f* transformation matrix
Transformationsoperation *f* transform operation, transformation procedure
Transformationspaar *n* transform pair
Transformationsparameter *m* transformation parameter
Transformationsstelle *f* transform location
Transformationstabelle *f* lookup table [memory], LUT; video lookup table
Transformationsverfahren *n* transformation method
Transformator *m* transformer
transformieren to transform; to morph, to warp; to deform
Transistor *m* transistor
Translation *f* translation *(geometrical transformation)*
~/**blockweise** blockwise translation *(video compression)*
Translationsbewegung *f* translatory movement, translational motion
translationsinvariant translation-invariant, shift-invariant *(image processing operation)*
Translationsinvarianz *f* translation (shift) invariance *(of an operator)*
Translationsmatrix *f* translation matrix
Translationsparallaxe *f* translation parallax
Translationsrichtung *f* translation direction
Translationssymmetrie *f* translational symmetry
Translationsvektor *m* translation vector
translatorisch translatory
transluzent translucent, lucid
Transluzenz *f* translucency
transluzid *s.* transluzent
Transmission *f* transmission
~/**optische** optical transmission

Transmissionsachse *f* transmission axis
Transmissionsbild *n* transmission image
Transmissionscomputertomografie *f s.* Transmissionstomografie
Transmissionsdensitometer *n* transmission densitometer
Transmissionsdichte *f* transmission density, Dt
Transmissions-Elektronenmikrografie *f* transmission electron micrograph
Transmissionselektronenmikroskop *n* transmission electron microscope, TEM
Transmissionselektronenmikroskopie *f* transmission electron microscopy, TEM
Transmissionsfaktor *m s.* Transmissionsgrad
Transmissionsfilter *n* transmission filter
Transmissionsfunktion *f* transmission function
Transmissionsgitter *n* transmission grid (grating), transmitting grating
Transmissionsgrad *m* transmittance [factor], transmission factor
~/**spektraler** spectral transmittance
Transmissionshologramm *n* transmission hologram
Transmissionskoeffizient *m* transmission coefficient
Transmissionskurve *f* transmission curve
Transmissionsmaske *f* transmission mask
Transmissionsneutronenradiografie *f* transmission neutron radiography
Transmissions-Röntgenmikroskop *n* transmission X-ray microscope, TXM
Transmissions-Röntgenmikroskopie *f* transmission X-ray microscopy
Transmissionssonografie *f* transmission sonography
Transmissionsspektrum *n* transmission spectrum
Transmissionsstufengitter *n* transmission echelon
transmissionstomografisch transmission tomographic
Transmissionsverlust *m* transmission loss
transmissiv transmissive
Transmissivität *f* transmittance, transmissivity
Transmitter *m* transmitter *(s.a. Sender)*
transmittieren to transmit
Transmodulation *f* transmodulation
Transmodulator *m* transmodulator
transparent transparent, pellucid; translucent
Transparentbild *n* transparency [image]
Transparentpapier *n* [semi]transparent paper; tracing paper
Transparentschirm *m* translucent screen
Transparenz *f* transparency, transparence
~/**interpolierte** interpolated transparency
Transparenzkanal *m* alpha (matte) channel *(video, computer graphics)*
Transponder *m* transponder *(satellite transmission)*

Transportdatenstrom *m* transport [data] stream
Transportgreifer *m* [pull-down] claw
~/doppelseitiger dual-fork claw
Transporthebel *m* [film] advance lever
Transportpaket *n* [data] transport packet
Transportprotokoll *n* transport [layer] protocol *(interactive television)*
Transportrolle *f* 1. [transport] sprocket; 2. shipping reel *(motion-picture film)*
Transportschicht *f* transport layer
Transportstrom *m* transport [data] stream
Transputer *m* transputer, transaction computer
Transversalfilter *n* transverse filter
Transversalmagnetisierung *f* transverse magnetization
Transversalrelaxationszeit *f* transverse (spin-spin) relaxation time, T-two [time constant], T2 *(magnetic resonance imaging)*
Transversalschichtbild *n s.* Transversalschnittbild
Transversalschnittbild *n* transverse sectional slice image, transverse axial tomographic image
Transversaltomografie *f* transverse tomography
Transversalverfahren *n* variable-area system *(optical sound recording)*
Transversalwelle *f* transverse wave
Trapezentzerrung *f*, **Trapezkorrektur** *f* keystone correction
Trapezverzeichnung *f*, **Trapezverzerrung** *f* trapezoidal distortion, keystone distortion (effect), keystoning
Trassierung *f* routing
Treatment *n* treatment *(as an outline of a screenplay)*
Trefferquote *f* bit rate *(e.g. in pattern recognition)*
Treiber *m* [device] driver *(software)*
Treiberelektronik *f* driving (control) electronics, drive[r] electronics
Treiberschaltung *f* drive circuit
Treibersoftware *f* driver software
Treibmittel *n* blowing agent
Trelliscodierer *m* trellis encoder
Trelliscodierung *f* trellis coding
Trellisdarstellung *f* trellis representation
Trellisdiagramm *n* trellis diagram
Trema *n* diaeresis *(diacritic mark)*
Trennanalyse *f* discriminant (discriminatory) analysis
Trennbild *n* peel-apart sandwich
Trennbildverfahren *n* peel-apart process
Trennfilter *n* separation (separating) filter
Trennlinie *f* part[ition]ing line
Trennschicht *f* spacer (spacing) layer, intermediate layer, interlayer
Trenn[ungs]strich *m* hyphen *(punctuation mark)*

Treppeneffekt *m* stair-stepping [artifact], staircasing, jaggedness, jaggies, spatial alias[ing]
Treppenpolygon *n* staircase polygon
Treppenstruktur *f* staircase structure (pattern), stair-step pattern
Treppenstufeneffekt *m s.* Treppeneffekt
Triac *m* Triac *(a bidirectional thyristor)*
triangulär triangular
Triangulation *f* triangulation [procedure]
~/aktive active [optical] triangulation
~/direkte direct triangulation
~/optische optical triangulation
Triangulationsmessung *f s.* Triangulation
Triangulationstaster *m* triangulation scanner
triangulieren to triangulate
Triangulierung *f s.* Triangulation
triboelektrisch triboelectric
Triboelektrizität *f* triboelectricity, static electricity
Triboluminseszenz *f* triboluminescence, piezoluminescence
Trichromasie *f* trichromacy, trichromatism *(e.g. of color vision)*
~/anomale anomalous trichromacy (trichromatism), color weakness *(color-vision deficiency)*
Trichromat *m* trichromat
~/anomaler anomalous trichromat
~/normaler normal trichromat
trichromatisch trichromatic
Trichromazität *f s.* Trichromasie
Trichter *m* funnel
Trick *m* [special] effect, trick effect *(s.a. Filmtrick)*
~/elektronischer digital (computer) special effect, computer-generated [special] effect
~/optischer optical [effect], special visual effect, montage
Trickabteilung *f* special effects department
Trickarbeit *f* special-effects [camera] work; [visual] effects work
Trickatelier *n s.* Trickstudio
Trickaufnahme *f* trick (VFX) shot, [special-]effects shot, process shot; special-effect[s] photograph
Trickbereich *m* effects area
Trickblende *f* wipe [transition]
Trickbühne *f* process stage *(cinema)*
Trickdrehbuch *n* storyboard
Trickfigur *f* animated character, creature
Trickfilm *m* trick (animated) film, [special-]effects film, special-effects movie, animation
Trickfilmanimator *m* animator
Trickfilmaufnahme *f s.* Trickaufnahme
Trickfilmen *n* animation production
Trickfilmkamera *f s.* Trickkamera
Trickfilmregisseur *m* animation director
Trickfilmsequenz *f* [/grafische] animation (animated) sequence
Trickfilmspezialist *m s.* Trickspezialist

Trickfilmstudio *n* s. Trickstudio
Trickfilmzeichner *m* s. Trickzeichner
Trickfilter *n* [special] effects filter, optical effects filter
Trickfotograf *m* visual effects photographer
Trickfotografie *f* trick photography; [special-]effects photography; rostrum photography
~/elektronische electronic trick photography, trick electronic photography
Trickgenerator *m*, **Trickgerät** *n* special-effects device (gear), effects machine
Trickgrafik *f* animation graphics
Trickkamera *f* animation camera, process motion-picture camera
Trickkameramann *m* animation camera operator
Trickkinematografie *f* trick (special-effects) cinematography
Trickkopieren *n* optical (special-effects) printing
Trickkopiermaschine *f* optical printer *(cinema)*
Tricklabor *n* [visual] effects house, optical house
Trickmaske *f* matte
Trickmuster *n* s. Stanzsignal
Trickperspektive *f* trick perspective
Trickprojektor *m* effects projector
Trickprozessor *m* effects processor
Trickregisseur *m* special effects supervisor, SFX sup[ervisor]; [visual] effects supervisor, VFX sup[ervisor]
Trickspezialist *m* visual effects professional; movie special-effects artist; optical printer operator
Trickstudio *n* [special] effects studio, effects facility (house); digital effects studio; special-effects company
Tricktechnik *f* 1. visual effects technology; 2. special-effects technique
Tricktechniker *m* special effects technician
Tricktisch *m* aerial image optical printer; [motion-picture] animation stand
Tricktischfotografie *f* animation stand photography
Tricktischplatte *f* compound [table]
Tricküberblendung *f* animation superimposition
Trickverfahren *n* special-effects technique
Trickzeichner *m* cartoonist, animator
Trieb *m* focusing mechanism *(microscope)*
Triebknopf *m* adjustment knob; focusing knob *(lens)*
Trifokaltensor *m* trifocal tensor
triggerbar triggerable
triggern to trigger
Triggerung *f*/**asynchrone** asynchronous trigger action
Triiodid *n* triiodide
trikubisch tricubic

Trimetallplatte *f* trimetal plate *(printing)*
Trimetrie *f* trimetric projection
Trinitron-Bildröhre *f* s. Streifenmaskenröhre
Trinokular *n* trinocular
Tripack-Film *m* tripack color [negative] film, [integral] tripack, monopack
Tripel *n* triple[t] triad *(s.a.* Farbtripel*)*
Tripelabstand *m* triad spacing
Tripelbildung *f* triplet production *(particle physics)*
Tripelprisma *n* corner [cube] reflector, corner cube [prism], retroreflector
Tripelpunkt *m* triad dot
Tripelreflektor *m*, **Tripelspiegel** *m* s. Tripelprisma
Triphenylamin *n* triphenylamine
Triplett *n* [optical lens] triple; triplet objective; [photographic] triplet lens
~/Cookesches (Taylorsches) Cooke triplet [lens]
Tristimuluswert *m* tristimulus value *(colorimetry)*
Tritanomalie *f* tritanomaly, decreased blue sensitivity *(color-vision deficiency)*
Tritanop *m* tritanope
Tritanopie *f* tritanopia, blue[-yellow color] blindness *(color-vision deficiency)*
Tritanstörung *f* s. Tritanomalie
Trixel *n* trixel, three-dimensional picture element
Trochlea *f* s. Seilschlinge
Trockenätzanlage *f* dry etching system
Trockenätzen *n* dry [dot-]etching
Trockenätztechnik *f* dry etching technique
Trockenbatterie *f* dry-cell battery
Trockenbereich *m* dry side (equipment) *(darkroom)*
Trockendruckverfahren *n* dry-process printing
Trockenentwickler *m* dry developer *(electrophotography)*
Trockenentwicklung *f* dry development
Trockenfilm *m* dry film
Trockenflachdruck *m* s. Trockenoffsetdruck
Trockenfleck *m* drying (water) mark, water spot [blemish]
Trockenfotografie *f* dry photography
Trockengestell *n* [print-]drying rack
Trockenkammer *f* drying chamber
Trockenklebepresse *f* dry-mount[ing] press *(for photographic prints)*; butt (guillotine) splicer *(for film material)*
Trockenkollodiumplatte *f* dry-collodion plate
Trockenkopierverfahren *n* dry [photo]copying process
Trockenobjektiv *n* dry objective (lens) *(optical microscopy)*
Trockenoffset[druck] *m* dry (letterpress) offset, letterset, waterless lithography, indirect letterpress [printing]
Trockenplatte *f* [dry] plate

Trockenplattenkamera f dry-plate camera
Trockenplattenmagazin n dry-plate magazine
Trockenplattenverfahren n dry-plate process
Trockenpresse f heated dryer (dry mounting press), [heated] print dryer
Trockenschrank m drying oven, [heated] drying cabinet
Trockenstoff m drier, siccative
Trockensystem n s. Trockenobjektiv
Trockenteil m dry side (equipment) *(darkroom)*
Trockentemperatur f drying temperature
Trockentintenverfahren n dry ink process *(printing)*
Trockentoner m dry toner
Trockentransfer-Elektrofotografie f xerography, xerographic printing
Trocken-Trocken-Zeit f dry-to-dry time *(machine processing)*
Trockenverarbeitung f dry[-to-dry] processing
trocknen to dry; to cure *(e.g. printing inks)*
Trocknung f**/wegschlagende** drying by absorption *(of printing inks)*
Trocknungstemperatur f drying temperature
Trocknungszeit f drying time
Troland n troland *(unit of retinal illuminance)*
~**/fotopisches** photopic troland *(photometry)*
~**/skotopisches** scotopic troland *(photometry)*
Trommel f**/fotoleitende** photoconductor drum
Trommeldrucker m drum (barrel) printer
Trommelentwicklung f drum processing
Trommelentwicklungsmaschine f drum processor
Trommelkamera f drum[-type] camera, rotating-drum camera
Trommelplotter m drum (rotary) plotter
Trommelscanner m drum[-type] scanner, rotary drum scanner, drum digitizer (digitizing system)
Trommeltrockner m drum dryer *(print finishing)*
Tropenentwickler m tropical developer
Tropenentwicklung f tropical processing
Tröpfchengröße f droplet size
Tropfenmodulationstechnologie f drop modulation technology *(ink-jet printing)*
Trübglas n, **Trübscheibe** f opal glass; milk glass
Trunkierung f truncation *(e.g. of a distribution)*
Tschebyschew-Filter n Chebyshev filter *(digital image processing)*
Tschebyschew-Polynom n Chebyshev polynomial

Tscherenkow-Licht n, **Tscherenkow-Strahlung** f Cerenkov radiation (light)
TTL-Belichtungsmessung f TTL (through-the-lens) metering
TTL-Blitzautomatik f TTL automatic flash
TTL-Lichtmessung f TTL (through-the-lens) light measurement
TTL-Phasenerkennung f TTL phase detection *(SLR camera)*
TTL-Sucher m through-the-lens [view]finder
Tubus m [extension] tube; barrel
~**/binokularer** binocular tube
~**/monokularer** monocular tube
Tubusauszug m tube extension
Tubuskamera f tube[-type] camera
Tubuslänge f tube length
~**/mechanische** mechanical tube length
~**/optische** optical tube length
Tubuslinse f tube lens
Tubusvorsatz m snoot *(e.g. of studio lights)*
~**/zylindrischer** straight snoot, top hat
Tüll m [tight] net *(e.g. as diffusing material)*
Tumordetektion f tumor detection
Tuner m tuner
Tungsten n tungsten
Tunnelblick m tunnel (tubular) vision *(visual aberration)*
Tunneleffekt m [**/quantenmechanischer**] [electric] tunnel effect
Tunnelmikroskop n [**/abtastendes**] scanning tunneling microscope, STM
~**/akustisches** tunneling acoustic microscope, TAM
Tunneln n [**/quantenmechanisches**] [quantum-mechanical] tunnel[l]ing, barrier penetration *(of particles)*
Tunnelspektroskopie f**/inelastische** inelastic tunneling spectroscopy
Tunnelstrom m tunneling current
Tunneltrockner m tunnel-type dryer *(e.g. in emulsion coating)*
Tupel n 1. tuple, two-dimensional vector *(morphological image processing)*; 2. -tuple *(e.g. as quintuple, sextuple)*
Tüpfeln n speckling *(digital image interference)*
Turbo-Gradientenecho n rapid gradient echo pulse sequence *(magnetic resonance imaging)*
Türkis n cyan *(subtractive primary color)*
TV-... s.a. Fernseh..., Video...
TV-Aufnahmeleiter m floor manager
TV-Karte f s. TV-Tunerkarte
TV-Shearografie f TV (electronic) shearography, electronic speckle pattern shearing interferometry, ESPSI
TV-Shearogramm n TV shearogram
TV-Tunerkarte f TV tuner card
Twain-Schnittstelle f Twain interface *(standard interface for scanners)*
Twain-Standard m Twain standard
Twain-Treiber m [standard] Twain driver

Tyndall-Effekt *m* Tyndall effect
Type *f* [piece of] type, type piece, printing type, letter
Typenbreite *f* set
Typendrucker *m* typeface-font printer
Typenguss *m* type casting
Typenkettendrucker *m* [horizontal] chain line printer
Typenkorbdrucker *m* thimble printer
Typenkörper *m* [type] body *(piece of type)*
Typenrad *n* daisy (type) wheel
Typenraddrucker *m* daisy wheel [printer], type wheel printer
Typensatz *m* type composition
Typenscheibe *f s.* Typenrad
Typenwalzendrucker *m* barrel printer
Typenzeile *f* type line; slug
Typizität *f* typicality, typicalness
Typograf *m* typographer, print designer
Typografie *f* typography
~/**digitale** digital typography
typografisch typographic[al]
Typoskript *n* typescript
T-Zahl *f* T-number *(of a lens)*

U

überabtasten to overscan; to oversample, to supersample
Überabtastung *f* oversampling, supersampling
Überallfernsehen *n s.* Fernsehen/digitales terrestrisches
Überanpassung *f* overfitting *(pattern recognition)*
Überätzen *n*, **Überätzung** *f* overetching
Überauflösung *f* 1. superresolution; 2. [visual] hyperacuity, vernier acuity
überbelichten to overexpose
Überbelichtung *f* [light] overexposure
Überbelichtungstoleranz *f* overexposure tolerance
Überblendart *f* transition type *(video, cinema)*
Überblendeffekt *m* transition effect
überblenden to dissolve *(images)*
Überblendprojektion *f* dissolve projection
Überblendprojektor *m* multiple [slide] projector
Überblendschau *f* multiple projector slide show, multiple slide projector presentation, multimedia slide show
Überblendung *f* [lap] dissolve, cross fade
~/**animierte** [image] morphing, polymorphic tweening *(animation technique)*
Überblendvorgang *m* changeover, projector change *(film screening)*
Überblendzeichen *n* cue dot (mark), changeover cue [mark], reel change mark
Überblick *m* overview
Überblicksaufnahme *f* establishing (wide-field-of-view) shot; master shot *(s.a.* Übersichtsaufnahme*)*
Überdeckung *f* overlap; occlusion
Überdeckungsgebiet *n* overlap area, overlapping region; occluded region
Überdeckungsperspektive *f* overlap
Überdrehen *n* overcranking *(filming)*
überdrucken to overprint, to surprint, to imprint
Übereinanderdruck *m* overprint
übereinanderdrucken *s.* überdrucken
Übereinanderdrucken *n* overprinting
übereinanderlegen to overlay, to super[impose] *(e.g. separation negatives)*
überentwickeln to overdevelop
Überentwicklung *f* overdevelopment, forced development (processing), push[ed] development, push [film] processing, pushing
Überfixieren *n*, **Überfixierung** *f* overfixing, overfixation

Überflugsbahn *f* flight strip (line), line of flight
Überflutungsalgorithmus *m* flood-fill algorithm
überfokussieren to overfocus
Überfokussierung *f* overfocusing
Überfüllen *n*, **Überfüllung** *f* trapping *(multicolor printing)*
Übergabetrommel *f*, **Übergabezylinder** *m* transfer drum (cylinder) *(printing machine)*
Übergang *m* transition
~/**allmählicher** gradual transition
Übergangseffekt *m* transition[al] effect
Übergangselement *n* fillet *(computer graphics)*
Übergangssehen *n* mesopic vision, dim-light vision
Überguss *m* supercoat, overcoat, topcoat, top layer *(photographic material)*
Überhang *m*, **Überhangzeile** *f* widow [line] *(printing)*
Überhorizontecho *n* transhorizon echo *(radar)*
Überhorizontradar *n* over-the-horizon radar, OTHR
Überkopfaufnahme *f* overhead shot
Überkorrektion *f* overcorrection *(of a lens)*
Überkorrektur *f*/**chromatische** chromatic overcorrection *(of a lens)*
überlagern to super[im]pose *(e.g. images)*; to heterodyne *(esp. frequencies)*
Überlagerung *f* super[im]position, superimposure; registration
~/**konturengleiche** registration
Überlagerungsbild *n* superposition (overlay) image
Überlagerungseffekt *m* layover effect
Überlagerungsfenster *n* pop-up window *(on a computer screen)*
Überlagerungsprinzip *n* principle of superposition *(wave optics)*
Überlappung *f* overlap *(e.g. between flight strips in aerial photogrammetry)*
Überlappungsfehler *m* aliasing error (defect)
überlappungsfrei disjunct
Überlauf *m* overflow *(in digitized images)*
Übermikroskop *m s.* Elektronenmikroskop
Übermittlungsgeschwindigkeit *f* transmission speed
Übermodulation *f* overmodulation
Überregenerierung *f* overreplenishment *(of processing solutions)*
Überreichweitenradar *n* over-the-horizon radar, OTHR
überschreiben to overwrite *(e.g. pixel values in computer graphics)*
Überschrift *f* headline
Überschwingen *n* ringing
Übersegmentierung *f* oversegmentation
Übersensibilisierung *f* oversensitization
Übersetzer *m* compiler
Übersetzungsprogramm *n* compiler

Übersicht *f* overview
Übersichtigkeit *f s.* Weitsichtigkeit
Übersichtsaufnahme *f* topogram; scout view *(tomography; s.a.* Überblicksaufnahme*)*
überspielen to dub; to overdub; to rerecord
Überspielgerät *n* dubber, dummy
Überspielsignal *n* playback signal
Überspielung *f* 1. dubbing; 2. dub
Überspielverstärker *m* enhancer, video processing amplifier
Übersprechdämpfung *f* cross talk attenuation
Übersprechen *n* cross talk
Übersprechstörung *f* cross talk
Übersteuerungsreserve *f* headroom
überstrahlen to outshine, to shine out
Überstrahlen *n* [image] blooming, blooming effect
Überstrahlfestigkeit *f* antiblooming
Überstrahlung *f*, **Überstrahlungseffekt** *m s.* Überstrahlen
übertragbar transferable; transmissible
Übertragbarkeit *f* transmissibility
übertragen to transmit; to transfer; to broadcast, to air *(e.g. images by television)*
~/**live** to broadcast live
Übertragung *f* transmission; transfer; broadcast
~/**asynchrone** asynchronous transmission
~/**digitale** digital transmission
~/**elektrostatische** electrostatic transfer *(of xerographic toner)*
~/**fehlerfreie** error-free transmission
~/**fotomechanische** photomechanical transfer, PMT
~/**quasi fehlerfreie** quasi error-free transmission
~/**sequentielle** sequential transmission
~/**terrestrische** terrestrial (over-the-air) transmission
~/**zeilensequentielle** line-sequential transmission
Übertragungsbandbreite *f* transmission bandwidth
Übertragungseinheit *f*/**mobile, Übertragungsfahrzeug** *n* outside broadcast vehicle
Übertragungsfehler *m* transmission error
Übertragungsfilter *n* transmission filter
Übertragungsformat *n* transmission format
Übertragungsfrequenz *f* transmission frequency
Übertragungsfunktion *f* transfer (transmission) function
~/**inkohärente** incoherent transfer function
~/**kohärente** coherent transfer function, CTF
~/**lineare** linear transfer function
~/**logarithmische** logarithmic transfer function
~/**optische** optical transfer function, OTF
Übertragungsgeschwindigkeit *f* transmission speed; transfer rate
Übertragungskanal *m* transmission channel; broadcast[ing] channel
Übertragungskapazität *f* transmission capacity *(s.a.* Bandbreite*)*
Übertragungskette *f* transmission chain
Übertragungsleitung *f* 1. transmission line; 2. *s.* Bus
Übertragungsmedium *n* transmission medium; transfer (conveying) medium
Übertragungsmodus *m* transfer (transmission) mode; broadcast mode
~/**asynchroner** asynchronous transfer (transmission) mode, ATM
~/**isochroner** isochronous transfer mode
~/**synchroner** synchronous transfer mode, STM
Übertragungsnorm *f* transmission standard
Übertragungsparameter-Pilot *m* transmission parameter signalling pilot, TPS
Übertragungsprotokoll *n* transfer (transmission) protocol
Übertragungsqualität *f* transmission quality; broadcast quality
Übertragungsrate *f s.* Übertragungsgeschwindigkeit
Übertragungsrauschen *n* transmission[-induced] noise
Übertragungsreihenfolge *f* transmission order
Übertragungssatellit *m* transmission satellite
Übertragungssicherheit *f* transmission reliability
Übertragungssignal *n* transmission signal
Übertragungsspektrum *n* transmission spectrum
Übertragungsstandard *m* transmission standard
Übertragungsstrecke *f* transmission link; transmission circuit
Übertragungssystem *n* transmission system
Übertragungstechnik *f* transmission technology
Übertragungsverhalten *n* transfer behavior
Übertragungsverlust *m* transmission loss
Übertragungsverzögerung *f* transmission delay
Übertragungswagen *m* outside broadcast vehicle
Übertragungsweg *m* transmission path, path of transmission
Übertragungszeit *f* transmission time; transfer time

Übertragungszylinder

Übertragungszylinder *m* 1. transfer roll[er] *(electrophotography)*; 2. s. Gummidrucktuchzylinder
übervergrößern to overenlarge
Übervergrößerung *f* 1. overenlargement *(e.g. of small negatives)*; 2. s. Vergrößerung/leere
Überwachungsaufnahmen *fpl* surveillance imagery
Überwachungsbild *n* surveillance image
Überwachungsflugzeug *n* surveillance aircraft
Überwachungsfoto *n* surveillance photo[graph]
Überwachungsfotografie *f* surveillance photography
Überwachungskamera *f* surveillance (security) camera, observation camera; spycam
Überwachungsmonitor *m* survey monitor
Überwachungsradar *n* surveillance radar
Überwachungssatellit *m* surveillance satellite
Überwachungssystem *n* monitoring system
Überwachungsvideo *n* surveillance (security camera) video
Überwasserfotografie *f* above-water photography
Überweitwinkelfotografie *f* ultrawide-angle photography
Überweitwinkelobjektiv *n* super wide-angle lens
UHF *s.* Frequenz/ultrahohe
Uhrwerksnachführung *f* clock drive *(of a telescope)*
Uhrzeigersinn *m* clockwise sense
UKW *s.* Ultrakurzwelle
Ulbricht-Kugel *f* integrating sphere *(photometry)*
Ultrafeinkornentwickler *m* ultrafine-grain developer, superfine-grain developer
Ultrafiltration *f* ultrafiltration
ultrahart ultra hard *(paper grade)*
Ultrahochauflösung *f* ultrahigh resolution
Ultrahochdruck-Quecksilberdampflampe *f* ultrahigh pressure mercury lamp
Ultrahochfrequenz *f* ultrahigh frequency, UHF
Ultrahochgeschwindigkeitsfotografie *f* ultrahigh-speed photography
Ultrahochgeschwindigkeitskamera *f* ultrahigh-speed [framing] camera
Ultrahochgeschwindigkeitskinematografie *f* ultrahigh-speed cinematography
Ultrakompaktkamera *f* ultracompact camera
Ultrakondensor *m* ultracondenser *(ultramicroscope)*
Ultrakurzpulslaser *m* ultrashort pulse laser
Ultrakurzwelle *f*, **Ultrakurzwellenbereich** *m* very high frequency, VHF [range], metric wavelength range
Ultrakurzzeitaufnahme *f* very-short-duration image
Ultrakurzzeitbelichtung *f* ultrashort time exposure
Ultrakurzzeitkamera *f* fast-shutter camera
Ultramikroelektrode *f* ultramicroelectrode, UME
Ultramikroskop *n* ultramicroscope, dark-field microscope
Ultramikroskopie *f* ultramicroscopy, dark-field microscopy
ultramikroskopisch ultramicroscopic[al], submicroscopic
Ultramikrotom *n* ultramicrotome
ultrarot *s.* infrarot
Ultraschall *m* ultrasound, supersound *(s.a. under* Schall*)*
~/**diagnostischer** diagnostic ultrasound
~/**digital codierter** digitally encoded ultrasound, DEU
~/**dreidimensionaler** three-dimensional ultrasound
~/**endoskopischer** endoscopic ultrasound, EUS
~/**medizinischer** medical ultrasound
~/**quantitativer** quantitative ultrasound [imaging]
Ultraschallabsorptionskoeffizient *m* ultrasonic absorption coefficient
Ultraschallaufnahme *f* 1. ultrasound image acquisition; 2. *s.* Ultraschallbild
Ultraschallausbreitungsgeschwindigkeit *f* ultrasound propagative speed
Ultraschallbild *n* ultrasound (ultrasonic) image, sonogram
~/**endoskopisches** endoscopic ultrasound image
~/**medizinisches** ultrasonic medical image
~/**räumliches** three-dimensional ultrasound image, 3-D ultrasound image
Ultraschallbildartefakt *n* ultrasound [imaging] artifact
Ultraschallbildauflösung *f* ultrasound image resolution
Ultraschallbildaufzeichnungsgerät *n s.* Ultraschallgerät
Ultraschallbildgebung *f* ultrasonic (sonographic) imaging, ultrasound [imaging technique], [ultra]sonography
~/**intravaskuläre** intravascular ultrasound imaging, IVUS
Ultraschallbildrekonstruktion *f* ultrasound image reconstruction
Ultraschallbildverarbeitung *f* ultrasonic image processing
Ultraschall-Computertomografie *f* ultrasonic computed tomography
Ultraschalldarstellung *f s.* Ultraschallbildgebung
Ultraschalldefektoskopie *f* ultrasonic inspection (examination)
Ultraschalldetektion *f* ultrasonic detection
Ultraschalldiagnostik *f* ultrasonic diagnosis, diagnostic ultrasound

Ultraschalldiagnostiker *m* sonographer, ultrasound clinician
Ultraschalldiagnostiksystem *n* ultrasound imaging system
Ultraschallecho *n* ultrasound echo
Ultraschallelastografie *f* sonoelasticity imaging, elastography, elasticity imaging [method]
Ultraschallempfänger *m* ultrasound receiver
Ultraschallendoskopie *f* endoscopic [ultra]sonography
Ultraschallenergie *f* ultrasonic energy
Ultraschallfrequenz *f* ultrasound frequency
Ultraschall-Gefäßdarstellung *f* vascular ultrasound imaging
Ultraschallgerät *n* ultrasonic sensing device; ultrasonic imager (image recorder), ultrasound unit (machine)
~/**tragbares** hand-carried ultrasound
Ultraschallholografie *f* ultrasound holography, sonoholography
Ultraschallhologramm *n* ultrasound hologram, sonohologram
Ultraschallimpuls *m* ultrasonic (ultrasound) pulse
Ultraschallintensität *f* ultrasound intensity
Ultraschallkardiografie *f* echocardiography
Ultraschallkartografie *f* ultrasound (US) cartography
Ultraschallkontrastmittel *n* ultrasound contrast agent (medium), sonographic contrast agent
Ultraschallkopf *m s.* Ultraschallmesskopf
Ultraschall-Kugelwelle *f* ultrasonic spherical wave
Ultraschall-Lichtablenkung *f* acousto-optic deflection
Ultraschallmesskopf *m* ultrasound scan head, ultrasound (ultrasonic) scanner, transducer
Ultraschallmikroskop *n* ultrasonic microscope
Ultraschallmikroskopie *f* ultrasonic microscopy
Ultraschall-Mikrospektrometer *n* ultrasonic microspectrometer
Ultraschallprüfgerät *n* ultrasonic test equipment (apparatus)
Ultraschallprüfkopf *m s.* Ultraschallmesskopf
Ultraschallprüfung *f* ultrasonic inspection (examination)
~/**zerstörungsfreie** ultrasonic nondestructive testing
Ultraschallreflexion *f* ultrasound reflection
Ultraschallreinigung *f* ultrasonic cleaning
Ultraschall-Reinigungsgerät *n* ultrasonic cleaner
Ultraschallscan *m* utrasound scan
Ultraschallscanner *m* ultrasonic (ultrasound) scanner
Ultraschall-Schnittbildmethode *f*, **Ultraschallschnittbildverfahren** *n s.* Ultraschalltomografie
Ultraschallschwinger *m s.* Ultraschallwandler
Ultraschallschwingung *f* ultrasonic vibration
Ultraschallsender *m* ultrasonic transmitter
Ultraschallsensor *m* ultrasonic (ultrasound) sensor
Ultraschallsichtverfahren *n* ultrasonic (acoustic) imaging
Ultraschallsignal *n* ultrasonic [echo] signal
Ultraschallsignalverstärker *m* ultrasonic signal amplifier
Ultraschallsonde *f* ultrasonic (ultrasound) probe
Ultraschall-Speckle *n* ultrasonic speckle
Ultraschallstrahl *m* ultrasonic beam, ultrasound ray (beam)
Ultraschalltechnik *f* ultrasonic technology; [ultra]sonography, ultrasound [imaging technique], ultrasonic (sonographic) imaging, echography
Ultraschalltomografie *f* ultrasound transmission tomography, transmissive ultrasonic computerized tomography, acousto-optical (ultrasound-modulated optical) tomography
Ultraschall-Transmissionskamera *f* ultrasonic transmission camera
Ultraschalluntersuchung *f* ultrasonic examination, ultrasound [exam] *(s.a.* Sonografie*)*
Ultraschallwandler *m* ultrasound (ultrasonic) transducer *(s.a.* Ultraschallmesskopf*)*
Ultraschallwelle *f* ultrasound wave, ultrasonic [sound] wave, high-frequency sound wave
~/**ebene** ultrasonic plane wave
Ultraschallwellenlänge *f* ultrasound wavelength
ultrasonisch ultrasonic
Ultrasonografie *f s.* Ultraschallbildgebung
Ultraspektrografie *f* ultraspectrography
Ultrastrahlung *f* cosmic radiation
ultraviolett ultraviolet *(s.a. under* UV-...*)*
Ultraviolett *n* ultraviolet, UV
~/**extremes** extreme ultraviolet, EUV
~/**fernes** far ultraviolet [radiation], far UV
~/**mittleres** medium-wave ultraviolet
ultraviolettdurchlässig UV-transmissive
ultraviolettempfindlich ultraviolet sensitive, UV-sensitive
Ultraviolettfilter *n* ultraviolet filter, UV filter
Ultraviolettfotografie *f* ultraviolet photography
Ultraviolettgitter *n* ultraviolet grating
Ultraviolettlampe *f* ultraviolet lamp
Ultraviolettlaser *m* ultraviolet (UV) laser
Ultraviolettmikrofotografie *f* ultraviolet photomicrography

Ultraviolettmikroskop *n* ultraviolet microscope
Ultraviolettmikroskopie *f* ultraviolet (UV light) microscopy
Ultraviolett-Objektiv *n* UV lens (optics)
Ultraviolettsperrfilter *n* ultraviolet-absorbing filter, UV-absorbing filter
Ultraweitwinkelkamera *f* ultra-wide-lens camera
Ultraweitwinkelobjektiv *n* ultrawide[-angle] lens, extreme wide-angle lens, ultrawide-angle focal-length lens
umbilden to remap
Umbildung *f* remapping
Umblättereffekt *m*, **Umblättertrick** *m* page flip, page-turn [effect] *(digital video)*
umbrechen to make up *(typeset matter for printing)*
Umbruch *m* [page] makeup, page assembly, composition *(printing)*
umcodieren to transcode
Umcodierung *f* transcoding
Umdruck *m* 1. transfer printing; 2. transfer print
Umdruckverfahren *n* autography
umentwickeln to redevelop
Umentwicklung *f*/**chromogene** chromogenic redevelopment
Umfahrt *f* rotation *(camera move in motion-picture photography)*
umfärben to recolor
Umfeldgeräusch *n* ambient noise
umfokussieren to refocus
Umfokussieren *n*, **Umfokussierung** *f* refocusing
Umformatieren *n*, **Umformatierung** *f* reformatting
Umgebung *f* environment, surroundings; surround[ing area]
~/computergestützte virtuelle computer-aided virtual environment, CAVE
~/elektromagnetische electromagnetic environment
~/künstliche artificial environment
~/vernetzte networked environment
~/verteilte virtuelle distributed virtual environment
~/virtuelle virtual environment
Umgebungsbeleuchtung *f* ambient illumination (lighting)
Umgebungsfarbe *f* surround[ing] color, ambient color
Umgebungsfilter *n s.* Faltungskern
Umgebungshelligkeit *f* surround (ambient) brightness; lightness of the surround
Umgebungsleuchtdichte *f* surround luminance
Umgebungslicht *n* ambient (surrounding) light
Umgebungslichtpegel *m* ambient light level

Umgebungslichtquelle *f* ambient [light] source
Umgebungsrauschen *n* ambient (surrounding) noise
~/thermisches ambient thermal noise
Umgebungsstrahlung *f* background radiation
Umkehrbad *n* reversed bath *(photoprocessing)*
Umkehrbarkeit *f*/**optische** optical reversibility
Umkehrbelichtung *f* reversal exposure
Umkehrbild *n* reversal (reversed) image
Umkehrbrille *f*/**prismatische** prism eyeglasses
Umkehrdruck *m* reversal image printing
umkehren to reverse [out]
Umkehrentwickler *m* reversal[-type] developer
Umkehrentwicklung[stechnik] *f* reversal development (processing)
Umkehrfarbfilm *m* reversal (transparency-type) color film, color reversal (transparency) film, color slide film
Umkehrfarbfilmverarbeitung *f* reversal color-film processing
Umkehrfehler *m* hysteresis *(e.g. in positioning)*
Umkehrfilm *m* reversal[-type] film, reversible film, reversal transparency (working) film, [reversal] positive film, knockout film; transparency (slide) film
Umkehrfilter *n* reversible filter
Umkehrintermediatefilm *m* reversal intermediate [film]
Umkehrlinse *f* [image] erecting lens, erector lens
Umkehrmaterial *n* reversal [photographic material, reversal [stock]
Umkehrmikroskop *n* inverted microscope
Umkehrokular *n* erecting (reversing) eyepiece
Umkehroriginal *n*, **Umkehr-Originalfilm** *m* reversal camera film, reversal [original] film
Umkehrpapier *n* reversal paper
Umkehrplanfilm *m* reversal sheet film
Umkehrpositiv *n* reversal positive image
Umkehrprisma *n* inversion (inverting) prism, reversing (derotation) prism
~/Dovesches Dove prism
Umkehrprojektion *f* reverse projection
Umkehrprozess *m* reversal process
Umkehrring *m* reversing (macro adapter) ring, lens reversing adapter
Umkehrspiegel *m* reversing mirror
Umkehrsystem *n* 1. inversion (image erecting) system *(optics)*; 2. reversal (negative-positive) system *(photography)*
Umkehrverarbeitung *f* reversal processing (development)
Umkehrverfahren *n* reversal process
Umklappung *f* 1. flop; layover *(radar)*

umkopieren to recopy
Umkopierung f optical printing
~/formatverkleinernde reduction printing
Umkristalisation f, **Umkristallisierung** f recrystallization
Umlaufblende f blade (multi-bladed) shutter, rotary (rotating) shutter, disk (sector-wheel) shutter, chopper
Umlaufsektorenblende f, **Umlaufverschluss** m s. Umlaufblende
Umlautzeichen n umlaut mark
umlenken to redirect; to deflect
Umlenkprisma n reflecting prism
Umlenkrolle f idle[r] roller, guide roller
Umlenkspiegel m reflecting mirror
umparametrisieren to reparamet[e]rize
Umrandung f boundary [line], borderline
Umriss m contour, outline (s.a. under Kontur)
Umrissbild n outline image
Umrisserkennung f contour detection
Umrisskarte f outline map
Umrisslinie f boundary line; contour line; outline [edge]
Umrisspolygon n circumscribing polygon
Umrisszeichnung f outline drawing
umrollen to rewind, to backwind, to rethread (e.g. a film)
Umroller m rewind[er]
Umrolltisch m rewind apparatus
Umschalter m, **Umschaltpult** n s. Videoumschalter
Umschalttaste f caps lock (keyboard)
Umschlagfoto n cover photo[graph], photographic cover
Umschlingungsgrad m wrap
Umschlingungswinkel m wrap angle
umschneiden to reedit
Umschnitt m reediting
Umschrift f runaround (typography)
Umsetzer m [television system] converter; translator; [television] transposer
Umskalierung f rescaling
umspielen to rerecord
Umspielraum m rerecording room, dubbing theater
Umspielung f rerecording
umspulen to rewind
Umspulzeit f rewind time
Umtastung f shift keying, SK
Umwälzpumpe f recirculating pump (e.g. of a machine processor)
umwandeln to convert
Umwandlungscodierung f s. Transformationscodierung
Umwandlungstabelle f für Pixelwerte lookup table [memory], LUT; video lookup table
umzeichnen to redraw
Unähnlichkeitsmaß n dissimilarity measure
unbedruckt unprinted
unbelichtet unexposed, nonexposed

unbeschnitten untrimmed (e.g. printed sheets)
unbunt uncolored, achromatic, neutral
Unbuntabgleich m s. Weißabgleich
Unbuntachse f gray line
Unbuntaufbau m gray component replacement, GCR, achromatic color removal
Unbuntempfindung f achromatic sensation
Unbuntgerade f gray line
Unbuntpunkt m achromatic (white) point (colorimetry)
Unbuntreiz m achromatic stimulus
uncodiert uncoded
UND n [/logisches] AND (logical operator)
undetektierbar undetectable
UND-Operation f/logische [logical] AND operation
Undulationstheorie f s. Wellentheorie des Lichts
Undulator m [beam] undulator, wiggler [magnet]
undurchsichtig opaque, lightproof
Undurchsichtigkeit f opacity, opaqueness
Unendlicheinstellung f infinity stop; infinity setting, infinity [focus] position; infinity (landscape) mode
Unendlich-Optik f infinity-corrected optics (microscope)
Unendlichverriegelung f infinity lock
unerkennbar unrecognizable
ungefalzt unfolded
ungekittet noncemented (lenses)
ungeradlinig curvilinear
ungleichachsig anaxial
ungleichfarbig heterochromatic
unhörbar inaudible
unidirektional unidirectional (e.g. data transmission)
Unikat n camera original (film)
Unipolartransistor m s. Feldeffekttransistor
Universalbus m aux[iliary] bus (switcher)
Universalemulsion f universal emulsion
Universalentwickler m universal (all-purpose) developer
Universalfarbfilm m universal color film
Universalfilm m general-purpose [photographic] film, all-around film
Universalfilter n general-purpose filter
Universalkamera f universal camera
Universalmagazin n slot magazine (slide tray)
Universalnetz n s. Digitalnetz mit Diensteintegration
Universalobjektiv n, **Universaloptik** f general-purpose [camera] lens, general-purpose photographic objective
Universalsucher m universal finder
Universalzoom[objektiv] n standard zoom; mid-range zoom
unkomprimiert unsqueezed, USQ (e.g. an image file)

unkorrigierbar uncorrectable *(optical aberration)*
unkorrigiert uncorrected
unlesbar unreadable
unleserlich illegible, indecipherable
unmagnetisch nonmagnetic
unperforiert unperforated, nonperforated, imperforate[d], sprocketless
unretuschiert unretouched
unscharf 1. unsharp, blurred, blurry, fuzzy; soft; out of focus; 2. fuzzy *(logic)*
Unschärfe f unsharpness, blur[riness], fuzziness
~/**Gaußsche** Gaussian blur
~/**geometrische** geometric blur, geometric[al] unsharpness
~/**innere** intrinsic (photographic) unsharpness *(radiography)*
~/**optische** optical blur
~/**projektive** projective geometric unsharpness
~/**zulässige** permissible unsharpness
Unschärfefunktion f blur[ring] function; point-spread function, PSF
Unschärfekreis m blur circle, circle of confusion
Unschärfekreisdurchmesser m, **Unschärfekreisgröße** f size of the blur circle
Unschärfemaskierung f s. Unscharfmaskierung
Unschärfematrix f blur matrix
Unschärfensteuerung f defocus image control
Unschärfeoperator m blurring (unsharp mask) operator
Unschärfepunkt m blur spot (point)
Unschärferadius m radius of blur spot
Unschärferelation f uncertainty relation[ship]; time-bandwidth product *(signal theory)*
~/**Heisenbergsche** Heisenberg's uncertainty relation (principle)
Unscharfmachen n blurring
Unscharfmaske f unsharp mask [filter], blur[ring] filter USM
Unscharfmaskieren n, **Unscharfmaskierung** f unsharp (soft-edge) masking, unsharp mask operation, Laplacian operation, peaking *(image-processing technique)*
Unscharfstellen n defocusing
unsensibilisiert unsensitized
unsichtbar invisible, nonvisible, viewless; extravisible
Unsichtbarkeit f/**quantitative** quantitative invisibility *(computer graphics)*
Unsymmetrie f dissymmetry; asymmetry
unsymmetrisch unsymmetric[al], dissymmetric; asymmetric[al]
unterabtasten to subsample, to undersample; to subscan, to underscan
Unterabtaster m subsampler
Unterabtastmuster n subsample (subsampling) pattern

Unterabtastrate f subsampling rate
Unterabtastung f subsampling [operation], undersampling, down-sampling; subscanning, underscanning
Unterabtastungsmatrix f subsampling matrix
Unterabtastungspyramide f subsampling pyramid
Unterbaum m subtree *(data structure)*
unterbelichten to underexpose
Unterbelichtung f underexposure
Unterbild n subimage *(e.g. in image analysis)*
Unterbrecherbad n stop bath, shortstop
Unterbrechungsanforderung f interrupt request (query), IRQ *(computer)*
Unterbrechungsfenster n preemption window *(multimedia operating system)*
Unterdrehen n undercranking *(filming)*
unterentwickeln to underdevelop; to pull *(esp. motion-picture film)*
Unterentwicklung f underdevelopment; pull development, pulling
Unterfarbenentfernung f, **Unterfarbenkorrektur** f, **Unterfarbenrücknahme** f undercolor removal, UCR, gray component replacement (removal), GCR *(reprography)*
Unterfarbenzugabe f undercolor addition, UCA *(reprography)*
Unterfenster n subwindow *(display)*
unterfixiert underfixed
Unterfixierung f underfixing
unterfokussieren to underfocus
Unterfokussierung f underfocusing
Untergraph m subgraph
Untergrundgeräusch n ambient sound, background sound[s]
Untergrundstrahlung f background radiation
Untergrundstreuung f background scattering *(laser spectroscopy)*
Unterguss m substrate *(film manufacture)*
Unterhaltungscomputer m entertainment computer
Unterhaltungselektronik f consumer (home) electronics
Unterhaltungsfernsehen n entertainment TV
Unterhaltungsfilm m entertainment feature film
Unterkante f bottom edge
Unterklasse f subclass, derived class
Unterkorrektion f undercorrection *(of a lens)*
Unterkorrektur f/**chromatische** chromatic undercorrection *(of a lens)*
Unterlage f, **Unterlagebogen** m, **Unterlagematerial** n packing *(of press cylinders)*
Unterlänge f 1. descender *(letterform)*; 2. descender depth

Unterlauf *m* underflow *(in digitized images)*
Untermalungsmusik *f* underscore *(s.a. Filmmusik)*
Untermenge *f* subset *(e.g. of features)*
Untermenü *n* submenu
Unternehmens-TV *n* business television, BTV, business video
Unterrahmen *m* subframe
Unterregenerierung *f* under-replenishment *(of processing solutions)*
Unterrichtsfernsehen *n* instructional television (TV), ITV
Unterrichtsfilm *m* educational film (motion picture), teaching (training) film, visual aid
unterscheidbar distinguishable, discernible, discernable
Unterscheidbarkeit *f* distinguishability
Unterscheidungsmerkmal *n* discriminating criterion (feature), distinguishing characteristic
Unterscheidungsvermögen *n* discriminability, discriminatory ability, discriminatory (discriminative) power
Unterschiedsschwelle *f* discrimination threshold
unterschneiden to kern (typography)
Unterschneiden *n* [character] kerning
~/paarweises pair-wise kerning
unterschnitten condensed, justified tight, narrow *(typeface)*
Unterschrift *f*/**elektronische (digitale)** *s.* Signatur/digitale
Unterschriftenerkennung *f* signature recognition
Unterschriftenprüfung *f*, **Unterschriftenverifizierung** *f* signature verification, signature image validation
~/visuelle visual signature verification
unterschwellig subliminal *(stimulus)*
Untersegment *n* subsegment
Untersegmentierung *f* undersegmentation
Unterseite *f* 1. bottom side, underside; 2. *s.* Subseite
Untersicht *f* bottom view
~/extreme worm's eye view, mouse eye's view
Untersichtaufnahme *f* low-angle shot
Untersteuerungsreserve *f* feetroom *(video signal)*
untertasten *s.* unterabtasten
Unterteilung *f* subdivision *(s.a. under Subdivision)*
Unterteilungsfläche *f* subdivision surface
Untertitel *m* subtitle, caption
untertiteln to subtitle, to caption
Untertitelnegativ *n* subtitle negative
Untertitelung *f* subtitling, captioning
Untertitelungsliste *f* subtitle cue sheet
Unterträger *m* subcarrier, auxiliary information carrier
Unterträgerfrequenz *f* subcarrier frequency

Unterverzeichnis *n* subdirectory *(computer)*
Unterwasseraufnahme *f* underwater shot; underwater photograph
Unterwasserblitzgerät *n* underwater electronic flash
Unterwasserfernsehkamera *f* underwater television camera
Unterwasserfotografie *f* underwater photography
Unterwassergehäuse *n* underwater housing (case)
Unterwasserkamera *f* underwater camera
Unterwasserkartierung *f* underwater mapping
Unterwasserkinematografie *f* underwater cinematography
Unterwasserobjektiv *n* underwater lens
ununterscheidbar indiscernible *(e.g. image features)*
~ indistinguishable
unvergrößert unmagnified
unvergütet uncoated *(optical glass)*
unverkittet uncemented
unverrauscht noiseless, noise-free
unverschlüsselt free-to-air, FTA
unverzeichnet, unverzerrt undistorted, distortion-free, orthoscopic *(lens)*; anastigmat[ic] *(lens)*
Unzialbuchstabe *m* uncial [letter]
Unziale *f*, **Unzialschrift** *f* uncial
Urbildpunkt *m s.* object point
Urethroskop *n* urethroscope
Urfarbe *f* pure color
Urheberidentifizierung *f* authentication
Urheberrecht *n* copyright
Urkamera *f* pinhole camera, camera obscura
Urlaubsfoto *n* vacation photograph
Urografie *f* urography
Ursprungsbild *n* source image (picture) *(image processing)*
USB *s.* Bus/universeller serieller
USB-Anschluss *m* USB connection (port)
USB-Schnittstelle *f* USB interface
UV-... *s.a.* Ultraviolett...
UV-Absorber *m* ultraviolet (UV) absorber
UV-Absorptionsfilterschicht *f* UV absorption (filter) layer
UV-Beleuchtung *f* ultraviolet illumination
UV-Belichtung *f* ultraviolet exposure
UV-Bereich *m* ultraviolet region
UV-Bild *n* ultraviolet-radiation image
UV-Diodenlaser *m* ultraviolet diode laser
UV-Emission *f* ultraviolet emission
UV-Filterschicht *f* UV-filter layer
UV-Filterung *f* ultraviolet filtration
UV-Fluoreszenz *f* ultraviolet fluorescence
UV-Fluoreszenzfotografie *f* ultraviolet [fluorescence] photography
UV-Fluoreszenzmikroskopie *f* ultraviolet fluorescence microscopy
UV-Foto *n* UV photograph

UV-Katastrophe f ultraviolet catastrophe *(theory of electromagnetic radiation)*
UV-Lackierung f UV coating *(of printed matter)*
UV-Laserlithografie f UV laser lithography
UV-Licht n ultraviolet (black) light
UV-Lichtquelle f ultraviolet (UV) source
UV-Linse f UV lens
UV-Lumineszenz f ultraviolet luminescence
UV-Photon n ultraviolet photon
UV-Schutz m ultraviolet radiation protection
UV-Sensor m UV sensor
UV-Spektrum n UV spectrum
UV-Strahl m ultraviolet ray
UV-Strahlung f ultraviolet radiation
~/**längerwellige** longer wavelength ultraviolet radiation
UV-Teleskop n ultraviolet telescope
Ü-Wagen m *s.* Übertragungswagen

V

Vakuum-CCD-Kamera f vacuum CCD camera
Vakuum-Fluoreszenzdisplay n vacuum [fluorescent] display, VFD
Vakuumfotozelle f vacuum photocell
Vakuumglühlampe f vacuum lamp
Vakuumkassette f vacuum cassette *(radiography)*
Vakuumkopierrahmen m vacuum frame, vacuum easel; [contact] platemaker
Vakuumröhre f [electronic] vacuum tube
Vakuumturmteleskop n vacuum tower telescope *(solar observation)*
Vakuum-Ultraviolett n, **Vakuum-UV** n vacuum ultraviolet radiation
Valenz f valence, valency
Valenzband n valence band
Valenzbandelektron n valence-band electron
Valenzelektron n valence (optical) electron
Valenzstufe f valence level (stage)
Validation f, **Validierung** f validation
Varianz f variance *(e.g. of a signal)*
~/**lokale** local variance
Varianzmatrix f variance matrix
Varianzoperator m variance operator (filter)
Variation f variation
Variationsbreite f range *(statistics)*
Variationskoeffizient f coefficient of variation
Variator m floating system, variator *(zoom lens)*
Variocolorfilter n variable-color filter
Varioobjektiv n variofocal (vario) lens, variable-focal-length lens, zoom [lens], pancratic [lens] system
Vase f/**Rubinsche** Rubin's vase [profile], Rubin's drawing, vase illusion *(ambiguous figure)*
Vaterknoten m parent node *(computer graphics)*
VCSEL-Laserdiode f vertical cavity surface emitting laser, VCSEL
Vegetationsdurchdringungsradar n foliage-penetration radar, FOPEN [radar]
Vektor m vector *(mathematical quantity)*
~/**charakteristischer** characteristic vector, eigenvector *(of an operator)*
~/**elektrischer** electrical vector
~/**magnetischer** magnetic vector
~/**orthogonaler** orthogonal vector
~/**orthonormaler** orthonormal vector
~/**repräsentativer** representative vector *(quantization)*
~/**topologischer** topological vector
Vektoraddition f vector addition
Vektoralgebra f vector algebra
Vektorbild n vector image
Vektorbildschirm m vector [graphic] display, calligraphic display
Vektorbildverarbeitungsalgorithmus m vector image processing algorithm
Vektordarstellung f vector[-based] representation
Vektordatei f vector file
Vektordaten pl vector data
Vektordiagramm n vector diagram
Vektorfeld n vector field
Vektorfeldoperator m vector field operator
Vektorfeldtopologie f vector field topology
Vektorfeldvisualisierung f vector field visualization
Vektorform f vector form
Vektorformat n vector format
Vektorfunktion f vector function
Vektorgenerator m vector generator
Vektorgradient m vector gradient
Vektorgradientenbild n vector gradient image
Vektorgrafik f 1. vector[-based] graphics, object-oriented graphics; 2. vector-based graphic
Vektorgrafikprogramm n vector-based [graphics] program
Vektorgraph m vector graph, vectograph
Vektorgröße f vector quantity; vector magnitude
vektorisieren to vectorize
Vektorisierung f vectorization, raster-to-vector conversion, tracing
Vektorkarte f vector map
Vektorlänge f vector length
Vektormatrix f vector matrix
Vektoroszillograf m vectorscope
Vektoroszillogramm n vectorscope presentation (display)
Vektorprinzip f vector principle
Vektorprodukt n vector [cross] product, cross product
Vektorquantisierer m vector quantizer
~/**lernender** learning vector quantizer
Vektorquantisierung f vector quantization, VQ
~/**baumstrukturierte** tree-structured vector quantization, TSVQ
~/**bildadaptive** image-adaptive vector quantization
~/**hierarchische** hierarchical vector quantization
~/**klassifizierte** classified vector quantization
~/**mehrstufige** multistage (residual) vector quantization
~/**mittelwertseparierende** mean separating vector quantization, MSVQ
~/**prädiktive** predictive vector quantization
~/**überwachte** supervised (learning) vector quantization

Vektorquantisierungsnetz *n* vector quantization network
Vektorraum *m* vector[-valued] space, linear space
Vektorraumdarstellung *f* vector-space representation (notation)
Vektorraumprojektion *f* vector space projection
Vektorrichtung *f* vector direction
Vektorskop *n* vectorscope
Vektorskopdarstellung *f* vectorscope presentation (display)
Vektortomografie *f* vector tomography
Vektorvisualisierungsverfahren *n* vector visualization technique
Vektor-Wavelet-Transformation *f* vector wavelet transform
Vektor-Zeichensatz *m* vector (outline) font
Vektorzeichnung *f* vector drawing
Vektroskop *n* vectorscope
Venenpulsbild *n* phlebogram
Venenröntgen[kontrast]bild *n* venogram
Venenverschlussplethysmografie *f* venous-occlusion plethysmography
Venografie *f* venography *(s.a.* Phlebografie*)*
venografisch venographic
Venogramm *n* venogram
Ventrikulografie *f* [X-ray] ventriculography
Ventrikulogramm *n* ventriculogram
Veränderungserkennung *f* change detection *(image merging)*
veranschaulichen to visualize
Veranschaulichung *f* illustration; visualization *(s.a. under* Visualisierung*)*
Verarbeitbarkeit *f* processibility
verarbeiten to process, to soup *(s.a.* entwickeln*)*
Verarbeitung *f* processing *(s.a. under* Bildverarbeitung*)*
~/**digitale** digital processing
~/**fotografische** photographic processing, photoprocessing
~/**geometrische** geometric[al] processing
~/**globale** domain processing
~/**punktweise** point-to-point processing
~/**sequentielle** sequential (serial) processing
~/**vergleichende** ensemble processing
~/**wasserlose** dry (washless) processing
Verarbeitungsabfolge *f* processing sequence
Verarbeitungsalgorithmus *m* processing algorithm
Verarbeitungsanstalt *f* [professional] processing lab, photofinishing lab[oratory]
Verarbeitungsautomat *m* automatic processor, automatic (automated) processing machine
Verarbeitungsbad *n* processing bath
Verarbeitungschemie *f* [photographic] processing chemistry
Verarbeitungschemikalie *f* processing chemical
Verarbeitungseinheit *f*/**zentrale** *s.* Zentraleinheit
verarbeitungsfähig developable
Verarbeitungsfehler *m* processing error; processing defect
Verarbeitungsfolge *f*, **Verarbeitungsgang** *m* processing sequence
Verarbeitungsgeschwindigkeit *f* processing speed
Verarbeitungslabor *n s.* Verarbeitungsanstalt
Verarbeitungsleistung *f* processing performance; processing power
Verarbeitungslösung *f* process[ing] solution, processing fluid *(photographic development)*
Verarbeitungsmaschine *f* processing machine, machine processor
Verarbeitungsmaterial *n* [photographic] processing material
Verarbeitungsplattform *f* processing platform
Verarbeitungsschale *f* processing tray (dish)
Verarbeitungsschritt *m* processing step
Verarbeitungsspielraum *m* development latitude
Verarbeitungsstufe *f* processing stage (step)
Verarbeitungssystem *n* processing system
Verarbeitungstank *m* processing tank
Verarbeitungstechnik *f* processing technique
Verarbeitungstemperatur *f* processing temperature
Verarbeitungstoleranz *f* development latitude
Verarbeitungsvorgang *m* processing procedure
Verarbeitungszeit *f* processing [cycle] time
Verarmungsschicht *f*, **Verarmungszone** *f* depletion layer (region), depletion zone, charge-depleted region *(photodiode)*
verbildlichen to picturize
Verbildlichung *f* picturization
Verbindungsgraph *m* junction graph
Verbindungshalbleiter *m* compound semiconductor
Verbindungskabel *n* connecting cord
Verbindungslinie *f* linking (connecting) line; join line
Verbindungspunkt *m* junction point
Verbindungsschicht *f* data link layer
Verbindungsstecker *m* 1. connector, connecting plug; 2. *s.* Brückenstecker
Verbindungsstrategie *f* linkage strategy *(e.g. in image segmentation)*
verblassen to fade
verbleichen to fade
Verbund *m* record *(digital image description)*

Verbunddokument *n* compound document
Verbundlinse *f* compound (complex) lens
Verbundsignal *n* composite [video] signal, composite color [video] signal, composite TV signal
verchromen to chromize, to chrome
verdecken to occult, to cover, to obscure; to occlude
Verdeckte-Flächen-Problem *n* hidden-surface problem
Verdeckte-Kanten-Problem *n* hidden-line problem
Verdeckung *f* occlusion, interposition; overlap
Verdeckungskante *f* occluding contour
Verdruckbarkeit *f* runability *(of printing paper)*
Verdunk[e]lung *f* blackout curtain *(e.g. in a darkroom)*
~[e]lungsstoff *m* dark cloth
Verdünnung *f* 1. dilution; 2. thinning, skeletonization *(binary image processing)*
~/topologische topological thinning
Verdünnungsalgorithmus *m* thinning (skeletonizing) algorithm
Verdünnungsoperation *f* thinning operation (procedure)
Verdünnungstransformation *f* thinning transformation
Vereinigung *f* [Boolean] union operation *(set-theoretic operation)*
~/unscharfe fuzzy union *(fuzzy set theory)*
Verfahren *n*/**bildgebendes** image-forming process, imaging process (procedure); imaging modality *(diagnostics)*
~/fotografisches photographic process; photographic process
Verfallsdatum *n* expiry (expiration) date *(e.g. of film material)*
verfärben to discolor, to stain
Verfärbung *f* discoloration
Verfeinerung *f*/**fortschreitende** progressive refinement, shooting *(radiosity technique)*
verfilmen to film, to picturize, to cinematize
Verfilmung *f* filmization, picturization
~/mehrteilige sequel
Verfolgungsalgorithmus *m* tracking algorithm *(video coding)*
Verfolgungsradar *n* [target] tracking radar
Verfolgungsschwenk *m* tracking, trucking, panning *(camera movement)*; tracking (follow) shot
Verfolgungsteleskop *n* tracking telescope
verformen to warp, to morph; to transform; to deform
Verfremdung *f*, **Verfremdungseffekt** *m* aliasing [effect], alias *(sampling artifact)*
Vergenz *f* [eye] vergence *(movement of the eyeballs)*
~/binokulare binocular vergence
~/relative relative vergence

Vergenzbewegung *f* vergence motion (eye movement)
Vergenzwinkel *m* vergence angle
vergilben to yellow
Vergilbung *f* yellowing
Vergleich *m* comparison, matching
~/paarweiser pairwise comparison
vergleichen to compare, to match
Vergleichsdensitometer *n* [/**visuelles**] comparator (visual) densitometer
Vergleichsfarbe *f* matching stimulus
Vergleichsfoto *n* comparative photograph
Vergleichskolorimeter *n* comparison colorimeter
Vergleichsmikroskop *n* comparison microscope
Vergleichsmuster *n* reference pattern
Vergleichsoperation *f* comparison operation
Vergleichspunkt *m* bench mark
Vergleichsspektroskop *n* comparison spectroscope
Vergleichsspektrum *n* comparison spectrum
Vergleichsstrahlungsquelle *f* comparison lamp
Vergleichswelle *f s.* Referenzwelle
Vergrauung *f* gray shading
Vergrößerer *m* [photographic] enlarger, photo-enlarger, enlarging projector, projection printer
~ mit diffuser Beleuchtung diffusion-type enlarger
Vergrößererkopf *m* enlarger head
Vergrößerer-Lichtquelle *f* enlarger light source
vergrößern to enlarge, to magnify, to blow up
~/optisch to enlarge optically
Vergrößerung *f* 1. enlargement, magnification; print magnification, blowup; scale [of reproduction]; 2. [photographic] enlargement, enlargement copy, enlarged print, blowup
~ auf Lebensgröße life-size magnification
~/förderliche *s.* Vergrößerung/nutzbare
~/laterale lateral (transverse) magnification
~/leere empty magnification *(microscopy)*
~/lineare linear magnification
~/longitudinale longitudinal magnification *(optics)*
~/nutzbare (nützliche) useful (usable) magnification *(microscopy)*
~/optische optical magnification
~/transversale transverse (lateral) magnification
~/visuelle visual magnification *(optics)*
Vergrößerungsapparat *m* enlarging projector, [photographic] enlarger, photo-enlarger, projection printer
~ mit diffuser Beleuchtung diffusion[-type] enlarger

Vergrößerungsarbeit *f* magnification work
Vergrößerungsautomat *m* automatic enlarger
Vergrößerungsbereich *m* magnification range
Vergrößerungsdifferenz *f*/**chromatische** 1. color magnification error *(optics)*; 2. *s.* Farbquerfehler
Vergrößerungseffekt *m* magnification effect
vergrößerungsfähig enlargeable
Vergrößerungsfähigkeit *f* magnifying ability, magnification power (capability), enlargeability
Vergrößerungsfaktor *m* magnification factor
Vergrößerungsfenster *n* magnifying window *(on a display)*
Vergrößerungsformel *f* magnification formula
Vergrößerungsgerät *n* 1. magnifying optical instrument; 2. *s.* Vergrößerungsapparat
Vergrößerungsgerätehersteller *m* enlarger manufacturer
Vergrößerungsgesetz *n* magnification law
Vergrößerungsglas *n* magnifying glass, magnifier
Vergrößerungsgrad *m* degree of enlargement (magnification)
Vergrößerungskassette *f* [multi-mask] enlarging easel, printing (masking) frame, [adjustable] masking easel, enlarging paper holder
Vergrößerungskopf *m* enlarger head, projection assembly
Vergrößerungskopie *f* blowup print
Vergrößerungskopieren *n* blowup printing
Vergrößerungslampe *f* magnifying lamp
Vergrößerungsleistung *f* magnifying (magnification) power
Vergrößerungslicht *n* enlarger (printing) light
Vergrößerungslichtquelle *f* enlarger light source
Vergrößerungslinse *f* magnifying (magnifier) lens
Vergrößerungsmaske *f* black mask
Vergrößerungsmaßstab *m* enlargement (magnification) scale, scale of enlargement
Vergrößerungsobjektiv *n* enlarging (enlarger) lens
Vergrößerungspapier *n* enlarging paper; print[ing] paper, photographic [printing] paper, photo paper *(s.a. under* Papier*)*
Vergrößerungsrahmen *m s.* Vergrößerungskassette
Vergrößerungsspiegel *m* magnifying mirror
Vergrößerungstechnik *f* magnification technique
Vergrößerungsverhältnis *n* magnification ratio

Vergrößerungszahl *f* enlargement factor
vergüten to coat
Vergütung *f* [optical] coating
~/**reflexionsmindernde** low-reflection coating
Vergütungsschichtdicke *f* coating thickness
Verhältnis *n*/**anamorphotisches** anamorphic ratio, compression (squeeze) factor
~/**gyromagnetisches** gyromagnetic (magnetogyric) ratio *(nuclear magnetic resonance)*
Verjüngen *n* tapering *(e.g. as transformation procedure in computer graphics)*
Verkehrsecho *n* traffic clutter *(radar)*
Verkehrsflussanalyse *f* traffic flow analysis
Verkehrssimulation *f* traffic simulation
Verkehrsüberwachung *f* traffic surveillance
Verkehrsüberwachungskamera *f* traffic monitoring camera
Verkettung *f* concatenation, chaining *(e.g. of codes)*
verkippbar tiltable
verkippen to tilt
Verkippung *f* tilt[ing], tilt movement
verkitten to cement [together]
Verkittung *f* cementing
verkleinern to reduce, to demagnify, to minify, to miniaturize
~/**fotografisch** to photoreduce, to reduce photographically
Verkleinerung *f* reduction, demagnification, minification
~/**optische** optical reduction
Verkleinerungsfaktor *m* demagnification factor; reduction ratio, ratio of reduction
Verkleinerungsglas *n* reduction lens, reducing (diminishing) glass
Verkleinerungskopie *f* reduction print
Verkleinerungskopieren *n* reduction printing
Verkleinerungskopiermaschine *f* reduction printer
Verkleinerungsmaßstab *m* scale of reduction
Verkleinerungsobjektiv *n* reduction lens
Verkleinerungsverhältnis *n* reduction ratio, ratio of reduction
Verknüpfung *f* link, connection, arc *(e.g. in a neural network)*
~/**Boolesche** Boolean operation
Verknüpfungsalgorithmus *m* linkage algorithm
Verknüpfungspunkt *m* tie point
Verkürzung *f*/**perspektivische** perspective foreshortening
Verkürzungseffekt *m* foreshortening [effect]
Verlängerungsbalgen *m* extension bellows
Verlängerungskabel *n* extension cord
Verlängerungsplatine *f* extender board
Verlängerungsschiene *f* rail *(view camera)*

Verlängerungstubus *m* extension tube
Verlauf *m*/**spektraler** spectral response
Verlauffilter *n* graduated filter, attenuator
Verleiher *m* distributor *(cinema)*
Verleihkopie *f* theatrical [projection] print, [exhibition] release print
verlustbehaftet lossy *(image compression)*
verlustfrei, verlustlos lossless, loss-free *(image compression)*
Vermessungskunde *f* geodesy
Vermessungstechnik *f* prospecting technique
Vermessungswesen *n* surveying
Vermittler *m* switch[er]
Vermittlungsknoten *m* switching node
Vermittlungsschicht *f* network layer
Vermittlungstechnik *f* switching technology
Vermittlungsverzögerung *f* switching delay
vernetzbar networkable
Vernetzbarkeit *f* networkability
vernetzen to network; to interconnect
Vernichtungsstrahlung *f* annihilation [radiation] *(particle physics)*
Vernier-Sehschärfe *f* vernier acuity, [visual] hyperacuity
Vernis mou *m s.* Weichgrundradierung
Verpackungsdruck *m* packaging printing
Verpackungsdruckmaschine *f* packaging press
Verpackungstiefdruck *m* packaging gravure
Verpackungstiefdruckmaschine *f* gravure packaging press
verrauschen to noise *(e.g. an image)*
verrauscht noisy, noised *(e.g. image signals)*
verreißen to jar *(e.g. a camera)*
Verriegelungshebel *m* lock lever
Verrollung *f* rolling *(e.g. camera rotation around the optical axis)*
Versal *m* capital (uppercase) letter, cap, majuscule
Versalhöhe *f* cap height (line)
Versandhauskatalog *m* mail order catalog
Versandrolle *f* shipping reel
Versatz *m* interleave
verschachteln to interleave *(signals)*
Verschachtelung *f* interleaving; scrambling; shuffling *(of signals)*
verschieben to shift; to translate
Verschiebung *f* shift; translation *(geometric transformation)*
~/bathochrome bathochromic shift
~/chemische chemical shift artifact, chemical shift [effect] *(magnetic resonance imaging)*
~/hypsochrome hypsochromic shift
Verschiebungsgesetz *n*/**Wiensches** Wien['s] displacement law, Wien's law *(thermal radiation)*

verschiebungsinvariant shift-invariant, translation-invariant *(image processing operator)*
~/linear linear shift-invariant, LSI
Verschiebungsinvarianz *f* shift (translation) invariance *(of an operator)*
Verschiebungskompensation *f* dechirping *(radar)*
Verschiebungsoperator *m* displacement operator
Verschiebungsvarianz *f* shift variance *(pattern recognition)*
Verschiebungsvektor *m* displacement vector; shift vector
Verschiebungsvektorfeld *n* displacement vector field
verschiedenfarbig differently colored, heterochromatic
verschleiern to fog *(film material)*
Verschleierung *f* fogging
Verschluss *m* [camera] shutter; shutter *(e.g. of a disk drive)*
~/akustooptischer acousto-optic shutter
~/elektrolytischer electrolytic shutter
~/elektromagnetischer electromagnetic shutter
~/elektromechanischer electromechanical shutter
~/elektronischer electronic (electronically controlled) shutter
~/elektrooptischer electro-optical shutter, Kerr cell [shutter]
~/fotografischer photographic shutter
~/magnetooptischer magneto-optical shutter, Faraday shutter
~/mechanischer mechanical shutter
~/nichtmechanischer nonmechanical shutter
Verschlussaufzug *m* shutter wind (cocking)
Verschlussauslösung *f* shutter release
Verschlussblende *f* [optical] obturator
Verschlussdurchmesser *m* shutter diameter
Verschlussebene *f* shutter plane
Verschlusseinrichtung *f* shutter mechanism
Verschlüsseler *m* encrypter
verschlüsseln to encrypt *(s.a. verwürfeln)*
Verschlüsselung *f* encryption *(of signals)*
Verschlussfehler *m* shutter fault
Verschlussgenauigkeit *f* shutter accuracy
Verschlussgeschwindigkeit *f* shutter speed (time)
Verschlusslamelle *f* [camera] shutter blade
verschlusslos shutterless
Verschlussmechanismus *m* shutter mechanism
Verschlussrollo *n s.* Verschlussvorhang
Verschlussspalt *m* shutter slit
Verschlussspannvorrichtung *f* shutter-cocking mechanism
Verschlussstellung *f* shutter setting
Verschlusstuch *n* shutter curtain material
Verschlusstuchband *n* shutter curtain tape

Verschlussvorhang *m* shutter curtain (blind)
Verschlussvorwahl *f* shutter priority
Verschlussvorwahlzeit *f* shutter release time lag
Verschlusszeit *f* shutter speed (time); shutter opening duration
Verschlusszeit-Blenden-Kombination *f* shutter speed and aperture combination, aperture and shutter speed combination
Verschlusszeitenbereich *m* range of shutter speeds
Verschlusszeiteneinstellung *f* [camera] shutter speed setting, shutter (speed) setting
Verschlusszeitenrad *n* shutter[-speed] dial, shutter-speed selector dial
Verschlusszeitenskale *f* shutter scale
Verschlusszyklus *m* shutter[-speed] cycle
Verschmelzung *f* fusion
~/**binokulare** binocular fusion
~/**zeitliche** temporal fusion
Verschmelzungsfrequenz *f* [critical] fusion frequency, critical flicker [fusion] frequency, CFF
Verschmelzungspunkt *m* recovery point *(human vision)*
Verschwärzlichung *f* black shading
Versetzungsbild *n* image of dislocation *(electron microscopy)*
Versetzungskontrast *m* dislocation contrast *(electron microscopy)*
Versetzungslinie *f* dislocation line
versilbern to silver
Verso *n* verso *(page)*; left-hand page *(layout)*
Versorgungsgebiet *n* serving (service) area, footprint *(television transmission)*
Versorgungsspannung *f* supply voltage
verspiegeln to mirrorize
verstärken 1. to intensify, to enhance *(e.g. image contrast)*; 2. to amplify, to boost *(e.g. signals)*
Verstärker *m* 1. intensifier *(negative processing)*; 2. amplifier, booster; enhancer *(video)*; regenerator, repeater *(esp. of fiber-optic links)*
~/**analoger** analog amplifier
~/**digitaler** digital amplifier
~/**faseroptischer** fiber-optic amplifier
~/**hochohmiger** high-impedance amplifier
~/**linearoptischer** linear-optical amplifier, LOA
~/**optischer** optical amplifier
~/**spannungsgesteuerter** voltage-controlled amplifier, VCA
Verstärkerfolie *f* intensifying screen *(radiography)*
Verstärkerkaskade *f* amplifier cascade
Verstärkerrauschen *n* amplifier noise; gain noise *(due to internal amplification)*
Verstärkung *f* 1. intensification; 2. amplification; gain *(amplifier)*
~/**differentielle** differential gain

~/**elektronische** electronic amplification
~/**lineare** linear amplification *(e.g. of scintillation signals)*
~/**optische** optical gain
~/**zeitabhängige** time-compensated gain *(of sound echo in ultrasound imaging)*
Verstärkungsfaktor *m* amplification factor; intensification factor
Verstärkungsfolie *f s.* Verstärkerfolie
Verstärkungsregelung *f*/**automatische** automatic gain control, AGC; [automatic] audio record level [control]
~/**selektive** time gain compensation, TGC
Verstellbarkeit *f* adjustability
Verstellmöglichkeit[en] *f[pl]* tilts and swings *(view camera)*
Verstümmelungsartefakt *n* Gibbs artifact (phenomenon), truncation (ringing) artifact *(magnetic resonance imaging)*
Versuchssendung *f* experimental transmission *(television)*
Vertauschbarkeit *f s.* Kommutativität
Verteiler *m* switcher *(video)*
Verteilersatellit *m* communication [technology] satellite, communications satellite
Verteilerverstärker *m* distribution amplifier *(video)*
Verteilung/**örtliche** spatial distribution
~/**spektrale** spectral [energy] distribution
Verteilungsdichte *f* distribution density
Verteilungsfunktion *f* [probability] distribution function, spread function
~/**kumulative** cumulative distribution function, CDF
~/**optische** optical spread function
Verteilungskurve *f* distribution curve
Verteilungsmuster *n* distribution pattern
Verteilungstemperatur *f* distribution temperature
Vertex *m* vertex, apex, pole
Vertiefung *f* pit *(compact disc)*
Vertikalablenkspule *f* field deflection coil
Vertikalablenkung *f* vertical deflection
Vertikalalias *m* vertical alias[ing]
Vertikalauflösung *f* vertical resolution
Vertikalaustastlücke *f* vertical blanking [interval], VBI, field blanking interval
Vertikalaustastung *f* vertical blanking
Vertikalen-Täuschung *f* tilt illusion
Vertikalfilter *n* vertical-pass filter
Vertikalfrequenz *f* vertical scanning frequency, vertical [sweep] frequency, vertical scan rate; field rate *(interlaced video)*; frame rate *(noninterlaced video)*
Vertikalhöhe *f* point size *(piece of type)*
Vertikalkamera *f* vertical camera *(process camera)*
Vertikalrücklauf *m* vertical retrace [time], frame flyback
Vertikalschwenk *m* tilt [move], camera tilt
Vertikalsynchronimpuls *m* vertical sync[hronization] pulse, vertical synchronizing signal, VSYNC

Vertikalsynchronisation f vertical sync[hronization] (monitor)
Vertikalvergrößerungsgerät n vertical enlarger
vertonen to dub
Vertonung f [audio] dubbing
Vertoskop n vertoscope
Vertreter m proxy (server)
verunschärfen to blur
Verunschärfung f blurring
vervielfältigbar reproducible
vervielfältigen to reproduce, to manifold; to copy; to duplicate
Vervielfältiger m duplicator
Vervielfältigung f 1. reproduction; duplication; 2. duplicate copy
~/**farbige** multicolor duplication
Vervielfältigungsapparat m, **Vervielfältigungsgerät** n manifolder, duplicator, duplicating device (machine)
Vervielfältigungsrecht n copyright
Vervielfältigungsverfahren n duplicating-printing process
Vervielfältigungsvorlage f master [copy]; master sheet
verwackeln to shake, to jar (e.g. a shot)
Verwacklung[sbewegung] f camera shake, [shaky] camera movement
Verwaschungsfunktion f s. Punktbildfunktion
Verweildauer f, **Verweilzeit** f dwell period (time) (e.g. of a detector)
Verweis m reference; reference mark
Verweißlichung f desaturation; white shading
Verweistabelle f lookup table, LUT, index map; video lookup table
Verwerfung f warp
Verwischeffekt m blurring effect
verwischen to blur
Verwischen n, **Verwischung** f blurring
Verwischungstomografie f blurring tomography
Verwürfeler m scrambler (signal processing)
verwürfeln to scramble (s.a. verschlüsseln)
Verwürfeln n, **Verwürfelung** f scrambling; shuffling (of signals)
verzeichnen to distort
Verzeichnis n directory (computer)
Verzeichnisdatei f directory file
Verzeichnung f distortion (s.a. under Verzerrung)
~/**anisotrope** anistropic distortion (magnetic aberration)
~/**kissenförmige** pincushion (negative) distortion (optics)
~/**radiale** radial [image] distortion
~/**relative** relative distortion
~/**sphärische** spherical aberration, SA
~/**tangentiale** tangential distortion
~/**tonnenförmige** barrel (positive) distortion (optics)
Verzeichnungsfehler m distortion error

verzeichnungsfrei distortion-free, undistorted, orthoscopic (lens); anastigmat[ic] (lens)
Verzeichnungsfreiheit f absence of distortion
Verzeichnungskorrektur f distortion correction
verzerren to distort
Verzerrung f 1. distortion (s.a. under Verzeichnung); 2. warp
~/**anamorphotische** anamorphic squeeze (distortion)
~/**epipolare** epipolar distortion
~/**geometrische** geometric[al] distortion
~/**harmonische** harmonic distortion
~/**lineare** linear distortion
~/**nichtlineare** nonlinear (curvilinear) distortion
~/**optische** optical distortion
~/**perspektivische** perspective distortion
~/**projektive** projective distortion
~/**radiometrische** radiometric distortion
~/**selbstaffine** self-affine distortion (computer graphics)
~/**spektrale** spectral distortion
~/**systematische** systematic distortion (remote sensing)
~/**topologische** topological distortion
Verzerrungsellipse f indicatrix (cartography)
verzerrungsfrei s. verzeichnungsfrei
Verzerrungsmaß n distortion measure
Verzögerer m restrainer, development inhibitor (s.a. Antischleiermittel)
Verzögerungsausgleich m delay equalization
verzögerungsempfindlich delay-sensitive (e.g. video signals)
Verzögerungsleitung f delay line (digital signal processing)
Verzögerungsmittel n s. Verzögerer
Verzögerungsplatte f [birefringent] wave plate, retardation plate, retarder s.a. Phasenplättchen)
~ **höherer Ordnung** multiple-order wave plate
~ **nullter Ordnung** zero-order wave plate
Verzögerungszeit f delay [time]
Verzweigungspunkt m branch point
Vesikularemulsion f vesicular emulsion
Vesikularfilm m vesicular film
Vesikular-Mikrofilm m vesicular microfilm
Vesikularverfahren n vesicular process
VGA-Grafikkarte f video graphics array, VGA
VGA-Monitor m VGA (video graphics array) display
VHS s. Video-Heimsystem
VHS-Band n VHS [analog] tape
VHS-Camcorder m VHS camcorder
VHS-Kassette f VHS cassette
Vibrograf m vibrograph
Vibrogramm n vibrogram

Video 426

Video *n* 1. video *(s.a.* Videografie, Videoband*)*; 2. *s.* Fernsehen
~/**analoges** analog (serial) video
~ **auf Abruf,** ~ **auf Bestellung** video-on-demand, VoD
~/**digitales** 1. digital (numerical) video; 2. *s.* Videoformat/digitales
~/**hochauflösendes** high-definition video, HD video
~/**interaktives** interactive video, IV
~/**interaktives digitales** digital video interactive, DVI
~/**komprimiertes** compressed (packet) video
~/**progressives** progressive (noninterlaced) video
~/**synthetisches** synthetic video *(e.g. of radar data)*
Videoabspielgerät *n* video player (playback device)
Videoabspielung *f* video playback (playout), replay
Videoabtaster *m* video scanner
Videoabtastrate *f* video scanning rate
Videoabtastung *f* video scanning (sampling)
Video-Abtastwert *m* video sample
Video-Abtastzeile *f* video scan line
Videoadapter *m s.* Videokarte
Videoamateur *m* video hobbyist
Videoanalyse *f* video analysis
Videoanalyser *m* video analyzer
Videoanimation *f* video animation
Videoanlage *f* video system
Videoanschluss *m* video port
Videoanwendung *f* video application
Videoanzeige *f* video display
Videoarbeit *f* video work
Videoarbeitsplatz *m* video workstation
Videoarchiv *n* video archive; video library
Videoarchivierung *f* video archiving (filing)
Video-Assistent *m* video operator *(filming)*
Videoastronomie *f* video astronomy
Videoauflösung *f* video [frame] resolution
Videoaufnahme *f* 1. video shooting; 2. video shot; 3. *s.* Videoaufzeichnung
Videoaufzeichnung *f* video [camera] recording, video capture
~/**digitale** digital video recording
~/**elektronische** electronic video recording, EVR
Videoaufzeichnungsformat *n* video recording format (standard)
Videoaufzeichnungsgerät *n* video[tape] recorder
Videoaufzeichnungsspur *f s.* Videospur
Videoaufzeichnungssystem *n* video recording system; video [imaging] system
Videoaufzeichnungstechnik *f* video recording technology
Videoausgabe *f* video output
Videoausgang *m*, **Video-Ausgangsbuchse** *f* video output

Videoausgangssignal *n* video output signal
Videoausrüstung *f* video equipment (gear)
Videoausstrahlung *f* video broadcast
Videoauthentifikation *f* video authentication
Videoband *n* 1. videotape, video[-recording tape], VT *(s.a.* Videomagnetband*)*; 2. *s.* Videofrequenzband
~/**bespieltes** [pre]recorded videotape
~/**metalldampfbeschichtetes** metal-evaporated tape, ME tape
Videobandabspielung *f* videotape playback
Videobandaufnahme *f* 1. videotape recording; 2. videotape record
Videobandaufzeichnung *f* videotape recording
Videoband-Aufzeichnungssystem *n*/**digitales** digital videotape recording system, DVTR
Videobandbreite *f* video bandwidth
Videobandformat *n* videotape format
Videobandgerät *n* videotape recorder, VTR; television tape machine
Videobandkassettensystem *n* **mit Schrägaufzeichnung** helical-scan videotape cassette system
Videobandkopie *f* dub
Videobandmaschine *f* videotape machine; videotape deck
Videobandmaterial *n* videotape[d] material, video[-captured] footage
Videobandrecorder *m* tape-based VCR
Videobandschleife *f* video loop
Videobandschnitt *m* videotape editing
Videobandspieler *m* videotape player
Videobandspule *f* video reel
Videobandtechnik *f* videotape technology
Videobasisband *n* video baseband
Videobeamer *m s.* Videoprojektor
Videobearbeitung *f* video processing; video editing
~/**digitale** digital video processing
Videobearbeitungsgerät *n* video manipulator
Videobearbeitungswerkzeug *n* video tool
Videobeleuchtung *f* video lighting
Videobereich *m* video domain (area)
Videobeschleunigerkarte *f* video accelerator chip
Videobestelldienst *m s.* Videodienst
Videobild *n* video image (picture); video frame
~/**analoges** video analog image
~/**stereoskopisches** stereoscopic video image
Videobildaufnehmer *m* video image recorder, video capture device
Videobildformat *n* video picture format
Videobildfrequenz *f* video [frame] rate, TV (television frame) rate, video frequency
Videobildqualität *f* video quality

Videofolge

~/**subjektive** subjective (user-perceived) video quality
Videobildrate f s. Videobildfrequenz
Videobildröhre f video [display] tube
Videobildschirm m video [display] screen, video [image] display, video display terminal, VDT
Videobildsegment n video picture segment
Videobildsensor m video-image sensor
Videobildspeicher m video display memory
Videobildspeicherplatte f video disk
Videobildsucher m video viewfinder
Videobildverarbeitung f video image processing
Videobildwandler m video imager
Video-Bitrate f video bit (data) rate
Videobrille f head-mounted (helmet-mounted) display, HMD
Videobuchse f video socket
Videobus m graphics bus, digital video link, DVL
Videocamcorder m video camcorder
~/**digitaler** DV camcorder
Video-CCD-Kamera f video [format] CCD camera
Video-CD f video compact disc, video CD, VCD, compact disc video, CDV, compact video disc, CVD
Videochip m video chip
Videoclip m video clip
Video-Codec m(n) [video] codec
Videocodierer m video [en]coder
Videocodierung f video [en]coding (s.a. under Codierung)
~/**inhaltsbasierte** content-based video coding
~/**modellbasierte** model-based video coding
~/**objektbasierte** object-based video coding
~/**robuste** robust video coding
Videocodierungsalgorithmus m video coding algorithm
Videocodierungsstandard m video [en]coding standard
Videocodierungssystem n video [en]coding system
Videodarstellung f video presentation
Videodatei f video file
Videodaten pl video (visual) data
~/**komprimierte** compressed video data
Videodatenbank f video database (library)
Videodatenblock m video data block
Videodatenformat n video data format
Videodatenkompression f, **Videokomprimierung** f video data compression
Videodatenkonvertierung f video conversion
Videodatenpaket n video packet
Videodatenrate f video data (bit) rate

Videodatenreduktion f video data reduction
Videodatenstrom m video data stream, video [bit] stream, stream of video data
Videodatenterminal n video data terminal
Videodatenübertragung f video data transmission
Videodecod[ier]er m video decoder
Videodecodierung f video decoding
Videodemodulation f video demodulation
Videodemodulator m video demodulator
Videodensitometrie f video densitometry
Videodienst m video[-on-demand] service, VOD service
Videodigitalisierer m,
Videodigitalisierkarte f s. Videodigitalisierungskarte
Videodigitalisierung f video digitization, frame capture (grab)
Videodigitalisierungskarte f [video] frame grabber, frame grabber (capture) card, video digitizer, digitizing board *(high-speed memory device)*
Videodiskette f still video floppy disk, video floppy, VF
Videodokumentation f video documentation
Videodreh m video shoot[ing], videotaping [session], recording session
Videodrucker m video printer
Videoduplikation f, **Videoduplizierung** f videotape duplication
Video-Echtzeitübertragung f video streaming
Videoeditor m 1. video editor *(as a profession)*; 2. s. Videoschnittcomputer
Videoeffekt m video [optical] effect
~/**digitaler** digital video effect, DVE
Videoeffektgerät n video effects device (unit)
Videoeinblendung f video insertion
Videoeingang m video input
Videoeingangssignal n video input signal
Videoeinzelbild n video frame
Videoelektronik f video electronics
Videoendoskop n electronic endoscope
Videoerweiterungskarte f video capture board (card)
Video-Farbdrucker m video color printer
Videofarbsignal n chroma signal, C [signal]
Videofenster n video window
Videofilm m video film; video movie
Videofilmen n videographing, taping
Videofilmer m videographer, videomaker
Videofilmkamera f motion video camera
Videofilmschnitt m s. Videoschnitt 1. and 2.
Videofilmsequenz f videotape sequence
Video-Film-Transfer m [video-to-]film transfer, tape-to-film transfer, printing to film
Videofilter n video filter
Videofluoroskopie f videofluoroscopy
Videofolge f s. Videosequenz

Videofon *n* videophone, VP, picturephone, video (visual) telephone, screen phone
Videofonie *f* videophony
Videoformat *n* video [recording] format
~/analoges analog video format
~/digitales digital video format, DV format
Videoformatierung *f* video formatting
Videofrequenz *f* video frequency, video [frame] rate, TV (television frame) rate
Videofrequenzband *n* video frequency band
Videofrequenzbandbreite *f* video bandwidth
Videofrequenzgang *m* video frequency response
Video-Füllsignal *n* video fill
Videofunktion *f* video function
Videogerät *n* video device
Videogleichrichter *m* video detector
Videograf *m* videographer, videomaker
Videografie *f* 1. videography, video photography; 2. videograph
~/ballistische ballistic videography
videografieren to videograph; to [video]tape
Videografik *f* video graphic
Video-Grafikadapter *m* video graphics array, VGA
Videografikkarte *f s.* Videokarte
videografisch videographic
Videohalbbild *n* video field
Video-Handy *n* video cell phone
Video-Heimsystem *n* Video Home System, VHS *(analog videotape recording format)*
Videoimpulsgeber *m* video pulse generator
Videoindexierungssystem *n* video indexing system
Videoindustrie *f* video industry
Videoinformation *f* video information
Video-Informationssystem *n* video information system
Videoingenieur *m* video engineer
Videoinhalt *m* video content
Videoinstrument *n* video instrument
Videojournalist *m* video journalist
Videokabel *n* video cable
Videokamera *f* [motion] video camera; videocassette camera
~/digitale digital video camera
Videokamerafilter *n* video camera filter
Videokameramann *m* video operator
Videokamerarecorder *m* camera-recorder, camcorder
Videokamerasystem *n* video camera system
Videokameratechnik *f* video camera technology
Videokanal *m* video channel
Videokarte *f* video [display] card, video capture card, video [graphics] board, video conversion board, video adapter (controller)
Videokartierung *f* video mapping

Videokassette *f* videocassette, videotape cassette, video cartridge
~/bespielte prerecorded videocassette
Videokassettenaufzeichnungssystem *n* videocassette recording system
Videokassettenband *n* videocassette tape
Videokassettenrecorder *m* videocassette recorder, VCR
~/analoger analog VCR (video cassette recorder)
~/digitaler digital VCR
Videokassettensystem *n* videocassette recording system
Videokassettenvorspann *m* video cassette leader
Videokommunikation *f* video communication
Videokommunikationssystem *n* video communication system
Videokompression *f* video [data] compression
~/bewegungskompensierte motion-compensated video compression
~/digitale digital video compression
Videokompressionsalgorithmus *m* video compression algorithm
Videokompressionsrate *f* video encode rate
Videokompressionssoftware *f* video compression software
Videokompressionsstandard *m* video compression standard
Videokompressionssyntax *f* video compression syntax
Videokompressionsverfahren *n* video compression technique (method)
Videokompressionsverhältnis *n* video compression ratio
Videokompressor *m* video compressor
Videokomprimierung *f s.* Videokompression
Videokonferenz *f* videoconference, video meeting (session)
Videokonferenzanlage *f* videoconference installation (facility)
Videokonferenzbandbreite *f* videoconferencing bandwidth
Videokonferenzbetrieb *m* [tele]videoconferencing
Videokonferenzdienst *m* video [tele]conferencing service
Videokonferenznetz *n* videoconferencing network
Videokonferenzraum *m* videoconference room
Videokonferenzsignal *n* videoconference[-type] signal
Videokonferenzsoftware *f* videoconferencing software
Videokonferenzstandard *m* vidoconferencing (video teleconferencing) standard
Videokonferenzstudio *n* videoconference room

Videokonferenzsystem *n* videoconferencing (videoconference) system, video teleconferencing system
~/**mobiles** rollabout [system]
Videokonferenztechnik *f* video teleconferencing, conference television (TV)
Videokonferenzteilnehmer *m* video conference party
Videokonferenzverbindung *f* videoconference connection
Videokonservierung *f* video preservation
Videokonsole *f* videotape deck
Videokonsum *m* video viewing
Videokonverter *m* video converter
Videokonvertierung *f* video [format] conversion
Videokopf *m* video[tape] head; VCR head
~/**rotierender** rotary head
Videokopfnachführung *f*/**automatische** automatic track following, ATF, auto tracking
Videokopfrad *n s.* Videokopftrommel
Videokopfreinigung *f* video head cleaning
Videokopftrommel *f* video recorder head drum, video scanning drum
Videokopie *f* video copy, [video] dub
Videokopierer *m* video printer
Videokopierung *f* videocassette duplication
Video-Koppelfeld *n*, **Video-Koppelsystem** *n* video patch panel
Videolabor *n* video laboratory
Video-Leihkassette *f* rental video
Videoleinwand *f* video wall
Videoleuchte *f* video light
~/**eingebaute (integrierte)** inbuilt [video] light
Videomagnetaufzeichnung *f* video tape recording
Videomagnetband *n* video magnetic tape, [magnetic] videotape *(s.a.* Videoband*)*
Videomakroskop *n* video macroscope
Video-Masterband *n* video master tape, master videotape
Videomaterial *n* video material (imagery); video[-captured] footage, videotape[d] material
Videomesstechnik *f*, **Videometrie** *f* videometry
Videomikroskop *n* video microscope, video magnification system
Videomikroskopie *f* video microscopy
Video-Mikrosonde *f* video microprobe
Videomischer *m*, **Videomischpult** *n* video switcher, video (vision) mixer; [studio] production switcher
Videomodellierung *f* video modeling
Videomodul *n* video module
Videomodulation *f* video modulation
Videomodulator *m* video modulator
Videomodus *m* video mode
Videomonitor *m* video [display] monitor

Videomultiplexer *m* video multiplexer, video multiplex [coder]
Videomuster *npl* video dailies
Videonachbearbeitung *f* video editing (postproduction), video postprocessing
~/**analoge** analog video editing
~/**digitale** digital video editing
~/**lineare** linear video editing
~/**nichtlineare** nonlinear video editing
Videonachbearbeitungsgerät *n* video editor
Videonachbearbeitungskarte *f* video capture board
Videonachbearbeitungsprogramm *n* video editing program
Videonorm *f* video [signal] standard
Videonutzer *m* video user
Videoobjekt *n* video object
Videoobjektcodierung *f* video object coding
Videoobjektebene *f* video object plane, VOP
Videoobjektiv *n* video [camera] lens
Videookulografie *f* videoooculography
Videooszillograf *m* video oscillograph
Videooszilloskop *n* video oscilloscope
Videoparameter *m* video parameter
Videopegel *m* video [signal] level, picture level picture level
Videoplatte *f* videodisc, videodisk; optical (laser) disk
~/**digitale** digital videodisc, *(comprehensive term, s.a. under* DVD*)*
Videoplatten-Abspielgerät *n*, **Videoplattenspieler** *m* videodisc player
Videopräsentation *f* video presentation
Videopräsentationsgerät *n* video (visual) presenter
Videoprinter *m* video printer
Videoprodukt *n* video product
Videoproduktion *f* video production
Videoproduktionsfirma *f* video production company (bureau)
Videoproduktionsstudio *n* [professional] video production house
Videoproduktionstechnik *f* 1. video production processing technology; video production technique; 2. video [production] equipment
~/**analoge** analog video production equipment
~/**digitale** digital video production equipment
Videoproduzent *m* video producer
Videoprogramm *n* video program
Videoprogrammierung *f* video programming
Videoprogrammsystem *n* video program system, VPS; videocassette recording system
Videoprojektion *f* video projection
Videoprojektionsgerät *n s.* Videoprojektor
Videoprojektionssystem *n* video projection system

Videoprojektionstechnik f video projection technology
Videoprojektor m video projector; [video] beamer *(esp. in advertising)*
Videoprozessor m video [signal] processor; video processing unit, VPU
Video-Pufferspeicher m s. Video-RAM
Videopuzzle[spiel] n video puzzle
Videoquantisierung f video quantization
Videoquelle f video [signal] source
Videoquellencodierer m video source coder
Videoquellencodierung f video source coding
Videoquellensignal n video source signal
Video-RAM n video RAM (random-access memory), VRAM
Videoraster m(n) video raster
Videorate f 1. video [frame] rate, TV (television frame) rate, video frequency; 2. s. Videodatenrate
Video-Raubkopie f bootleg video
Videorauschen n video noise
Videorauschunterdrückung f video noise reduction, VNR
Videorecorder m video[tape] recorder, VTR
~/**analoger** analog video recorder
~/**digitaler** 1. digital videotape recorder, DVTR; 2. hard disk [video] recorder, hard-drive-based consumer VCR
Video-Redundanzcodierung f video redundancy coding
Video-Reinigungskassette f video head cleaning cassette
Videorestauration f video restoration
Videoschaltkreis m video circuit
Videoschaltung f video circuit
Videoschirm m video [display] screen, video [image] display
Videoschlitten m torpedo *(underwater photography)*
Videoschnitt m 1. video[tape] editing; video postproduction *(s.a.* Videonachbearbeitung*)*; 2. video edit
~/**analoger** analog video editing
~/**digitaler** digital video editing
~/**nichtlinearer** nonlinear video editing
Videoschnittcomputer m, **Videoschnittgerät** n video editor
Videoschnittkarte f video capture board *(s.a.* Videodigitalisierungskarte*)*
Videoschnittliste f video edit decision list
Videoschnittprogramm n video editing program
Videoschnittsoftware f video-editing software
Videoschnittstelle f video interface [circuitry]
Videoschnittsteuergerät n video editor
Videoschnittsystem n video editing system
Videoschnitttechnik f video editing equipment

Videoschrägspuraufzeichnung f helical video recording
Videosegmentierungsalgorithmus m video segmentation algorithm
Videosektor m video domain (area)
Videosenke f video sink
Videosensor m video sensor
Videosequenz f video [image] sequence; videotape sequence
Videosequenzkompression f video sequence compression
Videoserver m [digital] video server, VOD (video-on-demand) server *(computer-based system)*
Videosignal n 1. video signal (waveform) *(s.a. under* Bildsignal*,* Signal*)*; 2. s. ~/zusammengesetztes
~/**aktives** active video [signal], active region
~/**analoges** analog video signal
~/**digitales** digital video signal
~/**komprimiertes** compressed video signal
~/**kontinuierliches** continuous video signal
~/**zusammengesetztes** composite [video] signal, composite TV signal; composite color [video] signal, color (RGB) video signal
Videosignalabtastung f video signal sampling
Videosignalbearbeitung f video [signal] processing
Videosignaleingang m video input
Videosignalformat n video signal format
Videosignalkette f video signal chain
Videosignal-Magnetband-Aufzeichnungsgerät n/**digitales** digital videotape recorder, DVTR
Videosignalpegel m video [signal] level, picture level
Videosignalprozessor m video [signal] processor
Videosignalstrom m s. Videostrom
Videosignalverarbeitung f video [signal] processing
Videosignalverzögerung f video signal delay
Videoskalierung f video scaling
Videosoftware f video software
Videospannung f video voltage
Videospeicher m video [storage] memory, video buffer, graphics card memory
Videospeicherformat n video storage format
Videospeicherung f video [data] storage
Videospiel n video game
~/**dreidimensionales** 3-D video game
~/**interaktives** interactive video game
Videospielautomat m [video] arcade game
Videospielhalle f video arcade
Videospielkassette f video game cartridge
Videospielkonsole f [video] game console, play station

Videospot *m s.* Videoclip
Videosprachgebrauch *m* video parlance
Videospur *f* videotape track, video [data] track
Videostandard *m* video [signal] standard
Videostandbild *n* still video frame, video still
Videostandbilddigitalisierer *m s.* Videodigitalisierungskarte
Videostativ *n* video tripod
Video-Steckkarte *f s.* Videokarte
Videostrom *m* video [bit] stream, video data stream, stream of video data
Videostudio *n* video [production] studio
Videostudiosystem *n* broadcast-quality video recording format
Videostudiotechnik *f* video studio equipment
Videosynchronisation *f,*
Videosynchronisierung *f* video synchronization
Videosyntax *f* video syntax
Videosystem *n* video [imaging] system
Videoszene *f* video scene
Videotechnik *f* 1. video technology (engineering); 2. *s.* Videoproduktionstechnik 1. *and* 2.
~/**professionelle** pro-video equipment
Videotechniker *m* video engineer
Video-Teilbild *n* video field
Videotelefon *n* video telephone, videophone, VP
Videotelefonie *f* video[tele]phony, video (visual) telephony
Videotext *m* 1. broadcast videotex, teletext; 2. *s.* ~/interaktiver
~/**interaktiver** [interactive] videotex; viewdata
Videotextdecoder *m* [broadcast] videotex decoder
Videotextdienst *m* videotex service
Videotext-Inhaltsübersicht *f* table of pages, TOP
Videotext-Untertitel *mpl* closed subtitles
Videotext-Zusammenschaltung *f* videotex interworking
Videothek *f* 1. video library; 2. video shop (store)
Videotitel *m* video caption
Videotitelgenerator *m* [title] character generator, caption generator, title writer, titler
Videotransfer *m* videotape transfer; video-to-film transfer
Videotrick *m* video [optical] effect
Video-Überspielverstärker *m* enhancer
Videoübertragung *f* video transmission
~ **im Internet** Webcasting
Videoübertragungsbandbreite *f* video transmission bandwidth, transmission video bandwidth
Videoüberwachung *f* video surveillance
~ **im Nahbereich** closed-circuit television, CCTV

Videoüberwachungsanlage *f* video surveillance system
Videoüberwachungsbild *n* surveillance video image
Videoüberwachungskamera *f* surveillance camera
Video-Umschalter *m* video switcher
Videounterhaltung *f* video entertainment
Videoverleih *m* video rental *(s.a.* Videoverteildienst)
Videoverstärker *m* video [processing] amplifier
Videoverteildienst *m* video distribution
Videoverteiler *m* [video] switcher
Videoverteilverstärker *m* video distribution amplifier, VDA
Videovertriebskette *f* video chain
Videovollbild *n* full frame video image, video frame, frame [of video]
Videovorverarbeitung *f* video preprocessing
Videowand *f* video wall
Videowandler *m* video converter
Videowiedergabe *f* video playback (reproduction), replay
~/**fließende** videostreaming
Video-Wiedergabeeinheit *f,*
Videowiedergabegerät *n* video display unit, VDU, video reproducer (terminal)
Videozeile *f* video line, line of video
Video-Zeitcode *m* video time code
Videozubehör *n* video accessories
Videozugang *m* video access
Videozuspieler *m* source [videotape] recorder, source (playback) VTR, [slave] playback machine, player
Vidicon-Aufnahmeröhre *f s.* Vidikon
Vidikon *n* vidicon [tube], vidicon camera tube
Vidikonkamera *f* vidicon[-type] camera
Vidikonröhre *f s.* Vidikon
Vielblattdruck *m* multi-copy printing
Vieleck *n* [/**geschlossenes**] polygon
~/**gleichmäßiges (regelmäßiges)** regular polygon
Vielfachauflösung *f* multiresolution
Vielfachecho *n* reverberation *(sonography)*
Vielfachreflexion *f* 1. multiple reflection; 2. *s.* Vielfachecho
Vielfachspaltspektrometer *n* multiple-slit spectrometer
Vielfachstreuung *f* multiple scatter[ing]
Vielfachzugriff *m* multiple access
~ **im Codemultiplex** code division multiple access, CDMA
~ **im Frequenzmultiplex** frequency division multiple access, FDMA
~ **im Zeitmultiplex** time division multiple access, TDMA
vielfarbig multicolor[ed], polychromatic
Vielfarbigkeit *f* polychromy
Vielflächner *m* polyhedron
vielgestaltig polymorphic

Vielkanalanalyse f/optische optical multichannel analysis
Viellochkollimator m parallel-hole[s] collimator *(gamma camera)*
Vielmodenlaser m multimode laser
Vielstrahlinterferenz f multiple-beam interference
Vieräquivalentkuppler m four-equivalent coupler *(color photography)*
vierdimensional four-dimensional
Viereck n quadrangle, quad
Viererbaum m quad (quartic) tree *(data structure)*
Viererbaum-Codierung f quad-tree coding
Viererbaumdarstellung f quad-tree representation *(of an image)*
Viererbaumknoten m quad-tree node
Viererbaumkompression f quad-tree compression
Viererbaumstruktur f quad-tree [data] structure
Vierernachbarschaft f, **Viererumgebung** f four-connectivity neighborhood, four-adjacency, 4-neighborhood *(of pixels)*
Vierfarbendruck m 1. [four-]color process printing, process (full color) printing, quadrichromatic printing; 2. four-color print
Vierfarbendrucker m four-color printer
Vierfarbendruckmaschine f four-color printing press
Vierfarbenprozess m 1. four-color process; 2. s. Vierfarbendruck 1.
Vierfarbenreproduktion f four-color [process] reproduction
Vierfarbenseparation f four-color separation *(color printing)*
vierfarbig four-color, quadrichromatic, tetrachromatic
Vierfarbmaschine f four-color [printing] press
Vierflächner m/**regelmäßiger** tetrahedron
Vierkanalton m four-channel sound
Vierlinser m four-element lens
Vierniveaulaser m four[-energy]-level laser
Vierpunkt-Abbildung f s. Projektion/perspektivische
vierseitig quadrilateral
Vierspur-Magnetton m four-track magnetic sound
Vierspur-Raumton m four-track stereophonic sound
Viertelbogengröße f quarto *(sheet folded twice)*
Viertelpixelgenauigkeit f quarter-pixel accuracy *(video coding)*
Viertelpixelinterpolation f quarter-pel interpolation
Viertelwellenkompensator m s. Viertelwellenplättchen
Viertelwellenlänge f one-quarter (one-fourth) wavelength
Viertelwellenlängenplatte f, **Viertelwellenplättchen** n quarter-wave[length] plate, quarter-wave retarder
Viertelwellenvergütung f quarter-wave [antireflection] coating
Viertelzeilenoffset m quarter-line offset
Viertelzollband n quarter inch tape, 1/4-inch [magnetic] tape
Vieth-Müller-Kreis m Vieth-Müller circle *(binocular vision)*
Vignette f vignette
vignettieren to vignette
Vignettierung f [peripheral] vignetting; vignetting effect
~/**künstliche** mechanical vignetting
~/**natürliche** natural vignetting
~/**optische** optical vignetting
Villard-Effekt m Villard effect
V-Impuls m vertical (field) sync[hronization] pulse, vertical synchronizing signal
Violett n magenta
Violettband n purple ribbon *(printer)*
Virage f colorization, coloring, tinting *(esp. of motion-picture films)*
viragieren to color[ize], to tint
Viragierung f s. Virage
virtual s. virtuell
Virtualität f virtuality
virtuell virtual
visibel visible, visual
Visibilität f visibility, visibleness
Visiereinrichtung f sighting device
visieren to sight; to aim [at], to point *(e.g. a camera)*
Visierfehler m aiming error
Visierfernrohr n sighting (aiming) telescope, telescope (telescopic) sight
Visionspersistenz f persistence of vision
Visitenkartenporträt n carte-de-visite [photograph]
Viskosität f viscosity
visualisieren to visualize
Visualisierer m visualizer
Visualisierung f visualization
~/**abstrakte** s. Diagramm
~/**dreidimensionale** three-dimensional visualization
~/**fotorealistische** rendering
~/**interaktive** interactive visualization
~/**mehrdimensionale** multidimensional visualization
~/**molekulare** molecular visualization
~/**objektbasierte** object-based visualization
~/**quantitative** quantitative visualization
~/**räumliche (stereoskopische)** stereoscopic visualization
~/**szenenbasierte** scene-based visualization
~/**wissenschaftliche** scientific visualization

Visualisierungsalgorithmus *m* visualization algorithm
Visualisierungsaufgabe *f* visualization task
Visualisierungsnetzwerk *n* visualization network
Visualisierungsobjekt *n* visualization object
Visualisierungsschritt *m* visualization step
Visualisierungssoftware *f* visualization software
Visualisierungstechnik *f* 1. visualization technology 2. visualization technique
Visualisierungsverfahren *n* visualization technique
Visualisierungswerkzeug *n* visualization tool
Visualistik *f* visualistics
visuell visual, optical
Visus *m* 1. visual sense, sense of sight, [sense of] vision; 2. [visual] acuity
Visusbestimmung *f* visual acuity measurement
Vitaskop *n* vitascope *(an early motion-picture projector)*
Viterbi-Algorithmus *m* Viterbi algorithm *(image data processing)*
Viterbi-Decod[ier]er *m* Viterbi decoder
Viterbi-Decodierung *f* Viterbi decoding
Vitrotypie *f* vitrotype
Viviskop *n* Viviscope *(early animated-picture machine)*
VLSI-Technik *f* VLSI (very large-scale integration) technology
Vogelperspektive *f* bird's-eye view
Voice-over-Verfahren *n* voice-over
Vollbelichtung *f* full (maximum) exposure
Vollbild *n* full-sized image, full [frame] image, complete (entire) image; image (complete) frame, frame-picture, [full-size] frame *(cinema, video)*
~/protokolliertes logged frame
Vollbildabtastung *f* progressive [video] scanning, sequential (noninterlaced) scanning, progressive scan mode
Vollbildaufzeichnung *f* progressive scan (video output)
Vollbilddauer *f* frame time
Vollbildfrequenz *f* frame rate, vertical sweep frequency *(noninterlaced video)*
Vollbildmodus *m* frame movie mode *(video)*
Vollbildprädiktion *f* frame[-based] prediction
Vollbildrate *f s.* Vollbildfrequenz
Vollbildspeicher *m* frame store
Vollbildtransformation *f* full-frame transform
Vollbildverarbeitung *f* frame processing
volldigital all-digital, fully (completely) digital
Vollduplexbetrieb *m* full duplex
Volleistungswarnung *f* full output warning *(photoflash)*
Vollerwerden *n s.* Tonwertzunahme

Vollfarbabtastung *f* full-color scanning
Vollfarbbild *n* full-color image (picture), true-color image; true-color photograph
Vollfarbbildverarbeitung *f* full-color image processing
Vollfarb-Digitalscanner *m* full-color digital scanner
Vollfarbdisplay *n* hicolor (full-color) display
Vollfarbdruck *m* full-color printing; block color printing
Vollfarbe *f* block (solid) color
Vollfarbenbild *n s.* Vollfarbbild
Vollfarb-Flachbildschirm *m* full-color flat-panel display
Vollfarbhologramm *n* full-color hologram
vollfarbig full-colored
Vollfarbkopie *f* full-color copy
Vollfarbkopierer *m* full-color copier
Vollfarbprojektion *f* full-color projection
Vollfarbsensor *m* full-color sensor
Vollfarbsignal *n* full-color signal
Vollglasfilter *n* [/**in der Masse gefärbtes**] dyed-in-the-mass glass filter
Vollgrafik *f* full graphics *(display technology)*
Vollkreisdetektor *m* ring detector *(computed tomography)*
Vollkulisse *f* set, setting *(film production)*
Vollleistungswarnung *f* full output warning
Volloffenzeit *f* wide-open time (period) *(photographic shutter)*
Vollpixelgenauigkeit *f* integer-pel accuracy
Vollsuche *f* full search; full-search method *(motion estimation)*
Volltextsuche *f* full-text search
Volltext-Suchmaschine *f* full-text search engine
Vollton *m s.* Volltonfläche
Volltondrucker *m* dye-diffusion printer
Volltonfarbe *f* nonprocess color ink *(printing)*
Volltonfläche *f* solid *(reprography)*
Vollverstärker *m* power amplifier *(motion-picture equipment)*
Vollwinkeltomografie *f* full-angle tomography
Volumen *n* volume *(e.g. as a three-dimensional array of points)*
~/interessierendes volume of interest, VOI
Volumenbeschreibung *f* volume description
Volumenbild *n* volume[tric] image, image volume
Volumenbilddaten *pl* volume image data
Volumenbildsegmentierung *f* volume image segmentation
Volumen-Computertomografie *f* volume computerized tomography
Volumendarstellung *f* [/**computergrafische**] 1. volume rendering; 2. volume rendition
Volumendaten *pl* volume (volumetric) data
Volumendatensatz *m* volume[tric] data set, 3-D (three-dimensional) data set

Volumeneinheit *f* unit volume
Volumenelement *n* volume [pixel] element, volume pixel, voxel
Volumenform *f* volume form
Volumengitter *n* volume grating (mesh)
Volumenholografie *f* volume holography
volumenholografisch volume holographic
Volumenhologramm *n* volume [transmission] hologram, thick hologram
Volumenintegral *n* volume (space) integral
Volumenmodell *n* solid (volume) model
Volumenmodellierung *f* solid modeling
Volumenpixel *n s.* Voxel
Volumenprimitiv *n* volumetric (solid) primitive, primitive solid
Volumenrekonstruktion *f* volume reconstruction
Volumenrepräsentation *f s.* Volumendarstellung
Volumenscan *m* volume scan
Volumenscanner *m* volume scanner
Volumenstreuung *f* bulk scatter[ing]; volume scattering
Volumenultraschall *m* three-dimensional ultrasound
Volumenvisualisierung *f* volume visualization
~/**direkte** direct volume visualization
Volumenwachstum *n* volume growing
Volumenwelle *f* volume wave
Volumetrie *f* measurement of volume
volumetrisch volumetric
Vorabansicht *f* preview
Vorabbild *n* before image, preimage; previous (preceding) frame *(video coding)*
Vorabdruck *m* preprint, press proof
vorabdrucken to preprint
Vorabscan *m* prescan
Voransicht *f* preview
Voraufführung *f* preview, advance screening (showing)
voraufzeichnen to prerecord, to prescore *(e.g. a television show)*
Vorausandruck *m* proof
vorausberechnen to precompute, to precalculate
vorausdrucken to preprint
voraussagbar *s.* vorhersagbar
Voraussichtradar *n* forward-looking radar
Vorbad *n* forebath, prebath *(photoprocessing)*
Vorbeifahrt *f* track *(camera motion)*
vorbelichten to preexpose, to [pre]flash *(film)*
Vorbelichtung *f* preexposure, [pre]flashing
Vorbereitungsgradient *m* preparation gradient *(magnetic resonance imaging)*
vorbeschichten to precoat *(e.g. printing plates)*
vorbespielen to prerecord *(videotape)*
Vorbetrachtung *f* preview

Vorbild *n* before image, preimage; previous (preceding) frame *(video coding)*
Vorblitz *m*, **Vorblitzfunktion** *f* [test] preflash; red-eye reduction flash
vorcodieren to precode
Vorcodierer *m* precoder
Vorcodierung *f* precoding
Vorderansicht *f* frontal view
Vorderblende *f* front-operating aperture
Vorderdeckel *m* front cover *(of a book)*
Vorderflächenspiegel *m* front-surface[d] mirror
Vorderflächenverspiegelung *f* front-surface coating
Vorderfolie *f s.* Vorderverstärkungsfolie
Vorderglied *n* front component, front element (optics) *(objective)*
~/**sammelndes** positive front element
Vordergrund *m* foreground
Vordergrundbeleuchtung *f* foreground lighting
Vordergrundbereich *m* foreground region
Vordergrundbild *n* foreground image
Vordergrundfarbe *f* foreground color
Vordergrundmaskenfilm *m* action (female) matte
Vordergrundmerkmal *n* foreground feature
Vordergrundobjekt *n* foreground object (subject), foreground element
Vordergrundpixel *n* foreground pixel
Vordergrundszene *f* foreground scene
Vorderkammer *f* anterior chamber *(of the eye)*
Vorderlicht *n* front light
~/**seitliches** area front light
Vorderlinse *f* front (foremost) lens
Vorderseite *f* 1. front side; 2. recto [page] *(layout)*
Vorderverstärkungsfolie *f* front intensifying screen *(X-ray cassette)*
Vordruck *m* preprint
voreinstellen 1. to preset; to preadjust; 2. *s.* vorfokussieren
Voreinstellung *f* default [setting], custom preset[ting] *(e.g. of a camera)*
Vorentzerrung *f* preemphasis
Vorfilter *n* prefilter, presampling filter; absorber *(X-ray attenuation)*
~/**optisches** optical prefilter
vorfiltern to prefilter
Vorfilterung *f* prefiltering [operation], preprocessing filtering
~/**mehrdimensionale** multidimensional prefiltering
vorfokussieren to prefocus
Vorfokussierung *f* prefocusing
Vorführapparatur *f* presentation system
vorführbar screenable *(film print)*
vorführen to screen
Vorführer *m* [motion-picture] projectionist, cinematographer
Vorführfrequenz *f* display rate *(cinema)*

Vorführgerät *n* [optical] projector
Vorführhilfe *f* projection aid
Vorführkabine *f* projection booth
Vorführkopie *f* projection print, [exhibition] release print, release
Vorführmaschine *f* theater projector, cinematograph
Vorführraum *m* 1. screening (projection) room; preview room; 2. *s.* Projektorraum 1.
Vorführstartband *n* projection leader
Vorführung *f* exhibition, showing; screening *(cinema)*
Vorführzeit[dauer] *f* screen time
Vorgängerbild *n* precursor image *(motion estimation)*
Vorhaltespeicher *m* cache [memory], data cache
Vorhärtebad *n* prehardening bath, prehardener [bath] *(photographic processing)*
vorhersagbar predictable
Vorhersagbarkeit *f* predictability
Vorhersage *f* prediction *(s.a. under* Prädiktion*)*
vorkomprimieren to precompress *(e.g. raw video data)*
Vorlage *f* copy *(esp. in reprography)*; template *(s.a.* Schablone*)*
~/**gerasterte** halftone copy
~/**grafische** artwork
~/**repro[duktions]fähige** camera-ready art[work]
~/**typografische** typographic copy
Vorlagenebene *f* copy plane
Vorlagenelement *n* copy element
Vorlagenfläche *f* copyboard *(graphic arts photography)*
Vorlagenhalter *m* copyholder, copyboard *(process camera)*
Vorlagenherstellung *f* copy preparation
Vorlagenmaterial *n* copy material
Vorlagenplatte *f*,**Vorlagenträger** *m s.* Vorlagenhalter
Vorlagentrommel *f* copy drum
Vorlauf *m* preroll
Vorlaufband *n* countdown cueing leader, [head] leader
Vorlauf-Federwerk *n s.* Selbstauslöser
Vorlaufspeicher *m* storage unit, reservoir
Vorlaufstreifen *m* [head] leader, leader [strip]
Vormagnetisierung *f* biasing; bias
Vormessblitz *m* [test] preflash
Vormischung *f* 1. premixing, submixing *(e.g. of motion-picture sound)*; 2. premix
Voronoi-Analyse *f* Voronoi analysis *(computational geometry)*
Voronoi-Bild *n* Voronoi image
Voronoi-Diagramm *n* Voronoi (Thiessen) diagram, Wigner-Seitz diagram, Blum transform *(s.a.* Voronoi-Mosaik*)*
Voronoi-Kante *f* Voronoi edge

Voronoi-Mosaik *n* [Poisson-]Voronoi tessellation, Voronoi tiling, Dirichlet tiling (tessellation) *(computer graphics)*
Voronoi-Punkt *m* Voronoi point, site, generator, source
Voronoi-Region *f s.* Voronoi-Zelle
Voronoi-Skelett *n* Voronoi skeleton
Voronoi-Zelle *f*, **Voronoi-Zone** *f* Voronoi [sur]face, Voronoi region (cell) *(computational geometry)*
Vorratsbehälter *m* storage container *(darkroom equipment)*
Vorratsgefäß *n* storage bottle
Vorratskassette *f* supply cassette
Vorratslösung *f* stock solution
Vorratsrolle *f*, **Vorratsspule** *f* supply reel (spool), feed reel (spool)
Vorsättigung *f* presaturation *(magnetic resonance imaging)*
Vorsättigungs[im]puls *m* presaturation pulse *(magnetic resonance imaging)*
Vorsatz *n* 1. endpaper[s] *(of a book)*; 2. *s.* Vorsatzblatt
~ *m* attachment *(optical instrumentation)*
~/**anamorphotischer** anamorphic
Vorsatzachromat *m* achromatic [doublet] supplementary lens, two-element achromat
Vorsatzblatt *n* flyleaf, free endpaper *(of a book)*
Vorsatzlinse *f* supplementary (supplemental) lens, auxiliary (diopter) lens
Vorsatzmodell *n* miniature
Vorsatzobjektiv *n s.* Vorsatzlinse
Vorsatzpapier *n* endpaper[s] *(of a book)*
Vorsatztubus *m* extension tube
Vorschau *f* preview
Vorschaubild *n* [display] thumbnail, miniature print *(photoprocessing)*
Vorschaubildschirm *m s.* Vorschaumonitor
Vorschaufenster *n* preview window
Vorschaumodus *m* preview mode
Vorschaumonitor *m* preview monitor (screen)
Vorschautaste *f* preview button
Vorschleifen *n* generating [process] *(lens manufacture)*
Vorsichtung *f* preview
Vorspann *m* 1. leader *(e.g. for threading a motion-picture machine)*; [movie] credits, opening credits; 2. header [information] *(of a digital image file)*
Vorspannband *n* leader tape
Vorspannfilm *m* 1. leader; 2. preview, trailer
Vorspannung *f* bias *(e.g. of a sensor)*
Vorspulen *n*/**schnelles** fast forward
Vorstufenbetrieb *m* prepress plant
Vortrabant *m* preequalizing pulse *(composite video signal)*
vorverarbeiten to preprocess *(e.g. image data)*

Vorverarbeitung *f* preprocessing *(e.g. of image data)*
Vorverarbeitungsschritt *m* preprocessing step
Vorverstärker *m* preamp[lifier]
Vorverstärkung *f* preamplification
vorverzerren to predistort *(e.g. a video signal)*
Vorverzerrung *f* predistortion; preemphasis *(frequency modulation)*
Vorvideosignal *n* pre-video signal
Vorwahlblende *f* preset iris
Vorwärtsabbildung *f* forward mapping *(geometric transformation)*
Vorwärtsanalyse *f* forward analysis *(image data compression)*
Vorwärtsfehlerbehebung *f* forward error recovery
Vorwärts-Fehlerkorrektur *f* forward[-acting] error correction, FEC
Vorwärts-Fehlerkorrekturcode *m* forward error-correction code
Vorwärtsfilter *n* forward filter
Vorwärtskanal *m* forward channel
Vorwärtskinematik *f* forward kinematics *(computer animation)*
vorwärtskompatibel forward compatible
Vorwärtskompatibilität *f* forward compatibility
Vorwärtsprädiktion *f* forward predicition *(image sequence coding)*
Vorwärtsstreuung *f* forward scatter[ing]
Vorwärtssuche *f* forward search
Vorwärtstransformation *f* forward transform[ation]
Vorwärtstransformationskern *m* forward transform kernel
Vorwärtstransformationsmatrix *f* forward transformation matrix
Vorwärtsverkettung *f* forward chaining
Vorwärtsvermittlungsnetz *n* feedforward network
Vorwässern *n*, **Vorwässerung** *f* preliminary rinse
Vorwickel[zahn]rolle *f*, **Vorwickler** *m* [upper] feed sprocket
Vorwissen *n* prior knowledge, a priori knowledge, foreknowledge *(image understanding)*
Vorzeichenfestlegung *f*, **Vorzeichenkonvention** *f*, **Vorzeichenvereinbarung** *f* sign convention *(optics)*
Voxel *n* voxel, volume pixel [element], volume [picture] element
Voxelauflösung *f* voxel resolution
Voxelbild *n* voxel image
Voxelgitter *n* voxel lattice (grid)
Voxelgröße *f* voxel size
Voxelmitte *f* voxel center
Voxelmodell *n* voxel model
Voxelprojektion *f* voxel projection
Voxelraum *m* voxel space

Voxelrekonstruktion *f* voxel[-based] reconstruction
Voxelvolumen *n* voxel volume
voxelweise voxel-by-voxel
Voxelwert *m* voxel value
Voxelwürfel *m* cubic voxel
VR *s.* Realität/virtuelle
VR-Bildschirm *m* VR (virtual-reality) display
VR-Modellierungssprache *f* virtual-reality modeling language, VRML

W

Wabenfilter *n* honeycomb filter
Wabenkondensor *m* honeycomb [grid], grid spot
Wabenlinse *f* fly's eye lens
Wachspapier *n* wax paper
Wachspapierverfahren *n* waxed-paper process *(photographic negative process)*
Wackeln *n* jitter
Wafer *m* [semiconductor] wafer
Wagenrücklauf *m* carriage return *(printer)*
Wahlrad *n*, **Wählscheibe** *f* selector (command) dial
Wahrheits[werte]tafel *f* truth table *(propositional logic)*
wahrnehmbar perceptible, perceivable
Wahrnehmbarkeit *f* perceptibility
wahrnehmen to perceive
Wahrnehmung *f* perception
~/**audiovisuelle** audiovisual perception
~/**bewusste** conscious perception
~/**menschliche** human perception
~/**optische** visual perception
~/**räumliche** space (depth) perception, perception of depth, stereopsis
~/**sinnliche** s. Sinneswahrnehmung
~/**unterschwellige** subliminal perception
~/**visuelle** visual perception
Wahrnehmungsabbild *n* perceptual image
Wahrnehmungsbereich *m* perception domain
Wahrnehmungseffekt *m* perceptual effect
Wahrnehmungseigenschaft *f* perceptual property
Wahrnehmungsexperiment *n* perceptual experiment
Wahrnehmungsfehler *m* perceptual defect, perception error, error of perception
Wahrnehmungsforschung *f* perceptual research
wahrnehmungsgemäß perceptual
Wahrnehmungskonstanz *f* perceptual constancy
Wahrnehmungsleistung *f* perceptual performance
Wahrnehmungsobjekt *n* perceptual object
Wahrnehmungsphänomen *n* perceptual phenomenon
Wahrnehmungsprozess *m* perceptual process
Wahrnehmungspsychologe *m* perceptual psychologist
Wahrnehmungspsychologie *f* perceptual psychology
Wahrnehmungsredundanz *f* perceptual redundancy
Wahrnehmungsschwelle *f* perceptual threshold
~/**absolute** [absolute] limen, absolute threshold
Wahrnehmungssemantik *f* perceptual semantics
Wahrnehmungssubjektivität *f* perceptive subjectivity
Wahrnehmungssyntax *f* perceptual syntax
Wahrnehmungssystem *n* perceptual system
Wahrnehmungsübelkeit *f* perceptual nausea
wahrnehmungsunabhängig perceptually independent
Wahrnehmungsvermögen *n* perceptivity, perceptiveness
Wahrnehmungsverzerrung *f* perceptual distortion
Wahrnehmungsvorgang *m* act of perception
Wahrscheinlicheit/unbedingte prior probability
Wahrscheinlichkeit *f* probability, likelihood
~/**bedingte** conditional (a posteriori) probability
~/**kumulative** cumulative probability, CP
~/**maximale** maximum likelihood
Wahrscheinlichkeitdichtefunktion *f* [probability] density function, PDF
Wahrscheinlichkeitsdichte *f* probability density
Wahrscheinlichkeitsdichteverteilung *f s.* Wahrscheinlichkeitsdichtefunktion
Wahrscheinlichkeitsfunktion *f* probability function
Wahrscheinlichkeitsmatrix *f* probability matrix
Wahrscheinlichkeitsmodell *n* probability (statistical source) model *(lossless symbol coding)*
Wahrscheinlichkeitsschätzung *f* probabilitics estimation
Wahrscheinlichkeitstheorie *f* [conventional] probability theory
~/**Bayessche** Bayesian probability theory
Wahrscheinlichkeitsverteilung *f* probability distribution
Wahrscheinlichkeitsverteilungsfunktion *f* [probability] distribution function, spread function
Waldkartierung *f* forest mapping
Walsh-Hadamard-Transformation *f*/**diskrete** discrete Walsh-Hadamard transform, DWHT
Walsh-Transformation *f*/**diskrete** discrete Walsh transform, DWT
Walzendrucker *m* barrel (drum) printer
Walzenentwicklungsmaschine *f* roller[-transport] processor, roller-transport machine
walzenfrisch roller fresh *(printing ink)*
Walzenplotter *m* drum (rotary) plotter
Walzentemperatur *f* roll temperature
Walzentransportmaschine *f s.* Walzenentwicklungsmaschine

Wanderbild *n* slow-running picture
Wanderfeldröhrenverstärker *m* traveling wave tube amplifier, TWTA
Wandermaske *f* traveling matte, articulate (rotoscope) matte *(cinema)*
Wandermaskenaufnahme *f* traveling matte [shot]
Wandermaskentrick *m*, **Wandermaskenverfahren** *n* traveling-matte process (procedure)
Wanderwellenantenne *f* traveling-wave antenna (aerial), slotted-pipe antenna *(television)*
Wanderwellenröhre *f* traveling-wave tube
Wanderwellenverstärker *m* traveling-wave amplifier
Wandler *m* 1. transducer; 2. converter
~/**elektrooptischer (lichtelektrischer)** photoelectric transducer, electrooptic converter
~/**mechanischer** mechanical transducer
~/**optisch-elektrischer (optoelektrischer)** optical converter
~/**optoelektronischer** optoelectronic transducer
~/**ortsfester** stationary transducer
~/**piezoelektrischer** piezo[electric] transducer; piezoelectric element
Wandleranordnung *f* transducer array
Wandlerebene *f* transducer plane
Wandlerelement *n* transducer element
Wandlerimpuls *m* transducer impulse
Wandlung *f*/**anamorphotische** anamorphotic conversion
~/**optoelektronische** optoelectronic conversion
Wärmeableitung *f* heat dispersal
Wärmeabstrahlung *f* heat emission, emission (radiation) of heat
Wärmeausdehnungskoeffizient *m* coefficient of thermal expansion, CTE, thermal expansion coefficient *(e.g. of optical glass)*
Wärmebild *n* heat (thermal) image, thermogram, thermal map, thermograph[ic image]
Wärmebildaufnahme *f* thermal (thermographic) imaging
Wärmebildaufzeichnung *f* temperature mapping, heat recording
Wärmebildauswertung *f* thermal analysis
Wärmebildgebung *f* thermal (thermographic) imaging *(s.a. Thermografie)*; temperature mapping
Wärmebildgerät *n* thermal imager (imaging device); forward-looking infrared device, FLIR *(esp. of tanks)*
Wärmebildkamera *f* infrared (thermographic recording) camera, thermal [image] camera, heat-sensing camera
Wärmebildsensor *m* thermal imaging sensor

Wärmebildspektrometer *n* thermal imaging spectrometer, thermal imager
Wärmebildsystem *n* thermal imaging system
Wärmebildtechnik *f* thermal imaging [technology], thermographic imaging
Wärmebild-Videosystem *n* thermal video system
Wärmefixierung *f* heat fusing *(copier)*
Wärmefixierwalze *f* [heated] fuser roll
Wärmekamera *f s.* Wärmebildkamera
Wärmekopierung *f* thermal printing
Wärmerauschen *n s.* Temperaturrauschen
Wärmeschutzfilter *n* heat[-absorbing] filter, diathermic (diathermal) filter; heat-reflection filter
Wärmespannung *f* thermal stress *(photoelastics)*
Wärmestrahl *m* heat ray
Wärmestrahler *m* heat (thermal) radiator
Wärmestrahlung *f* thermal (heat) radiation
Warmlichtspiegel *m* hot mirror
Warmprägung *f* hot embossing *(stereotypy)*
Warmstart *m* warm boot[ing], warm start, soft boot, restart *(of a computer)*
Warmstrahler *m s.* Wärmestrahler
Warmtonentwickler *m* warm-tone developer
Warmtonfilter *n* warm-up [diffusion] filter
Warmtonpapier *n* warm-tone paper
Warmwasserbad *n* tempered water bath
Warping-Technik *f* warping *(visualization technique)*
Warteschlange *f* queue, spooler *(data processing)*
wasserabstoßend, wasserabweisend water-repellent, hydrophobic
wasserannehmend, wasseraufnehmend water-receptive, hydrophilic
Wasserbad *n* water bath
Wasserbadentwicklung *f* water-bath development
wasserdicht watertight
Wasserenthärter *m* water softener
Wasserenthärtung *f* water softening
Wasser-Farb-Balance *f* ink-water balance *(printing)*
Wasserfenster *n* water window *(X-ray microscopy)*
wasserfest water-resistant
wasserfreundlich *s.* wasseraufnehmend
Wasserhärte *f* water hardness
Wasserimmersionsobjektiv *n* water immersion objective
Wassermantelbad *n* water jacket, water-bath temperature control
wässern to wash
Wasserphantom *n* water-equivalent mathematical phantom *(X-ray dosimetry)*
Wasserscheidenalgorithmus *m* watershed [segmentation] algorithm
Wasserscheidentransformation *f* watershed transform, watershed

segmentation [procedure], watersheds technique *(binary image processing)*
Wasserstoffblasenkammer *f* hydrogen [bubble] chamber
Wasserstoffdichte *f* hydrogen density *(magnetic resonance imaging)*
Wasserstoffionenkonzentration *f* hydrogen ion concentration
Wasserstoffkern *m* hydrogen nucleus; [water] proton
Wasserstofflaser *m* hydrogen laser
Wasserstoffperoxid *n* hydrogen peroxide
Wasserstoffsensibilisierung *f* hydrogen sensitization
Wassertiefenmessung *f* water depth measurement, bathymetry
Wässerung *f* water wash (rinse), washing
~/**fließende** [running water] rinse
Wässerungsdauer *f* washing time
Wässerungsflüssigkeit *f* washing fluid, wash water
Wässerungskaskade *f* cascade [print] washer
Wässerungstank *m* wash[ing] tank
Wässerungstechnik *f* washing technique
Wässerungstemperatur *f* wash water temperature
Wässerungsvorrichtung *f* washing apparatus
Wässerungswanne *f* [print] washing tray
Wässerungszeit *f* washing time
Wasserwaage *f* [/**eingebaute**] level bubble
Wasserzeichen *n* watermark
~/**digitales** digital watermark
~/**robustes** robust watermark
~/**sichtbares** visible watermark
~/**unsichtbares** invisible watermark
~/**zerbrechliches** fragile watermark
Wasserzeichenalgorithmus *m* watermarking algorithm
Wasserzeichenverfahren *n* watermarking technique
Watt *n* watt, W *(unit of power)*
Wattsekunde *f* watt-second
Wattzahl *f* wattage *(e.g. of a floodlamp)*
Wavelet *n* wavelet; mother wavelet
~/**biorthogonales** biorthogonal wavelet
~/**orthogonales** orthogonal wavelet
~/**symmetrisches** symmetrical wavelet, symlet
Wavelet-Analyse *f* wavelet analysis
Wavelet-Bildcodierung *f*, **Wavelet-Codierung** *f* wavelet [image] coding, wavelet-based coding
Wavelet-Darstellung *f* wavelet [image] representation, wavelet domain representation
Wavelet-Filter *n* wavelet (regular) filter, Gabor function filter
Wavelet-Filterbank *f* wavelet filter bank
Wavelet-Funktion *f* wavelet function
Wavelet-Koeffizient *m* wavelet [transform] coefficient, detail coefficient

Wavelet-Kompression *f*, **Wavelet-Kompressionsverfahren** *n* wavelet [transform] compression, wavelet[-transform]-based compression
Wavelet-Paket *n* wavelet packet
Wavelet-Pakettransformation *f* wavelet-packet transform
Wavelet-Radiosity *f* wavelet radiosity *(computer graphics)*
Wavelet-Rekonstruktion *f* wavelet reconstruction
Wavelet-Rücktransformation/schnelle inverse fast wavelet transform
Wavelet-Transformation *f* wavelet transform[ation] *(digital imaging)*
~/**baumstukturierte** tree-structured wavelet transform
~/**biorthogonale** biorthogonal wavelet transform
~/**diskrete** discrete wavelet transform, DWT
~/**dyadische** dyadic wavelet transform
~/**inverse** inverse wavelet transform
~/**kontinuierliche** continuous wavelet transform, CWT
~/**orthogonale** orthogonal wavelet transform
~/**schnelle** fast wavelet transform, Mallat's herringbone algorithm
Wavelet-Vektor *m* wavelet vector
Wavelet-Zerlegung *f* wavelet decomposition
Web *n* [World Wide] Web, WWW *(part of the Internet)*
Webbrowser *m* Web browser
Webcam *f s.* Webkamera
Webdesign *n* Web design
Webdesigner *m* Web page designer
Weber *n* weber, Wb *(unit of magnetic flux)*
Webgrafik *f* Web graphics
Webkamera *f* Webcam
Webkamera-Software *f* Webcam software
Webkante *f s.* woven edge *(inked ribbon)*
Webseite *f* Web page; [World Wide] Web site, Internet site
Webseitenadresse *f* uniform resource locator, URL
Website *f s.* Webseite
Wechseldatenträger *m* removable data carrier
Wechselfestplatte *f* removeable hard disk
Wechselfilmkassette *f s.* Wechselkassette
Wechselfilter *n* interchangeable filter
Wechselmagazin *n* interchangeable magazine (back), interchangeable film back (holder) *(medium-format SLR camera)*
Wechselmattscheibe *f* interchangeable [focusing] screen
Wechselobjektiv *n* interchangeable (removable) lens, detachable lens
Wechselobjektivkamera *f* interchangeable-lens camera
Wechseloptik *f s.* Wechselobjektiv

Wechselplatte

Wechselplatte f 1. removable [hard] disk; 2. s. Wechselplattenspeicher
Wechselplattenspeicher m exchangeable disk [store]
Wechselprismensucher m interchangeable pentaprism
Wechselrichter m inverter
Wechselsack m changing (black) bag
Wechselspeicher m auxiliary (backing) storage, removable storage [device]
Wechselstrom m alternating current, AC, ac
Wechselstrom-Bogenlampe f alternating current arc
Wechselstrom-Tunnelmikroskopie f/**nichtlineare** nonlinear alternating-current tunneling microscopy, NACTM
Wechselsucher m interchangeable viewfinder
Wechseltubus m interchangeable tube
wechselwirken to interact
Weg m/**optischer** optical path[way], light path[way]
wegbewegen to dolly out, to truck out *(the camera in filming)*
Wegdifferenz f/**optische** optical path difference, OPD
Wegeleitung f routing *(of data packages)*
Weglänge f/**optische** optical path length, optical distance
Wegsensor m displacement sensor
Wegwerfkamera f single (one-time) use camera, disposable (throw-away) camera, film-with-camera
Wehnelt-Spannung f Wehnelt voltage
Wehnelt-Zylinder m Wehnelt (cathode) cylinder, cathode-ray tube shield (grid)
weich soft *(paper grade)*; soft[-focus]; low-contrast, flat *(image)*
Weichentwickler m soft[-working] developer, low-energy (low-contrast) developer; compensating developer
Weichgewebekontrast m soft-tissue contrast *(radiography)*
Weichgrundradierung f soft-ground etching, vernis mou
Weichmacher m plasticizer
Weichstrahler m soft light
Weichstrahlröhre f soft [X-ray] tube
Weichteilaufnahme f soft-tissue roentgenogram
Weichteilkontrast m soft-tissue contrast *(radiography)*
Weichteilradiografie f soft-tissue radiography
weichzeichnen to soften
Weichzeichner m soft-focus attachment (filter); diffuser, diffusor; diffusion disk
~/**Gaußscher** Gaussian filter (kernel)
Weichzeichnereffekt m softening (soft-focus) effect, diffusing effect
Weichzeichnerfolie f, **Weichzeichnergaze** f diffuser (light-diffusing) screen
Weichzeichnerlinse f, **Weichzeichnerobjektiv** n soft-focus lens
Weichzeichnung f soft focusing
Weigert-Effekt m Weigert effect *(exposure phenomenon)*
Weinland-Effekt m Weinland effect *(exposure phenomenon)*
Weißabgleich m 1. white balance [correction], white-light balancing, WB *(video camera)*; 2. WB switch
~/**automatischer** automatic white balance (balancing), automatic white control, AWC
~/**digitaler** digital white balance
~/**fortwährender** auto-tracing white balancing, ATW
~/**manueller** manual white balance [correction]
Weißabgleichautomatik f automatic white balance feature *(s.a. Weißabgleich/automatischer)*
Weißabgleichfehler m white balance error
Weißausgleich m s. Weißabgleich
Weißbegrenzung f white limiting
Weiße f whiteness
Weißgehalt m white content *(colorimetry)*
weißlich whitish
Weißlichkeit f whitishness
Weißlicht n white (incandescent) light
Weißlichtabgleich m s. Weißabgleich
Weißlichthologramm n white-light hologram
Weißlichtinterferometrie f white-light interferometry; optical coherence tomography, OCT
Weißlicht-Leuchtdiode f white LED
Weißlichtquelle f incandescent (white) light source
Weißlicht-Reflexionsholografie f white-light reflection holography
Weißlicht-Reflexionshologramm n white-light reflection hologram
Weißlichtspektrum n white-light spectrum
Weißlichtstreifen m white-light fringe *(interferometry)*
Weißlicht-Transmissionshologramm n white-light transmission hologram
Weißnormal n reference white [color]
Weißpegel m s. Weißwert
Weißpunkt m white (achromatic) point *(colorimetry)*
Weißpunkteinstellung f white-point normalization
Weißraum m white space *(e.g. between characters)*
Weißsein n whiteness
Weißstandard m reflectance standard
Weißwert m white level; peak white [level] *(video signal)*
Weißzone f clear area *(page layout)*
Weitaufnahme f very long shot, VLS *(cinema)*
Weite f/**räumliche** spaciousness
Weitsehen n far vision

weitsichtig farsighted, farseeing, longsighted, hyper[metr]opic
Weitsichtigkeit f farsightedness, longsightedness, long sight, hyper[metr]opia
Weitverkehrsnetz n wide-area network, WAN
Weitwinkel m wide angle
Weitwinkelaufnahme f wide-angle shot
Weitwinkelbalgen m wide-angle bellows
Weitwinkelbild n wide-angle picture
Weitwinkelcharakteristik f wide-angle rendition
Weitwinkeleffekt m s. Weitwinkelverzerrung
Weitwinkelfotografie f wide-angle photography
Weitwinkel-Hochgeschwindigkeits-Spiegelkamera f wide-angle high-speed reflector-type camera *(astrophotography)*
Weitwinkelkamera f wide-angle camera
Weitwinkel-Kamerasystem n/**elektronisches** electronic wide-angle camera system, EWACS
Weitwinkelkonverter m wide-angle conversion lens
Weitwinkelobjektiv n wide-angle [photographic] lens, short lens
~/**extremes** extreme-wide-angle lens
~/**kurzbrennweitiges** short focal-length wide-angle lens
~/**mittelbrennweitiges** moderate wide-angle lens
~/**retrofokales** retrofocus wide-angle lens, reverse telephoto wide-angle lens
Weitwinkelokular n wide-angle eyepiece
Weitwinkelreflektor m wide-angle reflector
Weitwinkelspiegel m wide-angle mirror
Weitwinkel-Stereobild n wide-angle stereoimage
Weitwinkelstreuung f wide-angle scattering
Weitwinkelsucher m wide-angle [view]finder
Weitwinkelverzerrung f geometric (wide-angle) distortion, wide-angle effect
Weitwinkelvorsatz m wide-angle attachment
Weitwinkelvorsatzlinse f s. Weitwinkelvorsatz
Weitwinkelzoom n medium telephoto zoom
~**[objektiv]** n wide-angle zoom [lens]
weitwinklig wide-angle
Welle f wave
~/**akustische** acoustic (sound) wave
~/**ebene** plane wave
~/**ebene harmonische** harmonic plane wave
~/**elektromagnetische** electromagnetic wave
~/**gebeugte** diffracted wave
~/**gebrochene** refracted wave
~/**harmonische** harmonic wave
~/**Huygenssche** Huygens' wavelet
~/**kohärente** coherent wave
~/**kontinuierliche** continuous wave, CW
~/**monochromatische [elektromagnetische]** monochromatic wave
~/**optische** optical (light) wave
~/**periodische** periodic wave
~/**planare** s. ~/ebene
~/**rückgestreute** backscattered wave
~/**skalare** scalar wave
~/**stehende** standing (stationary) wave
~/**transmittierte** transmitted wave
Wellenaberration f wave[-front] aberration, wave-front error (deformation)
Wellenamplitude f wave amplitude
Wellenausbreitungsrichtung f direction of wave propagation
Wellenband n wave band
Wellenbewegung f wave motion
Wellenfeld n wave field
Wellenfeldsynthese f wave field synthesis
Wellenfläche f wave surface (front)
Wellenform f waveform, waveshape
Wellenformcodierung f waveform-based coding, waveform encoding
Wellenformeditor m waveform editor
Wellenformfilter n [/**variables**] wavelet (regular) filter
Wellenformmonitor m waveform monitor, scope
Wellenfrequenz f wave frequency
Wellenfront f wave front (surface)
Wellenfrontaberration f s. Wellenaberration
Wellenfrontamplitude f wave-front amplitude
Wellenfrontanalyse f wave-front analysis
Wellenfrontdeformation f s. Wellenaberration
Wellenfrontfehler m s. Wellenaberration
Wellenfrontinterferogramm n wave-front interferogram
Wellenfrontkorrektur f wave-front correction
Wellenfrontkrümmung f wave-front curvature
Wellenfrontrekonstruktion f wave-front reconstruction *(s.a. Holografie)*
Wellenfrontsensor m wave-front sensor
Wellenfrontverzerrung f wave-front distortion
Wellenfront-Zellenfeld n wave-front array
Wellenfunktion f wave function
~/**komplexe** complex wave function, complex analytic signal
Wellengeschwindigkeit f wave velocity
Wellengleichung f wave equation
Welleninterferenz f wave[length] interference
Wellenlänge f wavelength
~ **maximaler Beugungseffektivität** blaze wavelength

Wellenlänge 442

~/**dominante (dominierende)** dominant wavelength *(colorimetry)*
~/**farbtongleiche** s. ~/dominante
~/**räumliche** spatial wavelength
~/**spektrale** spectral wavelength
wellenlängenabhängig wavelength-dependent
Wellenlängenanalyse f wavelength analysis
Wellenlängenband n wavelength band, band of wavelengths
Wellenlängenbereich m wavelength range (region), wavelength regime
~/**optischer (sichtbarer)** visual (optical) wavelength range, optical wavelength regime
Wellenlängenfilter n wavelength filter
Wellenlängengruppe f wavelength (radiation) band
Wellenlängenintervall n wavelength interval
Wellenlängenmultiplexverfahren n wavelength multiplex technique, wavelength division multiplexing, WDM
wellenlängenselektiv dichroic
Wellenlängenspektrum n wavelength spectrum
wellenlängenunabhängig wavelength-independent, independent of wavelength
Wellenlängenverteilung f wavelength distribution
Wellenleiter m waveguide
~/**faseroptischer** fiber-optic waveguide
~/**planarer** planar waveguide
Wellenmuster n wave pattern; wavy pattern *(e.g. moiré)*
Wellennatur f des Lichts wave nature of light
Wellenoptik f [scalar] wave optics, physical optics
wellenoptisch wave optical, wave-optics
Wellenpaket n wave packet
Wellenperiode f period of wave
Wellenstrahlung f undulatory radiation
Wellentheorie f wave (undulatory) theory *(of light)*
Wellenvektor m wave vector
Wellenwiderstand m/**akustischer** [acoustic] impedance *(sonography)*
Wellenzahl f wave number, frequency
Wellenzahlspektrum n wave-number spectrum
Wellenzahlvektor m wave-number vector
Wellenzug m wave train
Welligkeit f waviness ; buckle *(of photographic material)*
Wellpappschachtel f corrugated box
Welt f/**virtuelle** virtual world
Weltkoordinate f world coordinate
Weltkoordinatenpunkt m world point
Weltkoordinatensystem n world (global) coordinate system, world reference frame, world (global) space, scene coordinate system
Weltprojektion f world projection
Weltraumbild n space image; orbital photograph
Weltraumfotografie f space photography
Weltraumteleskop n space telescope
Weltraumteleskopaufnahme f, **Weltraumteleskopbild** n space telescopic picture
Weltvertrieb m foreign release
Wendekassette f reversible cartridge *(printer)*
Wendelbild n filament image
Wendeprisma n reversing (derotation) prism, inversion (inverting) prism
Wendestange f turning bar *(roll-fed offset machine)*
Werbebeilage f newspaper advertising insert
Werbeeinblendung f commercial insertion
Werbefernsehen n commercial TV
Werbefernsehspot m TV commercial
Werbefilm m commercial
Werbefoto n advertising photo[graph]
Werbefotograf m advertising photographer
Werbefotografie f 1. advertising photography; 2. s. Werbefoto
Werbekurzfilm m, **Werbespot** m commercial, [commercial] spot, teaser
Werbesendungen fpl/**personalisierte** direct mail *(printed matter)*
Werbeunterbrechung f commercial break *(e.g. in television)*
Werkaufnahme f, **Werkbild** n s. Werkfoto
Werkdruckpapier n publishing (text) paper; book paper
Werkfoto n continuity still *(filming)*
Werk[satz]schrift f body face, bread-and-butter type *(typography, printing)*
Werkseinstellung f default [setting]
Werkstattmikroskop n [work]shop microscope
Werkstoff m/**optischer** optical (lens) material
Werkstoffprüfung f/**zerstörungsfreie** nondestructive evaluation, NDE, nondestructive testing [of materials]
Werkstückerkennung f, **Werkstückidentifikation** f workpiece recognition, components detection, industrial parts verification
Werkstückklassifizierung f workpiece classification
Werkstückkontrolle f parts inspection
Werkzeugleiste f toolbar *(strip of icons on a display)*
Werkzeugpalette f [set of] tools, tool palette *(computer graphics)*
Wertediskretisierung f s. Wertequantisierung

Wertequantisierung f quantization, quantizing *(digitizing the amplitude values of signals)*
Wertetabelle f lookup table [memory], LUT, index map
Wertgeber m valuator device
Wertigkeit f valence, valency
Wertpapierdruck m security printing
Wettbewerbslernen n competitive learning *(neuroinformatics)*
Wetterkarte f weather map
Wetterradar n weather [surveillance] radar, meteorological radar
~/**flugzeuggetragenes** aircraft meteorologicl radar
Wettersatellit m weather (meteorological) satellite
~/**geostationärer** geostationary meteorological satellite
Wettersatellitenbilder npl weather satellite imagery
Wettstreit m/**binokularer** binocular disparity
Whittaker-Funktion f Whittaker's [confluent hypergeometric] function *(signal processing)*
Wichtungsfaktor m weighting factor
~/**organspezifischer** tissue[-specific] weighting factor *(X-ray dosimetry)*
Wichtungsfunktion f weighting (modulation) function *(signal processing)*
Wichtungsmatrix f weighting matrix (kernel)
Wickel m pancake *(of magnetic tape)*
Wickelkern m [winding] core, take-up core, bobbin
Wickelplatte f wraparound [press] plate *(printing)*
Widerdruck m back-up printing, backing up
Widerdruckwerk n perfecting unit
widerspiegeln to reimage
Widerstand m 1. resistance; 2. resistor
~/**lichtmodulierter** light-modulated resistor
~/**temperaturabhängiger** thermal sensitive resistor, thermistor
Widerstandsmagnet m resistive magnet *(magnetic resonance imaging)*
Wiederabdruck m reprint
Wiederauffindbarkeit f retrievability *(e.g. of stored image data)*
Wiederauffinden n retrieval
wiederauffinden to retrieve
Wiederaufnahme f, **Wiederaufzeichnung** f rerecording
wiederausstrahlen to rebroadcast
Wiederausstrahlung f rebroadcast
wiederbeschreibbar rewritable
Wiederbeschreibbarkeit f rewritability, rewrite capability
wiederbespielbar rerecordable
wiederbespielen to rerecord
Wiederentwicklung f redevelopment

Wiedergabe f 1. reproduction; 2. display *(esp. of screen images)*; 3. rendering, rendition *(esp. of colors)*; 4. playback, replay *(video)*
~/**bildliche** pictorial rendition (rendering)
~/**fotografische** photographic reproduction
~/**fotomechanische** photomechanical reproduction
~/**magnetische** magnetic reproduction
~/**tiefenverkehrte** pseudoscopy
Wiedergabeanamorphot m anamorphic projector (projection) lens, anamorphic expansion lens, de-squeeze lens
Wiedergabebildschirm m display [screen], monitor screen
wiedergabefähig reproducible
Wiedergabefeinheit f resolution *(s.a. under Auflösung)*
Wiedergabeformat n presentation format; playback format
Wiedergabegerät n reproduction device, reproducer; display device
~/**magnetisches** magnetic reproducer
Wiedergabegeschwindigkeit f 1. playback speed; 2. rendering speed
Wiedergabekontrast m contrast of reproduction
Wiedergabekopf m reproducing (replay) head, play[back] head
~/**voreilender** advanced replay head
Wiedergabeleistung f reproduction (playback) performance *(e.g. of a videocassette recorder)*
Wiedergabemöglichkeit f rendering capability
Wiedergabeobjektiv n projection (projector) lens, projection optics
Wiedergabepause f playback pause mode *(video)*
Wiedergabequalität f reproduction quality, quality of reproduction
Wiedergaberöhre f reproducing (reproduction) tube; [television] picture tube
Wiedergabespalt m reproducing slit *(photographic sound)*
Wiedergabespule f [motion-picture] projection reel
Wiedergabetreue f fidelity [of reproduction]
wiedergebbar 1. displayable; 2. reproducible
wiedergeben to reproduce *(a copy image)*; to [re]display; to render
Wiederholfrequenz f repetition rate; refresh rate *(video)*
Wiederholfunktion f instant replay *(video)*
Wiederholsender m repeater, gap filler, intermediate broadcasting facility
Wiederholungsaufnahme f rerecording [session]; pickup [shot], retake *(s.a. Nachdreh)*

Wiederholungsecho *n* reverberation *(sonography)*
Wiederholungssendung *f* rebroadcast
Wiederholungszeichen *n* swung dash; tilde *(diacritic)*
Wiedervereinigungspunkt *m* recovery point *(human vision)*
Wiedervergrößerung *f* reenlargement
Wiederzugriff *m* retrieval, retrieve
Wiederzündung *f* reignition *(e.g. of a discharge lamp)*
Wiegendruck *m* incunabulum, incunable
Wiener-Filter *n* Wiener[-matrix] filter, least (minimum mean) square error filter *(image restoration)*
~/**lineares** linear Wiener filter
~/**parametrisches** parametric Wiener filter
Wiener-Filterung *f* Wiener filtration, minimum mean square error filtering
Wiener-Matrix *f* Wiener matrix
Wiener-Spektrum *n* Wiener [noise power] spectrum, noise power spectrum, NPS
Wiggler *m* wiggler [magnet], [beam] undulator
Winder *m* [power] winder
Windschutz *m* windscreen
Windschutzhülle *f* furry windscreen *(microphone)*
Windungsart *f* winding type *(cinematographic film)*
Winkel *m*/**azimutaler** azimuth[al] angle
~/**Brewsterscher** Brewster angle [of incidence], polarization (polarizing) angle *(optics)*
~/**ebener** plane angle
~/**kritischer** critical angle
~/**streifender** graze (grazing) angle
~/**tomografischer** tomographic angle
Winkelaberration *f* angular defect
Winkelabhängigkeit *f* angular (angle) dependence
Winkelablenkung *f* angular deflection (deviation)
Winkelabstand *m* angular distance
Winkelauflösung *f* angular resolution
Winkelbereich *m* angular region
Winkeldispersion *f* angular dispersion
Winkelfehler *m* angular defect
Winkelfehlsichtigkeit *f* heterophoria
Winkelfernrohr *n* elbow telescope
Winkelfluktuation *f* glint, specular flash *(radar)*
Winkelfrequenz *f* angular frequency
Winkelfunktion *f* trigonometric (circular) function
Winkelgenauigkeit *f* angular accuracy
Winkelgeschwindigkeit *f*/**konstante** constant angular velocity, CAV
Winkelhaken *m* composing stick *(typesetting)*
Winkelmaß *n* 1. angle gauge; 2. angular measure
Winkelminute *f* angular minute
Winkelmodulation *f* angle modulation

Winkelobjektiv *n* candid angle [lens] attachment
Winkelperspektive *f* angular (two-point) perspective
Winkelposition *f* angular position
Winkelprisma *n* optical square
Winkelprojektion *f* angular (angle) projection
Winkelrauschen *n* noise-equivalent angle *(mirror optics)*
Winkelspektrum *m* angular spectrum
Winkelspiegel *m* angled mirror
Winkelsucher *m* angle [view]finder, angled viewer, right-angle [viewing] attachment
Winkeltreue *f* conformality *(of a map projection)*
Winkelüberdeckung *f* angular subtense
Winkelvergrößerung *f* angular magnification *(optics)*
Winkelverteilung *f* angular distribution
Wippschalter *m* rocker switch
Wirbligkeit *f* vorticity
Wirksamkeit *f*/**relative biologische** relative biological effectiveness, RBE *(X-ray dosimetry)*
Wirkung *f*/**perspektivische** perspective effect
Wirkungsgrad *m*/**optischer** *s.* Modulationsübertragungsfaktor
Wirkungsquantum *n* [/**Plancksches**] Planck's constant *(quantum theory)*
Wirtsrechner *m* *s.* Hostrechner
Wischblende *f* [transitional] wipe *(motion-picture optical effect)*
Wischeffekt *m* wiping effect
Wischer *m* swish (whip) pan, flash pan *(filming)*
Wissen *f*/**apriorisches** a priori knowledge, prior knowledge *(image understanding)*
~/**lokales** local knowledge
Wissensakquisition *f* *s.* Wissenserwerb
Wissensbasis *f* knowledge base *(expert system)*
Wissenschaftsfotograf *m* scientific photographer
Wissenschaftsfotografie *f* 1. scientific photography; 2. scientific photograph
Wissensdarstellung *f* knowledge representation
Wissenserwerb *m* knowledge acquisition
Wissensrepräsentation *f* knowledge representation
Wochenschau *f* newsreel
Wölbspiegel *m* convex mirror
Wölbung *f* warp *(image processing routine)*
Wolfram *n* tungsten
Wolframfadenlampe *f* *s.* Wolframglühlampe
Wolframglühlampe *f* tungsten[-filament] lamp, incandescent tungsten-wire filament lamp
Wolframglühwendel *f* *s.* Wolframwendel

Wolframhalogenlampe f tungsten-halogen (tungsten-halide) lamp; quartz[-halogen] lamp, quartz filament lamp
Wolframlichtquelle f tungsten light source
Wolframwendel f tungsten[-wire] filament, tungsten lamp filament
Wolframwendellampe f s. Wolframglühlampe
Wolkenecho n cloud echo (clutter) *(radar)*
Wolkenradar n cloud radar
Wolkigkeit f mottle, sinkage; chalking, crocking *(printing defect)*
Wollaston-Prisma n Wollaston [polarizing] prism
Wolter-Teleskop n Wolter telescope *(X-ray telescope)*
Woodburytypie f 1. woodburytype [process]; 2. woodburytype *(print)*
World Wide Web n [World Wide] Web, WWW *(part of the Internet)*
WORM-Bildplatte f, **WORM-Datenträger** m WORM disk (platter), write-once read-many optical disk
Wortabstand m word spacing (space) *(layout)*
Wortzwischenraum m s. Wortabstand
Wrap-around-Platte f wraparound [press] plate *(printing)*
Wratten-Filter n Wratten filter, gelatin[-base] filter, dyed gelatin filter, gel
Wundertrommel f zoetrope, wheel of life *(early cinematography)*
Würfel m cube *(geometric primitive)*
würfelförmig cubic[al]; hexahedral
Wurfzettel f flyer
Wurzelknoten m root node *(binary tree)*; start (root) node *(graph)*

X

x-Achse f x-axis, horizontal (east/west) axis
(coordinate system)
X-Blitzsynchronisation X synchronization
(flash photography)
x-Höhe f s. Mittellänge
Xenonblitzlampe f xenon flash lamp
Xenonblitzröhre f xenon [flash] tube
Xenonbogenlampe f xenon arc lamp,
xenon burner
Xenongas n xenon gas
Xenon-Hochdruckgasentladungslampe f
xenon arc lamp, xenon burner
Xenon-Hochdruckionisationskammer f
xenon-filled chamber *(X-ray detector)*
Xenon-Hochdrucklampe f xenon
high-pressure lamp
Xenonlampe f xenon[-filled] lamp, xenon
bulb
~/**gepulste** pulsed xenon lamp
Xenonlicht n xenon [arc] light
Xenonlichtquelle f xenon halide light
source
Xerodruck m s. Xerografie
Xerodruckmaschine f Xerox copier
Xerogel n xerogel
Xerografie f xerography, xerographic
printing *(electrophotography)*
xerografieren to xerox
xerografisch xerographic
Xerogramm n xerogram, xeroradiograph
Xerokopie f xerographic copy
Xeromammografie f xeromammography
xeromammografisch xeromammographic
Xeroradiografie f xeroradiography,
radioxerography
xeroradiografisch xeroradiographic
X-Kontakt m X contact
X-Strahl m X-ray [beam], Roentgen ray
Xylografie f xylography, wood-engraving

Y

y-Achse *f* y-axis, vertical (north/south) axis *(coordinate system)*
Yagi-Antenne *f* yagi, Yagi[-Uda] antenna
YAG-Laser *m* YAG laser, yttrium aluminum garnet laser
Yellow *n* yellow *(subtractive primary color)*
YIQ-Farbmodell *n* YIQ (luminance, in-phase chromatic, quadratic chromatic) color coordinate system, YIQ color space
YMC-Modell *n*, **YMC-System** *n s.* Yellow-Magenta-Cyan-Modell
Young-Helmholtz-Theorie *f* Young-Helmholtz theory [of color vision], three-color theory [of light], trichromacy (trichromatic) theory
Y-Signal *n* luminance (luma) signal, black-[and-]white signal, Y [signal] *(video)*
Yttrium-Aluminium-Granat-Laser *m* yttrium aluminum garnet laser, YAG laser
YUV-Farbmodell *n* YUV color space
Y-Verstärker *m* video [processing] amplifier
Y-Videosignal *n s.* Y-Signal

Z

z-Achse f z-axis
Zackenschrift f variable-area sound track
Zähigkeit f tack *(of printing ink)*
Zahl f/**Abbesche** Abbe [V-]number, V value (number), Abbe constant, constringence, reciprocal relative dispersion *(optics)*
~/**Avogadrosche** Avogadro['s] number, Avogadro's constant *(number of atoms or molecules per mole)*
~/**Prandtlsche** Prandtl number *(flow imaging)*
~/**Reynoldssche** Reynolds number *(flow imaging)*
Zählwerk n counting mechanism
Zahnaufnahme f dental picture
Zahnfilm m dental film
Zahnkranz-Kopiermaschine f sprocket [drum] printer
Zahnräder-Hemmwerk n gear train *(mechanical shutter)*
Zahnrolle f, **Zahntrommel** f sprocket [wheel]
Zahnung f matrix teeth
Zäpfchen n s. Zapfen[/retinaler]
Zapfen m [/**retinaler**] [retinal] cone, visual cone, cone [photo]receptor
Zapfenapparat m cone system
Zapfenblindheit f achromatism, achromatopsia
Zapfendichte f cone density
Zapfenempfindlichkeit f cone sensitivity
Zapfenfarbenblindheit f, **Zapfenmonochromasie** f cone monochromacy (monochromatism)
Zapfenpigment n cone [photo]pigment
Zapfensehen n cone[-mediated] vision, photopic vision, daylight (daytime) vision, bright-light (light-adapted) vision
Zapfensystem n cone system
Zapfentyp m cone type
Zauberscheibe f s. Phenakistiskop
Zauberstab m wand *(computer graphics)*
Zebra n, **Zebrafunktion** f, **Zebrastreifen-Fehlbelichtungswarnung** f zebra-level indicator *(video signal processing)*
Zebramuster n zebra pattern
Zeeman-Effekt m Zeeman effect (splitting) *(of nuclear spin states)*
Zehntelbreite f full-width-at-tenth-maximum, FWTM *(of a line-spread function)*
Zeichen n character; sign, symbol; mark; glyph *(typography)*
~/**alphanumerisches** alphanumeric character
~/**diakritisches** diacritic, accent
~/**ikonisches** iconic sign
~/**typografisches** typographic[al] character, glyph
Zeichenabbild n character image
Zeichenabstand m character spacing (pitch)
Zeichenaufwärtsvektor m character up vector
Zeichenausgleich m [character] kerning *(typography)*
Zeichenbasisvektor m character base vector (width)
Zeichenbegrenzung f character boundary
Zeichenbild n character image
Zeichenbreite f character width
Zeichenbreitefaktor m character expansion factor
Zeichencodierung f character encoding
Zeichendichte f character density
Zeichendickte f [advance] width *(typography)*
Zeichendrucker m character printer
Zeichenerkennung f [alphanumeric] character recognition
~/**entscheidungstheoretische** decision-theoretic character recognition
~/**optische** optical character recognition, OCR
Zeichenfeld n character field (area)
Zeichenfilm m s. Zeichentrickfilm
Zeichenfilmfigur f animated figure
Zeichenfläche f tablet *(graphics tablet)*; drawing surface, viewport *(device coordinate system)*
Zeichenfolge f s. Zeichenkette
Zeichengenerator m character generator, CG
Zeichengerät n s. Zeichenmaschine
Zeichengröße f character size
Zeichenhöhe f character height
Zeichenkette f [character] string, series of characters, character sequence
Zeichenklasse f character class
Zeichenklassifikation f character classification
Zeichenklassifikator m character classifier
Zeichenkontext m rendering hints *(computer graphics)*
Zeichenkopf m plot head
Zeichenkörper m character body
Zeichenleser m [/**optischer**] optical character reader, OCR
Zeichenleuchtdichte f character luminance
Zeichenmaschine f [/**rechnergesteuerte**] [drafting] plotter, plotting machine; plotting instrument *(s.a. under Plotter)*
Zeichenmatrix f character matrix
Zeichenmittenabstand m character spacing (pitch)
Zeichenokular n drawing eyepiece
Zeichenpapier f drawing paper
Zeichenposition f character position
Zeichenprogramm n draw (graphic drawing) program; drafting program

Zeichensatz *m* font [set], type font (family), font of types (characters), typeface, character set (font)
~/codierter coded character set
Zeichenschärfe *f s.* Auflösungsvermögen
Zeichenspeicher *m* character memory
Zeichensprache *f* sign language
Zeichenstelle *f* character position
Zeichenstiftplotter *m* pen plotter
Zeichentrickfilm *m* cartoon film (movie), [animated] cartoon, animation
Zeichentrickfilmer *m* cartoonist
Zeichentrick-Spielfilm *m* full-length animated feature film
Zeichenübersprechen *n* intersymbol interference
Zeichenvorrat *m* [character] repertoire, alphabet
Zeichenwerkzeug *n* drawing tool
Zeichenzwischenraum *m* character distance
zeichnen to draw; to graph, to plot; to cartoon *(animation)*
Zeichnung *f* 1. drawing; 2. [image] definition
~/maßstäbliche scale drawing, drawing to scale
~/perspektivische perspective drawing
~/technische engineering drawing
Zeichnungserstellung f/computerunterstützte computer-aided drafting
Zeichnungsverfilmung *f* microfilming of engineering drawings
Zeigegerät *n* [graphic] pointing device, point-and-select device
Zeiger *m* pointer; hand *(on a dial)*
Zeigerliste *f* pointer list *(computational geometry)*
Zeile *f* line
~/aktive (bildgebende) active video line, active [scan] line *(video)*
~/ausgeschlossene justified line *(typesetting)*
~/digitale aktive digital active line
~/geradzahlige even-numbered line
~/sichtbare visible scanning line
~/ungeradzahlige odd-numbered line
Zeilenablenkspule *f* horizontal scanning (sweep) coil
Zeilenablenkung *f* line sweep, horizontal deflection (sweep)
Zeilenabstand *m* [inter]line spacing, leading
Zeilenabtaster *m* linear array scanner (digitizer), linear scanning device
Zeilenabtastfrequenz *f* line scanning frequency
Zeilenabtastrichtung *f* line scan direction
Zeilenabtastung *f* line[-by-line] scanning, single-line scan, horizontal scan
Zeilenanfang *m* start of a line, beginning of line
Zeilenanordnung *f* linear array

Zeilenauflösung *f* line resolution
Zeilenausfall *m* line dropout
Zeilenaustastlücke *f* line blanking
Zeilenbildwandler *n* linear array transducer, line[ar] array detector; single-line CCD, linear array charge-coupled device imager
Zeilendauer *f* [scanning] line time, line period, scan line duration
~/aktive active [picture] line time, unblanked line time, active line period
Zeilendetektor *m s.* Zeilenbildwandler
Zeilendichte *f* line density
Zeilendrucker *m* line (parallel) printer
Zeilendurchschuss *m* line gap, [external] leading *(typography)*
Zeilenelektrode *f* line electrode *(plasma display)*
Zeilenendbestimmung *f* end-of-line decision *(typesetting)*
Zeilenende *n* end of [a] line
Zeilenflimmern *n* line flicker (jitter)
Zeilenfrequenz *f* line frequency (rate), line (horizontal) scanning frequency, horizontal [sweep] frequency, horizontal scan rate
Zeilengießmaschine *f s.* Zeilengussmaschine
Zeilenguss *m* linecasting, slugcasting
Zeilengussmaschine *f* linecaster, slugcasting machine
~/tastaturgesteuerte keyboard[-operated] linecaster
Zeilenimpuls *m* line pulse
Zeileninterpolation[stechnik] *f* line[-to-line] interpolation, line averaging
Zeilenkamera *f* linear array (CCD) camera, line scan camera
Zeilenkennung *f* line identification
Zeilenklaffung *f* underscan *(remote sensing)*
Zeilenlänge *f* line length, length of line
~/aktive active line length *(television)*
Zeilenoszillogramm *n* color bar waveform (test signal) *(color television)*
Zeilenperiodendauer *f s.* Zeilendauer
Zeilenpufferspeicher *m* line store (memory)
Zeilenraster *m(n)* 1. line raster (screen) *(printing)*; 2. line-scanning pattern *(television)*
Zeilenrücklauf *m* line flyback, horizontal retrace [time]
Zeilensatz *m* slugcasting
Zeilenscanner *m* linear scanner (scanning device), linear array scanner (digitizer)
Zeilensegment *n* line segment
Zeilensensor *m* line (linear array) sensor, linear image sensor, linear detector array
~/optischer optical line sensor
Zeilensequenz *f* line sequence
Zeilensetz- und -gießmaschine *f* slugcasting compositor (typesetter)
Zeilenspeicher *m* line store (memory)

Zeilensprung

Zeilensprung *m* interlace
Zeilensprungabtastung *f* interlace[d] [video] scanning, interlaced scan[ning] system, interlacing
Zeilensprungartefakt *n* interlace (interlacing) artifact
Zeilensprungkamera *f* interlaced scan camera
Zeilensprungsignal *n* interlaced [raster] signal
Zeilensprungverfahren *n s.* Zeilensprungabtastung
Zeilenstruktur *f* line structure
Zeilensynchronisation *f* line synchronization
Zeilensynchronisierimpuls *m*, **Zeilensynchronsignal** *n* line sync[hronization] pulse, drive pulse *(s.a. Synchronisiersignal/horizontales)*
Zeilentransferstruktur *f* interline transfer [CCD] array
Zeilenüberdeckung *f* overscan *(remote sensing)*
Zeilenumbruch *m* word wrap
Zeilenumlauf *m* wraparound *(word processing)*
Zeilenvektor *m* row vector
Zeilenverdoppler *m* line-doubler, scaler *(monitor)*
Zeilenverdopplung *f* line-doubling
Zeilenversatz *m* line offset
Zeilenvorschub *m* line feed
Zeilenwähler *m* line selector *(oscilloscope)*
Zeilenwandern *n* line craw[ling] *(interlace artifact)*
Zeilenwechsel *m* line-to-line change
Zeilenwechselfrequenz *f s.* Zeilenfrequenz
zeilenweise line-by-line
Zeilenzahl *f* line number
Zeilenzwischenraum *m* line gap, [external] leading *(typography)*
Zeitachse *f* time (temporal) axis
Zeitauflösung *f* time (temporal) resolution
Zeitauslöser *m* time[-limit] release *(photography)*
Zeitautomatik *f* aperture priority [auto] *(exposure mode)*
Zeit-Bandbreiten-Produkt *n* time-bandwidth product *(signal theory)*
Zeitbasis *f* time base
Zeitbasisfehler *m* time base error
Zeitbasiskorrektor *m* time base corrector, TBC
Zeitbasiskorrektur *f* time base [error] correction; time base correction circuit
Zeitbasiskorrekturgerät *n s.* Zeitbasiskorrektor
Zeitbasisstabilität *f* time base stability
Zeitbelichtung *f* time exposure
Zeitbereich *m* time domain
Zeitbereichsdarstellung *f* time-domain representation
Zeit-Blenden-Kombination *f* shutter speed and aperture combination
Zeitcode *m* time code, TC
Zeitcodeeinblender *m* time code inserter
Zeitcodegenerator *m* time code generator
Zeitcodeinformation *f* time code information
Zeitcodeleser *m* time code reader
Zeitcodemarkierung *f*, **Zeitcodenummer** *f* time code number
Zeitcodespur *f* time code channel
Zeitcodierung *f* time coding
Zeitdehner *m* slow-motion device
Zeitdehnerkamera *f* slow-motion camera
zeitdiskret discrete-time
Zeitdiskretisierung *f* time direction discretization; scanning; sampling
Zeiteinstellung *f* time setting
Zeitenpriorität *f* shutter priority
Zeitfehler *m* timing error; time base error *(video recording)*
Zeitfehlerausgleicher *m* time base corrector, TBC
Zeitfenster *n* time (temporal) window, window of time
Zeitfunktion *f* temporal response function
Zeit-Gamma-Kurve *f* time-gamma curve, gamma-time curve
Zeitgeber *m* timer
zeitgenau duration-accurate
zeitgleich synchronous, in sync
Zeitintervall *n* time (temporal) interval
zeitinvariant time-invariant
Zeitkompression *f* time compression *(video signal processing)*
zeitkontinuierlich continuous-time
Zeitkoordinate *f* time coordinate
Zeitleiste *f* time line *(video editing)*
zeitlich temporal
Zeitlupe *f* slow motion, slo[w-]mo
~ **rückwärts** reverse slow motion
Zeitlupenaufnahme *f* slow-motion photography
Zeitlupeneffekt *m* slow-motion effect
Zeitlupengerät *n* slow-motion machine
Zeitlupenkamera *f* high-speed camera
Zeitlupenwiedergabe *f*, **Zeitlupenwiederholung** *f* slow-motion replay (playback)
Zeitmittelungsholografie *f* time average holography
Zeitmittelungsinterferometrie *f* time average interferometry
Zeitmittelungstechnik *f* time average method *(holographic interferometry)*
Zeitmultiplexen *n* time [division] multiplexing, TDM, time-multiplexing technique *(video)*
~/**statisches** *s.* ~/synchrones
~/**synchrones** synchronous time division multiplex, STDM
Zeitmultiplextechnik *f*/**optische** optical time multiplex technique, OTDM
Zeitmultiplexverfahren *n s.* Zeitmultiplexen
Zeitquantisierung *f* time quantization

Zeitraffer *m* fast motion
Zeitrafferaufnahme *f* time-lapse shot; time-lapse image
Zeitraffereffekt *m* fast-motion effect
Zeitrafferfilm *m* time-lapse film (movie)
Zeitrafferfotografie *f* 1. time-lapse photography; 2. time-lapse photograph
Zeitrafferkamera *f* time-lapse camera; time-lapse recorder
Zeitrafferkinematografie *f* time-lapse cinematography (filming)
Zeitraffung *f* time scaling
Zeitreferenzsignal *n* [video] timing reference code
Zeitreihe *f* time series; time line graph
Zeitreihenanalyse *f* time-series analysis
Zeitschalter *m s.* Zeitschaltuhr
Zeitschaltuhr *f* timer; darkroom timer
~/**eingebaute** built-in timer
Zeitschlitz *m* time slot *(signal processing)*
Zeitschriftendruck *m* magazine printing; publication [gravure] printing
Zeitschriftendruckmaschine *f* publication gravure press
Zeitschriftenfoto *n* magazine photo
Zeitschriftenfotograf *m* magazine photographer
Zeitschriftenfotografie *f* magazine photography
zeitsequentiell time-sequential, temporal-sequential *(e.g. data acquisition)*
Zeitskalierbarkeit *f* temporal scalability
Zeitstempel *m* [presentation] time stamp, PTS *(video transmission)*
Zeittakt *m* clock
Zeit-Temperatur-Kurve *f* time-temperature curve
Zeitung *f*/**elektronische** electronic newspaper
Zeitungsausschnitt *m* newspaper clipping
Zeitungsbeilage *f* newspaper supplement
Zeitungsbild *n* newspaper [halftone] image, newspaper picture (illustration)
Zeitungsbildredakteur *m* [daily] newspaper photo editor
Zeitungsdruck *m* newspaper print[ing]
Zeitungsdruckfarbe *f* newsprint ink
Zeitungsdruckmaschine *f* newspaper press
Zeitungsdruckpapier *n* newsprint
Zeitungsfoto *n* news photo[graph], press photo
Zeitungsfotograf *m* newspaper (daily news) photographer, press photographer
Zeitungsfotografie *f* 1. news photography; 2. *s.* Zeitungsfoto
Zeitungspapier *n* newsprint
Zeitungsrotationsmaschine *f* rotary newspaper press
Zeitungsseite *f* newspaper page
zeitveränderlich time-varying *(e.g. signal)*
Zeitversatz *m* time delay *(e.g. in ultrasound imaging)*
zeitversetzt time-delayed
Zeitversetzung *f* time shift
Zeitverzerrung *f*/**dynamische** dynamic time warping *(pattern recognition)*
Zeitwirkungsgrad *m* shutter efficiency
Zellbildanalyse *f* cell image analysis
Zelldaten *pl* cell data
Zelle *f* cell
~/**amakrine** amacrine cell *(of the retina)*
~/**elektrooptische** *s.* Zelle/lichtelektrische
~/**fotovoltaische** photovoltaic cell
~/**leere** idle cell *(asynchronous transfer mode)*
~/**lichtelektrische** photoelectric cell, photocell; Kerr cell
~/**verdrillt nematische** twisted nematic [liquid crystal] cell
Zellenfeld *n*/**systolisches** systolic array
Zellenzerlegung *f* cell decomposition *(computer graphics)*
Zellfehlerrate *f* cell error rate, CER
Zellhornfilm *m* cellulose nitrate film
Zellkopf *m* cell header *(asynchronous transfer mode)*
Zellmatrix *f* cell array *(computer graphics)*
Zelloidinpapier *n* celloidin paper
Zelluloid *n s.* Celluloid
Zellverlust *m* cell loss
Zener-Diode *f* Zener diode *(semiconductor)*
Zenitkamera *f* zenith camera
Zenitteleskop *n* zenith telescope (tube)
Zentralabschattung *f* central obscuration (obstruction) *(e.g. of an optical pupil)*
Zentraleinheit *f* central processing unit, CPU *(computer module)*; [master] processor, mainframe
Zentrallabor *n* central laboratory [facility]
Zentralperspektive *f* central (linear) perspective, convergence of parallels
zentralperspektivisch centered perspective
Zentralpixel *n* central (center) pixel, center pel, midpoint
Zentralprojektion *f* central projection
Zentralprojektionslinie *f* main projection line
Zentralprozessor *m s.* Zentraleinheit
Zentralrechner *m* 1. mainframe [computer], central computer; 2. *s.* Zentraleinheit
Zentralstrahl *m* central ray (beam)
Zentraltakt *m* gen lock
Zentralverschluss *m* central (center-opening) shutter; [central-opening] between-the-lens[-type] shutter; leaf[-type] shutter, diaphragm shutter
Zentralverschlusskamera *f* leaf-shutter camera
Zentralwellenlänge *f* center wavelength
Zentralwert *m* median [value], middle value *(statistics)*
zentrierbar centerable

zentrieren to center
Zentrierfehler *m* decentation aberration
Zentriermikroskop *n* centering microscope
Zentriertoleranz *f* centering tolerance
Zentrierung *f* centration, centering, alignment *(e.g. of lens elements)*
~/binokulare binocular centration
Zentrifugenmikroskop *n* centrifuge microscope
Zentrum *n*/**optisches** optical center
Zerfall *m*/**radioaktiver** radioactive decay (transformation)
Zerfallsreihe *f*/**radioaktive** radioactive disintegration series
Zerlegung *f* decomposition *(e.g. of image data)*
~/dyadische dyadic (octave) decomposition
~/rekursive recursive decomposition
~/spektrale spectral dispersion
Zerlegungsfilter *n* decomposition filter
Zernike-Polynomkoeffizient *m* Zernike polynomial *(wave optics)*
Zerrbild *n* distorted image
Zerrlinse *f*, **Zerroptik** *f* distorting (squeeze) lens, anamorphic [squeeze] lens, anamorphote [lens], anamorphic optics (system)
Zerr-Raum *m* Ames room *(optical illusion)*
Zerrspiegel *m* distorting mirror
Zerstörschwelle *f* damage threshold *(laser optics)*
Zerstrahlung *f* annihilation [radiation] *(particle physics)*
zerstreuen to scatter, to diffuse, to disperse *(e.g. light)*
Zerstreuung *f* scatter[ing], diffusion; dispersion *(of radiation)*
Zerstreuungsfigur *f* scattering image
Zerstreuungskreis *m* circle of confusion, blur circle
Zerstreuungskreisdurchmesser *m* blur diameter, diameter of circle of confusion
Zerstreuungslinse *f* diverging (dispersive) lens, negative (concave) lens
Zerstreuungsprisma *n* dispersing prism
Zerstreuungspunkt *m* center of dispersion, virtual focus
Zerstreuungsscheibchen *n* s. Punktbild
Zerstreuungsspiegel *m* convex mirror
Zeugmatografie *f* zeugmatography *(s.a. magnetic resonance imaging)*
Zickzackabtastung *f* zigzag scan[ning], zigzag sampling
Zickzackanordnung *f* zigzag [ordering] pattern *(e.g. of a compression algorithm)*
Zickzackfalz *m* concertina fold
Zickzackstapel *m* fanfolded paper
Ziehen-und-Ablegen *n* drag-and-drop [feature] *(to move objects on screen)*
Ziehpunkt *m* handle *(computer graphics)*
Zielabbildung *f* target imaging (mapping) *(radar)*

Zielbild *n* target (goal) image *(e.g. in image search and retrieval)*; target frame (picture) *(motion estimation)*
Zielentdeckung *f* target detection
Zielentfernung *f* target range
Zielerfassung *f* target acquisition
Zielerfassungsradar *n* acquisition radar
Zielerkennung *f* target recognition (identification)
Zielextraktion *f* target extraction *(radar)*
Zielfernrohr *n* telescope (telescopic) sight, sighting (aiming) telescope; [gun]sight, rifle (gun) scope; sniperscope
Zielfilmfotografie *f* photofinish photography
Zielfotografie *f* photofinish photography
Zielführung *f* guidance
Zielgerät *n* target device
Zielkamera *f* photofinish[-type] camera, racetrack photofinish camera
Zielknoten *m* goal node *(graph theory)*
Ziellinie *f* vanishing line
Zielmaschine *f* delivery engine
Zielmikroskop *n* sighting microscope
Zielobjekt *n* target object
Zielpunkt *m* target point
Zielradar *n* target radar
Zielsignatur *f* target signature
Zielsuchsystem *n*/**militärisches** targeting sight
Zielüberwachung *f* target surveillance
Zielunterscheidung *f* target discrimination
Zielverfolgungsradar *n* [target] tracking radar
Zielverfolgungsrechner *m* tracker *(radar)*
Zielvergenz *f* target vergence *(stereopsis)*
Zielvertauschung *f* target swap (swop) *(radar)*
Zielverweilzeit *f* time on target, dwell time *(radar)*
Zielwinkel-Entfernungsmesser *m* tachymeter
Zielzuweisungsgerät *n*/**lasergestütztes** ground laser locator designator, GLLD
Zierlinie *f* line of decoration
Zierstrich *m* flourish *(typography)*
Ziffer *f* digit
Ziffernanzeige *f* numerical display
Ziliarfortsatz *m* ciliary process
Ziliarkörper *m* ciliary body *(of the eye)*
Ziliarmuskel *m* ciliar (iris) muscle *(of the eye)*
Zimmerantenne *f* indoor antenna (aerial)
Zimmeraufnahme *f* indoor photograph (picture); interior shot
Zinkätzung *f* zinc etching *(s.a. Zinkflachdruck)*
Zinkdruckform *f* zincograph, zincotype
Zinkflachdruck *m*, **Zinkografie** *f* zincography
Zinkoxid *n* zinc oxide *(photoconductor)*
Zinkoxidpapier *n* zinc oxide paper
Zinksulfid *n* zinc sulfide *(phosphor)*
Zinnplatte *f* pewter (tin) plate

Zirconiumlampe f zirconium [arc] lamp
zirkular circular, round
Zirkularpol[arisations]filter n,
  Zirkularpolarisator m circular[ly]
  polarizing filter, circular polarizer
Zirkularpolarisation f circular polarization
Zirkumflex m circumflex accent *(diacritic)*
Zittern n jitter *(of digital signals)*
Zoetrop n Zoetrope, wheel of life *(early animated-picture machine)*
Zölostat m s. Heliostat
Zone f/**Fresnelsche** Fresnel zone (region), half-period zone *(wave optics)*
Zonenachse f zone axis *(crystallography)*
Zonenbelichtungsmessung f zone system *(exposure metering)*
Zonenfehler m zonal [spherical] aberration
Zonenfokussierung f zone focusing
Zonenlinse f s. Zonenplatte
Zonenmesssystem n s. Zonensystem
Zonenplatte f [/**Fresnelsche**] [Fresnel] zone plate, zone-plate lens *(diffractive focusing element)*
Zonenplattenmikroskop n zone-plate microscope
Zonenplattenmuster n zone plate pattern
Zonenplattenoptik f zone-plate optics
Zonenschraube f key *(printing- ink fountain)*
Zonensystem n zone system
Zonulafasern f zonule fiber
Zoom n(m) 1. zoom [lens], varifocal (vario) lens, variable-focal-length lens, pancratic [lens] system; 2. zoom *(act of zooming)*
~/**digitales** digital zoom [feature] *(video camera)*
~/**echtes** true zoom lens
~/**elektronisches** s. Zoom/digitales
~/**elektrooptisches** electro-optical zoom
~/**motorisches (motorisiertes)** motorized (power) zoom
~/**optisches** optical zoom
Zoomaufnahme f zoom shot
zoombar zoomable
Zoombereich m zoom[ing] range
Zoombewegung f zoom [movement]
Zoomblitz m zoom flash
Zoomeffekt m zoom effect *(s.a. Zoomfahrt)*
Zoomeinstellring m zoom ring
Zoomeinstellung f zoom setting
zoomen to zoom
Zoomfahrt f zoom shot (effect) *(filming)*
Zoomfaktor m zoom factor
Zoomgeschwindigkeit f rate of zoom
Zoomkamera f zoom[-lens] camera
Zoommikrofon n zoom microphone
Zoommotor m zooming motor
Zoomobjektiv n s. Zoom 1.
Zoomokular n zoom eyepiece
Zoomoptik f s. Zoom 1.
Zoomring m zoom ring
Zoomsteuerung f zoom [lens] control
Zoomsucher m zoom finder

Zoomvergrößerung f zoom magnification (enlargement)
Zoomverhältnis n zoom ratio
Zoomverriegelung f zoom lock mechanism
z-Puffer m z buffer, depth buffer *(computer graphics)*
z-Puffer-Algorithmus m z-buffering algorithm, depth buffer algorithm
z-Pufferspeicher m s. z-Puffer
z-Puffer-Verfahren n z-buffering, depth-buffering
Zubehörgerät n accessory device
Zubehörpalette f s. Zubehörsystem
Zubehörschuh m accessory shoe
Zubehörsystem n accessory system
Zubehörtasche f gadget bag
zubewegen to dolly in, to truck (push) in *(the camera in filming)*
Zuchtkristall m synthetic crystal
Zufälligkeit f randomness
zufallsbedingt random, stochastic
Zufallsfarbrauschen n random color noise
Zufallsfehler m random (accidental) error *(e.g. in image compression)*
Zufallsfeld n random field
~/**ergodisches** ergodic random field
~/**homogenes** homogeneous random field
~/**unkorreliertes** uncorrelated random field
Zufallsgröße f s. Zufallsvariable
Zufallsmuster n random pattern
Zufallspolygon n random polygon
Zufallspunktkinetogramm n random-dot kinetogram
Zufallspunktmuster n random-dot pattern
Zufallspunktstereogramm n random dot stereogram
Zufallsrasterung f stochastic (frequency-modulated) screening, [dot] diffusion dithering, error diffusion *(halftoning technique)*
Zufallsrauschen n 1. random noise; 2. s. ~/thermisches
~/**additives** additive random noise
~/**thermisches** random [thermal] noise, Johnson (system) noise, Nyquist noise
Zufallssignal n random signal
Zufallsstereogramm n random dot stereogram
Zufallsvariable f random (stochastic) variable, variate
~/**gaußverteilte** Gaussian-distributed random variable
~/**gleichverteilte** uniform-distributed random variable
~/**mittelwertfreie** zero-mean random variable
Zug m s. Zügigkeit
Zugangskontrollalgorithmus m admission control algorithm *(multimedia server)*
Zugangskontrollsystem n conditional access technology *(television)*
Zugband n drive tape

Zugehörigkeitsfunktion f membership (characteristic) function *(fuzzy logic)*
Zugfestigkeit f tensile strength
Zuggreifer m [pull-down] claw
Zügigkeit f tack *(of printing ink)*
Zugriff m/**bedingter** conditional access, CA
~/**sequentieller** sequential access
~/**wahlfreier** random (direct) access; nonlinear access
Zugriffseinheit f access unit
Zugriffseinheitsschicht f access unit layer *(video compression)*
Zugriffsgeschwindigkeit f access speed, speed of access
Zugriffskontrolle f access control
Zugriffsschlitz m s. Zeitschlitz
Zugriffssteuerfeld n access control field
Zugriffssteuerung f automatic coded access control
Zugriffsverzögerung f access delay
Zugriffszeit f access time *(data processing)*
~/**mittlere** average access time
Zündelektrode f ignition electrode
Zündpapier n touch paper *(for igniting flash powder)*
Zuordnung f assignment; matching
~/**flächenbasierte** area-based matching
~/**merkmalsbasierte** feature-based matching, FBM
Zuordnungseinheit f cluster *(data storage)*
Zuordnungsproblem n allocation (assignment) problem
Zurichten n makeready, setup *(printing)*
zurückprojizieren s. rückprojizieren
zurückspulen to rewind, to backwind, to rethread *(e.g. a film)*
zurückstrahlen to reradiate
Zurückstrahlung f reradiation
zurückstreuen s. rückstreuen
zurückverfolgen to retrace *(e.g. rays)*
Zusammenhang m connectedness
~/**unscharfer** fuzzy connectedness *(e.g. of voxels)*
Zusammenhangsbedingung f connectedness constraint
Zusammenlegungsverlust m collapsing loss *(radar)*
Zusammensetzung f/**spektrale** spectral composition (content) *(e.g. of light)*
zusammentragen to gather, to stack, to collate *(folded signatures)*
Zusatzbeleuchtung f additional lighting
Zusatzbelichtung f supplementary (additional) exposure
Zusatzdaten pl ancillary (auxiliary) data *(video)*
Zusätze mpl finals *(emulsion manufacture)*
Zusatzempfangsgerät n s. Set-Top-Box
Zusatzfarbe f spot color (varnish) *(printing)*
Zusatzfilter n supplementary filter
Zusatzgerät n/**peripheres** peripheral add-on

Zusatzlicht n additional light, supplementary (supplemental) light
Zusatzlichtquelle f additional light source
Zusatzlinse f supplementary (supplemental) lens, auxiliary (diopter) lens
Zusatzmikrofon n external microphone
Zusatzmodul n plug-in [module], add-in
Zusatzobjektiv n s. Zusatzlinse
Zusatzrauschen n additional noise *(e.g. in avalanche photodiodes)*
Zuschauer m viewer
Zuschauerperspektive f audience perspective
Zuschauerraum m auditorium
Zuschneiden n clipping *(computer graphics)*
zuschneiden to crop, to trim, to clip *(e.g. a photograph)*
Zuschuss m overrun, overs *(printing)*
Zusetzen n **der Druckform**, ~ **von Rastertonwerten** fill-up *(printing defect)*
Zuspielband n source (slave) tape
Zuspieler m, **Zuspielgerät** n, **Zuspielmaschine** f contributing device, source machine *(s.a. Zuspielrecorder)*
Zuspielmonitor m source monitor
Zuspielrecorder m source [videotape] recorder, source (playback) VTR, [slave] playback machine, player
Zuspielung f contribution *(video, television)*
Zustandsdiagramm n state (constellation) diagram
Zustandsraum m state space
Zustandsvektor m state [vector]
Zweiäquivalentkuppler m two-equivalent coupler *(color photography)*
Zweibadentwickler m two-solution developer
Zweibadentwicklung f two-bath development
Zweibadfixierung f two-bath fixation (fixing)
Zweibandverfahren n s. Zweistreifenverfahren
Zweibildmessung f stereophotogrammetry
Zweibuchstabenmatrize f two-letter matrix, duplex matrix
zweidimensional two-dimensional, bidimensional, 2-D, planar
Zweidimensionalität f two-dimensionality, bidimensionality
Zweiebenenangiogram n biplane angiogram
Zweifachabtastung f dual scan *(liquid crystal display)*
Zweifachkonverter m X2 converter
Zweifarbenbild n two-color image
Zweifarbenfotografie f two-color photography
Zweifarbenmaschine f two-color machine; two-color [rotary] press *(printing)*

Zweifarbenplatte f duotone plate
Zweifarben-Rasterbild n duotone [halftone image], two-color halftone image
Zweifarbensehen n dichromatic vision
Zweifarbentiefdruckpresse f two-color gravure press
zweifarbig two-color[ed], bicolor[ed], bichrome; dichromatic, dichroic
Zweiflügelblende f two-bladed shutter *(film projector)*
Zweikanalaufnahme f two-channel recording
Zweikanal-Stereofonie f two-channel stereophony, two-channel stereo audio
Zweikanalton m 1. second[ary] audio program, SAP *(television)*; 2. Zweiton *(television sound)*
Zweikomponentenentwickler m two-component developer
Zweikomponentensystem n two-component system *(e.g. in color photography)*
Zweikomponententoner m dual-component toner
Zweilinsensystem n two-lens system
Zweimagazinmaschine f double-distribution machine *(typesetting)*
Zwei-Nadel-Illusion f double-nail illusion *(stereopsis)*
Zweipartner-Videokonferenz f biparty (one-to-one) videoconference, point-to-point videoconferencing
Zweipegelbild n two-value picture
Zweiphasen-CCD-Bildsensor m two-phase CCD [image sensor]
Zweiphasen-CCD-Schieberegister n two-phase CCD shift register
Zweiphotonenmikroskop n two-photon excitation microscope
Zweiphotonenmikroskopie f two-photon [fluorescence] microscopy; two-photon laser scanning [fluorescence] microscopy
Zweiphotonenspektroskopie f two-photon spectroscopy
zweipolig bipolar
Zweipunktauflösung f two-point resolution
Zweipunktperspektive f two-point perspective, angular perspective
Zweiraumkamera f darkroom camera
Zweirichtungsthyristor m bidirectional thyristor
Zweiringzoom[objektiv] n two-touch zoom
Zweischalenfehler m astigmatism, astigmatic aberration (error)
Zweischichtencodierung f two-layer coding *(of video data)*
Zweischichtenfilm m duplitized (double-coated) film, double-emulsion film
Zweistärkenglas n bifocal [eyeglass] lens; split-field lens

Zweistrahlfall m two-beam case (situation) *(electron diffraction)*
Zweistrahlinterferenz f two-beam interference
Zweistrahlinterferometrie f two-beam interferometry
Zweistreifenverfahren n double-system recording (shooting)
Zweitbelichtung f second exposure
Zweitblitzgerät n slave [electronic] flash unit
Zweitentwickler m second developer, redeveloper
Zweitentwicklung f second development
Zweitnegativ n duplicate negative, dupe [negative]
Zweitontechnik f Zweiton *(television sound)*
Zweitourenmaschine f two-revolution [cylinder] press
Zweiwellenlängenmikroskop n two-wavelengths microscope
Zwei-Zoll-Band n two-inch [video]tape
Zwei-Zoll-Schrägspurmaschine f two-inch helical scan machine
Zwielicht n twilight
Zwillingsbild n twin image *(holography)*
Zwillingsgrenze f twin boundary *(electron microscopy)*
Zwipo n s. Zwischenpositiv
Zwischenabbildungssystem n intermediate lens [system] *(photomicrography)*
Zwischenablage f clipboard *(data processing)*
Zwischenaugenabstand m interocular distance
Zwischenbad n intermediate bath
Zwischenbelichtung f second exposure
Zwischenbild n intermediate (in-between) image, interim image; in-between frame; in-between drawing
~/**reelles** real intermediate image
Zwischenbildebene f intermediate [image] plane
Zwischenbilderzeugung f intermediate image formation
Zwischenbildplatte f intermediate plate *(photolithography)*
Zwischenbildposition f intermediate image position
Zwischenbildzeit f interframe time
Zwischenbrennpunkt m intermediate focus
Zwischenfarbe f intermediate color; intermediate hue
Zwischenfilter n intermediate filter
Zwischenflügel m anti-flicker blade *(projector shutter)*
Zwischenfrequenz f intermediate frequency, IF
Zwischengitterplatz m interstitial position
Zwischengitter-Silberion n interstitial silver ion

Zwischenknoten *m* internode *(binary tree)*
Zwischenkopie *f* intermediate print
Zwischenlinse *f* intermediate lens
Zwischennegativ *n* intermediate (dupe) negative, interneg[ative], dupe neg; color reversal intermediate, color internegative (duplicate negative)
Zwischenphasenberechnung *f* in-betweening
Zwischenphasenzeichner *m* in-betweener, assistant animator
Zwischenpixelabstand *m* interpixel spacing
Zwischenpixelinterpolation *f* interpixel inerpolation
Zwischenpixelkorrelation *f* interpixel correlation
Zwischenpixelposition *f* interpixel position
Zwischenpixelredundanz *f* interpixel redundancy
Zwischenpixelwert *m* intermediate pixel value
Zwischenpixelzeile *f* inter-pixel line
Zwischenpositiv *n* interpositive [film], intermediate positive, master positive; interpositive print; color master positive [print]
Zwischenprojektion *f* intermediate projection
Zwischenring *m* intermediate ring; [auto] extension tube, [extension] ring
Zwischenringsatz *m* extension-tube set
Zwischenschicht *f* 1. intermediate (spacer) layer, interlayer *(e.g. of a color film)*; 2. *s.* Schicht/verdeckte
Zwischenschichtabstand *m* interslice space, slice gap *(tomography)*
Zwischenschnitt *m* 1. intercutting *(motion-picture editing)*; 2. intercut, cutaway, cut-in; 3. *s.* Insertschnitt 1. *and* 2.)
Zwischenspaltenbetrieb *m* interline transfer
Zwischenspeicher *m* intermediate memory; cache [memory], data cache; buffer [store]
zwischenspeichern to cache; to buffer
Zwischenspeicherplatz *m* cache space
Zwischenspeicherung *f* caching; [intermediate] buffering
Zwischenspeicherverwaltung *f* buffer management
Zwischentitel *m* insert [title] *(cinema)*
Zwischenton *m* intermediate tone
Zwischentubus *m* [extension] tube
Zwischenüberschrift *f* subhead
Zwischenwässern *n*, **Zwischenwässerung** *f* intermediate rinse [stage]
Zwischenwertbestimmung *f* interpolation
Zwischenzeilenflimmern *n* interline flicker, twitter
Zwischenzeilentransfer *m* [frame] interline transfer
Zwischenzeilentransferkamera *f* interline transfer camera
Zwischenzeilentransferstruktur *f* interline transfer structure *(area array CCD)*
Zwischenzeilenverfahren *n s.* Zeilensprungverfahren
Zwölffingerdarmendoskopie *f* duodenoscopy
Zyan... *s.* Cyan...
Zylinder *m* cylinder *(geometric primitive)*
Zylinderdruckmaschine *f* cylinder press
Zylinder-Flachformmaschine *f* flatbed [printing] press
Zylinderhut-Transformation *f* top-hat transform *(morphological image processing)*
Zylinderlinse *f* cylindrical (cylinder) lens
Zylinderlinsenobjektiv *n* anamorphic
Zylinderoptik *f s.* Zylinderlinsenobjektiv
Zylinderprojektion *f* cylindrical projection, cylindrical [projection] mapping
Zylinderwelle *f* cylindrical wave
Zystoskop *n* cystoscope
Zytofluorogramm *n* cytofluorogram
Zytofotometer *n* cytophotometer
Zytofotometrie *f* cytophotometry
Zytometrie *f*/**bildgestützte** image cytometry

DICTIONARY

OF

IMAGING

PART II

ENGLISH-GERMAN

A

A mode Amplitudenmodus *m (Sonografie)*
A mode scan A-Scan *m (Sonografie)*
A mode ultrasound scanning
  A-Bild-Sonografie *f*, A-Mode-Verfahren
  n, eindimensionale Sonografie *f*
a posteriori probability
  a-posteriori-Wahrscheinlichkeit *f*,
  bedingte Wahrscheinlichkeit *f*,
  Rückschlusswahrscheinlichkeit *f*
  (Bayes-Statistik)
a priori information (knowledge)
  a-priori-Wissen *n*, Vorwissen *n*,
  apriorisches Wissen *n (Bildanalyse)*
A scan A-Scan *m (Sonografie)*
A-scan [image] A-Bild *n (Sonografie)*
A scan process A-Bild-Sonografie *f*,
  A-Mode-Verfahren *n*
A spline s. algebraic spline
A-to-D converter s. analog-digital
  converter
A type (wind) A-Wicklung *f (Kinefilm)*
AA-type alkaline battery
  Alkali-Mignonzelle *f*
AB cutting (editing) AB-Schnitt *m*,
  Schachbrettschnitt *m*
  (Videobearbeitung)
AB printing AB-Kopieren *n (Film, Video)*
Abat's wedge Abatischer Keil *m*
abaxial achs[en]fern, achsenentfernt,
  außeraxial, abaxial
~ **ray** achs[en]ferner Strahl *m*
Abbe condenser Abbe-Kondensor *m*
  (Lichtmikroskop)
~ **constant** s. ~ number
~ **invariant** Abbesche Invariante *f (Optik)*
~ **number** Abbe-Zahl *f*, Abbesche Zahl *f*
~ **prism** Abbe-Prisma *n*
~ **refractometer** Abbe-Refraktometer *n*
~ **sine condition** [Abbesche]
  Sinusbedingung *f*
~ **V-number** s. ~ number
Abbe's theory of the microscope
  Abbesche Mikroskoptheorie *f*
aberrated bildfehlerbehaftet, verzeichnet
~ **image** verzeichnetes Bild *n*
aberration Aberration *f*, Abbildungsfehler
  m
~ **coefficient** Aberrationskoeffizient *m*,
  Bildfehlerkoeffizient *m*
~ **compensation**
  Aberrationskompensation *f*
~-**corrected** aberrationskorrigiert
~ **correction** Bildfehlerkorrektur *f*,
  Aberrationskorrektion *f*,
  Aberrationskorrektur *f*, Fehlerkorrektur *f*
  (Optik)
~ **curve** von Rohrsche Darstellung *f (eines
  Objektivs)*
~-**free** aberrationsfrei, bildfehlerfrei,
  abbildungsfehlerfrei; verzeichnungsfrei
~-**free image** aberrationsfreies Bild *n*
~-**free lens** verzeichnungsfreies Objektiv *n*
~ **function** Aberrationsfunktion *f*
~ **theory** Bildfehlertheorie *f*, Seidelsche
  Fehlertheorie *f*, Aberrationstheorie *f*
~ **tolerance** Bildfehlertoleranz *f*
aberrationless s. aberration-free
ablation Ablation *f*, Abtragung *f*
Abney effect Bezold-Abney-Effekt *m*
  (Farbmetrik)
~ **law** Abneysches Gesetz *n (Fotometrie)*
above-water photography
  Überwasserfotografie *f*
abrasion Abrieb *m*
~ **mark** Schramme *f*, Kratzer *m*
~ **protection** Abriebschutz *m*
~ **resistance** Abriebfestigkeit *f*
~-**resistant** abriebfest, abriebbeständig
abrasive Schleifmittel *n*
~ **reduction** Schab[e]retusche *f*
abrupt cut harter Schnitt *m*, Hartschnitt *m*
  (Film, Video)
~ **serif** ungekehlte Serife *f*
  (Buchstabenbild)
~ **transition** s. ~ cut
absence of coma Komafreiheit *f (Optik)*
~ **of distortion** Verzeichnungsfreiheit *f*
~ **of flicker** Flimmerfreiheit *f*
absolute absorption absolute Absorption *f*
~ **address** absolute Adresse *f*
~ **limen** absolute Wahrnehmungsschwelle
  f
~ **quantum efficiency** absoluter
  Quantenwirkungsgrad *m*
~ **refractive index** absolute Brechzahl *f*
~ **temperature scale** Kelvin-Skala *f (der
  absoluten Temperatur)*
~ **threshold** s. ~ limen
absorb/to absorbieren
absorbance, absorbancy Absorbanz *f*,
  optische Dichte *f*
absorbed dose Energiedosis *f*, absorbierte
  Dosis *f (Röntgendosimetrie)*
~ **dose rate** Energiedosisleistung *f*
~ **absorber** Absorber *m*; Vorfilter *n*
  (Röntgenstrahlenschwächung)
absorptance Absorptionsgrad *m*;
  Absorptionsvermögen *n*
absorption Absorption *f*
~ **band** Absorptionsbande *f*
~ **coefficient** Absorptionskoeffizient *m*
  (eines Mediums)
~ **constant** Absorptionskonstante *f*
~ **contrast** Absorptionskontrast *m*
  (Röntgenmikroskopie)
~ **curve** Absorptionskurve *f (z.B. eines
  Filters)*
~ **density distribution**
  Absorptionsdichteverteilung *f*
~ **edge** Absorptionskante *f*

absorption

~ **edge jump ratio** Kantensprungverhältnis n
~ **efficiency** Absorptionseffizienz f
~ **energy** Absorptionsenergie f
~ **factor** Absorptionsfaktor m
~ **filter** Absorptionsfilter n, Massefilter n
~ **hologram** Absorptionshologramm n
~ **image** Absorptionsbild n
~ **index** Absorptionsindex m
~ **line** Absorptionslinie f
~ **line spectrum** Absorptionslinienspektrum n
~ **loss** Absorptionsverlust m
~ **maximum (peak)** Absorptionsmaximum n
~ **photometry** Absorptions[spektral]fotometrie f
~ **region** Absorptionsbereich m
~ **spectroscopy** Absorptionsspektroskopie f
~ **spectrum** Absorptionsspektrum n
absorptive absorptiv
absorptivity Absorptionsvermögen n
abstract class abstrakte Klasse f
~ **pattern** abstraktes Muster n
abstraction Abstraktion f
~ **hierarchy** Abstraktionshierarchie f *(logische Struktur)*
~ **layer (level)** Abstraktionsniveau n *(z.B. eines Multimediasystems)*
acacin[e] Akaziengummi n, Gummiarabikum n
academy aperture (format) Academy-Format n, Standardformat n, Normalfilmformat n *(Kinefilm)*
Academy ratio s. academy aperture
accelerated graphic[s] port beschleunigte Grafikschnittstelle f, beschleunigter Grafikanschluss m *(Datenbussystem)*
accelerating anode Beschleunigeranode f *(Katodenstrahlröhre)*
~ **electrode** Beschleunigungselektrode f
acceleration grid Beschleunigungsgitter n *(Katodenstrahlröhre)*
~ **potential** Beschleunigungspotential n
~ **voltage** Beschleunigungsspannung f, Röhrenspannung f *(Katodenstrahlröhre)*
accelerator Beschleuniger m
~ **card** Beschleunigerkarte f, Beschleunigungskarte f, Grafikbeschleuniger m
accent 1. Hervorhebung f *(z.B. im Layout)*; 2. s. diacritic
accented character Akzentbuchstabe m
accentuation Akzentuierung f
acceptance angle Akzeptanzwinkel m *(z.B. eines Objektivs)*
~ **of writing** Beschreibbarkeit f *(z.B. von Fotopapier)*
access control Zugriffskontrolle f
~ **control field** Zugriffssteuerfeld n
~ **delay** Zugriffsverzögerung f
~ **speed** Zugriffsgeschwindigkeit f
~ **time** Zugriffszeit f

~ **unit** Zugriffseinheit f
~ **unit layer** Zugriffseinheitsschicht f *(Videokompression)*
accessory device Zubehörgerät n
~ **shoe** Zubehörschuh m
~ **system** Zubehörsystem n, Zubehörpalette f
accidental error Zufallsfehler m *(Bilddatenkompression)*
accommodate/to akkommodieren, anpassen
accommodation Akkommodation f, Anpassung f, Brechwerteinstellung f [des Auges]
~ **condition** Akkommodationszustand m
~ **range** Akkommodationsbereich m, Akkommodationsgebiet n
~ **reflex (response)** Akkommodationsreflex m
~ **state** Akkommodationszustand m
~ **time** Akkommodationszeit f
~ **width** Akkommodationsbreite f
accommodative akkommodativ
~ **ability** Akkommodationsfähigkeit f
accompanying sound Begleitton m
accumulator Akkumulator m, Akku m
~ **array** s. Hough domain
accuracy in details Detailtreue f
~ **of focus** Fokussiergenauigkeit f
~ **of resolution** Auflösungsgenauigkeit f
acetate 1. Acetat n; 2. Celluloseacetat n; 3. s. animation cel
~ **base** Acetatunterlage f
~ **base filter** Acetatfilter n
~ **cel** s. animation cel
~ **film** 1. Acetatfilm m, Celluloseacetatfilm m; Sicherheitsfilm m, Safety-Film m; 2. Acetatfolie f
~ **roll film** Acetatrollfilm m
~ **sleeve [protector]** Klarsichthülle f, Sichthülle f, Klarsichttasche f, Acetatschlauch m
acetic acid Essigsäure f
acetone Aceton n, Dimethylketon n
acetylated cellulose Acetylcellulose f, Celluloseacetat n
achromat s. 1. achromatic lens; 2. achromatic objective
achromatic 1. achromatisch, unbunt *(Kolorimetrie)*; 2. achromatisch, farb[fehler]korrigiert *(Objektiv)*
~ **color** achromatische (unbunte) Farbe f, graue Farbe f
~ **color removal** Graustufenersatz m, Unbuntaufbau m
~ **condenser** achromatischer Kondensor m
~ **doublet [lens]** achromatisches Dublett n
~ **doublet supplementary lens** Vorsatzachromat m
~ **lens** achromatisches (farbkorrigiertes) Objektiv n, farb[fehler]korrigiertes Objektiv n
~ **light** achromatisches Licht n
~ **objective** achromatisches Objektiv n

~ **point** Weißpunkt *m*, Unbuntpunkt *m* *(Farbmetrik)*
~ **prism** achromatisches Prisma *n*
~ **sensation** Unbuntempfindung *f*
~ **stimulus** Unbuntreiz *m*
~ **telescope** achromatisches Teleskop *n*
achromatism 1. Achromatismus *m*, Farbfehlerfreiheit *f (Optik)*; 2. Achroma[top]sie *f*, Achromatismus *m*, Zapfenblindheit *f*, totale Farbenblindheit *f*
achromatization Achromatisierung *f*
achromatize/to achromatisieren, farbkorrigieren
achromatopsia *s.* achromatism 2.
acid- and lignin-free paper säure- und holzfreies Papier *n*
~-**free paper** säurefreies Papier *n*
acidity Säuregrad *m (z.B. eines Fixierbades)*
Acmade code Acmade-Codierung *f (von Kinefilm)*
~ **machine** Acmade-Nummeriermaschine *f*
~ **number** Acmade-Codierung *f*
acoustic beam Schallstrahl *m*
~ **coupler** Akustikkoppler *m* *(Telekommunikation)*
~ **dipole** akustischer Dipol *m*
~ **feedback** akustische Rückkopplung *f*
~ **field** Schall[wellen]feld *n*, Tonfeld *n*
~ **image** Schallbild *n*, akustisches Bild *n*
~ **imaging** akustische Bildgebung *f*, Ultraschallsichtverfahren *n*
~ **impedance** akustische Impedanz *f*, akustischer Wellenwiderstand *m*, Schallwellenwiderstand *m (Sonografie)*
~ **microscopy** akustische Mikroskopie *f*
~ **pulse** Schallimpuls *m*
~ **reflection** Schallreflexion *f*
~ **signal** akustisches Signal *n*, Tonsignal *n*, Audiosignal *n*, Schallsignal *n*
~ **speckle** Speckle-Störung *f (Radar, Sonografie)*
~ **surface wave** akustische Oberflächenwelle *f*
~ **tomography** akustische Tomografie *f*
~ **wave** Schallwelle *f*, akustische Welle *f*
~ **window** Schallfenster *n (Sonografie)*
acoustical energy Schallenergie *f*
~ **hologram** akustisches Hologramm *n*
~ **holography** akustische Holografie *f*
~ **imaging** Schallbildgebung *f*
~ **noise** akustisches Rauschen *n*
acousto-optic deflection akustooptische Lichtablenkung *f*, Ultraschall-Lichtablenkung *f*
~-**optic deflector** akustooptische Ablenkeinrichtung *f*
~-**optic diffraction** akustooptische Beugung *f*
~-**optic filter** akustooptisches Filter *n*
~-**optic modulator** akustooptischer Modulator *m (Lasertechnik)*
~-**optic Q-switch** akustooptischer Güteschalter *m (Lasertechnik)*
~-**optic scanner** akustooptischer Scanner *m*
~-**optic shutter** akustooptischer Verschluss *m*
~-**optic signal processing** akustooptische Signalverarbeitung *f*
~-**optic tunable filter** abstimmbares akustooptisches Filter *n*
~-**optical** akustooptisch
~-**optical beam splitter** akustooptischer Strahlenteiler *m*
~-**optical modulation** akustooptische Modulation *f*
~-**optical tomography** Durchschallungstomografie *f*, Ultraschalltomografie *f*, Sonotomografie *f*, Ultraschall-Schnittbildverfahren *n*
acoustooptics Akustooptik *f*
acoustothermometry Akustothermometrie *f*
acquire/to akquirieren, erfassen, aufnehmen; importieren *(z.B. Bilddaten)*
acquired color vision defect erworbene Farbsinnstörung *f*
acquisition Akquisition *f*, Erfassung *f*, Aufnahme *f*, Aufzeichnung *f*
~ **device** Aufnahmegerät *n*, Aufzeichnungsgerät *n*
~ **direction** Aufnahmerichtung *f*
~ **format** Aufzeichnungsformat *n*, Aufnahmeformat *n*
~ **radar** Zielerfassungsradar *n*, Erfassungsradar *n*
~ **rate** Aufnahmefrequenz *f*
~ **speed** Aufnahmegeschwindigkeit *f*
~ **time** Akquisitionsdauer *f*, Akquisitionszeit *f*; Bildakquisitionszeit *f*, Bildaufnahmezeit *f*
across the grain quer zur Faserrichtung (Papierlaufrichtung), Dehnrichtung *f (von Druckpapier)*
acrylic glass Acrylglas *n (optischer Werkstoff)*
act of perception Wahrnehmungsvorgang *m*
actinic aktinisch
~ **light** aktinisches Licht *n*
~ **radiation** aktinische Strahlung *f*
actinism, actinity Aktinität *f*
actinometer Aktinometer *n*
action button Schaltfläche *f (Computer)*
~ **matte** Vordergrundmaskenfilm *m (Trickkinematografie)*
~ **of light** Licht[ein]wirkung *f*
~ **photography** Ereignisfotografie *f*, Actionfotografie *f*
~ **potential** Aktionspotential *n (Neuroinformatik)*
~ **shot** Aktionsaufnahme *f*
~ **still** Standfoto *n*, Filmstandbild *n*, Szenenfoto *n*
actioner Aktionsfilm *m*

activation

activation energy Aktivierungsenergie f *(Fotodetektor)*
~ **level** Aktivierungszustand m *(neuronales Netz)*
activator Aktivator m
~ **bath (solution)** Aktivatorbad n
active amplifier Abzweigverstärker m *(Kabelfernsehen)*
~ **autofocus [system]** aktiver Autofokus
~ **camera** aktive Kamera f
~ **contour** aktive Kontur f *(Segmentierung)*
~ **contour model** aktives Konturmodell n
~ **filter** aktives Filter n
~ **illumination** aktive Beleuchtung f
~ **layer** aktive Schicht f *(Halbleiterlaser)*
~ **line** aktive (bildgebende) Zeile f *(Video)*
~ **line length** aktive Zeilenlänge f
~ **line period (time)** aktive Zeilendauer f
~ **loudspeaker** Aktivlautsprecher m
~ **matrix** aktive Matrix f *(Flüssigkristallanzeige)*
~-**matrix addressing** aktive Adressierung f
~-**matrix display** Aktivmatrixbildschirm m, aktiver Bildschirm m, aktives Display n, TFT-Bildschirm m, TFT-Monitor m
~-**matrix LCD (liquid-crystal display)** Aktivmatrix-Flüssigkristallanzeige f
~-**matrix thin-film transistor** Aktivmatrix-Dünnfilmtransistor m
~ **medium** aktives Medium n *(Laser)*
~ **memory** Arbeitsspeicher m, Hauptspeicher m
~ **optical triangulation** aktive Triangulation f
~ **optics** aktive Optik f *(Teleskopsteuerung)*
~ **picture area** aktive Bildfläche f *(Fernsehschirm)*
~ **picture information** aktiver Bildinhalt m
~ **picture portion** aktiver Bildbereich m *(Fernsehschirm)*
~ **pixel** aktives Pixel n
~ **pixel area** aktive Pixelfläche f
~ **pixel sensor** aktiver Pixelsensor m; CMOS-Bildsensor m
~ **radar** aktives Radar n
~ **Raman scattering** aktive Raman-Streuung f
~ **region** 1. aktiver Bereich m *(Halbleiterlaser)*; 2. s. ~ video signal
~ **scan line** s. active line
~ **sensor** aktiv sendender Sensor m
~ **snake** aktive Kontur f *(Segmentierung)*
~ **storage** Aktivspeicher m
~ **video line** aktive (bildgebende) Zeile f *(Video)*
~ **video signal** aktives Videosignal n, aktiver Bildinhalt m
~ **vision** aktives Sehen n
~ **window** aktives Fenster (Bildschirmfenster) n *(grafische Benutzerschnittstelle)*
activity s. radioactivity
actual focal spot wahrer Brennfleck m

~ **location** Originaldrehort m, Originalschauplatz m *(Filmarbeit)*
~ **resolution** reale Auflösung f *(Bildschirm)*
actuator Aktuator m, Aktor m, elektromechanisches Bauelement n
acuity Sehschärfe f, Schärfe f, Visus m
~ **distribution** Schärfeverteilung f
~ **of the eye** s. acuity
~ **test** Sehschärfetest m
~ **to detail** Detailerkennbarkeit f
acutance Schärfe f, Bildschärfe f, Abbildungsschärfe f; Kontur[en]schärfe f; Kantenschärfe f *(s.a. unter sharpness)*
~ **value** Schärfegrad m
acute accent Akut m *(Betonungszeichen)*
~ **triangle** spitzwinkliges Dreieck n
~ **vision** scharfes Sehen n
acyclic graph azyklischer Graph m
AD conversion s. analog-digital conversion [process]
adapt/to adaptieren, anpassen
adaptability Adaptationsvermögen n, Adaptabilität f
adaptation Adaptation f, Adaption f, Anpassung f
~ **field** Adaptations[daten]feld n
~ **field control** Adaptationsfeldsteuerung f
~ **luminance** Adaptationsleuchtdichte f
~ **parameter** Adaptationsparameter m
~ **state** Adaptationszustand m
adapter Adapter m
~ **cable** Adapterkabel n
~ **cassette** Adapterkassette f, Kassettenadapter m
~ **cord** Adapterkabel n
~ **ring** Adapterring m, Anpassring m
~ **tube** Adaptertubus m
adaption s. adaptation
adaptive adaptiv
~ **algorithm** adaptiver Algorithmus m
~ **antenna** adaptive Antenne f *(Radar)*
~ **arithmetic coding** adaptiv-arithmetische Codierung f
~ **block quantization** adaptive Blockquantisierung f
~ **coding** adaptive Codierung f
~ **compression** adaptive Kompression f
~ **DCT [coding]** adaptive diskrete Kosinustransformation f
~ **differential pulse code modulation** adaptive differentielle Pulscodemodulation f
~ **edge detection** adaptive Kantendetektion f
~ **filter** adaptives Filter n
~ **filtering** adaptive Filterung f
~ **Huffman [en]coding** adaptive Huffman-Codierung f
~ **image segmentation** adaptive Bildsegmentierung f
~ **median filter** adaptives Medianfilter n
~ **neighborhood filter** adaptives Nachbarschaftsfilter n

~ **noise suppression** adaptive Rauschunterdrückung *f*
~ **optics** adaptive (selbstkorrigierende) Optik *f*
~ **pattern recognition** adaptive Mustererkennung *f*
~ **prediction** adaptive Prädiktion *f*
~ **predictor** adaptiver Prädiktor *m*
~ **quantization** adaptive Quantisierung *f*
~ **segmentation** adaptive Segmentierung *f*
~ **signal processing** adaptive Signalverarbeitung *f*
~ **smoothing** adaptive Glättung *f*
~ **spatiotemporal filtering** adaptive raumzeitliche Filterung *f*
~ **surface data compression** adaptive Flächendatenkompression *f*
~ **threshold** adaptiver Schwellenwert *m*
~ **thresholding** adaptive Schwellenwertbildung *f*
~ **time** Adaptationszeit *f*
~ **transform coding** adaptive Transformationscodierung *f*
adaptivity Adaptivität *f*
adaptometer Adaptometer *n*
adaptor *s.* adapter
add-in Zusatzmodul *n*, Einsteckmodul *n*, Plug-In *n*
addition of matrices Matrixaddition *f*
additional dialog[ue] recording Nachsynchronisation *f*, Synchronbearbeitung *f*
~ **exposure** Zusatzbelichtung *f*
~ **light** Zusatzlicht *n*
~ **light source** Zusatzlichtquelle *f*
~ **lighting** Zusatzbeleuchtung *f*
~ **noise** Zusatzrauschen *n* *(z.B. in Lawinenfotodioden)*
~ **photography** Nachdreh *m* *(Filmarbeit)*
additive color Additionsfarbe *f*
~ **color film** additiver Farbfilm *m*
~ **color matching**, ~ **color mixing (mixture)** additive (optische) Farbmischung *f (Farbmetrik)*
~ **color photography** additive Farbfotografie *f*
~ **color process** Farbverfahren *n* mit additiver Farbmischung
~ **color system** additives Farbmodell *n*, RGB-Farbmodell *n*
~ **color viewer** Farbmischprojektor *m* *(analoge Bildbearbeitung)*
~ **composition** *s.* ~ color matching
~ **electronic noise** *s.* ~ noise
~ **filter** additives Filter *n*
~ **filtering** additive Filterung *f*
~ **lamphouse** additives Lampenhaus *n*
~ **matching** additive (optische) Nachmischung *f*
~ **noise** additives Rauschen *n*; additives weißes Rauschen *n*, Gaußsches (gaußverteiltes) Rauschen *n*
~ **primary [color]** additive (spektrale) Grundfarbe *f*, additive Primärfarbe *f*
~ **printer** additiver Kopierer *m*
~ **printing** additives Kopier[verfahr]en
~ **random noise** additives Zufallsrauschen *n*
~ **white Gaussian noise** additives weißes Gaußsches (gaußverteiltes) Rauschen *n*
additivity Additivität *f*
address Adresse *f*
~ **bus** Adressbus *m (Computer)*
~ **code** Adressencode *m*
~ **field** Adressfeld *n*
~ **reader (reading machine)** Anschriftenlesegerät *n*
~ **signal** Adressiersignal *n (Bildplatte)*
~ **track** Steuerspur *f*, Kontrollspur *f (Videoband)*
addressability Ansteuerbarkeit *f*, Adressierbarkeit *f*
addressable ansteuerbar, adressierbar
~ **pixel** ansteuerbares (adressierbares) Pixel *n*
addressing Adressierung *f*, Ansteuerung *f*
~ **space** Adressraum *m*
adhesion Adhäsion *f*
~ **force** Adhäsionskraft *f*
~ **promoter** Haftvermittler *m*
adhesive force Adhäsionskraft *f*
~ **layer** Haftschicht *f*, Substratschicht *f (Filmherstellung)*
~ **tape** Klebeband *n*, Klebestreifen *m*; Filmklebeband *n*
adjacency Nachbarschaft *f*, Adjazenz *f (Topologie)*
~ **algorithm** Nachbarschaftsalgorithmus *m*
~ **effect** Nachbareffekt *m*, Randeffekt *m*, Kanteneffekt *m*
~ **graph** Nachbarschaftsgraph *m*, Adjazenzgraph *m*
~ **matrix** Adjazenzmatrix *f*
adjacent adjazent, benachbart
~ **block** Nachbarblock *m*
~ **channel** Nachbarkanal *m*
~ **channel interference** Nachbarkanalstörung *f*
~ **pixel** Nachbarpixel *n*, Nachbarbildpunkt *m*
~ **polygon** Nachbarpolygon *n*
adjust/to [ad]justieren, einstellen, verstellen, einrichten *(s.a. align/to)*
adjustability Verstellbarkeit *f*
adjustable aperture variable Blende *f*
~ **aperture diaphragm** einstellbare (verstellbare) Aperturblende *f*
~ **disk shutter** verstellbare Sektorenblende *f*
~ **masking blade** verstellbare Formatblende *f*
~ **masking easel** Vergrößerungskassette *f*, Vergrößerungsrahmen *m*, Kopierrahmen *m*
~ **monopod** verstellbares Einbein[stativ] *n*
adjusting ring Stellring *m*
adjustment error Einstellfehler *m*

adjustment

~ **knob** Triebknopf *m*; Feintrieb *m*, Feinstellschraube *f*
~ **mark** Justiermarke *f*
admission control algorithm Zugangskontrollalgorithmus *m* *(Multimediaserver)*
ADR *s.* automatic dialogue replacement
adsorb/to adsorbieren
adsorbent, adsorber Adsorber *m*
adsorption Adsorption *f*
adsorptive adsorptiv
advance lever Transporthebel *m*
~ **screening (showing)** Vorauführung *f*
~ **television** Hochzeilenfernsehen *n*, hochzeiliges (hochauflösendes) Fernsehen *n*
~ **width** Zeichendicke *f*, Dicke *f* *(Typografie)*
advanced colorimetry höhere Farbmetrik *f*
Advanced Photo System *halbdigitales Kleinbild-Fotosystem mit verbessertem Komfort*
advanced replay head voreilender Wiedergabekopf *m*
~ **sync pulse** voreilendes Synchronisiersignal *n* *(Magnetbildaufzeichnung)*
Advanced Television Standards (System) Committee *US-Standardisierungsgremium im Bereich des hochauflösenden Fernsehens*
adventure game Abenteuerspiel *n* *(interaktives Video)*
advertising photo[graph] Werbefoto *n*, Reklamefoto *n*
~ **photographer** Werbefotograf *m*
~ **photography** Werbefotografie *f*
AE lock *s.* aperture-exposure lock
AE system *s.* autoexposure feature
aerial Antenne *f* *(s.a. unter* antenna*)*
~ **archaelogy** Luftbildarchäologie *f*
~ **camera** Luftbildkamera *f*
~ **camera lens** Luftbildobjektiv *n*
~ **color film** Luftbildfarbfilm *m*
~ **color photograph** Farb-Luftaufnahme *f*, Farb-Luftbild *n*
~ **film** Luftbildfilm *m*
~ **film speed** Luftbildfilmempfindlichkeit *f*
~ **frame camera** Reihenmesskamera *f*, Reihenmesskammer *f*
~ **haze** atmosphärischer Dunst m, Luftlicht *n*
~ **image** 1. Luftbild *n*, Luftaufnahme *f*; 2. Luftbild *n* *(Optik)*
~ **image location** Luftbildort *m* *(Optik)*
~ **image optical printer** Tricktisch *m*
~ **image segmentation** Luftbildsegmentierung *f*
~ **image sequence** Luftbildsequenz *f*
~ **imagery** Luftbildmaterial *n*
~ **imaging** Luftbildaufnahme *f*
~ **infrared image (photograph)** Infrarotluftaufnahme *f*

~ **map** Luftbildkarte *f*
~ **mapping** Luftbildkartierung *f*
~ **mapping photography** Luftbildfotogrammetrie *f;* Aerofotogrammetrie *f*
~ **mosaic** Bildskizze *f*; Bildplan *m* *(Luftbildmessung)*
~ **mosaic map** Bildplankarte *f*
~ **perspective** Luftperspektive *f*
~ **photo interpretation** Luftbildauswertung *f*, Luftbildinterpretation *f*
~ **photogrammetry** Aerofotogrammetrie *f*, Luftbildmessung *f*
~ **photography** Luftbildfotografie *f*, Aerofotografie *f*
~ **photography laboratory** Luftbildlabor[atorium] *n*
~ **reconnaissance** Luftaufklärung *f*, Lufterkundung *f*
~ **reconnaissance camera** Luftaufklärungskamera *f*
~ **reconnaissance picture** Luftaufklärungsfoto *n*
~ **reconnaissance survey** *s.* ~ reconnaissance
~ **shot** Luftbild *n*, Luftaufnahme *f*
~ **stereo pair** Stereo-Luftbild *n*
~ **surveillance** Luftüberwachung *f*
~ **surveillance photo[graph]** Luftbild *n*, Luftaufnahme *f*
~ **survey** Luftaufklärung *f*, Lufterkundung *f*
~ **survey film** Luftbildfilm *m*
~ **survey flight** Bildflug *m*
~ **technical camera** Luftbildkamera *f*
aerocartographer Aerokartograf *m*
aerographic film Luftbildfilm *m*
aerophoto Luftbild *n*, Luftaufnahme *f*
aerophotogrammetry Aerofotogrammetrie *f*, Luftbildmessung *f*
aerophotography Aerofotografie *f*, Luftbildfotografie *f*
aerotriangulation Luftbildtriangulation *f*, Aerotriangulation *f*
AF *s.* autofocus
AF area mode selector Messfeld-Betriebsartenwähler *m*
AF coupling AF-Kupplung *f*
AF start button AF-Starttaste *f*
affine camera affine Kamera *f (maschinelle Bilderkennung)*
~ **camera model** affines Kameramodell *n*
~ **image** affine Abbildung *f*
~ **invariance** affine Invarianz *f* *(Computergrafik)*
~ **mapping** affine (verwandte) Abbildung *f*, Dreipunkt-Abbildung *f (geometrische Datenverarbeitung)*
~ **model** affines Modell *n*
~ **motion** affine Bewegung *f*
~ **projection** affine Projektion *f*
~ **transformation** affine Transformation *f*
afocal afokal; brennpunktlos

~ **attachment** Televorsatz *m*, Televorsatzlinse *f*
~ **filter** afokales Filter *n*
~ **imaging** afokale Abbildung *f*
~ **lens** afokales Objektiv *n*
~ **system** afokales System *n*
aftereffect Nacheffekt *m (Sehen)*
afterglow Nachleuchten *n*, Persistenz *f*
afterimage [positives] Nachbild *n*
~ **effect** Nachbildwirkung *f*
afterripening Nachreifung *f*, Nachdigestion *f*, chemische Reifung (Sensibilisierung) *f (Emulsionsherstellung)*
aftertreatment Nachbehandlung *f (z.B. von Filmnegativen)*
against the grain quer zur Faserrichtung (Papierlaufrichtung), Dehnrichtung *f (von Druckpapier)*
~**-the-light effect** Gegenlichteffekt *m*
age resistance Alterungsbeständigkeit *f (z.B. von Filmmaterial)*
aged film gealterter Film *m*
agglomeration Agglomeration *f*, Zusammenballung *f (z.B. von Bildpunkten)*
aggregate object zusammengesetztes Objekt *n*
agitation [of the bath] Badbewegung *f (Fotoverarbeitung)*
AGP *s.* accelerated graphic port
AgX *s.* silver halide
AI *s.* artificial intelligence
aided eye bewaffnetes Auge *n*
aim [at]/to [an]visieren
aiming error Visierfehler *m*
~ **telescope** Zielfernrohr *n*, Visierfernrohr *n*
air/to ausstrahlen, senden, übertragen
air 1. Luft *f (s.a. under* aerial*)*; 2. *s.* blank space
~ **drying** Lufttrocknung *f (z.B. von Fotopapier)*
~ **gap** Luftspalt *m*, Interferrikum *n (z.B. zwischen Magnetpolen)*; Luftraum *m*, Luftabstand *m (zwischen Linsenelementen)*
~ **gap technique** Groedel-Technik *f (der Streustrahlenminderung in der Medizinbildgebung)*
~**-glass interface** Glas-Luft-Fläche *f*
~ **humidity** *s.* ~ moisture
~ **Kerma** Luftkerma *n (Röntgendosimetrie)*
~ **lens** Luftlinse *f (Objektiv)*
~ **mail stationery** Luftpostpapier *n (Papiersorte)*
~ **moisture** Luftfeuchte *f*, Luftfeuchtigkeit *f*
~ **photograph** Luftbild *n*, Luftaufnahme *f*
~ **photography** Luftbildfotografie *f*, Aerofotografie *f*
~ **route surveillance radar** Flugroutenüberwachungsradar *n*, Flugstreckenüberwachungsradar *n*
~ **surveillance** Luftüberwachung *f*
~**-surveillance radar** Luftraumüberwachungsradar *n*

~ **triangulation** Bildtriangulation *f (Aerofotogrammetrie)*
airborne camera Luftbildkamera *f*, Luftbildkammer *f*
~ **Doppler radar** Flugzeug-Doppler-Radar *n*
~ **imager** flugzeuggetragener Bildsensor *m*
~ **radar** Flugzeugradar *n*, flugzeuggetragenes Radar *n*
~ **scanner** Flugzeugscanner *m*
airbrush Aerograf *m*, Sprühpistole *f*, Feinsprüher *m*, Luftpinsel *m (Bildbearbeitungswerkzeug)*
airbrushing 1. Aerografie *f*, Airbrush-Technik *f*; 2. Spritzretusche *f*
aircraft image Flugzeugaufnahme *f*
~ **meteorological radar** flugzeuggetragenes Wetterradar *n*
~ **simulator** Flugsimulator *m*
airlight Himmelslicht *n*
airline ticket reader Flugscheinlesegerät *n*
airphoto interpretation Luftbildauswertung *f*, Luftbildinterpretation *f*
airport surveillance radar Flughafenüberwachungsradar *n*, Airport-Rundsichtradar *n*
airspace *s.* air gap
Airy disk [Airy-]Beugungsscheibchen *n*, Airy-Scheibe *f*, zentrales Beugungsmaximum *n (Optik)*
~ **function** Airy-Funktion *f*
~ **pattern** Airysches Beugungsbild *f*
Airy's tangent condition Airysche Tangensbedingung *f (Optik)*
Akima interpolation Akima-Interpolation *f (Computergrafik)*
Albada [view]finder Albada-Sucher *m*; Leuchtrahmensucher *m*, Spiegelrahmensucher *m*
albedo Albedo *f*, Rückstrahl[ungs]vermögen *n*, Rückstrahlungsgrad *m*, Reflektivität *f*
Albert effect Albert-Effekt *m (fotografische Umkehrbilderzeugung)*
albertype Albertotypie *f (Lichtdruckerzeugnis)*
Albertypy Albertotypie *f (Lichtdruckverfahren)*
album Album *n*
~ **page** Albumseite *f*
albumen glass plate Albuminplatte *f*
~ **negative process** Albuminverfahren *n*
~ **paper** Albuminpapier *n*, Eiweißpapier *n*
~ **print** Albumin[papier]abzug *m*
albumenized paper *s.* albumen paper
alcohol damping system Alkoholfeuchtung *f (Druck)*
alexandrite laser Alexandritlaser *m*
algebraic coding algebraische Codierung *f*
~ **distance** algebraischer Abstand *m*
~ **granulometry** algebraische Granulometrie *f*
~ **half-space** algebraischer Halbraum *m*

algebraic

~ **reconstruction** algebraische Rekonstruktion *f*
~ **spline** algebraische Spline-Kurve *f*
~ **transformation** algebraische Transformation *f*
algorithm Algorithmus *m*, Rechenvorschrift *f*
~ **animation** Algorithmenanimation *f*, Algorithmusanimation *f*
algorithmic algorithmisch
~ **image generation** algorithmische Bilderzeugung *f*
algorithmize/to algorithmieren
alias *s.* aliasing
~ **component** Aliaskomponente *f*
~-**free** aliasfrei
~-**free sampling** aliasfreie Abtastung *f*
aliased frequency Aliasing-Frequenz *f*, Faltungsfrequenz *f*
aliasing Aliasing *n*, Alias[effekt] *m*, Verfremdung *f*, Verfremdungseffekt *m*; Banduberlappungseffekt *m*; Rückfaltungsverzerrung *f* *(Abtastfehler)*
~ **artifact** Aliasstörung *f*, Aliasstruktur *f*
~ **defect** *s.* ~ error
~ **effect** *s.* aliasing
~ **error** Aliasfehler *m*, Überlappungsfehler *m*
~ **spectrum** Aliasspektrum *n*
align/to ausrichten *(s.a.* adjust/to*)*
align center Mittelachsensatz *m*, Mittelachse *f*, zentrierter Satz *m* *(Typografie)*
~ **left** linksbündiger Flattersatz *m*
~ **right** rechtsbündiger Flattersatz *m*
aligned bundle kohärentes Bündel *f* *(Faseroptik)*
alignment Ausrichtung *f*; Schriftausrichtung *f*; Passung *f (z.B. von Bildern);* Zentrierung *f (z.B. von Linsenelementen)*
~ **coil** Abstimmspule *f*, Justierspule *f* *(Katodenstrahlröhre)*
~ **laser** Ausrichtlaser *m*, Justierlaser *m*
~ **layer** Ausrichtungsschicht *f* *(Flüssigkristallanzeige)*
~ **level** Bezugspegel *m*
~ **microscope** Justiermikroskop *n*
~ **tape** Messband *n*, Betriebsmessband *n*, Bezugsband *n (Videotechnik)*
~ **telescope** Flucht[ungsprüf]fernrohr *n*
alkali Alkali *n*
~ **carbonate** Alkalicarbonat *n*
~ **halide** Alkalihalogenid *n*
~ **halide solution** Alkalihalogenidlösung *f*
~ **metal** Alkalimetall *n*
~ **nitrate** Alkalinitrat *n*
alkaline alkalisch
~ **battery** Alkalibatterie *f*
~ **paper** säurefreies Papier *n*
alkalinity Alkalität *f*
all-around film Universalfilm *m*

~ **capital letters** Kapitale *f*, Kapitalschrift *f*, Majuskelschrift *f*, Großbuchstabenschrift *f*
~-**color film** panchromatischer Film *m*, Panfilm *m*
~-**digital** volldigital
~-**electronic camera** vollelektronische Kamera *f*
~-**in-one device** *s.* multifunction printer
~-**metal camera** Ganzmetallkamera *f*
~-**metal housing** Ganzmetallgehäuse *n*
~-**mode depth-of-field preview button** Abblendtaste *f*
~ **points addressable** *Grafikmodus z.B. eines Laserdruckers, der es ermöglicht, sämtliche Bildpunkte zu adressieren*
~-**purpose developer** Universalentwickler *m*
~-**signal signal processing** volldigitale Signalverarbeitung *f*
~-**sky camera** Großfeldkamera *f* *(Astrofotografie)*
~-**text document** Textdokument *n*
alley Spaltenzwischenraum *m (Layout)*
allocation problem Zuordnungsproblem *n*
allpass filter Allpassfilter *n*
alpha blending Alpha-Blending *n* *(Computergrafik)*
~ **channel** Alphakanal *m*, Transparenzkanal *m*, Maskenkanal *m*, Schablonenkanal *m* *(Computergrafik, Video)*
~ **channeling** Alphakanalsteuerung *f*
~ **mix[ing]** *s.* ~ blending
~ **particle** Alphateilchen *n*
~ **radiation** Alphastrahlen *mpl*, Alphastrahlung *f*
~ **ray** *s.* alpha particle
~ **value** Alpha-Wert *m*
alphabet Alphabet *n*; Zeichenvorrat *m*
~ **letter** Buchstabe *m*
alphageometric[al] alphageometrisch
alphanumeric alphanumerisch, alphamerisch
~ **character** alphanumerisches Zeichen *n*
~ **character recognition** Zeichenerkennung *f*
~ **display (screen)** Datenbildschirm *m*
alphanumerical *s.* alphanumeric
alphanumerics Alphanumerik *f*
altazimuth Altazimut *m(n) (Astrooptik)*
~ **mounting** altazimutale Montierung *f* *(Teleskop)*
alternating burst Schwabbelburst *m*, alternierender Burst *m (Videosignal)*
~ **current** Wechselstrom *m*
~ **current arc** Wechselstrom-Bogenlampe *f*
aluminize/to aluminieren
aluminized mirror Aluminiumspiegel *m*
~ **screen** metallisierte Bildwand *f*
aluminizing Aluminierung *f*
aluminum case Alukoffer *m*
~ **chloride** Aluminiumchlorid *n*
~ **filter** Aluminiumfilter *n*
~ **mirror** Aluminiumspiegel *m*

~ **potassium sulfate**
Kaliumaluminiumsulfat *n*, Kalialaun *n*
(Gelatinehärtungsmittel)
~ **step tablet** Aluminiumtreppe *f*
(Helligkeitsnormierung)
alychne Alychne *f*, lichtlose Ebene *f*
(Kolorimetrie)
amacrine cell Amacrinzelle *f*, amakrine
Zelle *f (der Netzhaut)*
amateur astrophotography
Amateur-Astrofotografie *f*
~ **camera** Amateurkamera *f*
~ **camera lens** Amateurkameraobjektiv *n*
~ **cinematography**
Amateurkinematografie *f*
~ **color film** Amateurfarbfilm *m*
~ **color motion-picture film**
Farb-Schmalfilm *m*
~ **color photography**
Amateur-Farbfotografie *f*
~ **color picture** Amateurfarbfoto *n*
~ **developing tank** Entwicklungsdose *f*,
Filmentwicklungsdose *f*
~ **field** Amateurbereich *m*
~ **film** Amateurfilm *m*
~ **filmmaker** Amateurfilmer *m*,
Filmamateur *m*, Heimfilmer *m*
~ **filmmaking** Amateurfilmproduktion *f*
~ **home motion picture,** ~ **home movie**
Amateurschmalfilm *m*
~ **home moviemaking**
Amateurschmalfilmen *n*
~ **moviemaking** Amateurfilmen *n*
~ **photograph** Amateurfoto *f*
~ **photographer** Amateurfotograf *m*,
Fotoamateur *m*, Freizeitfotograf *m*
~ **photographic** amateurfotografisch
~ **photography** Amateurfotografie *f*
~ **production** Amateurfilmproduktion *f*
~ **snapshot camera**
Amateur-Schnappschusskamera *f*
~ **still film** Amateurfotofilm *m*
~ **studio** Amateurstudio *n*
~ **telescope** Amateurteleskop *n*
~ **video** Amateurvideo *n*
amaurosis Erblindung *f*, Amaurose *f*
amber screen Bernsteinbildschirm *m*
ambience Atmo[sphäre] *f*,
Originalgeräusch *n*, Realgeräusch *n*,
[allgemeines] Umgebungsgeräusch *n*
(Filmarbeit)
ambient brightness Umgebungshelligkeit *f*
~ **color** Umgebungsfarbe *f*
~ **illumination** Umgebungsbeleuchtung *f*
~ **light** Umgebungslicht *n*, Grundlicht *n*,
ambientes Licht *n*
~ **light level** Umgebungslichtpegel *m*
~ **light source** Umgebungslichtquelle *f*
~ **lighting** Umgebungsbeleuchtung *f*
~ **noise** Umgebungsrauschen *n*,
Hintergrundrauschen *n*
~ **reflection** ambiente Reflexion *f*

~ **sound** Untergrundgeräusch *n*,
Hintergrundgeräusch[e] *n[pl]*,
Umfeldgeräusch *n*, Nebengeräusch *n*
~ **thermal noise (sound)** thermisches
Umgebungsrauschen *n*
ambiguous design (figure) ambivalente
Figur *f*, Inversionsfigur *f*, Kippfigur *f*,
Kippbild *n (optische Täuschung)*
amblyopia Amblyopie *f*,
Schwachsichtigkeit *f*
amblyopic amblyop, schwachsichtig
ambrotype process Ambrotypie *f*,
Melanotypie *f*
American National Standards Institute
US-amerikanische Normungsbehörde
~ **Standard Code for Information
Interchange** Amerikanischer
Standardzeichensatz *m* zum
Informationsaustausch *(das
verbreitetste alphanumerische
digitaleTextaustauschformat)*
Ames room Zerr-Raum *m (optische
Täuschung)*
ametropia Ametropie *f*, Fehlsichtigkeit *f*,
Refraktionsanomalie *f*
ametropic fehlsichtig
Amici prism Amici-Prisma *n*,
Dachkant[en]prisma *n*,
Geradsichtprisma *n* [nach Amici]
aminophenol Aminophenol *n*
(Entwicklerchemikalie)
ammonia Ammoniak *n*
~ **fume (vapor)** Ammoniakdampf *m*
ammoniacal emulsion
Ammoniakemulsion *f (Filmherstellung)*
ammonium bichromate
Ammoniumbichromat *n*
~ **bromide** Ammoniumbromid *n*,
Bromammonium *n*
~ **chloride** Ammoniumchlorid *n*
~ **dichromate** *s*. ~ **bichromate**
~ **iodide** Ammoniumiodid *n*
~ **oxalate** Ammoniumoxalat *n*
(Entwicklerchemikalie)
~ **persulfate reducer**
Ammoniumpersulfat-Abschwächer *m*
~ **thiosulfate** Ammoniumthiosulfat *n*
(Fixiermittel)
amodal completion amodale Ergänzung *f*,
Kanisza-Täuschung *f (visuelle
Wahrnehmung)*
amorphous selenium amorphes Selen *n*
(Fotoleiter)
~ **semiconductor** amorpher Halbleiter *m*
~ **silicon** amorphes Silicium *n*
amount 1. Menge *f*; 2. Intensität *f (von
achromatischem Licht)*
~ **of data** Datenmenge *f*
~ **of light** Lichtmenge *f*, Lichtarbeit *f*
ampere Ampere *n (SI-Einheit der
elektrischen Stromstärke)*
ampersand Et-Zeichen *n*, &
amplification factor Verstärkungsfaktor *m*
amplifier Verstärker *m*

amplifier

~ **cascade** Verstärkerkaskade f
~ **noise** Verstärkerrauschen n
amplify/to verstärken (z.B. Signale)
amplitude Amplitude f
~ **analysis** Amplitudenanalyse f
  (Bodendurchdringungsradar)
~ **attenuation** Amplitudendämpfung f
~ **bias** Amplitudenverzerrung f
~ **contrast** Amplitudenkontrast m
  (Elektronenmikroskopie)
~-**contrast microscope**
  Amplitudenkontrastmikroskop n
~ **damping** Amplitudendämpfung f
~ **density** Amplitudendichte f
~ **density distribution**
  Amplitudendichteverteilung f
~ **difference** Amplitudendifferenz f
~ **diffraction grating** Amplitudengitter n
~ **distortion** Amplitudenverzerrung f
~ **distribution** Amplitudenverteilung f
~ **domain** Amplitudenbereich m
~ **Doppler** Amplituden-Doppler m
  (Sonografie)
~ **envelope** Amplituden-Hüllkurve f
~ **error** Amplitudenfehler m
~ **filtering** Amplitudenfilterung f
~ **fluctuation** Amplitudenfluktuation f,
  Amplitudenschwankung f
~-**frequency characteristic (response)**
  Amplituden[frequenz]gang m,
  Amplitudenverlauf m
~ **gradient** Amplitudengradient m
~ **histogram** Amplitudenhistogramm n
~ **hologram** Amplitudenhologramm n
~ **irrelevancy** Amplitudenirrelevanz f
~ **level** Amplitudenhöhe f
~ **limiter** Amplitudenbegrenzer m
~ **linearity** Amplitudenlinearität f
~-**mode ultrasound scanning**
  A-Bild-Sonografie f, A-Mode-Verfahren n, eindimensionale Sonografie f
~-**modulated carrier**
  amplitudenmodulierter Träger m
~-**modulated function**
  amplitudenmodulierte Funktion f
~-**modulated light** amplitudenmoduliertes Licht n
~-**modulated raster**
  amplitudenmodulierter (autotypischer) Raster m, herkömmlicher Raster m
~-**modulated sensor**
  amplitudenmodulierter Sensor m
  (Faseroptik)
~-**modulated signal**
  amplitudenmoduliertes Signal n
~ **modulation** Amplitudenmodulation f
~ **noise** Amplitudenrauschen n
~ **object** Amplitudenobjekt n
~-**phase diagram**
  Amplitude-Phasendiagramm n
  (Elektronenbeugung)
~ **predistortion** Amplitudenvorverzerrung f

~ **presentation** Amplitudenbild n,
  Amplitudendarstellung f
~ **projection** Amplitudenprojektion f
~ **quantization** Amplitudenquantisierung f
~ **range** Amplitudenbereich m
~ **ratio** Amplitudenverhältnis n
~ **reduction** Amplitudendämpfung f
~ **reflection coefficient**
  Amplitudenreflexionskoeffizient m
~ **resolution** Amplitudenauflösung f,
  Amplitudentiefe f
~ **response** Amplitudenverlauf m,
  Amplituden[frequenz]gang m
~ **sampling** Amplitudenabtastung f
~ **scale** Amplitudenskala f
~ **scaling** Amplitudenskalierung f
~ **separator** Amplitudensieb n
~ **shift keying** Amplituden[um]tastung f
~ **specimen** Amplitudenobjekt n
  (Hellfeldmikroskopie)
~ **spectrum** Amplitudenspektrum n
  (Fourier-Analyse)
~ **stability** Amplitudenstabilität f
~ **step** Amplitudenstufe f
~ **structure** Amplitudenstruktur f
~ **trace** Amplitudenschrift f (Filmton)
~ **transmission coefficient**
  Amplitudentransmissionskoeffizient m
~ **transmittance** Amplitudentransmission f
  (Holografie)
~ **value** Amplitudenwert m
~ **variation** Amplitudenschwankung f,
  Amplitudenfluktuation f
~ **vector** Amplitudenvektor m
~ **velocity** Amplitudengeschwindigkeit f
~ **zone plate** Amplitudenzonenplatte f
  (Röntgenmikroskopie)
anaglyph Anaglyphbild n
~ **glasses** Anaglyphenbrille f,
  Farb[filter]brille f, Rotgrünbrille f
~ **system, anaglyphic method**
  Anaglyphenverfahren n
  (Stereobildbetrachtung)
anaglyphic print Anaglyphendruck m
analog analog
~ **amplifier** analoger Verstärker m
~ **camera** Analogkamera f, analoge Kamera f
~ **circuit** analoger Schaltkreis m
~ **computer** Analogrechner m, analoger Computer m
~ **data** Analogdaten pl, analoge Daten pl
~-**digital conversion [process]**
  Analog-Digital-Umsetzung f,
  Analog-Digital-Wandlung f,
  Digitalisierung f
~-**digital converter**
  Analog-Digital-Signalwandler m,
  Analog-Digital-Umsetzer m
~-**digital interface**
  Analog-Digital-Schnittstelle f
~ **display** Analoganzeige f;
  Analogbildschirm m, analoger Bildschirm m

~ **domain** Analogbereich *m*
~ **filter** Analogfilter *n*, analoges Filter *n*; zeitkontinuierliches Filter *n*
~ **filtering** Analogfilterung *f*, analoge Filterung *f*
~ **Fourier transform** analoge Fourier-Transformation *f*
~ **image** Analogbild *n*, analoges Bild *n*
~ **image processing** analoge Bildverarbeitung *f*
~ **image transformation** analoge Bildtransformation *f*
~ **input** Analogeingang *m*; Analogeingabe[einheit] *f*
~ **interface** analoge Schnittstelle *f*
~ **magnetic tape recording** Analog-Tonbandaufzeichnung *f*
~ **modulation** analoge Modulation *f*
~ **monitor** Analogmonitor *m*; Analogbildschirm *m*, analoger Bildschirm *m*
~ **noise** analoges Rauschen *n*
~ **photography** Analogfotografie *f*
~ **proof** Analogproof *m (Druck)*
~ **receiver** Analogempfänger *m*
~ **recorder** Analogrecorder *m*
~ **recording** Analogaufzeichnung *f*
~ **scan converter** analoger Scankonverter *m*
~ **signal** Analogsignal *n*, analoges (analytisches) Signal *n*
~ **signal processing** Analogsignalverarbeitung *f*
~ **sound** Analogton *m*
~ **sound recording** analoge Tonaufnahme *f*
~ **sound track** Analogtonspur *f*
~ **stereoplotter** Stereoautograf *m*
~ **storage** analoge Speicherung *f*
~ **switcher** Analogmischer *m*, analoges Bildmischpult *m (Video)*
~ **tape** Analogband *n*
~ **technology** Analogtechnik *f*
~ **television** Analogfernsehen *n*, analoges Fernsehen *n*
~ **television set** analoges Fernsehgerät *n*
~ **television signal** analoges Fernsehsignal *n*
~ **television system** analoges Fernsehsystem *n*
~-**to-digital** *s.* analog-digital
~ **transmission** Analogübertragung *f*
~ **value** Analogwert *m*
~ **video** analoges Video *n*, Analogvideo *n*
~ **video cassette recorder** analoger Videokassettenrecorder *m*
~ **video editing** analoge Videonachbearbeitung *f*, analoger Videoschnitt *m*
~ **video format** analoges Videoformat *n*
~ **video production equipment** analoge Videoproduktionstechnik *f*
~ **video recorder** analoger Videorecorder *m*
~ **video signal** analoges Videosignal *n*

~ **vision mixer** *s.* ~ switcher
analysis Analyse *f*
~ **filter** Analysefilter *n*; Prädiktionsfehlerfilter *n*
~ **filter bank** Analysefilterbank *f*
~-**synthesis [image] coding** Analyse-Synthese-Codierung *f*, modellbasierte Bildcodierung *f*
~ **window** Analysefenster *n*
analytic geometry analytische Geometrie *f*
~ **phase** analytische Phase *f (z.B. eines Kompressionsalgorithmus)*
~ **signal** *s.* analog signal
~ **solid modeling** analytische Festkörpermodellierung *f*
analytical density analytische Farbdichte *f*
~ **electron microscope** analytisches Elektronenmikroskop *n*
~ **function** analytische Funktion *f*
~ **imaging technique** Bildanalyseverfahren *n*
~ **microscopy** analytische Mikroskopie *f*
~ **photogrammetry** analytische Fotogrammetrie *f*
~ **shading model** analytisches Schattierungsmodell *n*
~ **spectrometer** Analysenspektrometer *n*
analyzer Analysator *m*
anamorphic 1. anamorphotisch, anamorph, verzerrt; 2. *s.* ~ image; 3. *s.* ~ frame; 4. *s.* ~ lens
~ **[film] format** Breitwandformat *n*
~ **cinematography** anamorphotische Kinematografie *f*
~ **conversion** anamorphotische Wandlung *f*
~ **distortion** anamorphotische Verzerrung *f*
~ **expansion lens** [optischer] Entzerrungsvorsatz *m*, Wiedergabeanamorphot *m*
~ **frame** anamorphotisches Bild *n* (Kinefilm)
~ **image** anamorphotisches (verzerrtes) Bild *n*
~ **image formation** anamorphotische Abbildung *f*
~ **lens (optics)** anamorphotisches Objektiv (System) *n*, Anamorphot *m*, anamorphotischer Vorsatz *m*, Zerrlinse *f*, Zerroptik *f*, Zylinderlinsenobjektiv *n*, Zylinderoptik *f*
~ **photography** anamorphotische Fotografie *f*
~ **picture format** anamorphotisches Bildformat *n*
~ **prism pair** anamorphotisches Prismenpaar *n*
~ **projection (projector) lens** Wiedergabeanamorphot *m*, [optischer] Entzerrungsvorsatz *m*
~ **release print** anamorphotische Filmkopie *f*
~ **squeeze** anamorphotische Verzerrung *f*
~ **system** *s.* ~ lens

anamorphosed movie anamorphotischer Breitwandfilm *m*
anamorphosis Anamorphose *f*
anamorphote [lens] *s.* anamorphic lens
anamorphotic *s.* anamorphic 1.
anastatic printing [procedure] anastatischer Druck *m*
anastigmat *s.* anastigmatic lens
anastigmatic anastigmatisch; verzeichnungsfrei, unverzeichnet, unverzerrt, verzerrungsfrei *(Objektiv)*
~ **lens** anastigmatisches Objektiv *n*, Anastigmat *m(n)*
anatomic noise anatomisches Rauschen *n (medizinische Bildgebung)*
anaxial anaxial, ungleichachsig
anchor picture Stützbild *n (Bewegungsschätzung)*
~ **point** Ankerpunkt *m*, Kurvenpunkt *m (Computergrafik)*
anchorman Moderator *m (z.B. in Nachrichtensendungen)*
ancillary data Hilfsdaten *pl*, Zusatzdaten *pl*
~ **data packet** Hilfsdatenpaket *n*
~ **time code** Hilfszeitcode *m*
AND [logisches] UND *n*
~ **operation** logische UND-Operation *f*
anechoic echofrei
angel echo Engelecho *n (Radar)*
~ **hair** Engelshaar *n (Kinefilmbeschädigung)*
Anger[-type] camera Anger-Kamera *f*, [Einkristall-]Gammakamera *f*, Szintillationskamera *f*
angiocardiographic angiokardiografisch
angiocardiography Angiokardiografie *f*
angiogram Angiogramm *n*
angiographic angiografisch
~ **catheter** Angiografiekatheter *m*, angiografischer Katheter *m*
~ **imaging, angiography** Angiografie *f*
angiography cassette Angiografiekassette *f*
angioscope Angioskop *n*
angioscopy Angioskopie *f*
angle/to anwinkeln
angle bracket spitze Klammer *f (Druckzeichen)*
~ **finder** Winkelsucher *m*
~ **gauge** Winkelmaß *n (tool)*
~ **modulation** Winkelmodulation *f*
~ **of acceptance** Akzeptanzwinkel *m (z.B. eines Objektivs)*
~ **of arrival** Auftreffwinkel *m*
~ **of convergence** Konvergenzwinkel *m*
~ **of coverage** Bildwinkel *m (Objektiv)*
~ **of deflection** Ablenkwinkel *m*
~ **of diffraction** Beugungswinkel *m*
~ **of field** *s.* ~ of view
~ **of flash coverage** Blitzwinkel *m*, Leuchtwinkel *m*
~ **of illumination** Beleuchtungswinkel *m*
~ **of incidence** Einfallswinkel *m*; Auftreffwinkel *m*
~ **of intersection** Schnittwinkel *m*
~ **of opening** Öffnungswinkel *m (z.B. eines Verschlusses)*
~ **of radiation** Abstrahlwinkel *m*
~ **of reflection** Reflexionswinkel *m*; Ausfallswinkel *m*
~ **of refraction** Brechungswinkel *m*; Refraktionswinkel *m*
~ **of rotation** Drehwinkel *m*
~ **of spread** Streuwinkel *m*
~ **of tilt** Kippwinkel *m*
~ **of view** 1. Blickwinkel *m*; Beobachtungswinkel *m*, Betrachtungswinkel *m*, Sichtwinkel *m*; 2. Aufnahmewinkel *m*, Feldwinkel *m*
~ **of vision** Sehwinkel *m*, Gesichtswinkel *m*
~ **viewfinder** Winkelsucher *m*
angled mirror Winkelspiegel *m*
~ **viewer** Winkelsucher *m*
angstrom Ångström *n (veraltende Wellenlängeneinheit)*
angular angular, angulär
~ **accuracy** Winkelgenauigkeit *f*
~ **acuity** anguläre Sehschärfe *f*
~ **aperture** *s.* aperture angle
~ **defect** Winkelfehler *m*, Winkelaberration *f*
~ **deflection** Winkelablenkung *f*
~ **dependence** Winkelabhängigkeit *f*
~ **deviation** Winkelablenkung *f*
~ **disparity** anguläre Disparität *f*
~ **dispersion** Winkeldispersion *f*
~ **distance** Winkelabstand *m*
~ **distribution** Winkelverteilung *f*
~ **field** Bildfeldwinkel *m*
~ **frequency** Winkelfrequenz *f*
~ **magnification** Winkelvergrößerung *f (Optik)*
~ **measure** Winkelmaß *n*
~ **minute** Winkelminute *f*
~ **momentum** Drehmoment *n*
~ **perspective** Winkelperspektive *f*, Zweipunktperspektive *f*
~ **phase shift** Phasendrehung *f*
~ **position** Winkelposition *f*
~ **projection** Winkelprojektion *f*
~ **region** Winkelbereich *m*
~ **resolution** Winkelauflösung *f*
~ **spectrum** Winkelspektrum *m*
~ **subtense** Winkelüberdeckung *f*
angulation Angulierung *f (Radiologie)*
aniline dye Anilinfarbstoff *m*, Anilinfarbe *f*
~ **printing (process)** Anilin[gummi]druck *m*, Flexodruck *m*, Flexografie *f (Hochdruckverfahren)*
anilox inking system, ~ roll Aniloxfarbwerk *n*, Kurzfarbwerk *n*, Raster-Farbauftragswalze *f (Flexodruck)*
animacast Internet-Videoanimation *f*
animal glue Tierleim *m*
animatable animierbar
animate/to animieren
animated cartoon Zeichen[trick]film *m*
~ **character** Trick[film]figur *f*

~ **figure** Animationsfigur *f*; Zeichenfilmfigur *f*
~ **film** Animationsfilm *m*, Trickfilm *m*, Effektfilm *m*
~ **GIF** GIF-Animation *f*, animierte GIF-Datei *f*; Internet-Trickfilm *m*
~ **icon** animiertes Icon *n*
~ **image** animiertes Bild *n*, Animationsbild *n*
~ **sequence** *s.* animation sequence
~ **short** Animationskurzfilm *m*, Trickkurzfilm *m*
animation 1. Animation *f*; animierte Grafik *f*; 2. Zeichen[trick]film *m*; 3. *s.* animated film; 4. *s.* computer animation
~ **camera** Animationskamera *f*, Trick[film]kamera *f*
~ **camera operator** Trickkameramann *m*
~ **cel** 1. Cellofolie *f*, Folie *f* *(Zeichentrickfilmproduktion)*; 2. Phasenzeichnung *f (Trickfilmproduktion)*
~ **character** Animationsfigur *f*
~ **cinematography** Animationskinematografie *f*
~ **designer** Animationsdesigner *m*
~ **director** Trickfilmregisseur *m*
~ **effect** Animationseffekt *m*
~ **file** Animationsdatei *f*
~ **frame** *s.* ~ image
~ **graphics** Trick[film]grafik *f*
~ **image** Animationsbild *n*, animiertes Bild *n*
~ **model** Animationsmodell *n*
~ **motor** Einzelbildmotor *m*
~ **photography** Animationsfotografie *f*
~ **production** Trickfilmen *n*
~ **program** Animationsprogramm *n*
~ **puppet** Animationspuppe *f*
~ **sequence** Animationssequenz *f*, [grafische] Trickfilmsequenz *f*
~ **software** Animationssoftware *f*
~ **stand** Tricktisch *m*, Filmtricktisch *m*
~ **stand photography** Tricktischfotografie *f*
~ **studio** Animationsstudio *n*
~ **superimposition** Trickü̈berblendung *f*
~ **system** Animationssystem *n*
~ **technique** Animationsverfahren *n*; Animationstechnik *f*
animator Animator *m*, Animationsspezialist *m*; Trickfilmanimator *m*; Trick[film]zeichner *m*
animatronic Animationsfigur *f*
anion Anion *n*
~ **vacancy** Anionenleerstelle *f*
aniseikonia Aniseikonie *f (Sehfehler)*
aniseikonic aniseikonisch
anisometropia Anisometropie *f (Sehfehler)*
anisometropic anisometropisch
anisotropic anisotrop, richtungsabhängig
~ **astigmatism** anisotroper Astigmatismus *m (Abbildungsfehler)*
~ **coma** anisotrope Koma *f (Abbildungsfehler)*

~ **crystal** anisotroper Kristall *m*
~ **diffusion** anisotrope Diffusion *f (Musteranalyse)*
~ **distortion** anisotrope Verzeichnung *f (Magnetbildfehler)*
~ **filter** anisotropes Filter *n*
~ **mapping** verzerrte Abbildung *f (geometrische Datenverarbeitung)*
~ **medium** anisotropes Medium *n*
~ **reflection** anisotrope Reflexion *f*
~ **scaling** anisotrope Skalierung *f*
anisotropism *s.* anisotropy
anisotropy Anisotropie *f*, Richtungsabhängigkeit *f*
annihilation process Paarvernichtungsprozess *m (Teilchenphysik)*
~ **radiation** Vernichtungsstrahlung *f*, Zerstrahlung *f*, Annihilation *f*
annotation Annotation *f*
annular aperture Ringblende *f*, ringförmige Blende *f*
~ **electrode** Ringelektrode *f*
~ **magnet** Ringmagnet *m*
anode Anode *f*
~ **angle** Anodenneigungswinkel *m*
~-**cathode voltage** Beschleunigungsspannung *f*, Röhrenspannung *f (Katodenstrahlröhre)*
~ **cylinder** Anodenzylinder *m*
~ **disk** Anodenplatte *f*
~ **dissipation power** Anodenverlustleistung *f*
~ **grid** Anodengitter *n*
~ **material** Anodenmaterial *n*, Targetmaterial *n*
~ **panel** Anodenplatte *f*
~ **voltage** Anodenspannung *f*
anodized plate eloxierte Platte *f (Offsetdruck)*
anomaloscope Anomaloskop *n (Instrument zur Farbsinnprüfung)*
anomalous color vision Farb[en]fehlsichtigkeit *f*, Farbsinnstörung *f*
~ **dispersion** anomale Dispersion *f*
~ **propagation** Ausbreitungsanomalie *f (z.B. von Radarstrahlen)*
~ **trichromacy** anomale Trichromasie *f*, Farbenschwäche *f (Sehfehler)*
~ **trichromat** anomaler Trichromat *m*
~ **trichromatism** *s.* ~ trichromacy
anoopsia, anopsia Anop[s]ie *f*, Nichtsehen *n*
ANSI *s.* American National Standards Institute
~ **lumen** ANSI-Lumen *n (eine Einheit des Lichtstromes)*
answer print Nullkopie *f*, Erstkopie *f (Kinematografie)*
antenna Antenne *f*
~ **aperture** Antennenapertur *f*, Antennenfläche *f*, Apertur *f (Radar)*
~ **array** Antennenfeld *n (Radar)*

antenna 14

~ **beam** Antennen[strahlungs]keule f (Radar)
~ **beam width** Antennenstrahlbreite f
~ **cable** Antennenkabel n
~ **coil** Antennenspule f
~ **directivity diagram** Antennenrichtcharakteristik f (Radar)
~ **frequency** Antennenfrequenz f
~ **gain** Antennengewinn m
~ **geometry** Antennengeometrie f
~ **input** Antenneneingang m
~ **lead** Antennenkabel n
~ **lobe** Antennen[strahlungs]keule f (Radar)
~ **motion** Antennenbewegung f (Radar)
~ **noise** Antennenrauschen n
~ **orientation** Antennenausrichtung f
~ **[radiation] pattern** Antennencharakteristik f, Antennendiagramm n
~ **signal** Antennensignal n
~ **sweep** Antennenschwenkung f
~ **voltage** Antennenspannung f
anterior chamber vordere Augenkammer f, Vorderkammer f
anthropological photography Personenfotografie f, Menschenfotografie f
anthropometric anthropometrisch
anthropometry Anthropometrie f
anthropomorphic phantom Körperphantom n (Röntgendosimetrie)
anti-Newton mount, anti-Newton-ring glass Antinewtonglas n
antiabrasion coating, antiabrasive layer Schrammschutzschicht f, Abriebschutzschicht f
antialiasing Antialiasing n, Antialiasing-Technik f ; Kantenglättung f (Computergrafik)
~ **filter** Antialiasing-Filter n
antibacterial [agent] Bakterizid n (Entwicklerzusatz)
antiblooming Überstrahlfestigkeit f
anticlutter rain maximum maximale Regenenttrübung f (Radar)
~ **rain minimum** minimale Regenenttrübung f
~ **sea maximum** maximale Seegangsenttrübung f (Radar)
~ **sea minimum** minimale Seegangsenttrübung f
anticollision radar Abstandswarnradar n
anticurl backing (layer) Rollschutzschicht f, Antiroll[rück]schicht f, Anticurl-Schicht f, Gelatine-Rückguss m
antielectron Antielektron n, Positron n, positives Elektron n
antiflicker blade Zwischenflügel m (Projektorblende)
antifoaming agent s. antifrothing agent
antifog coating Antibeschlagschicht f
antifoggant [compound] Antischleiermittel n

antifogging effect Antischleiereffekt m
antifrothing agent Entschäumer m (Emulsionsherstellung)
antiglare/to entspiegeln
antiglare screen Blendschutz[schirm] m
~ **surface** blendarme Oberfläche f
antihalation coating s. ~ layer
~ **dye** Antihalofarbstoff m, Lichthofschutz-Farbstoff m, Schirmfarbstoff m
~ **layer** Lichthofschutzschicht f, Antihaloschicht f
~ **protection** Lichthofschutz m
antihalo backing s. antihalation layer
antimony trisulfide Antimontrisulfid n (Fotowiderstand)
antinous release Drahtauslöser m
antioxidant Antioxidans n, Oxidationsschutzmittel n
antique paper Antikdruckpapier n
antireflection coating (film) reflex[ions]mindernde Schicht f, Antireflex[ions]beschichtung f, Antireflex[ions]schicht f, Antireflexvergütung f, Antireflexbelag m; Entspiegelung[sschicht] f
~ **multiple coating** Antireflex-Mehrfachvergütung f
antireflective coating s. antireflection coating
antiscatter grid Streustrahlenraster m(n), Röntgenstreustrahlenraster m(n) (Röntgentechnik)
antistatic antistatisch
~ **agent** Antistatikmittel n
~ **backing** s. ~ coating
~ **cloth** Antistatiktuch n
~ **coating (layer)** Antistatikschicht f, antistatische Schutzschicht f
antistatical antistatisch
antivibration table optischer Tisch m
antivignetting filter Antivignettierungsfilter n
antivirus program Antivirenprogramm n (Software)
aortographic aortografisch
aortography Aortografie f
aperiodic image aperiodisches Bild n
apertometer Apertometer n
aperture Apertur f, Blende f
~ **adjustment** Blendeneinstellung f
~ **and shutter speed combination** Verschlusszeit-Blenden-Kombination f
~ **angle** Aperturwinkel m, Öffnungswinkel m
~ **annulus** 1. Blendenring m; 2. s. ~ ring
~ **card** Mikrofilmkarte f, Mikrofilm-Lochkarte f
~ **choice** Blendenwahl f
~ **control** Blendensteuerung f
~ **correction** Aperturkorrektur f, Kantenkorrektur f
~ **diameter** Blendendurchmesser m

~ **diaphragm** Aperturblende f, Öffnungsblende f, Diaphragma n
~ **diaphragm opening [size]** Aperturblendenöffnung f
~ **effect** Blendeneffekt m
~-**exposure lock** Bildschärfe- und Belichtungsspeicher m
~ **function** Blendenfunktion f; Pupillenfunktion f *(Strahlenoptik)*
~ **grating** Blendengitter n *(Farbbildröhre)*
~ **grille CRT** Streifenmaskenröhre f, Schlitzmaskenröhre f
~ **grille mask** Streifenmaske f, Schlitzmaske f *(Bildröhre)*
~ **grille monitor** Streifenmaskenmonitor m
~ **half-angle** Blendenhalbwinkel m
~ **image** Blendenbild n
~ **imaging** Aperturabbildung f
~ **jitter** Apertur-Jitter m *(Abtast-Halte-Glied)*
~-**limited** aperturbegrenzt, beugungsbegrenzt *(Objektiv)*
~-**limited optical microscopy** aperturbegrenzte optische Mikroskopie f
~ **mask** Blendenmaske f; Streifenmaske f, Schlitzmaske f, Schattenmaske f *(Farbbildschirm)*
~ **number** Blendenzahl f, Blendenwert m, f-Zahl f *(s.a.* ~ *stop)*; relative Apertur (Lichtstärke) f, Lichtstärkenverhältnis n *(Objektiv)*
~ **opening** Blendenöffnung f, Blendenloch n
~ **plane** Blendenebene f
~ **plate** Aperturblende f *(Kinokamera)*
~ **priority auto** Belichtungsautomatik f mit Blendenvorwahl, Zeitautomatik f
~ **priority mode** Blendenpriorität f, Schärfepriorität f
~ **probe** Apertursonde f
~ **problem** Aperturproblem n, Blendenproblem n *(des Bewegungssehens)*
~ **range** Blendenbereich m
~ **ratio** Öffnungsverhältnis n, relative Öffnung f, Öffnungszahl f, Blendenzahl f *(Objektiv)*
~ **ring** Blendeneinstellring m, Objektivblendenring m, Blendensteuerring m
~ **scale** Blendenskale f, Blendenzahl[en]reihe f
~ **setting** 1. Blendeneinstellung f; 2. s. ~ stop
~ **shape** Aperturform f
~ **shutter** Blendenverschluss m; Objektivverschluss m
~ **stop** Blendenstufe f, f-Blende f *(s.a.* ~ number, ~ diaphragm*)*
~ **synthesis** Apertursynthese f *(Radioastronomie)*
~ **transmission function** s. ~ function
~ **vignette** s. ~ diaphragm

apex Apex m, Spitze f; Vertex m, Scheitel[punkt] m
~ **angle** Scheitelwinkel m
aplanat [lens] Aplanat m(n), aplanatische Linse f
aplanatic aplanatisch
~ **condenser** aplanatischer Kondensor m
~ **imaging** aplanatische Abbildung f
~ **lens** s. aplanat [lens]
~ **lens system** aplanatisches System n
~ **meniscus** aplanatischer Meniskus m
aplanatism Aplanatismus m
apochromat [objective] Apochromat m, apochromatisches Objektiv n
apochromatic apochromatisch
~ **lens** 1. apochromatische Linse f; 2. s. apochromat [objective]
~ **refractor** apochromatischer Refraktor m
~ **system** apochromatisches System n
apodization Apodisation f *(Optik; Signalverarbeitung)*
apostilb Apostilb n *(SI-fremde Einheit der Leuchtdichte)*
apostrophe Apostroph m, Auslassungszeichen n *(Druckzeichen)*
apparent field of view scheinbares Gesichtsfeld n
~ **motion (movement)** scheinbare (abgetastete) Bewegung f, Phi-Bewegung f, Phi-Phänomen n *(Wahrnehmungsphysiologie)*
~ **visual angle** Sehwinkel m, Gesichtswinkel m
apparition Apparition f, [optische] Erscheinung f
appearance Erscheinungsbild n, visuelle Erscheinung f, Aussehen n
appliance Gerät n
application icon Anwendungssymbol n *(grafische Benutzerschnittstelle)*
~ **layer (level)** Anwendungsschicht f *(Datenübertragung)*
~ **program** Anwendungsprogramm n
~ **program interface** Anwendungsschnittstelle f
~ **programming interface** Anwendungsprogrammierschnittstelle f
~ **software** Anwendungssoftware f
~-**specific integrated circuit** anwendungsspezifisch integrierte Schaltung f
~ **window** Anwendungsfenster n
applied optics angewandte Optik f
~ **photography** angewandte Fotografie f
approval print Nullkopie f, Erstkopie f *(Kinematografie)*
approximate/to approximieren
approximate color temperature ähnlichste (korrelierte) Farbtemperatur f
approximating curve Näherungskurve f
~ **line** Approximationsgerade f
~ **spline** Näherungskurve f
approximation Approximation f, Näherung f

approximation

~ **approach** Näherungsansatz *m*
~ **coefficient** Skalierungskoeffizient *m*
~ **error** Approximationsfehler *m*
~ **filter** Approximationsfilter *n*
approximative approximativ, näherungsweise
APS *s.* Advanced Photo System
aquarelle paper Aquarellpapier *n*
aquarium photography Aquarienfotografie *f*
aquatint *s.* 1. ~ process; 2. aquatinta engraving
~ **process** Aquatinta[ätzung] *f*
aquatinta engraving Aquatinta[ätzung] *f*
aquatone printing Aquatondruck *m (ein Lichtdruckverfahren)*
aqueous coating Feuchtmittelfilm *m*
~ **coating process** Druckformfeuchtung *f*, Feuchtung *f*
~ **gelatin** wässrige Gelatine *f*
~ **humor** Kammerwasser *n (des Auges)*
arbitrarily-shaped object Freiformobjekt *n (Computergrafik)*
~-**shaped surface** Freiformfläche *f*
arbitrary object beliebiges Objekt *n*
~ **polygon** beliebiges Polygon *n*
~ **ray** beliebiger Strahl *m*
~-**shape wavelet transform** Freiform-Wavelettransformation *f*
arc 1. Bogen *m*; 2. Lichtbogen *m*; 3. *s.* ~ lamp; 4. *s.* connection; 5. *s.* polyline
~-**discharge lamp** Bogenentladungslampe *f*
~ **lamp** Lichtbogenlampe *f*, Bogenlampe *f*, Hochdrucklampe *f*
~ **lamp motion-picture projector** Lichtbogen-Filmprojektor *m*
~ **length** Bogenlänge *f*
~ **light** Bogenlicht *n*
~ **reference profile** Kreisbogen-Bezugsprofil *n (Filmzahnrolle)*
~ **second** Bogensekunde *f*
arcade game Videospielautomat *m*
archaeological photography Archäologiefotografie *f*
Archer's collodion wet plate process Nassbildplattenverfahren *n*
architectural perspective stürzende Linien *fpl*
~ **photogrammetry** Architekturfotogrammetrie *f*
~ **photograph** Architekturaufnahme *f*
~ **photographer** Architekturfotograf *m*
~ **photography** Architekturfotografie *f*
archival archivisch; archivalisch
~ **footage** Archivmaterial *n*
~ **image** Archivbild *n*
~ **image storage** Bildarchivierung *f*
~ **keeping** Archivierung *f*
~ **paper** Archivpapier *n*, Dokumentenpapier *n*
~ **photocopying** archivalisches Fotokopieren *n*
~ **photography** Archivfotografie *f*
~ **property** Archivierungseigenschaft *f*
~ **quality** Archivierbarkeit *f*, Archiv[ier]fähigkeit *f*
~ **stability** Archivfestigkeit *f*
~ **storage** Archivierung *f*
~ **theater** Reprisenkino *n*
archive/to archivieren
archive Archiv *n*
~ **file** Archivdatei *f*
~ **paper** *s.* archival paper
~ **photography** Archivfotografie *f*
~-**proof** archivfest, archivsicher
~ **server** Archiv-Server *m*
archiving Archivierung *f*
archivist Archivar *m*
area Fläche *f (Formmerkmal)*
~ **array** flächige (flächenhafte) Anordnung *f (z.B. von Fotodioden)*
~ **array camera** [CCD-]Matrixkamera *f*
~-**based matching** flächenbasierte Zuordnung *f*
~ **character coding** Blockcodierung *f*
~ **chart** Flächendiagramm *n*
~ **code** Ländercode *m (Digitalvideoproduktion)*
~ **detector** [Halbleiter-]Flächendetektor *m*, flächiger (flächenauflösender) Detektor *m*
~ **element** Flächenelement *n*
~ **feature** Flächenmerkmal *n*
~ **front light** seitliches Vorderlicht *n*
~ **function** Flächenfunktion *f*
~ **illumination** Flächenausleuchtung *f*
~ **image sensor** Flächen[bild]sensor *m*
~ **light** Flächenlicht *n*
~ **light source** Flächenlichtquelle *f*
~ **of illumination** Leuchtfläche *f*
~ **of interest** interessierender Bildausschnitt *m*, Arbeitsbereich *m (z.B. in der Bildanalyse)*
~ **sampling** Flächenabtastung *f*
~ **scan camera** Flächen[chip]kamera *f*, [CCD-]Matrixkamera *f*
~ **scanner** Flächenscanner *m*
~ **source** Flächenlichtquelle *f*
~ **subdivision** Gebietszerlegung *f*, regionenbasierte (regionenorientierte) Segmentierung *f (Computergrafik)*
~ **target** Flächenziel *n (Radar)*
~-**weighted measurement** Mehrfeld[belichtungs]messung *f*
areal moment of inertia Flächenträgheitsmoment *n*
areography Areografie *f*, Marsgeografie *f*
argentite Silberglanz *m*
argentothiosulfate Silberthiosulfat *n*
argon[-ion] laser Argon[ionen]laser *m*
aristotype Aristotypie *f*
arithmetic average arithmetisches Mittel *n*
~ **coder** arithmetischer Codierer *m*
~ **coding** arithmetische Codierung *f*
~ **compression** arithmetische Kompression *f*

~ **logic unit** Arithmetikeinheit *f*, arithmetisch-logische Einheit *f* *(Prozessor)*
~ **mean** arithmetisches Mittel *n*
~ **mean filter** arithmetisches Mittelwertfilter *n*
~ **operator** arithmetischer Operator *m*
~ **reconstruction technique** arithmetische Rekonstruktionstechnik *f*
arm Stativ *n (zusammengesetztes Mikroskop)*
armoring Armierung *f (z.B. von optischen Instrumenten)*
ARPA *s.* automatic radar plotting aid
array Array *n*, Anordnung *f*, Feld *n*; flächige (flächenhafte) Anordnung *f*
~ **camera** Flächen[chip]kamera *f*, [CCD-]Matrixkamera *f*
~ **CCD (charge-coupled device)** CCD-Flächenchip *m*, CCD-Flächensensor *m*
~ **detector** flächiger (flächenauflösender) Detektor *m*
~ **imager** Flächen[bild]sensor *m*
~ **of dots (pixels)** Pixelfeld *n*, Pixelanordnung *f*
~ **processor** Arrayprozessor *m*, Feldrechner *m*, parallel arbeitender Prozessor *m*
~ **sensor** Flächen[bild]sensor *m*
arrow Cursorpfeil *m*
~ **key** Pfeiltaste *f*
art *s.* artwork
~ **of cinematography** Filmkunst *f*
~ **of printing** Druckkunst *f*
~ **paper** Bilderdruckpapier *n*
~ **photograph** Kunstfotografie *f (Bildprodukt)*
~ **photographer** Kunstfotograf *m*
~ **photography** Kunstfotografie *f*
~ **print** Kunstdruck *m (Erzeugnis)*
~ **printing paper** Bilderdruckpapier *n*
~ **theater** Filmkunsttheater *n*
artboard Ganzseitenmontage *f (Druckvorstufe)*
artefact *s.* artifact
arterial imaging Arteriografie *f*
arteriogram Arteriogramm *n*
arteriographic arteriografisch
arteriography Arteriografie *f*
arthrogram Arthrogramm *n*
arthroscope Arthroskop *n*, Gelenkspiegel *m*
arthroscopic arthroskopisch
arthroscopy Arthroskopie *f*, Gelenkspiegelung *f*
articulate matte Wandermaske *f (Trickkinematografie)*
articulatory loop Seilschlinge *f*, Trochlea *f (Augenmuskulatur)*
artifact Artefakt *n*; Bildverfälschung *f*
~ **elimination** Artefaktbeseitigung *f*
~-**free signal** artefaktfreies Signal *n*
~ **of color reproduction** Farbwiedergabefehler *m*
~ **suppression** Artefaktreduktion *f*
artifactual signal loss artefaktbedingter Signalverlust *m*
artificial environment künstliche Umgebung *f*
~ **illumination** Kunstlichtbeleuchtung *f*, künstliche Beleuchtung *f*
~ **intelligence** künstliche Intelligenz *f (Informatik)*
~ **light** Kunstlicht *n*, künstliches Licht *n*
~-**light-balanced film** Kunstlichtfilm *m*
~-**light photography** Kunstlichtfotografie *f*
~ **light source** Kunstlichtquelle *f*
~ **lighting** *s.* ~ illumination
~ **midtone** Graukarte *f*
~ **neural network** künstliches neuronales Netz *n*
~ **neuron** künstliches (formales) Neuron *n*
~ **vision system** technisches (maschinelles) Sehsystem *n*
artistic photography künstlerische Fotografie *f*
artwork Druckvorlage *f*, grafische Vorlage *f*; Kopiervorlage *f*
aryl diazonium salt Aryldiazoniumsalz *n*
as-acquired image unverarbeitetes Bild *n*, Roh[daten]bild *n (s.a.* input image*)*
ASA film speed ASA-Empfindlichkeit *f*
~ **rating** ASA-Wert *m*
~ **scale** ASA-Skala *f*
ascender [height] Oberlänge *f (Typografie)*
ASCII *s.* American Standard Code for Information Interchange
~ **character** ASCII-Zeichen *n*
~ **code** ASCII-Code *m (Textaustauschformat)*
~ **database** ASCII-Datenbank *f*
~ **standard character set** ASCII-Zeichensatz *m*
ascorbic acid Ascorbinsäure *f (Entwicklerbestandteil)*
aspect *s.* ~ ratio
~ **angle** Aspektwinkel *m*
~ **graph** Aspektgraph *m*
~ **ratio** Aspektverhältnis *n*; Seitenverhältnis *n*; Bildseitenverhältnis *n*, Bildformat *n*
~ **ratio accommodation** Seitenverhältnistransformierung *f*, Bildseitenverhältniswandlung *f*
~ **source flag** Aspektanzeiger *m (Computergrafik)*
asphalt varnish Asphaltlack *m*
aspheric asphärisch
~ **lens corrector plate** Kompensatorplatte *f*, Schmidt-Platte *f*
~ **lens system** asphärisches System *n*
~ **optical surface** Asphäre *f*, asphärische Fläche *f*
~ **single-element lens** asphärisches Linsenelement *n*
aspherical asphärisch

aspherical 18

~ **correction** asphärische Korrektur *f*
~ **lens element** asphärisches Linsenelement *n*
~ **mirror** asphärischer Spiegel *m*
~ **photographic lens** Asphären-Objektiv *n*, asphärisches Objektiv *n*
~ **plate** asphärische Platte *f*
~ **surface** Asphäre *f*, asphärische Fläche *f*
aspherizing Asphärisierung *f*
assemble/to montieren *(Layout; Druckvorstufe)*
assemble edit[ing] Anfügeschnitt *m*, Montageschnitt *m*, Assemble-Schnitt *m*, aneinanderfügender Schnitt *m (Video)*
~ **list** Schnittliste *f*
assembly Montage *f (z.B. von Bildelementen)*
assess/to [ab]schätzen
assessment parameter Schätzparameter *m*
assignment Zuordnung *f*
~ **problem** Zuordnungsproblem *n*
assistant animator Zwischenphasenzeichner *m*
~ **cameraman (cameraperson)** [Erster] Kameraassistent *m*
~ **chief lighting technician** Beleuchtungsassistent *m*
~ **director** Erster Aufnahmeleiter *m*, Regieassistent *m*
~ **film (picture) editor** Schnittassistent *m*, Cutterassistent *m*
~ **production manager** Produktionsassistent *m*
association cell *s.* amacrine cell
associative hatching Assoziativschraffur *f*, assoziative Schraffur *f (Computergrafik)*
~ **memory (storage)** assoziativer (inhaltsadressierter) Speicher *m*, Assoziativspeicher *m*, Katalogspeicher *m*
associativity Assoziativität *f*
assortment of filters Filtersortiment *n*, Filtersatz *m*
assumption of stationarity Stetigkeitsbedingung *f*
asterisk Asteriskus *m (Hinweiszeichen)*
asthenopia Asthenopie *f*, Sehschwäche *f*
asthenopic asthenop, sehschwach
astigmat Astigmat *m*
astigmatic aberration (error) *s.* astigmatism
~ **lens** Astigmat *m*
~ **spectral line** astigmatische Spektrallinie *f*
astigmatical astigmatisch
astigmatism Astigmatismus *m*, Punktlosigkeit *f*, Zweischalenfehler *m (Optik)*
Aston's mass spectrograph Astonscher Massenspektrograf *m*
astrograph Astrograf *m*
~ **lens** Astrografenobjektiv *n*
astrometric astrometrisch

~ **astrograph** Messastrograf *m*, astrografische Messkamera *f*, Astrometrie-Astrograf *m*
astrometry Astrometrie *f*
astronomical camera astronomische Kamera *f*, Astrokamera *f*
~ **CCD camera** CCD-Astrokamera *f*
~ **mirror** astronomischer Spiegel *m*
~ **objective** Astroobjektiv *n*
~ **observation** Astrobeobachtung *f*
~ **observatory** astronomische Beobachtungsstation *f*, Sternwarte *f*, Observatorium *n*
~ **optics** astronomische Optik *f*, Astrooptik *f*
~ **photograph** Astrofoto *n*, Himmelsfoto *n*
~ **photography** Astrofotografie *f*, Sternbildfotografie *f*; Himmelsfotografie *f*
~ **plate** Astroplatte *f*
~ **spectrograph** Astrospektrograf *m*
~ **spectroscopy** Astrospektroskopie *f*
~ **telescope** astronomisches Teleskop (Fernrohr) *n*, Keplersches Fernrohr *n*
astrophotograph Astrofoto *n*
astrophotographer Astrofotograf *m*
astrophotographic astrofotografisch
~ **telescope** astrofotografisches Teleskop *n*
astrophotography Astrofotografie *f*, Sternbildfotografie *f*, Himmelsfotografie *f*
astrophysical optics astrophysikalische Optik *f*
astrospectroscopy Astrospektroskopie *f*
astrostereogram Astrostereogramm *n*
astrotelescope *s.* astronomical telescope
asymmetric echo asymmetrisches Echo *n (Sonografie)*
~ **filter** asymmetrisches Filter *n*
~ **sampling** asymmetrische Abtastung *f*
asymmetrical asymmetrisch, unsymmetrisch
~ **aberration** asymmetrische Aberration *f*
~ **algorithm** asymmetrischer Algorithmus *m*
~ **coding** asymmetrische Codierung *f*
~ **compression** asymmetrische Kompression *f*
~ **digital subscriber line** asymmetrisch digitale Teilnehmerleitung (Anschlussleitung) *f*
~ **lens** asymmetrisches (unsymmetrisches) Objektiv *n*
~ **model** asymmetrisches Modell *n*
~ **modeling** asymmetrische Modellierung *f*
~ **spectrum** asymmetrisches Spektrum *n*
asymmetry Asymmetrie *f*; Unsymmetrie *f*
asynchronism Asynchronität *f*
asynchronous asynchron
~ **time division multiplexing** statistisches Multiplexen *n (Signalverarbeitung)*
~ **transfer mode** asynchroner Übertragungsmodus *m*

~ **transfer mode network** ATM-Netz *n* *(Datenübertragung)*
~ **transmission** asynchrone Übertragung *f*
~ **trigger action** asynchrone Triggerung *f*
asynchrony Asynchronität *f*
at the receiving end empfangsseitig
at the transmitting end sendeseitig
ATA *s.* automated tracking aid
ATM *s.* asynchronous transfer mode
~ **network** ATM-Netz *n* *(Datenübertragung)*
atmosphere Atmosphäre *f (z.B. als Tiefeninformation in Bildern)*
atmospheric dispersion atmosphärische Dispersion *f*
~ **drying** Lufttrocknung *f (z.B. von Fotopapier)*
~ **extinction** atmosphärische Extinktion *f*
~ **fog** Atmosphärentrübung *f*, atmosphärischer Nebel *m*
~ **haze** atmosphärischer Dunst *m*, Ferndunst *m*, Luftlicht *n*
~ **humidity (moisture)** Luftfeuchte *f*, Luftfeuchtigkeit *f*
~ **perspective** Luftperspektive *f*
~ **radiation** Gegenstrahlung *f*
~ **refraction** atmosphärische Refraktion *f*
~ **scattering** atmosphärische Streuung *f*
~ **scintillation** Luftunruhe *f (Astrooptik)*
~ **spectral window** atmosphärisches Fenster *n*
atom optics Atomoptik *f*
atomic absorption spectrophotometry Atomabsorptionsspektrofotometrie *f*
~ **absorption spectroscopy** Atomabsorptionsspektroskopie *f*, AAS
~ **bond** Atombindung *f*
~ **electron shell** Elektronenhülle *f*
~ **emission spectrometry** Atomemissionsspektrometrie *f*
~ **emission spectroscopy** Atomemissionsspektroskopie *f*
~ **fluorescence spectroscopy** Atomfluoreszenzspektroskopie *f*, AFS
~ **force microscope** Rasterkraftmikroskop *n*, Kraftmikroskop *n*
~ **force microscopy** Rasterkraftmikroskopie *f*, [atomare] Kraftmikroskopie *f*
~ **mass** Atommasse *f*
~ **nucleus** Atomkern *m*
~ **number** Kernladungszahl *f*
~ **radius** Atomradius *m*
~ **resolution** atomare Auflösung *f*
~ **spectroscopy** Atomspektroskopie *f*
~ **weight** Atommasse *f*
ATSC *s.* Advanced Television Standards (System) Committee
attachment Vorsatz *m (optisches Bauteil)*
attentional blink Aufmerksamkeitszuwendung *f (Augenbewegung)*
attenuate/to abschwächen

attenuated total reflectance (reflection) abgeschwächte (gedämpfte) Totalreflexion *f*
attenuation Abschwächung *f*, Schwächung *f*, Dämpfung *f*
~ **artifact** Dämpfungsartefakt *n*
~ **coefficient** Schwächungskoeffizient *m*, Abschwächungskoeffizient *m*, Dämpfungskoeffizient *m*; Extinktionskoeffizient *m*
~ **constant** Dämpfungskonstante *f*; Dämpfungsmaß *n*
~ **contrast** Schwächungskontrast *m (Radiografie)*
~ **correction** Dämpfungskorrektur *f (Emissionstomografie)*
~ **effect** Abschwächungseffekt *m*
~ **image (map), ~ profile** Schwächungsbild *n*, Schwächungsprofil *n*
~ **value** Schwächungswert *m*
attenuator 1. Abschwächer *m (fotografische Entwicklung)*; 2. Verlauffilter *n*
attribute Attribut *n*; Merkmal *n (s.a. unter feature, descriptor)*
~ **element** Attributelement *n (Bilddateielement)*
~ **selection** Merkmalsauswahl *f*, Merkmalsselektion *f*
audible hörbar
~ **frequency range** *s.* audio frequency
~ **level** Hörschwelle *f*
~ **sound** Hörschall *m*
audience perspective Zuschauerperspektive *f*
audile auditiv
audio ... *s.a. unter* sound ...
~ **amplifier** Tonverstärker *m*
~ **carrier** Tonträger *m*
~ **cassette** Audiokassette *f*
~ **cassette [magnetic tape] recorder** Audiokassettengerät *n*, Audiokassettenrecorder *m*
~ **channel** Audiokanal *m*, Tonkanal *m*
~ **circuit** Tonleitung *f (Fernsehtechnik)*
~ **coding** Toncodierung *f*
~ **compression** Audiokompression *f*
~ **data** Audiodaten *pl*
~ **data track** Audiospur *f*, Ton[aufzeichnungs]spur *f*
~ **dubbing** Vertonung *f*; Nachvertonung *f*, Tonnachbearbeitung *f*, Audiopost[produktion] *f*
~ **effects device** Audioeffektgerät *n*
~ **encoder** Audiocodierer *m*
~ **encoding** Audiocodierung *f*
~ **file** Klangdatei *f*
~ **format** Audioformat *n*
~ **frequency** Tonfrequenz *f*, Audiofrequenz *f*
~ **-frequency signal** Tonfrequenzsignal *n*
~ **head** Tonkopf *m*
~ **input** Audioeingang *m*

audio 20

~ **jack** Audiobuchse *f*
~ **magnetic tape** Magnettonband *n*
~ **material** Tonmaterial *n*
~ **mix equipment** Tonmischanlage *f*
~ **mixer (mixing console)** Tonmischpult *n*, Audiomischer *m*, Audiomischpult *n*
~ **modulation** Tonmodulation *f*
~ **noise-reduction system** Rauschreduktionssystem *n*
~ **pickup** Tonaufnahme *f*, Tonaufzeichnung *f*
~ **processing unit** Audioprozessor *m* *(Fernsehtechnik)*
~ **recording** Tonaufnahme *f*, Tonaufzeichnung *f*, Schallaufzeichnung *f*
~ **recording ability** Tonaufnahmemöglichkeit *f*
~ **reproduction** Tonwiedergabe *f*, Schallwiedergabe *f*
~ **signal** Tonsignal *n*, Audiosignal *n*, akustisches Signal *n*
~ **signal processing** Tonsignalverarbeitung *f*
~ **slate** Synchronzeichengeber *m*
~ **subcarrier** Audio-Hilfsträger *m*
~ **system** Audiosystem *n*, Tonwiedergabesystem *n*
~ **tape machine** Tonbandmaschine *f*
~ **tape recorder** Tonbandgerät *n*
~ **technician** Tontechniker *m*
~ **technology** Tontechnik *f*
~ **time code** Audio-Zeitcode *m*
~-**video crosspoint** Audio-Video-Kreuzschiene *f*, Audio-Video-Kreuzschienenverteiler *m*
~-**video mixer** Audio-Video-Mischer *m*
~-**video output** Audio-Video-Ausgang *m*, AV-Ausgang *m*
~-**video synchronization** Audio-Video-Synchronisation *f*
~-**video technique** Audio-Video-Technik *f*
audiogram Audiogramm *n*
audiotape Tonband *n*
audiovision Audiovision *f*
audiovisual communication audiovisuelle Kommunikation *f*
~ **descriptor** audiovisueller Deskriptor *m*
~ **device** audiovisuelles Gerät *n*
~ **medium** audiovisuelles Medium *n*
~ **perception** audiovisuelle Wahrnehmung *f*
~ **presentation** audiovisuelle Darstellung (Präsentation) *f*
~ **recording** audiovisuelle Aufzeichnung *f*
~ **scene** audiovisuelle Szene *f*
~ **service** audiovisueller Dienst *m*
auditorium Zuschauerraum *m*
~ **loudspeaker** Saallautsprecher *m*
auditory auditiv
augmented reality erweiterte Realität *f*
aura *s.* ambience
aural aural, aurikulär
~ **signal** *s.* audio signal
auricular *s.* aural

authenticate/to authentifizieren, authentisieren
authentication Authentifizierung *f*, Authenti[fi]kation *f*, Authentizitätsprüfung *f*; Echtheitsbestätigung *f*; Urheberidentifizierung *f*
authenticity Authentizität *f*, Authentie *f*
authoring tool Autorensystem *n*, Autorenwerkzeug *n* *(Multimediagestaltung)*
authorization Autorisierung *f*
auto ... *s.a.* automatic ...
~ **assembly [edit]** computergesteuerter Schnitt *m*
~-**bracketing [function]** Belichtungsreihenautomatik *f*, Belichtungsreihenfunktion *f (Kamera)*
~ **channel programming** automatischer Sendersuchlauf *m*
~ **exposure** Belichtungsautomatik *f*
~ **flash** Automatikblitz *m*
~ **iris [control]** Blendenautomatik *f*, Automatikblende *f (Kamerafunktion)*
~ **iris lens** Autoirisobjektiv *n*
~ **knee** automatische Knieschaltung *f (elektronische Kamera)*
~ **locator** [automatische] Bandsuchlaufeinrichtung *f*
~ **macro function** automatische Makroeinstellung *f*, Makroautomatik *f*
~ **mode** Automatikmodus *m (Videokamera)*
~ **shutter priority** Verschlussvorwahl *f*, Belichtungsautomatik *f* mit Zeitvorwahl, Blendenautomatik *f (Belichtungsmodus)*
~-**tracing white balancing** fortwährender Weißabgleich *m*
~ **tracking** *s.* automatic track following
autoassociation Autoassoziation *f* *(Neuroinformatik; Mustererkennung)*
autoassociative memory autoassoziativer Speicher *m*
~ **neural network** autoassoziatives neuronales Netz *n*
autocalibrating display autokalibrierendes Display *n*
autocatalytic autokatalytisch *(Entwicklungsvorgang)*
autochrome [plate] Autochromplatte *f*
~ **process (system)** Autochromie *f*, Autochromplattentechnik *f* *(fotografisches Farbrasterverfahren)*
autocollimate/to autokollimieren
autocollimating microscope Autokollimationsmikroskop *n*
~ **spectrograph** Autokollimationsspektrograf *m*
autocollimation Autokollimation *f*
~ **prism** Autokollimationsprisma *n*
~ **telescope** Autokollimationsfernrohr *n*
autocollimator 1. Autokollimator *m*; 2. Autokollimationsfernrohr *n*
autocorrelation Autokorrelation *f*

~ **coefficient** Autokorrelationskoeffizient *m*
~ **function** Autokorrelationsfunktion *f*
~ **histogram** Autokorrelationshistogramm *n*
~ **image** Autokorrelationsbild *n*
~ **matrix** Autokorrelationsmatrix *f*
~ **theorem** Autokorrelationstheorem *n*
autocorrelator Autokorrelator *m*
autocovariance matrix Autokovarianzmatrix *f*
autocue Teleprompter *m*
autoexposure feature Belichtungsautomatik *f*, automatische Belichtungseinstellung *f*
autofluorescence Autofluoreszenz *f*
autofocus Autofokus *m*, AF, Fokussierautomatik *f*, Autofokuseinrichtung *f*
~ **accuracy** Autofokusgenauigkeit *f*
~ **camera** Autofokuskamera *f*
~ **capability** Autofokusfunktion *f*
~ **compact camera** Autofokus-Kompaktkamera *f*
~ **enlarger** Autofokusvergrößerer *m*
~ **illumination** Autofokushilfslicht *n*
~ **lens** Autofokusobjektiv *n*
~ **lock** Autofokussperre *f*
~ **mirror** Autofokusspiegel *m*
~ **module** Autofokusmodul *n*
~ **operation** Autofokusbetrieb *m*
~ **sensor** Autofokussensor *m*
~ **slide projector** Autofokus-Diaprojektor *m*
~ **speed** Autofokusgeschwindigkeit *f*
~ **system** Autofokussystem *n* (s.a. autofocus)
~ **zoom lens** Autofokus-Zoomobjektiv *n*
autofocusing automatische Fokussierung (Scharfeinstellung) *f*, Autofokussierung *f*
~ **device (system)** s. autofocus
autograph, autographic recorder Autograf *m* (Kartiergerät)
autographic[al] autografisch, autograf
autography Auto[litho]grafie *f*, Umdruckverfahren *n*
autoguider [automatische] Nachführkamera *f* (Astrofotografie)
autoguiding automatisches Nachführen *n*
autoluminescence Autolumineszenz *f*
automated image detection automatische Bilderkennung *f*
~ **machine printer** Kopierautomat *m*
~ **photofinishing** Großlaborverarbeitung *f*
~ **tracking aid** ATA-Radaranlage *f* (Navigationssystem)
automatic black control automatischer Schwarzabgleich *m*
~ **brightness control** automatische Helligkeitsregelung *f*
~ **camera** automatische Kamera *f*
~ **channel installation** automatische Programminstallation *f*

~ **chrominance control** automatische Farb[kontrast]regelung (Farbkontrolle) *f* (Video)
~ **classification** automatische Klassifikation *f*
~ **coded access control** Zugriffssteuerung *f*
~ **color control** s. ~ chrominance control
~ **contrast selection** automatische Kontrastwahl *f* (Video)
~ **convergence** automatische Konvergenzkorrektur *f*
~ **cut sheet feeder** automatischer Einzelblatteinzug *m*
~ **data transmission** automatische Datenübertragung *f*
~ **developing plant** Entwicklungsautomat *m*
~ **dialog[ue] replacement** Synchronbearbeitung *f*; Nachsynchronisation *f*
~ **dialog[ue] replacement editor** Synchronbearbeiter *m*
~ **diaphragm system** Blendenautomatik *f*, Automatikblende *f*
~ **document feeder** automatischer Dokumenteneinzug (Originaleinzug) *m*
~ **enlarger** Vergrößerungsautomat *m*
~ **exposure** automatische Belichtung *f*
~ **exposure control** automatische Belichtungssteuerung *f*
~ **exposure system** Belichtungsautomatik *f*, automatische Belichtungseinstellung *f*
~ **film processor** Filmverarbeitungsautomat *m*
~ **film transport (winding)** automatischer Filmtransport *m*
~ **fine-tuning** automatische Feinabstimmung *f*
~ **flash exposure control** Blitzautomatik *f*
~ **focus** s. autofocus
~ **focusing** automatische Fokussierung (Scharfeinstellung) *f*, Autofokussierung *f*
~ **frequency control** automatische Frequenzregelung (Frequenzsteuerung) *f*
~ **function** Automatikfunktion *f* (z.B. einer Kamera)
~ **gain control** automatische Verstärkungsregelung *f*
~ **iris mechanism** Blendenautomatik *f*, Automatikblende *f*
~ **machine vision system** Maschinen-Sichtsystem *n*
~ **macro function (setting)** automatische Makroeinstellung *f*, Makroautomatik *f*
~ **noise limiter** selbsttätiger Rauschbegrenzer *m*, automatische Rauschunterdrückung *f*
~ **pattern recognition** automatische Mustererkennung *f*
~ **phase control** automatische Phasenregelung *f*
~ **photometric telescope** automatisches fotometrisches Teleskop *n*

automatic

~ **picture finder** s. ~ program search
~ **picture transmission** automatische Bildübertragung f
~ **plate changing (loading)** [voll]automatischer Plattenwechsel (Druckplattenwechsel) m
~ **plate measuring machine** automatische Plattenmessmaschine f, APM-Maschine f *(Astrofotografie)*
~ **power-down mode** automatische Ausschaltung f *(z.B. einer Kamera)*
~ **processor** Verarbeitungsautomat m, Entwicklungsautomat m
~ **program search** automatische Bandstellensuche f *(Videotechnik)*
~ **radar plotting aid** automatisches Radarbildauswertegerät (Radarzeichengerät) n, ARPA-Anlage f, ARPA-Gerät n
~ **rewind** Rückspulautomatik f
~ **search tuning** automatischer Sendersuchlauf m
~ **start-up tuning** automatische Erstinstallation f *(z.B. eines Videorecorders)*
~ **track following** automatische Spurlagenregelung (Videokopfnachführung) f
~ **white balance [feature]**, ~ **white control** Weißabgleichautomatik f, automatischer Weißabgleich m *(Videokamera)*

autonomous segmentation autonome Segmentierung f
autoprocess transparency Sofortdiapositiv n
autoradiogram, autoradiograph [image] Autoradiogramm n
autoradiographic autoradiografisch
autoradiography Autoradiografie f
autoregressive model autoregressives Modell n *(Bildverarbeitung)*
autostereogram Autostereogramm n
autostereoscopic autostereoskopisch
~ **display** autostereoskopisches Display n
~ **panoramic image** autostereoskopisches Panoramabild n
autostereoscopy Autostereoskopie f
autotransformer Autotransformator m, Spartransformator m
autotype Autotypie f, Netzätzung f; Rasterätzung f *(Druckprodukt)*
autotypic autotypisch
autotypy Autotypie f, Netzätzung f; Rasterätzung f *(Verfahren)*
autowinder automatischer Filmtransport m
autoxidation Autoxidation f
auxiliary antenna Hilfsantenne f
~ **bulk storage** Hilfsmassenspeicher m
~ **bus** Universal[daten]bus m *(Verteiler)*
~ **data** Hilfsdaten pl, Zusatzdaten pl
~ **developer (developing agent)** Hilfsentwickler m

~ **information carrier** Hilfsträger m, Unterträger m
~ **lens** Zusatzlinse f, Vorsatzlinse f, Vorsatzobjektiv n, Zusatzobjektiv n
~ **oscillator** Hilfsoszillator m
~ **storage** Wechselspeicher m, externer Speicher m

AV out[put] Audio-Video-Ausgang m
available light verfügbares (vorhandenes) Licht n
avalanche photodiode Lawinenfotodiode f
avatar Avatar m, Computerfigur f; digitaler Sprecher (Darsteller) m *(Software-Programm)*
average/to mitteln
average Mittelwert m
~ **access time** mittlere Zugriffszeit f
~ **artificial daylight** künstliches mittleres Tageslicht n
~ **bit rate** mittlere Bitrate f
~ **brightness [level]** Durchschnittshelligkeit f, mittlere Helligkeit f
~ **code word length** mittlere Codewortlänge f
~ **contrast** mittlerer Kontrast m
~ **daylight** mittleres Tageslicht n
~ **gradient** mittlerer Gradient m, G-Strich m *(Densitometrie)*
~ **gray value** mittlerer Grauwert m
~ **image** Mittelwertbild n
~ **information content** mittlerer Informationsgehalt m
~ **noon daylight** mittleres Mittagslicht n
~ **observer** Normalbeobachter m, durchschnittlicher (normalsichtiger) Beobachter m
~ **optical density** mittlere optische Dichte f
~ **photographer** Durchschnittsfotograf m
~ **sensitivity** Normalempfindlichkeit f *(von Fotomaterial)*
~ **slope** s. ~ gradient

averaging Mittelwertbildung f, Mittelung f
~ **filter** Mittelwertfilter n
~ **operation** Mittelwertoperation f *(s.a. averaging)*
~ **operator** Erwartungsoperator m *(Bildquantisierung)*

averted vision gezieltes Danebenschauen n *(Beobachtungstechnik)*
Avogadro's constant, Avogadro['s] number Avogadro-Konstante f, Avogadrosche Zahl f *(Anzahl Atome oder Moleküle pro Mol)*
axal s. axial
axes of coordinates Koordinatenachsen f pl
axial axial
~ **astigmatism** axialer Astigmatismus m
~ **chromatic aberration**, ~ **color** axiale chromatische Aberration f, Farblängsfehler m, Farbortsfehler m, Farbschnittweitenfehler m, chromatische Längsaberration (Schnittweitendifferenz) f

~-flow laser längsgeströmter (axial durchströmter) Laser *m*
~ image dislocation axiale Bildversetzung *f*
~ point spread function *s.* ~ resolution
~ ray Achsenstrahl *m*
~ resolution axiale Auflösung *f*
~ resolving power axiales Auflösungsvermögen *n (s.a.* depth of field*)*
~ symmetry Axialsymmetrie *f*, axiale Symmetrie *f*, Achsensymmetrie *f*
axiality Axialität *f*
axially parallel achsenparallel
~ symmetrical system achsensymmetrisches System *n*
axis Achse *f*
~ of a lens 1. Linsenachse *f*; 2. Objektivachse *f*
~ of gaze Blickachse *f*
~ of polarization Polarisationsachse *f*
~ of precession Präzessionsachse *f (Magnetresonanzbildgebung)*
~ of rotation Drehachse *f*, Rotationsachse *f*
~ of shear Scher[ungs]achse *f*
~ of symmetry Symmetrieachse *f*
~-parallel achsenparallel
axisymmetric[al] achsensymmetrisch, axialsymmetrisch
axisymmetry *s.* axial symmetry
axonometric projection axonometrische Projektion *f*, Axonometrie *f*
~ representation axonometrische Darstellung *f*
azimuth Azimut *n(m)*, Richtungswinkel *m (s.a.* azimuthal angle*)*
~ adjustment Azimuteinstellung *f*
~ display Azimutdarstellung *f (Radar)*
~ error Azimutfehler *m*
~ loss Azimutverlust *m*
~ recording Schrägspuraufzeichnung *f (Video)*
~ resolution Azimutauflösung *f*, azimutale Auflösung *f (Radar)*
~ resolution cell Auflösungszelle *f*
~-scanning radar Rundsuchradar *n*
~ sweep Azimutdurchlauf *m*
azimuthal azimutal
~ angle Azimutwinkel *m*, azimutaler Winkel *m*, Horizontalwinkel *m*, Längenwinkel *m*
~ effect Azimuteffekt *m*
~ equidistant projection [mittabstandstreue] Azimutalprojektion *f*, äquidistante Projektion *f*
azo dye (pigment) Azofarbstoff *m*
azomethine dye Azomethinfarbstoff *m*

B

B frame B-Bild *n*, bidirektional [prädiktiv] codiertes Bild *n (Videocodierung)*
B mode image B-Mode-Bild *n*
B mode imaging B-Bild-Sonografie *f*, B-Bildverfahren *n*, zweidimensionale Sonografie *f*
B mode scanner B-Mode-Scanner *m (Sonografie)*
B scan imaging (modality) *s.* B mode imaging
B setting B-Einstellung *f (Fotoapparat)*
B spline [curve] B-Spline-Kurve *f*, B-Spline *n (Computergrafik)*
B spline surface patch B-Spline-Fläche *f*
B spline transform B-Spline-Transformation *f*
B type *s.* B wind
B wind B-Wicklung *f (Kinefilm)*
B-Y signal *s.* blue-minus-luma signal
Babinet['s] principle Babinets Prinzip *n*, Babinetsches Theorem *n (Beugungsoptik)*
baby legs *s.* ~ tripod
~ **light (spot)** Babyspot[scheinwerfer] *m*
~ **tripod** [Dreibein-]Kleinstativ *n*, Ministativ *n*
back buffer Hintergrund[farb]puffer *m*, Rückspeicher *m (Computergrafik)*
~-**coated mirror** Rückflächenspiegel *m*
~ **cover** Hinterdeckel *m (Buchherstellung)*
~ **focal distance** Bildschnittweite *f*, bildseitige Schnittweite (Brennpunktschnittweite) *f*, Auflagemaß *n (Objektiv)*
~ **focal length** Bildbrennweite *f*, bildseitige (hintere) Brennweite *f*
~ **focal plane** bildseitige (hintere) Brennebene *f*
~ **focus** *s.* ~ focal distance
~ **intensifying screen** Rück[verstärkungs]folie *f (Röntgenkassette)*
~ **light** *s.* background light
~ **lighting** Gegenlichtbeleuchtung *f*
~ **matter** Notenanhang *m (Layout)*
~ **of the eye** Augenhintergund *m*, Augenrückwand *f*
~ **of the film** Filmrückseite *f*, Blankseite *f*, Glanzseite *f*, emulsionsabgewandte Seite *f*
~ **plane** Hintergrund *m (s.a. background)*
~ **porch** hintere Schwarzschulter *f (Videosignal)*
~-**project/to** [zu]rückprojizieren
~-**projected image** Rückprojektionsbild *n*, rückprojiziertes Bild *n*
~ **projection** Rückprojektion *f*

~-**projection algorithm** Rückprojektionsalgorithmus *m*
~-**projection imaging (technique)** Rückprojektion[stechnik] *f*
~ **projector** Rückprojektor *m*, Rückprojektionsgerät *n*
~ **reflection** Rückreflexion *f*
~-**silvered mirror** Rückflächenspiegel *m*
~ **standard** Rückstandarte *f*, Filmstandarte *f*, Bildrückteil *n*, Filmrückwand *f*, Kamerarückteil *m(n)*, Rückteil *m(n) (Fachkamera)*
~-**surface mirror** Rückflächenspiegel *m*
~ **up/to** 1. sicherungskopieren; 2. beidseitig bedrucken
backbone Basisnetz *n (Netzwerkstruktur)*
backchannel Rückkanal *m (Datenübertragung)*
backdrop Hintergrundmaterial *n*, Hintergrund[vorhang] *m*, Rückhänger *m (Studioausrüstung; Filmhintergrund)*
backface culling (removal) Rückseitenentfernung *f (Computergrafik)*
background 1. Hintergrund *m*; 2. *s.* backdrop
~ **color** Hintergrundfarbe *f*
~ **countermatte** Hintergrundmaske *f*, Hintergrundmaskenfilm *m*, Gegenmaske *f*, Gegenkasch *m*
~ **density** Hintergrundrauschen *n*, Umgebungsrauschen *n*
~ **detail** Hintergrunddetail *n*
~ **drawing** Hintergrundzeichnung *f (Animationsfilm)*
~ **illumination** Hintergrundausleuchtung *f*
~ **image** Hintergrundbild *n*
~ **image noise** Gesamtrauschen *n*
~ **light** Hinter[grund]licht *n*, Horizontbeleuchtung *f*
~ **lighting** Hintergrundbeleuchtung *f*
~ **luminance** Hintergrundleuchtdichte *f*
~ **luminosity** Hintergrundhelligkeit *f*
~ **noise** Grundrauschen *n*, Hintergrundrauschen *n*, Hintergrundgeräusch[e] *n[pl]*; Geräuschuntermalung, Geräuschkulisse *f*
~ **object** Hintergrundobjekt *n*
~ **paper** Hintergrundkarton *m*, Papierhintergrund *m (Studioausrüstung)*
~ **pixel** Hintergrundpixel *n*
~ **plate** Hintergrundbild *n (Filmproduktion)*
~ **point** Hintergrundpunkt *m (Bildsegmentierung)*
~ **prediction** Hintergrundprädiktion *f*
~ **primitive** Hintergrundprimitiv *n*
~ **process** *s.* batch mode
~ **projection** Hintergrundprojektion *f*; Rückprojektion *f*, Durchprojektion *f*
~ **projector** Hintergrundprojektor *m*
~ **radiation** [kosmische] Hintergrundstrahlung *f*, Drei-Kelvin-Strahlung *f*;

Umgebungsstrahlung *f*;
Untergrundstrahlung *f*
~ **radiation noise** Grundrauschen *n*,
Hintergrundrauschen *n*,
Hintergrundgeräusch[e] *n[pl]*
~ **region** Hintergrundbereich *m*
~ **scattering** Untergrundstreuung *f*
(Laserspektroskopie)
~ **scene** Hintergrundszene *f*
~ **signal** Hintergrundsignal *n*
~ **sound[s]** Hintergrundgeräusch[e] *n[pl]*,
Untergrundgeräusch *n*
~ **subject** Hintergrundobjekt *n*
~ **subtraction** Hintergrundabzug *m*,
Hintergrundsubtraktion *f*
(Bildverarbeitung)
~ **table** Aufnahmetisch *m*
(Studioausrüstung)
backing Hintergrund[vorhang] *m*,
Hintergrundmaterial *n*
(Studioausrüstung; Filmhintergrund)
~ **color** Hintergrundfarbe *f*
~ **flat** Rücksetzer *m (Studioausrüstung)*
~ **layer** Rückguss *m (Filmherstellung)*
~ **paper** Papierschutzband *n (Rollfilm)*
~ **storage** Wechselspeicher *m*
~ **up** Widerdruck *m*
backlight/to hinterleuchten
backlight 1. Gegenlicht *n*; 2.
Gegenlichtquelle *f*; 3. *s.* background
light
~ **button** Gegenlichttaste *f (Camcorder)*
~ **compensation** Gegenlichtkompensation
f, Gegenlichtkorrektur *f*
~ **photography** Gegenlichtfotografie *f*
backlighted [camera] shot
Gegenlichtaufnahme *f*
backlighting Hinterleuchten *n*,
Hinterleuchtung *f*
~ **light source** Gegenlichtquelle *f*
backlit CCD (charge-coupled device)
rückseitenbestrahlter CCD-Sensor *m*
~ **LCD** hintergrundbeleuchtete
Flüssigkristallanzeige *f*
backlot Filmgelände *n*,
Produktionsgelände *n*
Studio[frei]gelände *n*
backpropagation Fehlerrückführung *f*,
Fehlerrückvermittlung *f*;
Fehlerrückmeldung *f*;
Fehlerrückverfolgung *f*
~ **network** Fehlerrückführungsnetz *n*
(Neuroinformatik)
backscatter/to [zu]rückstreuen
backscatter Rück[wärts]streuung *f*
~ **X-ray unit** Reflexionsröntgengerät *n*
backscattered electron Rückstreuelektron
n
~ **electron image** Rückstreuelektronenbild
n (Elektronenmikroskopie)
~ **light** rückgestreutes Licht *n*
~ **radiation** rückgestreute Strahlung *f*
~ **signal** Echosignal *n (Radar)*
~ **wave** rückgestreute Welle *f*

backscattering coefficient
Rückstreukoeffizient *m*
backslanting rückwärtsgeneigt
(Schriftschnitt)
backslash Rückschrägstrich *m*
backup 1. Datensicherung *f*; 2. *s.* ~ copy
~ **camera** Ersatzkamera *f*
~ **copy** Sicherungskopie *f*,
Sicherheitskopie *f*,
Datensicherungskopie *f*
~ **file** Sicherungsdatei *f*
~ **printing** Widerdruck *m*
backward-adaptive bit allocation
rückwärtsadaptive Bitzuordnung *f*
~-adaptive prediction
rückwärtsgesteuerte adaptive Prädiktion
f
~-adaptive quantization
rückwärtsadaptive Quantisierung *f*
~ **chaining** Rückwärtsverkettung *f*
~ **channel** Rückkanal *m*
(Datenübertragung)
~ **compatibility** Rückwärtskompatibilität *f*,
Abwärtskompatibilität *f*
~ **compatible** rückwärtskompatibel,
abwärtskompatibel
~ **difference operator**
Rückwärtsdifferenzenoperator *m*
~ **mapping** Rückwärtsabbildung *f*, inverse
Abbildung *f (geometrische
Transformation)*
~ **playout** Rückwärtsabspielen *n*,
Rückwärtsabspielung *f*
~ **predicition** Rückwärtsprädiktion *f*
(Bildsequenzcodierung)
~ **wave oscillator (tube)** Carcinotron *n*,
Karzinotron *n (eine Elektronenröhre)*
backwind/to [zu]rückspulen, umrollen *(z.B.
Bandmaterial)*
bactericide Bakterizid *n (Entwicklerzusatz)*
badge meter Filmdosimeter *n*,
Strahlenschutzplakette *f*, Filmplakette *f*
balance arm Führungsgriff *m*,
Führungshebel *m (Stativ)*
~ **stripe** Ausgleichsspur *f (Tonfilm)*
balanced line symmetrische Leitung *f*
~ **tree** ausgeglichener Baum *m*
(Datenstruktur)
balancing coating Rückkaschierung *f*
(eines Filmschichtträgers)
~ **filter** Ausgleichsfilter *n*;
Schwächungsfilter *n (Radiografie)*
ball and socket [tripod] head, ~ joint head
Kugel[gelenk]kopf *m*, Kugelgelenk *n*,
Kugelneiger *m (Stativ)*
~-point ink Kugelschreibertinte *f*
~ **printer** Kugelkopfdrucker *m*
~ **terminal** Kugelende *n (Buchstabenbild)*
Ballard process Ballard-Verfahren *n*
(Druckformaufkupferung)
ballistic electron emission microscope
ballistisches
Elektronenemissionsmikroskop *n*
~ **photography** ballistische Fotografie *f*

ballistic 26

~-**synchro camera** synchroballistische Kamera *f*
~ **videography** ballistische Videografie *f*
balloon Sprechblase *f (Typografie)*
band Band *n*, Frequenzband *n*; Kanal *m (Telekommunikation)*
~ **elimination filter** *s.* band-stop filter
~ **gap** Bandlücke *f*, Bandabstand *m (Fotodiode)*
~-**limit/to** das Frequenzband begrenzen
~ **limitation (limiting)** Bandbegrenzung *f*
~-**limited** band[breiten]begrenzt
~-**limited channel** bandbegrenzter Kanal *m*
~-**limited function** bandbreitenbegrenzte Funktion *f*
~-**limited functions tree** bandbreitenbegrenzter Funktionsbaum *m*
~-**limited signal** band[breiten]begrenztes Signal *n*
~-**limiting filter** Bandbegrenzungsfilter *n*
~ **model** Bändermodell *n*, Energiebändermodell *n*, Bänderschema *n (Halbleiterphysik)*
~ **of frequencies** Frequenzband *n*, Frequenzbereich *m*
~ **of wavelengths** Wellenlängenband *n*
~-**pass** Bandpass *m (s.a.* passband*)*
~-**pass characteristic** *s.* ~ response
~-**pass filter** Bandpassfilter *n*, Band[breiten]filter *n*
~-**pass filtering [operation]** Bandpassfilterung *f*
~-**pass function** Bandpassfunktion *f*
~-**pass pyramid** Laplace-Pyramide *f (Bildverarbeitung)*
~-**pass response** Bandpassverhalten *n*, Bandpasscharakterisitk *f*
~-**pass sampling** Bandpassabtastung *f*
~-**pass signal** Bandpassignal *n*
~ **printer** Banddrucker *m*, Kettendrucker *m*
~-**reject filter** *s.* band-stop filter
~ **spectrum** Bandenspektrum *n*
~-**stop filter** Bandsperrfilter *n*, Bandsperre *f*, Sperrfilter *n*
~-**stop filtering** Bandsperrfilterung *f*
~ **theory** *s.* ~ model
banding 1. Streifenartefakt *n*; 2. *s.* posterization; 3. *s.* amplitude quantization
bandwidth Bandbreite *f (Frequenzbereich)*
~ **availability** Bandbreitenverfügbarkeit *f*
~ **channel** Kanal *m (Kommunikationstheorie)*
~ **compression** Bandbreitenkompression *f*
~-**constrained (bandwidth-limited) system** bandbreitenbegrenztes System *n*
~ **consumption** Bandbreitenverbrauch *m*
~ **expansion** Bandbreitenexpansion *f*
~ **fluctuation** Bandbreitenschwankung *f*, Bandbreitenfluktuation *f*

~ **limitation (limiting)** Bandbreitenbegrenzung *f*, Bandbreitenbeschränkung *f*
~ **reduction** Bandbreitenreduktion *f*
~ **requirement** Bandbreitenbedarf *m*
~ **segment** Bandbreitensegment *n*
~ **use** Bandbreitenausnutzung *f*
bank of filters Filterbank *f*
~ **surveillance camera** Banküberwachungskamera *f*
bankcheck reader Scheckscanner *m*
banknote paper Banknotenpapier *n*
banner Schlagzeile *f*
~ **ad[vertising]** Bannerwerbung *f (Internet)*
~ **page** *s.* ~ screen
~ **printing** Bannerdruck *m*
~ **screen** Eröffnungsbildschirm *m*, Begrüßungsbildschirm *m*
bar chart *s.* ~ graph
~ **code** Strichcode *m*, Barcode *m*, Balkencode *m*
~-**code labeling** Strichcodierung *f*
~-**code pistol** Strichcode-Lesepistole *f*
~-**code reader** Strichcodeleser *m*, Barcodeleser *m*, Barcodescanner *m*
~-**code reading** Strichcodelesen *n*, Barcodelesen *n*
~-**code scanner** *s.* ~ reader
~ **coding** Strichcodierung *f*
~ **detector** Balkendetektor *m*
~ **graph** Säulendiagramm *n*, Balkendiagramm *n (s.a.* histogram*)*
~ **pattern** Balkenraster *m(n)*, Strichraster *m(n)*
bare tungsten filament bulb Klarglas[glüh]birne *f*, Klarglaslampe *f*
barite Baryt *m*, Schwerspat *m*
barium crown [glass] Baritkronglas *n*
~ **sulfate** Bariumsulfat *n*
Barlow lens Barlow-Linse *f (Teleskop)*
barn door Scheinwerfertor *n*, Lampentor *n*, Lichttor *n*, Lichtklappe *f*, Torblende *f*, Lichtblende *f*
barney Schallschutzgehäuse *n*, Schallschutzhaube *f (s.a.* blimp*)*
barrage jammer breitbandiger Störer *m (Radar)*
barrel Tubus *m*
~ **distortion** Tonnenverzeichnung *f*, Tonnenverzerrung *f*, tonnenförmige Verzeichnung *f (Abbildungsfehler)*
~ **printer** Typenwalzendrucker *m*, Walzendrucker *m*, Trommeldrucker *m*
barrier filter Sperrfilter *n (UV-Fluoreszenzfotografie)*
~ **layer** Sperrschicht *f*, Randschicht *f Halbleiterfotoelement)*
~ **layer cell** Sperrschicht-Fotoelement *n*, Sperrschicht[foto]zelle *f*, fotovoltaische Zelle *f*; Halbleiterfotoelement *n*
~ **penetration** [quantenmechanisches] Tunneln *n (Teilchenphysik)*

Bartlett window Bartlett-Fenster *n*, Bartlett-Filter *n*, Dreiecksfenster *n* *(Signalverabeitung)*
barycenter Baryzentrum *n*, Schwerpunkt *m*, Masseschwerpunkt *m*
barycentric coordinate baryzentrische Koordinate *f*
baryta Baryt *m*, Bariumsulfat *n (Pigment, Röntgenkontrastmittel)*
~-**coated** barytbeschichtet
~ **coating** Barytschicht *f*, Barytbeschichtung *f*
~ **paper** Barytpapier *n*; Barytfotopapier *n*
~ **white** Barytweiß *n*, Permanentweiß *n*
baryte[s] Baryt *m*, Schwerspat *m*
base 1. Basis *f*, Grundlage *f (s.a.* film base*);* 2. Base *f (Chemie)*
~ **bandwidth** Basisbandbreite *f*
~ **code** Basiscode *m (Bildkompression)*
~ **density** Grundschwärze *f*, Grundschwärzung *f*
~ **exposure time** Grundbelichtungszeit *f*
~ **line** Schriftlinie *f*
~ **map** Grundkarte *f (Kartografie)*
~ **memory** Arbeitsspeicher *m*
~ **number** Grundzahl *f*
~ **of the microscope** Mikroskopstativfuß *m*; Mikroskopstativ *n*
~ **plate** Grundplatte *f (Stativ)*
~-**plate electrode** Trägerelektrode *f*
~ **plus fog** Minimaldichte *f (Schwarzweißfilm)*
~ **side** Filmrückseite *f*
~ **thickness** Papierstärke *f*, Papierdicke *f*
~ **unit [in the International System of Units]** internationale Basiseinheit *f*, SI-Einheit *f*
~ **vector** Basisvektor *m*, Einheitsvektor *m*
~ **white** Grundweiß *n*
baseband Basisband *n (Frequenz)*
~ **filter** Basisbandfilter *n*
~ **modulation** Basisbandmodulation *f*
~ **signal** Basisbandsignal *n*
~ **transmission** Basisbandübertragung *f*
baseboard Grundbrett *n (Vergrößerungsgerät)*
baseline Grundlinie *f*, Schrift[grund]linie *f (Typografie)*
basic color s. basis color
~ **colorimetry** Farbvalenzmetrik *f*, niedere Farbmetrik *f*
~ **contrast** Grundkontrast *m*
~ **filter** Grundfilter *n*
~ **fog** Grundschleier *m*
~ **frequency** Grundfrequenz *f*
~ **noise level** Grundrauschpegel *m*
~ **shape [geometrische]** Grundform *f*
~ **stimulus** Mittelpunktsvalenz *f*
basis color Grundfarbe *f*, Primärfarbe *f*, Spektralhauptfarbe *f*; Normspektralfarbe *f*, Primärvalenz *f*, Primärfarbwert *m*
~ **function** Basisfunktion *f (digitale Bildverarbeitung)*
~ **image** Basisbild *n*
~ **matrix** Basisbild *n (digitale Bildverarbeitung)*
~ **spline** B-Spline-Kurve *f*, B-Spline *n (Computergrafik)*
~ **vector** Basisvektor *m*, Einheitsvektor *m*
~ **weight [of paper]** Papierflächengewicht *n*, Papierflächenmasse *f*
bass boosting Bassanhebung *f*
~ **loudspeaker** Tieftonlautsprecher *m*
batch capture s. ~ digitizing
~ **digitizing** Stapeldigitalisierung *f*, Stapelaufnahme *f (z.B. von Videomaterial)*
~ **file** Stapeldatei *f (Datenverarbeitung)*
~ **mode (processing)** Stapelverarbeitung *f*
bath temperature Badtemperatur *f (Fotoverarbeitung)*
bathochromic shift bathochrome Verschiebung *f*
bathochromism Bathochromie *f*
bathymetric map Gewässertiefenkarte *f*
bathymetry Bathymetrie *f*, Wassertiefenmessung *f*
battery Batterie *f*; Akku[mulator] *f*
~ **belt** Akkugürtel *m*, Batteriegürtel *m*
~ **charge tester** Batterietester *m*
~ **charger** Batterieladegerät *n*, [externes] Ladegerät *n*
~ **check** Batterieprüfung *f*, Batteriekontrolle *f*
~ **compartment** Batteriefach *m (z.B. einer Kamera)*
~ **cover** Batteriefachdeckel *m*
~ **holder** Batteriemagazin *n*
~ **mode** Batteriebetrieb *m*
~ **pack** Akkupack *m*
~ **power** Akkukapazität *f*
~-**powered** batteriebetrieben, batteriegespeist
~ **remaining indicator** Akkuanzeige *f*
batwing antenna Schmetterlingsantenne *f (Fernsehtechnik)*
baud Baud *n (Einheit der Datenübertragungsgeschwindigkeit)*
~ **rate** Baudrate *f*
~ **rate generator** Baudratengenerator *m*
Bauernfeind prism Bauernfeindsches Prisma *n*, Bauernfeind-Prisma *n*
Bayer pattern Bayer-Mosaik *n (CCD-Sensor)*
Bayes decision rule Bayes-Regel *f*
~ **optimal discriminant function** Bayes-Regel *f*
Bayes' theorem Bayes-Theorem *n*, Bayesscher Satz *m (Wahrscheinlichkeitsrechnung)*
Bayesian classification Bayes-Klassifikation *f (Mustererkennung)*
~ **classifier** Bayes-Klassifikator *m*, bayesoptimaler Klassifikator *m*
~ **estimation** Bayes-Schätzung *f*
~ **motion estimation** Bayessche Bewegungsschätzung *f*

Bayesian

~ **network** Bayes-Netz *n* *(Informationstheorie)*
~ **observer** idealer Betrachter *m* *(mathematisches Modell)*
~ **probability theory** Bayessche Wahrscheinlichkeitstheorie *f*
~ **statistics** Bayes-Statistik *f*

bayonet Bajonett *n*; Objektivhalterung *f*
~ **coupling** Bajonettanschluss *m*, Bajonettverschluss *m*
~ **holder** Bajonetthalterung *f*
~ **mount** *s.* ~ coupling

beacon Bake *f (z.B. in Navigationssystemen)*

beaded screen Perl[lein]wand *f*; Kristallperlwand *f*

beak terminal Dachansatz *m (Buchstabenbild)*

beam/to strahlen; abstrahlen

beam Strahlenbündel *n*, Bündel *n*, Strahl *m*; Strahlungskeule *f*
~ **angle** Strahlwinkel *m*
~ **aperture** 1. Bündelöffnung *f*; 2. Strahlenblende *f*, Strahlbegrenzungsblende *f*, bündelbegrenzende Blende *f*
~ **aperture angle** Bündelöffnungswinkel *m*
~ **area** Strahlquerschnitt *m*, Strahlquerschnittsfläche *f (Laser)*
~ **attenuation** Strahlabschwächung *f*
~ **attenuator** Strahlabschwächer *m*
~ **axis** Strahlachse *f*
~ **bending** Strahlenbeugung *f*, Strahlenumlenkung *f*
~ **collimation** Bündelkollimation *f*, Bündelkollimierung *f*
~ **combiner** Strahlmischer *m*
~ **control** Keulensteuerung *f (Radar)*
~ **convergence** Strahlkonvergenz *f*
~ **convergence misalignment** Konvergenzfehler *m*
~ **cross-sectional area** *s.* ~ area
~ **current** Strahlstrom *m*, Elektronenstrahlstrom *m*
~-**defining aperture** Strahlbegrenzungsblende *f*, Strahlenblende *f*, bündelbegrenzende Blende *f*
~ **deflection** Strahlablenkung *f*
~ **deflection cube** Strahlumlenkblock *m*
~ **deflector** Strahlablenker *m*; Strahlweiche *f*
~ **deviation** Strahlablenkung *f*
~ **diameter** Strahldurchmesser *m*
~ **direction** Strahlrichtung *f*
~ **displacement** Strahlversatz *m*
~ **divergence** Strahldivergenz *f*
~ **divider** Strahl[en]teiler *m*
~ **division** Strahlenteilung *f*, Strah[lauf]teilung *f*
~-**division prism** *s.* beam-splitting prism
~ **dump** Lichtfalle *f*
~ **energy** Strahlenergie *f*
~ **expander** Strahlaufweitung *f*
~ **expanding system** Strahlaufweitsystem *n*
~ **expansion** Strahlaufweitung *f*
~ **focus** Strahlfokus *m*
~ **focusing** Strahlfokussierung *f*; Bündelfokussierung *f*
~ **forming** Strahlformung *f*
~ **geometry** Strahlgeometrie *f*
~-**guiding system** Strahlführung *f*
~ **hardening** Strahlenaufhärtung *f*, Aufhärtung *f (Röntgenabsorption)*
~ **intensity** Strahlstärke *f*, Strahlintensität *f (Radiometrie)*
~ **limiting** Strahlbegrenzung *f*
~-**limiting aperture** *s.* beam-defining aperture
~ **matrix tube** Strahlmatrixröhre *f*
~ **modulation** Strahlmodulation *f*
~ **multiplexer** Strahlvervielfacher *m*
~ **multiplexing** Strahlvervielfachung *f*
~ **of rays** Strahlenbündel *n*, Bündel *n*, Strahlenbüschel *n*; Strahl *m*
~ **optics** Bündeloptik *f*
~ **partition** Strahlenteilung *f*, Strahl[auf]teilung *f*
~ **path** Strahlweg *m*, Strahlverlauf *m*, Strahlengang *m*
~ **path length** Strahllänge *f*
~ **position** Strahllage *f*
~ **position stability** Strahllagestabilität *f*
~ **power** Strahlleistung *f (Laser)*
~ **profile** Strahlprofil *n*
~ **profiling** Strahlprofilierung *f*
~ **projector** Parabolspiegelscheinwerfer *m*, Niedervoltscheinwerfer *m*
~ **propagation factor** Strahlpropagationsfaktor *m (Laser)*
~ **radius** Strahlradius *m*
~ **sampler** Strahlprober *m*
~ **sampling** Strahlprobung *f*
~ **scanning speed** Strahlgeschwindigkeit *f*
~ **shape loss** Keulenverlust *m (Radar)*
~ **shaper** Strahlformer *f*
~ **shaping** Strahlformung *f*
~ **source** Strahlquelle *f*
~ **splitter** Strahl[en]teiler *m*
~ **splitting** Strahlenteilung *f*, Strahl[auf]teilung *f*
~-**splitting camera** Strahlenteilerkamera *f*, Strahlenteilungskamera *f*
~-**splitting mirror** Teilerspiegel *m*, strahl[en]teilender Spiegel *m*
~-**splitting optics** Strahlenteilungsoptik *f*
~-**splitting prism** Strahlenteilungsprisma *n*, Teilerprisma *n*
~-**splitting ratio** Strahlenteilungsverhältnis *n*
~ **spread** Strahldivergenz *f*
~ **spreading** Strahlaufweitung *f*
~ **stability** Strahlstabilität *f (Laser)*
~ **steerer** Strahlumlenkung *f (optisches Bauteil)*
~ **steering** Strahlsteuerung *f*; Strahlumlenkung *f*

~ **symmetry** Strahlsymmetrie *f*
~ **thickness** Strahldicke *f*
~ **undulator** Undulator *m*
~ **velocity** Strahlgeschwindigkeit *f*
~ **voltage** Strahlspannung *f*
~ **waist** [Gaußsche] Strahltaille *f*, Gaußsche Strahlweite *f*, Fleckradius *m* *(paraxiale Optik)*
~ **waist diameter** Taillendurchmesser *m*
~ **waist radius** Taillenradius *m*
~ **width** Strahlbreite *f*
beamer elektronischer Bildwerfer *m*, Digitalprojektor *m*; Bildschirmprojektor *m*, LCD-Projektor *m*; Videoprojektor *m*, Multimediaprojektor *m*, Präsentationsprojektor *m*
bearer Messring *m (Druckformzylinder)*
beat Schwebung *f (Wellenoptik)*
~ **length** Schwebungslänge *f*
Beck effect Beck-Effekt *m (Optik)*
Becquerel effect Becquerel-Effekt *m (Belichtungseffekt)*
bed 1. Laufboden *m (Fachkamera)*; 2. Druckformträger *m (Buchdruck)*
Beer's law, Beer-Lambert [absorption] law Beersches Gesetz *n*, Beersche Formel *f*, Lambert-Beer[sches]-Gesetz *n (spektrale Absorption)*
before image Vor[ab]bild *n*, vorangehendes Bild *n (Videocodierung)*
begin edit point Schnittanfang *m (Filmbearbeitung, Videobearbeitung)*
beginning of a tape Bandanfang *m*
~ **of line** Zeilenanfang *m*
behavioral animation verhaltensbedingte Animation *f*
Bell and Howell barrel-shaped perforation Bell-Howell-Perforation *f*, Negativperforation *f (Kinefilm)*
bell-shaped curve (function) Glockenkurve *f (Statistik)*
~-**shaped pulse** Gauß-Impuls *m*
bellows 1. Balgen *m*; 2. *s*. ~ extension
~ **attachment** Balgen[einstell]gerät *n*
~ **camera** Balgenkamera *f*, Klappkamera *f*
~ **connection** Balgenzwischenstück *n*
~ **extension** Balgenauszug *m*; Kameraauszug *m*, Bildentfernung *f*, Bildweite *f*
belt printer Kettendrucker *m*, Banddrucker *m*
bench mark Vergleichspunkt *m*
bend/to beugen
bending Beugung *f*, Diffraktion *f*
~ **magnet** Beugungsmagnet *m*
bendy leg tripod Kleinstativ *n* mit flexiblen Beinen
Benham['s] disk Benham-Scheibe *f*, Benhamsche Scheibe *f (Farbpsychologie)*
bent contour Biegekontur *f (Elektronenmikroskopie)*
Benton hologram Benton-Hologramm *n*, Regenbogenhologramm *n*

benzene Benzol *n (Lösungsmittel)*
~ **derivative** Benzolderivat *n (Entwicklungschemikalie)*
benzotriazole Benztriazol *n (Antischleiermittel)*
Bernoulli distribution *s*. binomial distribution
Bernstein polynomial Bernstein-Polynom *n*, Bernstein-Basispolynom *n (Computergrafik)*
Bertrand lens Bertrand-Linse *f (Phasenkontrastmikroskopie)*
Bessel filter Bessel-Filter *n*, Thomson-Filter *n (Fernsehtechnik)*
~ **function** Bessel-Funktion *f (Frequenzmodulation)*
~ **function of order one, ~ function of the first kind** Bessel-Funktion *f* erster Ordnung
best boy [electric] Beleuchter *m*, Beleuchtungsassistent *m (Filmarbeit)*
beta Beta *n*, Betawert *m*, relativistische Geschwindigkeit *f (Densitometrie)*
~-**barium borate** Bariumbetaborat *n*, BBO
~ **decay** Betazerfall *m*
~ **fluorography** Betafluorografie *f*
~ **particle** Betateilchen *n*
~ **radiation** Betastrahlung *f*
~ **radiography** Betaradiografie *f*
betaluminescence Betalumineszenz *f*
betatron Betatron *n (Elektronenbeschleuniger)*
better-than-pixel resolution Subpixelauflösung *f*
between-the-lens[-type] shutter Zentralverschluss *m*, Objektivverschluss *m*
bevel 1. Fase *f*; 2. Konus *m (Drucktype)*
bevelled overlapped splice keilförmig überlappte Klebestelle *f (Film)*
bezel Bildschirmmaske *f*, Bildröhrenmaske *f*, Bildschirmrahmen *m*
Bézier approximation Bézier-Approximation *f (Computergrafik)*
~ **bicubic patch** bikubische Bézier-Fläche *f*
~ **curve** Bézier-Kurve *f*, Bézier-Funktion *f*, Bézier-Polynom *n*
~ **geometry vector** Bézier-Vektor *m*
~ **hyperpatch** Bézier-Hyperfläche *f*
~ **patch** Bézier-Flächensegment *n*
~ **segment** Bézier-Kurvensegment *n*, Bézier-Segment *n*
~ **spline** *s*. ~ curve
~ **surface** Bézier-Fläche *f*
Bezold-Brücke phenomenon Bezold-Brücke-Effekt *m*, Brücke-Bezoldsches Phänomen *n (Farbwahrnehmung)*
BH barrel-shaped perforation Bell-Howell-Perforation *f*, Negativperforation *f (Kinefilm)*

bias

bias Vorspannung f *(z.B. eines Sensors)*; Grundgrauwert m; Gleichanteil m; Bias m, Neigung f; Vormagnetisierung f
~ **current** Sperrstrom m
~ **light** seitliches Auflicht n
~ **voltage** Sperr[vor]spannung f *(z.B. an einer Transistorsteuerelektrode)*
biased detector vorgespannter Detektor m
biasing Vormagnetisierung f
biaxial crystal [optisch] zweiachsiger Kristall m
bichromated ... s. dichromated ...
bichrome, bicolor[ed] bichrom, zweifarbig
biconcave bikonkav
~ **lens** Bikonkavlinse f, bikonkave Linse f
biconcavity Bikonkavität f
biconvex bikonvex
~ **lens** Bikonvexlinse f, bikonvexe Linse f
biconvexity Bikonvexität f
bicubic bikubisch
~ **algorithm** bikubischer Algorithmus m
~ **B-spline surface patch** bikubische B-Spline-Fläche f
~ **interpolation** bikubische Interpolation f
~ **surface** bikubische Fläche f
bidimensional zweidimensional
bidimensionality Zweidimensionalität f
bidirectional bidirektional
~ **associative memory** bidirektionaler Assoziativspeicher m, bidirektionaler assoziativer Speicher m
~ **bus** bidirektionaler Bus m *(Datenübertragung)*
~ **frame** bidirektional [prädiktiv] codiertes Bild n, B-Bild n *(Videocodierung)*
~ **interface** bidirektionale Schnittstelle f
~ **microphone** zweiseitig gerichtetes Mikrofon n
~ **prediction** bidirektionale Prädiktion f
~ **printer** bidirektionaler Drucker m
~ **printing** bidirektionaler Druck m
~ **spectral reflectivity** bidirektionales Reflexionsvermögen n
~ **thyristor** Zweirichtungsthyristor m
bidirectionally predictive coded picture s. bidirectional frame
bifocal Bifokalbrille f
~ **[eyeglass] lens** Bifokallinse f, Bifokalglas n, Zweistärkenglas n *(Brillenoptik)*
~ **spectacles** Bifokalbrille f
big enlargement Großvergrößerung f
~ **viewfinder** Großbildsucher m
bilateral area track Doppelzackenschrift f *(Lichttonaufzeichnung)*
~ **filtering** bilaterale Filterung f
bilevel display Monochrombildschirm m, Schwarzweißbildschirm m
~ **graphics** Binärgrafik f
~ **image** 1. binäres Bild n, Binärbild n; 2. Doppeltonbild n, bitonales Bild n
~ **pixel** Binärbildpunkt m
bilinear filter bilineares Filter n
~ **filtering** bilineare Filterung f
~ **interpolation** bilineare Interpolation f

~ **mapping** bilineare Abbildung f
~ **motion** bilineare Bewegung f
~ **subdivision** bilineare Subdivision (Unterteilung) f
~ **transformation** bilineare Transformation f
billboard 1. Anzeigetafel f; 2. Trägerpolygon n *(Computergrafik)*
Billet's split lens Billetsche Halblinsen fpl
bimetal plate Bimetallplatte f *(Druck)*
bimodal bimodal
~ **histogram** bimodales Histogramm n
bimodality Bimodalität f
bin 1. Histogrammurne f; 2. s. film bin; 3. s. trim bin
binarization Binarisierung f, Binärisierung f
binarize/to binarisieren
binarized image binarisiertes Bild n
binarizing threshold Binarisierungsschwelle f
binary binär, zweiwertig
~ **alphabet** binäres Alphabet n
~ **arithmetic coding** binäre arithmetische Codierung f
~ **channel** Binärkanal m
~ **code** Binärcode m, binärer Code m, Dualcode m
~ **code word** binäres Codewort n
~ **coded information** binär codierte Information f
~ **coding** s. ~ encoding
~ **contour** binäre Kontur f
~ **convolution** binäre Faltung f
~ **data coding** Binärdatencodierung f
~ **digit** Binärzahl f, Binärzeichen n, Binärziffer f, Bit n, Dualzahl f, Dualziffer f *(s.a. unter bit)*
~ **digital image processing** Binärbildverarbeitung f
~ **dilation filter** Dilatationsoperator m
~ **display** Binäranzeige f
~ **edge detection** binäre Kantendetektion f
~ **edge image (map)** binäres Kantenbild n
~ **encoding** Binärcodierung f, binäre (zweiwertige) Codierung f
~ **entropy function** binäre Entropiefunktion f *(Bilddatenkompression)*
~ **error-correcting code** binärer Fehlerkorrekturcode m
~ **file** Binärdatei f, binäre Datei f
~ **filtering** binäre Filterung f
~ **graphics** Binärgrafik f
~ **group flag** Binärgruppenzeichen n
~ **hologram** binäres Hologramm n
~ **image** Binärbild n, binäres Bild n
~ **image analysis** Binärbildanalyse f
~ **image coding (compression)** Binärbildkompression f
~ **image data** binäre Bilddaten pl
~ **image processing** Binärbildverarbeitung f
~ **image representation** Binärbilddarstellung f

~ **image skeletonization** Binärbildskelettierung f, binäre Skelettierung f
~ **large object** s. blob
~ **mask** Binärmaske f
~ **mask image** Binärmaskenbild n
~ **matrix** Binärmatrix f, Boolesche Matrix f
~ **median filter** binäres Medianfilter n
~ **morphology** binäre Morphologie f
~ **noise** binäres Rauschen n
~ **number** Binärzahl f, Binärzeichen n, Binärziffer f, Bit n, Binärelement n, Dualzahl f, Dualziffer f (s.a. unter bit)
~ **number[ing] system** Binärsystem n, binäres System n, Dualsystem n
~ **object** Binärobjekt n, binäres Objekt n
~ **object detection** Binärobjekterkennung f
~ **optics** binäre Optik f
~ **pattern** Binärmuster n, Bitmuster n
~ **phase-shift keying** zweiwertige Phasenumtastung f
~ **picture** Binärbild n, binäres Bild n
~ **prefix code** binärer Präfixcode m
~ **printer** Rasterdrucker m
~ **processing** Binärverarbeitung f
~ **pulse-width modulation** binäre Pulsbreitenmodulation f
~ **representation** Binärdarstellung f, Binärrepräsentation f
~ **search tree** s. ~ tree
~ **segmentation** Bereichsdetektion f
~ **segmentation** Binärsegmentierung f
~ **signal** Binärsignal n, binäres Signal n
~ **space-partitioning tree** binärer Raumunterteilungsbaum m, BSP-Baum m (Datenstruktur)
~ **system** Binärsystem n, binäres System n, Dualsystem n
~ **threshold** Binärschwelle f
~ **thresholding** binäre Schwellenwertbildung f
~ **tree** Binärbaum m, binärer Baum (Suchbaum) m (Datenstruktur)
~ **unit** s. ~ number
~ **value** Binärwert m
~ **word** Binärwort n n
binaural effect Raumklangeffekt m
binder Bindemittel n
binding Bund m (eines mehrseitigen Druckerzeugnisses)
~ **agent (compound)** Bindemittel n
~ **energy** Bindungsenergie f
binning 1. Klasseneinteilung f (z.B. für Histogrammdarstellungen); 2. Pixelbinning n (CCD-Bildtechnik)
binocular binokular, beidäugig
~ **[binokulares] Fernglas** n, Binokular n, Binokel n, Doppelfernrohr n
~ **body** Binokularansatz m, Binokularaufsatz m (Mikroskop, Teleskop)
~ **camera** zweiäugige Kamera f
~ **cell** binokulares Neuron n (Sehsystem)
~ **centration** binokulare Zentrierung f

~ **collimation** binokulare Kollimation f
~ **contrast** binokularer Kontrast m
~ **depth perception** binokulare Tiefenwahrnehmung f, binokulares Stereosehen n
~ **disparity** binokulare Wettstreit m, binokulare Disparität f (Sehen)
~ **field [of view]** binokulares Blickfeld n
~ **fixation point** binokularer Fixationspunkt m
~ **fusion** binokulare Fusion (Verschmelzung) f
~ **luster** binokularer Glanz m
~ **magnifier** Lupenbrille f
~ **microscope** Binokularmikroskop n
~ **parallax** binokulare (stereoskopische) Parallaxe f
~ **rivalry** binokulare Rivalität f
~ **stereo vision, ~ stereopsis** binokulares Stereosehen n, binokulare Tiefenwahrnehmung f
~ **suppression** s. ~ rivalry
~ **telescope** Binokularteleskop n, Doppelteleskop n
~ **tube** Binokulartubus m, binokularer Tubus m
~ **vergence** binokulare Vergenz f
~ **viewing** beidäugige Betrachtung f (s.a. ~ vision)
~ **vision** Binokularsehen n, beidäugiges Sehen n, Simultansehen n
~ **visual field** binokulares Gesichtsfeld n
binocularity Beidäugigkeit f
binomial approximation binomiale Approximation f
~ **distribution** Binomialverteilung f, Bernoulli-Verteilung f
~ **filter** Binomialfilter n
biochemical imaging biochemische Bildgebung f
biocular s. binocular
bioinformatics Bioinformatik f
bioluminescence Biolumineszenz f
biomagnetic imaging biomagnetische Bildgebung f
biomedical imaging biomedizinische Bildgebung f
~ **signal processing** biomedizinische Signalverarbeitung f
biometric[al] biometrisch
biometrical feature biometrisches Merkmal n
~ **signature** biometrische Signatur f
biometrics, biometry Biometrik f, Biometrie f
biomicroscope Biomikroskop n
bionics Bionik f
biophotonic imaging biophotonische Bildgebung f
biorthogonal filter biorthogonales Filter n
~ **filter bank** biorthogonale Filterbank f
~ **transform[ation]** biorthogonale Transformation f
~ **wavelet** biorthogonales Wavelet n

biorthogonal 32

~ **wavelet transform** biorthogonale Wavelet-Transformation *f*
biorthogonality constraint (requirement) Biorthogonalitätsbedingung *f (Rekonstruktionsfilterung)*
bipack film Bipack *n(m) (Filmmaterial für Kombinationsaufnahmen)*
biparty videoconference Zweipartner-Videokonferenz *f*
biped Menschmodell *n (Computeranimation)*
biphasic gradient biphasischer Gradient *m*
biplane angiogram Zweiebenenangiogramm *n*
~ **angiography** biplane Angiografie *f*
bipolar bipolar, zweipolig
~ **cell** Bipolarzelle *f (Augennetzhaut)*
~ **gradient** bipolarer Gradient *m*
~ **image** bipolares Bild *n*
~ **impulse noise** bipolares Impulsrauschen *n*, Schrotrauschen *n*
~ **signal** Bipolarsignal *n*
biprism Doppelbildprisma *n*, [Fresnelsches] Biprisma *n*
biquadratic mapping biquadratische Abbildung *f*
bird *s.* satellite
bird's-eye view Vogelperspektive *f*, extreme Obersicht *f*
bireflection Bireflexion *f*
birefracting *s.* birefringent
birefraction *s.* birefringence
birefractive *s.* birefringent
birefringence Doppelbrechung *f*
birefringent [optisch] doppelbrechend
~ **crystal** doppelbrechender Kristall *m*
~ **filter** doppelbrechendes Filter *n*, Lyot-Filter *n*
~ **interference microscope** doppelbrechendes Interferenzmikroskop *n*
~ **wave plate** Verzögerungsplatte *f*
bispectrum Bispektrum *n*
bispheric lens [symmetrische] Bi-Linse *f*
bistability [optische] Bistabilität *f*
bistable bistabil
~ **image** *s.* bilevel image
~ **system** bistabiles System *n*
bistatic radar bistatisches Radar *n*
~ **radar receiver** bistatischer Radarempfänger *m*
bit Bit *n*, Binärzahl *f*, Binärzeichen *n*, Binärelement *n*, Dualzahl *f*
~ **allocation** Bitzuordnung *f (Bilddatenkompression)*
~ **array** Bitmatrix *f*
~ **assignment** Bitzuweisung *f*
~ **blit** *s.* ~ block transfer
~ **block transfer** Bitblocktransfer *m*, Bitblocktransport *m*
~ **clock rate** Bit-Takt *m*, Bittaktfrequenz *f*, Bitfolgefrequenz *f*
~ **density** Bitdichte *f*
~ **depth** Bittiefe *f*, Datentiefe *f*

~ **error** Bitfehler *m*
~ **error probability** Bitfehlerwahrscheinlichkeit *f*
~ **error rate** Bitfehlerhäufigkeit *f*, Bitfehlerquote *f*, Bitfehlerrate *f*, Bitfehlerzahl *f* pro Sekunde
~ **error ratio** Bitfehlerverhältnis *n*
~ **interleaving** Bitverschachtelung *f*, Bit-Umordnung *f*
~ **location** Bitposition *f*
~-**map** 1. Bitmap *f*, Pixelraster *m(n)*, Bildpunktraster *m(n) (logischer Bildspeicher)*; 2. *s.* bit-mapped image
~-**map animation** Bitmap-Animation *f*
~-**map-based shape coding** bitmapbasierte Formcodierung *f*
~-**map data** Bitmap-Daten *pl*
~-**map display** Rasterdisplay *n*, Rasterbildschirm *m*
~-**map file** Bitmap-Datei *f*, Pixelgrafikdatei *f*
~-**map format** Bitmap-Format *n*, BMP-Format *n*
~-**map representation** Bitmap-Darstellung *f*, Pixeldarstellung *f (s.a. bit-map)*
~-**map texture** Bitmap-Textur *f*
~-**mapped font** Bitmap-Schrift *f*, Bitmap-Zeichensatz *m*
~-**mapped graphics** Pixelgrafik *f*, Bit[muster]grafik *f*, Bitmap-Grafik *f*, Rastergrafik *f*
~-**mapped graphics program** Bitmap-Grafikprogramm *n*, pixelorientiertes Grafikprogramm *n*
~-**mapped image** Bitmap-Bild *n*, Pixelbild *n*, pixelorientiertes Bild *n*, Bitbild *n*, Bitmuster *n*
~-**mapping** Bitabbildung *f*
~ **mask** Bitmaske *f*
~ **masking** Bitmaskierung *f*
~ **matrix** Bitmatrix *f*
~ **parallel** bitparallel
~ **pattern** Bitmuster *n*, Binärmuster *n*
~ **per second** *s.* Baud
~ **period** Bitperiode *f*
~ **plane** Bitebene *f*
~-**plane coded image** bitebenencodiertes Bild *n*
~-**plane coding** Bitebenencodierung *f*
~-**plane decomposition** Bitebenenzerlegung *f*
~-**plane scaling** Bitebenenskalierung *f*
~ **position** Bitposition *f*
~ **rate** Bitrate *f*, Bitfrequenz *f*, mittlere Codewortlänge *f*; Trefferquote *f (Mustererkennung)*
~ **rate compression** Bitratenkompression *f*, Bitratenkomprimierung *f*
~ **rate control** Bitratensteuerung *f*
~ **rate minimization** Bitratenminimierung *f*
~ **rate profile** Bitratenprofil *n*
~ **rate reduction** Bitratenreduktion *f*, Bitratenreduzierung *f*
~ **rate variability** Bitratenvariabilität *f*
~ **rate variation** Bitratenvariation *f*

~ **resolution** Bitauflösung *f*
~ **reversal** Bitumkehr *f*
~ **reverse shuffling** Bitspiegelung *f*
~-**serial** bitseriell
~ **string** Bitfolge *f*
~ **stuffing** Bitstopfen *n*
~ **transfer rate** Bitrate *f*
~ **width** Bitbreite *f*
bitonal image Doppeltonbild *n*, bitonales Bild *n*
bitone ink Doppeltonfarbe *f (Typografie)*
bitonic sequence bitonische Sequenz *f*
bitoric lens bitorische Linse *f*
bits per second Bits *npl* pro Sekunde *(Maßzahl der Datenübertragungsgeschwindigkeit)*
bitstream Bitstrom *m*
~ **syntax** Bitstromsyntax *f*
bitumen of Judea Judäa-Asphalt *m (lichtempfindlicher Stoff)*
~ **process** Asphaltkopierverfahren *n*
Bjerrum screen Bjerrum-Schirm *m (zur Bestimmung der Sehfeldgrenzen)*
black-and-white schwarzweiß *(s.a.unter monochrome, monochromatic)*
~-**and-white camera** Schwarzweißkamera *f*, Monochromkamera *f*
~-**and-white cathode-ray tube** Schwarzweißbildröhre *f*
~-**and-white continuous-tone paper** Schwarzweiß-Halbtonpapier *n*
~-**and-white contrast** Schwarzweißkontrast *m*
~-**and-white copier** Schwarzweißkopierer *m*
~-**and-white copy** Schwarzweißkopie *f;* Schwarzweißvorlage *f*
~-**and-white developer** Schwarzweißentwickler *m*
~-**and-white development** Schwarzweißentwicklung *f*, Schwarzweißverarbeitung *f*
~-**and-white emulsion** Schwarzweißemulsion *f*
~-**and-white enlarger** Schwarzweißvergrößerer *m*, Schwarzweißvergrößerungsgerät *n*
~-**and-white enlarging** Schwarzweißvergrößern *n*
~-**and-white enlarging paper** Schwarzweißvergrößerungspapier *n*
~-**and-white film** Schwarzweißfilm *m*
~-**and-white film camera** Schwarzweißfilmkamera *f*
~-**and-white film developer** Schwarzweißfilmentwickler *m*
~-**and-white film image** Schwarzweißfilmbild *n*
~-**and-white film processing** Schwarzweißfilmverarbeitung *f*, Schwarzweiß[film]entwicklung *f*, Schwarzweißprozess *m*
~-**and-white illustration** Schwarzweißillustration *f*
~-**and-white image** Schwarzweißbild *n;* Schwarzweißaufnahme *f*
~-**and-white infrared film** Schwarzweiß-Infrarotfilm *m*
~-**and-white instant film** Schwarzweiß-Sofortfilm *m*
~-**and-white laser printer** Schwarzweiß-Laserdrucker *m*
~-**and-white mode** Schwarzweißmodus *m (CCD-Kamera)*
~-**and-white monitor** Schwarzweißmonitor *m*
~-**and-white motion-picture film** Schwarzweiß-Kinefilm *m*
~-**and-white negative** Schwarzweißnegativ *n*
~-**and-white negative film (material)** Schwarzweiß-Negativmaterial *n*
~-**and-white pan[chromatic] film** panchromatischer Schwarzweißfilm *m*
~-**and-white photographic image** Schwarzweißfoto *n*
~-**and-white photographic material** Schwarzweißmaterial *n*
~-**and-white photographic paper** Schwarzweiß[foto]papier *n*
~-**and-white photography** Schwarzweißfotografie *f*
~-**and-white photomicrography** Schwarzweißmikrofotografie *f*
~-**and-white pixel** Schwarzweißpixel *n*
~-**and-white positive** Schwarzweißpositiv *n*
~-**and-white positive film** Schwarzweißpositivfilm *m*
~-**and-white print** Schwarzweißabzug *m*, Schwarzweißkopie *f*, Monochromabzug *m*
~-**and-white print film** Schwarzweißpositivfilm *m*
~-**and-white printing** Schwarzweißkopieren *n*
~-**and-white processing** Schwarzweißverarbeitung *f*, Schwarzweißentwicklung *f*
~-**and-white projection transparency** Schwarzweißdia[positiv] *n*
~-**and-white receiver** Schwarzweiß-Fernsehempfänger *m*
~-**and-white reversal film** Schwarzweiß-Umkehrfilm *m*
~-**and-white reversal process** Schwarzweiß-Umkehrverfahren *n*
~-**and-white reversal processing** Schwarzweiß-Umkehrverarbeitung *f*
~-**and-white scanner** Schwarzweißscanner *m*
~-**and-white screen** Schwarzweißbildschirm *m*, Monochrombildschirm *m*
~-**and-white signal** Schwarzweißsignal *n*, Leuchtdichtesignal *n*, [Fernseh-]Luminanzsignal *n*, Helligkeitssignal *n*, Y-Videosignal *n*

black 34

~-and-white slide Schwarzweißdia[positiv] *n*
~-and-white television Schwarzweißfernsehen *n*
~-and-white television receiver (set) Schwarzweiß-Fernsehempfänger *m*
~-and-white thermal image Schwarzweiß-Wärmebild *n*
~-and-white transmission Schwarzweißübertragung *f*; Schwarzweißsendung *f (Fernsehen)*
~-and-white work Schwarzweißarbeit *f*
~ bag Dunkelsack *m*, Wechselsack *m*
~ balance Schwarzabgleich *m*
~ box Schnittstelle *f (s.a.* interface 2.*)*
~ burst Studio-Referenzsignal *n*, Schwarzbezugswert *m*, Black Burst *m (Video)*
~ cartridge Schwarzpatrone *f*
~ content Schwarzgehalt *m (Farbmetrik)*
~ emulsion leader Schwarzfilm *m*
~ filter Schwarz[licht]filter *n*
~ leader Schwarzfilm *m*
~ letter serifenlose Linearantiqua *f (Schriftgattung)*
~ level Schwarzpegel *m*, Schwarzwert *m (Videosignal)*
~-level clamp[ing] Schwarzwertklemmung *f (Videosignal)*
~-level setup Schwarzabhebung *f*, Austastwert *m (Videosignal)*
~ light ultraviolettes Licht *n*, UV-Licht *n*
~-light lamp Schwarzlichtlampe *f*
~-light photography Fluoreszenzfotografie *f*
~ lightning *s.* Clayden effect
~ mask Vergrößerungsmaske *f*
~ noise schwarzes Rauschen *n*
~ pedestal Austastwert *m*, Austastpegel *m*, Schwarzabhebung *f (Videosignal)*
~ point Schwarzpunkt *m*
~ porch Schwarzschulter *f*
~ separation Schwarzauszug *m (Reprografie)*
~ shading Verschwärzlichung *f*
~ stretch Schwarzdehnung *f (elektronische Kamera)*; Schwarzentzerrer *m (Filmabtaster)*
~ sun effect Solarisation *f*, Solarisationseffekt *m*
~ tape Schwarzband *n*, Bandvorlauf *m*
~-to-white transition Schwarzweißübergang *m*
~-white vision Schwarzweißsehen *n*, Grauwertsehen *n*
blackbody *s.* ~ radiator
~ emissive power spektrale spezifische Strahldichte *f* des Schwarzen Körpers
~ radiator Schwarzkörperstrahler *m*, Hohlraumstrahler *m*, Schwarzer Strahler (Körper) *m*, Planckscher Strahler *m*
~ thermal radiation Schwarzkörperstrahlung *f*, Hohlraumstrahlung *f*

blacked tape Schwarzband *n*, Bandvorlauf *m*
blacken/to schwärzen
blackening Schwärzung *f*; Dichte *f (s.a.* density*)*
~ effect Schwärzungseffekt *m*
blackline process *s.* brownline process
blackness Schwärze *f*
blackout curtain Verdunk[e]lung *f (z.B. als Dunkelraumausrüstung)*
blackprint Formproof *m (Druckvorstufe)*
blackset Gegenimpuls *m (elektronische Kamera)*
blade shutter Flügelblende *f*, Umlauf[sektoren]blende *f*, Umlaufverschluss *m (Kinotechnik)*
blanc fixe Permanentweiß *n*, Barytweiß *n (Pigment)*
blank [out]/to austasten, dunkeltasten, dunkelsteuern *(Videosignal)*
~ film Blankfilm *m*
~ line Leerzeile *f*
~ magnetic tape *s.* ~ tape
~ page Leerseite *f*
~ space Leerraum *m*, freier Raum *m (z.B. zwischen Druckzeichen)*
~ tape Leerband *n*, unbespieltes Band *n (s.a.* virgin stock*)*
~ timing control signal Austastsignal n, Austastzeichen *n*
blanket Drucktuch *n*
~ [-covered] cylinder Drucktuchzylinder *m*, Gummi[drucktuch]zylinder *m*
~-to-blanket press Schön- und Widerdruckmaschine *f*, Perfektormaschine *f*
blanking Austastung *f*, Dunkeltasten *n*
~ aperture Austastblende *f*
~ interval Austastlücke *f*, Schwarzlücke *f*
~ level Austastwert m, Austastpegel m, Schwarzabhebung *f*
~ period Austastzeit *f*
~ pulse Austastimpuls *m*
~ signal Austastsignal *n*, Austastzeichen *n*
~ time Austastzeit *f*
blaze angle Blaze-Winkel *m*
~ grid *s.* blazed grating
~ wavelength Blaze-Wellenlänge *f*, Wellenlänge *f* maximaler Beugungseffektivität
blazed grating Blaze-Gitter *n*, geblaztes Gitter *n*
bleach/to bleichen
bleach away/to ausbleichen
~ out/to ausbleichen
~ [chemical] *s.* bleaching agent
~-fix solution Bleichfixierlösung *f*
~-fixing bath Bleichfixage *f*, Bleichfixierbad *n*, Blix *n*
~-out process Bleichprozess *m*
~ regenerator Bleichbad-Auffrischlösung *f*
~ replenisher Bleichbad-Nachfüllösung *f*
~ starter Bleichbad-Starter *m*
bleacher *s.* bleaching agent

bleaching accelerator Bleichbeschleuniger *m*
~ **agent** Bleichmittel *n*, Bleicher *m*
~ **away** Ausbleichen *n*
~ **bath** Bleichbad *n*
~ **solution** Bleichlösung *f*
bled off [rand]abfallend, angeschnitten *(Layout)*
bleed Anschnitt *m (Typografie)*
~-**through** Durchscheinen *n (Druckschwierigkeit)*
blended light Mischlicht *n*
blimp [schalldichte] Kamerahülle *f*, Blimp *m (s.a. barney)*
blimped camera geräuschgedämpfte Filmkamera *f*
blind Rollo *n (Schlitzverschluss)*
~ **emboss/to** blindprägen
~ **image** Prägebild *n*
~ **speed** Blindgeschwindigkeit *f (von Radarzielen)*
~ **spot** blinder Fleck *m*, Papille *f (des Auges)*
~ **stamping** Prägedruck *m*
blinding *s.* blind stamping
~ **glare** Absolutblendung *f*
blindness Blindheit *f*
blindsight Restsehvermögen *n*
blink comparator Blinkkomparator *m (Astrooptik)*
blip 1. Echoanzeige *f (Radar)*; 2. Bildmarke *f (Mikrofilmtechnik)*
blister pack Blisterpackung *f (Druckerzeugnis)*
blix *s.* bleach-fixing bath
blob Blob *m*, Objektpixelgruppe *f*; Bereich *m*, Gebiet *n (digitale Bildverarbeitung)*
~ **coloring** Gebietsmarkierung *f*
~-**like** blobähnlich
Bloch's law Blochsches Gesetz *n (Lichtwahrnehmung)*
block [out]/to ausblenden; abblocken; abdecken, maskieren *(z.B. Bildelemente)*
~ 1. Block *m*; Datenblock *m*; 2. Tragkörper *m*, Linsentragkörper *m (Linsenfertigung)*
~ **artifact** Blockartefakt *n*
~-**based coding** *s.* block coding
~-**based DCT** blockbasierte diskrete Kosinustransformation *f*
~-**based motion compensation** blockbasierte Bewegungskompensation *f*
~-**based motion estimation** blockbasierte Bewegungsschätzung *f*
~-**based motion representation** blockbasierte Bewegungsdarstellung *f*
~-**based texture** blockbasierte Textur *f*
~-**based transform coding** blockweise Transformationscodierung *f*
~ **bit pattern** Blockbitmuster *n*
~ **boundary** Blockbegrenzung *f*
~ **center** Blockmitte *f*
~ **check** Blockprüfung *f*
~ **check character** Blockprüfzeichen *n*
~ **code** Blockcode *m*
~ **code bit** Blockcodebit *n*
~ **coder** Blockcodierer *m*
~ **coding** Blockcodierung *f*, blockweise Codierung *f*
~ **color** Vollfarbe *f*
~ **color printing** Vollfarbdruck *m*
~ **corner** Blockecke *f*
~ **cosine transform** Blockkosinustransformation *f*
~ **decomposition** Blockzerlegung *f*
~ **delimiter** Blockbegrenzer *m*
~ **diagram** Blockdiagramm *n*; Blockschaltbild *n*
~ **edge** Blockkante *f*
~-**encoded image** blockcodiertes Bild *n*
~ **entropy** Blockentropie *f*
~ **error correction** Blockfehlerkorrektur *f*
~ **error rate** Blockfehlerrate *f*
~ **gap** Blocklücke *f*
~ **graphic** Blockgrafik *f*
~ **header** Blockanfangskennsatz *m*
~ **layer** Blockebene *f*
~ **length error** Blocklängenfehler *m*
~ **letter** Blockbuchstabe *m*
~ **matching** Blockvergleich *m*, Blockanpassung *f*, Blockmatching[-Verfahren] *n*, Bereichszuordnung *f (Bildcodierung)*
~ **matching algorithm** Blockvergleichsalgorithmus *m*
~ **mean value** Blockmittelwert *m*
~ **of image data** Bilddatenblock *m*
~ **of memory** Speicherblock *m*
~ **of pixels** Pixelblock *m*
~ **overlapping** Blocküberlappung *f*
~ **printing** [direkter] Hochdruck *m*, Reliefdruck *m*; Buchdruck *m*
~ **quantization** Blockquantisierung *f*
~ **quantizer** Blockquantisierer *m*
~ **size** Blockgröße *f*
~ **sort** Blocksortierung *f*
~ **transfer** Blockübertragung *f*
~ **transform coding** Blocktransformationscodierung *f*
~ **transformation** Blocktransformation *f*
~ **variance** Blockvarianz *f*
blockiness Pixeligkeit *f*
blocking 1. Abblocken *n*, Block[ier]ung *f (z.B. von Strahlungsanteilen)*; 2. Blockstruktur *f (Digitalbildfehler)*
~ **artifact** Blockartefakt *n*
~ **of printed sheets** Kleben *n* der Druckbogen [im Stapel]
~ **press** Heißprägepresse *f*
blocks world Blockwelt *f*, Klötzchenwelt *f (Computergrafik)*
blockwise translation blockweise Translation *f (Videokompression)*
blocky pixelig
blood flow image Blutflussdarstellung *f (Sonografie)*
~ **oxygen level-dependent functional magnetic resonance imaging**

blooming 36

funktionelle Magnetresonanztomografie unter Einbeziehung des Blutsauerstoffgehaltes
blooming [effect] Überstrahlen *n*, Überstrahlungseffekt *m*, Blooming-Effekt *m*, Nachziehleuchtfahne *f*
blow up/to vergrößern
blower brush Blasepinsel *m*, Objektivpinsel *m* mit Blasebalg (Gummiball)
blowing agent Treibmittel *n*, Blähmittel *n* *(Entwicklerzusatz)*
blowup Vergrößerung *f*
~ **print** Vergrößerungskopie *f*
~ **printing** Vergrößerungskopieren *n*
blue Blau *n (Spektralhauptfarbe)*
~-**and-green-sensitive** orthochromatisch, tonwertrichtig *(Fotomaterial)*
~ **base** blaugefärbter Schichtträger (Filmschichtträger) *m*
~ **beam** Blaustrahl *m (Katodenstrahlröhre)*
~ **bias** Blaustich *m*
~-**blind** blaublind
~ **blindness** Blaublindheit *f*, Blau-Gelb-Blindheit *f*, Tritanopie *f* *(Farbsinnstörung)*
~ **box** Blauraum *m (Studioausrüstung; s.a. ~ screen)*
~ **cast** Blaustich *m*
~ **channel** Blaukanal *m*
~ **diode laser** blauer Diodenlaser *m*
~ **filter** Blaufilter *n*
~-**green** Blaugrün *n*; Cyan *n (subtraktive Grundfarbe)*
~-**green filter** Blaugrünfilter *n*
~ **light** Blaulicht *n*
~ **light filter** Blaufilter *n*
~ **light laser** blauer Laser *m*
~ **light record** *s.* ~ **record**
~ **light sensitivity** Blauempfindlichkeit *f*
~-**minus-luma signal** Farbdifferenzsignal *n* B-Y *(Video)*
~ **phosphor** Blauphosphor *m*
~ **record** Blauteilbild *n*, Blauauszug *m* *(Dreischichtenfarbfilm)*
~ **screen** Blauwand *f*, blaue Stanzwand *f* *(Trickkinematografie)*
~-**screen effect** Stanztrick *m (Trickkinematografie)*
~-**screen photography (process)** Bluescreen-Verfahren *n*, Blaustanze *f*
~-**screen shot** Bluescreen-Aufnahme *f*
~-**sensitive** blauempfindlich *(fotografische Emulsion)*
~-**sensitive layer** blauempfindliche Schicht *f*
~-**sensitive yellow [dye] layer** blauempfindliche Gelbschicht *f*
~ **sensitivity** Blauempfindlichkeit *f*
~ **signal** Blausignal *n (Video)*
~ **speed** *s.* ~ **sensitivity**
~ **toner** Blautoner *m*
~ **toning** Blautonung *f*

~-**yellow color blindness** *s.* **blue blindness**
blueline [proof] Blaupause *f*, Formproof *m* *(Druckvorstufe)*
blueprint/to blaupausen
blueprint 1. Blaupause *f*, Lichtpause *f*; Blaudruck *m (s.a.* blueline [proof]*)*; 2. Cyanotypie *f*
~ **paper** Pauspapier *n*
~ **process** Cyanotypie *f*, [negativer] Eisenblaudruck *m*
blueprinting lamp Lichtpauslampe *f*
bluish cast Blaustich *m*
~ **green** bläuliches Grün *n*
Blum transform *s.* **Voronoi diagram**
blur/to verwischen, verunschärfen
blur Unschärfe *f*, Bildunschärfe *f*
~ **circle** Unschärfekreis *m*, Streukreis *m*, Zerstreuungskreis *m*
~ **diameter** Zerstreuungskreisdurchmesser *m*
~ **filter** Unschärfmaske *f*, unscharfe Maske *f*
~-**free** [konturen]scharf *(Abbildung)*
~ **function** *s.* **blurring function**
~ **matrix** Unschärfematrix *f*
~ **point (spot)** Unschärfepunkt *m*, Nebelpunkt *m (Sehen)*
blurred unscharf
~ **edge** unscharfe Kante *f*
blurriness *s.* **blur**
blurring Verwischen *n*, Verwischung *f*, Verunschärfung *f*, Unscharfmachen *n*
~ **effect** Verwischeffekt *m*
~ **filter** *s.* **blur filter**
~ **function** Unschärfefunktion *f*; Punktbild[verwaschungs]funktion *f*, Punktstreufunktion *f*, Punktantwortfunktion *f*
~ **operator** Unschärfeoperator *m*
~ **tomography** Verwischungstomografie *f*
blurry unscharf
~ **image** unscharfes (verschwommenes) Bild *n*; verwischtes (verwackeltes) Bild *n*
BNC connector (pin), ~ **plug** BNC-Stecker *m (von Bayonet Neil-Concelman; Videotechnik)*
board 1. Ganzseitenmontage *f (Druckvorstufe)*; 2. *s.* ~ **paper**
~ **paper** Karton *m*, Pappe *f*
bobbin Wickelkern *m*, Aufwickelkern *m*, Spulenkern *m*, Rollenkern *m*, Filmkern *m*, Bobby *m*
body 1. Körper *m*; 2. Textkörper *m*; 3. Typenkörper *m (Drucktype)*
~ **animation** Körperanimation *f*
~ **cap** Gehäusedeckel *m*
~ **coil** Ganzkörperantenne *f*, Körperspule *f* *(Magnetresonanztomografie)*
~ **color** Körperfarbe *f*, Objektfarbe *f*, Oberflächenfarbe *f*
~ **cross-sectional image** Körperquerschnittsbild *n*

~ **face** Grundschrift f, Brotschrift f, Textschrift f, Werk[satz]schrift f, Mengensatz m *(Typografie)*
~ **mount adapter** Objektivadapter m
~ **size** Schriftgröße f, Schrifthöhe f, Glyphenhöhe f
~ **slice** Körperscheibe f *(Tomografie)*
Bohr atom model Bohrsches Atommodell n
boid Boid m(n), Schwarmelement n *(Computeranimation)*
boiler plate Textbaustein m
bold s. 1. boldfaced; 2. boldface
~ **italic typeface** fett-kursiver Schriftschnitt m
~ **typeface** fetter Schriftschnitt m
boldface Fettdruck m *(Typografie)*
boldfaced fett[gedruckt]
bolograph Bolograf m
bolometer [detector], ~ **element** Bolometer n
~ **film** Bolometerschicht f
~ **resistance** Bolometerwiderstand m
bolometric bolometrisch
~ **effect** bolometrischer Effekt m
Boltzmann constant Boltzmann-Konstante f
~ **factor** Boltzmann-Faktor m
~ **machine** Boltzmann-Maschine f *(einschichtiges neuronales Netz)*
~ **statistics** Boltzmann-Statistik f
bond paper Bankpostpapier n
bone scintigraphy Skelettszintigrafie f
book cover Buchdecke f, Buchdeckel m; Bucheinband m
~ **page** Buchseite f
~ **paper** Bücher[schreib]papier n; Werkdruckpapier n
~ **printing** Buchdruck m
~-**type cassette** Buchkassette f *(Schirmbildfotografie)*
bookmaking Buchfertigung f, Buchherstellung f
Boolean algebra Boolesche Algebra (Logik) f
~ **EX-OR** logisches EXKLUSIV-ODER n, EXKLUSIV-ODER-Verknüpfung f, Modulo-2-Addition f
~ **expression** Boolescher Ausdruck m
~ **filter** Boolesches Filter n
~ **function** Boolesche Funktion f
~ **logic** Boolesche Logik (Algebra) f
~ **matrix** Boolesche Matrix f, Binärmatrix f
~ **model** Boolesches Modell n
~ **operation** Boolesche Operation (Verknüpfung) f *(Modellierungsverfahren)*
~ **operator** Boolescher (logischer) Operator m
~ **retrieval (search)** Boolesche Suche f
~ **set operation** Boolesche Mengenoperation f *(Computergrafik)*
~ **union operation** [Boolesche] Vereinigung f

boom [arm] Mikrofonausleger m, Ausleger m, Tongalgen m, Mikrofongalgen m
~ **operator** Tonassistent m
~ **pole** Mikrofonangel f, Tonangel f, [Mikro-]Angel f, Perche f
boost/to verstärken *(z.B. Signale)*
booster Verstärker m
booth porthole Kabinenfenster n, Kabinenfensteröffnung f, Projektionsfenster n *(Filmvorführung)*
bootleg/to raubkopieren
bootleg software raubkopierte Software f
~ **video** Video-Raubkopie f
borax Borax n *(Entwicklerzusatz)*
border Rand m
~ **detection algorithm** Kantendetektionsalgorithmus m, Kantendetektor m, Kantenfinder m
~ **effect** Randeffekt m, Nachbareffekt m
~ **pixel** Randpixel n
~ **voxel** Randvoxel n
borderless print randloser Abzug (Fotoabzug) m
~ **printing** randloses Drucken n
borderline s. boundary line
borescope [lens] Industrieendoskop n, Technoskop n
boric acid Borsäure f *(Entwicklerzusatz)*
borosilicate crown [glass] Borsilikat-Kronglas n, Borkron m, BK
~ **glass** Borsilikatglas n
botanical photography Pflanzenfotografie f
bottom edge Unterkante f
~ **field** unteres Halbbild n
~ **sediment** Bodenkörper m *(z.B. einer Entwicklerlösung)*
~ **side** Unterseite f
~-**up segmentation** agglomerative Segmentierung f
~ **view** Untersicht f *(Kameraperspektive)*
Bouguer-Lambert law Bouguer-Lambertsches Gesetz n, Bouguersches Gesetz n *(Optik)*
~ **photometer** Bouguer-Fotometer n
bounce card Streuscheibe f; Blitzreflektor m
~ **flash** indirekter Blitz m
~ **flash adapter (adaptor)** Blitzneiger m, Bounce-Reflektor m, Bouncer m
~ **light** indirektes (reflektiertes) Licht n, Reflex[ions]licht n; indirektes Blitzlicht n
~ **lighting** indirekte Beleuchtung f
boundary Konturkante f; Umrandung f, Berandung f
~ **condition** Randbedingung f *(z.B. in der Computergrafik)*
~ **contour** umschreibende Konturlinie f
~ **curve** Randkurve f
~ **edge** Randkante f, begrenzende Kante f
~ **effect** Randeffekt m
~ **feature** Randmerkmal n
~ **gradient** Kantengradient m
~ **layer** Randschicht f, Sperrschicht f *(z.B. eines Halbleiterfotoelements)*

boundary 38

~ **layer microphone** Grenzflächenmikrofon n
~ **line** Umrisslinie f, Umrandung f, Konturlinie f, Randlinie f
~ **object** Randobjekt n
~ **pixel** Randpixel n
~ **point** Konturpunkt m, Randpunkt m
~ **representation** Randdarstellung f; Begrenzungflächenrepräsentation f (Computergrafik)
~ **representation list** B-Rep-Liste f
~ **segment** Randsegment n
~ **sharpness** Rand[bild]schärfe f
~ **surface** Begrenzungsfläche f (dreidimensionale Visualisierung)
bounding box s. ~ rectangle
~ **polyhedron** umschließendes Polyeder n
~ **rectangle** umgebendes (umschließendes, umschreibendes) Rechteck n, Darstellungsquader m, Quaderhülle f (Computergrafik)
~ **sphere** umhüllende (umschließende) Kugel f, Kugelhülle f, Hüllkugel f
~ **volume** Hüllkörper m, Objektumgebung f
bouquet Programmpaket n (Fernsehen)
Bouwers system s. Maksutov system
bowl Auge n (Buchstabenbild)
box Abhörlautsprecher m
~ **camera** Box[kamera] f
~ **filter** Rechteckfilter n, Spalttiefpass m; Mittelwertfilter n
~ **function** Rechteckfunktion f
brace Akkolade f, geschweifte Klammer f, Nasenklammer f (Druckzeichen)
Brachyt telescope Schiefspiegler m (Teleskopbauart)
bracketing function Belichtungsreihenautomatik f, Belichtungsreihenfunktion f
Bragg angle Bragg-Winkel m, Glanzwinkel m
~ **cell** akustooptischer Modulator m (Lasertechnik)
~ **diffraction** Braggsche Beugung f
~ **reflection** Bragg-Reflexion f
~ **reflection condition** Braggsche Reflexionsbedingung f
~ **reflector** Bragg-Reflektor m
~ **scattering** Bragg-Streuung f
brain imaging zerebrale Bildgebung f
~ **perfusion study** Hirnperfusionsuntersuchung f (Tomografie)
braking radiation s. bremsstrahlung [radiation]
branch point Verzweigungspunkt m
brass rule Messinglinie f, Setzlinie f (Handsatzgerät)
~ **type** Messingtype f
Braun tube Braunsche Röhre (Elektronenstrahlröhre) f
bread-and-butter type Brotschrift f, Grundschrift f, Textschrift f, Werk[satz]schrift f, Mengensatz m (Typografie)
break point Abreißpunkt m, Diplopiepunkt m (Augenoptik)
breakdown Drehbuchauszug m
breast imaging Mammografie f
breathing Atmen n, Atemeffekt m (Filmprojektion)
bremsstrahlung [radiation] Röntgenbremsstrahlung f, Bremsstrahlung f
~ **[X-ray] spectrum** Röntgenbremsspektrum n, kontinuierliches Röntgenspektrum n, [kontinuierliches] Bremsspektrum n
Bresenham's algorithm Bresenham-Algorithmus m, Kreisalgorithmus m von Bresenham (Kurvenrasterung, Computergrafik)
Brewster angle [of incidence] Brewster-Winkel m, Brewsterscher Winkel m, Polarisations[dreh]winkel m
~ **angle window,** ~ **window** Brewster-Fenster n (Laser)
Brewster's angle dispersing prism Brewster-Prisma n
~ **fringes** Brewstersche Streifen mpl (Interferenzmuster)
~ **law** Brewstersches Gesetz n, Brewster-Bedingung f (Optik)
bridge s. crossover
~ **camera** Bridgekamera f
bridger amplifier benutzerseitige Breitbandkabel-Verstärkerstelle f, B-Verstärker m
bridging Folgebildanschluss m
~ **error** Anschlussfehler m
~-**type filter** Durchschleiffilter n
bright hell
~ **color** brillante Farbe f
~-**field condenser** Hellfeldkondensor m
~-**field illumination** Hellfeldbeleuchtung f
~-**field image** Hellfeldbild n
~-**field microscope** Hellfeldmikroskop n
~-**field microscopy** Hellfeldmikroskopie f
~-**field observation** Hellfeldbeobachtung f
~-**field reflected-light illumination** Auflicht-Hellfeldbeleuchtung f
~-**field reflected-light microscopy** Hellfeld-Auflichtmikroskopie f
~-**frame [view]finder** Leuchtrahmensucher m, Spiegelrahmensucher m, Albada-Sucher f
~ **light** helles Licht n, Hellicht n
~-**light vision** Helligkeitssehen n, Tagessehen n, fotopisches Sehen n, Zapfensehen n
~ **point of Poisson** Poissonscher Fleck m (Fresnel-Beugung)
brighten [up]/to aufhellen
brightener optischer Aufheller m
brightening Aufhellung f

brightline viewfinder s. bright-frame [view]finder
brightly colored bunt
brightness Helligkeit f
~ **adaptation** Helligkeitsadaptation f
~ **change** Helligkeitsänderung f
~ **change constraint equation** Kontinuitätsgleichung f (Bewegungsanalyse)
~ **constancy** Helligkeitskonstanz f
~ **content** Helligkeitsgehalt m (eines Bildes)
~ **control** Helligkeitsregelung f, Helligkeitssteuerung f
~ **decrease** Helligkeitsabfall m
~ **difference** Helligkeitsunterschied m, Helligkeitsdifferenz f
~ **distribution** Helligkeitsverteilung f
~ **distribution curve** Helligkeitsverlauf m
~ **fluctuation** Helligkeitsschwankung f
~ **function** Helligkeitsfunktion f
~ **gain** Helligkeitsverstärkung f
~ **gradient** Helligkeitsgradient m
~ **histogramm** Helligkeitshistogramm n
~ **information** Helligkeitsinformation f
~ **level** Helligkeitsstufe f, Helligkeitsniveau n
~ **loss** Helligkeitsverlust m
~ **modulation** Helligkeitsmodulation f
~ **pattern** Helligkeitsmuster n
~ **perception** Helligkeitswahrnehmung f
~ **profile** Helligkeitsprofil n
~ **range** Helligkeitsbereich m; Helligkeitsumfang m (s.a. contrast)
~ **resolution** Helligkeitsauflösung f
~ **scale** Helligkeitsskala f
~ **scan** Helligkeitsabtastung f
~ **sensation** Helligkeitsempfindung f, Helligkeitsempfinden n
~ **sensitivity** Helligkeitsempfindlichkeit f
~ **setting** Helligkeitseinstellung f (z.B. eines Monitors)
~ **signal** Helligkeitssignal n
~ **value** Helligkeitswert m, Intensitätswert m
~ **variation** Helligkeitsschwankung f; Helligkeitsänderung f
brilliance, brilliancy Brillanz f
brilliant brillant
~ **color** brillante Farbe f
~ **finder** Brillantsucher m, Aufsichtssucher m, Lichtschachtsucher m
Brillouin scattering Brillouin-Streuung f (Quantenoptik)
bristol [board] Bristolkarton m
brittleness Brüchigkeit f (z.B. einer fotografischen Schicht)
broad s. ~ light
~**-beam lamp** Breitstrahler m
~ **light** 1. Flächenlicht n; 2. Flächenleuchte f, Lichtwanne f (s.a. Fluter)
~ **pulse** Haupttrabant m (Videosignal)
broadband Breitband n
~ breitbandig

~ **access** Breitbandzugang m
~ **amplifier** Breitbandverstärker m
~ **cable** Breitbandkabel n
~ **channel** Breitbandkanal m
~ **coating** Breitbandbeschichtung f
~ **coding** Breitbandcodierung f
~ **communication** Breitbandkommunikation f
~ **connection** Breitbandverbindung f, Breitbandanschluss m, Hochgeschwindigkeitsverbindung f
~ **electrical signal** Breitbandsignal n
~ **filter** Breitbandfilter n
Broadband Integrated Services Digital Network s. ~ ISDN
broadband interference filter Breitbandinterferenzfilter n
~ **Internet** Breitband-Internet n
Broadband ISDN Breitband-ISDN n, breitbandiges diensteintegrierendes Datennetz n
broadband medium Breitbandmedium n
~ **multilayer [antireflection] coating** breitbandige mehrlagige Entspiegelung f
~ **multimedia information retrieval service** Breitband-Multimedia-Informationsabrufdienst m
~ **network** Breitbanddatennetz; Breitband[kommunikations]netz n; Breitbandkabelnetz n, BK-Netz n
~ **noise** Breitbandrauschen n
~ **portal** Breitbandportal n
~ **reception** Breitbandempfang m
~ **service** Breitbanddienst m
~ **signal** Breitbandsignal n
~ **technology** Breitbandtechnik f
~ **transmission** Breitbandübertragung f
~ **user** Breitbandnutzer m
broadcast/to senden
broadcast live/to live senden; live übertragen
~ Sendung f, Übertragung f, Ausstrahlung f; Sendebeitrag m
~ **bandwidth** Sendebandbreite f
~ **day** Sendetag m
~ **digital videotape recorder** Rundfunk-Videorecorder m
~ **editing** Programmbearbeitung f
~ **engineer** Sendetechniker m
~ **engineering** Sendetechnik f
~ **equipment** Sendetechnik f
~ **facility** Sendeanlage f
~**-grade studio equipment** Sendetechnik f
~ **illumination level** Sendelicht n
~ **industry standard** Studiostandard m
~ **interface** Rundfunkschnittstelle f
~**-level** s. broadcast-quality
~ **mode** Übertragungsmodus m
~ **operation** Sendeeinrichtung f; Sendeanstalt f
~ **plant** Sendeanlage f
~ **program** Sendebeitrag m, Sendung f
~**-quality** sendefähig; sendefertig

broadcast 40

~ **quality** [technische] Studioqualität f, Übertragungsqualität f
~-**quality camera** Produktionskamera f; Studiokamera f
~-**quality format** Sendeformat n
~-**quality tape** Sendeband n
~-**quality video recording format** Videostudiosystem n
~ **satellite service** Satelliten-Rundfunkdienst m
~ **signal** Sendesignal n
~ **station** Sendestation f
~ **studio** Sendestudio n
~ **system** Sendesystem n
~ **television channel** Fernseh[programm]kanal m
~ **television network** Fernsehsendernetz n
~ **television receiver** Fernseh[empfäng]er m, Fernsehgerät n, Fernsehapparat m
~ **television signal** Fernseh-Sendesignal n
~ **television standard** Fernseh[übertragungs]norm f, Fernsehstandard m
~ **television system** Fernseh[rund]funk m
~-**type facility** Sendeeinrichtung f
~ **videotape** Sende[magnet]band n, sendefertiges Band (Videoband) n
~ **videotex** Videotext m, Fernsehtext m
~ **videotex decoder** Videotextdecoder m
broadcaster Sender m; Sendeanstalt f
broadcasting Rundfunk m (s.a. broadcast)
~ **channel** Sendekanal m, Übertragungskanal m
~ **company** Sendeanstalt f
~ **network** Sendernetz n
~ **standard** Sendenorm f
~ **technology** Sendetechnik f
~ **transmitter** Sender m
broadside Faltprospekt m
Brodatz texture Brodatz-Textur f (Computergrafik)
bromide 1. Bromid n; 2. s. ~ print
~ **drag** s. ~ streak
~ **emulsion** Bromidemulsion f
~ **ion** Bromion n
~ **paper** Bromidpapier n, Bromsilber[vergrößerungs]papier n, Silberbromidpapier n, Bromsilber-Gelatine-Papier n
~ **print** Bromidabzug m, Bromsilberdruck m
~ **printing** Bromsilberdruck m
~ **streak** Bromidfahne f, Bromidstreifen m
~-**streak effect** Bromablaufeffekt m
bromine acceptor Bromakzeptor m
bromoil printing (process) Bromöldruck m
~ **process photography** Bromöldruckfotografie f
bronchoscope Bronchoskop n
bronchoscopic bronchoskopisch
bronchoscopy Bronchoskopie f
bronzing Bronzieren n
Brownian motion Brownsche Bewegung f (z.B. von Strömungsteilchen)

brownline s. blueline [proof]
~ **process** Ozalidverfahren n (ein Diazo-Lichtpausverfahren)
browse/to durchsuchen
browser Browser m (Clientprogramm)
browsing Stöbern n (Multimedia)
brush Pinsel m (z.B. als elektronisches Bildbearbeitungswerkzeug)
~ **retouching** Pinselretusche f
~ **stroke** Pinselstrich m
bubble chamber Blasenkammer f
~ **chamber holography** Blasenkammerholografie f
~ **chamber optics** Blasenkammeroptik f
~ **chamber photograph** Blasenkammerfoto n
~ **chamber photography** Blasenkammerfotografie f
~ **chart** Blasengrafik f
~ **image** Bläschenbild n, Blasenbild n (Vesikularverfahren)
~ **jet** Dampfblasenstrahl m
~-**jet printer** Thermotintenstrahldrucker m
~-**jet printing** thermischer Tintendruck m
~-**jet process** Dampfblasenverfahren n (Tintenstrahldruck)
bucket brigade device Eimerkettenschaltung f (CCD-Sensor)
buckle Schleifenverziehen n; Welligkeit f (von Fotomaterial)
Bucky diaphragm Bucky-Raster m, bewegter Raster m (Radiografie)
buffer/to zwischenspeichern
buffer 1. Puffer m (z.B. als Fixiererzusatz); 2. s. ~ memory
~ **management** Zwischenspeicherverwaltung f
~ **memory** Puffer[speicher] m, Zwischenspeicher m (s.a. frame buffer [memory])
~ **solution** Pufferlösung f
~ **space** Pufferspeicherplatz m
~ **storage (store)** Puffer[speicher] m, Zwischenspeicher m
~ **substance** Puffersubstanz f
buffering Zwischenspeicherung f
bug Computerprogrammfehler m, Programmfehler m
build-up factor Dosiszuwachsfaktor m
built-in exposure meter eingebauter Belichtungsmesser m
~-**in flash [unit]** Gehäuseblitz m, eingebautes (integriertes) Blitzgerät n, eingebauter Blitz m, Kamerablitz m
~-**in font** eingebaute Schrift f (Computer)
~-**in light meter** Kamerabelichtungsmesser m
~-**in microphone** eingebautes Mikrofon n
~-**in speedlight** s. ~ flash [unit]
~-**in timer** eingebaute Zeitschaltuhr f
bulk-channel CCD MOS capacitor, ~ device Ladungsverschiebungsschaltung f

~ **eraser** Bandlöschgerät n, Magnetspulenlöschgerät n
~ **erasure** Gesamtlöschung f
~ **film** Meterware f (Film)
~ **film loader** Filmladegerät n, Filmlader m
~ **lengths** Meterware f (Film)
~ **scatter[ing]** Volumenstreuung f
bull's eye Lichtpunkt m, Butzen m, Pop[p]el m (Druckbildfehler)
bullet [point] Aufzählungspunkt m, Aufzählungszeichen n, Hervorhebungszeichen n (Typografie)
bump map eine Bitmapgrafik zur Texturierung von dreidimensionalen Körpern
~ **mapping**, ~ **texture mapping** computergrafische Texturerzeugung f, Bump-Mapping f
bundle Bündel n (s.a. ~ of light rays, ~ of rays)
~ **block** Bündelblock m
~ **block adjustment** Bündelblockausgleich m, Bündelblockausgleichung f, fotogrammetrische Bündelausgleichung f
~ **index** Bündelindex m (Computergrafik)
~ **of light rays** Licht[strahlen]bündel n
~ **of rays** Strahlenbündel n, Bündel n, Strahlenbüschel n
~ **table** Bündeltabelle f
~ **table entry** Bündeltabelleneintrag m
Bunsen photometer Bunsen-Fotometer n, Fettfleckfotometer n
~**-Roscoe [reciprocity] law** Bunsen[-Roscoesches] Gesetz n, Reziprozitätsgesetz n [nach Bunsen und Roscoe], Reziprozitätsregel f (fotografische Belichtung)
~ **screen** Fettblende f
Burgers vector Burgers-Vektor m (Elektronenmikroskopie)
buried channel abgedeckter Transferkanal m (Halbleiter-Lichtempfänger)
burn s. burn-in
~ **in/to** nachbelichten
~**-in** Einbrennen n, Einbrenneffekt n (bes. von Standbildern auf Bildschirmen)
~**-off paper** elektrosensitives Papier n
burning glass Brennglas n
burst 1. Burst m, Farbsynchronimpuls m, Farbsynchron[isier]signal n (Video); 2. Rauscheinbruch m
~ **amplitude** Burstamplitude f
~ **blanking** Bündelaustastung f
~ **capture** Serienauslösung f (Kleinbildkamera)
~ **error** Burstfehler m, Bündelfehler m, Blockfehler m, Büschelfehler m
~ **flag (gate)** Burst-Kennimpuls m, K-Impuls m
~ **generator** Burstgenerator m
~ **image** Serienaufnahme f
~ **images** Aufnahmesequenz f, Aufnahmeserie f, Aufnahmereihe f

~ **key** s. ~ flag
~ **noise** Burstrauschen n
~ **phase** Burstphase f
~ **signal** Burstsignal n
~ **synchronization** Burstsynchronisation f
~ **transmission** Bitbündelübertragung f
~**-type interference** Burststörung f
bursty stoßweise (z.B. ein Bitstrom)
bus Bus m, Hauptleitungsträger m
~ **address** Busadresse f
~ **arbitration** Busverwaltung f
~ **bandwidth** Busbandbreite f
~ **bar** Sammelschiene f
~ **electrode** Buselektrode f
~ **error** Busfehler m
~ **interface** Busschnittstelle f
~ **network** Busnetz n
~ **standard** Busstandard m
~ **system** Bussystem n
~ **width** Busbreite f
business form Geschäftsdrucksache f
~ **graphics** Geschäftsgrafik f
~ **paper** Bankpostpapier n
~ **printing** Geschäftsdrucksachenherstellung f
~ **television (video)** betriebliches Fernsehen n, Unternehmens-TV n, Firmen-TV n
bust shot Brustbild n; Halbporträt n, Halbporträtaufnahme f
butt fit (register) Farbpasser m (Farbdruck)
~ **splice** Stumpfklebestelle f
~ **splicer** Stumpfklebepresse f (für Filmmaterial)
~ **splicing** Stumpfkleben n
butterfly algorithm Schmetterlingsalgorithmus m (diskrete schnelle Fourier-Transformation)
Butterworth filter Butterworth-Filter n
~ **high-pass filter** Butterworth-Hochpass m
~ **low-pass filter** Butterworth-Tiefpass m
button Schaltfläche f (Bildschirm)
~ **bar** Symbolleiste f (Bildschirm)
buzz track Buzz-Track-Tonspur f (Lichttonspur)
byte Byte n (Dateneinheit)
~ **order** Bytefolge f
~ **size** Byteumfang m

C

C mount C-Anschluss *m*, C-Fassung *f*, C-Gewinde *n* *(genormtes Objektivgewinde)*
C programming language C *(höhere Programmiersprache)*
C signal *s.* chrominance signal
cabinet axonometry Kabinettprojektion *f*
cable authority television *s.* ~ television
~ **broadcaster** Kabelsender *m*
~ **channel (conduct)** Kabelkanal *m*
~ **connector** Kabelverbinder *m*
~ **customer** Kabelfernsehteilnehmer *m*
~ **digital video broadcasting** digitales Kabelfernsehen *n*
~ **headend** Kabel[fernseh]kopfstation *f*, Rundfunkempfangsstelle *f*
~ **junction** Kabelanschluss *m*
~ **modem** Kabelmodem *n(m)*
~ **modulator** Kabelmodulator *m*
~ **network** Kabelnetz *n*
~**-ready television receiver** kabelfähiges (kabeltaugliches) Fernsehgerät *n*
~ **receiver** Kabelempfänger *m*
~ **reception** Kabelempfang *m*
~ **release** Drahtauslöser *m*, Auslösekabel *n*
~ **remote control** Kabelfernbedienung *f*
~ **return path** Kabelrückkanal *m*
~ **signal** Kabelsignal *n*
~ **subscriber** Kabelfernsehteilnehmer *m*
~ **system operator** Kabel[netz]betreiber *m*
~ **television** Kabelfernsehen *n*
~ **television channel** Kabelfernsehkanal *m*
~ **television distribution system,** ~ **television network** Kabelfernseh-Verteilsystem *n*, Kabelfernsehnetz *n*
~ **television plant** Kabel[fernseh]anlage *f*
~ **television provider** Kabelfernsehanbieter *m*
~ **television relay service station** Kabelfernsehempfangsstation *f*
~ **television service** Kabelfernsehdienst *m*
~ **television signal** Kabelfernsehsignal *n*
~ **television system** Kabelfernsehsystem *n*; Breitbandkabelnetz *n*
~ **television transmission** Kabelfernsehübertragung *f*
~ **transmission** Kabelübertragung *f*
~ **TV** *s.* ~ television
cache/to zwischenspeichern
cache [memory] Cachespeicher *m*, Vorhaltespeicher *m*, Hintergrundspeicher *m*, schneller Pufferspeicher *m*, Zwischenspeicher *m*
~ **space** Zwischenspeicherplatz *m*
caching Zwischenspeicherung *f*
CAD *s.* computer-aided design

cadastral map Katasterkarte *f*; Flurkarte *f*
~ **survey** Katasteraufnahme *f*
cadmium sulfide meter Cadmiumsulfid-Belichtungsmesser *m*
~ **sulfide photocell (photoelectric cell)** Cadmiumsulfid-Widerstand *m*, CdS-Widerstand *m*
caesium ... *s.* cesium ...
calcareous spar, calcite Kalkspat *m*, Calcit *m*, Kalzit *m*
calcite interference microscope Calcit-Interferenzmikroskop *n*
~ **polarizer** Kalkspatpolarisator *m*
calcium fluoride Calciumfluorid *n*, Fluorit *m*, Flussspat *m* *(optisches Material)*
~ **fluoride glass** Fluoritglas *n*
~ **iodide** Calciumiodid *n*
~ **tungstate intensifying screen** Calciumwolframat-Verstärkerfolie *f* *(Radiografie)*
calculation time Rechenzeit *f*
calender/to kalandern, kalandrieren; satinieren *(Papier)*
calender [roller] Kalander *m*
calendered satiniert *(Papier)*
calibrate/to kalibrieren, eichen
calibrated atlas method Gleichheitsverfahren *n* *(Kolorimetrie)*
~ **focal length** Kammerkonstante *f* *(Fotogrammetrie)*
calibration Kalibrierung *f*, Eichung *f*
~ **constant** Eichkonstante *f*
~ **curve** Eichkurve *f*
~ **error** Eichfehler *m*
~ **film** Eichfilm *m*
~ **function** Eichkurve *f*
~ **lamp** Kalibrierungslampe *f* *(Spektroskopie)*
~ **tape** Bezugsband *n*, Eichband *n* *(Videotechnik)*
caliper 1. Papierstärke *f*, Papierdicke *f*; 2. Doppelbogenkontrolle *f* *(Druckmaschine)*
call sheet Tagesdisposition, Dispo[sition] *f* *(Filmarbeit)*
Callier coefficient Callier-Quotient *m*
~ **effect** Callier-Effekt *m* *(selektive Lichtstreuung)*
calligraphic display Vektorbildschirm *m*
calorescence Kaloreszenz *f*
calotype Kalotypie *f*, Talbotypie *f* *(Negativkopie)*
~ **process** Kalotypie *f*, Talbotypie *f* *(fotografisches Negativ-Verfahren)*
calotypist Kalotypist *m*
cam *s.* camera roll
camcorder Camcorder *m*, [mobile] Handvideokamera *f*, Kamerarecorder *m*, Videokamerarecorder *m*
~ **battery** Camcorderbatterie *f*
~ **cable** Camcorderkabel *n*
~ **cassette** Camcorderkassette *f*
~ **lens** Camcorderobjektiv *n*
camel's hair brush Kamelhaarpinsel *m*

cameo/to [erhaben] prägen
camera 1. Kamera *f*; 2. *s.* ~ obscura
~ **accessories** Kamerazubehör *n*
~ **adapter** Kameraadapter *m*
~ **adjustment** Kamerajustierung *f*, Kameraeinstellung *f*
~ **angle** Kamera[blick]winkel *m* (s.a. ~ axis)
~ **aperture** Kamerafenster *n*, Kamerablende *f*
~ **apparatus** Kamera *f*; Fotoapparat *m*
~ **assistant** [Erster] Kameraassistent *m* (Filmarbeit)
~ **axis** Kameraachse *f*, Aufnahmeachse *f* (s.a. ~ angle)
~ **back** Kamerarückwand *f*; Kamerarückteil *n*; Kamerarückseite *f*, Filmrückwand *f* (Fachkamera)
~ **back lock release lever** Rückwandentriegelung *f*
~ **backpack** Kamerarucksack *m*
~ **bag** Kameratasche *f*; Kamerabeutel *m*; Fototasche *f*
~ **barrel** Kameratubus *m*
~ **battery** Kamerabatterie *f*
~ **bellows** Balgen *m*
~ **body** Kamerakörper *m*, Kameragehäuse *n*
~ **boom** Kameraausleger *m*; Kamerakran *m*
~ **cable** Kamerakabel *n*
~ **cable release** Drahtauslöser *m*
~ **calibration** Kamerakalibrierung *f* (maschinelle Bilderkennung)
~ **car** selbstfahrender Kamerawagen *m*
~ **card** Digitalkamera-Speicherkarte *f*, Kamerakarte *f*
~ **care** Kamerapflege *f*
~**-carrying aircraft** Bildflugzeug *n* (Fernerkundung)
~ **case** Kameratasche *f*
~ **cell phone** Kamerahandy *n*, Foto-Handy *n*, Multimedia-Handy *n*
~ **clinic** Kameraklinik *f*
~ **constant** Kamerakonstante *f*
~ **control** 1. Kamerasteuerung *f*; 2. Kamera-Bedienelement *n*
~ **control feature** Kamera-Bedienelement *n*
~ **control unit** Kamerasteuereinheit *f*, Kamerakontrolleinheit *f*, Kamerakontrollgerät *n*, Basisstation *f* (Videoaufnahme)
~ **coordinate system** Kamerakoordinatensystem *n*
~ **crew** Kamerateam *n*, Kameraabteilung *f* (Filmarbeit)
~ **defect** Kamerafehler *m*
~ **design** Kamerakonstruktion *f*, Kamerabauart *f*; Kameradesign *n*
~ **designer** Kamerakonstrukteur *m*; Kameradesigner *m*
~ **diaphragm** Kamerablende *f*
~ **diaphragm opening** Kamerablendenöffnung *f*

~ **direction** Kamerarichtung *f*
~ **distance** Kameraabstand *m*
~ **documentation** Fotodokumentation *f*
~ **dolly** Dolly *m*, Fahrstativ *n*, fahrbares Stativ *n*, Rollstativ *n*, Stativwagen *m*; fahrbarer Stativuntersatz *m*, Fahrspinne *f*
~ **effect** Kameraeffekt *m*, Kameratrick *m*, Filmaufnahmetrick *m*
~ **electronics** Kameraelektronik *f*
~ **equipment** Kameraausrüstung *f*
~ **exposure** Kamerabelichtung *f*
~ **exposure chart** Negativbericht *m* (Filmproduktion); s.a. ~ report)
~ **exposure meter** Kamerabelichtungsmesser *m*
~ **exposure setting** Kamerabelichtungseinstellung *f*
~ **extension** Kameraauszug *m*, Bildentfernung *f*, Bildweite *f*
~ **feature** Kamerafunktionsmerkmal *n*, Kamerafunktion *f*
~ **field of view** Kamerablickfeld *n*, Kamerasichtfeld *n*, Kameragesichtsfeld *n*
~ **film** Kamerafilm *m*, Kameraoriginal *n*, Aufnahmefilm *m*, Unikat *n*
~-**film format** Kamerafilmformat *n*
~ **film plane** Kamerafilmebene *f*
~ **film speed** Kamerafilmempfindlichkeit *f*
~ **filter** Kamerafilter *n*, Aufnahmefilter *n*
~ **finder** Sucher *m*
~ **focal length** Kamerabrennweite *f*
~ **focal plane** Kamerabildebene *f*
~ **focal plane shutter** Kamerabildfensterverschluss *m*
~ **focal point**, ~ **focus** Kamerabrennpunkt *m*
~ **format** Kameraformat *n*
~ **frame-per-second rate** Aufnahmefrequenz *f*
~ **front** Kamerafront *f*
~ **function** Kamerafunktion *f*
~ **gate** Kamerafenster *n*, Bildbühne *f*
~ **gear** Kameraausrüstung *f*
~ **grip** Kameragriff *m*
~ **ground glass** Kameramattscheibe *f*
~ **handling** Kamerahandhabung *f*
~ **head** Kamerakopf *m*
~ **height** Kamerahöhe *f*
~ **history** Kamerageschichte *f*
~ **housing** Kameragehäuse *n*, Kamerakörper *m*
~ **instruction manual** Kameragebrauchsanweisung *f*
~ **interest** Kamerablickpunkt *m*
~ **interface** Kameraschnittstelle *f*
~ **interior** Kamerainnere *n*
~ **jam** Filmsalat *m*
~ **lens** Kameralinse *f*; Kameraobjektiv *n*, Fotokameraobjektiv *n*
~ **lens diaphragm** Kamerablende *f*
~ **lens distortion** Objektivverzeichnung *f*
~ **lens filter** Objektivfilter *n*

camera

~ **lens focal length** Kameraobjektivbrennweite *f*
~ **lens mount** Kameraobjektivhalter *m*
~ **loading** Filmladen *n*, Filmeinlegen *n*; Filmeinspulen *n*
~ **location** Kameraposition *f*, Kamerastellung *f*; Kamerastandort *m*, Kamerastandpunkt *m*
~ **look-at** Kamerablickpunkt *m*
~ **lucida** Camera *f* lucida *(frühes Zeichengerät)*
~-**made image** Kamerabild *n*
~ **magazine** Kameramagazin *n*
~ **maintenance** Kamerapflege *f*
~ **maker** s. ~ manufacturer
~ **manipulation** Kamerahandhabung *f*
~ **manufacture** Kamerabau *m*, Kamerafertigung *f*
~ **manufacturer** Kamerabauer *m*, Kamerahersteller *m*, Kameraproduzent *m*
~ **mechanism** Kameramechanismus *m*
~ **memory** Kameraspeicher *m*
~ **metering system** Kameramesssystem *n*
~ **mode** Kameramodus *m*
~ **model** Kameramodell *n*
~ **modeling** Kameramodellierung *f* *(Computergrafik)*
~ **module** Kameramodul *n*
~ **monitor** Kameramonitor *m*
~ **motion** Kamerabewegung *f*
~ **motor** Kameramotor *m*
~ **move[ment]** Kamerabewegung *f*
~ **neck strap** s. ~ strap
~ **negative** Kameranegativ *n*
~ **negative film** Kameranegativfilm *m*, Originalnegativ *n*
~ **noise** Kamera[lauf]geräusch *n*; Kamerarauschen *n*
~ **objective** Kameraobjektiv *n*, Fotokameraobjektiv *n*
~ **obscura** Camera *f* obscura, Loch[blenden]kamera *f*, Urkamera *f*
~ **operating noise** Kamera[lauf]geräusch *n*
~ **operation** Kameraführung *f*, Bildführung *f*
~ **operator** Kameramann *m*, Operateur *m*; Erster Kameraassistent *m*
~ **operator assistant** Materialassistent *m*, Zweiter Kameraassistent *m*, Loader *m*
~ **optics** Kameraoptik *f*
~ **orientation** Kameraausrichtung *f*, Kameraorientierung *f*
~ **original [film]** Kameraoriginal *n*, Kamerafilm *m*, Unikat *n*
~-**original footage** Original-Kamerafilmmaterial *n (s.a. camera original [film])*
~ **original negative** s. ~ negative
~ **output voltage** Kameraausgangsspannung *f*
~ **pan** Kameraschwenk *m*, Horizontalschwenk *m*, Schwenk *m*, Mitzieher *m*

~ **parameter** Kameraparameter *m*
~ **photograph** Kameraaufnahme *f*
~ **pickup (picture) tube** Bildaufnahmeröhre *f*, Aufnahme[bild]röhre *f*, Kameraröhre *f*
~ **plane** Kameraebene *f*
~ **point of view** Kameraperspektive *f*
~ **pointing** Kamerarichten *n*
~ **position** Kameraposition *f*, Kamerastellung *f*; Kamerastandort *m*, Kamerastandpunkt *m*
~ **pouch** Kamerabeutel *m*
~ **pressure plate** Andruckplatte *f*
~ **rain guard** Regenschutzhaube *f*
~-**ready** reprofähig, reproduktionsfähig, reproreif
~-**ready art[work]** repro[duktions]fähige Grafik *f*, Reprografik *f*
~-**ready copy** Reprovorlage *f*, Fotovorlage *f*
~ **record** Kameraaufnahme *f*
~-**recorder** Kamerarecorder *m*, Videokamerarecorder *m*; Camcorder *m*
~ **reference frame** Kamerakoordinatensystem *n*
~ **rental house** Kameraverleih *m*
~ **repair** Kamerareparatur *f*, Fotoapparatereparatur *f*
~ **repair technician** Kamerareparateur *m*
~ **report** Drehbericht *m*, Kamerabericht *m*, Kameraprotokoll *n*, Aufnahmebericht *m*, Negativbericht *m (Filmarbeit)*
~ **retaining screw** Kameraschraube *f*
~ **rig** Kameraaufbau *m (Filmarbeit)*
~ **roll** Kamera[film]rolle *f*
~ **rotation** Kamerarotation *f*
~ **running speed** Kamerageschwindigkeit *f*
~ **scanner** Kamerascanner *m*, Scannerkamera *f*
~ **scanning** Kameraabtastung *f*
~ **script** Filmskript *n (s.a. motion-picture screenplay)*
~ **self-calibration** Kamera-Selbstkalibrierung *f*
~ **sensitivity** Kameraempfindlichkeit *f*
~ **sensor** Kamerasensor *m*
~ **service** Reproanstalt *f*
~ **setting** Kameraeinstellung *f*
~ **setup** Kameraanordnung *f*; Kameraeinstellung *f*
~ **shake** Kameraerschütterung *f*; Verwacklung[sbewegung] *f*
~ **sheet** s. ~ report
~ **shot** Kameraaufnahme *f*
~ **shutter** Kameraverschluss *m*, Verschluss *m*
~ **shutter blade** Verschlusslamelle *f*
~ **shutter speed setting** Verschlusszeiteneinstellung *f*
~ **signal** Kamerasignal *n (Fernsehen)*
~ **size** Kameragröße *f*
~ **sling** Kamerakordel *f*
~ **space** Kamerakoordinatensystem *n*
~ **speed** Kamerageschwindigkeit *f*

~ **stability** Kamerastabilität f
~ **stabilization** Kamerastabilisierung f
~ **stabilization device** Kamerastabilisator m, Kamerastabilisierer m
~ **stabilizing system** Kamerastabilisierungssystem n
~ **stand** Kamerastativ n; Fotostativ n
~ **standard** Kamerastandarte f *(Fachkamera)*
~ **station** Aufnahmestandort m, Aufnahmestandpunkt m *(s.a. ~ position)*
~ **store** Fotofachgeschäft n
~ **strap** Kameragurt m, Kameratrag[e]riemen m, Kamerariemen m
~ **strap eyelet** Riemenhalterung f
~ **support [device]** Kameraabstützung f, Kamerastütze f, Kameraauflage f
~ **system** Kamerasystem n
~ **take** Kameraeinstellung f *(Filmarbeit)*
~ **target** Abbildungsebene f *(Videomodellierung)*
~ **team** Kamerateam n, Kameraabteilung f *(Filmarbeit)*
~ **technician** Kameratechniker m
~ **technique** Kameratechnik f
~ **technology** Kameratechnik f; Kameratechnologie f
~ **tilt** 1. Kameraneigung f; 2. Vertikalschwenk m
~**-to-object distance** Kamera-Objekt-Entfernung f
~**-to-subject axis** Kameraachse f, Aufnahmeachse f, Kamera[blick]winkel m
~ **top** Kameraoberseite f
~ **tracking** s. ~ travel
~ **translation** Kameratranslation f
~ **travel** Kamerafahrt f, Verfolgungsschwenk m *(Filmarbeit)*
~ **tripod** Kamerastativ n
~ **tube** Bild[speicher]röhre f
~ **type** Kameratyp m
~ **vibration** Kameravibration f
~ **video tube** s. ~ pickup tube
~ **view** Kamerablickfeld n, Kamerasichtfeld n
~ **viewfinder** Kamerasucher m
~ **viewpoint** Kamerablickpunkt m
~ **weight** Kameragewicht n
~ **window** Kamerafenster n
~ **work** Kameraarbeit f
~ **zoom [lens]** Kamerazoom n
camera's default setting Kameragrundeinstellung f
cameraless kameralos
~ **photograph** Fotogramm n, Fotografik f, Lichtgrafik f, Lichtmalerei f
~ **photography** kameralose Fotografie f
cameraman Kameramann m, Operateur m
cameraperson s. cameraman
camerist Fotograf m
camouflage detection photograph Infrarot-Farbfoto n

campimeter Gesichtsfeldmesser m, Perimeter n
campimetry Gesichtsfeldmessung f, Perimetrie f
can Filmdose f, Filmbüchse f
Canada balsam Kanadabalsam m, Kanadaterpentin n *(optischer Kitt)*
cancel key Löschtaste f
candela Candela f, Neue Kerze f *(SI-Basiseinheit der Lichtstärke)*
~ **per square meter** Candela f pro Quadratmeter, Nit n *(SI-Einheit der Leuchtdichte)*
candid s. ~ photograph
~ **angle [lens] attachment** Spiegelvorsatz m, Winkelobjektiv n
~ **camera** 1. verdeckte (versteckte) Kamera f; Geheimkamera f; 2. Kleinbildkamera f; Schnappschusskamera f, Schnellschusskamera f
~ **photograph (shot)** Knipsfoto n, ungestelltes Foto n, Schnappschuss m
candle s. candela
candlepower Lichtstärke f in Candela
Canny edge detector, ~ filter (operator) Canny-Filter n, Canny-Operator m *(maschinelle Bilderkennung)*
canonical camera kanonische Kamera f
~ **code** kanonischer Code m
~ **Huffman code** kanonischer Huffman-Code m
~ **perspective** kanonische Perspektive f
canvas Leinwand f
cap s. capital letter
~ **height** Versalhöhe f *(Typografie)*
~ **keeper** Objektivdeckelhalter m
~ **line** s. ~ height
capacitance Kapazität f
~ **pick-up** kapazitiver Lesekopf m
capacitive sensor kapazitiver Sensor m
capacitor Kondensator m
~ **microphone** Kondensatormikrofon n
capital letter Großbuchstabe m, Versal m, Majuskel f
Capri-blue effect Capriblaueffekt m *(Farbfotografie)*
caps lock Umschalttaste f *(Tastatur)*
capstan Bandantriebsachse f, Bandantriebswelle f; Bandtransportantrieb m
caption/to untertiteln
caption 1. Bildbeschriftung f, Bildunterschrift f, Legende f; Untertitel m, Fußtitel m, Filmuntertitel m; 2. Kennungsbild n, Signet n, Logo n
~ **generator** Videotitelgenerator m
captioned photo[graph] untertiteltes Foto n
captioning Untertitelung f
capture/to aufnehmen; in eine Datei aufnehmen; digitalisieren *(bes. Videobilddaten)*
capture Erfassung f *(z.B. von Bilddaten)*
~ **board** Nachbearbeitungskarte f *(Video)*

capture 46

~ **material** Aufnahmematerial n, Aufzeichnungsmaterial n
~ **medium** Aufnahmemedium n
~ **mode** Aufnahmemodus m, Aufzeichnungsmodus m
~ **rate** Aufnahmefrequenz f
~ **stage** Aufnahmestudio n (bes. für Trickaufnahmen)
captured motion video erfasstes Laufbildvideo n
capturing process Aufnahmevorgang m
car adapter (charger) Autoadapter m, Ladegerät n für Autoanschluss; Autoladekabel n, Autobatterie-Anschlusskabel n
~ **navigation system** Fahrzeugnavigationssystem n
carbocyanine Carbocyanin n (Farbstoff)
carbon arc Kohlelichtbogen m
~**-arc lamp** Kohlebogenlampe f
~**-arc light** Kohlebogenlicht n
~ **black** Ruß m (Pigment)
~ **copy** Durchschlag m
~**-dioxide [gas] laser** Kohlendioxidlaser m
~ **filament incandescent lamp** Kohlefaden[glüh]lampe f
~ **film** Kohle[aufdampf]schicht f (Elektronenmikroskopie)
~ **paper** Kohlepapier n
~ **print** Kohledruck m, Karbondruck m
~ **process** Kohledruck m, Karbondruck m, Kohlekopierverfahren n
~ **tetrachloride** Tetrachlorkohlenstoff m
~ **tissue** Pigmentpapier n
carbonate buffer Karbonatpuffer m (Entwicklerzusatz)
carbonless paper Selbstdurchschreibepapier n, selbstdurchschreibendes Papier n, SD-Papier n
carbro print Carbrodruck m (Erzeugnis)
~ **process** Carbrodruck m
carcinotron Carcinotron n, Karzinotron n (eine Elektronenröhre)
card adapter Kartenadapter m
~ **reader** Kartenlesegerät n, Kartenleser m
~ **slot** Kartensteckplatz m; Speicherkartenschlitz m, Speicherkarteneinschub m
cardboard Pappe f, Karton m
~ **mount** Papprähmchen n, Papprahmen m
cardiac angiography Kardioangiografie f
~ **cine MRI** Kinekoronarografie f
~ **gating** EKG-Steuerung f, EKG-Triggerung f (Magnetresonanzbildgebung)
~ **imaging** kardiologische Bildgebung f
cardinal plane [Gaußsche] Hauptebene f, Gaußsche Bildebene f (Optik)
~ **point** Kardinalpunkt m (Optik)
cardioangiogram Angiokardiogramm n
cardioangiography Angiokardiografie f
cardiogram Kardiogramm n
cardioid microphone Kardioidmikrofon n, Nierenmikrofon n

cardiological imaging s. cardiac imaging
caret [mark] [keilförmiges] Einfügungszeichen n, Einschaltungszeichen n (Typografie)
carriage return Wagenrücklauf m (Drucker)
carrier 1. Träger m; 2. Trägerfrequenz f; 3. s. ~ signal
~ **amplitude** Trägeramplitude f
~ **frequency** Trägerfrequenz f
~**-frequency system** Trägerfrequenzsystem n
~ **material** Trägermaterial n (Filmherstellung)
~ **modulation** Trägermodulation f
~ **signal** Trägersignal n
~ **suppression** Trägerunterdrückung f
~**-to-interference ratio** Träger-Störsignal-Verhältnis n
~**-to-noise ratio** Träger-Rauschabstand m, Träger-Rausch-Verhältnis n
~ **wave** Trägerwelle f, Trägerschwingung f
carrying agent (medium) Trägermedium n
carryover Bäderverschleppung f, Chemieverschleppung f (Filmverarbeitung)
carte-de-visite [photograph] Visitenkartenporträt n
Cartesian color space kartes[ian]ischer Farbraum m
~ **coordinate system** kartes[ian]isches Koordinatensystem n
~ **grid** kartes[ian]isches Gitter n
~ **matrix** kartesi[ani]sche Matrix f
~ **space** kartes[ian]ischer Raum m
cartographer Kartograf m
cartographic kartografisch
~ **rectification** kartografische Entzerrung f
~ **representation** kartografische Darstellung f
cartographical kartografisch
~ **pattern recognition** kartografische Mustererkennung f
cartography Kartografie f
cartometry Kartometrie f, Kartenmesskunde f
cartoon/to zeichnen
cartoon [film], ~ **movie** Zeichen[trick]film m
cartoonist Zeichentrickfilmer m; Trick[film]zeichner m
cartridge Kartusche f; Kassette f; Patrone f
~**-based tape machine** Kassettenbandmaschine f
~ **tape** Kassettenband n
cascadable kaskadierbar
cascade/to kaskadieren
cascade print washer Wässerungskaskade f
~ **processing** Kaskadenmethode f (des Wässerns von Fotomaterial)
cascaded amplifier Kaskadenverstärker m
~ **convolution** kaskadierte Faltung f
~ **filter bank** Filterbankkaskade f, kaskadierte Filterbank f

cascading Kaskadierung f
case study Fallstudie f
Cassegrain antenna Cassegrain-Antenne f
~-Coudé telescope
  Cassegrain-Coudé-Teleskop n
~ focus Cassegrain-Fokus m,
  Sekundärfokus m *(Teleskop)*
~ lens system Cassegrain-System n
~ mirror [system] Cassegrain-Spiegel m,
  Cassegrainscher Spiegel m
~ reflecting telescope
  Cassegrain-Spiegelteleskop n
~ spectrograph Cassegrain-Spektrograf m
cassette Kassette f
~ changer Kassettenwechsler m
~ compartment Kassettenfach n
~ entry slot Kassettenschlitz m
~ film Kassettenfilm m
~ film retriever Filmherauszieher m,
  Filmrückholer m
~ format Kassettenformat n
~ frame Kassettenrahmen m
~ loading section Kassettenladestation f
~ machine Kassettenmaschine f
~ memory Kassettenspeicher m
~ mouth Kassettenmaul n
~ opener Kassettenöffner m
~ recorder Kassettenrecorder m;
  Audiokassettengerät n,
  Audiokassettenrecorder m
~ recording format Kassettenformat n
~ size Kassettenformat n
~ tape Kassettenband n
~ tape player Kassettenbandgerät n
~-type film Kassettenfilm m
cast s. color cast
~-coated paper gussgestrichenes Papier
  n, Hochglanzpapier n
~ shadow Schlagschatten m, echter
  Schatten m
caster Gießmaschine f,
  Letterngießmaschine f
CAT s. computed axial tomography
~ scan Computertomogramm n,
  CT-Aufnahme f, CT-Bild n
~ scanner Computertomograf m
cat's-eye diaphragm Katzenaugenblende f
catacaustic s. caustic surface
catadioptric katadioptrisch
~ lens (system) katadioptrisches Objektiv
  (System) n, Spiegel[linsen]objektiv n,
  Spiegellinse f
catadioptrics Katadioptrik f
catalog photographer Katalogfotograf m
~ photography Katalogfotografie f
~ printing Katalogdruck m
catalyst Katalysator m
catalyze/to katalysieren
cataract Katarakt[a] f, grauer Star m
  (Augenlinsentrübung)
catchlight [effect] Spitzlicht n
catchment area Fangbereich m *(visuelle
  Navigation)*

catechol Brenzcatechin n
  (Entwicklersubstanz)
categorization s. classification
catheter angiography Katheterangiografie
  f
cathetometer Kathetometer n *(technisches
  Fernrohr)*
cathode Katode f
~ area Katodenfläche f
~ cylinder Katodenzylinder m,
  Wehnelt-Zylinder m
~ electron Katodenelektron n
~ luminescence s. cathodoluminescence
~ ray Katodenstrahl m
~-ray detection finding
  Elektronenstrahl-Richtungssuche f
~-ray graphic display Grafikdisplay n,
  grafikfähiges Display n, Grafikanzeige f;
  Grafikbildschirm m
~-ray oscillograph
  Katodenstrahloszillograf m
~-ray oscilloscope
  Katodenstrahloszilloskop n,
  Elektronenstrahloszilloskop n
~-ray picture tube Katodenstrahlbildröhre
  f, Elektronenstrahl[bild]röhre f
~-ray tube Katodenstrahlröhre f,
  Elektronenstrahl[bild]röhre f *(s.a. unter
  CRT)*
~-ray tube controller
  Bildröhrensteuereinheit f
~-ray tube envelope Röhrenkolben m
~-ray tube film recorder
  optomechanischer Filmabtaster m
~-ray tube mask Bildschirmmaske f
~-ray tube monitor Röhrenmonitor m,
  Bildröhrenmonitor m,
  Katodenstrahlmonitor m
~-ray tube phototypesetter
  CRT-Fotosetzanlage f,
  Katodenstrahl[rohr]maschine f
  (Druckvorstufe)
~-ray tube picture Bildschirmbild n;
  Monitorbild n
~-ray tube projector Röhrenprojektor m
  (Video)
~-ray tube scanner Kamera-Filmabtaster
  m, Speicher[röhren]abtaster m,
  Katodenstrahlbelichter m
~-ray tube shield Katodenzylinder m,
  Wehnelt-Zylinder m
~-ray viewing screen Röhrenbildschirm m
~ surface Katodenfläche f
~ voltage Katodenspannung f
cathodolithography
  Elektronenstrahllithografie f
cathodoluminescence Katodolumineszenz
  f, Katodenlumineszenz f
cathodoluminescent katodolumineszent,
  katodenlumineszent
catoptric light katoptrisches Licht n
~ system katoptrisches System n
catoptrics Katoptrik f
CATV amplifier Kabelverstärker m

CATV

~ **headend** Kabel[fernseh]kopfstation f, Rundfunkempfangsstelle f
~ **operator** Kabel[netz]betreiber m
~ **plant** Kabel[fernseh]anlage f
~ **subscriber** Kabelfernsehteilnehmer m
~ **system** Kabelfernsehsystem n
Cauchy formula Dispersionsformel f
causal filter kausales Filter n
~ **signal** kausales Signal n
caustic s. 1. ~ surface; 2. ~ soda
~ **alkalies** Ätzalkalien npl
~ **line** Brennlinie f, [kata]kaustische Linie f
~ **potash** Ätzkali n, Kaliumhydroxid n (Entwicklerbestandteil)
~ **soda** Ätznatron n (Entwicklerbestandteil)
~ **surface** Brennfläche f, Kaustik f, Katakaustik f (Optik)
cavalier axonometry (projection) Kavalierprojektion f, Kavalierperspektive f
CAVE s. computer-aided virtual environment
cavitation Kavitation f (Sonografie)
cavity 1. Hohlraum m; 2. Resonator m, Etalon n (Interferometrie, Laser); 3. s. Fabry-Perot cavity
~ **dumping** Auskoppelmodulation f, Pulsauskopplung f (Laser)
~ **radiation** Hohlraumstrahlung f, Schwarzkörperstrahlung f
~ **radiator** Hohlraumstrahler m, Schwarzkörperstrahler m, Planckscher (Schwarzer) Strahler m
CC filter CC-Filter n, Farbkorrekturfilter n; Farbkompensationsfilter n
CCD s. charge-coupled device
~ **array** CCD-Matrix f, CCD-Bauelementanordnung f, Matrix-CCD f
~ **camera** CCD-Kamera f, Halbleiterkamera f
~ **camera chip** s. ~ imaging chip
~ **color scanner** CCD-Farbscanner m
~ **column** CCD-Spalte f
~ **image sensor, ~ imager** CCD-Bildsensor m, CCD-Bildwandler m
~ **imaging chip** [CCD-]Bildwandlerchip m, Bildempfängerchip m, CCD-Chip m, Pixelchip m
~ **noise** Sensorrauschen n
~ **photodetector** s. ~ sensor
~ **pixel** CCD-Pixel n
~ **sensor** CCD-Sensor m, CCD-Detektor m, CCD-Wandler m
~ **shift register** [CCD-]Schieberegister n
~ **technology** CCD-Technik f, CCD-Technologie f
~ **telecine** CCD-Filmabtaster m, CCD-Abtaster m
~ **television (TV) camera** CCD-Fernsehkamera f
~ **video camera** CCD-Videokamera f
~ **wafer** CCD-Flächenchip m, CCD-Flächensensor m

CCIR standard CCIR-Norm f (digitales Video)
CCU s. camera control unit
CD CD[-Platte] f, Kompaktplatte f (s.a. unter compact disc)
CD burner CD-Brenner m, CD-Schreiber m
CD-I s. compact disc interactive
CD movie CD-Spielfilm m
CD-R s. compact disc recordable
CD-ROM s. compact disc read-only memory
CD-ROM drive CD-ROM-Laufwerk n
CD-RW s. compact disc rewritable
CD video s. compact disc video
CD writer CD-Brenner m
CdS exposure meter Cadmiumsulfid-Belichtungsmesser m
cedilla Cedille f (diakritisches Zeichen)
ceiling-mounted camera deckenmontierte Kamera f, Deckenkamera f
~-**mounted monitor** Deckenmonitor m
~ **rail system** Deckenschienensystem n, Laufschienensystem n (Studioausrüstung)
cel 1. Cellofolie f, Folie f (Zeichentrickfilmproduktion); 2. s. ~ drawing
~ **drawing** Phasenzeichnung f (Trickfilmproduktion)
celestial photograph Himmelsfoto n; Astrofoto n
~ **photography** Himmelsfotografie f, Astrofotografie f; Sternbildfotografie f
~ **radiation** Himmelsstrahlung f
cell 1. Zelle f; Rasternäpfchen n, Näpfchen n (Tiefdruck); 2. Feld n (Tabelle; Bildschirmmenü); 3. s. cel 1.
~ **array** Zellmatrix f (Computergrafik)
~ **data** Zelldaten pl
~ **decomposition** Zellenzerlegung f (Computergrafik)
~ **error rate** Zellfehlerrate f
~ **header** Zellkopf m (asynchroner Übertragungsmodus)
~ **image analysis** Zellbildanalyse f
~ **loss** Zellverlust m
~ **phone** Mobil[funk]telefon n, Handy n
~-**phone display** Handydisplay n
celloidin paper Zelloidinpapier n
cellular logic image processor Bildprozessor m mit zellularer Logikstruktur
~ **neural network** zellulares neuronales Netz n
~ **pattern** zelluläres Muster n
~ **telephone** Mobil[funk]telefon n, Handy n
celluloid Celluloid n, Zelluloid n
~ **[roll] film** Celluloidrollfilm m
cellulose Cellulose f (Polysaccharid)
~ **acetate** Celluloseacetat n, Acetylcellulose f
~ **acetate film** Celluloseacetatfilm m
~ **diacetate** Cellulosediacetat n
~ **ester** Celluloseester m

~ **nitrate** Cellulosenitrat n, Nitratcellulose f (Filmträger)
~ **nitrate film** Cellulosenitratfilm m, Nitrofilm m, Zellhornfilm m
~ **propionate** Cellulosepropionat n
~ **triacetate** Cellulosetriacetat n
~ **triacetate safety film** Sicherheitsfilm m, Safety-Film m, Acetatfilm m
cement [together]/to [ver]kitten
~ Klebekitt m; Filmkleber m
~ **splice** Nassklebestelle f
cemented filter gekittetes (verkittetes) Filter n
~ **lens** verkittete Linse f
~ **surface** Kittfläche f
cementing Verkittung f
center/to zentrieren
center axis Mittelachse f
~ **column** Mittelsäule f (Stativ)
~ **frequency** Mittenfrequenz f
~ **of curvature** Krümmungsmittelpunkt m, Krümmungszentrum n
~ **of dispersion** Zerstreuungspunkt m, virtueller Brennpunkt m
~ **of mass** Schwerpunkt m, Masseschwerpunkt m, Baryzentrum n
~ **of perspective** Perspektivitätszentrum n
~ **of projection** Projektionszentrum n
~ **of rotation of the eye** Augendrehpunkt m
~ **of the fovea** innere Netzhautgrube f, Foveola f
~**-opening shutter** Zentralverschluss m
~ **pel** Zentralpixel n, Mittenpunkt m (Binärbild)
~ **pillar** Mittelsäule f (Stativ)
~ **pixel** s. ~ pel
~ **speaker** Mittellautsprecher m (Kinotechnik)
~ **stop** Mittelblende f, Sternblende f (Objektiv)
~ **thickness** Mittendicke f (Linse)
~**-to-center distance (spacing)** Mittenabstand m
~ **track** Mittenspur f (Tonfilm)
~ **wavelength** Mittenwellenlänge f, Zentralwellenlänge f (Laser)
~**-weighted median filter** zentral gewichtetes Medianfilter n
~**-weighted metering** mittenbetonte Integralmessung (Belichtungsmessung) f, mittenbetonte Messung f
centerable zentrierbar
centered lens zentrierte Linse f
~ **lens system** zentriertes optisches System n
~ **perspective** zentralperspektivisch
~ **perspective projection** zentralperspektivische Projektion f
centering Zentrierung f
~ **control** Bildlageregelung f (Display)
~ **microscope** Zentriermikroskop n
~ **tolerance** Zentriertoleranz f
centerpost Mittelsäule f (Stativ)

central beam Zentralstrahl m
~ **computer** Zentralrechner m; Großrechner m, Großrechenanlage f
~ **definition** Mittenschärfe f
~ **laboratory [facility]** Zentrallabor n
~ **lobe, ~ main lobe** Hauptkeule f (Radar, Ultraschall)
~ **memory** Hauptspeicher m, Arbeitsspeicher m
~ **moment** zentrales Moment n
~ **obscuration (obstruction)** Zentralabschattung f, Mittenabschattung f (Optik)
~ **perspective** Zentralperspektive f, Linearperspektive f, lineare Perspektive f
~ **pixel** Zentralpixel n, Mittenpunkt n (Binärbild)
~ **processing unit** Hauptprozessor m, Zentraleinheit f, zentrale Verarbeitungseinheit f (Computermodul)
~ **projection** Zentralprojektion f
~ **ray** Zentralstrahl m
~ **retinal artery** [zentrale] Netzhautarterie f
~ **shutter** Zentralverschluss m
~ **speaker** Mittellautsprecher m (Kinotechnik)
~ **stop** Mittelblende f, Sternblende f (Objektiv)
~ **visual ray** Sehachse f
centralized structure store zentraler Strukturspeicher m (Computergrafik)
centration Zentrierung f
centrifuge microscope Zentrifugenmikroskop n
centripetal paramet[e]rization zentripetale Parametrisierung f
centroid Objektschwerpunkt m
~ **of the area** Flächenschwerpunkt m
CEPS s. color electronic prepress system
ceramic filter Keramikfilter n
cerebral cortex Großhirnrinde f
Cerenkov light (radiation) Tscherenkow-Licht n, Tscherenkow-Strahlung f
cerium oxide Ceriumoxid n (Poliermittel)
cesium iodide Cäsiumiodid n (Röntgenleuchtstoff)
~ **oxide cell** Caesiumoxidzelle f (Fotoemissionsdetektor)
~ **vapor lamp** Caesiumdampflampe f
CG s. 1. computer-generated; 2. computer graphics
CG imagery s. computer-generated imagery
CGA s. color graphics adapter
CGI s. computer-generated imagery
chaff Düppel m, Düppelecho n (Radar)
chain 1. Kette f; 2. Linienzug m (Computergrafik)
~ **cluster** Kettencluster m
~ **code** Kettencode m
~**-code representation** Kettencodedarstellung f
~ **coding** Kettencodierung f

chain 50

- ~ **decoding** Kettendecodierung f
- ~ **dot** elliptischer Rasterpunkt m
- ~ **line printer** Typenkettendrucker m
- **chaining** Verkettung f, Konkatenation f (z.B. von Codes)
- **chalcogenide glass** Chalkogenidglas n (optischer Werkstoff)
- **chalking** Wolkigkeit f, Perlen n, Mottling n (Druckschwierigkeit)
- **change detection** Änderungsdetektion f, Änderungserkennung f, Veränderungserkennung f
- ~ **list** Änderungsliste f (Filmschnitt)
- ~ **of scale** Maßstabsänderung f
- ~ **of the objective** Objektivwechsel m
- **changeover** Überblendvorgang m, Projektorwechsel m (Filmvorführung)
- ~ **cue [mark]** Überblendzeichen n; Ausblendzeichen n, Abfahrzeichen n
- **changing bag** Wechselsack m, Dunkelsack m
- **channel** Kanal m
- ~ **allocation** Kanalaufteilung f; Kanalzuordnung f
- ~ **bandwidth** Kanalbandbreite f
- ~ **buffer** Kanalspeicher m
- ~ **bundling** Kanalbündelung f
- ~ **capacity** Kanalkapazität f
- ~ **change** Kanalwechsel m
- ~ **code** Kanalcode m
- ~ **-coded data** kanalcodierte Daten pl
- ~ **coding** Kanalcodierung f
- ~ **combiner (combining unit)** Kanalweiche f
- ~ **constancy** Kanalkonstanz f
- ~ **decoder** Kanaldecod[ier]er m
- ~ **efficiency** Kanaleffizienz f
- ~ **encoder** Kanalcodierer m
- ~ **encoding** Kanalcodierung f
- ~ **error** Kanalfehler m
- ~ **filter** Kanalfilter n
- ~ **hierarchy** Kanalhierarchie f
- ~ **multiplexer** Kanalmultiplexer m
- ~ **multiplexing** Kanalvervielfachung f
- ~ **noise** Kanalrauschen n
- ~ **output** Kanalausgang m
- ~ **plate** Kanalplatte f
- ~ **separation** Kanaltrennung f
- ~ **structure** Kanalstruktur f
- ~ **transmission** Kanalübertragung f
- ~ **transmission error** Kanalfehler m
- ~ **width** Kanalbandbreite f
- **character** 1. Druckzeichen n; Schriftzeichen n; Buchstabe m; 2. Darsteller m, Filmfigur f
- ~ **area** Zeichenfeld n
- ~ **base vector (width)** Zeichenbasisvektor m
- ~ **block** Schriftzeichenblock m
- ~ **body** Zeichenkörper m
- ~ **boundary** Zeichenbegrenzung f
- ~ **class** Zeichenklasse f
- ~ **classification** Zeichenklassifikation f, Zeichenklassifizierung f
- ~ **classifier** Zeichenklassifikator m
- ~ **density** Zeichendichte f
- ~ **distance** Zeichenzwischenraum m
- ~ **encoding** Zeichencodierung f
- ~ **expansion factor** Zeichenbreitefaktor m
- ~ **field** Zeichenfeld n
- ~ **font** Zeichensatz m
- ~ **generator** Zeichengenerator m; Schriftgenerator m; Titelgenerator m, Titelgerät n, Videotitelgenerator m
- ~ **height** Zeichenhöhe f
- ~ **icon** s. ~ image
- ~ **image** Zeichen[ab]bild n; Schriftzeichenbild n
- ~ **kerning** Schriftunterschneidung f, Unterschneiden n, Zeichenausgleich m (Typografie)
- ~ **luminance** Zeichenleuchtdichte f
- ~ **matrix** Zeichenmatrix f
- ~ **memory** Zeichenspeicher m
- ~ **pitch** Zeichen[mitten]abstand m
- ~ **position** Zeichenposition f, Zeichenstelle f
- ~ **printer** Zeichendrucker m; Seriendrucker m
- ~ **reader** Klarschriftleser m
- ~ **recognition** Zeichenerkennung f; Schrift[zeichen]erkennung f; Klarschrifterkennung f, Klarschriftlesen n
- ~ **repertoire** Zeichenvorrat m
- ~ **sequence** Zeichenfolge f, Zeichenkette f
- ~ **set** Zeichensatz m
- ~ **size** Zeichengröße f
- ~ **spacing** Zeichen[mitten]abstand m
- ~ **string** Zeichenkette f, Zeichenfolge f
- ~ **up vector** Zeichenaufwärtsvektor m
- ~ **width** Zeichenbreite f
- **characteristic curve** Gradationskurve f, Schwärzungskurve f, Grauwertkennlinie f; [fotografische] Dichtekurve f, charakteristische Kurve (Filmkurve) f
- ~ **D-log H curve** s. ~ curve
- ~ **display curve** Bildröhrenkennlinie f
- ~ **function** Zugehörigkeitsfunktion f (Fuzzy-Logik)
- ~ **radiation** charakteristische Strahlung (Röntgenstrahlung) f, Eigenstrahlung f
- ~ **spectrum** charakteristisches Spektrum n
- ~ **value** Eigenwert m (z.B. eines Skalars)
- ~ **vector** charakteristischer Vektor m, Eigenvektor m (eines Operators)
- ~ **X-ray lines** Röntgenlinienspektrum n, charakteristisches Spektrum n
- **charge/to** [auf]laden (z.B. einen Akkumulator)
- **charge accumulation** Ladungsakkumulation f
- ~ **amplifier** Ladungsverstärker m
- ~ **carrier** Ladungsträger m
- ~ **carrier density** Ladungsträgerdichte f
- ~ **carrier injection** Ladungsträgerinjektion f
- ~ **-carrier layer** Ladungsträgerschicht f
- ~ **carrier recombination** Ladungsträgerrekombination f

chip

~**-carrier trapping** Ladungsträgereinfang *m*
~ **cloud** Ladungswolke *f*
~**-coupled detector** *s.* ~ device
~**-coupled device** ladungsgekoppeltes Halbleiterelement (Bauelement) *n*, ladungsgekoppelter Bildwandler *m*, Ladungstransferelement *n*, CCD-Element *n*, CCD *f*
~**-coupled MOS (metal-oxide semiconductor) capacitor** ladungsgekoppelter MOS-Kondensator *m*
~**-coupled photodiode** ladungsgekoppelte Fotodiode *f*
~**-coupled storage** Ladungsspeicher *m*
~ **coupling** Ladungskopplung *f*
~ **density** Ladungsdichte *f*
~**-density pattern** [elektrisches] Ladungsbild *n*, Ladungsmuster *n*
~**-depleted region** Verarmungsschicht *f*, Verarmungszone *f*, Raumladungszone *f* *(Fotodiode)*
~ **diffusion** Ladungsdiffusion *f*
~ **distribution** Ladungsverteilung *f*
~ **image** *s.* ~ pattern
~**-injection device** Ladungsinjektionswandler *m*, ladungsinjizierendes Bauelement *n*, CID-Sensor *m*
~ **integration** Ladungsintegration *f*
~ **packet** Ladungspaket *n* *(z.B. eines CCD-Sensors)*
~ **pair** Ladungs[träger]paar *n*
~ **pattern** [elektrisches] Ladungsbild *n*
~ **receiver** Ladungsempfänger *m*
~ **spectrograph** Ladungsspektrograf *m*
~ **spectrometer** Ladungsspektrometer *n*
~ **stabilization** Ladungsstabilisierung *f*
~ **storage** Ladungsspeicherung *f*
~ **storage capacity** Ladungsspeicherkapazität *f*
~ **storage location** Ladungsspeicherstelle *f*
~ **tester** Batterietester *m*
~ **transfer** Ladungsübertragung *f*, Ladungstransfer *m*, Ladungsverschiebung *f*
~ **transport** Ladungstransport *m*
~**-transport layer** Ladungstransportschicht *f*
~ **trapping** Ladungseinfang *m*
charged particle Ladungsteilchen *n*
~**-particle detection** Ladungsteilchendetektion *f*
~**-particle detector** Ladungsteilchendetektor *m*
~**-particle optics** Ladungsteilchenoptik *f*
charger [externes] Ladegerät *n*
charging current Ladestrom *m*
chart/to kartieren
chase Druckformträger *m* *(Hochdruck)*
Chebychev *s.* Chebyshev
Chebyshev filter Tschebyschew-Filter *n* *(Bildverarbeitung)*

~ **polynomial** Tschebyschew-Polynom *n*
check amount reading machine Scheckscanner *m*
~ **bit** Prüfbit *n*, Kontrollbit *n*
~ **point** Kontrollpunkt *m*
~ **print** Nullkopie *f*, Erstkopie *f* *(Kinematografie)*
~ **reader** Scheckscanner *m*
~ **sum** Prüfsumme *f*
checkerboard cutting Schachbrettschnitt *m*, AB-Schnitt *m* *(Videobearbeitung)*
cheek Filmteller *m*
chemical automixer Chemikalienmixer *m* *(Fotoverarbeitung)*
~ **darkroom** [fotografische] Dunkelkammer *f*; Dunkelraum *m*
~ **development** chemische Entwicklung *f*
~ **etching** chemisches Ätzen *n*
~ **fixer** Fixierer *m*, Fixiermittel *n*
~ **laser** chemischer Laser *m*
~ **microscopy** chemische Mikroskopie *f*
~ **photography** chemische Fotografie *f*
~ **reduction** chemische Reduktion *f*
~ **ripening (sensitization)** chemische Reifung (Sensibilisierung) *f*, Nachreifung *f*, Nachdigestion *f* *(Emulsionsherstellung)*
~ **shift [artifact]**, ~ **shift effect** chemische Verschiebung *f* *(Kernspinresonanz)*
~ **toner** chemischer Toner *m*
~ **toning** chemische Tonung *f*
chemiluminescence Chemilumineszenz *f*, Chemolumineszenz *f*
chemiluminescent chemilumineszent
chemisorption Chemisorption *f*
chemosphere *s.* mesosphere
chessboard distance Schachbrettdistanz *f* *(Binärbildgeometrie)*
chest microphone Krawattenmikrofon *n* *(s.a.* lapel [microphone]*)*
~ **radiograph** Thoraxaufnahme *f*
~ **radiography (X-ray)** Thoraxradiografie *f*
chestpod Bruststativ *n*
chi-square distribution Chi-Quadrat-Verteilung *f* *(Wahrscheinlichkeitsdichtefunktion)*
chief lighting technician Chefbeleuchter *m*, Oberbeleuchter *m*
~ **ray** Haupt[punkt]strahl *m*, Mittelpunktstrahl *m*; ausgezeichneter Strahl *m*
~ **set electrician** *s.* ~ lighting technician
Child-Langmuir current Child-Langmuir-Strom *m* *(Katodenstrahlröhre)*
child lock Kindersicherung *f* *(Fernsehgerät)*
~ **node** Kindknoten *m* *(Graphentheorie)*
chip Chip *m*; Halbleiterchip *m*; Mikroprozessor *m*
~ **camera** Chipkamera *f*, Halbleiterkamera *f*; CCD-Kamera *f*
~ **set** Chipsatz *m*
~ **surface** Chipoberfläche *f*

chirp

chirp radar monoton frequenzmoduliertes Radar *n*
~ **signal** Chirp *m*, linear frequenzmoduliertes Signal *m (Radar)*
chloride paper Chloridpapier *n*, Silberchloridpapier *n*, Chlorsilberpapier *n*, Kontaktpapier *n*
chlorine Chlor *n*
~ **ion** Chlorion *n*
chlorobromide emulsion Chlorbromemulsion *f*
~ **paper** Chlorbrom[silber]papier *n*, Silberchloridbromidpapier *n*
chloroiodide emulsion Chloriodidemulsion *f*
choice device Auswähler *m*
~ **of frequency** Frequenzwahl *f*
~ **of subject** Motivwahl *f*
choker close-up [shot] Ganzgroßaufnahme *f*
cholangiography Cholangiografie *f*, Gallenwegsröntgen[kontrast]darstellung *f*
choledochoscope Cholangioskop *n*, Choledochoskop *n*, Gallengangspiegel *m*
cholesteric phase cholesterinische Phase *f (Flüssigkristall)*
chopper Umlauf[sektoren]blende *f*, Sektorenblende *f*, Flügelblende *f*, Umlaufverschluss *m*, Flimmerblende *f (Kinotechnik)*
choppiness Bildruckeln *n*
choppy ruckelig
chord encoding Lauflängencodierung *f*
chordal paramet[e]rization chordale Parametrisierung *f*
choroid [coat] Aderhaut *f (des Auges)*
choropleth map choroplethische Karte *f*, Choroplethe *f*
Christiansen [effect] filter Christiansen-Filter *n*; Dispersionsfilter *n*
chroma Farbsättigung *f*, Sättigung *f (s.a. unter chrominance)*; Buntheit *f*, Chromatizität *f (Munsell-Farbordnungssystem)*
~ **black** Dunkelentsättigung *f*
~ **burst** s. color burst
~ **channel** Farbkanal *m (Fernsehen)*
~ **control** Farbregler *m (Fernsehen)*
~ **dark** s. ~ black
~ **delay** Farbverzögerung *f (Videorecorder)*
~ **demodulator** Farbdecod[ier]er *m*, Farbdemodulator *m*
~ **gain** Farbsättigungsregler *m*, Farbsignalverstärkung *f (Video)*
~ **key** Chromakey-Verfahren *n*, Farbstanze *f*, Farbstanztrick *m*, Farbschablonentechnik *f (Video)*
~ **key color** Stanzfarbe *f (Trickkinematografie)*
~ **keyer** Chromakey-Gerät *n*, Chromakey-Mischer *m*

~ **keying** Farbeingabe *f*, Farbeintastung *f (s.a. ~ key)*
~ **mapping** Farbwertrekonstruktion *f*
~ **noise** Farbrauschen *n*, farbiges Rauschen *n*, Chrominanz-Störabstand *m*
~ **signal** s. chrominance signal
chromate Chromat *n*, Chromsalz *n*
~ **process** Chromatverfahren *n*
chromatic chromatisch, farbig, bunt
~ **aberration** chromatische Aberration *f*, chromatischer Fehler *m*, Farb[abbildungs]fehler *m*
~ **aberration correction** Farb[fehler]korrektion *f*, Farbfehlerkorrektur *f*
~ **aberration-free** farbfehlerfrei
~ **adaptation** chromatische Adaptation *f*, Farbadaptation *f*, Farb[um]stimmung *f (z.B. des Auges)*
~ **aftereffect** farbiger Sukzessivkontrast *m (Sehen)*
~ **channel** Farbkanal *m (Gegenfarbentheorie)*
~ **color** bunte Farbe *f*, Buntfarbe *f*
~ **color constancy** Farbkonstanz *f*, Farbinvarianz *f*
~ **composition** Buntaufbau *m (Reprografie)*; Farbzusammensetzung *f (z.B. des Lichts)*
~ **content** Buntheit *f*, Chromatizität *f (s.a. colorfulness)*
~ **correction** s. ~ aberration correction
~ **defect** s. ~ aberration
~ **difference of magnification** Farbmaßstabsfehler *m*, Farbquerfehler *m*, chromatische Brennweitendifferenz (Queraberration) *f*
~ **dispersion** [chromatische] Dispersion *f*, Farbaufspaltung *f*, Regenbogeneffekt *m*
~ **equidensity line** Farbäquidensite *f*
~ **error** s. ~ aberration
~ **filter** chromatisches Filter *n*
~ **lens aberration** s. ~ aberration
~ **light** chromatisches Licht *n*
~ **overcorrection** chromatische Überkorrektur *f (eines Objektivs)*
~ **property** Farbeigenschaft *f*
~ **purity** Farbreinheit *f*
~ **resolution** Farbauflösung *f*
~ **resolving power** Farbauflösungsvermögen *n*
~ **selectivity** Farbunterscheidungsvermögen *n*
~ **sensation** Farbempfindung *f*, Farbempfinden *n*
~ **stimulus** Farbreiz *m*
~ **undercorrection** chromatische Unterkorrektur *f (eines Objektivs)*
~ **variation of focus** chromatische Schnittweitendifferenz (Längsaberration) *f*, Farbbrennweitenfehler *m*, Farblängsfehler *m*, Farbortsfehler *m*, axiale chromatische Aberration *f*

~ **variation of magnification** s.
~ difference of magnification
~ **variation of spherical aberration**
Gauß-Fehler m *(Optik)*
~ **vision** chromatisches Sehen n,
Farb[en]sehen n, Buntsehen n
chromatically corrected objective
farb[fehler]korrigiertes Objektiv n
chromaticity 1. Chromatizität f,
Normfarbwertanteil m, Farbverhältnis n,
Buntheit f; 2. Farbart f
~ **chart** s. ~ diagram
~ **coordinate** Chromatizitätswert m
~ **diagram** Farb[art]diagramm n,
Farb[art]tafel f, Farbkarte f
~ **discrimination** Farbartunterscheidung f
~ **value** Normfarbwert m, Normvalenz f
chromaticness Buntheit f, Chromatizität f
(s.a. colorfulness)
chromatics Chromatik f, Farb[en]lehre f
chromatopsia Chromatopsie f
chrome/to s. chromize/to
chrome alum Chromalaun n
(Gelatinehärter)
~ **alum fixer** Chromalaunfixierer m
chromic acid Chromsäure f
(Entwicklerbestandteil)
~ **potassium sulfate** s. chrome alum
chrominance Chrominanz f, Farbart f,
Farbdifferenzwert m *(s.a. unter chroma)*
~ **amplitude** Chrominanzamplitude f
~ **bandwidth** Chrominanzbandbreite f
~ **block** Chrominanzblock m
(Bildsequenzcodierung)
~ **carrier** Farbträger m
~ **carrier frequency** Farbträgerfrequenz f
~ **channel** Chrominanzkanal m,
Chromakanal m, Farbkanal m *(Video)*
~ **coefficient** Chrominanzkoeffizient m
~ **component** Chrominanzkomponente f
~ **detail** Farbdetail n, Farbeinzelheit f
~ **distortion** Chrominanzverzerrung f
~ **fidelity** Farbtreue f *(Video)*
~ **frame** Chrominanzbild n
~ **information** Chrominanzinformation f,
Farb[art]information f
~ **parameter** Chrominanzparameter m
~ **resolution** Chrominanzauflösung f
~ **signal** Chrominanzsignal n,
Chromasignal n, Videofarbsignal n,
Farb[art]signal n, Buntheitssignal n,
Gegenfarbsignal n
~ **signal-to-[random-]noise ratio**
Chrominanz-Störabstand m,
Farbrauschen n, farbiges Rauschen n
~ **subcarrier** Farbhilfsträger m
~ **video signal** Farbbildsignal n
chromium aluminum oxide laser
Rubinlaser m
~ **dioxide magnetic material**
Chromdioxidbandmaterial n
~ **salt** Chromsalz n, Chromat n
chromize/to verchromen *(z.B. Tiefdruckzylinder)*

chromogenic chromogen, farbbildend,
farbstoffaufbauend, pigmentbildend
~ **black-and-white film** chromogener
Schwarzweißfilm m
~ **development** chromogene Entwicklung
(Farbentwicklung) f,
Chromogenentwicklung f,
Fischer-Entwicklung f
~ **film** chromogener Film (Farbumkehrfilm)
m, Farbstoffaufbaufilm m
~ **photography** chromogene Fotografie f
~ **redevelopment** chromogene
Umentwicklung f
chromolithographic chromolithografisch
chromolithography Chromolithografie f
chromolytic chromolytisch,
farbstoffabbauend
~ **development** chromolytische
Entwicklung f
chromophore Chromophor n(m),
chromophore Gruppe f
chromoscope Chrom[at]oskop n
chromosome analysis
Chromosomenbildanalyse f
chronocinematography
Chronokinematografie f
chronophotographic chronofotografisch
chronophotography Chronofotografie f,
Reihenfotografie f
chunk Datenblock m
CI slot CI-Einschubschacht m
CI value CI-Wert m, Kontrastindex m
CID s. charge-injection device
~ **imager** CID-Bildaufnehmer m
CIE color-matching function
Normspektralwertfunktion f,
Normspektralwertkurve f
~ **color space** CIE-Farbraum m, CIE-Kegel
m [der sichtbaren Farben]
~ **source** CIE-Normlichtart f
~ **standard chromaticity diagram**
CIE-Normfarbtafel f, CIE-Farbdiagramm
n, CIE-Farbendreieck n
~ **standard illuminant** CIE-Normlichtart f
~ **[standard primary reference] system**
CIE-Normvalenzsystem n *(Kolorimetrie)*
~ **tristimulus value** Normfarbwert m,
Normvalenz f
CIELAB [color] space CIELAB-Farbmodell
n, CIELAB-Farbraum m
CIELUV color space CIELUV-Farbmodell n
CIF s. common intermediate format
ciliar muscle Ziliarmuskel m, Linsenmuskel
m *(des Auges)*
ciliary body Ziliarkörper m, Strahlenkörper
m *(des Auges)*
~ **process** Ziliarfortsatz m
Cinch connection Cinch-Verbindung f,
RCA-Verbindung f *(Video)*
cinch mark Laufschramme f, Laufstreifen m
(auf Film- oder Bandmaterial)
Cinch plug Cinch-Stecker m, RCA-Stecker
m

cine ... *s.a. unter* cinematographic[al], motion-picture
~ **camera** *s.* cinematographic camera
~ **camera lens** Filmkameraobjektiv *n*
~ **cement** Filmkleber *m*, Filmkitt *m*
~ **equipment** Filmausrüstung *f*
~ **film** Kinefilm *m*, kinematografischer Film *m*; Kinofilm *m*
~ **film printer** Filmkopiermaschine *f*
~ **film processor** Filmentwicklungsmaschine *f*
~ **film projector** Filmprojektor *m*, Filmvorführgerät *n*; Kinoprojektor *m*
~ **film recorder** Kinofilmbelichter *m*
~ **film size** Kinefilmformat *n*
~ **lens** Kino[projektions]objektiv *n*
~ **photographer** Filmfotograf *m*, Kinofotograf *m*
~ **projection equipment** Filmprojektionsanlage *f*
cineangiocardiography Kineangiokardiografie *f*
cineangiogram Kineangiogramm *n*
cineangiography Kineangiografie *f*
cineast Cineast *m*, Filmfachmann *m*
cinecoronary arteriography Kinekoronarografie *f*
cinedome Kugelkino *n*
cinefluorographic röntgenkinematografisch
cinefluorography Röntgenkinematografie *f*
cinema 1. Filmwesen *n*; 2. Kino *n*, Filmtheater *n (s.a. unter* motion picture, movie*)*; 3. *s.* cinematography
~ **digital sound** Kino-Digitalton *m*, digitaler Kinoton *m*
~ **editor** Filmeditor *m*, Filmcutter *m*, Cutter *m*, Schnittmeister *m*
~ **history** Filmgeschichte *f*
~ **industry** Filmindustrie *f*, Kinofilmindustrie *f*, Filmbranche *f*, Filmwirtschaft *f*
~ **laboratory** Filmkopierwerk *n*, Kopierwerk *n*, Kopieranstalt *f*, Filmbearbeitungsbetrieb *m*, Filmlabor *n*
~ **performance** Kinovorführung *f*
~ **production** Kinofilmproduktion *f*, Filmproduktion *f*
~ **projection** Kinoprojektion *f*
~ **screen** Filmleinwand *f*, Kinoleinwand *f*
~ **spectator** Kinozuschauer *m*
~ **technology** Kinotechnik *f*, Kinetechnik *f*
~ **tripod** Kinostativ *n*
~ **van** *s.* cinemobile
cinemacrography Makrokinematografie *f*
Cinemascope Cinemascope[verfahren] *n (ein Breitwandfilmverfahren)*
cinematheque Kinemathek *f*, Filmothek *f*; Filmarchiv *n*
cinematic kinematisch; filmisch
~ **illusion** Bewegungstäuschung *f*
~ **special effect** Filmtrick *m*
cinematize/to verfilmen
cinematograph/to filmen

cinematograph Kinoapparat *m*, Kinomaschine *f*, Vorführmaschine *f*, Kinematograf *m*; Laufbildprojektor *m*, Laufbildwerfer *m*; Filmprojektor *m*, Filmvorführgerät *n*
~ **lens** Kineobjektiv *n*, Kineoptik *f*, Filmobjektiv *n*, kinematografisches Objektiv *n*
cinematographer 1. Kameramann *m*, Filmkameramann *m*, Kinokameramann *m*, Operateur *m*; 2. *s.* motion-picture projectionist
cinematographic kinematografisch
~ **camera** kinematografische Kamera (Bildaufnahmekamera) *f*, Laufbildkamera *f*, Film[aufnahme]kamera *f*
~ **film** kinematografischer Film *m*, Kinefilm *m*; Kinofilm *m*
~ **image** kinematografisches Bild *n*
~ **imaging** kinematografische Abbildung *f*
cinematographical kinematografisch
cinematography Kinematografie *f*, Lichtspielwesen *n*
cinemicrographic camera mikrokinematografische Kamera *f*
cinemicrography Mikrokinematografie *f*
cinemobile Kinowagen *m*
cineoesophagography Kineösophagografie *f*
cinephile Cineast *m*, Filmfachmann *m*
cinephotography Bewegungsfotografie *f*
cinephotomicrography Mikrokinematografie *f*
cineplex Kinozentrum *n*, Multiplex[kino] *n*
cineradiogram Kineradiogramm *n*
cineradiographic kineradiografisch
cineradiography, cineroentgenography Kineradiografie *f*, Röntgenkinematografie *f*
cinescintigraphy Kineszintigrafie *f*
cinex strip Belichtungsreihe *f*, Belichtungsserie *f*, Belichtungsfächer *m*
circle Kreis *m (geometrisches Primitiv)*
~ **diagram (graph)** Kreisdiagramm *n*
~ **of confusion** Zerstreuungskreis *m*, Streukreis *m*, Unschärfekreis *m*
~ **of coverage** Bildkreis *m*
~ **of curvature** Krümmungskreis *m*
~ **of least confusion** Diffusionskreis *m*
~ **of vision** Gesichtskreis *m*, Sehkreis *m*, Betrachtungskreis *m*
circled take Kopierer *m (Kinofilmbearbeitung)*
circling Einkreisen *n (von Klappennummern im Negativbericht)*
circuit 1. Kreislauf *m*; 2. Stromkreis *m*; Schaltung *f*; 3. geschlossene Linie (Kurvenlinie)
~ **board** [gedruckte] Leiterplatte *f*, Elektronikplatine *f*, Platine *n*, gedruckter Schaltkreis *m*
~ **board inspection** Leiterplatteninspektion *f*

~ **board photolithography** Leiterplattenfotolithografie *f*
~ **board printing** Leiterplattendruck *m*
~ **image** Platinenfoto *n*
~ **noise** Schaltkreisrauschen *n*
~ **printer** Leiterplattendrucker *m*
~**-switched network** leitungsvermitteltes Netz *n (Videoübertragung)*
~ **switching** Leitungsvermittlung *f*
~**-type panoramic camera** Rundpanoramakamera *f*, Rotationskamera *f*, Rotorkamera *f*
circuits manufacturing Leiterplattenherstellung *f*
circular kreisförmig, [kreis]rund, zirkular, zirkulär
~ **aperture** Kreisblende *f*, kreisförmige Blende *f*
~ **artifact** 1. kreisförmiges Artefakt *n (Bildcodierung)*; 2. s. ringing artifact
~ **chart** Kreisdiagramm *n*, Tortendiagramm *n*
~ **color palette** Farbkreis *m (Kolorimetrie)*
~ **convolution** zirkulare (zyklische) Faltung *f*
~ **flash tube** Ringblitzleuchte *f*
~ **frequency** Kreisfrequenz *f*
~ **function** s. trigonometric function
~**-hole shadow mask** Lochmaske *f (Fernsehbildröhre)*
~ **Hough transform** Hough-Transformation *f* für Kreise
~ **motion** Kreisbewegung *f*
~ **polarization** Zirkularpolarisation *f*, zirkulare Polarisation *f*
~ **polarizer** s. circularly polarizing filter
~ **pupil** Kreispupille *f*, kreisförmige (ringförmige) Pupille *f*
~ **scale** Teilkreis *m*
~ **slide tray** Rundmagazin *n (Diaprojektor)*
~ **stop** Kreisblende *f*, kreisförmige Blende *f*
~ **symmetry** Kreissymmetrie *f*
~**-tray projector** Rundmagazin-Diaprojektor *m*, Rundmagazinprojektor *m*
circularity Kreisförmigkeit *f*, Rundheit *f (Formmerkmal)*
circularly polarized light zirkular polarisiertes Licht *n*
~ **polarizing filter** Zirkularpol[arisations]filter *n*, Zirkularpolarisator *m*
~ **symmetric[al]** kreissymmetrisch
circumflex accent Zirkumflex *m (ein Dehnungszeichen)*
circumscribing polygon Konturpolygon *n*, Umrisspolygon *n*, einfassendes (umschreibendes) Polygon *n*
civil evidence photography Beweismittelfotografie *f*, beweissichernde Fotografie *f*
cladded fiber ummantelte Faser *f (Faseroptik)*
cladding Schutzüberzug *m (Bildplatte)*

clamp-mount device Klemmstativ *n*
~**-on light (socket)** Klemmleuchte *f*
~ **table tripod** Tisch-Klemmstativ *n*
~ **tripod** Klemmstativ *n*
clamping Klemmung *f (Videosignalverarbeitung)*
~ **[circuit]** Klemmschaltung *f*
clandestine camera Geheimkamera *f*, Detektivkamera *f*
clapboard, clapper [board] Handklappe *f*, Synchronklappe *f*, Tonklappe *f*, Klappe *f (Filmarbeit)*
clapper/loader Materialassistent *m*, Zweiter Kameraassistent *m*, Loader *m (Filmteam)*
clapping slate Szenenklappe *f*
clapstick[s] s. clapboard
clarifier Klärmittel *n*
class/to s. classify/to
class Klasse *f*
~ **boundary** Klassengrenze *f*
~ **center** Klassenmitte *f*
~ **hierarchy** Klassenhierarchie *f*
~ **mean** Klassenmittelwert *m*
~ **membership** Klassenzugehörigkeit *f*
~ **of codes** Codeklasse *f*
~ **of filters** Filterklasse *f*
~ **of images** Bildklasse *f*
~ **of objects** Objektklasse *f*
~ **of pixels** Pixelklasse *f*
~ **separability** Klassentrennbarkeit *f*
~ **separation** Klassentrennung *f*
~**-specific linear projection** klassenspezifische Linearprojektion *f*
~ **structure** Klassenstruktur *f*
~ **subtree** Klassenunterbaum *m*
classical optics klassische Optik *f*
~ **Rayleigh scattering** klassische Rayleigh-Streuung *f*
~ **scattering** klassische Streuung *f*
classifiable klassifizierbar *(z.B. Muster)*
classification Klassifikation *f*, Klassifizierung *f*
~ **accuracy** Klassifikationsgenauigkeit *f*
~ **algorithm** Klassifikationsalgorithmus *m*, Klassifikator *m*
~ **capability** Klassifikationsvermögen *n*
~ **error** Klassifikationsfehler *m*
~ **method** Klassifizierungsverfahren *n*
~ **performance** Klassifikationsleistung *f*
~ **phase** Klassifikationsphase *f (Bildvorverarbeitung)*
~ **scheme** Klassifikationsschema *n*
~ **space** Klassifikationsraum *m*
~ **speed** Klassifizierungsgeschwindigkeit *f*
~ **success** Klassifikationserfolg *m*
~ **task** Klassifikationsaufgabe *f*
~ **technique** Klassifikationstechnik *f*; Klassifikationsverfahren *n*
~ **tree** s. decision tree
classified vector quantization klassifizierte Vektorquantisierung *f*
classifier Klassifikator *m*, Klassifikationsalgorithmus *m*

classifier

~-independent feature analysis klassifikatorunabhängige Merkmalsanalyse f
classify/to klassifizieren
claw Greifer m; Transportgreifer m, Zuggreifer m
~-type mechanism Greifergetriebe n, Greiferwerk n
clay animation Knettrick m *(Trickfilmproduktion)*
~-coated barytbeschichtet *(Fotopapier)*
Clayden effect Clayden-Effekt m, Clayden-Entwicklungseffekt m
claymation s. clay animation
clean image unverrauschtes Bild n
~ room Reinraum m
cleaning brush Reinigungsbürste f *(z.B. in Kopiergeräten)*
~ cassette Reinigungskassette f
clear aperture nutzbare Apertur f, förderliche Blende f
~ area Weißzone f *(Seitenlayout)*
~ base ungefärbter Schichtträger (Filmschichtträger) m
~-base film Klarsichtfilm m
~ film Blankfilm m
~ filter Kompensatorplatte f
~ glass Klarglas n
~ lamp Klarglas[glüh]birne f, Klarglaslampe f
~ leader Allonge f, Schutzfilm m *(Kinefilm)*
~ lightbulb s. lamp
~ vision deutliches Sehen n
clearing agent Klärmittel n
~ bath Klärbad n *(Umkehrverarbeitung)*
~ time Klärzeit f
click/to [an]klicken
click stop Rastpunkt m; Rast[sperr]e f, Rastung f; Rastblende f
clickable anklickbar
~ map anklickbare Grafik f *(World Wide Web)*
clicker Fernbedienung f
clinical endoscopy medizinische Endoskopie f
~ imaging medizinische (diagnostische) Bildgebung f, Medizinbildgebung f
~ photography klinische Fotografie f
~ scanner diagnostischer Scanner m
~ SPECT system SPECT-Gerät n, Einzelphotonen-Emissionstomograf m, Emissionscomputertomograf m
clinometer Klinometer n
clip/to abschneiden; zuschneiden; beschneiden
clip Clip m, Filmclip m, Filmausschnitt m
~ art Cliparts pl *(Symbolgrafiken)*
~ leg lock Stativbeinarretierung f, Stativbein-Schnellarretierung f
~ rectangle Clipping-Rechteck n *(Computergrafik)*
clipboard 1. Zwischenablage f *(Datenverarbeitung);* 2. Klemmbrett n

clipped p[ix]el array beschnittenes Pixelfeld n
clipping Abschneiden n; Zuschneiden n, Clipping n *(Computergrafik);* Beschneiden n, Beschneidung f, Beschnitt m
~ algorithm Clipping-Algorithmus m
~ indicator Clipping-Anzeiger m
~ mode Clipping-Modus m
~ operation Clipping-Operation f
clique Clique f *(z.B. als Struktur benachbarter Bildpunkte)*
clock/to takten
clock Zeittakt m, Takt m; Taktquelle f
~ accuracy Taktgenauigkeit f
~ control Taktsteuerung f
~ cycle Taktzyklus m, Taktperiode f
~ drive Uhrwerksnachführung f *(Teleskop)*
~-driven telescope Teleskop n mit Uhrwerksnachführung
~ frequency Takt[geber]frequenz f, Taktrate f
~ generator Taktgeber m, Takt[frequenz]generator m, Impulsgenerator m
~ jitter Taktjitter m
~ phase deviation Taktabweichung f
~ pulse generator s. ~ generator
~ rate s. ~ frequency
~ recovery Taktrückgewinnung f
~ skew Taktabweichung f
~ speed s. ~ frequency
clocked sampling getaktete Abtastung f
clocking Taktung f
~ signal Taktsignal n
clockwise sense Uhrzeigersinn m
cloning tool Klonwerkzeug n, Duplizierstempel m *(digitale Bildbearbeitung)*
close/to schließen
close box Schließfeld n
~ distance Nahentfernung f
~-down Geräteabschaltung f
~ focus Nahfokus m
~ focusing Naheinstellung f
~ focusing ability Nahfokussierungsfähigkeit f
~-focusing lens Makroobjektiv n
~-range attachment s. close-up attachment
~-range photogrammetry Nahbereichsfotogrammetrie f, Nahbildmessung f
~ shot s. close-up shot
~-up Nahaufnahme f, Nahe f; Großaufnahme f
~-up accessories Nah[aufnahme]zubehör n
~-up adjustment Naheinstellung f
~-up attachment Nahvorsatz m, Nah[vorsatz]linse f, Makro[vorsatz]linse f
~-up bellows Balgennaheinstellgerät n
~-up camera Nahaufnahmekamera f, Nah[aufnahme]gerät n

~-up equipment Nah[aufnahme]zubehör *n*
~-up focusing at infinity
  Nah-Unendlich-Einstellung *f*
~-up lens *s.* ~ attachment
~-up photograph Nahaufnahme *f*, Nahe *f*;
  Großaufnahme *f*
~-up photographer Nahfotograf *m*
~-up photography
  Nah[bereichs]fotografie *f*
~-up portrait Nahporträt *n*
~-up range Nahbereich *m*
~-up shot Nahaufnahme *f*, Nahe *f*;
  Großaufnahme *f*
~-up stereophotography
  Stereo-Nahfotografie *f*
~-up tube Balgennaheinstellgerät *n*
closed circuit geschlossener Stromkreis *m*
  (z.B. einer Fotodiode)
~-circuit television 1. Videoüberwachung *f*
  im Nahbereich; 2. *s.* cable television
~ contour geschlossene Kontur *f*
~ figure geschlossene Figur *f*
  (Computergrafik)
~ point set *s.* ~ set
~ polygon geschlossenes Polygon *n*
~ set abgeschlossene Menge *f*
~ shape geschlossene Form *f*
  (Objektbeschreibung)
~ subtitles Videotext-Untertitel *mpl*
~ surface geschlossene Fläche *f*
~ user group geschlossene
  Benutzergruppe *f*
closest focusing distance kürzeste
  Einstellentfernung *f*, Naheinstellgrenze *f*,
  Nah[fokussier]grenze *f*
closing Schließen *n*, Closing *n*,
  Closing-Operation *f*
  (Binärbildverarbeitung)
~ credits Titelabspann *m*, Abspann *m*,
  Nachspann *m*, End[e]titel *m*, Schlusstitel
  m (Film)
closure Abschließung *f*
  (Binärbildverarbeitung)
cloth tape Lassoband *n*, Textilklebeband *n*
cloud chamber Nebelkammer *f*
~ clutter (echo) Wolkenecho *n (Radar)*
~ radar Wolkenradar *n*
clumping *s.* clustering
cluster 1. Cluster *m*, Häufung *f*; 2.
  Zuordnungseinheit *f*
  (Datenspeicherung)
~ analysis Clusteranalyse *f*
~ analysis method
  Clusteranalyseverfahren *n*
~ center Clusterzentrum *n*
~ geometry Clustergeometrie *f*
clustering Clustern *n*, Clusterung *f*
~ algorithm Cluster[analyse]algorithmus
  m
CLUT *s.* color lookup table
clutter Clutter *m*, Fremdecho *n*, Störecho *n*
  (Radar)
~ equation Störechogleichung *f*
~ map Störechokarte *f*

~ spectrum Clutterspektrum *n*
~ suppression Clutterunterdrückung *f*
CMOS *s.* complementary metal oxide
  semiconductor
~ image sensor, ~ imager
  CMOS-Bildsensor *m*, CMOS-Sensor *m*
~ technology CMOS-Technologie *f*
CMY color space CMY-Farbmodell *n*,
  CMY-Farbraum *m*
CMYK color space, ~ model
  CMYK-Farbmodell *n*, CMYK-Farbraum
  m, Prozessfarbmodell *n*
co-occurence matrix
  Grauwertübergangsmatrix *f*,
  Paarhäufigkeitsmatrix *f*,
  Grauwertabhängigkeitsmatrix *f*
coarse adjustment knob, ~ focus control
  Grobtrieb *m*, Schnelltrieb *m (Mikroskop)*
~ focusing Grobfokussierung *f*
~ focusing mechanism Grobfokussierung *f*
~ grain grobes Korn *n*
~-grain[ed] film grobkörniger Film *m*
~ quantization grobe Quantisierung *f*
~ resolution grobe Auflösung *f*
~ saccade Blick[folge]bewegung *f*
~ scanning grobe Abtastung *f*
~ screen Grobraster *m(n)*, grober Raster *m*
  (Rasterdruck)
coat/to beschichten; vergüten
coated lens vergütete Linse *f*
~ paper gestrichenes Papier *n*
~ silver Schichtsilber *n*
coating Beschichtung *f*; Vergütung *f*
~ apparatus Begießanlage *f*
  (Filmherstellung)
~ head Gießkopf *m*
~ machine Gießmaschine *f*
~ thickness Vergütungsschichtdicke *f*,
  Schichtdicke *f*
coax[ial] koaxial
coaxial cable Koax[ial]kabel *n*
~ illumination koaxiale Beleuchtung *f*
cobalt glass Cobaltglas *n*
cocking device Spannvorrichtung *f (z.B.
  eines mechanischen Verschlusses)*
codability Codierbarkeit *f*
codable codierbar
code/to codieren
code Code *m*
~ alphabet Codealphabet *n*
~ bit Codebit *n*
~ block Codeblock *m*
~ compatibility Codekompatibilität *f*
~ division multiple access Vielfachzugriff
  m im Codemultiplex
~ efficiency Codier[ungs]effizienz *f*
~ element Codeelement *n*
~ extension Codeerweiterung *f*
~ extension character Codesteuerzeichen
  n
~ length Codelänge *f*
~ number Codenummer *f*
~ rate Coderate *f*
~ sequence Codefolge *f*

code 58

~ **set** Codesatz *m*
~ **signal** Codesignal *n*
~ **symbol** Codesymbol *n*
~ **table** Codetabelle *f*
~ **value** Codewert *m*
~ **vector** Codevektor *m*
~ **word** Codewort *n (Bitfolge)*
~ **word length** Codewortlänge *f*
codebook Codebuch *n*
codec Codierungs-Decodierungspaar *n*, [Video-]Codec *m(n)*
~ **filter** Codec-Filter *n*
coded character set codierter Zeichensatz *m*
~ **description** codierte Beschreibung *f*
~ **excitation** codierte Anregung *f (Sonografie)*
~ **representation** codierte Darstellung *f*
coder Codierer *m*, Coder *m*
~**-decoder** *s.* codec
coding Codierung *f (s.a. unter encoding, compression)*
~ **algorithm** Codier[ungs]algorithmus *m*
~ **approach** Codierungsansatz *m*
~ **artifact** Codier[ungs]artefakt *n*
~ **dictionary** Codebuch *n*
~ **efficiency** Codier[ungs]effizienz *f*
~ **error** Codier[ungs]fehler *m*
~ **gain** Codiergewinn *m*; Kompressionsfaktor *m*
~ **hierarchy** Codierhierarchie *f*
~ **layer** Codierungsschicht *f (z.B. eines neuronalen Netzes)*
~ **method** Codierungsmethode *f*
~ **mode** Codierungsmodus *m*
~**-mode decision** Codierungsentscheidung *f*
~ **order** Codier[ungsreihen]folge *f*
~ **parameter** Codierungsparameter *m*
~ **performance** Codierungsleistung *f*
~ **rate** *s.* bit transfer rate
~ **redundancy** Codierungsredundanz *f*
~ **rule** Codierungsregel *f*
~ **scheme** Codier[ungs]schema *n*
~ **sequence** Codefolge *f*, Codierungssequenz *f*
~ **standard** Codierstandard *m*
~ **step** Codierungsschritt *m*
~ **strategy** Codierungsstrategie *f*
~ **style** Codierungsstil *m*
~ **syntax** Codierungssyntax *f*
~ **system** Codierungssystem *n*
~ **table** Codierungstabelle *f*
~ **technique** Codier[ungs]technik *f*; Codierverfahren *n*
~ **theorem** Codierungstheorem *n*
~ **theory** Codierungstheorie *f*
~ **tool** Codierwerkzeug *n*
~ **type** Codierungsart *f*
~ **unit** Codier[ungs]einheit *f (z.B. einer Videosequenz)*
coefficient of thermal expansion Wärmeausdehnungskoeffizient *m (z.B. von optischem Glas)*

~ **of variation** Variationskoeffizient *f*
~ **quantization** Koeffizientenquantisierung *f*
coefficients matrix Koeffizientenmatrix *f*
coelostat *s.* heliostat
coercive force, coercivity Koerzitivfeldstärke *f*, Koerzitivkraft *f*
cognition Kognition *f*
cognitive kognitiv
~ **science** Kognitionswissenschaft *f*
coherence Kohärenz *f*
~ **bandwidth** Kohärenzbandbreite *f*
~ **function** Kohärenzfunktion *f*
~ **laser radar** Kohärenzradar *n*
~ **length** Kohärenzlänge *f (z.B. einer Lichtquelle)*
~ **matrix** Kohärenzmatrix *f (Teilpolarisation)*
~ **measure** Kohärenzmaß *n*
~ **time** Kohärenzzeit *f*
coherency *s.* coherence
coherent kohärent
~ **bundle** kohärentes Bündel *n (Faseroptik)*
~ **demodulation** kohärente Demodulation *f*
~**-fiber bundle** kohärentes Faserbündel *n*
~ **filtering** kohärente Filterung *f*
~ **illumination** kohärente Beleuchtung *f*
~ **image formation** kohärente Bildentstehung *f*
~ **imaging system** kohärentes Abbildungssystem *n*
~ **interference** kohärente Interferenz *f*
~ **length** *s.* coherence length
~ **light** kohärentes Licht *n*
~**-light imaging** kohärente Abbildung *f*
~ **light source** kohärente Lichtquelle *f*
~ **local oscillator** Kohärenzoszillator *m (Radar)*
~ **microscope** kohärentes Mikroskop *n*
~ **motion** zusammenhängende Bewegung *f*
~ **noise** kohärentes Rauschen *n*
~ **optical system** kohärentes [optisches] System *n*
~ **optics** kohärente Optik *f*
~ **point-spread function** kohärente Punktbildfunktion *f*
~ **radiation** kohärente (zusammenhängende) Strahlung *f*
~ **scattering** kohärente (lineare) Streuung *f*, Rayleigh-Streuung *f*, Luftstreuung *f*, elastische Lichtstreuung *f*
~ **signal** kohärentes Signal *n*
~ **transfer function** kohärente Übertragungsfunktion *f*
~ **wave** kohärente Welle *f*
cohesion Kohäsion *f*
cohesive force Kohäsionskraft *f*
coil current Spulenstrom *m (Elektronenlinse)*
~ **filament lamp** Spiralwendellampe *f*
coiled-coiled filament Doppelwendel *f*
~ **cord** Spiralkabel *n*
~ **filament** Glühwendel *f*

~ **sync[hronized] cord** Spiralsynchronkabel *n*
coin-operated copier Münzkopierer *m*
~ **photography** Münzfotografie *f*
coincidence camera Koinzidenz-Gammakamera *f*
~**[-type] rangefinder** Mischbildentfernungsmesser *m*, Koinzidenzentfernungsmesser *m*, Telemeter *n*
coincident koinzident
cold boot Kaltstart *m (Computer)*
~ **camera** Tiefkühlkamera *f (Astrofotografie)*
~**-cathode fluorescent display** Kaltkatodenfluoreszenzanzeige *f*
~**-cathode fluorescent light** Kaltkatodenfluoreszenz *f*, Fluoreszenz *f* bei Kaltkatode
~**-cathode fluorescent tube** Kaltlichtröhre *f*
~**-cathode lamp** Kaltkatodenlampe *f*
~ **embossing** Kaltprägung *f (Stereotypie)*
~ **laminating film** Kaltkaschierfolie *f*, Filmfolie *f*, Klebefolie *f*
~ **light** Kaltlicht *n*, kaltes Licht *n*
~ **light illumination** Kaltlichtbeleuchtung *f*
~**-light illuminator** Kaltlichtleuchte *f*
~**-light lamp** Kaltlichtlampe *f*
~ **light reflector**, ~ **mirror** Kaltlichtspiegel *m*, dichroitischer (farbzerlegender) Spiegel *m*
~**-light source** Kaltlichtquelle *f*
~ **mirror lamp** Kaltspiegellampe *f*
~**-tone paper** Kalttonpapier *n*
~**-type composition** Kaltsatz *m (Typografie)*
colinear *s.* collinear
collage/to collagieren
collage Collage *f*, Klebebild *n*
collagen Kollagen *n (Skleroprotein)*
collapsible stand Klappstativ *n*
collapsing loss Zusammenlegungsverlust *m (Radar)*
collate/to zusammentragen *(Falzbögen)*
collating table Stapeltisch *m (Druckweiterverarbeitung)*
collectible [camera] Sammlerkamera *f*
collecting mirror Sammelspiegel *m*, Konkavspiegel *m*, Hohlspiegel *m*
~ **optics** sammelndes System *n*, [optisches] Positivsystem *n*
collection electrode Sammelelektrode *f (Fotodetektor)*
~ **lens** Sammellinse *f*, Konvexlinse *f*, Positivlinse *f*
collector [lens] 1. Kollektor *m*; 2. *s.* collection lens
collimate/to kollimieren
collimated beam, ~ **bundle [of rays]** kollimierter Strahl *m*, kollimiertes (paralleles) Bündel *n*, Parallel[licht]bündel *n*
~ **color scale** kollimierte Farbskala *f*
~ **light** kollimiertes Licht *n*, Parallellicht *n*
~ **light source** kollimierte Lichtquelle *f*
~ **lighting** kollimierte Beleuchtung *f*
~ **radiation** kollimierte Strahlung *f*
collimating cylinder Kollimatorzylinder *m*
~ **lens** Kollimatorlinse *f*
~ **mark** Kollimatormarke *f*
~ **mirror** Kollimatorspiegel *m*
~ **module** Kollimiermodul *n*
~ **optics** Kollimationsoptik *f*
collimation Kollimation *f*
~ **error** Kollimationsfehler *m*
collimator Kollimator *m*, Soller-Blende *f*, Soller-Spalt *m (optisches System)*
~ **angle** Kollimatorwinkel *m*
~ **constant** Kollimatorkonstante *f*
~ **lens** Kollimatorlinse *f*
~ **objective** Kollimatorobjektiv *n*
~ **resolution** Kollimatorauflösung *f*
~ **slit** Kollimatorschlitz *m*
collinear kollinear
collinearity Kollinearität *f*
collineation projektive Transformation *f*
collision analysis Kollisionsanalyse *f*
~ **avoidance radar** Abstandswarnradar *n*
~ **detection technique** Kollisionserkennungstechnik *f*
collodion Kollodium *n*
~ **cotton** Kollodiumwolle *f*
~ **dry plate** trockene Kollodiumplatte *f*
~ **emulsion** Kollodiumemulsion *f*
~ **glass plate** Kollodiumplatte *f*
~ **photography** Kollodiumfotografie *f*
~ **plate** Kollodiumplatte *f*
~ **positive** Ambrotypie *f*, Melanotypie *f*
~ **print** Kollodiumabzug *m*
~ **process** Kollodiumverfahren *n*
~ **wet plate** nasse Kollodiumplatte *f*
collodium *s.* collodion
colloid Kolloid *n*
colloidal dispersion kolloide Dispersion *f*
~ **silver** kolloid[al]es Silber *n*
~ **solution** kolloidale Lösung *f*
~ **suspension** kolloidale Suspension *f*
collotype [process] Collotypeverfahren *n (ein Lichtdruckverfahren)*
colonoscope Koloskop *n*, Dickdarmspiegel *m*
colonoscopy Koloskopie *f*, Dickdarmspiegelung *f*
color/to färben
color Farbe *f (s.a. unter* colored, chromatic*)*
~ **aberration** Farb[abbildungs]fehler *m*, chromatische Aberration *f*, chromatischer Fehler *m*
~ **absorption** Farbabsorption *f*
~ **accuracy** Farbgenauigkeit *f*, Farbrichtigkeit *f*
~ **acquisition** Farberfassung *f*
~ **adaptation** *s.* chromatic adaptation
~ **adjustment** *s.* ~ matching
~ **aerial photograph** Luftbild-Farbaufnahme *f*
~ **aerial photography** Luftbild-Farbfotografie *f*

color 60

~ **analysis** Farbanalyse f
~ **analyzer** Farbanalysator m; Lichtbestimmungsgerät n
~ **appearance** Farberscheinung f, Farbeindruck m
~ **artifact** Farbfehler m (s.a. ~ defect)
~ **assignment** Farbzuordnung f
~ **asthenopia** Farbsehschwäche f (s.a. ~ weakness)
~ **atlas** Farbatlas m, Farbmusterbuch n, Farbmustersammlung f
~ **attribute** Farbmerkmal n
~ **balance** Farbbalance f, Farbgleichgewicht n
~ **balance filter** s. color-compensating filter
~ **balance memory** Farbbalancespeicher m
~ **balance shift** Farbbalanceverschiebung f
~ **band** Farbband n, Druckerfarbband n
~ **bandwidth** Farbsignalbandbreite f
~ **bar** 1. Farbbalken m; 2. Druckkontrolleiste f, Druckkontrollstreifen m, Farbmessstreifen m
~ **bar amplitude** Farbbalkenamplitude f
~ **bar generator** Farbbalkengenerator m
~ **bar test pattern** Farbbalken[test]bild n (s.a. ~ bar test signal)
~ **bar test signal**, ~ **bar waveform** Normfarbbalkenfolge f, Normfarbbalkenvorlage f; Farbbalken[prüf]signal n; Zeilenoszillogramm n
~ **bias** Farbstich m
~ **bit** Farbbit n
~ **bleaching process** Farbsilberbleich[verfahr]en n, Silberfarbbleichverfahren n, Farb[aus]bleichverfahren n
~ **blend** Farbmischung f
~ **blending** Farb[er]mischung f, Farberzeugung f
~ **-blind** 1. farbenblind; 2. s. blue-sensitive
~ **-blind person** Farbenblinder m
~ **blindness** [angeborene] Farbenblindheit f
~ **boundary** Farbrand m
~ **box** Farbpalette f (Grafikprogramm)
~ **brilliance** Farbbrillanz f
~ **broadcast** Farb[fernseh]sendung f
~ **broadcast TV** Farbfernsehrundfunk m
~ **broadcasting** Farbfernsehübertragung f
~ **burst [signal]** Farb[träger]burst m, Farbsynchronimpuls m, Farbsynchron[isier]signal n, Farbbündelung f, Burst m (Video)
~ **calibration** Farbkalibrierung f; Bildschirmkalibrierung f, Monitorkalibrierung f
~ **camera** Farbfotoapparat m, Farbkamera f, Naturfarbenkamera f
~ **capability** Farbfähigkeit f, Farbtüchtigkeit f
~ **-capable** farbfähig

~ **cartridge** Farbpatrone f
~ **cast** Farbstich m
~ **cathode-ray tube** [Mehrstrahl-]Farbbildröhre f, Farbbild-Elektronenstrahlröhre f
~ **CCD** CCD-Farbsensor m
~ **CCD camera** CCD-Farbkamera f, Farb-CCD-Kamera f
~ **change** Farbveränderung f, Farbwechsel m, Farbwandlung f
~ **channel** Farbkanal m (Fernsehen)
~ **chart** Farb[en]karte f (s.a. ~ control chart)
~ **check** Farbtest m
~ **choice** Farbwahl f
~ **chromatic adaptation** Farbadaptation f, Farbstimmung f
~ **cinematography** Farbkinematografie f
~ **circle** Farb[en]kreis m
~ **classification** Farbklassifikation f, Farbklassifizierung f
~ **classifier** Farbklassifikator m
~ **code** Farbcode m
~ **-code/to** farbcodieren
~ **-coded image** farbcodiertes Bild n
~ **-coded object** farbcodiertes Objekt n
~ **-coded signal** farbcodiertes Signal n
~ **coder** Farbcodierer m
~ **coding** Farbcodierung f
~ **coding system (table)** Farbcodiersystem n (Fernsehen)
~ **coherence vector** Farbkohärenzvektor m
~ **combination** Farbkombination f, Farbzusammenstellung f
~ **comparison** Farbvergleich m
~ **-compensating filter** Farbausgleichsfilter n, Farbkompensationsfilter n (s.a. color correction filter)
~ **-compensating filtration** Farbkorrekturfilterung f
~ **compensation** Farbausgleich m, Farbkompensation f
~ **complement** Farbkomplement n
~ **component** Farbanteil m, Farbkomponente f
~ **component signal** Farbkomponentensignal n
~ **composite** Farbkomposite f (analoge Bildverarbeitung)
~ **composition** Farbkomposition f, Farbzusammensetzung f (z.B. des Lichts)
~ **cone** Farb[en]kegel m
~ **conformance (conformity)** Farbübereinstimmung f
~ **consistency** Farbbeständigkeit f, Farbstabilität f
~ **-consistent** farbbeständig
~ **constancy** Farbkonstanz f, Farbinvarianz f
~ **contamination** Farbverunreinigung f
~ **content** Farbgehalt m (z.B. eines Suchbildes)
~ **continuity** Farbkontinuität f
~ **contrast** Farbkontrast m

~ **contrast filter** Farbkontrastfilter *n* *(Lichtmikroskopie)*
~ **contrast illusion** Farbkontrasttäuschung *f*
~ **control** Farbsteuerung *f*, Farbregelung *f*
~ **control bar** Druckkontrolleiste *f*, Druckkontrollstreifen *m*, Farbmessstreifen *m*
~ **control chart** Farb[kontroll]tafel *f*, Farbmesstafel *f*
~ **conversion** Farbkonversion *f*
~ **conversion filter** *s.* ~ correction filter
~ **converter** Farbkonverter *m* *(Videoprozessor)*
~ **coordinate system** Farbkoordinatensystem *n*
~ **copier** Farbkopierer *m*
~ **copy** 1. Farbkopie *f*; 2. Farbvorlage *f* *(Reprografie)*
~ **copying** Farbkopieren *n*
~-**correct** farbrichtig, farbgenau, farbkorrekt
~-**correct/to** farbkorrigieren, achromatisieren
~-**corrected** farb[fehler]korrigiert, achromatisch *(Objektiv)*
~-**corrected image** farbrichtiges (farbgetreues) Bild *n*
~-**corrected lens** farbkorrigierte (achromatische) Linse *f*; farb[fehler]korrigiertes Objektiv *n*
~ **correcting machine** Farbkorrekturmaschine *f*
~ **correction** Farb[gang]korrektur *f*
~ **correction filter** Farbkorrekturfilter *n*, Lichtausgleichsfilter *n*, CC-Filter *n*
~ **correction filtration** Farbkorrekturfilterung *f*
~-**correction layer** Farbkorrekturschicht *f*
~ **correction table** Farbkorrekturtabelle *f*
~ **correctness** Farbrichtigkeit *f*
~ **corrector** 1. Farbkorrekturgerät *n*; 2. Farbkorrekturfilter *n*, CC-Filter *n*
~ **coupler** Farb[stoff]kuppler *m*, Kuppler *m*
~ **coupling** Farbaufbau *m*
~-**coupling developer** Farbentwickler *m*
~-**coupling development** chromogene Entwicklung (Farbentwicklung) *f*, Chromogenentwicklung *f*, Fischer-Entwicklung *f*
~ **crossover** Farbübersprechen *n*, Farbüberstrahlung *f*, Farbüberlagerung *f*, Chrominanz-Übersprechen *n*, Cross-Color-Effekt *m*
~ **CRT monitor** Farb-Röhrenmonitor *m*
~ **cube** Farb[en]würfel *m*, RGB-Würfel *m*
~ **curve** Farb[korrektur]kurve *f*
~ **cycle** Farb[en]kreis *m*
~ **cycling** Farbrotation *f (Grafikprogramm)*
~ **darkroom** Farb[foto]labor *n*
~ **decoder** *s.* ~ demodulator
~ **decoding** Farbdecodierung *f*

~ **defect** Farb[abbildungs]fehler *m*, chromatischer Fehler *m*, chromatische Aberration *f*
~-**deficient** farbfehlsichtig
~ **definition** Farbdefinition *f (Rasterbild)*
~ **demodulator** Farbdemodulator *m*, Farbdecod[ier]er *m*
~ **densitometer** Farbdensitometer *n*
~ **densitometry** Farbdensitometrie *f*
~ **density** Farbdichte *f*
~ **density measurement** Farbdichtemessung *f*
~ **depth** Farbtiefe *f*
~ **description** Farbbeschreibung *f*, Farbspezifikation *f*
~ **descriptor** Farbdeskriptor *m*
~ **design** Farbgestaltung *f*
~ **designer** Farbgestalter *m*
~ **detail** Farbdetail *n*, Farbeinzelheit *f*
~ **developer additive** Farbentwicklerzusatz *m*
~ **developer bath** Farbentwicklerbad *n*
~ **developer starter** Farbentwickler-Starter *m*
~-**developing agent** Farbentwicklersubstanz *f*
~-**developing solution** Farbentwicklerbad *n*
~ **development** Farbentwicklung *f*
~ **deviation** Farbabweichung *f*; Farbverfälschung *f*
~ **device** Farbgerät *n*
~ **dialogue box** Farbauswahlfeld *n*
~ **difference** Farbunterschied *m*, Farbdifferenz *f*
~ **difference channel** Farbdifferenzkanal *m*
~ **difference component** *s.* ~ difference signal
~ **difference measure** Farbabstandsmaß *n*
~ **difference measurement** Farbdifferenzmessung *f*
~ **difference signal** Farbdifferenzsignal *n*, Farbunterschiedssignal *n (Video)*
~ **differentiation** Farbdifferenzierung *f*
~ **digital [electronic] image** Digitalfarbbild *n*
~ **discrimination** Farbunterscheidung *f*
~ **disk** Farb[en]kreis *m*
~ **dispersion** Farbzerlegung *f*, Farb[enzer]streuung *f*, chromatische Dispersion *f*
~ **display [terminal]** Farbdisplay *n*, Computerfarbbildschirm *m*, Farbbildschirm *m*
~ **distance** 1. Farbabstand *m*; 2. *s.* ~ difference
~ **distortion** Farbverzerrung *f (s.a.* ~ aberration*)*
~ **distribution** Farbverteilung *f*
~ **dithering** Farb-Dithering *n*
~ **document copier** Farb-Dokumentenkopierer *m*
~ **Doppler echocardiography** Farb-Doppler-Echokardiografie *f*

color 62

~ **Doppler sonography (ultrasound)** Farb-Doppler-Sonografie f
~ **dot** Farbpunkt m
~ **duplicate negative** Internegativ n, Zwischennegativ n
~ **edge** Farbkante f
~ **edge detection** Farbkantenerkennung f, Farbkantendetektion f
~ **edge detector** Farbkantendetektor m
~ **edge extraction** Farbkantenextraktion f
~ **edging** Farbsaumbildung f
~ **effect** Farbwirkung f, Farbeffekt m
~ **effect filter** Farbeffektfilter n
~ **eight-bit image** Acht-Bit-Farbbild n
~ **electroluminescence** Farbelektrolumineszenz f
~ **electrophotographic** farbxerografisch
~ **electrophotography** Farbxerografie f
~ **electrostatic plotter** elektrostatischer Farbplotter m
~ **emulsion** Farbemulsion f
~ **encoding system** Farbcodiersystem n
~**-enhanced roentgenogram** Röntgenfarbbild n
~ **enlarger** Farbvergrößerer m, Farbvergrößerungsgerät n
~ **enlarging** Farbvergrößern n, Farbvergrößerung f
~ **enlarging paper** Farbvergrößerungspapier n
~ **enlarging system** Farbvergrößerungssystem n
~ **equation** Farbgleichung f
~ **error** s. ~ defect
~ **etching** Farbätzung f
~ **evaluation lamp** Farbprüfleuchte f
~ **exposure system** Farbbelichtungssystem n
~ **facsimile transmission** Farbbildübertragung f
~ **fax** Farbfax n
~ **feature** Farbmerkmal n
~ **fidelity** Farbtreue f
~ **film** Farb[aufnahme]film m, Colorfilm m
~ **film bleach** Farbfilmbleicher m
~ **film emulsion** Farbfilmemulsion f
~**-film manufacturer** Farbfilmhersteller m
~**-film processing** Farbfilmverarbeitung f, Farbfilmentwicklung f
~ **film recorder** Farbfilmrecorder m
~ **film speed** Farbfilmempfindlichkeit f
~ **film stock** Farbfilmmaterial n
~**-film structure** Farbfilmaufbau m
~ **film technology** Farbfilmtechnik f
~ **filter** Farbfilter n, Colorfilter n
~ **filter disk** Farbfilterscheibe f
~ **filter mosaic** Farbfiltermosaik n (Flüssigkristallanzeige)
~ **filter wheel** Farbfilterrad n
~ **filtering (filtration)** Farbfilterung f
~ **flatbed scanner** Farb-Flachbettscanner m
~ **flicker** Farbflimmern n

~ **fluctuation** Farbvariation f, Farbschwankung f
~ **formation** Farbbildung f
~ **former** Farbbildner m (s.a. ~ coupler)
~**-forming agent** Farbbildner m (Colorfotografie)
~**-forming developer** Farbentwickler m
~**-forming development** s. color-coupling development
~ **fringe** Farbsaum m (Konvergenzfehler)
~ **fringing** Farbsaumbildung f
~ **gamut** Farb[raum]umfang m, Farbbereich m, Farbpalette f (z.B. eines Druckers)
~ **geometry** Farbgeometrie f
~ **glossy photo** Hochglanz-Farbfoto n
~ **gradation** Farbabstufung f; Farbübergang m
~**-grade** s. color-correct
~ **grader** s. ~ timer
~ **gradient** Farbgradient m
~ **grading** s. ~ timing
~ **grain** Farbkorn n
~ **graphics** Farbgrafik f
~ **graphics adapter** Farbgrafikkarte f, Farbgrafikadapter m, CGA-Grafikkarte f
~ **graphics array** Farbgrafikfeld n
~ **graphics library** Farbgrafik-Bibliothek f
~ **grating** Farbgitter n
~ **guide** Druckkontrolleiste f, Druckkontrollstreifen m, Farbmessstreifen m
~ **harmony** Farbharmonie f
~ **head** Farb[misch]kopf m (Vergrößerungsgerät)
~ **hexagon** Farbsechseck n
~ **histogram** Farbhistogramm n
~ **hologram** Farbhologramm n
~ **holography** Farbholografie f
~ **home video camera** Amateur-Farbvideokamera f
~ **hue** Buntton m, Farbton m, Farbfrequenz f
~ **identification** Farberkennung f
~ **illustration** Farbillustration f, farbige Illustration f
~ **image** Farbbild n
~ **image acquisition** Farbbildaufnahme f
~ **image analysis** Farbbildanalyse f
~ **image coding** Farbbildcodierung f
~ **image compression** Farbbildkompression f, Farbbildkomprimierung f
~ **image data** Farbbilddaten pl
~ **image digitizer** Farb-Bilderfassungskarte f
~ **image fidelity** Farbbildtreue f
~ **image filtering** Farbbildfilterung f
~ **image formation** Farbbildentstehung f
~ **image processing** Farbbildverarbeitung f
~ **image quantization** Farbbildquantisierung f
~ **image reproduction** Farbbildwiedergabe f

~ **image reproduction device** Farbbildwiedergabegerät n
~ **image restoration** Farbbildrestauration f
~ **image segmentation** Farbbildsegmentierung f
~ **image sensor** Farbbildsensor m
~ **image smoothing** Farbbildglättung f
~ **image transformation** Farbbildtransformation f
~ **image understanding** Farbbildverstehen n
~ **imagerelated color reproduction** farbbildbezogene Farbwiedergabe f (Druck)
~ **imagery** Farbbildmaterial n
~ **imaging** 1. Farbbildgebung f; 2. Farbbildbearbeitung f
~ **imbalance** Farbunausgeglichenheit f
~ **impression** Farb[sinnes]eindruck m
~ **impurity** Farbunreinheit f
~ **index** Farbindex m
~ **information** Farbinformation f; Farbartinformation f
~ **information processing** Farbinformationsverarbeitung f
~ **information signal** s. chrominance signal
~ **infrared film** Infrarotfarbfilm m, Farbinfrarotfilm m, Falschfarbenfilm m
~ **infrared image** Farbinfrarotbild n
~ **infrared photography** Infrarot-Farbfotografie f
~ **ink cartridge** Farbtintenpatrone f
~ **ink-jet printer** Farbtinten[strahl]drucker m, Tintenstrahl-Farbdrucker m
~ **-insensitive** farbunempfindlich
~ **insert** Farb[bild]teil m, Farbtafelteil m (z.B. in Büchern)
~ **inspection** Farbkontrolle f
~ **instant-picture film** Farbsofortbildfilm m
~ **intensity** Farbintensität f, Farbtiefe f
~ **-intensive** farbintensiv
~ **internegative** Internegativ n, Zwischennegativ n
~ **interpolation** Farbinterpolation f
~ **interpolation shading** Gouraud-Schattierung f (Computergrafik)
~ **judgment** Farbbeurteilung f, Farburteil n
~ **key** Farbstanze f, Farbstanztrick m, Farbschablonentechnik f (Kinematografie)
~ **killer** Farbabschalter m, Farbabschaltung f (Video)
~ **kinescope** [Mehrstrahl-]Farbbildröhre f
~ **kinescope screen** Farbbildschirm m
~ **labeling** Farbkennzeichnung f
~ **laboratory** Farblabor n, Buntlabor n
~ **laser copier** Farblaserkopierer m
~ **laser printer** Farblaserdrucker m
~ **layer** Farbschicht f
~ **light dispersion** Farbzerlegung f, Farb[enzer]streuung f, chromatische Dispersion f

~ **light source** Farblichtquelle f
~ **lightness** Farbhelligkeit f
~ **lock flag** Farbverkoppelungszeichen n (PAL-Zeitcode)
~ **locus** Farbort m, Spektralfarbzug m (Farbmetrik)
~ **lookup table** Farb[index]tabelle f, Farbzuordnungstabelle f, Farbabbildungstabelle f
~ **magnification error** Farbvergrößerungsfehler m, chromatische Vergrößerungsdifferenz f (Optik)
~ **management** Farbsteuerung f, Farbmanagement n
~ **management module** Farbmanagementmodul n
~ **management system** Farbsteuersystem n, Farbmanagementsystem n, Farbverwaltungssystem n
~ **manipulation** Farbmanipulation f
~ **map** 1. Farb[en]tafel f, Farbkarte f; 2. s. ~ lookup table
~ **-mapped image** indiziertes Farbbild n
~ **mask** Farbmaske f
~ **masking** Farbmaskierung f
~ **master positive [print]** Farbzwischenpositiv n, Interpositiv n, Zwischenpositiv n (Kinematografie)
~ **match** Farbgleichheit f
~ **matching** Farbabstimmung f, Farbangleichung f, Farbabgleich m, Ausmischung f, Farbanpassung f; Farbabmusterung f, Abmusterung f
~ **matching experiment** Farbmessung f nach dem Gleichheitsverfahren
~ **matching function** Spektralwertfunktion f, Spektralwertkurve f
~ **material** Colormaterial n, Farbmaterial n
~ **matrix** Farbmatrix f
~ **matrixing** Farbmatrizierung f
~ **measure** Farbmaß n
~ **measurement** Farbmessung f
~ **measurement laboratory** Farbmesslabor[atorium] n
~ **measurement method** Farbmessverfahren n
~ **memory** Farbgedächtnis n
~ **mesh** Farbgitter n
~ **meter** s. colorimeter
~ **metrics** Farbmetrik f, Kolorimetrie f
~ **microfilm** Farbmikrofilm m, Mikrofarbfilm m
~ **microscopy** Farbmikroskopie f
~ **mixing** Farb[er]mischung f, Farberzeugung f
~ **mixing law** Farbmischungsgesetz n
~ **mixture** Farbmischung f
~ **mixture curve (function)** Farbmischkurve f (Fernsehkamera); 2. s. ~ matching function
~ **mode** Farbmodus m (Bildbearbeitungssoftware)
~ **model** Farbmodell n

color

- ~ **modulation** Farbmodulation *f*
- ~ **modulation frequency** Farbmodulationsfrequenz *f*
- ~ **modulator** Farbmodulator *m*
- ~ **moiré pattern** Farbmoiré[muster] *n*
- ~ **moment** Farbmoment *n*
- ~ **monitor [display]** Farbmonitor *m*, Farbbildschirmgerät *n*, Farbbild-Kontrollempfänger *m*, Farbsichtgerät *n*
- ~ **motion picture** Farb[kine]film *m*, kinematografischer Farbfilm *m*
- ~ **motion-picture film** Farbkinefilm *m*
- ~ **motion-picture photography** Farbkinematografie *f*
- ~ **motion-picture processing** Farbkinefilmverarbeitung *f*
- ~ **movie** Farb[kino]film *m*
- ~ **naming** Farbbenennung *f*
- ~ **naming system** Farbbezeichnungssystem *n*
- ~ **naming system** Farbnomenklatur *f*
- ~ **negative** farbnegativ *(Film)*
- ~ **negative [image]** Farbnegativ *n*
- ~ **negative film** Farbnegativfilm *m*
- ~ **negative material** Farbnegativmaterial *n*
- ~ **negative motion-picture film** Farbnegativ-Kinefilm *m*
- ~ **negative process** Farbnegativentwicklung *f*
- ~ **negative processing** Farbnegativtechnik *f*, Farbnegativverarbeitung *f*
- ~ **negative stock** Farbnegativmaterial *n*
- ~ **noise** Farbrauschen *n*, farbiges Rauschen *n*, Chrominanz-Störabstand *m*
- ~ **nonuniformity** Farbunausgeglichenheit *f*
- ~ **normal observer** farbmetrischer Normalbeobachter *m*
- ~ **normalization** Farbnormierung *f*
- ~ **notation** Farbkennzeichnung *f*
- ~ **of light** Lichtfarbe *f*
- ~ **order system** Farb[ordnungs]system *n*
- ~ **output** Farbausdruck *m*, farbiger Ausdruck *m*
- ~ **palette** Farbpalette *f*, Palette *f*
- ~ **paper** Colorpapier *n*, Farb[foto]papier *n*
- ~ **pattern** 1. Farbmuster *n*; 2. Farbfiltermuster *n (CCD-Technologie)*
- ~ **perception** Farbwahrnehmung *f*
- ~ **perspective** Farbperspektive *f*
- ~ **photo** *s.* ~ photograph
- ~ **photocopier** Farbfotokopierer *m*, Farbfotokopiergerät *n*
- ~ **photocopy/to** farbfotokopieren
- ~ **photograph** Farbfoto *n*, Farbfotografie *f*, Farbaufnahme *f*, farbfotografisches Bild *n*
- ~ **photographer** Farbfotograf *m*
- ~ **photographic** farbfotografisch
- ~ **photographic film** Farb[aufnahme]film *m*, Colorfilm *m*
- ~ **photographic image** *s.* ~ photograph
- ~ **photographic paper** *s.* ~ paper
- ~ **photography** Farb[en]fotografie *f*, Buntfotografie *f*
- ~ **photography process** Farbfotoverfahren *n*
- ~ **photomicrography** Farbmikrofotografie *f*
- ~ **photoprint** *s.* ~ print 1.
- ~ **physics** Farbphysik *f*
- ~ **picker** Farbaufnehmer *m (Bildbearbeitungssoftware)*
- ~ **picture** Farbbild *n*
- ~ **picture screen** Farb[fernseh]bildschirm *m*
- ~ **picture signal** Farbbildsignal *n*
- ~ **picture tube** [Mehrstrahl-]Farbbildröhre *f*
- ~ **pigment** Farbpigment *n*, Pigment *n*, Farbkörper *m*
- ~ **pixel** Farbpixel *n*; Farbbildpunkt *m*
- ~ **plane** Farbebene *f*
- ~ **plate** Farb[en]tafel *f*, Farbkarte *f*
- ~ **plotter** Farbplotter *m*
- ~ **point** Farbpunkt *m*
- ~ **portion** Farbanteil *m (z.B. des Videosignals)*
- ~ **positive** Colorpositiv *n*, Farbpositiv *n*
- ~ **positive film** Farbpositivfilm *m*, Positiv-Farbfilm *m*, Farbkopierfilm *m*
- ~ **positive material** Farbpositivpapier *n*
- ~ **positive processing** Farbpositivtechnik *f*
- ~ **precision** Farbgenauigkeit *f*, Farbrichtigkeit *f*
- ~ **prepress** Farb-Druckvorstufenbereich *m*
- ~ **print** 1. Farbabzug *m*, Farb[papier]bild *n*, Coloraufsichtsbild *n*; Farbkopie *f*; 2. Farbdruck *m (Erzeugnis)*
- ~ **print film** Farbkopierfilm *m*
- ~ **print material (paper)** Colorpapier *n*, Farbpositivpapier *n*, Farb[foto]papier *n*; Farbkopierpapier *n*
- ~ **print processing** Colorpositivverarbeitung *f*
- ~ **printer** Farbdrucker *m*
- ~ **printing** 1. Farbkopierung *f*, Farbkopieren *n*; 2. Farbdruck *m*; 3. *s.* ~ print processing
- ~ **printing device** Farbdrucker *m*
- ~ **printing filter** Farbkopierfilter *n*
- ~ **printing material** Farbkopiermaterial *n*
- ~ **printing process** Farbkopierverfahren *n*
- ~ **printing system** Farbdrucksystem *n*
- ~ **process** Farbverfahren *n*; Farbfotoverfahren *n*
- ~ **process printing** Vierfarbendruck *m*
- ~ **processing** Farb[film]verarbeitung *f*, Farb[film]entwicklung *f*, Colorverarbeitung *f*
- ~ **processing lab[oratory]** Farblabor *n*, Buntlabor *n*
- ~ **profile** Farbprofil *n*
- ~ **program** Farb[fernseh]sendung *f*
- ~ **projection device, ~ projector** Farbprojektionsgerät *n*, Farbprojektor *m*
- ~ **proof** 1. Farbproof *m*, farbverbindlicher Proof *m*, Farbandruck *m*; 2. Farbsatzprüfgerät *n*

~ **proofing** Farbsatzprüfung f, Farbproofherstellung f
~ **proofing system** Farbproofsystem n (Reprografie)
~ **property** Farbeigenschaft f
~ **purity** Farbreinheit f
~ **purity adjustment** Farbreinheitseinstellung f (Fernsehtechnik)
~ **quality** Farbqualität f
~ **quality index** Farbwiedergabeindex m
~ **quantization** Farbquantisierung f
~ **radar image** Farbradarbild n
~ **radiography** Farbradiografie f
~ **range** Farb[raum]umfang m, Farbbereich m, Farbpalette f (z.B. eines Druckers)
~ **raster** Farbraster m(n)
~ **raster display** Rasterfarbbildschirm m
~ **receiver** Farbfernsehempfänger m, Farbfernsehgerät n
~ **reception** Farbempfang m
~ **receptor** Farbrezeptor m
~ **record** Teilfarbenbild n, Farbstoffteilbild n (Farbfotografie)
~ **reduction** Farbreduktion f
~ **reflection** Farbreflexion f
~ **region** Farbbereich m
~ **rendering index** Farbwiedergabeindex m
~ **rendering property** Farbwiedergabevermögen n
~ **rendition accuracy** Farbwiedergabegenauigkeit f
~ **rendition chart** Farb[en]tafel f, Farbkarte f
~ **replacer** Farbradierer m (elektronisches Bildbearbeitungswerkzeug)
~ **representation** Farbdarstellung f
~ **reproducibility** Farbwiedergabevermögen n
~ **reproduction** Farbwiedergabe f, Farbreproduktion f
~ **reproduction quality** Farbwiedergabequalität f
~ **reproduction range** Farbwiedergabebereich m
~ **reproduction technology** Farbwiedergabetechnik f
~ **restoration** Farbrestauration f
~ **retouching** Farbretusche f
~ **reversal** Farbumwandlung f, Farbumkehr f
~ **reversal film** Farbumkehrfilm m, Umkehrfarbfilm m, Farbdiafilm m
~ **reversal intermediate (internegative)** Original-Bildnegativ n, Internegativ n, Zwischennegativ n
~ **reversal material** Colorumkehrmaterial n
~ **reversal motion-picture film** Farbumkehr-Kinefilm m
~ **reversal printing paper** Farbumkehr[foto]papier n
~ **reversal process** Farbumkehrprozess m, Farbumkehrtechnik f
~ **ringing** Farbringbildung f
~ **sample** Farbprobe f, Farbmuster n
~ **sampling** Farbabtastung f
~-**saturated** farbsatt
~ **saturation** Farbsättigung f, Sättigung f
~ **scale** Farbskala f
~ **scan head** Farbscankopf m
~ **scanner** Farbscanner m
~ **scanning** Farbscannen n, Farbabtastung f
~ **schlieren photograph** Schlierenfarbfoto n
~ **science** Farbwissenschaft f; Farb[en]lehre f, Chromatik f
~ **scientist** Farbwissenschaftler m
~ **scission** Farbaufspaltung f (Wahrnehmungsphänomen)
~ **screen** 1. Farbbildschirm m; 2. Farbraster m(n); 3. s. ~ filter
~ **segmentation** Farbsegmentierung f
~ **selection** Farbwahl f, Farbselektion f
~ **selection mode** Farbauswahlmodus m
~ **sensation** Farbempfindung f, Farbempfinden n
~ **sense** Farb[en]sinn m
~ **sensitive** farbempfindlich
~ **sensitive layer** farbempfindliche Schicht f
~ **sensitivity** Farbempfindlichkeit f; spektrale Empfindlichkeit f, Spektralempfindlichkeit f
~ **sensitization** Farbsensibilisierung f
~-**sensitize/to** farbsensibilisieren
~-**sensitized** farbsensibilisiert
~ **sensitizer** Farbsensibilisator m
~ **sensitometry** Farbsensitometrie f
~ **sensor** Farbsensor m
~ **separation** 1. Farbtrennung f, Farbenzerlegung f, Farbseparierung f; 2. Farbauszug m
~ **separation film** Farbauszugsfilm m
~ **separation filter** Farbauszugsfilter n, Reproauszugsfilter m
~ **separation negative** Farbauszugsnegativ n, Separationsnegativ n
~ **separation photography** Farbauszugsfotografie f
~ **separation process** Farbauszugsverfahren n
~ **sequence** Farbreihenfolge f (Druck)
~ **setting file** Farbgrundeinstellungsdatei f (Dateinamenerweiterung)
~ **shade** 1. Farbnuance f; 2. s. ~ tone
~ **shading** Farbschattierung f
~ **shift** Farbverschiebung f
~ **shifting** bei seitlicher Betrachtung von Videobildwänden auftretender Farbstich
~ **shot** Farbaufnahme f
~ **signal** Farbsignal n
~ **signal processing** Farbsignalverarbeitung f
~ **similarity measure** Farbähnlichkeitsmaß n
~ **slide** Farbdia[positiv] n
~ **slide film** Farbdiafilm m, Farbumkehrfilm m, Umkehrfarbfilm m

color

~ **slide projector** Farbdiaprojektor *m*
~ **solid** 1. Farbkörper *m (Kolorimetrie)*; 2. *s.* ~ pigment
~ **space** Farbraum *m*
~ **space conversion** Farbraumkonvertierung *f*, Farbraumtransformation *f*, Farbraumumwandlung *f*
~ **space converter** Farbraumkonverter *m*
~ **space transformation** *s.* ~ space conversion
~-**specific** farbspezifisch
~ **specification** Farbspezifikation *f*, Farbbeschreibung *f*, Farbkennzeichnung *f*
~ **specification system** Farb[ordnungs]system *n*
~ **spectrometer** Farbspektrometer *n*
~ **spectrum** Farbspektrum *n*
~ **sphere** Farbenkugel *f*, kugelförmiger Farbkörper *m (Farbmetrik)*
~ **spill suppression** Farbunterdrückung *f*
~ **spindle** *s.* ~ solid
~ **splitter** Farbteiler *m*
~ **splitting** Farbaufspaltung *f (Wahrnehmungsphänomen)*
~ **stability** Farbstabilität *f*
~ **step** Farbstufe *f*
~ **stereographic slide** Stereo-Farbdia[positiv] *n*
~ **stimulus** Farbreiz *m*
~ **stimulus function** Farbreizfunktion *f*
~ **store** Farbspeicher *m*
~ **subcarrier** Farb[hilfs]träger *m (Video)*
~ **subcarrier frequency** Farb[hilfs]trägerfrequenz *f*
~ **subcarrier period** Farbträgerperiode *f*
~ **subsampling** Farb-Unterabtastung *f*
~ **synchronizing burst** Farbsynchron[isier]signal *n*, Farb[träger]burst *m*, Farbsynchronimpuls *m*, Farbvergleichssignal *n*, Burst *m*
~-**synchronizing burst** Farbsynchronimpuls *m*, Farbsynchron[isier]signal *n*, Farb[träger]burst *m*, Burst *m*, Farbbündelung *f (Video)*
~ **synthesis** Farbsynthese *f*
~ **system** Farbsystem *n*, Farbmodell *n*
~ **table** Farb[zuordnungs]tabelle *f*, Farbindextabelle *f*, Farbabbildungstabelle *f*
~ **technology** Farbtechnik *f*
~ **television** Farbfernsehen *n*
~ **television broadcast system** Farbfernsehsystem *n*
~ **television camera** Farbfernsehkamera *f*
~ **television CRT (cathode-ray tube)** Farbfernseh[bild]röhre *f*
~ **television display device** Farbfernseh[wiedergabe]gerät *n*
~ **television encoding system** Farbcodiersystem *n*

~ **television image** Farbfernsehbild *n*
~ **television monitor** Farbfernsehmonitor *m*
~ **television picture tube** Farbfernseh[bild]röhre *f*
~ **television receiver** Farbfernsehempfänger *m*, Farbfernsehgerät *m*
~ **television reception** Farbfernsehempfang *m*
~ **television signal** Farbfernsehsignal *n*
~ **television standard** Farbfernsehnorm *f*, Farbfernsehstandard *m*
~ **television technology** Farbfernsehtechnik *f*
~ **television test card** *s.* ~ test pattern
~ **television transmission** Farbfernsehübertragung *f*
~ **temperature** Farbtemperatur *f*
~ **temperature measurement** Farbtemperaturmessung *f*
~ **temperature meter** Farbtemperaturmesser *m*, Farbtemperaturmessgerät *n*
~ **temperature scale** Farbtemperaturskala *f*
~ **temperature shift** Farbtemperaturverschiebung *f*
~ **temperature value** Farbtemperatur[mess]wert *m*
~ **test** Farbtest *m*
~ **test chart** Farb[test]tafel *f*, Farbkarte *f*
~ **test pattern** [elektronisches] Farbtestbild *n*
~ **test strip** Testfarbstreifen *m*
~ **texture** Farbtextur *f*
~ **theory** Farbtheorie *f*
~ **thermal printer** Thermofarbdrucker *m*
~ **thermogram (thermograph)** Farbthermogramm *n*
~ **threshold** Farbschwelle *f*
~ **time/to** farblichtbestimmen
~ **timer** Farblichtbestimmer *m*, Filmlichtbestimmer *m*, Farbtechniker *m*
~ **timing** Filmlichtbestimmung *f*, Farb[licht]bestimmung *f*, Lichtbestimmung *f*, Farbkorrektur *f*
~ **tolerance** Farbtoleranz *f*
~ **tone** Farbton *m*, Buntton *m*, Farbfrequenz *f*
~ **toner image** Farbtonerbild *n*
~ **transform[ation]** Farbtransformation *f*
~ **transformation matrix** Farbtransformationsmatrix *f*
~ **transmission** Farbübertragung *f (Video)*
~ **transparency** Farbdia[positiv] *n*
~ **transparency film** Farbdiafilm *m*, Farbumkehrfilm *m*, Umkehrfarbfilm *m*
~ **transparency material** Farbdiamaterial *n*
~ **transparency processing** Farbdiafilmverarbeitung *f*
~ **triad** Farbtripel *n (Farbbildröhre)*
~ **triangle** Farbdreieck *n (Farbmetrik)*
~ **tube** [Mehrstrahl-]Farbbildröhre *f*, Farbbild-Elektronenstrahlröhre *f*

~ **tuning** Farbabstimmung f
~ **TV broadcast** Farb[fernseh]sendung f
~ **TV screen** Farbfernsehbildschirm m
~ **uniformity** Farbuniformität f
~ **value** 1. Farbwert m; 2. Pixelwert m (Bitmap-Bild)
~ **variation** Farbvariation f, Farbschwankung f
~ **vector** Farbvektor m
~ **vector space** Farbvektorraum m
~ **video** Farbvideo n
~ **video analyzer** Farbvideoanalysator m
~ **video camera** Farbvideokamera f
~ **video cassette player** Farbvideokassettenabspielgerät n
~ **video cassette recorder** Farbvideokassettenrecorder m
~ **video compression** Farbvideokompression f
~ **video format** s. ~ video standard
~ **video monitor** Farbvideomonitor m
~ **video projection** Farbvideoprojektion f
~ **video projector** Farbvideoprojektor m
~ **video recorder** Farbvideorecorder m
~ **video sequence** Farbvideosequenz f
~ **video signal** Farbvideosignal n, Farbwertsignal n, RGB-Signal n, RGB-Videosignal n
~ **video standard** Farbfernsehnorm f, Farbfernsehstandard m
~ **video transmission** Farbvideoübertragung f
~ **viewfinder** Farbsucher m
~ **viewing** Farbbetrachtung f
~ **vision** Farb[en]sehen n, chromatisches Sehen n, Buntsehen n
~ **vision defect (deficiency)** Farb[en]fehlsichtigkeit f, Farbsinnstörung f, Farbsehstörung f
~ **vision system** Farbsehsystem n (des Auges)
~ **vision test** Farbsehtest m
~ **visual field [of the eyes]** Farbgesichtsfeld n
~ **weakness** Farbenschwäche f, anomale Trichromasie f (Farbsinnstörung)
~ **wedge** Farb[mess]keil m
~ **wheel** Farb[en]kreis m
~ **xerography** Farbxerografie f
colorant Färbemittel n; Pigment n
coloration Färbung f
colorcast Farb[fernseh]sendung f
colored farbig (s.a. unter color ...)
~ **area** Farbfläche f
~ **filter** Farbfilter n, Colorfilter n
~ **foil** Farbfolie f
~ **gel** Gelatinefilter n
~ **glass filter** Farbglasfilter n
~ **image** farbiges Bild n, Farbbild n
~ **ink** Farbtinte f
~ **light** Farblicht n, farbiges Licht n
~ **masking coupler** gefärbter Maskenkuppler m

~ **noise** farbiges Rauschen n, Farbrauschen n, Chrominanz-Störabstand m
~ **paper** Buntpapier n
~ **polarizing filter** Polarisationsfarbfilter n
~ **ribbon** Farbband n, Druckerfarbband n
~ **toner** Farbtoner m
~ **vision** Chromatopsie f
~ **wax paper** Farbwachspapier n
colorfast farbecht, farbstabil
colorfastness Farbechtheit f
colorfulness Farbenmannigfaltigkeit f, Farbvielfalt f, Farbigkeit f
colorimeter Kolorimeter n, Farbmessgerät n, Tintometer n
colorimetric kolorimetrisch, farbmetrisch
~ **color reproduction** exakte (korrekte) Farbwiedergabe f
~ **fidelity** Farbtreue f
~ **measurement** Farbmessung f
~ **model** kolorimetrisches Modell n
~ **photometer** kolorimetrisches Fotometer n
~ **purity** kolorimetrische Reinheit f
colorimetrics, colorimetry Kolorimetrie f, Farbmetrik f
coloring 1. Farbgebung f, Färbung f; 2. s. colorization
~ **agent** Färbemittel n
~ **glass** Farbglas n, Buntglas n
~ **material** Färbemittel n
~ **technique** Farbgebungstechnik f
colorist Kolorist m (s.a. color timer)
coloristic farblich
colorization Einfärben n; Kolorierung f, Filmkolorierung f, Virage f, Viragierung f
colorize/to färben; einfärben, viragieren; kolorieren
colorless coupler farbloser Kuppler m (Farbfotografie)
colorlessness Farblosigkeit f
colorphoto Farbfoto n
colposcopic kolposkopisch
colposcopy Kolposkopie f, Scheidenspiegelung f
column 1. Säule f; Führungssäule f, Tragsäule f, Standsäule f (Vergrößerungsgerät); 2. Spalte f (Tabelle); Druckspalte f, Kolumne f
~ **break** Spaltenumbruch m (Druck)
~ **matrix** Spaltenmatrix f
~ **vector** Spaltenvektor m
~ **width** Spaltenbreite f (Typografie)
columnwise spaltenweise (z.B. Bildfilterung)
COM s. computer output microfilm
coma [blur] Koma f, Komafehler m (Abbildungsfehler)
~ **correction** Komakorrektur f
~ **-free mirror** komafreier Spiegel m
~ **patch (pattern)** Komafigur f
comatic aberration Komafehler m, Koma f
~ **circle** Komafigur f
comb filter Kammfilter n

comb 68

~ **filtering** Kammfilterung f
~ **function** Kammfunktion f
combat photography Kriegsfotografie f
combination filter Kombinationsfilter n
combined focal length Gesamtbrennweite f *(z.B. von Kameraobjektiv und Vorsatzlinse)*
~ **image** kombiniertes Bild n *(s.a. composite image)*
~ **negative** kombiniertes Negativ n *(Filmbearbeitung)*
~ **print** kombinierte Kopie (Filmkopie) f
~ **shot** Kombinationsaufnahme f *(Kinematografie)*
~ **X-ray spectrometer** kombiniertes Röntgenspektrometer n
combiner 1. Strahlvereiniger m, Strahlvereinigungsoptik f; 2. Kanalweiche f
comet tail Bildnachziehen n, Kometeneffekt m, Kometenschweif m *(Bewegungsartefakt)*; Resonanzartefakt n *(Sonografie)*
COMMAG, commag 1. Startbandaufdruck auf Bildfilmen mit Magnettonspur; 2. s. composite magnetic [sound]
command Befehl m, Anweisung f *(Computerprogramm)*
~ **button** Schaltfläche f *(Computer)*
~ **dial** [Betriebsarten-]Einstellrad n, Wählscheibe f, Wahlrad n
~ **language** Befehlssprache f
~ **menu** Befehlsmenü n
~ **set** Befehlsvorrat m
commercial Werbe[kurz]film m, Werbespot m
~ **break** Werbeunterbrechung f *(z.B. im Fernsehen)*
~ **darkroom** Foto[fach]labor n
~ **developer** handelsüblicher Entwickler m
~ **developing and printing** Fotofinishing n
~-**grade CCD** handelsüblicher (kommerzieller) CCD-Sensor m
~ **insertion** Werbeeinblendung f
~ **lab** Großlabor[atorium] n
~ **photographer** Fachfotograf m
~ **photography** Fachfotografie f, gewerbliche (kommerzielle) Fotografie f
~ **spot** s. commercial
~ **TV** Werbefernsehen n
~ **videotape** Kaufkassette f, Kaufvideo n
commissioned photography Auftragsfotografie f
common air interface Luftschnittstelle f *(Optik)*
~-**impression-cylinder principle** Satellit-Prinzip n *(Druckmaschine)*
~ **interface** einheitlich definierte Schnittstelle f
~-**interface slot** s. CI slot
~ **intermediate format** *ein digitales Bildformat für Bildtelefon- und Videokonferenzdienste*
~ **salt** Kochsalz n, Natriumchlorid n

communication engineering theory s. ~ theory
~ **signal** Kommunikationssignal n
~ **theoretic** informationstheoretisch, kommunikationstheoretisch
~ **theory** Informationstheorie f, Kommunikationstheorie f
~**[s] channel** Kommunikationskanal m
~**[s] channel noise** Kanalrauschen n
~**[s] engineering** Nachrichtentechnik f
~**[s] highway** Datenautobahn f
~**[s] interface** Kommunikationsschnittstelle f
~**[s] medium** Kommunikationsmittel n, Medium n
~**[s] network** Kommunikationsnetz n
~**[s] satellite** Fernmeldesatellit m, Nachrichtensatellit m, Verteilersatellit n, Kommunikationssatellit m
~**[s] technology** Kommunikationstechnik f
community antenna television (TV) Gemeinschaftsantennenfernsehen n; Kabelfernsehen n
~ **antenna TV system** Gemeinschaftsantenne[nanlage] f
commutative kommutativ, vertauschbar
commutativity Kommutativität f, Vertauschbarkeit f *(z.B. von Bildverarbeitungsoperatoren)*
COMOPT Startbandaufdruck auf Bildfilmen mit Lichttonspur
compact [camera] Kompaktkamera f
~ **cassette** Kompakt-Magnetbandkassette f
~ **code** kompakter Code m
~ **disc** CD-Platte f, CD f
~ **disc burner** CD-Brenner m
~ **disc erasable** löschbare CD f
~ **disc interactive** interaktive CD f, CD-I f
~ **disc read-only memory** CD-ROM f
~ **disc recordable** beschreibbare CD f, CD-R f
~ **disc rewritable** wiederbeschreibbare CD f, CD-RW f
~ **disc video** CD-Video n, Video-CD f
~ **flash card** Kompakt-Flash-Karte f
~ **instant camera** Sofortbild-Kompaktkamera f
~ **mass-market camera** Großserien-Kompaktkamera f
~ **video disc** s. ~ disc video
compaction Kompression f, Komprimierung f *(z.B. von Bilddaten; s.a. unter compression,* [en]coding*)*
compactness Kompaktheit f
companding technique [of quantization] logarithmische Quantisierung f
company logo Firmenlogo n
~ **photographic department** betriebliche Fotoabteilung f
comparative photograph Vergleichsfoto n
comparator Komparator m
~ **densitometer** [visuelles] Vergleichsdensitometer n
compare/to vergleichen

compare-and-swap module
Komparator-und-Vertauschungsmodul *n*
(Sortiernetzwerk)
comparison colorimeter
Vergleichskolorimeter *n*
~ **lamp** Vergleichsstrahlungsquelle *f*
~ **microscope** Vergleichsmikroskop *n*
~ **operation** Vergleichsoperation *f*
~ **photometer** visuelles Fotometer *n*
~ **spectroscope** Vergleichsspektroskop *n*
~ **spectrum** Vergleichsspektrum *n*
compass gradient Kompassgradient *m*
(Bildverarbeitungsoperator)
compatibility Kompatibilität *f*
compatible kompatibel
compendium hood Kompendium *n*,
Objektivkompendium *n*;
Balgenkompendium *n*
compensating developer
Ausgleichsentwickler *m*, weich
arbeitender Entwickler *m*,
Weichentwickler *m*
~ **eyepiece** Kompensationsokular *n*
(Mikroskop)
~ **filter** Kompensationsfilter *n*
~ **glass** Kompensatorplatte *f*
~ **wedge** Messkeil *m*
competitive learning kompetitives
(konkurrierendes) Lernen *n*,
Wettbewerbslernen *n (Neuroinformatik)*
compiler Compiler *m*, Übersetzer *m*,
Übersetzungsprogramm *n*
(Datenverarbeitung)
complanarity Komplanarität *f*
complanate komplanar
complement Komplement *n*
complementary komplementär, ergänzend
~ **angle** Ergänzungswinkel *m*
~ **binary code** komplementärer Binärcode *m*
~ **color** Komplementärfarbe *f*,
Ergänzungsfarbe *f*, komplementäre
Farbe *f*, Kompensationsfarbe *f*,
Kontrastfarbe *f*, Gegenfarbe *f*
~ **color filter** Komplementär[farb]filter *n*
~ **contrast** Komplementärkontrast *m*
~ **dye** Komplementärfarbstoff *m*
~ **filtration** Komplementärfiltrierung *f*
~ **image** Komplementärbild *n*
~ **metal-oxide semiconductor** integrierter
Halbleiterschaltkreis *m*
~ **metal oxide semiconductor [image] sensor** CMOS-Bildsensor *m*,
CMOS-Sensor *m*
complete color blindness totale
Farbenblindheit *f*, Einfarbensehen *n*,
Monochromasie *f*
~ **frame** Vollbild *n*
~ **image** [optisches] Ganzbild *n*, Vollbild *n*,
Komplettbild *n*
~ **picture signal** vollständiges Bildsignal *n*
~ **segmentation** vollständige
Segmentierung *f*

~ **sound track** Gesamttonspur *f*;
Endmischband *n*
completely digital volldigital
complex amplitude komplexe Amplitude *f*
(Wellenoptik)
~ **amplitude distribution** komplexe
Amplitudenverteilung *f*
~ **analytic signal** komplexe Wellenfunktion
f
~ **Fourier coefficient** komplexer
Fourier-Koeffizient *m*
~ **ion** Komplex-Ion *n*
~ **lens** 1. mehrlinsiges (viellinsiges)
Objektiv *n*, Mehrlinser *m*; 2.
Verbundlinse *f*, dicke Linse *f*
~ **salt** Komplexsalz *n*
~**-shaped contour** komplexe Kontur *f*
~**-valued function** komplexwertige
Funktion *f*
~ **wave function** komplexe Wellenfunktion
f
complexation Komplexbildung *f*
complexing agent Komplexbildner *m*,
Komplexierungsmittel *n*
(Entwicklerzusatz)
compliance, compliancy Kompatibilität *f*
component analog interface analoge
Geräteschnittstelle *f*
~ **analog video** analoges
Komponentenvideo *n*
~**-coded television signal**
komponentencodiertes Fernsehsignal *n*
~ **coding** Komponentencodierung *f*
(digitales Fernsehen)
~ **color** Teilfarbe *f*
~ **digital recording** digitale
Komponentenaufzeichnung *f (Video)*
~ **digital signal** digitales
Komponentensignal *n (Video)*
~ **image** Teilbild *n*, Komponentenbild *n*
~ **lens** *s.* complex lens
~ **signal recording**
Komponentenaufzeichnung *f*
~ **television** Komponentenfernsehen *n*
~ **vector** Komponentenvektor *m*
~ **video** Komponentenvideo *n*;
Komponentenfernsehen *n*
~ **video signal** [analoges]
Komponenten[video]signal *n*
components detection Teileerkennung *f*,
Bauteilidentifikation *f*,
Werkstückerkennung *f*
compose/to setzen *f (Druck)*
composer *s.* compositor
composing machine Satzmaschine *f*,
Setzmaschine *f*
~ **room** Setzerei *f*
~ **stick** Winkelhaken *m*
(Handsetzwerkzeug)
composite *s.* ~ image
~ **color** Mischfarbe *f*
~ **color [video] signal**
Farb-Bild-Austast-Synchron[isier]-Signal
n, FBAS-Signal *n*

composite

~ **daylight [film-handling] system** zentrales Tageslichtsystem n
~ **dup[licat]e negative** kombiniertes Duplikatnegativ n
~ **effect** Kombinationseffekt m
~ **encoded video signal** s. ~ video signal
~ **film** seitengroßer Film m, Ganzseitenfilm m *(Reprografie)*
~ **filter** zusammengesetztes Filter n
~ **focal length** Gesamtbrennweite f *(z.B. von Kameraobjektiv und Vorsatzlinse)*
~ **image** Kombinationsbild n, Bildkombination f, zusammengesetztes (kombiniertes) Bild n; Mischbild n
~ **lens** s. 1. ~ objective; 2. compound lens
~ **light** Mischlicht n
~ **magnetic** s. COMMAG
~ **magnetic sound** kombinierter Magnetton m
~ **objective** mehrlinsiges (viellinsiges) Objektiv n, Mehrlinser m
~ **optical** s. 1. COMOPT; 2. ~ optical sound
~ **optical sound** kombinierter Lichtton m
~ **photograph** Kombinationsaufnahme f; Fotomontage f
~ **print** kombinierte Filmkopie (Kopie) f *(Kinematografie)*
~ **printing** kombiniertes Kopieren n *(Kinefilmverarbeitung)*
~ **prism** zusammengesetztes Prisma n, Prismensystem n, Prismenkombination f
~ **proof** echter Andruck m *(Druckvorstufe)*
~ **scene** Mischbildszene f *(Trickkinematografie)*
~ **shot** Kombinationsaufnahme f *(Kinematografie)*
~ **signal** 1. zusammengesetztes Signal n; Summensignal n; 2. Audio-Video-Signal n, AV-Signal n
~ **sync[hronization] pulse** gemischtes Synchronisiersignal n
~ **TV signal** s. ~ video signal
~ **video signal** 1. zusammengesetztes Videosignal (Fernsehsignal) n, Verbundsignal n, Kompositsignal n, Bild-Austast-Synchron[isier]-Signal n, BAS-Fernsehsignal n; 2. s. ~ color [video] signal
compositing 1. Kombinationsaufnahmeverfahren n, Kombinationstrickverfahren n *(Kinematografie)*; 2. Schattierung f *(Computergrafik)*
composition Satz m *(Druck)*
~ **caster** Einzelbuchstabensetz- und -gießmaschine f
~ **effect** Kombinationseffekt m
~ **workstation** Satzrechner m, Satzcomputer m
compositor Schriftsetzer m, Setzer m
compound s. compound table
~ **document** Bild-Text-Dokument n, Verbunddokument n, zusammengesetztes Dokument n
~ **eyepiece** zusammengesetztes Okular n
~ **lens** 1. Verbundlinse f, dicke Linse f; Objektiv n; 2. s. composite objective
~ **light microscope** zusammengesetztes Mikroskop n
~ **primitive** zusammengesetztes Darstellungselement n
~ **semiconductor** Misch[ungs]halbleiter m, Verbundungshalbleiter m
~ **table** Tricktischplatte f
compress/to komprimieren
compressed data komprimierte Daten pl
~ **file** komprimierte (gepackte) Datei f
~ **image** komprimiertes Bild n
~ **signal** komprimiertes Signal n
~ **video** komprimiertes Video n
~ **video data** komprimierte Videodaten pl
~ **video signal** komprimiertes Videosignal n
compressibility Komprimierbarkeit f
compressible komprimierbar
compression Kompression f, Komprimierung f *(s.a. unter coding, encoding)*
~ **algorithm** Kompressionsalgorithmus m
~ **amplifier** Kompressionsverstärker m *(Ultraschallscanner)*
~ **artifact** Kompressionsartefakt n
~ **-based transcoding** kompressionsbasierte Transcodierung f
~ **cycle** Kompressionszyklus m
~ **distortion** Kompressionsverzerrung f
~ **efficiency** Kompressionseffizienz f
~ **error** Kompressionsfehler m
~ **factor** Kompressionsfaktor m, Reduktionsfaktor m, Datenreduktionsfaktor m
~ **format** Kompressionsformat n
~ **gain** Kompressionsgewinn m
~ **level** Kompressionsstufe f, Kompressionsrate f
~ **loss** Kompressionsverlust m
~ **method** Kompressionsverfahren n
~ **parameter** Kompressionsparameter m
~ **performance** Kompressionsleistung f
~ **process** Kompressionsvorgang m
~ **program** Kompressionssoftware f
~ **range** Kompressionsbereich m
~ **rate** Kompressionsstufe f, Kompressionsrate f
~ **ratio** Kompressionsverhältnis n *(s.a. ~ factor)*
~ **scheme** Kompressionssystem n
~ **standard** Kompressionsstandard m
~ **system** Kompressionssystem n
~ **technique** Kompressionsverfahren n
~ **technology** Kompressionstechnik f
~ **type** Kompressionsart f
compressor Kompressor m
Compton effect s. ~ scattering
~ **electron** Compton-Elektron n
~ **line** Compton-Linie f
~ **scattering** Compton-Streuung f, Compton-Effekt m, inkohärente

Streuung f, Streuabsorption f
(Röntgenstrahlenschwächung)
computation time Rechenzeit f
computational burden (cost), ~ effort
Rechenaufwand m
~ **fluid dynamics** numerische
Strömungssimulation f
~ **geometric** computergeometrisch
~ **geometry** Computergeometrie f,
algorithmische Geometrie f,
geometrische Datenverarbeitung f
~ **graphics** s. computer graphics
computationally expensive (intensive)
rechenaufwendig, rechenintensiv
~ **intensive algorithm** rechenintensiver
Algorithmus m
computed axial tomography
Computertomografie f
~ **radiography** Computerradiografie f,
digitale Projektionsradiografie f
~ **radiology** Computerradiologie f
~ **tomogram** Computertomogramm n,
CT-Aufnahme f, CT-Bild n
~ **tomographic** computertomografisch
~ **tomography** Computertomografie f, CT
~ **tomography angiography**
Computerangiografie f,
computertomografische Angiografie f
~ **tomography scanner**
Computertomograf m,
Computertomografiegerät n,
CT-Scanner m
computer Computer m, Rechner m
~**-aided design** 1. computergestütztes
Entwerfen (Konstruieren) n; 2.
computergestützter Entwurf m,
computerunterstützte Konstruktion f
~**-aided design display** CAD-Bildschirm m
~**-aided detection** computergestützte
Detektion f
~**-aided drafting** computerunterstützte
Zeichnungserstellung f
~**-aided engineering** rechnerunterstützte
Ingenieurarbeit f
~**-aided geometric design** geometrische
Modellierung f
~**-aided mammography**
computergestützte Mammografie f
~**-aided manufacturing**
rechnerunterstützte Fertigung f
~**-aided modeling** rechnergestützte
Modellierung f
~**-aided molecular design** Moleküldesign
n
~**-aided radiology** computergestützte
Radiologie f
~**-aided virtual environment**
computergestützte virtuelle Umgebung f
~ **algorithm** Computeralgorithmus m
~**-animated film** Computer[trick]film m,
computeranimierter Film m
~**-animated image** computeranimiertes
Bild n

~ **animation** Computeranimation f,
computererzeugte Animation f;
computerbasierte Animation f
~ **animation software**
Computeranimationssoftware f
~ **animation system**
Computeranimationssystem n
~ **animation technique**
Computeranimationtechnik f
~ **animator** Computeranimator m,
Computeranimateur m
~ **art** Computerkunst f
~**-assisted animation** s. computer
animation
~**-assisted image analysis**
computergestützte (digitale) Bildanalyse
f
~**-assisted image processing**
rechnergestützte Bildverarbeitung f
~**-assisted microscopy** computergestützte
Mikroskopie f
~**-assisted simulation** computergestützte
Simulation f
~**-assisted surgery** computergestützte
Chirurgie f
~**-assisted tomography**
Computertomografie f
~**-based edit system** computergestütztes
Schnittsystem n
~ **chip** Computerchip m
~ **command** Maschinenbefehl m
~ **connection accessories**
Computeranschlusszubehör n
~ **control** Computersteuerung f
~**-controlled camera** computergesteuerte
Kamera f (s.a. motion control camera)
~**-controlled editing** computergesteuerter
Filmschnitt m, computergesteuerter
Schnitt m
~**-controlled editing machine**
Schnittcomputer m
~**-controlled image manipulation**
coputergestützte Bildmanipulation f
~ **disk** Computerfestplatte f
~ **display** Computer[bild]schirm m,
Rechnerbildschirm m
~ **display monitor** Computermonitor m
~ **drive** Computerlaufwerk n
~ **editing suite** Schnittcomputer m
~**-enhanced animation** s. computer
animation
~**-enhanced imagery**
computerbearbeitetes Bildmaterial n
~ **enhancement** Computerretusche f
~ **file format** Computerdateiformat n
~ **flash** Computerblitz m
~ **game** Computer[grafik]spiel n
~**-generated** computergeneriert
~**-generated actor** Computerfigur f,
digitaler (virtueller) Darsteller m; Avatar
m
~**-generated animation**
Computeranimation f,

computererzeugte (computerbasierte) Animation *f*
~-**generated graphic** Computergrafik *f*, Computergrafikbild *n*
~-**generated hologram** Computerhologramm *n*, computererzeugtes Hologramm *n*
~-**generated holography** Computerholografie *f*
~-**generated image** computererzeugtes (computergeneriertes) Bild *n*, Computerbild *n*, synthetisches Bild *n*
~-**generated imagery** rechnererzeugtes (computergeneriertes) Bildmaterial *n*, künstliches Bildmaterial *n*
~-**generated movie** *s.* computer-animated film
~-**generated simulation** Computersimulation *f*
~-**generated special effect** Computertrick *m*, elektronischer Trick *m*, digitaler Spezialeffekt *m*
~-**generated volume hologram** Computervolumenhologramm *n*
~-**graphic** computergrafisch
~-**graphic display** grafikfähiges (grafisches) Display *n*, Grafikdisplay *n*, Grafikanzeige *f*; Grafikbildschirm *m*; Grafikmonitor *m*
~ **graphicist** Computergrafiker *m*
~ **graphics** Computergrafik *f*, grafische Datenverarbeitung *f (s.a. unter* graphics*)*
~ **graphics camera** virtuelle Kamera *f*
~ **graphics character** *s.* computer-generated actor
~ **graphics generator** Computerbildgenerator *m*
~ **graphics hardware** Computergrafikhardware *f*
~ **graphics image** Computergrafik *f*, Computergrafikbild *n (s.a.* computer-generated image*)*
~ **graphics interface** Computergrafikschnittstelle *f*, grafische Geräteschnittstelle *f*
~ **graphics metafile** Computergrafik-Metadatei *f*
~ **graphics practitioner (professional)** Computergrafiker *m*
~ **graphics program** Computergrafikprogramm *n*, Grafikprogramm *n*
~ **graphics system** Computergrafiksystem *n*
~ **graphics technology** *s.* ~ graphics
~ **graphics worker** Computergrafiker *m*
~ **graphics workstation** Computergrafikarbeitsplatz *m*
~ **hard drive** Festplattenlaufwerk *n*
~ **icon** Icon *n*, Programmsymbol *n*, Platzhalter-Pixelbild *n*, Platzhalter *n*
~ **image** Computerbild *n*, computererzeugtes (computergeneriertes) Bild *n*, synthetisches Bild *n*
~ **image analysis** Computerbildanalyse *f*
~ **image display** *s.* ~ display
~ **image file** Computerbilddatei *f*
~ **image generation** Computerbilderzeugung *f*
~ **image generator** Computerbildgenerator *m*
~ **image page** Computerbildseite *f*
~ **image processing** Computerbildverarbeitung *f*; Computerbildbearbeitung *f*
~ **image processing system** *s.* ~ imaging system
~ **image synthesis** Computerbildsynthese *f*
~ **imaging** Computerbildverarbeitung *f*
~ **imaging software** Bildverarbeitungssoftware *f*, bildverarbeitende Software *f*; Bildbearbeitungssoftware *f*
~ **imaging system** Computerbildverarbeitungssystem *n*; Computerbildbearbeitungssystem *n*
~ **input device** Computereingabegerät *n*
~ **instruction** Maschinenbefehl *m*
~-**integrated manufacturing** rechnerintegrierte Fertigung
~ **interface** Computerschnittstelle *f*, Rechnerschnittstelle *f*
~ **keyboard** Computertastatur *f*
~ **language** Computersprache *f*
~ **layout** Computerlayout *n*
~ **lingo** Computer[fach]sprache *f*
~ **link system** Computeranschluss *m*
~ **memory chip** Computerspeicherchip *m*, Speicherchip *m*, Speicherbaustein *m*
~ **memory device** Computerspeicher *m*
~ **model** Computermodell *n (Gleichungssystem)*
~ **modeler** Computermodellierer *m*
~ **modeling** Computermodellierung *f*
~ **modem** Computermodem *n*
~-**monitor CRT (cathode-ray tube)** Computerbildröhre *f*
~ **monitor resolution** Computerauflösung *f*
~ **motherboard** Computerplatine *f*, Hauptplatine *f*, Mutterplatine *f*, Systemplatine *f*
~ **mouse** Computermaus *f*, [PC-]Maus *f (Eingabegerät)*
~ **network** Computernetz *n*
~ **output** Computerausgabe *f*
~ **output microfilm** Computerausgabe-Mikrofilm *m*, COM-Film *m*
~ **output microfilm recorder** Computerausgabe-Mikrofilmrecorder *m*
~ **paint program (software)** [Computer-]Malprogramm *n*, Pixelgrafikprogramm *n*
~ **parlance** Computer[fach]sprache *f*
~ **printer** Computerdrucker *m*

~ **printing** Computerdruck m
~ **processing** Computerverarbeitung f (z.B. von Bilddaten)
~ **processing power** Computerleistung f
~-**produced** s. computer-generated
~ **programming language** Programmiersprache f
~-**readable** computerlesbar, maschinenlesbar (z.B. Bilddaten)
~ **representation** Computerdarstellung f (z.B. eines Objektsystems)
~ **science** Informatik f
~ **screen** Computer[bild]schirm m, Rechnerbildschirm m
~ **screen image** Computerschirmbild n
~ **screen photography** Bildschirmfotografie f
~-**simulated image** computersimuliertes Bild n
~ **simulation** Computersimulation f
~ **software program** Computerprogramm n
~ **special effect** digitaler Spezialeffekt m, elektronischer Trick m, Computertrick m
~ **storage** 1. Computerspeicherung f; 2. Computerspeicher m
~-**synthesized picture** s. computer-generated image
~ **technology** Computertechnologie f
~-**to-plate [system]** digitale Druckvorstufe f; filmlose Druckformherstellung f (Direktübertragung von Computerdaten auf Digitaldruckplatten)
~-**to-press** Bebilderung f in der Druckmaschine
~ **typesetting** Computersatz m
~ **typography** Computertypografie f
~ **video** Computervideo n
~ **vision** maschinelle Bilderkennung f, maschinelles Sehen n, Computersehen n, Rechnersehen n
~ **visualization** Computervisualisierung f
computer's operating system Computer-Betriebssystem n
computerese Computer[fach]sprache f
computerization Computerisierung f
computerized editing system computergestütztes Schnittsystem n
~ **image** s. computer-generated image
~ **output** Computerausgabe f
~ **tomography** s. computed tomography
~ **typesetting system** Computersatzsystem n
~ **X-ray tomography** Röntgencomputertomografie f
computing power Rechenleistung f
~ **time** Rechenzeit f
concatenation Verkettung f, Konkatenation f
concave konkav
~ **grating** Konkavgitter n, Rowland-Gitter n
~ **holographic grating** holografisches Konkavgitter n

~ **lens** konkave (negative) Linse f, Konkavlinse f, Negativlinse f, Zerstreuungslinse f, Streulinse f
~ **mirror** Konkavspiegel m, Hohlspiegel m, Sammelspiegel m
~ **polygon** konkaves Polygon n
~ **reflection grating** s. ~ grating
concavity Konkavität f
concavo-concave bikonkav
~-**convex** konkavkonvex
~-**convex lens** Konkavkonvexlinse f, positiver (sammelnder) Meniskus m
concealment Restfehlerverdeckung f (elektronische Bildgebung)
concentric meniscus konzentrischer Meniskus m
concentricity Konzentrizität f
conceptual pattern recognition konzeptionelle Mustererkennung f
concertina fold Leporellofalz m, Zickzackfalz m
concrete class konkrete Klasse f
~ **pattern** konkretes Muster n
condensation Kondensation f
condensed unterschnitten, schmal[laufend] (Schriftauszeichnung)
condenser 1. Kondensorlinse f, Kondensor m, Beleuchtungslinse f; 2. Kondensator m
~ **aperture [diaphragm]**, ~ **diaphragm** Kondensorapertur f, Kondensorblende f, Beleuchtungsapertur f (Mikroskopie)
~ **front lens** Kondensor-Frontlinse f
~ **lens** Kondensorlinse f, Beleuchtungslinse f
~ **microphone** Kondensatormikrofon n
~-**type enlarger** Kondensorvergrößerer m
condensor lens array Kondensorlinsengruppe f
condition/to konditionieren (z.B. Druckpapier)
condition of achromatism Achromasiebedingung f
~ **of aplanatism** Aplanasiebedingung f (Optik)
conditional access bedingter Zugriff m
~ **access technology** Zugangskontrollsystem n (Fernsehtechnik)
~ **probability** bedingte Wahrscheinlichkeit f
conditioner Konditionierungsbad n
conduction band Leitungsband n
~-**band electron** Leitungsbandelektron n
~ **electron** Leitungselektron n
conductive brush Ladungsbürste f (Elektrofotografie)
conductivity Leitfähigkeit f
cone 1. Kegel m; 2. Zapfen m, Netzhautzapfen m, Netzhautzäpfchen n, Sehzapfen m
~ **angle** Kegelwinkel m, Raumwinkel m
~ **beam** Kegelstrahl m, kegelförmiges Strahlenbündel n

cone

~-beam collimator konvergierender Kollimator *m*
~-beam imaging geometry Kegelstrahlgeometrie *f*
~-beam tomography Kegelstrahltomografie *f*
~ density Zapfendichte *f*
~-mediated vision Zapfensehen *n*, fotopisches Sehen *n*, Helligkeitssehen *n*, Tagessehen *n*
~ monochromacy (monochromatism) Zapfenfarbenblindheit *f*, Zapfenmonochromasie *f*
~ of illumination Beleuchtungskegel *m*
~ of light Lichtkegel *m*
~ of rays Strahlenkegel *m*
~ photopigment Zapfenpigment *n*
~ photoreceptor, ~ receptor s. cone 2.
~ sensitivity Zapfenempfindlichkeit *f*
~ system Zapfenapparat *m*, Zapfensystem *n*
~ type Zapfentyp *m*
~ vision s. cone-mediated vision
conference television Konferenzfernsehen *n*; Videokonferenztechnik *f*
confidence Hinterbandkontrolle *f*
configuration Konfiguration *f*
confocal konfokal
~ imaging konfokale Abbildung *f*
~ laser scanning microscopy konfokale Laserabtastmikroskopie *f*
~ microscope Konfokalmikroskop *n*, konfokales Mikroskop *n*
~ microscope image konfokalmikroskopisches Bild *n*
~ microscopic konfokalmikroskopisch
~ microscopy Konfokalmikroskopie *f*, konfokale Mikroskopie *f*
~ optical system konfokales optisches System *n*
~ resonator konfokaler Resonator *m*
~ scanning light microscope s. ~ microscope
~ theta microscopy konfokale Theta-Mikroskopie *f*
~ tomograph Konfokaltomograf *m*
conform/to anlegen *(Filmschnitt)*
conformal map winkeltreue Karte *f*
~ projection winkeltreue Projektion *f*
conformality Winkeltreue *f (einer Kartenprojektion)*
conformed negative kombiniertes Negativ *n (Filmbearbeitung)*
~ work print angelegte Arbeitskopie *f*
conforming Synchronschnitt *m*, [synchrones] Anlegen *n*, Anlegearbeit *f (Filmbearbeitung)*
congenital color vision defect angeborene Farbsinnstörung *f*
congruence, congruency Kongruenz *f*
congruent kongruent
conic projection Kegelprojektion *f (Kartografie)*
~ refraction konische Refraktion *f*

~ section Kegelschnitt *m*
conical diffraction konische Beugung *f*
~ lens konische Linse *f*
~ scan technique Kegelabtastverfahren *n (Radar)*
~ surface Kegelfläche *f*
coniometer s. konimeter
conjugate/to konjugieren
conjugate konjugierte Größe *f (Optik)*
~ amplitude konjugierte Amplitude *f (Holografie)*
~ eye movement konjugierte Augenbewegung *f*
~ holographic image konjugiertes Hologramm *n*
~ image konjugiertes Bild *n (Optik)*
~ image point zugehöriger Bildpunkt *m*
~ plane konjugierte Ebene *f*
~ point konjugierter Punkt *m*
~ quadrature filter Quadraturspiegelfilter *n*
~ quadrature filter bank konjugiertes Quadraturfilter *n (Bildcodierung)*
~ ratio Konjugationsverhältnis *n (Optik)*
connected component labeling Gebietsmarkierung *f f*
~ contour geschlossene Kontur *f*
connectedness Zusammenhang *m*
~ constraint Zusammenhangsbedingung *f*
connecting cord Verbindungskabel *n*, Anschlusskabel *n*
~ line Verbindungslinie *f*
~ plug Verbindungsstecker *m*
connection Verbindung *f*; Verknüpfung *f*
connectionism Konnektionismus *m*
connectionist model (network) konnektionistisches Modell (System) *n*, neuronales Netz (System) *n*, Neuronennetz *n*
connectivity Konnektivität *f*
connector Verbindungsstecker *m*
~ adapter Adapter *m* für Verbindungskabel
conoscope Konoskop *n*
conoscopic konoskopisch
~ image konoskopisches Bild *n*
conscious perception bewusste Wahrnehmung *f*
consecutive image Folgebild *n*, Nachfolgerbild *n*
conservative algorithm konservativer Algorithmus *m*
consistent interpolation konsistente Interpolation *f*
console Konsole *f (z.B. eines Elektronenmikroskops)*
constancy Konstanz *f*
~ of illumination Beleuchtungskonstanz *f*
~ testing Konstanzprüfung *f (Filmverarbeitung)*
constant angular velocity konstante Winkelgeschwindigkeit *f*
~ bit rate konstante Bitrate *f*
~-deviation prism doppelbrechendes (doppelreflektierendes) Prisma *n*

~ **error** systematischer Fehler *m*
~ **gray value** konstanter Grauwert *m*
~ **linear velocity** konstante Laufgeschwindigkeit (Lineargeschwindigkeit) *f*, linearkonstante Geschwindigkeit *f*
~ **neighborhood** konstante Nachbarschaft *f*
~ **shading** konstante Schattierung *f*
constellation diagram Zustandsdiagramm *n*
constrained feed Leitungsspeisung *f* *(Radar)*
constraint length Abhängigkeitslänge *f*, Beeinflussungslänge *f* *(Videosignalverarbeitung)*
constringence Abbe-Zahl *f* *(Optik)*
construction length Baulänge *f* *(Objektiv)*
constructive interference konstruktive Interferenz *f*
~ **solid geometry** konstruktive Körpergeometrie (Festkörpergeometrie) *f*
~ **solid geometry tree** CSG-Baum *m* *(Computergrafik)*
consumer camcorder Amateurcamcorder *m*
~ **camera** Amateurkamera *f*
~ **device** Heimgerät *n*
~ **electronics** Heimelektronik *f*, Unterhaltungselektronik *f*, Konsumelektronik *f*
~ **electronics industry** Heimelektronikindustrie *f*
~ **film** handelsüblicher Film *m*
~-**grade digital camera** Amateur-Digitalkamera *f*
~-**grade video player** Heimvideogerät *n*
~-**grade video recorder** Amateur-Videorecorder *m*, Heim[video]recorder *m*, Heimkassettenrecorder *m*
~ **image** Kundenfoto *n*
~ **imaging** Heimbildtechnik *f*
~ **interface** Nutzer-Netz-Schnittstelle *f*
~-**level video camera** Amateur-Videokamera *f*
~ **photography** Amateurfotografie *f*
~ **television set** Heimfernsehgerät *n*, Heimfernseher *m*, Fernseh-Heimempfänger *m*
~ **VCR** *s*. consumer-grade video recorder
~ **video** Heimvideo *n*
~ **video camcorder** Amateurcamcorder *m*
~ **video industry** Heimvideoindustrie *f*
~ **video recording technology** Heimvideotechnik *f*
~ **videotape** Amateurvideoband *n*
contact copy Kontaktkopie *f*
~ **exposure** Kontaktbelichtung *f*
~ **image sensor** Kontaktbildsensor *m*
~ **lens** Kontaktlinse *f*
~ **microphone** Kontaktmikrofon *n*

~ **microradiography** Kontaktmikroradiografie *f*, Mikroradiografie *f*
~ **microscopy** Kontaktmikroskopie *f*
~ **paper** Kontaktpapier *n*
~ **platemaker** Vakuumkopierrahmen *m*
~-**print/to** kontaktkopieren
~ **print** Kontaktkopie *f*; Kontaktabzug *m*
~ **printer** Kontaktkopierer *m*, Kontaktkopiergerät *n*, Kontaktbelichtungsgerät *n*
~ **printing** Kontaktkopieren *n*, Kontaktkopierung *f*; Kontaktdruck *m*
~ **printing device** *s*. ~ printer
~ **printing frame** Kontaktkopierrahmen *m*
~ **printing paper** Kontakt[kopier]papier *n*
~ **printing process** Kontaktkopierverfahren *n*
~ **process** Kontaktverfahren *n*
~ **profilometer** Kontaktprofilometer *n*
~ **proof** Probeabzug *m*
~ **screen** Kontaktraster *m(n)*
~ **sheet** Kontaktbogen *m*
~ **speed paper** *s*. ~ printing paper
~ **X-ray microscopy** Kontakt-Röntgenmikroskopie *f*
contacting *s*. contact printing
contained shadow Eigenschatten *m*
content-addressable memory inhaltadressierter (assoziativer) Speicher *m*, Assoziativspeicher *m*, Katalogspeicher *m*
~-**based arithmetic encoding** inhaltsbasierte arithmetische Codierung *f*
~-**based image retrieval** inhaltsbasierte Bildsuche *f*
~-**based scalability** inhaltsbasierte Skalierbarkeit *f*
~-**based video coding** inhaltsbasierte Videocodierung *f*
~ **insertion** Inhaltseinsetzung *f* *(interaktives Fernsehen)*
~ **provider** Programmanbieter *m*, Inhalteanbieter *m* *(elektronische Medien)*
~ **scrambling system** *ein Kopierschutz-Datenverschlüsselungssystem im DVD-Videobereich*
~ **server** *s*. ~ provider
context Kontext *m*
~-**based binary arithmetic coding** kontextbasierte binäre arithmetische Codierung *f*
~-**based classification** kontextabhängige Klassifikation *f*
~-**based image compression** kontextbasierte Bildkompression *f*
~-**based model** kontextbasiertes Modell *n*
~-**dependent modeling** kontextabhängige Modellierung *f*
~-**dependent operator** kontextabhängiger Operator *m*
~-**free grammar** kontextfreie Grammatik *f*

context

~-independent classification kontextunabhängige Klassifikation *f*
~ menu Kontextmenü *n*
contextual analysis Kontextanalyse *f* *(Zeichenerkennung)*
~ classification kontextabhängige Klassifikation *f*
~ information Kontextinformation *f*
~ segmentation kontextabhängige Segmentierung *f*
contiguous contour geschlossene Kontur *f*
contingency matrix Kontingenzmatrix *f* *(Klassifikation)*
~ table Kontingenztafel *f*
contingent color aftereffect McCollough-Effekt *m*
continual pilot ständiger Pilot *m* *(Fernsehsignal)*
continuity Kontinuität *f*, Stetigkeit *f*
~ constraint Kontinuitätsbedingung *f*
~ equation Kontinuitätsgleichung *f*
~ girl Skriptgirl *n* *(Filmarbeit)*
~ report Drehtagebuch *n*
~ still Werkaufnahme *f*, Werkbild *n*, Werkfoto *n* *(Filmarbeit)*
continuous amplitude kontinuierliche Amplitude *f*
~ autofocus kontinuierlicher Autofokus *m*
~ bit stream kontinuierlicher Bitstrom *m*
~-burning lamp Dauerlichtlampe *f*
~-burning light Dauerlicht *n*
~-burning light source Dauerlichtquelle *f*
~-contact printer Durchlauf-Kontaktkopiermaschine *f*, Durchlauf[kopier]maschine *f*
~ convolution kontinuierliche Faltung *f*
~ cosine transform kontinuierliche Kosinustransformation *f*
~ curve kontinuierliche Kurve *f*
~ dryer Durchlauftrockenmaschine *f*, Durchlauftrockner *m*
~ form Endlosvordruck *m*
~-form paper Endlospapier *n*
~ Fourier transform kontinuierliche (allgemeine) Fourier-Transformation *f*
~ frequency spectrum kontinuierliches Frequenzspektrum *n*
~-frequency spectrum frequenzkontinuierliches Spektrum *n*
~ image 1. Analogbild *n*, analoges (kontinuierliches) Bild *n*; 2. *s.* continuous-tone image
~ impulse function kontinuierliche Impulsfunktion *f*
~ jet kontinuierlicher Strahl *m* *(Tintenstrahldruck)*
~ loop Endlosschleife *f*; Bandschleife *f*, Endlosband *n*
~ loop projector Endlosprojektor *m*, Schleifenprojektor *m*
~ machine Durchlaufentwicklungsmaschine *f*
~ machine processing maschinelle Entwicklung *f*, Maschinenentwicklung *f*,

~ medium kontinuierliches Medium *n*
~-motion projector Projektor *m* mit kontinuierlichem Filmlauf
~ paper roll Papierbahn *f*, Bahn *f*, Rollenpapier *n* *(Druck)*
~ presence geteilter Bildschirm *m* *(Bildtelefonie)*
~ printing Durchlaufkopieren *n*
~ processing Durchlaufverarbeitung *f* *(von Fotomaterial)*
~ processor Durchlauf[kopier]maschine *f*, Durchlauf-Kontaktkopiermaschine *f*
~ radiator kontinuierlicher Strahler *m*, Kontinuumstrahler *m*, Dauerstrahler *m*
~ recording Endlosaufnahme *f*
~ relaxation kontinuierliche Relaxation *f*
~ repetitive projection Endlosprojektion *f*
~ shooting mode Serienbildfunktion *f*, Serienbildmodus *m*, Serienbildschaltung *f*, Reihenbildschaltung *f* *(Kamerafunktion)*
~ signal kontinuierliches Signal *n*
~ space kontinuierlicher Raum *m*
~-space ortskontinuierlich
~-space Fourier transform ortskontinuierliche Fourier-Transformation *f*
~-space image ortskontinuierliches Bild *n*
~-space signal ortskontinuierliches Signal *n*
~ spectrum kontinuierliches Spektrum *n*
~-spectrum light source Lichtquelle *f* mit kontinuierlichem Spektrum
~-strand (continuous-strip) processor Durchlaufentwicklungsmaschine *f*
~ text Fließtext *m*
~-time zeitkontinuierlich
~-time convolution zeitkontinuierliche Faltung *f*
~-time filter zeitkontinuierliches (analoges) Filter *n*, Analogfilter *n*
~-time Fourier transform zeitkontinuierliche Fourier-Transformation *f*
~-time signal Analogsignal *n*, analoges Signal *n*, zeitkontinuierliches Signal *n*
~ tone [echter] Halbton *m*
~-tone black-and-white copy Halbton-Schwarzweißvorlage *f* *(Druck)*
~-tone color print Halbton-Farbkopie *f*
~-tone copy Halbtonvorlage *f*
~-tone copy film Halbtonfilm *m*
~-tone development Halbtonentwicklung *f*
~-tone effect Halbtoneffekt *m*
~-tone image Halbtonbild *n*, Graustufenbild *n*
~-tone image coding Halbtonbildcodierung *f*
~-tone image compression Halbtonbildkompression *f*
~-tone negative Halbtonnegativ *n*
~-tone original Halbtonoriginal *n*
~-tone photographic film Halbtonfilm *m*

~-tone photographic image fotografisches Halbtonbild n
~-tone photography Halbtonfotografie f
~-tone positive Halbtonpositiv n
~-tone printer Halbtonkopierer m; Halbtondrucker m
~-tone printing Halbtondruck m
~-tone process Halbtonverfahren n (Druck)
~-tone process film Repro-Halbtonfilm m
~-tone representation Halbtondarstellung f
~-tone reproduction Halbtonreproduktion f, Halbtonwiedergabe f
~-tone slide Halbtondia[positiv] n
~-tone slide film Halbton-Diafilm m
~-tone still image Halbtonfestbild n
~-tone still image compression Halbtonfestbildkompression f
~-tone type developer Halbtonentwickler m
~-tone xerography Halbtonxerografie f
~-value signal wertkontinuierliches Signal n
~ video signal kontinuierliches Videosignal n
~ wave kontinuierliche Welle f
~-wave Doppler [ultrasound] CW-Doppler m (Sonografie)
~-wave irradiation kontinuierliche Strahlung f
~-wave laser Dauerstrichlaser m, CW-Laser m, kontinuierlicher Laser m
~-wave power Dauerstrichleistung f
~-wave radar Dauerstrichradar n, CW-Radar n
~ wavelet transform kontinuierliche Wavelet-Transformation f
~-zoom optical system Schiebezoom[objektiv] n
contone s. continuous tone
contour/to konturieren
contour Kontur f, Umriss m
~ analysis Konturanalyse f
~ approximation Konturapproximation f
~-based tracking s. contour tracing
~ classifier Konturklassifikator m
~ code Konturcode m
~-coded image konturcodiertes Bild n
~ coding algorithm Konturcodierungsalgorithmus m
~ correlation Konturkorrelation f
~ curvature Konturkrümmung f
~ curve Konturkurve f
~ decomposition Kontursegmentierung f
~ description Konturbeschreibung f
~ detection Umrisserkennung f
~ discontinuity Konturdiskontinuität f, Konturunterbrechung f
~ drawing Konturzeichnung f
~ extraction Konturextraktion f
~ feature Konturmerkmal n
~ film Konturenfilm m
~ fitting Konturanpassung f

~ generator Konturgenerator m
~ image Konturbild n
~ information Konturinformation f
~ length Konturlänge f
~ line Konturlinie f, Umrisslinie f
~-line image Konturbild n
~ line segment Konturliniensegment n
~ map Höhenlinienkarte f
~ noise Konturrauschen n
~ normal Konturnormale f
~ perception Konturwahrnehmung f
~ pixel Konturpixel n
~ plot Konturgrafik f
~ point Konturpunkt m, Randpunkt m
~ point detection Konturpunktauffindung f
~ projector Profilprojektor m
~ region Konturbereich m
~ representation Konturdarstellung f
~ segment Kontursegment n, Konturstück n
~ segmentation Kontursegmentierung f
~ sharpness Rand[bild]schärfe f
~ smoothing Konturglättung f
~ surface Isofläche f (Computergrafik)
~ tracing Konturverfolgung f, Konturfolgeverfahren n
contouring 1. Konturierung f; 2. Streifenartefakt n
contraction mapping theorem Banachscher Fixpunktsatz m, Fixpunktsatz m von Banach (fraktale Bildkompression)
contraharmonic mean filter kontraharmonisches Mittelwertfilter n
contrast/to kontrastieren
contrast Kontrast m
~ adaptation Kontrastanpassung f
~ adjustment Kontrasteinstellung f
~ agent Kontrastmittel n; Röntgenkontrastmittel n (Radiografie)
~ amplification s. ~ enhancement
~-amplified copy kontrastverstärkte Kopie f (Radiografie)
~ amplifier Kontrastverstärker m
~ angiography Kontrastangiografie f
~ booster Kontrast-Booster m (Teleskopfilter)
~ change Kontrast[ver]änderung f
~ compensation Kontrastausgleich m
~ constancy Kontrastkonstanz f
~ control Kontraststeuerung f, Kontrastregelung f, Kontrasteinstellung f
~ correction Kontrastkorrektur f
~ crispening Kontrastanhebung f, Kontrastanreicherung f
~ decomposition Kontrastzerlegung f
~ degradation Kontrastabnahme f, Kontrastabschwächung f
~-detail phantom Kontrast-Detail-Diagramm n (Bildgütebewertung)
~ detection Kontrasterkennung f
~ detection threshold Kontrastschwelle f
~ developer Kontrastentwickler m

contrast

~ **difference** Kontrastunterschied *m*
~ **display** Kontrastdarstellung *f*
~ **distortion** Kontrastverzerrung *f*
~ **distribution** Kontrastverteilung *f*
~ **editing** Kontrastbearbeitung *f*
~ **effect** Kontrastwirkung *f*
~-**enhanced MRA** kontrastverstärkte Magnetresonanzangiografie *f*
~ **enhancement** Kontrastverstärkung *f*, Kontrasterhöhung *f*, Kontraststeigerung *f*, Kontrastversteilerung *f*, Kontrastverschärfung *f*
~ **expansion** Kontrastdehnung *f*, Kontrastspreizung *f*
~ **feature** Kontrastmerkmal *m*
~ **fidelity** Kontrasttreue *f*
~ **filter** Kontrastfilter *n*
~ **grade** Papiergradation *f*
~ **gradient** Kontrastgradient *m*
~ **image** Kontrastbild *n*
~ **improvement** Kontrastverbesserung *f*
~ **increase** *s.* ~ enhancement
~ **index** Kontrastindex *m*
~-**index meter** Kontrastindexmeter *n*
~ **index value** Kontrastindex *m*, CI-Wert *m*
~ **intensification** *s.* ~ enhancement
~ **level** Kontraststufe *f*, Kontrastniveau *n*
~ **manipulation** Kontrastbeeinflussung *f*, Kontrastmanipulation *f*
~ **mask** Kontrastmaske *f*
~ **masking** Kontrastmaskierung *f*
~ **match[ing]** Kontrastangleich *m*, Kontrastangleichung *f*
~ **material** *s.* ~ agent
~ **measurement** Kontrastmessung *f*
~ **mechanism** Kontrastmechanismus *m*
~ **medium [fluid]** *s.* ~ agent
~ **modification** Kontrastmodifikation *f*
~ **modulation** Kontrastmodulation *f*
~ **normalization** Kontrastnormierung *f*
~ **of reproduction** Wiedergabekontrast *m*
~ **optimization** Kontrastoptimierung *f*
~ **perception** Kontrastwahrnehmung *f*
~ **photometer** Kontrastfotometer *n*
~ **radiogram** Röntgenkontrastbild *n*
~ **range** Kontrastbereich *m*; Kontrastumfang *m*, Objektumfang *m*, Objektdynamik *f*; Leuchtdichteumfang *m*
~ **ratio** Kontrastverhältnis *n*
~ **reduction** Kontrast[ver]minderung *f*, Kontrastreduzierung *f*, Kontrastverringerung *f*
~ **rendering (rendition),** ~ **reproduction** Kontrastwiedergabe *f*
~ **resolution** Kontrastauflösung *f*
~ **reversal** Kontrastumkehr *f*
~ **saturation** Kontrastsättigung *f*
~ **scaling** Kontrastskalierung *f*
~ **sensitivity** Kontrastempfindlichkeit *f (z.B. des Auges)*
~ **sensitivity function** *s.* ~ transfer function
~ **setting** Kontrasteinstellung *f*

~ **sonography** Kontrastsonografie *f*
~ **step** Kontraststufe *f*
~ **stretch[ing]** Kontrastdehnung *f*, Kontrastspreizung *f*
~ **threshold** Kontrastschwelle *f*
~ **transfer** Kontrastübertragung *f*
~ **transfer function** Kontrastübertragungsfunktion *f*, Kontrasttransferfunktion *f*, Modulationstransferfunktion *f*
~ **transferability** Kontrastübertragbarkeit *f*
~-**uptake imaging** Kontrastmitteldarstellung *f (Radiografie)*
~ **value** Kontrastwert *m*
~ **variation** Kontrastveränderung *f*
contrasting color Kontrastfarbe *f*
contrasty image kontrastreiches Bild *n*
contre-jour Gegenlichtaufnahme *f*
~-**jour lighting** Hinterlicht *n*
~-**jour photograph** Gegenlichtaufnahme *f*
~-**jour photography** Gegenlichtfotografie *f*
contributing device Zuspieler *m*, Zuspielgerät *n*, Zuspielmaschine *f*, Schnittzuspieler *m (Videobearbeitung)*
contribution Einspielung *f*; Zuspielung *f*; Programmzuspielung *f*
contrivance Gerät *n*
control Bedien[ungs]element *n*
~ **bit** Steuerungsbit *n*
~ **bus** Steuerbus *m*
~ **character** Steuerzeichen *n (z.B. eines alphanumerischen Codes)*
~ **circuit voltage** Steuerspannung *f*
~ **code** Steuercode *m*
~ **computer** Steuerrechner *m*
~ **electrode** Steuerelektrode *f*
~ **electronics** Steuer[ungs]elektronik *f*; Ansteuerelektronik *f*, Treiberelektronik *f*
~ **grid** Steuergitter *n (Katodenstrahlröhre)*
~ **grid interpolation** interpolative Bewegungsbeschreibung *f (Computergrafik)*
~ **grid voltage** Steuerspannung *f*
~ **image** Kontrollbild *n*
~ **interface** Steuerschnittstelle *f*
~ **key** Steuertaste *f*
~ **line** Meldeleitung *f (Fernsehübertragung)*
~ **module** Steuermodul *n*; Prozessormodul *n*
~ **network** Passpunktnetz *n (Fotogrammetrie)*
~ **panel** Bedienfeld *n*
~ **point** Passpunkt *m*, Passmarke *f*, Passelement *n (Fotogrammetrie)*; Steuerpunkt *m*, Kontrollpunkt *m (Computergrafik)*
~ **polygon** Kontrollpolygon *n (Computergrafik)*
~ **program** Steuerprogramm *n*
~ **pulse** Steuerimpuls *m*
~ **room** Regieraum *m*, Kontrollraum *m*
~ **signal** Steuersignal *n*

~ **strip** Kontrollstreifen *m* *(Filmentwicklung)*
~ **track** Steuerspur f, Kontrollspur *f* *(Videoband)*
~ **track editing** CTL-Schnitt *m*
~ **track pulse (signal)** Steuerspursignal *n*, CTL-Impuls *m (Videoband)*; Bildsynchronisierimpuls *m*, Bildsynchronisiersignal *n*
~ **vertex** Steuerpunkt *m*, Kontrollpunkt *m* *(Computergrafik)*
controlled photomosaic kontrolliertes Mosaik *n (Fotogrammetrie)*
controller Steuergerät *n*
conventional dot konventioneller (quadratischer) Rasterpunkt *m*
~ **film** Normalfilm *m*
~ **gravure** konventioneller (tiefenvariabler) Tiefdruck *m*
~ **microscope** Lichtmikroskop *n*, optisches Mikroskop *n*
~ **microscopy** konventionelle Mikroskopie *f*
~ **photography** konventionelle (herkömmliche) Fotografie *f*
~ **radiography** konventionelles Röntgen *n*
~ **silver halide still camera** Fotokamera f, Fotoapparat *m*
~ **X-ray image** konventionelles Röntgenbild *n*
~ **X-ray imaging** konventionelles Röntgen *n*
converge/to konvergieren
convergence Konvergenz *f*
~ **angle** Konvergenzwinkel *m*
~ **error** Konvergenzfehler *m*
~ **of parallels** *s*. central perspective
~ **pattern** Gittertestbild *n*, Gittertesttafel *f*
convergency *s.* convergence
convergent konvergent *(s.a. unter converging)*
~ **lens** *s*. convex lens
~ **mirror** Sammelspiegel *m*, Hohlspiegel *m*, Konkavspiegel *m*
converging bundle [of rays] konvergentes Bündel *n*
~ **collimator** konvergierender Kollimator *m*
~ **lens** *s*. convex lens
~ **lines** konvergierende Linien *fpl*
~ **medium** Übertragungsmedium *n*
~ **verticals** stürzende Linien *fpl*
conversion Konversion *f*, Konvertierung *f*, Umkehrung *f*
~ **filter** Konversionsfilter *n*
~ **gain** Konversionsgewinn *m* *(Fotodetektor)*
~ **matrix** Konversionsmatrix *f*
convert/to konvertieren, umwandeln
convert-to-binary signal Bild-Austast-Farb-Synchron[isier]-Signal *n*
converter Konverter *m*, Umsetzer *m*
~ **lens** Konverter *m (Optik)*
convertible lens (objective) Satzobjektiv *n*

convertor *s.* converter
convex konvex
~ **body** konvexer Körper *m*
~ **hull** konvexe Hülle *f (geometrische Mathematik)*
~ **hull property** Konvexe-Hülle-Eigenschaft *f*
~ **lens** Konvexlinse f, Sammellinse f, Positivlinse *f*
~ **mirror** Konvexspiegel *m*, Wölbspiegel *m*, Zerstreuungsspiegel *m*
~ **polygon** konvexes Polygon *n*
~ **polyhedron** konvexes Polyeder *n*
convexity Konvexität *f*
convexo-concave konvexkonkav
~**-concave lens** negativer Meniskus *m*
~**-convex** bikonvex
convolution Faltung *f* *(Signalverarbeitungsoperation)*
~ **algorithm** Faltungsalgorithmus *m*
~ **equation** Faltungsgleichung *f*
~ **filter** *s.* ~ kernel
~ **filtering** Faltung *f*
~ **function** Faltungsfunktion *f*
~ **integral** Faltungsintegral *n*
~ **kernel (mask)** Faltungskern *m*, Faltungsfilter *n*, Faltungsmaske *f*, Umgebungsfilter *n*
~ **matrix** Faltungsmatrix *f*
~ **operation** Faltungsoperation f, Faltungsprozess *m*
~ **product** Faltungsprodukt *n*
~ **result** Faltungsergebnis *n*
~ **routine** Faltungsroutine *f*
~ **sum** Faltungssumme *f*
~ **summation** Faltungssummierung *f*
~ **surface** Faltungsfläche *f*
~ **technique** Faltungstechnik *f*
~ **theorem** Faltungstheorem *n*, Faltungssatz *m (Signalanalyse)*
convolutional code Faltungscode *m*, Konvolutionscode *m*
~ **coding** Faltungscodierung *f*
~ **decoder** Faltungsdecodierer *m*
~ **encoder** Faltungscodierer *m*
~ **operator** Faltungsoperator *m*, Maskenoperator *m (s.a. ~ kernel)*
convolve/to falten *(z.B. Signale)*
convolving function Faltungsfunktion *f*
Cook and Torrance reflection (shading) model Cook-Torrance-Schattierungsmodell *n (Computergrafik)*
cookaloris *s.* cookie
Cooke lens (objective) Cooke-Objektiv *n*
~ **triplet [lens]** Cookesches (Taylorsches) Triplett *n*
cookie Schattenwerfer *m (Beleuchtungszubehör)*
cooking Reifung *f (Emulsionsherstellung)*
cool color kalte Farbe *f*
~**-down filter** Blaufilter *n*
cooled CCD camera gekühlte CCD-Kamera *f*

Coolidge tube Coolidge-Röhre f (Röntgenröhre)
coordinate Koordinate f
~ **axes** Koordinatenachsen fpl
~ **file** Koordinatendatei f
~ **geometry** analytische Geometrie f
~ **graphics** Liniengrafik f, Strichgrafik f
~ **grid** Koordinatengitter n
~ **measuring machine** Koordinatenmessgerät n
~ **measuring microscope** Koordinatenmessmikroskop n
~ **origin** Koordinatenursprung m
~ **pair** Koordinatenpaar n
~ **plane** Koordinatenebene f
~ **representation** Koordinatendarstellung f
~ **space** Koordinatenraum m
~ **system** Koordinatensystem n
~ **table** Koordinatenmesstisch m
~ **transform[ation]** Koordinatentransformation f (Computergrafik)
coordinatograph Koordinatograf m, Koordinator m (Fotogrammetrie)
cophasal phasengleich
copier Kopierer m, Kopiergerät n, Kopierapparat m
~ **film** Kopierfolie f
coplanar koplanar
copolarized light kopolarisiertes Licht n
copper chloride Kupferchlorid n (Bleichmittel)
~ **intensifier** Kupferverstärker m
~ **printing plate** Kupferdruckplatte f
~ **red toner** Kupfer[rot]toner m
~ **red toning** Kupfer[rot]tonung f
~ **vapor laser** Kupferdampflaser m
copperplate gravure Kupfer[tief]druck m
~ **intaglio engraving** gestochene Kupferplatte f
coprocessor Koprozessor m
copy/to kopieren; vervielfältigen
copy 1. Kopie f; Abdruck m; 2. Vorlage f; Repro[duktions]vorlage f; Satzvorlage f; Druckvorlage f
~ **camera** Repro[duktions]kamera f
~ **drum** Vorlagentrommel f
~ **element** Vorlagenelement n
~ **function** Kopierfunktion f (z.B. von Faxgeräten)
~ **image** Bildvorlage f
~ **lens** Reproduktionsobjektiv n
~ **machine** Kopierer m, Kopiergerät n, Kopierapparat m
~ **material** Vorlagenmaterial n
~ **negative** Negativkopie f
~ **paper** Kopiererpapier n
~ **photograph** 1. Fotokopie f, fotografische Kopie f; 2. Reproaufnahme f
~ **photography** Repro[duktions]fotografie f
~ **plane** Vorlagenebene f
~ **preparation** Vorlagenherstellung f
~ **prevention** Kopierschutz m
~ **prohibition bit** Kopierschutzbit n

~ **-protected** kopiergeschützt
~ **protection** Kopierschutz m
~ **protection mechanism** Kopierschutzvorrichtung f
~ **radiograph** Röntgenkopie f
~ **stand** Reprostativ n, Reprogestell n, Reproständer m
~ **-stand lighting** Reprostativbeleuchtung f
~ **tape** Bandkopie f
~ **tray** Kopieablage f, Papierablage f (Kopierer)
~ **work** Kopierarbeit f; Reproarbeit f
copyboard, copyholder Vorlagenfläche f (Reprofotografie); Vorlagenplatte f, Vorlagenhalter m; Vorlagenträger m
copying camera Repro[duktions]kamera f
~ **lens** Kopierobjektiv n
~ **machine** Kopiermaschine f
~ **material** Kopiermaterial n
~ **medium** Kopiermedium n
~ **paper** Kopierpapier n
~ **process** Kopierverfahren n
~ **technique** Kopiertechnik f
copyright Copyright n, Urheberrecht n; Vervielfältigungsrecht n
cordless mouse kabellose (schnurlose) Maus f
core Spulenkern m, Wickelkern m, Aufwickelkern m, Rollenkern m, Bobby m
~ **matrix** Speichermatrix f
~ **memory** Arbeitsspeicher m, Hauptspeicher m
cornea Hornhaut f, Augenhornhaut f, Cornea f, Kornea f
corneal curvature Hornhautkrümmung f
~ **microscope** Hornhautmikroskop n
corner Ecke f
~ **cube [prism]** Tripelprisma n, Tripelspiegel m, Retroreflektor m
~ **detection** Eckenerkennung f
~ **detector** Eckendetektor m
~ **frequency** Eckfrequenz f (eines aktiven Filters)
~ **mark** Beschnittmarke f, Beschnittzeichen n (Druckbogen)
~ **pixel** Eckpixel n
~ **point** Eckpunkt m
~ **-preserving diffusion** eckenerhaltende Diffusion f
~ **reflector** s. ~ cube [prism]
Cornu double prism Cornu-Doppelprisma n
corona charging Korona-Aufladung f
~ **charging apparatus** Aufladungsgerät n (Elektrofotografie)
~ **discharge** Koronaentladung f
~ **discharge photography** Kirlian-Fotografie f
~ **wire** Koronadraht m
coronagraph s. coronograph
coronary angiography Koronarangiografie f
~ **angioscopy** Koronarangioskopie f

~ **arteriography** Koronararteriografie f
coronograph Koronograf m [nach Lyot] (Spezialfernrohr)
coronographic camera koronografische Kamera f
corotron Korotron n (Elektrofotografie)
corpuscular korpuskular
~ **radiation** Korpuskularstrahlung f, Teilchenstrahlung f, Partikelstrahlung f
~ **theory [of light]** Korpuskulartheorie (Teilchentheorie) f des Lichts, Emissionstheorie f des Lichts
correct/to korrigieren (z.B. Linsenfehler)
correct-color film orthochromatischer Film m, Orthofilm m
~ **exposure** richtige Belichtung f
~-**reading image** seitenrichtiges (seitenkorrektes) Bild n
~ **top to bottom** höhenrichtig (Bild)
correctable korrigierbar
corrected lens korrigiertes Objektiv n
~ **print** farbkorrigierte Kopie f (Film)
~ **vision** Normalsichtigkeit f, Emmetropie f
correcting filter s. correction filter
correction Korrektur f, Korrektion f
~ **algorithm** Korrekturalgorithmus m
~ **filter** Korrekturfilter n, Korrektionsfilter n
~ **function** Korrekturfunktion f
~ **image** Korrekturbild n
~ **lens** Korrektionslinse f, Korrekturlinse f
~ **level** Korrekturstufe f (z.B. eines Objektivs)
~ **map** Korrekturmatrix f (Emissionstomografie)
~ **mark** Korrekturzeichen n
~ **matrix** Korrekturmatrix f
~ **of pincushion distortion** Kissenentzerrung f
~ **optics** Korrektionsoptik f
corrective filtering (filtration) Korrekturfilterung f
~ **lens** Korrektionslinse f, Korrekturlinse f
~ **training** korrektives Training n
corrector plate [Schmidtsche] Korrektionsplatte f
correlated color temperature korrelierte (ähnlichste) Farbtemperatur f
~ **jitter** korrelierter Jitter m (Signalstörung)
~ **noise** korreliertes Rauschen n
correlation Korrelation f
~ **coefficient** Korrelationskoeffizient m
~ **filtering** Korrelationsfilterung f (Schablonenabgleich)
~ **function** Korrelationsfunktion f
~ **matrix** Korrelationsmatrix f
~ **measure** Korrelationsmaß n
~ **spectroscopy** Korrelationsspektroskopie f
~ **theorem** Korrelationstheorem n
~ **time** Korrelationszeit f
correlogram Korrelogramm n
correspondence analysis Korrespondenzanalyse f
~ **matrix** Korrespondenzmatrix f

~ **problem** Korrespondenzproblem n (des Stereosehens)
corrigendum Erratum n, Druckfehler m
corrugated bellows Balgen m, Faltbalgen m, Faltenbalg m
~ **box** Wellpappschachtel f
corrupted signal verfälschtes Signal n
cortical module Sehrindenmodul n
cosine Kosinus m; Kosinusfunktion f, Kosinusschwingung f (Signalverarbeitung)
~-**corrected diffuser** Plandiffusor m (Beleuchtungsstärkemesser)
~ **filter** s. finite impulse response filter
~ **law [of illumination]** [Lambertsches] Kosinusgesetz n
~-**to-the-fourth law** Kosinus-hoch-vier-Gesetz n (Optik)
~ **transform** 1. Kosinustransformation f (Bildcodierung); 2. Kosinustransformierte f
~ **wave** Kosinuswelle f
~ **wave grating** Kosinusgitter n
cosinusoidal grating Kosinusgitter n
cosmic background radiation kosmische Hintergrundstrahlung f, Drei-Kelvin-Strahlung f
~ **noise** kosmisches Rauschen n
~ **radiation (rays)** [kosmische] Höhenstrahlung f, kosmische Stahlung f, Ultrastrahlung f
cost function Kostenfunktion f (Computergrafik)
coudé focus Coudé-Fokus m (Teleskop)
~ **optical system** Coudé-System n (Spiegelteleskop)
Coulomb force microscope elektrostatisches Kraftmikroskop n
~ **scattering** Coulomb-Streuung f (von Ladungsteilchen)
countdown cueing leader, ~ head leader Vorlaufband n, Normstartband n, Startband n; Filmstartband n (Vorführkopie)
counter Punze f (Buchstabenbild)
counterbalance Gegengewicht n (z.B. am Kamerastativ)
counterclockwise sense Gegenuhrzeigersinn m
counterfeit/to fälschen
counterion Gegenion n
countermatte Gegenmaske f, Gegenkasch m, Hintergrundmaske f, Hintergrundmaskenfilm m
counterrotating prisms (wedges) Drehkeilpaar n
counting mechanism Zählwerk n
country code Ländercode m (Digitalvideoproduktion)
couple in[to]/to einkoppeln (Faseroptik)
~ **out/to** auskoppeln (Faseroptik)
coupled range finder [objektiv]gekoppelter Entfernungsmesser m, Messsucher m

coupler

coupler [compound] Kuppler *m*,
Farb[stoff]kuppler *m (Farbfotografie)*
~ **molecule** Kupplermolekül *n*
coupling of light Lichteinkopplung *f*
course microscope Kursmikroskop *n*
~ **over ground** Kurs *m* über Grund *(GPS-Navigation)*
covalent bond[ing] kovalente Bindung *f* (z.B. von Silberhalogeniden)
covariance function Kovarianzfunktion *f*
~ **matrix** Kovarianzmatrix *f*
cover/to verdecken
cover glass Deckglas *n*, Deckgläschen *n (Mikroskopie)*
~ **glass thickness** Deckglasdicke *f*
~ **illustration** Titelillustration *f*
~ **image** Titelbild *n*
~ **photo[graph]** Titelfoto *n*, Umschlagfoto *n*
~ **set** Innendekoration *f*
~ **sheet** Deckblatt *n*
~ **shot** Reserveaufnahme *f (Filmarbeit)*
coverage 1. Farbdeckung *f*; 2. Reichweite *f (Radar)*; 3. Einstellungswiederholungen *fpl (Filmarbeit)*; 4. Berichterstattung *f*
coverslip *s.* cover glass
covert camera verdeckte (versteckte) Kamera *f*
coving Hohlkehle *f*, Rundkehle *f (Studioausrüstung)*
CP *s.* copy-protected
CPU *s.* central processing unit
crab dolly fahrbare Kameraplattform *f*, Dolly *m*
crane Kran *m*, Kamerakran *m*
~ **operator** Kamerakranführer *m*
~ **shot** Kranaufnahme *f*
crank/to drehen *(Filmarbeit)*
crawl Bildwandern *n (Bildstörung)*
crawling title Laufschrift *f*, Kriechschrift *f*, Rolltitel *m*
CRC *s.* cyclic redundancy check
crease/to rillen *(Druckweiterverarbeitung)*
creation engine Entwicklermaschine *f (Computergrafik)*
creative filter Kreativfilter *n*, Effektfilter *n*, Trickfilter *n*
~ **photography** gestaltende (kreative) Fotografie *f*
~ **silk-screen printmaking** Kunstsiebdruck *m*, künstlerischer Siebdruck *m*, Serigrafie *f*
creature Trick[film]figur *f*
credit card reader Kreditkartenlesegerät *n*
credits Titelabspann *m*, End[e]titel *m*, Schlusstitel *m (Film)*
crime scene photograph Tatortfoto *n*, Tatortaufnahme *f*
~ **scene photographer** Tatortfotograf *m*
~ **scene photography** Tatortfotografie *f*
~ **scene video** Tatortvideo *n*
crisp [konturen]scharf *(Abbildung)*
~ **filter** Schärfefilter *n*, Scharfzeichnungsfilter *n*

crispening Bild[ver]schärfung *f*; Konturkorrektur *f (Bildverarbeitung)*
crispness Schärfe *f*, Bildschärfe *f*; Konturenschärfe *f*
critical angle Grenzwinkel *m*, Totalreflexionswinkel *m*, kritischer Winkel *m*
~ **aperture** kritische Blende *f*
~ **flicker frequency** kritische Flimmerfrequenz *f*, Flimmergrenze *f*
~ **frequency** kritische Frequenz *f*
~ **fusion frequency** Flimmerverschmelzungsfrequenz *f*, Verschmelzungsfrequenz *f*
~ **pulse width** kritische Pulsbreite *f*
~ **stop** kritische Blende *f*
~ **temperature** kritische Temperatur *f*, Sprungtemperatur *f (Supraleiter)*
crocking *s.* chalking
crookedness Gekrümmtheit *f*
crop/to beschneiden; zuschneiden
crop mark Beschnittmarke *f*, Beschnittzeichen *n (Druck)*
cropping 1. Ausschnittvergrößern *n*; 2. Randbeschnitt *m*; Beschnitt *m*, Beschneidung *f*
cross brace Mittelstrebe *f (Stativ)*
~ **braced legs** Querstreben *fpl (Stativ)*
~-**color [artifact]**, ~ **effect** Farbübersprechen *n*, Farbüberstrahlung *f*, Farbüberlagerung *f*, Cross-Color-Effekt *m*; Farbschlieren *fpl (Videobildfehler)*
~-**correlation** Kreuzkorrelation *f*
~-**correlation function** Kreuzkorrelationsfunktion *f*
~-**correlation[al] image** Kreuzkorrelationsbild *n*
~ **covariance** Kreuzkovarianz *f*
~ **cutting** Kreuzschnitt *m*
~ **fade** Überblendung *f*, Bildüberblendung *f*, Durchblende *f*
~-**flow laser** quergeströmter Laser *m*
~ **grain** Dehnrichtung *f (von Druckpapier)*
~-**luma artifact, cross-luminance [artifact]** Helligkeitsübersprechen *n*, Luminanz-Übersprechen *n*, Cross-Luminanz-Effekt *m*
~ **luma**, ~ **luminance** Kreuzluminanz *f (Videodatenverarbeitung)*
~-**mod[ulation]** Kreuzmodulation *f*
~ **modulated synthesis filter** kreuzmoduliertes Synthesefilter *n*
~ **modulation test** Doppeltonprobe *f (Lichttontechnik)*
~ **polarization** Kreuzpolarisation *f*
~-**polarized light** kreuzpolarisiertes Licht *n*
~ **product** Vektorprodukt *n*
~-**range resolution** Querauflösung *f (Radar)*
~ **screen (star) filter** Gitterfilter *n*, Stern[effekt]filter *n*, Crossfilter *n*
~-**section[al] image** Querschnittsbild *n*
~ **talk** Übersprechstörung *f*, Übersprechen *n*, Nebensprechen *n*

~ **talk attenuation** Übersprechdämpfung f
~ **wire** s. crosshair
crossbar [distributor], ~ switch Kreuzschienenverteiler m
crossed-field tube Kreuzfeldröhre f *(Radar)*
~ **polarized illumination** kreuzpolarisierte Ausleuchtung f
~ **polarizer** Kreuzpolarisator m
~-**prism square** Prismenkreuz n
crosshair Fadenkreuz n
~ **cursor** Fadenkreuz-Cursor m
~ **eyepiece** Fadenkreuzokular n
crosslight gegenlichtiges Seitenlicht n
crossline halftone Kreuzraster m(n)
~ **screen** Kreuzraster m(n)
crossmark Pass[er]kreuz n
crossover angeschnittenes Bild n, [rand]abfallendes Bild n *(Layout)*
~ **effect** Durchbelichtungseffekt m *(Radiografie)*
crosspoint Bildanwahl f *(Videoschnitt)*
crowd scene Massenszene f *(Filmarbeit)*
crown flint glass Kronflint m
~ **glass** Kronglas n
crow's foot Stativspinne f
CRT s. cathode-ray tube
~-**based [film] recorder** Kamera-Filmabtaster m, Speicher[röhren]abtaster m
~ **faceplate** Bildröhrenfront f
~ **gamma** Bildröhrengamma n
~ **mask** Bildschirmmaske f, Bildröhrenmaske f, Bildschirmrahmen m
~ **monitor** Katodenstrahlmonitor m, Röhrenmonitor m
~ **neck** Bildröhrenhals m, Röhrenhals m
~ **raster** Röhrenraster m(n)
~ **screen** Röhrenbildschirm m, Bildröhrenmonitor m
~ **television [set]** Röhrenfernsehgerät n, Röhrenfernseher m, Bildröhrengerät n
crush Schramme f
cryoelectron microscopy Kryoelektronenmikroskopie f
~ **tomography** Kryoelektronentomografie f
cryomicroscopic kryomikroskopisch
cryospectroscopy Kryospektroskopie f
cryptogram, cryptograph Kryptogramm n
cryptographic kryptografisch
cryptography Kryptografie f
crystal Kristall m
~-**controlled motor** Quarzmotor m
~ **defect** Kristall[bau]fehler m
~ **growth** Kristallwachstum n
~ **imperfection** Kristall[bau]fehler m
~ **lattice constant** Kristallgitterkonstante f
~ **lattice defect** Kristallgitterfehler m
~ **lattice structure** Kristallgitterstruktur f
~ **microphone** Kristallmikrofon n
~ **nucleus** Kristallkeim m
~ **optics** Kristalloptik f
~ **oscillator** Querzgenerator m, Schwingquarz m
~ **quartz** Quarzkristall m

~ **spectrograph** Kristallspektrograf m
~ **spectrometer** Kristallspektrometer n
~ **surface** Kristalloberfläche f
~ **sync** Quarz-Synchrontechnik f; [elektronischer] Synchronverbund m *(Kinofilmtechnik)*
crystalline lattice Kristallgitter n
~ **lens** Augenlinse f, Kristallinse f
~ **structure** Kristallstruktur f
crystallogram Kristallogramm n
crystallographic kristallografisch
crystallography Kristallografie f
CSG tree s. constructive solid geometry tree
CSS s. content scrambling system
CT s. computed tomography
CT angiographic computerangiografisch
CT angiography Computerangiografie f, digitale Subtraktionsangiografie f
CT image s. ~ scan
CT machine Computertomograf m, Computertomografiegerät n, CT-Scanner m
CT number s. Hounsfield unit
CT scan, ~ slice [image] Computertomogramm n, CT-Aufnahme f, CT-Bild n
cube Würfel m, Kubus m, Hexaeder n *(geometrischer Grundkörper)*
~ **beam splitter** Strahlenteilerwürfel m, Teilerwürfel m, Teilungswürfel m
cubic kubisch, würfelförmig
~ **B-spline** kubische B-Spline-Kurve f
~ **B-spline interpolation** kubische B-Spline-Interpolation f
~ **convolution** kubische Faltung f
~ **convolution interpolation** kubische Faltungsinterpolation f *(Bildrestauration)*
~ **crystal** kubischer Kristall m
~ **interpolation** kubische Interpolation f
~ **lattice** kubisches Gitter n
~ **polynomial** kubisches Polynom n, Polynom n dritter Ordnung
~ **polynomial curve** kubische Kurve f
~ **spline [function]** kubische Spline-Kurve f
~ **voxel** Voxelwürfel m
cubical s. cubic
cue 1. Markierung f *(z.B. auf Filmmaterial)*; 2. Regiesignal n
~ **card** Neger m *(Filmstudiozubehör)*
~ **dot (mark)** Überblendzeichen n, Ausblendzeichen n; Abfahrzeichen n *(Filmvorführung)*
~ **sheet** Schnittliste f
~ **time** Suchlaufzeit f
~ **tone** Tonmarkierung f *(Videoschnitt)*
~ **track** Hilfstonspur f, Merkspur f
cueing Suchlauf m
~ **device** Regiegerät n
cuke s. cookie
cultural paper Feinpapier n, holzfreies Papier n
cumulative distribution function kumulative Verteilungsfunktion f

cumulative

~ **histogram** kumulatives Histogramm *n*
~ **probability** kumulative Wahrscheinlichkeit *f*
cupric chloride Kupferchlorid *n (Bleichmittel)*
curb Kabelverteiler *m*
cure/to 1. konditionieren *(z.B. Druckpapier)*; 2. trocknen *(z.B. Druckfarben)*; 3. [aus]härten *(z.B. Klebstoffe)*
curl Krümmung *f*, Welligkeit *f (z.B. von Fotopapier)*; Papierverzug *m (Druckschwierigkeit)*
curly bracket geschweifte Klammer *f*, Nasenklammer *f (Druckzeichen)*
current body size Grundschriftgröße *f*
~ **frame (picture)** aktuelles Bild *n*, Momentanbild *n (Bewegungsschätzung, Prädiktionscodierung)*
cursive kursiv; schräg[laufend]
~ **script (word) recognition, ~ handwriting recognition** Kursivschrifterkennung *f*
cursor Cursor *m*, Schreibmarke *f*, Einfügemarke *f*, Lichtmarke *f*, Positionsmarke *f*
~ **arrow** Cursorpfeil *m*
curvature-augmented tensor Krümmungstensor *m*
~ **energy** Krümmungsenergie *f*
~ **estimation** Krümmungsschätzung *f*
~ **measure** Krümmungsmaß *n*
~ **measurement** Krümmungsmessung *f*
~ **of field** Bildfeldwölbung *f*, Feldkrümmung *f*
~ **operator** Krümmungsoperator *m*
~ **point** Krümmungspunkt *m*
~ **vector** Krümmungsvektor *m*
curve Kurve *f (geometrische Modellierung)*
~ **approximation** Kurvenapproximation *f*
~ **chart** Kurvendiagramm *n*
~ **description** Kurvenbeschreibung *f*
~ **detection** Kurvendetektion *f*, Krümmungsdetektion *f*
~ **feature** Kurvenmerkmal *n*
~**-fitting technique** Kurvenanpassungstechnik *f*
~ **point** Kurvenpunkt *m*
~ **primitive** Kurvenprimitiv *n*
~ **representation** Kurvenbild *n*
~ **segment** Kurvensegment *n*, Kurvenstück *n*
~ **segment primitive** Kurvenprimitiv *n*
~ **shape description** Kurvengestaltbeschreibung *f*
~ **smoothing** Kurvenglättung *f*
curved-array scanner Konvexscanner *m*, Konvexschallkopf *m (Sonografie)*
~ **edge** gekrümmte Kante *f*
~ **lens** gekrümmte Linse *f*
~ **line** gekrümmte Linie *f*; Kurve *f*
~ **mirror** gekrümmter Spiegel *m*
~ **outward** *s.* convex
~ **surface** gekrümmte Fläche (Oberfläche) *f*

curvilinear ungeradlinig, krummlinig
~ **distortion** nichtlineare Verzerrung *f*
custom color lab Farblabor *n*, Buntlabor *n*
~ **finishing** Individualverarbeitung *f (von Fotomaterial)*
~**-finishing lab[oratory]** Kleinlabor *n*
~ **lab** *s.* custom-finishing lab[oratory]
~ **preset[ting]** Voreinstellung *f (z.B. einer Kamera)*
~ **setting** Individualfunktion *f*
customized printing personalisiertes Drucken *n*
cut/to schneiden; cutte[r]n *(Filmbearbeitung)*
cut into/to einschneiden
~ **off/to** abschneiden
~ **out/to** ausschneiden
~ Schnitt *m*
~**-and-paste** Ausschneiden *n* und Einfügen *n (Computergrafik)*
~ **effect** Schnitteffekt *m*
~ **film** Blattfilm *m*, Einzelblattfilm *m*; Planfilm *m*
~**-in [shot]** Einschnittszene *f*, Zwischenschnitt *m*, Cut-in *m (Filmschnitt)*
~ **list** Schnittliste *f (Filmbearbeitung)*
~ **plane** Schnittebene *f*
~**-sheet feeder** Einzelblatteinzug *m*
~**-sheet machine** Bogenmaschine *f*
cutaway *s.* cut-in [shot]
~ **diagram (view)** Schnittbild *n*, Schnittansicht *f*
cutline *s.* caption 1.
cutoff 1. Randvignettierung *f*; 2. Abschnittlänge *f (Rollendruck)*
~ **frequency** Grenzfrequenz *f*, Abschneidefrequenz *f (z.B. bei Bildfilterung)*
~ **wavelength** Grenzwellenlänge *f (z.B. eines Quantendetektors)*
cutout Ausschnittbild *n*
~ **animation** 1. Legetrick *m*; Schiebetrick *m (Trickkinematografie)*; 2. Scherenschnittfilm *m*
~ **image** Ausschnittbild *n*
~ **photograph** freistehende Fotografie *f (Typografie)*
cutter Cutter *m*, Filmcutter *m*, Schnittmeister *m*, Filmeditor *m*
cutting copy Schnittkopie *f*, Arbeitskopie *f*, Klatschkopie *f (Filmschnitt)*
~ **in the camera** Drehen *n* auf Schnitt, Schnitt *m* beim Drehen *(Filmarbeit)*
~ **machine** Schneidemaschine *f*
~ **mat** Schnittunterlage *f*
~ **point** Schnittpunkt *m*, Schnittstelle *f*
~ **reducer** Subtraktivabschwächer *m*, kontrasterhaltender Abschwächer *m*
~ **rhythm** Schnittrhythmus *m*
~ **room** Filmschneideraum *m*; Schnittbearbeitungsraum *m*
~ **table** Schneidetisch *m*, Filmschneidetisch *m*

cyan Cyan *n*, Blaugrün *n*, Türkis *n*;
  genormtes Blau *n* *(subtraktive Grundfarbe)*
~ **cyanblau**
~ **developer** Cyanentwickler *m* *(Farbfotografie)*
~ **dye** Cyanfarbstoff *m*
~ **dye developer** Cyanentwickler *m*
~ **dye forming layer** rotempfindliche Schicht *f* *(Farbfilm)*
~ **filter** Blaugrünfilter *n*
~-**forming coupler** Cyankuppler *m*, Blaugrünkuppler *m*
~-**magenta-yellow color space** CMY-Farbmodell *n*, CMY-Farbraum *m*, subtraktives Farbmodell *n*
~ **toner** Cyantoner *m*
cyanine [dye] Cyanin *n*, Cyaninfarbstoff *m*
cyanometer Cyanometer *n*
cyanometry Cyanometrie *f*
cyanotype process Cyanotypie *f*, [negativer] Eisenblaudruck *m*
cyber citizen *s.* cyborg
~ **glove** Datenhandschuh *m*, sensorischer Handschuh *m* *(Navigationswerkzeug)*
~ **citizen, cybernetic organism** *s.* cyborg
cybernetical kybernetisch
cybernetics Kybernetik *f*
cybersickness Cyberkrankheit *f*
cyberspace 1. Cyberspace *m*, virtueller Raum *m*; 2. *s.* Internet
cyborg Avatar *m*; Cyberianer *m*, Computerfigur *f* *(virtuelle Realität)*; digitaler Sprecher (Darsteller) *m* *(Software-Programm)*
cyc *s.* cyclorama
cyclic code zyklischer Code *m*
~ **convolution** zyklische (zirkulare) Faltung *f* *(Datenverarbeitung)*
~ **redundancy check** zyklische Redundanzprüfung (Blocksicherung) *f* *(Datenverarbeitung)*
cyclorama Filmhintergrund *m*, Diorama *n*; Rundhorizont *m*
cylinder Zylinder *m* *(geometrischer Grundkörper)*
~ **blanket** Drucktuch *n*
~ **lens** Zylinderlinse *f*
~ **press** Rotationspresse *f*, Rotations[druck]maschine *f*, Zylinderdruckmaschine *f*
cylindrical color space zylindrischer Farbraum *m*
~ **coordinate system** zylindrisches Koordinatensystem *n*
~ **lens** Zylinderlinse *f*
~ **plano-concave lens** zylindrisch-plankonkave Linse *f*
~ **plano-convex lens** zylindrisch-plankonvexe Linse *f*
~ **projection [mapping]** Zylinderprojektion *f*
~ **rectification** zylindrische Rektifizierung *f* *(Fotogrammetrie)*

~ **wave** Zylinderwelle *f*
cyphertext verschlüsselter Text *m*
cystoscope Zystoskop *n*, Blasenspiegel *m*
cytofluorogram Zytofluorogramm *n*
cytophotometer Zytofotometer *n*
cytophotometry Zytofotometrie *f*

D

D-cinema s. digital cinema
D-log H curve s. density curve
D-max s. maximum density
D-min s. minimum density
dacryocystography Dakryozystografie f, Tränensackröntgendarstellung f
dactylogram, dactylograph Daktylogramm n, Fingerabdruck m
dactyloscopic daktyloskopisch
dactyloscopist Daktyloskop m
dactyloscopy Daktyloskopie f
dagger Anmerkungszeichen n
daguerreotype/to daguerreotypieren
daguerreotype s. ~ image
~ **camera** Daguerreotypiekamera f, Daguerresche Kamera f
~ **image** Daguerreotypie f *(Bildprodukt)*
~ **photographic process** Daguerreotypie f
~ **plate** Daguerreotypieplatte f
daguerreotypist Daguerreotypist m
daguerreotypy Daguerreotypie f
dailies Tagesmuster npl, Filmmuster npl, Muster npl *(Filmproduktion)*
~ **screening** Mustervorführung f
daily news photographer Pressefotograf m, Zeitungsfotograf m, Bildreporter m, Fotoreporter m
daisy wheel Typenrad n, Druckrad n
~ **wheel printer** Typenraddrucker m
Daltonism Daltonismus m, [angeborene] Farbenblindheit f, Rotgrünblindheit f
damage detection Defekterkennung f
~ **threshold** Zerstörschwelle f *(Laseroptik)*
dammar varnish Dammarlack m
dampen/to feuchten *(Druck)*
dampener Feuchtmittel n
dampening roller Feucht[auftrags]walze f *(Druckmaschine)*
~ **solution** Feuchtmittel n
~ **system [rollers]** Feuchtwerk n
damping constant Dämpfungskonstante f
~ **force** Dämpfungskraft f
~ **matrix** Dämpfungsmatrix f
dance photography Tanzfotografie f, Ballettfotografie f
dark dunkel, lichtlos
~ **adaptation** Dunkeladaptation f, Dunkelanpassung f *(Sehen)*
~-**adapted eye** dunkeladaptiertes Auge n
~-**adapted vision** Dunkelsehen n, Nachtsehen n, skotopisches (dunkeladaptiertes) Sehen n, Stäbchensehen n
~ **box** Papiersafe m
~ **chamber** Dunkelkammer f *(s.a. unter darkroom)*
~ **charge** Dunkelladung f

~ **cloth** Verdunk[e]lungstuch n; Einstelltuch n *(Fotografie)*
~ **color** dunkle Farbe f
~-**colored** dunkelfarbig
~ **conductivity** Dunkelleitfähigkeit f
~ **current** Dunkelstrom m, Sättigungssperrstrom m *(Fotodetektor)*
~-**current [shot] noise** Dunkelstromrauschen n, Dunkel[ladungs]rauschen n
~ **current density** Dunkelstromdichte f
~ **discharge** Dunkelentladung f *(Fotodetektor)*
~ **field** Dunkelfeld n
~-**field condenser** Dunkelfeldkondensor m
~-**field illumination** Dunkelfeldbeleuchtung f
~-**field image** Dunkelfeldbild n *(Elektronenmikroskopie)*
~-**field microscope** Dunkelfeldmikroskop n, Ultramikroskop n
~-**field microscopy** Dunkelfeldmikroskopie n, Ultramikroskopie f
~-**field object** Dunkelfeldobjekt n
~-**field observation** Dunkelfeldbeobachtung f, Dunkelfeldbetrachtung f
~-**field photomicrography** Dunkelfeld-Mikrofotografie f
~-**field projection** Dunkelfeldprojektion f
~-**field reflected-light illumination** Auflicht-Dunkelfeldbeleuchtung f
~-**field stop** Dunkelfeldblende f
~ **focus** Dunkeladaptationszustand m
~-**ground** ... s. dark-field ...
~ **interval** s. ~ period
~ **noise** s. dark-current [shot] noise
~ **period** Dunkelperiode f, Dunkelphase f, Dunkelpause f *(Kinefilmtransport)*
~-**to-light [image] transition** Dunkel-Hell-Übergang m
darken/to abdunkeln
darkened room abgedunkelter (verdunkelter) Raum m, Dunkelraum m
darkening Abdunkelung f
darkness Dunkelheit f, Lichtlosigkeit f
darkroom Dunkelraum m, Dunkelkammer f
~ **accessories** Dunkelkammerzubehör n
~ **appliance** Dunkelkammergerät n
~ **camera** Zweiraumkamera f
~ **color analyzer** Farbanalysator m
~ **enthusiast** Selbstverarbeiter m, Selbstausarbeiter m
~ **equipment** Dunkelkammerausrüstung f
~ **facilities** Dunkelkammergerätschaften pl
~ **illumination** Dunkelraumausleuchtung f, Dunkelkammerbeleuchtung f
~ **lamp** Dunkelkammerlampe f, Dukalampe f *(s.a. ~ safelight 2.)*
~ **outfit** Dunkelkammerausrüstung f
~ **photography** s. ~ work
~ **photoprocessing** Dunkelkammerverarbeitung f
~ **practice** Dunkelkammerpraxis f

~ process camera Dunkelraumkamera *f*
~ safelight 1. Dunkelkammerlicht *n*, Schutzlicht *n*, Laborlicht *n*; 2. Dunkelkammerleuchte *f*, Dukaleuchte *f*, Fotolaborleuchte *f*, Laborleuchte *f*
~ safelighting *s.* ~ illumination
~ technician Fotolaborant *m*
~ timer Belichtungs[zeitschalt]uhr *f*, Zeitschaltuhr *f*, Schaltuhr *f*, Zeitschalter *m*
~ ventilation Dunkelraumbelüftung *f*
~ work Dunkelkammerarbeit *f*, Dunkelkammertätigkeit *f*
dash Gedankenstrich *m* *(Interpunktionszeichen)*; Geviertstrich *m*; Halbgeviertstrich *m* *(Typografie)*
data Daten *pl*
~ access time Datenzugriffszeit *f*
~ acquisition Datenerfassung *f*
~ acquisition device Datenerfassungsgerät *n*
~ acquisition system Datenerfassungssystem *n*
~ analysis Datenanalyse *f*
~ bank *s.* database
~ bit Datenbit *n*
~ bit stream Datenbitstrom *m*
~ block Datenblock *m*
~ broadcast[ing] Datenrundfunk *m*
~ broadcasting service DVB-Datenrundfunk *m*
~ buffer *s.* ~ cache
~ burst Datenbündel *n*, Datenburst *m*
~ bus Datenbus *m*, Hauptleitungsträger *m* *(s.a. unter bus)*
~ bus connector Busanschluss *m*
~ bus technology Datenbustechnik *f*
~ byte Byte *n*, Datenbyte *n*
~ cache Datenzwischenspeicher *m*, Zwischenspeicher *m*, Cachespeicher *m*, Hintergrundspeicher *m*, [schneller] Pufferspeicher *m*, Vorhaltespeicher *m*
~ capture Datenerfassung *f*
~ capture device Datenerfassungsgerät *n*
~ carrier Datenträger *m*
~ chaining Datenverkettung *f*
~ channel Datenkanal *m*
~ coding Datencodierung *f*
~ communication Datenübermittlung *f*, Datenkommunikation *f*
~ compatibility Datenkompatibilität *f*
~ compression Datenkompression *f*, Datenkomprimierung *f*, Datenverdichtung *f*
~ compression algorithm Datenkompressionsalgorithmus *m*
~ compression level Datenreduktionsrate *f*, Datenreduktionsstufe *f*
~ compression technique Datenkompressionsverfahren *n*
~ converter Datenwandler *m*
~ correction Datenkorrektur *f*
~ density Datendichte *f*

~ display Datenfeld *n*, Datendisplay *n*, optische Datenanzeige *f*; Datumsanzeige *f*
~ display terminal *s.* ~ terminal
~ element Datenelement *n*
~ encoding Datencodierung *f*
~ encryption Datenverschlüsselung *f*
~ entry Dateneingabe *f*
~ entry error Dateneingabefehler *m*
~ error Datenfehler *m*
~ exchange Datenaustausch *m*
~ extraction Datenextraktion *f*
~ field Datenfeld *n (z.B. einer Datenbank)*
~ file Datei *f*
~ file format Dateiformat *n*
~ flow Datenfluss *m*, Datenstrom *m*
~ flow diagram Datenflussplan *m*
~ format Datenformat *n*
~ frame Datenrahmen *m*
~ fusion Datenfusion *f*
~ glove Datenhandschuh *m*, sensorischer Handschuh *m*
~ grid Datennetz *n*
~ group Datengruppe *f*
~ imprinting Dateneinbelichtung *f*
~ input Dateneingabe *f*
~ interface Datenschnittstelle *f*, Schnittstelle *f*
~ interleaving Datenverschachtelung *f*
~ line Datenzeile *f*
~ link layer Verbindungsschicht *f (Datenübertragung)*
~ loss Datenverlust *m*
~ management Datenverwaltung *f*
~ matching Datenabgleich *m*
~ matrix Datenmatrix *f*
~ medium Datenträger *m*
~ model Datenmodell *n*
~ modeling Datenmodellierung *f*
~ monitor Datenmonitor *m (s.a. ~ display)*
~ multiplexer Datenmultiplexer *m*
~ network Datennetz *n*
~ object Datenobjekt *n*
~ package (packet) Datenpaket *n*
~-parallel architecture datenparallele Architektur *f*
~ partitioning Datenaufteilung *f*
~ path Datenpfad *m*
~ point Datenpunkt *m*
~ preprocessing Datenvorverarbeitung *f*
~ presentation Datendarstellung *f*
~ processing Datenverarbeitung *f*
~ processing technology Datenverarbeitungstechnik *f*
~ processing tool Datenverarbeitungswerkzeug *n*
~ processor Datenverarbeiter *m*
~ projection Datenprojektion *f*
~ projection system Datenprojektor *m*
~ rate *s.* data-transfer rate
~ rate reduction Datenreduktion *f*
~ readout Datenauslesung *f*
~ record Datensatz *m*
~ recorder Datenrecorder *m*

data

~ **recording** Datenaufzeichnung f, Datenerfassung f
~-**recording back** Datenrückwand f (Kamera)
~ **recovery** Datenrückgewinnung f, Datenwiedergewinnung f; Datenwiederherstellung f
~ **reduction** Datenreduktion f, Datenreduzierung f
~ **reduction factor** Datenreduktionsfaktor m
~ **reduction process** Datenreduktionsverfahren n
~ **redundancy** Datenredundanz f
~ **representation** Datendarstellung f
~ **resource** Datenobjekt n
~ **security** Datensicherheit f
~ **service** Datendienst m
~ **set** Datensatz m; Datenmenge f
~ **set attribute** Datensatzattribut n
~ **signal** Datensignal n
~ **sink** Datensenke f
~ **size** Datenumfang m
~ **source** Datenquelle f
~ **space** Datenraum m
~ **spectrum** Datenspektrum n
~ **station** Datenstation f
~ **storage** 1. Datenspeicherung f; 2. Datenspeicher m
~ **storage capacity** Daten[speicher]kapazität f
~ **storage card** Datenspeicherkarte f, Speicherkarte f
~ **storage density** Speicherdichte f
~ **storage device** Datenspeicher m
~ **storage format** Datenspeicherformat n
~ **storage medium** Datenspeichermedium n
~ **storage technology** Datenspeichertechnik f
~ **stream** Datenstrom m, Datenfluss m
~ **stream format** Datenstromformat n
~ **stream payload** Datenstrom-Nutzlast f, Nutzdatenrate f
~ **structure** Datenstruktur f
~ **suit** Datenanzug m (virtuelle Realität)
~ **switching** Datenvermittlung f
~ **terminal** Datenendstation f, Datensichtgerät n, Terminal n, Endgerät n
~ **throughput** Datendurchsatz m
~ **track** Datenspur f
~ **transducer** Datenwandler m
~ **transfer** Datentransfer m, Datenübertragung f
~ **transfer rate (speed)** Daten[übertragungs]rate f, Datenübertragungsgeschwindigkeit f; Datenübertragungskapazität f
~ **transmission** Datenübertragung f, Datentransfer m
~ **transmission equipment** Datenübertragungseinrichtung f
~ **transmission protocol** Datenübertragungsprotokoll n
~ **transmission system** Datenübertragungssystem n
~ **transport interface** Datenschnittstelle f
~ **transport packet** Transportpaket n
~ **truncation** Datenverstümmelung f
~ **type** Datentyp m
~ **unit** Dateneinheit f
~ **vector** Datenvektor m
~ **visualization** Datenvisualisierung f
~ **volume** Datenvolumen n
~ **word** Datenwort n

database Datenbank f; Datenbasis f
~ **format** Datenbankformat n
~ **image** Datenbankbild n
~ **language** Datenbanksprache f
~ **management** Datenbankverwaltung f
~ **management system** Datenbankverwaltungssystem n
~ **query language** Datenbank-Anfragesprache f
~ **search[ing]** Datenbanksuche f
~ **server** Datenbank-Diensterbringer m
~ **storage system** Datenbankspeichersystem n
~ **system** Datenbanksystem n

datacast[ing] 1. Internet-Datendienst m; 2. Datenrundfunk m
datagram Datagramm n (Paketdatenvermittlung)
date stamp Datums[auf]druck m
datum Datenobjekt n
Daubechies wavelet Daubechies-Wavelet n
Daubresse prism Daubresse-Prisma n (Optik)
daughter wavelet Tochter-Wavelet n (Signalverarbeitung)
Davis-Gibson [liquid] filter [Davis-Gibson-]Doppelflüssigkeitsfilter n
Dawes limit Dawes-Grenze f (des Auflösungsvermögens von Teleskopen)
day blindness Tagblindheit f, Hemeralopie f
~-**for-night [effect]** amerikanische Nacht f (Filmlicht)
daylight Tageslicht n
~-**balanced color film** Tageslichtfarbfilm m
~-**balanced film** Tageslichtfilm m; Hellraumfilm m, Raumlichtfilm m
~-**balanced filter** Tageslichtfilter n
~-**balanced lighting fixture** Tageslichtleuchte f
~ **color film** Tageslichtfarbfilm m
~ **color temperature** Tageslicht-Farbtemperatur f
~ **conditions** Tageslichtbedingungen fpl
~ **conversion light filter** Tageslichtfilter n
~ **correction gel** Tageslichtfilter n
~ **developer** Hellentwickler m
~ **developing (development) tank** Tageslicht[-Entwicklungs]dose f, Filmentwicklungsdose f, Entwicklungsdose f

~ emulsion Tageslichtemulsion *f*
~ **film** Tageslichtfilm *m*; Hellraumfilm *m*, Raumlichtfilm *m*
~ **film-handling system** Tageslicht[bearbeitungs]system *n* *(Schirmbildfotografie)*
~ **glare** Tageslichtblendung *f*
~ **illuminant** Tageslichtleuchte *f*
~ **illumination** Tageslichtbeleuchtung *f*
~ **lamp** Tageslichtlampe *f*
~ **-load roll cassette** Tageslichtkassette *f*
~ **loader** Tageslichtspule *f*
~ **-loading film roll** Tageslicht-Rollfilmspule *f*
~ **-loading magazine** Tageslichtkassette *f*
~ **-loading package** Tageslichteinlegepackung *f*
~ **magazine** Tageslichtmagazin *n*
~ **paper** Tageslichtpapier *n*
~ **photograph** Tageslichtfoto *n*
~ **photography** Tageslichtfotografie *f*
~ **processing** Tageslichtverarbeitung *f*
~ **screen** Tageslichtbildschirm *m*
~ **studio** Tageslichtatelier *n*
~ **-type film** *s.* daylight-balanced film
~ **-type illumination** Tageslichtbeleuchtung *f*
~ **vision** Tagessehen *n*, fotopisches Sehen *n*, Zapfensehen *n*
daytime solar observation Sonnenbeobachtung *f*
~ **vision** *s.* daylight vision
dB *s.* decibel
DC restoration *s.* clamping
de Casteljau algorithm de-Casteljau-Algorithmus *m* *(Computergrafik)*
de-ink/to entfärben *(z.B. Altpapier)*
de-inking Entfärben *n (von Altpapier)*
de-squeeze lens [optischer] Entzerrungsvorsatz *m*, Wiedergabeanamorphot *m*
dead sync Schnittsynchronisierung *f* *(Filmproduktion)*
~ **time** Totzeit *f (Signalverarbeitung)*
~ **time correction** Totzeitkorrektor *m*
~ **zone quantization** Totzonenquantisierung *f* *(Transformationscodierung)*
~ **zone quantizer** Totzonenquantisierer *m*
deanamorphotic printing Kopieren *n* mit anamorphotischer Entzerrung
deblurring Schärfung *f*, Aufschärfung *f* *(elektronische Bildbearbeitung)*
~ **filter** Schärfefilter *n*, Scharfzeichnungsfilter *n*
deboss/to prägen
Debot effect Debot-Effekt *m* *(Latentbildentstehung)*
Debye-Scherer X-ray camera Debye-Scherrer-Kamera *f*
~ **-Scherer X-ray film** Debye-Scherrer-Röntgenfilm *m*
decal Abziehbild *n*

~ **transfer paper** Abziehbilderpapier *n*
decaMIRED value Dekamired-Wert *m* *(Farbtemperaturmessung)*
decelerated radiation *s.* bremsstrahlung [radiation]
decentered lens nichtzentrierte Linse *f*
decentration Dezentrierung *f*
~ **aberration** Dezentrierungsfehler *m*, Zentrierfehler *m*
dechirping Verschiebungskompensation *f* *(Radar)*
decibel Dezibel *n*, dB *(logarithmische Messgröße)*
decimal digit Dezimalziffer *f*
decimate/to dezimieren
decimation Dezimation *f* *(Signalverarbeitung)*; Ausdünnen *n*, Ausdünnung *f (z.B. eines polygonalen Netzes)*
~ **algorithmus** Ausdünnungsalgorithmus *m*
~ **filter** Dezimationsfilter *n*, Dezimationstiefpass *m*, Dezimator *m*
~ **filtering** Dezimationsfilterung *f*
decimator *s.* decimation filter
decimeter wave range Dezimeterwellenbereich *m*
decipher/to entziffern
decipherable image entzifferbares Bild *n*
decision boundary Entscheidungsschwelle *f*
~ **box** Entscheidungssymbol *n* *(Flussdiagrammsymbol)*
~ **class** Entscheidungsklasse *f*
~ **classifier** Entscheidungsklassifikator *m*
~ **error** Entscheidungsfehler *m*
~ **feedback** Entscheidungsrückkopplung *f*
~ **function** Entscheidungsfunktion *f*, Diskriminanzfunktion *f* *(Objekterkennung)*
~ **level** Entscheidungsebene *f*
~ **making** Entscheidungsfindung *f*
~ **processor** Entscheidungsprozessor *m*
~ **region** Entscheidungsbereich *m*
~ **rule** Entscheidungsregel *f*
~ **space** Entscheidungsraum *m*
~ **surface** Entscheidungsfläche *f* *(Musterklassifikation, Bildsegmentierung)*
~ **-theoretic** entscheidungstheoretisch
~ **-theoretic character recognition** entscheidungstheoretische Zeichenerkennung *f*
~ **theory** [statistische] Entscheidungstheorie *f*
~ **threshold** Entscheidungsschwelle *f*
~ **tree** Entscheidungsbaum *m* *(Datenstruktur)*
~ **variable** Entscheidungsvariable *f*
decodability Decodierbarkeit *f*
decodable decodierbar, entschlüsselbar
decode/to decodieren
decoded signal decodiertes Signal *n*

decoder

decoder 1. Decoder *m*, Codeumsetzer *m*, Datenentschlüssler *m*; 2. s. decompression algorithm
~ **matrix** Decodiermatrix *f*
~ **output** Decoderausgang *m*
decoding Decodierung *f*, Rückcodierung *f*
~ **algorithm** Decodierungsalgorithmus *m*
~ **layer** Decodierungsschicht *f (neuronales Netz)*
~ **loop** Decodierungsschleife *f*
~ **process** Decodiervorgang *m*
~ **speed** Decodierungsgeschwindigkeit *f*
~ **step** Decodierungsschritt *m*
~ **system** Decodierungssystem *n*
decolorize/to entfärben
decomposition Zerlegung *f (z.B. von Bilddaten)*
~ **filter** Zerlegungsfilter *n*
decompress/to dekomprimieren *(z.B. Bilddaten)*
decompression Dekompression *f*, Dekomprimierung *f*
~ **algorithm (program)** Dekompressionsalgorithmus *m*
decompressor Dekompressor *m*
deconvolution Dekonvolution *f*, Entfaltung *f*, Inversfilterung *f*, inverse Filterung *f (Bildrekonstruktion)*
~ **filter** Restaurationsfilter *n*
deconvolve/to entfalten
decoration Dekoration *f*
decorrelate/to dekorrelieren *(z.B. Bilddaten)*
decorrelation Dekorrelation *f*
~ **filter** Dekorrelationsfilter *n*
~ **transform** Dekorrelationstransformation *f*
decrease in contrast Kontrastabnahme *f*, Kontrastabschwächung *f*
decreased blue sensitivity Blauschwäche *f*, Tritanomalie *f*, Tritanstörung *f*, angeborene Blau-Gelb-Störung *f (Farbsinnstörung)*
~ **green sensitivity** Grünschwäche *f*, Deuteranomalie *f (Farbsinnstörung)*
~ **red sensitivity** Rotschwäche *f*, Protanomalie *f (Farbsinnstörung)*
decrement/to dekrementieren *(Daten)*
decrypt/to entschlüsseln
decryptable entschlüsselbar, decodierbar
decrypter Entschlüsseler *m*
decryption Entschlüsselung *f*
deemphasis Deemphasis *m*, Höhenabsenkung *f*, Nachentzerrung *f (Frequenzmodulation)*
deep black tiefschwarz
~ **discharging** Tiefentladen *n (Batterie)*
~-**etch plate** Tiefätz[druck]platte *f*
~ **layer recording** Tiefenmultiplex *m (Videospeicherung)*
~-**sea photography** Tiefseefotografie *f*
~-**sky photography** Deep-Sky-Fotografie *f*
~ **tank** Hochtank *m (Fotoverarbeitung)*
~-**water camera** Tiefseekamera *f*

default [setting] Grundeinstellung *f*, Voreinstellung *f*, Werkseinstellung *f (eines Gerätes)*
defect electron Defektelektron *n*, Loch *n (Fotodetektor)*
~ **function** [Gaußsche] Fehlerfunktion *f*
defective color vision Farb[en]fehlsichtigkeit *f*, Farbsinnstörung *f*, Farbsehstörung *f*
defectoscope Defektoskop *n*
defectoscopy Defektoskopie *f*
deferral mode Aktualisierungsmodus *m (Grafikarbeitsplatz)*
deficient color vision s. defective color vision
definition Detailschärfe *f*, Bilddefinition *f*, Auflösungsfeinheit *f*, Scharfzeichnung *f*; Kontur[en]schärfe *f*; Kontrastschärfe *f*; Durchzeichnung *f*, Zeichnung *f*
deflect/to ablenken, umlenken
deflected ray abgelenkter Strahl *m*
deflecting capacitor Ablenkkondensator *m*
~ **coil** Ablenkspule *f*
~ **electrode** Ablenkelektrode *f*
deflection Ablenkung *f*
~ **aberration** Ablenkfehler *m*
~ **angle** Ablenkwinkel *m*
~ **circuit[ry]** Ablenkschaltung *f*
~ **coil** Ablenkspule *f*
~ **current** Ablenkstrom *m*
~ **mirror** Ablenkspiegel *m*
~ **plane** Ablenkebene *f*
~ **plate** Ablenkplatte *f*
~ **power** Ablenkvermögen *n*
~ **prism** Ablenkprisma *n*
~ **sensitivity** Ablenkempfindlichkeit *f*
~ **system** Ablenksystem *n*
~ **voltage** Ablenkspannung *f*
~ **yoke** Ablenkeinheit *f*, Ablenkjoch *n*; Ablenkspule *f (Bildröhre)*
deflectometry Deflektometrie *f*
deflector Deflektor *m*, Licht[strahl]ablenker *m*
~ **coil** Ablenkspule *f*
defoamer Entschäumer *m*
defocus/to defokussieren
defocus Brennweitenabweichung *f*
~ **image control** Unschärfensteuerung *f*
defocusing Defokussierung *f*; Fokusverlagerung *f*, Unscharfstellen *n*
deform/to deformieren, verformen
deformable contour verformbare Kontur *f*
~ **contour model** aktives Konturmodell *n*
~ **curve** verformbare Kurve *f*
~ **model** deformierbares Modell *n*
~ **object** verformbares Objekt *n*
~ **surface** deformierbare Fläche (Oberfläche) *f (Computergrafik)*
~ **surface model** deformierbares Oberflächenmodell *n*
deformation Deformation *f*, Deformierung *f*
defuzzification Defuzzifizierung *f*, Defuzzifikation *f*
defuzzify/to defuzzifizieren

degauss/to entmagnetisieren
degausser Entmagnetisierer *m*
degaussing Entmagnetisierung *f*
~ coil Entmagnetisierungsspule *f*, Entmagnetisierungswicklung *f* *(Katodenstrahlröhre)*
degradation of detail[s] Detailverlust *m*
degrade verlaufende Rasterfläche *f*
degree of acidity Säuregrad *m* *(z.B. eines Fixierbades)*
~ of coherence Kohärenzgrad *m*
~ of compression Kompressionsgrad *m*
~ of contrast Papiergradation *f*
~ of correction Korrektionsgrad *m*
~ of curvature Krümmungsgrad *m*
~ of diffusion Diffusionsgrad *m*
~ of enlargement Vergrößerungsgrad *m*
~ of focusing Fokussierungsgrad *m* *(Sonografie)*
~ of freedom Freiheitsgrad *m* *(Statistik)*
~ of glare Blendungsgrad *m*
~ of homogeneity Homogenitätsgrad *m*
~ of magnification Vergrößerungsgrad *m*
~ of polarization Polarisationsgrad *m*
~ of resolution Auflösungsgrad *m*
~ of saturation Sättigungsgrad *m*
~ of similarity Ähnlichkeitsgrad *m*
~ of transmittance Durchlässigkeitsgrad *m*
deinking Druckfarbenentfernung *f*
deionize/to entionisieren
dejagging Kantenglättung *f*, Antialiasing *n* *(digitale Filteroperation)*
del *s.* detector element
Delaunay mesh Delaunay-Netz *n*
~ triangle Delaunay-Dreieck *n*
~ triangulation Delaunay-Triangulation *f*, Delaunay-Triangulierung *f*
delay edit Bild-Ton-versetzter Schnitt *m*
~ equalization Verzögerungsausgleich *m*
~ line Verzögerungsleitung *f* *(digitale Signalverarbeitung)*
~-sensitive verzögerungsempfindlich *(z.B. Videosignale)*
~ time Verzögerungszeit *f*
~ variance (variation) *s.* ~ jitter
delayed action Auslöseverzögerung *f* *(Kamera)*
~-action self timer selbstrückstellender Selbstauslöser *m*
~ luminescence verzögerte Lumineszenz *f*
delete/to löschen *(Daten)*
delete key Löschtaste *f*
delimiter Begrenzer *m*
delimiting rectangle umgebendes (umschließendes, umschreibendes) Rechteck *n*, Darstellungsquader *m*, Quaderhülle *f* *(Formanalyse)*
delineate/to abbilden
delineation Abbildung *f*, Abbild *n*
delivery engine Zielmaschine *f*
~ stack Bogenauslage *f*, Stapelauslage *f* *(Druckmaschine)*
Delone ... *s.* Delaunay ...

delta compression Deltakompression *f*
~ frame Deltabild *n*
~ function [Diracsche] Deltafunktion *f*, Dirac-Funktion *f*, Deltafunktional *n*, Impulsfunktion *f* *(Signalverarbeitung)*
~ modulation Deltamodulation *f* *(Bilddatenkompression)*
~ modulator Deltamodulator *m*
~ rule Deltaregel *f* *(Vorwärtsvermittlungsnetz)*
~ tree Deltabaum *m*
~ tree representation Deltabaumdarstellung *f*
~ tube Deltaröhre *f*
~ vector Deltavektor *m*
demagnetization Entmagnetisierung *f*
demagnetize/to entmagnetisieren
demagnetizer Abmagnetisierungsdrossel *f*
demagnification factor Verkleinerungsfaktor *m*
demagnify/to verkleinern
demand file Abrufdatei *f*
demibold[faced] halbfett *(Schrift)*
demodulate/to demodulieren
demodulation Demodulation *f*
demodulator Demodulator *m*
Dempster-Shafer theory Dempster-Shafer-Theorie *f*, Evidenztheorie *f*
demultiplex/to demultiplexieren
demultiplexer Demultiplexer *m*, DEMUX *m*
demultiplexing Demultiplexierung *f*, Demultiplexen *n*
dendrogram Baum *m*, Baumdarstellung *f* *(Datenstruktur)*
denoising [procedure] Entrauschung *f*, Rauschbefreiung *f*, Rauschbeseitigung *f*, Störbefreiung *f*
dense barium crown [glass] Baritschwerkron *n*
~ black tiefschwarz
~ depth map *s.* depth map
~ flint glass Schwerflint *m*, Schwerflintglas *n*
densitometer Densitometer *n*, Dichtemesser *f* Dichtemessgerät *n*, Schwärzungsmesser *m*
~ error Densitometerfehler *m*
~ filter Densitometerfilter *n*
densitometric densitometrisch
densitometry Densitometrie *f*, Dichtemessung *f*
density Dichte *f*, Densität *f*; Farbdichte *f*, Deckung *f*; Grau[stufen]wert *m*, Dunkelwert *m*; Schwärzung *f*
~ change Dichteänderung *f*
~ correction Dichtekorrektur *f*
~ curve [fotografische] Dichtekurve *f*, Schwärzungskurve *f*, Gradationskurve *f*, Grauwertkennlinie *f*, charakteristische Kurve (Filmkurve) *f*
~ difference Dichteunterschied *m*
~ distribution Dichteverteilung *f*
~ fluctuation Dichteschwankung *f*

density

~ **function** Dichtefunktion *f*, Wahrscheinlichkeitsdichtefunktion *f*
~ **gradient** Dichtegradient *m*
~ **measurement** Dichtemessung *f*, Densitometrie *f*
~ **range** Dichteumfang *m*, Dichtebereich *m*, Schwärzungsumfang *m*, Schwärzungsbereich *m*
~ **scale** Dichteskala *f*
~ **slicing** Äquidensitenherstellung *f* *(Bildverarbeitung)*
~ **value** Dichtewert *m*
~ **variation** Dichteschwankung *f*
~ **wedge** Grau[stufen]keil *m*, Stufengraukeil *m*, Grauskala *f*
~-**weighted MR image** dichtegewichtetes (protonengewichtetes) Magnetresonanzbild *n*
dental film Dental[röntgen]film *m*, Zahnfilm *m*
~ **microscope** Dentalmikroskop *n*
~ **photographer** Dentalfotograf *m*
~ **photography** Dentalfotografie *f*
~ **picture** Zahnaufnahme *f*
~ **radiographic equipment** zahnärztliche Röntgeneinrichtung *f*
~ **radiography** Dentalradiografie *f*
~ **radiology** zahnärztliche Röntgenaufnahmetechnik *f*
~ **X-ray machine (unit)** Dentalröntgeneinrichtung *f*
dephase/to dephasieren
dephasing Dephasierung *f*
~ **effect** Dephasierungseffekt *m*
depict/to abbilden, bildlich darstellen
depiction 1. Bilddarstellung *f*, bildliche Darstellung *f*, Abbildung *f*; 2. Abbild *n*, Abbildung *f*
depletion layer (region), ~ **zone** Verarmungsschicht *f*, Verarmungszone *f*, Raumladungszone *f* *(Fotodiode)*
depolarization Depolarisation *f*
depolarize/to depolarisieren
depolarizer Depolarisator *m*
depression angle Depressionswinkel *m*
depth [räumliche] Tiefe *f*
~ **buffer** Tiefenpuffer *m* *(Computergrafik)*
~ **buffer algorithm** Tiefenpufferalgorithmus *m*, z-Puffer-Algorithmus *m*
~ **buffering** Tiefenpufferverfahren *n*, Tiefenspeicherverfahren *n*, z-Puffer-Verfahren *n*
~ **clue (cue)** Tiefenhinweis *m*, Tiefeninformation *f*
~ **discrimination** Tiefenunterscheidung *f*
~ **discrimination ability** Tiefenunterscheidungsvermögen *n*
~ **effect** Tiefenwirkung *f*, Tiefeneffekt *m*
~ **estimation** Tiefenabschätzung *f*
~-**first search** Tiefensuche *f*
~-**first search tree** Tiefensuchbaum *m*
~ **image** *s.* ~ **map**
~ **impression** Tiefeneindruck *m*

~ **information** Tiefeninformation *f*, Tiefenhinweis *m*
~ **judg[e]ment** Tiefenabschätzung *f*
~ **layer** Tiefenschicht *f*
~ **map** Tiefenkarte *f*, Tiefenbild *n* *(maschinelle Bilderkennung)*
~ **of field (focus)** Schärfebereich *m*, Schärfentiefe *f*, Tiefenschärfe *f*, Fokustiefe *f*, Abbildungstiefe *f*, axiales Auflösungsvermögen *n*
~-**of-field indicator** Schärfentiefenanzeige *f*, Schärfentiefenkontrolle *f*
~-**of-field parameter** Schärfentiefenparameter *m*
~-**of-field preview** Blendenvorwahl *f*
~-**of-field preview button** Abblendtaste *f*
~-**of-field scale** Schärfentiefenskale *f*, Schärfentiefenring *m*, Tiefenring *m*
~-**of-field table** Schärfentiefentabelle *f*
~-**of-field zone** Schärfentiefebereich *m*, Schärfenzone *f*, Schärferaum *m*
~ **of penetration** Eindringtiefe *f* *(z.B. von Ultraschall)*
~ **perception** Raum[bild]wahrnehmung *f*, räumliche Wahrnehmung *f*, Tiefenwahrnehmung *f*; Tiefensehvermögen *n*
~ **range** Tiefenbereich *m*
~ **reconstruction** Tiefenrekonstruktion *f*
~ **reproduction** Tiefenwiedergabe *f*
~ **resolution** Tiefenauflösung *f*
~ **scaling** Tiefenskalierung *f*
~ **scanning** Tiefenabtastung *f* *(Sonografie)*
~ **sensation** Tiefeneindruck *m*
~ **shading** Tiefenschattierung *f*
dequantization Dequantisierung *f*
dequantize/to dequantisieren
dequantizer Dequantisierer *m*
Deriche filter Deriche-Filter *n*, Deriche-Kantenfilter *n*
derivation Ableitung *f*
derivative Ableitung *f*
~ **operator** Ableitungsoperator *m*, Ableitungsfilter *n* *(Kantendetektion)*
derived class Unterklasse *f*
~ **feature** abgeleitetes Merkmal *n*
~ **quantization** abgeleitete Quantisierung *f*
derotation prism Wendeprisma *n*, Reversionsprisma *n*, Umkehrprisma *n*
desaturate/to entsättigen
desaturated color entsättigte Farbe *f*
desaturation Entsättigung *f*, Farbenentsättigung *f*, Verweißlichung *f*
descender [depth] Unterlänge *f* *(Typografie)*
descramble/to entschlüsseln, entwürfeln *(Signale)*
descrambler Entschlüsseler *m*, Entwürfeler *m*
descrambling Entschlüsselung *f*, Entwürfelung *f*
descreen/to entrastern
descreening Entrasterung *f*

descriptive geometry darstellende Geometrie *f*
descriptiveness Anschaulichkeit *f*
descriptor Deskriptor *m* *(Mustererkennung; s.a. unter* attribute, feature*)*
~ **element** beschreibendes Element *n (z.B. einer Metadatei)*
desensitization Desensibilisierung *f*
~ **effect** Desensibilisierungseffekt *m*
desensitize/to desensibilisieren
desensitizer Desensibilisator *m*
deserialize/to parallelisieren *(z.B. Abtastwerte)*
design pattern Entwurfsmuster *n*
desilverization Entsilberung *f*
desk microphone Tischmikrofon *n*
desktop color scanner Tischscanner *m*
~ **computer** Tischrechner *m*
~ **data display monitor** Datensichtgerät *n*, Datenendstation *f*
~ **device** Tischgerät *n*
~ **laser printer** Laser-Tischdrucker *m*
~ **monitor** externer Monitor (Bildschirm) *m*
~ **plotter** Tischplotter *m*, Tischzeichner *m*; Flachbettplotter *m*
~ **printer** Arbeitsplatzdrucker *m*, Einzelplatzdrucker *m*, Schreibtischdrucker *m*
~ **publishing** Desktoppublishing *n*, Publizieren *n* am Schreibtisch, DTP; digitaler Satz *m*
~ **scanner** Tischscanner *m*
~ **video** Desktop-Video *n*
~ **videoconference system** Desktop-Videokonferenzsystem *n*
desorption Desorption *f*
destriping Streifenbeseitigung *f*
destructive interference destruktive Interferenz *f*
detachable lens Wechselobjektiv *n*, [aus]wechselbares Objektiv *n*, Wechseloptik *f*
detail Detail *n*; Bilddetail *n*
~ **coefficient** Wavelet-Koeffizient *m*
~ **contrast** Detailkontrast *m*
~ **detectability** Detailerkennbarkeit *f*
~ **drawing** Detailzeichnung *f*
~ **enhancement** Detailrestaurierung *f*
~ **image** Detailbild *n*
~ **information** Detailinformation *f*
~ **loss** Detailverlust *m*
~-**preserving filter** detailerhaltendes Filter *n*
~ **rendering** Detailwiedergabe *f*
~ **resolution** Detailauflösung *f*
~ **shot** Detailaufnahme *f*; Ganzgroßaufnahme *f*; Detaileinstellung *f* *(Filmarbeit)*
detailed image (picture) detailliertes Bild *n*
detailing Detaillierung *f*; Konturkorrektur *f*
detect/to detektieren, nachweisen; erkennen *(s.a.* recognize/to, identify/to*)*

detectability Detektierbarkeit *f*, Nachweisbarkeit *f*; Erkennbarkeit *f*
~ **factor** Detektierbarkeitsfaktor *m*
detectable detektierbar, nachweisbar; erkennbar
detection Detektion *f*; Erkennen *n*, Erkennung *f*
~ **algorithm** Detektionsalgorithmus *m*, Erkennungsalgorithmus *m*
~ **bandwidth** Detektionsbandbreite *f*
~ **capability** *s.* detectivity
~ **cycle** Detektionszyklus *m*
~ **efficiency** Detektionseffizienz *f*
~ **filter** Detektionsfilter *n*
~ **layer** Sensorschicht *f (CCD-Element)*
~ **limit** Nachweisgrenze *f*
~ **mask** Detektionsmaske *f*
~ **of moving targets** Bewegtzielerkennung *f (Radar)*
~ **performance** Detektionsleistung *f*
~ **powder** Anzeigepulver *n*
~ **probability** Detektionswahrscheinlichkeit *f*, Entdeckungswahrscheinlichkeit *f*
~ **quality** Detektionsgüte *f*
~ **sensitivity** Detektionsempfindlichkeit *f*
~ **theoretic** erkennungstheoretisch
~ **threshold** Detektionsschwelle *f*
detective camera Detektivkamera *f*, Geheimkamera *f*
~ **quantum efficiency** *s.* detector quantum efficiency
detectivity Detektivität *f*, Nachweisvermögen *n (z.B. von Fotodetektoren)*
detector Detektor *m (s.a. unter* sensor*)*
~ **area** Detektorfläche *f*
~ **array** Detektormatrix *f*, Detektoranordnung *f*, Detektorarray *n*
~ **artifact** Detektorartefakt *n*
~ **bandwidth** Detektorbandbreite *f*
~ **current** Detektorstrom *m*
~ **dark current** Detektordunkelstrom *m*
~ **electronics** Detektorelektronik *f*
~ **element [diskretes]** Detektorelement *n*
~ **geometry** Detektorgeometrie *f*
~ **intrinsic noise** Detektorrauschen *n*
~ **material** Detektormaterial *n*
~ **noise** Detektorrauschen *n*
~ **noise current** Detektorrauschstrom *m*
~ **parameter** Detektorparameter *m*
~ **performance** Detektorleistung *f*
~ **pixel** Detektorpixel *n*
~ **plane** Detektorebene *f*
~ **quantum efficiency** Quantenwirkungsgrad *m*, Quanteneffizienz *f*
~ **resistance** Detektorwiderstand *m*
~ **resolution** Detektorauflösung *f*
~ **responsivity** Detektorempfindlichkeit *f*
~ **segment** Detektorsegment *n*
~ **sensitivity** Detektorempfindlichkeit *f*
~ **signal** Detektorsignal *n*
~ **surface** Detektoroberfläche *f*

detector

~ **system** Detektorsystem *n*
~ **voltage** Detektorspannung *f*
~ **window** Detektorfenster *n*
deterministic fractal deterministisches Fraktal *n*
~ **model** deterministisches Modell *n*
~ **prediction** deterministische Prädiktion *f*
~ **signal** determiniertes (deterministisches) Signal *n*
~ **texture** deterministische Textur *f*
deuteranomaly Deuteranomalie *f*, Grünschwäche *f (Farbsinnstörung)*
deuteranope Grünblinder *m*
deuteranopia Deuteranopie *f*, Deutanstörung *f*, Grünblindheit *f (Farbsinnstörung)*
deuteranopic deuteranop, grünblind
develop/to entwickeln
~ **out** ausentwickeln
developability Entwickelbarkeit *f*, Entwicklungsfähigkeit *f*
developable entwickelbar, entwicklungsfähig, verarbeitungsfähig
developed-out photograph ausentwickeltes Foto *n*
developer Entwickler *m*
~ **activity** Entwickleraktivität *f*
~ **alkali** Entwickleralkali *n*
~ **bath** Entwickleransatz *m*; Entwicklungsbad *n*
~ **component** Entwicklerbestandteil *m*
~ **composition** Entwicklerzusammensetzung *f*
~ **compound** Entwicklersubstanz *f*
~ **concentrate** Entwicklerkonzentrat *n*
~ **concentration** Entwicklerkonzentration *f*
~ **constituent** Entwicklerbestandteil *m*
~ **crystal** Entwicklerkristall *m*
~ **dye** Entwicklerfarbstoff *m*
~ **electron** Entwicklerelektron *n*
~ **exhaustion** Entwicklererschöpfung *f*
~ **formula** Entwicklerrezeptur *f*
~ **formulation** Entwicklerrezeptur *f*
~ **improver** Entwicklerzusatz *m*
~**-inhibitor-releasing coupler** DIR-Kuppler *m*, DIR-Farbkuppler *m*
~ **molecule** Entwicklermolekül *n*
~ **oxidation product** Entwickleroxidationsprodukt *n*
~ **powder** Entwicklerpulver *n*
~ **reaction** Entwicklerreaktion *f*
~ **replenisher** Entwickler-Nachfülllösung *f*
~ **restrainer** Entwicklungsverzögerer *m*
~ **roller** Entwicklertrommel *f*, Entwicklerwalze *f (Elektrofotografie)*
~ **solubility** Entwicklerlöslichkeit *f*
~ **solution** Entwicklerlösung *f*, Entwicklungsflüssigkeit *f*
~ **streak** Entwicklerfahne *f*
~ **tank** s. developing tank
~ **temperature** Entwicklertemperatur *f*
~ **tray** Entwicklerschale *f*
~ **unit** Entwicklereinheit *f (Kopierer)*

94

developing agent Entwicklersubstanz *f*, Entwicklerchemikalie *f*
~ **agent molecule** Entwicklermolekül *n*
~ **bath** Entwicklungsbad *n*
~ **chemical** Entwicklerchemikalie *f*, Entwicklersubstanz *f*
~ **dish** Entwicklerschale *f*
~**-out paper** Entwicklungspapier *f*
~**-out process** Auskopierprozess *m*, Ausentwicklung *f*
~ **procedure** Entwicklungsverfahren *n*
~ **solution** Entwicklerlösung *f*, Entwicklungsflüssigkeit *f*
~ **tank** Filmentwicklungstank *m*, Entwicklertank *m*; Entwicklungsdose *f*, Filmentwicklungsdose *f*
~ **technique** Entwicklungstechnik *f*; Entwicklungsverfahren *n*
~ **time** Entwicklungsdauer *f*, Entwicklungszeit *f*
~ **tray** Entwicklerschale *f*
development Entwicklung *f*
~ **acceleration** Entwicklungsbeschleunigung *f*
~ **accelerator** Entwicklungsbeschleuniger *m*, Beschleuniger *m*
~ **action** Entwicklungsvorgang *m*
~ **additive** Entwicklerzusatz *m*
~ **center** Entwicklungszentrum *n*
~ **contrast** Entwicklungskontrast *m*
~ **effect** Entwicklungseffekt *m*
~ **fog** Entwicklungsschleier *m*
~ **inhibitor** Entwicklungsverzögerer *m*, Entwicklungshemmer *m*, Verzögerungsmittel *n*, Verzögerer *m*, Bremsmittel *n*
~ **latitude** Entwicklungsspielraum *m*, Verarbeitungsspielraum *f*, Verarbeitungstoleranz *f*
~ **nucleus** Entwicklungskeim *m*, Latentbildkeim *m*, Latentbildzentrum *n*
~ **paper** Entwicklungspapier *n*
~ **process** Entwicklungsprozess *m*, Entwicklungsvorgang *m*
~ **rate** Entwicklungsgeschwindigkeit *f*
~ **reaction** Entwicklungsreaktion *f*
~ **roll** Entwicklertrommel *f*, Entwicklerwalze *f (Elektrofotografie)*
~ **step** Entwicklungsschritt *m*
~ **temperature** Entwicklungstemperatur *f*
~ **time** Entwicklungsdauer *f*, Entwicklungszeit *f*
deviate/to ablenken
deviated light abgelenktes (gebeugtes) Licht *n*
deviation Deviation *f*, Abweichung *f*, Ablenkung *f*
device Gerät *n*
~ **coordinate** Gerätekoordinate *f*
~ **coordinate system** Gerätekoordinatensystem *n*
~ **dependency** Geräteabhängigkeit *f*
~**-dependent bit-map** geräteabhängiges Pixelbild *n*

~-**dependent color space**
geräteabhängiger Farbraum *m*
~ **driver** Gerätetreiber *m*, Treiber *m*
(Software)
~-**independent bit-map**
geräteunabhängiges Pixelbild *n*
~-**independent color** geräteunabhängige
Farbe *f*
~-**independent color space**
geräteunabhängiger Farbraum *m*
~-**independent image data**
medienneutrale Bilddaten *pl*
~ **noise** Apparaterauschen *n*
~ **space** Gerätebereich *m*
~ **viewport** Gerätedarstellungsfeld *n*
devitrified glass Glaskeramik *f*
devoted amateur ambitionierter
(engagierter) Amateur *m*
dewarping Entzerrung *f*
dextro[gyrate], dextrorota[to]ry
rechtsdrehend
DH perf *s.* Dubray-Howell perforation
diabolos unteres Rollenpaket *n*
(Filmentwicklungsmaschine)
diacaustic diakaustisch *(Strahlenoptik)*
~ **line** diakaustische Linie *f*, Brennlinie *f*
~ **surface** Diakaustik *f*, Kaustik *f*
diacritic diakritisches Zeichen *n*
(Typografie)
diaeresis Trema *n (diakritisches Zeichen)*
diagnostic image diagnostisches Bild *n*
~ **imaging modality (procedure)**
diagnostisches Bildgebungsverfahren *n*,
bildgebendes Diagnoseverfahren *n*
~ **medical imaging** diagnostische
(medizinische) Bildgebung *f*,
Medizinbildgebung *f*
~ **monitor** Befundungsmonitor *m*
~ **radiography** diagnostische Radiografie *f*
~ **radiologist** Strahlendiagnostiker *m*
~ **radiology** Strahlendiagnostik *f*,
diagnostische Radiologie *f*
~ **scanner** diagnostischer Scanner *m*
~ **ultrasound** diagnostischer Ultraschall *m*;
Ultraschalldiagnostik *f*
~ **X-ray film** medizinischer Röntgenfilm *m*
~ **X-ray tube** Diagnostik-Röntgenröhre *f*
diagonal diagonal, schräg[laufend]
~ Diagonale *f*, Schräglinie *f*; Schrägstrich *m*
~ **matrix** Diagonalmatrix *f*, diagonale
Matrix *f*
~ **resolution** diagonale Auflösung *f*
~ **screen size** Bildschirmdiagonale
~ **through the film** Formatdiagonale *f*
(Kinefilm)
~ **track** Schrägspur *f (Videoband)*
diagonalization Diagonalisierung *f*
diagonalized matrix Diagonalmatrix *f*
diagram/to als Diagramm darstellen
diagram Diagramm *n*, Schaubild *n*
~ **of optical glasses** Glasdiagramm *n*
dialer [program] Einwahlprogramm *n*
(Internet)

dialog *s.* dialogue
dialogue Dialog *m*
~ **box** Dialogfeld *n*
~ **continuity** Textdrehbuch *n*
~ **editing** Dialogbearbeitung *f*
~ **line** *s.* ~ track
~ **looping** Nachsynchronisation *f*,
Synchronbearbeitung *f*
~ **track** Dialogspur *f*, Dialogband *n*,
Sprachband *n*, Sprachstreifen *m*
(Tonfilm)
~ **window** Dialogfenster *n*
dialyte prism Dialytprisma *n*
diamagnetic diamagnetisch
~ **contrast agent** diamagnetisches
Kontrastmittel *n*
diameter of circle of confusion
Zerstreuungskreisdurchmesser *m*
diaminophenol dihydrochloride
Hydroxydiaminobenzenhydrochlorid *n*,
Diamidophenylhydrochlorid *n*, Amidol *n*
(Entwicklersubstanz)
diamond lattice Quincunx-Raster *m(n)*
(Signalabtastung)
~-**[-tipped] stylus** Diamantstichel *m*
diaphaneity Diaphanität *f*
diaphanous diaphan, durchscheinend
~ **image** Diaphanbild *n*, Diaphanie *f*,
durchscheinendes Bild *n*
diaphanousness Diaphanität *f*
diaphragm/to abblenden
diaphragm Blende *f*, Diaphragma *n*
~ **control ring** Blendeneinstellring *m*,
Objektivblendenring *m*,
Blendensteuerring *m*
~ **f-number** Blendenzahl *f*, Blendenwert *m*,
f-Blende *f*, f-Zahl *f*, relative Apertur
(Lichtstärke) *f*, Lichtstärkenverhältnis *n*
(Objektiv)
~ **opening** Blendenöffnung *f*, Blendenloch *n*
~ **scale** Blendenskale *f*,
Blendenzahl[en]reihe *f*
~ **setting** Blendeneinstellung *f*
~ **setting device**
Blendeneinstellvorrichtung *f*
~ **setting ring** *s.* ~ control ring
~ **shutter** Blendenverschluss *m*;
Zentralverschluss *m*; Objektivverschluss *m*
diaphragming Abblenden *n*, Abblendung *f*
diapositive Diapositiv *n*,
durchscheinendes fotografisches Bild *n*
diascope Diaskop *n*
diascopic illumination
Durchlichtbeleuchtung *f*
~ **projection** diaskopische Projektion *f*
diathermal (diathermic) filter
Wärmeschutzfilter *n*
diathermic mirror Kaltlichtspiegel *m*
diazine Diazin *n (Entwicklerchemikalie)*
diazo coating Diazo-Kopierschicht *f*,
Diazobeschichtung *f (Druckplatte)*
~ **copy** Diazokopie *f*, Diazotypie *f*

diazo 96

~ **copying process** Diazoverfahren *n*, Diazotechnik *f*
~ **duplicating film** Diazofilm *m*
~ **emulsion** Diazoemulsion *f*
~ **film** Diazofilm *m*
~ **microfilm** Diazomikrofilm *m*
~ **plate** diazobeschichtete Druckplatte *f*, Diazoniumsalz-Druckplatte *f*
~**-treated paper** Diazopapier *n*
diazonium compound Diazoverbindung *f*
~ **salt** Diazoniumsalz *n*
diazotype Diazotypie *f*, Diazokopie *f*
~ **process, diazotyping [process]** Diazotypie *f*, Diazotechnik *f*
dibit Dibit *n*, Doppelbit *n*
dichoptic vision dichoptisches Sehen *n*
dichroic 1. dichroitisch; 2. wellenlängenselektiv; 3. *s.* dichromatic
~ **beam splitter** dichroitischer Strahlenteiler *m*
~ **[color] filter** dichroitisches Filter *n*, Dichroidfilter *n*; Interferenzfilter *n*
~ **fog** dichroitischer (zweifarbiger) Schleier *m*, Farbschleier *m*
~ **mirror** dichroitischer (farbzerlegender) Spiegel *m*, Kaltlichtspiegel *m*
~ **polarizer** dichroitischer Polarisator *m*
dichroism Dichroismus *m*
dichroitic *s.* dichroic
dichromat 1. Dichromat *m* *(optisches System)*; 2. Dichromat *m*, partiell Farbenblinder *m*
dichromate Dichromat *m*, Bichromat *n* *(Chromsalz)*
dichromated colloid Dichromatkolloid *n*
~**-colloid process** Dichromatverfahren *n* *(frühe Fotografie)*
~ **gelatin** Dichromatgelatine *f*, Chromgelatine *f*
dichromatic dichromatisch, zweifarbig, bichrom
~ **vision, dichromatism** Zweifarbensehen *n*, Dichroma[top]sie *f*, dichromatisches Farbensehen *n*, partielle Farbenblindheit *f*
dichroscope Dichroskop *n*, Haidingersche Lupe *f*
DICOM *s.* Digital Imaging and Communications in Medicine
dictionary-based compression wörterbuchbasierte Kompression *f*, Phrasencodierung *f*
Didot point Didot-Punkt *m*, typografischer Punkt *m*, p
didymium [glass] filter Didymfilter *n*
die Matrize *f*; Buchstabenform *f*
dielectric dielektrisch
~ Dielektrikum *n*
~ **anisotropy** dielektrische Anisotropie *f*
~ **coating** dielektrische Beschichtung *f*
~ **constant** Dielektrizitätskonstante *f*
~ **filter** dielektrisches Filter *n*
~ **interference filter** dielektrisches Interferenzfilter

~ **material** Dielektrikum *n*
~ **medium** dielektrisches Medium *n*
~ **mirror** dielektrischer Spiegel *m*
~ **printer** dielektrischer Drucker *m*
~ **reflection** dielektrische Reflexion *f*
difference block Differenzblock *m* *(Videokompression)*
~ **descriptor** Differenzdeskriptor *m*
~ **filter** Differenzenfilter *n*
~ **frequency** Differenzfrequenz *f*
~ **histogram** Differenzhistogramm *n*
~ **image** Differenzbild *n*, Subtraktionsbild *n*
~ **of Gaussians [filter]** DoG-Filter *n*
~ **operation** Differenzoperation *f*
~ **operator** Differenzoperator *m*
~ **signal** Differenzsignal *n* *(Differenzcodierung)*
~ **threshold** *s.* just noticeable difference
differencing 1. Differenzbildung *f*; 2. *s.* differential coding
~ **mask** Differenz[en]filter *n*
differential coding Differenzcodierung *f*, differentielle (relative) Codierung *f*, prädiktive Codierung *f*, Prädiktionscodierung *f*
~ **gain** differentielle Verstärkung *f*
~ **global positioning system** erweitertes (genaueres) GPS *n*, DGPS *n*
~ **image compression** differentielle Bildkompression *f*
~ **interference contrast microscopy** Differentialinterferenzkontrastmikroskopie *f*, Nomarski-Mikroskopie *f*
~ **interferometer** Differentialinterferometer *n*
~ **phase** differentielle Phase *f*
~ **phase detection** differentielle Phasendetektion *f*
~ **phase-shift keying** Phasendifferenzcodierung *f*
~ **pulse code modulation** Differenzpulscodemodulation *f*, differentielle Pulscodemodulation *f* *(Bilddatenkompressionsverfahren)*
~ **quadrature phase shift keying** differentielle vierwertige Phasenumtastung *f*
~ **quantum efficiency** differentieller Quantenwirkungsgrad *m*
~ **signal** Differenzsignal *n*
differently colored verschiedenfarbig
diffract/to beugen
diffracted beam gebeugter Strahl *m*, Beugungsstrahl *m*
~ **light** gebeugtes (abgelenktes) Licht *n*
~ **wave** gebeugte Welle *f*
diffracting edge Beugungskante *f*, beugende Kante *f*
~ **object** beugendes Objekt *n*
~ **system** beugendes System *n*
diffraction Beugung *f*, Diffraktion *f*; Lichtbeugung *f*
~ **amplitude** Beugungsamplitude *f*
~ **angle** Beugungswinkel *m*

~ **artifact** Beugungsfehler *m*
~ **blur** Beugungsunschärfe *f*
~ **by a double slit** Beugung *f* am Doppelspalt
~ **calculation** Beugungsberechnung *f*
~ **contrast** Beugungskontrast *m*, Orientierungskontrast *m* *(Elektronenmikroskopie)*
~-**contrast image** Beugungskontrastbild *n*
~ **diagram** Beugungsdiagramm *n*
~ **disk** [Airy-]Beugungsscheibchen *n*, Beugungsscheibe *f*, Airy-Scheibchen *n*, zentrales Beugungsmaximum *n (Optik)*
~ **effect** Beugungswirkung *f*, Beugungseffekt *m*
~ **efficiency** Beugungswirkungsgrad *m*, Beugungseffektivität *f*
~ **fan** Beugungsfächer *m*
~ **figure** Beugungsbild *n*, Beugungsmuster *n*
~ **fringe** Beugungssaum *m*, Beugungsstreifen *m*
~ **geometry** Beugungsgeometrie *f*
~ **grating** Beugungsgitter *n*, diffraktives Gitter *n*
~ **grating pattern** Gitterbeugungsbild *n*
~ **grating spectrograph** Gitterspektrograf *m*
~ **grid** *s.* ~ grating
~ **image** Beugungsbild *n*
~ **intensity** Beugungsintensität *f*
~ **interference** Beugungsinterferenz *f*
~ **limit** Beugungsgrenze *f*
~ **limitation** Beugungsbegrenzung *f*
~-**limited** beugungsbegrenzt
~-**limited aplanat [lens]** beugungsbegrenzter Aplanat *m*
~-**limited beam** beugungsbegrenzter Strahl *m*
~-**limited image** beugungsbegrenzte Abbildung *f*
~-**limited imaging system** beugungsbegrenztes Abbildungssystem *n*
~-**limited lens** beugungsbegrenztes Objektiv *n*
~-**limited modulation transfer function** beugungsbegrenzte Modulationsübertragungsfunktion *f*
~-**limited optical system** beugungsbegrenztes [optisches] System *n*
~-**limited point-spread function** beugungsbegrenzte Punktbildfunktion *f*
~-**limited resolution** beugungsbegrenzte Auflösung *f*
~ **maximum** Beugungsmaximum *n*
~ **microscope** Beugungsmikroskop *n*
~ **mode** Beugungsmodus *m*
~ **optic[s]** Beugungsoptik *f*, beugungsoptisches System *n*
~-**optical** beugungsoptisch
~ **order** Beugungsordnung *f*

~ **pattern** Beugungsmuster *n*, Beugungsbild *n*
~ **phenomenon** Beugungserscheinung *f*
~ **plane** Beugungsebene *f*
~ **resolution** Beugungsauflösung *f*
~ **ring** Beugungsring *m (s.a.* Newton's rings*)*
~ **spectrum** Beugungsspektrum *n*
~ **spot** Beugungsfleck *m*
~ **theory** Beugungstheorie *f*
~ **tomography** Diffraktionstomografie *f*
diffractive integral Beugungsintegral *n*
~-**optical** beugungsoptisch
~ **optical element** lichtbrechendes optisches Element *n*
~ **optics** Beugungsoptik *f*, diffraktive Optik *f*
diffractometer Diffraktometer *n*
diffractometric diffraktometrisch
diffractometry Diffraktometrie *f*
diffusable *s.* diffusible
diffuse/to diffundieren; [zer]streuen *(z.B. Licht)*
diffuse diffus
~ **color** diffuse Farbe *f*
~ **halo** Diffusionslichthof *m*
~ **illumination** diffuse Beleuchtung *f*
~ **light** diffuses (weiches) Licht *n*
~ **light source** diffuse Lichtquelle *f*
~ **modulation transfer function** diffuse Modulationsübertragungsfunktion *f*
~ **reflectance curve** Remissionskurve *f*
~ **reflection** diffuse (gestreute) Reflexion *f*, Lambertsche Reflexion *f*, Lichtremission *f*
~ **reflector** diffuser Reflektor *m*
~ **scattering** diffuse Streuung *f*
diffused light diffus reflektiertes Licht *n*, gestreutes (zerstreutes) Licht *n*, Streulicht *n*
~ **lighting** diffuse Beleuchtung *f*
diffuser Diffusor *m*
~ **disk** Streuscheibe *f*, Diffusorscheibe *f (Fotometer)*
~ **screen** Weichzeichnerfolie *f*, Weichzeichnergaze *f*
diffusibility Diffusionsfähigkeit *f*
diffusible diffusionsfähig
diffusing effect Weichzeichnereffekt *m*
~ **filter** *s.* diffusion filter
~ **material** Diffusionsmaterial *n (Beleuchtungszubehör)*
~ **screen** Streuschirm *m*
~ **sphere** Diffusionskugel *f*, Streukalotte *f*, Diffusorkalotte *f (Beleuchtungsstärkemesser)*
diffusion Diffusion *f*; Lichtdiffusion *f*, Streuung *f*, Zerstreuung *f*
~ **algorithm** Diffusionsalgorithmus *m*
~ **angle** Diffusionswinkel *m*
~ **coefficient** Diffusionskoeffizient *m*
~ **current** Diffusions[foto]strom *m (Fotodiode)*

diffusion

~ **dithering** Streurasterung f, Zufallsrasterung f, frequenzmodulierte (nichtperiodische) Rasterung f, FM-Rasterung f
~ **filter** Diffusionsfilter n, Streufilter n
~ **filtering** Diffusionsfilterung f
~ **gradient** Diffusionsgradient m
~ **imaging** Diffusionsbildgebung f *(Magnetresonanztomografie)*
~ **model** Diffusionsmodell n *(Bildmodellierung)*
~ **rate** Diffusionsgeschwindigkeit f
~ **sheet** Diffusionsfolie f
~ **tensor** Diffusionstensor m
~ **tensor imaging** Diffusionstensorbildgebung f
~ **transfer copying system, ~ transfer photographic process** Silbersalzdiffusionsverfahren n
~**-type enlarger** Vergrößerungsapparat m mit diffuser Beleuchtung
~ **velocity** Diffusionsgeschwindigkeit f

dig Laufschramme f, Laufstreifen m *(auf Filmmaterial)*

digestion Nachreifung f, Nachdigestion f, chemische Reifung (Sensibilisierung) f *(Emulsionsherstellung)*

digicam s. digital camera

digit Digit[alelement] n; Digitalzahl f, Ziffer f

digital digital
~ **active line** digitale aktive Zeile f
~ **amplifier** digitaler Verstärker m
~ **animation** digitale Animation f
~ **animator** Computeranimator m, Computeranimateur m
~ **audio** Digitalton m

Digital Audio Tape DAT-Band n *(Audiobandformat)*

digital broadcast[ing] Digitalausstrahlung f
~ **camcorder** Digitalcamcorder m, digitaler Camcorder m
~ **camera** Digitalkamera f, digitale Kamera f
~ **camera technology** Digitalkameratechnik f
~ **cinema** digitales Kino n, Digitalkino n; elektronische Filmproduktion f
~ **cinema projection** digitale Kinoprojektion (Projektion) f
~ **circuit** digitaler Schaltkreis m, Digitalschaltkreis m
~ **code** digitaler Code m
~ **color camera** Digital-Farbkamera f
~ **color printer** Digitalfarbdrucker m
~ **color printing** Digitalfarbdruck m
~ **comb filter** digitales Kammfilter n
~ **compact camera** Digitalkompaktkamera f
~ **component video** digitales Komponentenvideo n
~ **component video signal** digitales Komponentensignal n
~ **compression standard** digitaler Kompressionsstandard m
~ **computer** Digitalrechner m, digitaler Computer m
~ **convolution** digitale Faltung f
~ **copier** Digitalkopierer m
~ **copying** digitales Kopieren n
~ **cut** Digitalschnitt m, digitaler Schnitt m
~ **data** digitale Daten pl, Digitaldaten pl
~ **data storage** 1. digitaler Datenspeicher m; 2. Digitaldatenspeicherung f
~ **data transmission** digitale Datenübertragung f
~ **decoder** Digitaldecoder m
~ **decoding** digitale Decodierung f
~ **densitometry** digitale Densitometrie f
~ **detector** digitaler Detektor m
~ **display** digitale Anzeige f, Digitalanzeige f; digitaler Bildschirm m, Digitalbildschirm m
~ **domain** Digitalbereich m
~ **dot** digitaler Druckpunkt m
~ **edit bay** digitaler Filmschnittplatz m
~ **editing** Digitalschnitt m, digitaler Schnitt m
~ **editing system** nichtlineares [digitales] Schnittsystem n
~ **effects studio** [digitales] Effektstudio n, Trickstudio n
~ **electric signal** digitales Signal n, Digitalsignal n
~ **electronics** Digitalelektronik f
~ **elevation model** digitales Höhenmodell n *(Fotogrammetrie)*
~ **encoding** digitale Codierung f
~ **enlarger** Digitalvergrößerer m
~ **file** digitale Datei f
~ **film** Digitalfilm m
~ **film scanner** [digitaler] Filmabtaster m, Filmscanner m, FAT
~ **film technology** Digitalfilmtechnik f
~ **filter** Digitalfilter n, digitales Filter n; zeitdiskretes Filter n
~ **filter network** digitales Filternetzwerk n
~ **filtering** Digitalfilterung f, digitale Filterung f
~ **fluorographic imaging** digitale Fluoroskopie f
~ **fluoroscopic imaging** digitale Radiografie f
~ **format** Digitalformat n
~ **framestore [device]** Digitalbildspeicher m
~ **gradient** digitaler Gradient m, Digitalgradient m
~ **graphics** digitale Grafik f
~ **graphics format** digitales Grafikformat n
~ **halftoning** s. dither technique
~ **hard proof** materieller Digitalproof m *(Druckvorstufe)*
~ **high-speed camera** Hochgeschwindigkeits-Bildwandlerkamera f
~ **image** Digitalbild n, digitales Bild n, Szene f
~ **image acquisition** Digitalbildaufnahme f

digital

~ **image back** Digital[kamera]rückteil *n*
~ **image coding** Digitalbildcodierung *f*
~ **image communication** digitale Bildkommunikation *f*
~ **image compression** digitale Bildkompression *f*
~ **image correlation** digitale Bildkorrelation *f*
~ **image data** Digitalbilddaten *pl*
~ **image data set** Digitalbilddatensatz *m*
~ **image display** Digitalbildschirm *m*, digitaler Bildschirm *m*
~ **image file** Digitalbilddatei *f*
~ **image manipulation** Digitalbildmanipulation *f*
~ **image processing** Digitalbildverarbeitung *f*, digitale Bildverarbeitung *f*
~ **image-processing system** digitales Bildverarbeitungssystem *n*
~ **image-processing technique** Digitalbildbearbeitungstechnik *f*
~ **image-processing unit** Digitalbildverarbeitungseinheit *f*
~ **image resolution** Digitalbildauflösung *f*
~ **image service** digitale Bilddienstleistung *f*
~ **image stabilizer** digitaler (elektronischer) Bildstabilisator *m*
~ **image storage** Digitalbildspeicherung *f*
~ **image technique** Digitalbildtechnik *f*
~ **image transformation** digitale Bildtransformation *f*
~ **imager** Digitalbildbearbeiter *m*
~ **imaging** 1. digitale Bildaufnahme *f*; 2. digitale Bildverarbeitung *f*; digitale Bildbearbeitung *f*; 3. digitale Bebilderung *f (Druckvorstufe)*

Digital Imaging and Communications in Medicine *US-Kommunikationsstandard für den Austausch von medizinischen Bilddaten*

digital imaging camera Digitalkamera *f*, digitale Kamera *f*
~ **imaging chain** digitale Abbildungskette *f*
~ **imaging sensor** Digitalbildsensor *m*
~ **imaging system** digitales Abbildungssystem *n*
~ **imaging technology** Digitalbildtechnik *f*
~ **imaging workstation** digitale Bildverarbeitungsstation *f*
~ **input** Digitaleingang *m*
~ **input device** digitales Eingabegerät *n*
~ **interface** digitale Schnittstelle *f*, Digitalschnittstelle *f*
~ **interpolation** digitale Interpolation *f*
~ **light microscope** [optisches] Digitalmikroskop *n*
~ **luminescence radiography** digitale Lumineszenzradiografie *f*
~ **mammography** digitale Mammografie *f*
~ **map** digitale Karte *f*
~ **mapping** digitale Kartierung *f*

~ **memory** digitaler Speicher *m*, Digitalspeicher *m*
~ **micromirror device video projector** DMD-Projektor *m*, DMD-Videoprojektor *m*
~ **microscopy** Digitalmikroskopie *f*
~ **mirror projector** [digitaler] Spiegelprojektor *m*
~ **modulation** digitale Modulation *f*, Tastung *f (Signalverarbeitung)*
~ **multimedia** digitales Multimedia *n*
~ **multispectral classification** digitale multispektrale Klassifikation *f*
~ **noise** digitales Rauschen *n*
~ **noise reduction** digitale Rauschreduktion (Störunterdrückung) *f*
~ **nonlinear editor** nichtlineares [digitales] Schnittsystem *n*
~ **object** digitales Objekt *n*
~ **optical disk** digitaler Bildplattenspeicher *m*
~ **optical recording** digitale optische Aufzeichnung *f*
~ **output** Digitalausgang *m*
~ **photofinishing** digitale Fotoverarbeitung *f*
~ **photogrammetry** digitale Fotogrammetrie *f*
~ **photograph** Digitalfoto *n*
~ **photographer** Digitalfotograf *m*
~ **photography** digitale Fotografie *f*, Digitalfotografie *f*, Digigrafie *f*
~ **photomicrography** digitale Mikrofotografie
~ **picture** 1. Digitalbild *n*, digitales Bild *n*, Szene *f*; 2. Digitalfilm *m*
~ **picture card** [digitale] Bildspeicherkarte *f*, Bildaufnahmekarte *f*, Videodigitalisierungskarte *f*, Bildeinzugskarte *f*, Framegrabber *m*
~ **picture effect** digitaler Bildeffekt *m*, Digitaleffekt *m*
~ **picture manipulator** Digitalbildmanipulator *m*
~ **picture memory** digitaler Bildspeicher *m*
~ **plate** *s.* ~ printing plate
~ **plotter** digitaler Plotter *m*
~ **print** Digitalprint *n*, Digital[aus]druck *m*
~ **printer** Digitaldrucker *m*, digitaler Printer *m*
~ **printing** digitales Drucken *n*, Digitaldruck *m*, digitaler Druck *m*
~ **printing plate** digital zu bebildernde Druckplatte *f*, Digitaldruckplatte *f*
~ **processing** digitale Verarbeitung *f*
~ **projection** Digitalprojektion *f*
~ **projector** digitaler Projektor *m*
~ **proof** digitaler Proof (Prüfdruck) *m*, Digitalproof *m*, Digitalprüfdruck *m*
~ **proofing** digitale Proofanfertigung *f*
~ **radar** Digitalradar *m*
~ **radiography** digitale Radiografie *f*
~ **realm** Digitalbereich *m*
~ **receiver** Digitalempfänger *m*

digital

- ~ **record head** digitaler Aufnahmekopf *m*
- ~ **recording** digitale Aufzeichnung *f*, Digitalaufzeichnung *f*
- ~ **recording technique** digitales Aufnahmeverfahren *n*
- ~ **representation** digitale Darstellung *f*
- ~ **residual sideband modulator** digitaler Restseitenbandmodulator *m*
- ~ **resolution** digitale Auflösung *f*
- ~ **sampling** digitale Abtastung *f*
- ~ **satellite equipment control** digitales Steuerungsverfahren *f* für Satelliteneinrichtungen *(Datenübertragung)*
- ~ **satellite news gathering** digitale Satelliten-Berichterstattung *f*
- ~ **satellite receiver** digitaler Satellitenempfänger *m*
- ~ **satellite television** digitales Satellitenfernsehen *n*
- ~ **scan converter** Digitalscankonverter *m*
- ~ **scanner** Digitalscanner *m*
- ~ **sensor** digitaler Sensor *m*, Digitalsensor *m*
- ~ **serial components** digital-serielle Komponenten *fpl*
- ~ **shearography** Digital-Shearografie *f*, digitale Shearografie *f*
- ~ **signal** digitales Signal *n*, Digitalsignal *n*
- ~ **signal processing** digitale Signalverarbeitung *f*
- ~ **signal processor** digitaler Signalprozessor *m*, Digitalprozessor *m*
- ~ **signature** digitale (elektronische) Signatur *f*; digitale (elektronische) Unterschrift *f*
- ~ **soft proof** immaterieller Digitalproof *m (Druck)*
- ~ **sound** Digitalton *m*
- ~ **sound recording** digitale Tonaufnahme *f*
- ~ **special effect** digitaler Spezialeffekt *m*, elektronischer Trick *m*, Computertrick *m*
- ~ **still camera** Digitalfotoapparat *m*, Digitalfotokamera *f*, digitaler Fotoapparat *m*
- ~ **still imaging** Digitalfotografie *f*, digitale Fotografie *f*, Digigrafie *f*
- ~ **still output** digitale Standbildausgabe *f*
- ~ **still picture** Digitalfoto *n*, digitales Stehbild (Standbild) *n*
- ~ **still video photography** digitale Standbildfotografie *f*
- ~ **storage** digitale Speicherung *f*, Digitalspeicherung *f*
- ~ **storage medium** digitales Speichermedium *n*
- ~ **studio** digitales Studio *n*
- ~ **studio [production] standard** digitaler Studiostandard *m*
- ~ **subscriber line** digitale Teilnehmeranschlussleitung *f*
- ~ **subtraction angiography** digitale Subtraktionsangiografie *f*, Computerangiografie *f*
- ~ **subtraction radiography** digitale Subtraktionsradiografie *f*
- ~ **surface model** digitales Oberflächenmodell *n*
- ~ **switcher** digitales Bildmischpult *n*
- ~ **tape editor** Schnittsteuergerät *n*
- ~ **technology** Digitaltechnik *f*, digitale Technik *f*
- ~ **television [broadcasting]** digitales Fernsehen *n*, Digitalfernsehen *n*
- ~ **television signal** digitales Fernsehsignal *n*
- ~ **television standard** Digitalfernsehstandard *m*
- ~ **television station** Digitalfernsehsender *m*
- ~ **television technology** Digitalfernsehtechnik *f*
- ~ **terrain map** digitale Flurkarte *f*
- ~ **terrain model** digitales Geländemodell *n*
- ~ **terrestrial broadcast tuner** Digitaltuner *m (Fernsehtechnik)*
- ~ **terrestrial broadcasting** digital terrestrische Ausstrahlung *f*
- ~ **terrestrial reception** digital terrestrischer Empfang *m*
- ~ **terrestrial television** digitales terrestrisches Fernsehen *n*, terrestrisches Digitalfernsehen *n*, digitales Antennenfernsehen *n*, Überallfernsehen *n*
- ~ **terrestrial video broadcast system** digitaler terrestrischer Bildfunk *m*
- ~**-to-analog [signal] converter** Digital-Analog-Konverter *m*, Digital-Analog-Wandler *m (s.a. decoder)*
- ~**-to-analog conversion** Digital-Analog-Wandlung *f*
- ~**-to-plate process** digitale Druckbildübertragung *f*
- ~ **tomosynthesis** digitale Tomosynthese *f*
- ~ **topology** digitale Topologie *f*
- ~ **transmission** digitale Übertragung *f*, Digitalübertragung *f*
- ~ **TV set** Digitalfernsehgerät *n*, Digitalfernsehempfänger *m*
- ~ **TV system** Digitalfernsehsystem *n*
- ~ **TV transmitter** Digitalfernsehsender *m*
- ~ **typeface** digitale Schrift *f*
- ~ **typesetting** digitaler Satz *m (s.a. desktop publishing)*
- ~ **typography** digitale Typografie *f*
- ~ **versatile disk** DVD[-Scheibe] *f (s.a. unter DVD)*
- ~ **video** 1. digitales Video *n*, Digitalvideo *n*; 2. *s.* ~ television broadcasting [system]
- ~ **video broadcasting [system]** digitaler Fernsehrundfunk (Bildfunk) *m*, digitale Fernsehausstrahlung *f*; Digitalfernsehen *n*, digitales Fernsehen *n*
- ~ **video camera** digitale Videokamera *f*, Digitalvideokamera *f*
- ~ **video cartridge (cassette)** Digitalvideokassette *f*

~ **video cassette recorder** digitaler Videokassettenrecorder *m*
~ **video compression** digitale Videokompression *f*
~ **video editing** digitale Videonachbearbeitung *f*, digitaler Videoschnitt *m*
~ **video effect** digitaler Videoeffekt *m*
~ **video effects device** digitales Bildeffektgerät (Effektgerät) *n*, DVE-Gerät *n*
~ **video format** digitales Videoformat *n*, DV-Format *n*
~ **video interactive** interaktives digitales Video *n*
~ **video link** Video[daten]bus *m*
~ **video processing** digitale Videobearbeitung *f*
~ **video production equipment** digitale Videoproduktionstechnik *f*
~ **video recorder** Digitalvideorecorder *m*
~ **video recording** digitale Videoaufzeichnung *f*
~ **video signal** digitales Videosignal *n*
~ **video technology** Digitalvideotechnik *f*
~ **videodisc** 1. digitale Videoplatte (Bildplatte) *f*; 2. *s.* ~ versatile disk
~ **videotape** Digital[video]band *n*
~ **videotape recorder** digitaler Videorecorder *m*, digitales Videosignal-Magnetband-Aufzeichnungsgerät *n*
~ **videotape recording system** digitales Videoband-Aufzeichnungssystem *n*
~ **vision mixer** digitales Bildmischpult *n*
~ **visual interface** digitale Anzeigeschnittstelle *f (Grafikkarte)*
~ **visual interface connection port** *s.* DVI connection port
~ **watermark** digitales Wasserzeichen *n*
~ **white balance** digitaler Weißabgleich *m*
~ **X-ray detector** Röntgenpixeldetektor *m*
~ **X-ray suite** digitale Röntgenanlage *f*
~ **zoom [feature]** digitales (elektronisches) Zoom *n*, Digitalzoom *n(m)*, elektronische Lupe *f (Videokamera)*
digitalize/to *s.* digitize/to
digitally encoded ultrasound digital codierter Ultraschall *m*
digitization Digitalisierung *f*, Analog-Digital-Umsetzung *f*
~ **noise** Digitalisierungsrauschen *n*; Quantisierungsrauschen *n*
digitize/to digitalisieren
digitized data set Digitaldatensatz *m*
~ **font** digitalisierte Schrift *f*
~ **image** digitalisiertes Bild *n*; Bildmatrix *f*
~ **photo[graph]** digitalisiertes Foto *n*
~ **signal** digitalisiertes Signal *n*
~ **terrain model** digitales Geländemodell *n*
digitizer Digitalisierer *m*, Digitalisiereinheit *f*, Digitalisiergerät *n*

digitizing board Digitalisierungskarte *f*, Bildeinzugskarte *f*, Bildaufnahmekarte *f (s.a.* frame grabber [card]*)*
~ **interval** Abtastintervall *n*, Abtastperiode[ndauer] *f*
~ **pen** Digitalisierstift *m*, Grafikstift *m*
~ **tablet** Digitalisiertablett *n*, Eingabetablett *n*, Grafiktablett *n*, grafisches Tablett *n*, Digitalisiertisch *m*
digraph gerichteter Graph *m*
dilate/to dilatieren, ausdehnen
dilation Dilatation *f*, Ausdehnung *f (Binärbildverarbeitung)*
~ **filter** Dilatationsoperator *m*, Dilatationsfilter *n*
~ **gradient** Dilatationsgradient *m*
~ **operation** Dilatationsoperation *f*
dilution Verdünnung *f*
dim/to dimmen
dim lichtarm, lichtschwach
~ **image** lichtschwaches Bild *n*
~ **light** Dämmerlicht *n*
~-**light vision** 1. Dämmerungssehen *n*, Übergangssehen *n*, mesopisches Sehen *n*; 2. *s.* dark-adapted vision
dimensional checking Maßprüfung *f*
~ **stability** Dimensionsstabilität *f*, Maßhaltigkeit *f*
dimensionality Dimensionalität *f*
~ **reduction** Dimensionsreduzierung *f*
dimensionally stable maßhaltig, maßkonstant *(z.B. Filmmaterial)*
dimensioning Dimensionierung *f*
dimensionless quantity dimensionslose Größe *f*
dimethylketone Dimethylketon *n*, Aceton *n (Lösungsmittel)*
dimetric projection dimetrische Projektion (Axonometrie) *f*, Dimetrie *f*
diminished image verkleinertes Bild *n*
diminishing glass Verkleinerungsglas *n*
dimmable dimmbar
dimmed light gedämpftes Licht *n*
dimmer [switch] Dimmer *m*, Lichtdimmer *m*; stufenloser Helligkeitsregler *m*; Lichtsteuergerät *n*
dimming Dimmung *f*
dimness of sight Schwachsichtigkeit *f*, Amblyopie *f*
DIN film speed, ~ rating (speed value) DIN-Filmempfindlichkeit *f*
dingbat [typografisches] Sonderzeichen *n*
diode Diode *f*
~ **area array** flächige Diode *f*
~ **laser** Diodenlaser *m*
~ **matrix** Diodenmatrix *f*
~ **modulator** Diodenmodulator *m*
~-**pumped laser** diodengepumpter Laser *m*
diopter Dioptrie *f*
~ **adjustment knob** Dioptrieneinstellknopf *m*
~ **correction [lens]** Dioptrienkorrektur[linse] *f*

diopter

~ **lens** Vorsatzlinse f, Vorsatzobjektiv n, Zusatzlinse f, Zusatzobjektiv n
~ **number** 1. Dioptrienzahl f; 2. s. dioptric power
dioptometer Dioptrometer n, Dioptrienmesser m
dioptre s. diopter
dioptric dioptrisch, lichtbrechend, fotorefraktiv
~ **adjustment** Dioptrieneinstellung f
~ **compensation** Dioptrienanpassung f, Dioptrienausgleich m
~ **power** [optische] Brechkraft f
~ **system** dioptrisches System n
dioptrics Dioptrik f
diorama Diorama n, Durchscheinbild n
dip and dunk processor Hänger[entwicklungs]maschine f, Filmentwicklungsmaschine f nach dem Hängerprinzip
~ **coating** Tauchbeschichtung f
diplexer Diplexer m *(Fernsehtechnik)*
diplopia Diplopie f, Doppeltsehen n
dipole Dipol m
~ **antenna** Dipolantenne f
~ **moment** Dipolmoment n
DIR coupler DIR-Kuppler m, DIR-Farbkuppler m
Dirac delta Dirac-Delta n
~ **delta function** Dirac-Funktion f, [Diracsche] Deltafunktion f, Impulsfunktion f *(Signalverarbeitung)*
~ **filter** Dirac-Filter n, Impulsfilter n, Nächste[r]-Nachbar-Filter n
~ **pulse** Dirac-Impuls m, Dirac-Stoß m
direct access Direktzugriff m, wahlfreier Zugriff m
~-**access file** Direktzugriffsdatei f
~-**access storage [device]** Direktzugriffsspeicher m, Schreib-Lese-Speicher m, RAM f(n)
~ **addressing** direkte (absolute) Adressierung f
~ **broadcast by satellite** Satelliten-Direktausstrahlung f
~ **broadcast satellite** Rundfunksatellit m, Direktempfangssatellit m, direktstrahlender Satellit m
~ **broadcast satellite transmission** Satelliten-Direktübertragung f
~ **color** direkte Farbzuordnung f
~-**contact exposure** Kontaktbelichtung f
~ **copy** Direktkopie f
~ **copying** Direktkopierung f
~ **current** Gleichstrom m
~ **digital color proof** digitaler Farbproof m
~ **estimation** direkte Schätzung f
~ **exposure** Direktbelichtung f
~-**exposure film** folienloser Film (Röntgenfilm) m
~ **front projection** Direktprojektion f
~-**gap semiconductor** direkter Halbleiter m
~ **glare** Direktblendung f

~ **imaging** Direktbebilderung f [in der Druckmaschine], direkte Bebilderung (Druckbildübertragung) f
~ **light** direktes Licht n, Direktlicht n
~ **lighting** direkte Beleuchtung f
~ **mail** personalisierte Werbesendungen fpl
~ **memory access** direkter Speicherzugriff m
~ **method of rectification** direkte Entzerrung f
~ **photography** Direktfotografie f
~-**positive copy** Direktkopie f
~-**positive emulsion** Direktpositivemulsion f, Positivemulsion f
~ **positive film** Direktpositivfilm m
~ **positive image** Direktpositiv n
~ **positive paper** Direktpositivpapier n
~ **positive process** Direktpositivverfahren n
~-**positive silver halide emulsion** Direktpositiv-Silberhalogenidemulsion f
~ **print** Direktausdruck m
~ **printing** Direktdruck m, direkter Fotodruck m
~ **printing process** direktes Druckverfahren n
~ **projection** Direktprojektion f
~ **radiation** direkte Strahlung f
~ **radiography** Direktradiografie f, direkte Radiografie f
~ **ray** direkter Strahl m
~ **recording** Direktaufzeichnung f, Livemitschnitt m
~ **reflection** gerichtete (regelmäßige) Reflexion f, Fresnel-Reflexion f
~ **reversal** Direktumkehr f
~ **reversal color film** Direktumkehrfarbfilm m
~-**reversal emulsion** Direktumkehremulsion f
~-**reversal film** Direktumkehrfilm m
~ **satellite broadcast** Satelliten-Direktübertragung f
~ **scanning** Direktabtastung f
~ **sound** Originalton m, O-Ton m, Live-Ton m
~ **sound positive** Direkttonpositiv n *(Lichttonfilm)*
~ **thermal printer** Thermodrucker m
~-**to-home** Satellitendirektempfang m, Satelliten-Individualempfang m
~ **toner** Direkttoner m
~ **toning** Direkttonung f, direkte Tonung f
~ **transfer** Direktübertragung f
~-**transfer gravure** flächenvariabler (autotypischer) Tiefdruck m
~ **transmission** Direktübertragung f
~ **triangulation** direkte Triangulation f
~-**view display (storage tube)** Direktsichtdisplay n, Direktsichtspeicherröhre f, [bistabile] Speicherbildröhre f
~ **view storage tube** Direktadressierröhre f

~ **viewfinder** Linsendurchsichtssucher *m*, Fernrohrsucher *m*, [optischer] Durchsichtssucher *m*
~ **viewing** 1. Direktbetrachtung *f*; 2. Aufsicht *f*, Obersicht *f*
~-**vision camera** Kompaktkamera *f*
~-**vision optical viewfinder** *s.* direct viewfinder
~-**vision prism** Amici-Prisma *n*, Geradsichtprisma *n* [nach Amici]
~-**vision spectroscope** Geradsichtspektroskop *n*
~-**vision viewfinder** *s.* direct viewfinder
~ **visual observation** Direktbetrachtung *f*
~ **volume visualization** direkte Volumenvisualisierung *f*
~-**writing paper** Auskopierpapier *n*
directed acyclic graph gerichteter azyklischer Graph *m*
~ **graph** gerichteter Graph *m*
~ **light** gerichtetes Licht *n*, Richtungslicht *n*
direction 1. Richtung *f*; 2. Regie *f* *(Filmarbeit)*
~ **code** Richtungscode *m*
~ **detection** Richtungserkennung *f*, Richtungsdetektion *f*, Orientierungsdetektion *f*
~ **in space** Raumrichtung *f*
~ **of film travel** Filmlaufrichtung *f*
~ **of incidence** Einfallsrichtung *f*
~ **of incident light** Lichteinfallsrichtung *f*
~ **of light** Lichtrichtung *f*
~ **of magnetization** Magnetisierungsrichtung *f*
~ **of motion (movement)** Bewegungsrichtung *f*
~ **of projection** Projektionsrichtung *f*
~ **of propagation** Ausbreitungsrichtung *f*
~ **of propagation of light** Lichtausbreitungsrichtung *f*
~ **of radiation** Strahlungsrichtung *f*, Ausstrahlungsrichtung *f*
~ **of rotation** Drehrichtung *f*
~ **of scan** Abtastrichtung *f*
~ **of scatter** Streurichtung *f*
~ **of shooting** Aufnahmerichtung *f*
~ **of sound** Schallausbreitungsrichtung *f*
~ **of tape travel** Bandlaufrichtung *f*
~ **of view[ing]** Sehrichtung *f*, Beobachtungsrichtung *f*
~ **of wave propagation** Wellenausbreitungsrichtung *f*
~-**sensitive filter** richtungsempfindliches Filter *n*
~-**sensitive filtering** richtungsempfindliche Filterung *f*
~-**sensitive low-pass filter** richtungsempfindliches Tiefpassfilter *n*
~ **vector** Richtungsvektor *m*
directional *s.* directionally dependent
~ **anisotropy** Richtungsabhängigkeit *f*, Anisotropie *f*
~ **antenna** Richtantenne *f*, gerichtete Antenne *f*
~ **coding** Richtungscodierung *f*
~ **filter** Richtungsfilter *n*, gerichtetes Filter *n*
~ **filtering** Richtungsfilterung *f*
~ **light source** gerichtete Lichtquelle *f*
~ **lighting** gerichtete Beleuchtung *f*
~ **low-pass filter** gerichtetes Tiefpassfilter *n*
~ **mic[rophone]** Richtmikrofon *n*
~ **sensitivity** Richtungsempfindlichkeit *f*
~ **specular reflection** gerichtete (regelmäßige) Reflexion *f*
~ **television antenna** Fernseh-Richtantenne *f*
directionality Gerichtetheit *f*
directionally dependent richtungsabhängig, anisotrop
~ **independent** richtungsunabhängig, isotrop
~ **sensitive** richtungsempfindlich
~ **sensitive edge detector** richtungsempfindlicher Kantendetektor *m*
directivity pattern Richtcharakteristik *f*, Richtwirkung *f* *(Mikrofon)*
directly viewed material Aufsichtsmaterial *n*
director Regisseur *m*; Filmregisseur *m*
~ **of photography** Chefkameramann *m*, Zweiter Bildregisseur *m*, leitender (lichtbestimmender, verantwortlicher) Kameramann *m*
director's cut Schnittfassung *f* des Regisseurs, Regisseur-Fassung *f* *(Filmschnitt)*
directory Verzeichnis *n*; Dateiverzeichnis *n* *(Computer)*
~ **file** Verzeichnisdatei *f*
directrix [curve] Direktrix *f* *(Leitlinie von Kegelschnitten)*
Dirichlet tessellation (tiling) Dirichlet-Parkettierung *f*, Voronoi-Mosaik *n* *(Computergrafik)*
disability glare physiologische Blendung *f*
disambiguation Disambiguierung *f* *(Zeichenerkennung)*
disc Scheibe *f*; Platte *f* *(s.a. unter disk)*
~ **camera** Diskkamera *f*
~ **drive** Scheibenlaufwerk *n*
discarded electronics Elektronikschrott *m*
discernible pattern unterscheidbares Muster *n*
discerning perzeptiv
discharge current Entladestrom *m*
~ **curve** Entladekurve *f*
~ **cycle** Entladungszyklus *m*
~ **energy** Entladungsenergie *f*
~ **image** Entladungsbild *n*
~ **lamp** Entladungslampe *f*
~ **pattern** Entladungsbild *n*
discolor/to verfärben
discoloration Verfärbung *f*
discomfort glare psychologische Blendung *f*

discontinuous

discontinuous s. discrete
discrete diskret, diskontinuierlich
~ **algorithm** diskreter Algorithmus m
~ **amplitude** diskrete Amplitude f
~ **approximation** diskrete Approximation f
~ **channel** diskreter Kanal m
~ **color space** diskreter Farbraum m
~ **convolution** diskrete Faltung f
~ **correlation** diskrete Korrelation f
~ **cosine transform[ation]** diskrete Kosinustransformation f
~ **data** diskrete Daten pl; digitale Daten pl
~ **delta function** diskrete Deltafunktion (Impulsfunktion) f, Kroneckersches Delta n
~ **detector** diskreter Detektor m
~ **fast Fourier transform** diskrete schnelle Fourier-Transformation f
~ **feature** diskretes Merkmal n
~ **filter** diskretes Filter n
~ **Fourier transform** diskrete Fourier-Transformation f
~ **frequency** diskrete Frequenz f
~ **frequency spectrum** diskretes Frequenzspektrum n
~ **geometry** diskrete Geometrie f
~ **gradient operator** diskreter Gradientenoperator m
~ **grid** diskretes Gitter n
~ **Hadamard transform** diskrete Hadamard-Transformation f
~ **histogram** diskretes Histogramm n
~ **image** diskretes Bild n
~ **image function** diskrete Bildfunktion f
~ **image signal** diskretes Bildsignal n
~ **impulse function** s. ~ delta function
~ **linear filtering** diskret lineare Filterung f
~ **noise** diskretes Rauschen n
~ **object** diskretes Objekt n
~ **relaxation** diskrete Relaxation f
~ **sampling** diskrete Abtastung f
~ **signal** diskretes Signal n
~ **sine (sinusoidal) transform[ation]** diskrete Sinustransformation f
~-**space** ortsdiskret
~-**space Fourier transform** ortsdiskrete Fourier-Transformation f
~-**space image** ortsdiskretes Bild n
~-**space signal** ortsdiskretes Signal n
~ **spatial Fourier transform** zweidimensionale diskrete Fourier-Transformation f
~ **spectrum** diskretes (diskontinuierliches) Spektrum n, Linienspektrum n
~-**time** zeitdiskret
~-**time convolution** zeitdiskrete Faltung f
~-**time filter** zeitdiskretes Filter n; Digitalfilter n, digitales Filter n
~-**time Fourier transform** zeitdiskrete Fourier-Transformierte f
~-**time oscillator** zeitdiskreter Oszillator m
~-**time signal** zeitdiskretes Signal n, Abtastsignal n, Scansignal n

~-**time signal processing** zeitdiskrete Signalverarbeitung f
~-**time system** zeitdiskretes System n
~ **transformation** diskrete Transformation f
~-**value signal** wertdiskretes Signal n
~ **Walsh-Hadamard transform** diskrete Walsh-Hadamard-Transformation f
~ **Walsh transform** diskrete Walsh-Transformation f
~ **wavelet transform** diskrete Wavelet-Transformation f
discreteness Diskretheit f
discretization Diskretisierung f
~ **error** Diskretisierungsfehler m; Abtastfehler m
~ **noise** Diskretisierungsrauschen n
discretize/to diskretisieren
discriminability Unterscheidungsvermögen n, Diskriminationsfähigkeit f
discriminant analysis Diskriminanzanalyse f, Trennanalyse f
~ **function** Diskriminanzfunktion f, Entscheidungsfunktion f *(Objekterkennung)*
~ **method** Diskriminanzmethode f *(Schwellenwertbildung)*
discriminating criterion (feature) Unterscheidungsmerkmal n
discrimination threshold Unterschiedsschwelle f
discriminative s. discriminatory
discriminatory ability Unterscheidungsvermögen n, Diskriminationsfähigkeit f
~ **analysis** Diskriminanzanalyse f, Trennanalyse f
~ **power** s. ~ ability
dish 1. Schale f; 2. Satellitenschüssel f
~ **development** Schalenentwicklung f
~ **processing** Schalenverarbeitung f
dished konkav
dishwarmer beheizbare Entwicklerschale f
disjoint, disjunct disjunkt, überlappungsfrei *(z.B. Bildbereiche)*
disk Scheibe f; Platte f *(s.a. unter disc)*
~-**based camcorder** Speicherkartencamcorder m
~ **drive** Plattenlaufwerk n; Diskettenlaufwerk n, Laufwerk n; Speicherkartenlaufwerk n
~ **memory** Plattenspeicher m
~ **shutter** 1. Scheibenverschluss m; 2. s. chopper
~ **storage** Plattenspeicherung f
~ **telescope** Koronograf m [nach Lyot]
diskette Diskette f, Computerdiskette f, Floppydisk f
dislocation contrast Versetzungskontrast m *(Elektronenmikroskopie)*
~ **line** Versetzungslinie f
disorder of vision Sehstörung f; Fehlsichtigkeit f, Ametropie f
disparity Disparität f

~ **analysis** Disparitätsanalyse *f*
~-**compensated prediction**
  disparitätskompensierte Prädiktion *f*
~ **estimation** Disparitätsschätzung *f*
~ **range** Disparitätsbereich *m*
~ **ratio** Disparitätsverhältnis *n*
~ **vector** Disparitätsvektor *m*
dispenser cathode imprägnierte Katode *f* *(Bildröhre)*
dispersant Dispergierungsmittel *n*
disperse/to dispergieren; zerstreuen
disperse dispers
dispersed light dispergiertes Licht *n*
dispersible dispergierbar
dispersing agent Dispergierungsmittel *n*
~ **instrument** *s.* spectroscope
~ **prism** Dispersionsprisma *n*, Zerstreuungsprisma *n*
dispersion 1. [chromatische] Dispersion *f*, Farbaufspaltung *f*, Regenbogeneffekt *m*; 2. Dispersion *f*, Dispergierung *f (z.B: von optischen Werkstoffen)*; Zerstreuung *f (von Strahlung)*; Streuung *f (Statistik)*
~ **angle** Dispersionswinkel *m*
~ **coefficient** Dispersionskoeffizient *m*
~ **equation** Dispersionsformel *f*
~ **filter** Dispersionsfilter *n*, Christiansen-Filter *n*
~ **spectroscopy** Dispersionsspektroskopie *f*
dispersity Dispersität *f*
dispersive dispersiv
~ **lens** Zerstreuungslinse *f*, Streulinse *f*, konkave (negative) Linse *f*, Konkavlinse *f*, Negativlinse *f*
~ **medium** dispersives Medium *n*
~ **power** Dispersionsvermögen *n*
displacement operator Verschiebungsoperator *m*
~ **sensor** Wegsensor *m*
~ **vector** Verschiebungsvektor *m*, Geschwindigkeitsvektor *m*
~ **vector field** Verschiebungsvektorfeld *n*
display/to anzeigen; wiedergeben; darstellen
display 1. Display *n*, Anzeige *f*, Kontrollanzeige *f*, [optische] Datenanzeige *f (s.a.* display device*)*; 2. Darstellung *f*; Wiedergabe *f*
~ **ability** Darstellungsvermögen *n (z.B. eines Monitors)*
~ **adapter** Bildschirmkarte *f*, Bildschirmadapter *m*, Grafikkarte *f*
~ **addressing** Bildschirmansteuerung *f*
~ **area** Anzeigefläche *f*, Displayfläche *f*; Bildschirmfläche *f*
~ **attribute** Darstellungsattribut *n*
~ **board** Bildschirmkarte f, Bildschirmadapter *m*, Grafikkarte *f*
~ **build-up** Bildaufbau *m (Video)*
~ **characteristic curve** Displaykennlinie *f*
~ **control** Bildschirmsteuerung *f*
~ **controller** Bildschirmsteuereinheit *f*
~ **curve** Bildröhrenkennlinie *f*

~ **cycle** Bildschirmzyklus *m*
~ **device** Anzeigegerät *n*, Anzeigevorrichtung *f*; Bildschirm[sicht]gerät *n*, Bildschirmanzeigegerät *n*, Sichtgerät *n*, Wiedergabegerät *n*
~ **drive electronics,** ~ **driver** Bildschirmtreiber *m*
~ **duration** Anzeigedauer *f*
~ **electronics** Anzeigeelektronik *f*
~ **element** Darstellungselement *n*
~ **face** Auszeichnungsschrift *f (Typografie)*
~ **field** Anzeigefeld *n*
~ **file** Displayliste *f*
~ **frame rate** *s.* ~ rate
~ **function** Displaykennlinie *f*
~ **image** Bildschirmbild *n*; Monitorbild *n*
~ **map** Bildschirmmaske *f*, Bildröhrenmaske *f*, Bildschirmrahmen *m*
~ **matrix** Bildmatrix *f*
~ **medium** Darstellungsmedium *n*; Bildschirmmedium *n*
~ **memory** Bildschirmspeicher *m*
~ **menu** Bildschirmmenü *n*
~ **mode** Anzeigemodus *m*, Darstellungsmodus *m*
~ **monitor** Monitor *m*
~ **noise** Bildschirmrauschen *n*
~ **panel** Anzeigefeld *n*
~ **pixel** Monitorpixel *n*
~ **process** Bildschirmprozess *m*
~ **processor** Displayprozessor *m*; Bildschirmprozessor *m*
~ **rate** Vorführfrequenz *f*, Abspielgeschwindigkeit *f (von Film- oder Videosequenzen)*
~ **representation** Bildschirmdarstellung *f*
~ **research** Displayforschung *f*
~ **screen** Wiedergabebildschirm *m*
~ **screen page** Bildschirmseite *f*
~ **setting** Bildschirmeinstellung *f*
~ **signal** Bildschirmsignal *n*
~ **space** Darstellungsbereich *m*
~ **subroutine** Bildprozedur *f*
~ **surface** 1. Darstellungsfläche *f*; 2. Bildschirmoberfläche *f*, Sichtfläche *f*
~ **system** Anzeigesystem *n*, Displaysystem *n*
~ **technology** Displaytechnik *f*, Displaytechnologie *f*, Anzeigetechnik *f*; Bildschirmtechnik *f*
~ **terminal** Bildschirmterminal *n*, Bildendgerät *n*
~ **thumbnail** 1. Vorschaubild *n*; 2. Layoutausdruck *m*
~ **transparency** Großdia[positiv] *n*, Großbilddia *n*
~ **tube** Bild[wiedergabe]röhre *f*
~ **type** Auszeichnungsschrift *f (Typografie)*
~-**type holography** Displayholografie *f*
~ **window** Bildschirmfenster *n*, Monitorfenster *n*
~ **workstation** Bildschirmarbeitsplatz *m*, Monitorarbeitsplatz *m*

displayable

displayable anzeigbar; wiedergebbar; darstellbar
~ resolution darstellbare Auflösung *f*
disposable camera Einwegkamera *f*, Wegwerfkamera *f*
dissecting microscope Präpariermikroskop *n*
dissector tube Dissektorröhre *f*, Bildsondenröhre *f*
dissimilarity measure Unähnlichkeitsmaß *n*
dissociation Dissoziation *f*
dissolution Auflösung *f (z.B. von Chemikalien)*
dissolve/to 1. überblenden; 2. auflösen *(Chemikalien)*
dissolve Überblendung *f*, Bildüberblendung *f*, Durchblende *f*
~ projection Überblendprojektion *f*
dissymmetric unsymmetrisch
dissymmetry Unsymmetrie *f*; Asymmetrie *f*
distance error Entfernungsfehler *m*
~ estimation Entfernungsschätzung *f*
~ gauge Entfernungsmesser *m*
~ map Abstandsbild *n*
~ measure Abstandsmaß *n*, Distanzmaß *n*
~ measurement Entfernungsmessung *f*
~ measuring system Entfernungsmesssystem *n*
~ metric Abstandsmaß *n*, Distanzmaß *n*
~ of distinct vision Nahpunktabstand *m*
~ perception Entfernungswahrnehmung *f*
~ radar Abstandsmessradar *n*
~ range Entfernungsbereich *m*; Entfernungseinstellbereich *m (Objektiv)*
~ ratio Entfernungsverhältnis *n*
~ ring Distanzring *m*
~ scale Entfernungsskale *f*
~ setting Entfernungseinstellung *f*
~ shot *s.* distant shot
~ transform[ation] Abstandstransformation *f*, Distanztransformation *f (Binärbildverarbeitung)*
~ value Abstandswert *m*
~-versus-angle signature Polarabstandsprojektion *f*
distant shot Fernaufnahme *f*; Totalaufnahme *f*, Totale *f*
distinct *s.* discrete
distinguishability Unterscheidbarkeit *f*
distinguishable unterscheidbar
distinguishing characteristic Unterscheidungsmerkmal *n*
distort/to verzerren, verzeichnen
distorted image (picture) Zerrbild *n*, verzerrtes (anamorphotisches) Bild *n*
distorting lens Zerrlinse *f*, Zerroptik *f (s.a. anamorphic lens)*
~ mirror Zerrspiegel *m*
distortion Verzeichnung *f*, Verzerrung *f*, Distorsion *f*

~ correction Entzerrung *f*, Verzeichnungskorrektur *f*
~ error Verzeichnungsfehler *m*, Bildmaßstabsfehler *m*
~-free unverzeichnet, unverzerrt, verzeichnungsfrei, verzerrungsfrei
~-free image unverzerrtes Bild *n*
~-free imaging unverzerrte (verzerrungsfreie) Abbildung *f*
~-free lens verzeichnungsfreies Objektiv *n*
~-free reconstruction verzerrungsfreie Rekonstruktion *f*
~ measure Verzerrungsmaß *n*
distributed feedback verteilte Rückkopplung *f*
~ virtual environment verteilte virtuelle Umgebung *f*
distribution 1. Verteilung *f*, Distribution *f*; 2. Programmausstrahlung *f*
~ amplifier Verteilerverstärker *m (Videotechnik)*
~ curve Verteilungskurve *f*
~ density Verteilungsdichte *f*
~ function Verteilungsfunktion *f*, Wahrscheinlichkeitsverteilungsfunktion *f*
~ of radioactivity Radioaktivitätsverteilung *f*
~ pattern Verteilungsmuster *n*
~ temperature Verteilungstemperatur *f*
distributive distributiv
distributivity Distributivität *f*
distributor Verleiher *m (Filmwirtschaft)*
disturbance transfer function Störübertragungsfunktion *f*
disturbing field Störfeld *n*
dither/to aufrastern
dither pattern Dithermatrix *f*
~ technique, dithering Aufrasterung *f*, Bildaufrasterung *f*, Halbtonrasterung *f*, Halbtonapproximation *f*, Dithering-Technik *f*, Dithering *n (s.a.* dot diffusion dithering*)*
dithering matrix Dithermatrix *f*
diverge/to divergieren
divergence Divergenz *f*
~ angle Divergenzwinkel *m*
~ operator Divergenzoperator *m (nichtlineare Filterung)*
divergent divergent
~ meniscus lens negativer Meniskus *m*
diverging bundle divergentes Bündel *n*
~ collimator divergierender Kollimator *m*
~ lens Zerstreuungslinse *f*, Streulinse *f*, negative Linse *f*, Negativlinse *f*, Konkavlinse *f*
divide-and-conquer strategy Teile-und-herrsche-Ansatz *m (Computergrafik)*
divided circle Teilkreis *m*
~-circle spectrometer Teilkreisspektrometer *n*
division of amplitude Amplitudenteilung *f*
DLP projector system DLP-System *n (Großbildwiedergabe; digitales Kino)*

Doppler

DMD video projector DMD-Projektor *m*, DMD-Videoprojektor
Dobsonian telescope Dobson-Teleskop *n*
docket [konventionelle] Auftragstasche *f* *(Druckgewerbe)*
doctor off/to [ab]rakeln
~ **[blade]** Rakel *f*, Abstreifrakel *f*, Rakelmesser *n*, Stahlrakel *f*
~ **blade [oscillation] stroke** Rakelschlag *m*
~ **roll** Rakelwalze *f*
document/to dokumentieren
document capture Dokumentenerfassung *f*
~ **copier** Dokumentenkopierer *m*
~ **copying** Dokumentenvervielfältigung *f*
~-**copying camera** Dokumentenkamera *f*
~-**copying machine** Dokumentenkopierer *m*
~ **feed** Dokumentenzuführung *f*
~ **feeder** Dokumentenzuführung *f* *(Baugruppe)*
~ **image** Dokumentenbild *n*, Schriftabbild *n*, Schriftabbildung *f*
~ **image analysis** Dokumentenanalyse *f*
~-**imaging system** Dokumentablichtungssystem *n*
~ **mark** Bildmarke *f* *(Mikrofilmtechnik)*
~ **page** Dokumentseite *f*
~ **paper** Dokumentenpapier *n*
~ **reader** Dokumentenlesegerät *n*, Dokumentenleser *m*, Belegleser *m*
~ **recognition** Dokumentenerkennung *f*
~ **reproduction** Dokumentenvervielfältigung *f*
~ **scanner** Dokumentenscanner *m*
~ **transfer** Dokumentenübertragung *f*
~ **viewer** *s.* ~ reader
documentary *s.* 1. ~ film; 2. ~ production
~ **camera person** Dokumentarfilmer *m*
~ **crew** Dokumentar[film]team *n*
~ **film** Dokumentarfilm *m*
~ **film production** Dokumentarfilmproduktion *f*
~ **filmmaker** Dokumentarfilmer *m*
~ **photograph** Dokumentaraufnahme *f*, Dokumentationsaufnahme *f*
~ **photographer** Dokumentarfotograf *m*
~ **photographic** dokumentarfotografisch
~ **photography** Dokumentarfotografie *f*, dokumentierende Fotografie *f*
~ **production** dokumentarische Produktion *f* *(Film, Video)*
dodge [out]/to abwedeln, abhalten, partiell (teilweise) belichten
dodging Abwedeln *n*, Kontrastausgleich *m* *(fotografische Arbeitstechnik)*
~ **tool** Abwedelmaske *f*; Abdeckschablone *f*
dolly Dolly *m*, Fahrstativ *n*, fahrbares Stativ *n*, Rollstativ *n*; Rollwagen *m*; Stativwagen *m*, fahrbarer Stativuntersatz *m*, Fahrspinne *f*
~ **grip** Kabelhelfer *m*, Kabelzieher *m*, Kabelhilfe *f* *(Aufnahmeteam)*
~ **in/to** heranfahren, zubewegen *(Filmkamera)*
~ **out/to** wegbewegen *(Filmkamera)*
~ **pusher** Dollyfahrer *m*, Kamerawagenfahrer *m*
~ **shot** Fahraufnahme *f* *(Filmarbeit)*
domain Bereich *m*, Domäne *f* *(Datenverarbeitung)*
~ **labeling** Gebietsmarkierung *f*
~ **of definition** Definitionsbereich *m*
~ **processing** globale Verarbeitung *f* *(Computergrafik)*
domestic communication satellite ziviler Fernmeldesatellit *m*
~ **projection equipment** Heimprojektionsanlage *f*, Heimprojektor *m*
~ **television** Heimfernsehen *n*
~ **VCR (video cassette recorder)** Heim[video]recorder *m*, Amateur-Videorecorder *m*
dominance Dominanz *f*, Äugigkeit *f* *(Physiologie des Sehens)*
dominant eye Referenzauge *n*
~ **light source** Führungslichtquelle *f*, Hauptlichtquelle *f*, szenenbestimmende Lichtquelle *f*
~ **subject** Hauptmotiv *n* *(z.B. einer Fotografie)*
~ **wavelength** dominante (dominierende) Wellenlänge *f*, farbtongleiche Wellenlänge *f*, dominante Frequenz *f* *(Farbmetrik)*
dongle Kopierschutzstecker *m*
dopant Dotiermittel *n*, Dotierstoff *m*, Dotand *m*
dope/to dotieren *(Halbleitermaterial)*
dope sheet *s.* 1. camera report; 2. camera exposure chart
doping Dotierung *f*
Doppler angle Doppler-Winkel *m*
~ **broadening** Doppler-Verbreiterung *f*
~ **device** Doppler-Sonograf *m*
~ **dilemma** Doppler-Dilemma *n*
~ **domain** Doppler-Raum *m*
~ **echocardiography** Doppler-Echokardiografie *f*
~ **effect** Doppler-Effekt *m*
~ **frequency shift** Doppler-Frequenzverschiebung *f*, Doppler-Verschiebung *f*
~ **image** Doppler-Bild *n*
~ **imaging** Doppler-Bildgebung *f*
~ **information display** Doppler-Monitor *m*
~ **lidar** Doppler-Lidar *m(n)*
~ **power imaging** Amplituden-Doppler *m* *(Sonografie)*
~ **power spectrum** Doppler-Spektrum *n*
~ **principle** Doppler-Prinzip *n*
~ **radar** Doppler-Radar *n*
~ **reflector** Doppler-Reflektor *m*
~ **resolution** Doppler-Auflösung *f*
~ **shift** Doppler-Verschiebung *f*, Doppler-Frequenzverschiebung *f*

Doppler

~ shift frequency
   Doppler-Verschiebungsfrequenz *f*
~-shift frequency Doppler-Frequenz *f*
~-shifted spectrum Doppler-Spektrum *n*
~-shifted ultrasound Doppler-Ultraschall *m*
~ signal Doppler-Signal *n*
~ space Doppler-Raum *m*
~ spectroscopy Doppler-Spektroskopie *f*
~ technique Doppler-Verfahren *n*
~ tomography Doppler-Tomografie *f*
~ ultrasound imaging technology
   Doppler-Sonografie *f*
~ widening Doppler-Verbreiterung *f*
~ width Doppler-Breite *f*,
   Doppler-Linienbreite *f*
dosage meter Dosimeter *n*
dose absorbierte Dosis *f*
~ buildup Aufbaueffekt *m*
   (Röntgendosimetrie)
~ deposition versus depth
   Tiefendosiskurve *f (Röntgendosimetrie)*
~ of X radiation Röntgen[strahlen]dosis *f*
dosimeter Dosimeter *n*
dosimetric dosimetrisch
dosimetry Dosimetrie *f*
dot Punkt *m*; Rasterpunkt *m*;
   Belichtungspunkt *m*; Belichterpixel *n*;
   Druckpunkt *m*, Punkt *m (Rasterdruck)*
~ address IP-Adresse *f (Internet)*
~ area Flächendeckung *f*,
   Flächendeckungsgrad *m*; Rasterdichte *f*,
   Rastertonwert *m (Druck)*
~ clock Bildelementtakt *m*, Pixeltakt *m*
~ definition Rasterpunktschärfe *f*
~ density Punktdichte *f (z.B. eines Druckers)*
~ diffusion dithering Streurasterung *f*,
   Zufallsrasterung *f*, frequenzmodulierte
   (nichtperiodische) Rasterung *f*,
   FM-Rasterung *f*
~ element Rasterpunkt *m*
~-etching solution Punktätzlösung *f*
~ gain (growth) Rasterpunktverbreiterung
   f, Punktüberhang *m*, Punktzuwachs *m*,
   Druckpunktzuwachs *m*,
   Rastertonwertzunahme *f*,
   Tonwertzuwachs *m*
~ image Rasterbild *n*
~ matrix Punktmatrix *f*, Punktraster *m(n)*
~ matrix display Punktmatrixbildschirm *m*
~ matrix image Punktmatrixbild *n*
~ matrix printer Punktmatrixdrucker *m*,
   Matrixdrucker *m*, Nadelmatrixdrucker
   m, Mosaikdrucker *m*
~ matrix printhead Punktmatrix-Druckkopf *m*
~ matrix wire printer Matrix-Nadeldrucker *m*
~ pattern Punktmuster *n*
~ pitch 1. Lochmaskenabstand *m*, 2.
   Pixelabstand *m*, Punktabstand *m*
   (Bildschirm)
~ product Skalarprodukt *n*
~-scanning method Punktrasterverfahren *n*
~ size Rasterpunktgröße *f*
~ spread *s.* ~ gain
dots per [square] inch Punkte *mp/* pro Zoll
   (Auflösungsmaß)
double anastigmat [lens]
   Doppelanastigmat *m(n)*
~-anastigmatic objective
   Doppelanastigmat *m(n)*
~ anode [X-ray] tube Doppelanodenröhre *f*
~-beam deflection Doppelstrahlablenkung *f*
~ buffering doppelte Pufferung *f*,
   Doppelpufferung *f*
   (Bilddatenverarbeitung)
~-burn/to doppelbelichten *(Reprografie)*
~-click/to doppelklicken
~-click Doppelklick *m*
~-coated film Doppelschichtfilm *m*,
   Zweischichtenfilm *m*
~-coated X-ray film
   Doppelschicht-Röntgenfilm *m*,
   doppelseitig begossener (beschichteter)
   Röntgenfilm *m*
~ coating Doppelbeschichtung *f (z.B. von Videobändern)*
~-coiled filament Doppelwendel *f*
~-concave lens Bikonkavlinse *f*, bikonkave Linse *f*
~ contrast Doppelkontrast *m*
   (Fluoroskopie)
~-convex lens Bikonvexlinse *f*, bikonvexe Linse
~-crystal monochromator
   Doppelkristallmonochromator *m*
~ dagger Doppelkreuz *n (Sonderzeichen)*
~-distribution machine
   Zweimagazinmaschine *f (Satztechnik)*
~-door light lock Doppeltürschleuse *f*
   (Dunkelraum)
~-emulsion X-rax film Doppelschichtfilm
   m, doppelseitig begossener
   (beschichteter) Röntgenfilm *m*
~ exposure Doppelbelichtung *f*
~-exposure hologram
   Doppelbelichtungshologramm *n*
~-exposure holography
   Doppelbelichtungsinterferometrie *f*,
   holografische Interferometrie *f*,
   Hologramminterferometrie *f*
~-exposure lock (prevention device)
   Auslöserverriegelung *f*, Auslösesperre *f*,
   Doppelbelichtungssperre *f*
~-exposure mask
   Doppelbelichtungsmaske *f*
~-exposure method
   Doppelbelichtungstechnik *f*
   (holografische Interferometrie)
~-extension bellows doppelter
   Balgenauszug *m*
~ eyepiece Doppelokular *n*

~-face printing beidseitiger (doppelseitiger) Druck m, Duplexdruck m
~-faced paper Duplexpapier n
~ flash Doppelblitz m
~-focus tube (valve) Doppelfokus[röntgen]röhre f
~ focusing mass spectrometer doppeltfokussierendes Massenspektrometer n
~-Gauss lens Gauß-Doppelobjektiv n
~ grating prism Doppelgitterprisma n
~ heterostructure Doppel-Heterostruktur f (Leuchtdiode)
~ image Doppelbild n
~-image microscopy Doppelbildmikroskopie f
~ image prism Doppelbildprisma n
~ image splitter Doppelbildteiler m
~-jet emulsion Doppeleinlaufemulsion f
~-jet precipitation Doppeleinlauf m
~-layer filter Doppelschichtfilter n
~ modulation Doppelmodulation f
~-nail illusion Zwei-Nadel-Illusion f (Stereosehen)
~-perforated film doppelseitig (zweiseitig) perforierter Film m
~ perforation doppelseitige Perforation f
~-phase hologram Doppelphasenhologramm n
~ prism Doppelprisma n
~-prism square Prismenkreuz n
~ projection Doppelprojektion f
~ projector Doppelprojektor m
~-pulse laser Doppelimpuslaser m
~ reflection [effect] Doppelreflexion f
~ refraction Doppelbrechung f
~ refractive index Doppelbrechzahl f
~-run eight-mm Doppel-Acht-Film m
~ screen Doppelbildschirm m (Fernsehtechnik)
~-screen film cassette Film-Folien-Kombination f (Radiografie)
~ slit Doppelspalt m (Optik)
~-slit experiment Doppelspaltversuch m (Interferenzoptik)
~-system recording (shooting) Zweistreifenverfahren n, Zweibandverfahren n (Tonfilmschnitt)
~ vision Doppeltsehen n, Diplopie f
~-way printing beidseitiges Drucken n
~-weight kartonstark (Papier)
doublet [lens] 1. Doppelobjektiv n, Dualobjektiv n, Dublettlinse f, Dublett n; 2. Duplet n (zweilinsige Lupe)
~ lens system zweiteiliges Objektiv n
doubling Dublieren n (Druckschwierigkeit)
doubly logarithmic paper doppelt logarithmisches Papier
~ refract/to doppelbrechen
~ refracting crystal doppelbrechender Kristall m
doughnut, dount Lochblende f (bes. von Scheinwerfern)

douser Feuerschutzklappe f (Projektor, Scheinwerfer)
Dove prism Dove-Prisma n, Dovesches Umkehrprisma n
down-convert/to abwärtskonvertieren
~ path s. downlink
~-sample/to abwärtstasten
downconversion Abwärtskonvertierung f, Dezimation f (Signalverarbeitung)
downconverter Abwärtskonverter m
downlink Abwärtsstrecke f (Satellitenübertragung)
download/to herunterladen, fernladen (Daten)
download Herunterladen n; Download m
~ time Downloadzeit f
downloadable [herunter]ladbar
downsampler Abwärtstaster m
downsampling Abwärtstastung f, Unterabtastung f
downscaling Abwärtsskalierung f
downstream keyer Schrifteinblender m, Schriftzumischer m, Schriftzusetzer m (Video)
downward compatibility Abwärtskompatibilität f, Rückwärtskompatibilität f
~ compatible abwärtskompatibel, rückwärtskompatibel
~ looking infrared [system] abwärts gerichtetes Infrarotsystem n (Wärmebilderfassung)
dowser s. douser
DP s. director of photography
dpi, DPI s. dots per [square] inch
draft mode Entwurfsmodus m (Matrixdrucker)
~ quality Entwurfsqualität f (Matrixdrucker)
drafting plotter Plotter m, [rechnergesteuerte] Zeichenmaschine f
~ program Zeichenprogramm n
drag-and-drop [feature] Ziehen-und-Ablegen n (Computergrafik)
drain Senke f (Signalverarbeitung)
~ edge Ablaufkante f (geometrische Datenverarbeitung)
draw/to zeichnen
draw program Zeichenprogramm n
drawing Zeichnung f
~ eyepiece Zeichenokular n
~ paper Zeichenpapier n
~ program Illustrationsprogramm n
~ surface Zeichenfläche f (Gerätekoordinatensystem)
~ to scale maßstäbliche Zeichnung f
~ tool Zeichenwerkzeug n
drawtube Ausziehtubus m, Teleskoptubus m (s.a. telescope tube)
drier Trockenstoff m, Sikkativ n
drive Laufwerk n
~ circuit Treiberschaltung f
~-in theater Autokino n, Drive-in-Kino n
~ pulse Ansteuerimpuls m

drive

~ **tape** Zugband n
driver Treiber m
~ **assistance system** Fahrerassistenzsystem n
~ **electronics** s. driving electronics
~ **software** Treibersoftware f
driver's license photo Führerscheinfoto n
driving electronics Ansteuerelektronik f, Treiberelektronik f
~ **signal** Ansteuersignal n
~ **simulator** Fahrsimulator m
drop bed herabklappbarer Laufboden m
~ **cable** Hausanschluss m (Kabelfernsehen)
~ **cap[ital]** hineingestellte Initiale f (Typografie)
~-**in loading system** Drop-in-Ladeautomatik f
~ **modulation technology** Tropfenmodulationstechnologie f (Tintenstrahldruck)
~-**on-demand jet** pulsierender Strahl m (Tintenstrahldruck)
~ **shutter** Fallverschluss m
droplet size Tröpfchengröße f
dropout Signalausfall m, Signaleinbruch m; Aussetz[fehl]er m; Ausfallstelle f; Bildausfall m, Bildaussetzer m; Tonaussetzer m
~ **highlight** Glanzlicht n, Hochlicht n
drum color scanner Farbscanner m
~ **digitizer (digitizing system)** s. drum-type scanner
~ **dryer** Trommeltrockner m (Bildaufbereitung)
~ **plotter** Trommelplotter m, Walzenplotter m
~ **press** Satellit-Druckeinheit f
~ **printer** Trommeldrucker m, Walzendrucker m
~ **processing** Trommelentwicklung f
~ **processor** Trommelentwicklungsmaschine f
~-**type camera** Trommelkamera f
~-**type scanner** Trommelscanner m, Rollenscanner m
dry-cell battery Trockenbatterie f
~-**collodion plate** Trockenkollodiumplatte f, trockene Kollodiumplatte f
~-**collodion process** trockenes Kollodiumverfahren n
~ **developer** Trockenentwickler m (Elektrofotografie)
~ **development** Trockenentwicklung f
~ **dot-etching** Trockenätzen n
~ **equipment** Trockenbereich m, Trockenteil m (Dunkelkammer)
~ **etching system** Trockenätzanlage f
~ **etching technique** Trockenätztechnik f
~ **film** Trockenfilm m
~ **ink** Festtinte f, Trockentinte f
~ **ink process** Trockentintenverfahren n (Druck)

110

~ **lens (objective)** Trockenobjektiv n, Trockensystem n (Lichtmikroskopie)
~-**mount[ing] press** Trockenklebepresse f
~ **offset** Trockenoffset[druck] m, wasserloser Offsetdruck m, Trockenflachdruck m, Letter[off]setdruck m; indirekter Hochdruck m
~ **photocopying process** Trockenkopierverfahren n
~ **photography** Trockenfotografie f
~ **plate** Trockenplatte f
~-**plate camera** Trockenplattenkamera f
~-**plate magazine** Trockenplattenmagazin n
~-**plate process** Trockenplattenverfahren n
~-**process printing** Trockendruckverfahren n
~ **processing** wasserlose Verarbeitung (Fotoverarbeitung) f
~ **proof** Druckvorstufenproof m, Andruckersatz m
~ **side** Trockenteil m, Trockenbereich m (Dunkelkammer)
~-**to-dry processing** Trockenverarbeitung f (Fotoverarbeitung)
~-**to-dry time** Trocken-Trocken-Zeit f (Fotoverarbeitung)
~ **toner** Trockentoner m
~-**trap/to** nass auf trocken drucken
drying by absorption wegschlagende Trocknung f (von Druckfarben)
~ **cabinet** Trockenschrank m
~ **chamber** Trockenkammer f
~ **mark** Trockenfleck m (z.B. auf Filmmaterial)
~ **oven** Trockenschrank m
~ **rack** Trockengestell n
~ **temperature** Trocknungstemperatur f, Trockentemperatur f
~ **time** Trocknungszeit f
DTH s. direct-to-home
DTS s. digital theater sound
DTV, DTVB s. digital television [broadcasting]
dual apodization duale Apodisation f
~ **bus** Doppelbus m (Datenübertragung)
~-**component toner** Zweikomponententoner m
~ **condenser** Doppelkondensor m
~-**fork claw** doppelseitiger Transportgreifer m (Kinotechnik)
~ **graph** dualer Graph m
~-**image filter** Doppelgängerfilter n
~-**modulation** Doppelmodulation f
~ **operator** dualer Operator m
~ **prism** Doppelprisma n
~ **scan** Zweifachabtastung f (Flüssigkristallanzeige)
~ **track** Doppelspur f (Filmtonaufnahmetechnik)
duality Dualität f
dub/to 1. überspielen; 2. vertonen; nachvertonen; 3. kopieren (Videobandmaterial); 4. s. ~ in/to

dub in/to einspielen *(z.B. Toneffekte in eine Film- oder Videoproduktion)*
~ 1. Überspielung *f*; Einspielung *f*; 2. Video[band]kopie *f*
dubber Überspielgerät *n*
dubbing Überspielung *f*; Vertonung *f*; Nachvertonung *f*, Tonnachbearbeitung *f*, Audiopost[produktion] *f*
~ **print** Synchronkopie *f*
~ **stage** Tonstudio *n*, Tonatelier *n*
~ **theater** Umspielraum *m*
Dubray-Howell perforation Dubray-Howell-Lochung *f*
duct fresh kastenfrisch *(Druckfarbe)*
~ **roller** s. ductor [roller]
~ **tape** s. gaffer tape
ductor [roller] Duktor *m*, Farb[kasten]walze *f (Druckwerk)*
dull finish Satinage *f (Papier)*
~ **surface** matte Oberfläche *f*
dulling spray Mattspray *n*
Dultgen halftone intaglio process flächentiefenvariabler Tiefdruck *m*
dummy 1. Überspielgerät *n*; 2. Probelayout *n*
~ **camera** Kameraimitation *f*
~ **coordinate** Hilfskoordinate *f*
~ **duotone** unechter Duplexdruck *m*
dumpster [elektronischer] Papierkorb *m (Computer)*
duobinary duobinär
duodecimal digit Duodezimalziffer *f*
duodenoscope Duodenoskop *n*
duodenoscopy Duodenoskopie *f*, Zwölffingerdarmendoskopie *f*
duotone [halftone image] Zweifarben-Rasterbild *n*, Duotonabbildung *f*
~ **plate** Zweifarbenplatte *f*
~ **process** Duoton-Verfahren *n*, Duplexdruck *m*
dupe/to s. duplicate/to
dupe s. 1. duplicate [copy]; 2. duplicate film; 3. duplicate slide; 4. duplicate negative
~ **neg[ative]** s. duplicate negative
duplex bidirektional
~ **halftone** unechter Duplexdruck *m*
~ **matrix** Zweibuchstabenmatrize *f*
~ **mode (operation)** Duplexbetrieb *m (z.B. in der Ultraschallbildgebung)*
~ **paper** Duplexpapier *n*
~ **press** Schön- und Widerdruckmaschine *f*, Perfektormaschine *f*
~ **printing** beidseitiges Drucken *n*
~ **scanner** Duplexgerät *n (Ultraschallbildgebung)*
duplexer [switch] Duplexgerät *n*; Sende-Empfangs-Duplexer *m*, Sende-Empfangs-Umschalter *m*, Sende-Empfangs-Weiche *f*
duplica[ta]able duplizierbar
duplicate/to duplizieren; vervielfältigen

duplicate [copy] Duplikat *n*; Vervielfältigung *f*; Abzug *m*
~ **film** Duplikatfilm *m*, Dup[likat] *n*
~ **negative** Duplikatnegativ *n*, Dup-Negativ *n*, Zweitnegativ *n*; Zwischennegativ *n*, Internegativ *n*
~ **[relief] plate** Duplikatdruckform *f*, Duplikat[buch]druckplatte *f*, Abformung *f*, Stereotypplatte *f*, Stereo *n*, Klischee *n*, Druckklischee *n*, Hochdruckplattennachformung *f*
~ **slide (transparency)** Diakopie *f*, Diaduplikat *n*
duplicating color film Duplizierfarbfilm *m*
~ **device** Vervielfältigungsgerät *n*
~ **film** Duplizierfilm *m*
~ **machine** Bürodruckmaschine *f*
~ **-printing process** Vervielfältigungsverfahren *n*
~ **stock** Dupliziermaterial *n*
duplication Duplizierung *f*; Vervielfältigung *f*
~ **process** Duplizierprozess *m*
duplicator Dupliziergerät *n*; Vervielfältiger *m*, Bürodruckmaschine *f (s.a. manifolder)*; Kleinoffsetmaschine *f*, Offsetvervielfältiger *m*
duplitized film Zweischichtenfilm *m*, Doppelschichtfilm *m*
~ **X-ray film** Doppelschicht-Röntgenfilm *m*, doppelseitig begossener (beschichteter) Röntgenfilm *m*
duration-accurate zeitgenau
dust on/to aufstauben
~ **speck (spot)** Staubfleck *m*
Dutch telescope Galilei-Fernrohr *n*, Galilei-Teleskop *n*, Holländisches Fernrohr *n*
duty cycle Tastverhältnis *n (Signalverarbeitung)*
DV camcorder digitaler Videocamcorder *m*
DV camera Digitalvideokamera *f*
DV format digitales Videoformat *n*, DV-Format *n*
DVB s. digital video broadcasting
~ **receiver** DVB-Empfänger *m*, Digitalfernsehgerät *n*; Multimedia-Terminal *n*
~ **receiving card** DVB-Empfängerkarte *f*, DVB-Karte *f*
DVD DVD[-Scheibe] *f (s.a. digital versatile disk)*
~ **audio** DVD-Audio *n*
~ **audio disk** DVD-Tonträger *m*
~ **disk** s. DVD
~ **movie** DVD-Film *m*
~ **player** DVD-Spieler *m*, DVD-Videospieler *m*, DVD-Player *m*
~ **recorder** DVD-Recorder *m*, DVD-Videorecorder *m*
~ **scanning** DVD-Abtastung *f*
~ **technology** DVD-Technik *f*
~ **unit** DVD-Anlage *f*
~ **video** DVD-Video *n*

DVI connection port DVI-Anschluss m, DVI-Eingang m
dwell period Verweildauer f, Verweilzeit f (z.B. eines Detektors)
~ **time** Zielverweilzeit f (Radar)
DX code DX-Code m (Kleinbildfilm)
DX coding [system] DX-Codierung f
dyadic dyadisch (s.a. unter binary)
~ **decomposition** dyadische Zerlegung f (Bildverarbeitung)
~ **operator** dyadischer Operator m
~ **point operation** dyadische Punktoperation f
~ **set** dyadische Menge f (Wavelet-Transformation)
~ **wavelet transform** dyadische Wavelet-Transformation f
dye/to färben
dye-based ink Farbtinte f
~ **bath** Farbstoffbad n
~ **bleach [process]** Farbsilberbleich[verfahr]en n, Farbstoff[aus]bleichung f; Silberfarbbleichverfahren n, Farb[aus]bleichverfahren n (Colorpositivverarbeitung)
~ **bleach solution** Farbbleichbad n
~ **bleaching** s. ~ bleach [process]
~ **cloud** Farbstoffwolke f
~ **color** bunte Farbe f, Buntfarbe f
~ **concentration** Farbkonzentration f
~ **contrast** Farbstoffkontrast m
~ **coupler** Farb[stoff]kuppler m, Kuppler m (Farbfotografie)
~ **coupling** Farbkupplung f
~ **density** Farbstoffdichte f
~ **desensitization** Farbstoffdesensibilisierung f
~ **destruction** Farbstoffabbau m
~ **destruction process** Farbstoffabbauverfahren n, Farbbleichverfahren n (Farbfotografie)
~ **developer** s. developer dye
~ **diffusion** Farbstoffdiffusion f
~ **diffusion method** Farbstoffdiffusionsverfahren n
~ **diffusion printer** s. ~ sublimation printer
~ **diffusion thermal transfer printing,** ~ **diffusion transfer process** Farbstoffdiffusionsverfahren n
~ **donor ribbon** Farbband n, Druckerfarbband n
~ **fading** Farbstoffausbleichung f
~ **formation** Farbstoffbildung f
~ **formation reaction** Farbbildungsreaktion f
~ **former** Farbbildner m
~-**forming agent** Farbbildner m (Farbfotografie)
~-**forming coupler** Farb[stoff]kuppler m, Kuppler m (Farbfotografie)
~-**forming developer** Farbstoffentwickler m
~-**forming layer** farbstoffbildende Schicht f

~ **generation** Farbstoffbildung f
~ **globule** Farbstoffkügelchen n
~ **hue** Buntton m, Farbton m, Farbfrequenz f
~ **image** Farbstoff[teil]bild n
~ **imbibition print** Druckkopie f
~ **imbibition process** s. transfer [printing] process
~ **laser** Farbstofflaser m
~ **layer** Farbstoffschicht f
~ **mask** Farbstoffmaske f
~ **masking** Farbstoffmaskierung f
~ **molecule** Farbstoffmolekül n
~ **release** Farbstofffreisetzung f
~ **releaser** farbstoffabspaltender Precursor m (Farbfotografie)
~-**sensitized** farbsensibilisiert
~ **sensitizer** Farbsensibilisator m
~ **solution** Farbstofflösung f
~ **stability** Farbstoffstabilität f
~ **sublimation printer** Farb[thermo]sublimationsdrucker m, Thermosublimationsdrucker m, Thermotransferdrucker m, Farb-Thermoprinter m
~ **sublimation printing** Farbsublimationsdruck m, Thermosublimationsdruck m, Thermotransferdruck m, Thermodiffusionsdruck m
~ **transfer** Farbstoffübertragung f
~ **transfer [printing] process** Farbstoffübertragungsverfahren n
~ **transfer print** Druckkopie f (Farbfotografie)
dyed gelatin filter Gelatinefilter n
~-**in-the-mass glass filter** [in der Masse gefärbtes] Vollglasfilter n
dyeline process s. diazo copying process
dyestuff Farbstoff m
dynamic astigmatism dynamischer Astigmatismus m
~ **coding** dynamische (voll adaptive) Codierung f
~ **diffraction theory** dynamische Theorie f (Elektronenstrahlbeugung)
~ **elastography** dynamische Elastografie f
~ **focusing** dynamische Fokussierung f
~ **graphic simulation** grafisch-dynamische Simulation f
~-**graphic simulation** grafisch-dynamische Simulation f
~ **Huffman [en]coding** dynamische Huffman-Codierung f
~ **image** dynamisches Bild n
~ **image processing** Bewegtbildverarbeitung f
~ **Markov coding** dynamische Markow-Codierung f
~ **microphone** dynamisches Mikrofon m
~ **mosaic** dynamisches Mosaik n
~ **noise limiter** dynamischer Störbegrenzer m

~ **noise suppression** dynamische Rauschunterdrückung f
~ **picture control** dynamische Bildkorrektur f
~ **pixel management** *ein Verfahren des elektronischen Videoformatwechsels ohne Auflösungsverlust*
~ **programming** dynamische Programmierung f
~ **quantization** dynamische Quantisierung f
~ **random-access memory** dynamischer Schreib-Lese-Speicher m mit wahlfreiem Zugriff
~ **range** Dynamikbereich m, Dynamikumfang m; Leuchtdichtebereich m; Ruhegeräuschspannugsabstand m
~ **range compression** Dynamikkompression f
~ **range suppression** Dynamikreduktion f
~ **resolution** dynamische Auflösung f
~ **scanning** dynamische Abtastung f
~ **scanning force microscopy** dynamische Rasterkraftmikroskopie f
~ **scene** dynamische Szene f
~ **signal range** *s.* ~ range
~ **simulation** dynamische Simulation f
~ **spectroscopy** dynamische Spektroskopie f
~ **thresholding** adaptive Schwellenwertbildung f
~ **time warping** dynamische Zeitverzerrung f *(Mustererkennung)*
~ **track following** dynamische Spurlagenregelung f *(Magnetbandtechnik)*
dynamics 1. Dynamik f; 2. dynamische Animation f
dynode Dynode f, Prallelektrode f *(Fotoelektronenvervielfacher)*

E

E-cinema s. electronic cinema
e-form Online-Formular n
e-mail/to mailen
E-mail E-Mail f, elektronische Post f
e-text elektronischer Text m
early warning radar Frühwarnradar n
~ **warning radar system** Radar-Frühwarnsystem n
earphone Kopfhörer m
earth imaging (observation) satellite Erdbeobachtungssatellit m, Erderkundungssatellit m, Fernerkundungssatellit m
~ **station** Erdefunkstelle f, [empfangende] Bodenstation f *(Datenübertragung)*
ease of operation Bedien[ungs]komfort m, Handhabungskomfort m
easel Kopierrahmen m, Kontaktkopierrahmen m
EAV s. end of active video
EBCT scanner s. electron beam CT scanner
Eberhard effect Eberhard-Effekt m *(Fotoentwicklung)*
eccentric exzentrisch
eccentricity Exzentrizität f *(Formmerkmal)*
ECDIS s. electronic chart display and information system
echelette [grating] Echelettegitter n, Blaze-Gitter n, geblaztes Gitter n
echelle [grating] Echellegitter n
~ **spectrograph** Echellespektrograf m
echelon [grating] Stufengitter n
echo Echo n *(Sonografie, Radar)*
~ **brightening** Echoaufhellung f
~ **cancellation** Echoausblendung f
~ **enhancement** Echoverstärkung f, [künstliche] Echovergrößerung f
~ **field** Echofeld n
~ **formation** Echobildung f
~ **image** Echobild n
~ **intensity** Echointensität f
~ **leading edge** Eintrittsecho n *(Sonografie)*
~ **pattern** Echomuster n, Echostruktur f
~ **planar imaging** Echoplanarverfahren n
~**-planar imaging** echoplanare Bildgebung f *(Magnetresonanztomografie)*
~ **planar imaging sequence** Echoplanarsequenz f
~ **signal** Echosignal n, Reflexsignal n *(Sonografie, Radar)*
~ **signal amplitude** Echoamplitude f
~ **signal processing** Echosignalverarbeitung f
~ **sounder** Echolot n
~ **sounding** Echolotung f
~ **stretching** s. ~ enhancement
~ **suppression** Echounterdrückung f
~ **suppressor** Echounterdrücker m
~ **time** Echozeit f
~ **trailing edge** Austrittsecho n *(Sonografie)*
~ **train** Echozug m
~ **unit** Nachhallgerät n, Hallgenerator m
echocardiac image, echocardiogram Echokardiogramm n
echocardiographic echokardiografisch
echocardiography Echokardiografie f, Ultraschallkardiografie f
echocardiology Echokardiologie f
echoencephalographic echoenzephalografisch
echoencephalography Echoenzephalografie f
echogenic echobildend
echogram Echogramm n
echograph Echograf m
echographic echografisch
echography 1. Echografie f; 2. s. sonography f
echoscope Echoskop n
edge Kante f
~ **acuity (acuteness)** Kantenschärfe f
~**-adaptive filtering** kantenadaptive Filterung f
~ **angle** Kantenwinkel m
~ **approximation** Kantenapproximation f
~**-based segmentation** kantenbasierte (kantenorientierte) Segmentierung f
~ **block coding** Kantenblockcodierung f
~ **center** Kantenmittelpunkt m
~ **coherence** Kantenkohärenz f
~ **coloring** Kantenfärbung f
~ **contrast** Kantenkontrast m, Kantenschärfe f; Randkontrast m
~ **corruption** Kantenverschmierung f
~ **crispening** s. ~ enhancement
~ **curvature** Kantenkrümmung f
~ **damage** Randverletzung f
~ **definition** Kantenschärfe f; Rand[bild]schärfe f
~ **detail** Kantendetail n
~ **detectability** Kantenerkennbarkeit f
~ **detection** Kantenerkennung f, Kantendetektion f
~ **detection filter (operator)** Kantendetektionsfilter n
~ **detection operator** Kantenoperator m
~ **detector** Kantendetektor m, Kantenfinder m, Kantendetektionsalgorithmus m
~ **direction** Kantenrichtung f
~ **distortion** Kantenverzerrung f; Randverzeichnung f
~ **effect** Kanteneffekt m, Nachbareffekt m
~ **element** Kantenelement n, Kantenpixel n
~**-emitting LED** kantenemittierende Leuchtdiode (Lumineszenzdiode) f
~ **endpoint** Kantenendpunkt m
~**-enhanced image** kantenverstärktes Bild n

- ~ **enhancement** Kantenhervorhebung *f*, Kantenbetonung *f*, Kantenanhebung *f*, Kantenverstärkung *f*, Kantenanschärfung *f*, Bildkantenversteilerung *f*
- ~ **enhancement algorithm** Kantenverstärkungsalgorithmus *m*
- ~ **enhancer** kantenverstärkendes Filter *n*
- ~-**enhancing filter** kantenverstärkendes Filter *n*
- ~ **extraction** Kantenextraktion *f (Bildsegmentierung)*
- ~ **feature** Kantenmerkmal *n*
- ~ **filter** Kantenfilter *n*
- ~ **filter mask** Kantenfiltermaske *f*
- ~ **finding** Kantenfindung *f*
- ~-**finding technique** Kantenfindungstechnik *f*
- ~ **flag** Kantenanzeiger *m (Computergrafik)*
- ~ **flicker** Kantenflackern *n*
- ~ **following** Kantenverfolgung *f*
- ~-**following algorithm** Kantenverfolgungsalgorithmus *m*
- ~ **gradient** Kantengradient *m*
- ~ **gradient analysis** Kantenbildanalyse *f*
- ~ **guide** Anlagekante *f*, Führungskante *f*
- ~ **histogram** Kantenhistogramm *n*
- ~ **identification** Kantenidentifikation *f*, Kantenidentifizierung *f*
- ~ **image** *s.* ~ map
- ~ **intensity** Kantenintensität *f*
- ~ **intersection algorithm** Indexverfahren *n*
- ~ **kurtosis** Kantensteilheit *f*
- ~ **length** Kantenlänge *f*
- ~ **light** Kantenlicht *n*
- ~ **linking** Kantenverknüpfung *f*
- ~ **list** Kantenliste *f (polygonales Netz)*
- ~ **localization** Kantenlokalisation *f*, Kantenlokalisierung *f*
- ~ **locating behavior** Kantenlokalisierungsverhalten *n*
- ~ **location** Kantenort *m*
- ~ **map** Kantenbild *n (Bildsegmentierung)*
- ~ **margin** Kantenabstand *m*
- ~ **model** Kantenmodell *n*
- ~ **modeling** Kantenmodellierung *f*
- ~ **noise** Kantenrauschen *n*
- ~ **normal** Kantennormale *f*
- ~ **notch** Kerbmarkierung *f (z.B. von Blattfilm)*
- ~ **number** Randnummer *f*, [Negativ-]Fußnummer *f*, Randzahl *f (Film)*
- ~ **numbering** Randnummerierung *f*
- ~ **numbers** Randsignatur *f*
- ~ **operator** Kantenoperator *m*, Kantenfilter *n*
- ~ **orientation** Kantenausrichtung *f*, Kantenorientierung *f*
- ~-**perforated film** randperforierter Film *m*
- ~ **perforation** Randperforation *f*, Randlöcher *npl*
- ~ **pixel** Kantenpixel *n*
- ~ **point** Kantenpunkt *m*
- ~ **point linking** Kantenpunktverknüpfung *f*
- ~ **position** Kantenposition *f*
- ~ **preservation** Kantenerhaltung *f*
- ~-**preserving filter** kantenerhaltendes Filter *n*
- ~-**preserving median filter** hybrides Medianfilter *n*
- ~-**preserving smoothing** kantenerhaltende Glättung *f*
- ~ **profile** Kantenprofil *n*
- ~ **quality** Kantengüte *f*, Kantenqualität *f*
- ~ **ray** Randstrahl *m*, randnaher (randseitiger) Strahl *m*
- ~ **recognition** ~ detection
- ~ **region** Kantenregion *f*
- ~ **representation** Kantendarstellung *f*
- ~ **segment** Kantensegment *n*
- ~ **segmentation** Kantensegmentierung *f*
- ~-**sensitive prediction** kantensensitive Prädiktion *f*
- ~ **shadow** Randschatten *m*
- ~ **sharpening** *s.* ~ enhancement
- ~ **sharpness** Kantenschärfe *f*; Kontur[en]schärfe *f*
- ~ **signal** Kantensignal *n*
- ~ **slope** Kantenanstieg *m*
- ~ **smoothing** Kantenglättung *f*, Kantenbegradigung *f*
- ~ **softness** Randunschärfe *f*
- ~ **strength** Kantenstärke *f*
- ~ **stripe** *s.* ~ track
- ~ **structure** Kantenstruktur *f*
- ~ **table** Kantentabelle *f*
- ~ **template** Kantenschablone *f*
- ~ **thickness** Randdicke *f (z.B. einer Linse)*
- ~ **thinning** Kantenverdünnung *f*
- ~ **tracing** Kantenverfolgung *f*
- ~ **track** Randspur *f (Tonfilm)*
- ~ **transition** Kantenübergang *m*
- ~ **type** Kantentyp *m*
- ~ **width** Kantenbreite *f*, Kantenstärke *f*
- **edgel** *s.* edge element
- **edgeprint** Randkennzeichnung *f (an Filmmaterial)*
- **edit**/to editieren; bearbeiten; cutte[r]n, schneiden *(bes. Videomaterial)*
- **edit** Schnitt *m (s.a. unter* editing*)*
- ~ **bay** Schnittplatz *m*, Schneideplatz *m*
- ~ **bench** Schneidetisch *m*, Filmschneidetisch *m*
- ~ **control** Schnittsteuerung *f*, Schnittkontrolle *f*
- ~ **control system** Schnitt[steuer]system *n*
- ~ **controller** Schnittsteuergerät *n*
- ~ **controller software** Schnittsteuersoftware *f*
- ~ **decision** Schnittfestlegung *f*, Schnittbestimmung *f*
- ~ **decision list** [elektronische] Schnittliste *f (s.a.* ~ script*)*
- ~ **deck** Schnittpult *n*, Schneidepult *n*
- ~ **frame** Schnittbild *n*
- ~ **gap** Schnittlücke *f*
- ~ **monitor** Schnittmonitor *m*

edit

~ **point** Schnittpunkt m, Schnittstelle f
~ **pulse** Schneid[e]impuls m
~ **script** Schnittplan m
~ **suite** Nachbearbeitungsplatz m
~ **tape** Schnittband n, nachzubearbeitendes Band n
editable editierbar; schnittfähig
edited camera negative Schnittnegativ n, geschnittenes Negativ (Originalnegativ) n *(Filmbearbeitung)*
~ **work print** geschnittene Arbeitskopie f, Schnittkopie f
editing Nachbearbeitung f, Editierung f; Schnittbearbeitung f, Schnitt m *(s.a. unter* edit*)*
~ **accuracy** Schnittgenauigkeit f
~ **console** Mischpult n
~ **deck** Schnittpult n, Schneidepult n
~ **device** Schnitt[steuer]gerät n, Editiergerät n
~ **effect** Schnitteffekt m
~ **equipment** Schnitteinrichtung f, Schnittechnik f
~ **log** Einstellungsliste f *(Videografie)*
~ **machine** Schneidemaschine f
~ **method (mode)** Schnittmethode f, Bearbeitungsmodus m
~ **operation (process)** Schnittvorgang m, Schnittprozess m, Editiervorgang m
~ **program** Schnittprogramm n
~ **recorder** Schnittrecorder m, Aufnahmerecorder m
~ **room** Schneideraum m, Schnittbearbeitungsraum m; Filmschneideraum m
~ **software** Schnittprogrammsoftware f
~ **software package** Schnittsoftwarepaket n
~ **special-effects computer** Schnittcomputer m
~ **station** 1. Schnittplatz m, Schneideplatz m; 2. *s.* ~ **device**
~ **suite** *s.* ~ **room**
~ **system** Schnitt[steuer]system n
~ **table** Schneidetisch m, Filmschneidetisch m
~ **technique** 1. Schnittverfahren n; 2. Schnittechnik f
~ **technology** Schnittechnik f
~ **workstation** Schnittplatz m, Schneideplatz m
editor 1. Schnittmeister f, Filmcutter m, Cutter m, Filmeditor m; 2. Schnitteinrichtung f, Nachbearbeitungseinrichtung f; 3. Editor m *(Software-Werkzeug)*
editorial cut harter Schnitt m, Hartschnitt m
~ **department** Schnittabteilung f
~ **manipulation (refinement)** Schnittbearbeitung f
~ **script** Schnittplan m
~ **sync** Schnittsynchronisierung f
~ **work** Schnittarbeit f, Schnittausführung f

EDTV *s.* enhanced definition television
educational film (motion picture) Unterrichtsfilm m, Lehrfilm m, Schulungsfilm m
~ **television** Schulfernsehen n; Bildungsfernsehen n
EEG *s.* electroencephalogram
EEPROM *s.* electrically erasable programmable read-only memory
effect 1. Effekt m; Wirkung f; 2. Effekt m, Trick m *(Film, Video)*
~ **filter** Effektfilter n *(s.a.* special-effects filter*)*
~ **lighting** Effektbeleuchtung f
~ **of depth** Tiefenwirkung f
effective aperture effektive Apertur (Blendenöffnung) f, effektive Blende f, wirksame Öffnung f, Eintrittspupille f
~ **area** effektive Fläche f *(z.B. eines Spiegelteleskops)*
~ **bandwidth** wirksame Bandbreite f
~ **dose** effektive Dosis f
~ **echo time** effektive Echozeit f
~ **exposure time** effektive Belichtungszeit f, Effektivzeit f, Äquivalentzeit f *(fotografischer Verschluss)*
~ **f-number** effektive Blendenzahl (Öffnungszahl) f, T-Blende f
~ **focal length** effektive (tatsächliche) Brennweite f, Effektivbrennweite f, Gesamtbrennweite f, Äquivalentbrennweite f
~ **focal spot** optisch wirksamer Brennfleck m
~ **lens aperture** *s.* ~ **aperture**
~ **luminous flux** Nutzlichtstrom m
~ **relative aperture** *s.* ~ **f-number**
~ **tape speed** effektive Bandgeschwindigkeit f
~ **viewport** effektives Darstellungsfeld n *(Computergrafik)*
effects area Trickbereich m
~ **channel** Effektkanal m
~ **film** Effektfilm m, Trickfilm m, Animationsfilm m
~ **filter** Effektfilter n, Trickfilter n, Kreativfilter n
~ **house** Tricklabor n *(s.a.* ~ **studio***)*
~ **light** Effektlicht n
~ **machine** Effektgerät n, Trickgenerator m, Trickgerät n
~ **photography** Trickfotografie f
~ **processor** Trickprozessor m
~ **projector** Effektprojektor m, Trickprojektor m
~ **shot** Effektaufnahme f, Trick[film]aufnahme f
~ **studio** Effektstudio n, Trick[film]studio n, Trickatelier n
~ **supervisor** Trickregisseur m
~ **track** Geräuschtonspur f, Effektspur f
~ **work** Trickarbeit f
efficiency of detection Detektionseffizienz f

egg crate [grid] Gittervorsatz *m* (*Leuchtenzubehör*)
eidetic image eidetisches Bild *n*
eigen axis Eigenachse *f*
eigenemission Eigenemission *f*
eigenfunction Eigenfunktion *f* (*z.B. eines Abbildungssystems*)
eigenimage, eigenpicture Eigenbild *n*
eigenvalue Eigenwert *m* (*Skalar*)
~ **analysis** Eigenwertanalyse *f*
~ **matrix** Eigenwertmatrix *f*
eigenvector Eigenvektor *m*, charakteristischer Vektor *m* (*eines Operators*)
~ **matrix** Eigenvektormatrix *f*
~ **transform** Eigenvektortransformation *f*, Hauptkomponentenanalyse *f*, Karhunen-Loève-Transformation (*Merkmalserkennung*)
eight-adjacency *s.* eight-connection neighborhood
~**-bit codeword** Acht-Bit-Wort *n*
~**-bit color depth** Acht-Bit-Farbtiefe *f*
~**-bit image** Acht-Bit-Bild *n*
~**-bit quantization** Acht-Bit-Quantisierung *f*
~**-connection neighborhood** Achternachbarschaft *f*, Achterumgebung *f* (*von Bildpunkten*)
~ **millimeter (mm) film** Acht-Millimeter-Film *m*
~**-mm color movie film** Acht-Millimeter-Farbfilm *m*
~**-to-fourteen modulation** Acht-auf-Vierzehn-Modulation *f* (*Kanalcodierung*)
eikonal Eikonal *n* (*Strahlenoptik*)
Einstein's coefficient Einstein-Koeffizient *m* (*spontane Emission*)
EIRP *s.* effective isotropically emitted radio power
EISA *s.* Extended Industry Standard Architecture
eject Kassettenauswurf *m*
elastic scattering elastische Streuung *f*
~ **scattering spectroscopy** optische Biopsie *f*
elasticity imaging [method] *s.* elastography
elastogram Elastogramm *n*
elastography Elastografie *f*, Ultraschallelastografie *f*
elastostatic model elastostatisches Modell *n*
elbow telescope Winkelfernrohr *n*
electret Elektret *n*(*m*)
~ **[condenser] microphone** Elektret-Kondensatormikrofon *n*, Elektretmikrofon *n*
electric-charge carrier Ladungsträger *m*
~ **dipole** elektrischer Dipol *m*
~ **dipole moment** elektrisches Dipolmoment *n*

~ **dipole radiation** elektrische Dipolstrahlung *f*
~ **discharge lamp** Entladungslampe *f*
~ **erasable and programmable read-only memory** elektrisch lösch- und programmierbarer Festwertspeicher *m*
~ **eye** Fotozelle *f*
~**-field vector** Feldvektor *m*
~ **image** elektrisches Bild *n*
~**-impedance plethysmograph** Impedanzplethysmograf *m*
~ **lamp** elektrische Lampe *f*
~ **polarization** elektrische Polarisation *f*
~ **sensor** elektrischer Sensor *m*
~ **tunnel effect** [quantenmechanischer] Tunneleffekt *m*
electrical bandwidth elektrische Bandbreite *f*, Leistungsbandbreite *f* (*Fotodetektor*)
~ **filter** elektrisches Filter *n*
~ **impulse** elektrischer Impuls *m*
~ **noise** elektrisches Rauschen *n*
~ **signal** elektrisches Signal *n*
~ **vector** elektrischer Vektor *m*
electrically erasable programmable read-only memory elektrisch löschbarer [programmierbarer] Nurlesespeicher *m*
electro-optic converter elektrooptischer (lichtelektrischer) Wandler *m*
~**-optic crystal** elektrooptischer Kristall *m*
~**-optic double prism** elektrooptisches Doppelprisma *n*
~**-optic effect** elektrooptischer Effekt *m*
~**-optic imaging** elektrooptische Bildgebung *f*
~**-optic light modulation** elektrooptische Lichtmodulation *f*
~**-optic modulator** elektrooptischer Modulator *m*
~**-optic phase change** elektrooptische Phasenveränderung *f*
~**-optic phenomenon** elektrooptisches Phänomen *n*
~**-optic radar** elektrooptisches Radar *n*
~**-optic signal** elektrooptisches Signal *n*
~**-optical filter** elektrooptisches Filter *n*
~**-optical focusing** elektrooptische Fokussierung *f*
~**-optical imaging system** elektrooptisches Abbildungssystem *n*
~**-optical modulation** elektrooptische Modulation *f*
~**-optical photometer** lichtelektrisches Fotometer *n*
~**-optical scanner** elektrooptischer Scanner *m*
~**-optical sensor** elektrooptischer Sensor *m*
~**-optical shutter** elektrooptischer Verschluss *m*, Kerr-Zellenverschluss *m*
~**-optical switch** elektrooptischer Schalter *m*
~**-optical zoom** elektrooptisches Zoom *n*
~**-optics** Elektrooptik *f*

electrocardiogram Elektrokardiogramm *n*
electrocardiographic elektrokardiografisch
~ **gating** EKG-Steuerung *f*, EKG-Triggerung *f*
~ **imaging, electrocardiography** Elektrokardiografie *f*
electrochemical etching elektrochemisches Ätzen *n*
~ **impedance spectroscopy** elektrochemische Impedanzspektroskopie *f*
~ **microscopy** elektrochemische Mikroskopie *f*
~ **signal** elektrochemisches Signal *n*
electrode Elektrode *f*
electrodeless tube Nullode *f (eine Sperrröhre)*
electrodiagnosis s. electromyography
electrodynamic microphone dynamisches Mikrofon *n*
electroencephalogram Elektroenzephalogramm *n*, EEG
electroencephalograph Elektroenzephalograf *m*
electroencephalographic elektroenzephalografisch
electroencephalography Elektroenzephalografie *f*
Electrofax [process] Elektrografie *f (Elektrofotografie)*
electroholography Elektroholografie *f*
electroluminescence Elektrolumineszenz *f*
electroluminescent elektrolumineszierend, elektrolumineszent
~ **display** Elektrolumineszenzanzeige *f*, Elektrolumineszenzdisplay *n*, EL-Display *n*, ELD; Elektrolumineszenzbildschirm *m*
~ **lamp** Elektrolumineszenzlampe *f*
electrolysis Elektrolyse *f*
electrolytic elektrolytisch
~ **development** elektrolytische Entwicklung *f*
~ **shutter** elektrolytischer Verschluss *m*
~ **silver recovery** elektrolytische Silberrückgewinnung *f*
electromagnet Elektromagnet *m*
electromagnetic elektromagnetisch
~ **absorption** elektromagnetische Absorption *f*
~ **echo** elektromagnetisches Echo *n (Radar)*
~ **energy** elektromagnetische Energie *f*
~ **environment** elektromagnetische Umgebung *f*
~ **field** elektromagnetisches Feld *n*
~ **image** elektromagnetisches Bild *n*
~ **image tube** elektromagnetische Bildröhre *f*
~ **imaging** elektromagnetische Bildgebung *f*
~ **interference** elektromagnetische Interferenz *f*
~ **interference** elektromagnetische Störung *f*
~ **lens** elektromagnetische Linse *f*
~ **noise** elektromagnetisches Rauschen *n*
~ **optics** elektromagnetische Optik *f*
~ **pulse** elektromagnetischer Impuls *m*
~ **radiation** elektromagnetische Strahlung *f*
~ **release** elektromagnetischer Auslöser *m*
~ **shutter** elektromagnetischer Verschluss *m*; elektromagnetische Blende *f*
~ **signal** elektromagnetisches Signal *n*
~ **spectrum** elektromagnetisches Spektrum *n*
~ **wave** elektromagnetische Welle *f*
~ **wave spectrum** elektromagnetisches Spektrum *n*
electromechanical engraving elektromechanische Gravur *f*
~ **resolution** elektromechanische Auflösung *f*
~ **shutter** elektromechanischer Verschluss *m*
electromotive force Potentialdifferenz *f*
electromyogram Elektromyogramm *n*
electromyograph Elektromyograf *m*
electromyographic[al] elektromyografisch
electromyography Elektromyografie *f*
electron Elektron *n*
~ **acceleration** Elektronenbeschleunigung *f*
~ **acceptor** Elektronenakzeptor *m*
~ **beam coating** Elektronenstrahlvergütung *f (von Linsen)*
~ **beam computed tomography** Elektronenstrahl-Computertomografie *f*, Elektronen[strahl]tomografie *f*
~ **beam CT scanner** Elektronenstrahl-Computertomograf *m*
~ **beam current** Elektronenstrahlstrom *m*, Strahlstrom *m*
~ **beam deflection** Elektronenstrahlablenkung *f*
~ **beam energy** Elektronenstrahlenergie *f*
~ **beam engraving** Elektronenstrahlgravur *f*
~ **beam exposure** Elektronenstrahlbelichtung *f*
~ **beam film scanning** Elektronenstrahl-Filmabtastung *f*
~ **beam gravure** Elektronenstrahlgravur *f*
~ **beam gun** s. ~ gun
~ **beam image** Elektronenstrahlbild *n*
~ **beam microlithography** Elektronenstrahllithografie *f*
~ **beam modulation** Elektronenstrahlmodulation *f*
~ **beam probe** Elektronen[strahl]sonde *f*
~ **beam recording** Elektronenstrahlaufzeichnung *f*
~ **beam retrace** Strahlrücklauf *m*, Strahlrücksprung *m*
~ **beam scanner** Elektronenstrahlabtaster *m*
~ **beam scanning** Elektronenstrahlabtastung *f*

electronic

- ~ **beam source** Elektronenstrahlquelle f
- ~ **beam tomography** s. ~ beam computed tomography
- ~ **beam tube** Elektronenstrahl[bild]röhre f, Katodenstrahlröhre f
- ~ **beam writing** Elektronenstrahlschreiben n
- ~ **capture** Elektroneneinfang g
- ~ **cloud** Elektronenwolke f
- ~ **collector** Elektronenkollektor m
- ~ **column** Mikroskopsäule f (Elektronenmikroskop)
- ~ **current** Elektronenstrom m
- ~ **current density** Stromdichte f
- ~ **density** Elektronendichte f
- ~ **detector** Elektronendetektor m
- ~ **don[at]or** Elektronendonator m, Elektronenspender m
- ~ **emission microscope** Emissions[elektronen]mikroskop n
- ~ **emitter** Elektronenemitter m
- ~ **energy** Elektronenenergie f
- ~ **excitation** Elektronenanregung f
- ~ **exposure system** Elektronenbelichtungsanlage f (Mikrolithografie)
- ~ **flow** Elektronenstrom m
- ~ **gun** Elektronen[strahl]kanone f, Elektronenstrahlerzeuger m, Elektronenstrahlerzeugungssystem n, Strahlkanone f (Katodenstrahlröhre)
- ~ **gun beam current** Strahlstrom m
- ~ **hole** Elektronenfehlstelle f, Elektronenleerstelle f
- ~-**hole pair** Elektron-Loch-Paar n
- ~-**hole pair creation (production)** Elektron-Loch-Paarbildung f, Elektronenpaarbildung f (Elektrofotografie)
- ~ **holography** Elektronenholografie f
- ~ **image** Elektronenbild n
- ~ **image simulation** Elektronenbildsimulation f
- ~ **image tube** Elektronenbildröhre f
- ~ **lens** Elektronenlinse f
- ~ **metallography** Elektronenmetallografie f
- ~ **micrograph** Elektronenmikroskopaufnahme f, elektronenmikroskopische Aufnahme f, Elektronenmikrografie f, Elektronenmikrogramm n
- ~ **micrography** Elektronenmikrografie f
- ~ **microscope** Elektronenmikroskop n, Übermikroskop n
- ~ **microscope image** s. ~ micrograph
- ~ **microscope tomography** elektronenmikroskopische Tomografie f
- ~-**microscopic[al]** elektronenmikroskopisch
- ~ **microscopist** Elektronenmikroskopiker m
- ~ **microscopy** Elektronenmikroskopie f
- ~ **microscopy laboratory** Elektronenmikroskopie-Labor[atorium] n
- ~ **mirror** Elektronenspiegel m
- ~-**optical** elektronenoptisch
- ~-**optical interpolation** elektronenoptische Interpolation f
- ~ **optics** Elektronenoptik f
- ~-**pair bond (linkage)** Elektronenpaarbindung f
- ~ **pair production** s. electron-hole pair creation
- ~-**paramagnetic resonance** elektronenmagnetische Resonanz f, Elektronenspinresonanz f
- ~ **photomicrography** Elektronenmikrofotografie f
- ~-**positron annihilation** Elektron-Positron-Paarvernichtung f
- ~ **probe** Elektronen[strahl]sonde f
- ~ **shell** Elektronenhülle f
- ~ **source** Elektronenquelle f
- ~ **spectrometer** Elektronenspektrometer n
- ~ **spectroscopy** Elektronenspektroskopie f
- ~ **spin** Elektronenspin m
- ~ **spin resonance** Elektronenspinresonanz f, elektronenmagnetische Resonanz f
- ~ **storage ring** Elektronenspeicherring m (Röntgenmikroskopie)
- ~ **stream** Elektronenstrom m
- ~ **telescope** Elektronenteleskop n
- ~ **tomographic** elektronentomografisch
- ~ **tomographic microscopy** elektronentomografische Mikroskopie f
- ~ **tomography** Elekronen[strahl]tomografie f
- ~ **transfer** Elektronentransfer m, Elektronenübertragung f
- ~ **trap** s. ~ trapping site
- ~ **trapping** Elektroneneinfang m
- ~ **trapping site** Elektroneneinfangstelle f
- ~ **tube** Elektronenröhre f
- ~ **tunnelling** Elektronentunneln n, Elektronentunnelung f
- ~ **valve** s. ~ tube
- ~ **volt** Elektronenvolt n, eV (Energieeinheit)
- ~ **wave** Elektronenwelle f

electronic elektronisch
- ~ **amplification** elektronische Verstärkung f
- ~ **animation** elektronische Animation f
- ~ **archive** elektronisches Archiv n
- ~ **beam** Elektronenstrahl m
- ~ **camera** elektronische (elektrooptische) Kamera f, E-Kamera f
- ~ **charge** Elektronenladung f
- ~ **chart display and information system** elektronische Seekarte f
- ~ **cinema** digitales Kino n, Digitalkino n; elektronische Filmproduktion f
- ~ **cinematography** elektronische Kinematografie f
- ~ **circuit noise** Elektronikrauschen n

electronic

~ **clapper** elektronische Klappe f
~ **collimation** elektronische Kollimation f
~ **composition** Computersatz m
~ **cue card** elektronischer Textgeber n, Teleprompter m *(Studioausrüstung)*
~ **densitometer** fotoelektrisches Densitometer n
~ **digital imaging** Digitalbildtechnik f
~ **display** elektronische Anzeige f
~ **document image procssing** [elektronische] Dokumentenbildverarbeitung f
~ **dot generation** fotoelektronische Rasterung f
~ **editing** elektronischer Schnitt m, EB-Schnitt m
~ **editing tool** elektronisches Schnittwerkzeug n
~ **endoscope** Videoendoskop n
~ **engraving** elektronische Gravur f
~ **eraser** elektronischer Radiergummi m
~ **exposure meter** elektronischer Belichtungsmesser m
~ **field production** elektronische Außenproduktion f
~ **filter** elektronisches Filter n
~ **filtering** elektronische Filterung f
~ **flash** Elektronenblitz m, Elektronenblitzlicht n
~-**flash duration** Elektronenblitzdauer f
~-**flash head** Blitzkopf m
~ **flash lamp** Elektronenblitzlampe f
~ **flash meter** Blitzbelichtungsmesser m
~ **flash photography** Elektronenblitzfotografie f, Blitzfotografie f
~ **flash system (unit)** Elektronenblitzgerät n, Röhrenblitzgerät n
~ **focusing** elektronische Fokussierung f *(Sonografie)*
~ **form** Online-Formular n
~ **front end** Computersatz m
~ **hologram** elektronisches Hologramm n
~ **image** elektronisches Bild n, Elektronikbild n
~ **image distortion** [elektronische] Bildverfremdung f
~ **image file** Bild[bearbeitungs]datei f
~ **image processing** elektronische Bildverarbeitung f
~ **image scanning** elektronische Bildabtastung f
~ **image sensor** elektronischer Bildsensor m
~ **image stabilizer** elektronischer (digitaler) Bildstabilisator m
~ **image storage** elektronische Bildspeicherung f
~ **imaging** 1. elektronische Bildaufnahme f; 2. elektronische Bildbearbeitung f; 3. elektronische Bebilderung f *(Druckvorstufe)*
~-**imaging back** Digitalkamerarückteil n

~-**imaging camera** elektronische (elektrooptische) Kamera f, E-Kamera f
~ **imaging technology** elektronische Bildtechnik f
~ **impulse** elektronischer Impuls m
~ **ink** elektronische Tinte f
~ **intelligence** elektronische Aufklärung f
~ **mail** elektronische Post f, E-Mail f
~ **map** elektronische Karte f *(Radar)*
~ **matting** s. chroma key
~ **mechanical** elektronische Montage f *(Druckvorstufe)*
~ **medium** elektronisches Medium n
~ **news gathering** elektronische Berichterstattung f; Fernsehberichterstattung f
~ **newspaper** elektronische Zeitung f
~ **noise** elektronisches Rauschen n
~ **paper** elektronisches (digitales) Papier n
~-**photographic** elektronenfotografisch
~ **photography** Elektronenfotografie f
~ **prepress** elektronische Druckvorstufe f
~ **program[ming] guide** elektronischer Programmführer m, elektronische Programmzeitschrift f
~ **projection** elektronische Projektion f
~ **publishing** elektronisches Publizieren n
~ **pulse** elektronischer Impuls m
~ **recording** elektronische Aufzeichnung f
~ **retouching** elektronische Retusche f
~ **scanner** elektronischer Scanner m
~ **scanning** elektronische Abtastung f
~ **sensitometry** elektronische Sensitometrie f
~ **sensor** elektronischer Sensor m
~ **shearography** elektronische Shearografie f, TV-Shearografie f
~ **shutter** Elektronikverschluss m, elektronischer Verschluss m
~ **signal** elektronisches Signal n
~ **speckle pattern interferometry** elektronische Speckle-Interferometrie f, elektronische Holografie f
~ **speckle pattern shearing interferometry** s. ~ shearography
~ **spectroscopy** elektronische Spektroskopie f
~ **standing picture** elektronisches Standbild (Stehbild) n
~ **still camera** Standbildkamera f
~ **still photography** elektronische Fotografie (Stehbildfotografie) f
~ **still video camera** elektronische Stehbildkamera f, Stillvideokamera f
~ **storage** elektronische Speicherung f
~ **stroboscope** elektronisches Stroboskop n
~ **stylus** Digitalisierstift m, Tablettstift m, Grafikstift m *(Eingabetablett)*
~ **tablet** Digitalisiertablett n, Eingabetablett n, Grafiktablett n, grafisches Tablett n
~ **television** elektronisches Fernsehen n
~ **text** elektronischer Text m

~ **transition** Elektronenübergang *m (in einem Atom)*
~ **trick photography** elektronische Trickfotografie *f*
~ **trigger** elektronischer Auslöser *m*
~ **video recording** elektronische Videoaufzeichnung (Bildaufzeichnung) *f*
~ **viewfinder** elektronischer Sucher *m*; Suchermonitor *m (Filmkamera)*
~ **wide-angle camera system** elektronisches Weitwinkel-Kamerasystem *n*
~ **zoom** elektronisches Zoom *n*
electronically controlled shutter Elektronikverschluss *m*, elektronischer Verschluss *m*
electronics Elektronik *f*
~ **noise** Elektronikrauschen *n*
~**-to-electronics [mode]** Durchschleifbetrieb *m*, E-E-Betrieb *m (Videosignalverarbeitung)*
electronystagmograph Elektronystagmograf *m*
electrooculogram Elektrookulogramm *n*
electrophoresis Elektrophorese *f*
electrophotographic elektrofotografisch
~ **developer** elektrofotografischer Entwickler *m*
~ **development** elektrofotografische Entwicklung *f*
~ **imaging** Elektrofotografie *f*
~ **photoconductor (photoreceptor)** elektrofotografischer Fotoleiter *m*
~ **printer** elektrofotografischer (fotoelektrischer) Drucker *m*
~ **printing** elektrofotografischer Druck *m*
electrophotography Elektrofotografie *f*
electroradiographic elektroradiografisch, ionografisch
electroretinogram Elektroretinogramm *n*
electrostatic elektrostatisch
~ **charge** elektrostatische Ladung *f*
~ **charge pattern** elektrostatisches Ladungsbild *n*
~ **charging** elektrostatische Aufladung *f*
~ **copier** elektrostatischer Kopierer *m*
~ **copying** elektrostatisches Kopieren *n*
~ **deflection** elektrostatische Ablenkung *f*
~ **electron microscope** elektrostatisches Elektronenmikroskop *n*
~ **field** elektrostatisches Feld *n*
~ **focusing** elektrostatische Fokussierung *f*
~ **image** elektrostatisches Bild *n*
~ **latent image** elektrostatisches Latentbild *n*
~ **lens** elektrostatische Linse *f (Ionenoptik)*
~ **photoconductor** elektrostatischer Fotoleiter *m*
~ **plate** elektrostatische Druckplatte *f*
~ **plotter** elektrostatischer Plotter *m*, Rasterplotter *m*
~ **potential** elektrostatisches Potential *n*
~ **printer** elektrostatischer Drucker *m*
~ **printing [process]** elektrostatischer Druck *m*
~ **storage** elektrostatische Speicherung *f*
~ **transfer** elektrostatische Übertragung *f (von xerografischem Toner)*
electrothermography Elektrothermografie *f*
electrotype Galvano *n*, Hochdruckplattennachformung *f*
electrotyping Galvanoformung *f*
electrovalent bond heteropolare Bindung *f*, Ionenbindung *f*
element 1. Element *n*; 2. Einzellinse *f*
~ **splitting** Linsenaufspaltung *f*
elemental silver elementares Silber *n*
elementary bit stream Elementarbitstrom *m*, Elementardatenstrom *m*
~ **cell** Elementarzelle *f (Bildverarbeitung)*
~ **image** Elementarbild *n*
~ **particle** Elementarteilchen *n*
~ **wave** Elementarwelle *f*, Wavelet *n*
elevation 1. Keulenbreite *f (Radar)*; 2. s. ~ angle
~ **angle** Elevation *f*, Elevationswinkel *m*, Höhenwinkel *m*
elevator Kurbelmittelsäule *f (Stativ)*
elimination key Eliminationsschlüssel *m (Bildanalyse)*
elint s. electronic intelligence
ellipse scissors Ellipsenschere *f (Computergrafik)*
~ **tool** Ellipsenwerkzeug *n (Computergrafik)*
ellipsis Auslassungspunkte *mpl (Druckzeichen)*
ellipsoid Ellipsoid *n*
ellipsoidal mirror Ellipsoidspiegel *m*
~ **reflector floodlight** Ellipsenspiegelscheinwerfer *m*
~ **reflector spotlight** Profilscheinwerfer *m*, Verfolger *m*
ellipsometer Ellipsometer *n*
ellipsometric ellipsometrisch
ellipsometry Ellipsometrie *f*
elliptical coma elliptische Koma *f (Abbildungsfehler)*
~ **dot** elliptischer Rasterpunkt *m*
~ **filter** elliptisches Filter *n*
~ **mirror** elliptischer Spiegel *m*
~ **polarization** elliptische Polarisation *f*
~ **polarized radiation** elliptisch polarisierte Strahlung *f*
elliptically polarized light elliptisch polarisiertes Licht *n*
ellipticity Elliptizität *f*
elon s. methylaminophenol sulfate
em dash Geviertstrich *m (Typografie)*
em quad Geviert *n (Typografie)*
em rule s. ~ dash
emanate/to emanieren
emanation Emanation *f*
embedded movie integrierter Film *m (Multimedia)*
emboss/to [erhaben] prägen

embossed hologram Prägehologramm n
embossing press Prägepresse f
emergence (emergent) angle
Austrittswinkel m, Ausfallswinkel m
emergent beam, emerging ray
Austrittsstrahl m, austretender Strahl m
emission Emission f; Abstrahlung f
~ **characteristic** Emissionskennlinie f, Emissionskurve f (z.B. einer Lichtquelle)
~ **computed tomography** Emissions[computer]tomografie f, szintigrafische Tomografie f, tomografische Szintigrafie f
~ **current** Emissionsstrom m
~ **direction** Emissionsrichtung f
~ **electron microscope** Emissions[elektronen]mikroskop n
~ **energy** Emissionsenergie f
~ **filter** Emissionsfilter n (Fluoreszenzmikroskop)
~ **image** Emissionsbild n
~ **imaging** Emissionsbildgebung f
~ **ion microscope** Emissionsionenmikroskop n
~ **light** Emissionslicht n
~ **line spectrum** Emissionslinienspektrum n
~ **microscope** Emissions[elektronen]mikroskop n
~ **of heat** Wärmeabstrahlung f
~ **scanning electron microscope** Emissionsrasterelektronenmikroskop n
~ **spectrography** Emissionsspektrografie f
~ **spectroscopy** Emissionsspektroskopie f
~ **spectrum** Emissionsspektrum n
~ **theory of light** Emissionstheorie (Teilchentheorie) f des Lichts, Korpuskulartheorie f des Lichts
~ **tomographic** emissionstomografisch
~ **tomography** Emissionstomografie f, szintigrafische Tomografie f, tomografische Szintigrafie f
~ **wavelength** Emissionswellenlänge f
emissive emittierend
~ **color** emittierte Farbe f
~ **power** emittierte Strahlungsleistung f
emissivity [spezifisches] Emissionsvermögen n, [spezifische] Emissivität f, [spektraler] Emissionsgrad m; spezifische spektrale Abstrahlung (Ausstrahlung) f
emit/to emittieren; abstrahlen, ausstrahlen; aussenden
emit light/to leuchten
emittance s. emissivity
emitted light ausgestrahltes Licht n
~ **radiation** emittierte Strahlung f
~ **radiation spectral photometry** Emissionsspektralfotometrie f
emitter Emitter m; Strahler m
emitting surface Emissionsfläche f
EMM s. entitlement management message
emmetrope Normalsichtiger m

emmetropia Normalsichtigkeit f, Emmetropie f
emmetropic emmetrop, normalsichtig, rechtsichtig
empirical horopter empirischer Horopter m (Abbildungsgeometrie)
empty electron position Elektronenfehlstelle f, Elektronenleerstelle f
~ **interior style** leere Ausfüllung f (Computergrafik)
~ **line** Leerzeile f, Blindzeile f
~ **magnification** Leervergrößerung f, leere Vergrößerung f, Übervergrößerung f (Mikroskopie)
emulate/to emulieren; imitieren
emulation Emulation f, Nachbildung f
emulator Emulator m
emulsification Emulgierung f (s.a. emulsion making)
emulsion Emulsion f
~ **additive** Emulsionszusatz[stoff] m
~ **adhesion** Emulsionshaftung f
~ **batch** Emulsionscharge f
~ **coat** Emulsionsschicht f
~ **coating** Emulsionsbeguss m
~ **component** Emulsionsbestandteil m
~ **contrast** Emulsionskontrast m
~ **fog** Emulsionsschleier m
~ **grain** Emulsionskorn n
~ **grain size** Emulsionskorngröße f
~ **ingredient** Emulsionsbestandteil m
~ **laser storage** Emulsions-Laserspeicher m
~ **layer thickness** Emulsionsschichtdicke f
~ **layer** Emulsionsschicht f
~ **maker** Emulsionshersteller m
~ **making (manufacture)** Emulsionsherstellung f, Emulsionsbereitung f
~ **microcrystal** Emulsionskristall m
~ **number** Emulsionsnummer f
~ **precipitation** Emulsionsfällung f
~ **reactor** Emulsionsreaktor m
~ **sensitivity** Emulsionsempfindlichkeit f
~ **sequence** Schichtfolge f, Schichtaufbau m
~ **shred** Nudel f (Emulsionsherstellung)
~ **side** Emulsionsseite f, Schichtseite f, Mattseite f (Fotomaterial); Filmvorderseite f
~ **speed** Emulsionsempfindlichkeit f
~ **stabilizer** Emulsionsstabilisator m
~ **surface** 1. Emulsionsoberfläche f; 2. s. ~ side
~ **technology** Emulsionstechnik f
~ **thickness** Emulsionsdicke f
~ **washing** Emulsionswäsche f
en dash Halbgeviertstrich m (Typografie)
en-face optical coherence tomography transversale [optische] Kohärenztomografie f
en quad (rule), ~ space Halbgeviert n (Typografie)

Encapsulated PostScript file s. EPS file
encephalogram, encephalograph Enzephalogramm n
encephalographic enzephalografisch
encephalography Enzephalografie f
encircling Einkreisen n (von Klappennummern im Negativbericht)
encode/to codieren, encodieren
encoded data codierte (komprimierte) Daten pl
~ **image** codiertes Bild n
~ **signal** codiertes Signal n
encoder Codierer m; Kompressionsalgorithmus m
~**-decoder** [Video-]Codec m(n), Codierungs-Decodierungspaar n
~ **loop** Codiererschleife f
encoding Codierung f (s.a. unter coding)
~ **circuitry** Codierungsschaltung f
~ **delay** Codierverzögerung f
~ **function** Codierungsfunktion f
~ **loop** Codierungsschleife f
~ **procedure** Codiervorgang m
~ **process** Codierverfahren n
~ **software** Codierungssoftware f
encrypt/to verschlüsseln (Signale)
encrypter Verschlüsseler m
encryption Verschlüsselung f
end credits s. ~ title
~ **edit point** Schnittende n
~ **effector** Endeffektor m (Computeranimation)
~ **matter** Notenanhang m (Layout)
~ **of a line** Zeilenende n
~**-of-line decision** Zeilenendbestimmung f (Satzherstellung)
~ **of picture** Bildende n (Kinefilm)
~ **of tape** Bandende n
~ **search** Bandendeabschaltung f
~ **sheet** Spiegel m (Buchfertigung)
~ **slate** Schlussklappe f (Filmarbeit)
~ **title** End[e]titel m, Schlusstitel m, Titelabspann m; Abspann m, Nachspann m, Trailer m, Filmtrailer m
~**-to-end delay** Ende-zu-Ende-Verzögerung f (Datenkommunikation)
~**-to-end protocol** Ende-zu-Ende-Protokoll n
~ **user** Endanwender m
~ **window tube** Endfensterröhre f, Stirnfensterröhre f (Röntgentechnik)
endless loop Endlosschleife f; Bandschleife f, Endlosband n
~ **recording** Endlosaufnahme f
endoscope Endoskop n
~ **head** Endoskopspitze f
~ **image** Endoskopaufnahme f
~ **lens** Endoskopieobjektiv n
~ **probe** Endoskopsonde f
~ **tip** Endoskopspitze f
endoscopic endoskopisch
~ **camera** Endoskopiekamera f, endoskopische Kamera f
~ **field** endoskopisches Sichtfeld n
~ **image** Endoskopaufnahme f, endoskopisches Bild n
~ **photography** endoskopische Fotografie f
~ **sonography (ultrasonography)** Endosonografie f, Ultraschallendoskopie f
~ **ultrasound** endoskopischer Ultraschall m
~ **ultrasound image** endoskopisches Ultraschallbild n
endoscopist Endoskopierer m, Endoskopanwender m
endoscopy Endoskopie f
~ **suite** Endoskopieeinheit f
endpaper[s] Vorsatz[papier] n (Buchherstellung)
endpoint Endpunkt m
~ **node** Endknoten m (Graphenstruktur)
energize/to pumpen (Laser)
energy balance Energiebilanz f
~ **density** Energiedichte f
~**-density spectrum** spektrale Energiedichte f, Energiedichtespektrum n
~ **deposition versus depth** Tiefendosiskurve f (Röntgendosimetrie)
~ **dispersal** Energieverwischung f (Kanalcodierungsschritt)
~**-dispersive X-ray spectrometer** energiedispersives Röntgenspektrometer n
~ **distribution** Energieverteilung f
~ **flow (flux)** Energiefluss m
~ **flux density** Energieflussdichte f, Energiestromdichte f
~ **level** Energieniveau n
~ **quantum** Energiequant n
~ **resolution** Energieauflösung f (PET-Detektor)
~ **save mode** Energiesparschaltung f
~ **spectrum** Energiespektrum n, Leistungs[dichte]spektrum n, spektrale Leistungsdichte (Dichte) f
ENG s. electronic news gathering
engineer's drawing, engineering drawing technische Zeichnung f, Ingenieurzeichnung f
engrave/to 1. gravieren; 2. s. photoengrave/to
engraver Graveur m
engraving 1. Klischee n, Druckklischee n; 2. Gravur f
~ **head** Gravurkopf m
~ **stylus** Gravierstichel m
enhance/to verstärken (z.B. den Bildkontrast)
enhanced definition television Fernsehen n mit verbesserter Auflösung
~ **graphics adapter** EGA-Grafikkarte f
~ **reality** erweiterte Realität f
~ **television** verbessertes Fernsehen n
enhancement Hochpassfilterung f

enhancement

~ **filter** Schärfefilter *n*,
Scharfzeichnungsfilter *n*
enhancer [Video-]Überspielverstärker *m*,
Verstärker *m*
enhancing Hervorheben *n*
(Bildverarbeitung)
~ **filter** s. enhancement filter
enlarge/to vergrößern
~ **optically** optisch vergrößern
enlargeability Vergrößerungsfähigkeit *f*
enlargeable vergrößerungsfähig
enlarged image (print) vergrößertes Bild *n*,
Vergrößerung *f*
enlargement 1. Vergrößerung *f*; 2. *s.* ~
copy
~ **copy** Vergrößerung *f*
~ **factor** Vergrößerungszahl *f*
~ **scale** Vergrößerungsmaßstab *m*
enlarger Vergrößerer *m*,
Vergrößerungsgerät *n*,
Vergrößerungsapparat *n*
~ **column** Führungssäule *f*
~ **head** Vergrößerkopf *m*,
Vergrößerungskopf *m*
~ **lens** Vergrößerungsobjektiv *n*
~ **light** Vergrößerungslicht *n*
~ **light source** Vergrößererlichtquelle *f*,
Vergrößerungslichtquelle *f*
~ **manufacturer**
Vergrößerungsgerätehersteller *m*
~ **timer** Kopieruhr *f*
enlarging easel Vergrößerungskassette *f*,
Vergrößerungsrahmen *f*; Kopierrahmen
m
~ **exposure meter**
Kopierbelichtungsmesser *m*
~ **lens** Vergrößerungsobjektiv *n*
~ **paper** Vergrößerungspapier *n*,
Fotopapier *n*, fotografisches Papier *n*
~ **paper holder** *s.* ~ easel
~ **projector** *s.* enlarger
enrolment Ersterfassung *f*
(Authentifizierung)
ensemble processing vergleichende
Verarbeitung *f (Computergrafik)*
enter/to eingeben *(Daten)*
enter key Eingabetaste *f*
entering beam Eintrittsstrahl *m*,
Einfallsstrahl *m*
enteroscope Enteroskop *n*, Intestinoskop
n, Darmspiegel *m*; Dünndarmspiegel *m*
enteroscopic enteroskopisch
enteroscopy Enteroskopie *f*,
Darmspiegelung *f*
entertainment computer
Unterhaltungscomputer *m*
~ **feature film** Unterhaltungsfilm *m*
~ **television set** Heimfernsehgerät *n*,
Heimfernseher *m*
~ **TV** Unterhaltungsfernsehen *n*
entocentric perspective entozentrische
Perspektive *f*
entoptic entoptisch *(Seheindruck)*
entrance aperture Eintrittsblende *f*

~ **beam** Eintrittsstrahl *m*, Einfallsstrahl *m*
~ **field size** Eingangsfeldgröße *f*
~ **pupil** Eintrittspupille *f*,
Lichteinfallöffnung *f*, effektive
Blende[nöffnung] *f*, wirksame Öffnung *f*
~ **slit** Eintrittsspalt *m*
~ **spectrum** Eintrittsspektrum *n*
(Radiografie)
~ **stop** Eintrittsblende *f*
~ **to the darkroom** Dunkelkammereingang
m
~ **window** Eintrittsluke *f (Optik)*
entropy Entropie *f*, mittlerer
Informationsgehalt *m (eines
Quellsymbols)*
~**-based compression** *s.* entropy coding
~**-coded quantization** entropiecodierte
Quantisierung *f*
~ **coder** Entropiecodierer *m*
~ **coding** Entropiecodierung *f*, variable
Längencodierung *f*; statistische
Codierung *f*
~ **decoder** Entropiedecod[ier]er *m*
~ **encoder** Entropiecodierer *m*
entry Eingabe *f (Datenverarbeitung)*
~**-level camera** Einsteigerkamera *f*,
Einstiegskamera *f*
envelope 1. Hüllkurve *f*, einhüllende Kurve
f; Hüllfläche *f*; Einhüllende *f*, Enveloppe
f; 2. *s.* cathode-ray tube envelope
~ **demodulation** Hüllkurvendemodulation
f
~**-wrapped film** folienloser Film
(Röntgenfilm) *m*
environment Umgebung *f*
~ **mapping** Environment-Mapping *n*
(Computergrafik)
epi-illumination microscopy
Auflichtmikroskopie *f*
epidiascope Epidiaskop *n*
epifluorescence Epifluoreszenz *f*
~ **microscope** Epifluoreszenzmikroskop *n*
epipolar epipolar
~ **distortion** epipolare Verzerrung *f*
~ **geometry** Epipolargeometrie *f*
~ **line** Epipolarlinie *f*
(Bewegungsschätzung)
~ **plane** Epipolarebene *f*
episcope Episkop *n*, Epiprojektor *m*,
Auflichtprojektor *m*
episcopic projection episkopische
Projektion *f*, Epiprojektion *f*
~ **projector** *s.* episcope
epoxy cement Epoxidkitt *m*
EPROM *s.* erasable and programmable
read-only memory
EPS file EPS-Bilddatei *f*, EPS-Datei *f*
equal/to äqualisieren
equal-energy spectrum energiegleiches
Spektrum *n*
~**-energy stimulus**
Konstantenergie-Stimulus *m*
~**-energy white** Gleichenergieweiß *n*
(Farbmessung)

equality-of-brightness photometer Gleichheitsfotometer *n*
equalization Äqualisierung *f*, Äqualisation, Äquivalisierung *f* *(Bildverarbeitungsoperation)*; Entzerrung *f*
~ **pulse** Ausgleichsimpuls *m*, Trabant *m* *(Fernsehsignal)*
equalize/to entzerren; äqualisieren
equalizer Entzerrer *m*
~ **pulse** *s.* equalization pulse
equally distant gleichabständig, äquidistant *(z.B. Abtastwerte)*
equatorial mounting äquatoriale Montierung *f*, Äquatorialmontierung *f* *(Teleskop)*
equi-inclination contour Biegekontur *f* *(Elektronenmikroskopie)*
equibiconvex äquibikonvex *(Linsenelement)*
equiconcave äquikonkav
equiconvex äquikonvex
equidensitometry Äquidensitometrie *f*
equidensity film Äquidensitenfilm *m*
equidistance map Äquidistanzkarte *f*
equidistant äquidistant, gleichabständig
~ **paramet[e]rization** äquidistante (gleichmäßige) Parametrisierung *f*
~ **projection** äquidistante Projektion *f*
~ **quantization** äquidistante Quantisierung *f*
~ **scanning raster** äquidistanter Abtastraster *m*
~ **tristimulus value** gleichabständige Farbvalenz *f*
equilateral triangle gleichseitiges Dreieck *n*
equiluminant, equiluminous äquiluminant, gleichhell
equipment Ausrüstung *f*
~ **block diagram** Blockschaltbild *n*, Blockdiagramm *n*
equivalent Äquivalent *n*
~ **color reproduction** äquivalente Farbwiedergabe *f*
~ **color temperature** korrelierte (ähnlichste) Farbtemperatur *f*
~ **dose** Äquivalentdosis *f (Radiografie)*
~ **focal length** *s.* effective focal length
~ **lens** Äquivalentlinse *f*
~ **luminance** äquivalente Leuchtdichte *f*
~ **phot** *s.* lambert
~ **weight** äquivalente Menge *f (z.B. von Fotochemikalien)*
~ **width** Äquivalenzbreite *f*
erasability Löschbarkeit *f*
erasable löschbar
~ **and programmable read-only memory** lösch- und programmierbarer Festwertspeicher *m*
~ **laser optical disk** löschbare Bildplatte *f*
~ **memory** löschbarer Speicher *m*
~ **printing form** löschbare Druckform *f*
~ **programmable read-only memory** löschbarer programmierbarer Nurlesespeicher *m*
erase/to löschen
erase exposure Löschbelichtung *f* *(Elektrofotografie)*
~ **function** Löschfunktion *f*
~ **head** Löschkopf *m*
~-**head width** Löschkopfbreite *f*
eraser laser Löschlaser *m*
erasing current Löschstrom *m*
~ **head** Löschkopf *m*
erasure Löschung *f*
~ **protection** Löschschutz *m*
erect image aufrechtes (lotrechtes) Bild *n*
erecting eyepiece Umkehrokular *n*
~ **lens** Umkehrlinse *f*
~ **telescope** Erdfernrohr *n*, terrestrisches Fernrohr *n*, erdgebundenes Teleskop *n*
erection of image Bildaufrichtung *f*
erector lens Umkehrlinse *f*
Erfle eyepiece Erfle-Okular *n*
erg Erg *n (Basiseinheit der Energie)*
ergodic ergodisch
~ **random field** ergodisches Zufallsfeld *n*
ergodicity Ergodizität *f (stochastischer Prozesse)*
Erlang noise Erlang-Rauschen *n*, Gammarauschen *n*
erosion Erosion *f*, Abtragung *f* *(morphologische Bildverarbeitungsoperation)*
~ **gradient** Erosionsgradient *m*
~ **operation** Erosionsoperation *f*
~ **operator** Erosionsoperator *m*
erratum Erratum *n*, Druckfehler *m*
erroneous data fehlerhafte Daten *pl*
~ **exposure** Fehlbelichtung *f*
error Fehler *m*
~ **backpropagation** Fehlerrückführung *f*, Fehlerrückvermittlung *f*; Fehlerrückmeldung *f*, Fehlerrückverfolgung *f* *(Lernalgorithmus)*
~ **burst** Fehlerburst *m*
~ **concealment** Fehlerverdeckung *f*
~-**correcting algorithm** Fehlerkorrekturalgorithmus *m*
~-**correcting code** Fehlerkorrekturcode *m*, Fehlerschutzcode *m*, fehlerkorrigierender Code *m*
~-**correcting coding** Fehlerkorrekturcodierung *f*, Fehlerschutzcodierung *f*
~ **correction** Fehlerkorrektur *f*
~ **correction code** *s.* error-correcting code
~ **correction mode** Fehlerkorrekturmodus *m (Faxübertragung)*
~-**detecting code** Fehlererkennungscode *m*
~ **detection** Fehlererkennung *f*
~ **diffusion [rendering]** 1. Fehlerdiffusion *f* *(Halbtonapproximation)*; 2. *s.* dot diffusion dithering

~-**free compression** verlustlose (verlustfreie) Kompression f
~-**free transmission** fehlerfreie Übertragung f
~ **function** [Gaußsche] Fehlerfunktion f
~ **function curve** Fehlerfunktionskurve f
~ **gradient** Fehlergradient m
~ **image** Fehlerbild n *(Bilddatenkompression)*
~ **indicator** Fehlerkennung f *(Datenverarbeitung)*
~ **limit** Fehlergrenze f
~ **matrix** Fehlermatrix f
~ **measure (metric)** Fehlermaß n
~ **of perception** Wahrnehmungsfehler m
~ **propagation** Fehlerfortpflanzung f
~ **propagation law (theorem)** [Gaußsches] Fehlerfortpflanzungsgesetz n
~ **protection** Fehlerschutz m
~ **protection code** Fehlerschutzcode m
~ **rate** Fehlerrate f
~ **rate display** Fehlerratenanzeige f *(digitaler Videobandrecorder)*
~ **recognition** Fehlererkennung f
~ **resilience (robustness)** Fehlertoleranz f
~ **segmentation** Fehlersegmentierung f
~ **sequence** Fehlersequenz f
~ **signal** Fehlersignal n
escort jammer zielbegleitender Störer m *(Radar)*
esophagoscope Oesophagoskop n, Speiseröhrenspiegel m
espionage photography Spionagefotografie f
establishing shot Eröffnungseinstellung f, Überblicksaufnahme f, Einführungstotale f, Gesamtaufnahme f, Anfangsaufnahme f *(Film)*
estimate/to [ab]schätzen
estimate Schätzwert m
estimated image Schätzbild n
~ **motion parameter** Bewegungsschätzwert m
~ **parameter** geschätzter Parameter m, Schätzparameter m
estimation Schätzung f
~ **accuracy** Schätzgenauigkeit f
~ **algorithm** Schätzalgorithmus m
~ **of spectrum** Spektralschätzung f
~-**theoretic** schätztheoretisch
~ **theory** Schätztheorie f
etalon Etalon n, Resonator m *(Interferometrie, Laser)*
etch/to ätzen
etch depth Ätztiefe f
~ **pit** Ätzgrübchen n
etchant Ätzmittel n
etched printing plate geätzte Druckplatte f
etcher Radierer m
etching 1. Ätzen n, Ätzung f; 2. Radierung f *(grafisches Tiefdruckverfahren)*; 3. Radierung f *(Originaldruck)*
~ **bath** Ätzbad n
~ **chemical** Ätzchemikalie f

~ **ground** Ätzgrund m
~ **knife** Retuschiermesser n, Schabemesser n
~ **liquid** Ätzflüssigkeit f
~ **machine** Ätzmaschine f
~ **mask** Ätzmaske f
~ **needle** Radiernadel f
~ **process** Ätzverfahren n
~ **technique** Ätztechnik f
~ **technology** Ätztechnik f
Ethernet Ethernet n *(LAN-Standard)*
~ **adapter** Ethernet-Adapter m
~ **cable port** Ethernet-Kabelanschluss m
~ **connection (link)** Ethernet-Schnittstelle f, Ethernet-Verbindung f
ethylene glycol Ethylenglycol n
ethylenediaminetetraacetic acid Ethylendiamintetraessigsäure f, EDTA *(Bleichfixierbadzusatz)*
Euclidean algorithm Euklidischer Algorithmus m
~ **classifier** Euklidischer Klassifikator m
~ **distance** Euklidischer Abstand m, Euklidische Distanz f
~ **distance map** Abstandsbild n
~ **geometry** Euklidische Geometrie f
~ **granulometry** Euklidische Granulometrie f
~ **metric** Euklidische Metrik f; Euklidisches Abstandsmaß m
~ **norm** Euklidische Norm f *(eines Vektors)*
~ **space** Euklidischer Raum m
Euler number Euler-Zahl f *(Binärbildverarbeitung)*
~ **operation** Euler-Operation f *(Computergrafik)*
~ **operator** Euler-Operator m
Euler's equation (formula) Euler-Gleichung f, Eulerscher Polyedersatz m, Eulersche Formel f *(mathematische Morphologie)*
Euroconnector SCART-Stecker m, Euro-AV-Stecker m *(video)*
European Telecommunication Standard Europäische Telekommunikationsnorm f
EV s. exposure value
evaluating computer Auswerterechner m
evaluation Auswertung f
evaporograph Evaporograf m *(Sensor)*
evaporography Evaporografie f
even field geradzahliges Halbbild n
~ **illumination** gleichmäßige Ausleuchtung f
~-**numbered line** geradzahlige Zeile f
~-**numbered page** gerade Seite f, Verso n, Blattrückseite f
~ **parity** gerade Parität f
~ **signal** gerades Signal n
evenly lit picture gleichmäßig ausgeleuchtetes Bild n
event Ereignis n
~ **mode** Ereignismodus m *(Grafiksystem)*
~ **queue** Eingabewarteschlange f *(Grafiksystem)*

ever-ready [camera] case
Bereitschaftstasche *f*
evidence photograph Beweisfoto *n*
~ **photography** Beweismittelfotografie *f*, beweissichernde Fotografie *f*
~ **theory** Evidenztheorie *f* [von Dempster und Shafer], Dempster-Shafer-Theorie *f*
evidential classification evidenztheoretische Klassifikation *f*
evolutionary algorithm evolutionärer Algorithmus *m*
Ewald['s] sphere Ewald-Kugel *f (Elektronenbeugung)*
exact color reproduction exakte (korrekte) Farbwiedergabe *f*
~ **encoding** verlustfreie (verlustlose) Kompression *f*
~ **match query** Punktfrage *f (Computergrafik)*
~ **range query** Bereichs[ab]frage *f*, Bereichsanfrage *f*, reverse Aufspießanfrage *f (Computergrafik)*
example-based image analysis beispielsbasierte Bildanalyse *f*
~ **image** Beispiel[s]bild *n*, Bildbeispiel *n*
exchangeable disk [store] Wechselplattenspeicher *m*
excimer laser Excimerlaser *m*
excitable anregbar
excitation Anregung *f*, Exzitation *f*
~ **energy** Anregungsenergie *f*
~ **frequency** Anregungsfrequenz *f*
~ **integral** Anregungsintegral *n*
~ **pulse** Anregungsimpuls *m*
~ **purity** 1. Farbsättigung *f*, Sättigung *f (Farbmetrik)*; 2. spektrale Farbdichte *f (Fernsehen)*
~ **signal** Anregungssignal *n*
~ **temperature** Anregungstemperatur *f*
~ **volume** Anregungsvolumen *n*
excite/to anregen
excited electron angeregtes Elektron *n*
exciter lamp Tonlampe *f (Lichttonsystem)*
exciting radiation Anregungsstrahlung *f*
exclamation mark (point) Ausrufungszeichen *n*
exclusive NOR exklusives NOR *n (binärer Schaltkreis)*
exhausted developer verbrauchter Entwickler *m*
exhaustion Erschöpfung *f (z.B. von Fotochemikalien)*
exhibition Ausstellung *f*; Vorführung *f*
~ **chain** Kinokette *f*
~ **print** Ausstellungsbild *n*, Ausstellungsfoto *n*
~ **release print** Vorführkopie *f*, Kinokopie *f*, Theaterkopie *f*, Verleihkopie *f*, vorführbereite (vorführfertige) Filmkopie *f*
existing light vorhandenes (verfügbares) Licht *n*
exit angle Austrittswinkel *m*
~ **aperture** Ausrittsapertur *f*

~ **dose** Austrittsdosis *f (Radiologie)*
~ **pupil** Austrittspupille *f*
~ **pupil diameter** Austrittspupillendurchmesser *m*
~ **pupil plane** Austrittspupillenebene *f*
~ **tray** Kopieablage *f*, Papierablage *f (Kopierer)*
~ **wave** Austrittswelle *f*
~ **window** Austrittsfenster *n*, Austrittsluke *f (Röntgenröhre)*
exitance [spezifische spektrale] Abstrahlung *f*
exiting ray Austrittsstrahl *m*, austretender Strahl *m*
exotic optical glass extremes Glas *n*
expand/to 1. aufweiten, ausweiten; 2. *s.* decompress/to
expanded beam aufgeweiteter Strahl *m*
~ **laser beam** aufgeweiteter Laserstrahl *m*
~ **memory** Erweiterungsspeicher *m*
~ **type** gesperrte (breitlaufende) Schrift *f*
expanding lens Strahlaufweitsystem *n*
expansion Expansion *f*; Aufweitung *f (z.B. eines Laserstrahls)*
~ **board** Erweiterungs[steck]karte *f*, Steckkarte *f*, Einsteckkarte *f*, Einsteck-Chipkarte *f*, Extenderkarte *f*
~ **bus** Erweiterungsbus *m*
~ **card** *s.* ~ board
~ **ratio** Aufweitungsfaktor *m*, Aufweitungsverhältnis *n*, Expansionsverhältnis *n*
~ **slot** Erweiterungssteckplatz *m*, Steckplatz *m*, Steckschacht *m*, Modulschacht *m*
expectation operator Erwartungsoperator *m (Bildquantisierung)*
~ **value** Erwartungswert *m*
expected value Erwartungswert *m*
experimental photography Experimentalfotografie *f*, experimentelle Fotografie *f*
~ **transmission** Versuchssendung *f (Fernsehen)*
expert knowledge Expertenwissen *n*
~ **system** Expertensystem *n*, wissensbasiertes System *n (Datenverarbeitung)*
expiration (expiry) date Verfallsdatum *n (z.B. von Fotomaterial)*
explicit quantization explizite Quantisierung *f*
~ **representation** explizite Darstellung *f (von Bilddaten)*
exploded diagram, exploded-view [photograph] Explosionsdarstellung *f*, Explosionszeichnung *f*
exponential [function] Exponentialfunktion *f*
expose/to exponieren; belichten
expose/ to light/to belichten
exposed film belichteter Film *m*
exposing device Belichtungsgerät *n (Lithografie)*

exposing

- ~ **light** Aufnahmelicht *n*
- ~ **light intensity** Belichtungsintensität *f*
- ~ **optics** Belichtungsoptik *f*
- ~ **radiation** Belichtungsstrahlung *f*
- **exposure** 1. Exposition *f*; Belichtung *f*; Belichtungsmenge *f*; 2. [fotografische] Aufnahme *f*
- ~ **accuracy** Belichtungsgenauigkeit *f*, Belichtungspräzision *f*
- ~ **adjustment** Belichtungsanpassung *f*
- ~ **calculator** Blendenrechner *m*
- ~ **change** Belichtungsänderung *f*
- ~ **chart** Belichtungstabelle *f*
- ~ **check** Belichtungskontrolle *f*
- ~ **compensation** Belichtungsausgleich *m*, Belichtungskompensation *f*; Belichtungskorrektur *f*
- ~ **compensation button** Belichtungskorrekturtaste *f*
- ~ **compensation value** Belichtungskorrekturwert *m*
- ~ **computer** Belichtungscomputer *m*
- ~ **control** Belichtungssteuerung *f*, Belichtungsregelung *f*
- ~ **control system** Belichtungssteuerungssystem *n*
- ~ **controller** Belichtungssteuergerät *n*
- ~ **correction** Belichtungskorrektur *f*
- ~ **correction factor** Belichtungskorrekturfaktor *m*
- ~ **counter** Bildzähler *m*, Bildzählwerk *n* *(Kamera)*
- ~ **data** Belichtungsdaten *pl*
- ~ **device** Belichtungsgerät *n*
- ~ **distribution** Belichtungsverteilung *f*
- ~ **drum** Belichtungstrommel *f*
- ~ **duration** Belichtungsdauer *f*
- ~ **effect** Belichtungseffekt *m*
- ~ **error** Belichtungsfehler *m*
- ~ **factor** Belichtungsfaktor *m*
- ~ **film speed** Belichtungsempfindlichkeit *f*
- ~ **filter** Belichtungsfilter *n*
- ~ **focal length** Aufnahmebrennweite *f*
- ~ **gate** Belichtungsfenster *n*; Bildfenster *n*
- ~ **geometry** Aufnahmegeometrie *f*
- ~ **glass** Einlegefläche *f (Kopierer, Scanner)*
- ~ **increase** Belichtungszeitverlängerung *f*
- ~ **increase factor** Belichtungsverlängerungsfaktor *m*
- ~ **index** Belichtungsindex *m*
- ~ **index number** Belichtungsrichtzahl *f* *(Kinefilm)*
- ~**-induced fog** Belichtungsschleier *m*
- ~ **intensity** Belichtungsintensität *f*
- ~ **interval** Belichtungsintervall *n*, Aufnahmeintervall *n*, Aufnahme-Folgezeit *f*, Bildfolgezeit *f*
- ~ **lamp** Aufnahmelampe *f*
- ~ **latitude** Belichtungsumfang *m*, Belichtungsspielraum *m*
- ~ **level** Belichtungsstärke *f*; Belichtungsstufe *f*
- ~ **measurement** Belichtungsmessung *f*
- ~ **meter** Belichtungsmesser *m*, Belichtungsmessgerät *n*, Exposimeter *n*
- ~ **meter accuracy** Belichtungsmessergenauigkeit *f*
- ~ **meter coupling** Belichtungsmesserkupplung *f*
- ~ **metering** Belichtungsmessung *f*
- ~ **metering field** Belichtungsmessfeld *n*
- ~ **metering system** Belichtungsmesssystem *n*
- ~ **mode** Belichtungsmodus *m*, Belichtungsmessart *f*, Belichtungsfunktion *f*
- ~ **mode selection** Belichtungswahl *f*
- ~ **nucleus** Belichtungskeim *m*
- ~ **parameter** Belichtungsparameter *m*
- ~ **pattern** Belichtungsmuster *n*
- ~ **period** Belichtungszeitraum *m*
- ~ **phenomenon** Belichtungseffekt *m*
- ~ **process** Belichtungsvorgang *m*
- ~ **range** Belichtungsspielraum *m*, Belichtungszeitenbereich *m*, Belichtungsumfang *m*
- ~ **recommendation** Belichtungsempfehlung *f*
- ~ **screen** Aufnahmefolie *f (Radiografie)*
- ~ **sensitivity** Belichtungsempfindlichkeit *f*
- ~ **series** Belichtungsreihe *f*, Belichtungsserie *f*, Belichtungsfächer *m*
- ~ **setting ring** Belichtungszeiteneinstellring *m*, Belichtungszeitenwähler *m*
- ~ **slit** Belichtungsspalt *m*
- ~ **speed** 1. Belichtungsgeschwindigkeit *f*; 2. Belichtungsempfindlichkeit *f*
- ~ **step** Belichtungsstufe *f*
- ~ **stop** belichtungskorrekte Blendenzahl *f*
- ~ **system** Belichtungssystem *n*
- ~ **table** Belichtungstabelle *f*
- ~ **technique** Belichtungstechnik *f*
- ~ **test** Belichtungsprobe *f*, Belichtungstest *m*
- ~ **time** Expositionszeit *f*; Belichtungszeit *f*
- ~ **time determination** Belichtungszeitbestimmung *f*
- ~ **time setting** Belichtungs[zeit]einstellung *f*
- ~ **timer** Belichtungs[zeitschalt]uhr *f*
- ~ **timing** Belichtungs[zeit]einstellung *f*
- ~ **to light** Belichtung *f*, Lichtexposition *f*
- ~ **unit** Belichtungseinheit *f*
- ~ **value** [relativer] Belichtungswert *m*, Belichtungsgröße *f*, Blenden-Zeit-Stufe *f*
- ~ **value scale** Belichtungsskala *f*
- ~ **wavelength** Belichtungswellenlänge *f*
- ~ **wedge** *s.* ~ series
- **expression** [mathematischer] Ausdruck *m*
- **extendable bellows** Balgenauszug *m*
- **extended definition television** *s.* enhanced definition television
- ~ **graphics array** erweiterter Grafikbereich *m (Grafikstandard mit 1.024 x 768 Pixel Auflösung)*

~ **Huffman code** erweiterter Huffman-Code *m*
Extended Industry Standard Architecture *ein Datenbusstandard für den Anschluss von Videokarten*
extended light source ausgedehnte Lichtquelle *f*
~ **memory** Erweiterungsspeicher *m*
~ **RGB color space** erweiterter RGB-Farbraum *m*
~**-term keeping (storage)** Langzeitarchivierung *f*
~ **type** gesperrte (breitlaufende) Schrift *f*
extender board Verlängerungsplatine *f*
extensibility Erweiterbarkeit *f (z.B. von Datentransportformaten)*
extension Auszug *m (Kamera)*
~ **bellows** Balgen[einstell]gerät *n*; Verlängerungsbalgen *m*
~ **cord** Verlängerungskabel *n*
~ **in depth** Tiefenausdehnung *f*
~ **ring** Zwischenring *m (s.a. ~ tube)*
~ **tube** Auszugsverlängerung *f*, Verlängerungstubus *m*, Vorsatztubus *m*; Zwischentubus *m*, Tubus *m*
~**-tube set** Zwischenringsatz *m*
extent 1. Ausmaß *n*, Ausdehnung *f*; Bereich *m*; 2. Seitenzahl *f*
~ **in depth** Tiefenausdehnung *f*
exterior Außenaufnahme *f*
~ **location** Außendrehort *m*, Außenaufnahmeort *m*, Außenmotiv *n (Filmarbeit)*
~ **shooting** Außendreh *m*, Außendreharbeit *f*
external computer memory externer Speicher *m*
~ **drive** externes Laufwerk *n*
~ **drum recorder** Außentrommelbelichter *m*
~ **exposure meter** externer Belichtungsmesser *m*
~ **flash** externes Blitzgerät *n*
~ **leading** Zeilendurchschuss *m*, Zeilenzwischenraum *m*, Durchschuss *m (Typografie)*
~ **magnetic field** äußeres Magnetfeld *n*
~ **microphone** Zusatzmikrofon *n*, separates (externes) Mikrofon *n*
~ **peripheral** Peripheriegerät *n*, peripheres Gerät *n*
~ **photoeffect (photoelectric effect)** äußerer fotoelektrischer (lichtelektrischer) Effekt *m*, Fotoemissionseffekt *m*
~ **reflection** Reflexion *f* am optisch dichteren Medium
extinction Extinktion *f*, Auslöschung *f*; Deckung *f*
~ **coefficient** Extinktionskoeffizient *m*; Schwächungskoeffizient *m*, Abschwächungskoeffizient *m*, Dämpfungskoeffizient *m*

~ **[exposure] meter** Extinktionsbelichtungsmesser *m*
~ **ratio** Extinktionsverhältnis *n*, Auslöschungsverhältnis *n*
extra-axial außeraxial, achs[en]fern, achsentfernt, abaxial
~ **dense flint [glass]** Schwerstflint *m*
~ **hard** extrahart *(Fotopapier)*
~**-high-pressure mercury [vapor] lamp** Quecksilber-Höchstdrucklampe *f*
~**-high-voltage electron microscope** Höchstspannungselektronenmikroskop *n*
~ **soft** extraweich *(Fotopapier)*
extractor Abzug *m (Dunkelraumausrüstung)*
extrafoveal color vision extrafoveales (indirektes) Farbensehen *n*
extraneous environmental noise Fremdgeräusch *n (Filmproduktion)*
~ **light** Fremdlicht *n*
~ **radiation** Fremdstrahlung *f*
extraordinary ray außerordentlicher Strahl *m (Optik)*
extrapolate/to extrapolieren
extrapolation Extrapolation *f*
extraterrestrial telescope extraterrestrisches Teleskop *n*, Raumteleskop *n*
extravisible unsichtbar, invisibel
extreme and mean ratio goldener Schnitt *m*
~ **close-up** extreme Nahaufnahme *f*, Ganzgroßaufnahme *f*; Detailaufnahme *f*
~ **infrared** extremes Infrarot *n*
~ **long shot** Panoramaeinstellung *f*
~ **ultraviolet** extremes Ultraviolett *n*, EUV
~ **wide-angle lens** Superweitwinkelobjektiv *n*, Ultraweitwinkelobjektiv *n*, extremes Weitwinkelobjektiv *n*
extremum filter Extremwertoperator *m (Grauwertbildverarbeitung)*
extrinsic photoconduction äußerer Fotoeffekt *m*, Fotoemissionseffekt *m*, Störstellenfotoleitung *f*
~ **semiconductor** dotierter Halbleiter *m*
extruded surface Extrusionsfläche *f*, extrudierte Fläche *f (Flächenmodellierung)*
eye 1. Auge *n (s.a. unter ocular)* ; 2. Augenlicht *n*
~ **adaptation** Adaptation *f (des Auges)*
~ **base** Augenbasis *f*
~ **chart** Sehprobentafel *f*
~ **color** Augenfarbe *f*
~ **cornea** Augenhornhaut *f*, Hornhaut *f*, Cornea *f*, Kornea *f*
~ **cup** Augenmuschel *f*
~ **disorder** Augenstörung *f*
~ **distance** Augenabstand *m*
~ **fixation** Fixation *f (Sehen)*
~ **fundus** Augenhintergrund *m*, Augenrückwand *f*

eye

- ~ guard Augenmuschel f
- ~ injury Augenschädigung f
- ~ lens Augenlinse f *(eines Okulars)*
- ~ level Augenhöhe f
- ~-level viewing Durchsichtsbetrachtung f *(Spiegelreflexkamera)*
- ~ line Augenlinie f, Blicklinie f, Sichtlinie f, Gesichtslinie f, Sichtverbindung f
- ~ location Augenort m
- ~ motion Augenbewegung f
- ~ motion speed Augenbewegungsgeschwindigkeit f
- ~ motion tracking Augensteuerung f, Blicksteuerung f
- ~ movement Augenbewegung f
- ~ muscle Augenmuskel m
- ~ pattern Augendiagramm n
- ~ point Aug[en]punkt m; Austrittspupille f *(Köhlersche Beleuchtung)*
- ~ position Augenstellung f, Augenposition f
- ~ receptor Sehrezeptor m, Rezeptorzelle f, Fotorezeptor m
- ~-related disorder Augenstörung f
- ~ scintigraphy Augenszintigrafie f
- ~ sensitivity Augenempfindlichkeit f
- ~ shield Augenmuschel f
- ~ socket Augenkapsel f, Augenhöhle f, Orbita f
- ~ system Sehsystem n, visuelles System n
- ~ tracking Augensteuerung f, Blicksteuerung f
- ~ vergence Vergenz f *(Augenbewegung; s.a. unter vergence)*

eyeball Augapfel m, Augenbulbus m
eyedness Äugigkeit f
- ~ Äugigkeit f, Dominanz f *(Physiologie des Sehens)*

eyeglass s. eyepiece n
- ~ lens Brillenglas n

eyeglasses Brille f
eyehole s. eye socket
eyelid Augenlid n
eyelight 1. Augenlicht n, Kopflicht n *(Porträtfotografie)*; 2. Augenlichtlampe f
eyepiece Okular n
- ~ adapter Okularadapter m
- ~ camera Okularkamera f, Mikroskopkamera f, Ansetzkamera f, Aufsetzkamera f *(Mikrofotografie)*
- ~ correction lens Augenkorrektionslinse f, Augenkorrekturlinse f
- ~ diaphragm Okularblende f *(Mikroskop)*
- ~ draw tube Okularauszug m
- ~ filter Okularfilter n
- ~ graticule Okularskale f
- ~ housing Okulartubus m *(Mikroskop)*
- ~ lens Okularlinse f
- ~ magnification Okularvergrößerung f
- ~ measuring graticule, eyepiece micrometer Okularmikrometer n
- ~ optics Okularobjektiv n
- ~ projection Okularprojektion f
- ~ scale Okularskale f

eye's optics Augenoptik f; Brillenoptik f
eyesight Augenlicht n; Sehkraft f
eyestrain Augenermüdung f
eyetube Okulartubus m, Okularauszug m

F

f-number setting Blendeneinstellung *f*
f-number, F number Blendenzahl *f*,
Blendenwert *m*, f-Blende *f*, f-Zahl *f*,
relative Apertur (Lichtstärke) *f*,
Lichtstärkenverhältnis *n (Objektiv)*
f stop 1. Blendenstufe *f*; 2. *s.* f-number
f theta correction F-Theta-Korrektur *f (z.B.*
in Laserdruckern)
f theta lens F-Theta-Linse *f*,
F-Theta-Objektiv *n (eines*
Abtastsystems)
fabric blind Rollo *n (Schlitzverschluss)*
~ **printing** Textildruck *m*
~ **ribbon** Textilfarbband *n*,
Gewebefarbband *n*
Fabry-Perot cavity Fabry-Perot-Resonator
m
~**-Perot device** Fabry-Perot-System *n*
~**-Perot interferometer**
Fabry-Perot-Interferometer *n*,
Luftplattenspektroskop *n*
face 1. Flächenstück *n*; 2. Schriftbild *n (der*
Einzelletter); 3. *s.* typeface
~ **animation**
Gesichts[ausdrucks]animation *f*
~**-centered cubic** kubisch-flächenzentriert
(Kristallstruktur)
~ **detection** Gesichtserkennung *f*
~ **detection and recognition system**
Gesichtserkennungssystem *n*
~ **image** Gesichtsbild *n*
~ **perception** Gesichtswahrnehmung *f*
faceplate Frontplatte *f*; Frontscheibe *f*,
Frontglas *n*, Bildröhrenfront *f*;
Eintrittsfenster *n (Bildaufnahmeröhre)*
facet/to facettieren
facet Facette *f*
~ **model** Facettenmodell *n*
faceted mirror Facettenspiegel *m*
~ **shading** konstante Schattierung *f*
~ **surface** facettierte Oberfläche *f*
faceting Facettierung *f*,
Polyederapproximation *f*
(Computergrafik)
facial expressions animation
Gesichts[ausdrucks]animation *f*
~ **feature** Gesichtsmerkmal *n*
~ **image** Gesichtsbild *n*
~ **modeling** Gesichtsmodellierung *f*
~ **recognition feature**
Gesichtserkennungsmerkmal *n*
facsimile/to faksimilieren
facsimile 1. Faksimile *n*; Bildtelegramm *n*,
Fax *n*, Fernkopie *f (s.a. unter* fax*)*; 2. *s.*
phototelegraphy
~ **chart** Faxgrafik *f*, Faxbild *n*

~ **coding** Faksimilecodierung *f*,
Faxcodierung *f*
~ **compression** Faksimilekompression *f*;
Faxcodierung *f*
~ **copy** Fernkopie *f*, Fax *n*
~ **data** Faxdaten *pl*
~ **flatbed equipment**
Fernkopierer-Flachbettgerät *n*
~ **machine** *s.* ~ transceiver
~ **message** Faxmitteilung *f*
~ **printing** Faksimiledruck *m*
~ **radiograph** Röntgenkopie *f*
~ **representation** Faksimiledarstellung *f*
~ **transceiver** Faxgerät *n*, Telefax[gerät *n*,
Fernkopierer *m*
~ **transmission** Bildfernübermittlung *f*,
Bildfernübertragung *f*, Faxübertragung *f*
~ **transmission format**
Faxübertragungsformat *n*
factor analysis Faktorenanalyse *f*
factorial filtering faktorielle Filterung *f*
~ **space** faktorieller Raum *m*
fade/to verblassen, verbleichen,
ausbleichen
fade down/to abblenden
~ **in/to** [weich] einblenden; aufblenden
~ **out/to** weich ausblenden (abblenden)
~ **up/to** aufblenden
~ Blende *f*; Abblende *f*, Abblendung *f*
(Film, Video)
~ **button** Blendenschalter *m (Camcorder)*
~ **control** elektronische Blende *f*
~**-in** Aufblende *f*, Aufblendung *f*;
Einblendung *f (Film, Video)*
~**-in from black** Aufblende *f* aus Schwarz
~**-out** Abblende *f*, Abblendung *f*;
Ausblendung *f*
~**-out to black** Abblende *f* nach Schwarz
faded color verblasste Farbe *f*
~ **image** verblasstes Bild *n*
~ **photograph** verblichenes (vergilbtes)
Foto *n*
~ **print** verblasster (verblichener) Abzug *m*
fader 1. Doppelpol[arisations]filter *n*; 2. *s.*
~ control
~ **control** 1. Lichtregler *m*,
Lichtsteuerblende *f*, elektronische
Blende *f (Videorecorder)*; 2. Tonregler *m*,
Lautstärkeregler *m*, Einsteller *m*,
Schieberegler *m*
fading Ausbleichen *n (z.B. von*
Fotomaterial)
~ **down (out)** Abblende *f*, Abblendung *f*;
Ausblendung *f*
failure Ausfall *m*; Fehler *m*
faint lichtarm, lichtschwach; matt, flau
(Bildkontrast)
~ **color** flaue Farbe *f*
~ **detail** lichtschwaches Detail *n*
~ **image** lichtschwaches Bild *n*
~ **light** schwaches Licht *n*, Schwachlicht *n*
fairing *s.* smoothing
fake/to fälschen
faked picture gefälschtes Bild *n*

fall 132

fall time Abfallzeit *f (eines Impulses)*
falloff [of light] Lichtabfall *m*, Lichtschwund *m*
false acception rate Falschakzeptanzrate *f*, FAR *(Authentifizierung)*
~ **alarm rate** Falschalarmrate *f (Radar)*
~ **color** Falschfarbe *f (s.a. unter pseudocolor)*
~-**color film** Falschfarbenfilm *m*, Farbinfrarotfilm *m*, Infrarotfarbfilm *m*
~-**color image** Falschfarbenbild *n*
~-**color photograph** Infrarot-Farbfoto *n*
~-**color photography** Falschfarbenfotografie *f*
~-**color thermograph** Falschfarben-Wärmebild *n*
~ **duotone** unechter Duplexdruck *m*
~ **edge** falsche Kante *f*
~ **enrolment rate** Falscherfassungsrate *f*, FER *(Authentifizierung)*
~ **light** Falschlicht *n*
~ **rejection rate** Falschrückweisungsrate *f*, FRR, Abweisungsrate *f* berechtigter Personen *(Authentifizierung)*
~ **replies unsynchronous in time** *s.* fruit
family album Familienalbum *n*
~ **of curves** Kurvenfamilie *f*, Kurvenschar *f*
fan angle Fächerwinkel *m*
~ **beam** Fächerstrahl *m*, Strahlenfächer *m*, Fächerkeule *f (Radar)*
~ **beam collimation** Fächerstrahlkollimation *f*
~ **beam collimator** divergierender Kollimator *m*
~ **beam detector** Fächerstrahldetektor *m (Tomografie)*
~ **beam projection** Fächerstrahlprojektion *f*, fächerförmige Projektion *f (Tomografie)*
~-**cooled projector** gebläsegekühlter Projektor *m*
~ **fader** Fächerblende *f*
~-**like geometry** Fächerform *f (z.B. von Sonogrammen)*
~-**shaped beam** *s.* fan beam
~ **X-ray beam** Röntgenfächerstrahl *m*, Röntgenstrahlfächer *m*
fancy script font Effektschrift *f (Typografie)*
fanfolded paper Zickzackstapel *m*
fanned beam *s.* fan beam
fanout Papierverzug *m (Druckschwierigkeit)*
far-distance measurement Fernmessung *f*; Telemetrie *f*
~-**end camera** fernbedienbare (fernsteuerbare) Kamera *f*; robotergeführte Kamera *f*, Roboterkamera *f*
~-**field** Fernfeld *n (z.B. Ultraschall, Laser)*
~-**field diffraction** Fraunhofer-Beugung *f*
~-**field diffraction pattern** Fraunhofer-Beugungsbild *n*
~ **infrared [region]** fernes Infrarot *n*
~ **point** Fernpunkt *m (Sehschärfe)*
~ **red** nahes (fotografisches) Infrarot *n*
~ **ultraviolet [radiation]**, ~ **UV** fernes Ultraviolett *n*
~ **vision** Weitsehen *n*
Faraday cage Faraday-Käfig *m*
~ **effect** Faraday-Effekt *m*
~ **rotation** Faraday-Rotation *f*
~ **rotator** Faraday-Rotator *m*
~ **shutter** Faraday-Verschluss *m*, magnetooptischer Verschluss *m*
faradic current faradischer Strom *m*
Farmer's reducer Farmerscher Abschwächer *m (Fotochemikalie)*
farseeing, farsighted weitsichtig, übersichtig, hypermetropisch, hyperop
farsightedness Weitsichtigkeit *f*, Übersichtigkeit *f*, Fernsichtigkeit *f*, Hyper[metr]opie *f*
fashion photograph Modeaufnahme *f*
~ **photography** Modefotografie *f*
fast 1. schnell; 2. hoch[licht]empfindlich *(Filmmaterial)*; 3. lichtstark *(Objektiv)*
~-**acting developing agent** Schnellentwickler *m*, Rapidentwickler *m*, schnellarbeitender Entwickler *n*
~-**acting fixing agent** Schnellfixierer *m*, Express-Fixierbad *n*
~ **algorithm** schneller Algorithmus *m (z.B. für geometrische Transformationen)*
~-**drying ink** schnelltrocknende Druckfarbe *f*
~ **film** hoch[licht]empfindlicher Film *m*
~ **forward [movement]** schnelles Vorspulen *n*, Schnellvorlauf *m*; Schnellsuchlauf *m (Videokassettenrecorder)*
~ **Fourier transform[ation]** schnelle Fourier-Transformation *f*, Fourier-Schnelltransformation *f*
~ **image processing** schnelle Bildverarbeitung *f*
~ **imaging** schnelle Bildgebung *f*
~ **lens** lichtstarkes Objektiv *n*
~ **memory** schneller Speicher *m*
~ **motion** Zeitraffer *m*
~-**motion effect** Zeitraffereffekt *m*
~ **reverse (rewind)** Schnellrücklauf *m*, schneller Rücklauf *m*
~-**shutter camera** Ultrakurzzeitkamera *f*
~ **spin echo pulse sequence** schnelle Spinechosequenz *f (Sonografie)*
~ **transient thermal imaging**, ~ **transient thermography** Impulsthermografie *f (zerstörungsfreie Werkstoffprüfung)*
~ **wavelet transform** schnelle Wavelet-Transformation *f*
fat fiber Dickkernfaser *f (Faseroptik)*
~ **saturation (suppression)** Fettsättigung *f*, Fettsuppression *f (Magnetresonanztomografie)*
~-**tail coupler** Fettschwanzkuppler *m*, ölgeschützter Farbkuppler *m*, Ölkuppler *m (Farbfotografie)*

fata morgana Fata Morgana *f (optische Täuschung)*
fatigue *s.* eyestrain
fault Fehler *m (s.a. unter error)*
faulted crystal fehlgeordneter Kristall *m*
fax/to faxen, fernkopieren
fax 1. Fax *n*, Fernkopie *f*; 2. *s.* ~ terminal
~ **board (card)** Faxkarte *f*
~ **coding** Faxcodierung *f*
~ **cover page** Deckblatt *n*
~ **machine** *s.* ~ terminal
~ **map** Faxgrafik *f*, Faxbild *n*
~ **modem** Faxmodem *n*
~ **software** Fax-Software *f*
~ **telephony** Faxübertragung *f*
~ **terminal** Telefax[gerät] *n*, Faxgerät *n*, Fernkopierer *m*
~ **transmission** Faxübertragung *f*
FDMA *s.* frequency division multiple access
feature 1. Merkmal *n*; Ausstattungsmerkmal *n*; 2. *s.* descriptor
~ **analysis** Merkmalsanalyse *f*
~ **area** Merkmalsfläche *f*
~**-based classification** merkmalbasierte Klassifikation *f*
~**-based filtering** merkmalsbasierte Filterung *f*
~**-based image matching** merkmalsbasierte Bildzuordnung *f*
~**-based image metamorphosis** merkmalsbasierte Bildmetamorphose *f*
~**-based matching** merkmalsbasierte Zuordnung *f*
~**-based model** merkmalsgestütztes Modell *n (Objekterkennung)*
~**-based motion estimation** merkmalsbasierte Bewegungsschätzung *f*
~**-based reconstruction** merkmalsbasierte Rekonstruktion *f*
~**-based representation** merkmalsgestützte Darstellung *f*
~**-based segmentation** merkmalsbasierte Segmentierung *f*
~ **boundary** Merkmalsgrenze *f*
~ **cinematographer** Filmemacher *m*, Filmschaffender *m*
~ **class** Merkmalsklasse *f*
~ **classification** Merkmalsklassifikation *f*
~ **cluster** Merkmalscluster *m*
~ **code** Merkmalscode *m*
~ **correspondence** Merkmalskorrespondenz *f*
~ **descriptor** Merkmalsdeskriptor *m*
~ **detail** Merkmalsdetail *n*
~ **detection** Merkmalserkennung *f*, Merkmalsidentifikation *f*
~ **detector** Merkmalsdetektor *m*
~ **edge** Merkmalskante *f*
~ **enhancement** Merkmalsverstärkung *f*
~ **extraction** Merkmalsextraktion *f*
~ **extractor** Merkmalsextraktor *m*
~ **film** Spielfilm *m*, Hauptfilm *m*
~ **film camera** Kino[film]kamera *f*
~ **film editing** Spielfilmnachbearbeitung *f*
~ **film industry** Spielfilmindustrie *f*
~ **film production** Spielfilmproduktion *f*
~ **grouping** Merkmalsgruppierung *f*
~ **histogram** Merkmalshistogramm *n*
~ **identification** *s.* ~ detection
~ **image** Merkmalsbild *n*
~ **interval** Merkmalsintervall *n*
~**-length film (motion picture)** Großfilm *m*, Hauptfilm *m*, abendfüllender Film *m*
~ **localization** Merkmalslokalisierung *f*
~ **map** nachbarschaftserhaltende (topologieerhaltende) Abbildung *f*, Merkmalskarte *f (Mustererkennung)*
~ **matching** Merkmalszuordnung *f*
~ **measurement** Merkmalsmessung *f*
~ **modeling** Merkmalsmodellierung *f*
~ **motion picture** Hauptfilm *m*
~ **observation** Merkmalsbeobachtung *f*
~ **of interest** interessierendes Merkmal *n*
~ **orientation** Merkmalsausrichtung *f*
~ **overlap** Merkmalsüberlappung *f*
~ **parameter** Merkmalsparameter *m*
~ **pixel** Merkmalspixel *n*
~ **point** Merkmalspunkt *m*
~ **polygon** Merkmalspolygon *n*
~ **primitive** Merkmalsprimitiv *n*
~ **property** Merkmalseigenschaft *f*
~ **recognition** Merkmalserkennung *f*, Merkmalsidentifikation *f*
~ **reduction** Merkmalsreduktion *f*, Merkmalsreduzierung *f*
~ **resolution** Merkmalsauflösung *f*
~ **search** Merkmalssuche *f*
~ **selection** Merkmalsauswahl *f*, Merkmalsselektion *f*
~ **set** Merkmalssatz *m*
~ **shape** Merkmalsform *f*
~ **similarity** Merkmalsähnlichkeit *f*
~ **size** Merkmalsgröße *f*
~ **smoothing** Merkmalsglättung *f*
~ **space** Merkmalsraum *m*
~ **space analysis** Merkmalsraumanalyse *f*
~ **space image** *s.* scatter diagram
~ **tracking** Merkmalsverfolgung *f*
~ **value** Merkmalswert *m*
~ **vector** Merkmalsvektor *m*
~ **volume** Merkmalsvolumen *n*
Fechner's colors Fechner-Benhamsche Farben *fpl*, Benham-Farben *fpl*, Flimmerfarben *fpl*, subjektive Farben *fpl*
~ **law** [Weber-]Fechnersches Gesetz *n*, psychophysisches Grundgesetz *n (Wahrnehmungsphysiologie)*
feed magazine Abwickelmagazin *n*
~ **reel** Abwickelspule *f*, Vorratsspule *f*, Vorratsrolle *f*
~ **scanner** Einzugsscanner *m*
~ **spool** *s.* ~ reel
~ **sprocket** Vorwickel[zahn]rolle *f*, Vorwickler *m*
~ **tray** Eingabetisch *m (z.B. eines Entwicklungsautomaten)*

feed 134

~ **unit** Speiseeinheit *f*, Speisesystem *n* *(Satellitenempfangsanlage)*
feedback Rückkopplung *f*, Feedback *n*
~ **network** Rückkopplungsnetz[werk] *n*
~ **noise** Rückkopplungsrauschen *n*
feeder *s.* feeding unit
feedforward network Vorwärtsvermittlungsnetz *n*, Mitkopplungsnetz *n*, vorwärtsgekoppeltes Netz *n*
feedhorn *s.* feed unit
feeding edge Greiferkante *f*, Greiferrand *m* *(Bogendruck)*
~ **unit** Anlegeapparat *m*, Anleger *m*, Bogenanleger *m*, Bogenanlage *f* *(Druckmaschine)*
feeling of spaciousness Raumgefühl *n*
feetroom Untersteuerungsreserve *f* *(Videosignal)*
felt side Filzseite *f*, Schön[druck]seite *f* *(Papier)*
female matte Vordergrundmaskenfilm *m*
femtosecond laser Femtosekundenlaser *m*
Fermat's principle [of least time] Fermatsches Prinzip *n* *(Strahlenoptik)*
Fermi [energy] level Fermi-Energie *f*, Fermi-Niveau *n* *(Halbleiter)*
ferric ammonium citrate Ammoniumeisencitrat *n*, Ammoniumferricitrat *n*, Eisenoxidammoniak *n* *(Tonungsmittel)*
~ **chloride** Eisenchlorid *n* *(Ätzmittel)*
~ **oxide** Eisen-III-oxid *n*
~ **process** Eisensalzverfahren *n* *(frühe Fotografie)*
ferricyanide Cyanoferrat *n*, Hexacyanoferrat *n* *(Bleichmittel)*
ferrite core Ferritkern *m*
ferro-prussiate process Cyanotypie *f*, [negativer] Eisenblaudruck *m*
ferroelectric liquid ferroelektrische Flüssigkeit *f*
~ **liquid crystal** ferroelektrischer Flüssigkristall *m*
~ **liquid crystal display** FLC-Bildschirm *m*
ferromagnetic ferromagnetisch
ferromagnetism Ferromagnetismus *m*
ferrotype [process] Ferrotypie *f*
ferrotyper Ferrotypist *m*
ferrous oxalate developer Eisenoxalatentwickler *m*
FET *s.* field-effect transistor
fetal imaging, ~ [ultra]sonography, fetography Fetografie *f*
fetoscope Fetoskop *n*
fetoscopy Fetoskopie *f*
fiber-base[d] photographic paper Naturpapier *n*, ungestrichenes Papier *n*
~ **bundle** Faserbündel *n*, Lichtleiterbündel *n*
~ **cable** Faserkabel *n*
~ **core** Faserkern *m*
~-**coupled photodetector** fasergekoppelter Fotodetektor *m*

~ **coupler** Faserkoppler *m*
~ **interferometer** Faserinterferometer *n*
~ **laser** Faserlaser *m*
~-**linked array image formatter** lichtwellenleitergekoppeltes Bildausgabe-Array *n*
~-**optic** faseroptisch
~-**optic amplifier** faseroptischer Verstärker *m*
~-**optic bundle** Faserbündel *n*, Lichtleiterbündel *n*
~-**optic cable** Lichtleitkabel *n*, Glasfaserkabel *n*
~-**optic collimator** Faseroptikkollimator *m*
~-**optic connector** faseroptischer Stecker *m*
~-**optic coupler** faseroptisches Kopplungselement *n*
~-**optic coupling** faseroptische Lichteinkopplung *f*, Faserkopplung *f*
~-**optic element** faseroptisches Element *n*
~-**optic endoscope** Glasfaserendoskop *n*, Faserendoskop *n*, faseroptisches (flexibles) Endoskop *n*
~-**optic instrument** faseroptisches Instrument *n*
~-**optic light** faseroptisches Licht *n*
~-**optic light guide** faseroptischer Lichtleiter *m*, Licht[wellen]leiter *m*
~-**optic lighting** faseroptische Beleuchtung *f*
~-**optic plate** Faser[optik]platte *f*
~-**optic scanner** faseroptischer Scanner *m*
~-**optic sensor** faseroptischer Sensor *m*
~-**optic spectrometer** faseroptisches Spektrometer *n*
~-**optic strand** optische Faser *f*
~-**optic waveguide** faseroptischer Wellenleiter *m*
~-**optical** faseroptisch
~ **optics** Faseroptik *f*, Glasfaseroptik *f*, Fiberoptik *f*
~ **paper** Naturpapier *n*, ungestrichenes Papier *n*
~ **sensor** faseroptischer Sensor *m*
~ **spectrograph** Faserspektrograf *m*, faserabbildender Spektrograf *m*
fiberscope [device] Faseroptikinstrument *n* *(s.a. fiber-optic endoscope)*
fiction film Spielfilm *m*
fidelity Wiedergabetreue *f*; Detailtreue *f*
~ **of color reproduction** Farbwiedergabegenauigkeit *f*
~ **of reproduction** Wiedergabetreue *f*
fiducial frame Markenrahmen *m* *(Fotogrammetrie)*
~ **line** Markenlinie *f*
~ **mark** Rahmenmarke *f*, Bildrahmenmarke *f (Fotogrammetrie)*
field 1. Feld *n*; Datenfeld *n* 2. Halbbild *n* *(Video)*; 3. Textabschnitt *m (Typografie)*; 4. *s.* ~ of view
~-**accurate editing** bildgenauer Schnitt *m*
~ **amplitude** Feldamplitude *f*

~ **angle** Feldwinkel m, Bild[feld]winkel m
~-**based prediction** Halbbildprädiktion f, halbbildbasierte Prädiktion f
~ **blanking** Halbbildaustastung f, Bildaustastung f *(Video)*
~ **blanking interval** Bildaustastlücke f, Vertikalaustastlücke f, vertikale Austastlücke f
~-**blanking period** Halbbildaustastperiode f
~ **broadcast** Außenübertragung f
~ **coil** Feldspule f
~ **correction** Bildfeldkorrektur f
~ **coverage** Bildfeldgröße f; Feldgröße f *(Radiografie)*
~ **curvature [aberration]** Bildfeldwölbung f, Feldkrümmung f, Petzval-Krümmung f
~ **deflection coil** Vertikalablenkspule f
~ **diaphragm** Feldblende f, Bildfeldblende f, feldbegrenzende Blende f; Gesichtsfeldblende f; Sehfeldblende f
~ **distortion** Bildfeldverzerrung f
~ **divider** Frequenzteiler m *(Fernsehtechnik)*
~ **dominance** Halbbilddominanz f
~ **duration** s. ~ period
~ **effect transistor** Feldeffekttransistor m, Unipolartransistor m *(Lichtdetektor)*
~ **emission** Feldemission f *(von Elektronen)*
~ **emission current** Feldemissionsstrom m
~ **emission display [panel]** Feldemissionsanzeige f, Feldemissionsdisplay n
~ **emission microscope** Feldemissions[elektronen]mikroskop n, Feldelektronenmikroskop n
~ **emitter** Feldemitter m
~ **flattener [element]** Ebnungslinse f, Bildfeldebner m
~ **flattening** Bild[feld]ebnung f
~ **frequency** s. ~ rate
~ **glass[es]** Feldstecher m, Fernglas n, Doppel[hand]fernrohr n
~ **gradient** Feldgradient m
~ **heterogeneity** Feldheterogenität f
~ **homogeneity** Feldhomogenität f
~ **identification** Halbbildkennung f
~ **inhomogeneity** Feldinhomogenität f, Magnetfeldinhomogenität f
~ **interpolation** Halbbildinterpolation f
~ **ion microscope** Feldionenmikroskop n
~ **ion microscopy** Feldionenmikroskopie f
~ **lens** Feldlinse f, Kollektivlinse f
~ **memory** Halbbildspeicher m
~ **of coverage** Bildwinkel m *(Objektiv)*
~ **of view** Blickfeld n; Sichtfeld n
~ **of view of the camera** Kamerablickfeld n, Kamerasichtfeld n, Kameragesichtsfeld n
~ **of vision** Gesichtsfeld n, Sehfeld n
~ **period** Halbbilddauer f, Periodendauer f der Vertikalablenkung (des Halbbildwechsels)
~ **pickup unit** Richtfunkübertragungsanlage f
~ **plate** Feldplatte f *(Fotodiode)*
~ **processing** Halbbildverarbeitung f
~ **production** Außenproduktion f *(Film, Video)*
~ **pulse** Halbbildimpuls m
~ **rate** Halbbild[wechsel]frequenz f, Halbbildrate f, Bildkippfrequenz f, Vertikalfrequenz f *(Video)*
~ **rate conversion** Abtastratenkonversion f, Abtastratenumsetzung f
~ **recorder** Reportagekamera f
~ **recording** Außenaufnahme[n] f[pl], Dreharbeit f vor Ort, Außendreh m, Außendreharbeit f *(Video)*
~ **refresh rate** s. ~ rate
~ **repetition** Halbbildwiederholung f
~ **resolution** Halbbildauflösung f
~ **scan** Halbbildabtastung f
~ **scanning frequency** vertikale Ablenkfrequenz f *(Video)*
~ **size** Feldgröße f
~ **spectrograph** Feldspektrograf m
~ **stop** s. ~ diaphragm
~ **storage** Halbbildspeicherung f
~ **store** Halbbildspeicher m
~ **sync[hronization] pulse** V-Impuls m *(Video)*
~ **synchronization** Halbbildsynchronisation f
~ **television camera** Außenaufnahmekamera f
~ **time** s. ~ period
~ **tripod** Feldstativ n
~ **use** Außeneneinsatz m *(z.B. von Filmaufnahmetechnik)*
~ **vector** Feldvektor m
fifth-order aberration Bildfehler m fünfter Ordnung
figural shape s. figure 1.
figure/to berechnen *(z.B. optische Elemente)*
figure 1. Figur f; Gestalt n; 2. Abbild n, Abbildung f; 3. Ziffer f, Zahl f
~ **eight [shaped pattern]** Acht-Charakteristik f *(Mikrofon)*
~-**ground organization** Figur-Grund-Differenzierung f, Figur-Grund-Gliederung f *(Wahrnehmungspsychologie)*
~-**ground reversal** Figur-Grund-Differenzierung f, Figur-Grund-Gleichung f, Figur-Grund-Verhältnis n
filament image Glühwendelbild n, Wendelbild n
~ **lamp** Glüh[faden]lampe f, Glühbirne f
filamentary silver particle Silberfaden m, fadenförmige Silberstruktur f *(fotografischer Prozess)*
filar eyepiece Fadenkreuzokular n
file/to archivieren
file Datei f

file 136

~ **access** Dateizugriff *m*
~ **coordinates** Dateikoordinaten *fpl*
~ **element** Dateielement *n*
~ **format** Dateiformat *n*
~ **format extension** Dateinamenerweiterung *f*
~ **header** Dateivorspann *m*
~ **interchange format** Dateiaustauschformat *n*
~ **management** Dateiverwaltung *f*
~ **name** Dateiname *m*
~ **name extension** Dateinamenerweiterung *f*
~ **security** Dateisicherheit *f*
~ **server** Dateiserver *m*
~ **size** Dateigröße *f*
~ **storage** Dateispeicherung *f*
~ **structure** Dateistruktur *f*
~ **transfer protocol** Dateiübertragungsprotokoll *n* *(Clientsoftware)*
~ **type** Dateityp *m*
filing Archivierung *f*
~ **cabinet** Archivschrank *m*
~ **system** Archivierungssystem *n*
fill 1. Füllsignal *n*; 2. *s.* ~ light
~ **area** Füllfläche *f*, Füllgebiet *n* *(Computergrafik, Druck)*
~ **area bundle table** Füllgebietsbündeltabelle *f*
~ **area color index** Füllgebietsfarbindex *m*
~ **area set** Füllgebietsmenge *f*
~ **color** Füllfarbe *f*
~ **factor** Flächenfüllfaktor *m*, [optischer] Füllfaktor *m*
~-**flash photography** Aufhellblitzen *n*
~-**in** Aufhellen *n*
~-**in flash** Aufhellblitz *m*
~-**in light** *s.* fill light
~-**in lighting** Aufhellung *f*
~ **light** Aufhelllicht *n*, Fülllicht *n*
~ **primitive** Fülldarstellungselement *n*
~ **tool** Füllwerkzeug *n*, Farbrolle *f* *(Computergrafik)*
~-**up** 1. Zusetzen *n* der Druckform, Zusetzen *n* von Rastertonwerten *(Druckschwierigkeit)*; 2. Beifilm *m*
~-**up film** Beifilm *m*
fillet Übergangselement *n* *(Computergrafik)*
~ **surface** Ausrundungsfläche *f*
filling factor *s.* fill factor
film/to 1. filmen; 2. verfilmen
film off/to abfilmen
~ 1. Film *m (s.a. unter motion picture, cinema, movie)*; 2. Folie *f*
~ **advance** Film[weiter]transport *m*, Filmvorschub *m*
~ **advance knob** Aufzugsknopf *m*
~ **advance lever** Filmtransporthebel *m*, Aufzugshebel *m*, Transporthebel *m*
~ **advance mechanism** Filmtransporteinrichtung *f*, Filmtransportmechanismus *m*

~ **advance mode** Filmtransportart *f*
~ **advance mode dial** Filmtransportwähler *m*
~ **advance speed** Filmtransportgeschwindigkeit *f*
~ **analysis** Filmauswertung *f* *(Luftbildfotografie)*
~-**and-filter combination** Film-Filter-Kombination *f*
~ **animation** Filmanimation *f*
~ **aperture** Formatrahmen *m*
~ **architecture** Filmarchitektur *f*
~ **archive** Filmarchiv *n*; Filmbibliothek *f*, Kinemathek *f*
~ **archiving** Filmarchivierung *f*
~ **archivist** Filmarchivar *m*
~ **art** Filmkunst *f*
~ **aspect ratio** Filmbildseitenverhältnis *n*
~ **astrophotography** Film-Astrofotografie *f*
~ **badge** *s.* dosimeter
~ **base** Film[schicht]träger *m*, Filmunterlage *f*, Schichtträger *m*
~ **base material** Filmträgermaterial *n*
~-**based camera** fotografische Kamera *f*
~ **bin** Schleifenmagazin *n*, Schleifenschrank *m (Filmkopierung)*
~ **blackening** Filmschwärzung *f*
~ **blank** Imbitions-Kopierfilm *m*
~ **border** Filmrand *m*
~ **box** Filmschachtel *f*
~ **cabinet** Filmschrank *m*
~ **camera move** Kamerabewegung *f*
~ **can[ister]** Filmdose *f*, Filmbüchse *f*
~ **capture process** Filmaufnahmeverfahren *n*, Filmaufzeichnungsverfahren *n*
~ **care** Filmpflege *f*
~ **cartridge** Filmpatrone *f*
~ **cassette** Filmkassette *f*
~ **casting line** Filmgießanlage *f*
~ **cement** Filmkleber *m*, Filmkitt *m*
~ **chamber** Filmkammer *f*
~ **change[over]** Filmwechsel *m*
~ **characteristic** Filmcharakteristik *f*
~ **characteristic curve** Filmkennlinie *f*, Filmschwärzungskurve *f*
~ **choice** Film[aus]wahl *f*
~ **cleaner** Filmreiniger *m*
~ **clip** 1. Filmclip *m*, Filmausschnitt *m*; Klammerteil *n(m)*; 2. Film[aufhänge]klammer *f*
~ **coating** Filmschicht *f*, Beguss *m*
~ **coating machine** Filmgießmaschine *f*
~ **code** Filmcode *m*
~ **coding** Filmcodierung *f*
~ **coefficient of friction** Filmreibungskoeffizient *m*
~ **coil** Filmwindung *f*
~ **collection** Filmsammlung *f*
~ **color** Filmfarbe *f*
~ **color timer** Filmlichtbestimmer *m*, Farblichtbestimmer *m*, Farbtechniker *m*
~ **color timing** Filmlichtbestimmung *f*, Farb[licht]bestimmung *f*, Lichtbestimmung *f*, Farbkorrektur *f*

~ **confirmation window** Filmtypenfenster n *(Spiegelreflexkamera)*
~ **consumption** Filmverbrauch m
~ **container** Filmbehälter m
~ **contrast** Filmkontrast m
~ **copy** Filmkopie f
~ **core** Filmkern m
~ **counter** Filmzählwerk n, Bildzähler m
~ **crew** Filteam n, Filmcrew f, Drehteam n, Drehstab m
~ **curvature** Filmkrümmung f
~ **cut list** Filmschnittliste f
~ **cutting** Filmschnitt m
~ **cutting room** Filmschneideraum m, Schneideraum m
~ **dailies** Filmmuster npl, Tagesmuster npl, Muster npl *(Filmproduktion)*
~ **damage** Filmbeschädigung f, Filmschaden m
~ **darkening** Filmschwärzung f
~ **density** Filmschwärzung f
~ **developer** Filmentwickler m
~ **developing tank** Filmentwicklungsdose f, Entwicklungsdose f
~ **development** Filmentwicklung f
~ **digitization** Filmdigitalisierung f, Filmabtastung f
~ **digitizer** [digitaler] Filmabtaster m
~ **directing (direction)** Filmregie f
~ **director** Filmregisseur m, Regisseur m
~ **dispenser** Filmspender m
~ **documentation** Filmdokumentation f
~ **door lock** Filmkammerverriegelung f
~ **dosimeter** Filmdosimeter n, Filmplakette f, Strahlenschutzplakette f
~ **dosimetry** Filmdosimetrie f
~ **drive** Filmantrieb m
~ **drum** Filmtrommel f
~ **drying** Filmtrocknung f
~ **-drying cabinet** Filmtrockenschrank m
~ **dubbing** Filmvertonung f
~ **dubbing suite** Filmtonstudio n
~ **dye** Filmfarbstoff m
~ **edge** Filmrand m, Filmkante f
~ **edgeprint** Randkennzeichnung f *(an Filmmaterial)*
~ **editing** Filmbearbeitung f; Filmschnitt m
~ **editing machine** Filmschneidemaschine f
~ **editing room** Filmschneideraum m, Schneideraum m
~ **editor** Cutter m, Filmcutter m, Schnittmeister m
~ **ejection** Filmauswurf m
~ **emulsion** Filmemulsion f
~ **emulsion layer** Filmemulsionsschicht f
~ **end** Filmende n
~ **exposure** Filmbelichtung f
~ **exposure system** Filmbelichtungssystem n
~ **exposure time** Filmbelichtungszeit f
~ **extractor** Filmherauszieher m, Filmrückholer m
~ **feed** Filmeinzug m

~ **fixer** Filmfixierbad n
~ **fixing** Filmfixierung f
~ **fixing bath** Filmfixierbad n
~ **fogging** Schleierbildung f
~ **footage** Filmmaterial n; Filmmeter mpl
~ **format** Filmformat n
~ **format width** Filmbreite f
~ **fracture** Filmriss m
~ **frame** Filmbild n, Filmfeld n, Feld n, Filmkader m, Bildfeld n, Bildkader m, Kader m
~ **frame numeration** Filmbildnumerierung f
~ **frame rate** Filmbildfrequenz f
~ **friction** Filmreibung f
~ **gate** Filmfenster n, Bildfenster n, Feldblende f, Bildbühne f
~ **gate mask** Bildfenstermaske f
~ **gauge** 1. Filmformat n; 2. Filmdicke f
~ **grain** Filmkorn n
~ **grain noise** Film[korn]rauschen n
~ **graininess** Filmkörnigkeit f
~ **granularity** Filmkörnung f
~ **handling** 1. Filmbehandlung f, Filmhandhabung f; 2. Filmbearbeitung f
~ **handling device** Filmgerät n
~ **head** Filmkopf m
~ **holder** Filmhalter m; Filmrahmen m; Negativbühne f, Negativhalter m, Negativträger m *(Vergrößerungsgerät)*
~ **identification** Filmidentifizierung f
~ **identification camera** Aufbelichtungskamera f *(Radiografie)*
~ **illumination** Filmausleuchtung f
~ **image plane** Filmbildebene f
~ **image sequence** Filmbildsequenz f
~ **industry** Filmindustrie f, Kinofilmindustrie f, Filmbranche f, Filmwirtschaft f
~ **inspection apparatus** Filmkontrollgerät n
~ **lab[oratory]** Filmkopierwerk n, Kopierwerk n, Kopieranstalt f, Filmbearbeitungsbetrieb m, Filmlabor m
~ **laminate** Filmkaschierung f, Glanzfolienkaschierung f *(Erzeugnis)*
~ **laminating** Folienkaschierung f; Glanzfolienkaschierung f
~ **layer** Filmschicht f
~ **leader** Filmanfang m, Filmlasche f, Filmzunge f
~ **leader retriever** Filmherauszieher m, Filmrückholer m
~ **length** Filmlänge f
~ **library** Filmarchiv n; Filmbibliothek f, Kinemathek f
~ **lighting** Filmbeleuchtung f, Filmlicht n
~ **load** Filmvorrat m *(z.B. einer Kamera)*
~ **loader** Filmladegerät n, Filmlader m
~ **loading [procedure]** Filmladen n, Filmeinlegen n; Filmeinspulen n
~ **location** Drehort m, Aufnahmeort m, Spielstätte f
~ **loop** Filmschleife f
~ **luminaire** Filmaufnahmeleuchte f

film 138

- ~ **magazine** Filmmagazin *n*, Magazin *n*
- ~ **mammogram** Film-Mammogramm *n*
- ~ **manufacture** Filmherstellung *f*, Rohfilmherstellung *f*
- ~ **manufacturer** Filmhersteller *m*
- ~ **marking pen** Folienschreiber *m*
- ~ **material** Filmmaterial *n*
- ~ **motion (movement)** Filmbewegung *f*
- ~ **movement mechanism** *s.* ~ advance mechanism
- ~ **moving mechanism** Filmlaufwerk *n*
- ~ **negative** Filmnegativ *n*, Negativfilm *m*
- ~ **negative cut list** Negativschnittliste *f*
- ~ **noise** Film[korn]rauschen *n*
- ~ **notch** Kerbmarkierung *f (z.B. von Blattfilm)*
- ~ **pack** Filmpack *m*, Packfilm *m*
- ~ **package** Filmpackung *f*
- ~ **packet** Filmpack *m*
- ~ **passage** Filmdurchlauf *m*
- ~ **patch** perforiertes Filmklebeband *n*
- ~ **path** Filmkanal *m*, Filmweg *m (Kamera, Projektor)*
- ~ **perforation** Filmperforation *f*
- ~ **pickup** Filmscanner *m*, Filmabtaster *m*, FAT
- ~ **plane** Filmebene *f*; Bildebene *f*
- ~ **plane indicator** Bildebenenmarkierung *f*
- ~ **plate** Filmplatte *f*, Fotoplatte *f*, fotografische Platte *f*
- ~ **playback** Filmwiedergabe *f*
- ~ **postproduction** Film[nach]bearbeitung *f*
- ~ **practice** Filmpraxis *f*
- ~ **presentation** Filmvorführung *f*
- ~ **preservation** Filmkonservierung *f*
- ~ **preservationist** Filmrestaurator *m*
- ~ **pressure plate** Filmandruckplatte *f*, Platine *f*
- ~ **print** Filmkopie *f*
- ~ **printer** 1. Filmkopiermaschine *f*; 2. Filmdrucker *m*
- ~ **printing** Filmdruck *m*; Foliendruck *m*
- ~ **processing** Filmverarbeitung *f*, Filmentwicklung *f*
- ~ **processing chemical** Fotochemikalie *f*
- ~ **processing chemistry** Filmverarbeitungschemie *f*
- ~ **processing envelope** Fotoauftragstasche *f*, Auftragstasche *f*
- ~ **processing machine**, ~ **processor** Filmentwicklungsmaschine *f*, Filmprozessor *m*
- ~ **producer** Filmproduzent *m*
- ~ **product** Filmprodukt *n*
- ~ **production** Filmproduktion *f*, Filmherstellung *f*
- ~ **projection** Filmprojektion *f*
- ~ **projector** Filmprojektor *m*, Laufbildprojektor *m*, Filmvorführgerät *n*; Laufbildwerfer *m*
- ~ **radiograph** Röntgenfilmbild *n*
- ~ **reader** Filmlesekopf *m*
- ~ **record** Filmaufnahme *f*, Filmaufzeichnung *f*
- ~ **recorder** Filmaufzeichnungsanlage *f*, Filmbelichter *m*, Belichter *m*, Filmrecorder *m*
- ~ **recording** Filmaufzeichnung *f*, FAZ
- ~ **recording technique** Filmaufnahmetechnik *f*
- ~ **reel** Filmrolle *f*, Filmspule *f*
- ~ **resolution** Filmauflösung *f*
- ~ **restoration** Filmrestaurierung *f*
- ~ **rewind** Filmrückspulung *f*, Filmrücktransport *m*, Filmrückwicklung *f*
- ~ **rewind crank** Filmrückspulkurbel *f*, Rückspulkurbel *f*
- ~ **running speed** Film[lauf]geschwindigkeit *f*
- ~ **sample** Filmprobe *f*
- ~ **scanner** Filmscanner *m*, Filmabtaster *m*, FAT
- ~ **scanning** Filmabtastung *f*
- ~ **scene** Filmszene *f*
- ~ **scratch** Filmkratzer *m*, Filmschramme *f*
- ~ **screen** Filmleinwand *f*
- ~ **-screen combination** Film-Folien-Kombination *f (Radiografie)*
- ~ **-screen system** Film-Folien-System *n*
- ~ **screening** Filmvorführung *f*
- ~ **selection** Film[aus]wahl *f*
- ~ **sensitivity** Filmempfindlichkeit *f*
- ~ **sequence** Filmsequenz *f*
- ~ **sharpness** Filmschärfe *f*
- ~ **sheet** Filmblatt *n*
- ~ **shrinkage** Filmschrumpfung *f*
- ~ **size** Filmformat *n*
- ~ **slide** Dia[positiv] *n*
- ~ **sound** Film[begleit]ton *m*
- ~ **sound track** Filmtonspur *f*, Soundtrack *m*
- ~ **speed** Filmempfindlichkeit *f*
- ~ **speed dial** ISO-Einstellung *f*
- ~ **speed number (value)** Empfindlichkeitswert *m*
- ~ **speed range** Filmempfindlichkeitsbereich *m*
- ~ **speed setting** Filmempfindlichkeitseinstellung *f*, Empfindlichkeitseinstellung *f*
- ~ **speed standard** Filmempfindlichkeitsnorm *f*
- ~ **speed table** Filmempfindlichkeitstabelle *f*
- ~ **splice** Filmklebestelle *f*
- ~ **splicer** Filmklebepresse *f*, Filmklebeapparat *m*, Klebelade *f*, Klebelehre *f*
- ~ **spool** Filmspule *f*, Filmrolle *f*
- ~ **squeegee** Filmabstreifer *m*, Filmabstreifzange *f*
- ~ **standard** Filmstandarte *f*, Rückstandarte *f*, Bildrückteil *n*, Kamerarückteil *m(n)*, Filmrückwand *f (Fachkamera)*
- ~ **still** Filmstandbild *n*, Szenenfoto *n*, Standfoto *n*
- ~ **stock** Film[aufnahme]material *n*, Aufnahmefilmmaterial *n*, Rohfilm *m*; Filmvorrat *m*

~ **storage** Filmlagerung f, Filmspeicherung f
~ **store** Filmlager n
~ **storeroom** Filmlagerraum m
~ **strip** Filmband n
~ **structure** Filmaufbau m, Filmstruktur f
~ **support** Film[schicht]träger m, Schichtträger m, Filmunterlage f
~ **surface** Film[ober]fläche f
~ **technical** kinotechnisch
~ **technology** Filmtechnik f; Filmtechnologie f
~ **tension** Filmzug m
~ **test strip** Testfilmstreifen m
~ **threading** Filmeinfädelung f
~**-to-tape transfer** Film-zu-Band-Konversion f (s.a. film transfer)
~**-to-video transfer** s. film transfer
~ **tongue** Filmzunge f, Filmlasche f
~ **transfer** Filmtransfer m, Filmabtastung f; Film-zu-Band-Konversion f
~ **transfer system** Filmscanner m, Filmabtaster m, FAT
~ **transport** Film[weiter]transport m, Filmvorschub m
~ **transport system** Filmtransportsystem n
~ **travel** Filmweg m, Filmkanal m (Kamera, Projektor)
~ **treatment** Filmbehandlung f
~ **type** Filmart f; Filmtyp m; Filmsorte f
~ **velocity** Film[lauf]geschwindigkeit f
~ **viewer** 1. Filmzuschauer m, Filmbetrachter m; 2. Filmbetrachtungsgerät n
~ **viewing** Filmbetrachtung f
~ **viewing box** Filmbetrachtungsgerät n, Betrachtungskasten m
~ **weave** seitlicher Bildstandsfehler m
~ **weld** Heißklebestelle f
~ **width** Filmbreite f; Filmformat n
~ **work print** Arbeitskopie f, Schnittkopie f, Klatschkopie f
filmcard Mikrofiche n(m), Fiche n(m); Mikroplanfilm m
filmdom Filmindustrie f, Kinofilmindustrie f, Filmbranche f, Filmwirtschaft f
filmer Filmer m
filmgoer Kinobesucher m
filmic filmisch
filming of documents Schriftgutverfilmung f
filmization Verfilmung f
filmless filmlos
~ **imaging** filmlose Bildgebung f
~ **photography** filmlose Fotografie f
~ **platemaking** filmlose Druckplattenherstellung f
~ **radiology** filmlose Radiologie f
filmmaker Filmemacher m, Filmschaffender m
filmmaking Filmemachen n
~ **apparatus** Kinotechnik f
filmography Filmografie f

filmsetting Fotosatz m, Filmsatz m, Lichtsatz m
filmstill Filmstill n, Filmstillstand m
filmstrip Filmstreifen m, Bildband n; Diastreifen m
~ **projector** Filmstreifenprojektor m; Diastreifenprojektor m
filmwright Filmautor m, Drehbuchautor m
filter/to filtern
filter Filter n(m)
~ **absorption** Filterabsorption f
~ **adapter ring** Filteradapterring m
~ **architecture** Filterarchitektur f
~ **arrangement** Filteranordnung f
~ **bandwidth** Filterbandbreite f
~ **bank** Filterbank f
~ **bank analysis** Filterbankanalyse f
~ **bank channel** Filterbankkanal m
~ **behavior** Filterverhalten n
~ **change[over]** Filterwechsel m
~ **characteristic** Filtercharakteristik f
~ **choice** Filterwahl f
~ **circuit** Filterschaltung f
~ **clamp** Filterklemme f (s.a. ~ holder)
~ **coating** Filterschicht f
~ **coefficient** Filterkoeffizient m, Maskenkoeffizient m
~ **color** Filterfarbe f
~ **combination** Filterkombination f
~ **concept** Filterkonzept n
~ **cube** Filterwürfel m
~ **design** Filterdesign n, Filterentwurf m
~ **diameter** Filterdurchmesser m
~ **disk** Filterscheibe f
~ **drawer** Filterschublade f
~ **dye** Filterfarbstoff m
~ **error** Filterfehler m
~ **factor** Filterfaktor m
~ **foil** Filterfolie f
~ **frequency** Filterfrequenz f
~ **function** Filterfunktion f, Filterkurve f
~ **geometry** Filtergeometrie f
~ **glass** Filterglas n
~ **grating** Filtergitter n
~ **holder** Filterhalter m, Filterhalterung f; Filteradapter m
~ **impulse response** Filterimpulsantwort f
~ **kernel** s. filtering mask
~ **layer** Filterschicht f
~ **length** Filterlänge f
~ **line** Filterreihe f
~ **mask** s. filtering mask
~ **material** Filtermaterial n
~ **matrix** Filtermatrix f
~ **mount** Filterfassung f
~ **operation** Filtervorgang m, Filterprozess m
~ **operator** Filteroperator m
~ **order** Filterordnungsgrad m
~ **out/to** [her]ausfiltern
~ **output** Filterausgang m
~ **output signal** Filterausgangssignal n
~ **pack** Filterpaket n
~ **pair** Filterpaar n

filter 140

~ **parameter** Filterparameter *m*
~ **performance** Filterleistung *f*
~ **plane** Filterebene *f*
~ **pocket** Filteretui *n*
~ **polynomial** Filterpolynom *n*
~ **profile** Filterprofil *n*
~ **radius** Filterradius *m*
~ **raster** Filterraster *m(n)*
~ **recommendation** Filterempfehlung *f*
~ **response** Filterantwort *f*
~ **revolver** Filterrevolver *m*
~ **scale** Filterskale *f*
~ **selection** Filterwahl *f*
~ **set** Filtersatz *m*
~ **setting** Filtereinstellung *f*
~ **shape** Filterform *f*
~ **size** Filtergröße *f*
~ **slider** Filterschublade *f*
~ **slot** Filtereinschub *m*
~ **software** Filtersoftware *f*
~ **structure** Filterstruktur *f*
~ **system** Filtersystem *n*
~ **theory** Filtertheorie *f*
~ **thread** Filtergewinde *n*
~ **transfer function** Filterübertragungsfunktion *f*
~ **transmission** Filtertransmission *f*
~ **transmittance** Filter-Transmissionsgrad *m*
~ **turret** Filterrevolver *m*
~ **type** Filtertyp *m*
~ **-type equalizer** Entzerrerfilter *n*
~ **value** Filterwert *m*
~ **wheel** Filterrad *n*
~ **width** Filterausdehnung *f*
~ **window** Filterfenster *n*, Operatorfenster *n*

filtered back projection [reconstruction method] gefilterte Rückprojektion *f* *(Emissionstomografie)*
~ **block compression** gefilterte Blockcodierung *f*
~ **image** gefiltertes Bild *n*, Filterbild *n*
~ **Rayleigh scattering** gefilterte Rayleigh-Streuung *f*
~ **signal** gefiltertes Signal *n*
filtering Filterung *f*
~ **action** s. ~ effect
~ **algorithm** Filteralgorithmus *m*
~ **artifact** Filterungsartefakt *n*
~ **effect** Filtereffekt *m*, Filterwirkung *f*
~ **mask** Filtermaske *f*, Faltungsmaske *f*, Faltungskern *m*, Maskenoperator *m*, Filterkern *m*, Operatorkern *m* *(Grauwertbildverarbeitung)*
~ **operation** Filteroperation *f*
~ **power** Filterleistung *f*
~ **process (technique)** Filterverfahren *n*; Filterprozess *m*; Filtertechnik *f*
~ **result** Filterergebnis *n*
~ **time** Filterzeit *f*
~ **tool** Filterwerkzeug *n*
filtration Filterung *f*
final amplifier Endverstärker *m*

~ **cut** Endschnitt *m*, Feinschnitt *m* *(Film, Video)*
~ **format** Endformat *n* *(z.B. einer Vergrößerung)*
~ **image** Fertigbild *n*, Endbild *n*, Ergebnisbild *n*, Bildergebnis *n*, Bildresultat *n*, Resultatbild *n*, endgültiges Bild *n*
~ **image fluorescent screen** Endbild[leucht]schirm *m* *(Elektronenmikroskop)*
~ **image magnification** Endvergrößerung *f*
~ **layer** Schlussschicht *f*
~ **mixdown (mixing)** End[ab]mischung *f*, Tonendmischung *f*, Tonendfertigung *f* *(Filmton)*
~ **node** Endknoten *m* *(Graphendarstellung)*
~ **picture** s. ~ image
~ **print** Endkopie *f*
~ **printed product** Druckerzeugnis *n*, Druckprodukt *n*
~ **proof** echter Andruck *m*
~ **rinse** fließende Schlusswässerung *f*
~ **size** Endformat *n*
~ **wash[ing]** Schlusswässerung *f*, Endwässerung *f*
finality development Auswicklung *f*
finals Zusätze *mpl* *(Emulsionsherstellung)*
finder Sucher *m* *(s.a. unter viewfinder)*
~ **eyepiece** Sucherokular *n*
~ **lens** Sucherlinse *f*
~ **screen** Einstell[matt]scheibe *f*, Sucherscheibe *f*, Mattscheibe *f* *(Kamera)*
~ **system** Suchersystem *n*
fine-art paper Kunstdruckpapier *n*
~ **-art photographer** Kunstfotograf *m*
~ **-art photography** Kunstfotografie *f*
~ **-art print** Edeldruck *m*
~ **beam** Feinstrahl *m* *(bes. von Elektronen)*
~ **cut** Feinschnitt *m* *(Film, Video)*
~ **detail** feinstrukturiertes Detail *n*, kleines Objektdetail *n*
~ **filter** Feinfilter *n*
~ **-focus control (knob)** Feintrieb *m*, Feinstellschraube *f*
~ **focusing** Feinfokussierung *f*
~ **-focusing device (mechanism)** Feinfokussierung *f*
~ **grain** Feinkorn *n*
~ **-grain color film** Feinkornfarbfilm *m*
~ **-grain copy** Feinkornkopie *f*
~ **-grain developer** Feinkornentwickler *m*
~ **-grain development** Feinkornentwicklung *f*
~ **-grain emulsion** Feinkornemulsion *f*
~ **-grain print** Feinkornkopie *f*
~ **-grain print film** Feinkorn-Positivfilm *m*
~ **-grained film** Feinkornfilm *m*, feinkörniger Film *m*
~ **-grained image** feinkörniges Bild *n*
~ **image detail** feinstrukturiertes Bilddetail *n*
~ **line** Feinstrich *m*

fish

~-**line screen printing** Feinliniensiebdruck m
~ **paper** Fein[druck]papier n, holzfreies Papier n
~ **print** 1. Kleingedruckte n; 2. s. fine-art print
~ **resolution** Feinauflösung f, feine Auflösung f
~ **scanning** feine Abtastung f
~ **screen** Feinraster m(n), feiner Raster m
~ **structure** Feinstruktur f
~-**tune/to** feinabstimmen
fineness Feinheit f
~ **of detail** Detailschärfe f, Bilddefinition f
~ **of grain** Feinkörnigkeit f
finesse Finesse f *(Interferenzoptik)*
finest-grain film feinstkörniger Film m
finger grip Griffmulde f *(z.B. des Fokussierringes)*
fingerprint Fingerabdruck m, Dactylogramm n
~ **analysis** Fingerabdruckanalyse f
~ **camera** Fingerabdruckkamera f
~ **data** Fingerabdruckdaten pl
~ **image** Fingerabdruckbild n
~ **mark** Fingerabdruck m *(z.B. als Störung auf Filmmaterial)*
~ **matching** Fingerabdruckvergleich m
~ **reader** Fingerabdrucklesegerät n, Fingerabdruckscanner m
~ **recognition** Fingerabdruckerkennung f; Fingerabdruckanalyse f
~ **sensor** Fingerabdrucksensor m
~ **template** Fingerabdruckschablone f
finish 1. Ausrüstung f, Papierausrüstung f, Finish n; 2. Druckweiterverarbeitung f
finished art Reprovorlage f
~ **drawing** Reinzeichnung f
~ **picture** s. final image
~ **size** Endformat n, beschnittenes Format n *(z.B. eines Druckprodukts)*
finishing Druckweiterverarbeitung f
finite approximation finite Approximation f
~ **element analysis (method)** Finite-Elemente-Methode f, FEM *(mathematisches Analysenverfahren)*
~-**element modeling** Modellierung f finiter Elemente
~ **graph** finiter Graph m
~ **impulse response** begrenzte (endliche) Impulsantwort f
~ **impulse response filter** endliches Impulsantwortfilter n, nichtrekursives Filter n, FIR-Filter n
~ **ray** endlicher Strahl m *(Optik)*
~ **slit width** endliche Spaltbreite f
~-**state automaton (machine)** endlicher (finiter) Automat m
~ **topology** finite Topologie f
FIR filter s. finite-impulse-response filter
fire shutter Feuerschutzklappe f *(Projektor, Scheinwerfer)*
firewall Internet-Sicherheitsschleuse f *(Computersoftware)*

firewire interface Firewire-Schnittstelle f, Firewire-Buchse f *(Bilddatenübertragung)*
first answer print Nullkopie f, Erstkopie f *(Kinematografie)*
~ **assistant director** Erster Aufnahmeleiter m, Regieassistent m
~ **assistant editor** Schnittassistent m
~ **camera assistant** [Erster] Kameraassistent m
~ **cameraman** Erster Kameramann m, Kameraschwenker m, Schwenker m
~ **cut** Schnittfassung f des Regisseurs, Regisseur-Fassung f *(Filmschnitt; s.a.* rough cut*)*
~ **developer** Erstentwickler m *(fotografische Umkehrverarbeitung)*
~ **development** Erstentwicklung f
~ **exposure** Erstbelichtung f
~ **focal point** Objektbrennpunkt m, dingseitiger (objektseitiger) Brennpunkt m
~-**generation tape** Masterband n
~ **image** primäres Bild n *(Optik)*
~ **law of photochemistry** Grothus-Drapersches Gesetz n *(Fotochemie)*
~-**order Bessel function** Bessel-Funktion f erster Ordnung
~-**order entropy** Quellenentropie f, Signalentropie f *(Informationstheorie)*
~-**order interpolation** Interpolation f erster Ordnung *(Grauwertbildverarbeitung)*
~ **order of diffraction** erste Beugungsordnung f
~-**order optics** Optik f erster Ordnung, paraxiale (Gaußsche) Optik, Optik f des Paraxialgebietes
~-**order polynomial** Polynom n erster Ordnung
~-**order spectrum** Spektrum n erster Ordnung
~-**order statistics** Statistik f erster Ordnung, univariate Statistik f
~ **print** s. ~ trial print
~ **proof** Rohabzug m, Hauskorrektur f *(Druckvorstufe)*
~ **ripening** physikalische Reifung f, Ostwald-Reifung f *(Emulsionsherstellung)*
~ **run** Erstaufführung f
~-**run house (theater)** Premierenkino n, Erstaufführungskino n, Erstaufführungstheater n
~ **stage of latent-image formation** fotografischer Primärprozess m
~-**surface[d] mirror** Oberflächenspiegel m, oberflächenversilberter Spiegel m
~ **trial print** Nullkopie f, Erstkopie f *(Kinematografie)*
fish eye Lichtpunkt m, Butzen m, Pop[p]el m *(Druckbildfehler)*
~ **eye lens** Fischauge[nobjektiv] n, Fisheye[objektiv] n

fishpole 142

fishpole Angel *f*, Mikrofonangel *f*, Tonangel *f*, Perche *f*
fistulography Fistulografie *f*
fit/to anpassen
fit Anpassung *f*
five-axis spatial filter fünfachsiges Raumfilter *n*
~-sided prism Fünfseit[en]prisma *n*
fix/to fixieren *(z.B. Fotomaterial)*
fix out/to ausfixieren
fixable fixierbar
fixate/to fixieren *(ein Sehobjekt)*
fixation 1. Fixierung *f*, Fixage *f* *(Fotoverarbeitung)*; 2. Fixation *f (Sehen)*
~ distance Fixationsentfernung *f*
~ dwell time Fixationszeit *f*
~ point Fixierpunkt *m*, Fixationspunkt *m*
fixative Fixativ *n (Retuschierhilfsmittel)*
fixed bit rate konstante Bitrate *f*
~ diaphragm Festblende *f*
~ disk Festplatte *f*
~ eye raumfest ruhendes Auge *n*
~ focal distance (length) Festbrennweite *f*
~-focal-length lens *s.* fixed-focus lens
~-focus festbrennweitig
~ focus arrangement Fixfokuseinstellung *f*, Naheinstellung *f* auf Unendlich
~-focus camera Fixfokuskamera *f*
~-focus lens Fix[fokus]objektiv *n*, Fest[brennweiten]objektiv *n*, festbrennweitiges Objektiv *n*
~-focus snapshot camera Fixfokus-Schnappschusskamera *f*
~-focus[ed] color camera Fixfokus-Farbkamera *f*
~-grain film gradationsfester Film *m*
~ hard disk Festplatte *f*, Computerfestplatte *f*
~-length code Code *m* mit fester Symbollänge
~-lens camera starre Kamera *f*
~-lens-thirty-five-mm camera Fixfokus-Kleinbildkamera *f*
~-mirror reflex housing Lichtschacht *m* *(zweiäugige Spiegelreflexkamera)*
~-pattern noise eingefrorenes Rauschen *n*
~-point arithmetic Festpunktarithmetik *f*
~-point representation Festkommabild *n*
~-point sequence Root-Signal *n*
~-resolution projector Projektor *m* fester Auflösung
~-target suppression Festzielunterdrückung *f (Radar)*
fixer Fixierer *m*, Fixiermittel *n*
~ bath Fixierbad *n*
~ tray Fixierschale *f*
fixing Fixierung *f*, Fixage *f* *(Fotoverarbeitung)*
~ accelerator Fixierbeschleuniger *m*
~ agent Fixiermittel *n*, Fixierer *m*
~ and toning bath Tonfixierbad *n*
~ bath Fixierbad *n*
~ bath test Fixierbadkontrolle *f*
~ developer Fixierentwickler *m*

~ development Fixierentwicklung *f*
~ performance Fixierleistung *f*
~ process Fixiervorgang *m*, Fixierprozess *m*
~ rate Fixiergeschwindigkeit *f*
~ salt Fixiersalz *n*
~ solution Fixierlösung *f*
~ speed Fixiergeschwindigkeit *f*
~ time Fixierzeit *f*, Fixierdauer *f*
~ tray Fixierschale *f*
Fizeau interferometer Fizeau-Interferometer *n*
flag 1. Abdeckfahne *f*, Lichtblende *f*; Projektionsmaske *f*, Projektionsblende *f*; 2. Sonderzeichen *n*
flange Filmteller *m*
~ focal distance Anlagemaß *n*, Auflagemaß *n (Objektiv)*
flap Lampenklappe *f*, Lichtklappe *f*, Tor *n*
flare 1. Streustrahlung *f*; Streulicht *n*; 2. Lichtreflex *m*; Flimmern *n*
~ correction Streulichtkompensation *f* *(elektronische Kamera)*
~ factor Blendungszahl *f*, Streulichtfaktor *m*
~ light Streulicht *n*
~ spot Reflexionsfleck *m*
flash/to 1. blitzen; aufblitzen; 2. nachbelichten *(bes. Kinefilm)*; 3. *s.* preflash/to
flash Blitz *m*, Belichtungsblitz *m*
~ accessories Blitzzubehör *n*
~ adapter (adaptor) Blitzadapter *m*
~ bracket Blitzschiene *f*
~ bracketing Blitzbelichtungsreihe *f*
~ camera Blitzlichtkamera *f*
~ capacitor Blitzkondensator *m*
~ connector 1. Blitzlicht-Steckverbindung *f*; 2. *s.* ~ cord
~ contact Blitzkontakt *m*
~ control Blitz[licht]steuerung *f*
~ converter Parallelumsetzer *m*, Parallelwandler *m (Videoprozessor)*
~ cord Blitz[anschluss]kabel *n*, Synchronkabel *n*
~ cube Blitzwürfel *m*
~ curve Blitzkurve *f*
~ discharge Blitzentladung *f*
~ divider Blitzteiler *m*
~ duration Blitz[leucht]dauer *f*, Blitz[leucht]zeit *f*, Leuchtdauer *f*
~ effectiveness Blitz[licht]leistung *f*
~ equipment Blitzausrüstung *f*
~ exposure Blitzbelichtung *f*
~ exposure bracketing Blitzbelichtungsreihe *f*
~-exposure control Blitz[belichtungs]steuerung *f*
~ exposure measurement Blitzbelichtungsmessung *f*
~ extension lead Blitzverlängerungskabel *n*
~ factor *s.* ~ guide number
~ fixture Blitzanschluss *m*

~ **guide number** Blitzleitzahl f, Leitzahl f
~ **head** Blitzkopf m, Blitzreflektor m
~ **high-speed photography** Hochgeschwindigkeits-Blitzfotografie f
~ **ignition** Blitzzündung f
~ **illumination** Blitzbeleuchtung f, Blitzausleuchtung f
~ **illumination source** Blitzlichtquelle f
~ **intensity** Blitzintensität f
~ **lamp array** Blitzlampensystem n
~ **lighting** Blitzbeleuchtung f, Blitzausleuchtung f
~ **luminous intensity** Blitzlichtintensität f
~ **manufacturer** Blitzgerätehersteller m
~ **meter** Blitzbelichtungsmesser m
~ **mode** Blitzbetriebsart f, Blitz[synchronisations]modus m
~ **of light** Lichtblitz m
~ **on/off facility** Blitzabschaltung f
~ **operation** Blitzbetrieb m
~ **output [level]** Blitz[licht]leistung f
~ **pan** Reißschwenk m, schneller Schwenk m, Wischer m (Kamerabewegung)
~ **photography** Blitz[licht]fotografie f
~ **picture** s. ~ shot
~ **powder** Blitz[licht]pulver n
~ **range** Blitz[licht]reichweite f
~ **readylight** Blitzbereitschaftslampe f
~ **readylight indication** Blitzbereitschaftsanzeige f, Blitzkontrollanzeige f
~ **reflector** Blitzreflektor m
~ **sensor** Blitzsensor m
~ **sequencer** Multiblitzauslöser m
~ **shoe** Blitzschuh m
~ **shot** Blitz[licht]aufnahme f, Blitzlichtfoto n
~ **sync mode** Blitzbetriebsart f, Blitz[synchronisations]modus m
~ **sync socket** Blitzanschluss m
~ **synchronization** Blitzsynchronisation f
~ **synchronization cable** Blitz[anschluss]kabel n, Synchrokabel n
~ **time** Blitz[leucht]zeit f, Blitz[leucht]dauer f, Leuchtdauer f
~ **trigger** Blitzauslöser m
~ **triggering** Blitzauslösung f
~-**type stroboscope** Lichtblitzstroboskop n
~ **umbrella** Blitzschirm m, Reflexschirm m
~ **unit** Blitzgerät n
~ **use** Blitzeinsatz m
flashbulb Blitzbirne f; Blitz[licht]lampe; Kolbenblitz m, Kolbenblitzlampe f
~ **fixture** Blitzleuchte f
flashgun Blitz[licht]gerät n; Blitzleuchte f
flashing 1. Blinken n; 2. Nachbelichten n, Nachbelichtung f (bes. von Kinefilm); 3. s. preexposure; 4. s. latensification
~ **frequency (rate)** Blitzfrequenz f
flashlamp Blitz[licht]lampe f; Kolbenblitzlampe f, Kolbenblitz m
~ **performance** Blitzleistung f
~-**pulsed laser** Blitzlampenlaser m, blitzlampengepulster Laser m
~-**pumped dye laser** Blitzlampen-Farbstofflaser m, blitzlampengepumpter Farbstofflaser m
flashlight 1. Blitzlicht n; 2. s. ~ photograph
~ **battery** Blitzbatterie f
~ **exposure meter** Blitzbelichtungsmesser m
~ **photograph** Blitz[licht]aufnahme f, Blitzlichtfoto n
~ **powder** Blitz[licht]pulver n
~ **source** Blitzlichtquelle f
flashtube Blitzröhre f
flat 1. plan[ar], flächenhaft, flächig, eben; plano (Druckbogen); 2. flau, kontrastarm, kontrastschwach, weich; kontrastlos
~ 1. Plan[parallel]platte f, planparallele Platte f, Parallelplatte f (Optik); 2. Planobogen m
~ **color** flaue Farbe f
~ **crystal monochromator** Flachkristallmonochromator m
~ **diffuser** Plandiffusor m (Beleuchtungsstärkemesser)
~ **display** Flachdisplay n; Flachbildschirm m, flacher Bildschirm m
~-**field achromat** Planachromat m
~-**field camera** Slevogt-Kamera f, Slevogt-System n (Astrofotografie)
~-**field correction** Plankorrektur f (Optik)
~-**field lens** Planobjektiv n
~-**file database** Datenbanksystem n
~ **film** Planfilm m; Blattfilm m, Einzelblattfilm m
~ **glass** Planglas n
~ **gradation** flache Gradation f
~ **illumination** s. ~ lighting 1. und 2.
~ **image** flaues (kontrastarmes) Bild n
~ **lighting** 1. kontrastarme Beleuchtung f; 2. Frontalbeleuchtung f, frontale Ausleuchtung f
~ **mirror** Planspiegel m, Flachspiegel m, ebener Spiegel m
~-**panel active-matrix display** Matrix-Flachbildschirm m
~-**panel array (detector)** [Halbleiter-]Flächendetektor m, flächiger (flächenauflösender) Detektor m
~-**panel display (monitor)** s. flat-screen display
~-**screen display** Flachdisplay n; Flachbildschirm m, flacher Bildschirm m
~ **shading** konstante Schattierung f (Computergrafik)
~-**square tube** Flachbildröhre f
~ **surface** Planfläche f
~ **tint halftone** s. false duotone
flatbed 1. Laufboden m (Kamera); 2. s. ~ editing machine
~ **camera** Laufbodenkamera f, Reisekamera f
~ **device** Flachbettgerät n
~ **digitizer** s. ~ scanner

flatbed

~ **document scanner** Flachbett-Dokumentenscanner *m*
~ **editing machine (table)** Flachbettschneidetisch *m*
~ **offset press** Flachoffsetpresse *f*, Flachform-Offsetdruckmaschine *f*
~ **plotter** Flachbettplotter *m*; Tischplotter *m*
~ **print dryer** Flachpresse *f*
~ **printing press** Flachform-Druckmaschine *f*, Zylinder-Flachformmaschine *f*
~ **proof press** Flachoffsetpresse *f*
~ **scanner** Flachbettscanner *m*, Flachbettabtaster *m*
~ **table (viewer)** Flachbettschneidetisch *m*

flatness 1. Planlage *f*; Ebenheit *f*, Planheit *f*, Plan[ar]ität *f*; 2. Flauheit *f*, Kontrastarmut *f*; Kontrastlosigkeit *f*

flatten/to ebnen

flattening reducer kontrastmindernder Abschwächer *m*, Superproportionalabschwächer *m* *(Fotochemikalie)*

flaw analysis Defektanalyse *f*
~ **detection** Defektoskopie *f*

flesh tone Hautton[wert] *m*, Fleischfarbe *f*

flexible display flexibles (verformbares) Display *n*; flexibler Bildschirm *m*
~ **film printing** Foliendruck *m*
~ **imagescope** flexibles (faseroptisches) Endoskop *n*, Faserendoskop *n*, Glasfaserendoskop *n*
~ **object** flexibles Objekt *n* *(Computergrafik)*
~ **plate** flexible Druckplatte *f*; elastische Druckform *f*
~ **program mode** variable Programmautomatik *f*
~ **skeletonization** flexible Skelettierung *f*

flexographic flexografisch
~ **plate** Flexodruckplatte *f*
~ **printing press** Flexodruckmaschine *f*

flexography [process] Flexodruck *m*, Flexografie *f*, Anilin[gummi]druck *m*

flexopress Flexodruckmaschine *f*

flicker Flimmern *n*, Bildflimmern *n*
~ **artifact** Flimmerstörung *f*
~ **blade** Flimmerblende *f*
~ **correction** Flimmerkorrektur *f*
~ **effect** Flimmereffekt *m*
~-**free** flimmerfrei
~ **frequency** Flimmerfrequenz *f*; Flimmerverschmelzungsfrequenz *f*, Fusionsfrequenz *f*
~ **fusion** Flimmerverschmelzung *f*
~ **noise** Funkelrauschen *n*
~ **perception** Flimmerwahrnehmung *f*
~ **photometer** Flimmerfotometer *n*
~ **photometry** Flimmerfotometrie *f*
~ **rate** Flimmerfrequenz *f*
~ **threshold** kritische Flimmerfrequenz *f*, Flimmergrenze *f*

flickering *s.* flicker

flickerless image flimmerfreies Bild *n*

flight line Überflugsbahn *f*, Flugweg *m* über Grund *(Luftbildaufnahme)*
~-**line spacing** Bildstreifenbreite *f*
~ **map** Flugwegkarte *f*
~ **simulation** Flugsimulation *f*
~ **simulator** Flugsimulator *m*
~ **strip** Flugstreifen *m* *(s.a. flight line)*
~ **track** Flugbahn *f*

flint glass Flintglas *n*
~ **lens** Flintglaslinse *f*

flip angle Flipwinkel *m*, Pulswinkel *m* *(Magnetresonanztomografie)*
~-**book** Abblätterbuch *n*, Daumenkino *n*
~-**flop** Flipflop *n(m)*, bistabiler Schaltkreis *m*, bistabile [elektronische] Kippschaltung *f*
~-**out color LCD viewfinder** schwenkbarer LCD-Monitor *m* *(Camcorder)*
~ **photo album** Flipalbum *n*
~-**up flash** ausklappbarer Blitz *m*

float Bildunruhe *f* *(Kinefilmprojektion)*

floaters Mückensehen *n*, Mouches volantes *pl* *(Sehstörung)*

floating element axial verschiebbare Hinterlinse *f*; bewegliche Linsengruppe *f* *(Aufnahmeobjektiv)*
~ **lid** Flüssigkeitsdeckel *m* *(Entwicklerdose)*
~-**point arithmetic** Gleitkommaarithmetik *f*
~-**point calculation (computation)** Gleitkommarechnung *f*
~-**point filter** Gleitkommafilter *n*
~-**point operation** Gleitkommaoperation *f*
~-**point representation** Gleitkommabild *n*
~ **system** Variator *m* *(Optik)*

flood *s.* floodlight
~-**fill algorithm** Überflutungsalgorithmus *m*
~ **fill tool** Farbrolle *f*, Füllwerkzeug *n* *(Computergrafik)*

floodlamp Fotolampe *f*

floodlight 1. Flutlicht *n*; 2. Fluter *m*, Flutlichtscheinwerfer *m*, Flächenfluter *m*, [symmetrischer] Flächenscheinwerfer *m*

floor manager TV-Aufnahmeleiter *m*
~ **sheet** Auflagenpapier *n*
~ **spreader** Bodenspinne *f*, Spinne *f* *(Studiozubehör)*

flop Umklappung *f* *(geometrische Transformation)*

flopped seitenverkehrt, spiegelverkehrt

floppy [disk] Diskette *f*, Computerdiskette *f*, Floppydisk *f*, Folienspeicher *m*
~ **disk adapter** Diskettenadapter *m*
~ **disk drive** Diskettenlaufwerk *n*

flourish Zierstrich *m* *(Typografie)*

flow artifact Strömungsartefakt *n*, Flussartefakt *n* *(Magnetresonanzbildgebung)*
~ **compensation** Flusskompensation *f*
~ **diagram** *s.* flowchart
~ **field analysis** Strömungsfeldanalyse *f*

~ **imaging (mapping)** Strömungsvisualisierung f
~ **pattern** Strömungsbild n, Fließmuster n
~ **sheet** s. flowchart
~ **vector** Geschwindigkeitsvektor m
~ **visualization** Strömungsvisualisierung f
flowchart Flussdiagramm n, Programmablaufplan m
flowed text Fließtext m
fluid-dampened tripod head s. fluid head
~ **head** Fluidkopf m, Hydrokopf m, flüssigkeitsgedämpfter Stativkopf m
~ **ink** dünn[flüssig]e Druckfarbe f, niederviskose Druckfarbe f
~ **process** Hektografie f, Spirit-Umdruck m
~ **solvent ink** s. ~ ink
fluids motion analysis Strömungsanalyse f
fluoresce/to fluoreszieren
fluorescein isothiocyanate Fluoresceinisothiocyanat n (Fluoreszenzarbstoff)
fluorescence Fluoreszenz f
~ **confocal microscopy** Fluoreszenz-Konfokalmikroskopie f
~ **contrasting technique** Fluoreszenzkontrastverfahren n
~ **correlation spectroscopy** Fluoreszenzkorrelationsspektroskopie f
~ **effect** Fluoreszenzeffekt m
~ **excitation** Fluoreszenzanregung f
~ **image** Fluoreszenzbild n, Fluoreszenzaufnahme f
~ **imaging** Fluoreszenzbildgebung f
~ **intensity** Fluoreszenzintensität f
~ **light microscopy** Fluoreszenzmikroskopie f
~**-mediated tomography** fluoreszenzvermittelte Tomografie f
~ **microscope** Fluoreszenzmikroskop n
~ **photography** Fluoreszenzfotografie f
~ **photomicrography** Fluoreszenzmikrofotografie f
~ **scanner** Fluoreszenzscanner m
~ **spectrometry** Fluoreszenzspektrometrie f
~ **spectroscopy** Fluoreszenzspektroskopie f
~ **spectrum** Fluoreszenzspektrum n
~ **staining** Fluoreszenzfärbung f
~ **videomicroscopy** Fluoreszenzvideomikroskopie f
fluorescent fluoreszierend, fluoreszent
~ **color** fluoreszente Farbe f
~ **display** Fluoreszenzanzeige f
~ **dot** Phosphorleuchtpunkt m, Leucht[stoff]punkt m
~ **dye** Fluoreszenzfarbstoff m
~ **image** Fluoreszenzbild n, Fluoreszenzaufnahme f
~ **ink** Fluoreszenzdruckfarbe f
~ **lamp** Fluoreszenzlampe f, Leuchtstofflampe f
~ **layer** Fluoreszenzschicht f, Leuchtschicht f (z.B. einer Bildröhre)
~ **light** Fluoreszenzlicht n, fluoreszierendes Licht n; Leuchtstofflampenlicht n
~ **lighting** fluoreszierende Beleuchtung f
~ **material** Fluoreszenzstoff m
~ **paint** Leuchtfarbe f
~ **radiation** Fluoreszenzstrahlung f
~ **screen** Fluoreszenzschirm m, Leuchtschirm m
~ **screen image** Leuchtschirmbild n, Durchleuchtungsbild n
~ **screen material** Bildschirmleuchtstoff m
~ **substance** Fluoreszenzstoff m
~ **tube** Leucht[stoff]röhre f, Fluoreszenzröhre f
~ **yield** Fluoreszenzausbeute f
fluorescing screen Fluoreszenzfolie f; Salzverstärkerfolie f (Röntgenfilm)
~ **stain** Fluoreszenzfarbstoff m
fluoride glass Fluoridglas n
fluorite Fluorit m, Flussspat m, Calciumfluorid n (optisches Material)
~ **glass** Fluoritglas n
~ **objective** Fluoritobjektiv n, Fluoritlinse f
fluorochrome Fluoreszenzfarbstoff m
fluorographic schirmbildfotografisch, röntgenfotografisch
~ **film** Röntgenfilm m, radiografischer Film m
~ **roll film** Röntgenrollfilm m
fluorography Fluorografie f, Schirmbildfotografie f, Radiofotografie f
fluorometer Fluorometer n
fluorometry Fluorometrie f
fluorophore Fluoreszenzträger m, Fluorophor m
fluororadiography, fluororoentgenography Röntgen[strahlen]fotografie f, Röntgenografie f, Filmröntgen n
fluoroscope/to durchleuchten, röntgen
fluoroscope Röntgendurchleuchtungsanlage f, Durchleuchtungsgerät n
fluoroscopic fluoroskopisch
~ **image** Leuchtschirmbild n, Durchleuchtungsbild n
~ **image intensifier** Röntgenbildverstärker m, fluoroskopischer Bildverstärker m
~ **screen** Röntgenschirm m, Durchleuchtungsschirm m
~ **time** Durchleuchtungszeit f
fluoroscopist Durchleuchter m
fluoroscopy Fluoroskopie f, Durchleuchtung f
~ **frame** Leuchtschirmbild n, Durchleuchtungsbild n
fluorosensor Fluorosensor m
fluorspar s. fluorite
flush left 1. linksbündig; 2. linksbündiger Flattersatz m (Layout)
~ **right** 1. rechtsbündig; 2. rechtsbündiger Flattersatz m
flutter 1. Flackern n, Flackerstörung f; Helligkeitsschwankung f

flux

(Fernsehbildstörung); 2. Jaulen *n*, schnelle Gleichlaufschwankung *f (Bandlauffehler)*
flux density 1. Flussdichte *f*; 2. *s.* irradiation
~ **noise** Flussrauschen *n*
~ **quantum** [magnetisches] Flussquant *n*
~ **transition** Flusswechsel *m (Magnetismus)*
fluxon *s.* flux quantum
flyback Rücklauf *m*, Elektronenstrahlrücklauf *m*, Strahlrücklauf *m*, Strahlrücksprung *m*
~ **time** Rücklaufzeit *f*
flyer Flugblatt *n*, Wurfzettel *m (Druckerzeugnis)*
flying erase head fliegender (rotierender) Löschkopf *m*
~ **ink** Farbnebeln *n (Druckschwierigkeit)*
~ **optics** fliegende Optik *f*
~ **splice mechanism** Speicher-Rollenwechsler *m (Rollendruckmaschine)*
~**-spot scanner** Punktlichtabtaster *m*, Lichtpunkt[film]abtaster *m*, [Elektronenstrahl-]Leuchtfleck[bild]abtaster *m*, Flying-Spot-Abtaster *m*, aktiver Scanner *m*
~**-spot scanning** Punktlichtabtastung *f*
~**-spot telecine** *s.* ~ scanner
flyleaf Vorsatzblatt *n*, fliegendes Blatt *n (Buchfertigung)*
fly's eye lens Wabenlinse *f*, Fliegenaugenlinse *f*
FM radar *s.* frequency-modulated radar
FMCW radar FMCW-Radar *n*; frequenzmoduliertes Dauerstrichradar *n*
fMRI *s.* functional magnetic resonance imaging
focal fokal
~ **axis** Fokusachse *f*
~ **distance** *s.* ~ length
~ **length** Brennweite *f*; Kammerkonstante *f (Fotogrammetrie)*
~ **length of the eyepiece** Okularbrennweite *f*
~**-length ratio** Brennweitenverhältnis *n*
~ **length setting** Brennweiteneinstellung *f*
~ **lens system** fokales Linsensystem *n*
~ **line** Brennlinie *f*, [kata]kaustische Linie *f*
~ **plane** Brennebene *f*, Fokalebene *f*, Fokusfläche *f*, Fokus[sier]ebene *f*, Einstellebene *f*, Schärfenebene *f*, Bildebene *f*
~**-plane array imager** Infrarot-CCD *f*
~**-plane shutter** Bildfensterverschluss *m*, Lamellenschlitzverschluss *m*, Schlitzverschluss *m*
~ **point** *s.* focus 1.
~ **position** Fokuslage *f*
~ **power** Fokussierungswirkung *f (eines symmetrischen optischen Systems)*
~ **range** *s.* focus range

146

~ **ratio** Brennweitenverhältnis *n*, Öffnungsverhältnis *n*, relative Öffnung *f*, Öffnungszahl *f*, Blendenzahl *f (Objektiv)*
~ **ray** Brenn[punkt]strahl *m*
~ **reducer** Fokalreduktor *m (Astrooptik)*
~ **shift** Blendendifferenz *f*
~ **spot** Brennfleck *m (z.B. einer Röntgenröhre)*
~ **spot motion (movement)** Brennfleckbewegung *f*
~ **surface** Brennfläche *f*, Kaustik *f*, Katakaustik *f*
~ **system** fokales System *n*
~ **track** Brennfleckbahn *f*
~ **zone, focal-length range** *s.* focus range
focalize/to *s.* focus/to
focimeter *s.* focometer
focogram Fokogramm *n*
focometer Fokometer *n*, Brennweitenmesser *m*
focometry Fokometrie *f*, Brennweitenmessung *f*
focus/to fokussieren, scharfstellen
focus 1. Fokus[punkt] *m*, Brennpunkt *m*, fokaler Punkt *m (s.a. under* focusing, focal*)*; 2. *s.* focal length
~ **adjustment** Fokuseinstellung *f*, Brennweiteneinstellung *f*
~ **area selection** Messfeldwahl *f*
~ **area selector** Messfeldwähler *m*, Messfeldwippe *f*
~ **control** Fokussteuerung *f*; Scharf[ein]stellung *f*, Schärfenregulierung *f*, Fokussierung *f*
~ **control ring** Entfernungs[einstell]ring *m*
~ **correction** Fokuskorrektion *f*
~ **difference** Fokusdifferenz *f*
~ **distance** Fokaldistanz *f*
~**-film distance** Fokus-Film-Abstand *m*, Fokus-Bildebenen-Abstand *m (Radiografie)*
~ **finder** Scharfeinstellgerät *n*
~**-free camera** Fixfokuskamera *f*
~ **indication** Schärfe[n]indikator *m*
~ **lock** Schärfenspeicher *m*; Schärfenspeicherung *f*; Fixfokuseinstellung *f*; Nacheinstellung *f* auf Unendlich
~ **mechanism** Scharfsteller *m (Vergrößerungsgerät)*
~ **mode** Fokussier[betriebs]art *f*
~ **mode selector** Fokussierschalter *m*
~ **motor** Fokussiermotor *m*, Autofokusmotor *m*
~**-object distance** Fokus-Objekt-Abstand *m*
~ **of expansion** Expansionspunkt *m (optischer Fluss)*
~ **plane** Brennebene *f*
~ **priority** Schärfepriorität *f*, Belichtungsautomatik *f* mit Blendenvorwahl

~ **pull** Schärfennachführung *f*, Fokusnachführung *f*, Schärfeziehen *n*, Tracking *n*
~ **puller** Schärfezieher *m*, Schärfenassistent *m* *(Filmteam)*
~ **range** Brennweitenbereich *m*, Brennweitenspanne *f*, Fokusbereich *m*, Fokalbereich *m*, Schärfenbereich *m*
~ **sensor** Fokussensor *m*
~ **setting** Fokuseinstellung *f*, Brennweiteneinstellung *f*
~ **shift** Brennpunktverschiebung *f*
~ **solenoid** *s.* focusing coil
~ **tracking** *s.* ~ pull
focusability Fokussierbarkeit *f*, Fokussierfähigkeit *f*
focusable fokussierbar
focused light fokussiertes Licht *n*
focuser Fokussierer *m*
focusing Fokussierung *f*, Scharf[ein]stellung *f*, Schärfenregulierung *f*
~ **accuracy** Fokussiergenauigkeit *f*
~ **aid** Fokussierhilfe *f*, Scharfstellhilfe *f*, Einstellhilfe *f*
~ **anode** Fokussieranode *f*
~ **capability** Fokussierbarkeit *f*, Fokussierfähigkeit *f*
~ **cloth** Einstelltuch *n*
~ **coil** Fokussier[ungs]spule *f*
~ **control** Schärfensteuerung *f*
~ **distance** 1. Einstellentfernung *f*; 2. *s.* focal length
~ **electrode** Fokussierelektrode *f*
~ **error** Fokussierfehler *m*
~ **glass** *s.* ~ magnifier
~ **grid** Fokussierungsgitter *n*
~ **knob** Triebknopf *m* *(Objektiv)*
~ **lens** Fokussier[ungs]linse *f*; Sucherobjektiv *n* *(Mittelformatkamera)*
~ **light** Einstellicht *n*
~ **magnifier** Sucherlupe *f*, Einstellupe *f*, Scharfsteller *m*, Scharfeinstellgerät *n*; Standlupe *f*
~ **mechanism** Fokussiermechanik *f*, Fokussiereinrichtung *f*, Trieb *m* *(z.B. am Mikroskop)*
~ **microscope** fokussierendes Mikroskop *n*
~ **mirror** Fokussierspiegel *m*
~ **monochromator** fokussierender Monochromator *m*
~ **mount** Einstellfassung *f* *(Filmkameraobjektiv)*
~ **movement** Fokussierbewegung *f*
~ **optics** Fokussieroptik *f*
~ **range** Fokussierbereich *m* *(s.a. focus range)*
~ **ring** Brennweiten[einstell]ring *m*, Fokus[sier]ring *m*, Scharfeinstellring *m*, Schärfering *m*
~ **scale** Brennweitenskale *f*, Einstellstufung *f*
~ **screen** Sucherscheibe *f*, Einstell[matt]scheibe *f*, Mattscheibe *f*

~ **screen image** Mattscheibenbild *n*
~ **spotlight** Linsenscheinwerfer *m*
~ **system** Fokussiersystem *n*
~ **voltage** Fokussierspannung *f* *(Elektronenstrahlröhre)*
focusless brennpunktlos; afokal
fog/to verschleiern *(Filmmaterial)*
fog [fotografischer] Schleier *m*
~ **center** Schleierkeim *m*
~ **density** Schleierdichte *f*, Schleierschwärzung *f*; Negativdichte *f*, Negativschwärzung *f*
~ **filter** Nebel[effekt]filter *n* *(s.a.* diffusion filter*)*
~ **formation** Schleierbildung *f*
~**-free** schleierfrei
~ **increase** Schleieranstieg *m*
~ **inhibitor,** ~ **inhibiting agent** Antischleiermittel *n*
~ **level** Schleierwert *m*, Minimaldichte *f* *(Schwarzweißfilm)*
~ **limit** Schleiergrenze *f*
~ **machine** Nebelmaschine *f*
~ **measurement** Schleiermessung *f*
~ **screen** Nebelleinwand *f*
fogging Schleierbildung *f*, Verschleierung *f*
~ **agent** Schleiermittel *n*
~ **effect** Schleierwirkung *f*
fogless schleierfrei
foil Folie *f*
~ **emboss/to** heißprägen
~ **mirror** Folienspiegel *m*
~ **printing** Foliendruck *m*
~ **stamp/to** heißprägen
~ **stamping** Heißfolienprägung *f*, Prägefoliendruck *m*, Heißfolienprägedruck *m*
fold/to falten; falzen
fold Falz *m*, Bruch *m*
~ **mark** Falzmarke *f*
~**-out LCD screen** schwenkbarer LCD-Monitor *m*
folded optics Planoptik *f*
~ **signature** Falzbogen *m*
folder 1. Falzapparat *m*, Falzvorrichtung *f*, Falzmaschine *f*; 2. Faltprospekt *m*; Faltblatt *n*
folding Faltung *f* *(Signalverarbeitungsoperation; s.a. unter* convolution*)*
~ **bellows camera** Faltkamera *f*
~ **camera** Balgenkamera *f*, Klappkamera *f*
~ **carton printing** Faltschachteldruck *m*
~ **clip mount** Klappdiarahmen *m*
~ **flash bracket** abgewinkelte Blitzschiene *f*, Klapp-Winkelschiene *f*
~ **magnifier** Klapplupe *f*
~ **mirror** Faltreflektor *m*
~ **roll film camera** Spring[spreizen]kamera *f*; Klappkamera *f*
~ **succession** Falz[reihen]folge *f*
~ **system** *s.* folder 1.

folding 148

~ **viewfinder light shield,** ~ **viewing hood** Faltlichtschacht *m* *(Spiegelreflexkamera)*
foldout picture Ausklappbild *n*
Foley artist Geräuschemacher *m*
~ **editor** Geräuschetechniker *m*
~ **operator** Geräuschemacher *m*
~ **sound effect** Toneffekt *m*, Geräuscheffekt *m*
~ **stage** Geräuschstudio *n*
foliage-penetration radar Vegetationsdurchdringungsradar *n*
folio [number] Seitenzahl *f*, Pagina *f*
follow focus Schärfeziehen *n*, Schärfennachführung *f*, Fokusnachführung *f*, Tracking *n* *(Kinematografie)*
~**-focus assistant** Schärfenassistent *m*, Schärfezieher *m* *(Filmteam)*
~ **shot** 1. Mitschwenk *m*, Mitzieher *m*, Verfolgungsschwenk *m* *(Kameraführung)*; 2. Fahraufnahme *f* *(Filmarbeit)*
fond Tonfläche *f (Druck)*
font 1. Schriftart *f*; 2. Zeichensatz *m*
~ **family** Schrift[art]familie *f*, Schriftsippe *f*; Schrifttyp *m*; Zeichensatz *m*
~ **file** Schriftdatensatz *m*
~ **generator** Schriftgenerator *m (Software)*
~ **library** Schriftenbibliothek *f*
~ **metrics** Schriftartmetrik *f*
~ **of characters (types),** ~ **set** Zeichensatz *m*
~ **size** Schriftgrad *m*, Schrifthöhe *f*, Glyphenhöhe *f*
~ **style** Schriftschnitt *m*, Schriftstil *m*, Schriftart *f*, Schrift *f*
food photography Lebensmittelfotografie *f*
foot Durchhang *m*, Kurvenfuß *m*; Fußempfindlichkeit *f* *(Schwärzungskurve)*
~**-candle** Lumen *n* pro Quadratfuß
~ **margin** Fußsteg *m*, unterer Rand *m* *(Druckseite)*
~ **of the microscope** Mikroskopstativfuß *m*; Mikroskopstativ *n*
footage Filmmaterial *n*; Filmmeter *mpl*
~ **counter (indicator)** Filmzählwerk *n*, Filmlängenmesser *m*
~ **number** [Negativ-]Fußnummer *f*, Randnummer *f*, Randzahl *f (Film)*
footer Fußzeile *f (Datenstruktur)*
footlambert *eine SI-fremde Einheit der Leuchtdichte*
footnote Fußnote *f*
footprint Satellitenempfangsgebiet *n*, Versorgungsgebiet *n*, Ausleuchtzone *f* *(Fernsehübertragung)*
footswitch Fußschalter *m*
for position only image niedrigaufgelöstes Bild *n (Druckvorstufe)*
forbidden gap Bandlücke *f*, Bandabstand *m* *(Fotodiode)*

force card Patrize *f*, Prägestock *m (z.B. im Prägedruck)*
~ **feedback** Kraftrückkopplung *f*
~**-process/to** forcieren *(unterbelichteten Film)*
forced development (processing) forcierte (gesteigerte) Entwicklung *f*, Überentwicklung *f*, Pushentwicklung *f*
forcing *s.* forced development
forebath Vorbad *n*
foreground Vordergrund *m*
~ **color** Vordergrundfarbe *f*
~ **element** Vordergrundobjekt *n*
~ **feature** Vordergrundmerkmal *n*
~ **image** Vordergrundbild *n*
~ **lighting** Vordergrundbeleuchtung *f*
~ **object** Vordergrundobjekt *n*
~ **pixel** Vordergrundpixel *n*
~ **region** Vordergrundbereich *m*
~ **scene** Vordergrundszene *f*
foreign atom Fremdatom *n*
~ **language release** fremdsprachige Filmkopie *f*
~ **release** Weltvertrieb *m (Filmwirtschaft)*
foreknowledge Vorwissen *n*, a-priori-Wissen *n*, apriorisches Wissen *n* *(Neuroinformatik)*
foremost lens Frontlinse *f*, Vorderlinse *f*
forensic photogrammetry forensische Fotogrammetrie *f*
~ **photograph** Gerichtsfoto *n*
~ **photographer** Gerichtsfotograf *m*; kriminaltechnischer Fotograf *m*
~ **photographic** gerichtsfotografisch
~ **photography** kriminaltechnische (forensische) Fotografie *f*; Gerichtsfotografie *f*
foreshortening [effect] Verkürzungseffekt *m (Perspektive)*
forest mapping Waldkartierung *f*
~ **photogrammetry** forstliche Fotogrammetrie *f*
forge/to fälschen
forgery detection Fälschungserkennung *f*
form 1. Form *f (s.a. unter shape)*; 2. Formular *n*; 3. Druckform *f*
~ **factor** Formfaktor *m*
~ **feature** Formmerkmal *n*, Gestaltmerkmal *n*, formbeschreibendes (morphometrisches) Merkmal *n*
~ **feed** Seitenvorschub *m (Drucker)*
~ **reader (reading system)** Formularlesegerät *n*
~ **recognition** Formerkennung *f*
~ **roller** Farbauftrag[s]walze *f*
formaldehyde Formaldehyd *m*
formalin Formalin *f*
format/to formatieren
format Format *n*
~ **change** Formatänderung *f*; Formatumschaltung *f*
~ **conversion** Formatkonversion *f*, Formatkonvertierung *f*

~ **diagonal** Formatdiagonale f, Bildformatdiagonale f
~ **effector** Formatsteuerzeichen n
~ **originator** Formatersteller m
~ **selection** Formatauswahl f
formatted data formatierte Daten pl
~ **text** formatierter Text m
formatting Formatierung f
forme Druckform f
forming gas Formiergas n *(Astrofilmentwicklung)*
forms printing Formulardruck m
forward-acting error correction Vorwärts-Fehlerkorrektur f
~-**adaptive bit allocation** vorwärtsadaptive Bitzuordnung f
~ **adaptive prediction** vorwärtsgesteuerte adaptive Prädiktion f
~ **adaptive quantization** vorwärtsadaptive Quantisierung f
~ **analysis** Vorwärtsanalyse f *(Bilddatenkompression)*
~ **bias[-voltage]** Durchlassvorspannung f *(Leuchtdiode)*
~ **chaining** Vorwärtsverkettung f
~ **channel** Vorwärtskanal m, Hinkanal m
~ **compatibility** Vorwärtskompatibilität f
~ **compatible** vorwärtskompatibel
~ **error correction** Fehlervorwärtskorrektur f
~ **error-correction code** Vorwärts-Fehlerkorrekturcode m
~ **error recovery** Vorwärtsfehlerbehebung f
~ **filter** Vorwärtsfilter n
~ **Fourier transform** Fourier-Vorwärtstransformation f
~ **kinematics** Vorwärtskinematik f *(Computeranimation)*
~-**looking infrared device** Wärmebildgerät n *(bes. in Panzerfahrzeugen)*
~-**looking radar** Voraussichtradar n
~ **mapping** Vorwärtsabbildung f *(geometrische Transformation)*
~ **overlap** Längsüberdeckung f *(Aerofotogrammetrie)*
~ **predicition** Vorwärtsprädiktion f *(Bildsequenzcodierung)*
~ **scatter[ing]** Vorwärtsstreuung f
~ **search** Vorwärtssuche f
~ **transform kernel** Vorwärtstransformationskern m
~ **transformation** Vorwärtstransformation f
~ **transformation matrix** Vorwärtstransformationsmatrix f
Foucault knife[-edge] test [Foucaultsches] Schneiden[prüf]verfahren n, Foucaultsche Schattenprobe f, Messerschneidenmethode f [nach Foucault] *(Linsenprüfung)*
~ **prism** Foucaultsches Prisma n
foundry type Gussletter f
fount s. font 1. *und* 2.

fountain Farb[dosier]kasten m *(Druckmaschine)*
~ **solution** Feuchtmittel n
four-adjacency s. four-connectivity neighborhood
~-**channel sound** Vierkanalton m
~-**color** vierfarbig, tetrachromatisch
~-**color print** Vierfarbendruck m *(Erzeugnis)*
~-**color printer** Vierfarbendrucker m
~-**color printing press** Vierfarb[endruck]maschine f
~-**color process [printing]** Vierfarbenprozess m, Vierfarbendruck m
~-**color reproduction** Vierfarbenreproduktion f
~-**color separation** Vierfarbenseparation f
~-**connectivity neighborhood** Vierernachbarschaft f, Viererumgebung f *(von Bildpunkten)*
~-**dimensional** vierdimensional
~-**dimensional representation** vierdimensionale Darstellung f
~-**element lens** viergliedriges Objektiv n, Vierlinser m
~-**energy-level laser** Vierniveaulaser m
~-**equivalent coupler** vierwertiger Kuppler m, Vieräquivalentkuppler m *(Farbfotografie)*
~-**level laser** Vierniveaulaser m
~-**track magnetic sound** Vierspur-Magnetton m
~-**track stereophonic sound** Vierspur-Raumton m
Fourier analysis Fourier-Analyse f, Fourier-Transformation f, harmonische Analyse f
~-**based texture analysis** fourierbasierte Texturanalyse f
~ **coefficient** Fourier-Koeffizient m, Fourier-Konstante f
~ **component** Fourier-Komponente f
~ **decomposition** Fourier-Zerlegung f *(Wellenoptik)*
~ **description** Fourier-Beschreibung f
~ **descriptor** Fourier-Deskriptor m, Fourier-Merkmal n
~ **domain** Fourier-Raum m
~ **domain filtering** Fourier-Filterung f
~ **filter** Fourier-Filter n
~ **image** Fourier-Bild n
~ **image analysis** Fourier-Bildanalyse f
~ **integral** Fourier-Integral n
~ **inversion** Fourier-Rücktransformation f
~ **model** Fourier-Modell n
~ **optical** fourieroptisch
~ **optics** Fourier-Optik f
~-**optics** fourieroptisch
~ **power spectrum** Fourier-Spektrum n, Ortsfrequenzspektrum n
~ **reconstruction** Fourier-Rekonstruktion f
~ **sequence (series)** Fourier-Reihe f, trigonometrische Reihe f

Fourier 150

~ **series expansion**
Fourier-Reihenentwicklung *f*
~ **series representation**
Fourier-Darstellung *f*
~ **space** Fourier-Raum *m*
~ **synthesis** Fourier-Synthese *f*,
harmonische Synthese *f*
~ **theory** Fourier-Theorie *f*
~ **transform/to** fouriertransformieren
~ **transform** 1. Fourier-Transformation *f*,
Fourier-Analyse *f*, harmonische Analyse
f; 2. Fourier-Transformierte *f*
~ **transform coefficient** Fourier-Koeffizient
m, Fourier-Konstante *f*
~ **transform hologram** Fourier-Hologramm
n, Fourier-Transformationshologramm *n*
~ **transform holography**
Fourier-Holografie *f*
~ **transform image** fouriertransformiertes
Bild *n*
~ **transform imaging**
Fourier-Bildgewinnung *f*
~ **transform infrared spectroscopy**
Fourier-Transformations-Infrarotspektroskopie *f*
~ **transform lens**
Fourier-Transformations-Objektiv *n*
~ **transform pair**
Fourier-Transformationspaar *n*
~ **transform plane** Fourier-Ebene *f* *(s.a. focal plane)*
~ **transform spectrometer**
Fourier-Spektrometer *n*
~ **transform spectroscopy**
Fourier-Spektroskopie *f*
~ **transformation** Fourier-Transformation *f*
fourth-degree polynomial Polynom *n*
vierter Ordnung
fovea Fovea [centralis] *f*, Sehgrube *f*,
Netzhautgrube *f*
foveal foveal
~ **center** *s.* fovea
~ **viewing (vision)** foveales Sehen *n*
FPD *s.* flat-panel display
FPO image *s.* for position only image
fractal fraktal
~ Fraktal *n*, fraktales Objekt *n*
~ **analysis** Fraktalanalyse *f*
~**-based compression** fraktale
Kompression *f*, Fraktalkompression *f*
~**-based representation** fraktale
Darstellung *f*
~ **block coding** fraktale Blockcodierung *f*
~ **code** fraktaler Code *m*
~ **coding** fraktale Codierung *f*
~ **curve** fraktale Kurve *f*
~ **decoding** fraktale Decodierung *f*
~ **dimension** fraktale (fraktionäre)
Dimension *f*,
Hausdorff-Besikowitsch-Dimension *f*
(Computergrafik)
~ **encoding** fraktale Codierung *f*
~ **figure** *s.* ~ image
~ **geometric** fraktalgeometrisch

~ **geometry** fraktale Geometrie *f*,
Fraktalgeometrie *f*
~ **image** fraktales Bild (Muster) *n*,
Fraktalbild *n*
~ **image analysis** fraktale Bildanalyse *f*
~ **image coding** Fraktalbildcodierung *f*,
fraktale Bildcodierung *f*
~ **image compression**
Fraktalbildkompression *f*, fraktale
Bildkompression *f*
~ **imager** fraktaler Bildverarbeiter *m*
~ **model** fraktales Modell *n*
~ **object** fraktales Objekt *n*, Fraktal *n*
~ **pattern** fraktales Muster (Bild) *n*,
Fraktalbild *n*
~ **program** Fraktalprogramm *n*
~ **set** fraktale Menge *f*
~ **signature** fraktale Signatur *f*
~ **solid** fraktaler Körper *m*
~ **texture analysis** fraktale Texturanalyse *f*
~ **theory** Fraktaltheorie *f*
~ **transform[ation]** fraktale Transformation
f
fractional Brownian motion gebrochene
Brownsche Bewegung *f*
~**-pel accuracy** Subpixelgenauigkeit *f*
Fractur *s.* Fraktur
fragile watermark zerbrechliches
Wasserzeichen *n*
fragment Fragment *n*
~**[ize]/to** fragmentieren
Fraktur Fraktur[schrift] *f*, Bruchschrift *f*,
gebrochene Schrift *f*
frame/to kadrieren
frame 1. Rahmen *m*; Positionsrahmen *m*;
Bildausschnitt *m*; Bildfeld *n*; 2.
Datenübertragungsblock *m*; 3. Filmbild
n, Bildkader *m*, Kinobild *n*; Videobild *n*;
Fernseh[einzel]bild *n*; 4. Frame *m(n)*
(bes. als Computerbildausschnitt)
~ **accuracy** Bildgenauigkeit *f*
(Filmabtastung)
~**-accurate** [einzel]bildgenau
~**-accurate editing** bildgenauer Schnitt *m*
~**-accurate synchronization** bildgenaue
Synchronisation *f*
~ **area** Bildfläche *f*
~ **averaging** Bildmittelung *f*
~**-based prediction** Vollbildprädiktion *f*
~ **blanking** Bildaustastung *f* *(Video)*
~ **buffer [memory]** Bildpuffer[speicher] *m*,
Pufferspeicher *m*, Bildwiederholspeicher
m, Auffrischspeicher *m*,
Bildschirmspeicher *m*,
Rasterbildspeicher *m*, Einzelbildpuffer *m*
(Video)
~**-by-frame animation** ein[zel]bildweise
Animation *f*
~**-by-frame exposure** Einzelbildbelichtung
f
~**-by-frame recording (shooting)**
einzelbildweise Aufnahme *f*
~**-by-frame technique** Einzelbildtechnik *f*
~ **capture card** *s.* ~ grabber [card]

Fraunhofer

~ **check sequence** Blockprüfzeichenfolge f
~ **coil** Bildablenkspule f
~ **count** Bildzählung f; Bildnumerierung f
~ **counter** Bildzähler m, Bildzählwerk n (Kamera)
~ **counter** Bildzähler m, Bildzählwerk n
~ **coverage** Bildabdeckung f
~ **deflection** Bildablenkung f
~ **delay** Bildverzögerung f (Video)
~ **duration** Bilddauer f
~ **finder** Sportsucher m (Kamera)
~ **flyback** Bildrücklauf m, Vertikalrücklauf m
~ **frequency** Bild[folge]frequenz f
~ **gauge** Bildschritt m, Bildschritthöhe f
~ **grabber, ~ grabber board (card)** [digitale] Bildspeicherkarte f, Bilderfassungskarte f, Bildaufnahmekarte f, Bildeinzugskarte f, Framegrabber m, Videodigitalisierungskarte f, Digitalisierungskarte f, Bilddigitalisierer m
~ **grabbing** Videodigitalisierung f, Bilderfassung f; Einzelbildspeicherung f
~ **handles** Klappennachlauf m, Klappenvorlauf m (Film)
~ **header** Rahmenkopf m (Datenstruktur)
~ **height** Bildhöhe f
~ **interline transfer** Zwischenzeilentransfer m
~-**interline-transfer device** FIT-CCD-Bildwandler m, FIT-Chip m
~ **interpolation** Bildinterpolation f
~ **interval** Bildintervall n
~ **jitter** Bildzittern n, Bildwackeln n, Bildinstabilität f
~ **line** Filmsteg m, Bildstrich m
~ **loss** Bildverlust m
~ **memory** Einzelbildspeicher m
~ **memory depth** Bildspeichertiefe f
~ **movie mode** Vollbildmodus m (Video)
~ **noise** Bildrauschen n
~ **number** Bildnummer f
~ **of picture** s. frame 3.
~ **of reference** 1. Bezugsrahmen m; 2. Bezugsbild n, Referenzbild n (Videocodierung)
~-**per-second rate** Bildfrequenz f
~ **period** Bilddauer f
~ **picture** Fernseh[einzel]bild n
~ **prediction** Vollbildprädiktion f
~ **processing** Vollbildverarbeitung f
~ **pulse** Bildimpuls m; Schneid[e]impuls m (Videoschnitt)
~ **rate** 1. Bild[folge]frequenz f, Vollbildfrequenz f, Bildrate f, Einzelbildrate f; Laufbildgeschwindigkeit f, Filmbildfrequenz f; 2. s. framing rate
~-**rate conversion** Abtastratenkonversion f, Abtastratenumsetzung f
~-**rate difference** Bildfrequenzunterschied m
~-**rate flicker** Bildflimmern n

~ **record** Einzelbildaufnahme f
~ **refresh rate** s. ~ rate 1.
~ **resolution** Bildauflösung f
~ **roll** Bilddurchlauf m; [vertikales] Bildkippen n
~ **rotation** Bilddrehung f, Bildrotation f
~ **scanning time** Bildabtastzeit f
~ **sequence coder** Bildsequenzcodierer m
~ **size** 1. Bildfeldgröße f; 2. Filmbildformat n
~ **storage technique** Bildspeichertechnik f
~ **storage unit** Bildspeichereinheit f
~ **store [memory]** Vollbildspeicher m; Einzelbildspeicher m; Standbildspeicher m
~ **structure** Rahmenstruktur f
~ **synchronization** Bildsynchronisation f
~ **synchronizing pulse** Bildsynchronisierimpuls m, Bildsynchronsignal n
~-**synchronous** bildsynchron
~ **time** Vollbilddauer f, Bilddauer f
~-**to-frame coding** Bild-zu-Bild-Codierung f, Interframe-Codierung f
~-**to-frame correlation (redundancy)** zeitliche Redundanz f
~-**transfer CCD imager** Frame-Transfer-Bildaufnehmer m, CCD-Sensor m mit Bildauswahl, FT-CCD-Bildwandler m
~ **transfer imager** Frame-Transfer-Bildaufnehmer m, CCD-Sensor n mit Bildauswahl
~-**transfer structure** Bildtransferstruktur f
~ **type** Bildtyp m
~ **viewfinder** Rahmensucher m, Sportsucher m (Kamera)
~ **width** Bildbreite f

frames per second Bilder npl pro Sekunde (Kinematografie)
framing 1. Bildausschnittwahl f, Bildfeldauswahl f, Ausschnittbestimmung f; Bildeinstellen n, Bildeinstellung f; Kadrierung f, Cadrage f (Kinematografie); 2. Bildreihenaufnahme f
~ **accuracy** Einstellgenauigkeit f
~ **camera** Bildsequenzkamera f
~ **control** Bildsteuerung f, Bildregelung f
~ **error** Sucherfehler m
~ **eyepiece** Beobachtungsokular n, Einstellfernrohr n
~ **mask** Bildmaske f
~ **rate** 1. Bildaufnahmefrequenz f, Aufnahmefrequenz f, Bilderfassungsrate f; 2. s. frame rate 1.
~ **speed** 1. Aufnahmegeschwindigkeit f (Kinematografie); 2. s. ~ rate 1.

Fraunhofer diffraction Fraunhofer-Beugung f, Fraunhofersche Beugung f
~ **diffraction pattern** Fraunhofer-Beugungsbild n, Fraunhofersches Beugungsbild n

Fraunhofer

~ **equatorial mounting** deutsche Montierung f *(Teleskop)*
~ **hologram** Fraunhofer-Hologramm n
~ **holography** Fraunhofer-Holografie f
~ **lines** Fraunhofer-Linien *fpl*, Fraunhofersche Linien *fpl*
free aperture s. clear aperture
~ **carrier** freier Ladungsträger m
~ **charge** freie Ladung f
~ **electron** freies Elektron n
~-**electron laser** Freie-Elektronen-Laser m, FEL
~ **endpaper** Vorsatzblatt n, fliegendes Blatt n *(Buchfertigung)*
~-**form deformation** Freiformverformung f *(Computergrafik)*
~-**form surface** Freiformfläche f
~-**form surface representation** Freiformflächendarstellung f
~ **induction decay** freier Induktionszerfall m *(Kernspinresonanz)*
~ **radical** freies Radikal n
~ **sheet** Feinpapier n, holzfreies Papier n
~-**space laser** Freistrahllaser m
~-**space propagation** Freiraumübertragung f
~ **television (TV)** frei empfangbares Fernsehen n, Frei-Fernsehen n
~-**to-air** unverschlüsselt *(Fernsehprogramm)*
~-**to-air receiver** Free-to-Air-Empfänger m
freedom from chromatic aberration Farbfehlerfreiheit f
freeform object Freiformobjekt n
freehand drawing Freihandzeichnen n *(Computergrafik)*
~ **scanner** Handscanner m
~ **scanning** freie Schallkopfführung f *(Sonografie)*
~ **scissors** Freihandschere f, Lassowerkzeug n *(digitale Bildbearbeitung)*
Freeman chain Freeman-Kette f
~ **chain code** Freeman-Code m *(Bildanalyse)*
freeware frei herunterladbare (verfügbare) Software f
freeze buffer Standbildspeicher m
~-**drying microscope** Kryomikroskop n
~-**drying microscopy** Kryomikroskopie f
~ **frame** 1. Standbild n; stehendes (angehaltenes) Filmbild n; 2. Standkopierung f, Standverlängerung f
~ **frame mode** Standbildmodus m *(Camcorder)*
freezing [the movement] Einfrieren n [der Bewegung] *(Video)*
French fold Kreuzfaltung f *(von Druckbogen)*
Frenet frame Frenetsches Bezugssystem n *(geometrische Modellierung)*
Frenkel defect (disorder) Frenkel-Defekt m, Frenkel-Fehlstelle f *(fotografischer Elementarprozess)*

~ **equilibrium** Frenkel-Gleichgewicht n
frequency Frequenz f, Schwingungszahl f
~ **aliasing** Frequenzverzerrung f
~ **analysis** Frequenzanalyse f
~ **analyzer** Frequenzanalysator m
~ **axis** Frequenzachse f
~ **band** Frequenzband n, Frequenzbereich m
~ **bandwidth** Frequenzbandbreite f
~ **change** Frequenzänderung f, Frequenzschwankung f
~ **coefficient** Frequenzkoeffizient m
~ **component** Frequenzkomponente f, Frequenzanteil m *(z.B. einer Fourier-Transformation)*
~ **content** Frequenzgehalt m
~ **conversion** Frequenzkonversion f
~ **dependence** s. ~ masking
~-**dependent noise** Frequenzrauschen n
~ **difference** Frequenzdifferenz f
~ **distortion** Frequenzverzerrung f
~ **distribution** Frequenzverteilung f, Häufigkeitsverteilung f; Energieverteilungskurve f
~ **divider** Frequenzteiler m
~ **division multiple access** Vielfachzugriff m im Frequenzmultiplex
~-**division multiplexing** s. frequency multiplexing
~ **domain** Frequenzbereich m, Frequenzebene f
~-**domain analysis** Frequenzanalyse f
~-**domain filter** Frequenzbereichsfilter n
~-**domain filtering** Frequenzbereichsfilterung f
~-**domain function** Frequenzbereichsfunktion f
~-**domain image** Frequenzbereichsbild n
~-**domain representation** Frequenzbereichsdarstellung f
~-**domain resolution** Frequenzbereichsauflösung f
~-**domain signal** Frequenzbereichssignal n
~-**domain value** Frequenzbereichswert m
~ **doubler** Frequenzverdoppler m
~ **doubling** Frequenzverdopp[e]lung f
~ **encoding** Frequenzcodierung f *(z.B. in der Magnetresonanzbildgebung)*
~-**encoding direction** Frequenzcodierungsrichtung f
~-**encoding gradient** Frequenz[codier]gradient m, Auslesegradient m, Lesegradient m *(Magnetresonanzbildgebung)*
~ **filter** Frequenzfilter n
~ **function** Frequenzfunktion f, Amplitudenfunktion f; Spektralfunktion f
~ **interference** Frequenzinterferenz f
~ **interlace (interleaving)** Frequenzverkämmung f, Frequenzverschachtelung f
~ **interval** Frequenzintervall n
~ **inversion** Frequenzinversion f
~ **jitter** Frequenzschwankung[en] *f[pl]*

~ **masking** Frequenzmaskierung f
~ **mixer** Frequenzmischer m
~-**modulated** frequenzmoduliert
~-**modulated carrier** frequenzmodulierter Träger
~-**modulated continuous-wave radar** frequenzmoduliertes Dauerstrichradar n, FMCW-Radar n
~-**modulated radar** frequenzmoduliertes Radar n, FM-Radar n
~-**modulated screening** frequenzmodulierte (nichtperiodische) Rasterung f, Streurasterung f, Zufallsrasterung f, FM-Rasterung f
~-**modulated signal** frequenzmoduliertes Signal n
~ **modulation** Frequenzmodulation f
~ **multiplexing** Frequenzmultiplexen n, Frequenzmultiplextechnik f, Frequenzmultiplexverfahren n
~ **noise** Frequenzrauschen n
~ **of light** Lichtfrequenz f
~ **overlap** Frequenzüberlappung f
~ **plane** s. ~ domain
~ **range** Frequenzbereich m; Frequenzumfang m
~ **range capability** Bandbreite f
~ **raster** Frequenzraster m(n)
~ **resolution** Frequenzauflösung f
~ **response** Frequenzgang m, Frequenzverlauf m
~ **response curve (function)** Frequenzkurve f
~ **sampling** Frequenzabtastung f
~ **selection** Frequenzwahl f
~-**selective filter** frequenzselektives Filter n
~-**selective RF pulse** weicher Hochfrequenzimpuls m *(Magnetresonanztomografie)*
~ **separation** Frequenzzerlegung f
~ **shift** Frequenzverschiebung f
~ **shift keying** Frequenzumtastung f, Frequenzsprungmodulation f
~ **signal** Frequenzsignal n
~ **space** Frequenzraum m
~-**space representation** Frequenzraumdarstellung f
~ **span** s. ~ range
~ **spectrum** Frequenzspektrum n, Frequenzgemisch n
~ **stability** Frequenzstabilität f
~ **sweep** Frequenzhub m, Chirp m *(Laser)*
~ **synthesis** Frequenzsynthese f
~ **transform[ation]** Frequenztransformation f
~ **tripler** Frequenzverdreifacher m
~-**weighted quantization** frequenzgewichtete Quantisierung f
~ **weighting filter** Frequenzfilter n
Fresnel biprism [Fresnelsches] Biprisma n, Doppelbildprisma n

~ **diffraction** Fresnel-Beugung f, Fresnelsche Beugung f, Nahfeldbeugung f
~ **diffraction from a slit** Fresnel-Beugung f am Spalt
~ **diffraction pattern** Fresnelsches Beugungsbild n
~ **effect** Fresnel-Effekt m
~ **hologram** Fresnel-Hologramm n
~ **holography** Fresnel-Holografie f
~ **lens** Fresnel-Linse f, [Fresnelsche] Stufenlinse f
~-**lens spotlight** Stufenlinsenscheinwerfer m, Stufenlinser m
~ **loss** Fresnel-Verlust m
~ **mirror** Fresnel-Spiegellinse f
~ **number** Fresnel-Zahl f *(Wellenoptik)*
~ **reflection** Fresnel-Reflexion f, Fresnelsche Reflexion f
~ **reflection formula** Fresnelsche Reflexionsformel f
~ **reflection loss** Fresnel-Verlust m
~ **region** s. ~ zone
~ **rhomb** Fresnel-Rhomboid n
~ **screen** Fresnel-Scheibe f
~ **sine integral** Fresnelsches Integral n *(Beugungsoptik)*
~ **zone** Fresnelsche Zone f *(Wellenoptik)*
~ **zone plate** Fresnel-Platte f, [Fresnelsche] Zonenplatte f *(lichtbrechendes fokussierendes Element)*
Fresnel's equations Fresnelsche Gleichungen (Formeln) fpl *(Wellenoptik)*
friction clutch Reibungskupplung f, Friktionskupplung f
~ **drive** Friktions[an]trieb m
~ **head** Friktionskopf m *(Stativ)*
fringe Saum m; Farbsaum m; Hof m *(Rasterpunkt)*
~ **contrast** Streifenkontrast m *(Holografie, Elektronenmikroskopie)*
~ **effect** Saumeffekt m
~ **pattern** 1. Streifenmuster n; 2. Dehnungslinienbild n
~ **stability** Streifenstabilität f *(Holografie)*
fringing field Randfeld n *(CCD-Sensor)*
front camera standard Frontstandarte f, Objektivstandarte f *(Fachkamera)*
~ **component (element)** Frontglied n, Vorderglied n *(Objektiv)*
~ **cover** Vorderdeckel m *(Buchherstellung)*
~ **end** Kameraende n
~ **face** Frontscheibe f, Frontglas n, Bildröhrenfront f
~ **focal length** objektseitige (vordere) Brennweite f
~ **focal plane** objektseitige Brennebene f
~ **group** Frontgruppe f *(Objektiv)*
~ **intensifying screen** Vorder[verstärkungs]folie f *(Röntgenkassette)*
~ **lens** Frontlinse f, Vorderlinse f
~ **lens cap** Objektivkappe f, Objektivabdeckung f

front 154

~ **lens protective filter** Frontlinsenschutzfilter *n*
~ **lens standard** *s.* ~ camera standard
~ **light** Frontallicht *n*, Vorderlicht *n*
~ **lighting** Frontalbeleuchtung *f*, frontale Ausleuchtung *f*
~ **matter** Titelei *f (Buchherstellung)*
~ **nodal point** objektseitiger Knotenpunkt *m*
~-**operating aperture** Vorderblende *f*
~ **optics** *s.* ~ component
~ **panel** Bedienfeld *n*
~ **porch** vordere Schwarzschulter *f (Farbvideosignal)*
~ **principal point** objektseitiger (dingseitiger) Hauptpunkt *m*, Objekthauptpunkt
~ **projection [process]** Frontprojektion *f*, Auf[licht]projektion *f (Filmtrickverfahren)*
~-**projection screen** Frontprojektions[lein]wand *f*
~ **projection setup** Frontprojektionseinrichtung *f*
~ **projector** Frontprojektor *m*
~ **side** 1. Vorderseite *f*; 2. Mattseite *f*, Schichtseite *f*, Emulsionsseite *f (Fotomaterial)*
~-**side-illuminated CCD** frontbestrahlter CCD-Sensor *m*
~ **slate** Anfangsklappe *f (Film, Video)*
~ **standard** *s.* ~ camera standard
~-**surface coating** Vorderflächenverspiegelung *f*; Oberflächenverspiegelung *f*
~-**surface[d] mirror** Vorderflächenspiegel *m*; Oberflächenspiegel *m*, oberflächenversilberter Spiegel *m*
frontal nodal (principal) plane objektseitige Hauptebene *f*, Eingangshauptebene *f (dicke Linse)*
~ **view** Vorderansicht *f*, Frontansicht *f*
frontality Frontalität *f*
frosted diffusion filter Nebel[effekt]filter *n*
~ **glass** Mattglas *n*
~ **glass filter** Mattglasfilter *n*
~ **white bulb** mattierte Glühlampe *f*
fruit nichtsynchrone Störung (Empfangsstörung) *f (Radar)*
fulcrum Fulkrum *n*, Drehpunkt *m*
full-angle tomography Vollwinkeltomografie *f*
~ **aperture** maximale Blende (Öffnung) *f*, Maximalöffnung *f*, maximaler Blendendurchmesser *m*; Anfangsöffnung *f (Objektiv)*
~-**aperture exposure metering [system]** Offenblendenmessung *f (Spiegelreflexkamera)*
~ **CG feature** computeranimierter Film *m*, Computer[trick]film *m*
~-**coated magnetic film** voll beschichteter Magnetfilm *m*
~-**color copier** Vollfarbkopierer *m*

~-**color copy** Vollfarbkopie *f*
~-**color digital scanner** Vollfarb-Digitalscanner *m*
~-**color display** Vollfarbdisplay *n*
~-**color flat-panel display** Vollfarb-Flachbildschirm *m*
~-**color hologram** Vollfarbhologramm *n*
~-**color image** Vollfarbbild *n*
~-**color image processing** Vollfarbbildverarbeitung *f*
~-**color photograph** Echtfarbenbild *n*
~-**color picture** Vollfarbbild *n*
~-**color prepress proof** Farbproof *m (Druckvorstufe)*
~ **color printing** Vierfarbendruck *m*, Vierfarbenprozess *m*
~-**color printing** Vollfarbdruck *m*
~-**color projection** Vollfarbprojektion *f*
~-**color scanning** Vollfarbabtastung *f*
~-**color sensor** Vollfarbsensor *m*
~-**color signal** Vollfarbsignal *n*
~-**colored** vollfarbig
~ **development** Ausentwicklung *f*
~ **duplex** Vollduplexbetrieb *m*
~ **exposure** Vollbelichtung *f*
~-**frame image** [optisches] Vollbild *n*
~-**frame transform** Vollbildtransformation *f*
~-**frame video image** Videovollbild *n*
~-**front view** Frontalaufnahme *f*, En-face-Aufnahme *f*
~ **graphics** Vollgrafik *f (Bildschirmtechnik)*
~-**justification** Blocksatz *m (Typografie)*
~-**length animated feature film** Zeichentrick-Spielfilm *m*
~-**length feature movie**, ~ **film (picture)** Hauptfilm *m*, Langfilm *m*, Großfilm *m*, abendfüllender Film *m*
~-**length portrait** Ganzporträt *n*
~-**motion video** Bewegtbildvideo *n*, Laufbildvideo *n*
~-**output warning** Volleistungswarnung *f (Blitzelektronik)*
~-**page display** Ganzseitenanzeige *f*, Ganzseitenbildschirm *m*
~-**page illustration** ganzseitige Abbildung *f*
~-**page pagination** Ganzseitenumbruch *m*
~ **photograph** Ganzfoto *n*
~-**pixel precision** Vollpixelgenauigkeit *f*, Pixelgenauigkeit *f*
~-**scale histogram stretch** Kontrastdehnung *f*, Kontrastspreizung *f*
~ **search** Vollsuche *f (Bewegungsschätzung)*
~-**sheet** ganzseitig
~ **shot** Halbtotale *f*, halbtotale Einstellung *f*
~-**size frame** Vollbild *n (Film, Video)*
~-**sized image** *s.* full-frame image
~ **stop** Punkt *m (Satzzeichen)*
~-**text search** Volltextsuche *f*
~-**text search engine** Volltext-Suchmaschine *f*
~ **well capacity** Sättigungsladung *f (Bildsensor)*

~-width-at-half-maximum [spektrale] Halbwertsbreite *f (einer Linienbildfunktion)*
~-width-at-tenth-maximum Zehntelbreite *f (einer Linienbildfunktion)*
fully automatic camera vollautomatische Kamera *f*
~ automatic-thirty-five-mm camera vollautomatische Kleinbildkamera *f*
~ corrected lens ideal korrigiertes Objektiv *n*
~ digital volldigital
function Funktion *f*
~ call Funktionsaufruf *m*
~ key Funktionstaste *f*
~ memory Funktionsspeicher *m*
~ selection Betriebsartenwahl *m*
~ symbol Funktionssymbol *n*
functional calculus Prädikatenkalkül *n*
~ diagram Funktionalbild *n*
~ imaging funktionelle Bildgebung *f*, Funktionsuntersuchung *f*
~ MRI (magnetic resonance imaging) funktionelle Magnetresonanztomografie (Kernspintomografie) *f*
~ scintigraphy Funktionsszintigrafie *f*
fundamental difference Fundamentaldifferenz *f*
~ frequency Grundfrequenz *f*
~ law of photometry fotometrisches Grundgesetz *n*, fotometrisches (quadratisches) Entfernungsgesetz *n*, Abstandsquadratgesetz *n*
~ mode Grundmode *f (Laser)*
~ period fundamentale Periode *f (Signalverarbeitung)*
fundoscopic *s.* funduscopic
fundus Augenhintergrund *m*, Augenrückwand *f*
~ camera Funduskamera *f*, Netzhautkamera *f*, Retinakamera *f*
~ photography Fundusfotografie *f*
funduscopic fundoskopisch
funduscopy Fundoskopie *f*
fungal (fungi) attack Pilzbefall *m (z.B. von Filmmaterial)*
fungicide Fungizid *n (Entwicklerzusatz)*
funnel Trichter *m*
furry windscreen Fell-Windschutz *m*, Windschutzhülle *f (Mikrofon)*
fused quartz, ~ silica [glass] Quarzglas *n*, Kieselglas *n*
fuser roll[er] Heizrolle *f*, Heizwalze *f*, Fixierwalze *f*, Wärmefixierwalze *f (Elektrofotografie)*
fusing Aufschmelzen *n (von Tonerpulver auf Papier)*
fusion Fusion *f*, Verschmelzung *f*
~ frequency Verschmelzungsfrequenz *f*, Flimmerverschmelzungsfrequenz *f*
fusional area Panum-Raum *m*, Panum-Areal *n (binokulares Sehen)*
fuzzification Fuzzifizierung *f*, Fuzzifikation *f*
fuzzify/to fuzzifizieren

fuzziness Unschärfe *f*
fuzzy unscharf
~ classifier unscharfer Klassifikator *m*
~ cluster unscharfer Cluster *m*
~ cluster analysis Fuzzy-Clusteranalyse *f*
~ connectedness unscharfer Zusammenhang *m (z.B. von Volumenelementen)*
~ filter Fuzzy-Filter *n*
~ Hough transform unscharfe Hough-Transformation *f (Bildsegmentierung)*
~ image unscharfes Bild *n*
~ logic Fuzzy-Logik *f*, unscharfe (kontinuierlichwertige) Logik *f*
~ object unscharfes Objekt *n*
~ operator Fuzzy-Operator *m*
~ photo unscharfes Foto *n*; verwackeltes Foto *n*
~ rule Fuzzy-Regel *f*
~ segmentation unscharfe Segmentierung *f*
~ set Fuzzy-Menge *f*, unscharfe Menge *f*
~ set theory Fuzzy-Theorie *f*, Theorie *f* unscharfer Mengen
~ shadow weicher Schatten *m*
~ system Fuzzy-System *n*
~ technique Fuzzy-Technik *f*
~ union unscharfe Vereinigung *f*

G

G bar G-Strich *m*, mittlerer Gradient *m* *(Densitometrie)*
g-line g-Linie *f (Leiterplattenherstellung)*
GaAs laser GaAs-Laser *m*, Galliumarsenidlaser *m*
~ **photodiode** Galliumarsenid-Fotodiode *f*
Gabor analysis Gabor-Analyse *f (Binärbildverarbeitung)*
~ **filter** Gabor-Filter *n*
~ **filter bank** Gabor-Filterbank *f*
~ **function** Gabor-Funktion *f (Texturvisualisierung)*
~ **function filter** Wavelet-Filter *n*
~ **hologram** Einstrahlhologramm *n*
~ **texture** Gabor-Textur *f*
~ **wavelet** Gabor-Wavelet *n*
~ **wavelet transform** Gabor-Transformation *f*
Gabriel graph Gabriel-Graph *m (Mustererkennung)*
gadget Kleinzubehör *n*
~ **bag** Zubehörtasche *f*
gadolinium Gadolinium *n (Schwermetall)*
~ **diethylenetriamine pentaacetic acid** Gadolinium-DTPA *n (Röntgenkontrastmittel)*
gaffer Chefbeleuchter *m*, Oberbeleuchter *m (Filmarbeit)*
~ **tape** Lassoband *n*, Textilklebeband *n*
gain Signalverstärkung *f*, Verstärkung *f*; Gesamtverstärkung *f (Sonografie)*; Bildsignalverstärkung *f (Camcorder)*
~**-guided laser** gewinngeführter Laser *m*
~**-guided laser diode** verstärkungsgeführte Laserdiode *f*
~ **noise** Verstärkerrauschen *n*
galactography Galaktografie *f*
Galilean telescope Galilei-Fernrohr *n*, Galilei-Teleskop *n*, Holländisches Fernrohr *n*
gallery camera Einraumkamera *f*, Horizontalkamera *f (Reprografie)*
galley 1. Setzschiff *n*; 2. *s.* ~ proof
~ **proof** Druckfahne *f*, Korrekturfahne *f*, Fahne *f*, Fahnenabzug *m*
gallic acid Gallussäure *f*
gallium arsenide field effect transistor Galliumarsenid-Feldeffekttransistor *m*
~ **arsenide photodiode** Galliumarsenid-Fotodiode *f*
~ **arsenide semiconductor laser** GaAs-Laser *m*
~ **nitride laser** Galliumnitridlaser *m*
~ **phosphide** Galliumphosphid *n*
galvanography Galvanografie *f*
galvanometer Galvanometer *n*
game character Computerspielfigur *f*
~ **console** Spiel[e]konsole *f*, Videospielkonsole *f*, Telespielkonsole *f*
~ **designer** Spieledesigner *m*
~ **developer** Spieleentwickler *m*
~ **graphics** Computerspielgrafik *f*
~ **programming** Spieleprogrammierung *f*
gamma *s.* ~ value
~ **adjustment** 1. Gammawertanpassung *f*; 2. *s.* ~ correction
~ **calculation** Gammawertberechnung *f*
~ **camera** [Einkristall-]Gammakamera *f*, Szintillationskamera *f*, Anger-Kamera *f*
~ **camera image (picture)** Gamma[kamera]aufnahme *f*
~ **characteristic** Gammakurve *f*, Gammakennlinie *f (z.B. einer Elektronenstrahlbildröhre)*
~**-corrected luminance** gammakorrigierte Luminanz *f*
~**-corrected signal** gammakorrigiertes Signal *n*
~ **correction** Gammakorrektur *f*, Gammaschaltung *f*, Gradationsentzerrung *f (Videosignalverarbeitung)*
~ **correction algorithm** Gammakorrekturalgorithmus *m*
~ **correction factor** Gammakorrekturfaktor *m*
~ **correction table** Gammakorrekturtabelle *f*
~ **corrector** Gammakorrektor *m*
~ **densitometer** Gammadichtemesser *m*
~ **distortion** Gammaverzerrung *f*
~ **distribution** Gammaverteilung *f (von Zufallsvariablen)*
~ **error** Gammafehler *m*
~ **factor** *s.* ~ value
~ **function** *s.* ~ characteristic
~ **imaging Cerenkov telescope** Gammastrahlenteleskop *n*
~ **index** Kontrastindex *m*
~ **infinity** Gammagrenzwert *m*
~ **noise** Gammarauschen *n*, Erlang-Rauschen *n*
~ **quantum** Gammaquant *n*
~ **radiograph** Gammastrahlenbild *n*
~ **ray** Gammastrahl *m*
~ **ray beam** Gammastrahlenbündel *n*
~ **ray camera detector screen** Szintillationsschirm *m*
~ **ray detector** Gammadetektor *m*
~ **ray image (photograph)** Gammastrahlenbild *n*, Radiogramm *n*, Radiografie *f*, Strahlenbild *n*
~ **ray imaging** *s.* ~ ray radiography
~ **ray photon** Gammaquant *n*
~ **ray radiation** Gammastrahlung *f*
~ **ray radiography** Gammaradiografie *f*, Gammadurchstrahlung *f*
~ **ray spectrometer** Gammaspektrometer *n*
~ **ray spectrum** Gammaspektrum *n*

~ ray tomography
Gammastrahlentomografie f
~ spectroscopy
Gamma[strahlen]spektroskopie f
~-time curve Gamma-Zeit-Kurve f,
Zeit-Gamma-Kurve f
~ value Gammawert m, Gamma n,
Gradation f, Kontrast m (Densitometrie);
Bildröhrengamma n
gamut mapping Farbraumanpassung f
~ of colors Farb[raum]umfang m,
Farbbereich m, Farbpalette f (z.B. eines
Druckers)
gangliocyte s. ganglion cell
ganglion Ganglion n, Nervenknoten n
~ cell Ganglienzelle f, Ganglionzelle f (z.B.
der Netzhaut)
~ cell layer Ganglienzellschicht f
gantry Gantry f (Tomograf)
Gantt chart Gantt-Diagramm n
(Computergrafik)
gap depth Spalttiefe f
~ filler Füllsender m, Lückenfüllsender m,
Wiederholsender m (Fernsehen)
~ length Spaltlänge f
~ loss Spaltverlust m
~ width Spaltbreite f
garbling Schlüsselverwirrung f (Radar)
gas discharge Gasentladung f
~ discharge display
Gasentladungsbildschirm m,
Plasmabildschirm m, Plasmadisplay n
~ discharge lamp Gasentladungslampe f
~ discharge tube Gasentladungsröhre f
~ laser Gas[entladungs]laser m
~ plasma display Gasplasmabildschirm m
~ transport laser Gastransportlaser m
gaseous-burst agitation Durchsprudelung
f (Fotoverarbeitung)
gastroscope Gastroskop n, Magenspiegel
m
gastroscopic gastroskopisch
gastroscopy Gastroskopie f,
Magenspiegelung f
gate 1. Messtor n (Sonografie); 2. s. ~
electrode; 3. s. film gate; 4. s. camera
gate
~ circuit Gatterschaltung f
~ electrode Torelektrode f, Gate-Elektrode
f
~ line Abtastzeile f (Flüssigkristallanzeige)
~ positioning Filmfensterpositionierung f
~ weave seitlicher Bildstandsfehler m
gatefold 1. Ausklappbild n; 2. Fensterfalz m
gather/to zusammentragen, kollationieren
(Falzbögen)
gauss Gauß n (alte Maßeinheit der
magnetischen Induktion)
Gauss lens Gauß-Objektiv n, Gaußsches
Fernrohrobjektiv n
~ point s. nodal point
~-Seidel method Gauß-Seidel-Verfahren n
(zur Lösung linearer Gleichungen)
~-type lens Gauß-Typ-Objektiv n

Gaussian gaußförmig; gaußverteilt
~ aperture gaußförmige Apertur f
~ approximation Gaußsche
Approximation f
~ beam Gauß-Bündel n, Gauß-Strahl m,
Gaußscher Strahl m (Wellenoptik)
~ beam optics s. ~ optics
~ blur Gaußsche Unschärfe f
~ convolution Gauß-Faltung f
~ curvature Gaußsche Krümmung f
~ curve [Gaußsche] Glockenkurve f
(Normalverteilung)
~ density Gaußsche Dichte f
~-distributed gaußverteilt
~-distributed random variable
gaußverteilte Zufallsvariable f
~ distribution Gauß-Verteilung f,
Gaußsche Normalverteilung
(Amplitudendichteverteilung) f
~ edge Gaußsche Kante f
~ error distribution Gauß-Fehlerverteilung
f
~ error function [Gaußsche]
Fehlerfunktion f
~ filter Gauß-Filter n, Gauß-Maske f,
Gaußscher Weichzeichner m
~ filter function Gauß-Filterfunktion f
~ focal plane Gaußsche Brennebene f
~ function Gauß-Funktion f,
Gauß-Glocke[nkurve] f
~ highpass filter Gauß-Hochpass m
~ image Gaußsches Bild n, Gaußsche
Abbildung f
~ image formation Gaußsche (kollineare)
Abbildung f
~ image plane Gaußsche Bildebene f
~ image point Gaußscher Bildpunkt m
~ impulse function Gaußsche
Impulsfunktion f
~ intensity distribution Gaußsche
Intensitätsverteilung f
~ kernel s. ~ filter
~ lens equation (formula) Gaußsche
Linsengleichung f
~ low-pass filter Gauß-Tiefpass m,
Gaußsches Tiefpassfilter n
~ mode Grundmode f (Laser)
~ noise s. Gaussian-type noise
~ optics Gaußsche (paraxiale) Optik f,
Optik f des Paraxialgebietes, Optik f
erster Ordnung
~ plane Gaußsche Hauptebene f
~ pulse Gauß-Impuls m, Gaußsches Signal
n
~ pyramid Gauß-Pyramide f (lineare
Bildverarbeitung)
~ ray Gauß-Strahl m, Gaußscher Strahl m
~-shape function s. Gaussian function
~-shaped impulse response Gaußsche
Impulsantwort f
~ signal s. ~ pulse
~ smoothing kernel (operator) Gaußscher
Glättungskern (Glättungsoperator) m
~ spectrum gaußförmiges Spektrum n

Gaussian

~-**type noise** Gaußsches Rauschen n, Gauß-Rauschen n, gaußverteiltes (normalverteiltes) Rauschen n
~ **window** Gauß-Fenster n, Gaußsches Fenster n
gauze [filter] Gazefilter n *(Beleuchtungszubehör)*
gaze Blick m
~ **axis** Blickachse f
~ **duration** Blickdauer f
gear train Zahnräder-Hemmwerk n *(mechanischer Verschluss)*
geared center column Kurbelmittelsäule f *(Stativ)*
~ **head** Getriebe[neige]kopf m *(Stativ)*
Geiger-Müller [counting] tube Geiger-Müller-Zählrohr n, Geigerzähler m, Auslösezählrohr n *(Dosimetrie)*
~[-**Müller] counter** Geiger-Müller-Zähler m
gel 1. Gel n; 2. s. gelatin filter n
~ **coat** Lichthofschutzschicht f, Antihaloschicht f
gelatin Gelatine f
~-**base filter** s. gelatin filter
~-**based emulsion** Gelatineemulsion f
~ **binder** Gelatinebindemittel n
~ **bromide paper** Bromgelatinepapier n
~ **chloride printing-out paper** Chlorsilber-Gelatine-Emulsionspapier n, Aristopapier n
~-**coated** gelatinebeschichtet
~-**coated paper** gelatinebeschichtetes (gelatiniertes) Papier n
~ **coating** Gelatinebeschichtung f, Gelatineüberzug f, Gelatineschutzschicht f
~ **dye** Gelatinefarbstoff m
~ **effect** Gelatineeffekt m, Ross-Effekt m *(Fotoverarbeitung)*
~ **emulsion layer** Gelatineemulsionsschicht f
~ **film** Gelatinefolie f
~ **filter** Gelatinefilter n, Folienfilter n, Wratten-Filter n
~ **filter holder** Folienfilterhalter m
~ **hardening** Gelatinehärtung f
~-**hardening agent (compound)** Gelatinehärtungsmittel n
~ **interlayer** Gelatine-Zwischenschicht f
~ **layer** Gelatineschicht f
~ **matrix** Gelatinematrix f
~ **paper** Gelatineemulsionspapier n
~ **plate** Gelatineplatte f, Gelatinetrocken[bild]platte f
~ **process** Gelatineverfahren n
~ **relief [image]** Gelatinerelief n *(Druckverfahren der Farbfotografie)*
~-**silver bromide emulsion** Bromsilber-Gelatineemulsion f
~-**silver bromide glass dry plate** Bromsilber-Gelatine-Trockenplatte f, Bromsilber-Trockenplatte f auf Gelatinebasis

~-**silver chloride paper** Chlorsilber-Gelatine-Emulsionspapier n
~-**silver dry plate** s. gelatin plate
~ **silver print** Gelatinesilberabzug m, Silbergelatineabzug m
~ **solution** Gelatinelösung f
~ **swelling** Gelatinequellung f
gelatine s. gelatin
gelatinobromide Bromsilbergelatine f
gelatinochloride Chlorsilbergelatine f
general contrast Allgemeinkontrast m, Gesamtkontrast m
~ **lighting** Allgemeinbeleuchtung f
~ **photography** allgemeine Fotografie f
~ **point operation** allgemeine Punktoperation f
~-**purpose camera lens** Allzweckobjektiv n, Universalobjektiv n, Universaloptik f
~-**purpose collimator** Allzweckkollimator m *(Radiografie)*
~-**purpose developer** Normalentwickler m
~-**purpose film** Universalfilm m
~-**purpose filter** Universalfilter n, Allzweckfilter n
~-**purpose interface** GPI-Schnittstelle f
~-**purpose photography** Normalfotografie f
~-**purpose X-ray tube** Standardröntgenröhre f
generalized delta rule [for learning by backpropagation] Perzeptron-Lernregel f, generalisierte Deltaregel f *(Neuroinformatik)*
~ **drawing primitive** verallgemeinertes Darstellungselement n *(Computergrafik)*
generating [process] Vorschleifen n *(Linsenherstellung)*
generation Generation f
~[**al] loss** Kopierverlust m, Generationsverlust m
generative grammar generative Grammatik f
generic coding generische Codierung f
~ **model** generisches Modell n
genetic algorithm genetischer Algorithmus m *(stochastische Suche)*
Geneva cross Malteserkreuz n
~ **movement** Schrittschaltwerk n, Bildschrittschaltung f, Filmschaltwerk n, Filmfortschalteinrichtung f, Fortschaltmechanismus m
~ **wheel** Malteserscheibe f
genlock 1. Zentraltakt m; 2. s. ~ board; 3. s. sync generator
~ **board** PC-Video-Karte f, Genlock-Karte f *(zur Kombination von Video und Computergrafik)*
~ **device** PC-Video-Konverter m
geocoded data geocodierte Daten pl
geocoding Geocodierung f
geodesic s. geodetic[al]
~ **active contour** geodätische aktive Kontur f
geodesist Geodät m, Geometer m

geodesy Geodäsie f, Vermessungskunde f
geodetic geodätisch
~ **map** geodätische Karte f
~ **telescope** geodätisches Fernrohr n
geodetical geodätisch
geographic information system
  Geoinformationssystem n,
  geografisches Informationssystem n
~ **map** Landkarte f, geografische Karte f
geological map geologische Karte f
~ **photography** geologische Fotografie f
geometric geometrisch
~ **algebra** geometrische Algebra f
~ **average** geometrisches Mittel n
~ **blur** geometrische Unschärfe f
~ **camera calibration** geometrische
  Kamerakalibrierung f
~ **centroid of the area**
  Flächenschwerpunkt m
~ **classifier** geometrischer Klassifikator m
~ **continuity** geometrische Kontinuität f
~ **data structure** geometrische
  Datenstruktur f
~ **descriptor** geometrischer Deskriptor m
~ **distortion** geometrische Verzerrung f;
  Weitwinkelverzerrung f, Weitwinkeleffekt m
~ **distortion correction** geometrische
  Entzerrung f
~ **element** geometrisches Element n
~ **error** Geometriefehler m
~ **feature** geometrisches Merkmal n
~ **filter** geometrisches Filter n
~ **illumination model** geometrisches
  Beleuchtungsmodell n
~ **image** geometrisches Bild n
~ **image plane** geometrische Bildebene f
~ **image transformation** geometrische
  Bildtransformation f
~ **interpolation** geometrische
  Interpolation f
~ **map** nachbarschaftserhaltende
  (topologieerhaltende Abbildung f,
  Merkmalskarte f *(Mustererkennung)*
~ **mapping** geometrische Abbildung f
~ **mean** geometrisches Mittel n
~ **mean filter** geometrisches
  Mittelwertfilter n
~ **model** geometrisches Modell n
~ **modeling** geometrische Modellierung f,
  Geometriemodellierung f
~ **mosaicking** geometrische
  Mosaikbildung f
~ **object** geometrisches Objekt n
~ **object model** geometrisches
  Objektmodell n
~ **operator** geometrischer Operator m
~ **optics** geometrische Optik f,
  [geometrische] Strahlenoptik f
~ **perspective** geometrische Perspektive f
~ **primitive** geometrisches Primitiv n,
  geometrische Grundform f,
  [geometrisches] Elementarmuster n;
  Elementarobjekt n
~ **processing** geometrische Verarbeitung f
~ **projection** geometrische Projektion f
~ **redundancy** örtliche Redundanz f
~ **representation** geometrische
  Darstellung f
~ **resolution** geometrische Auflösung f
~ **scene reconstruction** geometrische
  Szenenrekonstruktion f
~ **transform[ation]** geometrische
  Transformation f
~ **unsharpness** geometrische (projektive)
  Unschärfe f
geometrical geometrisch
~ **aberration** geometrischer
  Abbildungsfehler (Fehler) m,
  geometrische Aberration f, Lagefehler m
~ **correction** geometrische Korrektur f
~ **horopter** geometrischer Horopter m
  (Abbildungsgeometrie)
~ **operation** geometrische Operation f
~-**optics** strahlenoptisch
~ **ray tracing** geometrische
  Strahlverfolgung f
geometrically deformed model
  geometrisch deformiertes Modell n
geometry Geometrie f
~-**based rendering** geometriebasiertes
  Rendering n *(Computergrafik)*
~ **compression** Geometriekompression f
~ **entity** Geometrieelement n
~ **of illumination** Beleuchtungsgeometrie f
~ **of stereo[psis]** Epipolargeometrie f
~ **of viewing** Betrachtungsgeometrie f
~ **processor** Geometrieprozessor m
geophysical tomography
  geophysikalische Tomografie f
georadar Georadar n,
  Bodendurchdringungsradar n,
  Oberflächendurchdringungsradar n
georeferencing Georeferenzierung f,
  absolute Entzerrung f *(Fotogrammetrie)*
geostationary meteorological satellite
  geostationärer Wettersatellit m
~ **(geosynchronous) satellite**
  geostationärer (geosynchroner) Satellit m
German [equatorial] mounting deutsche
  Montierung f *(Teleskop)*
germanium photoconductor
  Germanium-Fotoleiter m
Gestalt factor Gestaltfaktor m *(Sehen)*
gestalt information Gestaltinformation f
  (visuelle Wahrnehmung)
~ **law** Gestaltgesetz n
~ **psychology** Gestaltpsychologie f
~ **theory, gestaltism** Gestalttheorie f *(der
  menschlichen Wahrnehmung)*
gesture recognition Gestenerkennung f
getter Fangstoff m *(z.B. in
  Katodenstrahlröhren)*
ghost cancellation
  Geisterbildunterdrückung f
~ **echo** Geisterecho n *(Radar)*
~ **effect** s. ~ **image**

ghost 160

~ **halftone** s. ghosting 2.
~ **image** Geisterbild n, Phantombild n, Nebenbild n; überlagertes Fernsehbild n; Doppelkontur f
ghosting 1. Geisterbildentstehung f, Bildübersprechen n; 2. Geistereffekt m, Kontakterscheinung f *(Druckbildfehler)*; 3. s. ghost image
~ **artifact** s. ghost image
ghosts Systemrauschen n
giant format Großformat n
~ **screen** Großbildwand f, Riesenbildwand f, Riesenleinwand f
~ **screen theater** Großleinwandkino n
~ **telescope** Riesenradioteleskop n
~ **tripod** Großstativ n
Gibbs artifact Gibbs-Artefakt n, Gibbssches Phänomen n, Verstümmelungsartefakt n *(Bildverarbeitung)*
~ **distribution** Gibbs-Verteilung f, Gibbs-Zufallsfeld n *(Bildsegmentierung)*
~ **effect (phenomenon)** s. ~ artifact
GIF s. graphics interchange format
~ **file** GIF-Datei f
gigabyte Gigabyte n, Gb
gigahertz Gigahertz n, GHz
gigantic movie screen s. giant screen
gimbal [optical] mount kardanischer Optikhalter m
~ **head** Kugel[gelenk]kopf m, Kugelgelenk n, Kugelneiger m *(Stativ)*
Giroux camera Kastenkamera f
glacial acetic acid Eisessig m *(Unterbrecherbad)*
glamour photography Glamourfotografie f
glancing angle Glanzwinkel m
~ **incidence** schräger Einfall m
glare/to blenden
glare Blendung f; Spiegelung f, Spiegelreflexion f, spiegelnde Reflexion f
~ **angle** Blendwinkel m
~ **effect** Blendwirkung f
~ **filter** Entspiegelungsfolie f
~ **guard** Blendschutz[schirm] m *(Bildschirm)*
~ **index (number)** Blendungszahl f, Streulichtfaktor m
~ **reflection** Spiegelung f, Spiegelreflexion f, spiegelnde Reflexion f
~ **screen** Blendschutz[schirm] m *(Bildschirm)*
~ **stop [diaphragm]** Streulichtblende f
glaring light gleißendes (blendendes) Licht
glass Glas n
~-**beaded screen** Perl[lein]wand f; Kristallperlwand f
~ **blank** Glasrohling m
~ **block** Glasblock m
~ **catalog** Glaskatalog m
~ **ceramic** Glaskeramik f
~ **coverslip** Deckglas n, Deckgläschen n *(Mikroskopie)*

~ **envelope** Röhrenkolben m
~ **faceplate** Eintrittsfenster n
~ **filter** Glasfilter n, Massiv[glas]filter n
~ **formulation** Glasrezeptur f, Glaszusammensetzung f
~ **halftone screen** Glas[gravur]raster m(n), Distanzraster m(n)
~ **laminate** Glaslaminat n
~ **lens** Glaslinse f
~ **map** Glasdiagramm n
~ **melt** Glasschmelze f
~ **mirror** Glasspiegel m
~ **mount** Glas[dia]rahmen m, geglaster Diarahmen m
~-**mounted filter** s. glass filter
~-**mounted slide** Glasdia[positiv] n, glasgerahmtes (plangeglastes) Dia n
~ **negative** Glasnegativ n, Negativplatte f
~ **plate** Glasplatte f
~ **plate negative** Glasnegativ n, Negativplatte f
~ **prism** Glasprisma n
~ **screen** s. ~ halftone screen
~ **screen photography** Rasterfotografie f
~ **shot** Glas[vorsatz]aufnahme f, Spiegeltrick m *(Trickkinematografie)*
~ **slide** s. glass-mounted slide
~ **type** Glassorte f; Glastyp m
glasses Brille f
glassine Pergamin[papier] n
glassless [slide] mount glasloser Rahmen (Diarahmen) m
glazer Hochglanzpresse f
glint Glint m, Winkelfluktuation f *(Radar)*
glitch Störimpuls m *(Digital-Analog-Wandler)*
global algorithm globaler Algorithmus m
~ **binarization** globale Binarisierung f
~ **color correction** globale Farbkorrektur f
~ **coordinate system** Weltkoordinatensystem n, weltfestes Koordinatensystem n, Szenenkoordinatensystem n
~ **descriptor** globaler Deskriptor m
~ **feature** globales Merkmal n
~ **histogram** globales Histogramm n
~ **illumination** globale Beleuchtung f *(Computergrafik)*
~ **illumination algorithm** globaler Beleuchtungsalgorithmus m
~ **illumination model** globales Beleuchtungsmodell n
~ **motion analysis** globale Bewegungsanalyse f
~ **motion compensation** globale Bewegungskompensation f
~ **motion estimation** globale Bewegungsschätzung f
~ **motion representation** globale Bewegungsdarstellung f
~ **neighborhood operation** globale Nachbarschaftsoperation f
~ **operation** globale Operation f
~ **operator** globaler Operator m

~ **positioning system** [weltweites] Satellitennavigationssystem *n*, GPS *n*
~ **quantization** globale Quantisierung *f*
~ **radiation** Globalstrahlung *f*
~ **search** globale Suche *f (Bildcodierung)*
~ **shape feature** globales Formmerkmal *n*
~ **space** *s*. ~ coordinate system
~ **texture** globale Textur *f*
~ **thresholding** globale Schwellenwertbildung *f*
~ **transformation** globale Transformation *f*
gloss ink Glanzdruckfarbe *f*
glossy 1. glänzend; hochglänzend; 2. *s*. ~ print
~ **paper** Hochglanzpapier *n*, hochglänzendes (gussgestrichenes) Papier *n*
~ **print** Hochglanzfoto *n*, Hochglanzabzug *n*; Hochglanzkopie *f*
~ **surface** glänzende Oberfläche *f*
~**-surface paper** *s*. glossy paper
glove input device Datenhandschuh *m*, sensorischer Handschuh *m (Navigationswerkzeug)*
glow lamp Glimmlampe *f*
~ **time** Nachleuchtdauer *f*, Nachleuchtzeit *f (z.B. eines Fernsehbildschirms)*
glycerin[e], glycerol Glycerin *n*, Glycerol *n (Feuchthaltemittel)*
glycin Glycin *n (Entwicklersubstanz)*
glycol Ethylenglycol *n*
glyph Glyphe *f*; Schriftzeichen *n*, [typografisches] Zeichen *n*; grafisches Objekt *n (Visualisierung)*
gnomonic projection gnomonische Projektion *f (Kartennetzabbildung)*
goal-directed animation zielgerichtete Animation *f*
~**-directed motion** zielgerichtete Bewegung *f*, inverse Kinematik *f (Computeranimation)*
~ **image** Zielbild *n*
~ **node** Zielknoten *m (Graphenstruktur)*
gobo 1. Abdeckfahne *f*, Lichtblende *f*; Projektionsmaske *f*, Projektionsblende *f*; 2. Mikrofonhülle *f*
Golay cell Golay-Zelle *f*, Golay-Detektor *m (thermischer Detektor)*
gold and sulfur sensitization Gold-Schwefel-Reifung *f (fotografischer Prozess)*
~ **salt** Goldsalz *n*
~ **sensitization** Goldsensibilisierung *f*
~ **sensitizer** Goldsensibilisator *m*
~ **toner** Goldtoner *m*
~ **toning** Goldtonung *f*, Röteltonung *f*
Goldberg condition Goldberg-Bedingung *f*, Gammabedingung *f (Sensitometrie)*
~ **wedge** Goldberg-Keil *m*
golden ratio (section) goldener Schnitt *m*
golf ball printer Kugelkopfdrucker *m*
Golomb code Golomb-Code *m (Bilddatenkompression)*
goniometer Goniometer *n*

goniometric radiometer goniometrisches Radiometer *n*
~**[al]** goniometrisch
goniophotometer Goniofotometer *n*
goniophotometric goniofotometrisch
GOP *s*. group of pictures
gothic, Gothic Gotisch *f*, serifenlose Linearantiqua *f (Schriftgattung)*
Gouraud shading Gouraud-Schattierung *f (Computergrafik)*
GPR *s*. ground-penetrating radar
GPS *s*. global positioning system
gradation Gradation *f*, Härtegrad *m*, Kontrastfaktor *m*; Leuchtdichteabstufung *f*
~ **level** Gradationsstufe *f*
graded-index medium inhomogenes Medium *n*
~**-index optical fiber** Gradientenfaser *f*
~**-index optics** Gradientenoptik *f*
~ **paper** Gradationspapier *n*, gradationsfestes Papier *n*
~ **reflectance micromirror** Mikro-Gradientenspiegel *m*
gradient Gradient *m*
~ **amplifier** Gradientenverstärker *m (Magnetresonanzbildgebung)*
~ **amplitude** Gradientenamplitude *f*
~ **analysis** Gradientenanalyse *f*
~**-based edge detection** gradientenbasierte Kantendetektion *f*
~**-based search** gradientenbasierte Suche *f*
~ **coil** Gradientenspule *f (Magnetresonanzbildgebung)*
~ **descent** Gradientenabstieg *m*
~ **descent method (procedure)** Gradientenabstiegsmethode *f*, Gradientenabstiegsverfahren *n*
~ **detector** Gradientendetektor *m*
~ **direction** Gradientenrichtung *f*, Gradientenorientierung *f*
~ **echo** Gradientenecho *n*
~ **echo image** Gradientenechobild *n*
~ **echo pulse sequence** Gradientenechosequenz *f*
~ **estimation** Gradientenschätzung *f*
~ **filter** Gradientenfilter *m*
~ **illusion** Gradiententäuschung *f (optische Täuschung)*
~ **image** Gradientenbetragsbild *n*, Gradientenbild *n*
~ **index glass** Gradientenindexglas *n*
~ **index micro lens** Gradientenindex-Mikrolinse *f*
~ **magnetic field** [magnetisches] Gradientenfeld *n*
~ **magnitude** Gradientenbetrag *m*
~ **moment nulling** *s*. flow compensation
~ **operator** Gradientenoperator *m*, Nabla-Operator *m*
~ **pulse** Gradientenpuls *m*
~ **quantization** Gradientenquantisierung *f*

gradient 162

~-recalled (gradient-refocused) echo
Gradientenecho *n*
~ **refocusing** Gradientenrefokussierung *f*
~ **shading** Gradientenschattierung *f*, Grauwertgradientenschattierung *f*
~ **space** Gradientenraum *m*
~ **value** Gradientenbetrag *m*
~ **vector** Gradientenvektor *m*
grading Filmlichtbestimmung f, Farb[licht]bestimmung *f*, Lichtbestimmung *f*, Farbkorrektur *f*
~ **card** Lichtkarte *f*, Kopierkarte *f* *(Filmkopierung)*
~ **function** Gradationsfunktion *f*
~ **print** Nullkopie *f*, Erstkopie *f* *(Kinematografie)*
gradiometer Gradiometer *n*
gradual transition allmählicher Übergang *m*
graduate Messzylinder *m*, Messglas *n*, Messgefäß *n*, Mensur *f*
graduated circle Teilkreis *m*
~ **cylinder** *s.* graduate
~ **dial** Teilkreis *m*
~ **filter** Verlauffilter *n*
grain Korn *n*, Emulsionskristall *m* *(Silberfotografie)*
~ **cluster** Kornzusammenballung *f*
~ **direction** Papierlaufrichtung *f*, Maschinenrichtung *f*, Laufrichtung *f (Druck)*; Faserrichtung *f (in Druckpapier)*
~ **growth** Kornvergrößerung *f*
~ **long paper** Schmalbahnpapier *n (Druck)*
~ **noise** Kornrauschen *n*, Granularrauschen *n*
~ **ripening** Kornreifung *f*
~ **short paper** Breitbahnpapier *n*
~ **size** Korngröße *f*
~ **size distribution** Korngrößenverteilung *f*
~ **structure** Kornstruktur *f*
~ **surface** Kornoberfläche *f*
~ **volume** Kornvolumen *n*
grained screen Kornraster *m(n)* *(Reprografie)*
grainfree image kornloses Bild *n*
graininess Körnigkeit *f*
grainless kornlos
grainy image körniges Bild *n*
gram-atom, gram-atomic weight (mass) Grammatom *n*
~-molecular weight (mass), gram-molecule Grammmolekül *n*, Mol *n*
grammage Papierflächengewicht *n*, Papierflächenmasse *f*, flächenbezogene Masse *f*, Quadratmetergewicht *n*
grammar Grammatik *f*, syntaktische Darstellung *f (Bildbeschreibung)*
grams per square meter *s.* grammage
granular image körniges Bild *n*
~ **noise, ~ quantization noise** Kornrauschen *n*, Granularrauschen *n*
~ **structure** Kornstruktur *f*
granularity Körnung *f*
~ **level** Körnungswert *m*

graph/to grafisch darstellen, zeichnen
graph 1. Graph *m*; 2. grafisches Bild *n*, grafische Darstellung *f*
~ **algorithm** Graph-Algorithmus *n*
~ **paper** Millimeterpapier *n*
~ **representation** Graphendarstellung *f*, Graphbild *n*
~ **search[ing]** Graphsuche *f*
~-theoretic graphentheoretisch
~ **theory** Graphentheorie *f*
~ **transformation** Graphtransformation *f*
grapheme Graphem *n*
graphic Grafik *f*, grafische Darstellung *f*; grafisches Produkt (Erzeugnis) *n*
~ grafisch *(s.a. unter graphical)*
~ **arts** Druckgewerbe *n*, Polygrafie *f*, Druckkunst *f*
~ **arts camera** Repro[duktions]kamera *f*
~ **arts drum scanner** Grafikscanner *m*
~ **arts film** Druckfilm *m*, [litho]grafischer Film *m*, Lithfilm *m*; Kunstdruckfilm *m*
~ **arts halftone dot** Rasterbildpunkt *m*
~ **arts industry** Druckindustrie *f*
~ **arts photography** Repro[duktions]fotografie *f (s.a.* photomechanical reproduction)
~ **arts printing** Kunstdruck *m*
~-based computer operating system Grafikbetriebssystem *n*
~ **character** Schriftzeichen *n*
~ **design** Grafikdesign *n*, Grafikgestaltung *f*
~-design profession grafisches Gewerbe *n*
~ **designer** Grafikdesigner *m*
~ **display** Grafikbildschirm *m*, grafikfähiger Bildschirm *m*
~ **drawing program** Zeichenprogramm *n*
~ **element** Grafikelement *n*
~ **file format** Bilddateiformat *n*
~ **interchange format** Grafik-Austauschformat *n*
~-object recognition Grafikerkennung *f*
~ **paper** Feinpapier *n*, holzfreies Papier *n*; grafisches Papier *n*
~ **pointing device** Zeigegerät *n*
~ **presentation** Grafikdarstellung *f*, grafische Darstellung *f*
~ **production tool** Grafikwerkzeug *n*
~ **scanner** Grafikscanner *m*
~ **slide** Grafikdia[positiv] *n*
~ **technology** Drucktechnik *f*
graphical grafisch
~ **block diagram** Blockdiagramm *n*; Blockschaltbild *n*
~ **code** grafischer Code *m*
~ **compiler** Grafikcompiler *m*
~ **convolution** grafische Faltung *f*
~ **data** Grafikdaten *pl*, grafische Daten *pl*
~ **depiction** grafische Darstellung *f*, Grafikdarstellung *f*
~ **development environment** grafische Entwicklungsumgebung *f*
~ **device interface** grafische Geräteschnittstelle *f*
~ **display** *s.* graphics display

~ **editor** Grafikeditor *m*
~ **front-end** *s.* ~ interface
~ **icon** Icon *n*, Grafiksymbol *n*; Bildsymbol *n*, Bildzeichen *n*
~ **image** grafisches Bild *n*, grafische Abbildung *f*
~ **information** grafische Information *f*
~ **input device** grafisches Eingabegerät *n*
~ **interface** Grafikschnittstelle *f*, grafische Schnittstelle (Benutzerschnittstelle) *f*
~ **kernel system** grafisches Kernsystem *n*
~ **modeling** grafische Modellierung *f*
~ **object** Grafikobjekt *n*, grafisches Objekt *n*
~ **operating system** Grafikbetriebssystem *n*
~ **output** Grafikausgabe *f*
~ **output device** grafisches Ausgabegerät *n*
~ **performance (power)** Grafikleistung *f* *(eines Rechners)*
~ **primitive element** *s.* graphics primitive
~ **programming** Grafikprogrammierung *f*
~ **ray trace** Strahldurchzeichnung *f*
~ **representation** grafische Darstellung *f*, Grafikdarstellung *f*
~ **resolution** Grafikauflösung *f*
~ **symbol** *s.* ~ icon
~ **tool** Grafikwerkzeug *n*
~ **user interface** *s.* ~ interface
~ **workstation** grafische Arbeitsstation *f*
graphics Grafik *f*
~ **acceleration** Grafikbeschleunigung *f*
~ **accelerator [card]** Grafikbeschleuniger *m*, Beschleunigerkarte *f*, Beschleunigungskarte *f*
~ **adapter** *s.* ~ display card
~ **algorithm** Grafikalgorithmus *m*, Computergrafikalgorithmus *m*
~ **application** Grafikanwendung *f*
~ **application program** Grafikanwendungsprogramm *n*
~ **architecture** Grafikarchitektur *f*
~-**based software** *s.* graphics software
~ **board** *s.* ~ display card
~ **bus** Videobus *m*
~ **capability** Grafikfähigkeit *f* *(z.B. eines Computers)*
~ **card** *s.* ~ display card
~ **card memory** Grafik[karten]speicher *m*, Videospeicher *m*
~-**card performance** Grafikleistung *f* *(eines Rechners)*
~ **chip** Grafikchip *m*, Grafikprozessor *m*
~ **command** Grafikbefehl *m*
~ **computer** Grafikrechner *m*, Grafikcomputer *m*
~ **computer workstation** *s.* ~ workstation
~ **controller** Bildsteuereinheit *f*, Grafik-Controller *f* *(s.a.* ~ display card*)*
~ **controller interface** Grafikschnittstelle *f*, grafische Schnittstelle (Benutzerschnittstelle) *f*
~ **data** Grafikdaten *pl*, grafische Daten *pl*
~ **device** grafisches Gerät *n*

~ **display** Grafikdisplay *n*, grafikfähiges (grafisches) Display *n*; grafische Anzeige *f*; Grafikbildschirm *m*; Grafikmonitor *m*
~ **display card** [PC-]Grafikkarte *f*, Bildschirmkarte *f*, Grafikadapter *m*
~ **display controller** *s.* ~ controller
~ **display hardware** Grafikhardware *f*
~ **display screen** *s.* ~ display
~ **file** Grafikdatei *f*
~ **file format,** ~ **format** Grafik[datei]format *n*
~ **function** Grafikfunktion *f*
~ **image file** Bild[dokument]datei *f*
~ **instruction** Grafikbefehl *m*
~ **interchange format** GIF-Grafikformat *n*
~ **interchange format file** GIF-Datei *f*
~ **language** grafische Symbolsprache *f*, Grafiksprache *f*
~ **library** Grafikbibliothek *f*, Grafikdatenbank *f*
~ **mode** Grafikmodus *m*
~ **modeling** Grafikmodellierung *f*
~ **package** Grafikpaket *n*
~ **primitive** Grafikprimitiv *n*, grafisches Primitiv (Grundelement) *n*, [grafisches] Darstellungselement *n*
~ **printer** Grafikdrucker *m*, grafikfähiger Drucker *m*
~ **processing** Grafikverarbeitung *f*
~ **processor** Grafikprozessor *m*, Grafikchip *m*
~ **program** Grafikprogramm *n*
~ **programmer** Grafikprogrammierer *m*
~ **recognition** Grafikerkennung *f*
~ **screen** *s.* ~ display
~ **software** Grafiksoftware *f*, grafische Software *f*
~ **standard** Grafikstandard *m*
~ **system** Grafiksystem *n*
~ **tablet** Grafiktablett *n*, Eingabetablett *n*, grafisches Tablett *n*, Digitalisiertablett *n*
~ **transformation** Grafiktransformation *f*
~ **workstation** Grafikarbeitsplatz[rechner] *m*, grafischer Arbeitsplatz (Computerarbeitsplatz) *m*
Grassman's laws [of additive color mixture] Grassmannsche Gesetze *npl (Farbmetrik)*
gratic[u]le Strichgitter *n*, Rechteckgitter *n*; Gitternetz *n*; Retikel *n*, Strichplatte *f*, Netzgitterraster *m(n) (Optik)*
grating Gitter *n (s.a. unter* grid*,* lattice*,* mesh*)*
~ **aperture** Gitteröffnung *f*
~ **array** Gitteranordnung *f*
~ **efficiency** Gitterausbeute *f*
~ **equation** Gittergleichung *f*
~ **frequency** Gitterfrequenz *f*
~ **geometry** Gittergeometrie *f*
~ **imperfection** Gitterfehler *m*
~ **line** Gitterlinie *f*
~ **lobe** Rasterkeule *f*, sekundäre Nebenkeule *f (Radar)*
~ **order** Gitterordnung *f*

grating

~ **pattern** Gittermuster *n*
~ **prism** Gitterprisma *n*, Grisma *n* *(Astrospektroskopie)*
~ **profile** Gitterprofil *n*
~ **spectrograph** Gitterspektrograf *m*
~ **theory** Gittertheorie *f*
~ **vector** Gittervektor *m*
gravure *s.* 1. ~ printing; 2. photogravure
~ **cell** Tiefdrucknäpfchen *n*
~ **crosshatch screen** Tiefdruckraster *m(n)*
~ **cylinder** Tiefdruck[form]zylinder *m*, Rasterwalze *f*
~ **cylinder etching** Tiefdruckzylinderätzung *f*
~ **etching** Tiefdruckätzung *f*
~ **image** Tiefdruckbild *n*
~ **ink** Tiefdruckfarbe *f*
~ **machine** Tiefdruckmaschine *f*
~ **packaging press** Verpackungstiefdruckmaschine *f*
~ **plate** Tiefdruckplatte *f*
~ **prepress** Tiefdruckvorstufe *f*
~ **print** Tiefdruck *m (Erzeugnis)*
~ **printing** [konventioneller] Tiefdruck *m*, tiefenvariabler Tiefdruck *m*; Rakeltiefdruck *m*
~ **printing cylinder** *s.* ~ cylinder
~ **printing press** Tiefdruckpresse *f*
~ **printing process** Tiefdruckverfahren *n*
~ **proof** Tiefdruckproof *m*
~ **screen** Tiefdruckraster *m(n)*
gray Gray *n*, Gy *(SI-Einheit der Strahlungsenergiedosis)*
~ **balance** Graubalance *f*; Grauabgleich *m*
~ **board** *s.* ~ card
~ **body** Grauer Strahler *m*
~ **card** Graukarte *f*
Gray code Gray-Code *m (Fernsehen)*
gray component removal (replacement) Unbuntaufbau *m*, Graustufenersatz *m (Reprografie; s.a.* undercolor removal*)*
~ **filter** Graufilter *n*, Neutral[dichte]filter *n*, Dichtefilter *n*, Lichtreduktionsfilter *n*
~ **fog** Grauschleier *m*
~ **level** Grau[wert]wertstufe *f*
~-**level** ... *s.a. unter* gray-scale..., gray-value...
~-**level allocation** Grauwertzuordnung *f*
~-**level amplitude** Grauwertamplitude *f*
~-**level assignment** Grauwertzuordnung *f*
~-**level change** Grauwertänderung *f*
~-**level co-occurence matrix** Grauwertabhängigkeitsmatrix *f*, Grauwertübergangsmatrix *f*, Paarhäufigkeitsmatrix *f*
~-**level content** Grauwertgehalt *m*
~-**level difference** Grauwertdifferenz *f*
~-**level discontinuity** Grauwertdiskontinuität *f*
~-**level distribution** Grauwertverteilung *f*
~-**level dynamics** Grauwertdynamik *f*
~-**level gradient shading** Grauwertgradientenschattierung *f*, Gradientenschattierung *f*

~-**level image** Grau[wert]bild *n*, Graustufenbild *n*
~-**level image compression** Grauwertbildkompression *f*
~-**level image filter** Grauwertbildfilter *n*
~-**level interpolation** Grauwertinterpolation *f*
~-**level interval** Grauwertintervall *n*
~-**level mathematical morphology** Grauwertmorphologie *f*
~-**level median filter** Grauwert-Medianfilter *n*
~-**level modification** Grauwertmodifikation *f*, einstellige Operation *f*, Punktoperation *f (Pixelverarbeitung)*
~-**level pixel** Grauwertpixel *n*
~-**level profile** Grauwertprofil *n*
~-**level quantization** Grauwertquantisierung *f*
~-**level range** Grauwertbereich *m*
~-**level region** Grauwertbereich *m*
~-**level resolution** Grauwertauflösung *f*
~-**level rounding** Grauwertrundung *f*
~-**level scale** Grauskala *f*
~-**level scaling** Grauwertskalierung *f*
~-**level statistics** Grauwertstatistik *f*, Graubildstatistik *f*
~-**level threshold** Grau[wert]schwelle *f*
~-**level transition** Grauwertübergang *m*, Grauwertübergangsgebiet *n*
~-**level variance** Grauwertvarianz *f*
~ **line** Unbuntgerade *f*, Unbuntachse *f*
~ **midtone** mittlerer Grauwert *m*, Grauton *m*
~ **pattern** Grau[wert]bild *n*
~ **pixel value** Pixelgrauwert *m*
~ **range** Grauwertbereich *m*
~ **rendition** Grauwertdarstellung *f*
~ **scale** Grauskala *f*
~-**scale** ... *s.a. unter* gray-level..., gray-value...
~-**scale chart** Graubalkendiagramm *n*
~-**scale code** Grauwertcode *m*
~-**scale component** Grauwertkomponente *f*
~-**scale contouring** Grauwertkonturierung *f*
~-**scale depth** Grauwerttiefe *f*
~-**scale device** Graustufengerät *n*
~-**scale digital image** *s.* ~ image
~-**scale dilation** Grauwertdilatation *f*
~-**scale edge** Grauwertkante *f*
~-**scale edge detection** Grauwertkantendetektion *f*
~-**scale encoding** Grauwertcodierung *f*
~-**scale equalization** Grauwertäqualisation *f*, Grauwertäqualisierung *f*
~-**scale erosion** Grauwerterosion *f*
~-**scale histogram** Grauwerthistogramm *n*
~-**scale image** Grau[wert]bild *n*, Graustufenbild *n*; Halbtonbild *n*
~-**scale image analysis** Graustufenanalyse *f*, Halbtonbildanalyse *f*

grip

~-scale image processing Grau[wert]bildverarbeitung f, Grauwertverarbeitung f
~-scale intensity Grauwertintensität f
~-scale intensity value Grau[stufen]wert m, Dunkelwert m
~-scale morphology Grauwertmorphologie f
~-scale processing s. ~ image processing
~-scale rendition (reproduction) Grauwertwiedergabe f, Grauwertreproduktion f, Tonwertwiedergabe f, Tonreproduktion f
~-scale shading Grauwertschattierung f
~-scale skeletonization Grauwertskelettierung f
~-scale spread Grauwertintervall n
~-scale step Grau[wert]stufe f
~-scale threshold Intensitätsschwelle f
~-scale value Grau[stufen]wert m, Dunkelwert m (s.a. unter gray-value)
~-scale variation Grauwertvariation f
~-scale video signal Schwarzweiß[video]signal n, Bildhelligkeitssignal n (s.a. composite video signal)
~-scale wedge Graukeil m, Stufengraukeil m
~ screen Grauraster m(n)
~ shade Grauton m, Grauabstufung f
~-shaded color vergraute Farbe f
~ shading Vergrauung f
~ step Grau[wert]stufe f
~ step wedge Grau[stufen]keil m, Stufengraukeil m, Grauskala f
~-stepped scale Grauskala f
~ tone Grauton m
~ tone value, ~ value s. gray-scale value
~-value agglomeration Grauwertagglomeration f
~-value change Grauwertveränderung f
~-value difference Grauwertunterschied m
~-value evaluation Grauwertauswertung f
~-value gradient Grauwertgradient m
~-value image Grau[wert]bild n
~-value matrix Grauwertmatrix f
~-value transformation Grauwerttransformation f
graymap Grautonbild n
graze (grazing) angle streifender Winkel m
grazing incidence streifender Einfall m
grease pencil Fettstift m
~-receptive fettfreundlich, oleophil
~-repellent fettabweisend, oleophob
~-spot [photo]meter Fettfleckfotometer n, Bunsen-Fotometer f
greasy crayon Fettstift m
~ ink dick[flüssig]e Druckfarbe f
greedy algorithm Greedy-Algorithmus m, gieriger Algorithmus m (kombinatorische Optimierung; Computergrafik)
green Grün n (Grundfarbe)
~ beam Grünstrahl m (Farbbildröhre)
~ bias Grünstich m
~-blind grünblind, deuteranop
~ blindness Grünblindheit f, Deuteranopie f (Farbsinnstörung)
~ cast Grünstich m
~ channel Grünkanal m
~ film frische Kopie f (Kinefilm)
~ light filter Grünfilter n
~ light record, ~ record Grünauszug m, Grünteilbild n (Farbfotografie)
~ light sensitivity Grünempfindlichkeit f
~-sensitive emulsion grünempfindliche (orthochromatische) Emulsion f (Farbfotografie)
~-sensitive layer grünempfindliche Schicht f
greeting card paper Grußkartenpapier n
~ card printing Grußkartendruck m
Gregorian[-type] telescope Gregory-System n, Gregory-Teleskop n
grenz rays Grenzstrahlen mpl
grey s. gray
grid 1. Gitter n (s.a. unter grating, lattice, mesh); 2. Raster m(n); Gestaltungsraster m(n) (Typografie); 3. Netz n (z.B. von Fernsehstationen); 4. Beleuchterbrücke f (Film)
~ block Gitterblock m
~ cell Gitterzelle f
~ electrode Gitterelektrode f (Katodenstrahlröhre)
~ element spacing Rasterabstand m (Druck)
~ field Rasterfeld n (Typografie)
~ file Gitterdatei f (als Datenstruktur in der Bildsuche)
~ line Gitterlinie f
~-line intersection Gitterlinienschnittpunkt m
~ lines Gitternetz n
~ map Rasterkarte f
~ mask Gittermaske f
~ node Gitterknoten m
~ of lines Gitternetz n
~ of points Punktgitter n
~ pattern Gittermuster n
~ point Gitter[schnitt]punkt m; Stützpunkt m, Stützstelle f
~ scan order Abtastreihenfolge f
~ spacing Gitterabstand m
~ square Gitterquadrat n
~ system Rastersystem n (Typografie)
~ topology Gittertopologie f
~ vector Gittervektor m
~ voltage Gitterspannung f (Katodenstrahlröhre)
~ X-ray tube gittergesteuerte Röntgenröhre f
gridded cassette Rasterkassette f (Radiografie)
grille Schattenmaske f (Farbbildröhre)
grinding block Linsentragkörper m, Tragkörper m (Linsenfertigung)
grip Atelierarbeiter m

grip 166

~ **tape** Lassoband n, Textilklebeband n
~-**type flash** Stabblitz[licht]gerät n
gripper edge Greiferkante f, Greiferrand m (Bogendruck)
groove Fußrille f (einer Letter)
grooveless video disk rillenlose Bildplatte f
gross fog Grundschleier m
grotesque Grotesk f, serifenlose Linearantiqua f, Endstrichlose f (Schriftgattung)
Grothus-Draper law Grothus-Drapersches Gesetz n (Fotochemie)
ground attenuation Bodendämpfung f (Radar)
~-**based radar** Bodenradar n
~-**based receiving station** Erdefunkstelle f, [empfangende] Bodenstation f (Datenübertragung)
~-**based telescope** terrestrisches Fernrohr n, Erdfernrohr n, erdgebundenes Teleskop n
~ **clutter** Bodenclutter m, Bodenecho n (Radar)
~ **clutter map** Bodenclutterkarte f
~ **control point** Bodenkontrollpunkt m, Passpunkt m (Fernerkundung)
~ **coordinate system** Geländekoordinatensystem n
~ **glass** Einstellmattscheibe f
~-**glass focusing screen** Mattscheibe f, Einstell[matt]scheibe f, Sucherscheibe f
~-**glass image** Mattscheibenbild n
~-**glass plane** Mattscheibenebene f
~-**glass viewfinder** Mattscheibensucher m
~ **laser locator designator** lasergestütztes Zielzuweisungsgerät n
~-**mapping radar** Geländemessradar n
~ **noise** Grundrauschen n
~-**penetrating radar** Bodendurchdringungsradar n, Oberflächendurchdringungsradar n, Georadar n
~ **photograph** terrestrisches Messbild n
~ **point** Bodenkontrollpunkt m (Fernerkundung)
~ **radar** Bodenradar n
~ **range** Horizontalentfernung f (Radar)
~ **resolution** Bodenauflösung f
~ **station** s. ground-based receiving station
~ **swath** Bodenstreifen m (Aerofotogrammetrie, Radar)
~ **track** Flugweg m über Grund, Überflugsbahn f (Luftbildaufnahme)
~-**wave radar** Bodenwellenradar n
groundwood paper holzhaltiges Papier n
group code Gruppencode m (algebraische Codierung)
~ **coding** Gruppencodierung f
~ **delay** Gruppenverzögerung f, Gruppenlaufzeit f (Signalverarbeitung)
~ **node** Gruppierungsknoten m
~ **of blocks** Blockgruppe f
~ **of frames** s. ~ of pictures

~ **of pictures** Bild[er]gruppe f (z.B. als Datenstruktur der MPEG-Kompression)
~ **of pixels** Pixelgruppe f
~ **operator** Gruppenoperator m
~ **picture** Gruppenbild n
~ **portrait** Gruppenporträt n
~ **shot** Gruppenaufnahme f
~ **velocity** Gruppengeschwindigkeit f (Wellenphysik)
grouping of screens Bildschirminstallation f
guard band 1. Schutzband n (Fernsehübertragung); 2. Rasen m (Videoband)
guess Schätzwert m
GUI s. graphical user interface
guidance Zielführung f
~ **radar** Lenkradar n
guide number Leitzahl f, Blitzleitzahl f
~ **pin** Führungsstift m
~ **rail** Führungsschiene f; Andruckschiene f
~ **roller** Führungsrolle f; Laufrolle f; Umlenkrolle f
~ **wire** Führungsdraht m Angiografie)
guided edge Führungskante f, Anlagekante f
guidescope Leitfernrohr n (Astrofotografie)
guiding Nachführung f (Astrofotografie)
~ **beam** Leitstrahl m
~ **correction** Nachführkorrektur f
guillotine cutter Hebelschneidemaschine f
~ **splicer** Stumpfklebepresse f (für Filmmaterial)
~ **trimmer** Hebelschneidemaschine n
gum acacia (arabic) Gummiarabikum n, Akaziengummi n
~ **bichromate [printing] process** Gummi-Bichromat-Verfahren n
~ **bichromate print** Gummidruck m
~ **print process** Gummidruckverfahren n
gun pod Schulterstütze f (Kamerazubehör)
~ **scope** s. gunsight
guncotton Schießbaumwolle f
gunsight Gewehrzielfernrohr n, Zielfernrohr n
Gurney-Mott theory Gurney-Mott-Theorie f (der Latentbildentstehung)
gutter Bundsteg m, Papierrand m innen (Layout)
~ **bleed (jump)** angeschnittenes Bild n, [rand]abfallendes Bild n (Layout)
gyro s. gyroscope
~ **head** Kreiselkopf m (Stativ)
gyromagnetic precession gyromagnetische Präzession f (Kernspinresonanz)
~ **ratio** gyromagnetisches Verhältnis n
gyroscope 1. Gyroskop n, Kreiselkompass m; 2. s. gyrostabilizer
gyroscopic gyroskopisch
gyrostabilizer, gyrostat Kreiselstabilisator m

H

H unit s. Hounsfield unit
Haar transform Haar-Transformation f *(Bildcodierung)*
~ **wavelet** Haar-Wavelet n
hachure/to schraffieren
hachure Schraffur f
Hadamard matrix Hadamard-Matrix f
~ **transform** Hadamard-Transformation f
Haidinger brushes Haidinger-Büschel n *(entoptisches Phänomen)*
hair light Haarlicht n, Gloriole f
hairline Haarlinie f, Haarstrich m, Feinststrich m; Aufstrich m *(Buchstabenbild)*
hairpin filament Haarnadelkatode f *(Elektronenmikroskop)*
halation 1. Lichthofbildung f; Reflexionslichthof m, [fotografischer] Lichthof m; 2. s. halo effect
~ **protection** Lichthofschutz m
half-angular width Halbwinkelbreite f
~-**byte** Halbbyte n
~-**field angle** halber Feldwinkel m *(Objektiv)*
~-**frame** Halbbild n
~-**frame camera** Halbformatkamera f
~-**frame image** Halbbild n *(Kinematografie)*
~-**inch [magnetic] tape** Halbzollband n *(Video)*
~-**length portrait** Halbporträt n, Halbporträtaufnahme f, Brustbild n
~-**life [period]** Halbwertszeit f
~-**line** 1. Halbzeile f *(Video)*; 2. Mittellänge f, x-Höhe f *(Typografie)*
~-**line offset** Halbzeilen-Offset m, Halbzeilenversatz m
~-**period zone** Fresnelsche Zone f *(Wellenoptik)*
~-**pixel accuracy** Halbpixelgenauigkeit f *(Videocodierung)*
~-**pixel interpolation** Halbpixelinterpolation f
~-**reflecting mirror** halbdurchlässiger Spiegel m, Halbspiegel m
~-**serif terminal** Halbserife f *(Buchstabenbild)*
~-**shade** Halbschatten m; Penumbra f
~-**shade polarizer** Halbschattenpolarisator m
~ **shadow** Halbschatten m, Penumbra f
~-**silvered mirror** s. half-reflecting mirror
~-**space** Halbraum m *(Euklidische Geometrie)*
~-**track** Teilspur f
~-**value layer** Halbwertsschicht f *(Radiografie)*
~-**wave** Halbwelle f
~-**wave antenna** Halbwellenantenne f
~-**wave dipole [antenna]** Lambdahalbedipol m
~-**wave plate (retarder)** Lambdahalbeplatte f, Lambda-Halbe-Verzögerungsplatte f, Halbwellenlängenplättchen n, Halbwellenplatte f
~-**wave voltage** Halbwellenspannung f
halftone/to rastern
halftone 1. Rastertonwert m, unechter Halbton m; 2. s. ~ dot image
~ **cell** Rasterzelle f; Elementarquadrat n *(Digitaldruck)*
~ **color separation** Raster-Farbauszug m
~ **color synthesis** autotypische Farbmischung f
~ **copy** Rastervorlage f, gerasterte Vorlage f
~ **dot** Raster[bild]punkt m
~ **dot image** Rasterbild n, gerastertes Bild n
~ **dot pattern** Rasterpunktmuster n
~ **dot size** Rasterpunktgröße f
~ **film** Rasterfilm m, Strichfilm m *(Reprografie)*
~ **graphics** Rastergrafik f
~ **gravure** Rastergravur f, Tiefdruckgravur f; Rastertiefdruck m
~ **negative** Rasternegativ n
~ **photography** Rasterfotografie f
~ **pixel** Raster[bild]punkt m
~ **plate** Rasterplatte f
~ **positive** Rasterpositiv n
~ **principle** Rasterprinzip n
~ **printer** Rasterdrucker m
~ **printing** Rasterdruck m
~ **printing process, ~ process** Rasterdruckverfahren n, Halbtonverfahren n
~ **resolution** Rasterauflösung f
~ **screen** 1. Halbtonraster m(n), Autotypieraster m(n); Rastergitter n; 2. Rasterfolie f
~ **screened image** Rasterbild n, gerastertes Bild n
~ **screening** autotypische (amplitudenmodulierte) Rasterung f, AM-Rasterung f, Halbtonrasterung f
halftoning [technique] Halbtonapproximation f, Halbtonrasterung f, Aufrasterung f, Rasterung f, Dithering-Technik f *(elektronische Bildbearbeitung)*
halide [salt] Halogenid n; Halogensalz n
Hall coefficient Hall-Konstante f *(Magnetfeldvisualisierung)*
~ **effect** Hall-Effekt m
~ **generator (probe)** Hall-Sensor m
~ **voltage** Hall-Spannung f
halo Halo m, Lichthof m, Hof m *(s.a. halation)*

halo

~ **effect** Rasterpunkthof *m*, Rasterpunktunschärfe *m* *(Druckbildfehler)*
halogen Halogen *n*, Salzbildner *m*
~ **acceptor** Halogenakzeptor *m*
~ **bulb light** Halogenlicht *n*
~ **lamp** Halogen[glüh]lampe *f*
~ **light** Halogenlicht *n*
~ **receptor** Halogenrezeptor *m* *(z.B. Gelatine)*
halogenide *s.* halide [salt]
halving plane Halbebene *f (Euklidische Geometrie)*
Hamming code Hamming-Code *m*
~ **distance** Hamming-Distanz *f*, Hamming-Abstand *m*, Signalabstand *m* *(digitale Signalverarbeitung)*
~ **encoding** Hamming-Codierung *f*
~ **function** Hamming-Funktion *f*
~ **net** Hamming-Netz *n*
~ **window** Hamming-Fenster *n*
hand Zeiger *m* *(z.B. auf einer Einstellscheibe)*
~ **camera** Handkamera *f*
~-**carried ultrasound** tragbares Ultraschallgerät *n*
~-**color/to** handkolorieren
~-**coloring** Handkolorierung *f*
~-**coloring pen** Handkolorierstift *m*, Kolorierstift *m*
~ **colorist** Handkolorist *m*
~ **composition** Handsatz *m* *(Druckgewerbe)*
~-**eye calibration** Hand-Auge-Kalibrierung *f (Robotik)*
~ **gesture recognition** Gestenerkennung *f*
~ **glass** Handspiegel *m*
~-**holdable camera** bewegliche (mobile) Kamera *f*
~ **lens (magnifier)** Handlupe *f*; Leseglas *n*
~-**printed character** Druckzeichen *n*; Druckbuchstabe *m*; Handschriftzeichen *n*
~ **processing** Handverarbeitung *f*, Handentwicklung *f*, manuelle Entwicklung *f*
~ **retouching** Handretusche *f*
~ **spectroscope** Handspektroskop *n*
~-**tint/to** handkolorieren
~-**tinting** Handkolorierung *f*
handheld camera Handkamera *f*
~ **filming** Freihandfilmen *n*
~ **light meter** Handbelichtungsmesser *m*
~ **microphone** Handmikrofon *n*
~ **miniscanner** Handscanner *m*
~ **photograph** Handkameraaufnahme *f*
~ **photography** Freihandfotografie *f*
~ **scanner** Handscanner *m (Sonografie)*
~ **shooting** Freihandfilmen *n*; Aufnahme *f* aus der Hand
~ **shot** Freihandaufnahme *f*, Handaufnahme *f*
~ **telescope** Handfernrohr *n*
~ **transducer** *s.* ~ scanner

~ **TV** Taschenfernseher *m*
~ **video camera** [mobile] Handvideokamera *f*, Camcorder *m*
~ **work** Freihandeinsatz *m*
handiness Handlichkeit *f*
handle Anfasser *m*, Griff[punkt] *m*, Ziehpunkt *m (Computergrafik)*
handles Klappennachlauf *m*, Klappenvorlauf *m (Film)*
handset Fernbedienung *f*
~ **type** 1. Handsatzletter *f*, Handsatztype *f*; 2. Handsatzschrift *f*
handwriting analysis Handschriftanalyse *f*
~ **recognition** Handschrifterkennung *f*
handwritten character Handschriftzeichen *n*
~ **character recognition** Handschrifterkennung *f*
~ **text** handgeschriebener (handschriftlicher) Text *m*
handycam Einhand-Camcorder *m*, Hand[video]kamera *f*
hanger chip Aufhängeklammer *f*
hanging indent hängender Einzug *m*, negativer Erstzeileneinzug *m (Layout)*
~-**togetherness** Gestalt *f*
Hanning window Hanning-Fenster *n (Bildverarbeitung)*
haploscope Haploskop *n*
haploscopic haploskopisch
haptic interface haptische Schnittstelle *f*
hard hart *(Papiergradation)*
~ **boot** Kaltstart *m (Computer)*
~ **copy** Computerausdruck *m*, Papierausdruck *m*, Ausdruck *m*, Bildschirmausdruck *m*; Hardcopy *f*, stoffliche Kopie *f*; Schirmbildaufnahme *f*, Papierbild *n*
~ **copy camera** Bilddokumentationssystem *n*
~ **copy device** Hardcopygerät *n*
~ **copy output** Druck[er]ausgabe *f*, Papierausgabe *f*, permanente Bildausgabe *f*
~ **copy position proof** Formproof *m*
~ **copy print** Papierkopie *f*
~ **copy printer** Drucker *m*
~ **copy unit** Multiformatkamera *f (bes. in der Medizinbildgebung)*
~ **digital continuous-tone proof** materieller Halbton-Digitalproof *m*
~ **digital halftone proof** materieller Raster-Digitalproof *m*
~ **disk** Festplatte *f*, Computerfestplatte *f*
~ **disk camcorder** Festplattencamcorder *m*
~ **disk drive** Festplattenlaufwerk *n*, Plattenlaufwerk *n*
~ **disk storage device** Festplattenspeicher *m*
~ **disk video recorder** Festplatten[video]recorder *m*, digitaler Videorecorder *m*; Set-Top-Box *f* mit Aufzeichnungsfunktion
~ **dot** scharfer Rasterpunkt *m*

~ drive Festplattenlaufwerk *n*
~ drive-based consumer VCR *s.* hard disk video recorder
~ drive interface Festplattenschnittstelle *f*
~-edged shadow harter Schatten *m*
~ light hartes Licht *n*
~ lighting harte Beleuchtung *f*
~ mechanical Klebespiegel *m*, Klebelayout *n*, Klebeumbruch *m*, Papiermontage *f* *(Druckvorstufe)*
~ paper hart[zeichnend]es Papier (Fotopapier) *n*
~ proof Probeausdruck *m*, Testausdruck *m*; materieller Farbproof *m*
~ radiation harte Strahlung *f*
~ RF pulse harter Hochfrequenzimpuls *m*
~ shadow harter Schatten *m*
~ thresholding harte Schwellenwertbildung *f*
~ X rays harte (hochenergetische) Röntgenstrahlung *f*
hardened gelatin Hartgelatine *f*
hardener for emulsion incorporation Emulsionshärtungsmittel *n*
hardening agent Härtemittel *n*, Härtungsmittel *n*, Härter *m*, Antiquellmittel *n*
~ bath Härtebad *n*
~ developer gerbender Entwickler *m*, Gerbentwickler *m*
~ fixer Härtefixierer *m*
~ fixing bath Härtefixierbad *n*
hardware Hardware *f*
~ dependency Geräteabhängigkeit *f*
~ device Hardware *f*
harmonic Harmonische *f (Sinuswelle)*
~ analysis harmonische Analyse *f*, Fourier-Analyse *f*, Fourier-Transformation *f*
~ distortion harmonische Verzerrung *f*
~ distortion factor Klirrfaktor *m*
~ frequency harmonische Frequenz *f*
~ function (imaging) harmonische Funktion (Abbildung) *f (Strahlenoptik)*
~ mean filter harmonisches Mittelwertfilter *n*
~ noise harmonisches Rauschen *n*
~ oscillation harmonische Schwingung (Oberwelle) *f*
~ plane wave ebene harmonische Welle *f*
~ wave harmonische Welle *f*
harsh light hartes Licht *n*
~ lighting harte Beleuchtung *f*
~ shadow harter Schatten *m*
Hartley transform Hartley-Transformation *f*
Hartmann formula Dispersionsformel *f*
~-Shack [wave-front] sensor Hartmann-Shack-Sensor *m*
hashing gestreute Speicherung *f (Datenverarbeitung)*
hatch/to schraffieren
hatch Schraffe *f (Typografie, Computergrafik)*
~ style Schraffurart *f*

hatching Schraffur *f*
Hausdorff-Besicovitch dimension Hausdorff-Besikowitsch-Dimension *f*, fraktale (fraktionäre) Dimension *f (Computergrafik)*
haze filter Dunstfilter *n*, Haze-Filter *n*
HDTV *s.* high-definition television
~ format HDTV-Format *n*
head 1. Kopf *m (s.a.* Magnetkopf*)*; 2. Kopfsteg *m*, Papierrand *m* oben *(Layout)*
~ and shoulder close-up Großaufnahme *f*
~ azimuth Kopfazimut *n(m)*
~ cleaner tape Reinigungskassette *f (Video)*
~ clog Kopfzusetzer *m*
~ close-up [shot] Großaufnahme *f*
~ coil Kopfspule *f (Magnetresonanzbildgebung)*
~ drum Kopftrommel *f*, Kopfrad *n*, Kopfscheibe *f*, Bandführungsrolle *f (Videobandgerät)*
~ gap Kopfspalt *m*
~ leader Startband *n*; Filmstartband *n*, Vorlaufstreifen *m*; Vorlaufband *n*, Normstartband *n*
~-mounted display Daten[sicht]helm *m*, Datenbrille *f*, Bildschirmbrille *f*, Bildschirmhelm *m*, Videobrille *f*, Kopfmonitor *m*, Helmdisplay *n*
~ noise Kopfrauschen *n*
~ rotation Kopftrommelrotation *f*
~ servo Kopftrommel-Regeleinheit *f (Videobandmaschine)*
~ slate Anfangsklappe *f (Film, Video)*
~ switch Kopfumschaltung *f*
~ sync Tonstartmarke *f*
~ tilt Kopfneigung *f*
~-to-tape speed Aufzeichnungsgeschwindigkeit *f*, Schreibgeschwindigkeit *f*, Relativgeschwindigkeit *f (Bandmaschine)*
~ track Kopfspur *f*
~ tracker Orientierungsverfolger *m (virtuelle Realität)*
~ wear Kopfabrieb *m*
~ wheel *s.* ~ drum
headend Kabel[fernseh]kopfstation *f*, Rundfunkempfangsstelle *f*
header Kopfdatenbereich *m*, Anfangskennsatz *m*, Kopf *m*, Vorspann *m (Datenrahmen)*
~ data Kopfdaten *pl*, Paketkopfdaten *pl*
~ information (record) *s.* header
headline Headline *f*, Titelzeile *f*; Überschrift *f*; Schlagzeile *f*
headliner Titelsetzgerät *n (Satztechnik)*
headphone[s] Kopfhörer *m*
headroom Übersteuerungsreserve *f*
headscreen Abdeckfahne *f*, Lichtblende *f*, Neger *m*
headset [Hör-]Sprechgarnitur *f*, Mikrofonkopfhörer *m*, Kopfhörergeschirr *n*

hearing

hearing-impaired viewer hörgeschädigter Betrachter *m*
heat-absorbing filter Wärmeschutzfilter *n*
~-activated laminating material Heißklebefolie *f*
~-copying paper Thermopapier *n*, thermoaktives (wärmeempfindliches) Papier *n*; Telefaxpapier *n*
~ dispersal Wärmeableitung *f*
~-drying printing ink unter Hitzeeinwirkung verdunstende Druckfarbe *f*
~ emission Wärmeabstrahlung *f*
~-fixable image wärmefixierbares Bild *n* *(Elektrofotografie)*
~ fusing Wärmefixierung *f (Kopierer)*
~ image Wärmebild *n*, Thermogramm *n*, Thermografiebild *n*
~ of projection Projektionswärme *f*
~ radiation Wärmestrahlung *f*, Thermalstrahlung *f* Temperaturstrahlung *f*
~ radiator Wärmestrahler *m*, Warmstrahler *m*, Temperaturstrahler *m*
~ ray Wärmestrahl *m*
~ recording Wärmebildaufzeichnung *f*
~-reflecting mirror Infrarotspiegel *m*
~ reflection filter Wärmeschutzfilter *n*
~-sensing camera Wärme[bild]kamera *f*, Thermografiekamera *f*, Infrarotkamera *f*
~-sensitive paper Thermopapier *n*, wärmeempfindliches (thermoaktives) Papier *n*; Telefaxpapier *n*
~-set web [press] Heat-set-Rollenoffsetpresse *f*
~ splicer Heißklebepresse *f*
~-transfer printing Thermotransferdruck *m*, indirekte Thermografie *f*, Transferthermografie *f*
heated dry mounting press, ~ dryer *s*. ~ print dryer
~ drying cabinet Trockenschrank *m*
~ filament Glühfaden *m*
~ fuser roll Heizrolle *f*, Heizwalze *f*, Fixierwalze *f*, Wärmefixierwalze *f (Elektrofotografie)*
~ pressure roller beheizte Andruckwalze *f (Elektrofotografie)*
~ print dryer Trockenpresse *f*, Heißtrockenpresse *f*
heating microscope Erhitzungsmikroskop *n*
heavy spar Schwerspat *m*, Baryt *m*
Hebb's rule Hebbsche Lernregel *f*, Hebb-Regel *f (des unüberwachten Lernens)*
hectograph/to hektografieren
hectograph Hektograf *m*; Spirit-Umdruckapparat *m*
heel effect Heel-Effekt *m*, anodenseitiger Intensitätsabfall *m (Radiografie)*
Hefner candle Hefner-Kerze *f (Fotometrie)*
height adjustment *s*. ~ control
~ contour curve Höhenliniendarstellung *f*

~ control Höhenverstellung *f (z.B. eines Vergrößerungsgeräts)*
~ field Höhennetz *n (Fotogrammetrie)*
~-finding radar Höhenmessradar *n*, Höhensuchradar *n*
~ map *s*. depth map
~-to-width proportion (ratio) Seitenverhältnis *n*, Bildseitenverhältnis *n*
Heisenberg's uncertainty principle (relation) Heisenberg-Unschärfe *f*, Heisenbergsche Unschärferelation *f*
held frame angehaltenes (stehendes) Filmbild *n*
helical computed tomography Spiral-Computertomografie *f*, Spiral-CT *f*
~ CT scanner Spiralscanner *m* *(Tomografie)*
~ focusing mount Schneckenführung *f*, Schneckengang *m*, Schneckengangfassung *f*; Fokussierschnecke *f*, Fokussierschneckengang *m (Objektiv)*
~ scan Spiralscan *m*
~ scan data Spiral-[CT-]Datensatz *m*
~-scan machine Schrägspurmaschine *f*
~-scan magnetic recording *s*. helical video recording
~-scan videotape cassette system Videobandkassettensystem *n* mit Schrägaufzeichnung
~ scanning [system] Schrägspur[aufzeichnungs]verfahren *n*
~ video recording Videoschrägspuraufzeichnung *f*, Schrägspuraufzeichnung *f*
~ videotape machine Schrägspurmaschine *f*
helicoid extension tube Einstellschnecke *f*
helicopter simulator Hubschraubersimulator *m*
heliochromy Heliochromie *f*
heliograph 1. Heliograf *m*; 2. Heliografie *f (Druckerzeugnis)*
heliographic heliografisch
~ ink Lichtpausfarbe *f*
~ process, heliography Heliografie *f (s.a.* Chemigrafie*)*
heliogravure Heliogravüre *f*, Fotogravüre *f*, Lichtgravüre *f*, Heliogravurtechnik *f*
helioseismic holographhy helioseismische Holografie *f*
heliostat Heliostat *m*, Zölostat *m (zur Sonnenbeobachtung)*
helium-neon laser Helium-Neon-Laser *m*
helmet-mounted display *s*. head-mounted display
Helmholtz equation Helmholtz-Gleichung *f (Wellenoptik)*
~ invariant Helmholtz[-Lagrange]-Invariante *f*, [Huygens-]Helmholtz-Invariante *f*, optische Invariante *f*

~-Lagrange relationship
Helmholtz-Lagrangesche Gleichung f
(diffraktive Optik)
hemeralopia Hemeralopie f, Tagblindheit f
hemicube Halbwürfel m; Halbquader m
(Computergrafik)
~ prism Halbwürfelprisma n
hemispherical diffuser sphärischer
Diffusor m
Henderson process flächenvariabler
(autotypischer) Tiefdruck m
henry Henry n *(Maßeinheit der Induktivität)*
Hering's opponent theory of color vision
Gegenfarbentheorie f
Hermann grid illusion Hermann-Gitter n
(optische Täuschung)
Hermitian interpolation
Hermite-Interpolation f *(geometrisches Modellieren)*
~ matrix hermitische Matrix f
~ transform hermitische Transformation f
Herschel effect Herschel-Effekt m
(fotografischer Entwicklungseffekt)
Herschelian telescope Herschel-Teleskop n
hertz Hertz n, Hz *(Frequenzmaß)*
Hessian matrix Hesse-Matrix f, Hessesche
Matrix f *(Netzwerkoptimierung)*
hetero-associative memory
heteroassoziativer Speicher m
heterochromatic heterochromatisch,
ungleichfarbig, verschiedenfarbig,
farbungleich
~ light verschiedenfarbiges Licht n
~ photometer heterochromes Fotometer n
~ photometry heterochrome Fotometrie f
heterodyne/to überlagern *(bes. Frequenzen)*
heterogeneous sensor heterogener
Sensor m
heterojunction Heteroübergang m
(Halbleiter)
~ diode [array] s. heterostructure
photodiode
heterophoria Heterophorie f,
Winkelfehlsichtigkeit f
heteropolar bond heteropolare Bindung f,
Ionenbindung f
heterostructure laser Heterostrukturlaser m
~ photodiode Heterostruktur-Fotodiode f
heuristic heuristisch
~ search heuristische Suche f
heuristics Heuristik f
hexadecimal Hexadezimalzahl f,
Hexadezimalziffer f
~ [numbering] system
Hexadezimalsystem n
hexagon Hexagon n, Sechseck n
hexagonal hexagonal, sechseckig
~ grid (lattice) Hexagonalgitter n,
hexagonales Gitter n; Hexagonalraster m(n), hexagonaler Raster m
~ sampling hexagonale Abtastung f
hexahedral sechsflächig; würfelförmig

hexahedron Hexaeder n, [regelmäßiger]
Sechsflächner m *(geometrisches Primitiv)*
hexcone HSV color model Farbsechseck n
HF s. high frequency
hi-hat Bodenstativ n, Froschstativ n, Frosch m
hickey Lichtpunkt m, Butzen m, Pop[p]el m
(Druckbildfehler)
hicolor display Vollfarbdisplay n
hidden layer verdeckte (versteckte) Schicht
f, verborgene Ebene f *(künstliches neuronales Netz)*
~ line verdeckte Linie f; verdeckte Kante f
~-line problem Verdeckte-Kanten-Problem n
~-line removal Elimination f verdeckter
Kanten (Linien)
~ Markov model Hidden-Markow-Modell n
(Mustererkennung)
~ surface verdeckte Fläche f
~-surface elimination (removal)
Elimination f verdeckter Flächen
~-surface problem
Verdeckte-Flächen-Problem n
hierarchic[al] hierarchisch
hierarchical algorithm hierarchischer
Algorithmus m
~ ascendant classification hierarchisch
aufsteigende Klassifikation f
~ block matching hierarchischer
Blockvergleich m
~ classification hierarchische
Klassifikation f
~ classifier hierarchischer Klassifikator m,
Baumklassifikator m
~ clustering algorithm hierarchischer
Cluster[analyse]algorithmus m
~ coding hierarchische Codierung f
~ data structure hierarchische
Datenstruktur f
~ image description hierarchische
Bildbeschreibung f
~ interpolation hierarchische Interpolation f
~ modeling hierarchische Modellierung f
~ modulation hierarchische Modulation f
~ neural network hierarchisches
neuronales Netz n
~ object hierarchisches Objekt n
~ prediction hierarchische Prädiktion f
~ representation hierarchische
Darstellung f
~ search hierarchische Suche f
~ storage hierarchische Speicherung f
~ thresholding hierarchische
Schwellenwertbildung f
~ tree hierarchischer Baum m
~ tree structure hierarchische
Baumstruktur f
~ vector quantization hierarchische
Vektorquantisierung f
hieroglyphic[s] Bilderschrift f
high-acuity vision scharfes Sehen n

high

~-acutance image gestochen scharfes Bild *n*
~-altitude aerial photograph Luftbildaufnahme *f* aus großer Höhe, Höhenbild *n*
~-altitude observatory Höhenobservatorium *n*
~-aperture lens lichtstarkes Objektiv *f*
~ band oberes Band *n (z.B. als Satellitenempfangs-Frequenzbereich)*
~-bandwidth breitbandig
~-bit-rate connection Breitbandverbindung *f*, Hochgeschwindigkeitsverbindung *f*
~-brightness monitor lichtstarker Monitor *m*
~ color *bezeichnet die 15-Bit-Farbtiefe eines Displaysystems*
~-contrast kontrastreich, kontraststark, hart
~-contrast developer Kontrastentwickler *m*, Hochkontrastentwickler *m*; hart arbeitender Entwickler *m*
~-contrast emulsion kontrastreiche Emulsion *f*
~-contrast film Hochkontrastfilm *m*, kontrastreicher Film *m*
~-contrast image kontrastreiches Bild *n*
~-contrast lighting Hochkontrastbeleuchtung *f*, kontrastreiche Beleuchtung *f*
~-contrast paper hart[zeichnend]es Papier (Fotopapier) *n*
~-contrast resolution Hochkontrastauflösung *f*
~-definition developer hochauflösender Entwickler *m*, Feinkornentwickler *m*
~-definition digital television hochauflösendes Digitalfernsehen *n*
~-definition lens scharfzeichnendes Objektiv *n*
~-definition screen hochauflösender Bildschirm *m*
~-definition signal hochaufgelöstes Signal *n*
~-definition television hochauflösendes (hochzeiliges) Fernsehen *n*, Hochzeilenfernsehen *n*
~-definition video hochauflösendes Video *n*
~-dimensionality *s.* multidimensional
~-efficiency printer Hochleistungsdrucker *m*
~-end amateur ambitionierter (engagierter) Amateur *m*
~-energy developer hart arbeitender Entwickler *m*
~-energy physics Teilchenphysik *f*
~-energy radiation Hochenergiestrahlung *f*
~-energy X rays harte (hochenergetische) Röntgenstrahlung *f*
~ fidelity Highfidelity *f*
~ filter *s.* low-pass filter

~ frequency Hochfrequenz *f*
~-frequency hochfrequent
~-frequency channel Hochfrequenzkanal *m*
~-frequency cut-off obere Grenzfrequenz *f*
~-frequency loudspeaker Hochfrequenzlautsprecher *m*
~-frequency noise hochfrequentes Rauschen *n*
~-frequency radar Hochfrequenzradar *n*
~-frequency radar wave hochfrequente Radarwelle *f*
~-frequency signal hochfrequentes Signal *n*
~-frequency sound wave Ultraschallwelle *f*
~-frequency ultrasound Hochfrequenz-Ultraschall *m*
~ gloss Hochglanz *m*
~-gloss surface Hochglanzoberfläche *f*, hochglänzende Oberfläche *f*
~-granularity image grobkörniges Bild *n*
~-impedance amplifier hochohmiger Verstärker *m*
~ in chroma farbsatt
~-index glass hochbrechendes (starkbrechendes) Glas *n*
~-index medium hochbrechendes Medium *n*
~-intensity discharge lamp Quecksilberdampflampe *f*
~-intensity reciprocity failure Kurzzeitfehler *m*
~ key heller Bildton *m*
~-key effect High-Key-Effekt *m*
~-key photo[graph], ~ picture High-Key-Bild *n*
~-level programming language höhere Programmiersprache *f*
~-line-rate camera Hochzeilenkamera *f*
~-luminosity lichtstark *(z.B. Projektor)*
~-oblique photograph Schrägluftbild *n*, Schrägaufnahme *f (Aerofotogrammetrie)*
~-order convolutional interpolation function Faltungsinterpolationsfunktion *f* höherer Ordnung
~-pass decomposition filter Hochpass-Zerlegungsfilter *n*
~-pass filter Hochpassfilter *n*, Hochpass *m*; Schärfefilter *n*
~-pass filtering Hochpassfilterung *f*
~-pass image Hochpassbild *n*
~-performance camera Hochleistungskamera *f*
~-performance graphics Hochleistungsgrafik *f (Computergrafik)*
~-performance instrument Hochleistungsinstrument *n*
~-performance lens Hochleistungsobjektiv *n*, Hochleistungsoptik *f*
~-performance MRI scanner Hochleistungs-Kernspintomograf *m*, Hochleistungs-Magnetresonanztomograf *m*

~-**power laser** Hochleistungslaser *m*, Hochenergielaser *m*
~-**power microscope** Hochleistungsmikroskop *n*
~-**power objective** lichtstarkes Objektiv *n*
~-**powered light source** Starklichtquelle *f*
~-**pressure [gas-]discharge lamp** Hochdruck-Entladungslampe *f*
~-**pressure lamp** Hochdrucklampe *f*, Lichtbogenlampe *f*
~-**pressure mercury vapor lamp** Hochdruck-Quecksilberdampflampe *f*
~-**pressure sodium lamp** Hochdruck-Natriumdampflampe *f*
~-**pressure sodium lamp** Natriumhochdrucklampe *f*
~-**quality camera** Präzisionskamera *f*
~-**quality color printing** Qualitätsfarbdruck *m*
~-**quality optics** Feinoptik *f*, Präzisionsoptik *f*
~-**quality photographic lens** Präzisionsobjektiv *n*, Spitzenobjektiv *n*
~-**quality printing** Qualitätsdruck *m*
~-**rate multimedia transmission** hoch[bit]ratige Multimediaübertragung *f*
~-**rating X-ray tube** Hochleistungs[röntgen]röhre *f*
~ **resolution** Hochauflösung *f*
~-**resolution camera** hochauflösende Kamera *f*
~-**resolution collimator** hochauflösender Kollimator *m*
~-**resolution detector** hochauflösender Detektor *m*
~-**resolution display** hochauflösendes Display *n*; hochauflösender Bildschirm *m*
~-**resolution electron microscopy** hochauflösende Elektronenmikroskopie *f*
~-**resolution film** hochauflösender Film *m*
~-**resolution image** hochauflösendes Bild *n*; hochaufgelöstes Bild *n*
~-**resolution imaging** hochauflösende Bildgebung (Abbildung) *f*
~-**resolution lens** hochauflösendes Objektiv *n*
~-**resolution monitor** hochauflösender Monitor *m*
~-**resolution radar** hochauflösendes Radar *n*
~-**resolution screen** 1. hochauflösender Bildschirm *m*; 2. feinzeichnende Folie *f* *(Radiografie)*
~-**resolution stereo camera** hochauflösende Stereokamera *f*
~-**resolution storage medium** hochauflösendes Speichermedium *n*
~-**resolution tomography** hochauflösende Tomografie *f*
~-**saturation color** hochgesättigte Farbe *f*
~-**sensitivity CCD camera** hochempfindliche CCD-Kamera *f*

~-**spee photograph** Hochgeschwindigkeitsbild *n*
~-**speed bus** Hochgeschwindigkeitsbus *m* *(Datenübertragung)*
~-**speed camera** Zeitlupenkamera *f*
~-**speed cinematography** Hochgeschwindigkeitskinematografie *f*, Hochfrequenzkinematografie *f*
~-**speed color copier** Farb-Schnellkopierer *m*
~-**speed copier** Schnellkopierer *m*
~-**speed data network** schnelles Datennetz *n*
~-**speed digital camera** Hochgeschwindigkeits-Bildwandlerkamera *f*
~-**speed emulsion** hochempfindliche Emulsion *f*
~-**speed film** hoch[licht]empfindlicher Film *m*
~-**speed framing camera** Hochgeschwindigkeitskamera *f*, Hochfrequenzkamera *f*
~-**speed interface** Hochgeschwindigkeitsschnittstelle *f*
~-**speed lens** hochlichtstarkes Objektiv *n*
~-**speed memory device** Hochgeschwindigkeitsspeicher *m*
~-**speed motion-picture camera** Hochgeschwindigkeitsfilmkamera *f*, Hochfrequenz-Filmkamera *f*
~-**speed motion-picture photography** Hochgeschwindigkeitskinematografie *f*
~-**speed network** Hochgeschwindigkeitsnetz *n* *(Datenübertragung)*
~-**speed photographic** hochgeschwindigkeitsfotografisch
~-**speed press** Schnellpresse *f* *(Druckmaschine)*
~-**speed printer** Schnelldrucker *m*
~-**speed printing** Schnelldruck *m*, Hochgeschwindigkeitsdruck *m*
~-**speed printing plate** Schnelldruckplatte *f (Reprografie)*
~-**speed processing** Schnellverarbeitung *f*, Schnellentwicklung *f (von Filmmaterial)*
~-**speed radiography** Hochgeschwindigkeitsradiografie *f*
~-**speed recording** Hochgeschwindigkeitsaufnahme *f*
~-**speed scanner** Hochgeschwindigkeitsscanner *m*
~-**speed screen** hochempfindliche (hochverstärkende) Folie *f (Radiografie)*
~-**speed shutter** Hochgeschwindigkeitsverschluss *m*
~-**speed still photography** Hochgeschwindigkeitsfotografie *f*, Hochfrequenzfotografie *f*, Kurzzeitfotografie *f*
~-**speed still picture** Hochgeschwindigkeitsbild *n*

high 174

~-speed sync[hronization] Kurzzeitsynchronisation f
~-speed video camera Hochgeschwindigkeits-Videokamera f
~-temperature microscope s. heating microscope
~-temperature processing Hochtemperaturverarbeitung f
~-voltage electron microscopy Hochspannungselektronenmikroskopie f
~-voltage lamp Hochvoltlampe f
~-volume copier Massenkopierer m
~-volume lab Großlabor[atorium] n (Fotoverarbeitung)
higher-order aberration Bildfehler m höherer Ordnung
~-order polynomial Polynom n höherer Ordnung
highest-resolution monitor höchstauflösender Monitor
~-speed film höchstempfindlicher Film m
highlight Hochlicht n; Spitzlicht n; Glanzlicht n
~ contrast Lichtkontrast m
~ dot Lichterpunkt m (Rasterdruck)
~ exposure Hochlichtaufnahme f
highlighting 1. Hervorheben n; 2. Helltastung f (Tomografie, Radar)
highlights Lichtpartie f, Lichter pl
highly corrected lens (objective) hochkorrigiertes Objektiv n
~ polished paper Hochglanzpapier n, hochglänzendes (gussgestrichenes) Papier n
~ resolved image hochaufgelöstes Bild n
~ saturated color hochgesättigte Farbe f
Hilbert curve Hilbert-Kurve f
~ filter Hilbert-Filter n, Hilbert-Operator m (Signalverarbeitung)
~ space Hilbert-Raum m
~ transform Hilbert-Transformation f
hi-peaker Aussteuerungsinstrument n (am Studiokamerasucher)
hippus Hippus m, Iriszittern n
histogram Histogramm n, Staffelbild n (s.a. bar graph)
~ adjustment Histogrammeinstellung f
~ analysis Histogrammanalyse f
~ backprojection Histogrammrückprojektion f
~-based cluster analysis histogrammbasierte Clusteranalyse f
~-based processing Histogrammverarbeitung f
~-based segmentation histogrammgestützte Segmentierung f
~ bin Histogrammurne f
~ comparison Histogrammvergleich m
~ compression (contraction) Histogrammkompression f
~ difference Histogrammdifferenz f
~ equalization Histogrammausgleich m, Histogramm[ein]ebnung f, Histogrammegalisierung f, Histogrammäqualisation f (nichtlineare Punktoperation)
~ estimation Histogrammschätzung f
~ expansion Histogrammdehnung f, Histogrammspreizung f
~ flattening s. ~ equalization
~ function Histogrammfunktion f, Histogrammkurve f
~ hyperbolization Histogrammhyperbolisation f, Histogrammhyperbolisierung f
~ intersection Histogrammzerlegung f, Histogrammschnitt m
~ manipulation Histogrammanipulation f
~ matching Histogrammangleich m
~ modification Histogrammmodifikation f
~ parametrization Histogrammparametrisierung f
~ peak Histogrammberg m
~ plot Histogrammdarstellung f
~ pyramid Histogrammpyramide f
~ segmentation Histogrammsegmentierung f
~ sharpening [operation] Histogrammverschärfung f
~ smoothing s. ~ equalization
~ specification Histogrammspezifikation f
~ statistics Histogrammstatistik f
~ stretching Histogrammdehnung f, Histogrammspreizung f
~ transform[ation] Histogrammtransformation f
~ valley Histogrammtal n
~ value Histogrammwert m
~ window Histogrammfenster n
histogramming Histogrammbildung f
historadiography Historadiografie f
historical photography historische Fotografie f
history of photography Foto[grafie]geschichte f
hit-and-miss transform s. hit-or-miss transform[ation]
~-or-miss operator Hit-Miss-Operator m (morphologische Bildverarbeitung, Objekterkennung)
~-or-miss transform[ation] Hit-Miss-Transformation f, Alles-oder-nichts-Transformation f (Binärbildverarbeitung)
~ rate Trefferquote f (Mustererkennung)
HLS color space, ~ coordinate system s. hue-lightness-saturation color space
HMD s. head-mounted display
HMI lamp (light) HMI-Brenner m, HMI-Lampe f, Hochdruck-Halogenmetalldampflampe f
Hoegh meniscus [lens] Hoeghscher Meniskus m
Hofmeister series Hofmeistersche Ionenreihe f
hold back/to abhalten, abwedeln, partiell (teilweise) belichten

~ **element** Halteglied *n*
(Signalverarbeitung)
~ **frame** *s.* held frame
holdback sprocket Nachwickel[zahn]rolle *f*, Nachwickler *m*
holding capacitor Haltekondensator *m*
hole 1. Loch *n*; 2. *s.* electron hole; 3. *s.* defect electron
~ **mask** Lochmaske *f*
hollow cathode source Hohlkatodenlampe *f (Atomabsorptionsspektroskopie)*
~ **interior style** leere Ausfüllung *f (Computergrafik)*
hologram Hologramm[bild] *n*, holografisches Bild *n* Speicherbild *n*
~ **grating** holografisches Gitter *n*
holograph/to holografieren
holograph *s.* hologram
holographer Holograf *m*
holographic holografisch
~ **beam sampler** holografischer Strahlabtaster *m*
~ **camera** holografische Kamera *f*, Hologrammkamera *f*
~ **data storage** holografische Datenspeicherung *f*
~ **emulsion** holografische Emulsion *f*
~ **exposure** holografische Belichtung *f*
~ **film** holografischer Film *m*
~ **filter** holografisches Filter *n*
~ **image** *s.* hologram
~ **image recording** holografische Bildaufzeichnung *f*
~ **imaging** holografische Abbildung *f*
~ **interferogram** holografisches Interferogramm *n*
~ **interferometry** holografische Interferometrie *f*, Hologramminterferometrie *f*, Doppelbelichtungsinterferometrie *f*
~ **lattice** holografisches Gitter *n*
~ **layer** holografische Schicht *f*
~ **line grating** holografisches Liniengitter *n*
~ **lithography** holografische Lithografie *f*
~ **mass storage** holografischer Massenspeicher *m*
~ **memory** Holografiespeicher *m*
~ **microscopy** holografische Mikroskopie *f*
~ **optical element** holografisch-optisches Element *n*
~ **optics** holografische Optik *f*
~ **plane** Hologrammebene *f*
~ **plate** Hologrammplatte *f*, holografische Platte *f*
~ **reconstruction** holografische Rekonstruktion *f*
~ **reconstruction** Hologrammrekonstruktion *f*, Hologrammwiedergabe *f*
~ **recording** Hologrammaufnahme *f*, holografische Aufnahme *f*
~ **recording setup** holografische Aufnahmeanordnung *f*
~ **reference beam** Bezugsstrahl *m*

~ **scanning** holografische Abtastung *f*
~ **stereogram** holografisches Stereogramm *n*
holography Holografie *f*, Laserfotografie *f*
holoplate Hologrammplatte *f*, holografische Platte *f*
home antenna Hausantenne *f*, Dachantenne *f*
~ **appliance** Heimgerät *n*
~ **cinema** Heimkino *n*
~ **cinema installation** Heimkinoanlage *f*
~ **cinema receiver** Heimkinoempfänger *m*
~ **cinema screen** Heimkinobildwand *f*
~ **cinema system** Heimkinoanlage *f*
~ **darkroom** Heimlabor *n*, Hobbylabor *n*
~ **darkroom enthusiast** Hobbylaborant *m*, Selbstverarbeiter *m*, Selbstausarbeiter *m*
~ **electronics** Unterhaltungselektronik *f*
~ **game** Heim-Videospiel *n*
~ **movie** 1. Heimkino *n*; 2. Heimkinofilm *m*
~ **movie camera** Schmalfilmkamera *f*
~ **movie film** Heimkinofilm *m*; Amateurfilm *m*
~ **movie format** Heimkinoformat *n*
~ **page** Startseite *f (World Wide Web)*
~ **PC (personal computer)** Heimcomputer *m*, Heim-PC *m*
~ **processing** Heimverarbeitung *f*, Selbstverarbeitung *f (z.B. von Fotomaterial)*
~ **receiver** Heimempfänger *m*
~ **reception** Heimempfang *m*
~ **screen** *s.* ~ television receiver
~ **screening** Heimprojektion *f*
~ **studio** Heimstudio *n*
~ **surveillance** Hausüberwachung *f*
~ **television** Heimfernsehen *n*
~ **television receiver (set)** Fernseh-Heimempfänger *m*, Fernseh-Heimgerät *n*, Heimfernsehgerät *n*, Heimfernseher *m*, Fernseh[empfäng]er *m*
~ **theater projector** Heimkinoprojektor *m*
~ **-use projector** Heimprojektor *m*, Heimprojektionsanlage *f*
~ **video** Heimvideo *n*
~ **video camera** Heimvideokamera *f*
~ **video cassette recorder,** ~ **video recorder** Heim[video]recorder *m*, Amateur-Videorecorder *m*
~ **videotape** Amateurvideoband *n*
homocentric beam homozentrisches Bündel *n*
homochromatic homochromatisch, isochromatisch, gleichfarbig, farbgleich
~ **light** gleichfarbiges Licht *n*
homogeneity Homogenität *f (z.B. von Bildbereichen)*
~ **criterion** Homogenitätskriterium *n*
homogeneous coordinate homogene Koordinate *f*
~ **fractal** homogenes Fraktal *n*
~ **matrix** homogene Matrix *f*

homogeneous 176

~ **medium** homogenes Medium *n*
~ **point operation** homogene Punktoperation *f*
~ **point operator** homogener Punktoperator *m*
~ **random field** homogenes Zufallsfeld *n*
homogenous class homogene Klasse
~ **illumination** gleichmäßige Ausleuchtung *f*
homography projektive Transformation *f*
homojunction Homoübergang *m* *(Halbleiter)*
~ **diode [array]** Homodiode *f*
homologous point gemeinsamer (homologer) Punkt *m* *(dreidimensionale Abbildung)*
homomorphic filter homomorphes Filter *n*
~ **filtering** homomorphe Filterung *f*
homophotic image homophotisches Bild *n*
honeycomb filter Wabenfilter *n*
~ **grid** Wabenkondensor *m*
Hopfield net[work] Hopfield-Netz[werk] *n* *(Bildcodierung, Mustererkennung)*
hopper coating Kaskadenguss *m* *(Filmherstellung)*
horizon line Horizontlinie *f*
~ **plane** Horizontebene *f*
horizontal axis Abszissenachse *f*, x-Achse *f* *(Koordinatensystem)*
~ **blanking** horizontale Austastung *f*, Horizontalaustastung *f*
~ **blanking interval (period)** horizontale Austastlücke *f (Bildröhre)*
~ **cell** Horizontalzelle *f (der Augennetzhaut)*
~ **chain line printer** Typenkettendrucker *m*
~ **decimation** horizontale Dezimation *f*
~ **deflection** *s.* ~ sweep
~ **enlarger** Horizontalvergrößerungsgerät *n*
~ **format** Querformat *n*
~ **linear polarization** horizontale Polarisation *f (Radar)*
~ **orientation** Querformat *n*
~ **parallax** horizontale Parallaxe *f*
~ **process camera** Horizontalkamera *f (Reprografie)*
~ **resolution** Horizontalauflösung *f*, horizontale (waagerechte) Auflösung *f*
~ **retrace [time]** Horizontalrücklauf *m*, Zeilenrücklauf *m (Bildröhre)*
~ **scan** Zeilenabtastung *f*
~ **scan rate** horizontale Abtastfrequenz (Ablenkfrequenz) *f*, Horizontalfrequenz *f*, Zeilen[abtast]frequenz *f*, Zeilenwechselfrequenz *f*
~ **scanning coil** Zeilenablenkspule *f*
~ **scanning frequency** *s.* ~ scan rate
~ **sweep** Zeilenablenkung *f*, Horizontalablenkung *f*
~ **sweep coil** Zeilenablenkspule *f*
~ **sweep frequency** *s.* ~ scan rate
~ **sync[hronization]** Horizontalsynchronisation *f*, horizontale Synchronisation *f*

~ **sync[hronization] pulse, ~ synchronizing signal** Horizontal[synchron]impuls *m*, H-Impuls *m*, horizontales Synchronisiersignal *n*
Horn constraint equation Hornsche Bedingung *f (Bewegungsdetektion)*
horn[-type] radiator Hornstrahler *m (Radar)*
horopter Horopter *m (Abbildungsgeometrie)*
horseshoe[-shaped] mounting Hufeisenmontierung *f (Teleskop)*
host bus Hostbus *m*
~ **computer** Hostcomputer *m*, Hostrechner *m*, Hauptrechner *m*, Wirtsrechner *m*
hot cathode [electron] tube Glühkatodenröhre *f*
~ **embossing** Warmprägung *f (Stereotypie)*
~ **filter** *s.* infrared-blocking filter
~ **foil printing** Heißfolienprägedruck *m*, Heißfolienprägung *f*, Prägefoliendruck *m*
~ **foil stamp/to** heißprägen
~ **foil stamping** *s.* ~ foil printing
~ **foil transfer** Thermokaschieren *n*
~ **light** Heißlicht *n*, Glühlicht *n*
~ **light source** Glühlichtquelle *f*
~ **-melt** [thermoplastischer] Schmelzklebstoff *m*
~ **mirror** Warmlichtspiegel *m*, Interferenz-Wärmeschutzfilter *n*; Infrarotspiegel *m*
~ **roll** *s.* heated fuser roll
~ **shoe [contact]** Blitzschuh *m*; Aufsteckschuh *m*, Aufsteckfuß *m*
~ **shoe flash** Aufsteckblitz *m*, Aufsteckblitzgerät *n*
~ **splice** Heißklebestelle *f*
~ **splicer** Heißklebepresse *f*
~ **spot** heller Fleck *m*, fokale Anreicherung *f (Bildfehler; s.a.* hickey*);* Randhelligkeitsabfall *m (Fernsehbildstörung)*
Hotelling transform Hauptkomponentenanalyse *f*, Eigenvektortransformation *f*, Karhunen-Loève-Transformation *f (Merkmalserkennung)*
Hough domain (space) Hough-Raum *m*
~ **transform** 1. Hough-Transformierte *f*; 2. *s.* ~ transformation
~ **transform plane** *s.* ~ domain
~ **transformation** Hough-Transformation *f (Bildsegmentierung)*
Hounsfield scale Hounsfield-Skale *f*
~ **unit** Hounsfield-Einheit *f (Maß der computertomografischen Amplitudenauflösung)*
house black (reference) Studio-Referenzsignal *n*, Schwarzbezugswert *m*, Black Burst *m (Video)*
~ **sheet** Auflagenpapier *n*
~ **style** Hausschrift *f (Typografie)*
~ **sync** *s.* ~ black

household light[bulb], house-lighting bulb
  Haushaltsglühbirne *f*,
  Haushaltsglühlampe *f*
howl round akustische Rückkopplung *f*
HSI space (system) *s.*
  hue-saturation-intensity color system
HSL (HSV) color model *s.*
  hue-saturation-intensity color system
HTML *s.* Hypertext Markup Language
hub Hub *m*, Sternverteiler *m*
Hubble Space Telescope, ~ telescope
  Hubble-Teleskop *n*,
  Hubble-Weltraumteleskop *n*
hue Farbton *m*, Buntton *m*, Farbfrequenz *f*,
  Farbe *f*; Farbnuance *f*
~ **accuracy** Farbgenauigkeit *f*,
  Farbrichtigkeit *f*
~ **angle** Farbtonwinkel *m*, Bunttonwinkel *m*
~ **circle** Farbtonkreis *m*; Farb[en]kreis *m*
~ **constancy** Farbtonkonstanz *f*
~ **control** Farbregler *m* *(Fernsehen)*
~ **difference** Farbtonunterschied *m*,
  Farbtondifferenz *f*
~ **error** Farbfehler *m*
~ **image** Farbtonbild *n*, Bunttonbild *n*
~**-lightness-saturation color space** *s.*
  hue-saturation-intensity color system
~**-saturation-intensity color system**
  Farbton-Sättigungs-Helligkeits-
  Farbsystem *n*, HSI-Merkmalsraum *m*,
  HSI-Raum *m*, HLS-Farbmodell *n*,
  HSV-Farbraum *m*
~**-saturation-value space** *s.*
  hue-saturation-intensity color system
~ **scale** Farb[ton]skala *f*, Farbtonabstufung *f*
~ **step** Bunttonstufe *f*
~ **wheel** *s.* ~ circle
Hueckel operator Hueckel-Operator *m*
  (Kantendetektion)
Huffman code Huffman-Code *m*
  (Bilddatenkompression)
~ **code table** Huffman-Tabelle *f*
~ **coder** Huffman-Cod[ier]er *m*
~ **coding** Huffman-Codierung *f*,
  Entropiecodierung *f* nach Huffman
~ **coding algorithm** Huffman-Algorithmus *m*
~ **shift code** Huffman-Code *m*
~ **tree** Huffman-Baum *m*,
  Huffman-Codierbaum *m*
hum trouble Brummstörung *f*
human body animation Körperanimation *f*
  (Computergrafik)
~**-body counter** Ganzkörperzähler *m*
  (Dosimetrie)
~**-computer interaction**
  Mensch-Maschine-Kommunikation *f*
~ **expertise** Expertenwissen *n*
  (Neuroinformatik)
~ **eye** Menschenauge *n*, menschliches
  Auge *n*
~ **interface**
  Mensch-Maschine-Schnittstelle *f*

~ **perception** menschliche Wahrnehmung *f*
~ **vision** menschliches Sehen *n*
~ **visual perception** Sehwahrnehmung *f*
~ **visual system** menschlicher Sehapparat
  m, menschliches Sehsystem (visuelles
  System) *n*
humectant Feuchthaltemittel *n*
humidity of [the] air Luftfeuchte *f*,
  Luftfeuchtigkeit *f*
Huygenian [microscope] eyepiece
  Huygens-Okular *n*, Huygenssches
  Okular *n*, Negativokular *n*, Einheitsokular
Huygens' principle Huygenssches Prinzip *n*
  (Wellentheorie)
~ **wavelet** Huygenssche Welle
  (Elementarwelle) *f*
hyaloid canal Glaskörperkanal *m* *(des Auges)*
hyalotype Hyalotypie *f*
  (Albuminplattenfotografie)
hybrid coding hybride Codierung *f*,
  Hybridcodierung *f*
~ **database** hybride Datenbank
~ **device** Hybridgerät *n*
~ **filter** Hybridfilter *n*
~ **glass-polymer lens** Hybridobjektiv *n*
~ **image coder** Hybrid[bild]codierer *m*
~ **lens** Hybridobjektiv *n*
~ **median filter** hybrides Medianfilter *n*
~ **modeling** hybride Modellierung *f*,
  Hybridmodellierung *f*
~ **recorder** Hybridrecorder *m*
~ **set** Hybridgerät *n*
~ **transform coding** hybride
  Transformationscodierung *f*
~ **transform/waveform coding** *s.* ~ coding
hydraulic head Hydrokopf *m*,
  Hydraulikkopf *m*, Fluidkopf *m*,
  flüssigkeitsgedämpfter Stativkopf *m*
hydrazine Hydrazin *n* *(Entwicklerzusatz)*
hydrofluoric acid Flusssäure *f*
hydrogen [bubble] chamber
  Wasserstoffblasenkammer *f*
~ **density** Wasserstoffdichte *f*
  (Magnetresonanzbildgebung)
~ **ion concentration**
  Wasserstoffionenkonzentration *f*,
  pH-Wert *m*
~ **laser** Wasserstofflaser *m*
~ **nucleus** Wasserstoffkern *m*; Proton *n*,
  Nukleon *n*
~ **peroxide** Wasserstoffperoxid *n*
~ **sensitization**
  Wasserstoffsensibilisierung *f*
hydrological map hydrologische Karte *f*
hydrophilic hydrophil, wasserannehmend,
  wasseraufnehmend, wasserfreundlich,
  feuchtfreundlich, feuchtigkeitsführend
hydrophilicity Hydrophilie *f*
hydrophobic hydrophob,
  wasserabweisend, wasserabstoßend,
  feuchtfeindlich, feuchtigkeitsabstoßend
hydrophobicity Hydrophobie *f*

hydroquinone Hydrochinon *n*
 (Entwicklerchemikalie)
~ **developer** Hydrochinonentwickler *m*
hydroxylammonium sulfate
 Hydroxylaminsulfat *n*
 (Farbentwicklerzusatz)
hyperacuity Nonius-Sehschärfe *f*,
 Vernier-Sehschärfe *f*, Überauflösung *f*
hyperbolic filter hyperbolisches Filter *n*
~ **geometry** hyperbolische Geometrie *f*
~ **mirror** hyperbolischer Spiegel *m*,
 Hyperbolspiegel *m*
~ **projection** hyperbolische Projektion *f*
~ **reflection** hyperbolische Reflexion *f*
 (Radar)
~**[al]** hyperbolisch, hyperbelförmig
hyperbolical *s.* hyperbolic
hyperboloid Hyperboloid *n*
 (Elementarobjekt)
hypercardioid microphone
 Superkardioid-Mikrofon *n*
~ **polar pattern** Nierencharakteristik *f*,
 Supernierencharakteristik *f (Mikrofon)*
hypercentric perspective hyperzentrische
 Perspektive *f*
hyperfocal distance Hyperfokaldistanz *f*,
 hyperfokale Distanz *f*,
 Nahunendlichpunkt *m (Optik)*
~ **position** Hyperfokaleinstellung *f*
hyperlink Hyperlink *m(n)*
hypermedia [system] Hypermediasystem
 n (Datenbankformat)
hypermetropia, hyperopia
 Hyper[metr]opie *f*, Weitsichtigkeit *f*,
 Übersichtigkeit *f*, Fernsichtigkeit *f*
hyperopic hypermetropisch, hyperop,
 weitsichtig, übersichtig
hyperpanchromatic hyperpanchromatisch
 (fotografische Emulsion)
hyperpatch Hyperfläche *f (Computergrafik)*
hyperplane Hyperfläche *f*
hyperpolarization Hyperpolarisation *f*
hyperpolarize/to hyperpolarisieren
hypersensitization Hypersensibilisierung *f*
hypersensitize/to hypersensibilisieren
hyperspectral hyperspektral
~ **image** hyperspektrales Bild *n*,
 Hyperspektralaufnahme *f*
~ **image data** hyperspektrale Bilddaten *pl*,
 Hyperspektraldaten *pl*
~ **imaging** Hyperspektralaufnahme *f*
~ **sensor** Hyperspektralsensor *m*,
 hyperspektraler Sensor *m*
hypersphere Hyperkugel *f*
hyperstereoscopy Hyperstereoskopie *f*
hypersurface Hyperfläche *f*
hypertext Hypertext *m*, nichtlinearer Text
 m (Datenbankformat)
~ **abstract machine** abstrakte
 Hypertextmaschine *f*
 (Hypermediasystem)
~ **markup language** *die im World Wide
 Web benutzte
 Seitenbeschreibungssprache
 (Dokumentenauszeichnungssprache)*
hypervoxel Hypervoxel *n (Computergrafik)*
hyphen Bindestrich *m*; Trenn[ungs]strich
 m, Divis *n*
hypo 1. Fixierbad *n*; 2. *s.* hyposulfite
hypochromia Hypochromasie *f (Optik)*
hypoechoic echoschwach, echoarm
hypostereoscopy Hypostereoskopie *f*
hyposulfite Hyposulfit *n*, Natriumthiosulfat
 n, unterschwefligsaures Natrium
 (Natron) *n*, Fixiernatron *n*
hypothetical primary imaginäre
 Primärfarbe *f*
hypothetize-and-test Hypothetisieren *n*
 und Testen *n (Bilderkennung)*
hypsochromic shift hypsochrome
 Verschiebung *f (Lichtabsorption)*
hysteresis Hysterese *f*, Umkehrfehler *m*
 (z.B. bei Positionierungen)
~ **loop** Hystereseschleife *f*
~ **thresholding** Hysterese-Binarisierung *f*
hysterosalpingography
 Hysterosalpingografie *f*,
 Röntgenkontrastdarstellung *f* von
 Gebärmutter und Eileitern

I

I frame (picture) I-Bild *n*, Intrabild *n*, intracodiertes Bild *n* *(Video)*
IC *s.* integrated circuit [chip]
ICCD camera *s.* intensified charge-coupled device camera
icon Icon *n*, Bildsymbol *n*, Grafiksymbol *n*; Anwendungssymbol *n*
~ **bar** Symbolleiste *f* *(Bildschirm)*
iconic ikonisch, bildhaft
~ **data** ikonische Daten *pl*
~ **image** ikonisches Bild *n*
~ **image description** ikonische (konkrete) Bildbeschreibung *f*
~ **image processing** ikonische Bildverarbeitung *f*, Bild-zu-Bild-Verarbeitung *f*
~ **indexing** Ikonenindexieren *n* *(Mustererkennung)*
~ **information** ikonische Information *f*
~ **memory** ikonischer Speicher *m*; Bildspeicher *m*
~ **model** ikonisches Modell *n*
~ **operation** ikonische Operation *f*
~ **sign** ikonisches Zeichen *n*
~ **store** *s.* ~ memory
iconicity Ikonizität *f*; Bildhaftigkeit *f*; Anschaulichkeit *f*
iconography Ikonografie *f*
iconoscope Ikonoskop *n* *(eine Bildspeicherröhre)*
ID card security Ausweis-Fälschungssicherheit *f*
ideal diffuse surface Lambertsche Fläche (Oberfläche) *f* *(Fotometrie)*
~ **filter** ideales Filter *n*
~ **high-pass filter** ideales Hochpassfilter *n*
~ **image** ideale [geometrisch-optische] Abbildung *f*, ideales Bild *n*, Idealbild *n*
~ **imagery** ideales Bildmaterial *n*
~ **isotropic diffuser** ideal matte (weiße) Fläche *f*, vollkommen matte Oberfläche *f* *(Farbmetrik)*
~ **Lambertian reflector** Lambertscher Strahler (Reflektor) *m*, Lambert-Strahler *m*
~ **lens** ideale (perfekte) Linse *f*
~ **low-pass filter** ideales Tiefpassfilter *n*
~ **observer** idealer Betrachter *m* *(mathematisches Modell)*
~ **optical system** ideales optisches System *n*
~ **radiator** idealer Strahler *m*
~ **sampling** ideale Abtastung *f*
idempotence Idempotenz *f*
idempotent idempotent
~ **operator** Idempotentfilter *n* *(morphologische Bildverarbeitung)*

identifiability Identifizierbarkeit *f*
identifiable identifizierbar
identification Identifizierung *f*, Identifikation *f*
~ **caption** Bildkennung *f*
~ **leader** Kennzeichnungsband *n*
~ **photo[graph]** Erkennungsfoto *n*; Fahndungsfoto *n*, Fahndungsbild *n*
~ **photography** Ausweisfotografie *f*
~ **picture** Erkennungsbild *n*
~ **trailer** Kennzeichnungsband *n*
identifier Bezeichner *m*
identify/to identifizieren
identity matrix Identitätsmatrix *f*
ideogram Ideogramm *n*
idiot card Neger *m* *(Filmstudiozubehör)*
idle cell leere Zelle *(asynchroner Übertragungsmodus)*
~**[r] roller** Laufrolle *f*, Leerlaufrolle *f*; Umlenkrolle *f*; Führungsrolle *f*
ignition electrode Zündelektrode *f*
IIR filter IIR-Filter *n*
ike *s.* iconoscope
ILA *s.* image light amplifier
illegal color illegale Farbe *f* *(Video)*
~ **copy** Raubkopie *f*
illegible unleserlich
illuminance Beleuchtungsstärke *f*, Illuminanz *f*
~ **meter** Beleuchtungs[stärke]messer *m*, Beleuchtungsstärkemessgerät *n*, Luxmeter *n*
~ **ratio** Beleuchtungsstärkeverhältnis *n*
illuminant 1. Lichtart *f*; 2. Leuchtkörper *m*; Beleuchtungsgerät *n*
illuminate/to beleuchten, ausleuchten, illuminieren
illuminated area Leuchtfläche *f*
~ **display** Leuchtanzeige *f*
~ **field diaphragm** Leuchtfeldblende *f* *(Lichtmikroskop)*
~ **lens viewfinder frame** Sucherleuchtrahmen *m*
~ **view box** Lichtkasten *m*, Leuchtkasten *m*
illuminating aperture Beleuchtungsapertur *f* *(Mikroskopie)*
~ **apparatus (device)** Beleuchtungseinrichtung *f*; Beleuchtungsgerät *n*
~ **engineer** Beleuchtungsingenieur *m*
~ **engineering** Beleuchtungstechnik *f*; Lichttechnik *f*
~ **light** Beleuchtungslicht *n*
~ **light cone** Beleuchtungslichtkegel *m*
~ **light path** Beleuchtungslichtweg *m*
~ **mirror** Beleuchtungsspiegel *m*
~ **pulse** Beleuchtungsimpuls *m*
~ **ray path** Beleuchtungsstrahlengang *m*
illumination 1. Beleuchtung *f*, Ausleuchtung *f*, Illumination *f* *(s.a. unter lighting)*; 2. Belichtung *f* *(s.a. unter exposure)*; 3. *s.* illuminance
~ **angle** Beleuchtungswinkel *m*

illumination

- ~ **box** Lichtkasten *m*, Leuchtkasten *m*, Beleuchtungskasten *m*
- ~ **bundle** Beleuchtungsbündel *n*
- ~ **change** Beleuchtungsänderung *f*
- ~ **color** Beleuchtungsfarbe *f*
- ~ **compensation** Beleuchtungskompensation *f*
- ~ **cone** Beleuchtungskegel *m*
- ~ **correction** Beleuchtungskorrektur *f*
- ~ **direction** Beleuchtungsrichtung *f*, Leuchtrichtung *f*
- ~ **distribution** Beleuchtungsstärkeverteilung *f*
- ~ **effect** Beleuchtungseffekt *m*
- ~ **geometry** Beleuchtungsgeometrie *f*
- ~ **intensity** Beleuchtungsintensität *f*
- ~ **level** Beleuchtungsniveau *n*
- ~ **model** Beleuchtungsmodell *n* *(Computergrafik)*
- ~ **modeling** Beleuchtungsmodellierung *f*
- ~ **patch** Ausleuchtzone *f*
- ~ **screen** Leuchtschirm *m*
- ~ **source** Beleuchtungsquelle *f*
- ~ **spectrum** Beleuchtungsspektrum *n*
- ~ **system** Beleuchtungssystem *n*
- ~ **system optics** Beleuchtungsoptik *f*
- ~ **technique** Beleuchtungstechnik *f*
- ~ **transfer** Lichtübertragung *f*
- ~ **unit** Beleuchtungseinheit *f*
- ~ **variation** Beleuchtungsänderung *f*

illuminator 1. Illuminator *m*; 2. Diabetrachter *m*

illuminometer Beleuchtungs[stärke]messer m, Beleuchtungsstärkemessgerät *n*, Luxmeter *n*

illusion Täuschung *f*, Illusion *f*
- ~ **of motion (movement)** Bewegungstäuschung *f*

illusionistic projection täuschende Projektion *f*

illusory movement Bewegungstäuschung *f*

illustrate/to illustrieren, bebildern

illustration Illustration *f*, Bebilderung *f*; Veranschaulichung *f*, Visualisierung *f*
- ~ **photography** Illustrationsfotografie *f*

illustrative material (matter) Bildmaterial *n* *(Typografie)*

illustrator Illustrator *m*

image/to abbilden; projizieren

image onto itself/to ineinander abbilden, ineinanderkopieren

- ~ Bild *n*, Abbildung *f* *(s.a. unter* picture, frame, imaging*)*
- ~ **aberration** Abbildungsfehler *m*, Bildfehler *m*, Aberration *f*
- ~ **accuracy** Bildgenauigkeit *f*
- ~ **acquisition** Bilderfassung *f*, Bildgewinnung *f*, Bildakquisition *f*
- ~ **acquisition computer** Bildrechner *m*
- ~ **acquisition device** Bilderfassungsgerät *n*
- ~ **acquisition hardware** Bilderfassungshardware *f*, Bildaufnahmetechnik *f*
- ~ **acquisition rate** Bildaufnahmefrequenz *f*, Bilderfassungsrate *f*
- ~ **acquisition speed** Bilderfassungsgeschwindigkeit *f*
- ~ **acquisition time** Bildakquisitionszeit *f*, Bildaufnahmezeit *f*
- ~-**adaptive vector quantization** bildadaptive Vektorquantisierung *f*
- ~ **address** Bildadresse *f*
- ~ **algebra** Bildalgebra *f*
- ~ **alignment** Bildausrichtung *f*
- ~ **alteration** Bildveränderung *f*
- ~ **amplification** Bildverstärkung *f*
- ~ **amplification device**, ~ **amplifier** [fotoelektrischer] Bildverstärker *m*
- ~ **amplitude** Bildamplitude *f*
- ~ **amplitude histogram** Bildamplitudenhistogramm *n*
- ~ **amplitude range** Bildamplitudenbereich *m*
- ~ **analysis** Bildanalyse *f*
- ~ **analysis algorithm** Bildanalysealgorithmus *m*
- ~ **analysis computer** Bildanalysecomputer *m*
- ~ **analysis function** Bildanalysefunktion *f*
- ~ **analysis program** Bildanalyseprogramm *n*
- ~ **analysis software** Bilderkennungssoftware *f*
- ~ **analysis system** Bildanalysesystem *n*
- ~ **analysis tool** Bildanalysewerkzeug *n*
- ~ **analysis workstation** Bildanalysearbeitsplatz *m*
- ~-**analytical** bildanalytisch
- ~ **analyzer** Bildauswerter *m*, Bildanalysator *m*, Bildanalytiker *m*
- ~ **angle** Bildwinkel *m* *(s.a.* field angle*)*
- ~ **animation** Bildanimation *f*
- ~ **annotation** Bildannotation *f*
- ~ **appearance** Bildeindruck *m*
- ~ **archive** Bildarchiv *n*
- ~ **archiving** Bildarchivierung *f*
- ~ **area** Bildfläche *f*, Bildareal *n*; Bildteil *m(n)*; Bildstelle *f*; Bildbereich *m*, Bildregion *f*; Bildpartie *f*, Bildspiegel *m* *(Layout)*
- ~ **arithmetic** bildarithmetisch
- ~ **arithmetic** Bildberechnung *f*
- ~ **arithmetics** Bildarithmetik *f*
- ~ **arrangement (array)** Bildanordnung *f*
- ~ **artifact** Bildartefakt *n*; Bildfehler *m*
- ~ **aspect ratio** Bildseitenverhältnis *n*, Bildformat *n*
- ~ **assembly** Bildmontage *f*, Montage *f* *(Druckvorstufe)*
- ~ **asset management** Bilddatenverwaltung *f*
- ~ **assets** Bildbestand *m*
- ~ **attribute** Bildeigenschaft *f*, Bildattribut *f*
- ~ **authentication** Bildauthentifikation *f*, Bildauthentifizierung *f*
- ~ **averaging** Bildmittelung *f (inhomogene Punktoperation)*

image

- ~ **axis** Bildachse *f*
- ~ **background** Bildhintergrund *m*
- ~ **backup** Bild[daten]sicherung *f*
- ~ **bandwidth** Bildbandbreite *f*
- ~ **bank** Bildbank *f*
- ~-**based graphics** bildbasierte Grafik *f*
- ~-**based modeling** bildbasierte Modellierung *f*
- ~-**based object recognition** bildbasierte Objekterkennung *f*
- ~-**based rendering** bildbasiertes Rendering *n (Computergrafik)*
- ~-**based representation** bildbasierte Darstellung *f*
- ~-**bearing plate** Bildplatte *f*
- ~-**bearing side** Schichtseite *f (Fotomaterial)*
- ~-**bearing support** Bildträger *m*
- ~ **binarization** Bildbinarisierung *f*
- ~ **blooming** Überstrahlen *n*, Überstrahlungseffekt *m*, Blooming-Effekt *m*, Nachziehleuchtfahne *f*
- ~ **blur** 1. Bildunschärfe *f*; 2. *s.* ~ blurring
- ~ **blurring** Bildverschmierung *f*
- ~ **border (boundary)** Bildabgrenzung *f*, Bildbegrenzung *f*, Bildrand *m*; Bildkante *f*
- ~ **brightness** Bildhelligkeit *f*
- ~ **brilliance** Bildbrillanz *f*
- ~ **buffer** *s.* frame buffer [memory]
- ~ **calibration** Bildkalibrierung *f*
- ~ **capture** Bilderfassung *f*, Bildgewinnung *f*, Bildakquisition *f*, Bildaufnahme *f*
- ~ **capture material** Bildaufnahmematerial *n*
- ~-**capturing device** Bildaufzeichnungsgerät *n*, Bildaufnahmegerät *n*, Bilderfassungsgerät *n*
- ~-**capturing system** Bilderfassungssystem *n*
- ~ **carrier** Bildträger *m*
- ~-**carrying ray** Abbildungsstrahl *m*
- ~ **center** Bildmitte *f*, Bildzentrum *n*, Bildmittelpunkt *m*
- ~ **chain** *s.* ~ processing chain
- ~ **change** Bildwechsel *m*
- ~ **change principle** Bildwechselprinzip *n (grafisch-dynamische Simulation)*
- ~ **characteristic** Bildmerkmal *n*
- ~ **characterization** Bildcharakterisierung *f*
- ~ **circle** Bildkreis *m*
- ~ **circle diameter** Bildkreisdurchmesser *m*
- ~ **class** Bildklasse *f*
- ~ **class** Bildklasse *f*
- ~ **classification** Bildklassifikation *f*, Bildklassifizierung *f*, Bildeinordnung *f*
- ~ **clipping** Bildbeschneidung *f*, Bildbeschnitt *m*
- ~ **code** Bildcode *m*
- ~ **coder** Bildcodierer *m*
- ~ **coding** Bildcodierung *f*
- ~ **coding algorithm** Bildcodieralgorithmus *m*
- ~ **coding scheme** Bildcodierungsschema *n*
- ~ **coding standard** Bildcodierungsstandard *m*
- ~ **coding system** Bildcodierungssystem *n*
- ~-**coding technique** Bildcodierungsverfahren *n*
- ~ **coincidence** Bildkoinzidenz *f*
- ~ **collection** Bildsammlung *f*
- ~ **color** Bildfarbe *f*; farbiger Bildton *n*
- ~ **coloration** Bildkolorierung *f*
- ~ **combination** Bildkombination *f*
- ~ **communication** Bildkommunikation *f*
- ~ **communication system** Bildkommunikationssystem *n*
- ~ **comparison** Bildvergleich *m*
- ~ **completion** Bildaufbau *m (z.B. in der Sofortbildfotografie)*
- ~ **component** Bildbestandteil *m*, Bildkomponente *f*
- ~ **composition** Bildzusammensetzung *f*, Bildkomposition *f*
- ~ **compressibility** Bildkomprimierbarkeit *f*
- ~ **compression** Bild[daten]kompression *f*
- ~ **compression algorithm** Bildkompressionsalgorithmus *m*
- ~ **compression method** Bildkompressionsverfahren *n*
- ~ **compression standard** Bildkompressionsstandard *m*
- ~ **computation** Bildberechnung *f*
- ~ **conjugate** Bildweite *f*, Bildentfernung *f*, Kameraauszug *m*
- ~ **construction** Bildaufbau *m*, Bildkonstruktion *f*, Listingsche Strahlenkonstruktion *f (Optik)*
- ~-**containing film** Bildfilm *m (Kinematografie)*
- ~ **content** Bildinhalt *m*
- ~ **content analysis** Bildinhaltsanalyse *f*
- ~ **content feature** Bildinhaltsmerkmal *n*
- ~ **contour** Bildkontur *f*
- ~ **contrast** Bildkontrast *m*
- ~ **contrast amplification** Bildkontrastverstärkung *f*
- ~ **contrast comparison** Bildkontrastvergleich *m*
- ~ **contrast measurement** Bildkontrastmessung *f*
- ~ **control** Bildkontrolle *f*
- ~ **conversion** Bild[um]wandlung *f*
- ~ **converter** Bildwandler *m*
- ~ **converter camera** Bildwandlerkamera *f*
- ~ **converter tube** Bildwandlerröhre *f*, Elektronenstrahlwandlerröhre *f*
- ~ **convolution** Bildfaltung *f*
- ~ **coordinate** Bildkoordinate *f*
- ~ **coordinate measurement** Bildkoordinatenmessung *f*
- ~ **coordinate system** Bildkoordinatensystem *n*
- ~ **copy** Bildkopie *f*
- ~ **correction** Bildkorrektur *f*
- ~ **correlation** Bildkorrelation *f*, Bildzuordnung *f*,

image

~ **correlation filtering** Bildkorrelationsfilterung *f*
~ **correlation spectroscopy** Bildkorrelationsspektroskopie *f*
~ **correlation technique** Bildkorrelationstechnik *f*
~ **corruption** Bild[ver]fälschung *f*
~ **coupling** Bildverknüpfung *f*
~ **coverage** Bildabdeckung *f*
~ **creation** Bildgestaltung *f (s.a. ~ generation)*
~ **crispening** Bild[ver]schärfung *f*
~ **cross talk** Bildübersprechen *n*, Geisterbildentstehung *f*
~ **curvature** Bildkrümmung *f (Optik)*
~ **curve** Bildkurve *f*
~ **cycle** Bildzyklus *m*
~ **cytometry** bildgestützte Zytometrie *f*
~ **data** Bilddaten *pl*
~ **data acquisition** Bilddatenerfasssung *f*
~ **data analysis** Bilddatenanalyse *f*
~ **data bus** Bilddatenbus *m*
~ **data compression** Bild[daten]kompression *f*
~ **data format** Bilddatenformat *n*
~ **data interface** Bilddatenschnittstelle *f*
~ **data matrix** Bild[daten]matrix *f*
~ **data preprocessing** Bilddatenvorverarbeitung *f*
~ **data processing** Bilddatenverarbeitung *f*
~ **data representation** Bilddatendarstellung *f*
~ **data set** Bilddatensatz *m*
~ **data store** Bilddatenspeicher *m*
~ **data structure** Bilddatenstruktur *f*
~ **data transfer (transmission)** Bilddatenübertragung *f*
~ **database** Bilddatenbank *f*
~ **database [management] routine** Bilddatenbankprogramm *n*
~ **database developer** Bilddatenbankentwickler *m*
~ **database interface** Bilddatenbankschnittstelle *f*
~ **database management** Bilddatenbankverwaltung *f*
~ **database system** Bilddatenbanksystem *n*
~ **decoding** Bilddecodierung *f*
~ **decomposition** Bildzerlegung *f*, Bilddekomposition *f*
~ **decompression** Bilddekompression *f*, Bilddekomprimierung *f*
~ **deconvolution** Bild[daten]rekonstruktion *f*, lineare Bildrestauration *f*
~ **defect** Bildfehler *m*
~ **definition** Bildfeinheit *f*, Bildauflösung *f*, Bilddefinition *f*, Detailschärfe *f*; Kontur[en]schärfe *f*; Durchzeichnung *f*, Zeichnung *f*
~ **deflection** Bildablenkung *f*
~ **deformation** Bilddeformation *f*
~ **degradation** Bildverschlechterung *f*, Bilddegradation *f*

~ **demodulation** Bilddemodulation *f*
~ **density** Bilddichte *f*, Bildschwärzung *f*
~ **depth** Bildtiefe *f*
~ **description** Bildbeschreibung *f*
~ **description language** Bildbeschreibungssprache *f*
~ **descriptor** Bilddeskriptor *m*
~ **detail** Bilddetail *n*, Bildeinzelheit *f*
~ **detail contrast** Detailkontrast *m*
~ **detection scheme** Bilderkennungssystem *n*
~ **development** Bildentwicklung *f*
~ **diagonal** Bilddiagonale *f*
~ **difference** Bildunterschied *m*, Bilddifferenz *f*
~ **differencing (differentiation)** Bilddifferenzierung *f*
~ **digitization** Bilddigitalisierung *f*
~ **digitizer** Bilddigitalisierer *m*
~ **digitizing** Bilddigitalisierung *f*
~ **dimension** Bildmaß *n*, Bildabmessung *f*
~ **dimensionality** Bilddimensionalität *f*
~ **direction** Bildrichtung *f*
~ **discrimination** Bildunterscheidung *f*
~ **displacement** Bildversatz *m*
~ **display** 1. Bilddarstellung *f*, Bildanzeige *f*; Bildwiedergabe *f*; 2. *s.* ~ **display device**
~ **display device** Bildschirmgerät *n*, Bildwiedergabegerät *n*, Bildanzeige *f*
~ **display medium** Bildwiedergabemedium *n*
~ **display monitor** Bildmonitor *m*
~ **display noise** Bildschirmrauschen *n*
~ **display system** Bildwiedergabesystem *n*
~ **dissection** Bildzerlegung *f*, Bilddekomposition *f*
~ **dissector tube** Bilddissektorröhre *f*, Bildsondenröhre *f*
~ **distance** Bildweite *f*, Bildentfernung *f*, Kameraauszug *m*; Projektionsentfernung *f*
~ **distortion** 1. Bildverzeichnung *f*, Bildverzerrung *f*; 2. Bildverfremdung *f*
~ **distortion correction** Bildentzerrung *f*, Bildrektifikation *f*
~ **disturbance** Bildstörung *f*
~ **document** Bilddokument *n*
~ **documentation** Bilddokumentation *f*
~ **domain** Bildbereich *m*
~ **dot** Bildpunkt *m (Reprografie)*
~ **doubling** Bildverdopp[e]lung *f*
~ **dropout** Bildausfall *m*, Bildaussetzer *m*
~ **dye release** Bildfarbstofffreisetzung *f*
~ **edge** Bildkante *f*; Bildrand *m*
~ **editing** Bildbearbeitung *f*; Bildaufbereitung *f*
~ **-editing software** Bildbearbeitungssoftware *f*
~ **editor** 1. Bildbearbeiter *m*; Bildaufbereiter *m*, Bildeditor *m (Software)*
~ **element** Bildelement *n*
~ **energy** Bildenergie *f*

~ **enhancement** Bildverbesserung f, Bildverdeutlichung f
~ **enhancer** [fotoelektrischer] Bildverstärker m
~ **enlargement** Bildvergrößerung f
~ **environment** Bildumgebung f
~ **erasure** Bildlöschung f
~ **erecting lens** Umkehrlinse f
~-**erecting prism** Aufrichteprisma n
~ **erecting system** Umkehrsystem n
~ **error** Bildfehler m
~ **error measure** Bildfehlermaß n
~ **evaluation** Bildbewertung f
~ **exploitation algorithm** Bildauswertungsalgorithmus m
~ **exposure** Bildbelichtung f
~ **fault** Bildfehler m
~ **feature** Bildmerkmal n
~ **feature analysis** Bildmerkmalsanalyse f
~ **feature extraction** Merkmalsextraktion f
~ **feature point** Bildmerkmalspunkt m
~ **fidelity** Bildgenauigkeit f; Bildwiedergabequalität f, Abbildungstreue f
~ **field** 1. Bildfeld n; 2. Halbbild n *(Video)*
~ **field angle** Bildfeldwinkel m
~ **field dissection** Bildfeldzerlegung f
~ **file** Bild[dokument]datei f
~ **file directory** Bilddateiverzeichnis n
~ **file format** Bilddateiformat n
~ **file function** Bilddateifunktion f
~ **filter** Bildfilter n
~ **filtering** Bildfilterung f
~ **filtering technique** Bildfilterungsverfahren n
~ **flicker[ing]** Bildflimmern n
~ **focus** Bildschärfe f
~ **fog** Bildschleier m
~ **footage** Filmmaterial n, Bildmaterial n
~ **foreground** Bildvordergrund m
~ **format** Bildformat n
~ **format conversion** Bildformatkonversion f
~ **format parameter** Bildparameter m
~ **formation** Bildentstehung f; Abbildung f; Bilderzeugung f, Bildgenerierung f
~ **formation model** Bildentstehungsmodell n
~ **formation process** Bildentstehungsprozess m
~ **formation technique** Bildgebungstechnik f, Bilderzeugungstechnik f, Abbildungstechnik f; Abbildungsverfahren n
~ **formatting** Bildformatierung f
~-**forming** bildgebend, bilderzeugend, bildzeichnend, bildaufbauend
~-**forming beam** Abbildungsstrahl m
~-**forming conjugate plane** Abbildungsebene f
~-**forming contrast** bildgebender Kontrast m
~-**forming dye** Bildfarbstoff m

~-**forming exposure** bildmäßige Belichtung f
~-**forming layer** bildgebende Schicht f
~-**forming light** bildformendes Licht n
~-**forming light path** Abbildungslichtweg m
~-**forming optical system** abbildendes optisches System n
~-**forming plane** Abbildungsebene f
~-**forming process** Bilderzeugungsprozess m; Bildentstehungsprozess m
~-**forming property** Abbildungseigenschaft f *(z.B. eines Objektivs)*
~-**forming radiation** bilderzeugende Strahlung f
~-**forming ray [of light]** Abbildungsstrahl m
~-**forming ray path** Abbildungsstrahlengang m
~-**forming silver** Bildsilber n, bildaufbauendes Silber n
~-**forming system** 1. Abbildungssystem n, abbildendes System n; 2. bilderzeugendes (bildgebendes) System n
~ **frame** Vollbild n *(Video)*
~ **frame addition** Bildaddition f
~ **frame rate**, ~ **frequency** Bildfrequenz f
~ **function** Bildfunktion f
~ **fusing** Bildfixierung f *(Elektrofotografie)*
~ **fusion** Bildfusion f, Bildverschmelzung f
~ **fuzziness** Bildunschärfe f
~ **gate** Bildfenster n *(Kamera)*
~ **gathering** Bilderfassung f, Bildgewinnung f, Bildakquisition f, Bildaufnahme f
~-**gathering device** Bilderfassungsgerät n
~ **gathering process** Bilderfassungsprozess m, Bildgewinnungsprozess m
~ **generation** Bildgenerierung f, Bilderzeugung f
~ **generator** Bildgenerator m
~ **geometry** Bildgeometrie f
~ **gradient** Bildgradient m
~ **grain** Bildkorn n
~ **graininess** Bildkörnigkeit f
~ **granularity** Bildkörnung f
~ **graph** Bildgraph m
~ **gray-level [value]** Bildgrauwert m
~ **guidance** Bildführung f *(z.B. chirurgischer Operationen)*
~ **guide** Bildleitung f
~-**guided neurosurgery** bildgeführte Neurochirurgie f
~-**guided surgery** bildgeführte (bildgestützte) Chirurgie f
~ **half** Bildhälfte f
~ **halftoning** Bildrasterung f
~ **handling** Bildbehandlung f
~ **height aberration of skew rays** Bildhöhenaberration f windschiefer Strahlen

image

- **~ histogram** Bildhistogramm *n*
- **~ iconoscope** Superikonoskop *n (Bildspeicherröhre)*
- **~ identification** Bildidentifizierung *f (Bildanalyse)*
- **~ illuminance** Bildbeleuchtungsstärke *f*
- **~ illumination** Bildbeleuchtung *f*, Bild[feld]ausleuchtung *f*
- **~ impairment** Bildbeeinträchtigung *f*
- **~ imperfection** Bildfehler *m*
- **~ impression** Bildeindruck *m*, Bildanmutung *f*
- **~ improvement** Bildverbesserung *f*
- **~ inclination** Bildneigung *f*
- **~ indexing** Bildindexierung *f*
- **~ infidelity** Bilduntreue *f*
- **~ informatics** Bildinformatik *f*
- **~ information** Bildinformation *f*, bildliche (bildhafte) Information *f*
- **~ input** Bildeingabe *f*
- **~ input device** Bildeingabegerät *n*
- **~ integration** Bildintegration *f*
- **~ intelligibility** Bildverständlichkeit *f*
- **~ intensification** Bildverstärkung *f*
- **~ intensification fluoroscopy** Bildverstärkerfluoroskopie *f*
- **~ intensifier** [fotoelektrischer] Bildverstärker *m*; Röntgenbildverstärker *m*
- **~ intensifier input phosphor** Bildverstärkereingangsschirm *m*, Eingangs[leucht]schirm *m*, Röntgenleuchtschirm *m*
- **~ intensifier output phosphor** Bildverstärkerausgangsschirm *m*, Ausgangs[leucht]schirm *m*
- **~ intensifier television** Bildverstärkerfernsehen *n*
- **~ intensifier tube** Bildverstärkerröhre *f*
- **~ intensity** Bildintensität *f*
- **~ interpolation** Bildinterpolation *f*
- **~ intensity histogram** Bildintensitätshistogramm *n*
- **~ interpretation** Bildauswertung *f*; Bildinterpretation *f*, Bilddeutung *f*
- **~ inversion** Bildinversion *f*, Bildumkehr[ung] *f*
- **~ irradiance** Bildverteilung *f (Radiometrie)*
- **~ irradiance equation** Reflektivitätsgleichung *f (Schattierungsanalyse)*
- **~ jitter** Bildzittern *n*, Bildwackeln *n*
- **~ judgment** Bildbeurteilung *f*
- **~ labeling** Bildkennzeichnung *f*, Bildmarkierung *f*
- **~ lag** Bildverzögerung *f*, Bildübersprechen *n (Video)*
- **~ language** Bildsprache *f*
- **~ layer** Bildschicht *f*
- **~ library** Bildbibliothek *f*
- **~ light amplifier** *lichtstarker Video-Großbildprojektor mit optisch-fotoelektrischer Ansteuerung der Flüssigkristallschicht*
- **~ light exposure** bildmäßige Belichtung *f*
- **~ limitation** Bildbegrenzung *f*
- **~ line** Bildlinie *f*; Bildzeile *f (Fernsehen)*
- **~ linearity** Bildlinearität *f*
- **~ location** Bildort *m*, Bildstelle *f (Optik)*
- **~ longevity** Bildbeständigkeit *f*, Bildhaltbarkeit *f*
- **~ luminance** Bildleuchtdichte *f*; Bildhelligkeit *f*
- **~ magnification** Bildvergrößerung *f*
- **~ maker** Bildner *m*
- **~ -making** Bilderzeugung *f*, Bildgenerierung *f*, Bildnerei *f*
- **~ management** Bildverwaltung *f*
- **~ management and communication system** Bildverwaltungs- und kommunikationssystem *n*
- **~ management program** Bildverwaltungsprogramm *n*
- **~ management system** Bildverwaltungssystem *n*
- **~ -manipulating software** Bildbearbeitungssoftware *f*
- **~ manipulation** Bildmanipulation *f*
- **~ manipulation [software] program** Bildbearbeitungsprogramm *n*, Bildmanipulationsprogramm *n*
- **~ manipulator** Bildmanipulator *m*
- **~ map** *s.* clickable map
- **~ masking** Bildmaske *f (digitale Bildverarbeitung)*
- **~ masking** Bildmaskierung *f*
- **~ matching** Bildabgleich *m*; Bildvergleich *m*; Bildzuordnung *f*
- **~ material** Bildmaterial *n*
- **~ matrix** Bildmatrix *f*; digitalisiertes Bild *n*
- **~ measurement** Bild[ver]messung *f*
- **~ medium** Bildmedium *n*
- **~ memory** Bild[daten]speicher *m*
- **~ mensuration** Bild[ver]messung *f*
- **~ merging** Bildmischen *n*; Bildkombination *f*
- **~ minification** Bildverkleinerung *f*
- **~ mixing** Bildmischen *n*
- **~ mode** Bildmodus *m*
- **~ model** Bildmodell *n*
- **~ modeling** Bildmodellierung *f*
- **~ modification** Bildmodifikation *f*
- **~ modulation** Bildmodulation *f (s.a. unter modulation)*
- **~ moiré** Moiré *n*
- **~ morphing** computeranimierter Gestaltwandel (Gestaltwechsel) *m*, animierte Überblendung *f*, Morphing *n*, Formen *n*
- **~ mosaic** Bildmosaik *n*
- **~ motion** Bildbewegung *f*, Bildwanderung *f*
- **~ motion blur** Bildbewegungsunschärfe *f*
- **~ motion compensation** Bildstandsausgleich *m*, Bildbewegungsausgleich *m* Bildwanderungsausgleich *m*
- **~ move[ment]** Bildbewegung *f*

image

- ~ movement accuracy Bildbewegungsgenauigkeit *f*
- ~ multiplication Bildvervielfachung *f*
- ~ navigation Bildnavigation *f*
- ~ navigation system Bildnavigationssystem *n*
- ~ negation Bildumkehr[ung] *f*, Bildinversion *f*
- ~ negation *s.* ~ inversion
- ~ negative Bildnegativ *n*
- ~ noise source Bildrauschquelle *f*
- ~ object Bildgegenstand *m*, Bildobjekt *n*
- ~ observation Bildbeobachtung *f*
- ~ of dislocation Versetzungsbild *n* *(Elektronenmikroskopie)*
- ~ operation Bildoperation *f*
- ~ operator Bildoperator *m (s.a. unter operator)*
- ~ optical noise Bildrauschen *n*
- ~ optically/to optisch abbilden
- ~ optimization Bildoptimierung *f*
- ~ orientation Bildorientierung *f*, Bild[aus]richtung *f*
- ~ orthicon [tube] Bildorthikon *n*, Superorthikon *n*, Fernseh-IOT-Röhre *f* *(Bildaufnahmeröhre)*
- ~ output Bildausgabe *f*; Bildwiedergabe *f*
- ~ output device Bildausgabegerät *n*
- ~ output unit Bildausgabeeinheit *f*
- ~ overlap Bildüberlappung *f*
- ~ overlay Bildmontage *f*, Bildsandwich *n*
- ~ pair Bildpaar *n*
- ~-parallel rasterization bildparallele Rasterung *f*
- ~ parallelism Bildparallelität *f*
- ~ parameter Bildparameter *m*
- ~ part Bildteil *m(n)*
- ~ partition Bildaufteilung *f*
- ~ partitioning Bildteilung *f*
- ~ patch Bildstelle *f*, Bildfleck *m*
- ~ pattern Bildmuster *n*
- ~ pattern contrast Bildmusterkontrast *m*
- ~ pattern recognition Bildmustererkennung *f*
- ~ perception Bildwahrnehmung *f*, Bildperzeption *f*
- ~ performance 1. Bildleistung *f (z.B. einer Bildröhre)*; 2. *s.* ~ quality
- ~ periphery Bildrand *m*
- ~ periphery Bildrand *m*
- ~ permanence Bildbeständigkeit *f*, Bildhaltbarkeit *f*
- ~ perturbation Bildstörung *f*
- ~ pixel Bildpixel *n*
- ~ plane Bildebene *f*, Brennebene *f*
- ~ point Bildpunkt *m*
- ~ point operation Bildpunktoperation *f*
- ~ portion Bildabschnitt *m*, Bildsektor *m*
- ~ position Bildposition *f*, Bildlage *f*
- ~ position shift Bildlageänderung *f*
- ~ positioning Bildpositionierung *f*
- ~ postprocessing Bildnachbearbeitung *f*, Bildnachverarbeitung *f*
- ~ power Bildenergie *f*

- ~ preprocessing Bildvorverarbeitung *f*
- ~ presentation Bilddarbietung *f*, Bildpräsentation *f*, Bildvorführung *f*
- ~ primitive Bildprimitiv *n*
- ~ printer Grafikdrucker *m*
- ~ printing Bilderdruck *m*
- ~ printing technology Bilderdrucktechnik *f*
- ~ processing Bildverarbeitung *f*
- ~ processing algorithm Bildverarbeitungsalgorithmus *m*
- ~ processing application Bildverarbeitungsanwendung *f*
- ~ processing architecture Bildverarbeitungsarchitektur *f*
- ~ processing chain Bildverarbeitungskette *f*, Abbildungskette *f*
- ~ processing code Bildcode *m*
- ~ processing computer Bildbearbeitungscomputer *m*; Bildverarbeitungscomputer *m*, Bild[verarbeitungs]rechner *m*
- ~ processing device Bildverarbeitungsgerät *n*
- ~ processing engineer Bildverarbeiter *m*, Bildverarbeitungsfachkraft *f*, Bildverarbeitungsingenieur *m*
- ~ processing filter Bildverarbeitungsfilter *n*
- ~ processing function Bildverarbeitungsfunktion *f*
- ~ processing hardware Bildverarbeitungshardware *f*
- ~ processing instruction Bildverarbeitungsbefehl *m*
- ~ processing laboratory Bildverarbeitungslabor[atorium] *n*
- ~ processing library Bildverarbeitungsbibliothek *f*
- ~ processing module Bildverarbeitungsmodul *n(m)*
- ~ processing operation Bildverarbeitungsoperation *f*
- ~ processing operator Bildverarbeitungsoperator *m (s.a. unter operator)*
- ~ processing parameter Bildverarbeitungsparameter *m*
- ~ processing performance Bildverarbeitungsleistung *f*
- ~ processing procedure Bildverarbeitungsverfahren *n*
- ~ processing program Bildverarbeitungsprogramm *n*; Bildbearbeitungsprogramm *n*
- ~ processing programming Bildverarbeitungsprogrammierung *f*
- ~ processing routine Bildverarbeitungsroutine *f*
- ~ processing software Bildverarbeitungssoftware *f*, bildverarbeitende Software *f*
- ~ processing software package Bildverarbeitungssoftwarepaket *n*

image

- ~ **processing step** Bildverarbeitungsschritt m
- ~ **processing system** Bildverarbeitungssystem n, bildverarbeitendes System n; Bildbearbeitungssystem n
- ~ **processing task** Bildverarbeitungsaufgabe f
- ~ **processing technique** Bildverarbeitungsverfahren n
- ~ **processing technology** Bildverarbeitungstechnik f
- ~ **processing time** Bildverarbeitungszeit f
- ~ **processing tool** Bildverarbeitungswerkzeug n
- ~ **processing workstation** Bildverarbeitungsanlage f
- ~ **processor** Bild[verarbeitungs]prozessor m, Bildverarbeiter m
- ~ **product** Bilderzeugnis n
- ~ **production** Bild[h]erstellung f, Bildproduktion f, Bilderzeugung f, Bildgenerierung f
- ~ **projecting system** Bildprojektionssystem n
- ~ **projection** Bildprojektion f
- ~ **projection device** Bildprojektor m
- ~ **projection profile** Bildprofil n, Bildsignatur f *(Binärbildanalyse)*
- ~ **property** Bildeigenschaft f
- ~ **protection** Bildschutz m
- ~ **pyramid** Bildpyramide f
- ~ **quadrant** Bildquadrant m, Bildviertel n
- ~ **quality** Bildqualität f, Bildgüte f, Abbildungsqualität f
- ~ **quality assessment** Bildgütetest m, Bildgüteuntersuchung f, Bildqualitätsbeurteilung f
- ~ **quality assurance** Bildqualitätssicherung f
- ~ **quality characteristic** Bildgütemerkmal n
- ~ **quality characterization** Bildqualitätskennzeichnung f
- ~ **quality control phantom** Bildgüteprüfkörper m *(Durchstrahlungsprüfung)*
- ~ **quality criterion** Bildgütemerkmal n
- ~ **quality evaluation** Bildqualitätsbeurteilung f
- ~ **quality improvement** Bildqualitätsverbesserung f
- ~ **quality indicator** Bildgüteprüfkörper m *(Durchstrahlungsprüfung)*
- ~ **quality loss** Bildgüteverlust m
- ~ **quality measure (metric)** Bildgütemaß n, Bildqualitätsmaß n
- ~ **quality requirement** Bildgüteanforderung f
- ~ **quality value** Bildgütezahl f
- ~ **quantization** Bildquantisierung f
- ~ **query** Bildabfrage f
- ~ **raster** Bildraster m(n)
- ~ **ray** Bildstrahl m
- ~ **readout [process]** Bildauslesung f

- ~ **rearrangement** Bildumsortierung f
- ~ **receiver** Bildempfänger m
- ~ **receiving (reception)** Bildempfang m
- ~-**receiving layer** Bildempfangsschicht f Tagesmuster npl
- ~ **receptor** Bildaufnehmer m; Bildempfänger m
- ~ **recognition** Bilderkennung f
- ~ **reconstruction** Bild[daten]rekonstruktion f
- ~ **reconstruction algorithm** Bildrekonstruktionsalgorithmus m
- ~ **reconstruction filter** Bildrekonstruktionsfilter n
- ~ **reconstruction technique** Bildrekonstruktionstechnik f
- ~ **reconstruction time** Bildrekonstruktionszeit f; Bildentstehungszeit f *(Computertomografie)*
- ~ **recorder** Bildaufzeichnungsgerät n
- ~ **recording** Bildaufzeichnung f, Bildaufnahme f
- ~-**recording device** Bildaufnahmegerät n, Bildaufzeichnungsgerät n
- ~-**recording medium** Bildaufnahmemedium n
- ~-**recording system** Bildaufnahmesystem n, Bildaufzeichnungssystem n
- ~ **recovery** 1. Bildwiedergewinnung f; 2. s. ~ restoration
- ~ **rectification** Bildentzerrung f, Bildrektifikation f
- ~ **rectifier** Entzerrungsgerät n
- ~ **reduction** Bildverkleinerung f
- ~ **redundancy** Bildredundanz f
- ~ **reference frame** Bildkoordinatensystem n
- ~ **regeneration** Bildwiedergewinnung f
- ~ **region** Bildregion f, Bildbereich m
- ~ **registering (registration)** Bildregistration f, Bildregistrierung f, relative Entzerrung f *(Fotogrammetrie)*; Bildjustierung f
- ~ **registration technique** Bildregistrationstechnik f
- ~ **rendering (rendition)** Bildwiedergabe f
- ~ **replication** Bildwiederholung f
- ~ **representation** Bilddarstellung f
- ~ **reproduction** Bildreproduktion f; Bildwiedergabe f
- ~ **reproduction system** Bildwiedergabesystem n
- ~ **resolution** Bildauflösung f
- ~ **restitution** Bildauswertung f
- ~ **restitution machine** Bildauswertegerät n
- ~ **restoration** Bildrestauration f, Bildrestaurierung f
- ~ **restoration algorithm** Bildrestaurationsalgorithmus m
- ~ **restoration filter** Restaurationsfilter n
- ~ **retrieval** Bildwiederauffindung f, Bildretrieval n, Bildaufruf m; Bildrecherche f, Bildsuche f

image

~ **retrieval algorithm** Bildsuchalgorithmus m
~ **retrieval system** Bildrecherchesystem n
~ **reversal** Bildumkehr[ung] f, Bildinversion f
~ **rotation** Bilddrehung f, Bildrotation f
~ **row** Bildreihe f
~ **sampling** Bildabtastung f, Bilddiskretisierung f
~ **sampling pattern** Bildabtastmuster n
~ **scale [of reproduction]** Bild[wiedergabe]maßstab m, Abbildungsmaßstab m
~ **scaling** Bildskalierung f
~ **scan** s. ~ scanning
~ **scanner** Bildscanner m, Bildabtaster m, Bildabtastgerät n, Scanner m
~ **scanning** Bildabtastung f, Bilddiskretisierung f
~ **scene** Bildszene f, Szene f
~ **scenery** Bildszenerie f
~ **science** Bildwissenschaft f
~ **screen** Bildschirm m
~ **search and retrieval** Bildrecherche f, Bildsuche f
~ **search and retrieval technology** Bildrecherchetechnik f
~ **search engine** Bildsuchmaschine f
~ **search process** Bildsuchvorgang m
~ **section (sector)** Bildsektor m, Bildabschnitt m, Bildausschnitt m
~ **segment** Bildsegment n
~ **segmentation** Bild[objekt]segmentierung f (s.a. unter segmentation)
~ **segmentation algorithm** Bildsegmentierungsalgorithmus m
~ **semantics** Bildsemantik f
~**-sensing CCD** CCD-Bildsensor m, CCD-Bildwandler m
~ **sensor** Bild[aufnahme]sensor m, bildaufnehmender (bildgebender) Sensor m
~ **separation** Bildtrennung f
~ **sequence** Bild[er]folge f, Bildsequenz f
~ **sequence analysis** Bildfolgenanalyse f
~ **sequence coding (compression)** Bildsequenzcodierung f
~ **sequence filter** Bildfolgenfilter n
~ **sequence filtering** Bildfolgenfilterung f
~ **sequence processing** Bildsequenzverarbeitung f
~ **sequence stabilization** Bildfolgenstabilisierung f
~ **set** Bildmenge f
~ **shading** Bildabschattung f
~ **shape** Bildform f
~ **sharpening** Bild[ver]schärfung f
~ **sharpness** Bildschärfe f, Abbildungsschärfe f
~ **sharpness adjustment** Bildschärferegulierung f
~ **shift** Bildverschiebung f
~**-side** bildseitig

~ **side** Bildseite f (z.B. eines Papierabzugs)
~ **side length** Bildseitenlänge f
~ **signal** Bildsignal n
~ **signal amplifier** Bildsignalverstärker m
~ **signal model** Bildsignalmodell n
~ **signal-to-noise ratio** Bildrauschabstand m
~ **signature** Bildsignatur f, Bildprofil n (Binärbildanalyse)
~ **silver** Bildsilber n, bildaufbauendes Silber n
~ **similarity** Bildähnlichkeit f
~ **simplification** Bildvereinfachung f
~ **simulation** Bildsimulation f
~ **size** Bildgröße f, Bildformat n
~ **skeletonization** Bildskelettierung f
~ **slice** Schnittbild n, Bildschicht f; Tomogramm n
~ **smear[ing]** Bildverschmierung f
~ **smoothing** Bildglättung f
~**-smoothing filter** Bildglättungsfilter n
~ **source** Bildquelle f
~ **space** Bildraum m
~ **space algorithm** Bildraumalgorithmus m
~ **space coordinate system** Bildraumkoordinatensystem n
~ **space method** Bildraumverfahren n (Computergrafik)
~ **space principal plane** Bildraum-Hauptebene f
~ **space refractive index** Bildraumbrechzahl f
~ **space representation** Bildraumdarstellung f
~ **spacing** Bildabstand m
~ **specimen** Bildmuster n
~ **spectrum** Bildspektrum n
~ **splitter** Bildteiler m, Strahlenteiler-Vorsatz m (Stereokamera)
~ **stability** Bildstabilität f
~ **stabilization** Bildstabilisierung f, Bildstabilisation f
~ **stabilization system** Bildstabilisierungssystem n, Antiverwacklungssystem n
~ **stabilizer** Bildstabilisator m
~ **stack** Bild[er]stapel m
~ **state** Bildzustand m
~ **statistical** bildstatistisch
~ **statistics** Bildstatistik f (Bilddatenverarbeitung)
~ **storage** Bildspeicherung f
~ **storage device** Bildspeichervorrichtung f
~ **storage function** Bildspeicherfunktion f
~ **storage space** Bildspeicherraum m
~ **storage system** Bildspeichersystem n
~ **storage technology** Bildspeichertechnik f
~ **storage unit** Bildspeichereinheit f
~ **store** Bild[daten]speicher m
~ **store addressing** Bildspeicheradressierung f
~ **stream** Bildfluss m; Bilderfluss m
~ **strength** Bildstärke f

~ **stretching** Bilddehnung f
~ **strip** Bildstreifen m
~ **structure** Bildstruktur f; Bildaufbau m
~ **subtraction** Bildsubtraktion f
~ **superimposition** Bildüberlagerung f
~ **surface** 1. Bildoberfläche f; 2. Bildschale f (Optik)
~-**synchro camera** synchroballistische Kamera f
~ **synchronization** Bildsynchronisation f
~ **synthesis** Bildsynthese f
~ **synthesizer** Bildsynthetisierer m
~ **taking** s. ~ capture
~ **technique** Bildtechhnik f
~ **textural feature** Bildtexturmerkmal n
~ **texture** Bildtextur f
~ **texture analysis** Bildtexturanalyse f
~ **texture classification** Bildtexturklassifikation f
~ **texture descriptor** Bildtexturdeskriptor m
~-**to-image transformation** Bild-zu-Bild-Transformation f
~-**to-image variation** Bild-zu-Bild-Variation f
~ **tone** Bildton m (von Fotopapier)
~ **toner** Tonungsmittel n
~ **topography** Bildtopografie f
~ **topology** Bildtopologie f
~ **track** Bildspur f
~ **transcoding** Bildumcodierung f
~ **transfer** Bildübertragung f, Bildtransfer m
~ **transfer process** Bildübertragungsverfahren n
~ **transfer system** Bildübertragungssystem n
~ **transform[ation]** Bildtransformation f, Bildveränderung f
~ **transition** Bildübergang m
~ **translation** Bildtranslation f, Bildverschiebung f
~ **transmission** Bildübertragung f
~ **transmission chain** Bildübertragungskette f
~ **transmission technique** Bildübertragungstechnik f
~ **tube** Bild[wiedergabe]röhre f
~ **tube camera** Röhrenkamera f
~ **type** Bildart f
~ **understanding** Bildverstehen n
~ **unsharpness** Bildunschärfe f
~ **value** Bildwert m
~ **variability** Bildvariabilität f
~ **variable** Bildvariable f
~ **variation principle** Bildänderungsprinzip n
~ **vector** Bildvektor m
~ **vector quantization** Bildvektorquantisierung f
~ **velocity** Bildgeschwindigkeit f
~ **vibration** Bildvibration f
~ **viewing** Bildbetrachtung f
~ **visualization** Bildvisualisierung f

~ **volume** Volumenbild n
~ **warping** Bildwölbung f (s.a. ~ distortion)
~ **wave** Bildwelle f (Holografie)
~ **widening** Bildverbreiterung f
~ **width** Bildbreite f
~ **wrap** Einfaltung f, Einfaltungsartefakt n (Binärbildverarbeitung)
imaged object Abbildungsobjekt n
imager 1. Bildgeber m, Bilderzeuger m (s.a. image sensor); 2. s. image processor
imagery Bildmaterial n, Bilder npl; Bilddaten pl
imagesetter Belichter m; Laserbelichter m
imagewise [einzel]bildweise; bildmäßig
~ **exposure** bildmäßige Belichtung f
imaginary primary imaginäre Primärfarbe f, irreale Farbe f
imaging 1. Abbilden n, Abbildung f; 2. Bilderfassung f, Bildaufnahme f; Bildgebung f; 3. Bebilderung f (bes. von Druckformen); 4. s. ~ technology
~ bildgebend, bilderzeugend, bildzeichnend, bildaufbauend (s.a. unter image-forming); bildnerisch
~ **aberration** Abbildungsfehler m, Aberration f
~ **ability** Abbildungsvermögen n
~ **algebra** Abbildungsalgebra f
~ **algorithm** Abbildungsalgorithmus m
~ **apparatus** Abbildungsapparat m
~ **behavior** Abbildungsverhalten n (z.B. eines Objektivs)
~ **camera** Aufnahmekamera f, Bildaufnahmekamera f
~ **capability** Abbildungsvermögen n
~ **chain** Abbildungskette f, bilderzeugende Kette f; Bildverarbeitungskette f
~ **chip** Bild[aufnahme]chip m
~ **command** Bildverarbeitungsbefehl m
~ **computer** Bildverarbeitungscomputer m, Bild[verarbeitungs]rechner m; Bildbearbeitungscomputer m
~ **computer workstation** Grafikarbeitsplatz[rechner] m, grafischer Arbeitsplatz m, Bildarbeitsplatz m
~ **conditions** Abbildungsbedingungen fpl
~ **contrast agent** s. contrast agent
~ **data mining** Bilddatenfilterung f
~ **depth** Abbildungstiefe f
~ **detector** bildgebender Detektor m (s.a. image sensor)
~ **device** 1. Bildgerät n, Bildgeber m, bildgebendes Gerät n; Abbildungsvorrichtung f; 2. s. image-recording device
~ **device coordinate system** Gerätekoordinatensystem n Tagesmuster npl
~ **diagnostics** Bilddiagnostik f, bildgebende Diagnostik f
~ **direction** Abbildungsrichtung f
~ **efficiency** Abbildungsleistung f
~ **equation** Abbildungsgleichung f
~ **equipment** Bildgebungsausrüstung f

~ **fiber bundle** Bild[leit]kabel *n*, Bildleitbündel *n (Faseroptik)*
~ **geometry** Abbildungsgeometrie *f*
~ **grating** abbildendes Gitter *n*
~ **infrared** abbildendes Infrarot *n*
~ **instrument** Bildverarbeitungsmessgerät *n*
~ **laser scanner** abbildender Laserscanner *m*
~ **law** Abbildungsgesetz *n*
~ **lens** 1. Abbildungslinse *f*, Bildgebungslinse *f*; 2. bilderzeugendes Objektiv *n*
~ **light** bildformendes Licht *n*
~ **material** Bildgebungsmaterial *n*
~ **medical diagnostics** Bilddiagnostik *f*, bildgebende Diagnostik *f*
~ **medium** Bildmedium *n*; Abbildungsmedium *n*
~ **method** 1. Abbildungsmethode *f*; Bildgebungsmethode *f*; 2. Bildbearbeitungsmethode *f*
~ **modality** Bildgebungsverfahren *n*, bildgebendes Verfahren *n*, Abbildungsverfahren *n (Diagnostik)*
~ **mode** Abbildungsmodus *m*, Abbildungsmode *f*
~ **operation** Bildoperation *f*
~ **optical system** abbildendes optisches System *n*
~ **optics** Abbildungsoptik *f*, abbildende Optik *f*
~ **order** Darstellungsreihenfolge *f*
~ **performance** Abbildungsleistung *f*
~ **photodetector** bildgebender Strahlungsempfänger *m*
~ **plane** Abbildungsebene *f (Optik)*
~ **polarimeter** abbildendes Polarimeter *n*
~ **precision** Abbildungsgenauigkeit *f*
~ **principle** Abbildungsprinzip *n*
~ **procedure (process)** Abbildungsprozess *m*, Bildgebungsprozess *m*; Abbildungsvorgang *m*; Abbildungsverfahren *n*, Bildgebungsverfahren *n*
~ **property** Abbildungseigenschaft *f (z.B. eines Objektivs)*
~ **purpose** Bildgebungszweck *m*
~ **quality** Abbildungsqualität *f*, Abbildungsgüte *f*
~ **radar** Bild[aufnahme]radar *n*, abbildendes Radar *n*
~ **radar sensor** bildgebender Radarsensor *m*
~ **ray** Abbildungsstrahl *m*
~ **satellite** Aufklärungssatellit *m*
~ **scenario** Abbildungsszenario *n*
~ **science** Bildwissenschaft *f*
~ **scientist** Bildwissenschaftler *m*
~ **signal** bildgebendes Signal *n*
~ **situation** Abbildungssituation *f*
~ **software** Bildbearbeitungssoftware *f*; Bildverarbeitungssoftware *f*, bildverarbeitende Software *f*

~ **space** Abbildungsraum *m*
~ **spectrograph** abbildender Spektrograf *m*
~ **spectrometer** Bildspektrometer *n*, abbildendes Spektrometer *n*; hyperspektraler Scanner *m*
~ **spectrometry** Bildspektrometrie *f*
~ **speed** Abbildungsgeschwindigkeit *f*
~ **surface** Abbildungsfläche *f*
~ **system** 1. Abbildungssystem *n*, abbildendes System *n*; 2. Bildgebungssystem *n*, bilderzeugendes (bildgebendes) System *n*; 3. Bildverarbeitungssystem *n*; Bildbearbeitungssystem *n*
~ **task** Abbildungsaufgabe *f*
~ **technique** Bildgebungstechnik *f*, Bilderzeugungstechnik *f*
~ **technology** Bildtechnik *f*, Abbildungstechnik *f*
~ **telescope** abbildendes Teleskop *n*
~ **theory** Abbildungstheorie *f*
imbibe/to imbibieren
imbibition print Imbibitionskopie *f*
~ **process** Quellreliefverfahren *n (fotografische Chemie)*
immersed microscope objective Immersionsobjektiv *n*
immersion electron microscope Immersionsmikroskop *n*
~ **grating** Immersionsgitter *n*
~ **lens** Immersionslinse *f*
~ **medium** Immersionsmedium *n*
~ **objective** Immersionsobjektiv *n*
~ **oil** Immersionsöl *n (Mikroskopie)*
~ **printing** Nasskopierung *f*, Nasskopierverfahren *n (Filmverarbeitung)*
immersive television immersives Fernsehen *n*
immobile coupler diffusionsfester Farb[stoff]kuppler *m (Farbfotografie)*
immunofluorescence microscopy Immunfluoreszenzmikroskopie *f*
impact dot-matrix printer Anschlagdrucker *m*, anschlagender (mechanischer) Drucker *m*
~ **ionization** Stoßionisation *f*
~ **printer** Anschlagdrucker *m*, anschlagender (mechanischer) Drucker *m*
~ **printing process** mechanisches Druckverfahren *n*
impedance 1. Impedanz *f*, [elektrischer] Scheinwiderstand *m*; 2. *s.* acoustic impedance
~-**cardiographic** impedanzkardiografisch
~ **cardiography** Impedanzkardiografie *f*
~ **converter** Impedanzwandler *m*
~ **mismatch** Impedanzsprung *m*
~ **plethysmography** Impedanzplethysmografie *f*
~ **tomography** Impedanztomografie *f*
imperceptible imperzeptibel

imperfect

imperfect crystal fehlgeordneter Kristall *m*
imperforate[d] unperforiert
impinging beam auftreffender Strahl *m*
~ **light** auftreffendes Licht *n*
implant mask Implantationsmaske *f*
implicit modeling implizite Modellierung *f*
~ **quantization** implizite Quantisierung *f*
~ **representation** implizite Darstellung *f (von Bilddaten)*
implode/to implodieren
implosion Implosion *f*
impose/to ausschießen *(Satzherstellung)*
imposer Titelspeicher *m (Camcorder)*
imposition Ausschießen *n*, Druckbogenmontage *f*, Bogenmontage *f*
~ **proof** echter Andruck *m (Druckvorstufe)*
~ **scheme** Ausschießschema *n*
impostor Trägerpolygon *n (Computergrafik)*
imprecise focusing ungenaue Fokussierung *f*
impregnated cathode imprägnierte Katode *f (Bildröhre)*
impress *s.* imprint
impression Eindruck *m*; Abdruck *m*
~ **cylinder** Druckzylinder *m*, Druckwalze *f*; Gegendruckzylinder *m*, Presseur *m (Druckmaschine)*
~ **density** Druckdichte *f*
~ **of depth** Tiefeneindruck *m*
~ **roll[er]** *s.* ~ cylinder
imprimatur Imprimatur *n(f)*, Druckerlaubnis *f*, Druckfreigabe[erklärung] *f*
imprint/to aufdrucken; über[einander]drucken
imprint Aufdruck *m*
improper frame fehlerhafter Datenübertragungsblock *m*
improved-definition television Fernsehen *n* mit verbesserter Auflösung, verbessertes Fernsehen *n*
impulse Impuls *m (s.a. unter* pulse*)*
~ **filter** Impulsfilter *n*, Dirac-Filter *n*, Nächste[r]-Nachbar-Filter *n*
~ **function** Impulsfunktion *f*, [Diracsche] Deltafunktion *f*, Dirac-Funktion *f (Signalverarbeitung)*
~ **generator** Taktgeber *m*, Takt[frequenz]generator *m*
~ **invariance** Impulsinvarianz *f*
~ **noise** Impulsrauschen *n*, impulsförmiges Rauschen *n*, Impulsstörung *f*
~ **response** Impulsantwort *f*, Stoßantwort *f*
~ **response function** Impulsantwortfunktion *f*
~ **train** Kammfunktion *f (Signalverarbeitung)*
impulselike impulsähnlich
impulsive noise *s.* impulse noise
impurity Störstelle *f*
in-between image Zwischenbild *n*
in-betweener Zwischenphasenzeichner *m*
in-betweening Zwischenphasenberechnung *f*
in-camera kameraintern
in-camera editing Drehen *n* auf Schnitt; Schnitt *m* beim Drehen
in-camera effect Kameraeffekt *m*, Kameratrick *m*, Filmaufnahmetrick *m*
in-camera exposure meter eingebauter Belichtungsmesser *m*
in-home studio Heimstudio *n*
in-line hologram Einstrahlhologramm *n*, Geradeaushologramm *n*, In-line-Hologramm *n*, Gabor-Hologramm *n*
in-line holography Geradeausholografie *f*
in-line system Fließfertigungssystem *n (z.B. der Drucksachenherstellung)*
in-line tube In-line-Röhre *f*, In-line-Farbbildröhre *f*, Streifenmaskenröhre *f*, Schlitzmaskenröhre *f*, Trinitron-Bildröhre *f*
in-motion radiography dynamische [industrielle] Radiografie *f*
in-phase phasenrichtig, phasengleich
in point Einstiegspunkt *m (Bandschnitt)*
in register pass[er]genau, passgerecht
in situ microscopy In-situ-Mikroskopie *f*
in sync synchron, zeitgleich
in vivo imaging In-vivo-Abbildung *f*
inaudible unhörbar
inbuilt [video] light eingebaute (integrierte) Videoleuchte *f*
incandescent halogen lamp Halogen[glüh]lampe *f*
~ **lamp** Glühlampe *f*, Glühbirne *f*
~ **light** Glüh[lampen]licht *n*; Weißlicht *n*, weißes (unbuntes) Licht *n*
~ **light source** Glühlichtquelle *f*; Weißlichtquelle *f*
~ **tungsten-wire filament lamp** Wolframwendellampe *f*, Wolframglühlampe *f*
incidence Einfall *m*, Inzidenz *f (von Strahlen)*
~ **angle** Einfallswinkel *m*; Auftreffwinkel *m*
~ **normal** Einfallslot *n*
incident inzident
~ **angle** *s.* incidence angle
~ **bundle** einfallendes Bündel *n*
~ **irradiance** Bestrahlungsstärke *f*, Irradianz *f (Radiometrie)*
~ **light** Auflicht *n*; einfallendes Licht *n*
~-**light [exposure] meter** Beleuchtungs[stärke]messer *m*, Beleuchtungsstärkemessgerät *n*, Luxmeter *n*
~-**light illumination** Auflichtbeleuchtung *f*
~-**light metering** Lichtmessung *f*
~-**light microscopy** Auflichtmikroskopie *f*
~-**light ray** einfallender Lichtstrahl *m*
~ **medium** Eingangsmedium *n*
~ **path** Einfallsweg *m*

~ **radiation** Einfallsstrahlung f, einfallende Strahlung f
~ **ray** Einfallsstrahl m, einfallender Strahl m
inclinable stand Kippstativ n
inclination Neugung f, Inklination f
~ **angle** Neigungswinkel m
inclined schräg
inclinometer Klinometer n
inclusion updating information Inklusionsinformation f *(geometrische Datenverarbeitung)*
incoherence Inkohärenz f
incoherent bundle inkohärentes Bündel n
~ **demodulation** inkohärente Demodulation f
~ **illumination** inkohärente Beleuchtung f
~ **imaging** inkohärente Abbildung f
~ **light** inkohärentes Licht n
~ **radiation** inkohärente (unzusammenhängende) Strahlung f
~ **scattering** inkohärente Streuung f, Compton-Streuung f, Compton-Effekt m *(Röntgenstrahlenschwächung)*
~ **transfer function** inkohärente Übertragungsfunktion f
incoming clock rate Eingangstaktfrequenz f
~ **light** einfallendes Licht n
~ **light ray** einfallender Lichtstrahl m
~ **signal** Eingangssignal n
incompatibility Inkompatibilität f
incompatible inkompatibel
incorporated [color] coupler eingebetteter (eingelagerter) Farbkuppler m
increase in contrast Kontrasterhöhung f, Kontraststeigerung f
~ **in sensitivity** Empfindlichkeitssteigerung f, Empfindlichkeitsgewinn m
increment/to inkrementieren
increment Inkrement n
incremental inkrementell
incunabulum, incunable Inkunabel f, Wiegendruck m, Frühdruck m
indecipherable unleserlich
indent/to einziehen, einrücken *(z.B. Drucktext)*
indent, indent[at]ion 1. Einzug m, Einrückung f *(Layout)*; 2. Abdruck m, Eindruck m
independent frame intracodiertes Bild n, Intrabild n, I-Bild n *(Video)*
~ **identically distributed picture element** unabhängig identisch verteilter Bildpunkt m
~ **of wavelength** wellenlängenunabhängig *(Detektor)*
index/to indexieren
index Index m
~ **ellipsoid** Indexellipsoid n, optische Indikatrix f *(Kristalloptik)*
~-**guided laser** indexgeführter Laser m, indexgeführte Laserdiode f
~ **map** s. lookup table [memory]

~ **matching** Brechzahlanpassung f, Phasenanpassung f *(nichtlineare Optik)*
~-**matching fluid** Immersionsflüssigkeit f
~ **of metamerism** Metamerie-Index m
~ **of refraction** Brechzahl f, Brechungsindex m, Brechwert m, Lichtbrechungsindex m
~-**of-refraction gradient** Brechzahlgradient m
~ **print** Indexbild n, Indexprint m, Fotoindex m
~ **search** Index-Suchlauf m
~ **signal** Indexsignal n *(Video)*
indexed color indizierte Farbe f *(Digitalbildverarbeitung)*
~-**color image** indiziertes Farbbild n
indication Index m
indicator dye Indikator[farbstoff] m
~ **element** Anzeigeelement n
~ **strip** Indikatormessstreifen m
~ **test paper** Indikatorpapier n
indicatrix Indikatrix f, Verzerrungsellipse f *(Kartografie)*
indirect color s. indexed color
~ **estimation** indirekte Schätzung f
~ **illumination** indirekte Beleuchtung f
~ **letterpress [printing]** indirekter Hochdruck m, Letter[off]setdruck m; Trockenoffset[druck] m, wasserloser Offsetdruck m
~ **light** indirektes Licht n
~ **lighting** indirekte Beleuchtung f
~ **method of rectification** indirekte Entzerrung f *(Fotogrammetrie)*
~ **printing process** indirektes Druckverfahren n
~ **radiography** indirekte Radiografie f
~ **reflection** ungerichtete Reflexion f
~ **toning** indirekte Tonung f
indiscernible, indistinguishable ununterscheidbar *(z.B. Bildmerkmale)*
indium antimonide Indiumantimonid n *(Photonendetektor)*
~ **gallium arsenide** Indiumgalliumarsenid n *(Photonendetektor)*
~ **tin oxide** Indiumzinnoxid n *(Elektrodenmaterial)*
individual detector Einzelsensor m
~ **image** Einzelbild n
~ **image slice** Einzelschichttomogramm n
~ **scene** Einzelszene f
~ **shot** Einzelaufnahme f
indoor antenna Zimmerantenne f, Innenraumantenne f
~ **illumination** Innenbeleuchtung f, Innenausleuchtung f
~ **light** Innenraumlicht n
~ **photograph (picture)** Innen[raum]aufnahme f, Interieuraufnahme f, Zimmeraufnahme f
~ **portrait shot** Innenraum-Porträtaufnahme f
~ **scene** Innenszene f
~ **setting** Innendekoration f

induce/to

induce/to induzieren
induced dipole moment induziertes Dipolmoment *n*
inductance Induktivität *f*
induction Induktion *f*
~ **coil** Induktionsspule *f*
~ **period** Induktionsperiode *f*, Inkubationszeit *f*, Latenzzeit *f*
inductive induktiv
industrial camera Industriekamera *f*, industrielle Kamera *f*
~ **comput[eriz]ed tomography** industrielle Computertomografie *f*
~ **endoscopy** industrielle (technische) Endoskopie *f*
~ **film** Industriefilm *m*
~ **image processing** industrielle Bildverarbeitung *f*
~ **machine vision** maschinelles Sehen *n*, Maschinensehen *n*, Computersehen *n*, maschinelle Bilderkennung *f*; industrielles Sichtsystem *n*
~ **microscopy** Industriemikroskopie *f*
~ **photogrammetry** Industriefotogrammetrie *f*
~ **photographer** Industriefotograf *m*
~ **photographic** industriefotografisch
~ **photographic department** betriebliche Fotoabteilung *f*
~ **photography** Industriefotografie *f*
~ **radiography** industrielle Radiografie (Durchstrahlungsprüfung) *f*
~ **robot** Industrieroboter *m*
~ **telescope** technisches Fernrohr *m*
~ **television** Industriefernsehen *n*, industrielles Fernsehen *n*
~ **tomography** industrielle Tomografie *f*
~ **X-ray film** Industrie-Röntgenfilm *m*, industrieller Röntgenfilm *m*
inelastic scattering unelastische (inelastische) Streuung *f*
~ **tunneling spectroscopy** inelastische Tunnelspektroskopie *f*
inertia matrix Trägheitsmatrix *f*
~ **tensor** Trägheitstensor *m*
inexpensive camera Billigkamera *f*
inference engine (machine) Inferenzmaschine *f* *(künstliche Intelligenz)*
infinite impulse response infinite (unbegrenzte) Impulsantwort *f*
~ **impulse response filter** unendliches Impulsantwortfilter *n*, IIR-Filter *n*, rekursives Filter *n*
~ **loop** Endlos[band]schleife *f*, Bandschleife *f*, Endlosband *n*
infinity-corrected objective (optics) Objektiv *n* mit unendlicher Bildweite, Unendlich-Optik *f (Mikroskop)*
~ **focus position** Unendlicheinstellung *f*
~ **lock** Unendlichverriegelung *f*
~ **mode (setting)**, ~ **stop** Unendlicheinstellung *f*
inflow angiography Inflow-Angiografie *f*

informatics Informatik *f*
information Information[en] *f[pl]*
~ **carrier** Informationsträger *m*
~ **channel** Informationskanal *m*
~ **content** Informationsgehalt *m (z.B. eines Bildes)*
~ **density** Informationsdichte *f*
~ **display** Informationsanzeige *f*
~ **efficiency** Informationseffizienz *f*
~ **graphics** Informationsgrafik *f*, Infografik *f*
~ **loss** Informationsverlust *m*
~ **measure** Informationsmaß *n*
~ **pit** Informations-Pit *n*
~ **preservation** Informationserhaltung *f*
~-**preserving differential coding** informationserhaltende Differenzcodierung *f*
~ **processing** Informationsverarbeitung *f*
~ **rate** Informationsgeschwindigkeit *f*
~ **retrieval** Informationswiedergewinnung *f*
~ **science** Informatik *f*
~ **storage** Informationsspeicherung *f*
~ **storage capacity** Informationsspeichervermögen *n*
~ **storage system** Informationsspeichersystem *n*
~ **technology** Informationstechnik *f*
~-**theoretic[al]** informationstheoretisch, kommunikationstheoretisch
~ **theory** Informationstheorie *f*, Kommunikationstheorie *f*
~ **transfer (transmission)** Informationsübertragung *f*
~ **transmission system** Informationsübertragungssystem *n*
~ **visualization** Informationsvisualisierung *f*
infrared infrarot, ultrarot
~ Infrarot *n*, Ultrarot *n*
~ **absorber** Infrarotabsorber *m (Thermodruck)*
~-**absorbing filter** Infrarotsperrfilter *n*
~ **absorption spectroscopy** Infrarotabsorptionsspektroskopie *f*
~ **aerial photography** Infrarot-Luftbildfotografie *f*
~ **astronomy** Infrarot-Astronomie *f*
~ **autofocus** Infrarot-Autofokus *m*
~ **band** Infrarotbande *f*
~ **band-pass filter** Infrarot-Bandpassfilter *n*
~ **beam** Infrarot[licht]strahl *m*
~ **beam splitter** Infrarotstrahl[en]teiler *m*
~ **black-and-white film** Schwarzweiß-Infrarotfilm *m*
~-**blocking filter** Infrarotsperrfilter *n*
~ **camera** Infrarotkamera *f*, Wärme[bild]kamera *f*, Thermografiekamera *f*
~ **channel** Infrarotkanal *m*
~ **cinematography** Infrarotkinematografie *f*
~ **color aerial photograph** Infrarot-Farbluftbild *n*

~ **color film** Infrarotfarbfilm *m*, Farbinfrarotfilm *m*
~ **color photograph** Infrarot-Farbfoto *n*
~ **detection device,** ~ **detector** *s.* ~ photodetector
~ **device** Infrarotgerät *n*
~ **diode** Infrarotdiode *f*
~ **dryer** Infrarottrockner *m*
~ **emission** Infrarotemission *f*
~ **emitter** Infrarotsender *m*
~ **emitting diode** Infrarotemitterdiode *f*
~ **emitting lamp** Infrarotlampe *f*
~ **emulsion** Infrarotemulsion *f*
~ **endoscopy** Infrarotendoskopie *f*
~ **energy** Infrarotenergie *f*
~ **exposure** Infrarotbelichtung *f*
~ **false-color film** Falschfarbenfilm *f*, Farbinfrarotfilm *m* Kornea *f*
~ **film** Infrarotfilm *m*, infrarotempfindlicher Film *m*
~ **filter** Infrarotfilter *n*, Infrarot-Transmissionsfilter *n*
~ **flash** Infrarotblitz *m*, Dunkelblitz *m*
~ **flash photography** Infrarotblitzfotografie *f*
~ **fluorescence** Infrarotfluoreszenz *f*
~ **fluorescence photography** Infrarotfluoreszenzfotografie *f*
~ **focusing index** *s.* ~ mark
~ **handset** *s.* ~ remote control [unit]
~ **illumination** Infrarotbeleuchtung *f*
~ **image** Infrarotbild *n*, infrarotes Bild *n*
~ **image converter** Infrarotbildwandler *m*
~ **image data** Infrarotbilddaten *pl*
~ **image processing** Infrarotbildverarbeitung *f*
~ **imager** Infrarotbildsensor *m*
~ **imaging** Infrarotbildaufnahme *f*
~ **interface** Infrarotschnittstelle *f*
~ **laser** Infrarotlaser *m*
~ **light** Infrarotlicht *n*
~ **luminescence** Infrarotlumineszenz *f*
~ **mark** Infrarotmarke *f*, Infrarotmarkierung *f (Kamera)*
~ **microscope** Infrarotmikroskop *n*
~ **microscopy** Infrarotmikroskopie *f*
~ **mirror** Infrarotspiegel *m*
~ **motion-picture film** Infrarotkinefilm *m*
~ **observation satellite** Infrarot-Beobachtungssatellit *m*
~-**optical** infrarotoptisch
~ **optics** Infrarotobjektiv *n*, Infrarotoptik *f*, infrarotkorrigiertes Objektiv *n*
~ **photodetector (photon detector)** Infrarotdetektor *m*, Infrarotstrahlungssensor *m*
~ **photograph** Infrarotaufnahme *f*, Infrarotfoto *f*
~ **photographic film** Infrarotfilm *m*, infrarotempfindlicher Film *m*
~ **photographic material** Infrarot-Fotomaterial *n*
~ **photography** Infrarotfotografie *f*, Dunkelfotografie *f*
~ **photon** Infrarotquant *n*
~ **photosensitive plate** Infrarotplatte *f*
~-**polarizing filter** Infrarotpolarisationsfilter *n*
~ **portion of the spectrum** infraroter Spektralbereich *m*
~ **pyrometer** Infrarotpyrometer *n*
~ **radiation** Infrarotstrahlung *f*, infrarote Strahlung *f*
~ **radiation source** Infrarot[strahlungs]quelle *f*
~ **range** Infrarotbereich *m*
~ **receptor** *s.* ~ photodetector
~-**reflecting filter** Infrarotsperrfilter *n*
~ **reflectographic** infrarotreflektografisch
~ **reflectography** Infrarotreflektografie *f*
~ **regime (region)** Infrarotbereich *m*
~ **remote control [unit]** Infrarot-Fernbedienung *f*, Infrarotfernsteuerung *f*
~ **satellite image** Infrarot-Satellitenbild *n*
~ **scanner** Infrarotscanner *m*, Thermalscanner *m*
~ **scanning** Infrarotabtastung *f*
~ **scope** Infrarotsichtgerät *n*
~-**sensitive** infrarotempfindlich
~-**sensitive emulsion** infrarotempfindliche Emulsion *f*
~-**sensitive film** infrarotempfindlicher Film *m*, Infrarotfilm *m*
~ **sensitivity** Infrarotempfindlichkeit *f*
~ **sensor** Infrarotsensor *m*
~ **signature** Infrarotsignatur *f*
~ **slave** Infrarot[fern]auslöser *m*
~ **spectroscopy** Infrarotspektroskopie *f*
~ **spectrum** Infrarotspektrum *n*
~ **technology** Infrarottechnik *f*
~ **telescope** Infrarotteleskop *n*
~ **thermal imaging technique** *s.* ~ thermography
~ **thermographic** infrarotthermografisch
~ **thermographic system** Infrarotbildsensor *m*
~ **thermography** Infrarotthermografie *f*, Infrarot-Wärmebildverfahren *n*
~ **transmission** Infrarotübertragung *f*
~ **transmitter** Infrarotsender *m*
~-**transmitting** infrarotdurchlässig, infrarottransparent
~-**transmitting filter** Infrarot-Transmissionsfilter *n*, Infrarotfilter *n*
~ **trigger** Infrarot[fern]auslöser *m*
~ **video camera** Infrarot-Videokamera *f*
~ **visual display unit** Infrarotsichtgerät *n*
~ **wavelength** Infrarotwellenlänge *f*
infrasonic frequency range Infraschall[bereich] *m*
inherent noise Eigenrauschen *n*
inhibition Hemmung *f*, Inhibition *f*
inhibitor Hemmstoff *m*, Inhibitor *m*
inhomogeneous diffusion inhomogene Diffusion *f (Bildmodellierung)*
~ **medium** inhomogenes Medium *n*

inhomogeneous 194

~ **point operation** inhomogene Punktoperation *f*
inhomogenous contrast inhomogener Kontrast *m*
initial *s.* ~ capital letter
~ **alignment control** Synchronisationssteuerzeichen *n*
~ **capital letter** Anfangsbuchstabe *m*, Initialbuchstabe *m*, Initial *n*, Initiale *f*
~ **contrast** Anfangskontrast *m*
~ **exposure** Erstbelichtung *f*
~ **image** *s.* input image
~ **phase** Anfangsphase *f (z.B. einer Lichtwelle)*
~ **point** Anfangspunkt *m*, Ausgangspunkt *m*, Startpunkt *m*, Initialpunkt *m*; Keimpunkt *m (Bereichswachstumsverfahren)*
initialization file Initialisierungsdatei *f*
initialize/to initialisieren; formatieren *(z.B. Datenträger)*
injection laser Injektionslaser *m*, Halbleiterlaser *m*, Halbleiterlaserdiode *f*
ink/to einfärben *(eine Druckform)*
ink 1. Tinte *f*; 2. Druckfarbe *f*
~ **balance** Farbbalance *f*
~ **cartridge** Tintenkartusche *f*, Tinten[druck]patrone *f*
~ **coverage** Farbdeckung *f (Druck)*
~ **density control** Farbdichteregelung *f (Druckmaschine)*
~ **dot** Druckpunkt *m*
~ **film** Farbschicht *f*
~ **flooding mechanism** Farbwerk *n (Druckmaschine)*
~ **fountain** Farb[dosier]kasten *m (Druckmaschine)*
~-**jet head** Tintenstrahlkopf *m*
~-**jet paper** Tintendruckerpapier *n*, Tintenstrahlpapier *n*
~-**jet plotter** Tintenstrahlplotter *m*, Farbdüsenplotter *m*
~-**jet print** Tintenstrahlausdruck *m*
~-**jet printer** Tinten[strahl]drucker *m*, Ink-Jet-Drucker *m*; Ink-Jet-Druckmaschine *f*
~-**jet printing** Tinten[strahl]druck *m*, Farbstrahldruck *m*
~-**jet printing technology** Tintenstrahldrucktechnik *f*
~ **nozzle** Tintendüse *f*; Farbdüse *f*
~ **number printer** Acmade-Numeriermaschine *f (Kinefilmbearbeitung)*
~ **pan** Farbwanne *f (Druckmaschine)*
~ **reception** Farbannahme *f (Druck)*
~-**receptive** farbannehmend, farbfreundlich, farbführend
~ **receptivity** Farbannahmefähigkeit *f*, Farbannahmevermögen *n*, Druckfarbenaufnahmevermögen *n*
~-**repellent** farbabstoßend, farbabweisend
~ **reservoir** Tintentank *m*
~ **roller** Farbwalze *f*, Farbauftrag[s]walze *f*

~ **tank** Tintentank *m*
~ **transfer** Farbübertragung *f (Druck)*
~-**water balance** Druckfarbe-Feuchtmittel-Balance *f*, Farb-Wasser-Gleichgewicht *n*
inked ribbon Farbband *n*, Druckerfarbband *n*
~ **ribbon cartridge** Farbbandkassette *f*
inking Einfärbung *f (von Druckplatten)*
~ **mechanism** *s.* ~ system
~ **roller** Farbwalze *f*, Farbauftrag[s]walze *f*
~ **system** Farbwerk *n (Druckmaschine)*
inner error correction innerer Fehlerschutz *m*
~ **error correction code** innerer Fehlerkorrekturcode *m*
~ **form** innere Druckform *f*
~ **noise** Eigenrauschen *n*
inorganic photoconductor anorganischer Fotoleiter *m*
inplant firmeneigene (hauseigene) Druckerei *f*, Hausdruckerei *f*
inpolygon eingeschriebenes Polygon *n*
input/to eingeben *(Daten)*
input Eingabe *f*
~ **amplifier** Eingangsverstärker *m*
~ **bandwidth** Eingangsbandbreite *f*
~ **beam** Eintrittsstrahl *m*
~ **brightness** Eingangshelligkeit *f (elektronische Bildaufnahme)*
~ **clock** Eingangstakt *m*
~ **data matrix** Eingabedatenmatrix *f*
~ **data set** Eingangsdatensatz *m*
~ **device** Eingabegerät *n*
~ **field** Eingabefeld *n*
~ **fluorescent screen** Eingangs[leucht]schirm *m*, Bildverstärkereingangsschirm *m*, Röntgenleuchtschirm *m*
~ **format** Eingabeformat *n*
~ **frequency** Eingangsfrequenz *f*
~ **function** Eingabefunktion *f*
~ **histogram** Eingabehistogramm *n*
~ **image** Bildvorlage *f*; Eingabebild *n*, Eingangsbild *n*; Roh[daten]bild *n*, unverarbeitetes Bild *n*
~ **image data** Eingangsbilddaten *pl*
~ **image resolution** Eingangsbildauflösung *f*
~ **image signal** Eingangsbildsignal *n*
~ **image size** Eingangsbildgröße *f*
~ **interface** Eingangsschnittstelle *f*
~ **layer** Eingabeschicht *f*, Eingangsschicht *f (neuronales Netz)*
~ **mask** Eingabemaske *f*
~ **multiplex filter** Eingangs-Multiplexfilter *n*
~ **noise** Eingangsrauschen *n*
~ **pattern** Eingangsmuster *n*, Eingabemuster *n (Mustererkennung)*
~ **phosphor [screen]** *s.* ~ fluorescent screen
~ **pulse** Eingangsimpuls *m*

~ **queue** Eingabewarteschlange *f* *(Grafiksystem)*
~ **scanner** Eingabescanner *m*
~ **scene** Aufnahmeszene *f*
~ **signal** Eingangssignal *n*
~ **stimulus** Eingangsreiz *m*
~ **vector** Eingabevektor *m*, Eingangsvektor *m*
~ **vector space** Eingabevektorraum *m*
~ **video picture** Eingangs-Videobild *n*
~ **video signal** Eingangsvideosignal *n*
inquiry function Erfragefunktion *f*
inscribed circle Inkreis *m*
~ **polygon** eingeschriebenes Polygon *n*
insensitivity to noise Rauschunempfindlichkeit *f*
insert/to einfügen
insert 1. Insert *n*; 2. Beilage *f*, Druckbeilage *f*; 3. Bildeinblendung *f*; 4. *s.* ~ sequence; 5. *s.* ~ title
~ **editing** Einfügeschnitt *m*, einfügender Schnitt *m*, Insertschnitt *m* *(Videografie)*
~ **key** Einfügetaste *f*
~ **mode** Einfügemodus *m*
~ **sequence** Einschnittszene *f*, eingeschnittene Filmszene *f*, Einblendung *f*
~ **title** Texteinblendung *f*; Zwischentitel *m*
insertion point Einfügemarke *f*, Schreibmarke *f*
~ **test signal** Prüfzeilensignal *n*
inset/to einstecken, sammeln *(Falzbogen)*
inside margin[s] Papierrand *m* innen, Bundsteg *m* *(Layout)*
insonify/to [an]schallen, beschallen *(Sonografie)*
insonifying frequency Anschallfrequenz *f*
inspection light Prüflicht *n*
install/to installieren
instant camera Sofortbildkamera *f*
~-**color film** Sofortbild-Farbfilm *m*, Farbsofortbildfilm *m*
~-**color image** Farbsofortbild *n*, Colorsofortbild *n*
~-**color photography** Sofortbild-Farbfotografie *f*, Farbsofortbildfotografie *f*
~ **color print** Farbsofortbild *n*, Colorsofortbild *n*
~-**color slide** Sofortbild-Farbdia[positiv] *n*
~-**color transparency film** Sofortbild-Farbdiafilm *m*
~ **endoscopy** Sofortbildendoskopie *f*
~-**film picture** Sofortbild *n*, Sofortfoto *n*
~-**image system** Sofortbildsystem *n*
~ **lettering** Abreibeschrift *f*
~ **of exposure** Belichtungszeitpunkt *m*
~ **photograph** Sofortbild *n*, Sofortfoto *n*
~-**photographic print** Sofortbildabzug *m*
~ **photography** Sofortbildfotografie *f*, Instantfotografie *f*
~ **photomacrography** Sofortbild-Makrofotografie *f*
~-**picture camera** Sofortbildkamera *f*
~-**picture film** Sofortbildfilm *m*
~-**picture material** Sofortbildmaterial *n*
~-**picture photography** Sofortbildfotografie *f*, Instantfotografie *f*
~-**picture process** Sofortbildverfahren *n*
~-**print color film** Sofortbild-Papierfilm *m*
~ **print film** Direktpositivfilm *m*
~ **replay** Wiederholfunktion *f* *(Videokamera)*
~-**return iris** [automatische] Springblende *f*
~-**return[-type reflex] mirror** Rückschwingspiegel *m*, Schnellrücklaufspiegel *m*, Klappspiegel *m* *(Spiegelreflexkamera)*
~-**slide film** Sofortbild-Dia[positiv]film *m*, Sofortdiafilm *m*
~ **transparency** Sofortbild-Diapositiv *n*
instantaneous field of view (vision) momentanes Gesichtsfeld *n*
~ **record** Momentaufnahme *f*
~ **shutter** Momentverschluss *m*
~ **viewing** Echtzeitbetrachtung *f*
instantaneously decodable code Präfixcode *m*, präfixfreier (sofort decodierbarer) Code *m*
instantiate/to instantiieren, instanziieren
instantiation Instantiierung *f*, Instanzierung *f* *(Computergrafik)*
instruction Anweisung *f*, Befehl *m* *(Computerprogramm)*
~ **set** Befehlsvorrat *m*
instructional television (TV) Unterrichtsfernsehen *n*
instrumental resolving power instrumentelles Auflösungsvermögen *n*
intaglio cell Rasternäpfchen *n*, Näpfchen *n* *(Tiefdruck)*
~ **image carrier** Tiefdruckform *f*, Intaglioplatte *f*
~ **printing [process]** Tiefdruck *m*; Tiefdruckverfahren *n*
~ **printing plate** Tiefdruckplatte *f*
intake device *s.* input device
integer-pixel accuracy Pixelgenauigkeit *f*, Vollpixelgenauigkeit *f*
integrability Integrierbarkeit *f*
~ **constraint** Integrationsbedingung *f*
integral color density integrale Farbdichte *f*
~ **film** Integralfilm *m*
~ **tripack** Tripack-Film *m*, Monopack *n* *(Farbfotografie)*
~ **tripack color film** Dreischichtenfarbfilm *m*
integrated circuit [chip] integrierte Schaltung *f*, integrierter Schaltkreis *m*, Mikrochip *m*
~ **circuit technology** Leiterplattentechnik *f*
~ **daylight film-handling system** dezentrales (modulares) Tageslichtsystem *n* *(Röntgenfotografie)*
~ **flash** Kamerablitz *m*, eingebauter Blitz *m*, Gehäuseblitz *m*
~ **optics** integrierte Optik *f*

integrated

~ **receiver-decoder** digitaler Empfangsdecoder *m*
Integrated Services Digital Network diensteintegrierendes Digitalnetz *n*, diensteintegrierendes digitales Kommunikationsnetz *n*, ISDN
integrating meter Integralbelichtungsmesser *m*
~ **metering** Integral[belichtungs]messung *f*, integrale Belichtungsmessung *f*
~ **sphere** Kugelfotometer *n* [nach Ulbricht], Ulbricht-Kugel *f*, Ulbrichtsche Kugel *f* *(Fotometrie)*
integration control Belichtungssteuerung *f* *(CCD-Technologie)*
~ **period (time)** Integrationszeit *f* *(CCD-Technologie; Analog-Digital-Wandlung)*
intelligence Aufklärung *f*
~-**bearing signal** Nutzsignal *n*, Nachrichtensignal *n*
intelligent character recognition Handschrifterkennung *f*
~ **robot** KI-Roboter *m*
intensification Verstärkung *f*
intensified CCD (charge-coupled device) camera verstärkende CCD-Kamera *f*
intensifier Verstärker *m* *(Fotonegativverarbeitung)*
intensify/to intensivieren, verstärken
intensifying screen Verstärkerfolie *f*, Verstärkungsfolie *f*, Folie *f* *(Radiografie)*
~ **screen-film system** Film-Folien-System *n* *(Radiografie)*
intensity 1. Intensität *f*; 2. Sättigung *f*, Farbsättigung *f* *(Kolorimetrie)*; 3. Helligkeit *f* *(HSI-Merkmalsraum)*; 4. *s.* illuminance; 5. *s.* sound pressure
~ **distortion** Intensitätsverzerrung *f*
~ **distribution** Intensitätsverteilung *f*; Lichtstärkeverteilung *f*
~ **edge** Intensitätskante *f*
~ **function** Intensitätsfunktion *f*
~ **gradient** Intensitätsgradient *m*
~ **histogram** Intensitätshistogramm *n*
~ **image** Intensitätsbild *n*
~ **interpolation shading** Gouraud-Schattierung *f* *(Computergrafik)*
~ **interval** Intensitätsintervall *n*
~ **map** Intensitätsbild *n*
~ **modulation** Intensitätsmodulation *f*
~ **noise** Intensitätsrauschen *n* *(einer Lichtquelle)*
~ **of light** Lichtintensität *f*, Lichtstromdichte *f*
~ **pattern** Intensitätsmuster *n*
~ **picture** Schwarzweißbild *n*
~ **plane** Intensitätsebene *f* *(Grauwertbild)*
~ **plot** Intensitätsbild *n*
~ **profile** Intensitätsprofil *n*
~ **range** Intensitätsbereich *m*
~ **resolution** Intensitätsauflösung *f*; Helligkeitsauflösung *f*
~ **scale** Intensitätsskala *f*
~ **scaling** Intensitätsskalierung *f*
~ **threshold** Intensitätsschwelle *f*
~ **transformation** Intensitätstransformation *f*; Grauwerttransformation *f*
~ **transition** Intensitätsübergang *m*
~ **value** Intensitätswert *m*; Grauwert *m*, Helligkeitswert *m*
interact/to interagieren; wechselwirken
interaction channel Interaktionskanal *m* *(Fernsehen)*
interactive interaktiv
~ **computer graphics** interaktive Computergrafik *f*
~ **data service** interaktiver Datendienst *m*
~ **display [device]** Dialogmonitor *m*
~ **graphics** interaktive Grafik *f*
~ **graphics system** interaktives Grafiksystem *n*
~ **image processing** interaktive Bildverarbeitung *f*
~ **input device** Interaktionsgerät *n*
~ **interface** interaktive Schnittstelle *f*
~ **lighting** interaktive Beleuchtung *f*
~ **multimedia** interaktives Multimedia *n*
~ **program[ming] guide** interaktiver Programmführer *m*
~ **surface modeling** interaktive Flächenmodellierung *f*
~ **television** interaktives Fernsehen *n*, Fernsehen *n* mit Zuschauerbeteiligung
~ **text transmission system** interaktives Textübertragungssystem *n*
~ **video** interaktives Video *n*
~ **video game** interaktives Videospiel *n*
~ **videotex** Bildschirmtext[dienst] *m*, BTX; interaktiver Videotext *m* Lichtbestimmer *m*
~ **visualization** interaktive Visualisierung *f*
interactivity Interaktivität *f*
interaxial distance Achsenabstand *m*
interblock gap Blocklücke *f*
interception plane Auffangebene *f* *(Optik)*
~ **radar** Abfangradar *n*
interchange format Austauschformat *n*, Bildaustauschformat *n*
interchangeable back, ~ film back (holder) auswechselbare Kamerarückwand *f*, Wechselmagazin *n* *(Spiegelreflexkamera)*
~ **filter** Wechselfilter *n*
~ **focusing screen** Wechselmattscheibe *f*
~ **lens** Wechselobjektiv *n*, [aus]wechselbares Objektiv *n*, Wechseloptik *f*
~-**lens camera** Wechselobjektivkamera *f*
~ **magazine** Wechselmagazin *n*
~ **pentaprism** Wechselprismensucher *m*
~ **screen** Wechselmattscheibe *f*
~ **tube** Wechseltubus *m*
~ **viewfinder** Wechselsucher *m*
intercode/to intercodieren

intercom (intercommunication) system
Intercomeinrichtung f, Sprechanlage f
(Studioausrüstung)
~ **signal** Intercomsignal n
~ **speaker** Intercomlautsprecher m
interconnect/to zusammenschalten;
vernetzen
interconnection technology
Anschlusstechnik f
intercut/to einspielen, einschneiden *(z.B.
kontrastierende Einstellungen in eine
Filmszene)*
intercut Einspielung f, Zwischenschnitt m
intercutting Zwischenschnitt m
(Filmbearbeitung)
interdot distance Punktabstand m;
Rasterpunktabstand m
interface/to anschließen
interface 1. Grenzfläche f; 2. Schnittstelle f,
Interface n
~ **cable** Schnittstellenkabel n
~ **card** Schnittstellenkarte f
~ **control word** Schnittstellen-Steuerwort
n
~ **device** s. interface 2.
~ **integration** Schnittstellenintegration f
~ **multiplier** Schnittstellenvervielfacher m
~ **speed** Schnittstellengeschwindigkeit f
~ **technology** Schnittstellentechnologie f
interfaceable anschlussfähig
interfacing device s. interface 2.
interfere/to interferieren
interference Interferenz f; Bildstörung f
~ **coating** Interferenzschicht f
~ **color** Interferenzfarbe f
~ **contrast** Interferenzkontrast m
~ **effect** Interferenzeffekt m
~ **equation** Interferenzgleichung f
~ **field** Interferenzfeld n, Störfeld n
~ **figure** s. ~ pattern
~ **filter** Interferenzfilter f; Dichroidfilter n,
dichroitisches Filter n
~ **fringe** Interferenzstreifen m,
Interferenzlinie f
~ **grating** Interferenzgitter n
~ **holography** Interferenzholografie f
~ **level** Störpegel m
~ **microscope** Interferenzmikroskop n
~ **microscopy** Interferenzmikroskopie f
~ **noise** Rauschen n
~ **pattern** Interferenz[streifen]muster n,
Interferenzbild n, Stör[ungs]muster n
~ **phenomenon** Interferenzerscheinung f
~ **photography** Interferenzfotografie f
~ **pulse** Störimpuls m
~ **signal** Störsignal n
~ **spectrum** Interferenzspektrum n
~ **suppression** Störunterdrückung f
~ **-to-noise ratio** Stör-Rausch-Abstand m
~ **tube microphone** Richtmikrofon n,
Rohrrichtmikrofon n, Keulenmikrofon n
interfering signal Störsignal n
interferogram Interferogramm n
interferograph Interferograf m

interferographic interferografisch
interferography Interferografie f
interferometer Interferometer n
interferometric interferometrisch
~ **camera** interferometrische Kamera f
~ **light microscope** Interferenzmikroskop n
~ **lithography** interferometrische
Lithografie f
~ **tomography** interferometrische
Tomografie f
interferometry Interferometrie f
interframe correlation s. ~ redundancy
~ **differential coding** prädiktive
Interframe-Codierung f
~ **encoding** Interframe-Codierung f,
Intercodierung f, Bild-zu-Bild-Codierung
f
~ **predictive coding** s. ~ differential coding
~ **redundancy** zeitliche Redundanz f *(von
Videobilddaten)*
~ **time** Zwischenbildzeit f
interim image Zwischenbild n
interimage effect vertikaler
Eberhard-Effekt m, Interimage-Effekt m
interior location Innendrehort m
~ **recording** Innenaufnahme f
~ **scene** Innenszene f
~ **set** Innendekoration f
~ **shooting** Innendreh m, Innendreharbeit f
~ **shot** Innen[raum]aufnahme f,
Interieuraufnahme f; Zimmeraufnahme f
interlace Zeilensprung m
~ **artifact** Zeilensprungartefakt n
~ **flicker** Kantenflimmern n
interlaced mode Halbbildmodus m
~ **raster signal** Zeilensprungsignal n
~ **scan camera** Zeilensprungkamera f
~ **video scanning (system), interlacing**
Zeilensprungabtastung f,
Halbbildverfahren n, Abtastung f im
Zeilensprungverfahren
(Zwischenzeilenverfahren),
Halbbildverkämmung f
interlayer Zwischenschicht f, Trennschicht
f *(z.B: im Colorfilm)*
interleave/to verschachteln *(Signale)*
interleave Versatz m
interleaves Druckbeilage f; Beilage f *(z.B. in
Zeitschriften)*
interleaving 1. Verschachtelung f; 2.
Codespreizung f, räumliche
Datenspreizung f
interlens shutter Objektivverschluss m
interline flicker Zwischenzeilenflimmern n
~ **spacing** Zeilenabstand m,
Grundzeilenabstand m *(Typografie)*
Lichtbestimmer m
~ **transfer** Zwischenspaltenbetrieb m
~ **transfer camera**
Zwischenzeilentransferkamera f
~ **transfer device (imager)**
Interline-Transfer-Bildaufnehmer m,
IL-Sensor m

interline

~ **transfer structure**
Zwischenzeilentransferstruktur f
(CCD-Flächensensor)
intermediate bath Zwischenbad n
~ **broadcasting facility** Wiederholsender m, Füllsender m, Lückenfüllsender m *(Fernsehen)*
~ **buffering** Zwischenspeicherung f
~ **color** Zwischenfarbe f
~ **film** Intermediatefilm m
~ **filter** Zwischenfilter n
~ **focus** Zwischenbrennpunkt m
~ **frequency** Zwischenfrequenz f
~ **hue** Zwischenfarbe f
~ **image** Zwischenbild n
~ **image formation** Zwischenbilderzeugung f
~ **image plane** Zwischenbildebene f
~ **image position** Zwischenbildposition f
~ **layer** Zwischenschicht f, Trennschicht f, *(z.B. im Colorfilm)*; verdeckte (versteckte) Schicht f, verborgene Ebene f *(künstliches neuronales Netz)*
~ **lens** Zwischenlinse f
~ **lens system** Zwischenabbildungssystem n *(Mikrofotografie)*
~ **memory** Zwischenspeicher m
~ **negative** Zwischennegativ n, Internegativ n
~ **pixel value** Zwischenpixelwert m
~ **plate** Zwischenbildplatte f *(Fotolithografie)*
~ **positive** Interpositiv n, Zwischenpositiv n, Zwipo n *(Kinematografie)*
~ **print** Zwischenkopie f
~ **projection** Zwischenprojektion f
~ **ring** Zwischenring m
~ **rinse [stage]** Zwischenwässern n, Zwischenwässerung f
~ **tone** Zwischenton m
~**-weighted image** intermediär gewichtetes Bild n, protonengewichtetes Bild n *(Magnetresonanztomografie)*
intermittency effect Intermittenzeffekt m
intermittent s. ~ **movement**
~**-action motion-picture camera** Kamera f mit diskontinuierlichem Filmtransport
~ **exposure** intermittierende Belichtung f
~ **film movement** ruckweiser Filmtransport (Bildtransport) m
~ **movement** Filmschaltwerk n, Bildschrittschaltung f, Schrittschaltwerk n, Filmfortschalteinrichtung f, Fortschaltmechanismus m
~ **printing** Schrittkopierung f *(Filmkopierung)*
~ **shoe** Andruckrolle f
~ **sprocket** [gezähnte] Schaltrolle f, Filmschaltrolle f *(Filmprojektor)*
intermodulation Intermodulation f
~ **distortion** Intermodulationsverzerrung f
~ **noise** Intermodulationsstörung f
~ **product** Intermodulationsprodukt n

internal barrier layer Sperrschicht f, Randschicht f *(Halbleiterfotoelement)* Hornhaut f
~ **development** Tiefenentwicklung f
~ **focusing** Innenfokussierung f
~ **focusing objective** innenfokussiertes Objektiv n
~ **image [emulsion] reversal process** Innenbildumkehrverfahren n
~ **memory** interner Speicher m
~ **mirrored** innenverspiegelt
~ **ocular surfaces** Augeninnere n
~ **photoeffect (photoelectric effect)** innerer Fotoeffekt m, innerer fotoelektrischer Effekt m, Halbleiterfotoeffekt m
~ **reflection** Reflexion f am optisch dünneren Medium
~ **transmittance** [spektraler] Reintransmissionsgrad m
international exchange of programs, ~ program distribution internationaler Programmaustausch m
~ **sound track** Internationales Tonband (Band) n, IT-Band n, IT-Fassung f, IT-Mischung f *(Filmsynchronisation)*
International System[s] unit SI-Einheit f, internationale Basiseinheit f
international tape s. ~ **sound track**
interneg[ative] Internegativ n, Zwischennegativ n
internegative film Internegativfilm m
Internet Internet n *(s.a. unter Web)*
~ **access** Internetzugang m, Internetzugriff m
~ **animation** Internet-Videoanimation f
~ **application** Internetanwendung f
~ **connection** Internetverbindung f, Internetanschluss m
~ **content** Internetinhalt m
~ **domain** Internetbereich m
~**-enabled (Internet-ready) television set** internetfähiges (internettaugliches) Fernsehgerät n
~ **image** Internetbild n
~ **multimedia** Internet-Multimedia n
~ **port** Internetanschluss m
~ **protocol** Internetprotokoll n
~ **provider** s. ~ **service provider**
~ **screen** Internetbildschirm m
~ **service** Internetdienst m
~ **service provider** Internetdienstanbieter m, Internet-Dienstleister m
~ **site** Internetseite f, Webseite f
~ **video** Internetvideo n
~ **videoconferencing** Internet-Videokonferenzbetrieb m
internetwork s. **Internet**
internode Zwischenknoten m *(Binärbaum)*
interocular distance Augenabstand m, Zwischenaugenabstand m
interoperability Interoperabilität f *(z.B. von Bilddatenbanken)*
interpicture coding s. **interframe encoding**

interpixel correlation
Zwischenpixelkorrelation f
~ **interpolation**
Zwischenpixelinterpolation f
~ **line** Zwischenpixelzeile f
~ **position** Zwischenpixelposition f
~ **redundancy** Zwischenpixelredundanz f
~ **spacing** Zwischenpixelabstand m
interpolate/to interpolieren
interpolated resolution interpolierte
Auflösung f
~ **shading** interpolierte (interpolative)
Schattierung f
~ **transparency** interpolierte Transparenz f
interpolating curve Interpolationskurve f
~ **filter** Interpolationsfilter n
~ **function** Interpolationsfunktion f
interpolation Interpolation f,
Zwischenwertbestimmung f
~ **accuracy** Interpolationsgenauigkeit f
~ **algorithm** Interpolationsalgorithmus m
~ **approach** Interpolationsansatz m
~ **artifact** Interpolationsartefakt n
~ **coefficient** Interpolationskoeffizient m
~ **error** Interpolationsfehler m
~ **filter** Interpolationsfilter n
~ **function** Interpolationsfunktion f
~ **kernel** Interpolationskern m
~ **lattice** Interpolationsgitter n
~ **mask** Interpolations[faltungs]maske f
~ **matrix** Interpolationsmatrix f
~ **operator** Interpolationsfilter n
~ **passband** Interpolationspassband n
~ **polynomial** Interpolationspolynom n
interpolative coding
Interpolationscodierung f, interpolative
Codierung f
~ **shading** interpolative (interpolierte)
Schattierung f
interpolator Interpolator m;
Interpolationsfilter n
interposition Verdeckung f, Okklusion f
interpositive [film], ~ **print** Interpositiv n,
Zwischenpositiv n, Zwipo n
(Kinematografie)
interpret/to interpretieren, auswerten (z.B.
Bildmaterial)
interpretability Auswertbarkeit f,
Interpretierbarkeit f
interpretable auswertbar, interpretierbar
~ **image** auswertbares Bild n
interpretation Interpretation f, Auswertung
f
~ **element** Interpretationsfaktor m
~ **key** Interpretationsschlüssel m
(Bildanalyse)
~ **of maps** Karteninterpretation f
interpretoscope Interpretoskop n
(Fotogrammetrie)
interpupillary distance Pupillenabstand m,
Pupillendistanz f
interreflection Interreflexion f
interrogation point Fragezeichen n
interrogator Sekundärradarabfragegerät n

interrupt query (request)
Unterbrechungsanforderung f
(Computer)
intersect/to sich schneiden (z.B. Linien)
intersection point Durchstoßpunkt m
(Optik)
interslice gap (space)
Schichtzwischenraum m,
Zwischenschichtabstand m (Tomografie)
interstitial position Zwischengitterplatz m
~ **silver ion** Zwischengitter-Silberion n
intersymbol interference
Zeichenübersprechen n,
Impulsinterferenz f
interval Intervall n
~ **scale** Skala f
~ **tree** Intervallbaum m (geometrische
Datenstruktur)
intervalometer Intervallometer n,
Bildfolgeregler m
interventional angiography
interventionelle Angiografie f
~ **fluoroscopy** interventionelle
Fluoroskopie f
~ **magnetic resonance imaging, ~ MRI**
interventionelle Kernspintomografie
(Magnetoresonanztomografie) f
intracode/to intracodieren
intracoded frame s. intraframe coded
picture
intraframe coded picture intracodiertes
Bild n, Intrabild n, I-Bild n (Video)
~ **encoding** Intraframe-Codierung f,
Intracodierung f
~ **redundancy** örtliche Redundanz f
intragranular nucleus Innenkeim m,
Entwicklungsinnenkeim m
(fotografischer Elementarprozess)
intranet Intranet n, unternehmensinternes
Computernetz n
intraocular lens Intraokularlinse f
(Ophthalmologie)
intravascular ultrasound imaging
intravaskuläre Ultraschallbildgebung f
intrinsic conductivity Eigenfotoleitung f
(Fotodiode)
~ **font** eingebaute Schrift f (Computer)
~ **gray** Eigengrau n
~ **hue** freie Farbe f
~ **image** intrinsisches Bild n
~ **photoconduction** innerer Fotoeffekt m,
Halbleiterfotoeffekt m
~ **region** intrinsische (eigenleitende)
Schicht f (Fotodiode)
~ **semiconductor** intrinsischer
(undotierter) Halbleiter m
~ **unsharpness** innere Unschärfe f,
Bildempfängerunschärfe f (Radiografie)
invalid color ungültige Farbe f
invariance Invarianz f
invariant invariant
~ Invariante f
~ **feature** invariantes Merkmal n
~ **pattern** invariantes Muster n

invariant

~ **pattern recognition** invariante Mustererkennung *f*
invercone Kalotte *f (Belichtungsmesser)*
inverse amplification factor Durchgriff *m (Elektronenröhre)*
~ **discrete cosine transform** inverse diskrete Kosinustransformation *f*
~ **discrete Fourier transform** inverse diskrete Fourier-Transformation *f*, diskrete Fourier-Rücktransformation *f*
~ **fast wavelet transform** schnelle Wavelet-Rücktransformation *f*
~ **filter** inverses Filter *n*
~ **filtering** inverse Filterung *f*, Inversfilterung *f*, Entfaltung *f*, Dekonvolution *f (Bildrekonstruktion)*
~ **Fourier transform** inverse (umgekehrte) Fourier-Transformation *f*, Fourier-Rücktransformation *f*
~ **halftone gravure** flächenvariabler (autotypischer) Tiefdruck *m*
~ **kinematics** inverse Kinematik *f (Computeranimation)*
~ **Laplace transform** inverse Laplace-Transformation *f*
~ **mapping** inverse Abbildung *f*, Rückwärtsabbildung *f (geometrische Transformation)*
~ **piezoelectric effect** reziproker (umgekehrter) Piezoeffekt *m*, umgekehrter piezoelektrischer Effekt *m*
~ **quantization** Requantisierung *f*, Rückquantisierung *f (Videokompression)*
~ **quantizer** Rückquantisierer *m (Videokompression)*
~ **Raman scattering** inverse Raman-Streuung *f*
~ **square law [of distance]** Abstandsquadratgesetz *n*, fotometrisches Grundgesetz *n*, fotometrisches (quadratisches) Entfernungsgesetz *n*
~ **synthetic-aperture radar** Radar *n* mit inverser synthetischer Apertur
~ **transform** 1. Rücktransformierte *f*; 2. *s.* ~ transformation
~ **transform kernel** Rücktransformationskern *m*
~ **transformation** Rücktransformation *f*, inverse Transformation *f*
~ **transformation matrix** Rücktransformationsmatrix *f*
~ **wavelet transform** inverse Wavelet-Transformation *f*, Wavelet-Rücktransformation *f*
inversion Inversion *f*, Umkehrung *f*
~ **prism** Umkehrprisma *n*, Wendeprisma *n*, Reversionsprisma *n*
~ **pulse** Inversionsimpuls *m (Magnetresonanzbildgebung)*
~ **recovery** Inversionsrückkehr *f (Magnetresonanzbildgebung)*
~ **system** Umkehrsystem *n (Optik)*
invert/to invertieren

inverted fluorescence microscope inverses Fluoreszenzmikroskop *n*
~ **image** kopfstehendes (vollständig umgekehrtes) Bild *n*, Kehrbild *n*
~-**image rangefinder** Kehrbildentfernungsmesser *m*, Invertentfernungsmesser *m*
~ **laterally** seitenverkehrt, spiegelverkehrt
~ **matte** Gegenmaske *f*, Gegenkasch *m*, Hintergrundmaske *f*, Hintergrundmaskenfilm *m (Trickkinematografie)*
~ **microscope** Umkehrmikroskop *n*, inverses Mikroskop *n*
~ **spectral line** umgekehrte Spektrallinie *f*
inverter Wechselrichter *m*
invertible invertierbar, umkehrbar
inverting pentagonal prism Pentadachkantenprisma *n*
~ **prism** *s.* inversion prism
~ **telescope** astronomisches Teleskop (Fernrohr) *n*
invisible unsichtbar, invisibel
~ **image** 1. unsichtbares Bild *n*; 2. *s.* latent image
~ **light** unsichtbares Licht *n*
~ **radiation** unsichtbare Strahlung *f*
~ **spectrum** unsichtbares Spektrum *n*
~ **watermark** unsichtbares Wasserzeichen *n*
involatile memory nichtflüchtiger Speicher *m*, Permanentspeicher *m*
inward rotation Einwärtsdrehung *f (Augenbewegung)*
iodate Iodat *n*
iodide Iodid *n*
iodin[e] Iod *n*
iodochloride emulsion Chloriodidemulsion *f*
iodopsin Iodopsin *n (Netzhautpigment)*
ion Ion *n*
~ **beam** Ionenstrahl *m*
~ **beam lithography** Ionenstrahllithografie *f*
~ **chamber** Ionenkammer *f*
~ **conductance** Ionenleitfähigkeit *f*
~-**deposition printer** Ionen[beschuss]drucker *m*
~-**deposition printing, ion-flow electrophotography** *s.* ionography
~ **emission** Ionenemission *f*
~ **exchange** Ionenaustausch *m*
~ **microscope** Ionenmikroskop *n*
~ **microscopy** Ionenmikroskopie *f*
~-**optical** ionenoptisch
~-**optical imaging** ionenoptische Abbildung *f*
~ **optics** Ionenoptik *f*
~ **pair** Ionenpaar *n*
~-**selective electrode** ionenselektive Elektrode *f*
~-**sensitive field-effect transistor** ionensensitiver Feldeffekttransistor *m*

ionic bond[ing] Ionenbindung f, heteropolare Bindung f
~ **concentration** Ionenkonzentration f
~ **conductivity** Ionenleitfähigkeit f
~ **crystal** Ionenkristall m, polarer Kristall m
~ **lattice** Ionengitter n
~ **product** Ionenprodukt n
ionization Ionisierung f, Ionisation f
~ **chamber** Ionisationskammer f
ionize/to ionisieren
ionized gas ionisiertes Gas n
ionizing radiation ionisierende Strahlung f
ionographic ionografisch, elektroradiografisch
ionography Ionografie f, Elektroradiografie f
IR s. infrared
iridium sensitization Iridiumsensibilisierung f
iris in/to aufblenden *(Filmkamera)*
~ **out/to** abblenden
~ Regenbogenhaut f, Iris f, Augeniris f
~ **blade** Blendenlamelle f
~ **closing lever** Blendenschließhebel m
~ **diaphragm** Irisblende f
~ **lever** Blendenschließhebel m
~ **mount** Blendenkörper m
~ **muscle** Linsenmuskel m, Ziliarmuskel m *(des Auges)*
~ **pigmentation** Irispigmentierung f
~ **ring** Blendeneinstellring m, Objektivblendenring m, Blendensteuerring m
~ **scan** Iris-Scan m, Augen-Scan m
~ **scanner** Iris-Scanner m, Iris-Erkennungsgerät n
~ **wipe** Kreisblende f *(Filmeffekt)*
iron oxide Eisenoxid n
~ **process**, ~ **salt process** Eisensalzverfahren n *(frühe Fotografie)*
irradiance Bestrahlungsstärke f, Einstrahlung f, Irradianz f, Flussdichte f *(Radiometrie)*
irradiate/to bestrahlen
irradiation 1. Bestrahlung f; 2. s. irradiance
irregular astigmatism unregelmäßiger Astigmatismus m *(Bildfehler)*
~ **data** unstrukturierte Daten pl
~ **polygon** unregelmäßiges Polygon n
~ **topology** unregelmäßige Topologie f
irrelevance, irrelevancy Irrelevanz f
irrelevant irrelevant
irreversible compression verlustbehaftete Kompression f
ISAR s. inverse synthetic aperture radar
isarithm Isarithme f, Isolinie f
isarithmic map Isarithmenkarte f, Isolinienkarte f
ISDB s. Integrated Services Digital Broadband Network
ISDN s. Integrated Services Digital Network
Ishihara plate Ishihara-Tafel f *(Farbsehprüfung)*

iso-elevation contour line Höhenlinie f, Niveaulinie f, Isohypse f
ISO film speed ISO-Empfindlichkeit f, Empfindlichkeitsangabe f nach ISO
~ **index (rating)** ISO-Grad m, ISO-Wert m, ISO-Zahl f
isochromat s. isochromatic line
isochromatic farbgleich, gleichfarbig, isochrom[atisch], orthochromatisch; farbtonrichtig
~ **light** gleichfarbiges Licht n
~ **line** isochromatische Linie f, Isochromate f *(fotoelastische Spannungsanalyse)*
isochronous isochron
~ **signal** isochrones Signal n
~ **transfer mode** isochroner Übertragungsmodus m
isoclinic line Isokline f
isodensitometry Isodensitometrie f
isodensity line Äquidensite f
isoelectric point isoelektrischer Punkt m
isogram s. isoline
isohelie Isohelie f
isoline Isolinie f, Isarithme f
isoluminant gleichhell, äquiluminant
isolux s. isophote
isomagnetic isomagnetische Linie f
isomeric color isomere (unbedingt gleiche) Farbe f
isomerization Isomerisierung f
isometric isometrisch
~ **projection** isometrische Projektion f
isometry Isometrie f
isomorph[ic] isomorph, gleichgestaltig
isomorphism 1. Isomorphie f, Gleichgestaltigkeit f; 2. Isomorphismus m
isomorphous s. isomorph[ic]
isopach Isopache f *(Linie konstanter Spannungssumme)*
isoparametric interpolation isoparametrische Interpolation f
isophote Isophote f *(Linie gleicher Helligkeit)*
isoplanatic isoplanatisch, ortsinvariant
isoplanatism Isoplanasie f, Ortsinvarianz f
isopleth map Isoplethenkarte f
isosceles triangle gleichschenkliges Dreieck n
isosurface Isofläche f *(Computergrafik)*
~ **algorithm** Isoflächenalgorithmus m
~ **extraction algorithm** Isoflächen-Extraktionsalgorithmus m
isosurfacing Isoflächenbildung f *(Bildvorverarbeitungsoperation)*
isotope Isotop n
~ **decay** Isotopenzerfall m
isotropic isotrop, richtungsunabhängig
~ **crystal** isotroper Kristall m
~ **diffusion** isotrope Diffusion f
~ **filter** isotropes (rotationssymmetrisches) Filter n

isotropic

~ **mapping** 1. unverzerrte Abbildung *f*; 2. Ähnlichkeitstransformation *f* *(Computergrafik)*
~ **medium** isotropes Medium *n*
~ **motion** isotrope Bewegung *f*
~ **pattern** isotropes Muster *n*
~ **radiator** isotroper Strahler *m*
~ **resolution** isotrope Auflösung *f*
~ **scaling** isotrope Skalierung *f*
isotropy Isotropie *f*, Richtungsunabhängigkeit *f*
isovalue surface *s.* isosurface
ISP *s.* Internet service provider
italic *s.* 1. italicized; 2. ~ typeface
~ **type** Kursiv[e] *f*, Kursivschrift *f*
~ **typeface** kursiver Schriftschnitt *m*
italicize/to kursiv setzen; kursiv drucken
italicized kursiv, schräg[laufend]
iterate/to iterieren
iteration Iteration *f*
~ **loop** Iterationsschleife *f*
iterative algorithm iterativer Algorithmus *m*, Iterationsalgorithmus *m*
~ **decoding** iterative Decodierung *f*
~ **motion estimation** iterative Bewegungsschätzung *f*
~ **object classification** iterative Objektklassifikation *f*
~ **reconstruction** iterative Rekonstruktion *f*
~ **relaxation** iterative Relaxation *f*
~ **search** iterative Suche *f*
~ **transformation** iterative Transformation *f*

J

jack Klinkenbuchse f
~ **plug** Klinkenstecker m
jagged boundary (edge) stufige Kante f
jaggedness, jaggies Treppen[stufen]effekt m, Stufeneffekt m, Stufenfehler m, Stufigkeit f, Sägezahneffekt m *(Binärbild)*
jam/to stören *(z.B. Radarsignale)*
Jamin interferometer Jamin-Interferometer n
jammer Störsender m, Störer m *(Radar)*
jamming Filmsalat m
~ **signal** Störsignal n *(Radar)*
jar/to verreißen *(die Kamera)*; verwackeln *(eine Aufnahme)*
JBIG s. Joint Bi-level Image Experts Group
jellied processing agent Entwicklerpaste f
jerk-free ruckelfrei
jerkiness [of motion] Bildruckeln n *(Video)*
jerky ruckelig
jet Strahl m *(von Gasen oder Flüssigkeiten)*
~ **printing** Tintenstrahldruck m, Farbstrahldruck m
jewelers' rouge Polierrot n *(Linsenfertigung)*
jib arm Ausleger m *(s.a.* boom [arm]*)*
jitter 1. Signaldegeneration f, Signalschwankung f, Zittern n, Jitter m; 2. Bildwackeln n, Bildzittern n, Bildinstabilität f, Bildschwankung[en] f[pl]
JND s. just-noticeable difference
job Druckauftrag m, Druckjob m
~ **composition** Akzidenzsatz m *(Druck)*
~ **printing** Akzidenzdruck m, Kleinseriendruck m
~ **ticket** Druckauftrag m, [konventionelle] Auftragstasche f
jobbing [printing] press Akzidenzmaschine f
jog/to rütteln, glattstoßen, geradestoßen, schütteln *(Druckbogen)*
jog dial s. jogwheel
~**-shuttle** Jog-Shuttle-Regler m
jogging Einzelbild[fort]schaltung f *(Videoschnitt)*
jogwheel Einzelbild[fort]schaltung f *(Videokamera)*; Suchlaufrad n
Johnson noise Johnson-Rauschen n, Nyquist-Rauschen n, thermisches Zufalsrauschen n
join/to kleben *(z.B. Filmstücke)*
join line Verbindungslinie f
Joint Bi-level Image Experts Group 1. *US-Normierungsgremium zur Bilddatenkompression;* 2. *Norm für die Kompression von Schwarzweißbildern*
~ **Photographic Experts Group** 1. *US-Normierungsgremium zur Bilddatenkompression;* 2. *Norm für die Kompression und Speicherung von Festbilddaten*
Josephson [tunnel] junction Josephson-Kontakt m, Josephson-Tunnelelement n *(Quanteninterferometer)*
joule Joule n, J *(SI-Einheit für Arbeit und Energie)*
journalistic photography journalistische Fotografie f; Pressefotografie f
joystick Steuerknüppel m, Steuerungshebel m, Joystick m
JPEG s. Joint Photographic Experts Group
~ **compression algorithm** JPEG-Algorithmus m
~ **compression technique** JPEG-Verfahren n *(der verlustbehafteten Bilddatenkompression)*
~ **file** JPEG-Datei f
~ **file interchange format** JPEG-Dateiformat n, JPEG-Format n
~ **image compression** JPEG-Kompression f
~ **image compression standard** JPEG-Standard m
judder Bewegungsruckeln n
juke-box Nickelodeon n *(frühe Kinematografie)*
jumbo slide Großdia[positiv] n, Großbilddia n
jump cut springender Schnitt m, Sprungschnitt m *(Videoeffekt)*; Bildsprung m *(Kinematografie)*
jumper (kleiner) Brückenstecker m *(Leiterplatte)*
junction graph Verbindungsgraph m
~ **point** Verbindungspunkt m
just noticeable difference Ebenunterscheidbarkeit f
justification [process] 1. Ausschließen n, Ausschließvorgang m, Spationierung f; 2. Blocksatz m *(Druck)*
~ **wedge** Ausschließkeil m, Spatienkeil m, Keil m
justified [full-out] ausgeschlossen *(Schriftauszeichnung)*
~ **loose** gesperrt
~ **tight** unterschnitten, schmal[laufend], eng
~ **type** ausgeschlossener Satz m, Blocksatz m
justify/to ausschließen, spationieren, spatiieren
justifying spacer Ausschließkeil m, Spatienkeil m, Keil m *(Satzherstellung)*
jutter s. judder
juxtaposition Nebeneinanderstellung f, Juxtaposition f

K

k-space K-Raum *m (mathematischer Datenraum)*
Kaiser window Kaiser-Fenster *n (Signalverarbeitung)*
kaleidoscope Kaleidoskop *n*
kaleidoscopic kaleidoskopisch
Kalman filter Kalman-Filter *n (Bildanalyse)*
~ **filtering** Kalman-Filterung *f*
Kalvar process Kalvar-Verfahren *n*
Karhunen-Loève transformation (expansion) Karhunen-Loève-Transformation *f*, Hauptkomponentenanalyse *f*, Kompressionstransformation *f*, Eigenvektortransformation *f (Merkmalserkennung)*
karyogram Karyogramm *n*
Keck telescope Keck-Teleskop *n*
keen eyesight Sehschärfe *f*
keeping quality Haltbarkeit *f*, Langzeithaltbarkeit *f*, Langlebigkeit *f*, Langzeit-Lagereigenschaft *f (z.B. von Bildmaterial)*
Kell factor Kell-Faktor *m (Videobildauflösung)*
Kellner eyepiece Kellner-Okular *n*
kelvin Kelvin *n*, K *(Maßeinheit der Farbtemperatur)*
Kelvin [temperature] scale Kelvin-Skale *f*, Temperaturskale *f* nach Kelvin *f*
Kepler telescope finder Keplerscher Teleskopsucher *m*
Keplerian telescope Keplersches Fernrohr *n*, astronomisches Teleskop (Fernrohr) *n*
kept take Kopierer *m (Kinefilmbearbeitung)*
keratometer Ophthalmometer *n*
keratoscope Keratoskop *n*
keratoscopic keratoskopisch
Kerma Kerma *n (Röntgendosimetrie)*
~ **in air** Luftkerma *n*
kern/to unterschneiden *(Satzherstellung)*
kerned text unterschnittener Text *m (Typografie)*
kernel Kern *m*; Faltungskern *m*, Faltungsfilter *n*, Faltungsmaske *f*, Maskenoperator *m*, lokaler Operator *m (Bildverarbeitung)*
~ **operation** *s.* linear operation
kerning Unterschneiden *n*, Schriftunterschneidung *f*, Zeichenausgleich *m (Typografie)*
Kerr cell Kerr-Zelle *f*, Karolus-Zelle *f*, lichtelektrische (elektrooptische) Zelle *f (Hochgeschwindigkeitsfotografie)*
~ **cell shutter** Kerr-Zellenverschluss *m*, elektrooptischer Verschluss *m*
~ **effect** Kerr-Effekt *m*
key [in]/to 1. einstanzen; 2. *s.* keyboard/to
~ 1. Lichtcharakter *m*, Lichtstimmung *f*, Stimmung *f*, Tonigkeit *f (einer Fotografie)*; 2. Stanze *f*, Trickmaske *f*, Maske *f (Kinematografie)*; 3. Zonenschraube *f (des Farbkastens einer Druckmaschine)*; 4. *s.* ~ light source
~ **animator** Hauptphasenzeichner *m (Zeichentrickfilm)*
Key code [number] Keycode-Codierung *f (von Filmmaterial)*
~ **code reader** Keycode-Lesegerät *n*
key color Stanzfarbe *f*
~ **fill** Stanzfläche *f*, Stanzhintergrund *m*, Füllmuster *n (Video)*
~ **frame** 1. Schlüsselbild *n*, Basisbild *f (Videocodierung)*; 2. Bezugsbild *n*, Referenzbild *n (Computergrafik)*
~ **frame animation,** ~ **framing** Hauptphasenanimation *f*, Keyframe-Animation *f*
~ **image** *s.* ~ frame
~ **invert** Stanzsignal-Umkehrung *f*
~ **light** 1. Führungslicht *n*, Hauptlicht *n*; 2. *s.* ~ light source
~ **light source** Führungslichtquelle *f*, Hauptlichtquelle *f*, szenenbestimmende Lichtquelle *f*
~ **number** Randnummer *f*, [Negativ-]Fußnummer *f*, Randzahl *f (Film)*
~ **panel** Tastenfeld *n*
~ **point** Schlüsselpunkt *m (z.B. in der Objekterkennung)*
~ **signal (source)** Stanzsignal *n*; Trickmuster *n*
~ **type** Tonwertbereich *m*, Tonwertumfang *m (eines Bildes)*
keyboard/to [per Tastatur] eingeben
keyboard Tastatur *f (Eingabegerät)*
~ **lockup** Tastatursperre *f*
~**-operated linecaster** tastaturgesteuerte Zeilengussmaschine *f*
~**-operated photocomposition** tastaturgesteuerter Fotosatz *m*
~**-operated typesetting** tastaturgesteuerter Maschinensatz *m*
~**-operated typesetting machine** tastaturgesteuerte Setzmaschine *f*
keying 1. Tastung *f*, digitale Modulation *f (Signalverarbeitung)*; 2. *s.* ~ technique; 3. *s.* chroma key
~ **signal** Stanzsignal *n (Trickkinematografie)*
~ **technique** Kombinationsaufnahmeverfahren *n*, Kombinationstrickverfahren *n*; Stanz[verfahr]en *n*
keypad Tastenfeld *n*
keystone correction Trapezentzerrung *f*, Trapezkorrektur *f*

~ **distortion (effect), keystoning**
Trapezverzeichnung f, Trapezverzerrung
f, Parallaxenverzerrung f
kicker Kicker[scheinwerfer] m
kilobit Kilobit n, kb, Kb
kilobyte Kilobyte n
kilohertz Kilohertz n, kHz *(Frequenzmaß)*
kind of glass Glasart f
~ **of lighting** Beleuchtungsart f
kinematic analysis Bewegungsanalyse f
~ **model** kinematisches Modell n
~ **optical mount** kinematischer Optikhalter m
kinematical [diffraction] theory
kinematische Theorie f
(Elektronenstrahlbeugung)
kinematics Kinematik f
kinematography s. cinematography
kinescope Kineskop n;
Bild[wiedergabe]röhre f; Fernsehröhre f
kinetic energy released in media s. Kerma
~ **unsharpness** Bewegungsunschärfe f
kinetograph Kinetograf m *(eine frühe kinematografische Kamera)*
kinetophone Kinetophon n *(Kombination von Kinetoskop und Schallplattenspieler)*
kinetoscope Kinetoskop n
(Guckkastenapparat)
kink mark Knickstelle f *(z.B. in Fotomaterial)*
Kirchhoff['s] formula Kirchhoffsche Beugungsformel f
Kirchhoff's law Kirchhoffsches Gesetz (Strahlungsgesetz) n
Kirlian electrophotography
Kirlian-Fotografie f, Aurafotografie f, Koronafotografie f, Hochspannungsfotografie f
~ **generator** Kirlian-Generator m
~ **photograph** Kirlian-Fotogramm n
Kirsch [edge] operator Kirsch-Operator m *(Kantenhervorhebung)*
kiss impression leichter Druck m *(Druckarbeit)*
~ **register** Farbpasser m *(Farbdruck)*
klystron 1. Klystron n *(Elektronenröhre)*; 2. Hilfsoszillator m *(Radar)*
knee correction Kniefunktion f *(Videosignalbearbeitung)*
knife-edge technique
Messerschneidenmethode f [nach Foucault], [Foucaultsches] Schneiden[prüf]verfahren n, Foucaultsche Schattenprobe f *(Linsenprüfung)*
knock out/to abdecken, maskieren *(z.B. Bildelemente)*
knockout film Umkehrfilm m
knowledge acquisition Wissenserwerb m, Wissensakquisition f *(Neuroinformatik)*
~ **base** Wissensbasis f *(Expertensystem)*

~-**based analysis-synthesis coding**
wissensbasierte Analyse-Synthese-Codierung f
~-**based coding** wissensbasierte Codierung f
~-**based image analysis** wissensbasierte (wissensgestützte) Bildanalyse f
~-**based image processing**
wissensbasierte Bildverarbeitung f
~-**based model** wissensbasiertes Modell n
~-**based pattern recognition**
wissensbasierte Mustererkennung f
~-**based scene analysis** wissensbasierte Szenenanalyse f
~-**based segmentation** wissensbasierte Segmentierung f
~-**based system** wissensbasiertes System n, Expertensystem n *(Datenverarbeitung)*
~-**guided segmentation** vollständige Segmentierung f
~ **representation** Wissensdarstellung f, Wissensrepräsentation f *(Bildanalyse)*
Kochanek-Bartels spline
Kochanek-Bartels-Spline n, TCB-Spline n *(geometrisches Modellieren)*
Köhler illumination [technique]
Köhlersche Beleuchtung f, Köhlersches Beleuchtungsverfahren n *(Mikroskopie)*
Kohonen map (network) Kohonen-Karte f, Kohonen-Netz n, selbstorganisierende Merkmalskarte (Karte) f, selbstorganisierendes Tableau n *(Mustererkennung)*
konimeter Konimeter n *(Staubteilchenmessung)*
Kostinsky effect Kostinsky-Effekt m *(fotografischer Effekt)*
Kron effect Kron-Effekt m *(fotografischer Effekt)*
Kronecker delta [function] Kroneckersches Delta n, diskrete Deltafunktion (Impulsfunktion) f
krypton laser Kryptonlaser m
~-**[-filled incandescent] lamp**
Krypton[entladungs]lampe f
Ku band Ku-Band n *(Satellitenübertragung)*
Kundt effect s. magnetic rotation
~ **prism** Farbstoffprisma n
kurtosis Exzess m *(Histogrammanalyse)*
Kuwahara filter Kuwahara-Filter n *(Binärbildverarbeitung)*
kymogram Kymogramm n
kymograph Kymograf m
kymographic kymografisch
kymography Kymografie f

L

L cone L-Zapfen *m (Netzhautrezeptor)*
lab *s.* laboratory
L*a*b* color coordinates
  L*a*b*-Farbmodus *m*, LAB-Farbraum *m*
lab roll Kopierwerksrolle *f*
label 1. Etikett *n*; Aufdruck *m*; 2. Tracer *m*
  (Nuklearmedizin); 3. Bezeichner *m*
  (Computergrafik)
~ **image** Regionenbild *n*
~ **inspection** Aufdruckkontrolle *f*,
  Aufdruckprüfung *f*
~ **printing** Etikettendruck *m*
laboratory apparatus Laborgerät *n*
~ **assistant** Laborant *m*
~**-based photography** Laborfotografie *f*
~ **bottle** Laborflasche *f*
~ **enlarger** Laborvergrößerer *m*
~ **equipment** Laborausrüstung *f*,
  Laborausstattung *f*, Laboreinrichtung *f*
~ **image analysis** Laborbildanalyse *f*
~ **microscope** Labormikroskop *n*
~ **parlance** Laborsprache *f*
~ **product** Kopierwerkserzeugnis *n*
~ **report** Laborbericht *m*
~ **technician** Labortechniker *m*
~ **test** Kopierwerktest *m*
~ **timer** *s.* film color timer
~ **X-ray microscope**
  Labor-Röntgenmikroskop *n*
labyrinth entrance Labyrintheingang *m*,
  Labyrinthschleuse *f (Dunkelraum)*
lacing Abschnüren *n (einer Filmleinwand)*
lack of coma Komafreiheit *f (Optik)*
~ **of contrast** Kontrastarmut *f*;
  Kontrastlosigkeit *f*
lacking in contrast kontrastarm;
  kontrastlos
lacquer Drucklack *m*
ladar *s.* laser radar
lag effect Nachzieheffekt *m (Bildröhre)*
Lagrange interpolation
  Lagrange-Interpolation *f*
  (Computergrafik)
~ **invariant** Helmholtz-Lagrangesche
  Invariante *f*, optische Invariante *f*
~ **multiplier** Lagrangescher Multiplikator *m*
  (Bildrestaurierung)
~ **polynomial** Lagrange-Polynom *n*
Lagrangean factor *s.* Lagrange multiplier
Lainer effect Lainer-Effekt *m*
lambert Lambert *n (SI-fremde Einheit der
  Leuchtdichte)*
Lambert's cosine law [of illumination]
  [Lambertsches] Kosinusgesetz *n*
  (geometrische Optik)
Lambertian diffuser (emitter)
  Lambert-Strahler *m*, Lambertscher
  Strahler *m*, Lambert-Reflektor *m*,
  Lambertsche Fläche (Oberfläche) *f*
~ **reflection** Lambertsche Reflexion *f*,
  diffuse (gestreute) Reflexion *f*,
  Lichtremission *f*
~ **reflector**, ~ **source (surface)** *s.* ~ diffuser
~ **surface reflectance model**
  Lambert-Reflexionsmodell *n*
laminar flow Laminarströmung *f*, laminare
  Strömung *f*
~ **grating** Laminargitter *n*
laminate/to laminieren; kaschieren
laminate Laminat *n*; Kaschierung *f*
laminated collimator Lamellenkollimator
  m
laminating film Aufziehfolie *f*, Kaschierfolie
  f; Glanzfolie *f*
~ **press** Laminierpresse *f*;
  Folienkaschiermaschine *f*
lamination [process] Laminierung *f*,
  Kaschierung *f*
lamp Lampe *f*
~ **age** Lampenalter *n*
~ **condenser** Lampenkondensor *m*
~ **dimmer** Dimmer *m*, Lichtdimmer *m*,
  stufenloser Helligkeitsregler *m*
~ **filament** Lampenwendel *f*
~ **filter** Lampenfilter *n*
~ **head** Lampenkopf *m*
~ **house** *s.* lamphouse
~ **life** Lampenlebensdauer *f*
~ **wattage** Lampenleistung *f*
lampblack Ruß *m (Pigment)*
lamphouse Lampenhaus *m (Projektor)*
lamplight Lampenlicht *n*
LAN *s.* local area network
land 1. Steg *m*, Nichtvertiefung *f*
  (CD-Platte); 2. Rastersteg *m*
  (Tiefdruckform)
~ **use map** Bodennutzungskarte *f*
landmark Landmarke *f (Bildregistrierung)*
Landolt C (ring) Landolt-Ring *m*
  (Normsehzeichen)
landscape querformatig
~ **display** Querformatanzeige *f*
~ **film** Landschafts-Rückprofilm *m*
  (Kinematografie)
~ **lens** Landschaftslinse *f*
~ **mode** 1. Querformat *n*; 2.
  Unendlicheinstellung *f*
~ **photograph** Landschaftsfoto *n*
~ **photographer** Landschaftsfotograf *m*
~ **photography** Landschaftsfotografie *f*
~ **picture** Landschaftsbild *n*
~ **shot** Landschaftsaufnahme *f*
lantern Stehbildprojektor *m*,
  Stehbildwerfer *m*, Dia[positiv]projektor
  m
~ **plate** Dia[positiv]platte *f*
~ **slide** Dia[positiv] *n*
lanthanum hexaboride electron gun
  Lanthanhexaborid-Kristallelektrode *f*
  (Elektronenmikroskop)

lap dissolve Überblendung f, Bildüberblendung f, Durchblende f
laparoendoscopic laparoendoskopisch
laparoscope Laparoskop n, Bauchhöhlenspiegel m
laparoscopic laparoskopisch
laparoscopy Laparoskopie f, Bauch[höhlen]spiegelung f
lapel [microphone] Ansteckmikrofon n (s.a. lavalier[e] microphone)
Laplace distribution Laplace-Verteilung f (einer Zufallsvariablen)
~ **transform** 1. Laplace-Transformation f (Signalverarbeitung); 2. Laplace-Transformierte f
Laplacian Laplace-Ableitung f
~ **filter** Laplace-Filter n, Laplace-Operator m
~-**filtered image** laplacegefiltertes Bild n
~ **filtering** Laplace-Filterung f
~ **gradient** Laplace-Gradient m
~ **image** laplacegefiltertes Bild n
~ **mask (operator)** s. ~ filter
~-**of-Gaussian [operator]** Laplace-Gauß-Operator m, Sombrerofilter n, LoG-Filter n, Laplace-Filter n mit Tiefpasswirkung, Marr-Hildreth-Operator m (Bildverarbeitung)
~ **processing** s. deblurring
~ **pyramid** Laplace-Pyramide f (z.B. in der Bewegungsanalyse)
laptop [computer] Laptop-Computer m, Laptop m(n)
~ **computer screen,** ~ **display** Laptop-Bildschirm m
large-area continuous photoconductor Flächenbildwandler m
~-**area flicker** Großflächenflimmern n
~-**format** großformatig
~ **format** Großformat n
~-**format camera** Großformatkamera f, Großbildkamera f
~-**format color copier** Großformat-Farbkopierer m
~-**format display** s. large-screen display
~-**format enlarger** Großformat-Vergrößerungsapparat m
~-**format lens** Großformatobjektiv n
~-**format negative** Großformatnegativ n
~-**format photography** Großformatfotografie f, Großbildfotografie f
~-**format photomicrography** Großformatmikrofotografie f
~-**format portrait** Großporträt n
~-**format print** großformatiger Abzug m
~-**format printer** Großformatdrucker m
~-**format rangefinder camera** Großformat-Sucherkamera f
~-**format single-lens reflex camera** großformatige Spiegelreflexkamera f
~-**format transparency** Großdia[positiv] n, Großbilddia n

~ **observatory** Großobservatorium n
~ **photographic enlargement** Großvergrößerung f
~ **plasma display** Plasma-Großbildschirm m
~ **print** Großkopie f
~-**print book** Großdruckausgabe f
~-**scale** großmaßstäbig, großmaßstäblich
~-**scale lab[oratory]** Großlabor[atorium] n
~-**scale projection** Großprojektion f
~-**scale telescope** Großteleskop n
~-**screen display** Großbildschirm m, großflächiger Bildschirm m, großflächiges Display n
~-**screen monitor** Großbildmonitor m
~-**screen projection** Großbildprojektion f
~-**screen projection television** Großbild-Projektionsfernsehen n
~-**screen projection unit** Großbildprojektor m
~-**screen television** Großbildfernsehen n
~-**screen television projector** Fernseh-Großbildprojektor m
~-**size[d]** großformatig
~-**surface-area imager** Flächenbildwandler m
~-**volume photofinishing lab[oratory]** Großlabor[atorium] n
largest aperture s. maximum aperture
Larmor equation Larmor-Gleichung f, Larmor-Beziehung f (Kernspinresonanz)
~ **frequency** Larmor-Frequenz f, Präzessionsfrequenz f
~ **precession** Larmor-Präzession f
~ **precessional frequency** s. ~ frequency
~ **relationship** s. ~ equation
laryngoscope Laryngoskop n, Kehlkopfspiegel m
laryngoscopic laryngoskopisch
laryngoscopy Laryngoskopie f, Kehlkopfspiegelung f
lase/to lasern, kohärentes Licht emittieren
laser Laser m, Lichtverstärkung f durch angeregte (stimulierte) Strahlungsemission
~ **ablation** Ablation f mit Lasern
~ **absorption spectrometer** Laserabsorptionsspektrometer n
~ **action** Laserwirkung f
~-**active material** laseraktives Medium n
~ **all-dome projection system** Laser-Ganzkuppelprojektionssystem n
~ **assembly** Laseranordnung f
~-**based remote sensing** Laserfernerkundung f
~ **beam** Laser[licht]strahl m, Laserbündel n
~ **beam expander** Laserstrahlaufweiter m
~ **beam expansion** Laserstrahlaufweitung f
~ **beam exposure** Laserbelichtung f
~ **beam noise** Laserstrahlrauschen n
~ **beam optics** Laseroptik f
~ **beam recording** Laserabtastung f (Video-Film-Transfer)
~ **beam scanning** Laser[strahl]abtastung f

laser

~ **beam source** Laserstrahlquelle *f*
~ **beam stabilization** Laserstrahlstabilisierung *f*
~ **bond [paper]** Laser[druck]papier *n*
~ **capture microscopy** Lasermikroskopie *f*
~ **cavity** Laserresonator *m*
~ **collimator** Laserkollimator *m*
~ **copier** Laserkopierer *m*
~ **crystal** Laserkristall *m*
~ **device** Lasergerät *n*
~ **diode** Laserdiode *f*
~ **diode beam** Laserdiodenstrahl *m*
~ **diode collimator** Laserdiodenkollimator *m*
~ **diode controller (driver)** Laserdiodensteuergerät *n*, Laserdiodentreiber *m*
~ **diode exposure** Laserdiodenbelichtung *f*
~ **disk** Laserplatte *f*, Laserdisk *f*, Bild[speicher]platte *f*; analoge [optische] Bildplatte *f (s.a.* videodisc*)*
~ **disk objective** Abtastobjektiv *n*, Abtastoptik *f*
~ **disk player** Laserplattenspieler *m*
~ **display** Laserdisplay *n*
~ **Doppler anemometry** Laser-Doppler-Anemometrie *f*
~ **dot** Laserpunkt *m*; Belichterpixel *n*
~ **dye** Laserfarbstoff *m*
~ **effect** Lasereffekt *m*
~ **efficiency** Laserwirkungsgrad *m*
~-**electrophotographic** laserelektrofotografisch
~ **emission** Laseremission *f*
~ **energy** Laserenergie *f*
~ **engraving** Lasergravur *f*
~ **etching** Laserätzen *n*
~ **exposure unit** Laserbelichter *m*
~ **film recorder (scanner)**, ~ **film printer** Laserfilmabtaster *m*, Laserfilmbelichter *m*, Laserfilmrecorder *m*
~ **focus** Laserfokus *m*
~ **force microscope** Laser-Kraft-Mikroskop *n*
~ **frequency** Laserfrequenz *f*
~ **gas** Lasergas *n*
~ **gravure** Lasergravur *f*
~ **grid** Laserraster *m(n)*
~ **head** Laserkopf *m*
~ **head ophthalmoscope** Laserkopfophthalmoskop *n*
~ **illumination** Laserbeleuchtung *f*
~ **imager (imagesetter)** Laserbelichter *m*, Laserkamera *f*
~ **imaging** Laserabbildung *f*
~-**induced fluorescence** laserinduzierte Fluoreszenz *f*
~-**induced fluorescent spectroscopy** laserinduzierte Fluoreszenzspektroskopie *f*
~-**induced plasma spectroscopy** laserinduzierte Plasmaspektroskopie *f*
~ **intensity** Laserlichtstärke *f*
~ **interferometer** Laserinterferometer *n*

~ **interferometry** Laserinterferometrie *f*
~ **jet** Laser[licht]strahl *m*, Laserbündel *n*
~ **light** Laserlicht *n*
~ **light beam** Laserstrahl *m*, Laserbündel *n*
~ **light energy** Laserlichtenergie *f*
~ **light source** Laserlichtquelle *f*
~ **line** Laserlinie *f*
~ **marker** Laserbeschrifter *m*, Lasermarkierer *m*
~ **marking** Laserbeschriften *n*, Laserbeschriftung *f*
~ **material** Lasermaterial *n*
~ **measuring microscope** Lasermessmikroskop *n*
~ **micrometer** Lasermikrometer *n*
~ **microscope** Lasermikroskop *n*
~ **microscopy** Lasermikroskopie *f*
~ **mirror** Laserspiegel *m*
~ **mode** Lasermode *f*
~ **modulator** Lasermodulator *m*
~ **mount** Laserhalter *m*
~ **noise** Laserrauschen *n*
~ **objective** Laserobjektiv *n*
~-**optical** laseroptisch
~ **optics** Laseroptik *f*
~ **output mirror** Auskoppelspiegel *m*
~ **paper** Laser[druck]papier *n*
~ **performance** Laserleistung *f*
~ **photon** Laserphoton *n*
~ **physics** Laserphysik *f*
~ **plotter** [elektrostatischer] Laserplotter *m*, Fotoplotter *m*
~ **point** Laserpunkt *m*; Belichterpixel *n*
~ **pointer** Laserstift *m*, Laserpointer *m*
~ **power** Laserleistung *f*
~ **printer** Laserdrucker *m*, Laserprinter *m*
~ **printer cartridge** Laserdruckerpatrone *f*
~ **printing** Laserdruck *m*
~ **probe** Lasersonde *f*
~ **projection** Laserprojektion *f*
~ **protective eyewear** Laserschutzbrille *f*
~ **protective glass** Laserschutzglas *n*
~ **pulse** Laser[im]puls *m*
~ **pulse duration (width)** Laserpulsdauer *f*
~ **pump** Laserpumpe *f*
~ **radar** Laserradar *n*, Lichtradar *n*, optisches Radar *n*, Lidar *n*
~ **radiation** Laserstrahlung *f*
~ **Raman spectroscopy** Laser-Raman-Spektroskopie *f*
~ **rangefinder (ranger)** Laser-Entfernungsmesser *m*
~ **recorder** *s.* ~ film recorder
~ **resonator** Laserresonator *m*
~ **rod** Laserstab *m*
~ **saturation spectroscopy** Laser-Sättigungsspektroskopie *f*
~ **scan microscope** Laserrastermikroskop *n*, Lichtrastermikroskop *n*
~-**scanned playback** laserabgetastete Abspielung *f*
~ **scanner** Laserabtaster *m*, Laserscanner *m*
~ **scanning** Laser[strahl]abtastung *f*

~ **scanning confocal microscope** Laserkonfokalmikroskop *n*
~ **scanning confocal microscopy** konfokale Laserabtastmikroskopie *f*
~ **scanning microscope** Laserabtastmikroskop *n*
~ **scribing** *s.* ~ marking
~ **sensor** Lasersensor *m*
~ **sheet** aufgeweiteter Laserstrahl *m*
~ **show** Lasershow *f*
~ **signal** Lasersignal *n*
~ **sintering** Lasersintern *n*
~ **spectroscopic** laserspektroskopisch
~ **spectroscopy** Laserspektroskopie *f*
~ **spike** Laserblitz *m*
~ **spot** Laserfleck *m*; Laserpunkt *m*
~ **stroboscope** Laserstroboskop *n*
~ **stroboscopy** Laserstroboskopie *f*
~ **system** Lasersystem *n*
~ **technology** Lasertechnik *f*
~ **telescope** Laserteleskop *n*
~ **tracker** Laserziel[verfolgungs]gerät *n*
~ **triangulation** Lasertriangulation *f*
~ **triangulation sensor** Lasertriangulationssensor *m*
~ **tube** Laserrohr *n*
~ **unit** Laseranlage *f*
~ **videodisk** Laserplatte *f*, Laserdisk *f*, Bild[speicher]platte *f*
~ **wavelength** Laserwellenlänge *f*
laserjet paper Laser[druck]papier *n*
~ **printer** Laserdrucker *m*, Laserprinter *m*
lasing action Laserwirkung *f*
~ **medium** Lasermedium *n*
lasso tool Lassowerkzeug *n*, Freihandschere *f (digitale Bildbearbeitung)*
last frame of action (picture) Bildende *n (Kinefilm)*
Last Supper format Abendmahlsformat *n (Bildtelefonie)*
latency 1. Ende-zu-Ende-Verzögerung *f (Datenkommunikation)*; 2. *s.* ~ time
~ **time** Latenzzeit *f*, Induktionsperiode *f (Fotoentwicklung)*
latensification Latensifikation *f*
latensify/to latensifizieren
latent charge[d] image latentes Ladungsbild *n*
~ **edge number** [Negativ-]Fußnummer *f*
~ **image** Latentbild *n*, latentes (verborgenes) Bild *n*
~ **image center** *s.* ~ image nucleus
~ **image destruction effect** Intensitätsumkehreffekt *m*
~ **image formation** Latentbildentstehung *f*
~ **image intensification** Latensifikation *f*
~ **image keeping [performance]** Latentbildstabilität *f*
~ **image nucleus** Latentbildkeim *m*, Latentbildzentrum *n*, Entwicklungskeim *m*
~ **image silver** Latentbildsilber *n*
~ **image stability** Latentbildstabilität *f*

~ **image theory** Latentbildtheorie *f*
~ **photographic image** *s.* ~ image
lateral aberration Queraberration *f*, Querabweichung *f*, außeraxialer Abbildungsfehler *m*
~ **adaptation** Simultankontrast *m (Sehen)*
~ **chromatic aberration (error)**, ~ **color** Farbquerfehler *m*, chromatische Queraberration (Brennweitendifferenz) *f*, lateraler Farbfehler *m*
~ **coma** seitliche Koma *f (Abbildungsfehler)*
~ **geniculate nucleus** [seitlicher] Kniehöcker *m*, Sehstrahlung *f*
~ **inhibition** laterale Inhibition *f (Sehen)*
~ **magnification** laterale (transversale) Vergrößerung *f*, Lateralvergrößerung *f*, Seitenvergrößerung *f*
~ **resolution** Lateralauflösung *f*, laterale Auflösung *f*, Seitenauflösung *f*
~ **reversal** 1. Seitenumkehr[ung] *f*; 2. Seitenverkehrtheit *f*
laterally correct seitenrichtig
~ **correct[ed] image** seitenkorrektes (seitenrichtiges) Bild *n*
~ **reversed** seitenverkehrt, spiegelverkehrt
~ **reversed image** seitenverkehrtes (einseitig umgekehrtes) Bild *n*
Latham loop Ausgleichsschleife *f*, Beruhigungsschleife *f*, Latham-Schlaufe *f (Kinotechnik)*
latitude Belichtungsumfang *m*; Dynamikbereich *m (Silberfotografie)*
lattice Gitter *n*
~ **arrangement** Gitteranordnung *f (z.B. von Atomen)*
~ **binding** Gitterbindung *f (von Elektronen)*
~ **constant** Gitterkonstante *f*
~ **coupling** *s.* ~ binding
~ **defect** Gitterbaufehler *m*, Gitterbaufehlstelle *f*
~ **image** Gitterbild *n*
~ **imperfection** Gitterfehler *m*
~ **impurity** Störstelle *f*
~ **ion** Gitterion *n*
~ **line** Gitterlinie *f*
~ **plane** Gitterebene *f*
~ **point** Gitter[schnitt]punkt *m*
~ **position (site)** Gitterstelle *f*
~ **spacing** Gitterabstand *f*
~ **spectrum** Gitterspektrum *n*
~ **structure** Gitterstruktur *f*
~ **-theoretic** gittertheoretisch
~ **theory** Gittertheorie *f*
~ **vibration** Gitterschwingung *f*
Laue method Laue-Verfahren *n (Kristallografie)*
~ **pattern (photograph)**, **Lauegram** Laue-Diagramm *n*
lavalier[e] microphone Ansteckmikro[fon] *n*; Krawattenmikrofon *n*, Lavaliermikrofon *n*

lavender

lavender print Lavendel *n*, Lavendelkopie *f*, Duplikatpositiv *n*, Duplikatpositivkopie *f* *(Kinefilmverarbeitung)*

law of inverse squares fotometrisches Grundgesetz *n*, quadratisches Entfernungsgesetz *n*, Abstandsquadratgesetz *n*

~ **of reflection** Reflexionsgesetz *n*, Spiegelgesetz *n*

~ **of refraction** Brechungsgesetz *n*

laydown sequence Farbreihenfolge *f* *(Druck)*

layer 1. Schicht *f*; 2. Bildebene *f* *(Trickkinematografie)*

~ **arrangement** *s.* ~ order

~ **exposure** Schichtentwicklung *f*

~ **order** Schichtfolge *f*, Schichtaufbau *m*

~ **thickness** Schichtdicke *f*

layered coding mehrstufige Codierung *f*

layout 1. Layout *n*, Makrotypografie *f*; 2. Layout *n*, Gestaltungsvorlage *f*

~ **grid** Einteilungsbogen *m*, Standbogen *m*

~ **man** Layouter *m*

~ **sheet** Layoutfolie *f*, Montagefolie *f*

~ **work** Layoutgestaltung *f*

~ **workstation** Layout-Arbeitsstation *f*

layover [effect] 1. Umklappung *f* *(geometrische Transformation)*; 2. Überlagerungseffekt *m* *(Radar)*

lazy eye Schwachsichtigkeit *f*, Amblyopie *f*

LCD *s.* liquid crystal display

~ **color monitor** LCD-Farbmonitor *m*

~ **pixel** LCD-Pixel *n*

~ **projector** LCD-Projektor *m*, Flüssigkristallprojektor *m*, Flüssigkristall-Projektionsgerät *n*

~ **screen** LC-Bildschirm *m*, Flüssigkristallbildschirm *m*

LCOS display *s.* liquid crystal on silicon display

LD chip LCD-Chip *m*

lead composition Bleisatz *m*

~ **crystal glass** Bleikristallglas *n*

~ **equivalent** Bleigleichwert *m*

~ **foil** *s.* ~ intensifying foil

~ **glass** Bleiglas *n*

~-**in area** Einlaufbereich *m* *(Bildspeicherplatte)*

~ **intensifying foil**, ~ **screen** Blei[verstärker]folie *f* *(Radiografie)*

~-**lined film pouch** Filmschutzbeutel *m*

~-**out area** Auslaufbereich *m* *(Bildspeicherplatte)*

~ **oxide camera tube**, ~ **oxide vidicon** Plumbikon *n* *(Bildröhre)*

~ **shielding** Bleiabschirmung *f*

~ **type** Bleitype *f*

leader 1. Filmanfang *m*, Filmlasche *f*, Filmzunge *f*; 2. Anfangsallonge *f*, Vorspann[film] *m*; 3. Vorlaufband *n*, Anfangsband *n*, Normstartband *n*

~ **strip** Vorlaufstreifen *m*, Startband *n* *(Kinematografie)*

~ **tape** Vorspannband *n*

leading Zeilenabstand *m*, Grundzeilenabstand *m*; Durchschuss *m*, Zeilendurchschuss *m*, Zeilenzwischenraum *m* *(Typografie)*

~ **edge** Greiferkante *f*, Greiferrand *m* *(Bogendruck)*

leaf Blatt *n*, Einzelblatt *n* *(Papier)*

~ **node** Blattknoten *m* *(Binärbaum)*

~ **shutter** Lamellenverschluss *m*, Segmentverschluss *m*; Zentralverschluss *m*

~-**shutter camera** Zentralverschlusskamera *f*

leakage current Leckstrom *m* *(z.B. eines Halbleiters)*

learnability Lernfähigkeit *f* *(Neuroinformatik)*

learnable lernfähig

learning Lernen *n*, Training *n* *(s.a. unter training)*

~ **algorithm** Lernalgorithmus *m*, Trainingsalgorithmus *m*, lernender Algorithmus *m*

~ **classifier** lernender Klassifikator *m*

~ **set** Lerndatensatz *m*, Trainingsdatensatz *m*, Lernmenge *f*, Lernstichprobe *f*

~ **vector quantization** überwachte Vektorquantisierung *f*

~ **vector quantizer** lernender Vektorquantisierer *m*

least expensive camera Einfachstkamera *f*

~ **mean square approximation** Fehlerquadratminimierung *f*

~ **significant bit** niederwertigstes Bit *n* *(sequentielle Kompression)*

~ **significant bit plane** niederwertige Bitebene *f*

~ **squares error** minimales Fehlerquadrat *n*

~ **squares error filter** Wienersches Optimalfilter *n*, Wiener-Filter *n* *(Bildrestaurierung)*

~ **squares matching** Kleinste-Quadrate-Ausgleichung *f*, Kleinste-Quadrate-Bildzuordnung *f*

~ **squares method** Methode *f* der kleinsten Quadrate

leather facing Gehäusebezug *m*, Belederung *f* *(Fotoapparat)*

LED *s.* light-emitting diode

~ **display** LED-Anzeige *f*, Leuchtdiodenanzeige *f*

~ **line** LED-Linienlicht *n*

left-adjusted, left-aligned linksbündig *(Typografie)*

~-**circularly polarized light** linkszirkular polarisiertes Licht *n*

~ **click** Linksklick *m*

~ **clicking** Linksklicken *n*

~-**elliptically polarized light** linkselliptisch polarisiertes Licht *n*

~-**eye image** linksäugiges Bild *n*

~-**eye view** linksäugiger Blick *m*

~-**eyed** linksäugig

~-hand page Verso n, Blattrückseite f, gerade Seite f *(Layout)*
~-hand[ed] polarization linksdrehende (linkszirkulare) Polarisation f
~-handed coordinate system linkshändiges Koordinatensystem n
legend s. caption 1.
legibility Leserlichkeit f; Lesbarkeit f
legible leserlich; lesbar
Leica thread Leica-Gewinde n *(Vergrößerungsgerät)*
Lempel-Ziv coding Lempel-Ziv-Codierung f
~-Ziv-Welch coding Lempel-Ziv-Welch-Codierung f, LZW-Codierung f
length of line Zeilenlänge f
lens/to filmen
lens 1. Linse f; 2. Objektiv n; 3. Augenlinse f
~ **aberration** Linsenfehler m
~ **accessories** Objektivzubehör n
~ **adapter** Objektivadapter m
~ **angle** Objektivwinkel m
~ **aperture** Objektivapertur f, Objektivöffnung f, Objektivblende f frequenzmodulierte Rasterung f
~-aperture setting Blendeneinstellung f
~ **area** Linsenfläche f
~ **arrangement** Linsenanordnung f
~ **artifact** Objektivfehler m
~ **assembly** Linsenkombination f, Linsensystem n
~ **attachment** Objektivvorsatz m, Objektivzusatz m
~ **axis** 1. Linsenachse f; 2. Objektivachse f
~ **barrel** Objektivtubus m, Objektivstutzen m
~ **bench** optische Bank f
~ **blank** Rohlinse f, Linsenrohling m
~ **block holder** Linsentragkörper m, Tragkörper m
~ **board** optische Bank f; Objektivträger m
~ **brush** Objektivpinsel m
~ **cap** Objektiv[schutz]deckel m, Objektiv[schutz]kappe f
~ **case** Objektivköcher m
~ **cement** optischer Kitt m; Feinkitt m
~ **center** Linsenmittelpunkt m
~-changing system Objektivwechselsystem n
~ **choice** Objektivwahl f
~ **cleaning cloth** Linsenputztuch n, Objektivreinigungstuch n
~ **cleaning fluid** Linsenreinigungsflüssigkeit f
~ **cleaning tissue** Objektivreinigungspapier n, Linsenpapier n
~ **coating** Linsenvergütung f, Linsenoberflächenbehandlung f; Objektivvergütung f
~ **combination** Linsenkombination f, Linsensystem n; Objektivsystem n
~ **compatibility** Objektivkompatibilität f
~ **configuration** Objektiv[auf]bau m

~ **conjugate equation** s. ~ equation
~ **correction** Linsenkorrektur f
~ **coverage** Gesichtsfeld n *(Objektiv)*
~ **coverage** Objektivabdeckung f
~ **current** Linsenstrom m *(Elektronenmikroskop)*
~ **curvature** Linsenkrümmung f
~ **defect** Linsenfehler m
~ **design** Objektivkonstruktion f, Objektivaufbau m, Objektivausführung f
~ **designer** Objektivkonstrukteur m, Optikkonstrukteur m, Optikmodellierer m
~ **diameter** Objektivdurchmesser m
~ **diaphragm** Objektivblende f, Blende f, Diaphragma n
~ **diaphragm scale** Blendenskale f, Blendenzahl[en]reihe f
~ **distortion** Objektivverzeichnung f
~ **doublet** Doppelobjektiv n, Dualobjektiv n, Dublettlinse f, Dublett n
~ **drawing** Linsenzeichnung f, Linsenschnitt m
~ **element** Linsenelement n, Einzellinse f; Objektivelement n, Objektivglied n
~ **entrance pupil** Objektiveintrittspupille f
~ **equation** Gaußsche Linsengleichung f
~ **error** Linsenfehler m
~ **extender** Objektivvorsatz m, Objektivzusatz m
~ **extension** Objektivauszug m
~ **fabrication** s. ~ manufacture
~ **filter** Objektivfilter n
~ **filter ring straightening block** Filterrichtblock m
~ **filter thread** Filtergewinde n
~ **filtration** Objektivfilterung f
~ **flare** Linsenstreuung f
~ **focal length** Objektivbrennweite f
~ **focus** Objektivbrennweite f
~ **glass** Linsenglas n
~ **grinder** Linsenschleifer m
~ **group** Linsengruppe f
~ **guard** Objektivschutz m
~ **holder** Linsenhalter m
~ **hood** Gegenlichtblende f, Gegenlichttubus m, Sonnenblende f; Streulichtblende f
~ **housing** Objektivtubus m, Objektivstutzen m
~ **imperfection** Linsenfehler m
~ **interface** Linsengrenzfläche f
~ **length** Objektivlänge f; Objektivbrennweite f
~ **line** Objektivreihe f, Objektivsatz m
~ **manufacture** Linsenfertigung f, Objektivbau m, Objektivherstellung f
~ **material** Linsenwerkstoff m, optischer Werkstoff m, Linsenmaterial n
~ **microprocessor** Objektivmikroprozessor m
~-mirror system Spiegellinse f
~ **mount** Objektivanschluss m, Objektivfassung f; Objektivhalter m

lens

~ **nomogram** Linsennomogramm *n*
~ **opening** Objektivöffnung *f*, Objektivapertur *f*; Objektivblende *f*
~ **pair** Linsenpaar *n*
~ **paper** Linsenpapier *n*, Linsenputztuch *n*
~ **parameter** Objektivparameter *m*
~ **path** Objektivlichtweg *m*
~ **pen** Linsenreinigungsstift *m*
~ **performance** Objektivleistung *f*
~ **plane** Linsenebene *f*; Objektivebene *f*
~ **plane swing** Objektivverschwenkung *f*
~ **pole** Linsenscheitel *m*
~ **producer** Objektivhersteller *m*, Optikhersteller *m*
~ **quality** Objektivqualität *f*
~ **release button** Objektiventriegelung[staste] *f*
~ **resolution** Objektivauflösung *f*, Objektivauflösungsvermögen *n*
~ **reversing adapter** Umkehrring *m*
~ **ring** Objektivring *m*
~ **ring straightening pliers** Filterring-Richtzange *f*
~ **selection** Objektivwahl *f*
~ **set** Objektivsatz *m*, Objektivreihe *f*
~ **setting** Objektiveinstellung *f*
~ **shade** *s.* ~ hood
~ **shape** Linsenform *f*
~ **shutter** Objektivverschluss *m*
~ **-shutter camera** Objektivverschlusskamera *f*
~ **speed** Objektivlichtstärke *f*
~ **stage** Objektivträger *m*; Objektivplatine *f* *(Vergrößerungsgerät)*
~ **standard** Objektivstandarte *f* *(Fachkamera)*
~ **suction cup** Linsensaugnapf *m*
~ **surface** Linsen[ober]fläche *f*
~ **system** Linsensystem *n*, Linsenkombination *f*; Objektivsystem *n*
~ **testing** Objektivprüfung *f*
~ **thickness** Linsendicke *f*
~ **tissue** Linsenputztuch *n*, Linsenpapier *n*
~ **-to-film distance (spacing)** Bildweite *f*, Bildentfernung *f*, Objektiv-Film-Abstand *m*; Balgenauszug *m*
~ **tool** Objektivwerkzeug *n*
~ **turret** Objektivrevolver *m*, Revolverkopf *m*
~ **type** Objektivtyp[us] *m*
~ **vertex** Linsenscheitel *m*
lensless linsenslos, linsenfrei
lensmaker's formula Linsenmachergleichung *f* *(Brennweitenbestimmung)*
lensman Kameramann *m*; Fotograf *m*
lenticular linsenförmig, lentikulär
~ **additive color amateur motion-picture film** Linsenrasterschmalfilm *m*
~ **color photography** Linsenrasterfarbfotografie *f*
~ **color process** Linsenrasterverfahren *n*
~ **film** Linsenrasterfilm *m*

~ **screen (sheet display)** Linsenrasterschirm *m*, geprägte Bildwand *f*, Riffelwand *f*
lenticulated *s.* lenticular
lerping *s.* linear interpolation
letter/to drucken
letter Buchstabe *m*, Letter *f*; Schriftzeichen *n*; Druckbuchstabe *m*; Drucktype *f*
~ **image** Buchstabenbild *n*
~ **paper** Briefpapier *n*
~ **quality** Briefqualität *f*, Korrespondenzqualität *f* *(Papier; Druckbild)*
~ **space/to** sperren, spationieren, spatiieren *(Layout, Satzherstellung)*
~ **spacing** Laufweite *f*, Buchstabenabstand *m*
letterbox [format], ~ **picture format** Letterbox-Format *n* *(Fernsehen, Video)*
letterboxed picture Letterbox-Bild *n*
letterboxing Letterbox-Verfahren *n*; Letterbox-Wiedergabe *f*
letterform Buchstabenbild *n*
letterhead 1. Briefkopf *m*; Firmenaufdruck *m*, Firmenkopf *m*; 2. Kopfbogen *m*
lettering Beschriftung *f*
letterpress *s.* ~ printing
~ **composition** Schriftsatz *m*
~ **offset** *s.* letterset
~ **paper** Hochdruckpapier *n*
~ **plate** Buchdruckplatte *f*; Hochdruckplatte *f*, Reliefdruckplatte *f*
~ **printing** Buchdruck *m*; [direkter] Hochdruck *m*, Reliefdruck *m*
~ **printing machine (press)** Buchdruckmaschine *f*; Hochdruckmaschine *f*
~ **rotary** Buchdruck-Rotationsmaschine *f*
letterset Letter[off]setdruck *m*; Trockenoffsetdruck *m*, wasserloser Offsetdruck *m*; indirekter Hochdruck *m*
leuco dye Leuco[cyan]farbstoff *m*
level bubble Libelle *f*, Libellennivellier *n*, [eingebaute] Wasserwaage *f*
~ **contour line** Höhenlinie *f*, Niveaulinie *f*, Isohypse *f*
~ **control** Tonregler *m*, Lautstärkeregler *m*
~ **curve** Konturkurve *f*
~ **of correction** Korrektionsgrad *m*
~ **of detail** Genauigkeitsstufe *f*, Detaillierungsebene *f* *(Computergrafik)*
~ **of hierarchy** Hierarchieebene *f*, Hierarchiestufe *f*
~ **sync** 1. Schnittsynchronisierung *f*; 2. Synchronmarke *f* *(Kinematografie)*
leveling instrument Nivellierinstrument *n*
~ **telescope** Nivellierfernrohr *n*
levo, levorota[to]ry linksdrehend
LFOA *s.* last frame of action
library of type fonts Schriftenbibliothek *f*
~ **shot** Archivaufnahme *f*
Lichtenberg figure (image) Lichtenbergsche Figur *f* *(Ladungsbild)*

lidar Lidar n, Laserradar n, Lichtradar n, optisches Radar n
life size 1. Lebensgröße f; 2. s. life-sized
~-size magnification Vergrößerung f auf Lebensgröße
~-sized image lebensgroßes Bild n
ligature Ligatur f, Doppelbuchstabe m
light/to beleuchten
light 1. hell; 2. mager *(Schriftauszeichnung)*
~ 1. Licht n *(s.a. unter* optical, luminous*)*; 2. s. lighting fixture
~ **absorber** Lichtabsorber m
~**-absorbing dye** lichtabsorbierender Farbstoff m
~ **absorption** Lichtabsorption f, optische Absorption f; Lichtfang m *(bes. zwischen Rasterbildpunkten)*
~ **acceptance angle** Akzeptanzwinkel m *(Objektiv)*
~ **action** Lichtwirkung f
~ **adaptation** Helladaptation f
~**-adapted** helladaptiert; fotopisch
~**-adapted eye** helladaptiertes Auge n
~**-adapted vision** Helligkeitssehen n, Tagessehen n, fotopisches Sehen n
~ **alternating frequency** Lichtwechselfrequenz f
~ **amplification** Lichtverstärkung f
~ **amplification by stimulated emission of radiation** Lichtverstärkung f durch angeregte (stimulierte) Strahlungsemission *(s.a. unter* Laser*)*
~ **amplification unit**, ~ **amplifier** Lichtverstärker m
~ **arc** Lichtbogen m
~ **areas** Lichter pl *(Fotografie)*
~ **arrangement** Lichtarrangement n
~ **attenuation** Licht[ab]schwächung f
~ **axis** Lichtachse f
~**-balancing filter** Lichtausgleichsfilter n, Konversionsfilter n
~ **bank** Lichtbank f
~ **barium crown [glass]** Baritleichtkronglas n
~ **beam** Licht[strahlen]bündel n; Lichtstrahl m
~ **beam pointer** Lichtzeiger m
~ **box** Lichtkasten m, Leuchtkasten m, Beleuchtungskasten m; Leuchtpult n; Diasortierpult n
~ **bundle** Lichtbündel n
~ **change** Lichtwechsel m
~ **collection** Lichtsammlung f
~ **color** 1. Lichtfarbe f; 2. helle Farbe f
~**-colored** hellfarbig
~ **composition** Lichtzusammensetzung f
~ **conditions** Lichtverhältnisse pl
~ **conduit** Licht[wellen]leiter m
~ **cone** Lichtkegel m
~ **control** Lichtsteuerung f
~ **control system** Lichtsteuersystem n
~**-controlling device** Lichtsteuereinrichtung f

~ **conversion** Lichtwandlung f
~ **decay time** Lichtabklingzeit f *(eines PET-Szintillators)*
~ **decomposition** Lichtzerlegung f
~ **deflection** Lichtablenkung f
~ **deflector** Licht[strahl]ablenker m
~ **degradation** Lichtdegradation f
~ **detector** Lichtdetektor m, optischer Detektor m, Fotodetektor m
~ **diffraction** Lichtbeugung f
~ **diffuser** Lichtdiffusor m
~**-diffusing screen** Weichzeichnerfolie f, Weichzeichnergaze f
~ **diffusion** Lichtdiffusion f, Diffusion f
~ **direction** Lichtrichtung f
~ **dissipation** Lichtabfall m, Lichtschwund m
~ **distribution curve** Lichtverteilungskurve f
~ **distribution solid** Lichtverteilungskörper m, fotometrischer Körper m
~ **disturbance** Lichtstörung f
~ **drawing** s. ~ graphics
~ **effect** Lichteffekt m
~ **efficiency** Lichtausbeute f; Lichtleistung f *(z.B. von Elektronenblitzgeräten)*
~ **emission** Lichtemission f, Lichtaussendung f, Lichtausstrahlung f, Lichtabstrahlung f
~ **emitter** Lichtemitter m
~**-emitting diode** Leuchtdiode f, Lichtemitterdiode f, Lumineszenzdiode f, lichtemittierende Diode f, LED
~**-emitting diode display** Leuchtdiodenanzeige f
~ **energy** Lichtenergie f
~ **entry** Lichteinlass m
~ **equivalent** [fotometrisches] Lichtäquivalent n
~ **excitation** Lichterregung f
~ **exit** Lichtaustritt m
~ **exit port** Lichtaustrittsöffnung f
~**-exposed film** belichteter Film m
~ **exposure** Lichtexposition f, Belichtung f *(s.a. unter* exposure*)*
~ **exposure test** Belichtungstest m
~ **falloff** Lichtabfall m, Lichtschwund m
~ **field** Lichtfeld n
~ **field rendering** [computergrafische] Beleuchtungsberechnung f
~ **filter** 1. optisches Filter n, Lichtfilter n; 2. s. color filter
~ **filtration** Lichtfilterung f
~ **flash** Lichtblitz m
~ **flint glass** Leichtflintglas n
~ **flow** Lichtfluss m
~ **flux** Lichtstrom m; Lichtleistung f
~ **flux density** Lichtstromdichte f
~ **fog** Lichtschleier m
~ **from subject** Motivlicht n
~ **gate** Lichtschranke f
~**-gathering ability** Lichtsammelfähigkeit f
~**-gathering power [of a lens]** Lichtstärke f, Objektivlichtstärke f

light 214

- ~ **generation** Lichterzeugung f
- ~ **gradation** Lichtabstufung f
- ~ **graphics** Fotografik f, Lichtgrafik f, Lichtmalerei f
- ~ **guide** Licht[wellen]leiter m
- ~ **guide cable** Lichtleitkabel n, Glasfaserkabel n
- ~ **image** Lichtbild n, optisches Bild n, optische Abbildung f
- ~ **impulse** Licht[im]puls m
- ~-**insensitive** lichtunempfindlich
- ~-**integrating timer** Belichtungsautomat m (Typografie)
- ~ **intensification** Lichtverstärkung f
- ~ **intensifier** Lichtverstärker m
- ~ **intensity** Lichtintensität f, Lichtstärke f
- ~ **interference** Lichtinterferenz f
- ~ **interruption** Lichtunterbrechung f
- ~ **irradiation** Lichteinstrahlung f
- ~ **leakage** Lichtundichtheit f
- ~ **level** Lichtniveau n, Lichtpegel m (s.a. illuminance)
- ~ **loss** Lichtverlust m
- ~ **loss factor** Lichtverlustfaktor m
- ~ **measure** Lichtmaß n
- ~ **measurement** Lichtmessung f
- ~ **meter** 1. Lichtmessgerät n, Fotometer n; 2. Belichtungsmesser m, Belichtungsmessgerät n, Exposimeter n
- ~ **metering** 1. Lichtmessung f; 2. Belichtungsmessung f
- ~ **microscope** Lichtmikroskop n
- ~ **microscope image** Lichtmikroskopaufnahme f, Lichtmikroskopbild n
- ~ **microscopy** Lichtmikroskopie f, lichtoptische Mikroskopie f
- ~-**mixing box** Lichtmischschacht m, Mischschacht m (Vergrößerungsgerät)
- ~-**modulated resistor** lichtmodulierter Widerstand m
- ~-**modulated signal current** lichtmodulierter Signalstrom m
- ~ **modulation** Lichtmodulation f
- ~ **modulator** Lichtmodulator m
- ~ **negative** dünnes Negativ n
- ~-**operated switch** optischer Schalter m
- ~-**optical** lichtoptisch, fotooptisch
- ~ **optics** Lichtoptik f
- ~ **output** Lichtabgabe f; Lichtausbeute f
- ~ **overexposure** Überbelichtung f
- ~ **panel** Leuchtplatte f
- ~ **particle** Lichtteilchen n, Lichtquant n
- ~ **patch** Lichtfleck m
- ~ **path[way]** Lichtweg m, optischer Weg m
- ~ **pen** Lichtgriffel m, Lichtstift m
- ~ **perception** Lichtwahrnehmung f
- ~ **physics** Physik f des Lichts, Fotophysik f
- ~ **plane** Lichtfläche f
- ~ **pointer** Lichtzeiger m
- ~ **polarization** Lichtpolarisierung f
- ~ **polarizer** Lichtpolarisator m
- ~ **pollution** Lichtverschmutzung f, Lichtverseuchung f (Astrofotografie)
- ~ **power** Lichtleistung f, Lichtstrom m (Fotometrie)
- ~ **pressure** Lichtdruck m
- ~ **probe** Lichtsonde f (konfokale Mikroskopie)
- ~-**produced charge carrier** fotogenerierter Ladungsträger m
- ~-**producing** lichterzeugend
- ~-**producing phosphor** Leuchtstoff m, Leuchtphosphor m, Phosphor m, Luminophor m
- ~ **production** Lichterzeugung f
- ~ **propagation** Lichtausbreitung f, Lichtfortpflanzung f
- ~-**protecting paper** Lichtschutzpapier n
- ~ **protecting varnish** Lichtschutzlack m
- ~ **protection** Lichtschutz m
- ~ **pulse** Licht[im]puls m
- ~ **quality** Lichtqualität f
- ~ **quantum** Lichtquant n, Lichtteilchen n; Strahlungsquant n, Photon n
- ~ **ray** Lichtstrahl m
- ~ **ray deflection** Lichtablenkung f
- ~ **rays bending** Lichtbeugung f
- ~ **receiver** Lichtempfänger m
- ~ **receptor** 1. Lichtrezeptor m, Fotorezeptor m, [lichtempfindlicher] Rezeptor m; 2. Lichtsinneszelle f; Lichtsinnesorgan n
- ~ **reflection** Lichtreflexion f
- ~ **reflector** Lichtreflektor m
- ~ **refraction** Lichtbrechung f
- ~ **regulation** Lichtregulierung f
- ~ **resistance** s. ~ stability
- ~ **right-hand rule** Rechte-Hand-Regel f (Optik)
- ~ **scatter[ing]** Licht[zer]streuung f
- ~ **scattering image** Streubild n
- ~-**section method** Lichtschnittverfahren n (Topometrie)
- ~-**section microscope** Lichtschnittmikroskop n
- ~ **sensing** Lichtempfindung f
- ~ **sensing cell** Lichtsinneszelle f
- ~-**sensitive** lichtempfindlich, fotoempfindlich, fotosensibel
- ~-**sensitive diode** lichtempfindliche Diode f, Fotodiode f
- ~-**sensitive emulsion** lichtempfindliche Emulsion f
- ~-**sensitive material** lichtempfindliches Material n
- ~-**sensitive sensor** lichtempfindlicher Sensor m
- ~ **sensitivity** Lichtempfindlichkeit f, Fotoempfindlichkeit f
- ~ **sensitization** Fotosensibilisierung f
- ~ **sensor** Lichtsensor m, Optosensor m, optischer Sensor m, Fotosensor m
- ~ **shield[ing]** Lichtabschirmung f
- ~ **signal** Lichtsignal n
- ~ **situation** Lichtsituation f
- ~ **slit** Lichtspalt m
- ~ **source** Lichtquelle f, Lichtstrahler m

~ **source color** Lichtquellenfarbe f
~-**source color** Lichtfarbe f
~ **source distance** Lichtquellenabstand m
~ **source image** Lichtquellenbild n
~ **source optics** Beleuchtungsoptik f
~ **spectrum** Lichtspektrum n
~ **splitter** Strahl[en]teiler m
~ **spot** Lichtpunkt m, Lichtfleck m, Leuchtfleck m; Spiegelfleck m
~ **spread** Lichtausbreitung f
~ **stability** Lichtechtheit f, Lichtbeständigkeit f, Fotostabilität f
~ **stand** Leuchtenstativ n, Lichtständer m
~ **stimulus** Lichtreiz m
~-**stripe method** s. light-section method
~ **sum** Lichtsumme f
~ **support** Leuchtenstativ n, Lichtständer m
~ **table** Lichttische m, Leuchttisch m
~-**to-dark [image] transition** Hell-Dunkel-Übergang m
~ **transmission** Lichttransmission f, Lichtübertragung f; Lichtdurchgang m
~ **transmittance** Lichttransmissionsgrad m, Lichtdurchlass[grad] m
~ **trap** Lichtschleuse f; Lichtfalle f
~ **trap labyrinth** Labyrintheingang m, Labyrinthschleuse f *(Dunkelraum)*
~-**trapped opening** lichtdichte Eingießöffnung f *(Entwicklungsdose)*
~-**travel distance** Lichtweg m
~ **tube** Lichtröhre f *(Optik)*
~ **unit** lichttechnische Einheit f
~ **utilization** Lichtausnutzung f
~ **value** Lichtwert m
~ **valve** Lichtventil n; Lichtschranke f; Lichtmodulator m
~ **valve projector** Lichtventilprojektor m
~ **vector** Lichtvektor m
~ **velocity** Lichtgeschwindigkeit f
~ **wave** Lichtwelle f, optische Welle f
~ **wave propagation** Lichtwellenausbreitung f
~ **wavelength** Lichtwellenlänge f
~ **yield** Lichtausbeute f, [fotometrisches] Strahlungsäquivalent n
lightbulb Glühbirne f, Glühlampe f
lighten/to aufhellen
lightening Aufhellung f
lightfast lichtecht, lichtbeständig, lichtstabil
lightfastness Lichtechtheit f, Lichtbeständigkeit f, Fotostabilität f
lighting 1. Beleuchtung f *(s.a. unter illumination)*; Lichtführung f, Lichtsetzung f; 2. s. pre-lighting
~ **accessories** Beleuchtungszubehör n
~ **angle** Beleuchtungswinkel m
~ **arrangement** s. ~ setup
~ **axis** Beleuchtungsachse f
~ **board** s. ~ console
~ **bridge** Beleuchtungsbrücke f

~ **cameraman** Chefkameramann m, leitender (lichtbestimmender, verantwortlicher) Kameramann m
~ **color** Beleuchtungsfarbe f
~ **conditions** Beleuchtungsbedingungen fpl
~ **console** Lichtstellanlage f, Lichtstellpult n, Lichtorgel f
~ **contrast** Beleuchtungskontrast m
~ **control board** Lichtsteuereinrichtung f
~ **design** Lichtgestaltung f, Lichtdesign n; Lichtregie f
~ **direction** Beleuchtungsrichtung f, Leuchtrichtung f
~ **effect** Beleuchtungseffekt m
~ **electrician** Lichttechniker m, Beleucht[ungstechnik]er m
~ **engineering** Lichttechnik f, Beleuchtungstechnik f
~ **environment** Beleuchtungsmilieu n
~ **equipment** Lichtausrüstung f; Beleuchtungsanlage f
~ **filter** Beleuchtungsfilter n
~ **fixture** Leuchte f, Beleuchtungskörper m
~ **hours** Brenndauer f *(Lampe)*
~ **installation** Beleuchtungsanlage f
~ **instrument** s. ~ fixture
~ **kit** Beleuchtungsanlage f
~ **level** Beleuchtungsintensität f, Beleuchtungsniveau n
~ **model** Beleuchtungsmodell n *(Computergrafik)*
~ **module** Beleuchtungsmodul n
~ **plan** Beleuchtungsplan m
~ **practice** Beleuchtungspraxis f
~ **ratio** Beleuchtungsverhältnis n
~ **rig (setup)** Beleuchtungsaufbau m, Licht[auf]bau m, Beleuchtungsanordnung f, Beleuchtungseinrichtung f
~ **situation** Beleuchtungssituation f
~ **source** Beleuchtungsquelle f
~ **stand** Leuchtenstativ n, Lichtständer m
~ **style** Beleuchtungsstil m, Lichtstil m; Beleuchtungsart f
~ **supervisor** Chefbeleuchter m, Oberbeleuchter m
~ **system** Beleuchtungssystem n
~ **technician** Lichttechniker f, Beleucht[ungstechnik]er m
~ **technique** Beleuchtungstechnik f
~ **tent** Lichtzelt n
~ **umbrella** Schirmreflektor m, Studioschirm m; Streuschirm m
~ **unit** Beleuchtungseinheit f
lightless lichtlos, dunkel
lightlessness Lichtlosigkeit f, Dunkelheit f
lightness Helligkeit f *(reflektierender Objekte; s.a. unter brightness)*
~ **of the surround** Umgebungshelligkeit f
lightning location Blitzortung f
~ **locator (position system)** Blitzortungssystem n
~ **sensing** Blitzüberwachung f

lightning 216

~ **warning system** Blitzwarnsystem n
lightproof lichtdicht, lichtundurchlässig, opak, undurchsichtig
lightproofness Lichtdichtheit f, Lichtundurchlässigkeit f, Opazität f
lighttight s. lightproof
lightweight paper leichtes Papier n
~ **tripod** Leichtstativ n
like-colored farbgleich, gleichfarbig, isochrom[atisch], orthochromatisch
likelihood Wahrscheinlichkeit f
~ **function** Likelihood-Funktion f *(Wahrscheinlichkeitsrechnung)*
limb Stativ n *(zusammengesetztes Mikroskop)*
limen absolute Wahrnehmungsschwelle f
limit of resolution Auflösungsgrenze f
limited accommodation Alters[weit]sichtigkeit f, Presbyopie f
~-**angle tomography** Teilwinkeltomografie f
~-**bit-depth CG image** bittiefenbegrenztes Computerbild n
~-**definition television** Fernsehen n mit begrenzter Auflösung
~-**resolution image** auflösungsbegrenztes Bild n
limiter Begrenzer m, Spitzenwertbegrenzer m; Lautstärkebegrenzung f
limiting frequency Grenzfrequenz f *(z.B. in der Bildfilterung)*
~ **resolution** Grenzauflösung f
linac s. linear accelerator
line 1. Linie f; Strich m; 2. Zeile f; Textzeile f
~ **adjacency graph** Liniennachbarschaftsgraph m
~ **approximation** Linienapproximation f
~ **array detector** s. linear array detector
~ **art** Strichgrafik f, Liniengrafik f; Koordinatengrafik f; Strichvorlage f
~ **averaging** Zeileninterpolation[stechnik] f
~-**based image segmentation** linienbasierte Bildsegmentierung f
~ **blanking** Horizontalaustastung f; Zeilenaustastlücke f
~-**by-line** zeilenweise
~-**by-line phase reversal** zeilenweise Phasenumkehr f
~-**by-line scanning** Zeilenabtastung f, zeilenweise Abtastung f
~ **chart** Kurvendiagramm n, Liniendiagramm n
~ **coding** Liniencodierung f
~ **contrast** Linienkontrast m
~ **copy** 1. Strichvorlage f; 2. Strichkopie f
~ **copy print** Strichkopie f
~ **craw[ling]** Zeilenwandern n *(Zeilensprungartefakt)*
~ **crossover** Linienkreuzung f
~ **density** Zeilendichte f
~ **detection** Liniendetektion f *(Bildsegmentierung)*
~ **detector** Liniendetektor m
~ **diagram** s. ~ chart

~ **doubler** Zeilenverdoppler m *(Monitortechnik)*
~ **doubling** Zeilenverdopp[e]lung f
~ **drawing** Strichzeichnung f
~-**drawing image** Linienbild n; Strichbild n, Strichabbildung f
~ **dropout** Störzeile[n] f*[pl]*
~ **dropout** Zeilenausfall m
~ **edge** Strichkante f
~ **electrode** Zeilenelektrode f *(Plasmabildschirm)*
~ **element** Linienelement n
~ **end[ing]** Linienende n; Linienendpunkt m
~ **etching** Strichätzung f
~ **feed** Zeilenvorschub m
~ **film** Strichfilm m, Rasterfilm m *(Reprografie)*
~ **fitting** Linienanpassung f
~ **flicker** Zeilenflimmern n
~ **flyback** Zeilenrücklauf m, Horizontalrücklauf m *(Elektronenstrahl)*
~ **following** Linienverfolgung f; sequentielle Kantenextraktion f
~ **frequency** s. ~ scanning frequency
~ **gap** Zeilendurchschuss m, Durchschuss m, Zeilenzwischenraum m
~ **graphics** Strichgrafik f, Liniengrafik f; Koordinatengrafik f
~ **grating** Liniengitter n
~ **hum** Netzbrumm m, Netzbrummen n
~ **identification** Zeilenkennung f *(Video)*
~ **illustration (image)** Linienbild n; Strichbild n, Strichabbildung f
~ **integral** Linienintegral n
~ **interpolation** Zeileninterpolation[stechnik] f
~ **jitter** Zeilenflimmern n
~ **length** Zeilenlänge f
~ **memory** Zeilen[puffer]speicher m
~ **negative** Strichnegativ n
~ **noise** Linienrauschen n
~ **number** Zeilenzahl f
~ **object** Linienobjekt n
~ **of cameras** Kameraserie f
~ **of decoration** Zierlinie f
~ **of dialog[ue]** Dialogpassage f, Dialogstück n
~ **of flight** Überflugsbahn f, Flugstreifen m *(Aerofotogrammetrie)*
~ **of intersection** Schnittlinie f
~ **of pixels** Pixelzeile f
~ **of print** Druckzeile f
~ **of response** Koinzidenzlinie f *(Positronenemissionstomografie)*; Messstrahl m *(Radiografie)*
~ **of sight** Blicklinie f, Sichtlinie f, Gesichtslinie f, Augenlinie f, Sichtverbindung f
~-**of-sight propagation** quasioptische Ausbreitung f *(von Signalen)*
~-**of-sight registration** Blicklinienmessung f, Blickzieluntersuchung f

linear

~-of-sight telescope Flucht[ungsprüf]fernrohr *n*
~-of-sight vector Blicklinienvektor *m*
~ of text Textzeile *f*
~ of video Videozeile *f*
~ of vision *s.* ~ of sight
~ offset Zeilenversatz *m*
~ orientation Linienrichtung *f*
~ original Strichvorlage *f*
~ pair Linienpaar *n (Auflösungsmaß)*
~ pattern Linienmuster *n*
~ period Zeilen[perioden]dauer *f*
~ printer Zeilendrucker *m*, Paralleldrucker *m*; Textdrucker *m*
~ producer Aufnahmeleiter *m (Filmteam)*
~ pulse Zeilenimpuls *m*
~ radiator Linienstrahler *m*
~ raster Linienraster *m(n)*; Zeilenraster *m(n)*; Druckraster *m(n)*
~ rastering Linienrasterung *f*
~ rate *s.* ~ scanning frequency
~ representation Liniendarstellung *f*
~ resolution Zeilenauflösung *f*
~ scan Linienscan *m*
~ scan camera Zeilenkamera *f*
~ scan direction Zeilenabtastrichtung *f*
~ scanner Linienscanner *m*
~ scanning Zeilenabtastung *f*, zeilenweise Abtastung *f*
~ scanning frequency Zeilen[abtast]frequenz *f*, Zeilenwechselfrequenz *f*, horizontale Abtastfrequenz (Ablenkfrequenz) *f*, Horizontalfrequenz *f*
~-scanning frequency Zeilenabtastfrequenz *f*, Zeilen[wechsel]frequenz *f*, horizontale Ablenkfrequenz *f*, Horizontalfrequenz *f*
~-scanning method Strichrasterverfahren *n (Rastergrafik)*
~-scanning pattern Zeilenraster *m(n)*, Linienraster *m(n) (Video, Fernsehen)*
~ screen *s.* ~ raster
~-screen process Linienrasterverfahren *n (Farbfotografie)*
~ segment Liniensegment *n*, Linienabschnitt *m*, Linienstück *n*; Zeilensegment *n*
~ segmentation Liniensegmentierung *f*
~ selector Zeilenwähler *m (Oszilloskop)*
~ sensor Sensorzeile *f*, Zeilensensor *m*
~ sequence Zeilensequenz *f*
~-sequential transmission zeilensequentielle Übertragung *f*
~ sharpness Strichschärfe *f*
~ slide Strichdia *n*
~ source Linien[licht]quelle *f*; Linienquelle *f (Emissionstomografie)*
~-space resolution Linienauflösung *f*
~ spacing Linienabstand *m*; Zeilenabstand *m*, Grundzeilenabstand *m*
~ spectrum Linienspektrum *n*, diskretes Spektrum *n*

~-spread [response] function [eindimensionale] Linienbildfunktion *f*, Lininenverbreiterungsfunktion *f*, Linienstreufunktion *f*
~ store Zeilen[puffer]speicher *m*
~ structure Linienstruktur *f*; Zeilenstruktur *f*
~ style Linientyp *m*
~ sweep Zeilenablenkung *f*, Horizontalablenkung *f*
~ synchronization Zeilensynchronisation *f*
~ synchronization pulse Zeilensynchronisierimpuls *m*, Zeilensynchronsignal *n*
~ termination Linienende *n*; Linienendpunkt *m*
~ thickness *s.* ~ width
~ time Zeilen[perioden]dauer *f*
~-to-line change Zeilenwechsel *m*
~-to-line interpolation Zeileninterpolation[stechnik] *f*
~ type Linientyp *m*
~ width Linienbreite *f*; Strichstärke *f*, Strichdicke *f*
~ width scale factor Linienbreitenfaktor *m*
~ work Strichvorlage *f*
linear absorption coefficient linearer Absorptionskoeffizient *m*
~ accelerator Linearbeschleuniger *m*, Linac *m (Gammastrahlenerzeugung)*
~ amplification lineare Verstärkung *f (z.B. von Szintillationssignalen)*
~ anisotropy lineare Anisotropie *f*
~ approximation lineare Approximation *f*
~ array lineare Anordnung *f*, Zeilenanordnung *f*
~ array CCD camera [CCD-]Zeilenkamera *f*
~ array CCD imager CCD-Zeile *f*, CCD-Zeilensensor *m*; Zeilenbildwandler *m*,
~ array detector (sensor) Zeilensensor *m*, Sensorzeile *f*, zeilenauflösender Detektor *m*
~ array transducer Zeilenbildwandler *n*
~ attenuation coefficient linearer Schwächungskoeffizient *m*
~ audio track Audiolängsspur *f*, Längstonspur *f*
~ CCD [detector array] *s.* ~ array CCD imager
~ classifier linearer Klassifikator *m*
~ color space linearer Farbraum *m*
~ convolution lineare (aperiodische) Faltung *f*
~ detector array *s.* ~ array detector
~ difference operator linearer Differenzoperator *m*
~ dispersion lineare Dispersion *f*
~ distortion lineare Verzerrung *f*
~ editing system lineares Schnitt[steuer]system *n*
~ electro-optic effect Pockels-Effekt *m*
~ encoding lineare Codierung *f*
~ filter lineares Filter *n*

linear

- **~ filtering** lineare Filterung *f*
- **~ frequency-modulated signal** linear frequenzmoduliertes Signal *n*
- **~ frequency modulation** lineare Frequenzmodulation *f*
- **~ histogram** lineares Histogramm *n*
- **~ Hough transform** Hough-Transformation *f* für Geraden
- **~ image processing** lineare Bildverarbeitung *f*
- **~ image restoration** lineare Bildrestauration *f*
- **~ imaging** lineare Abbildung *f*
- **~ interpolation** lineare Interpolation *f*, Lerping *n*
- **~ interpolator** linearer Interpolator *m*
- **~ key** lineare Stanze *f*
- **~ low-pass filter** lineares Tiefpassfilter *n*
- **~ magnification** lineare Vergrößerung *f*
- **~ mapping** *s.* ~ encoding *f*
- **~ motor** Linearmotor *m*
- **~ operation** lineare Operation *f*
- **~ operator** linearer Operator *m*
- **~-optical amplifier** linearoptischer Verstärker *m*
- **~ optics** lineare Optik *f*
- **~ perspective** Linearperspektive *f*, lineare Perspektive *f*, Zentralperspektive *f*
- **~ photodiode array** Diodenreihe *f*, Diodenzeile *f*
- **~ point operation** lineare Punktoperation *f*
- **~ polarization** Linearpolarisation *f*, lineare Polarisation *f*
- **~ polarizer** Linearpolarisator *m*, Linearpolarisationsfilter *n*
- **~ prediction** lineare Prädiktion *f*
- **~ predictive coding** lineare Prädiktionscodierung *f*, LPC
- **~ predictor** linearer Prädiktor *m*
- **~ programming** lineare Programmierung *f* *(Optimierungsverfahren)*
- **~ projection** lineare Projektion *f*
- **~ quantization** lineare Quantisierung *f*
- **~ quantizer** linearer Quantisierer *m*
- **~ relaxation** lineare Relaxation *f*
- **~ resolution** lineare Auflösung *f*
- **~ response function** lineare Antwortfunktion *f*
- **~ scaling** lineare Skalierung *f*
- **~ scan** linearer Scan *m*
- **~ scanner (scanning device)** Zeilenscanner *m*, Zeilenabtaster *m*; Parallelstrahlgerät *n* *(Tomografie)*
- **~ shading** *s.* intensity interpolation shading
- **~ shift-invariant** verschiebungsinvariant
- **~ skeletonization** lineare Skelettierung *f*
- **~ space** Vektorraum *m*
- **~-systems theory** Theorie *f* linearer Systeme
- **~ time counter** Echtzeitzählwerk *n* *(Videotechnik)*
- **~ time-invariant discrete-time system** linear zeitinvariantes diskretes System *n*, [zeit]diskretes LTI-System *n* *(digitale Filterung)*
- **~ tomography** lineare Tomografie *f*
- **~ transfer function** lineare Übertragungsfunktion *f*
- **~ transformation** lineare Transformation *f*
- **~ video editing** linearer Videoschnitt (Schnitt) *m*, lineare Videonachbearbeitung *f*, Online-Schnitt *m*
- **~ Wiener filter** lineares Wiener-Filter *n*

linearity Linearität *f*, Geradlinigkeit *f*
linearization Linearisierung *f*
linearize/to linearisieren
linearly encoded signal linear codiertes Signal *n*
- **~ polarized light** linear polarisiertes Licht *n*, planpolarisiertes Licht *n*
- **~ polarizing filter** Linearpolarisationsfilter *n*, Linearpolarisator *m*
- **~ separable class** linear separierbare Klasse *f*

lineation Lineament *n*, Lineation *f* *(Bildinterpretation)*
linecaster Zeilengussmaschine *f*, Zeilengießmaschine *f*
linecasting Zeilenguss *m*
lined script Stäbchenplan *m* *(Filmproduktion)*
linen finish Leinenprägung *f* *(z.B. auf Werkdruckpapier)*
- **~ tester** Fadenzähler *m*

lines per inch Linien *fpl* pro Zoll *(Maß der Rasterweite)*
lineup Fernseh-Programmplan *m*
- **~ table** Montagetisch *m* *(Satzherstellung)*

link Verknüpfung *f*
linkage algorithm Verknüpfungsalgorithmus *m*
- **~ strategy** Verbindungsstrategie *f* *(Bildsegmentierung)*

linked list verknüpfte Liste *f*
linking line Verbindungslinie *f*
Linotype Linotype-Setzmaschine *f*
lip-sync/to lippensynchronisieren
~-sync lippensynchron
~-sync animation lippensynchrone Animation *f*
~-sync band Synchron-Leitband *n*
~ sync relationship Lippensynchronität *f*
~-synch/to *s.* lip-sync/to
~ synchronization Lippensynchronisation *f*, lippensynchrone Nachvertonung *f*
~-synchronized sound lippensynchroner Ton *m*
lipophilic lipophil, oleophil, fettfreundlich
Lippmann emulsion Lippmann-Emulsion *f*
- **~ process** Lippmannsche Farbfotografie *f*, Fotografie *f* in natürlichen Farben

lipstick lens brush Lippenstift-Objektivpinsel *m*
liquid crystal Flüssigkristall *m*

~ **crystal cell** Flüssigkristallzelle f
~ **crystal diode** Flüssigkristalldiode f
~ **crystal display** Flüssigkristallanzeige f, Flüssigkristalldisplay n, LC-Display n
~ **crystal display projector** Flüssigkristallbildschirm m
~ **crystal filter** Flüssigkristallfilter n
~ **crystal light valve** Flüssigkristall-Lichtventil n
~ **crystal matrix** Flüssigkristallmatrix f
~ **crystal on silicon display** LCOS-Display n, LCOS-Bildschirm m
~ **crystal optics** Flüssigkristalloptik f
~ **crystal readout** Flüssigkristallanzeige f, LC-Display n
~ **crystal shutter** Flüssigkristallschiene f
~ **crystalline** flüssigkristallin
~ **crystallinity** Flüssigkristallinität f
~ **developer** Flüssigentwickler m
~ **development** Feuchtentwicklung f
~ **emulsion** Flüssigemulsion f
~ **filter** Flüssigkeitsfilter n
~ **gate** Nasskopierfenster n, Flüssigkeits-Kopierfenster n *(Filmentwicklungsmaschine)*
~-**gate [optical] printing** Nasskopierung f, Nasskopierverfahren n
~ **ink-jet print** Flüssigtintenstrahldruck m
~ **ink-jet printer** Flüssigtintenstrahldrucker m
~ **laser** Flüssig[keits]laser m
~ **plasma display** plasmaadressierte Flüssigkristallanzeige f
~ **scintillation counter** Betaprobenwechsler m *(Nuklearmedizin)*
~ **toner** Nasstoner m, Flüssigtoner m
~ **toning** Nasstonung f
list Liste f *(z.B. als Folge von Bildelementen)*
lith developer Lithentwickler m
~ **development** Lithentwicklung f
~-**film photography** Lithfilmfotografie f
~-**type film** s. lithographic film
lithium battery (cell) Lithiumbatterie f
~-**ion battery** Lithium-Ionen-Akku[mulator] m
litho s. 1. lithograph; 2. lithography
~-**offset** Offsetdruck m, Offsetlithografie f, indirekter Flachdruck m
lithograph/to lithografieren
lithograph Litho n, Lithografie f
lithographer Lithograf m; Steindrucker m
lithographic lithografisch
~ **color print** Farblithografie f
~ **film** [litho]grafischer Film m, Lithfilm m, Druckfilm m
~ **film developer** Lithentwickler m
~ **image** Litho n, Lithografie f
~ **ink** Lithofarbe f
~ **paper** Lithografiepapier n
~ **plate** 1. Steindruckform f; 2. Offset[druck]platte f
~ **press** Stein[druck]presse f

~ **printing** 1. Steindruck m, Lithografie f, lithografischer Druck m; 2. Offsetdruck m
~ **screen** Offsetraster m(n)
~ **stone** Lithografiestein m, Lithografenstein m
lithography 1. Lithografie f, Steindruck m *(Erzeugnis)*; 2. s. lithographic printing; 3. [indirekter] Flachdruck m *(s.a. unter offset printing)*
litmus Lackmus m(n) *(Indikatorfarbstoff)*
live live; editierbar
~ **action** Originalszene f *(Filmarbeit)*
~-**action character** Realdarsteller m
~-**action feature (film)** Realfilm m
~-**action footage (material)** Realfilmmaterial n
~-**action movie** Realfilm m
~ **action scene** Realszene f *(Filmarbeit)*
~-**action shoot[ing]** Realdreh m, Live-Dreh m
~-**action shot** Realaufnahme f
~ **actor** Realdarsteller m
~ **broadcast** Livesendung f, Live-Übertragung f, Direktübertragung f, Originalsendung f
~ **check** Lebenderkennung f *(Authentifizierung)*
~ **filming** Realdreh m, Live-Dreh m
~ **recording** Liveaufzeichnung f
~ **satellite TV** Satellitenfernsehen n
~ **shoot** Realdreh m, Live-Dreh m
~ **show production** Live-Produktion f
~ **telecast (TV broadcast)** Fernsehdirektsendung f, Fernseh-Livesendung f
~ **television** Live-Fernsehen n
~ **television camera** Aufnahmekamera f, Bildaufnahmekamera f
~ **video** Echtzeitvideo n
liveness test s. live check
load/to 1. laden, einlegen *(z.B. eine Bandkassette)*; 2. [ein]laden, eindigitalisieren *(z.B. Daten in einen Speicher)*
load into/to [ein]laden, eindigitalisieren
~ **resistance** Lastwiderstand m
loading procedure Einlegevorgang m
~ **slot** Kassettenschlitz m
local analysis lokale Analyse f
~ **area network** lokales Computernetz (Rechnernetz) n; lokales Datennetz (Netz) n; hausinternes Netz n
~ **broadcast station** Lokalsender m
~ **bus** lokaler Bus m
~ **coil** Oberflächenspule f, Lokalantenne f *(Magnetresonanztomografie)*
~ **contrast** lokaler Kontrast m; Detailkontrast m, Gradation f
~ **coordinate system** Objektkoordinatensystem n
~ **feature** lokales Merkmal n
~ **Fourier transform** lokale Fourier-Transformation f

local

~ **gradient** lokaler Gradient *m*
~ **gradient operator** lokaler Gradientenoperator *m*
~ **histogram** lokales Histogramm *n*
~ **illumination model** lokales Beleuchtungsmodell *n*
~ **image contrast** lokaler Bildkontrast *m*
~ **impulse response** lokale Impulsantwort *f*
~ **knowledge** lokales Wissen *n*
~ **neighborhood** lokale Nachbarschaft *f*
~ **neighborhood operation** lokale Nachbarschaftsoperation *f*
~ **noise** lokales Rauschen *n*
~ **operation** lokale Operation *f (Grauwertbildverarbeitung)*
~ **operator** lokaler Operator *m*, Maskenoperator *m*
~ **orientation** lokale Orientierung *f*
~ **oscillator** Lokaloszillator *m (Fernsehtechnik)*
~ **prediction** lokale Prädiktion *f*
~ **shape feature** lokales Formmerkmal *n*
~ **television** Lokalfernsehen *n*, lokales Fernsehen *n*
~ **television broadcasting station** lokaler Fernsehsender *m*, Regionalstudio *n*
~ **thresholding** lokale Schwellenwertbildung *f*
~ **TV station** lokaler Fernsehsender *m*, Regionalstudio *n*
~ **variance** lokale Varianz *f*
locality Lokalität *f (z.B. von Bildstrukturen)*
localization Lokalisierung *f*
~ **accuracy** Lokalisierungsgüte *f*
locally adaptive compression lokal adaptive Kompression *f*
locatable ortbar
locate/to orten
location 1. Ortung *f (Radar)*; 2. Produktionsort *m*, Drehort *m*, Spielstätte *f (Filmarbeit)*
~ **accuracy** Ortungsgenauigkeit *f*
~ **manager** Aufnahmeleiter *m (Filmteam)*
~ **of fixation** Fixationsstelle *f*
~ **photographer** studiounabhängiger Fotograf *m*; Standfotograf *m (Filmarbeit)*
~ **photography** mobile Fotografie *f*
~ **production** Außenproduktion *f (Film, Video)*
~ **recording** Originaltonaufnahme *f*
~ **scouting** Schauplatzsuche *f (Filmarbeit)*
~ **shoot[ing]** Außenaufnahme[n] *f[pl]*, Dreharbeit *f* vor Ort, Außendreharbeit *f*, Außendreh *m*
locator device Lokalisierer *m (Eingabegerät)*
lock-in thermography Phasenthermografie *f*
~ **lever** Verriegelungshebel *m*
lockdown shot Standaufnahme *f*
locked audio bildsynchroner Ton *m*
~-**off camera** statische (unbewegte) Kamera *f (Kinematografie)*
lockout Tastatursperre *f*

lockup 1. Mettage *f (Druckformherstellung)*; 2. Metteur *m* 3. Tastatursperre *f*
locus of spectral colors Farbort *m*, Spektralfarbenzug *m (Farbmetrik)*
lofted surface Regelfläche *f (geometrisches Modellieren)*
log exposure range Belichtungsspielraum *m*, Belichtungsumfang *m*, Belichtungszeitenbereich *m*
LoG filter (operator) Laplace-Gauß-Operator *m*, Sombrerofilter *n*, LoG-Filter *n (Kantendetektion)*
log sheet Schnittliste *f*
logarithmic color space logarithmischer Farbraum *m*
~ **data** logarithmische Daten *pl*
~ **image processing** logarithmische Bildverarbeitung *f*
~ **pixel** logarithmisches Pixel *n*
~ **point operation** logarithmische Punktoperation *f*
~ **pulse code modulation** logarithmische Pulscodemodulation *f*
~ **quantization** logarithmische Quantisierung *f*
~ **search** logarithmische Suche *f*
~ **transfer function** logarithmische Übertragungsfunktion *f*
logged frame protokolliertes Vollbild *n*
logger Messwertdrucker *m*
logic-based interpolation logische Interpolation *f*
~ **board** Hauptplatine *f*, Systemplatine *f*, Computerplatine *f*, Mutterplatine *f*
~ **circuit** logische Schaltung *f*
~ **memory** Logikspeicher *m*
logical AND operation logische UND-Operation *f*
~ **data unit** logische Dateneinheit *f*
~ **expression** logischer Ausdruck *m*
~ **image** logisches Bild *n*
~ **interpolation** logische Interpolation *f*
~ **operation** logische Operation *f*
~ **operator** logischer (Boolescher) Operator *m*
~ **topology** logische Topologie *f*
~ **tree** logischer Baum *m (Datenstruktur)*
logo 1. Logo *n(m)*, Bildmarke *f (z.B. eines Unternehmens)*; 2. *s.* logotype
logotype Logotype *f*, Silbenzeichen *n*
long-bellows camera Großformat-Fachkamera *f*
~-**distance [aerial] photography** Fernfotografie *f*
~-**distance infrared photography** Infrarot-Fernfotografie *f*
~-**exposure photograph** lang[zeit]belichtete Aufnahme *f*
~ **focal-length lens** langbrennweitiges Objektiv *n*
~ **focal-length macro lens** langbrennweitiges Makroobjektiv *n*

~ **focal-length telephoto lens** langbrennweitiges Teleobjektiv *n*, Supertele[objektiv] *n*
~**-focus lens** *s.* long focal-length lens
~**-grain paper** Schmalbahnpapier *n (Druck)*
~**-line transmission** Fernübertragung *f*
~**-lived phosphorescence** Nachleuchten *n*, Persistenz *f*
~ **pass [filter]** Langpassfilter *n*
~**-persistence phosphor display screen** Speicherbildschirm *m*
~**-persistent screen** langnachleuchtender Bildschirm *m*
~ **pitch** Positiv-Perforationslochabstand *m*, Positiv-Perforationsschritt *m (Filmmaterial)*
~ **play mode** Langspielmodus *m (Video)*
~ **shot** Halbtotale *f*, halbtotale Einstellung *f*
~ **sight** *s.* longsightedness
~ **telephoto zoom** Telezoom[objektiv] *n*
~**-term archival use** Langzeitarchivierung *f*
~**-term exposure [to light]** *s.* long-time exposure
~**-term illumination** Dauerbeleuchtung *f*
~**-term memory** Langzeitspeicher *m*
~**-term permanence (stability)** Langlebigkeit *f*, Langzeithaltbarkeit *f*, Langzeit-Lagereigenschaft *f (z.B. von Bildmaterial)*
~**-term visual memory** visuelles Langzeitgedächtnis *n*
~**-time exposure** Langzeitbelichtung *f*, Zeitbelichtung *f*, Dauerbelichtung *f*; Langzeitaufnahme *f*
~ **tom** Fernobjektiv *n*, Tele[foto]objektiv *n*, Fernbildlinse *f*, Teleoptik *f*
~ **wave band** Langwellenband *n*
~**-wave[length]** langwellig
~**-wavelength infrared [region]** langwelliges Infrarot *n*
~**-wavelength light** langwelliges Licht *n*
~**-wavelength pass filter** Langpassfilter *n*
~**-wavelength radar** langwelliges Radar *n*
~**-wavelength radiation** langwellige Strahlung *f*
~**-wavelength-sensitive cone** L-Zapfen *m (Netzhautrezeptor)*
longer focal-length lens längerbrennweitiges Objektiv *n*
~ **wavelength ultraviolet radiation** längerwellige UV-Strahlung *f*
longevity Langlebigkeit *f*, Langzeithaltbarkeit *f*, Langzeit-Lagereigenschaft *f (z.B. von Bildmaterial)*
longitudinal aberration Längsaberration *f*, Längsabweichung *f*, axialer Abbildungsfehler *m*
~ **angularity** Längswinkligkeit *f (Bandfehler)*
~ **chromatic aberration** Farblängsfehler *m*, Farbortsfehler *m*, Farbschnittweitenfehler *m*, chromatische Längsaberration (Schnittweitendifferenz) *f*, axiale chromatische Aberration *f*
~ **chromatic aberration correction** Farblängsfehlerkorrektur *f*
~ **color** *s.* ~ chromatic aberration
~ **Doppler effect** longitudinaler Doppler-Effekt *m*
~ **magnetization** Längsmagnetisierung *f*, Longitudinalmagnetisierung *f*
~ **magnification** longitudinale Vergrößerung *f (Optik)*
~ **mode** longitudinale Mode *f (Laser)*
~ **redundancy check** Längsparitätsprüfung *f*
~ **relaxation time** Längsrelaxationszeit *f*, longitudinale Relaxationszeit *f*, Spin-Gitter-Relaxationszeit *f (Magnetresonanztomografie)*
~ **ripple** Längswelligkeit *f (Bandfehler)*
~ **spherical aberration** sphärische Längsaberration *f*
~ **time code** Längsspur-Zeitcode *m*
~ **twist** Längsdrehung *f (Bandfehler)*
~ **video recording** Längsspuraufzeichnung *f*, Längsspurverfahren *n*
~ **wave** Longitudinalwelle *f*
longsighted übersichtig, weitsichtig, hypermetropisch, hyperop
longsightedness Weitsichtigkeit *f*, Übersichtigkeit *f*, Fernsichtigkeit *f*, Hyper[metr]opie *f*
look/to 1. blicken; 2. aussehen
look 1. Blick *m*; 2. Aussehen *n*; Erscheinungsbild *n*
~ **direction** Blickrichtung *f*; Beobachtungsrichtung *f*; Betrachtungsrichtung *f*; Sehrichtung *f*
looking glass Spiegel *m*
lookup table [memory] Lookup-Tabelle *f*, Transformationstabelle *f*, Koordinatenliste *f*, Verweistabelle *f*, Speichertabelle *f*, Wertetabelle *f*, Umwandlungstabelle *f* für Pixelwerte
loop Schleife *f*; Bandschleife *f*; Filmschleife *f*
~ **[low-pass] filter** Schleifenfilter *n*, Schleifen-Tiefpassfilter *n (Videocodierer)*
~ **through [filter]** Durchschleiffilter *n*
looping Nachvertonung *f*, Tonnachbearbeitung *f*, Audiopost[produktion] *f*
loose proof Rohabzug *m*, Hauskorrektur *f (Druckvorstufe)*
Lorentz [electromagnetic] force Lorentz-Kraft *f*
loss-free *s.* lossless
~ **of contrast** Kontrastabfall *m*; Kontrastverlust *m*
~ **of detail[s]** Detailverlust *m*
~ **of image information** Bildinformationsverlust *m*
~ **of image quality** Bildgüteverlust *m*
~ **of information** Informationsverlust *m*

~ **of light** Lichtverlust *m*
~ **of resolution** Auflösungsverlust *m*
~ **of sharpness** Schärfeverlust *m*
~ **of signal** Signalverlust *m*
lossless coding verlustfreie (verlustlose) Codierung *f*
~ **compression** verlustfreie (verlustlose) Kompression *f*
~ **format conversion** verlustlose Formatkonversion *f*
lossy [en]coding verlustbehaftete Codierung *f*
~ **[image] compression** verlustbehaftete Bildkompression (Komprimierung) *f*
lot Studio[frei]gelände *n*, Studioareal *n*, Produktionsgelände *n*
loudness Lautheit *f*; Lautstärke *f*
loudspeaker Lautsprecher *m*
loupe Lupe *f*; Fadenzähler *m (Typografie)*
~ **magnification** Lupenvergrößerung *f*
low-angle shot Untersichtaufnahme *f*
~ **band** unteres Band *n (Frequenzbereich)*
~-**bandwidth network** schmalbandiges Netz *n*
~-**battery warning** Batteriewarnanzeige *f*
~-**bit-rate** niederbitratig *(Datenkanal)*
~-**bit-rate coding** Codierung *f* mit kleiner Bitrate
~-**bit-rate telecommunication** visuelle Kommunikation *f*
~-**contrast** kontrastarm, kontrastschwach, weich, flau *(Bild)*
~-**contrast developer** *s.* low-energy developer
~-**contrast emulsion** kontrastarme Emulsion *f*
~-**contrast resolution** Niederkontrastauflösung *f*
~-**cost camera** Billigkamera *f*
~-**definition television** niedrigauflösendes (niedrigzeiliges) Fernsehen *n*
~-**delay coding** verzögerungsarme Codierung *f*
~-**density range negative** abgeschwächtes Negativ *n*
~-**energy developer** weich arbeitender Entwickler *m*, Weichentwickler *m*, Ausgleichsentwickler *m*
~-**energy X rays** weiche Röntgenstrahlung *f*
~-**frequency** niederfrequent, tieffrequent
~-**frequency cut-off** untere Grenzfrequenz *f*
~-**frequency drop** Nullpunktabfall *m (Modulationsübertragungsfunktion)*
~-**frequency loudspeaker** Tieftonlautsprecher *m*
~-**frequency noise** niederfrequentes (tieffrequentes) Rauschen *n*
~-**frequency pattern** tieffrequentes Muster *n*
~-**frequency signal** tieffrequentes (niederfrequentes) Signal *n*

~-**index** niedrigbrechend, tiefbrechend *(optisches Glas)*
~-**index medium** niedrigbrechendes Medium *n*
~-**intensity reciprocity failure** Langzeitfehler *m (Fotoentwicklung)*
~ **key** dunkler Bildton *m*
~-**key effect** Low-Key-Effekt *m*
~-**key picture** Low-Key-Bild *n*, lichtschwaches Bild *n*
~-**level computer vision** Ikonik *f*
~-**level echo** schwaches Echo *n*
~-**level image processing** ikonische Bildverarbeitung *f*, Bild-zu-Bild-Verarbeitung *f*
~-**level light** Schwachlicht *n*, schwaches Licht *n*
~-**level noise** schwaches Rauschen *n*
~-**level programming language** Maschinencode *m*
~ **light** Schwachlicht *n*, schwaches Licht *n*
~-**light-level** lichtschwach
~-**light-level camera** Restlichtkamera *f*
~-**light mode** Nachtaufnahmemodus *m (Camcorder)*
~-**luminance subject** lichtschwaches Objekt *n*
~-**noise** rauscharm
~-**noise block converter** [rauscharmer] Blockumsetzer *m (Satellitenfernsehen)*
~-**noise CCD camera** rauscharme CCD-Kamera *f*
~-**noise image** rauscharmes Bild *n*
~-**numerical-aperture objective** lichtschwaches Objektiv *n*
~-**pass-filter/to** tiefpassfiltern
~-**pass filter** Tiefpassfilter *n*, Tiefpass *m*; Glättungsfilter *n*
~-**pass filtered image** tiefpassgefiltertes Bild *n*
~-**pass filtering** Tiefpassfilterung *f*
~-**pass frequency filter** *s.* ~ filter
~-**pass image** Tiefpassbild *n*
~-**pass linear filtering** lineare Tiefpassfilterung *f*
~-**pass pre-filter** Tiefpass-Vorfilter *n*
~-**pass pre-filtering** Tiefpass-Vorfilterung *f*
~-**pass smoothing** *s.* ~ filtering
~-**power detector** Niederleistungsdetektor *m*
~-**power lens (objective)** lichtschwaches Objektiv *n*
~-**power X-ray tube** Niederleistungs[röntgen]röhre *f*
~-**pressure gas discharge lamp** Niederdruck[gas]entladungslampe *f*
~-**pressure lamp** Niederdrucklampe *f*
~-**pressure sodium lamp** Natriumniederdrucklampe *f*
~-**priced camera** Billigkamera *f*; Einfachkamera *f*
~-**radiation screen** strahlungsarmer Bildschirm *m*
~-**reflection** reflex[ions]arm

~-reflection coating reflexionsmindernde Vergütung f
~-reflective screen reflex[ions]armer Bildschirm m
~-resolution camera niedrigauflösende Kamera f
~-resolution display niedrigauflösendes Display n; niedrigauflösender Bildschirm m
~-resolution electromagnetic tomography niedrigauflösende elektromagnetische Tomografie f
~-resolution image niedrigaufgelöstes Bild n
~-resolution quantization grobe Quantisierung f
~ side light flaches Seitenlicht n
~-signal signalschwach
~-speed film niedrigempfindlicher Film m
~-viscosity ink niederviskose Druckfarbe f, dünn[flüssig]e Druckfarbe f
~ vision Schwachsichtigkeit f, Amblyopie f
~-voltage lamp Niedervoltlampe f
lower-energy X-rays niederenergetische Röntgenstrahlung f
~ feed sprocket Nachwickel[zahn]rolle f, Nachwickler m
~ magazine Aufwickelmagazin n
~ sideband unteres Seitenband n
lowercase letter Kleinbuchstabe m, Minuskel f, Gemeine f
lowpass reconstruction filter Tiefpass-Rekonstruktionsfilter n
LP mode Langspielmodus m *(Video)*
lpi *s.* lines per inch
lubricant Gleitmittel n
lubricate/to covalieren *(Kinefilmmaterial)*
lucid 1. durchscheinend, transluzent, halbopak; 2. *s.* luminous
luma 1. gammakorrigierte Luminanz f *(Video)*; 2. *s.* luminance
luma/chroma separation [technique] Luminanz-Chrominanz-Trennung f *(Videosignalverarbeitung)*
lumen Lumen n, lm *(SI-Einheit der Lichtleistung)*
~ hour Lumenstunde f
~ per square centimeter Phot n *(Einheit der Beleuchtungsstärke)*
~ per square foot Lumen n pro Quadratfuß *(Einheit der Beleuchtungsstärke)*
~ per square meter *s.* lux
~ second Lumensekunde f *(Einheit der Lichtmenge)*
~-second per square meter Luxsekunde f *(Belichtungseinheit)*
luminaire Leuchte f, Beleuchtungskörper m
luminance Luminanz f, Leuchtdichte f; Flächenhelligkeit f; Farbhelligkeit f
~ amplitude Luminanzamplitude f
~ band Luminanzband n
~ bandwidth Luminanzbandbreite f
~ block Luminanzblock m *(Bildsequenzcodierung)*
~ channel Luminanzkanal m
~ component Luminanzkomponente f
~ contrast Leuchtdichtegegensatz m, Leuchtdichtekontrast m, Helligkeitskontrast m
~ difference sensitivity Leuchtdichteunterschiedsempfindlichkeit f, Lichtunterschiedsempfindlichkeit f
~ distribution Leuchtdichteverteilung f
~ edge Helligkeitskante f
~ factor Leuchtdichtefaktor m
~ filter Luminanzfilter n
~ flicker Helligkeitsflimmern n
~ histogram Luminanzhistogramm n
~ image Luminanzbild n
~ information Luminanzinformation f, Helligkeitsinformation f *(Video)*
~ keying Helligkeits-Stanztrick m *(Kinematografie)*
~ level Luminanzpegel m
~ low-pass filter Luminanztiefpassfilter n
~ masking Luminanzmaskierung f
~ measure Luminanzmaß n
~ measurement Leuchtdichtemessung f
~ meter Leuchtdichtemesser m, Leuchtdichtemessgerät n
~ noise Luminanzrauschen n
~ perception Helligkeitswahrnehmung f
~ pixel Helligkeitspixel n
~ profile Luminanzprofil n
~ range Leuchtdichtebereich m maschinelle Entwicklung f
~ ratio Luminanzverhältnis n, Leuchtdichteverhältnis n; Leuchtdichteumfang m, Objektumfang m, Objektdynamik f; Kontrastumfang m
~ resolution Luminanzauflösung f
~ reversal Negativ-Positiv-Umschaltung f, Inversschaltung f *(Video)*
~ signal Luminanzsignal n, Leuchtdichtesignal n, Y-Signal n, Fernsehluminanzsignal n, Bildhelligkeitssignal n, Helligkeitssignal n, Schwarzweißsignal n
~ spectrum Leuchtdichtespektrum n
~ standard Leuchtdichtenormal n
~ value Leuchtdichtewert m
luminesce/to lumineszieren
luminescence Lumineszenz[strahlung] f
~ light Lumineszenzlicht n
~ microscopy Lumineszenzmikroskopie f
~ modulation spectroscopy Lumineszenzmodulationsspektroskopie f
~ screen Lumineszenzschirm m
~ spectroscopy Lumineszenzspektroskopie f
luminescent lumineszierend
~ diode Lumineszenzdiode f, Lichtemitterdiode f, Leuchtdiode f, Lichtemissionsdiode f, lichtemittierende Diode f, LED *(Halbleiterelement)*
~ dye Lumineszenzfarbstoff m
~ material *s.* luminophor

luminescent   224

~ **radiator** Lumineszenzstrahler *m*,
  Nichttemperaturstrahler *m*, selektiver
  Strahler *m*
~ **screen** Leuchtschirm *m*
luminescing lumineszierend
luminiferous lichterzeugend
luminogram Röntgenarteriogramm *n*
luminometer Beleuchtungs[stärke]messer
  m, Beleuchtungsstärkemessgerät *n*,
  Luxmeter *n*
luminophor Luminophor *m*, Leuchtstoff *m*,
  Leuchtphosphor *m*, Phosphor *m*
luminosity Leuchtstärke *f*, Leuchtkraft *f*;
  Hellempfindlichkeit *f*; relative Helligkeit *f*
~ **curve (function)**
  Hellempfindlichkeitskurve *f*
luminous [hell] leuchtend, luminös,
  luminos *(s.a. unter light)*
~ **efficacy (efficiency)** 1. Lichtausbeute *f*,
  [fotometrisches] Strahlungsäquivalent
  n; Hellempfindlichkeitsgrad *m*,
  Hellempfindungsgrad *m*; 2. s.
  Lichtleistung *f (z.B. von
  Elektronenblitzgeräten)*
~ **efficiency function** spektrale
  Hellempfindlichkeitskurve *f*
~ **electron** strahlendes Elektron *n*,
  Leuchtelektron *n*
~ **energy** Lichtarbeit *f*, Lichtmenge *f*
  (Fotometrie)
~ **exitance** spezifische Lichtausstrahlung *f*
~ **field** Leuchtfeld *n*
~ **flux** *s*. ~ power
~**-flux density** Lichtstromdichte *f*
~ **image** Leuchtbild *n*
~ **intensity** Lichtstärke *f*, Lichtintensität *f*
~ **paint** Leuchtfarbe *f*
~ **power** Leuchtkraft *f*, Leuchtstärke *f*;
  Lichtleistung *f*, Lichtstrom *m*
  (Fotometrie)
~ **power per area** spezifische
  Lichtausstrahlung *f (Fotometrie)*
~ **radiation** leuchtende (luminöse)
  Strahlung *f*
~ **row** Leuchtband *n*
~ **sensitivity** Helligkeitsempfindlichkeit *f*
~ **source** Leuchtquelle *f*, Lichtquelle *f*,
  Lichtstrahler *m*
~ **spot** Leuchtfleck *m (Katodenstrahlröhre)*
~ **value** Helligkeitswert *m (Farbmetrik)*
Lummer-Brodhun cube (photometer)
  Lummer-Brodhun-Würfel *m*,
  Fotometerwürfel *m*
lumophor *s.* luminophor
lunar caustic Höllenstein *m*
~ **probe camera** Mondsondenkamera *f*
luster Glanz *m*; Oberflächenglanz *m*
~ **number** visuelle Glanzzahl *f (Polygrafie)*
lustre *s.* luster
lustrous glänzend
LUT *s.* lookup table [memory]
lux Lux *n (SI-Einheit der
  Beleuchtungsstärke)*

~ **second** Luxsekunde *f*
  (Belichtungseinheit)
~**[o]meter** Luxmeter *n*,
  Beleuchtungsstärkemesser *m*,
  Beleuchtungsstärkemessgerät *n*
lymph[angi]ogram Lymphangiogramm *n*
~**[angi]ographic** lymphangiografisch
~**[angi]ography** Lymphangiografie *f*
lyotropic series Hofmeistersche
  Ionenreihe *f*
LZW [data] compression
  Lempel-Ziv-Welch-Codierung *f*

M

M cone M-Zapfen *m (Netzhautrezeptor)*
M mode Bewegungsmodus *m (Sonografie)*
M mode imaging, M mode scanning (ultrasound method) M-Bildverfahren *n*, M-Mode-Verfahren *n*
M scan *s.* M mode
MAC *s.* multiplexed analog components
MacAdam ellipse MacAdam-Ellipse *f*, Schwellenellipse (Farbunterschiedsschwelle) *f* nach MacAdam *(Farbmetrik)*
Mach band Mach-Band *n*, Machscher Streifen *m*
~ band effect, ~ banding Mach[-Band]-Effekt *m*, Mach-Täuschung *f (Wahrnehmungsphänomen; s.a.* edge contrast*)*
~-Zehnder interferometer Mach-Zehndersches Interferometer *n*
machine classification automatische Klassifikation (Klassifizierung) *f*
~ code Maschinencode *m*
~ composition Maschinensatz *m (Typografie)*
~ direction Maschinenrichtung *f*, Papierlaufrichtung *f*, Laufrichtung *f (Druckpapier)*
~-glazed paper [einseitig] satiniertes Papier *n*
~ intelligence künstliche Intelligenz *f (Informatik)*
~ language Computersprache *f*, Maschinencode *m*
~-printed text gedruckter Text *m*
~ printer Kopiermaschine *f*
~-processable maschinenverarbeitungsfähig
~ processing Maschinenentwicklung *f*, Maschinenverarbeitung *f*,
~ processor Maschinenentwickler *m*, Verarbeitungsmaschine *f*, Entwicklungsmaschine *f*
~-readable maschinenlesbar, computerlesbar
~-specific code Maschinencode *m*, Computersprache *f*
~ vision maschinelle Bilderkennung *f*, industrielle Bildverarbeitung *f*, maschinelles Sehen *n*, Maschinensehen *n*, Computersehen *n*
~ vision system Maschinen-Sichtsystem *n*
~-written maschinenschriftlich
macro Makro *m (Computertechnik)*
~ adapter ring Umkehrring *m*
~ facility *s.* macro
~ image *s.* macrophotograph
~ lens Makroobjektiv *n*
~ mode Makromodus *m*
~-zoom lens Makrozoom[objektiv] *n*
macroblock Makroblock *m (Videokompression)*
~ address Makroblockadresse *f*
macrocinematographic makrokinematografisch
macrocinematography Makrokinematografie *f*
macrofeature Makromerkmal *n (z.B. in der Bildklassifizierung)*
macrofocusing Makrofokussierung *f*
macromolecule Makromolekül *n*
macron Längestrich *m (diakritisches Zeichen)*
macrophotograph Makroaufnahme *f*, Lupenaufnahme *f*
macrophotographic lens Makroobjektiv *n*
macrophotography Makrofotografie *f*, Lupenfotografie *f*
macropsia, macropsy Makropsie *f (Sehfehler)*
macroscopic image makroskopisches Bild *n*
~ magnetization makroskopische Magnetisierung *f*
macrostage Makrotisch *m (Mikroskop)*
macula [lutea] Makula *f* lutea, gelber Fleck *m (der Augennetzhaut)*
macular degeneration [altersbedingte] Makuladegeneration *f*
~ pigment Makulapigment *n*
~ pigmentation Makulapigmentierung *f*
mag *s.* magnetic
magazine Magazin *n*; Filmdose *f*, Filmbüchse *f*; Filmvorratsraum *m*
~ camera Magazinkamera *f*
~ photo Zeitschriftenfoto *n*
~ photographer Zeitschriftenfotograf *m*
~ photography Zeitschriftenfotografie *f*
~ printing Zeitschriftendruck *m*, Magazindruck *m*
~ take-up Magazinaufwicklung *f*
magenta Magenta *n*, Purpur *n*, Anilinrot *n*, Rosarot *n*; genormtes Rot *n (subtraktive Grundfarbe)*
~ magentarot, magentafarben, magentafarbig
~ coupler Magentakuppler *m*, Purpur[farb]kuppler *m*
~ dye Magentafarbstoff *m*
~ dye developer Magentaentwickler *m*
~ dye-forming coupler *s.* ~ coupler
~ dye-forming layer grünempfindliche Schicht *f (Colorfilmmaterial)*
~ filter Magentafilter *n*, Purpurfilter *n*
~ filter layer Magentafilterschicht *f*
~ screen Magentaraster *m(n)*
magic-eye stereogram Autostereogramm *n*
~ lantern Laterna *f* magica *(ein früher Standbildprojektor)*
~ lasso aktive Kontur *f (Computergrafik)*

~ **wand approach** Bereichswachstum[sverfahren] *n*, Regionenwachstum *n*, Flächenwachstum *n* *(Bildsegmentierung)*
magnesium flash Magnesiumblitz *m*, Magnesiumblitzlicht *n*
~ **flash powder** Magnesium-Blitzpulver *n*
~ **fluoride** Magnesiumfluorid *n* *(optischer Werkstoff)*
~ **light** *s.* ~ flash
~ **oxide** Magnesiumoxid *n*
magnetic aberration magnetischer Bildfehler *m* *(Elektronenoptik)*
~ **anisotropy** magnetische Anisotropie *f*
~ **audio recording** Magnettonaufnahme *f*
~ **audio track** Magnettonspur *f*
~ **brush [roll]** Magnetbürste *f*
~ **bubble memory** Magnetblasenspeicher *m*
~ **coating** Magnetschicht *f*
~ **cord** Magnetfilmband *n*
~ **crack detection** Magnetpulver-Rissprüfung *f*
~ **deflection** magnetische Ablenkung *f*
~ **deflection coil pair** Ablenkeinheit *f*, Ablenkjoch *n*; Ablenkspule *f* *(Bildröhre)*
~ **dipole** magnetischer Dipol *m*
~ **dipole moment** magnetisches Dipolmoment (Moment) *n*
~ **disk** Magnetplatte *f*
~ **disk drive** Magnetplattenlaufwerk *n*, Plattenlaufwerk *n*
~ **disk memory** Magnetplattenspeicher *m*
~ **electron microscope** magnetisches Elektronenmikroskop *n*
~ **energy** magnetische Energie *f*
~ **field** Magnetfeld *n*
~ **field coil** Magnetspule *f*
~ **field gradient** Magnetfeldgradient *m*
~ **field inhomogeneity** Magnetfeldinhomogenität *f*, Feldinhomogenität *f*
~ **field line** Magnetfeldlinie *f*
~ **field sensor** Magnetfeldsensor *m*
~ **field strength** Magnetfeldstärke *f*, [magnetische] Feldstärke *f*
~ **field vector** Magnetfeldvektor *m*
~ **film** 1. Magnetfilm *m*; 2. *s.* ~ coating
~ **film memory** Magnetfilmspeicher *m*
~ **film recorder** Magnetfilmaufzeichnungsgerät *n*, Magnettonkamera *f*
~ **film stock** Magnetfilmmaterial *n*
~ **film stripe** Magnetfilmstreifen *m*
~ **film transport** Magnetfilmlaufwerk *n*
~ **flaw detection powder** Anzeigepulver *n* *(Magnetpulverprüfung)*
~ **flux** Magnetfluss *m*, magnetischer Fluss *m*
~ **flux density** Magnetflussdichte *f*, magnetische Flussdichte (Induktion) *f*
~ **focusing** magnetische Fokussierung *f*

~ **force microscope** Magnet-Kraft-Mikroskop *n*
~ **head** Magnetkopf *m*
~ **head core** Magnetkopfkern *m*
~ **head gap** Magnetkopfspalt *m*, Kopfspalt *m*
~ **image recording** magnetische Bildaufzeichnung *f*, Magnetbildaufzeichnung *f*, MAZ
~ **image storage** magnetische Bildspeicherung *f*
~ **imaging** Magnetografie *f*
~ **impulse** magnetischer Impuls *m*
~ **induction** magnetische Induktion *f*
~ **ink** magnetische Druckfarbe *f*
~ **ink character recognition** magnetische Schriftzeichenerkennung *f*
~ **lens** Magnetlinse *f*, magnetische Linse *f*
~ **memory** Magnetspeicher *m*
~ **moment** magnetisches Moment (Dipolmoment) *n*
~ **particle examination (inspection)** Magnetpulverprüfung *f*
~ **ray deflection** magnetische Strahlablenkung *f*
~ **recorder** Magnetaufzeichnungsgerät *n*
~ **recording** magnetische Aufzeichnung *f*, Magnetaufzeichnung *f*
~ **recording head** Aufnahmekopf *m*
~ **recording medium** magnetisierbarer Aufzeichnungsträger *m*
~ **recording/reproducing head** Aufzeichnungs-Wiedergabe-Kopf *m*
~ **recording system** Magnetaufzeichnungssystem *n*
~ **reproducer** magnetisches Wiedergabegerät *n*; Magnettonwiedergabegerät *n*
~ **reproduction** magnetische Wiedergabe *f*
~ **resonance** Magnetresonanz *f*, magnetische Resonanz *f*
~ **resonance angiography** Magnetresonanzangiografie *f*, MRA *f*
~ **resonance endoscopy** Magnetresonanzendoskopie *f*
~ **resonance image** Magnetresonanzbild *n*, Magnetresonanzaufnahme *f*, Kernspinbild *n*, Kernspintomogramm *n*
~ **resonance imaging** Magnetresonanztomografie *f*, Magnetresonanzbildgebung *f*, Kernspin[resonanz]tomografie *f*
~ **resonance imaging system** Magnetresonanzanlage *f*, Magnetresonanzgerät *n*
~ **resonance measurement** Magnetresonanzmessung *f*
~ **resonance microscopy** Magnetresonanzmikroskopie *f*
~ **resonance phenomenon** Magnetresonanzphänomen *n*
~ **resonance signal** Magnetresonanzsignal *n*

~ **resonance spectrometer** Magnetresonanzspektrometer *n*
~ **resonance spectroscopic** magnetresonanzspektroskopisch
~ **resonance spectroscopy** Magnetresonanzspektroskopie *f*, Kernspin[resonanz]spektroskopie *f*
~ **resonance tomographic** magnetresonanztomografisch, kernspintomografisch
~ **rotation** Faraday-Rotation *f*
~ **sensor** Magnetfeldsensor *m*
~ **sound** Magnetton *m*
~ **sound film** Magnettonfilm *m*
~ **sound head** Magnettonkopf *m*; Magnettonabtastgerät *n*
~ **sound reproduction** Magnettonwiedergabe *f*
~ **sound stripe** Magnet[ton]streifen *m*, Magnetrandspur *f*
~ **sound tape** Magnettonband *n*
~ **sound track** Magnettonspur *f*
~ **sprocketed film** perforierter Magnetfilm *m*
~ **storage** 1. Magnetspeicherung *f*, magnetische Speicherung *f*; 2. *s*. ~ storage medium
~ **storage disk** Magnetplatte *f*
~ **storage medium** Magnetspeicher *m*
~ **strip[e]** *s*. ~ sound stripe
~ **striping** Magnetbespurung *f*
~ **susceptibility** magnetische Suszeptibilität *f*
~ **susceptibility artifact** Suszeptibilitätsartefakt *n* *(Magnetresonanzbildgebung)*
~ **tape** Magnetband *n*
~ **tape cartridge (cassette)** Magnetbandkassette *f*
~ **tape medium** Magnetbandmedium *n*
~ **tape recording** Magnetbandaufzeichnung *f*
~ **tape sound recorder** Magnetband-Tonaufnahmegerät *n*
~ **tape storage capacity** Magnetbandspeicherkapazität *f*
~ **tape storage device** Magnetbandgerät *n*
~ **tape technology** Magnetbandtechnik *f*
~ **tape video recorder** Magnetband-Videorecorder *m*
~ **track** Magnetspur *f*
~ **vector** magnetischer Vektor *m*
~ **videotape** Video[magnet]band *n*, MAZ-Band *n*
magnetically recorded sound Magnetton *m*
magnetizability Magnetisierbarkeit *f*
magnetizable magnetisierbar
magnetization curve Magnetisierungskurve *f*
~ **direction** Magnetisierungsrichtung *f*
~ **transfer contrast** Magnetisierungstransferkontrast *n*
~ **vector** Magnetisierungsvektor *m*

magnetize/to magnetisieren
magneto-optic[al] magnetooptisch
~-**optical disk** magnetooptische Platte *f*; magnetische Bildplatte *f*
~-**optical recording** magnetooptische Aufzeichnung *f*
~-**optical rotation** Magnetorotation *f*
~-**optical shutter** magnetooptischer Verschluss *m*, Faraday-Verschluss *m*
~-**optical storage** magnetooptischer Speicher *m*
~-**optical technology** Magnetooptik *f*
~-**optics** Magnetooptik *f*
magnetocardiogram Magnetokardiogramm *n*
magnetocardiography Magnetokardiografie *f*
magnetoelectroencephalogram, magnetoencephalogram Magnet[o]enzephalogramm *n*
magnetoencephalography Magnet[o]enzephalografie *f*
magnetographic printing magnetografischer Druck *m*
~ **toner** magnetografischer Toner *m*
magnetography Magnetografie *f*
magnetogyric ratio gyromagnetisches Verhältnis *n (Kernspinresonanz)*
magnetometer Magnetometer *n*
magnetometry Magnetometrie *f*
magnetoresistivity effect magnetoresistiver Effekt *m*
magnetostriction Magnetostriktion *f*
magnetostrictive magnetostriktiv
magnetron Magnetron *n (Oszillatorröhre)*
magnification Vergrößerung *f*
~ **effect** Vergrößerungseffekt *m*
~ **factor** Vergrößerungsfaktor *m*; Linearmaßstab *m*, Linearfaktor *m*
~ **formula** Vergrößerungsformel *f*
~ **law** Vergrößerungsgesetz *n*
~ **power** Vergrößerungsleistung *f*; Vergrößerungsfähigkeit *f*
~ **range** Vergrößerungsbereich *m*
~ **ratio** Vergrößerungsverhältnis *n*
~ **scale** Vergrößerungsmaßstab *m*
~ **technique** Vergrößerungstechnik *f*
~ **work** Vergrößerungsarbeit *f*
magnified image vergrößertes Bild *n*
magnifier Vergrößerungsglas *n*; Lupe *f*
~ **lens** Vergrößerungslinse *f*
magnify/to vergrößern
magnifying ability Vergrößerungsfähigkeit *f*
~ **glass** Vergrößerungsglas *n*; Lupe *f*
~ **lamp** Vergrößerungslampe *f*
~ **lens** Vergrößerungslinse *f*
~ **mirror** Vergrößerungsspiegel *m*
~ **optical instrument** Vergrößerungsgerät *n*
~ **power** Vergrößerungsleistung *f*
~ **window** Vergrößerungsfenster *n (auf Bildschirmen)*

magnitude

magnitude 1. Größe f; Größenklasse f; 2. Magnitude f *(Maß der Sternhelligkeit)*
~ **response** Amplitudenfrquenzgang m
magoptical print Magnetton-Lichtton-Kopie f
Mahalanobis classifier Mahalanobis-Klassifikator m *(Musterklassifikation)*
~ **distance [measure]** Mahalanobis-Abstand m, Mahalanobis-Distanz f
mail order catalog Versandhauskatalog m
~ **sorting** Postsortierung f
main and credit title Haupttitel m, Anfangstitel m, Titelvorspann m *(Kinofilm)*
~ **beam** Hauptstrahl m *(Radiografie)*
~ **bus** Hauptleitungsträger m, Bus m *(in einem Computersystem)*
~ **camera** Hauptkamera f *(Filmarbeit)*
~ **clock** Haupttaktgeber m
~ **computer** Hauptrechner m, Hostcomputer m, Hostrechner m
~ **computer circuit board** Hauptplatine f, Systemplatine f, Computerplatine f, Mutterplatine f
~ **exposure** Hauptbelichtung f
~ **field** Hauptmagnetfeld n, Grund[magnet]feld n *(Magnetresonanztomografie)*
~ **film** Hauptfilm m *(Kino)*
~ **flash** Hauptblitz m
~ **header** Hauptkopf m *(Bilddatenstruktur)*
~ **image** Hauptbild n
~ **lens** Grundobjektiv n, Hauptobjektiv n
~ **light** Hauptlicht n, Führungslicht n
~ **light source** Hauptlichtquelle f, Führungslichtquelle f, primäre Lichtquelle f
~ **lighting** Hauptbeleuchtung f
~ **lobe** Hauptkeule f *(Radar)*
~ **memory** Hauptspeicher m, Arbeitsspeicher m
~ **mirror** Hauptspiegel m, Primärspiegel m *(z.B. eines katadioptrischen Systems)*
~ **object** Hauptobjekt n
~ **projection line** Zentralprojektionslinie f
~ **subject** Hauptmotiv n
~ **telescope** Hauptteleskop n *(Astrofotografie)*
~ **unit shoot** Hauptdreh m *(Filmarbeit)*
mainframe s. 1. master processor; 2. ~ computer
~ **computer** Zentralrechner m, Großrechenanlage f, Großrechner m
mains adapter Netz[strom]adapter m, Netzladeadapter m, Netzgerät n
major axis Hauptachse f *(z.B. einer Ellipse)*
~ **axis orientation** Hauptachsen[aus]richtung f
majority filter binäres Medianfilter n
majuscule Majuskel f, Großbuchstabe m, Versal m

make up/to umbrechen *(zu druckendes Material)*
makegood korrigierter (verbesserter) Nachdruck m
makeready 1. Einrichten n, Zurichten n, Rüsten n *(Druckvorbereitung)*; 2. s. ~ paper
~ **paper** Makulatur f
~ **time** Rüstzeit f
makeup Umbruch m, Mettage f *(Druck)*
Maksutov-Cassegrain telescope Maksutow-Cassegrain-Teleskop n
~ **system** Maksutow-System n *(Spiegelobjektiv)*
~ **telescope** Maksutow-Teleskop n
male die Patrize f, Prägestock m *(z.B. im Prägedruck)*
~ **matte** Gegenmaske f, Gegenkasch m, Hintergrundmaske f, Hintergrundmaskenfilm m *(Trickkinematografie)*
Mallat's herringbone algorithm s. fast wavelet transform
Maltese cross Malteserkreuz n
~ **cross mechanism** Malteserkreuzgetriebe f, Malteserkreuzschaltung f
Malus' theorem (law) Malusscher Satz m *(Strahlenoptik)*
mammogram Mammogramm n
mammographic mammografisch
~ **film** Mammografiefilm m
~ **image** Mammogramm n
~ **X-ray unit** Röntgenmammografiegerät n
mammography Mammografie f
~ **device (equipment)** Mammografiegerät n
~ **film** Mammografiefilm m
~ **viewer** Mammografiegerät n
MAN s. metropolitan arc network
man-machine interface Mensch-Maschine-Schnittstelle f
~**-made illumination** Kunstlichtbeleuchtung f, künstliche Beleuchtung f
~**-made noise** künstliches Rauschen n
Manchester code Manchester-Code m
Mandelbrot set Mandelbrot-Menge f *(fraktale Geometrie)*
Mangin [mirror] Mangin-Spiegel m *(katadioptrisches System)*
manifold/to vervielfältigen
manifold paper Durchschlagpapier n
manifolder Vervielfältigungsapparat m, Vervielfältigungsgerät n
manipulability Manipulierbarkeit f *(z.B. von Bildern)*
manipulable manipulierbar
manipulated photograph manipuliertes Foto n
manipulative error Bedienungsfehler m; Handhabungsfehler m
manual backlight control button Gegenlichttaste f *(Camcorder)*
~ **camera** mechanische Kamera f

~ **copperplate intaglio engraving** gestochene Kupferplatte *f*
~ **editing** manuell gesteuerter Schnitt *m*
~ **enlarging system** Handvergrößerungssystem *n*
~ **exposure** Handauslösung *f*
~ **film transport** manueller Filmtransport *m*
~ **focusing** manuelle Fokussierung (Scharfeinstellung) *f*
~ **override** manuelle Einstellmöglichkeit (Eingriffsmöglichkeit) *f*
~ **printing process** Handdruckverfahren *n*
~ **processing** Handverarbeitung *f*, Handentwicklung *f*, manuelle Entwicklung *f*
~ **retouching** Handretusche *f*
~ **setting** Handeinstellung *f*
~ **white balance [correction]** manueller Weißabgleich *m*
manufacturer of motion picture equipment Filmgerätehersteller *m*
many-sided prism Mehrfachprisma *n*
map/to 1. kartografieren; kartieren; 2. abbilden
map onto/to aufeinander abbilden
~ 1. Karte *f*; Landkarte *f*; 2. Abbild *n*, Abbildung *f (s.a. unter Bild)*
~-**based semantic model[l]ing** bildbasierte semantische Modellierung *f*
~ **coordinates** Kartennetzentwurf *m*, Netzentwurf *m*
~ **digitization** Kartendigitalisierung *f*
~ **image** Kartenbild *n*
~ **plane** Kartenebene *f*
~ **projection** Kartenprojektion *f*
~ **scale** Kartenmaßstab *m*
~ **sheet** Kartenblatt *n*
~ **symbol** Kartenzeichen *n*
~ **table** Kartentisch *m*
mapmaker Kartograf *m*
mapmaking *s.* mapping 2.
mapper *s.* mapmaker
mapping 1. Abbildung *f*; 2. Kartierung *f*, Kartenaufnahme *f*
~ **accuracy** Kartierungsgenauigkeit *f*
~ **algorithm** Abbildungsalgorithmus *m*
~ **camera** Messbildkamera *f*, [fotogrammetrische] Messkammer *f*
~ **function** Abbildungsfunktion *f*
~ **geometry** Abbildungsgeometrie *f*
~ **photograph** [fotografisches] Messbild *n*, Messaufnahme *f*, fotogrammetrisches Bild *n*
~ **principle** Abbildungsprinzip *n*
~ **radar** Bildradar *n*, abbildendes Radar *n*
~ **science** Kartografie *f*
~ **space** Abbildungsraum *m*
~ **transformation** *s.* intensity transformation
~ **value** Abbildungsgröße *f (Fotogrammetrie)*

marching cubes [contouring] algorithm Marching-Cubes-Algorithmus *m (Visualisierung)*
margin Rand *m*; Papierrand *m*
marginal entropy Quellenentropie *f*, Signalentropie *f (Informationstheorie)*
~ **fog** Randschleier *m*
~ **ray** Randstrahl *m*, randnaher (randseitiger) Strahl *m*
~ **resolution** Randauflösung *f*
~ **veil** Randschleier *m*
marine chart Seekarte *f*
~ **photography** Meeresfotografie *f*
mark up/to auszeichnen *(Druckvorlagenerstellung)*
~**[ing]** Markierung *f*; Zeichen *n*
marking compound Markersubstanz *f*
~ **laser** Beschriftungslaser *m*, Markierlaser *m*
Markoff ... *s.* Markov ...
Markov chain Markow-Kette *f*
~ **model** Markow-Modell *n*
~ **process** Markow-Prozess *m*
~ **random field** Markow-Zufallsfeld *n*
Markovian analysis Markow-Analyse *f*
markup-language Dokumentenauszeichnungssprache *f*, Auszeichnungssprache *f*, Markierungssprache *f*, Beschreibungssprache *f (Datenverarbeitung)*
Marr-Hildreth operator *s.* Mexican hat filter
married print kombinierte Filmkopie (Kopie) *f (Kinematografie)*
mask/to maskieren
mask off (out)/to abdecken, kaschieren, abkaschen
~ 1. Maske *f*, Abdeckmaske *f*; Fotomaske *f*; Filmmaske *f*, Filmkasch *m*, Kaschblende *f*, Kasch *m*, Cache *m*, Schablone *f*; 2. Maskenoperator *m*, lokaler Operator *m (Bildverarbeitung)*; 3. abgeschwächtes Negativ *n (Reprografie)*
~ **aperture** Maskenloch *n (Farbbildröhre)*
~ **coefficient** Maskenkoeffizient *m*, Filterkoeffizient *m*
~ **exposure** Maskenbelichtung *f*
~ **fabrication** Maskenherstellung *f*, Maskenfertigung *f*
~ **film** Maskenfilm *m*
~ **holder** Maskenhalter *m*
~ **image** Maskenbild *n*
~ **processing** Filterung *f*, Digitalbildverarbeitung)
~ **set** Maskensatz *m*
maskable maskierbar
masking 1. Maskierung *f*; 2. *s.* ~ off
~ **coupler** Maskenkuppler *m (Colorfilm)*
~ **dye** Maskierungsfarbstoff *m*
~ **easel** *s.* ~ frame
~ **effect** Maskierungseffekt *m*
~ **film** Abdeckfilm *m*, Abdeckfolie *f*, Maskierfolie *f (z.B. für Negativmontagen)*

masking

~ **frame** Kopierrahmen *m*; Vergrößerungskassette *f*, Vergrößerungsrahmen *m*
~ **ink** Abdeckfarbe *f*
~ **lacquer** Abdecklack *m*, Abziehlack *m*
~ **method** Maskenverfahren *n*, fotomechanisches Korrekturverfahren *n*
~ **off** Abkaschen *n*, Abkaschung *f*
~ **pen** Abdeckstift *m* *(Retuschierwerkzeug)*
~ **sheet** *s*. ~ film
~ **tape** Abdeckband *n*
~ **technique** Maskierungstechnik *f*
mass attenuation coefficient Massenschwächungskoeffizient *m*, Massenabsorptionskoeffizient *m*
~ **data storage medium** Massenspeicher *m*
~ **density** Dichte *f*
~ **energy absorption (transfer) coefficient** *s*. ~ attenuation coefficient
~ **printing** Massenkopierung *f*
~ **radiography** Röntgenreihenuntersuchung *f*
~ **release print** Massen[projektionskopie]kopie *f* *(Film)*
~ **spectrograph** Massenspektrograf *m*
~ **spectrometry** Massenspektrometrie *f*
~ **storage [device]** Massenspeicher *m*
master Original *n*, Master *m*
~ **antenna television** Gemeinschaftsantennenfernsehen *n*
~ **clock [signal] generator** Haupttaktgeber *m*
~ **control** Bildregie *f*, Senderegie *f* *(Fernsehen)*
~ **control room** Bildregieraum *m*
~ **copy** Vervielfältigungsvorlage *f*
~ **film** Originalfilm *m*
~ **flash** Hauptblitz *m*
~ **hologram** Masterhologramm *n*
~ **original** ungeschnittene Originalaufzeichnung *f*
~ **oscillator power amplifier laser** MOPA-Laser *m*
~ **photographer** Meisterfotograf *m*
~ **positive** Duplikatpositiv *n*, Duplikat-Positivkopie *f*; Lavendelkopie *f*, Lavendel *n* *(Kinefilmverarbeitung)*
~ **processor** Hauptprozessor *m* *(s.a. Zentraleinheit)*
~ **recorder** Aufnahmerecorder *m*
~ **sheet** Vervielfältigungsvorlage *f*
~ **shot** Mastereinstellung *f*; Überblicksaufnahme *f* *(Filmarbeit)*
~ **strip** Referenzstreifen *m*
~ **tape** Master[misch]band *n*; Aufnahmeband *n*
~ **unit** Hauptgerät *n* *(Blitzausrüstung)*
~ **videotape** Video-Masterband *n*
masthead Impressum *n*
mat *s*. matrix 2.
match/to angleichen, anpassen; abgleichen *(z.B. Farben)*; vergleichen
match Angleich *m*; Anpassung *f*

~ **frame edit** Pseudoschnitt *m* *(Video)*
matched color gleichaussehende Farbe *f*
~ **filter** [signal]angepasstes Filter *n*; optimales Suchfilter *n*; Korrelationsfilter *n*
~ **filtering** 1. [signal]angepasste Filterung *f*; 2. Mustervergleich *m*, Schablonenabgleich *m*, Schablonenanpassung *f* *(Mustererkennung)*
matching 1. Abgleich *m*, Abgleichung *f*; Vergleich *m*; Zuordnung *f*; 2. Farbabgleich *m*, Ausmischung *f*
~ **problem** Korrespondenzproblem *n* *(maschinelles Sehen)*
~ **stimulus** Vergleichsfarbe *f*
materials microscopy Materialmikroskopie *f*
mathematical filter mathematisches Filter *n*
~ **modeling** mathematische Modellierung *f* *(z.B. in der Bildrestaurierung)*
~ **morphology** mathematische Morphologie *f*
matrix/to matrizieren
matrix 1. Matrix *f*; 2. Matrize *f*; Buchstabenform *f*
~ **addition** Matrixaddition *f*
~ **algebra** Matrixalgebra *f*
~ **array** Matrixanordnung *f*
~ **array camera** Flächen[chip]kamera *f*, [CCD-]Matrixkamera *f*
~ **character** Matrixzeichen *n*
~ **coefficient** Matrixkoeffizient *m*
~ **computation** Matrixberechnung *f*
~-**controlled display** *s*. matrix display
~ **conversion** Matrixkonversion *f*
~ **detector** Matrixsensor *m*
~ **diagonalization** Matrixdiagonalisierung *f*
~ **display** Matrixanzeige *f*, Matrixdisplay *n*
~ **element** Matrixelement *n*
~ **equation** Matrixgleichung *f*
~ **film** Matrixfilm *m*, Matrizenfilm *m* *(Farbfotografie)*
~ **form** Matrixform *f* *(z.B. eines transformierten Bildes)*
~ **frame** Matrizenrahmen *m* *(Satzherstellung)*
~ **inversion** Matrixinversion *f*
~ **manipulation** Matrixoperation *f*
~ **matching** Schablonenabgleich *m*, Schablonenanpassung *f*; Mustervergleich *m*
~ **metering** Matrixmessung *f*
~ **multiplication** Matrixmultiplikation *f*
~ **notation** Matrixschreibweise *f*
~ **of coefficients** Koeffizientenmatrix *f*
~ **of pixels** Pixelmatrix *f*
~ **operation** Matrixoperation *f*
~ **optics** Matrixoptik *f*
~ **printer** Matrixdrucker *m*, Punktmatrixdrucker *m*, Nadel[matrix]drucker *m*, Mosaikdrucker *m*, Rasterdrucker *m*

~ **product** Matrixprodukt *n*
~ **representation** Matrixdarstellung *f*
~ **sensor** Matrixsensor *m*
~ **size** Matrixgröße *f*
~ **teeth** Zahnung *f (Buchstabenmatrize)*
~ **transformation** Matrixtransformation *f*
~ **transposition** Matrixtransponierung *f*
matrixing [operation] Matrizierung *f*
matt-black mattschwarz
~ **gray** mattgrau
~ **screen** diffuse Bildwand *f*
~ **spray** Mattspray *n*
~-**surface paper** Mattglanzfotopapier *n*
~-**surface print** Mattglanzkopie *f*
~ **varnish** Mattlack *m*
~-**white** mattweiß
matte 1. Farbflächengenerator *m*; 2. Trickmaske *f*, Filmmaske *f*, Maske *f (Kinematografie)*; 3. *s.* mask 1.
~ **artist** Mattemaler *m*
~ **box** Objektivkompendium *n*; Balgenkompendium *n*, Kompendium *n*; Maskeneinschub *m (Trickfilmkamera)*
~ **channel** Alphakanal *m*, Transparenzkanal *m*, Maskenkanal *m*, Schablonenkanal *m (Computergrafik, Video)*
~ **effect** Stanztrick *m (Trickkinematografie)*
~ **extraction technique** Maskenverfahren *n (Kinematografie)*
~-**finished** mattiert
~ **generation** Maskenaufbau *m*
~ **image** Maskenbild *n*
~ **line** Kontaktlinie *f*
~ **painting** gemalter Hintergrund *m*, Mattebild *n*, Tafelbild *n*, Prospekt *m*
~ **paper** mattes (mattgestrichenes) Papier *n*
~ **photography** Schablonentrickverfahren *n*, Kombinationsaufnahmeverfahren *n*, Maskenverfahren *n (Trickkinematografie)*
~ **shot** Maskenaufnahme *f (Filmtrick)*
matter to be printed Bedruckmaterial *n*, Bedruckstoff *m*
matting [process] *s.* matte extraction technique
~ **agent** Mattiermittel *n*
mature/to konditionieren *(z.B. Druckpapier)*
maximum aperture Maximalöffnung *f*, maximale Öffnung *f*, Anfangsöffnung *f (Objektiv)*; maximaler Blendendurchmesser *m* , maximale Blende *f*
~ **contrast** Maximalkontrast *m*
~ **density** maximale Dichte (Schwärzung) *f*, Maximaldichte *f*, Maximalschwärzung *f*, Höchstdichte *f (Densitometrie)*
~ **diaphragm opening** *s.* ~ aperture
~ **exposure** Vollbelichtung *f*
~ **filter** Maximumfilter *n*
~ **filtering** Maximumsfilterung *f*
~ **intensity projection** Maximumsprojektion *f*, Maximum-Intensitäts-Profil *n (Visualisierung)*
~ **likelihood** maximale Wahrscheinlichkeit *f*
~ **likelihood classification** Maximum-Likelihood-Klassifikation *f*
~ **luminance** maximale Leuchtdichte *f*, Spitzenleuchtdichte *f*
~ **phase deviation** Phasenhub *m* Maschinenverarbeitung *f*
Maxwell-Boltzmann statistics Boltzmann-Statistik *f*
~ **disk** [Maxwellscher] Farbkreisel *m*, Maxwellsche Scheibe *f (additive Farbmischung)*
~ **fish-eye** Maxwellsches Fischauge *n*
~ **triangle** Maxwellsches Dreieck *n (Farbartdiagramm)*
Maxwell's equations Maxwell-Gleichungen *fpl (elektromagnetische Strahlung)*
maze [light trap] Labyrintheingang *m*, Labyrinthschleuse *f (Dunkelraum)*
McCollough effect McCollough-Effekt *m (Farbeffekt)*
ME tape *s.* metal-evaporated tape
mealy image wolkiges Druckbild *n (Druckschwierigkeit)*
mean [arithmetisches] Mittel *n*; Mittelwert *m*
~ **absolute difference** mittlerer absoluter Fehler *m (Verzerrungsmaß)*
~ **curvature** mittlere Krümmung *f*
~ **filter** Mittelwertfilter *n*
~ **noon sunlight** mittleres Mittagslicht *n*
~ **opinion score** subjektive Beurteilung z.B. der Bildqualität durch Versuchspersonen
~ **separating vector quantization** mittelwertseparierende Vektorquantisierung *f*
~-**square deviation (error)** mittlere quadratische Abweichung *f*, mittleres Abweichungsquadrat *n*, mittlerer quadratischer Fehler *m*, mittlere quadratische Abweichung *f*, mittleres Fehlerquadrat *n (Schätzparameter)*
~-**square error** mittlerer quadratischer Fehler *m*, mittlere quadratische Abweichung *f*, mittleres Fehlerquadrat *n*
~-**square quantization error** mittlerer quadratischer Quantisierungsfehler *m*
~-**squared** ... *s.* mean-square ...
~ **value filtering** Mittelwertfilterung *f*
~ **value operator** Mittelwertoperator *m*
measure 1. Maß *n*; 2. Textblockbreite *f*
measurement aperture Messblende *f*
~ **geometry** Messgeometrie *f*
~ **gratic[u]le** Messkreuz *n (s.a.* gratic[u]le*)*
~ **of brightness** Helligkeitsmessung *f*, Fotometrie *f*
~ **of volume** Volumenmessung *f*, Volumetrie *f*
measuring beaker Messglas *n*, Messgefäß *n*, Messzylinder *m*, Mensur *f*

measuring

~ **beam** Messstrahl *m*
~ **diaphragm** Messblende *f*
~ **eyepiece** Messokular *n*
~ **head** Messkopf *m*
~ **magnifier** Messlupe *f*
~ **mark** Messmarke *f*
~ **microscope** Messmikroskop *n*
~ **projector** Messprojektor *m*
~ **stereoscope** Messstereoskop *n*
~ **telescope** Messfernrohr *n*
~ **wedge** Messkeil *m*
mechanical Ganzseitenmontage *f*, Montage *f (Druckvorstufe; s.a.* hard mechanical*)*
~ **birefringence** Spannungsdoppelbrechung *f*
~ **dot gain** Rasterpunktverbreiterung *f*, Rastertonwertzunahme *f*
~ **focusing** mechanische Fokussierung *f (Sonografie)*
~ **mouse** mechanische Maus *f*
~ **noise** mechanisches Rauschen *n*
~ **noise of the camera** Kamera[lauf]geräusch *n*
~ **radiation equivalent** mechanisches Strahlungsäquivalent *n*
~ **scanner** mechanischer Abtaster (Scanner) *m*
~ **scanning** mechanische Abtastung *f*
~ **shutter** mechanischer Verschluss *m*
~ **stage** Kreuztisch *m (Mikroskop)*
~ **stroboscope** mechanisches Stroboskop *n*
~ **television** mechanisches Fernsehen *n*
~ **tint** Einkopierraster *m(n) (Druckvorstufe)*
~ **transducer** mechanischer Wandler (Schallkopf) *m (Sonografie)*
~ **tube length** mechanische Tubuslänge *f*
~ **typesetting** maschinelle Satzherstellung *f*
~ **vignetting** künstliche Vignettierung *f*
mechanized processing Maschinenverarbeitung *f*, maschinelle Entwicklung *f (von Fotomaterial)*
media archive Medienarchiv *n*
~ **data throughput** Mediendatendurchsatz *m*
~ **file** Mediendatei *f*; Multimediadatei *f*
~ **installation** Multimediainstallation *f*
~ **integration** Medienintegration *f*
~ **management** [angewandte] Medienwirtschaft *f*
~ **object** Medien[daten]objekt *n*, Multimediaobjekt *n*
~ **object identifier** Objektidentifikator *m*
~ **processor** Multimediaprozessor *m*
~ **service** Mediendienst *m*
~ **stream** Mediendatenstrom *m*
~ **technology** Medientechnik *f*, Medientechnologie *f*
~ **translation** Medienumsetzung *f*, Medienwechsel *m*

medial axis transform[ation] Mittelachsentransformation *f*; Symmetrieachsentransformation *f*
medialness Mittigkeit *f*
median Medianwert *m*, Zentralwert *m*
~ **cut algorithm** Medianschnittverfahren *n (Farbquantisierung)*
~ **filter** Medianfilter *n*, Medianoperator *m (Bildoperator)*
~ **filter mask** Medianfiltermaske *f*
~ **filtering** Medianfilterung *f*
~ **gray** mittelgrau
~ **line** Mittellinie *f*
~ **operation** Medianoperation *f*
~ **pixel** Medianpixel *n*
~-**type filter** *s.* median filter
~ **value** Median[wert] *m*, Zentralwert *m*
medical endoscopy medizinische Endoskopie *f*
~ **image analysis** medizinische Bildanalyse *f*
~ **image diagnosis** Bilddiagnose *f*
~ **image diagnostic** bilddiagnostisch
~ **image informatics** medizinische Informatik *f*
~ **image processing** medizinische Bildverarbeitung *f*
~ **imagery** medizinisches Bildmaterial *n*
~ **imaging** Medizinbildgebung *f*, medizinische (diagnostische) Bildgebung *f*; medizinische Bildverarbeitung *f*
~ **imaging department** Schnittbildzentrum *n*
~ **imaging modality** medizinisches Bildgebungsverfahren *n*
~ **imaging technology** Medizinbildtechnik *f (s.a.* ~ imaging*)*
~ **photographer** Medizinfotograf *m*
~ **photography** Medizinfotografie *f*, medizinische Fotografie *f*
~ **radiography** medizinische Radiografie *f*
~ **tomography** medizinische Tomografie *f*
~ **ultrasound** medizinischer Ultraschall *m*
~ **X-ray film** medizinischer Röntgenfilm *m*
medium Medium *n*
~ **access control** Medienzugriffskontrolle *f*
~ **close-up** Halbnahe *f*, Halbnaheinstellung *f*
~ **close-up shot** Halbgroßaufnahme *f*
~-**distance shot** Halbnahaufnahme *f*
~-**faced** halbfett *(Schriftauszeichnung)*
~ **format** Mittelformat *n*
~-**format camera** Mittelformatkamera *f*
~-**format lens** Mittelformatobjektiv *n*
~-**format photography** Mittelformatfotografie *f*
~-**format projector** Mittelformatprojektor *m*
~-**format rangefinder camera** Mittelformat-Sucherkamera *f*
~-**format roll-film camera** Mittelformat-Rollfilmkamera *f*

~-format single-lens reflex camera Mittelformat-Spiegelreflexkamera *f*
~-format slide Mittelformatdia[positiv] *n*
~ gray mittelgrau
~ interchange Medienumsetzung *f*, Medienwechsel *m*
~ shot Halbnahaufnahme *f*
~-speed film mittelempfindlicher Film *m*
~ telephoto lens mittellangbrennweitiges Teleobjektiv *n*
~ telephoto zoom Weitwinkelzoom *n*
~ tone Mittelton *m*
~-wave[length] infrared mittleres Infrarot *n*
~-wave[length] ultraviolet mittleres Ultraviolett *n*
megabit Megabit *n*, Mb
megabyte Megabyte *n*, MB
megahertz Megahertz *n*, MHz *(Frequenzmaß)*
megapixel Megapixel *n*
~ camera Megapixelkamera *f*
megascopic makroskopisch
melanin Melanin *n (Pigment)*
membership function Zugehörigkeitsfunktion *f*
membrane model Membranmodell *n*
memoriless speicherfrei
memory Speicher *m*
~ access Speicherzugriff *m*
~ address Speicheradresse *f*
~ addressing Speicheradressierung *f*
~ bandwidth Speicherbandbreite *f*
~ bit Speicherbit *n*
~ block Speicherblock *m*
~ board Speicherplatine *f*
~ bus Speicherbus *m*
~ card slot Speicherkartenschlitz *m*, Speicherkarteneinschub *m*
~ cell Speicherzelle *f*
~ chip Speicherchip *m*, Speicherbaustein *m*, Computerspeicherchip *m*
~ content Speicherinhalt *m*
~ control Speichersteuerung *f*
~ device Speicher *m*
~ expansion Speichererweiterung *f*
~ file Speicherdatei *f*
~ interface Speicherschnittstelle *f*
~ location Speicherstelle *f*
~ management Speicherverwaltung *f*
~ matrix Speichermatrix *f*
~ medium Speichermedium *n*
~ module Speichermodul *n*
~ occupation Speicherbelegung *f*
~ organization Speicherorganisation *f*
~ performance Speicherleistung *f*
~ readout process Speicherlesen *n*, Speicherabfrage *f*, sekundäres Erkennen *n*
~ space Speicherplatz *m*, Speicherraum *m*
~ stick Digitalkamera-Speicherkarte *f*, Kamerakarte *f*
~ stick slot Speicherkartenschlitz *m*
~ storage Speicherung *f*
~ storage card Speicherkarte *f*, Datenspeicherkarte *f*
~ system Speichersystem *n*
~ technology Speichertechnik *f*
memoryless coding speicherlose Codierung *f*
meniscus [lens], meniscus-type lens Meniskus *m*, Meniskuslinse *f*
menu Menü *n*
~ bar Menüleiste *f*, Menübalken *m*
~ box Menübox *f*, Menüfenster *n*
~ control Menüführung *f*, Menüsteuerung *f*
~-driven [operator] prompting menügesteuerte Bedienerführung *f*
~ function Menüfunktion *f*
~ instruction Menübefehl *m*
~ key Menütaste *f*
~ selection Menüauswahl *f*
~ tree Menübaum *m*
Mercator projection Mercatorprojektion *f*, Mercator-Zylinderprojektion *f (Kartografie)*
~ projection map Mercator-Karte *f*
mercuric chloride intensifier Quecksilberverstärker *m*
mercury arc lamp Quecksilberdampflampe *f*
~ fume Quecksilberdampf *m*
~ high-pressure arc-discharge lamp Quecksilberhochdruck[entladungs]lampe *f*
~ intensifier Quecksilberverstärker *m*
~ salt Quecksilbersalz *n*
~ vapor lamp Quecksilberdampflampe *f*
merging bit Koppelbit *n*
meridional coma meridionale Koma *f*, Meridionalkoma *f*, Asymmetriefehler *m (Optik)*
~ curvature of field meridionale Bildfeldwölbung *f*
~ image height aberration meridionale Bildhöhenaberration *f*
~ image surface meridionale Bildschale *f*
~ plane Meridionalebene *f*, Meridionalschnitt *m*; Tangentialebene *f (Optik)*
~ ray Meridionalstrahl *m*, meridionaler Strahl *m*
merit function [Gaußsche] Fehlerfunktion *f*
merocyanine [dye] Merocyanin *n*, Merocyaninfarbstoff *m*
mesh Gitter *n*; Gitternetz *n*
~-based representation Gitternetzdarstellung *f (Computergrafik, Texturverarbeitung)*
~ optimization Gitteroptimierung *f*
~ pocket Netztasche *f (z.B. in einer Kameratasche)*
~ point Gitter[schnitt]punkt *m*
~ representation Gitterdarstellung *f (z.B. von Oberflächen)*
~ simplification algorithm Gittervereinfachungsalgorithmus *m (Bildanalyse)*

mesopic mesopisch
~ **vision** mesopisches Sehen n, Übergangssehen n, Dämmerungssehen n
mesosphere Mesosphäre f *(Schicht der Erdatmosphäre)*
mesostructure Mesostruktur f
message signal Nutzsignal n, Nachrichtensignal n, artefaktfreies Signal n
meta-search engine Metasuchmaschine f
metadata Metadaten pl
metafile Metadatei f
~ **element** Bilddateielement n
~ **generator** Bilddateigenerator m
~ **interpreter** Bilddateiinterpreter m
metal camera Metallkamera f
~ **detector** Metalldetektor m
~**-evaporated tape** metalldampfbeschichtetes Videoband n, ME-Band n
~ **frame** Metallrahmen m
~ **halide gas-discharge arc lamp** s. HMI lamp
~ **halide lamp** Metallhalogen[id]lampe f, MH-Lampe f, Halogen-Metalldampflampe f
~ **oxide semiconductor** Metalloxidhalbleiter m
~ **oxide semiconductor capacitor** MOS-Kondensator m
~ **oxide semiconductor field-effect transistor** Isolierschicht-Feldeffekttransistor m, Metalloxid-Feldeffekttransistor m, MOSFET
~ **particle tape** Metall[partikel]band n, Reineisenband n, MP-Band n; Metalltonband n
~ **semiconductor diode** Metall-Halbleiter-Diode f
~ **semiconductor diode** MOS-Diode f
~ **tripod** Metallstativ n
~ **vapor lamp** Metalldampf[entladungs]lampe f
metalized screen metallisierte Bildwand f
metallic ink Metall[druck]farbe f
~ **mirror** Metallspiegel m
~ **paper** metallbedampftes Etikettenpapier n
~ **silver** metallisches Silber n
metallograph Metallograf m
metallographic metallografisch
~ **microscope** metallografisches Mikroskop n
metallography Metallografie f
metamer s. 1. metameric color; 2. metameric [color] stimulus
metameric metamer
~ **color** metamere (bedingt gleiche) Farbe f
~ **[color] stimulus** metamerer Farbreiz f
metamerism Metamerie f
~ **index** Metamerie-Index m
metamery s. metamerism

meteorological radar Wetterradar n
~ **satellite** Wettersatellit m
meter-candle-second s. lux second
~ **sensor** Messfühler m, Sensor m
metering cell Messzelle f
~ **feature** Messcharakteristik f
~ **field** Messfeld n
~ **range** Messbereich m
~ **system** Messsystem n
~ **system selector** Messcharakteristikwähler m *(Spiegelreflexkamera)*
method of least squares Methode f der kleinsten Quadrate
~ **of recording** Aufnahmeverfahren n
~ **of total least squares** Methode f der totalen kleinsten Quadrate
methylaminophenol sulfate, metol Methylaminophenolsulfat n, Monomethyl-p-aminophenolsulfat n, Metol n *(Entwicklersubstanz)*
metol-hydroquinone developer Metol-Hydrochinon-Entwickler m
metric camera Messkamera f
~ **space** metrischer Raum m
~ **wavelength range** Meterwellenbereich m, Meterwellenfrequenz f, Ultrakurzwellenbereich m, Ultrakurzwelle f, UKW
metrology Metrologie f, Messtechnik f
metropolitan arc network Stadtbereichsnetz n *(Datenübertragung)*
Mexican hat filter (kernel) Mexikanerhut-Operator m, Sombrerofilter n, Laplace-Gauß-Operator m, LoG-Filter n *(Kantendetektion)*
mezzograph screen Kornraster m(n) *(Reprografie)*
mezzotint Mezzotinto n *(Druckerzeugnis)*
~ **technique** Mezzotinto n, Schabmanier f *(Druckformherstellung)*
MHP s. Multimedia Home Platform
~ **device** MHP-Endgerät n, MHP-Gerät n
~ **standard** s. Multimedia Home Platform standard
MHz s. megahertz
mic s. microphone
Michelson interferometer Michelson-Interferometer n
micon s. motion icon
MICR s. magnetic ink character recognition
micro-CT scanner Mikrotomograf m, Mikro-Computertomograf m
~ **raster** Mikroraster m(n)
~ **zone plate** Mikrozonenplatte f *(Röntgenmikroskopie)*
~ **zone plate objective** Mikrozonenplattenobjektiv n
microadapter Mikroskopadapter m
microammeter Mikroamperemeter n
microanalysis Mikroanalyse f
microanalytical mikroanalytisch

microbolometer Mikrobolometer n
(Photonenabsorber)
microcapsule Mikrokapsel f
microcard Mikrokarte f
microcassette Mikrokassette f
microchannel image intensifier
Mikrokanal-Bildverstärker m
~ **plate** Mikrokanalplatte f,
Mikrokanal-Elektronenvervielfacherplatt
e f, Kanalelektronenvervielfacherplatte f
microchip Mikrochip m, integrierte
Schaltung f, integrierter Schaltkreis m
microcinematographic camera
mikrokinematografische Kamera f
microcinematography
Mikrokinematografie f
microcircuit production
Mikroschaltkreisherstellung f
microcomputer Mikrocomputer m
microcopier Mikrokopierer m
microcopy/to mikrokopieren
microcopy Mikrokopie f,
Mikroreproduktion f
microcopying Mikroverfilmung f
microcrystal Mikrokristall m
microcrystalline grain mikrokristallines
Korn n
microdensitometer Mikrodensitometer n
microdensitometric mikrodensitometrisch
microdensitometrie Mikrodensitometrie f
microdisplay Mikrodisplay n
microelectronic mikroelektronisch
~ **circuit** Mikroschaltkreis m
microelectronics Mikroelektronik f
microfacet Mikrofacette f
microfeature Mikromerkmal n
microfiche 1. Mikrofiche n(m), Fiche n(m);
2. s. ~ film
~ **camera** Mikrofiche-Kamera f
~ **film** s. microfilm
microfilm/to mikroverfilmen
microfilm Mikro[plan]film m,
Kleinstbildfilm m; Dokumentenfilm m
~ **aperture card** Mikrofilmkarte f,
Mikrofilm-Lochkarte f
~ **camera** Mikrofilmkamera f,
Mikrografiekamera f,
Mikroverkleinerungskamera f
~ **copy** Mikrofilmkopie f
~ **documentation**
Mikrofilm-Dokumentationsfotografie f
~ **duplicate** Mikrofilmduplikat n
~ **enlarger** Mikrofilm-Vergrößerungsgerät
n
~ **image** Mikrofilmbild n
~ **jacket** Mikrofilmtasche f
~ **reader** Mikrofilm[lese]gerät n
~ **recording** Mikrofilmaufnahme f,
Mikrofilmaufzeichnung f
~ **storage** Mikrofilmspeicher m
~ **strip** Mikrofilmstreifen m
~ **technics (technology)** Mikrofilmtechnik f
microfilming Mikroverfilmung f

~ **of engineering drawings**
Zeichnungsverfilmung f
microfilter Mikrofilter n
microflash Mikroblitz m
microfocal mikrofokal
microfocus radiography
Mikrofokusradiografie f
~ **X-ray tube** Mikrofokus-Röntgenröhre f
microform Mikroaufnahme m;
Mikroreproduktion f, Mikrokopie f
~ **reader** Mikrofilm[lese]gerät n
micrograph mikroskopisches Bild n,
Mikroskopbild n
micrographer Mikrofotograf m
micrographic mikrografisch
~ **film technology** Mikrofilmtechnik f
~ **storage** mikrografischer Speicher m
micrographics Mikrografie f
microimage Mikrobild n, Kleinstbild n;
Mikroaufnahme f, Mikrofoto n,
Mikrofotografie f
microlaser Mikrolaser m
microlens Mikrolinse f
microlithographic mikrolithografisch
microlithography Mikrolithografie f
micrometer 1. [optisches] Mikrometer n; 2.
Mikrometer n, Mikron n
~ **ocular** Mikrometerokular n
~ **resolution** Mikrometerauflösung f
micromirror Mikrospiegel m, Kleinspiegel
m
~ **projector** Mikrospiegelprojektor m
micromophology Mikrostruktur f
micromotor Mikromotor m
micron Mikrometer n
microopaque s. microcard
microoptic[al] mikrooptisch
microoptics Mikrooptik f
microoptoelectronics Mikrooptoelektronik
f
microphone Mikrofon n
~ **boom [apparatus]** Mikrofongalgen m,
Mikro-Galgen m, Tongalgen m,
Mikrofonausleger m, Ausleger m
~ **cable (cord)** Mikrofonkabel n
~ **input** Mikrofoneingang m (Videokamera)
~ **jack** Mikrofonbuchse f
~ **mixer** Mikrofonmischer m,
Audiomischer m, Tonmischpult n
~ **multiplexer** Mikrofonmultiplexer m
~ **polar pattern** Mikrofoncharakteristik f,
Aufnahmecharakteristik f,
Richtcharakteristik f, Richtwirkung f
~ **pole** Mikrofonangel f, [Mikro-]Angel f,
Tonangel f, Perche f
~ **stand** Mikrofonständer m
microphotodiode Mikrofotodiode f
microphotogrammetry
Mikrofotogrammetrie f
microphotograph mikrofotografische
Aufnahme f
microphotography Mikrofotografie f,
Fotomikrografie f
microphotometer Mikrofotometer n

microphotometry Mikrofotometrie f
micropixel Mikropixel n
micropolarizer Mikropolarisator m
micropolygon Mikropolygon n
microprism Mikroprisma n
~ **area (array)** Mikroprismenfeld n
~ **focus finder** Mikroprismenentfernungsmesser m
~ **grid** Mikroprismenraster m(n)
microprocessing unit, microprocessor Mikroprozessor m
microprocessor control Mikroprozessorsteuerung f
~-**controlled camera** mikroprozessorgesteuerte Kamera f
microprojection Mikroprojektion f
microprojector Mikroprojektionsgerät n, Mikroprojektor m
micropsia, micropsy Mikropsie f (Sehfehler)
microradiogram, microradiograph Röntgenmikroaufnahme f
microradiographic mikroradiografisch
microradiography Mikroradiografie f, Kontakt-Röntgenmikroskopie f
microreader Mikrofilm[lese]gerät n
microreciprocal degree Mikroreziprokgrad n, Mired n (Farbtemperaturmessung)
microreduction camera Mikroverkleinerungskamera f, Mikrofilmkamera f, Mikrografiekamera f (Mikrofotografie)
microreproduction Mikroreproduktion f, Mikrodokumentation f, Mikrokopie f
microscope/to mikroskopieren
microscope Mikroskop n
~ **adapter** Mikroskopadapter m
~ **body tube length** Mikroskoptubuslänge f
~ **camera** Mikroskopkamera f, Okularkamera f, Ansetzkamera f, Aufsetzkamera f
~ **condenser** Mikroskopkondensor m
~ **eyepiece** Mikroskopokular n
~ **fine-adjustment knob** Feintrieb m, Feinstellschraube f
~ **illumination** Mikroskopbeleuchtung f
~ **illumination source,** ~ **illuminator** Mikroskoplichtquelle f (s.a. ~ lamp)
~ **image** Mikroskopbild n, mikroskopisches Bild n, Mikroskopaufnahme f
~ **image analysis** Mikroskopbildanalyse f
~ **image processing** Mikroskopbildverarbeitung f
~ **imaging** mikroskopische Abbildung f
~ **lamp** Mikroskopierlampe f, Mikroskopierleuchte f
~ **light source** Mikroskoplichtquelle f
~ **monitor** Mikroskopmonitor m
~ **objective** Mikroskopobjektiv n, Mikroobjektiv n
~ **objective barrel** Mikroskoptubus m
~ **objective mount** Mikroskopobjektivhalter m
~ **ocular** Mikroskopokular n
~ **optics** Mikroskopoptik f
~ **photometer** Mikroskopfotometer n
~ **photometry** Mikroskopfotometrie f
~ **resolution** Mikroskopauflösung f
~ **setting** Mikroskopeinstellung f
~ **slide** Objektträger m
~ **specimen** mikroskopisches Objekt n
~ **stage** Objekttisch m
~ **stage micrometer** Mikroskopmikrometer n
~ **stand** Mikroskopstativ n; Mikroskopstativfuß m
~ **tube** Mikroskoptubus m
microscopic analysis mikroskopische Analyse f
~ **filter** Mikroskopfilter n
~ **image** mikroskopisches Bild n, Mikroskopbild n, Mikroskopaufnahme f
~ **image formation** mikroskopische Abbildung f
~ **object** mikroskopisches Objekt n
microscopical s. unter microscopic
microscopist Mikroskopist m, Mikroskopiker m, Mikroskopierer m
microscopy Mikroskopie f
microsensitometry Mikrosensitometrie f
microsensor Mikrosensor m
microspectrofluorescence Mikrospektrofluoreszenz f
microspectrometer Mikrospektrometer n
microspectrophotometer Mikrospektrofotometer n
microspectrophotometry Mikrospektrofotometrie f
microspectroscopy Mikrospektroskopie f
microstereoscopy Mikrostereoskopie f
microstructure Mikrostruktur f
microtelescope Mikroteleskop n
microtexture mask Mikrotexturmaske f
microtome Mikrotom n (Mikroskopie)
microtomography Mikrotomografie f
microwave Mikrowelle f
~ **band** Mikrowellenband n
~ **channel** Mikrowellenkanal m
~ **energy** Mikrowellenenergie f
~ **frequency** Mikrowellenfrequenz f
~ **holography** Mikrowellenholografie f
~ **image** Mikrowellenbild n
~ **imager** Mikrowellensensor m
~ **imaging** Mikrowellen-Bildgebung f
~ **optics** Mikrowellenoptik f
~ **photonics** Mikrowellenphotonik f
~ **pulse** Mikrowellenpuls m
~ **radiation** Mikrowellenstrahlung f
~ **ranging radar** Mikrowellenradar n
~ **receiver** Mikrowellenempfänger m
~ **remote sensing** Mikrowellen-Fernerkundung f
~ **sensor** Mikrowellensensor m
~ **signal** Mikrowellensignal n
~ **surveillance radar** Mikrowellen-Überwachungsradar n
~ **thermography** Mikrowellenthermografie f

~ **tube** Mikrowellenröhre f
mid-IR region mittleres Infrarot n
~**-range zoom** Standardzoom[objektiv] n, Normalzoom[objektiv] n, Universalzoom[objektiv] n
~**-roll change** das Wechseln von teilbelichtetem Filmmaterial
~**-roll rewind** Rückspulung f teilbelichteter Filme, vorzeitige Rückspulung f
~**-scale gray** mittlerer Grauwert m
~**-scale region** geradliniger Gradationskurvenbereich (Kurventeil) m
~**-wavelength infrared** mittleres Infrarot n
midday daylight Mittagslicht n
middle distance Mittelgrund m
~ **gray** mittelgrau
~ **ground** Mittelgrund m
~**-key image** Mitteltonbild n
~ **layer** Mittelguss m (Filmherstellung)
~ **tone** s. midtone
~ **value** Mittelwert m; Zentralwert m
~**-wavelength-sensitive cone** M-Zapfen m (Netzhautrezeptor)
midline Mittellinie f
midpoint Mittenpunkt m; Zentralpixel n
~ **reconstruction** Mittenpunktrekonstruktion f
midtone Mittelton m
~ **area** Mitteltonbereich m
~ **contrast** Mitteltonkontrast m
~ **image** Mitteltonbild n
~ **region** Mitteltonbereich m
Mie scattering Mie-Streuung f (von Licht)
mike s. microphone
military photography Militärfotografie f
milk glass Milchglas n, Trübglas n; Opalglas n
milkiness Entwicklungsschleier m
millimicron Nanometer n(m), nm
milliradian Milliradian n (Auflösungsmaß)
mimic/to simulieren; emulieren
mini flash illumination Mini-Blitzausleuchtung f
miniature Vorsatzmodell n; Miniaturdekoration f (Trickkinematografie)
~ **camera** Kleinkamera f, Miniaturkamera f
~ **camera lens** Kleinbildobjektiv n
~ **camera work** Kleinbildfotografie f
~**-format camera** Kleinbildkamera f
~**-format photography** Kleinbildfotografie f
~ **negative** Kleinbildnegativ n
~ **print** Miniaturabzug m, Vorschaubild n (Fotoverarbeitung)
~ **set** Miniaturdekoration f, Miniaturkulisse f (Filmarbeit)
~ **shot** Modellaufnahme f
~ **slide projector** Kleinbild[dia]projektor m
~ **transducer** Miniaturwandler m (Sonografie)
miniaturization Miniaturisierung f
miniaturize/to miniaturisieren, verkleinern
miniaturized optics Mikrooptik f

minicamcorder Minicamcorder m
minicomputer Minicomputer m
minification Verkleinerung f
minified image verkleinertes Bild n
minify/to verkleinern
minilab Minilab[or] n (Fotoverarbeitung)
~ **photofinishing equipment** Minilabzubehör n
minimum aperture kleinste Blende f
~ **coded unit** kleinste Codiereinheit f
~ **density** Minimaldichte f, Mindestdichte f, minimale Dichte f, Minimalschwärzung f (Densitometrie)
~ **distance classification** Minimaldistanzklassifikation f (Objekterkennung)
~ **distance classifier** Minimaldistanzklassifikator m
~ **distinct border** Minimum n separabile (Sehen)
~ **exposure** Minimalbelichtung f
~ **exposure time** Mindestbelichtungszeit f
~ **filter** Minimumfilter n
~ **filtering** Minimumfilterung f
~ **focus[ing distance]** Nahfokussiergrenze f, Nah[einstell]grenze f, kürzeste Einstellentfernung f
~ **luminance** minimale Leuchtdichte f
~ **mean square error filter** Wienersches Optimalfilter n, Wiener-Filter n (Bildrestaurierung)
~ **mean square error filtering** Wiener-Filterung f
~ **perceptible color difference** Ebenunterscheidbarkeit f
~ **redundancy code** kompakter Code m
~ **resolution** Mindestauflösung f
~ **resolvable temperature difference** minimale auflösbare Temperaturdifferenz f (Wärmebildgebung)
~ **Steiner spanning tree** Steiner-Baum m (Computergrafik)
~ **viewing distance** Mindestbetrachtungsabstand m
minipod [Dreifuß-]Kleinstativ n, Ministativ n
miniscule s. minuscule
Minkowski distance Minkowski-Abstand m, Minkowski-Distanz f
~ **operator** Minkowski-Operator m
~ **set addition** Minkowski-Addition f, Dilatation f (Binärbildverarbeitung)
~ **set subtraction** Minkowski-Subtraktion f, morphologische Erosion f
~ **sum** Minkowski-Summe f
minority carrier Minoritätsträger m (Fotodetektor)
minus color Minusfarbe f
~ **first order of diffraction** minus erste Beugungsordnung f
minuscule Minuskel f, Kleinbuchstabe m, Gemeine f
minute of arc Bogenminute f

mip mapping Mip-Mapping *n* *(Computergrafik, Texturverarbeitung)*
mirage Fata Morgana *f*
MIRED Mired *n*, Mikroreziprokgrad *n* *(Farbtemperaturmessung)*
~ **value** Mired-Wert *m*
mirror/to spiegeln
mirror Spiegel *m*
~ **alignment** Spiegelausrichtung *f*
~ **aperture** Spiegelapertur *f*
~ **arrangement** Spiegelanordnung *f*
~ **bounce** Spiegelschlag *m* *(Spiegelreflexkamera)*
~ **box** Spiegelkasten *m*
~ **camera** Spiegelkamera *f*
~ **curvature** Spiegelkrümmung *f*
~ **diameter** Spiegeldurchmesser *m*
~ **direction** Spiegelrichtung *f*
~ **drum scanning** Spiegelradabtastung *f*
~ **edge** Spiegelkante *f*
~ **effect** Spiegelungseffekt *m*
~ **face** Spiegelfläche *f*
~ **facet** Spiegelfacette *f*
~ **figure** Spiegelgestalt *f*
~ **galvanometer** Spiegelgalvanometer *n*
~ **glass** Spiegelglas *n*
~ **image** Spiegelbild *n*, gespiegeltes Bild *n*
~-**image ray** Spiegelbildstrahl *m*
~-**image relationship** Spiegelbildlichkeit *f*
~-**image symmetrical** spiegelbildlich
~ **imaging** spiegelbildliche Darstellung *f*
~ **lens** Spiegel[linsen]objektiv *n*, Spiegellinse *f*, katadioptrisches Objektiv (System) *n*
~ **lock[up feature]** Spiegelvorauslösung *f* *(Spiegelreflexkamera)*
~ **master tape** spiegelbildliches Masterband *n* *(Video)*
~ **microscope** Spiegelmikroskop *n*
~ **mount** Spiegelhalter *m*
~ **optics** Spiegeloptik *f*
~ **plane** Spiegelebene *f*
~ **plate** Spiegelglas *n*
~ **reflection** Spiegelung *f*, Spiegelreflexion *f*, spiegelnde Reflexion *f*, Fresnel-Reflexion *f*
~ **reflector** Spiegelreflektor *m*, spiegelnder Reflektor *m*
~ **shot** Spiegeltrick *m* *(Trickkinematografie)*
~ **shutter** Spiegel[umlauf]blende *f* *(Filmkamera)*
~ **slap** Spiegelschlag *m* *(Spiegelreflexkamera)*
~ **stereoscope** Spiegelstereoskop *n*
~ **surface** Spiegel[ober]fläche *f*
~ **symmetry** Spiegelsymmetrie *f*
~ **system** Spiegelsystem *n*
mirrored ball Spiegelkugel *f*, Diskokugel *f*
~ **end** Endspiegel *m* *(Laser)*
~ **image** gespiegeltes Bild *n*, Spiegelbild *n*
~ **prism** Spiegelprisma *n*
mirrorize/to verspiegeln

misadjustment Fehleinstellung *f* *(z.B. eines Objektivs)*
misalign/to dejustieren
misalignment Fehlausrichtung *f*, Dejustage *f*
miscibility Mischbarkeit *f*, Ermischbarkeit *f* *(z.B. von Farben)*
miscible color [er]mischbare Farbe *f*
misclassification Fehlklassifizierung *f*, Fehlklassifikation *f*
~ **error** Klassifikationsfehler *m*
misclassify/to fehlklassifizieren
misconvergence Konvergenzfehler *m*
misexposure Fehlbelichtung *f*
misfit s. misregistration
misfocus Fehlfokussierung *f*, falsche Fokuseinstellung *f*
misidentification Fehlidentifikation *f*
misinterpretation Fehlinterpretation *f*
misrecognition Fehlerkennung *f*
misregister Fehlpassung *f*; Passerungenauigkeit *f (Druck)*
misregistration 1. Fehlregistration *f*, Fehlausrichtung *f*; Farbdeckungsfehler *m (Farbbildröhre)*; 2. s. misregister
missing dots fehlende Bildstelle *f* *(Druckschwierigkeit)*
misting Farbnebeln *n (Druckschwierigkeit)*
mistracking Fehlabtastung *f*; Spurlagenfehler *m*, Trackingfehler *m* *(Bandaufnahmetechnik)*
mit out sound Drehen *n* ohne O-Ton *(Filmarbeit)*
mix/to mischen; abmischen *(z.B. Tonspuren)*
mixdown Abmischen *n*, Abmischung *f*
mixed color Mischfarbe *f*
~ **crystal** Mischkristall *m*
~ **illumination** Mischbeleuchtung *f*
~ **image** Mischbild *n*
~ **light** Mischlicht *n*
~-**light situation** Mischlichtbeleuchtung *f*
~-**light source** Mischlichtquelle *f*
~-**media** multimedial *(s.a. unter multimedia)*
~-**media document** Multimediadokument *n*, multimediales Dokument *n*
~-**media personal computer** Multimediacomputer *m*, Multimedia-PC *m*
~-**mode object** s. multimedia object
~ **reflection** gemischte Reflexion *f*
~ **semiconductor** Misch[ungs]halbleiter *m*, Verbindungshalbleiter *m*
~ **signature** Mischsignatur *f (Bildanalyse)*
mixing Mischen *n*, Mischung *f*
~ **board** Mischpult *n*
~ **box** Mischschacht *m*, Lichtmischschacht *m (Vergrößerungsgerät)*
~ **console** Mischpult *n*
mixture density Mischverteilung *f* *(Wahrscheinlichkeitstheorie)*
mobile camera bewegliche (mobile) Kamera *f*

~ **multimedia** mobiles Multimedia *n*
~ **phone** Mobil[funk]telefon *n*, Handy *n*
~ **printer** Mobildrucker *m*
~ **radar** mobiles Radar *n*
~ **radio** Mobilfunk *m*
Möbius strip Möbius-Band *n*
mock-up Probelayout *n*
MOCO camera s. motion control camera
modal noise Modenrauschen *n*
~ **value** Modalwert *m*, Dichtemittel *n* *(Statistik)*
mode 1. Mode *f(m) (Laser)*; 2. s. ~ of operation; 3. s. modal value
~ **competition noise** Modenverteilungsrauschen *n (Laser)*
~ **diaphragm** Modenblende *f (Laser)*
~ **locking** Modensynchronisation *f*, Phasensynchronisation *f (Laser)*
~ **of microscopy** Mikroskopiermethode *f*
~ **of operation** Betriebsart *f*, Betriebsmode *f (z.B. eines Lasers)*
~ **selector** Betriebsartenschalter *m*
~ **structure** Modenstruktur *f*
model/to modellieren
model Modell *n (z.B. in der Bildanalyse)*
~ **acquisition** Modellakquisition *f*
~**-based coding** modellbasierte Codierung *f*
~**-based feature extraction** modellgestützte Merkmalsextraktion *f*
~**-based image analysis** modellbasierte (modellgesteuerte) Bildanalyse *f*
~**-based image coding** modellbasierte Bildcodierung *f*
~**-based image processing** modellbasierte Bildverarbeitung *f*
~**-based object recognition** modellbasierte Objekterkennung *f*
~**-based pattern recognition** modellbasierte Mustererkennung *f*
~**-based segmentation** modellbasierte Segmentierung *f*
~**-based signal processing** modellbasierte Signalverarbeitung *f*
~**-based video coding** modellbasierte Videocodierung *f*
~**-based vision** modellbasiertes Sehen *n*
~ **building** 1. Modellbau *m*; 2. s. model generation
~ **coordinate system** Modellkoordinatensystem *n*
~ **effect** Modelltrick *m (Kinematografie)*
~ **feature** Modellmerkmal *n*
~**-free motion tracking** modellfreie Bewegungsverfolgung *f*
~ **generation** Modellbildung *f*, Modellerstellung *f*
~ **geometry** Modellgeometrie *f*
~ **hierarchy** Modellhierarchie *f*
~ **illumination** Modellbeleuchtung *f (Videomodellierung)*
~ **image** Modellbild *n*
~ **method** Modellmethode *f*

~ **object** Modellobjekt *n (Videomodellierung)*
~ **parameter** Modellparameter *m*
~ **projection** Modellprojektion *f*
~ **representation** Modellrepräsentation *f*
~ **scene** Modellszene *f (Videomodellierung)*
~ **shot** Modellaufnahme *f (Filmarbeit)*
~ **simplification** Modellvereinfachung *f*
~ **space** Modellraum *m*
~ **structure** Modellstruktur *f*
~ **texture** Modelltextur *f (Videomodellierung)*
modeling Modellierung *f*, Modellieren *n*
~ **coordinate system** Objektkoordinatensystem *n*
~ **error** Modellierungsfehler *m*
~ **flash** Blitzeinstelllicht *n*
~ **light** Modellierlicht *n*; Einstelllicht *n*, Pilotlicht *n*
~ **program** Modellierungsprogramm *n*, Modellierer *m*
~ **technique** Modellierungsverfahren *n*; Modelliermethode *f*; Modellierungstechnik *f*
~ **tool** Modellierungswerkzeug *n*
modelling s. modeling
modem Modem *n(m)*, Modulator-Demodulator *m (Signalverarbeitung)*
~ **board** Modemkarte *f*
~ **line** Modemleitung *f*
moderate wide-angle lens mittelbrennweitiges Weitwinkelobjektiv *n*
modified Cassegrain focus modifizierter Cassegrain-Fokus *m*
~ **Huffman code** modifizierter Huffman-Code *m (Faxübertragung)*
modular modular
~ **camera** Systemkamera *f*
~ **daylight film-handling system** dezentrales (modulares) Tageslichtsystem *n (Röntgenfotografie)*
modularity Modularität *f*
modulate/to modulieren
modulate [up]on/to aufmodulieren
modulated light moduliertes Licht *n*
~ **signal** moduliertes Signal *n*
modulation Modulation *f*
~ **analysis** Modulationsanalyse *f*
~ **characteristic** Modulationskennlinie *f*
~ **contrast** Modulationskontrast *m*
~ **current** Modulationsstrom *m*
~ **depth** Modulationstiefe *f*
~ **electrode** Steuerelektrode *f*
~ **factor** Modulationsgrad *m*
~ **frequency** Modulationsfrequenz *f*
~ **function** Wichtungsfunktion *f (Signalverarbeitung)*
~ **index** Modulationsindex *m*
~ **limit** Modulationsgrenze *f*
~ **matrix** Modulationsmatrix *f*
~ **modeling** Modulationsmodellierung *f*

modulation

~ **noise** Modulationsrauschen *n*
~ **rate** Modulationsgeschwindigkeit *f*
~ **scheme** Modulationsschema *n*; Modulationsart *f*; Modulationsverfahren *n*
~ **signal** Modulationssignal *n*
~ **technique** Modulationstechnik *f*
~ **transfer factor** Modulationsübertragungsfaktor *m*, Modulationsübertragungswert *m*; optischer Wirkungsgrad *m*
~ **transfer function** Modulationsübertragungsfunktion *f*, Modulationstransferfunktion *f*, Kontrastübertragungsfunktion *f*
~ **voltage** Modulationsspannung *f*
modulator Modulator *m*
~**-demodulator** Modem *n(m) Signalumformer)*
module Modul *n(m)*
moiré [effect] Moiré[muster] *n*, Moiré-Effekt *m*, Moiré-Erscheinung *f*, Flimmereffekt *m*
~ **fringes** Moiréstreifen *mpl*
~ **fringing** Moiréstörung *f*
~ **grating** Moirégitter *n*
~ **interference pattern** Moiré[muster] *n*
~ **interferometry** Moiré-Interferometrie *f*
~ **method** Moirétechnik *f*
~ **pattern effect** *s.* ~ [effect]
~ **sensor** Moirésensor *m*
~ **technique** Moirétechnik *f (z.B. in der Materialprüfung)*
moistening Feuchtung *f*, Druckformfeuchtung *f*
~ **system** Feuchtwerk *n*
mol *s.* mole
molar absorption coefficient molarer Absorptionskoeffizient *m*
~ **concentration, molarity** Stoffmengenkonzentration *f*, Molarität *f*
molded rubber plate Gummiklischee *n*, Gummistereo *n*, Gummi[duplikat]druckplatte *f*
mole Mol *n (SI-Einheit der Stoffmenge)*
molecular gas laser Molekülgaslaser *m*
~ **imaging** molekulare Bildgebung *f*
~ **mass** Molekülmasse *f*
~ **medicine** Molekularmedizin *f*
~ **modeling** Moleküldesign *n*
~ **motion** Molekularbewegung *f*
~ **spectroscopy** Molekülspektroskopie *f*
~ **visualization** molekulare Visualisierung *f*
molecule Molekül *n*
moment Moment *n (z.B. einer Funktion)*
~ **invariant** Momentinvariante *f*
~ **of exposure** Belichtungszeitpunkt *m*
MOMS filter *s.* multiscale filter
monaural monaural, monofon
~ **sound** Monoton *m*
~ **sound track** Monotonspur *f*, monaurale Tonspur *f*
monitor 1. Monitor *m*, Bildkontrollempfänger *m*; 2. Kontrollbildschirm *m*, Wiedergabebildschirm *m*; Bildschirm *m*, Monitor *m (s.a. unter display, screen)*
~ **alignment (calibration)** Bildschirmkalibrierung *f*, Monitorkalibrierung *f*, Monitoreinstellung *f*
~ **color** Bildschirmfarbe *f*
~ **display** Monitorbildröhre *f*
~ **engineer** Bildschirmtechniker *m*
~ **gamma** Bildröhrengamma *n*
~ **image** Monitorbild *n*; Bildschirmbild *n*
~ **noise** Monitorrauschen *n*
~ **performance** Monitorleistung *f*
~ **phosphor** Bildschirmphosphor *m*
~ **photodiode** Monitor-Fotodiode *f*
~ **pixel** Monitorpixel *n*
~ **pre-flash** Messblitz *m*
~ **resolution** Monitorauflösung *f*
~ **screen** *s.* monitor 2.
~ **setting** Monitoreinstellung *f (s.a. monitor alignment)*
~ **white** Monitorweiß *n*
monitoring system Überwachungssystem *n*
mono-Si *s.* monocristalline silicon
~ **sound track** *s.* monaural sound track
monobath developer[-fixer] Einbad-Fixierentwickler *m*
monocentric eyepiece monozentrisches Okular *n*
monochromacy Monochromasie *f*, Einfarbensehen *n*, totale Farbenblindheit *f*
monochromat Monochromat *m*
monochromatic monochrom[atisch], einfarbig *(s.a. unter monochrom)*
~ **aberration** monochromatische Aberration *f*, monochromatischer Abbildungsfehler *m*
~ **color** monochromatische Farbe *f*
~ **emulsion** monochromatische Emulsion *f*
~ **illumination** monochromatische Beleuchtung *f*
~ **laser** Monochromlaser *m*
~ **light** monochromatisches (einfarbiges) Licht *n*
~ **primary** Primärfarbe *f*, Spektralhauptfarbe *f*, Grundfarbe *f*; Elementarfarbe *f*; Normspektralfarbe *f*, Primärvalenz *f*, Primärfarbwert *m*
~ **radiation** monochromatische (monoenergetische) Strahlung *f*
~ **sensitometer** monochromatisches Sensitometer *n*
~ **sodium light** monochromatisches Natriumlicht *n (zur Dunkelraumbeleuchtung)*
~ **vision** Monochromasie *f*, Einfarbensehen *n*, totale Farbenblindheit *f*
~ **wave** monochromatische [elektromagnetische] Welle *f*

monochromaticity Monochromie f, Einfarbigkeit f
monochromatism s. monochromatic vision
monochromatization Monochromatisierung f
monochromator Monochromator m
monochrome 1. monochrom, einfarbig; schwarzweiß *(s.a. unter monochromatic; black-and-white)*; 2. s. ~ image
~ **broadcast** Schwarzweißsendung f, Schwarzweißübertragung f *(Fernsehen)*
~ **camera** Monochromkamera f, Schwarzweißkamera f
~ **color** monochromatische Farbe f
~ **developer** Monochromentwickler m
~ **device** Monochromgerät n
~ **electronic image scanner** Schwarzweiß-Scanner m
~ **emulsion** Monochromemulsion f
~ **film** Monochromfilm m
~ **image** monochromes (einfarbiges) Bild n, Monochrombild n
~ **image encoding** Schwarzweißbildcodierung f
~ **image processing** Monochrombildverarbeitung f
~ **imager** Schwarzweißbildgeber m
~ **laser printer** Schwarzweißlaserdrucker m
~ **monitor** Schwarzweißmonitor m
~ **photographic process** Schwarzweißprozess m
~ **photography** Schwarzweißfotografie f
~ **picture tube** Monochrombildröhre f, Schwarzweißbildröhre f
~ **print** Monochromabzug m, Schwarzweißabzug m
~ **printer** Schwarzweißdrucker m
~ **printing** Schwarzweißdruck m
~ **screen** Monochrombildschirm m, Schwarzweißbildschirm m
~ **signal** Schwarzweiß[video]signal n, Bildhelligkeitssignal n, Luminanzsignal n
~ **stock** Monochromfilmmaterial n
~ **television** Schwarzweißfernsehen n
~ **television camera** Schwarzweißfernsehkamera f
~ **television set** Schwarzweißfernsehgerät n
~ **transparency** Schwarzweißdia[positiv] n
~ **video** Schwarzweißvideo n
~ **video signal** Schwarzweiß[video]signal n, Bildhelligkeitssignal n
~ **viewfinder** Schwarzweißsucher m
~ **vision** Grauwertsehen n, Schwarzweißsehen n
monochromic s. monochromatic
monocomparator Monokomparator m *(Fernerkundung)*
monocomponent developer Einkomponententoner m *(Xerografie)*
~ **system** Einkomponentensystem n

monocrystal Einkristall m
monocrystalline einkristallin, monokristallin
~ **silicon** einkristallines (monokristallines) Silicium n
monocular monokular, einäugig
~ **field [of view]** monokulares Blickfeld n
~ **observation** einäugige Beobachtung f
~ **tube** monokularer Tubus m
~ **viewing (vision)** monokulares (einäugiges) Sehen n
~ **visual field** monokulares Gesichtsfeld n
monoculous s. monocular
monodisperse emulsion monodisperse Emulsion f
monoenergetic radiation monoenergetische (monochromatische) Strahlung f
~ **X-ray spectrum** monoenergetisches (monochromatisches) Röntgenspektrum n
monolithic mirror Massivspiegel m
monometal plate Monometallplatte f *(Offsetdruck)*
monometric projection monometrische Projektion f
monomial Mon[on]om n, eingliedriger Ausdruck m
monomode [optical] fiber Monomodefaser f, Einmodenfaser f
~ **step-index fiber** Monomode-Stufenindexfaser f
monopack Monopack n, Tripack-Film m *(Farbfotografie)*
monophonic monofon
~ **movie** Monotonfilm m
~ **signal** monofones Signal n
~ **sound** Monoton m
monopod Einbein[stativ] n, Monostativ n
monopulse secondary surveillance radar Monopuls-Sekundärradar n
monorail Führungsschiene f *(Fachkamera)*
~ **view camera** Optische-Bank-Kamera f, Kamera f auf optischer Bank
monoscope Monoskop n
monoscopic monoskopisch
monospaced dicktengleich *(Typografie)*
monostatic radar monostatisches Radar n
monotint s. monochrome 1.
monotone image s. monochrome image
~ **polygon** monotones Polygon n
monotonic function monotone Funktion f
~ **operator** monotoner Operator m
monotype composing machine Einzelbuchstabensetzmaschine f
~ **composition caster** Einzelbuchstaben-Setz- und -gießmaschine f
montage optischer Effekt (Trick) m *(Kinematografie)*
Monte Carlo method Monte-Carlo-Methode f *(Simulationsverfahren)*
~ **Carlo model** Monte-Carlo-Modell n

mood Stimmung *f*
~ **of light** Lichtstimmung *f*; Lichtcharakter *m*
moon illusion Mondtäuschung *f* *(Wahrnehmungsphänomen)*
MOPA laser *s.* master oscillator power amplifier laser
morning light Morgenlicht *n*
morph/to verformen; transformieren
morph Musterprimitiv *n*
morphing computeranimierter Gestaltwandel (Gestaltwechsel) *m*, Morphing *n*, Formen *n*, animierte Überblendung *f*
~ **animation effect** Morphingeffekt *m*
morphological algorithm morphologischer Algorithmus *m*
~ **analysis** Formanalyse *f*
~ **closing** Schließen *n*, Closing *n*, Closing-Operation *f* *(Binärbildverarbeitung)*
~ **edge detection** morphologische Kantendetektion *f*
~ **erosion** morphologische Erosion *f* *(Binärbildverarbeitung)*
~ **filter** morphologisches Filter *n*
~ **filtering** morphologische Filterung *f*
~ **gradient** morphologischer Gradient *m*
~ **image analysis** morphologische Bildanalyse *f*
~ **image processing** morphologische Bildverarbeitung *f*
~ **image segmentation** morphologische Bildsegmentierung *f*
~ **imaging** morphologische Bildgebung *f*
~ **operation** morphologische Operation *f*
~ **operator** morphologischer Operator *m*
~ **reconstruction** morphologische Rekonstruktion *f*
~ **skeleton** morphologisches Skelett *n*
~ **smoothing** morphologische Glättung *f*
morphology Morphologie *f*
morphometric image analysis morphometrische Bildanalyse *f*
~ **map** morphometrische Karte *f*
~ **parameter** morphometrischer Parameter *m*
morphometry Morphometrie *f*
MOS *s.* 1. metal oxide semiconductor; 2. mean opinion score; 3. mit out sound
~ **capacitor** MOS-Kondensator *m*
~ **footage** stumm gedrehtes Filmmaterial *n*
mosaic/to mosaikieren
mosaic Mosaik *n*; Mosaikbild *n*; Bildskizze *f* *(Fotogrammetrie)*
~ **construction** Mosaikbildung *f*
~ **detector array** Flächen[bild]sensor *m*
~ **filter** Mosaikfilter *n*
~ **filtering** Mosaikfilterung *f*
~ **image** Mosaikbild *n*
mosaicking 1. Mosaikeffekt *m*, digitale Blockbildung *f*; 2. Mosaikbildung *f* *(Luftbildkartierung)*

MOSFET *s.* metal oxide semiconductor field effect transistor
mosquito noise Kantenrauschen *n*
Mössbauer effect Mößbauer-Effekt *m*
most significant bit höchstwertiges Bit *n* *(sequentielle Kompression)*
mother wavelet Basis-Wavelet *n*, Mutter-Wavelet *n*
motherboard Hauptplatine *f*, Systemplatine *f*, Mutterplatine *f*, Computerplatine *f*
motif Motiv *n*; Motivobjekt *n* *(s.a. unter subject, object)*
motion Bewegung *f*
~-**adaptive code** bewegungsadaptiver Code *m*
~-**adaptive filter** bewegungsadaptives Filter *n*
~-**adaptive image processing** bewegungsadaptive Bildverarbeitung *f*
~-**adaptive interpolation** *s.* motion-dependent interpolation
~-**adaptive signal processing** bewegungsadaptive Signalverarbeitung *f*
~ **analysis** Bewegungsanalyse *f*
~ **analysis technique** Bewegungsanalysetechnik *f*
~ **artifact** Bewegungsartefakt *n*
~-**based segmentation** bewegungsbasierte Segmentierung *f*
~ **blur** Bewegungsunschärfe *f*
~-**blurred** bewegungsunscharf
~ **camera** *s.* motion-picture camera
~ **capture (capturing)** Bewegungserfassung *f*
~ **coding** Bewegungscodierung *f*
~-**compensated coding** bewegungskompensierende Codierung *f*
~-**compensated filtering** bewegungskompensierte Filterung *f*
~-**compensated interpolation** bewegungskompensierte Interpolation *f*
~-**compensated noise reduction** bewegungskompensierte Rauschreduktion *f*
~-**compensated prediction** bewegungskompensierte Prädiktion *f*
~-**compensated prediction error** bewegungskompensierter Prädiktionsfehler *m*
~-**compensated predictive coding** bewegungskompensierte Prädiktionscodierung *f*
~-**compensated predictor** bewegungskompensierter Prädiktor *m*
~-**compensated video compression** bewegungskompensierte Videokompression *f*
~ **compensation** Bewegungskompensation *f*
~ **compensation filter** Bewegungskompensationsfilter *n*

~ **component** Bewegungskomponente f
~ **constancy** Bewegungskonstanz f, Geschwindigkeitskonstanz f *(Wahrnehmungsphänomen)*
~ **control camera** Motion-Control-Kamera f, computergesteuerte Kamera f
~-**dependent interpolation** bewegungsadaptive Interpolation f *(schmalbandige Bildübertragung)*
~-**detecting neuron** bewegungserkennendes Neuron
~ **detection** Bewegungsdetektion f, Bewegungserkennung f
~-**detection filter** Bewegungsdetektionsfilter n
~ **detector** Bewegungsdetektor m, Bewegungsmelder m *(s.a. ~ sensor)*
~ **direction** Bewegungsrichtung f
~ **estimate** Bewegungsschätzwert m
~ **estimation** Bewegungsschätzung f
~ **estimation accuracy** Bewegungsschätzgenauigkeit f
~ **estimation algorithm** Bewegungsschätzalgorithmus m
~ **estimator** Bewegungsschätzer m
~ **field** Bewegungsfeld n, Geschwindigkeitsfeld n
~ **film** Kinefilm m
~ **gradient** Bewegungsgradient m
~ **icon** animiertes Icon n
~ **image compression** Bewegtbildkompression f
~ **information** Bewegungsinformation f
~ **interpolation** Bewegungsinterpolation f
~ **judder** Bewegungsruckeln n
~ **model** Bewegungsmodell n *(Bewegungsdetektion)*
~ **parallax** Bewegungsparallaxe f
~ **parameter** Bewegungsparameter m
~ **path** Bewegungspfad m
~ **perception** Bewegungswahrnehmung f
~ **perspective** Bewegungsperspektive f
~ **picture** 1. Laufbild n, Bewegtbild n, bewegtes Bild n; 2. Kinofilm m, Spielfilm m, Film m *(s.a. unter film, movie)*
~-**picture animation** Filmanimation f
~-**picture animation stand** Filmtricktisch m, Tricktisch m
~-**picture animation technique** Filmtrickverfahren n
~-**picture art** Filmkunst f
~-**picture camera** Laufbildkamera f, Film[aufnahme]kamera f, kinematografische Kamera f, Aufnahmekamera f; Kino[film]kamera f
~-**picture camera lens** Filmkameraobjektiv n
~-**picture camera technique** Kinokameratechnik f
~-**picture cameraman** Filmkameramann m, Spielfilmkameramann m, Kinokameramann m, Kameramann m
~-**picture coding** Bewegtbildcodierung f
~-**picture contact printer** Kontaktkopiermaschine f
~-**picture crew** Filmteam n, Filmstab m
~-**picture director** Filmregisseur m
~-**picture display** Bewegtbilddarstellung f
~-**picture duplicate** Duplikatfilm m
~-**picture duplicating process** Filmkopierverfahren n
~-**picture editing** Filmbearbeitung f, Filmschnitt m
~-**picture editing machine** Filmschneidemaschine f
~-**picture editing room** Filmschneideraum m, Schneideraum m, Schnittbearbeitungsraum m
~-**picture editor** Filmcutter m, Cutter m, Schnittmeister m, Filmeditor m
~-**picture engineer** Filmtechniker m; Kinotechniker m
~-**picture equipment** Filmausrüstung f; Kinotechnik f
~-**picture film** Kinefilm m, kinematografischer Film m
~-**picture film cleaner** Kinofilmreiniger m
~-**picture film exposure** Filmbelichtung f
~-**picture film format (gauge)** Kinefilmformat n; Kinofilmformat n
~-**picture film manufacture** Kinefilmherstellung f
~-**picture film processing** Kinofilmverarbeitung f
~-**picture film scanner** Filmgeber m, Laufbildgeber m, Filmtransfergerät n
~-**picture film stock** Kinefilmmaterial n, Filmaufnahmematerial n, Aufnahmefilmmaterial n
~-**picture format** Kinefilmformat n
~-**picture frame** Filmbild n, Filmfeld n, Feld n, Filmkader m, Bildkader m, Kader m
~-**picture image** filmisches Bild n, Kino[film]bild n, Filmbild n
~-**picture industry** Filmindustrie f, Kinofilmindustrie f, Filmbranche f, Filmwirtschaft f
~-**picture laboratory** Filmkopierwerk n, Kopierwerk n, Kopieranstalt f, Filmbearbeitungsbetrieb m, Filmlabor n
~-**picture lighting source** Filmlicht n
~-**picture machine** Filmmaschine f
~-**picture machine operator** s. ~ projectionist
~-**picture negative** Filmnegativ n
~-**picture negative film** Kinenegativfilm m
~-**picture optical effect** optischer Filmtrick m, filmischer Effekt m
~-**picture optical printing technique** Kopiertrickverfahren n
~-**picture photogrammetry** Kinefotogrammetrie f
~-**picture photographer** Filmfotograf m
~-**picture photography** Laufbildfotografie f, Kinefotografie f, Filmfotografie f, Kinematografie f

motion 244

~-**picture print film** Kopier[film]material *n*, Kopierfilm *m*, Kopier-Rohfilm *m*
~-**picture printer** Filmkopiermaschine *f*
~-**picture printing** Filmkopierung *f*
~-**picture printing technique** Filmkopierverfahren *n*
~-**picture processing laboratory** s. ~ laboratory
~-**picture production** Filmproduktion *f*; Kinofilmproduktion *f*
~-**picture production crew** Filmcrew *f*, Aufnahmestab *m*, Drehstab *m*
~-**picture production technique** Filmproduktionstechnik *f*
~-**picture projection** Laufbildprojektion *f*, Filmprojektion *f*; Kinoprojektion *f*
~-**picture projection objective** Kino[projektions]objektiv *n*
~-**picture projection reel** Wiedergabespule *f*
~-**picture projectionist** Filmvorführer *m*, Vorführer *m*, Filmoperateur *m*
~-**picture projector** Laufbildprojektor *m*, Filmprojektor *m*, Filmvorführgerät *n*, Laufbildwerfer *m*
~-**picture recording** Laufbildaufnahme *f*; Filmaufnahme *f*
~-**picture release print** Kinokopie *f*, Theaterkopie *f*, Vorführkopie *f*, vorführbereite (vorführfertige) Filmkopie *f*
~-**picture restoration** Filmrestaurierung *f*
~-**picture roll** Filmrolle *f*, Filmakt *m*, Akt *m*
~-**picture scene** Filmszene *f*
~-**picture science** Filmwissenschaft *f*, Filmkunde *f*, Filmologie *f*
~-**picture screen** Filmleinwand *f*
~-**picture screening** Filmvorführung *f*
~-**picture screenplay** Drehbuch *n*, Regiebuch *n*
~-**picture script** Filmskript *n*
~-**picture set** Filmset *m*, Set *m*; Filmkulisse *f*, Filmdekoration *f* (s.a. location)
~-**picture shot** Filmaufnahme *f*
~-**picture show[ing]** Filmvorführung *f*
~-**picture sound** Film[begleit]ton *m*
~-**picture sound dubbing** Filmvertonung *f*
~-**picture sound record[ing]** Filmtonaufnahme *f*, Filmtonaufzeichnung *f*
~-**picture sound reproduction** Tonfilmwiedergabe *f*
~-**picture sound track** Filmtonspur *f*, Soundtrack *m*
~-**picture special effect** Filmtrick *m*
~-**picture studio** Filmstudio *n*, Filmatelier *n*, Spielfilmatelier *n*
~-**picture subtitle** Filmuntertitel *m*, Fußtitel *m*
~-**picture technology** Kinotechnik *f*, Filmtechnik *f*
~-**picture theater** Lichtspielhaus *n*, Lichtspieltheater *n*, Filmtheater *n*, Kino *n*

~-**picture wide-screen process (system)** Breitbildverfahren *n*, Breitwand[film]verfahren *n*
~ **portrayal** Bewegungsdarstellung *f*
~ **prediction** Bewegungsprädiktion *f*
~ **record** Bewegungsaufnahme *f*
~ **rendering (rendition)** [computergrafische] Bewegungswiedergabe *f*
~ **representation** Bewegungsdarstellung *f*
~ **reproduction** Bewegungswiedergabe *f*
~ **resolution** Bewegungsauflösung *f*
~ **segmentation** Bewegungssegmentierung *f*
~ **sensor** Bewegungssensor *m*
~ **signal** Bewegungssignal *n*
~ **simulation** Bewegungssimulation *f*
~ **smear** Bewegungsunschärfe *f*
~ **study** Bewegungsstudie *f*
~ **tracking** Bewegungsverfolgung *f*
~ **trajectory** Bewegungstrajektorie *f*
~ **unsharpness** Bewegungsunschärfe *f*
~ **vector** Bewegungsvektor *m*
~ **vector coder** Bewegungsvektorcodierer *m*
~ **vector coding** Bewegungsvektorcodierung *f*
~ **vector estimation** Bewegungsvektorschätzung *f*
~ **vector field** Bewegungsvektorfeld *n*
~ **vector histogram** Bewegungsvektorhistogramm *n*
~ **video** Laufbildvideo *n*, Bewegtbildvideo *n*
~ **video camera** Video[film]kamera *f*
~ **video sequence** Bewegtbildfolge *f*, Bewegtbildsequenz *f*
motor drive Motorantrieb *m* (z.B. zum Filmweitertransport)
motorized-driven zoom flash head Motorzoomblitz *m*
~ **film advance** motorischer (motorisierter) Filmtransport *m*
~ **zoom** Motorzoomobjektiv *n*, motorisches (motorisiertes) Zoom *n*
mottle Wolkigkeit *f*, Perlen *n* (Offsetdruckschwierigkeit)
mottled image wolkiges Druckbild *n*
mottling s. mottle
mount/to 1. rahmen (z.B. Diapositive); 2. aufkleben, aufziehen (z.B. Fotos)
mount Montierung *f* (Teleskop)
~ **board** s. mounting board 1. und 2.
mountaintop observatory Höhenobservatorium *n*
mounting 1. Gitteraufstellung *f* (Gitterspektrografie); 2. s. mount
~ **board** 1. Fotokarton *m*; Aufziehkarton *m*; 2. Aufziehblock *m*; Montagebogen *m*, Montageunterlage *f*
~ **head** Anschlussgewinde *n* (Objektiv)
~ **machine** Rahmungsmaschine *f*
~ **of photographs** Aufziehen *n* von Fotos
~ **press** Klebepresse *f*

~ **ring** Anschlussring *m*
~ **spray** Sprühkleber *m*
mouse [PC-]Maus *f*, Computermaus *f*
~ **button** Maustaste *f*
~ **click** Mausklick *m*
~ **control** Maussteuerung *f*
~**-controlled cursor** mausgesteuerter Cursor *m*
~ **cursor** Mauszeiger *m*
~ **eye's view** extreme Untersicht *f*, Froschperspektive *f*
~ **mat (pad)** Mausunterlage *f*
~ **pointer** Mauszeiger *m*
movable letter, ~ type [character] bewegliche Letter *f*
move/to bewegen *(z.B. geometrische Elemente)*
movement adaptation Bewegungsanpassung *f*
~ **aftereffect** Bewegungsnacheffekt *m (Bewegungssehen)*
~ **blur** Bewegungsunschärfe *f*
~ **detector** Bewegungsmelder *m*, Bewegungsdetektor *m*
~ **unsharpness** Bewegungsunschärfe *f*
movie Kinofilm *m*; Spielfilm *m*, Film *m (s.a unter motion picture, film)*
~ **aspect ratio** Kinobildseitenverhältnis *n*
~ **audience** Kinopublikum *n*
~ **camera** Kino[film]kamera *f*, Filmkamera *f*
~ **camera objective** Filmkameraobjektiv *n*
~ **channel** Filmkanal *m (eines Fernsehsenders)*
~ **clip** Filmclip *m*, Filmausschnitt *m*
~ **copy** Spielfilmkopie *f*
~ **distribution** Filmverleih *m*, Kinoverleih *m*
~ **file format** Film-Datenformat *n*
~ **film** Kinefilm *m*, kinematografischer Film *m*
~ **footage** Kinofilmmaterial *n*
~ **frame** Kinobild *n*
~ **house** s. ~ theater
~ **lighting** Filmbeleuchtung *f*
~ **miniature** Miniaturdekoration *f*, Miniaturkulisse *f (Filmarbeit)*
~ **palace** Filmpalast *m*
~ **photography** Filmfotografie *f*, Kinofotografie *f*
~ **picture** Filmbild *n*, filmisches Bild *n*, Kinobild *n*
~ **poster** Filmplakat *n*
~ **program** Kinoprogramm *n*
~ **projection** Kinofilmprojektion *f*
~ **projector** Kinofilmprojektor *m*
~ **review room** Filmbewertungsraum *m*
~ **screen** Kinoleinwand *f*; Filmleinwand *f*
~ **set** Filmset *m(n)*, Set *m(n)*, Filmdekoration *f*
~ **shoot[ing]** Filmdreh *m*
~ **shot** Filmaufnahme *f*
~ **special-effects artist** Trick[film]spezialist *m*

~ **still** Filmstandbild *n*, Szenenfoto *n*, Standfoto *n*
~ **studio** Filmstudio *n*, Filmatelier *n*, Spielfilmatelier *n*
~ **theater** Filmtheater *n*, Kino *n*, Lichtspielhaus *n*, Lichtspieltheater *n*
~ **theater screen** Kinoleinwand *f*
~ **theater showing** Kino[film]vorführung *f*
~ **trailer** Filmtrailer *m*, Kinotrailer *m*, Trailer *m*
~ **video** Bewegtbildvideo *n*, Laufbildvideo *n*
moviedom, movies Filmwesen *n*; Filmindustrie *f*, Kinofilmindustrie *f*, Filmbranche *f*; Filmwirtschaft *f*
moviemaker Filmemacher *m*
moviemaking Filmemachen *n*
moving caption Laufschrift *f*, Rolltitel *m*
~**-coil microphone** Tauchspulenmikrofon *n*
~**-image coding** Bewegtbildcodierung *f*
~**-image communication** Bewegtbildkommunikation *f*
~**-image compression** Bewegtbildkompression *f*
~**-image digital storage** digitale Bewegtbildspeicherung *f*
~**-image encoder** Bewegtbildcodierer *m*
~**-image photography** Laufbildfotografie *f*
~**-image sequence** Bewegtbildfolge *f*, Bewegtbildsequenz *f*
~**-image transmission** Bewegtbildübermittlung *f*, Bewegtbildübertragung *f*
~ **optics** fliegende Optik *f*
~ **picture** Bewegtbild *n*, bewegtes Bild *n*, Laufbild *n*
Moving Picture Experts Group *ISO-Normierungsgremium zur Bildsignalverarbeitung*
moving-picture telecommunication Bewegtbildkommunikation *f*
~**-picture transmission** Laufbildübertragung *f*
~ **resolution** dynamische Auflösung *f*
~ **sequence** s. moving-image sequence
~**-target detection** Bewegtzieldetektion *f (Radar)*
~**-target detector** Bewegtzieldetektor *m*
~**-target indication** Bewegtzielanzeige *f*
~**-target indicator** Bewegtzielanzeiger *m*
MPEG s. Moving Pictures Experts Group
~ **compression (encoding)** MPEG-Kompression *f (von Videosequenzen)*
~ **standard** MPEG-Standard *m*
MQ developer Metol-Hydrochinon-Entwckler *m*
MR s. magnetic resonance
MR angiogram Magnetresonanzangiogramm *n*
MR image (slice) MRT-Bild *n*, Kernspinbild *n*, Kernspinaufnahme *f*, Kernspintomogramm *n*, Magnetresonanztomogramm *n*,

Magnetresonanzbild *n*,
Magnetresonanzaufnahme *f*
MR spectroscopic
magnetresonanzspektroskopisch
MRI *s.* magnetic resonance imaging
~ **acquisition** Kernspinaufnahme *f*
~ **machine** Magnetresonanzanlage *f*
~ **mammogram** Kernspinmammogramm *n*
~ **scanner** Magnetresonanztomograf *m*, Kernspintomograf *m*
MRS *s.* magnetic resonance spectroscopy
MSE *s.* mean square error
muddying Farbentsättigung *f*, Entsättigung *f*
muffled sound dumpfer Ton *m*
mug photography Fahndungsfotografie *f*
~ **shot** Fahndungsfoto *n*, Erkennungsfoto *n*, Fahndungsbild *n*; erkennungsdienstliche Personenaufnahme *f*
~ **shot database** Fahndungsdatei *f*
multi-access module Multi-Access-Modul *n*
~-**bladed shutter** Flügelblende f, Sektorenblende *f*, Umlaufblende *f*
~-**copy printing** Vielblattdruck *m*
~-**digit binary number** Binärwort *n*
~-**field measurement** Mehrfeld[belichtungsmessung *f*
~-**frame averaging** Mehrbildfeldmittelung *f*
~-**image processing** Mehrbildtechnik *f*, Mehrbildverfahren *n* *(Fotogrammetrie)*
~-**image screen** Mehrbildschirm *m*
~-**image slide-tape program** Multivisionsschau *f*
~-**mask enlarging easel** Vergrößerungskassette *f*, Vergrößerungsrahmen *m*; Kopierrahmen *m*
~-**pattern metering** Mehrfeld[belichtungs]messung *f*
~-**program flash** Multiprogrammblitz *m*
~-**user computer system** Mehrbenutzer-Betriebssystem *n*
~-**zone autofocus** Mehrfeld-Autofokus *m*
multiband camera Multispektralkamera *f*
~ **filter** Mehrbandfilter *n*
~ **image** *s.* multichannel image
multibeam autofocus mehrstrahliger Autofokus *m*
multicamera television production Mehrkameraproduktion *f*
multicarrier modulation Multiträgermodulation *f*
~ **signal** Multiträgersignal *n*
~ **system** Multiträgerverfahren *n*, Mehrträgermodulation *f* *(Signalübertragung)*
multichannel mehrkanalig
~ **amplifier** Mehrkanalverstärker *m*
~ **array** Mehrkanalanordnung *f* *(CCD-Technologie)*
~ **coding** Mehrkanalcodierung *f*

~ **filtering** Mehrkanalfilterung *f*
~ **image** Multispektralbild *n*, Mehrkanalbild *n*, multispektrales (mehrkanaliges) Bild *n*, vektorielles Eigenschaftsbild *n*
~ **magnetography** Mehrkanalmagnetografie *f*
~ **multiplier** Mikrokanalvervielfacher *m*
~ **multiplier plate** *s.* ~ plate
~ **plate** Mikrokanalplatte *f*, Mikrokanal-Elektronenvervielfacherplatte *f*, Kanalelektronenvervielfacherplatte *f*
~ **point operation** Mehrkanal-Punktoperation *f*, Mehrkomponenten-Punktoperation *f*
~ **receiver** Mehrkanalempfänger *m*
~ **signal** Mehrkanalsignal *n*
~ **sound** Mehrkanalton *m*
~ **spectrometer** Mehrkanalspektrometer *n*, Simultanspektrometer *n*
~ **SQUID system** SQUID-Vielkanalsystem *n*
~ **stereophony** Mehrkanalstereofonie *f*
~ **surround sound** Mehrkanal-Surroundton *m*
~ **television sound** Fernseh-Mehrkanalton *m*
~ **UV spectrophotometry** Mehrkanal-UV-Spektrofotometrie *f*
multichip camera Multichipkamera *f*
multicoated mehrfachvergütet, mehrschicht[en]vergütet
~ **lens** mehrschichtenvergütetes Objektiv *n*
multicoating Mehrfachvergütung *f*, Mehrschicht[en]vergütung *f*, mehrlagige Beschichtung *f*
multicolor mehrfarbig, vielfarbig, polychrom[atisch]
~ **display** Farbdisplay *n*, Computerfarbbildschirm *m*; Farbbildschirm *m*
~ **duplication** farbige Vervielfältigung *f*
~ **gravure printing** Mehrfarbentiefdruck *m*
~ **halftone image** Mehrfarben-Rasterbild *n*
~ **image** Mehrfarbenbild *n*
~ **photometry** Mehrfarbenfotometrie *f*
~ **press** Mehrfarbendruckmaschine *f*
~ **printer** Mehrfarbdrucker *m*
~ **printing** Mehrfarbendruck *m*, mehrfarbiger Druck *m*
~ **sheet-fed press** Mehrfarben-Bogendruckmaschine *f*
~ **web press** Mehrfarbentiefdruckrotationsmaschine *f*
multicolored mehrfarbig, vielfarbig, polychrom[atisch]
~ **image** vielfarbiges Bild *n*
~ **light** polychromatisches Licht *n*
~ **ribbon** Mehrfarbenband *n*
multicore Mehraderkabel *n*
multicrystal camera Multikristallkamera *f*, Autofluoroskop *n*
multideflection Mehrfachablenkung *f* *(z.B. eines Tintenstrahls)*

multidetector computed tomography
Multidetektor-Computertomografie f
~ **system** Multidetektorensystem n
multidimensional mehrdimensional
~ **coding** mehrdimensionale Codierung f
~ **convolution** mehrdimensionale Faltung f
(Binärbildverarbeitung)
~ **discrete Fourier transform**
mehrdimensionale (multidimensionale)
diskrete Fourier-Transformation f
~ **filter** mehrdimensionales Filter n
~ **filtering** mehrdimensionale Filterung f
~ **histogram** mehrdimensionales
Histogramm n
~ **image** mehrdimensionales Bild n
~ **image analysis** mehrdimensionale
Bildanalyse f
~ **image data** mehrdimensionale
(multidimensionale) Bilddaten pl
~ **image processing** multidimensionale
Bildverarbeitung f
~ **imaging** mehrdimensionale Abbildung f
~ **object** mehrdimensionales Objekt n
~ **prefiltering** mehrdimensionale
Vorfilterung f
~ **representation** mehrdimensionale
Darstellung f
~ **sampling** mehrdimensionale Abtastung f
~ **signal** mehrdimensionales Signal n
~ **signal processing** mehrdimensionale
Signalverarbeitung f
~ **space** mehrdimensionaler Raum m
~ **visualization** mehrdimensionale
Visualisierung f
multidimensionality Mehrdimensionalität f
multielement lens mehrlinsiges Objektiv n,
Mehrlinser m
~ **system** mehrlinsiges System n
multiexposure camera Bildserienkamera f
~ **photograph** mehrfachbelichtetes Foto n
multifeed Mehrfachspeisung f
(Satellitenempfang)
multiflash Mehrfachblitz m
~ **photography** Multiblitzfotografie f
multifocal multifokal
multiformat[ting] camera
Multiformatkamera f
multifractal Multifraktal n
multifrequency holography
Multifrequenzholografie f
~ **network** Mehrfrequenznetz n
multifunction board Multifunktionskarte f
~ **display** Multifunktionsmonitor m
~ **printer** Multifunktionsdrucker m,
Multifunktionsgerät n,
Fax-Scan-Kopier-Laserdrucker m,
Scandruckfaxkopierer m
~ **radar** Multifunktionsradar n
multigraded paper
Mehrgradationenpapier n
multihierarchical graph search
multihierarchische Graphsuche f

multilayer antireflection coating
[antireflex-]Mehrschichtvergütung f,
mehrlagige Beschichtung f
~ **artificial neural network**
mehrschichtiges künstliches neuronales
Netz n
~**-coated** mehrschicht[en]vergütet,
mehrfachvergütet
~**-coated mirror** mehrschichtvergüteter
Spiegel m
~ **coating** Mehrschicht[en]vergütung f,
mehrlagige Beschichtung f,
Mehrfachvergütung f
~ **color film** Mehrschichtenfarbfilm m
~ **film** Mehrschichtenfilm m
~ **polarizer** Mehrfachschichtpolarisator m
~ **toner image** Mehrschicht-Tonerbild n
multilayered mirror Mehrschichtenspiegel
m
~ **perceptron** mehrschichtiges Perzeptron
n *(Neuroinformatik)*
multilevel thresholding
Mehrschwellenverfahren n
(Punktoperation)
multimedia multimedial *(s.a. unter
mixed-media)*
~ Multimedia n
~ **application** Multimediaanwendung f,
Multimediaapplikation f
~ **application developer**
Multimediadesigner m
~**-based presentation**
Multimediapräsentation f
~ **card** Multimediakarte f
~ **cell phone** Multimedia-Handy n,
Foto-Handy n, Kamera-Handy n
~ **coding** Multimediacodierung f
~ **communications**
Multimediakommunikation f
~ **communications network**
Multimedianetz n, multimediales Netz n
~ **content** Multimediainhalt m
~ **data** Multimediadaten pl
~ **database** Multimediadatenbank f,
multimediale Datenbank f,
Multimediadatei f
~ **design** Multimediadesign n
~ **designer** Multimediadesigner m
~ **device** Multimediagerät n
~ **display** Multimediadisplay n
~ **document** Multimediadokument n,
multimediales Dokument n
~ **engineering** Multimediatechnik f
~ **field** Multimediabereich m,
Multimediasektor m
~ **file format** Multimediaformat n
~ **format file** Multimediadatei f
~ **home platform** System n für interaktive
Anwendungen
Multimedia Home Platform [standard]
MHP-Standard m *(ein offener
Digitalfernsehstandard)*
multimedia information retrieval service
Multimedia-Informationsabrufdienst m

multimedia 248

- ~ **interface** Multimediaschnittstelle *f*
- ~ **machine** Multimediamaschine *f*
- ~ **material** Multimediamaterial *n*
- ~ **messaging service** Bildversand *m* per Mobilfunk
- ~ **mode** Multimediamodus *m*
- ~ **object** Multimediaobjekt *n*, Medien[daten]objekt *n*
- ~ **offering** Multimediaangebot *n*
- ~ **operating system** Multimediabetriebssystem *n*
- ~ **PC (personal computer)** Multimediacomputer *m*, Multimedia-PC *m*
- ~ **presentation system** Multimediasystem *n*
- ~ **printer** Multimediadrucker *m*
- ~ **product** Multimediaprodukt *n*
- ~ **production** Multimediaproduktion *f*
- ~ **program** Multimediaprogramm *n*
- ~ **receiver** Multimediagerät *n*
- ~-**related** multimedial
- ~ **server** Multimedia-Server *m*
- ~ **service** Multimediadienst *m*, multimedialer Dienst *m*
- ~ **signal processing** Multimediasignalverarbeitung *f*
- ~ **slide show** Multimediaschau *f*; Diaüberblendschau *f*, Überblendschau *f*
- ~ **software** Multimediasoftware *f*
- ~ **standard** Multimediastandard *m*
- ~ **studio** Multimediastudio *n*
- ~ **system** Multimediasystem *n*
- ~ **technology** Multimediatechnik *f*
- ~ **television [set]** Multimediafernseher *m*
- ~ **terminal** Multimedia-Terminal *n*, Multimedia-Endgerät *n*, DVB-Empfänger *m*
- ~ **video processor** Multimedia-Videoprozessor *m*

multimetal plate metallische Mehrschichtplatte *f (Offsetdruck)*

multimirror telescope Mehrspiegelteleskop *n*

multimodal histogram multimodales Histogramm *n*

- ~ **image data** multimodale Bilddaten *pl*
- ~ **interaction** multimodale Interaktion *f*

multimodality Multimodalität *f*

multimode laser Multimodelaser *m*, Vielmodenlaser *m*

- ~ **optical fiber** Multimodefaser *f*
- ~ **step-index fiber** Multimode-Stufenindexfaser *f*

multinomial distribution Polynomverteilung *f*

multiorientation filter *s.* multiscale filter

multiparametric image data multiparametrische Bilddaten *pl*

multiparty videoconference Mehrparteien-Videokonferenz *f*

multipath echo Mehrwegeecho *n (Radar)*
- ~ **propagation** Mehrwegeausbreitung *f*

multiphoton spectroscopy Multiphotonenspektroskopie *f*

multipin connector mehrpoliger Stecker *m*

multiplanar multiplanar, mehrschichtig

- ~ **gradient echo** multiplanares Gradientenecho *n (Magnetresonanztomografie)*
- ~ **reconstruction** multiplanare Rekonstruktion *f*

multiple multipel, multiplex, mehrfach, vielfach

- ~ **access** Vielfachzugriff *m*
- ~ **accidental exposure** unbeabsichtigte (versehentliche) Mehrfachbelichtung *f*
- ~ **beam** Mehrfachbündel *n (Optik)*
- ~-**beam interference** Mehrstrahlinterferenz *f*, Vielstrahlinterferenz *f*
- ~ **camera operation** Mehrkameraproduktion *f (Fernsehen)*
- ~-**capture mode** Reihenbildschaltung *f*, Serienbildschaltung *f (Kamerafunktion)*
- ~ **carrier system** Multiträgerverfahren *n*, Mehrträgermodulation *f (Signalübertragung)*
- ~ **coating** Mehrfachvergütung *f*, Mehrschicht[en]vergütung *f*, mehrlagige Beschichtung *f*
- ~-**component lens** mehrgliedriges Objektiv *n*
- ~ **copy** Mehrfachkopie *f*
- ~ **diffraction** Mehrfachbeugung *f*
- ~ **echo** Mehrfachecho *n (Radar)*
- ~ **encoding** Mehrfachcodierung *f*, mehrstufige Codierung *f*
- ~ **exposure** Mehrfachbelichtung *f*; Mehrfachexposition *f*
- ~ **exposure procedure** Mehrfachbelichtungsverfahren *n*
- ~ **flash terminal** Multiblitzbuchse *f*
- ~ **image** Mehrfachbild *n*, Mehrfachaufnahme *f*
- ~ **media** *s.* multimedia
- ~ **media archive** Multimediaarchiv *n*, multimediales Archiv *n*
- ~ **neighborhood** mehrfache Nachbarschaft *f*
- ~-**order wave plate** Verzögerungsplatte *f* höherer Ordnung
- ~-**page printing** Mehrseitendruck *m*
- ~ **projection** Mehrfachprojektion *f*
- ~ **projector slide show** Diaüberblendschau *f*, Überblendschau *f*
- ~ **reflection** Mehrfachreflexion *f*, Vielfachreflexion *f*
- ~ **scatter[ing]** Vielfachstreuung *f*
- ~ **slice image** Mehrschichtaufnahme *f (Magnetresonanztomografie)*
- ~ **slice imaging** Mehrschichtaufnahme *f (Vorgang)*
- ~ **slide projector** Überblendprojektor *m*
- ~-**slit spectrometer** Vielfachspaltspektrometer *n*

~ **switch** Multischalter *m* (*Satellitenempfang*)
~-**track recording** Mehrspuraufzeichnung *f*
~-**track sound record** Mehrspur-Tonaufzeichnung *f*
multiplex/to multiplexen; gleichzeitig senden
multiplex 1. multiplex *(s.a.* multiple*)*; 2. *s.* ~ cinema
~ **cinema** Multiplex[kino] *n*, Kinozentrum *n*
~ **hologram** Multiplexhologramm *n*
~ **mode** Multiplexbetrieb *m*
~ **operation** Multiplexbetrieb *m*
~ **theater** *s.* ~ cinema
~ **transmission** Multiplexübertragung *f*
multiplexed analog components *ein Zeitmultiplexformat zur Codierung analoger Farbfernsehsignale*
~ **signal** Multiplexsignal *n*
multiplexer Multiplexer *m*, Mehrfachumschalter *m*
~ **hierarchy** Multiplexhierarchie *f*
multiplexing Multiplexbildung *f*, Multiplexen *n*, Multiplexierung *f*
~ **equipment** Multiplexeinrichtung *f*
~ **method (technique)** Multiplexverfahren *n*
multiplexor *s.* multiplexer
multiplicative noise multiplikatives Rauschen *n*
~ **scaling** multiplikative Skalierung *f*
multiplier phototube Foto[elektronen]vervielfacher *m*, Fotomultiplier *m*, Foto-Sekundärelektronenvervielfacher *m*, Elektronenvervielfacher *m*
multipoint videoconferencing Mehrparteien-Videokonferenz *f*
multiprojector large-image system Multiprojektor-Großbildsystem *n*
multiresolution Mehrfachauflösung *f*, Vielfachauflösung *f*
~ **analysis** Mehrfachauflösungsanalyse *f*
~ **filter** Mehrfachauflösungsfilter *n*
~ **pyramid** Mehrfachauflösungspyramide *f*
multirow detector CT machine Mehrzeilen-Computertograf *m*
multiscalar multiskalar
multiscale filter Multiskalenfilter *n* (*Mustererkennung*)
multisearch engine Metasuchmaschine *f*
multisection cassette Simultanschichtkassette *f* (*Röntgentechnik*)
multisensor processing Multisensorverarbeitung *f*
multisensoral data acquisition multisensorale Datenerfassung (Aufnahme) *f*
~ **method** Multisensoralverfahren *n* (*Bildkombination*)
multisensorial camera multisensorische Kamera *f*

multislice acquisition (imaging) Mehrschichtaufnahme *f* (*Magnetresonanztomografie*)
~ **X-ray CT scanner** Mehrschicht[-Spiral]-Computertomogra f *m*
multispectral multispektral
~ **analysis** Multispektralanalyse *f*
~ **camera** Multispektralkamera *f*
~ **classification** Multispektralklassifizierung *f*, multispektrale Klassifikation *f*
~ **data acquisition** Multispektralaufnahme *f*
~ **image** Multispektralbild *n*, Mehrkanalbild *n*, Multispektralfotografie *f*, multispektrales (mehrkanaliges) Bild *n*, vektorielles Eigenschaftsbild *n*
~ **image data** multispektrale Bilddaten *pl*
~ **image processing** multispektrale Bildverarbeitung *f*
~ **imaging** multispektrale Abbildung *f*
~ **photograph** *s.* ~ image
~ **photography** Multispektralfotografie *f*, multispektrale Fotografie *f*
~ **remote sensing** multispektrale Fernerkundung *f*
~ **scanner (scanning system)** Multispektralscanner *m*
~ **sensor** Multispektralsensor *m*, multispektraler Sensor *m*
~ **thresholding** multispektrale Schwellenwertbildung *f*
multistage vector quantization mehrstufige Vektorquantisierung *f*
multistandard equipment Multinormgerät *n*; Mehrnormenempfänger *m*
multistatic radar multistatisches Radar *n*
multistep image processing Mehrschrittbildverarbeitung *f*
multiswitch *s.* multiple switch
multisync [display], ~ monitor Mehrfrequenzbildschirm *m*, Multifrequenzmonitor *m*, Multiscan-Monitor *m*
multitemporal data acquisition multitemporale Aufnahme *f*
~ **image data** multitemporale Bilddaten *pl*
~ **method** Multitemporalverfahren *n* (*Bildkombination*)
multitrack mehrspurig
~ **audio** Mehrspur-Tontechnik *f*
~ **machine** Mehrspurbandmaschine *f*
~ **recording** Mehrspuraufzeichnung *f*
~ **tape** Mehrspurband *n*
~ **tape recorder** Mehrspur-Recorder *m*
multivariate Gaussian data multivariate Gauß-Daten *pl*
~ **image** multivariates Bild *n*
Munsell chroma Buntheit *f*, Chromatizität *f*
~ **color-order system, ~ system of color notation, ~ system of perceptual color** Munsell-Farb[ordnungs]system *n*, Munsell-System *n* [der Farbordnung]

Munsell

~ **color tree** Munsell-Farbbaum *m*
museum photographer Museumsfotograf *m*
music and effect track Internationales Tonband (Band) *n*, IT-Band *n*, IT-Fassung *f*, IT-Mischung *f (Filmsynchronisation)*
~ **track** Musikspur *f*; Musikband *n*
~ **video** Musikvideo *n*, Musikclip *m*
musical score Filmmusik *f*
mute 1. Stummschaltungsfunktion *f*, Stummtaste *f*; 2. Stummfilm *m*
~ **head** Bildbetrachter *m (Kinotechnik)*
~ **print** stumme Kopie *f*, Bildkopie *f (Kinematografie)*
mutual illumination gegenseitige Beleuchtung *f*
mux *s.* multiplexer
myelography Myelografie *f*, Rückenmarkröntgendarstellung *f*
myocardial infarct imaging Myokardszintigrafie *f*
~ **perfusion imaging** Myokardszintigrafie *f*
~ **perfusion study** Myokardperfusionsmessung *f (Einzelphotonenemissionstomografie)*
~ **scintigram** Myokardszintigramm *n*, Herzmuskelszintigramm *n*
myopia Myopie *f*, Kurzsichtigkeit *f*
myopic myop, kurzsichtig

N

n-ary encoding n-wertige Codierung f
nadir image Nadiraufnahme f *(Aerofotogrammetrie)*
naked eye unbewaffnetes Auge n
nano-scale imaging Nanobildgebung f
~-scale optics Nanooptik f
~-structuring technology Nanostrukturierungstechnologie f
nanodetector Nanodetektor m
nanoelectrics Nanoelektronik f
nanoimaging Nanobildgebung f
nanomechanics Nanomechanik f
nanometer Nanometer n(m), nm
nanophotonics Nanophotonik f
nanoscopic nanoskopisch
nanosecond Nanosekunde f, ns
nanostructure Nanostruktur f
nanotechnology Nano[verfahrens]technik f, Nanotechnologie f
naphthol coupler Naphtholkuppler m *(Farbfotografie)*
narcissus s. back reflection
narrow schmal[laufend], eng, unterschnitten *(Schriftauszeichnung)*
~-angle lens Schmalwinkelobjektiv n, schmalwinkliges Objektiv n
~-angle tomography Engwinkeltomografie f, Kleinwinkeltomografie f
~-bandwidth s. unter narrowband
~-beam geometry Schmalstrahlgeometrie f
~-field instrument Kleinfeldinstrument n *(Astrooptik)*
~-gauge cine film Schmalfilm m
~-line laser Schmalbandlaser m
narrowband channel Schmalbandkanal m
narrow-web paper Schmalbahnpapier n *(Druck)*
narrowband coating schmalbandige Beschichtung f
~ filter Schmalbandfilter n, schmalbandiges Filter n, Linienfilter n
~ filtering Schmalbandfilterung f
~ laser Schmalbandlaser m
~ medium Schmalbandiges Medium n
~ noise Schmalbandrauschen n
~ picture transmission schmalbandige Bildübertragung f
~ radiation schmalbandige Strahlung f
~ signal Schmalbandsignal n
~ television Schmalbandfernsehen n
National Television Standards (System) Committee US-dominierter Normenausschuss zur Fernseh- und Videosignalverarbeitung

natural binary code natürlicher Binärcode m
~ color naturgetreue (natürliche) Farbe f
~ color image Naturfarbenbild n
~ color system NCS-Modell n *(Farbordnungssystem)*
~ diaphragm natürliche Blende
~ image natürliches (reales) Bild n
~ light Naturlicht n, natürliches Licht n
~ paper Naturpapier n, ungestrichenes Papier n
~ radiation Eigenstrahlung f
~ resident s. cybercitizen
~ scene natürliche Szene f
~ vignetting natürliche Vignettierung f
nature photographer Naturfotograf m
~ photography Naturfotografie f
navigate/to navigieren
navigation Navigation f
~ key Steuertaste f *(Computer)*
~ radar Navigationsradar n
navigational aid Navigationshilfe f
~ tool Navigationswerkzeug n
ND filter s. neutral-density filter
Nd glass laser Nd-Glaslaser m, Nd-Laser m
Nd:YAG laser s. neodymium in yttrium-aluminum garnet laser
near-axis ray achsennaher (paraxialer) Strahl m, Paraxialstrahl m
~ distance Nahentfernung f
~-distance measurement Nahmessung f
~ field Nahfeld n *(Gaußsche Optik)*
~-field acoustic holography [akustische] Nahfeldholografie f
~-field diffraction Nahfeldbeugung f, Fresnel-Beugung f, Fresnelsche Beugung f
~-field focusing Nahfeldfokussierung f
~-field hologram Nahfeldhologramm n
~-field optical scanning microscope optisches Nahfeld-Rastermikroskop n
~-field optics Nahfeldoptik f
~-field scanning Nahfeldabtastung f
~-field scanning optical microscopy optische Nahfeldmikroskopie f, nahfeldoptische Mikroskopie f
~-field thermal microscope Raster-Wärme-Mikroskop n
~ focus Nahfokus m
~ focusing limit Nahfokussiergrenze f, Nah[einstell]grenze f, kürzeste Einstellentfernung f
~-infrared nahes (fotografisches) Infrarot n
~-infrared light infrarotnahes Licht n
~-infrared photography Fehlfarbenfotografie f, Infrarotreflektografie f
~-infrared radiation infrarotnahe Strahlung f
~-infrared spectrum infrarotnahes Spektrum n
~ limit s. ~ point
~-lossless coding nahezu verlustlose Codierung f

near 252

~-**photographic image quality** fotorealistische (fotoähnliche) Bildqualität *f*
~-**photographic printer** fotorealistischer Drucker *m*
~-**photographic quality image** fotoähnliches Bild *n*
~-**photographic representation** fotorealistische Darstellung *f*
~ **photography** Nah[bereichs]fotografie *f*
~ **point** Akkommodationsnahpunkt *m*, Nah[abstands]punkt *m (Optik)*
~-**point distance** Nahpunktabstand *m*
~-**real-time** echtzeitnah
~-**to-lossless compression** verlustarme Kompression *f*
~ **video on demand** Form der zeitversetzten Programmverteilung an Kabel- oder Satellitenhaushalte
~ **vision** Nahsehen *n*
nearest-neighbor classifier Nächste[r]-Nachbar-Klassifikator *m*
~-**neighbor decision rule** Nächste[r]-Nachbar-Regel *f*
~-**neighbor distance** Nächste[r]-Nachbar-Abstand *m*
~-**neighbor filter** Nächste[r]-Nachbar-Filter *n*, Dirac-Filter *n*, Impulsfilter *n*
~-**neighbor gray-level interpolation** Nächste[r]-Nachbar-Interpolation *f*
~-**neighbor multichannel filter** Nächste[r]-Nachbar-Multikanalfilter *n*
~-**neighbor pattern classification** Nächste[r]-Nachbar-Klassifikation *f*
~-**neighbor problem** Nächste[r]-Nachbar-Problem *n*
~-**neighbor query** Nachbarschaftsfrage *f (Computergrafik)*
~-**neighbor search[ing]** Nächste-Nachbar-Suche *f*
nearsighted kurzsichtig, myop
nearsightedness Kurzsichtigkeit *f*, Myopie *f*
nebular filter Nebelfilter *n (Astrofotografie)*
neck Konus *m (Drucktype)*
~ **strap** Tragegurt *m*, Trageriemen *m*
needle printer Nadeldrucker *m*
negation Bildumkehr[ung] *f*
negative [fotografisches] Negativ *n*, Fotonegativ *n*, Gegenbild *n*
~-**acting film** Negativfilm *m*
~ **carrier** Negativträger *m*, Negativhalter *m*, Negativbühne *f (Vergrößerungsgerät)*
~ **color film** Farbnegativfilm *m*
~ **color material** Color-Negativmaterial *n*
~ **color photography** Negativ-Farbfotografie *f*
~ **color processing** Farbnegativtechnik *f*, Farbnegativverarbeitung *f*
~ **coma** Außenkoma *f (Optik)*
~ **contrast** Negativkontrast *m*; Schwärzungsumfang *m*
~ **cut list** Negativschnittliste *f*
~ **cutter** Negativcutter *m*

~ **cutting** Negativschnitt *m*, Negativmontage *f*, Negativabziehen *n (Filmbearbeitung)*
~ **defect** Negativfehler *m*
~ **density** Negativdichte *f*, Negativschwärzung *f*; Schleierdichte *f*
~ **developer** Negativentwickler *m*; Filmentwickler *m*
~ **development** Negativentwicklung *f*
~ **distortion** Kissenverzeichnung *f*, Kissenverzerrung *f*, kissenförmige Verzeichnung *f*, Kissenfehler *m (Abbildungsfehler)*
~ **emulsion** Negativemulsion *f*
~ **eyepiece** Negativokular *n*, Huygenssches Okular *n*, Huygens-Okular *n*, Einheitsokular *n*
~ **file binder** Negativvordner *m*
~ **filing page** Negativ-Ablageblatt *n*, Negativtasche *f*, Negativhülle *f*
~ **film** Negativfilm *m*
~ **fixer** Negativfixierer *m*
~ **footage** *s.* ~ **material**
~ **grader** Filmlichtbestimmer *m*, Farblichtbestimmer *m*, Farbtechniker *m*; Lichtbestimmer *m*
~ **grading** Negativ-Lichtbestimmung *f (Filmkopierung)*
~ **holder** Negativhalter *m*, Negativträger *m*, Negativbühne *f (Vergrößerungsgerät)*
~ **image** Negativbild *n*
~ **lens** negative (konkave) Linse *f*, Negativlinse *f*, Konkavlinse *f*, Zerstreuungslinse *f*
~ **material** [fotografisches] Negativmaterial *n*, Aufnahmematerial *n*
~ **meniscus lens** negativer Meniskus *m*
~ **modulation** Negativmodulation *f (Fernsehen)*
~ **motion-picture film,** ~ **movie film** Kinenegativfilm *m*
~ **number** Negativ-Fußnummer *f (Kinefilm)*
~ **original** Originalnegativ *n*
~ **parallax** negative Parallaxe *f*
~ **perf[oration]** Negativperforation *f*, Bell-Howell-Perforation *f (von Kinefilm)*
~ **photograph** *s.* negative
~ **photographic material** *s.* ~ **material**
~ **pictorial film** Bildnegativfilm *m*
~ **plate** Negativplatte *f*, Glasnegativ *n*
~ **pocket** *s.* ~ **filing page**
~-**positive material** Negativ-Positiv-Material *n*
~-**positive photographic process** [fotografisches] Negativ-Positiv-Verfahren *n*
~-**positive system** Umkehrsystem *n (Fotografie)*
~ **printing material** Negativkopiermaterial *n*
~ **processing** Negativverarbeitung *f*
~ **raw stock** Negativ-Rohfilmmaterial *n*

~ **rear element** zerstreuendes Hinterglied n; Telenegativ n
~ **retouching** Negativretusche f
~ **scanner** Negativscanner m
~ **scratch** Negativschramme f
~ **size** Negativformat m
~ **sleeve** Negativstreifentasche f, Streifentasche f, Hüllenstreifen m
~ **sound film** Tonnegativfilm m
~ **stage** Negativbühne f (s.a. ~ holder)
~ **staining** Negativkontrastierung f (Elektronenmikroskopie)
~ **storage sheet** Negativ-Ablageblatt n, Negativtasche f, Negativhülle f
~ **technique** Negativtechnik f
~ **timing** Negativ-Lichtbestimmung f (Filmkopierung)
~-**to-negative process** [farbfotografisches] Negativ-Negativ-Verfahren n
~-**type material** Negativmaterial m
~-**working emulsion** Negativemulsion f
~-**working paper** Negativpapier n
~-**working photoresist** negativer Fotolack m, Negativlack m
~-**working process** [fotografischer] Negativprozess m, Negativverfahren n
negatron Negat[r]on n (s.a. electron)
neighbor pixel Nachbarpixel n, Nachbarbildpunkt m
neighborhood Nachbarschaft f (z.B. von Bildpunkten)
~ **analysis** Nachbarschaftsanalyse f
~ **graph** Nachbarschaftsgraph m, Adjazenzgraph m
~ **operation** Nachbarschaftsoperation f, Koppelfeldprozess m
~ **operator** Nachbarschaftsoperator m
~ **process** s. ~ operation
~ **relation** Nachbarschaftsrelation f
~ **structure** Nachbarschaftsstruktur f
nematic liquid crystal nematischer Flüssigkristall m
~ **phase** nematische Phase f (Flüssigkristall)
neocognitron Neocognitron n (Mustererkennung)
neodymium glass laser Nd-Glaslaser m, Nd-Laser m
~ **in yttrium-aluminum garnet laser** Neodym-YAG-Laser m
~-**type laser** Neodym[ium]laser m
neon [glow] lamp Neonlampe f
~ **light** Neonlicht n
nephrogram Nephrogramm n, Nierenröntgendarstellung f
nephrography Nephrografie f, Nierenröntgendarstellung f
nerve cell Nervenzelle f, Neuron n
~ **ganglion** Nervenknoten m, Ganglion n m
~ **impulse** Aktionspotential n (Neuroinformatik)
nest/to einstecken, sammeln (Falzbogen)

net 1. Netz n (s.a. unter network); 2. Diffusionsmaterial n; Tüll m (zur Lichtbeeinflussung); 3. s. Internet
~ **bit rate** Nettobitrate f, Nutzbitrate f
~ **magnetization** Nettomagnetisierung f (Magnetresonanzbildgebung)
~ **model** Netzmodell n, Gittermodell n, Drahtgittermodell n (Computergrafik)
network/to vernetzen
network Netzwerk n
~ **access** Netzwerkanbindung f, Netzwerkeinbindung f
~ **architecture** Netzwerkarchitektur f
~ **bandwidth** Netzbandbreite f
~ **computer** Netzwerkrechner m
~-**independent protocol** netzunabhängiges Protokoll n (Digitalfernsehen)
~ **interface** Netz[werk]schnittstelle f
~ **layer** Vermittlungsschicht f (Datenübertragung)
~ **node** Netzknoten m
~ **operator** Netz[werk]betreiber m
~ **printer** Netzwerkdrucker m
~ **topology** Netzwerktopologie f
~ **transmission** Netzübertragung f
networkability Vernetzbarkeit f; Netzwerkfähigkeit f
networkable vernetzbar; netzwerkfähig
networked environment vernetzte Umgebung f
~ **multimedia** vernetztes Multimedia n
~ **printer** vernetzter Drucker m
neural adaptation neuronale Adaptation f
~ **cell** Nervenzelle f, Neuron n
~ **classifier** neuronaler Klassifikator m
~ **computer** Neurocomputer m
~ **excitation** neuronale Erregung f
~ **filter** neuronales Filter n
~ **memory** neuronales Gedächtnis n
~-**net architecture** neuronale Netzwerkarchitektur f
~ **net[work]** neuronales Netz (System) n, Neuronennetz n, konnektionistisches System (Modell) n
~ **resolution** neuronale Auflösung f
~ **signal** neuronales Signal n
neuroangiography Neuroangiografie f
neuroimaging zerebrale Bildgebung f
neuroinformatics Neuroinformatik f
neuromorphic system s. neural net[work]
neuron Neuron n, Nervenzelle f; Elementareinheit f (Neuroinformatik)
~ **model** neuronales Modell n
neurone s. neuron
neurophysiologic[al] neurophysiologisch
neurophysiology Neurophysiologie f
neutral 1. [chemisch] neutral; 2. unbunt, achromatisch (Kolorimetrie)
~ **beam splitting coating** Neutralteilerschicht f
~ **black** neutralschwarz
~ **color** unbunte (achromatische) Farbe f, graue Farbe f

neutral

~ **density** Neutraldichte f
~-**density card** Graufeld n
~-**density filter** Neutral[dichte]filter n, Neutralgraufilter n, Graufilter n, Dichtefilter n, ND-Filter n, Lichtreduktionsfilter n, Helligkeitskorrekturfilter n
~-**density filtration** Neutralfilterung f
~ **density graduated filter** Neutraldichte-Verlauffilter n
~-**density step wedge** Grau[stufen]keil m, Stufengraukeil m, Grauskala f
~ **filter** s. neutral-density filter
~ **glass** Neutralglas n, Grauglas n, Panglas n
~ **gray** neutralgrau
~-**gray wedge** Neutralgraukeil m (Sensitometrie)
~ **pH paper** säurefreies Papier n
~ **test card** Graukarte f
~ **tone** Neutralton m; Grautonwert m
~ **white** neutralweiß
neutralization Neutralisation f
neutralizer Neutralisator m
neutrino Neutrino n
~ **spectroscopy** Neutrinospektroskopie f
~ **telescope** Neutrinoteleskop n
neutron Neutron n
~ **absorption** Neutronenabsorption f
~ **activation autoradiography** Neutronenaktivierungsautoradiografie f
~ **beam** Neutronenstrahl m
~ **diffraction** Neutronenbeugung f
~ **radiograph (radiographic image)** Neutronenradiogramm n
~ **radiographic** neutronenradiografisch
~ **radiography** Neutronenradiografie f
~ **scintillator** Neutronenszintillator m
~ **tomogram** Neutronentomogramm n
~ **tomographic** neutronentomografisch
~ **tomography** Neutronentomografie f
new candle s. candela
news broadcast Nachrichtensendung f
~ **camera** Reportagekamera f
~ **coverage** Berichterstattung f
~ **photo[graph]** Zeitungsfoto n, Pressefoto n
~ **photography** Zeitungsfotografie f, Pressefotografie f
~ **video** Nachrichtenvideo n
newscast Nachrichtensendung f
newspaper advertising insert Werbebeilage f, Prospektbeilage f
~ **clipping** Zeitungsausschnitt m
~ **halftone image, ~ illustration** Zeitungsbild n
~ **page** Zeitungsseite f
~ **photo editor** Zeitungsbildredakteur m
~ **photographer** Zeitungsfotograf m, Pressefotograf m, Fotoreporter m, Bildreporter m, Bildberichterstatter m
~ **press** Zeitungsdruckmaschine f
~ **print[ing]** Zeitungsdruck m
~ **supplement** Zeitungsbeilage f

newsprint Zeitungs[druck]papier n
~ **ink** Zeitungsdruckfarbe f
newsreel Wochenschau f
Newton finder Newton-Sucher m
Newton's rings Newton-Ringe mpl, Newtonsche Ringe mpl, kreisförmige Fizeau-Linien fpl (Interferenzmuster)
Newtonian lens equation Newtonsche Linsengleichung (Abbildungsgleichung) f
~ **reflector (telescope)** Newton-Teleskop n
nibble Nibble n, Halbbyte n
NiCad battery s. nickel-cadmium battery
nick Signatur f (Drucktype)
nickel-cadmium battery Nickel-Cadmium-Batterie f
~ **metal hydride battery** Nickel-Metallhydrid-Akku[mulator] m, Ni-MH-Akku m
nickelodeon Nickelodeon n (frühe Kinematografie)
Nicol [prism] Nicol[-Prisma] n, Nicolsches Prisma n
night blindness Nachtblindheit f, Nyktalopie f
~ **exposure** Nacht[sicht]aufnahme f
~ **exterior** Außenaufnahme f bei Nacht
~ **interior** Innenaufnahme f bei Nacht
~ **light** Nachtlicht n
~ **photograph** Nachtaufnahme f
~ **photography** Nachtfotografie f
~ **portrait modus** Nachtporträtmodus m
~ **sequence** Nachtszene f, Nachtszenerie f (Kinematografie)
~ **shot** Nacht[sicht]aufnahme f
~ **vision** Nachtsehen n, Dunkelsehen n, skotopisches (dunkeladaptiertes) Sehen n, Stäbchensehen n
~ **vision device** Nachtsichtgerät n
~ **vision equipment** Nachtsichttechnik f
~ **vision goggles** Nachtsichtbrille f
nightscope Nachtsichtgerät n
nighttime aerial photograph Luft-Nachtaufnahme f
nine-track tape Neunspurband n
Nipkow disk Nipkow-Scheibe f, Nipkow-Spirallochscheibe f (mechanische Bildabtastung)
nit Nit n, Candela f pro Quadratmeter (SI-Einheit der Leuchtdichte)
nitrate[-based] film Nitrofilm m, Nitratfilm m, Cellulosenitratfilm m
nitric acid Salpetersäure f
nitrocellulose Nitratcellulose f, Nitrocellulose f, Cellulosenitrat f
nitrogen burst agitation Stickstoffagitation f (Fotoverarbeitung)
~ **laser** Stickstofflaser m
NMR s. nuclear magnetic resonance
~ **imaging** Magnetresonanztomografie f, Kernspintomografie f; Kernspinresonanzabbildung f
~ **signal** Kernresonanzsignal n
no bias mode s. photovoltaic mode

no-parallax focusing parallaxenfreie Fokussierung *f*
noble-gas halide Edelgashalogenid *n*
nodal plane Knotenpunktebene *f (Optik)*
~ **point** Knotenpunkt *m*, Nodalpunkt *m*, Nodus *m*
~ **point separation** Hauptpunktabstand *m*
~ **point shift** Knotenpunktversatz *m*
~ **space** Hauptpunktabstand *m*
~ **vector** Knotenvektor *m*, Trägervektor *m* *(Bewegungsschätzung; B-Spline-Technik)*
nodding-beam radar Nickradar *n*
node Knoten *m (Graphentheorie, Computergrafik)*
noise/to rauschen; verrauschen *(z.B. ein Bild)*
noise Rauschen *n*, Geräusch *n*, Störgeräusch *n*; Fremdspannung *f*; Streuechos *npl (Radar; Sonografie)*
~ **accumulation** Rauschakkumulation *f*
~**-adaptive** rauschadaptiv
~ **amplification** Rauschverstärkung *f*
~ **amplitude** Rauschamplitude *f*, Störamplitude *f*
~ **attenuation** Rauschdämpfung *f*
~ **bandwidth** Rauschbandbreite *f*
~ **bump** Rauscheinbruch *m*
~ **cancel[l]ing**, ~ **cleaning** Rauschbefreiung *f*, Störbefreiung *f*, Rauschbeseitigung *f*, Entrauschung *f*
~ **coefficient** Rauschkoeffizient *m*
~ **component** Rauschanteil *m*
~ **content** Rauschgehalt *m*
~ **contribution (contributor)** Rauschbeitrag *m*
~**-corrupted image** verrauschtes Bild *n*
~ **current** Rauschstrom *m*
~ **current source** Rauschstromquelle *f*
~ **density** Rauschdichte *f*
~ **disturbance** Rauschstörung *f*
~ **effect** Rauscheffekt *m*
~ **electron** Rauschelektron *n*
~ **environment** Rauschumgebung *f*
~ **equalization** Rauschglättung *f*
~**-equivalent angle** Winkelrauschen *n (Spiegeloptik)*
~**-equivalent bandwidth** rauschäquivalente Bandbreite *f*
~**-equivalent power** äquivalente Rauschleistung *f*, Rauschäquivalentleistung *f*; rauschäquivalente Strahlungsleistung *f*
~**-equivalent power** rauschäquivalente Leistung *f*, Eigenrauschleistungsdichte *f*
~**-equivalent quantum** rauschäquivalentes Quant *n*
~**-equivalent temperature difference** rauschäquivalente Temperaturdifferenz *f (Wärmebildgebung)*
~ **error** Rauschfehler *m*
~ **factor** Rauschfaktor *m*
~ **feature** Rauschmerkmal *n*
~ **figure** Rauschzahl *f*, Rauschmaß *n*

~ **filter** Rausch[bewertungs]filter *n*
~ **filtering** Rauschfilterung *f*
~ **floor** Grundrauschpegel *m*
~**-free** unverrauscht, rauschfrei
~**-free image** unverrauschtes (rauschfreies) Bild *n*
~**-free medium** rauschfreies Medium *n*
~ **frequency** Rauschfrequenz *f*
~ **gain** Rauschverstärkung *f*
~ **gate** Störgeräuschregler *m*
~ **generator** Rauschgenerator *m (Radar)*
~ **gray-level value** Rauschgrauwert *m*
~ **immunity** Rauschunempfindlichkeit *f*; Rauschfreiheit *f*
~ **impulse** Rauschimpuls *m*, Rauschsignal *n*
~ **insensitivity** Rauschunempfindlichkeit *f*
~ **interference pattern** Rauschmuster *n*
~ **jitter** unkorrelierter Jitter *m*
~ **level** Rauschpegel *m*, Rauschniveau *n*, Störsignalpegel *m*; Geräuschpegel *m*
~**-like** rauschähnlich *(Signal)*
~ **limit** Rauschgrenze *f*
~**-limited** rauschbegrenzt
~ **limiter** Rauschbegrenzer *m*
~ **matrix** Rauschmatrix *f*
~ **measurement** Rauschmessung *f*
~ **meter** Psophometer *n*
~ **model** Rauschmodell *n*
~ **parameter** Rauschparameter *m*
~ **part** Rauschanteil *m*
~ **pattern** Rauschmuster *n*
~ **peak** Rauschspitze *f*
~ **performance** Rauschleistung *f*, Störleistung *f*; Rauschverhalten *n*
~ **pixel** Rauschpixel *n*
~ **point** Rauschpunkt *m*
~ **power** Rauschleistung *f*, Störleistung *f*
~ **power [spectral] density** Rauschleistungsdichte *f*
~ **power spectrum** Rauschleistungsspektrum *m*, Wiener-Spektrum *n*
~ **process** Rauschvorgang *m*
~ **propagation** Rauschausbreitung *f*
~ **reducer** Rauschminderer *m*
~ **reduction** Rauschreduktion *f*, Rauschreduzierung *f*, Rausch[ver]minderung *f (s.a. ~ removal)*
~ **reduction algorithm** Rauschreduktionsalgorithmus *m*
~ **reduction filter** Rauschreduktionsfilter *n*
~ **reduction filtering** Rauschreduktionsfilterung *f*
~ **reduction system** Rauschreduktionssystem *n*
~ **removal** Rauschbefreiung *f*, Störbefreiung *f*, Rauschbeseitigung *f*, Entrauschung *f*
~**-resistant** rauschunempfindlich
~**-sensitive** rauschempfindlich
~ **sensitivity** Rauschempfindlichkeit *f*
~ **signal** Rauschsignal *n*
~ **signature** Rauschsignatur *f*

noise

- ~ **smoothing** Rauschglättung *f*
- ~ **smoothing filter** Rauschglättungsfilter *n*
- ~ **source** Rausch[stör]quelle *f*
- ~ **spectrum** Rauschspektrum *n*
- ~ **spike** Rauschspitze *f*
- ~ **suppression** Rauschunterdrückung *f*, Stör[signal]unterdrückung *f*; Bildrauschunterdrückung *f*
- ~ **temperature** Rauschtemperatur *f*
- ~ **threshold** Rauschschwelle *f* *(eines Empfängers)*
- ~ **transfer (transmission)** Rauschübertragung *f*
- ~ **value** Rauschwert *m*
- ~ **variance** Rauschvarianz *f*
- ~ **voltage** Rauschspannung *f*

noised *s.* noisy
noiseless camera geräuschlose Kamera *f*
- ~ **image** unverrauschtes (rauschfreies) Bild *n*
- ~ **source coding theorem** rauschfreies Codierungstheorem *n*

noiselessness Rauscharmut *f*
noisy verrauscht, rauschbehaftet
- ~ **[channel] coding theorem** rauschbehaftetes Codierungstheorem *n*
- ~ **edge** verrauschte Kante *f*
- ~ **image** verrauschtes Bild *n*
- ~ **signal** verrauschtes Signal *n*

Nomarski [interference] microscope Nomarski-Mikroskop *n*
- ~ **[interference] microscopy** Nomarski-Mikroskopie *f*, Differentialinterferenzkontrastmikroskopie *f*

nominal [anode] input power Eingangsnennleistung *f (Röntgenröhre)*
- ~ **scale** Skale *f*, Skala *f*

nomogram, nomograph Nomogramm *n*
non-emulsion side Blankseite *f*, Glanzseite *f*, Filmrückseite *f*, emulsionsabgewandte Seite *f (Filmmaterial)*
~-Euclidean geometry nichteuklidische Geometrie *f*
~-frequency-selective RF pulse harter Hochfrequenzimpuls *m*
~-image-forming light nichtabbildendes Licht *n*
~-return-to-zero signal NRZ-Signal *n (Digitalsignalverarbeitung)*
- ~ **return zero inverse code** NRZI-Code *m (digitale Signalspeicherung)*

~-screen [X-ray] film folienloser Film *m*
~-self-luminous nichtselbstleuchtend
~-self-luminous source (surface) Nichtselbstleuchter *m*, Fremdleuchter *m*
nonachromatic *s.* chromatic
nonactinic nichtaktinisch *(Strahlung)*
nonadaptive transform coding nichtadaptive Transformationscodierung *f*
noncausal filter nichtkausales Filter *n*
noncemented ungekittet, unverkittet *(Linsen)*

noncircled take Nichtkopierer *m (Filmbearbeitung)*
noncoherent inkohärent
noncolor material Schwarzweißmaterial *n*
noncompressed image unkomprimiertes Bild *n*
nonconducting medium dielektrisches Medium *n*
noncontact atomic force microscopy Nicht-Kontakt-Rasterkraftmikroskopie *f*
- ~ **inspection** berührungslose Prüfung *f*
- ~ **measurement** berührungslose Messung *f*

noncontextual segmentation kontextunabhängige Segmentierung *f*
noncontinuous spectrum diskontinuierliches (diskretes) Spektrum *n*
noncurl backing (coat) Antiroll[rück]schicht *f*, Gelatinerückguss *m*, Anticurl-Schicht *f*, NC-Schicht *f (Fotofilm)*
nondestructive evaluation, ~ testing [of materials] zerstörungsfreie Materialprüfung (Werkstoffprüfung) *f*
nondiffusing coupler diffusionsfester Farbkuppler *m*
nondirectional filter ungerichtetes Filter *n*
- ~ **gradient** ungerichteter Gradient *m*
- ~ **illumination** ungerichtete Ausleuchtung *f*
- ~ **light** ungerichtetes Licht *n*

nonerasable nichtlöschbar
nonexposed unbelichtet, nichtbelichtet
nonglare glass blendfreies Glas *n*
nonharmonic signal unharmonisches Signal *n*
noniconic image nichtikonisches Bild *n*
nonideal lens nichtideale Linse *f*
nonimage bildfrei; druckbildfrei
- ~ **area** Nichtbildpartie *f*, Nichtbildstelle *f*, nichtdruckende Bildstelle *f*
- ~ **silver** *s.* fog

nonimpact printer anschlagfreier (aufschlagfreier) Drucker *m*, nichtmechanischer Drucker *m*
- ~ **printing [process]** nichtmechanisches Druckverfahren *n*, anschlagfreies Drucken *n*

noninterlaced scanning progressive Abtastung *f*, Folgeabtastung *f*, Vollbildabtastung *f*, Vollbildaufzeichnung *f (Video)*
- ~ **video** progressives Video *n*

nonintrusive testing eindringfreie Prüfung *f*
noninvasive imaging nichtinvasive Bildgebung *f*
nonionizing optical tomography nichtionisierende optische Tomografie *f*
- ~ **radiation** nichtionisierende Strahlung *f*

nonisotropic anisotrop, richtungsabhängig
nonlinear access Direktzugriff *m*, wahlfreier Zugriff *m*

~ **alternating-current tunneling microscopy** nichtlineare Wechselstrom-Tunnelmikroskopie *f*
~ **color space** nichtlinearer Farbraum *m*
~ **convolution** nichtlineare Faltung
~ **correlation** nichtlineare Korrelation *f*
~ **diffusion** nichtlineare Diffusion *f*
~ **distortion** nichtlineare Verzerrung *f*
~ **editing** nichtlinearer Schnitt (Videoschnitt) *m*, Offline-Schnitt *m*, Layout-Schnitt *m*
~ **editing system** nichtlineares [digitales] Schnittsystem *n*
~ **editing workstation** nichtlinearer Schnittplatz *m*
~ **encoding** nichtlineare Codierung *f*
~ **filter** nichtlineares Filter *n*
~ **filtering** nichtlineare Filterung *f*
~ **holography** nichtlineare Holografie *f*
~ **image processing** nichtlineare Bildverarbeitung *f*
~ **imaging** nichtaffine (nichtlineare) Abbildung *f*
~ **operator** nichtlinearer Operator *m*
~ **optics** nichtlineare Optik *f*
~ **point operation** nichtlineare Punktoperation *f*
~ **prediction** nichtlineare Prädiktion *f*
~ **quantization** nichtlineare Quantisierung *f*
~ **quantizer** nichtlinearer Quantisierer *m*
~ **smoothing** nichtlineare Glättung *f*
~ **spectroscopy** nichtlineare Spektroskopie *f*
~ **tomography** nichtlineare Tomografie *f*
~ **transformation** nichtlineare Transformation *f*
~ **video editing** nichtlinearer Videoschnitt *m*, nichtlineare Videonachbearbeitung *f*
nonlinearity Nichtlinearität *f*
nonlossy compression verlustfreie (verlustlose) Kompression *f*
nonluminous nichtleuchtend
nonmagnetic unmagnetisch, amagnetisch
nonmechanical shutter nichtmechanischer Verschluss *m*
nonmetric nichtmetrisch
nonmoving image stehendes (unbewegtes) Bild *n*, Stehbild *n*, Festbild *n*, Standbild *n*
nonnormal incidence nichtsenkrechter Einfall *m*
nonoriented graph ungerichteter Graph *m*
nonorthonormal filter nichtorthonormales Filter *n*
nonparametric classification nichtparametrische Klassifikation *f*
~ **classifier** nichtparametrischer Klassifikator *m*
~ **decision theoretic classifier** nichtparametrischer entscheidungstheoretischer Klassifikator *m*
~ **model** nichtparametrisches Modell *n*

nonparaxial ray achs[en]ferner Strahl *m*
nonpareil Nonpareille *f (Schriftgrad)*
nonperforated unperforiert
~ **film** unperforierter Film *m*
~ **tape** unperforiertes Band *n*
nonperiodic function nichtperiodische Funktion *f*
~ **signal** nichtperiodisches Signal *n*
nonperspective imaging nichtperspektivische Abbildung *f*
nonphotorealistic rendering nichtfotorealistisches Rendering *n (Computergrafik)*
nonplanar surface nichtplanare Oberfläche *f*
nonpolarized light unpolarisiertes (nichtpolarisiertes) Licht *n*
nonprimary color Sekundärfarbe *f*
nonprintable nichtdruckbar
nonprinting area nichtdruckende Fläche *f*
nonprocess color ink Sonderfarbe *f*, Volltonfarbe *f (Mehrfarbendruck)*
nonprofessional camera Amateurkamera *f*
nonreal time Nichtechtzeit *f*
nonrecursive convolution filter nichtrekursiver Faltungskern *m*
~ **filter** nichtrekursives Filter *n*
nonredundant relevant
nonreflecting reflex[ions]frei
nonreflection Reflexfreiheit *f*
nonreflective reflex[ions]frei
nonreversal film Negativfilm *m*
nonseparable class nichtseparierbare Klasse *f*
~ **filter** nichtseparierbares Filter *n*
nonserif[ed] serif[en]los *(Schriftschnitt)*
nonsharp vision unscharfes Sehen *n*
nonsilver film silberfreier (silberloser) Film *m*
~ **photography** silberfreie Fotografie *f*
~ **process** Nichthalogensilberverfahren *n*, NHS-Verfahren *n*
nonslip pad Riemengleitschutz *m*
nonspectral color (hue) nichtspektrale Farbe *f*, Purpurfarbe *f*
nonspecular nichtspiegelnd
nonspherical asphärisch
nonsquare pixel rechteckiges (nichtquadratisches) Pixel *n*
nonstationarity Instationarität *f*, Nichtstationarität *f (z.B. von Bildern)*
nonstationary instationär, nichtstationär, nichtstatisch
nonsymmetric half-plane filter asymmetrisches Halbebenenfilter *n (Bildmodellierung)*
nonsymmetrical amplitude nichtsymmetrische Amplitude *f*
nonsynched sound asynchroner Ton *m*; separat aufgenommener Ton *m*
nonsynchronous asynchron
nonsystematic jitter unkorrelierter Jitter *m*
nonthermal radiation nichtthermische Strahlung *f*

nonthermal 258

~ **radiator** Kaltstrahler *m*
nonuniform illumination ungleichmäßige Ausleuchtung *f*
~ **lighting** ungleichmäßige Beleuchtung *f*
~ **QAM** ungleichförmige Quadraturamplitudenmodulation *f*
~ **quantization** ungleichförmige (ungleichmäßige) Quantisierung *f*
~ **rational B-spline** rationale B-Spline-Kurve *f*, NURBS-Kurve *f*, approximierende Kurve *(Computergrafik)*
nonvisible image unsichtbares (invisibles) Bild *n*
nonvolatile memory nichtflüchtiger Speicher *m*, Permanentspeicher *m*
nonzero-power system fokales System *n*
noodle Emulsionsnudel *f*, Nudel *f*
noon daylight Mittagslicht *n*
normal Normale *f*, Einfallslot *n* *(Einheitsvektor)*
~ normal *(Papiergradation)*
~-**angle camera** Normalwinkelkammer *f*, Normalwinkelkamera *f* *(Fotogrammetrie)*
~ **color** naturgetreue (natürliche) Farbe *f*
~ **color film** Normalfarbfilm *m*
~ **color photograph** Normalfarbfoto *n*
~ **color vision** Normalfarbsichtigkeit *f*, Farbnormalsichtigkeit *f*, normales Farbensehen *f*
~ **contrast** Normalkontrast *m*
~ **curve** [Gaußsche] Glockenkurve *f* *(Normalverteilung)*
~-**definition TV** normalauflösendes Fernsehen *n*
~ **design lens** Normalobjektiv *n*, Standardobjektiv *n*
~ **development** Normalentwicklung *f*
~ **dispersion** Normaldispersion *f*, normale Dispersion *f*
~ **distribution** [Gaußsche] Normalverteilung *f*, Gauß-Verteilung *f*, Gaußsche Amplitudendichteverteilung *f*
~ **exposure** Normalbelichtung *f*
~ **film** Normalfilm *m*
~ **film processing** Normalfilmverarbeitung *f*
~ **focal length** Normalbrennweite *f*
~ **focal-length lens**, ~ **focus lens** normalbrennweitiges Objektiv *n*
~ **frequency distribution** *s.* ~ distribution
~ **human observer** durchschnittlicher (normalsichtiger) Beobachter *m*, Normalbeobachter *m*
~ **incidence** rechtwinkliger Einfall *m*; senkrechter Einfall *m*
~ **light** Normallicht *n*
~ **magnification** Normalvergrößerung *f* *(Mikroskopie)*
~ **noise** normalverteiltes (gaußverteiltes) Rauschen *n* Gaußsches Rauschen *n*, Gauß-Rauschen *n*
~ **perspective** Normalperspektive *f*

~ **photography** Normalfotografie *f*
~ **solution** Normallösung *f*
~ **sync[hronization]** Normalsynchronisation *f*
~ **to the surface** Flächennormale *f*
~ **trichromat** normaler Trichromat *m*, Normalfarbsichtiger *m*
~-**type lens** Normalobjektiv *n*, Standardobjektiv *n*
~ **vector** Normal[en]vektor *m* *(Computergrafik)*
~-**vector interpolation [shading]** Phong-Schattierung *f (Computergrafik)*
~ **viewing distance** Normsehweite *f*, Bezugssehweite *f*, konventionelle (deutliche) Sehweite *f*
~ **vision** Normalsichtigkeit *f*, Emmetropie *f*
normalization 1. Normalisierung *f*; 2. Normierung *f*
~ **factor** Normierungsfaktor *m*
~ **matrix** Normierungsmatrix *f*
~ **transformation** Normierungstransformation *f*
normalize/to 1. normalisieren; 2. normieren
normalized convolution normalisierte Faltung *f*
~ **device coordinate** normierte Koordinate *f*
~ **gradient vector** normalisierter Gradientenvektor *m*
~ **histogram** normiertes Histogramm *n*
~ **line-spread function** normierte Linienbildfunktion *f*
~ **optical transfer function** Ortsfrequenzgang *m*
normalizing constant Normierungsfaktor *m*
nosepiece turret Okularrevolver *m*
not in focus fokusfern
notch Randkerbe *f*
~ **filter** Lochfilter *n*
notebook [computer] Notebook *n*, Personalcomputer *m* im Buchformat
NRZ *s.* non-return-to-zero
NTSC *s.* National Television Standards (System) Committee
~ **process** NTSC-Verfahren *n* *(Farbfernsehen)*
~ **standard** NTSC-Norm *f*
~ **video** NTSC-Fernsehen *n*
nuance Nuance *f*, Abtönung *f*, Schattierung *f*, Abstufung *f*
nuclear binding energy Bindungsenergie *f*
~ **emulsion** Kern[spur]emulsion *f*
~ **emulsion plate** Kernspurenplatte *f*, Kernfotoplatte *f*
~ **fusion** Kernfusion *f*, Kernverschmelzung *f*
~ **magnetic dipole moment** kernmagnetisches Dipolmoment *n*
~ **magnetic resonance** Kernspinresonanz *f*, nuklearmagnetische (kernmagnetische) Resonanz *f*, NMR

~ **magnetic resonance imaging** Kernspinresonanzabbildung f
~ **magnetic resonance signal** Kernresonanzsignal n
~ **magnetic resonance spectroscopy** kernmagnetische Resonanzspektroskopie f, NMR-Spektroskopie f
~ **magnetic resonance tomography** NMR-Tomografie f
~ **magnetism** Kernmagnetismus m
~ **medical** nuklearmedizinisch
~ **medical camera** nuklearmedizinische Kamera
~ **medicine** Nuklearmedizin f
~-**medicine image** nuklearmedizinisches Bild n
~ **medicine imaging** nuklearmedizinische Bildgebung f
~-**medicine scanning instrument** nuklearmedizinischer Scanner m
~ **photography** Kernfotografie f
~ **radiation** Kernstrahlung f
~ **resonance signal** Kernresonanzsignal n
~ **spin** Kernspin m, Spin m, Eigendrehimpuls m
~-**track photography** Kernspurfotografie f
~-**track recording** Kernspuraufzeichnung f
nucleating agent Keimbildner m
nucleation Keimbildung f *(fotografischer Elementarprozess)*
~-**and-growth model** Keim-Korn-Modell n, Silberkeimtheorie f
nucleon Nukleon n, Proton n; Wasserstoffatom n
nucleus 1. Nukleus m, Kern m; 2. Nervenknoten m
null densitometer Nulldensitometer n
~ **frequency** Nullfrequenz f
~ **matrix** Nullmatrix f
nullode Nullode f *(eine Sperrröhre)*
number board Szenenklappe f, Szenentafel f, Handklappe f *(Filmarbeit)*
~ **theoretic transform** zahlentheoretische Transformation f
numerical aperture numerische Apertur f
~ **classification** numerische Klassifikation f
~ **display** Ziffernanzeige f
~ **feature** numerisches Merkmal n
~ **model** numerisches Modell n
~ **objective aperture** numerische Objektivapertur f
~ **pattern recognition** numerische Mustererkennung f
~ **representation** numerische Darstellung f
~ **simulation** numerische Simulation f
~ **video** digitales Video n, Digitalvideo n
~ **visualization** Datenvisualisierung f
NURBS s. nonuniform rational B-spline
nyctalope Nachtblinder m
nyctalopia Nyktalopie f, Nachtblinheit f
nyctalopic nachtblind
Nyquist band limit Nyquist-Bandbegrenzung f

~ **bandwidth** Nyquist-Bandbreite f
~ **condition** Nyquist-Bedingung f
~ **criterion** Nyquist-Kriterium n
~ **filter** Nyquist-Filter n
~ **frequency** Nyquist-Frequenz f, Nyquist-Wellenzahl f, Grenzwellenzahl f, Grenzabtastfrequenz f
~ **interval** Nyquist-Intervall n
~ **limit** Nyquist-Grenze f
~ **noise** Nyquist-Rauschen n, Johnson-Rauschen n, Systemrauschen n, thermisches Zufallsrauschen n
~ **rate** s. ~ frequency
~ **rule** Nyquist-Theorem n
~ **sample** Nyquist-Punkt m
~ **sample spacing** Nyquist-Bereich m
~ **sampling** Nyquist-Abtastung f
~ **sampling theorem** Nyquist-Theorem n
~ **slope** Nyquist-Flanke f
nystagmic nystagmisch
nystagmus [movement] Nystagmus m, Augenzittern n

O

obie Augenlichtlampe f *(Porträtfotografie)*
object 1. Objekt n; Aufnahmeobjekt n, Aufnahmegegenstand m *(s.a. unter subject)*; 2. Bildelement n *(bes. in Vektordateien)*
~ **area** Objektfläche f
~-**based analysis-synthesis coding** objektbasierte Analyse-Synthese-Codierung f
~-**based classification** objektbasierte Klassifikation f
~-**based coding** objektbasierte Codierung f
~-**based image coding** objektbasierte Bildcodierung f
~-**based image matching** objektbasierte Bildzuordnung f
~-**based interpolation** objektbasierte Interpolation f
~-**based motion analysis** objektorientierte Bewegungsanalyse f
~-**based registration** objektbasierte Registrierung f
~-**based representation** objektbasierte Darstellung f
~-**based scalability** objektbasierte Skalierbarkeit f
~-**based temporal scalability** objektbasierte zeitliche Skalierbarkeit f
~-**based video coding** objektbasierte Videocodierung f
~-**based visualization** objektbasierte Visualisierung f
~ **beam** Objektstrahl m, Gegenstandsstrahl m; Objektwelle f, Gegenstandswelle f, Signalwelle f *(Holografie)*
~ **boundary** Objektrand m, Objektgrenze f
~ **boundary detection** Objektranderkennung f
~ **brightness** Objekthelligkeit f
~ **category** Objektklasse f
~-**centered coordinate system** objektzentriertes Koordinatensystem n
~-**centered model** objektorientiertes Modell n
~ **characteristic** Objektmerkmal n
~ **circle diameter** Objektkreisdurchmesser m *(Objektiv)*
~ **class** Objektklasse f
~ **classification** Objektklassifikation f
~ **clipping** Objekt-Clipping n *(Computergrafik)*
~ **code** Maschinencode m
~ **coding** Objektcodierung f
~ **color** Objektfarbe f, Körperfarbe f, Oberflächenfarbe f
~ **conjugate** s. ~ distance
~ **constancy** Objektkonstanz f
~ **contour** Objektkontur f
~ **contour tracking** Objektkonturverfolgung f
~ **contrast** Objektkontrast m; Motivkontrast m
~ **coordinate system** Objektkoordinatensystem n
~ **description** Objektbeschreibung f
~ **detail** Objektdetail n
~ **detectability** Objekterkennbarkeit f
~ **detection** Objekterkennung f, Objektdetektion f
~ **discrimination** Objektunterscheidung f
~ **displacement** Objektverschiebung f
~ **distance** Dingweite f, Gegenstandsweite f, Objektweite f, Objektabstand m, Objektentfernung f, Objektdistanz f
~ **edge** Objektkante f
~ **extraction** Objektextraktion f
~ **feature** Objektmerkmal n
~ **field** Objektfeld n
~ **field angle** Objektfeldwinkel m
~ **field stop** Objektfeldblende f
~ **frequency** Objektfrequenz f
~ **geometry** Objektgeometrie f
~ **height** Objekthöhe f
~ **hierarchy** Objekthierarchie f
~ **identification** Objektidentifikation f
~ **identifier** Objektidentifikator m
~ **illumination** Objektausleuchtung f
~ **image** Objektbild n, Gegenstandsbild n
~ **isolation** Objektisolierung f
~ **localization** Objektlokalisation f, Objektlokalisierung f
~ **location** Objektort m; Objektzuordnung f
~ **luminance** Objektleuchtdichte f, Objektluminanz f
~ **magnification** Objektvergrößerung f
~ **menu** Kontextmenü n
~ **micrometer** Objektmikrometer n
~ **model** Objektmodell n *(Computergrafik; maschinelle Bilderkennung; s.a. unter model)*
~ **modeling** Objektmodellierung f
~ **modeling system** Objektmodellierungssystem n
~ **modulation** Objektmodulation f
~ **motion (movement)** Objektbewegung f
~ **occlusion** Objektverdeckung f
~ **of fixation** Fixationsobjekt n
~ **of interest** interessierendes Objekt n
~ **orientation** Objektausrichtung f, Objektorientierung f
~-**oriented coding** objektorientierte Codierung f
~-**oriented database** objektorientierte Datenbank f
~-**oriented graphics** objektorientierte (vektororientierte) Grafik f
~-**oriented motion estimation** objektorientierte Bewegungsschätzung f
~-**oriented programming** objektorientierte Programmierung f
~ **outline** Objektumriss m

~ **pattern** Objektmuster *n*
~ **perception** Objektwahrnehmung *f*
~ **photography** Objektfotografie *f*, Sachfotografie *f*
~ **pixel** Objektpixel *n*
~ **plane** Dingebene *f*, Objektebene *f*
~ **point** Objektpunkt *m*, Dingpunkt *m*, Gegenstandspunkt *m*; Urbildpunkt *m*, Originalpunkt *m*, Deltapunkt *m*
~ **position** Objektlage *f*, Objektposition *f*
~ **radiance** Objektverteilung *f* *(Radiometrie)*
~ **recognition** Objekterkennung *f*, Objektdetektion *f*
~ **reconstruction** Objektrekonstruktion *f*
~ **reflectance** Objektreflexion *f*
~ **region** Objektbereich *m*
~-**related feature** objektbezogenes Merkmal *n*
~-**related image analysis** objektbezogene Bildanalyse *f*
~ **representation technique** Objektdarstellungstechnik *f*
~ **resolution** Objektauflösung *f*
~ **scanner** Objektabtaster *m*
~ **scanning** Objektabtastung *f*
~ **scene** Objektszene *f*, Szene *f*
~ **segmentation** Objektsegmentierung *f*
~ **segregation** Objekttrennung *f*
~ **shape** Objektform *f*
~ **shape analysis** Objektformanalyse *f*
~-**shaped feature** objektförmiges Merkmal *n*
~ **side** Objektseite *f* *(z.B. eines Objektivs)*
~-**side** dingseitig, objektseitig, gegenstandsseitig
~ **signature** Objektsignatur *f (Bildanalyse)*
~ **simplification algorithm** Objektvereinfachungsalgorithmus *m*
~ **size** Objektgröße *f*
~ **space** Dingraum *m*, Objektraum *m*, Gegenstandsraum *m*, objektseitiger Strahlenraum *m*
~-**space algorithm** Objektraumalgorithmus *m*
~-**space filtering** Objektraumfilterung *f*
~ **speed** Objektgeschwindigkeit *f*
~ **structure** Objektstruktur *f*
~ **surface** Objektoberfläche *f*
~ **system** Objektsystem *n*
~-**to-film distance** Objekt-Film-Abstand *m*
~-**to-image distance** Objekt-Bild-Abstand *m*, Konjugationsabstand *m*
~ **tracking** Objektverfolgung *f (maschinelles Sehen)*
~ **visualization** Objektvisualisierung *f*
~ **wave** Objektwelle *f*, Gegenstandswelle *f*, Signalwelle *f (Holografie)*
objectionable pattern Stör[ungs]muster *n*, Interferenzmuster *n*
objective Objektiv *n*
~ **back focal plane** Austrittspupille *f* des Objektivs *(Köhlersche Mikroskopbeleuchtung)*

~ **barrel** Objektivtubus *m*, Objektivstutzen *m*
~ **changer** Objektivwechseleinrichtung *f*
~ **color** objektive Farbe *f*
~ **contrast** objektiver (fotometrischer) Kontrast *m*, relativer Leuchtdichteunterschied *m*
~ **design** Objektivaufbau *m*, Objektivausführung *f*
~ **front lens** Objektivfrontlinse *f*
~ **lens** Objektivlinse *f*
~ **magnification** Objektivvergrößerung *f*
~ **prism** Objektivprisma *n*
~ **screw thread** Objektivanschlussgewinde *n*
~ **zone plate** Objektiv-Zonenplatte *f (Rastermikroskop)*
objectness Objektzugehörigkeit *f (z.B. eines Pixels oder Voxels in der Bildanalyse)*
oblique schräg
~ **aerial photograph** Schrägluftbild *n*, Schrägaufnahme *f*
~ **bundle** schiefes (schräges) Bündel *n*
~ **illumination** Schräg[auf]lichtbeleuchtung *f*, Schrägbeleuchtung *f*, schiefe (schräge) Beleuchtung *f*
~ **imaging** Schrägbildaufnahme *f*
~ **incidence** schräger Einfall *m*
~ **light** Schräglicht *n*, schräg auffallendes Licht *n*
~ **lighting** *s.* ~ illumination
~ **parallel projection** schiefwinklige Parallelprojektion *f*
~ **perspective** Dreipunktperspektive *f*
~ **projection** schief[winklig]e Projektion *f*, Schrägprojektion *f*
~ **ray** Schrägstrahl *m*, schräger (windschiefer) Strahl *m*
~ **stroke** Schrägstrich *m*
~ **view** schräger Aufblick *m*
~ **viewing** Schrägbetrachtung *f*
obliqueliy-incident light schräg auffallendes Licht *n*, Schräglicht *n*
obliquity Schiefe *f*, Schiefheit *f (z.B. eines Lichtstrahls)*
obscure/to 1. abdunkeln; 2. verdecken
observability Beobachtbarkeit *f*
observable beobachtbar
observation angle Beobachtungswinkel *m*, Betrachtungswinkel *m*, Blickwinkel *m*, Sichtwinkel *m*
~ **by reflected light** Auflichtbeobachtung *f*, Auflichtbetrachtung *f*
~ **camera** Überwachungskamera *f*
~ **microscope** Beobachtungsmikroskop *n*, Betrachtungsmikroskop *n*
~ **parallax** Betrachtungsparallaxe *f*
~ **plane** Beobachtungsebene *f*
~ **point** Beobachtungsort *m*, Beobachtungspunkt *m*
~ **position** Betrachtungsposition *f*
~ **site** *s.* ~ point

observational

observational satellite Beobachtungssatellit *m*
~ **tool** Beobachtungsgerät *n*
observatory Observatorium *n*
~ **telescope** Beobachtungsfernrohr *n*, Betrachtungsfernrohr *n*
observe/to beobachten, betrachten
observer Beobachter *m*, Betrachter *m*, Beschauer *m*
~ **metamerism** Beobachtermetamerie *f (Kolorimetrie)*
observer's flicker threshold kritische Flimmerfrequenz *f*, Flimmergrenze *f*
obstacle avoidance Hindernisvermeidung *f*
~ **recognition** Hinderniserkennung *f*
obturator Verschlussblende *f*
obtuse triangle stumpfwinkliges Dreieck *n*
occipital cortex (lobe) Hinterhauptlappen *m (des Gehirns)*
occlude/to verdecken
occluded edge verdeckte Kante *f*
~ **image** verdecktes Bild *n*
~ **region** Okklusionsbereich *m*, Überdeckungsgebiet *n*
occluding contour Verdeckungskante *f*
occlusion Okklusion *f*, Verdeckung *f*, Überdeckung *f*
occult/to verdecken
ocean mapping Meeresbodenkartierung *f*
OCR *s.* optical character recognition
OCT image Kohärenztomogramm *n*
octagonal median filter achteckiges Medianfilter *n*
~ **neighborhood** Achternachbarschaft *f*, Achterumgebung *f*
octal digit Oktalziffer *f*
~ **numbering system** Oktalsystem *n*
octant Oktant *m*
octave band analysis Oktavbandanalyse *f*, Oktavbandzerlegung *f*
~ **decomposition** dyadische Zerlegung *f (Bildverarbeitung)*
octavo Oktav *n*, Oktavbogen *m*, Dreistrichbogen *m*
octet 1. Oktett *n*; 2. *s.* byte
~ **theory** Oktettregel *f*, Oktetttheorie *f*
octree Oktagonbaum *m*, Oktalbaum *m*, Achterbaum *m (Datenstruktur; Computergrafik)*
~ **encoding [procedure]** Achterbaumcodierung *f*
~ **quantization** Achterbaumquantisierung *f*
~ **representation** Achterbaumdarstellung *f*
ocular okular
~ Okular *n*
~ **accommodation** Akkommodation *f*, Anpassung *f (des Auges)*
~ **filter** Okularfilter *n*
~ **fundus** Augenhintergrund *m*, Augenrückwand *f*
~ **lens** Okularlinse *f*
~ **measuring graticule** Okularmikrometer *n*
~ **optics** Augenoptik *f*

~ **tremor** Augenzittern *n*, Nystagmus *m*
oculist Augenoptiker *m*
oculomotor okulomotorisch, augenmotorisch
~ **function** Augenmuskelfunktion *f*
~ **system** okulomotorisches System *n*
odd field ungeradzahliges Halbbild *n*
~**-numbered line** ungeradzahlige Zeile *f*
~ **parity** ungerade Parität *f*
~ **signal** ungerades Signal *n*
off-axis achsenentfernt, achs[en]fern, außeraxial, abaxial
~**-axis aberration** außeraxialer Abbildungsfehler *m*, Querabweichung *f*, Queraberration *f*
~**-axis coma** sagittale Koma *f*, Rinnenfehler *m (Abbildungsfehler)*
~**-axis hologram** außeraxiales Hologramm *n*, Off-axis-Hologramm *n*, Leith-Upatniek-Hologramm *n*
~**-axis holography** Trägerfrequenzholografie *f*
~**-axis image** achs[en]fernes Bild *n*, außeraxiale Abbildung *f*
~**-axis object point** außeraxialer Dingpunkt (Objektpunkt) *m*
~**-axis ray** achs[en]ferner Strahl *m*
~**-axis reflector** Herschel-Teleskop *n*
~**-camera** Off *n (Kinematografie)*
~**-camera flash control** kabellose Blitzsteuerung *f*
~**-camera flash unit** externes Blitzgerät *n*
~**-color** Farbfehler *m (Video)*
~**-line holography** Seitenbandholografie *f*
~**-press proof** Druckvorstufenproof *m*, Andruckersatz *m*
~**-screen photograph** Bildschirmfoto *n*, Bildschirmaufnahme *f*, Fernsehschirmbild *n*
~**-specular reflection** nichtspiegelnde Reflexion *f*
~**-the-cuff shooting** Freihandfilmen *n*
~**-the-shelf camera** handelsübliche Kamera *f*
~**-the-shelf image-handling software** Standard-Bildbearbeitungssoftware *f*
office color-printing device Bürofarbdrucker *m*
~ **communication** Bürokommunikation *f*
~ **copier** Bürokopierer *m*, Bürokopiergerät *n*
~ **copy** Bürokopie *f*
~ **copying** Bürokopiertechnik *f*, Bürokopierverfahren *n*; Bürovervielfältigung *f*
~ **document architecture** Bürodokumente-Architektur *f*
~ **document interchange format** Bürodokumente-Austauschformat *n*
~ **graphics** Bürografik *f*
~ **photocopier** Bürokopierer *m*, Bürokopiergerät *n*
~ **printer** Bürodrucker *m*
~ **printing** Büroduck *m*

offline editing Offline-Schnitt *m*, nichtlinearer Schnitt (Videoschnitt) *m*, Layout-Schnitt *m*
~ **media composer** Offline-Schnittsystem *n*
offset/to abliegen, ablegen *(Druckschwierigkeit)*
offset Ablegen *n*
~ **cylinder** Drucktuchzylinder *m*, Gummi[drucktuch]zylinder *m*
~ **duplicating machine** Offsetvervielfältiger *m*, Kleinoffsetmaschine *f*
~ **ink** Offsetdruckfarbe *f*
~ **lithographic press** Offset[druck]maschine *f*
~ **lithographic process** Flachdruckverfahren *n*
~ **lithography** *s.* ~ printing
~ **paper** Offset[druck]papier *n*, Flachdruckpapier *n*; maschinenglattes (ungestrichenes) Papier *n*
~ **plate** Offsetdruckplatte *f*
~ **plate making** Offsetdruckplattenherstellung *f*
~ **principle** Offset-Prinzip *n*
~ **print shop** Offsetdruckerei *f*
~ **printer** Offsetdrucker *m*
~ **printing** Offsetdruck *m*, Offsetdruckverfahren *n*, Offsetlithografie *f*; [indirekter] Flachdruck *m*
~ **printing machine** Offset[druck]maschine *f*
~ **product** Offseterzeugnis *n*
~ **production** Offsetherstellung *f*
~ **rotary** Offsetrollendruckmaschine *f*, Offsetrotations[druck]maschine *f*, Rollenoffset[druck]maschine *f*
ohm Ohm *n (Einheit des elektrischen Widerstandes)*
oil immersion microscopy Ölimmersionsmikroskopie *f*
~ **immersion objective (optics)** Ölimmersionsobjektiv *n*, Ölimmersionsoptik *f*
~ **printing process** Öldruck *m*
~**-protected coupler** ölgeschützter Farbkuppler *m*, Fettschwanzkuppler *m*, Ölkuppler *m*
~**-receptive** fettfreundlich, oleophil
~**-repellent** fettabweisend, oleophob
OLC *s.* on-lens chip
old chemistry tank Altchemietank *m*
~ **eye** Alters[weit]sichtigkeit *f*, Presbyopie *f*
~ **movie restoration** Filmrestaurierung *f*
~**-style roman type[face]** [klassizistische] Antiqua *f*, Antiqua[druck]schrift *f*
OLED *s.* organic light-emitting diode
oleophilic oleophil, fettfreundlich
oleophobic oleophob, ölabweisend, fettabweisend
omnidirectional camera omnidirektionale Kamera
~ **microphone** ungerichtetes Mikrofon *n*, Kugelmikrofon *n*
~ **microphone pattern** Kugelcharakteristik *f*
on air auf Sender (Sendung)
on-air broadcast use Direktsendebetrieb *m*
on-axis aberration Längsaberration *f*, Längsabweichung *f*, axialer Abbildungsfehler *m*
on-axis bundle Achsparallelbündel *n*, achsparalleles Bündel *n*
on-board radar Bordradar *n*
on-camera flash (gun) Aufsteckblitz *m*, Aufsteckblitzgerät *n*
on-camera microphone [eingebautes] Kameramikro[fon] *n*
on-line editing Filmmontage *f*, Online-Schnitt *m*, linearer Schnitt *m*
on-line memory Online-Speicher *m*
on-line storage Online-Speicherung *f*
on-location filming (shooting) Außendreh *m*, Außendreharbeit *f*, Außenaufnahme[n] *f[pl]*, Dreharbeit *f* vor Ort
on-location industrial photography Industriefotografie *f*
on-location recording Originaltonaufnahme *f*
on-screen display Bildschirmanzeige *f*, Bildschirmmenü *n*
on-screen graphics Bildschirmgrafik *f*
on-screen icon Icon *n*, Programmsymbol *n*, Platzhalter-Pixelbild *n*, Platzhalter *m*
on-screen menu Bildschirmmenü *n*
on-screen object Bildschirmobjekt *n*
on-set sound recording Originaltonaufnahme *f*
on-stage picture Bühnenfoto *n*
one-bit image Monochrombild *n*
~**-bit quantization** Ein-Bit-Quantisierung *f*
~**-button tuning** Einknopf-Abstimmungssystem *n*
~**-dimensional convolution** eindimensionale Faltung *f*
~**-dimensional filter** eindimensionales Filter *n*
~**-dimensional Fourier transform** eindimensionale Fourier-Transformation *f*
~**-dimensional image** eindimensionales Bild *n*
~**-dimensional signal** eindimensionales Signal *n*
~**-dimensional space** eindimensionaler Raum *m*
~**-dimensionality** Eindimensionalität *f*
~**-fourth wavelength** Viertelwellenlänge *f*
~**-half-inch cassette** Halbzollkassette *f*
~**-half wavelength** Halbwellenlänge *f*
~**-hand camcorder** Einhand-Camcorder *m*, Hand[video]kamera *f*
~**-hour [processing] lab** Foto-Stundenservice *m*

~-inch tape Ein-Zoll-Band *n* *(Filmbearbeitung)*
~-light print Einlichtkopie *f*, Musterkopie *f* *(Kinefilmbearbeitung)*
~-point perspective Einpunktperspektive *f*, Parallelperspektive *f*, telezentrische Perspektive *f*
~-quarter wavelength Viertelwellenlänge *f*
~-shot camera Strahlenteilerkamera *f*, Strahlenteilungskamera *f*
~-shot developer Einmalentwickler *m*
~-sided Laplace transform einseitige Laplace-Transformation *f*
~-time-use camera Einwegkamera *f*, Wegwerfkamera *f*
~-to-one printing Eins-zu-eins-Kopieren *n*
~-to-one videoconference Zweipartner-Videokonferenz *f*
~-track [sound] record[ing] Einspur-Tonaufzeichnung *f*
~-use developer Einmalentwickler *m*
~-wavelength optical system kohärentes [optisches] System *n*
~-way interface unidirektionale Schnittstelle *f*
onion skin Luftpostpapier *n*
opacity Opazität *f*, Undurchsichtigkeit *f*, Lichtundurchlässigkeit *f*
opal filament lamp Opal[glas]lampe *f*
~ glass Opalglas *n*, Trübglas *n*, Trübscheibe *f*
opalesce/to opaleszieren, opalisieren
opalescence Opaleszenz *f*
opalized lamp [bulb] Mattglasglühbirne *f*, Mattglaslampe *f*
opaque/to abdecken, maskieren *(s.a.* block out/to*);* ausflecken *(s.a.* spot/to*)*
opaque opak, lichtundurchlässig, undurchsichtig, nichttransparent; gedeckt *(Druckwesen)*
~ projector Auflichtprojektor *m*, Epiprojektor *m*
~ to X rays röntgenundurchlässig
opaqueness *s.* opacity
opaquing paint Abdeckfarbe *f*, Deckfarbe *f* *(Retuschiermittel)*
~ pen Abdeckstift *m*
open-circuit voltage Leerlaufspannung *f* *(Fotodiode)*
~ curve offene Kurve *f*
~-flash [procedure] Offenblitz *m*, Offenblitzmethode *f*
~ polygon offenes Polygon *n*
~ portion [of the shutter] Hellsektor *m* *(Verschluss)*
~ prepress interface *ein* Schnittstellensystem *der digitalen Druckvorstufe*
~ reel tape freies (freilaufendes) Band *n*
~ X-ray spectrometer offenes Röntgenspektrometer *n*
opening [morphologisches] Öffnen *n*; Opening-Operation *f (Bildverarbeitung)*

~ angle Öffnungswinkel *m (z.B. eines Verschlusses)*
~ credits (title) Titelvorspann *m*, Vorspann *m*, Anfangstitel *m (Film)*
~ operation *s.* opening
opera glass[es] Opernglas *n*, Theaterglas *n*
operability Bedienbarkeit *f*, Handhabbarkeit *f*
operating interface Benutzerschnittstelle *f*, Benutzungsoberfläche *f*
~ memory Operativspeicher *m*
~ microscope Operationsmikroskop *n*
~ system Betriebssystem *n*
operation Operation *f*
operational amplifier Operationsverstärker *m (Signalverarbeitung)*
~ state Betriebsstatus *m*
operative cameraman Erster Kameramann *m*, Kameraschwenker *m*, Schwenker *m*
operator Bediener *m*, Operator *m*, Operateur *m*; Auswerter *m*
~ console Bedienfeld *n*
~ error Bedienfehler *m*
~ interface Bedienerschnittstelle *f*
~ kernel Operatorkern *m*, Filterkern *m (Grauwertbildverarbeitung)*
~ window Operatorfenster *n*, Filterfenster *n*
ophthalmic ophthalmisch
~ camera Funduskamera *f*, Netzhautkamera *f*, Retinakamera *f*
~ optics Augenoptik *f*; Brillenoptik *f*
ophthalmology Ophthalmologie *f*, Augenheilkunde *f*
ophthalmometer Ophthalmometer *n*
ophthalmoscope Ophthalmoskop *n*, Augenspiegel *m*
ophthalmoscopic ophthalmoskopisch
ophthalmoscopy Ophthalmoskopie *f*
opponent color Gegenfarbe *f*, Komplementärfarbe *f*, komplementäre Farbe *f*
~-colors theory, opponent [process] theory Gegenfarbentheorie *f*
opposite color *s.* opponent color
opsin Opsin *n (Protein)*
optic 1. optisch; 2. *s.* optical system; 3. *s.* optical instrument
~ axis 1. optische Achse *f (Kristallografie; s.a.* optical axis*);* 2. [optische] Augenachse *f*
~ chiasm[a] Chiasma *n*, Sehnervenkreuzung *f*
~ disk blinder Fleck *m*, Papille *f (des Auges)*
~ disk *s.* retinal blind spot
~ nerve Sehnerv *m*, Optikus *m*
~ nerve fiber Sehnervenfaser *f*
~ rod Netzhautstäbchen *n*, Sehstäbchen *n*, Stäbchen *n*, Rhabdom *f*
optical 1. optisch; visuell; 2. *s.* ~ effect
~ aberration optische Aberration *f*, optischer Fehler (Abbildungsfehler) *m*

optical

- ~ **absorption** optische Absorption f, Lichtabsorption f, Lichtfang m
- ~ **activity** optische Aktivität f, optisches Drehvermögen n
- ~ **add/drop filter** optisches Add/Drop-Filter n
- ~ **add/drop multiplexer** optischer Add/Drop-Multiplexer m
- ~ **aid** Sehhilfe f
- ~ **alignment** optische Ausrichtung f
- ~ **amplifier** optischer Verstärker m
- ~ **aperture** optische Blende f
- ~ **artifact** optischer Fehler m (s.a. ~ aberration)
- ~ **astronomy** optische Astronomie f
- ~ **attenuation** s. reflectance
- ~ **attenuator** optischer Abschwächer n
- ~ **audio track** Lichttonspur f
- ~ **axis** optische Achse f (Linsenoptik); Aufnahmeachse f (s.a. optic axis)
- ~ **bandwidth** optische Bandbreite f, Spannungsbandbreite f (Fotodetektor)
- ~ **beam splitter** optischer Strahlenteiler m
- ~ **bench** optische Bank f
- ~ **biopsy** optische Biopsie f
- ~ **bistability** [optische] Bistabilität f
- ~ **blur** optische Unschärfe f
- ~ **brightener** optischer Aufheller m
- ~ **calculation[s]** Optikrechnen n, Optikrechnung f
- ~ **camera length** [optische] Kameralänge f
- ~ **cavity** Laserresonator m
- ~ **center** optisches Zentrum n, optischer Mittelpunkt m; Einrichtemitte f (Layout)
- ~ **center of the eye** optischer Augenmittelpunkt m
- ~ **character reader** [optischer] Zeichenleser m
- ~ **character recognition** optische Zeichenerkennung (Schriftzeichenerkennung) f, Klarschrifterkennung f, Klarschriftlesen n
- ~ **coating** Optikvergütung f, Vergütung f, optische Entspiegelung f
- ~ **coherence** optische Kohärenz f
- ~ **coherence tomography** [optische] Kohärenztomografie f; Weißlichtinterferometrie f
- ~ **color filter** optisches Farbfilter n
- ~ **communication** optische Kommunikation f
- ~ **communications technology** optische Kommunikationstechnik f
- ~ **comparator** Komparator m
- ~ **component** Optikkomponente f, Optik[bau]teil n, optisches Teil n (s.a. ~ element)
- ~ **computation** Optikrechnen n, Optikrechnung f
- ~ **computer** [kohärenter] optischer Computer m
- ~ **contact** optischer Kontakt m
- ~ **contrast** optischer Kontrast m
- ~ **contrast ratio** Kontrastverhältnis n
- ~ **converter** optisch-elektrischer (optoelektronischer) Wandler m
- ~ **correction** optische Korrektion (Korrektur) f
- ~ **coupling** Lichteinkopplung f
- ~ **coupling element** optisches Kopplungselement n
- ~ **crystal** optischer Kristall m
- ~ **cube beam splitter** Strahlenteilerwürfel f
- ~ **data processing** optische Datenverarbeitung f
- ~ **data storage** optische Datenspeicherung f
- ~ **defect** optischer Fehler (Abbildungsfehler) m, optische Aberration f
- ~ **density** optische Dichte f, Schwärzung f
- ~ **design** Optik-Konstruktion f; optischer Aufbau m
- ~ **detection** optische Detektion f
- ~ **detector** optischer Detektor m, Lichtdetektor m, Fotodetektor m
- ~ **device** optisches Gerät n
- ~ **diffusion** Lichtdiffusion f
- ~ **disk** optische Speicherplatte (Platte) f; analoge [optische] Bildplatte f, Bildspeicherplatte f, Laserdisk f (s.a. videodisc)
- ~ **disk drive** Bildplattenlaufwerk n
- ~ **disk memory** Bildplattenspeicher m
- ~ **disk storage** 1. optischer Plattenspeicher m; 2. Bildplattenspeicherung f
- ~ **dispersion** optische Dispersion f
- ~ **display** optische Anzeige f
- ~ **distance** s. ~ path
- ~ **distortion** optische Verzerrung f
- ~ **dot gain** Tonwertzunahme f, Tonwertzuwachs m, Rasterpunktverbreiterung f, Vollerwerden n
- ~ **effect** optischer Effekt m; optischer Spezialeffekt (Trick) m, Filmaufnahmetrick m, [In-]Kamera-Effekt m, Kameratrick m
- ~ **effects filter** Effektfilter n, Trickfilter n, Kreativfilter n
- ~ **electron** Valenzelektron n
- ~ **element** optisches (optisch abbildendes) Bauelement n, optisches Element n
- ~ **endoscopic instrument** Endoskop n
- ~ **error** optischer Fehler m
- ~ **feedback** optische Rückkopplung f
- ~ **fiber** Lichtleitfaser f, optische Faser f, Glasfaser f; Lichtwellenleiter m
- ~ **fiber cable** Lichtleitkabel n, Glasfaserkabel n
- ~ **fiber coupler** faseroptisches Kopplungselement n
- ~ **fiber network** Glasfasernetz n
- ~ **field converter** optischer Feldkonverter m
- ~ **filter** optisches Filter n, Lichtfilter n
- ~ **filtering (filtration)** optische Filterung f
- ~ **flash** Belichtungsblitz m

optical

~ **flat** Plan[parallel]platte f, Parallelplatte f, planparallele Platte f
~ **flow** optischer Fluss m, Lichtleitwert m
~ **flow field** optisches Strömungsfeld (Flussfeld) n
~ **flow segmentation** Bewegungssegmentierung f
~ **fog** Belichtungsschleier m
~ **Fourier transform** optische Fourier-Transformation f
~ **frequency** optische Frequenz f
~ **gain** optische Verstärkung f, optischer Gewinn m
~ **geometry** optische Geometrie f
~ **glass** optisches Glas n
~ **glass chart** Glasdiagramm n
~ **glass prism** Glasprisma n
~ **gradient** optischer Gradient m
~ **grating** optisches Gitter n
~ **hologram** optisches Hologramm n
~ **holography** optische Holografie f
~ **house** Tricklabor n; Trickstudio n
~ **illusion** optische Täuschung f
~ **image** optisches Bild n, optische Abbildung f; Lichtbild n
~ **image formation** optische Bildentstehung f
~ **image processing** optische Bildverarbeitung f
~ **image recording** optische Bildaufzeichnung f
~ **image stabilizer** optischer Bildstabilisator m
~ **imaging** optische Abbildung (Bildgebung) f
~ **imaging system** optisches Abbildungssystem n
~ **indicatrix** optische Indikatrix f, Indexellipsoid n *(Kristalloptik)*
~ **information** optische Information f
~ **instrument** optisches Instrument n, Optik f
~ **interference** optische Interferenz f, Lichtinterferenz f
~ **invariant** optische (Helmholtz-Lagrangesche) Invariante f
~ **isolator** optischer Isolator m
~ **laser disk** Laserplatte f
~ **lens** optische Linse f
~ **lens coupling** linsenoptische Lichteinkopplung f
~ **lens triplet** Triplett n, Dreilinser m, dreilinsiges Objektiv n
~ **light microscope** s. ~ microscope
~ **line grating** optisches Liniengitter n
~ **line sensor** optischer Zeilensensor m
~ **lithography** Fotolithografie f, Lichtlithografie f, [licht]optische Lithografie f
~ **magnification** optische Vergrößerung f
~ **mammography** optische Mammografie f
~ **material** optischer Werkstoff m; Linsenwerkstoff m, Linsenmaterial n
~ **measurement** optische Messung f

~ **measuring instrument** optisches Messinstrument n
~-**mechanical** optomechanisch
~-**mechanical scanner** optomechanischer Abtaster m
~ **medium** optisches Medium n
~ **memory** optischer Speicher m
~ **metrology** optische Metrologie f
~ **micrometer** optisches Mikrometer n
~ **microscope** Lichtmikroskop n, optisches Mikroskop m
~ **microscope image** Lichtmikroskopaufnahme f, Lichtmikroskopbild n
~ **microscopic** lichtmikroskopisch
~ **microscopy** lichtoptische Mikroskopie f, Lichtmikroskopie f
~ **microsensor** optischer Mikrosensor m
~ **mirror** optischer Spiegel m
~ **modulator** Lichtmodulator m, optischer Modulator m
~ **module** Optikmodul n, optisches Modul n
~ **mount** Optikhalter m, Halter m
~ **mouse** optische (optomechanische) Maus f
~ **multichannel analysis** optische Vielkanalanalyse f
~ **multiplexer** optischer Multiplexer m
~ **noise** optisches Rauschen n
~ **obturator** Verschlussblende f
~ **parallax** optische Parallaxe f
~ **parametric oscillator** parametrischer Oszillator m
~ **path** optischer Pfad (Strahlengang) m, optischer Weg m, Lichtweg m
~ **path difference** optische Wegdifferenz f, optischer Gangunterschied m, Lichtwegunterschied m
~ **path length** optische Weglänge f *(s.a. ~ path)*
~ **pathway** s. ~ path
~ **pattern recognition** optische Mustererkennung f
~ **performance** optische Leistung f
~ **phase change** optischer Phasenwechsel m *(DVD-Technik)*
~ **phenomenon** optische Erscheinung f; Apparition f
~ **pickup** optischer Aufnehmer m
~ **plastic** optischer Kunststoff m
~ **point-spread function** optische Punktbildfunktion f
~ **polarization** optische Polarisation f
~ **polygon** optisches Polygon n
~ **polymer** optischer Kunststoff m
~ **prefilter** optisches Vorfilter n
~ **printer** optische Kopiermaschine f, optischer Printer m; Trickkopiermaschine f *(Kinematografie)*
~ **printer operator** Trick[film]spezialist m
~ **printing** 1. optisches Kopieren n; 2. Umkopierung f; 3. Trickkopieren n
~ **printing effect** Kopiertrick m

~ **projection** optische Projektion f
~ **projector** Lichtbildwerfer m, Bildwerfer m, Vorführgerät n; Projektor m, Projektionsapparat m
~ **pulse** optischer Puls (Impuls) m, Licht[im]puls m
~ **pumping** optisches Pumpen n *(Spektroskopie)*
~ **radiation** optische Strahlung f, Lichtstrahlung f
~ **radiation filter** optisches Strahlungsfilter n
~ **rail** optische Schiene f
~ **ray** optischer Strahl m
~ **read head** optischer Lesekopf m
~ **receiver** optischer Empfänger m
~ **recognition** optische Erkennung f
~ **reduction** optische Verkleinerung f
~ **reflective videodisc** optisch reflektierende Bildplatte f
~ **refraction** [optische] Brechung f, Refraktion f
~ **resolution** optische Auflösung f
~ **resonance** optische Resonanz f
~ **resonator** optischer Resonator m; Laserresonator m
~ **return loss** optische Rückflussdämpfung f *(Fotodetektor)*
~ **reversibility** optische Umkehrbarkeit f
~ **rotation** optische Drehung f
~ **scanner** optischer Scanner m
~ **scanning** optische Abtastung f
~ **scatter[ing]** optische Streuung f
~ **scattering power** optisches Streuvermögen n
~ **sensitization** optische (spektrale) Sensibilisierung f
~ **sensitizer** optischer Sensibilisator m
~ **sensor** Optosensor m, optischer Sensor m, Lichtsensor m, Fotosensor m
~ **sight** Diopter n
~ **signal** optisches Signal n
~ **signal processing** optische Signalverarbeitung f
~ **signature** optische Signatur f
~ **snake track** Partial-Lichttonspur f
~ **sound** Lichtton m
~ **sound head** Lichtton[abtast]gerät n
~ **sound negative** Lichttonnegativ n, Lichttonnegativfilm m
~ **sound print** Lichttonkopie f
~ **sound quality** Lichttonqualität f
~ **sound reading equipment** Lichtton[abtast]gerät n
~ **sound recording** Lichttonaufnahme f, Lichttonaufzeichnung f
~ **sound reproducer** Lichttonwiedergabegerät n
~ **sound reproduction** Lichttonwiedergabe f
~ **sound track** Lichttonspur f
~ **spectroscopy** optische Spektroskopie f
~ **spectrum** optisches Spektrum n
~ **speed** Lichtempfindlichkeit f *(von Fotomaterial)*
~ **spread function** optische Verteilungsfunktion f
~ **square** Winkelprisma n
~ **step printer** optische Schrittkopiermaschine f *(Filmkopierung)*
~ **stimulation** optische Anregung f
~ **storage** optische Speicherung f
~ **storage medium** optisches Speichermedium n
~ **stylus** optischer Lesekopf m
~ **surface** optische Fläche (Oberfläche) f, optisch wirksame Fläche f
~ **switch** optischer Schalter m
~ **system** optisches System n, Optik f
~ **table** optischer Tisch m
~ **technology** Optotechnik f
~ **telescope** optisches Teleskop n, Lichtteleskop n
~ **thickness** optische Dicke f
~ **time multiplex technique** optische Zeitmultiplextechnik f
~ **tomographic imaging**, ~ **tomography** optische Tomografie f
~ **track** Lichttonspur f
~ **train** optischer Pfad (Strahlengang) m
~ **transfer function** optische Übertragungsfunktion f
~ **transmission** optische Transmission f
~ **triangulation** optische Triangulation f
~ **tube length** optische Tubuslänge f, optisches Intervall n *(Mikroskop)*
~ **viewfinder** optischer Sucher m
~ **vignetting** optische Vignettierung f
~ **wave** Lichtwelle f, optische Welle f
~ **waveguide** Lichtwellenleiter m
~ **wavelength range (regime)** optischer (sichtbarer) Wellenlängenbereich m
~ **wedge** optischer Keil m *(Sensitometrie)*
~ **window** optisches Fenster n
~ **zoom** optisches Zoom n

optically active medium optisch aktives Medium n
~ **flat surface** Planfläche f
~ **induced charge** lichtinduzierte Ladung f
~ **isotropic medium** optisch isotropes Medium n
~ **navigated robot** optisch navigierter Roboter m
~ **pumped laser** optisch gepumpter Laser m

optician Optiker m
optics 1. Optik f, Lehre f vom Licht, Lichtlehre f; 2. s. optic 2.
~ **cleaning tissue (wipe)** Linsenputztuch n, Linsenpapier m, Objektivreinigungstuch n
~ **laboratory** Optiklabor n
~ **table** optischer Tisch m

optimal color stimulus [Schrödingersche] Optimalfarbe f *(Farbmetrik)*
~ **filter** optimales Filter n, Optimalfilter n *(Bildrestaurierung)*

optimal 268

~ **filtering** optimale Filterung f, Optimalfilterung f
~ **morphological operator** s. ~ filter
~ **operator** optimaler Operator m
~ **predictor** optimaler Prädiktor m
optimization Optimierung f
~ **algorithm** Optimierungsalgorithmus m
optimize/to optimieren
optimized interpolation optimierte Interpolation f
optimum aperture förderliche Blende f, nutzbare Apertur f
~ **code** kompakter Code m
~ **color** Optimalfarbe f
~ **exposure** optimale Belichtung f
~ **filter** Optimalfilter n, optimales Filter n (Bildrestaurierung)
~ **filtering** optimale Filterung f, Optimalfilterung f
~ **quantization** optimale Quantisierung f
~ **scalar quantizer** optimaler Quantisierer m
optoacoustic effect optoakustischer Effekt m
optocoupler Optokoppler m
optoelectronic optoelektronisch
~ **component** optoelektronisches Bauelement n
~ **conversion** optoelektronische Wandlung f
~ **integrated circuit** optoelektronische integrierte Schaltung f
~ **scanner** optoelektronischer Scanner m
~ **semiconductor** Optohalbleiter m, optoelektronischer Halbleiter m
~ **sensor** optoelektronischer Sensor m
~ **transducer** optoelektronischer Wandler m
optoelectronics Optoelektronik f, Optronik f
optoisolator Optokoppler m
optokinetic optokinetisch
~ **nystagmus** optokinetischer Nystagmus m
~ **reflex** optokinetischer Reflex m
optomechanical scanner optomechanischer Scanner m
optometer Optometer m, Sehweitenmesser m
optometric[al] optometrisch, augenoptisch
optometrist Augenoptiker m
optometry Optometrie f, Sehkraftbestimmung f
optotypes Optotypen pl, Sehzeichen npl (Sehschärfebestimmung)
optronics Optronik f, Optoelektronik f
OR [logisches] ODER n (Operator)
OR gate ODER-Gatter n
orange cast Orangefarbstich m
~ **filter** Orangefilter n
orbit Augenhöhle f, Augenkapsel f, Orbita f
orbital Orbital n(m)

~ **electron** Bahnelektron n, Hüllenelektron n
~ **photograph** Weltraumbild n
order envelope Auftragstasche f (Fotoservice)
~ **n Bessel function** Bessel-Funktion f nullter Ordnung
~ **of diffraction** Beugungsordnung f
ordered tree geordneter Baum m (Datenstruktur)
ordinary camera lens Standardobjektiv n, Normalobjektiv n
~ **developer** Normalentwickler m
~ **light** Normallicht n
~ **paper** Normalpapier n, Standardpapier n
~ **photography** konventionelle (herkömmliche) Fotografie f, Normalfotografie f
~ **ray** ordentlicher Strahl m
organ imaging bildliche Organdarstellung f
~ **of sight** Sehorgan n
organic display organisches Display n
~ **dye** organischer Farbstoff m
~ **glass** organisches Glas n
~ **light-emitting diode** organische Leuchtdiode (Lichtmitterdiode) f, organische lichtemittierende Diode f
~ **matrix display** organisches Matrixdisplay n
~ **photoconductor** organischer Fotoleiter m
~ **thin film transistor** organischer Dünnschichttransistor m
orient/to orientieren, ausrichten
orientability Orientierbarkeit f
orientate/to s. orient/to
orientation Orientierung f, Ausrichtung f
~ **angle** Richtungswinkel m
~ **contrast** Orientierungskontrast m, Beugungskontrast m (Elektronenmikroskopie)
~ **detection** Richtungserkennung f, Richtungsdetektion f, Orientierungsdetektion f
~ **information** Richtungsinformation f
~ **-selective filter** richtungsempfindliches Filter n
~ **sensing device**, ~ **sensor** Richtungssensor m
~ **vector** Orientierungsvektor m
oriented filter Richtungsfilter n, gerichtetes Filter n
~ **pattern** gerichtetes Muster n
original 1. Original n; Bildvorlage f; 2. Originalfilm m; 3. Primärton m (Tonfilm)
~ **camera film** Kameraoriginal n
~ **camera negative** Originalnegativ n, Kameranegativ n
~ **color** Originalfarbe f
~ **color photograph** Originalfarbfoto n
~ **copy** 1. Originalkopie f; 2. Originalvorlage f (Druck)
~ **data** Rohdaten pl
~ **film** 1. Originalfim m; 2. Schreibfolie f

~ **film footage** Originalfilmmaterial n, [originales] Drehmaterial n
~ **image** Originalbild n
~ **image data** Originalbilddaten pl
~ **location** Originaldrehort m, Originalschauplatz m *(Filmarbeit)*
~ **motion-picture image** Originalfilmbild n
~ **negative [film]** Originalnegativ n
~ **photoengraving** [fotomechanische] Original-Hochdruckplatte f
~ **photograph** Originalfoto n, Originalaufnahme f
~ **print** Originalabzug m; Originalvergrößerung f
~ **production sound** s. ~ sound
~ **recording** Originalaufzeichnung f
~ **scene** Originalszene f
~ **shot** Originalaufnahme f
~ **signal** Originalsignal n
~ **sound** Originalton m, O-Ton m, Live-Ton m
~ **sync-sound production recording** Originaltonfilmaufnahme f
~ **wave** Objektwelle f, Gegenstandswelle f, Signalwelle f *(Holografie)*
ornamental capital Initiale f, [verzierter] Anfangsbuchstabe m
orphan [line] Schusterjunge m *(Druckfehler)*
orthicon Orthikon n, CPS-Emitron n *(Bildwandlerröhre)*
ortho s. orthochromatic
~ **image** Orthobild n *(Fotogrammetrie)*
orthochromatic orthochromatisch, farbtonrichtig, tonwertrichtig
~ **emulsion** orthochromatische Emulsion f
~ **film** orthochromatischer Film m, Orthofilm m
orthochromatism Orthochromasie f, Tonwertrichtigkeit f
orthocorrection Orthorektifizierung f
orthodiagram Orthodiagrafie f, Orthoröntgenografie f
orthogonal orthogonal; achsenparallel; rechtwinklig
~ **filter** orthogonales Filter n, Orthogonalfilter n
~ **frequency division modulation** orthogonale Frequenzmodulation f
~ **frequency division multiplex** orthogonales Frequenzmultiplexen n
~ **matrix** orthogonale Matrix f
~ **polarization** orthogonale Polarisation f
~ **polygon** orthogonales Polygon n
~ **projection** Orthogonalprojektion f, Normalprojektion f, orthogonale Projektion f (Parallelprojektion) f
~ **sampling (scanning)** orthogonale Abtastung f
~ **transformation** orthogonale Transformation f
~ **vector** orthogonaler Vektor m
~ **view** orthogonale Ansicht f
~ **wavelet** orthogonales Wavelet n

~ **wavelet transform** orthogonale Wavelet-Transformation f
orthogonality Orthogonalität f; Rechtwinkligkeit f
~ **condition** Orthogonalitätsbedingung f
~ **principle** Orthogonalitätsprinzip n
orthographic [parallel] projection s. orthogonal projection
orthomorphic map winkeltreue Karte f
orthonormal filter orthonormales Filter n
~ **matrix** orthonormale Matrix f
~ **transform** orthonormale Transformation f
~ **vector** orthonormaler Vektor m
orthonormality Orthonormalität f
orthopanchromatic orthopanchromatisch
orthophenylenediamine Orthophenylendiamin n *(Entwicklersubstanz)*
orthophoto Orthofoto n, entzerrte Fotografie f
~ **element** Orthofotoelement n
~ **map** Orthofotokarte f
~ **mosaic** Orthofotomosaik n
orthophotograph s. orthophoto
orthophotography Orthofotografie f
orthoprojector Orthoprojektor m, Differentialentzerrungsgerät n *(Fotogrammetrie)*
~ **system** Orthoprojektorsystem n
orthorectification Orthorektifizierung f
orthoscope Orthoskop n *(Optik)*
orthoscopic orthoskopisch, unverzeichnet, verzeichnungsfrei, unverzerrt, verzerrungsfrei; entzerrt
~ **eyepiece** orthoskopisches Okular n
~ **illumination** orthoskopische Beleuchtung f
~ **image** orthoskopisches (unverzeichnetes) Bild n, Orthobild n *(s.a. ortho image)*
~ **lens** verzeichnungsfreies Objektiv n
~ **observation (viewing)** orthoskopische Beobachtung f
orthoscopy Orthoskopie f
oscillate/to oszillieren
oscillation amplitude Schwingungsamplitude f
~ **plane** Schwingungsebene f
~ **train** Schwingungszug m
oscillator Oszillator m
~ **frequency** Oszillatorfrequenz f
~ **noise** Oszillatorrauschen n
~ **tube (valve)** Oszillatorröhre f
oscillatory amplitude Schwingungsamplitude f
oscillogram Oszillogramm n
oscillograph Oszillograf m, Schwingungsschreiber m
~ **screen** Oszillografenschirm m
~ **valve** Oszillografenröhre f
oscillographic oszillografisch
oscillography Oszillografie f

oscilloscope Oszilloskop *n*; Elektronenstrahloszilloskop *n*
~ **camera** Oszilloskopkamera *f*
~ **photography** Oszilloskopfotografie *f*
~ **screen** Oszillografenschirm *m*
oscilloscopic oszilloskopisch
OSD s. on-screen display
OSI s. open system interconnection
Ostwald color system Ostwald-System *n* *(Farbmetrik)*
~ **ripening** Ostwald-Reifung *f*, physikalische Reifung *f* *(Emulsionsherstellung)*
otoscope Otoskop *n*, Ohrspiegel *m*
otoscopic otoskopisch
otoscopy Otoskopie *f*, Ohrspiegelung *f*
Otsu's method Diskriminanzmethode *f* *(Schwellenwertbildung)*
out of focus fokusfern; extrafokal, unscharf
~-**of-focus image** unscharfes Bild *n*
~ **of phase** phasenverschoben
~ **of sync** asynchron
~ **point** Ausstiegspunkt *m* *(Videobandschnitt)*
outdent negativer Einzug *m* *(Layout)*
outdoor antenna Außenantenne *f*
~ **color film** Tageslichtfarbfilm *m*
~ **daylight picture** Tag-Außenaufnahme *f*
~ **exposure** Außenaufnahme *f*
~ **landscape photography** Landschaftsfotografie *f*
~ **lighting** Außenbeleuchtung *f*
~ **location** Außendrehort *m*, Außenaufnahmeort *m*, Außenmotiv *n* *(Filmarbeit)*
~ **photograph** Außenaufnahme *f*
~ **photographer** Freilichtfotograf *m*
~ **photography** Freilichtfotografie *f*
~ **picture** Freilichtaufnahme *f*
~ **scene** Außenszene *f*
~ **setting** Außendekoration *f*
~ **unit** Außeneinheit *f*
outer edge Außenkante *f*
~ **error correction** äußerer Fehlerschutz *m*
~ **error-correction code** äußerer Fehlerkorrekturcode *m*
~ **form** äußere Druckform *f*
~-**shell electron** Außenhüllenelektron *n*
outlier Ausreißer *m* *(Statistik)*
~ **detection** Ausreißererkennung *f*
outline Umriss *m* *(s.a. contour)*
~ **drawing** Umrisszeichnung *f*
~ **edge** Konturlinie *f*, Umrisslinie *f*
~ **font** Vektor-Zeichensatz *m*
~ **image** Umrissbild *n*
~ **map** Umrisskarte *f*
output Ausgabe *f*
~ **amplifier** Ausgangsverstärker *m*
~ **amplifier noise** Ausgangsverstärkerrauschen *n*
~ **angle** Austrittswinkel *m*
~ **beam** Austrittsstrahl *m*
~ **brightness** Ausgangshelligkeit *f* *(elektronische Bildbearbeitung)*
~ **buffer** Ausgangspuffer *m*, Ausgabepuffer[speicher] *m*
~ **clock** Ausgangstakt *m*
~ **coupler [mirror]** Auskoppelspiegel *m* *(Laser)*
~ **device** Ausgabegerät *n*
~ **film** Endfilm *m* *(Reprografie)*
~ **fluorescent screen** s. ~ phosphor screen
~ **format** Ausgabe[datei]format *n*
~ **frame** Ausgabebild *n* *(Video)*
~ **frequency** Ausgangsfrequenz *f*
~ **histogram** Ausgabehistogramm *n*
~ **house** Reproanstalt *f*
~ **image** 1. Ausgangbild *n*; 2. Ausgabebild *n*
~ **interface** Ausgangsschnittstelle *f*
~ **layer** Ausgabeschicht *f*, Ausgangsschicht *f*, Kohonen-Schicht *f* *(Neuroinformatik)*
~ **lens** Austrittslinse *f*
~ **material** Ausgabematerial *n*
~ **medium** Ausgabemedium *n*
~ **mirror** Auskoppelspiegel *m* *(Laser)*
~ **multiplex filter** Ausgangs-Multiplexfilter *n*
~ **pattern** Ausgangsmuster *n* *(Musterklassifikation)*
~ **phosphor screen** Bildverstärkerausgangsschirm *m*, Ausgangs[leucht]schirm *m* *(Röntgenbildverstärker)*
~ **pixel** Ausgangspixel *n*
~ **plane** Ausgangsebene *f* *(Strahlenoptik)*
~ **polarization axis** Ausgangspolarisation *f*
~ **primitive [element]** Ausgabeprimitiv *n*, Ausgabeelement *n* *(Bildbeschreibung)*
~ **pulse** Ausgangsimpuls *m*
~ **resolution** Ausgabeauflösung *f*
~ **scene** Ausgangsszene *f*
~ **screen** s. ~ phosphor screen
~ **signal** Ausgangssignal *n*
~ **symbol** Ausgangssymbol *n* *(Codierung)*
~ **tray** Papierausgabefach *n* *(Kopierer)*
~ **vector** Ausgangsvektor *m*, Ausgabevektor *m*
~ **video image** Ausgangsvideobild *n*
~ **window** Auskoppelfenster *n* *(Laser)*
outs s. outtakes
outshine/to überstrahlen
outside broadcast Außenübertragung *f*
~ **broadcast vehicle** Übertragungswagen *m*, Übertragungsfahrzeug *n*, Ü-Wagen *m*, mobile Übertragungseinheit *f*
outtakes Reste *mpl*, Schnittabfall *m* *(Filmbearbeitung)*
oval scissors Ellipsenschere *f* *(Computergrafik)*
~ **tool** Ellipsenwerkzeug *n* *(Computergrafik)*
over-the-air broadcast terrestrische Ausstrahlung *f*
~-**the-air broadcasting** Terrestrik *f* *(Sendetechnik)*

~-**the-air transmission** terrestrische Übertragung f
~-**the-horizon radar** Überreichweitenradar n, Überhorizontradar n, weitsichtiges Radar n
overall aberration [optischer] Gesamtfehler m
~ **brightness** Gesamthelligkeit f (z.B. eines Bildschirms)
~ **contrast** Allgemeinkontrast m, Gesamtkontrast m
~ **exposure** Gesamtbelichtung f, Gesamtbelichtungszeit f
~ **image** Gesamtbild n
~ **light** Allgemeinlicht n, Gesamtaufhellung f, Grundhelligkeit f, Grundlicht n
~ **magnification** Gesamtvergrößerung f
~ **noise** Gesamtrauschen n
~ **processing time** Gesamtverarbeitungszeit f
~ **resolution** Gesamtauflösung f
~ **sensitivity** Allgemeinempfindlichkeit f (z.B. einer fotografischen Emulsion)
~ **sharpness** Allgemeinschärfe f, Gesamtschärfe f
overcast sky bedeckter Himmel m
overcoat [layer] Oberguss m, Überguss m, Emulsionsdeckschicht f, Schutzschicht f (Filmherstellung)
overcorrection Überkorrektion f (von Objektiven)
overcranking Überdrehen n (Kinematografie)
overdevelop/to überentwickeln
overdevelopment Überentwicklung f, Pushentwicklung f, forcierte (gesteigerte) Entwicklung f
overdub/to überspielen
overenlarge/to übervergrößern (z.B. kleinformatige Negative)
overenlargement Übervergrößerung f
overetching Überätzen n, Überätzung f
overexpose/to überbelichten
overexposure Überbelichtung f
~ **tolerance** Überbelichtungstoleranz f
overfitting Überanpassung f (Mustererkennung)
overfixation, overfixing Überfixieren n, Überfixierung f
overflow Grauwertüberlauf m, Überlauf m (Digitalbild)
overfocus/to überfokussieren
overfocusing Überfokussierung f
overhead s. ~ projector
~ **camera** Deckenkamera f, deckenmontierte Kamera f
~ **image** Luftbild n, Luftaufnahme f
~ **projected image** Overheadprojektion f
~ **projection** Overheadprojektion f
~ **projector** Overheadprojektor m, Tageslichtprojektor m, Arbeitsprojektor m, Diaskop f
~ **reconnaissance image** Luftaufklärungsfoto n

~ **shot** Überkopfaufnahme f
~ **surveillance** Luftraumüberwachung f
~ **surveillance camera** Luftaufklärungskamera f
~ **transparency** Overheadfolie f
~ **transparency adapter** Durchlichtaufsatz m, Durchlichteinheit f (Scanner)
overlap 1. Überlappung f, Überdeckung f, Okklusion f; 2. Bildüberdeckung f; 3. Überdeckungsperspektive f
~ **area** Überdeckungsgebiet n, Okklusionsbereich m
~ **splice** überlappte Klebestelle f
overlapping region s. overlap area
overlay/to übereinanderlegen, überlagern, superponieren
overlay 1. Auflegemaske f, Aufleger m (Layout); 2. Bildsandwich n
~ **board** Overlay-Karte f (Video)
~ **cel** Folie f (Animationsfilm)
~ **image** Überlagerungsbild n
overmodulation Übermodulation f
overprint/to über[einander]drucken, aufdrucken
overprint Übereinanderdruck m, Aufdruck m
~ **color** Sekundärfarbe f
overprinting Übereinanderdrucken n
overreplenishment Überregenerierung f (Fotochemie)
override [manuelle] Einstellmöglichkeit f
overrun, overs Zuschuss m (Druck)
oversample/to überabtasten
oversampling Überabtastung f
oversaturated color übersättigte Farbe f
overscan/to überabtasten
overscan Zeilenüberdeckung f
oversegmentation Übersegmentierung f
oversensitization Übersensibilisierung f
overtable [X-ray] tube Obertischröhre f (Radiografie)
overview Überblick m, Übersicht f
overwrite/to überschreiben (z.B. Pixelwerte)
oxidant Oxidationsmittel n
oxidation Oxidation f
~ **product** Oxidationsprodukt n
oxidative fog Entwicklungsschleier m
oxide cathode Oxidkatode f
oxidizing agent Oxidationsmittel n
Ozalid process Ozalidverfahren n (ein Diazo-Lichtpausverfahren)

P

P-bus interface P-Bus-Schnittstelle f
P-frame prädiziertes (prädiktiv codiertes) Bild n, P-Bild n *(Video)*
P frame (picture) s. predicted frame
p-i-n photodiode pin-Fotodiode f
p-n boundary pn-Grenzschicht f *(Fototransistor)*
p-n junction pn-Übergang m
p-n junction electroluminescence Rekombinationsstrahlung f *(Leuchtdiode)*
p-n junction photodiode pn-Fotodiode f
p-phenylenediamine p-Phenylendiamin n *(Entwicklersubstanz)*
pack film Packfilm m
~ **shot** Produktaufnahme f, Produktfoto n, Sachaufnahme f, Gegenstandsaufnahme f
packaging gravure Verpackungstiefdruck m
~ **press** Verpackungsdruckmaschine f
~ **printing** Verpackungsdruck m
packet Paket n; Datenpaket n
~ **identification** Paketidentifikation f
~ **length** Paketlänge f
~ **loss** Paketverlust m
~-**switched network** paketvermitteltes Datennetz n
~-**switched videophony** paketvermittelte Bildtelefonie f
~ **switching** Paket[daten]vermittlung f, Datenpaketvermittlung f
~ **video** komprimiertes Video n
~ **video transmission** Paketvideoübertragung f
packetization Paketierung f
~ **delay** Paketierungsverzögerung f
packetize/to paketieren *(z.B. Bilddaten)*
packetized data transfer paketweise Datenübertragung f
~ **elementary stream** paketierter Elementarbitstrom m
packing Unterlage f, Unterlagebogen m, Unterlagenmaterial n *(von Druckplattenzylindern oder Gummituchzylindern)*
PACS s. picture archiving and communication[s] system
pad printing Tampondruck m, Tampondruckverfahren n, Rotationstampondruck m, Transferdruck m
~ **roller** Andruckrolle f
~ **transfer printing** s. ~ printing
padding Klappennachlauf m, Klappenvorlauf m *(Film)*
page/to paginieren

page Seite f, Druckseite f
~ **area memory** Seitenspeicher m
~ **assembly** s. ~ makeup
~ **break** Seitenwechsel m *(Typografie)*
~ **catching** Blättern im Videotext
~ **count** Seitenzahl f
~ **description command** Seitenbeschreibungsbefehl m *(Computersatz)*
~ **description language** Seitenbeschreibungssprache f
~ **designer** Layouter m
~ **flip** Umblättereffekt m, Umblättertrick m, Seitenblättern n *(Videoeffekt)*
~ **format** Seitenformat n
~ **header** Kopfzeile f *(Videotext)*; lebender Kolumnentitel m *(Druckseite)*
~ **imposition** Ausschießen n *(Druckvorstufe)*
~ **layout** Seitenlayout n, Seitengestaltung f
~ **layout program (software)** Seitenlayoutprogramm n, Layoutsoftware f
~ **makeup** Seitenumbruch m, Umbruch m, Mettage f, Seitenmontage f
~ **number** Seitenzahl f, Pagina f
~ **of text** Textseite f
~ **of type** Druckseite f
~ **printer** Seitendrucker m, Blattdrucker m
~ **proof** Seitenproof m
~ **table** Seitentabelle f, Seitentafel f *(Grafikdatei)*
~ **turn [effect]** s. ~ flip
paginate/to paginieren
pagination, paging Paginierung f, Seitennumerierung f
paint Farbe f
~ **mode** Malmodus m *(Computergrafik)*
~ **pigment** Farbpigment n
~ **program (software)** [Computer-]Malprogramm n, Pixelgrafikprogramm n
~ **tool** Malwerkzeug n *(Computergrafik)*
painted glass shot Glas[vorsatz]aufnahme f *(Trickkinematografie)*
painter's algorithm Painter's-Algorithmus m, Prioritätenlistenalgorithmus m *(Computergrafik)*
pair of binoculars Doppelfernrohr n, binokulares Fernrohr n
~ **of bits** Bitpaar n
~ **of glasses** Brille f
~ **of images** Bildpaar n
~ **of prisms** Prismenpaar n
~ **of stereo pictures** Stereobildpaar n
~ **production process** Paarbildung f, Paarerzeugungsprozess m *(Teilchenphysik)*
~-**wise comparison [technique]** paarweiser Vergleich m
~-**wise kerning** paarweises Unterschneiden n *(Typografie)*
PAL s. phase alternating line

~ **decoder** PAL-Auftrennstufe *f*, PAL-Decoder *m*
~ **standard** PAL-Norm *f*
~ **system** *s.* phase alternating line system
~ **television (video)** PAL-Fernsehen *n*
pale color blasse Farbe *f*; Pastellfarbe *f*
palette Farbpalette *f*
palladiotype Palladiotypie *f*
palladium Palladium *n*
~ **[printing] process** Palladiotypie *f*
~ **print** Palladiumabzug *m*
PALplus standard PALplus-Norm *f*, PALplus-Format *n*
~ **television [system]** PALplus-Fernsehen *n*, erweitertes PAL-Fernsehen *n*
pan/to schwenken *(Kameraarbeit)*
pan *s.* 1. ~ move; 2. panchromatic
~**-and-tilt head** Neigekopf *m (Stativ)*
~ **focus arrangement** Fixfokuseinstellung *f*, Naheinstellung *f* auf Unendlich
~ **head** *s.* panoramic head *m*
~ **move (shot)** Schwenk *m*, Mitschwenk *m*, Mitzieher *m*, Horizontalschwenk *m (Kameraführung)*
Panavision Panavision *n (kinematografisches Breitbildverfahren)*
pancake Bandwickel *m*, Wickel *m*; Magnetbandrolle *f*
panchromatic panchromatisch, rotempfindlich *(fotografische Emulsion)*
~ **black-and-white film** panchromatischer Schwarzweißfilm *m*
~ **film** panchromatischer Film *m*, Panfilm *m*
~ **imaging** panchromatische Abbildung *f*
~ **plate** panchromatische Platte *f*
~ **separation film** Farbauszugsfilm *m*
~ **silver halide emulsion** panchromatische Emulsion *f*
~ **vision filter** Betrachtungsfilter *n*
pancratic [lens] system pankratisches System (Objektiv) *n*, Zoomoptik *f*, Zoom[objektiv] *n*, Gummilinse *f*, Varioobjektiv *n*
~ **telescope** pankratisches Fernrohr *n*
panel point Passpunkt *m*, Passmarke *f*, Passelement *n (Fotogrammetrie)*
panic button Panikknopf *m (Spiegelreflexkamera)*
panmyelography Panmyelografie *f (Röntgenkontrastdarstellung des Spinalkanals)*
panning Mitziehen *n* [der Kamera]
panorama Panorama *n*
~ **shot** Panoramaaufnahme *f*
panoramic camera Panoramakamera *f*
~ **distortion** Panoramaverzerrung *f*
~ **film** Panoramafilm *m*
~ **head** Panoramakopf *m*, Schwenkkopf *m (Stativ)*
~ **image** Panoramabild *n*
~ **photograph** Panoramafoto *n*, Panoramaaufnahme *f*
~ **photography** Panoramafotografie *f*
~ **slide** Panoramadia[positiv] *n*

~ **view** Rundumsicht *f*
pantograph Pantograf *m*, Storchschnabel *m (Zeichengerät)*
pantographic pantografisch
Pantone matching system Pantone-Matching-System *n (ein Farbmischsystem)*
Panum's fusional area Panum-Raum *m*, Panum-Areal *n (binokulares Sehen)*
paper Papier *n*
~ **advance** Papiervorschub *m*, Papiertransport *m (Drucker)*
~ **backdrop** Papierhintergrund *m*, Hintergrundkarton *m (Atelierausrüstung)*
~ **base** Papier-Schichtträger *m*, Papierträger *m*, Papierunterlage *f*
~ **base thickness** Papierstärke *f*, Papierdicke *f*
~ **cassette** Papier[vorrats]kassette *f*
~ **color** Papierfarbe *f*
~ **contrast** Papierkontrast *m*
~ **contrast grade** Papiergradation *f*, Papierhärtegrad *m*
~ **copy** Papierkopie *f*; Papierausdruck *m*, Bildschirmausdruck *m*, Computerausdruck *m*, Ausdruck *m*
~ **copy image** Papierbild *n*
~ **developer** Papierentwickler *m*, Positiventwickler *m*
~ **development** Papierentwicklung *f*, Papierverarbeitung *f*
~ **emulsion** Papieremulsion *f*
~ **exposure** Papierbelichtung *f*
~ **exposure error** Papierbelichtungsfehler *m*
~ **feed** Papiereinzug *m*, Papierzuführung *f*, Papiervorschub *m*, Papiertransport *m (Drucker)*
~ **fiber** Papierfaser *f*
~ **finish** Papierausrüstung *f*
~ **fixer** Papierfixierer *m*
~ **grade** Papiergradation *f*, Papierhärtegrad *f*
~ **hard copy** *s.* ~ copy
~ **holder** Papierhalter *m (Fachkamera)*
~ **image** Papierbild *n*
~ **input** *s.* ~ feed
~ **jam[ming]** Papierstau *m*
~ **negative** Papiernegativ *n*
~ **path** Papierdurchlauf *m*, Papierweg *m*
~ **photograph** Papierfoto *n*
~ **positive print**, ~ **print** Papier[bild]abzug *m*, Bildabzug *m*, Fotoabzug *m*, Papierpositiv *n*
~ **print developer** *s.* ~ developer
~ **processing** Papierverarbeitung *f*
~ **processor** Papierentwicklungsmaschine *f*
~ **reproduction** *s.* ~ positive print
~ **roll** *s.* ~ web
~ **scanner** Papierscanner *m*
~ **sensitivity** Papierempfindlichkeit *f*
~ **size** Papierformat *n*

paper 274

~ **speed** Papierempfindlichkeit *f*
~ **stock tint** Papierton *m*, Papiertönung *f*
~ **support** Papier-Schichtträger *m*, Papierträger *m*, Papierunterlage *f*
~ **surface** Papieroberfläche *f*
~ **thickness** *s*. ~ weight
~ **throughput** Papierdurchsatz *m*
~ **train** Papierführung *f (Drucker)*
~ **tray** Papier[vorrats]kassette *f*
~ **type** Papiersorte *f*, Papierart *f*; Papiertyp *m*
~ **web** Papierbahn *f*, Bahn *f*, Rollenpapier *n (Druck)*
~ **weight** Papierstärke *f*, Papierdicke *f*
~ **white** Papierweiß *n*
paperboard Pappe *f*, Karton *m*
papier collé Collage *f*, Klebebild *n*
PAR light *s*. parabolic aluminized reflector light
para-aminophenol developer Paraaminophenol-Entwickler *m*
parabolic parabolisch
~ **aluminized reflector light** PAR-Lampe *f*, PAR-Scheinwerfer *m*
~ **antenna** Parabol[empfangs]antenne *f*, Parabolspiegelantenne *f*
~ **geometry** Euklidische Geometrie *f*
~ **index profile** parabelförmiges Indexprofil *n*
~ **mirror (reflector)** Parabolspiegel *m*, Parabolreflektor *m*
parabolize/to parabolisieren *(z.B. einen Teleskopspiegel)*
paraboloid Paraboloid *n*
paraboloidal mirror Parabolspiegel *m*
paracatadioptric camera calibration parakatadioptrische Kamerakalibrierung *f*
paradigm-based filter paradigmenbasiertes Filter *n*
paragraph Absatz *m (Textlayout)*
~ **indent** Absatzeinzug *m*, Einrückung *f*
parallactic axis parallaktische Achse *f*
~ **error** Parallaxenfehler *m*
parallax Parallaxe *f*
~ **angle** Parallaxenwinkel *m*
~ **correction [system]** Parallaxenausgleich *m*, Parallaxenkorrektur *m*
~ **difference** Parallaxenunterschied *m*
~ **displacement** Parallaxenverschiebung *f*
~ **error** Parallaxenfehler *m*
~ **error correction** Parallaxenausgleich *m*, Parallaxen[fehler]korrektur *f*
~-**free** parallaxenfrei
~ **shift** Parallaxenverschiebung *f*
~ **stereogram** Parallaxenstereogramm *n*
parallel beam Parallelstrahl *m*
~ **beam projection** Parallelstrahlprojektion *f*, Parallelstrahlverfahren *n Tomografie)*
~ **bundle [of rays]** Parallel[strahlen]bündel *n*, paralleles Bündel *n*
~ **bus** Parallelbus *m*
~ **computer** Parallelrechner *m*
~ **data stream** paralleler Datenstrom *m*

~ **data transfer** parallele Datenübertragung *f*
~ **displacement** *s*. ~ shift
~ **distributed processing model** konnektionistisches Modell (System) *n*, neuronales Netz (System) *n*, Neuronennetz *n*
~ **edge extraction** parallele Kantenextraktion *f*
~ **fold** Parallelbruchfalz *m*
~ **hole[s] collimator** Parallellochkollimator *m*, Viellochkollimator *m (Gammakamera)*
~ **image processing** parallele Bildverarbeitung *f*
~ **image processor** parallel arbeitender Bildprozessor *m*
~ **interface** Parallelschnittstelle *f*, parallele Schnittstelle *f*, Parallel-Anschlussbuchse *f*
~ **light** paralleles Licht *n*
~ **perspective** Parallelperspektive *f*, telezentrische Perspektive *f*, Einpunktperspektive *f*
~-**polarized image** parallel polarisiertes Bild *n (Radar)*
~ **port** Parallelschnittstelle *f*, parallele Schnittstelle *f*, Parallel-Anschlussbuchse *f*
~ **printer** Paralleldrucker *m*, Zeilendrucker *m*
~ **processing** Parallelverarbeitung *f*
~ **processor** Parallelprozessor *m*, parallel arbeitender Prozessor *m*
~ **projection** 1. Parallelprojektion *f*, parallele (orthogonale) Projektion *f*, Orthogonalprojektion *f*, Normalprojektion *f*; 2. *s*. ~ beam projection
~ **ray** Parallelstrahl *m*
~ **scan[ning]** Parallelabtastung *f*, Parallel-Scan *m*
~ **shift** Parallelverschiebung *f*, Parallelversetzung *f*
~ **transmission** Parallelübertragung *f*
parallelepiped Parallelepiped[on] *n*, Parallelflach *n*
~ **classification** Parallelepipedklassifikation *f*, Quaderklassifikation *f*, Quadermethode *f (Mustererkennung)*
parallelism Parallelität *f*
parallelization Parallelisierung *f*
parallelize/to parallelisieren
parallelogram Parallelogramm *n*
paramagnet Paramagnet *m*
paramagnetic paramagnetisch
~ **contrast agent** paramagnetisches Kontrastmittel *n*
paramagnetism Paramagnetismus *m*
parameter Parameter *m*
~ **[en]coding** Parametercodierung *f*
~ **estimation** Parameterschätzung *f*
~ **matrix** Parametermatrix *f*
~ **optimization** Parameteroptimierung *f*

~ **space** Parameterraum *m*, Merkmalsraum *m*
~ **vector** Parametervektor *m*
parameterization Parametrisierung *f*
parameterize/to parametr[is]ieren
parametral *s.* parametric
parametric parametrisch
~ **classification** parametrische Klassifikation *f*
~ **classifier** parametrischer Klassifikator *m*
~ **continuity** parametrische Kontinuität *f*
~ **curve** Parameterkurve *f*
~ **curve interpolation** parametrische Kurveninterpolation *f*
~ **description** parametrische Beschreibung *f*
~ **downconversion** parametrische Fluoreszenz *f*
~ **feature** parametrisches Merkmal *n*
~ **image** parametrisches Bild *n*
~ **image processing** parametrische Bildverarbeitung *f*
~ **model** parametrisches Modell *n*
~ **motion model** parametrisches Bewegungsmodell *n*
~ **oscillator** parametrischer Oszillator *m*
~ **polynomial curve** Parameterkurve *f*
~ **representation** Parameterdarstellung *f*, parametrische (parametrisierte) Darstellung *f*
~ **signature** parametrische Signatur *f*
~ **space** Parameterraum *m*
~ **Wiener filter** parametrisches Wiener-Filter *n*
parametrical parametrisch
parametrizable parametri[si]erbar
parametrization *s.* parameterization
paraminophenol *s.* para-aminophenol developer
paraperspective paraperspektivisch
paraphenylenediamine Paraphenylendiamin *n (Entwicklersubstanz)*
paraphotography silberfreie Fotografie *f*
paraxial paraxial, achsennah
~ **approximation** paraxiale Näherung *f (Strahlenoptik)*
~ **domain** *s.* ~ region
~ **focal plane** paraxiale Brennebene *f*
~ **focusing** paraxiale Fokussierung *f*
~ **geometric optics** *s.* ~ optics
~ **image** paraxiales Bild *n*, achs[en]nahes Bild *n*
~ **image formation** paraxiale Bildentstehung *f*
~ **image location** paraxialer Bildort *m*
~ **image plane** paraxiale (Gaußsche) Bildebene *f*
~ **marginal ray** paraxialer Randstrahl *m*
~ **optics** paraxiale (Gaußsche) Optik *f*, Optik *f* des Paraxialgebietes, Optik *f* erster Ordnung
~ **pupil ray** paraxialer Pupillenstrahl *m*

~ **ray** Paraxialstrahl *m*, paraxialer (achsennaher) Strahl *m*
~ **region** Paraxialgebiet *n*, achsnahes (paraxiales) Gebiet *n*, achs[en]naher Raum *m*, Gaußscher (fadenförmiger) Raum *m*
parent-child relationship Eltern-Kind-Beziehung *f (Grafikprogrammierung)*
~ **node** Vaterknoten *m (Computergrafik)*
parental control Kindersicherung *f (Fernsehgerät)*
parfocal parfokal
parietal lobe Parietallappen *m*, Scheitellappen *m (der Großhirnrinde)*
parity 1. Parität *f*; 2. *s.* ~ check bit
~ **check** Paritätsprüfung *f*, Plausibilitätsprüfung *f*
~ **check bit** Paritätsbit *n (Codierungsredundanz)*
parquetry Parkettierung *f*, Kachelung *f*, Mosaik *f (geometrische Datenverarbeitung)*
Parseval's theorem Parseval-Theorem *n*, Parsevalsche Regel *f (Signalverarbeitung)*
partial absorption Teilabsorption *f*, teilweise Absorption *f*
~ **beam** Teilstrahl *m*
~ **coherence** Teilkohärenz *f*, partielle Kohärenz *f*
~ **color blindness** partielle Farbenblindheit *f*, Zweifarbensehen *n*, dichromatisches Farbensehen *n*, Dichroma[top]sie *f*
~ **darkness** Halbdunkel *n*
~ **dispersion** Teildispersion *f (Optik)*
~ **exposure** Teilbelichtung *f*
~ **image** Teilbild *n*
~ **luminous flux** Teillichtstrom *m*
~ **match query** Teilpunktfrage *f (Computergrafik)*
~ **mirror** Teilspiegel *m*
~ **picture** Teilbild *n*
~ **polarization** Teilpolarisation *f*, teilweise Polarisation *f*
~ **range query** Teilbereich[sab]frage *f (Computergrafik)*
~ **reflection** Teilreflexion *f*
~ **segmentation** Teilsegmentierung *f*
~ **shadow** Halbschatten *m*
~ **silvering** Teilverspiegelung *f*
~ **volume effect** Partialvolumeneffekt *m (Bildsegmentierung)*
~ **wave** Teilwelle *f*
partially coherent teilkohärent
~ **coherent illumination** teilkohärente Beleuchtung *f*
~ **coherent imaging** partiell kohärente Abbildung *f*
~ **coherent light** teilkohärentes (partiell kohärentes) Licht *n*
~ **coherent lighting** partiell kohärente Beleuchtung *f*

partially

- ~ **color-blind person** partiell Farbenblinder *m*
- ~ **exposed film** teilbelichteter Film *m*
- ~ **mirrored** teilverspiegelt
- ~ **polarized light** teilpolarisiertes Licht *n*
- ~ **polarized radiation** teilpolarisierte Strahlung *f*
- ~ **reflecting (silvered) mirror** teildurchlässiger Spiegel *m*
- ~ **suppressed sideband** *s.* vestigial sideband
- ~ **transmitting mirror** teildurchlässiger Spiegel *m*
- ~ **transparent** teildurchsichtig

particle accelerator Teilchenbeschleuniger *m*
- ~ **mechanics** Teilchenmechanik *f*
- ~ **optics** Korpuskularoptik *f*
- ~ **physics** Teilchenphysik *f*
- ~ **radiation** Teilchenstrahlung *f*, Korpuskularstrahlung *f*, Partikelstrahlung *f*
- ~ **theory of light** Teilchentheorie (Korpuskulartheorie) *f* des Lichts
- ~ **tracing** Partikelverfolgung *f* *(Visualisierung)*

particulate scattering Teilchenstreuung *f*
parting line Trennlinie *f*
partition/to [auf]teilen, segmentieren
partition Partition *f*, Bildaufteilung *f*, Segmentierung *f (s.a. unter segmentation)*
partitioning line Trennlinie *f*
parts inspection Werkstück[güte]kontrolle *f*
Pascal [language] PASCAL *n (eine höhere Programmiersparache)*
passage of light Lichtdurchgang *m*
passband Durchlassband *m*, Passband *n (s.a. band-pass)*
- ~ **frequency** Durchlassfrequenz *f*
- ~ **range (width)** Durchlassbereich *m (eines Filters)*

passe-partout Passepartout *n*
passivation [layer] Passivierung *f (Fotodiode)*
passive addressing passive Ansteuerung *f*
- ~ **autofocus [device]** passiver Autofokus *m*
- ~ **display** passive Anzeige *f*
- ~ **filter** passives Filter *n*
- ~ **matrix** passive Matrix *f (Flüssigkristallanzeige)*
- ~ **matrix addressing** passive Adressierung *f*
- ~ **matrix display** Passivmatrixbildschirm *m*
- ~-**matrix LCD (liquid-crystal display)** Passivmatrix-Flüssigkristallanzeige *f*
- ~ **microwave system** passives Mikrowellensystem *n*
- ~ **pixel sensor** passiver Pixelsensor *m*
- ~ **radar** passives Radar *n*
- ~ **remote sensing** passive Fernerkundung *f*
- ~ **sensor** passiver Sensor *m*

passively addressed display passives Display *n*; passiver Bildschirm *m*
passport paper Passbildpapier *n*
- ~ **photo** Passbild *n*
- ~ **portrait** Passfotoporträt *n*
- ~ **[-size] photograph** Passbild *n*

past picture Folgebild *n*, Nachfolgerbild *n*
paste/to einfügen *(Computergrafik)*
paste Pflanzenleim *m*
- ~ **ink** Druckpaste *f*

pastedown Spiegel *m (Buchfertigung)*
pastel 1. pastellfarben, pastellig; 2. *s.* ~ color
- ~ **color** Pastellfarbe *f*
- ~-**colored** *s.* pastel 1.
- ~ **hue (shade)** Pastellton *m*

pasteup Klebespiegel *m*, Klebelayout *n*, Klebeumbruch *m*, Papiermontage *f*, Montage *f*; Ganzseitenmontage *f (Druckvorstufe)*
- ~ **process** Aufsichtmontage *f*, Klebemontage *f*, Papiermontage *f*, Montage *f*

patch ebenes Polygon *n (Radiosity-Verfahren; Computergrafik)*
- ~ **cable** Steckkabel *n*
- ~ **panel** Steckfeld *n*, Steckverteiler *m*, Koppelfeld *n*

path Pfad *m*; Weg *m (Computergrafik)*
- ~ **iterator** Pfaditerator *m*
- ~ **of transmission** Übertragungsweg *m*

patient couch *s.* ~ table
- ~-**image retrieval** Patientenbildrecherche *f*
- ~ **table** Patientenlagerungstisch *m*, Lagerungstisch *m*, Patientenliege *f*

pattern Muster *n*
- ~ **analysis** Musteranalyse *f*
- ~ **arrangement** Musteranordnung *f*
- ~ **associator** Musterassoziator *m*, Musterverknüpfer *m*
- ~ **class** Musterklasse *f*
- ~ **class separator** Musterklassenseparator *m*
- ~ **classification** Musterklassifikation *f*, Musterklassifizierung *f*
- ~ **classifier** Musterklassifikator *m*
- ~ **completion** Musterergänzung *f*, Mustervervollständigung *f*
- ~ **description language** Musterbeschreibungssprache *f*
- ~ **discriminability** Musterunterscheidbarkeit *f*
- ~ **distribution** Musterverteilung *f*
- ~ **generation** Mustererzeugung *f*
- ~ **identification** *s.* ~ recognition
- ~ **jitter** korrelierter Jitter *m*
- ~ **library** Musterbibliothek *f*
- ~ **mapping** Texturabbildung *f*, Textur-Mapping *n (Computergrafik)*
- ~ **mask** Projektionsmaske *f*; Schattenwerfer *m*
- ~ **matching** Mustervergleich *m*, Musterabgleich *m*; Musterzuordnung *f*
- ~ **morphology** Mustermorphologie *f*

~ **noise** Festmusterrauschen *n*
~ **point** Musterpunkt *m*
~ **primitive** Musterprimitiv *n*
~ **projector** Musterprojektor *m*
~ **recognition** Mustererkennung *f*
~ **recognition algorithm** Mustererkennungsalgorithmus *m*
~ **recognition engineering** Mustererkennungstechnik *f*
~ **recognition robot** Mustererkennungsroboter *m*
~ **recognition software** Mustererkennungssoftware *f*; Mustererkennungsprogramm *n*
~ **recognition system** Mustererkennungssystem *n*
~ **recognition task** Mustererkennungsaufgabe *f*
~ **recognition technique** Mustererkennungsverfahren *n*; Mustererkennungstechnik *f*
~ **reconstruction** Musterrekonstruktion *f*
~ **reference point** Musterreferenzpunkt *m*
~ **representation** Musterdarstellung *f*
~ **retrieval** Musterwiederauffindung *f*
~ **scanning** Musterabtastung *f*
~ **segmentation** Mustersegmentierung *f*
~ **size** Mustergröße *f*
~ **space** Musterraum *m*
~ **spectrum** Musterspektrum *n*
~ **structure** Musterstruktur *f*
~ **table** Mustertabelle *f*
~ **vector** Mustervektor *m*
patterning Musterbildung *f*
pause feature Pausenfunktion *f (Camcorder)*
~ **mode** Bereitschaftsmodus *m*, Bereitschaftsschaltung *m* Stand-by-Betrieb *m*, Stand-by *n*
pay-cable Kabel-Bezahlfernsehen *n*
~ **channel** Bezahl[fernseh]sender *m*
~**-per-channel** Bezahlung *f* pro Programmkanal
~**-per-package** Bezahlung *f* pro Programmpaket
~**-per-view** Bezahlung *f* pro Programmbeitrag
~**-TV** Bezahlfernsehen *n*
~**-TV receiver** Pay-TV-Empfänger *m*
PC PC *m*, Personalcomputer *m*
PC card PC-Karte *f (Standardschnittstelle)*
PC card adapter PC-Kartenadapter *m*
PC card slot PC-Kartenschlitz *m*
PC connector *s.* pin cylinder connector
PC lens PC-Objektiv *n*, Perspektivekorrekturobjektiv *n*, Shiftobjektiv *n*
PC terminal *s.* pin cylinder connector
PC user PC-Nutzer *m*, Computer[be]nutzer *m*
PCI slot *s.* peripheral component interconnect slot
PCM *s.* pulse code modulation
PE paper polyesterbeschichtetes Papier *n*

peak lokales Maximum *n*
~ **amplitude** Spitzenamplitude *f*
~ **bit rate** Spitzenbitrate *f*
~ **brightness** Spitzenleuchtdichte *f*, maximale Leuchtdichte *f*
~ **detection** Spitzendetektion *f*
~ **limiter** Spitzenwertbegrenzer *m*
~ **limiting** Spitzenwertbegrenzung *f*
~ **luminance** maximale Leuchtdichte *f*, Spitzenleuchtdichte *f*
~ **meter** Spitzenwertanzeiger *m*; Spitzenspannungsmesser *m*
~ **noise** Punktrauschen *n*
~ **pulse power** Pulsspitzenleistung *f*
~ **sensitivity** maximale Empfindlichkeit *f*
~ **shift** Impulsspitzenverschiebung *f*
~ **signal-to-noise ratio** Spitzen-Signal-Rausch-Verhältnis *n*
~ **white [level]** Weißwert *m*, Weißpegel *m* *(Videosignal)*
pearl seidenmatt *(z.B. Fotopapier)*
~ **screen** Perl[lein]wand *f*; Kristallperlwand *f*
pec cell *s.* photocell
pedestal 1. Pumpstativ *n*; pneumatisches Stativ *n*; Studiokamerastativ *m*, Studio[pump]stativ *n*, Studiopumpe *f*; 2. Schwarzabhebung *f*, Austastwert *m* *(Videosignal)*
peel-apart film Abziehfilm *m*, Stripping-Film *m (Reprografie)*
~**-apart process** Trennbildverfahren *n*
~**-apart sandwich** Trennbild *n*
peeling [off] Abziehen *n*
peep show Guckkasten *m*
~ **show machine** Guckkastenapparat *m*
~ **sight** Diopter *n*
peephole Guckloch *n*
pel *s.* pixel
pellicle beam splitter Dünnschicht-Strahl[en]teiler *m*, Folienstrahlteiler *m*
pellucid durchsichtig, lichtdurchlässig, transparent
Peltier-cooled camera peltiergekühlte Kamera *f*
~ **cooler** Peltier-Element *n*, Peltier-Kühler *m*
pen plotter Zeichenstiftplotter *m*, Stiftplotter *m*
pencil beam Bleistiftkeule *f*, Nadelstrahl *m (Radar)*
~ **retouching** Bleistiftretusche *f*
penetrating-type radiation durchdringende Strahlung *f*
penetration depth Eindringtiefe *f (z.B. von Ultraschall)*
~ **power** Durchdringungsfähigkeit *f*, Durchdringungsvermögen *n (z.B. von Röntgenstrahlung)*
pentagonal prism, pentaprism Penta[gon]prisma *n*, Fünfseit[en]prisma *n*

pentaprism

pentaprism finder, ~ viewfinder [system] Pentaprismensucher *m*, Prismensucher *m*
penthouse Tonlaufwerk *n*, Magnettonwiedergabegerät *n*
penumbra, penumbral shadow Penumbra *f*, Halbschatten *m*
people photography Personenfotografie *f*, Menschenfotografie *f*
perceivable *s.* perceptible
perceive/to wahrnehmen, perzipieren
perceived brightness wahrgenommene (empfindungsgemäße) Helligkeit *f*, subjektive Helligkeit *f*
~ **color** wahrgenommene Farbe *f*
~ **depth** wahrgenommene Tiefe *f*
~ **hue** wahrgenommene Farbe *f*
~ **image** wahrgenommenes Bild *n*
~ **lightness** *s.* ~ brightness
perceptibility Wahrnehmbarkeit *f*
perceptible wahrnehmbar, perzeptibel
perception Wahrnehmung *f*
~-based image coding wahrnehmungsbasierte Bildcodierung (Codierung) *f*
~ **domain** Wahrnehmungsbereich *m*
~ **error** Wahrnehmungsfehler *m*
~ **of color[s]** Farbwahrnehmung *f*
~ **of depth** *s.* ~ of space
~ **of detail** Detailwahrnehmung *f*
~ **of flicker** Flimmerwahrnehmung *f*
~ **of motion** Bewegungswahrnehmung *f*
~ **of shape** Formwahrnehmung *f*; Gestaltwahrnehmung *f*, Figurwahrnehmung *f*, Dingwahrnehmung *f*
~ **of space** Raum[bild]wahrnehmung *f*, räumliche Wahrnehmung *f*, Tiefenwahrnehmung *f*; Tiefensehvermögen *n*
~ **of visual motion** Bewegungssehen *n*
perceptive perzeptiv
~ **subjectivity** Wahrnehmungssubjektivität *f*
perceptiveness, perceptivity Wahrnehmungsvermögen *n*
perceptron Perzeptron *n*, Perzeptor *m* *(neuronales Netz)*
perceptual wahrnehmungsgemäß
~ **brightness sensation** Helligkeitsempfindung *f*, Helligkeitsempfinden *n*
~ **coding** wahrnehmungsbasierte Codierung *f*
~ **color difference** empfindungsgemäße Farbdifferenz *f*
~ **color space** empfindungsgemäßer (perzeptueller) Farbraum *m*
~ **constancy** Wahrnehmungskonstanz *f*
~ **defect** Wahrnehmungsfehler *m*
~ **discrepancy** perzeptuelle Diskrepanz *f* *(Robotik)*
~ **distortion** Wahrnehmungsverzerrung *f*
~ **effect** Wahrnehmungseffekt *m*
~ **experiment** Wahrnehmungsexperiment *n*
~ **image** Wahrnehmungsabbild *n*
~ **nausea** Wahrnehmungsübelkeit *f* *(s.a. simulator sickness)*
~ **object** Wahrnehmungsobjekt *n*
~ **performance** Wahrnehmungsleistung *f*
~ **phenomenon** Wahrnehmungsphänomen *n*
~ **process** Wahrnehmungsprozess *m*
~ **property** Wahrnehmungseigenschaft *f*
~ **psychologist** Wahrnehmungspsychologe *m*
~ **psychology** Wahrnehmungspsychologie *f*
~ **redundancy** Wahrnehmungsredundanz *f*
~ **research** Wahrnehmungsforschung *f*
~ **semantics** Wahrnehmungssemantik *f*
~ **sensation** Sinneswahrnehmung *f*, sinnliche Wahrnehmung *f*
~ **syntax** Wahrnehmungssyntax *f*
~ **system** Wahrnehmungssystem *n*
~ **threshold** Wahrnehmungsschwelle *f*
perceptually independent wahrnehmungsunabhängig
~ **optimized quantization** wahrnehmungsoptimierte Quantisierung *f*
perf *s.* perforation
perfect crystal idealer Kristall *m*
~ **diffuser** ideal matte (weiße) Fläche *f*, vollkommen matte Oberfläche *f* *(Farbmetrik)*
~ **grating** vollkommenes Gitter *n*
~ **lens** 1. ideale (perfekte) Linse *f*; 2. verzeichnungsfreies Objektiv *n*
~ **mirror** perfekter Spiegel *m*
~ **radiator** idealer Strahler *m*
perfecting cylinder press, ~ machine Schön- und Widerdruckmaschine *f*, Perfektormaschine *f*
~ **unit** Widerdruckwerk *n*
perfector [press] *s.* perfecting cylinder press
perforate/to perforieren
perforated film perforierter Film *m*
~ **paper tape** *s.* ~ tape
~ **screen** akustisch [hoch]transparente Bildwand *f*
~ **tape** Lochstreifen *m*, Lochband *n*
perforating machine Perforiermaschine *f*
perforation Perforation *f*
~ **damage** Perforationsschaden *m*
~ **hole** Perforationsloch *n*
~ **pitch** Perforationslochabstand *m*, Perforationsschritt *m*
~ **type** Perforationsart *f*
perforator Perforator *m*
performance photograph Bühnenfoto *n*
perfusion image Perfusionsbild *n*
~ **imaging** Perfusionsbildgebung *f*
~ **scintigram** Perfusionsszintigramm *n*
~ **scintigraphy** Perfusionsszintigrafie *f*

perimeter Perimeter n, Gesichtsfeldmesser m
perimetric[al] perimetrisch
perimetry Perimetrie f, Gesichtsfeldmessung f
period 1. Periode f; Periodendauer f; 2. Punkt m *(Satzzeichen)*
~ **of wave** Wellenperiode f
periodic convolution periodische Faltung f
~ **data** periodische Daten pl
~ **filter** periodisches Filter n
~ **filtering** periodische Filterung f
~ **function** periodische Funktion f
~ **image** periodisches Bild n
~ **noise** periodisches Rauschen n
~ **pattern** periodisches Muster n
~ **signal** periodisches Signal n
~ **spectrum** periodisches Spektrum n
~ **texture** periodische Textur f
~ **wave** periodische Welle f
periodicity Periodizität f *(z.B. einer Fourier-Transformation)*
peripheral [add-on] s. ~ **device**
~ **brightness** Randhelligkeit f
~ **component interconnect bus** PCI-Bus m
~ **definition** Rand[bild]schärfe f
~ **device** Peripheriegerät n, peripheres Gerät (Zusatzgerät) n
~ **equipment** Peripherie f *(Computer)*
~ **illumination** Randausleuchtung f
~ **node** Endknoten m *(Graphenstruktur)*
~ **pixel** Randpixel n
~ **ray** Randstrahl m, randnaher (randseitiger) Strahl m
~ **retina** periphere Netzhaut (Retina) f
~ **vignetting** Randabschattung f, Vignettierung f
~ **vision** peripheres Sehen n
periphery Peripherie f
periscope Periskop n, Sehrohr n
periscopic periskopisch
Peritel connector s. SCART connector
permanence, permanency Haltbarkeit f, Langzeithaltbarkeit f, Langlebigkeit f, Langzeit-Lagereigenschaft f *(z.B. von Bildmaterial)*
permanent permanent, [be]ständig; haltbar
~ **connection** Festanschluss m
~ **file** permanente Datei f
~ **image** bleibendes (beständiges) Bild n, dauerhaftes Bild n
~ **magnet** Dauermagnet m
~**-magnetic field** Dauermagnetfeld n
permeability Permeabilität f *(Magnetismus)*
permissible unsharpness zulässige Unschärfe f
permittivity Dielektrizitätskonstante f
peroxide Peroxid n
perpendicular orthogonal; rechteckig
persistence 1. Persistenz f; 2. s. ~ **time**; 3. s. persistent luminescence

~ **of vision [effect]** Nachbildwirkung f, Visionspersistenz f, Trägheit f des Auges
~ **time** Nachleuchtdauer f, Nachleuchtzeit f *(z.B. eines Fernsehbildschirms)*
persistent image [positives] Nachbild n
~ **luminescence** Nachleuchten n, Persistenz f
personal assistant Regieassistent m *(Filmteam)*
~ **computer** Personalcomputer m, PC m
~ **computer connecting cord** PC-Anschlusskabel n
~ **darkroom** Heimlabor n
perspective perspektivisch
~ Perspektive f
~ **center** Perspektivitätszentrum n
~ **compensation** s. ~ **control**
~ **control (correction)** Perspektivekorrektur f
~**-control lens** Perspektivekorrekturobjektiv n, PC-Objektiv n, Shiftobjektiv n
~ **distortion** perspektivische Verzerrung f
~ **drawing** perspektivische Zeichnung f
~ **effect** perspektivische Wirkung f
~ **foreshortening** perspektivische Verkürzung f
~ **illusion** perspektivische Täuschung f
~ **image** perspektivisches Bild n
~ **mapping** perspektivische Abbildung f
~ **plot** s. ~ **representation**
~ **projection** perspektivische Projektion f, Vierpunkt-Abbildung f; perspektivische Abbildung f
~ **representation** perspektivische Darstellung f
~ **view** perspektivische Sicht (Ansicht) f
perspectivity Perspektivität f
PET s. 1. positron emission tomography; 2. polyethylene terephthalate
~ **camera** Positronenkamera f
~ **scanner** PET-Scanner m, PET-Gerät n, Positronen[emissions]tomograf m
Petzval contribution Petzval-Bedingung f
~ **curvature,** ~ **field curvature** Petzval-Krümmung f, Petzval-Wölbung f, Feldkrümmung f, Bildfeldwölbung f
~ **objective (portrait lens)** Petzval-Objektiv n
~ **sum** Petzval-Summe f
~ **surface** Petzval-Schale f
pewter plate Zinnplatte f
pH [value] pH[-Wert] m, pH-Zahl f, Wasserstoffionenexponent m, Protonenaktivitätsexponent m
phantom Phantom n
~ **image** Phantombild n, Geisterbild n, Nebenbild n
pharmacoangiography Pharmakoangiografie f
phase Phase f *(einer Welle oder eines Signals)*
~ **alternating line** zeilenweise wechselnde Phasenlage f

phase

~ **alternating line system (television)** PAL-System *n*, PAL-Fernsehen *n*
~ **analysis** Phasenanalyse *f*
~ **angle** Phasenwinkel *m*, Phasenspektrum *n*
~ **change** Phasenwechsel *m*, Phasenänderung *f*
~ **change printer** Phasenwechseldrucker *m*
~ **change RAM (random-access memory)** Phasenwechselspeicher *m*
~-**coded radar** phasengetastetes Radar *n*
~ **coefficient** Phasenkonstante *f*
~ **coherence** Gleichphasigkeit *f*, Phasenkohärenz *f*
~-**coherent** phasenkohärent
~ **comparison** Phasenvergleich *m*
~ **compensation** Phasenkompensation *f*
~ **congruency** Phasenkongruenz *f*
~-**conjugating mirror** phasenkonjugierender Spiegel *m*
~ **conjugation** Phasenkonjugation *f*
~ **contrast** Phasenkontrast *m*
~ **contrast fluorescence microscope** Phasenkontrast-Fluoreszenzmikroskop *n*
~ **contrast illumination** Phasenkontrastbeleuchtung *f*
~ **contrast image** Phasenkontrastbild *n*
~ **contrast imaging (method)** Phasenkontrastverfahren *n*
~ **contrast magnetic resonance angiography** Phasenkontrastangiografie *f*
~ **contrast microscope** Phasenkontrastmikroskop *n*
~ **contrast microscopy** Phasenkontrastmikroskopie *f*
~ **contrast objective** Phasenkontrastobjektiv *n*
~ **contrast optics** Phasenkontrastoptik *f*
~ **contrast X-ray microscope** Phasenkontrast-Röntgenmikroskop *n*
~ **control** Phasensteuerung *f*
~ **corrector** Phasenkorrektor *m*
~ **correlation function** Phasenkorrelationsfunktion *f*
~ **delay** Phasenlaufzeit *f* *(Signalverarbeitung)*
~ **detector** Phasendetektor *m*
~ **deviation** Phasenhub *m*
~ **difference** Phasendifferenz *f*
~ **direction** Phasenrichtung *f*
~ **distribution** Phasenverteilung *f*
~-**encoded amplitude** phasencodierte Amplitude *f*
~ **encoding** Phasencodierung *f*
~-**encoding direction** Phasencodierungsrichtung *f*
~-**encoding field gradient** Phasencodiergradient *m*
~-**encoding gradient** Phasengradient *m* *(Magnetresonanzbildgebung)*
~-**encoding step** Phasencodierschritt *m*
~ **error** Phasenfehler *m*

~ **factor** Phasenfaktor *m*
~ **filter** Phasenfilter *n*
~ **filtering** Phasenfilterung *f*
~ **fluctuation** Phasenfluktuation *f*
~ **frequency response** Phasen[frequenz]gang *m*
~ **gradient** Phasengradient *m* *(Magnetresonanzbildgebung)*
~ **grating** Phasengitter *n*
~ **hologram** Phasenhologramm *n*
~ **image** Phasenbild *n*
~ **information** Phaseninformation *f*
~ **interference** Phaseninterferenz *f*
~ **jump** Phasensprung *m*
~ **linearity** Phasenlinearität *f*
~-**locked loop** Phasenregelkreis *m*
~ **map** Phasenbild *n*
~ **mask** Phasenmaske *f*
~ **matching** Phasenanpassung *f*; Brechzahlanpassung *f* *(nichtlineare Optik)*
~ **modifier** Phasenschieber *m*
~ **modulation** Phasenmodulation *f*
~ **modulator** Phasenmodulator *m*
~ **noise** Phasenrauschen *n*
~ **object** Phasenobjekt *n*
~ **oversampling** Einfaltungsunterdrückung *f*, Phasen-Oversampling *n* *(Magnetresonanztomografie)*
~ **plate** Phasenplättchen *n*, Phasenplatte *f*, doppelbrechende planparallele Platte *f* *(Phasenkontrastmikroskopie)*
~ **position** Phasenlage *f*
~-**preserving filter** Nulldurchgangsoperator *m*
~-**preserving reconstruction** phasenerhaltende Rekonstruktion *f*
~ **problem** Phasenproblem *n* *(Beugungsoptik)*
~ **relationship** Phasenbeziehung *f*
~ **retarder** *s.* ~ plate
~ **separation** Phasentrennung *f*
~ **shift** Phasenverschiebung *f*
~ **shift keying** Phasenumtastung *f*
~ **shifter** Phasenschieber *m*
~-**shifting shearography** [bildgebende] Phasenschiebe-Shearografie *f*
~ **spectrum** Phasenspektrum *n*, Phasenwinkel *m*
~ **structure** Phasenstruktur *f*
~ **swing** Phasenhub *m*
~ **telescope** Phasenteleskop *n*
~ **transfer function** Phasenübertragungsfunktion *f*
~ **transition** Phasenübergang *m*
~ **velocity** Phasengeschwindigkeit *f* *(einer Welle)*

phased-array antenna 1. phasengesteuerte Gruppenantenne (Antenne) *f (Radar)*; 2. Synergiespule *f* *(Magnetresonanztomografie)*
~-**array transducer** Schallkopf *m* mit [elektronisch] variierbarem Schallfeld *(Sonografie)*

phasor Drehzeiger m, komplexe Exponentialfunktion f *(Signalverarbeitung)*
phenakistoscope Phänakistiskop n, Zauberscheibe f
phenol Phenol n
~ **coupler** Phenolkuppler m
phenylenediamine Phenylendiamin n *(Entwicklersubstanz)*
phenylpyrazolid[in]one Phenylpyrazolidon n, Phenidon n *(Entwicklersubstanz)*
phi motion (phenomenon) Phi-Bewegung f, Phi-Phänomen n; scheinbare (abgetastete) Bewegung f
phlebogram Phlebogramm n, Venenpulsbild n
phlebographic phlebografisch
phlebography Phlebografie f
phon Phon n *(Lautstärkemaß)*
phone directory Rufnummernverzeichnis n *(Faxgerät)*
Phong interpolation (shading) Phong-Schattierung f
Phong's illumination model Phongsches Beleuchtungsmodell n
phonocardiogram Phonokardiogramm n
phonocardiographic phonokardiografisch
phonocardiography Phonokardiografie f
phonograph record[ing] Schallplatte f
phonon Phonon n, quantisierte Gitterschwingung f; Schallquant n
phorometer Phorometer n
phosphene Phosphen n *(Lichtempfindung)*
phosphor Phosphor m, Leuchtphosphor m, Leuchtstoff m, Luminophor m
~ **aging** Leuchtstoffalterung f
~-**coated screen** s. phosphor screen
~ **coating** 1. Phosphorschicht f, Leuchtstoffschicht f; 2. s. ~ screen
~ **dot** Phosphor[leucht]punkt m, Leucht[stoff]punkt m
~ **image** Leuchtstoffbild n
~ **layer** s. ~ coating
~ **persistence** Nachleuchtdauer f, Nachleuchtzeit f *(z.B. eines Fernsehbildschirms)*
~ **screen** Phosphoreszenzschirm m, Farbtripel-Leuchtschicht f, Speicherschicht f
~ **stripe** Phosphorleuchtstreifen m
~ **wear** Leuchtstoffalterung f
phosphore s. phosphor
phosphoresce/to phosphoreszieren
phosphorescence Phosphoreszenz f
phosphorescent radiator Phosphoreszenzstrahler m
~ **screen** s. phosphor screen
~ **substance** Phosphor m
phosphorus Phosphor m *(nichtmetallisches Element)*
phot Phot n *(Einheit der Beleuchtungsstärke)*
photic stimulus Lichtreiz m
photo/to s. photograph/to

photo 1. Foto n, Fotografie f, Lichtbild n *(s.a. unter photographic)*; 2. s. photographer
~ **agency** Fotoagentur f
~-**aquatint process** Gummi-Bichromat-Verfahren n
~ **archiving system** Bildarchivierungssystem n
~ **backpack** Fotorucksack m
~ **bag** Fototasche f
~ **button** Fotoauslöser m
~ **CD (compact disk)** Foto-CD f
~ **contest** Fotowettbewerb m
~ **control point** Passpunkt m, Passmarke f, Passelement n *(Fotogrammetrie)*
~-**crosslinkable polymer** fotovernetzbares Polymer n
~ **design** Fotodesign n
~ **development minilab** Minilab[or] n
~ **editing** Fotobearbeitung f
~-**editing software** Bildbearbeitungssoftware f
~ **editor** Fotoredakteur m, Bildredakteur m
~ **enlarger** Vergrößerer m, Vergrößerungsapparat m, Vergrößerungsgerät n
~ **equipment technician** Foto[geräte]techniker m
~ **essay** Fotoessay m(n)
~ **evaluation** Fotoauswertung f
~ **fakery** Fotofälschung f
~ **finish** Fotofinish n
~ **flashlamp** Blitz[lichtlampe f, Kolbenblitzlampe f, Kolbenblitz m
~ **frame** Fotorahmen m
~ **function** s. ~ mode
~ **industry** Fotoindustrie f
~ **lamp** Fotolampe f
~ **linen** Fotoleinen n
~ **luminaire** Fotoaufnahmeleuchte f
~ **material** Fotomaterial n, fotografisches Material n
~-**mechatronics** Fotomechatronik f
~ **mode** Fotomodus m *(Videokamera, Kopierer)*
~ **mounting corner** Fotoecke f
~-**narrative** Fotobericht m, Fotoerzählung f
~ **paper** Fotopapier n, Vergrößerungspapier n
~ **paper glue** Fotoleim m
~ **pocket** Foto-Sichthülle f
~ **print** Fotoabzug m, Bildabzug m, Papierpositiv n, Abzug m
~ **printer** Fotodrucker m, Filmdrucker m, Fotoprinter m
~ **processing machine** Entwicklungsmaschine f, Maschinenentwickler m, Verarbeitungsmaschine f
~ **quality** Fotoqualität f *(als Gütemerkmal digitaler Bildwiedergabe)*
~-**quality CG image** fotorealistische Computergrafik f, Computerfoto n
~ **reconnaissance** Fotoaufklärung f

photo 282

~ **retailer** Foto[fach]händler *m*
~-**retouching software** Fotobearbeitungssoftware *f*
~ **scale** Bildmaßstab *m*
~ **shoot** Fotosession *f*, Fotositzung *f*
~ **shot** Fotoaufnahme *f*
~ **stock agency** Fotoagentur *f*
~ **supply store** Fotofachgeschäft *n*
~-**technical** fototechnisch
~ **vest** Fotografenweste *f*
photoacoustic tomography fotoakustische Tomografie *f*
photoanalytical fotoanalytisch
photobooth picture Automatenfoto *n*
photocathode Fotokatode *f*
photocell Fotozelle *f*, lichtelektrische (elektrooptische) Zelle *f*
photoceramics Fotokeramik *f*
photochemical fotochemisch
~ **absorption** fotochemische Absorption *f*
~ **equivalent** fotochemisches Äquivalent *n*
~ **etching** fotochemisches Ätzen *n*
~ **polymerization** Fotopolymerisation *f*, Fotovernetzung *f*
~ **reaction** fotochemische Reaktion *f*, Lichtreaktion *f*, Fotoreaktion *f*
photochemist Fotochemiker *m*
photochemistry Fotochemie *f*
photochromic dye fotochromer Farbstoff *m*
photochromism Fotochromie *f*
photochromoscope Fotochromoskop *n*
photoclinometer Fotoinklinometer *n*
photocollage Fotocollage *f*
photocomposer 1. Fotosetzer *m*; 2. Fotosatzgerät *n*, Fotosatzdrucker *m*, Satzbelichter *m*
photocomposition Fotosatz *m*, Lichtsatz *m*, Filmsatz *m*
~ **system** Lichtsatzsystem *n*
photoconducting layer Fotoleiterschicht *f*
photoconduction Fotoleitung *f*
photoconductive fotoleitend; fotoleitfähig
~ **cell** Fotowiderstandszelle *f* (Sensor)
~ **detector** Fotodetektor *m*, Lichtdetektor *m*, optischer Detektor *m*
~ **diode** Halbleiterfotodiode *f*
~ **effect** Fotoleitungseffekt *m*
~ **element** Fotoleiter *m*
~ **layer** fotoleitende (fotoleitfähige) Schicht *f*
~ **material** Fotoleiter *m*
~ **mode** Fotoleitungsbetrieb *m* (Fotodiode)
~ **polymer** fotoleitfähiges Polymer *n*
~ **polymeric layer** Fotopolymerschicht *f*
~ **rotating drum** *s.* photoconductor drum
photoconductivity Fotoleitfähigkeit *f*
~ **effect** Fotoleitungseffekt *m*
photoconductor Fotoleiter *m*
~ **detector** Fotoleitungssensor *m*
~ **drum** Foto[leiter]trommel *f*, Fotoleiterwalze *f*, fotoleitende Trommel *f*; Belichtungstrommel *f* (Laserdrucker)
~ **layer** Fotoleiterschicht *f*

~ **surface** Fotoleiter[ober]fläche *f*
photoconversion Lichtwandlung *f*
photoconverter Lichtwandler *m*
photocopier Fotokopiergerät *n*, Fotokopierautomat *m*, Fotokopierer *m*
photocopy/to fotokopieren
photocopy Fotokopie *f*; Lichtbildabzug *m*; elektrofotografische Kopie *f*
~ **machine industry** Fotokopiererindustrie *f*
~ **paper** Fotokopierpapier *n*
photocopying Fotokopieren *n*
~ **machine** Fotokopiermaschine *f* (s.a. photocopier)
~ **shop** Kopierservice *m*
photocurrent Fotostrom *m*, fotoelektrischer Strom *m*
photodegradation Fotodegradation *f*
photodetection Lichtdetektion *f*
photodetector Fotodetektor *m*, Lichtdetektor *m*, optischer Detektor *m*
~ **imaging array** Fotodiodenarray *n*
~ **noise** Fotodetektorrauschen *n*
photodiode Fotodiode *f*, lichtempfindliche Diode *f*
~ **array** Fotodiodenarray *n*
~ **detector** Fotodiodendetektor *m*
photodischarge Fotoentladung *f*
photodissociation Fotolyse *f*
photoduplicate/to fotokopieren
photoduplicate Fotokopie *f*, fotografische Kopie *f*; Lichtbildabzug *m*
photoeffect Fotoeffekt *m*, fotoelektrischer (lichtelektrischer) Effekt *m*
photoelastic fotoelastisch, spannungsoptisch
~ **stress analysis** [fotoelastische] Spannungsanalyse *f*
photoelasticity, photoelastics Fotoelastizität *f*, Spannungsoptik *f*
photoelectric fotoelektrisch, lichtelektrisch, elektrooptisch
~ **absorption** fotoelektrische Absorption *f*
~ **absorption coefficient** fotoelektrischer Absorptionskoeffizient *m*
~ **cell** lichtelektrische (elektrooptische) Zelle *f*, Fotozelle *f*
~ **colorimeter** fotoelektrisches (lichtelektrisches) Kolorimeter *n*
~ **current** fotoelektrischer Strom *m*, Fotostrom *m*
~ **densitometer** fotoelektrisches Densitometer *n*
~ **detector** fotoelektrischer (lichtelektrischer) Detektor *m*, fotoelektrischer Empfänger *m*
~ **device** fotoelektrisches Gerät *n*
~ **effect** fotoelektrischer (lichtelektrischer) Effekt *m*, Fotoeffekt *m*
~ **emission** lichtelektrische Emission *f*, Fotoemission *f*
~ **exposure meter** fotoelektrischer (lichtelektrischer) Belichtungsmesser *m*

~ **image converter** fotoelektrischer Bildwandler *m*
~ **photometer** lichtelektrisches Fotometer *n*
~ **reader** fotoelektrischer Leser *m*
~ **receiver** Fotoempfänger *m*
~ **scanning** fotoelektrische Abtastung *f*
~ **sensor** fotoelektrischer Sensor *m*
~ **signal** fotoelektrisches (lichtelektrisches) Signal *n*
~ **transducer** lichtelektrischer (elektrooptischer) Wandler *m*
photoelectricity Fotoelektrizität *f*
photoelectromagnetic effect fotoelektromagnetischer (fotomagnetoelektrischer) Effekt *m*, PEM-Effekt *m*
photoelectron Fotoelektron *n*
~ **current** Fotoelektronenstrom *m*
~ **emission** *s.* photoelectric emission
~ **noise** Fotoelektronenrauschen *n*
photoelectronic fotoelektronisch
~ **metrology** fotoelektronische Messtechnik *f*
photoelectrophoresis Fotoelektrophorese *f*
photoemission Fotoemission *f*, lichtelektrische Emission *f*
~ **microscope** Fotoemissionsmikroskop *n*
photoemissive fotoemittierend
~ **detector (sensor)** Fotoemissionsdetektor *m*
photoemitter Fotoemitter *m*
photoemulsion Fotoemulsion *f*, fotografische Emulsion *f*
~ **[micro]crystal** Emulsionskristall *m*, fotografisches Korn *n*
photoengrave/to lichtelektrisch gravieren
photoengraved plate Chemiegrafie *f*, Hochdruckätzplatte *f*
photoengraver Chemiegraf *m*
photoengraving 1. Chemiegrafie *f*, Hochdruckätzung *f (Druckerzeugnis)*; 2. *s.* ~ process; 3. *s.* photoengraved plate
~ **process** Chemiegrafie *f*, Hochdruckätzung *f*, fotomechanische Klischeeherstellung *f*
photoetch/to fotoätzen
photofabrication Fotoproduktion *f*
photofinish camera Zielkamera *f*
~ **photography** Ziel[film]fotografie *f*
photofinisher 1. Fotodienstleister *m*, Fotofinisher *m*, Finisher *m*; 2. Foto[medien]laborant *m*; 3. Entwicklungsanstalt *f*
photofinishing Fotoausarbeitung *f*, Fotofinishing *n*; Großlaborverarbeitung *f*
~ **industry** Fotoverarbeitungsindustrie *f*
~ **lab[oratory]** Fotofachlabor[atorium] *n*, Entwicklungslabor *n*, Verarbeitungslabor *n*, Verarbeitungsanstalt *f*
~ **service** Fotoservice *m*, Fotodienstleistung *f*
~ **technology** Fotoverarbeitungstechnik *f*

photofit Phantomfoto *n*
photoflash device Blitzlichtgerät *n*, Fotoblitzgerät *n*
~ **lamp** Blitz[licht]lampe *f*
~ **source** Blitzlichtquelle *f*
photoflood [bulb], ~ **lamp** Fotolampe *f*; Fotoleuchte *f*; Fotoscheinwerfer *m*
photofluorogram Schirmbildaufnahme *f*
photofluorographic schirmbildfotografisch
~ **camera** Schirmbildkamera *f*
~ **film** Röntgenfilm *m*, radiografischer Film *m*
~ **image** Schirmbildaufnahme *f*
photofluorography Schirmbildfotografie *f*, Radiofotografie *f*, Fluorografie *f*; Röntgen[strahlen]fotografie *f*, Röntgenografie *f*, Filmröntgen *n*
photogalvanic fotogalvanisch
photogalvanography Fotogalvanografie *f*
photogelatin ink Lichtdruckfarbe *f*
~ **process** 1. Lichtdruck *m*; 2. Collotypeverfahren *n (ein Lichtdruckverfahren)*
photogenerated charge carrier lichtinduzierter (fotogenerierter) Ladungsträger *m*
~ **hole** *s.* defect electron
photogenic 1. fotogen, bildwirksam; 2. lichterzeugend
~ **drawing, photogenics** 1. Fotografik *f*, Lichtgrafik *f*, Fotozeichnen *n*, Lichtmalerei *f*; 2. *s.* photogram
photogeologic[al] fotogeologisch
photogeology Luftbildgeologie *f*, Fotogeologie *f*, Aerogeologie *f*
photogoniometer Fotogoniometer *n*
photogram, photogrammatic image 1. Fotogramm *n*, Fotografik *f*, Lichtgrafik *f*, Lichtmalerei *f*; 2. *s.* photogrammetric image
photogrammetric apparatus Bildmessgerät *n*
~ **camera** Messbildkamera *f*, Bildkammer *f*, fotogrammetrische Kamera (Messkammer) *f*
~ **film** Bildmessfilm *m*
~ **image** fotogrammetrisches Bild *n*, [fotografisches] Messbild *n*, Messaufnahme *f*
~ **mapping** fotogrammetrische Kartierung *f*
~ **objective** Messobjektiv *n*
~ **plotter** fotogrammetrischer Plotter *m*
~ **rectification** fotogrammetrische Entzerrung *f*
~ **triangulation** Bildtriangulation *f*
photogrammetrical restitution fotogrammetrische Auswertung *f*
photogrammetrist Fotogrammeter *m*
photogrammetry Fotogrammetrie *f*, Bildmesswesen *n*, Fototopografie *f*
photograph/to fotografieren
photograph Fotografie *f*, Foto *n*, Lichtbild *n* *(s.a.* photographic image*)*

photograph

- ~ **album** Fotoalbum *n*
- ~ **collector** Fotosammler *m*
- ~ **format** Fotoformat *n*
- ~ **restoration** Fotorestaurierung *f*
- ~ **scanner** Fotoscanner *m*
- **photographable** fotografierbar
- **photographer** Fotograf *m*, Lichtbildner *m*
- **photographic** fotografisch
- ~ **accessories** Fotozubehör *n*
- ~ **adhesive** Fotokleber *m*, Fotoklebstoff *m*
- ~ **aerial survey** Luftvermessung *f*
- ~ **agency** Fotoagentur *f*
- ~ **aircraft** Bildflugzeug *n*
- ~ **apparatus** Fotoapparat *m*
- ~ **archival** fotoarchivisch
- ~ **archive** Fotoarchiv *n*
- ~ **archivist** Fotoarchivar *m*
- ~ **art** Fotokunst *f*
- ~ **artist** Fotokünstler *m*
- ~ **background** Hintergrund[vorhang] *m* *(Studiozubehör)*
- ~ **badge** Filmdosimeter *n*, Strahlenschutzplakette *f*, Filmplakette *f*
- ~ **base paper** Fotorohpapier *n*
- ~ **book** Fotobuch *n*
- ~ **camera** fotografische Kamera *f*, Fotokamera *f*, Fotoapparat *m*
- ~ **chemical** Fotochemikalie *f*
- ~ **chemistry** fotografische Chemie *f*
- ~ **collage** Fotocollage *f*
- ~ **color film** Farb[aufnahme]film *m*, Colorfilm *m*
- ~ **color image** Farbfoto *n*, Farbfotografie *f*, fotografisches Farbbild *n*
- ~ **color material** Colormaterial *n*
- ~ **color paper** Farbfotopapier *n*
- ~ **color print** Farbabzug *m*
- ~ **color transparency** Farbdiapositiv *n*
- ~ **comparison** Fotovergleich *m*
- ~ **contrast** fotografischer Kontrast *m*
- ~ **copy** fotografische Kopie *f*, Fotokopie *f*; Fotovorlage *f*, Reprovorlage *f* *(Reprografie)*
- ~ **copying** Fotokopieren *n*
- ~ **coupler** fotografischer Kuppler *m*, Farb[stoff]kuppler *m*
- ~ **cover** Umschlagfoto *n*, Titelfoto *n*
- ~ **craft** Fotogewerbe *n*
- ~ **darkroom** Dunkelraum *m*, Dunkelkammer *f*
- ~ **daylight** fotografisches Tageslicht *n*
- ~ **dealer** Foto[fach]händler *m*
- ~ **density** fotografische Dichte *f*, Schwärzungsdichte *f*, D
- ~ **density wedge** Grau[stufen]keil *m*, Stufengraukeil *m*, Grauskala *f*
- ~ **department** Fotoabteilung *f*
- ~ **depiction** fotografische Darstellung *f*
- ~ **developer** [fotografischer] Entwickler *m*
- ~ **development** [fotografische] Entwicklung *f*
- ~ **device** Fotogerät *n*
- ~ **document** Fotodokument *n*
- ~ **documentation** Fotodokumentation *f*
- ~ **effect** fotografischer Effekt *m*
- ~ **effluent** Fotoabwasser *n*
- ~ **emulsion** Fotoemulsion *f*, fotografische Emulsion *f*
- ~ **emulsion manufacture** Emulsionsherstellung *f*
- ~ **emulsion technology** Emulsionstechnik *f*
- ~ **engineer** Fotoingenieur *m*
- ~ **engineering** Fototechnik *f*
- ~ **engraving** s. photogravure [process]
- ~ **enlargement** Vergrößerung *f*
- ~ **enlarger** Vergrößerer *m*, Vergrößerungsapparat *m*, Vergrößerungsgerät *n*
- ~ **enthusiast** Fotoenthusiast *m*
- ~ **equipment** Fotoausrüstung *f*
- ~ **exhibition** Fotoausstellung *f*
- ~ **expert** Fotofachmann *m*, Fotosachverständiger *m*
- ~ **exposure** [fotografische] Belichtung *f*
- ~ **film** Foto[grafie]film *m*, fotografischer Film *m*
- ~ **film base** Film[schicht]träger *m*, Filmunterlage *f*, Schichtträger *m*
- ~ **film box** Filmschachtel *f*
- ~ **film camera** Fotokamera *f*
- ~ **film manufacturer** Filmhersteller *m*
- ~ **filter** fotografisches Filter *n*
- ~ **flashlamp array** Blitzlampensystem *n*
- ~ **fraud** Fotofälschung *f*
- ~ **gallery** Fotogalerie *f*
- ~ **gelatin** Fotogelatine *f*
- ~ **gradation** Gradation *f*
- ~ **grain** fotografisches Korn *n*, Emulsionskristall *n*
- ~ **grain noise** Film[korn]rauschen *n*
- ~ **gun** Fotogewehr *n*
- ~ **historian** Fotohistoriker *m*
- ~ **historical** fotohistorisch
- ~ **history** Foto[grafie]geschichte *f*
- ~ **illustration** Fotoillustration *f*
- ~ **image** fotografisches Bild *n*, fotografische Abbildung *f*, Fotobild *n* *(s.a. photograph)*
- ~ **image compression algorithm** Fotokompressionsalgorithmus *m*
- ~ **industry** Fotoindustrie *f*
- ~ **instrumentation** Fotogerätetechnik *f*
- ~ **interpreter** Bildauswerter *m*
- ~ **journal** Fotozeitschrift *f*, Fotojournal *n*, Fotomagazin *n*
- ~ **lab[oratory]** [professionelles] Fotolabor *n*
- ~ **layer** fotografische Schicht *f*, Fotoschicht *f*
- ~ **lens** Fotoobjektiv *n*, fotografisches Objektiv *n*
- ~ **library** Foto[biblio]thek *f*, Lichtbildsammlung *f*
- ~ **literature** Fotoliteratur *f*
- ~ **magazine** Fotomagazin *n*, Fotozeitschrift *f*, Fotojournal *n*
- ~ **manufacturer** Fotogerätehersteller *m*
- ~ **map** Bildkarte *f* *(Fotogrammetrie)*

~ **marker** Aufbelichtungskamera *f* *(Radiografie)*
~ **mask** Fotomaske *f*
~ **masking** fotografische Maskierung *f*
~ **material** Fotomaterial *n*, fotografisches Material *n*, Aufnahmematerial *n*
~ **mensuration** Bildmessung *f*
~ **metrology** fotografische Messtechnik *f*
~ **microscope** *s.* photomicroscope
~ **monitoring** Fotoüberwachung *f*
~ **motion analysis** fotografische Bewegungsanalyse *f*
~ **negative** Fotonegativ *n*, Negativ *n*, fotografisches Negativ *n*, Gegenbild *n*
~ **objective** Fotoobjektiv *n*, fotografisches Objektiv *n*
~ **optics** fotografische Optik *f*, Fotooptik *f*
~ **original** Originalfoto *n*, Originalaufnahme *f*
~ **paper** fotografisches Papier *n*, Fotopapier *n*, Kopierpapier *n*, Vergrößerungspapier *n*
~ **paper developer** Papierentwickler *m*, Positiventwickler *m*
~ **paper emulsion** Papieremulsion *f*
~ **paper print** fotografisches Papierbild *n*
~ **parlance** Fotofachsprache *f*
~ **perspective** fotografische Perspektive *f*
~ **photometry** fotografische Fotometrie *f*
~ **physics** fotografische Physik *f*
~ **picture** fotografisches Bild *n*, fotografische Abbildung *f*, Fotobild *n*
~ **plate** fotografische Platte *f*, Fotoplatte *f*, Filmplatte *f*
~ **polymer film** Fotopolymerfilm *m*
~ **portrait** Fotoporträt *n*
~ **portrait studio** Porträtstudio *n*, Porträtatelier *n*
~ **postcard** Fotopostkarte *f*
~ **practice** Fotopraxis *f*
~ **printing paper** *s.* ~ paper
~ **printing process** fotografisches Druckverfahren *n*
~ **printing technology** Fotodrucktechnik *f*
~ **procedure** Fotoprozess *m*, fotografisches Verfahren *n*
~ **process** 1. fotografischer Prozess (Elementarprozess) *m*; 2. *s.* ~ procedure
~ **processing** Fotoverarbeitung *f*, fotografische Verarbeitung *f*
~ **processing chemistry** Verarbeitungschemie *f*
~ **processing material** Verarbeitungsmaterial *n*
~ **product** Fotoerzeugnis *n*
~ **project** Fotoprojekt *n*
~ **proof** fotografischer Proof *m* *(Druckvorstufe)*
~ **publisher** Fotoverlag *m*
~ **pyrometry** fotografische Pyrometrie *f*
~ **realism** Fotorealismus *m*
~ **record[ing]** fotografische Aufnahme *f*
~ **reportage** Fotoreportage *f*

~ **reproduction** Fotoreproduktion *f*, fotografische Wiedergabe *f*
~ **response curve** [fotografische] Dichtekurve *f*, Schwärzungskurve *f*, Gradationskurve *f*, charakteristische Kurve (Filmkurve) *f*
~ **retouching** Fotoretusche *f*
~ **school** Fotoschule *f*
~ **sensitivity** fotografische Empfindlichkeit *f*
~ **series** Fotoserie *f*, Fotoreihe *f*, Bild[er]folge *f*, Fotosequenz *f*
~ **service** Fotodienst *m*, Fotoservice *m*; Fotodienstleistung *f*
~ **session** Fotosession *f*, Fotositzung *f*
~ **shutter** fotografischer Verschluss *m*, Fotoverschluss *m*
~ **silver image** Silberbild *n*
~ **single-emulsion film** Einschichtfilm *m*
~ **sitting** Fotositzung *f*, Fotosession *f*
~ **situation** Aufnahmesituation *f*
~ **slide** Dia[positiv] *n*
~ **sound** Lichtton *m* *(Kinematografie)*
~ **sound recorder** Lichttonaufzeichnungsgerät *n*
~ **sound recording** Lichttonaufnahme *f*, Lichttonaufzeichnung *f*
~ **sound test film** Lichtton-Testfilm *m*
~ **sound track** Lichttonspur *f*
~ **special effect** Fototrick *m*
~ **spectrophotometry** fotografische Spektralfotometrie *f*
~ **speed** fotografische Empfindlichkeit *f*
~ **spotting pen** Fleckretuschierstift *m*
~ **stereogram (stereograph)** Stereofoto *n*, Stereofotografie *f*
~ **storage** fotografischer Speicher *m*
~ **store** Fotofachgeschäft *n*
~ **studio** Fotoatelier *n*, Fotostudio *n*
~ **style** Fotostil *m*
~ **subject** Fotomotiv *n*, fotografisches Motiv *n*; Fotoobjekt *n*
~ **system** Fotosystem *n*
~ **technician** Fototechniker *m*
~ **technique** fotografische Aufnahmetechnik *f*, Fototechnik *f*
~ **technology** Fototechnik *f*; Fototechnologie *f*
~ **telescope** Fototeleskop *n*
~ **thermometry** fotografische Thermometrie *f*
~ **trade fair (show)** Fotomesse *f*
~ **transparency** Fotopositiv *n*
~ **triplet lens** dreilinsiges Objektiv *n*, Dreilinser *m*, Triplett *n*
~ **unsharpness** Bildempfängerunschärfe *f*, innere Unschärfe *f*
~ **work** Fotoarbeit *f*
photographically active light aktinisches Licht *n*
photographist Fotograf *m*
photographlike fotoähnlich *(Bild)*
photography Fotografie *f*
~ **collection** Fotosammlung *f*

photography

~ **dealer** Foto[fach]händler *m*
~ **gallery** Fotogalerie *f*
~ **museum** Fotomuseum *n*
~ **periodical** Fotozeitschrift *f*
~ **portfolio** Fotomappe *f*
~ **teacher** Fotopädagoge *m*
photogravure, ~ printing (process) 1. Fotogravüre *f*, Heliogravüre *f*; 2. Rastertiefdruck *m*; Rakeltiefdruck *m*
photogravure rotary machine Rollenrotationstiefdruckmaschine *f*
photoguide Foto-Fibel *f*
photoheadliner Titelsetzgerät *n* *(Satztechnik)*
photoheliograph Heliograf *m*
photohistorian Fotohistoriker *m*
photoimaging Lichtbildwesen *n*, Lichtbildnerei *f*
photoinstrumentation Fotogerätetechnik *f*
~ **engineer** Fotogerätetechniker *m*
photointerpretation Bildauswertung *f*, Bildinterpretation *f*, Fotoauswertung *f*
photointerpreter Bildauswerter *m*
photointerview Fotointerview *n*
photoionization Fotoionisation *f*
photojournalism Fotojournalismus *m*, Bildjournalismus *m*
photojournalist Fotojournalist *m*, Bildjournalist *m*
photojournalistic fotojournalistisch
photolab [professionelles] Fotolabor *n*, Fotofachlabor *n*
photolabile lichtunbeständig
photolability Lichtunbeständigkeit *f*
photolens Fotoobjektiv *n*, fotografisches Objektiv *n*
photolitho Fotolithografie *f* *(Druckerzeugnis)*
photolithographer Fotolithograf *m*
photolithographic fotolithografisch
~ **lens** fotolithografisches Objektiv *n*
~ **mask** Fotolithografiemaske *f*
~ **plate** fotolithografische Platte *f*
photolithography 1. Fotolithografie *f*, Lichtlithografie *f*, [licht]optische Lithografie *f*; 2. *s.* photolitho
photology Lichtlehre *f*
photoluminescence Fotolumineszenz *f*
photoluminescent fotolumineszierend
photolysis Fotolyse *f*
photolytic fotolytisch
~ **silver** fotolytisches Silber *n*
photomacrograph Makroaufnahme *f*, Lupenaufnahme *f*, makrofotografische Aufnahme *f*
photomacrographic makrofotografisch
~ **camera** makrofotografische Kamera *f*
~ **lens (objective)** Makroobjektiv *n*
~ **stand** Makrostativ *n*
photomacrography Makrofotografie *f*, Lupenfotografie *f*
photomap Bildkarte *f (Fotogrammetrie)*
photomask Fotomaske *f*, Fotoschablone *f*

photomaton booth Fotoautomat *m*; Passbildautomat *m*
photomechanical fotomechanisch
~ **copy** fotomechanische Kopie *f*, Fotodruck *m*
~ **printing** Fotodruck *m*, Fotografiedruck *m*
~ **printing plate** fotomechanische Druckplatte *f*
~ **printing process** fotomechanisches Druckverfahren *n*
~ **reproduction** fotomechanische Reproduktion (Wiedergabe) *f*, fotomechanische Bildreproduktion *f*; Repro[duktions]fotografie *f*
~ **transfer** fotomechanische Übertragung *f*; Ablichtung *f*
~ **worker** Fototechniker *m*
photomechanics 1. Fotomechanik *f*; 2. *s.* platemaking
photomensuration Bildmessung *f*
photometer Fotometer *n*, Lichtmessgerät *n*
~ **bench** Fotometerbank *f*
~ **head** Fotometerkopf *m*
~ **lamp** Fotometerlampe *f*
photometric fotometrisch, licht[mess]technisch
~ **accuracy** fotometrische Genauigkeit (Richtigkeit) *f*
~ **brightness** Farbhelligkeit *f*; Leuchtdichte *f*, Luminanz *f (s.a. unter* luminance*)*
~ **color contrast** fotometrischer Farbkontrast *m*
~ **cube** Fotometerwürfel *m*, Lummer-Brodhun-Würfel *m*
~ **digitization** fotometrische Digitalisierung *f*
~ **equivalent** fotometrisches Äquivalent *n*
~ **field** Fotometerfeld *n*
~ **lamp** Fotometerlampe *f*
~ **measurement** fotometrische Messung *f*
~ **quantity** lichttechnische Größe *f*
~ **radiation equivalent** [fotometrisches] Strahlungsäquivalent *n*, Lichtausbeute *f*
~ **unit** fotometrische Einheit *f*
photometrical *s.* photometric
~ **feature** fotometrisches Merkmal *n*
photometrology Bildmesswesen *n*
photometry Fotometrie *f*, Lichtmesstechnik *f*, Lichtmessung *f*; Helligkeitsmessung *f*
photomicrograph/to mikrofotografieren
photomicrograph Mikrofoto *n*, Mikrofotografie *f*, mikrofotografische Aufnahme *f*
photomicrographer Mikrofotograf *m*
photomicrographic mikrofotografisch
~ **camera** mikrofotografische Kamera *f*
~ **lens (objective)** mikrofotografisches Objektiv *n*
~ **setup** mikrofotografischer Aufbau *m*
photomicrography Mikrofotografie *f*, Fotomikrografie *f*
photomicroscope Kameramikroskop *n*, Fotomikroskop *n*

photomicroscopy Mikrofotografie f, Fotomikrografie f
photomontage Fotomontage f
photomosaic Fotomosaik n, Mosaik n (Luftbildmessung)
photomultiplier [tube] Foto[elektronen]vervielfacher m, Elektronenvervielfacher m, Sekundärelektronenvervielfacher m, Fotomultiplier m
photomural Fotowand f, Fotopete f
photon Photon n, Lichtquant n, Lichtteilchen n; Strahlungsquant n
~ **absorber** Photonenabsorber m
~ **absorption** Photonenabsorption f, Fotoabsorption f
~ **beam** Photonenstrahl m
~ **catch** Quantenausbeute f (z.B. eines Bildsensors)
~ **correlation spectroscopy** Photonenkorrelationsspektroskopie f
~ **counter** Photonenzähler m
~ **counting** Photonenzählung f
~-**counting detector** Photonenzähler m
~-**counting efficiency** Quanteneffizienz f
~ **current** Photonenstrom m
~ **[current] density** Photonendichte f
~ **detection** Photonendetektion f
~ **detector** Photonendetektor m, Quantendetektor m (s.a. photodetector)
~ **effect** Photoneneffekt m
~ **emission** Photonenemission f
~ **energy** Photonenenergie f
~ **excitation** Photonenanregung f
~ **flux** Photonenstrom m, Photonenfluss m, Quantenfluss m
~-**flux density** Photonendichte f
~-**generated charge** lichtinduzierte Ladung f
~ **noise** Photonenrauschen n
~ **quantum** s. photon
~ **radiation** Photonenstrahlung f
~ **scanning tunneling microscope** Photonenrastertunnelmikroskop n
~ **shot noise** Photonenrauschen n
~ **source** Photonenquelle f
~ **spectrum** Photonenspektrum n
~ **stream** s. ~ flux
photonic photonisch
~ **network** Photoniknetz n
photonics Photonik f
photooptical fotooptisch, lichtoptisch
photooptics Fotooptik f, fotografische Optik f
photooxidation Fotooxidation f
photooxidative fotooxidativ
photophone Lichttelefon n, Photophon n
photophoresis Fotophorese f
photophysical fotophysikalisch
photophysics Fotophysik f, Physik f des Lichts f
photopia Tagessichtigkeit f
photopic fotopisch, helladaptiert (Auge)

~ **spectral sensitivity** fotopische Hellempfindlichkeit f
~ **troland** fotopisches Troland n (Fotometrie)
~ **vision** fotopisches Sehen n, Helligkeitssehen n, Tagessehen n, Zapfensehen n
photopigment Fotopigment n
photoplate Fotoplatte f, fotografische Platte f, Filmplatte f
photoplay Spielfilm m
photoplethysmograph Fotoplethysmograf m
photoplethysmographic fotoplethysmografisch
photoplethysmography Fotoplethysmografie f
photopolymer Fotopolymer n
~ **coating** Fotopolymerschicht f
~ **film** Fotopolymerfilm m
~ **gravure** Fotopolymergravur f
~ **gravure plate** fotopolymere Tiefdruckplatte f
~ **holographic film** holografischer Fotopolymerfilm m
~ **image carrier** Druckfolie f (Tiefdruck)
~ **[printing] plate** Fotopolymer[druck]platte f, Fotopolymerklischee n; fotopolymere Hochdruckplatte f
~ **resist** Foto[kopier]lack m, fotoempfindlicher Lack m, Fotoresist m
~ **technology** Fotopolymertechnik f
photopolymerizable fotopolymerisierbar
photopolymerization Fotopolymerisation f, Fotovernetzung f
photopolymerize/to fotopolymerisieren
photoprinting lamp Lichtpauslampe f
photoprocessing fotografische Verarbeitung f, Fotoverarbeitung f
photoproduct Fotoerzeugnis n
photoradiogram s. radiophotograph
photoradiography Röntgen[strahlen]fotografie f, Röntgenografie f, Filmröntgen n
photoreaction Fotoreaktion f, fotochemische Reaktion f
photoreal[istic] fotorealistisch
photorealism Fotorealismus m
photorealistic image fotorealistisches Bild n
~ **rendering (rendition)** fotorealistische Darstellung f (Computergrafik)
photoreceiver Fotoempfänger m
photoreception Fotorezeption f
photoreceptor Fotorezeptor m, Lichtrezeptor m, [lichtempfindlicher] Rezeptor m
~ **cell** Rezeptorzelle f, Sehrezeptor m
photoreconnaissance Bildaufklärung f, Lichtbildaufklärung f fotografische Aufklärung f; Luftbildaufklärung f
~ **satellite** Aufklärungssatellit m
photorecord fotografische Aufnahme f

photorecorder Bildaufzeichnungsgerät *n*
photoreduce/to fotografisch verkleinern
photorefractive [foto]refraktiv, lichtbrechend, dioptrisch, brechkraftändernd
~ **crystal** lichtbrechender Kristall *m*
photoreport Bildbericht *m*
photoreportage Fotoreportage *f*
photoreporting Reportagefotografie *f*, Live-Fotografie *f*
photoreproduction Fotokopie *f*; elektrofotografische Kopie *f*
photoresist Foto[kopier]lack *m*, Fotoresist *m*, fotoempfindlicher Lack *m*, fotoresistives Material *n*
photoresistive fotoresisitiv
photoresistor Fotowiderstand *m*, Fotowiderstandszelle *f*; Halbleiterfotowiderstand *m*
photoscanner Fotoscanner *m*
photosculpture Fotoplastik *f*, Fotoskulptur *f*
photosensitive lichtempfindlich, fotoempfindlich
~ **cell** Fotozelle *f*
~ **foil** lichtempfindliche Folie *f*
~ **layer** lichtempfindliche Schicht *f*
~ **material** lichtempfindliches Material *n*
~ **paper** lichtempfindliches Papier *n*
~ **pigment** Fotopigment *n*
~ **polymer** lichtempfindliches Polymer *n*, Fotopolymer *n*
~ **resist** *s.* photoresist
photosensitivity Fotoempfindlichkeit *f*, Lichtempfindlichkeit *f*
photosensitization Fotosensibilisierung *f*
photosensitize/to fotosensibilisieren
photosensitizer Fotosensibilisator *m*
photosensor Fotosensor *m*, Lichtsensor *m*, Optosensor *m*, optischer Sensor *m*
photostability Fotostabilität *f*, Lichtbeständigkeit *f*
photostat/to ablichten
photostat, photostat[ic] copy Ablichtung *f*
photostimulable phosphor Speicherleuchtstoff *m*, Speicherphosphor *m*
photostimulated luminescence lichtangeregte Lumineszenz *f*
phototechnology Fototechnik *f*; Fototechnologie *f*
phototelegram Bildtelegramm *n*
phototelegraphy Bildtelegrafie *f*
phototheodolite Fototheodolit *m*
photothermal fotothermisch
photothermographic fotothermografisch
photothermography Fotothermografie *f*
photothermometry Fotothermometrie *f*
phototopography Fotogrammetrie *f*, Bildmesswesen *n*, Fototopografie *f*
phototransformer Entzerrungsgerät *n* *(Fotogrammetrie)*
phototransistor Fototransistor *m*, Fotohalbleiter *m*
phototropic fototrop

~ **glass** fototropes Glas *n*
phototropism, phototropy Fototropie *f*
phototube Röhrenfotozelle *f*
phototypesetter 1. Fotosatzgerät *n*, Fotosatzdrucker *m*, Satzbelichter *m* *(s.a.* phototypesetting machine*)*; 2. Fotosetzer *m*
phototypesetting Lichtsatz *m*, Fotosatz *m*, Filmsatz *m*
~ **film** Fotosatzfilm *m*
~ **machine** Fotosatzmaschine *f*, Lichtsatzmaschine *f*, Lichtsetzmaschine *f* *(s.a.* phototypesetter*)*
~ **paper** Fotosatzpapier *n*
phototypography *s.* phototypesetting
photovoltage Fotospannung *f*
photovoltaic fotovoltaisch
~ **cell** [Sperrschicht-]Fotoelement *n*, Sperrschicht[foto]zelle *f*, fotovoltaische Zelle *f*; Halbleiterfotoelement *n*
~ **detector** fotovoltaischer Detektor *m*
~ **effect** Foto-Volta-Effekt *m*, Sperrschicht-Fotoeffekt *m*
~ **mode** fotovoltaischer Betrieb *m* *(Fotodetektor)*
photovoltaics Fotovoltaik *f*
photozincography Fotozinkografie *f*
phthalocyanine Phthalocyanin *n* *(Pigment)*
physical camera Realkamera *f*
~ **contrast** physikalischer Kontrast *m*
~ **developer** physikalischer Entwickler *m*
~ **development** physikalische Entwicklung *f*
~ **effect** mechanischer Spezialeffekt *m* *(Kinematografie)*
~ **etching** Schab[e]retusche *f*
~ **image** physikalisches Bild *n*
~ **image formation** physikalische Bildentstehung *f*
~ **layer** physikalische Schicht *f*
~ **length** Baulänge *f* *(z.B. eines Objektivs)*
~ **location** Realdekoration *f* *(Filmarbeit)*
~ **optics** physikalische Optik *f*, Wellenoptik *f*
~ **photometer** physikalisches Fotometer *n*
~ **photometry** physikalische (objektive) Fotometrie *f*
~ **reduction** Schab[e]retusche *f*
~ **resolution** physikalische Auflösung *f*
~ **ripening** physikalische Reifung *f*, Ostwald-Reifung *f* *(Emulsionsherstellung)*
~ **topology** physikalische Topologie *f*
physics of color Farbphysik *f*
physiogram Lichtpendelgrafik *f*, Pendelfotogramm *n*, Rhythmogramm *n*
physiological nystagmus physiologischer Nystagmus *m*
~ **optics** physiologische Optik *f*
physiopsychologic[al] psychphysiologisch
pica Pica *f* *(typografische Maßeinheit)*
picking Farbrupfen *n*, Rupfen *n* *(Druckschwierigkeit)*
pickup Aufnehmer *m*

~ **coil** Antennenspule f *(z.B. eines Quanteninterferometers)*
~ **device** Aufnehmer m
~ **head** Hörkopf m *(Magnettonwiedergabe)*
~ **pattern** Richtcharakteristik f, Richtwirkung f *(Mikrofon)*
~ **reel** Aufwickelrolle f, Aufwickelspule f, Aufwickeltrommel f
~ **shot** Nachaufnahme f; Korrekturaufnahme f, Wiederholungsaufnahme f *(Filmarbeit)*
~ **system** Aufnahmesystem n
~ **tube** Aufnahme[bild]röhre f, Bildaufnahmeröhre f

picometer Pikometer m
picosecond laser Pikosekundenlaser m
pictogram, pictograph Piktogramm n
pictographic piktografisch
pictoralism Piktoralismus m
pictorial bildlich; bildmäßig; bildhaft
~ **archive** Bildarchiv n
~ **character** Bildzeichen n *(s.a.* icon, pictogram*)*
~ **color copy** Farbbildkopie f
~ **color printer** Farbbilddrucker m
~ **composition** Bildgestaltung f, Bildkomposition f
~ **continuity** Bildzusammenhang f
~ **contrast** Bildkontrast m
~ **database** Bilddatenbank f
~ **depth cue** Tiefenhinweis m
~ **detail** Bilddetail n
~ **documentary representation** bilddokumentarische Darstellung f
~ **effect** 1. Bildwirkung f, Bildeffekt m; 2. Bildtrick m *(Film, Video)*
~ **element** Bildelement n
~ **example** Bildbeispiel n
~ **icon** Bildsymbol n, Icon n *(s.a.* unter icon*)*
~ **illustration** Bebilderung f, Illustration f; Abbildung f
~ **image** Abbildung f
~ **information** Bildinformation f, bildhafte (bildliche) Information f
~ **information processing** Bildinformationsverarbeitung f
~ **information system** Bilddatenbanksystem n
~ **material** Bildmaterial n
~ **negative** Bildnegativ n
~ **negative film** Bildnegativfilm m
~ **noise** Bildrauschen n
~ **noise** Bildrauschen n
~ **object** Bildgegenstand m; Bildmotiv n *(s.a. unter* object*)*
~ **pattern recognition** Bildmustererkennung f
~ **perspective** Bildperspektive f
~ **photography** abbildende (bildgebende) Fotografie f, bildmäßige Fotografie f; bildnerische Fotografie f, Piktoralismus m

~ **rendering (rendition)** bildliche Wiedergabe f
~ **representation** bildliche Darstellung f, Bilddarstellung f
~ **segment** Bildsegment n
~ **statistics** Bildstatistik f *(Visualisierung)*
~ **subject** s. ~ object
~ **works** Bildnerei f
pictorialization bildliche Darstellung f; Bebilderung f
pictorialize/to 1. bildlich darstellen; 2. bebildern, illustrieren
pictorialness Bildmäßigkeit f; Bildhaftigkeit f
picture/to 1. abbilden; 2. bebildern, illustrieren
picture 1. Bild n, Abbild n, Abbildung f *(s.a. unter image)*; 2. Spielfilm m
~ **agency** Bildagentur f
~ **aperture** Bildfenster n *(Projektor)*
~ **archiving** Bildarchivierung f
~ **archiving and communication[s] system** Bildarchivierungs- und -kommunikationssystem n *(bes. im medizinischen Bereich)*
~ **area** Bildfläche f; Bildpartie f, Bildspiegel m *(Layout)*
~ **black** Bildschwarz n
~ **block** Bildblock m
~ **book** Bildband m, Bilderbuch n
~ **breakup** Bildausfall m, Bildaussetzer m
~ **camera** s. motion-picture camera
~ **-capture rate** Bildaufnahmefrequenz f, Bilderfassungsrate f
~ **carrier frequency** Bildträgerfrequenz f
~ **CD (compact disc)** Bild-CD f
~ **cell** Bildzelle f
~ **complexity** Bildkomplexität f
~ **control** Bildsteuerung f
~ **corner** Bildecke f
~ **credit** Bildnachweis m
~ **cropping** Bildbeschneidung f, Bildbeschnitt m
~ **cut** Bildschnittstelle f
~ **-data storage** Bilddatenspeicherung f
~ **defect** Bildfehler m
~ **degradation** Bildverschlechterung f, Bilddegradation f
~ **disruption** Bildunterbrechung f
~ **edge** Bildkante f
~ **edit** Bildschnittstelle f
~ **editing [process]** Bildschnitt m, Bildbearbeitung f *(Film, Video)*
~ **-editing program** Bildbearbeitungsprogramm n
~ **editor** Bildbearbeiter m; Bildredakteur m; Fotoredakteur m
~ **effect** s. pictorial effect 1. *und* 2.
~ **element** 1. Bildelement n; 2. s. pixel n
~ **field** Bildfeld n
~ **field rate** Halbbild[wechsel]frequenz f, Halbbildrate f, Vertikalfrequenz f *(Video)*
~ **file** Bild[dokument]datei f
~ **filing software** Bildspeichersoftware f

~ **film** Bildfilm *m*
~ **format** Aufnahmeformat *n*
~ **frame** Bildrahmen *m*
~ **frequency** Bildfrequenz *f*
~ **gate** *s.* ~ aperture
~**-goer** Kinobesucher *m*
~ **grid** Bildraster *m(n)*
~ **head** Projektorkopf *m*
~ **height** Bildhöhe *f*
~ **hierarchy** Bildhierarchie *f*
~ **image** filmisches Bild *n*
~**-in-picture mode** Bild-in-Bild-Technik *f*; Bild-in-Bild-Modus *m*, Bild-in-Bild-Funktion *f (Video, Fernsehen)*
~ **information** Bildinformation *f*, bildliche (bildhafte) Information *f*
~ **insertion processor** Bild-in-Bild-Prozessor *m*
~ **jitter** Bildschwankung[en] *f[pl] (Film, Video)*
~ **level** Bildpegel *m*, Video[signal]pegel *m*
~ **line** Bildzeile *f*
~ **making** Bildaufnahme *f*
~**-making situation** Bildaufnahmesituation *f*, Aufnahmesituation *f*
~ **matrix** Bildmatrix *f*
~ **memory** 1. Bild[daten]speicher *m*; 2. Bildgedächtnis *n*
~ **message** Bildmitteilung *f*
~ **monitor** Bildkontrollempfänger *m*
~ **negative** 1. Bildnegativ *n*; 2. Negativfilm *m (Kinematografie)*
~ **number** Bildnummer *f*
~ **only print** Bildkopie *f*, stumme Kopie *f (Kinematografie)*
~ **palace** Filmpalast *m*
~ **performance** Bildleistung *f*
~ **plane** Bildebene *f*
~ **point** Bildpunkt *m*
~ **postcard** Bildpostkarte *f*
~ **preparation** Bildaufmachung *f*, Bildpräparation *f*
~**-processing service** Bilderdienst *m*
~**-processing unit** Bildverarbeitungseinheit *f*
~ **projector** Bildprojektor *m*; Filmprojektor *m*, Filmvorführgerät *n*
~ **quality** Bildqualität *f*, Bildgüte *f*
~ **quality constraint** Bildqualitätseinbuße *f*
~ **quality enhancement (improvement)** Bildqualitätsverbesserung *f*
~ **receiver** Bildempfangsgerät *n*
~ **recording** Bildaufnahme *f*
~ **repetition rate** Bildwiederholfrequenz *f*, Bildwiederholrate *f*, Bildwechselfrequenz *f*, Bilderneuerungsfrequenz *f*
~ **rest [period]** Bildstillstand *m*
~ **sameness** Bildgleichheit *f*
~ **scene** Bildszene *f*
~ **script** Bilderschrift *f*
~ **segmentation** Bild[objekt]segmentierung *f*

~ **series** Bildserie *f*, Bildreihe *f*, Bild[er]folge *f*
~ **service** Bilddienst *m*
~ **sharpness** Bildschärfe *f*, Abbildungsschärfe *f*
~ **sharpness control** Bildschärferegulierung *f*
~ **signal** Bildsignal *n*
~ **size** Bildgröße *f*
~ **space** Bildraum *m*
~ **steadiness** Bildruhe *f*, Bildstand *m*
~ **surface** Bildoberfläche *f*
~**-taking conditions** Aufnahmebedingungen *fpl*, Bildaufnahmebedingungen *fpl*
~**-taking film** Aufnahmefilm *m*, Kamerafilm *m*, Kameraoriginal *n*, Unikat *n*
~**-taking lens** Aufnahmeobjektiv *n*, Aufnahmeoptik *f*, bilderzeugendes Objektiv *n*
~**-taking process** Bildaufnahme *f*
~**-taking situation** Aufnahmesituation *f*
~**-taking technique** Bildaufnahmetechnik *f*, fotografische Aufnahmetechnik *f*
~ **tape** Bildband *n*
~ **telegraphy** Bildtelegrafie *f*
~**-to-sound offset** Bild-Ton-Versatz *m*, Bild-Ton-Abstand *m (Tonfilm)*
~ **track** Bildspur *f*
~ **trimming** *s.* ~ cropping
~ **tube** Bild[wiedergabe]röhre *f*, Wiedergaberöhre *f*
~ **tube deflection circuitry** Bildröhren-Ablenkschaltung *f*
~ **tube diagonal** Bildröhrendiagonale *f*
~ **tube recycling** Bildröhrenrecycling *n*
~ **type** Bildart *f*
~ **viewer** Bildbetrachter *m*
~ **viewing** Bildbetrachtung *f*
~ **white** Bildweiß *n*

picturephone Bildtelefon *n*, Videofon *n*, Bildfernsprecher *m*
picturization 1. Verbildlichung *f*; 2. Verfilmung *f*
picturize/to 1. verbildlichen, bildlich darstellen; 2. verfilmen
PID *s.* packet identification
pie chart Tortendiagramm *n*, Kreisdiagramm *n*
piece of film Filmstück *n*
~ **of type** Type *f*, Einzelletter *f*; Drucktype *f*, Druckbuchstabe *m*
piezoceramic filter Keramikfilter *n*
piezoelectric piezoelektrisch
~ **actuator** Piezoantrieb *m*
~ **crystal** Piezokristall *m*, piezoelektrischer Kristall *m*
~ **effect** Piezoeffekt *m*, piezoelektrischer Effekt *m*
~ **element** Piezoelement *n*, piezoelektrisches Element *n (s.a.* ~ transducer*)*
~ **foil** piezoelektrische Folie *f*

~ **generator** Quarzgenerator *m*
~ **ink-jet printer** Piezo-Tintenstrahldrucker *m*, piezoelektrischer Tintenstrahldrucker *m*
~ **oscillator** Quarzgenerator *m*
~ **printer head** piezoelektrischer Druckkopf *m*
~ **scanner** piezoelektrischer Scanner *m*
~ **sensor** piezoelektrischer Sensor *m*
~ **transducer** piezoelektrischer Wandler *m*, Piezowandler *m*
piezoelectricity Piezoelektrizität *f*
piezoluminescence Triboluminesenz *f*
pigment Pigment *n*
~ **image** Pigmentbild *n*
~ **layer** Pigmentschicht *f*
~ **process** Pigmentdruck *m*
pigmentation Pigmentierung *f*
pigmented pigmentiert
~ **color** Buntfarbe *f*, bunte Farbe *f*
~ **dye** pigmentierter Farbstoff *m*
~ **epithelium** Pigmentepithel *n* *(des Auges)*
~ **gelatin** Pigmentgelatine *f*
~ **ink** pigmentierte Druckfarbe *f*; pigmentierte Tinte *f*
~ **print** Pigmentdruck *m* *(Erzeugnis)*
PIL tube *s.* precision in-line tube
pile of sheets Bogenstapel *m*
piling Pelzen *n* *(Druckschwierigkeit)*
pilot Pilotsignal *n*
~ **frequeny recording** Pilotfrequenzaufzeichnung *f*
~ **laser** Positionierlaser *m*
~ **pin** 1. Registerstift *m*; 2. Justiergreifer *m*, Sperrgreifer *m* *(Kinofilmtechnik)*
~ **program** Pilotsendung *f*
~ **tone** Pilotton *m*
pin cylinder connector PC-Buchse *f* *(einer Kamera)*
~ **reader** Lesestift *m*
~**-registering mechanism** Sperr-Justier-Greifer *m*
~**-sharp image** gestochen scharfes Bild *n*
pinch roller Andruckrolle *f*
pincushion distortion Kissenverzeichnung *f*, Kissenverzerrung *f*, kissenförmige Verzeichnung *f*, Kissenfehler *m* *(Abbildungsfehler)*
ping-pong buffering doppelte Pufferung *f*, Doppelpufferung *f* *(Bilddatenverarbeitung)*
pinhole [aperture] Lochblende *f*
~ **camera** Loch[blenden]kamera *f*, Urkamera *f*, Camera *f* obscura
~ **camera image** Lochkamerabild *n*
~ **camera model** Lochkameramodell *n* *(Videomodellierung)*
~ **collimator** Einlochkollimator *m*, Pinhole-Kollimator *m* *(Gammakamera)*
~ **diaphragm** Lochblende *f*
~ **perspective** *s.* central perspective
~ **perspective** Zentralperspektive *f*, Linearperspektive *f*, lineare Perspektive *f*
pinholes Blitzer *mpl* *(Druckschwierigkeit)*

pink filter Rosafilter *n*
~ **noise** rosa Rauschen *n*
pinpoint digital zoom Punkt-Digital-Zoom *n*
pipe/to leiten *(z.B. Licht)*
pipe processing Röhrenentwicklung *f* *(Fotoverarbeitung)*
pipette Pipette *f*
pirate/to raubkopieren
pirate Raubkopierer *m*
~ **copy** Raubkopie *f*
pirated software raubkopierte Software *f*
pistol grip Pistolengriff *m*, Kameragriff *m* *(Kamerazubehör)*
pit Vertiefung *f* *(CD-Platte)*
pitch 1. Mittenabstand *m* *(z.B. von Pixeln)*; 2. Perforationslochabstand *m*, Perforationsschritt *m*; 3. Rastermaß *n*; 4. Druckweite *f*; 5. Tonhöhe *f*
~ **button** Kittkörper *m* *(Linsenfertigung)*
pivot point Drehpunkt *m*, Fulkrum *m*
pivoting mirror Drehspiegel *m*
pixel Pixel *n*, Bildpixel *n*, Bildpunkt *m*, Bildelement *n*
~ **accuracy** Pixelgenauigkeit *f*
~ **address** Pixeladresse *f*, Bildpunktadresse *f*
~ **addressing** Pixeladressierung *f*
~ **amplifier** Pixelverstärker *m* *(CMOS-Sensor)*
~ **amplitude** Pixelamplitude *f*
~ **anomaly** *s.* ~ error
~ **area** Pixelfläche *f*
~ **arrangement** Pixelanordnung *f* *(s.a.* ~ array*)*
~ **array** Pixelfeld *n*, Bildelementmatrix *f*
~ **aspect ratio** Pixelseitenverhältnis *n*
~ **averaging** Pixelmittelung *f*
~**-based image processing** pixelbasierte Bildverarbeitung *f*
~**-based motion compensation** pixelbasierte Bewegungskompensation *f*
~**-based motion estimation** pixelbasierte Bewegungsschätzung *f*
~**-based output device** Rastergerät *n*, rasterorientiertes Ausgabegerät *n*
~**-based representation** *s.* pixel representation
~**-based segmentation** pixelbasierte (punktorientierte) Segmentierung *f*
~**-based textural feature** pixelbasiertes Texturmerkmal *n*
~ **block** Pixelblock *m*
~ **boundary** Pixelrand *m*
~ **brightness** Bildpunkthelligkeit *f*
~**-by-pixel classification** pixelbasierte (pixelweise) Klassifikation *f*
~**-by-pixel image coding algorithm** pixelbasierter (pixelweiser) Bildcodieralgorithmus *m*
~**-by-pixel operation** pixelweise Operation *f*
~ **cache** Pixelcache[speicher] *m*

pixel

~ **center** Pixelmitte *f*, Pixelmittelpunkt *m*
~ **chain** Pixelkette *f*
~ **charge** Pixelladung *f*
~ **clock** Pixeltakt *m*, Bildelementtakt *m*
~ **clock rate** Pixeltaktrate *f*
~ **cluster** Pixelcluster *m*
~ **clustering** Pixelclusterung *f*
~ **color** Pixelfarbe *f*, Bildpunktfarbe *f*
~ **color value** Pixelfarbwert *m*
~ **column** Pixelspalte *f*
~ **comparison** Pixelvergleich *m*
~ **connection** Pixelverbindung *f*
~ **contrast** Pixelkontrast *m*
~ **coordinate** Pixelkoordinate *f*
~ **count** 1. Pixelnumerierung *f*; 2. Pixelzahl *f*
~ **data** Pixeldaten *pl*
~ **density** Pixeldichte *f*
~ **depth** Pixeltiefe *f*, Datentiefe *f*, Bittiefe *f* *(s.a. color depth)*
~ **dimension** Pixelgröße *f*
~ **distance** Pixelabstand *m*, Bildpunktdistanz *f*
~ **distribution** Pixelverteilung *f*
~ **domain** Pixelbereich *m*
~-**domain representation** Pixelbereichsdarstellung *f*
~ **dropout** Pixelausfall *m*; Störpixel *n*
~ **duplication** Pixelverdopp[e]lung *f*
~ **edge** Pixelrand *m*
~ **editing** Pixelbearbeitung *f*
~ **electrode** Pixelelektrode *f* *(Flüssigkristallanzeige)*
~ **encoding** Pixelcodierung *f*
~ **error** Pixelfehler *m*, Pixeldefekt *m*
~ **frequency** Pixelfrequenz *f*
~ **graphics** Pixelgrafik *f*, Rastergrafik *f*
~ **gray level (value)** Pixelgrauwert *m*, Pixeldichtewert *m*
~ **grid** Pixelgitter *n*
~ **group** Pixelgruppe *f*
~ **image** Pixelbild *n*, Einzelbitbild *n* *(s.a. ~ map)*
~ **independence** Pixelunabhängigkeit *f*
~ **intensity [value]** Pixelgrauwert *m*, Pixeldichtewert *m (s.a. ~ luminosity)*
~ **interpolation** Pixelinterpolation *f*
~ **interval** *s.* ~ **spacing**
~ **jitter** Pixeljitter *m*
~ **level** Pixelebene *f*
~ **linking** Pixelverbindung *f*
~ **location** Pixelposition *f*, Bildpunktposition *f*
~ **loss** Pixelverlust *m*
~ **luminance [value]** Pixelluminanz *f*
~ **luminosity** Bildpunkthelligkeit *f*
~ **map** Bitmap-Bild *n*, Bitmap *f*; Bitmuster *n* *(s.a. ~ image)*
~ **matrix** Pixelmatrix *f*
~ **neighborhood** Pixelnachbarschaft *f*, Punktnachbarschaft *f*
~ **noise** Pixelrauschen *n*
~ **offset** Pixelverschiebung *f*
~ **optimization** Pixeloptimierung *f*

~ **pair** Pixelpaar *n*
~ **pattern** Pixelmuster *n*
~ **per inch** Bildpunkte *mpl* pro Zoll *(Auflösungsmaß)*
~ **pitch** *s.* ~ **spacing**
~ **plane** Pixelebene *f*
~ **position** Pixelposition *f*, Bildpunktposition *f*
~-**precise** pixelgenau
~ **processing** Pixelverarbeitung *f*
~-**recursive motion estimation** pixelrekursive Bewegungsschätzung *f*
~-**related** pixelbezogen, bildpunktbezogen
~-**related operator** bildpunktbezogener Operator *m*
~ **replication** Pixelverdopp[e]lung *f*
~ **representation** Pixeldarstellung *f*, Bildpunktdarstellung *f*, pixelorientierte Darstellung *f*, Pixelrepräsentation *f*
~ **resolution** Pixelauflösung *f*
~ **sensor** Pixelsensor *m*
~ **separation [distance]** *s.* ~ **spacing**
~ **shift** Pixelverschiebung *f*
~ **shifting** Bildpunktverschiebung *f*
~ **signature** Pixelsignatur *f*
~ **site** *s.* ~ **location**
~ **size** Pixelgröße *f*, Pixelabmessung *f*
~ **space** Pixelraum *m*
~ **spacing** Pixelabstand *m*, Bildpunktdistanz *f*
~ **structure** Pixelstruktur *f*
~ **subsampling** Pixel-Unterabtastung *f*
~-**synchronous** pixelsynchron
~-**synchronous scan[ning]** pixelsynchrone Abtastung *f*
~ **table** Pixeltabelle *f*
~ **tile** Makropixel *n*, Parkettstein *m* *(grafische Datenverarbeitung)*
~ **topology** Pixeltopologie *f*
~ **value** Pixelwert *m*, Pixelinhalt *m*
~ **variation** Pixelschwankung *f*
~ **vector** Pixelvektor *m*
~ **voltage** Pixelspannung *f* *(Flüssigkristallanzeige)*
~ **width** Pixelbreite *f*
pixelate/to aufrastern
pixelated pixelig; gepixelt
~ **image** gepixeltes Bild *n*
pixelation Pixeligkeit *f*
pixels per inch Punkte *mpl* pro Zoll *(Auflösungsmaß)*
pixelwise pixelweise, bildpunktweise, bildelementweise
~ **classification** pixelbasierte (pixelweise) Klassifikation *f*
pixilated *s.* **pixelated**
pixmap *s.* **pixel map**
placeholder Platzhalter *m*, Platzhalter-Pixelbild *n*; Programmsymbol *n*, Icon *n*
placement accuracy Positionier[ungs]genauigkeit *f*
plain paper Normalpapier *n*, Standardpapier *n*

~-**paper copier** Normalpapierkopierer *m*
~ **photographic film** Normalfilm *m*
~ **text** unformatierter Text *m*
~ **typeface** normaler (aufrechter) Schriftschnitt *m*
plaintext Klartext *m*, unverschlüsselter Text *m*
plan achromat [objective] Planachromat *m*
~ **apochromatic objective** Planapochromat *m*
~-**corrected objective** plankorrigiertes Objektiv *n*
~ **correction** Plankorrektur *f*
~ **objective** Planobjektiv *n*
~ **position indication** Polarkoordinatendarstellung *f (Radar)*
~ **position indicator [device]** Rundsichtanzeige *f*, PPI-Sichtgerät *n (Radar)*
planapochromat Planapochromat *m*
planar flächig, flächenhaft, plan[ar], eben; zweidimensional *(s.a. unter plane)*
~ **anisotropy** planare Anisotropie *f*
~ **contour** planare Kontur *f*
~ **detector** flächiger (flächenauflösender) Detektor *m*, [Halbleiter-]Flächendetektor *m*
~ **element** Flächenelement *n*
~ **graph** planarer Graph *m*
~ **image** flächiges (ebenes) Bild *n*
~ **imaging** flächige Abbildung *f*, planare Bildgebung *f*
~ **integral** Flächenintegral *n*
~ **mirror** *s.* plane mirror
~ **photodiode** flächige Fotodiode *f*
~ **picture** flächiges (ebenes) Bild *n*
~ **plate** Plan[parallel]platte *f*, Parallelplatte *f*, planparallele Platte *f*
~ **polarization** Planpolarisation *f*
~ **polygon** Flächenpolygon *n*
~ **projection** Flächenprojektion *f*
~ **scintigraphy** planare Szintigrafie *f*
~ **waveguide** planarer Wellenleiter *m*
planarity Ebenheit *f*, Planheit *f*, Plan[ar]ität *f*; Flächigkeit *f (Formmerkmal)*
Planckian radiation Hohlraumstrahlung *f*, Schwarzkörperstrahlung *f*
~ **radiator** Planckscher (Schwarzer) Strahler *m*, Schwarzkörperstrahler *m*, Hohlraumstrahler *m*, Schwarzer Körper *m*
Planck's constant Plancksche Konstante *f*, [Plancksches] Wirkungsquantum *n (Teilchenphysik)*
~ **formula** *s.* ~ radiation law
~ **function** Plancksche Kurve *f (Kolorimetrie, Farbtemperaturmessung)*
~ **radiation law** Plancksches Strahlungsgesetz *n*, Plancksche Strahlungsformel *f*
plane eben, plan[ar] *(s.a. unter planar)*; plano *(Druckbogen)*
~ ebene (planare) Oberfläche *f*
~ **angle** ebener Winkel *m*

~ **chart** Flächendiagramm *n*
~ **grating** Plangitter *n*, ebenes Gitter *n*
~ **grating spectrograph** Plangitterspektrograf *m*
~ **mirror** Planspiegel *m*, Flachspiegel *m*, ebener Spiegel *m*
~ **object** Flächenobjekt *n*, flächenhaftes Objekt *n*
~ **of focus** Brennebene *f*, Schärfeebene *f*; Einstellebene *f*
~ **of incidence** Einfallsebene *f*
~ **of light** Lichtfläche *f*
~ **of observation** Beobachtungsebene *f*
~ **of polarization** Polarisationsebene *f*
~ **of reflection** Reflexionsebene *f*
~ **of rotation** Rotationsebene *f*
~ **of symmetry** Symmetrieebene *f*
~ **of vibration** Schwingungsebene *f*
~-**parallel** planparallel
~ **parallel plate** Plan[parallel]platte *f*, Parallelplatte *f*, planparallele Platte *f (Optik)*
~ **parallelism** Planparallelität *f*
~-**polarized light** planpolarisiertes (linear polarisiertes) Licht *n*
~ **polarizer** Planpolarisator *m*
~ **reflection grating** Plangitter *n*, planes Reflexionsgitter *n*
~ **screen** ebene Bildwand *f*
~ **surface** Planfläche *f*, ebene (planare) Oberfläche *f*
~-**sweep algorithm** Durchlaufalgorithmus *m*
~-**table sheet** Messtischblatt *n*
~ **tomography** planares Röntgen *n*
~ **wave** ebene (planare) Welle *f*
planetarium Planetarium *n*
planetary camera Schrittkamera *f*
planigram, planigraph Planigramm *n*
planigraphy Planigrafie *f (röntgenografisches Verfahren)*
planimeter Planimeter *n*, Flächenmesser *m*
planimetric planimetrisch
~ **map** planimetrische Karte *f*
~ **projection** planimetrische Projektion *f*
planimetry Planimetrie *f*, ebene Geometrie *f*, Flächenmessung *f*
plano-concave plankonkav
~-**concave lens** Plankonkavlinse *f*
~-**convex** plankonvex
~-**convex lens** Plankonvexlinse *f*
planographic plate Flachdruckplatte *f*
~ **printing process** Flachdruckverfahren *n*
planography Flachdruck *m*
plasma Plasma *n*
~ **display [panel]** Plasma[bild]schirm *m*, Plasma-Flachbildschirm *m*; Plasmaanzeige *f*, Plasmadisplay *n*
~ **dry etching** Plasmatrockenätzen *n*
~ **photography** Kirlian-Fotografie *f*
~ **screen** *s.* ~ display [panel]
~ **source** Plasmaquelle *f*
plasmon Plasmon *n*
plastic duplicate plate Kunststoffstereo *n*

plastic

~ **filter** Kunststofffilter n
~-**laminated paper** kunststoffbeschichtetes Papier n, Kunststoffpapier n
~ **lens** 1. Kunststofflinse f, Plastiklinse f; 2. Kunststoffobjektiv n
~ **mount** Kunststoffrähmchen n, Kunststoffrahmen m
~ **optical material** optischer Kunststoff m
plasticizer Weichmacher m
plate 1. Platte f; Tafel f; 2. Druckplatte f; Druckstock m; 3. s. background plate
~ **beam splitter** Teilerplatte f
~-**bearing cylinder** Druckformzylinder m, Formzylinder m, Plattenzylinder m (Druckmaschine)
~ **camera** Plattenkamera f
~ **etching** Druckplattenätzung f
~ **exposure** Plattenbelichtung f, Druckplattenbelichtung f
~ **glass** Tafelglas n, Flachglas n
~ **gravure printing** Plattentiefdruck m
~ **imposition** Ausschießen n, Druckbogenmontage f, Bogenmontage f
~ **printing process** mechanisches Druckverfahren n
plateless printing process nichtmechanisches Druckverfahren n
platemaking Druckformherstellung f, Druckplattenfertigung f, Plattenherstellung f
platen Einlegefläche f (Kopierer, Scanner)
~ **drum** s. ~ roller
~ **press** Tiegeldruckmaschine f, Tiegel[druck]presse f
~ **roller** Druckwalze f (z.B. eines Thermotransferdruckers)
platinotype s. platinum print
~ **paper** Platinpapier n
~ **process** Platindruckverfahren n, Platinotypie f
platinum print Platinabzug m, Platindruck m
~ **printing paper** Platinpapier n
Platonic body (solid) platonischer Körper m, regelmäßiges Polyeder n (geometrisches Primitiv)
platter [system] Flachbettprojektor m, Filmtellereinrichtung f (Kinotechnik)
play/to [ab]spielen
play back (out)/to abspielen
~ **head** Abspielkopf m, Wiedergabekopf m
~ **list** Titelliste f
~ **mode** Abspielmodus m (z.B. eines Camcorders)
~ **station** Spiel[e]konsole f, Videospielkonsole f, Telespielkonsole f
playability Abspielbarkeit f
playable abspielbar
playback Abspielung f, Abspielvorgang m, Wiedergabe f
~ **device** Abspielgerät n, Abspielmaschine f, Abspieler m
~ **electronics** Abspielelektronik f

~ **format** Wiedergabeformat n
~ **frame rate** Abspielgeschwindigkeit f
~ **head** Abspielkopf m, Wiedergabekopf m
~ **mode** Abspielmodus m (Camcorder)
~-**only format** Abspielformat n
~-**only machine** Abspielgerät n, Abspielmaschine f, Abspieler m
~ **pause mode** Wiedergabepause f, Standbildmodus m (Video)
~ **performance** Wiedergabeleistung f
~ **process** Abspielung f, Abspielvorgang m
~ **quality** Abspielqualität f
~ **rate** Abspielgeschwindigkeit f
~ **signal** Überspielsignal n
~ **speed** Wiedergabegeschwindigkeit f, Abspielgeschwindigkeit f
~ **time** Abspielzeit f, Spielzeit f, Spieldauer f (z.B. einer Bildplatte)
player [device] Abspieler m, Abspielgerät n, Abspielmaschine f
playing time s. playback time
PLED display PLED-Display n, Polymerdisplay n
plenoptic modeling plenoptische Modellierung f
pleochroism Pleochroismus m
plesiochronous plesiochron
~ **multiplexer** plesiochroner Multiplexer m
plethysmogram Plethysmogramm n
plethysmograph Plethysmograf m
plethysmographic plethysmografisch
plethysmography Plethysmografie f
Plössl eyepiece Plössl-Okular n, symmetrisches Okular n
plot/to 1. plotten, [maschinell] zeichnen; 2. abtragen (Diagrammwerte)
plot Plot m(n), grafische Darstellung f (Abbildung)
~ **head** Zeichenkopf m
plotter Plotter m, [rechnergesteuerte] Zeichenmaschine m; Zeichengerät n
~ **display** Plotterdisplay n (Navigationsdatenanzeige)
~ **operator** Auswerter m
plotting camera Auswertekamera f, Auswertekammer f
~ **instrument (machine)** s. plotter
~ **pencil** Plotterstift m
plug-in s. ~ module
~-**in board (card)** Einsteck-Chipkarte f, Einsteckkarte f, Steckkarte f, Erweiterungs[steck]karte f
~-**in computer board** Computersteckkarte f
~-**in module** Einsteckmodul n, Zusatzmodul n, Einschub m, Plug-In n
pluggable einsteckbar
plumbicon [tube] Plumbikon n (Bildspeicherröhre)
plus s. supplementary close-up lens
~ **first order of diffraction** plus erste Beugungsordnung f
PMT s. photomultiplier tube

pneumatic bulb release
Luftdruck-Fernauslöser *m*,
pneumatischer Fernauslöser *m*
Pockels cell Pockels-Zelle *f*
(elektrooptisches Gerät)
~ **effect** Pockels-Effekt *m (elektrooptischer Effekt)*
pocket binocular Taschenfernglas *n*
~ **camera** Taschenkamera *f*, Pocketkamera *f*
~ **digicam** digitale Taschenkamera *f*
~ **magnifier** Taschenlupe *f*
~**-size camera** Taschenkamera *f*, Pocketkamera *f*
~**-size[d] video recorder**
Taschenvideorecorder *m*
~ **slide viewer** Taschendiabetrachter *m*
~ **stereoscope** Taschenstereoskop *n*
~ **television** Taschenfernseher *m*
POD *s.* printing on demand
Poggendorff illusion
Poggendorff-Täuschung *f (geometrische optische Täuschung)*
point/to [an]visieren
point Punkt *m*; typografischer Punkt *m*, Didot-Punkt *m*, p
~ **acuity** Punktsehschärfe *f*
~**-and-select device** Zeigegerät *n*
~**-and-shoot camera**
Schnappschusskamera *f*,
Schnellschusskamera *f*, Knipskamera *f*
~**-and-shoot photographer**
Gelegenheitsfotograf *m*
~ **beam** Punktstrahl *m (Elektronenstrahl)*
~ **brilliance** Punkthelligkeit *f*
~**-by-point scanning** bildpunktsequentielle (bildpunktweise) Abtastung *f*
~ **cloud** Punktwolke *f*
~ **contact microscope**
Punktkontaktmikroskop *n*
~ **coordinate** Punktkoordinate *f*
~ **data set** Punktdatensatz *m*
~ **defect** Punktstörung *f*
~ **density** Punktdichte *f*
~ **detection** Punkterkennung *f*
~ **determination** Punktbestimmung *f*
~ **diffraction interferometer**
Punktdiffraktionsinterferometer *n*
~ **distribution** Punktverteilung *f*
~ **image** Punktbild *n*, punktförmige Abbildung *f*, Zerstreuungsscheibchen *n*, Spotdiagramm *n (Optik)*
~ **image formation** Punktbildentstehung *f*
~**-in-polygon location**
Punkt-im-Polygon-Test *m (geometrische Datenverarbeitung)*
~ **light** Punktlicht *n*
~ **light source** Punktlichtquelle *f*, punktförmige Lichtquelle *f*
~ **location** Punktlokalisierung *f*, Punktlokalisation *f*
~ **logarithmic operation** logarithmische Punktoperation *f*
~ **object** Punktobjekt *n (Optik)*

~ **of convergence** Konvergenzpunkt *m*
~ **of fixation** Fixierpunkt *m*, Fixationspunkt *m (Sehen)*
~ **of incidence** Auftreffpunkt *m*
~ **of intersection** Schnittpunkt *m*
~**-of-sale scanner** Kassenscanner *m*
~ **of sharpest focus** Scharfpunkt *m*
~ **of view** Blickpunkt *m*
~ **operation** Punktoperation *f*, einstellige Operation *f*, Grauwertmodifikation *f (Pixelverarbeitung)*
~ **operator** Punktoperator *m*
~ **pattern** Punktmuster *n*
~ **processing** Pixelverarbeitung *f*
~ **resolution** Punktauflösung *f*
~ **scan[ning]** Punktabtastung *f*, punktweise Abtastung
~ **scatterer** Punktstreuer *m*, punktförmiger Streukörper *m*
~ **set** Punktmenge *f*
~ **signature** Punktsignatur *f*
~ **size** 1. Punktgröße *f*; Schriftgrad *m (Typografie)*; 2. Kegel *m*, Vertikalhöhe *f (der Einzelletter)*
~ **source** Punktquelle *f*
~ **source illumination**
Punktlichtbeleuchtung *f*
~ **source object** Punktobjekt *n (Optik)*
~ **source of light** Punktlichtquelle *f*
~ **source spectroscopy**
Punktquellenspektroskopie *f*
~**-spread function**
Punktbild[verwaschungs]funktion *f*,
Punktstreufunktion *f*,
Punktantwortfunktion *f*,
Unschärfefunktion *f*
~**-symmetric convolution kernel**
punktsymmetrischer Faltungskern *m*
~**-to-multipoint distribution system**
Punkt-zu-Multipunkt-Verteilsystem *n*
~**-to-point distribution system**
Punkt-zu-Punkt-Verteilsystem *n*
~**-to-point processing** punktweise Verarbeitung *f*
~**-to-point videoconferencing**
Zweipartner-Videokonferenz *f*
~ **transform[ation]** Punkttransformation *f*
~ **visibility** Punkterkennbarkeit *f (Auflösungsmaß)*
pointer 1. Zeiger *m*, Punktzeiger *m*; 2. Hinweiszeichen *n*; 3. Cursor *m*, Positionsmarke *f (Bildschirm)*
~ **list** Zeigerliste *f (geometrische Datenverarbeitung)*
pointing Kamerarichten *n*
~ **device** Zeigegerät *n*
pointwise punktweise, bildpunktweise
Poisson counting noise Poisson-Rauschen *n*, poissonverteiltes weißes Rauschen *n*
~**-distributed** poissonverteilt
~**-distributed white noise** *s.* Poisson counting noise
~ **[probability density] distribution**
Poisson-Verteilung *f*

Poisson

~ **process** Poisson-Prozess *m*
~ **statistics** Poisson-Verteilung *f*
~**-Voronoi tessellation**
 [Poisson-]Voronoi-Mosaik *n*,
 Dirichlet-Parkettierung *f*
 (Computergrafik)
pola screen *s.* polarizing filter
polar angle Polarwinkel *m*
~ **axis** Polarachse *f*, Stundenachse *f*
 (Astrooptik)
~ **coordinate axis** Polarkoordinatenachse *f*
~ **coordinate[s] system**
 Polarkoordinatensystem *n*, polares
 Koordinatensystem *n*
~ **coordinates** Polarkoordinaten *fpl*
~ **crystal** polarer Kristall *m*, Ionenkristall *m*
~ **diagram (graph)** polares
 Lichtstärkeverteilungsdiagramm *n*
~ **pattern** Richtcharakteristik *f*,
 Richtwirkung *f (Mikrofon)*
~ **planimeter** Polarplanimeter *n*
~ **projection** *s.* perspective projection
~ **vector** Richtungsvektor *m*
polarimeter Polarimeter *n*
polarimetric radar polarimetrisches Radar *n*
polarimetry Polarimetrie *f*
polariscope Polariskop *n*
polarity Polarität *f*
polarizability Polarisierbarkeit *f*
polarizable polarisierbar
polarization Polarisation *f*
~ **analyzer** Polarisationsanalysator *m*
~ **angle** Polarisations[dreh]winkel *m*,
 Brewster-Winkel *m*, Brewsterscher
 Winkel *m*
~ **axis** Polarisationsachse *f*
~ **capability** Polarisationsvermögen *n*
~ **characteristic** Polarisationseigenschaft *f*
~ **coating** Polarisationsbeschichtung *f*
~ **control** Polarisationskontrolle *f*
~ **degree** Polarisationsgrad *m*
~ **device** Polarisationsgerät *n*,
 Polarisationseinrichtung *f*
~ **direction** Polarisationsrichtung *f*
~ **diversity radar** Multipolarisationsradar *n*
~ **effect** Polarisationseffekt *m*
~ **ellipse** Polarisationsellipse *f*
~ **ellipticity** Polarisationselliptizität *f*
~ **hologram** Polarisationshologramm *n*
~ **holography** Polarisationsholografie *f*
~ **interferometry**
 Polarisationsinterferometrie *f*
~ **measurement** Polarisationsmessung *f*
~ **microscopy** Polarisationsmikroskopie *f*
~ **mode dispersion**
 Polarisationsmodendispersion *f*
~ **noise** Polarisationsrauschen *n*
~ **optics** Polarisationsoptik *f*
~ **orientation** Polarisationsrichtung *f*
~ **pattern** Polarisationsmuster *n*
~ **photomicrography**
 Polarisationsmikrofotografie *f*
~ **plane** Polarisationsebene *f*

~ **purity** Polarisationsreinheit *f*
~ **ratio** Polarisationsverhältnis *n*
~ **rotation** Polarisationsdrehung *f*
~ **rotator** Polarisationsrotator *m*
~ **state** Polarisationszustand *m*
~ **vector** Polarisationsvektor *m*
polarize/to polarisieren
polarized excitation X-ray spectrometer
 Polarisations-Röntgenspektrometer *n*
~ **glasses** Polarisations[filter]brille *f*,
 Polfilterbrille *f*
~ **image** polarisiertes Bild *n*
~ **light** polarisiertes Licht *n*
~**-light microscope**
 Polarisationsmikroskop *n*
~**-light microscopy**
 Polarisationsmikroskopie *f*
~**-light photography**
 Polarisationsfotografie *f*
~ **reflection** polarisierte Reflexion *f*
polarizer Polarisator *m (s.a.* polarizing filter*)*
polarizing angle *s.* polarization angle
~ **axis** Polarisationsachse *f*
~ **effect** Polarisationseffekt *m*
~ **filter** Pola[risations]filter *n*, Polfilter *n*
~ **foil** *s.* ~ sheet
~ **goggles** *s.* polarized glasses
~ **lens** Polarisationslinse *f*
~ **optical system** Polarisationsoptik *f*
~ **optics** Polarisationsoptik *f*
~ **plate** Polarisationsplatte *f*
~ **prism** Polarisationsprisma *n*,
 Prismenpolarisator *m*
~ **sheet** Polarisationsfilterfolie *f*,
 Pol[arisations]folie *f*, Folienpolarisator *m*,
 Flächenpolarisator *m*
pole Pol *m (Überragungsfunktion)*; Vertex *m*, Scheitel[punkt] *m*
police photograph Polizeiaufnahme *f*,
 Polizeifoto *n*
~ **photographer** Polizeifotograf *m*
polishing material Poliermittel *n*
~ **pitch** Polierpech *n (Linsenfertigung)*
polling Faxpollen *n*
poly-Si *s.* polycrystalline silicon
polybézier curve Polybézierkurve *f*
 (Computergrafik)
polychromatic polychrom[atisch],
 mehrfarbig, vielfarbig
~ **light** polychromatisches (mehrfarbiges)
 Licht *n*
~ **radiation** polychromatische Strahlung *f*
~ **X-ray spectrum** polyenergetisches
 Röntgenspektrum *n*
polychromaticity Polychromasie *f*
polychrome image Mehrfarbenbild *n*
~ **printing** Mehrfarbendruck *m*,
 mehrfarbiger Druck *m*
~ **rotary**
 Mehrfarben-Rotationsdruckmaschine *f*
polychromy Polychromie *f*, Mehrfarbigkeit *f*, Vielfarbigkeit *f*

polycrystalline silicon polykristallines Silicium *n*, Polysilicium *n*
polydisperse emulsion polydisperse Emulsion *f*
polyenergetic X-ray spectrum polyenergetisches Röntgenspektrum *n*
polyester Polyester *m*
~-based film Polyesterfilm *m*
~-coated paper polyesterbeschichtetes Papier *n*, PE-Papier *n*
~ film base Polyesterfilmträger *m*
~ plate Polyesterdruckfolie *f*
~ resin Polyester *m*
polyethylene Polyethylen *n*
~ azine Polyethylenazin *n* *(Entwicklerzusatz)*
~-coated paper polyethylenkaschiertes Papier *n*
~ terephthalate Polyethylenterephthalat *n* *(Filmträgermaterial)*
polygon Polygon *n*, [geschlossenes] Vieleck *n*
~-based shape coding polygonbasierte Formcodierung *f*
~ boundary Polygonkontur *f*, Polygonumrandung *f*, Polygonkante *f*
~ decomposition Polygonzerlegung *f*
~ filling algorithm Polygonfüllalgorithmus *m*
~ intersection Polygondurchdringung *f*
~ mesh (net) Polygonnetz *n*, polygonales Netz *n*
~ optimization Polygonoptimierung *f*
~ reduction [technique] Polygonreduktion *f*
~ rendering [computergrafische] Polygondarstellung *f*
~ scanner Polygonabtaster *m*
~ section point Polygonschnittpunkt *m*
~ set Polygonmenge *f*
~ table Polygontabelle *f*
~ thinning Polygonreduktion *f*
~ triangulation Polygontriangulation *f*
~ vertex Polygoneckpunkt *m*, Polygonecke *f*
polygonal polygonal
~ approximation Polygonapproximation *f*, polygonale Approximation *f*
~ contour *s.* polygon boundary
~ curve Polygonzug *m*
~ face Polygonfläche *f*, Polygonebene *f*
~ mirror Polygonspiegel *m*
~ model Polygonmodell *n*, polygonales Modell *n* *(Computergrafik)*
~ modeling Polygonmodellierung *f*
~ net[work] polygonales Netz *n*, Polygonnetz *n*
~ prism Polygon[al]prisma *n*
~ representation Polygondarstellung *f*
~ scene polygonale Szene *f*
~ subdivision Polygonzerlegung *f*
polygonalization Polygonbildung *f*, Polygonalisierung *f*
polygonalize/to polygonalisieren

polyhedral face Polyederfläche *f*
~ object Polyederobjekt *n*
polyhedron Polyeder *n*, Vielflächner *m*
~ representation Polyederdarstellung *f*
polyline Linienzug *m*
~ color index Linienzugfarbindex *m*
polymarker Polymarke *f*
polymer Polymer *n*
~-based OLED display *s.* polymer display
~ display Polymerdisplay *n*, PLED-Display *n*
~ film Polymerfolie *f*
~ light-emitting diode display *s.* ~ display
~ thin-film layer polymere Dünnschicht *f*
polymerizable polymerisierbar
polymerization Polymerisation *f*
polymerize/to polymerisieren
polymesh *s.* polygon mesh
~ representation *s.* polygonal representation
polymethine dye Polymethin[imin]farbstoff *m (Sensibilisator)*
polymethyl methacrylate Polymethylmethacrylat *n (optischer Kunststoff)*
polymorphic polymorph, vielgestaltig
~ tweening *s.* morphing
polynomial Polynom *n*, mehrgliedriger Ausdruck *m*
~ polynomisch, polynomial
~ classification Polynomklassifikation *f*
~ classifier Polynomklassifikator *m*, polynomialer Klassifikator *m*
~ coefficient Polynomkoeffizient *m*
~ curve polynomische (polynomiale) Kurve *f*
~ distribution Polynomverteilung *f*
~ filter Polynomfilter *n (Bildverarbeitung)*
~ interpolation polynomiale (polynomische) Interpolation *f*, Polynominterpolation *f*
~ mapping polynomiale Abbildung *f*
~ transform polynomische Transformation *f*
polyphase filter Polyphasenfilter *n*
polypropylene Polypropylen *n (Foliengrundstoff)*
polysilicon Polysilicium *n*, polykristallines Silicium *n*
polyvinyl chloride Polyvinylchlorid *n*, PVC *(z.B. als Filmträger)*
polyvinylcinnamate polymer Polyvinylzimtsäurepolymer *n*
pop Piepser *m (Filmschnitt)*
POP *s.* printing-out paper
pop-up flash ausklappbarer Blitz *m*
~-up window Überlagerungsfenster *n*, Pop-up-Fenster *n (Bildschirmdarstellung)*
~ video Musikvideo *n*
popularity algorithm Popularitätsmethode *f (Farbquantisierung)*
population inversion Besetzungsinversion *f (Laser)*

porous printing Durchdruck *m*
Porro prism of the first type Porro-Prisma *n* erster Art
~ **prism of the second type** Porro-Prisma *n* zweiter Art
port Anschluss *m*; Schnittstelle *f*
portable computer Mobilcomputer *m*, tragbarer Computer *m*
~ **document format** plattformunabhängiges Datenformat *n*
~ **networks graphics** *ein lizenzfrei nutzbares Pixelgrafik-Speicherformat*
~ **projector** Kofferprojektor *m*
~ **television [set]**, ~ **TV** tragbares Fernsehgerät *n*
portal Internetportal *n*, Portal *n*
portfolio Fotomappe *f*; Präsentationsmappe *f*
portography Portografie *f*, Pfortaderangiografie *f*
portrait hochformatig
~ 1. Porträt *n*; 2. Hochformat *n*
~ **attachment lens** Nah[vorsatz]linse *f*, Nahvorsatz *m*
~ **en face** Frontalporträt *n*
~ **fashion** Hochformat *n*
~ **film** Porträtfilm *m*
~ **lens** Porträtobjektiv *n*, Porträt-Teleobjektiv *n*
~ **lighting** Porträtbeleuchtung *f*
~ **mode** 1. Porträtfunktion *f (Kleinbildkamera)*; 2. *s*. ~ orientation
~ **-mode monitor** Hochformatmonitor *m*
~ **orientation** Hochformat *n*
~ **photographer** Porträtfotograf *m*
~ **photography** Porträtfotografie *f*
~ **setting** Porträteinstellung *f*
~ **shot** Porträtaufnahme *f*
~ **studio** Porträtstudio *n*, Porträtatelier *n*
~ **subject** Porträtmotiv *n*
~ **zoom** Porträtzoom *n*
portraiture Porträtfotografie *f*
portray/to porträtieren; abbilden
portrayability Abbildbarkeit *f*
portrayable abbildbar
portrayal Abbildung *f*; [bildliche] Darstellung *f*
portrayer Porträtist *m*
position/to 1. positionieren; 2. orten
position constancy Lagekonstanz *f*, Ortskonstanz *f*, Lokalzeichenkonstanz *f (Wahrnehmungsphysiologie)*
~ **coordinate** Ortskoordinate *f*
~ **data** Lagedaten *pl*
~ **-dependent system** lageabhängiges System *n*
~ **display** Positionsdisplay *n (Navigationsdatenanzeige)*
~ **finding (fixing)** Lagebestimmung *f*
~ **function** Ortsfunktion *f*
~ **-independent system** lageunabhängiges System *n*
~ **invariance** Ortsinvarianz *f*
~ **-invariant** ortsinvariant

~ **mark** Positionsmarke *f*; Pass[er]kreuz *n*
~ **proof** Formproof *m*
~ **sensing** Lageerkennung *f*
~ **sensing device**, ~ **sensor** Lagesensor *m*, Positionsgeber *m*
~ **signal** Ortssignal *n*
~ **vector** Ortsvektor *m*, Positionsvektor *m*
positional accuracy Positionsgenauigkeit *f (Objekterkennung)*
~ **astronomy** Himmelskartierung *f*
~ **control** Positionsregelung *f*
~ **error** Lagefehler *m*
~ **resolution** Orts[frequenz]auflösung *f*, Raumauflösung *f*, örtliche (räumliche) Auflösung *f*
~ **symmetry** Lagesymmetrie *f*
positioning Positionierung *f*
~ **error** Positionierungsfehler *m*
~ **stage** Positioniertisch *m*
~ **system** Positionierungssystem *n*
~ **table** Positioniertisch *m*
~ **tool** Positionierungswerkzeug *n*
positive Positiv *n*
~ **color film** Positiv-Farbfilm *m*, Farbpositivfilm *m*
~ **color image** Colorpositiv *n*, Farbpositiv *n*
~ **coma** Innenkoma *f*
~ **copy** Positivkopie *f*
~ **development** Positiventwicklung *f*
~ **distortion** Tonnenverzeichnung *f*, Tonnenverzerrung *f* tonnenförmige Verzeichnung *f (Abbildungsfehler)*
~ **emulsion** Positivemulsion *f*, Direktpositivemulsion *f*
~ **eyepiece** Ramsden-Okular *n*
~ **film** Positivfilm *m*, Umkehrfilm *m*
~ **film material** Positivmaterial *n*
~ **film print** Positivkopie *f*
~ **front element** Telepositiv *n*, sammelndes Vorderglied *n*
~ **image** Bildpositiv *n*, Positiv *n*
~ **layer** Positivschicht *f (Sofortbildfilm)*
~ **lens** positive Linse *f*, Positivlinse *f*, Konvexlinse *f*, Sammellinse *f*
~ **material** Positivmaterial *n (Fotografie)*
~ **meniscus [lens]** positiver (sammelnder) Meniskus *m*, Konkavkonvexlinse *f*
~ **modulation** Positivmodulation *f (Fernsehen)*
~ **on glass** Ambrotypie *f*, Melanotypie *f*
~ **paper** Positivpapier *n*
~ **parallax** positive Parallaxe *f*
~ **perforation** Positivperforation *f*
~ **photograph** Positiv *n*
~ **photographic material** Positivmaterial *n*
~ **photoresist** *s*. positive-working photoresist
~ **picture** Bildpositiv *n*, Positiv *n*
~ **plate** Positivplatte *f (Farbfotografie)*
~ **-positive procedure** Positiv-Positiv-Verfahren *n (Colorpositivverarbeitung)*

~ **print** Papierpositiv *n*, Positivabzug *m*, Bildabzug *m*, Abzug *m*, Fotoabzug *m* *(s.a.* ~ film print*)*
~ **raw stock** Positiv-Rohfilm *m*
~ **retouching** Positivretusche *f*
~ **stock** *s.* ~ photographic material
~ **transparency** transparentes Positiv *n*, durchscheinendes fotografisches Bild *n*; Dia[positiv] *n*
~ **work print** Positivkopie *f*; Arbeitskopie *f*, Klatschkopie *f*, Schnittkopie *f* *(Filmbearbeitung)*
~-**working emulsion** *s.* positive emulsion
~-**working photoresist** Positiv-Fotolack *m*, Positivlack *m*, positiver Fotolack *m*
~-**working process** Positivverfahren *n*, Positivprozess *m* *(Silberfotografie)*
positron Positron *n*, positives Elektron *n*, Antielektron *n*
~ **camera** Positronenkamera *f*
~ **decay** Positronenzerfall *m*
~-**emission image** Positronenemissionstomogramm *n*
~-**emission tomograph** Positronen[emissions]tomograf *m*, PET-Scanner *m*, PET-Gerät *n*
~-**emission tomography** Positronenemissionstomografie *f*, PET
~ **emitter** Positronenstrahler *m*
~ **radiator** Positronenstrahler *m*
post-dub/to nachvertonen
~-**dubbing** Nachvertonung *f*, Tonnachbearbeitung *f*, Audiopost[produktion] *f*
~-**emphasis** Deemphasis *f*, Nachentzerrung *f* *(Frequenzmodulation)*
~ **house** *s.* postproduction house
~ **press (printing) operations** Druckweiterverarbeitung *f*
~-**scoring** *s.* post-dubbing
postal mail sorter Postsortieranlage *f*
postcard photography Postkartenfotografie *f*
~ **picture** Postkartenfoto *n*
~ **size** Postkartenformat *n*
postdetection integration inkohärente Impulsintegration *f*
postequalization *s.* post-emphasis
postequalizing pulse Nachtrabant *m* *(BAS-Fernsehsignal)*
poster Poster *n(m)*, Plakat *n*
~ **color (paint)** Plakatfarbe *f*
posterior chamber hintere Augenkammer *f*
posterization Postereffekt *m*, Ton[wert]trennung *f*
postexposure Nachbelichtung *f*
postfilter/to nachfiltern
postfilter Nachfilter *n*
postfiltering Nachfilterung *f*
postfixation development physikalische Entwicklung *f* *(fotografischer Prozess)*
postflashing Nachbelichten *n*, Nachbelichtung *f* *(bes. von Kinefilm)*

postprocess/to nachbearbeiten *(z.B. Film- oder Videomaterial)*
postprocessing Nachbearbeitung *f* *(s.a.* postproduction*)*
~ **algorithm** Nachbearbeitungsalgorithmus *m*
postproduction Filmnachbearbeitung *f*, Produktionsnachbearbeitung *f*, Postproduktion *f*, Endfertigung *f*, Filmschnitt *m*
~ **device** Nachbearbeitungsgerät *n*
~ **editing** *s.* postproduction
~ **effect** Nachbearbeitungseffekt *m*, Nachbearbeitungstrick *m*
~ **effects generator** Effektgenerator *m*, Spezialeffektgenerator *m*
~ **facility** Nachbearbeitungseinrichtung *f*
~ **house** Schnittstudio *n*, Postproduktionsfirma *f*
~ **phase** Endfertigungsphase *f*
~ **work** *s.* postproduction
postrecord/to nachaufnehmen, nachträglich aufnehmen
postroll 1. Nachlauf *m (Bandgerät)*; 2. *s.* ~ time
~ **time** Nachlaufzeit *f*, Bremszeit *f*
postsync[hronization] Nachsynchronisation *f*
~[**hronize**]/**to** nachsynchronisieren
posttreatment Nachbehandlung *f (z.B. von Negativen)*
pot *s.* potentiometer
potassium alum Kalialaun *n*, Kaliumaluminiumsulfat *n* *(Gelatinehärtungsmittel)*
~ **bichromate** *s.* ~ dichromate
~ **bromide** Kaliumbromid *n (Verzögerer)*
~ **carbonate** Kaliumcarbonat *n* *(Entwicklerbestandteil)*
~ **cyanide** Kaliumcyanid *n*
~ **dichromate** Kaliumdichromat *n*, Kaliumbichromat *n (Bleichmittel)*
~ **ferricyanide (ferrocyanide)** Kaliumferricyanid *n*, rotes Blutlaugensalz *n (Bleichmittel)*
~ **hydroxide** Kaliumhydroxid *n* *(Entwicklerbestandteil)*
~ **iodide** Kaliumiodid *n (Verzögerer)*
~ **metabisulfite** Kaliumdisulfit *n*, Kaliummetabisulfit *n (Fixierzusatz)*
~ **nitrate** Kaliumnitrat *n*
~ **oxalate** Kaliumoxalat *n*
~ **permanganate reducer** Kaliumpermanganat-Abschwächer *m*
~ **rhodanide (thiocyanate)** Kaliumrhodanid *n*, Kaliumthiocyanat *n* *(Entwicklerzusatz)*
potential difference Potentialdifferenz *f*
~ **well** Potentialmulde *f*, Potentialsenke *f*, Potentialtopf *m (Fotodetektor)*
potentially visible set potentiell sichtbare Objektmenge *f (Computergrafik)*
potentiometer Potentiometer *n*, Spannungsteiler *m*

powder

powder diffractometer
   Pulverdiffraktometer *n*
~ **image** Pulverbild *n (Elektrofotografie)*
power 1. [optische] Wirkung *f*;
   Vergrößerungsvermögen *m*; 2.
   Äquivalentbrennweite *f*,
   Effektivbrennweite *f*, effektive
   Brennweite *f*; 3. sphärischer Fehler *m*
   (Objektiv)
~ **amplifier** Leistungsverstärker *m*,
   Vollverstärker *m (Kinotechnik)*
~ **bandwidth** elektrische Bandbreite *f*,
   Leistungsbandbreite *f (Fotodetektor)*
~-**complementary filter**
   Quadraturspiegelfilter *n*
~ **density** Leistungsdichte *f*
~ **distribution** Energieverteilung *f*
~ **Doppler [imaging]** Amplituden-Doppler
   m (Sonografie)
~ **grip [kit]** Batteriehandgriff *m*
   (Kamerazubehör)
~ **line frequency** Netzfrequenz *f*
~-**line hum** Netzbrumm *m*, Netzbrummen
   n
~ **of accommodation**
   Akkommodationskraft *f*
~ **of vision** Sehkraft *f*
~ **pan and tilt** motorgetriebener Neigekopf
   m
~ **reflection** Leistungsreflexion *f*
~ **saving mode** Stromsparschaltung *f*,
   Energiesparschaltung *f*
~-**spectral density** spektrale Energiedichte
   f, Energiedichtespektrum *n*; spektrale
   Leistungsdichte (Dichte) *f*
~ **spectrum** 1. Leistungs[dichte]spektrum
   n, Energiespektrum *n*; 2. *s*. amplitude
   spectrum
~ **switch** Hauptschalter *m*
~ **transmission** Leistungstransmission *f*
~ **winder** Winder *m*
~ **zoom** Motorzoomobjektiv *n*,
   motorisches (motorisiertes) Zoom *n*
powerful lens lichtstarkes Objektiv *m*
Poynting vector Poynting-Vektor *m*
   (Energiefluss)
PPI display *s*. plan position indicator
   [device]
practicability Bedienbarkeit *f (z.B. einer
   Kamera)*
practical effect Sachtrick *m*
   (Kinematografie)
Prandtl number Prandtlsche Zahl *f*
   (Strömungsvisualisierung)
praxinoscope Praxinoskop *n (frühes
   Bildwiedergabegerät)*
pre-etch/to anätzen
~-**groove** Führungsrille *f (Plattenspeicher)*
~-**knee** Gammavoreinstellung *f*,
   Gammavorentzerrung *f*
~-**light/to** einleuchten *(eine Filmkulisse)*
~-**lighting** Einleuchten *n*, Einleuchtung *f*
~-**moistening solution**
   Anfeuchtungslösung *f (Retusche)*

~-**thinned image** vorverdünntes Bild *n*
~-**video signal** Vorvideosignal *n*
preadjust/to voreinstellen
preamp[lifier] Vorverstärker *m*
preamplification Vorverstärkung *f*
preamplifier for optical sound
   Lichtton-Vorverstärker *m*
preattentive vision unverzügliches Sehen
   n (Wahrnehmungsphysiologie)
prebath Vorbad *n (Fotoverarbeitung)*
preblacked tape Bandvorlauf *m*,
   Schwarzband *n*
precalculate/to vorausberechnen
preceding frame vorangehendes Bild *n*,
   Vor[ab]bild *n (Videocodierung)*
precess/to präzedieren *(Protonen)*
precession Präzession *f*
~ **angle** Präzessionswinkel *m*
~ **cone** Präzessionskegel *m*
~ **frequency** Präzessionsfrequenz *f*,
   Larmor-Frequenz *f (Kernspinresonanz)*
~ **matrix** Präzessionsmatrix *f*
precessional motion
   Präzessionsbewegung *f*
precipitate [out]/to [aus]fällen
precipitation Fällung *f (z.B. in der
   Emulsionsherstellung)*
~ **radar** Niederschlagsradar *n*
precision-approach radar
   Präzisionsanflugradar *n*
~ **camera** Präzisionskamera *f*
~-**ground mirror** Präzisionsspiegel *m*
~-**in-line tube** In-line-Röhre *f*;
   Schlitzmaskenröhre *f*,
   Streifenmaskenröhre *f*,
   Trinitron-Bildröhre *f*
~ **mirror** Präzisionsspiegel *m*
~ **optical** präzisionsoptisch
~ **optical device** optisches Präzisionsgerät
   n
~ **optical equipment** Präzisionsoptik *f*
~ **optics** Feinoptik *f*, Präzisionsoptik *f*
~ **photomicrography**
   Präzisionsmikrofotografie *f*
~ **printing** Präzisionsdruck *m*
precoat/to vorbeschichten *(z.B.
   Druckplatten)*
precode/to vorcodieren
precoder Vorcodierer *m*
precoding Vorcodierung *f*, Präcodierung *f*
precompress/to vorkomprimieren *(z.B.
   Video-Rohdaten)*
precompute/to vorausberechnen
precursor image Vorgängerbild *n*
   (Bewegungsschätzung)
predetection integration kohärente
   Impulsintegration *f*
predicate Prädikat *n (mathematische
   Logik)*
~ **calculus** Prädikatenkalkül *n*
~ **logic** Prädikatenlogik *f*
predictability Prädiktabilität *f*,
   Vorhersagbarkeit *f*

predictable prädiktabel, vorhersagbar, voraussagbar
predicted frame (image) prädiziertes (prädiktiv codiertes) Bild *n*, P-Bild *n* *(Video)*
prediction Prädiktion *f*, Vorhersage *f*
~ **accuracy** Prädiktionsgenauigkeit *f*
~ **block** Prädiktionsblock *m*
~ **coefficient** Prädiktionskoeffizient *m*
~ **difference** Prädiktionsdifferenz *f*
~ **error** Prädiktionsfehler *m*
~ **error block** Prädiktionsfehlerblock *m*
~ **error image** Prädiktionsfehlerbild *n*
~ **error signal** Prädiktionsfehlersignal *n*
~ **error spectrum** Prädiktionsfehlerspektrum *n*
~ **gain** Prädiktionsgewinn *m*
~ **image** Prädiktionsbild *n*
~ **process** Prädiktionsverfahren *n*
~ **value** Prädiktionswert *m*
predictive prädiktiv
~**-coded picture** prädiziertes (prädiktiv codiertes) Bild *n*, P-Bild *n* *(Video)*
~ **coding** Prädiktionscodierung *f*, prädiktive Codierung *f*, Differenzcodierung *f*, differentielle (relative) Codierung *f*
~ **encoder** Prädiktionscodierer *m*
~ **frame** *s.* predicted frame
~ **image coding** prädiktive Bildcodierung *f*
~ **motion field segmentation** prädiktive Bewegungsfeldsegmentierung *f*
~ **quantizer** prädiktiver Quantisierer *m*
~ **vector quantization** prädiktive Vektorquantisierung *f*
predictor Prädiktor *m*
predistort/to vorverzerren *(Signale, Frequenzen)*
predistortion Vorverzerrung *f*, Signalvorverzerrung *f*; Vorentzerrung *f* *(Frequenzmodulation; s.a.* preemphasis*)*
preemphasis Höhenanhebung *f*, Preemphasis *f*
preemption window Unterbrechungsfenster *n* *(Multimedia-Betriebssystem)*
preequalizing pulse Vortrabant *m* *(Video-Verbundsignal)*
preexpose/to vorbelichten *(bes. Kinefilm)*
preexposure Vorbelichtung *f*
prefilter/to vorfiltern
prefilter Vorfilter *n*
prefiltering [operation] Vorfilterung *f*
prefix code Präfixcode *m*, präfixfreier (sofort decodierbarer) Code *m*
preflash/to *s.* preexpose/to
preflash Vor[mess]blitz *m*, Probeblitz *m*; Vorblitzfunktion
preflight procedure[s] drucktechnische Eingangsdatenkontrolle *f*
prefocus/to vorfokussieren
prefocused camera voreingestellte Kamera *f*
prefocusing Vorfokussierung *f*

prehardener [bath], prehardening bath Vorhärtebad *n* *(Fotoverarbeitung)*
preliminary rinse Vorwässern *n*, Vorwässerung *f*
premarked point Passpunkt *m*, Passmarke *f*, Passelement *f* *(Fotogrammetrie)*
premium run Erstaufführung *f*
premixing Vormischung *f* *(z.B. von Filmton)*
prep service Reproanstalt *f*
preparation 1. Präparation *f* *(z.B. von mikroskopischen Objekten)*; 2. *s.* prepress [area]
~ **gradient** Vorbereitungsgradient *m* *(Magnetresonanzbildgebung)*
prepress [area] Druckvorstufe *f*
~ **photographic proof** fotografischer Proof *m*
~ **plant** Druckvorstufenbetrieb *m*, Vorstufenbetrieb *m*
~ **printing process** Druckvorstufe *f*
~ **proof** Probeandruck *m*, Prüfandruck *m*, Andruckersatz *m*, Druckvorstufenproof *m*
~ **system** Druckvorstufensystem *n*
~ **work** Druckvorbereitung *f*
preprint/to vorabdrucken, vorausdrucken
preprint Vor[ab]druck *m*
preprocess/to vorverarbeiten *(z.B. Bilddaten)*
preprocessing Vorverarbeitung *f*
~ **filtering** Vorfilterung *f*
~ **step** Vorverarbeitungsschritt *m*
prerecord/to 1. vorbespielen; voraufzeichnen; aufzeichnen; 2. *s.* prescore/to
prerecorded videocassette bespielte Videokassette *f*
~ **videotape** bespieltes Videoband *n*
preroll 1. Vorlauf *m*; 2. *s.* ~ time
~ **time** Hochlauf *m*, Hochlaufzeit *f*, Anlaufzeit *f* *(Bandgerät)*
presampling filter Vorfilter *n*
presaturation Vorsättigung *f* *(Magnetresonanzbildgebung)*
~ **pulse** Vorsättigungs[im]puls *m*
presbyopia Presbyopie *f*, Alters[weit]sichtigkeit *f*
presbyopic alters[weit]sichtig
prescan Vorabscan *m*
prescore/to [vor]aufzeichnen *(z.B. eine Fernsehsendung)*
prescreened film vorgerasterter Film *m*
prescription glasses verordnete Brille *f*
presence Originalgeräusch *n*, Realgeräusch *n*, Atmo[sphäre] *f*, [allgemeines] Umgebungsgeräusch *n* *(Filmarbeit)*
presensitized plate vorsensibilisierte Druckplatte *f*, vorbeschichtete Platte *f* *(Offsetdruck)*
presentation Präsentation *f*, Vorführung *f*; Darstellung *f*
~ **format** Wiedergabeformat *n*
~ **graphics** Präsentationsgrafik *f*

presentation 302

~ **layer** Darstellungsschicht *f*
~ **medium** Darstellungsmedium *n*
~ **software** Präsentationssoftware *f* *(Multimedia)*
~ **surface** Darstellungsfläche *f*
~ **system** Vorführapparatur *f*, Präsentationssystem *n*
~ **technology** Präsentationstechnik *f*
~ **time stamp** Zeitstempel *m* *(Videoübertragung)*
~ **window** Darstellungsfenster *n*, Abbildungsfenster *n (Bildschirm; Computergrafik)*
preservative Konservierungsmittel *n (Entwicklerzusatz)*
preset/to voreinstellen
preset diaphragm Blendenvorwahl *f*
~ **iris** Vorwahlblende *f*
~ **shutter** Spannverschluss *m*
press Druck[er]presse *f*
~ **form** Druckform *f*
~ **gain** Rasterpunktverbreiterung *f*, Punktüberhang *m*, Punktzuwachs *m*, Druckpunktzuwachs *m*, Rastertonwertzunahme *f*, Tonwertzuwachs *m*
~ **photo** Pressefoto *n*, Zeitungsfoto *n*
~ **photographer** Pressefotograf *m*, Zeitungsfotograf *m*, Fotoreporter *m*, Bildreporter *m*, Bildberichter[statter] *m*
~ **photography** Pressefotografie *f*
~ **proof** 1. Proof *m*, Andruck *m*, Vorabdruck *m*; 2. s. repro proof *m*
~ **sheet** Druckbogen *m*
~-**type camera** Laufbodenkamera *f*
pressing Pressling *m (Linsenfertigung)*
pressman Drucker *m*, Auflagendrucker *m*, Drucktechniker *m*
pressroom Drucksaal *m*
pressrun 1. Druck[durch]gang *m*; 2. Auflage *f*, Druckauflage *f*
pressure Druck *m*
~ **diaphragm** Druckblende *f*
~ **mark** Druckstelle *f (z.B. auf Fotomaterial)*
~ **microphone** Druckmikrofon *n*, Druckempfänger *m*
~ **pad** *s*. ~ plate
~ **plate** Andruckplatte *f*
~ **printing process** mechanisches Druckverfahren *n*
~ **roller** Andruckrolle *f*
~-**sensitive pen** Grafikstift *m*, Digitalisierstift *m*, Tablettstift *m*
~-**sensitive screen** Berührungsbildschirm *m*, berührungssensitiver Bildschirm *m*, berührungsempfindliches (haptisches) Display *n*
~-**set ink** Absorptionsdruckfarbe *f*
~-**zone microphone** Grenzflächenmikrofon *n*
pressureless printer anschlagfreier (aufschlagfreier) Drucker *m*, nichtmechanischer Drucker *m*

~ **printing process** nichtmechanisches Druckverfahren *n*
presswork Druck *m*
preventive policing präventive Regulierung *f (Videoübertragung)*
preview 1. Vorschau *f*, Bildvorschau *f*, Vor[ab]ansicht *f*, Vorbetrachtung *f*; Vorsichtung *f*; Voraufführung *f*; 2. Druckbildvorschau *f*, Druckbildanzeige *f*; 3. Vorspannfilm *m*; Filmtrailer *m*
~ **button** Vorschautaste *f*
~ **mode** Vorschaumodus *m*
~ **monitor (screen)** Vorschaumonitor *m*; Vorschaubildschirm *m*
~ **room** Vorführraum *m*
~ **screen** Vorschaubildschirm *m*
~ **trailer** *s*. movie trailer
~ **window** Vorschaufenster *n*
previewer Druckvoranzeigeprogramm *n*
previous frame vorangehendes Bild *n*, Vor[ab]bild *n (Videocodierung)*
~-**pixel coding** *s*. predictive coding
previsualization Prävisualisierung *f (Filmarbeit)*
previsualize/to prävisualisieren
previz *s*. previsualization
prevue *s*. preview 3.
Prewitt edge gradient operator, ~ filter (kernel), ~ mask Prewitt-Filter *n*, Prewitt-Operator *m*
PRF *s*. pulse repetition frequency
primary *s*. ~ color
~ **aberration** Seidel-Aberration *f*, Seidelscher Abbildungsfehler (Bildfehler) *m (Optik)*
~ **beam** Primärstrahl *m (z.B. eines Lasers)*
~ **beam filter** Primärstrahlfilter *n*
~ **cell** Batterie *f*; Akku[mulator *m*]
~ **color** Primärfarbe *f*, Spektralhauptfarbe *f*, Hauptfarbe *f*, Grundfarbe *f*; Elementarfarbe *f*; Normspektralfarbe *f*, Primärvalenz *f*, Primärfarbwert *m*
~ **color filter** Primärfarbenfilter *n*, Grundfarbenfilter *n*
~ **color image** Primärfarbenbild *n*
~ **color stimulus** Grundfarbwert *m*, Primärfarbreiz *m*
~-**colored light** primärfarbiges Licht *n*
~ **electron beam** Primärelektronenstrahl *m (Elektronenmikroskop)*
~ **excitation** Primäranregung *f (Röntgenfluoreszenz)*
~ **fluorescence** Autofluoreszenz *f*
~ **image** primäres Bild *n (Optik)*
~ **image defect** *s*. ~ aberration
~ **light** 1. Führungslicht *n*, Hauptlicht *n*; 2. *s*. dominant light source
~ **light source** Hauptlichtquelle *f*, Führungslichtquelle *f*, primäre Lichtquelle *f*
~ **memory** Kurzzeitspeicher *m*
~ **mirror** Primärspiegel *m*, Hauptspiegel *m (eines katadioptrischen Systems)*
~ **mouse button** linke Maustaste *f*

~ **photochemical process** fotochemischer Primärprozess m, fotochemische Primärreaktion f
~ **radiation** Primärstrahlung f (z.B. einer Röntgenquelle)
~ **radiator** Primärstrahler m, Selbststrahler m, Selbstleuchter m, selbstleuchtendes Objekt n
~ **reflection** Primärreflexion f
~ **surveillance radar** Primärradar n
~ **visual cortex** Hinterhauptlappen m (des Gehirns)
~ **X-rays** primäre Röntgenstrahlung f
prime coat s. primer
~ **focus** Primärfokus m
~ **lens** Grundobjektiv n, Hauptobjektiv n, Primärobjektiv n
~ **time** Hauptsendezeit f (Fernsehen)
primer Primer m, Grundierungslack m (Druckweiterverarbeitung)
primitive [element] Primitiv n, Elementarobjekt n, [geometrisches] Elementarmuster n, [geometrische] Grundform f; strukturloses Objekt n
~ **solid** Primitivkörper m, [elementarer] Grundkörper m, Raumprimitiv n
principal axis Hauptachse f (z.B. einer Ellipse)
~ **axis of inertia** Hauptträgheitsachse f
~ **axis transformation** Hauptachsentransformation f
~ **cameraperson** Erster Kameramann m, Kameraschwenker m, Schwenker m (Filmteam)
~ **color** Hauptfarbe f
~ **component axis** Hauptkomponentenachse f
~**-component image** Hauptkomponentenbild n
~ **components analysis (transform)** Hauptkomponentenanalyse f, Eigenvektortransformation f (Merkmalserkennung)
~ **focus** Fokus m, Brennpunkt m
~ **hue** Hauptfarbton m (Munsell-Farbordnungssystem)
~ **index of refraction** Hauptbrechzahl f
~ **light** Hauptlicht n, Führungslicht m
~ **maximum** Hauptmaximum n (z.B. einer Punktbildfunktion)
~ **object** Hauptobjekt n (z.B. eines Bildes)
~ **photography** Hauptdreh m
~ **plane** [Gaußsche] Hauptebene f, Gaußsche Bildebene f (Optik)
~ **point** Hauptpunkt m; Linsenhauptpunkt m
~ **printing process** Hauptdruckverfahren n
~ **ray** Haupt[punkt]strahl m, Mittelpunktstrahl m; ausgezeichneter Strahl m
~ **refractive index** Hauptbrechzahl f
~ **subject** Hauptmotiv n (z.B. einer Fotografie)

principle of reciprocity Reziprozitätsprinzip n
~ **of superposition** Superpositionsprinzip n, Überlagerungsprinzip n (Wellenoptik)
print/to 1. drucken; bedrucken; 2. kopieren (Filmmaterial)
print in/to 1. einkopieren; 2. nachbelichten
~ **on/to** bedrucken
~ **out/to** 1. ausdrucken; 2. auskopieren
~ 1. Abzug m; Fotoabzug m, Papierabzug m; Kopie f (s.a. unter printing); 2. Druck m, Abdruck m; 3. Drucksache f
~ **cartridge** Tintenkartusche f, Tinten[druck]patrone f, Druckkassette f
~ **characteristic** Druckkennlinie f
~ **command** Druckbefehl m
~ **competition** Fotowettbewerb m
~ **contrast** [relativer] Druckkontrast m
~ **damage** Kopiebeschädigung f (Kinefilm)
~ **designer** Schriftgrafiker m, Typograf m, gestaltender Schriftsetzer m
~ **developer** Positiventwickler m
~ **direction** Druckrichtung f
~ **drum** Entwicklungstrommel f, Papiertrommel f
~ **dryer** Papiertrockner m
~**-drying rack** Trockengestell n
~ **enlargement** Abzugsvergrößerung f
~ **file** Druckdatei f
~ **film** Kopierfilm m; Bildfilm m
~ **finishing** Bildaufbereitung f
~ **format** Kopierformat n; Abzugsformat n
~ **graphic** druckgrafisch
~ **graphics** Druckgrafik f
~ **magnification** Vergrößerung f
~ **manager** Druckmanager m (Steuerprogramm)
~ **marking pen** Folienschreiber m
~ **material** Kopierfilmmaterial n, Kopier-Rohfilm m
~ **medium** Printmedium n
~ **on demand** bedarfsweiser Druck m
~ **paper** Vergrößerungspapier n, Fotopapier n, Kopierpapier n
~ **permanence** Bildbeständigkeit f, Bildhaltbarkeit f
~ **presenter** Präsentationsmappe f; Fotomappe f
~ **preview** Druckvoranzeige f
~ **processing** Papierverarbeitung f, Papierentwicklung f
~ **quality** Druckqualität f, Druckgüte f
~ **queue** Druckwarteschlange f, Druckerschlange f
~ **reel** Filmkopierolle f
~ **run** Druckdurchgang m
~ **scanner** Flachbettscanner m, Flachbettabtaster m
~ **server** Druckserver m
~ **service** Druckservice m
~ **sheet** Foto-Sichthülle f
~ **side** Emulsionsseite f (Fotopapier)
~ **size** Kopierformat n; Abzugsformat n
~ **squeegee** Papierabstreifer m

print

~ **stock** Kopier[film]material n, Kopier-Rohfilm m
~ **storage** Druckspeicher m
~ **support material** Bedruckmaterial n, Bedruckstoff m
~-**technical** drucktechnisch
~ **through** Kopiereffekt m (Magnetbandtechnik)
~ **tongs** Laborzange f, Entwicklerzange f, Bild[er]zange f, Papierzange f
~ **trimmer** Schneidemaschine f
~ **washer** Bilderwascher m
~ **washing tray** Wässerungswanne f
printability Bedruckbarkeit f; Abdruckbarkeit f; Druckfähigkeit f; Kopierfähigkeit f
printable bedruckbar; [ab]druckbar, druckfähig; kopierbar, kopierfähig
printed board [gedruckte] Leiterplatte f, Elektronikplatine f, Platine n, gedruckter Schaltkreis m
~ **both sides** beidseitig bedruckt
~ **character** Druckzeichen n; Druckbuchstabe m
~ **circuit board** [gedruckte] Leiterplatte f, Elektronikplatine f, Platine n, gedruckter Schaltkreis m
~-**circuit manufacture** Leiterplattenherstellung f
~-**circuit technology** Leiterplattentechnik f
~ **color reproduction** Farbdruck m (Erzeugnis)
~ **font** Druckzeichensatz m
~ **image** gedrucktes Bild n, Druckbild n
~ **image control** Druckbildinspektion f, Druckbildkontrolle f
~ **image store** Druckbildspeicher m
~ **letter** Druckbuchstabe m
~ **material** Druckerzeugnis n, Druckprodukt n
~ **page** Druckseite f
~ **piece** Drucksache f
~ **product** Druckerzeugnis n, Druckprodukt n
~ **sheet** Druckbogen m, gedruckter Bogen m
~ **take** Kopierer m (Kinefilmbearbeitung)
~ **type** Druckschrift f, gedruckte Schrift f
printer 1. Drucker m, Printer m; Kopiergerät n, Kopierer m; 2. s. pressman
~ **aperture** Kopierfenster n
~ **buffer** Druckpufferspeicher m, Druckerspeicher m, Druckerpuffer m
~ **cable** Druckerkabel n
~ **calibration** Druckerkalibrierung f
~ **card** Kopierkarte f, Lichtkarte f (Filmkopierung)
~ **cartridge** Druckerpatrone f
~ **command (control) language** Drucker[steuer]sprache f
~ **description file** Druckerbeschreibungsdatei f

304

~ **driver** Druckertreiber m
~ **emulation** Druckeremulation f
~ **error** Druckfehler m
~ **font** Druckerschrift f
~ **head** Kopierkopf m
~ **interface** Druckeranschluss m, Druckerschnittstelle f
~ **lamphouse** Kopiermaschinenlampenhaus n
~ **language** Drucker[steuer]sprache f
~ **light** s. printing light
~ **output** Druck[er]ausgabe f, Papierausgabe f, permanente Bildausgabe f
~ **paper** Druckerpapier n
~ **performance test** Druckerleistungstest m
~ **point** Kopierlichtwert m
~ **port** Druckeranschluss m, Druckerschnittstelle f
~ **queue** Druck[er]warteschlange f, Druckerschlange f (s.a. ~ buffer)
~ **resolution** Druckerauflösung f
~ **software** Druckersoftware f
~ **startmark** Kopierstartmarke f
~ **technology** Druckertechnik f
printer's copy Druckvorlage f
~ **ink** Druckerschwärze f
printery Druckerei f
printhead Druckkopf m
~ **control** Druckkopfsteuerung f
printing 1. Drucken n; Druck m; Drucklegung f; 2. Druckwesen n; 3. Kopieren n, Kopierung f
~ **additive** Druckhilfsmittel n
~ **aperture** Kopierfenster n
~ **area** druckende Fläche f, Druckzone f
~ **black** Druckerschwärze f
~ **block** Druckstock m
~ **card** s. printer card
~ **color** Druckfarbe f
~ **company** Druckbetrieb m
~ **contrast** Kopierkontrast m
~ **defect** Druckschwierigkeit f
~ **density** Kopierdichte f
~ **device** Drucker m, Printer m
~ **dot** Druckpunkt m
~ **drum** Kopiertrommel f
~ **easel** Kopierrahmen m
~ **effect** Kopiereffekt m
~ **error** Kopierfehler m
~ **exposure** Kopierbelichtung f
~ **exposure time** Kopierbelichtungszeit f
~ **filter** Kopierfilter n, Korrektorfilter n
~ **firm** Druckbetrieb m
~ **form** Druckform f
~ **format** Druckformat n
~ **frame** Kopierrahmen m, Kontaktkopierrahmen m
~ **image area** druckende Bildstelle f, Druckbildelement n
~ **in** Einkopieren n
~ **industry** Druckindustrie f
~ **ink** Druckfarbe f; Druck[er]tinte f, Tinte f

probabilistic

~ **ink pigment** Druckfarbenpigment *n*
~ **job** Druckauftrag *m*, Druckarbeit *f*, Druckjob *m*
~ **lamp** Kopierlampe *f*
~ **light** Kopierlicht *n*; Vergrößerungslicht *n*
~ **light value** Kopierlichtwert *m*
~ **line** Druckzeile *f*
~ **machine** Druckmaschine *f*; Kopiermaschine *f*
~ **mask** Kopiermaske *f*, Abdeckmaske *f*
~ **master** Gesamttonspur *f*; Endmischband *n*
~ **material** Kopiermaterial *n*
~ **medium** Druckmedium *n*
~ **method** Druckverfahren *n*
~ **needle** Drucknadel *f*
~ **negative** Negativkopie *f*
~ **nip** Druckzone *f*, Druckstreifen *m*
~ **nozzle** Druckdüse *f*
~ **office** Druckerei *f*, Druckbetrieb *m*
~ **oil** Drucköl *n*
~ **on demand** Drucken *n* nach Bedarf, bedarfsweises Drucken *n*
~ **operation** Druckvorgang *m*
~ **order** Druckauftrag *m* (s.a. ~ job)
~ **-out paper** Auskopierpapier *n*
~ **-out process** Auskopierprozess *n*
~ **paper** 1. Druckpapier *n*; 2. Fotopapier *n*, Vergrößerungspapier *n*
~ **pass** Kopierdurchlauf *m*
~ **paste** Druckpaste *f*
~ **plane** Kopierebene *f*
~ **plant** s. ~ office
~ **plate** Druckplatte *f*; Druckstock *m*
~ **-plate fabrication** Druckformherstellung *f*, Druckplattenfertigung *f*, Druckplattenherstellung *f*, Plattenherstellung *f*
~ **press** Druck[er]presse *f*
~ **principle** Druckprinzip *n*
~ **procedure (process)** Druckprozess *m*; Kopierprozess *m*, Kopiervorgang *m*; Kopierverfahren *n*
~ **rate** s. ~ speed
~ **result** Druckergebnis *n*
~ **shop** Druckerei *f*
~ **slit** Kopierspalt *m*
~ **speed** Druckgeschwindigkeit *f*; Kopiergeschwindigkeit *f*
~ **stage** Kopiertisch *m*
~ **station** Druckwerk *n*
~ **step** Druckgang *m*
~ **stock** Auflagenpapier *n*
~ **substrate** Bedruckmaterial *n*, Bedruckstoff *m*
~ **system** Drucksystem *n*
~ **tape** Licht[steuer]band *n* (Filmkopierung)
~ **technique** 1. Druckverfahren *n*; 2. Drucktechnik *f*; 3. Kopiertechnik *f*
~ **technology** 1. Drucktechnik *f*; 2. Kopiertechnik *f*
~ **time** Druckzeit *f*; Kopierzeit *f*
~ **to film** Video-Film-Transfer *m*
~ **type** Drucktype *f*, Type *f*, Druckbuchstabe *m*
~ **unit** Druckwerk *n*; Druckeinheit *f*
~ **width** Druckbreite *f*
printout Bildschirmausdruck *m*, Computerausdruck *m*, Ausdruck *m*
~ **device** Ausdruckvorrichtung *f*, Drucker *m*, Printer *m*
~ **emulsion** Auskopieremulsion *f*
prior knowledge Vorwissen *n*, a-priori-Wissen *n*, apriorisches Wissen *n* (Bildanalyse)
~ **probability** a-priori-Wahrscheinlichkeit *f*, unbedingte Wahrscheinlichkeit *f*, Rückschlusswahrscheinlichkeit *f* (Bayes-Statistik)
prioritization Priorisierung *f*
priority queue Prioritätswarteschlange *f* (Datenverarbeitung)
~ **search tree** Prioritätensuchbaum *m* (Datenstruktur)
prism Prisma *n*
~ **angle** Prismenwinkel *m*
~ **beam splitter** Strahlenteilungsprisma *n*, Teilerprisma *n*
~ **binocular[s]** Prismenfeldstecher *m*, Prismenfernglas *n*
~ **block** Prismenblock *m*
~ **clamp** Prismenklemme *f*
~ **combination** Prismenkombination *f*
~ **eyeglasses** Prismenbrille *f*, prismatische Umkehrbrille *f*
~ **face** Prismenfläche *f*
~ **filter** Prismenfilter *n*
~ **finder** Prismensucher *m*
~ **interface angle** Prismenwinkel *m*
~ **interferometer** Prismeninterferometer *n*
~ **polarizer** Prismenpolarisator *m*, Polarisationsprisma *n*
~ **reflex camera** Spiegelreflexkamera *f*
~ **spectrograph** Prismenspektrograf *m*
~ **spectrometer** Prismenspektrometer *n*
~ **spectroscope** Prismenspektroskop *n*
~ **system** Prismensystem *n*
~ **table** Prismentisch *m*, Prismenhalter *m*
~ **table clamp** Prismenklemme *f*
~ **telescope** Prismenfernrohr *n*
prismal prismatisch
prismatic beam splitter Prismenstrahl[en]teiler *m*
~ **plane** Prismenfläche *f*
~ **spectrum** Prismenspektrum *n*
prismatical prismatisch
pro-video equipment professionelle Videotechnik *f*
probabilistic classifier probabilistischer Klassifikator *m*
~ **Hough transform** probabilistische Hough-Transformation *f*
~ **model[l]ing** probabilistische Modellierung *f*
~ **relaxation technique** probabilistische Relaxationstechnik *f*

probabilitics

probabilitics estimation Wahrscheinlichkeitsschätzung *f*
probability Wahrscheinlichkeit *f*
~ **density** Wahrscheinlichkeitsdichte *f*
~ **density function** Wahrscheinlichkeitsdichtefunktion *f*, Wahrscheinlichkeitsdichteverteilung *f*, Dichtefunktion *f*
~ **distribution function** Wahrscheinlichkeitsverteilungsfunktion *f*, Verteilungsfunktion *f*
~ **function** Wahrscheinlichkeitsfunktion *f*
~ **matrix** Wahrscheinlichkeitsmatrix *f*
~ **model** Wahrscheinlichkeitsmodell *n (Symbolcodierung)*
~ **of detection** Detektionswahrscheinlichkeit *f*, Erkennungssicherheit *f*
~ **of error** Fehlerwahrscheinlichkeit *f*
~ **of occurence** Auftrittswahrscheinlichkeit *f (statistische Codierung)*
~ **of occurrence** Auftrittswahrscheinlichkeit *f*
~ **of target detection** Zielentdeckungswahrscheinlichkeit *f (Radar)*
~ **theory** Wahrscheinlichkeitstheorie *f*
probe/to abtasten
probe Sonde *f*; Messkopf *m*
~ **lens** Industrieendoskop *n*
~ **microscopy** Sondenmikroskopie *f*
~ **motion artifact** Sondenbewegungsartefakt *n (Sonografie)*
~ **tip** Sondenspitze *f*
probing Abtastung *f*
proc amp *s.* processing amplifier
procedural texture prozedurale Textur *f*
process/to verarbeiten
process blue Cyan *n (Druckfarbe)*
~ **camera** Repro[duktions]kamera *f*
~ **color** Prozessfarbe *f (Druck)*
~ **color printing** Vierfarbendruck *m*
~ **copy camera** Repro[duktions]kamera *f*
~ **engraving** Chemiegrafie *f*, Hochdruckätzung *f*, fotomechanische Klischeeherstellung *f*
~ **film** Reprofilm *m*, [foto]technischer Film *m*
~ **ink** Prozess[druck]farbe *f*
~ **lens** Reproduktionsobjektiv *n*
~ **material** Repro-Aufnahmematerial *n*
~ **monitoring** Prozessüberwachung *f*
~ **motion-picture camera** Trick[film]kamera *f*, Animationskamera *f*
~ **photography** Repro[duktions]fotografie *f*
~ **printing** Vierfarbendruck *m*, Vierfarbenprozess *m*
~ **projection** Rückprojektion *f*, Durchprojektion *f*
~ **projector** Rückprojektor m, Rückprojektionsgerät *n (Trickkinematografie)*
~ **red** Magenta *n (Vierfarbdruck)*

~ **shot** Projektionstrick *m*; Trick[film]aufnahme *f*, Effektaufnahme *f*; Kombinationsaufnahme *f (Kinematografie)*
~ **stage** Trickbühne *f (Kinematografie)*
~ **work** Reproarbeit *f*
processed film verarbeiteter Film *m*
processibility Verarbeitbarkeit *f*
processing Verarbeitung *f*
~ **algorithm** Verarbeitungsalgorithmus *m*
~ **amplifier** Stabilisier[ungs]verstärker *m (Videosignalverarbeitung)*
~ **bath** Verarbeitungsbad *n*
~ **chemical** Verarbeitungschemikalie *f*
~ **chemistry** Verarbeitungschemie *f*
~ **cycle time** Verarbeitungszeit *f*
~ **defect** Verarbeitungsfehler *m*
~ **dish** Verarbeitungsschale *f*, Fotoschale *f*
~ **effect** Entwicklungseffekt *m*
~ **envelope** Auftragstasche *f*, Fotoauftragstasche *f*
~ **error** Verarbeitungsfehler *m*
~ **fluid** *s.* ~ solution
~ **lab** Verarbeitungsanstalt *f*, Verarbeitungslabor *n*, Entwicklungslabor *n*
~ **machine** Verarbeitungsmaschine *f*, Entwicklungsmaschine *f*, Maschinenentwickler *m*
~ **material** Verarbeitungsmaterial *n*
~ **performance** Verarbeitungsleistung *f*
~ **platform** Verarbeitungsplattform *f*
~ **procedure** Verarbeitungsvorgang *m*
~ **sequence** Verarbeitungs[ab]folge *f*, Verarbeitungsgang *m*
~ **solution** Verarbeitungslösung *f*, Arbeitslösung *f*, Gebrauchslösung *f*
~ **speed** Verarbeitungsgeschwindigkeit *f*
~ **stage** Verarbeitungsstufe *f*
~ **step** Verarbeitungsschritt *m*
~ **system** Verarbeitungssystem *n*
~ **tank** Verarbeitungstank *m*
~ **technician** Labortechniker *m*
~ **technique** Verarbeitungstechnik *f*
~ **temperature** Verarbeitungstemperatur *f*
~ **time** Verarbeitungszeit *f*
~ **tray** Verarbeitungsschale *f*, Fotoschale *f*
processor Prozessor *m*; Hauptprozessor *m*, Zentraleinheit *f*, zentrale Verarbeitungseinheit *f (Computermodul)*
~ **array** Prozessorfeld *n*
~ **speed** Prozessorgeschwindigkeit *f*
product assembly analysis Fertigungskontrolle *f*
~ **photography** Produktfotografie *f*; Sachfotografie *f*
production camera Aufnahmekamera *f*
~ **company** Produktionsfirma *f*; Filmproduktionsfirma *f*
~ **control** Fertigungssteuerung *f*
~ **crew** Produktionsteam *n*; Filmcrew *f*, Filmteam *n*, Drehstab *m*, Aufnahmestab *m*
~ **manager** Produktionsleiter *m*

progressive

~ **measuring technology** Fertigungsmesstechnik f
~ **press** Fortdruckmaschine f
~ **printing (run)** Auflagendruck m, Fortdruck m
~ **shooting** Dreharbeit f, Film[aufnahme]arbeit f
~ **sound** Originalton m, O-Ton m, Live-Ton m
~ **sound log** Tonbericht m
~ **sound mixer** 1. Tonmischanlage f; 2. s. ~ sound recordist
~ **sound recording** Originaltonaufnahme f
~ **sound recordist** Filmtontechniker m, Tontechniker m
~ **still** Standfoto n, Szenenfoto n, Filmstandbild n
~ **still photography** Standfotografie f
~ **studio** Produktionsstudio n
~ **supervisor** Aufnahmeleiter m
~ **switcher** Produktionsmischer m, Videomischer m, Videomischpult n
~ **team** Produktionsteam n
~**-type press** Fortdruckmaschine f
production's director Produktionsleiter m
professional broadcast equipment Sendetechnik f
~ **broadcast operation** Sendeeinrichtung f
~ **camcorder** Proficamcorder m
~ **color laboratory** Fachfarblabor[atorium] n, Farblabor n, Buntlabor n
~ **film format** Berufsfilmformat n
~**-grade equipment** Profiausrüstung f
~**-level camera** Profikamera f, professionelle Kamera f
~ **motion-picture camera** professionelle Filmkamera f; Kino[film]kamera f
~ **photofinisher** Fotomedienlaborant m
~ **photographer** Berufsfotograf m, Fachfotograf m
~ **photography** Berufsfotografie f, professionelle Fotografie f
~ **processing lab** Verarbeitungsanstalt f, Verarbeitungslabor n, Entwicklungslabor n
~**-quality lens** Profiobjektiv n
~ **tape** Sendeband n
profile close-up shot Profil-Nahaufnahme f
~ **of intensity** Intensitätsprofil n
~ **photograph (portrait)** Profilaufnahme f
~ **projector** Profilprojektor m
~ **shot** Profilaufnahme f
~ **spot** Profilscheinwerfer m, Verfolger m
~ **view** Profilansicht f
profilometer Profilmessgerät n, Profilometer n
profilometry Profilometrie f
program 1. Programm n; Anwendungsprogramm n; 2. Programmbeitrag m, Sendebeitrag m, Sendung f
~ **area** Programmbereich m (Bildplatte)
~ **channel** Programmkanal m

~ **clock reference** Programmtaktreferenz f (Fernsehtechnik)
~ **duration** Spieldauer f, Abspielzeit f, Spielzeit f (z.B. einer Bildplatte)
~ **editing** Programmbearbeitung f
~ **end signal area** Auslaufbereich m (Bildspeicherplatte)
~ **error** Programmfehler m
~ **exposure system** Belichtungsprogrammautomatik f, Programmautomatik f
~ **file** Programmdatei f
~ **instruction** Programmbefehl m
~ **line** Tonleitung f (Fernsehtechnik)
~ **material** Programmmaterial n
~ **memory** Programmspeicher m
~ **mode selector** Programmwählscheibe f (Kompaktkamera)
~ **monitor** Programmmonitor m
~ **origination (production)** Programmproduktion f (z.B. einer Fernsehanstalt)
~ **shift** Programmverschiebung f (automatische Belichtung)
~ **signal** Programmsignal n
~ **sound** Programmton m, Sendeton m
~**-specific information** programmspezifische Information f
~ **stream** s. ~ transport stream
~ **structure chart** Struktogramm n
~ **transport stream** Programm[daten]strom m (digitales Video)
~ **window** Programmfenster n (als Teil des Bildschirms)
programmable programmierbar
~ **filter** programmierbares Filter n
~ **gate array** programmierbarer Logikbaustein m
~ **image processor** programmierbarer Bildprozessor m
~ **logical array (device)** programmierbares logisches Feld n
~ **read-only memory** programmierbarer Nurlesespeicher (Festwertspeicher) m
programmed auto[matic] exposure Belichtungsprogrammautomatik f, Programmautomatik f
~ **electronic shutter** elektronischer Programmverschluss m
programmer's hierarchical interactive graphics system hierarchisch-interaktives Grafiksystem n des Programmierers
~ **interface** Programmierschnittstelle f
programming Programmmaterial n (z.B. eines Fernsehsenders)
~ **information** Programminformation[en] f[pl]
~ **language** Programmiersprache f
progressive coding progressive Codierung f
~ **compression** progressive Kompression f

progressive 308

- ~ **image compression** progressive Bildkompression f
- ~ **image transmission** progressive Bildübertragung f
- ~ **proof** Andruckskala f, Skalen[an]druck m, Farbsatz m *(Farbdruckvorbereitung)*
- ~ **refinement** fortschreitende Verfeinerung f *(Radiosity-Verfahren, Computergrafik)*
- ~ **scan [mode]** s. ~ video scanning
- ~ **video** progressives Video n
- ~ **video scanning** progressive Abtastung f, Folgeabtastung f, Vollbildabtastung f, Vollbildaufzeichnung f

progressives, progs s. progressive proof
project/to projizieren
projectability Projizierbarkeit f
projectable projizierbar
projected background Hintergrundprojektion f

- ~ **frame-per-second rate** Projektionsfrequenz f
- ~ **image** Projektionsbild n, projiziertes Bild n; Diaprojektionsbild n

projecting light ray Projektionslichtstrahl m

- ~ **microscope** Projektionsmikroskop n

projection Projektion f, Projizierung f
- ~ **aid** Vorführhilfe f
- ~ **angle** Projektionswinkel m
- ~ **aperture** Projektor[bild]fenster n
- ~ **area** Projektionsfläche f
- ~ **assembly** Projektionseinheit f, Vergrößerungskopf m *(Vergrößerungsgerät)*
- ~ **axis** Projektionsachse f
- ~ **beam** Projektionsstrahl m; Projektionslichtstrom m
- ~ **booth (box)** Projektorraum m, Projektionskabine f, Vorführkabine f; Bildwerferraum m
- ~ **cart** fahrbarer Projektortisch m
- ~ **cathode-ray tube** Projektionsröhre f
- ~ **center** Projektionszentrum n
- ~ **condenser** Projektionskondensor m
- ~ **cone** Projektionskegel m; Projektionslichtkegel m
- ~ **data** Projektionsdaten pl
- ~ **data set** Projektionsdatensatz m
- ~ **device** Projektionsgerät n
- ~ **direction** Projektionsrichtung f
- ~ **display [device]** Projektionsdisplay n, Projektionsbildschirm m
- ~ **distance** Projektionsabstand m, Projektionsentfernung f, Projektionsdistanz f
- ~ **enlargement** Projektionsvergrößerung f
- ~ **equation** Projektionsgleichung f
- ~ **eyepiece** Fotookular n
- ~ **facility** Projektionsanlage f
- ~ **format** Projektionsformat n
- ~ **frame rate** Projektions[bild]frequenz f
- ~ **geometry** Projektionsgeometrie f
- ~ **image** Projektionsbild n
- ~ **image formation** Projektionsbildentstehung f
- ~ **image plane** Projektionsbildebene f
- ~ **imaging** projektive Abbildung f
- ~ **jitter** Bildwackeln n
- ~ **jump** vertikaler Bildstandsfehler m
- ~ **lamp** Projektionslampe f, Projektorlampe f
- ~ **leader** Vorführstartband n
- ~ **lens** Projektionsobjektiv n, Projekt[orobjekt]iv n, Projektionsoptik f, Wiedergabeobjektiv n; Projektionslinse f
- ~ **line** Projektionslinie f
- ~ **lithography** Projektionslithografie f
- ~ **material** Projektionsmaterial n
- ~ **matrix** Projektionsmatrix f *(maschinelle Bilderkennung)*
- ~ **microfilm reader** Mikrofilmlesegerät n
- ~ **microscope** Projektionsmikroskop n
- ~ **mirror** Projektionsspiegel m
- ~ **model** Projektionsmodell n
- ~ **optical** projektionsoptisch
- ~ **optics** s. ~ lens
- ~ **path** Projektionslichtweg m
- ~ **plane** Projektionsebene f
- ~ **point** Projektionspunkt m
- ~ **port** Projektionsfenster n; Kabinenfensteröffnung f, Kabinenfenster n *(Projektorraum)*
- ~ **print** Projektionskopie f, Vorführkopie f, vorführbereite (vorführfertige) Filmkopie f
- ~ **printer** Vergrößerungsapparat m, Vergrößerer m
- ~ **printing** Projektionsbelichtung f, Projektionskopierung f, Projektionskopieren n, optisches Kopieren n
- ~ **profile** Projektionsprofil n
- ~ **radiograph** Projektionsradiogramm n
- ~ **radiography** Projektionsradiografie f, Projektionsröntgentechnik f
- ~ **raw data** Projektionsrohdaten pl
- ~ **ray** Projektionsstrahl m
- ~ **reader** Projektionslesegerät n
- ~ **reconstruction** Projektionsrekonstruktion f *(Magnetresonanztomografie)*
- ~ **reel** Wiedergabespule f
- ~ **room** Projektorraum m, Projektionsraum m, Vorführraum m
- ~ **screen** Projektions[lein]wand f, Projektionsschirm m, Lichtbildwand f, Bildwand f
- ~ **slide** Projektionsdia[positiv] n
- ~ **slide plate** Dia[positiv]platte f
- ~ **source** Projektionslichtquelle f
- ~ **space** Projektionsraum m
- ~ **speed** Projektionsgeschwindigkeit f
- ~ **surface** Projektionsfläche f
- ~ **system** Projektionssystem n
- ~ **technique** Projektionstechnik f
- ~ **technology** Projektionstechnik f
- ~ **television** Projektionsfernsehen n

~ **television system** Projektionsfernsehsystem n
~ **theorem** Projektionstheorem n, Fourier-Scheibentheorem n
~ **transparency** Projektionsdia[positiv] n
~ **tube** Projektionsröhre f
~ **TV set** Projektionsfernseher m, Projektionsfernsehgerät n, Projektionsempfänger m
~ **type** Projektionsart f
~-**type film** Projektionsfilm m
~ **unit** s. ~ assembly
~ **wall** Bildwand f
~ **X-ray angiogram** Röntgenangiogramm n
projectionist 1. Vorführer m, Filmvorführer m, Filmoperateur m; 2. Kartograf m
projective distortion projektive Verzerrung f
~ **geometry** projektive Geometrie f
~ **imaging** projektive Abbildung f; Projektionsrekonstruktion f *(Magnetresonanzbildgebung)*
~ **invariant** projektive Invariante f
~ **mapping** s. ~ imaging
~ **plane** Projektionsebene f
~ **transformation** projektive Transformation f
projector Projektor m, Projektionsapparat m; Bildwerfer m, Lichtbildwerfer m, Vorführgerät n
~ **aperture** Projektor[bild]fenster n
~ **bulb** s. ~ lamp
~ **case** Projektorkoffer m
~ **change** Projektorwechsel m, Überblendvorgang m *(Filmvorführung)*
~ **equiment** Projektionsapparatur f
~ **format** Projektorformat n
~ **gate** Projektorbildfenster n
~ **head** Projektorkopf m
~ **intermittent** Projektorlaufwerk n
~ **lamp** Projektorlampe f, Projektionslampe f
~ **lamphouse** Lampenhaus n
~ **lens** Projektorobjektiv n, Projekt[ionsobjekt]iv n, Wiedergabeobjektiv n
~ **light** Projektorlicht n, Projektionslicht n
~ **luminosity** Projektionslichtstärke f
~ **magazine** Projektormagazin n
~ **shutter** Projektorblende f
~ **stand** Projektorstativ f
~ **table** Projektortisch m, Projektionstisch m
prompt 1. Eingabeaufforderung f, Aufforderung f *(Mensch-Maschine-Kommunikation)*; 2. s. ~ character
~ **character** Bereitschaftszeichen n
proof/to andrucken
proof s. ~ print
~ **correction mark** Korrekturzeichen n
~ **paper** Andruckpapier n
~ **print** Proof[druck] m, Andruck m, Vorausandruck m, Probeandruck m, Prüf[an]druck m
~ **printer, proofer** Proofdrucker m
proofing Proofanfertigung f, Proofherstellung f
~ **press** Andruckmaschine f
~ **result** Andruckergebnis n
~ **scale** Andruckskala f, Skalen[an]druck m, Farbsatz m *(Farbdruckvorbereitung)*
~ **system** Proofsystem n
proofreader mark Korrekturzeichen n
prop Filmrequisit n
propagation constant Ausbreitungskonstante f
~ **delay** Ausbreitungsverzögerung f
~ **direction** Ausbreitungsrichtung f
~ **medium** Ausbreitungsmedium n
propagative direction Ausbreitungsrichtung f
~ **distance** Reichweite f
~ **speed (velocity)** Ausbreitungsgeschwindigkeit f
proper exposure richtige Belichtung f
properties s. props
property man Requisiteur m *(Filmarbeit)*
propman s. property man
proportional counter Proportionalzählrohr n *(Detektor)*
~ **font** Proportionalschrift f *(Typografie)*
~ **reducer** Proportionalabschwächer m, Farmerscher Abschwächer m *(Fotochemie)*
~ **spacing (typefont)** Proportionalschrift f *(Typografie)*
propositional calculus Aussagenkalkül n(m)
~ **logic** Aussagenlogik f
proprietary file format herstellerspezifisches (proprietäres) Dateiformat n
props Bauten mpl, Requisiten pl *(Filmarbeit)*
prospecting technique Vermessungstechnik f
prosumer digital camera semiprofessionelle Digitalkamera f
protan rotblind
protanomaly Protanomalie f, Rotschwäche f *(Farbsinnstörung)*
protanope Protanop m, Rotblinder m
protanopia Protanopie f, Protanstörung f, Rotblindheit f *(Farbsinnstörung)*
protanopic rotblind
protected coupler geschützter Farbkuppler m
protection bit Schutzbit n
~ **master** Sicherheitskopie f
protective coat[ing] Schutzschicht f
~ **colloid** Schutzkolloid n
~ **eyewear** Schutzbrille f
~ **filter** Schutzfilter n
~ **layer** Schutzschicht f
~ **leader** Allonge f, Schutzfilm m *(Kinefilm)*

protective

~ **overcoat** Schutzüberzug *m*
~ **track** Sicherheitstonband *n* *(Filmproduktion)*
protein crystallography Proteinkristallografie *f*
protocol Protokoll *n (Datenaustausch)*
~ **data unit** Protokolldateneinheit *f*
proton Proton *n*, Nukleon *n*; Wasserstoffkern *m*
~ **density** Protonendichte *f*
~-**density-weighted image** protonengewichtetes (dichtegewichtetes) Bild *n (Magnetresonanztomografie)*
~ **don[at]or**, ~ **emitter** Protonendonator *m*, Protonenspender *m*
~ **magnetic resonance spectroscopy** Protonen-Magnetresonanzspektroskopie *f*
~ **microscope** Protonenmikroskop *n*
~ **spectroscopy** Protonenspektroskopie *f*
prototype Prototyp *m*, Mustermaske *f*, Klassenrepräsentant *m (Mustererkennung)*
~ **classification** Prototypenklassifikation *f*, Prototypenklassifizierung *f*
prototypical prototypisch
proximity fuze Annäherungszünder *m (Radar)*
~ **printing** Schattenprojektion *f (Halbleiterfertigung)*
~ **problem** Nächste[r]-Nachbar-Problem *n*
proxy [server] Proxy *m*, Vertreter *m (z.B. als Server in Datenübertragungssystemen)*
Prussian-blue process Cyanotypie *f*, [negativer] Eisenblaudruck *m*
pseudo-edge Pseudokante *f*
~-**Laplacian [operator]** Pseudo-Laplace-Operator *m*
~-**Laplacian edge detection** pseudolaplacesche Kantendetektion *f*
~-**perspective mapping** pseudoperspektivische Abbildung *f*
~-**perspective transformation** pseudoperspektivische Transformation *f*
~ **real-time animation** Pseudo-Echtzeitanimation *f*
~-**three-dimensional** pseudodreidimensional
pseudocolor Pseudofarbe *f*
~ **coding** Pseudofarbcodierung *f*
~ **display** Pseudofarbbildschirm *m*
~ **image** Pseudofarbbild *n*
~ **image processing** Pseudofarbbildverarbeitung *f*
~ **map (rendition)** Pseudofarbdarstellung *f*
~ **sequence** Pseudofarbfolge *f*
pseudocoloring Pseudofarbdarstellung *f*, Pseudokolorierung *f*
pseudohalide Pseudohalogenid *n*
pseudoinverse filter pseudoinverses Filter *n*
~ **operator** pseudoinverser Operator *m*

pseudoisochromatic pseudoisochromatisch
~ **plate (test target)** pseudoisochromatische Tafel *f*, Farbtesttafel *f*, Farbflecktafel *f (zur Prüfung des Farbsehvermögens)*
pseudomedian filter Pseudomedianfilter *n*
pseudooptics Pseudooptik *f*
pseudorandom binary sequence binäre Pseudozufallsfolge *f*
~ **code** Pseudozufallscode *m*
~ **noise** Pseudozufallsrauschen *n*
~ **number (sequence) generator** Pseudozufallsfolgengenerator *m*
pseudorelief Pseudorelief *n*
pseudoscope Pseudoskop *n*
pseudoscopic pseudoskopisch, tiefenverkehrt
~ **image** pseudoskopisches Bild *n (Holografie)*
pseudoscopy Pseudoskopie *f*, tiefenverkehrte Wiedergabe *f*
pseudostereoscopic pseudostereoskopisch
pseudosteroscopy Pseudostereoskopie *f*
pseudotriangulation Pseudotriangulation *f*
PSF *s.* point-spread function
psophometer Psophometer *n*
psophometric psophometrisch
~ **voltage** Geräuschspannung *f*
psychoacoustic[al] psychoakustisch
psychoacoustics Psychoakustik *f*
psychological primary [color] psychologische Primärfarbe *f*
psychometric psychometrisch
psychometrics, psychometry Psychometrie *f*
psychophysical psychophysikalisch
~ **color** psychophys[iolog]ische Farbe *f*
~ **scaling** psychophysikalische Skalierung *f (Bildgütemessung)*
psychophysicist Psychophysiker *m*
psychophysics Psychophysik *f*
psychophysiologic[al] psychophysiologisch
psychovisual psychovisuell, psychooptisch
~ **redundancy** psychooptische (psychovisuelle) Redundanz *f*
public [service] television öffentliches Fernsehen *n*
publication gravure press Zeitschriftendruckmaschine *f*
~ **gravure printing** Zeitschriftendruck *m*, Magazindruck *m*
publicity photo (still) Standfoto *n*, Szenenfoto *n*, Filmstandbild *n*; Promotionsfoto *n*
publishing paper Werkdruckpapier *n*
puck Computermaus *f*, [PC-]Maus *f (Eingabegerät)*
Pulfrich effect Pulfrich-Effekt *m (Stereoskopie)*

~ **photometer** Pulfrich-Fotometer *n*, Stufenfotometer *n*
pull/to unterentwickeln *(bes. Kinefilm)*
pull development Unterentwicklung *f*
~**-down claw** Transportgreifer *m*, Zuggreifer *m*, Greifer *m (Kinotechnik)*
~**-down mechanism** Greifergetriebe *n*
~**-down menu** Abrollmenü *n (Bildschirm)*
~**-up** Bild-Ton-Versatz *m*, Bild-Ton-Abstand *m (Tonfilm)*
pulling *s.* pull development
~ **[the] aperture** Nachziehen *n* der Blende
pullout Ausklappbild *n*
pulse/to pulsen
pulse Impuls *m*, Puls *m (s.a. unter impulse)*
~ **amplitude** Pulsamplitude *f*
~ **amplitude modulation** Pulsamplitudenmodulation *f*
~ **broadening** Pulsverbreiterung *f*
~ **characteristic** Pulscharakteristik *f*
~ **code modulation** Pulscodemodulation *f*
~ **counting** Impulszählung *f*
~ **dispersion** Pulsdispersion *f*
~ **Doppler radar** Impuls-Doppler-Radar *n*
~ **duration** Impulsdauer *f*, Pulsdauer *f*
~ **duration modulation** *s.* ~ width modulation
~ **echo behavior** Impuls-Echo-Verhalten *n*
~ **echo image** Impuls-Echo-Bild *n*
~ **echo imaging** Impuls-Echo-Verfahren *n*, Pulsreflexionsverfahren *n*, Impulsschallverfahren *n (Sonografie)*
~ **echo imaging transducer** Impuls-Echo-Bildwandler *m*
~ **echo principle** Impuls-Echo-Prinzip *n*
~ **echo signal** Impuls-Echo-Signal *n*
~ **echo ultrasonic image** Impuls-Echo-Bild *n*
~ **echo ultrasonic scanner** Impuls-Echo-Bildwandler *m*
~ **edge** Impulsflanke *f*
~ **energy** Pulsenergie *f*
~ **frequency** Impulsfrequenz *f*
~ **generator** Impulsgeber *m*, Impulsgenerator *m*; Taktgeber *m*, Takt[frequenz]generator *m*
~ **height** Impulsamplitude *f*
~ **height analysis** Impulshöhenanalyse *f*
~ **height analyzer** Impulshöhenanalysator *m*, Impulshöhendiskriminator *m (Gammakamera)*
~ **height analyzer window** Energiefenster *n (Gammakamera)*
~ **height discrimination** Impulshöhendiskriminierung *f*
~ **height distribution** Impulshöhenverteilung *f*
~ **height equalization** Impulshöhenangleichung *f*
~ **length** Pulslänge *f*
~ **length modulation** *s.* ~ width modulation
~ **lengthening** Pulsverlängerung *f*
~ **mode** Pulsbetrieb *m (Laser)*

~ **modulation** Impulsmodulation *f*, Pulsmodulation *f*
~ **modulator** Impulsmodulator *m*, Pulsmodulator *m*
~ **of light** Licht[im]puls *m*, optischer Puls (Impuls) *m*
~ **of radar energy** Radar[im]puls *m*
~ **peak power** Pulsspitzenleistung *f*
~ **position modulation** Pulsphasenmodulation *f*
~ **power** Pulsleistung *f*
~ **propagation** Impulsausbreitung *f*
~ **rate** Impulsfrequenz *f*
~ **recurrence (repetition) frequency** *s.* ~ repetition rate
~ **repetition frequency** Pulswiederholfrequenz *f*, Pulswiederholrate *f*
~ **repetition interval** Pulsabstand *m (Radar)*
~ **repetition rate** Impulsfolgefrequenz *f*, Pulsfolgefrequenz *f*, Impulswiederhol[ungs]frequenz *f*, Folgefrequenz *f (Laser, Ultraschall, Radar)*
~ **sequence** Impulsfolge *f*, Pulsfolge *f*, Impulssequenz *f*
~ **shaping filter** Impulsformungsfilter *n*
~ **spreading** Pulsverbreiterung *f*
~ **suppression** Impulsunterdrückung *f*
~ **train** *s.* ~ sequence
~ **wave** Pulswelle *f*
~ **wave Doppler [ultrasound]** Pulsschallverfahren *n*, PW-Doppler-Verfahren *n*
~ **width** Pulsbreite *f*
~ **width measurement** Pulsbreitenmessung *f*
~ **width modulation** Pulsbreitenmodulation *f*, Pulsweitenmodulation *f*, Pulsdauermodulation *f*
pulsed action Pulsbetrieb *m (Laser)*
~ **dye laser** gepulster Farbstofflaser *m*
~ **lamp** gepulste Lampe *f*
~ **laser** Pulslaser *m*, Impulslaser *m*, gepulster Laser *m*
~ **laser light** gepulstes Laserlicht *n*
~ **light** gepulstes Licht *n*
~ **light source** Impulslichtquelle *f*
~ **magnetron** Impulsmagnetron *n (Radar)*
~ **radar** Pulsradar *n*, Impulsradar[verfahren] *n*
~ **radiation** gepulste Strahlung *f*
~ **semiconductor laser** Halbleiterpulslaser *m*
~ **xenon lamp** gepulste Xenonlampe *f*
pulser *s.* pulse generator
pump/to pumpen, anregen *(z.B. Atome oder Moleküle)*
pump mirror Pumpspiegel *m (Laser)*
pumped laser Pumplaser *m*
pumping light Pumplicht *n*
~ **light source** Pumplichtquelle *f*

pumping

~ **pulse** Pumppuls *m*
punched-tape reader Lochstreifenleser *m*
punctuation mark Satzzeichen *n*,
Interpunktionszeichen *n*
pupil Pupille *f*, Augenpupille *f*, Sehloch *n*
~ **aberration** Pupillenaberration *f*,
Öffnungsfehler *f* der Pupille
~ **area** Pupillenfläche *f*
~ **diameter** Pupillendurchmesser *m*
~ **function** Pupillenfunktion *f*,
Blendenfunktion *f (Strahlenoptik)*
~ **location** Pupillenposition *f*
~ **plane** Pupillenebene *f*
~ **position** Pupillenposition *f*
~ **radius** Pupillenradius *m*
~ **ray** Pupillenstrahl *m*, Hauptpunktstrahl *m*
~ **shape** Pupillenform *f*
~ **size** Pupillengröße *f*, Pupillenöffnung *f*
pupillary magnification (ratio)
Pupillen[abbildungs]maßstab *m*
pupillometrics Pupillometrie *f*
puppet Animationspuppe *f*
~ **animation** Puppen[trick]film *m*,
Puppenfilmanimation *f*, Marionettenfilm *m*
pure color reine Farbe *f*, Urfarbe *f*
purity Reinheit *f (z.B. von Farben; s.a.* color saturation*)*
Purkinje effect (phenomenon), ~ **shift**
Purkinje-Phänomen *n (Sehen)*
purple boundary Purpurlinie *f*,
Purpurgerade *f (Farbmetrik)*
~ **color** Purpurfarbe *f*, nichtspektrale Farbe *f*
~ **filter** Purpurfilter *n*
~ **ribbon** Violettband *n (Drucker)*
pursuit eye movement
Blickfolgebewegung *f*
~ **movement** Folgebewegung *f*,
Führungsbewegung *f (der Augen)*
push Schiebeblende *f (digitaler Videoeffekt)*
~ **button** Schaltfläche *f*
~ **development (film processing)**
Pushentwicklung *f*, forcierte
(gesteigerte) Entwicklung *f*,
Überentwicklung *f*
~ **in/to** heranfahren, zubewegen
(Filmkameraarbeit)
~-**pull system** *s.* variable-density [sound] track
~-**pull track** Gegentakttonspur *f*
pushbroom scanner optoelektronischer Scanner *m*
pushing *s.* push development
pyelofluoroscopy Pyelofluoroskopie *f*,
Nierenbeckendurchleuchtung *f*
pyelography Pyelografie *f*,
Nierenbeckenaufnahme *f*
pyramid Pyramide *f*
~ **coding** Pyramidencodierung *f*,
progressive Codierung *f*
~ **data structure** pyramidenförmige
Datenstruktur *f*

~ **decomposition** Pyramidenzerlegung *f*
~ **interpolation** Pyramideninterpolation *f*
pyrazolone coupler Pyrazolonkuppler *m*
(Farbfotografie)
pyro *s.* 1. pyrocatechol; 2. pyrogallol developer
pyrocatechol Brenzcatechin *n*
(Entwicklersubstanz)
pyroelectric detector pyroelektrischer Detektor *m*
~ **effect** pyroelektrischer Effekt *m*
pyrogallol developer Pyrogallolentwickler *m*
pyroxylin Kollodiumwolle *f*
Pythagoras' theorem (theory)
Pythagoreischer Lehrsatz *m*

Q

Q-switch Güteschalter *m*, Gütemodulation *f (Laser)*
Q-switched laser gütegeschalteter Laser *m*
Q-switched laser cavity gütegeschalteter Resonator *m*
Q-switching Q-Switch-Betrieb *m (Laser)*
QCIF *s.* quarter common intermediate format
quad 1. Quadrat *n*; 2. *s.* quadrangle
~ **subdivision** bilineare Subdivision (Unterteilung) *f*
~ **tree** Viererbaum *m*, quaternärer Baum *m*, quartärer Bildbaum *m (Datenstruktur)*
~**-tree-based textural segmentation** viererbaumbasierte Textursegmentierung *f*
~**-tree coding** Viererbaum-Codierung *f*
~**-tree compression** Viererbaumkompression *f*
~**-tree data structure** Viererbaumstruktur *f*
~**-tree method** *s.* split-and-merge algorithm
~**-tree node** Viererbaumknoten *m*
~**-tree representation** Viererbaumdarstellung *f (eines Bildes)*
quadrangle Viereck *n*; Geviert *n*, Quadrangel *n*
~**-based motion compensation** interpolative Bewegungsbeschreibung *f*
quadrant Quadrant *m*
quadrat[e] Quadrat *n*
quadratic electro-optic[al] effect Kerr-Effekt *m*
~ **polynomial** Polynom *n* zweiter Ordnung
quadrature amplitude modulation Quadratur[amplituden]modulation *f*
~ **coil** Quadraturspule *f (Magnetresonanzbildgebung)*
~ **demodulation** Quadraturdemodulation *f*
~ **detection** Quadraturdetektion *f (Magnetresonanzbildgebung)*
~ **detector** Quadraturdetektor *m*
~ **filter** Quadraturfilter *n*
~ **filter pair** Quadraturfilterpaar *n*
~ **mirror filter** Quadraturspiegelfilter *n (Bilddatenkompression)*
~ **mirror filter bank** Quadraturspiegelfilterbank *f*
~ **modulation** Quadraturmodulation *f*, QAM
~ **modulator** Quadraturmodulator *m*
~ **phase shift keying** Quadraturphasenumtastung *f*, vierwertige Phasenumtastung *f (digitales Fernsehen)*
~ **technique** Quadraturtechnik *f*

quadric [surface] Quadrik *f*, algebraische Fläche *f* zweiter Ordnung *(Euklidische Geometrie)*
quadrichromatic tetrachromatisch, vierfarbig
~ **printing** Vierfarbendruck *m*, Vierfarbenprozess *m*
quadrifocal tensor quadrifokaler Tensor *m*
quadrilateral vierseitig
quadrophony Quadrofonie *f*
quadruple extended graphics array Grafikstandard mit 2.048 x 1.536 Pixel Auflösung
qualitative descriptor qualitativer Deskriptor *m*
~ **map** qualitative Karte *f*
quality of reproduction Wiedergabequalität *f*, Reproduktionsqualität *f*
~ **print** Qualitätsdruck *m (Erzeugnis)*
quantitative descriptor quantitativer Deskriptor *m*
~ **image analysis** quantitative Bildanalyse *f*
~ **invisibility** quantitative Unsichtbarkeit *f*, Index *m (Computergrafik)*
~ **map** quantitative Karte *f*
~ **ultrasound [imaging]** quantitativer Ultraschall *m*
~ **visualization** quantitative Visualisierung *f*
quantity of illuminance Belichtung *f*
~ **of light** Lichtmenge *f*, Lichtarbeit *f*
~ **printing** Massenkopierung *f*
~ **release printing** Massenkopierung *f (von Kinefilm)*
quantization Quantisierung *f*, Wertequantisierung *f*, Wertediskretisierung *f*, Quantelung *f*
~ **accuracy** Quantisierungsgenauigkeit *f*
~ **algorithm** Quantisierungsalgorithmus *m*
~ **curve** Quantisierungskennlinie *f*
~ **effect** Quantisierungseffekt *m*
~ **error** Quantisierungsfehler *m*
~ **error distortion** Quantisierungsfehlerverzerrung *f*
~ **error measure** Quantisierungsfehlermaß *n*
~ **function** Quantisierungsfunktion *f*
~ **index** Quantisierungsindex *m*
~ **interval** Quantisierungsintervall *n*
~ **level** Quantisierungsstufe *f*
~ **matrix** Quantisierungsmatrix *f*
~ **noise** Quantisierungsrauschen *n*
~ **operator** Quantisierungsoperator *m*
~ **parameter** Quantisierungsparameter *m*
~ **scheme** Quantisierungsschema *n*
~ **step** Quantisierungsschritt *m*
~ **step size** Quantisierungsstufenhöhe *f*
~ **table** Quantisierungstabelle *f*, Teilertabelle *f*
~ **techniqe** Quantisierungsverfahren *n*
quantize/to quantisieren
quantized image quantisiertes Bild *n*
~ **signal** quantisiertes Signal *n*

quantizer

quantizer Quantisierer *m*
quantizing distortion Quantisierungsverzerrung *f*, Quantisierungsrauschen *n*
~ **range** Quantisierungsbereich *m*
quantum [elektromagnetisches] Quant *n*; Strahlungsquant *n*
~ **detection efficiency** *s.* ~ efficiency
~ **detector** Quantendetektor *m*, Photonendetektor *m*
~ **efficiency** Quantenwirkungsgrad *m*, Quanteneffizienz *f*
~ **electrodynamics** Quantenelektrodynamik *f*, Quantentheorie *f*
~ **energy** Quantenenergie *f*
~ **flux** Quantenfluss *m*
~ **jump** Quantensprung *m*
~-**mechanical tunnel[l]ing** [quantenmechanisches] Tunneln *n*
~ **mechanics** Quantenmechanik *f*
~ **mottle (noise)** Quantenrauschen *n*
~ **of flux** [magnetisches] Flussquant *n*
~ **of radiation** Strahlungsquant *n*
~ **optics** Quantenoptik *f*
~ **physics** *s.* ~ theory
~ **sensor** Quantensensor *m*
~ **state** Röntgenniveau *n*
~ **theory** Quantentheorie *f*
~ **theory of light** [Einsteinsche] Lichtquantenhypothese *f*, Lichtquantentheorie *f*, Photonenhypothese *f*
~ **well** Quantentopf *m*
~ **yield** Quantenausbeute *f*
quarter-common intermediate format *ein digitales Videobildformat niedriger Datenrate*
~-**inch tape** Viertelzollband *n*
~-**line offset** Viertelzeilenoffset *m (Farbfernsehsignal)*
~-**pel interpolation** Viertelpixelinterpolation *f*
~-**pixel accuracy** Viertelpixelgenauigkeit *f (Videocodierung)*
~-**wave [antireflection] coating** Viertelwellenvergütung *f*
~-**wave retarder, quarter-wavelength plate** Lambda-Viertelplättchen *n*, Lambda-Viertelplatte *f*, Lambda-Viertel-Verzögerungsplatte *f*, Viertelwellenlängenplatte *f*, Viertelwellenplättchen *n*, Viertelwellenkompensator *m*
quartic polynomial Polynom *n* vierter Ordnung
~ **tree** *s.* quad tree
quarto Quart[o] *n*, Viertelbogengröße *f*
quartz Quarz *m*
~ **crystal** Quarzkristall *m (optisches Material)*
~ **filament lamp** *s.* ~ lamp
~ **filter** Quarzfilter *n*
~ **glass** Quarzglas *n*

~ **halogen [filament] lamp** 1. Halogenglühlampe *f*; 2. *s.* ~ lamp
~ **lamp** Quarzlampe *f*, Quarzhalogen[glüh]lampe *f*; Wolframhalogenlampe *f*
~ **lens** Quarzlinse *f*
~ **oscillator** Schwingquarz *m*
quasi-Cassegrain system Quasi-Cassegrain-System *n (Teleskop)*
~ **error-free transmission** quasi fehlerfreie Übertragung *f*
~-**imaging** quasiabbildend
~-**monochromatic light** quasimonochromatisches Licht *n*
~-**monostatic radar** quasimonostatisches Radar *n*
~-**optical** quasioptisch
~-**symmetrical lens** quasisymmetrisches Objektiv
quaternion Quaternion *f(n)*, Quaternio *m (z.B. als Vektor aus vier Elementen)*
quenching Quenching *n*, Tilgung *f (Fotoleitung)*
~ **coil** Löschdrossel *f*
query/to anfragen; abfragen *(z.B. eine Bilddatenbank)*
query Suchanfrage *f*, Datenbankabfrage *f*
~ **image** Anfragebild *n*, Suchbild *n (Datenbanksystem)*
~ **language** Anfragesprache *f*, Abfragesprache *f (Datenbanksystem)*
~ **window** Suchfenster *n*
question mark Fragezeichen *n*
queue Warteschlange *f (Datenverarbeitung)*
quick-change bayonet Schnellwechselbajonett *n*
~ **mechanism** Schnellstartlaufwerk *n*
~ **photography** Schnellfotografie *f*
~ **printing** Schnelldruck *m*
~-**release adapter (device)** Schnellkupplung *f (Stativ)*
~-**release platform** Schnellkupplungsplatte *f*, Schnellspannkameraplatte *f*, Schnellwechselplatte *f*
quincunx lattice Quincunx-Raster *m(n) (Signalabtastung)*
~ **sampling** Quincunx-Abtastung *f*
quoin/to schließen *(Handsatz)*
quoin Schließkeil *m (Handsatz)*
quotation (quote) mark Anführungszeichen *n*
QXGA *s.* quadruple extended graphics array

R-Y signal s. red-minus-luma signal
racetrack photofinish camera Zielkamera f
rack-over [viewfinder] Parallaxenausgleich m
racon s. radar beacon
rad Rad n *(Dosiseinheit ionisierender Strahlung)*
radar Radar n
~ **altimeter** Radarhöhenmesser m
~ **antenna** Radarantenne f
~ **astronomy** Radarastronomie f
~ **backscatter** Radarrückstreuung f
~ **backscatter coefficient** Radarrückstreufaktor m
~ **bandwidth** Radarbandbreite f
~ **beacon** Radar[antwort]bake f
~ **beam** Radarstrahl m, Radarkeule f
~ **bearing** Radarpeilung f
~ **cathode-ray tube** Radarbildröhre f
~ **cell** Radarzelle f
~ **chain** Radarkette f
~ **clutter** Clutter m, Fremdecho n, Störecho n
~ **cross section** Radarquerschnitt m, Echoquerschnitt m, Rückstrahlquerschnitt m, Rückstreufläche f
~ **data** Radar[bild]daten pl
~ **data processor** Radardatenprozessor m
~ **detection** Radarortung f
~ **device** Radargerät n
~ **display** Radarschirm m
~ **display image** Radarbild n
~ **display indicator** Radarsichtgerät n
~ **dome** Radarkuppel f, Radom m
~ **echo** Radarecho n
~ **electronics** Radarelektronik f
~ **energy** Radarenergie f
~ **energy frequency** Radarfrequenz f
~ **engineering** Radartechnik f
~ **equation** Radargleichung f
~ **facility** Radaranlage f
~ **footprint** Radar-Ausleuchtzone f
~ **frequency** Radarfrequenz f
~ **horizon** Radarhorizont m
~ **hydrography** Radarhydrografie f
~ **illumination** Radarausleuchtung f
~ **image** Radar[schirm]bild n
~ **image processing** Radarbildverarbeitung f
~ **imagery** Radaraufzeichnung f
~ **imaging** Radarabbildung f
~ **impulse** Radar[im]puls m
~ **indicator** Radarsichtgerät n
~ **information** Radarinformation f
~ **interferometer** Radarinterferometer n
~ **interferometry** Radarinterferometrie f
~ **jamming** Radarstörung f
~ **location** Radarortung f
~ **map** Radarkarte f
~ **meteorological** radarmeteorologisch
~ **meteorologist** Radarmeteorologe m
~ **meteorology** Radarmeteorologie f
~ **mode** Radarmodus m
~ **modulator** Radarmodulator m
~ **navigation** Radarnavigation f
~ **network** Radarnetz n
~ **observation** Radarbeobachtung f
~ **observer** Radarbeobachter m
~ **operation** Radarbetrieb m
~ **operator** Radartechniker m
~ **pattern** Radarcharakteristik f
~ **pulse** Radar[im]puls m
~ **range** Radarreichweite f; Radarabstand m
~ **range equation** Radargleichung f
~ **raw data** Radarrohdaten pl
~ **receiver** Radarempfänger m
~ **reconnaissance** Radaraufklärung f
~ **reflection** Radarrückstreuung f
~ **reflectivity** Radarreflektivität f
~ **reflectivity factor** Radarrückstreufaktor m
~ **reflector** Radarreflektor m
~ **remote sensing** Radarfernerkundung f
~ **return** Radarecho n
~ **satellite** Radarsatellit m
~ **scanner** Radarkopf m
~ **scatter** Radarstreuung f
~ **screen** Radarschirm m
~ **screen picture** Radarbild n
~ **sensor** Radarsensor m
~ **set** Radargerät n
~ **shadow** Radarschatten m
~ **signal** Radarsignal n
~ **signature** Radarsignatur f
~ **simulator** Radarsimulator m
~ **station** Radarstation f
~ **surveillance** Radarüberwachung f
~ **surveying** Radarvermessung f
~ **system** Radarsystem n
~ **target** Radarziel n
~ **technology** Radartechnik f
~ **telescope** Radarteleskop n
~ **tracking** Radarverfolgung f
~ **transmitter** Radarsender m
~ **triangulation** Radartriangulation f
~ **tube** Radar[bild]röhre f
~ **unit** Radaranlage f
~ **warning receiver** Radarwarnempfänger m
~ **wave** Radarwelle f
~ **wave front** Radarwellenfront f
~ **wavelength** Radarwellenlänge f
radargrammetry Radargrammetrie f
radarscope photography Radarschirmfotografie f
radial basis functions [neural] network Radial-Basis-Funktions-Netzwerk n, radiales Basisfunktionsnetz n, RBF-Netz n *(Musterklassifizierung)*

radial

- ~ **distortion** radiale Verzeichnung f
- ~ **plane** Sagittalebene f
- ~ **resolution** radiale Auflösung f *(Radar)*
- ~ **resolving power** radiales Auflösungsvermögen n *(Radar)*
- ~ **signal** Radialsignal n *(Bildspeicherplatte)*
- ~ **speed (velocity)** Radialgeschwindigkeit f *(Radar)*

radian Radiant m *(Winkeleinheit)*

radiance, radiancy Strahl[ungs]dichte f *(Radiometrie)*

radiant strahlend, radiant
- ~ **efficiency** Strahlungsausbeute f
- ~ **emittance** s. ~ exitance
- ~ **energy** Strahlungsenergie f
- ~ **exitance** spezifische spektrale Ausstrahlung (Abstrahlung) f, Strahlungsflussdichte f
- ~ **exposure** 1. Exposition f; Belichtung f *(s.a. unter exposure)*; 2. Bestrahlung f *(Radiometrie)*
- ~ **flux** Strahlungsfluss m, Strahlungsleistung f
- ~ **flux density** Strahlungsflussdichte f
- ~ **heat** Strahlungswärme f
- ~ **intensity** Strahl[ungs]intensität f, Strahl[ungs]stärke f *(Radiometrie)*
- ~ **power** Strahlungsleistung f
- ~ **sensitive area** bestrahlungsempfindliche Fläche f *(Fotodiode)*
- ~ **source** Strahlungsquelle f, Strahlenquelle f

radiate/to [ab]strahlen; ausstrahlen

radiate out/to ausstrahlen

radiating antenna Sendeantenne f
- ~ **efficiency** Strahlungsausbeute f
- ~ **temperature** Strahlungstemperatur f

radiation Strahlung f, Ausstrahlung f; Abstrahlung f
- ~ **absorbed dose** s. rad
- ~ **absorption** Strahlungsabsorption f
- ~ **angle** Ausstrahlungswinkel m, Ausstrahlwinkel m, Abstrahlwinkel m
- ~ **attenuation** Strahlungs[ab]schwächung f, Strahlenschwächung f
- ~ **band** Wellenlängengruppe f
- ~ **burden** Strahlenbelastung f
- ~ **damage** Strahlenschaden m
- ~ **damping** Strahlungsdämpfung f
- ~ **detection** Strahlungsdetektion f, Strahlungsnachweis m
- ~ **detector** Strahlungsdetektor m, Strahlungsempfänger m
- ~ **dose** Strahlendosis f
- ~ **energy** Strahlungsenergie f
- ~ **exposure** Strahlenexposition f *(z.B. von Patienten)*
- ~ **field** Strahlungsfeld n
- ~ **flux** Strahlungsfluss m *(s.a. ~ power)*
- ~ **hazard** Strahlenrisiko n
- ~ **imaging** Radiografie f
- ~ **lobe** Strahlungskeule f
- ~ **loss** Strahlungsverlust m
- ~-**monitoring film** Monitorfilm m
- ~ **of heat** Wärme[ab]strahlung f
- ~ **pattern** Strahlungsdiagramm n *(z.B. einer Antenne)*
- ~ **physics** Strahlungsphysik f
- ~ **power** Strahlungsleistung f *(s.a. ~ flux)*
- ~ **pressure** Strahlungsdruck m
- ~-**produced image** s. radiogram
- ~ **protection cabinet** Strahlenschutzkabine f
- ~ **quantity** Strahlungsmenge f
- ~ **receiver** Strahlungsempfänger m
- ~ **safety** Strahlensicherheit f
- ~-**sensitive film** strahlungsempfindlicher Film m
- ~ **sensitivity** Strahlungsempfindlichkeit f
- ~ **sensor** Strahlungssensor m
- ~ **source** Strahlungsquelle f, Strahlenquelle f
- ~ **spectrum** Strahlungsspektrum n
- ~ **transmission** Strahlungsdurchgang m
- ~ **type** Strahlungsart f
- ~ **wavelength** Strahlungswellenlänge f
- ~ **yield** Strahlungsausbeute f

radiative field Strahlungsfeld n
- ~ **loss** Strahlungsverlust m
- ~ **pattern** Strahlungsdiagramm n *(z.B. einer Antenne)*
- ~ **spectrum** Strahlungsspektrum n

radiator Strahler m

radical Radikal n

radio astronomer Radioastronom m
- ~ **astronomical** radioastronomisch
- ~ **astronomy** Radioastronomie f
- ~ **astronomy observatory** Radioobservatorium n
- ~ **camera** Funkkamera f
- ~ **detection and ranging** s. radar
- ~ **frequency** Radiofrequenz f
- ~-**frequency antenna (coil)** Hochfrequenzspule f, Hochfrequenzantenne f *(Magnetresonanztomografie)*
- ~-**frequency energy pulse** Hochfrequenzimpuls m
- ~-**frequency identification** Radiofrequenzidentifizierung f
- ~-**frequency magnetic field** Hochfrequenzfeld n
- ~-**frequency pulse** Hochfrequenzimpuls m
- ~-**frequency radiation** Radio[frequenz]strahlung f
- ~-**frequency range** Hochfrequenzbereich m
- ~-**frequency signal** Hochfrequenzsignal n
- ~-**frequency spectroscopy** Radiofrequenzspektroskopie f
- ~ **image** Strahlenbild n, Radiogramm n
- ~ **interferometer** Radiointerferometer n
- ~ **interferometry** Radiointerferometrie f
- ~ **location** Funkortung f
- ~ **microphone** Funkmikrofon n, kabelloses (drahtloses) Mikrofon n, Mikroport n
- ~ **mouse** Funkmaus f *(Eingabegerät)*
- ~-**opaque** strahlenundurchlässig

~ **position finding** Funkortung f
~ **regime** Radiowellenbereich m
~ **silence** Funkstille f
~ **slave** Funk[fern]auslöser m
~ **telescope** Radioteleskop n
~ **transmission** Funkübertragung f
~ **wave** Radiowelle f
~**-wave frequency** Radiofrequenz f, Hochfrequenz f
~ **wavelength regime** Radiowellenbereich m *(des elektromagnetischen Spektrums)*
~ **window** Radiofenster n
radioactive radioaktiv
~ **decay** radioaktiver Zerfall m
~ **disintegration series** radioaktive Zerfallsreihe f
~ **isotope** Radioisotop n
~ **radiation** radioaktive Strahlung f
~ **tracer** Radiopharmakon n
~ **transformation** radioaktiver Zerfall m
radioactivity Radioaktivität f
radioangiography Röntgenkontrastangiografie f
radioautograph Autoradiogramm n
radiodiagnostic strahlendiagnostisch
radiogram s. radiograph
radiograph/to radiografieren, durchstrahlen; röntgen
radiograph Radiogramm n, Radiografie f, Strahlenbild n; Durchstrahlungsaufnahme f, Durchstrahlungsbild n, Durchleuchtungsbild n, Strahlungsabbildung f, radiografische Aufnahme f
radiographer Radiograf m
radiographic radiografisch
~ **cassette** radiografische Kassette f; Röntgenkassette f
~ **contrast** radiografischer Kontrast m
~ **equipment manufacturer** Röntgengerätehersteller m
~ **exposure** 1. Röntgenbelichtung f; 2. Röntgen[bild]aufnahme f
~ **film** radiografischer Film m, Röntgenfilm m
~ **grid** Röntgenstreustrahlenraster m(n), Streustrahlenraster m(n)
~ **image** s. radiogram
~ **photography** Röntgen[strahlen]fotografie f, Röntgenografie f, Filmröntgen n
~ **projection** radiografische Projektion f
~ **screen** Röntgenschirm m, Durchleuchtungsschirm m
~ **sensitivity** radiografische Empfindlichkeit f
~ **shadow** Röntgenschatten m
~ **test report** Durchstrahlungsprotokoll n
radiography Radiografie f
~ **department** Röntgenabteilung f, Röntgenstation f, Röntgenbetrieb m
radioisotope Radioisotop n

~ **camera** Radioisotopenkamera f
radiologic film radiologischer Film m
radiological image radiologisches Bild n
~ **imaging workstation** radiologischer Bildarbeitsplatz m
~ **information system** radiologisches Informationssystem n
~ **technologist** Röntgentechniker m
radiologist Radiologe m
radiology Radiologie f, Strahlenkunde f
~ **department** s. radiography department
radiolucency Strahlendurchlässigkeit f
radiolucent strahlendurchlässig
radioluminescence Radiolumineszenz f
radiometer Radiometer n
radiometric calibration radiometrische Kalibrierung f
~ **correction** radiometrische Korrektur f
~ **distortion** Radiometrieverzerrung f, radiometrische Verzerrung f
~ **image transformation** radiometrische Bildtransformation f
~ **imaging** radiometrische Abbildung f
~ **mosaicking** radiometrische Mosaikbildung f
~ **quantity** Strahlungsgröße f, strahlungsphysikalische Größe f
~ **resolution** radiometrische Auflösung f
radiometry Radiometrie f, Strahlungsmessung f
radionuclide Radionuklid n, strahlendes Nuklid n
~ **emission tomography** Emissionstomografie f, szintigrafische Tomografie f, tomografische Szintigrafie f
radiopacity Strahlenundurchlässigkeit f
radiopaque strahlenundurchlässig
radiopharmaceutical Radiopharmakon n
radiophoto 1. Funkbildübertragung f; 2. s. radiophotograph
radiophotogram Radiofotogramm n
radiophotograph Funkbild n, Radiofoto n
radiophotography 1. Bildfunk m, drahtlose Bildtelegrafie f; 2. Radiofotografie f, Schirmbildfotografie f; Röntgen[strahlen]fotografie f, Röntgenografie f, Filmröntgen n
radioprotection Strahlenschutz m
radioscopic[al] testing radioskopische Prüfung f
radioscopy Radioskopie f
radiosensitive strahlungsempfindlich
~ **layer** strahlungsempfindliche Schicht f
radiosensitivity Strahlungsempfindlichkeit f
radiosity Radiosity f, Lichtenergiekalkül n
~ **image generation** s. ~ technique
~ **matrix** Radiosity-Matrix f
~ **technique** Radiosity-Verfahren n *(Computergrafik)*
radiotelephone Funktelefon n
radioxerography Xeroradiografie f
radius of blur spot Unschärferadius m

~ **of curvature** Krümmungsradius *m*
~ **vector** Radiusvektor *m*
radome [protective covering] Radom *m*, Radarkuppel *f*
Radon space Radon-Raum *m* *(Objektklassifizierung)*
~ **transform[ation]** Radon-Transformation *f* *(Tomografie)*
rag paper Hadernpapier *n*
ragged left Flattersatz *m* links; rechtsbündig
~ **right** Flattersatz *m* rechts; linksbündig
~ **setting** Flatterrand *m*
RAID array RAID-Konfiguration *f*
rail Verlängerungsschiene *f* *(Fachkamera)*
rain clutter (echo) Regenclutter *m*, Regenecho *n* *(Radar)*
rainbow hologram Regenbogenhologramm *n*, Benton-Hologramm *n*
raised cap[ital] herausgestellte Initiale *f* *(Typografie)*
~ **printing** Thermografie *f*
raking light schräg auffallendes Licht *n*, Schräglicht *n*
RAM *s.* random-access memory
Raman laser Raman-Laser *m*
~ **scattering** Raman-Streuung *f*
~ **spectrometer** Raman-Spektrometer *n*
~ **spectroscopy** Raman-Spektroskopie *f*
ramp edge Rampenkante *f*
~ **filter** Rampenfilter *n*
~ **function** Rampenfunktion *f*
Ramsden circle Austrittspupille *f*, Ramsdenscher Kreis *m* *(Optik)*
~ **microscope eyepiece** Ramsden-Okular *n*
random zufallsbedingt, stochastisch
~ **access** wahlfreier Zugriff *m*, Direktzugriff *m*
~-**access capability** Direktzugriffsmöglichkeit *f*
~-**access file** Direktzugriffsdatei *f*
~-**access memory** Direktzugriffsspeicher *m*, Schreib-Lese-Speicher *m*, Arbeitsspeicher *m*, Hauptspeicher *m*, RAM *f(n)*
~ **color noise** Zufallsfarbrauschen *n*
~-**dot kinetogram** Zufallspunktkinetogramm *n*
~-**dot pattern** Zufallspunktmuster *n*
~-**dot stereogram** Zufalls[punkt]stereogramm *n*
~ **error** Zufallsfehler *m* *(Bilddatenkompression)*
~ **field** Zufallsfeld *n*
~ **model** zufälliges Modell *n*
~ **noise** Zufallsrauschen *n*
~ **noise pixel** Rauschpixel *n*
~ **pattern** Zufallsmuster *n*
~ **polygon** Zufallspolygon *n*
~ **signal** Zufallssignal *n*
~ **thermal noise** thermisches Zufallsrauschen *n*, Johnson-Rauschen *n* *(s.a. thermal noise)*

~ **variable** Zufallsvariable *f*, Zufallsgröße *f*
randomized Hough transform randomisierte Hough-Transformation *f*
randomly addressable wahlfrei addressierbar
~ **polarized radiation** unpolarisierte (willkürlich polarisierte) Strahlung *f*
randomness Zufälligkeit *f*
range 1. Variationsbreite *f*; 2. Reichweite *f*; Bereich *m*; 3. Frequenzband *n*, Band *n*
~ **curvature** Entfernungskrümmung *f* *(Radar)*
~-**height indicator [display]** RHI-Sichtgerät *n* *(Radar)*
~ **image** Tiefenbild *n* *(maschinelle Bilderkennung)*
~ **imaging sensor** Entfernungssensor *m*
~ **of shutter speeds** Verschlusszeitenbereich *m*
~ **of tones** Tonwertbereich *m*, Tonwertumfang *m* *(eines Bildes)*
~ **query** Bereichs[ab]frage *f*, Bereichsanfrage *f* *(Computergrafik)*
~ **rate** Radialgeschwindigkeit *f* *(Radar)*
~ **resolution** Entfernungsauflösung *f* *(Radar)*
~ **sensor** Entfernungssensor *m*
ranged left linksbündig *(Flattersatz)*
rangefinder Entfernungsmesser *m*; Messucher *m*
~ **camera** Messucherkamera *f*, Suchkamera *f*, Entfernungsmesserkamera *f*
~ **error** Messucherfehler *m*, Sucherfehler *m*
~ **image** Messucherbild *n*, Sucherbild *n*
~ **optics** Sucheroptik *f*
ranging system Entfernungsmesssystem *n*
rank operator, rank-order filter Rangordnungsfilter *n*, Rang[ordnungs]operator *m*
~-**order filtering** Rangordnungsfilterung *f*, Rang[folge]operation *f*, Rangordnungsverfahren *n*
~-**order similarity** Rangordnungsähnlichkeit *f*
rapid-access developer *s.* rapid-working developer
~-**access memory** Schnellzugriffsspeicher *m*
~-**acting fixer** Schnellfixierer *m*, Express-Fixierbad *n*
~-**advance lever** Schnellaufzugshebel *m*
~ **copying** Schnellkopierung *f*
~ **film changer** Filmwechsler *m* *(Röntgentechnik)*
~ **fixing bath** Schnellfixierbad *n*
~ **gradient echo pulse sequence** schnelle Gradientenechosequenz *f*, Turbo-Gradientenecho *n* *(Magnetresonanztomografie)*
~ **processing** Schnellverarbeitung *f*, Schnellentwicklung *f* *(von Filmmaterial)*

~-**processing paper** Schnellverarbeitungspapier *n*
~ **prototyping** digitaler Prototypenbau *m*, Stereolithografie *f*
~-**sequence camera** Filmwechsler *m* *(Röntgentechnik)*
~-**working developer** Schnellentwickler *m*, Rapidentwickler *m*, schnellarbeitender Entwickler *m*
rare-earth glass Seltenerdglas *n*
raster/to rastern
raster Raster *m(n)*, Bildpunktraster *m(n)*, Röhrenraster *m(n)*, Bildschirmraster *m(n)*; Pixelraster *m(n)* *(s.a. unter bit-map)*
~-**based monitor** Rasterbildschirm *m*, Rasterdisplay *n*
~-**based printing device** Rasterdrucker *m*
~-**based representation** Rasterdarstellung *f*
~ **beam** Rasterstrahl *m*, Abtaststrahl *m*, Scanstrahl *m*
~ **cathode-ray tube output device** Rastersichtgerät *n*
~ **command** Rasterbefehl *m*
~ **coordinate** Rasterkoordinate *f*
~ **data** Rasterdaten *pl*
~ **display screen** Rasterbildschirm *m*, Rasterdisplay *n*
~ **distance** Rasterabstand *m*
~ **effect** Rastereffekt *m*
~ **format** Rasterformat *n*
~ **frequency** Rasterfrequenz *f*, Rasterzahl *f*, Rasterfeinheit *f*, Rasterweite *f*
~ **geometric error** Rastergeometriefehler *m*
~ **geometry** Rastergeometrie *f*
~ **graphics** Rastergrafik *f*, Pixelgrafik *f*
~ **graphics display** Rasterbildschirm *n*, Rasterdisplay *n*
~ **graphics package (system)** Rastergrafiksystem *n*
~ **grid** Rasternetz *n*, Rastergitter *n* *(Computergrafik)*
~ **hard copy device** Rasterdrucker *m*
~ **image** Rasterbild *n* *(s.a. pixel image)*
~ **image data** Rasterbilddaten *pl*
~ **image file** Raster[bild]datei *f*
~ **image file format** Rasterbilddateiformat *n*
~ **image format** Rasterbildformat *n*
~ **image processing** Rasterbildverarbeitung *f*
~ **image processor** Raster[bild]prozessor *m*, Rasterbildrechner *m*
~ **input scanner** Rasterscanner *m*, Mehrstrahlscanner *m*
~ **line** Rasterlinie *f*; Rasterzeile *f*, Abtastzeile *f*, Scannerzeile *f*
~ **line printer** Rasterdrucker *m*
~ **line spacing** Rasterzeilenabstand *m*
~ **modulation** Rastermodulation *f*
~ **operation** Rasteroperation *f*
~-**order search** Rastersuche *f*

~ **output device** Rastergerät *n*, rasterorientiertes Ausgabegerät *n*
~ **point** Rasterpunkt *m* *(Elektrofotografie)*
~ **printing system** Rasterdrucksystem *n*
~ **rotation** Rasterdrehung *f*
~ **scan/to** abrastern
~ **scan** Rasterabtastung *f*
~-**scan format** Rasterscanformat *n*
~ **scan[-type] pattern** Abtastmuster *n*
~-**scanned display** Rasterdisplay *n*, Rasterbildschirm *m*
~ **scanner** *s.* ~ input scanner
~ **screen** Rasterbildschirm *m*, Rasterdisplay *n*
~ **search** Rastersuche *f*
~ **signal** Rastersignal *n*
~ **spacing** Rasterabstand *m*
~ **system** Rastersystem *n*
~-**to-vector conversion** Vektorisierung *f*
~ **video signal** Rastervideosignal *n*
rasterization Rasterung *f*, Rasterisierung *f*
~ **algorithm** Rasteralgorithmus *m*
rasterize/to rastern
rasterized image data Rasterbilddaten *pl*
~ **photograph** gerastertes Foto *n*
rasterizing Rastern *n*
RATAN system RATAN-System *n* *(ein Radar-Video-Navigationssystem)*
rate of development Entwicklungsgeschwindigkeit *f* *(von Silberhalogenidkristallen)*
~ **of fixation (fixing)** Fixiergeschwindigkeit *f*
~ **of zoom** Zoomgeschwindigkeit *f*
ratio image Ratiobild *n* *(Fernerkundung)*
~ **of distances** Entfernungsverhältnis *n*
~ **of image sizes** Bildgrößenverhältnis *n*
~ **of object distances** Objektweitenverhältnis *n*
~ **of reduction** Verkleinerungsverhältnis *n*, Verkleinerungsfaktor *m*
~ **of sizes** Größenverhältnis *n*
~ **scale** Skala *f*
ratioing Ratioverfahren *n* *(Fernerkundung)*
raw data Rohdaten *pl*
~ **data rate** Rohdatenrate *f*
~ **film** Rohfilm *m*
~ **film stock** Rohfilmmaterial *n*
~ **footage** Originalfilmmaterial *n*, [originales] Drehmaterial *n*
~ **image data** Bildrohdaten *pl*, Rohbilddaten *pl*
~ **segmentation** Rohsegmentierung *f*
~ **stock** Rohfilmmaterial *n*; Rohfilm *m*
~ **video** Rohvideo *n*
ray Strahl *m*
~ **aberration** Strahlaberration *f*
~ **angle** Strahlwinkel *m*
~ **bending** Strahlbeugung *f*
~ **bundle** Strahlenbündel *n*, Strahlenbüschel *n*; Strahl *m*
~ **casting** 1. vereinfachte Strahlverfolgung *f*; 2. *s.* ~ tracing
~ **data** Strahldaten *pl*

ray 320

~ **deflection** Strahlablenkung f
~ **deflection angle** Strahlablenkwinkel m
~ **deflector** Strahlablenker m
~ **direction** Strahlrichtung f
~ **equation** Strahlgleichung f
~ **intersection** Strahldurchstoß[ungs]punkt m
~ **merging** Strahlintegration f
~ **of light** Lichtstrahl m
~ **optics** [geometrische] Strahlenoptik f, geometrische Optik f
~-**optics** strahlenoptisch
~ **parallel to the axis** Achsenparallelstrahl m, achs[en]paralleler Strahl m
~ **path** Strahlengang m, Strahlverlauf m
~ **projection** Strahlprojektion f
~ **propagation** Strahlausbreitung f
~ **segment** Strahlsegment n
~ **theory of light** Strahlentheorie f des Lichts
~ **trace** Strahldurchzeichnung f
~ **tracing** Strahlverfolgung f; Strahlenrückverfolgung f; Strahldurchrechnung f
~ **tracing algorithm** Strahlverfolgungsalgorithmus m
~ **tracing model** Strahlverfolgungsmodell n
~ **trajectory** Strahlengang m, Strahlverlauf m
~ **transfer matrix** Strahlmatrix f, ABCD-Matrix f

Rayleigh condition (criterion) Rayleigh-Kriterium n, Rayleighsches Auflösungskriterium n *(Abbildungsoptik, Radar)*
~ **distribution** Rayleigh-Verteilung f
~ **equation** Rayleigh-Gleichung f *(Farbsehen)*
~ **length** Rayleigh-Länge f *(Laser)*
~ **noise** Rayleigh-Rauschen n
~ **range** Rayleigh-Bereich m *(Gaußsche Optik)*
~ **scattering** Rayleigh-Streuung f, elastische Lichtstreuung f, Luftstreuung f, kohärente (lineare) Streuung f

razor-sharp picture gestochen scharfes Bild n
RC paper RC-Papier n, kunstharzbeschichtetes Papier n
RCA [phono] connector, ~ plug RCA-Stecker m, Cinch-Stecker m
reacquire/to reakquirieren
reaction time Reaktionszeit f, Ansprechzeit f, Antwortzeit f *(z.B. eines Fotodetektors)*
read s. readout process
~ **clock** Lesetakt m *(Zeitkompression)*
~ **cycle** Auslesezyklus m
~ **in[to]/to** einlesen *(z.B. Signale oder Bilddaten)*
~ **off (out)/to** auslesen
~-**only [electronic] memory** Festwertspeicher m, Nurlesespeicher m, Lesespeicher m, ROM n
~ **pen** Lesestift m
~-**write cycle** Schreib-Lese-Zyklus m
~-**write head** Schreib-Lese-Kopf m
~-**write memory** Schreib-Lese-Speicher m
readability Lesbarkeit f, Ablesbarkeit f
readable [ab]lesbar
readableness s. readability
readaptation Readaptation f
reader 1. Leser m; Lesegerät n; 2. Eingabeprogramm n
~-**printer** Lese-Kopiergerät n
reading beam Lesestrahl m
~ **device** Lesegerät n
~ **distance** Leseabstand m
~ **from memory** Speicherlesen n, Speicherabfrage n, sekundäres Erkennen n
~ **glass** Leseglas n
~ **glasses** Lesebrille f
~ **head** Lesekopf m
~ **lamp** Leselampe f
~ **speed** Lesegeschwindigkeit f
~ **telescope** Ablesefernrohr n
readjust/to nachjustieren
readout 1. Auslesen n, Auslesung f *(z.B. von Bilddaten)*; 2. Anzeige f, Kontrollanzeige f *(s.a. display)*
~ **amplifier** Ausleseverstärker m
~ **bandwidth** Auslesebandbreite f
~ **beam** Auslesestrahl m
~ **CCD** Auslese-CCD f
~ **circuitry** Ausleseelektronik f
~ **device** Auslesevorrichtung f; Anzeigegerät n *(s.a. display device)*
~ **direction** Ausleserichtung f
~ **electrode** Ausleseelektrode f
~ **electronics** Ausleseelektronik f
~ **error** Anzeigefehler m
~ **gradient** Lesegradient m, Auslesegradient m; Frequenz[codier]gradient m *(Magnetresonanzbildgebung)*
~ **line** Auslesezeile f
~ **mode** Auslesemodus m
~ **multiplexer** Auslesemultiplexer m
~ **noise** Ausleserauschen n
~ **period (phase)** Auslesephase f
~ **process** Auslesevorgang m
~ **pulse** Ausleseimpuls m
~ **rate** Auslesefrequenz f; Auslesegeschwindigkeit f
~ **[shift] register** Ausleseregister n
~ **speed** Auslesegeschwindigkeit f
~ **time** Auslesezeit f
~ **value** Auslesewert m
ready for [the] press druckfertig
~ **for exposure** aufnahmebereit *(Kamera)*
~-**light contact** Bereitschaftslampenkontakt m
~-**made frame** Passepartout n
~ **to record** aufnahmebereit
~-**to-record mode** Aufnahmemodus m, Aufzeichnungsmodus m
readylight Bereitschaftslampe f

~ **indication** Blitzbereitschaftsanzeige f, Blitzkontrollanzeige f
real antenna reale Antenne f *(Radar)*
~ **aperture (beam) radar** Radar n mit realer Apertur (Antennenapertur)
~ **camera** Realkamera f
~ **color** 1. Echtfarbe f, originalgetreue (reale) Farbe f; 2. s. high color
~ **edge** reale (echte) Kante f *(Computergrafik)*
~ **holographic image** konjugiertes Hologramm f
~ **image** reelles (reales) Bild n, wahres Bild n *(Optik)*
~-**image optical [view]finder** optischer Echtbildsucher m
~-**image viewfinder** Echtbildsucher m, Realbildsucher m
~-**image zoom [view]finder** Echtbildzoomsucher m
~ **imagery** reales Bildmaterial n
~ **intermediate image** reelles Zwischenbild n
~ **location** 1. Originaldrehort m, Originalschauplatz m *(Filmarbeit)*; 2. s. ~ setting
~ **scene** Realszene f
~ **setting** Realdekoration f *(s.a. ~ location1.)*
~ **space** realer Raum m
~ **time** Echtzeit f, Realzeit f
~-**time access** Echtzeitzugriff m
~-**time animation** Echtzeitanimation f
~-**time camera** Echtzeitkamera f
~-**time capture** Echtzeitaufnahme f
~-**time computer** Echtzeitcomputer m
~-**time conferencing** Echtzeit[tele]konferenz f
~-**time digitization** Echtzeitdigitalisierung f
~-**time disparity estimator** Echtzeit-Disparitätsschätzer m
~-**time display** s. ~ rendering
~-**time encoding** Echtzeitcodierung f
~-**time gray-scale image** Echtzeit-Grauwertbild n
~-**time holography** Echtzeitholografie f, Sofortbildholografie f
~-**time image** Echtzeitbild n
~-**time image coding (compression)** Echtzeit-Bildcodierung f
~-**time image processing system** Echtzeit-Bildverarbeitungssystem n
~-**time imager** Echtzeitbildgeber m
~-**time imaging** Echtzeit-Bilddarstellung f
~-**time medium** Echtzeitmedium n
~-**time method** Echtzeittechnik f *(holografische Interferometrie)*
~-**time microscopy** Echtzeitmikroskopie f
~-**time mode** Echtzeitmodus m
~-**time motion segmentation** Echtzeit-Bewegungssegmentierung f
~-**time motion tracking** Echtzeit-Bewegungsverfolgung f
~-**time on-site video** Live-Fernsehen n

~-**time operating system** Echtzeit-Betriebssystem n
~-**time photogrammetry** Echtzeitfotogrammetrie f
~-**time playback** Echtzeitwiedergabe f *(Video)*
~-**time processing** Echtzeitverarbeitung f
~-**time processing capability** Echtzeitfähigkeit f *(z.B. von Bildverarbeitungssystemen)*
~-**time radiography** Echtzeitradiografie f
~-**time readout** Echtzeitauslesung f
~-**time recording** Echtzeitaufnahme f
~-**time rendering (rendition)** [computergrafische] Echtzeit[bild]darstellung f, Rendering n in Echtzeit
~-**time scanner** Echtzeitscanner m *(Sonografie)*
~-**time sensor** Echtzeitsensor m
~-**time shutter release** Echtzeitauslösung f
~-**time simulation** Echtzeitsimulation f
~-**time spectrum analyzer** Echtzeit-Spektralanalysator m
~-**time speed** Echtzeitgeschwindigkeit f
~-**time system** Echtzeitsystem n
~-**time tomographic** echtzeittomografisch
~-**time tomographic image** Echtzeittomogramm n
~-**time transform coding** Echtzeit-Transformationscodierung f
~-**time transmission** Echtzeitübertragung f
~-**time ultrasonic scanner** Echtzeit-Ultraschallgerät n
~-**time video** Echtzeitvideo n; Echtzeitfernsehen n
~-**time video signal processor** Echtzeit-Videosignalprozessor m
~-**time viewing** Echtzeitbetrachtung f
~-**time visualization** Echtzeitvisualisierung f
~-**world camera** Realkamera f
~-**world image** natürliches Bild n
~-**world scene (video sequence)** Realweltszene f, Realweltbildfolge f
realistic image realistisches Bild n
realized edge begrenzende Kante f
realm Bereich m, Domäne f
ream Ries n *(Papiermaß)*
rear component (element) Hinterglied n *(Objektiv)*
~-**curtain synchronization** Synchronisation f auf den zweiten Verschlussvorhang
~ **focal length** Bildbrennweite f, bildseitige (hintere) Brennweite f
~ **focal plane** bildseitige (hintere) Brennebene f
~ **focal point** bildseitiger Brennpunkt m, Bildbrennpunkt m
~ **focusing** Hintergliedfokussierung f
~ **lens cap** Objektivrückdeckel m
~-**lit screen** hinterleuchtete Bildwand f
~ **member** Hinterglied n *(Objektiv)*

~ **nodal plane** s. ~ principal plane
~ **nodal point** bildseitiger (hinterer) Knotenpunkt m
~ **principal plane** Ausgangshauptebene f, bildseitige Hauptebene f *(dicke Linse)*
~ **principal point** Bildhauptpunkt m, bildseitiger Hauptpunkt m
~-**project/to** [zu]rückprojizieren
~ **projection** Rückprojektion f, Durchprojektion f
~ **projection camera** Rückprojektionskamera f
~ **projection display** Rückprojektionsschirm m
~ **projection microfilm reader** Durchlicht-Mikrofilmlesegerät n
~ **projection process** Rückprojektionsverfahren n
~ **projection screen** Rückprojektionsleinwand f, Durchlichtwand f
~ **projection table** Rückprojektionstisch m
~ **projection unit** Rückprojektionsanlage f
~ **projection video wall** Rückprojektionsvideowand f
~ **projection viewing screen** Rückprojektionsschirm m
~ **projector** Rückprojektor m, Rückprojektionsgerät n
~ **screen lens** Rückprojektionsobjektiv n
~ **screen process** Rückprojektionsverfahren n
~ **screen projection** Rückprojektion f, Durchprojektion f
~ **shutter** Hinterlinsenverschluss m
~ **standard** Rückstandarte f, Filmstandarte f, Bildrückteil n, Kamerarückteil n, Filmrückwand f *(Fachkamera)*
~ **view** Rückansicht f
~ **view camera** Rückfahrkamera f
rebroadcast/to wiederausstrahlen, erneut senden
rebroadcast Wiederholungssendung f, Wiederausstrahlung f
receivability Empfangbarkeit f
receivable empfangbar
receive/to empfangen *(z.B. Signale)*
received image Empfangsbild n
~ **signal** Empfangssignal n
receiver Empfänger m; Empfangsgerät n; Rezeptor m *(s.a. receptor)*
~ **amplifier** Empfangsverstärker m
~ **bandwidth** Empfängerbandbreite f
~ **circuit noise** Empfängerrauschen n
~ **coil** Empfängerspule f *(Magnetresonanzbildgebung)*
~ **sensitivity** Empfängerempfindlichkeit f
~ **side** Empfangsseite f
receiving amplifier Empfangsverstärker m
~ **antenna** Empfangsantenne f, empfangende Antenne f
~ **channel** Empfangskanal m
~ **converter** Empfangskonverter m
~ **dish** Satellitenschüssel f, Parabol[empfangs]antenne f
~ **end** Empfangsseite f
~ **frequency** Empfangsfrequenz f
~ **layer** Empfangsschicht f, Bildempfangsschicht f
~-**path side lobe suppression** Nebenkeulenunterdrückung f auf dem Empfangsweg *(Radar)*
~ **set** Empfangsgerät n
~ **station** Empfangsstation f
recenter/to nachzentrieren
reception Empfang m
receptive field rezeptives Feld n *(der Netzhaut)*
receptor 1. Rezeptor m, Aufnehmer m; Empfänger m *(s.a. light receptor)*; 2. Sinnesorgan n
~ **layer** 1. Rezeptorschicht f; Bildempfangsschicht f *(Sofortbildfotografie)*
~ **pigment** Rezeptorpigment n
~ **signal** Rezeptorsignal n
recess printing Tiefdruck m
recharge unit [externes] Ladegerät n
rechargeable battery wiederaufladbare Batterie f
reciprocal antenna reziproke Antenne f *(Radar)*
~ **lattice** reziprokes Gitter n *(Kristallografie)*
~-**lattice point** Relpunkt m
~-**lattice rod** Relstab m
~ **relative dispersion** Abbe-Zahl f *(Optik)*
~ **space** reziproker Raum m
reciprocity Reziprozität f
~ **behavior** Reziprozitätsverhalten n
~ **correction** Reziprozitätskorrektur f
~ **effect** s. ~ law failure
~ **law** Reziprozitätsgesetz n [nach Bunsen und Roscoe], Bunsen-Roscoesches Gesetz n, Reziprozitätsregel f
~ **law failure** Reziprozitätsfehler m, Schwarzschild-Verhalten n, Reziprozitätseffekt m
recirculating pump Umwälzpumpe f *(z.B. einer Entwicklungsmaschine)*
reclassification Reklassifikation f, Reklassifizierung f
reclassify/to reklassifizieren
reclocking Taktrückgewinnung f
recode/to nachcodieren
recognition Erkennung f, Erkennen n
~ **accuracy** Erkennungsgenauigkeit f
~ **algorithm** Erkennungsalgorithmus m
~ **capability** Erkennungsvermögen n
~ **error** Erkennungsfehler m
~ **performance** Erkennungsleistung f
~ **process** Erkennungsvorgang m
~ **rate** Erkennungsrate f
~ **speed** Erkennungsgeschwindigkeit f
~ **task** Erkennungsaufgabe f
~ **technique** Erkennungsverfahren n
recognizability Erkennbarkeit f; Identifizierbarkeit f

recognizable erkennbar; identifizierbar
recognize/to erkennen
recognized color wahrgenommene Farbe *f*
recolor/to umfärben
recombination Rekombination *f*
~ **radiation** Rekombinationsstrahlung *f* *(Leuchtdiode)*
recombine/to rekombinieren
recompress/to rekomprimieren *(z.B. Bilddaten)*
recompression Rekompression *f*, Rekomprimierung *f*, Neukomprimierung *f*
recondensation Rekondensation *f* *(z.B. von Druckfarbe)*
reconnaissance Aufklärung *f*
~ **aircraft** Aufklärungsflugzeug *n*
~ **camera** Aufklärungskamera *f*
~ **image** Aufklärungsbild *n*
~ **photo[graph]** Aufklärungsfoto *n*
~ **photography** Aufklärungsfotografie *f*
~ **satellite** Aufklärungssatellit *m*
reconstruct/to rekonstruieren
reconstructed image Rekonstruktionsbild *n*, rekonstruiertes Bild *n*
~ **signal** rekonstruiertes Signal *n*
~ **wave** Rekonstruktionswelle *f*
reconstruction Rekonstruktion *f* *(z.B. von Bilddaten)*
~ **accuracy** Rekonstruktionsgenauigkeit *f*
~ **algorithm** Rekonstruktionsalgorithmus *m*
~ **color** Rekonstruktionsfarbe *f* *(Laser)*
~ **error** Rekonstruktionsfehler *m*
~ **fidelity** Rekonstruktionsgenauigkeit *f*
~ **filter** Rekonstruktionsfilter *n*
~ **filter bank** Rekonstruktionsfilterbank *f*
~ **grid** Rekonstruktionsmatrix *f*
~ **level** *s.* quantization level
~ **matrix** Rekonstruktionsmatrix *f*
~ **operator** Rekonstruktionsfilter *n*
~ **performance** Rekonstruktionsleistung *f*
~ **result** Rekonstruktionsergebnis *n*
~ **time** Rekonstruktionszeit *f*
reconstructive algorithm Rekonstruktionsalgorithmus *m*
reconversion Rückwandlung *f*
recopy/to umkopieren
record/to aufnehmen; aufzeichnen
record 1. Aufnahme *f*; Aufzeichnung *f* *(s.a. unter recording)*; 2. Registrat *n*, Verbund *m* *(Farbfotografie)*; 3. Schallplatte *f*; 4. Datensatz *m*
~ **button** Aufnahmetaste *f*
~ **circuit** *s.* ~ line
~ **function** Aufnahmefunktion *f*
~-**head width** Aufnahmekopfbreite *f*
~ **in point** Aufnahmestart *m* *(Bandaufnahme)*
~ **line** Meldeleitung *f* *(Fernsehübertragung)*
~ **machine** *s.* recorder
~ **performance** Aufnahmeleistung *f*
~ **photography** Aufnahmefotografie *f*
~-**playback head** Schreib-Lese-Kopf *m* *(Computer)*
~ **signal** Aufzeichnungssignal *n*
~ **speed** Aufzeichnungsgeschwindigkeit *f*
~ **start** Aufnahmestart *m* *(Bandaufnahme)*
~ **stop** Aufnahmestopp *m*
recordable 1. aufnehmbar, aufzeichenbar *(z.B. Signale)*; 2. beschreibbar, bespielbar *(Datenträger)*
~ **compact disc** beschreibbare CD *f*
~ **DVD** beschreibbare DVD *f*
recorded material Aufzeichnungsmaterial *n*, Aufnahmematerial *n*
~ **track** Aufzeichnungsspur *f*
~ **videotape** bespieltes Videoband *n*
recorder 1. Recorder *m*, Aufnahmegerät *n*, Aufzeichnungsgerät *n*; 2. Filmrecorder *m*, Filmbelichter *m*, Belichter *m*
~ **noise** Recorderrauschen *n*
recording Aufnahme *f*; Aufzeichnung *f*
~ **amplifier** Aufzeichnungsverstärker *m*
~ **angle of view** Aufnahmewinkel *m*
~ **artifact** Aufzeichnungsstörung *f*
~ **camera** Aufnahmekamera *f*, Bildaufnahmekamera *f*
~ **capability** Aufnahmevermögen *n*
~ **densitometer** Densograf *m*
~ **density** Aufzeichnungsdichte *f*
~ **device** Aufnahmegerät *n*, Aufzeichnungsgerät *n*, Recorder *m*
~ **electronics** Aufnahmeelektronik *f*
~ **engineer** Tontechniker *m*
~ **equipment** Aufnahmeapparatur *f*
~ **exposure** Aufnahmebelichtung *f*
~ **film** Aufnahmefilm *m*, Kameraoriginal *n*, Unikat *n*
~ **format** Aufnahmeformat *n*, Aufzeichnungsformat *n*
~ **galvanometer** registrierendes (schreibendes) Galvanometer *n*
~ **head** Aufnahmekopf *m*
~ **image size** Aufnahmebildgröße *f*
~ **key** Aufnahmetaste *f*
~ **layer** Aufnahmeschicht *f*
~ **level indication** Aussteuerungsanzeige *f*
~ **machine** Tonaufnahmegerät *n*
~ **material** Aufzeichnungsmaterial *n*, Aufnahmematerial *n*
~ **medium** Aufzeichnungsmedium *m*, Aufnahmemedium *n*
~ **mode** Aufnahmemodus *m*, Aufzeichnungsmodus *m*
~ **paper** [fotografisches] Registrierpapier *n*
~ **pause** Aufzeichnungspause *f* *(Video)*
~ **process** Aufnahmevorgang *m*
~ **quality** Aufnahmequalität *f*, Aufzeichnungsqualität *f*
~ **rate** Aufnahmefrequenz *f*
~ **sensitivity** Aufnahmeempfindlichkeit *f*
~ **spectrophotometer** registrierendes Spektralfotometer *n*
~ **speed** Aufnahmegeschwindigkeit *f*
~ **standard** Aufzeichnungsnorm *f*

recording

~ **studio** Aufnahmestudio n; Synchronstudio n, Synchronatelier n
~ **system** Aufnahmesystem n
~ **tape** Aufnahmeband n
~ **technique** Aufnahmeverfahren n, Aufzeichnungsverfahren n
~ **technology** Aufnahmetechnik f
~ **time** Aufnahmezeit f; Aufnahmedauer f
~ **track** Aufzeichnungsspur f
~ **wavelength** Aufnahmewellenlänge f (Holografie)
recordist Aufnahmetechniker m
recovering silver from used fixer solution Fixierbadentsilberung f
recovery point Wiedervereinigungspunkt m, Verschmelzungspunkt m, Fusionspunkt m (Sehen)
~ **time** Diawechselzeit f
recrystallization Rekristallisation f; Umkristallisation f, Umkristallisierung f
rectangle function s. rectangular impulse function
rectangular rechtwinklig; rechteckig
~ **aperture** rechteck[förm]ige Apertur (Blende) f, Rechteckblende f, Rechteckapertur f
~ **coordinate** rechtwinklige Koordinate f
~ **coordinate system** rechtwinkliges Koordinatensystem n
~ **grid** 1. Rechteckgitter n; 2. s. ~ raster
~ **impulse function** Rechteckfunktion f, rechteckförmige Impulsfunktion f (digitale Signalverarbeitung)
~ **lattice** s. ~ grid
~ **pixel** rechteckiges (nichtquadratisches) Pixel n
~ **pulse** Rechteck[im]puls m
~ **raster** rechteck[förm]iger Abtastraster (Raster) m, Rechteckraster m(n)
~ **sampling** rechteckförmige Abtastung f
~ **signal** Rechtecksignal n
~ **wave** Rechteckwelle f
rectangularity Rechtwinkligkeit f
rectification Entzerrung f, Rektifizierung f
~ **photogrammetry** Entzerrungsfotogrammetrie f
rectifier 1. Entzerrungsgerät n; 2. Gleichrichter m
rectify/to entzerren, rektifizieren
rectilinear rektilinear; rechtwinklig; geradlinig
~ **coordinate** rechtwinklige Koordinate f
~ **grid** rechtwinkliges Gitter n (Datenstruktur)
~ **polygon** orthogonales Polygon n
~ **scanner** rektilinearer Scanner m
recto [page] Rekto n; Blattvorderseite f, Vorderseite f, ungerade Seite f (Layout)
recursion Rekursion f
~ **depth** Rekursionstiefe f
recursive convolution rekursive Faltung f
~ **decomposition** rekursive Zerlegung f
~ **digital filter** s. ~ filter
~ **estimation** rekursive Schätzung f

~ **filter** rekursives Filter n, Rekursivfilter n
~ **filter structure** rekursive Filterstruktur f
~ **filtering** rekursive Filterung f
~ **ray tracing** rekursive Strahlverfolgung f
recut/to nachschneiden (z.B. Filmmaterial)
recycle time Aufladezeit f (Akkumulator)
recycled paper Recyclingpapier n
red Rot n (Grundfarbe)
~ **and bluish green confusion** s. ~ blindness
~ **beam** Rotstrahl m (Katodenstrahlröhre)
~ **bias** Rotstich m
~-**blind** rotblind
~ **blindness** Rotblindheit f, Protanstörung f (Farbsinnstörung)
~ **cast** Rotstich m
~ **channel** Rotkanal m
~-**eye effect** Rote-Augen-Effekt m (Blitzfotografie)
~-**eye pen** Antirotaugenstift m
~-**eye reduction** Rote-Augen-Reduktion f, Rote-Augen-Korrektur f
~-**eye reduction flash** Vorblitz m; Vorblitzfunktion f
~-**eye remover** Antirotaugenstift m
~ **filter** Rotfilter n
~ **filter layer** Rotfilterschicht f
~-**green blindness** Rotgrünblindheit f, Grünblindheit f, Deuteranopie f, Daltonismus m (Farbsinnstörung)
~-**green-blue ...** s. RGB
~-**green goggles** Rotgrünbrille f, Farb[filter]brille f; Anaglyphenbrille f
~-**insensitive** rotunempfindlich
~ **lamp** Rotlampe f
~ **light** Rotlicht n
~ **light laser** roter Laser m
~ **light record** Rotteilbild n, Rotauszug m (Farbfotografie)
~ **light sensitivity** Rotempfindlichkeit f (von Filmmaterial)
~ **light sensitivity** Rotlichtempfindlichkeit f
~-**minus-luma signal** Farbdifferenzsignal n R-Y (Video)
~ **prussiate of potash** rotes Blutlaugensalz n, Kaliumferricyanid n (Bleichmittel)
~ **record** s. ~ light record
~ **sable brush** Rotmarderhaarpinsel m (Retuschierwerkzeug)
~ **safety window** Bildnummernfenster n (Kamera)
~-**sensitive** rotempfindlich
~-**sensitive emulsion** rotempfindliche Emulsion f
~-**sensitive layer** rotempfindliche Schicht f (Blaugrünschicht)
~ **signal** Rotsignal n (Video)
~ **speed** s. ~ light sensitivity
redevelop/to nachentwickeln; umentwickeln
redeveloper Zweitentwickler m
redevelopment Nachentwicklung f; Wiederentwicklung f
redigitze/to redigitalisieren

redirect/to umlenken *(z.B. Strahlen)*
redisplay/to [erneut] wiedergeben
redox potential Redoxpotential *n*
~ **reaction** Redoxprozess *m*, Redoxreaktion *f*, Redoxvorgang *m*
redraw/to umzeichnen
reduce/to reduzieren; verkleinern; abschwächen
reduce photographically/to fotografisch verkleinern
reduced silver reduziertes Silber *n*
reducer Abschwächer *m (Fotochemikalie)*
reducing agent Reduktionsmittel *n*
~ **glass** Verkleinerungsglas *n*
reductant Reduktionsmittel *n*
reduction Reduktion *f*, Reduzierung *f*; Verkleinerung *f*; Abschwächung *f*, Abschwächen *n (Fotoverarbeitung)*
~ **camera** Reduktionskamera *f*
~ **in contrast** Kontrastverminderung *f*, Kontrastverringerung *f*
~ **lens** Verkleinerungsobjektiv *n*; Verkleinerungsglas *n*
~**-oxidation property** Redoxeigenschaft *f*
~ **print** Verkleinerungskopie *f*
~ **printer** Verkleinerungskopiermaschine *f*
~ **printing** Verkleinerungskopieren *n*, formatverkleinernde Umkopierung *f*
~ **process** Reduktionsvorgang *m*
~ **ratio** Verkleinerungsverhältnis *n*, Verkleinerungsfaktor *n*
~ **sensitization** Antisensibilisierung *f*
redundancy Redundanz *f*
~**-free** redundanzfrei
~ **reduction** Redundanzreduktion *f*, Redundanzreduzierung *f*
~ **removal** Redundanzbeseitigung *f*
redundant redundant
~ **code** redundanter Code *m*
~ **data** redundante Daten *pl*
~ **image** redundantes Bild *n*
~ **information** redundante Information *f*
Reed-Solomon [block] code Reed-Solomon-Blockcode *m*, Reed-Solomon-Code *m (digitales Fernsehen)*
~**-Solomon [en]coding** Reed-Solomon-Codierung *f*
reedit/to umschneiden, nachschneiden, nachbearbeiten *(z.B. Film- oder Videomaterial)*
reediting Umschnitt *m*
reel Spiraleinsatz *m*, Filmspirale *f*, Aufwickeldorn *m*, Spuleneinsatz *m (Entwicklungsdose)*
~ **case** Filmvorratsraum *m*; Filmdose *f*, Filmbüchse *f*
~ **change mark** Ausblendzeichen *n*; Überblendzeichen *n*; Abfahrzeichen *n (Filmvorführung)*
~ **container** Spulendose *f*
~**-fed press** Rollendruckmaschine *f*
~**-to-reel tape recorder** Spulentonbandgerät *n*
~**-to-reel video machine** Spulenvideobandgerät *n*
reemit/to reemittieren
reencode/to nachcodieren
reencoding Nachcodierung *f*
reenlarge/to nachvergrößern; rückvergrößern
reenlargement Nachvergrößerung *f*, Rückvergrößerung *f*, Wiedervergrößerung *f*
reexpose/to nachbelichten
reexposure Nachbelichtung *f*
reference area Bezugsfläche *f*
~ **beam** Referenzstrahl *m*, Bezugsstrahl *m*, Referenzwelle *f (Holografie)*
~ **black** Schwarzbezugswert *m*, Studio-Referenzsignal *n*, Black Burst *m (Video)*
~ **color** Bezugsfarbe *f*
~ **color model** Referenz-Farbmodell *n*
~ **coordinate system** Bezugskoordinatensystem *n*
~ **direction** Bezugsrichtung *f*
~ **edge** Bezugskante *f*
~ **flat** Referenzplatte *f (Optik)*
~ **frame** Referenzbild *n*, Bezugsbild *n*; Schlüsselbild *n*, Basisbild *n (Videocodierung)*
~ **frequency** Bezugsfrequenz *f*
~ **illuminant** Bezugslichtart *f*
~ **image** Bezugsbild *n*, Referenzbild *n*
~ **mark** 1. Rahmenmarke *f*, Bildrahmenmarke *f (Fotogrammetrie)*; 2. Hinweiszeichen *n*, Verweis *m*; Anmerkungszeichen *n*
~ **matrix** Referenzmatrix *f*
~ **model** Referenzmodell *n*
~ **monitor** Referenzmonitor *m*
~ **object** Bezugsobjekt *n*
~ **orientation** Bezugs[aus]richtung *f*
~ **oscillator** Referenzoszillator *m (Fernsehtechnik)*
~ **pattern** Vergleichsmuster *n*, Referenzmuster *n*
~ **phase** Bezugsphase *f*
~ **picture** Bezugsbild *n*, Referenzbild *n*
~ **pixel** Bezugspixel *n*, Referenzpixel *n (differentielle Bildkompression)*
~ **plane** Bezugsebene *f*
~ **point** Bezugspunkt *m*, Referenzpunkt *m*
~ **print** Abnahmekopie *f*, Korrekturkopie *f (Filmproduktion)*
~ **radar** Referenzradar *n*
~ **ray** Bezugsstrahl *m*
~ **signal** Bezugssignal *n*, Referenzsignal *n*
~ **sphere** Bezugskugel *f (Wellenoptik)*
~ **system** Bezugssystem *n*
~ **tape** Referenzleerband *n*, Bezugsband *n (Video)*
~ **track** Bezugsspur *f*
~ **vector** Referenzvektor *m*
~ **wave** Referenzwelle *f*, Referenzstrahl *m*, Vergleichswelle *f (Holografie)*

reference 326

~ **wave front** Bezugswellenfront *f (z.B. eines Interferometers)*
~ **white [color]** Bezugsweiß *n*, Normweiß *n*, Normweißwert *m*, Weißnormal *n*
refillable auffüllbar *(z.B. Druckertinte)*
refix/to nachfixieren
reflect/to reflektieren
reflect into/to einspiegeln
reflectance Reflexionsgrad *m*, Remission *f*, Reflektivität *f*, Rückstrahlungsgrad *m*, Rückstrahl[ungs]vermögen *n*, Albedo *f*, Reflexionsvermögen *n*
~ **curve** Remissionskurve *f*
~ **factor** *s.* reflectance
~ **glare reduction** Reflexminderung *f*
~ **model** Reflexionsmodell *n (Bildanalyse, Computergrafik)*
~ **spectrometer** Reflexionsspektrometer *n*
~ **spectroscopy** Reflexionsspektroskopie *f*
~ **standard** Weißstandard *m*
reflected amplitude reflektierte Amplitude *f*
~ **exposure** Reflexbelichtung *f*
~ **glare** indirekte Blendung *f*, Reflexblendung *f*
~ **image** reflektiertes Bild *n*, Reflex[ions]bild *n*
~ **light** reflektiertes Licht *n*, Reflex[ions]licht *n*; Auflicht *n*
~-**light fluorescence microscopy** Auflicht-Fluoreszenzmikroskopie *f*
~-**light illumination** Auflichtbeleuchtung *f*
~-**light image** Auflichtbild *n*
~-**light meter** Leuchtdichtemesser *m*, Leuchtdichtemessgerät *n*
~-**light metering** Objektmessung *f*
~-**light microscope** Auflichtmikroskop *n*
~-**light microscopy** Auflichtmikroskopie *f*
~-**light photographic exposure meter** *s.* ~ meter
~ **luminance** remittierte Leuchtdichte *f*
~ **ray** reflektierter Strahl *m*, Reflexionsstrahl *m*
reflecting reflektierend *(s.a. unter reflection)*
~ **finder** Spiegelreflexsucher *m*
~ **lens** Spiegel[linsen]objektiv *n*, Spiegellinse *f*, katadioptrisches Objektiv (System) *n*
~ **light source** Fremdstrahler *m*
~ **microscope** Auflichtmikroskop *n*, Spiegelmikroskop *n*
~ **mirror** Umlenkspiegel *m*
~ **power** Reflexionsvermögen *n*, Reflexionsfähigkeit *f (s.a. reflectivity)*
~ **prism** Reflexionsprisma *n*, Rücksichtprisma *n*; Umlenkprisma *n*
~ **screen** 1. reflektierende Bildwand *f*, Reflektorwand *f*, Reflexwand *f*; 2. Aufhellschirm *m*, Aufheller *m (s.a. reflector board)*
~ **telescope** Spiegelteleskop *n*, Spiegelfernrohr *n*
~ **telescope optics** Spiegelteleskopoptik *f*

~ **viewfinder** Spiegelreflexsucher *m*
reflection 1. Reflexion *f*; 2. *s.* ~ image
~ **angle** Reflexionswinkel *m*; Ausfallswinkel *m*, Austrittswinkel *m*
~ **beam** reflektierter Strahl *m*, Reflexionsstrahl *m*
~ **coefficient** Reflexionskoeffizient *m (s.a. reflectance)*
~ **color print** Aufsicht-Farbkopie *f*
~ **copy** *s.* reflective copy
~ **curve** Reflexionskurve *f*
~ **densitometer** Auflichtdensitometer *n*, Aufsichtdensitometer *n*, Reflexionsdensitometer *n*
~ **densitometry** Auflichtdensitometrie *f*, Reflexionsdensitometrie *f*
~ **density** Reflexionsdichte *f*
~ **diffraction grating** Reflexions[beugungs]gitter *n*
~-**diminishing** reflex[ions]mindernd
~ **display material** Aufsichtsmaterial *n*
~ **echelon** Reflexionsstufengitter *n*
~ **electron microscopy** Reflexionselektronenmikroskopie *f*
~ **factor** 1. Reflexionsfaktor *m*, Remissionsfaktor *m*, Remissionsgrad *m (bei diffuser Reflexion)*; 2. *s.* reflectance
~ **filter** Reflexionsfilter *n*
~ **grating** Reflexions[beugungs]gitter *n*
~ **halation** Reflexionslichthof *m*
~ **holographic** reflexionsholografisch
~ **image** Reflex[ions]bild *n*, reflektiertes Bild *n*
~ **law** Reflexionsgesetz *n*, Spiegelgesetz *n*
~ **loss** Reflexionsverlust *m*
~ **matrix** Reflexionsmatrix *f*
~ **model** *s.* reflectance model
~ **polarizer** Reflexionspolarisator *m*
~ **print** Aufsichtsbild *n*, Aufsichtkopie *f*
~ **seismology** Reflexionsseismik *f*
~ **spectrophotometric** reflexionsspektrofotometrisch
~ **spectrum** Reflexionsspektrum *n*
~-**type electron microscope** Reflexionselektronenmikroskop *n*
~-**type hologram** Reflexionshologramm *n*
~ **vector** Reflexionsvektor *m*
reflective ability Reflexionsfähigkeit *f*, Reflexionsvermögen *n*
~ **copy** Aufsichtsvorlage *f*, Auflichtvorlage *f*, Epivorlage *f*; Aufsichtsbild *n*
~ **layer** Reflexionsschicht *f*, reflektierende Schicht *f (z.B. einer Röntgenverstärkerfolie)*
~ **loss** Reflexionsverlust *m*
~ **material** Aufsichtsvorlage *f*, Auflichtvorlage *f*, Epivorlage *f*
~ **modeling** symmetrische Modellierung *f*
~ **power** *s.* reflectivity
~ **print** *s.* reflection print
~ **projection** Spiegelprojektion *f*
~ **substratum layer** *s.* ~ layer
~ **surface** Reflexionsfläche *f*
reflectivity *s.* reflectance

reflectography Reflektografie f
reflectometer Reflektometer n
reflector 1. Reflektor m; 2. Spiegelteleskop n, Spiegelfernrohr n
~ **board** Reflektorwand f, Reflex[ions]wand f, Reflextafel f
~ **floodlight** Flutlichtscheinwerfer m, Fluter m
~ **lamp** Reflektorlampe f
~ **prism** Reflexionsprisma n, Rücksichtprisma n; Umlenkprisma n
~**-type camera** Spiegelkamera f
reflex 1. Reflex m; 2. Reflex[ions]bild n, reflektiertes Bild n, Spiegelbild n
~ **autocollimator** Autokollimator m, Reflexautokollimator m
~ **camera** Spiegelreflexkamera f
~ **copy** s. 1. reflective copy; 2. reflection print
~ **exposure** Reflexbelichtung f
~ **finder** s. ~ viewfinder
~ **mirror** Ablenkspiegel m, Schwingspiegel m, Rückschwingspiegel m, Klappspiegel m, Rapidspiegel m (Spiegelreflexkamera)
~ **prism** s. reflector prism
~ **projection** Auf[licht]projektion f, Frontprojektion f (Filmtrickverfahren)
~ **radiography** Reflexradiografie f
~ **viewfinder** Reflexsucher m, Spiegelreflexsucher m
reflexion s. reflection
refocus/to nachfokussieren, die Schärfe nachstellen; umfokussieren; akkommodieren
refocusing Umfokussieren n, Umfokussierung f
reformatting Umformatieren n, Umformatierung f
refract/to brechen
refracted ray gebrochener Strahl m
~ **wave** gebrochene Welle f
refractile s. refractive
refracting edge brechende Kante f
~ **power** [optische] Brechkraft f
~ **prism** brechendes Prisma n
~ **surface** brechende Fläche (Oberfläche) f
~ **telescope** Linsenfernrohr n, Refraktor m
refraction [optische] Brechung f, Strahl[en]brechung f, Refraktion f
~ **angle** Refraktionswinkel m, Brechungswinkel m
~ **error** Brechungsfehler m
~ **invariant** Brechungsinvariante f
~ **law** Snell[ius]sches Brechungsgesetz n
refractive lichtbrechend, [foto]refraktiv, brechkraftändernd, dioptrisch (s.a. unter refracting)
~ **condition** Refraktionszustand m (des Auges)
~ **error** Brechungsfehler m
~ **index** Brechzahl f, Brechungsindex m, Brechwert m, Lichtbrechungsindex m

~ **index determination** Brechzahlbestimmung f
~ **index difference** Brechzahldifferenz f
~ **index distribution** Brechzahlverteilung f, Brechzahlprofil n
~ **index gradient** Brechzahlgradient m
~ **index ratio** Brechungsverhältnis n
~ **medium** brechendes Medium n
~ **optical** linsenoptisch
~ **optics** refraktive Optik f, Linsenoptik f
~ **power** [optische] Brechkraft f
~ **state** Refraktionszustand m (des Auges)
refractivity Lichtbrechungsvermögen n
refractometer Refraktometer n, Brechzahlmesser m
refractometric refraktometrisch
refractometry Refraktometrie f, Brechzahlmessung f
refractor Refraktor m, Linsenfernrohr n
reframing Formatumschaltung f
refresh buffer s. ~ memory
~ **cycle** Bildschirmzyklus m
~ **memory** Auffrischspeicher m, Bildpuffer[speicher] m, Bildwiederholspeicher m, Rasterbildspeicher m
~ **rate** Bildelementwiederholfrequenz f, Wiederholfrequenz f (Video)
refringence Lichtbrechung f
regenerate/to regenerieren
regeneration Regenerierung f
region Region f, Bereich m
~ **adjacency** Regionennachbarschaft f
~ **adjacency graph** Gebietsnachbarschaftsgraph m, Regionennachbarschaftsgraph m
~ **analysis** Bereichsanalyse f
~**-based motion estimation** bereichsbasierte Bewegungsschätzung f
~**-based motion representation** bereichsbasierte Bewegungsdarstellung f
~**-based representation** bereichsbasierte Darstellung f, Regionendarstellung f
~**-based segmentation** bereichsbasierte (bereichsorientierte) Segmentierung f, regionenbasierte (regionenorientierte) Segmentierung f
~ **border (boundary)** Bereichskontur f
~ **characterization** Bereichscharakterisierung f
~ **classification** Regionenklassifikation f
~ **classifier** Bereichsklassifikator m
~ **contour** Bereichskontur f
~ **corner point** Bereichseckpunkt m
~ **correction algorithm** Bereichskorrekturalgorithmus m (Binärbildverarbeitung)
~ **description** Bereichsbeschreibung f
~ **descriptor** Bereichsdeskriptor m
~ **detection** Bereichsdetektion f
~ **encoding** Bereichscodierung f
~ **extraction** Bereichsextraktion f
~ **filling [method]** Bereichsauffüllung f

~ **finding** Bereichsdetektion f
~-**growing method (procedure)** Bereichswachstum[sverfahren] n, Regionenwachstum n, Flächenwachstum n *(Bildsegmentation)*
~ **identification** Regionenidentifikation f
~ **isolation** Bereichsisolierung f
~ **labeling** Gebietsmarkierung f
~ **merging** Bereichsverschmelzung f
~ **model** Bereichsmodell n
~ **of convergence** Konvergenzgebiet n *(Signaltheorie)*
~ **of interest** interessierender Bildbereich (Bildausschnitt) m, interessierender (signifikanter) Bereich m, interessierende Region f, Arbeitsbereich m *(Bildanalyse)*
~-**oriented image segmentation** s. region-based segmentation
~ **point** Bereichspunkt m
~ **primitive** Bereichsprimitiv n
~ **segmentation** Regionensegmentierung f, Gebietszerlegung f *(Bildverarbeitung)*
~ **shape feature** Bereichsmerkmal n
~ **splitting algorithm** Bereichsunterteilungsalgorithmus m

regional contrast regionaler Kontrast m
~ **descriptor** regionaler Deskriptor m

register/to registrieren, ausrichten, justieren

register Register n; Passer m, Bildpasser m *(Drucktechnik)*
~ **accuracy** Passergenauigkeit f
~ **control** Passerkontrolle f
~ **error** Registerfehler m
~ **mark** Pass[er]kreuz n
~ **pin** 1. Passstift m, Registerstift m, Arretierstift m; 2. Justiergreifer m, Sperrgreifer m *(Kinofilmtechnik)*
~ **sheet** Einrichtebogen m *(Druck)*
~ **system** Passsystem n
~ **unit** Bogenanlage f, Bogenanleger m, Anleger m *(Druckmaschine)*

registration 1. Registrierung f, Passung f; Ausrichtung f; [konturengleiche] Überlagerung f, Super[im]position f; 2. Farbdeckung f *(Farbbildröhre)*
~ **accuracy** Registergenauigkeit f
~ **pin** s. register pin

reglet Blindmaterial n, Reglette f *(Typografie)*

regression analysis Regressionsanalyse f

regular astigmatism regelmäßiger Astigmatismus m
~ **data** strukturierte Daten pl
~ **eight mm** Acht-Millimeter-Film m *(Heimkinoformat)*
~ **filter** Wavelet-Filter n, [variables] Wellenformfilter n
~ **graph** regulärer Graph m
~ **grid (mesh)** gleichmäßiges Gitter n *(Datenstruktur)*
~ **polygon** gleichmäßiges (regelmäßiges) Vieleck n, reguläres Polygon n
~ **polyhedron** regelmäßiges Polyeder n, platonischer Körper m

regularization Regularisierung f

regulated brightness source Leuchtdichtenormal n

regulation circuitry Regelschaltkreis m

rehalogenation Rehalogenierung f

rehalogenizing agent Rehalogenierungsmittel n

reignition Wiederzündung f *(z.B. einer Entladungslampe)*

reimage/to widerspiegeln

reimage onto itself/to ineinander abbilden, ineinanderkopieren

reimaging Neubebilderung f *(z.B. einer Kopiertrommel)*

reinitialization Reinitialisierung f

reject films Altfilmmaterial n

rejection band Sperrbereich m *(eines Filters)*

related color bezogene Farbe f

relational relational
~ **database** relationale Datenbank f
~ **descriptor** relationaler Deskriptor m
~ **graph** relationaler Graph m
~ **image description** relationale Bildbeschreibung f
~ **model[l]ing** relationale Modellierung f
~ **object** relationales Objekt n, Relationenobjekt n

relationship of figure to ground Figur-Grund-Verhältnis n *(Wahrnehmungspsychologie)*

relative absorption coefficient relativer Absorptionskoeffizient m
~ **address** relative Adresse f
~ **address coding** relative Adressencodierung f *(Bilddatenkompression)*
~ **aperture** relative Lichtstärke f, Lichtstärkenverhältnis n, Öffnungsverhältnis n, relative Öffnung f, Öffnungszahl f *(Objektiv)*
~ **biological effectiveness** relative biologische Wirksamkeit f *(Röntgendosimetrie)*
~ **brightness** relative Helligkeit f
~ **coding** relative (differentielle) Codierung f, Differenzcodierung f, prädiktive Codierung f, Prädiktionscodierung f
~ **contrast** relativer Kontrast m
~ **distortion** relative Verzeichnung f
~ **hue** gebundene Farbe f
~ **humidity [of the air]** relative Luftfeuchte (Luftfeuchtigkeit) f
~ **intensity noise** relatives Intensitätsrauschen n
~ **irradiance** relative Bestrahlungsstärke f
~ **luminance** relative Leuchtdichte f
~ **luminosity** relative Hellempfindlichkeit f
~ **luminous efficiency** relativer Hellempfindlichkeitsgrad m
~ **neighborhood graph** relativer Nachbarschaftsgraph m

~ **partial dispersion** relative Teildispersion f
~ **quantum efficiency** relativer Quantenwirkungsgrad m
~ **refractive index** Brechungsverhältnis n, relative Brechzahl f
~ **sensitivity** relative Empfindlichkeit f
~ **spectral power** relative spektrale Strahlungsleistung f
~ **spectral power distribution** relative spektrale Energieverteilung f, Strahlungsfunktion f
~ **spectral sensitivity** relative spektrale Empfindlichkeit f
~ **speed** relative Empfindlichkeit f
~ **tape-to-head speed** Aufzeichnungsgeschwindigkeit f, Schreibgeschwindigkeit f, Relativgeschwindigkeit f (Bandmaschine)
~ **vergence** relative Vergenz f (Physiologie des Sehens)
relativistic velocity relativistische Geschwindigkeit f, Betawert m, Beta n (Densitometrie)
relax/to relaxieren
relaxation Relaxation f (Bildverarbeitungsoperation)
~ **algorithm** Relaxationsalgorithmus m
~ **matrix** Relaxationsmatrix f
~ **method** Relaxationsverfahren n
~ **time** Relaxationszeit f
relay 1. Relais n; 2. s. servomotor
~ **broadcasting** Fernabfrage f (Faxbetrieb)
~ **lens** Relaisoptik f
~ **reception** Ballempfang m (Fernsehübertragung)
~ **transmitter** Relaissender m
relayed beam verketteter Strahlengang m
release/to auslösen
release s. ~ print
~ **button** Auslöseknopf m, Auslösetaste f
~ **cable** Fernauslösekabel n
~ **contact** Auslösekontakt m
~ **print** Massenkopie f, Kinokopie f, Vorführkopie f, vorführbereite (vorführfertige) Filmkopie f, Verleihkopie f
~ **priority** Auslösepriorität f, Belichtungsautomatik f mit Zeitvorwahl
relevant relevant
relief displacement Höhenversatz m (Fotogrammetrie)
~ **embossing** Blindprägung f, Farbloseprägung f, Blinddruck m, farblose Prägung f
~ **image** Reliefbild n
~ **map** Reliefkarte f
~ **printing** [direkter] Hochdruck m, Reliefdruck m; Buchdruck m
~ **printing plate** Hochdruckplatte f, Reliefdruckplatte f
~ **printing process** Hochdruckverfahren n
relrod s. reciprocal-lattice rod

remaining tape counter Bandrestanzeige f, Restbandanzeige f
~ **toner** Resttoner m
remanence Remanenz f, remanente Magnetisierung f, Restmagnetisierung f
remap/to umbilden
remapping Umbildung f
Rembrandt lighting Rembrandt-Beleuchtung f
remit/to remittieren
remix/to nachmischen
remjet backing Lichthofschutzschicht f, Antihaloschicht f
remote access Fernzugriff m
~ **camera control** Kamerafernauslösung f; Kamerafernbediensystem n
~ **control** Fernsteuerung f; Fernbedienung f
~ **control accessories** Fernsteuerungszubehör n
~ **control cable** Fernbedienungskabel n
~ **control camera** Roboterkamera f, Kameraroboter m, fernbedienbare (fernsteuerbare) Kamera f, robotergeführte Kamera f
~ **control composing** Fernsatz m
~ **control composing equipment** telegrafische Fernsetzmaschine f
~ **control device (unit)**, ~ **controller** Fernbedienung f
~ **cord** Fernauslöse[r]kabel n; Kabel[fern]auslöser m
~ **data transmission** Datenfernübertragung f
~ **flash unit** Tochterblitz m
~ **operation** Fernbedienung f
~ **printer** Netzwerkdrucker m
~ **proof** Fernproof m (Digitaldruck)
~ **release** Fernauslöser m
~ **release cable** s. ~ cord
~ **sensing camera** Fernerkundungskamera f
~ **sensing data** Fernerkundungsdaten pl
~ **sensing image** Fernerkundungsbild n
~ **sensing multispectral image** Multispektral-Fernerkundungsbild n
~ **sensing multispectral photography** Fernerkundungs-Multispektralfotografie f
~ **sensing satellite** Fernerkundungssatellit m
~ **sensing system** Fernerkundungssystem n
~ **sensing technology** Fernerkundung f, Fernerkennung f, Erdbeobachtung f
~ **surgery** Fernchirurgie f, Telechirurgie f
~ **surveillance** Fernüberwachung f (Video)
~ **terminal** Fernsteuerungsbuchse f
~ **trigger** Fernauslöser m
~ **triggering** Fernauslösung f
~ **video surveillance** Fernüberwachung f
remotely controllable fernsteuerbar
~ **controlled robot** ferngesteuerter Roboter m

remotely

~ **sensed** ... s. remote sensing ...
removable data carrier Wechseldatenträger m
~ **storage [device]** Wechselspeicher m
removal of artifacts Artefaktbeseitigung f
removeable hard disk [storage device] Wechsel[fest]platte f, Mobilfestplatte f, herausnehmbare Festplatte f
~ **lens** Wechselobjektiv n, [aus]wechselbares Objektiv n, Wechseloptik f
render/to [erneut] wiedergeben; generieren, rendern, computergrafisch darstellen; bildlich darstellen
rendering 1. Wiedergabe f (bes. von Farben); 2. fotorealistische Bilderzeugung (Visualisierung) f, Bildberechnung f, Bildsynthese f, Rendering n, Rendern n, computergrafische Simulation f
~ **algorithm** Rendering-Algorithmus m
~ **capability** Wiedergabemöglichkeit f
~ **equation** Rendering-Gleichung f
~ **hints** Zeichenkontext m (Computergrafik)
~ **of detail** Detailwiedergabe f
~ **of flesh tones** Hauttonwiedergabe f
~ **pipeline** Betrachtungstransformation f
~ **software** Rendering-Software f
~ **speed** Wiedergabegeschwindigkeit f
~ **subdivision** s. polygonal subdivision
~ **technique** Rendering-Technik f
rendition s. rendering
renogram Renogramm n
renographic renografisch
renography Renografie f, Isotopenrenografie f
rental video [Video-]Leihkassette f, Leihvideo n
reparamet[e]rization Reparametrisierung f
~[e]rize/to umparametrisieren f
repeater 1. Füllsender m, Lückenfüllsender m, Wiederholsender m (Fernsehen); 2. Signalverstärker m (lokales Computernetz); 3. Verstärker m (bes. von faseroptischen Kopplungen)
repetition frequency (rate) Wiederholfrequenz f, Folgefrequenz f (s.a. picture repetition rate)
~ **time** Repetitionszeit f (Magnetresonanzbildgebung)
repetitive flash photography Strobo[blitz]fotografie f, Phasenfotografie f
~ **signal** periodisches Signal n
rephase/to rephasieren
rephasing Rephasierung f
~ **gradient** Rephasierungsgradient m
rephotograph/to nachaufnehmen; fotokopieren; nachdrehen (Filmarbeit)
replay/to abspielen
replay Abspielung f, Abspielvorgang m; Wiedergabe f; Videoabspielung f, Videowiedergabe f

~ **head** Wiedergabekopf m, Abspielkopf m
replenish/to regenerieren (fotografische Verarbeitungslösungen)
replenisher [solution] Regenerator m, Regeneratorlösung f, Nachfülllösung f
replenishment rate Regenerierungsrate f
~ **tank** Regeneratortank m
replica Abdruck m (s.a. reprint)
~ **film** Abdruckfilm m
reportage camera Reportagekamera f
~ **photography** Reportagefotografie f
reposition Reposition[ierung] f (z.B. von Bildelementen)
represent/to darstellen
representable darstellbar
representation Darstellung f, Repräsentation f
~ **quality** Darstellungsqualität f
~ **space** Darstellungsraum m (z.B. audiovisueller Objekte)
~ **technique** Darstellungstechnik f
representational goal Darstellungsziel n
~ **structure** Darstellungsstruktur f
representative vector repräsentativer Vektor m (Quantisierung)
reprint/to nachdrucken; nachkopieren
reprint Nachdruck m, Wiederabdruck m, Reprint m
repro Repro f(n)
~ **page** Reproseite f
~ **proof** Repro f(n)
reprocess/to nachbearbeiten (z.B. Fotomaterial)
reproduce/to reproduzieren, wiedergeben; vervielfältigen
reproducer Reproduktionsgerät n, Wiedergabegerät n
reproducibility Reproduzierbarkeit f
reproducible reproduzierbar, wiedergebbar; wiedergabefähig; vervielfältigbar; reprofähig
~ **color** reproduzierbare Farbe f
~ **color gamut** Farbwiedergabebereich m
reproducing head Wiedergabekopf m, Abspielkopf m
~ **slit** Wiedergabespalt m (Lichttontechnik)
~ **tube** Wiedergaberöhre f
reproduction Wiedergabe f, Reproduktion f; Vervielfältigung f
~ **accuracy** Kopiergenauigkeit f
~ **camera** Repro[duktions]kamera f
~ **copy** Reprovorlage f
~ **device** Wiedergabegerät n
~ **objective** Reproduktionsobjektiv n
~ **performance** Wiedergabeleistung f
~ **process** Reproduktionsverfahren n
~ **quality** Wiedergabequalität f, Reproduktionsqualität f
~ **ratio** Reproduktionsverhältnis n, Abbildungsmaßstab m
~-related photography Repro[duktions]fotografie f (s.a. photomechanical reproduction)
~ **technology** Reprotechnik f

~ **tube** Wiedergaberöhre f
reproductionist Reprohersteller m
reprogrammable read-only memory s. erasable programmable read-only memory
reprographer Reprograf m
reprographic reprografisch
~ **camera** Repro[duktions]kamera f
~ **film** Reprofilm m, [foto]technischer Film m
~ **technology** Repro[duktions]technik f
reprographics Reprografik f
reprography Reprografie f
reproject/to rückprojizieren
requantization filter Rückquantisierungsfilter n
requantization, requantizing Requantisierung f, Rückquantisierung f
requantize/to requantisieren, rückquantisieren
reradiate/to zurückstrahlen
reradiation Rückstrahlung f, Zurückstrahlung f
rerecord/to 1. wiederbespielen; umspielen; überspielen; 2. nachaufnehmen, nachträglich aufnehmen
rerecordable wiederbespielbar
rerecording Wieder[holungs]aufnahme f, Wiederaufzeichnung f; Neuaufzeichnung f, Neubespielung f; Umspielung f; Nachaufnahme f
~ **room** Umspielraum m
resample/to nachabtasten
resampling Nachabtastung f; Neuabtastung f
rescale/to umskalieren, reskalieren (z.B. Daten)
rescaling Umskalierung f
research-grade microscope Forschungsmikroskop n
~ **observatory** Forschungsobservatorium n
~ **photography** Forschungsfotografie f
~ **radar system** Forschungsradaranlage f
reseau camera Reseau-Kamera f (Fotogrammetrie)
~ **marks** Reseau-Gitter n
~ **plate** Reseau-Platte f
resel s. resolution element
reservoir Reservoir n; Vorlaufspeicher m
resetting Neusatz m (Druck)
reshoot/to nachdrehen (Filmarbeit)
reshoot[ing] Nachdreh m
resident storage dauerhafter Speicher m
residual aberration Restbildfehler m, Restverzeichnung f, Restaberration f, Restverzerrung f, Abbildungsfehlerrest m
~ **astigmatism** Restastigmatismus m
~ **chromatic aberration** Restfarbfehler m, Farbrestfehler m, sekundäres Spektrum n

~ **coma[tic aberration]** Restkoma f, Komarestfehler m (Abbildungsfehler)
~ **electrostatic charge** Restladung f
~ **electrostatic image** Rest[ladungs]bild n (Elektrofotografie)
~ **image** [positives] Nachbild n
~ **light** Restlicht n
~ **light amplifier** Restlichtverstärker m
~ **luminance** Restleuchtdichte f
~ **magnetism** Restmagnetisierung f, remantente Magnetisierung f
~ **reflection** Restreflexion f
~ **uncorrected spherical aberration** Restöffnungsfehler m
~ **visual capability** Restsehvermögen n
residue Rest m
resin-coated [photographic] paper kunstharzbeschichtetes Papier n, RC-Papier n
resist Resist m, Fotoresist m, Foto[kopier]lack m, fotoempfindlicher Lack m
~ **layer** Resistschicht f
~ **mask** Resistmaske f
resistance Widerstand m
resistive magnet resistiver Magnet m, Widerstandsmagnet m
resistor Widerstand m (Bauelement)
resize/to skalieren
resolution Auflösung f, Zeichenschärfe f, Wiedergabefeinheit f
~ **artifact** Auflösungsfehler m
~ **bandwidth** Auflösungsbandbreite f
~ **capability** s. resolving [cap]ability
~ **cell** Auflösungszelle f (Radar)
~ **chart** Testplatte f
~ **degradation** Auflösungsverlust m
~ **enhancement** Auflösungssteigerung f, Auflösungserhöhung f
~ **error** Auflösungsfehler m
~ **independence** Auflösungsunabhängigkeit f (z.B. von Grafiksoftware)
~**-independent compression** auflösungsunabhängige Kompression f
~ **level** Auflösungsstufe f
~ **limit** Auflösungsgrenze f
~**-limited** auflösungsbegrenzt
~ **loss** Auflösungsverlust m
~ **measure (metric)** Auflösungsmaß n
~ **measurement** Auflösungsmessung f
~ **of detail** Detailauflösung f
~ **pyramid** Auflösungspyramide f
~ **reduction** Auflösungsverminderung f
~ **test target** Testplatte f (zur Prüfung der optischen Auflösung)
~ **wedge** Auflösungskeil m
resolvability Auflösbarkeit f
resolvable auflösbar
resolve/to auflösen
resolving [cap]ability, ~ power Auflösungsvermögen n, Auflösungsfähigkeit f (z.B. von Bildschirmen)

resonance 332

resonance Resonanz f
~ **absorption** Resonanzabsorption f
~ **amplitude** Resonanzamplitude f
~ **condition** Resonanzbedingung f
  (Magnetresonanzbildgebung)
~ **curve** Resonanzkurve f
~ **filter** Resonanzfilter n
  (Nachbarschaftsoperator)
~ **frequency** Resonanzfrequenz f *(z.B. eines piezoelektrischen Kristalls)*; Präzessionsfrequenz f, Larmor-Frequenz f *(Kernspinresonanz)*
~ **image** Resonanzbild n
~ **scattering** Resonanzstreuung f
~ **signal** Resonanzsignal n
resonant cavity s. resonator
~ **fluorescence** Resonanzfluoreszenz f
~ **frequency** s. resonance frequency
resonate/to resonieren
resonator Resonator m, Etalon n; Hohlraumresonator m *(Laser, Interferometrie)*
~ **mirror** Resonatorspiegel m
respiratory compensation Atemkompensation f *(Magnetresonanztomografie)*
~ **motion artifact** Atemartefakt n
~ **phase reordering, respiratory-ordered phase encoding** s. ~ compensation
response Reizantwort f
~ **function** Antwortfunktion f
~ **propagative time** Buslaufzeit f
~ **signal** Antwortsignal n
~ **time** Antwortzeit f, Raktionszeit f, Ansprechzeit f *(z.B. eines Fotodetektors)*
responsive emission stimulierte (induzierte) Emission f *(Laser)*
responsivity Ansprechempfindlichkeit f *(Fotodetektor)*
rest Auflage f *(z.B. zur Kamerastabilisierung)*
~ **magnetism** s. residual magnetism
restart Warmstart m *(Computer)*
resting state of accommodation Dunkeladaptationszustand m
restitution camera Auswertekamera f, Auswertekammer f
~ **machine** Bildauswertegerät n
restoration algorithm Restaurationsalgorithmus m
~ **filter (operator)** Restaurationsfilter n
~ **of photographs** Fotorestaurierung f, Fotorestauration f
restore/to restaurieren *(z.B. Bilddaten)*
restrainer Verzögerer m, Verzögerungsmittel n, Bremsmittel n, Entwicklungshemmer m
result image Ergebnisbild n, Resultatbild n
resynchronization Nachsynchronisation f; Neusynchronisation f, Neusynchronisierung f, Resynchronisation f
resynchronize/to nachsynchronisieren; resynchronisieren

retained image Nachwirkungsbild n *(Fernsehbildstörung)*
retake/to nachaufnehmen; nachdrehen *(Filmarbeit)*
retake Nachaufnahme f, Korrekturaufnahme f, Wiederholungsaufnahme f *(Filmarbeit)*
retardant Inhibitor m, Hemmstoff m
retardation plate Verzögerungsplatte f
~ **sheet** Retarderfolie f *(Flüssigkristallanzeige)*
retarder 1. Hemmkörper m; 2. s. retardation plate
rethread/to zurückspulen, umrollen *(z.B. Filmstreifen)*
reticle Strichplatte f, Retikel n; Netzgitterraster m(n), Rechteckgitter n
reticulated screen Gittermattscheibe f
reticulation Runzelkorn n
reticule s. reticle
retigraphy Siebdruck m, Durchdruck m
retina Retina f, Netzhaut f, Augennetzhaut f
retinal 1. retinal; 2. s. retinaldehyde
~ **area** Netzhautbereich m, Netzhautareal n
~ **bipolar cell** Bipolarzelle f
~ **blind spot** blinder Fleck m, Papille f *(der Netzhaut)*
~ **camera** Retinakamera f, Netzhautkamera f, Funduskamera f
~ **cone** Netzhautzapfen n, Netzhautzäpfchen m, Zapfen m, Sehzapfen m *(s.a. unter cone)*
~ **densitometry** Netzhautdensitometrie f
~ **disparity** retinale Disparität f, Netzhautrivalität f, Querdisparität f, Querdisparation f
~ **eccentricity** Netzhautexzentrizität f
~ **fovea** Netzhautgrube f, Sehgrube f, Fovea [centralis] f
~ **fundus photography** Fundusfotografie f
~ **ganglion [cell]** Netzhaut-Ganglienzelle f, retinale Ganglienzelle f, retinales Neuron n
~ **illuminance** Netzhautbeleuchtungsstärke f, Pupillenlichtstärke f
~ **image** Netzhautbild n, Retinabild n, retinales Bild n
~ **image quality** Netzhautbildqualität f
~ **image size** Netzhautbildgröße f
~ **imaging** Netzhautabbildung f
~ **location (locus)** Netzhautort m, Netzhautstelle f
~ **neuron** Netzhautnervenzelle f, Netzhautneuron n
~ **pattern detector** Netzhautscanner m, Retinascanner m
~ **periphery** Netzhautperipherie f, Netzhautrand m
~ **photoreceptor** Netzhautrezeptor m
~ **pigment** Netzhautpigment n
~ **pigment epithelium** Netzhautpigmentepithel n
~ **plane** Netzhautebene f

~ **position** s. ~ location
~ **projection** Netzhautprojektion f
~ **purple** Sehpurpur m, Rhodopsin n, Stäbchenpigment n
~ **rivalry** s. ~ disparity
~ **rod** Netzhautstäbchen n, Sehstäbchen n, Stäbchen n, Rhabdom n
~ **scanner** Netzhautscanner m, Retinascanner m
~ **sensor, ~ sensory receptor** Netzhautrezeptor m
~ **surface** Netzhautoberfläche f
retinaldehyde, retinene Retinal n
retinex theory Retinextheorie f (des Farbensehens)
retinoscope Retinoskop n, Skiaskop n
retinoscopic retinoskopisch
retinoscopy Retinoskopie f
retinotopic mapping retinotope Abbildung f

retouch/to retuschieren
retouch Retusche f
retoucher Retuscheur m
retouching brush Retuschierpinsel m
~ **color** Retuschefarbe f, Retuschierfarbe f
~ **colorant** Retuschefarbstoff m
~ **desk** Retuschierpult n
~ **dye** Retuschefarbstoff m
~ **knife** Retuschiermesser n, Schabemesser n
~ **lacquer** Retuschelack m
~ **machine** Retuschiermaschine f
~ **pen** Retuschier[blei]stift m
~ **software** Retuschiersoftware f
~ **specialist** Retuscheur m
~ **spray** Retuschierspray n
~ **work** Retusche f
retrace/to zurückverfolgen (z.B. Strahlen)
retrace Rücklauf m, Elektronenstrahlrücklauf m
~ **blanking** Dunkeltasten n, Rücklaufaustastung f
~ **line** Rücklaufzeile f
~ **time** Rücklaufzeit f
retransform/to rücktransformieren, retransformieren
retransformation Retransformation f
retransmission Rückübertragung f (z.B. von Bilddaten)
retrievability Wiederauffindbarkeit f
retrieval, retrieve Retrieval n, Wiederauffinden n; Wiederzugriff m; Recherche f
retrieve/to wiederauffinden; abrufen
retrofocus construction (design) Retrofokuskonstruktion f
~ **lens** Retrofokusobjektiv n, umgekehrtes Teleobjektiv n
~ **wide-angle lens** Retrofokus-Weitwinkelobjektiv n, retrofokales Weitwinkelobjektiv n
retroreflective retroreflektierend
~ **foil** Reflexfolie f, Aufhellfolie f

retroreflector Retroreflektor m, Tripelprisma n, Tripelspiegel m
return Echo n (Sonografie, Radar; s.a. echo)
~ **beam** Rückstrahl m
~ **channel** Rückkanal m
~ **key** Eingabetaste f
returned echo (signal) rücklaufendes Echo n
reverberation Hall m, Nachhall m; Vielfachecho n, Wiederholungsecho n (Sonografie)
~ **time** Hallzeit f, Nachhallzeit f
reverberator Hallgenerator m, Nachhallgerät n
reversal black-and-white film Schwarzweiß-Umkehrfilm m
~ **camera film** Umkehroriginal n, Umkehr-Originalfilm m, Originalumkehrfilm m
~ **color development** Farbumkehrentwicklung f
~ **color film** Umkehrfarbfilm f, Farbumkehrfilm m
~ **color-film processing** Umkehrfarbfilmverarbeitung f
~ **color paper** Farbumkehr[foto]papier n
~ **color process** Farbumkehrprozess m, Farbumkehrtechnik f
~ **development** Umkehrentwicklung[stechnik] f
~ **exposure** Umkehrbelichtung f
~ **film** 1. Umkehrfilm m; Positivfilm m; Dia[positiv]film m; 2. s. ~ original film
~ **image** Umkehrbild n
~ **image printing** Umkehrdruck m
~ **intermediate [film]** Umkehrintermediatefilm m, Reversalintermediatefilm m
~ **of tones** Tonwertumkehr f
~ **original film** Originalumkehrfilm m, Umkehroriginal n
~ **paper** Umkehr[foto]papier n
~ **photographic material** [fotografisches] Umkehrmaterial n
~ **positive film** Umkehrfilm m
~ **positive image** Umkehrpositiv n
~ **process** Umkehrverfahren n, Umkehrprozess m
~ **processing** Umkehrverarbeitung f
~ **sheet film** Umkehrplanfilm m
~ **stock** Umkehrmaterial n
~ **system** Umkehrsystem n (Fotografie)
~ **transparency film** Dia[positiv]film m, Positivfilm m
~-**type black-and-white developer** Schwarzweiß-Umkehrentwickler m
~-**type developer** Umkehrentwickler m
reverse [out]/to umkehren (z.B. bei Negativ-Positiv-Umkehr)
~ **action** Rückwärtslauf m, Filmablaufumkehrung f
~ **bias** Sperr[vor]spannung f (Fotodiode)
~ **biased mode** Fotoleitungsbetrieb m

reverse 334

~ **channel** Rückkanal *m*
~ **current** Leckstrom *m* *(z.B. eines Halbleiters)*
~ **direction** Gegenrichtung *f*
~ **playback** Rückwärtsabspielen *n*, Rückwärtsabspielung *f*, Rückwärtswiedergabe *f*
~ **printing** Kontern *n*, Spiegeln *n*
~ **projection** Umkehrprojektion *f*
~ **run** *s*. ~ action
~ **slow motion** Zeitlupe *f* rückwärts
~ **telephoto lens** Retrofokusobjektiv *n*, umgekehrtes Teleobjektiv *n*
~ **telephoto wide-angle lens** Retrofokus-Weitwinkelobjektiv *n*, retrofokales Weitwinkelobjektiv *n*
~ **transform[ation]** Rücktransformation *f*, inverse Transformation *f*
~ **voltage** *s*. ~ bias
reversed bath Umkehrbad *n* *(Fotoverarbeitung)*
~ **Galilean finder** Galilei-Sucher *m*, umgekehrter Galiläischer Echtbildsucher *m*
~ **Galilean telescope** umgekehrtes Galileisches Fernrohr *n*
~ **image** Umkehrbild *n*, spiegelverkehrtes Bild *n*
~ **lens** Retroobjektiv *n*
reversibility principle Reversibilitätsprinzip *n* *(geometrische Optik)*
reversible cartridge Wendekassette *f* *(Drucker)*
~ **compression** verlustfreie (verlustlose) Kompression *f*, reversible Kompression *f*
~ **film** *s*. reversal film
~ **filter** Umkehrfilter *n*
reversing eyepiece Umkehrokular *n*
~ **mirror** Umkehrspiegel *m*
~ **prism** Wendeprisma *n*, Reversionsprisma *n*, Umkehrprisma *n*
~ **ring** Umkehrring *n*
reverted image seitenverkehrtes (einseitig umgekehrtes) Bild *n*
revolving diaphragm Revolverblende *f*
~ **nosepiece** Objektivrevolver *m* *(Mikroskop)*
~ **shutter** Rotationsverschluss *m*
rewind/to [zu]rückspulen; umspulen; umrollen
rewind 1. Rückspulung *f*; Umspulung *f*; Bandrücklauf *m*, Rücklauf *m*; 2. Rückspulvorrichtung *f*
~ **apparatus** Umrolltisch *m*
~ **crank** Rückspulkurbel *f*
~ **knob** Rückspulknopf *m*
~ **speed** Rückspulgeschwindigkeit *f*
~ **time** Umspulzeit *f*
~**[er]** Umroller *m*
rewinding device (mechanism) Rückspulvorrichtung *f*
rewritability Wiederbeschreibbarkeit *f*
rewritable wiederbeschreibbar, mehrfach bespielbar

~ **optical disk** wiederbeschreibbare optische Speicherplatte *f*
rewrite capability Wiederbeschreibbarkeit *f*
Reynolds number Reynoldssche Zahl *f* *(Strömungsvisualisierung)*
RF *s*. radio frequency
RFID *s*. radio frequency identification
RGB color cube RGB-Würfel *m*, Farb[en]würfel *m*
~ **color matching method** Spektralverfahren *n* *(Farbmessung)*
~ **color space** RGB-Farbraum *m*
~ **cube** *s*. ~ color cube
~ **image** RGB-Bild *n*
~ **laser** RGB-Laser *m*
~ **model** RGB-Farbmodell *n*, additives Farbmodell *n*
~ **picture signal** RGB-Bildsignal *n*
~ **pixel** RGB-Pixel *n*
~ **primary color system** *s*. ~ model
~**-related color space** RGB-verwandter Farbraum *m*
~ **signal** RGB-Signal *n*, RGB-Videosignal *n*, Farbwertsignal *n*, Farbvideosignal *n*
~ **system** RGB-System *n*, RGB-Schema *n*
~ **triple[t]** Farbtripel *n*; Leuchtpunkttripel *n* *(Farbbildröhre)*
~ **video signal** *s*. ~ signal
rhabdom[e] Rhabdom *n*, Sehstäbchen *n*, Netzhautstäbchen *n*, Stäbchen *n* *(Fotorezeptor)*
Rheinberg illumination Rheinberg-Beleuchtung *f* *(Mikroskopie)*
rheostat Rheostat *m*
RHI display *s*. range-height indicator [display]
rhodamine Rhodamin *n* *(Fluoreszenzfarbstoff)*
rhodopsin Rhodopsin *n*, Sehpurpur *m*, Stäbchenpigment *n*
rhombic prism rhombisches Prisma *n*
ribbon cartridge Farbbandkassette *f*
~ **ink** Farbbandfarbe *f*
~ **microphone** Bändchenmikrofon *n*
Ricco's law Riccoscher Satz *m*, Riccos Gesetz *n* *(visuelle Wahrnehmung)*
Rice coding Rice-Codierung *f* *(Bilddatenkompression)*
ridge laser Streifenlaser *m*
Riemannian geometry Riemannsche Geometrie *f*
Riemann's curvature tensor Riemannscher Krümmungstensor (Tensor) *m*
rifle grip Schulterstütze *f* *(Kamerazubehör)*
~ **microphone** Keulenmikrofon *n*; Richtmikrofon *n*, Rohrrichtmikrofon *n*
~ **scope** Gewehrzielfernrohr *n*
rig wires Drahtstaffage *f* *(Filmdekoration)*
right-adjusted, right-aligned rechtsbündig *(Textdruck)*
~**-angle fold** Kreuzfalz *m*
~**-angle mirror** Rechtwinkelspiegel *m*

~-angle viewing attachment
 Winkelsucher *m*
~-angled prism Rechtwinkelprisma *n*,
 rechtwinkliges Prisma *n*
~-circularly polarized light rechtszirkular
 polarisiertes Licht *n*
~-click/to rechtsklicken
~ click Rechtsklick *m*
~ clicking Rechtsklicken *n*
~-elliptically polarized light
 rechtselliptisch polarisiertes Licht *n*
~-eye image rechtsäugiges Bild *n*
~-eye view rechtsäugiger Blick *m*
~-eyed rechtsäugig
~-hand page Rekto *n*, Blattvorderseite *f*,
 ungerade Seite *f (Layout)*
~-hand rule Rechte-Hand-Regel *f (Optik)*
~-handed coordinate system
 rechtshändiges Koordinatensystem *n*
~-handed polarization rechtsdrehende
 (rechtszirkulare) Polarisation *f*
~ reading leserichtig, seitenrichtig
 (Drucktext)
~-reading image seitenrichtiges
 (seitenkorrektes) Bild *n*
~ triangle rechtwinkliges Dreieck *n*
~-triangle prism *s.* right-angled prism
rigid body *s.* ~ solid
~-body transformation
 Starrkörpertransformation *f*
 (geometrische Modellierung)
~ camera case Fotokoffer *m*
~ endoscope starres Endoskop *n*
~ object starres Objekt *n*
~ solid starrer Körper *m (Computergrafik)*
~ transformation starre Transformation *f*
rim lighting Randaufhellung *f*
~ lighting effect Lichtkranz *m*
~ of light Lichtsaum *m*, Lichtrand *m*,
 Lichtkante *f*
~ ray Randstrahl *m*, randnaher
 (randseitiger) Strahl *m*
ring aperture Ringblende *f*, ringförmige
 Blende *f*
~ artifact Ringartefakt *n*, kreisförmiges
 Artefakt *n*
~ binder *s.* ringed binder
~ demodulator Ringdemodulator *m*
 (Videomodulation)
~ detector Ringdetektor *m*,
 Vollkreisdetektor *m*, Detektorring *m*,
 Detektorkranz *m (Tomografiegerät)*
~-flash [unit] Ringblitzgerät *n*
~ modulator Ringmodulator *m*
 (Videomodulation)
~ of detectors *s.* ~ detector
~-shaped artifact Ringartefakt *n*,
 kreisförmiges Artefakt *n (Bildcodierung)*
~-shaped electrode Ringelektrode *f*
ringed binder Ringordner *m*,
 [Foto-]Ringalbum *n*
ringing 1. Überschwingen *n*
 (Bildsignalfilterung); 2. *s.* ~ artifact

~ **artifact** 1. Verstümmelungsartefakt *n*,
 Gibbs-Artefakt *n*, Gibbssches Phänomen
 n (Bildverarbeitung); 2. *s.* ring-shaped
 artifact
ringlight Ring[blitz]leuchte *f*, Ringlicht *n*
rinse fließende Wässerung *f*
 (Fotoverarbeitung)
RIP *s.* raster image processor
ripener *s.* ripening agent
ripening Reifung *f (Emulsionsherstellung)*
~ **agent** Reifmittel *n*
 (Emulsionsherstellung)
~ **center** Reif[e]keim *m*, Subkeim *m*
 (Latentbildentstehung)
ripple Brummspannung *f*
rise [movement] Hochverstellung *f*
 (Fachkamera)
~ **time** Anstiegszeit *f*, Impulsanstiegszeit *f*
riser Steiger *m (Beleuchtungsausrüstung)*
Risley prisms Drehkeilpaar *n*
rms, RMS *s.* root-mean-square
road map Straßenkarte *f*
Roberts [edge] operator
 Roberts-Kantendetektor *m*,
 Roberts-Operator *m*
Robinson's operator Robinson-Operator *m*
robot camera Roboterkamera *f*,
 Kameraroboter *m*, robotergeführte
 Kamera *f*, fernbedienbare
 (fernsteuerbare) Kamera *f*
~ **navigation** Roboternavigation *f*
~ **telescope** Roboterteleskop *n*
~**[ic] vision** Robotersehen *n*
robotics Robotik *f*, Robotertechnik *f*
robust algorithm robuster Algorithmus *m*
~ **estimation** robuste Schätzung *f*
~ **model[l]ing** robuste Modellierung *f*
~ **to noise** rauschunempfindlich
~ **video coding** robuste Videocodierung *f*
~ **watermark** robustes Wasserzeichen *n*
robustness Robustheit *f*
rocker switch Schaltwippe *f*, Wippschalter
 m
rod 1. Stab *m*; 2. Stäbchen *n*, Sehstäbchen
 n, Netzhautstäbchen *n*, Rhabdom *n*
~ **adaptation** Dunkeladaptation *f*,
 Dunkelanpassung *f (Sehen)*
~ **anode** Stabanode *f*
~ **antenna** Stabantenne *f*
~ **monochromacy (monochromatism)**
 Stäbchenmonochromasie *f*
~ **photopigment (pigment)**
 Stäbchenpigment *n*, Sehpurpur *m*,
 Rhodopsin *n*
~ **receptor** *s.* rod 2. *n*
~ **system** Stäbchensystem *n*
~ **vision** Stäbchensehen *n*, Dunkelsehen *n*,
 Nachtsehen *n*, skotopisches
 (dunkeladaptiertes) Sehen *n*
roentgen Röntgen *n*, Röntgeneinheit *f*
 *(Einheit der Röntgen- oder
 Gammastrahlung)*
Roentgen diffraction apparatus
 Röntgendiffraktometer *n*

roentgen 336

roentgen examination
Röntgenuntersuchung f;
Röntgen[durchstrahlungs]prüfung f
Roentgen ray Röntgenstrahl m, X-Strahl m
(s.a. unter X-ray)
roentgenogram Röntgenogramm n,
Röntgenbild n
roentgenographic röntgen[fot]ografisch
~ **visualization** Röntgenbilddarstellung f,
röntgenografische Darstellung f
roentgenography Röntgen[fot]ografie f
roentgenologic[al] röntgenologisch
roentgenological image
röntgenologisches Bild n
roentgenologist Röntgenologe m
roentgenology Röntgenologie f,
Röntgenkunde f
roentgenoscopy Röntgenoskopie f,
Röntgendurchleuchtung f, Fluoroskopie
f
rogue Ausreißer m (Statistik)
ROI s. region of interest
roll-fed press Rollendruckmaschine f
~-**fed printing** Rollendruck m
~-**fed rotary [press], ~ web press**
Rollenrotationsmaschine f
~ **film** Rollfilm m
~-**film camera** Rollfilmkamera f
~-**film cassette** Rollfilmkassette f
~-**film format** Rollfilmformat n
~-**film holder** Rollfilmhalter m
~-**film magazine** Rollfilmmagazin n
~-**film material** Rollfilmmaterial n
~-**film negative** Rollfilmnegativ n
~-**film size** Rollfilmformat n
~-**film tank** Rollfilmtank m
~-**film transport** Rollfilmtransport m
~ **of background paper** Hintergrundrolle f
(Studiozubehör)
~ **of photographic paper** Fotopapierrolle f
~ **paper** Rollenpapier n
~ **temperature** Walzentemperatur f
rollabout [system] mobiles
Videokonferenzsystem n
roller fresh walzenfrisch (Druckfarbe)
~-**transport machine (processor)**
Walzenentwicklungsmaschine f,
Walzentransportmaschine f,
Rollentransportmaschine f
(Filmverarbeitung)
rolling Verrollung f (Kamerabewegung)
~-**ball filter** Top-Hat-Filter n
~-**ball technique** Top-Hat-Transformation f
(morphologische Bildverarbeitung)
~ **title** Rolltitel m
ROM s. read-only [electronic] memory
roman steil (Typografie)
~ Steilschrift f
~ **type** [klassizistische] Antiqua f,
Antiqua[druck]schrift f
roof antenna Dachantenne f, Hausantenne
f
~ **pentaprism** Pentadachkantenprisma n

~ **prism** Dachkant[en]prisma m,
Geradsichtprisma n [nach Amici],
Amici-Prisma n
~ **track system** Deckenschienensystem n,
Laufschienensystem n
(Studioausrüstung)
room illumination Raumausleuchtung f
~ **light** Raumlicht n
~ **lighting** Raumbeleuchtung f
~ **sound (tone)** 1. Raumton m; 2. s.
presence
root-mean-square quadratisches Mittel n
~-**mean-square error** mittlere
quadratische Abweichung f, mittlerer
quadratischer Fehler m, mittleres
Fehlerquadrat (Abweichungsquadrat) n
(Schätzparameter)
~-**mean-square granularity** RMS-Körnung
f, RMS-Wert m (Densitometrie)
~ **node** Wurzelknoten m (Datenstruktur)
rosette pattern Rosettenmuster n (von
Rasterpunkten)
Ross effect Ross-Effekt m, Gelatineeffekt m
(gerbender Entwickler)
rostrum camera Schnorchelkamera f
~ **photography** Trickfotografie f
rotary camera Durchlaufkamera f
(Reprografie)
~ **diaphragm** Drehblende f
~ **drum scanner** Trommelscanner m,
Rollenscanner m
~ **filter** Drehfilter n
~ **head** rotierender Videokopf m
~ **intaglio press**
Rotationstiefdruckmaschine f,
Tiefdruckrotationsmaschine f
~ **lamellar shutter**
Rotationslamellenverschluss m
~ **letterpress printing** Rotationshochdruck
m
~ **magazine** Rundmagazin n
~ **motion** s. rotational motion
~ **newspaper press**
Zeitungsrotationsmaschine f
~ **perfecting machine** Schön- und
Widerdruckmaschine f,
Perfektormaschine f
~ **plotter** Trommelplotter m, Walzenplotter
m
~ **press** s. rotary-type [printing] press
~ **printing** Rotationsdruck m
~ **printing process**
Rotationsdruckverfahren n
~ **processing** Rotationsentwicklung f
~ **processor** Rotationsentwicklunganlage f,
Rotationsentwicklungsmaschine f
~ **production-type press**
Fortdruckmaschine f
~ **scanner** Rotationsscanner m
~ **sheet-fed offset press**
Bogenoffset[druck]maschine f
~ **shutter** Umlauf[sektoren]blende f,
Flügelblende f, Umlaufverschluss m
(Kinotechnik)

~ **trimmer** Rollenschneidemaschine f, Rollenschneider m
~**-type [printing] press** Rotationspresse f, Rotations[druck]maschine f, Zylinderdruckmaschine f
~**-type proofing press** Rotationsandruckmaschine f
~ **vane pump** Drehschieberpumpe f *(Elektronenmikroskop)*
~ **web-fed offset machine** Offsetrollendruckmaschine f, Rollenoffset[druck]maschine f, Offsetrotations[druck]maschine f
rotate effect Rotationstrick m *(Videoeffekt)*
rotating anode Drehanode f *(Röntgenröhre)*
~**-anode X-ray generator** Drehanoden-Röntgengenerator m
~**-anode X-ray tube** Drehanoden[röntgen]röhre f
~**-door entrance** Drehtürschleuse f *(Dunkelraum)*
~**-drum camera** Trommelkamera f
~ **filter** Drehfilter n
~ **mirror** Drehspiegel m
~**-mirror camera** Drehspiegelkamera f
~**-mirror shutter** Spiegelumlaufblende f
~**-mirror system** Drehspiegelsystem n
~ **nosepiece** Okularrevolver m *(Mikroskop)*
~ **prism** Drehprisma n
~ **shutter** *s.* rotary shutter
rotation 1. Rotation f, Drehung f *(geometrische Transformation)*; Drehbewegung f; 2. Kamerakreisfahrt f, Umfahrt f; 3. Panoramaschwenk m, Rundumschwenk m; 4. *s.* laydown sequence
~**-invariant** rotationsinvariant
~ **matrix** Rotationsmatrix f
rotational angle Drehwinkel m
~ **axis** Rotationsachse f, Drehachse f
~ **invariance** Rotationsinvarianz f, Dreh[ungs]invarianz f *(Mustererkennung)*
~ **motion** rotatorische Bewegung f, Drehbewegung f *(s.a. rotation)*
~ **scanning** rotierende Abtastung f *(Sonografie)*
~ **symmetry** Rotationssymmetrie f
~ **variance** Rotationsvarianz f
rotationally symmetric edge filter (operator) rotationssymmetrischer (isotroper) Kantenoperator m
~ **symmetric low-pass filter** rotationssymmetrisches Tiefpassfilter n
~ **symmetric object** rotationssymmetrisches Objekt n
~ **symmetrical system** rotationssymmetrisches System n
rotogravure Rotationstiefdruck m; konventioneller (tiefenvariabler) Tiefdruck m
~ **paper** Tiefdruckpapier n
~ **[printing] process** *s.* rotogravure

~ **rotary** Rollenrotations-Tiefdruckmaschine f
rotoscope Rotoskop n *(Trickkinematografie)*
~**[d] matte** Wandermaske f
rough cut Rohschnitt m, Grobschnitt m *(Kinematografie)*
~ **sketch** Skizze f, Handskizze f, Gedankenskizze f; Scribble n
round [kreis]rund, kreisförmig, zirkular, zirkulär
rounding Rundung f
roundness Rundheit f, Kreisförmigkeit f *(Formmerkmal)*
routine microscope Routinemikroskop n
~ **microscopy** Routinemikroskopie f
routing Trassierung f, Wegeleitung f *(z.B. von Datenpaketen)*
row matrix Reihenmatrix f
~ **scanning** Reihenabtastung f
~ **vector** Reihenvektor m, Zeilenvektor m
rowwise reihenweise *(z.B. Bildfilterung)*
rub-proof ink scheuerfeste (abriebfeste) Druckfarbe f
rubber armoring Gummiarmierung f *(Kamera, Fernglas)*
~ **blanket** Gummi[druck]tuch n *(Offsetdruckmaschine)*
~ **blanket image transfer cylinder** Gummi[drucktuch]zylinder m, Drucktuchzylinder m
~ **duplicate [plate]** *s.* ~ stereo[type]
~ **eyecup** Gummi-Augenmuschel f
~ **foot with [a] retractable spike** Gummifuß m mit einstellbarem Dorn
~ **gloves** Gummihandschuhe mpl
~ **lens hood** Gummisonnenblende f
~ **printing plate** Gummidruckplatte f
~ **sheet transformation, ~ sheeting** geometrische Transformation f; Bildverzerrung f, Bildverzeichnung f, Bildwölbung f *(Computergrafik)*
~ **squeegee** Gummiabstreifer m
~ **stamp maker** Stempelschneider m
~ **stamp making** Stempelfertigung f
~ **stamp tool** Duplizierstempel m, Klonwerkzeug n *(digitale Bildbearbeitung)*
~ **stereo[type]** Gummiklischee n, Gummistereo n, Gummi[duplikat]druckplatte f
~**-tipped leg** Gummifuß m *(Stativ)*
Rubin's drawing, ~ vase [profile] Rubinsche Vase f *(Kippfigur)*
ruby [chromium aluminum] laser Rubinlaser m
rule 1. Linie f *(Setzmaterial)*; 2. Regel f; Vorschrift f; 3. Skale f; 4. *s.* ruler
~**-based expert system** regelbasiertes Expertensystem n *(Neuroinformatik)*
~ **of thirds** Dreierregel f *(Bildkomposition)*
ruled screen Distanzraster m(n), Glas[gravur]raster m(n)
ruler Lineal n

run

run Auflage *f*, Druckauflage *f*
~-length code Lauflängencode *m* *(Bilddatenkompression)*
~-length encoder Lauflängencodierer *m*
~-length encoding Lauflängencodierung *f*
~-length-limited code Code *m* mit fester Symbollänge
~ mode Lauflängenmodus *m*
~-out trailer Endband *n*, Endallonge *f*, Schlussband *n* *(Tonfilmkopie)*
~-time error Laufzeitfehler *m*
~-time layer Laufzeitschicht *f* *(Hypermediasystem)*
runability Verdruckbarkeit *f* *(von Papier)*
runaround Rundsatz *m*, Konturensatz *m*, Formsatz *m*, Figursatz *m*, Umschrift *f* *(Layout, Typografie)*
running speed Laufgeschwindigkeit *f*
~ time Laufzeit *f*; Filmlaufzeit *f*
~ water rinse fließende Wässerung *f* *(Fotoverarbeitung)*
rushes *s.* film dailies

S

S cone S-Zapfen *m*, K-Zapfen *m* *(Netzhautrezeptor)*
S-VHS *s.* Super Video Home System
S-video S-Video *n (Signalformat)*
Sabattier effect Sabattier-Effekt *m*, Pseudosolarisation *f (Belichtungseffekt)*
saccade Sakkade *f*, ruckartige (sakkadierte) Augenbewegung *f*, Blickzielbewegung *f*, Blicksprung *m*
saccadic sakkadiert
~ **[eye] movement** *s.* saccade
saddle coil Sattelspule *f*, Pantoffelspule *f (Katodenstrahlröhre)*
~ **surface** Sattelfläche *f (Computergrafik)*
safelamp Dunkelkammerlampe *f*
safelight 1. Dunkelkammerlicht *n*, Schutzlicht *n*, Laborlicht *n*; 2. Dunkelkammerleuchte *f*, Dukaleuchte *f*, Fotolaborleuchte *f*, Laborleuchte *f*
~ **filter** Dunkelkammer[schutz]filter *n*, Schutzfilter *n*
~ **illumination** Dunkelkammerbeleuchtung *f*, Dunkelkammerausleuchtung *f*, Sicherheitsbeleuchtung *f*
~ **lamp** Dunkelkammerlampe *f*
safety base Sicherheitsunterlage *f (Filmträgermaterial)*
~ **[base] film** Sicherheitsfilm *m*, Safety-Film *m*, Acetatfilm *m*
~ **goggles** Schutzbrille *f*
~ **margin** Sicherheitskasch *m*
sag[itta] Pfeilhöhe *f (Optik)*
sagittal sagittal
~ **coma** sagittale Koma *f*, Rinnenfehler *m (Abbildungsfehler)*
~ **curvature of field** sagittale Bildfeldwölbung *f*
~ **focus** Sagittalbrennpunkt *m*
~ **image height aberration** sagittale Bildhöhenaberration *f*
~ **image plane** sagittale Bildebene *f*
~ **image surface** sagittale Bildschale *f*
~ **plane** Sagittalebene *f*
~ **principal section** Sagittalschnitt *m*
~ **ray** sagittaler Strahl *m*
Sagnac interferometer Sagnac-Interferometer *n*
salon photography Salonfotografie *f*
salt Salz *n*; Kochsalz *n*
~**-and-pepper noise** Impulsrauschen *n*, impulsförmiges Rauschen *n*, Impulsstörung *f*, Speckle-Rauschen *n*
~ **intensifying screen** Salz[verstärker]folie *f*
~ **print** *s.* salted-paper print
salted paper Salzpapier *n*
~**-paper print** Salzpapierabzug *m*, Salzpapierkopie *f*

~**-paper process** Salzkopierverfahren *n*
same-size image maßstabgerechtes (maßstabsgleiches) Bild *n*
sample/to abtasten; abrastern
sample 1. Probe *f*, Stichprobe *f*; Muster *n*; Objekt *n*, Präparat *n (Mikroskopie)*; 2. Abtastwert *m*
~ **and hold** Halteglied *n* nullter Ordnung
~**-and-hold circuit** Abtast-Halte-Schaltung *f*, Abtast-Halte-Stufe *f*
~**-and-hold unit** Abtast-Halte-Glied *n*
~ **chamber** Probenkammer *f (Elektronenmikroskop)*
~ **clock** Abtasttakt *m*
~ **image** Musterbild *n*
~ **interval** Abtastperiode[ndauer] *f*, Abtastintervall *n*
~ **plane** Präparatebene *f*, Objektebene *f (Mikroskopie)*
~ **point** Abtastpunkt *m*
~ **rate clock** Abtasttakt *m*
~ **sequence** Abtastfolge *f*
~ **spacing** Abtastabstand *m*
~ **stage** Objekttisch *m (Mikroskop)*
~ **value** Abtastwert *m*
~ **volume** Messvolumen *n (Sonografie)*
sampled data filter Abtastfilter *n*
~ **signal** abgetastetes (zeitdiskretes) Signal *n*, Abtastsignal *n*, Scansignal *n*
sampler Abtaster *m*
samples per inch Abtastpunkte *mpl* pro Zoll
sampling Abtastung *f (s.a. unter scanning)*; Signalumsetzung *f*; Diskretisierung *f*; Zeitdiskretisierung *f*
~ **algorithm** Abtastalgorithmus *m*
~ **bandwidth** Abtastbandbreite *f*
~ **control** Abtaststeuerung *f*
~ **density** Abtastdichte *f*
~ **depth** Abtasttiefe *f*
~ **distance** Abtastabstand *m*
~ **efficiency** Abtasteffizienz *f*, Scan-Effizienz *f*
~ **error** Abtastfehler *m*
~ **format** Abtastformat *n*
~ **function** Abtastfunktion *f*
~ **geometry** Abtastgeometrie *f*
~ **grid** Abtastgitter *n*
~ **imperfection (inaccuracy)** Abtastungenauigkeit *f*
~ **instant** Abtastzeitpunkt *m*
~ **lattice** Abtastgitter *n*
~ **matrix** Abtastmatrix *f*
~ **moment** Abtastzeitpunkt *m*
~ **passband** Abtastpassband *n*
~ **pattern** Abtastmuster *n*
~ **period** Abtastperiode[ndauer] *f*, Abtastintervall *n*
~ **precision** Abtastgenauigkeit *f*, Abtastpräzision *f*
~ **pulse** Abtastimpuls *m*
~ **raster** Abtastraster *m(n)*
~ **rate conversion** Abtastratenkonversion *f*, Abtastratenumsetzung *f*

sampling 340

- **~ rate converter** Abtastratenwandler *m*
- **~ ratio** Abtastverhältnis *n*
- **~ resolution** Abtastauflösung *f*
- **~ series** Abtastreihe *f*
- **~ site** Abtastort *m*
- **~ spectrum** Abtastspektrum *n*
- **~ step size** Abtastschrittweite *f*
- **~ structure** Abtastratenverhältnis *n*
- **~ theorem** Abtasttheorem *n*, Sampling-Theorem *n (Signaltheorie)*
- **~ theory** Abtasttheorie *f*
- **~ time** Scanzeit *f*
- **~ volume** Abtastvolumen *n*

sand proof sanddicht *(Kamera)*
sans [serif], ~ serif font (type) serif[en]lose Schrift *f*
satellite Satellit *m*
- **~ antenna** Satellitenantenne *f*
- **~-based photography** Satellitenfotografie *f*
- **~-borne radar** Satellitenradar *n*, satellitengetragenes Radar *n*, Raumfahrzeugradar *n*
- **~ broadcaster** Satellitensender *m*
- **~ broadcasting** Satellitenausstrahlung *f*, Satellitenübertragung *f*
- **~ broadcasting technology** Satelliten[übertragungs]technik *f*
- **~ channel** Satellitenkanal *m*
- **~ color photograph** Satellitenfarbfoto *n*
- **~ digital video broadcasting** digitales Satellitenfernsehen *n*
- **~ dish [receiver]** Satellitenschüssel *f*
- **~-equipped household** Satellitenhaushalt *m*
- **~ image** Satellitenbild *n*
- **~ image analysis** Satellitenbildanalyse *f*
- **~ image classification** Satellitenbildklassifizierung *f*
- **~ image data** Satellitenbilddaten *pl*
- **~ image database** Satellitenbilddatenbank *f*
- **~ imager** Satellitenbildgeber *m*
- **~ imagery** Satellitenbildmaterial *n*
- **~ imaging technology** Satellitenbildtechnik *f*
- **~ infrared image** Infrarot-Satellitenbild *n*
- **~ lens** Satellitenkameraobjektiv *n*
- **~ link** Satellitenverbindung *f*
- **~ modulator** Satellitenmodulator *m*
- **~ news gathering** [elektronische] Berichterstattung *f* via Satellit
- **~ operator** Satellitenbetreiber *m*
- **~ photo interpretation** Satellitenbildauswertung *f*
- **~ photo[graph]** Satellitenfoto *n*
- **~ photography** Satellitenfotografie *f*
- **~ picture** Satellitenbild *n*
- **~ radar image** Satellitenradarbild *n*
- **~ receiver** Satellitenempfänger *m*, Satellitenempfangsgerät *n*
- **~ reception** Satellitenempfang *m*
- **~ reconnaissance** Satellitenaufklärung *f*
- **~ remote sensing** Satellitenfernerkundung *f*
- **~ scanner** Satellitenscanner *m*
- **~ scene** Satellitenbild *n*
- **~ signal** Satellitensignal *n*
- **~ surveillance system** Satellitenüberwachungssystem *n*
- **~ technology** Satellitentechnik *f*
- **~ television** Satellitenfernsehen *n*, Orbitalfernsehen *n*
- **~ television broadcasting** Satellitenfernsehübertragung *f*
- **~-tracking camera** Satellitenkamera *f*
- **~ transmission equipment** Satellitenübertragungsanlage *f*
- **~ transmission signal, satellite-transmitted signal** Satellitensignal *n*
- **~ video transmission** Satellitenfernsehübertragung *f*

saticon [tube] Satikon *n (Röhrenbildwandler)*
satin finish Satinage *f*
saturated absorption spectroscopy Sättigungsabsorptionsspektroskopie *f*
- **~ color** gesättigte (satte) Farbe *f*, kräftige Farbe *f*
- **~ solution** gesättigte Lösung *f*

saturation 1. Sättigung *f (z.B. einer Lösung)*; 2. Farbsättigung *f*, Saturation *f*
- **~ constancy** Sättigungskonstanz *f*
- **~ pulse** Sättigungspuls *m*
- **~ range** Sättigungsbereich *m (z.B. einer Schwärzungskurve)*
- **~ region** s. ~ range
- **~ spectroscopy** Sättigungsspektroskopie *f*
- **~ value** Sättigungswert *m*

save/to [ab]speichern *(z.B. Bilddaten)*
sawtooth generator Sägezahngenerator *m*
- **~ waveform** Sägezahnkurve *f*

scalability Skalierbarkeit *f*
scalable skalierbar
- **~ coding** skalierbare Codierung *f*
- **~ compression** skalierbare Kompression *f*
- **~ SNR encoding** skalierbare SNR-Codierung *f*

scalar skalar
- **~** Skalar *m (zahlenwertbestimmte Größe)*
- **~ diffraction** skalare Beugung *f*
- **~ field** skalares Feld *n*, Skalarfeld *n*
- **~ image** skalares Bild *n*
- **~ operator** skalarer Operator *m*
- **~ point operation** skalare Punktoperation *f*
- **~ product** Skalarprodukt *n*
- **~ quantization** skalare Quantisierung *f*
- **~ quantizer** Skalarquantisierer *m*
- **~ wave** skalare Welle *f*
- **~ wave optics** Wellenoptik *f*, physikalische Optik *f*

scale/to skalieren
scale 1. Skale *f*, Graduierung *f*; Skala *f*; 2. Maßstab *m*; Vergrößerungsmaßstab *m (s.a. image scale)*

~ **bar** Maßstabsleiste *f*, Maßstabs-Messstrecke *f*
~ **change** Maßstabsänderung *f*
~ **drawing** maßstäbliche Zeichnung *f*
~ **error** Maßstabsfehler *m*
~ **model** maßstab[s]gerechtes Modell *n*; Miniaturdekoration *f*, Miniaturkulisse *f* *(Filmarbeit)*
~ **of enlargement** Vergrößerungsmaßstab *m*
~ **of hues** Farbtonabstufung *f*
~ **of reduction** Verkleinerungsmaßstab *m*
~ **of reproduction** Abbildungsmaßstab *m*, Bildmaßstab *m*; Reproduktionsmaßstab *m*; Vergrößerung *f*
~ **ratio** Abbildungsverhältnis *n*
~ **space** Skalenraum *m*
~-**space filtering** Skalenraumfilterung *f*
scaled map maßstäbliche (maßstäbige) Karte *f*
~ **object** skaliertes Objekt *n*
~ **orthography** s. weak perspective
scalene triangle ungleichseitiges Dreieck *n*
scaling Skalierung *f*
~ **coefficient** Skalierungskoeffizient *m*
~ **constant** Skalierungskonstante *f*
~ **device** s. scintillation counter
~ **factor** Skalierungsfaktor *m*; Maßstabsfaktor *m*
~ **function** Skalierungsfunktion *f*
~ **matrix** Skalierungsmatrix *f*
~ **operator** Skalierungsoperator *m*, Skalierungsfilter *n*
~ **transformation** Skalierungstransformation *f*
~ **vector** Skalierungsvektor *m*
scamp s. scribble
scan/to 1. scannen; 2. s. ~ off/to
scan in/to einscannen
~ **off/to** abscannen, abtasten; abrastern
~ Abtastung *f*, Scan *m* *(s.a. unter scanning)*
~ **area** Scanfläche *f*, Rasterfläche *f*
~ **coil** Ablenkspule *f* *(Katodenstrahlröhre)*
~ **conversion** Rasterkonversion *f*, Rasterkonvertierung *f*
~ **converter** Scankonverter *m* *(Sonografie)*
~ **direction** Abtastrichtung *f*
~ **electrode** Abtastelektrode *f*
~ **format converter** Fernsehnormwandler *m*
~ **generator** Rastergenerator *m* *(Elektronenmikroskop)*
~ **header** Scankopf *m* *(Bilddatenstruktur)*
~ **line** Abtastzeile *f*, Scannerzeile *f*; Scanlinie *f*, Rasterzeile *f*, Rasterlinie *f*
~-**line algorithm** Scanline-Algorithmus *m*
~ **line duration** Zeilen[perioden]dauer *f*
~ **matrix** Abtastmatrix *f*
~ **operation** Scanvorgang *m*, Abtastvorgang *m*
~ **pattern** Abtastmuster *n*, Rastermuster *n*
~ **phase** Abtastintervall *n*
~ **position** Abtastposition *f*, Abtastort *m*
~ **rate** s. scanning rate

~~-**rate conversion** Abtastratenkonversion *f*, Abtastratenumsetzung *f*
~ **signal** Abtastsignal *n*, Scansignal *n*, abgetastetes (zeitdiskretes) Signal *n*
~ **size** Scangröße *f*
~ **time** Abtastzeit *f*, Scanzeit *f*; Bildakquisitionszeit *f*, Bildaufnahmezeit *f* *(Magnetresonanzbildgebung)*
~ **velocity** Abtastgeschwindigkeit *f*, Scangeschwindigkeit *f*
~ **volume** Abtastvolumen *n* *(Tomografie)*
scannable abtastbar, scanbar
scanned image gescanntes (abgetastetes) Bild *n*
~ **point** Abtastpunkt *m*
~ **projection radiography** digitale Projektionsradiografie *f*
scanner 1. Scanner *m*, Bildscanner *m*, Abtaster *m*, Bildabtaster *m*, Bildabtastgerät *n*; 2. s. telecine scanner
~ **coordinate system** Scannerkoordinatensystem *n*
~ **illuminant** Scannerlampe *f*
~ **image** Scannerbild *n*
~ **interface** Scannerschnittstelle *f*
~ **mirror** Scannerspiegel *m*
~ **module** Scannermodul *n*
~ **monitor** Scannerbildschirm *m*
~ **resolution** Scannerauflösung *f*
scanning 1. Abtastung *f* *(s.a. unter sampling)*; Zeitdiskretisierung *f*; Bildabtastung *f*, Bilddiskretisierung *f* *(s.a. unter scan)*; 2. Rasterung *f* (z.B. von Spektren)
~ **acoustic microscopy** akustische Rastermikroskopie *f*
~ **angle** Abtastwinkel *m*
~ **aperture** Abtastblende *f*
~ **area** Abtastfläche *f*, Abtastgebiet *n*, Abtastbereich *m*
~ **artifact** Abtastfehler *m*
~ **beam** Abtaststrahl *m*, Rasterstrahl *m*, Scan-Strahl *m*
~ **beam slit** Abtaststrahlapertur *f*
~ **behavior** Abtastverhalten *n*
~ **capacitance microscope** Rasterkapazitätsmikroskop *n*
~ **circuit[ry]** Abtastschaltung *f*
~ **control circuit** Abtaststeuer[schalt]ung *f*
~ **copy** Scanvorlage *f*, Abtastvorlage *f*
~ **cycle** Abtastzyklus *m*
~ **cylinder** Abtastzylinder *m*
~ **data** Scandaten *pl*
~ **density** Abtastdichte *f*
~ **depth** Abtasttiefe *f* *(Sonografie)*
~ **device** Abtastgerät *n*, Abtastvorrichtung *f* *(s.a. scanner)*
~ **diaphragm** Abtastblende *f*
~ **effect** Abtasteffekt *m*
~ **electrochemical microscope** elektrochemisches Rastermikroskop *n*
~ **electrochemical microscopy** elektrochemische Rastermikroskopie *f*

scanning

- ~ **electron beam** Abtaststrahl *m*, Rasterstrahl *m*, Scan-Strahl *m*
- ~ **electron beam lithography** Rasterelektronenstrahllithografie *f*
- ~ **electron microscope** Rasterelektronenmikroskop *n*, Abtastelektronenmikroskop *n*
- ~ **electron microscope photograph** rasterelektronenmikroskopische Aufnahme *f*, REM-Aufnahme *f*
- ~ **electron[ic] microscopy** Rasterelektronenmikroskopie *f*
- ~ **error** Abtastfehler *m*; Diskretisierungsfehler *m*
- ~ **force microscope** Rasterkraftmikroskop *n*
- ~ **format** Abtastformat *n*
- ~ **frequency** s. ~ rate
- ~ **gantry** Gantry *f (Tomografie)*
- ~ **head** Abtastkopf *m*
- ~ **impulse** Abtastimpuls *m*
- ~ **interval** Abtastintervall *n*, Abtastperiode[ndauer] *f*
- ~ **ion microscope** Rasterionenmikroskop *n*
- ~ **ion microscopy** Rasterionenmikroskopie *f*
- ~ **laser** Abtastlaser *m*
- ~ **laser ophthalmoscope** Laserophthalmoskop *n*
- ~ **light source** Abtastlichtquelle *f*
- ~ **light spot** Abtastlichtpunkt *m*
- ~ **line frequency (rate)** Abtastzeilenfrequenz *f*
- ~ **line time** Zeilen[perioden]dauer *f*
- ~ **luminescence microscope** Raster-Lumineszenzmikroskop *n*
- ~ **machine** s. scanner 1.
- ~ **matrix** Rastermatrix *f*
- ~ **mechanism** Abtastmechanismus *m*
- ~ **method** Abtastverfahren *n*; Abtastmethode *f*
- ~ **microscope** 1. Rastermikroskop *n*; 2. s. scanning electron microscope
- ~ **microscopy** Rastermikroskopie *f*
- ~ **microwave microscope** Rastermikrowellenmikroskop *n*
- ~ **mirror** Abtastspiegel *m*
- ~ **mode** Abtastmodus *m*, Scanmodus *m*
- ~ **motion (movement)** Abtastbewegung *f*
- ~ **near-field optical microscope** optisches Nahfeldmikroskop *n*
- ~ **near-field optical microscopy** optische Nahfeldmikroskopie *f*, nahfeldoptische Mikroskopie *f*
- ~ **noise** Abtastrauschen *n*, Abtastgeräusch *n*
- ~ **optics** Abtastobjektiv *n*, Abtastoptik *f*, Scanning-Objektiv *n*
- ~ **order** Abtastfolge *f*
- ~ **parameter** Abtastparameter *m*
- ~ **path** Abtastweg *m*
- ~ **photoemission microscope** Raster-Fotoemissionsmikroskop *n*
- ~ **photomacrography** Rastermakrofotografie *f*
- ~ **plane** Scanebene *f*
- ~ **principle** Abtastprinzip *n*
- ~ **printer** Rasterdrucker *m*
- ~ **prism** Abtastprisma *n*
- ~ **probe** Abtastsonde *f*
- ~ **probe microscope** Rastersondenmikroskop *n*
- ~ **probe microscopy** Rastersondenmikroskopie *f*
- ~ **probe microscopy image** rastersondenmikroskopisches Bild *n*
- ~ **probe tip** Sondenspitze *f (Elektronenmikroskop)*
- ~ **process** Abtastvorgang *m*, Scanvorgang *m*
- ~ **raster** Abtastraster *m(n)*, Raster *m(n) (Bildschirm)*
- ~ **rate** Abtastrate *f*, Abtastfrequenz *f*, Scanfrequenz *f*
- ~ **resolution** Abtastauflösung *f*, Scanauflösung *f*; Rasterauflösung *f*
- ~ **scheme** Abtastschema *n*
- ~ **sequence** Abtastfolge *f*
- ~ **slit** Abtastspalt *m*
- ~ **speed** Abtastgeschwindigkeit *f*, Scangeschwindigkeit *f*
- ~ **spot** Abtastpunkt *m*
- ~ **SQUID microscope** Raster-SQUID-Mikroskop *n*
- ~ **standard** Abtaststandard *m*, Abtastnorm *f*
- ~ **structure** Abtaststruktur *f*
- ~ **system** Abtastsystem *n*
- ~ **technique** Abtasttechnik *f*
- ~ **thermograph** Abtastthermograf *m*
- ~ **transmission electron microscope** Durchlicht-Rasterelektronenmikroskop *n*, Durchstrahlungs-Rasterelektronenmikroskop *n*, Rastertransmissionselektronenmikroskop *n*
- ~ **transmission electron microscopy** Durchlicht-Rasterelektronenmikroskopie *f*, Rastertransmissionselektronenmikroskopie *f*
- ~ **transmission ion microscope** Rastertransmissionsionenmikroskop *n*
- ~ **transmission X-ray microscope** Rastertransmissionsröntgenmikroskop *n*
- ~ **tube** Abtaströhre *f*
- ~ **tunneling microscope** Rastertunnelmikroskop *n*, [abtastendes] Tunnelmikroskop *n*
- ~ **tunneling microscopy** Rastertunnelmikroskopie *f*
- ~ **unit** Abtasteinheit *f*
- ~ **width** Scanbreite *f*
- ~ **X-ray microscope** Rasterröntgenmikroskop *n*

SCART cable SCART-Kabel *n*

~ **connection** SCART-Anschluss *m*,
Peri[tel]-Anschluss *m*,
Euro-AV-Anschluss *m (Videotechnik)*
~ **connector** SCART-Stecker *m*,
Euro-AV-Stecker *m*
~ **socket** SCART-Buchse *f*, Euro-AV-Buchse *f*
scatter/to [zer]streuen
scatter back/to [zu]rückstreuen
~ Streuung *f*; Zerstreuung *f*
~ **diagram** Punktdiagramm *n*,
Streuungsdiagramm *n*, Streubild *n*
~ **electron** Streuelektron *n*
~ **fraction** *s.* scattering fraction
~**-free** streuungsfrei
~ **matrix** Streuungsmatrix *f*
scattered amplitude Streuamplitude *f*
~ **data** gestreute (verteilte) Daten *pl*
~ **illumination** ungerichtete Ausleuchtung *f*
~ **light** gestreutes (zerstreutes) Licht *n*, Streulicht *n*
~ **pilot** verstreuter Pilot *m (Videosignal)*
~ **radiation** Streustrahlung *f*
scatterer Streukörper *m*, Streuer *m*;
Elementarreflektor *m (Radar)*
scattergram, scattergraph *s.* scatter diagram
scattering Streuung *f*; Zerstreuung *f*
~ **angle** Streuwinkel *m*
~ **center** Streuzentrum *n*
~ **coefficient** Streukoeffizient *m*
~ **cone** Streukegel *m*
~ **direction** Streurichtung *f*
~ **foil** Streufolie *f*
~ **fraction** Streustrahlenanteil *m*;
Streulichtanteil *m*
~ **image** Zerstreuungsfigur *f*
~ **loss** Streuverlust *m*
~ **matrix** Streumatrix *f*
~ **medium** [zer]streuendes Medium *n*
~ **of light** Licht[zer]streuung *f*,
Lichtdiffusion *f*
~ **power** Streuvermögen *n*
~ **process** Streuprozess *m*
~ **strength** Streuvermögen *n*
~ **surface** streuende Oberfläche *f*
scatterometer Fotogoniometer *n*
scatterplot *s.* scatter diagram
scenario Drehbuch *n*, Regiebuch *n*
scene 1. Szene *f*, Bildszene *f*;
mehrdimensionales Bild *n*; digitales Bild *n*; 2. Satellitenbild *n*; 3. Einstellung *f*,
Filmeinstellung *f*
~**-adaptive block matching**
szenenadaptiver Blockvergleich *m*
~**-adaptive coder** szenenadaptiver Codierer *m*
~ **analysis** Szenenanalyse *f*
~ **background** Szenenhintergrund *m*
~**-based interpolation** szenenbasierte Interpolation *f*
~**-based registration** szenenbasierte Registrierung *f*

~**-based segmentation** szenenbasierte Segmentierung *f*
~**-based surface rendering** szenenbasierte Oberflächendarstellung *f*
~**-based visualization** szenenbasierte Visualisierung *f*
~ **brightness** Motivhelligkeit *f*, Szenenhelligkeit *f*
~ **characteristic** Szenenmerkmal *n*
~ **color** Szenenfarbe *f*
~ **content** Szeneninhalt *m*
~ **contrast** Szenenkontrast *m*
~ **coordinate system**
Szenenkoordinatensystem *n*,
Weltkoordinatensystem *n*, weltfestes Koordinatensystem *n*
~ **depth** Szenentiefe *f*
~ **description** Szenenbeschreibung *f*
~ **description language**
Szenenbeschreibungssprache *f*
~ **distance** Szenenentfernung *f*
~ **domain** Szenenbereich *m*
~ **duration** Szenendauer *f*
~ **editor** Szeneneditor *m (Computergrafik)*
~ **element** Szenenelement *n*
~ **geometry** Szenengeometrie *f*
~ **graph** Szenegraph *m*
~ **heterogeneity** Szenenheterogenität *f*
~ **illumination** Szenenausleuchtung *f*
~ **information** Szeneninformation *f*
~ **intensity gradient**
Szenenintensitätsgradient *m*
(dreidimensionale Visualisierung)
~ **interpolation** Szeneninterpolation *f*
~ **luminance** Szenenhelligkeit *f*
~ **model** Szenenmodell *n*
~ **modeling** Szenenmodellierung *f*
~ **number** Szenennummer *f (Filmarbeit)*
~ **object** Szenenobjekt *n*
~ **parameter** Szenenparameter *m*
~ **point** Szenenpunkt *m*
~ **recognition** Szenenerkennung *f*
~ **segmentation** Szenensegmentierung *f*
~ **space** Szenenraum *m (Visualisierung)*
~ **structure** Szenenstruktur *f*
~ **transformation** Szenentransformation *f*
scenery Szenerie *f*
~ **change** Szenenwechsel *m*
scenic image Szenenbild *n*
~ **photography** Landschaftsfotografie *f*
Schadograph Schadografie *f*; Fotografik *f*,
Lichtgrafik *f*, Lichtzeichnung *f*,
Lichtmalerei *f*
schedulability Einplanbarkeit *f*
(Multimediadatenverarbeitung)
scheduling Drehplanung *f (Filmarbeit)*
Scheimpflug condition (law) *s.* ~ rule
~ **rule** Scheimpflugsche Regel (Bedingung) *f*, Scheimpflugsches Gesetz *n (Optik)*
Scheiner speed Scheiner-Grade *npl*
schematic [diagram] schematische Darstellung *f*
~ **drawing** Schemazeichnung *f*
~ **eye** schematisches Auge *n*

schematical 344

schematical representation schematische Darstellung *f*
schliere Schliere *f*
schlieren effect Schliereneffekt *m*
~ **image** Schlierenbild *n*
~ **interferometer** Schliereninterferometer *n*
~ **method** [Toeplersches] Schlierenverfahren *n* *(räumliche Filterung)*
~-**optical** schlierenoptisch
~ **optics** Schlierenoptik *f*
~ **pattern** Schlierenbild *n*
~ **photo[graph]** Schlierenbild *n*
~ **photography** Schlierenfotografie *f*
~ **setup** Schlierenaufnahmeanordnung *f*
Schlippe's salt Schlippesches Salz *n*
Schmidt camera s. ~ telescope camera
~-**Cassegrain telescope** Schmidt-Cassegrain-Teleskop *n*
~ **correcting (corrector) plate** Schmidt-Platte *f*, [Schmidtsche] Korrektionsplatte *f*, Kompensatorplatte *f*
~ **objective, Schmidt [projection] system** Schmidt-Optik *f*, Schmidt-Spiegel *m*
~ **telescope** Schmidt-Teleskop *n*
~ **telescope camera** Schmidt-Kamera *f* *(Astrofotografie)*
school photographer Schulfotograf *m*
~ **photography** Schulfotografie *f*
Schottky barrier pn-Übergang *m* *(Fotodiode)*
~ **barrier [photo]diode** Schottky-Diode *f*
~ **defect** Schottky-Defekt *m* *(Kristallbaufehler)*
~ **effect** Schottky-Effekt *m*
Schrödinger's [wave] equation Schrödinger-Gleichung *f* *(Quantenmechanik)*
Schufftan process Spiegeltrickverfahren *n*, Schüfftan-Verfahren *n*, Schüfftansches Einspiegelungsverfahren *n* *(Kinematografie)*
Schumann emulsion Schumann-Emulsion *f*
Schwarzschild behavior Schwarzschild-Verhalten *n*, Reziprozitätseffekt *m*
~ **camera** Schwarzschild-Kamera *f*
~ **effect** Schwarzschild-Effekt *m* *(Belichtungseffekt)*
~ **objective** Schwarzschild-Objektiv *n*
sciascopy Retinoskopie *f*
science of colors Farbwissenschaft *f*; Farb[en]lehre *f*, Chromatik *f*
scientific-grade CCD wissenschaftlicher CCD-Sensor *m*
~-**grade digital camera** wissenschaftliche Digitalkamera *f*
~ **image analysis** wissenschaftliche Bildanalyse *f*
~ **image processing** wissenschaftliche Bildverarbeitung *f*
~ **laser** wissenschaftlicher Laser *m*
~ **photographer** Wissenschaftsfotograf *m*
~ **photography** Wissenschaftsfotografie *f*, wissenschaftliche Fotografie *f*
~ **visualization** wissenschaftliche Visualisierung *f*
scintigraphic imaging szintigrafische Bildgebung *f*
scintigraphy Szintigrafie *f*
scintillate/to szintillieren
scintillation Szintillation *f*
~ **camera** Szintillationskamera *f*, [Einkristall-]Gammakamera *f*, Anger-Kamera *f*
~ **camera image** Szintigramm *n*
~ **counter** Szintillationszähler *m*
~ **crystal** Szintillationskristall *m*
~ **detector** Szintillationsdetektor *m*, Szintillationsscanner *m*
~ **grid** szintillierendes Gitter *n* *(optische Täuschung)*
~ **head** s. ~ probe
~ **layer** Szintillationsschicht *f*
~ **light** Szintillationslicht *n*
~ **probe** Szintillationsmesskopf *m*, Szintillationsmessonde *f*
~ **screen** Szintillationsschirm *m*, Szintillatofolie *f*
~ **signal** Szintillationssignal *n*
~ **time** Szintillationszeit *f*
scintillator Szintillator *m*
scissoring Beschneidung *f*, Beschnitt *m* *(Computergrafik)*
sclera, sclerotic [coat] Sklera *f*, Lederhaut *f*, harte Augenhaut *f*
scoop Oberlicht *n* *(Flächenleuchte)*
scope 1. Sichtgerät *n*; Betrachtungsgerät *n*; 2. Wellenformmonitor *m*; 3. Radarschirm *m*
score/to rillen *(Druckweiterverarbeitung)*
score Filmmusik *f*, Soundtrack *m*
~ **image** Eigenbild *n*
scorotron Skorotron *n* *(Elektrofotografie)*
scotoma Skotom *n*, Gesichtsfelddefekt *m*
scotopia Nachtsichtigkeit *f*
scotopic skotopisch, dunkeladaptiert
~ **troland** skotopisches Troland *n* *(Fotometrie)*
~ **vision** skotopisches (dunkeladaptiertes) Sehen *n*, Dunkelsehen *n*, Stäbchensehen *n*
scout view Übersichtsaufnahme *f*; Topogramm *n* *(Tomografie)*
scramble/to verwürfeln; verschachteln
scrambled signal verwürfeltes [digitales] Signal *n*
~ **text** verschlüsselter Text *m*
scrambler Verwürfler *m*
scrambling Verwürfelung *f*; Verschachtelung *f*
~ **non return zero code** S-NRZ-Code *m* *(digitale Signalspeicherung)*
scrap films Altfilmmaterial *n*
scrape [off]/to [ab]rakeln *(z.B. Druckfarbe)*

scraper Rakel f, Rakelmesser n, Abstreifrakel f, Stahlrakel f *(Tiefdruck)*
scratch Schramme f, Kratzer m
~ **resistance** Schrammenfestigkeit f, Kratzfestigkeit f *(z.B. von Filmmaterial)*
screen/to 1. rastern; 2. vorführen *(Kinefilm)*
screen 1. Bildschirm m; Bildwand f *(s.a. unter* display, monitor*);* 2. Leinwand f; 3. Stellwand f; 4. Raster m(n); Autotypieraster m(n), Kontaktraster m(n)
~ **angle** 1. Rasterwinkel m; 2. Bildschirmwinkel m *(Radar)*; 3. Projektionswinkel m
~ **area** Leinwandfläche f
~ **aspect ratio** Leinwandbildseitenverhältnis n
~ **background** Bildschirmhintergrund m
~ **base** Trägerschicht f *(radiografische Verstärkungsfolie)*
~ **blur** Folienunschärfe f *(Radiografie)*
~ **border** Bildschirmrand m
~ **brightness** Bildschirmhelligkeit f; Leinwandhelligkeit f
~ **center** Bildschirmmitte f
~ **change effect** Bildtrick m, Bildeffekt m *(Video)*
~ **color** Bildschirmfarbe f
~ **color process** Farbrasterverfahren n, Siebverfahren n *(frühe Farbfotografie)*
~ **content** Bildschirminhalt m
~ **coordinate** Bildschirmkoordinate f
~ **coordinate system** Bildschirmkoordinatensystem n
~ **corner** Bildschirmecke f
~ **credit** Titelrolle f
~ **cursor** Cursor m, Schreibmarke f, Einfügemarke f
~ **curvature** Bildschirmkrümmung f
~ **density** Rasterdichte f; Flächendeckung f, Flächendeckungsgrad m, Rastertonwert m *(Druck)*
~ **design** Bildschirmdesign n
~ **diagonal [size]** Bildschirmdiagonale f, Schirmdiagonale f
~ **distance** 1. Bildschirmabstand m; 2. Rasterabstand m *(Druck)*
~ **driver** Bildschirmtreiber m
~ **editor** Bildschirmeditor m
~-**film combination** Film-Folien-Kombination f *(Radiografie)*
~-**film mammography** Film-Folien-Mammografie f
~-**film radiography** Film-Folien-Radiografie f
~ **flare (flicker)** Bildschirmflimmern n; Leinwandflimmern n
~ **fluorescence** Bildschirmfluoreszenz f
~ **focusing camera** Mattscheibenkamera f
~ **font** Bildschirmschrift f
~ **format** 1. Bildschirmformat n; 2. Leinwandformat n
~ **frequency** *s.* ~ ruling

~ **glare** Bildschirmspiegelung f, Reflexion f am Bildschirm
~ **graphics** Bildschirmgrafik f
~ **grid** Schirmgitter n
~ **height** Bildschirmhöhe f
~ **illumination** Bildschirmausleuchtung f
~ **image** 1. Bildschirmbild n; Monitorbild n; Schirmbild n; 2. Leinwandbild n
~-**image aspect ratio** Leinwandbildseitenverhältnis n
~ **line** Bildschirmzeile f
~ **luminance** Bildschirmleuchtdichte f; Leinwandhelligkeit f; Bildwandleuchtdichte f, Bildwandausleuchtung f
~ **management** Bildschirmgestaltung f
~ **mask** 1. Bildschirmmaske f, Bildröhrenmaske f, Bildschirmrahmen m; 2. Bildwandabdeckung f *(Filmprojektion)*
~ **miniaturization** Bildschirm-Miniaturisierung f
~ **object** Bildschirmobjekt n
~ **page** Bildschirmseite f
~ **pattern** Rastermuster n
~ **percentage** Flächendeckung f, Flächendeckungsgrad m, Rastertonwert m *(Druck)*
~ **phone** Bildtelefon n, Bildfernsprecher m, Videofon n
~ **phosphor** Bildschirmphosphor m
~ **photography** Rasterfotografie f
~ **picture** 1. Schirmbild n; 2. Leinwandbild n
~ **pixel** Bildschirmpixel n, Monitorpixel n
~ **plane** Bildschirmebene f
~ **plate** Rasterplatte f
~ **pointer** Cursor m, Positionsmarke f *(Bildschirm)*
~ **presentation** Bildschirmdarstellung f
~ **press** Siebdruckpresse f
~ **printing** 1. Rasterdruck m; 2. Siebdruck m, Durchdruck m
~ **printing ink** Siebdruckfarbe f
~ **process** Rasterverfahren n *(frühe Farbfotografie)*
~ **projection** Leinwandprojektion f
~ **radiation** Bildschirmstrahlung f
~ **refresh rate** Bildwiederholfrequenz f, Bildwiederholrate f, Bilderneuerungsfrequenz f, Bildwechselfrequenz f
~ **resolution** Bildschirmauflösung f, bildschirmbedingte Auflösung f
~ **rolling** Bildrollen n
~ **ruling** Rasterweite f, Rasterzahl f, Rasterfeinheit f, Rasterfrequenz f
~ **saver** Bildschirmschoner m
~ **shot** Bildschirmaufnahme f, Fernsehschirmbild n, Bildschirmfoto n, Schirmbildaufnahme f
~ **size** Bildschirmgröße f

screen

~ **space** 1. Bildschirmfläche *f*; 2. Bildkoordinatensystem *n* *(Computergrafik)*
~ **speaker** Bühnenlautsprecher *m*
~ **split** Bildschirmteilung *f*
~ **splitter** Bildschirmteiler *m*
~ **splitting** Bildschirmaufteilung *f*, Bildschirm-Splitting *n*
~ **store** Bildschirmspeicher *m*
~ **surface** Leindwandfläche *f*
~ **texture** Siebdruckgewebe *n*
~ **tilt** Bildschirmneigung *f*
~ **time** Vorführzeit[dauer] *f*, Filmlaufzeit *f*
~ **tint** Rasterton *m*
~**-to-audience distance** Betrachterabstand *m*, Betrachtungsabstand *m*, Betrachtungsentfernung *f*
~ **tone** Rasterton *m*
~**-type film** Schirmbildfilm *m*
~**-type X-ray film** Röntgenfolienfilm *m*, Folienfilm *m*
~ **viewfinder** Mattscheibensucher *m*
~ **width** Bildschirmbreite *f*
~ **window** Bildschirmfenster *n*, Monitorfenster *n*
~ **work** Bildschirmarbeit *f*
screenable vorführbar, spielbar *(Filmkopie)*
screened digital hard proof materieller Raster-Digitalproof *m*
~ **image** gerastertes Bild *n*, Rasterbild *n* *(Reprografie)*
~ **offset plate** gerasterte Offsetdruckplatte *f*
~ **photograph** gerastertes Foto *n*
screening 1. Rastern *n*; 2. Projektionsdurchlauf *m*; Projektion *f*; Filmvorführung *f*, Vorführung *f*; 3. Filmbetrachtung *f*
~ **algorithm** Rasteralgorithmus *m*
~ **room** Vorführraum *m*, Filmvorführraum *m*, Projektorraum *m*
~ **study** Siebtest *m* *(z.B. in der Radiografie)*
screenland Filmindustrie *f*, Kinofilmindustrie *f*, Filmbranche *f*, Filmwirtschaft *f*
screenless lithography rasterlose Lithografie *f*
~ **printing process** rasterloses Druckverfahren *n*
screenplay Drehbuch *n*, Regiebuch *n*
screenwrighter, screenwriter Drehbuchautor *m*, Filmautor *m*
screw dislocation Schraubenversetzung *f* *(Elektronenmikroskopie)*
~**-in filter** *s.* screw-type filter
~ **thread** *s.* screw-type lens mount
~**-type filter** Einschraubfilter *n*, eindrehbares Filter *n*
~**-type lens mount** Schraubfassungsanschluss *m*, Gewindeanschluss *m*, Fassungsanschluss *m*, Einschraubfassung *f* *(Objektiv)*

scribble Ideenskizze *f*, Gedankenskizze *f*, Handskizze *f*, Schmierskizze *f*, Planungsskizze *f*, Skizze *f*, Rohzeichnung *f*, Scribble *n*
scrim Drahtgaze *f*; Diffusionsfolie *f*; Streufolie *f* *(Filmlichtsteuerung)*
script 1. Filmskript *n*; Drehprotokoll *n*; Cutterbericht *m*; 2. *s.* ~ typeface
~ **girl (supervisor)** Skriptgirl *n*
~ **typeface** Schreibschrift *f*, Schrift *f*
scroll/to blättern, navigieren *(Bildschirmarbeit)*
scroll arrow Bildlaufpfeil *m*
~ **bar** Bildlaufleiste *f*, Rollbalken *m* *(Display)*
~ **box** Bildlauffeld *n*
scrolling Bildrollen *n*
SCSI device SCSI-Gerät *n*
~ **hard disk** SCSI-Festplatte *f*
sea clutter Seeclutter *m*, Seegangecho *n* *(Radar)*
seamless impression roll nahtloser Druckzylinder *m* *(Druckmaschine)*
~ **roll** Hintergrundrolle *f* *(Atelierausrüstung)*
search Suche *f* *(Datenverarbeitung)*
~ **algorithm** Suchalgorithmus *m*
~ **area** Suchbereich *m*
~ **capacity** Suchkapazität *f*
~ **criterion** Suchkriterium *n*
~ **effort** Suchaufwand *m*
~ **engine** Suchmaschine *f*, Datenbankserver *m*
~ **file** Suchdatei *f*
~ **function** Suchfunktion *f*
~ **graph** Suchgraph *m*
~ **image** Suchbild *n*
~ **movement** Suchbewegung *f* *(z.B. der Augen)*
~ **pattern** Suchmuster *n*
~ **point** Suchpunkt *m*
~ **precision** Suchgenauigkeit *f*
~ **procedure** Suchverfahren *n*
~ **radar** Suchradar *m*
~ **range** Suchbereich *m*
~ **region** Suchbereich *m*
~ **result** Suchergebnis *n*
~ **run** Suchlauf *m*
~ **space** Suchraum *m*
~ **square** Suchquadrat *n*
~ **step** Suchschritt *m*
~ **strategy** Suchstrategie *f* *(z.B. in der Mustererkennung)*
~ **task** Suchaufgabe *f*
~ **term** Suchbegriff *m*
~ **time** Suchzeit *f*
~ **tool** Suchwerkzeug *n*
~ **tree algorithm** Suchbaumalgorithmus *m*
~ **window** Suchfenster *n*
searchlight Suchscheinwerfer *m*
season/to konditionieren *(z.B. Druckpapier)*
SECAM field identification bottles SECAM-Identifikationssignale *npl*

~ **process** SECAM-Verfahren *n* (Farbfernsehen; abgeleitet von Sequential Couleur A Mémoire)
SECM *s.* scanning electrochemical microscope
second assistant cameraman Zweiter Kameraassistent *m*, Materialassistent *m*, Loader *m* (Filmteam)
~**-curtain synchronization** Synchronisation *f* auf den zweiten Verschlussvorhang
~ **developer** Zweitentwickler *m*
~ **development** Zweitentwicklung *f*
~ **exposure** Zweitbelichtung *f*; Zwischenbelichtung *f*
~ **focal point** bildseitiger Brennpunkt *m*, Bildbrennpunkt *m*
~ **of arc** Bogensekunde *f*
~**-order gradient** Gradient *m* zweiter Ordnung
~**-order polynomial** Polynom *n* zweiter Ordnung
~**-order statistics** Statistik *f* zweiter Ordnung
~ **ripening** chemische Reifung (Sensibilisierung) *f*, Nachreifung *f*, Nachdigestion *f* (Emulsionsherstellung)
~**-trip echo** Geisterecho *n* (Radar)
secondary audio program Zweikanalton *m* (Fernsehtechnik)
~ **cell** Akkumulator *m*, Akku *m*
~ **color** Sekundärfarbe *f*
~ **electron** Sekundärelektron *n*
~**-electron image** Sekundärelektronenbild *n*
~ **electron imaging** Sekundärelektronenabbildung *f*
~ **emission** Sekundäremission *f*
~ **excitation** Sekundäranregung *f* (Röntgenfluoreszenz)
~ **feature** Sekundärmerkmal *n*
~ **fluorescence** sekundäre Fluoreszenz *f*
~ **image** sekundäres Bild *n*
~ **ion mass spectrometer** Sekundärionen-Massenspektrometer *n*
~ **ion mass spectrometry** Sekundärionen-Massenspektrometrie *f*
~ **light source** Fremdstrahler *m*, Sekundärlichtquelle *f*, sekundäre Lichtquelle *f*
~ **maximum** Nebenmaximum *n* (Beugungsoptik)
~ **mirror** Sekundärspiegel *m*, Fangspiegel *m* (z.B. eines Spiegellinsenobjektivs)
~ **radar** Sekundärradar *n* (s.a. synthetic aperture radar)
~ **radiation** Sekundärstrahlung *f*, sekundäre Streustrahlung *f*
~ **radiator** Sekundärstrahler *m*
~ **reaction** Sekundärreaktion *f*
~ **reflection** Sekundärreflexion *f*
~ **spectrum** sekundäres Spektrum *n*; Farbrestfehler *m* (Optik)
~ **storage** Sekundärspeicher *m*

~ **surveillance radar** *s.* ~ radar
~ **target** Sekundärtarget *n* (Röntgenfluoreszenz)
secret camera Geheimkamera *f*, Detektivkamera *f*
section Schnitt *m*
~ **image** Schnittbild *n*, Tomogramm *n*
~ **plane** Schnittebene *f*
sectional image Schnittbild *n*
~ **view** Schnittansicht *f*
sector aperture Sektorenblende *f*, Flügelblende *f*, Umlauf[sektoren]blende *f*, Sektor[en]verschluss *m* (Kinotechnik)
~ **disk** Sektorenscheibe *f* (z.B. eines Sensitometers)
~ **image** Sektorbild *n* (Sonografie)
~ **scanner** Sektorscanner *m* (Sonografie)
~ **scanning** Sektorabtastung *f* (Radar)
~ **wheel shutter** *s.* ~ aperture
security camera Überwachungskamera *f*
~ **camera video** Überwachungsvideo *n*
~ **printing** Wertpapierdruck *m*
~ **X-ray machine** Röntgen-Videosichtgerät *n*
seed crystal Kristallkeim *m*
~ **pixel** Anfangsbildpunkt *m*
~ **point** Keimpunkt *m*, Saatpunkt *m* (Bereichswachstumsverfahren der Bildsegmentierung)
seeing 1. Sehen *n*; 2. Seeing *n* (Astrooptik, Astrofotografie)
seek time Suchzeit *f*
segment/to segmentieren
segment Segment *n*
~ **boundary** Segmentkontur *f*
segmentable segmentierbar
segmental 1. segmental; 2. segmentweise
segmentation Segmentierung *f*, Segmentation *f*
~ **accuracy** Segmentierungsgenauigkeit *f*
~ **algorithm** Segmentierungsalgorithmus *m*
~ **approach** Segmentierungsansatz *m*
~ **error** Segmentierungsfehler *m*
~ **feature** Segmentierungsmerkmal *n*
~ **line** Segmentierungslinie *f*
~ **mask** Segmentierungsmaske *f*
~ **model** Segmentierungsmodell *n*
~ **object** Segmentierungsobjekt *n*
~ **performance** Segmentierungsleistung *f*
~ **process** Segmentierungsprozess *m*
~ **result** Segmentierungsergebnis *n*
~ **technique** Segmentierungstechnik *f*
segmented coding segmentierte Codierung *f*
~ **feature** segmentiertes Merkmal *n*
~ **image** segmentiertes Bild *n*
segue Szenenübergang *m* (Filmarbeit)
Seidel [monochromatic] aberration Seidel-Aberration *f*, Seidelscher Bildfehler (Abbildungsfehler) *m*
seismic imaging seismische Bildgebung *f*
~ **tomography** seismische Tomografie *f*
seismogram Seismogramm *n*

seismograph Seismograf *m*
seismographic seismografisch
seismography Seismografie *f*
selected-area diffraction
Feinbereichsbeugung *f*
(Elektronenmikroskopie)
selection tool Auswahlwerkzeug *n (digitale Bildbearbeitung)*
selective absorption selektive Absorption *f*
~ **angiography** selektive Angiografie *f*
~ **color correction** selektive Farbkorrektur *f*
~ **color filtering** selektive Farbfilterung *f*
~ **enlargement** Ausschnittvergrößerung *f*, Bildausschnittvergrößerung *f*
~ **excitation** selektive Anregung *f (Magnetresonanzbildgebung)*
~ **filtering (filtration)** selektive Filterung *f*
~ **focusing** selektive Fokussierung *f*
~ **key** Auswahlschlüssel *m (Bildanalyse)*
~ **radiator** Lumineszenzstrahler *m*, Nichttemperaturstrahler *m*, selektiver Strahler *m*
~ **reflection** selektive Reflexion *f*
~ **smoothing** selektive Glättung *f*
selectivity Selektivität *f*
selector aperture Selektorblende *f (Elektronenmikroskop)*
~ **dial** Wahlrad *n*, Wählscheibe *f*, [Betriebsarten-]Einstellrad *n*
selenium Selen *n*
~ **[photo]cell, ~ photovoltaic cell** Selenzelle *f*, Selenfotoelement *n*
~ **powder** Selenpulver *n*
~ **toner** Selentoner *m*
~ **toning** Selentonung *f*
self-adhesive strip Selbstklebeband *n*
~**-affine distortion** selbstaffine Verzerrung *f (Computergrafik)*
~**-blimped camera** selbstgeblimpte Kamera *f*
~**-calibration** Selbstkalibrierung *f*, Simultankalibrierung *f (von Kamerasystemen)*
~**-clocking** selbsttaktend *(z.B. Videodaten)*
~**-cocking shutter** Automatverschluss *m*
~**-convolution** Selbstfaltung *f*
~**-developing film** selbstentwickelnder Film *m*
~**-emitting** selbstemittierend
~**-filtering** Eigenfilterung *f (von Röntgenstrahlen)*
~**-focusing** Selbstfokussierung *f*
~**-focusing fiber** selbstfokussierende [optische] Faser *f*
~**-illuminate/to** selbstleuchten
~**-illuminating** selbstleuchtend
~**-illumination** Selbstleuchten *n*
~**-imaging** selbstabbildend
~**-luminous display** selbstleuchtender Bildschirm *m*
~**-luminous object** selbstleuchtendes Objekt *n*, Selbstleuchter *m*, Selbststrahler *m*, Primärstrahler *m*

~**-organizing feature map** selbstorganisierende Karte (Merkmalskarte) *f*, selbstorganisierendes Tableau *n*, Kohonen-Karte *f*, Kohonen-Netz *n (Mustererkennung)*
~**-organizing neural network** selbstorganisierendes neuronales Netz *n*
~**-oxidation** Autoxidation *f*
~**-scanned photodiode** selbstabtastende Fotodiode *f*
~**-shadow** Eigenschatten *m*
~**-similar fractal** selbstähnliches Fraktal *n*
~**-similar image** selbstähnliches Bild *n*
~**-similar object** selbstähnliches Objekt *n*
~**-similar pattern** selbstähnliches Muster *n*
~**-similarity** Selbstähnlichkeit *f*
~**-sticking tape** Selbstklebeband *n*
~**-timer indicator LED (light-emitting diode)** Selbstauslöser-Leuchtdiode *f*
~**-timer shutter release** Selbstauslöser *m*, Vorlauf-Federwerk *n*
~**-transformation** Selbsttransformation *f (Bildcodierung)*
Selwyn granularity Selwyn-Körnigkeit *f*, Selwyn-Körnung *f*
SEM photograph REM-Aufnahme *f*, rasterelektronenmikroskopische Aufnahme *f*
semantic class semantische Klasse *f*
~ **coding** semantische Codierung *f*
~ **descriptor** semantischer Deskriptor *m*
~ **model** semantisches Modell *n*
~ **modeling** semantische Modellierung *f*
~ **network** semantisches Netz *n (Datenstruktur)*
~ **primitive** semantisches Primitiv *n*
semi-closeup Halbnahe *f*, Halbnaheinstellung *f*
~**-continuous hidden Markov model** semikontinuierliches Hidden-Markow-Modell *n*
semiactive radar halbaktives Radar *n*
semiadaptive [en]coding semiadaptive Codierung *f*
~ **compression** semiadaptive Kompression *f*
semiangle Halbwinkel *m*
semiapochromatic halbapochromatisch
~ **objective** Halbapochromat *m*, Fluoritobjektiv *n*, Fluoritlinse *f*
semiautomatic camera halbautomatische Kamera *f*
~ **flash-exposure control** autofokusgekoppelte Blitzsteuerung *f*
~ **interpretation** halbautomatische Auswertung *f*
semiconducting film Halbleiterfolie *f*
~ **laser** *s.* semiconductor laser [diode]
semiconductive material Halbleitermaterial *n*
semiconductor Halbleiter *m*
~**-based detector** Halbleiterdetektor *m*
~**-based photodetector** Halbleiterfotodetektor *m*

~ **cell** Sperrschicht-Fotoelement *n*, Sperrschicht[foto]zelle *f*
~ **crystal** Halbleiterkristall *m*
~ **device** Halbleiter[bau]element *n*, Halbleiterbaustein *m*
~ **device fabrication** Halbleiterherstellung *f*
~ **diode** Halbleiterdiode *f*
~ **display** Halbleiterdisplay *n*; Halbleiterbildschirm *m*
~ **electronics industry** Halbleiterelektronikindustrie *f*
~ **integrated chip** Halbleiterchip *m*
~ **laser [diode]** Halbleiterlaser *m*, Halbleiterlaserdiode *f*, Injektionslaser *m*
~ **LED (light-emitting diode)** Halbleiter-Leuchtdiode *f*
~ **material** Halbleitermaterial *n*
~ **matrix** Halbleitermatrix *f*
~ **memory** Halbleiterspeicher *m*
~ **memory card** Halbleiter-Speicherkarte *f*
~ **optical** halbleiteroptisch
~ **optics** Halbleiteroptik *f*
~ **optoelectronics** Halbleiter-Optoelektronik *f*
~ **photocell** Halbleiterfotoelement *n*, Halbleiterfotozelle *n*
~ **photodiode [detector]** Halbleiterfotodiode *f*
~ **photoemissive detector** Halbleiterfotodetektor *m*
~ **radiation detector** Halbleiter-Strahlungsdetektor *m*
~ **resistor** Halbleiterwiderstand *m*
~ **technology** Halbleitertechnik *f*, Halbleitertechnologie *f*
~ **wafer** Halbleiterscheibe *f*, Wafer *m*
semidarkened room halbdunkler Raum *m*
semidarkness Halbdunkel *n*
semifield angle halber Feldwinkel *m* *(Objektiv)*
semigloss paper *s.* semimatt[e] paper
semigraphics Semigrafik *f*
semilogarithmic halblogarithmisch
semimatt[e] paper halbmattes (seidenmattes) Papier *n*
semimetal Halbmetall *n*
semipro[fessional] camera semiprofessionelle Kamera *f*, Semiprofikamera *f*
semiprofessional photographer semiprofessioneller Fotograf *m*
semiquinone Semichinon *n*
semireflecting mirror *s.* semitransparent mirror
semisilhouette profile portrait Halbprofil-Aufnahme *f*
semisilvered mirror *s.* semitransparent mirror
semitransparent semitransparent, halbtransparent, halbdurchsichtig
~ **mirror** halbdurchlässiger Spiegel *m*, Halbspiegel *m*
~ **paper** Transparentpapier *n*
send/to [aus]senden

send by telex/to telexen
~ **out/to** [aus]senden
sender Sender *m*
senior animator Hauptphasenzeichner *m* *(Zeichentrickfilm)*
sensation Sinneseindruck *m*, [sinnliche] Empfindung *f*, Sinnesempfindung *f*
~ **of brightness** Helligkeitsempfindung *f*, Helligkeitsempfinden *n*
~ **of color** Farbempfindung *f*, Farbempfinden *n*
~ **of light** Lichtempfindung *f*
sense/to detektieren *(s.a.* detect/to*)*
sense impression Sinneseindruck *m (s.a.* sensation*)*
~ **of depth** Tiefeneindruck *m*
~ **of distance** Entfernungseindruck *m*
~ **of perspective** Raumsinn *m*
~ **of rotation** Drehsinn *m*
~ **of scale** Proportionsempfinden *n*
~ **of sight (vision)** Gesichtssinn *m*, Sehsinn *m*, Visus *m*
~ **organ** Sinnesorgan *n*
~ **perception** Sinneswahrnehmung *f*, sinnliche Wahrnehmung *f*
sensible phenomenon Empfindungsphänomen *n*
sensing device Sensor *m*, Messfühler *m*
~ **element** Sensorelement *n*
~ **head** Aufnahmekopf *m*
~ **material** Sensormaterial *n*
~ **platform** Aufnahmeplattform *f*
~ **probe** Messkopf *m*, Sonde *f*
sensitive empfindlich; lichtempfindlich
~ **electronics** Sensorelektronik *f*
~ **to infrared light** infrarotempfindlich
~ **to light** lichtempfindlich, fotoempfindlich, fotosensibel
~ **to X-rays** röntgen[strahlen]empfindlich
sensitiveness, sensitivity Empfindlichkeit *f*; Bildrauschabstand *m*; Ansprechempfindlichkeit *f (Fotodetektor)*
sensitivity center Empfindlichkeitszentrum *n*
~ **curve [of the eye]** Augenempfindlichkeitskurve *f*, Empfindlichkeitskurve *f*
~ **function** Empfindlichkeitskurve *f*
~ **increase** Empfindlichkeitssteigerung *f*, Empfindlichkeitsgewinn *m*
~ **limit** Empfindlichkeitsgrenze *f*
~ **loss** Empfindlichkeitsverlust *m*
~ **of film** Filmempfindlichkeit *f*
~ **of the [human] eye** Augenempfindlichkeit *f*
~ **peak** Empfindlichkeitsmaximum *n*
~ **range** Empfindlichkeitsbereich *m*; Empfindlichkeitsspielraum *m*
~ **speck** Empfindlichkeitspunkt *m*
~ **spectrum** Empfindlichkeitsspektrum *n*
~ **time control** Nahechodämpfung *f (Radar)*

sensitivity 350

~ **to light** Lichtempfindlichkeit f, Fotoempfindlichkeit f
~ **to noise** Rauschempfindlichkeit f
~ **vector** Empfindlichkeitsvektor m
sensitizable sensibilisierbar
sensitization Sensibilisierung f, Sensibilisation f
sensitize/to sensibilisieren
sensitized emulsion sensibilisierte Emulsion f
~ **paper** lichtempfindliches (sensibilisiertes) Papier n
sensitizer, sensitizing agent Sensibilisator m
sensitizing center Reif[e]keim m, Subkeim m *(Latentbildentstehung)*
~ **dye** Sensibilisatorfarbstoff m, Sensibilisierfarbstoff m
~ **power** Sensibilisierungsvermögen n
~ **reagent** Sensibilisator m
sensitometer Sensitometer n, Empfindlichkeitsmesser m, Lichtempfindlichkeitsmesser m
sensitometric sensitometrisch
~ **curve** sensitometrische Kurve f
~ **exposure** sensitometrische Belichtung f
~ **strip** Sensitometerstreifen m
sensitometry Sensitometrie f, Empfindlichkeitsmessung f, Lichtempfindlichkeitsmessung f
sensor Sensor m, Messfühler m *(s.a. unter detector)*
~ **accuracy** Sensorgenauigkeit f
~ **amplifier** Sensorverstärker m
~ **architecture** Sensorarchitektur f
~ **area** Sensorfläche f
~ **array** Sensor-Array n, Sensortablett n, Sensorfläche f; Flächen[bild]sensor m, flächiger Sensor m
~ **auto flash** Sensorblitzgerät n
~ **chip** Sensorchip m
~ **circuitry** Sensorschaltung f
~ **current** Sensorstrom m
~ **data** Sensordaten pl
~ **element** Sensorelement n, Sel n
~ **engineering** Sensortechnik f, Sensorik f
~ **glove** Datenhandschuh m, Codehandschuh m, sensorischer Handschuh m *(Navigationswerkzeug)*
~ **head** Sensorkopf m
~ **material** Sensormaterial n
~ **model** Sensormodell n
~ **noise** Sensor[eigen]rauschen n
~ **pixel** Sensorpixel n
~ **plane** Sensorebene f
~ **position** Sensorposition f
~ **spectrum** Sensorspektrum n
~ **technology** Sensortechnik f, Sensorik f
sensorial s. sensory
sensory sensorisch, sensoriell
~ **fusion** sensorische Fusion f
~ **perception** Sinneswahrnehmung f, sinnliche Wahrnehmung f
~ **performance** Sinnesleistung f

~ **physiology** Sinnesphysiologie f
~ **psychology** Sinnespsychologie f
~ **stimulus** sensorischer Reiz m, Sinnesreiz m
~ **system** Sinnesorgan n
sentential calculus Aussagenkalkül n(m)
separability Separierbarkeit f
separable filter separierbares Filter n
~ **flash unit** externes Blitzgerät n
~ **mask** s. ~ filter
~ **signal** separierbares Signal n
separate/to separieren
separate-component coding Komponentencodierung f *(digitales Fernsehen)*
~ **video** S-Video n *(Signalformat)*
separated magnetic [sound] Magnetfilm m mit Tonaufzeichnung
separately recorded sound separat aufgenommener Filmton m, asynchroner Ton m
separating filter s. separation filter
~ **surface** Hyperfläche f *(Musterklassifikation)*
separation color Auszugsfarbe f
~ **film** Farbauszugsfilm m
~ **filter** Auszugsfilter n, Trennfilter n
~ **master** s. ~ positive
~ **negative** Separationsnegativ n, Auszugsnegativ n, Farbauszugsnegativ n
~ **of tones** Tonwerttrennung f
~ **positive** Auszugspositiv n, Farbauszugspositiv n
~ **printing** Farbauszugskopieren n
sepia 1. sepia[braun]; 2. s. ~ print
~ **effect** Sepiaeffekt m
~ **paper** Sepiapapier n
~ **print** Sepiaabzug m
~ **tone** Sepiaton m
~ **tone filter** Sepiafilter n
~ **toner** Sepiatoner m
~ **toning** Sepiatonung f, Sulfidtonung f
SEPMAG s. separated magnetic [sound]
sequel mehrteilige Verfilmung f
sequence Sequenz f, Folge f
~ **analysis** Sequenzanalyse f
~ **camera** Serienkamera f
~ **number** Szenennummer f *(Filmarbeit)*
~ **of instructions** Befehlsfolge f
~ **of photographs** Fotosequenz f, Fotoserie f, Fotoreihe f
~ **of pictures** Bildsequenz f, Bildfolge f
~ **of pulses** Pulssequenz f, Pulsfolge f
~ **of scenes** Szenenfolge f
~ **photograph** Serienfotografie f *(s.a. sequential image)*
sequencing Sequentialisierung f
sequency s. sequence
sequential access sequentieller Zugriff m
~ **code** sequentieller Code m
~ **coding (data compression)** progressive Codierung f, sequentielle Kompression f
~ **edge extraction** sequentielle Kantenextraktion f, Linienverfolgung f

~ **exposure** Reihenbelichtung *f*
~ **file** sequentielle Datei *f*
~ **frequency modulation** sequentielle Frequenzmodulation *f*
~ **image** Reihenbild *n*, Serienaufnahme *f*
~ **image processing** sequentielle (serielle) Bildverarbeitung *f*
~ **processing** sequentielle Verarbeitung *f* *(z.B. von Bilddaten)*
~ **scanning** progressive Abtastung *f*, Folgeabtastung *f*, Vollbildabtastung *f*, Vollbildaufzeichnung *f (Video)*
~ **spectrometer** Sequenzspektrometer *n*
~ **storage** sequentieller Speicher *m*
~ **transmission** sequentielle Übertragung *f*
sequesterant, sequestering agent (compound) Entkalkungsmittel *n*, Kalkschutzmittel *n (Entwicklerzusatz)*
serial [impact] printer Seriendrucker *m*
~ **bitstream** serieller Bitstrom *m*
~ **cable** serielles Kabel *n*
~ **camera** Filmwechsler *m (Röntgendiagnostik)*
~ **data** serielle Daten *pl*
~ **data interface (port)** serielle Schnittstelle *f*
~ **data stream** serieller Datenstrom *m*
~ **data transfer** serielle Datenübertragung *f*
~ **digital interface** seriell-digitale Schnittstelle *f*
~ **image** *s.* sequential image
~ **interface** serielle Schnittstelle *f*
~ **photograph** Serienfotografie *f*
~ **port [connection]** serieller Anschluss *m (Datenübertragung)*
~ **processing** sequentielle Verarbeitung *f* *(z.B. von Bilddaten)*
~ **radiography** Schnellserienaufnahmetechnik *f*, Seriografie *f*
~ **scanning** Seriellabtastung *f*, Serienabtastung *f*
~ **section images** Schnittbildserie *f*
~ **video** analoges Video *n*
serialize/to serialisieren
serializer Parallel-Seriell-Umsetzer *m*
series Serie *f*; Reihe *f*
~ **camera** Serienkamera *f*
~ **expansion** Reihenentwicklung *f*
~ **of characters** Zeichenkette *f*, Zeichenfolge *f*
~ **of diodes** Diodenreihe *f*, Diodenzeile *f*
~ **of images** Bildserie *f*, Bildreihe *f*, Bild[er]folge *f*
~ **of photographs** Fotoserie *f*, Fotoreihe *f*, Fotosequenz *f*
~ **of pulses** Impulsfolge *f*, Impulssequenz *f*, Pulsfolge *f*
~-**produced lens** Serienobjektiv *n*
serif Serife *f*, Serif *n*, Fußstrich *m (Typografie)*
~ **font** Serifenschrift *f*, serifenbehaftete Schrift *f*
~ **shape** Serifenform *f*

~ **type[face]** *s.* ~ font
serigraphic serigrafisch
~ **printing** Siebdruck *m*
serigraphy Serigrafie *f*, Kunstsiebdruck *m*, künstlerischer Siebdruck *m*
seriography *s.* serial radiography
serious amateur ambitionierter (engagierter) Amateur *m*
serration pulse Sägezahnimpuls *m (Fernsehsignal)*
server [machine] Server *m (Computer)*
~ **software** Server-Software *f*
service area *s.* serving area
~ **bureau** Reproanstalt *f*
~ **information** dienstebezogene Information *f*
~ **provider** Diensteanbieter *m*; Dienst[e]erbringer *m (Datenkommunikation)*
serving area Versorgungsgebiet *n*, Satellitenempfangsgebiet *n (Fernsehübertragung)*
servo *s.* servomechanism
~ **lockup time** Servo-Hochlaufzeit *f (Magnetbildtechnik)*
servomechanism Servoregelung *f*, servomotorische Steuerung *f*
servomotor Servomotor *m*, Stellmotor *m*
session layer Steuerungsschicht *f (Datenübertragung)*
set/to [aus]härten *(z.B. Klebstoffe)*
set off/to abliegen *(Druckschwierigkeit)*
~ 1. Menge *f*; 2. Set *m*, Filmset *m*, Produktionsort *m*; Filmkulisse *f*, Filmdekoration *f*, Vollkulisse *f*; 3. Typenbreite *f (Typografie)*
~ **designer** Filmarchitekt *m*, Filmszenenbildner *m*
~ **exposure time** eingestellte Belichtungszeit *f*
~ **light** Dekorationslicht *n*
~ **lighting fixture** Dekorationsleuchte *f*
~ **lighting technician** Beleucht[ungstechnik]er *m*, Lichttechniker *m*
~ **of attributes** Attributmenge *f*
~ **of curves** Kurvenschar *f*, Kurvenfamilie *f*
~ **of data** Datenmenge *f*
~ **of filters** Filtersatz *m*, Filtersortiment *n*
~ **of instructions** Befehlsvorrat *m*
~ **of lenses** Objektivsatz *m*
~ **of prisms** Prismensatz *m*
~ **of projection data** Projektionsdatensatz *m*
~ **of tools** Werkzeugpalette *f (Computergrafik)*
~ **of type** Schriftart *f*
~ **operator** Mengenoperator *m*
~ **piece** Dekorationsteil *n*
~ **size** Dickte *f*, Zeichendickte *f*, Buchstabenbreite *f (Handsatzletter)*
~ **square** Messwinkel *m*
~-**theoretic** mengentheoretisch

~-theoretic operation mengentheoretische Operation *f*
~ theory Mengentheorie *f (mathematische Morphologie)*
~-top appliance Beistellgerät *n*
~-top box [decoder], **~ converter** Beistelldecoder *m*, Set-Top-Box *f*, digitaler Empfangsdecoder *m*, Zusatzempfangsgerät *n (Digitalfernsehen)*
~ turnover Dekorationswechsel *m*
setoff Ablegen *n (Druck)*
setting 1. Einstellung *f (z.B. der Kamera)*; 2. *s.* set 2.
~ error Einstellfehler *m*
~ range Einstellbereich *m*
~ ring Einstellring *m*, Stellring *m*
~ to zero Nullsetzen *n*
setup 1. Einstellung *f*; Kameraeinstellung *f (Filmarbeit)*; 2. *s.* makeready
~ level Schwarzpegel *m*, Schwarzwert *m (Videosignal)*
seven-element lens Siebenlinser *m (Objektiv)*
~-ink printing Siebenfarbendruck *m*
~-track magnetic sound Siebenspur-Magnetton *m*
sexadecimal digit Sedezimalziffer *f*
SFN *s.* single-frequency network
SFX sup[ervisor] Trickregisseur *m*
shade/to schattieren, abschatten
shade 1. Schatten *m*; Bildschwarz *n*; 2. Schattierung *f*, Nuance *f*, Abtönung *f*, Abstufung *f*
~ of gray Grauton *m*, Grauabstufung *f*
shaded side Schattenseite *f*
~ type schattierte Schrift *f*
shading Schattierung *f*; Abschattung *f*; Schummerung *f (Kartografie)*
~ algorithm Schattierungsalgorithmus *m*
~ analysis Schattierungsanalyse *f*
~ calculation *s.* shadow computation
~ computation *s.* shadow computation
~ correction Schattierungskorrektur *f*
~ effect Schattenwurfeffekt *m*, Abschattungseffekt *m*
~ function Schattierungsfunktion *f*
~ model Schattierungsmodell *n*
~ operation *s.* shading
~ pattern Schattierungsmuster *n*
~ technique Schattierungsverfahren *n*
~ tool Abwedelmaske *f*; Abdeckschablone *f*
shadow Schatten *m*
~ area Schattenpartie *f*, Schattenzone *f*
~ calculation *s.* ~ computation
~ cast Schattenwurf *m*
~ computation Schattenberechnung *f*, Schattierungsberechnung *f (Computergrafik)*
~ contrast Schattenkontrast *m*
~ definition Schatten[durch]zeichnung *f*
~ density Schattendichte *f*, Schattenschwärzung *f*
~ detail Schattendetail *n*
~ edge Schattenkante *f*
~ effect Schatteneffekt *m*, Schattenwirkung *f*
~ formation (generation) Schattenbildung *f (Computergrafik)*
~ image Schattenbild *n*; Silhouette *f*
~ line Schattenlinie *f*
~ mask Schattenmaske *f (Farbbildschirm)*
~ mask [color picture] tube, **~ mask CRT** Schattenmaskenröhre *f*
~ microscope Röntgenstrahlschattenmikroskop *n*
~ pattern Schattenmuster *n*
~ projection Schattenprojektion *f*
~ puppeteer Schattenspieler *m*
~ side Schattenseite *f*
~ silhouette Schattenriss *m*
shadowed object abgeschattetes (schattiertes) Objekt *n*
shadowgram Schattenwurfhologramm *n*
shadowgraph [fotografisches] Schattenbild *n*
~ technique Schattenaufnahmetechnik *f*, Schattenverfahren *n (Schlierenfotografie)*
shadowing Abschattung *f*, Beschattung *f*
~ effect Schattenwirkung *f*, Schatteneffekt *m*
shadowless schattenfrei, schattenlos
~ illumination schattenfreie Ausleuchtung *f*
~ light schattenfreies Licht *n*
~ lighting schattenlose Beleuchtung *f*
shadows Tiefen *pl*, Schattenpartie *f (Densitometrie)*
shadowy light schattenreiches Licht *n*
shah function Kammfunktion *f (Signalverarbeitung)*
shake/to verwackeln
shaky camera movement Verwackelung[sbewegung] *f*
Shannon-Fano-Huffman coding *s.* Huffman coding
~ sampling theorem Shannon-Theorem *n (Abtasttheorie)*
shape Form *f (s.a. unter form)*; Gestalt *f*
~ analysis Formanalyse *f*
~-based interpolation formbasierte Interpolation *f*
~-based model formbasiertes Modell *n*
~ characteristic *s.* ~ feature
~ classification Formklassifikation *f*, Formklassifizierung *f*
~ coding Formcodierung *f*
~ constancy Form[en]konstanz *f*
~ description Formbeschreibung *f*
~ factor Formfaktor *m*
~ feature Formmerkmal *n*, Gestaltmerkmal *n*, formbeschreibendes (morphometrisches) Merkmal *n*
~-from-shading [technique] Formbestimmung *f* aus Grauwertverteilungen, Gestalt *f* aus

Schattierung, fotometrisches Stereosehen *n*
~-from-texture [technique] Gestalt *f* aus Textur
~ invariance Forminvarianz *f*
~ model[l]ing Gestaltmodellierung *f*, Geometriemodellierung *f*, geometrische Modellierung *f*
~ parameter Formparameter *m*
~ perception Formwahrnehmung *f*, Gestaltwahrnehmung *f*
~-preserving formerhaltend
~ recognition Formerkennung *f*
~ reconstruction Formrekonstruktion *f*
~ representation Formdarstellung *f*
~ segmentation Formsegmentierung *f*
~ shifting Formwandlung *f*, Formveränderung *f*
~ similarity Formähnlichkeit *f*
shaping Formgebung *f*
shared memory gemeinsam genutzter Speicher *m*; prozessübergreifender Speicher *m*
sharp scharf; konturenscharf
~ edge scharfe Kante *f*
~-focus lens scharfzeichnendes Objektiv *n*
~ image (picture) scharfes Bild *n*, scharfe Abbildung *f*
sharpening Schärfung *f*, Aufschärfung *f* *(Bildbearbeitung)*
~ coefficient Schärfungskoeffizient *m*
~ [spatial] filter Schärfefilter *n*, Scharfzeichnungsfilter *n*
sharpness Schärfe *f*, Kontur[en]schärfe *f*
~ adjustment Bildschärferegulierung *f*, Scharfeinstellung *f*, Schärfenregulierung *f*
~ control Schärfensteuerung *f*, Schärfekontrolle *f*
~ degradation (loss) Schärfeverlust *m*
~ distribution Schärfeverteilung *f* *(in einem Bild)*
~ performance Schärfeleistung *f*
~ value Schärfewert *m*
shear[ing] Scherung *f* *(geometrische Transformation)*
shearing interferometer Scher-Interferometer *n*
shearographic shearografisch
~ interferogram shearografisches Interferogramm *n*
~ interferometry shearografische Interferometrie *f*
shearography Shearografie *f*
sheen Glanz *m*, Oberflächenglanz *m*
sheer diaphan, durchscheinend
sheet counter Bogenzähler *m*
~-fed gravure Bogentiefdruck *m*
~-fed gravure press Bogentiefdruckmaschine *f*, Tiefdruckbogenmaschine *f*
~-fed machine Bogen[druck]maschine *f*
~-fed offset machine (press) Bogenoffset[druck]maschine *f*

~-fed press Bogen[druck]maschine *f*
~-fed printing Bogendruck *m*
~-fed printing machine Bogen[druck]maschine *f*
~-fed rotary [press] Bogenrotationsmaschine *f*
~-fed scanner Einzugsscanner *m*
~ feed[er] Einzelblatteinzug *m*
~ feeding Blattzuführung *f*; Bogenzuführung *f*
~ film Planfilm *m*; Blattfilm *m*, Einzelblattfilm *m*
~ film camera Planfilmkamera *f*
~ film hanger Planfilmhalter *m* *(Tankverarbeitung)*
~ film holder Planfilmhalter *m*, Planfilmkassette *f*
~ film tank Hochtank *m*
~ glass Flachglas *n*, Tafelglas *n*
~ of letterhead Kopfbogen *m*
~ of light Lichtfläche *f*
~ polarizer Flächenpolarisator *m*, Folienpolarisator *m*, Polarisations[filter]folie *f*; Polarisationsplatte *f*
~ transfer cylinder Auslagetrommel *f* *(Druckmaschine)*
shell electron Außenhüllenelektron *n*
shield Störlichtblende *f*
shift/to verschieben
shift Verschiebung *f*
~ invariance Verschiebungsinvarianz *f*, Translationsinvarianz *f (eines Operators)*
~-invariant verschiebungsinvariant, translationsinvariant *(Operator)*
~ keying Umtastung *f*, Tastung *f*
~ lens Shiftobjektiv *n*, Perspektivekorrekturobjektiv *n*, PC-Objektiv *n*
~ register Schieberegister *n*, Ladungsschieberegister *n (CCD-Sensor)*
~ variance Verschiebungsvarianz *f* *(Mustererkennung)*
~ vector Verschiebungsvektor *m*
shine out/to überstrahlen
shininess Glanz *m*, Oberflächenglanz *m*
shiny surface glänzende Oberfläche *f*
shipborne radar Schiffsradar *n*
shipping reel Versandrolle *f*, Transportrolle *f (Film)*
shock wave Schockwelle *f*
shoot/to aufnehmen *(Fotos)*; drehen *(Film)*
shoot *s.* shooting
shooting 1. Dreh *m*, Dreharbeit *f*; 2. *s.* progressive refinement
~ aperture Aufnahmeblende *f*
~ break Drehpause *f*
~ crew Aufnahmeteam *n*
~ day Drehtag *m*
~ location Drehort *m*, Aufnahmeort *m*, Spielstätte *f*, Motiv *n*
~ medium Aufnahmemedium *n*
~ notes Drehbericht *m*

shooting

~ **order** Drehfolge f, Einstellungsfolge f, Klappenreihenfolge f
~ **platform** Aufnahmeplattform f
~ **position** Aufnahmeposition f
~ **ratio** Drehverhältnis n
~ **schedule (script)** Drehplan m
~ **script** Filmskript n (s.a. screenplay)
~ **situation** Aufnahmesituation f; Drehsituation f
~ **speed** Aufnahmegeschwindigkeit f (Kinematografie)
~ **technique** fotografische Aufnahmetechnik f
~ **time** Drehzeit f

shop microscope Werkstattmikroskop n
short Kurzfilm m
~-**circuit flux** Kurzschlussfluss m (Magnetband)
~-**duration exposure** Kurzzeitbelichtung f, kurzzeitige Belichtung f
~-**duration flash** Kurzzeitblitz m
~ **exposure** Kurzzeitbelichtung f, kurzzeitige Belichtung f
~-**exposure photograph** kurz[zeit]belichtetes Foto n, kurz[zeit]belichtete Aufnahme f
~ **film** Kurzfilm m
~ **focal-length** kurzbrennweitig (Objektiv)
~-**focus eyepiece** kurzbrennweitiges Okular n
~-**focus lens** kurzbrennweitiges Objektiv n
~-**grain paper** Breitbahnpapier n
~-**haul transmission** Kurzstreckenübertragung f
~ **ink** kurze Druckfarbe f
~ **lens** Weitwinkelobjektiv n
~ **pass [filter]** Kurzpassfilter n
~-**persistent screen** kurznachleuchtender Bildschirm m
~ **pitch** Kurzschrittperforation f
~-**pulse detector** Kurzpulsdetektor m
~-**pulse laser** Kurzpulslaser m
~-**range photogrammetry** Nahbereichsfotogrammetrie f, Nahbildmessung f
~-**range radar** Nahbereichsradar n
~-**run color printing** Akzidenzfarbdruck m, kleinauflagiger Farbdruck m
~-**run lithographic press** Akzidenzmaschine f
~-**run work** Akzidenzdruck m, Kleinseriendruck m
~ **sight** Kurzsichtigkeit f, Myopie f
~ **tau inversion recovery** Pulssequenz zur Unterdrückung des Fettsignals in der Magnetresonanzbildgebung
~ **tau inversion recovery pulse sequence** STIR-Pulssequenz f (Magnetresonanztomografie)
~-**term** ... s. short-time ...
~-**time Fourier transform** Kurzzeit-Fourier-Transformation f, gefensterte Fourier-Transformation f
~-**time memory (store)** Kurzzeitspeicher m
~-**time visual memory** visuelles Kurzzeitgedächtnis n
~-**wave** s. short-wavelength
~-**wave band** Kurzwellenband n
~-**wave pass filter** Kurzpassfilter n
~-**wavelength** kurzwellig; hochfrequent
~-**wavelength infrared** kurzwelliges Infrarot n
~-**wavelength light** kurzwelliges Licht n
~-**wavelength radar** kurzwelliges Radar n
~-**wavelength radiation** kurzwellige Strahlung f
~-**wavelength-sensitive cone** S-Zapfen m, K-Zapfen m (Netzhautrezeptor)
~ **X-ray exposure** kurz[zeit]belichtete Aufnahme f

shortsighted kurzsichtig, myop
shortstop s. stop bath
shot Szenenaufnahme f; Filmszene f; Einstellung f (Kinematografie); [fotografische] Aufnahme f
~ **change detector** Szenenwechselerkenner m (Filmabtaster)
~ **list** Einstellungsliste f (Film)
~ **noise** Schrotrauschen n, bipolares Impulsrauschen n
~ **sheet** Einstellungsliste f (Film)
~ **transition** Szenenübergang m (Film)

shotgun microphone Keulenmikrofon n; Richtmikrofon n, Rohrichtmikrofon n
shoulder camera Schulterkamera f, aufgeschulterte Kamera f
~ **pad** Riemengleitschutz m
~ **part** Schulter f (Schwärzungskurve)
~ **pod** Schulterstativ n, Kameraschulterstativ n, [gepolsterte] Schulterauflage f
~ **region** s. ~ part
~ **rest** Schulterstütze f
~ **strap** Schulterriemen m, Trageriemen m, Tragegurt m (z.B. einer Kameratasche)

show-color proof Rohabzug m, Hauskorrektur f (Druckvorstufe)
showing Vorführung f
~-**through** Durchscheinen n (z.B. von Gedrucktem)
shrinkage Schrumpfung f (z.B. von Fotoschichten)
shuffling Verwürfeln n, Verwürfelung f, Verschachtelung f (von Signalen)
shutter 1. Verschluss m; Kameraverschluss m; 2. Blende f (Kinotechnik); Blendenschieber m (Scheinwerfer); 3. s. ~ button
~ **accuracy** Verschlussgenauigkeit f
~ **blade** Verschlusslamelle f
~ **blind** Verschlussvorhang m, Verschlussrollo n
~ **button** Auslöser m, Auslöseknopf m
~ **cocking** Verschlussaufzug m
~-**cocking mechanism** Verschlussspannvorrichtung f
~ **curtain** s. ~ blind

~ **curtain material** Verschlusstuch n
~ **curtain tape** Verschlusstuchband n
~ **dial** Verschlusszeitenrad n
~ **diameter** Verschlussdurchmesser m
~ **efficiency** Zeitwirkungsgrad m
~ **fault** Verschlussfehler m
~ **glasses** Shutterbrille f *(Stereosehen)*
~ **lag** Auslöseverzögerung f
~ **mechanism** Verschlussmechanismus m, Verschlusseinrichtung f
~ **opening duration** Verschlusszeit f
~ **plane** Verschlussebene f
~ **priority [mode]** Verschlussvorwahl f, Zeitpriorität f, Auslösepriorität f, Belichtungsautomatik f mit Zeitvorwahl
~ **release** Verschlussauslösung f, Auslösung f
~ **release button** Auslöser m, Auslöseknopf m
~ **release time lag** Verschlussvorwahlzeit f
~ **scale** Verschlusszeitenskale f
~ **setting** Verschluss[zeitenein]stellung f
~ **slit** Verschlussspalt m
~ **speed** Verschlussgeschwindigkeit f, Verschlusszeit f
~ **speed and aperture combination** Verschlusszeit-Blenden-Kombination f, Zeit-Blenden-Kombination f
~ **speed cycle** Verschlusszyklus m
~ **speed selector dial** Verschlusszeitenrad n
~ **speed setting** Verschlusszeiteneinstellung f
~ **time** s. ~ speed
~ **wind** Verschlussaufzug m
shutterless verschlusslos
shuttle dial Suchlaufdrehknopf m *(Videorecorder)*
shuttling Hin- und Herfahren n des Videobandes
SI unit SI-Einheit f, internationale Basiseinheit f
siccative Sikkativ n, Trockenstoff m
side Seite f
~ **light** Seitenlicht n
~ **lighting** seitliche Beleuchtung f
~ **lobe** Nebenkeule f, Seitenkeule f, Seitenzipfel m *(Radar, Sonografie)*
~ **lobe blanking (cancellation)** Nebenkeulenaustastung f
~ **lobe echo** Nebenkeulenecho n
~ **lobe level** Nebenkeulenpegel m
~-**looking airborne radar** Flugzeug-Seitensichtradar n
~-**looking radar** Seiten[sicht]radar n
~ **orientation** Seitenrichtung f
~-**scan[ned] sonar** Seitensicht-Sonarverfahren n
~ **view** Seitenansicht f
~-**viewing endoscope** Seitblickendoskop n
~ **window [X-ray] tube** Seitenfensterröhre f
sideband Seitenband n

Siemens star resolution chart Siemensstern m *(zur Ermittlung des Auflösungsvermögens)*
sievert Sievert n, Sv *(Einheit der Röntgenstrahlenexposition)*
SIF s. standard intermediate format
sight/to [an]visieren
sight 1. Sicht f; Sehen n; Sehkraft f; 2. Blick m; 3. Gewehrzielfernrohr n; Diopter n
~ **impaired** sehbehindert
~ **line** Sichtlinie f, Gesichtslinie f, Blicklinie f, Augenlinie f, Sichtverbindung f
sighting device Visiereinrichtung f, Visier n
~ **hole** Diopter n
~ **microscope** Zielmikroskop n
~ **telescope** Zielfernrohr n, Visierfernrohr n
sigma filter Sigma-Filter n
sigmoidoscope Sigmaspiegel m, Sigmoidoskop n
sign Zeichen n
~ **convention** Vorzeichenfestlegung f, Vorzeichenkonvention f, Vorzeichenvereinbarung f *(Optik)*
~ **language** Zeichensprache f
signal/to signalisieren
signal Signal n
~ **acquisition** Signalerfassung f, Signalgewinnung f
~-**adapted (signal-adaptive) filtering** [signal]angepasste Filterung f
~ **aliasing** Signalverfälschung f
~ **amplification** Signalverstärkung f
~ **amplifier** Signalverstärker m
~ **amplitude** Signalamplitude f
~ **analysis** Signalanalyse f
~ **attenuation** Signaldämpfung f, Signalabschwächung f
~ **average** Signalmittelwert m
~ **bandwidth** Signalbandbreite f
~ **brightness** Signalhelligkeit f
~ **charge** Signalladung f
~ **code** Signalcode m
~ **component** Signalkomponente f
~ **compression** Signalkompression f
~ **content** Signalinhalt m
~ **contrast** Signalkontrast m
~ **control** Signalkontrolle f; Signalsteuerung f
~ **conversion** Signalwandlung f, Signalkonvertierung f, Signaltransformation f
~ **converter** Signalumformer m
~ **correction** Signalkorrektur f
~ **corruption** Signalverfälschung f
~ **current** Signalstrom m
~ **decoding** Signaldecodierung f
~ **decomposition** Signalzerlegung f
~ **decorrelation** Signaldekorrelation f
~ **degradation** Signalverschlechterung f
~ **density** Signaldichte f
~-**dependent noise** signalabhängiges Rauschen n
~ **detection** Signaldetektion f
~ **detector** Signaldetektor m

signal

~ **diagnosis** Signalauswertung f
~ **distance** Signalabstand m, Hamming-Abstand m, Hamming-Distanz f
~ **distortion** Signalverzerrung f
~ **distribution** Signalverteilung f
~ **dropout** Signalausfall m
~ **edge** Signalflanke f
~ **element** Signalelement n
~ **encoder** Signalcodierer m
~ **encoding** Signalcodierung f
~ **encryption** Signalverschlüsselung f
~ **energy** Signalenergie f
~ **fidelity** Signaltreue f
~ **filtering** Signalfilterung f
~ **flux** Signalfluss m
~ **frequency** Signalfrequenz f
~ **frequency response** Signalfrequenzgang m
~ **gain** Signalverstärkung f
~ **generation** Signalerzeugung f
~ **generator** Signalgenerator m
~ **gradient amplitude** Signalgradientenamplitude f
~-**induced noise** Signalrauschen n
~ **input** Signaleingang m
~ **intensity** Signalintensität f, Signalstärke f
~ **interpolation** Signalinterpolation f
~ **level** Signalpegel m
~ **loss** Signalverlust m
~ **memory** Signalspeicher m
~ **model** Signalmodell n
~ **modeling** Signalmodellierung f
~ **modulation** Signalmodulation f
~ **parameter** Signalparameter m
~ **path** Signalweg m
~ **performance** Signalleistung f
~ **period** Signalperiode f
~ **plate** Signalplatte f, Schirmplatte f, Target n *(Bildaufnahmeröhre)*
~ **portion** Signalanteil m
~ **power** Signalleistung f
~ **prediction** Signalprädiktion f
~ **preprocessing** Signalvorverarbeitung f
~ **processing** Signalverarbeitung f, Signalbearbeitung f
~-**processing chain** Signalverarbeitungskette f
~ **processing technology** Signalverarbeitungstechnik f
~ **processing theory** *s.* ~ theory
~ **processor** Signalrechner m
~ **propagation** Signalausbreitung f
~ **quality** Signalqualität f
~ **quantization** Signalquantisierung f
~ **range** Signalbereich m
~ **readout** Signalauslesung f
~ **reconstruction (recovery)** Signalrekonstruktion f, Signalrückgewinnung f
~ **reflection** Signalreflexion f
~ **regeneration** Signalregeneration f
~ **region** Signalbereich m
~ **representation** Signaldarstellung f

~ **reproduction** Signalwiedergabe f
~ **resolution** Signalauflösung f
~ **response** Signalwert m
~ **sampling** Signalabtastung f
~ **scaling** Signalskalierung f
~ **scrambling** Signalverwürfelung f
~ **sequence** Signalfolge f, Signalsequenz f
~ **shuffling** Signalverwürfelung f
~ **source** Signalquelle f
~ **space** Signalraum m
~ **spectrum** Signalspektrum n
~ **step** Signalsprung m
~ **step-down** Signaldämpfung f, Signalabschwächung f
~ **storage** Signalspeicherung f
~ **strength** Signalstärke f
~ **suppression** Signalunterdrückung f
~ **synthesis** Signalsynthese f
~ **theory** Signaltheorie f, Theorie f der Signalverarbeitung
~-**to-clutter ratio** Signal-Störecho-Verhältnis n *(Radar)*
~-**to-noise ratio** Signal-Rausch-Verhältnis n, Rauschabstand m, Störabstand m, Fremdspannungsabstand m
~ **transducer** Signalwandler m
~ **transduction** Signalwandlung f
~ **transform** Signaltransformation f
~ **transmission** Signalübertragung f
~ **uniformity** Signalgleichförmigkeit f
~ **value** Signalwert m
~ **variance** Signalvarianz f
~ **variation** Signalvariation f
~ **vector** Signalvektor m
~ **voltage** Signalspannung f
~ **wavelength** Signalwellenlänge f

signature 1. Signatur f, Unterschrift f; 2. Falzbogen m
~ **image validation** *s.* ~ verification
~ **recognition** Unterschriftenerkennung f
~ **verification** Unterschriftenprüfung f, Unterschriftenverifizierung f

signet Signet n; Kennungsbild n; Logo n

silent [camera] Stummkamera f, stumme Kamera f
~ **era** Stummfilmzeit f
~ **film** Stummfilm m
~ **film days** Stummfilmzeit f
~ **motion picture** Stummfilm m
~ **print** stumme Kopie f, Bildkopie f *(Kinematografie)*

silhouette animation Silhouettentrickfilm m, Scherenschnittfilm m
~ **image** Silhouette f, Schattenbild n

silica gel Silicagel n, Kieselgel n *(Trocknungsmittel)*

silicate glass Silicatglas n

silicon cell Siliciumzelle f
~ **chip** Siliciumchip m
~-**controlled rectifier** Siliciumgleichrichter m
~ **crystal** Siliciumkristall m
~ **detector** Siliciumsensor m
~ **diode** Siliciumdiode f

~ **imaging sensor** Silicium-Bildsensor *m*
~ **photoconductive cell** Siliciumzelle *f*
~ **photodiode** Siliciumfotodiode *f*
~ **photoelectric cell** Siliciumzelle *f*
~ **photovoltaic cell** Solarzelle *f*
~ **rubber** Silikonkautschuk *m*
~ **semiconductor** Siliciumhalbleiter *m*
~ **wafer** Siliciumwafer *m*, Siliciumscheibe *f*
silk screen Seidenraster *m(n)*
silkscreen printing Siebdruck *m*, Durchdruck *m*
silver/to versilbern
silver Silber *n*
~ **aggregate** Silberaggregat *n*, Silbercluster *m*
~ **atom** Silberatom *n*
~ **atom cluster** *s.* ~ aggregate
~ **-based film** Silber[halogenid]film *m*, Chemiefilm *m*
~ **bleach** Silberbleichbad *n*
~ **bleaching [stage]** Silberbleichung *f*
~ **bromide** Silberbromid *n*, Bromsilber *n*
~ **bromide collodion plate** Bromsilber-Kollodium-Platte *f*
~ **bromide crystal** Bromsilberkristall *m*, Silberbromidkristall *m*
~ **bromide emulsion** Silberbromidemulsion *f*, Bromsilberemulsion *f*
~ **bromide gelatin plate** Bromsilber-Gelatine-Platte *f*
~ **bromide paper** Bromsilber[vergrößerungs]papier *n*, Bromidpapier *n*
~ **bromide print** Bromsilberdruck *m*, Bromidabzug *m*
~ **bromochloride** Chlorbromsilber *n*
~ **chloride** Silberchlorid *n*, Chlorsilber *n*
~ **chloride collodion** Chlorsilberkollodium *n*
~ **chloride emulsion** Silberchloridemulsion *f*
~ **chloride gelatin** Chlorsilbergelatine *f*
~ **chloride paper** Silberchloridpapier *n*, Chlorsilberpapier *n*, Chloridpapier *n*
~ **chlorobromide** Chlorbromsilber *n*
~ **cluster** Silberaggregat *n*, Silbercluster *m*
~ **complex** Silberkomplex *m*
~ **compound** Silberverbindung *f*
~ **content** Silbergehalt *m*
~ **crystal** Silberkristall *m*
~ **density** Silberschwärzung *f*, Silberdichte *f*
~ **deposit** Silberniederschlag *m*
~ **development** Silberentwicklung *f*
~**-dye-bleach process** Silberfarbbleichverfahren *n*, Farbsilberbleich[verfahr]en *n*
~ **emulsion** Silberemulsion *f*
~ **filament** Silberfaden *m*
~ **film layer** Silberfilmschicht *f*
~ **formation** Silberbildung *f*
~ **gelatin** Silbergelatine *f*

~ **gelatin print** Gelatinesilberabzug *m*, Silbergelatineabzug *m*
~ **glance** Silberglanz *m*
~ **grain** Silberkorn *n*
~ **halide** Silberhalogenid *n*, Halogensilber[salz] *n*, AgX
~ **halide-based film** Silber[halogenid]film *m*, Chemiefilm *m*
~ **halide-based photograph** Silber[halogenid]fotografie *f*
~ **halide-based printing plate** Silberhalogenid[druck]platte *f*
~ **halide color photography** Silberhalogenid-Farbfotografie *f*
~ **halide crystal** Silberhalogenidkristall *m*
~ **halide developer** Silberhalogenidentwickler *m*
~ **halide emulsion** Silberhalogenidemulsion *f*, AgX-Emulsion *f*
~ **halide film** Silber[halogenid]film *m*, Chemiefilm *m*
~ **halide grain** Silberhalogenidkorn *n*, Halogensilberkorn *n*
~ **halide image** Silberbild *n*
~ **halide instant film** Silberhalogenid-Sofortbildfilm *m*
~ **halide lattice** Silberhalogenidgitter *n*
~ **halide microcrystal** Silberhalogenidmikroskristall *m*
~ **halide microfilm** Silberhalogenidmikrofilm *m*
~ **halide photographic** silberfotografisch
~ **halide photographic emulsion** Silberhalogenidemulsion *f*
~ **halide photographic film** Silber[halogenid]film *m*, Chemiefilm *m*
~ **halide photography** Silber[halogenid]fotografie *f*
~ **halide precipitation** Silberhalogenidausfällung *f*
~ **halide print** Fotoabzug *m*, Bildabzug *m*
~ **halide process** Silberhalogenidverfahren *n*, Halogensilberverfahren *n*
~ **halide salt** Silberhalogenidsalz *n*
~ **halide solvent** Silberhalogenidlösungsmittel *n*
~ **image** Silberbild *n*
~ **image formation** Silberbildentstehung *f*
~ **intensifier** Silberverstärker *m*
~ **iodide** Silberiodid *n*, Iodsilber *n*
~ **iodide emulsion** Silberiodidemulsion *f*
~ **iodide paper** Iodsilberpapier *n*
~ **iodochloride emulsion** Silberiodchloridemulsion *f*
~ **ion concentration** Silberionenkonzentration *f*
~ **layer** Silberschicht *f*
~ **metal filament** Silberfaden *m*, fadenförmige Silberstruktur *f* *(fotografischer Prozess)*
~ **mirror** Silberspiegel *m*
~ **negative [image]** Silbernegativ *n*
~ **nitrate** Silbernitrat *n*

silver

~ **nitrate paper** Silbernitratpapier *n*
~ **nitrate solution** Silbernitratlösung *f*
~ **nucleus** Silberkeim *m*
~-**on-glass mirror** silberbeschichteter (versilberter) Spiegel *m*
~ **oxide** Silberoxid *n*
~ **photographic** silberfotografisch
~ **photographic image** silberfotografisches Bild *n*
~ **plate** Silberplatte *f*
~ **print** Silberbild *n*
~ **reclamation (recovery)** Silberrückgewinnung *f*
~ **recovery by metallic replacement** Metallaustauschverfahren *n*
~ **rhodanate (rhodanide)** *s.* ~ thiocyanate
~ **salt** Silbersalz *n*
~ **salt crystal** Silbersalzkristall *m*
~ **salt diffusion** Silbersalzdiffusion *f*
~ **salt diffusion transfer process** Silbersalzdiffusionsverfahren *n*
~ **screen** Silber[lein]wand *f*; metallisierte Bildwand *f*
~ **selenide** Silberselenid *n*
~-**solubilizing agent** Silberlösungsvermittler *m*
~ **solvent** Silberlösungsmittel
~ **sulfide** Silbersulfid *n*, Silberglanz *m*
~ **thiocyanate** Silberthiocyanat *n*, Silberrhodanid *n*
similarity constraint Ähnlichkeitsbedingung *f (Bildmodellierung)*
~ **distribution** Ähnlichkeitsverteilung *f*
~ **function** Ähnlichkeitsfunktion *f*
~ **matrix** Ähnlichkeitsmatrix *f*
~ **measure** Ähnlichkeitsmaß *n*
~ **measurement** Ähnlichkeitsmessung *f*
~ **metrics** Ähnlichkeitsmetrik *f*
~ **model** Ähnlichkeitsmodell *n*
~ **recognition** Ähnlichkeitserkennung *f*
~ **search** Ähnlichkeitssuche *f*
~ **term** Ähnlichkeitsterm *m*
~ **theorem** Ähnlichkeitssatz *m*
~ **transform[ation]** Ähnlichkeitstransformation *f*
simple camera Einfachkamera *f*
~ **lens** einfache Linse *f*
~ **microscope** einfaches Mikroskop *n*
~ **polygon** einfaches Polygon *n*
~ **printer** Einfachdrucker *m*
simulate/to simulieren
simulation Simulation *f*
~ **algorithm** Simulationsalgorithmus *m*
~ **display** Simulationsbildschirm *m*
~ **model** Simulationsmodell *n*
~ **program** Simulationsprogramm *n*
~ **result** Simulationsergebnis *n*
~ **technology** Simulationstechnologie *f*
simulator Simulator *m*
~ **sickness** Simulator[en]krankheit *f (subjektives Missbefinden in virtuellen Umgebungen)*
simulcast/to gleichzeitig (parallel) senden

simulcast gleichzeitige (parallele) Ausstrahlung *f*, Parallelbetrieb *m (Fernsehen)*
simultaneous broadcast *s.* simulcast
~ **color contrast** simultaner Farbkontrast *m*
~ **computer** Parallelrechner *m*
~ **contrast** Simultankontrast *m (Sehen)*
~ **exposure** Simultanbelichtung *f*
~ **shutter release** Simultanauslösung *f*
~ **spectrometer** Simultanspektrometer *n*, Mehrkanalspektrometer *n*
sinc filter Spaltmaske *f (digitale Signalverarbeitung)*
~ **function** Spaltfunktion *f*, sinc-Funktion *f*
sine condition [Abbesche] Sinusbedingung *f (Optik)*
~ **curve** Sinuskurve *f*
~ **function** Sinusfunktion *f*
~-**phase filter** Sinusphasenfilter *n*
~ **transform[ation]** Sinustransformation *f (Bildcodierung)*
~ **wave** Sinuswelle *f*
~-**wave amplitude** Sinuswellenamplitude *f*
~-**wave grating** Sinusgitter *n*
~-**wave signal** sinusförmiges Signal *n*
single-area AF mode Einzelfeld-Autofokus *m*
~-**beam spectrophotometer** Einstrahlspektrofotometer *n*
~-**bit error** Einzelbitfehler *m*
~ **canceller** Einfach-MIT[-Filter] *n (Radarsignalprozessor)*
~-**CCD camera** Ein-Chip-Videokamera *f*
~-**channel carrier** Einzelträger *m (Signalübertragung)*
~-**channel signal** einkanaliges Signal *n*
~-**chip camera** Ein-Chip-Videokamera *f*
~-**clicking** Einfachklicken *n (Computermaus)*
~-**coated** einfachvergütet
~-**coated X-ray film** einseitig beschichteter Röntgenfilm *m*, Einschichtfilm *m*
~-**color** *s.* single-colored
~-**color press** Einfarbenmaschine *f (Druck)*
~-**colored** einfarbig, monochrom
~-**column stand** Säulenstativ *n*
~-**component developer** Einkomponententoner *m (Xerografie)*
~-**component magnetic toner** Einkomponententoner *m (Ionenbeschussdruck)*
~-**component system** Einkomponentensystem *n*
~ **crystal** Einkristall *m*
~-**crystal gamma camera** [Einkristall-]Gammakamera *f*, Szintillationskamera *f*, Anger-Kamera *f*
~-**crystal monochromator** Einkristallmonochromator *m*
~-**crystal photodetector** Einkristall-Fotodetektor *m*
~-**crystal semiconductor** Einkristallhalbleiter *m*
~-**emulsion film** Einschichtfilm *m*

~ **frame** Einzelbild n *(Film, Video)*
~-**frame advance** Einzelbildtransport m
~-**frame camera** Einzelbildkamera f
~-**frame exposure (shooting)** Einzelbildaufnahme f, Einzelbildbelichtung f, Einzelbild[fort]schaltung f, Einergang m
~-**frequency laser** s. single-mode laser
~-**frequency network** Gleichwellennetz n, Gleichfrequenznetz n *(Fernsehen)*
~-**frequency semiconductor laser** Einfrequenz-Halbleiterlaser m
~ **image** Einzelbild n
~-**image analysis** Einzelbildanalyse f
~-**image display** Einzelbildanzeige f
~-**image random dot stereogram** Autostereogramm n
~-**image stereogram** Ein[zel]bildstereogramm n
~-**image storage** Einzelbildspeicherung f
~-**jet emulsion** Einzeleinlaufemulsion f
~-**jet method (scheme)** [konventioneller] Monoeinlauf m, Einzeleinlauf m
~-**layer disk** einschichtige Bildplatte f
~-**layer low-reflection coating** Einschichtvergütung f
~-**layer neural network** einschichtiges neuronales Netz n
~-**layer perceptron** Einschicht-Perzeptron n, einschichtiges Perzeptron n *(Neuroinformatik)*
~ **lens** Einzellinse f, Linsenelement n
~-**lens** einlinsig; einäugig *(Kamera)*
~-**lens imaging system** einlinsiges Abbildungssystem n
~-**lens reflex [camera]** einäugige Spiegelreflexkamera f, SLR-Kamera f
~-**lens-reflex photography** Reflexfotografie f
~-**line CCD** CCD-Sensorzeile f, CCD-Zeilensensor m, CCD-Zeile f, Zeilenbildwandler m
~-**line scan** Zeilenabtastung f
~-**mode fiber** Einmodenfaser f, Monomodefaser f *(Faseroptik)*
~-**mode laser** Einmodenlaser m, Einfrequenzlaser m, Monomodelaser m
~-**mode laser beam** Einmodenlaserstrahl m
~ **neighborhood** einfache Nachbarschaft f
~-**pass scanner** Einpass-Scanner m
~-**perforated film** einseitig perforierter Film m
~-**perforation** einseitige Perforation f
~-**photograph measurement** Einbildmessung f *(Fotogrammetrie)*
~-**photon emission-computed tomography** Einzelphotonen-Emissionstomografie f, Emissionscomputertomografie f *(s.a. unter SPECT)*
~-**pixel operation** Einzelpixeloperation f
~-**point auto focus** Einzel-Autofokus m
~-**pole filter** einpoliges Filter n

~-**post stand** Säulenstativ n
~ **pulse** Einzelimpuls m
~ **quotation mark** halbes Anführungszeichen n *(Druckzeichen)*
~-**revolution press** Eintouren[druck]maschine f *(Hochdruck)*
~-**sheet color film** Einblatt-Farbfilm m
~-**sheet film** Einblattfilm m, Integralfilm m
~-**sheet proof** Blankodruck m *(Farbdruck)*
~ **shot** 1. Einzelaufnahme f, Take m(n) *(s.a. shot)*; 2. Bildeinstellung f *(Film, Video)*
~-**sideband modulation** Einseitenbandmodulation f
~-**sideband transmission** Einseitenbandübertragung f
~-**sided film** s. single-coated X-ray film
~-**slice [CT] scanner** Einschicht-Spiral-Computertomograf m
~-**slit diffraction** Einzelspaltbeugung f
~-**sprocket stock** einseitig perforierter Film m
~-**surface lamination** einseitige Kaschierung f
~-**system cinematography, ~ recording (shooting)** Einstreifen-Ton-Bild-Aufzeichnung f, Einstreifenverfahren n
~-**track record[ing]** Einspur-Tonaufzeichnung f
~-**track sound reproducer** Einspur-Tonwiedergabegerät n
~-**type composing machine** Einzelbuchstabensetzmaschine f
~-**use camera** Einwegkamera f, Wegwerfkamera f
~-**wavelength color** monochromatische Farbe f
~-**weight** papierstark *(Papierstärkeklasse)*
singlet state Singulettzustand m
sink Senke f
sinkage Wolkigkeit f, Perlen n *(Offsetdruckschwierigkeit)*
sinogram Sinogramm n *(Projektionsdatensatz der Emissionstomografie)*
sinusoid Sinusfunktion f; Sinuskurve f
sinusoidal sinusförmig
~ **diffraction grating** Sinusgitter n
~ **function** Sinusfunktion f
~ **noise** sinusförmiges Rauschen n
~ **oscillation** Sinusschwingung f
~ **signal** sinusförmiges Signal n
~ **transform[ation]** Sinustransformation f, sinusförmige Transformation f *(Bildcodierung)*
~ **vibration** Sinusschwingung f
~ **wave** Sinuswelle f
six-channel sound Sechsspurmagnetton m
~-**color (six-ink) printing** Sechsfarbendruck m
~-**track [magnetic] sound** Sechsspurmagnetton m

size 1. Größe f; Format n (z.B. von Druckprodukten); 2. Streichmasse f, Streichpaste f (Papierherstellung)
~ **constancy** Größenkonstanz f
~ **illusion** [optische] Größentäuschung f
~**-invariant** größeninvariant
~ **of the blur circle** Unschärfekreisdurchmesser m, Unschärfekreisgröße f
~ **of type** Schriftgrad m; Schriftgröße f, Glyphenhöhe f (Typografie)
sized paper [maschinen]gestrichenes Papier n
sizing Papierleimung f
skeleton Skelett n, linienhaftes Elementargerüst n
~ **black** Skelettschwarz n (Reprografik)
~ **line** Skelettlinie f
~ **transform[ation]** Skeletttransformation f
skeletonization Skelettierung f, Verdünnung f (Binärbildverarbeitung)
~ **algorithm** Skelettierungsalgorithmus m
~ **operator** Skelettierungsoperator m
~ **technique** Skelettierungsverfahren n
skeletonize/to skelettieren
skeletonized pattern skelettiertes Muster n
skeletonizing algorithm Verdünnungsalgorithmus m
sketch/to skizzieren
sketch Skizze f, Handskizze f, Gedankenskizze f; Scribble n
~ **map** Kartenskizze f
skew 1. Bandzug m, Bandzugkraft f, Bandzugspannung f; 2. Spurwinkel m
~ **error** Bandzugfehler m
~ **ray** windschiefer Strahl m
skewness Schiefe f, Schiefheit f (z.B. von Bildsignalen)
skiagram s. radiograph
skid Andruckkufe f
~ **plate** Filmbühne f (Filmabtaster)
skin tone Hautton[wert] m, Fleischfarbe f
skip Sprungsuchlauf m
skivings Engelshaar n (Kinefilmbeschädigung)
sky blue Himmelsblau n
~ **coloring** Himmelsfärbung f
~ **fog** Atmosphärentrübung f
~ **glow** Himmelsleuchten n
~ **irradiance** Himmelsstrahlung f
~ **map** Höhennetz n
~ **mapping** Himmelskartierung f
skylight Himmelslicht n
~ **filter** Skylightfilter n
slab laser Bandleiterlaser m
~ **serif** Blockserife f (Buchstabenbild)
slant range Schrägentfernung f (Radar)
~**-track recording** Schrägspuraufzeichnung f (Videoband)
~ **transform** Slanttransformation f (eine spezielle Orthogonaltransformation)
slanted azimuth Azimut-Versatz m
~ **light** Schräglicht n, schräg auffallendes Licht n
~ **typeface** Schrägschrift f, geneigte Schrift f
slanting schräg[laufend]; kursiv
slash [mark] Schrägstrich m
slate Szenenklappe f, Szenentafel f, Klappe f; Klappenbeschriftung f (Film, Video)
slave cell Slave-Auslöser m (Blitzzubehör)
~ **flash unit** Zweitblitzgerät n, Slave-Blitzgerät n
~ **playback machine** Zuspielrecorder m, Videozuspieler m
~ **tape** Zuspielband n
sleep timer Abschaltautomatik f (z.B. eines Fernsehgeräts)
slice 1. Objektschicht f, Schicht f; 2. Scheibe f (Bildsequenzcodierung); 3. s. ~ image
~**-by-slice** schichtweise (Schnittbildgewinnung)
~ **gap** Zwischenschichtabstand m (Tomografie)
~ **image** Schichtbild n, Schichtaufnahme f, Tomogramm n
~ **interval** Schichtintervall n
~ **plane** Schnittebene f (Tomografie)
~ **selection** Schichtwahl f, Schichtselektion f
~ **selection gradient** Schichtwahlgradient m (Magnetresonanzbildgebung)
~ **spacing** Schichtabstand m
~ **thickness** Schichtdicke f; Schichttiefe f
slide Dia[positiv] n
~ **archive** Diaarchiv n
~ **archive cassette** Diaarchivkassette f
~ **box** Diakasten m
~ **change** Diawechsel m
~**-changing mechanism** Diawechsler m
~ **converter** Diascanner m, Diaabtaster m
~ **copier** Diakopierer m
~ **copying adaptor** Diakopieradapter m, Diakopiervorsatz m
~**-copying device** Diakopiergerät n
~ **cutter** Diaschneidegerät n
~ **digitizer** Diascanner m, Diaabtaster m
~ **duplicate** Diakopie f
~ **duplication** Diaduplikation f, Diavervielfältigung f
~**-duplication film** Diaduplikatfilm m
~ **duplicator** Diaduplikator m
~ **film** Dia[positiv]film m, Umkehrfilm m
~ **format** Diaformat n
~ **frame** Diarahmen m
~ **gate** Diafenster n
~ **holder** Dia[präsentations]hülle f
~ **image** Diabild n
~ **lever** Schieberegler m
~ **magazine** Diamagazin n
~ **making** Diaherstellung f
~ **mount** Diarahmen m, Diarähmchen n
~ **mount aperture (window)** Deckmaske f
~ **mounting** Diarahmung f
~ **plate** Dia[positiv]platte f
~ **presentation** Diavorführung f, Diapräsentation f, Diaschau f

~ **projection distance** Diaprojektionsabstand *m*
~ **projection system** Diaprojektionsanlage *f*
~ **projector** Diaprojektor *m*
~ **projector zoom lens** Diaprojektions-Zoomobjektiv *n*
~ **scanner (scanning equipment)** Diascanner *m*, Diaabtaster *m*
~ **series (set)** Diaserie *f*
~ **sheet** Dia[archiv]hülle *f*
~ **show** Diavorführung *f*, Diapräsentation *f*, Diaschau *f*
~-**show lecturer** Diavorführer *m*
~ **storage** Dia-Aufbewahrung *f*
~ **storage box** Diakasten *m*
~ **storage page (sheet)** Dia[archiv]hülle *f*
~ **switch** Schiebeschalter *m*
~-**to-video conversion** Diaüberspielung *f*
~-**to-video converter** Diascanner *m*, Diaabtaster *m*
~ **transparency** gerahmtes Dia *n*
~ **tray** Diamagazin *n*
~ **viewer** Diabetrachter *m*
slider Schieberegler *m*
slideway Gleitbahn *f*
sliding box camera Laufbodenkamera *f*, Reisekamera *f*
~ **masking blade** verstellbare Formatblende *f*
~ **prism** Schiebeprisma *n*
slip-on filter Aufsteckfilter *n*
slippage Schlupf *m*
slit 1. Spalt *m*; Schlitz *m*; 2. Tonspalt *m*
~ **aperture** Schlitzblende *f*, Spaltblende *f*
~ **camera** Spaltkamera *f* *(Hochgeschwindigkeitsfotografie)*
~ **collimator** Spaltkollimator *m*
~ **image** [optisches] Spaltbild *n*
~ **lamp** Spaltlampe *f*
~ **opening** Spaltöffnung *f*
~ **shutter** *s.* slot shutter
~ **spectrograph** Spaltspektrograf *m*
~ **width** Spaltbreite *f*
slitting Splitten *n (Rohfilmbearbeitung)*
slo-mo *s.* slow motion
slope Steilheit *f (z.B. einer Schwärzungskurve)*
~ **error** Tangensfehler *m*, Tangentenfehler *m*
~ **steepness** Flankensteilheit *f*
slot 1. Schlitz *m*; 2. Steckplatz *m*, Erweiterungssteckplatz *m*, Steckschacht *m*, Modulschacht *m*
~ **antenna** Schlitzantenne *f (Radar)*
~ **magazine** Universalmagazin *n (für Diapositive)*
~ **shutter** Schlitzverschluss *m*, Lamellenschlitzverschluss *m*
slotted pipe antenna (aerial) Wanderwellenantenne *f (Fernsehtechnik)*
~ **shadow mask** Schlitzmaske *f*, Streifenmaske *f (Bildröhre)*

slow 1. niederempfindlich, niedrigempfindlich *(Filmmaterial)*; 2. lichtschwach *(Objektiv)*
~ **lens** lichtschwaches Objektiv *n*
~ **motion** Zeitlupe *f*
~-**motion camera** Zeitdehnerkamera *f*
~-**motion device** Zeitdehner *m*
~-**motion effect** Zeitlupeneffekt *m*
~-**motion machine** Zeitlupengerät *n*
~-**motion photography** Zeitlupenaufnahme *f*
~-**motion playback (replay)** Zeitlupenwiedergabe *f*, Zeitlupenwiederholung *f*
~ **rewind** langsamer Rücklauf *m*
~-**running picture** Wanderbild *n*
~-**speed** *s.* slow 1. *und* 2.
~-**speed emulsion** niederempfindliche Emulsion *f*
~-**speed film** niederempfindlicher (niedrigempfindlicher) Film *m*
~ **sync[hronizaion]** Langzeitsynchronisation *f (Blitzsynchronisationsmodus)*
SLR [camera] *s.* single-lens reflex [camera]
slug Gusszeile *f*, Typenzeile *f*
slugcasting Zeilenguss *m*, Zeilensatz *m*
~ **compositor** *s.* ~ typesetter
~ **machine** Zeilengussmaschine *f*, Zeilengießmaschine *f*
~ **typesetter** Zeilensetz- und -gießmaschine *f*
small-angle scattering Kleinwinkelstreuung *f*
~ **camera** Kleinkamera *f*
~ **cap[ital]** Kapitälchen *n (Typografie)*
~ **cassette** Minikassette *f*
Small Computer Systems Interface SCSI-Schnittstelle *f*
small enlarger Kleinbildvergrößerer *m*, Kleinbildvergrößerungsgerät *n*
~-**format camera** Kleinbildkamera *f*
~-**format film** Kleinbild[aufnahme]film *m*
~-**format negative** Kleinbildnegativ *n*
~ **letter** Kleinbuchstabe *m*, Minuskel *f*, Gemeine *f*
~ **movie house** Kleinkino *n*
~ **offset duplicating machine** Kleinoffsetmaschine *f*
~-**scale** kleinmaßstäbig, kleinmaßstäblich
~-**size[d]** kleinformatig
~ **studio** Kleinstudio *n*
~ **tank processing** Dosenentwicklung *f*
~ **theater** Kleinkino *n*
~ **tripod** [Dreifuß-]Kleinstativ *n*, Ministativ *n*
~ **TV receiver** Minifernseher *m*
smart camera intelligente Kamera *f (mit integriertem Prozessor)*
~ **card** Chipkarte *f*
smear effect Schmiereffekt *m*
smeared image verschmiertes Bild *n*
smectic liquid crystal smektischer Flüssigkristall *m*

smectic

~ **phase** smektische Phase *f* (Flüssigkristall)
smooth/to glätten *(z.B. ein Binärbild)*
smooth curve glatte Kurve *f*
~ **gradation** weiche Gradation *f*
~ **pursuit eye movement** Folgebewegung *f*, Führungsbewegung *f (Sehen)*
smoother *s.* smoothing filter
smoothing Glättung *f (s.a. blurring)*
~ **algorithm** Glättungsalgorithmus *m*
~ **effect** Glättungswirkung *f*
~ **filter** Glättungsfilter *n*, Glättungsmaske *f*
~ **[filter] function** Glättungsfunktion *f*
~ **kernel (mask)** *s.* ~ filter
~ **matrix** Glättungsmatrix *f*
~ **operation** Glättungsoperation *f*
~ **parameter** Glättungsparameter *m*
smoothness Glattheit *f (z.B. einer Kurve)*
~ **constraint** Glattheitsbedingung *f* (Bildmodellierung)
~ **measure** Glattheitsmaß *n*
~ **term** Glattheitsterm *m*
SMPTE *s.* Society of Motion Picture and Television Engineers
~ **time code** Studio-Zeitcode *m*, SMPTE[/EBU]-Code *m*
snake aktive Kontur *f (Segmentierung)*
~ **track** Partial-Lichttonspur *f*
snap/to auslösen *(z.B. den Kameraverschluss)*
snap Schnappschuss *m*
snapshooter Schnappschussfotograf *m*, Schnappschussjäger *m*
snapshot Schnappschuss *m*
~ **camera** Schnappschusskamera *f*, Schnellschusskamera *f*, Knipskamera *f*
~ **mode** Schnappschusseinstellung *f*
~ **photograph** Schnappschuss *m*
~ **photographer** Schnappschussfotograf *m*
~ **photography** Schnappschussfotografie *f*
Snell's law [of refraction], ~ **refraction law** Snellius-Brechungsgesetz *n*, Snell[ius]sches Brechungsgesetz *n*
Snellen eye (test) chart, ~ **chart** Snellensche Sehtafel *f*; Sehprobentafel *f*
SNG *s.* satellite news gathering
sniperscope Gewehrzielfernrohr *n*, Zielfernrohr *n*
SNOM *s.* scanning near-field optical microscopy
snoot Scheinwerfertubus *m*, Tubusvorsatz *m*
snorkel camera Schnorchelkamera *f* (Trickkinematografie)
snow Schnee *m*, Schneegestöber *n* (Bildstörung); Bildrauschen *n*
snowflake curve Koch-Kurve *f (fraktale Geometrie)*
snowstorm [effect] *s.* snow
snowy picture verschneites Bild *n* (Bildstörung)
SNR scalability Rausch-Skalierbarkeit *f*
Sobel edge detecting mask *s.* ~ operator

~ **filter (gradient operator)** *s.* ~ operator
~ **kernel** *s.* ~ operator
~ **operation** Sobel-Filterung *f*
~ **operator** Sobel-Operator *m*, Sobel-Filter *n*, Sobel-Kantendetektor *m*, Sobel-Maske *f*
~ **transform** Sobel-Transformation *f*
Society of Motion Picture and Television Engineers *im Videobereich tätiges Standardisierungsgremium*
socket mount Anschlusssockel *m*
soda *s.* sodium carbonate
sodium acetate Natriumacetat *n*
~ **arc lamp** Natriumdampflampe *f*
~ **bisulfite** Natriumdisulfit *n*, Natriumbisulfit *n*, Metabisulfit *n* (Fixierbadzusatz)
~ **borate** Natriumborat *n* (Entwicklungsbeschleuniger)
~ **carbonate** Natriumcarbonat *n*, Soda *f(n)* (Entwicklerzusatz)
~ **chloride** Natriumchlorid *n*, Kochsalz *n*
~ **citrate** Natriumcitrat *n*
~ **dithionite** Natriumdithionit *n*
~ **hydroxide** Natriumhydroxid *n* (Entwicklerbestandteil)
~ **iodide crystal scintillation detector** Natriumiodidkristall *m (Gammakamera)*
~ **metabisulfite** Natriummetabisulfit *n*
~ **metaborate** Natriummetaborat *n* (Entwicklerzusatz)
~ **metaphosphate** Natriummetaphosphat *n (Entwicklerzusatz)*
~ **sulfate** Natriumsulfat *n* (Entwicklerzusatz)
~ **sulfite** Natriumsulfit *n (Entwicklerzusatz)*
~ **tetraborate** Borax *n (Entwicklerzusatz)*
~ **thiosulfate** Natriumthiosulfat *n*, Natriumhyposulfit *n*, unterschwefligsaures Natrium (Natron) *n*, Fixiernatron *n*
~ **vapor lamp** Natriumdampflampe *f*
soft 1. weich *(Papiergradation)*; 2. unscharf
~ **body** elastischer Körper *m (z.B. in der Computergrafik)*
~ **boot** Warmstart *m (Computer)*
~ **camera case** Fototasche *f*
~ **copy** flüchtiges (nichtpermanentes) Bild *n*, Softcopy *f*
~ **copy display** Bildschirmausgabe *f*; Bildschirmanzeige *f*
~ **copy system** Anzeigesystem *n*
~ **digital proof** *s.* ~ proof
~ **dot** unscharfer Rasterpunkt *m*
~ **edge** unscharfe Kante
~-**edge masking** Unscharfmaskierung *f*, Unschärfemaskierung *f*, unscharfe Maskierung *f*
~-**focus attachment (filter)** Diffusionsfilter *n*; Weichzeichner *m*
~-**focus lens** Weichzeichnerobjektiv *n*, Weichzeichnerlinse *f*, Softfokusobjektiv *n*, Softlinse *f*
~ **focusing** Weichzeichnung *f*

~-**ground etching** Weichgrundradierung f, Vernis mou m
~ **keying** weiches Einstanzen n (Trickkinematografie)
~ **lens pouch** Objektivbeutel m
~ **light** 1. weiches (diffuses) Licht n; 2. Weichstrahler m
~ **lighting** weiche Beleuchtung f
~ **mechanical** elektronische Montage f (Druckvorstufe)
~ **object** verformbares Objekt n
~ **paper** weiches Papier n
~ **proof** Softproof m, immaterieller Farbproof m (Druckvorstufe)
~ **radiation** weiche Strahlung f
~ **radio frequency pulse**, ~ **RF pulse** weicher Hochfrequenzimpuls m (Magnetresonanztomografie)
~ **shadow** weicher Schatten m
~ **thresholding** weiche Schwellenwertbildung
~-**tissue contrast** Weichteilkontrast m, Weichgewebekontrast m
~-**tissue radiography** Weichteilradiografie f
~-**tissue roentgenogram** Weichteilaufnahme f
~ **touch tyre** Gumminoppenlaufrolle f (Filmentwicklungsmaschine)
~ **viewing** Schirmbildbetrachtung f
~-**working developer** weich arbeitender Entwickler m, Weichentwickler m; Ausgleichsentwickler m
~ **X-ray tube** Weichstrahlröhre f
~ **X rays** weiche Röntgenstrahlung f
soften/to weichzeichnen, soften
softening effect Weichzeichnereffekt m
software Software f
~ **driver** Softwaretreiber m
~ **failure** Programmabsturz m
~ **package** Softwarepaket n
~ **pirate** Raubkopierer m
~ **program** Softwareprogramm n
~ **programmer** Softwareprogrammierer m
~ **theft** Raubkopierung f
soil map Bodenkarte f
solar angle Sonnenwinkel m
~ **cell** Solarzelle f
~ **filter** Sonnenfilter n
~ **irradiance** Sonneneinstrahlung f
~ **microscope** Solarmikroskop n
~ **observation** Sonnenbeobachtung f
~ **photography** Sonnenfotografie f
~ **radiation** Sonnenstrahlung f, Solarstrahlung f
~ **spectrum** Sonnenspektrum n, solares Spektrum n
~ **telescope** Sonnenteleskop n
solarization [effect] Solarisation f, Solarisationseffekt m
solarize/to solarisieren
solarizing filter Solarisationsfilter n
solenoid [coil] Solenoid n (Magnetresonanzbildgebung)

solid 1. [geometrischer] Körper m; 2. s. solid-fill area
~ **angle** Raumwinkel m
~ **area** s. solid-fill area
~ **color** Vollfarbe f
~ **fill area** Füllfläche f, Füllgebiet n, Volltonfläche f (Druck, Computergrafik)
~ **glass filter** Massiv[glas]filter n, Glasfilter n
~ **ink** Festtinte f
~-**ink printer** Festtintendrucker m
~ **model** Volumenmodell n, Körpermodell n
~ **modeling** Volumenmodellierung f, Körpermodellierung f, Festkörpermodellierung f
~ **object** räumliches Objekt n
~ **of luminous intensity distribution** Lichtverteilungskörper m, fotometrischer Körper m
~ **of revolution** Rotationskörper m
~ **primitive** Primitivkörper m, [elementarer] Grundkörper m, Raumprimitiv n
~-**state camera** Halbleiterkamera f, Chipkamera f
~-**state component** Festkörperbauelement n, Halbleiterelement n
~-**state detector** Halbleiterdetektor m
~-**state electronics** Halbleiterelektronik f
~-**state imager**, ~ **imaging chip (sensor)** Halbleiterbildsensor m, Halbleiterbildwandler m, Festkörperbildwandler m
~-**state laser** Festkörperlaser m
~-**state memory [device]** Festspeicher m
~-**state photodetector** Festkörper-Fotoempfänger m, Halbleiter-Lichtempfänger m
~-**state physics** Festkörperphysik f
~-**state sensor** Festkörpersensor m, Halbleitersensor m
~-**state technology** s. semiconductor technology
~ **tint** Farbfläche f (Typografie)
solidity Räumlichkeit f
solidus Schrägstrich m
solubility Löslichkeit f
solution-physical development halbphysikalische Entwicklung f
solve/to auflösen (z.B. eine Gleichung)
solvent Lösungsmittel n
~ **ink** Lösemittelfarbe f, Toluol[druck]farbe f
sombrero filter Sombrerofilter n, Mexikanerhut-Operator m, Laplace-Gauß-Operator m, LoG-Filter n
sonar autofocus Sonarautofokus m
~ **backscatter** Sonarecho n
~ **device** Sonargerät n
~ **image** Sonarbild n
~ **pulse** Sonarimpuls m
~ **sensor** Sonarsensor m
~ **technology** Sonartechnik f
sonic image Schallbild n, akustisches Bild n

~ **sounding** Echolotung f
~ **speed** Schallgeschwindigkeit f
sonoelasticity imaging
Ultraschallelastografie f, Elastografie f
sonogram Sonogramm n, Ultraschallbild n, sonografisches Bild n, Echogramm n
sonograph Sonograf m
sonographer Ultraschalldiagnostiker m
sonographic sonografisch
~ **contrast agent** Ultraschallkontrastmittel n
~ **imaging, sonography** Sonografie f, Ultraschallbildgebung f, Ultraschalltechnik f
sonohologram Sonohologramm n, Ultraschallhologramm n
sonoholography Sonoholografie f, Ultraschallholografie f
sonolucent schalldurchlässig
sonoluminescence Sonolumineszenz f
sonoluminescent sonolumineszent
~ **tomography** Sonolumineszenztomografie f
sonometer Sonometer n
sonophotography Schallwellenfotografie f
soot Ruß m *(Pigment)*
sort algorithm Sortieralgorithmus m
sorting problem Sortierproblem n
sound Schall m; Ton m; Geräusch n *(s.a. unter audio, ultrasound)*
~-**absorbent** schallschluckend
~ **absorbing box** Schallschutzgehäuse n, Schallschutzhaube f
~ **advance** Bild-Ton-Versatz m, Bild-Ton-Abstand m *(Tonfilm)*
~ **amplification** Tonverstärkung f
~ **aperture** Academy-Format n, Standardformat n *(Kinefilm)*
~ **attenuation** Schalldämpfung f, Schallschwächung f
~ **beam** Schallstrahl m
~ **board** Soundkarte f, Audiokarte f *(Computer)*
~ **burst** Schallimpuls m
~ **camera** Bild-Ton-Kamera f, Lichttonkamera f, Tonkamera f
~ **card** s. ~ board
~ **carrier** Tonträger m
~ **channel** Tonkanal m, Audiokanal m
~ **conductivity** Schalleitfähigkeit f
~ **conforming** Tonanlegearbeit f, Tonanlegen n *(Filmproduktion)*
~ **crew** Tonmannschaft f *(Filmproduktion)*
~ **data** Audiodaten pl
~ **design** Tongestaltung f
~ **detection** Schalldetektion f
~ **diffraction** Schallbeugung f
~ **editing** Tonschnitt m, Audiobearbeitung f, Tonbearbeitung f
~ **editor** Tonmeister m; Toncutter m, Tonschneider m
~ **effect** Geräuscheffekt m, Toneffekt m; Effektgeräusch n
~ **effects editing** Ton[effekt]schnitt m

~ **effects house** Tonstudio n, Tonatelier n
~ **effects library** Geräuscharchiv n
~ **energy** Schallenergie f
~ **engineer** Toningenieur m; Ton[aufnahme]techniker m
~ **engineering** Tontechnik f
~ **equipment** Tonanlage f, Tonausrüstung f
~ **field** Schall[wellen]feld n, Tonfeld n
~ **file** Klangdatei f
~ **film** Ton[negativ]film m
~ **film print** Tonfilmkopie f
~ **frequency range** Schallfrequenzbereich m
~ **head** Tonkopf m
~ **impulse** s. ~ pulse
~ **information** Toninformation f
~ **intensity** s. ~ pressure
~ **level** Schall[druck]pegel m; Lautstärke f
~ **level meter** Schalldruckmessgerät n
~ **log** Tonbericht m
~ **mixer** s. ~ mixing
~ **mixer** Tonschneider m, Toncutter m
~ **mixing** Ton[ab]mischung f
~ **mixing console** Tonmischpult n, Audiomischer m
~ **modulation** Tonmodulation f
~ **motion picture**, ~ **movie** Tonfilm m
~ **navigation and ranging device** Sonargerät n
~ **negative** Tonnegativ n *(Filmproduktion)*
~-**on-disk recording** Nadeltonverfahren n *(Kinematografie)*
~-**on-film system** Lichttonverfahren n
~ **pickup** s. ~ recording
~ **picture** Tonfilm m
~ **playback** Tonabspielung f
~ **positive** Tonpositiv n *(Filmproduktion)*
~ **postproduction** Nachvertonung f, Tonnachbearbeitung f, Audiopost[produktion] f
~ **premix[ing]** Tonvormischung f *(Filmbearbeitung)*
~ **pressure** Schalldruck m
~ **pressure level** Schalldruckpegel m
~ **processing** Tonbearbeitung f
~ **projector** Tonfilmprojektor m
~ **propagation** Schallausbreitung f
~ **propagative direction** Schallausbreitungsrichtung f
~ **pulse** Tonimpuls m, Schallimpuls m, Synchron[isier]impuls m *(Filmarbeit)*
~ **quality** Tonqualität f
~ **record** Tonaufnahme f, Tonaufzeichnung f *(Produkt)*
~ **recorder** Tonaufnahmegerät n, Audiorecorder m
~ **recording** Tonaufnahme f, Tonaufzeichnung f, Schallaufzeichnung f, Audioaufzeichnung f
~-**recording equipment** Tonaufnahmetechnik f
~-**recording process** Tonaufnahmeverfahren n

~-**recording technique** Tonaufzeichnungstechnik f
~ **recordist** Ton[aufnahme]techniker m, Toningenieur m; Filmtontechniker m
~ **report** Tonbericht m
~ **reproducer** Tonwiedergabegerät n
~ **reproduction** Tonwiedergabe f, Schallwiedergabe f
~ **reproduction system** Tonwiedergabesystem n
~ **roll** Tonrolle f *(Filmproduktion)*
~ **scanner** Tonabtaster m
~ **scanning** Tonabtastung f *(Kinotechnik)*
~ **shadow** Schallschatten m
~ **signal** Tonsignal n, Audiosignal n, akustisches Signal n
~-**slide program** Diatonbildschau f
~ **source** Schallquelle f
~ **speaker** Lautsprecher m
~ **stripe** Bespurungsband n, Schmal[spur]band n, Senkel m *(Kinefilm)*; Ton-Original n *(Magnetton)*
~ **studio** Tonstudio n, Tonatelier n
~ **synchronization** Tonsynchronisation f, Synchronisation f *(Filmproduktion)*
~ **system** Tonwiedergabesystem n
~ **take** Tonaufnahme f
~ **tape** Tonband n
~ **technician** Tontechniker m
~ **technology** Tontechnik f
~ **test** Tonprobe f
~ **track** 1. Ton[aufzeichnungs]spur f, Audiospur f *(s.a. ~ stripe)*; Filmtonspur f, Soundtrack m; 2. Filmmusik f
~ **track developer** Tonspurentwickler m
~ **track negative** Tonspurnegativ n
~ **track printer** Tonspurkopiergerät n
~ **transmission** Schallübertragung f, Tonübertragung f
~ **transmitter** Tonsender m *(Fernsehen)*
~ **velocity** Schallgeschwindigkeit f
~ **volume** Lautstärke f
~ **wave** Schallwelle f, akustische Welle f
soundman Tontechniker m; Filmtontechniker m
soundperson Tontechniker m; Filmtontechniker m
soundproof schalldicht
soundstage Aufnahmestudio n *(s.a. sound studio)*
soundwave photography Schallwellenfotografie f
soup/to verarbeiten, entwickeln *(Fotomaterial)*
soup Entwicklungsbad n
source code Quellencode m
~-**coding theorem** Quellencodierungstheorem n
~ **decoder** Quellendecodierer m
~ **decoding** Quellendecodierung f
~ **encoder** Quellencodierer m
~ **encoding** Quellencodierung f
~ **entropy** Quellenentropie f, Signalentropie f *(Informationstheorie)*
~ **file** Quelldatei f
~ **image** Bildvorlage f, Ausgangsbild n, Quell[en]bild n, Ursprungsbild n
~ **input (intermediate video) format** s. SIF-Format
~ **laser** Quellenlaser m
~ **machine** Zuspielmaschine f, Schnittzuspieler m, Zuspieler m
~ **material** [originales] Drehmaterial n *(Video)*
~ **model** Quellenmodell n *(Videocodierung)*
~ **model[l]ing** Quellenmodellierung f
~ **monitor** Zuspielmonitor m
~ **of clocking** Taktquelle f
~ **of illumination** Beleuchtungsquelle f
~ **of imagery** Bildquelle f
~ **of noise** Rausch[stör]quelle f
~ **of radiation** Strahlungsquelle f, Strahlenquelle f
~ **point** Quellpunkt m
~ **recorder** Zuspielrecorder m
~ **reel** Abwickelspule f
~ **signal** Quellensignal n
~ **tape** Zuspielband n, Originalband n *(Video)*
~ **videotape recorder, ~ VTR** Videozuspieler m, Zuspielrecorder m
space ... *s.a.* spatial ...
~ **charge** Raumladung f
~ **curve** Raumkurve f
~ **division multiplex** Raummultiplex n *(Signalübertragung)*
~ **domain** Orts[signal]bereich m, Ortsraum m
~ **feed** Strahlungsspeisung f *(Radarantenne)*
~-**frequency quantization** Ortsfrequenzquantisierung f
~ **function** Ortsfunktion f
~ **group symmetry** Raumgruppensymmetrie f *(Kristallografie)*
~ **image** Satellitenbild n; Weltraumbild n
~ **imaging** Satellitenbildaufnahme f
~ **integral** Volumenintegral n
~ **invariance** Rauminvarianz f
~-**invariant filter** ortsinvariantes Filter n
~ **multiplex** Raummultiplex m
~ **perception** Raum[bild]wahrnehmung f, räumliche Wahrnehmung f, Tiefenwahrnehmung f
~ **photography** Raumfahrtfotografie f, Weltraumfotografie f
~ **point** Raumpunkt m
~ **probe picture** Raumsondenaufnahme f
~ **quantization** Richtungsquantisierung f *(Magnetresonanztomografie)*
~ **subdivision** Raumteilung f *(Computergrafik)*
~ **telescope** Weltraumteleskop n, Raumteleskop n, extraterrestrisches Teleskop n

space 366

~ **telescopic picture** Weltraumteleskopaufnahme *f*, Weltraumteleskopbild *n*
~-**time** ortszeitlich, raumzeitlich
~-**variant apodization** ortsvariante Apodisation *f*
~-**variant image processing** ortsvariante Bildverarbeitung *f*
~-**variant resolution** ortsabhängige Auflösung *f*
spaceband Ausschließkeil *m*, Spatienkeil *m*, Keil *m* *(Satzherstellung)*
spaceborne satellitengestützt
~ **radar** Raumfahrzeugradar *n*; Satellitenradar *n*, satellitengetragenes Radar *n*
spacer layer Trennschicht *f*, Zwischenschicht *f* *(z.B. im Colorfilm)*
spacial *s.* spatial
spacing layer Trennschicht *f*
~ **loss** Abstandsverlust *m* *(Bandaufzeichnung)*
~ **ratio** Abstandsverhältnis *n*
spaciousness Räumlichkeit *f*, räumliche Weite *f*
spare camera Reservekamera *f*, Ersatzkamera *f*
~ **film** Reservefilm *m*
spark illumination Funkenbeleuchtung *f*
~ **illumination (light) source** Funkenlichtquelle *f*
spatial räumlich, örtlich *(s.a. unter space ...)*
~ **alias[ing]** Treppen[stufen]effekt *m*, Stufeneffekt *m* *(Bildfehler)*
~ **averaging filter** Mittelwertfilter *n*
~ **coding** Ortscodierung *f*
~ **coherence** räumliche Kohärenz *f*
~ **contrast** räumlicher Kontrast *m*
~ **convolution** räumliche Faltung *f*
~ **coordinate** Ortskoordinate *f*, Raumkoordinate *f*
~ **correlation** räumliche Korrelation *f*
~ **data** räumliche Daten *pl*
~ **data structure** räumliche Datenstruktur *f*
~ **decimation** räumliche Dezimation *f*
~ **depth** Raumtiefe *f*, räumliche Tiefe *f*
~ **discretization** Ortsdiskretisierung *f*
~ **discretization** räumliche Diskretisierung *f*, Ortsdiskretisierung *f*
~ **dispersion** räumliche Dispersion *f*
~ **distribution** örtliche Verteilung *f*
~ **domain** Ortsraum *m*, Orts[signal]bereich *m*
~-**domain convolution** Ortsbereichsfaltung *f*
~-**domain filter** Ortsbereichsfilter *n*
~-**domain frequency** Ortsbereichsfrequenz *f*
~-**domain image** Ortsbereichsbild *n*
~-**domain neighborhood** Ortsbereichsnachbarschaft *f*

~-**domain representation** Ortsbereichsdarstellung *f* *(z.B. von Bildsignalen)*
~ **encoding** räumliche Codierung *f*
~ **filter [mask]** Raumfilter *n*, Ortsfrequenzfilter *n*
~ **filtering (filtration)** räumliche Filterung (Frequenzfilterung) *f*, Ortsfrequenzfilterung *f*, Pupillenfilterung *f*
~ **Fourier transform** räumliche Fourier-Transformation *f*
~ **frequency** Ortsfrequenz *f*, Raumfrequenz *f*, räumliche Frequenz *f*, Objektfeinheit *f*
~-**frequency analysis** Ortsfrequenzanalyse *f*
~-**frequency axis** Ortsfrequenzachse *f*
~-**frequency bandwidth** ortsfrequente Bandbreite *f* *(z.B. des Auges)*
~-**frequency channel** Ortsfrequenzkanal *m*
~-**frequency content** Ortsfrequenzgehalt *m*
~-**frequency coordinate** Ortsfrequenzkoordinate *f*
~-**frequency dependence** Ortsfrequenzabhängigkeit *f*
~-**frequency-dependent** ortsfrequenzabhängig
~-**frequency direction** Ortsfrequenzrichtung *f*
~-**frequency distribution** Ortsfrequenzverteilung *f*
~-**frequency domain** Ortsfrequenzraum *m*, Ortsfrequenzbereich *m*
~-**frequency domain representation** Ortsfrequenzdarstellung *f*
~-**frequency filter** Ortsfrequenzfilter *n*, Raumfilter *n*
~-**frequency filtering** Ortsfrequenzfilterung *f*
~-**frequency pattern** Ortsfrequenzbild *n*
~-**frequency range** Ortsfrequenzbereich *m*
~-**frequency response** Ortsfrequenzgang *m*
~-**frequency spectrum** Ortsfrequenzspektrum *n*, Fourier-Spektrum *n*
~-**frequency vector** Ortsfrequenzvektor *m*
~ **gradient** räumlicher Gradient *m*
~ **gradient vector** räumlicher Gradientenvektor
~ **image** räumliches Bild *n*
~ **image sequence** dreidimensionale (räumliche) Bildfolge *f*
~ **interpolation** räumliche Interpolation *f*
~ **interval** räumliches Intervall *n*
~ **low-pass filtering** örtliche Tiefpassfilterung *f*
~ **map** räumliche Abbildung *f*
~ **masking** *s.* texture masking
~ **model** räumliches Modell *n*
~ **neighborhood** räumliche Nachbarschaft *f*
~ **noise** räumliches Rauschen *n*

~ **noise reduction** örtliche Rauschreduktion *f*
~ **occupancy enumeration** räumliches Enumerationsverfahren *n (Computergrafik)*
~ **orientation** räumliche Ausrichtung *f*
~ **pattern** räumliches Muster *n*
~ **perspective** räumliche Perspektive *f*
~ **quantization** örtliche Quantisierung *f*
~ **redundancy** örtliche (räumliche) Redundanz *f*
~ **representation** räumliche (raumbildliche) Darstellung *f*, Ortsbereichsdarstellung *f*
~ **resolution** Raumauflösung *f*, Orts[frequenz]auflösung *f*, räumliche (örtliche) Auflösung *f*
~ **resolving power** räumliches (örtliches) Auflösungsvermögen *n*
~ **response** Punktbildfunktion *f*
~ **response function** Ortsfunktion *f*
~ **sampling** räumliche Abtastung *f*
~ **scalability** räumliche Skalierbarkeit *f*, Orts-Skalierbarkeit *f*
~ **scaling** räumliche Skalierung *f*
~ **set operation** Boolesche Operation *f (Modellierungsverfahren)*
~ **signal** örtliches Signal *n*
~ **space** Ortsraum *m*
~ **subband** örtliches Teilband *n*
~ **transformation** örtliche Transformation *f*
~ **variable** Ortsvariable *f*
~ **vision** räumliches (stereoskopisches) Sehen *n*, dreidimensionales Sehen *n*, Raumsehen *n*, Tiefensehen *n*, Stereosehen *n*
~ **wavelength** räumliche Wellenlänge *f*
spatiality Räumlichkeit *f*
spatially continuous ortskontinuierlich
~ **dependent noise** räumliches Rauschen *n*
~ **invariant** ortsinvariant
~ **scalable profile** räumlich skalierbares Profil *n*
~ **variant apodization** ortsvariante Apodisation *f*
~ **varying signal** ortsvariantes Signal *n*
spatiotemporal raumzeitlich, ortszeitlich, örtlich-zeitlich
~ **curvature** ortszeitliche Krümmung *f*
~ **filter** raumzeitliches Filter *n*
~ **filtering** raumzeitliche Filterung *f*
~ **image** Orts-Zeit-Bild *n*, raumzeitliches (ortszeitliches) Bild *n*
~ **image processing** raumzeitliche Bildverarbeitung *f*
~ **masking** raumzeitliche Maskierung *f*
~ **noise** ortszeitliches Rauschen *n*
~ **prediction** ortszeitliche Prädiktion *f*
~ **sampling** zeitlich-räumliche Abtastung *f*
~ **signal** raumzeitliches (örtlich-zeitliches) Signal *n*
~ **spectrum** raumzeitliches Spektrum *n*
~ **window** raumzeitliches Fenster *n*
speaker 1. Sprecher *m*; 2. Lautsprecher *m*

~-**driven handset** sprachgesteuerte Fernbedienung *f*
special effect Spezialeffekt *m*, Bildeffekt *m*, Effekt *m*, Bildtrick *m*, Trick *m (Film, Video)*
~-**effects camera work** Trickarbeit *f*
~-**effects cinematography** Trickkinematografie *f*
~-**effects department** Trickabteilung *f*
~-**effects device** Effektgerät *n*, Trickgenerator *m*, Trickgerät *n*
~-**effects film** Effektfilm *m*, Trickfilm *m*, Animationsfilm *m*
~-**effects filter** Effektfilter *n*, Trickfilter *n*, Kreativfilter *n*
~-**effects generator** Effektgenerator *m*, Spezialeffektgenerator *m*
~-**effects movie** *s.* ~ film
~-**effects photograph** Trickaufnahme *f*
~-**effects photography** Trickfotografie *f*
~-**effects printing** Trickkopieren *n*
~-**effects procedure** Effektverfahren *n*, Trickverfahren *n*
~-**effects shot** Effektaufnahme *f*, Trick[film]aufnahme *f*
~-**effects studio** Effektstudio *n*, Trick[film]studio *n*, Trickatelier *n*
~-**effects supervisor** Trickregisseur *m*
~-**effects technician** Tricktechniker *m*
~-**effects technique** Trickverfahren *n*; Tricktechnik *f*
~-**effects work** Trickarbeit *f*
~ **filter** Spezialfilter *n*, Sonderfilter *n*
~-**formula developer** Spezialentwickler *m*
~-**interest channel** Spartenkanal *m*, Themenkanal *m (Fernsehen)*
~ **optics** Spezialoptik *f*
~ **picture effect** *s.* ~ effect
~-**purpose camera** Spezialkamera *f*
~-**purpose film** Spezialfilm *m*
~-**purpose lens** Spezialobjektiv *n*, Sonderobjektiv *n*
~-**purpose monitor** Spezialmonitor *m*
~-**purpose photography** Spezialfotografie *f*
~ **spectacles** Spezialbrille *f (z.B. für räumliches Sehen)*
~ **visual effect** optischer Effekt (Trick) *m (Kinematografie)*
specialized glass [optisches] Sonderglas *n*, Spezialglas *n*
~ **interest cable channel** Spartenkabelkanal *m*
~ **photographic paper** Spezial[foto]papier *n*, Sonderpapier *n*
specially equipped lab Speziallabor *n*
~ **treated paper** *s.* specialty paper
specialty filter Spezialfilter *n*, Sonderfilter *n*
~ **lens** Sonderobjektiv *n*, Spezialobjektiv *n*
~-**model enlarger** Spezialvergrößerer *m*
~ **paper** Spezialpapier *n*, Sonderpapier *n*
~ **printing process** Sonderdruckverfahren *n*
specific model spezifisches Modell *n*

specification of color Farbspezifikation f, Farbbeschreibung f
specimen 1. Prüfobjekt n, Prüfling m; Objekt n, Präparat n *(Mikroskopie)*; 2. Muster n; Probe f
~ **contrast** Objektkontrast m *(Mikroskopie)*
~ **detail** Objektdetail n
~ **illumination** Objektausleuchtung f
~ **image** Objektbild n, Gegenstandsbild n
~ **photography** Präparatefotografie f
~ **plane** Objektebene f, Präparatebene f, Gegenstandsebene f *(Mikroskopie)*
~ **point** Objektpunkt m *(Mikroskopie)*
~ **preparation** Präparation f
~ **radiography** Präparateradiografie f
~ **sharpness** Objektschärfe f
~ **slide** Objektträger m
~ **space** Objektraum m, Dingraum m, Gegenstandsraum m, objektseitiger Strahlenraum m *(Mikroskopie)*
~ **stage** Objekttisch m
speckle decorrelation Speckle-Dekorrelation f
~ **filter** Speckle-Filter n
~ **filtering** Speckle-Filterung f
~ **holography** Speckle-Holografie f
~ **interference [artifact]** Speckle-Störung f *(Radar, Sonografie)*
~ **interferogram** Speckle-Interferogramm n
~ **interferometer** Speckle-Interferometer n
~-**interferometric** speckleinterferometrisch
~ **metrology** Speckle-Messtechnik f
~ **noise** Impulsrauschen n, impulsförmiges Rauschen n; Schrotrauschen n, Speckle-Rauschen n
~ **pattern** Speckle-Muster n, Granulationsmuster n *(z.B. in Ultraschallbildern)*
~ **pattern interferometry** Speckle-Interferometrie f
~ **pattern shearing interferometry** Shearografie f
~ **phenomenon** Speckle-Effekt m
~ **photography** Speckle-Fotografie f
speckling Tüpfeln n *(Digitalbildstörung)*
specs Satzanweisung f *(Druckgewerbe)*
SPECT s. single-photon emission-computed tomography
~ **image** SPECT-Bild n
~ **imaging** SPECT f, Einzelphotonen-Emissionstomografie f, Emissionscomputertomografie f
~ **study** SPECT-Untersuchung f
~ **system** SPECT-Gerät n, Einzelphotonen-Emissionstomograf m, Emissionscomputertomograf m
spectacle lens Brillenglas n
~ **lens optics** Brillenoptik f
~ **wearer** Brillenträger m
spectacles Brille f
spectator Betrachter m, Beschauer m; Zuschauer m

spectral spektral
~ **absorptance** spektraler Absorptionsgrad n
~ **absorption** spektrale Absorption f
~ **analysis** Spektralanalyse f, spektrale Analyse f
~ **apparatus** Spektralapparat m
~ **band** Spektralband n, Spektralbande f
~ **bandwidth** spektrale Bandbreite f
~ **brightness** spektrale Helligkeit f
~ **channel** Spektralkanal m
~ **coefficient** Spektralkoeffizient m
~ **color** Spektralfarbe f, spektrale Farbe f
~ **color density** spektrale Farbdichte f
~ **color photography** Spektralfarbenfotografie f
~ **color stimulus** spektrale Farbvalenz f
~ **component** Spektralkomponente f
~ **composition (content)** spektrale Zusammensetzung f, Spektralzusammensetzung f *(z.B. des Lichts)*
~ **curve** Spektralverteilungskurve f
~ **data** spektrale Daten pl
~ **density** spektrale Dichte f, Spektraldichte f, Leistungsdichtespektrum n
~ **density curve** Spektraldichtekurve f
~ **dispersion** spektrale Zerlegung f
~ **distortion** spektrale Verzerrung f
~ **distribution** s. ~ power distribution
~ **efficiency** spektrale Effizienz f, Bandbreiteneffizienz f, Bandbreitenausnutzung f
~ **emission** spektrale Emission f
~ **energy distribution** spektrale Energieverteilung (Verteilung) f, Spektralverteilung f; spektrale Strahlungsverteilung f
~ **energy distribution chart (curve)** Spektralverteilungskurve f
~ **error** Spektralfehler m
~ **exposure** spektrale Belichtung f
~ **filter** Spektralfilter n, optisches Strahlungsfilter n
~ **filtering** spektrale Filterung f, Spektralfilterung f
~ **flux density** spektrale Flussdichte f
~ **illumination model** spektrales Beleuchtungsmodell n
~ **image** Spektralbild n, spektrales Bild n
~ **image analysis** spektrale Bildanalyse f
~ **incident luminous (radiant) flux** auffallender spektraler Strahlungsfluss m
~ **information** spektrale Information f
~ **internal transmittance** [spektraler] Reintransmissionsgrad m
~ **lamp** Spektrallampe f
~ **light** Spektrallicht n, spektrales Licht n
~ **line** Spektrallinie f
~ **line analysis** Spektrallinienanalyse f
~ **line distribution** Spektrallinienverteilung f

specular

~ **lines** Fraunhofer-Linien *fpl*, Fraunhofersche Linien *fpl*
~ **locus** Farbort *m*, Spektralfarbenzug *m*
~ **luminosity** spektrale Hellempfindlichkeit *f*
~ **luminosity curve (function)** spektrale Hellempfindlichkeitskurve *f*
~ **luminous efficiency** spektraler Hellempfindlichkeitsgrad *m*
~ **luminous flux** *s*. ~ radiant flux
~ **measurement** Spektralmessung *f*
~ **model** spektrales Modell *n*
~ **optical coherence tomography** spektraloptische Kohärenztomografie *f*
~ **plate** Spektralplatte *f*
~ **power distribution** spektrale Strahlungsverteilung (Verteilung) *f*, Spektralverteilung *f*
~ **primary** spektrale Primärvalenz *f (Kolorimetrie)*
~ **purity** spektrale Reinheit *f*
~ **quantization** spektrale Quantisierung *f*
~ **radiance** spektrale Strahldichte *f*
~ **radiance contrast** *s*. Planck's function
~ **radiance factor** spektraler Strahldichtefaktor (Strahldichtewert) *m*
~ **radiant flux** spektraler Strahlungsfluss *m*, spektrale Dichte *f* der Strahlungsleistung
~ **radiant intensity** spektrale Strahlstärke *f*
~ **radiation** spektrale Strahlung *f*
~ **range** Spektralbereich *m*
~ **redundancy** spektrale Redundanz *f*
~ **reflectance** spektraler Reflexionsgrad *m*
~ **reflected luminous (radiant) flux** reflektierter spektraler Strahlungsfluss *m*
~ **reflection** Spektralreflexion *f*
~ **region** Spektralbereich *m*, Spektralgebiet *n*
~ **representation** Spektraldarstellung *f*
~ **resolution** spektrale Auflösung *f*
~ **resolving power** spektrales Auflösungsvermögen *n*
~ **response** Spektralantwort *f*, Spektralverhalten *n*, spektraler Verlauf *m (s.a.* ~ sensitivity*)*
~ **response function** Spektralfunktion *f*
~ **responsivity** *s*. ~ sensitivity
~ **sample** spektraler Abtastwert *m*
~ **sampling** spektrale Abtastung *f*
~ **sensitivity** spektrale Empfindlichkeit *f*, Spektralempfindlichkeit *f*; spektrale Fotoempfindlichkeit *f*; Farbempfindlichkeit *f*
~ **sensitivity curve** spektrale Empfindlichkeitskurve (Empfindlichkeitsverteilung) *f*, Augenkurve *f*
~ **sensitization** spektrale (optische) Sensibilisierung *f*
~ **sensitized emulsion** spektralsensibilierte Emulsion *f*
~ **sensitizer** spektraler Sensibilisator *m*, Spektralsensibilisator *m*
~ **sensitizing dye** Sensibilisatorfarbstoff *m*, Sensibilisierfarbstoff *m*
~ **separation** Spektralzerlegung *f*
~ **shift** Spektralverschiebung *f*
~ **signature** spektrale Signatur *f*
~ **transform** Spektraltransformation *f*
~ **transmittance** spektraler Transmissionsgrad *m*, spektrale Durchlässigkeit *f*
~ **wavelength** spektrale Wellenlänge *f*
~ **window of absorption** Absorptionsspektrum *n*
spectrofluorimeter *s*. spectrofluorometer
spectrofluorometer Spektrofluorometer *n*
spectrofluorometric spektrofluorometrisch
spectrofluorometry Spektrofluorometrie *f*
spectrogram Spektrogramm *n*
spectrograph Spektrograf *m*
spectrographic spektrografisch
~ **imaging** Bildspektroskopie *f*
spectrography Spektrografie *f*
spectroheliogram Spektroheliogramm *n*
spectroheliograph Spektroheliograf *m*
spectroheliography Spektroheliografie *f*
spectrohelioscope Spektrohelioskop *n*
spectrometer Spektrometer *n*
spectrometric spektrometrisch
spectrometry Spektrometrie *f*
spectromicroscopy Spektromikroskopie *f*
spectrophotography Spektrofotografie *f*
spectrophotometer Spektralfotometer *n*
spectrophotometric[al] spektralfotometrisch
spectrophotometry Spektralfotometrie *f*, Spektrofotometrie *f*
spectroradiometer Spektralradiometer *n*
spectroradiometric spektralradiometrisch
spectroradiometry Spektralradiometrie *f*, Spektroradiometrie *f*
spectroscope Spektroskop *n*
spectroscopic spektroskopisch
~ **ellipsometer** spektroskopisches Ellipsometer *n*
~ **film** spektroskopischer Film *m*
~ **image** spektroskopisches Bild *n*
~ **imaging** spektroskopische Bildgebung *f*
~ **lamp** Spektrallampe *f*
~ **optics** spektroskopische Optik *f*
~ **photography** spektroskopische Fotografie *f*
~ **plate** spektroskopische Platte *f*
spectroscopist Spektroskopiker *m*
spectroscopy Spektroskopie *f*
spectrosensitogram Spektrosensitogramm *n*
spectrum Spektrum *n*, Ortsfrequenzverteilung *f (s.a. unter* spectral*)*
~ **analyzer** Spektralanalysator *m*, Spektrumanalysator *m*
specular spiegelnd
~ **color** spiegelnde Farbe *f*
~ **direction** Spiegelungsrichtung *f*

specular 370

~ **flash (glint)** Glint m, Winkelfluktuation f (Radar)
~ **highlight** Glanzlicht n; Hochlicht n
~ **light** hartes Licht n
~ **lighting** spiegelnde Beleuchtung f
~ **point** Glanzpunkt m
~ **reflection** Spiegelung f, Spiegelreflexion f, spiegelnde Reflexion f; gerichtete (regelmäßige) Reflexion f, Fresnel-Reflexion f
~ **reflector** spiegelnder Reflektor m, Spiegelreflektor m
~ **screen** Silber[lein]wand f; metallisierte Bildwand f
~ **surface** spiegelnd reflektierende Oberfläche f, spiegelnde Oberfläche (Fläche) f
~ **symmetry** Spiegelsymmetrie f
specularly reflected beam spiegelreflektierter Strahl m
~ **reflected light** spiegelnd (regulär) reflektiertes Licht n
speculum Spekulum n
~ **metal** Spiegelmetall n
~ **mirror** Metallspiegel m (bes. älterer Teleskope)
speech intelligibility Sprachverständlichkeit f
~ **visualization** Sprachvisualisierung f
speed 1. Geschwindigkeit f; 2. Empfindlichkeit f (von Fotomaterial); 3. Lichtstärke f (Objektiv)
~ **increase** Empfindlichkeitssteigerung f, Empfindlichkeitsgewinn m
~ **loss** Empfindlichkeitsverlust m
~ **of access** Zugriffsgeschwindigkeit f
~ **of film** Filmempfindlichkeit f
~ **of light** Lichtgeschwindigkeit f
~ **of motion** Bewegungsgeschwindigkeit f
~ **of sound** Schallgeschwindigkeit f
~ **printer** Schnellkopiermaschine f
~ **reduction** Empfindlichkeitsreduktion f
~ **setting** Verschluss[zeitenein]stellung f
~ **value** Empfindlichkeitswert m
speedflash, speedlight Elektronenblitz m; Blitzgerät n
spell check[er] Rechtschreibprüfprogramm n (Textverarbeitung)
spherical sphärisch, kugelförmig
~ **aberration** sphärische Aberration (Verzeichnung) f, Kugelgestaltsfehler m, Öffnungsfehler m (Optik)
~-**aberration-limited system** öffnungsfehlerbegrenztes [optisches] System n
~ **doublet [lens]** sphärisches Dublett n
~ **error** sphärischer Fehler m (Objektiv)
~ **geometry** Kugelgeometrie f
~ **lens** 1. sphärische Linse f, Kugellinse f; 2. sphärisch korrigiertes Objektiv n
~ **linear interpolation** sphärische lineare Interpolation f, SLERP (Computeranimation)

~ **mirror** sphärischer Spiegel m, Kugelspiegel m
~ **primary [mirror]** sphärischer Hauptspiegel m (z.B. eines Teleskops)
~ **projection** sphärische Projektion f
~ **reflector** s. ~ mirror
~ **surface** sphärische Fläche f, Kugelfläche f
~ **symmetry** Kugelsymmetrie f
~ **wave** Kugelwelle f
~ **wave front** Kugelwellenfront f
spherically corrected objective sphärisch korrigiertes Objektiv n
sphericity Kugelförmigkeit f
spherochromatism Gauß-Fehler m
spherometer Sphärometer n
spider Bodenspinne f, Spinne f (Stativzubehör)
spike Aktionspotential n (Neuroinformatik)
~ **edge** Stiftkante f (Bildverarbeitung)
~ **filter** Schmalbandfilter n, schmalbandiges Filter n, Linienfilter n
~ **noise** Schrotrauschen n, bipolares Impulsrauschen n
spill light Nebenlicht n
spin Spin m, Eigendrehimpuls m
~ **density** Spindichte f
~ **density-weighted image** Spindichtebild n
~ **echo** Spinecho n
~ **echo acquisition** Spinechoerfassung f
~ **echo imaging** Spinechoverfahren n
~ **echo MR image** Spinechobild n
~ **echo sequence** Spinechosequenz f
~-**lattice relaxation time** Spin-Gitter-Relaxationszeit f, Längsrelaxationszeit f, Longitudinalrelaxation f, T1 (Magnetresonanztomografie)
~ **mapping** Resonanzbildgebung f
~ **precession frequency** Präzessionsfrequenz f
~ **precession speed** Spinpräzessionsgeschwindigkeit f
~ **signal** Spinsignal n
~-**spin relaxation time** Spin-Spin-Relaxationszeit f, Querrelaxation[szeit] f, Transversalrelaxationszeit f, Querrelaxationszeitkonstante f (Magnetresonanztomografie)
~ **state** Spinzustand m
~ **system** Spinsystem n
spine Rückgrat n (z.B. in geometrischen Modellen)
spinning mirror Drehspiegel m
spinthariscope Spinthariskop n
spiral computed tomography Spiral-Computertomografie f, Spiral-CT f
~ **CT angiography** Spiral-Computerangiografie f
~ **reel** Spiraleinsatz m, Filmspirale f, Aufwickeldorn m, Spuleneinsatz m (Entwicklungsdose)
~ **scan** Spiralscan m, Helicalscan m

~ **scanner** Spiralscanner *m*
~ **volumetric computerized tomography** *s.* ~ computed tomography
spirit bubble Nivellierlibelle *f*
~ **duplicating (duplication)** Spirit-Umdruck *m*, Hektografie *f*
~ **duplicator** Spirit-Umdruckapparat *m*, Spirit-Umdrucker *m*; Hektograf *m*
~ **level** Nivellierlibelle *f*
splenic scintigraphy Milzszintigrafie *f*
splice/to kleben
splice Klebestelle *f*; Filmklebestelle *f*
splicer Klebelade *f*, Klebelehre *f*, Klebepresse *f*, Filmpresse *f*
splicing tape Klebeband n, Klebestreifen *m*; Filmklebeband *n*, Filmklebefolie *f*
spline [curve] Spline-Kurve *f*, Spline-Funktion *f*, Spline *n(m)*, stückweise polynomische Kurve *f*
~**-driven animation** Spline-Animation *f* *(geometrische Modellierung)*
~ **fitting** aktive Kontur *f (Computergrafik)*
~ **fitting** Spline-Anpassung *f*
~ **function** *s.* spline [curve]
~ **interpolation** Spline-Interpolation *f*
~ **surface** Spline-Oberfläche *f*, Spline-Fläche *f*
split-and-merge algorithm (approach) Split-and-Merge-Algorithmus *m* *(Bildsegmentierung)*
~ **edit** Bild-Ton-versetzter Schnitt *m*
~ **exposure** Teilbelichtung *f*
~**-field filter** Teilnahlinse *f*, Split-Linse *f*
~**-field lens** Bifokallinse *f*, Bifokalglas *n*, Zweistärkenglas *n (Brillenoptik)*
~**-field microscope** Doppelmikroskop *n*
~ **fountain** nebenwirkungsfreie Farbdosiereinrichtung *f* *(Druckmaschine)*
~**-image rangefinder (wedge), split-prism rangefinder** Schnittbildentfernungsmesser *m*, Schnittbildindikator *m*, Messkeil *m* *(Fokussierhilfe)*
~ **screen** 1. geteilte Leinwand *f*; 2. geteilter Bildschirm *m*; 3. Mehrfachbild *n*
~ **screen effect** Bildteilungstrick *m* *(Filmarbeit)*
~ **screen shot** Mehrfachbild *n*
spoilage Papierausschuss *m (Druck)*
spontaneous development Spontanentwicklung *f*
~ **emission** spontane Emission *f*
~ **Raman scattering** spontane Raman-Streuung *f*
spool/to spulen
spool Spule *f*; Filmrolle *f*, Filmakt *m*, Akt *m*
~ **box** Aufwickelmagazin *n*, Magazin *n*, Filmmagazin *n*
spooler Warteschlange *f* *(Datenverarbeitung)*
sports photographer Sportfotograf *m*
~ **photography** Sportfotografie *f*
~ **shooter** Sportfotograf *m*

~ **viewfinder** Sportsucher *m*, Rahmensucher *m*
spot/to ausflecken
spot 1. Fleck *m*; Punkt *m*; 2. Werbespot *m*, Werbekurzfilm *m*; 3. *s.* spotlight
~ **color** Schmuckfarbe *f*, Effektfarbe *f*; Zusatzfarbe *f (Druckwesen)*
~ **diagram (image)** Punktbild *n*, punktförmige Abbildung *n*, Zerstreuungsscheibchen *n*, Spotdiagramm *n (Optik)*
~**-film camera** Filmwechsler *m* *(Röntgendiagnostik)*
~ **jammer** schmalbandiger Störer *m* *(Radar)*
~ **lamp** Punktlichtlampe *f (s.a.* spotlight*)*
~ **meter** Punktbelichtungsmesser *m*, Spot[foto]meter *n*, Spotbelichtungsmesser *m*, Partialbelichtungsmesser *m*
~ **metering** Punktmessung *f*, Spot[belichtungs]messung *f*, Selektivmessung *f*, punktuelle Belichtungsmessung *f*
~ **noise** Punktrauschen *n*
~ **of light** Lichtpunkt *m*, Lichtfleck *m*, Leuchtfleck *m*
~ **projection** Lichtpunktprojektion *f* *(Triangulation)*
~**-scanning apparatus** Punktabtaster *m*
~ **size** Fleckgröße *f*
~ **spread** Punktausbreitung *f*
~ **varnish** *s.* ~ color
spotlight/to anstrahlen
spotlight 1. Scheinwerfer *m*; Punkt[licht]scheinwerfer *m*, Spotlight *n*, Spot *m*; Spotlampe *f*; 2. Punktlicht *n*, Scheinwerferlicht *n*
~ **mode** Scheinwerfermodus *m* *(synthetisches Aperturradar)*
spotlighting Spotbeleuchtung *f*, Punktlichtbeleuchtung *f*
spotting Ausfleckretusche *f*, Ausfleckarbeit *f*, Ausflecken *n*
~ **color (compound)** Ausfleckfarbe *f*
~ **pen** Fleckretuschierstift *m*
SPR *s.* surface-penetrating radar
spray adhesive Sprühkleber *m*
~ **can** Sprühdose *f* *(Bildbearbeitungswerkzeug)*
spread Doppelseite *f (Layout)*
~ **function** Verteilungsfunktion *f*, Wahrscheinlichkeitsverteilungsfunktion *f*
spreading Aufweitung *f (z.B. eines Laserstrahls)*
~ **agent** Netzmittel *n*, Entspannungsmittel *n*
spreadsheet Tabellenblatt *n*
spring constant Federkonstante *f* *(Rasterkraftmikroskopie)*
~ **mechanism** Federwerk *n*
sprocket Transportrolle *f*; [Film-]Zahnrolle *f*, Zahntrommel *f*

sprocket 372

~ **drum printer** Zahnkranz-Kopiermaschine f
~ **hole** Perforationsloch n
~ **hole area** Perforationsbereich m
~ **noise** Perforationsgeräusch n
~ **wheel** s. sprocket
sprocketed film perforierter Film m
~ **magnetic film** perforierter Magnetfilm m
~ **magnetic tape** perforiertes Magnetband n, Perfoband n, Perfo-Tonband n, Cordband n
~ **printing drum** Kopierzahntrommel f
sprocketless unperforiert
spurious echo Fehlecho n *(Sonografie, Radar)*
spy camera Spionagekamera f, Agentenkamera f; Überwachungskamera f
~ **plane** Spionageflugzeug n
spyglass Kleinteleskop n
spycam s. spy camera
spyware Spionagesoftware f *(Internet)*
square Quadrat n
~ **aperture** rechteck[förm]ige Apertur (Blende) f, Rechteckblende f, Rechteckapertur f
~ **bracket** eckige Klammer f *(Druckzeichen)*
~ **dot** quadratischer (konventioneller) Rasterpunkt m
~ **dot screen** quadratischer Raster m, Quadratraster m *(Druck)*
~ **grid (lattice)** 1. quadratisches Gitter n; Rechteckgitter n 2. s. ~ dot screen
~ **matrix** quadratische Matrix f
~ **pixel** quadratisches Pixel n
~ **root intensity image** quadratisches Amplitudenbild n
~ **screen** s. square dot screen
~ **serif** Blockserife f *(Buchstabenbild)*
~ **wave** Rechteckwelle f
~ **wave amplitude** Rechteckwellenamplitude f
~ **wave function** Rechteckwellenfunktion f
~ **wave signal** Rechtecksignal n
squawk box Intercomlautsprecher m
squeegee/to abquetschen, abstreifen
squeegee 1. Abquetscher m, Abstreifer m; 2. Siebdruckrakel f
~ **roll[er]** Abquetschrolle f, Quetschroller m
~ **rollers** Rollenquetscher m
squeegeeing Abquetschung f
squeeze Pressung f *(z.B. zwischen Druckzylindern)*
~ **lens** Zerrlinse f, Zerroptik f *(s.a. anamorphic lens)*
squeezed image verzerrtes (anamorphotisches) Bild n, Zerrbild n
SQUID [magnetometer], ~ sensor SQUID n, supraleitendes Quanteninterferometer n
~ **electronics** SQUID-Elektronik f
squint/to schielen
squint Schielen n, Strabismus m

stabbing problem Aufspießanfrage f *(grafische Datenverarbeitung, Schnittbestimmung)*
stabilizer, stabilizing agent Stabilisator m
stabilizing bath Stabilisatorbad n, Stabilisierungsbad n, Schlussbad n *(Fotoverarbeitung)*
stable filter stabiles Filter n
~ **resonator** stabiler Resonator m
~ **to light** lichtstabil, lichtbeständig, lichtecht
stacking fault Stapelfehler m *(Kristallografie)*
staff photographer Redaktionsfotograf m
stage light Bühnenscheinwerfer m
~ **lights** Bühnenbeleuchtung f
~ **loudspeaker** Bühnenlautsprecher m *(Kinotechnik)*
~ **micrometer** Mikroskopmikrometer n, Objektmikrometer n
~ **projection** Bühnenprojektion f
staged photo[graph] arrangiertes (gestelltes) Foto n
staggered grid versetztes Gitter n *(Visualisierung)*
stain/to [ver]färben
stained glass Farbglas n, Buntglas n
staircase pattern Treppenstruktur f
~ **polygon** Treppenpolygon n
~ **structure** Treppenstruktur f
staircasing, stair-stepping [artifact] Treppen[stufen]effekt m, Stufeneffekt m, Stufenfehler m, Sägezahneffekt m *(Binärbild)*
stamp/to aufdrucken
stamp Aufdruck m
stand Stativ n
~ **-alone computer** Einzelrechner m
~ **-alone monitor** externer Monitor (Bildschirm) m
~ **-alone workstation** Einzelrechner m
~ **leg** Stativbein n
~ **-mounted flash** Stativblitz m
standard 1. Norm f, Standard m; 2. Standarte f *(Fachkamera)*
~ **camera** Standardkamera f
~ **candle** Candela f, Neue Kerze f *(SI-Basiseinheit der Lichtstärke)*
~ **cassette** Standardkassette f *(Video)*
~ **chromaticity diagram** Normfarb[wert]tafel f
~ **color** Normfarbe f
~ **color bar** Normfarbbalken m
~ **color space** Normfarbraum m
~ **colorimetric observer** farbmetrischer Normalbeobachter m
~ **definition television** normalauflösendes Fernsehen n
~ **developer** Normalentwickler m
~ **deviation** Standardabweichung f
~ **double-eight-mm film** Doppel-Acht-Film m
~ **equipment eyepiece** Standardokular n
~ **file format** Standarddateiformat n

stationary

- ~ **focal length** Normalbrennweite *f*, Standardbrennweite *f*
- ~ **form map** Musterblattkarte *f* *(Fotogrammetrie)*
- ~ **format** Standardformat *n*
- ~ **human observer** fotometrischer Normalbeobachter *m*
- ~ **illuminant** Normlichtart *f*, Standardlichtquelle *f*
- ~ **input format** SIF-Format *n* *(Video)*
- ~ **interface** Standardschnittstelle *f*, normierte Schnittstelle *f*
- ~ **intermediate** *digitales Bildformat mit der Wiederholfrequenz von 30 Bildern pro Sekunde*
- ~ **light meter** Standardbelichtungsmesser *m*
- ~ **light source** *s.* ~ illuminant
- ~ **lighting** Standardbeleuchtung *f*
- ~ **objective** Normalobjektiv *n*, Standardobjektiv *n*
- ~ **observer** Normalbeobachter *m*, durchschnittlicher (normalsichtiger) Beobachter *m*
- ~ **offset color bar** Druckkontrolleiste *f*, Druckkontrollstreifen *m*, Farbmessstreifen *m*
- ~ **paper** Normalpapier *n*, Standardpapier *n*
- ~ **photographic lens** *s.* ~ objective
- ~ **photography** Normalfotografie *f*
- ~ **photometric observer** fotometrischer Normalbeobachter *m*
- ~ **picture format** Standarbildformat *n*
- ~ **reflector** Standardreflektor *m*
- ~ **resolution** Standardauflösung *f*
- ~ **sampling** Standardabtastung *f*
- ~ **size cassette** Standardkassette *f* *(Video)*
- ~ **software** Standardsoftware *f*
- ~ **tone** Normalton *m*
- ~ **TV receiver** Standard-Fernsehgerät *n*
- ~ **video signal** Standardvideosignal *n*
- ~ **zoom** Normalzoom[objektiv] *n*, Standardzoom[objektiv] *n*, Universalzoom[objektiv] *n*

standardized color-matching function Normspektralwertfunktion *f*, Normspektralwertkurve *f*

standards conversion Normenwandlung *f*
- ~ **conversion equipment**, ~ **converter** Normenwandler *m*

standby mode Bereitschaftsmodus *m*, Bereitschaftsschaltung *f*, Stand-by-Betrieb *m*, Stand-by *n*
- ~ **position** Bereitschaftsstellung *f*

standing light wave stehende Lichtwelle *f*
- ~ **magnifier** Standlupe *f*
- ~ **wave** Stehwelle *f*, stehende Welle *f*

star brightness Sternhelligkeit *f*
- ~ **field photography** Sternfeldfotografie *f*
- ~ **filter** *s.* starburst filter
- ~ **image** Sternabbildung *f*, Sternaufnahme *f*
- ~**-shaped polygon** Sternpolygon *n*

starburst filter Stern[effekt]filter *n*, Gitterfilter *n*, Crossfilter *n*

starch Stärke *f* *(Polysaccharid)*
- ~ **grain (granule)** Stärkekorn *n*, Stärkekörnchen *n*

starlight Sternenlicht *n*

start code Startcode *m* *(Videobitstrom)*
- ~ **leader** Startband *n*, Startstreifen *m*
- ~ **mark** Startkreuz *n*, Startzeichen *n*, Startmarkierung *f*, Bildstart *m* *(Filmschnitt)*
- ~ **menu** Startmenü *n*
- ~ **node** Startknoten *m*, Wurzelknoten *m* *(Graphstruktur)*
- ~ **of a line** Zeilenanfang *m*

starting point Startpunkt *m*, Anfangspunkt *m*, Ausgangspunkt *m*, Initialpunkt *m*; Keimpunkt *m* *(Bereichswachstumsverfahren)*

startup screen Eröffnungsbildschirm *m*, Begrüßungsbildschirm *m*

stat Ablichtung *f*
- ~ **camera** kleinformatige Reprokamera *f*

state diagram Zustandsdiagramm *n*
- ~ **of adaptation** Adaptationszustand *m*
- ~ **of aggregation** Aggregationszustand *m*
- ~ **of correction** Korrektionszustand *m*
- ~ **of polarization** Polarisationszustand *m*
- ~ **space** Zustandsraum *m*, Phasenraum *m*
- ~ **vector** Statusvektor *m*, Zustandsvektor *m*
- ~ **vector** Zustandsvektor *m*

statement Anweisung *f*, Befehl *m* *(Computerprogramm)*

static camera statische (unbewegte) Kamera *f* *(Kinematografie)*
- ~ **charge** elektrostatische Ladung *f*
- ~ **elastography** statische Elastografie *f*
- ~ **electricity** statische Elektrizität *f*, Reibungselektrizität *f*, Triboelektrizität *f*
- ~ **Huffman [en]coding** statische Huffman-Codierung *f*
- ~ **image** *s.* still image
- ~ **magnetic field** statisches Magnetfeld *n*
- ~ **mark** Blitzfigur *f* *(auf Radiogrammen)*
- ~ **mosaic** statisches Mosaik *n*
- ~ **neutralizer** Entelektrisator *m* *(z.B. an Druckmaschinen)*
- ~ **object** statisches Objekt *n*
- ~ **photograph** Standfoto *n*
- ~ **representation** statische Darstellung *f*
- ~ **resolution** statische Auflösung *f*
- ~ **subject** statisches Motiv *n*

station ID (identification) Senderkennung *f*

stationarity Stationarität *f*
- ~ **assumption** Stetigkeitsbedingung *f*
- ~ **condition** Stationaritätsbedingung *f*

stationary stationär
- ~ **anode** Festanode *f* *(Röntgenröhre)*
- ~ **detector** stationärer Detektor *m*
- ~ **image** statisches Bild *n*
- ~ **light wave** stehende Lichtwelle *f*
- ~ **ray** ordentlicher Strahl *m* *(Optik)*
- ~ **signal** stationäres Signal *n*

stationary

~ **transducer** ortsfester Wandler *m*
~ **wave** Stehwelle *f*, stehende Welle *f*
stationery Briefpapier *n*
stationpoint Blickpunkt *m*
statistic texture statistische Textur *f*
statistical classification statistische Klassifikation *f*
~ **classifier** statistischer Klassifikator *m*
~ **coding** statistische Codierung *f*
~ **decision theory** [statistische] Entscheidungstheorie *f*
~ **descriptor** statistischer Deskriptor *m*
~ **image analysis** statistische Bildanalyse *f*
~ **image compression** statistische Bildkompression *f*
~ **model** statistisches Modell *n*
~ **model[l]ing** statistische Modellierung *f*
~ **multiplexing** statistisches Multiplexen *n*
~ **noise** statistisches Rauschen *n*
~ **optics** statistische Optik *f*
~ **pattern analysis** statistische Musteranalyse *f*
~ **pattern recognition** statistische Mustererkennung *f*
~ **redundancy** statistische Redundanz *f*
~ **signal processing** statistische Signalverarbeitung *f*
~ **source model** Wahrscheinlichkeitsmodell *n* *(Symbolcodierung)*
~ **textural analysis** statistische Texturanalyse *f*
status filter Statusfilter *n (Densitometrie)*
STB *s.* set-top box
STDM *s.* synchronous time division multiplex
Steadicam [abgefedertes] Tragstativ *n*, Schwebestativ *f*
~ **operator** Steadicam-Kameramann *m*
steadiness of the air Luftruhe *f (Astrooptik)*
~ **of the image** Bildruhe *f*, Bildstand *m*
steady-state [IR] thermography Modulationsthermografie *f (zerstörungsfreie Werkstoffprüfung)*
steel film Stahlfilm *m*
steepness Steilheit *f*
steerable filter steuerbares (einstellbares) Filter *n*
Stefan-Boltzmann constant Stefan-Boltzmann-Konstante *f*
~-**Boltzmann equation (law)** Stefan-Boltzmannsches Gesetz *n*
steganographic steganografisch
steganography Steganografie *f*
Steiner tree Steiner-Baum *m (Computergrafik)*
stellar photography Stellarfotografie *f (s.a. astrophotography, star field photography)*
~ **spectrography** Sternspektrografie *f*
~ **spectroscope** Sternspektroskop *n*
~ **spectroscopy** Sternspektroskopie *f*

stem 1. Stamm *m*, Grundstrich *m (Buchstabenbild)*; 2. Tonkanal *m (als Teil einer Endabmischung)*
STEM *s.* scanning transmission electron microscopy
stencil Sieb[druck]schablone *f*
~ **printing** Schablonendruck *m*
step-and-repeat camera Schrittkamera *f*
~-**by-step printing** Schrittkopierung *f*
~ **edge** Stufenkante *f*
~ **filter** Stufenfilter *n (Sensitometrie)*
~ **function** Schrittfunktion *f (Signalverarbeitung)*
~-**index fiber** Stufenindexfaser *f*
~ **optical printer** optische Schrittkopiermaschine *f*
~ **photometer** Stufenfotometer *n*, Pulfrich-Fotometer *n*
~ **printer** Schrittkopiermaschine *f*
~ **printing** Schrittkopierung *f*
~ **tablet** *s.* stepped [optical] wedge
~-**tablet exposure** Stufenbelichtung *f*
~ **wedge, stepped [optical] wedge** Grau[stufen]keil *m*, Stufengraukeil *m*, Grauskala *f*
stepper (stepping) motor Schrittmotor *m*
stepwise approximation sukzessive Approximation *f*
steradian Steradiant *m*, Einheitsraumwinkel *m*
stereo ... *s.a. unter* stereoscopic, sterophonic
~ **acuity** stereoskopische Sehschärfe *f*
~ **attachment** Stereovorsatz *m*
~ **audio channel** Stereotonkanal *m*
~ **audio dubbing** Stereonachvertonung *f*
~ **base** stereoskopische Basis *f*, Stereobasis *f*
~-**blind** stereoblind
~ **calibration** Stereokalibrierung *f*
~ **camera** Stereokamera *f*, Raumbildkamera *f*, Doppelkamera *f*
~ **channel** Stereokanal *m*
~ **computer graphics** Stereo-Computergrafik *f*
~ **computer tomography** Stereo-Computertomografie *f*
~ **correspondence** Stereokorrespondenz *f*
~ **cross talk** Stereoübersprechen *n*
~ **daguerreotype** Stereodaguerreotypie *f*
~ **decoder** Stereodecoder *m*
~ **display** 1. Stereobildschirm *m*; 2. Raumbildwiedergabe *f*
~ **effect** Stereoeffekt *m*
~ **glasses** Stereobrille *f*
~ **image analysis** Stereobildanalyse *f*
~ **image coder** Stereobildcodierer *m*
~ **magnifier** Stereolupe *f*
~ **mode** Stereomodus *m*
~ **model** Stereomodell *n*
~ **pair** Stereobildpaar *n*, [stereoskopisches] Halbbildpaar *n (s.a. stereogram)*
~ **pair camera** *s.* ~ camera

~ **perception** Stereowahrnehmung f
~ **photograph** Stereofoto n
~ **photomacrography** Makro-Stereofotografie f
~ **picture** Stereo[skop]bild n, stereoskopisches Bild n, Raumbild n
~ **picture archive** Stereobildarchiv n
~ **projection** Raumbildprojektion f
~ **projection surface** Stereoprojektionsfläche f
~ **reconstruction** Stereorekonstruktion f
~ **resolution** Stereoauflösung f
~ **satellite image** Stereosatellitenbild n
~ **sensor** Stereosensor m
~ **sequence** Stereobildfolge f
~ **signal** Stereosignal n
~ **slide** Stereo-Diapositiv n
~ **slide viewer** Stereo-Diabetrachter m
~ **sound** Stereoton m
~ **sound track** Stereotonspur f
~ **television show** Stereofernsehsendung f
~ **video coder** Stereobildcodierer m
~ **view** Stereoansicht f
~ **viewer** Stereobildbetrachter m, Stereoskop n
~ **viewing** Stereo[bild]betrachtung f, stereoskopische Betrachtung f
~ **viewing device** s. ~ viewer
~ **vision** s. 1. stereoscopic vision; 2. stereopsis
~ **visualization** Stereovisualisierung f
stereoanaglyph image Anaglyphenbild n
stereoautograph Stereoautograf m
stereobinocular Stereobrille f
stereoblindness Stereoblindheit f
stereocomparator Stereokomparator m
stereodepth [räumliche] Tiefe f
stereofluoroscope Stereofluoroskop n
stereofluoroscopic stereofluoroskopisch
stereogram Stereogramm n, Körperdiagramm n; Raumbild n, Stereobild n; Stereobildpaar n
stereogrammetry s. stereophotogrammetry
stereograph s. stereogram
stereographic stereografisch, raumbildlich
~ **hologram** stereografisches Hologramm n
~ **motion picture** stereoskopischer (dreidimensionaler) Film m, Raumfilm m
~ **projection** stereografische Projektion f
stereographical s. stereographic
stereoimage display Stereobildanzeige f
stereokinetic effect stereokinetischer Effekt m
stereolical stereologisch
stereolithographic stereolithografisch
~ **model** stereolithografisches Modell n
stereolithography Stereolithografie f
stereology Stereologie f
stereometric stereometrisch
stereometry Stereometrie f
stereomicrography Stereomikrofotografie f

stereomicrometer Stereomikrometer n
stereomicroscope Stereomikroskop n
stereomicroscopic stereomikroskopisch
stereomicroscopy Stereomikroskopie f, stereoskopische Mikroskopie f
stereomovie Stereo[spiel]film m
stereophonic stereofon[isch]
~ **effect** Raumklangeffekt m
~ **microphone** Stereomikrofon n
stereophony Stereofonie f
stereophotogrammetric stereofotogrammetrisch
stereophotogrammetry Stereofotogrammetrie f, Stereobildmessung f, Raumbildmessung f, Doppelbildmessung f, Zweibildmessung f
stereophotograph stereoskopisches Halbbild (Teilbild) n
stereophotographic stereofotografisch
stereophotography Stereofotografie f, dreidimensionale Fotografie f
stereoplanigraph Stereoplanigraf m
stereoplastic plate Kunststoffstereo n
stereoplotter Stereoplotter m, Stereoauswertegerät n
stereoprojection Stereoprojektion f
stereopsis s. stereoscopic vision
stereopticon s. stereoscope
stereoradiography Stereoradiografie f, stereoskopische Radiografie f
stereoscope Stereoskop n, Stereobildbetrachter m
stereoscopic stereoskopisch *(s.a. unter stereo)*
~ **aerial photograph** Stereo-Luftbildaufnahme f
~ **beam splitter** stereoskopischer Strahlenteiler m
~ **cinema** stereoskopisches Kino n
~ **cinematography** Stereokinematografie f
~ **computer screen** Stereobildschirm m
~ **depth** [räumliche] Tiefe f
~ **depth effect** stereoskopischer Tiefeneffekt m
~ **depth perception** stereoskopische Tiefenwahrnehmung f
~ **disparity** Stereodisparität f
~ **display** stereoskopisches Display n; dreidimensionaler Bildschirm m
~ **endoscopy** stereoskopische Endoskopie f
~ **film** Stereofilm m
~ **image** stereoskopisches Bild n, Stereo[skop]bild n, Raumbild n
~ **image pair** Stereobildpaar n, [stereoskopisches] Halbbildpaar n *(s.a. stereogram)*
~ **image sequence** Stereobildfolge f
~ **imagery** Stereobildmaterial n
~ **imaging** Stereobildgebung f
~ **microscopy** stereoskopische Mikroskopie f

stereoscopic

~ **motion picture** Stereofilm *m*
~ **parallax** stereoskopische (binokulare) Parallaxe *f*
~ **photography** Stereofotografie *f*, dreidimensionale Fotografie *f*
~ **plotting instrument** *s*. stereoplotter
~ **projection** stereoskopische Projektion *f*, Steroprojektion *f*
~ **radiography** stereoskopische Radiografie *f*, Stereoradiografie *f*
~ **rangefinder** Raumbild-Entfernungsmesser *m*
~ **telescope** Stereoteleskop *n*
~ **television** stereoskopisches (räumliches) Fernsehen *n*, dreidimensionales Fernsehen *n*, Sterofernsehen *n*
~ **tomography** stereoskopische Tomografie *f*
~ **video image** stereoskopisches Videobild *n*
~ **vision** stereoskopisches (räumliches) Sehen *n*, dreidimensionales Sehen *n*, Stereosehen *n*, Tiefensehvermögen *n*, Raumsehen *n*, Stereopsis *f*, querdisparates Tiefensehen *n*
~ **visualization** räumliche (stereoskopische) Visualisierung *f*
stereoscopical *s*. stereoscopic
stereoscopy Stereoskopie *f*, Raumbildwesen *n*
stereotactic[al] stereotaktisch
stereotactical coordinate system stereotaktisches Koordinatensystem *n*
stereotaxic stereotaktisch
stereotaxis, stereotaxy Stereotaxie *f*
stereotelescope Scherenfernrohr *n*
stereotype/to stereotypieren
stereotype [plate] Stereotypplatte *f*, Stereo *n*, Duplikatdruckform *f*, Duplikat[buch]druckplatte *f*, Abformung *f*, Klischee *n*, Druckklischee *n*
stereotypy Stereotypie *f*
Sterry effect Sterry-Effekt *m* *(Gradationsverminderung)*
~ **process** Sterry-Verfahren *n* *(Kontrastreduzierung)*
stick figure Strichmännchen *n* *(Animationsfigur)*
stiffness matrix Steifigkeitsmatrix *f*
stigmatic stigmatisch
~ **image** stigmatisches Bild *n*
~ **imaging** stigmatische Abbildung *f*
stigmator Stigmator *m*, Korrekturfeld *n* *(Elektronenmikroskop)*
stilb Stilb *n* *(SI-fremde Einheit der Leuchtdichte)*
Stiles-Crawford effect Stiles-Crawford-Effekt *m* *(Physiologie des Sehens)*
still *s*. 1. ~ image; 2. ~ frame
~ **camera** Stehbildkamera *f*, Standbildkamera *f*
~ **camera film** Foto[grafie]film *m*, fotografischer Film *m*
~ **camera format** Fotokameraformat *n*
~ **electronic photography** elektronische Stehbildfotografie *f*
~ **frame** angehaltenes (stehendes) Filmbild *n*, Standfoto *n*
~ **image** stehendes (unbewegtes) Bild *n*, statisches Bild *n*, Stehbild *n*, Festbild *n*, Standbild *n*
~ **image archiving** Standbildarchivierung *f*
~ **image coding** Festbildcodierung *f*
~ **image communication** Festbildkommunikation *f*
~ **image compression standard** Festbildkompressionsstandard *m*
~ **image transmission** Festbildübertragung *f*, Standbildübertragung *f*
~ **life photograph** Stillebenaufnahme *f*
~ **life photographer** Stilllebenfotograf *m*
~ **life photography** Objektfotografie *f*, Sachfotografie *f*
~ **life photography** Stilllebenfotografie *f*
~ **photograph** Standfoto *n*, Fotografie *f*, Foto *n*
~ **photographer** Stehbildfotograf *m*, Standfotograf *m*, Fotograf *m*
~ **photography** Stehbildfotografie *f*
~ **photography equipment** Fotoausrüstung *f*
~ **picture camera** Stehbildkamera *f*, Standbildkamera *f*; Fotokamera *f*, Fotoapparat *m*
~ **picture database** Standbilddatenbank *f*
~ **picture mode** Standbildmodus *m* *(Videocodierung)*
~ **picture projection** Standprojektion *f*, Stillstandsprojektion *f*, Stehbildprojektion *f*
~ **picture projector** Stehbildprojektor *m*, Stehbildwerfer *m*, Standbildprojektor *m*, Diapositivprojektor *m*
~ **picture recording** Einzelbildaufnahme *f* *(Video)*
~ **picture transceiver** Festbild-Sende-Empfangs-Gerät *n*
~ **picture transmission** Festbildübertragung *f*, Standbildübertragung *f*
~ **projector** *s*. ~ picture projector
~ **store** Standbildspeicher *m*
~ **video** Standbild-Video *n*
~ **video camera** Stillvideokamera *f*, elektronische Stehbildkamera *f*
~ **video floppy disk** Videodiskette *f*
~ **video frame** Videostandbild *n*
~ **X-ray picture** Röntgenbild *n*, Röntgenogramm *n*
stimulate/to anregen
stimulated echo stimuliertes Echo *n*
~ **emission** stimulierte (induzierte) Emission *f* *(Laser)*
~ **Raman scattering** induzierte Raman-Streuung *f*
stimulation Stimulation *f*, Anregung *f*

stimulus Reiz *m*, Stimulus *m*
~ **duration** Reizdauer *f*
~ **increase** Reizsteigerung *f*
~ **intensity** Reizintensität *f*
~ **processing** Reizverarbeitung *f*
~ **response** Reizantwort *f*
STIR *s.* short tau inversion recovery
~ **pulse sequence** STIR-Pulssequenz *f* *(Magnetresonanztomografie)*
stirnparallel fronto-parallel
stitching *streifenweises Scannen einer breiten Vorlage mittels xy-Abtastung*
stochastic stochastisch, zufallsbedingt
~ **edge model** stochastisches Kantenmodell *n*
~ **geometry** stochastische Geometrie *f*
~ **grammar** stochastische Grammatik *f*
~ **halftone rendering** stochastisches Rendering *n*
~ **image model** stochastisches Bildmodell *n*
~ **model** stochastisches Modell *n*
~ **modeling** stochastische Modellierung *f*
~ **relaxation** stochastische Relaxation *f*
~ **sampling** stochastische Abtastung *f*
~ **screening** Streurasterung *f*, Zufallsrasterung *f*, frequenzmodulierte (nichtperiodische) Rasterung *f*, FM-Rasterung *f*
~ **signal** stochastisches Signal *n*
~ **variable** Zufallsvariable *f*
stock Film[aufnahme]material *n*, Aufnahmefilmmaterial *n*; Filmvorrat *m*
~ **footage** Archivmaterial *n*; vorgedrehtes Bildmaterial *n*
~ **house** Bildagentur *f*
~ **photograph** *s.* stock picture
~ **photographer** Agenturfotograf *m*
~ **picture** Agenturaufnahme *f*, Agenturfoto *n*; Archivfoto *n*
~ **picture agency** Bildagentur *f*
~ **shot** Archivaufnahme *f* *(s.a.* stock picture*)*
~ **solution** Vorratslösung *f*; Stammlösung *f*
stop Blendenstufe *f*
~-**action** ... *s.* stop-motion ...
~ **and hardening bath** Härtestoppbad *n*
~ **band** Sperrbereich *m* *(eines Filters)*
~ **bath** Stoppbad *n*, Unterbrecherbad *n*
~ **bath tank** Stoppbadtank *m*
~ **bath tray** Stoppbadschale *f*
~ **code** Stoppcode *m*
~-**cylinder press (printing machine)** Stoppzylinder[druck]maschine *f*
~ **down/to** abblenden
~ **frame** Standbild *n*; angehaltenes (stehendes) Filmbild *n*
~ **frequency** Sperrfrequenz *f*
~ **image** Blendenbild *n*
~-**motion animation (photography)** Stopptrick *m*, Einzelphasentrick *m*, Einzelbildtechnik *f* *(Kinematografie)*; dreidimensionale Animation *f*
~-**motion puppet** Stopptrickfigur *f*

~ **number** Blendenzahl *f*, Blendenwert *m*, f-Blende *f*, relative Apertur *f*
~ **spot** Blendenfleck *m*
~ **time** Stoppzeit *f*
stopping down Abblendung *f*
storable speicherbar
storage 1. Speicherung *f*; Abspeicherung *f*; 2. Speicher *m* *(s.a. unter* memory*)*
~ **architecture** Speicherorganisation *f*
~ **bandwidth** Speicherbandbreite *f*
~ **bit** Speicherbit *n*
~ **bottle** Vorratsgefäß *n*
~ **camera tube** Bildspeicherröhre *f*
~ **capability** Speicherfähigkeit *f*
~ **capacitor** Speicherkondensator *m*
~ **capacity** Speicherkapazität *f*; Speichervolumen *n*
~ **card** Speicherkarte *f*, Datenspeicherkarte *f*
~ **cell** Speicherzelle *f*
~ **container** Vorratsbehälter *m* *(Dunkelkammerzubehör)*
~ **demand** Speicher[platz]bedarf *m*
~ **density** Speicherdichte *f*
~ **depth** Speichertiefe *f*
~ **device** Speichergerät *n*
~ **disk** Speicherplatte *f*; Speicherdiskette *f*
~ **facility** Speicher *m*
~ **format** Speicherformat *n*
~ **key** Speichertaste *f*
~ **layer** Speicherungsschicht *f*, Speicherungsebene *f*, Datenbankebene *f* *(Hypermediasystem)*
~ **location** Speicherstelle *f*
~ **medium** Speichermedium *n*
~ **mesh** Speichergitter *n*
~ **oscilloscope** Speicheroszilloskop *n*
~ **phosphor** Speicherleuchtstoff *m*, Speicherphosphor *m*
~ **phosphor screen** Speicherbildschirm *m*, Speicherschicht *f*, Phosphorschicht *f* *(Katodenstrahlröhre)*
~ **plate** *s.* ~ target
~ **power** Speicherleistung *f*; Speicherkapazität *f*
~-**proof** archivfest, archivsicher
~ **register** Speicherregister *n* *(CCD-Matrix)*
~ **requirement[s]** Speicher[platz]bedarf *m*
~ **sheet** Ablageblatt *n*, Ablagehülle *f* *(z.B. für Diapositive)*
~ **site** Speicherstelle *f*
~ **space** Speicherraum *m*, Speicherplatz *m*
~ **target** Speicherplatte *f* *(Bildspeicherröhre)*
~ **technology** Speichertechnik *f*
~ **tube** Speicherröhre *f*, speichernde Fernsehaufnahmeröhre *f*
~ **tube display** Speicherbildschirm *m*
~ **unit** Vorlaufspeicher *m*
store/to [ab]speichern *(z.B. Bilddaten)*
store in/to einspeichern
~ Speicher *m*
stored image gespeichertes Bild *n*

storyboard Storyboard n, [illustriertes] Kurzdrehbuch n, Ablaufplan m (Filmproduktion); Trickdrehbuch n
strabismus Strabismus m, Schielen n
straight geradlinig
~ **binary code** natürlicher Binärcode m
~ **cartridge** Geradmagazin n (Diaprojektion)
~ **cut** harter Schnitt m, Hartschnitt m (Film, Video)
~ **edge** geradlinige Kante f
~ **flash bracket** gerade Blitzschiene f
~ **line** Gerade f, gerade Linie f
~-**line approximation** Geradenapproximation f
~-**line mechanism** Geradführung f
~ **line of the characteristic curve** geradliniger Gradationskurvenbereich (Kurventeil) m (Schwärzungskurve)
~-**line polynomial** Polynom n erster Ordnung
~-**line portion (region)** s. ~ line of the characteristic curve
~-**line recognition** Geradenerkennung f
~-**line segment** Geradenstück n (Grafikprimitiv)
~ **snoot** zylindrischer Tubusvorsatz m (Scheinwerferzubehör)
straightforward processing Direktverarbeitung f
straightness [of lines] Geradheit f, Geradlinigkeit f (Formmerkmal)
strain contrast Spannungskontrast m (Elektronenmikroskopie)
~-**free lens (objective)** spannungsfreies Objektiv n
~ **pattern** Spannungsfigur f
strap Trageschlaufe f; Hand[gelenk]schlaufe f; Trageriemen m
stratification Schichtung f (z.B. von Spektraldaten)
stratigraphic stratigrafisch
stratigraphy Stratigrafie f
stray/to streuen (z.B. reflektiertes Licht)
stray electron Streuelektron n
~ **field** Streufeld n
~ **light** Streulicht n, diffus reflektiertes Licht n; Störlicht n
~ **light measurement** Streulichtmessung f
~ **light source** Streulichtquelle f
~ **magnetic field** [magnetisches] Streufeld n
~ **radiation** Streustrahlung f
~ **ray** Streulichtstrahl m
streak 1. Schliere f; 2. Lumineszenzspur f
~ **camera** Streakkamera f, fotoelektrische Streakröhre f
~ **camera record** Streakkameraufzeichnung f
~ **effect** Nachzieheffekt m (Bildröhre)
~ **image** Streakaufnahme f, Streakbild n
~ **photography** Streakfotografie f
streaking Fahnenziehen n (Fernsehbildstörung)

streaky streifig (z.B. unterentwickelte Fotoabzüge)
stream of video data Video[daten]strom m, Bilddatenstrom m
~ **ribbon** Stromband n (Visualisierung)
~ **surface** Strömungsfläche f
streamer Magnetbandgerät n; [schnelles] Bandlaufwerk n, [schnelles] Magnetbandlaufwerk n
streaming Internet animation Internet-Videoanimation f
~ **multimedia** multimedialer Datenstrom m
street photographer Straßenfotograf m
~ **photography** Straßenfotografie f
Strehl definition, ~ [intensity] ratio [Strehlsche] Definitionshelligkeit f (Bildgütemerkmal)
stress birefringence Spannungsdoppelbrechung f
~ **pattern** Spannungsmuster n
stria s. striation
striate cortex Sehrinde f (des Gehirns)
striation Schliere f
~-**free** schlierenfrei
strike off proof Proof m, Andruck m (Druckvorstufe)
~-**through** Durchschlagen n (Druckschwierigkeit)
string Zeichenkette f, Zeichenfolge f; lineare Liste f (Bildanalyse)
~ **of bits** Bitfolge f
~ **of data** Datenfolge f
~ **of text** Textzeile f; Textabschnitt m
strip/to montieren (Layout; Druckvorstufe)
strip camera Streifenkamera f
~ **film projector** Filmstreifenprojektor m; Diastreifenprojektor m
~ **of film** Filmstreifen m
~ **test** Streifentest m (Belichtungsmessung)
stripe Schmal[spur]band n, Senkel m; Ton-Original n (Magnetton)
~ **mask** Streifenmaske f, Schlitzmaske f (Bildröhre)
~ **raster monitor** Streifenrastermonitor m
striped aperture s. stripe mask
~ **filter** Streifenfilter n
~ **pattern** Streifenmuster n
~ **tape** Bandvorlauf m, Schwarzband n
stripmap mode Streifenmodus m (synthetisches Aperturradar)
stripping 1. Montage f (Layout; Druckvorstufe); 2. s. ~ off
~ **film** Abziehfilm m, Stripping-Film m
~ **lacquer** Abziehlack m (Reprografie)
~ **off** Abziehen n
~ **operation** Bildmontage f (Reprografie)
~ **proof** echter Andruck m (Druckvorstufe)
~ **varnish** s. ~ lacquer
strobe 1. stroboscopic; 2. stroboscope; 3. stroboscopic light; 4. stroboscopic flash
stroboscope Stroboskop n

stroboscopic stroboskopisch
~ **apparent motion** s. ~ motion
~ **effect** Stroboskopeffekt m, stroboskopischer Effekt m, stroboskopische Bewegungstäuschung f
~ **flash** Strobo[skop]blitz m, stroboskopischer Blitz m
~ **flash unit** Stroboblitzgerät n
~ **illumination** Stroboskopbeleuchtung f, stroboskopische Beleuchtung f
~ **light** stroboskopisches Licht n (s.a. ~ flash)
~ **microscopy** stroboskopische Mikroskopie f
~ **motion** scheinbare (abgetastete) Bewegung f; Phi-Bewegung f, Phi-Phänomen n (Wahrnehmungsphysiologie)
~ **motion analysis** stroboskopische Bewegungsanalyse f
~ **photograph** Stroboskopaufnahme f, Stroboskopbild n
~ **photography** Strobo[blitz]fotografie f; Stroboskopfotografie f, Phasenfotografie f
~ **shearography** stroboskopische Shearografie f
stroboscopy Stroboskopie f
stroke Strich m; Linie f; Buchstabenlinie f
~ **device** Liniengeber m (logisches Eingabegerät)
~ **width** Strichstärke f, Strichdicke f
strong color kräftige (gesättigte) Farbe f, satte Farbe f
~ **edge** scharfe Kante f
Stroop effect Stroop-Effekt m (Wahrnehmungsstörung)
structural analysis Strukturanalyse f; linienhafte Gliederung f
~ **classification** strukturelle Klassifikation f
~ **feature** Strukturmerkmal n, strukturelles Merkmal n
~ **image description** strukturelle Bildbeschreibung f
~ **information theory** Codierungstheorie f
~ **magnetic resonance imaging** strukturelle Magnetresonanztomografie (Kernspintomografie) f
~ **model** strukturelles Modell n
~ **pattern recognition** strukturelle Mustererkennung f
~ **resolution** Punktauflösung f
structure Struktur f
~**-based object recognition** strukturbasierte Objekterkennung f
~ **chart** Struktogramm n, Strukturdiagramm n
~ **factor contrast** Massenkontrast m, Streuabsorptionskontrast m (Elektronenmikroskopie)
~ **from motion** kinetischer Tiefeneffekt m
~ **from shading** s. shape-from-shading [technique]
~ **level** Strukturebene f
~ **recognition** Strukturerkennung f
~ **tensor** Strukturtensor m
structured data strukturierte Daten pl
~ **illumination** strukturierte Beleuchtung f
~ **light** strukturiertes Licht n
~ **noise** strukturiertes Rauschen n
~ **points** gleichmäßiges Gitter n (Datenstruktur)
structuring Strukturieren n, Strukturierung f (Datenverarbeitungsoperation)
~ **element** Strukturelement n (morphologische Bildverarbeitung)
student-grade microscope Schülermikroskop n
~ **microscope** Ausbildungsmikroskop n, Kursmikroskop n
studio Studio n; Atelier n
~ **accessories** Studiozubehör n
~ **animation** Studioanimation f
~ **archive** Studioarchiv n
~ **backlot** Filmgelände n, Produktionsgelände n, Studio[frei]gelände n
~ **broadcast** Studiosendung f
~ **business** Studiobetrieb m
~ **cable** Studiokabel n
~ **camera** Studiokamera f
~ **ceiling** Studiodecke f
~ **deck** Studiobandmaschine f, Studiolaufwerk n
~ **device** Studiogerät n
~ **editing** Studioschnitt m
~ **editing environment** Bildtechnik f (als Teil des Studiobetriebs)
~ **electronic flash** Studioblitz m
~ **engineering** Studiotechnik f
~ **equipment** Studioausrüstung f, Studiotechnik f
~ **facility** Studioeinrichtung f
~ **flash system** Studioblitzanlage f
~ **flash unit** Studioblitz[licht]gerät n
~ **footage** Studiofilmmaterial n
~ **format** Studioformat n (z.B. von Bandmaterial)
~**-grade device** Studiogerät n
~ **illumination** Studioausleuchtung f (s.a. ~ lighting)
~ **lamp** Studiolampe f
~ **light** 1. Studiolicht n; 2. Studioscheinwerfer m; Studioleuchte f
~ **light source** Atelierlichtquelle f
~ **lighting** Studio[raum]beleuchtung f; Atelierbeleuchtung f
~ **machine** Studiobandmaschine f, Studiolaufwerk n
~ **microphone** Studiomikrofon n
~ **monitor** Studiomonitor m
~ **operation** Studiobetrieb m
~ **photographer** Studiofotograf m
~ **photography** Studiofotografie f
~ **picture** Studiobild n
~ **portrait** Studioporträt n

studio 380

~ **portrait photographer,** ~ **portraitist** Studioporträtfotograf *m*
~ **portraiture** Studioporträtfotografie *f*
~ **production** Studioproduktion *f*
~ **production standard** Studiostandard *m*
~ **production switcher** Produktionsmischer *m*, Videomischer *m*, Videomischpult *n*
~ **quality** [technische] Studioqualität *f*
~ **record** Studioaufzeichnung *f*, Studioaufnahme *f*
~ **recorder** Studiorecorder *m*
~ **recording** Studioaufzeichnung *f*
~ **scene** Studioszene *f*, Atelierszene *f*
~ **setting** Studiodekoration *f*
~ **shot** Studioaufnahme *f*; Atelieraufnahme *f*
~ **sound** Studioton *m*
~ **sound recording** Studiotonaufzeichnung *f*
~ **stand** Studiostativ *n*
~ **standard** Studiostandard *m*, Studionorm *f*
~ **structures** Studio[auf]bauten *pl*
~ **supplier** Studioausrüster *m*
~ **technician** Studiotechniker *m*
~ **television** Studiofernsehen *n*
~ **-type camera stand** Studiokamerastativ *n*
~ **-type electronic flash unit** Studioblitz[licht]gerät *n*
~ **-type lighting unit** Studioleuchte *f*
~ **video camera** Studio-Videokamera *f*
~ **video equipment** Fernsehstudiotechnik *f*; Studio-Videotechnik *f*
~ **view camera** Studio-Fachkamera *f*, Atelierkamera *f*
~ **work** Studioarbeit *f*
stuffing bit Stopfbit *n*, Ausgleichsbit *n*, Füllbit *n*
~ **byte** Stopfbyte *n*
stuttery ruckelig *(Bewegtbilder)*
style Druckformat *n*
~ **sheet** Druckformatvorlage *f*, Formatvorlage *f*; Dokumentvorlage *f*; Formblatt *n*
stylus Tablettstift *m*, Grafikstift *m*, Digitalisierstift *m* *(Eingabetablett)*
subband Teilband *n*
~ **analysis** Teilbandanalyse *f*
~ **analysis filter** Teilband-Analysefilter *n*
~ **coder** Teilbandcodierer *m*
~ **coding** Teilbandcodierung *f*, selektive Frequenztransformation *f*
~ **coding filter bank** Teilbandcodierungsfilterbank *f*
~ **coefficient** Teilbandkoeffizient *m*
~ **compression** *s.* ~ coding
~ **decomposition** Teilbandzerlegung *f*
~ **filter** Teilbandfilter *n*
~ **filtering** Teilbandfilterung *f*
~ **image** Teilbandbild *n*
~ **image coding** Teilband-Bildcodierung *f*
~ **signal** Teilbandsignal *n*
~ **synthesis** Teilbandsynthese *f*

subbing layer Substratschicht *f*, Haftschicht *f* *(Filmherstellung)*
subcarrier Hilfsträger *m*, Subträger *m*, Unterträger *m*
~ **frequency** Hilfsträgerfrequenz *f*, Subträgerfrequenz *f*, Unterträgerfrequenz *f*
~ **modulation** Hilfsträgermodulation *f*
~ **phase** Hilfsträgerphase *f*
~ **signal** Hilfsträgersignal *n*
subclass Unterklasse *f*
subdirectory Unterverzeichnis *n* *(Computer)*
subdivision Unterteilung *f*, Subdivision *f*
~ **surface** Unterteilungsfläche *f*
subdued light gedämpftes Licht *n*
~ **lighting** gedämpfte Beleuchtung *f*
subframe Unterrahmen *m* *(Datenstruktur)*
subgraph Untergraph *m*, Subgraph *m*
subhead Zwischenüberschrift *f*
subimage Teilbild *n*, Unterbild *n* *(Bildanalyse)*
~ **area** Teilbildfläche *f*
~ **decomposition** Teilbildzerlegung *f*
~ **format** Teilbildformat *n*
~ **processing** Teilbildverarbeitung *f*
~ **size** Teilbildgröße *f*
~ **transform** Teilbildtransformation *f*
subject Motiv *n*; Motivobjekt *n*; Bildobjekt *n*, Aufnahmegegenstand *m*; Bildgegenstand *m* *(s.a. unter object)*
~ **area** Motivstelle *f*; Motivbereich *m*
~ **beam** Gegenstandswelle *f*, Signalwelle *f* *(Holografie)*
~ **brightness** Motivhelligkeit *f*
~ **color** Körperfarbe *f*, Objektfarbe *f*, Oberflächenfarbe *f*
~ **color value** Objektfarbwert *m*
~ **contrast** Motivkontrast *m*; Objektkontrast *m*
~ **detail** Motivdetail *n*; Objektdetail *n*
~ **distance** 1. Kameraabstand *m*, Motivdistanz *f*, Motiventfernung *m*; 2. *s.* object distance
~ **lighting** Objektbeleuchtung *f*
~ **luminance** Motivhelligkeit *f*
~ **matter** *s.* subject
~ **motion** Motivbewegung *f*
~ **part** Objektteil *n(m)*
~ **plane** Dingebene *f*, Gegenstandsebene *f*, Objektebene *f*; Motivebene *f*
~ **point** Dingpunkt *m*, Gegenstandspunkt *m*
~ **size** Objektgröße *f*
~ **slide** Objektträger *m* *(Mikroskopie)*
~ **space** Dingraum *m*, Objektraum *m*, Gegenstandsraum *m*, objektseitiger Strahlenraum *m*
subjective brightness wahrgenommene (empfindungsgemäße) Helligkeit *f*, subjektive Helligkeit *f*
~ **colors** subjektive (Fechner-Benhamsche) Farben *fpl*, Benham-Farben *fpl*, Flimmerfarben *fpl*

~ **contrast** subjektiver (physiologischer) Kontrast *m*, Kontrastempfindung *f*
~ **percept[ion] of brightness** subjektive Helligkeitswahrnehmung *f*, subjektiver (psychophysiologischer) Helleigkeitseindruck *m*
~ **video quality** subjektive Video[bild]qualität *f*
sublimable dye sublimierbarer Farbstoff *m*
sublimation printer Sublimationsdrucker *m*
subliminal subliminal, unterschwellig *(Reiz)*
~ **perception** unterschwellige Wahrnehmung *f*
submatrix Teilmatrix *f*
submenu Untermenü *n*, Submenü *n*
submicroscopic submikroskopisch, ultramikroskopisch
submillimeter array Submillimeter-Array *n*, Submillimeter- Interferometer *n*, SMA *(Teleskop)*
subminiature camera Kleinst[bild]kamera *f*
submixing Vormischung *f (z.B. von Filmton)*
submount Bildumrandung *f*
subobject Teilobjekt *n*
suboptimum transform suboptimale Transformation *f*
subpattern Teilmuster *n*
subpixel Subpixel *n*, Teilpunkt *m*
~ **accuracy** Subpixelgenauigkeit *f*
~ **estimation** Subpixelschätzung *f*
~ **interpolation** Subpixelinterpolation *f*
~-**precision edge detection** subpixelgenaue Kantendetektion *f*
~ **resolution** Subpixelauflösung *f*
subproportional reducer Subproportionalabschwächer *m*, kontraststeigernder Abschwächer *m*
subreflector Fangspiegel *m (Teleskop)*
subregion Teilbereich *m (z.B. eines Bildes)*
subsample/to unterabtasten
subsample pattern Unterabtastmuster *n*
subsampled signal unterabgetastetes Signal *n*
subsampler Unterabtaster *m*
subsampling Unterabtastung *f*; Dezimation *f (Videosignalverarbeitung)*
~ **matrix** Unterabtastungsmatrix *f*
~ **operation** Unterabtastung *f*
~ **pattern** Unterabtastmuster *n*
~ **pyramid** Unterabtastungspyramide *f*
~ **rate** Unterabtastrate *f*
subscan/to unterabtasten
subscanning Unterabtastung *f*
subscene Teilszene *f*
subscriber Endteilnehmer *m*
~ **drop cable,** ~ **line** Teilnehmeranschlussleitung *f*
~ **management** Teilnehmerverwaltung *f*, Kundenverwaltung *f*
subscript Index *m*

subscription television (TV) Abofernsehen *n*, Abonnement[s]fernsehen *n*
subsegment Untersegment *n*
subsequent picture Folgebild *n*, Nachfolgerbild *n*
subset Teilmenge *f*, Untermenge *f (z.B. von Merkmalen)*
subsidiary absorption Nebenabsorption *f*, Fehlabsorption *f (Farbfotografie)*
subspace Subraum *m*
subspectrum Teilspektrum *n*
substage Kondensorträger *m (Mikroskop)*
substance weight Papierflächengewicht *n*, Papierflächenmasse *f*
substandard film Schmalfilm *m*
substantive color (coupler) film chromogener Farbumkehrfilm (Film) *m*, Farbstoffaufbaufilm *m*
substrate 1. Substrat *n*; Unterguss *m (Filmherstellung)*; 2. Bedruckmaterial *n*, Bedruckstoff *m*
~ **layer, substratum** Substratschicht *f*, Haftschicht *f (Filmherstellung)*
substring code Teilkettencode *m*
subsurface radar Oberflächendurchdringungsradar *n*, Bodendurchdringungsradar *n*, Georadar *n*
subtitle/to untertiteln
subtitle Untertitel *m*, Fußtitel *m (Film)*
~ **cue sheet** Untertitelungsliste *f*
~ **negative** Untertitelnegativ *n*
subtitled film untertitelter Film *m*
subtitling Untertitelung *f*
subtraction angiogram Subtraktionsangiogramm *n*
~ **image** Subtraktionsbild *n*, Differenzbild *n*
~ **operation** Differenzoperation *f (Pixelverarbeitung)*
subtractive color subtraktive Farbe *f*
~ **color film** subtraktiver Farbfilm *m*
~ **color matching** subtraktive Farbmischung *f (Farbmetrik)*
~ **color mixing (mixture)** subtraktive (multiplikative) Farbmischung *f*, substantielle Farbmischung *f*
~ **color photography** subtraktive Farbfotografie *f*
~ **color process** subtraktives Farbverfahren *n*
~ **color system** subtraktives Farbmodell *n*, CMY-Farbraum *m*
~ **dye** subtraktiver Farbstoff *m*
~ **filter** subtraktives Filter *n*
~ **filtering** subtraktive Filterung *f*
~ **image dye** subtraktiver Bildfarbstoff *m*
~ **instant color film** subtraktiver Farbsofortbildfilm *m*
~ **noise** subtraktives Rauschen *n*
~ **primary [color]** subtraktive Grundfarbe (Primärfarbe) *f*
~ **printing** subtraktives Kopieren *n*

subtractive

~ **reducer** Subtraktivabschwächer m, kontrasterhaltender Abschwächer m (Fotochemikalie)
subtree Unterbaum m, Subbaum m, Teilbaum m (Datenstruktur)
subwave Teilwelle f
subwindow Unterfenster n (Bildschirm)
subwoofer Tiefbasslautsprecher m; Subbasskanal m
succession of images Bild[er]folge f, Bildsequenz f
successive approximation sukzessive (schrittweise) Approximation f
~ **contrast** Sukzessivkontrast m
~ **image** Folgebild n, Nachfolgerbild n
sulfide toning Sulfidtonung f, Sepiatonung f
sulfite developer Sulfitentwickler m
sulfonamide coupler Sulfonamidkuppler m
sulfur-plus-gold sensitization Gold-Schwefel-Reifung f
~ **sensitization** Schwefelsensibilisierung f
~ **toner** Schwefeltoner m
~ **toning** Schwefeltonung f
sulfuric acid Schwefelsäure f
sum image Additionsbild n, Summationsbild n (Radiografie)
summation Rückprojektion f (Radiografie)
sun angle Sonnenwinkel m
~ **arc** Jupiterlampe f
~ **gun** Akkuscheinwerfer m
~ **viewing** Sonnenbeobachtung f
sunlight Sonnenlicht n
sunshade Sonnenblende f; Gegenlichtblende f; Streulichtblende f; Gegenlichttubus m
super/to s. superimpose/to
super class Oberklasse f (objektorientierte Modellierung)
~**-eight camera** Super-Acht-Kamera f
~**-eight mm film** Super-Acht-Film m (Heimkinoformat)
~ **extended graphics array** Grafikstandard mit 1.280 x 1.024 Pixel Auflösung
~**-speed developer** höchstempfindlicher Entwickler m
~ **telephoto [lens]** Supertele[objektiv] n, langbrennweitiges Teleobjektiv n
~ **video graphics array** Grafikstandard mit 800 x 600 Pixel Auflösung
Super Video Home System Super-VHS n (Norm für Heim-Videorecorder)
super visual graphics array monitor SVGA-Monitor m
~ **wide-angle lens** Superweitwinkelobjektiv n, Überweitwinkelobjektiv n
superachromat Superachromat m
superachromatic superachromatisch
~ **lens** Superachromat m
superadditive development superadditive Entwicklung f (fotografischer Prozess)
superadditivity Superadditivität f
superblack tiefschwarz

supercalendered paper hochsatiniertes Papier n
supercoat[ing] Oberguss m, Überguss m, Emulsionsdeckschicht f; Schrammschutzschicht f (Filmherstellung)
superconducting magnet supraleitender (supraleitfähiger) Magnet m, Supraleitungsmagnet m
~ **quantum interference device** supraleitendes Quanteninterferometer n, SQUID n (s.a. unter SQUID)
superconductor Supraleiter m
superfine-grain developer Feinstkornentwickler m, Ultrafeinkornentwickler m
superglossy superglänzend
superhigh resolution ultrahohe Auflösung f
superimpose/to überlagern, übereinanderlegen, superponieren (z.B. Bilder)
superimposed-image rangefinder Koinzidenzentfernungsmesser m
superimposition, superimposure Überlagerung f, Superimposition f; Bildüberlagerung f
superior lens Hochleistungsobjektiv n, Hochleistungsoptik f
supermarket scanner terminal Kassenscanner m
superpanchromatic superpanchromatisch
superparamagnetic superparamagnetisch
superpose/to s. superimpose/to
superposition s. superimposition
~ **image** Überlagerungsbild n
~ **principle** Superpositionsprinzip n (Wellenoptik)
superproportional reducer Superproportionalabschwächer m, Lichterabschwächer m, kontrastmindernder Abschwächer m
superresolution Superauflösung f, Überauflösung f
supersample/to überabtasten
supersampling Überabtastung f
supersaturated solution übersättigte Lösung f
superselective angiography superselektive Angiografie f
supersensitization Supersensibilisierung f
supersensitizer Supersensibilisator m
superslide Großdia[positiv] n, Großbilddia n
supersound Ultraschall m (s.a. ultrasound)
supervised classification überwachte Klassifikation f
~ **image segmentation** überwachte Bildsegmentierung f
~ **learning (training)** überwachtes Lernen n (Mustererkennung)
~ **vector quantization** überwachte Vektorquantisierung f
supervising sound editor Tonmeister m

superwhite hochweiß
superwide-field eyepiece
Supergroßfeldokular *n*
(Lichtmikroskopie)
supplemental lens *s.* supplementary lens
supplementary angle Supplementwinkel *m*
~ **close-up lens** Nah[vorsatz]linse, Nahvorsatz *m*, Makro[vorsatz]linse *f*
~ **exposure** Zusatzbelichtung *f*
~ **film** Beifilm *m* *(Kinoprogramm)*
~ **filter** Zusatzfilter *n*
~ **lens** Vorsatzlinse *f*, Zusatzlinse *f*, Vorsatzobjektiv *n*, Zusatzobjektiv *n*
~ **light** Zusatzlicht *n*
supply cassette Vorratskassette *f*
~ **magazine** Abwickelmagazin *n*
~ **reel (spool)** Vorratsrolle *f*, Vorratsspule *f*, Abwickelspule *f*
~ **voltage** Versorgungsspannung *f*
support 1. Träger *m*; Trägermaterial *n*; Schichtträger *m*; Film[schicht]träger *m*, Filmunterlage *f*; 2. Auflage *f* *(z.B. zur Kamerastabilisierung)*
supporting foil Trägerfolie *f*
suppressing filter Tiefpassfilter *n*, Tiefpass *m*; Glättungsfilter *n*
suppression of aliasing Aliasunterdrückung *f*
~ **of contrast** Kontrastunterdrückung *f*
surface Oberfläche *f*; Fläche *f*
~ **acoustic wave** akustische Oberflächenwelle *f*
~ **acoustic wave filter** Oberflächenwellenfilter *n*
~-**active agent** *s.* surfactant
~ **analysis** Oberflächenanalyse *f*
~ **approximation** Flächenapproximation *f*
~ **area** Oberfläche *f*
~-**based segmentation** oberflächenbasierte Segmentierung *f*
~ **charge** Oberflächenladung *f* *(Elektrofotografie)*
~ **charge density** Oberflächenladungsdichte *f*
~ **coil** Oberflächenspule *f*, Lokalantenne *f* *(Magnetresonanztomografie)*
~ **color** Oberflächenfarbe *f*, Körperfarbe *f*, Objektfarbe *f*
~ **contour** Oberflächenprofil *n*
~ **contrast** Binnenkontrast *m*
~ **curvature** Oberflächenkrümmung *f*, Flächenkrümmung *f*
~ **defect** Oberflächenfehler *m*
~ **description** Oberflächenbeschreibung *f*
~ **detail** Oberflächeneinzelheit *f*
~ **detection** Oberflächendetektion *f*
~ **developer** Oberflächenentwickler *m*, Schichtoberflächenentwickler *m*
~ **development** Oberflächenentwicklung *f*
~ **development center** oberflächlicher Entwicklungskeim *m*, Oberflächenkeim *m*
~ **diffuser** diffuse Bildwand *f*

~ **electron microscope** Oberflächenelektronenmikroskop *n*
~ **element** Oberflächenelement *n*, Flächenelement *n*
~ **emitter** Flächenstrahler *m* *(Leuchtdiodentyp)*
~ **extraction** Flächenextraktion *f*
~ **fitting** Flächenanpassung *f*
~ **flatness** Oberflächenebenheit *f*
~ **flattening** Flächenebnung *f*
~ **fragment** Flächenfragment *n*
~ **geometry** Oberflächengeometrie *f*
~ **gradient** Oberflächengradient *m*
~ **inspection** Oberflächenprüfung *f*
~ **luster** Oberflächenglanz *m*
~ **mesh** Oberflächengitter *n*
~ **model** Flächenmodell *n*, Oberflächenmodell *n*
~ **modeling** Flächenmodellierung *f*, Oberflächenmodellierung *f*
~ **modification** Flächenmodifikation *f*
~ **normal** Flächennormale *f*, Oberflächennormale *f*
~ **normal estimation** Oberflächennormalenschätzung *f*
~ **normal vector** Oberflächennormalenvektor *m*
~ **of revolution** Rotationsfläche *f*
~ **orientation** Oberflächenorientierung *f*
~ **overlap** Flächenüberlappung *f*
~ **patch** Flächenstück *n*
~-**penetrating radar** Bodendurchdringungsradar *n*, Oberflächendurchdringungsradar *n*, Georadar *n*
~ **picking** Rupfen *n*, Farbrupfen *n* *(Druckschwierigkeit)*
~ **plot** Flächendiagramm *n*
~ **point** Oberflächenpunkt *m* *(Computergrafik)*
~ **primitive** Oberflächenprimitiv *n*
~ **profile** Oberflächenprofil *n*
~ **projection** Flächenprojektion *f*
~ **reconstruction** Oberflächenrekonstruktion *f*, Flächenrekonstruktion *f*
~ **reflectance model** Reflexionsmodell *n* *(Bildanalyse, Computergrafik)*
~ **reflection** Oberflächenreflexion *f*
~ **relief** Oberflächenrelief *n*
~ **rendering (rendition)** computergrafische Oberflächendarstellung *f*
~ **representation** Oberflächendarstellung *f*, Flächendarstellung *f*
~ **roughness** Oberflächenrauh[igk]eit *f*
~ **scanner** Flächenscanner *m*
~ **scattering** Oberflächenstreuung *f*
~ **scratch** Schramme *f*, Kratzer *m* *(z.B. auf Filmmaterial)*
~ **segment** Oberflächensegment *n*
~ **segmentation** Oberflächensegmentierung *f*
~ **shading** Oberflächenschattierung *f*
~ **shape** Oberflächenform *f*

surface 384

~ **sheen (shininess)** Oberflächenglanz *m*
~-**silvered** oberflächenverspiegelt
~-**silvered mirror** Oberflächenspiegel *m*, oberflächenversilberter Spiegel *m*
~ **simplification algorithm** Flächenvereinfachungsalgorithmus *m* *(Computergrafik)*
~ **smoothing** Flächenglättung *f*
~ **smoothness** Oberflächenglattheit *f*
~ **structure** Oberflächenstruktur *f*
~ **texture** Oberflächentextur *f*
~ **topography** Oberflächentopografie *f*
~ **triangulation** Flächentriangulation *f*
~ **wave** Oberflächenwelle *f*
~-**wave propagation** Oberflächenwellenausbreitung *f*
~-**wave radar** Oberflächenwellenradar *n*
surfactant Netzmittel *n*, Entspannungsmittel *n*
surgical endoscopy chirurgische Endoskopie *f*
~ **navigational system** chirurgisches Navigationssystem *n*
~ **tomography** chirurgische Tomografie *f*
surprint/to über[einander]drucken
surreptitious photography Aufklärungsfotografie *f*
surrogate image Ersatzbild *n*
~ **traveling** Pseudo-Reisen *n* *(Multimediaanwendung)*
surround Hintergrundlicht *n* *(Mikroskopie)*
~ **brightness** Umgebungshelligkeit *f*
~ **luminance** Umgebungsleuchtdichte *f*
~ **sound** Raumklang *m*, Rundumton *m*, Surround-Ton *m* *(Stereotonsystem)*
~ **speaker** Raumlautsprecher *m*
surrounding area Randfeld *n* *(z.B. eines Bildschirms)*
~ **color** Umgebungsfarbe *f*
~ **light** Umgebungslicht *n*, Grundlicht *n*, ambientes Licht *n*
~ **noise** Umgebungsrauschen *n*, Untergrundgeräusch *n*, Umfeldgeräusch *n*, Nebengeräusch *n*
~ **polygon** einfassendes (umschreibendes) Polygon *n*, Umrisspolygon *n*, Konturpolygon *n*
surroundings Umgebung *f*
surveillance aircraft Überwachungsflugzeug *n*
~ **camera** Überwachungskamera *f*, Videoüberwachungskamera *f*
~ **image** Überwachungsbild *n*
~ **imagery** Überwachungsaufnahmen *fpl*
~ **photo[graph]** Überwachungsfoto *n*
~ **photography** Überwachungsfotografie *f*
~ **radar** Überwachungsradar *n*; Rundsichtradar *n*, Panoramaradar *n*
~ **satellite** Überwachungssatellit *m*
~ **video** Überwachungsvideo *n*
~ **video image** Videoüberwachungsbild *n*
survey flight Bildflug *m*
~ **monitor** Überwachungsmonitor *m*

~ **traverse** Polygonzug *m* *(Fotogrammetrie)*
surveying Vermessungswesen *n*
susceptibility artifact Suszeptibilitätsartefakt *n* *(Magnetresonanzbildgebung)*
suspended-frame finder Leuchtrahmensucher *m*, Spiegelrahmensucher *m*, Albada-Sucher *m*
suspension Suspension *f*
~ **bridge** Hängebrücke *f* *(Beleuchtungsausrüstung)*
~ **file** Hängeregistratur *f*
~ **points** Auslassungspunkte *mpl* *(Druckzeichen)*
sustained illumination Dauerbeleuchtung *f*
SVGA *s.* super video graphics array
~ **display (monitor)** SVGA-Monitor *m*
swap file Auslagerungsdatei *f*, Auslagerungsspeicher *m*, virtueller Speicher *m*
swath Bodenstreifen *m* *(Aerofotogrammetrie)*
~ **width** Messstreifenbreite *f*, Schwadbreite *f* *(Fernerkundung)*
sweep Spurkörper *m*, Sweep-Modell *n* *(Computergrafik)*
~ **generator** Ablenkgenerator *m*
~ **stage** Hohlkehle *f*, Rundkehle *f* *(Studioausrüstung)*
~ **surface** Austragungsfläche *f* *(Flächenmodellierung)*
sweeping Sweep-Operation *f* *(dreidimensionale Modellierung)*
~ **pan** Mitschwenk *m*, Mitzieher *m*, Verfolgungsschwenk *m* *(Kameraführung)*
sweepline Lauflinie *f* *(Datenstruktur)*
~ **algorithm** Scanline-Algorithmus *m*
sweetening *s.* sound effects editing
swell[ing] Quellung *f* *(z.B. von Gelatine)*
swept frequency generator Kippgenerator *m*
~ **jammer** wobbelnder Störer *m* *(Radar)*
swinging mirror Schwingspiegel *m*, Rückschwingspiegel *m*, Klappspiegel *m*, Rapidspiegel *m* *(Spiegelreflexkamera)*
swish pan Reißschwenk *m*, schneller Schwenk *m*, Wischer *m* *(Kamerabewegung)*
switch *s.* switcher
switchable coding schaltbare Codierung *f*; geschaltete Codierung *f*
switcher Verteiler *m*, Vermittler *m*; Kreuzschiene *f* *(s.a. video switcher)*
switching circuit Schaltkreis *m*
~ **delay** Vermittlungsverzögerung *f*
~ **element** Schaltelement *n*
~ **node** Vermittlungsknoten *m*
~ **rate** Schaltgeschwindigkeit *f*
~ **technology** Vermittlungstechnik *f*
~ **transistor** Schalttransistor *m*
~ **tube** Schaltröhre *f*

swivel head Drehkopf *m*, Panoramakopf *m*, Schwenkkopf *m* *(Stativ)*
swung dash Wiederholungszeichen *n*, Tilde *f*
SXGA *s.* super extended graphics array
symbol Symbol *n*; Zeichen *n*
~ **alphabet** Symbolalphabet *n*
~ **code** Symbolcode *m*
~ **decoder** Symboldecodierer *m*
~ **encoder** Symbolcodierer *m*
~ **error** Symbolfehler *m*
symbolic image symbolisches Bild *n*
~ **image description** symbolische (abstrakte) Bildbeschreibung *f*
~ **model** symbolisches Modell *n*
~ **representation** symbolische (relationale) Darstellung *f*
symlet *s.* symmetrical wavelet
symmetric axis Symmetrieachse *f*
~ **axis transform[ation]** Symmetrieachsentransformation *f*; Mittelachsentransformation *f*
~ **difference operator** symmetrischer Differenzoperator *m*
~ **filter** symmetrisches Filter *n*
~ **Fourier transform** diskrete Fourier-Transformation *f*
~ **recurrent network** *s.* Hopfield net[work]
symmetrical anastigmat symmetrischer Anastigmat *m*
~ **compression** symmetrische Kompression *f*
~ **digital filter** *s.* symmetric filter
~ **eyepiece** symmetrisches Okular *n*, Plössl-Okular *n*
~ **lens** symmetrisches Objektiv *n*
~ **matrix** symmetrische Matrix *f*
~ **modeling** symmetrische Modellierung *f*
~ **objective** symmetrisches Objektiv *n*
~ **tensor** symmetrischer Tensor *m*
~ **wavelet** symmetrisches Wavelet *n*
symmetry Symmetrie *f*
~ **assumption** Symmetriebedingung *f* *(z.B. der Quantisierung)*
~ **axis** Symmetrieachse *f*
~ **detection** Symmetriedetektion *f* *(z.B. zur Mustererkennung)*
~ **perception** Symmetriewahrnehmung *f*
sync Synchronismus *m*, Synchronität *f* *(s.a. unter* synchronization, synchronizing, synchronous*)*
~ **beep** Synchron[isier]impuls *m*, Tonimpuls *m* *(Filmarbeit)*
~ **block** Synchronisationsblock *m*
~ **byte** Synchronisationsbyte *n*
~ **contact** Synchronkontakt *m*
~ **cord** Blitz[anschluss]kabel *n*, Synchronkabel *n*
~ **error** Synchronfehler *m*
~ **generator** Synchron[isations]generator *m*, Takt[frequenz]generator *m*, Taktgeber *m*, Impulsgeber *m*, Impulsgenerator *m*
~ **lead** *s.* ~ cord
~ **leader** Synchronstartband *n*
~ **level** Synchronpegel *m* *(Videosignal)*
~ **mark** Startkreuz *n*, Startmarkierung *f*, Bildstart *m* *(Filmschnitt)*
~-**pop** Piepser *m* *(Filmschnitt)*
~ **pulse** Synchronisiersignal *n*
~ **separator** Amplitudensieb *n*
~ **sound** Synchronton *m*, bildsynchroner Ton *m*
~-**sound** Tonanlegearbeit *f*, Tonanlegen *n*, Anlegen *n* von Ton zu Bild
~ **sound recording** Synchrontonaufnahme *f*, Synchrontonaufzeichnung *f*
~ **stick** Synchronklappe *f*, Tonklappe *f*; Handklappe *f* *(Filmarbeit)*
~ **terminal** Blitzkontakt *m*
~ **track** Synchronspur *f*
synch *s.a. unter* synchronization, synchronizing, synchronous
synchroballistic camera synchroballistische Kamera *f*
~ **photography** synchroballistische Fotografie *f*
synchrometer Synchronumroller *m* *(Filmschnittgerät)*
synchroneity *s.* synchronism
synchronism Synchronismus *m*, Synchronität *f*; Gleichlauf *m*
synchronization Synchronisation *f*, Synchronisierung *f*
~ **delay** Synchronisationsverzögerung *f*
~ **mark** Synchronzeichen *n*, Synchronmarke *f*
~ **point** Synchronpunkt *m* *(Filmschnitt)*
~ **speed** Synchron[isations]zeit *f*
synchronize/to synchronisieren
synchronized flash Synchronblitz *m*
~ **sound** Synchronton *m*
~ **sound-slide program** Diatonbildschau *f*
synchronizer Synchronisierer *m*, Synchronisator *m*; Synchronumroller *m*
synchronizing pulse generator *s.* sync generator
~ **signal** Synchron[isier]signal *n*, Synchronisationsimpuls *m*, Synchronisationssignal *n*, Gleichlaufsignal *n* *(Video, Fernsehen)*
synchronous synchron, zeitgleich
~ **edit** Duettschnitt *m* *(Video)*
~ **motor** Synchronmotor *m*
~ **recording** Synchronaufzeichnung *f*
~ **sound** Synchronton *m*, bildsynchroner Ton *m*
~ **time division multiplex** synchrones (statisches) Zeitmultiplexen *n*
~ **transfer mode** synchroner Übertragungsmodus *m*
synchrotron emission Synchrotronstrahlung *f*
~ **radiation** Synchrotronstrahlung *f*
~ **radiation facility** Synchrotron *n*
~ **radiation source** Synchrotron[strahlungs]quelle *f*
~ **radiation storage ring** Synchrotron-Speicherring *m*

synchrotron 386

~ **X rays** Synchrotron-Röntgenstrahlung *f*
syncing-up [synchrones] Anlegen *n*, Synchronschnitt *m*, Anlegearbeit *f* *(Filmbearbeitung)*
synesthesia Synästhesie *f*
synesthetic synästhetisch
syntactic description syntaktische Beschreibung *f (z.B. in der Objektklassifizierung)*
~ **pattern recognition** syntaktische Mustererkennung *f*
syntax-based arithmetic coding syntaxbasierte arithmetische Codierung *f*
synthesis filter Synthesefilter *n*, inverses Prädiktionsfehlerfilter *n*
~ **filter bank** Synthesefilterbank *f*
synthesized motion video synthetisiertes Laufbild *n*
~ **still image** synthetisiertes Standbild *n*
synthetic antenna synthetische Antenne *f (Radar)*
~ **aperture** synthetische Apertur *f (Radar, Röntgenteleskop)*
~ **aperture focusing technique** Synthetische-Apertur-Fokussierungstechnik *f*
~ **aperture radar** Radar *n* mit synthetischer Apertur (Antennenapertur), synthetisches Aperturradar (Radar) *n*
~ **aperture radar image data** SAR-Bilddaten *pl*
~ **camera** virtuelle Kamera *f (Computergrafik)*
~ **crystal** Zuchtkristall *m*
~ **fused silica** synthetischer Quarz *m*
~ **hologram** synthetisches Hologramm *n*
~ **observer** synthetischer Betrachter *m (Computergrafik)*
~ **picture** synthetisches Bild *n (s.a. computer-generated image)*
~ **polymer** synthetisches Polymer *n*
~ **texture** synthetische Textur *f*
~ **video** synthetisches Video *n (Radardatenverarbeitung)*
system accessories Systemzubehör *n*
~ **bus** Systembus *m*, lokaler Bus *m (Computer)*
~ **camera** Systemkamera *f*
~ **clock** Systemtakt *m*, Systemzeit *f*
~ **error (fault)** Systemfehler *m*
~ **file** Systemdatei *f (Computer)*
~ **input-output bus** Erweiterungs[daten]bus *m*
~ **memory** Systemspeicher *m*
~ **noise** Systemrauschen *n*, Johnson-Rauschen *n*, Nyquist-Rauschen *n*, thermisches Zufallsrauschen *n*
~ **time clock** Systemtakt *m*, Systemzeit *f*
systematic distortion systematische Verzerrung *f Fotogrammetrie)*
~ **error** systematischer Fehler *m*
~ **jitter** korrelierter Jitter *m*
~ **noise** *s.* system noise

systems description language Systembeschreibungssprache *f*
systolic array systolisches Zellenfeld *n*
~ **filter** systolisches Filter

T

T grain s. tabular crystal
T number T-Zahl f (eines Objektivs)
T one [time constant] s. spin-lattice relaxation time
T ray Terahertz-Welle f
T-ray image Terahertz-Bild n
T-ray imaging modality Terahertz-Bildgebungsverfahren n
T setting T-Einstellung f (Kamera)
T-stop, t-stop T-Blende f, effektive Blendenzahl f
T two [time constant] Transversalrelaxationszeit f, Querrelaxation[szeit] f, Querrelaxationszeitkonstante f (Magnetresonanzbildgebung)
table feed Tischverschiebung f (Spiral-Computertomografie)
~ **of pages** Videotext-Inhaltsübersicht f, TOP-System n
tablet 1. Zeichenfläche f; 2. Digitalisiertablett n, Grafiktablett n
tabletop microphone Tischmikrofon n
~ **photography** Tabletop-Fotografie f
~ **printer** Arbeitsplatzdrucker m, Einzelplatzdrucker m, Tischdrucker m
~ **processor** Tischprozessor m
~ **slide viewer** Diabetrachter m
~ **tripod** Tischstativ n
tabloid Tabloid[format] n (Zeitungsdruck)
taboo channel Tabukanal m (Fernsehen)
tabular crystal Tafelkristall m, Flachkristall m, T-Kristall m (Silberfotografie)
~ **grain emulsion** T-Kristall-Emulsion f
~ **photoemulsion microcrystal** s. ~ crystal
~ **setting** Tabellensatz m
tachistoscope Tachistoskop n (Wahrnehmungsforschung)
tachistoscopic tachistoskopisch
tachometer Tachometer m(n)
tachymeter Tachymeter n, Zielwinkel-Entfernungsmesser m
tachymetry Tachymetrie f (geodätisches Messverfahren)
Tachyscope Tachyskop n (frühe Kinematografie)
tack Zähigkeit f, Zügigkeit f, Zug m (von Druckfarben)
tactile interface haptische Schnittstelle f (Mensch-Maschine-Kommunikation)
~ **screen** s. touch screen [monitor]
tag Markierung f; Auszeichnungsbefehl m, beschreibendes Sprachelement n (Datenstruktur)
~ **tree** Minimalwertbaum m
tagged image file format TIF-Format n (Bilddatenspeicherung)

tail-cueing leader s. tail leader
~ **leader** Schlussband n, Endband n, Endallonge f, Nachlaufstreifen m (Filmkopie)
~ **margin** Fußsteg m, unterer Rand m (Druckseite)
~ **slate** Schlussklappe f
tailflash synchronization Synchronisation f auf den zweiten Verschlussvorhang
tailing Fahnenziehen n (Fernsehbildstörung)
take/to aufnehmen (Fotos)
take Einstellung f, Filmeinstellung f, Szenenabschnitt m, Einzelsequenz f, Einzelszene f, Take m(n), Szenenaufnahme f, Aufnahme f (Dreharbeit)
~ **number** Einstellungsnummer f
~**-up core** Aufwickelkern m, Wickelkern m, Rollenkern m, Spulenkern m, Bobby m
~**-up magazine** Aufwickelmagazin n
~**-up reel** Aufwickelrolle f, Aufwickelspule f; Filmaufwickelspule f, Filmauffangspule f
~**-up spool** s. ~ reel
taking aperture Arbeitsblende f, gewählte Blende f
~ **camera** Aufnahmekamera f
~ **distance** Aufnahmedistanz f, Aufnahmeentfernung f, Aufnahmeabstand m
~ **lens** Aufnahmeobjektiv n, Aufnahmeoptik f
~ **scale** Aufnahmemaßstab m
Talbot s. lumen second
~ **effect** Talbot-Effekt m (Optik)
talbotype Talbotypie f, Kalotypie f (Negativkopie)
talkie, talking picture Tonfilm m
tally light Kamera[rot]licht n
tamper resistance Fälschungssicherheit f
tampering detection Fälschungserkennung f
tamperproof fälschungssicher
tangent Tangente f
~ **tangential**
~ **handle** Tangentenvektor m (Computergrafik)
~ **surface** Tangentenfläche f, Torse f
~ **vector** Tangentenvektor m
tangential coma tangentiale Koma f (Abbildungsfehler)
~ **distortion** tangentiale Verzeichnung f
~ **image height aberration** tangentiale Bildhöhenaberration f
~ **image plane** tangentiale Bildebene f
~ **image surface** tangentiale Bildschale f
~ **plane** Tangentialebene f
~ **ray** Meridionalstrahl m, meridionaler Strahl m
~ **signal** Tangentialsignal n (Bildspeicherplatte)
tank processing Tankverarbeitung f, Tankentwicklung f

tank 388

~ **solution** Arbeitslösung f, Verarbeitungslösung f (Fotoverarbeitung)
tannin[-coated collodion] plate Tanninplatte f, Kollodiumtanninplatte f
tanning action Gerbwirkung f
~ **developer** gerbender Entwickler m, Gerbentwickler m
~ **development** Gerbentwicklung f, gerbende Entwicklung f
tape/to auf Band aufnehmen (aufzeichnen); videografieren
tape 1. Band n; 2. Bandaufnahme f
~ **abrasion** Bandabrieb m
~**-and-slide presentation** Tonbildschau f
~ **archive** Bandarchiv n
~**-based device** Bandgerät n
~**-based storage** Bandspeicherung f
~**-based VCR** Videobandrecorder m
~ **breakage** Bandriss m
~ **cartridge (cassette)** Bandkassette f
~ **change** Bandwechsel m
~ **coating** Bandbeschichtung f
~ **consumption** Bandverbrauch m
~ **counter** Band[längen]zählwerk n
~ **deck** Tapedeck n; Bandmaschine f; Bandlaufwerk n, Laufwerk n
~ **defect** Bandfehler m
~ **drive** Bandlaufwerk n, Laufwerk n; Bandantrieb m
~ **edge** Bandkante f
~ **edit controller** Schnittsteuergerät n
~ **editing** Bandschnitt m
~ **erasure** Bandlöschung f
~ **format** Bandformat n
~ **guide** Bandführung f
~ **head** Bandkopf m
~ **installation process** Bandeinlegen n
~ **library** Bandarchiv n
~ **machine** Bandmaschine f (s.a. ~ recorder)
~ **machine counter** Band[längen]zählwerk n
~ **noise** Bandrauschen n
~**-operated typesetting** lochstreifengesteuerter Maschinensatz m
~ **pass** Banddurchlauf m
~ **path** Bandweg m
~ **path friction** Bandreibung f
~ **playback speed** Bandabspielgeschwindigkeit f
~ **playback system** Bandabspielsystem n
~ **player** Bandspieler m (s.a. ~ recorder)
~ **pressure** Bandandruck m
~**-record/to** auf Band aufnehmen (aufzeichnen)
~ **record time** Bandaufnahmezeit f
~ **recorder** Bandaufnahmegerät n, Bandrecorder m, Bandmaschine f; Tonbandgerät n
~ **recording** Bandaufnahme f
~ **reel** Bandspule f; Bandteller m
~ **review** Bildsuchlauf m
~ **rewind** Bandrücklauf m
~ **run** Bandlauf m
~ **scanning** Bandabtastung f
~ **slippage** Bandschlupf m
~ **speed** Band[lauf]geschwindigkeit f, Bandtransportgeschwindigkeit f
~ **splice** 1. Bandklebestelle f; 2. Stumpfklebestelle f
~ **splicer** Folienklebepresse f
~ **stock** Bandmaterial n
~ **store** Bandspeicher m
~ **stretch** Banddehnung f
~ **support** Bandträger m
~ **surface** Bandoberfläche f
~ **tension** Bandzug f, Bandzugkraft f, Bandzugspannung f
~ **thickness** Banddicke f
~**-to-film transfer** s. video-to-film transfer
~**-to-head speed** Aufzeichnungsgeschwindigkeit f, Schreibgeschwindigkeit f, Relativgeschwindigkeit f (Bandmaschine)
~ **track** Bandspur f
~ **transport** Bandtransport m, Laufwerk n
~ **transport mechanism** Bandtransportmechanismus m
~ **transport system** Bandtransportsystem n
~ **travel** Bandlauf m
~ **utilization** Bandausnutzung f
~ **velocity** s. ~ speed
~ **width** Bandbreite f
~ **wrap** Bandumschlingung f
taped material Bandmaterial n
tapeless recording bandlose Aufzeichnung f
tapering Verjüngen n (z.B. als computergrafische Transformation)
taping Bandaufnahme f (Vorgang); Videofilmen n
~ **location** Drehort m, Spielstätte f, Produktionsort m (Videoproduktion)
target 1. Ziel n; 2. Target n, Schirmplatte f, Signalplatte f (Bildaufnahmeröhre); 3. s. ~ material
~ **acquisition** Zielerfassung f
~ **detection** Zielentdeckung f (Radar)
~ **device** Zielgerät n
~ **discrimination** Zielunterscheidung f
~ **extraction** Zielextraktion f (Radar)
~ **frame** Zielbild n (Bewegungsschätzung)
~ **identification** Zielerkennung f
~ **image** 1. Zielbild n; 2. Testtafel f, Testbild n
~ **imaging (mapping)** Zielabbildung f (Radar)
~ **material** Targetmaterial n, Anodenmaterial n (Bildaufnahmeröhre)
~ **object** Zielobjekt n
~ **point** Zielpunkt m
~ **radar** Zielradar n
~ **range** Zielentfernung f
~ **recognition** Zielerkennung f

~ **signature** Zielsignatur *f*
~ **surveillance** Zielüberwachung *f*
~ **swap (swop)** Zielvertauschung *f (Radar)*
~ **tracking** Objektverfolgung *f* *(Bildsequenzcodierung)*
~ **tracking radar** Zielverfolgungsradar *n*, Verfolgungsradar *n*
~ **trail** Nachleuchtschleppe *f (Radar)*
~ **vergence** Zielvergenz *f (Stereosehen)*
~ **voltage** Anodenspannung *f*
targeting sight militärisches Zielsuchsystem *n*
task bar Taskleiste *f*
Taylor['s] series Taylor-Reihe *f (Funktionalanalysis)*
TBC *s.* time base corrector
TCB spline TCB-Spline *n*, Kochanek-Bartels-Spline *n (geometrisches Modellieren)*
teach-in Belehrung *f*, Einlernen *n*, Einlernvorgang *m*, Speicherschreiben *n*, primäres Erkennen *n (Neuroinformatik)*
teaching film Lehrfilm *m*, Unterrichtsfilm *m*, Schulungsfilm *m*
~ **microscope** Ausbildungsmikroskop *n*, Kursmikroskop *n*
tear resistance Reißfestigkeit *f (z.B. von Fotopapier)*
~ **sheet** Abreißblatt *n*
teaser Werbekurzfilm *m*, Werbespot *m*
technical camera technische Kamera *f*; Fachkamera *f*; Großformatkamera *f*
~ **image** technisches Bild *n*
~ **image system** technisches Bildsystem *n*
~ **imaging** bildtechnisch
~ **optics** technische Optik *f*
~ **photographer** technischer Fotograf *m*
~ **photographic** fototechnisch
~ **photography** technische Fotografie *f*
~ **television** Industriefernsehen *n*, industrielles Fernsehen *n*
tele lens *s.* telephoto lens
telecamera Fernsehkamera *f*
telecast Fernsehübertragung *f*; Fernsehsendung *f*, Fernsehbeitrag *m*
telecaster Fernsehsender *m*; Fernsehstation *f*; Fernsehanstalt *f*
telecentric lens telezentrisches Objektiv *n*
~ **path of rays** telezentrischer Strahlengang *m*
~ **perspective** telezentrische Perspektive *f*, Parallelperspektive *f*, Einpunktperspektive *f*
telecine *s.* ~ scanner
~ **projector** Fernsehbildprojektor *m*
~ **scanner** Filmgeber *m*, Laufbildgeber *m*, Filmtransfergerät *n*
~ **transfer** Filmtransfer *m*, Filmabtastung *f*; Film-zu-Band-Konversion *f*
telecommunication interface Netz[werk]schnittstelle *f*
telecommunications industry Telekommunikationsindustrie *f*
~ **network** Telekommunikationsnetz *n*

teleconverter [lens] Telekonverter *m*
telecopy *s.* telefacsimile
telefacsimile Telefax *n*, Fax *n*
telefilm Fernseh[spiel]film *m*
telegame Telespiel *n*
telegenic fernsehwirksam, telegen
telemacro lens Telemakroobjektiv *n*, Makro-Teleobjektiv *n*
telemammography Telemammografie *f*
telemedicine Telemedizin *f*
telemetric telemetrisch
~ **radar** Telemetrieradar *n*
telemetry Telemetrie *f*, Fernmessung *f*; Entfernungsmessung *f*
telemicroscope Telemikroskop *n*
telemicroscopic[al] telemikroskopisch
telemicroscopy Telemikroskopie *f*
teleobjective *s.* telephoto lens
teleoperated camera fernbediente (ferngesteuerte) Kamera
~ **camera** *s.* telerobotic camera
telephoto 1. Telefoto *n*, Fernbild *n*; 2. *s.* ~ lens
~ **attachment** Televorsatz *m*, Televorsatzlinse *f*
~ **lens** [echtes] Tele[foto]objektiv *n*, Fernobjektiv *n*, Fernbildlinse *f*, Teleoptik *f*
~ **power (ratio)** Televerhältnis *n*
telephotograph Teleaufnahme *f*
telephotographic telefotografisch
telephotography Telefotografie *f*
telephotometer Spotfotometer *n*
telepresence Telepräsenz *f (virtuelle Realität)*
teleprinter Fernschreiber *m*, Ferndrucker *m*, Telexgerät *n*, Ticker *m*
teleprompter Teleprompter *m*, [elektronischer] Textgeber *m (Studioausrüstung)*
teleradiologic[al] teleradiologisch
teleradiology Teleradiologie *f*
telerecording Fernsehschirmbildaufzeichnung *f*, Filmaufzeichnung *f*
telerobotic camera robotergeführte Kamera *f*, Roboterkamera *f*; fernbedienbare (fernsteuerbare) Kamera *f*
telerobotics Telerobotik *f*
teleroentgen diagnosis Tele-Röntgendiagnose *f*, Röntgen-Ferndiagnose *f*
telescope Teleskop *n*, Fernrohr *n*; Radioteleskop *n*
~ **aperture** Teleskopöffnung *f*
~ **attachment** Teleskopvorsatz *m*
~ **diameter** Teleskopdurchmesser *m*
~ **electronics** Teleskopelektronik *f*
~ **eyepiece** Teleskopokular *n*, Fernrohrokular *n*
~ **guiding** Teleskopnachführung *f*
~ **image** Teleskopbild *n*
~ **mirror** Teleskopspiegel *m*, Fernrohrspiegel *m*

telescope 390

- ~ **mount[ing]** Teleskopmontierung *f*
- ~ **objective** Teleskopobjektiv *n*, Fernrohrobjektiv *n*
- ~ **optics** Teleskopoptik *f*
- ~ **resolution** Teleskopauflösung *f*
- ~ **sight** Zielfernrohr *n*, Visierfernrohr *n*
- ~ **stand** Teleskopstativ *n*
- ~ **tube** Fernrohrtubus *m*

telescopic teleskopisch
- ~ **adapter** Teleskopadapter *m*
- ~ **attachment** Televorsatz *m*, Televorsatzlinse *f*
- ~ **imaging** teleskopische Abbildung *f*
- ~ **magnification** Fernrohrvergrößerung *f*
- ~ **magnifier** Fernrohrlupe *f*
- ~ **rangefinder** Teleskopsucher *m*
- ~ **sight** Zielfernrohr *n*
- ~ **tripod** Ausziehstativ *n*

telescoping leg Teleskopbein *n (Stativ)*
- ~ **tube** Teleskoptubus *m*, Ausziehtubus *m*

telescreen Fernseh[bild]schirm *m*
teleseismic tomography teleseismische Tomografie *f*
telespectroradiometry Telespektroradiometrie *f*
telestereoscope Scherenfernrohr *n*, Telestereoskop *n*
telesurgery Fernchirurgie *f*
teletext Videotext *m*, Fernsehtext *m*
teletypesetter Fernsetzmaschine *f*
teletypesetting Fernsatz *m*
teletypewriter Fernschreiber *m*, Fernschreibgerät *n*, Telexgerät *n*, Ferndrucker *m*, Ticker *m*
televideoconferencing Videokonferenzbetrieb *m*
teleview/to fernsehen
televiewer Fernsehzuschauer *m*
television Fernsehen *n*, Television *f (s.a. unter TV, video)*
- ~ **ad[vertising]** Fernsehwerbung *f*
- ~ **antenna** Fernsehantenne *f*
- ~ **archive[s]** Fernseharchiv *n*
- ~ **archiving** Fernseharchivierung *f*
- ~ **aspect ratio** Fernseh-Bildseitenverhältnis *n*
- ~ **band** Fernsehband *n*
- ~ **broadcast** Fernsehausstrahlung *f*; Fernsehsendung *f*, Fernsehbeitrag *f*
- ~ **broadcast band** Fernsehrundfunkband *n*
- ~ **broadcast program** Fernsehprogramm *n*
- ~ **broadcast transmission** Fernsehrundfunksendung *f*
- ~ **broadcast transmission standard** Fernseh[übertragungs]norm *f*, Fernsehstandard *m*
- ~ **broadcaster** Fernsehanstalt *f*; Fernsehsender *m*
- ~ **broadcasting** Fernseh[rund]funk *m*; Fernsehausstrahlung *f*
- ~ **broadcasting station** Fernsehstation *f (s.a. ~ broadcaster)*
- ~ **broadcasting system** Fernsehsendeanlage *f*
- ~ **cable** Fernsehkabel *n*
- ~ **cable network** Fernsehkabelnetz *n*, Kabelfernsehnetz *n*
- ~ **camera picture** Fernsehkamerabild *n*
- ~ **camera truck** Fernsehaufnahmewagen *m*
- ~ **camera tube** Fernsehkameraröhre *f*, Fernseh[bild]aufnahmeröhre *f*, Aufnahmeröhre *f*, Kameraröhre *f*, Fernseh-Bildspeicherröhre *f*
- ~ **cathode-ray tube** Fernsehröhre *f*
- ~ **chain** Fernsehkette *f*
- ~ **channel** Fernseh[programm]kanal *m*
- ~ **company** Fernsehgesellschaft *f*
- ~ **copy** Fernsehkopie *f*, Sendekopie *f*
- ~ **coverage** Fernsehberichterstattung *f*
- ~ **display** 1. Fernsehwiedergabe *f*; 2. Fernseh[bild]schirm *m*
- ~ **documentary** Fernsehdokumentation *f*
- ~ **editor** Fernsehcutter *m*
- ~ **engineer** Fernsehtechniker *m*
- ~ **engineering** Fernsehtechnik *f*
- ~ **equipment** Fernsehausrüstung *f*
- ~ **field** Fernseh-Halbbild *n*
- ~ **film** Fernseh[spiel]film *m*
- ~ **fluoroscopy system** Bildverstärker-Fernsehkette *f*
- ~ **format** Fernsehformat *n*
- ~ **frame** Fernseh[einzel]bild *n*
- ~ **frame rate** Fernsehfrequenz *f*, Video[bild]frequenz *f*, Video[bild]rate *f*
- ~ **household** Fernsehhaushalt *m*
- ~ **image** Fernsehbild *n*
- ~ **image contrast** Fernsehbildkontrast *m*
- ~ **image processing** Fernsehbildverarbeitung *f*
- ~ **image quality** Fernsehbildqualität *f*
- ~ **image resolution** Fernsehbildauflösung *f*
- ~ **image tube** Fernsehbildröhre *f*
- ~ **industry** Fernsehindustrie *f*
- ~ **journalism** Fernsehjournalismus *m*
- ~ **journalist** Fernsehjournalist *m*
- ~ **license-holder** Fernsehteilnehmer *m*
- ~ **line** Fernseh[bild]zeile *f*
- ~ **link** Fernsehverbindung *f*
- ~ **live broadcast** Fernseh-Direktsendung *f*, Fernseh-Livesendung *f*
- ~ **microscope** Fernsehmikroskop *n*
- ~ **microscopy** Fernsehmikroskopie *f*
- ~ **monitor** Fernsehmonitor *m*
- ~ **motion picture** Fernseh[spiel]film *m*
- ~ **network** Fernsehnetz *n*
- ~ **newscast** Fernseh-Nachrichtensendung *f*
- ~ **noise** Fernsehrauschen *n*
- ~ **operation** Fernsehbetrieb *m*; Fernsehanstalt *f*
- ~ **picture recording** Fernsehbildaufzeichnung *f*
- ~ **picture reproduction** Fernsehbildwiedergabe *f*
- ~ **picture signal** Fernsehbildsignal *n*

~ **picture tube** Fernsehbildröhre f; Bild[wiedergabe]röhre f, Wiedergaberöhre f
~ **pixel** Fernsehpixel n
~ **portal** Fernsehportal n
~ **print** Fernsehkopie f, Sendekopie f
~ **probe** Fernsehsonde f
~ **production** Fernsehproduktion f
~ **production equipment** Fernsehproduktionstechnik f, Fernsehsendertechnik f
~ **program** Fernsehprogramm n; Fernsehsendung f, Fernsehbeitrag m
~ **programming** Fernseh-Programmmaterial n
~ **programming schedule** Fernseh-Programmplan m
~ **projection** Fernsehprojektion f
~ **projector** Fernsehprojektor m
~ **raster** Fernseh[zeilen]raster m(n)
~ **receiver (receiving set)** Fernsehgerät n, Fernseh[empfäng]er m, Fernsehapparat m
~ **reception** Fernsehempfang m
~ **recording** Fernsehaufzeichnung f, Fernsehaufnahme f
~ **remote control[ler]** Fernseh-Fernbedienung f
~ **reproduction** Fernsehwiedergabe f
~ **resolution** Fernsehauflösung f
~ **satellite** Fernsehsatellit m
~ **scan line** Fernseh[bild]zeile f
~ **scanner** Fernsehabtaster m
~ **scanning** Fernsehabtastung f
~ **scene** Fernsehszene f
~ **screen** Fernseh[bild]schirm m
~ **screen photography** Bildschirmfotografie f
~ **sequence** Fernsehsequenz f
~ **series** Fernsehserie f
~ **service** Fernsehdienst m
~ **set** 1. Fernsehgerät n, Fernseh[empfäng]er m, Fernsehapparat m; 2. Fernsehdekoration f
~ **set manufacturer** Fernsehgerätehersteller m
~ **set speaker** Fernsehgerätlautsprecher m
~ **show** Fernsehsendung f
~ **sound** Fernseh[begleit]ton m
~ **sound transmission** Fernsehtonübertragung f
~ **sound transmitter** Fernsehtonsender m
~ **storage tube** Speicherröhre f, speichernde Fernsehaufnahmeröhre f
~ **studio** Fernseh[aufnahme]studio n
~ **studio camera** Fernsehstudiokamera f
~ **supply chain** Fernsehkette f
~ **system** Fernsehsystem n
~ **system converter** Fernsehnormwandler m, Umsetzer m, Konverter m
~ **tape machine** Videobandgerät n
~ **technical** fernsehtechnisch
~ **technology** Fernsehtechnik f
~ **test pattern** Fernsehtestbild n

~ **test pattern generator** Fernsehbildmustergenerator m
~ **tower** Fernsehturm m
~ **transmission** Fernsehausstrahlung f; Fernsehübertragung f
~ **transmission center** Fernseh-Großsender m, Sendezentrale f
~ **transmission channel** Fernsehübertragungskanal m
~ **transmission technology** Fernsehübertragungstechnik f
~ **transmitting antenna** Fernseh-Sendeantenne f
~ **transposer** Fernsehumsetzer m, Fernseh-Füllsender m, Umsetzer m
~ **tube** Fernsehröhre f
~ **tuner** Fernsehtuner m
~ **videotape** Sende[magnet]band n, sendefertiges Videoband (Band) n
~ **viewer** Fernsehzuschauer m
~ **viewing** Fernsehen n
~ **weather forecast** Fernseh-Wettervorhersage f
televisionary televisuell
televisor Fernsehzuschauer m
televisual televisuell
telex/to telexen
telex Telex n
~ **network (system)** Fernschreibnetz n
telly s. television set
TEM s. transmission electron microscopy
temperature coefficient Temperaturkoeffizient m
~ **exposure effect** Temperatureffekt m
~ **field** Temperaturfeld n
~ **mapping** Wärmebildaufzeichnung f, Wärmebildgebung f
~ **noise** s. thermal noise
~ **radiator** Temperaturstrahler m
tempered water bath Warmwasserbad n
template 1. Schablone f; Muster[teil] n; Prototyp m; Mustervorlage f, Vorlage f, Mustermaske f; Klassenrepräsentant m *(Mustererkennung)*; 3. Dokumentvorlage f
~ **matching** Schablonenabgleich m, Schablonenanpassung f; Mustervergleich m
~ **pattern** Schablonenmuster n *(Mustererkennung)*
temporal 1. zeitlich, temporal; 2. temporal, schläfenwärts
~ **alias[ing]** zeitliches Aliasing n
~ **axis** Zeitachse f
~ **coherence** zeitliche Kohärenz f
~ **correlation** zeitliche Korrelation f
~ **filtering** zeitliche Filterung f
~ **frequency** zeitliche Frequenz f
~ **fusion** zeitliche Verschmelzung f
~ **image sequence** zeitliche Bildfolge f
~ **inhibition** zeitliche Inhibition f *(Sehen)*
~ **interpolation** zeitliche Interpolation f
~ **interval** Zeitintervall n, Intervall n
~ **lobe** Schläfenlappen m *(des Gehirns)*

temporal

- **~ low-pass filtering** zeitliche Tiefpassfilterung *f*
- **~ noise reduction** zeitliche Rauschreduktion *f*
- **~ predicition** zeitliche Prädiktion *f*
- **~ quantization** zeitliche Quantisierung *f*
- **~ rate conversion** Abtastratenkonversion *f*, Abtastratenumsetzung *f*
- **~ redundancy** zeitliche Redundanz *f*
- **~ resolution** zeitliche Auflösung *f*, Zeitauflösung *f*
- **~ response function** Zeitfunktion *f*
- **~ sampling** zeitliche Abtastung *f*
- **~ scalability** Zeitskalierbarkeit *f*, zeitliche Skalierbarkeit *f*
- **~ window** Zeitfenster *n*, zeitliches Fenster *n*

tensile strength Zugfestigkeit *f*
tensor Tensor *m* *(generalisierter Vektor; generalisierte Matrix)*
- **~ ellipsoid** Tensorellipsoid *n*
- **~ field** Tensorfeld *n*
- **~ of inertia** Trägheitstensor *m*
- **~ product** Tensorprodukt *n*

terabyte Terabyte *n*, Tb, TB *(Maßeinheit des Datenspeichervermögens)*
terahertz gap Terahertz-Lücke *f*
- **~ image** Terahertz-Bild *n*
- **~ portion [of the spectrum]** Terahertzbereich *m*
- **~ radiation** Terahertz-Strahlung *f*
- **~ time-domain spectroscopy** Terahertz-Spektroskopie *f*
- **~ wave** Terahertz-Welle *f*
- **~ wave microscope** Terahertz-Mikroskop *n*

term [mathematischer] Ausdruck *m*
terminal 1. Anschluss *m*; 2. Endstrich *m* *(Buchstabenbild)*; 3. *s.* ~ node; 4. *s.* ~ device
- **~ amplifier** Endverstärker *m*
- **~ device** Endgerät *n*, Terminal *n*; Daten[end]station *f*, Datensichtgerät *n*
- **~ equipment manufacturer** Endgerätehersteller *m*
- **~ node** Endknoten *m*, Rechnerendknoten *m*
- **~ screen** Bildschirmterminal *n*

ternary signal ternäres Signal *n*
terrain-following radar Geländefolgeradar *n*
- **~ map** Flurkarte *f*
- **~ point** Geländepunkt *m*
- **~ recognition system** Geländeerkennungssystem *n*

terrestrial terrestrisch
- **~ antenna** terrestrische Antenne *f*
- **~ broadcast[ing]** terrestrische Ausstrahlung *f*
- **~ camera** Erdbildmesskammer *f*, terrestrische Messkammer *f*
- **~ digital video broadcasting** digitales terrestrisches Fernsehen *n*, terrestrisches Digitalfernsehen *n*
- **~ eyepiece** terrestrisches Okular *n*
- **~ photogram** terrestrisches Messbild *n*
- **~ photogrammetric camera** Erdbildmesskammer *f*, terrestrische Messkammer *f*
- **~ photogrammetry** Erdbildmessung *f*, terrestrische Fotogrammetrie *f*
- **~ receiver** terrestrischer Empfänger *m*
- **~ reception** terrestrischer Empfang *m*
- **~ telescope** Erdfernrohr *n*, terrestrisches Fernrohr *n*, erdgebundenes Teleskop *n*
- **~ television** terrestrisches (erdgebundenes) Fernsehen *n*
- **~ television broadcasting** terrestrische Fernsehausstrahlung *f*
- **~ transmission** terrestrische Übertragung *f*
- **~ transmitter** terrestrischer Sender *m*

tertiary color Drittfarbe *f*, Tertiärfarbe *f*
- **~ spectrum** tertiäres Spektrum *n*

tesla Tesla *n*, T *(Einheit der Magnetflussdichte)*
tessellation Parkettierung *f*, Kachelung *f*, Polygonzerlegung *f*; Mosaik *n* *(Computergrafik)*
test Test *m*, Prüfung *f*, Probe *f*; Versuch *m*; Experiment *n*; Nachweis *m*
- **~ chart** Testtafel *f*, Testbild *n*
- **~ color** Testfarbe *f*
- **~ color reproduction** Farbprüfdruck *m*
- **~ exposure** Probebelichtung *f*, Testbelichtung *f*
- **~ film** Testfilm *m*, Prüffilm *m*
- **~ glass** Probeglas *n* *(Linsenfertigung)*
- **~ image** Testtafel *f*, Testbild *n*
- **~ lens** Prüfobjektiv *n*
- **~ light** Testlicht *n* *(Farbabmusterung)*
- **~ line** Prüfzeile *f* *(Fernsehen)*
- **~ negative** Testnegativ *n*
- **~ object** Testobjekt *n*
- **~ paper** Prüfpapier *n*, Testpapier *n*
- **~ pattern** Prüfmuster *n*, Testmuster *n*, Testbild *n*
- **~ pattern generator** Testbildgenerator *m*, Bildmustergenerator *m*
- **~ photographic print** Probeabzug *m*
- **~ preflash** Vor[mess]blitz *m*, Probeblitz *m*; Vorblitzfunktion *f*
- **~ print** Probeabzug *m*
- **~ screening** Probevorführung *f* *(von Filmmaterial)*
- **~ series** Testreihe *f*
- **~ shot** Testaufnahme *f*, Probeaufnahme *f*
- **~ signal** Testsignal *n*
- **~ specimen** Prüfobjekt *n*, Prüfling *m*
- **~ strip** Teststreifen *m*, Probestreifen *m*, Kontrollstreifen *m* *(Filmentwicklung)*
- **~ strip printer** Mehrfachbelichtungskassette *f*, Mehrfachbelichtungsrahmen *m*
- **~ tape** Pilot-Bezugsband *n*
- **~ target** Test[bild]vorlage *f*, Testbild *n*, Testttafel *f*

testing telescope Prüffernrohr *n*
tetrachloromethane Tetrachlorkohlenstoff *m*

tetrachromatic tetrachromatisch, vierfarbig
tetrahedron Tetraeder *n*, regelmäßiger Vierflächner *m*
texel Texel *n*, Texturelement *n*, Texturpunkt *m*, Texton *n*
text Text *m*
~ **alignment** Textausrichtung *f*
~ **block** Textblock *m*
~ **character** Textzeichen *n*
~ **color index** Textfarbenindex *m*
~ **compression** Textkompression *f*
~ **contrast** Textkontrast *m*
~ **database** Textdatenbank *f*
~ **display** Textanzeige *f*
~ **document** Textdokument *n*
~ **element** Textelement *n*
~ **entry** Texterfassung *f*
~ **field** Textfenster *n*
~ **file** Textdatei *f*
~ **image** Textbild *n*
~ **legibility** Textlesbarkeit *f*
~ **line** Textzeile *f*
~ **mode** Textmodus *m*
~ **page** Textseite *f*
~ **paper** 1. Werkdruckpapier *n*; 2. geprägtes Papier *n*
~ **path** Schreibrichtung *f*
~ **printer** Textdrucker *m*
~ **processing** Textverarbeitung *f*
~ **recognition** Texterkennung *f*
~ **resolution** Textauflösung *f*
~ **search engine** Textsuchmaschine *f*
~ **track** Textspur *f (Video)*
~ **type** Grundschrift *f*, Brotschrift *f (Typografie)*
~ **vectorization algorithm** Textvektorisierungsalgorithmus *m*
~ **window** Textfenster *n*
textile press Textildruckpresse *f*
~ **printer** Stoffdrucker *m*
~ **printing** Textildruck *m*, Stoffdruck *m*
~ **ribbon** Textilfarbband *n*, Gewebefarbband *n*
texton *s.* texture element
textual textlich
~ textuell
~ **data** Textdaten *pl*
~ **graphics** Textgrafik *f*
~ **information** Textinformation *f*
textural texturell *(s.a. unter texture)*
~ **description** Texturbeschreibung *f*
~ **feature** Texturmerkmal *n*
~ **feature vector** Texturmerkmalsvektor *m*
~ **image** Texturbild *n*; Musterfeld *n (Computergrafik)*
~ **measure** Texturmaß *n*
~ **model** Texturmodell *n*
~ **representation** Texturdarstellung *f*
~ **vector** Texturvektor *m*
texture/to texturieren
texture Textur *f (s.a. unter textural)*
~ **algorithm** Texturalgorithmus *m*
~ **analysis** Texturanalyse *f*

~ **animation** Texturanimation *f*
~-**based classification** texturbasierte Klassifikation (Klassifizierung) *f*
~-**based segmentation** texturbasierte Segmentierung
~ **buffer** Texturpufferspeicher *m*
~ **characterization** Texturbestimmung *f*
~ **classification** Texturklassifikation *f*
~ **coder** Texturcodierer *m*
~ **coding** Texturcodierung *f*
~ **content** Texturgehalt *m*
~ **contrast** Texturkontrast *m*
~ **coordinate** Texturkoordinate *f*
~ **decoding** Texturdecodierung *f*
~ **descriptor** Texturdeskriptor *m*
~ **deviation** Texturabweichung *f (Codierungsartefakt)*
~ **discrimination** Texturunterscheidung *f*
~ **element** Texturelement *n*, Texturpunkt *m*, Texel *n*, Texton *n*
~ **extraction** Texturextraktion *f*
~ **filtering algorithm** Texturfilterungsalgorithmus *m*
~ **generation** Texturerzeugung *f*
~ **gradient** Texturgradient *m*
~ **homogeneity** Texturhomogenität *f*
~ **identification** Texturidentifikation *f*
~ **image segmentation** Textursegmentierung *f*
~ **information** Texturinformation *f*
~ **map** Texturbild *n*; Musterfeld *n (Computergrafik)*
~ **mapping** Texturabbildung *f*, Textur-Mapping *n (Rendering-Technik)*
~ **masking** Texturmaskierung *f*
~ **model[l]ing** Texturmodellierung *f*
~ **operator** Texturoperator *m*, Texturfiltermaske *f*
~ **parameter** Texturparameter *m*
~ **pattern** Texturmuster *n*
~ **pattern recognition** Texturmustererkennung *f*
~ **perception** Texturwahrnehmung *f*
~ **primitive** Texturprimitiv *n*
~ **processing** Texturverarbeitung *f*
~ **resolution** Texturauflösung *f*
~ **segmentation** Textursegmentierung *f*
~-**sensitive filter** Texturfiltermaske *f*
~ **shadow** Texturschatten *m*
~ **similarity** Texturähnlichkeit *f*
~ **synthesis** Textursynthese *f*
~ **tree** Texturbaum *m (Datenstruktur)*
textured laminating material, texturizing film material Strukturfolie *f*, Effektfolie *f*
TFT *s.* thin-film transistor
thalamus Thalamus *m*, Sehhügel *m*
thallous iodide Thalliumiodid *n*
thaumatrope Thaumatrop *n (frühes Projektionsgerät)*
theater Lichtspielhaus *n*, Lichtspieltheater *n*
~ **chain** Kinokette *f*
~ **digital sound** Kino-Digitalton *m*

theater

- ~ **distribution** Kino[film]verleih *m*, Filmverleih *m*
- ~ **installer** Kinoausstatter *m*
- ~ **loudspeaker** Raumlautsprecher *m*
- ~ **owner** Kinobetreiber *m*
- ~ **projectionist** Filmvorführer *m*, Filmoperateur *m*
- ~ **projector** Kinoprojektor *m*, Kinomaschine *f*, Vorführmaschine *f*
- ~ **screen** Kinoleinwand *f*
- ~ **sound** Kinoton *m*, Kinoklang *m*
- ~ **sound system** Kinotonanlage *f*, Kinotonsystem *n*
- ~ **speaker** Kinolautsprecher *m*
- ~ **technician** Bühnentechniker *m*

theatrical aspect ratio Kinobildseitenverhältnis *n*
- ~ **exhibition** Kinovorführung *f*
- ~ **feature (film)** Kino[spiel]film *m*
- ~ **film production** Kinofilmproduktion *f*
- ~ **format** Kinofilmformat *n*
- ~ **lighting** Bühnenbeleuchtung *f*
- ~-**lighting filter** Bühnenlichtfilter *n*
- ~ **motion picture** Kinofilm *m*
- ~ **motion picture projector** Kinofilmprojektor *m*
- ~ **movie** Kino[spiel]film *m*
- ~ **movie's sound** Kinofilmton *m*
- ~ **moviemaking** Kinofilmproduktion *f*, Filmproduktion *f*
- ~ **photography** Bühnenfotografie *f*, Theaterfotografie *f*
- ~ **presentation** Kinovorführung *f*
- ~ **print** Verleihkopie *f*, Kino[film]kopie *f*, Theaterkopie *f*, Massenkopie *f*
- ~ **projection** Kinoprojektion *f*, Spielfilmprojektion *f*
- ~ **projection print** *s*. ~ print
- ~ **projector** Kino[film]projektor *m*
- ~ **release** *s*. ~ print
- ~ **showing** Kino[film]vorführung *f*
- ~ **spotlight** Bühnenscheinwerfer *m*

thematic map thematische Karte *f*, Themakarte *f*

theoretical light source theoretische Lichtquelle *f* *(Computergrafik)*

theory of color[s] Farb[en]theorie *f*
- ~ **of light** Lichttheorie *f*

thermal analysis Wärmebildauswertung *f*
- ~ **bubble ink-jet printer** Tintenstrahldrucker *m* nach dem Bubble-Jet-Verfahren
- ~ **camera** *s*. ~ image camera
- ~ **conductance noise** *s*. ~ noise
- ~ **development** thermische Entwicklung *f* *(z.B. in Bläschenkopierverfahren)*
- ~ **diffusion printing** *s*. ~ dye-sublimation printing
- ~ **dye-sublimation printer** Thermosublimationsdrucker *m*, Farb[thermo]sublimationsdrucker *m*, Farb-Thermoprinter *m*, Thermotransferdrucker *m*
- ~ **dye-sublimation printing** Thermosublimationsdruck *m*, Farbsublimationsdruck *m*, Thermodiffusionsdruck *m*
- ~ **dye-transfer printing** *s*. ~ transfer printing
- ~ **emission** thermische Emission *f*
- ~ **expansion coefficient** Wärmeausdehnungskoeffizient *m* *(z.B. von optischem Glas)*
- ~ **fax machine** Thermofaxgerät *n*
- ~ **filament** Glühfaden *m*
- ~ **focal area** thermischer Brennfleck *m*
- ~ **gradient** thermischer Gradient *m*
- ~ **image** Wärmebild *n*, Thermalbild *n*; Infrarotbild *n*
- ~ **image camera** Wärme[bild]kamera *f*, Thermografiekamera *f*, Infrarotkamera *f*
- ~ **imager** Wärmebildgerät *n*; Wärmebildspektrometer *n*
- ~ **imaging** Wärmebildaufnahme *f*, Wärmebildgebung *f*
- ~ **imaging device** Wärmebildgerät *n*
- ~ **imaging sensor** Wärmebildsensor *m*
- ~ **imaging spectrometer** Wärmebildspektrometer *n*
- ~ **imaging system** Wärmebildsystem *n*
- ~ **imaging technology** Wärmebildtechnik *f*
- ~ **infrared** thermales (thermisches) Infrarot *n*
- ~ **infrared sensor** Infrarot-Wärmesensor *m*
- ~ **light source** thermische Lichtquelle *f*
- ~ **map** Wärmebild *n*, Thermogramm *n*, Thermo[grafie]bild *n*
- ~ **noise** thermisches Rauschen *n*, Wärmerauschen *n*, Temperaturrauschen *n* *(s.a. random thermal noise)*
- ~ **paper** Thermopapier *n*, thermoaktives (wärmeempfindliches) Papier *n*; Telefaxpapier *n*
- ~ **print** Thermokopie *f*
- ~ **print head** Thermodruckkopf *m*
- ~ **printer** Thermodrucker *m*, Thermokopierer *m*
- ~ **printing** Thermodruck *m*, Wärmekopierung *f*
- ~ **printing process** Thermodruckverfahren *n*, Thermokopierverfahren *n*
- ~ **printing technology** Thermokopiertechnik *f*
- ~ **profile** *s*. ~ gradient
- ~ **radiation** Wärmestrahlung *f*, Thermalstrahlung *f*, Temperaturstrahlung *f*
- ~ **radiation detector** thermischer Detektor (Sensor) *m*
- ~ **radiator** Temperaturstrahler *m*, Wärmestrahler *m*, Warmstrahler *m*
- ~ **resolution** thermische Auflösung *f*
- ~ **sensitive resistor** *s*. thermistor
- ~ **sensor** thermischer Sensor (Detektor) *m*
- ~ **stress** Wärmespannung *f* *(Spannungsoptik)*
- ~ **sublimation** Thermosublimation *f*

~ **sublimation dye transfer printer** s. ~ dye-sublimation printer
~ **transfer printing** Thermotransferdruck m, Transferthermografie f, indirekte Thermografie f
~ **transfer ribbon** Thermofarbband n
~ **video system** Wärmebild-Videosystem m
~ **wax printer** Thermowachsdrucker m
thermionic cathode Glühkatode f
~ **emission** Glühemission f, thermionische Emission f
~ **tube** Glühkatodenröhre f
thermistor Thermistor m, Heißleiter m, temperaturabhängiger Widerstand m (Wärmesensor)
thermochromism Thermochromie f
thermocouple Thermoelement n
thermoelectric cooler Peltier-Element n, Peltier-Kühler m
~ **photometer** thermoelektrisches Fotometer n
~ **sensor** thermoelektrischer Sensor m
thermogram, thermograph Thermogramm n, Thermo[grafie]bild n, Wärmebild n
thermographer Thermograf m
thermographic thermografisch
~ **image** s. thermogram
~ **imaging** Wärmebildaufnahme f, Wärmebildgebung f, Wärmebildtechnik f
~ **printer** s. thermal printer
~ **process** Thermodruckverfahren n, Thermokopieverfahren n
~ **recording camera** Wärme[bild]kamera f, Infrarotkamera f, Thermografiekamera f
thermography Thermografie f
thermolamination Thermokaschieren n
thermoluminescence Thermolumineszenz f
thermoluminescent dosemeter Thermolumineszenzdosimeter n
thermolysis Thermolyse f
thermolytic thermolytisch
thermoplastic film Thermoplastfilm m
~ **ink** thermoplastische Druckfarbe f
~ **layer** thermoplastische Schicht f
thermostat Thermostat m, [automatischer] Temperaturregler m
thick-film screen printing Dickfilm-Siebdruck m
~ **greasy ink** dick[flüssig]e Druckfarbe f, zähflüssige (hochviskose) Druckfarbe f
~ **hologram** Tiefenhologramm n, Volumenhologramm n
~ **lens** dicke Linse (Einzellinse) f
Thiessen diagram s. Voronoi diagram
thigh shot amerikanische Einstellung f (Filmarbeit)
thimble printer Typenkorbdrucker m
thin electron microscope section elektronenmikroskopischer Dünnschnitt m

~-**film capacitor** Dünnschichtkondensator m
~-**film electroluminescence display** Dünnschichtelektronenlumineszenzdisplay n
~-**film optical filter** Dünnschichtfilter n
~-**film polarizer** Dünnschichtpolarisator m
~-**film technology** Dünnschichttechnik f
~-**film transistor** Dünnschichttransistor m
~-**film transistor display** TFT-Bildschirm m, TFT-Monitor m, Aktivmatrixbildschirm m, aktives Display n
~-**layer photographic film** Dünnschichtfilm m
~ **lens** dünne Linse (Einzellinse) f
~ **line** dünne Linie f
~ **mirror telescope** Dünnspiegelteleskop n
~ **negative** dünnes Negativ n
~ **prism** dünnes Prisma n
~ **section** Dünnschnitt m, dünner Schnitt m (Mikroskopie)
thinning Verdünnung f, Skelettierung f (Binärbildverarbeitung)
~ **algorithm** Verdünnungsalgorithmus m
~ **method** Dünnungsverfahren n (Elektronenmikroskopie)
~ **operation (procedure)** Verdünnungsoperation f
~ **transformation** Verdünnungstransformation f
thiosulfate solution Thiosulfatlösung f (Fixiermittel)
third-order aberration Seidel-Aberration f, Seidelscher Abbildungsfehler (Bildfehler) m (Optik)
~-**order polynomial** Polynom n dritter Ordnung, kubisches Polynom n
thirty-five millimeter camera Kleinbildkamera f
~-**five-millimeter cassette (magazine)** Kleinbildpatrone f
~-**five millimeter film** Fünfunddreißig-Millimeter-Film m
~-**five-millimeter miniature film** Kleinbildfilm m
~-**five millimeter single-lens reflex camera** Kleinbild-SLR-Kamera f, Kleinbildspiegelreflexkamera f
~-**five-millimeter still photography** Kleinbildfotografie f
~-**five millimeter systems camera** Kleinbild-Systemkamera f
~-**five-millimeter viewfinder camera** Kleinbildsucherkamera f
thixotropic [printing] ink thixotrope Druckfarbe f
thixotropy Thixotropie f
Thomson scattering Thomson-Streuung f (Röntgenstrahlung)
thread/to einlegen (einen Film)
threaded filter Schraubfilter n

threaded

~ **mount** Gewindeanschluss *m*, Schraubfassungsanschluss *m*, Fassungsanschluss *m* *(Objektiv)*
threading mechanism Einfädelmechanismus *m*
three-bath tray processing Dreibadprozess *m* *(Fotopapierverarbeitung)*
~-**bladed shutter** Dreiflügel[zangen]blende *f* *(Filmprojektor)*
~-**CCD [imaging-array color] camera** *s.* three-chip DV camcorder
~-**channel sound** Dreikanalton *m*
~-**chip DV camcorder**, ~ **video camera** Dreichipkamera *f*, Dreisensorenkamera *f*
~-**color** dreifarbig *(s.a. unter tricolor)*
~-**color cinematography** Dreifarbenkinematografie *f*
~-**color filter** RGB-Filter *n*
~-**color image** Dreifarbenbild *n*
~-**color meter** Dreifarbenkolorimeter *n*
~-**color photography** Dreifarbenfotografie *f*
~-**color printing [process]** Dreifarbendruck *m*
~-**color projection [method]** Dreifarbenprojektion *f*
~-**color separation record** Dreifarbenauszug *m*
~-**color subtractive reversal film** subtraktiver Dreifarbenfilm *m*; chromogener Dreischichtenfarbfilm *m*
~-**color theory [of light]** Dreifarbentheorie *f* des Lichts, Young-Helmholtz-Theorie *f* [des Farbensehens]
~-**colored phosphor dot** Leuchtpunkttripel *n*, Farbtripel *n* *(Farbbildröhre)*
~-**cylinder offset press** Dreizylinder-Offsetpresse *f*
~-**detector color-temperature meter** Dreibereichs-Farbtemperaturmesser *m*
~-**dimensional** dreidimensional, räumlich
~-**dimensional analysis** dreidimensionale Analyse *f*
~-**dimensional animation** dreidimensionale Animation *f*, Modellanimation *f*
~-**dimensional array** dreidimensionales Array *n*
~-**dimensional cinematography** Stereokinematografie *f*
~-**dimensional color space** dreidimensionaler Farbraum *m*
~-**dimensional computer vision** technisches dreidimensionales Sehen *n*
~-**dimensional data set** dreidimensionaler Datensatz *m*, Volumendatensatz *m*
~-**dimensional Fourier transform** dreidimensionale Fourier-Transformation *f*
~-**dimensional geometry** dreidimensionale Geometrie *f*

~-**dimensional graphics** dreidimensionale Computergrafik *f*
~-**dimensional hologram** dreidimensionales Hologramm *n*
~-**dimensional image** dreidimensionales (räumliches) Bild *n*
~-**dimensional image processing** dreidimensionale Bildverarbeitung *f*
~-**dimensional imaging** dreidimensionale Abbildung *f*; dreidimensionale Bildgebung *f*
~-**dimensional imaging technique** Raumbildtechnik *f*
~-**dimensional matrix** dreidimensionale Matrix *f*
~-**dimensional microscopy** dreidimensionale Mikroskopie *f*
~-**dimensional model** dreidimensionales Modell *n*
~-**dimensional model[l]ing** dreidimensionale Modellierung *f*
~-**dimensional motion picture** Stereofilm *m*
~-**dimensional photography** dreidimensionale Fotografie *f*, Stereofotografie *f*
~-**dimensional picture element** Trixel *n*
~-**dimensional prediction** dreidimensionale Prädiktion *f*
~-**dimensional printing** dreidimensionaler Druck *m*, Stereolithografie *f*
~-**dimensional radar** dreidimensionales Radar *n*
~-**dimensional reconstruction** dreidimensionale Rekonstruktion *f*
~-**dimensional representation** dreidimensionale Darstellung *f*
~-**dimensional scene** dreidimensionale (räumliche) Szene *f*
~-**dimensional signal** dreidimensionales Signal *n*
~-**dimensional solid angle** Raumwinkel *m*
~-**dimensional space** dreidimensionaler Raum *m*
~-**dimensional spectrum** raumzeitliches Spektrum *n*
~-**dimensional television** dreidimensionales (räumliches) Fernsehen *n*, stereoskopisches Fernsehen *n*, Stereofernsehen *n*
~-**dimensional tomography** dreidimensionale Tomografie *f*
~-**dimensional transform[ation]** dreidimensionale Transformation *f*
~-**dimensional ultrasound** dreidimensionaler Ultraschall *m*, Volumenultraschall *m*
~-**dimensional ultrasound image** räumliches Ultraschallbild *n*
~-**dimensional viewing** stereoskopische Betrachtung *f*
~-**dimensional vision** dreidimensionales (räumliches) Sehen *n*, stereoskopisches

Sehen *n*, Raumsehen *n*, Tiefensehen *n*, Stereosehen *n*
~-**dimensional visualization** dreidimensionale Visualisierung *f*
~-**dimensionality** Dreidimensionalität *f*
~ **emulsion layer film** Dreischichtenfilm *m*
~-**gun cathode-ray tube** Dreistrahl-Lochmaskenbildröhre *f*, Dreistrahlröhre *f*
~-**gun shadow-mask color picture tube** Lochmaskenbildröhre *f*, Lochmasken[farbbild]röhre *f*
~-**knife trimmer** Dreischneider *m*, Dreimesserautomat *m* *(Druckweiterverarbeitung)*
~-**layer color film** Dreischichtenfarbfilm *m*
~-**layer film** Dreischichtenfilm *m*
~-**layer negative film** Dreischichten-Negativfilm *m*
~-**layer perceptron** dreischichtiges Perzeptron *n*
~-**legged stand** Dreibein[stativ] *n* *(s.a. unter tripod)*
~-**lens turret** Revolverkopf *m* für drei Projektionsobjektive
~-**level laser** Dreiniveaulaser *m*
~-**light method** Dreipassmethode *f* *(Abtastung)*
~-**phase CCD image sensor** Drei-Phasen-CCD-Bildsensor *m*
~-**pixel neighborhood** Drei-Bildpunkte-Nachbarschaft *f* *(Bildverarbeitung)*
~-**point perspective** Dreipunktperspektive *f*
~-**quarter face view** Dreiviertelporträt *n*, Dreiviertelprofil *n*
~-**quarter-inch cassette** Dreiviertelzoll-Kassette *f*
~-**quarter-inch tape** Dreiviertelzollband *n* *(Video)*
~-**quarter lighting** Dreiviertel-Frontallichtführung *f*
~-**sensor [professional] camera** Dreichipkamera *f*, Dreisensorenkamera *f*
~-**strip process** Dreistreifenverfahren *n* *(frühe Kinematografie)*
~-**tube [television color] camera** Dreiröhren[farb]kamera *f*, RGB-Kamera *f*
~-**way head** Dreiwegekopf *m* *(Stativ)*
~-**way video fluid effect head** Dreiweg-Fluideffekt-Videokopf *m*
threshold Schwelle *f*, Schwellenwert *m*
~-**based image segmentation** schwellenwertbasierte Bildsegmentierung *f*
~ **coding** Schwellenwertcodierung *f*
~ **current** Schwellenstrom *m* *(Laserdiode)*
~ **decomposition** Schwellenwertzerlegung *f*
~ **dithering** Schwellenwert-Dithering *n* *(Computergrafik)*
~ **exposure** Schwellenwert *m* *(Schwärzungskurve)*
~ **function** Schwellenwertfunktion *f*
~ **modulation** Schwellenmodulation *f*
~ **of audibility (hearing)** Hörschwelle *f*
~ **of vision** Sehschwelle *f*
~ **procedure (process)** *s.* thresholding
~ **range** Schwellenintervall *n*
~ **segmentation** Schwellenwertsegmentierung *f*
~ **setting** Schwellenfestlegung *f*
~ **value** Schwellenwert *m*
thresholding Schwellenwertverfahren *n*, Schwellenwertbildung *f*, Schwellenwertfestlegung *f* *(Bildverarbeitungsoperation)*
~ **operation** Schwellen[wert]operation *f*
through-focus series Fokusserie *f*
~-**the-lens light measurement** TTL-Lichtmessung *f*
~-**the-lens metering** TTL-Belichtungsmessung *f*, Belichtungsinnenmessung *f*, Innen[licht]messung *f*, Belichtungsmessung *f* durch das Objektiv
~-**the-lens viewfinder** TTL-Sucher *m*
throughput Durchsatz *m*
throw Bildentfernung *f*, Projektinsentfernung *f*
~-**away camera** Einwegkamera *f*, Wegwerfkamera *f*
~ **ratio** Projektionsverhältnis *n*
thumbnail 1. Vorschaubild *n*; Miniaturbild *n*, Miniaturfoto *n*; 2. Layoutausdruck *m*
~ **image** Miniaturbild *n*, Miniaturfoto *n*
~ **screen display** Miniaturansicht *f*
thumbnails Bildübersicht *f*, Fotoindex *m*, Indexbild *n*
thumbwheel Daumenrad *n*, Rändelrad *n*
thunder effect Donnereffekt *m* *(Lichttonstörung)*
thunderstorm echo Gewitterecho *n* *(Radar)*
thyratron Thyratron *n*, Stromtor *n* *(eine Glühkatodenröhre)*
thyristor Thyristor *m* *(Halbleiterelement)*
THz wave radiation Terahertz-Strahlung *f*
ticker Ticker *m*, Fernschreiber *m*, Fernschreibgerät *n*, Ferndrucker *m*
~ **tape** Fernschreibband *n*
tie point Verknüpfungspunkt *m*
tied letters Ligatur *f*, Doppelbuchstabe *m*
~-**mixture hidden Markov model** semikontinuierliches Hidden-Markow-Modell *n*
TIFF *s.* tagged image file format
tight close-up Ganzgroßaufnahme *f*
~ **net** Tüll *m* *(Diffusionsmaterial)*
tilde Tilde *f*, Wiederholungszeichen *n*
tile Parkettstein *m*, Makropixel *n* *(geometrische Datenverarbeitung)*
tiled display gekachelter Bildschirm *m*
tiling Parkettierung *f*, Kachelung *f*, Mosaik *f* *(Computergeometrie)*
tilt/to verkippen; neigen

tilt 1. Kippung f, Verkippung f, Neigung f; Achsenverschwenkung f; 2. s. ~ move; 3. s. ~ angle
~ **angle** Kippwinkel m
~ **illusion** Vertikalentäuschung f (geometrische Täuschung)
~ **move** Vertikalschwenk m
~ **top** Neigekopf m
tiltable [ver]kippbar; neigbar
tilted mirror Schrägspiegel m
tilting s. tilt 1. und 2.
~ **angle** Kippwinkel m
~ **mirror** Kippspiegel m
tilts and swings Verstellmöglichkeit[en] f[pl] (Fachkamera)
time average method Zeitmittelungstechnik f (holografische Interferometrie)
~-**averaged holography** Zeitmittelungsholografie f
~-**averaged interferometry** Zeitmittelungsinterferometrie f
~ **axis** Zeitachse f
~-**bandwidth product** Zeit-Bandbreiten-Produkt n (Signaltheorie)
~ **base** Zeitbasis f
~ **base corrector** Zeitbasiskorrektor m, Zeitbasiskorrekturgerät n, Zeitfehlerausgleicher m (Videotechnik)
~ **base error** Zeit[basis]fehler m
~ **base error correction** Zeitbasiskorrektur f
~ **base stability** Zeitbasisstabilität f
~-**based** ... s. time base ...
~ **code** Zeitcode m
~-**code channel** Zeitcodespur f, Adressspur f
~-**code editing** Kopierschnittverfahren n; zeitcodierter Schnitt m (Video)
~-**code generator** Zeitcodegenerator m
~-**code information** Zeitcodeinformation f
~-**code inserter** Zeitcodeeinblender m
~-**code number** Zeitcodemarkierung f, Zeitcodenummer f
~-**code reader** Zeitcodeleser m
~-**coded tape** codiertes Band n
~ **coding** Zeitcodierung f
~-**compensated gain** zeitabhängige Verstärkung f (Sonografie)
~ **compression** Zeitkompression f (Videosignalverarbeitung)
~-**contrast index curve** Kontrastindex-Zeit-Kurve f
~ **coordinate** Zeitkoordinate f
~ **delay** Zeitversatz m
~-**delayed** zeitversetzt
~-**dependent amplitude** zeitabhängige Amplitude f
~ **direction discretization** zeitliche Diskretisierung f, Zeitdiskretisierung f
~ **division multiple access** Vielfachzugriff m im Zeitmultiplex
~ **domain** Zeitbereich m

~-**domain representation** Zeitbereichsdarstellung f
~ **exposure** Langzeitbelichtung f, Zeitbelichtung f, Dauerbelichtung f; Langzeitaufnahme f
~ **gain compensation** selektive Verstärkungsregelung f, Tiefenausgleich m (Sonografie)
~-**gain compensation** Tiefenausgleich m
~-**gamma curve** Zeit-Gamma-Kurve f, Gamma-Zeit-Kurve f
~ **interval** Zeitintervall n, Intervall n
~-**invariant filter** zeitinvariantes Filter n
~-**lapse camera** Zeitrafferkamera f
~-**lapse cinematography** Zeitrafferkinematografie f
~-**lapse film (movie)** Zeitrafferfilm m
~-**lapse photography** Zeitrafferfotografie f
~-**lapse recorder** Zeitrafferkamera f
~-**lapse shot** Zeitrafferaufnahme f
~-**lapse video recorder** Langzeit-Videorecorder m
~-**limit release** Zeitauslöser m
~ **line** Zeitleiste f (Videobearbeitung)
~ **line graph** Zeitreihe f
~ **multiplexing** Zeitmultiplexen n
~-**multiplexing technique** Zeitmultiplexverfahren n (Videotechnik)
~ **of flight** Laufzeit f (von Impulsen)
~-**of-flight angiography** Inflow-Angiografie f
~-**of-flight diffraction method** Beugungslaufzeittechnik f
~-**of-flight tomography** Laufzeittomografie f
~ **on target** Zielverweilzeit f (Radar)
~ **quantization** Zeitquantisierung f
~ **release** Zeitauslöser m
~ **resolution** zeitliche Auflösung f, Zeitauflösung f
~-**resolved fluorescence spectroscopy** zeitaufgelöste Fluoreszenzspektroskopie f
~-**resolved microscopy** zeitaufgelöste Mikroskopie f
~-**resolved spectroscopy** zeitaufgelöste Spektroskopie f
~ **resolving limit** zeitliches Auflösungsvermögen n
~-**sampled motion portrayal** zeitdiskrete Bewegungsdarstellung f
~ **scaling** Zeitraffung f
~-**sequential image** zeitsequentielles Bild n
~ **series** Zeitreihe f
~-**series analysis** Zeitreihenanalyse f
~ **setting** Zeiteinstellung f
~ **shift** Zeitversetzung f
~ **slot** Zeitschlitz m, Zugriffsschlitz m (Signalverarbeitung)
~ **stamp** Zeitstempel m (Videoübertragung)
~-**temperature curve** Zeit-Temperatur-Kurve f

~ **to clear** Klärzeit f *(Fotoverarbeitung)*
~**-varying filter** zeitveränderliches Filter n
~**-varying image** zeitveränderliches Bild n
~**-varying image processing** zeitveränderliche Bildverarbeitung f
~**-varying magnetic field** zeitveränderliches Magnetfeld n
~**-varying signal** zeitveränderliches Signal n
~ **window** Zeitfenster n
timed print farbkorrigierte Kopie f *(Film)*
timer Zeitschaltuhr f, Schaltuhr f, Zeitschalter m; Zeitgeber m; Belichtungs[zeitschalt]uhr f
~ **duration** Selbstauslöser-Vorlaufzeit f
timing 1. Timing n, zeitliche Abstimmung f; 2. Filmlichtbestimmung f, Farb[licht]bestimmung f, Farbkorrektur f
~ **card** Lichtkarte f, Kopierkarte f *(Filmkopierung)*
~ **curve** Farbkorrekturkurve f
~ **error** Zeitfehler m
~ **list** s. ~ card
~ **recovery** Taktrückgewinnung f
~ **reference code** Zeitreferenzsignal n *(Video)*
~ **sequence** Selbstauslöserablaufzeit f
~ **signal** Taktsignal n
~ **tape** Licht[steuer]band n *(Filmkopierung)*
tin plate Zinnplatte f
tinge Färbung f
tint/to färben, kolorieren; viragieren
tint 1. Farbton m, Buntton m, Farbfrequenz f; getrübte Farbe f; 2. Tonfarbe f; Tonung f
~ **control** Farbregler m *(Fernsehen)*
tinted paper Buntpapier n
tinting Kolorierung f; Einfärben n, Filmkolorierung f, Virerung f, Virage f
tintype Ferrotypie f *(Positiv)*
~ **process** Ferrotypie f
tip [in]/to einkleben *(zusätzliche Buchseiten)*
~ **angle** Flipwinkel m, Pulswinkel m *(Magnetresonanztomografie)*
tissue characterization Gewebecharakterisierung f
~ **classification** Gewebeklassifikation f
~ **contrast** Gewebekontrast m
~ **discrimination** Gewebediskriminierung f
~ **overlay** Abdeckfolie f, Abdeckfilm m, Maskierfolie f *(z.B. für Negativmontagen)*
~**[-specific] weighting factor** Gewebewichtungsfaktor m, organspezifischer Wichtungsfaktor m *(Röntgendosimetrie)*
title card Titelvorlage f *(Kinematografie)*
~ **character generator** Titelgenerator m, Titelgerät n, Videotitelgenerator m
~ **embossing** Titelprägung f
~ **insertion** Titeleinkopierung f
~ **page** Titelseite f
~ **writer, titler** s. ~ character generator

titling Titelherstellung f, Titelerzeugung f, Betitelung f
TM scan s. time motion scan
to scale maßstäblich, maßstabsgerecht, maßstabsgleich
toe Durchhang m, Kurvenfuß m; Fußempfindlichkeit f *(Schwärzungskurve)*
Toepler schlieren technique (method) [Toeplersches] Schlierenverfahren n *(räumliche Filterung)*
Toeplitz matrix Töplitz-Matrix f
toggle frequency Kippfrequenz f
token 1. Marke f, Zeichen n; 2. s. symbol
tomochemistry s. biochemical imaging
tomogram Tomogramm n, Schichtbild n, Schnittbild n
tomograph Tomograf m, Tomografiegerät n
tomographic tomografisch
~ **angle** tomografischer Winkel m
~ **image** Schnittbild n, Schichtbild n, Tomogramm n
~ **imaging** s. tomography
~ **machine** Tomografiegerät n, Tomograf m
~ **mapping** s. tomography
~ **plane** Schnittbildebene f, tomografische Ebene f
~ **reconstruction** tomografische Rekonstruktion f
~ **slice** 1. tomografische Schicht f; 2. s. ~ image
tomography Tomografie f, tomografische Bildgebung (Abbildung) f, Schnitt[bild]darstellung f; schichtweises Röntgen n
tomophoto[fluoro]graphy Tomofotografie f
tomosynthesis Tomosynthese f
tonal assessment Tonwertbeurteilung f
~ **contrast** tonaler Kontrast m
~ **control** Tonwertsteuerung f
~ **differentiation** Tonwertabstufung f
~ **gradation** Ton[wert]abstufung f
~ **image** Halbtonbild n, Graustufenbild n
~ **modification** Tonwertkorrektur f
~ **quality** Tonwertreichtum m
~ **range** Tonwertbereich m, Tonwertumfang m
~ **rendition** Tonwertwiedergabe f
~ **separation** Ton[wert]trennung f, Postereffekt m
~ **value** Tonwert m, Farbwert m
~ **variation** Tonwertverteilung f, Tonwertschwankung f
tonality Tonigkeit f, Lichtcharakter m, Stimmung f *(z.B. einer Fotografie)*
tone/to tonen
tone Farbton m, Buntton m, Farbfrequenz f; Farbcharakter m
~ **copy** Halbtonvorlage f
~ **correction** Tonwertkorrektur f
~ **difference** Tonwertunterschied m
~ **distortion** Tonwertverzerrung f

tone 400

~ **gradation** Ton[wert]abstufung f; Tonwertübergang m
~ **of gray** Grauton m, Grauabstufung f
~ **range** s. tonal range
~ **reproduction** Grauwertreproduktion f
~ **reversal** Tonwertumkehr f
~ **scale** Tonwertskala f (s.a. ~ gradation)
~ **scale reproduction** Tonwertwiedergabe f, Tonreproduktion f
~ **separation** Ton[wert]trennung f
~ **value** Tonwert m, Farbwert m
~ **wedge** Grau[stufen]keil m, Grauskala f
toner [additive] Toner m
~ **adhesion** Tonerhaftung f
~ **cartridge** Tonerkartusche f, Tonerkassette f, Tonerpatrone f
~ **charge** Tonerladung f
~ **color** Tonerfarbe f
~ **concentration** Tonerkonzentration f
~ **deposition** Tonerauftrag m
~ **development** Tonerentwicklung f
~ **dispersion** Tonerdispersion f
~ **drum** Toner[transport]walze f
~ **image** Tonerbild n
~ **layer** Tonerschicht f
~ **layer thickness** Tonerschichtdicke f
~ **particle** Tonerpartikel n(f), Toner[farb]teilchen n
~ **particle image** Tonerbild n
~ **polymer** Tonerpolymer n
~ **powder** Tonerpulver n, Tonerstaub m
~ **solution** Tonerlösung f
~ **sticking** Tonerhaftung f
~ **support** Tonerträger m
~ **transfer** Tonerübertragung f
toning Tonung f, Bildtonung f
~ **bath** Ton[ungs]bad n
~ **method** Tonungsverfahren n
~ **solution** Tonungslösung f
~ **technique** Tonungstechnik f
tool/to prägen
tool Werkzeug n; Steuerelement n (Computersoftware)
~ **palette** Werkzeugpalette f (Computergrafik)
toolbar Symbolleiste f, Werkzeugleiste f (Bildschirm-Icons)
top-down segmentation divisive Segmentierung f
~ **edge** 1. Oberkante f; 2. Kopfsteg m, Papierrand m oben (Layout)
~ **electrode** Deckelektrode f (Fotoleiter)
~ **emulsion layer** Emulsionsdeckschicht f, Oberguss m, Überguss m (Fotomaterial)
~ **field** oberes Halbbild n
~ **hat** 1. Bodenstativ n, Froschstativ n, Frosch m; 2. s. straight snoot
~ **hat filter** Top-Hat-Filter n
~ **hat transform** Top-Hat-Transformation f, Zylinderhut-Transformation f (morphologische Bildverarbeitung)
~ **light[ing]** Oberlicht n
~ **side** Oberseite f

~-**to-bottom reversed image** höhenverkehrtes Bild n
~ **view** Draufsicht f
topcoat s. top emulsion layer
topogram Topogramm n, Übersichtsaufnahme f
topographer Topograf m
topographic topografisch
~ **feature** topografisches Merkmal n
~ **image** topografisches Bild n
~ **map** 1. topografische Karte f; topografisches Bild n; 2. s. topology-preserving map
~ **mapping** 1. topografische Abbildung f; 2. s. retinotopic mapping
~ **pixel classification** topografische Pixelklassifikation f
topographical topografisch
~ **projection** topografische Projektion f
topography Topografie f
topological topologisch
~ **classification** topologische Klassifikation f
~ **descriptor** topologischer Deskriptor m
~ **dimension** topologische Dimension f
~ **distortion** topologische Verzerrung f
~ **feature** Topologiemerkmal n, topologisches Merkmal n; Kontextmerkmal n
~ **filtering** topologische Filterung f
~ **graph** topologischer Graph m
~ **map** topologische Karte f
~ **mesh** topologisch (räumlich) organisiertes Netz n (Computergrafik)
~ **operation** topologische Operation f
~ **segmentation** topologische Segmentierung f
~ **space** topologischer Raum m
~ **thinning** topologische Verdünnung f
~ **vector** topologischer Vektor m
topology Topologie f
~ **matching** Topologievergleich m
~ **of networks** Netzwerktopologie f
~ **preservation** Topologieerhaltung f
~-**preserving map** 1. nachbarschaftserhaltende (topologieerhaltende) Abbildung f; 2. s. self-organizing feature map
~ **visualization** Topologievisualisierung f
topometric topometrisch
topometry Topometrie f
toric lens torische (toroidale) Linse f
toroid, toroidal [resistance] coil Toroidspule f, Ringspule f, Toroid n (Bildröhre)
torpedo Videoschlitten m (Unterwasserfotografie)
torus Torus m, Kreisring m
total aberration [optischer] Gesamtfehler m
~-**body plethysmograph** Ganzkörperplethysmograf m
~ **brightness** Gesamthelligkeit f (z.B. eines Bildschirms)

~ **conjugate distance** Konjugationsabstand *m*, Objekt-Bild-Abstand *m (Optik)*
~ **contrast** Gesamtkontrast *m*, Allgemeinkontrast *m*
~ **development time** Gesamtentwicklungszeit *f*
~ **exposure** Gesamtbelichtung *f*, Gesamtbelichtungszeit *f*
~ **external reflection** äußere Totalreflexion *f*
~ **focal length** Gesamtbrennweite *f*
~ **harmonic distortion** Gesamtklirrfaktor *m*
~ **illumination** Gesamtausleuchtung *f*, Gesamtbeleuchtung *f*
~ **image** Gesamtbild *n*
~ **image noise** Gesamtrauschen *n*
~ **image unsharpness** Gesamtunschärfe *f*
~ **internal reflection** innere Totalreflexion *f*
~ **line time** Gesamtzeilendauer *f (Fernsehsignal)*
~ **luminosity** Gesamtleuchtkraft *f*, Gesamtleuchtstärke *f*
~ **magnification** Gesamtvergrößerung *f (z.B. eines Mikroskops)*
~ **noise** Gesamtrauschen *n*
~ **radiation** Globalstrahlung *f*
~ **reflectance** Gesamtreflexionsgrad *m*
~ **reflection** Totalreflexion *f*, totale Reflexion *f*, Gesamtreflexion *f*
~ **reflection factor** Gesamtreflexionsgrad *m*
~ **reflection monochromator** Totalreflexionsmonochromator *m*
~ **reflection X-ray spectrometer** Totalreflexions-Röntgenspektrometer *n*
~ **spin** Gesamtspin *m*
totally reflecting prism totalreflektierendes Prisma *n*
touch pad Sensortastenfeld *n*
~ **paper** Zündpapier *n (frühe Blitzfotografie)*
~ **screen [monitor], touch-sensitive screen** berührungsempfindlicher (berührungssensitiver) Bildschirm *m*, Berührungsbildschirm *m*, Kontaktbildschirm *m*, Sensorbildschirm *m*; berührungsempfindliches (haptisches) Display *n*
trace/to [ab]pausen, durchzeichnen
tracer Tracer *m (Nuklearmedizin)*
tracing 1. Durchzeichnung *f*; 2. Vektorisierung *f*
~ **paper** Pauspapier *n*, Transparentpapier *n*
~ **table** Kartiertisch *m*, Messtisch *m*, Mensel *f (Fotogrammetrie)*
track 1. Spur *f*; 2. Vorbeifahrt *f*, Parallelfahrt *f (Kameraarbeit)*
~ **angle** Spurwinkel *m*
~ **configuration** Spurlage *f*
~ **density** Spurdichte *f*
~ **format** Spurformat *n*
~ **guard** Schutzwulstring *m*
~ **layout** Spurlagenanordnung *f*

~ **length** *s.* total conjugate distance
~ **lighting system** Beleuchtungsgerüst *n*, Deckenschienensystem *n*, Laufschienensystem *n (Studioausrüstung)*
~ **pitch** Spurabstand *m*
~ **position** Spurlage *f*
~ **spacing** Spurabstand *m*
~ **width** Spurbreite *f*
trackball Steuerkugel *f*, Rollkugel[einheit] *f*, Positionierungskugel *f (Eingabegerät)*
tracker Zielverfolgungsrechner *m (Radar)*
tracking 1. Objektverfolgung *f (Bildsequenzcodierung)*; Nachführung *f (Radar)*; 2. Kamerafahrt *f*, Mitziehen *n* [der Kamera], Verfolgungsschwenk *m*; 3. Laufweitenänderung *f (Typografie)*; 4. *s.* ~ adjustment
~ **adjustment** Spur[lagen]regelung *f*, Spureinstellung *f*, Spurnachführung *f (Bandgerät)*
~ **algorithm** Verfolgungsalgorithmus *m (Videocodierung)*
~ **control** Spursteuerung *f*
~ **edit** Pseudoschnitt *m (Video)*
~ **error** Spurlagenfehler *m*, Trackingfehler *m*
~ **eye** bewegtes Auge *n (Sehen)*
~ **mechanism** Spurlagenregler *m*
~ **movement of the eye** Augenfolgebewegung *f*
~ **pit** Führungs-Pit *n(m) (Bildspeicherplatte)*
~ **radar** Verfolgungsradar *n*, Zielverfolgungsradar *n*
~ **shot** 1. Fahraufnahme *f (Filmarbeit)*; 2. *s.* sweeping pan
~ **telescope** Verfolgungsteleskop *n*
tractrix Traktrix *f*, Schleppkurve *f*
trade camera service, ~ shop Reproanstalt *f*
traditional animation Animation *f*
~ **film editing** konventioneller (traditioneller) Filmschnitt *m*
traffic clutter Verkehrsecho *n (Radar)*
~ **flow analysis** Verkehrsflussanalyse *f*
~ **map** Straßenkarte *f*
~ **monitoring camera** Verkehrsüberwachungskamera *f*
~ **simulation** Verkehrssimulation *f*
~ **surveillance** Verkehrsüberwachung *f*
trailer 1. Abspann *m*, Nachspann *m*, Trailer *m*, Filmtrailer *m*; Allonge *f (Kinefilm)*; 2. Vorspannfilm *m*; 3. Endmarke *f (Datenübertragung)*
~ **tape** Nachspannband *n*
trailing edge schließende Kante *f*
train of prisms Prismenkombination *f*, Prismensystem *n*
~ **of pulses** Impulsfolge *f*, Impulssequenz *f*, Pulsfolge *f*
trainable lernfähig
traing video Schulungsvideo *n*

training 402

training Training *n*, Lernen *n* *(Neuroinformatik)*
~ **algorithm** Trainingsalgorithmus *m*, Lernalgorithmus *m*
~ **area (field)** Trainingsgebiet *n*
~ **film** Lehrfilm *m*, Unterrichtsfilm *m*, Schulungsfilm *m*
~ **object** Trainingsobjekt *n*
~ **pattern** Lernmuster *n*, Trainingsbild *n*
~ **period (phase)** Trainingsphase *f* *(Bildvorverarbeitung)*
~ **picture** Trainingsbild *n*
~ **population** *s.* ~ set
~ **rule** Lernregel *f*
~ **set** Lerndatensatz *m*, Trainingsdatensatz *m*, Lernstichprobe *f*, Lernmenge *f*
~ **vector** Trainingsvektor *m* *(Quantisierung)*
~ **video** Schulungsvideo *n*
trajectory Trajektorie *f*, Bahn[kurve] *f*, Phasenkurve *f*
transaction computer Dialogrechner *m*, Transputer *m*
transcode/to umcodieren, transcodieren
transcoder Transcoder *m*
transcoding Transcodierung *f*, Umcodierung *f*
transducer 1. Wandler *m*, Signalwandler *m*; 2. Ultraschall[mess]kopf *m*
~ **array** Wandleranordnung *f*
~ **element** Wandlerelement *n*
~ **field pattern** Schallfeldgeometrie *f*
~ **geometry** Schallkopfgeometrie *f*
~ **impulse** Wandlerimpuls *m*
~ **plane** Wandlerebene *f*
transfer/to übertragen, transferieren
transfer Übertragung *f*, Transfer *m*
~ **behavior** Übertragungsverhalten *n*
~ **cylinder (drum)** Übergabetrommel *f*, Übergabezylinder *m* *(Druckmaschine)*
~ **function** Transferfunktion *f*, Übertragungsfunktion *f*
~ **lettering** Abreibeschrift *f*
~ **medium** Übertragungsmedium *n*
~ **mode** Übertragungsmodus *m*
~ **paper** Abziehbilderpapier *n*
~ **print** Umdruck *m* *(Vervielfältigungsprodukt)*
~ **printing** Umdruck *m (Verfahren)*
~ **process** Transferverfahren *n* *(Elektrofotografie, Thermografie)*
~ **protocol** Übertragungsprotokoll *n*
~ **rate** Übertragungsrate *f*; Übertragungsgeschwindigkeit *f*
~ **register** Ladungsschieberegister *n*, Schieberegister *n (CCD-Sensor)*
~ **roll[er]** Übertrag[ungs]zylinder *m* *(Elektrofotografie)*
~ **time** Übertragungszeit *f*
transferable übertragbar
transfinite interpolation transfinite Interpolation *f*
transflective transflektiv *(Display)*

transform/to transformieren, umformen, verformen
transform 1. Transformierte *f*; 2. Transformation *f*
~ **analysis** Transformationsanalyse *f*
~-**based compression method** transformationsbasiertes Kompressionsverfahren *n*
~-**based image processing** transformationsbasierte Bildverarbeitung *f*
~-**based textural analysis** transformationsbasierte Texturanalyse *f*
~ **code/to** transformationscodieren
~ **code** Transformationscode *f*
~ **coder** Transformationscodierer *m*
~ **coding** Transformationscodierung *f*, Umwandlungscodierung *f*
~ **coding error** Transformationscodierungsfehler *m*
~ **domain** Ortsfrequenzraum *m*
~ **location** Transformationsstelle *f*
~ **operation** Transformationsoperation *f*
~ **pair** Transformationspaar *n*
~ **plane** Transformationsebene *f*
transformation Transformation *f*
~ **algorithm** Transformationsalgorithmus *m*
~ **block** Transformationsblock *m*
~ **coefficient** Transformationskoeffizient *m*
~ **function** Transformationsfunktion *f*
~ **kernel** Transformationskern *m*
~ **matrix** Transformationsmatrix *f*
~ **method** Transformationsverfahren *n*
~ **of coordinates** Koordinatentransformation *f* *(Computergrafik)*
~ **parameter** Transformationsparameter *m*
~ **procedure** Transformationsoperation *f*
transformational equation Transformationsgleichung *f*
~ **invariance** Transformationsinvarianz *f*
transformed image Transformationsbild *n*, transformiertes Bild *n*
transformer Transformator *m*
transhorizon echo Überhorizontecho *n* *(Radar)*
transient storage temporärer (transienter) Speicher *m*
transilluminate/to durchleuchten
transillumination Durchleuchtung *f*
transilluminator Durchleuchtungsgerät *n*
transistor Transistor *m*
transition Übergang *m*; Szenenübergang *m (Film, Video)*
~ **effect** Übergangseffekt *m*; Überblendeffekt *m*
~ **rate** Blenddauer *f*
~ **temperature** Sprungtemperatur *f*, kritische Temperatur *f (Supraleiter)*
~ **type** Überblendart *f*, Blendart *f*
transitional wipe Wischblende *f*, Schiebeblende *f*, Blendeneffekt *m* *(Filmtrick)*

translate/to [parallel] verschieben
translation Translation f, Verschiebung f (geometrische Transformation)
~ **direction** Translationsrichtung f
~ **invariance** Translationsinvarianz f, Verschiebungsinvarianz f (eines Operators)
~**-invariant** translationsinvariant, verschiebungsinvariant (Operator)
~ **matrix** Translationsmatrix f
~ **parallax** Translationsparallaxe f
~ **vector** Translationsvektor m
translational motion Translationsbewegung f, translatorische Bewegung f
~ **motion compensation** translatorische Bewegungskompensation f
~ **symmetry** Translationssymmetrie f
translator Umsetzer m
translatory translatorisch
translucency Transluzenz f, Lichtdurchlässigkeit f
translucent transluzent, transluzid, durchscheinend, halbopak, lichtdurchlässig (s.a. transparent)
~ **screen** Durchlichtbildschirm m, Durchlichtbildwand f, Transparentschirm m, durchscheinende Bildwand f
transmissibility Übertragbarkeit f
transmissible übertragbar
transmission 1. Übertragung f; Transmission f; 2. Sendung f; 3. Durchstrahlung f
~ **antenna** Sendeantenne f
~ **axis** Transmissionsachse f
~ **band** Durchlassbereich m
~ **bandwidth** Übertragungsbandbreite f
~ **capacity** Übertragungskapazität f
~ **center** Sendezentrale f
~ **chain** Übertragungskette f
~ **channel** Übertragungskanal m; Sendekanal m
~ **circuit** Übertragungsstrecke f
~ **coefficient** Transmissionskoeffizient m
~ **curve** Durchlasskurve f, Transmissionskurve f
~ **delay** Übertragungsverzögerung f
~ **densitometer** Transmissionsdensitometer n, Durchsichtdensitometer n
~ **density** Transmissionsdichte f
~ **echelon** Transmissionsstufengitter n
~ **electron micrograph** Transmissions-Elektronenmikrografie f
~ **electron microscope** Transmissionselektronenmikroskop n, Durchstrahlungselektronenmikroskop n
~ **electron microscopy** Transmissionselektronenmikroskopie f, Durchstrahlungselektronenmikroskopie f
~ **error** Übertragungsfehler m
~ **factor** Transmissionsgrad m
~ **filter** Übertragungsfilter n, Transmissionsfilter n
~ **format** Übertragungsformat n
~ **frame** Datenübertragungsblock m
~ **frequency** Übertragungsfrequenz f; Sendefrequenz f
~ **function** Übertragungsfunktion f, Transmissionsfunktion f
~ **grating** Transmissionsgitter n
~ **gray-scale** Durchsichts-Grauskala f
~ **grid** Transmissionsgitter n
~ **hologram** Transmissionshologramm n, durchlässiges Hologramm n, Lippmann-Bragg-Hologramm n
~ **image** Transmissionsbild n, Durchlichtbild n, Durchscheinbild n
~**-induced noise** s. transmission noise
~ **line** Übertragungsleitung f
~ **link** Übertragungsstrecke f
~ **loss** Übertragungsverlust m, Transmissionsverlust m
~ **mask** Transmissionsmaske f
~ **medium** Übertragungsmedium n
~ **microscope** 1. Durchlichtmikroskop n; 2. s. transmission electron microscope
~ **microscopy** Durchlichtmikroskopie f
~ **mode** Übertragungsmodus m
~ **neutron radiography** Transmissionsneutronenradiografie f
~ **noise** Übertragungsrauschen n, Transferrauschen n, Ladungstransferrauschen n
~ **optics** Durchstrahlungsoptik f
~ **order** Übertragungsreihenfolge f
~ **parameter signal[l]ing pilot** Übertragungsparameter-Pilot m
~ **path** Übertragungsweg m
~ **path delay** Buslaufzeit f (Datenübertragung)
~ **protocol** Übertragungsprotokoll n
~ **quality** Übertragungsqualität f
~ **radiography** Röntgenoskopie f, Fluoroskopie f, Röntgendurchleuchtung f, Durchleuchtung f
~ **reliability** Übertragungssicherheit f
~ **satellite** Übertragungssatellit m
~ **signal** Übertragungssignal n
~ **sonography** Transmissionssonografie f
~ **spectrum** Transmissionsspektrum n, Übertragungsspektrum n
~ **speed** Übertragungsgeschwindigkeit f, Übermittlungsgeschwindigkeit f
~ **standard** Übertragungsstandard m, Übertragungsnorm f
~ **step tablet** Durchsichts-Grauskala f
~ **system** Übertragungssystem n
~ **technology** Übertragungstechnik f
~ **time** Übertragungszeit f
~ **tomographic** transmissionstomografisch
~ **video bandwidth** Videoübertragungsbandbreite f
~ **X-ray microscope** Transmissions-Röntgenmikroskop n

transmission 404

~ **X-ray microscopy** Transmissions-Röntgenmikroskopie *f*
transmissive transmissiv, durchlässig
~ **display** Durchlichtanzeige *f*
~ **ultrasonic computerized tomography** Durchschallungstomografie *f*, Ultraschalltomografie *f*, Sonotomografie *f*, Ultraschall-Schnittbildverfahren *n*
transmissivity *s.* transmittance
transmit/to übertragen, transmittieren; [aus]senden
transmit-receive device Sende-Empfangs-Umschalter *m*, [Sende-Empfangs-]Duplexer *m*, Sende-Empfangs-Weiche *f*
~-**to-receive delay** Sende-Empfangs-Verzögerung *f*
transmittance 1. Transmissivität *f*, Durchlässigkeit *f*; 2. *s.* ~ factor
~ **factor** Durchlässigkeitsgrad *m*, Transmissionsgrad *m*, Transmissionsfaktor *m*
transmitted illumination Durchlichtbeleuchtung *f*
~ **light** Durchlicht *n*, transmittiertes Licht *n*
~ **light fluorescence** Durchlichtfluoreszenz *f*
~-**light holography** Durchlichtholografie *f*
~-**light image** Durchlichtbild *n*
~-**light objective** Durchlichtobjektiv *n* *(Lichtmikroskopie)*
~-**light observation** Durchlichtbetrachtung *f*
~-**light photomacrography** Durchlichtmakrofotografie *f*
~-**light photomicrography** Durchlichtmikrofotografie *f*
~-**light technique** Durchlichtverfahren *n*
~ **medium** Ausgangsmedium *n*
~ **pulse** Sende[im]puls *m*
~ **radiation** transmittierte Strahlung *f*, Durchlassstrahlung *f*
~ **ray** transmittierter Strahl *m*
~ **wave** transmittierte Welle *f*
transmittent illumination Durchlichtbeleuchtung *f*
transmitter Transmitter *m*; Sender *m*
~ **end (side)** Sende[r]seite *f*
transmitting amplifier Sendeverstärker *m*
~ **antenna** Sendeantenne *f*
~ **engineering** Sendetechnik *f*
~ **facility** Sendeanlage *f*
~ **power** Sendeleistung *f*
~ **tower** Sendeturm *m*
~ **tube** Senderöhre *f*
transmodulation Transmodulation *f*
transmodulator Transmodulator *m*
transparency 1. Transparenz *f*, Lichtdurchlässigkeit *f*, Durchsichtigkeit *f*; 2. Fotopositiv *n*, Diapositiv *n*, transparentes Positiv *n*, durchscheinendes fotografisches Bild *n* *(s.a. unter slide)*

~ **film** 1. Dia[positiv]film *m*, Umkehrfilm *m*; 2. Kopierfolie *f*
~ **format** Diaformat *n*
~ **illuminator** Diabetrachter *m*
~ **image** 1. Durchsichtbild *n*, Durchlichtbild *n*, Transparentbild *n*; 2. *s.* transparency 2.
~ **printer** Diakopierer *m*, Diakopiergerät *n*
~ **projection** Diaprojektion *f*
~ **retouching** Diapositivretusche *f*
~ **scanner** Diascanner *m*, Diaabtaster *m*
~-**type color film** Umkehrfarbfilm *m*, Farbumkehrfilm *m*
~ **viewer** Diabetrachter *m*
transparent transparent, durchsichtig, lichtdurchlässig *(s.a. translucent)*
~ **color** durchscheinende (lasierende) Farbe *f*
~ **compression** verlustarme Kompression *f*
~ **copy** Durchsichtvorlage *f*
~ **electrode** transparente [leitende] Signalelektrode *f (Bildspeicherröhre)*
~ **ink** lasierende (durchscheinende) Druckfarbe *f*
~ **paint** Lasurfarbe *f*
~ **paper** Transparentpapier *n*
~ **to X rays** röntgendurchlässig
transponder Transponder *m* *(Satellitenübertragung)*
transport bitstream Bitstrom *m*
~ **data stream** Transport[daten]strom *m*
~ **layer** Transportschicht *f*
~ **layer protocol** Transportprotokoll *n* *(interaktives Fernsehen)*
~ **sprocket** Transportrolle *f*
~ **stream** Transport[daten]strom *m*
transposer Umsetzer *m (Fernsehtechnik)*
transprint Diaabzug *m*
transputer Transputer *m*, Dialogrechner *m*
transversal optical coherence tomography transversale [optische] Kohärenztomografie *f*
transverse aberration Queraberration *f*, Querabweichung *f*, außeraxialer Abbildungsfehler *m*
~ **axial tomographic image** *s.* ~ sectional slice image
~ **chromatic aberration** chromatische Queraberration (Brennweitendifferenz) *f*, Farbquerfehler *m*, lateraler Farbfehler *m*, Farbvergrößerungsfehler *m*
~ **curl** Querkräuselung *f (Bandfehler)*
~ **diffusion** Querdiffusion *f*
~ **Doppler effect** transversaler Doppler-Effekt *m*
~ **filter** Transversalfilter *n*
~ **magnetization** Quermagnetisierung *f*, Transversalmagnetisierung *f*, transversale Magnetisierung *f*
~ **magnification** Breitenvergrößerung *f*, transversale (laterale) Vergrößerung *f*, Seitenvergrößerung *f*
~ **mode** transversale Mode *f (Laser)*

~ **relaxation [time]** Querrelaxation[szeit] f, Transversalrelaxationszeit f, Querrelaxationszeitkonstante f, transversale Relaxation[szeit] f, Spin-Spin-Relaxationszeit f, T2
~ **resolution** Querauflösung f
~ **sectional slice image** Transversalschnittbild n, Transversalschichtbild n
~ **spherical aberration** sphärische Queraberration f
~ **tape recording** Querspuraufzeichnung f, Querspurverfahren n; Schrägspuraufzeichnung f
~ **tomography** Transversaltomografie f
~ **tomosynthesis** transversale Tomosynthese f
~ **wave** Transversalwelle f
trapezoidal distortion Trapezverzeichnung f, Trapezverzerrung f, Parallaxenverzerrung f
trapping Überfüllen n, Überfüllung f, Farbüberlappung f (Mehrfarbdruck)
~ **noise** Generations-Rekombinations-Rauschen n (Fotodetektor)
~ **site** Elektroneneinfangstelle f
trash can [elektronischer] Papierkorb m
travel photograph Reisefoto n
~ **photography** Reisefotografie f
~**-ray radiography** dynamische [industrielle] Radiografie f
~ **shot** Fahraufnahme f (Filmarbeit)
~ **tripod** Reisestativ n
traveling matte Wandermaske f (Trickkinematografie)
~**-matte process** Wandermaskenverfahren n, Wandermaskentrick m
~**-matte shot** Wandermaskenaufnahme f
~ **photographer** Reisefotograf m
~**-wave amplifier** Wanderwellenverstärker m
~**-wave antenna** Wanderwellenantenne f (Fernsehtechnik)
~**-wave tube** Wanderwellenröhre f
~**-wave tube amplifier** Wanderfeldröhrenverstärker m
travelling ... s. traveling ...
tray development Schalenentwicklung f (Fotoverarbeitung)
~ **processing** Schalenverarbeitung f
~ **rocking** Kippentwicklung f, Kippmethode f (Fotoverarbeitung)
~ **washing** Schalenwässerung f
treatment Treatment n, Rohdrehbuch n, Drehbuch-Vorstufe f
tree Baum m (Datenstruktur)
~ **[en]coding** Baumcodierung f
~**-and-branch architecture (design)** Baumstruktur f (Kabelfernsehsystem)
~**-based code** Baumcode m
~**-like data structure** s. tree structure
~ **node** Baumknoten m
~ **representation** Baumdarstellung f

~ **search [technique]** Baumsuche f (Vektorquantisierung)
~ **structure** Baumstruktur f, baumartige Datenstruktur f
~**-structured quantization** baumstrukturierte Quantisierung f
~**-structured vector quantization** baumstrukturierte Vektorquantisierung f
~**-structured wavelet transform** baumstrukturierte Wavelet-Transformation f
trellis-coded modulation trelliscodierte Modulation f
~**-coded quantization** trelliscodierte Quantisierung f
~ **coding** Trelliscodierung f
~ **diagram** Trellisdiagramm n, Netzdiagramm n, Spalierdiagramm n
~ **encoder** Trelliscodierer m
~ **representation** Trellisdarstellung f
tremor of the iris Iriszittern n, Hippus m
tri-receptor theory of color vision s. trichromatic theory of color vision
Triac Triac m (ein Zweirichtungsthyristor)
triacetate cellulose Cellulosetriacetat n (Filmmaterial)
~ **film base** Acetatunterlage f
triad Tripel n; Farbtripel n; Leuchtpunkttripel n (Farbbildröhre)
~ **dot** Tripelpunkt m
~ **spacing** Tripelabstand m
trial composite print Nullkopie f, Erstkopie f (Kinematografie)
~ **proof** Proof m, Andruck m (Druckvorstufe)
triangle 1. Dreieck n; 2. Bodenspinne f, Stativspinne f, Spinne f
~ **lattice (mesh)** s. triangular mesh
triangular dreieckig, triangulär
~ **B-spline surface patch** dreieckige B-Spline-Fläche f (Computergrafik)
~ **dot pattern** Dreiecksraster m(n) (Reprografie)
~ **mesh (network)** Dreiecksgitter n, Dreiecksnetz n
~ **prism** Dreikantprisma n
~ **waveform** Sägezahnkurve f
triangulate/to triangulieren
triangulation Triangulation[smessung] f, Triangulierung f; Kreuzpeilung f
~ **rangefinder** Spiegelsucher m
~ **scanner** Triangulationstaster m
triboelectric triboelektrisch
triboelectricity Triboelektrizität f, Reibungselektrizität f
triboluminescence Triboluminszenz f
trichromacy Trichromasie f, Trichromazität f, Dreifarbensehen f
~ **of vision** s. trichromatic vision
~ **theory of light** 1. Dreifarbentheorie f des Lichts; 2. s. trichromatic theory of color vision
trichromat Trichromat m
trichromatic trichromatisch, dreifarbig

trichromatic

~ **color photography** Dreifarbenfotografie f
~ **colorimetric** dreifarbenkolorimetrisch
~ **light** trichromatisches Licht n
~ **print** Dreifarbendruck m *(Erzeugnis)*
~ **printing** Dreifarbendruck m
~ **system** Dreifarbensystem n
~ **theory of color vision** Dreikomponententheorie f des Farbensehens, trichromatische (Young-Helmholzsche) Theorie f des Farbensehens
~ **vision** trichromatisches Farbensehen n, Dreifarbensehen n

trichromatism s. trichromacy

trick Trick m; optische Täuschung f
~ **cinematography** Trickkinematografie f
~ **electronic photography** elektronische Trickfotografie f
~ **film** Trickfilm m, Animationsfilm m, Effektfilm m
~ **perspective** Trickperspektive f
~ **photography** Trickfotografie f
~ **shot** Trick[film]aufnahme f, Effektaufnahme f

tricolor cathode-ray tube, ~ CRT Dreifarbenröhre f
~ **image** Dreifarbenbild n
~ **ink-jet print cartridge** Dreikammer-Farbdruckpatrone f, Dreikammer-Farbtintenpatrone f
~ **system** Dreifarbensystem n

tricubic trikubisch
tridimensional dreidimensional, räumlich
tridimensionality Dreidimensionalität f
trifocal tensor Trifokaltensor m, trifokaler Tensor m
trigger/to auslösen, triggern
trigger Auslöser m, Auslöseknopf m
~ **circuit** Steuerimpulsgeber m *(Radar)*
~ **pulse** Auslöseimpuls m
triggerable triggerbar
triggering device Auslösevorrichtung f
~ **system** Auslösesystem n
trigonometric function trigonometrische Funktion f, Winkelfunktion f
~ **polynomial** trigonometrisches Polynom n
triiodide Trijodid n *(fotografische Chemie)*
trilinear interpolation trilineare Interpolation f
trim/to beschneiden, zuschneiden *(z.B. Fotos)*
trim off/to abschneiden
~ **bin** Filmgalgen m *(Schneideraum)*
~ **mark** Beschnittmarke f, Beschnittzeichen n
~ **point** Schnittpunkt m, Schnittstelle f
~ **size** s. trimmed size
trimetal plate Trimetallplatte f *(Drucktechnik)*
trimetric projection trimetrische Projektion (Axonometrie) f, Trimetrie f

trimmed size Endformat n, beschnittenes Format n *(z.B. eines Druckprodukts)*
trimmer Schneidemaschine f
trimming Beschneidung f, Beschnitt m
~ **edge** Beschnittkante f
trims Filmschnitzel npl, Ausschnitte mpl, Herausschnitt m *(Filmbearbeitung)*
trinocular Trinokular n
~ **camera** dreiäugige Kamera f
~ **stereo vision** trinokulares Stereosehen n
~ **vision** dreiäugiges Sehen n
trip/to auslösen *(z.B. den Kameraverschluss)*
tripack, ~ color [negative] film Tripack-Film m, Monopack n
triphenylamine Triphenylamin n
triple 1. Tripel n; 2. s. triplet [lens]
~ **coating** Dreifachvergütung f
~ **extension** Dreifachauszug m *(Fachkamera)*
~ **extension bellows** dreifacher Balgenauszug m
~**-layer color film** Dreischichtenfarbfilm m
~ **mirror** Tripelspiegel m
~ **reflector** Tripelreflektor m
~ **self-timer** Dreifach-Selbstauslöser m *(Digitalkamera)*
~ **sensor scanner** Dreipassscanner m
~**-take** Schnitt m beim Drehen, Drehen n auf Schnitt *(Filmarbeit)*
~ **zoom** Dreifachzoom[objektiv] n
triplet [lens], ~ objective Triplett n, Dreilinser m, dreilinsiges Objektiv n
~ **production** Tripelbildung f *(Teilchenphysik)*
tripod Dreibein[stativ] n; Stativ n
~ **case** Stativtasche f
~ **clamp** Stativklemme f
~ **column** Stativsäule f
~ **connection (coupler)** Stativanschluss m
~ **head** Statikopf m, Stativaufsatz m
~ **head control arm** Stativschwenkarm m
~ **holder** Stativhalterung f
~ **leg** Stativbein n
~ **mount** Stativanschluss m, Stativkupplung f
~**-mounted camera** Stativkamera f
~ **platform** Stativkopfplatte f
~ **screw** Stativschraube f
~ **shot** Stativaufnahme f
~ **socket** Stativgewinde n; Stativbuchse f
~ **spreader** Bodenspinne f, Spinne f *(Stativzubehör)*
~ **strap** Stativtraggurt m
~ **tray** Stativablage f
trispectral image RGB-Bild n
tristimulus colorimeter Dreibereichs-Farbmessgerät n
~ **method** Dreibereichsverfahren n, Helligkeitsverfahren n *(Farbmetrik)*
~ **value** Tristimuluswert m, Farbvalenz f, Farbwert m, trichromatische Farbmaßzahl f

~ **value calculation** Farbvalenzberechnung f
tritanomaly Tritanomalie f, Tritanstörung f, Blauschwäche f, angeborene Blau-Gelb-Störung f *(Farbsinnstörung)*
tritanope Tritanop m
tritanopia Tritanopie f, Blaublindheit f, Blau-Gelb-Blindheit f *(Farbsinnstörung)*
tritanopic blaublind
trixel Trixel n *(dreidimensionales Bildelement)*
troland Troland n *(Einheit der Netzhautbeleuchtungsstärke)*
tropical developer Tropenentwickler m
~ **processing** Tropenentwicklung f
truck [höhenverstellbarer] Kamerawagen m; Fahrstativ n, fahrbares Stativ n, Rollstativ n, Fahrspinne f, Stativwagen m
~ **in/to** heranfahren, zubewegen *(Filmkameraarbeit)*
~ **out/to** wegbewegen *(Filmkameraarbeit)*
~ **shot** Fahraufnahme f *(Filmarbeit)*
trucking Kamerafahrt f, Verfolgungsschwenk m, Mitziehen n [der Kamera] *(Filmarbeit)*
true absorption wahre Absorption f
~ **color** 1. Echtfarbe f, originalgetreue Farbe f; 2. *bezeichnet die 24-Bit-Farbtiefe eines Displaysystems*
~-**color holography** Echtfarbenholografie f
~-**color image (picture)** Echtfarbenbild n
~ **edge** echte (reale) Kante f
~ **fish-eye** Fischaugenobjektiv n
~ **image** wahres Bild n
~ **panoramic camera** echte Panoramakamera f
~ **photographic quality** Fotoqualität f *(digitaler Bildwiedergabe)*
~ **signal** Nutzsignal n, Nachrichtensignal n, artefaktfreies Signal n
~ **telephoto[graphic] lens** [echtes] Tele[foto]objektiv n, Fernobjektiv n, Fernbildlinse f, Teleoptik f
~ **to scale** maßstäblich, maßstabsgerecht, maßstabsgleich
~ **zoom lens** echtes Zoom[objektiv] n
trueness to scale Maßstabstreue f
truncate/to stutzen, kappen, abschneiden
truncation Abschneiden n, Stutzung f, Trunkierung f *(digitale Filterung; Computergrafik)*
~ **artifact** Verstümmelungsartefakt n, Gibbs-Artefakt n, Gibbssches Phänomen n *(Bildverarbeitung)*
~ **error** Abschneidefehler m
truth table Wahrheits[werte]tafel f *(Aussagenlogik)*
TTL ... s. through-the-lens ...
~ **automatic flash** TTL-Blitzautomatik f
~ **full-aperture exposure metering [system]** Offenblenden-Innenmessung f
~ **metering** Innen[licht]messung f
~ **phase detection** TTL-Phasenerkennung f *(Spiegelreflexkamera)*

tube Tubus m, Zwischentubus m
~ **characteristic** Bildröhrenkennlinie f
~ **current** Röhrenstrom m
~ **drive voltage** Röhrenspannung f
~ **envelope** Röhrenkolben m
~ **extension** Tubusauszug m
~ **face** Bildröhrenoberfläche f
~ **imager** Röhrenbildwandler m, Röhrensensor m
~ **kilovoltage** s. ~ voltage
~ **length** Tubuslänge f
~ **lens** Tubuslinse f
~ **neck** Röhrenhals m
~ **processing** Röhrenentwicklung f *(Fotoverarbeitung)*
~-**type camera** 1. Tubuskamera f; 2. s. tube-type video camera
~-**type video camera** Röhren[video]kamera f
~ **voltage** Röhrenspannung f, Beschleunigungsspannung f *(Katodenstrahlröhre)*
tubular fluorescent lamp Leucht[stoff]röhre f, Fluoreszenzröhre f
~ **lamp** Soffitte[nlampe] f
~ **vision** Tunnelblick m, Röhrensehen n *(Sehstörung)*
tumor detection Tumordetektion f
tunability Durchstimmbarkeit f, Abstimmbarkeit f *(z.B. von Lasern)*
tunable durchstimmbar, abstimmbar
~ **dye laser** abstimmbarer Farbstofflaser m
~ **filter** einstellbares (steuerbares) Filter n
~ **frequency** abstimmbare Frequenz f
~ **infrared laser** abstimmbarer Infrarotlaser m
~ **laser** abstimmbarer Laser m
~ **semiconductor laser** [frequenz]abstimmbarer Halbleiterlaser m
tune/to abstimmen, durchstimmen
tuner Tuner m
~ **dial** Kanalwähler m *(Fernsehgerät)*
tungsten Wolfram n, Tungsten n
~-**balanced film** Kunstlichtfilm m
~-**balanced reversal film** Kunstlichtdiafilm m
~ **color film** Kunstlichtfarbfilm m
~ **conditions** Kunstlichtbedingungen pl
~ **filament lamp** s. ~ lamp
~ **halide (halogen) lamp** Wolframhalogenlampe f, Halogenglühlampe f, Quarz[halogenglüh]lampe f
~ **lamp** Glühlampe f, Glühbirne f; Wolframglühlampe f, Wolframwendellampe f; Wolframfadenlampe f
~ **light** Glüh[lampen]licht n
~ **light source** Wolframlichtquelle f
~ **wire filament** Wolfram[glüh]wendel f
tuning Abstimmung f
~ **range** Abstimmbereich f

tunnel

tunnel effect [quantenmechanischer] Tunneleffekt *m*
~-type dryer Tunneltrockner *m* *(Filmherstellung)*
~ vision Tunnelblick *m*, Röhrensehen *n* *(Sehstörung)*
tunneling [quantenmechanisches] Tunneln *n*
~ acoustic microscope akustisches Tunnelmikroskop *n*
~ current Tunnelstrom *m*
~ electron tunnelndes Elektron *n*
tupel, tuple Tupel *n (morphologische Bildverarbeitung)*
turbulation Durchsprudelung *f (Filmverarbeitung)*
turn off/to austasten, dunkeltasten, dunkelsteuern *(Videosignal)*
turning bar Wendestange *f (Rollendruckmaschine)*
turnstile antenna Schmetterlingsantenne *f (Fernsehtechnik)*
turntable Plattenteller *m*
turret Objektivrevolver *m*, Revolverkopf *m*
~ eyepiece Revolverokular *n*
~-front camera Aufnahmekamera *f* mit Revolverkopf
TV ... *s.a. unter* television
TV aerial Fernsehantenne *f*
TV broadcast signal Fernseh-Sendesignal *n*
TV broadcast technology Fernsehtechnik *f*
TV camera Fernsehkamera *f*
TV camera operator Fernsehkameramann *m*
TV channel Fernseh[programm]kanal *m*
TV commercial Fernsehspot *m*, Fernseh-Werbefilm *m*
TV-enabled PC fernsehtauglicher Personalcomputer *m*
TV field Fernseh-Teilbild *n*
TV image sequence Fernsehbildsequenz *f*, Fernsehbildserie *f*, Fernsehbildfolge *f*
TV mask Fernseh-Kasch *m*
TV motion-picture film, TV movie Filmsendekopie *f*; Fernseh[spiel]film *m*
TV news Fernsehnachrichten *fpl*
TV newsroom Fernsehnachrichtenstudio *n*
TV pickup tube Fernsehkameraröhre *f*, Fernseh[bild]aufnahmeröhre *f*, Fernseh-Bildspeicherröhre *f*
TV-picture enhancement Fernsehbildverbesserung *f*
TV picture projection Fernsehbildprojektion *f*
TV rate Videobildfrequenz *f*, Videorate *f*
TV screen format Fernsehbild[schirm]format *n*
TV screen image Fernsehbild *n*
TV set Fernseh[empfäng]er m, Fernsehgerät *n*, Fernsehapparat *m*
TV set antenna Fernsehantenne *f*
TV set image Fernsehbild *n*
TV sharpness Fernsehbildschärfe *f*

TV shearogram TV-Shearogramm *n*
TV shearography TV-Shearografie *f*
TV signal Fernsehsignal *n*
TV sound Fernseh[begleit]ton *m*
TV station Fernsehstation *f*; Fernsehsender *m*
TV tuner card Fernseh[tuner]karte *f*, TV-Tunerkarte *f*, TV-Karte *f*
TV user Fernsehkonsument *m*
TV vacuum tube Fernsehröhre *f*
TV video channel Fernseh-Videokanal *m*
Twain-compliant program Twain-kompatibles Programm *n (Scannersoftware)*
~ driver Twain-Treiber *m*
~ interface Twain-Schnittstelle *f (Scannertechnik)*
~ standard Twain-Standard *m*
tweezers Pinzette *f (z.B. als Handsatzwerkzeug)*
twilight Dämmerung *f*, Zwielicht *n*
~ efficiency Dämmerungsleistung *f (Teleskop)*
~ factor Dämmerungszahl *f (Fernglas)*
twin boundary Zwillingsgrenze *f (Elektronenmikroskopie)*
~ drive Doppellaufwerk *n*
~ image Zwillingsbild *n (Holografie)*
~-lens camera Doppelkamera *f*, Raumbildkamera *f*, Stereokamera *f*
~-lens-reflex [camera] zweiäugige Spiegelreflexkamera *f*
~-sprocket stock doppelseitig (zweiseitig) perforierter Film *m*
twisted nematic liquid crystal gedrillter nematischer Flüssigkristall *m*
~ nematic liquid crystal cell verdrillt nematische Zelle *f*
~ nematic liquid crystal display Feldeffekt-Flüssigkristallanzeige *f*
twitter Zwischenzeilenflimmern *n*
two-bath development Zweibadentwicklung *f*
~-bath fixation (fixing) Zweibadfixierung *f*
~-beam case Zweistrahlfall *m (Elektronenbeugung)*
~-beam interference Zweistrahlinterferenz *f*
~-beam interferometry Zweistrahlinterferometrie *f*
~-bladed shutter Zweiflügelblende *f (Filmprojektor)*
~-button reset Schnellrückstellung *f (Kamera)*
~-channel recording Zweikanalaufnahme *f*
~-channel stereophony Zweikanal-Stereofonie *f*
~-color zweifarbig, bichrom; dichromatisch
~-color gravure press Zweifarbentiefdruckpresse *f*
~-color halftone image Duotonabbildung *f*, Zweifarben-Rasterbild *n*
~-color image Zweifarbenbild *n*

~-**color machine** Zweifarbenmaschine *f (Druck)*
~-**color photography** Zweifarbenfotografie *f*
~-**color rotary press** *s.* ~ machine
~-**component developer** Zweikomponentenentwickler *m*
~-**component system** Zweikomponentensystem *n (z.B. der Farbfotografie)*
~-**dimensional** zweidimensional
~-**dimensional animation** zweidimensionale Animation *f*
~-**dimensional array detector** [Halbleiter-]Flächendetektor *m*, flächiger (flächenauflösender) Detektor *m*
~-**dimensional convolution** zweidimensionale Faltung *f*
~-**dimensional DCT** zweidimensionale diskrete Kosinustransformation *f*
~-**dimensional discrete convolution** diskrete zweidimensionale Faltung *f*
~-**dimensional echo** zweidimensionales Echo *n*
~-**dimensional filter** zweidimensionales Filter *n*
~-**dimensional Fourier transform** zweidimensionale Fourier-Transformation *f*
~-**dimensional function** zweidimensionale Funktion *f*
~-**dimensional graphics** zweidimensionale Computergrafik *f*
~-**dimensional histogram** zweidimensionales Histogramm *n*
~-**dimensional hologram** zweidimensionales Hologramm *n*
~-**dimensional image** zweidimensionales Bild *n*
~-**dimensional image processing** zweidimensionale Bildverarbeitung *f*
~-**dimensional Markov process** zweidimensionaler Markow-Prozess *m*
~-**dimensional object** zweidimensionales Objekt *n*
~-**dimensional photodiode array** Diodenmatrix *f*
~-**dimensional representation** zweidimensionale Darstellung *f*
~-**dimensional scanning** zweidimensionale Abtastung *f*
~-**dimensional signal** zweidimensionales Signal *n*
~-**dimensional transform coding** zweidimensionale Transformationscodierung *f*
~-**dimensionality** Zweidimensionalität *f*
~-**element achromat** Vorsatzachromat *m*
~-**equivalent coupler** Zweiäquivalentkuppler *m*, zweiwertiger Kuppler *m (Farbfotografie)*
~-**eyed vision** beidäugiges (binokulares) Sehen *n*, Binokularsehen *n*, Simultansehen *n*

~-**inch helical scan machine** Zwei-Zoll-Schrägspurmaschine *f*
~-**inch videotape** Zwei-Zoll-Band *n*
~-**layer coding** Zweischichtencodierung *f (von Videodaten)*
~-**lens Abbe condenser** zweistufiger Kondensor *m*
~-**lens microscope** zusammengesetztes Mikroskop *n*
~-**lens system** Zweilinsensystem *n*
~-**letter matrix** Zweibuchstabenmatrize *f*
~-**level image** 1. binäres Bild *n*, Binärbild *n*; 2. bitonales Bild *n*, Doppeltonbild *n*
~-**mirror planar resonator** Fabry-Perot-Resonator *m*
~-**page spread** Doppelseite *f (Layout)*
~-**part compound lens** zweiteiliges Objektiv *n*
~-**phase CCD [image sensor]** Zwei-Phasen-CCD-Bildsensor *m*
~-**phase CCD shift register** Zweiphasen-CCD-Schieberegister *n*
~-**photon excitation microscope** Zweiphotonenmikroskop *n*
~-**photon [laser scanning] fluorescence microscopy** Zweiphotonenmikroskopie *f*
~-**photon spectroscopy** Zweiphotonenspektroskopie *f*
~-**point perspective** Zweipunktperspektive *f*, Winkelperspektive *f*
~-**point probability density function** Grauwertabhängigkeitsmatrix *f*, Paarhäufigkeitsmatrix *f*, Grauwertübergangsmatrix *f*
~-**point resolution** Zweipunktauflösung *f*
~-**revolution [cylinder] press** Zweitourenmaschine *f (Hochdruck)*
~-**shot self-timer** Doppelselbstauslöser *m*
~-**sided copy** doppelseitige Kopie *f*
~-**slit interference** Doppelspaltinterferenz *f*
~-**slit interference pattern** Doppelspalt-Interferenzbild *n*
~-**solution developer** Zweibadentwickler *m*
~-**state system** bistabiles System *n*
~-**tone paper** Duplexpapier *n*
~-**touch zoom** Zweiringzoom[objektiv] *n*
~-**value picture** Zweipegelbild *n*
~-**wavelengths microscope** Zweiwellenlängenmikroskop *n*
~-**way interface** bidirektionale Schnittstelle *f*
~-**way trap** Schleusengang *m (Dunkelraumzugang)*
Tyndall effect Tyndall-Effekt *m (Lichtstreuung an kleinsten Teilchen)*
type 1. Schrift *f*; Druckschrift *f*, gedruckte Schrift *f*; 2. Type *f*, Drucktype *f*; Druckbuchstabe *m*, Letter *f*
~ **area** Satzbild *n*, Satzspiegel *m*
~ **body** Typenkörper *m*, Letter *f*
~ **casting** Typenguss *m*
~ **character** Druckzeichen *n*
~ **composition** Typensatz *m*

type 410

~ **cutter** Schriftschneider *m*
~ **design** Schriftdesign *n*
~ **family** Schrift[art]familie *f*, Schriftsippe *f*; Schrifttyp *m*
~ **font** Schriftart *f*; Zeichensatz *m*
~ **height** Schrifthöhe *f*
~ **line** Typenzeile *f*
~ **of editing** Schnittart *f*
~ **of file** Dateityp *m*
~ **of film** Filmtyp *m*; Filmart *f*; Filmsorte *f*
~ **of glass** Glassorte *f*
~ **of light** Lichtart *f*
~ **of paper** Papiersorte *f*
~ **page** *s.* ~ area
~ **piece** Type *f*, Drucktype *f*, Druckbuchstabe *m*, Letter *f*
~ **size** Schriftgrad *m*; Schrifthöhe *f*, Schriftgröße *f*, Glyphenhöhe *f*
~ **wheel** Typenrad *n*, Typenscheibe *f*, Druckrad *n*
~ **wheel printer** Typenraddrucker *m*
typecase Setzkasten *m*
~ **frame** Matrizenrahmen *m*
typecaster 1. Schriftgießer *m*; 2. Buchstabengießmaschine *f*, Letterngießmaschine *f*, Gießmaschine *f*
typecasting Schriftguss *m*
~ **compositor** Buchstabensetz- und -gießmaschine *f*
~ **machine** *s.* typecaster
typeface 1. Schriftbild *n*, Schriftschnitt *m*, Schriftstil *m*, Schrift *f*; 2. Schriftgattung *f*, Schrift *f*; Zeichensatz *m*; 3. Druckformoberfläche *f*
~ **alphabet** Schriftalphabet *n*
~ **designer** *s.* typographer
~-**font printer** Typendrucker *m*
typefounder Schriftgießer *m*
typefounding Schriftguss *m*
typefoundry Schriftgießerei *f*
typescript Typoskript *n*; Maschinenschrift *f*
typeset/to setzen
typesetter 1. Setzer *m*, Schriftsetzer *m*, Satzgestalter *m*; *s.* typesetting machine
typesetting Satz *m*, Satzherstellung *f*
~ **department** Setzerei *f (Druckbetrieb)*
~ **machine** Satzmaschine *f*, Setzmaschine *f*
~ **system** Setzsystem *n*
~ **technology** Satztechnik *f*
~ **unit** Satzsystem *n*
typestyle *s.* typeface 1.
typewriter Schreibmaschine *f*
typicality, typicalness Typizität *f*
typing paper Schreibmaschinenpapier *n*, SM-Papier *n*
typo *s.* typographical error
typographer Typograf *m*, Schriftgrafiker *m*, gestaltender Schriftsetzer *m*
typographic typografisch; drucktechnisch
~ **color** typografische Farbe *f*
~ **copy** typografische Vorlage *f*
~ **grid** typografischer Raster *m*
typographical character typografisches Zeichen *n*, Glyphe *f*

~ **error** Druckfehler *m*, Erratum *n*
~ **point** typografischer Punkt *m*, Didot-Punkt *m*, p
~ **point system** typografisches Punktsystem *n*, Didot-System *n*
typography 1. Typografie *f*; 2. Buchdruck *m*

U

UHF s. ultrahigh frequency
ultor s. anode
ultra bold extrafett *(Schriftauszeichnung)*
~ extended graphics array Grafikstandard mit 1.600 x 1.200 Pixel Auflösung
~ hard ultrahart *(Fotopapiergradation)*
ultracompact camera Ultrakompaktkamera f
ultracondenser Ultrakondensor m *(Elektronenmikroskop)*
ultrafast computed tomography, ~ CT ultraschnelle Computertomografie f
~ imaging ultraschnelle Bildgebung f
~ laser Kurzpulslaser m
~ lens ultralichtstarkes Objektiv n
~ spectroscopy ultraschnelle Spektroskopie f
ultrafiltration Ultrafiltration f
ultrafine-grain developer Ultrafeinkornentwickler m, Feinstkornentwickler m
~ resolution Höchstauflösung f
ultrahard X-rays ultraharte Röntgenstrahlung f
ultrahigh frequency Ultrahochfrequenz f, ultrahohe Frequenz f, UHF
~ frequency wave range Dezimeterwellenbereich m
~ pressure mercury lamp Ultrahochdruck-Quecksilberdampflampe f
~ resolution Ultrahochauflösung f
~-speed camera Ultrahochgeschwindigkeitskamera f
~-speed cinematography Ultrahochgeschwindigkeitskinematografie f
~-speed film ultrahochempfindlicher Film m
~-speed photography Ultrahochgeschwindigkeitsfotografie f
ultramicroelectrode Ultramikroelektrode f
ultramicroscope Ultramikroskop n
ultramicroscopic[al] ultramikroskopisch
ultramicroscopy Ultramikroskopie f, Dunkelfeldmikroskopie f
ultramicrotome Ultramikrotom n
ultraminiature camera Kleinst[bild]kamera f
~ projector Kleinstprojektor m
ultrarapid lens ultralichtstarkes Objektiv n
ultrared ultrarot, infrarot *(s.a. unter infrared)*
ultrashort framing exposure ultrakurze Belichtungszeit f
~ pulse laser Ultrakurzpulslaser m
~ time exposure Ultrakurzzeitbelichtung f

ultrasonic ultrasonisch *(s.a. unter ultrasound)*
~ absorption coefficient Ultraschallabsorptionskoeffizient m
~ beam Ultraschallstrahl m
~ cleaner Ultraschall-Reinigungsgerät n
~ cleaning Ultraschallreinigung f
~ computed tomography Ultraschall-Computertomografie f
~ detection Ultraschalldetektion f
~ diagnosis Ultraschalldiagnostik f
~ echo signal Ultraschallsignal n
~ energy Ultraschallenergie f
~ examination s. ~ inspection
~ image processing Ultraschallbildverarbeitung f
~ image recorder, ~ imager Ultraschall[bildaufzeichnungs]gerät n, Sonografiegerät n
~ imaging Ultraschallbildgebung f, Ultraschallsichtverfahren n, Ultraschalldarstellung f, Ultrasonografie f, Sonografie f
~ inspection Ultraschallprüfung f, Ultraschalluntersuchung f, Ultraschalldefektoskopie f
~ medical image medizinisches Ultraschallbild n
~ microscope Ultraschallmikroskop n
~ microscopy Ultraschallmikroskopie f
~ microspectrometer Ultraschall-Mikrospektrometer n
~ nondestructive testing zerstörungsfreie Ultraschallprüfung f
~ plane wave ebene Ultraschallwelle f
~ pulse Ultraschallimpuls m
~ sensing device Ultraschallgerät n, Sonografiegerät n
~ sensor Ultraschallsensor m
~ signal Ultraschallsignal n
~ signal amplifier Ultraschallsignalverstärker m
~ speckle Ultraschall-Speckle n
~ spherical wave Ultraschall-Kugelwelle f
~ technology Ultraschalltechnik f
~ test equipment Ultraschallprüfgerät n
~ transmission camera Ultraschall-Transmissionskamera f
~ transmitter Ultraschallsender m, Schwinger m
~ vibration Ultraschallschwingung f
ultrasonogram Echogramm n, Sonogramm n, sonografisches Bild n
ultrasonographic sonografisch
ultrasonography Ultraschalltechnik f, Sonografie f *(s.a. ultrasonic imaging)*
ultrasound 1. Ultraschall m *(s.a. unter ultrasonic)*; 2. Ultraschalltechnik f, Sonografie f
~ B mode image B-Mode-Bild n
~ B mode imaging B-Bild-Sonografie f, B-Bildverfahren n, zweidimensionale Sonografie f
~ cartography Ultraschallkartografie f

ultrasound 412

~ **clinician** Ultraschalldiagnostiker *m*
~ **color Doppler system** farbcodierte Doppler-Sonografie *f*
~ **contrast agent (medium)** Ultraschallkontrastmittel *n*
~ **echo** Ultraschallecho *n*
~ **echo leading edge** Eintrittsecho *n* *(Sonografie)*
~ **echo trailing edge** Austrittsecho *n* *(Sonografie)*
~ **frequency** Ultraschallfrequenz *f*
~ **hologram** Ultraschallhologramm *n*, Sonohologramm *n*
~ **holography** Ultraschallholografie *f*, Sonoholografie *f*
~ **image** Ultraschallbild *n*, sonografisches Bild *n*, Sonogramm *n*
~ **image acquisition** Ultraschallaufnahme *f*
~ **image reconstruction** Ultraschallbildrekonstruktion *f*
~ **image resolution** Ultraschallbildauflösung *f*
~ **imaging artifact** Ultraschallbildartefakt *n*
~ **imaging system** Ultraschalldiagnostiksystem *n*
~ **imaging technique** s. ultrasonic imaging
~ **intensity** Ultraschallintensität *f*
~ **M-mode imaging** M-Bildverfahren *n*, M-Mode-Verfahren *n* *(Sonografie)*
~**-modulated optical tomography** s. ultrasound transmission tomography
~ **probe** Ultraschallsonde *f*, Schallsonde *f*
~ **propagative speed** Ultraschallausbreitungsgeschwindigkeit *f*
~ **ray** Ultraschallstrahl *m*
~ **receiver** Ultraschallempfänger *m*
~ **reflection** Ultraschallreflexion *f*
~ **scan** Ultraschallscan *m*
~ **scan head,** ~ **scanner** Ultraschallmesskopf *m*, Ultraschallscanner *m*, Ultraschall[prüf]kopf *m*, Schallkopf *m*, Schallsonde *f*
~ **transducer** Ultraschallwandler *m*, Schallwandler *m*, Ultraschallschwinger *m*, Ultraschallgeber *m*
~ **transmission tomography** Ultraschalltomografie *f*, Durchschallungstomografie *f*, Sonotomografie *f*, Ultraschall-Schnittbildverfahren *n*
~ **unit** Ultraschall[bildaufzeichnungs]gerät *n*, Sonografiegerät *n*
~ **wave** Ultraschallwelle *f*
~ **wavelength** Ultraschallwellenlänge *f*
ultraspectral sensor ultraspektraler Sensor *m*
ultraspectrography Ultraspektrografie *f*
ultraspeed film höchstempfindlicher Film *m*
ultraviolet ultraviolett
~ Ultraviolett *n*
~ **absorber** UV-Absorber *m*

~**-absorbing filter** Ultraviolettsperrfilter *n*
~**-absorbing glass** UV-absorbierendes Glas *n*
~ **absorption layer** UV-Absorptionsfilterschicht *f*, UV-Filterschicht *f*
~ **catastrophe** UV-Katastrophe *f* *(Theorie der elektromagnetischen Strahlung)*
~ **coating** UV-Lackierung *f* *(von Druckerzeugnissen)*
~ **diode laser** UV-Diodenlaser *m*
~ **emission** UV-Emission *f*
~ **exposure** UV-Belichtung *f*
~ **filter** Ultraviolettfilter *n*
~ **filter layer** s. ~ absorption layer
~ **filtration** UV-Filterung *f*
~ **fluorescence** UV-Fluoreszenz *f*
~ **fluorescence microscopy** UV-Fluoreszenzmikroskopie *f*
~ **fluorescence photography** UV-Fluoreszenzfotografie *f*
~ **grating** Ultraviolettgitter *n*
~ **illumination** UV-Beleuchtung *f*
~ **lamp** Ultraviolettlampe *f*
~ **laser** Ultraviolettlaser *m*
~ **laser lithography** UV-Laserlithografie *f*
~ **lens** Ultraviolett-Objektiv *n*, UV-Linse *f*
~ **light** ultraviolettes Licht *n*, UV-Licht *n*
~ **light microscopy** Ultraviolettmikroskopie *f*
~ **luminescence** UV-Lumineszenz *f*
~ **microscope** Fluoreszenzmikroskop *n*
~ **microscope** Ultraviolettmikroskop *n*, Fluoreszenzmikroskop *n*
~ **photograph** UV-Foto *n*
~ **photography** Ultraviolettfotografie *f*
~ **photomicrography** Ultraviolettmikrofotografie *f*
~ **photon** UV-Photon *n*
~ **radiation** UV-Strahlung *f*
~**-radiation image** UV-Bildwandler *n*
~ **radiation protection** UV-Schutz *m*
~ **ray** UV-Strahl *m*
~ **region** UV-Bereich *m*
~**-sensitive** ultraviolettempfindlich
~**-sensitive contact film** UV-empfindlicher Kontaktfilm *m*
~ **sensor** UV-Sensor *m*
~ **source** UV-Lichtquelle *f*
~ **spectrograph** Ultraviolettspektrograf *m*
~ **spectrum** UV-Spektrum *n*
~ **telescope** UV-Teleskop *n*
ultrawide-angle [focal-length] lens Ultraweitwinkelobjektiv *n*, Superweitwinkelobjektiv *n*, extremes Weitwinkelobjektiv *n*
~**-angle photography** Überweitwinkelfotografie *f*
~**-lens camera** Ultraweitwinkelkamera *f*
umbra Kernschatten *m*
umbrella Schirmreflektor *m*, Studioschirm *m*
umlaut mark Umlautzeichen *n*

unaberrated aberrationsfrei, abbildungsfehlerfrei, bildfehlerfrei
unaccommodated eye fernakkommodiertes Auge *n*
unaided eye unbewaffnetes Auge *n*
unamplified signal unverstärktes Signal *n*
unauthorized copy Raubkopie *f*
~ **duplication** Raubkopierung *f*
unbiased estimation erwartungstreue Schätzung *f*
unblanked line time aktive Zeilendauer *f*
uncemented unverkittet
uncertainty relation[ship] Unschärferelation *f*
uncial Unziale *f*, Unzialschrift *f*; Unzialbuchstabe *m*
~ **letter** Unzialbuchstabe *m*
uncoated glass unvergütetes Glas *n*
~ **paper** maschinenglattes (ungestrichenes) Papier *n*; Naturpapier *n*
~ **printing paper** ungestrichenes Druckpapier *n*
uncoded uncodiert
uncolored unbunt, achromatisch *(Farbmetrik)*
uncompress/to dekomprimieren; entzerren *(anamorphotische Bilder)*
uncompressed signal unkomprimiertes Signal *n*
uncorrectable error unkorrigierbarer Fehler *m*
uncorrected lens unkorrigiertes Objektiv *n*
uncorrelated jitter unkorrelierter Jitter *m*
~ **noise** unkorreliertes Rauschen *n*
~ **random field** unkorreliertes Zufallsfeld *n*
uncut original negative ungeschnittenes Originalnegativ *n*
under-replenishment Unterregenerierung *f* *(von Verarbeitungslösungen)*
undercolor addition Unterfarbenzugabe *f*, Buntfarbenaddition *f (Reprografie)*
~ **removal** Unterfarbenentfernung *f*, Unterfarbenkorrektur *f*, Unterfarbenrücknahme *f (Reprografie)*
undercorrection Unterkorrektion *f (eines Objektivs)*
undercranking Unterdrehen *n (Filmarbeit)*
underdevelop/to unterentwickeln
underdevelopment Unterentwicklung *f*
underexpose/to unterbelichten
underexposure Unterbelichtung *f*
underfixed unterfixiert
underfixing Unterfixierung *f*
underflow Unterlauf *m*, Grauwertunterlauf *m (Digitalbild)*
underfocus/to unterfokussieren
underfocusing Unterfokussierung *f*
undersample/to unterabtasten
undersampling Unterabtastung *f*
underscan/to unterabtasten
underscan Zeilenklaffung *f (Fernerkundung)*
underscanning Unterabtastung *f*

underscore Musikuntermalung *f*; Untermalungsmusik *f*
undersegmentation Untersegmentierung *f*
underside Unterseite *f*
underwater camera Unterwasserkamera *f*
~ **case** Unterwassergehäuse *n*
~ **cinematography** Unterwasserkinematografie *f*
~ **electronic flash** Unterwasserblitzgerät *n*
~ **housing** Unterwassergehäuse *n*
~ **lens** Unterwasserobjektiv *n*
~ **mapping** Unterwasserkartierung *f*
~ **photograph** Unterwasseraufnahme *f*
~ **photography** Unterwasserfotografie *f*
~ **shot** Unterwasseraufnahme *f*
~ **sonar image** Sonarbild *n*
~ **television camera** Unterwasserfernsehkamera *f*
undetectable undetektierbar
undeveloped film unentwickelter Film *m*
undeviated light ungebeugtes (direktes) Licht *n*
undirected graph ungerichteter Graph *m*
undispersed light unzerlegtes Licht *n*
undistorted unverzeichnet, unverzerrt, verzeichnungsfrei, verzerrungsfrei
~ **image (picture)** unverzerrtes Bild *n*, unverzerrte Abbildung *f*
undulator Undulator *m*, Wiggler *m (Magnet)*
undulatory radiation Wellenstrahlung *f*
~ **theory [of light]** Wellentheorie (Undulationstheorie) *f* des Lichts
unencoded date Rohdaten *pl*
unequal error protection ungleicher Fehlerschutz *m*
uneven illumination (lighting) ungleichmäßige Beleuchtung *f*
unexposed unbelichtet, nichtbelichtet
~ **film** unbelichteter Film *m*
~ **film stock** unbelichtetes Filmmaterial *n*
unfolded ungefalzt *(Druckbogen)*
uniaxial crystal [optisch] einachsiger Kristall *m*
unidimensional sampling eindimensionale Abtastung *f*
unidimensionality Eindimensionalität *f*
unidirectional bus unidirektionaler Bus *m (Datenübertragung)*
~ **interface** unidirektionale Schnittstelle *f*
~ **prediction** unidirektionale Prädiktion *f*
~ **reflectivity** unidirektionales (ambientes) Reflexionsvermögen *n*
uniform color space uniformer Farbraum *m*
~ **-distributed random variable** gleichverteilte Zufallsvariable *f*
~ **distribution** Gleichverteilung *f*
~ **filter** Rechteckfilter *n*, Spalttiefpass *m*; Mittelwertfilter *n*
~ **fractal** homogenes Fraktal *n*
~ **grid** gleichmäßiges Gitter *n (Datenstruktur)*

~ **illumination** gleichmäßige Ausleuchtung *f*
~ **noise** uniformes Rauschen *n*
~ **quadrature amplitude modulation** gleichförmige Quadraturamplitudenmodulation *f*
~ **quantization** gleichmäßige (uniforme) Quantisierung *f*, lineare Quantisierung *f*
~ **quantizer** linearer Quantisierer *m*
~ **resource locator** Webseitenadresse *f*
unilateral Laplace transform einseitige Laplace-Transformation *f*
unimodal histogram unimodales Histogramm *n*
uninverted top-to-bottom image höhenrichtiges Bild *n*
union operation Vereinigung *f (mengentheoretische Operation)*
unipod Einbein[stativ] *n*, Monostativ *n*
unipolar impulse noise unipolares Impulsrauschen *n*
unit Druckwerk *n*
~ **cell** Einheitszelle *f*, Elementarzelle *f (Elektronenbeugung)*
~ **cube** Einheitswürfel *m (Farbraumdarstellung, Computergrafik)*
~ **impulse** Einheits[im]puls *m*, diskreter Dirac-Impuls *m*, Dirac-Stoß *m* (Signalverarbeitung)
~ **impulse function** Einheitsimpulsfunktion *f*
~ **of resolution** Auflösungsmaß *n*
~ **production manager** Produktionsleiter *m (Filmarbeit)*
~ **pulse** *s.* ~ impulse
~-**radius circle** Einheitskreis *m*
~ **sample sequence** diskrete Deltafunktion (Impulsfunktion) *f*, Kroneckersches Delta *n*
~ **solid angle** Einheitsraumwinkel *m*, Raumwinkeleinheit *f*, Raumwinkelelement *n*, Steradiant *m*
~ **sphere** Einheitskugel *f*
~ **step** Einheitsschritt *m (kausales Signal)*
~ **vector** Einheitsvektor *m*, Basisvektor *m*
~ **volume** Volumeneinheit *f*
unitary color psychologische Primärfarbe *f*
~ **matrix** Einheitsmatrix *f*
~ **transform[ation]** unitäre Transformation *f*
universal camera Universalkamera *f*
~ **coding** adaptive Entropiecodierung *f*
~ **color film** Universalfarbfilm *m*
~ **developer** Universalentwickler *m*
~ **emulsion** Universalemulsion *f*
~ **serial bus** universeller serieller Bus *m*, universeller Serienbus *m*, USB *(zum Anschließen von Peripheriegeräten)*
~ **thread** Leica-Gewinde *n (Vergrößerungsgerät)*
~ **viewfinder** Universalsucher *m*, Mehrfachsucher *m*
unjustified matter Flattersatz *m (Typografie)*

unmagnified unvergrößert
unmodulated light unmoduliertes Licht *n*
unmoving camera unbewegte (statische) Kamera *f (Kinematografie)*
unperforated tape unperforiertes Band *n*
unpolarized light unpolarisiertes (nichtpolarisiertes) Licht *n*
~ **radiation** unpolarisierte Strahlung *f*
unposed photograph ungestelltes Foto *n*, Knipsfoto *n*
unprintable color nichtdruckbare Farbe *f*
unprinted unbedruckt
unreadable unlesbar
unrecognizable nichterkennbar, unerkennbar
unreel/to abspulen
unrelated color unbezogene Farbe *f*
unretouched unretuschiert
unsaturated color ungesättigte Farbe *f*
unscaled map nichtmaßstäbliche Karte *f*
unscattered light ungestreutes Licht *n*
unscreened photograph ungerastertes Foto *n*
unsensitized emulsion unsensibilisierte Emulsion *f*
unsharp image unscharfes Bild *n*
~ **mask [filter]** Unscharfmaske *f*, unscharfe Maske *f (Bildverarbeitungsoperator)*
~ **mask operator** Unschärfeoperator *m*
~ **masking** Unscharfmaskierung *f*, Unschärfemaskierung *f*, unscharfe Maskierung *f*
~ **vision** unscharfes Sehen *n*
unsharpness Unschärfe *f*
unsophisticated camera user Gelegenheitsfotograf *m*
unsqueeze/to entzerren *(anamorphotische Bilder)*
unsqueezed unkomprimiert; entzerrt
~ **[release] print** entzerrte Filmkopie *f*
unsqueezing 1. anamorphotische Entzerrung (Bildentzerrung) *f*; 2. Kopieren *n* mit anamorphotischer Entzerrung
unstable nuclide strahlendes Nuklid *n*, Radionuklid *n*
~ **resonator** instabiler Resonator *m (Laser)*
unsteadiness Bildunruhe *f*
~ **of the air** Luftunruhe *f (Astrofotografie)*
unstructured data unstrukturierte Daten *pl*
~ **grid** unstrukturiertes Gitter *n*
unsupervised automatic classification unüberwachte automatische Klassifikation *f*
~ **classification** unüberwachte (untrainierte) Klassifikation *f*
~ **learning (training)** unüberwachtes Lernen *n (Neuroinformatik)*
unsymmetric[al] unsymmetrisch
unsymmetrical lens unsymmetrisches (asymmetrisches) Objektiv *n*
untrimmed unbeschnitten *(z.B. Druckbogen)*

unwanted absorption Nebenabsorption *f*, Fehlabsorption *f* *(Farbfotografie)*
~ **light** Nebenlicht *n*
unweighted area sampling ungewichtete Flächenabtastung *f* *(Bildsynthese)*
unwind/to abspulen
unwind brake [system] Einzugwerk *n* *(Rollenrotationsdruckmaschine)*
up-conversion Aufwärtskonvertierung *f*
up-convert/to aufwärtskonvertieren
up path Aufwärtsverbindung *f* *(Signalübertragung)*
update Korrekturstern *m* *(Prädiktionsvektor)*
uplink Aufwärtsstrecke *f*, Aufwärtsverbindung *f* *(Satellitenübertragung)*
upload/to heraufladen, hochladen *(Daten auf Web-Seiten)*
upper band oberes Band *n* *(z.B. als Satellitenempfangs-Frequenzbereich)*
~ **feed sprocket** Vorwickel[zahn]rolle *f*, Vorwickler *m*
~ **sideband** oberes Seitenband *n*
uppercase letter Großbuchstabe *m*, Versal *m*, Majuskel *f*
upright steil *(Schriftschnitt)*
~ **fluorescence microscope** aufrechtes Fluoreszenzmikroskop *n*
~ **image** aufrechtes (lotrechtes) Bild *n*
upsample/to aufwärtstasten
upsampler Aufwärtstaster *m*
upsampling Aufwärtstastung *f*
upscaling Aufwärtsskalierung *f*
upside down image kopfstehendes (vollständig umgekehrtes) Bild *n*, Kehrbild *n*
upspeed Bildbeschleunigung *f* *(Filmprojektion)*
upward compatibility Aufwärtskompatibilität *f*
~ **compatible** aufwärtskompatibel
urethroscope Urethroskop *n*, Harnröhrenspiegel *m*
urography Urografie *f*, Harnwegsröntgendarstellung *f*
usable magnification *s.* useful magnification
~ **signal** *s.* useful signal
USB connection USB-Anschluss *m*
~ **interface** USB-Schnittstelle *f*
~ **port** USB-Anschluss *m*
used camera Gebrauchtkamera *f*
~ **electronics** Elektronikschrott *m*
~ **tape** bespieltes Band *n*
useful aperture nutzbare Apertur *f*, förderliche Blende *f*
~ **data** Nutzdaten *pl*
~ **data rate** Nutzdatenrate *f*
~ **density** nutzbarer Bildumfang *m* *(Radiografie)*
~ **focal length** nutzbare Brennweite *f*
~ **information** Nutzinformation *f*

~ **magnification** nutzbare (nützliche) Vergrößerung *f*, förderliche Vergrößerung *f* *(Mikroskopie)*
~ **signal** Nutzsignal *n*, Nachrichtensignal *n*, artefaktfreies Signal *n*
user agent *s.* ~ interface
~-**computer interface** *s.* user interface
~ **control** Bedien[ungs]element *n*
~ **convenience** Benutzerfreundlichkeit *f*; Benutzerkomfort *m*
~-**defined data** anwenderbestimmte (benutzerdefinierte) Daten *pl*
~-**friendly** [be]nutzerfreundlich
~-**friendly control** nutzerfreundliches Bedienelement *n*
~-**input device** Eingabegerät *n*
~ **interface** Bedienoberfläche *f*, Benutzerschnittstelle *f*, Benutzungsoberfläche *f*, Benutzungsschnittstelle *f*
~ **interface technology** Schnittstellentechnologie *f*
~ **menu** Benutzermenü *n*
~-**network interface** Nutzer-Netz-Schnittstelle *f*
~-**perceived video quality** subjektive Video[bild]qualität *f*
~-**processable, user-processible** selbstverarbeitbar *(Fotomaterial)*
~-**processing** Selbstverarbeitung *f*, Heimverarbeitung *f* *(z.B. von Fotomaterial)*
~ **program** Anwendungsprogramm *n*
~ **programmable** frei programmierbar
~ **prompting** Benutzerführung *f*
~ **setting** Benutzereinstellung *f*
~ **tracking** Nutzerermittlung *f*
UV *s.* ultraviolet
UV-transmissive ultraviolettdurchlässig
UXGA *s.* ultra extended graphics array

V

V number (value) Abbe-Zahl *f*, Abbesche Zahl *f*
vacancy Elektronenfehlstelle *f*, Elektronenleerstelle *f*
vacation photograph Urlaubsfoto *n*
vacuum back (board) Saugkassette *f*, Saugmattscheibe *f (Reprokamera)*
~ **cassette** Vakuumkassette *f (Radiografie)*
~ **CCD camera** Vakuum-CCD-Kamera *f*
~ **easel** *s.* 1. ~ frame; 2. ~ back
~ **fluorescent display** Vakuum-Fluoreszenzdisplay *n*
~ **frame** Vakuumkopierrahmen *m*
~ **lamp** Vakuumglühlampe *f*
~ **photocell** Vakuumfotozelle *f*
~ **tower telescope** Vakuumturmteleskop *n (Sonnenbeobachtung)*
~ **tube** Vakuumröhre *f*
~ **ultraviolet radiation** Vakuum-Ultraviolett *n*, Vakuum-UV *n*, Quarz-Ultraviolett *n*
valence Valenz *f*, Wertigkeit *f*
~ **band** Valenzband *n*
~ **band electron** Valenz[band]elektron *n*
~ **level (stage)** Valenzstufe *f*
valency *s.* valence
valid color gültige Farbe *f*
validation Validation *f*, Validierung *f*
valuator device Wertgeber *m*
value 1. Wert *m*; 2. Dunkelstufe *f (Farbmetrik)*; Tonwert *m*; Helligkeit *f (Munsell-Farbordnungssystem)*
valve *s.* electron tube
van Albada [view]finder Albada-Sucher *m*
vanishing line Fluchtgerade *f*, Fluchtlinie *f*, Ziellinie *f*
~ **point** Fluchtpunkt *m*
vantage point Blickpunkt *m*
variable-area sound track Zackenschrift *f*, Amplitudenschrift *f (Lichtton)*
~-**area system** Transversalverfahren *n (Lichttonaufzeichnung)*
~ **bit rate** variable Bitrate *f*
~ **bit rate [en]coding** variable Bitratencodierung *f*
~ **bit rate transmission** variable Bitratenübertragung *f*
~ **camera shutter** verstellbare Sektorenblende *f*
~-**color filter** Variocolorfilter *n*
~-**contrast black-and-white paper** kontrastvariables Schwarzweißpapier *n*
~-**contrast paper** Kontrastwandelpapier *n*, Gradationswandelpapier *n*, gradationsvariables Papier *n*
~ **data printing** variabler Datendruck *m*
~-**density sound track** Intensitätsschrift *f*, [Lichtton-]Sprossenschrift *f (Lichtton)*
~-**density system** Intensitätsverfahren *n (Lichttonaufzeichnung)*
~-**focal-length lens** *s.* varifocal lens
~-**gain film** gradationsvariabler (gammavariabler) Film *m*
~-**length code** längenvariabler (größenvariabler) Code *m*
~-**length code word** längenvariables Codewort *n*
~-**length coding** variable Längencodierung *f*, Codierung *f* mit variabler Wortlänge, Huffman-Codierung *f*
~ **program mode** variable Programmautomatik *f*
~-**resolution projector** Projektor *m* variabler Auflösung
~-**size code** *s.* variable-length code
~ **thresholding** variable Schwellenwertbildung *f*
variance Varianz *f (z.B. eines Signals)*
~ **filter** *s.* ~ operator
~ **matrix** Varianzmatrix *f*
~ **operator** Varianzoperator *m*
variant feature variantes Merkmal *n*
variate Zufallsvariable *f*
variation Variation *f*
~ **of image size** Bildgrößenschwankung *f*
variator Variator *m (Zoomobjektiv)*
varicolored verschiedenfarbig, bunt
varifocal lens Varioobjektiv *n*, variofokales Objektiv *n*, Zoom *n(m)*, Zoomobjektiv *n*, Zoomoptik *f*, Gummilinse *f*, pankratisches System (Objektiv) *n*
vario lens *s.* varifocal lens
varnish Lack *m*, Drucklack *m*
varnishing Lackierung *f (Druckveredelung)*
vascular imaging Angiografie *f*
~ **ultrasound imaging** Ultraschall-Gefäßdarstellung *f*
vase illusion Rubinsche Vase *f (Kippfigur)*
VBR transmission *s.* variable bit rate transmission
VC paper *s.* variable-contrast paper
VCD *s.* video compact disc
VCR *s.* videocassette recorder
~ **head** Videokopf *m*
VDU *s.* video display unit
vectograph *s.* vector graph
vector Vektor *m*
~ **addition** Vektoraddition *f*
~ **algebra** Vektoralgebra *f*
~-**based graphics** Vektorgrafik *f*, Objektgrafik *f*, vektororientierte (objektorientierte) Grafik *f*
~-**based graphics program** Vektorgrafikprogramm *n*
~-**based representation** Vektordarstellung *f*, vektorielle (vektororientierte) Darstellung *f*
~ **cross product** Vektorprodukt *n*
~ **data** Vektordaten *pl*
~ **diagram** Vektordiagramm *n*
~ **direction** Vektorrichtung *f*
~ **display** Vektorbildschirm *m*

~ **drawing** Vektorzeichnung f
~ **field** Vektorfeld n
~ **field operator** Vektorfeldoperator m
~ **field topology** Vektorfeldtopologie f
~ **field visualization** Vektorfeldvisualisierung f
~ **file** Vektordatei f
~ **font** Vektor-Zeichensatz m
~ **form** Vektorform f
~ **format** Vektorformat n
~ **function** Vektorfunktion f
~ **generator** Vektorgenerator m
~ **gradient** Vektorgradient m
~ **gradient image** Vektorgradientenbild n
~ **graph** Vektorgraph m
~ **graphic display** Vektorbildschirm m
~ **graphics** s. vector-based graphics
~ **image** Vektorbild n, vektorielles Bild n, vektorielle Abbildung f
~ **image processing algorithm** Vektorbildverarbeitungsalgorithmus m
~ **length** Vektorlänge f
~ **magnitude** Vektorgröße f
~ **map** Vektorkarte f
~ **matrix** Vektormatrix f
~ **principle** Vektorprinzip f
~ **product** Vektorprodukt n
~ **quantity** Vektorgröße f
~ **quantization** Vektorquantisierung f
~ **quantization network** Vektorquantisierungsnetz n
~ **quantizer** Vektorquantisierer m
~ **space** Vektorraum m
~-**space projection** Vektorraumprojektion f
~-**space representation** Vektorraumdarstellung f
~ **tomography** Vektortomografie f
~ **visualization technique** Vektorvisualisierungsverfahren n
~ **wavelet transform** Vektor-Wavelet-Transformation f
vectorial representation s. vector-based representation
vectorization Vektorisierung f
vectorize/to vektorisieren
vectorized file vektorisierte Datei f
vectorscope Vektoroszillograf m, Vektorskop n
~ **display (presentation)** Vektoroszillogramm n, Vektorskopdarstellung f
vegetable adhesive (glue) Pflanzenleim m
vehicle navigation system Fahrzeugnavigationssystem n
veil s. fog
velocity Geschwindigkeit f
~ **constancy** Geschwindigkeitskonstanz f, Bewegungskonstanz f (Wahrnehmungsphänomen)
~ **encoding** Geschwindigkeitscodierung f (Phasenkontrastangiografie)
~ **error** Geschwindigkeitsfehler m

~ **error compensator** Geschwindigkeitsfehlerausgleicher m, Geschwindigkeitsfehlerkorrektor m
~ **field** Geschwindigkeitsfeld n, Bewegungsfeld n
~ **image** Doppler-Bild n
~ **of light** Lichtgeschwindigkeit f
~-**recording camera** Streak-Kamera f
~ **vector** Geschwindigkeitsvektor m
venogram Venogramm n, Venenröntgen[kontrast]bild n
venographic venografisch
venography Venografie f
venous-occlusion plethysmography Venenverschlussplethysmografie f
ventriculogram Ventrikulogramm n
ventriculography Ventrikulografie f
vergence 1. Vergenz f (Augenbewegung); 2. Konvergenz f
~ **angle** Vergenzwinkel m
~ **eye movement** Vergenzbewegung f
vernier Nonius m
~ **acuity** Nonius-Sehschärfe f, Vernier-Sehschärfe f, Überauflösung f
vernis mou Vernis mou m, Weichgrundradierung f
verso [page] Verso n, Blattrückseite f, gerade Seite f (Layout)
vertex Vertex m, Scheitel m, Scheitelpunkt m; Eckpunkt m; Endpunkt m (Liniensegment)
~ **angle** Scheitelwinkel m
~ **focal length [of a lens]** Objektivschnittweite f, Schnittweite f, Schnittlänge f, Scheitelbrennweite f
~ **length** s. ~ focal length [of a lens]
~ **value** Scheitelwert m
vertical aerial photograph Senkrecht[bild]aufnahme f, Senkrechtluftbild n
~ **alias[ing]** Vertikalalias m
~ **axis** Ordinatenachse f, y-Achse f (Koordinatensystem)
~ **blanking** Vertikalaustastung f, vertikale Austastung f
~ **blanking interval** Vertikalaustastlücke f, vertikale Austastlücke f, Bildaustastlücke f
~ **camera** Vertikalkamera f (Reprokamera)
~ **cavity surface emitting laser** VCSEL-Laserdiode f
~ **deflection** Vertikalablenkung f
~ **disparity** vertikale Disparität f (Parallaxe) f (dreidimensionale Abbildung)
~ **enlarger** Vertikalvergrößerungsgerät n
~ **format** Hochformat n
~ **format picture** Hoch[format]aufnahme f
~ **frequency** s. ~ scan rate
~ **image amplitude** vertikale Bildamplitude f
~ **interval control address signal** Adressiersignal n
~ **linear polarization** vertikale Polarisation f (Radar)

vertical

~ **orientation** Hochformat *n*
~ **parallax** vertikale Parallaxe *f*
~**-pass filter** Vertikalfilter *n*
~ **redundancy check** Querparitätsprüfung *f*
~ **resolution** Vertikalauflösung *f*, vertikale (senkrechte) Auflösung *f*
~ **retrace [time]** Vertikalrücklauf *m*, Bildrücklauf *m*
~ **scan rate**, ~ **scanning (sweep) frequency** vertikale Abtastfrequenz (Ablenkfrequenz) *f*, Vertikalfrequenz *f*, Vollbildfrequenz *f*, Bildkippfrequenz *f* *(progressives Video)*
~ **sync[hronization]** Vertikalsynchronisation *f (Monitor)*
~ **sync[hronization] pulse**, ~ **synchronizing signal** Vertikalsynchronimpuls *m*, V-Impuls *m*, vertikales Synchronisiersignal *n*
~ **time-base generator** Bildablenkgenerator *m*
~**-travel focal-plane shutter** vertikal ablaufender Schlitzverschluss *m*
vertoscope Vertoskop *n*
very fine line Feinststrich *m*, Haarstrich *m*, Haarlinie *f*
~ **glossy image** Hochglanzbild *n*
~ **hard X-rays** ultraharte Röntgenstrahlung *f*
~ **high frequency** Ultrakurzwelle *f*, Ultrakurzwellenbereich *m*, Meterwellenbereich *m*, Meterwellenfrequenz *f*, UKW
~ **large-scale integrated circuit** höchstintegrierte Schaltung *f*
~ **large-scale integration technology** VLSI-Technik *f*
~ **large telescope interferometer** Sterninterferometer *n*
~ **long shot** Weitaufnahme *f* *(Kinematografie)*
~ **low-bit-rate coding** Codierung *f* mit sehr kleiner Bitrate
~**-short-duration image** Ultrakurzzeitaufnahme *f*
vesicular emulsion Vesikularemulsion *f*
~ **film** Vesikularfilm *m*
~ **image** Bläschenbild *n*, Blasenbild *n* *(Vesikularverfahren)*
~ **microfilm** Vesikular-Mikrofilm *m*
~ **process** Vesikularverfahren *n*, Bläschenkopierverfahren *n*
vestigial sideband Restseitenband *n*
~ **sideband demodulator** Restseitenband-Demodulator *m*
~ **sideband filter** Restseitenbandfilter *n*
~ **sideband method** Restseitenbandverfahren *n*
~ **sideband modulation** Restseitenbandmodulation *f*
VFX ... *s. under* visual effects ...
VGA *s.* video graphics array
~ **display** VGA-Monitor *m*
VHF [range] *s.* very high frequency

VHS *s.* Video Home System
~ **analog tape** VHS-Band *n*
~ **camcorder** VHS-Camcorder *m*
~ **cassette** VHS-Kassette *f*
vibrant color kräftige Farbe *f*, satte (gesättigte) Farbe *f*
vibration analysis Schwingungsanalyse *f*
~**-free table, vibration-isolated optical table** optischer Tisch *m*
~ **node** Schwingungsknoten *m*
vibrational direction Schwingungsrichtung *f*
~ **energy** Schwingungsenergie *f (z.B. eines Elektrons)*
~ **plane** Schwingungsebene *f*
vibrogram Vibrogramm *n*, Schwingungsmuster *n*, Schwingungsbild *n*
vibrograph Vibrograf *m*
video Video *n*; Fernsehen *n*, Television *f* *(s.a. unter* television*)*
~ **accelerator** Grafikbeschleuniger *m*, Beschleunigerkarte *f*, Beschleunigungskarte *f*
~ **accelerator chip** Videobeschleunigerkarte *f*
~ **access** Videozugang *m*
~ **accessories** Videozubehör *n*
~ **adapter** Videoadapter *m*, Video[grafik]karte *f*, Videosteckkarte *f*
~ **amplifier** Videoverstärker *m*, Luminanzverstärker *m*, Y-Verstärker *m*
~ **analog image** analoges Videobild *n*
~ **analysis** Videoanalyse *f*
~ **analyzer** Videoanalyser *m*
~ **animation** Videoanimation *f*
~ **application** Videoanwendung *f*
~ **arcade** Videospielhalle *f*
~ **arcade game** Videospielautomat *m*
~ **archive** Videoarchiv *n*
~ **archiving** Videoarchivierung *f*
~ **area** Videobereich *m*, Videosektor *m*
~ **assist [monitor]** Suchermonitor *m (der Filmkamera)*
~ **astronomy** Videoastronomie *f*
~ **authentication** Videoauthentifikation *f*
~ **bandwidth** Video[frequenz]bandbreite *f*
~ **baseband** Videobasisband *n*
~**-based pattern recognition** videobasierte Mustererkennung *f*
~ **beamer** Videoprojektor *m*, Präsentationsprojektor *m*
~ **bit rate** Video-Bitrate *f*, Videodatenrate *f*
~ **bit stream** Videostrom *m*, Bilddatenstrom *m*
~ **blanking** Bildaustastung *f*
~ **brightness level** Luminanzpegel *m*
~ **broadcast** Videoausstrahlung *f*
~ **broadcasting** Fernseh[rund]funk *m*
~ **broadcasting decoder** Fernsehrundfunkdecoder *m*
~ **broadcasting network** Fernsehnetz *n*
~ **buffer** Videospeicher *m*, Grafik[karten]speicher *m*

video

~ **cable** Videokabel *n*
~ **camcorder** Videocamcorder *m*
~ **camera** Videokamera *f*
~ **camera filter** Videokamerafilter *n*
~ **camera lens** Videoobjektiv *n*
~ **camera system** Videokamerasystem *n*
~ **camera technology** Videokameratechnik *f*
~ **caption** Videotitel *m*
~ **capture** Videoaufzeichnung *f*
~ **capture board (card)** Videonachbearbeitungskarte *f*, Videoerweiterungskarte *f*, Video[schnitt]karte *f*
~ **capture device** Videobildaufnehmer *m*
~ **cartridge** Videokassette *f*
~ **CD** *s.* ~ compact disc
~ **cell phone** Video-Handy *n*
~ **chain** Videovertriebskette *f*
~ **channel** Fernsehbildkanal *m*, Bildkanal *m*, Videokanal *m*
~ **chip** Videochip *m*
~ **circuit** Videoschaltung *f*, Videoschaltkreis *m*, Fernsehleitung *f*, Bildleitung *f*
~ **clip** Videoclip *m*, Kurzvideo *n*, Videospot *m*
~ **codec** Video-Codec *m(n)*
~ **coding** Videocodierung *f*, Bewegtbildcodierung *f*
~ **coding algorithm** Videocodierungsalgorithmus *m*
~ **coding standard** Videocodierungsstandard *m*
~ **color printer** Farbvideodrucker *m*, Video-Farbdrucker *m*
~ **communication** Videokommunikation *f*
~ **communication system** Videokommunikationssystem *n*
~ **compact disc** Video-CD *f*, CD-Video *n*
~ **compression** Videokompression *f*, Videokomprimierung *f*
~ **compression algorithm** Videokompressionsalgorithmus *m*
~ **compression ratio** Videokompressionsverhältnis *n*
~ **compression software** Videokompressionssoftware *f*
~ **compression standard** Videokompressionsstandard *m*
~ **compression syntax** Videokompressionssyntax *f*
~ **compression technique** Videokompressionsverfahren *n*
~ **compressor** Videokompressor *m*
~ **conference party** Videokonferenzteilnehmer *m*
~ **content** Videoinhalt *m*
~ **controller** *s.* ~ adapter
~ **conversion** Videodatenkonvertierung *f*
~ **conversion board** Video[grafik]karte *f*, Videosteckkarte *f*, Videoadapter *m*
~ **converter** Videokonverter *m*, Videowandler *m*

~ **copy** Videokopie *f*
~ **dailies** Videomuster *npl*
~ **data** Videodaten *pl*
~ **data block** Videodatenblock *m*
~ **data compression** Videodatenkompression *f*, Videokomprimierung *f*
~ **data format** Videodatenformat *n*
~ **data rate** Videodatenrate *f*, Video-Bitrate *f*
~ **data reduction** Videodatenreduktion *f*
~ **data storage** Videospeicherung *f*
~ **data stream** Video[daten]strom *m*, Bilddatenstrom *m*
~ **data terminal** Videodatenterminal *n*
~ **data track** Videospur *f*
~ **data transmission** Videodatenübertragung *f*
~ **database** Videodatenbank *f*
~ **decoder** Videodecod[ier]er *m*
~ **decoding** Videodecodierung *f*
~ **demodulation** Videodemodulation *f*
~ **demodulator** Videodemodulator *m*
~ **densitometry** Videodensitometrie *f*
~ **detector** Videogleichrichter *m*
~ **device** Videogerät *n*, Bildgerät *n*
~ **digitization** Videodigitalisierung *f*
~ **digitizer** Videodigitalisierer *m*, Videodigitalisier[ungs]karte *f*, Framegrabberkarte *f*, Bilderfassungskarte *f*
~ **display** Video[bild]schirm *m*, Videoanzeige *f*
~ **display card** Videokarte *f*
~ **display controller** Bildschirmsteuereinheit *f*
~ **display driver** Bildschirmtreiber *m*
~ **display memory** Videobildspeicher *m*
~ **display screen** Video[bild]schirm *m*
~ **display terminal** *s.* ~ display
~ **display tube** Videobildröhre *f*
~ **display unit** Video-Wiedergabeeinheit *f*, Videowiedergabegerät *n*
~ **distribution** Videoverteildienst *m*; Videoverleih *m*
~ **distribution amplifier** Videoverteilverstärker *m*
~ **documentation** Videodokumentation *f*
~ **domain** Videobereich *m*, Videosektor *m*
~ **dub** Video[band]kopie *f*
~ **edit decision list** Videoschnittliste *f*
~ **editing** Video[nach]bearbeitung *f*; MAZ-Bearbeitung *f*, Videoschnitt *m*
~ **editing equipment** Videoschnitttechnik *f*
~ **editing program** Videonachbearbeitungsprogramm *n*, Videoschnittprogramm *n*
~ **editing software** Videoschnittsoftware *f*
~ **editing system** Videoschnittsystem *n*
~ **editor** 1. Videoschnitt[steuer]gerät *n*, Videoschnittcomputer *m*, Videonachbearbeitungsgerät *n*; 2. Videoeditor *m* *(Beruf)*
~ **effect** Videoeffekt *m*, Videotrick *m*

video 420

- ~ **effects device (unit)** Videoeffektgerät *n*, DVE-Gerät *n*, digitales Effektgerät *n*
- ~ **electronics** Videoelektronik *f*
- ~ **encode rate** Videokompressionsrate *f*
- ~ **encoder** Videocodierer *m*, Bewegtbildcodierer *m*
- ~ **encoding system** Videocodierungssystem *n*
- ~ **engineer** Videotechniker *m*, Videoingenieur *m*
- ~ **engineering** Videotechnik *f*
- ~ **entertainment** Videounterhaltung *f*
- ~ **equipment** Videoausrüstung *f*
- ~ **field** Videohalbbild *n*, Videoteilbild *n*
- ~ **file** Videodatei *f*
- ~ **filing** Videoarchivierung *f*
- ~ **fill** Video-Füllsignal *n*
- ~ **film** Videofilm *m*
- ~ **filter** Videofilter *n*
- ~ **floppy** Videodiskette *f*
- ~ **footage** Video[band]material *n*
- ~ **format** Videoformat *n*
- ~ **format CCD camera** Video-CCD-Kamera *f*
- ~ **format conversion** Videokonvertierung *f*
- ~ **formatting** Videoformatierung *f*
- ~ **frame** Video[einzel]bild *n*; Videovollbild *n*
- ~ **frame grabber** Framegrabberkarte *f*, Videodigitalisier[ungs]karte *f*, Bilderfassungskarte *f*, Videostandbilddigitalisierer *m*, Digitalisierungskarte *f*
- ~ **frame rate, ~ frequency** Video[bild]frequenz *f*, Video[bild]rate *f*; Fernsehfrequenz *f*
- ~ **frequency band** Videofrequenzband *n*
- ~ **frequency response** Videofrequenzgang *m*
- ~ **function** Videofunktion *f*
- ~ **game** Videospiel *n*, Bildschirmspiel *n*
- ~ **game cartridge** Videospielkassette *f*
- ~ **game console** Videospielkonsole *f*, Telespielkonsole *f*, Spiel[e]konsole *f*
- ~ **gear** Videoausrüstung *f*
- ~ **graphic** Videografik *f*
- ~ **graphics array** 1. *Grafikstandard mit 640 x 480 Pixel Auflösung*; 2. VGA-Grafikkarte *f*, Video-Grafikadapter *m*
- ~ **graphics board** Video[grafik]karte *f*, Videosteckkarte *f*, Videoadapter *m*
- ~ **head cleaning** Videokopfreinigung *f*
- ~ **head cleaning cassette** Video-Reinigungskassette *f*
- ~ **hobbyist** Videoamateur *m*
- **Video Home System** Video-Heimsystem *n*, VHS *(analoges Amateurvideoformat)*
- **video home theater** Heimkino *n*
- ~ **image** Videobild *n*
- ~ **image display** *s*. ~ display
- ~ **image processing** Videobildverarbeitung *f*
- ~ **image recorder** Videobildaufnehmer *m*
- ~ **image sensor** Videobildsensor *m*
- ~ **imager** Videobildwandler *m*; Multiformatkamera *m*
- ~ **imagery** Videomaterial *n*
- ~ **imaging system** Video[aufzeichnungs]system *n*
- ~ **indexing system** Videoindexierungssystem *n*
- ~ **industry** Videoindustrie *f*
- ~ **information** Videoinformation *f*
- ~ **information system** Video-Informationssystem *n*
- ~ **input** Video[signal]eingang *m*
- ~ **input signal** Videoeingangssignal *n*
- ~ **insertion** Videoeinblendung *f*
- ~ **instrument** Videoinstrument *n*
- ~ **interface [circuitry]** Videoschnittstelle *f*
- ~ **journalist** Videojournalist *m*
- ~ **laboratory** Videolabor *n*
- ~ **level** *s*. ~ signal level
- ~ **library** Videodatenbank *f*; Videothek *f*; Videoarchiv *n*
- ~ **light** Videoleuchte *f*
- ~ **lighting** Videobeleuchtung *f*
- ~ **line** Videozeile *f*
- ~ **lookup table** Speichertabelle *f*, Verweistabelle *f*, Tabellenspeicher *m*, Lookup-Tabelle *f*, Umwandlungstabelle *f* für Pixelwerte, Transformationstabelle *f*
- ~ **loop** Videobandschleife *f*
- ~ **macroscope** Videomakroskop *n*
- ~ **magnetic tape** Videomagnetband *n*, MAZ-Band *n*
- ~ **magnification system** *s*. ~ microscope
- ~ **manipulator** Videobearbeitungsgerät *n*
- ~ **mapping** Videokartierung *f*
- ~ **master tape** Video-Masterband *n*
- ~ **material** Videomaterial *n*
- ~ **meeting** Videokonferenz *f*, Bildkonferenz *f*
- ~ **memory** Videospeicher *m*, Grafik[karten]speicher *m*
- ~ **microprobe** Video-Mikrosonde *f*
- ~ **microscope** Videomikroskop *n*
- ~ **microscopy** Videomikroskopie *f*
- ~ **mixer** Bildmischer *m*, Videomischer *m*, Mischer *m*, Bildmischpult *n*, Bildmischeinrichtung *f*
- ~ **mode** Videomodus *m*
- ~ **model[l]ing** Videomodellierung *f*
- ~ **modulation** Videomodulation *f*
- ~ **modulator** Videomodulator *m*
- ~ **module** Videomodul *n*
- ~ **monitor** Videomonitor *m*
- ~ **movie** Videofilm *m*
- ~ **multiplex [coder], ~ multiplexer** Videomultiplexer *m*
- ~-**near-demand** *s*. near video-on-demand
- ~ **noise** Videorauschen *n*
- ~ **noise reduction** Videorauschunterdrückung *f*
- ~ **object** Videoobjekt *n*
- ~ **object coding** Videoobjektcodierung *f*
- ~ **object plane** Videoobjektebene *f*

video

~-on-demand Video n auf Abruf (Bestellung)
~-on-demand server Videoserver m
~-on-demand service Videodienst m
~ operator Videokameramann m; Videoassistent m *(Filmteam)*
~ optical effect Videoeffekt m, Videotrick m
~ oscillograph Videooszillograf m
~ oscilloscope Videooszilloskop n
~ output 1. Video[signal]ausgang m; Video-Ausgangsbuchse f; 2. Videoausgabe f
~ output signal Videoausgangssignal n
~ output stage Bildendstufe f
~ overlay *das Kombinieren von Video und Computergrafik oder Text*
~ overlay board Overlay-Karte f
~ packet Videodatenpaket n
~ parameter Videoparameter m
~ parlance Videosprachgebrauch m
~ patch panel Video-Koppelfeld n, Video-Koppelsystem n
~ pel Fernsehpixel n
~ photography Videografie f
~ picture Videobild n
~ picture format Videobildformat n
~ picture segment Videobildsegment n
~ playback Videoabspielung f, Videowiedergabe f
~ playback device, ~ player Videoabspielgerät n
~ port Videoanschluss m
~ postprocessing (postproduction) Videonachbearbeitung f; MAZ-Bearbeitung f; Videoschnitt m
~ postproduction facility Nachbearbeitungseinrichtung f
~ preprocessing Videovorverarbeitung f
~ presentation Videopräsentation f, Videodarstellung f
~ presenter Videopräsentationsgerät n
~ preservation Videokonservierung f
~ printer Videokopierer m, Videoprinter m; Videodrucker m
~ processing Videobearbeitung f; Videoverarbeitung f
~ processing amplifier Videoverstärker m, Luminanzverstärker m; Überspielverstärker m; Y-Verstärker m
~ processor Video[signal]prozessor m
~ producer Videoproduzent m
~ product Videoprodukt n
~ production Videoproduktion f
~ production bureau (company) Videoproduktionsfirma f
~ production house Videoproduktionsstudio n
~ production processing technology Videoproduktionstechnik f
~ production studio Videostudio n
~ program Videoprogramm n
~ program system Videoprogrammsystem n
~ programming Videoprogrammierung f
~ projection Videoprojektion f
~ projection system Videoprojektionssystem n
~ projection technology Videoprojektionstechnik f
~ projector Videoprojektor m, Videoprojektionsgerät n, Videobeamer m
~ pulse generator Videoimpulsgeber m
~ puzzle Videopuzzle[spiel] n
~ quality Video[bild]qualität f
~ quantization Videoquantisierung f
~ RAM (random-access memory) Video-RAM n, Video-Pufferspeicher m
~ raster Videoraster m(n)
~ rate Video[bild]rate f, Video[bild]frequenz f; Fernsehfrequenz f
~ receiver Bildempfangsgerät n
~ recorder 1. Videorecorder m; 2. *s.* videotape recorder
~ recorder head drum Videokopftrommel f, Videokopfrad n
~ recording Videoaufzeichnung f
~ recording format (standard) Videoaufzeichnungsformat n
~ recording system Videoaufzeichnungssystem m
~ recording technology Videoaufzeichnungstechnik f
~ redundancy coding Video-Redundanzcodierung f
~ reel Videobandspule f
~ refresh rate Bildwiederholfrequenz f, Bildwiederholrate f, Bilderneuerungsfrequenz f, Bildwechselfrequenz f
~ rental Videoverleih n
~ reproduction *s.* ~ playback
~ resolution Videoauflösung f
~ restoration Videorestauration f
~ sample Video-Abtastwert m
~ sampling Videoabtastung f
~ scaling Videoskalierung f
~ scan line Video-Abtastzeile f
~ scanner Videoabtaster m
~ scanning Videoabtastung f
~ scanning drum Videokopftrommel f, Videokopfrad n
~ scanning rate Videoabtastrate f
~ scene Videoszene f
~ screen Video[bild]schirm m
~ segmentation algorithm Videosegmentierungsalgorithmus m
~ sensor Videosensor m
~ sequence Videosequenz f, Video[bild]folge f
~ sequence compression Videosequenzkompression f
~ server Videoserver m
~ service Video[bestell]dienst m
~ session Videokonferenz f, Bildkonferenz f
~ set-top unit digitaler Empfangsdecoder m, Beistelldecoder m, Set-Top-Box f,

video 422

Zusatzempfangsgerät *n (Digitalfernsehtechnik)*
~ **shoot[ing]** Videodreh *m*; Videoaufnahme *m*
~ **shop** Videothek *f*
~ **shot** Videoaufnahme *f*
~ **signal** Videosignal *n*, Bildsignal *n*
~ **signal chain** Videosignalkette *f*
~ **signal delay** Videosignalverzögerung *f*
~ **signal format** Videosignalformat *n*
~ **signal level** Video[signal]pegel *m*, Bildpegel *m*
~ **signal processing** Videosignalbearbeitung *f*; Videosignalverarbeitung *f*
~ **signal sampling** Videosignalabtastung *f*
~ **signal standard** Videostandard *m*, Videonorm *f*
~ **sink** Videosenke *f*
~ **socket** Videobuchse *f*
~ **software** Videosoftware *f*
~ **source** Videoquelle *f*
~ **source coder** Videoquellencodierer *m*
~ **source coding** Videoquellencodierung *f*
~ **source signal** Videoquellensignal *n*
~ **standard** Videostandard *m*, Videonorm *f*
~ **still** Videostandbild *n*
~ **storage** Videospeicherung *f*
~ **storage format** Videospeicherformat *n*
~ **storage memory** Videospeicher *m*, Grafik[karten]speicher *m*
~ **store** Videothek *f*
~ **stream** Video[signal]strom *m*
~ **streaming** Video-Echtzeitübertragung *f*, fließende Videowiedergabe *f*
~ **studio equipment** Videostudiotechnik *f*
~ **surveillance** Videoüberwachung *f*
~ **surveillance system** Videoüberwachungsanlage *f*
~ **switcher** 1. Videoverteiler *m*, Videoumschalter *m*, Umschalter *m*, Umschaltpult *n*, Kreuzschiene *f*; 2. Videomischer *m*, Videomischpult *n*, Bildmischpult *n*, Mischer *m*
~ **switching matrix** Bildschaltmatrix *f*
~ **synchronization** Videosynchronisation *f*, Videosynchronisierung *f*
~ **syntax** Videosyntax *f*
~ **system** Videoanlage *f*
~ **tap** Suchermonitor *m (Filmkamera)*
~ **technology** Videotechnik *f*
~ **teleconferencing** *s.* videoconferencing
~ **telephone** Videotelefon *n*
~ **telephone service** Bildtelefondienst *m*
~ **telephony** Videotelefonie *f*, Bildtelefonie *f*
~ **terminal** Video-Wiedergabeeinheit *f*, Videowiedergabegerät *n*
~ **time code** Video-Zeitcode *m*
~ **-to-film transfer** Video-Film-Transfer *m*, Videotransfer *m*
~ **tool** Videobearbeitungswerkzeug *n*
~ **track** Video[aufzeichnungs]spur *f*
~ **transfer** Videotransfer *m*, Filmtransfer *m*
~ **transmission** Videoübertragung *f*
~ **transmission bandwidth** Videoübertragungsbandbreite *f*
~ **transmitter** Fernsehbildsender *m*, Bildsender *m*
~ **tripod** Videostativ *n*
~ **tube** *s.* ~ display tube
~ **tube-type camera** Röhren[video]kamera *f*
~ **user** Videonutzer *m*
~ **viewfinder** Videobildsucher *m*, elektronischer Sucher *m*
~ **viewing** Videokonsum *m*
~ **voltage** Videospannung *f*
~ **wall** Video[lein]wand *f*
~ **waveform** Videosignal *n*
~ **window** Videofenster *n*
~ **work** Videoarbeit *f*
~ **workstation** Videoarbeitsplatz *m*
videobeam Großbild-Videoprojektor *m*
videocassette Videokassette *f*
~ **camera** Videokamera *f*
~ **duplication** Videokopierung *f*
~ **leader** Videokassettenvorspann *m*
~ **recorder** Videokassettenrecorder *m*, Kassetten-Videobandgerät *n*
~ **recording system** Videokassetten[aufzeichnungs]system *n*, Videoprogrammsystem *n*
~ **tape** Videokassettenband *n*
videoconference Videokonferenz *f*, Bildkonferenz *f*
~ **connection** Videokonferenzverbindung *f*
~ **facility (installation)** Videokonferenzanlage *f*
~ **room** Videokonferenzraum *m*, Videokonferenzstudio *n*
~ **signal** Videokonferenzsignal *n*
videoconferencing Konferenzfernsehen *n*; Videokonferenzbetrieb *m*; Videokonferenztechnik *f*
~ **bandwidth** Videokonferenzbandbreite *f*
~ **network** Videokonferenznetz *n*
~ **software** Videokonferenzsoftware *f*
~ **standard** Videokonferenzstandard *m*
~ **system** Videokonferenzsystem *n*
videodisc Video[bildspeicher]platte *f*, Bild[speicher]platte *f*, Laserdisk *f (s.a. unter DVD)*
~ **player** Videoplatten-Abspielgerät *n*, Videoplattenspieler *m*, Bildplattenspieler *m*, Bildplattengerät *n*
videodisk *s.* videodisc
videofluoroscopy Videofluoroskopie *f*
videograph/to videografieren
videograph Videografie *f (Erzeugnis)*
videographer Videograf *m*, Videofilmer *m*; Hobbyvideofilmer *m*
videographic videografisch
videographing Videofilmen *n*
videography Videografie *f*
videoland Fernsehindustrie *f*
videomaker *s.* videographer

videometry Videomesstechnik f, Videometrie f
videooculography Videookulografie f
videophone Video[tele]fon n, Bildtelefon n, Bildfernsprecher m
~ **service** Bildtelefondienst m
~ **transmission** Bewegtbildübermittlung f, Bewegtbildübertragung f
videophony Bildtelefonie f, Bildfernsprechen n, Video[tele]fonie f
~ **terminal** Bildtelefongerät n
videotape/to auf Videoband aufzeichnen, videografieren
videotape Video[magnet]band n; MAZ-Band n
~ **cassette** Videokassette f
~ **deck** Videokonsole f; Videobandmaschine f
~ **duplication** Videoduplikation f, Videoduplizierung f
~ **editing** Video[band]schnitt m, Videofilmschnitt m, MAZ-Schnitt m
~ **format** Videobandformat n
~ **head** Videokopf m
~ **machine** Videobandmaschine f, MAZ-Maschine f, Bildbandgerät n
~ **material** Video[band]material n
~ **playback** Videobandabspielung f
~ **player** 1. Videobandspieler m, Videobandgerät n; 2. s. ~ recorder
~ **recorder** Videoaufzeichnungsgerät n, Magnetbildaufzeichnungsgerät n
~ **recording** Videobandaufnahme f, Videobandaufzeichnung f, Videomagnetaufzeichnung f
~ **sequence** Video[film]sequenz f
~ **technology** Videobandtechnik f
~ **track** Video[aufzeichnungs]spur f
~ **transfer** Videotransfer m, Filmtransfer m
videotaping [session] Videodreh m; Videoaufnahme f
videotelephony s. videophony
videotex [interaktiver] Videotext m (s.a. videotext)
~ **decoder** Videotextdecoder m
~ **interworking** Videotext-Zusammenschaltung f
~ **service** Videotextdienst m
videotext Fernsehtext m, Videotext m, Teletext m, Bildschirmzeitung f; Bildschirmtext[dienst] m, BTX
vidicon [camera tube] Vidikon n, Vidikon[aufnahme]röhre f, Resistron n, Endikon n
~**-type camera** Vidikonkamera f
Vieth-Müller circle Vieth-Müller-Kreis m (beidäugiges Sehen)
view/to betrachten
view Ansicht f, Sicht f (s.a. unter viewing); Blick m
~ **axis** Sehachse f
~ **camera** Fachkamera f, technische Kamera f; Großformatkamera f
~ **camera back** Fachkamera-Rückteil n

~ **camera lens** Fach[kamera]objektiv n
~**-dependent** blickpunktabhängig (z.B. Objektformen)
~ **field** Blickfeld n; Gesichtsfeld n, Sichtfeld n
~ **field diameter** Sehfelddurchmesser m (Objektiv)
~ **index** Abbildungsindex m (Computergrafik)
~ **line** Blicklinie f, Sichtlinie f, Gesichtslinie f, Augenlinie f, Sichtverbindung f
~ **mapping matrix** Abbildungsprojektionsmatrix f (Computergrafik)
~ **orientation matrix** Abbildungsorientierungsmatrix f (Computergrafik)
~ **reference coordinate system** Abbildungsreferenzkoordinatensystem n (Computergrafik)
~ **reference point** Abbildungsreferenzpunkt m
~ **representation** Abbildungsbeschreibung f (Computergrafik)
~ **surface** Sichtfläche f
~ **table** Darstellungstabelle f, Abbildungstabelle f (Computergrafik)
~**-up vector** Abbildungsaufwärtsvektor m (Szenenkoordinatensystem)
~ **volume** 1. Sichtvolumen n (Computergrafik, Bildschirm) 2. Abbildungskörper m, Darstellungskörper m (Computergrafik)
~ **window** Abbildungsfenster n, Darstellungsfenster n
viewable beobachtbar; sichtbar
~ **screen diagonal** sichtbare Bildschirmdiagonale f
viewbox Schaukasten m; Betrachtungskasten m
viewdata interaktiver Videotext m (s.a. videotext)
viewer 1. Betrachter m, Beschauer m; Zuschauer m; 2. Betrachtungsgerät n; 3. Dateibetrachter m
~**-centered coordinate system** betrachterzentriertes Koordinatensystem n
~**-centered perspective** Betrachterperspektive f
~ **position** Betrachterposition f, Betrachterstandpunkt m
~**-to-screen distance** Bildschirmabstand m
viewfinder Sucher m
~ **accessories** Sucherzubehör n
~ **axis** Sucherachse f
~ **camera** Sucherkamera f
~ **error** Sucherfehler m
~ **focusing** Suchereinstellung f
~ **focusing** Sucherfokussierung f
~ **frame** Sucher[bild]rahmen m

viewfinder 424

~ **frame coverage** Sucher[gesichts]feld *n*, Sucherfeldgröße *f*
~ **image** Sucherbild *n*
~ **information** Sucheranzeige *f*
~ **lens** Sucherobjektiv *n*
~ **light path** Sucherlichtweg *m*
~ **magnification** Suchervergrößerung *f*
~ **mirror** Sucherspiegel *m*
~ **optics** Sucheroptik *f*
~ **performance** Sucherleistung *f*
~ **prism** Sucherprisma *n*
~ **system** Suchersystem *n*
~ **window** Sucherfenster *n*
viewing Betrachtung *f*; Sehen *n*
~ **aid** Betrachtungshilfe *f*
~ **angle** Betrachtungswinkel *m*; Beobachtungswinkel *m*; Blickwinkel *m*; Sichtwinkel *m*
~ **aparatus** Betrachtungsgerät *n*
~ **aperture** Beobachtungsapertur *f*
~ **area** Betrachtungsfeld *n*
~ **axis** Betrachtungsachse *f*
~ **box** Leuchtpult *n*
~ **conditions** Betrachtungsbedingungen *pl*
~ **cone** Betrachtungskegel *m*
~ **device** Betrachtungsgerät *n*
~ **direction** Blickrichtung *f*; Sehrichtung *f*; Beobachtungsrichtung *f*, Betrachtungsrichtung *f*
~ **distance** Sehabstand *m*, Sehentfernung *f*; Betrachtungsabstand *m*, Betrachtungsentfernung *f*; Beobachtungsentfernung
~ **environment** Abbildungsumgebung *f*; Betrachtungsumgebung *f* *(Computergrafik)*
~ **equipment** Betrachtungstechnik *f*
~ **filter** Betrachtungsfilter *n*
~ **geometry** Betrachtungsgeometrie *f*
~ **hood** Lichtschacht *m* *(Spiegelreflexkamera)*
~ **illuminant** Betrachtungslicht *n*
~ **lens** Sucherobjektiv *n*
~ **medium** Betrachtungsmedium *n*
~ **mode** Betrachtungsmodus *m*, Ansichtsmodus *m*
~ **parallax** Betrachtungsparallaxe *f*
~ **parameter** Betrachtungsparameter *m*
~ **pipeline** Betrachtungstransformation *f*
~ **plane** Ansichtsebene *f*; Darstellungsebene *f*, Abbildungsebene *f*
~ **point** Betrachtungsposition *f*
~ **position** Betrachtungsposition *f*
~ **print** Ansichtskopie *f*
~ **process** Betrachtungsvorgang *m*
~ **range** Beobachtungsbereich *m*
~ **ray** Blickstrahl *m*; Sehstrahl *m*
~ **screen** 1. Mattscheibe *f*, Sucherscheibe *f*, Einstellscheibe *f*; 2. Beobachtungsschirm *m*, Sichtschirm *m*; Bildschirm *m* *(s.a. unter* display, screen, monitor*)*
~ **situation** Betrachtungssituation *f*
~ **surface** Bildschirmfläche *f*

~ **system** Suchersystem *n*
~ **technique** Betrachtungstechnik *f*
~ **telescope** Betrachtungsfernrohr *n*, Beobachtungsfernrohr *n*
~ **time** Betrachtungszeit[dauer] *f*
~ **tube** Empfängerbildröhre *f*
~ **vector** Sichtvektor *m*
~ **window** Bildnummernfenster *n* *(Kamera)*
viewless unsichtbar, invisibel
viewmeter Ausschnittsucher *m*
viewpoint Blickpunkt *m*
~ **difference** Sucherparallaxe *f*, Parallaxe *f*
viewport Ansichtsfenster *n*, Darstellungsfeld *n*; Zeichenfläche *f* *(Gerätekoordinatensystem)*
vignette/to vignettieren
vignette Vignette *f*
~ **halftone** verlaufende Rasterfläche *f*
vignetting [effect] Vignettierung *f*, Randabschattung *f*
Villard effect Villard-Effekt *m* *(Röntgen-Doppelbelichtungseffekt)*
vintage [photographic] print Originalabzug *m*; Originalvergrößerung *f*
virgin stock (tape) Frischband *n* *(s.a.* blank tape*)*
virgule Schrägstrich *m*
virtual virtuell, virtual
~ **angioscopy** virtuelle Angioskopie *f*
~ **camera** virtuelle (synthetische) Kamera *f*
~ **classroom** virtuelles Klassenzimmer *n*
~ **device** virtuelles Gerät *n*
~ **device coordinate** virtuelle Koordinate *f*
~ **endoscopy** virtuelle Endoskopie *f*
~ **environment** virtuelle Umgebung *f*
~ **focus** virtueller Brennpunkt *m*, Sekundärfokus *m*, Zerstreuungspunkt *m*
~ **image** virtuelles (scheinbares) Bild *n*, Luftbild *n* *(Optik)*
~ **interface** virtuelle Schnittstelle *f*
~ **light source** virtuelle Lichtquelle *f*
~ **memory** virtueller Speicher *m*, Auslagerungsspeicher *m*, Auslagerungsdatei *f*
~ **microscopy** virtuelle Mikroskopie *f*
~ **mirror** virtueller Spiegel *m*
~ **model** virtuelles Modell *n*
~ **object** virtuelles Objekt *n*
~ **primary** virtuelle Primärvalenz *f*
~ **reality** virtuelle Realität *f*, Computerbildwelt *f*, betretbare Raumbilder *npl*
~ **-reality display** VR-Bildschirm *m*
~ **-reality helmet** Bildschirmhelm *m*, Daten[sicht]helm *m*, Helmdisplay *n*, Kopfmonitor *m*
~ **-reality model[l]ing language** VR-Modellierungssprache *f*
~ **-reality system** *s.* virtual space
~ **set** computergenerierte (virtuelle) Kulisse *f*, virtuelle Dekoration *f*
~ **space** virtueller Raum *m*, Cyberspace *m*

~ **storage** virtueller Speicher *m*
~ **studio** virtuelles Studio (Fernsehstudio) *n*
~ **world** virtuelle Welt *f*
virtuality Virtualität *f*
viscosity Viskosität *f*
viscous ink dick[flüssig]e Druckfarbe *f*, zähflüssige (hochviskose) Druckfarbe *f*
~ **processing** Pastenentwicklung *f*
visibility Sichtbarkeit *f*, Visibilität *f*; Sichtweite *f*, Sicht *f*
~ **computation** Sichtbarmachen *n*, Sichtbarmachung *f (Computergrafik)*
~ **of detail[s]** Detailerkennbarkeit *f*
~ **operation** Sichtbarkeitsverfahren *n (Computergrafik)*
~ **processing** Sichtbarkeits-Vorberechnung *f (Computergrafik)*
~ **range** Sichtbereich *m*
~ **threshold** Sehschwelle *f*
visible sichtbar, visibel
~ **color** sichtbare Farbe *f*
~ **image** sichtbares Bild *n*
~ **light** sichtbares Licht *n*
~-**light image** Lichtbild *n*, optisches Bild *n*, optische Abbildung *f*
~-**light microscopy** Lichtmikroskopie *f*, lichtoptische Mikroskopie *f*
~-**light photon** Lichtquant *n*, Photon *n*
~-**light spectrum** sichtbares Spektrum *n*
~-**light telescope** Lichtteleskop *n*
~-**line determination** Sichtbarkeitsentscheid *m*
~ **noise** sichtbares Rauschen *n*
~ **radiation** sichtbare Strahlung *f*
~ **scanning line** sichtbare Zeile *f (Video, Fernsehen)*
~ **screen diagonal** sichtbare Bildschirmdiagonale *f*
~ **search** sichtbarer Suchlauf *m*
~ **spectral region** sichtbarer Spektralbereich *m*
~ **sunlight** sichtbares Sonnenlicht *n*
~-**surface algorithm** Sichtbarkeitsalgorithmus *m (Computergrafik)*
~-**surface determination** Sichtbarkeitsentscheid *m (Computergrafik)*
~-**surface identification** Elimination *f* verdeckter Flächen
~ **watermark** sichtbares Wasserzeichen *n*
visibleness *s.* visibility
vision 1. Sehen *n*; 2. *s.* visual sense
~ **application** Bildverarbeitungsanwendung *f*
~ **carrier [frequency]** Bildträgerfrequenz *f*
~ **cone** Betrachtungskegel *m*
~ **control** Bildregie *f*, Senderegie *f (Fernsehen)*
~ **control room** Bildregieraum *m*
~ **defect** Sehfehler *m*
~ **mixer** *s.* video mixer

~ **module** Bilderkennungsmodul *m*
~ **persistence** Nachbildwirkung *f*
~ **process** Sehprozess *m*, Sehvorgang *m*
~ **research (science)** Sehforschung *f*
~ **test** Sehtest *m*, Sehprobe *f*
visual 1. visuell; 2. *s.* visible
~ **ability** Sehvermögen *n*, Sehfähigkeit *f*
~ **accommodation** Akkommodation *f*
~ **acuity** Sehschärfe *f*, Visus *m*
~ **acuity measurement** Sehschärfebestimmung *f*, Visusbestimmung *f*
~ **adaptation** Adaptation *f (des Auges)*
~ **aid** 1. Sehhilfe *f*; 2. *s.* teaching film
~ **analysis** visuelle Analyse *f*
~ **angle** Sehwinkel *m*, Gesichtswinkel *m*
~ **appearance** visuelle Erscheinung *f*, Erscheinungsbild *n*
~ **attention** visuelle Aufmerksamkeit *f*
~-**aural separation** Bild-Ton-Trägerabstand *m*, Bildträger-Tonträger-Abstand *m (Fernsehsignal)*
~ **axis** Sehachse *f*, visuelle Achse *f*
~ **behavior** Sehverhalten *n*
~ **brightness** gesehene Helligkeit *f*
~ **capability** Sehvermögen *n*, Sehfähigkeit *f*
~ **capture** visuelle Erfassung *f*
~ **cell** Sehzelle *f*
~ **center** Sehzentrum *n (des Gehirns)*
~ **communication** visuelle Kommunikation *f*
~ **completion** amodale Ergänzung *f*, Kanisza-Täuschung *f (visuelle Wahrnehmung)*
~ **cone** Sehzapfen *m*, Netzhautzapfen *m*, Netzhautzäpfchen *n*, [retinaler] Zapfen *m* *(s.a. unter* cone*)*
~ **contrast** visueller Kontrast *m*
~ **cortex** visueller Cortex *m*, Sehrinde *f (des Gehirns)*
~ **defect** Sehfehler *m*
~ **densitometer** [visuelles] Vergleichsdensitometer *n*, optisches Densitometer *n*
~ **detection task** Sehaufgabe *f*
~ **discomfort** Sehbeeinträchtigung *f*
~ **display** Sichtschirm *m*
~ **display terminal (unit)** Sichtgerät *n*, Bildschirmgerät *n*
~ **effect** visueller Effekt *m*; Filmtrick *m*
~ **effects company (house)** Tricklabor *n*
~ **effects photographer** Trickfotograf *m*
~ **effects production** Effektgestaltung *f*
~ **effects professional** Trick[film]spezialist *m*
~ **effects technology** Tricktechnik *f*
~ **effects work** Trickarbeit *f*
~ **error** Sehfehler *m*
~ **estimate** Augenmaß *n*
~ **experience** Seherfahrung *f*
~ **feature** visuelles Merkmal *n*
~ **fidelity** Abbildungstreue *f*
~ **field** Sehfeld *n*; Gesichtsfeld *n*

visual

~ **field size** Gesichtsfeldgröße f
~ **focusing** visuelle Fokussierung f
~ **function** Sehfunktion f
~ **hyperacuity** Nonius-Sehschärfe f, Vernier-Sehschärfe f, Überauflösung f
~ **illusion** optische Täuschung f
~ **image** [visuelles] Bild n *(s.a. unter image, picture)*
~ **image interpretation** visuelle Bildinterpretation f
~ **impairment** Sehbehinderung f
~ **impression** Seheindruck m
~ **information** visuelle Information f
~ **information processing** visuelle Informationsverarbeitung f
~ **inspection** Sichtkontrolle f, Sichtprüfung f
~ **interpolation** visuelle Interpolation f
~ **kinematics** visuelle Kinematik f
~ **light** sichtbares Licht n
~ **line** s. view line
~ **look** s. ~ appearance
~ **magnification** visuelle Vergrößerung f *(Optik)*
~ **mechanism** Sehmechanismus m
~ **memory** visuelles Gedächtnis n
~ **motion perception** visuelle Bewegungswahrnehmung f
~ **nervous system** Sehnervensystem n
~ **object** Sehding n, Sehobjekt n, visuelles Objekt n
~ **observation** visuelle Beobachtung f
~ **organ** Sehorgan n
~ **pathway** Sehbahn f
~ **pattern discrimination** visuelle Musterunterscheidung f
~ **perception** visuelle (optische) Wahrnehmung f, Sehwahrnehmung f, Gesichtswahrnehmung f
~ **performance** Sehleistung f
~ **phosphene** Phosphen n *(Lichtempfindung)*
~ **photometer** visuelles Fotometer n
~ **photometry** visuelle (subjektive) Fotometrie f
~ **physiology** Physiologie f des Sehens
~ **pigment** Sehpigment n, Sehfarbstoff m
~ **presentation** visuelle Darstellung f
~ **process** Sehprozess m, Sehvorgang m
~ **purple [pigment]** Sehpurpur m, Rhodopsin n
~ **range** Sehweite f, Sichtweite f
~ **ray** Sehstrahl m
~ **receptor** Sehrezeptor m, Rezeptorzelle f
~ **recognition** visuelles Erkennen n
~ **representation** visuelle Darstellung f
~ **resolution** visuelle Auflösung f
~ **scanner** Sichtscanner m
~ **scene** visuelle Szene f
~ **sensation** Seheindruck m, Gesichtsempfindung f
~ **sense** Sehsinn m, Gesichtssinn m, Visus m
~ **sensitivity** visuelle Empfindlichkeit f

~ **sensor** visueller Sensor m
~ **signal** visuelles Signal n
~ **signature verification** visuelle Unterschriftenprüfung f
~ **simulation** visuelle Simulation f
~ **space** Sehraum m
~ **spectrum** sichtbares Spektrum n
~ **stimulus** Sehreiz m, visueller (optischer) Reiz m
~ **storage system** Bildspeichersystem n
~ **system** Sehsystem n, visuelles System n, Sehapparat m
~ **telephony** Bildtelefonie f, Videotelefonie f, Bildfernsprechen n
~ **telephony installation** Bildtelefonanalage f
~ **telephony kiosk** Bildtelefonzelle f
~ **telephony link** Bildtelefonverbindung f
~ **telephony signal** Bildtelefonsignal n
~ **telescope** Lichtteleskop n
~ **test** Sehtest m, Sehprobe f
~ **test target** Sehzeichen n
~ **threshold** Sehschwelle f
~ **violet** Iodopsin n *(Netzhautpigment)*
~ **wavelength range** sichtbarer (optischer) Wellenlängenbereich m
visualistics Visualistik f
visualization Visualisierung f, Sichtbarmachung f, optische Darstellung f, Sichtbarmachen n, Veranschaulichung f

~ **algorithm** Visualisierungsalgorithmus m
~ **network** Visualisierungsnetzwerk n
~ **object** Visualisierungsobjekt n
~ **software** Visualisierungssoftware f
~ **step** Visualisierungsschritt m
~ **task** Visualisierungsaufgabe f
~ **technique** Visualisierungsverfahren n; Visualisierungstechnik f
~ **technology** Visualisierungstechnik f
~ **tool** Visualisierungswerkzeug n
visualize/to visualisieren, veranschaulichen, optisch darstellen
visualizer Visualisierer m
visually impaired sehbehindert
vitamin A aldehyde Retinal n
vitascope Vitaskop n *(frühes Filmprojektionsgerät)*
Viterbi algorithm Viterbi-Algorithmus m *(Bilddatenverarbeitung)*
~ **decoder** Viterbi-Decod[ier]er m
~ **decoding** Viterbi-Decodierung f
vitreous [body], ~ **humor** Glaskörper m *(des Auges)*
~ **silica** Kieselglas n
vitrotype Vitrotypie f *(Albuminplattenfotografie)*
vivid farbsatt
~ **color** kräftige (satte) Farbe f, gesättigte Farbe f
vividness [of color] Farbsättigungsgrad m, Sättigungsgrad m
Viviscope Viviskop n *(frühe Kinematografie)*

VLSI circuit s. very large-scale integrated circuit
~ **technology** s. very large-scale integration technology
VOD s. video-on-demand
Vogl interferometer Voglsches Interferometer n
voice activation (actuation), ~ input control Sprachsteuerung f *(z.B. eines Fernsehgerätes)*
~**-over** Voice-over-Verfahren n *(Filmton)*
volatile memory (storage) flüchtiger Speicher m
voltage bandwidth Spannungsbandbreite f; optische Bandbreite f *(Fotodetektor)*
~ **contrast** Spannungskontrast m *(Elektronenmikroskopie)*
~**-controlled amplifier** spannungsgesteuerter Verstärker m
~**-controlled oscillator** spannungsgesteuerter Oszillator m
~**-dependent scanning tunneling microscopy** spannungsabhängige Rastertunnelmikroskopie f
~ **divider** Spannungsteiler m
~ **pulse** Spannungsimpuls m
~ **regulator** Spannungsstabilisator m
~ **signal** Spannungssignal n
~ **spike** Spannungsspitze f
~ **stabilizer** Spannungsstabilisator m, Spannungskonstanthalter m
volume 1. Volumen n; 2. Lautstärke f; 3. s. data carrier
~ **brightness** Raumhelligkeit f
~ **computerized tomography** Volumen-Computertomografie f
~ **data** Volumendaten pl
~ **description** Volumenbeschreibung f
~ **element** s. voxel
~ **form** Volumenform f
~ **grating** Volumengitter n
~ **growing** Volumenwachstum n
~ **hologram** Volumenhologramm n, Tiefenhologramm n
~ **holographic** volumenholografisch
~ **holography** Volumenholografie f, Tiefenholografie f
~ **image** s. volumetric image
~ **image data** Volumenbilddaten pl
~ **image segmentation** Volumenbildsegmentierung f
~ **integral** Volumenintegral n
~ **mesh** Volumengitter n
~ **model** Volumenmodell n
~ **of interest** interessierendes Volumen n
~ **picture element, ~ pixel [element]** s. voxel
~ **printing** Massenkopierung f
~ **range** Lautstärkebereich m
~ **reconstruction** Volumenrekonstruktion f
~ **rendering** [computergrafische] Volumendarstellung f *(Vorgang)*
~ **rendition** [computergrafische] Volumendarstellung f *(Resultat)*
~ **scan** Volumenscan m
~ **scanner** Volumenscanner m
~ **scattering** Volumenstreuung f
~ **set** Datenträgersatz m
~ **transmission hologram** Volumenhologramm n, Tiefenhologramm n
~ **visualization** Volumenvisualisierung f
~ **wave** Volumenwelle f
volumetric volumetrisch, maßanalytisch
~ **data set** Volumendatensatz m
~ **image** Volumenbild n, volumetrisches Bild n
~ **image analysis** volumetrische Bildanalyse f
~ **image navigation** volumetrische Bildnavigation f
~ **object** räumliches Objekt n
~ **primitive** Primitivkörper m, [elementarer] Grundkörper m, Raumprimitiv n, Volumenprimitiv n
~ **segmentation** volumetrische Segmentierung f
von Hann window s. Hanning window
~ **Koch snowflake curve** Koch-Kurve f *(fraktale Geometrie)*
~ **Seidel aberration** Seidel-Aberration f, Seidelscher Abbildungsfehler (Bildfehler) m
Voronoi analysis Voronoi-Analyse f *(geometrische Datenverarbeitung)*
~ **diagram** Voronoi-Diagramm n, Thiessen-Diagramm n
~ **edge** Voronoi-Kante f
~ **image** Voronoi-Bild n
~ **point** Voronoi-Punkt m
~ **region** s. ~ surface
~ **skeleton** Voronoi-Skelett n
~ **surface** Voronoi-Zelle f, Voronoi-Zone f, Voronoi-Region f, Voronoi-Gebiet n
~ **tessellation (tiling)** [Poisson-]Voronoi-Mosaik n, Dirichlet-Parkettierung f
vorticity Wirbligkeit f *(Strömungsvisualisierung)*
voxel Voxel n, Volumenpixel n, Normzelle f, Volumenelement n, räumliches Pixel n, Elementarquader m
~**-based object** voxelbasiertes Objekt n
~**-based reconstruction** Voxelrekonstruktion f, voxelbasierte Rekonstruktion f
~**-based representation** voxelbasierte Darstellung f
~**-based surface rendering** voxelbasierte Oberflächendarstellung f
~**-by-voxel** voxelweise
~ **center** Voxelmitte f
~ **grid** Voxelgitter n
~ **image** Voxelbild n
~ **lattice** Voxelgitter n
~ **model** Voxelmodell n
~ **projection** Voxelprojektion f
~ **resolution** Voxelauflösung f

voxel

~ **size** Voxelgröße *f*
~ **space** Voxelraum *m*
~ **value** Voxelwert *m*
~ **volume** Voxelvolumen *n*
VP *s.* videophone
VR *s.* virtual reality
VR display VR-Bildschirm *m*
VSD imaging *neurologisches Bildgebungsverfahren unter Verwendung von spannungsempfindlichen Farbstoffen (voltage-sensitive dyes)*
VTR *s.* videotape recorder

W

wafer Wafer *m*, Halbleiterscheibe *f*
wagon Rollwagen *m*
waist diameter Taillendurchmesser *m* *(Strahlenoptik)*
~-level finder Aufsichtssucher *m*, Lichtschachtsucher *m*, Brillantsucher *m*
~ radius Taillenradius *m*
waldo s. remotely controlled robot
wall screen Feldnetz *n* *(Katodenstrahlröhre)*
walled garden Internetportal *n*, Portal *n*
wallpaper illusion Tapetenillusion *f* *(Stereosehen)*
WAN s. wide area network
wand 1. Strichcodeleser *m*, Barcodeleser *m*, Barcodescanner *m*; 2. Zauberstab *m* *(Bildbearbeitungswerkzeug)*
war photographer Kriegsfotograf *m*
warm boot[ing] Warmstart *m* *(Computer)*
~ color warme Farbe *f*
~ light warmes Licht *n*
~ start Warmstart *m* *(Computer)*
~-tone developer Warmtonentwickler *m*
~-tone paper Warmtonpapier *n*
~-up [diffusion] filter Warmtonfilter *n*
~-up time Anlaufzeit *f* *(z.B. eines Kopierers)*
warp/to verformen, deformieren, transformieren
warp Wölbung *f*, Verwerfung *f* *(z.B. von Filmmaterial)*; Verzerrung *f*
warping Warping-Technik *f* *(Visualisierungsverfahren zur Bewegungsschätzung)*
wash/to wässern *(Fotoverarbeitung)*
wash away/to auswaschen *(z.B. Offsetdruckplatten)*
~ out/to auswässern
~ up/to auswaschen
~ water Wässerungsflüssigkeit *f*
~ water temperature Wässerungstemperatur *f*
washed-out picture verwaschenes Bild *n*
washing Wässerung *f*, Auswässerung *f*, Auswässern *n* *(Fotoverarbeitung)*
~ apparatus Wässerungsvorrichtung *f*
~ fluid Wässerungsflüssigkeit *f*
~ tank Wässerungstank *m*
~ technique Wässerungstechnik *f*
~ time Wässerungsdauer *f*, Wässerungszeit *f*
~ tray Wässerungswanne *f*
~ water Spülwasser *n*
washless processing wasserlose Verarbeitung (Fotoverarbeitung) *f*
waste Makulatur *f* *(Druckwesen)*
~ electronics Elektronikschrott *m*

watch/to beobachten
watch television (TV)/to fernsehen
water bath Wasserbad *n*
~-bath development Wasserbadentwicklung *f*
~ depth measurement Wassertiefenmessung *f*, Bathymetrie *f*
~-equivalent mathematical phantom Wasserphantom *n* *(Röntgendosimetrie)*
~ hardness Wasserhärte *f*
~ immersion objective Wasserimmersionsobjektiv *n* *(Mikroskopie)*
~ jacket Wassermantelbad *n*
~ mark Trockenfleck *m* *(z.B. auf Filmmaterial)*
~ proton Wasserstoffkern *m*
~-receptive wasserannehmend, wasseraufnehmend, wasserfreundlich, feuchtfreundlich, hydrophil, feuchtigkeitsführend
~-repellent wasserabstoßend, wasserabweisend, feuchtfeindlich, hydrophob
~-resistant wasserfest; spritzwassergeschützt
~ rinse Wässerung *f*, Auswässern *n*, Auswässerung *f*
~ roller Feucht[auftrags]walze *f* *(Druckmaschine)*
~ softener Wasserenthärter *m*
~ softening Wasserenthärtung *f*
~ spot [blemish] Trockenfleck *m* *(auf Fotomaterial)*
~ wash Wässerung *f*, Auswässern *n*, Auswässerung *f*
~ window Wasserfenster *n* *(Röntgenmikroskopie)*
Waterhouse stop Steckblende *f* *(Lochblendenvariante)*
waterless lithography Trockenoffsetdruck *m*, Trockenflachdruck *m*, Letter[off]setdruck *m*, indirekter Hochdruck *m*
watermark Wasserzeichen *n*
watermarking algorithm Wasserzeichenalgorithmus *m*
~ technique Wasserzeichenverfahren *n*
waterproof camera housing wasserdichtes Kameragehäuse *n*
~ paper wasserfestes Papier *n*
watershed segmentation algorithm Wasserscheidenalgorithmus *m* *(Binärbildverarbeitung)*
~ transform, watersheds technique Wasserscheidentransformation *f*
watertight wasserdicht
watt Watt *n* *(Einheit der physikalischen Leistung)*
~-second Wattsekunde *f*
wattage Wattzahl *f* *(z.B. eines Scheinwerfers)*
wave Welle *f*
~ aberration s. wave-front aberration

wave

- ~ amplitude Wellenamplitude *f*
- ~ band Wellenband *n*
- ~ equation Wellengleichung *f*
- ~ field Wellenfeld *n*
- ~ field sythesis Wellenfeldsynthese *f*
- ~ frequency Wellenfrequenz *f*
- ~ front Wellenfront *f*, Wellenfläche *f*
- ~-front aberration Wellen[front]aberration *f*, Wellenfrontfehler *m*, Wellenfrontdeformation *f*
- ~-front amplitude Wellenfrontamplitude *f*
- ~-front analysis Wellenfrontanalyse *f*
- ~-front array Wellenfront-Zellenfeld *n*
- ~-front correction Wellenfrontkorrektur *f*
- ~-front curvature Wellenfrontkrümmung *f*
- ~-front deformation *s*. ~ aberration
- ~-front distortion Wellenfrontverzerrung *f*
- ~-front error *s*. ~ aberration
- ~-front interferogram Wellenfrontinterferogramm *n*
- ~-front reconstruction Wellenfrontrekonstruktion *f*, Wellenfrontumkehr *f*
- ~-front sensor Wellenfrontsensor *m*, Phasenfrontsensor *m*
- ~ function Wellenfunktion *f*
- ~ interference Welleninterferenz *f*
- ~ motion Wellenbewegung *f*
- ~ nature of light Wellennatur *f* des Lichts
- ~ number Wellenzahl *f*
- ~ number domain Frequenzraum *m*
- ~-number spectrum Wellenzahlspektrum *n*
- ~-number vector Wellenzahlvektor *m*
- ~ optical, wave-optics wellenoptisch
- ~ optics Wellenoptik *f*, physikalische Optik *f*
- ~ packet Wellenpaket *n*
- ~ pattern Wellenmuster *n*
- ~ plate doppelbrechende planparallele Platte *f*, Verzögerungsplatte *f*
- ~ surface Wellenfläche *f*, Wellenfront *f*
- ~ theory [of light] Wellentheorie (Undulationstheorie) *f* des Lichts
- ~ train Wellenzug *m*
- ~ vector Wellenvektor *m*
- ~ velocity Wellengeschwindigkeit *f*

waveform Wellenform *f*

- ~-based coding Wellenformcodierung *f*
- ~ editor Wellenformeditor *m*
- ~ encoding Wellenformcodierung *f*
- ~ monitor Wellenformmonitor *m*

waveguide Wellenleiter *m*

wavelength Wellenlänge *f*

- ~ analysis Wellenlängenanalyse *f*
- ~ band Wellenlängenband *n*, Wellenlängengruppe *f*
- ~-dependent refractive index wellenlängenabhängige Brechzahl *f*
- ~-dispersive X-ray spectrometer wellenlängendispersives Röntgenspektrometer *n*
- ~ distribution Wellenlängenverteilung *f*
- ~ division multiplexing *s*. ~ multiplex technique
- ~ filter Wellenlängenfilter *n*
- ~-independent wellenlängenunabhängig *(Detektor)*
- ~ interference Welleninterferenz *f*
- ~ interval Wellenlängenintervall *n*
- ~ multiplex technique Wellenlängenmultiplexverfahren *n*
- ~ range (region) Wellenlängenbereich *m*
- ~ spectrum Wellenlängenspektrum *n*

wavelet Wavelet *n*, Elementarwelle *f*

- ~ analysis Wavelet-Analyse *f*
- ~-based coding waveletbasierte Codierung *f*, Wavelet-Bildcodierung *f*, Wavelet-Codierung *f*
- ~-based edge detection waveletbasierte Kantendetektion *f*
- ~-based image coding waveletbasierte Bildcodierung *f*
- ~-based texture coding waveletbasierte Textcodierung *f*
- ~-based transform[ation] waveletbasierte Transformation *f*
- ~ basis Basis-Wavelet *n*
- ~ coefficient Wavelet-Koeffizient *m*
- ~ compression waveletbasierte Kompression *f*
- ~ decomposition Wavelet-Zerlegung *f*
- ~ domain representation Wavelet-Darstellung *f*
- ~ filter Wavelet-Filter *n*, [variables] Wellenformfilter *n*
- ~ filter bank Wavelet-Filterbank *f*
- ~ function Wavelet-Funktion *f*
- ~ image coding Wavelet-Bildcodierung *f*, Wavelet-Codierung *f*
- ~ packet Wavelet-Paket *n*
- ~-packet transform Wavelet-Pakettransformation *f*
- ~ radiosity Wavelet-Radiosity *f* *(Computergrafik)*
- ~ reconstruction Wavelet-Rekonstruktion *f*
- ~ representation Wavelet-Darstellung *f*
- ~-transform-based compression waveletbasierte Kompression *f*
- ~ transform coefficient Wavelet-Koeffizient *m*
- ~ transform compression Wavelet-Kompression *f*, Wavelet-Kompressionsverfahren *n*
- ~ transformation Wavelet-Transformation *f* *(Digitalbildverarbeitung)*
- ~ vector Wavelet-Vektor *m*

waveshape Wellenform *f*

waviness Welligkeit *f*

wavy edge Kantenwelligkeit *f*

- ~ pattern Wellenmuster *n* *(z.B. Moiré)*

wax-melt printer Thermowachsdrucker *m*

- ~ paper Wachspapier *n*

waxed-paper process Wachspapierverfahren *n* *(fotografisches Negativverfahren)*

wayfinding Navigation *f*

weak color ungesättigte Farbe *f*
~ **echo** schwaches Echo *n* *(Radar, Sonografie)*
~ **edge** unscharfe Kante *f*
~ **light** schwaches Licht *n*, Schwachlicht *n*
~ **perspective** flache Perspektive *f*
weather map Wetterkarte *f*
~ **satellite** Wettersatellit *m*
~ **satellite imagery** Wettersatellitenbilder *npl*
~ **surveillance radar** Wetterradar *n*
weatherized camera Allwetterkamera *f*
web 1. Papierbahn *f*, Bahn *f*, Rollenpapier *n* *(Druck)*; 2. *s.* Web
Web [World Wide] Web *n* *(s.a. unter Internet)*
~ **broadcasting** Internet-Fernsehen *n*
~ **browser** Webbrowser *m*
~ **camera** *s.* Webcam
~ **design** Internetgestaltung *f*, Webdesign *n*
web-fed gravure printing Rollentiefdruck *m*
~**-fed letterpress machine** Hochdruckrotationsmaschine *f*
~**-fed rotary press** Rollenrotationsmaschine *f*
~**-fed rotogravure** Rollenrotationstiefdruck *m*
Web graphics Webgrafik *f*
web offset press Offsetrollendruckmaschine *f*, Offsetrotations[druck]maschine *f*, Rollenoffset[druck]maschine *f*
~ **offset printing** Rollenoffsetdruck *m*
Web page Internetseite *f*, Webseite *f*
~ **page designer** Internetgestalter *m*, Webdesigner *m*
web press Rollendruckmaschine *f*
~ **printing** Rollendruck *m*
Web site Webseite *f*, Internetseite *f*
web tension Bahnspannung *f*
Web TV Internet-Fernsehen *n*
web width Rollenpapierbreite *f*
Webcam Internetkamera *f*, Webkamera *f*, Webcam *f*
~ **software** Webkamera-Software *f*
webcast video Internetvideo *n*
Webcasting Videoübertragung *f* im Internet
weber Weber *n*, Wb *(Einheit des magnetischen Flusses)*
Weber photometer Webersches Fotometer *n*
Weber's law, Weber-Fechner law [Weber-]Fechnersches Gesetz *n*, psychophysisches Grundgesetz *n* *(Wahrnehmungsphysiologie)*
wedding photograph Hochzeitsfoto *n*
~ **photographer** Hochzeitsfotograf *m*
~ **photography** Hochzeitsfotografie *f*
wedge Keil *m*
~ **photometer** Graukeilfotometer *n*
~ **spectrogram** Keilspektrogramm *n*
~ **spectrograph** Keilspektrograf *m*

wedged optical plate Keilplatte *f*, keilförmige Platte *f*
~ **spaceband** Ausschließkeil *m*, Spatienkeil *m*, Keil *m* *(Satzherstellung)*
Wehnelt cylinder Wehnelt-Zylinder *m*, Katodenzylinder *m* *(Katodenstrahlröhre)*
~ **voltage** Wehnelt-Spannung *f*
Weigert effect Weigert-Effekt *m* *(Belichtungseffekt)*
weight 1. Gewicht *n*; Masse *f*; 2. Wertigkeit *f*; 3. Schriftschnitt *m*; Schriftauszeichnung *f* *(Typografie)*
~ **matrix** *s.* weighting kernel
~ **vector** Gewichtsvektor *m*
weighted Euclidean distance gewichteter Euklidischer Abstand *m*
~ **filter** gewichtetes Filter *n*
~ **finite automaton** gewichteter endlicher Automat *m*
~ **graph** gewichteter Graph *m*
~ **median [filter]** gewichtetes Medianfilter *n*
~ **SNR** gewichtetes Signal-Rausch-Verhältnis *n*
weighting factor Wichtungsfaktor *m*
~ **function** Wichtungsfunktion *f*, Gewichtsfunktion *f* *(Signalverarbeitung)*
~ **kernel (matrix)** Wichtungsmatrix *f*, Gewichtsmatrix *f*
Weinland effect Weinland-Effekt *m* *(Belichtungseffekt)*
weld image Schweißnahtabbildung *f*
well Rasternäpfchen *n*, Näpfchen *n* *(Tiefdruck)*
~**-developed image** ausentwickeltes Bild *n*
wet-chemical etching nasschemisches Ätzen *n*
~ **chemical processing** *s.* ~ film processing
~**-collodion camera** Nasskollodiumkamera *f*
~**-collodion photography** Nasskollodiumverfahren *n*, nasses Kollodiumverfahren *n*
~**-collodion plate** nasse Kollodiumplatte *f*
~**-collodion stereograph camera** Nasskollodium-Stereokamera *f*
~ **development** Nassentwicklung *f*
~ **dot-etching** Nassätzen *n* *(Druckformherstellung)*
~ **equipment** *s.* ~ side
~ **etching** Nassätzen *n* *(Halbleiterverarbeitung)*
~ **film** Nassfilm *m*
~ **film processing** Nassverarbeitung *f*
~ **gate** Nasskopierfenster *n*
~**-gate printer** Nasskopiermaschine *f*, Nasskopiereinrichtung *f*
~**-gate printing** Nass[fenster]kopierung *f*, Nasskopierverfahren *n*
~**-gate scanning** Nassabtastung *f*
~**-plate [negative-positive] process** Nass[bild]plattenverfahren *n*

wet

~ **processing** Nassverarbeitung f, Nassbearbeitung f
~ **side** Nassbereich m, Nassteil m (Dunkelkammer)
~ **strength** Nassreißfestigkeit f (z.B. von Fotopapier)
~ **time** Nasszeit f
~**-trap/to** nass in nass drucken
wetting Feuchtung f, Druckformfeuchtung f
~ **agent** Netzmittel n, Entspannungsmittel n
~ **roller** Feucht[auftrags]walze f (Druckmaschine)
~ **system** Feuchtwerk n (Druckmaschine)
what you see is what you get bezeichnet die annähernd druckbildgerechte Bildschirmanzeige vor Druckausgabe
wheel mouse Radmaus f (Eingabegerät)
~ **of life** Bildertrommel f, Lebensrad n (frühe Kinematografie)
whip pan Reißschwenk m, schneller Schwenk m, Wischer m (Kamerabewegung)
white balance [correction] Weiß[licht]abgleich m, Weißausgleich m, Unbuntabgleich m, Grauabgleich m (Videokamera)
~ **balance error** Weißabgleichfehler m
~ **balance switch** Weißabgleichtaste f
~ **content** Weißgehalt m (Farbmetrik)
~ **Gaussian noise** weißes Gaußsches Rauschen n
~ **LED** Weißlicht-Leuchtdiode f, weiße Leuchtdiode f
~ **level** Weißwert m, Weißpegel m (Videosignal)
~ **light** Weißlicht n, weißes (unbuntes) Licht n
~**-light balancing** s. white balance [correction]
~**-light fringe** Weißlichtstreifen m (Interferometrie)
~**-light hologram** Weißlichthologramm n
~**-light interferometry** Weißlichtinterferometrie f
~**-light printing [method]** subtraktives Kopieren n
~**-light reflection hologram** Weißlicht-Reflexionshologramm n
~**-light reflection holography** Weißlicht-Reflexionsholografie f
~**-light source** Weißlichtquelle f
~**-light spectrum** Weißlichtspektrum n, sichtbares Spektrum n
~**-light transmission hologram** Weißlicht-Transmissionshologramm n
~ **limiting** Weißbegrenzung f
~ **noise** weißes Rauschen n, Breitbandrauschen n
~ **of the eye** harte Augenhaut f, Lederhaut f, Sklera f
~ **point** Weißpunkt m, Unbuntpunkt m (Farbmetrik)

~**-point normalization** Weißpunkteinstellung f
~ **shading** Verweißlichung f
~ **space** Weißraum m, unbedruckter Raum m (einer Druckseite)
whitener optischer Aufheller m
whiteness Weiße f, Weißsein n
whitening agent s. whitener
whitish weißlich
whitishness Weißlichkeit f
Whittaker's [confluent hypergeometric] function Whittaker-Funktion f (Signalverarbeitung)
whole-body coil Körperspule f (Magnetresonanztomografie)
~**-body counter** Ganzkörperzähler m (Dosimetrie)
~**-body dose** Körperdosis f (Radiometrie)
~**-body imaging system** Ganzkörper-Abbildungssystem n
~**-body scan** Ganzkörperscan m
~**-body scanner** Ganzkörperscanner m
wide-angle weitwinklig
~ **angle** Weitwinkel m
~**-angle attachment** Weitwinkelvorsatz m, Weitwinkelvorsatzlinse f
~**-angle bellows** Weitwinkelbalgen m
~**-angle camera** Weitwinkelkamera f
~**-angle conversion lens** Weitwinkelkonverter m
~**-angle distortion (effect)** Weitwinkelverzerrung f, Weitwinkeleffekt m
~**-angle effect** Weitwinkelverzerrung f
~**-angle eyepiece** Weitwinkelokular n
~**-angle high-speed reflector-type camera** Weitwinkel-Hochgeschwindigkeits-Spiegelkamera f (Astrofotografie)
~**-angle lens** Weitwinkelobjektiv n
~**-angle mirror** Weitwinkelspiegel m
~**-angle photographic lens** Weitwinkelobjektiv n
~**-angle photography** Weitwinkelfotografie f
~**-angle picture** Weitwinkelbild n
~**-angle reflector** Weitwinkelreflektor m
~**-angle rendition** Weitwinkelcharakteristik f
~**-angle scattering** Weitwinkelstreuung f
~**-angle shot** Weitwinkelaufnahme f
~**-angle stereoimage** Weitwinkel-Stereobild n
~**-angle viewfinder** Weitwinkelsucher m
~**-angle zoom [lens]** Weitwinkelzoom[objektiv] n
~**-area network** Weitverkehrsnetz n, Fernnetz n
~**-bandwidth** breitbandig
~**-bandwidth connection** Breitbandverbindung f, Hochgeschwindigkeitsverbindung f
~ **canvas** Breitwand f (Kinotechnik)
~**-field astronomical photography** Großfeldfotografie f

~-**field camera** Großfeldkamera f
~-**field lens** Großfeldobjektiv n
~-**field of view eyepiece** Großfeldokular n
~-**field-of-view shot** Eröffnungseinstellung f, Überblicksaufnahme f Anfangsaufnahme f *(Film)*
~-**field photograph (picture)** Großfeldaufnahme f *(Astrofotografie)*
~-**field Schmidt telescope** Großfeld-Schmidt-Teleskop n
~-**field telescope** Großfeldteleskop n
~-**format film** Breitwandfilm m
~-**format printer** Großformatdrucker m
~-**open period (time)** Volloffenzeit f *(fotografischer Verschluss)*
~ **picture** Breitbild n
~-**picture format** Breitbildformat n
~-**screen** breitwandig
~ **screen** Breitwand f; Breitbildschirm m
~-**screen camera** Breitwandkamera f
~-**screen cinema** Breitwandkino n, Breitbildkino n
~-**screen format** Breitbildformat n
~-**screen motion picture, ~ movie** Breitwandfilm m, Breitbild-Kinofilm m
~-**screen movie format** Breitwandformat n
~-**screen movie photography** Breitwandkinematografie f
~-**screen picture** 1. Breitwandbild n; 2. s. ~ motion picture
~-**screen presentation** Breitbilddarstellung f, Breitwandvorführung f
~-**screen process** Breitbildverfahren n, Breitwand[film]verfahren n, Breitfilmverfahren n
~-**screen projection** Breitwandprojektion f
~-**screen ratio** Breitwand-Bildseitenverhältnis n
~-**screen receiver** Breitbildfernseher m, Breitformatfernseher m, Breitbildfernsehgerät n, Breitbildempfänger m
~-**screen system** Breitwandsystem n
~-**screen television** Breitbildfernsehen n
~-**screen television standard** Fernsehbreitbildstandard m
~-**web paper** Breitbahnpapier n
wideband 1. Breitband n *(s.a. unter* broadband*)*; 2. s. wide-bandwidth
~ **cable** Breitbandkabel n
widest aperture Maximalöffnung f *(Objektiv)*
widget Interaktionsbaustein m *(Computergrafik)*
widow [line] Überhang m, Überhangzeile f, Hurenkind n *(Druckfehler)*
width 1. Breite f; Weite f; 2. Zeichendickte f, Dickte f *(Typografie)*
~ **of a text block** Textblockbreite f
~ **of column** Spaltenbreite f *(Typografie)*
~ **table** Dicktentabelle f, Breitentabelle f *(Typografie)*

~-**to-height ratio** Bildseitenverhältnis n; Bildformat n
Wien's displacement (radiation) law Wiensches Verschiebungsgesetz (Gesetz) n *(Wärmestrahlung)*
Wiener filter Wiener-Filter n, Wienersches Optimalfilter n
~ **filtration** Wiener-Filterung f
~ **matrix** Wiener-Matrix f
~ **matrix filter** s. ~ filter
~ **noise-power spectrum** Wiener-Spektrum n, Rauschleistungsspektrum n *(z.B. einer fotografischen Schicht)*
wiggler [magnet] Wiggler m, Undulator m
Wigner-Seitz diagram s. Voronoi diagram
wild footage stumm gedrehtes Filmmaterial n
~ **lines** asynchroner Dialog m *(Kinematografie)*
~ **motor** Asynchronmotor m *(Kinotechnik)*
~ **sound** asynchroner Ton m; separat aufgenommener Filmton m
~ **take** Aufnahme f mit nichtsynchronisierter Kamera
~ **track** s. ~ sound
wildlife photographer Tierfotograf m
~ **photography** Tierfotografie f
Winchester drive Festplattenlaufwerk n
wind/to spulen
winder Aufspuleinrichtung f, Winder m
winding core Wickelkern m, Spulenkern m, Rollenkern m, Bobby m
~ **knob** Aufzugsknopf m
~ **lever** Aufzugshebel m, Filmtransporthebel m
~ **type** Wicklungsart f, Windungsart f *(Kinefilm)*
~ **type** Windungsart f *(Kinefilm)*
window 1. Fenster n; Bildfenster n; Monitorfenster n; Bildausschnitt m; 2. s. chaff
~ **coefficient** Fensterkoeffizient m
~ **Fourier transform** Fenster-Fourier-Transformation f
~ **glass** Fensterglas n
~-**level transformation** Fenstertechnik f, Fensterung f
~ **light** Fensterlicht n
~ **management** Fensterverwaltung f
~ **mat (mount)** Passepartout n
~ **technique** s. window-level transformation
windowed Fourier transform gefensterte Fourier-Transformation f, Kurzzeit-Fourier-Transformation f
windowing function Fensterfunktion f *(Signalverarbeitung)*
windscreen Windschutz m
windup Kurbelstativ n
winterized camera Allwetterkamera f
wipe [transition] Wischblende f, Schiebeblende f, Blendeneffekt m *(Trickkinematografie)*

wiping

wiping effect Wischeffekt *m*
wire antenna Drahtantenne *f*
~ **frame** 1. Gittergrafik *f*; 2. *s.* ~ frame model *f*
~ **frame model (object)** Gittermodell *n*, Draht[gitter]modell *n*, Skelettmodell *n*, Netzmodell *n* *(Computergrafik)*
~ **frame viewfinder** Rahmensucher *m*, Sportsucher *m* *(Kamera)*
~ **side** Siebseite *f (Papier)*
~ **target [phantom]** Drahtsteg *m* *(Radiografie)*
wireless drahtlos, kabellos
~ **LAN (local area network)** kabelloses lokales Netz *n*
~ **microphone** kabelloses (drahtloses) Mikrofon *n*, Funkmikrofon *n*, Mikroport *n*
~ **modem** kabelloses Modem *n*
~ **mouse** kabellose (schnurlose) Maus *f*, Funkmaus *f*
~ **network** kabelloses Netz *n*
~ **remote release** kabelloser Fernauslöser *m*
~ **TV [set]** kabelloses Fernsehgerät *n*
within-class variability Intraklassenvarianz *f*
~**-component layer** Komponenteninhaltsschicht *f* *(Hypermediasystem)*
~**-frame coding** Intraframe-Codierung *f*
witness point Anhaltspunkt *m*
Wollaston [polarizing] prism Wollaston-Prisma *n*
Wolter telescope Wolter-Teleskop *n*, abbildendes Röntgenteleskop *n*
wood-engraving Xylografie *f*
~**-free paper** holzfreies Papier *n*, Feinpapier *n*
woodburytype [process] Woodburytypie *f*
woods glass Cobaltglas *n*
woofer Tieftonlautsprecher *m*
word processing Textverarbeitung *f*
~ **processing program** Textverarbeitungsprogramm *n*
~ **space (spacing)** Wortabstand *m*, Wortzwischenraum *m* *(Layout)*
~ **wrap** Zeilenumbruch *m*
wordlength Datenwortbreite *f*
work print Arbeitskopie *f*, Klatschkopie *f*; Schnittkopie *f (Filmarbeit)*
~ **tape** Masterband *n (Videobearbeitung)*
working aperture Arbeitsblende *f*, gewählte Blende *f*
~ **channel** Arbeitskanal *m (Endoskop)*
~ **distance** 1. Aufnahmedistanz *f*, Aufnahmeentfernung *f*, Aufnahmeabstand *m*, Dingweite *f*, Gegenstandsweite *f*; 2. [freier] Arbeitsabstand *m (Mikroskopie)*
~ **light** Arbeitslicht *n*
~**-strength solution** Gebrauchslösung *f*, Arbeitslösung *f*
~ **wavelength** Arbeitswellenlänge *f* *(konfokale Mikroskopie)*

workpiece classification Werkstückklassifizierung *f*
~ **recognition** Werkstückerkennung *f*, Werkstückidentifikation *f*, Bauteilidentifikation *f*, Teileerkennung *f*
workshop microscope Werkstattmikroskop *n*
workstation Arbeitsplatzcomputer *m*, Arbeitsplatzrechner *m*
~ **transformation** Gerätetransformation *f*
~ **viewport** Gerätedarstellungsfeld *n*
~ **window** Gerätefenster *n*
world coordinate Weltkoordinate *f*
~ **coordinate system** Weltkoordinatensystem *n*, weltfestes Koordinatensystem *n*, Szenenkoordinatensystem *n*
~ **point** Weltkoordinatenpunkt *m*
~ **projection** Weltprojektion *f*
~ **reference frame, ~ space** *s.* ~ coordinate system
World Wide Web [World Wide] Web *n* *(Informationsdienst im Internet; s.a. unter Web)*
WORM disk (platter) WORM-Bildplatte *f*, WORM-Datenträger *m*
worm's-eye view Froschperspektive *f*, extreme Untersicht *f*
worming Kriecheffekt *m (zeitliches Aliasing)*
woven edge Webkante *f (Farbband)*
wow langsame Gleichlaufschwankung *f*
~ **and flutter** Jaulen *n*, Gleichlaufschwankung *f (Bandlauffehler)*
wrap 1. Umschlingungsgrad *m*; 2. Drehende *n*, Drehschluss *m (Filmarbeit)*; 3. *s.* wraparound artifact
~ **angle** Umschlingungswinkel *m*; Kopftrommelumschlingungswinkel *m* *(Bandgerät)*
wraparound Zeilenumlauf *m (Layout, Druck)*
~ **artifact** Einfaltung *f*, Einfaltungsartefakt *n* *(Binärbildverarbeitung)*; Aliasing *n* *(Magnetresonanzbildgebung)*
~ **convolution** zyklische Faltung *f*
~ **lighting** Rundumbeleuchtung *f*
~ **movie screen** Panoramafilmleinwand *f*
~ **[press] plate** Wickel[druck]platte *f*, Wraparound-Platte *f*, flexible Druckplatte *f*
wrapping paper Einwickelpapier *n*
Wratten filter Wratten-Filter *n*, Gelatinefilter *n*
wrist strap Hand[gelenk]schlaufe *f*; Trageschlaufe *f*
~ **support** Handauflage *f z.B. einer Computertastatur)*
write clock Schreibtakt *m* *(Zeitkompression)*
~ **cycle time** Schreib-Zyklus-Zeit *f* *(Direktzugriffsspeicher)*
~ **head** Schreibkopf *m*

~-once read-many optical disk WORM-Bildplatte *f*, WORM-Datenträger *m*
~-protect tab Schreibschutzschalter *m* *(Videokassette)*
~-protected schreibgeschützt
~ rate (speed) Schreibgeschwindigkeit *f*
writing Schrift *f*
~ beam Schreibstrahl *m*
~ operation Schreibvorgang *m*
~ paper Schreibpapier *n*
~ speed Schreibgeschwindigkeit *f*
~ to memory Speicherschreiben *n*
written script Schreibschrift *f*
wrong-reading image seitenverkehrtes (einseitig umgekehrtes) Bild *n*
WWW *s.* World Wide Web
WYSIWYG *s.* what you see is what you get

X

x-axis x-Achse f, Abszissenachse f *(Koordinatensystem)*
X contact X-Kontakt m
X-irradiation Röntgenstrahlung f
x-line Mittellinie f *(Typografie)*
X-radiation Röntgenstrahlung f
X-radiation safety Strahlensicherheit f
X-radiograph Röntgenbild n
X-radiograph device Röntgengerät n
X-radiographic röntgenografisch
X-radiographic examination Röntgenuntersuchung f
X-radiological röntgenradiologisch
X-ray/to röntgen
X-ray 1. Röntgenstrahl m, X-Strahl m; 2. s. ~ photograph
X-ray absorber Röntgenabsorber m
X-ray absorption Röntgen[strahl]absorption f
X-ray absorption profile Röntgenabsorptionsbild n
X-ray absorption tomography Röntgenabsorptionstomografie f
X-ray analysis Röntgenanalyse f
X-ray angiogram Röntgenangiogramm n
X-ray angiographic röntgenangiografisch
X-ray angiography Röntgenangiografie f
X-ray apparatus Röntgenapparat m, Röntgenapparatur f
X-ray arteriogram Röntgenarteriogramm n
X-ray astronomer Röntgenastronom m
X-ray astronomy Röntgenastronomie f
X-ray attenuation Röntgenstrahlenschwächung f
X-ray attenuation coefficient Röntgenschwächungskoeffizient m
X-ray band Röntgen[strahlen]bereich m *(des elektromagnetischen Spektrums)*
X-ray beam Röntgenstrahl m, X-Strahl m, Röntgenstrahlenbündel n
X-ray camera Röntgenkamera f
X-ray cassette Röntgen[film]kassette f
X-ray cine camera Röntgenkinokamera f
X-ray cinematography Röntgenkinematografie f
X-ray compute[rize]d tomography Röntgencomputertomografie f
X-ray computed tomographic röntgencomputertomografisch
X-ray contact microscopy Röntgenkontaktmikroskopie f
X-ray continuum kontinuierliches Röntgenspektrum (Brennspektrum) n
X-ray contrast agent Röntgenkontrastmittel n, Kontrastmittel n
X-ray contrast angiography Röntgenkontrastangiografie f
X-ray coronary angiogram Röntgenkoronarangiogramm m
X-ray crystallography Röntgenkristallografie f
X-ray CT device (scanner) Röntgen[computer]tomograf m
X-ray department Röntgenabteilung f, Röntgenstation f; Röntgenbetrieb m
X-ray depiction Röntgendarstellung f
X-ray detection Röntgendetektion f
X-ray detection material (medium) Röntgendetektor m
X-ray detector Röntgendetektor m, Röntgensensor m
X-ray diagnostic röntgendiagnostisch
X-ray diagnostics Röntgendiagnostik f
X-ray diffraction Röntgenbeugung f
X-ray diffraction analysis Röntgenbeugungsanalyse f
X-ray diffraction camera Röntgenbeugungskamera f
X-ray diffraction pattern Röntgenbeugungsaufnahme f, Röntgenbeugungsbild n
X-ray diffraction spectrum Röntgenbeugungsspektrum n
X-ray diffractometer Röntgendiffraktometer n
X-ray dose Röntgen[strahlen]dosis f
X-ray dosimetry Röntgendosimetrie f
X-ray emissiography Reflexradiografie f
X-ray emission Röntgenemission f
X-ray emulsion Röntgenemulsion f
X-ray energy Röntgen[strahlungs]energie f
X-ray energy spectrum Röntgenspektrum n
X-ray equipment Röntgeneinrichtung f
X-ray examination Röntgenuntersuchung f
X-ray-exposed film röntgenbelichteter Film m
X-ray exposure 1. Röntgen[bild]aufnahme f; 2. Röntgenbelichtung f; 3. Röntgenbestrahlung f, Röntgenstrahlenexposition f
X-ray exposure time Röntgenbelichtungszeit f
X-ray fan beam angle Röntgenfächerstrahlwinkel m
X-ray film Röntgenfilm m, radiografischer Film m
X-ray film base Röntgenfilmträger m
X-ray film developer Röntgenfilmentwickler m, Röntgenfilm-Entwicklungsmaschine f
X-ray film digitization Röntgenfilmdigitalisierung f
X-ray film digitizer Röntgenfilmdigitalisierungsgerät n, Röntgenfilmdigitalisierer m
X-ray film radiography Filmröntgen n, Röntgenografie f

X-ray film-screen combination Film-Folien-Kombination f
X-ray film shield Filmschutzbeutel m
X-ray filtration Röntgenstrahlenfilterung f
X-ray flash Röntgenblitz m
X-ray fluorescence Röntgenfluoreszenz f
X-ray fluorescence imaging Röntgenfluoreszenzbildgebung f
X-ray fluorescence microprobe Röntgenfluoreszenz-Mikrosonde f
X-ray fluorescence radiation Röntgenfluoreszenzstrahlung f
X-ray fluorescence spectrum Röntgenfluoreszenzspektrum n
X-ray fluorescent hologram Röntgenfluoreszenzhologramm n
X-ray fluorescent holographic röntgenfluoreszenzholografisch
X-ray fluorescent image Röntgendurchleuchtungsbild n, Röntgendurchstrahlungsbild n, Röntgenfluoreszenzbild n
X-ray fluoroscope Röntgendurchleuchtungsanlage f
X-ray fluoroscopy Röntgen[fluor]oskopie f, Röntgendurchleuchtung f
X-ray fog Röntgenschleier m
X-ray gear Röntgengerät n; Röntgenanalage f
X-ray generator Röntgengenerator m, Röntgenstrahlenerzeuger m
X-ray grating Röntgenstrahlgitter n
X-ray holographic microscopy röntgenholografische Mikroskopie f
X-ray holography Röntgenholografie f
X-ray image Röntgenbild n
X-ray image formation Rötgenbildentstehung f
X-ray image intensifier Röntgenbildverstärker m
X-ray image intensifier tube Röntgen-Bildverstärkerröhre f
X-ray image pickup apparatus Röntgenbildaufnehmer m
X-ray imaging Röntgen n, Röntgenbildgebung f; Röntgenabbildung f, Röntgenbilddarstellung f
X-ray imaging detector Röntgenstrahlbildwandler m, Röntgenwandler m
X-ray imaging technology Röntgenbildtechnik f
X-ray inspection Röntgeninspektion f
X-ray intensifying screen Röntgen-Verstärkerfolie f
X-ray intensity Röntgenintensität f
X-ray interference Röntgeninterferenz f
X-ray interference pattern Röntgeninterferenzbild n
X-ray interferometer Röntgeninterferometer n
X-ray interferometric röntgeninterferometrisch
X-ray interferometric telescope röntgeninterferometrisches Teleskop n
X-ray interferometry Röntgeninterferometrie f
X-ray laser Röntgenlaser m
X-ray lens Röntgenlinse f
X-ray lithographic röntgenlithografisch
X-ray lithography Röntgenlithografie f
X-ray machine Röntgenapparat m, Röntgenapparatur f
X-ray mammogram Röntgenmammogramm n
X-ray mammography Röntgenmammografie f
X-ray map Röntgenbild n
X-ray microanalysis Röntgenmikroanalyse f
X-ray microdiffraction Röntgenmikrobeugung f
X-ray micrograph Röntgenmikroaufnahme f
X-ray micrography Mikroradiografie f, Kontaktmikroradiografie f
X-ray microlithography Röntgenmikrolithografie f
X-ray microprobe Röntgen-Mikrosonde f
X-ray microscope Röntgenmikroskop n
X-ray microscopy Röntgenmikroskopie f
X-ray microtomograph Röntgenmikrotomograf m
X-ray microtomography Röntgenmikrotomografie f
X-ray mirror Röntgenspiegel m
X-ray monochromator Röntgenmonochromator m
X-ray motion-picture film Röntgenkinefilm m
X-ray motion-picture photography Röntgenkinematografie n
X-ray observatory Röntgenobservatorium n
X-ray optical röntgenoptisch
X-ray optics Röntgenoptik f
X-ray phosphor Röntgenleuchtstoff m
X-ray photoemission spectroscopy Röntgenfotoemissionsspektroskopie f
X-ray photograph 1. Röntgenfoto n, Filmröntgenbild n, Strahlenbild n; 2. s. ~ picture
X-ray photographic röntgen[fot]ografisch
X-ray photography Röntgen[fot]ografie f, Filmröntgen n
X-ray photon Röntgenphoton n
X-ray photon energy Röntgen[strahlungs]energie f
X-ray physics Röntgenphysik f
X-ray picture Röntgenbild n, Röntgenogramm n
X-ray planar image planares Röntgenbild n
X-ray plate Röntgenplatte f
X-ray powder camera Röntgenpulverkamera f
X-ray practice Röntgenpraxis f
X-ray print Röntgenkopie f

X-ray production Röntgenstrahlenerzeugung f
X-ray projection Röntgenprojektion f
X-ray projection image (radiograph) Projektionsradiogramm n
X-ray projection radiography Projektionsradiografie f
X-ray protective clothing Röntgenschutzkleidung f
X-ray pulse Röntgen[im]puls m
X-ray quantum Röntgenquant n
X-ray quantum absorption Röntgen[strahl]absorption f
X-ray regime (region) Röntgen[strahlen]bereich m *(des elektromagnetischen Spektrums)*
X-ray room Röntgenraum m
X-ray scanner Röntgenscanner m
X-ray scattering Röntgenstreuung f
X-ray scintillating screen Röntgenszintillationsschirm m
X-ray scintillator Röntgenszintillator m
X-ray screen-type film Röntgenfolienfilm f, Folienfilm m
X-ray sensitive röntgen[strahlen]empfindlich
X-ray-sensitive emulsion röntgenstrahlenempfindliche Emulsion f
X-ray sensor Röntgensensor m
X-ray shadow Röntgenschatten m
X-ray sheet film Röntgenplanfilm m
X-ray source Röntgenquelle f
X-ray spectral line Röntgenspektrallinie f
X-ray spectrometer Röntgenspektrometer n
X-ray spectrometry Röntgenspektrometrie f
X-ray spectrophotometer Röntgenspektrofotometer n
X-ray spectroscopic röntgenspektroskopisch
X-ray spectroscopy Röntgenspektroskopie f
X-ray suite Röntgenanlage f
X-ray system Röntgensystem n
X-ray table Röntgentisch m
X-ray technician Röntgentechniker m
X-ray technology Röntgentechnik f
X-ray telescope Röntgenteleskop n
X-ray tomograph Röntgentomograf m
X-ray tomographic röntgentomografisch
X-ray tomography Röntgentomografie f, dreidimensionales Röntgen n
X-ray transmission microscope Röntgentransmissionsmikroskop n
X-ray tube Röntgen[strahl]röhre f
X-ray tube cable Röntgenröhrenkabel n
X-ray tube current Röntgenröhrenstrom m
X-ray tube kilovoltage Röntgenröhrenspannung f
X-ray-type film Röntgenfilm m
X-ray unit Röntgenanlage f; Röntgengerät n
X-ray ventriculography Ventrikulografie f

X-ray viewing box Betrachtungskasten m
X-ray wave Röntgenwelle f
X-ray wavelength Röntgenwellenlänge f
X-rays Röntgenstrahlung f
X synchronization X-Blitzsynchronisation f *(Blitzfotografie)*
xenon arc lamp, ~ burner Xenonbogenlampe f, Xenon-Hochdruckgasentladungslampe f
~ bulb Xenonlampe f
~-filled chamber Xenon-Hochdruckionisationskammer f *(Röntgendetektor)*
~-filled lamp Xenonlampe f
~ flash lamp Xenonblitzlampe f
~ flash tube Xenonblitzröhre f
~ gas Xenongas n
~ halide light source Xenonlichtquelle f
~ high-pressure lamp Xenon-Hochdrucklampe f
~ lamp Xenonlampe f
~ light Xenonlicht n
xerogel Xerogel n
xerogram Xerogramm n
xerographic xerografisch
~ copier xerografischer Kopierer m
~ copy Xerokopie f
~ image xerografisches Bild n
~ printer xerografischer Drucker m
~ printing s. xerography
~ toner xerografischer Toner m
xerography Xerografie f, Xerodruck m, xerografischer Druck m, indirekte Elektrofotografie f, Trockentransfer-Elektrofotografie f
xeromammographic xeromammografisch
xeromammography Xeromammografie f
xeroradiograph Xerogramm n
xeroradiographic xeroradiografisch
~ plate xeroradiografische Platte f
xeroradiography Xeroradiografie f
xerox/to xerografieren
Xerox copier Xerodruckmaschine f
XGA s. extended graphics array
XML s. Extended Markup Language
xylography Xylografie f
xyz map Tiefenbild n *(maschinelle Bilderkennung)*

Y

y-axis y-Achse *f*, Ordinatenachse *f*
Y-C separation
　Luminanz-Chrominanz-Trennung *f*
Y-C video *s.* S-video
Y signal *s.* luminance signal
YAG laser *s.* yttrium aluminum garnet laser
yagi, Yagi[-Uda] antenna Yagi-Antenne *f*
　(Fernsehtechnik)
yaw/to gieren
yaw angle Gierwinkel *m (z.B. einer*
　Kamera)
yellow/to vergilben
yellow Gelb *n*, Yellow *n (subtraktive*
　Grundfarbe)
~ **bias (cast)** Gelbstich *m*
~**-colored coupler** Gelbkuppler *m*
~ **dye** Gelbfarbstoff *m (Farbfotografie)*
~ **dye developer** Gelbentwickler *m*
~ **dye-forming coupler** Gelbkuppler *m*
~ **dye-forming layer** blauempfindliche
　Schicht *f (Colorfilmmaterial)*
~ **filter** Gelbfilter *n*
~ **filter layer** Gelbfilterschicht *f*
~ **spot** gelber Fleck *m*, Makula *f* lutea *(der*
　Augennetzhaut)
yellowed image vergilbtes Bild *n*
yellowing Vergilbung *f*
YIQ color coordinate system, ~ color
　space YIQ-Farbmodell *n*
Young-Helmholtz theory [of color vision]
　Young-Helmholtz-Theorie *f* [des
　Farbensehens], trichromatische theorie *f*
　des Farbensehens, Dreifarbentheorie *f*
　des Lichts
yttrium aluminum garnet laser
　Yttrium-Aluminium-Granat-Laser *m*,
　YAG-Laser *m*
YUV color space YUV-Farbmodell *n*

Z

z-axis z-Achse f
z-buffer z-Puffer[speicher] m, Tiefenpuffer m *(Computergrafik)*
z-buffering z-Puffer-Verfahren n, Tiefenpufferverfahren n
z-buffering algorithm z-Puffer-Algorithmus m, Tiefenpufferalgorithmus m, Tiefenspeicherverfahren n
zebra level indicator Zebra n, Zebrafunktion f, Zebrastreifen-Fehlbelichtungswarnung f *(Videosignalverarbeitung)*
~ **pattern** Zebramuster n *(Video)*
Zeeman effect (splitting) Zeeman-Effekt m *(Kernmagnetresonanz)*
Zener diode Zener-Diode f *(Halbleiter)*
zenith camera Zenitkamera f
~ **telescope (tube)** Zenitteleskop n
Zernike polynomial Zernike-Polynomkoeffizient m *(Wellenoptik)*
zero Nullstelle f *(Übertragungsfunktion)*
~ **crossing** Nulldurchgang m
~ **crossover** Nullpunktsteilheit f *(Fotodiode)*
~ **frequency** Nullfrequenz f
~-**mean random variable** mittelwertfreie Zufallsvariable f
~-**order interpolation** Nächste[r]-Nachbar-Interpolation f *(Bildrestaurierung)*
~-**order interpolation [reconstruction] filter** Interpolationsfilter n nullter Ordnung
~-**order spectrum** Spektrum n nullter Ordnung
~-**order wave plate** Verzögerungsplatte n nullter Ordnung
~ **padding** Aufwärtstastung f *(Bildfilterung)*
~ **parallax** Nullparallaxe f
~-**phase filter** Nulldurchgangsoperator m
~-**phase-shift filter** nullphasiges Filter n
~ **plane** Nullebene f
~-**power system** afokales System n
~ **suppression** Nullenunterdrückung f
~ **vector** Nullvektor m
zeroing Nullsetzen n *(z.B. eines Gradienten)*
zeroth-order light Licht n nullter Ordnung
~ **order of diffraction** nullte Beugungsordnung f
~ **place** Nullstelle f *(Übertragungsfunktion)*
zeugmatography [NMR-Fourier-]Zeugmatografie f *(s.a. Magnetresonanztomografie)*
zigzag [ordering] pattern Zickzackanordnung f *(z.B. von Kompressionsalgorithmen)*
~ **sampling, ~ scan[ning]** Zickzackabtastung f
zinc etching Zinkätzung f *(s.a. zincography)*
~ **oxide** Zinkoxid n *(Fotoleiter)*
~ **oxide paper** Zinkoxidpapier n
~ **sulfide** Zinksulfid n *(Leuchtstoff)*
zincograph Zinkdruckform f
zincography Zinkflachdruck m, Zinkografie f
zincotype s. zincograph
zirconium [arc] lamp Zirconiumlampe f
zoetrope Zoetrop n, Wundertrommel f, Lebensrad n *(frühe Kinematografie)*
zonal aberration Zonenfehler m *(optisches System)*
~ **coding** zonale Codierung f
~ **high-pass filter** zonales Hochpassfilter n
~ **low-pass filter** zonales Tiefpassfilter n
~ **spherical aberration** Zonenfehler m *(optisches System)*
zone axis Zonenachse f *(Kristallografie)*
~ **focusing** Zonenfokussierung f
~ **of focus** Schärfenzone f, Schärfentiefe f, Schärfebereich m, Tiefenschärfe f, axiales Auflösungsvermögen n
~ **plate [lens]** [Fresnelsche] Zonenplatte f, Fresnel-Platte f, Zonenlinse f
~ **plate microscope** Zonenplattenmikroskop n
~ **plate optics** Zonenplattenoptik f
~ **plate pattern** Zonenplattenmuster n
~ **system** Zonen[mess]system n, Zonenbelichtungsmessung f
zonule fibers Zonulafasern fpl, Zonula-Zinnii-Fasern fpl *(des Auges)*
zoom/to zoomen
zoom in/to heranzoomen, aufzoomen, einzoomen
~ **out/to** auszoomen
~ s. 1. ~ lens; 2. ~ movement
~ **camera** Zoomkamera f
~ **control** Zoomsteuerung f
~ **effect** 1. Zoomeffekt m; 2. s. ~ shot
~ **enlargement** Zoomvergrößerung f
~ **eyepiece** Zoomokular n
~ **factor** Zoomfaktor m
~ **finder** Zoomsucher m
~ **flash** Zoomblitz m
~ **lens** Zoom n(m), Zoomobjektiv n, Zoomoptik f, Gummilinse f, pankratisches Objektiv (System) n, Varioobjektiv n, Transfokator m
~ **lens camera** Zoomkamera f
~ **lens control** Zoomsteuerung f
~ **lock mechanism** Zoomverriegelung f
~ **magnification** Zoomvergrößerung f
~ **microphone** Zoommikrofon n
~ **movement** Zoombewegung f
~ **range** Zoombereich m
~ **ratio** Zoomverhältnis n

~ **ring** Zoom[einstell]ring *m*;
Brennweiten[einstell]ring *m*,
Scharfeinstellring *m*, Fokus[sier]ring *m*,
Schärfering *m*
~ **scale** Brennweitenskale *f*
~ **setting** Zoomeinstellung *f*
~ **shot** Zoomaufnahme *f*; Zoomfahrt *f*,
Brennweitenfahrt *f*, Fahreffektaufnahme
f, Fahreffekt *m*, optische Fahrt *f*
(Filmeffekt)
zoomable zoombar
zooming Skalierung *f (geometrische
Transformation)*
~ **motor** Zoommotor *m*
~ **range** Zoombereich *m*
Zweiton Zweitontechnik *f*
(Fernsehbegleitton)

Verzeichnis internationaler Fachorganisationen

ACM	Association for Computing Machinery
AIIM	Association for Information and Image Management
AIME	European Society for Artificial Intelligence in Medicine
AIPAD	Association of International Photography Art Dealers
AMII	Association for Multi-Image International
API	Associated Photographers International
ASIFA	International Animated Film Association, Internationals Animation Association
BECT	European Cinema and Television Office
CCIF	International Telephone Consultative Committee
CCIR	International Radio Consultative Committee Internationaler Beratender Ausschuss für den Funkdienst
CCITT	Consultative Committee for International Telephone and Telegraph International Telegraph and Telephone Consultative Committee
CEPT	European Conference of Postal and Telecommunications Administrations
CERN	European Laboratory for Particle Physics
CIE	International Commission on Illumination, ICI Commission Internationale de l'Eclairage Internationale Beleuchtungskommission, IBK
CVPR	International Conference on Computer Vision and Pattern Recognition
EACEM	European Association of Consumer Electronics Manufacturers Europäische Vereinigung der Hersteller von Unterhaltungselektronik Europäischer Verband der Heimgeräteindustrie
EANM	European Association of Nuclear Medicine
EAVA	European Audio-Visual Association
EBU	European Broadcasting Union Union der Europäischen Rundfunkorganisationen, UER, Europäische Rundfunkunion
ECCV	European Conference on Computer Vision
ECI	European Color Initiative
ECITC	European Committee for Information Technology Testing and Certification Europäische Kommission für die Prüfung und Zertifizierung nach ISO 9001
ECMA	European Computer Manufacturers Association Europäische Vereinigung der Computerindustrie
EDCF	European Digital Cinema Forum
EDVBC	European Digital Video Broadcasting Consortium Europäische Gesellschaft für Digitalfernsehen
EFOC	European Fiber Optics Conference Europäische Fachkonferenz für Faseroptik
EISA	European Image and Sound Association
ELMI	European Light Microscopy Initiative
EMF	European Multimedia Forum
EOS	European Optical Society Europäische Gesellschaft für Optik
EPCI	European Photographic Chemicals Industry Group
EPIC	Evidence Photographers International Council
EPMI	European Printer Manufacturers and Importers Vereinigung Europäischer Druckerhersteller und -Importeure

ERC	European Radio Committee
	Europäischer Ausschuss für Funkangelegenheiten
ESA	European Space Agency
	Europäische Weltraumorganisation,
	Europäische Raumfahrtbehörde
ESHPh	European Society for the History of Photography
ETNO	European Public Telecommunications Network Operators Association
	Verband der Europäischen Betreiber von Telekommunikationsnetzen
ETSI	European Telecommunications Standards Institute
	Europäisches Normungsinstitut für Telekommunikation
EURESCOM	European Institute for Research and Strategy Studies
	In Telecommunications
	Europäisches Institut für Forschung und Strategische Studien zur
	Telekommunikation
EUTELSAT	European Telecommunications Satellite Organization
EVN	Eurovision News
EVS	European Videoconferencing Service
	Europäischer Videokonferenzdienst
FTA	Flexographic Technical Association
GSTA	Giant Screen Theater Association
IAPR	International Association for Pattern Recognition
IAU	International Astronomical Union
ICA	International Cartographic Association
ICC	International Color Consortium
	Internationales Farbkonsortium
ICCV	International Conference on Computer Vision
ICHSPP	International Congress on High-Speed Photography & Photonics
ICI	s. CIE
ICIA	International Communications Industries Association
ICIP	International Conference on Image Processing
ICO	International Commission for Optics
ICOM	International Committee for Audiovisual and Image and Sound New
	Technologies
ICP	International Center of Photography
ICPR	International (Joint) Conference on Pattern Recognition
ICR	International Council for Reprography
ICSID	International Council of Societies of Industrial Design
ICSP	International Committee for the Science of Photography
IEC	International Electrotechnical Commission
	Internationale Elektrotechnische Kommission
IEEE	[The] Institute of Electrical and Electronics Engineers
IFIP	International Federation for (of) Information Processing
	Internationaler Verband für Datenverarbeitung
IFORS	International Federation of Operations Research Societies
IFPA	International Fire Photographers Association
IFSM	International Federation of Societies of Microscopy
IFTA	International Federation of Television Archives
IFTC	International Council for Film, Television and
	Audiovisual Communication
IFVC	International Federation of Visual Communication
IHMA	International Hologram Manufacturers Association
IIPC	India International Photographic Council
IJCAI	International Joint Conference on Artificial Intelligence
IMACS	International Association for Mathematics and Computing in Simulation
IMIA	International Medical Informatics Association

IMLA	International Minilab Association
IMPA	International Museum Photographers Association
IMTC	International Multimedia Teleconferencing Consortium
INIRC	International Non-Ionizing Radiation Committee
	Internationales Komitee für nichtionisierende Strahlung
INTELSAT	International Telecommunications Satellite Organization
IPA	International Prepress Association
IPC	International Photographic Council
IPOSA	International Photo-Optical Show Association
IPTC	International Press Telecommunication Council
IQ	International Quorum of Film and Video Producers
IRPA	International Radiation Protection Association
	Internationaler Strahlenschutzverband
IS & T	Society for Imaging Science and Technology
ISO	International Organization for Standardization
ISP	International Society for Photogrammetry
ISPRS	International Society of Photogrammetry and Remote Sensing
ISU	International Stereoscopic Union
ITU	International Typographical Union
ITU	International Telecommunication[s] Union
	Internationale Fernmeldeunion, IFU
ITU-R	International Telecommunications Union – Radio Sector
ITU-T	International Telecommunications Union – Telecom[munications Sector]
ITVA	International Television Association
IVLA	International Visual Literacy Association
JBIG	Joint Bilevel Image Experts Group
JPEG	Joint Photographic Expert Group
MPEG	Motion Pictures Experts Group
	Expertengruppe für Bewegtbildübertragung
OIRT	International Radio and Television Organization
OPS	Ophthalmic Photographers Society
PCMCIA	Personal Computer Memory Card International Association
SIGGRAPH	Special Interest Group for Graphics
SMPTE	Society of Motion Picture and Television Engineers
SPIE	International Society for Optical Engineering
UNIATEC	International Union of Technical Cinematograph Associations
VESA	Video Electronics Standards Association
WARC	World Administrative Radio Conference
WPI	Wedding Photographers International
WRC	World Radio Communication Conference